Oxford Dictionary of
National Biography

Volume 58

Oxford Dictionary of National Biography

IN ASSOCIATION WITH

The British Academy

From the earliest times to the year 2000

Edited by

H. C. G. Matthew

and

Brian Harrison

Volume 58

Wellesley–Wilkinson

OXFORD

UNIVERSITY PRESS

Great Clarendon Street, Oxford OX2 6DP

Oxford University Press is a department of the University of Oxford.
It furthers the University's objective of excellence in research, scholarship,
and education by publishing worldwide in

Oxford New York

Auckland Bangkok Buenos Aires Cape Town
Chennai Dar es Salaam Delhi Hong Kong Istanbul Karachi
Kolkata Kuala Lumpur Madrid Melbourne Mexico City Mumbai Nairobi
São Paulo Shanghai Taipei Tokyo Toronto

Oxford is a registered trade mark of Oxford University Press
in the UK and in certain other countries

Published in the United States
by Oxford University Press Inc., New York

© Oxford University Press 2004

British Library Cataloguing in Publication Data
Data available

Library of Congress Cataloging in Publication Data
Data available: for details see volume 1, p. iv

ISBN 0-19-861408-X (this volume)
ISBN 0-19-861411-X (set of sixty volumes)

Text captured by Alliance Phototypesetters, Pondicherry
Illustrations reproduced and archived by
Alliance Graphics Ltd, UK
Typeset in OUP Swift by Interactive Sciences Limited, Gloucester
Printed in Great Britain on acid-free paper by
Butler and Tanner Ltd,
Frome, Somerset

LIST OF ABBREVIATIONS

1 General abbreviations

AB	bachelor of arts
ABC	Australian Broadcasting Corporation
ABC TV	ABC Television
act.	active
A$	Australian dollar
AD	*anno domini*
AFC	Air Force Cross
AIDS	acquired immune deficiency syndrome
AK	Alaska
AL	Alabama
A level	advanced level [examination]
ALS	associate of the Linnean Society
AM	master of arts
AMICE	associate member of the Institution of Civil Engineers
ANZAC	Australian and New Zealand Army Corps
appx *pl.* appxs	appendix(es)
AR	Arkansas
ARA	associate of the Royal Academy
ARCA	associate of the Royal College of Art
ARCM	associate of the Royal College of Music
ARCO	associate of the Royal College of Organists
ARIBA	associate of the Royal Institute of British Architects
ARP	air-raid precautions
ARRC	associate of the Royal Red Cross
ARSA	associate of the Royal Scottish Academy
art.	article / item
ASC	Army Service Corps
Asch	Austrian Schilling
ASDIC	Antisubmarine Detection Investigation Committee
ATS	Auxiliary Territorial Service
ATV	Associated Television
Aug	August
AZ	Arizona
b.	born
BA	bachelor of arts
BA (Admin.)	bachelor of arts (administration)
BAFTA	British Academy of Film and Television Arts
BAO	bachelor of arts in obstetrics
bap.	baptized
BBC	British Broadcasting Corporation / Company
BC	before Christ
BCE	before the common (*or* Christian) era
BCE	bachelor of civil engineering
BCG	bacillus of Calmette and Guérin [inoculation against tuberculosis]
BCh	bachelor of surgery
BChir	bachelor of surgery
BCL	bachelor of civil law

BCnL	bachelor of canon law
BCom	bachelor of commerce
BD	bachelor of divinity
BEd	bachelor of education
BEng	bachelor of engineering
bk *pl.* bks	book(s)
BL	bachelor of law / letters / literature
BLitt	bachelor of letters
BM	bachelor of medicine
BMus	bachelor of music
BP	before present
BP	British Petroleum
Bros.	Brothers
BS	(1) bachelor of science; (2) bachelor of surgery; (3) British standard
BSc	bachelor of science
BSc (Econ.)	bachelor of science (economics)
BSc (Eng.)	bachelor of science (engineering)
bt	baronet
BTh	bachelor of theology
bur.	buried
C.	command [identifier for published parliamentary papers]
c.	*circa*
c.	*capitulum pl. capitula*: chapter(s)
CA	California
Cantab.	Cantabrigiensis
cap.	*capitulum pl. capitula*: chapter(s)
CB	companion of the Bath
CBE	commander of the Order of the British Empire
CBS	Columbia Broadcasting System
cc	cubic centimetres
C$	Canadian dollar
CD	compact disc
Cd	command [identifier for published parliamentary papers]
CE	Common (*or* Christian) Era
cent.	century
cf.	compare
CH	Companion of Honour
chap.	chapter
ChB	bachelor of surgery
CI	Imperial Order of the Crown of India
CIA	Central Intelligence Agency
CID	Criminal Investigation Department
CIE	companion of the Order of the Indian Empire
Cie	Compagnie
CLit	companion of literature
CM	master of surgery
cm	centimetre(s)

Cmd	command [identifier for published parliamentary papers]
CMG	companion of the Order of St Michael and St George
Cmnd	command [identifier for published parliamentary papers]
CO	Colorado
Co.	company
co.	county
col. *pl.* cols.	column(s)
Corp.	corporation
CSE	certificate of secondary education
CSI	companion of the Order of the Star of India
CT	Connecticut
CVO	commander of the Royal Victorian Order
cwt	hundredweight
$	(American) dollar
d.	(1) penny (pence); (2) died
DBE	dame commander of the Order of the British Empire
DCH	diploma in child health
DCh	doctor of surgery
DCL	doctor of civil law
DCnL	doctor of canon law
DCVO	dame commander of the Royal Victorian Order
DD	doctor of divinity
DE	Delaware
Dec	December
dem.	demolished
DEng	doctor of engineering
des.	destroyed
DFC	Distinguished Flying Cross
DipEd	diploma in education
DipPsych	diploma in psychiatry
diss.	dissertation
DL	deputy lieutenant
DLitt	doctor of letters
DLittCelt	doctor of Celtic letters
DM	(1) Deutschmark; (2) doctor of medicine; (3) doctor of musical arts
DMus	doctor of music
DNA	dioxyribonucleic acid
doc.	document
DOL	doctor of oriental learning
DPH	diploma in public health
DPhil	doctor of philosophy
DPM	diploma in psychological medicine
DSC	Distinguished Service Cross
DSc	doctor of science
DSc (Econ.)	doctor of science (economics)
DSc (Eng.)	doctor of science (engineering)
DSM	Distinguished Service Medal
DSO	companion of the Distinguished Service Order
DSocSc	doctor of social science
DTech	doctor of technology
DTh	doctor of theology
DTM	diploma in tropical medicine
DTMH	diploma in tropical medicine and hygiene
DU	doctor of the university
DUniv	doctor of the university
dwt	pennyweight
EC	European Community
ed. *pl.* eds.	edited / edited by / editor(s)
Edin.	Edinburgh
edn	edition
EEC	European Economic Community
EFTA	European Free Trade Association
EICS	East India Company Service
EMI	Electrical and Musical Industries (Ltd)
Eng.	English
enl.	enlarged
ENSA	Entertainments National Service Association
ep. *pl.* epp.	*epistola(e)*
ESP	extra-sensory perception
esp.	especially
esq.	esquire
est.	estimate / estimated
EU	European Union
ex	sold by (*lit.* out of)
excl.	excludes / excluding
exh.	exhibited
exh. cat.	exhibition catalogue
f. *pl.* ff.	following [pages]
FA	Football Association
FACP	fellow of the American College of Physicians
facs.	facsimile
FANY	First Aid Nursing Yeomanry
FBA	fellow of the British Academy
FBI	Federation of British Industries
FCS	fellow of the Chemical Society
Feb	February
FEng	fellow of the Fellowship of Engineering
FFCM	fellow of the Faculty of Community Medicine
FGS	fellow of the Geological Society
fig.	figure
FIMechE	fellow of the Institution of Mechanical Engineers
FL	Florida
fl.	*floruit*
FLS	fellow of the Linnean Society
FM	frequency modulation
fol. *pl.* fols.	folio(s)
Fr	French francs
Fr.	French
FRAeS	fellow of the Royal Aeronautical Society
FRAI	fellow of the Royal Anthropological Institute
FRAM	fellow of the Royal Academy of Music
FRAS	(1) fellow of the Royal Asiatic Society; (2) fellow of the Royal Astronomical Society
FRCM	fellow of the Royal College of Music
FRCO	fellow of the Royal College of Organists
FRCOG	fellow of the Royal College of Obstetricians and Gynaecologists
FRCP(C)	fellow of the Royal College of Physicians of Canada
FRCP (Edin.)	fellow of the Royal College of Physicians of Edinburgh
FRCP (Lond.)	fellow of the Royal College of Physicians of London
FRCPath	fellow of the Royal College of Pathologists
FRCPsych	fellow of the Royal College of Psychiatrists
FRCS	fellow of the Royal College of Surgeons
FRGS	fellow of the Royal Geographical Society
FRIBA	fellow of the Royal Institute of British Architects
FRICS	fellow of the Royal Institute of Chartered Surveyors
FRS	fellow of the Royal Society
FRSA	fellow of the Royal Society of Arts

FRSCM	fellow of the Royal School of Church Music
FRSE	fellow of the Royal Society of Edinburgh
FRSL	fellow of the Royal Society of Literature
FSA	fellow of the Society of Antiquaries
ft	foot *pl.* feet
FTCL	fellow of Trinity College of Music, London
ft-lb per min.	foot-pounds per minute [unit of horsepower]
FZS	fellow of the Zoological Society
GA	Georgia
GBE	knight or dame grand cross of the Order of the British Empire
GCB	knight grand cross of the Order of the Bath
GCE	general certificate of education
GCH	knight grand cross of the Royal Guelphic Order
GCHQ	government communications headquarters
GCIE	knight grand commander of the Order of the Indian Empire
GCMG	knight or dame grand cross of the Order of St Michael and St George
GCSE	general certificate of secondary education
GCSI	knight grand commander of the Order of the Star of India
GCStJ	bailiff or dame grand cross of the order of St John of Jerusalem
GCVO	knight or dame grand cross of the Royal Victorian Order
GEC	General Electric Company
Ger.	German
GI	government (*or* general) issue
GMT	Greenwich mean time
GP	general practitioner
GPU	[Soviet special police unit]
GSO	general staff officer
Heb.	Hebrew
HEICS	Honourable East India Company Service
HI	Hawaii
HIV	human immunodeficiency virus
HK$	Hong Kong dollar
HM	his / her majesty('s)
HMAS	his / her majesty's Australian ship
HMNZS	his / her majesty's New Zealand ship
HMS	his / her majesty's ship
HMSO	His / Her Majesty's Stationery Office
HMV	His Master's Voice
Hon.	Honourable
hp	horsepower
hr	hour(s)
HRH	his / her royal highness
HTV	Harlech Television
IA	Iowa
ibid.	*ibidem*: in the same place
ICI	Imperial Chemical Industries (Ltd)
ID	Idaho
IL	Illinois
illus.	illustration
illustr.	illustrated
IN	Indiana
in.	inch(es)
Inc.	Incorporated
incl.	includes / including
IOU	I owe you
IQ	intelligence quotient
Ir£	Irish pound
IRA	Irish Republican Army
ISO	companion of the Imperial Service Order
It.	Italian
ITA	Independent Television Authority
ITV	Independent Television
Jan	January
JP	justice of the peace
jun.	junior
KB	knight of the Order of the Bath
KBE	knight commander of the Order of the British Empire
KC	king's counsel
kcal	kilocalorie
KCB	knight commander of the Order of the Bath
KCH	knight commander of the Royal Guelphic Order
KCIE	knight commander of the Order of the Indian Empire
KCMG	knight commander of the Order of St Michael and St George
KCSI	knight commander of the Order of the Star of India
KCVO	knight commander of the Royal Victorian Order
keV	kilo-electron-volt
KG	knight of the Order of the Garter
KGB	[Soviet committee of state security]
KH	knight of the Royal Guelphic Order
KLM	Koninklijke Luchtvaart Maatschappij (Royal Dutch Air Lines)
km	kilometre(s)
KP	knight of the Order of St Patrick
KS	Kansas
KT	knight of the Order of the Thistle
kt	knight
KY	Kentucky
£	pound(s) sterling
£E	Egyptian pound
L	lira *pl.* lire
l. *pl.* ll.	line(s)
LA	Lousiana
LAA	light anti-aircraft
LAH	licentiate of the Apothecaries' Hall, Dublin
Lat.	Latin
lb	pound(s), unit of weight
LDS	licence in dental surgery
lit.	literally
LittB	bachelor of letters
LittD	doctor of letters
LKQCPI	licentiate of the King and Queen's College of Physicians, Ireland
LLA	lady literate in arts
LLB	bachelor of laws
LLD	doctor of laws
LLM	master of laws
LM	licentiate in midwifery
LP	long-playing record
LRAM	licentiate of the Royal Academy of Music
LRCP	licentiate of the Royal College of Physicians
LRCPS (Glasgow)	licentiate of the Royal College of Physicians and Surgeons of Glasgow
LRCS	licentiate of the Royal College of Surgeons
LSA	licentiate of the Society of Apothecaries
LSD	lysergic acid diethylamide
LVO	lieutenant of the Royal Victorian Order
M. *pl.* MM.	Monsieur *pl.* Messieurs
m	metre(s)

m. *pl.* mm.	membrane(s)
MA	(1) Massachusetts; (2) master of arts
MAI	master of engineering
MB	bachelor of medicine
MBA	master of business administration
MBE	member of the Order of the British Empire
MC	Military Cross
MCC	Marylebone Cricket Club
MCh	master of surgery
MChir	master of surgery
MCom	master of commerce
MD	(1) doctor of medicine; (2) Maryland
MDMA	methylenedioxymethamphetamine
ME	Maine
MEd	master of education
MEng	master of engineering
MEP	member of the European parliament
MG	Morris Garages
MGM	Metro-Goldwyn-Mayer
Mgr	Monsignor
MI	(1) Michigan; (2) military intelligence
MI1c	[secret intelligence department]
MI5	[military intelligence department]
MI6	[secret intelligence department]
MI9	[secret escape service]
MICE	member of the Institution of Civil Engineers
MIEE	member of the Institution of Electrical Engineers
min.	minute(s)
Mk	mark
ML	(1) licentiate of medicine; (2) master of laws
MLitt	master of letters
Mlle	Mademoiselle
mm	millimetre(s)
Mme	Madame
MN	Minnesota
MO	Missouri
MOH	medical officer of health
MP	member of parliament
m.p.h.	miles per hour
MPhil	master of philosophy
MRCP	member of the Royal College of Physicians
MRCS	member of the Royal College of Surgeons
MRCVS	member of the Royal College of Veterinary Surgeons
MRIA	member of the Royal Irish Academy
MS	(1) master of science; (2) Mississippi
MS *pl.* MSS	manuscript(s)
MSc	master of science
MSc (Econ.)	master of science (economics)
MT	Montana
MusB	bachelor of music
MusBac	bachelor of music
MusD	doctor of music
MV	motor vessel
MVO	member of the Royal Victorian Order
n. *pl.* nn.	note(s)
NAAFI	Navy, Army, and Air Force Institutes
NASA	National Aeronautics and Space Administration
NATO	North Atlantic Treaty Organization
NBC	National Broadcasting Corporation
NC	North Carolina
NCO	non-commissioned officer

ND	North Dakota
n.d.	no date
NE	Nebraska
nem. con.	*nemine contradicente*: unanimously
new ser.	new series
NH	New Hampshire
NHS	National Health Service
NJ	New Jersey
NKVD	[Soviet people's commissariat for internal affairs]
NM	New Mexico
nm	nanometre(s)
no. *pl.* nos.	number(s)
Nov	November
n.p.	no place [of publication]
NS	new style
NV	Nevada
NY	New York
NZBS	New Zealand Broadcasting Service
OBE	officer of the Order of the British Empire
obit.	obituary
Oct	October
OCTU	officer cadets training unit
OECD	Organization for Economic Co-operation and Development
OEEC	Organization for European Economic Co-operation
OFM	order of Friars Minor [Franciscans]
OFMCap	Ordine Frati Minori Cappucini: member of the Capuchin order
OH	Ohio
OK	Oklahoma
O level	ordinary level [examination]
OM	Order of Merit
OP	order of Preachers [Dominicans]
op. *pl.* opp.	opus *pl.* opera
OPEC	Organization of Petroleum Exporting Countries
OR	Oregon
orig.	original
OS	old style
OSB	Order of St Benedict
OTC	Officers' Training Corps
OWS	Old Watercolour Society
Oxon.	Oxoniensis
p. *pl.* pp.	page(s)
PA	Pennsylvania
p.a.	per annum
para.	paragraph
PAYE	pay as you earn
pbk *pl.* pbks	paperback(s)
per.	[during the] period
PhD	doctor of philosophy
pl.	(1) plate(s); (2) plural
priv. coll.	private collection
pt *pl.* pts	part(s)
pubd	published
PVC	polyvinyl chloride
q. *pl.* qq.	(1) question(s); (2) quire(s)
QC	queen's counsel
R	rand
R.	Rex / Regina
r	recto
r.	reigned / ruled
RA	Royal Academy / Royal Academician

RAC	Royal Automobile Club
RAF	Royal Air Force
RAFVR	Royal Air Force Volunteer Reserve
RAM	[member of the] Royal Academy of Music
RAMC	Royal Army Medical Corps
RCA	Royal College of Art
RCNC	Royal Corps of Naval Constructors
RCOG	Royal College of Obstetricians and Gynaecologists
RDI	royal designer for industry
RE	Royal Engineers
repr. *pl.* reprs.	reprint(s) / reprinted
repro.	reproduced
rev.	revised / revised by / reviser / revision
Revd	Reverend
RHA	Royal Hibernian Academy
RI	(1) Rhode Island; (2) Royal Institute of Painters in Water-Colours
RIBA	Royal Institute of British Architects
RIN	Royal Indian Navy
RM	Reichsmark
RMS	Royal Mail steamer
RN	Royal Navy
RNA	ribonucleic acid
RNAS	Royal Naval Air Service
RNR	Royal Naval Reserve
RNVR	Royal Naval Volunteer Reserve
RO	Record Office
r.p.m.	revolutions per minute
RRS	royal research ship
Rs	rupees
RSA	(1) Royal Scottish Academician; (2) Royal Society of Arts
RSPCA	Royal Society for the Prevention of Cruelty to Animals
Rt Hon.	Right Honourable
Rt Revd	Right Reverend
RUC	Royal Ulster Constabulary
Russ.	Russian
RWS	Royal Watercolour Society
S4C	Sianel Pedwar Cymru
s.	shilling(s)
s.a.	*sub anno*: under the year
SABC	South African Broadcasting Corporation
SAS	Special Air Service
SC	South Carolina
ScD	doctor of science
S$	Singapore dollar
SD	South Dakota
sec.	second(s)
sel.	selected
sen.	senior
Sept	September
ser.	series
SHAPE	supreme headquarters allied powers, Europe
SIDRO	Société Internationale d'Énergie Hydro-Électrique
sig. *pl.* sigs.	signature(s)
sing.	singular
SIS	Secret Intelligence Service
SJ	Society of Jesus

Skr	Swedish krona
Span.	Spanish
SPCK	Society for Promoting Christian Knowledge
SS	(1) Santissimi; (2) Schutzstaffel; (3) steam ship
STB	bachelor of theology
STD	doctor of theology
STM	master of theology
STP	doctor of theology
supp.	supposedly
suppl. *pl.* suppls.	supplement(s)
s.v.	*sub verbo* / *sub voce*: under the word / heading
SY	steam yacht
TA	Territorial Army
TASS	[Soviet news agency]
TB	tuberculosis (*lit.* tubercle bacillus)
TD	(1) *teachtaí dála* (member of the Dáil); (2) territorial decoration
TN	Tennessee
TNT	trinitrotoluene
trans.	translated / translated by / translation / translator
TT	tourist trophy
TUC	Trades Union Congress
TX	Texas
U-boat	*Unterseeboot*: submarine
Ufa	Universum-Film AG
UMIST	University of Manchester Institute of Science and Technology
UN	United Nations
UNESCO	United Nations Educational, Scientific, and Cultural Organization
UNICEF	United Nations International Children's Emergency Fund
unpubd	unpublished
USS	United States ship
UT	Utah
v	verso
v.	versus
VA	Virginia
VAD	Voluntary Aid Detachment
VC	Victoria Cross
VE-day	victory in Europe day
Ven.	Venerable
VJ-day	victory over Japan day
vol. *pl.* vols.	volume(s)
VT	Vermont
WA	Washington [state]
WAAC	Women's Auxiliary Army Corps
WAAF	Women's Auxiliary Air Force
WEA	Workers' Educational Association
WHO	World Health Organization
WI	Wisconsin
WRAF	Women's Royal Air Force
WRNS	Women's Royal Naval Service
WV	West Virginia
WVS	Women's Voluntary Service
WY	Wyoming
¥	yen
YMCA	Young Men's Christian Association
YWCA	Young Women's Christian Association

2 Institution abbreviations

All Souls Oxf.	All Souls College, Oxford
AM Oxf.	Ashmolean Museum, Oxford
Balliol Oxf.	Balliol College, Oxford
BBC WAC	BBC Written Archives Centre, Reading
Beds. & Luton ARS	Bedfordshire and Luton Archives and Record Service, Bedford
Berks. RO	Berkshire Record Office, Reading
BFI	British Film Institute, London
BFI NFTVA	British Film Institute, London, National Film and Television Archive
BGS	British Geological Survey, Keyworth, Nottingham
Birm. CA	Birmingham Central Library, Birmingham City Archives
Birm. CL	Birmingham Central Library
BL	British Library, London
BL NSA	British Library, London, National Sound Archive
BL OIOC	British Library, London, Oriental and India Office Collections
BLPES	London School of Economics and Political Science, British Library of Political and Economic Science
BM	British Museum, London
Bodl. Oxf.	Bodleian Library, Oxford
Bodl. RH	Bodleian Library of Commonwealth and African Studies at Rhodes House, Oxford
Borth. Inst.	Borthwick Institute of Historical Research, University of York
Boston PL	Boston Public Library, Massachusetts
Bristol RO	Bristol Record Office
Bucks. RLSS	Buckinghamshire Records and Local Studies Service, Aylesbury
CAC Cam.	Churchill College, Cambridge, Churchill Archives Centre
Cambs. AS	Cambridgeshire Archive Service
CCC Cam.	Corpus Christi College, Cambridge
CCC Oxf.	Corpus Christi College, Oxford
Ches. & Chester ALSS	Cheshire and Chester Archives and Local Studies Service
Christ Church Oxf.	Christ Church, Oxford
Christies	Christies, London
City Westm. AC	City of Westminster Archives Centre, London
CKS	Centre for Kentish Studies, Maidstone
CLRO	Corporation of London Records Office
Coll. Arms	College of Arms, London
Col. U.	Columbia University, New York
Cornwall RO	Cornwall Record Office, Truro
Courtauld Inst.	Courtauld Institute of Art, London
CUL	Cambridge University Library
Cumbria AS	Cumbria Archive Service
Derbys. RO	Derbyshire Record Office, Matlock
Devon RO	Devon Record Office, Exeter
Dorset RO	Dorset Record Office, Dorchester
Duke U.	Duke University, Durham, North Carolina
Duke U., Perkins L.	Duke University, Durham, North Carolina, William R. Perkins Library
Durham Cath. CL	Durham Cathedral, chapter library
Durham RO	Durham Record Office
DWL	Dr Williams's Library, London
Essex RO	Essex Record Office
E. Sussex RO	East Sussex Record Office, Lewes
Eton	Eton College, Berkshire
FM Cam.	Fitzwilliam Museum, Cambridge
Folger	Folger Shakespeare Library, Washington, DC

Garr. Club	Garrick Club, London
Girton Cam.	Girton College, Cambridge
GL	Guildhall Library, London
Glos. RO	Gloucestershire Record Office, Gloucester
Gon. & Caius Cam.	Gonville and Caius College, Cambridge
Gov. Art Coll.	Government Art Collection
GS Lond.	Geological Society of London
Hants. RO	Hampshire Record Office, Winchester
Harris Man. Oxf.	Harris Manchester College, Oxford
Harvard TC	Harvard Theatre Collection, Harvard University, Cambridge, Massachusetts, Nathan Marsh Pusey Library
Harvard U.	Harvard University, Cambridge, Massachusetts
Harvard U., Houghton L.	Harvard University, Cambridge, Massachusetts, Houghton Library
Herefs. RO	Herefordshire Record Office, Hereford
Herts. ALS	Hertfordshire Archives and Local Studies, Hertford
Hist. Soc. Penn.	Historical Society of Pennsylvania, Philadelphia
HLRO	House of Lords Record Office, London
Hult. Arch.	Hulton Archive, London and New York
Hunt. L.	Huntington Library, San Marino, California
ICL	Imperial College, London
Inst. CE	Institution of Civil Engineers, London
Inst. EE	Institution of Electrical Engineers, London
IWM	Imperial War Museum, London
IWM FVA	Imperial War Museum, London, Film and Video Archive
IWM SA	Imperial War Museum, London, Sound Archive
JRL	John Rylands University Library of Manchester
King's AC Cam.	King's College Archives Centre, Cambridge
King's Cam.	King's College, Cambridge
King's Lond.	King's College, London
King's Lond., Liddell Hart C.	King's College, London, Liddell Hart Centre for Military Archives
Lancs. RO	Lancashire Record Office, Preston
L. Cong.	Library of Congress, Washington, DC
Leics. RO	Leicestershire, Leicester, and Rutland Record Office, Leicester
Lincs. Arch.	Lincolnshire Archives, Lincoln
Linn. Soc.	Linnean Society of London
LMA	London Metropolitan Archives
LPL	Lambeth Palace, London
Lpool RO	Liverpool Record Office and Local Studies Service
LUL	London University Library
Magd. Cam.	Magdalene College, Cambridge
Magd. Oxf.	Magdalen College, Oxford
Man. City Gall.	Manchester City Galleries
Man. CL	Manchester Central Library
Mass. Hist. Soc.	Massachusetts Historical Society, Boston
Merton Oxf.	Merton College, Oxford
MHS Oxf.	Museum of the History of Science, Oxford
Mitchell L., Glas.	Mitchell Library, Glasgow
Mitchell L., NSW	State Library of New South Wales, Sydney, Mitchell Library
Morgan L.	Pierpont Morgan Library, New York
NA Canada	National Archives of Canada, Ottawa
NA Ire.	National Archives of Ireland, Dublin
NAM	National Army Museum, London
NA Scot.	National Archives of Scotland, Edinburgh
News Int. RO	News International Record Office, London
NG Ire.	National Gallery of Ireland, Dublin

NG Scot.	National Gallery of Scotland, Edinburgh
NHM	Natural History Museum, London
NL Aus.	National Library of Australia, Canberra
NL Ire.	National Library of Ireland, Dublin
NL NZ	National Library of New Zealand, Wellington
NL NZ, Turnbull L.	National Library of New Zealand, Wellington, Alexander Turnbull Library
NL Scot.	National Library of Scotland, Edinburgh
NL Wales	National Library of Wales, Aberystwyth
NMG Wales	National Museum and Gallery of Wales, Cardiff
NMM	National Maritime Museum, London
Norfolk RO	Norfolk Record Office, Norwich
Northants. RO	Northamptonshire Record Office, Northampton
Northumbd RO	Northumberland Record Office
Notts. Arch.	Nottinghamshire Archives, Nottingham
NPG	National Portrait Gallery, London
NRA	National Archives, London, Historical Manuscripts Commission, National Register of Archives
Nuffield Oxf.	Nuffield College, Oxford
N. Yorks. CRO	North Yorkshire County Record Office, Northallerton
NYPL	New York Public Library
Oxf. UA	Oxford University Archives
Oxf. U. Mus. NH	Oxford University Museum of Natural History
Oxon. RO	Oxfordshire Record Office, Oxford
Pembroke Cam.	Pembroke College, Cambridge
PRO	National Archives, London, Public Record Office
PRO NIre.	Public Record Office for Northern Ireland, Belfast
Pusey Oxf.	Pusey House, Oxford
RA	Royal Academy of Arts, London
Ransom HRC	Harry Ransom Humanities Research Center, University of Texas, Austin
RAS	Royal Astronomical Society, London
RBG Kew	Royal Botanic Gardens, Kew, London
RCP Lond.	Royal College of Physicians of London
RCS Eng.	Royal College of Surgeons of England, London
RGS	Royal Geographical Society, London
RIBA	Royal Institute of British Architects, London
RIBA BAL	Royal Institute of British Architects, London, British Architectural Library
Royal Arch.	Royal Archives, Windsor Castle, Berkshire [by gracious permission of her majesty the queen]
Royal Irish Acad.	Royal Irish Academy, Dublin
Royal Scot. Acad.	Royal Scottish Academy, Edinburgh
RS	Royal Society, London
RSA	Royal Society of Arts, London
RS Friends, Lond.	Religious Society of Friends, London
St Ant. Oxf.	St Antony's College, Oxford
St John Cam.	St John's College, Cambridge
S. Antiquaries, Lond.	Society of Antiquaries of London
Sci. Mus.	Science Museum, London
Scot. NPG	Scottish National Portrait Gallery, Edinburgh
Scott Polar RI	University of Cambridge, Scott Polar Research Institute
Sheff. Arch.	Sheffield Archives
Shrops. RRC	Shropshire Records and Research Centre, Shrewsbury
SOAS	School of Oriental and African Studies, London
Som. ARS	Somerset Archive and Record Service, Taunton
Staffs. RO	Staffordshire Record Office, Stafford

Suffolk RO	Suffolk Record Office
Surrey HC	Surrey History Centre, Woking
TCD	Trinity College, Dublin
Trinity Cam.	Trinity College, Cambridge
U. Aberdeen	University of Aberdeen
U. Birm.	University of Birmingham
U. Birm. L.	University of Birmingham Library
U. Cal.	University of California
U. Cam.	University of Cambridge
UCL	University College, London
U. Durham	University of Durham
U. Durham L.	University of Durham Library
U. Edin.	University of Edinburgh
U. Edin., New Coll.	University of Edinburgh, New College
U. Edin., New Coll. L.	University of Edinburgh, New College Library
U. Edin. L.	University of Edinburgh Library
U. Glas.	University of Glasgow
U. Glas. L.	University of Glasgow Library
U. Hull	University of Hull
U. Hull, Brynmor Jones L.	University of Hull, Brynmor Jones Library
U. Leeds	University of Leeds
U. Leeds, Brotherton L.	University of Leeds, Brotherton Library
U. Lond.	University of London
U. Lpool	University of Liverpool
U. Lpool L.	University of Liverpool Library
U. Mich.	University of Michigan, Ann Arbor
U. Mich., Clements L.	University of Michigan, Ann Arbor, William L. Clements Library
U. Newcastle	University of Newcastle upon Tyne
U. Newcastle, Robinson L.	University of Newcastle upon Tyne, Robinson Library
U. Nott.	University of Nottingham
U. Nott. L.	University of Nottingham Library
U. Oxf.	University of Oxford
U. Reading	University of Reading
U. Reading L.	University of Reading Library
U. St Andr.	University of St Andrews
U. St Andr. L.	University of St Andrews Library
U. Southampton	University of Southampton
U. Southampton L.	University of Southampton Library
U. Sussex	University of Sussex, Brighton
U. Texas	University of Texas, Austin
U. Wales	University of Wales
U. Warwick Mod. RC	University of Warwick, Coventry, Modern Records Centre
V&A	Victoria and Albert Museum, London
V&A NAL	Victoria and Albert Museum, London, National Art Library
Warks. CRO	Warwickshire County Record Office, Warwick
Wellcome L.	Wellcome Library for the History and Understanding of Medicine, London
Westm. DA	Westminster Diocesan Archives, London
Wilts. & Swindon RO	Wiltshire and Swindon Record Office, Trowbridge
Worcs. RO	Worcestershire Record Office, Worcester
W. Sussex RO	West Sussex Record Office, Chichester
W. Yorks. AS	West Yorkshire Archive Service
Yale U.	Yale University, New Haven, Connecticut
Yale U., Beinecke L.	Yale University, New Haven, Connecticut, Beinecke Rare Book and Manuscript Library
Yale U. CBA	Yale University, New Haven, Connecticut, Yale Center for British Art

3 Bibliographic abbreviations

Adams, *Drama* — W. D. Adams, *A dictionary of the drama*, 1: *A–G* (1904); 2: *H–Z* (1956) [vol. 2 microfilm only]

AFM — J O'Donovan, ed. and trans., *Annala rioghachta Eireann / Annals of the kingdom of Ireland by the four masters*, 7 vols. (1848–51); 2nd edn (1856); 3rd edn (1990)

Allibone, *Dict.* — S. A. Allibone, *A critical dictionary of English literature and British and American authors*, 3 vols. (1859–71); suppl. by J. F. Kirk, 2 vols. (1891)

ANB — J. A. Garraty and M. C. Carnes, eds., *American national biography*, 24 vols. (1999)

Anderson, *Scot. nat.* — W. Anderson, *The Scottish nation, or, The surnames, families, literature, honours, and biographical history of the people of Scotland*, 3 vols. (1859–63)

Ann. mon. — H. R. Luard, ed., *Annales monastici*, 5 vols., Rolls Series, 36 (1864–9)

Ann. Ulster — S. Mac Airt and G. Mac Niocaill, eds., *Annals of Ulster (to AD 1131)* (1983)

APC — *Acts of the privy council of England*, new ser., 46 vols. (1890–1964)

APS — *The acts of the parliaments of Scotland*, 12 vols. in 13 (1814–75)

Arber, *Regs. Stationers* — F. Arber, ed., *A transcript of the registers of the Company of Stationers of London, 1554–1640 AD*, 5 vols. (1875–94)

ArchR — *Architectural Review*

ASC — D. Whitelock, D. C. Douglas, and S. I. Tucker, ed. and trans., *The Anglo-Saxon Chronicle: a revised translation* (1961)

AS chart. — P. H. Sawyer, *Anglo-Saxon charters: an annotated list and bibliography*, Royal Historical Society Guides and Handbooks (1968)

AusDB — D. Pike and others, eds., *Australian dictionary of biography*, 16 vols. (1966–2002)

Baker, *Serjeants* — J. H. Baker, *The order of serjeants at law*, SeldS, suppl. ser., 5 (1984)

Bale, *Cat.* — J. Bale, *Scriptorum illustrium Maioris Brytannie, quam nunc Angliam et Scotiam vocant: catalogus*, 2 vols. in 1 (Basel, 1557–9); facs. edn (1971)

Bale, *Index* — J. Bale, *Index Britanniae scriptorum*, ed. R. L. Poole and M. Bateson (1902); facs. edn (1990)

BBCS — *Bulletin of the Board of Celtic Studies*

BDMBR — J. O. Baylen and N. J. Gossman, eds., *Biographical dictionary of modern British radicals*, 3 vols. in 4 (1979–88)

Bede, *Hist. eccl.* — *Bede's Ecclesiastical history of the English people*, ed. and trans. B. Colgrave and R. A. B. Mynors, OMT (1969); repr. (1991)

Bénézit, *Dict.* — E. Bénézit, *Dictionnaire critique et documentaire des peintres, sculpteurs, dessinateurs et graveurs*, 3 vols. (Paris, 1911–23); new edn, 8 vols. (1948–66), repr. (1966); 3rd edn, rev. and enl., 10 vols. (1976); 4th edn, 14 vols. (1999)

BIHR — *Bulletin of the Institute of Historical Research*

Birch, *Seals* — W. de Birch, *Catalogue of seals in the department of manuscripts in the British Museum*, 6 vols. (1887–1900)

Bishop Burnet's History — *Bishop Burnet's History of his own time*, ed. M. J. Routh, 2nd edn, 6 vols. (1833)

Blackwood — *Blackwood's [Edinburgh] Magazine*, 328 vols. (1817–1980)

Blain, Clements & Grundy, *Feminist comp.* — V. Blain, P. Clements, and I. Grundy, eds., *The feminist companion to literature in English* (1990)

BL cat. — *The British Library general catalogue of printed books* [in 360 vols. with suppls., also CD-ROM and online]

BMJ — *British Medical Journal*

Boase & Courtney, *Bibl. Corn.* — G. C. Boase and W. P. Courtney, *Bibliotheca Cornubiensis: a catalogue of the writings … of Cornishmen*, 3 vols. (1874–82)

Boase, *Mod. Eng. biog.* — F. Boase, *Modern English biography: containing many thousand concise memoirs of persons who have died since the year 1850*, 6 vols. (privately printed, Truro, 1892–1921); repr. (1965)

Boswell, *Life* — *Boswell's Life of Johnson: together with Journal of a tour to the Hebrides and Johnson's Diary of a journey into north Wales*, ed. G. B. Hill, enl. edn, rev. L. F. Powell, 6 vols. (1934–50); 2nd edn (1964); repr. (1971)

Brown & Stratton, *Brit. mus.* — J. D. Brown and S. S. Stratton, *British musical biography* (1897)

Bryan, *Painters* — M. Bryan, *A biographical and critical dictionary of painters and engravers*, 2 vols. (1816); new edn, ed. G. Stanley (1849); new edn, ed. R. E. Graves and W. Armstrong, 2 vols. (1886–9); [4th edn], ed. G. C. Williamson, 5 vols. (1903–5) [various reprs.]

Burke, *Gen. GB* — J. Burke, *A genealogical and heraldic history of the commoners of Great Britain and Ireland*, 4 vols. (1833–8); new edn as *A genealogical and heraldic dictionary of the landed gentry of Great Britain and Ireland*, 3 vols. [1843–9] [many later edns]

Burke, *Gen. Ire.* — J. B. Burke, *A genealogical and heraldic history of the landed gentry of Ireland* (1899); 2nd edn (1904); 3rd edn (1912); 4th edn (1958); 5th edn as *Burke's Irish family records* (1976)

Burke, *Peerage* — J. Burke, *A general [later edns A genealogical] and heraldic dictionary of the peerage and baronetage of the United Kingdom [later edns the British empire]* (1829–)

Burney, *Hist. mus.* — C. Burney, *A general history of music, from the earliest ages to the present period*, 4 vols. (1776–89)

Burtchaell & Sadleir, *Alum. Dubl.* — G. D. Burtchaell and T. U. Sadleir, *Alumni Dublinenses: a register of the students, graduates, and provosts of Trinity College* (1924); [2nd edn], with suppl., in 2 pts (1935)

Calamy rev. — A. G. Matthews, *Calamy revised* (1934); repr. (1988)

CCI — *Calendar of confirmations and inventories granted and given up in the several commissariots of Scotland* (1876–)

CCIR — *Calendar of the close rolls preserved in the Public Record Office*, 47 vols. (1892–1963)

CDS — J. Bain, ed., *Calendar of documents relating to Scotland*, 4 vols., PRO (1881–8); suppl. vol. 5, ed. G. G. Simpson and J. D. Galbraith [1986]

CEPR letters — W. H. Bliss, C. Johnson, and J. Twemlow, eds., *Calendar of entries in the papal registers relating to Great Britain and Ireland: papal letters* (1893–)

CGPLA — *Calendars of the grants of probate and letters of administration* [in 4 ser.: *England & Wales, Northern Ireland, Ireland,* and *Éire*]

Chambers, *Scots.* — R. Chambers, ed., *A biographical dictionary of eminent Scotsmen*, 4 vols. (1832–5)

Chancery records — chancery records pubd by the PRO

Chancery records (RC) — chancery records pubd by the Record Commissions

CIPM	Calendar of inquisitions post mortem, [20 vols.], PRO (1904–); also Henry VII, 3 vols. (1898–1955)
Clarendon, Hist. rebellion	E. Hyde, earl of Clarendon, The history of the rebellion and civil wars in England, 6 vols. (1888); repr. (1958) and (1992)
Cobbett, Parl. hist.	W. Cobbett and J. Wright, eds., Cobbett's Parliamentary history of England, 36 vols. (1806–1820)
Colvin, Archs.	H. Colvin, A biographical dictionary of British architects, 1600–1840, 3rd edn (1995)
Cooper, Ath. Cantab.	C. H. Cooper and T. Cooper, Athenae Cantabrigienses, 3 vols. (1858–1913); repr. (1967)
CPR	Calendar of the patent rolls preserved in the Public Record Office (1891–)
Crockford	Crockford's Clerical Directory
CS	Camden Society
CSP	Calendar of state papers [in 11 ser.: domestic, Scotland, Scottish series, Ireland, colonial, Commonwealth, foreign, Spain [at Simancas], Rome, Milan, and Venice]
CYS	Canterbury and York Society
DAB	Dictionary of American biography, 21 vols. (1928–36), repr. in 11 vols. (1964); 10 suppls. (1944–96)
DBB	D. J. Jeremy, ed., Dictionary of business biography, 5 vols. (1984–6)
DCB	G. W. Brown and others, Dictionary of Canadian biography, [14 vols.] (1966–)
Debrett's Peerage	Debrett's Peerage (1803–) [sometimes Debrett's Illustrated peerage]
Desmond, Botanists	R. Desmond, Dictionary of British and Irish botanists and horticulturists (1977); rev. edn (1994)
Dir. Brit. archs.	A. Felstead, J. Franklin, and L. Pinfield, eds., Directory of British architects, 1834–1900 (1993); 2nd edn, ed. A. Brodie and others, 2 vols. (2001)
DLB	J. M. Bellamy and J. Saville, eds., Dictionary of labour biography, [10 vols.] (1972–)
DLitB	Dictionary of Literary Biography
DNB	Dictionary of national biography, 63 vols. (1885–1900), suppl., 3 vols. (1901); repr. in 22 vols. (1908–9); 10 further suppls. (1912–96); Missing persons (1993)
DNZB	W. H. Oliver and C. Orange, eds., The dictionary of New Zealand biography, 5 vols. (1990–2000)
DSAB	W. J. de Kock and others, eds., Dictionary of South African biography, 5 vols. (1968–87)
DSB	C. C. Gillispie and F. L. Holmes, eds., Dictionary of scientific biography, 16 vols. (1970–80); repr. in 8 vols. (1981); 2 vol. suppl. (1990)
DSBB	A. Slaven and S. Checkland, eds., Dictionary of Scottish business biography, 1860–1960, 2 vols. (1986–90)
DSCHT	N. M. de S. Cameron and others, eds., Dictionary of Scottish church history and theology (1993)
Dugdale, Monasticon	W. Dugdale, Monasticon Anglicanum, 3 vols. (1655–72); 2nd edn, 3 vols. (1661–82); new edn, ed. J. Caley, J. Ellis, and B. Bandinel, 6 vols. in 8 pts (1817–30); repr. (1846) and (1970)
DWB	J. E. Lloyd and others, eds., Dictionary of Welsh biography down to 1940 (1959) [Eng. trans. of Y bywgraffiadur Cymreig hyd 1940, 2nd edn (1954)]
EdinR	Edinburgh Review, or, Critical Journal
EETS	Early English Text Society
Emden, Cam.	A. B. Emden, A biographical register of the University of Cambridge to 1500 (1963)
Emden, Oxf.	A. B. Emden, A biographical register of the University of Oxford to AD 1500, 3 vols. (1957–9); also A biographical register of the University of Oxford, AD 1501 to 1540 (1974)
EngHR	English Historical Review
Engraved Brit. ports.	F. M. O'Donoghue and H. M. Hake, Catalogue of engraved British portraits preserved in the department of prints and drawings in the British Museum, 6 vols. (1908–25)
ER	The English Reports, 178 vols. (1900–32)
ESTC	English short title catalogue, 1475–1800 [CD-ROM and online]
Evelyn, Diary	The diary of John Evelyn, ed. E. S. De Beer, 6 vols. (1955); repr. (2000)
Farington, Diary	The diary of Joseph Farington, ed. K. Garlick and others, 17 vols. (1978–98)
Fasti Angl. (Hardy)	J. Le Neve, Fasti ecclesiae Anglicanae, ed. T. D. Hardy, 3 vols. (1854)
Fasti Angl., 1066–1300	[J. Le Neve], Fasti ecclesiae Anglicanae, 1066–1300, ed. D. E. Greenway and J. S. Barrow, [8 vols.] (1968–)
Fasti Angl., 1300–1541	[J. Le Neve], Fasti ecclesiae Anglicanae, 1300–1541, 12 vols. (1962–7)
Fasti Angl., 1541–1857	[J. Le Neve], Fasti ecclesiae Anglicanae, 1541–1857, ed. J. M. Horn, D. M. Smith, and D. S. Bailey, [9 vols.] (1969–)
Fasti Scot.	H. Scott, Fasti ecclesiae Scoticanae, 3 vols. in 6 (1871); new edn, [11 vols.] (1915–)
FO List	Foreign Office List
Fortescue, Brit. army	J. W. Fortescue, A history of the British army, 13 vols. (1899–1930)
Foss, Judges	E. Foss, The judges of England, 9 vols. (1848–64); repr. (1966)
Foster, Alum. Oxon.	J. Foster, ed., Alumni Oxonienses: the members of the University of Oxford, 1715–1886, 4 vols. (1887–8); later edn (1891); also Alumni Oxonienses … 1500–1714, 4 vols. (1891–2); 8 vol. repr. (1968) and (2000)
Fuller, Worthies	T. Fuller, The history of the worthies of England, 4 pts (1662); new edn, 2 vols., ed. J. Nichols (1811); new edn, 3 vols., ed. P. A. Nuttall (1840); repr. (1965)
GEC, Baronetage	G. E. Cokayne, Complete baronetage, 6 vols. (1900–09); repr. (1983) [microprint]
GEC, Peerage	G. E. C. [G. E. Cokayne], The complete peerage of England, Scotland, Ireland, Great Britain, and the United Kingdom, 8 vols. (1887–98); new edn, ed. V. Gibbs and others, 14 vols. in 15 (1910–98); microprint repr. (1982) and (1987)
Genest, Eng. stage	J. Genest, Some account of the English stage from the Restoration in 1660 to 1830, 10 vols. (1832); repr. [New York, 1965]
Gillow, Lit. biog. hist.	J. Gillow, A literary and biographical history or bibliographical dictionary of the English Catholics, from the breach with Rome, in 1534, to the present time, 5 vols. [1885–1902]; repr. (1961); repr. with preface by C. Gillow (1999)
Gir. Camb. opera	Giraldi Cambrensis opera, ed. J. S. Brewer, J. F. Dimock, and G. F. Warner, 8 vols., Rolls Series, 21 (1861–91)
GJ	Geographical Journal

Gladstone, *Diaries*	*The Gladstone diaries: with cabinet minutes and prime-ministerial correspondence*, ed. M. R. D. Foot and H. C. G. Matthew, 14 vols. (1968–94)
GM	*Gentleman's Magazine*
Graves, *Artists*	A. Graves, ed., *A dictionary of artists who have exhibited works in the principal London exhibitions of oil paintings from 1760 to 1880* (1884); new edn (1895); 3rd edn (1901); facs. edn (1969); repr. [1970], (1973), and (1984)
Graves, *Brit. Inst.*	A. Graves, *The British Institution, 1806–1867: a complete dictionary of contributors and their work from the foundation of the institution* (1875); facs. edn (1908); repr. (1969)
Graves, *RA exhibitors*	A. Graves, *The Royal Academy of Arts: a complete dictionary of contributors and their work from its foundation in 1769 to 1904*, 8 vols. (1905–6); repr. in 4 vols. (1970) and (1972)
Graves, *Soc. Artists*	A. Graves, *The Society of Artists of Great Britain, 1760–1791, the Free Society of Artists, 1761–1783: a complete dictionary* (1907); facs. edn (1969)
Greaves & Zaller, *BDBR*	R. L. Greaves and R. Zaller, eds., *Biographical dictionary of British radicals in the seventeenth century*, 3 vols. (1982–4)
Grove, *Dict. mus.*	G. Grove, ed., *A dictionary of music and musicians*, 5 vols. (1878–90); 2nd edn, ed. J. A. Fuller Maitland (1904–10); 3rd edn, ed. H. C. Colles (1927); 4th edn with suppl. (1940); 5th edn, ed. E. Blom, 9 vols. (1954); suppl. (1961) [see also *New Grove*]
Hall, *Dramatic ports.*	L. A. Hall, *Catalogue of dramatic portraits in the theatre collection of the Harvard College library*, 4 vols. (1930–34)
Hansard	*Hansard's parliamentary debates*, ser. 1–5 (1803–)
Highfill, Burnim & Langhans, *BDA*	P. H. Highfill, K. A. Burnim, and E. A. Langhans, *A biographical dictionary of actors, actresses, musicians, dancers, managers, and other stage personnel in London, 1660–1800*, 16 vols. (1973–93)
Hist. U. Oxf.	T. H. Aston, ed., *The history of the University of Oxford*, 8 vols. (1984–2000) [1: *The early Oxford schools*, ed. J. I. Catto (1984); 2: *Late medieval Oxford*, ed. J. I. Catto and R. Evans (1992); 3: *The collegiate university*, ed. J. McConica (1986); 4: *Seventeenth-century Oxford*, ed. N. Tyacke (1997); 5: *The eighteenth century*, ed. L. S. Sutherland and L. G. Mitchell (1986); 6–7: *Nineteenth-century Oxford*, ed. M. G. Brock and M. C. Curthoys (1997–2000); 8: *The twentieth century*, ed. B. Harrison (2000)]
HJ	*Historical Journal*
HMC	Historical Manuscripts Commission
Holdsworth, *Eng. law*	W. S. Holdsworth, *A history of English law*, ed. A. L. Goodhart and H. L. Hanbury, 17 vols. (1903–72)
HoP, *Commons*	*The history of parliament: the House of Commons* [*1386–1421*, ed. J. S. Roskell, L. Clark, and C. Rawcliffe, 4 vols. (1992); *1509–1558*, ed. S. T. Bindoff, 3 vols. (1982); *1558–1603*, ed. P. W. Hasler, 3 vols. (1981); *1660–1690*, ed. B. D. Henning, 3 vols. (1983); *1690–1715*, ed. D. W. Hayton, E. Cruickshanks, and S. Handley, 5 vols. (2002); *1715–1754*, ed. R. Sedgwick, 2 vols. (1970); *1754–1790*, ed. L. Namier and J. Brooke, 3 vols. (1964), repr. (1985); *1790–1820*, ed. R. G. Thorne, 5 vols. (1986); in draft (used with permission): *1422–1504, 1604–1629, 1640–1660*, and *1820–1832*]
IGI	*International Genealogical Index*, Church of Jesus Christ of the Latterday Saints
ILN	*Illustrated London News*
IMC	Irish Manuscripts Commission
Irving, *Scots.*	J. Irving, ed., *The book of Scotsmen eminent for achievements in arms and arts, church and state, law, legislation and literature, commerce, science, travel and philanthropy* (1881)
JCS	*Journal of the Chemical Society*
JHC	*Journals of the House of Commons*
JHL	*Journals of the House of Lords*
John of Worcester, *Chron.*	*The chronicle of John of Worcester*, ed. R. R. Darlington and P. McGurk, trans. J. Bray and P. McGurk, 3 vols., OMT (1995–) [vol. 1 forthcoming]
Keeler, *Long Parliament*	M. F. Keeler, *The Long Parliament, 1640–1641: a biographical study of its members* (1954)
Kelly, *Handbk*	*The upper ten thousand: an alphabetical list of all members of noble families*, 3 vols. (1875–7); continued as *Kelly's handbook of the upper ten thousand for 1878* [1879], 2 vols. (1878–9); continued as *Kelly's handbook to the titled, landed and official classes*, 94 vols. (1880–1973)
LondG	*London Gazette*
LP Henry VIII	J. S. Brewer, J. Gairdner, and R. H. Brodie, eds., *Letters and papers, foreign and domestic, of the reign of Henry VIII*, 23 vols. in 38 (1862–1932); repr. (1965)
Mallalieu, *Watercolour artists*	H. L. Mallalieu, *The dictionary of British watercolour artists up to 1820*, 3 vols. (1976–90); vol. 1, 2nd edn (1986)
Memoirs FRS	*Biographical Memoirs of Fellows of the Royal Society*
MGH	Monumenta Germaniae Historica
MT	*Musical Times*
Munk, *Roll*	W. Munk, *The roll of the Royal College of Physicians of London*, 2 vols. (1861); 2nd edn, 3 vols. (1878)
N&Q	*Notes and Queries*
New Grove	S. Sadie, ed., *The new Grove dictionary of music and musicians*, 20 vols. (1980); 2nd edn, 29 vols. (2001) [also online edn; see also Grove, *Dict. mus.*]
Nichols, *Illustrations*	J. Nichols and J. B. Nichols, *Illustrations of the literary history of the eighteenth century*, 8 vols. (1817–58)
Nichols, *Lit. anecdotes*	J. Nichols, *Literary anecdotes of the eighteenth century*, 9 vols. (1812–16); facs. edn (1966)
Obits. FRS	*Obituary Notices of Fellows of the Royal Society*
O'Byrne, *Naval biog. dict.*	W. R. O'Byrne, *A naval biographical dictionary* (1849); repr. (1990); [2nd edn], 2 vols. (1861)
OHS	Oxford Historical Society
Old Westminsters	*The record of Old Westminsters*, 1–2, ed. G. F. R. Barker and A. H. Stenning (1928); suppl. 1, ed. J. B. Whitmore and G. R. Y. Radcliffe [1938]; 3, ed. J. B. Whitmore, G. R. Y. Radcliffe, and D. C. Simpson (1963); suppl. 2, ed. F. E. Pagan (1978); 4, ed. F. E. Pagan and H. E. Pagan (1992)
OMT	Oxford Medieval Texts
Ordericus Vitalis, *Eccl. hist.*	*The ecclesiastical history of Orderic Vitalis*, ed. and trans. M. Chibnall, 6 vols., OMT (1969–80); repr. (1990)
Paris, *Chron.*	*Matthaei Parisiensis, monachi sancti Albani, chronica majora*, ed. H. R. Luard, Rolls Series, 7 vols. (1872–83)
Parl. papers	*Parliamentary papers* (1801–)
PBA	*Proceedings of the British Academy*

Pepys, *Diary*	*The diary of Samuel Pepys*, ed. R. Latham and W. Matthews, 11 vols. (1970–83); repr. (1995) and (2000)
Pevsner	N. Pevsner and others, Buildings of England series
PICE	*Proceedings of the Institution of Civil Engineers*
Pipe rolls	*The great roll of the pipe for . . .* , PRSoc. (1884–)
PRO	Public Record Office
PRS	*Proceedings of the Royal Society of London*
PRSoc.	Pipe Roll Society
PTRS	*Philosophical Transactions of the Royal Society*
QR	*Quarterly Review*
RC	Record Commissions
Redgrave, *Artists*	S. Redgrave, *A dictionary of artists of the English school* (1874); rev. edn (1878); repr. (1970)
Reg. Oxf.	C. W. Boase and A. Clark, eds., *Register of the University of Oxford*, 5 vols., OHS, 1, 10–12, 14 (1885–9)
Reg. PCS	J. H. Burton and others, eds., *The register of the privy council of Scotland*, 1st ser., 14 vols. (1877–98); 2nd ser., 8 vols. (1899–1908); 3rd ser., [16 vols.] (1908–70)
Reg. RAN	H. W. C. Davis and others, eds., *Regesta regum Anglo-Normannorum, 1066–1154*, 4 vols. (1913–69)
RIBA Journal	*Journal of the Royal Institute of British Architects* [later *RIBA Journal*]
RotP	J. Strachey, ed., *Rotuli parliamentorum ut et petitiones, et placita in parliamento*, 6 vols. (1767–77)
RotS	D. Macpherson, J. Caley, and W. Illingworth, eds., *Rotuli Scotiae in Turri Londinensi et in domo capitulari Westmonasteriensi asservati*, 2 vols., RC, 14 (1814–19)
RS	Record(s) Society
Rymer, *Foedera*	T. Rymer and R. Sanderson, eds., *Foedera, conventiones, literae et cuiuscunque generis acta publica inter reges Angliae et alios quosvis imperatores, reges, pontifices, principes, vel communitates*, 20 vols. (1704–35); 2nd edn, 20 vols. (1726–35); 3rd edn, 10 vols. (1739–45); facs. edn (1967); new edn, ed. A. Clarke, J. Caley, and F. Holbrooke, 4 vols., RC, 50 (1816–30)
Sainty, *Judges*	J. Sainty, ed., *The judges of England, 1272–1990*, SeldS, suppl. ser., 10 (1993)
Sainty, *King's counsel*	J. Sainty, ed., *A list of English law officers and king's counsel*, SeldS, suppl. ser., 7 (1987)
SCH	Studies in Church History
Scots peerage	J. B. Paul, ed. *The Scots peerage, founded on Wood's edition of Sir Robert Douglas's Peerage of Scotland, containing an historical and genealogical account of the nobility of that kingdom*, 9 vols. (1904–14)
SeldS	Selden Society
SHR	*Scottish Historical Review*
State trials	T. B. Howell and T. J. Howell, eds., *Cobbett's Complete collection of state trials*, 34 vols. (1809–28)
STC, 1475–1640	A. W. Pollard, G. R. Redgrave, and others, eds., *A short-title catalogue of . . . English books . . . 1475–1640* (1926); 2nd edn, ed. W. A. Jackson, F. S. Ferguson, and K. F. Pantzer, 3 vols. (1976–91) [see also Wing, *STC*]
STS	Scottish Text Society
SurtS	Surtees Society
Symeon of Durham, *Opera*	*Symeonis monachi opera omnia*, ed. T. Arnold, 2 vols., Rolls Series, 75 (1882–5); repr. (1965)
Tanner, *Bibl. Brit.-Hib.*	T. Tanner, *Bibliotheca Britannico-Hibernica*, ed. D. Wilkins (1748); repr. (1963)
Thieme & Becker, *Allgemeines Lexikon*	U. Thieme, F. Becker, and H. Vollmer, eds., *Allgemeines Lexikon der bildenden Künstler von der Antike bis zur Gegenwart*, 37 vols. (Leipzig, 1907–50); repr. (1961–5), (1983), and (1992)
Thurloe, *State papers*	*A collection of the state papers of John Thurloe*, ed. T. Birch, 7 vols. (1742)
TLS	*Times Literary Supplement*
Tout, *Admin. hist.*	T. F. Tout, *Chapters in the administrative history of mediaeval England: the wardrobe, the chamber, and the small seals*, 6 vols. (1920–33); repr. (1967)
TRHS	*Transactions of the Royal Historical Society*
VCH	H. A. Doubleday and others, eds., *The Victoria history of the counties of England*, [88 vols.] (1900–)
Venn, *Alum. Cant.*	J. Venn and J. A. Venn, *Alumni Cantabrigienses: a biographical list of all known students, graduates, and holders of office at the University of Cambridge, from the earliest times to 1900*, 10 vols. (1922–54); repr. in 2 vols. (1974–8)
Vertue, *Note books*	[G. Vertue], *Note books*, ed. K. Esdaile, earl of Ilchester, and H. M. Hake, 6 vols., Walpole Society, 18, 20, 22, 24, 26, 30 (1930–55)
VF	*Vanity Fair*
Walford, *County families*	E. Walford, *The county families of the United Kingdom, or, Royal manual of the titled and untitled aristocracy of Great Britain and Ireland* (1860)
Walker rev.	A. G. Matthews, *Walker revised: being a revision of John Walker's Sufferings of the clergy during the grand rebellion, 1642–60* (1948); repr. (1988)
Walpole, *Corr.*	*The Yale edition of Horace Walpole's correspondence*, ed. W. S. Lewis, 48 vols. (1937–83)
Ward, *Men of the reign*	T. H. Ward, ed., *Men of the reign: a biographical dictionary of eminent persons of British and colonial birth who have died during the reign of Queen Victoria* (1885); repr. (Graz, 1968)
Waterhouse, *18c painters*	E. Waterhouse, *The dictionary of 18th century painters in oils and crayons* (1981); repr. as *British 18th century painters in oils and crayons* (1991), vol. 2 of *Dictionary of British art*
Watt, *Bibl. Brit.*	R. Watt, *Bibliotheca Britannica, or, A general index to British and foreign literature*, 4 vols. (1824) [many reprs.]
Wellesley index	W. E. Houghton, ed., *The Wellesley index to Victorian periodicals, 1824–1900*, 5 vols. (1966–89); new edn (1999) [CD-ROM]
Wing, *STC*	D. Wing, ed., *Short-title catalogue of . . . English books . . . 1641–1700*, 3 vols. (1945–51); 2nd edn (1972–88); rev. and enl. edn, ed. J. J. Morrison, C. W. Nelson, and M. Seccombe, 4 vols. (1994–8) [see also *STC, 1475–1640*]
Wisden	*John Wisden's Cricketer's Almanack*
Wood, *Ath. Oxon.*	A. Wood, *Athenae Oxonienses . . . to which are added the Fasti*, 2 vols. (1691–2); 2nd edn (1721); new edn, 4 vols., ed. P. Bliss (1813–20); repr. (1967) and (1969)
Wood, *Vic. painters*	C. Wood, *Dictionary of Victorian painters* (1971); 2nd edn (1978); 3rd edn as *Victorian painters*, 2 vols. (1995), vol. 4 of *Dictionary of British art*
WW	*Who's who* (1849–)
WWBMP	M. Stenton and S. Lees, eds., *Who's who of British members of parliament*, 4 vols. (1976–81)
WWW	*Who was who* (1929–)

Wellesley [*formerly* Wesley]**, Arthur, first duke of Wellington** (1769–1852), army officer and prime minister, was the third surviving son of Garret *Wesley, first earl of Mornington (1735–1781), and his wife, Anne (1742–1831), eldest daughter of Arthur Hill, first Viscount Dungannon. The family name was altered from Wesley to the older form Wellesley by Richard Wellesley, second earl, who used this spelling from 1789. Arthur did not sign himself Wellesley until May 1798. There is disagreement over the date and place of his birth, but 1 May 1769 and 6 Merrion Street (later 24 Upper Merrion Street), Dublin, have been accepted by modern biographers. The register of St Peter's Church, Dublin, records his christening under the date 30 April 1769. This is reconcilable with the alternative birth date of 29 April preferred by some earlier authorities, including the *Dictionary of National Biography*, but it would imply a degree of haste in the ceremony unusual except in cases of imminent danger, for which there is no evidence. Both parents subsequently attested to the date 1 May and this was the day kept as his birthday by Arthur himself.

Childhood and early military career Arthur Wesley lost his father at the age of twelve and was thought by his imperious mother to be foolish and dull in comparison with his elder brothers, Richard *Wellesley, second earl of Mornington, and William Wellesley-*Pole, later Baron Maryborough and third earl of Mornington. His only talents seemed to be for playing the violin (which may have come from his father, who was an accomplished amateur musician) and arithmetical calculation. But these minor gifts were obscured by his physical indolence and social awkwardness: signs perhaps of an unhappy and lonely childhood. His education was disjointed and his record undistinguished. As a small boy he attended the diocesan school at Trim, co. Meath, near the family seat at Dangan. He was then taken by his parents to London, where he became a pupil at Brown's Seminary, Chelsea. In 1781 he went to Eton College with his younger brother Gerald, who soon surpassed him scholastically. The little evidence that survives suggests that he was an unsociable and occasionally aggressive schoolboy who made little effort to learn. As a result he was removed from the college in the summer of 1784 to make way for the more promising fourth son, Henry *Wellesley (later Baron Cowley). When his mother moved to the cheaper society of Brussels in 1785 he accompanied her and received lessons in French from their landlord, a lawyer (*avocat*), Jacobus Foubert (not apparently Goubert as usually stated). On Lady Mornington's departure to England she dispatched him to the Academy of Equitation at Angers in preparation for the military career which seemed the only possible employment for such an unpromising boy.

The academy, where Arthur arrived in January 1786, was less a military college than an international finishing school for young men, which had been run for generations by the Pignerolle family; nearly a third of the intake that year came from the British Isles. In addition to fencing, horsemanship, and the science of fortification (none of which seems to have left much mark on him),

Arthur Wellesley, first duke of Wellington (1769–1852), by Sir Thomas Lawrence, *c.*1815–16

there were lessons in mathematics, grammar, and dancing. Out of school, besides drinking, gambling, and youthful rowdiness, there were occasional invitations from the local nobility. At the end of the year, when Arthur reappeared in London, he had visibly improved in manners and social deportment, with a command of fluent if old-fashioned French.

Lord Mornington, after the manner of the Ascendancy aristocracy, took seriously the duty of providing for the family of which he had become the youthful head. In March 1787 a commission was obtained for Arthur as ensign in the 73rd foot, a Highland regiment then in India. Further solicitation procured him an appointment as aide-de-camp to the lord lieutenant of Ireland, Lord Buckingham. To facilitate this (and possibly avoid his being sent to India) a commission as lieutenant in the 76th foot was secured in December. This was quickly followed by an exchange first into the 41st foot in January 1788 and then into the 12th light dragoons in June 1789. As part of Mornington's political ambitions his brother William was found a seat at Westminster, and Arthur replaced him in 1790 as MP for the family borough of Trim (where Arthur is commemorated by a fine obelisk). More military promotion followed. In June 1781 he was commissioned as captain in the 58th foot, exchanging to the 18th light dragoons in October 1792. In little more than five years he had held commissions in six different regiments, though there is no evidence that he served with any of them. As aide-de-camp in Dublin, member of the Irish House of Commons, and manager of the family estate at Dangan, he had more than sufficient occupation. His leisure pursuits were more conventional: drinking, gambling, and getting into debt. But he still played his violin and was showing an interest in serious reading.

The year 1793, which saw the start of the long war with revolutionary France, was also a turning point in Arthur Wesley's private life. In April he obtained a commission as major in the 33rd foot and about the same time proposed to Lady Catherine Sarah Dorothea Pakenham (d. 1831), sister of the young Lord Longford, whom he had been courting since 1792. The offer was declined by her brother on the grounds that Wesley lacked the prospect of being able to support her properly. This blow to his sensitive pride was harder to bear since (perhaps for not unconnected reasons) he had been displaying more activity in the Irish House of Commons, making his maiden speech when seconding the address in January. His emotional response to the snub was to apply himself more single-mindedly to his military profession. He gave up music and (in one of his not uncharacteristic dramatic gestures) burnt his violin. To familiarize himself with drill, he obtained leave from the new lord lieutenant, the duke of Richmond, to attend his military parades; and later that summer he asked Mornington to help him get a posting to one of the corps being formed for service abroad. Nothing came of that, but in September he was promoted to lieutenant-colonel and commanding officer of his regiment.

With this last step Wesley had risen as far up the military ladder as his brother's money and influence could take him. He was now caught in what a contemporary biographer called the 'seniority groove' (Gleig, *Life of Wellington*, 7), from which he could hope to escape only by active service. His chance came in 1794 when his regiment was assigned to an expeditionary force under Lord Moira sent out as reinforcement for the duke of York in the Netherlands. Having embarked at Cork early in June, the 33rd landed at Ostend nineteen days later. Wesley, given command of a rear-guard of three battalions, on his own initiative took them round to Antwerp by boat, arriving somewhat unconventionally before the main column. The outcome of the campaign, however, was virtually decided by the timidity and divisions of Britain's allies. The Austrians withdrew from the Netherlands after the battle of Fleurus (26 June), and Prussian co-operation had been half-hearted from the start. The small British contingent retreated therefore into Holland. In the new year, when the French were able to cross the frozen waterways, the isolated British troops moved off, starving and demoralized, into Hanover, to be evacuated to England in the early spring of 1795. Wesley had earned an official commendation for checking a French column in a minor engagement in September 1794 at Boxtel, but for the British force as a whole the campaign had been a miserable experience, made worse by defective organization and poor leadership. Individual regiments had behaved well, but it was clear to the young Colonel Wesley that nobody on the staff knew how to command an army. His laconic verdict many years later was that it had at least

taught him 'what one ought *not* to do; and that is always something!' (Stanhope, 182).

Early Indian campaigns, 1797–1802 Disillusioned by his first experience of active service Wesley turned his thoughts to civil employment. An optimistic application to his elder brother (now in the government) for the administrative post of secretary at war had no result; nor did a more despairing one to the new lord lieutenant, Lord Camden, for an appointment in the Irish administration. In the autumn of 1795 his regiment joined an expeditionary force destined for the West Indies. Wesley, whose health had suffered in the Netherlands campaign, was ill with fever at the time and the fleet sailed from Portsmouth without him. This was good fortune for him, since it ran straight into a channel gale and seven transports were wrecked on Chesil Beach with great loss of life. When it was sent out again in December it was once more hit by bad weather and Wesley's ship was one of the lucky ones that found their way back to England in February 1796. After a short stay at Poole the 33rd left in April for India, leaving its colonel, again seriously ill, to follow it out. Wesley, now a brevet colonel, eventually sailed from Portsmouth in June 1796.

To occupy himself on the voyage Wesley took with him a library of several hundred volumes. Nearly half of them, including a number on the history, languages, and government of India, he bought in London before he sailed. Others, brought from Ireland, indicated the seriousness with which he had already been studying his profession. Among them were works on military history and the art of war by Frederick the Great, Marshal Saxe, the contemporary French general Dumouriez, and the cosmopolitan soldier General H. Lloyd. Eton had presumably given Wesley enough Latin to read Caesar in the original since his *Commentaria* was among the London purchases. Methodical, strong-willed, and ambitious, Wesley was clearly bent on making the most of the opportunities which India offered.

Having caught up with his convoy at the Cape, Wesley arrived at Calcutta in February 1797. A few months later he received the welcome news that his brother Lord Mornington had been offered an Indian appointment, and at once wrote urging him to accept. Meanwhile he and his regiment went off on an abortive expedition to Manila, in the Spanish Philippines, only to be recalled half way because of the worsening military situation in both Europe and southern India. Early next year he visited Madras and remained there, at the instance of the local British commander General Harris, to act as adviser to the new governor, the reputedly dull and obstinate Lord Clive.

In May Wesley's brother, now Lord Wellesley, arrived in India as governor-general and commander-in-chief, bringing their younger brother Henry as his private secretary. In view of this sudden irruption of the Wellesley family into Indian affairs, it is possible that Harris's noticeable partiality towards Colonel Wesley was not uninfluenced by his connection with the new administration in Calcutta, since otherwise the two men did not get on well. For most of 1798, therefore, Wesley remained at Madras in the slightly equivocal role of unofficial representative of the governor-general, working surreptitiously to secure Lord Clive's co-operation (against the views of his local advisers) with the expansionist plans favoured by his ambitious elder brother.

The immediate problem was Tipu Sultan of Mysore, who was believed to be plotting, with French encouragement, the overthrow of British influence in southern India. Though Colonel Wellesley (as he now signed himself) counselled his brother against precipitate action, in the absence of General Harris he organized the Madras forces in readiness for a conflict. On his advice the friendly nizam of Hyderabad was forcibly extricated from the control of the French officers in his army, and a treaty made to assure the neutrality of the powerful Maratha confederacy further north. When war broke out in February 1799 Wellesley was given command of the native Hyderabad army, stiffened by the attachment of his own 33rd regiment. This appointment brought a sharp protest from General Baird who, despite being senior in rank, had been given an inferior command. General Harris, however, had been impressed by Wellesley's careful preparations for the campaign, and the nizam's prime minister had specifically requested that Wellesley should be in charge of his ruler's contingent.

During the advance against the great fortress town of Seringapatam the 33rd distinguished itself in a skirmish at Malavalli on 27 March against a column of Tipu's French-trained troops. This was followed, however, by an ignominious failure of a night attack in difficult enclosed country outside Seringapatam. Wellesley, suffering from dysentery at the time, was momentarily shaken by this reverse, though he took the position without difficulty next day. The rueful moral he drew was never to attack a prepared position by night that had not been reconnoitred. In the assault of 4 May on Seringapatam he was in command of the reserves but after its capture was appointed governor. This brought another protest from the peppery General Baird. It was, however, a defensible choice, since Wellesley enjoyed good relations with the local Indians and Baird notoriously did not. His share of prize money for this campaign was £4000, a sum which just covered the advances his brother had made to him from time to time for the purchase of commissions: but Lord Wellesley regally refused his offer of repayment. For the rest of 1799 and 1800 he was busy repressing looting, enforcing on his own men respect for Indian customs, and breaking up marauding bands of former enemy soldiers. The most formidable and elusive of these was led by the guerrilla leader Dhundia Wagh, who was chased first into Maratha territory and then back again into Hyderabad before he was defeated and killed. In an unconventional act of compassion Wellesley made himself responsible for the welfare and upbringing of Dhundia's four-year-old son, discovered among the enemy's baggage.

At the end of 1800 Wellesley became increasingly involved in the plans of the governor-general, now the Marquess Wellesley, to intensify the war against the French dominions overseas, and in December he went to Trincomalee in Ceylon to organize a sea-borne expeditionary force. The original idea was to attack the French naval base on the Île de France (Mauritius). Nothing came of this, however, because of the refusal of the local British naval commander to participate. Then, in January 1801, Wellesley was warned by the governor-general that if his force had to be employed against a more important target it would be necessary to appoint a more senior officer, probably General Baird, leaving him in as second in command. It was now Wellesley's turn to protest, at what he chose to regard as his supersession, in language understandable between candid brothers but hardly fitting in a colonel addressing his commander-in-chief. Worse followed. In February he learned from Lord Clive in Madras that the government in London had decided to send the expeditionary force to the Red Sea port of Mocha (in modern Yemen) to assist the current operations against the French in Egypt. Without waiting for orders from Calcutta, Wellesley sailed off with his force, intending first to revictual at Bombay and then proceed to the Red Sea. It is difficult to interpret this remarkable action as anything other than an attempt to forestall Baird's assumption of command. At Bombay, however, he fell victim to an attack of the distressing skin complaint known as the Malabar itch. The delay gave Baird time to catch up with his errant expeditionary force and take it on to Mocha. Wellesley was left behind to endure the heroic remedy of acid baths and vent his frustration in angry letters to Lord Wellesley and to another of his brothers, the discreet Henry. It was painfully obvious that he had set his heart on having an independent command, which would bring him both promotion and prize money, and that he had allowed his ambition to overcome his judgement. Though he soon made his peace with Baird, his resentment against his elder brother took some time to cool.

Defeat of the Marathas, 1802–1805 In April 1802, on his return to Mysore, Wellesley was finally promoted to the rank of major-general, but only on the Indian strength. More importantly, at the end of the year quarrels between the Maratha chiefs of the Deccan forced the peshwa of Poona to seek protection from the Bombay presidency. This created a welcome opportunity for Lord Wellesley to break the power of the formidable Maratha confederacy. His brother assumed, this time correctly, that he would be in charge of the military operation, and his appointment ended the breach with the governor-general. In June 1803, having without difficulty restored the peshwa to his throne, he received plenary political and military authority to pacify the Deccan. When negotiations broke down in August, he declared war on Sindhia and Berar, the two leading Maratha states, and in a surprise attack captured almost without loss the great fortress of Ahmadnagar, regarded as one of the strongest in India. Pushing another 120 miles north-east he made contact with the Maratha forces on 23 September.

Expecting, on the basis of Indian intelligence, to meet a body of only some 20,000 infantry, Wellesley found himself in the presence of the whole Maratha army of some 50,000, drawn up in a strong position behind the River

Kaitna. His force, reduced by his questionable decision to send Colonel Stevenson's Hyderabad contingent round by a different route, numbered only 7000. His men had already marched 20 miles that day and retreat would have been almost as hazardous as an advance. He took the bolder course. Guessing correctly that there must be a ford between two villages on opposite sides of the river, he crossed below the left flank of the Maratha position and placed his force in a narrow angle between the Kaitna and a tributary river, the Juah: a position which shortened his front and protected his flanks, but would have been a death-trap had he been beaten. The Marathas, under their French officers, skilfully changed front to meet him, and a desperate battle followed before victory was assured. Wellesley's right flank advanced too far and came under heavy artillery fire near Assaye village. Of approximately 5000 men who crossed the Kaitna over a third became casualties, a disproportionate number being among the British troops. Wellesley contributed by his personal example to the result. In the thick of the fighting throughout, he had one horse killed under him and another wounded.

Assaye was a remarkable victory, in which audacity and aggressiveness succeeded against a well-trained and numerically greatly superior enemy. Given the situation in which he found himself (partly his own fault), Wellesley's decision to risk a battle was perhaps unavoidable, certainly defensible, but it was hardly a textbook battle. The only justification is that he won it: a consideration which commonly outweighs all academic criticisms. Many years later he said that Assaye was the finest thing he had ever done in the fighting line—meaning, no doubt, that it was a triumph against all the odds. It undoubtedly made his reputation and ended all the talk of unfair family favouritism.

It also broke the morale of the Marathas. At Argaon on 29 November they were routed with only minor British casualties and early in December the raja of Berar's fortress of Gawilgarh fell after a weak resistance. Before the end of the year peace was made with both Sindhia and Berar. By the summer of 1804, however, Wellesley was anxious to get back to England. He was aggrieved by the failure of the authorities at home to confirm his last promotion and felt that as long as he remained in India he would be professionally in a disadvantageous position. In any case he did not want to stay after the expiry of Lord Wellesley's term of office. A further consideration was that he had suffered constantly in India from minor tropical illnesses, even though in later life he stoutly affirmed that India had toughened his previously weak constitution. From every point of view Europe offered a more promising field for his intensely ambitious nature. On 10 March 1805 he sailed for home. He was now Sir Arthur, having been made KB the previous August, and he had accumulated a fortune of £42,000, enough to give him financial independence. Success had turned him into a supremely confident man, convinced that nothing was impossible if the will-power and attention to details were present. His professional education, he felt, was now complete. He returned from India, he said afterwards, understanding 'as much of military matters as I have ever done since' (Guedalla, 117–18).

Return to England and marriage, 1806–1807 During Wellesley's homeward voyage he learned that Lord Wellesley had been recalled because of official dissatisfaction with his Maratha policy. As soon as he arrived, therefore, on 10 September, he began to lobby the government on Richard's behalf. It was when engaged on this task that he had his solitary meeting with Nelson in the anteroom of the old war and Colonial Office in Downing Street a few days later. He had much talk with most of the leading ministers, including Pitt and Castlereagh, though they were evidently more impressed by Richard's brother than by Richard's policy. Wellesley soon found himself in the congenial position of advising the government on Indian politics and European strategy. In December, however, he was selected to command a brigade in the abortive expedition to Hanover and wasted six weeks in the neighbourhood of Bremen before returning to England in February 1806. Despite Pitt's death the previous month, the formation of a coalition ministry, and his friend Castlereagh's consequent loss of office, Wellesley's career continued to progress. His 1802 promotion to major-general was confirmed and in January 1806 he was given the colonelcy of the 33rd, made vacant by the death of Lord Cornwallis. These two appointments made him a comparatively rich man. He was posted to a brigade near Hastings, and in the autumn of that year wrote the first of a series of mainly critical memoranda for the government on various projects that had been suggested for helping the independence movements in the Spanish colonies. To add to his responsibilities, in April 1806, at the instance of the new prime minister, Lord Grenville, he was elected MP for Rye so that he could defend his brother in the House of Commons against charges of maladministration and fraud.

In the middle of these preoccupations came one of the most inexplicable actions of Wellesley's life: his marriage to Catherine Pakenham. They had not met for twelve years and he had never written to her in all the time he had been away, though they had received news of each other through a common friend, Lady Olivia Sparrow. It is not easy to tell from his friendly remarks about Kitty (as she was generally known) and references to the disappointment he had suffered in 1793 what his feelings really were. Certainly by 1802 Kitty had decided that the affair was over, became engaged to another man, broke it off, and suffered a nervous breakdown which destroyed her youthful charm and self-confidence. On Wellesley's return in 1805, however, Olivia Sparrow threw herself into her matchmaking role with renewed energy. Having first revived Kitty's faltering hopes, she reminded Wellesley of her continued devotion to him and his continued duty to marry her. He obediently sent off a written proposal which Kitty accepted, with the timid suggestion that he should wait until he saw her before committing himself. That was in November 1805, and was followed, on his own confession, by considerable misgivings on his part.

However, when he returned from Germany he secured a week's leave, crossed to Ireland, and the wedding took place in Dublin on 10 April 1806. His wife subsequently joined him in London, and Arthur, the first of their two sons, was born in Harley Street on 3 February 1807, followed by Charles in January 1808. His motives for the marriage can only be guessed, but it was to turn out an unhappy relationship for both of them.

Chief secretary for Ireland, 1807–1808 In October 1806 parliament was dissolved and Wellesley was without a seat until one was found for him with Treasury assistance at Mitchell, a Cornish pocket borough, in January 1807. In March, however, the Portland ministry, containing several of his friends, took office and through the instrumentality of Lord Hawkesbury he was offered the post of chief secretary for Ireland. He accepted on condition it should not be allowed to interfere with his army career. Though re-elected for Mitchell he transferred in May to a cheaper seat at Newport, Isle of Wight. Learning soon afterwards of plans for a Baltic expedition, he put in an immediate application to serve. In due course he was given command of a division in the force under Lord Cathcart which was sent at the end of July to impound the Danish fleet. During the subsequent siege of Copenhagen he defeated a diversionary force at Kjöge on 29 August with no difficulty and little loss. By the beginning of October he was back in Dublin where his post had been kept open for him despite his request to be relieved. Unexciting as the Danish campaign had been, it confirmed his Indian reputation and earned him the thanks of the House of Commons. He had no great enthusiasm for the South American plans of the government on which he was still working, but at least his growing intimacy with the ministers gave him confidence of early employment in the field. As he wrote to a friend in India, since he had returned to England 'I have got pretty high up the tree' (Maxwell, 1.90).

Meanwhile Wellesley applied himself with his customary assiduity to his duties in Dublin and at Westminster. Courteous and firm, he brought to the multifarious tasks of a chief secretary a brisk efficiency which won him general respect. The larger part of his work lay in the unedifying field of Irish patronage, particularly demanding in the early summer of 1807 because of the imminent general election. He found time, however, to reorganize the Dublin police and introduce an Irish Insurrection Bill. Though pessimistic about the ultimate success of the recent union between England and Ireland, he took the view that government policy should at least aim at obliterating the distinction between protestant and Catholic. There was little room in his sceptical mind for religious partisanship. Back in London he dutifully conferred at ministerial request with General Miranda, the envoy of the revolutionary party in South America, but privately suggested to ministers that it made more strategic sense to strike a blow at Napoleon in Europe. In May 1808, within a week of his promotion to lieutenant-general, that opportunity came with the popular uprising in Spain against the French military occupation. It was, he told ministers, 'a crisis in which a great effort might be made

with advantage' (Guedalla, 151). The government, and indeed public opinion in general, were of the same mind. In June, to his great satisfaction, Wellesley was ordered to take a force already assembled in Ireland to the Peninsula to co-operate with the Portuguese and Spanish armies.

The Peninsular War: Vimeiro and the convention of Cintra The expedition, 9000 strong, left Cork on 12 July. It was weak in cavalry and transport, but contained some of the best infantry in the army. Sailing ahead in a fast frigate Wellesley called at Corunna to talk to the Spanish and at Oporto to the Portuguese authorities before going on to confer with the commander of the British naval squadron in the Tagus. The advice he received confirmed his view that the best place to disembark was Mondego Bay, 100 miles north of Junot's force in Lisbon. On 30 July he received the unwelcome news that since the French army in Portugal was larger than had previously been assumed, the British expeditionary force was to be reinforced by another 15,000 men and placed under the command of Sir Hew Dalrymple, the governor of Gibraltar, with General Burrard as his second in command, who were to be joined later by General Moore. Wellesley, already strengthened by 5000 men under General Spencer from Cadiz, decided to beat Junot, if he could, before his seniors arrived. The disembarkation of his force was carried out in the first week of August and he then moved off south by the coastal road. His first encounter with French troops came at Roliça on 17 August when contact was made with General Delaborde's corps. Enjoying a considerable numerical advantage, Wellesley launched a neat enveloping attack marred only by the rashness of some of the regiments in his centre. Delaborde made an adroit retreat and Wellesley's deficiencies in cavalry prevented him from making an effective pursuit.

Nevertheless, British losses were few and Wellesley's troops, most of them under fire for the first time, were impressed by what they saw of their new commander. Moving on south he halted at Vimeiro to cover the landing of two more brigades from England. A less welcome arrival on 20 August was General Burrard, who forbade any further advance until they were joined by General Moore, then at Mondego. When Junot, coming up from Lisbon, attacked the following day, however, Wellesley was still in command.

Vimeiro was the first of Wellesley's classic defensive battles. Though inferior in cavalry and artillery, he had nearly 19,000 men against the 14,000 which Junot brought into the field. He arranged his force in a shallow arc with the right flank bent back towards the sea and his left on a high ridge north of Vimeiro village. In a forward central position on Vimeiro Hill he placed a strong detachment covered by enfilade fire from the high ground on his left. Attacking in column in their usual manner the French were driven back (as most British military experts including Wellesley thought they would always be) by musketry volleys followed by bayonet charges from the British infantry drawn up in lines two deep. On the left, two French brigades attempting an outflanking movement were pushed northwards away from their main body.

Only Wellesley's lack of cavalry and the belated appearance of Burrard on the battlefield saved Junot from a crushing defeat. Next day he sent Kellermann to propose an armistice to the recently arrived Dalrymple. This was followed by the so-called convention of Cintra, ratified on 30 August. By its terms Lisbon and the French-held fortresses in Portugal were to be surrendered and the French troops conveyed back to France in British vessels. At Dalrymple's request Wellesley signed the armistice document, though he did not approve of it and had no hand in drawing it up. Not surprisingly his relations with Dalrymple were frosty and, like the troops he had just led, he was angry that so little advantage had been taken of the victory. Rather insubordinately he let his opinions be known in London and did his best to get Moore appointed commander in Portugal. Snubbing various suggestions for his own further employment in the Peninsula, Wellesley obtained leave to return to Dublin and resume his neglected duties as chief secretary.

Apart from the failure to exploit the victory, the convention of Cintra was not without advantages. It secured not only the removal of the main French army from Portugal but the surrender of the two strong fortresses of Elvas and Almeida, commanding the great roads into Portugal guarded on the Spanish side by Badajoz and Ciudad Rodrigo. The outraged British public, however, was blind to everything except the inexcusable caution, amounting to culpable timidity, which had thrown away the fruits of a rare victory over the French. Bowing to the universal indignation the government instituted a court of inquiry at which Wellesley, as well as Dalrymple and Burrard, was called to give evidence. Wellesley wisely confined himself to a defence of his own actions. Though the report of the inquiry, dated 22 December, was bland and inconclusive, the two senior generals were never employed on active service again.

The Peninsular War: Talavera For Wellesley, by contrast, the episode was a disguised piece of good fortune. In the middle of January 1809 Sir John Moore was killed at Corunna in a battle which successfully covered the embarkation of his shattered army. In a matter of weeks, therefore, three senior generals with Peninsular experience, including the ablest of them all, had been removed from Wellesley's path. The cabinet were still determined to pursue their interventionist policy, and even before the Corunna evacuation they had signed an alliance with the provisional government in Spain. They were heartened by Wellesley's confident advice that Portugal, with its long sea coast and short land communications, offered an advantageous base for operations against Napoleon. At the beginning of April he was appointed commander of yet another expeditionary force to the Peninsula. A degree of realism, however, had entered into ministerial strategy. His instructions in 1808 had been to liberate Portugal and Spain, and secure the expulsion of French forces from the Peninsula. In 1809 his letter of service laid down more soberly that his principal object was the defence of Portugal.

Having resigned both his Irish secretaryship and his seat in parliament, Wellesley arrived on 22 April in Lisbon, where there was still a small British garrison. He reorganized his 21,000-strong force into integrated, self-sufficient divisions, with Portuguese battalions brigaded with British regiments, and then rapidly moved north to secure Oporto. Soult, leisurely preparing to withdraw from his isolated position in the city, was surprised by an improvised crossing of the Douro River. Evacuating the port on 12 May he made a precipitate retreat into Spain, losing a fifth of his men and all his guns on the way. Wellesley then turned his attention to Spain, and after negotiations with the Spanish commander Cuesta a joint advance was planned against Madrid.

After Vimeiro, Wellesley had advised his government that little reliance could be placed on the Spanish army and that, though an advance into Spain might be attempted as a strategic method of defending Portugal, it would have to be on the assumption of a quick withdrawal if faced by a large concentration of French troops. Despite this, the campaign of 1809 was in many respects a recapitulation of Moore's ill-fated operations of 1808 and with nearly the same catastrophic outcome. It rested on delusive assurances of Spanish support and was undertaken with inadequate knowledge of the strength and movements of the opposing forces. Wellesley moved into Spain at the end of June along the valley of the Tagus. Overestimating the time it would take Soult to reorganize, he thought that the Portuguese forces under Beresford would be sufficient to protect his northern flank. His southern flank was to be covered by a second Spanish army under Venegas which had been ordered up to the Madrid area.

In the event everything went wrong. Venegas's march was countermanded by the supreme junta; Spanish promises of transport and food were not kept. Between 20 July and 20 August the British army received only ten days' rations. Meanwhile Victor's forces in front of Venegas were reinforced from Madrid and Soult was ordered south from Salamanca to cut the British lines of communication. When contact was made with the French, Cuesta's obstinacy frustrated Wellesley's wish for an immediate attack, and when they joined battle a few days later it was on less favourable terms.

Talavera was Wellesley's second great defensive battle, comparable to Waterloo and almost as hard fought. His disposition of the allied army and choice of ground were admirable. The naturally strong position on his right, resting on the River Tagus and Talavera village and protected in front by olive groves and irrigation channels, was allotted to the suspect Spanish troops. His centre was behind a stream and shallow ravine, with a half-finished gun emplacement occupying a prominent site. His left was withdrawn along high ground overlooking a valley. The fighting started on 27 July with an unsuccessful French night attack and continued more fiercely on the 28th. The allied army numbered some 52,000 men (21,500 being Wellesley's Anglo-Portuguese), compared with the 46,000 French of Victor and Jourdan, under the nominal command of King Joseph. On the evening of the second day, after desperate fighting, the French began to retreat even though they had not used their reserves. Wellesley's men by that time were too exhausted to follow up. Allied casualties, at about 7000, were almost as heavy as the French, and a disproportionate share was borne by the British regiments. This was not all. Shortly afterwards Wellesley learned of the formidable threat of Soult's army coming down from the north. He therefore left his sick and wounded at Talavera under the protection of Cuesta (who promptly abandoned them), recrossed the Tagus, and took his famished and disorderly troops back to the shelter of Badajoz on the Portuguese frontier.

Wellesley had escaped the French trap by the narrowest of margins. It was a sharp lesson and he drew the natural but mistaken moral. Writing to Castlereagh on 25 August he listed all the shortcomings of his Spanish allies and concluded savagely that 'I can only tell you that I feel no inclination to join in cooperation with them again' (Maxwell, 1.174). Talavera has been criticized as a useless battle; certainly it was a victory that would have been impossible to exploit. Yet, as with Moore's campaign, it yielded a measure of political, if not military, profit. The British cabinet and public had been longing for a success in Spain which would avenge Corunna, and the Spanish authorities had been given tangible evidence of British readiness to give them support. The victory earned Wellesley a peerage (4 September) and a pension as Viscount Wellington. But opinion at home was divided, and the whig parliamentary opposition was becoming sceptical of the whole concept of defending Portugal.

From August 1809 to February 1810 Wellington's army saw no fighting. For their general, however, it was an anxious period in which the future of his command hung in the balance. The defeat of Austria at Wagram in July 1809 set Napoleon free to turn his immense military resources against Spain and in December he announced his intention to lead an army of 140,000 veterans to drive the British from the Peninsula. At home a political crisis in the autumn weakened the ministry and brought about the resignation of Castlereagh, the only minister in whom Wellington had any trust. When parliament met in January 1810 the whig opposition mounted a fierce attack on Perceval's depleted administration. The Talavera campaign was described as a disaster and Wellington's motives in undertaking it impugned. Many of his own officers were openly critical of their chief, and an atmosphere of defeatism was detectable in both London and Lisbon.

Not surprisingly the new secretary of state for war, Lord Liverpool, in a lengthy correspondence from the autumn of 1809 to the spring of 1810, made it his business to elicit from Wellington his considered views on the basic problems which confronted him in the Peninsula. Could he defend Portugal against the vastly superior forces likely to be brought against him? Would Cadiz be a better base than Lisbon? If he could not maintain himself in Portugal, when and in what circumstances should he consider evacuation? Much of what Liverpool wrote was probably designed to obtain information and arguments which could be used against criticism in parliament and at court.

He invariably accepted Wellington's view of what was the right strategy and did his best to convince him of the cabinet's confidence in his leadership. Nevertheless, ministers were gravely concerned for the safety of Wellington's force. Liverpool felt it right to emphasize that it was not one of Britain's armies, but its only army, and that its destruction would have profound political as well as military consequences.

While Wellington returned firm and confident, if not always very specific, answers, his occasionally testy letters (and still more the intemperate and sometimes unreasonable language he used about the government privately) showed the strain he was under. In their different spheres both he and the cabinet were fighting for their professional existence. But though Wellington was irritated by what seemed to him the unnecessary caution of the ministers, he did not ignore the points raised by Liverpool. Indeed, his actions in the twelve months after Talavera were marked by the caution and avoidance of desperate battles which the secretary for war enjoined. In the autumn and winter of 1809, while the Spanish armies were being systematically routed by the French, he moved his own troops to the Mondego valley in northern Portugal. Unknown to the cabinet he had already surveyed the Torres Vedras district in front of Lisbon and given detailed orders for the construction of initially two and finally three lines of defences: the first of which would at least delay, the second halt, and the third (if the worst came to the worst) cover an embarkation. In July 1809 he had been appointed marshal-general of Portugal. Using his new powers to the limit, in March 1810 he revived the old Portuguese laws which authorized in a national emergency the mobilization of the entire male population. Simultaneously he issued a proclamation directing the inhabitants of the districts through which the French would advance to fall back towards Lisbon, taking their goods and cattle with them.

The Peninsular War: Busaco, Almeida, and Badajoz In the event Napoleon's divorce and his marriage to Marie-Louise of Austria in the spring of 1810 made him delegate the command of a much reduced army of Portugal to Masséna, one of his ablest commanders. Wellington, while detaching 12,000 men under Hill to stiffen Spanish resistance against a possible advance south of the Tagus, remained on the defensive in the north where he judged the main attack would come. He refused to weaken his force by sending assistance to the Spanish garrison of Ciudad Rodrigo and the fortress eventually surrendered to Masséna in July. This was followed by the unexpectedly early capture by the French of Almeida on the Portuguese side of the frontier. As Masséna advanced Wellington fell back, issuing another appeal to the civil population to remove or destroy everything that might be of use to the French invaders. On 21 September Hill's corps rejoined him to bring the army up to 25,000. With these, and about the same number of Portuguese, he had to face Masséna's 65,000.

Wellington's eventual decision to stand and fight at

Busaco was probably influenced by a number of considerations: the political panic in Lisbon as refugees came pouring in, the increasing doubts among his own officers, and the demoralizing effect on his men of continuous retreat, from which Moore had suffered in 1808. Masséna clinched the issue by choosing, through ignorance, the most westerly and worst road to Lisbon through Viseu and Coimbra. Aligning his force from north to south along the Busaco Ridge, a natural defensive feature he had previously noted, Wellington met the French attack on 27 September. The main weakness of his position, apart from his chronic insufficiency of cavalry and guns, was the sheer length (over 5 miles) of his front. In the opening attacks Reynier's corps actually pierced his line before being thrown back. But skilful use of the reverse slope and a recently improved lateral road, which enabled him to reinforce quickly any threatened point, gave Wellington in the end an emphatic victory. French casualties at 4500 were heavy compared with the allied total of 1200 shared equally between the Portuguese, who fought excellently, and the British.

Any hope Wellington might have had of stopping Masséna was disappointed. The French found a way round his left and Wellington was forced to resume his retreat southward. When Masséna reached the Torres Vedras defences in October, however, a brief examination was enough to convince him of the impossibility of his task: he had no stomach for a second Busaco. After waiting for a month with his supplies steadily diminishing, he made a masterly retreat to Santarem, 30 miles to the north-east, and in the spring returned to Spain. Wellington's drastic and comprehensive preparations, though gaining only the partial co-operation of the Portuguese population, had brought him a strategic success which permanently shaped the course of the war. After 1810 little doubt remained on either side that Portugal could be held against any French attack.

Wellington's next objective was to prevent such attacks by capturing the Spanish fortresses which commanded the only two roads into central Portugal suitable for the passage of large armies: Ciudad Rodrigo in the north and Badajoz in the south, separated by some 130 miles. Beresford, whom he had detached with 22,000 men in March to operate on the River Guadiana, was ordered in April to undertake the siege of Badajoz. He himself invested Almeida, the only Portuguese fortress in French hands, as a preliminary to moving against Ciudad Rodrigo. His Indian experience, as he once admitted, had perhaps made him trust too much to rapidity of attack and underestimate the potential for resistance of fortresses manned by resolute troops under a resourceful commander. The chief problem, however, was his numerical weakness. Against superior French manpower his best weapons were speed and surprise. Sieges pinned his army down to a particular locality and gave time for his opponents to concentrate against him. Wellington's simultaneous operations in the summer of 1811 demonstrated these inherent weaknesses as well as the self-willed streak in his own character.

Before Almeida fell Masséna, showing unanticipated resilience, launched an attack on the covering British force east of the town. With inferior numbers and a disparity of one to three in cavalry, Wellington's dispositions at the battle of Fuentes d'Oñoro fell short of his usual standards. Though his centre and left were securely posted along a ridge, his extreme right hung somewhat in the air on the edge of a level plain. Moreover, the units posted there included a newly arrived British division and some Spanish irregulars. In the battle which followed on 5 May his left flank, against which there had been a French feint on 3 May, was hardly engaged. In the centre, the village of Fuentes d'Oñoro was the scene of savage street fighting in which the French gave as good as they got. On the right his inexperienced troops were completely broken by French cavalry attacks. In this critical situation Wellington made a bold decision to pull back that part of his line to a more defensible position at right angles to his original front. This risky manoeuvre, skilfully covered by the light division, enabled him to keep between Masséna's army and Almeida, though at the cost of uncovering his own lines of communication back through Sabugal. In the night of 7–8th, however, frustrated by the insubordination of his senior commanders, Masséna disengaged. For Wellington it was a lucky escape. Writing to his brother William a month later he confessed it had been the most difficult battle he had ever fought: 'If Bony had been there we should have been beaten' (Maxwell, 1.228).

Almeida fell a few days later, though poor staff work permitted the French garrison to escape. Worse news came from the south. The battle of Albuera, fought by Beresford on 16 May against Soult's relieving force, resulted in some of the most murderous casualties of the war. The British lost some 4000 out of their total of 7600; the Spanish and Portuguese 2000; the French 7000 out of 24,000. Napoleon could afford such losses; Wellington could not. 'Another such battle would ruin us,' he wrote grimly to his brother Henry, the British attaché at Cadiz (Longford, *Years of the Sword*, 258). On arriving at Badajoz three days later he decided to renew the attack on the fortress, but made the double mistake of relying on ancient Portuguese siege guns and assuming he could capture Badajoz (a stronger fortress than Almeida with a larger garrison) before Soult could recover from his defeat. Two attempts in June failed before he abandoned the siege and in the face of the advancing French returned to Ciudad Rodrigo. His disease-ridden army, however, was too weak to permit more than a blockade of the town, and in September Marmont (Masséna's successor) was able to revictual the garrison. After some inconclusive manoeuvring both sides then drew apart.

In midwinter, however, having learned that Marmont had detached part of his force to aid French operations in Valencia, Wellington resumed the offensive, despite the lateness of the season. Three months' rest in cantonments, better preparations, and a modern siege-train which arrived during the summer had transformed the capabilities of his army. After a brief investment the under-garrisoned fortress of Ciudad Rodrigo was stormed in January 1812. It was the only siege undertaken by Wellington which went according to plan, though with heavy casualties and their usual aftermath, looting and violence. The success encouraged him to attempt another quick operation against Badajoz. Preparations started in mid-March, but since the first siege the defences had been improved, the garrison resupplied, and time was running short. It was not impossible that Marmont might move south to reinforce Soult, who himself was only three days' march away. When the assault took place on the night of 6–7 April the three breaches in the fortifications were far from adequate. The main storming-parties suffered enormous casualties and ironically victory came only as a result of following up diversionary attacks against lightly held points not previously bombarded. British losses were nearly 5000, and when the following day Wellington saw the steaming piles of corpses in front of the main breach his self-control momentarily broke down. The ferocious animal courage shown by his men had its blacker side in two days of looting, arson, rape, and drunkenness which followed the capture of the town.

Campaigning in Spain, 1812 Nevertheless, in the space of three months the two strong fortresses opening the way into Spain had been captured in the face of 80,000 French troops, and this was followed in mid-May by the destruction of the bridge of boats at Almaraz on the Tagus, which was the link between the French army of Portugal and its army of the south. It was a series of successes which strengthened the moral ascendancy that Wellington was already beginning to impose on the French marshals and confirmed his own army's faith in his leadership.

Wellington himself in the early summer of 1812 was full of confidence. He had received substantial reinforcements from England while the French armies had been reduced in numbers and quality by withdrawals for Napoleon's Russian campaign. Towards the end of May he wrote to Lord Liverpool that he was prepared to advance into Castile and bring Marmont to a general action. Though the French still had some 280,000 men in the Peninsula, their armies were divided by rivers, mountain ranges, and the mutual antipathies of their generals, and weakened by difficulties in supply, the continued existence of pockets of Spanish regular troops, and widespread harassment by Spanish guerrillas. Wellington hoped that further distraction would be provided by a British sea-borne expedition under Bentinck to be launched from Sicily against Valencia, attacks from the Spanish army under Ballesteros in the south-west, and naval demonstrations along the Biscayan coast.

As things turned out, there was little synchronization between the different parts of this ambitious strategy. Sicilian politics and Bentinck's vacillations delayed the landing in Valencia until late summer and Ballesteros signally failed to mount any serious threat. When Wellington moved into Spain in mid-June he was held up at Salamanca by recently improved defences and was unwilling to provoke a battle. Marmont, on the other hand, still in the process of concentrating his forces, refused to attack

Wellington in a prepared position. As a result there were several weeks of cautious movement in which the more lightly equipped French infantry outmarched, and Marmont outmanoeuvred, their British opponents. At one point there was even a threat to Wellington's line of communication with his base at Ciudad Rodrigo. On 22 July, however, with both armies moving west on parallel lines, Marmont allowed a gap to open up between his vanguard and his centre which Wellington immediately exploited. The 3rd division, which unknown to Marmont had been ordered up from Salamanca, rolled back the leading French divisions while Wellington developed a Frederician oblique attack from left to right. Marmont was wounded early in the engagement and had to relinquish command; an initially successful attack by Clausel on the allied centre was first stopped and then crushed by Wellington's reserves. Though he later claimed that the abandonment by the Spanish of a bridge across the River Tormes alone prevented a stubborn French retreat from developing into a rout, in fact there was no vigorous pursuit on his part. As it was, the French suffered some 7000 casualties and had about the same number taken prisoner, compared with only about 5000 casualties on the allied side. Salamanca, Wellington's greatest victory so far and one which the military historian Napier judged to be the most skilful of all his battles, brought him a marquessate (3 October 1812) to outrank the earldom (18 February 1812) conferred on him after the capture of Ciudad Rodrigo.

More important than this rapid ascent through the peerage was the problem of Wellington's next step: to pursue the defeated French army under Clausel or reap an easy political success by entering Madrid. He chose the latter: partly to rest and resupply his own army, which was suffering from sickness, unusually heavy losses among its senior officers, and shortages of food and money; partly to assist his home government (still precariously holding on to office despite Perceval's assassination in May) with a spectacular event more likely to catch the attention of Europe than the victory that made it possible. Having entered the Spanish capital to a tumultuous welcome on 12 August 1812, Wellington spent three weeks there before turning north against Clausel. The French, however, prudently fell back past Valladolid and Burgos to make contact with their remaining army behind the River Ebro. Lacking adequate artillery, Wellington's hasty siege of the castle at Burgos at the end of September failed ignominiously after five assaults. With the French beginning to concentrate against him once more, Wellington was now in a dangerously exposed position. Having lost 2000 men to no purpose he called off the siege and on 21 October began a long and disorderly retreat to the shelter of Ciudad Rodrigo, pressed hard by greatly superior French forces. At the end of the month he was back in familiar territory on the River Tormes, where he was joined by Hill's troops recalled from Madrid.

It was a disappointing end to a year that had promised so much. Wellington's hopes of pushing the French behind the Ebro had vanished and both he and his army were out of humour. A caustic circular letter he sent to his divisional and brigade commanders denouncing the indiscipline of their men during the retreat was evidence of his bad temper but did nothing to improve theirs. Moore's campaign of 1808, the Talavera campaign of 1809, and now the retreat from Salamanca in 1812 seemed part of a pattern he could not break. For this the fundamental reason was that the French armies in aggregate were always too strong to allow Wellington to exploit any of his local victories, however brilliant. Out of this realization came a new approach to the role of the Spanish armed forces. It amounted, in fact, to a change of heart among both allies.

The liberation of Spain, 1812–1814 In Spain, a larger and more decentralized country than Portugal, the government was weakened by deep provincial jealousies and constant friction between the successive regency councils and the Cortes. The larger part of Spain was under French occupation, thus depriving the Spanish government of revenue and manpower. The ill-trained Spanish professional army was never able to stand up to the French in battle; the guerrilla bands in the countryside could harass but not drive away the French invaders. As a result Spanish administration was paralysed to an extent that perhaps Wellington never fully realized. What was clear to him, however, was the need for Spain to make a greater contribution to a war which seemed impossible for him to win by himself. For this some impetus from above was required.

To obtain for Wellington command of the Spanish armies had been an object of British diplomacy ever since 1809. National pride, provincial autonomy, liberal jealousy of military authority, and the reluctance of the Spanish regency to part with power had all conspired to frustrate it. Nevertheless, the entry into Madrid finally converted the Cortes, and in September they offered Wellington the post of generalissimo of the Spanish armies. In this there was a degree of self-deception on both sides. The primary purpose of the Cortes was to secure Wellington and his army for the service of Spain, not to transfer to him the fundamental military control which by the liberal constitution of 1812 belonged to the civil authority. For Wellington the only value of the post was that it promised a more unified and authoritative direction of the Spanish military effort. In a letter to the Spanish war minister early in December 1812 he made a number of sweeping demands: the right to approve senior appointments in the Spanish army and the allocation of the military budget; the transmission through his headquarters of all orders to the Spanish armies in the field; and powers for the Spanish military commanders to obtain supplies without having to go through civilian authorities. He followed this up by going himself to Cadiz at the end of the month. By dint of threatening to resign his appointment he obtained the grudging consent of both the regency council and the Cortes to his demands.

Though he used his new powers circumspectly and the regency rarely fulfilled their side of the compact, the new arrangement at least gave Wellington hope that in future the Spanish armies would prove a more efficient ally. With Soult's retirement towards Madrid, Hill's force in south-west Spain was free to join the main army, and further reinforcements from England arrived during the winter of 1812–13, including five cavalry regiments. By the spring Wellington had under his command an effective force of over 100,000 men, comprising 55,000 British, 31,000 Portuguese, and 21,000 Spanish. By contrast the French forces had been further depleted by the withdrawal of 15,000 of their best troops to make good Napoleon's terrible losses in Russia, and their ablest general, Soult, had been recalled to Paris.

This was a decidedly more hopeful outlook than in any previous year, and Wellington improved on it by adopting a totally new strategy. Up to that point everything he had done in the Peninsula had been conditioned by his primary object, the defence of Portugal, and by the periodic opportunities to advance into Spain which that successful defence had created. The liberation of Spain, however, was a different kind of military problem. The whole French position in the Peninsula depended on the great high road from Bayonne through Burgos to Madrid. In 1808, in a different set of circumstances, Wellington had argued in a memorandum for the government that the only effective way to carry on operations against the French armies in Spain was to strike down from the Asturias against the flank and rear of the French line of communication, using the Biscayan ports as a base. In the early part of 1813, in fact, the protection of this vital link was becoming an increasing concern for King Joseph and his generals. Their strategy was to hold the northern part of Spain, using the River Douro as a defensive front on the left flank of any allied advance from the Ciudad Rodrigo sally-port. The bulk of their troops was concentrated in this sector, the rest being in the south-east guarding the Mediterranean coast against the Anglo-Sicilian threat.

This policy assumed that Wellington would, as in previous years, make his advance from central Portugal south of the Douro. In fact his new strategy, a modification of his 1808 ideas, was to outflank the French defensive position by crossing the Douro inside Portugal and make his main thrust against the French line of communication running north-east from the Douro to Bayonne. In doing so he proposed to use the Biscayan ports for his own communications and supplies. It was at this point that the defence of Portugal was transformed into the liberation of Spain. His theatrical gesture of farewell when he crossed the Portuguese frontier marked his sense that the war had taken on a new shape. In May 60,000 men under Graham began their march through the mountainous terrain of the Tras-os-Montes, emerging into northern Spain. As a blind, Wellington remained with Hill's smaller force which started out along the familiar route from Ciudad Rodrigo towards Salamanca. There Wellington left them to join Graham. The two halves of the army were reunited at Toro, north of the Douro, at the beginning of June. The surprise had been complete and the French, abandoning first Valladolid and then, surprisingly, Burgos, fell back towards the Ebro.

Wellington's tactics were to hustle, as he put it, the

French towards Bayonne by continuously outflanking them to the north and giving them no time to regroup. Meanwhile he shifted his base from Lisbon and Corunna to Santander on the Biscayan coast. It was a remarkable logistic achievement. Between mid-May and mid-June he moved 100,000 men, with 100 guns and a pontoon bridge train, 250 miles to within striking distance of the French frontier. The decisive engagement came on 21 June at Vitoria where the Madrid–Bayonne highway was joined by roads going north to Bilbao and east to Pamplona, the fortress guarding the pass of Roncesvalles through the Pyrenees into France.

Wellington, with a superiority of numbers, planned the battle as a classic enveloping movement with three separate parts of his army converging on the French position between the great bend of the River Zamorra and the town of Vitoria. It did not quite achieve classic perfection. Varying difficulties of terrain and distances to be covered upset the symmetry of his concentric attack. The French left and centre were broken after hard fighting but the stubborn resistance of their right wing under Reille saved them from being totally encircled. Nevertheless, not only was Joseph's army sent in disorderly retreat towards Pamplona but 150 guns, an immense store of ammunition, almost all his baggage, and a war chest of about £1 million (most of which disappeared into the pockets of the soldiers) fell into allied hands. Only an orgy of looting by the victorious troops prevented even more prisoners from being taken. As it was, though Joseph suffered 6000 casualties and had another 3000 captured, he was able to lead the wreckage of his army back into France. The usual disorganizing effect of protracted fighting and difficult country prevented Wellington from making any serious pursuit. Allied losses were 5000, mainly British: a relatively moderate price to pay for a victory that echoed round Europe.

The extraordinary success of the campaign had carried Wellington's army faster and further into the northeastern corner of Spain than he had expected. His immediate thought was more to protect what he had gained than to prepare for another forward leap. An invasion of France would mean that he would face a hostile population as well as French armies better supplied, more easily reinforced, and with shorter lines of communication than in Spain. He had no confidence in Britain's allies in central Europe and felt it not impossible that the armistice they had signed in June 1813 might end in a permanent peace which would set Napoleon free to turn south against him. He had equally little confidence in the Spanish government. The regency had been appointing and removing military commanders without consulting him and was conspicuously failing either to pay or provision the Spanish forces serving in his army. He was so exasperated at their conduct that at the end of August he resigned his command of the Spanish forces and consented to continue only until the next meeting of the Cortes. His difficulties in supplying his Portuguese and Spanish allies were further reasons for remaining on the defensive. In

the event the Cortes in December requested him to stay in office; but this made little practical difference.

There were in any case military reasons for Wellington to consolidate his position rather than advance into France. The fortresses of San Sebastian and Pamplona were still in French hands; in Catalonia, where the Anglo-Sicilian effort was petering out, Suchet with his 20,000 French was a potential threat to his right flank. Not surprisingly Wellington saw as his primary task the reduction of the two fortresses and the elimination of the last pockets of French resistance in Spain. This proved a longer and more difficult operation than could have been anticipated. Soult, sent down after Vitoria to take command in the south of France, proved as always a skilful and aggressive opponent. The allied front, stretching nearly 40 miles from San Sebastian to Pamplona, with poor lateral communications, was difficult for Wellington to supervise personally. In July Graham's attempt on San Sebastian was a miserable failure and Soult's simultaneous and unexpected attack through the Pyrenean passes involved Wellington in awkward and costly fighting until the French finally withdrew. The renewed siege of San Sebastian in August proved, like most of Wellington's sieges, a protracted and bloody operation. Despite the large new battering-train at Graham's disposal, the fortress did not yield until 8 September; in all it had resisted for seventy-three days.

There followed four weeks of inactivity on both sides. Only when he was confident of the imminent fall of Pamplona (which finally surrendered to the blockading Spanish force at the end of October) did Wellington reluctantly give way to the pressures of his own government and the wishes of the allied powers in Germany to invade France. On 7 October he forced the passage of the River Bidassoa and the French retreated to Bayonne. At the battle of the Nivelle a month later Soult's army, dispirited by the news of Napoleon's defeat at Leipzig, was both outnumbered and outmanoeuvred. Fighting gradually died down in December and when it resumed in the spring of 1814 the outcome was hardly in doubt. Soult's army, weakened by desertion and troop withdrawals, was defeated at Orthez in February and retired eastward. This allowed Wellington to send Beresford to make a formal entry into Bordeaux where a royalist party was already active. Wellington personally favoured a Bourbon restoration but he was tied by his government which, with their European allies, still recognized Napoleon. By the time the last engagement took place at Toulouse on 10 April, however, Napoleon had abdicated. Nine days later Wellington signed a separate convention with Soult and Suchet for the cessation of hostilities and the removal of all French forces from Spain.

Aspects of Wellington's generalship, 1808–1814 The Peninsular War was over at last and part, at least, of the credit for its successful outcome was due to the ministers at home. They had supported Wellington when he had been under severe parliamentary attack, given him great latitude of action, and had made immense efforts to supply him with the manpower and money needed to sustain his campaigns. Wellington's frequent grumblings and occasional threats in the early years did not so much reflect a lack of government support as illustrate the customary vehemence he employed on matters important to him. Nevertheless, the language of some of his official dispatches, coupled with the whig bias of Napier's monumental *History of the War in the Peninsula* (1828–40), subsequently created a false impression which was slow to disappear. But Wellington flatly denied in 1834 that he had ever offered to resign, though as he put it, 'I dare say I may have said as often as fifty times, "Damn it, if you don't do this or that you may as well give up the war at once"' (Stanhope, 58–9). And writing of the cabinet on another occasion, he said 'it is not true that they did not, in every way in their power, as individuals, as Ministers, and as a Government, support me' (ibid., 83).

Even so, that does not explain why Wellington was able to maintain his small force in the Peninsula in the face of the French armies ten times its size. In the proverbial phrase he himself quoted on occasion, Spain was a country where small armies were defeated and large armies starved. That Wellington's army suffered neither fate was primarily because he understood the peculiarities of that region better than Napoleon ever did. In Spain, as in Russia, the French encountered conditions quite unlike the civilized, populous, fertile states of central Europe in which they had previously campaigned. A country with great barren mountainous tracts, few good roads, a harsh climate, strong provincial autonomy, and a primitive, vengeful peasantry, Spain could hardly have been more unfavourable to the French system, often brutally enforced, of living off the land. For both political and logistical reasons the French forces had to become an army of occupation, spread over a large area, rather than a military organization dedicated to winning a war. This inherent disadvantage was compounded by jealousies between French marshals, who often behaved like proconsuls in their own territory, and the stream of injunctions and criticisms which came from the distant emperor, too late to be useful but irritating and oppressive. At bottom, therefore, the factor which made Wellington's victories possible was the steadfast Spanish national resistance. The outcome of the war, he wrote some years later:

> may be attributed to the operations of the Allied Armies in the Peninsula, but those would form a very erroneous notion of the facts who should not attribute a fair proportion of it to the effect of the enmity of the people of Spain. (Wellington MS 1/644/7, 16 April 1820)

Wellington tried from the start to enforce on his troops respect for the religion, customs, and property of the peoples of Portugal and Spain. It was a lesson the value of which he had learned in India, though he was not always successful in imparting it to others. Between his men, their officers included, and the inhabitants of the Peninsula was a gulf of prejudice, suspicion, and incomprehension. Even apart from the brutalities which accompanied the British captures of Ciudad Rodrigo, Badajoz, and San

Sebastian, the endemic problems of looting and theft required constant attention, and among Wellington's many innovations was an improved system of military police. But occasional shootings and hangings would have been useless had he not adopted a system of feeding his army that was completely different from that of the French. He could see all the military disadvantages of their methods. Not only did they antagonize the peasant population but they were difficult to operate when their armies were concentrated, or in rapid movement, or had stayed too long in one district.

Wellington, on the other hand, secured the co-operation of the civilian population by purchasing what he needed. He even dispensed with such powers of requisitioning as he legally possessed. Supplies which did not come directly from England were bought from contractors in the large towns or from local merchants. Regimental forage parties were strictly controlled to prevent waste, provide proper distribution, and ensure due payment to the owners. Depots were built up inside Portugal; for operations in Spain he organized a huge ancillary force of drivers, muleteers, waggoners, and draught animals to bring supplies up to his marching troops. It was a task for which India had provided him with considerable practice. A further refinement was his creation by 1810 of divisional transport to give additional mobility to his forward troops. This self-supporting system added a large and costly administrative tail to his army and explains his continual demands to his home government for ever-increasing amounts of gold and silver coinage. The system broke down from time to time, usually because of bad weather or rapid movement, but this was the inevitable friction of war. For all its expense and difficulty it was immensely superior in both military and political terms to the French practice.

One reward for Wellington's considerate policy towards the civilian population came in the form of continuous information about the French armies. This was a valuable supplement to the intelligence gathered by his patrols and outposts. Individuals at every level of Spanish society assisted in this way, often at great personal risk. Dr Curtis, rector of the Irish College at Salamanca, organized his clerical seminarists to report on French dispositions and movements. Guerrilla bands which intercepted French couriers gave or sold their dispatches to the British. In 1809 British military intelligence was patchy, much of it out of date, and its genuineness sometimes suspect. It steadily improved, however, and by 1811 Wellington was able to boast to Lord Liverpool that he knew all that passed in the French armies. As always the mass of miscellaneous reports coming to him had to be carefully assessed to be of operational value. Nevertheless, it is evident that Wellington placed a high value on his intelligence service and that his sources were superior to those of the French generals. He created a secret intelligence staff under his direct control, mainly British but including some Portuguese and Spanish officers. He also possessed a highly efficient mapping and sketching section under his quartermaster-general, which as early as 1810 provided him with better maps of central Portugal than were available to the French or even the Portuguese government. Without its work Graham's surprise advance in 1813 through the Tras-os-Montes over 150 miles of mountains and rivers would have been impossible. Even in Spain, Wellington was never hampered by inadequate knowledge of the terrain or seriously misled by faulty topographical information as Masséna had been in the Busaco campaign.

The increasingly systematic gathering of topographical and military intelligence was only part of the general structural reforms Wellington carried out in his army. His primary purpose was to impose uniformity, method, and discipline on his force so that it responded directly to his leadership. By 1814 the staff of his army, from the general headquarters down to divisional level, was not only larger proportionately but probably more efficient than that of any continental army, not excluding the French. The printed volumes of his *General Orders* offer impressive evidence of the comprehensive attention to detail which was at the heart of his generalship. From the additional training given to new divisions arriving from England and the raising of a corps of guides to direct the marches of his formations, down to the issue of tents, blankets, and tin kettles to the individual soldier, nothing that affected the efficiency or welfare of his troops seems to have escaped his attention. The mastery of logistics which he had acquired in India explains much of his success in Spain.

The final test of any general, however, is on the battlefield and it was here that Wellington displayed his supreme qualities. Though he won the reputation among French marshals of being primarily a master of defensive tactics, this was largely because his habitual inferiority in numbers forced those tactics on him. But Salamanca and Vitoria are proofs of his talents as an attacking commander. One important feature was his continuous control and tactical flexibility once the battle had started. 'I made my campaigns of ropes' he once remarked. 'If anything went wrong I tied a knot; and went on' (Longford, *Years of the Sword*, 442). The same was true of his conduct of battle. He had the faculty (the product of both instinct and experience) of being at the crucial point at the decisive moment.

Wellington's inexhaustible energy and powers of physical endurance enabled him to cover the whole area of most of his battles, and his unruffled manner (the product of will-power and self-discipline) had a moral effect on both officers and men. As with Napoleon, his presence on the battlefield came to be regarded by his troops as a guarantee of success. He has been criticized for exposing himself too much in action and delegating too little to his commanders in the field, but with armies as small as those he habitually led, and battlefields which could usually be kept under his direct observation, he would have regarded it as irresponsible not to exercise personal leadership. It was never his way to leave anything to chance. This type of generalship demanded complete and rigid obedience from his subordinates, and he was notably harsh, on some occasions to the point of injustice, on any apparent disregard of his orders.

A disciplinarian to his army, Wellington was equally disciplined with himself. He had the invaluable gift of being able to do with little sleep, and this, together with his methodical habits, enabled him to get through a load of administrative work which would have taxed most men and broken some. His normal routine was to rise at six and write letters until nine. He then appeared for breakfast, shaved and trimly dressed, and spent the rest of the morning seeing his senior staff officers. In the afternoon he would go off on horseback to visit various units and any places that called for particular attention. But, though busy, his life was not austere. The atmosphere at his headquarters was relaxed and informal. He enjoyed the society of his young, high-spirited, mainly aristocratic aides-de-camp, and there were usually a number of casual visitors at his mess dinners. Here the attraction was the conversation rather than the cuisine; Wellington had notoriously little interest in food. During the winter he hunted with his own pack, and he encouraged his officers to organize balls and concerts at which he would put in an appearance even if he took little part in the proceedings.

Nicknamed by his officers the Beau and later the Peer, to his more irreverent men he was Atty (for Arthur) or Nosey. They saw his neat figure in grey frock coat and plain cocked hat often enough, both on the battlefield and in cantonments, since he believed in seeing things for himself. It was fortunate for the army, in an age when brigadiers led their men into action and generals were not infrequently killed or wounded, that he was never a casualty himself. He was hit twice by spent bullets (in India and at Salamanca), slightly wounded once (at Orthez), and nearly captured on at least two occasions. After a narrow escape on the bridge at Sorauren during the battles of the Pyrenees, he wrote with a certain wryness to his brother William, 'I begin to believe that the finger of God is upon me' (Longford, *Years of the Sword*, 330). He had one other piece of good luck. Unlike his unfortunate predecessor, Sir John Moore, he was never obliged to face Napoleon (until 1815). Unkindly reminded of this in Paris after the war, he replied with the honesty which was one of his characteristics, 'no, and I am very glad I never was. I would at any time rather have heard that a reinforcement of 40,000 men had joined the French army, than that he had arrived to take the command' (ibid., 348–9).

Paris and Vienna, 1814–1815 With the war over, Wellington on 21 April 1814 accepted an invitation from Castlereagh to act as British ambassador in Paris. The appointment was less strange than might appear. Never a democrat, Wellington had looked to a Bourbon restoration even before the allies abandoned their negotiations with Napoleon, and he consistently held the view that one of the objects of an allied occupation of France was to protect the monarchy against republicans and Bonapartists. For himself he felt that the natural sequel to his military career would be some high post under the government. Castlereagh, for his part, was anxious to exercise a major influence on the eventual peace settlement and believed that to have Wellington in Paris during the negotiations would give unique weight to British diplomacy. 'His military name', he wrote to Lord Liverpool, 'would give him and us the greatest ascendancy' (Hinde, *Castlereagh*, 214).

On 4 May Wellington, having been made a duke the previous day, arrived in Paris: an object of interest to all, despite his deliberately inconspicuous civilian attire. Soon afterwards, at Castlereagh's request, he went back to Spain with a memorandum for the new king, Ferdinand VII, recommending him to adopt a degree of liberalism in the future government of his kingdom. But, as he reported to Castlereagh, 'I fear that I have done but little good' (Maxwell, 1.380). Returning to France he stopped at Bayonne to issue a general order on 14 June, taking leave of his Peninsular army in a few brief but dignified paragraphs. By 23 June he was back in England for the first time in over five years to meet a hero's welcome. He went down to Portsmouth to pay his respects to the prince regent and his distinguished guests, the emperor of Russia and the king of Prussia, and then back to London to take his seat in the House of Lords and receive the congratulations of the House of Commons, which had just voted him £400,000 for the purchase of an estate to support his new title. In July came a thanksgiving service at St Paul's, at which he carried the sword of state, and a fête at Carlton House.

By August Wellington was on the continent again, inspecting the defences of Belgium on behalf of the allies and then moving on to Paris to resume his diplomatic duties. These consisted mainly in an attempt to induce the French government to abolish the slave trade: a task almost as unpromising as persuading the Spanish king to embrace liberalism. By the time the Congress of Vienna opened in the autumn, however, the jealousy of some of the Bourbon princes and assassination threats from outraged Bonapartists were already causing concern to the British government. The only decent pretext for recalling Wellington from France was either to appoint him deputy to Castlereagh or give him a command in the field in the war against the USA that had broken out in 1812. Liverpool chose the latter as the more convincing excuse, though it is unlikely that he had any intention of sending Wellington across the Atlantic except possibly to negotiate peace. In the end, when Castlereagh returned home to assist the ministry in the House of Commons, Wellington took his place at the congress, arriving in Vienna on 3 February 1815.

Preparing to face Napoleon When Napoleon escaped from Elba it was the general desire of the allied sovereigns that Wellington should take charge of the forces in the Netherlands. As soon as a new treaty of alliance was signed towards the end of March, therefore, he left for Brussels, arriving in the first week of April. Politically and militarily his situation there was strewn with difficulties. A large part of the Belgian troops had recently served under Napoleon and their loyalty was suspect. King William of the Netherlands was jealous of his authority and only tardily surrendered control of the Dutch army. The duke's responsibilities included guarding the seat of government in Brussels, protecting the court of the fugitive

French king at Ghent, and liaising with the Prussian military headquarters at Namur. These different needs imposed on him a strategically awkward deployment of his motley allied army. His line of communication from Brussels to his base at Ostend, contrary to all orthodox theory, ran parallel to his front against Napoleon and not at right angles to it. Geographically the French frontier was only 27 miles from Brussels, less than 50 by the paved road through Hal, Mons, and Maubeuge, and he had little faith in either the ability or the fidelity of the barrier-fortress garrisons. There would be little space for manoeuvre once the French invaded and he was precluded by political considerations from sending patrols into France until Napoleon actually declared war. Both British and Prussian intelligence were dangerously ill-informed about what was going on behind the strict security screen Napoleon enforced along the frontier.

Militarily the British force placed under his command drew from Wellington the sour comment on 8 May that 'I have got an infamous army, very weak and ill-equipped, and a very inexperienced staff' (Maxwell, 1.394). Over the next six weeks, however, its quality gradually improved with the dispatch of many of his Peninsular generals and staff officers, and the last-minute arrival at Brussels on 17 June of a further 2000 of what he called his Spanish (that is, Peninsular) infantry. By that date his army had risen to about 95,000, composed of just over 33,000 British troops (only 7000 of whom had served in Spain), nearly 8000 of the King's German Legion (equal in value to the best British units), some 27,000 Brunswick, Hanoverian, and Nassau troops of varying quality, together with 20,000 Dutch and nearly 6000 Belgians of doubtful reliability. It was an uneven and heterogeneous array which spoke four languages and had no common training or equipment. Wellington was not even supreme commander in his own theatre of war, since he shared responsibility for the defence of the Netherlands with the Prussian commander, the 73-year-old Blücher.

Wellington's hope that an allied offensive would be launched before Napoleon completed his preparations disappeared when the allied sovereigns decided on a methodical mobilization to be followed in July by an invasion of France on a broad front. In the interval he and Blücher were left to guard the Netherlands against a possible (but by no means certain) French attack. Conscious of the vulnerability of his own position, the duke thought (and for the rest of his life believed) that the best strategy for Napoleon was to attack from the south-west up the great road from Paris to Brussels through Mons and Hal. This, if successful, would cut the British army off from its base: in effect a strategy comparable to his own in the Vitoria campaign. For that reason he kept the bulk of his force in his western sector rather than close to the Prussian zone. On 3 May he met Blücher at Tirlemont and came to a general understanding with him on their joint strategy if Napoleon invaded Belgium. Outwardly he remained (or took care to give the impression of being) calm and confident in the face of the feverish excitement in Brussels. Nevertheless, the initiative lay with Napoleon, and not until 13

June did it become clear that French military activity in the western sector of the frontier was a feint.

Preparations for Waterloo Very early on 15 June 1815 the French army invaded Belgium on a narrow front moving in the direction of Charleroi in the Prussian zone. When, later that day, Wellington learned that Blücher had committed himself to battle around Sombresse, he gave preparatory orders for an eastward movement towards Nivelles. What he did not know was that the Prussians had uncovered the high road from Charleroi to Brussels, and only at supper on the 15th (at the famous duchess of Richmond's ball) was he informed that French units had advanced up that road to the vicinity of Quatre Bras, only 20 miles from the capital. 'Napoleon has humbugged me, by God', he exclaimed to the duke of Richmond; 'he has gained twenty-four hours' march upon me' (Longford, *Years of the Sword*, 421). Early next morning he left for Quatre Bras, which in the meantime had been occupied by two brigades of the prince of Orange's corps on the initiative of his able chief of staff, Constant-Rebecque, and General Perponcher, commander of his 2nd division. Later he went on to meet Blücher at Brye, half way to Sombresse, and agreed to assist him if not attacked himself. By 3 p.m. he was back at Quatre Bras where stiff fighting had already started. With allied reinforcements steadily arriving Wellington was able to stabilize the situation, and at dusk the allies still held their position.

Early next day Wellington learned that the Prussians had been worsted at Ligny and were withdrawing towards Wavre, some 14 miles by road south-east of Brussels. The direction of their retreat was crucial since it kept the Prussians in touch with the allied army. To conform to their new alignment Wellington retired north to the ridge of Mont St Jean which he had previously reconnoitred. It lay just south of the village of Waterloo and about 10 miles from Brussels. In the small hours of the next morning (18th) a message came from Blücher informing him that two Prussian army corps would move towards his left flank and the duke promised in return to hold his ground until the Prussians arrived. The position he had selected was a classic example of his defensive skill. Along the Mont St Jean Ridge the Ohain road, partly hedged, partly sunken between high banks, constituted a considerable, in places an impassable, obstacle to cavalry. In front standing fields of rye provided further concealment from an enemy advancing across the shallow, undulating basin that lay to the south. It had rained heavily during the night and the thick Brabant clay soil was a further advantage to the defence. Wellington placed the bulk of his force, and his best troops, on his right wing where the road bent south-west towards the high road to Nivelles. It was in this obtuse angle that the most desperate fighting and heaviest casualties occurred. About 400 yards in front was the large walled enclosure of Hougoumont, consisting of a manor house, chapel, and farm buildings, into which he put four companies of the foot guards, later reinforced.

Wellington's weaker left flank, where the Prussians would arrive, was protected by the marshy ground of the Smohain stream to the east and the farm buildings of Papelotte and La Haye in front. In the centre, about 300 yards to the south, was the most exposed of all his forward defences, the farm and sandpits of La Haye-Sainte commanding the road from Quatre Bras, the axis of the French advance. The entire front was just over 2 miles long. To hold it he had (though estimates differ slightly) some 68,000 troops (of whom 24,000 were British) and 156 guns to oppose Napoleon's army of some 72,000 with 246 guns. About 80 of these were massed in the 'grande batterie' which Napoleon established in his centre, though almost at the limit of their range.

The battle of Waterloo, 18 June 1815 The battle which followed on Sunday, 18 June, was a savage and bloody encounter which with some intermissions lasted from the opening cannonade of the French guns at 11.30 a.m. until dusk fell soon after 8 p.m. Napoleon's fundamental mistake was to underestimate his opponent. Snubbing those of his marshals with Peninsular experience who cautioned him against attacking Wellington in a prepared position, he mounted a series of massive but unco-ordinated onslaughts without any preliminary manoeuvring. It was Vimeiro all over again on a larger scale. The French cavalry were met by allied squares, their infantry columns by allied troops in line, concealed until the last moment on the reverse side of the ridge. Wellington, slightly surprised by Napoleon's bludgeoning tactics, described the battle afterwards as a 'pounding match' (Longford, *Years of the Sword*, 488); this is often recalled as 'Hard pounding, gentlemen; let's see who will pound longest' (W. Scott, *Paul's Letters*, 1816, letter 8). On Wellington's right the Hougoumont garrison held out all day against almost continual attack, pinning down forces of ten times their number. At the other end of the line Papelotte and La Haye remained in allied hands until relieved by the advancing Prussians. In the afternoon, however, La Haye-Sainte was captured when its ammunition ran out, enabling French troops to reach the crest of the ridge. But by then it was too late; by 4.30 p.m. Wellington knew that the Prussians were engaging the right flank of the French position. Papelotte, in fact, became the hinge joining the allied front running from east to west with the Prussian front from north to south, between which the French were increasingly compressed as the evening wore on. Wellington himself was constantly on the move, encouraging his troops at each crisis, rallying wavering units (not always successfully), and meeting the inevitable set-backs and misfortunes of the fluctuating fighting with the uncomplaining good humour which was one of his greatest qualities on the battlefield. Though he had been nearly captured at Quatre Bras, his remarkable personal immunity continued. Frequently caught up in the fighting, the duke, riding Copenhagen, went through the day without injury while men were struck down at his side and all but one of his personal staff were killed or wounded. When Lord Uxbridge was hit, the following exchange took place: '"By God! I've lost my leg," cried Uxbridge. "Have you, by God" was all the Duke's reply' (Maxwell, 2.90).

Had he been forced to retire, Wellington would have moved west towards the coast, abandoning Brussels. On his way he would have picked up a detachment of 17,000 men, under the nominal command of Prince Frederick of the Netherlands, which (in a decision often criticized since) he left unused at Hal 8 miles away. This, however, was clearly one of his defensive precautions. That line of retreat would have taken him back along his lines of communication and not away from them. He might have been defeated at Waterloo but not routed. In any case he did not think that Napoleon, with the Prussians in his rear, would have been in a position to pursue him. In reality Napoleon himself, though operating on interior lines, had little room for manoeuvre, and Wellington's superbly organized defence presented his opponent with little choice but a frontal attack. Despite heavy casualties, mainly from French artillery fire, Wellington's thinning lines held out. Though the Prussians (chiefly because of the suspicious caution of Gneisenau, Blücher's chief of staff) arrived later and in smaller numbers than Wellington expected, the Anglo-Prussian strategy held firm. As early as 2.30 p.m. Wellington had seen the Prussian vedettes in the distance, heralding the approach of their main body; by 4 p.m. he could hear their guns in action. Relieved of anxiety on that flank he was able to move units from his left wing to strengthen his centre and right. To the end he always had reserves in hand.

Imperturbable as he seemed during the battle, Wellington admitted afterwards, as he put it next day to Thomas Creevey, 'It has been a damned nice thing—the nearest run thing you ever saw' (*Creevey Papers*, 236). 'I never took so much trouble about any Battle,' he wrote, 'and never was so near being beat' (Longford, *Years of the Sword*, 490). But with the failure of Napoleon's last futile effort—the attack at about 7 p.m. by five battalions of the middle guard against the reinforced centre-right of the allied position—the battle was over. The French troops, as always, had fought with immense courage and tenacity. Now, for the first time in Wellington's experience, their morale collapsed. What started as a retreat turned into a rout. Soon after 9 p.m. he met Blücher near the Belle Alliance crossroads and relinquished further pursuit to the Prussians. On both sides casualties had been very heavy: about 17,000 in Wellington's army, nearly 7000 among the Prussians, about 26,000 among the French, with a further 9000 taken prisoner and up to 10,000 missing or deserted. 'I hope to God', the duke said sombrely to Lady Shelley when talking to her not long afterwards, 'that I have fought my last battle' (*Diary of Frances, Lady Shelley*, 1.102). But that last battle, the most famous in European history, had done its work. Advancing rapidly into France, Wellington and Blücher secured an armistice on 3 July and three days later their troops entered Paris.

With this Wellington had reached the summit of his career. No man, certainly no Briton, had ever been in such a situation before in Europe, the object of universal hero-worship and gratitude. Honours and tributes poured in from every side. The king of the Netherlands conferred on him the title of prince of Waterloo, accompanied by an estate in Belgium to add to those presented to him during the Peninsular War by the governments of Portugal and Spain. Chivalric orders of knighthood came from Russia and from lesser European states—Savoy, Denmark, Naples, Saxony, Bavaria, Hesse-Cassel, and Württemberg. This international prestige gave him, in turn, an influence on the post-Waterloo settlement of Europe far surpassing that of any single military leader at the end of the two world wars in the following century. Though there was no enthusiasm either among the allied sovereigns or in the French provisional government for the Bourbon monarchy, Wellington believed that there was no practical alternative. He paved the way for a second restoration by persuading the king to take into his service the cynical and time-serving Fouché as minister of police. On the question of a final peace settlement he considered that financial reparations enforced by an army of occupation were preferable to permanent cessions of territory which would create lasting hostility and immediately discredit the restored monarchy. His military reputation, together with his integrity and common sense, gave his opinion peculiar weight.

Occupation of France, 1815–1818 By the second treaty of Paris, signed in November 1815, France was to be occupied by an allied force of 150,000 for five years, the cost to be borne by the French government, in addition to a general indemnity of 700 million francs. Wellington was appointed commander-in-chief of the allied occupation force and principal intermediary between the council of ambassadors in Paris and the French government. He was further charged with the responsibility for supervising the reconstruction of the barrier fortresses along the Belgian frontier. For this purpose, in a separate agreement signed in October 1816 between the British and Netherlands governments, he was given control of the financial arrangements for these works. He was soon on good terms with the French ministers, especially their leading figure, the duc de Richelieu, and showed himself unusually sympathetic to their problems.

As early as June 1816 Richelieu was pressing for a reduction in the size of the occupation forces, and though Wellington took the view that reparations and occupation were inseparable, he took steps to reduce the inflated allied armies to their proper treaty numbers. Financially, however, the French government was still in great difficulty and in November suspended its treaty payments. In a quick change of policy Wellington recommended to the council of ambassadors a reduction in the occupation forces of one-fifth on the grounds that the stability of the Bourbon monarchy, which it was an essential allied interest to preserve, was being endangered by the continued allied presence in France. He himself, as commander-in-chief, was the target of resentment from all parties in France. Besides a stream of threatening letters there were two, admittedly blundering, attempts on his life: one by arson and explosives at his house in June 1816, the other by pistol in February 1818. After the second incident the cabinet and the prince regent ordered him to withdraw to his military headquarters at Cambrai: a command which the duke, showing an indifference to superior authority which he would never have tolerated in a subordinate of his own, urbanely rejected.

An additional financial difficulty in the last years of the occupation was the repayment of the debts incurred by the French army abroad, which threatened to produce an avalanche of claims from both states and individuals. On the initiative of the tsar the whole problem was remitted to Wellington for arbitration in the autumn of 1817. His solution was to fix a maximum total of 240 million francs, together with accrued interest, and assign the decisions on individual claims to the respective states concerned. By that date he had concluded that a prolongation of the period of occupation was pointless, that the French government could be trusted to meet its remaining obligations, and that France should be admitted on equal footing to the European congress system established in 1815. To facilitate a shortening of the occupation he promoted negotiations between the French ministers and two British banks, Barings and Rothschilds, for a private loan to pay off the balance of the treaty indemnity. This paved the way for a general agreement in the autumn of 1818 at the Congress of Aix-la-Chapelle for the final evacuation of France and her readmittance to the councils of Europe. The allied powers accepted an immediate sum of 265 million francs in lieu of the 332 million still outstanding under the peace treaty. In October Wellington issued his last general order to the departing British occupation troops, thanking them for 'their uniform good conduct', and by the end of November, two years ahead of schedule, the last foreign armies had left French soil. As a final salute the tsar of Russia, the emperor of Austria, and the king of Prussia created him a field marshal in their respective armies.

A decision on Wellington's future had already been taken. The prime minister had for some time been considering what employment could be found for the most illustrious subject of the crown since Marlborough. At the age of fifty it was unthinkable that the duke should be relegated to a routine military post. To bring him into the government for which he had long been an influential adviser seemed the most straightforward solution. A vacancy was created for him by Lord Mulgrave, who gave up his position as master-general of the ordnance, the one cabinet office of a specifically military character. The unexpected demur came from the intended recipient. Wellington, with a soldier's distrust of politicians, showed a distinct unwillingness to enter the cabinet. Only his sense of duty to the crown and loyalty to the ministers who had supported him in the early difficulties of the Peninsular War persuaded him to accept. It was his old friend Castlereagh who seems to have overcome his final scruples with the argument that a refusal would weaken the government and leave him as a possible rallying point for the opposition. Even so, Wellington stipulated that if at any time the ministry was changed, he must be free to choose his own future, since 'my long service abroad has convinced me that a factious opposition to the Government is highly injurious to the interests of the country'

(Yonge, 2.378). It was as a great servant of the state, therefore, not as a party politician, that the duke joined the government. This was certainly the view taken by the prime minister. When discussing in March 1821 the prospects of the administration, Liverpool and Castlereagh were united in thinking that though Wellington had become an important member of the cabinet, he was too great a national figure to be placed in any post where he would be exposed to party animosity or be disqualified from resuming his active professional career.

Private life, 1818–1835 The return to England at the end of 1818 enabled Wellington for the first time to establish a settled domestic life. In 1817 he had paid a deliberately generous price for his brother Richard's residence, Apsley House at Hyde Park Corner, and this now became his London home, soon being known as No. 1, London. Eleven years later he employed the fashionable architect Benjamin Wyatt at considerable expense to enlarge and reshape the appearance of the house to make it a fitting depository for all the war trophies, pictures, statues, and other immense and elaborate presents (mainly gold, silver, and porcelain) given to him by foreign governments and public authorities at home. The year 1817 also saw the acquisition of a country seat. In November the parliamentary commissioners purchased for him Lord Rivers's estate at Stratfield Saye near Basingstoke for the sum of £263,000. The pleasant, unpretentious mansion on the River Loddon became the preferred home of the duchess and a place where her husband could assemble regular house parties. His new status as a Hampshire landowner was marked in December 1820 by appointment as lord lieutenant of the county, a position he held for the rest of his life.

From this time Wellington lived almost permanently in England with only a rare excursion abroad on official business. Not once during the Peninsular War had he returned home or suggested that his wife should join him. Though she had gone across to Paris in 1815, no more children were born to them. Closer proximity did nothing to improve their relationship. The duchess lacked confidence, found it difficult to manage her servants and finances, and because of her short sight dreaded large social gatherings. The duke wanted a poised, intelligent woman to organize his household and be hostess to his guests. Her clinging devotion was a burden to him and her tactlessness a recurrent irritation. He did not tell her (or many other people) of his movements; she resorted to questioning his attendants. At one point in the early summer of 1821 she angered him so much that he threatened to cease living in the same house with her. Though at times he tried to cultivate the society of their two sons, he remained apprehensive of the effect of their mother's weak and over-affectionate upbringing on their characters. Only when Kitty was dying in April 1831 did he show a belated tenderness towards her. Wellington in fact was at his worst and most ungracious in his dealings with his wife. His harshness and outbursts of blazing temper were signs of how little the marriage had come to mean (or perhaps had ever meant) to him. Talking about it with Mrs

Arbuthnot in 1822 he exclaimed 'Would you have believed that anybody could have been such a damned fool? I was not the least in love with her. I married her because they asked me to do it' (*Journal of Mrs Arbuthnot*, 1.169). That was not necessarily the reason, but the other possible explanation—that he did it to erase the slight of his rejection in 1793—is hardly more complimentary.

Both before and after marrying Kitty Pakenham, Wellington had had relations with other women. One of them was the well-known London courtesan Harriette *Wilson (1786–1845?), who later tried to blackmail him. Sexual affairs for Wellington were a form of physical relaxation, not a serious matter. Though suggestions of various brief liaisons in India and the Peninsula are largely anecdotal, there is too much to be ignored. Curiosity about his private life increased as his fame grew. To judge from cartoonists and the more scurrilous journals, both British and foreign, he had an established reputation after 1815 as a womanizer. No doubt more women were reputed to have enjoyed his attentions than were entitled to be. In Paris the singer Grassini and the actress Mlle Georges both claimed to have been his mistress. The allegation in the *St James's Gazette* in 1815 of intimacy with Lady Frances Webster seems to have been groundless. The evidence of an affair with Lady Charlotte Greville (*d.* 1862) about 1820 is more plausible, though not completely proved. After that date the duke appears to have been content with the platonic hero-worship of various pretty, aristocratic, preferably intelligent, and safely married women like Lady Shelley, Mrs Arbuthnot (a granddaughter of the eighth earl of Westmorland), and later the young marchioness of Salisbury. He also found much domestic pleasure in the society of his elder son's wife, Lady Douro, as well as in the children of his second son. His deepest feminine friendship, however, was with the devoted, discreet, but not uncritical Harriet Arbuthnot, wife of a junior tory minister. Their open companionship was such that many of the duke's colleagues believed her to be his mistress—not unreasonably, but certainly wrongly. After her death in 1834 her grieving husband came to join the equally grieving duke and lived with him until his death in 1850.

Cabinet minister, 1818–1827 In his first years as cabinet minister nothing indicated that Wellington's new and slightly ambiguous position in public life would prove unsustainable. Besides his departmental duties he soon fell into the familiar role of general adviser to the government on all military matters: imperial defence, peacetime economies in army establishments, affairs in India, and deployment of troops in disturbed districts at home. Together with Castlereagh he acted as governmental representative in the abortive negotiations with the queen's advisers on issues between the royal couple, and when the collapse of the parliamentary divorce bill in 1820 threatened the existence of Liverpool's administration he took the remarkable step of warning the king privately against any precipitate dismissal of the ministry. He was regularly involved in discussions on foreign policy, and after Castlereagh's suicide in 1822 took his place at the Congress of Verona. Before leaving England he was instrumental in

persuading George IV to agree to Lord Liverpool's desire to appoint Canning as the new foreign secretary.

The main problem for the congress was the constitutional conflict in Spain. British policy was already moving towards disengagement from collective action on the continent and Wellington's instructions left him with little latitude of action. Ironically therefore it fell to him, the most European of the British cabinet, to make the first breach in the congress system. In expressing British reservations about French intervention in Spain he found himself completely isolated, and an offer of mediation which he was told to make in Paris on his way home was, as he expected, politely refused. He arrived back in December decidedly out of humour. With the changes in the international scene it was clear that his old personal influence in Europe was a thing of the past.

While agreeing with the principle of non-intervention abroad, Wellington soon came to dislike both the style of Canning's diplomacy and the man himself. In his resentment and inexperience he allowed himself to be identified more than was wise with the anti-Canning faction at court, the so-called Cottage Coterie (which included the Russian, Austrian, and French ambassadors) that clustered round George IV and his favourites at Windsor. The king's frequently proclaimed partiality for Wellington was the more unfortunate since it was accompanied by royal criticisms of the prime minister. When in the spring of 1824 it seemed that Lord Liverpool might retire because of ill health, the duke was already being spoken of as a potential successor. In June the king and his brother, the duke of York, heir presumptive to the throne, both dropped hints that he should be in readiness for such a possibility. Though he protested his unfitness for such a post, his mind was certainly not closed on the matter. He was already emerging as the chief opponent of Canning within the cabinet, and since Liverpool regarded Canning as his obvious successor any rivalry between the two men had implications for the future.

The two matters of policy on which they differed were the recognition of the independent republics of the former Spanish and Portuguese colonies, and the domestic issue of Catholic emancipation. With his respect for legitimate authority and dislike of democracy, the duke thought it wrong to sanction independence movements abroad while repressing one in Ireland. Behind Canning, however, stood Lord Liverpool and the majority of his ministerial colleagues. In the end Wellington became so restive at his near isolation in the cabinet that early in December 1824 he offered to resign. Liverpool replied with a friendly remonstrance, and the duke was finally won over to the South American policy by the argument that British maritime and commercial power needed to be strengthened in this way. On the other issue the difference between Canning and Wellington was less than appeared. Always cosmopolitan, rational, and tolerant in his attitude to religion, the duke had enjoyed friendly personal relations with the Roman Catholic church in Spain and at home had been considerably influenced by Castlereagh's liberal views. Lord Liverpool's ministry, however, had been formed on the basis of neutrality on the Catholic issue and it was clear that there could be no departure from that position as long as he remained prime minister. What Wellington disliked was Canning's suspected connivance with members of the opposition in promoting emancipation, and even more his apparent readiness to risk breaking up the administration on the issue. When in April 1825, following the success of Burdett's Catholic Relief Bill in the House of Commons, both Liverpool and Peel, the home secretary, indicated their readiness to resign Wellington used all his influence to prevent such a political catastrophe. Though he objected to Burdett's bill, he believed nevertheless that the time had come to settle the dispute and produced a plan of his own for legalizing and endowing the Roman church in Ireland by means of a concordat with the pope.

The cabinet crisis ended in May with the defeat of Burdett's bill in the House of Lords and the failure of Canning's attempt to persuade the cabinet to abandon its neutrality on the issue. In subsequent discussion of the timing of the general election, due not later than 1826, Wellington headed the 'protestant' group in the ministry, which argued for an early election in 1825 to take advantage of the current anti-Catholic feeling in the country. Characteristically he attached more importance to the immediate need to strengthen the ministry than to any consistency of principle over Catholic emancipation. The fact remained, however, that by 1826 Wellington's political position had become curiously involved and illogical. Entering the government in 1818 as a non-partisan public figure, he had become deeply involved in controversial issues. On foreign policy, where he differed fundamentally from Canning, he had little support, especially after the king in the course of 1825 became reconciled to the foreign secretary. On Catholic emancipation, however, where he differed from Canning only on tactics, he had become the figurehead, if not the leader, for tory-Anglican politicians, both peers and commoners, who opposed the measure. It was a deceptive and dangerous position, though neither Wellington nor the political world at large realized it. For another year his ambiguous role as elder statesman remained intact. At the start of 1826 he was chosen by Canning for a special mission to Russia to congratulate the new Tsar Nicholas on his accession and to use his influence to prevent war between Russia and Turkey over the issue of Greek independence. It is doubtful whether his presence made any difference to Russian foreign policy. The protocol of 4 April that he was persuaded to sign went in some respects beyond his instructions and against his private inclinations. It provided for the establishment of Greece as a virtually autonomous state under nominal Turkish suzerainty and for joint Anglo-Russian mediation.

The wider implications were probably not realized by Wellington until he had returned home. To others it was apparent that another blow had been struck at the congress system and that the traditional British strategy of preserving the Ottoman empire as a counterpoise to Russian strength in the east had been compromised. Peace, however, had been preserved, and this after all had been the main object of his mission. He remained intensely critical of Canning's methods and felt that he himself was being excluded from foreign affairs. Nevertheless, the fragile truce between the two men lasted through 1826. Wellington supported the cabinet decision of 9 December to meet a Portuguese request for military assistance against a threatened Spanish invasion, though he thought (with the prime minister) that the British force should be withdrawn as soon as practicable. At the turn of the year two new appointments emphasized once again Wellington's dual position in public life. In December he was made constable of the Tower of London and in January 1827, following the death of the duke of York, he became commander-in-chief of the forces.

Declining to serve under Canning, 1827 Lord Liverpool's stroke on 17 February 1827 which ended the prime minister's political life marked an important stage in Wellington's career. Though many tories at once thought of him as a successor, the duke refused to make any response. He disliked the appearance of angling for Liverpool's office while he was still alive or of doing anything which might seem to limit the king's freedom of choice. To his friends he argued that his position as commander-in-chief was sufficient to exclude him from the premiership. This did not prevent him, however, from warning the king in emphatic terms of the disruptive effect on the administration if he appointed Canning. On 10 April, when Canning was formally commissioned to form a new government, he invited Wellington to continue as member of the cabinet. A frosty exchange of letters ended in Wellington's resignation not only as master-general of the ordnance but as commander-in-chief as well. Canning had taken no pains to be tactful or friendly; Wellington was sensitive and distrustful. Since his resignation was followed by that of six of his cabinet colleagues, the Liberal press accused him of heading a cabal against Canning. The duke's resentment at this baseless charge found an outlet in a vehement speech in the House of Lords on 2 May in which he said that he was not qualified to be head of government and would have been mad to think of such a thing. A further exchange of letters with Canning did nothing to remove the duke's angry conviction that he had been personally insulted by the new prime minister.

Between two proud and touchy men, with a record of mutual hostility and distrust, reconciliation was hardly to be expected, but the incident established Wellington even more firmly as titular leader of the 'protestant' anti-Canning party in politics. This impression was strengthened when the government's Corn Bill was defeated in June on an amendment moved by the duke, largely because of a genuine misunderstanding between Wellington and Huskisson and weak handling by Lord Goderich, the new leader of the House of Lords. After Canning's death in August and his succession by Goderich, Wellington at the king's invitation resumed command of the army. Although some of his close friends thought this might be interpreted as support for the ministry, any such impression must have been removed by a subsequent trip by the duke to the north of England which was converted by his tory hosts into a series of political demonstrations.

Prime minister, 1828–1830 When the weak Goderich cabinet collapsed on 8 January 1828, Wellington was commissioned by George IV to form an administration on the old basis of neutrality on the Catholic question. In consultation with Peel, who in effect became the duke's second in command in the House of Commons, it was agreed to reconstruct the old Liverpool party with a slightly more liberal flavour. Three of the more tory members of Liverpool's former cabinet—Eldon, Bexley, and Westmorland—were omitted. Two new young peers—Aberdeen and Ellenborough—together with Lyndhurst, Canning's supple lord chancellor, were recruited from the upper house. Four Canningites—Huskisson, Grant, Dudley, and Palmerston—joined Peel, Goulburn, and Herries to make up the House of Commons contingent. With seven 'Catholics' and six 'protestants' the cabinet returned to the balanced central position favoured by Lord Liverpool. Under pressure from his colleagues the duke also resigned his command of the army, though he grumbled unreasonably at having to submit to a constitutional requirement which he had implicitly accepted less than a year earlier. His main difficulty, however, lay in his inability to adjust his mind to the political outlook demanded of a prime minister.

Foreign affairs In foreign affairs Wellington was able to have his own way, since neither Dudley, the incompetent Canningite he had taken over from the Goderich ministry, nor the younger but more experienced Aberdeen, who succeeded as foreign secretary in May 1828, was temperamentally disposed to challenge his considerable authority in that field. But the duke's increasingly old-fashioned views made much of his diplomacy hesitant and ineffective, responding to events rather than anticipating them. He upheld the principle of non-intervention by withdrawing the British force from Portugal as soon as possible; but his handling of the issue of Greek independence, the main problem confronting him when he took office, amounted to little more than the abandonment of one position after another. He had already come to regret the concessions he had made at St Petersburg and had little enthusiasm for the 1827 treaty of London which had embodied them. Admiral Codrington's destruction of the Turco-Egyptian fleet at Navarino in October 1827, though a predictable consequence of armed allied intervention, had been profoundly unwelcome to the duke since it ran counter to his settled view that the Ottoman empire must be preserved as an essential element of the balance of power in the Middle East.

The king's speech of January 1828, drawn up by Wellington's cabinet, referred to Navarino as 'a collision wholly unexpected' and 'an untoward event'. The duke hoped even so to keep the question of Greek independence separate from the larger issue of Russian expansion, but he was unable either to get the support of France, which had ambitions of its own in the eastern Mediterranean, or to

prevent the war which broke out between Russia and Turkey in April. The fatuity and intransigence of the Ottoman government in fact made any pro-Turkish policy singularly difficult to sustain. The moderate terms of the treaty of Adrianople which ended hostilities in September were due to Russian calculation and not the duke's influence. In the subsequent delimitation of Greek territory Wellington and Aberdeen found it hard to make up their minds whether the new state should be kept small, on the assumption that it would fall under Russian domination, or made large in the hope of establishing it as a genuinely independent power. In the end the Greek frontiers laid down in the London protocol of February 1830 represented an unsatisfactory compromise which was to be a source of much later trouble. For the rest, Wellington's proposal for an international guarantee of Turkish territorial integrity, though supported by Austria, proved impracticable in the face of the studied indifference of the Russian government, which demonstrated its newly acquired influence over both the Ottoman empire and the fledgeling Greek state by persuading both to accept the diplomatic settlement. Even Metternich, the European statesman most sympathetic to Wellington's outlook, by now regarded him as a spent force. In reality, both these survivors of the Congress of Vienna had been left behind by the emergence of new personalities and objectives in European politics.

Domestic affairs In domestic affairs the optimism with which the duke had taken up his office barely survived the first few months of his administration. He was particularly incensed by the four Canningite ministers, who not only criticized his views but showed a disconcerting readiness to offer their resignations when thwarted. The duke had to accept a more free-trade version of Liverpool's Corn Bill than he would have liked and a surrender to the House of Commons over the repeal of the Test and Corporation Acts. His annoyance with the Canningites came to a head in May when Huskisson's impulsive offer of resignation over his equally impulsive departure from agreed cabinet policy on the East Retford Disfranchisement Bill was accepted by the prime minister with no attempt at conciliation. The resignation of the other three which followed not only destroyed the balance of the cabinet but left the government painfully short of front-bench talent in the House of Commons. The appointment of two of his Peninsular staff officers, Sir George Murray and Sir Henry Hardinge, to help fill the vacancies did nothing to assist Peel in the lower house, while strengthening the impression that the ministry was both illiberal and militaristic.

Catholic emancipation Meanwhile the state of Ireland was urgently demanding attention. In May 1828 the House of Commons had voted in favour of a settlement of the Catholic question. In subsequent debate in the Lords, Wellington based his objections entirely on expediency, arguing that concessions to Roman Catholics must be accompanied by guarantees for protestants. In private he was urged by Peel to say nothing that would prevent him from taking up the question at a later date. In July the election of Daniel O'Connell, a Roman Catholic and therefore ineligible to take the oath, in the County Clare by-election (another consequence of the Huskissonite resignations) brought a new danger. Having discussed the situation at length with Peel, the duke sent a memorandum to the king dated 1 August pointing out that the threat of a repetition of the County Clare election effectively paralysed Irish administration, and requesting permission to embark on a confidential review of the whole Catholic problem with Peel and the lord chancellor. His own ideas for a settlement, laid out in a memorandum for Peel, envisaged payment of Irish Catholic priests, suspension rather than abolition of the penal laws, and a reduction in the size of the Irish county electorate.

Apart from these internal discussions, the summer passed away with no progress on the main issue. Wellington felt that he could not depart from the principle of government neutrality without the king's permission; the king, physically ill and temperamentally irresolute, evaded any positive commitment. In Ireland the mounting expectation was heightened by an indiscreet letter from the prime minister to his old Peninsular friend Curtis, now the Roman Catholic archbishop of Armagh, which was leaked to the Irish press. On 10 January 1829 the continued indiscretions of another Peninsular veteran, now marquess of Anglesey and lord lieutenant of Ireland, resulted in his peremptory recall. The increasing atmosphere of crisis and alarm convinced Peel of the need to remain at the duke's side rather than persist with the provisional resignation he had tendered in May. For Wellington this helped to unblock the whole situation, and after interviewing three cabinet ministers previously opposed to emancipation George IV reluctantly gave permission on 15 January for the cabinet to take the Irish problem into consideration.

There were now less than three weeks before parliament met in which to settle the details of a settlement of the Catholic issue. In the course of intensive discussion most of Wellington's securities were dropped, because of the feeling in the cabinet that they were either technically impracticable or politically unacceptable. After a last-minute show of resistance by George IV, the ministerial plan, foreshadowed in the king's speech on 5 February, was placed before parliament in the course of February and March. It included the suppression of the Catholic Association; the admission of Roman Catholics to parliament, to all but a few offices under the crown, and to all civil and municipal offices without restriction; and a limitation of the Irish county franchise qualification. There was no veto on Roman Catholic episcopal appointments, no concordat with the pope, in fact none of the safeguards which Wellington had formerly considered necessary. He had been persuaded of their inutility partly by Henry Phillpotts, later bishop of Exeter, partly by Peel and his other cabinet colleagues. The bill represented, as he admitted in his speech in the Lords on the second reading

on 2 April, a great change of opinion on his part; but in politics as in war, the duke never found it difficult to abandon untenable positions.

The anger of the tory Anglicans at what appeared to be a complete surrender to the emancipation party was deep and bitter. It found expression in gross personal abuse of the principal authors of the bill, the prime minister and the home secretary, and resulted in a duel between Wellington and one of his most insulting critics, Lord Winchilsea, at Battersea Fields on 21 March, when both men carefully fired wide. The duke maintained afterwards that he fought to vindicate not his personal honour but the right of a public figure to change his opinions; but not everyone accepted this high-minded explanation. The resentment of the ultra-protestants could not, however, be dispersed by a couple of pistol shots. Two considerations in particular made Wellington's political conduct seem an unforgiveable betrayal: the general ignorance of his long-standing opinions on the Catholic question and the secrecy with which he had shrouded his actions following the County Clare election. The upshot was that, having given hostages to fortune by shedding the liberal Huskissonites, the duke had now alienated the ultra-tory wing of his supporters.

It is probable that in the existing political circumstances only the duke could have broken the deadlock over emancipation. In so doing he got rid of an issue which every administration since 1801 had found both insoluble and disruptive. In a sense it was a solution imposed on both the monarch and parliament by an authoritarian prime minister using to the full his executive power. But it was an act which further diminished the parliamentary basis of his government. The damage was mainly felt by Peel in the House of Commons; the duke could never be brought to believe that his ministry lacked numerical support in the lower house, only that it was weak in debating talent, to which he did not attach much importance. In this, as in other respects, he showed his lack of political sense. Years of military command and unbroken success had hardened his self-confidence and autocratic outlook. He despised public opinion because he had seen it so often prove unstable and misguided, and he was not a good manager of men because what had counted in his military life was leadership and discipline, not management and persuasion. Even in the cabinet he tended to interpret disagreement and criticism as indications of personal hostility, and the longer his ministry lasted the more peevish and disillusioned he became. So conscious was he of the alien character of the office he had taken on, that in the early summer of 1830, when George IV was clearly dying, he wrote a memorandum for Peel suggesting that the new reign should be made the occasion for his own retirement and Peel's succession to the premiership. The document was never sent, however, probably because of the objections raised by his over-partial friends the Arbuthnots.

Disintegration of the government At the same time the duke's innate conservatism inhibited him from accepting any of the new economic and financial policies which his former Liverpool cabinet colleagues were pressing on him. The proposal of the chancellor of the exchequer, Goulburn, in the spring of 1830 to revive the wartime income tax in modified form, though supported by the House of Commons members of the cabinet, found no sympathy with the prime minister. He thought the tax would press heavily on the landed aristocracy and that to resort to such an expedient would damage the credit of the country in the eyes of foreign powers. The consequent lack of apparent government initiatives in the 1830 session led to a steady erosion of its authority, and the general election in the summer caused by the king's death did nothing to improve matters. News of the July revolution in Paris, which came during the later stage of the polling, while it did not affect the outcome, added to the disorder of British domestic politics. The ultra-tory press seized the occasion to charge Wellington with being an accomplice of the overthrown Bourbon regime, and coupled this with Peel's recently introduced Metropolitan Police to accuse the duke of planning a military dictatorship. This was pure party vindictiveness. In fact there was immediate British recognition of the new French ruler, Louis Philippe, and when a similar revolution took place in Brussels shortly afterwards Wellington acted in concert with the French government to calm the situation.

Wellington in reality had no great opinion of the evicted Bourbon monarchy he had helped to put on the throne. The new French government was anxious to secure British friendship, and the arrival in London of the aged but familiar figure of Talleyrand as French ambassador was welcomed by the prime minister. While he regretted the break-up of the kingdom of the Netherlands, he soon realized that it could not be stopped. He concentrated instead on securing a member of the house of Orange as a ruler of the new state and preventing French military intervention. He refused Dutch appeals for assistance and sought a compromise settlement with the French government. They were more than ready to meet him halfway. While prepared for intervention to protect the rebellious Belgians against their former Dutch masters, French diplomacy had as its main object the preservation of peace. Wellington was able therefore to get general agreement for the issue to be submitted to the European powers responsible for the 1815 treaties, and for London rather than Paris to be the place for a conference. Though the detailed settlement of the Belgian question was ultimately left for his successors to negotiate, it was the duke who constructed the foundation for their work. His achievement owed something to the inability of Russia and the reluctance of Austria and Prussia to intervene, and even more to the needs of the fragile new regime in France. Nevertheless, in this final belated success for his diplomacy the duke showed realistic common sense in his handling of what was the first great breach that had so far been made in the 1815 territorial settlement.

Little domestic credit, however, accrued to Wellington on that account. By November 1830 it was obvious that the ministry was neither popular nor influential, and that there was a general feeling in the country in favour of more government economies, tax reduction, and parliamentary reform. Under pressure from his colleagues Wellington in September reluctantly agreed to explore the possibility of bringing back some of Canning's old followers. But after Huskisson's death in September the rest of his group were unwilling to return without a pledge of parliamentary reform and the inclusion in the cabinet of some of the whigs. This Wellington was not prepared to accept. It was in these uncertain circumstances that the duke made his celebrated declaration, in the debate on the king's speech at the beginning of November, that the constitution needed no improvement and that he would resist any measure of parliamentary reform as long as he was in office. Couched in his usual peremptory and uncompromising style, his statement was probably intended not so much to win back the ultra-tories (the usual interpretation placed on it at the time) as to make his own attitude plain and so put a stop to all the talk of parliamentary reform which had been going on, both outside and inside the administration, for several weeks. The speech was followed a few days later by the much derided decision to cancel the attendance of the king and his ministers at the lord mayor's banquet on 9 November for fear of public demonstrations. The final event in a suddenly worsening crisis was the defeat of the government in the House of Commons on 15 November on a hostile motion to submit its civil list to the scrutiny of a parliamentary committee. This unprecedented and offensive demand demonstrated more clearly than anything else that the ministry had lost control of the legislature. With Brougham's long-advertised parliamentary reform motion due to be debated the following day, the cabinet decided to avoid further humiliation. Next day Wellington laid his resignation before the king and by 22 November had ceased to hold office.

The duke later attributed the fall of his ministry to two adventitious factors: the duke of Cumberland's activity in stirring up ultra-tory opposition to him, and the effect of the July revolution in France in creating a temporary enthusiasm for parliamentary reform among the British public. What he would not admit was that either Catholic emancipation or his anti-reform speech had been a direct cause. It is clear, however, that neither before nor after the general election did his administration enjoy firm support in the Commons and that to survive the 1830–31 session would require imaginative leadership and parliamentary skill. Wellington was incapable of either, and the growing realization of his defects as prime minister had by 1830 demoralized his cabinet. Most of his colleagues were resigned to their fate; some, including Peel, welcomed it. The duke himself was probably not sorry to go. For three years he had been playing a role for which he was not suited either by temperament or training, and the strain was beginning to tell. It was a final irony that his own political limitations brought about the end of the parliamentary system of which he had made himself the champion.

The crisis of reform, 1831–1832 During the protracted reform crisis of 1831–2 Wellington's attitude was shaped by two considerations. He thought that the whig Reform Bill would be the ruin of the constitution and that the excitement in its favour was an artificial product not supported by the solid majority of his countrymen. His tactics were based on the belief that the government would not pin its existence to the bill and that the opposition should aim at gaining time for the true feeling in the country to assert itself. He therefore tried to restore good relations with the ultra-tories and discourage those Conservative peers (the so-called Waverers) anxious to negotiate a compromise. As always he felt that his primary duty was to the throne, and as early as November 1831, when advising the king to suppress the Birmingham Political Union, he let William IV know that if he wished to escape from his whig ministers he could count on the duke's assistance. Impervious to the hostility of the London mob, which twice smashed the windows of Apsley House, he planned his political battle with care. The decision to oppose the second reading of the bill was taken at a meeting of peers at Apsley House on 21 September 1831. When the bill was duly rejected by a decisive majority of 199 votes to 158, he hoped for a respite of six months in which both the nation and the ministers would come to their senses. During the autumn, however, the violence in the country, the resolution of the ministry, and the activity of the Waverers undermined the solidarity of the opposition peers. When a revised bill came to the Lords in April 1832 it passed by 184 votes to 175, though the duke both spoke and voted against it.

Wellington's tactics now became increasingly confused. He realized that reform of some sort was inevitable. Nevertheless, he still wanted to retain the support of the ultra-tory peers so that he could continue to influence events. The success, however, of an opposition amendment on 7 May to postpone the disfranchising clauses of the bill merely served to reveal the determination of the cabinet to force it through, if necessary by large peerage creations, or else resign. The startled duke and his colleagues felt obliged to make a disclosure of how far they themselves were ready to reform. But this in turn simply uncovered the ambivalent nature of the opposition without shaking the cabinet's resolve to bring the whole reform issue to a head.

The resignation of the ministry on 9 May placed Wellington in an extraordinary position. To take office with the king's stipulation that he must be prepared to carry an extensive measure of reform involved him in a display of public inconsistency, a sacrifice of cherished convictions, and a loss of personal dignity which few public men would have contemplated. Only the refusal of Peel and most of his former colleagues in the Commons saved him from that degrading spectacle. After five days of anger, uproar, and agitation in the country and desperate efforts behind the scene to discover presentable politicians ready to join him, Wellington on 15 May resigned his commission and privately assured the king that he would drop any further opposition to the bill. He was now convinced that there was no credible alternative to Lord Grey's ministry and that further struggle was useless. Though he continued for several years to believe that the Reform Act of 1832 was a revolution by due force of law, this conviction in itself made him all the more reluctant to engage in systematic hostility to the whig ministries. Stable, preferably also strong, government was to the duke a more important consideration than party advantage or temporary triumphs.

Conservative statesman, 1833–1846 Nevertheless, Wellington was still an influential figure in politics, and when early in 1834 he was elected chancellor of Oxford University his installation in June was marked by noisy tory celebrations. The duke, who conspicuously lacked academic credentials, at one point suggested to his supporters that they should unite behind Peel, whose claims were stronger and who had substantial backing in the university. His failure to communicate this to his sensitive colleague in the Commons increased the coolness which had grown up between them since their disagreement over taking office in 1832. However, they sensibly acted in concert when declining an overture for a coalition with the whigs made at the king's direction in July 1834 following Lord Grey's resignation.

William IV's dismissal of the whigs in November 1834 brought Wellington back for the last time to the centre of the political stage. With Peel absent in Italy, the duke was sworn in as first lord of the Treasury and secretary of state on 17 November to act as temporary head of a new government until his colleague's arrival three weeks later. He then became foreign secretary. But while insisting from the start that Peel must be the prime minister, the duke unwittingly presented him with an embarrassing *fait accompli*. Left to himself Peel might have refused a commission which promised little success; the preparations for a general election which he found in full swing on his return made it virtually impossible for him to meet parliament and explain his policies before appealing to the electorate. At the same time the extraordinary omnicompetent role of the duke in the first few weeks of the new administration alienated many moderate politicians, in particular the recently seceded members of Grey's cabinet—Stanley, Graham, Ripon, and Richmond—whom Peel wished to recruit.

Nevertheless, Peel's 'hundred days' raised the morale of the Conservative Party and perceptibly improved the relations of the two leaders. In the following years the duke's influence in the upper house did much to secure a degree of unity among opposition peers and to prevent any serious divergence from the line taken by Peel in the Commons. It was not always possible for Wellington to control ultra-tory peers like Cumberland and Londonderry, and the issue of municipal reform in 1835 in particular placed a severe strain on party unity. Wellington's language in the House of Lords often suggested a more extreme opposition to the government than was borne out by his subsequent actions, and age, deafness, and recurrent ill health increased his dislike of formal party gatherings. With the accession of the young Victoria in 1837, moreover, the duke became markedly more reluctant to have a Conservative ministry thrust upon her. When Melbourne resigned over the Jamaican crisis of 1839, the queen on his advice sent for Wellington and it was he who counselled her to summon Peel. In the difficulties with Victoria over the ladies of the bedchamber he supported Peel, but the fiasco strengthened his scepticism about taking office. He himself showed remarkable restraint during the years 1839–41 in subordinating his private views to the decisions taken by the House of Commons on such issues as the Hansard case, Irish corporations, and the Canadian question. Despite occasional trepidation among his party colleagues over his inconsistent or perhaps devious tactics, he remained faithful to his principle of avoiding clashes either between the two branches of the legislature or between the two Conservative oppositions. In contrast to his military career, Wellington in politics rendered his best services as a second in command.

When Peel formed his cabinet in September 1841 the duke became a minister without portfolio. At seventy-two he was the oldest man in the cabinet and the decision not to burden him with departmental duties was clearly right. In the autumn of 1842, when Lord Hill resigned as commander of the forces because of ill health, Wellington was the only conceivable successor. Though he offered to resign from the cabinet and the leadership of the House of Lords, his object was clearly to remove any constitutional objection to his appointment; he knew his cabinet colleagues would not wish to see him go. He continued, therefore, to serve as expert adviser to the prime minister on various aspects of national policy, especially India, disorder in Ireland, and home defence. On the latter the advantage given to France by the development of steam power loomed large in his mind, and in 1845 he made a personal tour of the fortifications in the Strait of Dover. His presence in the government, however, was never more valuable to the prime minister than in the corn law crisis of 1845–6. Though disagreeing with Peel over the need to repeal the corn laws, he urged his cabinet colleagues in a memorandum of 30 November 1845 to support the prime minister since 'a good Government for the country is more important than Corn Laws or any other consideration' (*Memoirs of Sir Robert Peel*, ed. Lord Mahon and Edward Cardwell, 1858, 2.200). After the failure of Lord John Russell to form a ministry in December, the issue for the duke became then a simple matter of loyalty to the queen and her prime minister. At the crucial second reading of the Corn Bill on 25 May 1846 he told the peers bluntly that they could not afford to isolate themselves from the crown and the majority in the House of Commons, and he later advised Peel, in the event of defeat on the Irish Coercion Bill, to dissolve parliament and go to the country.

The end of Peel's ministry, however, in June 1846, marked the effective end of the duke's political career. Though he believed it important that a strong Conservative Party should continue to exist, he felt it inconsistent with his public position to act as leader of opposition in the Lords. As a 'retained servant of the Sovereign', to use his own phrase (*Croker Papers*, 3.51), and commander-in-chief of the army, his allegiance was to something higher than party. As late as 1851, when informed confidentially by Prince Albert of the cabinet crisis in late February, he expressed the view that it was better to have the Liberals in office rather than joining the opposition radicals in attacks on the country's institutions. The last time his services were called upon in any extraordinary fashion, however, was in 1848 on the occasion of the great Chartist demonstration in London. Wellington organized the military preparations with all his old vigour; but in the event the Metropolitan Police maintained control of the streets with no need for assistance.

Commander-in-chief and other appointments, 1820–1852
Wellington's ten-year period as head of the army from 1842 to 1852 not surprisingly showed him at his most conservative. He saw little reason to change either the organization or the equipment of the army with which he had beaten Napoleon. Never a lover of technical innovation, he regarded the old Brown Bess musket as the most serviceable infantry weapon so far produced. Even when he sanctioned a partial issue of the new Minié rifle, he insisted on modifications so that the existing stock of smooth-bore ammunition could be used. He was only reluctantly brought to acquiesce in Lord Grey's scheme in 1847 to reduce the minimum period for service in regiments of the line to ten years, and to the last defended the retention of flogging as a necessary disciplinary sanction. In the 1830s and 1840s he opposed whig attempts to simplify the complicated and inefficient system of army administration by amalgamating the Ordnance department with the office of commander-in-chief, and was equally adamant against the creation of a chief of staff.

Wellington's general attitude towards the army was paradoxically that of a civilian aristocrat rather than of a professional soldier. He shared the traditional view that a standing army was an anomaly in the British constitution, justified only by the needs of imperial defence and internal order, and was reluctant to bring it unnecessarily under public scrutiny. Given its unpopularity and the absence of conscription, his argument was that the quality of the recruits on entry was bound to be poor, and that long-service engagements were the only way to ensure efficiency. What troubled him was not the old-fashioned structure but the inadequate size of the standing army. The parsimony of successive governments since 1815 had brought the armed forces of the crown to a point in the 1840s when he believed with sombre intensity that the country was incapable of defending itself. Since he knew that there was little hope of reversing this tendency, he paid increasing attention in his later years to plans for fortifying harbours and dockyards, and for the revival of the old militia system. He lived to see the passage of the Derby ministry's Militia Bill of 1852, which he thought superior to that for a purely local militia proposed by the whigs in 1851. The fact remained, however, that in the more restricted area of internal army reform, where he might have brought about useful changes, he was disinclined to act; in the wider field of national defence his anxieties (revealed to the public through his famous leaked letter of 1847 to the inspector-general of fortifications, Sir John Burgoyne) made little impression. The outcome was the obsolescent Waterloo army which went to the Crimea two years after his death.

Chancellor of Oxford University Ironically, Wellington's robust common sense was seen at its best in his dealings as chancellor with the arcane world of Oxford University. In the controversies which followed the appointment of the theologically suspect Dr Hampden as regius professor in 1836, the duke invariably recommended the avoidance of personal feuds and the preservation of at least an outward appearance of academic harmony. He was less kindly disposed towards the Tractarians, since he thought their movement smacked of schism. In religion as in politics the duke believed in authority and discipline. He was particularly incensed when their party challenged his nomination of an evangelical vice-chancellor in 1844. His disconcerting proposal to make a personal appearance at the induction ceremony was tactfully evaded, however, and a satisfyingly orthodox vote in convocation in support of his candidate made further action unnecessary. A larger issue loomed up in the movement for university reform heralded by Lord Radnor's parliamentary activities in the 1830s. When the prospect of a public inquiry into the internal regulations of the colleges began increasingly to take shape, Wellington took the sensible view that it would be best for the university to anticipate compulsory reform from without by voluntary change from within. He could only, however, advise and warn; he could not command the academic society over which he incongruously presided. It was not his fault that reform, foreshadowed in the report of a royal commission in 1852, was in the end imposed on Oxford by parliament.

Other offices The three other important offices Wellington filled in the latter part of his life lay in more familiar territory. As constable of the Tower of London and lord lieutenant of the Tower Hamlets from 1826 he had to deal not only with patronage and military security but with the corrupt and lawless population of the Tower liberties and their endemic problems of civil order and public health. The post of constable of Dover Castle and lord warden of the Cinque Ports, to which he was appointed in 1829, involved an even wider range of responsibilities: harbour works, salvage, channel pilotage, appointments of local officials, and recommendations to the magistracy. The perquisites, however, included a residence at Walmer Castle, a domesticated Tudor fortress in Kent which became his favourite country residence. Though he treated neither of these quasi-honorary posts as sinecures, the most onerous of his subsidiary appointments was the lord lieutenancy of Hampshire, which he held for thirty-two years. The office, traditionally held by one of the titled landowners of the county, was still one of the most influential positions in local government. For Wellington it was an instrument for maintaining the traditional hierarchy of county society against the forces of

electoral democracy. His recommendations for the magistracy, one of his most important duties, showed a clear preference for men who were politically Conservative, and a distaste, amounting to a virtual veto, for manufacturers, attorneys, brewers, and (for different reasons) clergy. Nevertheless, though not a reformer, the duke demonstrated a readiness to improve, a regard to economy, and a liking for efficiency which almost ranks him as a Peelite. He did much to revive the county yeomanry after the agricultural riots of 1830 and at the very end of his life he was encouraging the organization of the county militia under the terms of the 1852 act. Unlike many tory gentry he supported the Poor Law Amendment Act of 1834 from a conviction of the weakness of the old system, and though he was opposed to a compulsory national police force he welcomed the permissive act of 1839, which in effect placed control of any new local police force in the hands of the magistracy. Hampshire, in fact, was the second county to adopt the act.

Character and personality These latter years, with a widening circle of friends (few of them military men other than his old Spanish crony Alava), allowed Wellington to display the other aspects of his complex nature. The epithet Iron Duke, which was current even in his lifetime, was a curiously misleading description and its origin is obscure. *Punch* used the term Wrought-Iron Duke as early as 1842. In October of that year his irreverent great-nephew Richard called him the Iron Duke when describing the funeral of the Marquess Wellesley, as though it were an already accepted nickname. In the duke's obituary in the *Annual Register* for 1853 the term appears three times, though always in an ironical sense, to point the difference between the real man and his public image.

It is unlikely that many of Wellington's contemporaries regarded him as the impassive, unfeeling man that the sobriquet suggests. It is true that he had schooled himself during his army career to control, if not entirely to suppress, his emotions, and long habit easily becomes second nature. A youthful introvert who had found fulfilment as a man of action, he always had two sides to his temperament. In later life, with ambition sated, his basic nature reasserted itself. It was essentially a warm and lively one. His fondness for playing with small children, his continued interest in music, his indiscriminate generosity, his wry humour, his unassuming friendliness towards ordinary people all testified to that. So too did his occasional gusts of anger, his resentment at presumed slights, and his partiality for sarcasm and irony. There was fire beneath the surface, not to speak of other emotions. His continuing interest in young women, when coupled with his compulsive urge to answer letters, led to some curious relationships. The intermittent correspondence with the religious-minded Miss Jenkins, nearly forty-five years his junior, was pursued in nearly 400 letters on his side between 1834 and 1851. Another sentimental and mainly epistolary friendship was with the equally youthful Angela Burdett-Coutts, wealthy heir of the banker Thomas Coutts, to whom he wrote over 800 letters and who (like Miss Jenkins) did her best to become his duchess: an outcome which the duke steadfastly avoided.

Little of this was known in Wellington's lifetime. To the outside world the image he presented was that of a less complicated, more soldierly figure. He was seen as the archetypal servant of the state, whose watchwords were duty and service. He contributed to the making of this legend, which in any case embodied a substantial truth, by increasingly referring to himself in the third person, as though his extraordinary career had created a kind of separate personality, a national figure of whom he was the living guardian. As he wrote to Croker in 1834, 'I am Duke of Wellington and, *bon gré mal gré*, must do as the Duke of Wellington doth' (*Croker Papers*, 2.224). The conventions of written correspondence served to strengthen this concept, since the duke was the recipient of a large, varied, and incessant flow of letters from the general public. Much of it was unsolicited, much of it personal, but rarely going unanswered. Though he devised standard lithographed forms to lighten the load on his secretaries, he often could not refrain from adding a few pungent comments of his own. He complained bitterly of the burden of letter writing, but he would not have wished it to stop. It had become almost a psychological necessity for him to feel that he was universally consulted on matters of importance, personal and public, by the highest and lowest. His life had been full of action and responsibility, and it would have been hard for him not to have had at least the semblance of these things in his old age.

Unlike his unhappy wife, Wellington was a sociable man who loved to fill his house with congenial company. He was, moreover, a lively and inexhaustible conversationalist with a fund of stories from his unique experiences which became more polished and witty with countless repetitions. Yet he jealously guarded his privacy and would have been outraged had he known how many of his guests were secretly recording his remarks for posterity. Even the inevitable decline in his physical powers he tried to conceal as long as possible. To the end he protested that, deafness apart, he was as fit as he had ever been. In his later years he drove a curricle at alarming speeds both in London and along the narrow lanes of Kent, and he hunted regularly in Hampshire despite being (on the authority of R. S. Surtees, the austere hunting correspondent of the *New Sporting Magazine* in the 1830s) a clumsy rider who suffered countless falls. He was also a keen though indifferent and (for bystanders) an occasionally dangerous shot. Being susceptible to colds, he had a variety of strange shooting coats and galoshes to fend off the English climate, of which after so many years in warmer climes he had the lowest opinion. Gadgets of all kinds, in fact, had a fascination for him, from patent teapots and finger-stalls to a sword-umbrella and the formidable central-heating system he installed at Stratfield Saye.

Physical characteristics, illnesses, and death Though neat and almost dandyish in his dress on formal occasions, Wellington remained spartan in his personal habits, frugal in his diet, and notoriously indifferent to the quality of the food and wine he consumed. Physically he was a trim

but never a handsome man. His great nose and long, protruding jaw gave his profile something of the appearance of Punch, a resemblance joyfully seized on by the cartoonists though tactfully toned down in his many portraits, with the notable exception of the sketch by R. B. Haydon in 1839. In height Wellington was about 5 feet 9 inches, with brown hair that later turned silvery white, penetrating eyes usually described as blue though by some as grey, and a physique that even at the age of eighty-two impressed Thomas Carlyle as all muscle and bone. His voice was light, and when he spoke in public apt to be indistinct. This was partly due to loss of teeth in early life which was later remedied by a set of false teeth made of walrus ivory.

Wellington was most famously painted by Goya, whose chalk drawing of 1812 was said by Goya's grandson in 1862, when it was bought by the British Museum, to have been done the day after the battle of Salamanca, though this seems unlikely. All three of the oil portraits subsequently painted by Goya may derive from this drawing. Two very probably do; the portrait in the National Gallery was painted in August 1812 at the time when the duke entered Madrid and was probably, at least in part, done from life.

Wellington's general health began to deteriorate perceptibly after 1818, not surprisingly in view of the extraordinary demands of his soldierly career, his neglect of proper food, and the human vanity which led him to conceal any symptoms of physical weakness. Rheumatism in his neck and shoulders made his figure droop, and an attack of giddiness was reported as early as 1838. In November 1839, at Walmer, he suffered a severe stroke from which he only slowly recovered. More attacks came in the next few years, including one while riding in London in February 1840 and another a year later in the House of Lords, which were not easy to hide from public knowledge. After that there seems to have been an intermission, though the effects of the earlier seizures were evident in his changed appearance and failing energies. He resumed his sporting activities but in a more cautious fashion, and except for his deafness he seemed in better health as time went on. Active to the last, he died at Walmer Castle in the afternoon of 14 September 1852 following a stroke early that morning. His body lay in state at Walmer and then at Chelsea Hospital. His burial at St Paul's Cathedral on 18 November was the occasion for probably the most ornate and spectacular funeral ever seen in England, the procession from Horse Guards via Constitution Hill to St Paul's being witnessed, it was estimated, by a million and a half people (*LondG*, 3 Dec 1852; *Annual Register*, 1852, 482–92). Alfred Stevens's monument to the duke was later erected in an arch in the north side of the cathedral's nave.

Retrospect Wellington's funeral marked, for all its florid pomposity, the general sense among his countrymen that they had lost a great man: 'the only great man of the present time', wrote Greville (*The Greville Memoirs, 1814–1860*, ed. G. L. Strachey and R. Fulford, 8 vols., 1938, 18 Sept 1852), who had no reason to be friendly. 'The last great Englishman is low' lamented Tennyson in his fine funerary *Ode on the Death of the Duke of Wellington* (1852). In the years that followed Wellington's name was commemorated in almost every imaginable way, from articles of clothing, streets (fifty-seven in London), barracks, towers, waterfalls, and warships to a public school near Sandhurst, the capital city of New Zealand, and the great Californian redwood tree *Sequoia gigantica*. Already in his lifetime anecdotes had begun to cluster around him—some true, some (like 'publish and be damned') highly doubtful, others (like 'try sparrow-hawks, ma'am') demonstrably fictitious. That he remains one of the best-known characters in English history is not solely due to his military achievements, though these were greater than those of his only two rivals, Cromwell and Marlborough, nor to his unwavering sense of public duty, though it was the general recognition of this that enabled him to ride out his crisis of personal unpopularity in 1829–32 with undiminished reputation. Besides these outward virtues were the more human and endearing aspects: his lack of conceit, his ability to reflect with humorous detachment on his astonishing life, and a fundamental simplicity which charmed his friends and disarmed his enemies.

Earlier assessments of Wellington's professional career tended to be coloured by personal or patriotic prejudices, with British as with continental historians. Subsequent studies have enabled his military achievements to be seen in a more objective light than was possible in the first fifty years after his death. They have not, however, resulted in any substantial reversal of judgement, only a more discriminating analysis of his qualities. Moreover, they have revealed something which the earlier historians, concentrating on battles and campaigns, tended to overlook: the crucial importance of his organization and administration of the Peninsular army. Family influence and his elder brother's money gave Wellington invaluable advantages at the outset of his career, but what he made of those advantages was the work of no ordinary man. He was fortunate in the opportunities which came his way; yet he was active, in his early years aggressively so, in seeking them out. He had remarkable luck in escaping death by shipwreck or on the battlefield, but in the hazardous profession of war few rise to the top without a measure of luck. It has been said of him that he lacked the brilliance of Marlborough or Napoleon; but if as a general he was not a supreme artist, he was a supreme professional. His was the sober form of genius defined by Carlyle as the 'transcendent capacity of taking trouble'. If chance seemed to favour him, it was because he left so little to chance.

Wellington was successful in so many things that he came to believe that he could undertake anything. What is surprising is how well his integrity, common sense, and attention to detail carried him through even in positions for which he was patently unsuited. The world of politics which he entered in 1818 was, as it is for most soldiers, alien and uncomfortable. Yet no account of early nineteenth-century political history is complete that does not take into account his positive contribution. His premiership, disastrous in most respects, was vindicated by the single achievement of Catholic emancipation. His influence in the House of Lords helped to consolidate the Conservative Party in the 1830s and sustain Peel's ministry in the 1840s. Like all men he had his weaknesses. He could be unduly secretive in his actions, unduly prejudiced in his opinions. There was more than a touch of egotism in his nature and he was often insensitive to the feelings of others. But these defects were redeemed by his innate kindness and sense of justice. His idiosyncrasies were for the most part harmless while his virtues were solid as rock. A military commander of rare and comprehensive ability, a dedicated servant of the state, Wellington was also a remarkable human being whose personality left an imprint on his countrymen equalled only by that of Winston Churchill a century after him.   NORMAN GASH

Sources CORRESPONDENCE *The dispatches of … the duke of Wellington … from 1799 to 1818*, ed. J. Gurwood, 13 vols. in 12 (1834–9) · *Despatches, correspondence, and memoranda of Field Marshal Arthur, duke of Wellington*, ed. A. R. Wellesley, second duke of Wellington, 8 vols. (1867–80) · *Supplementary despatches (correspondence) and memoranda of Field Marshal Arthur, duke of Wellington*, ed. A. R. Wellesley, second duke of Wellington, 15 vols. (1858–72) · *Political correspondence: Wellington*, ed. J. Brooke and J. Gandy, 1: *1833 – November 1834* (1975) · *Political correspondence: Wellington*, ed. R. J. Olney and J. Melvin, 2: *November 1834 – April 1835* (1986) · U. Southampton L., Wellington MSS

BIOGRAPHICAL STUDIES M. S. Partridge, *The Duke of Wellington, 1769–1852: a bibliography* (1990) · E. Longford [E. H. Pakenham, countess of Longford], *Wellington*, 1: *The years of the sword* (1969) · E. Longford [E. H. Pakenham, countess of Longford], *Wellington*, 2: *Pillar of state* (1972) · H. E. Maxwell, *The life of Wellington: the restoration of the martial power of Great Britain*, 2 vols. (1899) · G. R. Gleig, *The life of Arthur, duke of Wellington* (1864) · P. Guedalla, *The duke* (1931) · N. Thompson, *Wellington after Waterloo* (1986) · E. A. Smith, *Wellington and the Arbuthnots* (1994) · N. Gash, ed., *Wellington: studies in the military and political career of the first duke of Wellington* (1990) · C. M. Woolgar, ed., *Wellington studies*, 1 (1996) · R. W. Davis, 'Wellington and the resurgence of the House of Lords', *Lords of parliament*, ed. R. W. Davis (1995)

MILITARY CAREER W. F. P. Napier, *History of the war in the Peninsula and in the south of France*, rev. edn, 6 vols. (1860) · D. Gates, *The Spanish ulcer: a history of the Peninsular War* (1986) · M. Glover, *Wellington's Peninsular victories* (1962) · S. G. P. Ward, *Wellington's headquarters: a study of the administrative problems in the Peninsula, 1809–14* (1957) · H. Bernard, *Le duc de Wellington et la Belgique* (1987) · T. D. Neve, *The duke of Wellington and the British army of occupation in France, 1815–1818* (1992)

PERSONAL LIFE *Diary of Frances, Lady Shelley*, ed. R. Edgcumbe, 2 vols. (1912–13) · *The journal of Mrs Arbuthnot, 1820–1832*, ed. F. Bamford and the duke of Wellington [G. Wellesley], 2 vols. (1950) · C. Oman, *The Gascoyne heiress: life and diaries of Frances Mary Gascoyne-Cecil, 1802–1839* (1968) · *The Creevey papers*, ed. H. Maxwell, 3rd edn (1905); repr. (1923) · *The Croker papers: the correspondence and diaries of … John Wilson Croker*, ed. L. J. Jennings, 3 vols. (1884) · T. Raikes, *Portion of a diary kept by Thomas Raikes, 1831–47*, 4 vols. (1856–7) · G. W. Chad, *The conversations of the first duke of Wellington with George William Chad*, ed. A. Wellesley, seventh duke of Wellington (1856) · W. A. Fraser, *Words on Wellington* (1892) · F. Egerton, first earl of Ellesmere, *Personal reminiscences of the duke of Wellington*, ed. Alice, countess of Strafford (1903) · P. H. Stanhope, *Notes of conversations with the duke of Wellington, 1831–1851*, 3rd edn (1889) · G. R. Gleig, *Personal reminiscences of the duke of Wellington* (1904) · N. Gash, *Wellington anecdotes: a critical survey* (1992)

CONTEMPORARY STATESMEN I. Butler, *The eldest brother: the Marquess Wellesley, the duke of Wellington's eldest brother* (1973) · A. Alison, *Lives of Lord Castlereagh and Sir C. Stewart*, 3 vols. (1861) · W. Hinde, *Castlereagh* (1981) · *The letters of King George IV, 1812–1830*, ed. A. Aspinall, 3 vols. (1938) · C. D. Yonge, *The life and administration of Robert Banks, second earl of Liverpool*, 3 vols. (1868) · N. Gash, *Lord Liverpool* (1984) · C. S. Parker, ed., *Sir Robert Peel: from his private papers*, 3 vols. (1891–9) · N. Gash, *Mr Secretary Peel: the life of Sir Robert Peel to 1830* (1961) · N. Gash, *Sir Robert Peel: the life of Sir Robert Peel after 1830* (1972) · W. Hinde, *Canning* (1983) · R. G. Thorne, 'Wellesley, Sir Arthur', HoP, *Commons, 1790–1820*, 5.503–6

WORKS OF REFERENCE A. Braham, 'Goya's portrait of the duke of Wellington in the National Gallery', *Burlington Magazine*, 108 (1966), 78–83 · G. Wellesley and J. Steegmann, *The iconography of the first duke of Wellington* (1935) · *Annual Register* (1852) · *Annual Register* (1853) · parish register (baptism), Dublin, St Peter · *LondG* (3 Dec 1852)

Archives Badminton House, Gloucestershire, corresp. relating to Cadiz · BL, corresp., Add. MS 63090 · BL, letters, papers, and dispatches from Peninsular War, Add. MS 64131 · BL, letters to civil and military officers in Madras, Add. MS 29238 [copies] · BL, Waterloo dispatch, Add. MS 69850 · BL OIOC, corresp. and papers relating to India · BL OIOC, letter-book of corresp. with residents at Poona, MS Eur E 216 · Duke U., Perkins L., corresp. · FM Cam., letters · McGill University, Montreal, McLennan Library, political and military letters · NL Scot., corresp. · NL Scot., letters on Scottish garrisons and Peninsular War · NRA, corresp. relating to Tralee borough · NRA, letters on Hampshire lieutenancy matters · Stratfield Saye House, Hampshire, personal, family, legal, and estate papers · Suffolk RO, Bury St Edmunds, copies of peninsula and Waterloo dispatches · U. Southampton L., political, military, and official papers · Walmer Castle, Kent | Balliol Oxf., letters to David Urquhart · Beds. & Luton ARS, corresp. with Earl de Grey · BL, corresp. with fourth earl of Aberdeen, Add. MSS 43056–43060 · BL, corresp. with third Earl Bathurst, loan 57 · BL, corresp. with Viscount Beresford, Add. MSS 21504, 36306 · BL, letters to William Draper Best, first Baron Wynford, Add. MS 63084 · BL, letters to J. W. Croker, Add. MS 38078 · BL, corresp. with W. E. Gladstone, Add. MSS 44086–44835 · BL, corresp. with Viscount Goderich, Add. MSS 40306–40877 · BL, corresp. with Sir James Willoughby Gordon, Add. MS 49481 · BL, letters to Lord Grenville, Add. MS 58990 · BL, corresp. with John Charles Herries, Add. MS 57368 · BL, corresp. with Sir Rowland Hill, Add. MSS 35059–35060 · BL, corresp. with W. Huskisson, Add. MSS 38738–38756 · BL, corresp. with Prince Lieven, Add. MS 47259 · BL, letters to earls of Liverpool, Add. MS 38196, loan 72 · BL, corresp. with third Viscount Melbourne, Add. MSS 60411–60415 · BL, letters to Sir Thomas Munro, Add. MS 29239 · BL, letters to Sir Robert Peel, Add. MSS 40306–40310, 40549–40561 · BL, corresp. with Marquess Wellesley, Add. MSS 13669–13674, 13772–13778, 37288–37315 · BL OIOC, letters to Sir Thomas Munro · BL OIOC, letters to James George Scott, MS Eur D 828 · BL OIOC, letters to Lord Tweeddale, MS Eur F 96 · Bodl. Oxf., corresp. with Sir William Napier, with other corresp. [copies] · Bodl. Oxf., letters mainly to the North family · Bodl. Oxf., letters to Benjamin Symons · Bodl. Oxf., corresp. with Philip Wynter · Bucks. RLSS, corresp. with first Baron Cottesloe, with related papers · Bucks. RLSS, papers and corresp. with Sir W. H. Fremantle · Bucks. RLSS, letters to Viscount Goderich · CKS, corresp. with first Marquess Camden and second Marquess Camden · CKS, corresp. with first Viscount Hardinge and others relating mainly to Ireland · CKS, corresp. with fifth earl of Stanhope · Cleveland Public Library, Ohio, letters mainly to James Stuart · Cornwall RO, letters to Charles Yorke · Cumbria AS, Carlisle, corresp. with Sir James Graham · Cumbria AS, Carlisle, letters to first earl of Lonsdale · Derbys. RO, letters to Sir R. J. Wilmot-Horton · Devon RO, letters to first Viscount Sidmouth · Durham RO, corresp. with third marquess of Londonderry · Exeter Cathedral, letters to Henry Phillpotts · Flintshire RO, Hawarden, letters to duchess of Northumberland · Glos. RO, corresp. with first earl of Redesdale ·

Gwent RO, Cwmbrân, corresp. with Lord Mornington · Gwent RO, Cwmbrân, corresp. with Lord Raglan · Hants. RO, corresp. with George Tierney and his father · Hatfield House, Hertfordshire, letters to marchioness of Salisbury · Hunt. L., letters to Viscount Beresford · Hunt. L., letters to J. H. Erlington · Hunt. L., letters to the Grenville family · ING Barings, London, letters to Lord Ashburton · ING Barings, London, letters to Sir John Macdonald and Lady Macdonald · Inst. CE, letters to James Walker re Dover Harbour · JRL, letters to Sir Henry Clinton · Keele University Library, letters to second earl of Clare and his mother · Lincs. Arch., Revensby Abbey MSS · Lincs. Arch., letters to Emily, countess of Stanhope · LMA, letters to Sarah, countess of Jersey · Lpool RO, corresp. with fourteenth earl of Derby · McGill University, Montreal, McLennan Library, military corresp. with Sir Edward Blakeney and others · McGill University, Montreal, McLennan Library, letters to first Viscount Hardinge · NA Scot., corresp. with ninth earl of Dalhousie, eleventh earl of Dalhousie, and marquess of Dalhousie · NA Scot., corresp. with Sir Alexander Hope and G. W. Hope · NA Scot., letters to Sir Andrew Leith-Hay · NA Scot., letters to second Viscount Melville · NAM, corresp. with Sir Benjamin D'Urban [copies] · NAM, corresp. with Frederick Maitland, with other corresp. [copies] · Niedersächsisches Hauptstaatsarchiv Hannover, Hanover, corresp. with duke of Cumberland · NL Ire., corresp. with fourth duke of Richmond · NL Scot., corresp. with first Baron Lynedoch · NL Scot., letters to Sir George Murray · NL Scot., corresp. with Baron Stuart de Rothesay · NL Scot., corresp. with Alexander Walker · NL Scot., letters to Sir David Wilkie · NL Wales, letters to William Lloyd and Louisa Lloyd · NL Wales, corresp. with earl of Powis · NRA, priv. coll., corresp. with first marquess of Anglesey · NRA, priv. coll., letters to fifth duke of Buccleuch, Lord Montagu, and Lady Montagu · NRA, priv. coll., corresp. with first Earl Cathcart, second Earl Cathcart, and Sir George Cathcart · NRA, priv. coll., military and personal corresp. with Sir Galbraith Lowry Cole and Lady Frances Cole · NRA, priv. coll., letters to Sir Charles Colville and Viscount Colville · NRA, priv. coll., letters to first Marquess Conyngham, his wife, and second Marquess Conyngham · NRA, priv. coll., letters to the Drummond family · NRA, priv. coll., letters to first earl of Eldon · NRA, priv. coll., corresp. with Maurice Fitzgerald · NRA, priv. coll., letters to Harriet Hatton and Elizabeth Frances Hatton · NRA, priv. coll., letters to fourth earl of Hopetoun · Oriel College, Oxford, letters to R. D. Hampden · Pembroke College, Oxford, corresp. with G. W. Hall and Francis Jeune · priv. coll., Canning MSS · priv. coll., Castlereagh MSS · PRO, corresp. with first earl of Ellenborough, PRO 30/9, PRO 30/12 · PRO, corresp. with first Earl Granville, PRO 30/29 · PRO, corresp. with Sir George Murray, Wo80 · PRO, corresp. with Lord John Russell, PRO 30/22 · PRO NIre., corresp. with first marquess of Anglesey · PRO NIre., corresp. with John de la Poer Beresford · PRO NIre., corresp. with Viscount Castlereagh · PRO NIre., letters to Helen, countess of Dufferin · PRO NIre., corresp. with third marquess of Londonderry · Royal College of Surgeons, Edinburgh, corresp. with John Robert Hume · Sandon Hall, Staffordshire, Harrowby Manuscript Trust, letters to first earl of Harrowby, etc. · Sheff. Arch., corresp. with first Baron Wharncliffe · Shetland Archives, corresp. with Thomas Edmonston · Surrey HC, letters to Cuthbert Ellison · Surrey HC, letters to Henry Goulburn, with related papers · Trinity Cam., letters mainly to Lord Lyndhurst · U. Durham L., corresp. with third Earl Grey · U. Nott. L., corresp. with Lord William Bentinck · U. Nott. L., corresp. with fourth duke of Newcastle and fifth duke of Newcastle · U. Southampton L., personal corresp. with Christopher Collins, confidential servant, and related papers · U. Southampton L., corresp. with John Gurwood, editor of his dispatches · U. Southampton L., corresp. with William Holmes relating to Wellesley's health · U. Southampton L., corresp. with Sir John Malcolm · U. Southampton L., corresp. with third Viscount Palmerston · UCL, corresp. with first Baron Brougham · V&A NAL, letters to Lord De Blaquiere · V&A NAL, corresp. with B. D. Wyatt relating to Apsley House · W. Sussex RO, letters to A. F. Greville · W. Sussex

RO, letters to fifth duke of Richmond · W. Yorks. AS, Leeds, Yorkshire Archaeological Society, letters to Colonel Hervey · W. Yorks. AS, Leeds, Yorkshire Archaeological Society, letters to Lady Wellesley · W. Yorks. AS, Leeds, corresp. with George Canning · Warks. CRO, letters to Sir Alexander George Woodford

Likenesses J. Hoppner, oils, c.1795, Stratfield Saye, Hampshire · R. Home, oils, 1804, NPG · miniature, 1804, NPG · R. Home, oils, c.1805, Royal Collection · R. Cosway, miniature, c.1806, V&A · D. Pellegrini, oils, 1809, National Museum of Fine Arts, Lisbon · F. Bertolozzi, stipple, 1810 (after D. Pellegrini), BM, NPG · M. Place, stipple, 1811 (after Captain Raria), BM, NPG · F. Goya, chalk drawing, 1812, BM · F. Goya, oils, c.1812, National Gallery, London · T. Heaphy, two watercolour sketches, 1813–14, NPG · G. Clint, mezzotint, pubd 1814 (after J. Hoppner), NG Ire. · T. Phillips, oils, 1814, Stratfield Saye, Hampshire · W. Say, mezzotint, pubd 1814 (after T. Phillips), BM, NPG · T. Lawrence, oils, 1814–15, Royal Collection · P. E. Ströhling, oils, c.1815, NAM · P. Turnerelli, marble bust, 1815, Gov. Art Coll. · etching, pubd 1815 (after unknown artist), NPG · line engraving, pubd 1815 (after unknown artist), NPG · T. Lawrence, oils, c.1815–1816, Wellington Museum, London [*see illus.*] · T. Lawrence, chalk drawing, c.1816, NPG · R. Page, stipple, pubd 1816 (after unknown artist), BM, NPG · C. Turner, mezzotint, pubd 1816 (after J. Banzil), NG Ire. · P. Turnerelli, marble bust, 1816, NG Ire. · J. B. Isabey, miniature, 1818, Wallace Collection, London · R. Dighton, etching, 1819 (after his earlier work), BM, NPG · G. Hayter, group portrait, oils, 1820 (*The trial of Queen Caroline, 1820*), NPG · G. Jones, group portrait, oils, 1822 (*The battle of Vittoria*), Royal Collection · F. Chantrey, marble bust, 1824, Petworth House, Sussex · J. W. Pieneman, group portrait, oils, 1824 (*The battle of Waterloo*), Rijksmuseum, Amsterdam · F. Chantrey, marble bust, 1828, Royal Collection · D. Lucas, mezzotint, pubd 1828 (after T. Lawrence), BM, NPG · W. W. D., etching, 1830 (after unknown artist), NPG · J. Doyle, lithograph, pubd 1831–4 (after his earlier work), NG Ire. · D. Wilkie, oils, 1835, Hatfield House, Hertfordshire · J. Hall, two chalk drawings, 1836, Scot. NPG · J. Lucas, oils, 1838, Trinity House, London · D. Wilkie, group portrait, oils, 1838 (*The first council of Queen Victoria*), Royal Collection · H. P. Briggs, oils, c.1839, Scot. NPG · B. R. Haydon, oils, 1839, NPG · W. O. Burgess, mezzotint, pubd 1842 (after T. Lawrence), NPG · F. X. Winterhalter, oils, 1843, Royal Collection · J. Harris, aquatint, pubd 1844 (after H. de Daubrawa), BM, NPG · W. Tell, wood-engraving, pubd 1844 (after his earlier work), NG Ire. · H. P. Bone, enamel miniature, 1845 (after T. Lawrence), NPG · S. Cousins, mezzotint, pubd 1845 (after oil painting by T. Lawrence), NG Ire. · J. Steell, marble bust, 1845, Scot. NPG · J. P. Lassouquèra, lithograph, pubd 1849 (after his earlier work), NG Ire. · lithograph, pubd 1852 (after unknown artist), BM, NPG · T. H. Ellis, line engraving, pubd 1853 (after F. Shephard), BM, NPG · J. Miller, oils, 1853, Scot. NPG · G. Baxter, baxter print (after unknown artist), BM, NPG · H. Cook, line engraving (after R. Scanlan), BM, NPG · J. Doyle, caricature drawings, BM · J. Doyle, lithograph (after his earlier work), NG Ire. · Baron Gérard, oils, Gov. Art Coll. · F. Goya, oils, Wellington Museum, London · G. Hayter, group portrait, oils (*The House of Commons, 1833*), NPG · T. Hazelhurst, watercolour on paper, NG Ire. · J. Henning, medallion, Scot. NPG · JPS or JCP, pen-and-ink drawing, NPG · J. Lucas, oils, NG Ire. · B. Pearce, silhouette, NPG · H. W. Pickersgill, oils, Oriental Club, London · W. Salter, group portrait, oils (*Waterloo banquet at Apsley House*), Wellington Museum, London · E. Smith, line engraving (after oil painting by T. Lawrence), NG Ire. · R. Thorburn, group portrait (with grandchildren), Stratfield Saye, Hampshire · D. Wilkie, oils, Aberdeen Art Gallery · D. Wilkie, pencil and watercolour, Scot. NPG · F. X. Winterhalter, group portrait, oils (*1st of May, 1851*), Royal Collection · etching (after unknown artist), NPG · lithograph (after unknown artist), BM, NPG · lithograph (after unknown artist), NPG · mezzotint (after T. Lawrence), NPG · plaster cast of death mask, NPG · watercolour on paper (after C. R. Leslie), NG Ire.

Wealth at death gross annual rental of Stratfield Saye (£16,873): 1873 return of owners of land

Wellesley [*née* Ashton], **Dorothy Violet**, duchess of Wellington (1889–1956), poet, was born on 30 July 1889 at Heywood Lodge, White Waltham, Berkshire, the only daughter of Robert Ashton, of Croughton, Cheshire, and his wife, Lucy Cecilia, *née* Dunn-Gardner (d. 1931). After her father's death when she was about seven years old, her mother married, in 1899, Aldred Beresford Lumley (1857–1945), the tenth earl of Scarbrough. Dorothy suffered from tuberculosis in adolescence, a disease which killed her twenty-year-old brother. On 30 April 1914 she married Lord Gerald Wellesley (1885–1972), secretary in the diplomatic service, who succeeded his nephew as seventh duke of Wellington in 1943. The Wellesleys spent the early part of their married life in Constantinople before returning to England prior to the outbreak of war. They had one son, Marquess Douro, and one daughter, Lady Elizabeth Clyde. Wellesley largely lived apart from her husband and he is an obscure presence in her autobiography *Far Have I Travelled* (1952).

Privately educated, Wellesley started writing poetry at a very young age and published *Early Poems* in 1913. She took a flat of her own in Hyde Park and became a friend of Vita Sackville-West, and to a far lesser extent, Virginia Woolf; Sackville-West dedicated *The Land* (1926) to Wellesley, and they almost certainly had a brief romantic attachment. Woolf found Wellesley 'pecking and exacting' of Vita, and Wellesley thought Woolf perverse, intellectually intolerant, and teasing (Lee; Wellesley, 153). Wellesley's later *Poems* (1920) had a lukewarm reception, and she was judged to be 'languishing through weary lines in quest of a dimly pagan paradise' (*The Times*, 12 July 1956). Sackville-West surmised that a university education might have disciplined Wellesley's often careless and unrevised work, and, one might add, her romantic capriciousness. Nevertheless *Genesis* (1926), the poem-sequence *Deserted House* (1931), 'a luminous, if grotesque, revisitation of childhood' (Hamilton), and a collection, *Poems of Ten Years* (1934), brought Wellesley to the attention of a wider public. She was praised for her rich detailing of nature in 'Shells', 'Birds', and 'Moths', and for the energy of her anguish over the subjugation of the natural world by commercialism. In his introduction to her *Selections from the Poems of Dorothy Wellesley* (1936), W. B. Yeats noted that 'she can unite a modern subject and vocabulary with traditional richness'.

Wellesley's reputation was only truly established owing to Yeats's support; they had become intimate friends in the last years of his life. He included her poem 'Horses' in his *Oxford Book of Modern Verse* (1936) and he also singled out for particular attention 'Walled Garden'; 'Matrix', a curious, philosophical vision of the womb as the source of the masculine soul; and 'Fire', which Yeats saw as expressing 'frenzied grandeur'. They also collaborated on a sequence of poems entitled 'The Three Bushes', a meditation upon the grave of a trio of lovers. Yeats's *Letters on Poetry* written to Wellesley were published in 1940, and she returned the favour with *Beyond the Grave* (c.1950), a collection of elegiac letters and poems addressed to him after his death.

Later volumes of Wellesley's poetry included *Lost Planet* (1942), *The Poets* (1943), *Desert Wells* (1946), and *Rhymes for Middle Years* (1954), the last a book of verses dedicated to 'the middle-aged'. Her prose works included a discursive and elusive autobiography, and a biography of childhood friend Sir George Goldie. She also edited the Living Poets series for the Hogarth Press; the English Poets in Pictures series (1941–2); and the 1937 series of Cuala Press broadsides with Yeats. She collected her poems in *Early Light* (1956).

In 1928, on the advice of Sackville-West, Wellesley had purchased Penns-in-the-Rocks at Withyham, Sussex, the dining room of which was designed by Vanessa Bell and Duncan Grant. She lived here with Hilda *Matheson ('amica amicarum') and Yeats considered it his English home. She also entertained other major literary figures and gave poetic and dramatic readings. Throughout her life Wellesley travelled widely in Egypt, India, Russia, and Persia with Sackville-West, and she was with Yeats in Roquebrune when he died (she read a few lines of her verse at his graveside).

Sackville-West described Wellesley as 'slight of build, almost fragile, with blazing blue eyes, fair hair, [and] transparently white skin' (*DNB*). George Goldie, who had an interest in phrenology, had felt her skull when Wellesley was a child, and had informed her then that she had overdeveloped bumps of temper, pride, and combativeness, and, indeed, she proved to be a self-styled iconoclast. She died on 11 July 1956 at Penns-in-the-Rocks.

Wellesley's literary reputation is contested. Kathleen Raine, editor of the 1964 version of *Letters on Poetry*, judged her to be a 'minor poet, [and] a not always perceptive judge of Yeats' poems', while Sackville-West felt that owing to Wellesley's half-formed philosophy, a weight was imposed upon her verse which 'it should never have been asked to carry' (*DNB*). Nevertheless the 'passionate precision' ascribed to her by Yeats perhaps best encapsulates Wellesley's work.

VITA SACKVILLE-WEST, rev. CLARE L. TAYLOR

Sources D. Wellesley, *Far have I travelled* (1952) · J. Shattock, *The Oxford guide to British women writers* (1993) · Blain, Clements & Grundy, *Feminist comp.* · H. Lee, *Virginia Woolf* (1997) · *The Times* (12 July 1956) · I. Hamilton, ed., *The Oxford companion to twentieth-century poetry in English* (1994) · W. B. Yeats, introduction, in *Selections from the poems of Dorothy Wellesley* (1936) · K. Raine, introduction, in *Letters on poetry from W. B. Yeats to Dorothy Wellesley* (1964), ix–xiii · Burke, *Peerage* (1999) · b. cert. · m. cert. · d. cert.
Archives State University of New York, Buffalo, corresp. and literary MSS | Emory University, Atlanta, Georgia, W. B. Yeats MSS, corresp. · U. Sussex, Monks House MSS, corresp.
Likenesses R. Whistler, pencil drawing, 1933, Stratfield Saye House, Hampshire · H. Coster, photograph, repro. in Wellesley, *Far have I travelled* · W. Rothenstein, drawing, repro. in Yeats, ed., *Selections* · W. Rothenstein, two drawings, Stratfield Saye House, Hampshire · Madame Yevonde, photograph, NPG
Wealth at death £20,467 12s. 7d.: probate, 16 Oct 1956, *CGPLA Eng. & Wales*

Wellesley, Garrett. *See* Wesley, Garrett, first earl of Mornington (1735–1781).

Wellesley, Sir George Greville (1814–1901), naval officer, born on 2 August 1814, was the third and youngest son of Gerald Valerian Wellesley DD (1770–1848), prebendary of Durham (the youngest brother of the duke of Wellington), and his wife, Lady Emily Mary (d. 1839), eldest daughter of Charles Sloane Cadogan, first Earl Cadogan. He entered the navy in 1828, taking the course at the Royal Naval College, Portsmouth. He passed his examination in 1834, and received his commission as lieutenant on 28 April 1838. In January 1839 he was appointed to the flagship in the Mediterranean for disposal, and on 30 March was sent to the frigate *Castor*, in which he served for over two years, ending as first lieutenant. In her he took part in the 1840 operations on the coast of Syria, including the attacks on Caiffa, Jaffa, Tyre, and Acre; he was twice gazetted. In November 1841 he was appointed to the frigate *Thalia*, going out to the East Indies; and on 16 April 1842 was promoted commander and appointed to the brig *Childers*, which he paid off two years later. On 2 December 1844 he was promoted captain, and in that rank was first employed in the *Daedalus*, which he commanded in the Pacific from 1849 to 1853. He married, on 25 January 1853, Elizabeth Doughty (d. 9 Jan 1906), youngest daughter of Robert Lukin. They had one daughter, Olivia Georgiana.

In February 1855 Wellesley was appointed to the *Cornwallis* (60 guns) for the Baltic, and commanded a squadron of the fleet at the bombardment of Sveaborg on 9 August. He was made CB in February 1856. The *Cornwallis* then went for a year to the North American station, after which, for five years, Wellesley commanded the Indian navy, which was then abolished. He was promoted rear-admiral on 3 April 1863, and in June 1865 was appointed admiral superintendent at Portsmouth, and held the post for four years. He was appointed, on 30 June 1869, commander-in-chief on the North America and West Indies station, and on 26 July following became vice-admiral. He returned home in September 1870, and from October 1870 to September 1871 was in command of the channel squadron; he was relieved after a court martial on the grounding of the *Agincourt* off Gibraltar in July. In May 1871 he had taken part in the Admiralty committee on ship designs, demonstrating a preference for high freeboard broadside armed ships, and a keen practical insight into the problems created by new designs. At the time he noted that he had not been at sea two nights since taking command the previous October.

In September 1873 Wellesley again became commander-in-chief on the North American station, where he remained until his promotion to admiral on 11 December 1875. From November 1877 to August 1879 he was first sea lord in W. H. Smith's Board of Admiralty. With the three obvious choices as senior naval lord out of the running, by refusal or alternative posts, Smith had few suitable officers to chose from. Wellesley was experienced, and in good health. He may well have been idle, by comparison with his workaholic successor Key, and ineffective, but that was the character of any Admiralty board of the time. He did secure a considerable increase in naval construction, though the ships were of dubious quality. In June

1879 he was awarded a good service pension, and he reached retirement age on 2 August of the same year. He was made KCB in April 1880, and GCB in 1887. In 1888 he became a commissioner of the Patriotic Fund. He died at his London home, 17 Chester Square, on 6 April 1901.

A brave officer, although not over-blessed with intellect, Wellesley was misplaced at the Admiralty. However, he was far from alone in that sad distinction. In an age of low estimates and arbitrary changes in policy, it took far stronger minds than his to resist the pressure for economy.　　L. G. C. LAUGHTON, rev. ANDREW LAMBERT

Sources P. H. Colomb, *Memoirs of Admiral the Right Honble. Sir Astley Cooper Key* (1898) · A. C. Dewar, ed., *Russian war, 1855, Black Sea: official correspondence*, Navy RS, 85 (1945) · B. M. Gough, *The Royal Navy and the north-west coast of North America, 1810–1914* (1971) · C. R. Low, *History of the Indian navy, 1613–1863*, 2 vols. (1877) · A. D. Lambert, 'Dalhousie: the last flagship of the Indian navy', in A. D. Lambert, *Warship '93: Fourth International Symposium on Naval Submarines* [London 1993] (1993), 9–18 · C. P. Fitzgerald, *Memories of the sea* (1913) · N. A. M. Rodger, 'The dark ages of the admiralty, 1869–1885: change and decay, 1874–1880', *Mariner's Mirror*, 62 (1976), 33–46 · N. A. M. Rodger, 'The dark ages of the admiralty, 1869–1885: peace, retrenchment and reform, 1880–1885', *Mariner's Mirror*, 62 (1976), 121–8 · J. Wells, *The immortal warrior* (1987) · 'Committee on designs for ships of war', *Parl. papers* (1872), 14.501, C. 477; 14.581, C. 477-I · *CGPLA Eng. & Wales* (1901)
Likenesses photograph, repro. in *ILN*, 118 (1901), 560
Wealth at death £8514 12s. 10d.: probate, 8 May 1901, *CGPLA Eng. & Wales*

Wellesley, Gerald Valerian (1809–1882), dean of Windsor, was the third son of Henry *Wellesley, first Baron Cowley (1773–1847), and his first wife, Lady Charlotte Cadogan (c.1781–1853), whom he divorced in 1810. He was born in London, and educated at Eton College and Trinity College, Cambridge, from whence he graduated MA in 1830. He was ordained in 1831, was rector of the family living of Stratfield Saye from 1836 to 1854, and dean of Windsor from 1854 until his death. On 16 September 1856, at St Mary's, Bryanston Square, London, he married the Hon. Magdalen 'Lily' Montagu (1831–1919), daughter of Henry Montagu, sixth Baron Rokeby, and his wife, Magdalen Huxley. They had one son, who died at the age of eighteen in 1883.

Wellesley was appointed resident chaplain to the queen in 1849, which, along with his appointment to the deanery of Windsor, brought him into close and regular contact with the royal family. His tact and gentlemanly demeanour made him one of Victoria's most valued advisers. In religious matters, he suited the queen, as he preached short sermons, and did 'everything on all sad and happy occasions to make me comfortable' (Fulford, 125). He was an essential conduit between Gladstone and the queen (not only on ecclesiastical matters), and the former frequently sought his advice on patronage questions. On his death, Gladstone noted in his diary: 'I reckoned his life the most valuable in the Church of England'. He died at Hazelwood, near Watford, on 17 September 1882, and was buried in St George's Chapel, Windsor. His wife was appointed extra woman of the bedchamber in the November following his death. The queen's requirements for his replacement summed up his character:

Gerald Valerian Wellesley (1809–1882), by John & Charles Watkins

a tolerant, liberal minded broad church clergyman who at the same time is pleasant socially & is popular with all Members and classes of her Household,—who understands her feelings not only in ecclesiastical but also in social matters—a good kind man without pride.　(Ponsonby, 62–3)

K. D. REYNOLDS

Sources W. A. Lindsay, *The royal household* (1898) · *Beloved mama: private correspondence of Queen Victoria and the German crown princess, 1878–1885*, ed. R. Fulford (1981) · Gladstone, *Diaries* · E. Longford, *Victoria RI* (1964) · Venn, *Alum. Cant.* · *The letters of Queen Victoria*, ed. A. C. Benson, Lord Esher [R. B. Brett], and G. E. Buckle, 9 vols. (1907–32) · A. Ponsonby, *Henry Ponsonby, Queen Victoria's private secretary: his life from his letters* (1942) · Burke, *Peerage*
Archives Royal Arch. · St George's Chapel, Windsor, corresp. and papers | BL, corresp. with W. E. Gladstone, Add. MSS 44339–44340 · BL, letters to Charles Kingsley, his wife, and his daughter, Add. MS 41299 · Bodl. Oxf., letters to Wilberforce family · LPL, corresp. with A. C. Tait · St George's Chapel, Windsor, letters to H. J. Ellison · St George's Chapel, Windsor, letters to Sir Henry Ponsonby · U. Durham L., letters to Charles Grey · U. Southampton L., letters to first duke of Wellington
Likenesses E. M. Ward, group portrait, oils, 1855 (*Queen Victoria investing Napoleon III with the order of the Garter at Windsor Castle*), Royal Collection · G. G. Adams, monument, 1882, Stratfield Saye House, Hampshire · H. von Angeli, oils, Royal Collection · Spy [L. Ward], caricature, chromolithograph, NPG; repro. in *VF* (8 April 1876) · J. & C. Watkins, photograph, NPG [*see illus.*] · woodcut (after photograph by S. A. Walker), NPG; repro. in *Pictorial World* (30 Sept 1882)

Wealth at death £9592 13s. 6d.: probate, 7 Nov 1882, *CGPLA Eng. & Wales*

Wellesley [*formerly* Wesley], **Henry**, **first Baron Cowley** (1773–1847), diplomatist, born at Dangan Castle, co. Meath, on 20 January 1773, was the youngest son of Garrett *Wesley, first earl of Mornington (1735–1781), and Anne (1742–1831), daughter of Arthur Hill, first Viscount Dungannon. He was brother of Richard *Wellesley, Marquess Wellesley, of Arthur *Wellesley, duke of Wellington, and of William Wellesley-*Pole, Baron Maryborough (afterwards third earl of Mornington). After being educated at Eton College (1783–9) and then studying languages and military science at the court of Brunswick in Germany (1789–90), he served in the army, where he exchanged from the 40th foot into the 1st foot guards in April 1791. He adopted the surname Wellesley some time after his eldest brother did so in 1789.

Wellesley's diplomatic career began with his appointment in 1791 as attaché to the British embassy at The Hague. The following year he went to Stockholm as secretary of legation. The year 1793 found him with his regiment in Flanders; it would prove to be his first and last encounter with military life. In February 1794 he left for Lisbon to accompany his sister Anne, recently widowed, to Britain. On the return trip their ship was seized by the French and passengers and crew were taken as prisoners of war, just as the terror entered its most violent stage. In January 1795, after Anne's release, Wellesley contrived his escape. He reached Britain's shores only after a harrowing crossing in which three men died. The experience confirmed the Wellesley family's antipathy for revolutionary France.

Wellesley subsequently was given a post in the Foreign Office as a précis writer and in July 1797 he accompanied Lord Malmesbury to Lille as his secretary. In November of the same year he sailed for India as private secretary to his brother, then Lord Mornington, afterwards Marquess Wellesley, the newly appointed governor-general. While in India, Henry Wellesley rendered important special services. Together with his brother Sir Arthur Wellesley (afterwards duke of Wellington), he acted as one of the commissioners for the settlement of Mysore after the defeat of Tipu Sultan. He was then dispatched to Britain to provide a firsthand account of the war and the treaties that concluded it. Lord Wellesley described him as 'next to himself most completely informed on these topics'. Henry Wellesley left India on 15 August 1799, and returned in February 1801. Soon after he was sent to Lucknow to negotiate a treaty requiring the vizier of Oudh to cede territory sufficient to defray the cost of the increased subsidized force dispatched to Oudh by the governor-general, and to act in conformity with the East India Company's instructions. On the treaty's conclusion Wellesley was appointed governor of the ceded territory. The court of directors of the company, though acknowledging his services, objected to the appointment because Wellesley was not a member of the service. They revoked the appointment but were subsequently overruled by the Board of Control, who pointed out that the Oudh mission was an

extraordinary service, and that Wellesley had declined all emoluments except his salary as private secretary to the governor-general. He resigned the governorship in March 1802, and returned to Europe. The following November the directors wrote to the governor-general a full acknowledgement of his brother's services in Oudh. Wellesley's years in India were not without controversy. On Lord Wellesley's return to Britain an attack on his governor-generalship was launched in parliament and Henry Wellesley's work was scrutinized along with the marquess's; though the inquiry lingered longer than expected, the brothers emerged with their reputations intact.

On 20 September 1803 Wellesley married Charlotte Sloane (c. 1781–1853), daughter of Charles Sloane, first Earl Cadogan. Together they had four children, three sons and a daughter. The eldest son, Henry Richard Charles *Wellesley, second Baron and first Earl Cowley, is separately noticed, as is the third son, Gerald Valerian *Wellesley. The second son, William Henry George, served as a captain in the Royal Navy. The daughter, Charlotte Arbuthnot, married Robert Grosvenor, first Lord Ebury. Wellesley was appointed a lord of the Treasury in 1804, a post he shortly afterwards resigned to take up an appointment as envoy to Spain. The outbreak of war with Spain prevented his going out and left him without employment. Subsequently, he was returned to parliament for Eye on 20 April 1808 and again appointed to the Treasury. In 1809 his marriage with Charlotte Sloane broke up in scandalous fashion, when Charlotte ran off with Henry Paget, the future first marquess of Anglesey. Wellesley was divorced by act of parliament on 22 February 1810, after an action for criminal conversation, in which he received £20,000 from Paget, who married Charlotte that same year. The event had two important consequences: Wellesley again resigned from the Treasury, and his brother Arthur refused to employ Paget in the Peninsular War, where cavalry officers of his calibre were much in demand.

In December 1809 Wellesley was again appointed envoy to Spain, this time by his brother the marquess, who had taken up the seals of office as foreign secretary. Accordingly, Wellesley was sworn of the privy council on 20 December 1809 and received his credentials as envoy-extraordinary on 3 January 1810. His appointment to the Spanish embassy put in place the remarkable arrangement whereby one family controlled the central places in Great Britain's prosecution of the war in Iberia: Arthur as commander-in-chief of the expeditionary forces, Richard as foreign secretary, and Henry as envoy and then (from 1 October 1811) ambassador to Spain. Together they worked to sustain the war effort throughout its most difficult stage. In 1812 Wellesley was knighted, and in January 1815 created GCB. In 1814 he prevailed upon the king of Spain to sign a treaty relinquishing for ever the scheme of a Bourbon alliance. After the peace he concluded a treaty with Spain containing an article by which Anglo-Spanish commercial relations were restored to those of 1796. In August 1815 he left Spain for Britain on leave. It was then that he married on 27 February 1816 his second wife, Georgiana Charlotte Augusta Cecil (1786–1860), eldest daughter of James Cecil, first marquess of Salisbury. Their only child, Georgiana Charlotte Mary, married William Henry Lytton Earle Bulwer, Baron Dalling and Bulwer. On his return to Spain, Wellesley negotiated in 1817 a treaty abolishing the slave trade.

Wellesley left Spain in April 1821 and on 3 February 1823 was named ambassador at Vienna. He remained in Austria for eight years. In August 1827 he told Wellington that he thought he had more than once prevented a rupture between Britain and Austria. But he complained that Canning never recognized his services. Although the two had known one another for years, and Canning had even asked Wellesley to be his second in the infamous duel with Lord Castlereagh, Wellesley was too conciliatory to please his aggressive minister.

In 1827 Wellington approached Canning's successor, Lord Goderich, concerning a peerage for his brother and on 21 January 1828 Wellesley was created a peer, with the title of Baron Cowley of Wellesley. On Palmerston's appointment to the Foreign Office at the end of 1830, Cowley offered to resign, and in July 1831 he left Vienna. On 13 March 1835 he was named ambassador at Paris by Peel's tory government, but he retired in May when the whigs returned to office.

Cowley was reappointed by Peel in October 1841. The appointment was unexpected in that the new ambassador was sixty-eight years old and there were those who questioned both his stamina and his hearing. None the less, Cowley presided successfully over the embassy in Paris until his resignation in August 1846 after the tories went out of office.

A handsome man of average height and build, Cowley possessed a gentle disposition which made him the most endearing of the Wellesley brothers. Metternich, the Austrian chancellor, characterized Cowley as a straightforward man with an eye for affairs. He lacked the brilliance of his brothers the marquess and the duke, but he was steady and sensible. He died in Paris on 27 April 1847. He was buried in Grosvenor Chapel, South Audley Street, London. Lady Cowley died at Hatfield House on 18 January 1860. G. LE G. NORGATE, rev. JOHN K. SEVERN

Sources The diary and correspondence of Henry Wellesley, first Lord Cowley, ed. F. A. Wellesley (1930) • The despatches, minutes and correspondence of the Marquess Wellesley … during his administration in India, ed. M. Martin, 5 vols. (1836–40) • Supplementary despatches (correspondence) and memoranda of Field Marshal Arthur, duke of Wellington, ed. A. R. Wellesley, second duke of Wellington, 15 vols. (1858–72) • The dispatches of … the duke of Wellington … from 1799 to 1818, ed. J. Gurwood, 13 vols. in 12 (1834–9) • I. Butler, The eldest brother: the Marquess Wellesley, the duke of Wellington's eldest brother (1973) • R. R. Pearce, Memoirs and correspondence of the most noble Richard Marquess Wellesley, 3 vols. (1846) • E. Longford [E. H. Pakenham, countess of Longford], Wellington, 1: The years of the sword (1969) • E. Longford [E. H. Pakenham, countess of Longford], Wellington, 2: Pillar of state (1972) • The Wellesley papers: the life and correspondence of Richard Colley Wellesley, Marquess Wellesley, ed. [L. S. Benjamin], 2 vols. (1914) • Memoirs and correspondence of Viscount Castlereagh, second marquess of Londonderry, ed. C. Vane, marquess of Londonderry, 12 vols. (1848–

53) • J. Severn, A Wellesley affair (1981) • Burke, Peerage • GEC, Peerage • PRO, Cowley MSS
Archives BL, copies of official corresp. as lieutenant-governor in Oudh, Add. MSS 13545, 13547–13554, 13556–13575, 13779 • BL OIOC, Indian corresp., MSS Eur. 172–181 • Essex RO • PRO, diplomatic and misc. corresp. and papers, FO 519/17–88, 290–291 | All Souls Oxf., corresp. with Sir Charles Richard Vaughan • Badminton House, Gloucestershire, letters to C. C. Smith, muniments • BL, corresp. with Lord Aberdeen, Add. MSS 43080, 43091–43093, 43129–43130 • BL, letters to Sir William A'Court, Add. MSS 41512–41513, 41553 • BL, corresp. with Lord Wellesley, Add. MSS 13537–13575, 37291–37312, 37415, passim • Hants. RO, corresp. with third earl of Malmesbury • Hatfield House, Hertfordshire, Salisbury MSS • NL Scot., corresp. with Lord Lynedoch • PRO, corresp. with Stratford Canning, FO 352 • PRO, corresp. with Lord Granville, PRO 3029 • PRO NIre., corresp. with Lord Castlereagh, D 3030 • U. Nott. L., corresp. with Lord William Bentinck • U. Southampton L., Carver MSS • U. Southampton L., corresp. with Lord Palmerston • U. Southampton L., corresp. with duke of Wellington • U. Southampton L., drafts and copies of letters to duke of Wellington and others
Likenesses J. Downman, watercolour drawing, 1783, Badminton, Gloucestershire • J. Hoppner, oils, Stratfield Saye House, Hampshire • miniature, Stratfield Saye House, Hampshire
Wealth at death under £12,000: GEC, Peerage

Wellesley, Henry (1794–1866), college head and art connoisseur, was born on 20 January 1794 at Park Lane in the parish of St George Hanover Square, London, the third son and youngest of five illegitimate children of Richard *Wellesley, second earl of Mornington and later first Marquess Wellesley (1760–1842), statesman, and Hyacinthe Gabrielle Roland (1760?–1816) daughter of Pierre Roland, of Paris. His parents married in November 1794 but were formally separated in 1810 after his father's long absence in India as governor-general (1797–1806). Wellesley was educated at the Revd Richard Roberts's Preparatory School in Mitcham, Surrey (1800–06), and Eton College (1806–11) before going up in October 1811 to Christ Church, Oxford, where he held a studentship until 1828. He graduated BA in 1816, with second class honours in classics, and MA in 1818. He was briefly enrolled at Lincoln's Inn in 1816 but was ordained at Oxford in 1823, and after travelling extensively in Europe he was appointed vicar of Flitton-with-Silsoe, Bedfordshire, in 1827. He was subsequently rector of Dunsfold in Surrey (1833–8), Woodmancote in Sussex (1838–60), and Herstmonceaux in Sussex (1860–66). In 1835 he married Charlotte Anne Mackenzie Vandyck (1817?/1818–1845), the stepdaughter of the Revd William Mackenzie DD, rector of Hascombe in Surrey. They had three sons, one of whom died at birth, and a daughter.

Although he remained a partially resident incumbent until his death, Wellesley was not entirely suited to the life of a country clergyman and was keen to return to Oxford. He unsuccessfully sought a canonry at Christ Church in 1830 and the regius professorship of modern history and modern languages in 1842, but in the latter year he was appointed vice-principal of New Inn Hall and in 1847 succeeded to the principalship on the nomination of his uncle the duke of Wellington, then chancellor of the university. In the same year he took the degrees of BD and DD and was appointed as a select preacher in the university. A connoisseur of old master prints and drawings with contacts in the art trade, he was one of the original curators of the university galleries and the leading figure in the campaign which acquired by public subscription the Raphael and Michelangelo drawings, delivered to Oxford in 1845, from the collection of Sir Thomas Lawrence. His own remarkable collection was largely broken up at sales in London and Paris, both before and after his death. Noted for his linguistic ability and especially his mastery of Italian dialects, he promoted the study of modern European languages in the university by the donation of books to the Taylor Institution, of which he was a curator from 1855; he was examiner in Italian for the scholarships offered there from 1858. His most substantial publication, *Anthologia polyglotta: a selection of versions in various languages chiefly from the Greek anthology* (1849), was intended to stimulate interest in the same field, then in the very early stages of development at Oxford. Elected a curator of the Bodleian Library in 1856, he represented it in negotiations to improve the copyright deposit procedure and devised a scheme for the enlargement of the library's storage capacity which, although not implemented, influenced designs for its expansion until the end of the century. He was also a delegate of the University Museum and one of the four members of the sub-delegacy which in 1854 steered the university towards choosing a Gothic design for that building.

Wellesley's other publications included an edition of the catalogue of the Bodleian's Canonici Italian manuscripts by his friend Count Alessandro Mortara and antiquarian papers in the *Collections* of the Sussex Archaeological Society, of which he was a founder member. Portraits suggest that Wellesley, who was considered to resemble his uncle, the duke of Wellington, was tall and of medium build; he was admired for his sociability, courteous and agreeable manner, and the light way he carried his learning. He died of prostatic disease at New Inn Hall, Oxford, on 11 January 1866 and was buried five days later at Iffley. SIMON BAILEY

Sources I. Butler, *The eldest brother: the Marquess Wellesley, the duke of Wellington's eldest brother* (1973) · *Jackson's Oxford Journal* (13 Jan 1866) · *Oxford Chronicle and Berks and Bucks Gazette* (13 Jan 1866) · *Oxford University Herald* (20 Jan 1866) · H. Farmar, *A Regency elopement* (1969) · S. L. Ollard, *Dunsfold and its rectors* (1919) · K. T. Parker, *The Italian schools* (1956), vol. 2 of *Catalogue of the collection of drawings in the Ashmolean Museum* · GM, 4th ser., 1 (1866), 440 · H. H. E. Craster, *History of the Bodleian Library, 1845–1945* (1952) · F. Lugt, *Les marques de collections de dessins et d'estampes* (Amsterdam, 1921) · Ordination papers, Oxfordshire Archives, Dioc. c. 221 · Baptism and fee registers of St George Hanover Square, City Westm. AC, 1324/5 and 1324/103 · G. L. Hennessy, *Chichester diocese clergy lists* (1900) · A. J. C. Hare, *The story of my life*, 2 (1896) · entrance book, Eton, archives, SCH/HMI/2 · Hascombe marriage register, Surrey RO · minutes of the curators of the Taylor Institution, Oxf. UA, TL/A/1/1 · d. cert. · d. cert. [Charlotte Wellesley] · Family correspondence of first Marquess Wellesley, BL, Add. MSS 37315–37316 · correspondence of Revd P. Bliss, BL, Add. MSS 34575–34581 · Foster, *Alum. Oxon.* · letters to Richard Wellesley, U. Southampton L., Carver MSS, SN 63/77 · minutes of the delegates and sub-delegates of the University Museum, Oxf. UA, UM/M/1/1 · letter to the Duke of Wellington, U. Southampton L., Wellington MSS, WP2/255/7 · parish register, Penkridge, Staffs. RO, F1354/1/21 [burial], p. 19

Archives BL, family corresp. of first Marquess Wellesley, Add. MSS 37315–37316, *passim* · BL, letters to P. Bliss, Add. MSS 34575–34581, *passim* · Staffs. RO, Littleton MSS · U. Southampton L., letters to Richard Wellesley

Likenesses S.-J. Rochard, watercolour, 1845, priv. coll.; repro. in Parker, *Italian schools* · A. Munro, medallion, 1856, AM Oxf. · oils, *c.*1860, U. Oxf., Taylor Institution · F. C. Lewis, stipple (after J. Slater; Grillion's Club series), BM, NPG · imitation of a drawing, BM · portraits, priv. coll.; repro. in Butler, *Eldest brother* · portraits, priv. coll.; repro. in Farmar, *Regency elopement*

Wealth at death under £14,000: resworn probate, Aug 1866, *CGPLA Eng. & Wales*

Wellesley, Henry Richard Charles, first Earl Cowley (1804–1884), diplomatist, was born in Hertford Street, Mayfair, Westminster, on 17 June 1804, the eldest son of Henry *Wellesley, first Baron Cowley (1773–1847), and his first wife, Charlotte Cadogan (1781–1853), daughter of the first Earl Cadogan. Gerald Valerian *Wellesley was his younger brother; Lord Clarence *Paget and Lord George *Paget were his half-brothers. His father was a diplomatist of note, ambassador at Vienna and, twice, at Paris. Educated at Eton College (1817–20) and Brasenose College, Oxford (where he matriculated in January 1822), Wellesley left the university without taking his degree to be an unpaid attaché at the Viennese embassy, then headed by his father. He was promoted paid attaché at The Hague in 1829 and secretary of legation at Stuttgart in 1832, and married on 23 October 1833 the Hon. Olivia Cecilia (1807–1885), daughter of Charlotte, *suo jure* Baroness de Ros, and her husband, Lord Henry Fitzgerald. They had three sons and two daughters. His wife's good looks and social gifts were to make her a notable ambassadress. From the diplomatic backwater of Württemberg, Wellesley eventually went to Constantinople (1843) as secretary of embassy, and served as minister *ad interim* in 1846–8. On his father's death in 1847, he succeeded to his peerage, and in February 1848 was appointed minister to Switzerland.

Although Cowley's politics were tory and he remained a member of the Carlton Club to his death, his career flourished under Liberal foreign secretaries. He was also a favourite at court, trusted, unlike his Liberal masters, by Queen Victoria and her dominant husband, Prince Albert. These connections notwithstanding, he proved himself a serviceable instrument of Palmerstonian policy. He did not take up his post at Bern, but proceeded instead on a special mission to observe the Frankfurt parliament's constitution-making for a liberal Germany. After the parliament's dissolution, and the defeat of the hopes it embodied, he became minister at Frankfurt to the old Germanic confederation (June 1851); a CB since 1848, he was made KCB (1 March 1851). In the following February Lord Granville chose him to succeed Lord Normanby at the Paris embassy; Palmerston had previously suggested him for St Petersburg, but Paris was a surprising promotion for a career diplomat without an established reputation.

The Bonapartist restoration in France in the person of Louis Napoleon as president and, from December 1852, as Emperor Napoleon III was an event of tremendous

Henry Richard Charles Wellesley, first Earl Cowley (1804–1884), by Auguste Charles Lemoine, 1856

importance. Handing over the Foreign Office to Lord Malmesbury in 1859, Lord Clarendon told him that 'the chief employment of the foreign secretary was to make bridges for the Emperor of the French' (Martin, 4.406). Cowley made himself indispensable in that context, helped by the fact that Napoleon III was an Anglophile, and Franco-British relations were central to his domestic as well as his foreign policy. He declared that his long-term aim was the gradual liberalization of the imperial dictatorship until it bore some resemblance to a parliamentary monarchy 'à l'anglaise'. Although by no means pro-British in other respects, educated opinion in France tended to measure his internal achievements by British standards of personal and political freedom. At the same time the expansion of French power in continental Europe, dictated by the Bonapartist legend, needed Britain to abstain from making the coalitions faced by the first Napoleon. Cowley's dispatches and correspondence depict the complementary themes of French and British policy as Palmerston, above all, exploited the emperor's inclinations and his needs for British purposes.

A typical Englishman of his class and time in his bearing and outlook, although quite at home in a cosmopolitan world, Cowley was close to Napoleon by the time the Crimean War broke out. 'I am not generally of a confiding character in regard to foreigners', he wrote a little later, 'but there is something about that man that always imbues me with a feeling of his sincerity' (Wellesley and Sencourt, 93). Nevertheless, he was acutely sensitive to the ambiguities and contradictions of the man and his

policies: the emperor was 'the sole depositary of his intentions' (Wellesley, 3). While the cynicism and corruption of the regime appalled Cowley—'the jobbery … amongst the Emperor's entourage exceeds all belief' (ibid., 110)—he was susceptible to Napoleon's appeals in their conversations for British tolerance and understanding of his problems as ruler of France. His authoritarian rule would change its nature once 'time and a settled government' had done their work: 'I cannot say what an impression his words and manner … made upon me', reported the ambassador (Wellesley and Sencourt, 117). Cowley responded to Napoleon's candour in private: 'there is a great charm in doing business with him, even when we do not agree' (ibid., 120). He was sympathetic to constantly reiterated complaints of British press hostility, accompanied as those imperial remonstrances were by reminders of what the French alliance was worth in great power politics. Cowley exemplified his countrymen's gratitude to Napoleon for having tamed the revolutionary France of 1848, 'not only a terror to herself but to all civilized governments' (Wellesley, 2–3).

Cowley's diplomatic successes were concentrated in the 1850s. The influence he then enjoyed with the emperor was instrumental in persuading him to reject the terms of peace brokered by Austria in the spring of 1855, when the Crimean campaign was not going well for Britain and France. Cowley enlisted the support of the French war minister against the foreign minister, Drouyn de Lhuys. The three argued in the emperor's presence: 'the decision lay with Napoleon and depended on whether Drouyn or Cowley would possess his soul' (Schroeder, 277). The latter prevailed, and determined the outcome of the war: without the deployment of France's large conscript army the Crimean operations could not have been sustained. Cowley had pressed the government to see that Napoleon, always conscious of being a parvenu among monarchs, received the highest honour in the queen's gift, although Prince Albert shuddered at the mere thought: 'Sebastopol is well worth the Garter' (Wellesley and Sencourt, 62). Once Sevastopol was taken in September 1855, however, Napoleon's liking for Cowley and respect for his judgement did not prevent him from bringing the war to an end, as the army and public opinion in France desired. As one of Britain's plenipotentiaries at the Congress of Paris, Cowley was disappointed with the peace treaty (March 1856), which he considered too favourable to Russia. It was an indication of his standing that ministers brought him over to testify in the Lords that no better terms could have been obtained. A privy councillor from 1852 (2 February) and a GCB (21 February 1853), he declined a step in the peerage at this time, but on 4 April 1857 became Earl Cowley. The earlier refusal, like the wish to retire he expressed in 1855, was prompted by his relative poverty in an expensive post. His plight was eased by £2000 paid annually from secret service money.

Cowley was entrusted with the negotiations, moved from Constantinople to Paris, that ended (March 1857) the Anglo-Persian War begun the year before. Apprised by the French of Russian intrigues to delay a settlement in the hope of embarrassing the Palmerston ministry at Westminster, Cowley indulged in some undiplomatic language to his Russian colleague: 'There is nothing like showing contempt for these bears, it brings them to reason sooner than anything' (Wellesley, 107). He could not take that tone with the emperor when Napoleon seized the opportunity presented by Britain's preoccupation with the Indian mutiny (May 1857) to get his way in the matter of Romanian union, with some sharp practice, after an international conference (Paris, May–August 1858) at which Cowley represented his country. Afraid of losing his privileged position with Napoleon—'Sometimes … he will barely condescend to speak to me' (Wellesley and Sencourt, 114)—he warned that the emperor resented Britain's independent diplomacy: 'it galls him to see that we do not … obey his behests' (ibid., 127).

Against this background, the attempted assassination of Napoleon and his empress in January 1858 by conspirators based in Britain introduced a period of Anglo-French tension that tested Cowley's abilities to the full. The Palmerston ministry fell in February, overturned for proposing legislation on refugee conspirators designed to appease French indignation. The tory foreign secretary in 1858–9, Lord Malmesbury, who relied heavily on the ambassador's advice, pursued for many months a distinctly conciliatory policy towards France, in order to buy time while Britain's navy was strengthened. Victoria and her husband were induced to grace a celebration of French power at the naval base of Cherbourg, flattered by Cowley's assurance that 'nothing does the Emperor so much moral good as seeing the Queen and Prince …' (Martin, 4.256–7).

Behind Napoleon's own desire for the restoration of the Crimean friendship lay his maturing plans to extrude Austria from Italy. Cowley's toryism was evident in the scepticism with which he contemplated a federal, or a unitary, Italian state. Malmesbury authorized him to approach Palmerston in search of an understanding between the parties to resist, by diplomatic means, the drift to war over Italy (Wellesley, 173–4). The overture was fruitless, as was Cowley's mission to Vienna in March 1859, frustrated by the emperor's 'ambiguous words and dark dealings' (Wellesley and Sencourt, 164–5). Napoleon was bent on war, and Palmerston on supporting him by an active and friendly diplomacy. But the second Palmerston administration (June 1859) saw renewed strain upon the Anglo-French relationship: Cowley himself could not forgive the emperor for the deceptions that French policy in Italy involved. The realization of Napoleon's duplicity over the French acquisition of Savoy and Nice in 1860 completely disillusioned him: 'You will never find me ask you to trust … him again', he told Lord John Russell (ibid., 181). Emperor and ambassador clashed in public at a function in March 1860, when Napoleon's 'tone and manner were really offensive' (*Letters of Queen Victoria*, ed. A. C. Benson, Lord Esher, and G. E. Buckle, 2nd ser., 1926–8, 3.390). Although the queen and foreign secretary approved of his behaviour on this occasion, the British court found

Cowley still too ready to make excuses for Napoleon, while Palmerston and Russell felt he was too pro-Austrian. He now carried less weight with Palmerston, and complained, at an important juncture, that for all he knew of the premier's thinking, 'I might as well be in California' (Maxwell, ii). Yet, if he currently predicted that a united Italy would have to resort to military rule in the south, he welcomed the reduction of papal authority and prestige: 'If the Pope is driven from Rome … the blessings to mankind will overrule everything else …' (Wellesley and Sencourt, 186).

As both Liberal ministers at home and the emperor recognized, Cowley's first priority was unchanging: the avoidance of dangerous frictions between their two countries. If the technicalities were outside his competence, he helped to negotiate the Anglo-French commercial treaty of 1860 as a contribution to repairing a relationship damaged by the invasion scare of 1859 and by France's annexations. The clumsiness of Russell's language and actions at the Foreign Office was agony to him. After the crude rejection of Napoleon's proposed European congress in 1863 was followed by Britain's humiliating isolation in the Schleswig-Holstein crisis, Cowley was '*broken hearted*' (Burghclere, 74). The transformation of his personal finances by the unexpected inheritance of a cousin's estate made him anxious to retire, but on the tories' return to office in 1866 their foreign secretary, Lord Stanley, appealed to him to stay in his post. Before he left in 1867, Cowley did a weak government in London and the Emperor, but particularly the latter, a final service by his part in defusing the politically explosive Franco-Prussian dispute over Luxembourg.

While Cowley lost confidence in the emperor, and consequently influence with him, he had interpreted Bonapartist France and Palmerstonian Britain to each other at critical moments, reminding both that it would be 'insane' if they were to come to blows, and cutting British fears of a sudden invasion down to size (Wellesley, 165; Wellesley and Sencourt, 200–205). No Francophile— he thought the French were not a moral people—he preferred Napoleon III's France to Bismarck's Germany, whose victory over Austria in 1866 he observed with misgiving: 'if ever she becomes a naval power, she will give us trouble' (Wellesley and Sencourt, 303). His large private correspondence is a major source for the diplomatic historian. It shows Cowley for what he was: a pragmatist in the best sense, as little cynical as was possible for someone in his calling; temperate and humane, an often amused and amusing observer, who seldom lost sight of the realities he was there to describe, and to reconcile. Some of the praise he received was not disinterested. The best estimate, perhaps, is Stanley's: 'Though not a man of first-rate talent, he knows the country and the people thoroughly, and can be relied on' (Vincent, 258).

Further honours came to Cowley after his earldom: KG (1866) and DCL from Oxford University (1870). He died at his London house, 20 Albemarle Street, on 15 July 1884, after an uneventful retirement, devoted to his property and the social round, and was buried at Draycot parish church, near Chippenham, on 18 July. He was succeeded by his eldest son, William, Viscount Dangan.

DAVID STEELE

Sources F. A. Wellesley, ed., *The Paris embassy during the second empire: selections from the papers of … 1st Earl Cowley, 1852–67* (1928) · V. Wellesley and R. Sencourt, eds., *Conversations with Napoleon III* (1934) · PRO, Cowley MSS · T. Martin, *The life of … the prince consort*, 5 vols. (1875–80) · *A great lady's friendships: letters to Mary, marchioness of Salisbury, countess of Derby, 1862–1876*, ed. W. A. Gardner, Baroness Burghclere (1933) · H. E. Maxwell, *Life and letters of George William Frederick, fourth earl of Clarendon*, 2 vols. (1913) · P. W. Schroeder, *Austria, Great Britain and the Crimean War: the destruction of the European concert* (1972) · D. E. D. Beales, *England and Italy, 1859–60* (1961) · A. L. Kennedy, ed., *My dear duchess: social and political letters to the duchess of Manchester, 1858–1869* (1956) · *Disraeli, Derby and the conservative party: journals and memoirs of Edward Henry, Lord Stanley, 1849–1869*, ed. J. R. Vincent (1978) · E. D. Steele, *Palmerston and liberalism, 1855–1865* (1991) · M. R. D. Foot, 'Great Britain and Luxemburg, 1867', *EngHR*, 67 (1952), 352–79 · GEC, *Peerage* · *The Times* (21 July 1884) · K. Weigand, *Österreich, die Westmächte und das europäische Staatensystem nach dem Krimkrieg, 1856–1859* (1997)

Archives PRO, papers, FO 519 · U. Southampton L., diary | BL, corresp. with Lord Aberdeen, Add. MSS 43131, 43239–43251 · BL, letters to Richard Cobden, Add. MS 43666 · BL, corresp. with W. E. Gladstone, Add. MSS 44374–44418 · BL, corresp. with Sir A. H. Layard, Add. MSS 38977–39135 · BL, corresp. with Lord Palmerston, Add. MSS 48514–48516, 48573 · BL OIOC, letters to Lord Elphinstone, MSS Eur. F 87–89 · Bodl. Oxf., letters to Lord Clarendon · Bodl. Oxf., corresp. with Lord Kimberley, MSS Eng. a 2013–2014, b 2047–2049, c 3933–4514, e 2790–2797 · Hants. RO, corresp. with Lord Malmesbury · LPL, corresp. with A. C. Tait · Lpool RO, corresp. with fifteenth earl of Derby while ambassador to France · NAM, corresp. with Lord Raglan · Norfolk RO, corresp. with Sir Henry Lytton Bulwer · NRA, priv. coll., letters to Lord Hammond · PRO, corresp. with Stratford Canning, FO 352 · PRO, letters to Lord Granville, PRO 30/29 · PRO, corresp. with Lord Hammond, FO 391 · PRO, letters to Odo Russell, FO 918 · PRO, corresp. with Lord John Russell, PRO 30/22 · U. Nott. L., corresp. with duke of Newcastle · U. Southampton L., Broadlands MSS · U. Southampton L., letters to Lord Palmerston · W. Sussex RO, corresp. with Richard Cobden

Likenesses A. C. Lemoine, photogravure, 1856, NPG [*see illus.*] · A. Lemoine, lithograph, BL · photograph (as ambassador at Paris), repro. in Wellesley and Sencourt, eds., *Conversations* · photograph (in old age), repro. in Wellesley, ed., *Paris embassy*, frontispiece

Wealth at death £38,640 10s. 5d.: resworn probate, Feb 1886, *CGPLA Eng. & Wales* (1885)

Wellesley [*formerly* Wesley], **Richard, Marquess Wellesley (1760–1842)**, governor-general of Bengal, was born on 20 June 1760, probably at Dangan Castle, co. Meath, though he later referred to himself as a 'native' of Dublin (*Wellesley Papers*, 1.4), and spent much of his early life at the family town house in Grafton Street, Dublin, opposite the Irish government buildings. The eldest of the six sons (one of whom died in infancy) and one daughter of Garret *Wesley (1735–1781), who was created earl of Mornington in October 1760, Richard became Viscount Wellesley, though he did not adopt Wellesley (in place of Wesley) as his surname until 1789. His mother was Anne (1742–1831), eldest daughter of Arthur Hill of Belvoir, co. Down, first Viscount Dungannon. His younger brothers were William Wellesley-*Pole, first Baron Maryborough and third earl of Mornington (1763–1845), Arthur *Wellesley, duke of Wellington (1769–1852), the Revd Gerald Wellesley (1770–

Richard Wellesley, Marquess Wellesley (1760–1842), by Sir Thomas Lawrence, 1812

1848), and Henry *Wellesley, Baron Cowley (1773–1847). The Wesleys had originated in Somerset, but members of the family held minor office in Ireland from the thirteenth century onward. The Colley family, into which they married, was descended from Richard Colley, who had been sent to Ireland in the reign of King Henry VII to watch the conduct of the earl of Kildare, lord-deputy of the country. The Wellesleys settled to a career as typical country gentlemen of the protestant ascendancy, mostly shunning active politics, though Richard *Wesley (or Wellesley, formerly Colley), grandfather of the subject of this article, sat in the Irish parliament as member for Trim until 1746, when he was raised to the peerage of Ireland as the first Baron Mornington. Garret Wesley, his son, was an amateur musician and poet whose artistic interests did little to repair the crumbling family fortunes. Richard Wellesley's relations with his demanding and embittered mother were poor. He was later to remark of his parents, with typical condescension, that they were 'frivolous and careless personages, like most of the Irish nobility of that time' (Butler, 27).

Education and early political career Viscount Wellesley was educated at Miss Towers's private school in Portarlington, a Huguenot settlement, where he learned fluent French. He was sent to Harrow when he was ten years old. As the result of taking too active a part in a schoolboy revolt against a newly appointed headmaster, Wellesley was removed from Harrow after eighteen months and sent to Eton, where he excelled in the classics, an interest which he retained in his later years. He matriculated as a nobleman at Christ Church, Oxford, in December 1778, and achieved early distinction by winning the chancellor's prize for Latin verse on the subject of the death of Captain Cook. But his career in the university was cut short when he returned to Ireland following the death of his father in May 1781 and succeeded as second earl of Mornington. Young Mornington took on the responsibility of paying his father's debts, running the estate, and educating his brothers. His brief period in the Irish House of Lords did, however, consolidate one important political connection, his friendship with William Grenville, later Baron Grenville, a friend from Eton. Grenville was chief secretary for Ireland at the time. More importantly, Grenville was William Pitt's first cousin: perpetually short of money, Mornington could at least count on productive 'connections'. Grenville eased Mornington's route into English politics, and in April 1784 he was returned to the House of Commons as member for Bere Alston in Devon. He was later returned as member for Windsor (19 July 1787 and 16 June 1790), and Old Sarum (13 May 1796). He was one of the original knights of St Patrick when the order was founded in 1783 and was made junior lord of the Treasury in 1786. In this year Mornington also made one of the most momentous decisions of his life: he entered his younger brother Arthur, who had not excelled academically at Eton, as a cadet in the Royal Academy of Equitation at Angers in Anjou. He later bought a colonelcy for Arthur, who was immediately posted to India, so becoming precursor to his brother.

Already a liberal whig in politics, Mornington had admired the Irish patriot Henry Grattan during his period in the politics of Dublin. Despite private cynicism about 'popery', he argued vigorously in the Irish House of Lords for Catholic emancipation. He also demanded an end to corruption in the disbursement of Irish government funds. On the other hand, his reverence for property and the constitution made him increasingly suspicious of the Irish armed volunteering movement of 1779–83. He had once 'revered' (*Wellesley Papers*, 1.12) its leaders but came to fear that it would tend in a democratic direction and infringe on the powers of the monarchy and the Irish parliament. In English politics, similarly, he now aligned himself with William Pitt in support of the radical agenda of free trade; he asserted the need to place England on 'the throne of commerce of the world' (ibid., 1.15) some ten years before he embarked for India. He also supported and began a lifelong friendship with William Wilberforce in opposition to the slave trade, which he regarded as a 'disgrace to Great Britain' (ibid., 1.18). Yet, suspicious of constitutional innovation, he was lukewarm to parliamentary reform, and his views against it hardened as the effects of the French Revolution gathered pace. Once the republican danger had passed by 1820, however, in contrast to his brother, by then the duke of Wellington, he was to become a firm advocate of reform.

At this time Mornington was also ambivalent about the consequences of British imperial expansion. He admired

Burke, and his maiden speech in the Commons was, ironically, an attack on the ministry for supporting the wars of Warren Hastings in India. He was not, however, opposed to territorial annexations as such, and early on he had read and absorbed Robert Orme's *Military Transactions of the British Nation in Indostan* (2 vols., 1763, 1778), which provided a justification for Robert Clive's conquest of Bengal. Growing expertise in Indian affairs resulted in his transfer in June 1793 from the Treasury to the Board of Control for India, where he worked with Henry Dundas, Viscount Melville, in a close but contentious partnership which was to continue during his governor-generalship of India. Mornington also became a confidant of Lord Cornwallis, who was expected to be reappointed to the post of governor-general, with Mornington as governor of Madras. In 1797 Cornwallis was indeed appointed governor-general, but the gathering Irish rising forced the administration to keep him in Ireland as lord lieutenant, while Mornington himself was unexpectedly appointed governor-general. He sailed for India in November 1797, leaving in England a wife, Hyacinthe Gabrielle (1760?–1816), purported daughter of Pierre Roland of Paris, whom he had married on 29 November 1794. To the distaste of some members of his family, he had already been living with Hyacinthe for nine years and had had five children with her.

Governor-general of Bengal Mornington's period of governor-generalship was to be the decisive phase in the establishment of British dominion over the Indian subcontinent and witnessed the beginnings of the projection of British military and maritime power into the Middle East and south-east Asia. As late as 1798 the East India Company was faced with a series of powerful enemies in the subcontinent who had been driven by the imminent threat to their own independence to revitalize their administrations and create more effective military forces on partly European lines. In the south the Muslim ruler Tipu Sultan of Mysore had been defeated by Cornwallis in 1792, but had quickly set about rebuilding his power. Having earlier founded his own armaments industry and centrally organized army, he now strengthened his hold on the rich, revenue-bearing districts which he had retained after the settlement of 1792, and embarked upon a more active foreign policy, seeking allies throughout India, in the Ottoman empire, and in France, to which he had recently sent an embassy. The French republic, while in no position to help Britain's Indian enemies directly, provided moral support and expertise and, in a piece of piquant symbolism, Tipu had planted a 'liberty tree' at his capital, Seringapatam.

In western India the Hindu states were also attempting to narrow the gap in military technology between themselves and the East India Company, developing powerful artillery and infantry forces to complement their already formidable capacity in mobile light-cavalry warfare. In retrospect the dangers to the British position were much less than contemporaries feared. And these were anyway exaggerated by officials such as William Kirkpatrick, later

Mornington's military secretary, who favoured an aggressive policy, in part because they hoped it would increase their own wealth and glory. But there is no doubt that the situation was highly fluid when Mornington reached Madras in January 1798. In the north-west the Afghan ruler Zaman Shah was threatening to repeat the destructive foray into the Indian plains made by his predecessor, Ahmad Shah Durrani, in 1759–61. Meanwhile, in those successor states to the Mughal empire—Oudh, Hyderabad, and Arcot—where the British had established overwhelming political influence, dissident factions still flourished, making overtures to the distant French or seeking the nearer support of Tipu Sultan. Worse was the social and economic decline of the company's allies. Caused in the main by excessive British demands for military subsidies, it threatened the company with the prospect of going to war against Maratha and Mysore troops, whose officers were French advisers, while the forces of their own clients melted away in disarray.

Lord Cornwallis and Sir John Shore, the previous governors-general, had been cautious about direct annexation. The one was forced by logistical weakness to allow Tipu Sultan to retain much of his power-base; the other placed a British supporter on the throne of Oudh in 1797, rather than directly annexing the territory. But Mornington's arrival heralded a new attitude to the balance of power in India. In London, Henry Dundas, Lord Melville, president of the Board of Control of the East India Company, was keen to use India as a source of tribute for the British government; the classic strategy of the Hanoverian minister had always been to seize as many foreign territories as possible during time of war in order to display a good hand of cards during peace negotiations. But there had been a deeper change; Dundas averred that 'We are in truth become an armed nation' (*Two Views*, 50), and resolute defence of the United Kingdom had to be complemented by the entrenchment of the British position in India, the loss of which would be a 'death-wound' (ibid.). The dangerous Irish rising of 1797–8 was accompanied by Bonaparte's thrust to the East. In England the landed classes were disturbed by the spread of radical societies, while Mornington's Irish correspondents, notably his brother William Wellesley-Pole, wrote to him of the 'spirit of insurrection and treason' (*Wellesley Papers*, 1.71) which manifested itself throughout Ireland. The sense of national emergency which pervaded Mornington's governor-generalship undoubtedly predisposed him to a more aggressive policy against the Indian powers, and one which was thoroughly welcomed by the group of able and intransigent young civil and military officers he gathered around him. These included William Kirkpatrick, Neil Edmonstone, John Malcolm, and William Palmer. Contemptuous of the 'weakness and langour of the late governor-general' (*Two Views*, 79), Sir John Shore, Mornington soon announced his intention of establishing complete British suzerainty in southern Asia.

War with Tipu Sultan Tipu Sultan's Mysore was no doubt a formidable potential enemy of the company's power, but it is clear that Mornington was determined to force him

into war as quickly as possible. Malartic, the French governor of Mauritius, had unwisely issued a proclamation inviting volunteers 'to serve under the banners of Tippoo' (Moon, 278), who, he asserted, was aiming to drive the British out of India. During the summer of 1798 Mornington regretfully heeded the advice of his senior officials and his brother Arthur Wellesley that the company was unprepared for war. His vigorous diplomatic and military preparations for a campaign over the next few months indicate, however, that the protestations that he wished to compromise with the sultan were false. As he wrote to Grenville at the onset of the war, 'I have had the satisfaction to succeed completely in drawing the beast of the jungle [Tipu] into the toils' (ibid., 285). They also give credence to the view of Joshua Uhthoff, resident at Mysore, that the tardy military preparations which Tipu himself made were no more than an expression of 'common prudence and self-defence' (W. Kirkpatrick to J. Uhthoff, 8 March 1799, BL, Add. MS 13587), a phrase which the governor-general and his military secretary, William Kirkpatrick, edited out of the envoy's dispatches.

As he made preparations for the final conflict with Tipu, Mornington reached an accommodation with the Marathas in the north and galvanized into action the sluggish authorities in Madras, whom he had despised since he first made landfall there during his voyage out from England. Wellesley also engineered a coup against the anti-British party in the Mughal successor state of Hyderabad to the north of Mysore. Here the ageing nizam, its ruler, fearing attack from Tipu and the Marathas and feeling that his French officers were getting above themselves, agreed that his French-led corps of 14,000 men should be disbanded and replaced with a British subsidiary force. This was effected without bloodshed, and the military and logistical support of Hyderabad proved critical in the forthcoming war.

Taxing Tipu with his relations with France, Mornington managed finally to harry the sultan into war in February 1799. General Harris, who had served under Cornwallis in the Second Anglo-Mysore War, marched into the kingdom. In contrast to the earlier occasion, the invading army was properly provisioned by the Madras authorities. Slightly outnumbered by the combined company and Hyderabad force and betrayed by two of his ministers, Tipu was unable to halt the resolute British advance on his capital, Seringapatam. On 4 May 1799 the final assault was launched and Tipu Sultan, vowing to 'die like a soldier', was killed defending the breach.

Extension of British authority in India Mornington's rapid victory over his most formidable Indian opponent shifted the balance of power in the subcontinent. His armies were strengthened by the access of a huge number of pack bullocks seized from the Mysorean troops, Madras was relieved from the danger of imminent revolt, and the Maratha states were now surrounded by British-controlled territory on three sides. Most importantly, the governor-general's success emboldened him to overawe the subordinate presidencies and appoint his own supporters to critical military and political positions. Henceforward, his relations with the cost-conscious directors of the East India Company were to deteriorate rapidly. Mornington himself was rewarded by being created Marquess Wellesley in December 1799.

In south India, it is true, Wellesley secured a settlement which seemed financially and politically favourable. He restored what Mark Wilks, the new Mysore resident, regarded as the ancient Hindu constitution of the state by returning to power a young prince of the Wodeyar dynasty, which had formally retained sovereignty during the reigns of the Muslim sovereigns. The effective ruler was the Maratha Brahman Purniya, who had served and later betrayed Tipu, but who quickly put the state on a strong financial footing, allowing it to pay a large subsidy to the British. The subsidy continued to be paid throughout the period of British rule in India, even in times of famine. Further to the south Wellesley was also able to terminate the irritating system of dual government which had since the 1760s split authority in Madras between the company and another sub-Mughal regime, the government of the nawab of Arcot. In the archives of Seringapatam the British had discovered letters from the nawab of Arcot to Tipu dating from Cornwallis's war of 1792. The Arcot authorities held, perfectly correctly, that these letters were merely aspects of the normal diplomatic relations among Indian states and did not constitute any betrayal of Arcot's treaty obligations. But the British deemed them treasonable and the Arcot dynasty was abruptly deprived of its remaining political power and pensioned off.

Hereafter Wellesley's policies towards the Indian rulers formed a common pattern; he wished to limit what he conceived of, following Cornwallis, as the corruption of oriental government and at the same time improve the company's financial position by annexing territories or negotiating generous subsidies in return for 'protection' by the company's forces. In October 1799 the small but rich state of Tanjore was effectively annexed to the Madras presidency, though its raja was afforded a substantial pension, which allowed him to sustain a large court and many religious and charitable institutions. More importantly, the large northern state of Oudh, which had been in alliance with the British since 1765, was partitioned. The governor-general sought 'not merely to secure the subsidiary funds, but to extinguish the Vizier's [ruler's] military power, substituting in its place a considerable British force' (Edmonstone to Scott, 27 May 1801, BL, Add. MS 13527). Oudh's central tracts around Lucknow were to remain semi-independent until 1856, but the commercial districts along the Ganges passed under a new British administration, the head of which for a time was another of the governor-general's brothers, Henry Wellesley. Cornwallis, hostile to further territorial expansion by the company, had sought to exclude British private interests from the state under a treaty of 1788. But it proved impossible to stabilize the frontier of British India; as many contemporaries observed, the very terms of the subsidiary alliances created by the company undermined

Indian states. The huge payments required to support company contingents on their own territory drained away the resources of the rajas and nawabs. In turn their desperate attempts to raise money and pay off their powerful creditor caused revolts which reinforced the appearance of 'native misgovernment'.

War against the Marathas and other conquests Indian rulers were only too well aware of this. Tipu and the major Maratha rulers, Daulat Rao Sindhia, the raja of Berar, and Jaswant Rao Holkar, had all resolutely refused to negotiate subsidiary treaties with the company, fearing an inevitable loss of their independence. To Wellesley, the alliance system was, by contrast, a financial and strategic panacea. When conflicts in Poona, capital of the peshwa, nominal head of the Maratha confederacy, drove Peshwa Baji Rao into British territory in 1802, Wellesley saw a chance to settle finally the affairs of Britain's only remaining formidable potential enemy in peninsular India, the Marathas. Deeming the peshwa to be ruler of an actual Maratha 'empire', and the great chieftains such as Sindhia and Holkar a mere territorial nobility, he thought that binding the former with a rigid treaty would tame the latter. The opposite turned out to be the case. In mid-1803, in a violent reaction to the treaty Wellesley had made with the peshwa at Bassein, the raja of Berar and Sindhia took to the field against the company. Opinion in Britain was generally hostile to Wellesley's diplomatic harassment of the Marathas. British power was already firmly entrenched in India, and, barring a small number of French soldiers employed by Sindhia, no significant European enemy remained in the subcontinent. Most important, both the now enraged directors of the company and the government feared that a further round of wars would be extremely costly. This was to prove perfectly correct. Over his governor-generalship, far from stabilizing the Indian finances, Wellesley managed virtually to treble the company's debt.

In the short term, however, Wellesley's war against the Marathas went brilliantly. Secure in the alliance and resources of the nizam of Hyderabad, the puppet state of Mysore, and the newly partitioned Oudh, the British were able to launch a two-pronged attack on the Marathas' redoubts in the western Indian uplands. The company, in addition, was lucky in that its forces were led by two soldiers of unusual ability for the Indian theatre. The southern army was commanded by Sir Arthur Wellesley, a ruthless officer in dealing with his Indian subordinates, but one who had early learned the importance of proper commissary and logistical arrangements. The army of the north, which moved from the Ganges valley against the Maratha armies poised south and west of Delhi, was led by the stolid and methodical General Gerard Lake (1744–1808), who had proved himself one of the best British commanders during the Irish rising of 1797–8.

Arthur Wellesley won a famous victory against the most powerful of the Maratha chieftains, Daulat Rao Sindhia, at Assaye in September 1803. Next he turned and defeated the army of the raja of Berar, which had a less powerful cavalry wing to deploy against the British. In the north,

Lake and the Bengal army defeated Sindhia's French-led army, taking Delhi and Agra, ancient centres of the Mughal empire. Wellesley was able to claim that he had eradicated residual French interest in north India, in the guise of Sindhia's French military advisers. This was a view which accorded well with opinion at home now that European hostilities had recommenced.

The year 1803 was to prove the high point of his Indian career, when Wellesley believed he had achieved his main aims in India. The company's government had, moreover, begun to flex its muscles on the broader Asian scene, foreshadowing the thrust of nineteenth-century imperial policies. Indian military and marine contingents had taken part in a British expeditionary force to Egypt in order to force a French withdrawal; John Malcolm's mission to Persia had marked out British antipathy to both French and Russian advances in the region; diplomatic relations with Burma seemed on the point of being established; and the company had exploited a further commercial bridgehead in south-east Asia which had appeared following the cession of the hinterland of Penang in 1798. Hereafter, the pace of military and diplomatic success slowed, and political difficulties between the governor-general and the directors became insurmountable.

The British had managed to force the major Maratha rulers into a dependent status because the armies of Lake and Arthur Wellesley had combined strict infantry discipline with a superiority in heavy cavalry. After the defeat of the main forces of the raja of Berar and Sindhia, however, they were faced with a more elusive and subtle enemy in the form of the 'predatory' light cavalry of Jaswant Rao Holkar, a Maratha chief who had abandoned the attempt to defeat the European armies in direct confrontations. Holkar's nuisance value was increased by the dispersal throughout central and western India of cavalry war bands, released from the defeated Indian armies, who plundered settled agriculture and frustrated the British attempt to revive agriculture and trade following the man-made food shortages of the previous two years. Colonel William Monson's attempt to trap Holkar in Rajputana failed miserably, and the British were drawn deeper into a war of light cavalry movement against him. They were simultaneously alarmed by the movements of the Muslim chieftain Amir Khan and pinned down by an ineffectual siege of the Jat stronghold of Bharatpur, southwest of Delhi. Worse, future military strategy was imperilled by the soaring debt of the company and the increasing unwillingness of native Indian capitalists to finance it.

Until 1804 the British government, and Castlereagh in particular, had generally favoured Wellesley, drawing credit from his suppression of the supposed French threat to India. The directors, however, had become bitterly hostile, resenting alike the cost of the governor-general's victories, his scarcely concealed contempt for their residual monopolies of trade and public office, and the proconsular style of his government. The set-backs against Holkar and Bharatpur turned the ministry against Wellesley too, and in 1805 he was, to all intents and purposes,

recalled. Hereafter the legacy of his Indian administration was to come under increasing attack in the British press, in parliament, and from the court of directors. Old radicals such as Philip Francis joined forces with anti-annexationist evangelicals like Charles Grant and 'new' radicals, who disliked the influence of the 'Irish cabal' in both domestic and imperial politics.

Civil government in India Wellesley's style of Indian government had been a particular source of suspicion across the political spectrum. Early in his governor-generalship he had announced his desire to revamp the stately dimension of Indian government and model his court on that of the lord lieutenant of Ireland. He rebuilt government house, Calcutta, in Palladian style and introduced a round of rituals, ceremonies, and levees. He hoped this would impress Indian rulers and subjects, but also instil discipline into the British master race in Calcutta, which had hitherto shown a marked preference for gambling, peculation, and extramarital affairs, including liaisons with Indian or Indo-Portuguese women. He clamped down on the scurrilous and outspoken English-language press in Calcutta, and sent two of its editors back home, charging them with 'Jacobin' sympathies. Wellesley was far from being an evangelical Christian; indeed, one of his sternest enemies, Charles Grant, a director of the company, charged his administration with being idolatrous. But Wellesley felt that, in India as in Ireland, the Anglican church itself should be on parade, as it were, an embodiment of the morality and pageantry of British rule. He insisted on regular Sunday observance and attendance at chapel or church for company servants and military officers. While he discountenanced active proselytization against Hinduism and Islam on the part of the Baptist missionaries established at the Danish station of Serampore, near Calcutta, he established better relations with its scholarly evangelists, who had once been classed with political radicals, and associated them with the government's plan to translate Sanskrit and Persian classics. These policies created many enemies. The increased ceremoniousness of government irritated the crown at home, while the new puritanism annoyed the lethargic Calcutta and Madras 'society'.

More damaging to Wellesley's political future, however, was the struggle between the governor-general and the directors over the education and control of junior civil servants. Wellesley's liking for efficiency and his distaste for the lax lifestyles of many 'griffins' (newly arrived servants of the company) quickly convinced him of the need to establish a training academy in Calcutta. Fort William College, which he opened in July 1799, married features of Oxford and Cambridge, such as the study of theology, and classical and oriental languages, with the discipline and sense of cadre common in the military academies of France, to one of which he had sent his brother and on which he specifically modelled the institution ('College of Fort William', BL, Add. MS 13862, fol. 29). A regular routine of teaching in secluded circumstances would also, he hoped, keep the company's youthful servants off the hunting field and out of the clutches of 'native women' (ibid., fol. 17b), corrupt Indian secretaries, or *munshis*, and other representatives of what Wellesley regarded as native corruption. The college did, indeed, train, if sometimes only briefly, a spectacular group of young men, including Mountstuart Elphinstone, Charles Metcalfe, Richard Jenkins, and E. C. Bayley, who went on to high office in the administrative and political services of the company. It also embarked upon a programme of teaching and translation of classical and modern south Asian languages which gave a considerable impetus to oriental studies worldwide. John Gilchrist, who standardized and explained Urdu, the Indian lingua franca, to the West, was professor there. Many learned Indians who played a prominent role in the recovery of Indian religious texts and history and their dissemination to the indigenous population were also associated with the college.

The directors, however, felt that Wellesley had exceeded his authority in establishing Fort William College. Alongside his creation of a private secretariat, his denomination of certain topics too secret to be readily discussed in home correspondence, and patronage of young military and civil officers directly dependent on him, Wellesley's actions smacked of an attempt to elevate the governor-general's authority over that of the company. The directors were particularly incensed by his promotion of his youngest brother, Henry, to the office of resident at Lucknow and the generous staff salary which he sanctioned for his brother Arthur. Wellesley's economic policies did not recommend themselves to the directors either. The huge expansion of the company's debt as a result of costly wars and shortfalls in the collection of land revenue provided a dismal background to his drive to create a more efficient government. The governor-general broadly approved Cornwallis's policy of creating an Indian landed class by fostering large landowners or *zamindars*, who, like the Anglo-Irish gentry, he believed could be cajoled into acting benignly towards their tenants. He would probably have tipped the balance against the favoured small farmer (*ryotwari*) strategy of south Indian officials which was beginning to gather support among the directors if he had finished his second term. In trade policy, however, Wellesley's attempt to have as much bullion pumped into India as possible in order to finance his military activities and his resolute championing of free trade on both intercontinental and Asian routes offended the mercantilist majority and the monopolist 'shipping interest' of the company which still prevailed among directors, if not among ministers.

The returned proconsul Wellesley returned to England in early 1806. Here he had to contend with a dramatic loss of status in comparison with his Indian days. This affected him so badly that he petulantly withdrew from his first dinner on English soil with his family and friends at an inn in Dover. His relationship with his wife did not survive his return for very long. In 1808 he separated from her and began a series of affairs with young ladies about town, which many, including Arthur Wellesley, thought damaged his ministerial ambitions: the Iron Duke once wrote furiously of his brother's manifold liaisons: 'I wish that

Wellesley was *castrated*' (Severn, 133). But, despite the scandals, the support of the friends of the recently dead William Pitt would probably have ensured Wellesley office but for the eruption of a noisy political controversy about his Indian government. Radicals and personal enemies of the Wellesley family combined to denounce his governor-generalship in parliament. They based their charges on the evidence of one James Paull, an old-style 'nabob', now MP, who charged him with ruining his trade in Oudh and undermining the nawab's authority in 1801–2. The change in attitudes to Asian territorial empire since the impeachment of Warren Hastings ensured, however, that the motion was finally defeated (182 to 31) in 1808.

Wellesley, once despot of 150 million people, like Warren Hastings before him and George Curzon after, proved a difficult, indeed embarrassing, figure to fit back into the intricate pattern of British politics and high office. His haughty refusal of office in 1807 when under attack in parliament worried his financially embarrassed family. Ultimately a position was found for him, and in 1809 he was dispatched as ambassador-extraordinary to the embattled Spanish junta in Seville. Here, he found himself once again in the same theatre of military and diplomatic activity as his brother Sir Arthur Wellesley. His main aim being to support his brother's army in the Peninsula, Wellesley objected strongly to Castlereagh's attempt to open a second front against Napoleon through his Walcheren expedition to Belgium. To Wellesley, ever alert in protection of Britain's international trading position, a Napoleonic conquest of Spain was a direct threat to Britain's growing trade with Spanish America. Equally, he believed that British support for a weakened Spain would help further prise open the Spanish monopoly of its colonial trade. Furious at the vacillation of the ministry in regard to the Spanish war, he tendered his resignation from his post at Seville and only withdrew it when ministers agreed to reinforce Arthur's military position against the French. Wellesley's main diplomatic effort was a prolonged battle to squeeze supplies and support out of an impoverished Spanish regime by threatening the withdrawal of British forces into Portugal. He also reinforced Canning's attempt to broaden the basis of the Spanish junta's support by having called a general representative assembly, or cortes.

Foreign secretary, 1810–1812 In 1810 Wellesley joined Spencer Perceval's ministry as foreign secretary, following Canning's open breach and duel with Castlereagh and their joint resignation. The moment was not propitious: the Peninsular campaign was bogged down, Napoleon pushed victorious into Poland and Russia, and war loomed with the United States over the operation of the British embargo on European trade. The British situation in the Iberian peninsula was also complicated by the rise of the Venezuelan independence movement. Wellesley, always distrustful of radical nationalism, hoped that the freeing of Spanish colonial trade would dissipate the grievances of the Latin American patriots and still their clamour for independence while also benefiting Britain. At the same time he kept his lines open to Bolívar and the Creole nationalists. By comparison with his negative attitudes to Indian self-government, Wellesley always displayed a shrewd understanding of the power of European and American nationalisms. In Europe he supported with finance and munitions the national movements against Napoleon in Russia and Sweden.

While the outlines of Wellesley's policies were clear enough, his execution of them left something to be desired. Perceval, the prime minister, was regarded as a weak leader attempting to hold together a fractious administration. In this he was not helped by Wellesley, who ran foreign policy without reference to his colleagues, rarely attended cabinet meetings, and also failed to support his friends vigorously in the Lords on the grounds of his 'nervousness'. Despite the pleas of the prince regent and the offer of the lord lieutenancy of Ireland, Wellesley finally broke with Perceval and resigned from the ministry in January 1812. But he was drawn back into the heart of politics in May of that year when Perceval was assassinated. Instructed by the prince regent to try to form a ministry, his attempt foundered on personal animosities and the two great divisive issues of the day: Catholic emancipation and the extent to which military and financial resources ought to be poured into the Peninsula. Liverpool refused to serve under Wellesley; Grey and Grenville disagreed with him on military policy. In the event Liverpool and his supporters formed a government, which, despite initial failures, was preserved by Wellington's victory at Salamanca and went on to last for more than a decade.

From 1812 to 1821 Wellesley was out of office. His vigorous support for Catholic emancipation alienated many important political figures, including Wellington, who opposed it. At the same time Wellesley's stance on the European war changed. He opposed the treaty of Fontainebleau and later the campaign which ended at Waterloo, arguing that Napoleon ought to be recognized as a constitutional monarch following his return from Elba. Wellesley also pressed for free trade and opposed the policy of protecting British wheat producers, another difference with Wellington and the ministry. After the end of the war he argued for an immediate reduction in military charges and taxation to palliate popular discontent, though he ultimately rallied behind the ministry when it came under fierce attack as a consequence of the Peterloo massacre.

Lord lieutenant of Ireland, and second marriage On the death of George III in 1820 and Grenville's move to support the ministry, Wellesley was again offered and this time accepted the post of lord lieutenant of Ireland. This was an astute move on the part of Liverpool, who consolidated the *rapprochement* with Grenville, while at the same time maintaining that this appointment was good for Ireland. Wellesley's support for Catholic emancipation suggested that, in the short run, he was in a position to allay the religious and social discontent which spread rapidly in the aftermath of the war. At the same time he was popular with Irish protestants, who saw him and Wellington as

two of their own, and had conspicuously benefited from the military and political offices created by the brothers all over the British empire and in the Iberian peninsula. This fund of goodwill was, however, rapidly exhausted in a country lurching again towards political violence, where the clandestine resistance of Ribbonmen and Whiteboys was matched by the public display of power of the Orange lodges. A few months after his arrival in January 1822 Wellesley was already in bad odour in Dublin when he attempted, through the lord mayor of the city, to prohibit the annual garlanding of the statue of William III, which constituted the classic demonstration of Orange triumphalism. A riot followed and troops were called out. Later, Wellesley was insulted in public and narrowly missed injury from a flying bottle thrown at him in the theatre. He responded by prosecuting those he regarded as responsible for these incidents. But the Dublin grand jury threw out the charges and the Irish administration very nearly stood condemned for its policy in the Commons.

Wellesley's Irish policies aimed at a compromise which would preserve social hierarchy and order: 'Ireland tranquillised' instead of the 'polemical clamour of conflicting religious zealots' (*Wellesley Papers*, 2.149), as he wrote to Liverpool. He attempted to alleviate the immediate economic crisis of 1821–2 with famine relief. He sought to limit the element of compulsion in the payment of tithes by the Catholic peasantry to the Church of Ireland and actually secured a bill for the composition of tithes in 1823. He modified the Insurrection Act, and sought to curb the arbitrary operation of the magistracy and petty sessions. Over his period in office he did his best to remove extremist protestants from major office; these included, ironically enough, Sir David Baird, commander of the final assault on Seringapatam a quarter of a century before, who was ousted as commander-in-chief of the Irish forces.

All these initiatives, however, were doomed to failure. In the first place the political nation in Britain, as well as the Irish administration, was fundamentally split on the issue of the future of the protestant ascendancy. Wellesley's Irish chief secretary, Henry Goulbourn, was ambivalent about further concessions to the Catholics, while in Britain powerful figures such as Peel and Wellington deplored every move of the Irish administration towards compromise. Wellesley's public relations were also poor. He failed to consult the Church of Ireland clergy about the planned reduction of tithes, which they saw as a raid on their property. He also allowed to spiral out of control a controversy about a measure allowing Catholics burial in protestant churchyards according to their own rites. Worse, Wellesley's grip over business was visibly weakening. His 'pretentious yet penurious' administration (Jenkins, 185) courted public ridicule. In a pathetic throwback to his Indian durbars, he dressed up his attendants in silver lace and required heralds to accompany him to the viceregal chapel in Dublin Castle. His natural son Edward Johnston (probably the product of a liaison which had predated even Hyacinthe) intervened openly in the distribution of jobs. As Brian Jenkins puts it:

> Sound, sensible and liberal as his position was, Wellesley's ability to shape a programme of reform was seriously impaired by those foibles and administrative failings which quickly undermined his authority and realised all the misgivings harboured at the time of his appointment. (ibid.)

It is doubtful, of course, whether even a more dynamic and less self-indulgent politician could have proceeded much further. The artificial boom which had concealed Irish poverty during the French wars had ended abruptly in 1816. Irish manufacturing was withering away without tariff protection, its food supply dangerously dependent on a single crop, the potato. The shift of political power to London following the union had only exacerbated the kingdom's sense of marginality and malaise.

Indeed, the fusion of social and religious grievances had proceeded too far for social peace to be easily assured by any viceregal measure. The founding of O'Connell's Catholic Association in 1824 saw Wellesley striving uneasily to balance his instinctive concern for social order with his longer-term aim of Catholic advancement. In the event he passed vigorous legislation against both protestant and Catholic secret societies which pleased no one. Wellesley's own alienation from his brother Arthur and from the protestant establishment was further confirmed by his marriage on 29 October 1825 to Marianne Paterson (d. 1853), née Caton, widow of Robert Paterson, a Baltimore merchant. (His estranged first wife, Hyacinthe, had died in 1816.) Marianne Paterson was a Catholic, and the marriage was solemnized by the lord primate of Ireland and by the Roman Catholic archbishop of Ireland. They had no children.

Wellesley held the position of lord lieutenant until 1828, when, after Canning's death, his brother became prime minister with the main intention of upholding the protestant ascendancy, and he left the ministry. Ironically, the opposition of Wellington and Peel to Catholic emancipation was soon afterwards abandoned as the country slid towards civil war. Supporting the Reform Bill, his adherence to the moderate whig party brought Wellesley a number of offices in the last years of his life. He became lord steward of the household under Lord Grey. He then resumed the lord lieutenancy of Ireland for two years (early 1832 to April 1834), during which time he again tried to promote Catholics to civil and judicial office. He left office with the whigs in April 1834, but when they returned to power in the next year, he took the office of lord chamberlain only briefly before finally retiring from public affairs at the age of seventy-five. He spent the last seven years of his life at Kingston House, Brompton, immersed once again in the classics.

Reassessments of Wellesley Wellesley's reputation, as has been seen, suffered a partial eclipse in the 1810s and 1820s, when a reaction set in against the cost of his Indian conquests, and he managed to alienate both factions in the Irish conflict. But as the generation of Indian officers whom he had promoted, such as Malcolm and

Edmonstone, wrote memoirs and achieved power among the directors, Wellesley began to be seen as a guarantor of the British destiny in India as notable as Robert Clive and Warren Hastings. The first stage of his rehabilitation culminated with Montgomery Martin's edition of Wellesley's *Despatches, Minutes and Correspondence* (1836) and the erection of a marble statue in his honour in the company's premises at Leadenhall Street. Wellesley's extension of British dominion in the subcontinent now seemed a marvellous thing to tories who had once been suspicious of him. Equally, his commitment to free trade and education ensured that whig radicals of the reform era did not view him with total hostility. After Wellesley's death the machine of Victorian biographical deification took over, producing the works of W. McCullagh Torrens (1880), Colonel G. B. Malleson (1889), and the Revd W. H. Hutton (1893). Malleson's work, written in the light of his own collaboration on Kaye's history of the Indian mutiny, set the stage for a full-blown imperialist interpretation of Wellesley which emphasized the French 'threat' to British India and the depravity of Tipu Sultan. Malleson was one of the first historians to compare Wellesley favourably with the supposedly unimaginative and impolitic Iron Duke. Wellesley's strict dealings with the Indian states also appealed to the experts of the later Victorian age, who saw domesticated Indian princes as a guarantee of the British Indian empire. Hereafter, the 'glorious little man' was generally applauded for his public policies but berated for his arrogance and impetuousness; a veil was drawn over his affairs with Drury Lane actresses and other concubines between the breakdown of his marriage in 1807 and his remarriage in 1825. At the end of the nineteenth century Lord Curzon's viceroyalty seemed like an avatar of Wellesley's government. Curzon's *British Government in India* (1925), volume 2, spent a whole chapter on Wellesley's new government house in Calcutta. By a delicious chance of fate, Wellesley's plans of 1799 had been based on Kedleston Hall, the Curzon family seat. Yet by the 1920s imperialist jingo was matched by nationalist and liberal deprecation of Wellesley's 'forward policy' against Tipu and the Marathas. Edward Thompson's and G. T. Garrett's *The Rise and Fulfilment of British Rule in India* (1934) was decidedly hostile to him.

In recent years Wellesley and his family have sometimes been seen as embodiments of the spirit of the 'second British empire', arch-exponents of 'military fiscalism', and upholders of the balance of power in Asia. This characterization, however, raises some difficulties. Wellesley was certainly an expansionist and a domineering governor-general. Iris Butler, in her perceptive *The Eldest Brother* (1973), the most recent biography of Wellesley, makes a vain effort to protect him against charges of aggression in India. She claims that the state of the subcontinent demanded action and implies that Wellesley was forming the basis for Indian nationality by his forced unification of the country (Butler, 417). In other respects, however, she does succeed in showing that the marquess was a more interesting and complex figure than the duke, and a most ambivalent Conservative and imperialist. It is clear that any attempt to paint a picture of a monolithic 'new imperialism' of the period of the Napoleonic war looks problematic after an examination of this powerful family alone, whose opinions were at variance on almost every major issue. In Europe, at least, Wellesley, unlike Wellington and Wellesley-Pole, was a free-trading liberal whig. He argued for representative government in Spain, Catholic emancipation, and, ultimately, for the reform of the British parliament. Both a lover and a hater of France from his youth, he seems to have had some admiration for the rationality of Napoleon's administration, and in 1814 preferred a constitutional government under the emperor to the antiquated absolutism of the Bourbons. He was an exponent abroad of the imperialism of free trade, buttressed by Indian territorial empire, and of whig modernization at home. He anticipated Peel in trying to impart vigour and professionalism to his Indian administrations and was more radical than Peel in his support for the Catholic cause in Ireland. Despite his origins among the Anglo-Irish rentier cabals of the eighteenth century, Wellesley anticipated many leading ideas and policies of the early Victorian generation.

Character and death Even in his own personality Wellesley displayed manifold contradictions. A small man of no more than 5 foot 7 inches in height, his charisma and classical features made him attractive to both sexes. A stern public moralist in India, who did not himself drink or gamble, he was soon to launch himself into a new series of sexual adventures which astounded even the relaxed Regency age. In India he was regarded as a hard-driving workaholic who personally penned hundreds of lengthy and percipient minutes. By contrast, at the Foreign Office and in Ireland he was noted for laziness and inattention to his duties. These contradictions seem to have come to a head in 1807 and 1808, when, as Iris Butler plausibly surmises, he may have suffered some kind of mental collapse.

Wellesley died at Kingston House, Brompton, on 26 September 1842, at the age of eighty-three, and was buried in the chapel of Eton College on 8 October. He composed his own Latin funerary ode, affirming the importance of the school in his early development. This epitaph was later placed over the inner archway of the north transept of the chapel by the duke of Wellington. Always impecunious, despite an *ex gratia* grant of £20,000 from the East India Company in 1837, he seems to have left little to his family. Wellesley's second wife, Marianne, lady of the bedchamber to the queen dowager Adelaide, died at Hampton Court Palace on 17 December 1853. He was survived at least by one illegitimate son, the Revd Henry Wellesley (1794–1866), and his illegitimate daughters Anne, Lady Charles Bentinck (1788–1875), and Hyacinthe Mary, Lady Hatherton (1789–1849). His eldest son, Richard (*b.* 1787), who had led a relatively unsuccessful parliamentary career, predeceased him in 1831. His second son, Gerald (1799–1833), was for a time the East India Company's resident at Indore. Wellesley's relations with his male offspring were not close, although he acknowledged his

paternity. The marquessate became extinct on his death, and the earldom of Mornington descended to his brother William.

C. A. BAYLY

Sources BL OIOC, Home misc. • BL, Wellesley MSS, Add. MSS • Neil Edmonstone's memoir on his Indian career, U. Cam., Centre of South Asian Studies • I. Butler, *The eldest brother: the Marquess Wellesley, the duke of Wellington's eldest brother* (1973) • *The Wellesley papers: the life and correspondence of Richard Colley Wellesley, Marquess Wellesley*, ed. [L. S. Benjamin], 2 vols. (1914) • *The despatches, minutes and correspondence of the Marquess Wellesley ... during his administration in India*, ed. M. Martin, 5 vols. (1836–40) • *The despatches and correspondence of the Marquess Wellesley ... during his lordship's mission to Spain as ambassador extraordinary to the supreme junta in 1809*, ed. M. Martin (1838) • J. K. Severn, *A Wellesley affair: Richard Marquess Wellesley and the conduct of Anglo-Spanish diplomacy, 1809–1812* (1981) • B. Jenkins, *Era of emancipation: British government of Ireland, 1812–1830* (1988) • *Two views of British India: the private correspondence of Mr. Dundas and Lord Wellesley, 1798–1801*, ed. E. Ingram (1969) • E. Ingram, *Commitment to empire* (1981) • M. Hasan, *History of Tipu Sultan*, 2nd edn (1971) • S. Gordon, *The Marathas, 1600–1818* (1993) • W. M. Torrens, *The Marquess Wellesley, architect of empire: an historic portrait* (1880) • *The diary and correspondence of Henry Wellesley, first Lord Cowley*, ed. F. A. Wellesley (1930) • G. Annesley [Viscount Valentia], *Voyages and travels in India, Ceylon, the Red Sea, Abyssinia, and Egypt*, 3 vols. (1809) • Lord Curzon of Kedleston, *British government in India*, 2 vols. (1925) • G. B. Malleson, *Life of the Marquess Wellesley* (1889) • J. Malcolm, *The political history of India, from 1784 to 1823*, 2 vols. (1826) • E. Thomson and G. T. Garrett, *The rise and fulfilment of British rule in India* (1934) • V. T. Harlow, *The founding of the second British empire, 1763–1793*, 2 vols. (1952–64) • F. Madden and D. Fieldhouse, *Imperial reconstruction, 1763–1840* (1987) • J. Ehrman, *The younger Pitt*, 1–2 (1969–83) • *A selection from the despatches, memoranda, and other papers relating to India of ... the duke of Wellington*, ed. S. J. Owen (1880) • P. Moon, *The British conquest and dominion of India* (1989) • W. H. Hutton, *The Marquess Wellesley* (1893) • GEC, *Peerage*

Archives BL, corresp. and papers, Add. MSS 12564–13915, 37274–37318, 37414–37416, 49979–49992, 51728 • BL OIOC, Bengal political and secret consultations • BL OIOC, corresp., dispatches, and papers relating to India • BL OIOC, dispatches and minutes, MS Eur. D 623 • Duke U., Perkins L., corresp. • Hunt. L., letter-books relating to Turkey and Persia • Lpool RO, corresp. • NL Ire., draft dispatches, memoranda, etc., letter-book • PRO, letter-book and copies of letters received • U. Southampton L., family and misc. corresp., and papers | BL, corresp. with Lord Grenville, Add. MSS 58910–58913, 70927–70928 • BL, Jenkinson MSS • BL, letters to Lord Liverpool, loan 72 • BL, corresp. with first and second earls of Liverpool, Add. MS 38103 • BL, letters to Sir Robert Peel, Add. MS 40324 • BL OIOC, letters to Thomas Cockburn, MS Eur. C 165 • BL OIOC, Henry Wellesley's papers, Eur. MSS • Bucks. RLSS, corresp. with Scrope Bernard • Bucks. RLSS, letters to Lord Hobart • CKS, letters to Lord Hobart • CKS, letters to William Pitt • Devon RO, corresp. with Lord Sidmouth • Herefs. RO, Brydges MSS • Herefs. RO, corresp. with Sir Harford Jones • JRL, letters to Henry Dundas and Robert Dundas • Morgan L., corresp. with George Canning • NA Scot., letters to Henry Dundas • NL Wales, corresp. with Clive family • NL Wales, letters to second Lord Clive • NRA, priv. coll., letters to Lord Anglesey • NRA, priv. coll., letters to Lord Elgin • NRA, priv. coll., corresp. with Spencer Perceval • priv. coll., Wellesley MSS • PRO, corresp. with Lord Cornwallis, PRO 30/11 • PRO, letters to William Pitt, PRO 30/8 • PRO NIre., corresp. with Lord Castlereagh, D 3030 • Royal Arch., letters to George III • Scottish United Services Museum, Edinburgh, corresp. with Sir David Baird • Staffs. RO, Hatherton MSS • Suffolk RO, Bunbury MSS • Surrey HC, corresp. with Henry Goulburn • TCD, corresp. with Lord Donoughmore • U. Durham L., Grey MSS, letters to second Earl Grey • U. Southampton L., corresp. with Henry Dundas • U. Southampton L., corresp. with duke of Wellington • UCL, corresp. with Lord Brougham • University of Minnesota, Minneapolis, Ames Library of South Asia, corresp. with Henry Dundas • W. Yorks. AS, Leeds, Yorkshire

Archaeological Society, letters to Lady Wellesley · W. Yorks. AS, Leeds, Osborne MSS

Likenesses D. Gardner, drawing, 1775, Badminton, Gloucestershire · G. Romney, oils, 1781, Eton · O. Humphry, pencil, chalk, and watercolour drawing, 1783, NPG · E. Walker, photogravure, 1783 (after R. Cosway), NPG · K. A. Hickel, oils, 1793 (study for NPG), Stratfield Saye House, Hampshire · R. Home, oils, c.1805, Wellington Museum, London · J. Nollekens, marble bust, 1808, Royal Collection · J. Bacon jun., statue, 1809, Calcutta · T. Lawrence, oils, 1812, Royal Collection [*see illus.*] · T. Lawrence, chalk drawing, c.1813, NG Ire. · J. Bacon, marble bust, NPG · C. F. Bates, oils, Christ Church Oxf. · attrib. M. Brown, oils, Stratfield Saye House, Hampshire · C. F. Bute, portrait, priv. coll. · J. P. Davis, oils, NPG · J. P. Davis, watercolour drawing, NPG · J. Downman, pencil and watercolour drawing, Stratfield Saye House, Hampshire · K. A. Hickel, group portrait, oils (*The House of Commons, 1793*), NPG · T. Hickey, oils, Wellington Museum, London · J. Hopner, portrait, priv. coll. · S. C. Smith, oils, Wellington Museum, London

Wellesley, Sir **Victor Alexander Augustus Henry** (1876–1954), diplomatist, was born at the British embassy, St Petersburg, on 1 March 1876, the only child of Colonel Frederick Arthur Wellesley (1844–1931), army officer in the Coldstream Guards, then serving as military attaché at the St Petersburg embassy, and his first wife, Emma Anne Caroline Bloomfield, daughter of Lord Augustus William Frederick Spencer *Loftus, ambassador in Berlin and St Petersburg. Wellesley's father was the third and youngest son of Henry Richard Charles *Wellesley, first Earl Cowley, ambassador to Paris, and the grandson of Henry *Wellesley, first Baron Cowley, ambassador in Vienna and Paris, and the youngest brother of the first duke of Wellington. Wellesley was a page of honour to his godmother Queen Victoria from 1887 to 1892. His parents divorced in 1882 and he was educated in Germany, first at Wiesbaden, where his mother lived, and later at Heidelberg. He returned to England when he was about twenty and lived with his maternal grandfather, Lord Augustus Loftus, at Leatherhead. He passed into Sandhurst but was then rejected on account of his eyesight, and instead entered the Foreign Office in April 1899.

Wellesley's early career included serving as acting second secretary at Rome from May 1905 to July 1906, as secretary to the British delegation to the Bern Labour Conference in September 1906, and as commercial attaché for Spain from January 1908. On 20 July 1909 he married Alice Muriel (*d.* 1949), eldest daughter of Oscar Leslie Stephen, of Eaton Terrace, London. They had one daughter, Anne Muriel (1913–1919). Wellesley returned to the Foreign Office in June 1913 and was promoted to senior clerk in November 1913. In September 1916 he became controller of commercial and consular affairs. He was promoted assistant secretary in April 1919 and made an important tour of inspection of the Latin American missions and consulates from November 1919 to April 1920. The post of controller was abolished in 1919 and on his return to the Foreign Office in 1920 Wellesley became head of the Far Eastern department. He remained closely involved in Far Eastern affairs for the remainder of his career, during which he was involved with the end of the Anglo-Japanese alliance, the Washington treaty of 1922, the British reaction to revolution in China, the dispatch of British troops

to Shanghai, and the Manchurian crisis. His role was controversial both to contemporaries and to historians. Supporters of the League of Nations saw him as hindering action against Japanese aggression. On the other hand he was among the first to warn, as early as 1921, of the growing divergence of interests between London and Tokyo. While often expressing astringent views about the United States, he viewed strong Anglo-American relations as the cornerstone of British foreign and security policy.

In January 1924 Wellesley was promoted as assistant under-secretary and when, in May the following year, Sir William Tyrrell became permanent under-secretary, he chose Wellesley as deputy under-secretary. Wellesley had already been unusual in identifying the importance of economic factors in Japan's actions, and his early exposure to economic issues while doing commercial work now led him to launch what would be a long campaign to integrate economic analysis into the Foreign Office's work. He proposed that this could be accomplished through creating a Foreign Office section to consider politico-economic intelligence, assisted by an external advisory body. Having noted the frustration of the consular service over the failure to co-ordinate foreign policy with commerce and industry, he made his first effort to reform the handling of overseas trade issues while he was controller of commercial and consular affairs. Together with Sir Eyre Crowe and Lord Eustace Percy he argued that after the First World War commercial issues would become central and that the Foreign Office should lead in promoting overseas trade. His plans were strongly opposed by the Board of Trade and the Treasury, and an unhappy compromise was reached through the creation in 1917 of a new department of overseas trade, responsible to both the Foreign Office and the Board of Trade, which also took over the commercial work of the Foreign Office.

Wellesley, though, had been arguing for the need to consider all the economic factors in external affairs, not just those concerning trade. He could only note the failure of communication between the Bank of England and the Foreign Office, which had to go via the Treasury, as well as the disagreements between the Treasury and the Foreign Office, which were such a characteristic of the 1920s, over the appropriate policy to follow on reparations and war debts. It was only the great economic crisis of 1929 that again opened the possibility of implementing Wellesley's ideas. In 1930 Wellesley proposed the creation of a politico-economic intelligence department within the Foreign Office. The idea was supported by the new Labour parliamentary under-secretary Hugh Dalton, and by the permanent under-secretary Sir Robert Vansittart, but it was blocked in 1931 by Sir Warren Fisher, head of the civil service, who was able to convince the prime minister, Ramsay MacDonald, that the plan was unsound. Wellesley bided his time, and at last succeeded in having a small economic relations section established in 1933. It was this tenacity which saw his proposal survive through the rapid succession of three foreign secretaries. Wellesley also succeeded in having economics made a compulsory subject for the diplomatic and consular services' entrance examinations. Ultimately he paid the price of his advocacy when, in a shake-up in the wake of Samuel Hoare's resignation as foreign secretary, he was retired on 1 October 1936. He was briefly employed during the Second World War in the Ministry of Economic Warfare (1939–40).

In retirement Wellesley did not lose interest in the conduct of foreign policy. Reflecting on his battle with Fisher, he wrote a notable letter to *The Times* in the summer of 1942 which warned of the danger being caused by the weakening of the Foreign Office through the interference of the head of the civil service. This led to a debate in parliament on the potential for confusion in the central machinery of government. In 1944 Wellesley published *Diplomacy in Fetters*, a trenchant but typically unsensational analysis of the impediments under which British diplomacy suffered. A pessimist, he once minuted 'The situation is hopeless and we are helpless' (Strang, 59). None the less his career was notable for its sustained effort to integrate economic concerns and analytical capacity into the structure of the Foreign Office. Wellesley was a fine amateur painter of landscapes and portraits, with his work often being exhibited at the Royal Academy. He edited his father's autobiography, *Recollections of a Soldier Diplomat* (1947) as well as *Conversations with Napoleon III* (1934). He was appointed CB in 1919 and KCMG in 1926.

Wellesley was an invalid after 1948 and, for the last two to three years of his life, almost blind. He died at his home, 12 Ranelagh Grove, Ebury Bridge, London, on 20 February 1954, and his funeral service was held nearby, at St Michael's, Chester Square. ERIK GOLDSTEIN

Sources F. T. Ashton-Gwatkin, 'Thoughts on the foreign office, 1918–1939', *Contemporary Review*, 188 (1955), 374–8 · R. Sencourt, 'Sir Victor Wellesley', *Heirs of tradition: tributes of a New Zealander* (1949), 120–37 · D. Boadle, 'The formation of the foreign office economic relations section', *HJ*, 20 (1977), 919–36 · Lord Strang, *Home and abroad* (1956) · *WWW, 1951–60* · Burke, *Peerage* · FO List · *CGPLA Eng. & Wales* (1954)
Archives CUL, minutes to diplomatic corresp.
Likenesses L. Powles, portrait
Wealth at death £28,434 6s. 2d.: probate, 8 July 1954, *CGPLA Eng. & Wales*

Wellesley, William Pole-Tylney-Long-, fourth earl of Mornington (1788–1857). *See under* Pole, William Wellesley-, third earl of Mornington (1763–1845).

Wellesz, Egon Joseph (1885–1974), composer and music scholar, was born in Vienna on 21 October 1885, the only child of (Solomon) Josef Wellesz, textile manufacturer, and his wife, Ilona Lövenyi. He was educated at Hegel Gymnasium in Vienna and studied musicology at Vienna University under Guido Adler. He started composing at the age of thirteen and six years later became a private composition-pupil of Arnold Schoenberg. The greatest musical influence in his early life was that of Gustav Mahler, whose musical personality and methods he was able to study by frequently attending his rehearsals at the opera. This double interest in the remoter past of music, as research student, and in the modern development of the art, as composer, was to mark the whole of his long life

and to impart a quite unusual breadth of interest and vision to his work not only as composer but also as teacher.

Wellesz's first researches were into the music, and particularly the opera, of the baroque period in Venice and in Vienna itself. But the subject that was to be his life-work was the history of Byzantine ecclesiastical chant and its relationship to the Gregorian chant of the western church. His earliest publications on the subject date from 1914, and his successful deciphering of Middle Byzantine musical notation (1918) gave him a unique authority, of which the non-specialist musician can appreciate something in his *A History of Byzantine Music and Hymnography* (1949; 2nd edn, 1961). On the other hand his earliest published book (1921) was a study of Schoenberg's music, which had a marked though by no means exclusive influence on the five operas and four ballets that Wellesz wrote between 1918 and 1930. If Richard Strauss was a strong influence in these works, their subject matter and character owed even more to Strauss's librettist, Hugo von Hofmannsthal, a close friend who provided Wellesz himself with librettos for the ballet *Achilles auf Skyros* (1926) and the opera *Alkestis* (1924).

Ballet particularly interested Wellesz at this time, both as an avenue of escape from the Wagnerian conception of opera and also as a form related to the Byzantine liturgy, conceived as a terrestrial reflection of the court of the divine *pantokrator*. This establishment of widely drawn parallels was an essential characteristic of Wellesz's mentality and explains his instinctive sense of the essential similarity between the new movements in all the arts of the day. His song-texts included poems by Stefan George and Francis Jammes and his friends included the writer Jacob Wassermann and the painter Oskar Kokoschka, whose portrait of Wellesz dates from 1911. The ballets and operas of these years were successful on German stages but, despite Wellesz's deep sense of belonging to a native Viennese tradition—both baroque and classical—he assiduously cultivated links with both France and England (which he visited for the first time in 1906, attending lectures at Cambridge) and he was active in the foundation and administration of both the International Society of Contemporary Music (1922) and the International Musicological Society. In 1932 he was the first Austrian composer since Haydn to receive an honorary doctorate of music from Oxford University. During these years (1929–38) he was professor of music history at Vienna University. In 1908 he married Emmy Franzisca, daughter of Ludwig Stross, with whom he had two daughters.

It was not wholly unexpected that when, in 1938, Hitler annexed Austria, it should have been England that offered Wellesz a new home. In that year Bruno Walter had conducted a major orchestral work based by Wellesz on *The Tempest* (*Prosperos Beschwörungen*), but the sudden and violent interruption of his career, and exile from the centre of new musical developments to the still musically insular atmosphere of England, caused a break of years in his development as a composer. During the 1930s he had taken an active interest in a movement aimed at the renewal, enlargement, and *aggiornamento* of the Catholic tradition in Austria; and this, with his Jewish origins and known hostility to national socialism, would have made him an inevitable victim of persecution had he remained in Vienna. Through Henry Colles, the chief music critic of *The Times*, and other friends he was able to settle with his family in Oxford, where in 1939 he was made a fellow of Lincoln College and later university lecturer in the history of music (1944) and university reader in Byzantine music (1948). He was naturalized in 1946. It was now that his career as teacher assumed a primary importance, and it seemed for a time as though this and his Byzantine studies might well occupy the rest of his life. In 1957 appeared volume 1, which he edited, of *The New Oxford History of Music*, of which he was one of the four editors. Instead of this, however, Wellesz entered a new and extremely prolific period of creative activity. This began in 1944 with a chamber work based on Gerard Manley Hopkins's 'The Leaden Echo and the Golden Echo'; and during the next thirty years he was to write a large quantity of music of all kinds, bringing the number of his string quartets (the first of which is dated 1911–12) to nine and including, most importantly, nine symphonies, written between 1945 and 1971. In all these works Wellesz, whose attitude to Schoenberg's serialism had never been that of a doctrinaire, was clearly concerned to continue and expand the Viennese symphonic tradition, as represented particularly by Schubert, Bruckner, and above all Mahler. These works interested and were championed by a number of English musicians and, taken with Wellesz's activities as teacher, lecturer, and writer, played an important part in what may be called the 'de-insulation' of English music. On the continent, however, and particularly in his native Vienna, enthusiasm for the music of first Schoenberg and then Anton von Webern was inextricably associated with hostility to the ideas of defeated national socialism: so that Wellesz's more traditionally based and basically eclectic 'Austro-European' music found at first little favour. Although he was made a fellow of the Royal Danish Academy of Science and Letters in 1946, became a fellow of the British Academy in 1953, and was appointed CBE in 1957, it was not until 1961 that he received the Austrian great state prize. In the same year he was also made a knight of the order of Saint Gregory the Great.

He spent the rest of his long life in Oxford, though returning regularly to Austria during the summer months. He remained active until two years before his death, when he had a severe stroke. He died in Oxford on 9 November 1974. If the specialist nature of his Byzantine studies (of which his greatest work was editing the *Monumenta musicae Byzantinae*) has made it hard for the general musical world to appreciate fully his quality as a scholar, his activities as teacher, writer, and inspirer of a generation of musicians in Britain and his part in bringing British music 'into Europe' will always be remembered; and the profusion, variety, and craftsmanship of his music remain to reflect the warmth and generosity of his personality and the scope of his artistic interests.

MARTIN COOPER, *rev.*

Sources R. Schollum, *Egon Wellesz* (1963) • E. Wellesz and E. Wellesz, *Egon Wellesz: Leben und Werke*, ed. F. Endler (Vienna, 1981) • C. C. Benser, *Egon Wellesz* (1985) • R. Layton, 'Wellesz, Egon', *New Grove* • W. Oakeshott, 'Egon Wellesz', *PBA*, 61 (1975), 567–87 • *The Times* (11 Nov 1974) • *CGPLA Eng. & Wales* (1975)
Archives Bodl. Oxf., letters to his daughter | SOUND BL NSA, documentary recordings • BL NSA, 'Egon Wellesz', 1970, M2089R, M2091W C1 • BL NSA, *Mining the archives*, 1995, H6161/3 • BL NSA, oral history interview • BL NSA, performance recording • BL NSA, recorded talks • BL NSA, *Talking about music*, 144, 1LP0153900 S2 BD3 BBC TRANSC
Likenesses O. Kokoschka, portrait, 1911 • J. E. Cooke, oils, *c.*1970, Lincoln College, Oxford • photograph, repro. in Oakeshott, 'Egon Wellesz'
Wealth at death £5417: probate, 4 Feb 1975, *CGPLA Eng. & Wales*

Wellington. For this title name *see* Wellesley, Arthur, first duke of Wellington (1769–1852); Wellesley, Dorothy Violet, duchess of Wellington (1889–1956).

Wellington, Hubert Lindsay (1879–1967), artist and art teacher, was born on 14 June 1879 in Gloucester, the elder of the two sons of Caleb Joseph Wellington, the eponymous proprietor of a large printing firm in that city, and his wife, Katherine Potter. Like his father, Hubert Wellington was educated at the Crypt Grammar School, Gloucester. In spite of some parental misgivings Wellington transferred at the age of sixteen from the Crypt to the Gloucester School of Art and in 1897 enrolled at the art school in Birmingham. Here he spent more time in the city's central library than in the school's cast room, discovering the *Mercure de France*, the *Revue Blanche*, the lithographs of Steinlen, and, in the *Saturday Review*, the art criticism of D. S. MacColl who later became his staunch champion. A year later he entered the more sympathetic atmosphere of the Slade School of Fine Art in London.

Wellington arrived at the Slade on the same day as Wyndham Lewis and Everard Meynell, with whom he spent many fruitful hours in the print room of the British Museum under the encouraging eye of Laurence Binyon. However, his closest friends came from the Camden Town Group, which centred around Spencer Gore and Harold Gilman and, somewhat later, Charles Ginner, with Walter Sickert as an enigmatic father figure.

In 1900, at the age of twenty-one and without an income, Wellington married Nancy Charlotte Boughtwood (*d.* 1943). At over 6 feet tall, with a halo of reddish-golden hair and a small Vandyke beard, he was a strikingly romantic and charismatic figure. For four years, after leaving the Slade, he worked sporadically, which included assisting Henry Payne, in Birmingham in 1902, with stained-glass commissions. In order to support his wife and two young sons, (Reginald Everard) Lindsay Wellington and Robert Michael Wellington, he secured a full-time teaching post at the Stafford School of Art in 1904, where the family stayed until 1916. He kept in touch with Gore and Gilman, who came to stay with him and to paint in the countryside near Stafford, and he in turn visited and travelled with them. In his own words:

> for my painting, one of the crucial points was undoubtedly in the summer of 1906, when I joined Gore at Dieppe. Walter Sickert had invited Gore to use his house at Neuville, and I joined them for an immensely stimulating six weeks. Sickert

was most generous and encouraging, with endless talk of great practitioners of 'la bonne peinture'. (H. Wellington, 5)

As a landscape painter Wellington remained faithful to the neo-impressionist style and to 'the divided touch', but as the years went by his sympathies moved further from the world of Camille Pissarro towards the monumental style of Paul Cézanne. In 1926 he wrote: 'Cézanne has changed the face of the world of painting by fundamental constructive and technical perceptions.' This comment gives a clue to his increasingly firm orientation towards Paris and contemporary French culture. Beyond the world of painters, he was a subscriber to the *Nouvelle Revue Fran-çaise* and so an early admirer of Marcel Proust.

The premature deaths of Gore in 1914 (at the Goupil Gallery memorial auction Wellington bought a work by Thér-èse Lessore to support Gore's family) and Gilman in 1919, together with the upheavals of the First World War (during which he went to France with the survey battalion of the Royal Engineers as a map draughtsman), left Wellington at forty still unestablished. Charles Holmes at the National Gallery, prompted by Charles Aitken and J. B. Manson from the Tate, spotted the potentialities of the articulate and enthusiastic painter–teacher, however, and proposed in the spring of 1919 that he should launch a new experiment of informal guide lecturing. For two hours each morning six days a week, he talked about the old masters as a painter rather than as an art historian. By the time he retired from this field in 1923, his pioneer work, together with that of W. G. Constable at the Wallace Collection and Edwin Fagg at the Tate Gallery, had established a pattern of guide lecturing which has since blossomed into the diverse educational activities now seen in today's museums and galleries. Although he had acquired a reputation for expertise about old masters, Wellington had also in occasional art criticism for the *Saturday Review*, *The Nation*, and the *Manchester Guardian* established himself as a spokesman for his contemporaries, such as Matthew Smith, Paul Nash and his brother John, and Ivon Hitchens. His monograph on Jacob Epstein, published in 1924, was regarded by the sculptor as one of the fairest assessments of his aims and work, as was his appreciation of his old acquaintance William Rothenstein, published in the same series in 1923. He contributed the entry on Sir William Orpen to the *Dictionary of National Biography*.

It was the production of the Rothenstein book which brought Wellington back into the world of art schools. Rothenstein, impressed by his tact and common sense, invited him, in his own words, to become his 'chief of staff' at the Royal College of Art, where as registrar and lecturer for ten years (1923–32) he provided a sympathetic link between the establishment and the younger generation of Henry Moore, John Piper, and Ceri Richards. In 1932 he moved from Kensington to become principal (1932–42) of the Edinburgh College of Art. Among the first there to take up a Grant scholarship in painting was the subsequent director of the Tate Gallery, Norman Reid, who wrote that:

One of Wellington's aims was to open our eyes to the world outside Scotland—in his own words to make us 'good Europeans'. To this end he inaugurated a programme of vacation scholarships which enabled students to travel abroad for a fortnight. … It was an experience that certainly blew a fresh wind through a number of minds.   (N. Reid to A. Glew, 12 Jan 1998, priv. coll.)

Perhaps, in instituting this programme, Wellington was remembering the gift of £15 awarded to him, towards expenses to travel to Italy, by the National Gallery in 1922. At Edinburgh he also arranged for outside lecturers to visit the college, notably Eric Gill, 'who came dressed in a priest's soutane' (ibid.). It was during this period that Wellington, influenced by the neo-Thomist writings of Charles Péguy and Jacques Maritain, embraced the Roman Catholic church.

Upon his wife's death in 1943, after more than forty years of exceptionally close partnership, Wellington retired from Edinburgh to Oxfordshire. Unexpectedly in 1946 he was invited by his old colleague Randolph Schwabe to stand in as lecturer in the history of art at the Slade School; this overlapped William Coldstream's appointment as professor in 1949. His favourite admonition to the young, taken from Francis of Sales, was 'live generously', advice which he followed in his own life. After his fingers had grown too arthritic and his eyesight too uncertain to paint, he selected, edited, and introduced for Phaidon Press a version of one of his own favourite books, *The Journals of Eugène Delacroix*, translated (1951) by Lucy Norton. His connections with art education were not entirely severed, as, from 1949 to 1959, he was examiner at the Ruskin School of Art, Oxford. The last twenty-three years of his life were made happier by the companionship and care of one of his former students at the Royal College of Art, the distinguished calligrapher and favoured pupil of Edward Johnston, Irene Bass [*see* Wellington, Irene], whom he married in November 1944.

Wellington exhibited at the Allied Artists' Association (1908–10) and the New English Art Club (1916), and with the London Group (1916–32). He was never a subscribing member of the Camden Town Group, though Gore at one time pressed him to leave Stafford to take up a position as their resident secretary. One of Wellington's paintings was shown at the Venice Biennale in 1928, yet it was only in 1963 that he had his first solo exhibition, at Thomas Agnew & Sons Ltd in London. This show, and a memorial exhibition held at the City Art Gallery, Gloucester, in 1968, confirmed him as a significant British lyrical artist of the early twentieth century. Examples of his work are in the collections, among others, of the Tate, the Contemporary Arts Society, the Arts Council, the Department of the Environment, the Ashmolean Museum, Oxford, and the Gloucester and Southampton art galleries. Hubert Wellington died at his home, the White House, North End, Henley-on-Thames, Oxfordshire, on 3 November 1967.

WILLIAM COLDSTREAM, rev. ADRIAN GLEW

Sources R. Wellington, *Hubert Wellington memorial exhibition* (1968) [exhibition catalogue, City Museum and Art Gallery, Gloucester, 8 Aug – 14 Sept 1968] · H. Wellington, foreword, *Retrospective exhibition of paintings and drawings (1900–1945) by Hubert Wellington* (1963) [exhibition catalogue, Thomas Agnew and Sons, London, 13 May – 8 June 1963] · *The Times* (7 Nov 1967) · E. Newton, 'Herbert [*sic*] Wellington', *The Guardian* (13 May 1963) · personal knowledge (1981) · private information (1981, 2004)

Archives Tate collection, TGA 881.16 | Tate collection, Lucy Norton, TGA 706 · Tate collection, The London Group, TGA 7713 · Tate collection, John Rothenstein, TGA 8726 · Tate collection, Goupil Gallery, TGA 8314

Likenesses D. Foggie, chalk drawing, 1934, Scot. NPG

Wealth at death £640: probate, 1968, *CGPLA Eng. & Wales*

Wellington [*née* Bass; *other married name* Sutton], **Irene** (1904–1984), calligrapher, was born on 29 October 1904, at Tourney Hall, Lydd, Kent youngest of the nine children of Charles Bass (1860–1944), a farmer, and his wife, Julia, *née* Goble (1864–1949). Irene grew up on the family farm in Kent, her early life revolving round farming and the countryside, from which she drew inspiration throughout her life. Her parents were strict Methodists, and the chapel and local school provided the major outside influences during her formative years. Later she attended Ashford county school, where two of her favourite subjects were English and drawing—significantly perhaps, as her love of the meaning and visual imagery of words informed her particular gift as a calligrapher. At Maidstone School of Art in 1921 she first started to learn and become fascinated by calligraphy. There she was introduced to Edward Johnston's book *Writing and Illuminating, and Lettering* and in 1925 won a scholarship to the Royal College of Art where Johnston was teaching. Irene found Johnston an inspirational teacher. She said later 'He was of anyone I have ever met, the one to have the strongest influence on me, in both my life and my work. I learnt from what he was' (Cockerell and others, 23). However, her time at the Royal College of Art was not easy. The unaccustomed freedom of art-school life contrasted strongly with her Methodist upbringing, creating unresolvable tensions that led to a severe breakdown. The bursar, the painter Hubert Lindsay *Wellington (1879–1967), who later became her second husband, secured her place; and after a year she was able to return and gain her diploma.

Marriage on 11 September 1930 to her cousin Ernest John (Jack) Sutton, an income tax officer, took Irene to Edinburgh. There, away from Johnston's immediate influence, she began to develop her own way of working. She delighted in exploring and interpreting the meaning of words through calligraphy, using different styles, colour, and arrangements of writing to reflect her own personal response to the text, and in doing so she created her own visual language, which she continued to evolve throughout her life. It was her unswerving search for the truth, within a landscape of great personal complexity of character and in a life full of contradictions and tensions, that made her work so authentic and alive. Within the personal domain lay Irene's great gift. Acutely aware of the people around her, she was always ready to engage her whole self with their ideas; often forgetful of time or other commitments, she would talk at length with serious depth and integrity, which was lit by a warm and rather quirky sense of humour.

Irene Sutton also taught at Edinburgh College of Art.

Hubert Wellington was principal there, and on Johnston's recommendation had invited her to teach. Both Hubert and his wife Charlotte became good friends, and after Charlotte's death in 1942 and the annulment of her own marriage to Jack Sutton in September 1944, she married Hubert Wellington on 11 November 1944 and moved with him to the White House near Henley-on-Thames, Oxfordshire.

Here, in what she described as her happiest time, Wellington undertook her major commissions. 'The Wykehamist roll of honour' (1948), 'The accession address' (1952), and 'The coronation address' (1953), the latter two both commissioned by the London county council for presentation to the queen, were among the many pieces she created during this productive time. She also taught part-time at the Central School of Arts and Crafts in London. After Hubert Wellington's death, on 3 November 1967, she lived in London for some years, then returned to Lydd to live with her brother. She died at Wray Common Nursing Home, Reigate, Surrey, on 18 September 1984, was cremated, and then buried at Old Romney church, Kent, on 26 September.

Irene Wellington was a key figure in the development of calligraphy in the twentieth century. She profoundly influenced the transformation of calligraphy from a medieval craft to a modern art form. A talented student of Edward Johnston, the founder of the modern calligraphic revival, she stretched the whole concept of calligraphy from Johnston's pioneer work in traditional formal writing to the freedom of personal expression.

ANN HECHLE

Sources H. Collins, 'Irene Wellington: a background', in H. Child and others, *More than fine writing: Irene Wellington, calligrapher, 1904–1984* (1986), 17–27 · personal knowledge (2004) · private information (2004) [Jean Bushby, niece] · S. C. Cockerell and others, *Tributes to Edward Johnston* (privately printed, Kent, 1948) · *CGPLA Eng. & Wales* (1986) · m. cert.

Archives Surrey Institute of Art and Design, Farnham, Crafts Study Centre, collection and archive · Surrey Institute of Art and Design, Farnham, Crafts Study Centre, Irene Wellington Educational Trust collection · University of Minnesota, Minneapolis

Likenesses photograph, Surrey Institute of Art and Design, Farnham, Surrey, Crafts Study Centre collection and archive

Wealth at death under £40,000: administration with will, 8 July 1986, *CGPLA Eng. & Wales*

Wells. *See also* Welles.

Wells, Charles Jeremiah (*c*.1800–1879), lawyer and poet, was born probably in London, the elder of the two children of James Turner Wells and Jane, *née* Sayers (*d*. 1832). Little is known of his parents, though his mother may have been an actress, and they appear to have been reasonably well off and planned for their son to become a solicitor. Wells is now remembered, if at all, for a practical joke which he played on the brother of the poet John Keats and for a belated period of fame among Pre-Raphaelite circles for his biblical verse-drama *Joseph and his Brethren* (1824).

From at least 1803 until Wells's departure from London about 1830, the family lived at Featherstone Buildings, Holborn, London. As a youth Wells met Tom Keats, and his brother John who, in the summer of 1816, wrote for him the sonnet 'To a Friend who Sent me some Roses'. After leaving school, he was apprenticed to a solicitor, and Keats's letters of 1817–18 show that during this period he moved in the Keats circle at dinners, parties, the theatre, and other social occasions. Wells comes across from these and other accounts as lively and high-spirited, witty and irrepressible, if somewhat lazy and irresponsible and even, at least as far as the details of his own life are concerned, untrustworthy. After the death of Tom in December 1818, Keats discovered that Wells had played what he saw as a cruel joke on his brother, a 'diabolical scheme' as he called it (*Letters of John Keats*, 2.90), which he believed had exacerbated his brother's illness and even hastened his death. Wells had written a series of admiring and amorous letters to Tom, signed by a fictitious Frenchwoman named Amena Bellafilla, in highly stylized and poeticized language full of cliché and mock-archaism, much of which was borrowed from the early pseudo-medieval poetry of Keats himself. Tom Keats appears to have been taken in by this patent prank and was deeply hurt when the truth became clear. On discovering the deception, and in mourning for his brother, Keats declared that 'I do not think death too bad' (ibid.) for Wells and that 'I will harm him all I possibly can' (ibid., 2.91). Having been dropped by the Keats circle, Wells undertook two literary projects which were, nevertheless, heavily indebted to the style of his erstwhile friend. The first was a series of prose stories modelled on Boccaccio, *Stories after Nature*, published anonymously in 1822: this volume rivalled a volume of verse-translations of Boccaccio planned by Keats and J. H. Reynolds. The second project was the dramatic poem *Joseph and his Brethren*, published in December 1823 (with 1824 on the title-page) under the name H. L. Howard. It was written, so Wells later claimed, in six weeks, 'to compel Keats to esteem me and admit my *power*' (Johnston, 81). Both projects were almost entirely ignored by the literary reviews—a fate which Wells apparently accepted with equanimity: throughout his life he exhibited what H. Buxton Forman described as 'a superb indifference to fame' (Forman, 294).

About 1827 Wells married Emily Jane Hill (*d.* 1874), daughter of a schoolmaster, Francis Hill, and his wife, Margaret, *née* Powell, from Broxbourne in Hertfordshire. Between 1827 and 1841 the couple had three daughters and a son, all born in Broxbourne, which suggests that despite the fact that Wells continued working as a solicitor in London until 1830, he may have been living at least part of the time in Hertfordshire. Possibly for reasons of health and no doubt afflicted by what Forman called 'a constitutional indolence' (Tatchell, 16), Wells retired to Hertfordshire, and possibly also to Wales, about 1830, where he seems to have devoted his time to hunting, fishing, and boating as well as horticulture and bee-keeping. In 1841 he moved with his family to France, where he lived until his death in 1879, first in Brittany where he taught English at a college in Quimper, and later in Marseilles.

Meanwhile, however, developments in England were slowly beginning to give Wells a cult status among certain poets and artists. In 1837 Thomas Wade, in his poem 'Contention of Love and Death', named him as one of the unjustly neglected poets; in 1841 Richard Henry Horne, an old schoolfriend, included Wells's 'Sonnet to Chaucer' (written in 1823) in his edition of *The Poems of Geoffrey Chaucer Modernised* and in 1844 made favourable mention of him in his *New Spirit of the Age*. In 1842 the magazine editor W. J. Linton reprinted a number of Wells's *Stories after Nature* in his *Illuminated Magazine*; and in 1846–7 two essays by Wells, on field sports and the local gentry in Brittany, were published in *Fraser's Magazine*. Through these and other public notices Dante Gabriel Rossetti was alerted to his work and read one of the few remaining copies of *Joseph and his Brethren* in the British Library. Convinced that he had discovered a neglected genius, Rossetti began to proselytize among his friends to the extent that it was said that reading Wells's verse-narrative became compulsory for entry into the Pre-Raphaelite circle. Edmund Gosse commented that reading the poem became a 'kind of shibboleth—a rite of passage into the true poetic culture' (*Encyclopaedia Britannica*). Over the next twenty-odd years attempts were made by Rossetti, Algernon Charles Swinburne, Theodore Watts-Dunton, George Meredith, and others to have *Joseph* republished, until eventually Chatto and Windus took an interest after Swinburne published an appreciation of Wells entitled 'An unknown poet' in the *Fortnightly Review* in February 1875. The poem was republished in 1876, edited by Forman with a revised version of Swinburne's essay as an introduction, and with corrections and revisions by Wells himself. This time the poem was reviewed more widely and favourably and for a brief period there seemed to be a chance that Wells would become a famous poet. But since he had burnt a series of manuscripts in 1874 after the death of his wife (including, he claimed, a novel, three volumes of stories, a number of lyric poems, and an epic), he was unable to capitalize on his new-found popularity, such as it was, to any significant extent. Wells, as Watts-Dunton remarked, seemed to have an 'instinct for "not getting on"' (Watts-Dunton, xlvi).

What appears to have attracted Rossetti, Swinburne, and others to Wells's poetry and to have made them believe that they had discovered another Keats, was a certain derivative richness of imagery, a facility with rhythm and poetic form, and an easy eloquence combined with a once-fashionable pseudo-Elizabethan manner which allowed his work to be compared favourably with that of Shakespeare, Webster, and Cyril Tourneur, as well as with Keats and other nineteenth-century poets such as Wordsworth and Blake. Wells remains, however—and despite attempts to revive his work—a curiosity of literary history: even the hyperbolic reviews of the second edition of *Joseph* by the Pre-Raphaelite circle were unable to generate significant sales for his poem, and he remains today little known and even less read.

Wells died at 2 Montée des Oblats, Barthélemy, Marseilles, on 17 February 1879 after a long illness. Some time before his death he had converted to the Roman Catholic church. He had also dabbled in spiritualism and claimed to have raised a young lady from the dead by means of prayer, a 'faculty which is', as Watts-Dunton comments, 'rare among modern poets' (Watts-Dunton, xlvii). Wells's son Charles, an engineer by profession and gambler by inclination, had his own moment of fame as the subject of Fred Gilbert's popular song 'The Man who Broke the Bank at Monte Carlo' (sung by Charles *Coborn).

ANDREW BENNETT

Sources M. Tatchell, 'Charles Jeremiah Wells (1800–1879)', *Keats-Shelley Memorial Bulletin*, 22 (1971), 7–17 · P. Johnston, 'Charles Jeremiah Wells: an early Keatsian poet', *Keats–Shelley Journal*, 26 (1977), 72–87 · T. Watts-Dunton, 'Rossetti and Charles Wells: a reminiscence of Kelmscott Manor', in C. Wells, *Joseph and his brethren: a dramatic poem* (1908), xix–lviii · A. C. Swinburne, 'An unknown poet', *Fortnightly Review*, 23 (1875), 217–32 · E. Gosse, 'Wells, Charles Jeremiah', *Encyclopaedia Britannica*, 11th edn (1910–11), vol. 28, pp. 513–14 · H. B. Forman, introduction to Charles Jeremiah Wells's 'A dramatic scene', *Literary anecdotes of the nineteenth century*, ed. W. R. Nicoll and T. J. Wise, 1 (1895), 291–5 · *The letters of John Keats, 1814–1821*, ed. H. E. Rollins, 2 vols. (1958)

Archives BL, letters to Richard Henry Horne, RP794

Likenesses T. C. Wageman, miniature, c.1822, Keats House, Hampstead, London

Wells, Edward (1667–1727), Church of England clergyman and educationist, was the eldest child of Edward Wells (*d*. 1677), vicar of Corsham, Wiltshire, and his wife, Elizabeth. He was admitted into Westminster School, London, in 1680, and was thence elected to a scholarship at Christ Church, Oxford, from where he matriculated on 16 December 1686. Wells was tutored by Thomas Burton, later canon of Gloucester, and held two exhibitionerships (in 1691–2 and 1699). He graduated BA on 10 July 1690 and was elected a praelector in the same year. He proceeded MA on 1 June 1693. From 1691 to 1702, Wells was a tutor at Christ Church, and among his pupils was Thomas Bennet, who later presented Wells to the living at Cotesbach, Leicestershire, into which he was inducted on 2 January 1702. He accumulated the degrees of BD and DD on 5 April 1704, the year in which his studentship at Christ Church became void. In March 1716 he was inducted to the rectory of Bletchley, Buckinghamshire, on the presentation of Browne Willis, another former pupil. He took the opportunity in sermons there 'to mark out by slander his benefactor, the very man who by mistake, in an uncommon manner, gave him the stand and opportunity of his behaviour' (Nichols, *Lit. anecdotes*, 6.187).

Wells published copiously from 1698 until his death, and his output can be divided into five main categories: two religious and three educational. As a divine, Wells achieved some notoriety for his polemical high-church tracts. Thus Wells attacked Presbyterianism in his *Letter from Minister of the Church of England to a Dissenting Parishioner* (1706; four subsequent editions and several replies), which was followed up by a similar *Letter* to a Presbyterian minister (1706; three subsequent editions and several replies) and a tract on *The Invalidity of Presbyterian Ordination* (1707). He also attacked the Anglican divine Samuel Clarke in his *Remarks* (1713) and the exchange which followed, Clarke's scepticism over Christ's status in Trinitarian doctrine rousing his ire (Wells had already written an *Essay* on the Trinity and Christ's divinity in 1712). In the

realm of church politics, Wells also wrote *Forty-Six Propositions* (1717), asserting the legality of the Hanoverian succession and supporting the removal of the nonjurors from their parishes. Second, Wells published several more eirenic religious works later in life in the form of catechismal and pastoral tracts: most popular was his *Letter Concerning the Sin of Taking Christ's Name in Vain* (1710; nine further editions). He also wrote *Of Children's Capacities to Receive Religious Instructions* (1717) and three works for such a juvenile audience: a catechism, *The Common Christian Rightly and Plainly Instructed* (1707); and a pair of instructional manuals of devotion, a *Help for the More Easy Understanding of the Holy Scripture* (1724) and a *Help for the Right Understanding of the Several Divine Laws and Covenants* (1729).

Wells's publications as an educationist dovetail neatly with his catechismal and pastoral writings, but also make occasional forays into religious polemics. First, he published a series of mathematical works, including the *Elementa arithmeticae* (1698), which was followed by a series of interconnected works: the *Young Gentleman's Astronomy, Chronology and Dialling* (1712), *Young Gentleman's Arithmetick and Geometry* (1713), *Young Gentleman's Course of Mathematicks* (1714), and *Young Gentleman's Trigonometry, Mechanicks and Opticks* (1714). These volumes treated, *inter alia*, the mathematical element of geography (the use of globes, determination of latitude and longitude, and so on), but Wells also, and secondly, published a series of descriptive geographies, largely cribbed from other sources, but widely recommended at schools and universities in the period. His *Treatise of Antient and Present Geography* (1701; and four further editions) was a popular gazetteer intended for students reading classics, while his *Historical Geography of the New Testament* (1708) and the companion *Historical Geography of the Old Testament* (1711–12) plagiarized travellers to the Near East and biblical scholars to give a description of the Holy Land, but also attacked Roman Catholicism and Presbyterianism in passing. Connected with his geographical books, and thirdly, Wells published translations and editions of classical and Christian texts: he contributed geographical notes to editions of Xenophon's *Hellenica* (1690) and of Eusebius's *History of the Church* (1709), and translated Dionysius the Guide's *Periegetes* (1704) from Greek into Latin, adding a series of notes in the light of sixteen centuries of subsequent geographical discoveries.

Wells's writings are more voluminous than distinguished. While uncharitable in tone, Thomas Hearne's assessment of Wells's *œuvre* is substantially accurate:

> [he] writ & scribbled many books, on purpose to scrape up money … The truth is, he was a man of great industry, but the books he hath writ & published, as they are very many, so they are inaccurate, & contain very little that is curious. (*Remarks*, 9.330)

Wells never married; he died at Cotesbach on 11 July 1727, and was buried on 15 July there. ROBERT J. MAYHEW

Sources Wood, *Ath. Oxon.*, new edn · Wood, *Ath. Oxon.: Fasti* · J. Nichols, *The history and antiquities of the county of Leicester*, 4 vols. (1795–1815) · parish register, Cotesbach, Leics. RO, DE 2095/1 & 2 · parish records, Corsham, Wilts. & Swindon RO · *Remarks and collections of Thomas Hearne*, ed. C. E. Doble and others, 9, OHS, 65 (1914) ·

Nichols, *Lit. anecdotes* · Christ Church Oxf., chapter book, D & C i.b.4 · J. Welch, *The list of the queen's scholars of St Peter's College, Westminster*, ed. [C. B. Phillimore], new edn (1852) · R. Butlin, 'Ideological contexts and the reconstruction of biblical landscapes in the seventeenth and early eighteenth centuries: Dr Edward Wells and the historical geography of the Holy Land', *Ideology and landscape in historical perspective*, ed. A. Baker and G. Biger (1992), 31–62 · R. J. Mayhew, *Enlightenment geography: the political languages of British geography, 1650–1850* (2000)
Wealth at death died a wealthy man: *Remarks*, ed. Doble and others

Wells, Francis (1606/7–1684x9), Church of England clergyman, was the son of Francis Wells, vicar of Mickleton, Gloucestershire. He attended Oxford University, matriculating from Gloucester Hall on 14 March 1623 aged sixteen and graduating BA on 20 November 1626 and MA on 25 June 1629. Instituted as curate of the chapelry of Bodicote in the parish of Adderbury, Oxfordshire, he was charged in 1634 with preaching there against the Book of Sports, though he claimed actually to have warned against church ales. He was also presented for failing to wear a surplice during the traditional perambulation of the parish bounds, and there were complaints that both his two Sunday sermons typically ran to an hour and a quarter. It seems that he supported parliament during the civil war and his enemies claimed in 1680 that he had been 'formerly preacher to a regiment of the late rebels', though this seems unlikely and cannot be confirmed. As occupant of the rectory of Weston Turville, Buckinghamshire, in 1645, he was ordered on 9 August to pay a fifth of the tithes to Mary Vintner, wife of the sequestered rector, a matter he disputed until his resignation on 15 March 1647.

In May of that year Wells was a lecturer at St Giles Cripplegate, London, but by early 1649 he was at the Oxfordshire vicarage of Adderbury, following the successive sequestration of two royalists, William Oldys and William Barker, at the urging of a strong section of their more puritan-minded parishioners. On the first Sunday in February 1649 (according to an exchequer deposition of 1 October 1661), after the execution of Charles I, Wells preached on the subject of the execution of St John the Baptist, and did not fail to spell out the significance of his choice: 'he had read of kings putting saints to death but never of saints putting kings to death. He was also said to have described the king's execution as "a most horrid act" and those responsible as "bloody minded men"' (*VCH Oxfordshire*, 9.33). Yet it was also suggested that he had preached against the king. So it was that Wells found himself at odds not only with royalists, but also with radical puritans who opposed political compromise and resented presbyterian discipline. In 1661 he was embroiled in a chancery dispute in which it was charged that he withheld the sacrament from some parishioners, and let it be administered 'in an indecent and irreverent manner' by a 'mere lay parson' (ibid., 9.37). As a result of these and other grievances sixty residents went elsewhere to church. Later that year Wells was removed from the living. He was probably the Francis Wells MA instituted as rector of Colby, Norfolk, on 25 February 1663; a successor there was

instituted on 7 February 1671. By this time Wells had married a wife, Lucy; their eldest child, Francis, died in 1756 at the age of ninety, and three girls, Elizabeth, Sarah, and Lucy, were aged under twenty-one in 1684.

Certainly Wells became curate of Tewkesbury in Gloucestershire, where the vicarage had been held until the Restoration by his brother John, and was charged in 1671 with refusing to wear the surplice. It was at Tewkesbury that he became involved in a labyrinthine *cause célèbre*, settled only after many years on the authority of Archbishop Sancroft himself. There were close to the town two chapelries, Tredington and Walton Cardiff, which were of uncertain formal status, but each could point to many years' *de facto* independence from the impropriate rectory of Tewkesbury. The rectorial leaseholder, Henry Dobbins, and the town authorities wanted to claim the tithes and to be able to levy rates, especially in Tredington. In 1674, with help in London from the member for Tewkesbury, Sir Francis Russell (*c*.1638–1706), Francis Wells was able to secure letters patent for the possession of the vicarage, and the town supported his claim as a means to assert control over Tredington and its curate, Wriggan. Wells was instituted to the vicarage in May 1677; although the town had been unable to secure a form of words for his presentation which included the chapelries within parishional control, it was in a strong position. Wells was installed as curate of Tredington and was paid the stipend which had been withheld from Wriggan. If the burgesses felt justified in celebrating, however, they soon had reason to repent.

On 13 November 1678 parliament called a fast to implore God to discover the truth about the Popish Plot. It was reported that in his sermon on this occasion Wells had discoursed largely upon the sins of England, and of Tewkesbury. Furthermore, the churchwardens claimed, after urging humility upon the townspeople he added 'that they should be humbler still "for the adultery, fornication and whoredom of the King"'; for this 'the land did mourne', and he marvelled out loud, despite efforts by the senior bailiff to stop him, that the king had not earlier been 'cut off in the midst of his sins' by such plots as Oates now revealed (Beaver, 305). Wells protested that he had spoken 'out of real love and true loyalty to his majesty, and out of zeal for God, and discharge of a good conscience toward God and man' (ibid.). But opposition was gathering. Next Sunday in church Wells felt it necessary to deny that his words had been seditious. He had opened old wounds, and had provided his religious and political opponents with an opportunity. The churchwardens presented articles against him at the consistory court on 3 December 1678 and the strongly anti-puritan chancellor of Gloucester diocese, Richard Parsons, suspended him on the same day. Parsons was a close ally of the town clerk, James Simpson, and although Wells had his supporters his appeals on the grounds of age and infirmity were ignored and the council brought new preachers to supply his place. The response of the redoubtable Wells was to attend services, but to remain seated and hatted throughout, signalling his view that the use of such 'supply preachers' was in breach of God's law, subverting the bond between pastor and flock. In January the town council asked him to resign, offering compensation in the hope of avoiding an expensive law suit (Russell appears to have acted as an intermediary in these negotiations); on 7 February Wells agreed, but he retracted his consent the next day.

In August 1680 Wells was deprived by Bishop Pritchett of Gloucester; following an immediate appeal to the court of arches he was reinstated pending its decision. It became ever clearer that the dispute involved much more than the vicar's musings on the sins of Charles II. As his opponents suggested, his outlook reflected a spirit of nonconformity, both among sections of his parishioners and in himself. He was accused of refusing to conduct funerals according to the Book of Common Prayer and of failing to consecrate the communion wine according to the rubric. He was said to be in the habit of making impromptu changes to other services, and of frequently omitting parts deemed to be superstitious. It is also clear that Parsons and his allies in the town were determined to oust their vicar by all means. Parsons was 'able to run the diocesan courts as his private preserve and did numerous favours for friends', including the burgesses; between them they were able to make a travesty of the hearings held locally by the court of arches in October 1681 (Beaver, 322). In December the court upheld Wells's deprivation on the grounds that he had been improperly inducted. The decision probably came as no surprise to the vicar; the previous month, during a visit of the new bishop of Gloucester, Robert Frampton (d. 1708), Wells had hoped for other means to vindication, urging that his right to the ministry be put 'to common vote of the whole town'—including nonconformists and separatists—a proposal which the burgesses rejected as 'a tumultuary way' (ibid., 315).

Eventually it was Frampton who framed the settlement, confirmed by Archbishop Sancroft, in which the sentence of deprivation upon Wells was confirmed, but the burgesses were to pay him the compensation they had originally offered. Francis Wells spent the last years of his life in Essex, at or near the home of his brother Michael in Hornchurch, where his wife, Lucy, was buried on 30 October 1683. When Wells drew up his will on 14 April 1684 he was officiating at the chapel of Havering, in the parish of Hornchurch; the date of his death is unknown, but it occurred before the grant of probate on 25 June 1689.

STEPHEN WRIGHT

Sources Calamy rev. · VCH Oxfordshire, vol. 9 · D. Beaver, 'Conscience and context: the Popish Plot and the politics of ritual, 1678–1682', HJ, 34 (1991), 297–327 · will, PRO, PROB 11/395, fols. 339–40 · Foster, Alum. Oxon. · Walker rev. [William Oldys and William Barker] · H. Carter, Norfolk incumbents for the period 1660–1720 (1936)

Wealth at death scattered property, fairly substantial: will, PRO, PROB 11/395, fols. 339–40

Wells [married name Whitford], **Helena** (1761?–1824), novelist and educationist, was born in South Carolina, America, the daughter of Robert *Wells (1727/8–1794) and his wife, Mary. She had a sister and an elder brother, the physician William Charles *Wells. Her parents were Scottish and had settled in Charlestown, Carolina, where her father, a printer and publisher who wrote verse, gained a certain standing as a man of letters. Loyalists, they returned to England at the outbreak of the War of Independence, and her father became a merchant in Fleet Street. From 1789 she and her sister ran a school in London. In 1799 she published Letters on Subjects of Importance to the Happiness of Young Females, indicating a change of career to governess. The Letters were in keeping with the female epistolary tradition, including advice on appropriate reading and behaviour, with the usual declaratory preface that the work was not self-promotional but was intended to promote religion and draw young ladies away from frivolous pursuits. In the preface to the second edition (1807) she wrote that her intentions had broadened, so that she was no longer simply offering herself as an instructor of children, but also as a guide to youth. However, she broke with the tradition of completely discouraging girls from reading novels, believing that there were even some excellent romances, and also advocated the reading of history and epic poetry, both of which she believed strengthened the mind without making it 'masculine'. She accepted that a woman, in contrast to a man, could not make her own way in the world unaided, and that 'woman has too often no protector but virtuous principle,—no support but what she derives from her industry' (Letters, 2nd edn, 1807, 128).

Helena Wells also published novels which were critically well received even by the conservative Anti-Jacobin Review. Thus The Step-Mother: a Domestic Tale from Real Life (2 vols., 1799) was seen as safe, moral reading for the young, a form of conduct book. Her later novel, published in 1800, Constantia Neville, or, The West Indian (3 vols.) was again intended as an edifying alternative to the light reading of the circulating libraries. Indeed, Constantia Neville was to serve as an example of a young lady overcoming misfortunes, with the help of others, maintaining her modesty and respectability, and becoming a useful member of society. As in The Step-Mother, it was argued that reading would strengthen rather than weaken the mind. Helena wrote that her style was realist, rather than romantic, and her work of observation rather than imagination. There is humour in the work, but also an underlying motive of focusing attention on the impoverished young lady who has to protect her virtue in the face of considerable adversity during a period of political tumult and war; she had herself to seek financial assistance from the Royal Literary Fund in 1801. She cited the example of Mary Wollstonecraft, regretting rather than totally condemning Wollstonecraft's radical moral and political beliefs. She argued that, had Wollstonecraft practised self-discipline, her literary work might have benefited society. Helena called on women to support each other and help such unfortunates earn a respectable living. She expressed concern that the established church was not alive to the dangers presented by the Roman Catholic church, which had established institutions to protect young ladies fallen on hard times. In addition, her novel, with its subtitle The West Indian, may be seen as part of the anti-slavery literature, with Constantia as the white colonial outsider in English society.

On 31 October 1801, described as resident at Warminster, Wiltshire, Helena Wells married Edward Whitford of Broad Street Buildings, and set up house in Salisbury Square, London. Following the birth of her fourth and last child, in 1806, Helena Whitford spent a long period of illness considering the plight of 'unportioned' young ladies. In what appears to have been her last publication, *Thoughts and remarks on establishing an institution for the support and education of unportioned respectable females* (1809), she returned to the themes of women supporting each other and of the need for improved education for young ladies. She recalled the criticisms of the fashionable education in the social graces made by Hannah More (1745–1833), and wrote of the precarious social as well as financial position of the governess, who often led a lonely, isolated life in contrast to the male tutor. Describing her own difficulties in hiring suitable staff for the school which she had established before her marriage, she pointed to the irony that the children of the lower orders received a more appropriate education (through charity schools, for example) than the daughters of the middle and upper classes. Thus she advocated the establishment in Yorkshire (with its cheap costs, clean air, and central location) of a type of protestant nunnery (though she had been forced to drop any reference to 'nunnery' from her title because of its links with Roman Catholicism), which she envisaged as a national house of refuge for respectable females who needed help, either to equip them for a teaching career or to shelter them in old age. While dismissing any demands for the rights of women, she was acutely aware of the precarious position of the spinster, perhaps because she married late in life. Helena Whitford died at her home in Mapledon Place, Burton Crescent, London, on 6 July 1824. Her husband survived her. Her eldest son, Robert Wells Whitford (1804–1879), educated at St Edmund Hall, Oxford, which was much favoured by evangelical parents, became a chaplain in India.

JANE MCDERMID

Sources *GM*, 1st ser., 94/2 (1824), 569 · *GM*, 1st ser., 71 (1801), 1052 · Blain, Clements & Grundy, *Feminist comp.* · C. Buck, ed., *Bloomsbury guide to women's literature* (1992) · *GM*, 1st ser., 64 (1794), 677
Archives BL, Evelyn collection · BL, Royal Literary Fund MSS

Wells, Henry Lake (1850–1898), army officer, son of Thomas Bury Wells, rector of Portlemouth, Devon, and his wife, Catharine Frances, daughter of the Revd William Stockdale (fellow of Jesus College, Cambridge), was born on 8 March 1850. After attending the Royal Military Academy at Woolwich he was commissioned lieutenant into the Royal Engineers on 2 August 1871, was captain in 1883, major in 1889, and lieutenant-colonel on 6 November 1896. He was specially employed in the War Office in 1873 and 1874, and went to India in 1875.

Wells served in the Afghan campaign of 1878–9, raised a corps of Ghilzai labourers, and constructed a road across the Khojak Pass, and was for some time in sole charge of the public works department at Quetta. He commanded

detachments of Punjab cavalry and Sind horse in an engagement near the Khojak, where he was wounded. He accompanied General Biddulph's force down the Thal-Chotiali route, took part in the action at Baghao, served with the Khyber line force, was present at the action of Majina, and had charge of the positions at the crossing of the Kabul River. He was five times mentioned in dispatches, Sir Donald Stewart recommending him 'for conspicuous gallantry and bravery'.

Wells surveyed routes in 1879–80 in Kashmir and Gilgit for a telegraph line, and in the latter year was appointed to the government Indo-European telegraph service in Persia as assistant director. During many years spent in Persia he surveyed routes between Dezful and Shiraz, and contributed papers to the Royal Geographical Society, the Society of Arts, and to the Royal Engineers' professional papers. He was repeatedly thanked for his services, especially for those rendered in the delimitation of the Afghan frontier in 1886, the army remount operations for India in 1887, in the cholera epidemic, and during the revolt in Shiraz in 1893. Wells married, on 15 January 1885, in London, Alice Bertha, daughter of the Revd Hugh Bacon.

Wells became director of the Persian telegraph service in 1891. He was presented by Shah Nasir al-Din with a sword of honour, and by Shah Muraffer with a diamond ring. On 1 January 1897 he was made CIE. He died suddenly at Karachi on 31 August 1898.

R. H. VETCH, *rev.* JAMES FALKNER

Sources *Army List* · *Royal Engineers Journal* (Oct 1898) · *Royal Engineers Journal* (Dec 1898) · *The Times* (Sept 1898) · *Hart's Army List* · F. J. Goldsmid, 'Lieutenant-Colonel H. L. Wells', *GJ*, 12 (1898), 530–32 · Boase, *Mod. Eng. biog.* · Venn, *Alum. Cant.*
Wealth at death £4840 15s. 5d.: probate, 8 Oct 1898, *CGPLA Eng. & Wales*

Wells, Henry Tanworth (1828–1903), miniature and portrait painter, was born on 12 December 1828 in Marylebone, Middlesex, and baptized on 18 January 1829 in St Pancras Old Church, the only son of Henry Tanworth Wells, merchant, and his wife, Charlotte Henman. One sister, Augusta, was an exhibitor at the Royal Academy, and another sister, Sarah, married the sculptor Henry Hugh Armstead. Educated at Lancing College, Sussex, Wells was apprenticed in 1843 as a lithographic draughtsman to Messrs Dickinson, with whom he soon, however, began work as a miniature painter. His studies were continued in the evening at J. M. Leigh's school and in 1850 he spent six months in the studio of Thomas Couture, a history and portrait painter, in Paris. At first he practised exclusively as a miniature painter, much in the manner of Sir William Ross, the principal miniaturist of the period. Between 1846 and 1860 Wells exhibited over seventy miniatures, chiefly of women and children, at the Royal Academy, including one of Princess Mary of Cambridge, commissioned by Queen Victoria (1853; Royal Collection). Several of his miniatures were exhibited at the South Kensington exhibition of portrait miniatures in 1865.

Wells counted among his friends many of the Pre-Raphaelites, and was sympathetic to their approach to their own art, although his own work remained uninfluenced by them. He also joined a drawing society which met every evening in Clipstone Street, London, and which counted D. G. Rossetti, C. Keene, J. R. Clayton, F. Smallfield, the brothers E. and G. Dalziel, and G. P. Boyce, the watercolour artist, among its members. On 9 December 1857 he married, in Rome, Joanna Mary *Boyce (1831–1861), a gifted painter and writer for the *Saturday Review* and the sister of G. P. Boyce.

From 1861 Wells, driven by the advent of photography, abandoned miniature painting in favour of full-scale oil portraiture. Over the next decade he specialized in depicting regimental and presentation portraits, including *Volunteers at the Firing Point* (1866; RA, London), engraved by T. L. Atkinson; *The Queen and her Judges Opening the Royal Courts of Justice* (1887); *The Duke of Devonshire* for the Iron and Steel Institute (1872); and *Lord Chancellor Selborne* (1874) for the Mercers' Company. His portrait of Earl Spencer was engraved by Samuel Cousins.

The most popular of Wells's works was, however, a painting of Queen Victoria, receiving the news of her accession, exhibited in 1887 at the Royal Academy as *Victoria regina* (versions in the Tate collection and the Royal Collection). He also produced about fifty crayon portraits of distinguished political and society figures in his capacity as limner to Grillion's Club, many of which were etched or engraved. His portraits were usually signed with his monogram and dated.

In 1870 Wells was elected a member of the Royal Academy having been an associate since 1866. He was an active member of the council, and in the agitation for reform, initiated in 1886 in *The Times* by Holman Hunt, he was the most vigorous defender of the existing order of affairs, supporting the constitutional rights and privileges of the academy. He was nominated by Lord Leighton to act as his deputy on certain occasions during the president's absence abroad in 1895. In 1879, at the time of the royal commission, and again in connection with the bill in 1900, he worked hard for the cause of artistic copyright.

Wells continued to exhibit oil paintings in the Royal Academy's exhibitions until his death at his home, Thorpe Lodge, Campden Hill, Kensington, on 16 January 1903. He was buried at Kensal Green cemetery. Wells was survived by his two daughters, Alice Joanna Street and Joanna Margaret Hadley. His son, Sidney Boyce, died in 1869.   J. D. MILNER, rev. V. REMINGTON

Sources *The Times* (19 Jan 1903) · *The Athenaeum* (24 Jan 1903), 122 · *Art Journal*, new ser., 23 (1903), 96 · J. Maas, *Victorian painters* (1988), 200, 216 · D. Millar, *The Victorian watercolours and drawings in the collection of her majesty the queen*, 2 vols. (1995), 282–3 · Graves, *RA exhibitors* · personal knowledge (1912) · D. Foskett, *Miniatures: dictionary and guide* (1987), 674 · B. S. Long, *British miniaturists* (1929), 457 · L. R. Schidlof, *The miniature in Europe in the 16th, 17th, 18th, and 19th centuries*, 2 (1964), 874 · *CGPLA Eng. & Wales* (1903) · B. Stewart and M. Cutten, *The dictionary of portrait painters in Britain up to 1920* (1997) · parish register, 1829, St Pancras Old Church, London [baptism]
Likenesses H. T. Wells, self-portrait, oils, 1882, Aberdeen Art Gallery · J. E. Boehm, bust, 1888; formerly in possession of A. J. Street · H. T. Wells, self-portrait, oils?, 1897; formerly in possession of A. J. Street; reproduction, Courtauld Inst., Witt Library · Lock and

Whitfield, photograph, woodburytype, NPG; repro. in T. Cooper, *Men of mark: a gallery of contemporary portraits* (1878) · G. G. Manton, group portrait, watercolour (*Conversazione at the Royal Academy, 1891*), NPG · R. W. Robinson, photograph, NPG; repro. in *Members and associates of the Royal Academy of Arts* (1891) · H. T. Wells, self-portrait; formerly in possession of Mrs Street · H. T. Wells, self-portrait, on ivory; formerly in possession of Mrs Hadley · wood-engraving, NPG; repro. in *ILN* (30 June 1866)
Wealth at death £52,977 19s. 10d.: resworn probate, Aug 1903, *CGPLA Eng. & Wales*

Wells, Herbert George (1866–1946), novelist and social commentator, was born on 21 September 1866 at Atlas House, 47 High Street, Bromley, Kent, the youngest of the four children of Joseph (Joe) Wells (1827/8–1910), a shopkeeper and professional cricketer, and his wife, Sarah (1822–1905), daughter of George Neal, an innkeeper at Midhurst in Sussex. Joseph's father was head gardener at Penshurst Place, and Joseph found employment as a gardener at Uppark, the country house of the Fetherstonhaughs on the South Downs near Midhurst, where Sarah was a lady's maid. Wells's parents were married in 1853. Two years later Joseph bought Atlas House, with its unsuccessful china business. Wells's earliest memories were of the dark subterranean kitchen, the bug-infested bedrooms, and the dingy parlour behind the shop. As a child he witnessed the growing discord between his parents as the family declined into insolvency.

Education and apprenticeships Joseph Wells, a legendary fast bowler, was happiest on the cricket field. On 26 June 1862 he took four wickets in four balls for Kent against Sussex at Brighton. He sold cricket goods from his shop, and coached schoolboys every summer until 1877, when he broke his thigh by falling from a ladder in his backyard on a Sunday morning while the rest of the family were at church. Officially he had been pruning a vine, but local gossip alleged that the church service ended earlier than usual and that he was caught helping a lady friend to escape over the back wall. Joe Wells was irresponsible, irresolute, and happy-go-lucky; Sarah was anxious, devout, long-suffering, and scrupulous in recording her complaints against Joe in the diary that she kept. Between them, Wells's parents did much to shape the contradictions of their son's character and outlook. As a writer and political thinker Wells was by turns optimist and pessimist, libertarian and authoritarian, hedonist and puritan. Born 'blasphemous and protesting', he reacted against his mother's fervent Anglicanism by becoming a 'prodigy of Early Impiety' (Wells, *Experiment in Autobiography*, vol. 1). Later his arguments for scientific materialism would often fall back on the prophetic urgings and symbolism of the low-church sermons of his childhood.

Bertie, as he was known to his family, was taught to read and write by his mother, and then attended Mrs Knott's dame-school at 8 South Street, Bromley. At the age of seven he was laid up with a broken leg and his father brought home library books, including Wood's illustrated *Natural History* and the bound volumes of *Punch*. He was a pupil for some years at the Bromley Academy, a private school for tradesmen's sons run by Thomas Morley, where

Herbert George Wells (1866–1946), by George Charles Beresford, 1920

bookkeeping, arithmetic, and copperplate handwriting were the principal subjects of study. At the age of twelve or thirteen he produced *The Desert Daisy* (1957), a humorous comic-strip narrative attributed to 'the immortal Buss' (his family nickname, but doubtless a reference to the 'inimitable Boz') and 'Edited by H. G. Wells'. By this time he was Morley's star pupil, being placed first in all England in the College of Preceptors examination in bookkeeping. But his school fees were increasingly in arrears, and in 1880 he was sent out into the world, like his two elder brothers, to become a draper.

Wells's first, probationary apprenticeship was brief. Messrs Rodgers and Denyer of Windsor judged that their thirteen-year-old shop assistant was too unrefined for the task. Instead, what seemed a far better opportunity presented itself. A remote relative, Alfred Williams, had become master of a national school at Wookey in Somerset, and he offered Wells the place of pupil teacher. Unfortunately Williams had misrepresented his teaching qualifications and was found to have obtained the post on false pretences. By now, Wells's mother had left the family home at Bromley to become resident housekeeper at Uppark, where Miss Fetherstonhaugh, pitying the Wells family's misfortunes, had charitably taken her on. Her youngest son stayed in the servants' quarters at Uppark while waiting to begin his next start in life, a post in a chemist's shop at Church Hill, Midhurst. In those days a pharmaceutical assistant was required to know Latin, so

Wells took lessons with Horace Byatt, the headmaster of Midhurst grammar school. Byatt liked his pupil, found him an avid learner, and sought to take advantage of the system of payment by results which was then being used to encourage technical and further education. He steered Wells away from Latin to study for the state examinations in elementary science, and every time his pupil gained a certificate, Byatt earned a grant.

Wells found the chemist's shop much more congenial than the draper's, but he soon realized that his family could not afford for him to be trained as a pharmacist. So he left after a few weeks and, for two years from the spring of 1881, he was apprenticed at Hyde's Drapery Emporium, Southsea, working a thirteen-hour day and sleeping in a dormitory with the other assistants. He was resentful and rebellious, and was ceaselessly (and, he later thought, deservedly) bullied by the shop manager. Somehow he kept alive the hope of escape, pursuing a course of rigorous self-discipline and devoting whatever time he could spare to self-education. He made it a rule never to read a work of fiction or play a game. Eventually he wrote to Byatt, begging for a place as a pupil teacher, and Byatt made an offer which he could only accept if his mother would pay to cancel his indentures. At first she refused, but Wells forced the issue by leaving the shop one Sunday morning to walk the 17 miles to Uppark and waylay her as she was returning from church in the servants' procession. Sarah backed down and purchased his freedom with her life savings. In September 1883 Wells was back as a pupil teacher at Midhurst grammar school, and a year later he entered T. H. Huxley's biology class at the Normal School (later Royal College) of Science, South Kensington, London, on a government scholarship for trainee teachers. Like his hero Mr Polly, he had thrown off the servitude of the draper's life and discovered that 'If the world does not please you, *you can change it*' (H. G. Wells, *The History of Mr Polly*, 1910, chap. 9).

Science student and teacher, 1884–1893 Thomas Huxley, then at the height of his fame, was dean of the Normal School, a title which reassured Sarah Wells, who had heard of him as a notorious freethinker. He was Wells's greatest teacher, and the influence of his course in elementary biology and zoology can be felt in almost everything that Wells subsequently wrote. As Wells noted, 'It was a grammar of form and a criticism of fact' (*Experiment in Autobiography*, vol. 1). But Huxley soon fell ill, and the other professors were more humdrum. Wells ended the year with a first in biology, and had his scholarship renewed. As he went on to take a year's physics course and then a year of geology, his appetite for the hard grind of examination successes suddenly left him. He plunged into student life, branched out into literature and politics, and rebelled against the technical and utilitarian bias of the college curriculum. His irreverence and wit brought him a circle of admiring companions, some of whom, such as Richard Gregory, became lifelong friends. He preached socialism at the student debating society and, on another occasion, brought the house down with a demonstration of a perpetual motion machine. He wore a red tie as a sign of his political convictions, and he attended William Morris's meetings at Hammersmith. He founded and edited the *Science Schools Journal*, in which he published both his first efforts at scientific romance and an attack on the Normal School ethos thinly disguised as an essay on Socrates. Meanwhile, he neglected his studies and abandoned any dreams he may have had of becoming an experimental scientist. In 1887, partly for disciplinary reasons, he failed his final examination in geology.

During his student years Wells was undernourished, shabbily dressed, and usually half-starved on the days before his weekly maintenance of 1 guinea was paid out. He spent much of his time reading in the South Kensington libraries when he should have been in the laboratory. Romantic poetry, Enlightenment satire, and classical utopian thought, together with evolutionary science, were his intellectual passions. His study of Plato and Swift had begun at Uppark, where he had been given the run of the library collected earlier in the century by the freethinker Sir Harry Fetherstonhaugh. In an attic there were forgotten books of engravings of Renaissance art, as well as the pieces of a telescope which he laboriously fitted together. The great house embodying the ideals of the whig aristocracy furnished him with an abiding image of the liberal education which, after Huxley's retirement, the Normal School failed to provide.

In the summer of 1887 Wells left South Kensington without a degree and took a teaching post at Holt Academy, north Wales, an impoverished boarding-school. Within a few weeks he was badly fouled by one of his pupils during a game of football, resulting in a crushed kidney and a series of lung haemorrrhages. Tuberculosis was diagnosed (though the diagnosis was never confirmed), and he was forced to resign from Holt and to spend several months convalescing at Uppark. He was to suffer further lung haemorrhages in 1891, 1893, and 1898. The experience of illness and the prognosis of an early death quickened his imagination, as is clear from the apocalyptic and visionary starkness of his early scientific romances, beginning with *The Time Machine* (1895). During his first convalescence he wrote copiously and dreamed of achieving fame as a social prophet, though as yet he was 'the Prophet of the Undelivered Spell' (*Correspondence*, 1.102–3).

Wells returned to London in the autumn of 1888 and became a teacher at Henley House School, Kilburn, where A. A. Milne was one of his pupils. In 1890 he took his London University BSc, with a first class in zoology and a second in geology, and then joined William Briggs's University Correspondence College, preparing students for matriculation in biology at the Tutorial College in Red Lion Square. He had fallen in love with Isabel Mary Wells (*c*.1866–1930), his pretty but conventional cousin at whose home he had lodged during his student years. They married on 30 October 1891 and set up house at 28 Haldon Road, Wandsworth. Soon Wells was supplementing his income by writing for the educational press, editing Briggs's *University Correspondent*, contributing to the *Educational Times*, and writing his *Textbook of Biology* (1893) which, much revised by other hands, remained in print for thirty

years. In 1893 his health again collapsed and he had to give up class teaching for the insecurity of freelance journalism.

Fiction and prophecy, 1893–1914 'The Chronic Argonauts', the early version of *The Time Machine* published in the *Science Schools Journal* (April–June 1888), was a stilted performance in the manner of Nathaniel Hawthorne and Edgar Allan Poe. In 1891 Wells had been summoned by Frank Harris, the editor of the *Fortnightly Review*, only to have one of his most carefully written scientific articles brutally rejected. Now he determined to achieve literary recognition, and suddenly hit on the formula for success with short stories and light-hearted essays. He wrote fiction and drama reviews for the *Saturday Review* and *Pall Mall Gazette*, and, encouraged by W. E. Henley, recast his time-travelling tale first as a series of newspaper prophecies and then as the haunting adventure story which appeared in book form in 1895. 'It's my trump card', he wrote to his friend Elizabeth Healey, '& if it does not come off very much I shall know my place for the rest of my career' (*Correspondence*, 1.226). *The Time Machine* won instant acclaim, and he produced in quick succession *The Island of Doctor Moreau* (1896), *The Invisible Man* (1897), *The War of the Worlds* (1898), *The First Men in the Moon* (1901), and several volumes of short stories.

Boldly melodramatic and intellectually provocative, Wells's early scientific romances (as they came to be called) remain unsurpassed for their imagination and visionary power. They reveal his profound grasp of the changes—perhaps the diminution—in the meaning and sense of purpose of human life brought about by Darwinian evolutionary theory. Their pessimism is at one with the *fin de siècle* mood, but the passing of time has not dimmed their assault on human complacency. Where Wells's contemporaries saw him as adding what Tyndall had called the 'scientific imagination' to nineteenth-century romance, the twentieth century regarded him as the greatest of the forerunners of modern science fiction. His tales of future evolution, alien intelligence, interplanetary warfare, and technological dystopia anticipated most of the genre's thematic repertory. He stands midway between the older traditions of the learned satire, the utopia, and the marvellous voyage, and the twentieth-century growth of mass-entertainment technological fantasy.

But Wells had little wish to be remembered as the founder of science fiction or as a rival of Jules Verne and Edgar Allan Poe. He had larger ambitions, craving recognition both as a serious novelist and as a public intellectual urging his readers towards a new world. At the turn of the century he produced *Love and Mr Lewisham* (1900), the first of a long series of semi-autobiographical novels, and *Anticipations* (1901), a book of social and technological forecasts arguing for a rationally planned 'New Republic' to supersede existing monarchies and nation states. Queen Victoria's long reign came to an end in 1901, and Wells's emergence as a futurological essayist in *Anticipations* and in his Royal Institution lecture *The Discovery of the Future* (1902) matched the public mood. He became a member of the Fabian Society and of the Coefficients, a political dining club which included R. B. S. Haldane, Bertrand Russell, and Sidney Webb among its members. His most considerable contribution to political thought was *A Modern Utopia* (1905), a 'shot-silk' narrative combining the traditional traveller's report from Utopia with a critical commentary and a synthesis of earlier utopian ideas. His 'good place' is an evolving socialist world state, not a picture of settled perfection, and it is ruled by a voluntary élite (an updated version of Plato's Guardians), the Samurai.

Wells continued to write scientific romances, but these were now semi-realistic 'fantasies of possibility' closely linked to his futurological writings. They included *The Sleeper Awakes* (1899; rev. 1910), *The Food of the Gods* (1904), *In the Days of the Comet* (1906), *The War in the Air* (1908), and *The World Set Free* (1914). All but *The Food of the Gods* contain a vision of future world war, and in *The World Set Free*, inspired by Frederick Soddy's work on radium, he prophesied the atomic bomb. 'The Land Ironclads' (1903), the short story acknowledged by Winston Churchill as originating the idea of the tank, also belongs to this period. Wells portrayed mass destruction as the apocalyptic prelude to a new, more rational world order. It is hard to say whether these forebodings were taken very seriously. A novel such as *The War in the Air* is enlivened by his gifts for picaresque narrative, humour, and farce; in *The World Set Free* and his later novel *The Shape of Things to Come* (1933) he adopts the sibylline pose of a future historian.

In nearly all the scientific romances, the unknown is let loose upon the placid communities of south-east England. Wells's realistic comedies written in the Edwardian period portray the same landscape, seen from the perspective of the frustrated and rebellious 'little man' who is a draper's apprentice or shopkeeper. *Kipps* (1905) and *The History of Mr Polly* (1910) show their heroes escaping from drudgery, while *Tono-Bungay* (1909), a much more ambitious novel, traces the rise and fall of a chemist's apprentice whose uncle becomes a patent-medicine tycoon. *Tono-Bungay*, with its sharp social satire and panoramic sweep, revives and reinvents the 'Condition-of-England' novel of Dickens and his contemporaries; but its successors, such as *The New Machiavelli* (1911)—a novel of high politics— became increasingly didactic and discursive. Moreover, after *Tono-Bungay* Wells had largely exhausted the vein of autobiographical fiction which drew heavily on his painful experiences in adolescence and young manhood. He now began to draw the material of his fiction from his life as a successful and prosperous writer.

'A Don Juan among the intelligentsia' Wells's marriage to Isabel lasted barely two years. In January 1894 he set up house with (Amy) Catherine Robbins (1871/2–1927), who had been his student at the Tutorial College in Holborn. After becoming divorced from Isabel in January 1895, he married Catherine on 27 October of that year; the couple had two sons, George Philip (Gip), who became a zoologist, and Frank Richard, who worked in films. H. G. and Jane, as Wells and his second wife were usually known, lived at first in lodgings at Camden Town and Sevenoaks, and later at Woking and Worcester Park in Surrey. Their

Worcester Park household was portrayed by Dorothy Miller Richardson, a schoolfriend of Catherine Wells, in her novel *Pilgrimage* (1915). After a renewed episode of ill health in 1898, Wells was advised to leave the London area and prepare for a life of possible invalidism. He moved to Sandgate in Kent, and to Spade House, a house on the cliffs designed by C. F. A. Voysey for wheelchair use. Here he became intimate with such literary neighbours as Joseph Conrad, Ford Madox Ford, and Henry James, and was visited by Arnold Bennett, George Gissing, and Bernard Shaw. As his health quickly improved, he resorted to the bicycle rather than the wheelchair, and entered a restless and turbulent phase. He and Catherine moved back to London, where they lived at 17 Church Row, Hampstead, from 1909 to 1913, and in 1912 they acquired Easton Glebe at Little Easton, Essex. The Wellses' hospitality at Easton Glebe was renowned, as were the violent games of hockey played to a set of rules which only Wells seemed to understand. In his fifties he suffered from bronchitis and began to winter abroad, but his physical vigour remained undiminished until the onset of diabetes and heart disease in old age.

'The literary life', Wells wrote in 1911, 'is one of the modern forms of adventure'; his fame as a writer had brought him 'the utmost freedom of movement and intercourse' ('My Lucky Moment'). He ridiculed the English class system in *Kipps* and *Tono-Bungay* and neither forgot nor forgave the stringencies of his youth. Now that he was successful he all but abandoned the self-denial and self-discipline which he believed to be necessary for the building of a new socialist world. A fascinating talker with arresting blue eyes, he was deeply attractive to women, and his numerous love affairs (and Catherine's apparent complaisance in them) became the talk of literary London. His utopian ideal of free love, as expressed in *In the Days of the Comet*, made him a prime target in the 'war against socialism' waged by the tory press in 1906–7. Before 1914 his lovers included the novelists Dorothy Miller *Richardson (1873–1957) and Elizabeth von *Arnim (1866–1941), as well as a young Fabian just down from Cambridge, Amber Reeves. Wells had recently failed in a political battle within the Fabian Society to overturn the old guard of Shaw and the Webbs, and Amber's pregnancy and hurried marriage to Rivers Blanco-White caused great offence within the society. Anna-Jane Blanco-White, born in 1909, was acknowledged twenty years later by Wells as his daughter. A further scandal resulted from his liaison with a young feminist journalist, Rebecca West [*see* Andrews, Dame Cicily Isabel (1892–1983)], who gave birth to his third son, Anthony West, on the day after war was declared in 1914. Wells and West remained lovers for some years, but Anthony was told that he was their nephew. Anthony grew up to revere his father and to blame much of his unhappiness on his mother. His autobiographical novel *Heritage* (1955) portrays the relative ease with which his prosperous and usually absent father was able to put the sufferings of his second family on one side.

Although the details of his love affairs were kept out of print until nearly all the participants were dead, Wells was committed to greater openness about sexual behaviour. He spoke of his reputation as a 'Don Juan among the intelligentsia' (Wells, *Experiment in Autobiography*, vol. 2), and he wrote a third volume of autobiography which was posthumously published as *H. G. Wells in Love* (1984). *Ann Veronica* (1909), whose heroine was a feminist, was the first of a series of novels aimed at the taboos surrounding sexual desire in Edwardian England. His commitment to the 'discussion novel', dealing provocatively with social themes and sexual relationships, brought him into conflict with Henry James, whom he satirized in *Boon* (1915). James wrung from Wells the admission that 'I had rather be called a journalist than an artist, that is the essence of it' (Edel and Ray, 264). To Wells's disadvantage, their quarrel in 1915 would come to symbolize the conflict between artistic autonomy and political engagement in twentieth-century literature.

War, education, and human rights, 1914–1946 Wells was unwise to renounce any claims on the word 'art', but he was an increasingly passionate and influential journalist, especially during the war years. *The War that will End War* (1914) set out his case for supporting the allies. His novel *Mr Britling Sees it Through* (1916) is a vivid evocation of the war as seen from the home front. In 1918 he was recruited by Lord Northcliffe's ministry of propaganda at Crewe House, where his task was to work on a statement of war aims, chief among which was the setting up of the League of Nations. The league fell far short of his hopes, however, and he soon became one of its most vociferous critics.

Wells viewed the First World War as the inevitable outcome of the rivalries between modern nation states. Popular nationalism and imperialism reflected the prejudices and misunderstandings sowed by the teaching of national history in each country. He envisaged a new kind of history textbook and, at the end of the war, assembled a team of specialist advisers and wrote his 'Plain History of Life and Mankind', *The Outline of History* (1920). Against all expectations, the *Outline* was both a critical success and an international best-seller. He wrote three more encyclopaedic works—*A Short History of the World* (1922), *The Science of Life* (with Julian Huxley and G. P. Wells, 1930), and *The Work, Wealth and Happiness of Mankind* (1931)—and these inspired the work of other popular educationists such as Lancelot Hogben.

The Outline of History brought Wells new fame, though his activities as a propagandist and commentator on world affairs rapidly undermined his standing as a novelist. From time to time he used his position to secure interviews with the world's political leaders, interpreting their ideas for an international readership and urging them to find common ground in the quest for world order. On his first visit to the United States in 1906 he had met President Theodore Roosevelt; in 1920 he had the meeting with Lenin described in his book *Russia in the Shadows* (1921); and in 1934 he spoke with Franklin Roosevelt in the White House and with Stalin in the Kremlin. Although never a party man, he stood as a Labour candidate for the London University seat in 1922. His favoured project was an 'Open Conspiracy' to work towards world peace and global reorganization. George Orwell and others would later accuse him of political naïvety between the wars, though he was an early and persistent critic of both fascism and communism. In fact, his outlook had become more liberal and less authoritarian than it had been when he wrote *Anticipations* and *A Modern Utopia*. He became president of PEN, the international writers' organization founded by John Galsworthy, and was a founder member of the National Council for Civil Liberties. As the Second World War approached he formed a new committee to draft a fundamental statement of human rights. Throughout the war he showed almost fanatical persistence in getting agreement on an international charter of rights, which led directly to the universal declaration of human rights adopted by the United Nations in 1948. He refused to take personal credit for what now seems his most significant political achievement.

In *The Outline of History* Wells had summed up modern life as a 'race between education and catastrophe'. As he entered old age his attempts to educate took the form of an endless, repetitive stream of books and articles. His epic *Experiment in Autobiography* (1934) began with a vivid account of his early struggles and ended with his crusades for 'world education' and 'world revolution'. His later novels were far less triumphal than this. Two of the best of them, *Mr Blettsworthy on Rampole Island* (1928) and *The Croquet Player* (1936), are haunting fables of the psychic forces which threaten to bring humanity to collective suicide. His film *Things to Come* (produced by Alexander Korda in 1936) begins with a spectacular bombing raid and shows world war and pestilence as the prelude to utopian reconstruction by airborne revolutionaries. Dismissed by the literary avant-garde, he succeeded in exploiting the new medium of cinema as a forum for his ideas.

The end of Wells's relationship with Rebecca West in 1923, and Catherine Wells's death from cancer in 1927, brought about great changes in his personal life. During the late twenties he spent half the year with Odette Keun in Lou Pidou, the house they had built at St Mathieu, near Grasse in the Alpes-Maritimes in France. He and Odette parted acrimoniously, and Baroness Moura Budberg, whom he had met at Maksim Gorky's house in Moscow in 1920, became his most constant companion. After Easton Glebe was sold he moved permanently to central London, living first in a flat at 47 Chiltern Court, Clarence Gate, off Baker Street, and then at 13 Hanover Terrace, Regent's Park. It was at Hanover Terrace that he lived throughout the Second World War, though his windows were shattered by the flying-bomb attacks.

As a young man Wells was slim and pinched, with fiery eyes and a wispy moustache. Later his moustache was well trimmed, his face filled out, and he tended, as he put it, to embonpoint. His short, unimpressive figure and high, piping voice made him a disastrous platform speaker, though he was more effective in his numerous broadcasts for BBC radio. His best writing in the 'prophetic' style has a simple grandeur and austerity of phrase, and most of it was produced early. Then there came the warm, wistful, anarchic mood of the comic romances such as *Mr Polly*. Once again this phase was short-lived, and in some of his later fiction and non-fiction he tried, and usually failed, to recapture his earlier magic. But much of his output was deliberately ephemeral. He never tired of controversy and was a life-long scourge of those aspects of capitalism, communism, nationalism, imperialism, Zionism, and Roman Catholicism which could not be reconciled with his vision of a scientific world order. His last writings are among his most vehement; Wells in old age did not mellow. He was notoriously irascible, and his impatience and emotionalism ruined some of his political interventions, though his capacity for penetrating self-criticism saved him from the worst of his follies. His ebullience, generosity, and kindness to the young won him many friends, and his candour and warmth shine through his voluminous correspondence. He wanted to guide humanity to a better world, but it is as a novelist, and especially as the founder of modern science fiction, that he is best remembered. His short last prophetic book, *Mind at the End of its Tether* (1945), was dismayingly pessimistic, but its predecessor was *The Happy Turning*, published in the same year, and he angrily denied a newspaper report that he was plunged into the depths of despair. He died in his sleep at his home at Hanover Terrace, in Regent's Park, London on 13 August 1946, a month short of his eightieth birthday, and was cremated at Golders Green three days later.

PATRICK PARRINDER

Sources H. G. Wells, *Experiment in autobiography*, 2 vols. (1934) · N. Mackenzie and J. Mackenzie, *The time traveller: the life of H. G. Wells*, rev. 2nd edn (1987) · G. West, *H. G. Wells: a sketch for a portrait* (1930) · D. C. Smith, *H. G. Wells: desperately mortal* (1986) · *The correspondence of H. G. Wells*, ed. D. C. Smith, 4 vols. (1998) · *H. G. Wells in love*, ed. G. P. Wells (1984) · The H. G. Wells Society, *H. G. Wells: a comprehensive bibliography*, rev. 4th edn (1986) · *DNB* · A. H. Watkins, *The catalogue of the H. G. Wells Collection in the Bromley Public Libraries* (1974) · L. Edel and G. N. Ray, eds., *Henry James and H. G. Wells: a record of their friendship, their debate on the art of fiction, and their quarrel* (1958) · M. Mullin, ed., *H. G. Wells: reality and beyond* (1986) · B. Loing, *H. G. Wells à l'oeuvre: les débuts d'un écrivain* (1984) · C. Rollyson, *Rebecca West: a saga of the century* (1995) · Bromley Public Libraries, H. G. Wells MSS · P. Parrinder, ed., *H. G. Wells: the critical heritage* (1972) · A. West, *Heritage*, 2nd edn (1984) · J. R. Hammond, *An H. G. Wells chronology* (1999) · b. cert. · m. cert. [H. G. Wells and Amy Catherine Robbins] · d. cert. [Joseph Wells]

Archives Boston University, literary papers · Bromley Central Library, London, corresp. and papers · McMaster University, Hamilton, Ontario, literary papers · Milwaukee Public Library, corresp. and literary papers · NRA, corresp. and literary papers · Sheff. Arch., notes and sketches · University of Illinois, Urbana-Champaign, corresp., literary MSS, and papers · University of Virginia, Charlottesville, corresp. relating to his publications · Yale U., Beinecke L., papers | BBC WAC, corresp. with BBC staff · BL, letters to Lady Aberconway, Add. MSS 52551–52553 · BL, corresp. with G. K. Chesterton and others, Add. MS 73199 fols. 17–44 · BL, letters to Holbrook Jackson, Add. MS 62992 · BL, letters to S. S. Koteliansky, Add. MSS 48973–48974 · BL, corresp. with Macmillans, Add. MSS 54943–54945 · BL, corresp. with Lord Northcliffe, Add. MS 62161 · BL, corresp. with George Bernard Shaw and Charlotte Shaw, Add. MS 50552 · BL, corresp. with Society of Authors, Add. MS 56843–56844, 63342–63345 · BL, corresp. with Marie Stopes, Add. MS 58496 · BL, corresp. with Geoffrey West, Add. MS 60571 · BLPES, letters to Fabian Society · BLPES, letters to Graham Wallas · BLPES, letters to Sidney Webb and Beatrice Webb · Bodl. Oxf., corresp. with Sibyl Colefax · Bodl. Oxf., corresp.

with H. A. Gwynne · Bodl. Oxf., letters to Francis Marvin · Bodl. Oxf., corresp. with Gilbert Murray · Harvard U., Houghton L., letters to Herbert Greenhough Smith · HLRO, corresp. with Lord Beaverbrook · Internationaal Instituut voor Sociale Geschiedenis, Amsterdam, corresp. with Dora Russell · Keele University Library, LePlay Collection, corresp. and minute book entries as member of Sociological Society committees · Man. CL, corresp. with J. L. Hodson · McMaster University, Hamilton, Ontario, corresp. with Siegfried Sassoon · Ransom HRC, corresp. with John Lane · Rice University, Houston, Texas, Woodson Research Center, corresp. with Sir Julian Huxley · Richmond Local Studies Library, London, corresp. with Douglas Sladen · U. Edin., corresp. with Charles Sarolea · U. Leeds, Brotherton L., letters to Edmund Gosse · U. Newcastle, Robinson L., corresp. with Frederic Whyte · U. Sussex, corresp. with Leonard Woolf | FILM BFI NFTVA, *Bookmark*, BBC2, 24 Aug 1996 · BFI NFTVA, 'Whoosh: an outline of H. G. Wells', BBC1, 15 Sept 1966 · BFI NFTVA, current affairs footage · BFI NFTVA, documentary footage · BFI NFTVA, home footage | SOUND BL NSA, 'H. G. Wells', 20 Oct 1993, C125/246 BD1 · BL NSA, 'Herbert George Wells—a portrait', MP1035 W&R · BL NSA, performance recording

Likenesses W. Rothenstein, lithograph, 1896, Bradford City Art Gallery · M. Beerbohm, caricature, 1903, Yale U. · W. Rothenstein, lithograph, 1904, NPG · A. L. Coburn, photogravure, 1905, NPG · W. Rothenstein, chalk, 1912, NPG · oils, *c*.1915, U. Texas · G. C. Beresford, four photographs, *c*.1920, NPG [*see illus.*] · E. Kapp, 1921, Barber Institute of Fine Arts, Birmingham · T. Spicer-Simson, plasticine medallion, *c*.1922, NPG · W. Stoneman, two photographs, 1925–35, NPG · R. S. Sherriffs, ink caricature, 1928, NPG · E. Kapp, portrait, 1930, Barber Institute of Fine Arts, Birmingham · M. Beerbohm, caricature, 1931, *The Spectator* offices, London · H. Coster, prints, 1934, NPG · R. S. Sherriffs, pencil and ink caricature, 1934, NPG · Mrozewski, wood-engraving, 1935, NPG · D. Low, cartoon, 1936, Boston University Library · G. Freund, colour print, 1939, NPG · Y. Karsh, bromide print, 1943, NPG · W. Stoneman, oils, 1943, NPG · F. Topolski, oils, 1943, NPG · J. Davidson, bust, repro. in F. Swinnerton, *The Georgian literary scene* (1935) · C. L. Fraser, charcoal and wash caricature, NPG · D. Low, two pencil caricatures, NPG · B. Thomas, ink caricature, NPG · engraving (after D. Low), NPG; repro. in *New Statesman* (16 Jan 1926) · photograph (as a student), ICL · two prints (as a young man), NPG

Wealth at death £59,811 9s.: probate, 19 Nov 1946, *CGPLA Eng. & Wales*

Wells, Hugh of (*d.* 1235), bishop of Lincoln, was the eldest son of Edward of Wells, and was a native of the cathedral city in Somerset from which he took his name. It is not known in which year he was born but it is probable that he was an old man at the time of his death—as far as can be determined from the extant sources, he never left his episcopal residence of Stow Park near Lincoln after March 1233, and this long period of immobility would seem to suggest incapacity due to old age or physical infirmity. Hugh began his ecclesiastical career in the service of Bishop Reginald Fitzjocelin of Bath (1174–91)—he first occurs in witness lists in the late 1180s—and after the latter's death, he is found as a clerk in the household of his successor, Bishop Savaric (1192–1205). He first occurs as a canon of Wells Cathedral at the end of the century. Hugh maintained close links with his native diocese throughout his life, and drew on many clerks from the region for his own episcopal *familia*. His younger brother, Jocelin of *Wells (*d.* 1242), became bishop of Bath in 1206. There is no evidence to suggest that Hugh spent any time at a university, and unlike his brother he is never once styled *magister*.

With the accession of King John in 1199 Hugh entered the royal chancery. It may be conjectured that his entry into the royal administration was connected with Simon of Wells (alias Fitzrobert), archdeacon of Wells (d. 1207), a close adherent of Hubert Walter, archbishop of Canterbury (d. 1205). When Archbishop Hubert was appointed royal chancellor in May 1199, Archdeacon Simon and Hugh were brought into the chancery, the former acting as datary and deputy of the chancellor, in which capacity Hugh eventually succeeded him, when Simon was elevated to the bishopric of Chichester in 1204. Hugh spent the years from 1199 to 1209 in active service to the king, both in England and abroad, and it is probable that he was one of the administrators responsible for the implementation of Archbishop Hubert's chancery innovations, an experience that probably led to the systematic registration of documents at Lincoln during his episcopate.

Loyal service to the king produced its expected rewards in ecclesiastical preferment, including prebends at Lincoln Cathedral and St Paul's, London, and the archdeaconry of Wells, as well as parochial benefices; in addition Hugh was granted the Somerset manors of Cheddar and Axbridge and the hundreds of Cheddar and Winterstoke in fee-farm. He was also a royal custodian of the vacant bishopric of Lincoln between 1200 and 1203, and served in a similar capacity in the diocese of Bath and Glastonbury during the vacancy of 1205–6. Early in 1209 Pope Innocent III (r. 1198–1216) commanded the cathedral chapter of Lincoln to elect a new bishop in place of William de Blois, who had died in 1206, and by 12 April 1209 Hugh is found styled as bishop-elect of Lincoln. The election of a prominent royal official aroused papal suspicions that the king had exerted pressure on the chapter, and the pope commissioned the exiled Archbishop Stephen Langton of Canterbury (d. 1228) to examine the elect and the form of the election. As well as possible election irregularities, the archbishop was charged with investigating allegations of incontinence against the bishop-elect, namely that he had daughters. But it is evident that these charges were not well founded. Hugh broke with the now excommunicate King John later in the year, and on 20 December at Melun he was confirmed and consecrated as bishop of Lincoln by Langton. The new bishop remained in exile for three and a half years during the papal interdict on England. Of the intervening period little is known. Apart from his consecration the only other recorded appearance Hugh made during his enforced stay abroad was in November 1212, at St Martin de Garenne near Paris, when he drew up his (first recorded) testament. He returned to England in June or July 1213, and his active episcopate dates from then, the temporalities of his see being restored on 20 July. Hugh was present when Magna Carta was issued, and he joined his episcopal colleagues in protesting when the barons refused to honour their promise to give surety for the maintenance of the peace. In September 1215 he again left England, this time to attend the Fourth Lateran Council, and was abroad for eighteen months.

After Hugh's return from exile during the interdict years the task of restoring normality to diocesan government, and introducing new methods in administrative practice and procedure, consumed his energies for the rest of his episcopate. His tenure of the see was marked by transition and innovation in the sphere of episcopal government. He introduced episcopal registration at Lincoln, very much on the lines of his experience in the royal chancery: a general institutions roll gave way to separate rolls defined by archdeaconry, and other developments included charter rolls (only one has survived) and memoranda rolls (all of which have since disappeared), together with surveys of vicarage endowments. While he was, of course, ably assisted by a group of household clerks, all the indications are that he was a man with a remarkable talent for administration.

Yet Hugh did not cease to be active in public life during the royal minority of Henry III and afterwards. His itinerary indicates that he was regularly in attendance upon the king and his regents. In 1218–19 he headed the names of the justices on eyre for Lincolnshire, Nottinghamshire, and Derbyshire, and he was again employed as an itinerant justice in 1226. In 1225 he was present at Westminster when the charters were confirmed and reissued, and later he was one of the English ambassadors engaged in negotiations with Louis VIII of France over Normandy and Poitou. He was also naturally active in the proceedings leading to the canonization of his predecessor and namesake, Hugh of Avalon (d. 1200), in 1219–20. Marks of royal favour at this time included the gift of timber and stone to assist the construction of the hall and kitchen at the episcopal palace in Lincoln, work begun by the first Hugh.

Matthew Paris (Historia Anglorum, 2.375–6) bestowed upon Bishop Hugh a questionable but enduring reputation as 'monachorum gravator indefessus canonicorum, sanctimonialium et omnium religiosorum malleus' ('the untiring persecutor of monks, the hammer of canons, nuns and all the religious'), but in fact there is no evidence that Hugh was particularly inimical to the interests of the regular clergy, as long as these did not conflict with his own diocesan obligations. Matthew Paris's exempt abbey of St Albans had been obliged to conclude an agreement with the bishop over the appointment of priors to the abbey's dependencies in the Lincoln diocese, and over the ordination of a perpetual vicarage at Luton, and this may have been the cause of the chronicler's resentment. In his dealings with other non-exempt houses the bishop was concerned with the routine examination and confirmation of new superiors, and with their vacation of office (the only head he is known to have deposed is Abbot Adam of Eynsham, the biographer of St Hugh). There is some little evidence for his visitations of religious houses from 1220 onwards, and towards the end of his episcopate he was employing his official to conduct such visitations in his name. In respect of parochial visitations there is no evidence that the bishop undertook them (the articles of inquiry once attributed to Bishop Hugh are now accepted as belonging to his immediate successor, Robert Grosseteste), and it is likely that Grosseteste (d. 1253) was the first bishop of Lincoln to visit his parishes systematically.

Hugh has in the past enjoyed renown for his energy in respect of appropriations of parish churches and the ordination of perpetual vicarages, and this is partly based on the extant archival material including vicarage rolls and a survey volume of vicarage endowments and appropriation deeds known as the *Liber antiquus*. It is also partly based on the misinterpretation of this abundant evidence. It has been shown beyond doubt that the endowment of perpetual vicarages was a development of the twelfth century, well before the enactments of the Fourth Lateran Council of 1215. Many of the vicarages Bishop Hugh was once thought to have ordained for the first time have since proved to be mere reassessments of existing provisions, augmenting inadequate vicarage endowments; nevertheless, this should not lead modern interpreters to diminish his role in the more systematic approach to appropriations and pastoral responsibilities.

Hugh died at his residence of Stow Park on 7 February 1235 and was buried in the north aisle of his cathedral three days later. His (second recorded) testament, dated 1 June 1233, is a lengthy document. In addition to bequests to his family (including his brother the bishop of Bath, and a niece called Agatha) and to his household clerks and staff, the fabric of Lincoln Cathedral, many religious houses in the diocese, and the poor received generous benefactions. The residue of his estate was to be divided between the poor religious houses and leper houses of the diocese, the masters and scholars of Oxford, converts from Judaism in his diocese, and poor men on his episcopal manors.   DAVID M. SMITH

Sources W. P. W. Phillimore and others, eds., *Rotuli Hugonis de Welles, episcopi Lincolniensis*, 3 vols., CYS, 1, 3–4 (1907–9) · W. P. W. Phillimore and others, eds., *Rotuli Hugonis de Welles*, 3 vols., Lincoln RS, 3, 6, 9 (1912–14) · A. W. Gibbons, ed., *Liber antiquus de ordinationibus vicariarum tempore Hugonis Wells, Lincolniensis episcopi, 1209–1235* (1888) · D. M. Smith, 'The administration of Hugh of Wells, bishop of Lincoln, 1209–1235', PhD diss., U. Nott., 1970 [incl. edn of 400 *acta* of the bishop] · D. M. Smith, 'The rolls of Hugh of Wells, bishop of Lincoln, 1209–35', *BIHR*, 45 (1972), 155–95 · F. M. R. Ramsey, ed., *Bath and Wells, 1061–1205*, English Episcopal Acta, 10 (1995) · *The book of John de Schalby: canon of Lincoln, 1299–1333, concerning the bishops of Lincoln and their acts*, trans. J. H. Srawley, another edn (1966) · J. A. Robinson, 'Jocelin of Wells and members of his family', *Somerset Historical Essays* (1921), 156–9 · *Calendar of the manuscripts of the dean and chapter of Wells*, 2 vols., HMC, 12 (1907–14) · *Matthaei Parisiensis, monachi Sancti Albani, Historia Anglorum, sive … Historia minor*, ed. F. Madden, 3 vols., Rolls Series, 44 (1886–9) · *Gir. Camb. opera*, 7.223–30

Archives Lincs. Arch., episcopal records

Wells, Jocelin of (*d.* 1242), bishop of Bath and Wells, was a son of Edward of Wells (also known as Edward Troteman or Tortesmains), of Wells and younger brother of Hugh of *Wells, bishop of Lincoln (*d.* 1235). He was born and educated at Wells, whose canons later said he 'had grown up in the bosom of their church from infancy' (*Wells MSS*, 1.63). He may have had a son named Nicholas of Wells. Jocelin attested two charters for Bishop Reginald Fitzjocelin (*d.* 1191), evidently as a layman, but by 28 January 1200 he was among the Wells canons who, with some laymen, brought back several monks from Glastonbury as prisoners for opposing the claim of Bishop Savaric (*d.* 1205) to the

abbey. Jocelin remained a member of the Wells chapter, in deacon's orders, until his consecration as bishop in 1206.

In 1202 Jocelin was in royal service, paying cash to the exchequer from the vacant see of Lincoln of which his brother Hugh was one of the keepers. He himself was keeper of the see in 1204. From that year also he was active in government administration, hearing fines at Westminster, sitting as a justice in the *curia regis*, and assessing and collecting tallages in south-west England. From the summer of 1204 until the spring of 1206 he was in regular attendance on the king, described simply as clerk, but often sealing letters close and charters and witnessing letters patent. About 1204 the prior of Bath, evidently for services rendered, gave Jocelin an annuity of £5, and soon afterwards, in fulfilment of a promise, presented him to the priory living of Dogmersfield, Hampshire. In the same year the king gave him the church of Lugwardine, Herefordshire, from which he negotiated a pension, and in 1206 he received, also from the crown, the Somerset living of Winsham.

On 3 February 1206 Jocelin was elected bishop by the monks of Bath and the canons of Wells in succession to Savaric. Whether the initiative in his promotion was taken by the king or by the chapter it is impossible to tell. The temporalities were restored on 3 May and he was consecrated at Reading by William de Ste Mère-Église, bishop of London (*d.* 1224), in the absence of Stephen Langton, archbishop of Canterbury (*d.* 1228). He was often in attendance on the king until early in 1208, and continued with his brother Hugh in royal service after the publication of the interdict and the exile of most of the bishops. He was one of a group who conferred in London with Langton on behalf of the king in March 1209, and he and his brother were present at Dover in the following July when the threat of excommunication against the king was temporarily withdrawn. Jocelin remained engaged in negotiation until early October, and was probably still in England until the end of that year, leaving when Hugh had been consecrated by Langton at Melun. Jocelin did not escape contemporary criticism for his long-continued support for the king.

Jocelin was with his brother at St Martin de Garenne near Bordeaux in November 1212, and returned with him and the other bishops in May 1213. He resumed his support for the king, and was one of John's councillors named in the preamble to Magna Carta. It is likely that he remained loyal to John thereafter, since he was one of the bishops who crowned Henry III at Gloucester in October 1216, and he was also present at the battle with Eustace the Monk in the following year. In 1218–19 he was a justice itinerant in the south-western counties, and he presided over forest cases in Wiltshire, Somerset, and Dorset. A major figure in the administration of the realm in the mid-1220s, alongside the justiciar, Hubert de Burgh (*d.* 1243), and Richard Poore, bishop of Salisbury (*d.* 1237), Jocelin was given temporary custody of the county of Somerset and the castles of Sherborne, Dorset, and Bristol in the winter of 1223–4, and he was closely involved in the action against Falkes de Bréauté (d. 1226) in 1224. When the garrison of Bréauté's castle at Bedford surrendered and was sent to the gallows, Jocelin is said to have remarked, in words more characteristic of a government officer than a bishop, that if the same thing had happened after the siege of Bytham, Lincolnshire, three years earlier, no such thing would have been necessary now. When Falkes de Bréauté complained to the pope of his ill usage, the bishop of Wells was singled out for criticism. In 1225 Jocelin's prominence was underlined when he was set in charge of one of the two special exchequers established for the receipt of that year's fifteenth. He continued to be an occasional witness to government business until 1233, acted as arbitrator in ecclesiastical disputes at Bristol and Worcester, and in 1237 witnessed the confirmation of Magna Carta.

In Jocelin's own diocese the dispute with Glastonbury begun under Savaric, who had tried to bring the abbey under direct episcopal control by himself becoming its abbot, was resumed in 1217, but was settled in the following year when the monastery's brief union with the see was dissolved. Thenceforward Jocelin's title was bishop of Bath and Wells. In 1234 he deprived the abbot of Glastonbury for misconduct. On 23 October 1239 Jocelin dedicated the cathedral at Wells. The work had been in progress since the time of Reginald Fitzjocelin, but most of the nave and the fabric of the west front is attributable to Jocelin's time. He is also credited with domestic buildings at Wells and Wookey, with the foundation (jointly with his brother Hugh) of St John's Hospital at Wells, with the creation or increased endowment of cathedral offices, prebends, and common fund, and with the cathedral's constitutional arrangements.

Jocelin died at Wells on 19 November 1242 'full of days and commendable in life and character' (Paris, Chron., 4.233). He was buried in the middle of the choir at Wells, as befitted a founder, under a marble tomb, which he had prepared during his life, with a flat brass said to be one of the earliest monuments of its kind in England.

ROBERT W. DUNNING

Sources J. A. Robinson, 'Bishop Jocelin and the interdict', Somerset historical essays (1921), 141–59 · Calendar of the manuscripts of the dean and chapter of Wells, 1, HMC, 12 (1907) · Chancery records · Pipe rolls · D. A. Carpenter, The minority of Henry III (1990) · J. Hunter, ed., Fines sive pedes finium, 2 vols. (1835–44) · Curia regis rolls preserved in the Public Record Office (1922–) · W. Hunt, ed., Two chartularies of the priory of St Peter at Bath, Somerset RS, 7 (1893) · Ann. mon., vols. 1, 2, 4 · Paris, Chron. · J. A. Robinson, ed., 'Historia major', Collectanea I, ed. T. F. Palmer, Somerset RS, 39 (1924), 57–71 · J. A. Robinson, ed., 'Historia minor', Collectanea I, ed. T. F. Palmer, Somerset RS, 39 (1924), 54–6 · [H. Wharton], ed., Anglia sacra, 2 vols. (1691) · A. Way, 'Sepulchral brasses, and incised slabs', Archaeological Journal, 1 (1844), 197–212 · R. C. Stacey, Politics, policy and finance under Henry III, 1216–1245 (1987) · L. S. Colchester, ed., Wells Cathedral: a history (1982)

Likenesses effigy; now lost

Wells [Wellys], **John** (d. **1388**), Benedictine monk and theological controversialist, was already a monk of Ramsey Abbey, Huntingdonshire, when he was ordained priest on 7 June 1365. From at least 1374 he studied at Gloucester College, the Benedictine hall in Oxford. While at Gloucester College he was for thirteen years prior studentium, a position he still held in 1381. He incepted as DTh about 1376.

As a member of a religious order, Wells seems always to have been implacably opposed to John Wyclif (d. 1384) and his followers. Indeed, so determined was he in his opposition that he acquired the title Malleus Haereticorum ('Hammer of Heretics'). He was almost certainly the Wellys that the compiler of Fasciculi zizaniorum identifies as 'quidam canis niger de ordine Benedicti' ('a black dog of the Benedictine order'; Fasciculi zizaniorum, 239), who argued with Wyclif concerning the religious orders; although the rubricator of the only extant copy of the compilation gives Wellys's first name as William, John Bale corrected the rubric to John. John Wells was also very probably the opponent Wyclif refers to as dompnus niger (Wyclif, Sermones, 3.252), as well as the one he dismisses as speaking elaborately and diffusely, just like a monk. In 1380–81 he was on William Barton's committee of twelve doctors of theology who condemned Wyclif's views on the eucharist. In 1382 he and the Carmelite Peter Stokes (d. 1399) complained to the new chancellor of Oxford, Robert Rygge (d. 1410), about a sermon Nicholas Hereford had preached in St Mary's, in which he had asserted that members of religious orders could not take degrees in the university without apostatizing. Wells was also the first to speak at the council convened in that year by Archbishop William Courtenay (d. 1396) at Blackfriars, London, which condemned ten of Wyclif's views as heretical and fourteen as erroneous; three of the errors correspond with views Wyclif seems to have maintained specifically against Wells. A satirical song describes Wells's arguments on this occasion as windy and feeble, just what might be expected of someone with a face the colour of gall; in words Wyclif would mockingly echo, the song then describes how Wells had been completely outargued by Hereford in the schools.

On 9 July 1387 the English Benedictines sent Wells as their general proctor to Pope Urban VI, with instructions to intercede for the deprived and imprisoned Cardinal Adam Easton (d. 1397). Wells must have pleaded on behalf of Easton either at Lucca, where the pope was resident until 23 September, or at Perugia, where the pope then took up residence; as Easton was not reinstated until 18 December 1389, Wells's pleas were evidently unsuccessful. Wells himself died in Perugia in 1388 and was buried in the church of Santa Sabina.

John Bale credits Wells with De socii sui ingratitudine, Epistolae ad diversos, Pro religione privata (probably identical with the De religione perfectorum some later authorities refer to), Super cleri prerogativa, Super eucharistiae negotio, and Contra Nicolaum Herefordium. John Pits notes that Wells wrote many further works, almost always against heresies and heretics. All that has survived of Wells's writing is Wyclif's account of his Pro religione privata (in Fasciculi zizaniorum, 239–41).

On folio 6v of Bodl. Oxf., MS Bodley 851 (SC 3041), a fifteenth-century illumination indicates that this manuscript belonged to someone almost certainly identifiable with Wells: 'Iste liber constat fratri Johanni de Wellis, monacho Ramseye'. Because the manuscript contains, among other items, the 'Z' text of Piers Plowman, it has been suggested that Wells is the first known owner of any text of Piers Plowman. However, scholars are still debating whether the relevant part of the manuscript is early enough to have been his. The part of the manuscript he could have owned contains mainly texts by Walter Map.

John Wells of Ramsey should be distinguished from various contemporaries and near contemporaries with the same name, including a John Wells, also a DTh, but a Franciscan, who had goods stolen from him in London in 1377, and who may or may not have also been the John Wells who sought to procure the election of Doctor John Wylyot as chancellor of Oxford in 1349. He should also be distinguished from the Master John Wells who on 26 June 1410 moved a decree in Oxford against the works of Wyclif, and who spoke at the Council of Constance.

CHRISTINA VON NOLCKEN

Sources Emden, Oxf., 1.620–21 [Adam Easton]; 3.1616–17 [Robert Rygge], 2008 [John Welles] · Tanner, Bibl. Brit.-Hib., 757 · Bale, Cat., 1.496–7 · J. Pits, Relationum historicarum de rebus Anglicis, ed. [W. Bishop] (Paris, 1619), 540, no. 677 · [T. Netter], Fasciculi zizaniorum magistri Johannis Wyclif cum tritico, ed. W. W. Shirley, Rolls Series, 5 (1858) · J. Wycliffe, Sermones, ed. J. Loserth, 4 vols. (1887–90), vol. 3, pp. 224–57 · John Wiclif's Polemical works in Latin, ed. R. Buddensieg, 2 (1883), 485–536 · J. Wyclif, Tractatus de blasphemia, ed. M. H. Dziewicki, Wyclif Society (1893), 90 · J. Wyclif, Tractatus de apostasia, ed. M. H. Dziewicki, Wyclif Society (1889), 57–8 · T. Wright, ed., Political poems and songs relating to English history, 1, Rolls Series, 14 (1859), 260 · DNB · H. B. Workman, John Wyclif, 2 (1926), 123–4, 412 · J. Raine, ed., Historical papers and letters from the northern registers, Rolls Series, 61 (1873), 423–4 · W. A. Pantin, ed., Documents illustrating the activities of … the English black monks, 1215–1540, 3 vols., CS, 3rd ser., 45, 47, 54 (1931–7), vol. 3, p. 232 · CClR, 1392–6, 524 · Registrum Simonis de Sudbiria, diocesis Londoniensis, AD 1362–1375, ed. R. C. Fowler, 2, CYS, 38 (1938), 35 · M. Creighton, A history of the papacy from the Great Schism to the sack of Rome, new edn, 1 (1897); repr. (1969), 1.89–105

Wells, John (1623–1676), nonconformist minister, son of Hugh Wells of London, was born on 29 January 1623. He must be distinguished from the John Wells of Mickleton, Gloucestershire, who later became vicar of Tewkesbury and for some time lived at St Ives, Huntingdonshire. John Wells of London was admitted to Merchant Taylors' School on 11 September 1634. He matriculated from St John's College, Oxford, on 3 July 1640, was elected a fellow in 1643, and took the degree of BA on 7 May 1644. In November 1646 Wells was acting as chaplain at Ilford Hospital, in Essex, but he returned to Oxford and was created MA on 14 April 1648; his submission to the parliamentary visitors is not recorded, and it seems that he took up his rights as a fellow in response to their call. Certainly he was one of those appointed on 10 August 1648 'to take care of all the affairs of St John Baptist College in the absence of Mr Cheynell' (Burrows, 182). Wells was minister of St Olave Jewry by January 1649, signing together with many others A Vindication of the Ministers of the Gospel in and about London in opposition to the trial of Charles I. He was a leader with Edmund Calamy of the City's sixth classis and

acted as scribe of the London Provincial Assembly in November 1654.

Wells was ejected from St Olave's in 1662. On 3 May 1665 he was reported to be preaching at his house in Moorfields, and in 1669 another report had him preaching at the Blackamore, in Wood Street. On 1 July 1670 the governor of the Tower, Sir John Robinson, reported that the Moorfields house was no longer used as a meeting-place, but on 17 April 1672 Wells took out a licence to preach as a presbyterian there. He died on 18 June 1676 when, as the administration of his property records, he was resident in the parish of St Leonard, Shoreditch. In his sermon at the funeral of Wells on 2 July 1676, Thomas Watson, former minister at St Stephen Walbrook, recalled a minister who 'preached intelligibly to the capacity of his auditory', who was 'charitable and of a forgiving spirit', a man of 'candour and courtesy', 'not morose but affable' (Watson, 33–4). Wells's wife, Maria, survived him, but Sarah, the daughter of a minister named John Wells, was buried at St Giles Cripplegate on 25 July 1664.

STEPHEN WRIGHT

Sources Calamy rev. · Foster, Alum. Oxon. · M. Burrows, ed., The register of the visitors of the University of Oxford, from AD 1647 to AD 1658, CS, new ser., 29 (1881) · T. Watson, A sermon preached the 2 July at the funeral of Mr John Wells, late minister of St Olave's Jewry (1676) · C. J. Robinson, ed., A register of the scholars admitted into Merchant Taylors' School, from AD 1562 to 1874, 2 vols. (1882–3) · Tai Liu, Puritan London: a study of religion and society in the City parishes (1986)

Wells, John (1761–1848). See under Wells, William (1729–1805).

Wells, John Campbell (1936–1998), writer and actor, was born at Christchurch parsonage, Glover Road, Ashford, Kent, on 17 November 1936, the only child of the Revd Eric George Wells, rural dean of Bognor, and his wife, Dorothy Amy (née Thompson). During the Second World War his father served as a hospital chaplain, and Wells was evacuated to live with his grandmother in Shropshire. He went on to Eastbourne College, where the first target of his mimicry was 'a master who was very fat and poised on two tiny feet and spoke in a ridiculous maiden-aunt voice'. When Wells was caught doing his imitation, the master, far from being angry, offered him the part of Mrs Candour in The School for Scandal. Before taking up a scholarship in modern languages, at St Edmund Hall, Oxford, in 1957 he did his national service as a second lieutenant in the Royal Sussex Regiment. He was posted to Korea, and during a visit to headquarters at Inchon he first clapped eyes on his future collaborator Richard Ingrams, playing the harmonium in the garrison chapel.

After notable success in Oxford cabaret, Wells played a leading part in launching a satirical magazine, Mesopotamia, the forerunner of Private Eye. On leaving Oxford in 1961 with a second in German and French, he spent two years teaching modern languages at Eton College. At the same time he was contributing to the early issues of Private Eye under the pseudonym J. Campbell Murdoch and appearing on stage at the opening night of the Establishment Club, from which he would return to Eton just in

John Campbell Wells (1936–1998), by Lewis Morley, mid-1960s

time for early school at 7.30 a.m. This prompted the newspaper headline 'Eton master peddles smut in Soho'. In 1963 he joined *Private Eye* to work with Ingrams, the cartoonist William Rushton, Peter Cook, and Claud Cockburn, a revered link with the pre-war left-wing satire of *The Week*. The following year he collaborated with Cockburn on a play, *Listen to the Knocking Bird*, performed at John Neville's Nottingham Playhouse. But his first great success was his collaboration with Ingrams on *Mrs Wilson's Diary*, a spoof account of domestic life at 10 Downing Street, which *Private Eye* ran from 1964 until Harold Wilson's retirement in 1976.

Joan Littlewood, always a great influence on Wells, commissioned a play based on the *Diary*, which opened at the Theatre Royal, Stratford, and later transferred to the Criterion, where it ran for several months. Three years later he and Ingrams repeated the feat with even greater éclat in the 'Dear Bill' letters, which began on 15 May 1979, immediately after Margaret Thatcher came to power. This alleged correspondence between the new prime minister's husband and his long-standing golfing partner, widely assumed to be W. F. Deedes (later Lord Deedes), the politician and journalist, invented a memorable persona, somewhere between Malvolio and Bertie Wooster, of a henpecked husband always longing to escape the Fleet Street reptiles and sink a few quiet tinctures with his cronies.

Wells turned this fantasy into a play, *Anyone for Denis?*, which ran for more than a year at the Whitehall Theatre. The Thatchers themselves were persuaded to attend a special charity performance, from which they emerged with forced smiles, but in truth the play humanized them in the public eye and Wells himself, rather reluctantly playing the part of Denis, the put-upon buffoon who is really shrewder than his persecutors, was not so far from the reality. These popular successes helped to revive the tradition of mocking public figures which had been more or less defunct since the Regency.

Wells was also hyperactive in the theatre, appearing at the National Theatre in *Bartholomew Fair* and at Wyndham's in *The Philanthropist* and playing the lead part in Graham Greene's *Travels with my Aunt*. On the screen he played cameo parts in *Casino Royale*, *For Your Eyes Only*, the Tarzan film *Greystoke*, and finally in a charming film he co-wrote, *Princess Caraboo* (1994), based on a true story about a girl who turned up in Bristol in 1817 claiming to be an oriental princess. During these later years he was already suffering from the lymphoma which finally killed him but never slowed him up. He married on 24 June 1982, after a long courtship, Teresa Gatacre, *née* Chancellor (*b*. 1933), with whom he had a daughter, Dolly, who also became an actor. He wrote a delightful history of the London Library, *Rude Words* (1991), and at the end of his life *The House of Lords: an Unofficial History* (1997), as well as a novel, adaptations of Lewis Carroll for radio, and many librettos and songs for cabaret and musicals.

The little crusader with the crumpled sword on the masthead of *Private Eye* (drawn by his old friend Rushton) immortalizes Wells's peculiar appearance, with his protuberant upper lip, beaky nose, and floppy forelock. He tended to speak in a hesitant mutter, interrupted by a wild cackle when struck by some passing absurdity. Whether walking on Sussex Downs or paddling through Soho, he was invariably dressed like a shabby schoolmaster in dung-coloured tweed jacket, thick jersey, and trousers too heavy for the time of year. He was enormously loved by men and women alike, including many of the targets of his acute but affectionate satire. While being treated in the Charing Cross Hospital he was attended by everyone from the prince of Wales and Lord Runcie to decayed actors and mysterious figures from the heyday of the Third Programme. He was indifferent to his reputation, and his only career aim was to amuse himself and others.

Wells died at his home, 44 Victoria Road, Kensington, on 11 January 1998 and was buried in the churchyard at East Chiltington, Sussex, just over the hedge from his country home and in the lee of the South Downs. His wife survived him. FERDINAND MOUNT

Sources *The Times* (12 Jan 1998) · *Daily Telegraph* (12 Jan 1998) · *The Independent* (12 Jan 1998) · *The Guardian* (12 Jan 1998) · WWW · personal knowledge (2004) · private information (2004) · b. cert. · m. cert. · d. cert. · *Supplement to the historical register of 1900*, University of Oxford (1970)

Archives E. Sussex RO, corresp. and papers

Likenesses L. Morley, bromide print, 1963–7, NPG [*see illus.*] · L. Morley, group portrait, bromide print, 1965, NPG · photograph, 1991, repro. in *Daily Telegraph* · photograph, repro. in *The Times* · photograph, repro. in *The Guardian* · photograph, repro. in *The Independent*

Wealth at death £886,646: probate, 29 June 1998, *CGPLA Eng. & Wales*

Wells [*née* Davies; *other married name* Sumbel], **Mary Stephens** (1762–1829), actress, one of the three daughters of Thomas Davies, a carver and gilder in Birmingham, was born in that city on 16 December 1762. Her father died in a madhouse while she was a small child. Her mother kept a tavern frequented by actors, including Richard Yates, under whose management both mother and daughter appeared on the stage. Mary Davies's early roles at the Birmingham theatre included the Duke of York in *Richard III*, Cupid in Whitehead's *A Trip to Scotland*, and Arthur in *King John*. After visiting Bath and York she went to Gloucester, where she played Juliet to the Romeo of an actor named Ezra Wells. They were married on 22 November 1778 in St Chad's Church, Shrewsbury, but Wells shortly afterwards deserted her.

After provincial performances in Bristol and Plymouth, Mary Wells made her first appearance at the Haymarket on 1 June 1781, as Madge in Bickerstaffe's *Love in a Village* and Mrs Cadwallader in Foote's *Author*. On 3 September, in O'Keeffe's *The Agreeable Surprize*, she was the first Cowslip, a name that stuck to her (although she was occasionally spoken of as Becky Wells). Genest thought her acting as Cowslip was superior. On 25 September 1781, as Nancy in *The Camp*, she made her début at Drury Lane, where she remained for four seasons. Her roles included Mrs Oakley in Colman's *The Jealous Wife*, Widow Brady in Garrick's *The Irish Widow*, and Jacintha in Benjamin Hoadley's *The Suspicious Husband*. At the Haymarket in 1782 she appeared as Molly in *The English Merchant*, and Bridget in *The Chapter of Accidents*. She also replaced Ann Cargill, after that lady's elopement, as Macheath in *The Beggar's Opera*, with the male characters played by women and vice versa. She made from the first a distinguished success, and was received with great enthusiasm.

As the title character in Nicholas Rowe's *Jane Shore*, Mary Wells made her first appearance at Covent Garden on 14 December 1785, in what she considered her best performance. She also played Laura in Edward Topham's farce *The Fool* and a variety of other comic and tragic characters. She remained at Covent Garden for the following winter season, and continued her summer performances at the Haymarket. James Leigh, in *The New Rosciad*, complimented her 'magic smile' and 'enchanting form', admitting that he was as pleased with her attempt at tragedy as he had previously been with her comic characters. When John Palmer made his ill-starred experiment at the Royalty Theatre, Wellclose Square, in 1787, Wells gave her imitations of Sarah Siddons and other famous actresses, in *Ourselves, or, The Realities of the Stage*, which proved highly popular. She returned to Covent Garden, where she played Mrs Page in *The Merry Wives of Windsor*, Lady in Milton's *Comus*, and Fatima in Garrick's *Cymon*. Here she remained until 1792, while acting in the summers at Cheltenham, Brighton, and Weymouth.

Meanwhile Wells's domestic affairs had become complicated. She had begun a liaison with Edward *Topham (1751–1820), who was concerned in a daily newspaper called *The World*, which she assisted in producing. It served

Mary Stephens Wells (1762–1829), by John Downman

as a medium for complimentary criticisms of her performances. However, by 1792 Topham had taken their three daughters and left her for another woman. Wells had, moreover, backed bills for a considerable amount for her brother-in-law, Emmanuel Samuel, the husband of Anna Davies, who appeared at the Haymarket on 28 July 1786. This last indiscretion involved her in endless trouble. More than once she was a prisoner in the Fleet and in other places of detention in England and Ireland. Frederick Reynolds, who described her as the most beautiful actress of her day, tells of her eccentricities and erratic behaviour. In her own memoirs, she denied the charge of madness, but resorted to staying with Dr Francis Willis in Lincolnshire to avoid her creditors.

This was to little avail, and it was in the Fleet that Wells met her second husband, Joseph Sumbel, who was confined there for contempt of court. Sumbel was a Moorish Jew, and secretary to the ambassador from Morocco. Their reputedly lavish wedding was performed in the Fleet in October 1797 to the amusement of contemporary newspapers, which recorded that the bride had converted to Judaism and changed her name to Leah. Evidently a man of morbid temperament, Sumbel seems to have alternately made passionate love to her and disowned her and left her to starve. A year later he sought unsuccessfully to have the marriage dissolved, declaring that on account of failure to follow the prescribed ceremony she was not his wife. He apparently died abroad in 1804. After their separation, she reverted to Christianity.

The three volumes of her rambling autobiography, initially advertised in Brighton in 1792 and published in 1811 as *Memoirs of the Life of Mrs Sumbel, Late Wells*, are occupied principally with details of travels in search of her children and denunciations of Topham, Sumbel, and Samuel. The third volume is composed largely of printed compliments on her performances and correspondence from Topham and Reynolds.

Although the actress had no permanent engagement in London after 1792, she made occasional appearances under the name Mary Sumbel in London into the nineteenth century. After a final benefit performance, in 1815, she spent her later years in lodgings with her aged mother. She also applied to the Covent Garden Theatrical Fund, and received an annuity of £55 until her death in London on 23 January 1829. She was buried in St Pancras, London.   K. A. CROUCH

Sources Highfill, Burnim & Langhans, *BDA* · C. B. Hogan, ed., *The London stage, 1660–1800*, pt 5: 1776–1800 (1968) · Genest, *Eng. stage* · M. D. Wells, *Memoirs of the life of Mrs Sumbel, late Wells*, 3 vols. (1811) · F. Reynolds, *The life and times of Frederick Reynolds, written by himself*, 2 vols. (1826) · A. Pasquin [J. Williams], *The pin basket to the children of Thespis* (1796) · [J. Haslewood], *The secret history of the green rooms: containing authentic and entertaining memoirs of the actors and actresses in the three theatres royal*, 2 vols. (1790) · M. J. Young, *Memoirs of Mrs Crouch*, 2 vols. (1806) · *Memoirs of Mrs Inchbald*, ed. J. Boaden, 2 vols. (1833) · J. Leigh, *The new Rosciad* (1785)
Archives Garr. Club, Smith collection, appeal to Covent Garden theatrical fund; letter
Likenesses J. H. Ramberg, two Indian ink drawings, 1785, BM · E. Scott, stipple, pubd 1788 (after J. Singleton), NPG · J. Downman, chalk and watercolour drawing, 1792, BM · W. Hamilton, portrait, 1802, Royal Shakespeare Theatre, Stratford upon Avon, picture gallery · J. R. Smith, mezzotint, pubd 1802, BM · M. Brown, oils, Garr. Club · S. De Wilde, oils (as Anne Lovely in *A bold stroke for a wife*), Garr. Club · S. De Wilde, sketch, Yale U. CBA · J. Downman, chalk and watercolour, priv. coll. [*see illus.*] · J. Downman, drawing (as Cowslip in *The agreeable surprize*, with John Edwin as Lingo), Yale U. CBA · W. Leney, line engraving (after S. De Wilde), BM; repro. in J. Bell, *Bell's British theatre* (1791) · W. Ridley, engraving (after Naish), repro. in J. Parsons, *The minor theatre*, 7 vols. (1794) · T. Stothard, drawing (as Belinda in *The provok'd wife*), BM · engraving (after Stothard), repro. in *Lady's Magazine* (1783)

Wells, Nathaniel (1779–1852), slave owner and landowner, was born on St Kitts in the Leeward Islands on 10 September 1779, one of at least six children of William Wells (1730–1794), a St Kitts sugar planter and merchant. His mother was Juggy (d. 1811), one of his father's African house slaves. His father, born in Cardiff, went to St Kitts about 1749 with his younger brother Nathaniel (b. 1732). He eventually acquired three sugar plantations, the largest of which was Vambells. His first wife, Elizabeth, died and was buried at Basseterre with their son and daughter. Their surviving daughter, Elizabeth, married John Taylor of Nevis. William Wells had children by at least three of his house slaves. In his will he granted manumission to some of the slaves who had borne him children. He left bequests to his daughters, both legitimate and illegitimate, but the bulk of his estate was left to his only surviving son, Nathaniel. At the time that his father made his will in 1789, the young Nathaniel was at school at Newington, near London, and living under the care of his uncle Nathaniel. It was his father's wish that he should attend Oxford University, but this does not appear to have happened. William Wells died in 1794, leaving his son Nathaniel his three plantations and money amounting to an estimated £120,000.

Wells remained under the care and supervision of his uncle until about the age of twenty-one, when he moved to Bath. He did not stay there long and seems to have moved quickly back to London, where he resided first at Baker Street and then at Pall Mall. On 9 June 1801 he married Harriet Este (1780–1820), the only daughter of the Revd Charles Este, former chaplain to King George II, and his wife, Cordelia, of St George Row, Hanover Square. Vambells plantation, St Kitts, was part of their marriage settlement. His mother, Juggy, and at least two other female slaves granted manumission by his father appear on the plantation's inventory. On being freed Juggy adopted the name Joardine Wells.

In 1802 Wells bought the Piercefield estate at Chepstow for £90,000 from Mark Wood (created a baronet in 1808). The estate stood at the mouth of the River Wye below Tintern Abbey and had been extensively landscaped into one of the most renowned in Britain by Valentine Morris before he became governor of St Vincent. The estate attracted numerous visitors, including Coleridge, William Gilpin, and Thomas Gray. During his time at Piercefield, Wells continued the tradition of allowing visitors to tour the grounds. Among these was the landscape and topographical painter Joseph Farington, who visited Piercefield in 1803. He described Wells as 'a West Indian of large fortune, a man of very gentlemanly manners, but so much a man of colour as to be little removed from a Negro' (Farington, *Diary*, 6.2017).

Wells appeared to be assimilated into Monmouthshire society. He was appointed a justice of the peace in 1806 and sheriff of Monmouthshire in 1818, and was later appointed a deputy lieutenant for the county. He was also active in the local church at St Arvan's, where he acted as churchwarden from 1804 until 1843 and, with the duke of Beaufort, paid for improvements to the building.

Wells had ten children with his first wife. Following her death he married, on 30 January 1823, Esther Owen (1803/4–1871), daughter of the Revd John Henry Owen, rector of Paglesham, Essex, and his wife, Charlotte. They had a further ten children. Of the children of his first marriage, Nathaniel Armstrong Wells (1806–1846), who was also described as black, became an author and lived for part of his time at Caen, Normandy; Charles Rush Wells (*bap.* 1807), entered the church and became the incumbent at Nicholaston, Glamorgan; and John Tighe Wells (*bap.* 1808), followed him, becoming incumbent at Newman Street, Oxford Street, Middlesex. Wells moved to Bath about 1844. He died at 9 Park Street, Lansdown, Bath, on 13 May 1852, of fever, and was buried in Walcot cemetery, Bath.   J. A. H. EVANS

Sources will of William Wells, PRO, PROB 11/1253, fols. 273r–275r · will of Nathaniel Wells, PRO, PROB 11/2157, fols. 47v · Farington, *Diary* · St Arvan's parish registers, Gwent RO, D.Pa.2.2 & D.Pa.2.3 · marriage settlement, Gwent RO, Piercefield Collection, D412/52 & 53 · R. T. W. Denning, J. B. Davies, and G. H. Rhys, eds.,

The diary of William Thomas, 1762–1795, of Michaelston-super-Ely, near St Fagans, Glamorgan (1995) • Piercefield Collection, Gwent RO, D412/72 • Piercefield Collection, Gwent RO, D412/45 • A. M. Cuyler, 'Recollections of a visit to Llanbeder in county of Brecon', 1807, NL Wales, MS 784A, 136–44 • *DNB* • d. cert.

Wealth at death owned Piercefield estate

Wells [*née* Perry], **Nesta Helen** (1892–1986), physician and police surgeon, was born on 9 July 1892 at 71 Waterloo Road, Wolverhampton, the daughter of Herbert Edward Perry, a mineral water manufacturer who later became a Unitarian minister, and his wife, Edith Grafton Hopkins. She became a medical student at the University of Manchester, graduating MB ChB in 1916.

Perry's first medical post was as house surgeon at the General Hospital, Nottingham, but by 1918 she had returned to Manchester, where she began her long and devoted work among children and women. She held a number of local appointments: resident medical officer at the Manchester Children's Hospital at Pendlebury; house surgeon at the Beckett Hospital in Barnsley; medical officer to the Salvation Army's Crossley Maternity Hospital; and honorary registrar at the Manchester Babies' Hospital, a women-run hospital founded by Catherine Chisholm in 1914 and devoted to the care of infants. By the mid-1920s she had resigned from all but the babies' hospital, where she became honorary physician and remained throughout the rest of her career, publishing occasional reports of interesting clinical cases (*BMJ*, 1939, 1948; *Archives of Disease in Childhood*, 1947). On 28 December 1923 she married Lionel Wraith Wells (*b.* 1897/8), a mechanical engineer, the son of John Nugent Wells, a grain merchant; they had two daughters, Helen and Ruth.

Known as Dr Wells or Dr Perry Wells, she was an early member of the Medical Women's Federation (founded 1917), which in the 1920s advocated that women victims of indecent assault should be examined only by female doctors. It was well known that many cases involving children were not reported to the police for various reasons, including the reluctance of parents to allow an examination by a male police surgeon. In Manchester, Councillor Annie Lee, the only female member of the watch committee, was aware of public feeling in this regard, and succeeded in persuading the committee to appoint a female doctor to undertake such examinations. As a result Wells was the first woman in Britain (and, she believed, in the world) to be appointed as a police surgeon, on 1 August 1927.

Wells's duties consisted in examination of cases of indecent assault on women, girls, and young children, incest, rape, common assault, concealed abortion, abandoned babies, and other 'odd cases'. By far the largest number of cases involved sexual assaults on children, and the examinations were usually carried out at her house. Wells was paid a fee by the watch committee for each case examined (usually one or two each week), and a separate fee (paid by the court) for each court appearance (one or two each month). In addition she was responsible for examining female police recruits, and for their treatment when ill, but she felt that it was her work with victims of sexual assault that was most important.

Wells's work as a police surgeon was essentially part time: she was paid a retaining fee of £50 per year (later raised to £60 when more women had joined the police force) and was able to arrange her other medical posts accordingly. She advocated the creation of more such part-time appointments in other large cities, where women doctors tended to be consulted on an irregular basis. She kept careful figures concerning each case examined and published several short accounts of her work, stressing particularly her experiences with child victims: *Shield* (December 1937); *Medical Press and Circular* (22 October 1941); *Journal of the Medical Women's Federation* (April 1947); and *BMJ* (6 December 1958, 16 December 1961).

In addition to her work at the babies' hospital (renamed the Duchess of York Hospital for Babies in 1935) and as surgeon to the Manchester city police, Wells was sometimes called upon by the local courts when girls who had appeared before them needed a medical examination before going to homes or special schools. She was the medical officer for Bury grammar school, the Manchester Girls' Remand Home, and Afflecks and Browns Ltd. She was a fellow of the Manchester Medical Society, and a member of both the North of England Obstetrics and Gynaecological Society and the Manchester and District Medico-Legal Association.

Wells retired in 1954, and her replacement at the Duchess of York Hospital was a man, Duncan Macauley. The campaign for the appointment of more designated woman police surgeons continued, as there were still only one or two in England. She worked for a few years as a part-time medical officer to the Manchester Child Welfare Clinic, and lived throughout her long retirement in Cheshire. She died at the home of her daughter, 38 Alumbrook Avenue, Holmes Chapel, on 17 February 1986, from cerebral thrombosis and heart disease, and was survived by her husband and children.   K. D. WATSON

Sources P. D. Mohr, 'Women-run hospitals in Britain: a historical survey focusing on Dr Catherine Chisholm (1878–1952) and the Manchester Babies' Hospital (Duchess of York Hospital)', PhD diss., University of Manchester, 1995 • *Medical Directory* • M. M. Reekie, 'Nesta Helen Wells, MB ChB', *Medical Woman*, 5/2 (summer 1986), 33–4 • Wellcome L., SA/NWF/D15; SA/NWF/D18; SA/MWF/ C66, C67 • b. cert. • m. cert. • d. cert. • N. H. Wells, 'Sexual offences as seen by a woman police surgeon', *BMJ* (6 Dec 1958), 1404–8 • N. H. Wells, 'Ten years as a woman police surgeon', *The Shield* (Dec 1937), 117–22 • S. Jeffreys, *The spinster and her enemies: feminism and sexuality, 1880–1930* (1985)

Archives Wellcome L., Medical Women's Federation MSS

Wealth at death £7802: probate, 2 June 1986, *CGPLA Eng. & Wales*

Wells, Robert (1727/8–1794), printer and bookseller, was born in Dumfries. After schooling at the Dumfries Academy, where he became a fair Latin scholar, and after his apprenticeship as a bookbinder and bookseller, he moved in 1749 at the age of twenty-one to Glasgow. There, in the following year, he married Mary, daughter of the merchant John Rowand; they had five children, including William Charles *Wells, physician, and Helena *Wells, novelist and educationist.

All five of Wells's children were born in Charlestown, South Carolina, where the family had emigrated in 1752, joining Robert's brother, John, a planter, and several of Mary's family. In his new home Robert Wells began as a general merchandiser, going into temporary partnerships with his brothers-in-law before starting his own bookshop and, in 1757, a bindery. In the following year he moved his growing business to 'the great Stationery and Book Shop on the Bay', opposite the town's lower market, where he conducted sales as the vendue master or public auctioneer.

Embedded in the Scottish community centred on the First (Scots) Presbyterian Church and the St Andrew's Society, Wells developed various business ties with fellow Scots, among them John Stuart, who became superintendent of Indian affairs for the southern district in 1763. Despite his multiple engagements Wells never assimilated into the colony. He insisted his sons wear 'blue scotch bonnet[s]' with tartan coats, and that they return to Scotland to be educated. He disparaged plantation life, the low country environment, and the practice of keeping African slaves. Lastly, he consistently took the part of the royal government against the local assembly through his weekly newspaper, the *South Carolina and American General Gazette*, which he began in 1758 with government backing.

While these choices in some ways set Wells apart, they also helped him to rise in South Carolina society. His commission as a marshal of the colony's vice-admiralty court and his appointment as provincial grand secretary of the freemasons (both 1758) were indications of his improving status. Such activities were not what most struck his pastor, however. In his history of South Carolina and Georgia, published in 1779, Alexander Hewat chose to emphasize how Wells had 'introduced many of the most distinguished authors' as a bookseller, as a printer, and lastly in 1774–5 as a co-operative publisher of perhaps twenty reprint editions of belletristic and scientific titles. Among these were plays by Hannah More, novels by Frances Brooke, Henry Mackenzie, and Oliver Goldsmith, poems by James Beattie, and histories and memoirs by Thomas Leland and John Dalrymple, all of which were then also being reprinted in Philadelphia and New York. Wells seems to have acquired limited numbers of unbound copies of such reprints to which he added his own title-pages, so becoming among the most active reprinters in the American colonies.

As one of at least fourteen Scottish-born printers to set up shop in America in the quarter century before the American War of Independence, and one of a dozen or so printers and booksellers substantially involved in the colonial reprint trade, Wells shared his disposition to loyalism with many in the trade at this time. However, his role in South Carolina public affairs and his active engagement in trade with Britain also gave him more reason to leave America after news of the battles of Concord and Lexington arrived late in the spring of 1775. Hoping to return, he left his wife and children behind, though most soon followed him to London. The last of his children to leave Charlestown after a fire consumed the family business in 1778 found her parents and siblings in straitened circumstances. Within two years, however, Robert's fortunes as a Baltic and West Indian merchant in Fleet Street had improved considerably; as a result, the government reduced the family's refugee aid from £150 to £60 per annum.

Wells's prosperity was to be short-lived. The additional loss of all his South Carolina property, the speculations of his Georgia correspondents, and the dishonesty of associates in the West Indies forced him into bankruptcy in 1787. Four years later he was paralysed by his second stroke. Months before Wells's death in 1794, the South Carolina legislature awarded the Wells family some compensation for its confiscated property. By then a son and daughter were living in the West Indies; another son and two daughters were resident in England, far from their Scottish heritage and Carolina upbringing. However, what did survive was the network of personal and professional bonds that had long sustained the family's success. In 1800, South Carolinians, Baltic merchants, loyalists resident in Britain, and old Scottish connections all subscribed to help publish the second novel of Wells's daughter Helena.   DAVID MOLTKE-HANSEN

Sources D. Moltke-Hansen, 'The empire of Scotsman Robert Wells, loyalist South Carolina printer–publisher', MA diss., University of South Carolina, 1984 · L. S. Wells, *The journal of a voyage from Charlestown, S.C. to London undertaken during the American Revolution*, reprinted (1906) · W. C. Wells, *Two essays ... with a memoir of his life* (1818) · C. Gould, 'Robert Wells, colonial Charleston printer', *South Carolina Historical Magazine*, 79 (1978), 23–49 · loyalist claims commission, PRO, AO 12/51 · commissioners of forfeited estates, account book, 1782–3, and general assembly petitions, South Carolina Department of Archives, Columbia, South Carolina · R. Wells, correspondence, Mass. Hist. Soc. · C. Winton, 'The colonial South Carolina book trade', *Proof*, 2 (1972), 71–87
Archives Mass. Hist. Soc.
Wealth at death declared bankrupt 1787

Wells, Samuel (1614–1678), nonconformist minister, was born on 18 August 1614 in St Peter-in-the-East, Oxford, and baptized there on 24 August, the son of William Wells of Oxford. He matriculated from Magdalen Hall, Oxford, on 11 May 1632, graduated BA from New College on 27 June 1633, and proceeded MA from Magdalen Hall on 3 May 1636. He was ordained as deacon in Salisbury on 25 September 1636 as curate at Ashbury, Berkshire, and was for some time a schoolmaster at Wandsworth, Surrey. In 1637 he married Dorothy Doyley of Wiltshire; the couple had ten or eleven children, including a son, William, and daughter, Martha (*d.* 1669). During the civil war Wells served as chaplain to Colonel Charles Essex's regiment in 1642. After his chaplaincy he was made vicar of Wendover, Buckinghamshire, on 9 October 1643. Subsequently he was given, by the Westminster assembly, on 1 July 1646, the lucrative sequestered rectory of Remenham, Berkshire, where, with only about twenty households in the parish, he had little work to do yet £200 per annum of living. Therefore when the House of Lords ordered, on 13 September 1648, that 'Dr Bennet give Institution and

Induction unto Sam. Wells clerk, to the vicarage of Banbury, in the County of Oxon.' (*JHL*, 10, 1647–8, 501), although it carried far less remuneration Wells took this ministry opportunity with enthusiasm and eager expectation.

One of Wells's early accomplishments in Banbury was organizing an anti-regicide campaign in which he, along with eighteen other ministers in Oxfordshire and Northamptonshire, condemned the proceedings of the high court of justice against Charles I. This resulted in a pamphlet, *The humble advice and earnest desires of certain well-affected ministers ... of Banbury in the county of Oxon ... to his Excellency Tho. Fairfax: presented 25 January 1649 by two of the subscribers* (1649). The two presenting subscribers were Wells and John Bayley of Fringford, Oxfordshire. In 1654 Wells, along with John Owen, Thomas Goodwin, and others, was appointed a member of the commission for Oxfordshire to reject incompetent and scandalous ministers. Moreover, the trustees for maintenance of ministers granted an annual augmentation of £30 to his salary. As the Quakers gained greater numbers of converts, including some within Oxfordshire, Wells became affected by this overtly anti-clerical movement. In 1654 he brought charges against Anne Audland, who had called Wells a 'false prophet' and was incarcerated for blaspheming against the Lord's servant. In a letter dated 27 July 1655 Thomas Curtis, a former captain in the parliamentary army, accused Wells of being unnecessarily severe in his dealings with Audland. The same year Wells was reprimanded by a certain Sarah Timms who called him to 'fear the Lord'; in return Timms was imprisoned for six months.

On 20 May 1661 Wells wrote to Richard Baxter enquiring of Baxter's view on the imminent and increased pressure to conform exerted by the Restoration Church of England, so as to 'reduce the publick worship of God to the forme of that Liturgy which was formerly in use in England' (Keeble and Nuttall, 2.15). Eventually, refusing the terms of conformity set forth by the Restoration church settlement, Wells was ejected from his living in November 1662. However, he soon became the leader of the group which, having seceded from the parish church, formed a presbyterian conventicle. He continued to live and minister in Banbury until the Five Mile Act of 1665, which prohibited former parish incumbents from coming within a 5 mile distance of their parishioners, forced him to move to Deddington, Oxfordshire. Although removed from Banbury he wrote weekly letters of encouragement and spiritual counsel to his erstwhile congregation, and in 1669 he was preaching at Adderbury, Bicester, and elsewhere in Oxfordshire. Wells's farewell sermon at Banbury, *The Spiritual Remembrancer*, based on Acts 20: 27 was published in 1676, along with the regular letters to his former flock. *The Spiritual Remembrancer* shows the typical puritan casuistical genre of epistolary counselling and pastoral guidance.

After Charles II issued the indulgence of religion on 15 March 1672, Wells returned to Banbury and, being a man of considerable means, bought a house and took a licence to preach as presbyterian at his residence or that of James Sutton of Banbury, on 20 April 1672. He is said to have kept a cordial relationship with the new incumbent of Banbury, Dr Richard White, maintaining a 'very fair and friendly correspondence' in which White said, 'I pray God bless your Labours in private, and mine in publick'. Wells died in June or July 1678 in Banbury, and was buried there on 7 July. His wife survived him.   PAUL C-H LIM

Sources S. W. [S. Wells], *The spiritual remembrancer* (1676) · *The humble advice and earnest desires of certain well-affected ministers ... of Banbury in the county of Oxon* (1649) · *Calamy rev.* · letter to Baxter, 20 May 1661, DWL, Richard Baxter correspondence, MS 59 [vol. 4, fol. 153] · W. Kennett, *A register and chronicle ecclesiastical and civil* (1728), 896 · *CSP dom.*, 1654, 355 · *JHL*, 10 (1647–8), 501 · A. Beesley, *History of Banbury* (1842), 289–90, 435–6, 451, 464–6, 623–4 · *VCH Oxfordshire*, 10.99, 112 · BL, Add. MS 15670, fol. 132 · will, PRO, PROB 11/357, fol. 395r · *DNB* · *Calendar of the correspondence of Richard Baxter*, ed. N. H. Keeble and G. F. Nuttall, 2 (1991)
Archives DWL, Richard Baxter letters, MS 59
Wealth at death see will, PRO, PROB 11/357, fol. 395r

Wells, Simon of [Simon fitz Robert; Simon de Camera] (*d.* 1207), bishop of Chichester, was probably a Somerset man, the son of Robert of Whatley, who held land of William Fitzjohn's fee in Harptree, Somerset, which was confirmed to Simon by King John in 1201. It is doubtful whether, as has been claimed, he was related to Hugh of Wells, bishop of Lincoln (though the two men were linked professionally), or to Jocelin, bishop of Bath and Wells. He owed the advancement of his career in church and royal service entirely to Archbishop Hubert Walter and the first evidence of him comes about 1192, when Hubert, still bishop of Salisbury, collated to him a Salisbury prebend newly formed out of the churches of Lyme and Halstock. It is in this connection that he is called, in the Salisbury register, Simon Fitzrobert.

Simon attested a number of Hubert's *acta* as archbishop of Canterbury. By 1198 he was archdeacon of Wells, and he obtained the provostship of Beverley in 1199. With his archdeaconry he held the churches of Huish and South Brent in Devon, and as archdeacon he often occurs as the datary of royal documents (the official who organized their issue). He was with King John in Normandy in 1199 and in 1203 during the campaigns against Philip Augustus of France which ended in the loss of the duchy. In 1201 he is recorded as receiving money into the king's chamber from the knights of the archbishopric of Canterbury, thereby giving substance to his title of Simon de Camera, or clerk of the chamber. He was elected bishop of Chichester in early April 1204, being consecrated by Hubert Walter at Westminster on 11 July 1204. The temporalities had been restored by 3 August.

Once he was bishop the royal grants to Simon and his own charters suggest a strong concentration on his pastorate (ordination of vicarages, visitation of monasteries) and on exploiting the material assets of his see—holding the royal farm of Chichester, supervising Chichester mints, building shops round the cathedral cemetery, walling Chichester city, and recovering alienated lands of the see by judgment of his own court. He also received the right to transport marble from Purbeck to Chichester for the repair of his cathedral, thereby showing his interest in the fabric of the building, and also his participation in the architectural aesthetic of the time, which favoured the use of this dark marble against light-coloured stone. His royal service did not immediately cease, for in 1204 he supervised the valuation of Gilbert de l'Aigle's fee, and he was active in the purveyance of supplies for the king's (abortive) Poitevin expedition in 1205, but there is no more evidence of royal service after Hubert Walter's death in July 1205. Bishop Simon died at St Gilles in southern France on 21 August 1207, apparently returning from a pilgrimage to Santiago de Compostela; he left in his will 100 marks towards a chantry for Archbishop Hubert.

HENRY MAYR-HARTING

Sources H. Mayr-Harting, *The bishops of Chichester, 1075–1207: biographical notes and problems* (1963) · H. Mayr-Harting, ed., *The acta of the bishops of Chichester, 1075–1207*, CYS, 56 (1964)

Wells, Sir Thomas Spencer, first baronet (1818–1897), gynaecological surgeon, was born at St Albans, Hertfordshire, on 3 February 1818, the eldest of the four sons and one daughter of builder Joseph William Wells (1794–1856) and his wife, Harriet (d. 1846), daughter of William Wright, of Bermondsey. Wells's formal education began at St Albans Abbey School. On leaving St Albans in 1835, Wells decided on a surgical career, undertaking a year's pupillage with Dr Michael Sadler in Barnsley. Wells followed Sadler on rounds, used his mentor's library, and learned medical bookkeeping and dispensing. Wells then moved to Leeds and was apprenticed to the parish surgeon Mr Marsden. Attending the poor, Wells, still only nineteen, gained substantial surgical experience and assisted in numerous childbirths. He also attended Leeds medical school for lectures and demonstrations, including those of Joseph Garlick, William Hey, and Thomas Pridgin Teale senior. Like many ambitious would-be surgeons, Wells recognized the importance of travelling to hospitals and schools to broaden his education. Despite limited moneys, he went to Trinity College, Dublin, in the summer of 1837 to study with physicians Robert Graves and William Stokes, surgeon Philip Crampton, and ophthalmologist Arthur Jacob.

At Dublin, one of the leading British medical schools, the traditional emphasis on identification of symptoms was giving way to revolutionary changes generated from the Paris clinics, where prognoses and diagnoses were increasingly based on correlations between physical signs and autopsy findings. These French methods helped to elevate the status of surgery just as Wells entered the profession. He absorbed this new approach and in 1839 received recognition for his prize-winning essay on bronchotomy (tracheotomy) delivered at the Dublin Medico-Chirurgical Society.

After two years in Dublin, Wells moved to London to walk the wards of St Thomas's Hospital. During his two years there, he amassed experience in hospital practice and surgery. He was congratulated for completing the best series of post-mortem reports for 1839–40, and in 1841 was admitted as a member of the Royal College of Surgeons.

Sir Thomas Spencer Wells, first baronet (1818–1897), by Rudolph Lehmann, 1884

Wells was enamoured of the London medical environment, but on leaving St Thomas's he still lacked the financial and social resources to acquire a metropolitan appointment. In September 1841 he accepted the Royal Navy post of assistant surgeon, with a guaranteed salary and the opportunity to hone his skills. Wells was dispatched to Britain's main foreign naval hospital in Malta, where he treated a wide range of infectious diseases and injuries, as well as establishing a civilian practice and publishing in Britain's leading medical journals. In 1844 he became a fellow of the Royal College of Surgeons.

Wells left Malta in 1846, and for the next decade led a nomadic life. From mid-1846 until mid-1848 he undertook several voyages aboard HMS *Ceylon*, *Locust*, *Hibernia*, and *Trafalgar*—and compiled reports that were published in British medical journals. On shore leave Wells reinforced his professional profile by presenting foreign findings to his London colleagues. In 1848 he was promoted to surgeon and granted two months' leave in Paris to study the treatment of gunshot wounds. At this point his career took a noticeable turn toward civilian practice.

Following his initial Parisian stint, Wells requested a further six months' break for continental travel. In Paris he attended Dupuytren's and Malgaigne's clinics and became interested in the work of Bernard and Magendie, especially in pathology and ophthalmology. Wells also visited Vienna and other leading centres of clinical and laboratory medicine. Shortly afterwards the navy again granted him leave, this time to accompany the ailing marquess of Northampton to Egypt, where Wells became interested in malaria. By then he was clearly looking beyond the navy and towards a more comfortable London existence. Nevertheless, in 1851 he was commissioned as surgeon and sanitary officer to HMS *Modeste* with the Mediterranean Fleet. Again, Wells made the best of the opportunity and further developed his interest in public health, becoming a strong proponent of quarantine and vaccination.

By 1853, however, Wells had tired of naval life. On 16 July that year he married Elizabeth Lucas Wright, daughter of James Wright, a solicitor; they had five daughters and a son, Arthur Spencer Wells, private secretary to the chancellor of the exchequer from 1893 to 1895. Ambitious and accomplished, Wells wanted to return to London permanently. Furthermore, his health was poor, and he obtained leave to visit mineral springs in Germany. On his return to London he continued to receive half pay from the navy while establishing a private practice in prestigious Grosvenor Square, where he at first concentrated on ophthalmic surgery. What Wells still lacked at this time was one of the highly desirable hospital appointments that usually guaranteed metropolitan success. Wells, it appears, lacked the necessary social connections. However, in 1854, he received two lesser, but crucial, appointments: he became attached to the Grosvenor Place school of medicine (affiliated with St George's Hospital) as lecturer in surgery and gained a position as surgeon to the dispensary of the Samaritan Free Hospital for Women and Children.

The Samaritan was Wells's making. There, over the next two decades, Wells developed a reputation as Britain's leading 'women's surgeon', as well as helping to develop gynaecology as a distinct medical specialism. The Samaritan was one of the first generation of small hospitals that specialized in the treatment of women. They were commonly started as shoestring affairs and, in this instance, the hospital had no in-patient facilities. Wells's professional standing enabled him to experiment, carrying out innovative surgery that would eventually place the Samaritan among the world's leading gynaecological institutions. In addition, he became editor of the *Medical Times and Gazette*, a position that further enhanced his professional standing.

At this juncture, then, it seems curious that Wells should have volunteered for a civilian posting with the army in the Crimean War. Perhaps an annual salary of £1500 appealed to a young man whose other positions were chiefly honorary. He and his wife went initially to the large hospital in Smyrna and later to Renkioi in the Dardanelles. Their first child, Helen, was born there in 1855. This sojourn was curtailed in April 1856, when the British Admiralty discovered that while still receiving half pay Wells was in full army employ. Ordered back to London to prepare for duty, he resigned.

During his time at the military front line Wells had come to rethink the limits of surgery. He now saw the abdomen as operable. In civilian practice, abdominal surgery was largely viewed as tantamount to murder, yet in battle the abdomen was frequently ripped open, and the surgical attempts to save lives sometimes succeeded. Wells returned to the Samaritan with a new confidence in the potential of abdominal surgery and the conviction that new approaches could be applied to the treatment of women.

Wells's place in medical history is most securely attached to his pioneering work in abdominal surgery, particularly in the development of ovariotomy, an operation that entailed removing diseased ovaries and Fallopian tubes. While a handful of surgeons had previously attempted this dangerous procedure with minimal success, Wells placed it within the surgical canon. Although ovariotomy was highly controversial, in a small hospital like the Samaritan Wells had greater autonomy than would have been the case in one of the larger, more hierarchical teaching hospitals. On his return from the Crimea he obtained his own hospital beds. The Samaritan was beginning to draw attention from leading consultants such as Sir William Fergusson and Wells was willing to demonstrate his techniques to them. Enormous ovarian cysts had been beyond the surgical scope and were frequently treated palliatively by repeated tapping. Wells sought a cure and turned to ovariotomy, a move that won him the backing of James Young Simpson, the renowned Edinburgh obstetrician who himself had already attempted ovariotomy.

Wells had witnessed his first ovariotomy while assisting Isaac Baker Brown at the Middlesex Hospital in 1854. The patient died, and Wells was discouraged, but nevertheless he attempted his own ovariotomy in December 1857. The operation was disappointing because the consulting surgeons Wells had gathered to observe and assist persuaded him to abandon the procedure when they discovered the extent of adnexal masses. That woman died from the cyst and on autopsy Wells decided the tumour would have been operable. He improved his technique, and shortly afterwards in February 1858 a patient of his survived the operation. This launched Wells on a series of operations that would over three decades establish ovariotomy as an acceptable procedure. He utilized the *Medical Times and Gazette* to publicize his own and other cases, applying cumulative medical statistics to demonstrate that mortality rates resulting from the surgery were declining and that ovariotomy was a justifiable, life-saving procedure. Wells was meticulous about presenting his failures as well as his successes. By 1880 Wells had completed his thousandth ovariotomy and had made an immense contribution to the development of gynaecology.

Although ovariotomy continued to be a controversial procedure, it came to be used as a 'cure' for a variety of female maladies. By the 1870s and 1880s some surgeons began to carry out oöphorectomies, the removal of healthy ovaries, in the belief that these could cure uterine fibromata, dysmenorrhoea, and 'menstrual epilepsy' (Moscucci, 157). Opponents argued that this led to the 'unsexing' of women, as it 'deprived women of their true essence and prevented them from fulfilling their proper role in society as mothers and moral leaders' (Moscucci, 159). Wells, too, denounced oöphorectomy, claiming in 1891 that 'The oöphorectomists of civilization touch hands with the aboriginal spayers of New Zealand'

(Moscucci, 158). He was also vociferously opposed to the salpingo-oöphorectomy (removal of the ovaries and fallopian tube) devised by Robert Lawson Tait. The two were bitter rivals and the dispute over 'Tait's operation' did nothing to help matters; it also divided the medical profession for many years.

Wells also maintained his interest in public health. In London he pleaded for legislation to govern waste disposal, water supply, and housing. He also became a prominent proponent of cremation as a more efficient, hygienic method of disposing of the dead. In surgery, he adopted Listerian antisepsis from 1878.

Although Wells performed controversial surgery and supported such causes as cremation, he was none the less a man of the establishment. In 1871 he became a member of the council of the Royal College of Surgeons, was the Hunterian professor in 1877, vice-president in 1879, and president in 1883, when he gave the Hunterian oration. In Ireland in 1886 he was made an honorary fellow of the King and Queen's College of Physicians and of the Royal College of Surgeons. Leiden and Bologna universities presented him with honorary medical degrees. Wells, who was acutely mindful of social as well as professional conventions, was awarded a baronetcy in 1883. From 1863 to 1896 he served as surgeon to Queen Victoria's household. Wells's publications include *Diseases of the Ovaries* (1865), *Diagnosis and Surgical Treatment of Abdominal Tumours* (1885), *Surgery Past, Present and Future* (1872), *The Revival of Ovariotomy …* (1884), and *Modern Abdominal Surgery: with an Appendix on the Castration of Women* (1891).

In addition to his house in London, Wells owned a country house with substantial gardens at Golder's Hill, North End, Hampstead, and became an accomplished horseman. He died from an apoplectic fit at the Hotel du Cap d'Antibes, near Cannes, on 31 January 1897. Wells's body was cremated at Woking and his ashes were buried in Brompton cemetery. JANE ELIOT SEWELL

Sources J. A. Shepherd, *Spencer Wells: the life and work of a Victorian surgeon* (1965) · F. M. L. Thompson, *St Alban's School in the abbey*, Abbey Papers, Fraternity of the Friends of Saint Alban's Abbey, 2 [n.d.] · J. J. Keevil, J. L. S. Coulter, and C. Lloyd, *Medicine and the navy, 1200–1900*, 4: *1815–1900* (1963) · *DNB* · F. G. Parsons, *The history of St Thomas's Hospital*, 3 (1936) · A. W. Oxford, *The history of the Samaritan Free Hospital* (1931) · O. Moscucci, *The science of woman: gynaecology and gender in England, 1800–1929* (1990) · M. Lewis, *The navy in transition, 1814–1864: a social history* (1965) · Z. Cope, *The Royal College of Surgeons of England: a history* (1959) · Burke, *Peerage* (1894) · m. cert. · d. cert.

Archives PRO, Admiralty archives · Royal College of Surgeons, Edinburgh, corresp. with James Young Simpson · St Alban's Abbey School

Likenesses R. Liebreich, bust, 1879, priv. coll. · R. Liebreich, marble bust, exh. RA 1879, Royal Naval Hospital, Haslar · plaster statuette, exh. RA 1879, RCS Eng. · A. P. Tilt, group portrait, oils, 1882 (*The Baroness Burdett-Coutt's garden party*), repro. in Shepherd, *Spencer Wells*, p. 117 · R. Lehmann, oils, 1884, RCS Eng. [*see illus.*] · mezzotint, 1898 (after R. Lehmann), Wellcome L. · Barraud, photograph, Wellcome L. · Beynon and Co., group lithograph (*Buildings and famous alumni of St. Thomas's Hospital*), Wellcome L. · H. J. Brooks, group portrait, oils (*Council of the Royal College of Surgeons of England, 1884–85*), RCS Eng. · S. J. Solomon, oils, Wellcome L. · lithograph (after

R. Lehmann), Wellcome L. · portrait, St Thomas's Medical School, London

Wealth at death £56,377 4s. 4d.: resworn probate, March 1898, *CGPLA Eng. & Wales* (1897)

Wells, William (1729–1805), shipbuilder, was born at Canister House, Chislehurst, Kent, the eldest son of Abraham Wells (*c.*1690–1755), also a shipbuilder, and his wife, Elizabeth, daughter of Samuel Buttall of Topsham, Devon. One of a long line associated with shipbuilding, he was a direct descendant of John Wells (*d.* 1635), paymaster of his majesty's navy. Little is known of William Wells's early years, but it seems likely that he would have acquired the experience of management and shipbuilding skills through entry into the family shipbuilding yards of Rotherhithe and Deptford, both of which were under his father's ownership. In 1758 William took control of the Deptford yard, which he managed in partnership with his brother John. When Abraham Wells died in 1755 the partnership was extended to encompass the Rotherhithe yard with the Deptford yard sold to William Dedman & Co. In due course William also inherited the family estates of Canister House and further lands at Holme and Glatton in Huntingdonshire, these latter sited close to Hinchinbrooke, owned by the fourth earl of Sandwich. The business partnership now expanded to include a John Hallett (*b.* 1744), a banker and navy agent who was also associated with ships built for the East India trade.

With William Wells the clear driving force, contracts were signed for the building of numerous ships for various individual charterers to the East India Company. Between 1769 and 1773 the Rotherhithe yard, which was considerably expanded and became one of the largest on the Thames, saw the annual launch of at least one new East Indiaman. In addition, though there is no evidence to verify this, it is probable that many merchant vessels were built for the West Indian, Baltic, and other trades. The partnership with Hallett appears to have been disbanded in the mid-1770s with the two Wells brothers continuing to trade as John and William Wells.

This partnership proved even more successful. A further arrangement with East India Company charterers resulted in the launch of twenty-one ships during the period 1777 to 1792. At the time of the partnership with Hallett a number of ships had also been constructed for the Admiralty, these including one of the largest 74-gun ships built for the navy, the *Invincible*, which was launched in 1765. Doubtless further ships would have been built for the navy upon the outset of the American War of Independence (1775) but for William Wells's determination to receive a price higher than laid down by the Navy Board. Obviously a more profitable arrangement than the board's standard fee of £17 10s. per ton existed with those chartering to the East India Company. Wells's stance eventually came to the attention of the House of Commons, which recommended that a higher rate should be set, so encouraging private yards, chief among them Wells's, to undertake contract work for the navy at a time when a desperate demand existed for warships.

In spearheading this campaign, Wells was ideally situated, being a close friend of the fourth earl of Sandwich, first lord of the Admiralty (1771–82). Following a lengthy period of negotiation, a higher sum was eventually established, with Wells contracting for three 74-gun warships, the *Terrible*, *Thunderer*, and *Swiftsure*, launched in the years 1783, 1785, and 1787. In the following year William's son, **John Wells** (1761–1848), shipbuilder and politician, entered into the shipbuilding partnership. John was the second of three sons born to William and his wife, Susanna (*d.* 1810), daughter of James Neave and sister of Sir R. Neave, baronet, governor of the Bank of England (1780). Following the death of the elder John Wells in 1794, the firm came under the control of William and John junior, with William inheriting John's estate at Bickley, Kent, purchased in 1759 and considerably improved with the building of a new mansion, Bickley Hall, designed by Robert Mylne (demolished 1963), in 1780. John and William entered into partnership with the Perrys of Blackwall in 1798, this arrangement also coinciding with a series of complex land deals, mostly involving John, who had now emerged as a property developer in the Blackwall area. On the north bank of the Thames, the new shipbuilding partnership traded as Perry, Wells, and Green while that on the Rotherhithe side traded as Wells, Perry, and Green. Although Philip Banbury indicates that the Rotherhithe yard ceased to build after 1798, this seems incorrect, since the partnership continued to pay rates until 1805. However, owing to age and increasing infirmity, William Wells was less committed to the enterprise, while John's interest had always been more limited.

William Wells died in 1805. Thereafter the family's influence within the partnership sharply declined, John attending just one day a week to deal with the political business of the firm. In 1810 even this connection ceased, with John removing himself from the partnership, the Blackwall yard becoming Wigram and Green and the Rotherhithe yard apparently sold. In 1812 John became high sheriff of Kent, and in 1820 and in 1826 he was elected one of the two members of parliament for Maidstone. A high tory, he opposed Roman Catholic emancipation in a number of speeches made before the house. John Wells died in 1848. William Wells was survived by two other sons: Thomas, an admiral in the navy, whose early promotions had been eased by his father's friendship with the earl of Sandwich; and William *Wells, who used part of his father's fortune to become a patron of the arts and owner of a fine estate near Penshurst, Kent.

PHILIP MacDOUGALL

Sources P. Banbury, *Shipbuilders of the Thames and Medway* (1971) · E. L. S. Horsburgh, *Bromley, Kent* (1929) · E. A. Webb, G. W. Miller, and J. Beckwith, eds., *The history of Chislehurst: its church, manors, and parish* (1899) · N. Dews, *The history of Deptford*, 2nd edn (1884) · parish register, Deptford, St Nicholas · Deptford parish rate book, Lewisham Library, Lewisham, Lewisham local studies and archives · Rotherhithe parish rate book, Lewisham Library, Lewisham, Lewisham local studies and archives
Likenesses S. W. Reynolds, engraving (after H. Edridge, 1798), priv. coll. · engraving (John Wells; after unknown portrait), repro. in Horsburgh, *Bromley, Kent*

Wealth at death estates in Huntingdon, Bromley, and Chislehurst

Wells, William (1768–1847), shipbuilder and art collector, was born at Canister House, Chislehurst, Kent, the second of the four children of William *Wells (1729–1805), shipbuilder, and Susanna Neave (*d.* 1810). His ancestors had been connected with shipbuilding from the seventeenth century. Wells loved the sea and cultivated a rollicking sea captain's walk, even though he only once commanded a ship, on a voyage to China in 1794–5. Joseph Farington, the noted diarist, explained that it was not lack of opportunity that led Wells to give up his career on the high seas, but family obligations—he was needed to supervise the building of battleships at his family's shipyards at the Blackwall docks during the Napoleonic wars and to supervise their investment in Meux brewery. Wells sold his shipbuilding interests in 1811 and retired with his wife, Mary Hughes (*d.* 1818), to Redleaf, Penshurst, Kent, where he spent his time gardening, hunting, and adding to his art collection. He was an active member of the Church of England.

Wells inherited paintings from his grandfather, who had commissioned marine subjects from Charles Brooking, and from his father (whose portrait was engraved by Sir Joshua Reynolds). He added a large selection of old masters, on which he spent over £18,000. He began to add modern pictures to his collection after his retirement, purchasing paintings directly from William Mulready, Thomas Webster, and David Wilkie. Most of his attention, however, was directed at Edwin Landseer, from whom he bought almost thirty pictures, and at the young landscape painter Frederick Richard Lee, who provided nearly fifty. Wells selected paintings which were compatible with what he already owned: for instance, his animal scenes by Landseer harmonized with the bovine and equine subjects he had acquired by such Dutch seventeenth-century artists as Cuyp, Wouwerman, and Berchem, while Lee's untroubled landscapes blended in with the Hobbemas and Claude Lorrains which were already in place at Redleaf. His insistence on measuring his contemporary purchases against his old masters rankled with John Constable. The artist vented his frustration in a letter written to his friend C. R. Leslie on 2 March 1833: 'I had, on Friday, a long visit from Mr. Wells alone. He saw hundreds of my things—I sincerely believe nothing amongst them made any impression upon him or did they come into his rules, or whims, of the art' (*Constable's Correspondence*, 94).

Wells shared many of the biases of his class in preferring art that did not deviate too far from the traditional norm. A trustee of the National Gallery and a director of the British Institution, he preferred artists such as Landseer, who had trained himself to model his habits after those of the upper classes. Landseer became a permanent fixture at Redleaf, where his patron had a special painting seat constructed for him in his garden. Landseer's deeply toned paintings were more in accord with Wells's taste than anything in Constable's studio, or in Turner's for that matter. Wells told Constable that he thought 'Turner was "quite gone"—lost and possessed by a yellow which he could not see himself, therefore could not avoid' (*Constable's Correspondence*, 97). Yet the fact that Wells collected the works of contemporary artists at all indicates that he was sensitive to the emerging dynamism of the early-Victorian middle class which was beginning to make its mark in matters of taste, politics, and finance. Childless, Wells died at Redleaf on 7 August 1847, aged seventy-nine years, leaving his estate to his grandnephew, William *Wells (1818–1889), whose agricultural experiments depleted most of his fortune. Following his death, Wells's collection was sold at Christies on 10–14 May 1890.

DIANNE SACHKO MACLEOD

Sources priv. coll. · private information (2004) · *GM*, 2nd ser., 29 (1848), 87 · *Art Union*, 9 (1847), 335 · *The Farington diary*, ed. J. Greig, 8 vols. (1922–8) · Burke, *Gen. GB* (1964) · *John Constable's correspondence*, ed. R. B. Beckett, 3, Suffolk RS, 8 (1965), 94, 97 · P. Banbury, *Shipbuilders of the Thames and Medway* (1971) · Wells file, Kent County Library and Museums Service · d. cert. · CKS, Redleaf estate papers · census returns, 1841
Archives CKS, file · CKS, Redleaf estate MSS · NRA, priv. coll. | V&A, Landseer corresp.
Likenesses H. Edridge, pen and wash drawing, *c.*1800, Antique Collectors' Club, Woodbridge, Suffolk; repro. in H. L. Mallalieu, *Understanding watercolours* (1895)

Wells, William (1818–1889), agriculturist and politician, was born on 15 March 1818, the eldest son of Captain William Wells RN, of Holme, Huntingdonshire, and Elizabeth, daughter of John Joshua *Proby, first earl of Carysfort. After being educated at Harrow School he went to Balliol College, Oxford, where he matriculated on 16 June 1836 and graduated BA (1839) and MA (1842). He then entered the army, holding a commission in the 1st Life Guards.

In 1826 Wells inherited an estate of 8000 acres in the fens. He is chiefly remembered for his efforts as a practical agriculturist to improve and develop this area, and especially for the draining of Whittlesea Mere. This was a shallow sheet of stagnant water, a little more than 1000 acres in extent, surrounded by another 2000 acres of bog and marsh. The drainage of the mere was begun by Wells in 1851. In the following year, as a result of heavy rain, the mere flooded on 12 November. All the water was, however, discharged a second time with the help of an 'Appold' centrifugal pump, which Wells was one of the first to utilize for land drainage. By the autumn of 1853 the bed of the mere was under cultivation. The surrounding peatland proved more intractable, however, and it was found necessary to go through a process of warping, or overlaying with fertile soil. This work had hardly begun when Wells contributed his account of the draining operations to the *Journal of the Royal Agricultural Society*, in 1860. On 7 December 1854 Wells married Louisa, daughter of Francis Wemyss-Charteris-Douglas, seventh earl of Wemyss.

The operations at Whittlesey were brought to an end about 1866, after fifteen years of incessant labour. Much of the cultivation of the reclaimed land, and most of that of the two home farms reserved by Wells, was performed by means of steam power. With the object of encouraging the intelligent use of steam for agricultural purposes, Wells offered annual prizes, beginning in 1864, at the

meetings of the Peterborough Agricultural Society; these were awarded to the drivers of agricultural portable steam engines, for skill and care in the management of the machines, coupled with a clear record with regard to accidents.

Wells became a member of council of the Royal Agricultural Society in 1861. In December 1862 he was a member of the chemical committee, of which he was elected chairman in 1866. This post he continued to hold up to the time of his death. He was president of the Royal Agricultural Society in 1880, and of the Shire Horse Society in 1885. He represented Beverley in parliament from 1852 to 1857, and Peterborough from 1868 to 1874. He was justice of the peace for Kent and Huntingdonshire, and high sheriff of the latter county in 1876.

Wells died at his London residence, 12 North Audley Street, Grosvenor Square, on 1 May 1889, and was buried at Holme, Huntingdonshire, on 6 May. He had no sons and was succeeded by his brother, Grenville Granville Wells.

ERNEST CLARKE, *rev.* JOHN MARTIN

Sources *The Times* (6 May 1889) · *Annual Register* (1889), 144 · *Agricultural Gazette* (6–13 May 1889), 415, 452 · *Mark Lane Express and Agricultural Journal*, 688 · *Bell's Weekly Messenger* (13 May 1889) · *Journal of the Royal Agricultural Society of England*, 2nd ser., 25 (1889), xlviii · Burke, *Gen. GB* · Walford, *County families* · Foster, *Alum. Oxon.* · d. cert. · *CGPLA Eng. & Wales* (1889)
Wealth at death £96,681 12*s.* 5*d.*: probate, 28 Sept 1889, *CGPLA Eng. & Wales*

Wells, William Charles (1757–1817), physician, the second son of Robert *Wells (1727/8–1794), and Mary Wells, who had emigrated from Scotland, was born in Charles Town, South Carolina, on 24 May 1757. The author Helena *Wells (1761?–1824) was his sister. His father, who had settled in Carolina in 1753, was a printer and bookseller. A fervent loyalist, he made his son wear a tartan coat and blue bonnet, so that he might be known to be a Scot at heart and not an American. Wells was sent to school at Dumfries in 1768, and then went to the University of Edinburgh in 1770, but in 1771 returned to Carolina, and was apprenticed to Alexander Garden, a physician and botanist in Charles Town, with whom he remained until the American War of Independence broke out in 1775. Wells then returned to Britain and began regular medical studies at Edinburgh, where he lived until 1778. He attended William Hunter's lectures on anatomy and midwifery in London, and became a student of St Bartholomew's Hospital. He went to the Netherlands in 1779 as surgeon to a Scottish regiment in the Dutch service, but resigned, owing to a disagreement with the colonel. He studied medicine at Leiden in 1780 for three months, and prepared a thesis, 'De frigore', before graduating MD at Edinburgh on 24 July 1780.

Wells returned to Carolina in 1781 to look after his father's property, and went from there in December 1782 to St Augustine, East Florida, where he put together a press, which he had brought in pieces, and published a weekly newspaper. He was also a volunteer captain, and acted, from his recollection of Garrick's performance of the role, the part of Lusignan in *Zara*.

Wells returned to England in May 1784, and, after three months in Paris in 1785, borrowed money to set up a practice in London. He passed several years without receiving a fee, and at the end of ten years had an income of £250. He was admitted a licentiate of the Royal College of Physicians in 1788, was elected physician to the Finsbury Dispensary in 1789, and held office until 11 December 1799. In 1795 he was elected assistant physician to St Thomas's Hospital and in 1800 physician, an office which he held until his death. Wells published in 1792 *An Essay upon Single Vision with Two Eyes*, and in November 1793 he was elected FRS, becoming a fellow of the Royal Society of Edinburgh in 1814.

Wells published widely, including *An Essay on Dew* in 1814, for which he received the Rumford medal of the Royal Society, and in 1818, an *Account of a Female of the White Race of Mankind, Part of whose Skin Resembles that of a Negro*, in which he has been thought to anticipate Darwin.

The largest annual income Wells received was £764. He never had a bank account and left about £600, including his books, furniture, and gold medal. Wells's struggle to build a practice meant that he lived very frugally, but he managed to maintain a keen interest in his research. Astley Cooper considered him to be 'ingenious but irritable' (Cooper, 307). Wells had a difference with the College of Physicians, the grounds of which he explained in a published letter to Lord Kenyon, and never became a fellow. However, Matthew Baillie, David Pitcairn, and William Lister, all fellows of the college, were his friends, and they helped him as much as was possible in practice.

Wells died of hydrothorax on 18 September 1817 in London, at his lodgings in Serjeants' Inn, Chancery Lane, and was buried in St Bride's, Fleet Street, where a tablet was erected to his memory. He was unmarried. During his final illness he dictated to his friend Samuel Patrick an autobiography, which was published with his chief works in 1818.   NORMAN MOORE, *rev.* CATHERINE BERGIN

Sources Munk, *Roll* · R. W. Innes Smith, *English-speaking students of medicine at the University of Leyden* (1932) · E. Bartlett, *A brief sketch of the life, character and writings of William Charles Wells* (1849) · F. A. Willins and T. E. Keys, *Cardiac classics* (1941) · F. G. Parsons, *The history of St Thomas's Hospital*, 3 (1936) · F. L. Pleadwell, 'That remarkable philosopher and physician, Wells of Charleston', *Annals of Medical History*, new ser., 6 (1934), 128–42 · B. B. Cooper, *The life of Sir Astley Cooper*, 1 (1843), 307 · J. H. S. Green, 'William Charles Wells (1757–1817)', *Nature*, 179 (1957), 997–9
Wealth at death approx. £600: Parsons, *History*

Wells, William Frederick (*bap.* 1764, *d.* 1836), watercolour painter, was baptized at Chislehurst, Kent, on 24 April 1764, the son of William Wells (*d.* in or after 1815) and his wife, Ann (*d.* 1815). He was educated at Robert Harper's school in Queen Anne Street, London—premises later owned by J. M. W. Turner—and by the age of eleven he was being taught drawing by either John James Barralet or his brother John Melchior Barralet. Wells married his wife, Mary (*d.* 1807), about 1786 and lived for a period in Northampton, where four of his nine children (three sons and six daughters) were born; two children died in infancy. By 1795 he had returned to London and was living at 34 Mount Street. In 1796 he published *A New and Compendious*

Treatise of Anatomy, 'designed principally for … ladies'. A set of studies of female heads, by Wells, was engraved by George Townley Stubbs in 1800; between 1802 and 1805 Wells and the artist John Laporte made a series of seventy-two etchings after drawings by Thomas Gainsborough; and about 1809–10 Wells etched the Revd Joseph Wilkinson's views of the Lake District.

Wells was a successful drawing-master; his pupils included two of the daughters of the duke of Clarence (later William IV). In 1792 a former pupil, Robert Ker Porter, introduced Wells to Turner, who was then aged about seventeen, and the two became intimate friends. Wells's daughter Clara recalled: 'Turner loved my father with a son's affection—to me he was an elder brother' (Hamilton, 41). It was Wells who, in 1806, suggested to Turner the idea for the *Liber Studiorum*, which Turner began at the cottage that Wells owned at Knockholt in Kent. Wells travelled extensively, his pictures including English, Scottish, and Welsh scenes; after the peace of Amiens, in 1802, which made it possible to travel abroad again, he went on a sketching tour of Norway, Sweden, and Denmark, an undertaking which was exceptional at the time.

Wells was 'a sound though not brilliant painter' (Hardie, 3.132); his drawings were nearly all landscapes in the tradition of Claude, and show a feeling for nature but his work is marred by poorly drawn figure groups. The Victoria and Albert Museum holds four of his works, two signed W. F. Wells. Wells is more significant as the instigator, in 1804, of the Society of Painters in Water Colours, which he founded in an effort to raise the status of watercolour painting, since drawings in the medium were poorly presented at Royal Academy exhibitions. He served from 1806 to 1807 as its second president, but resigned from the society in 1813, when its exhibition began to include oil paintings. In all Wells exhibited ninety-one pictures with the society (thirty-seven of Scandinavian scenes) and, between 1795 and 1813, forty-two drawings at the Royal Academy. His pictures were priced from 2 to 15 guineas.

In 1813 Wells was appointed the first drawing-master for the East India Company's cadets at Addiscombe College, near Croydon in Surrey; it was said that he had difficulty in controlling his students. Portraits of Wells from middle age show a round-faced, genial man, clean-shaven, his domed head nearly bald. The Italian poet Ugo Foscolo wrote that he had seen Wells in a blue overcoat, *habillé en dandy* (Wheeler, *Old Water-Colour Society*, 1971, 18). Highly hospitable, Wells frequently hosted parties, often fancy dress ones. The Revd Robert Finch recorded in his diary that he had 'Conversed upon the subject of Twelfth Night at Wells's. He [Wells] will support the characters of a Chinese Mandarin, Mr. Noodle or Doodle, and a Beau of Fashion' (Wheeler, *Old Water-Colour Society*, 1971, 14). Wells also gave music lessons and played the piano and the 'harmonica' (or musical glasses).

Wells moved from 33 York Buildings to a house on Mitcham Common in 1819. In 1829 he was commissioned by Finch to do a series of drawings of English scenery (now mostly lost), and in 1832 he made a sketching tour of Jersey. He died, at his home, on 16 November 1836 and was buried in Mitcham churchyard. To the elder of his sons he left only 5s. and the hope 'that he would see the error of his ways'; each of Wells's three surviving daughters was bequeathed £100 by Turner on his death in 1851.

SIMON FENWICK

Sources J. M. Wheeler, *The family and friends of William Frederick Wells* (privately printed, 1970) · J. M. Wheeler, 'William Frederick Wells', *Old Water-Colour Society's Club*, 46 (1971), 9–24 · J. M. Wheeler, 'William Frederick Wells: postscript to the article on Wells that appeared in the 1971 volume', *Old Water-Colour Society's Club*, 51 (1976), 45–7 · M. Hardie, *Water-colour painting in Britain*, ed. D. Snelgrove, J. Mayne, and B. Taylor, 3 vols. (1966–8) · B. Long, 'William Frederick Wells', *Old Water-Colour Society's Club*, 13 (1935–6), 1–9 · Bankside Gallery, London, Royal Watercolour Society MSS · J. Hamilton, *Turner: a life* (1997)
Archives priv. coll. | Bankside Gallery, London, Royal Watercolour Society MSS · Bodl. Oxf., Finch MSS
Likenesses Barralet, pencil drawing, 1775, repro. in Wheeler, *Family and friends* · Barralet, watercolour drawing, c.1780 · W. Sherlock senior, portrait, 1806 · H. P. Briggs, oils, c.1814 · G. R. Ward, pencil drawing, 1836, V&A; repro. in Long, 'William Frederick Wells' · Mrs G. R. Ward, portrait on ivory, 1836

Wells, William Nathan [Jinky] (1868–1953), morris dancer and musician, was born on 30 January 1868 at Mill Arches, Weald, Bampton, Oxfordshire, the illegitimate elder son of Sarah Ann Taylor (1849–1932). Born into a complex of interrelated morris-dancing families, within his own community he was known as Jingy, but became known universally among morris dancers as Jinky Wells. His mother being in service, he spent his childhood with his grandmother, whose father, second husband, and sons all danced the morris. He had eight years' schooling in Bampton (five at a private school), and after four years doing casual work in the village, spent two years with his mother in London. His private schooling and London experience gave him wider appreciation and ability than his fellows, but his working life was spent doing odd jobs, including growing and selling vegetables, acting as scrap merchant, and delivering newspapers.

Wells returned to Bampton in 1887 and was dragooned into being the Fool at the morris dancers' traditional Whitsun performance—clearing room for them, entertaining between dances, dancing jigs, and collecting money. He filled this role for a decade, although for one year illness rendered him blind. The sight in one eye recovered, but blindness afflicted him again in later life. About 1892 he married Ellen, daughter of Charles Shewry (a descendant of a musician for the Bampton dancers), of Buckland, Berkshire; two sons and one daughter were born in the next six years.

From 1897, in a typical manifestation of his eccentricity, Wells toured local towns and villages at Whitsuntide as a one-man morris, in Fool's costume, simultaneously dancing and playing his fiddle. This earned good money—£1 a day—but sometimes he had to endure indignities, as when in Witney a university student held him off the ground by his earlobes. Wells, a small, wiry man, was helpless until he explained himself and was rewarded with 5s.

About 1899 (he gives contradictory dates) Wells became fiddler for the team. One story of the event has the previous musician breaking his fiddle accidentally, whereupon, being exasperated by the dancers' drinking and fighting, he went home with relief, leaving Wells to step in. Wells himself was often equally aggrieved by his dancers' attitudes, and twenty years later fell out with them in turn. Instead of ending his involvement with the morris, however, he formed a rival team, which first danced in 1927. This was initially a youths' side, with costumes made entirely by Wells and his wife. Although the old team continued at first, its appearances after 1933 were sporadic, while Wells's team survived, and he increased their repertory of dances.

During Wells's stewardship a revival of the dance form took place nationally, to which he himself contributed greatly. In 1909 Cecil Sharp encountered him in Bampton and invited him to his lodgings at Stow on the Wold, where Wells demonstrated some dances. Sharp had further meetings with Wells and travelled to Bampton to see the whole team dance. As most teams had stopped dancing in the nineteenth century, Sharp rarely saw a full team. He published the Bampton dances, but warned his colleagues that the dancing there was 'degenerate'; perhaps because it differed from the Headington Quarry style which he promoted as the norm, perhaps because he was unused to the natural variation in a full team. Moreover, Wells did not identify strongly with Sharp's ideals. He publicized his team's claim to be the 'oldest' in a letter to the *Daily News* in 1910, much reprinted; and continued to perform for Mary Neal's rival organization after her and Sharp's public estrangement, including performances at the Globe, London, and Reading regatta.

Wells stopped playing regularly in 1948, but, though wheelchair-bound, emerged to play a few tunes in later years. The non-standard pitch of his fiddle, and his habit of humming as he played, were the despair of sound engineers who recorded him; but he is one of just a few traditional dance musicians of his time to be recorded. He died on 27 November 1953 at his home, 18 Fox Close, Bampton, and was buried at his parish church.

MICHAEL HEANEY

Sources private information (2004) · K. Chandler, *Morris dancing at Bampton until 1914* (1983) · *William Wells, 1868–1953: morris dancer, fiddler and fool* (1957) · *English Dance and Song*, 18/4 (1954), 115–16 · *Constant Billy: music and memories of a morris man II: William Wells*, Folktracks, FSA–90–084, 1975 [cassette recording] · 'Writings of "Jinky" Wells', *Folk Music Journal*, 2 (1970–74), 3–11 · K. Chandler, *Morris dancing in the south midlands, 1660–1900* (1993) · R. Judge, 'Cecil Sharp and Morris, 1906–1909', *Folk Music Journal*, 8 (2001–5), 195–228 · d. cert. · 'Revival of the morris', *Daily News* (4 June 1910)
Archives FILM Morris Ring Archive, *Traditional dance sides*, film 26 · Vaughan Williams Memorial Library, London, *Bampton traditional morris dancers*, 1936, film 25 | SOUND BL NSA, performance recording
Likenesses C. J. Sharp, photograph, 1911, Vaughan Williams Memorial Library, London, mo/Bam/1948, 10977 · W. Rothenstein, pencil drawing, 1931, Cecil Sharp House, London · E. M. Bateman, watercolour, c.1935, Cecil Sharp House, London · photograph, c.1946, repro. in *English Dance and Song*, cover · photograph, c.1946, repro. in *William Wells, 1868–1953*, frontispiece · J. J. Clarke, photograph, 1948, Vaughan Williams Memorial Library, London,

mo/Bam/1948, 10538 · F. R. Maddison, photograph, 1948, priv. coll.

Wells, William Thomas [called Bombardier Billy Wells] (1887–1967), boxer, was born on 31 August 1887 at 250 Cable Street, Stepney, London, the eldest of five brothers, and one of nine children of the musician William Thomas Wells (b. 1862) and his wife, Emily Rhoda Farrier (b. 1867), a laundress. Both parents came from waterside families and the significance of music and sport in their lives was considerable. He attended Broad Street elementary school, Shadwell, until about 1901.

Billy Wells was a reluctant boxer. East End board schools were keen on competitive football and swimming, and he shone at both. However, the local university settlement club in Broad Street, where his father taught fife and drums, encouraged boxing through the amateur London federation of working boys' clubs for 14- to 18- year-olds. A tall lad weighing 10 stones was uncommon and the gymnastics instructor pushed amiable Billy into the ring to represent the club. The annual federation championships were keenly contested and he never won a title.

In 1906, at the age of eighteen, Wells relinquished the messenger-boy jobs which he held after leaving school to join the Royal Artillery as a gunner. He was posted to Rawalpindi, where he found that boxing was *the* sport among the 80,000 strong British garrison of India, and he won his divisional heavyweight championship (Quetta, 1908), and the prestigious All India title at Poona and Lucknow in succeeding years. Wells, now promoted bombardier, was training full-time and prompted by his civilian coach, Jim Maloney, a former world title contender, bought himself out of the army in 1910 to return to Britain, already tipped as a boxing prospect. Maloney followed to manage Wells's professional boxing career, and between them they earned prolifically as boxing lifted off as a spectator sport in the USA, France, and Britain. Boxing's increased takings were led by heavyweights as 'white hopes' were sought to beat the first black world champion of that division, Jack Johnson, who reigned from 1908 to 1915.

On 24 April 1911, in his eighth professional contest, Wells won the British title and the first heavyweight Lonsdale belt, defeating the title-holder, Iron Hague, at the National Sporting Club in Covent Garden. Thereafter he drew packed houses as hero on the music hall circuit. Matched with Johnson for the world title in London in October 1911, religious opponents of excessive prize money and inter-racial contests, led by the Baptist minister Frederick Brotherton Meyer, caused the fight to be blocked. Subsequently, Wells twice travelled to New York city (June 1912 and March 1913), where on both occasions he lost decisively. Between trips to the USA, Wells married sixteen-year-old Ellen Kilroy, daughter of Luke Kilroy, a publican, on 7 September 1912. They had five children before parting.

Bombardier Wells held the British heavyweight boxing championship for eight years between 1911 and 1919 and he defended the title fourteen times. He was an exciting boxer; of his forty-eight professional contests only two went the distance, then set at twenty rounds. His straight

William Thomas Wells [Bombardier Billy Wells] (1887–1967), by unknown photographer, 1922

left followed by a right cross was exquisite to watch, and his matches turned suddenly, often against the bookmakers' odds.

Wells joined up for military service in May 1915, was promoted to sergeant, and in 1917 went to France, where he organized physical training. After demobilization he resumed his boxing career, but lost his British heavyweight title against Joe Beckett on 27 February 1919. He retired from the ring after defeat by Jack Bloomfield in October 1922 but made a brief comeback between November 1924 and April 1925, when he finally retired. Shortly after his title victory in 1911 he published *Modern Boxing: a Practical Guide to Present-Day Methods*, which went through eight editions.

Wells's extraordinary popularity between 1910 and 1922 rested partly upon his own physical prowess and partly on three converging social trends. Sport, particularly football and boxing, had rapidly become the pastime of everyman; an extended range of personalities covered in the press allowed women a refracted interest in boxing; and in a decade of advancing democracy the Bombardier epitomized the common people. He died at his home, The Studio, 1b Florence Road, Ealing, London, on 11 June 1967 and was cremated at Ruislip.   STAN SHIPLEY

Sources S. Shipley, *Bombardier Billy Wells* (1993) · *Thomson's Weekly News* (17 April–11 Sept 1920) · *Boxing News* (16 June 1967) · *Boxing News* (23 Aug 1991) · *Ring Boxing Encyclopedia and Record Book* (1968), 332 · private information (2004) · b. cert. · m. cert. · d. cert.
Archives FILM BFI NFTVA, news footage · BFI NFTVA, performance footage · BFI NFTVA, sports footage
Likenesses photographs, 1911–45, Hult. Arch. · photograph, 1922, Hult. Arch. [see illus.] · photograph, repro. in *Boxing* (10 Aug 1912)
Wealth at death £773: administration with will, 18 Jan 1968, *CGPLA Eng. & Wales*

Wellsted, James Raymond (1805–1842), surveyor and traveller, was in 1828–9 secretary to Sir Charles Malcolm, superintendent of the Bombay marine. In 1830 he was appointed second-lieutenant of the East India Company's ship *Palinurus*, then engaged, under Captain Moresby, in making a detailed survey of the Gulf of 'Aqabah and the northern part of the Red Sea. She returned to Bombay early in 1833, and was then sent, under the command of Captain Haines, to survey the southern coast of Arabia, Wellsted being still her second-lieutenant. In January 1834 she crossed over to Socotra, and on the 10th anchored in the Bay of Tamarida. Wellsted spent the following two months travelling in the island, returning to his ship on 7 March. He published the results of his journey as 'Memoir on the island of Socotra' (*JRGS*, 5, 1835, 129).

In November 1835 Wellsted had permission to travel in Oman, and went to Muscat on the 21st with Lieutenant F. Whitelock, also of the Indian navy. The imam gave them every assistance in his power, but their fever and the disturbed state of the country curtailed their plans. None the less, the two reached areas which no European had previously seen and which were not visited again by Europeans for another hundred years. Wellsted published preliminary results of this journey in the *Journal of the Royal Geographical Society* (7, 1837, 102).

Wellsted seems to have made another attempt to explore Oman in the following winter, and to have arrived at Muscat in April 1837 in an acute stage of fever. 'In a fit of delirium he discharged both barrels of his gun into his mouth, but the balls, passing upwards, only inflicted two ghastly wounds in the upper jaw'. He was carried to Bombay, and thence returned to Europe on leave. He retired from the service in 1839, 'and dragged on a few years in shattered health and with impaired mental powers, chiefly residing in France' (Low, 2.85–6). He died on 25 October 1842 at his father's house in Molineux Street, London, aged thirty-seven.

Wellsted's papers read before the Royal Geographical Society procured him immediate recognition in the scientific world, and he was elected a fellow of the Royal Society on 6 April 1837. He was also a fellow of the Royal Astronomical Society. As well as writing several scientific papers, he was the author of *Travels in Arabia* (2 vols., 1838) and *Travels to the City of the Caliphs* (2 vols., 1840), an account of the travels of his friend Lieutenant Ormsby. Wellsted was an acute observer and not blinded by prejudice or ignorance in his description of the local people. His accounts of the geography of Oman, particularly the irrigation systems and the way of life in remote mountain tracts, continue to be important as a unique description of the country at an early date.

J. K. LAUGHTON, *rev.* ELIZABETH BAIGENT

Sources *Journal of the Royal Geographical Society*, 13 (1842), xliii · *The Times* (12 Nov 1842) · C. R. Low, *History of the Indian navy, 1613–1863*, 2 vols. (1877) · C. R. Markham, *A memoir on the Indian surveys*, 2nd edn (1878) · *GM*, 2nd ser., 20 (1843), 102 · J. B. Kelly, *Britain and the Persian Gulf, 1795–1880* (1968)

Wellwood, Sir Henry Moncreiff, eighth baronet (1750–1827), Church of Scotland minister, was born Henry Moncreiff at his father's manse on 6 February 1750, the eldest of seven children of Sir William Moncreiff, seventh baronet (1706–1767), Church of Scotland minister of Blackford, Strathearn, Perthshire, and Katherine Wellwood (*d.* 1768), the eldest daughter of Robert Wellwood of Garvock. He was educated at the parish school of Blackford, and at the universities of Glasgow (1763–7) and Edinburgh (1767–

Sir Henry Moncreiff Wellwood, eighth baronet (1750–1827), by Sir Henry Raeburn, exh. RA 1811

71), where he prepared for the ministry. At his father's death on 9 December 1767 he succeeded to the title of baronet. The patron and other leading men of Blackford parish agreed to keep his father's living vacant until Henry was qualified for it. He was licensed to preach by the presbytery of Auchterarder on 8 May 1771, and was ordained to the ministry of Blackford on 15 August 1771. On 16 November 1772 he married his cousin, Susan Robertson (*d.* 1826), the eldest daughter of James Robertson Barclay of Keavil, a writer to the signet; the couple had seven children, including Sir James Wellwood *Moncreiff. Moncreiff added the name Wellwood to his own when his greatuncle, Henry Wellwood, settled on him the estate of Tulliebole, in Kinross-shire. In 1775, at the request of the property owners in the parish, the crown presented him to one of the two collegiate charges of the Edinburgh parish of St Cuthbert.

With a vigorous mind and broad interests, Moncreiff Wellwood became active in the Edinburgh Enlightenment and made minor contributions in philosophy and history. His publications included a sermon *The Connexion betwixt Natural and Revealed Religion* (1777), which appears to have been well received, and he edited the fourth volume of Robert Henry's *History of Great Britain* (1771–93). At the same time Moncreiff Wellwood preserved the dignity and independence of a Presbyterian minister, and gained a reputation as a forceful preacher of the Calvinist orthodoxy. He was soon one of the city's most influential ministers. His influence became national when, in 1784, he was elected by the trustees to be joint collector and principal manager of the fund for the widows and children of the ministers of the Church of Scotland—a collection made up of regular contributions from the ministers. The office gave him an intimate knowledge of the circumstances of every parish living and every minister in the church. He demonstrated a capacity for practical business, combined with a sincere compassion in dealing with bereaved families. During his forty-three years in office, he apparently made not a single error in the accounts, nor was there one complaint against him of severity or injustice. His concern for clerical families found further expression in 1790, when he became a founding member of the Society for the Benefit of the Sons of the Clergy of the Church of Scotland. The church elected him moderator of the general assembly in 1785, and the University of Glasgow awarded him the degree of doctor of divinity in the same year. In 1793 he was appointed a chaplain-in-ordinary to George III.

Moncreiff Wellwood was an old-style whig Presbyterian, who spoke in broad Scots and combined pride in his title of baronet with a genuine commitment to defend the traditional liberties and religion of the Scottish people. He took a leading role in the ecclesiastical courts of the Church of Scotland. There he associated with the popular party, which upheld Calvinist orthodoxy and opposed church patronage—calling for a greater popular voice in the selection of ministers. They confronted the more patrician moderate party, proponents of cultural improvement and keen defenders of the rights of church patrons. Following the death of the popular party leader, John Erskine, in 1805, Moncreiff Wellwood was generally acknowledged as the party's leader. In this position he endeavoured to ease the tensions between the two ecclesiastical parties, especially over the contentious issue of church patronage. He maintained that whatever the popular party's views of patronage, it had now been confirmed as the law of the land, and continued resistance to it would be both futile and divisive. He also worked to overcome the suspicion that many popular ministers felt towards intellectual culture and worldly improvement. In 1806 he embraced the cause of church extension, urging the building of new churches in response to Scotland's growing population. Through his influence the two parties drew closer together and the church exhibited a new unity. His main publication, the *Account of the Life and Writings of John Erskine*, appeared in 1818, and included a masterly concise description of the Church of Scotland. Moncreiff Wellwood was, in the words of an observer in 1819, a man of commanding presence, with a smile of 'courtly suavity' and an air of 'sheer honesty'—'a very amiable master of the great art of rule' (Lockhart, 3.47). His health began to fail in 1825, and he died on 9 August 1827 after a long illness. He was buried at St Cuthbert's (West Church) churchyard, Edinburgh.   STEWART J. BROWN

Sources J. W. Moncreiff, 'Memoir of Sir Henry Moncreiff Wellwood', in H. M. Wellwood, *Sermons*, 3, ed. J. W. Moncreiff (1831), viii–xxiv · Chambers, *Scots.*, rev. T. Thomson (1875), 6.513–15 · J. Kay, *A series of original portraits and caricature etchings … with biographical sketches and illustrative anecdotes*, ed. [H. Paton and others],

2 (1838) · *Fasti Scot.*, new edn, 1.98 · S. Macgill, 'Character of Sir Henry Moncreiff Wellwood', *Principal acts of the general assembly of the Church of Scotland for 1828* (1828), 34–5 · [J. G. Lockhart], *Peter's letters to his kinsfolk*, 2nd edn, 3 (1819) · H. Cockburn, *Life of Lord Jeffrey, with a selection from his correspondence*, 1 (1852) · Burke, *Peerage*
Archives NRA, priv. coll., corresp. and papers · U. Edin. L., prayers | U. Edin., New Coll. L., letters to Thomas Chalmers
Likenesses J. Kay, etching, 1793, BM; repro. in Kay, *Series of original portraits*, vol. 2, facing p. 267 · J. Henning, pencil sketch, 1808, Scot. NPG · J. Henning, porcelain medallion, 1809, Scot. NPG · H. Raeburn, oils, exh. RA 1811, priv. coll. [*see illus.*] · W. K. Munro, engraving, 1812 (after H. Raeburn), U. Edin., New Coll. L. · C. Turner, engraving, 1812 (after H. Raeburn), U. Edin., New Coll. L. · S. Joseph, plaster bust, 1822, Scot. NPG · S. Joseph, marble bust, 1825, Scot. NPG · J. Caw, repro. in J. Caw, *Scottish portraits*, 5 vols. (1903), pl. xciv · A. Edouart, silhouette, Scot. NPG · S. Freeman, engraving (after H. Raeburn), NPG · E. Scriven, stipple (after H. Raeburn), BM, NPG; repro. in *Contemporary portraits* (1812) · C. Thomson, engraving (after H. Raeburn), NPG

Welsbourne, Sir John (c.1498–1548). *See under* Henry VIII, privy chamber of (*act.* 1509–1547).

Welsby, William Newland (1803–1864), legal writer, was born at Acton, near Nantwich in Cheshire, the only son of William Welsby, a barrister of the Middle Temple and land agent, and his wife, formerly Miss Newland. He received his schooling at Acton grammar school and Dr Doncaster's, Oakham, before being admitted on 28 October 1818 as a pensioner at St John's College, Cambridge, where he graduated BA in 1823 and MA in 1827. On 22 April 1823 he was admitted as student at the Middle Temple, and was called to the bar on 10 November 1826. He went the north Wales and Chester circuit, in time becoming the leader, and in 1841 was appointed recorder of Chester by Lord Cottenham, to whom his father was agent. He became junior counsel to the Treasury and was chosen to hold an inquiry into Birmingham borough prison in 1853. He enjoyed the reputation of being an accomplished scholar and lawyer, but while contemporaries acknowledged that he was just and upright, they found 'a certain roughness of manner and indifference to general opinion which at times caused him to be misunderstood' (*Law Times*, 418).

An industrious and prolific writer, Welsby edited, with Roger Meeson, seventeen volumes of *Exchequer Reports*, beginning with 1837, and collaborated with E. T. Hurlstone and J. Gordon in nine subsequent volumes ranging from 1849. In conjunction with John Horatio Lloyd he published in three parts *Reports of Mercantile Cases in the Courts of Common Law* in 1829 and 1830, and with Edward Beavan he edited the second edition of Chitty's *Collection of Statutes* (1851–4, 4 vols.), superintending also the third edition, which appeared in 1865, after his death. He 'seemed to have a peculiar talent for re-arranging and improving old textbooks and adapting them to existing needs' (*Law Times*, 418). Among works which benefited from his attentions were *Archbold's Summary of the Law on Pleading and Evidence in Criminal Cases* (tenth and fifteenth editions) and Jervis's *Treatise on the Office of Coroner* (1854). Welsby also edited a volume of sixteen *Lives of Eminent English Judges of the Seventeenth and Eighteenth Centuries*, which originally came out in the *Law Magazine*; nine of them were from his pen.

Renowned for his capacity for hard work, Welsby eventually overtaxed his strength. On 1 July 1864 he died at his home, 19 Holland Villas Road, Kensington, London. He left a widow, Mary, but no children.

W. P. COURTNEY, rev. PATRICK POLDEN

Sources Law Times (16 July 1864), 418 · GM, 3rd ser., 17 (1864), 260 · Venn, Alum. Cant. · Boase, Mod. Eng. biog. · J. Hutchinson, ed., A catalogue of notable Middle Templars: with brief biographical notices (1902) · H. A. C. Sturgess, ed., Register of admissions to the Honourable Society of the Middle Temple, from the fifteenth century to the year 1944, 2 (1949) · The Times (5 July 1864) · J. Whishaw, Synopsis of the modern English bar (1835) · J. W. Wallace, The reporters, 4th edn (1882) · Allibone, Dict. · CGPLA Eng. & Wales (1864) · private information (1899) · Holdsworth, Eng. law, vol. 15
Likenesses G. Black, lithograph, 1847, NPG
Wealth at death under £20,000: probate, 20 July 1864, CGPLA Eng. & Wales

Welsford, Enid Elder Hancock (1892–1981), literary scholar, was born on 26 February 1892 at Harrow on the Hill, Middlesex. She was the daughter of Joseph William Wilson Welsford (1856–1909), mathematics master at Harrow School and a fellow of Gonville and Caius College, Cambridge, and Mildred Laura Hancock (d. 1935), a painter of some note. Until 1909 Enid Welsford was educated at the Conamur School in Sandgate, Kent. A creative and sensitive child, she was the author of a book of poetry, The Seagulls and other Poems, which her parents had published and placed in the Cambridge University Library in 1904. At seventeen Welsford began her literary studies with W. P. Ker at University College, London, taking her first degree in 1911. In that year she went to Newnham College, Cambridge, where in 1914 she earned first-class honours in the medieval and modern languages tripos, with a distinction in Old English. At Newnham, Welsford met Nora Kershaw, later Chadwick, who became a lifelong friend. In 1915 Welsford was awarded a Marion Kennedy studentship at Newnham which she used to study comparative literature with Professor H. M. Chadwick, her friend's husband, beginning what she described as 'a long and delightful initiation into research' (Welsford, viii). Welsford continued her research with Chadwick until about 1917 or 1918, when she decided to concentrate on a later period of literature. She began teaching at Newnham in 1916.

In 1918 Welsford was awarded an associate research fellowship at Newnham, where she spent the rest of her career. She was elected a fellow in 1921 and served as director of studies in English from 1929 to 1952, as a lecturer in the faculty of English from 1923, and university lecturer from 1928 to 1959. Demonstrating her versatility, Welsford also served as director of studies in archaeology and anthropology from 1939 to 1952, and in moral sciences from 1941 to 1952. Conscious of the cold climate for women scholars in Cambridge, Welsford founded the University Women's Research Club in 1919 with M. D. Haviland, and served as its president several times.

Welsford's early publications included an article in the Modern Language Review, 'Italian influence on the English court masque', in 1923, and four articles in the Encyclopedia of Religion and Ethics (1917–21). Her first book, The Court Masque, was published in 1927. She acknowledged the influence of Professor Chadwick and her Newnham colleague Jane Ellen Harrison, describing the masque as 'strangely like those pantomimic ritual dances of which we hear so much from the students of comparative religion' (Welsford, viii). Extremely erudite, wide-ranging, well written and researched, The Court Masque was awarded the Rose Mary Crawshay prize of the British Academy in 1928, and has been reissued many times. Welsford dedicated it to her only brother, Geoffrey, who was killed in the First World War.

Welsford's most important work, The Fool: his Social and Literary History, was published in 1935. She delighted in recounting how the publisher commissioned the work, telling her that she was the ideal person to write on the subject. Well reviewed in its time, the book has remained influential, as a source for theatrical production, and inspired a Festschrift, The Fool and the Trickster: Studies in Honour of Enid Welsford, in 1979.

At Newnham Welsford was a popular if demanding teacher. She established lifelong friendships with many of her students, including literary scholars Elsie Duncan-Jones, Sita Narasimhan, and Dorothea Krook. She founded the Informal Club, where students, liberally provided by her with sweets and cigarettes, discussed literary issues of the day. As well as a respected scholar and teacher, Welsford was known for her engaging personality, absent-mindedness, and sense of humour. She relished the amusing anecdotes that were often told about her, and she loved to argue and debate. A colleague recalled examining with her for the English tripos: 'Miss Welsford once prolonged a meeting for three hours by her objections to one question. Of course she won' (Duncan-Jones, 219). Welsford's intellectual engagement extended into religion. An active and committed Anglican, she was, however, closely connected with the Franciscan community of St Benet's in Cambridge. She was strongly ecumenical in outlook, serving as a member of the committees of the Christian Frontier Council and the Student Christian Movement for the inter-denominational conference of university teachers from 1950 to 1959. Welsford was also remarkable for her diminutive size; she had to have clothes specially made and had some difficulty doing ordinary tasks (although she was fond of skiing, skating, and more daringly fencing).

Welsford remained active in the Newnham and Cambridge communities after her retirement. She continued her research, publishing Salisbury Plain, a Study in the Development of Wordsworth's Mind and Art in 1966, and an edition of Spenser's Fowre Hymnes, Epithalamion in 1967. She suffered a stroke in 1978. After several years of struggle, she died at her home, 7 Grange Road, Cambridge, on 4 December 1981. She was cremated; on 26 March 1982, as she requested, her ashes were interred in her mother's grave at Harrow.

FERNANDA HELEN PERRONE

Sources E. Duncan-Jones, 'Enid Welsford, 1892–1981', Cambridge women: twelve portraits, ed. E. Shils and C. Blacker (1996), 203–19 · The Times (10 Dec 1981) · S. Narasimhan, 'Miss E. E. H. Welsford', Newnham College Roll Letter (1983), 52–5 · A. B. White and others, eds., Newnham College register, 1871–1971, 2nd edn, 3 vols. (1979) ·

A. Phillips, ed., *A Newnham anthology*, 2nd edn (1988) · E. Welsford, *The court masque* (1962) · Venn, *Alum. Cant.* · *CGPLA Eng. & Wales* (1982)

Archives Newnham College, Cambridge

Likenesses photograph, *c.*1970, Newnham College, Cambridge; repro. in Duncan-Jones, 'Enid Welsford', facing p. 234 · B. Gaye, photograph, repro. in Narasimhan, 'Miss E. E. H. Welsford'

Wealth at death £134,875: probate, 15 March 1982, *CGPLA Eng. & Wales*

Welsh, Alexander (1929–1982), trumpeter and band leader, was born at the Royal Maternity Hospital, Edinburgh, on 9 July 1929, the eldest child of Alexander Welsh (*d. c.*1965), a coal merchant, and his wife, Ann Livingstone Plank (*d. c.*1978). He had a sister, Anne. His father was Roman Catholic, but his mother was Presbyterian and he was brought up in the Church of Scotland, and was in the Boys' Brigade. The family lived at 2 Lawn Square, Leith, and Welsh attended Broughton secondary school, where he played the accordion; he left at eighteen to work as a clerk in the Ministry of Works. He had cornet lessons from Bill Taverner, and played in a local silver band, but he became interested in jazz and modelled his style on the legendary Bix Beiderbecke.

In 1951 Welsh joined clarinettist Archie Semple's band, with whom he made his first recordings that year for S. & M. (Swarbrick and Mossman). In 1952 he moved to the Nova Scotia Jazz Band with Archie Semple and trombonist Dave Keir. Both of these played Chicago-style jazz, in the style associated with Eddie Condon, with Semple echoing Condon's clarinettist, Edmund Hall. In 1953 Welsh replaced Al Fairweather in Sandy Brown's band and recorded with them for S. & M., Fairweather having departed for London. The following year Welsh too left for London, to join Dave Keir's band, which had been booked by the National Jazz Federation to play at the Royal Festival Hall. This band was based on the Duke Ellington–Johnny Hodges small groups of the 1930s, with Keir on alto saxophone, but as Welsh was not familiar with the tight arrangements, Keir's band pulled out of the engagement, and Welsh was asked if he would fill the spot with a Chicago-style Dixieland band. This was Welsh's great opportunity, and he used Roy Crimmins on trombone. After the concert the band stayed together, and Welsh became leader by picking the short straw. The band was not really settled, however, until Archie Semple came in on clarinet, a player of great creative individuality, now playing in a style closer to that of Pee Wee Russell, also associated with Condon.

The band recorded for Decca, Nixa, and Columbia, and broadcast for the BBC. In 1957 American trombonist Jack Teagarden invited Welsh to join his band but he declined out of loyalty to his bandsmen. In 1962 the band toured Britain with the Louis Armstrong band. About this time Semple left the band owing to illness, and Roy Crimmins too left in 1965. Welsh's style had broadened under the influence of other musicians such as Condon, trumpeter Wild Bill Davison, and Henry Red Allen, and a new combination came into being with Al Gay on clarinet and tenor saxophone, John Barnes on clarinet and alto and baritone saxophone, and Roy Williams on trombone. Fred

Hunt continued on piano from the old band. Welsh was short and dapper, with a perky demeanour. He and his first wife, Vicky, were divorced. In 1977 he married Margaret Collins (*b.* 1947), a secretary; they lived at Herlwyn Avenue, Ruislip.

The band featured at the Newport jazz festival, USA, in 1968. They accompanied many visiting American musicians, including Earl Hines, Red Allen, Wild Bill Davison, Ruby Braff, and Bud Freeman. By now the band was playing in a much more 'mainstream' style, with the tenor and baritone saxes featured more prominently. They toured Australia in 1978, but Welsh's health began to fail. He played in Switzerland in April 1982 and led the band for the last time in Nottingham on 10 June. He died in Hillingdon Hospital, Middlesex, on 25 June 1982. He was buried in Ruislip cemetery, Ruislip, and was survived by his second wife.

Welsh was Britain's leading trumpeter in the Chicago–Dixieland style. Though not the most inventive of musicians, he could play movingly beautiful solos, of which 'Sleepy Time Girl' (1959) and 'Davenport Blues' (1966) are good examples. However, his real contribution was in holding together for more than twenty years a band of the highest professional quality, and providing a platform for other more creative but volatile personalities.

A. J. H. LATHAM

Sources J. Chilton, *Who's who of British jazz*, 2nd edn (1998) · G. Bielderman, *Alex Welsh discography*, 4th edn (1990) · B. Kernfeld, ed., *The new Grove dictionary of jazz* (1994) · J. Latlam, 'Archie Semple (1928–74): Roy Crimmins remembers …', *Jazz Rag* (March–April 1998), 16–17 · M. Richards, 'John Barnes talks to Martin Richards', *Jazz Journal International* (Nov 1998), 6–9 · M. Richards, 'John Barnes talks to Martin Richards', *Jazz Journal International* (Dec 1998), 8–11 · b. cert. · d. cert.

Likenesses photographs, priv. coll.

Wealth at death £8000: probate, 21 Jan 1983, *CGPLA Eng. & Wales*

Welsh, David (1793–1845), Free Church of Scotland minister and author, youngest son of David Welsh, sheep farmer, of Earlshaugh and Tweedshaws, was born at Braefoot, Moffat, on 11 December 1793. He was educated at Moffat parish school, the high school of Edinburgh, and Edinburgh University, and on 7 May 1816 was licensed to preach by the presbytery of Lochmaben. On 22 March 1821 he was ordained minister of the parish of Crossmichael in Kirkcudbrightshire, and on 6 September 1827 he was translated to St David's Church, Glasgow. He married, probably in 1830, Isabel, sister of William Hamilton, provost of Glasgow. In 1825 Welsh published a biography of Thomas Brown MD, following it with an edition of Brown's philosophical lectures in 1834. In October 1831 he was appointed professor of ecclesiastical history in the University of Edinburgh, and, on leaving Glasgow, received from the university the degree of DD. He was a painstaking lecturer. In 1834 he visited Germany and in 1844 published *Elements of Church History*. He wrote articles on Jesus and on the Jews for the *Encyclopaedia Britannica* (1841).

At the meeting of the general assembly of 1842 Welsh was chosen moderator of the assembly, which adopted 'the claim of right', and he was one of the leaders of those who, on 18 May 1843, formed themselves into 'the general assembly of the Free Protesting Church of Scotland', with Dr Thomas Chalmers as its first moderator. It was Welsh who laid their protest on the table of the assembly. *The Limits and Extent of the Right of Private Judgement* (1843) records his opinions. He had to resign his chair, and his appointment as secretary to the Bible board, made in 1839, was cancelled. In two months he collected £21,000 for building New College at Edinburgh for the education of Free Churchmen. In 1844 he was appointed librarian of the college and professor of church history; he left his books to the library. Also in 1844 he was first editor of the *North British Review*, the Free Church's journal. He died suddenly at Camis Eskin on the Clyde on 24 April 1845, survived by his wife and four children.

GEORGE STRONACH, *rev.* H. C. G. MATTHEW

Sources *Fasti Scot.* · D. Welsh, *Sermons, with a memoir by A. Dunlop*, ed. [A. Dunlop] (1846) · J. A. Wylie, *Disruption worthies: a memorial of 1843*, ed. J. B. Gillies, new edn (1881) · *DSCHT* · J. Shattock, 'Problems of parentage: the *North British Review* and the Free Church of Scotland', in J. Shattock and M. Wolff, *The Victorian periodical press* (1982), 145–66

Archives NL Scot., corresp. with George Combe · NL Scot., corresp. with Lord Rutherford · U. Edin., New Coll. L., letters to Thomas Chalmers

Likenesses F. A. Roberts, stipple (after G. Harvey), NPG

Wealth at death £1968 13s. 11d.: inventory, 1845, Edinburgh

Welsh, Elizabeth (1843–1921), college head, was born on 3 March 1843 in co. Down, Ireland, eldest of the four daughters of John Welsh (a descendant of John Knox) of Portaferry, co. Down, and of Eliza (or Elizabeth) Dalzell of Ards, co. Down. She had the conventional education of her day, at home, at private schools, and at classes, all in Ireland. She later acknowledged how much she owed to the clergyman of her parish church who taught her Greek and Latin. She went to Girton College, Cambridge, in 1872, where she read for the classical tripos to which women were informally admitted. She may well have heard of the college through her compatriot, Isabella Townshend, who was one of the six 'pioneer' students of the new institution. With her Irish wit, charm, and high spirits, Elizabeth Welsh was a popular student. That she remained so was no mean feat, at a time when the student body was rent with factions, personal and religious. It was said that a number of critical outbursts between students and the governing body were averted by her tact in the early days.

Elizabeth Welsh was offered a college classical lectureship in 1875 but refused it on principle because the previous holder's position was still in question. Instead, she took a teaching post at Manchester high school, on what was then the very good salary of £200 per annum. When she did return to Girton as a lecturer in 1876, she showed unexpected spirit in arguing for a salary as good as the one she had just resigned. That she was a good teacher is attested by her proud record that no student of hers had ever failed the 'little-go' examination: a considerable achievement in the days when many girls had never studied Latin before their arrival in Cambridge.

As the college grew larger, Marianne Bernard, the mistress, devolved some of her responsibilities, Elizabeth

Elizabeth Welsh (1843–1921), by Sir John Lavery, 1904

Welsh becoming vice-mistress in 1880 and garden steward in 1883, a feature of the college which she made peculiarly her own. Much of the landscaping of the grounds was her work. She became mistress of the college in 1885, the obvious successor to Miss Bernard. Although there were critics of this 'automatic' appointment, on the grounds that it was 'dull', it met the long-held demands of many former students who had lobbied for a mistress who was an Old Girtonian of graduate status. During her term of office, a third major building programme further extended student accommodation, from 70 places in 1884 to 120, and gave the college a chapel. No more building took place thereafter until 1932.

Elizabeth Welsh's capacity for taking a personal interest in others proved a valuable asset as mistress, and the students found her a kindly adviser; her skilfully written testimonials revealed a shrewd judgement. Plagued since her student days by illness, she was increasingly wracked by neuralgia which forced her withdrawal from much of the social life of the college. Since there were still few resident fellows, student life particularly suffered from the loss of her influence, which had once made such a lively impression on her contemporaries; a steady flow of entrants to the college from newly established girls' schools brought with them many school customs and attitudes, stamping college life with a rather immature ethos bound by team games and student-run societies. She was, however, active in the movement among schools and universities to establish settlements in areas of social need, being associated with the foundation by the Oxford and Cambridge women's colleges of the Women's University Settlement in Southwark. Nearer home, also under her aegis, a subscription fund was mounted by lecturers and a few students to provide a nurse to work in the village of Girton, then the home of many impoverished farm labourers and their families.

The portrait painted by James Lavery on Elizabeth Welsh's retirement in 1903 is a fitting comment on her devoted contribution to the college over forty-two years. Compared with earlier photographs of her, it reveals the toll taken by illness and years of work. There is no sign here of the lively girl who, it was said, would kilt up her skirts to perform an Irish reel or lead her friends in singing the college songs, for which she had composed many of the words. On retirement, she appears to have returned to Ireland, to Londonderry, and in 1916 had an address in Lyme Regis, Dorset, when she finally resigned her membership of the Girton college council. Three years before she died, however, she moved to Edinburgh, the home of her forebears. There, with her flair for personal sympathy undimmed, she became a focal point for former students living in the area. She died, unmarried, at her home, 55 Morningside Park, Edinburgh, on 13 February 1921, of a heart condition, following a bronchial attack, and was buried in Girton village churchyard.

BARBARA E. MEGSON

Sources K. T. Butler and H. I. McMorran, eds., *Girton College register, 1869–1946* (1948) · Girton Cam. · *Girton Review*, Lent term (1921), 2–4 · B. Stephen, *Girton College, 1869–1932* (1933) · B. Megson and J. Lindsay, *Girton College, 1869–1959: an informal history* (1961), 27–48 · *CGPLA Eng. & Wales* (1921)

Archives CUL, introductions for students of Girton College to attend Lord Acton's lectures | Girton Cam., annual reports, council minutes, mistresses' corresp.

Likenesses J. Lavery, oils, 1904, Girton Cam. [*see illus.*] · photographs, Girton Cam.

Wealth at death £1689 19s. 7d.: confirmation, 17 May 1921, *CCI* · £190 16s. 7d.: additional estate, 6 Sept 1921, *CCI*

Welsh, Freddie [*formerly* Frederick Hall Thomas] (1886–1927), boxer, was born on 5 March 1886 at The Bridge inn, Pontypridd, the son of John Thomas (*d.* 1898), auctioneer, and his wife, Elizabeth, *née* Hall. Despite being a product of the South Wales mining valleys he was never a hungry fighter, and his parents were sufficiently well-off to send him to a boarding-school in Long Ashton, near Bristol. There, tired of being the butt of stronger schoolfellows, he devoted himself to body-building and the study of physical culture, and won the school boxing championship. He worked as an apprentice boilermaker and engineer at the Pentre (Rhondda) foundry of Llewellyn and Cubitt, but with characteristic self-confidence and independence left at sixteen years of age to seek a new life in North America.

After landing in Montreal in 1902 Thomas made his way to New York, where he worked for a year in various machine shops and enrolled at Macfadyean's College of Physical Training. He moved on to spend his late teens as a hobo, living as a tramp and riding the rails across the Midwest, a harsh environment that forced him to learn to look after himself. He finally settled in Philadelphia, where he was employed first as a salesman and demonstrator of sporting goods in a newly opened department store; he then taught boxing in an evening school in physical education. At this point he decided to take up boxing on his own account as a more profitable activity; after identifying himself with the land of his birth by changing his name to Freddie Welsh, he fought his first bout in Philadelphia in December 1905.

Welsh boxed in Australia in 1906 and on returning to Wales fought in Jack Scarrott's boxing booths, where he was spotted by the shrewd Harry Marks of Cardiff, who became his manager. He made his first official British appearance on 13 February 1907 at the National Sporting Club (NSC) in Covent Garden, where he defeated Seaman Arthur Hayes on points over six rounds; in a rematch the following year he knocked him out in the fifth. On 21 May 1907 at Pontypridd he knocked out Johnny Owen of Aberaman in the seventh round to become lightweight champion of Wales, and in September that year he fought Joe White, a Canadian domiciled in Cardiff and a rated welterweight who, though taller and a stone heavier than Welsh, retired after sixteen rounds. Welsh then returned to the USA, where he suffered only one defeat in sixty-two contests before his next visit to the UK in 1909.

At 5 feet 7 inches in height and weighing 9½ stone, Welsh had a rapier-like straight left and a virtually impregnable defence, but his reputation was built on the trademark techniques he had acquired in the US and which were viewed with suspicion in Britain: crouching, clinching, vicious two-handed fighting, punching his opponent's kidneys, and flagrant use of the elbows and head. By these methods he forced the Frenchman Henri Piet to retire in the twelfth round of their bout at Mountain Ash in August 1909 in front of 15,000 spectators, the largest crowd to watch a boxing match in Wales up to that time. On 8 November that year he defeated Johnny Summers of Canning Town over twenty rounds at the NSC for the lightweight championship of Britain, a title he successfully defended against his fellow Welshman Jim Driscoll in a controversial bout at Cardiff on 20 December 1910. In the tenth round of their scheduled twenty-round contest Driscoll, goaded beyond endurance by Welsh's constant and surreptitious fouling, lost his self-control and repeatedly butted him under the chin and across the ring, giving referee A. F. Bettinson no option but to award the fight to Welsh on a disqualification.

Welsh lost his British title on 27 February 1911 to Matt Wells, but gained revenge in a return bout the following year, when he also beat Hughie Mehegan of Australia for the British empire title. He was denied an opportunity to fight for the world lightweight title in November 1911, when the reigning champion Ad Wolgast, 'the Michigan wildcat', suffered appendicitis the day before the fight.

Not until 7 July 1914 did Welsh get his next big chance and he seized it with both fists to defeat Willie Ritchie of San Francisco, who had taken the title from Wolgast two years earlier, over twenty rounds at London's Olympia in front of 14,000, including 2000 women. By the end of the year he had defended his championship against Wolgast, Charley White of Chicago, Jimmy Duffy of Buffalo, and Joe Shugrue of Jersey City, all of whom he fought within the space of two months (November–December 1914).

During the First World War Welsh served in the US army sanitary corps, helping to rehabilitate wounded soldiers at the Walter Reed Hospital, Washington. He continued to box and fought thirty-seven bouts in 1915 and 1916, including two defences of his world title: against Wolgast in Denver in July 1916 and Charley White in Colorado Springs two months later. He lost his title on 28 May 1917, when he was knocked out in the ninth by the 21-year-old Benny Leonard, whom he had beaten on two previous occasions, at the Manhattan Casino, New York.

A points defeat by Archie Walker in Brooklyn in April 1921 ended Welsh's career. In retirement he cashed in on his fads of physical culture and vegetarianism—he was routinely described in the press as 'the fruitarian' and 'the vegetarian phenom' (Welsh scrapbooks)—to become a professional medicine man. He founded a health farm in New Jersey, where he lectured on physical education to businessmen and lawyers anxious to regain their lost youth and where one of his sparring partners was the writer F. Scott Fitzgerald. Welsh himself appeared to have wider literary interests than the average professional boxer; 'the prize-fighter who trains on Ibsen's plays' and 'an ardent student of John Ruskin' (Corri, 35), he impressed even cynical fight correspondents by his familiarity with the works of Browning, Shaw, Maeterlinck, and Tolstoy (Los Angeles Times, 8 March 1914, and other cuttings in Welsh scrapbooks, vol. 3).

For all his bombast and famed business acumen, Welsh's health club collapsed as his clients forsook Sparta for the fleshpots of the 'roaring twenties' and he was apparently penniless when found dead on 28 July 1927 in a seedy New York apartment. At his funeral in New York on 30 July Benny Leonard, who had retired undefeated in 1923, was one of the pallbearers. Freddie Welsh, world lightweight champion from 1914 to 1917, was survived by his wife, Fanny (née Weston), whom he married in 1907, and their two children Elizabeth and Fred junior.

GARETH WILLIAMS

Sources Freddie Welsh scrapbooks, 4 vols., NL Wales, ex 1806 · Freddie Welsh cuttings, Cardiff Central Library · D. Smith, *Aneurin Bevan and the world of south Wales* (1993), chap. 12 · E. Corri, *Gloves and the man* (1927) · *Western Mail* [Cardiff] (21 June 1909) · *Western Mail* [Cardiff] (29 July 1927) · *Western Mail* [Cardiff] (11 Nov 1949) · A. Richards, *Days of absence* (1986) · G. Williams, *1905 and all that: essays on rugby football, sport and Welsh society* (1991)
Archives Cardiff Central Library, cuttings · NL Wales, cuttings books | FILM BFI NFTVA, news footage · BFI NFTVA, sports footage
Likenesses photographs, c.1900–1924, Hult. Arch. · J. Gronow, photograph, 1910, repro. in J. Huntington-Whiteley, *The book of British sporting heroes* (1998), 90 · photograph, repro. in N. Fleischer and S. Andre, *A pictorial history of boxing* (1979)
Wealth at death supposedly penniless: *Western Mail* (29 July 1927) · according to brother, real estate and property value over $100,000: *The Times*, (1 Aug 1927), 6

Welsh, James (1775–1861), army officer in the East India Company, the son of John Welsh, a Scot, was born in Scotland on 12 March 1775. He obtained a commission as ensign in the army of the East India Company on 22 May 1790, and arrived at Madras on 23 January 1791. He joined the 3rd European regiment at Vellore, and in November went with Colonel Floyd's detachment to serve in the grand army under Lord Cornwallis.

Welsh was promoted to be lieutenant in the 24th native infantry on 1 November 1792, and took part with it in the siege of Pondicherry in July and August 1793. He married at Calcutta, in 1794, a daughter of Francis *Light, first governor of Prince of Wales's Island, Penang. They had a numerous family, and his wife survived him.

Transferred in 1795 to the 9th native infantry at Mandura, Welsh served at the capture of Colombo and Ceylon in February 1796, and remained at Point-de-Galle as fort-adjutant until the end of 1798, when he was transferred in the same capacity to Masulipatam.

On 10 December 1799 Welsh was promoted to be captain, and appointed adjutant and quartermaster of the 3rd native infantry, which in 1803 formed part of a force under Major-General Arthur Wellesley to operate against the Marathas. He marched with it across India to Poona, and was present at the assault on the great hill fort at Ahmednagar, which was captured on 12 August 1803.

Welsh served on the staff at the battle of Argaon (29 November) and in the siege and assault (15 December) of Gawilgarh, and led a body of 250 men, after a forced march of 54 miles, to the capture of Mankarsir on 6 February 1804. He was appointed judge-advocate and assistant surveyor to the Poona subsidiary force, and with it on 10 August 1804 took part in the assault and capture of Chandur, and the occupation of Dhurp on 14 October. He commanded a party of 300 men at the capture of Galna on 26 October, and on 13 November went with a small force to open communications with Surat, where he arrived on 25 November. In December Welsh was sent on a mission to a Bhil chief by an unexplored pass to the northward, and caught a malignant fever from which he suffered for many years.

On 15 May 1805 Welsh succeeded to the command of his battalion of native infantry at Poona, continuing to hold his staff appointment until the end of the year, when he marched with his regiment to Palamcottai in the Carnatic, arriving on 27 March. He was in command there on 19 November, when, as the garrison were assembling under arms, he discovered a plot among the sepoys to murder the Europeans at the station. Acting with promptitude he seized the leaders, disarmed the sepoys, and expelled trouble-makers from the fort. He was tried by court martial for precipitate conduct in having disarmed the sepoy garrison with insufficient cause, but was honourably acquitted on 20 March 1807, and congratulated by government on this vindication. Welsh was promoted major on 22 May 1807, and went home on furlough.

Welsh rejoined his regiment on 5 February 1809 before the lines of Travancore, where it formed part of a force under Colonel St Leger, and led the storming party in the successful assault on the formidable defences on the night of 10 February. He was mentioned in dispatches, and the court of directors of the East India Company praised his services on the occasion. On 19 February 1809, leading the advance from the south, Welsh was successful in capturing several hill forts, arriving at Trivandrum, the capital of Travancore, on 2 March. In April 1812 he commanded a small force sent to quell a rising in the Wainad, which he accomplished after a month of heavy marching and desultory fighting. He was promoted lieutenant-colonel on 25 January 1813, and was appointed deputy judge-advocate-general, residing at Bangalore.

On 6 February 1821 Welsh was appointed to command the troops in the provinces of Malabar and Kanara; on 6 May 1823 to command at Vellore; on 23 January 1824 to command in Travancore and Cochin; and on 1 August 1826 to command the Doab field force. He arrived at Belgaum in September, and was immediately engaged with the resident in measures which were successful in preventing a threatened rising at Kolhapur.

Early in 1829 Welsh went to England on furlough and was promoted colonel on 5 June. He published his informative *Military Reminiscences* (2 vols., 1830) with more than ninety illustrations.

Welsh did not return to India until his promotion to major-general on 10 January 1837. He was appointed on 1 June to the command of the northern division, Madras presidency, to which was added, in November 1838, the command in Cuttack. He was promoted lieutenant-general on 9 November 1846, and relinquished his command on 16 February 1847. When he left India the governor in council praised his gallantry and zeal in his remarkable service of fifty-eight years. He was promoted general on 20 June 1854. He died at his home, 10 North Parade, Bath, on 24 January 1861.

R. H. VETCH, rev. JAMES FALKNER

Sources *East-India Register and Directory* (1830–60) • *Indian Army and Civil Service List* (1861) • *Annual Register* (1861) • J. Philippart, ed., *The royal military calendar*, 3rd edn, 5 vols. (1820) • *London Monthly Review* (1830) • J. Welsh, *Military reminiscences: 40 years' active service in the East Indies* (1830) • *CGPLA Eng. & Wales* (1861)
Archives BL OIOC, journal, MS Eur. D 168
Wealth at death under £800: probate, 9 Feb 1861, *CGPLA Eng. & Wales*

Welsh, John (1568/9–1622), Church of Scotland and French Reformed minister, was born in Dumfriesshire, one of five children and the second son of John Welsh (*d.* 1600), laird of Collieston in Dunscore, and his wife, Marion Greir. He attended school locally, although he was a truant and, on leaving this first period of education, fell in with a band of border reivers. Falling on hard times he threw himself

on the mercy of his parents, who sent him to the fledgeling college at Edinburgh where he matriculated in 1585 under the regency of Adam Colt and graduated MA in 1588, along with another twenty-nine students, eleven of whom were later ministers. Being ordained into the parish of Selkirk in 1589 he distinguished himself as the first Edinburgh graduate to enter the ministry. In this capacity, on 6 March 1590 the privy council appointed him to a commission to preserve the 'true religion' in Ettrick Forest and Tweeddale. According to an early biography his spiritual zeal aroused 'the malice of the wicked' in Selkirk and he was forced to leave after one local laird killed two of his horses (Tweedie, 1.3). He was last recorded as minister of Selkirk on 11 March 1594 and was then translated to Kirkcudbright, where he remained for six years, also taking on the nearby charges of Galtaway, Dunrod, and Kilchrist. At about the time of leaving Selkirk he married Elizabeth, daughter of the reformer John Knox (*d.* 1572). They had six children, four sons and two daughters, although only three appear still to have been alive in January 1625 at their mother's death.

Welsh had an active career in the kirk. He was appointed by the general assembly of March 1596 'to visit and try the doctrine, life, diligence and fidelitie' (Calderwood, 5.420) of ministers and to plant clergy in areas with no presbyteries in Nithsdale, Annandale, Lauderdale, Easdale, and Ewesdale. In December of that year he was in Edinburgh when its ministers fled after a confrontation with the king. Occupying the pulpit, he was himself suspended from the ministry for speaking in their support, for 'ellegeing that his Majestie was possest with a devill' and for suggesting that, just as sons may restrain an insane father, so subjects might 'bind his Majestie' (*Reg. PCS*, 5.359). He was outlawed for failing to appear before the privy council in January 1597, but was restored after a request from the general assembly. In 1598 he was appointed to a commission of the general assembly charged with examining complaints against the standing commission of the kirk and, in 1600 and 1602, was reappointed as a visitor in Nithsdale by the assembly. In 1599 he wrote the only one of his works to be published in Scotland during his life, *Popery Anatomized* (1602). Dedicated to James VI, it was a reply to criticisms of the kirk by Gilbert Brown, former abbot of the Cistercian house of Newabbey, taking the form of a 28-section, 440-page attack on Catholicism.

In August 1600 Welsh was translated to Ayr to be assistant to the ageing John Porterfield. On Porterfield's death in 1604 the people of Ayr called on the burgh council to confirm Welsh as his successor, which they formally did on 12 June. His daily preaching was said to be so popular that the council resolved to build a new kirk to accommodate the increased attendances, a plan which was, however, not carried out until long after Welsh's death. He took an active role in quelling factional violence which troubled Ayr on his arrival, even intervening in disturbances with only a helmet for protection and, once quarrels were quelled, staging public acts of reconciliation. There survive from his time at Ayr a number of stories which endow him with great spiritual gifts. People 'saw clearly a strange light surround him' (Tweedie, 1.12) while he was praying in his garden at night. In 1604, when plague was rife but Ayr was free of disease, he is said to have discerned, through prayer, that two merchants wishing to enter the town were carrying infection. They were sent away and were admitted to Cumnock where plague struck and 'the living were hardly able to bury their dead' (ibid., 1.13).

Welsh's service at Ayr came to a premature end in 1605. The king had not permitted the general assembly to meet since 1602, and many feared severe curtailment of ecclesiastical freedom, so when the assembly scheduled to meet at Aberdeen in July was also prorogued fourteen presbyteries, including Ayr, sent commissioners anyway. Although Welsh arrived in Aberdeen two days after the bulk of commissioners had already constituted and dissolved the assembly, he formally declared his support for their actions. He was the first to reach Edinburgh after the meeting. Summoned before the privy council he was warded in Blackness Castle and, after languishing there for three months, he again appeared before the privy council and, along with five others, rejected its competence in what they argued was an ecclesiastical matter. They were sent back to Blackness and the king demanded that they be tried for treason. This duly went ahead in the following January. John Forbes and Welsh, described at the time by the secretary of state, Lord Balmerino, as 'the strongest pillaris of that disorder', were appointed by the others to speak for all (Reg. PCS, 1st ser., 7.478). Welsh warned the packed jury that they were usurping the jurisdiction of Christ, and thus, he said, 'yee … bring upon yourselves … the guiltines of our innocent blood' (Forbes, 485–8). All six were found guilty and sentence was remitted to the king who, in October 1606, ordered that they be banished from his dominions. At two o'clock on the morning of 7 November they took ship at Leith after 'Mr Johne Welsche conceivit a prayer, quhilk bred great motioune in the heartis of all the heareres' (Autobiography and Diary of … Melvill, 670). The burgh council of Ayr continued to pay 'their weilbelovit pastor' his stipend for a number of years after he was exiled, even though he was never to return (Fasti Scot., 2.6).

Welsh sailed to Bordeaux, immediately set to learning the language, and was able, within fourteen weeks, to preach in French. He soon took up a ministerial charge at Nerac, then moved to Jonzac, where he published another anti-Catholic work, L'Armageddon de la Babylon apocalyptique (1612). Some time after 1613 he settled at St Jean-d'Angely. In 1620 the Huguenot town was besieged by Louis XIII and Welsh is said to have rallied the people and aided the gunners on the walls. Louis sought terms and it was agreed that St Jean would keep its walls, civic privileges, and religious freedom. Welsh was summoned before the king for his preaching but he impressed Louis by pointing out that his priests placed him under papal authority while Welsh argued that none on earth was the king's superior. After a subsequent siege the town was

taken by the king, whereupon Welsh was given his freedom and transport to La Rochelle for himself and his family.

Welsh obtained permission to enter England where, pleading ill health, he attempted to get leave to return to Scotland. The dean of Winchester, John Young, tried to get Welsh to approve the Scottish ecclesiastical status quo as a condition of his return but he refused. Elizabeth Knox's pleadings before the king himself were similarly fruitless. James sought the same condition for his return and she replied, holding out her apron, 'Please your Majesty, I'd rather kep his head there' (McCrie, 396). Welsh was not granted liberty to preach in London until he was too frail to do so. He died there on 2 April 1622 aged fifty-three and was buried in the churchyard of St Botolph without Bishopsgate two days later. Subsequent to his death two collections of his sermons were published, Thirty-Five Sermons (1744) and Forty-Eight Select Sermons (1811), as well as Discourses (1752) and A Cry to the Whole Earth (1785).

ALAN R. MACDONALD

Sources W. K. Tweedie, ed., Select biographies, 2 vols., Wodrow Society, 7 (1845–7) · Fasti Scot., new edn · J. Forbes, Certaine records touching the estate of the kirk in the years MDCV & MDCVI, ed. D. Laing and J. Anderson, Wodrow Society, 19 (1846) · D. Laing, ed., The miscellany of the Wodrow Society, Wodrow Society, [9] (1844) · D. Calderwood, The history of the Kirk of Scotland, ed. T. Thomson and D. Laing, 8 vols., Wodrow Society, 7 (1842–9) · T. McCrie, The life of John Knox (1812) · T. Thomson, ed., Acts and proceedings of the general assemblies of the Kirk of Scotland, 3 pts, Bannatyne Club, 81 (1839–45) · commissary court records, NA Scot., CC8, CC9 · Reg. PCS, 1st ser. · The autobiography and diary of Mr James Melvill, ed. R. Pitcairn, Wodrow Society (1842)

Archives Ayr Archives, Ayr kirk session book, CH 2/751/1

Welsh, John (d. 1681), covenanter field preacher, was the son of Josiah Welsh (d. 1634), minister at Temple-Kirkpatrick, co. Antrim, Ireland, and the grandson of John *Welsh (1568/9–1622), Church of Scotland and French reformed minister, and the great-grandson of the illustrious Scottish reformer, John *Knox (d. 1572). Little is known about his early years. He graduated MA from the University of Glasgow in 1647, and was admitted and ordained minister of the parish of Kirkpatrick-Irongray, Kirkcudbrightshire, on 21 January 1653 at the instigation of David M'Brear of Newark and Almagill (MP for the stewarty of Kirkcudbright and patron of that charge). On 18 February the same year he married Elizabeth Somerville (d. before 1674), at Holyrood, Edinburgh.

Welsh vehemently opposed the reimposition of Erastian episcopacy at the Restoration and was ejected from his incumbency and deprived of his living in 1662. Notwithstanding repeated and sustained attempts by the state to have him apprehended and silenced, Welsh sustained a long and popular itinerant ministry throughout the south-west of Scotland, the Lothians, and into Fife and Perthshire, preaching in vacant pulpits and in the open air for some nineteen years. The civil authorities forfeited him in 1667 for having been present at the Pentland rising the previous November. By 1674 the government was offering a reward of 2000 merks for his apprehension. The intensity of the campaign to eradicate conventicling was such that by August he was forced to seek refuge over the border in Northumberland. His first wife having died, Welsh was able to remarry, and did so probably in that year; his second wife's name is unknown.

Sir George Mackenzie of Rosehaugh, the king's advocate in Scotland, who earned the infamous sobriquet Bloody Mackenzie for his severe persecution of the covenanters, described Welsh as a 'person of much courage, but no parts' (Wodrow, 2.244n.). It was testimony to his indefatigable courage and commitment to presbyterian principles that Welsh was back preaching and serving those who shared his beliefs in the south-west early in 1675. On account of his appeal and influence right across the social spectrum throughout lowland Scotland, Charles II, in his determination to have Welsh detained and prosecuted, ordered that the sum on his head be raised to a staggering 9000 merks in February 1679. Welsh continued to serve the covenanters in the wake of Drumclog and Bothwell Bridge, but he championed moderation and cautioned Richard Cameron and those of like conviction against separation from those ministers who had accepted the indulgence.

Some time after Bothwell Bridge, in defiance of the price on his head Welsh went to London, where he died on 9 January 1681. He was buried in the churchyard of St Botolph without Bishopsgate. A number of his sermons were published posthumously. These include: *A Preface, Lecture, and a Sermon* (1686); *Fifty and Two Directions to his Parish of Irongray* (1703); *A Sermon Preached at Nemphlar Brae in Clidsdale* (1703); and *An Alarm to the Impenitent: the Great Gospel Sumonds to Close with Christ* and *The Church's Paradox* in 1710.   A. S. WAYNE PEARCE

Sources *Fasti Scot.*, 2.287–8 · R. Wodrow, *The history of the sufferings of the Church of Scotland from the Restoration to the revolution*, ed. R. Burns, 2 (1840); 3 (1840) · I. B. Cowan, *The Scottish covenanters, 1660–1688* (1976) · *Reg. PCS*, 3rd ser., vols. 5–6 · *DSCHT*, 861 · M. Grant, *The lion of the covenant: the story of Richard Cameron* (1997)

Welsh, John (1824–1859), meteorologist, eldest son of George Welsh of Craigenputtoch, and his wife, Margaret Kissock, was born at Boreland, Kirkcudbrightshire, on 27 September 1824. His father, who held a small estate which had been long in the family, died in 1835 and his mother settled at Castle Douglas, where Welsh received his early education. In November 1839 he entered the University of Edinburgh with a view to becoming a civil engineer, and studied under professors Philip Kelland, James David Forbes, and Robert Jameson. In December 1842 Sir Thomas Brisbane, on the advice of Forbes, engaged Welsh as an observer at his magnetical and meteorological observatory at Makerstoun under John Allan Broun, then director. In 1850, the magnetic observations being terminated, Welsh was appointed assistant to Francis Ronalds, superintendent at Kew observatory. Welsh read, at the Ipswich meeting of the British Association in October 1851, a report on Ronalds's three magnetographs, and described two sliding rules which he had devised for reducing hygrometrical and magnetic observations. In 1852 he read an important report on the methods used in graduating

and comparing standard instruments at the Kew observatory, and subsequently standard thermometers and barometers destined for scientific use were verified and certificated at the observatory.

Ronalds retired in 1852 and Welsh succeeded him as superintendent of the observatory. Between August and November 1852 Welsh and Charles Green made four balloon ascents from Vauxhall in order to make meteorological observations. In March and May 1854 Welsh and the barometer maker Alexander Adie made several voyages to investigate and remedy the pumping, or motion, of mercury in marine barometers. In 1855 Welsh supervised at the Paris Exhibition the exhibit of magnetic and meteorological instruments used at Kew. In 1856 he began at Kew a series of monthly determinations of absolute magnetic intensity and magnetic dip with instruments provided by General Edward Sabine. In the same year a set of self-recording magnetic instruments was constructed, based on the models devised originally by Ronalds and improved by Welsh.

In 1857 Welsh was elected FRS. In the same year, the society's Kew committee having decided on a magnetic survey of the British islands, Welsh was appointed to undertake the north British division, and he spent part of the summers of 1857 and 1858 on this work. But he suffered from lung disease during the intervening winter and this became worse during the following year. Acting under medical advice he spent the winter of 1858–9, accompanied by his mother, at Falmouth, and died there, at Woodlane Terrace, on 11 May 1859.

P. J. HARTOG, *rev.* ANITA MCCONNELL

Sources *PRS*, 10 (1859–60), xxxiv–xxxviii · b. cert. · d. cert. · *CGPLA Eng. & Wales* (1859)
Archives PRO, corresp. as superintendent of Kew observatory, BJ1 · UCL, corresp. | U. St Andr. L., corresp. with James David Forbes
Wealth at death under £1500: probate, 27 June 1859, *CGPLA Eng. & Wales*

Welsh [*née* Dalzell], Dame (**Ruth**) **Mary Eldridge** (1896–1986), director of the Women's Auxiliary Air Force, was born on 2 August 1896 at 22 Slatey Road, Claughton, Birkenhead, one of two children of William Robert Dalzell, a medical practitioner, and his wife, Ruth Mary Frances Annie Elizabeth Goldsworth Kirkpatrick (*b.* 1872). She attended a local high school, but the First World War precluded attendance at a French finishing school. Instead she went to France in October 1918 as a driver in the First Aid Nursing Yeomanry, remaining until June 1919.

On 2 October 1922 she married Squadron Leader William Lawrie Welsh (1891–1962) of the Royal Air Force, and in 1926 her only child, Michael, was born. She travelled widely with her husband's RAF postings, and also gained six years' business experience. When in 1937 her husband was promoted to the Air Council, she joined the Emergency Service, a body, set up in response to the growing German threat, to train women as officers in case of war. The 1938 Munich crisis precipitated the forming of the Auxiliary Territorial Service, for which she volunteered in December 1938. Shortly afterwards she was appointed senior commandant, with thirty-two London companies under her command. Welsh later recalled watching the women 'in dusty unromantic drill halls, drilling in high heels and tight skirts … I really did admire them' (Welsh, 12).

When war broke out, Mary Welsh transferred in October 1939 to the newly formed Women's Auxiliary Air Force (WAAF), initially as squadron officer responsible for recruiting, then as staff officer to a London balloon group. In spring 1940—the eve of the battle of Britain—she became senior WAAF officer to Fighter Command, where her husband described her, at the start, as 'looking like a hunted hare' (Welsh, 14). Nevertheless, by 1942 she was able triumphantly to outface a critic on the Marham committee inquiring into WAAF conditions. The strain of continual travel throughout the country necessitated three months' sick leave. After her husband's knighthood in 1941 she also became sensitive to accusations of nepotism in her career.

Despite her misgivings, Mary Welsh was appointed to the newly created office of inspector-general WAAF, in December 1942. The post took her to commands up and down the country, where she had to break down a wall of suspicion and mistrust. However, being now experienced, conscientious, extremely smart in uniform, having an easy and approachable manner, and with a saving sense of humour, she proved to be very effective. Welsh thus became the natural choice as director of the WAAF, in succession to Air Chief Commandant Katherine Trefusis-Forbes, who was being seconded to special duties overseas. The latter kept her rank as senior officer, which was not achieved by Mary Welsh until August 1944. Nor did Welsh accept the post willingly, refusing it twice before it was finally gazetted on 4 October 1943. By this time she was in her forty-eighth year, tall and slim, with dark eyes and hair, and a husband head of the RAF delegation in Washington, DC.

Plans were already afoot for airwomen to be posted overseas, a move bitterly resisted by the Air Ministry. In January 1944 a tri-service agreement settled shipping, conditions, and accommodation abroad for women. This in turn led to controversy on overseas warm-weather WAAF uniforms. The army could not understand why airwomen objected to wearing khaki, but khaki it became, until autumn 1945, when the director won her case.

'Concern for women serving overseas was very real', Welsh later wrote (Beauman, 232); and her duties necessitated frequent inspections of units and stations at home and abroad. She was involved also in discussions about the continuation of women's services after the war, to provide a nucleus of trained women for expansion against future emergencies. As the war drew to a close, the director also had to consider demobilization arrangements for the WAAF, and was to oversee the gradual reduction of a force of 180,339 when she took over to about 32,590 when she left. She turned the new advisory council into a powerful instrument of administration, and gradually strengthened the director's role. The myriad of other matters with which she dealt included a general merging of messing, and sometimes living accommodation, for the WAAF and the RAF, the further extension of the duties of specialist officers and non-commissioned officers into administration and welfare, and the substitution in trades of WAAF for RAF (which was almost 100 per cent in mechanical transport and meteorology).

By late 1946, aged fifty, tiring from the strain, often putting in a seventeen-hour day, and with her marriage falling apart, Mary Welsh asked to be relieved of her post. She was sometimes criticized for preferring the status quo to reform, and being overinfluenced by her staff; but she had seen the WAAF through three momentous years covering the transition from war to peace, and under her the WAAF had settled down and matured. Welsh retired on 30 November 1946, being created a DBE that year. Her marriage was dissolved in October 1947. Later Dame Mary settled in Odiham, Hampshire, where she was secretary of the local British Legion and first president of the Odiham Society; in the latter role she helped to save the pest house, used during the great plague of 1665, from demolition. She died from bronchopneumonia aged eighty-nine on 25 June 1986, at 26 Fleet Road, Cove, Farnborough.

BERYL E. ESCOTT

Sources M. Welsh, 'Our directors, no. 3', *WRAF Officers Gazette* (1961) [autobiography] · *The Aeroplane* (25 Oct 1946) · *Flight Magazine* (7 Oct 1943) · *Flight Magazine* (16 Dec 1943) · B. E. Escott, *Women in air force blue* (1989) · K. B. Beauman, *Partners in blue* (1971) · F. Peake, *Pure chance* (1993) · D. Collett-Wadge, *Women in uniform* (1946) · *WWW*, 1961–70 · *Women's auxiliary air force, 1939–45* (1953) [AP, 3234; addition 1946–9 pubd later] · *The Times* (27 June 1986) · *CGPLA Eng. & Wales* (1986) · b. cert. · m. cert. · d. cert. · private information (2004)

Likenesses photographs, 1943–6, Gov. Art Coll. · photographs, IWM

Wealth at death £124,595: probate, 21 Oct 1986, *CGPLA Eng. & Wales*

Welsh, Robert (*b.* in or before **1506**, *d.* **1549**), priest and rebel, is known for his leading role in the siege of Exeter during what contemporaries called 'the Commotion' and modern historians term the 'western' or 'prayer-book' rebellion of 1549. According to the *Description of the Citie of Excester* by Welsh's younger contemporary John Hooker, he was born at Penryn, Cornwall, 'of good honest parentage', at a date that can be conjectured as 1506 or a year or two earlier. This follows from his ordination as priest in 1530, which required an age of at least twenty-four. By the latter date Welsh may have had connections with east Cornwall and west Devon since he was ordained to all three grades of major holy orders at Bodmin Priory, with an ordination title provided by Launceston Priory, and was admitted to the vicarage of St Thomas in Cowick, near Exeter, on 9 March 1537, a benefice belonging to Tavistock Abbey. Hooker describes him as a manly outdoor man, 'of no great stature, but well sett and mightelie compacte', who excelled in wrestling, hunting, and shooting with longbow, crossbow, or gun. He was 'suche a one as wolde not geve his hed for the pollinge nor his bearde for the washeinge', in other words of unkempt appearance, yet sociable in all sports 'and of a courtuose and gentle behavior' (Vowell, 2.91).

Welsh came to prominence when opponents of the new Book of Common Prayer rebelled in Cornwall and Devon, and laid siege to Exeter on 2 July 1549. Hooker calls him 'an archecapytayn and a pryncypall doer' (Vowell, 2.92) in the rebellion, but Welsh does not appear among the leaders who signed the rebels' demands to the crown, and his influence seems to have been confined to events in Exeter. He is said to have encouraged the rebels to attack the city (his own church and parish lay outside its walls), but to have intervened to stop a project to burn it within by firing missiles from a gun. After the king's forces relieved the siege on 6 August, Welsh was arrested and tried under martial law. He was charged, according to Hooker, with being a principal leader of the rebellion, persuading people to support the old religion against the new, and causing a tinner of Chagford named Kingewell to be hanged for carrying letters on behalf of the crown. He was condemned to death and, despite some local sympathy, was duly hanged in chains from a gallows erected on the tower of his parish church. As an example to others, he was dressed in what Hooker later called 'his popishe apparell, and havinge a holye water bucket, a sprinkle, a sacringe bell, a payre of beddes [a rosary], and such other lyke popyshe trashe hangued aboute him'. He took his death patiently, according to Hooker, who believed that he would have been a good member of the commonwealth 'had not the weedes overgrowne the good corne, and his foule vices overcomed his vertewes' (ibid., 94).

NICHOLAS ORME

Sources J. Vowell [J. Hooker], *The description of the citie of Excester*, ed. W. J. Harte, J. W. Schopp, and H. Tapley-Soper, 3 pts in 1, Devon and Cornwall RS (1919–47), pt 2, pp. 91–4 · episcopal register of John Veysey, Devon RO, Charter XIV, vol. 1, fol. 87r and ordination lists · F. Rose-Troup, *The western rebellion of 1549* (1913) · J. Youings, 'The south-western rebellion of 1549', *Southern History*, 1 (1979), 99–122

Welsh, Thomas (1781–1848), singer, was born at Wells, Somerset, the son of John Welsh and his wife, who was a daughter of the elder Thomas *Linley. At the age of six he became a chorister at Wells Cathedral, where his singing soon attracted an eager audience. Sheridan heard of him, and persuaded Linley to engage him for the 1792 Bath concerts. His first opera appearance was in 1792 in Thomas Attwood's *The Prisoner*, written especially for him, and he performed at Drury Lane Theatre in 1795 in Attwood's *The Adopted Child* and Storace's version of *Lodoiska*. John Kemble promoted him as an actor, and coached him in the part of Prince Arthur in Shakespeare's *King John*. Meanwhile Welsh was continuing his musical education under Karl Friedrich Horn, Johann Baptist Cramer, and Karl Friedrich Baumgarten. In 1802 he was admitted as a gentleman of the Chapel Royal.

Welsh, who was a bass, was most renowned as a singing teacher. His pupils included John Sinclair, Charles Edward Horn, and Catherine Stephens. **Mary Ann Wilson** (1802–1867), who was also his pupil, became his second wife on 9 June 1827. They had one daughter, who married the cellist Alfredo Piatti. Mary Ann Wilson had made her début as Mandane in Arne's *Artaxerxes* at Drury Lane in January

1821, and had created a great sensation. Her career was lucrative but short, as her exertions led to a breakdown in her health and the ruin of her voice. Welsh produced two farces at the Lyceum Theatre, an opera, *Kamskatka*, at Covent Garden, and music for several plays. He also wrote several songs, glees, partsongs, and duets. His song 'Harry Bluff' was popular, and his glee 'Hark! 'tis the whistling wind' won a prize in 1813. He published a *Vocal Instructor* in 1825. He died in Brighton on 31 January 1848.

J. C. HADDEN, *rev.* ANNE PIMLOTT BAKER

Sources *New Grove* · Brown & Stratton, *Brit. mus.* · D. Baptie, *A handbook of musical biography* (1883) · Grove, *Dict. mus.* · private information (1899) · *GM*, 2nd ser., 29 (1848), 554–5

Welsted, Leonard (*bap.* 1688, *d.* 1747), poet, baptized on 3 June 1688 at Abington, Northamptonshire, was the eldest child of Leonard Welsted (1649?–1694), rector of Abington, and Anne Staveley (*bap.* 1663, *d.* 1694), daughter of Thomas *Staveley (*bap.* 1626, *d.* 1684), the Leicester antiquary. Both parents died in 1694, two years after the father became vicar of St Nicholas, Newcastle upon Tyne: Anne was buried on 18 July, her widower on 15 November; so the orphaned Leonard and his younger brother and sister were brought up by Staveley relatives in Leicestershire. Leonard followed his father to Westminster School (queen's scholar, 1703) and Trinity College, Cambridge (admitted pensioner on 12 June 1707), but, unlike his father, he never graduated. In late 1707 or early 1708 he married Frances Purcell (*bap.* 1688), daughter and residuary legatee of Henry *Purcell. The only offspring of this (hasty?) union of under-age orphans was a daughter, Frances, baptized on 2 September 1708.

Welsted's first wife died young. On 4 December 1712 he married Anna Maria Walker (*d.* 1747), sister of Admiral Sir Hovenden Walker; she was called Zelinda in poems by Welsted and his friends, and was said to be a great beauty. There were no children from the second marriage. Welsted's daughter, Frances, died in her eighteenth year and was mourned in his fine *Hymn to the Creator* (1727).

Welsted said that 'Apple-pye' was his first-written poem: this engaging little georgic was printed in *The Northern Atlantis* (1713) attributed to William King (1663–1712), but is included in Welsted's collected *Epistles, Odes, &c.* (1724). His earliest published works were two verse eulogies of the duke of Marlborough and an elegy on John Philips in 1709, and a version of Longinus's *On the Sublime* in 1712 which Swift, with some justice, alleged was translated from Boileau's translation. Two of the 1709 publications were dedicated to tory ministers (Harley and St John) but by 1714, when Welsted published *The Prophecy*, a satire on Harley, and *An Epistle to Mr. Steele on the King's Accession*, he had shifted to the whigs. He became Steele's secretary or assistant and in that capacity carried £500 of government secret service money to Steele, though Pope, in *The Dunciad*, falsely claimed that Welsted received the money for himself. Welsted contributed to such whig periodicals as Steele's *Town-Talk* (1715–16) and Ambrose Philips's *Free-Thinker* (1718–19); he wrote a prologue and epilogue for

Steele's *The Conscious Lovers* (1722). Bezaleel Morrice's satirical verse *Epistle to Mr. Welsted* (1721) characterizes him as a smooth, lightweight, fashionable love poet.

Between 1720 and 1726 Welsted addressed complimentary poems to the duke of Chandos, the duke of Dorset, Earl Cadogan, General Wade, Dr Garth, and the countess of Warwick (on her marriage to Addison). Welsted's comedy, *The Dissembled Wanton*, was acted with James Quin in the lead in December 1726, at Lincoln's Inn Fields; it earned the author £138 7s., together with £60 for the printed copy. In 1727 Welsted published proposals for editing and translating the whole works of Horace in five volumes by subscription at a guinea a volume; a few specimens were published, but he soon abandoned the project.

Samuel Garth included Welsted's work in the well-known collective translation of Ovid's *Metamorphoses* which he edited in 1717. In April of that year Garth asked the duke of Newcastle to find an allowance or a place worth £100 a year in the custom house for Welsted—'a scholar and very modest, your Schoolfellow, and has dedicated things to you' (BL, Add. MS 32658, fol. 12)—but Welsted's place, secured by 1725 and worth £50 p.a., proved to be an extraordinary clerkship in the Ordnance office and was probably owing to the favour of Earl Cadogan, master-general of the ordnance, to whom the poet had also dedicated things.

Welsted described his official residence at the Tower of London in *Oikographia* (1725), an engaging poem in octosyllabic couplets where he dwells with relish on his furniture, the family portraits (including his bewhiskered grandsire, the antiquary), the view from an alcove on the roof, and the parlour furnished for a levée of humble bards: altogether a well-appointed dwelling except for the emptiness of its cellar. In 1730 Welsted was advanced to the post of clerk-in-ordinary at the Ordnance office (£70 p.a.), probably through the interest of Bishop Hoadley; in May 1731 he became a commissioner and manager of the national lottery (£150 p.a.), by the favour of Bubb Dodington.

In 1717 Welsted published *Palaemon to Caelia, or, The Triumvirate*, a lively verse satire on Pope, Gay, and Arbuthnot's *Three Hours after Marriage*; in 1724 Welsted's 'Dissertation', prefacing *Epistles, Odes, &c.*, contained a slighting reference to a line in Pope's *Essay on Criticism*; a year later Welsted was introduced as Pope's main antagonist in Thomas Cooke's *The Battel of the Poets*. As a result Welsted's verse and servility to patrons were ridiculed in Pope's *Peri Bathous* (1728) and in text and notes of *The Dunciad* (1728, 1729): most memorably in the Denham parody beginning: 'Flow Welsted, flow! like thine inspirer, Beer' (A. Pope, *The Dunciad*, 3). Welsted responded with *One Epistle to Mr. A. Pope* (1730), *Of Dulness and Scandal*, and *Of False Fame* (both 1732): the first of these was a collaboration with another *Dunciad* victim, James Moore Smythe. Pope had the last word in his *Epistle to Arbuthnot* (1735).

Welsted's verse address to the princess of Wales in 1737, at the height of the prince's quarrel with his father, suggests that he was flirting with the whig opposition, but he wrote very little thereafter. He turned to prose in *The Scheme and Conduct of Providence* (1736), a conventional vindication of the justice and goodness of God.

Welsted is best known today as a Pope dunce. His complimentary poems are obsequious, his translations, verse tales, and love lyrics are, at best, competent; he was massively outgunned by Pope in satire; but there is merit in his relaxed, conversational, convivial poems, such as 'The Invitation' (*Free-Thinker*, 124, 1719), *Oikographia*, and his last published work, *The Summum bonum, or, Wisest Philosophy* (1741), a poem in praise of simple pleasures, such as the sociable drinking of wine and spirits. Apart from such invitations, and the complaint in *Oikographia* that he lacked wine for his spacious cellar in the Tower, there is no evidence for Pope's libel that Welsted was a drunkard or even a beer drinker. John Nichols wrote, 'a gentleman now living recollects hearing of Welsted's fame as a chess-player at the Temple coffee-house' (*Works*, xxii). Welsted died intestate at the Tower in August 1747; his second wife survived him only for a few months; his brother, Thomas, had died in 1713, so letters of administration were granted on 24 May 1748 to his unmarried sister, Anne (*d.* 1757).

JAMES SAMBROOK

Sources *The works in verse and prose of Leonard Welsted*, ed. J. Nichols (1787) · Nichols, *Lit. anecdotes*, 9.32–5 · D. Fineman, *Leonard Welsted, gentleman poet of the Augustan age* (1950) · J. Chamberlayne, *Magnae Britanniae notitia, or, The present state of Great Britain*, 37th edn (1748) · R. Shiels, *The lives of the poets of Great Britain and Ireland*, ed. T. Cibber, 4 (1753), 205–9 · J. Duncombe, *Letters by several eminent persons deceased … with notes explanatory and historical*, 2nd edn, 3 vols. (1773) · *Report on manuscripts in various collections*, 8 vols., HMC, 55 (1901–14), vol. 6, pp. 9–10 · *IGI* · undated letter from Garth to Newcastle, BL, Add. MS 32658, fol. 12 · *GM*, 1st ser., 56 (1786), 940 · *GM*, 1st ser., 58 (1788), 235–7 · *GM*, 1st ser., 62 (1792), 395 · *GM*, 1st ser., 73 (1803), 495–6 · *London Magazine*, 16 (1747), 388 · F. B. Zimmerman, *Henry Purcell, 1659–1695: his life and times*, rev. edn (1983), 340 · *The correspondence of Richard Steele*, ed. R. Blanchard (1941) · D. F. Foxon, ed., *English verse, 1701–1750: a catalogue of separately printed poems with notes on contemporary collected editions*, 2 vols. (1975) · *Old Westminsters*, 2.979 · Venn, *Alum. Cant.* · *Richard Steele's periodical journalism, 1714–1716*, ed. R. Blanchard (1959)

Welsted, Robert (1670/71–1735), physician, was the son of Leonard Welsted of Bristol. He matriculated from St Edmund Hall, Oxford, on 4 December 1687, aged sixteen, and was elected in 1689 to a demyship at Magdalen College, which he held until 1698, graduating BA on 25 June 1691, and MA on 12 May 1694. He was admitted an extra-licentiate of the Royal College of Physicians on 11 December 1695.

Welsted was then practising medicine at Bristol, where he remained for some years, but eventually moved to London, and was admitted a licentiate of the college on 3 September 1710. Welsted was one of 'the oldest and heartiest' friends of Bishop Hugh Boulter, primate of Ireland, who described him as a true Hanoverian and supporter of the revolution, and thought that because of this 'he has been distressed in his business by the disaffected' (*Letters*, 1.94). He was the author of a number of philosophical works and was admitted a fellow of the Royal Society on 20 March 1718. With Richard West (1671–1716), the father of

Gilbert West (1703–1756), Welsted edited the works of Pindar with notes and a paraphrase (1692). His practice was not successful in his later years and he was obliged to rely on the generosity of Bishop Boulter, who allowed him £200 a year and maintained his son at Hart Hall, Oxford (*Letters*, 1.94). Welsted died at Tavistock Street, London, on 1 February 1735.   E. I. CARLYLE, *rev.* PATRICK WALLIS

Sources Foster, *Alum. Oxon.* · Munk, *Roll* · *GM*, 1st ser., 5 (1735), 107 · [H. Boulter], *Letters written by … Hugh Boulter … to several ministers of state*, ed. [A. Philips and G. Faulkner], 2 vols. (1769–70)

Welton, Richard (1671/2–1726), clergyman of the nonjuring Church of England, was born at Framlingham, Suffolk, the son of Thomas Welton, druggist, of Woodbridge, Suffolk. First educated at Woodbridge, he was admitted on 3 March 1688 to Gonville and Caius College, Cambridge, aged sixteen, and graduated BA (1692), MA (1695), and DD (1708). He was married to Temperance Goodwyn, and they had at least one child, Richard, who was baptized at Whitechapel in 1708.

Welton was ordained in 1695 and served as rector of St Mary's, Whitechapel, London, from 1697 to 1715. To his rectory, the vicarage of East Ham, Essex, was added in 1710. A friend and supporter of fellow London minister Henry Sacheverell, in 1710 Welton preached the controversial sermon *The Wise Man's Counsel upon the Test*, which attacked occasional conformity, which he claimed 'abused and perverted' the Lord's supper 'to countenance and secure the PATRIOTS of Resistance, in places of great station and power' (R. Welton, *The Wise Man's Counsel upon the Test*, 1710, Preface). The sermon also defended absolute monarchy and urged active obedience to the monarchy, except where contrary to God's word, in which circumstances one 'must submit and yield Passive Obedience unto them', withstanding the government only with tears and prayers (ibid., 9). The sermon drew an anonymous response entitled *Solomon Against Welton* (1710), which raised the spectre of Jacobitism. Further controversy arose in 1713 when Welton had the portrait painter James Fellowes create a new altarpiece for Whitechapel which portrayed Bishop White Kennett as Judas at the last supper. Kennett appealed to the bishop of London to have the painting removed and in April 1714 he succeeded, despite Welton's claim that the bishop's own chancellor had asked only that minor changes be made to the painting. Welton's response to the controversy, a sermon entitled *Church Ornament without Idolatry Vindicated* (1714), defended the piece, suggesting that opposition to it was political in nature for it had offended 'the very scum of a whiggfaction' (Welton, Preface). Welton's Jacobite sympathies were also expressed in his sermon 'The shipwreck of faith', preached in honour of Queen Anne's memory. There he spoke of the Stuart name being 'hateful to our Enemies, but the glory of our Country' (R. Welton, *The Substance of the Christian Faith and Practice*, 1724, 261–2). He then suffered deprival from his clerical positions on 3 March 1715 after he failed to appear and take the oath of allegiance in October 1714.

After his deprival Welton led a nonjuring congregation in Whitehall, London. In 1717 government agents raided his chapel in Goodman's Fields, finding there a gathering of 250 people. Those assembled were requested to take the oaths of abjuration, which Welton and forty others refused. Consecrated irregularly to the nonjuring episcopate in 1722 by Ralph Taylor of the nonusager party, he went to America in 1724 and was called as rector of Christ Church, Philadelphia, on 27 July 1724. There he published a collection of eighteen sermons, including a reprinting of 'Church ornament without idolatry vindicated', published at the request of the Whitechapel congregation, under the title *The Substance of the Christian Faith and Practice* (1724). Welton also translated, as *The Sufferings of the Son of God* (1720), the *Trabalhos de Jesus* written by the Portuguese mystic Thomas of Jesus (1529–1582). He served at Christ Church, despite the objections of William Keith, the governor of Pennsylvania, until he was requested to return to England by royal writ in January 1726. There is no evidence that he exercised episcopal jurisdiction, and at his request the church in Philadelphia prepared a testimonial to his conduct. He went instead to Lisbon, in Portugal, where he seems to have had some connections. He died there on 22 July 1726.   ROBERT D. CORNWALL

Sources *A biographical history of England, from the revolution to the end of George I's reign: being a continuation of the Rev. J. Granger's work*, ed. M. Noble, 3 (1806), 151 · J. Venn and others, eds., *Biographical history of Gonville and Caius College*, 1: 1349–1713 (1897), 1.484 · Venn, *Alum. Cant.*, 1/4.365 · W. S. Perry, ed., *Historical collections relating to the American colonial church*, 2 (1871); repr. (1969), 136–53 · W. S. Perry, ed., *The history of the American Episcopal church*, 2 vols. (1885), 1.234–7, 541–60 · R. Welton, *Church ornament without idolatry vindicated* (1714) · *A full and true account of the apprehending and taking Dr Welton* (1720) · *Solomon against Welton* (1710) · [W. Shippen], *The case of not taking the oaths* (1717) · J. G. Wilson and J. Fiske, eds., *Appleton's cyclopaedia of American biography*, rev. edn, 6 (1899), 434 · J. H. Overton, *The nonjurors: their lives, principles, and writings* (1902), 283 · *N&Q*, 2 (1850), 355 · *N&Q*, 4th ser., 5 (1870), 519 · *N&Q*, 5th ser., 12 (1879), 221–3 · *N&Q*, 6th ser., 10 (1884), 377 · G. V. Bennett, *White Kennett, 1660–1728, bishop of Peterborough* (1957) · *IGI* · P. Fritz, *The English ministers and Jacobitism between the rebellions of 1715 and 1745* (1975) · G. Holmes, *The trial of Doctor Sacheverell* (1973) · T. Lathbury, *A history of the nonjurors* (1845) · H. Broxap, *The later nonjurors* (1924)

Likenesses line engraving, BM, NPG · portrait, repro. in R. Welton, *The substance of the Christian faith and practice* (1724)

Welwitsch, Friedrich Martin Josef (1806–1872), botanist, was born at Maria-Saal, near Klagenfurt, Carinthia, Austria, on 5 February 1806, to a large family of a prosperous farmer and surveyor. While at school he was encouraged by his father in the study of botany, and when sent to the University of Vienna with a view to the legal profession, he was so devoted to the study of natural history as to make no progress in the study of the law. His father thereupon withdrew his allowance, but Welwitsch transferred to the medical faculty of the university, continued with his botanical studies, and supported himself by writing critiques of theatrical productions. In 1834 he gained a prize, offered by the mayor of Vienna, for his 'Beiträge zur cryptogamischen Flora Unter-Oesterreichs', and his appointment about the same time to report on the cholera in Carinthia reconciled his father to his new profession. After travelling as tutor to a nobleman, he returned

Friedrich Martin Josef Welwitsch (1806–1872), by unknown engraver

to Vienna, and graduated MD in 1836, his thesis being published in that year as *Synopsis Nostochinearum Austriæ inferioris.*

Welwitsch spent much of his time in the botanical museum at Vienna, and became intimate with Fenzl and other botanists. In 1839, 'an act of youthful indiscretion on his part, in the course of enjoying too freely the gaieties of Vienna, rendered it expedient for him to leave Austria' (Hiern, 1.xvii) and he accepted a commission from the Unio Itineraria of Württemberg to collect the plants of the Azores and Cape Verde Islands. With this object he travelled to England, from where he sailed to Lisbon, arriving in July 1839. He learned Portuguese in six weeks, and, becoming attached to Portugal, he did not leave that country until 1853, except for short visits to Paris and London. During these years he had charge of the botanical gardens at Lisbon and Coimbra, and of those of the duke of Palmela at Cintra, Alemtejo, and elsewhere. He was also engaged as demonstrator and curator at the Lisbon Polytechnic. He explored most of Portugal, forming a herbarium of nine thousand species fully represented by specimens in all stages of growth, with descriptive notes and synonymy; he sent eleven thousand specimens to the Unio Itineraria and deposited sets with the academies of Lisbon and Paris. In 1841 Welwitsch had a three days' excursion to the Valle de Zebro with Robert Brown (1773–1858), and in 1847 and 1848, with Count Descayrac, he explored the southern province of Algarve, then little known to botanists. Between 1847 and 1852 he added 250 species of the larger fungi from the neighbourhood of Lisbon to those enumerated in Brotero's *Flora*, while in his

zeal for algae (of which in 1850 he published a list in the second volume of the *Actas* of the Lisbon Academy) he spent hours day after day up to his waist in water. In 1851 he sent twelve thousand specimens of flowering plants and six thousand cryptogams to England for sale; the fungi and mosses collected by him were described by Miles Joseph Berkeley and Mr Mitten in *Some Notes upon the Cryptogamic … Plants Collected in Portugal, 1842–50* (1853). He also studied and collected molluscs and insects, especially Coleoptera and Hymenoptera, and in 1844 was one of the founders of the Horticultural Society of Lisbon.

In 1851 Welwitsch was engaged to prepare the Portuguese collections for the Great Exhibition, and accompanied them to London, where he sought the advice of Robert Brown and others as to the exploration of Portuguese West Africa, for which he had been chosen by the government of his adopted country. He started from Lisbon on this seven years' journey on 8 August 1853, visited Madeira, the Cape Verde Islands and Freetown, Sierra Leone (where he spent nine days in making his first acquaintance with tropical vegetation), and reached Luanda on 30 September. Nearly a year was devoted to the exploration of the coast zone from the mouth of the Quizembo, lat. 8°15′ S, to that of the Cuanza, lat. 9°20′ S. He had been given £270 for his scientific equipment and voyage, and was paid £45 a month, but finding that bearers and other expenses of his fieldwork far exceeded this allowance, he sent large collections of insects, seeds, living plants, and dried specimens to England for sale. In September 1854 he ascended the River Bengo to Sange in Golungo Alto, 125 miles from the coast, where he met David Livingstone, living with him some time, and remaining in this district of dense jungle in all for about two years, during which he suffered much from fever, scurvy, and ulcerated legs. In 1856 he travelled south-westward to Pungo Andongo in the Presidio das Pedras Nigras. After eight months' exploration from this centre he returned to Luanda, having in the course of three years explored a triangular area with 120 miles of coast as its base, and its apex at Quisonde on the Cuanza, and collected over 3200 species of plants.

Welwitsch drew up a summary of his geographical and botanical findings under the title of 'Apontamentos phyto-geographicos sobre a flora da provincia de Angola', which was published at Lisbon in 1859 in the *Annaes do Conselho Ultramarino*. In this work he divided Angola into three botanical regions: the coast, up to an altitude of 1000 feet, the mountain woodland, from 1000 to 2500 feet; and the highland, above 2500 feet. In September 1858 he took a trip to Libongo, to the north of Luanda, and in June 1859 went to Benguela and thence by sea to Mossamedes. There the subtropical climate did much to reinvigorate him, and he found a flora near the coast more like that of Cape Colony, though only a mile inland it was more purely tropical. As he approached Cape Negro (in lat. 15°40′ S) the coast rose as a plateau of tufaceous limestone, covered with sandstone shingle, 300 or 400 feet high and 6 miles across, and it was there that Welwitsch discovered that remarkable plant which he named *Tumboa*, but which J. D.

Hooker later renamed *Welwitschia* in his honour. This unique plant is made up of an enormous underground stem, and a pair of strap-shaped leaves that lie along the ground. Welwitsch was so amazed by his discovery 'that he could do nothing but kneel down on the burning soil and gaze at it, half in fear lest a touch should prove it a figment of the imagination' (Hiern, 1.xiii).

Welwitsch collected more than two thousand specimens in Benguela, but a tribal rebellion stopped his work; fifteen thousand Munanos attacked the colony of Lopollo in Huila, where he then was, and blockaded it for two months. After this Welwitsch, wounded and in bad health, returned to Mossamedes and Luanda, and from there in January 1861, he sailed to Lisbon, taking with him what was undoubtedly the best and most extensive herbarium ever collected in tropical Africa (Hiern, 1.xiv). He was placed on Portuguese government committees for the improvement of cotton cultivation in Angola and for collecting the products of Portuguese colonies for the London International Exhibition of 1862, in connection with which he published one of his more important independent works, *Synopse explicativa de madeiras e drogas medicinaes* (1862). In November 1861 his patron King Dom Pedro V died, leaving Welwitsch at the mercy of the Portuguese bureaucracy. Finding it necessary to compare his specimens, a very large proportion of which were new to science, with those in English collections, he obtained permission from the Portuguese government in 1863 to take his collections, which are estimated to have comprised five thousand species of plants and three thousand species of insects, to England. He arrived in London on 20 October 1863, and devoted the remaining nine years of his life to the task of studying and arranging his collections. In connection with this work he maintained an extensive correspondence with many of the leading specialists among the naturalists of Europe, and received honourable recognition from many learned societies. However, the Portuguese government became impatient with his rate of progress, and ultimately, in February 1866, suspended his salary of £2 a day. Welwitsch worked on in London, paying out of his own means the expenses of various publications which he had begun, the most important of which was his 'Sertum Angolense' (*Transactions of the Linnean Society*, 27, 1869, 1–94), which cost him £130.

Poverty eventually forced him to consider returning to Portugal, but he had insufficient funds for the voyage. His health deteriorated further, and he died on 20 October 1872 at his home at 15 Fitzroy Street, London, and was buried on 24 October in Kensal Green cemetery, where he is described on his tomb as 'Botanicus eximius, florae Angolensis investigatorum princeps'. By his will, dated three days before his death, Welwitsch directed that the study set of his African plants should be offered to the British Museum (whose natural history departments were soon to be accommodated separately in the Natural History Museum, South Kensington), for purchase. The Portuguese government, however, claimed the whole of the collections, a claim which was resisted by the executors. The resulting chancery suit, the *King of Portugal* v.

Carruthers and Justen, was eventually settled, the study set being returned to Lisbon, and the museum receiving the next best set with a copy of the explanatory notes and descriptions made by Welwitsch. A highly regarded catalogue of the collection, edited by William Philip Hiern (2 vols., 1896–1901), contains an engraved portrait, biography, and full bibliography not only of Welwitsch's own work, but also of that of others relating to his collections.

Although Welwitsch's achievements in economic botany disappointed his Portuguese employers, and as a man he could be 'difficult … impatient, and tactless' (Swinscow, 278–9), his collections 'far exceeded in number, quality and documentation any made before then in tropical Africa and remain a valuable source of information' (Stearn, 101).

Of Welwitsch's many papers the more important were the 'Apontamentos', the *Synopsis nostochienearum*, the *Synopse explicativa*, and the 'Sertum Angolense' already referred to. His most important other work concerned the cultivation of cotton in Angola, and a translation by A. R. Saraiva was published in London in 1862.

G. S. BOULGER, *rev.* ANDREW GROUT

Sources T. D. V. Swinscow, 'Friedrich Welwitsch, 1806–72. A centennial memoir', *Biological Journal of the Linnean Scoiety*, 4 (1972), 269–89 · F. A. Stafleu and R. S. Cowan, *Taxonomic literature: a selective guide*, 2nd edn, 7, Regnum Vegetabile, 116 (1988), 174–8 · W. T. Stearn, *The catalogue of the African plants collected by Dr Friedrich Welwitsch (1896–1901) and its litiginous background*, Garcia de Orta Botany Series, 1 (1973), 101–4 · W. P. Hiern, *Catalogue of the African plants collected by Dr Friedrich Welwitsch in 1853–1861*, 1 (1896), 7–25 · P. I. Edwards, 'Friedrich Welwitsch, 1806–1872. His manuscripts and correspondence in the Departments of Botany and Zoology, British Museum (Natural History), the Linnean Society of London, and the Royal Botanic Garden, Kew', *Biological Journal of the Linnean Society*, 4 (1972), 291–303 · *CGPLA Eng. & Wales* (1872)
Archives Linn. Soc. · NHM · RBG Kew | NHM, plants
Likenesses lithograph, 1865, RBG Kew; repro. in E. Nelmes, ed., *Curtis's Botanical Magazine dedications, 1827–1927* (1931), facing p. 147 · engraving, repro. in Hiern, *Catalogue of the African plants* · engraving, RBG Kew [*see illus.*] · photograph, NHM
Wealth at death under £200: resworn probate, May 1876, *CGPLA Eng. & Wales* (1872)

Welwood, James (*fl.* 1652–1727). *See under* Welwood, James (1652–1727).

Welwood, James (1652–1727), physician and writer on politics, was born in Dunfermline, Fife, Scotland, the third son of John Welwood (*c*.1603–*c*.1680) and Margaret Dury (*c*.1620–1659). Formerly a teacher, the elder Welwood began preaching on a rota basis at Leuchars in 1643, and by 1659 had procured a parish near Annandale, Dumfriesshire. Mrs Welwood died that same year. In 1663 the Revd John Welwood, an ardent Presbyterian, was dismissed for refusing to accept episcopacy in Scotland. Both of James Welwood's older brothers, John and Andrew, became irreconcilable covenanters. In 1668 Welwood enrolled at St Andrews University (St Salvator's College), receiving his BA and MA degrees by 25 July 1671. He probably taught at a school in Fife for a few years. Welwood later acknowledged that his brother John's sermons against Archbishop James Sharp implicated the Welwood family in

Sharp's murder in 1679, forcing him to flee Scotland (appendix to *Mercurius Reformatus*, 1692).

Welwood studied medicine on the continent, apparently at Leiden and Paris, and spent some time at the court of William of Orange in the Hague before graduating MD from Rheims in 1684. His experience in France during the years when the government of Louis XIV eroded the policy of religious toleration and persecuted Huguenots instilled in him a desire for religious accommodation under a protestant king. On his return to Scotland that year Welwood was arrested for corresponding with Scottish exiles in the Netherlands, but he was released and practised medicine for a time in Edinburgh. In 1685 he married Barbara Armor (*c.*1665–*c.*1700), who in 1686 gave birth to Mary Welwood Maxwell, the first of their three daughters.

Welwood moved across the border to Newcastle upon Tyne in 1687 and after the arrival in England of William of Orange the following year, engaged in a published war of words with John March, vicar of Newcastle. Their letters appeared in March's *Vindication of the Present Great Revolution in England* (1689). Welwood strongly supported the revolution of 1688, mainly because he viewed the Dutch prince as a champion of protestantism against the twin dangers of the Roman church and Catholic France. In the first weeks of 1689 Welwood migrated to London and began publication of the twice-weekly Williamite journal *Mercurius Reformatus*. He caught the attention of Bishop Gilbert Burnet, who admired his writing style and political views; Welwood proved useful in the campaign to deflect Jacobite propaganda emanating from the continent. Welwood was appointed an extra-physician to William and Mary in March 1690, and elevated to physician to the person by warrant from the lord chamberlain in April of that year. Accordingly the Royal College of Physicians welcomed him as a royal doctor when he became a fellow in 1690 (annals, RCP Lond.). In January 1691 he was named superintendent of surgeons in the fleet, the first of many government medical appointments. From the spring of 1691 he also functioned as a reformist commissioner for the sick and wounded, and as principal physician to the forts along the Thames.

Despite the favour shown him by William and Mary, Welwood and his printer, Richard Baldwin, were castigated by the House of Commons in November 1691 for criticizing in *Mercurius Reformatus* the parliamentary management of war appropriations. Welwood ceased publication of the paper immediately thereafter, and, at the request of Queen Mary, started to write a history of the reign of Charles I. Disturbed by a number of critical works on her grandfather's life, the queen charged Welwood with writing for her private edification an honest account, which he expanded to a hundred-year survey after her death, and published in 1700. *Memoirs of the most Material Transactions*, generally sympathetic to Charles I, went through multiple editions and influenced later whig historians.

Welwood's first wife died about the turn of the century and in 1703 he married Elizabeth Tregonwell Seymour (*c.*1670–1732), daughter of John Tregonwell, and widow of Henry Seymour. The Welwoods lived in the York Buildings just off the Strand. During the next two decades he wrote an almanac (1705); authenticated Bulstrode Whitelocke's manuscript on early English history (1709); translated Xenophon's *Symposium* as *The Banquet* (1710); and wrote a lengthy preface to an English verse rendition of Lucan by Nicholas Rowe (1718). Welwood was also active in the Royal College of Physicians, becoming a censor and an elector in 1722. In 1726 he acted as a go-between in the tumultuous triangle that included Prince George, his mistress and friend of the Welwood family Henrietta Howard, and her husband Charles. Before a settlement was reached Welwood died, on 2 April 1727 at his home in York Buildings, and was buried in the vault of his parish church, St Martin-in-the-Fields. He was preceded in death by his daughter Barbara Welwood Molesworth, but nominated his unmarried daughter Jane Welwood as executor of the estate. Most of Welwood's wealth was distributed to family and friends. His wife's dowry was returned to her as part of a pre-nuptial agreement; she died in 1732.

The James Welwood of this article should not be confused with the **James Welwood** (*fl.* 1652–1727) who was the son of Robert Wellwood, of Touch, and his wife, Jean Livingstone, and who has often been wrongly credited with Welwood's works. ELIZABETH LANE FURDELL

Sources E. L. Furdell, *James Welwood MD* (1998) • *DNB* • P. Chalmers, *Historical and statistical account of Dunfermline*, 2 (1859) • R. Sibbald, *History, ancient and modern, of the sheriffdoms of Fife and Kinross* (1804) • wills, PRO, PROB 11/615, sig. 101; PROB 11/651, sig. 125 [Elizabeth Welwood] • annals, RCP Lond., 5.125b • *Mercurius Reformatus* (1692), appx, ed. J. Welwood • *Corrections and additions to the Dictionary of National Biography*, Institute of Historical Research (1966) • J. C. Sainty and R. Bucholz, eds., *Officials of the royal household, 1660–1837*, 1: *Department of the lord chamberlain and associated offices* (1997)
Archives BL, Sloane MSS
Wealth at death approx. £5000: will, PRO, PROB 11/615, sig. 101

Welwood, William (*fl.* 1566–1624), legal writer and mathematician, was the eldest son of Thomas Welwood (*d.* 1583), a prominent merchant burgess of St Andrews, and his wife, Janet Geddie (*d.* 1616); he had at least four sisters and three brothers. He matriculated at St Leonard's College, St Andrews, in 1566 and graduated BA in 1569 and MA in 1570. In October 1573 he matriculated at the University of Wittenberg, where he may have taken the degree of LLD. In the early 1570s, his family was high in the favour of the regime of the regent, James Douglas, earl of Morton, and on 26 December 1575 he was gifted the office of third master in St Mary's College. His duty was to teach the mathematical sciences. At an unknown date he married Christina Cunningham; they had at least one son, David.

Welwood belonged to a cultivated group of scientists in the university and taught not only arithmetic, geometry, geography, and astronomy, but also map making, the use of the astrolabe, calendars, and horology, practical disciplines of interest to the son of a merchant. It is possible that he was an early influence on the distinguished map maker Timothy Pont, then a student at St Andrews. In 1577, with John Geddie, former servitor to George Buchanan, a skilled mathematician and probably a relative, he gained a patent for an improved method of raising water from wells, about which he later published *Guilielmi Velvod de aqua in altum per fistulas plumbeas facile exprimenda apologia demonstratiua* (1582). Dedicated to the earl of Bothwell, *De aqua* probably gained Welwood the title 'his hienes mathematicien' that he held by 1583, when, with Edward Bruce, advocate and future courtier of James VI, he gained a licence for an engine to pump out coalmines.

This success came in the context of attempts by the masters of St Mary's, who had been opposed to Welwood's admittance, to remove him from his post. A visitation of the university in 1579 transferred the mathematician and lawyer to St Salvator's College, but here too the appointment was unpopular with the masters, this time ostensibly because of its financial implications. However, while there may have been genuine grounds for grievance here, the unremitting hostility he encountered from the provost, James Martin, seems to have derived from or been intensified by a feud between Martin's family and that of Welwood. The origins of the feud are unknown. On one side were the Arthurs, who included several sons of Margaret Martin, the provost's cousin. These brothers were also the brothers-in-law of the new archbishop of St Andrews, Patrick Adamson; they were supported by the powerful Learmonth of Dairsie family, whose members were regularly elected as provosts of the burgh. On the other side were the Welwoods, with their relatives the Geddies and the Smiths. Enriching the brew of hostility was the Welwoods' strong support for Andrew Melville, the noted advocate of presbyterianism in the reformed kirk in Scotland and powerful reforming principal of St Mary's College, who had also provided introductory verses for Welwood's *De aqua*.

In 1584 the Black Acts had asserted crown authority over the kirk, marking the temporary eclipse of the Melville faction. In 1587 Welwood transferred to the chair of law, replacing John Arthur, one of the brothers; whether this move had any connection with the feud is unknown. In the hothouse atmosphere of religious and family tension in St Andrews, however, these political and local developments resulted in the attempt of Henry Hamilton, servitor to the archbishop, to murder Welwood (whom he had earlier assaulted) as he went to lecture. In the general tumult, James Arthur, one of the brothers, was killed. The dispute between the families was put to arbitration, resulting in the banishment from Scotland of James Smith, John Welwood, and John Geddie and the banishment of some others from St Andrews, including Thomas Geddie. This was a severe punishment on a set of families who made their living as merchants; John Geddie, for example, had six children to support.

In 1590 Welwood published in Edinburgh *The sea law of Scotland. Shortly gathered and plainly dressit for the reddy use of all seafairing men*. In a dedication to King James, this short work called for a reformation of justice. Indeed legal reform was much in the air in Scotland at this time and Welwood's convinced presbyterianism induced him no doubt to hope for a godly reform. The work is essentially aimed at explaining the law underpinning the type of trading carried on in the small vessels that characterized

Scottish shipping, focusing on the duties of the master of the vessel. Politics now favoured the Welwoods. In 1592 Archbishop Adamson died, while parliament recognized the Melvillian structure of the kirk. The financial disputes between Martin and Welwood and Homer Blair (the new mathematician) were settled. The municipal elections of 1593 in St Andrews favoured the supporters of Melville. In 1594 James Melville, nephew of Andrew, solicited the king for the return of John Welwood and James Smith from exile, although the men had either to submit to trial or to satisfy the Arthurs with compensation. In 1595 King James recommended to the provost and council of St Andrews that there should be a reconciliation between the Welwoods and the Arthurs. By September 1596 it appears that considerable progress had been made in this through negotiations involving the presbytery of St Andrews.

In 1594 Welwood published a number of works abroad, perhaps to escape the control of the privy council. That summer he spent time in Leiden, where he issued two works concerned with the relationship between Jewish law and Roman law. *Juris divini Judaeorum, ac juris civilis Romanorum parallela*, dedicated to John Kennedy, earl of Cassillis, and John Lindsay, Lord Lindsay, supporters of the presbyterians, had an appendix on ecclesiastical law. This appendix contained a letter to Welwood from Franciscus Junius while the two radical ministers of St Andrews, David Black and Robert Wallace, were addressed by Welwood in a letter. *Filios Lucis esse prudentiores filiis huius seculi*, dedicated to the great Dutchman Oldenbarnevelt, devoted considerable attention to the issue of sale. These works of Welwood deserve further study but evince a concern with the links between *jus scripturae* (biblical law), *jus scriptum* (written law), and *jus humanum* (human law), connecting his study of Roman law with certain biblical and religious concerns. In the same year he also published, this time at Middleburg, *Ars Domandarum perturbationum ex solo Dei verbo quais transcripto constructa*, a theological treatise also dedicated to the earl of Cassillis.

The tide now turned once more against the Melvilles and their supporters, bringing further problems for Welwood and his family. In 1596 Black and Wallace were removed from their charge; in the aftermath of the resulting disturbances, Welwood's brother Andrew and brother-in-law Henry Smith were among the men in St Andrews who had to find caution for their good behaviour. In 1597 there was a royal visitation of St Andrews, the main object of which was to curb the authority of Andrew Melville. Welwood was removed from the chair in law which was suppressed. At almost the same time, the general assembly moved against Black, Wallace, and Melville, with a series of charges. Black in particular was charged with usurping the power of the civil magistrate in dealing with the blood feud between the Welwoods and the Arthurs. At this point the Welwoods once more found themselves under physical threat in St Andrews. William Welwood's brother-in-law James Smith was murdered in September 1597, the day before a meeting arranged to seek a settlement of the feud. There ensued difficult negotiations involving the kirk session, which evidently favoured the Arthurs, and the presbytery, which sympathized with the Welwoods. In this tense period Esther Welwood, William's sister, was shot at. The Welwoods eventually succeeded in securing the excommunication of some of the Arthurs and their relatives. By late 1599 pressure had succeeded in securing another arbitration and decreet-arbitral settling the disputes between the two families, although relationships clearly remained tense. Probably as part of the negotiated settlement, King James restored Welwood to the chair of law in St Salvator's College, but he had to sign a bond for his good behaviour. No more is heard of the blood feud.

In 1605 Welwood published in London an elementary work on Roman law dealing briefly with the topic *de verborum obligationibus* in Justinian's compilation. This was dedicated to Chancellor Seton as Welwood manoeuvred for supporters. The following year saw the beginning of a concerted attack on the presbyterians, involving treason trials, the deprivation and imprisonment of Andrew Melville, and the re-erection of a full diocesan episcopacy. By 1611 one of Welwood's earlier opponents was an archbishop of St Andrews, now with full powers to complement his position as chancellor of the university. Welwood's resignation from the chair of law was engineered that year and he departed for England. His years there are obscure. In 1613, in the hope of patronage, he published, with a dedication to the king, *An abridgement of all sealawes; gathered forth of all writings and monuments, which are to be found among any people or nations, upon the coasts of the great ocean and Mediterranean Sea*. This work contained an early attack on Grotius's *Mare liberum* of 1609. Patronage came, and Welwood was employed on behalf of Queen Anne to expand this attack into *De dominio maris, juribusque ad dominium praecipue spectantibus assertio brevis et methodica* (1616). This contributed to the considerable legal debate over freedom of the seas at this period; its reprinting in 1653 elicited a reply the same year from the Dutchman Dirk Graswinkel.

By 1619 Welwood was ill and seeking patronage from Lancelot Andrews, bishop of Winchester. He may have singled out this Arminian-leaning cleric, who was a member of both the Scottish and English privy councils, because his brother was currently involved in an international legal dispute over a ship attacked by the Dutch in 1618. Welwood's final work, *Dubiorum quae tam in foro poli quam in foro fori occurrere solent, brevis expeditio* (1622), appeared in London and was dedicated to Sir Julius Caesar and John Williams, bishop of Lincoln. Welwood obviously had some association with Caesar, a devout Calvinist, as the latter's papers contain an opinion by Welwood dated 7 May 1624 on the legal status of ambassadors. By mid-1630 Welwood was dead: on 4 June his son David was retoured as heir to his grandfather in lands in Fife and was settling other aspects of the family affairs.   JOHN W. CAIRNS

Sources J. W. Cairns, 'Academic feud, blood feud, and William Welwood: legal education in St Andrews, 1560–1611', *Edinburgh Law Review*, 2 (1998), 158–79, 255–87 • J. H. Baxter, 'William Welwood of St. Mary's College', *Ecclesia: een bundel opstellen aangeboden aan Prof. Dr. Bakhuizen van den Brilk* (The Hague, 1959), 241–51 • D. H. Fleming, ed., *Register of the minister, elders, and deacons of the Christian congregation of St Andrews*, 2 vols., Scottish History Society, 4, 9 (1889–1990) • A. I. Dunlop, ed., *Acta facultatis artium universitatis Sanctiandree, 1413–1588*, 2 vols., Scottish History Society, 3rd ser., 54–5 (1964) • U. St Andr. L. • commissary court records and registers of deeds, and registers of sasines, NA Scot. • NL Scot., Balcarres MS Adu. MS 29.2.7

Archives NL Scot., Balcarres papers • U. St Andr.

Wemyss. For this title name *see* individual entries under Wemyss; *see also* Douglas, Francis Wemyss-Charteris-, eighth earl of Wemyss and sixth earl of March (1818–1914); Charteris, Mary Constance, countess of Wemyss (1862–1937).

Wemyss, David, second earl of Wemyss (1610–1679). *See under* Wemyss, David, fourth earl of Wemyss (*bap.* 1678, *d.* 1720).

Wemyss, David, fourth earl of Wemyss [*formerly* Lord Elcho] (*bap.* **1678**, *d.* **1720**), politician, was the eldest son of Margaret, countess of Wemyss and Cromartie (1659–1705), only surviving daughter of David Wemyss, second earl [*see below*], and her first husband, Sir James Wemyss of Caskieberran (*d.* 1682), who was created a life peer as Lord Burntisland in 1672. He was baptized on 29 April 1678 and was styled Lord Elcho until his mother's death in 1705.

Elcho was descended from a distinguished Fife family, which included Sir David Wemyss, who signed the letter to the pope in 1320 asserting the independence of Scotland, Sir John Wemyss, who assisted in repulsing an attempt by the English to land in Fife in 1547, and Sir John Wemyss (1586–1649), high commissioner to the general assembly, who was created earl of Wemyss, on 25 June 1633.

The first earl of Wemyss's only son, the grandfather of the fourth earl, was **David Wemyss**, second earl of Wemyss (1610–1679), army officer, whose mother was Jean Gray (*d.* 1640), daughter of Lord Gray. He was born on 6 September 1610. As Lord Elcho, a title he held between 1633 and 1649, he commanded a regiment of Fife infantry in the Scottish army which reached Newcastle upon Tyne in August 1640. On 1 September 1644, at the head of about 6000 men, he was routed by Montrose at Tippermuir, and in August 1645, as supernumerary commander to Lieutenant-General William Baillie, again suffered defeat by Montrose's forces at Kilsyth.

The second earl was married three times: in July 1625 to Anna (*d.* 1649), daughter of Robert *Balfour, second Lord Balfour of Burleigh; in April 1650 to Helenor (*d.* 1652), daughter of John *Fleming, second earl of Wigtown; and on 13 January 1653 to Margaret (*d.* 1688), daughter of John *Leslie, sixth earl of Rothes, and widow of Francis Scott, second earl of Buccleuch. The third marriage produced one daughter, Margaret, the only child to outlive her father. He died in July 1679 at Wemyss Castle, whose estate he had done much to develop.

The fourth earl of Wemyss, in succession to his mother, entered parliament on 28 June 1705 and was the same year sworn of the privy council and named one of the commissioners for the treaty of Union with England. In 1706 he was appointed high admiral of Scotland, and this office having been abolished at the Union, he was then constituted vice-admiral of Scotland, and nominated one of the council of Prince George of Denmark, high admiral of Great Britain. Following the Union he was on 13 February 1707 chosen as one of the sixteen representative Scottish peers; he was re-elected in 1708.

The fourth earl was also married three times. His first wife, Anne (d. 23 Feb 1700), whom he married on 13 August 1697, was the only daughter of William Douglas, first duke of Queensberry. The marriage produced two sons, David, Lord Elcho (d. 1715), and James (1699–1756), who became fifth earl of Wemyss. He remarried on 5 January 1709 at St Martin-in-the-Fields, London. His second wife was Mary (d. 1711/12), daughter of Sir John Robinson and his wife, Mary Dudley. His third wife, whom he married in July 1716, was Elizabeth (d. 1721), daughter of Henry, Lord Sinclair; they had two daughters: Elisabeth, who married William Sutherland, seventeenth earl of Sutherland, and Margaret, who married James Stewart, eighth earl of Moray.

Wemyss, whom Macky described as 'a fine personage and very beautiful', being a 'man of honour' with 'good sense' (*Memoirs of the Secret Services*, 250), died at Wemyss Castle on 15 March 1720.   JANET SORENSEN

Sources GEC, *Peerage* · *Memoirs of the secret services of John Macky*, ed. A. R. (1733) · *DNB*
Archives NA Scot., GD50

Wemyss, David, styled sixth earl of Wemyss [*known as* Lord Elcho] (**1721–1787**), Jacobite army officer, was born on 21 August 1721, probably at Wemyss Castle, Fife, the first son and heir of James, fifth earl of Wemyss (1699–1756), and his wife, Janet (d. 1778), daughter of the notorious Colonel Francis Charteris and Helen Swinton. The parents of Wemyss, who was known by his father's subsidiary title Lord Elcho, separated in 1732. Educated at Winchester College, which he attended from 1734 to 1738, and at the military academy at Angers, Elcho was in Rome from October 1740 until April 1741. There, like many young visitors to the city, he met James Stuart (Stuart claimant to the throne). However, unlike the audiences obtained by many such visitors, Elcho's sprang not from mere curiosity nor a wish to experience the frisson arising from the knowledge that he was committing an act of treason. Rather his two interviews were an expression of his family's traditional loyalty to the house of Stuart. Elcho's commitment had at one time in his youth wavered under the influence of the master of Sinclair, a third cousin of his father, who tried to persuade him to abandon the Jacobite cause and obtain a government post. It seems that Elcho considered this idea but was dissuaded from it by Sir James Stuart of Coltness and Goodtrees. The Pretender's response to Elcho's visits was to appoint him a colonel of dragoons in February 1744, having already admitted him a member of the Royal Company of Archers on 12 July 1741. He returned to England in October 1741 but was back in France again from September 1743 to April 1744, during which time orders were 'sent to Scotland to take up the earl of Wemys' son, and 'tis said, some others will be seized, to the number of 15' (*Egmont Diary*, 3.287).

Elcho's Jacobitism led him to join Prince Charles Edward at Gray's Mill, near Edinburgh, on 16 September 1745, when he became the prince's first aide-de-camp and an original member of his council. Elcho fought at the battle of Prestonpans on 21 September 1745 and was very likely in command of the 1st troop of the Horse Guards, which he had raised and then commanded throughout the time Charles was campaigning in England. Consisting of about 100 'gentleman of family and fortune … their uniform all blew and reed and all extreamly well mounted' (*Memorials of John Murray*, 226), these Horse Guards formed the prince's personal bodyguard. Elcho was one of the majority who at a council of war held at Derby in December 1745 advised the prince to return to Scotland rather than advance further into England and face almost certain death. Later Elcho was present on 17 January 1746 at the siege of Falkirk and on 16 April 1745 at the battle of Culloden, at which Charles's army was defeated by English forces under the command of the duke of Cumberland. Elcho was of the same mind as Lord George Murray, lieutenant-general in the Jacobite army and Charles's second in command, in attributing this defeat to the prince's lack of military acumen. While there appears to be little basis for the story that Elcho vilified the prince as he left the field of battle as 'a damned cowardly Italian' (Marshall, 146), Elcho clearly had little regard for him and believed that he placed too great a trust in Irish advisers such as Sir Thomas Sheridan. Whatever the truth of this, the defeat marked for the time being the end of the hope that Charles would secure his father's succession to the British throne, and Elcho, together with the duke of Perth and other leaders of the Jacobite forces, escaped to France in the frigate *Mars* on 3 May 1746. Elcho's *Short Account of the Affairs of Scotland in the Years 1744, 1745, 1746*, based on his manuscript journal, was published in 1907.

Elcho never returned to England, and for his part in the rising he was subject to the act of attainder passed in 1746 and his titles and lands were forfeited. In spite of this legal bar, he assumed the title of sixth earl of Wemyss on his father's death on 21 March 1756, although he continued generally to be known as Lord Elcho.

Elcho continued his military career in France, where he entered the service of Louis XV and held two unpaid offices. On 3 May 1756 he became a captain in Fitzjames's regiment, and from July 1756 until some time in 1763 held the rank of colonel in the Royal Scots. In the latter post Elcho was with his regiment at Gravelines from June to October 1757 and then at Dunkirk in 1758. Although he held no other military command, Louis XV conferred the order of military merit upon him in July 1770. Elcho divided his time between France and Switzerland, becoming naturalized in Neûchatel and purchasing a property there named La Prie. Although he had settled in France Elcho tried at various times to have his name removed from the act of attainder, and wrote from Paris on 27 June 1747 to the lord justice clerk 'if his Majesty will allow me to come home, I will give any assurance whatever for my making his Majesty a most loyall subject for the future' (*Memorials of John Murray*, 414). These unsuccessful attempts to have the attainder lifted created an enduring sense of bitterness between the prince and Elcho. This feeling was reinforced on Elcho's side by the prince's failure to repay the moneys he had advanced to him in support of his campaign in England.

On 9 September 1776 Elcho married at Beûtal in Switzerland the daughter (*b.* 1756) of Baron d'Uxhull. She died in childbirth on 26 November 1777. Elcho himself died in Paris on 29 April 1787, aged sixty-five, and was buried with his wife at Bôle in Switzerland. ROGER TURNER

Sources DNB · H. Tayler, *A Jacobite miscellany* (1948), 125–71 · GEC, *Peerage*, new edn, 12/2.471–2 · *Manuscripts of the earl of Egmont: diary of Viscount Percival, afterwards first earl of Egmont*, 3 vols., HMC, 63 (1920–23), vol. 3, p. 287 · *Memorials of John Murray of Broughton*, ed. R. F. Bell, Scottish History Society, 27 (1898), 226, 414 · C. W. Holgate and H. Chitty, eds., *Winchester long rolls, 1723–1821* (1904), 32, 35, 38, 40 · W. B. Blaikie, ed., *Itinerary of Prince Charles Edward Stuart*, Scottish History Society, 23 (1897) · R. K. Marshall, *Bonnie Prince Charlie* (1988) · David, Lord Elcho, *A short account of the affairs of Scotland in the years 1744, 1745, 1746*, ed. E. Charteris (1907)
Archives NRA, priv. coll., MS of his account of the Jacobite rising of 1745
Likenesses D. Dupra?, portrait, priv. coll.; repro. in Marshall, *Bonnie Prince Charlie* · A. Lalauze, etching (after A. Ramsay), BM · portrait, Wemyss Castle, Fife
Wealth at death act of attainder deprived him of estates and titles

Wemyss, David Douglas (1760–1839), army officer, went by the name of Douglas until about 1790, when he took the additional name of Wemyss, to the noble family of which name he belonged. He was commissioned ensign in the 49th foot on 27 April 1777, and joined them that year in North America, where he served first under General Howe, and then under Sir Henry Clinton, in the operations of the American war. In November 1778 he sailed with the 49th from New York in the expedition under Admiral Hotham and Major-General Grant to the West Indies. He took part in the capture of St Lucia on 13 December, and in the defence of the Vigie against the French under D'Estaing on the 18th. He was also in the naval engagement off the island of Grenada on 6 July 1779, and was promoted lieutenant on 15 August 1779. He returned to England in 1781.

Wemyss was promoted captain on 31 May 1783, and shortly after, on reduction of his regiment, was placed on half pay. He was brought into the 3rd foot (the Buffs) on 9 June 1786, joining the headquarters at Jamaica. He was required by ill health to return home in 1789. On 16 March 1791 he was promoted major in the 37th foot. In 1793 he served with them under the duke of York in Flanders, where he took part in the affair of Saultain, the battle of Famars (22 May), and the siege of Valenciennes, which capitulated on 28 July. For his services he was promoted lieutenant-colonel in the 18th foot (Royal Irish) from 12 April 1793. He was aged thirty-three. He had purchased every step in rank from ensign to colonel.

Wemyss commanded his new regiment in 1794, with the force under Sir Charles Stuart at the capture of Corsica, taking part in the sieges of Fiorenza in February, of Bastia in April, and of Calvi, where he was wounded, in

David Douglas Wemyss (1760–1839), by Henry R. Cook, pubd 1814 (after Thomas Stewardson)

August. He was mentioned in dispatches, and in 1795 was appointed governor of Calvi and its dependencies. He was promoted brevet colonel on 3 May 1796. On the evacuation of Corsica in October he accompanied the troops to Porto Ferrajo in Elba, whence he commanded a force (including the 18th) which landed on the Italian coast on 7 November, and succeeded in driving the French from Piombino, Campiglia, and Castiglione, but, the enemy receiving considerable reinforcements, the British troops were withdrawn from Italy and returned to Elba. On the evacuation of the Mediterranean in 1797 Wemyss took his regiment to Gibraltar, where he was employed as a brigadier-general on the staff until promoted major-general on 29 April 1802, when he returned to England.

In April 1803 Wemyss was appointed to the command of the forces in Ceylon. He returned home in 1806, was promoted lieutenant-general on 25 April 1808, and on 27 May 1809 was appointed governor of Tynemouth Castle and Cliffe Fort. He was promoted general on 12 August 1819. He died on 5 September 1839 at his residence, Upper Gore House, Kensington, and was buried at Kensal Green cemetery. R. H. VETCH, *rev.* JAMES LUNT

Sources *The Times* (3 Sept 1839) · J. Philippart, ed., *The royal military calendar*, 3rd edn, 5 vols. (1820) · *GM*, 2nd ser., 12 (1839), 652–3 · R. Cannon, ed., *Historical record of the eighteenth, or the royal Irish regiment of foot* (1848) · Burke, *Peerage* · H. Calvert, *Campaigns in Flanders and Holland* (1853) · Fortescue, *Brit. army*, vol. 4 · S. Griffith, *In defense of the public liberty* (1977) · P. Mackesy, *The war for America, 1775–1783* (1964)
Archives Morgan L., letters to Sir James Murray-Pulteney
Likenesses H. R. Cook, stipple, pubd 1814 (after T. Stewardson), NPG [*see illus.*] · Stewardson, portrait; formerly priv. coll.

Wemyss, James, of Caskieberran (*c.*1610–1667), army officer, was the son of James Wemyss, laird of Caskieberran, Fife, and his wife, Janet Durie, lady of Cardan in the parish of Auchterderran, Fife. He moved to London in the winter of 1629–30 with his uncle Colonel Robert *Scott (*d.* 1631), probably receiving a grant of denization at the same time as his uncle's family. Scott, while in Swedish and Danish service, had developed a type of leather-covered cannon or leather gun, and Wemyss, who may also have served in the army of Gustavus Adolphus, an innovator in field artillery, was to refine his uncle's invention and more generally devote himself to gunnery and associated skills.

At some point Wemyss married Katherine, widow of John Guilliams and daughter of Thomas Rayment, poulterer of St Botolph without Bishopsgate, with whom he had his son and heir, James, and other children, before her death in February 1649. On 26 February 1634 Charles I granted a warrant to the lieutenant-general of the ordnance, Sir John Heydon, 'for carrying such quantity of earth to Mr Wemyss's garden at Foxhall [Vauxhall] as should suffice for making a butt to prove ordnance at' (*DNB*). Three years later Wemyss's house was burnt down, leading to the loss of his scientific instruments and tools he had personally purchased to further his inventions. In the pursuit of his knowledge Wemyss had amassed debts of £2000 by 1637. The king, who had supported Wemyss for seven years, appears to have relieved him from his most pressing debts, and in 1638 made him master-gunner of England. 'Weemes, a Scotchman', Clarendon later sourly noted, 'had been as much obliged by the King as a man of his condition could be, and in a manner very unpopular'. His appointment as master-gunner, with 'a pension of three hundred pounds *per annum* for his life, … was looked upon as some disrespect to the English nation' (Clarendon, *Hist. rebellion*, 3.367).

In the middle of 1638 Wemyss gained a contract to hire a ship and load it with light guns and powder to reinforce the royal garrison at Dumbarton Castle. On 12 February 1639, when the king was preparing militarily to suppress the Scottish covenanters, Wemyss explained to the king that England lacked gunners who understood the ranges of ordnance or the use of mortars. Wemyss accompanied the train of artillery which followed the royal army to Berwick in the summer of 1639. He also served with the army raised in 1640 to oppose the covenanters.

The failure of the royal armies to defeat the parliamentarians, and the Scottish decision to ally with the latter, persuaded Wemyss to transfer his services to the English parliament (or as Clarendon glossed the defection, 'having never done the King the least service, he took the first opportunity to disserve him' (Clarendon, *Hist. rebellion*, 3.367–8). Wemyss was appointed master of the ordnance to Sir William Waller. When Wemyss left London for Waller's army on 5 December 1643 his artillery train included the leather guns which he had developed from his uncle's invention: 'leatherne Musquets shooting bullets of one lb weight' (Sheffield University Library, Hartlib MSS, Ephermerides, 1643: 30/4/86a–93b). 'These leather pieces',

a newsletter observed, predicting their value to Sir William's army, 'are of very great use, and very easie and light of carriage. One horse may draw a piece, which will carry a bullet of a pound and a halfe weight, and do execution very farre' (*The True Informer*, 9 Dec 1643). In the event the royalist forces at the battle of Cropredy Bridge on 29 June 1644 captured both Wemyss and his eleven cannon, 'with two barricadoes of wood, which were drawn upon wheels, and in each seven small brass and leather guns, charged with case-shot' (Clarendon, *Hist. rebellion*, 3.367). The leather guns at the time had a higher reputation than they generally have had since, and one royalist later claimed that the pieces captured at Cropredy 'proved very serviceable to the king' (J. Gwynne, *Memoirs of the Great Civil War*, 1822, 42). Nevertheless they seem to have had a relatively slight impact in the English context, one reason for which is probably the prolonged imprisonment of the inventor.

The earl of Essex, Sir John Meldrum, Sir William Waller, and Sir Arthur Hesilrige made every effort to have Wemyss (whom Clarendon called 'a confessed good soldier') exchanged, but he remained a prisoner for many months (Clarendon, *Hist. rebellion*, 5.489). The king told Wemyss that the post of master-gunner remained vacant, and offered to reinstate him. By 12 June 1645 Wemyss had regained his freedom. Now an officer in the earl of Leven's Scottish army, he proved the ordnance and gunpowder for the English parliamentarian navy, and fitted out three new frigates with 100 pieces of cannon in 1646, for which he received £50. In March 1648 the navy commissioners awarded him the same sum for similar work done in the summer of 1647.

In March 1648 Wemyss returned to Scotland. On 27 March the Scottish parliament passed an act 'granting to Colonel James Wemyss the privilege of making leather ordnance for three terms of nineteen years, with power to enforce secresy' (*APS*, 6/2, 18–19). As an adherent of the anti-republican kirk party regime, Wemyss lost his post of master-gunner of England to Richard Wollaston after 5 February 1649.

On 10 July 1649 the Scottish parliament appointed Wemyss general of artillery and engineering, and master of the ordnance of Scotland, replacing the senile engager Alexander 'Dear Sandy' Hamilton. Wemyss's pay was fixed at 600 Scots merks monthly. In July 1650 he received command of a regiment of foot. He fought at the battle of Dunbar (3 September 1650), but escaped the debacle that overtook most of the infantry. After the defeat he scoured Scotland for artillery, and produced a train of 29 field and 42 leather pieces for the Worcester campaign of August–September 1651. Wemyss fell prisoner at the battle of Worcester on 3 September. He was confined at Windsor Castle, and was bound over in £2000 in order to attend to private business in London for a few days in the summer of 1652. Early in 1654 he was permitted six months' leave for his health in Scotland. In May 1658 he petitioned the lord protector for an act to enable 'him to provide a place to erect his works for the making and practising certain inventions of light ordnance and engines of war, the fruits of his study and labour for thirty years' (*CSP dom.*, 1658–9, 35–

7). The petition included a list of his scientific inventions for naval and military gunnery, which allowed Britain to make considerable advances in ordnance. The dislocation of governmental functions following Cromwell's death delayed matters, but in 1660 Charles II granted a patent

> to James Wemyss, senior, and James Wemyss, junior, of the invention of the former for making light ordnance, and of a way whereby all motions caused by the force of a river, wind, or horses may be done by one or two men, and may be useful for lifting of weights, draining of mines, &c. (*DNB*)

Charles II restored Wemyss to the post of master-gunner of England and general of artillery in Scotland in 1660. On 1 March 1661 the Scottish parliament renewed his monopoly of leather ordnance for fifty-seven years. That April he received a Scottish monopoly of mine draining equipment. In 1663 Wemyss received a royal patent for light ordnance. Owing to the cost of maintaining the affairs of these offices Wemyss resigned from them in 1666, and retired to Scotland on the king's permission. He received a payment for resigning the English position to Captain Valentine Pyne. Wemyss died in December 1667.

Wemyss's son James inherited the estate of Caskieberran. On 15 April 1672 he was created Baron Burntisland for life, following his marriage on 25 December 1671 to Margaret Wemyss (1659-1705), countess of Wemyss in her own right. At his death in December 1682 he left a son David, who succeeded his mother as fourth earl of Wemyss. EDWARD M. FURGOL

Sources *CSP dom.*, 1630–67 · *Scots peerage* · *APS*, 1643–69 · NA Scot., PA.11.11, fol. 86 · J. Turner, *Memoirs of his own life and times, 1632–1670*, ed. T. Thomson, Bannatyne Club, 28 (1829) · Clarendon, *Hist. rebellion* · E. M. Furgol, *A regimental history of the covenanting armies, 1639–1651* (1990) · C. Dalton, ed., *The Scots army, 1661–1688* (1909) · private information (2004) [S. Murdoch] · *DNB* · *The letters and journals of Robert Baillie*, ed. D. Laing, 3 vols., Bannatyne Club, 73 (1841–2)

Wemyss, John. *See* Weemes, John (c.1579–1636).

Wemyss, Rosslyn Erskine, Baron Wester Wemyss (1864–1933), naval officer, was born in London on 12 April 1864, fifth child of James Hay Erskine Wemyss (1829–1864)—who had died only two weeks before—and Millicent Ann Mary Kennedy Erskine (1830–1895). He was connected by birth to most of the old Scottish aristocracy and on his mother's side was a great-grandson of William IV and the actress Mrs Dorothy Jordan.

Early career Wemyss's connections and charm stood him in good stead during his initial naval training in the *Britannia* and he was selected to accompany princes Albert Victor (later duke of Clarence) and George (later George V) on their training cruise around the world from 1879 until 1882. A friendship developed between Wemyss and Prince George which was nurtured by later service together and by Wemyss's repeated appointments to the royal yachts. In 1918–19 this relationship was to prove important in sustaining Wemyss's position as first sea lord.

Wemyss proved a capable and clever officer, securing good results in examinations—for which he seems to have done sufficient study to do well, but no more—and

Rosslyn Erskine Wemyss, Baron Wester Wemyss (1864–1933), by Sir William Orpen, 1919

possessing considerable practical skills. He refused to specialize, preferring to serve in the royal yachts, interspersed with fleet appointments as a flag lieutenant and ship's officer. Yacht service not only gave Wemyss exposure to the highest royal and political circles, but also gave him time to enjoy social and sporting life ashore. Although a youngest son, his allowance of £250 a year was sufficient to liberate him from the cares of living on service pay.

Wemyss's approach brought him early but not exceptional advancement to commander with a 'yacht promotion' on leaving the *Victoria and Albert* in 1898. His real chance came as second in command of the liner *Ophir*, fitted out for Prince George's visit to Australia for the opening of the first federal parliament in 1901. The tour was a great success and Wemyss received a special promotion to captain and appointment as MVO.

The start of the Selborne scheme for officer training in 1902 made it vital that the first captain of the new junior naval college at Osborne be universally acceptable. Wemyss had the charm and connections to reassure anxious parents and the energy and tact to implement a wholly new curriculum without disruption or controversy. On 21 December 1903 he married Victoria Mary Alice (d. 1945), only daughter of the diplomat Sir Robert Burnet David *Morier. A formidable personality in her own right, Victoria Wemyss remained closely engaged with European diplomatic circles and was to be an important influence in Wemyss's development as a naval statesman. They had one daughter.

Wemyss followed Osborne with command of the cruiser *Suffolk* in the Mediterranean, succeeding Captain

David Beatty. Although Wemyss's biography, written by his widow, was to allege that Wemyss found the ship defective and in a poor state of morale, there is no evidence of this in contemporary letters or Wemyss's diary. He enjoyed his command immensely. In late 1908 Wemyss saw an opportunity to serve as naval secretary to the first lord, succeeding Captain Hugh Evan Thomas, but the price for the support of the first sea lord, Sir John Fisher, in securing this post seemed to be total acquiescence to the latter's policies. Wemyss spurned the idea and from this moment was out of the 'Fish Pond'. His career was in no real danger of interruption, however, and in 1909 he took command of the battleship *Albion*. After completing the necessary sea time for promotion to flag rank, Wemyss was appointed commodore of the naval barracks at Devonport. In 1910 he commanded the liner *Balmoral Castle*, conveying the duke and duchess of Connaught to the opening of the first parliament of the Union of South Africa. After his return Wemyss was appointed CMG and soon afterwards promoted rear-admiral.

Wemyss expected to receive the plum command of the Mediterranean cruiser squadron but to his indignation the job went instead to Rear-Admiral Thomas Troubridge. Wemyss's resignation followed and he was only persuaded to withdraw after a stormy interview with Winston Churchill which concluded with the first lord's promise of the first suitable appointment. This came in late 1912 as second in command of the 2nd battle squadron in the super-dreadnought *Orion*.

War-time commands Wemyss left the squadron in October 1913 and settled down to a period of half pay, spent largely in France and Germany. At this stage his future was uncertain. Wemyss had long hankered for the Mediterranean command, the station for 'an officer of splendour', but he would not have this prospect unless he could first secure a primary command, such as the 1st or 2nd battle squadrons. With no technical expertise or Admiralty experience, Wemyss's fate was more likely to be a subsidiary overseas station, or else the royal yachts—either of which would finish his active career. Matters were not helped by the fact that his wife was playing an active role in the Ulster crisis and serving as a conduit for anti-government feeling within the senior ranks of the navy at the time of the Curragh incident. Whether Wemyss himself would have taken part in organizing mass refusals to serve is uncertain, but he clearly intended to return to the United Kingdom as matters in Ireland were coming to a head.

On mobilization in 1914, Wemyss went in command of cruiser force I, responsible for protecting merchant traffic in the western channel in conjunction with the French. This was not glamorous work, but Wemyss's mastery of French made him ideal for the job. In the circumstances, any seagoing post was better than none. After several months of tedious and increasingly dangerous convoy and trade protection duties, Wemyss's patience was rewarded when he was sent as base commander at Lemnos in the Aegean, in preparation for the forthcoming assault on the Dardanelles.

Installed in the town of Mudros before the end of February 1915, Wemyss soon encountered all the confusion which marked the early operations against Turkey. Lemnos was Greek and thus neutral, but Wemyss was expected to act as governor and senior naval officer with no formal instructions and no legal authority. More critically, he had no depot ships, little physical plant, and very few administrative staff to organize a base. Wemyss succeeded in matching conflicting service and national priorities with his necessarily hand-to-mouth organization by relying almost wholly on his personal influence. Mudros proved a miracle of improvisation and the ability of the allies to sustain the long Dardanelles campaign of 1915–16 depended very largely upon it.

The illness of the senior officer afloat, Vice-Admiral Sackville Carden, seemed to give Wemyss the chance for great distinction, but he stepped aside in favour of Rear-Admiral John De Robeck, who was junior to him. Wemyss agreed that De Robeck, who had been closely involved in the early attacks on the Dardanelles, was much more familiar with the operational situation and thus more qualified for the overall command. Wemyss's behaviour confirmed his reputation in the navy for probity and disinterest and was to have important consequences in making him an acceptable successor to J. R. Jellicoe in the difficult circumstances of the latter's dismissal as first sea lord.

Wemyss played an active role in the remainder of the Dardanelles campaign, both at sea and from Mudros. He sometimes deputized for De Robeck and supported Commodore Roger Keyes when the latter sought approval in Whitehall for a renewal of the naval assault at the end of 1915. Wemyss was also bitterly opposed to the evacuation of the land forces in the new year, but played a leading part in the almost casualty-free withdrawal. His services were recognized by a KCB and appointment to the East Indies and Egypt station. Here Wemyss continued to focus on co-operation with forces ashore, supporting T. E. Lawrence and the Arab uprising, as well as attempts to relieve the British troops besieged at Kut. His difficulties in achieving properly co-ordinated efforts made him acutely conscious of the need for joint organizations to develop strategic plans.

Sea lord In the middle of 1917 submarines were taking such a toll in the Mediterranean that the allies finally agreed to the appointment of a British commander-in-chief to reorganize the fragmented and largely unsuccessful anti-submarine efforts in the theatre. Wemyss was offered the post and, in July 1917, set off to Paris to discuss the new arrangements. Here he found himself caught up in changes being forced on the Board of Admiralty. The new first lord, Sir Eric Geddes, asked Wemyss to serve as second sea lord and as deputy to the first sea lord, Jellicoe. The hidden agenda, as Wemyss soon discovered from his own sources, was that Geddes and Lloyd George were considering him as a possible successor to Jellicoe. Wemyss believed that duty required him to accept the Admiralty post, despite his preference for the Mediterranean, but he indicated his disapproval of the prime minister's intent by refusing the latter's invitation to accompany him back to London. His motives were honourable, but Wemyss's behaviour did not augur well for his relationship with Lloyd George.

Wemyss became progressively more frustrated by Jellicoe's refusal to delegate any serious work or responsibility to him, despite his success in persuading Geddes to select a new second sea lord and reappoint Wemyss solely as deputy first sea lord. With Geddes himself also finding Jellicoe's working methods and chronic pessimism an increasing trial, it took only until Christmas 1917 for matters to come to a head. Just as Wemyss himself was considering resignation, Geddes sacked Jellicoe and asked Wemyss to take his place. Geddes' method and timing could hardly have been worse, but Wemyss could neither deny the first lord's constitutional right to choose the first sea lord nor the fact that he considered himself to be a better man for the job at this point than his predecessor was. It required all Wemyss's considerable tact to placate an outraged board in particular and the flag list in general, but he succeeded in doing so and within a few months had restored a measure of confidence in the Admiralty.

Wemyss's differences from Jellicoe lay more in manner than in matter. Although he reorganized the naval staff to give himself three effective functional deputies, he could not wholly overcome the general lack of expertise in higher staff duties. He did not change the employment of the Grand Fleet and, although he enthusiastically encouraged attacks on the German submarine bases on the Belgian coast, plans for the raids on Zeebrugge and Ostend were already in train when Wemyss came into office. He was not a wholehearted enthusiast for convoy, sharing the misconception of his generation that it was inferior to 'offensive' measures against submarines, but the first sea lord did not interfere with the progressive development of the convoy system.

If Wemyss was fortunate in reaping the benefits of work done by his predecessors, he made an important contribution in 1918 to improving co-operation between the Royal Navy and the British army and between the United Kingdom and its allies. He convinced the French high command of the need to defend the remaining channel ports at the height of the German spring offensive and even made some progress in persuading the Italians to operate more effectively with the other allies in the Mediterranean. Wemyss also worked very closely with Admiral William Sims of the United States Navy and encouraged the American naval contribution to the war in Europe, despite his suspicions as to that navy's long-term intent.

Post-war difficulties Wemyss's personal relations with Admiral Beatty in the Grand Fleet were more problematic and friction between the commander-in-chief and the first sea lord, which Wemyss himself did his best to avoid, became an increasing problem. Wemyss displayed a remarkable grasp of the strategic problems resulting from the collapse of the central powers, not only in northern Europe but in the Mediterranean, Black Sea, and Near East. Most of his time was taken up by increasingly complicated negotiations but matters were not helped by

Beatty's efforts to involve himself in the decision-making processes, however inappropriately.

Wemyss played a vital part in securing the terms in the armistice with Germany which the navy felt were essential to prevent a revival of German naval power. This required considerable education of allied senior military officers, particularly the French, in the issues involved. The latter were inclined to discount any need to deal with the U-boat force and the high seas fleet. Wemyss succeeded in securing the continuation of the blockade and the internment of all German submarines and most of the major surface units in neutral ports. Wemyss had wanted outright surrender of the German fleet and his failure to gain this point was immediately treated as a sign of weakness by Beatty, who did not understand the issues or the pressures involved. In the event, no neutral ports were available and the German ships were sent into British anchorages. Bringing news of the signing of the armistice, Wemyss incurred Lloyd George's wrath by reporting first to the king, rather than the prime minister, thus depriving him of political capital with the opportunity to break the news in parliament.

Despite the apparent triumph of British naval power, 1919 was not a happy year for Wemyss. He was dogged by the petulance and impatience of Beatty, who was determined to bundle Wemyss out of office at the earliest possible moment. Negotiations for the final peace treaty required Wemyss's near continuous presence in Paris, while crises in the Balkans and the Baltic, as well as the continuing intervention operations in Russia, made heavy calls on the Royal Navy's diminishing strength. At the same time, mobilization proceeded apace and the Admiralty, led by Wemyss, had to fight hard for an equitable settlement of pay scales which recognized the inflation of the war years. Wemyss regarded a just solution to ratings' pay as one of his most important goals, but Treasury intransigence meant that a solution was not achieved until well on into 1919.

Some progress was made with a much more sophisticated naval staff organization, the brain child of Captain Herbert Richmond, which Wemyss approved almost in its entirety; but the truth was that the pressures of the day and the ever increasing pressures of financial restraint meant that the Admiralty's approach to planning was reactive and disjointed. This was not wholly Wemyss's fault, since the job he was doing was too much for one man. Thus, Jellicoe was dispatched on a tour of the dominions to advise on naval development with few instructions as to the Admiralty's strategy for the empire. The whole question of naval policy for the Far East had yet to be considered, let alone resolved, and the future of Anglo-American naval relations appeared increasingly murky. Wemyss disliked the concept of the League of Nations and was determined not to surrender British naval supremacy or belligerent rights for any reason. His concerns at American attempts to build a fleet 'second to none' brought him into spectacular conflict with the United States Navy's chief of naval operations, Admiral Benson.

His one clear success was to secure practically all that Britain wanted in the naval terms for the final peace treaty with Germany.

Final years All these problems remained extant and Wemyss's own future uncertain when his exclusion from the July 1919 victory honours list embittered him to the point of resignation. Having secured an earldom for Beatty, to match that conferred on Field Marshal Haig, Wemyss sought a viscountcy but this was viewed by Lloyd George as being more than his due. While the other chiefs of staff received money grants and baronetcies, Wemyss got nothing. Already appointed GCB in June 1918 and confirmed as an admiral only in 1919, his sights were probably set too high. In the event, Wemyss was persuaded by the first lord, Walter Long, to wait for a better moment to go, which he did at the end of October. His departure was sweetened by promotion to admiral of the fleet and his creation as Baron Wester Wemyss, but he was offered no further employment. An earlier proposal to go to the Mediterranean as naval commander-in-chief and governor of Malta was scotched by the army's insistence that the latter post belonged to them. No other naval billet had much attraction and Wemyss was never given the diplomatic or vice-regal posts he sought. Whether there was a political animus against the admiral and his wife is uncertain; Wemyss never had much regard for Lloyd George or his successor, Bonar Law, but he was clearly greatly disappointed and a number of directorships and presidency of the Institution of Naval Architects were little compensation. He published *The Navy in the Dardanelles Campaign* in 1924 and spoke in the House of Lords on a number of occasions, but most of his time was spent in France. It is significant that Wemyss's happiest moment in retirement was the occasion in 1922 on which he was awarded the French médaille militaire in recognition of his services. He died at the Villa Monbrilliant, in Cannes, on 24 May 1933 and was buried in Scotland in the chapel at Wemyss Castle, Kirkcaldy, Fife, on 1 June.

Wemyss was in no way a naval intellectual, but he possessed great common sense, good humour, and moral courage, as well as reserves of strength which allowed him to sustain responsibility with little apparent stress. Lloyd George pointed out that his two greatest virtues were that he was not a factionalist and that he would listen to his juniors. A man with more interest in reform might have achieved more in setting the Royal Navy on a better course for the post-war years, but it is unlikely that anyone could have done better than Wemyss to make sense of the maze of strategic problems which Britain faced in the 1918–19 period. He was a naval statesman in a sense which was to become much more clearly understood in the coalition operations of the Second World War.   JAMES GOLDRICK

Sources V. M. A. Wemyss, *The life and letters of Lord Wester Wemyss, GCB, CMG, MVO, admiral of the fleet* (1935) · J. Goldrick, 'Admiral Sir Rosslyn Wemyss, 1917–1919', *The first sea lords: from Fisher to Mountbatten*, ed. M. H. Murfett (1995), 113–25 · R. E. Wemyss [Lord Wester Wemyss], *The navy in the Dardanelles campaign* (1924) · CAC Cam., Wemyss MSS · U. Cal., Irvine, Wemyss MSS and Marder MSS ·

I. F. W. Beckett and K. Jeffery, 'The Royal Navy and the Curragh incident', *Historical Research*, 62 (1989), 54–69 · S. W. Roskill, *The period of Anglo-American antagonism, 1919–1929* (1968), vol. 1 of *Naval policy between the wars* · A. J. Marder, *From the Dreadnought to Scapa Flow: the Royal Navy in the Fisher era, 1904–1919*, 5 vols. (1961–70) · S. W. Roskill, 'The dismissal of Admiral Jellicoe', *Journal of Contemporary History*, 1 (1966), 69–83 · D. Lloyd George, *War memoirs*, 3 (1934) · *The Beatty papers: selections from the private and official correspondence of Admiral of the Fleet Earl Beatty*, ed. B. Ranft, 1, Navy RS, 128 (1989) · private information (2004) [Alice Cunnack] · A. J. Marder, *Portrait of an admiral: the life and papers of Sir Herbert Richmond* (1952) · D. F. Trask, *Captains and cabinets: Anglo-American naval relations, 1917–1918* (Columbia, MO, 1972) · B. D. Hunt, *Sailor–scholar: Admiral Sir Herbert Richmond, 1871–1946* (1982) · C. Petrie, *Walter Long and his times* (1936) · P. G. Halpern, *The naval war in the Mediterranean, 1914–1918* (1987) · *The Jellicoe papers*, ed. A. T. Patterson, 2, Navy RS, 111 (1968) · CGPLA Eng. & Wales (1934) · L. G. Pine, *The new extinct peerage, 1884–1971: containing extinct, abeyant, dormant, and suspended peerages with genealogies and arms* (1972) · DNB

Archives CAC Cam., corresp. and papers | BL, corresp. with Arthur James Balfour, Add. MSS 49714, *passim* · BL, Jellicoe MSS · BL, corresp. with R. J. B. Keyes · CAC Cam., corresp. with Sir John De Robeck · HLRO, letters to David Lloyd George · IWM, corresp. with Sir Henry Wilson · NMM, letters to David Beatty · NMM, corresp. with Sir Julian S. Corbett · PRO, ADM 1 (papers), esp. ADM 1/1770–ADM 1/1850 · PRO, war histories, ADM 137 · PRO, war ops and policy, ADM 116 (cases), esp. ADM 116/1348–1351 · Royal Arch., King George V MSS · U. Cal., Irvine, Marder MSS, M. 000185, reel 0001

Likenesses F. Dodd, charcoal and watercolour drawing, 1917, IWM · W. Stoneman, photograph, 1918, NPG · W. Orpen, oils, 1919, NPG [*see illus.*] · A. S. Cope, group portrait, oils, 1921 (*Some sea officers of the Great War*), NPG · photographs, CAC Cam., Wester Wemyss MSS, WMYS 10/1–10/8

Wealth at death £2915 19s. 7d. in England: probate, 7 March 1934, *CGPLA Eng. & Wales*

Wendover, Richard of (d. 1252), physician, was an ecclesiastic who became a canon of St Paul's, London, and came to hold several prebends in the London area. In 1239 the manor of Sandon in Essex was demised to him by the dean and chapter. Richard may have become physician to Pope Gregory IX, perhaps between 1239 and 1241 when English records are silent about him. Matthew Paris wrote that 'Magister Ricardus de Wendovre … phisicus praelectus' (Paris, *Chron.*, 5.299) left to the monastery of St Albans an ivory cross containing relics that was willed to his dear physician by Gregory when he died. After the pope's death in 1241, Richard reappeared in England, witnessing London charters at St Paul's and at St Bartholomew's Hospital. From 1244 until his death he may have been in attendance upon Bishop Suffield of Norwich, who at his own death in 1257 willed 20 marks to be distributed to the poor for the soul of Richard of Wendover, his companion.

Toward the end of his life, in 1250, Richard of Wendover gave a psalter in two volumes, the epistles of St Paul, an altar, and an altar-cloth to St Bartholomew's Priory and 30 marks to the priory of Holy Trinity. He also established a chantry at Thremhall Priory in Essex. The inventories of St Paul's record that he gave the cathedral a red silk cope with a round onyx at its centre. He died in 1252; his obit was celebrated at the cathedral on 5 March.

That Richard of Wendover was a physician is attested by cathedral documents. Whether this Richard the physician is identifiable with any of the other of his contemporaries called Richard to whom writings on medicine have been attributed—Richardus de Montepessulano; Master Richardus; Master Richardus Anglicus; Richard Wendover, bishop of Rochester; Richard, bishop of Durham; and Richardus Anglicus the jurist—is a source of scholarly dispute that may admit of no firm solution. The last three may be dismissed out of hand because they were not known to have been physicians. But the others were all authors of medical texts. However, no evidence linking Richard of Wendover to any of these men has yet been found, nor do papal records suggest that Richard of Wendover, physician to Gregory IX, was the author of any medical text. Matthew Paris failed to mention that his Richard wrote anything. Clerical physicians were the rule rather than the exception during the twelfth and thirteenth centuries in learned circles, and many English scholars trod a well-worn path to the papal court in Wendover's lifetime. Whether Richard of Wendover, canon and papal physician, was responsible for any medical texts is open to conjecture.

The identity of **Richardus Anglicus** ($fl.$ $c.$1180), physician and medical writer, is equally problematic. It would appear that someone calling himself Richardus Anglicus assembled a learned medical compendium in Latin. He called the work $Micrologus$, and wrote it at the famous medical university of Montpellier at the behest of Lancelinus de l'Isle-Adam, dean of Beauvais from 1178 to 1190. But if Richardus actually composed this work when Lancelinus was dean of Beauvais, it could not have been written after about 1190, a date surely far too early for the $Micrologus$ to have been the work of Richard of Wendover, who died in 1252. That there may indeed have been two Richards is attested as early as the first quarter of the thirteenth century. Gilles de Corbeil ($d.$ 1224), Montpellier professor and famous versifier on the subject of urines and pulses, wrote warmly of a Richardus senior, also of Montpellier. He does not call him Anglicus.

The $Micrologus$ does not survive intact, but its preface suggests that texts circulating separately under the authorship of Richardus Anglicus originally belonged together. These parts, named as topics in the preface to the $Micrologus$, include a 'Practica' or general practice of medicine, several uroscopies, an anatomy, a collection of 'violently laxative' medicines, and prognostic signs of diseases. Numerous other texts are attributed to Richardus Anglicus, or to him in one manuscript and to others in other manuscripts. They include works on fevers, pulses, bloodletting, times a disease reaches crisis, and the adornment of women. Their authenticity as the work of the author of the $Micrologus$ is doubtful.

The $Micrologus$ contains little of the theory that characterizes medicine as it was later expounded by the titans of scholastic science, under the influence of the Persian physician Avicenna. Instead, the $Micrologus$ collection presents the reader with an earlier style of medicine, a deliberate distillation of large amounts of medical material into a simple, straightforward, and practical format. Like so many other clerical physicians—Petrus Hispanus, Gilbert the Englishman, and John Gaddesden—Richardus

wanted to make the best of learned medicine easily accessible to the poor scholar. The writer arranges his material from the head downward, making it simple to locate. His diagnoses are easy to understand, and the treatments suggested are herbal in nature. The large number of surviving manuscripts is ample testimony to the writer's wide popularity.

A reading of the $Micrologus$ collection suggests that its author was a well-travelled scholar typical of his time. He wrote of his presence in Montpellier, Bologna (or possibly Poland; the evidence is ambiguous), and Spoleto, and he may of course have attended the pope. As for his associations, a Master Richardus was mentioned with unparalleled admiration by his near-contemporary Gilbert the Englishman, also the author of a medical compendium, as 'of all the doctors the most learned and experienced' (Gilbertus Anglicus, fol. 47). Gilbert wrote a commentary of his own on Gilles de Corbeil's poem on urines and may merely have reflected Gilles's praise of Richardus, and not personal acquaintance.   FAYE GETZ

Sources H. H. Beusing, $Leben$ und $Werke$ des $Richardus$ $Anglicus,$ $samt$ $einem$ $erstmaligen$ $Abdruck$ $seiner$ $Schrift$ $'Signa'$ (1922) · K. Sudhoff, 'Richard der Engländer', $Janus,$ 28 (1924), 397–403 · L. Thorndike and P. Kibre, A $catalogue$ of $incipits$ of $mediaeval$ $scientific$ $writings$ in $Latin,$ rev. edn (1963) · A. Paravicini Bagliani, $Medicina$ e $scienze$ $della$ $natura$ $alla$ $corte$ dei $papi$ nel $duecento$ (1991) · $Fasti$ $Angl.,$ $1066–1300,$ [St Paul's, London] · C. H. Talbot and E. A. Hammond, The $medical$ $practitioners$ in $medieval$ $England:$ a $biographical$ $register$ (1965) · $Paris,$ $Chron.,$ vol. 5 · E. Wickersheimer and D. Jacquart, $Dictionnaire$ $biographique$ des $médecins$ en $France$ au $moyen$ $âge,$ new edn, ed. G. Beaujouan, 3 vols. (Geneva, 1979) · H. Hellriegel, Die $'Practica'$ aus dem $'Micrologus'$ $Richards$ des $Engländers,$ I (Zeulenroda, [1936]) · K. Sudhoff, 'Der $Micrologus$: text der 'Anatomia' Richards des Engländers', $Sudhoffs$ $Archiv,$ 19 (1927), 209–39 · Aegidius Corboliensis, $Carmina$ $medicina,$ ed. L. Choulant (1826) · Gilbertus Anglicus, $Compendium$ $medicinae$ (1510)

Wendover, Roger of ($d.$ 1236), historian and prior of Belvoir, was a monk of St Albans, who was probably associated with Wendover in Buckinghamshire and possibly a kinsman of Richard of *Wendover, a physician to Pope Gregory IX ($r.$ 1227–41). Roger became prior of Belvoir, a Leicestershire cell of St Albans, but was deposed in consequence of a visitation, conducted in or shortly after 1219, during which his abbot, William of Trumpington, is said to have concluded that Roger 'had wasted the property of the church in careless prodigality' ($Gesta$ $abbatum,$ 1.270). After his departure from Belvoir, Roger of Wendover presumably returned to the monastic community at St Albans, where he died on 6 May 1236. It was probably in this last period of his life that he established himself as one of the most significant members of the St Albans school of historiography.

From the available evidence it can only be demonstrated that Roger of Wendover started to write his $Flores$ $historiarum$ at some date between 1204 and 1231, and that he had not ceased to work on the text by 1234. It is, however, probable that he was actually involved in the compilation of his chronicle in the period between about 1220 and his death in 1236.

The $Flores$ $historiarum$ is a work that can be divided into three sections whose analysis reveals that Roger of

Wendover's original contribution to the text grew as its production became more contemporaneous with the events it describes. In the first section, the coverage of the period from the creation to 1202 is essentially based on a compilation of well-known authorities, such as Bede, Henry of Huntingdon, Roger of Howden, and Ralph de Diceto, which Roger of Wendover may have inherited from a single St Albans text to which one or more St Albans historians had already contributed. In the second section, which basically involves the description of John's reign after 1202, Roger of Wendover began to make his own mark on the *Flores historiarum* by interlacing at least some of his own observations with those that he borrowed from such other works as the lost source that he shared with the thirteenth-century author of the *Annales sancti Edmundi*, and another set of annals which he found at the end of what is now BL, Royal MS 13 E. vi, the St Albans copy of the work of Ralph de Diceto. It is therefore only in the third and final section of the text, which covers the period from near the end of John's reign to May 1234, that there is unambiguous evidence that the chronicle is primarily based on Roger of Wendover's own historiographical approach.

Commentators on Roger of Wendover's *Flores historiarum* have often expressed their disappointment with the quality of various aspects of his historical writing. Inaccuracies in his identification of people and places and in his transmission of documents, such as Magna Carta, have been painstakingly indicated. His style has been described as clear, but bald. His learning has been denounced as shallow. His narrative has been found to be lacking in vigour. Such criticisms have largely arisen from the succession of comparisons that have been made between the *Flores historiarum* and the work of Matthew Paris who succeeded Roger of Wendover as St Albans' principal historian. Although there can be little argument that the *Chronica majora* of Matthew Paris is a more interesting piece of historiography than Roger of Wendover's *Flores historiarum*, it is, however, equally evident that Matthew Paris owed much to a predecessor whose work not only provided him with a wealth of material, which was similarly used by other authors, such as the anonymous annalists of Norwich and Waverley and Nicholas Trevet, but also introduced him to certain historiographical techniques which became important features of his own chronicle. It was, for example, through Roger of Wendover's knowledge of Roger of Howden's writing that Matthew Paris came to adopt the convention of beginning each annal with a record of where the king spent Christmas and ending each annal with a summary of the events of the year.

Matthew Paris did not, however, only learn 'his profession, as a historian, from Roger of Wendover' (Vaughan, 34), for his reading of the *Flores historiarum* also shaped Paris's political outlook by encouraging him to develop that set of grievances and beliefs that he parades so emphatically in his writings. On occasions the examination of these prejudices has been clouded by anachronistic attempts to endow them with the sort of constitutional coherence, as a systematic apologia for baronial opposition to Plantagenet despotism, that has given the St Albans scriptorium an undeserved place in the development of political theory. There can, nevertheless, be little doubt that Matthew Paris's homiletic defence of the Benedictinism of St Albans was, in part, a product of the inspiration that he derived from the intense interest shown by Roger of Wendover in miracles and other spiritual matters. The unqualified reverence accorded to St Francis in the *Flores historiarum* is, for example, more than matched in the *Chronica majora* in which, despite his growing hostility towards the mendicant orders, Matthew Paris chose to add a moving picture of the receipt of the stigmata to Roger of Wendover's unequivocally sympathetic account of the saint and his canonization.

These common spiritual concerns have attracted relatively little attention from those historians who have committed themselves to detailed analyses of the extent to which Matthew Paris's anti-governmental attitudes were foreshadowed in the writing of Roger of Wendover. Such historians have, however, successfully demonstrated that, although the highly critical view of King John in the *Flores historiarum* may well have been paralleled in a lost early version of Ralph of Coggeshall's *Chronicon Anglicanum*, and was certainly present in embryo in the works of such authors as Roger of Howden, Richard of Devizes, and Gervase of Canterbury, who did not have the benefit of knowing the later events of the reign, it was essentially Roger of Wendover's literary portrait of John that had most influence on Matthew Paris. That portrait was of a king who was so incapable of controlling himself that, shortly after the granting of Magna Carta, he went, dumbfounded and in great consternation, to the Isle of Wight, where he stayed for three months on the sea-shore and in the company of sailors, pondering how he might revenge himself upon his barons. This particular story is totally fictitious in that John never went near the Isle of Wight in the relevant period. Nevertheless it constitutes one of the most impressive images of John that St Albans produced. Furthermore, its treatment, in the *Chronica majora*, exemplifies the way in which Matthew Paris reacted to Roger of Wendover's work, in that the tale is as it is in the *Flores historiarum* except that John now 'burns with rage', and 'plots' rather than 'ponders' his revenge.

Matthew Paris's approach to Henry III was equally dependent upon Roger of Wendover's initial depiction of John's successor, since the basic elements of the *Flores historiarum*'s description of the king as a simple man who showed too much favour to foreigners and refused to live off his customary revenues are again adopted and then embellished, sometimes through the *Chronica majora*'s use of an apt quotation or an illustrative verse, but, more often, through its employment of a cluster of pejorative adjectives. As the *Chronica majora*'s coverage of events approaches the period during which Matthew Paris was himself active as a historian, his editorial enhancement of the *Flores historiarum* becomes more substantial. It is nevertheless evident, from any comprehensive comparison of the two texts, that Roger of Wendover was the most influential mentor of the most readable, if not the most gifted, of England's late medieval chroniclers.

Roger of Wendover's *Flores historiarum* survives, in its own right, in Bodl. Oxf., MS Douce 207, of *c*.1300, and BL, Cotton MS Otho B.v, of *c*.1350. Important derivatives are, however, also extant in the first two of the three original manuscripts of Matthew Paris's *Chronica majora*—Cambridge, Corpus Christi College, MS 26, and Cambridge, Corpus Christi College, MS 16—and in the shortest of Matthew Paris's abridged versions of the *Chronica majora*, of which a text, closely associated with its author, survives in BL, Cotton MS Vitellius A.xx.

There is no complete printed edition of the *Flores historiarum*. It has been edited from *c*.447 onwards by H. O. Coxe and from 1154 onwards by H. G. Hewlett. H. R. Luard's edition of Matthew Paris's *Chronica majora* also attempts to identify what the editor assumed to be its author's borrowings from the *Flores historiarum*. None of these editions is, however, totally satisfactory, since it is clear that both the common source of the texts of the *Flores historiarum* in Bodl. Oxf., MS Douce 207, and BL, Cotton MS Otho B.v, and the text that survives in the first two original manuscripts of the *Chronica majora*, share a lost common source in an early recension of the *Flores historiarum*, and this can only be reconstructed through the resolution of every conflict between the texts derived from it, and through a detailed analysis of the status of the borrowings from Roger of Wendover's work in BL, Cotton MS Vitellius A.xx. DAVID CORNER

Sources *Rogeri de Wendoveri chronica, sive, Flores historiarum*, ed. H. O. Coxe, 5 vols., EHS (1841–4) · *Rogeri de Wendover liber qui dicitur flores historiarum*, ed. H. G. Hewlett, 3 vols., Rolls Series, [84] (1886–9) · Paris, *Chron.* · R. Vaughan, *Matthew Paris*, Cambridge Studies in Medieval Life and Thought, new ser., 6 (1958) · A. Gransden, *Historical writing in England*, 1 (1974) · R. Vaughan, *Chronicles of Matthew Paris* (1984) · V. H. Galbraith, *Roger Wendover and Matthew Paris* (1944) · C. Jenkins, *The monastic chronicler and the early school of St Albans* (1922) · F. M. Powicke, 'The compilation of the *Chronica majora* of Matthew Paris', *PBA*, 30 (1944), 147–60 · F. M. Powicke, 'Roger of Wendover and the Coggeshall Chronicle', *EngHR*, 21 (1906), 286–96 · J. C. Holt, 'The St Albans chroniclers and Magna Carta', *TRHS*, 5th ser., 14 (1964), 67–88 · R. Kay, 'Wendover's last annal', *EngHR*, 84 (1969), 779–85 · *Gesta abbatum monasterii Sancti Albani, a Thoma Walsingham*, ed. H. T. Riley, 3 vols., pt 4 of *Chronica monasterii S. Albani*, Rolls Series, 28 (1867–9)
Archives BL, Cotton MS Otho B.v · Bodl. Oxf., MS Douce 207

Wendy, Thomas (1499/1500–1560), physician, born between May 1499 and May 1500, was the second son of Thomas Wendy of Clare, Suffolk. He was educated at Cambridge, graduating BA in 1519. In the same year he became a fellow of Gonville Hall (afterwards Gonville and Caius College), and continued as such until 1524. He proceeded MA in 1522, and then went abroad to study medicine. He graduated MD at Ferrara, and was incorporated in this degree at Cambridge in 1527.

Wendy was able to build a lucrative medical practice and became a substantial landowner. In 1534 his services were retained by Henry Percy, sixth earl of Northumberland. As part of his duties for Northumberland he carried letters to Thomas Cromwell in 1536, and attended the earl during his final illness in 1537.

Wendy was subsequently appointed physician to Henry VIII, who on 12 June 1541 granted to him and his wife, Margery, the manor of Haslingfield, Cambridgeshire.

According to John Foxe, Wendy played some part in thwarting Stephen Gardiner's scheme to have Queen Katherine Parr condemned for heresy. Wendy was appointed physician to the queen in 1546. He attended Henry VIII on his deathbed, was one of the witnesses to his will, and was bequeathed £100 by the king. He was continued as royal physician with a salary of £100 by Edward VI, who made him further grants of land.

On 12 November 1548 Wendy was appointed one of the ecclesiastical visitors of Oxford, Cambridge, and Eton College, and on 6 May 1552 was again commissioned to visit Eton. He was admitted fellow of the College of Physicians on 22 December 1551, and became an elect in 1552. In the same year he married his second wife, Margaret (*d.* 1570), daughter of John Porter of London, and widow of Thomas Atkins of London. Wendy attended Edward VI on his deathbed, and was continued as royal physician by Mary, to whom he performed a similar service.

On 26 March 1554 Wendy became member of parliament for St Albans, and on 10 October 1555 for Cambridgeshire. He was appointed an ecclesiastical visitor by Elizabeth in 1559.

Wendy died at Haslingfield on 11 May 1560, in his sixty-first year, and was survived by his wife. He was buried at Haslingfield on 27 May. Having been a benefactor of Gonville and Caius College, he is commemorated there by a service held on 11 May. The college library has his collection of medical and classical books. Wendy had a stepson, but his nephew Thomas, son of his elder brother, John, was his heir. Thomas was sheriff of Cambridgeshire and Huntingdonshire in 1573–4, 1585–6, and 1602–3; in 1586–7 he was in trouble with the privy council for refusing the oath. He added his lands at Barrington, Cambridgeshire, to his uncle's endowment of Gonville and Caius College.

A. F. POLLARD, *rev.* SARAH BAKEWELL

Sources Venn, *Alum. Cant.* · Munk, *Roll* · J. Venn and others, eds., *Biographical history of Gonville and Caius College*, 1: *1349–1713* (1897), 24 · BL, Sloane MSS, 1301 fol. 151, 3562 fol. 51 · *CSP dom.*, *1547–80* · BL, Add. MS 19154 · *APC*, *1542–1631* · S. R. Maitland, *Essays on subjects connected with the Reformation in England* (1849), 319–21 · *Literary remains of King Edward the Sixth*, ed. J. G. Nichols, 1, Roxburghe Club, 75 (1857), cxcvii · Cooper, *Ath. Cantab.*, vol. 1 · HoP, *Commons*, *1558–1603*
Wealth at death extensive property

Wenham, Brian George (1937–1997), broadcasting executive, was born on 9 February 1937 at 153 Lower Clapton Road, Hackney, London, the only child of George Frederick Wenham (1907–1939), a stockbroker's clerk, and his wife, Harriet, *née* Farr (*b.* 1905), a shop manager. He was educated (following the early death of his father) at the Royal Masonic School at Bushey, and subsequently at St John's College, Oxford (1957–60), where he took a first in modern history. One of the last generation to be called up for national service, his experience—which included the loss of a Bren gun in the Welsh mountains—left him with a healthy scepticism for over-rigid hierarchies and management by diktat.

Between 1962 and 1969 Wenham learned the skills of television production and editing at Independent Television News (ITN). It was a fruitful and rewarding period in which his fascination with the political process coincided with the flowering of a fresher style of television journalism. At ITN he met Elisabeth Downing Woolley (b. 1942), a production assistant, daughter of Keith and Margery Woolley, whom he married on 18 November 1966. They had two daughters. In 1967 ITN launched News at Ten, a ground-breaking half-hour news programme in prime time, which for over thirty years was the nation's premier news bulletin. Wenham was one of the programme's first editors, and claimed authorship of its title. Throughout this period he also served as the London correspondent of the Washington weekly the New Republic.

In 1969, at the age of only thirty-two, Wenham was recruited by the BBC to edit its flagship current affairs programme, Panorama. It was a challenging time for political coverage, not least with the developing crisis in Ulster, which was becoming increasingly violent and dangerous. Within two years Wenham was promoted to become head of the BBC television current affairs group, and seven years later, in 1978, he was appointed to the controllership of BBC2.

Running BBC2 was the job which perhaps gave Wenham the greatest pleasure in broadcasting. He called on a wider range of skills and interests than most broadcasting journalists possess: a love of music (particularly opera), drama, and good writing. Fortunately, his lack of pretentiousness and the challenge of the launch of the 'alternative' Channel 4 in 1981 insured against any retreat into élitism. Wenham's BBC2 was a lively and intelligent channel of broad appeal, its operas and serious journalism skilfully complemented by adventurous satire and televised snooker. During this period he edited The Third Age of Broadcasting (1982), a collection of substantial essays which painted a prophetic vision of the future of multichannel television. Wenham correctly identified the central dilemma of the new distribution technologies: how to reconcile the apparent benefits of burgeoning channel capacity with the concomitant fragmentation of audiences, and the consequent problem of funding and sustaining high levels of programme quality. 'The new services of satellite and cable' he wrote, 'carry both the promise of enrichment and the threat of deprivation. ... Constant vigilance will be required, for the greatest danger is that of gradual disenfranchisement by stealth' (Wenham, Third Age, 26–7).

As director of programmes, BBC television, between 1982 and 1985 Wenham made his most significant contribution to British broadcasting. Margaret Thatcher's second election victory in 1984 brought free-market theory to the centre of policy making. The BBC was not immune: indeed, its exclusive enjoyment of the compulsory licence fee, and the Thatcherite perception of in-built left-wing bias, made it an obvious candidate for the bracing disciplines of market forces. Consequently, in 1985 the home secretary, Leon Brittan, appointed a committee under the chairmanship of Sir Alan Peacock to review the corporation's funding. It was widely anticipated that the committee would recommend that the BBC be required to seek funding—in whole or in part—from commercial advertising. Wenham organized the BBC's submission to the Peacock committee, using his analytical skills and political knowledge. It was a clear statement of the principle that public-service broadcasting must remain separately funded if Britain were to escape the market failure manifest in wholly commercial systems like that of the United States. Peacock did not recommend commercial funding for the BBC, which continued to provide a benchmark of quality and diversity for existing commercial channels, and for the many more which followed. This crucial outcome owed much to the cogency and persuasiveness of Wenham's contribution.

In other times such a critical role and successful track record might have led ultimately to the director-generalship of the BBC. But although Wenham was further promoted to become managing director of BBC radio (1986–7), the political climate remained hostile to his kind. Dissembling his formidable intelligence behind a laconic manner and acerbic wit was perhaps also contrary to the temper of the times. In 1987 the board of governors appointed the deputy director-general, Michael Checkland, an accountant, to the top job. Wenham saw the writing on the wall, and went his own way. In his last decade he advised numerous media companies, wrote regularly on broadcasting matters, and enjoyed to the full the breadth of his interests and the company of his many friends.

Wenham's professional life was spent in broadcasting, progressing from programme production to senior managerial roles in BBC television and radio, and latterly becoming a consultant and commentator on a wide range of broadcasting issues. His career spanned a period in which British broadcasting moved from the tightly regulated duopoly of the BBC and ITV of the early 1960s to the commercially driven plurality of channels of the late 1990s. His analytical intelligence, foresight, and an ability to recruit and inspire talent made him a significant and influential figure in this period of transition. Throughout he remained a firm but undogmatic champion of public-service broadcasting, and a forceful critic of the fashionable ideologies and management techniques which he identified as enemies of creativity. He died of a heart attack at St Thomas's Hospital, Lambeth, London, on 8 May 1997, and was buried on 19 May at St James's Church, Weybridge, Surrey. He was survived by his wife and daughters. PETER IBBOTSON

Sources A. Briggs, The history of broadcasting in the United Kingdom, rev. edn, 5 (1995) · B. Appleyard, 'Programming the life of Brian', The Times (15 May 1986) · A. Leslie, 'Men in charge', Harpers and Queen (Feb 1971), 64–7 · The Times (10 May 1997) · The Independent (10 May 1997) · WWW · b. cert. · m. cert. · d. cert. · private information (2004)

Archives SOUND BL NSA, performance recordings

Likenesses photograph, repro. in *The Times* · photograph, repro. in *The Independent*
Wealth at death £555,225: probate, 14 Aug 1997, *CGPLA Eng. & Wales*

Wenham, Jane (*d.* 1730), last person convicted of witchcraft in England, details of whose upbringing are unknown, lived in Church Lane, Walkern, Hertfordshire, and for many years endured a reputation in the village not only for witchcraft but also for swearing, cursing, idleness, thievery, and whoredom. She was married twice, and had a number of children, but was a widow by the time of her prosecution in March 1712. Earlier that year a farmer named John Chapman called her a 'Witch and Bitch', blaming her for a spate of deaths among his livestock. Wenham decided to nip any further accusations in the bud, and on 9 February she applied to the local justice, Sir Henry Chauncy, for a warrant against Chapman for defamation. Chauncy declined to take any legal action, and instead the local minister, Godfrey Gardiner, was obliged to arbitrate. Much to Wenham's annoyance, Gardiner merely ordered Chapman to pay her a shilling in compensation, and took no further action. As she left the meeting Jane was heard to say 'if she could not have justice here she would have it elsewhere'. These were dangerous words for any suspected witch to utter, and, not surprisingly, when Gardiner's servant, a young woman named Ann Thorn, was subsequently afflicted with terrible fits and delusions Wenham was immediately identified as the culprit.

Chauncy issued a warrant for her arrest and Wenham was searched for teats, which would prove her bond with the devil. None being found, Jane then offered to be swum in order to prove her innocence. Chauncy refused, but the vicar of the neighbouring parish of Ardley, Robert Strutt, proposed another test: to repeat the Lord's prayer, which it was thought no witch could achieve. Unfortunately, Jane faltered in her recitation. Her guilt was confirmed in the eyes of those present, and she was sent to Hertford prison to await trial at the next assizes. Her case was heard on 4 March before Sir John Powell. There were sixteen witnesses for the prosecution, including Gardiner, Strutt, and the Revd Francis Bragge, Chauncy's grandson and a friend of Gardiner. Bragge told the court that Wenham had confessed to him that she had practised witchcraft for sixteen years. Other villagers gave accounts of how she had bewitched them. Elizabeth Field, for example, stated how nine years earlier Wenham had cast a spell over a child in her care, and Thomas Adams swore that she had bewitched some of his sheep. Despite many damning testimonies and proofs, including the discovery under her pillow of a magic concoction said to be made from rendered corpses, the only indictment which the assize lawyers would accept was that she had conversed with the devil in the form of a cat.

After hearing all the evidence Wenham could only say that 'she was a clear woman'. The court was adjourned and when it reconvened several hours later the jury announced that they found her guilty as charged. The punishment was death by hanging, but on Powell's orders the sentence was reprieved until further notice. The high-churchman Francis Bragge, who subsequently wrote three pamphlets on the case, asserted that even 'her nearest relations thinks she deserves to die, and that upon other accounts than witchcraft' (Bragge, *Full and Impartial Account*, 33). However, Powell, who throughout the trial had expressed his scepticism at the evidence, managed to obtain a royal pardon for Wenham. She was removed from Walkern for her own safety, and was given a home on the estate of a whig landowner, Colonel Plumer at Gilston. There she was visited by the Revd Francis Hutchinson, later bishop of Down and Connor, who thought her a good, pious woman. After Plumer's death she was looked after by Earl and Countess Cowper on their estate at Hertingfordbury. She died there on 11 January 1730, and was buried in Hertingfordbury churchyard.

OWEN DAVIES

Sources [F. Bragge], *A full and impartial account of the discovery of sorcery and witchcraft practis'd by Jane Wenham of Walkerne in Hertfordshire* (1712) · [F. Bragge], *Witchcraft further display'd* (1712) · *The case of the Hertfordshire witchcraft consider'd* (1712) · *A full confutation of witchcraft* (1712) · F. Hutchinson, *A historical essay concerning witchcraft* (1718) · J. Guskin, 'The context of English witchcraft: the case of Jane Wenham (1712)', *Eighteenth-Century Studies*, 15 (1981–2), 48–71 · W. B. Gerish, *Hertfordshire folk-lore* (1970) · I. Bartridge, *Witchcraft and its transformations, c.1650–c.1750* (1997)

Wenlock, John, first Baron Wenlock (*d.* 1471), diplomat and administrator, was the second son of William Wenlock (*d.* in or after 1415), a Bedfordshire landowner, and his wife, Margaret Briton. John Wenlock inherited the family properties in 1429, following the death of his elder brother, Sir Thomas Wenlock. Before then he served in France under Henry V, and in 1422 was constable of Vernon-sur-Seine (Eure). Appropriately for a future diplomat, he proved adroit in securing powerful patrons at home; the first of these was Sir John Cornewall, Lord Fanhope (*d.* 1443), a royal kinsman and Bedfordshire magnate, whom Wenlock was to support during the 1430s in a series of confrontations with Reynold, Lord Grey of Ruthin, and whose executor Wenlock later became. By then Wenlock was an usher in the king's chamber, and had begun to be active as a diplomat; closely identified with the peace policy of the duke of Suffolk, he took part from 1441 in the exchanges that in 1444 culminated in a two-year truce with France and, at a ceremony at Tours which Wenlock attended, in the betrothal of Henry VI to Margaret of Anjou. His rewards for his services included a number of offices on former Beauchamp estates in south Wales, and appointment as usher, and later as chamberlain, to the queen. Wenlock was knighted in 1447, while in the following year, when granted the office of constable of Bamburgh Castle, he was described as a 'king's knight'. Despite his membership of the royal household and association with Suffolk, he escaped attack by Cade's rebels in 1450, and managed to gain exemption from that year's Act of Resumption. He sat as knight of the shire for Bedfordshire in six parliaments during Henry VI's reign—those of 1433, 1437, 1439–40, 1447, 1449, and 1455–6.

During the 1450s Wenlock's loyalty to Lancaster seems

to have diminished somewhat; he probably shared the disgust felt by many veteran soldiers at the mismanagement of the French wars, and he had great difficulty in obtaining repayment of a substantial loan made to the crown in 1449. A letter from Henry VI, probably dating from 1453, castigated him for partiality to the duke of York, and suspended him from his office of queen's chamberlain while he went on pilgrimage. Although Wenlock fought for the king at St Albans in 1455 and was wounded, being afterwards carried 'in a carte sore hurt' (Gairdner, *Paston Letters*, 1.331), he may have owed his election as speaker of the Commons in 1455 to his not being firmly allied to either side; indeed, at that time he was associated in the foundation of a chantry at Staines, Middlesex, with John Bourchier, Lord Berners, a member of a family that favoured reconciliation. That in 1458 he went as an envoy with Viscount Bourchier and the Neville earls of Warwick and Salisbury to treat with Burgundy over breaches of a truce may point to further links with York, but he was ostensibly more impartially employed in late 1458 and early 1459, when he headed an embassy to arrange marriages for the prince of Wales, the earl of March (York's eldest son), and the duke of Somerset's son with either French or Burgundian princesses. But no marriages were negotiated, and in October 1459 Wenlock declared himself for York by joining the duke at Ludlow. He subsequently followed Warwick and March to Calais, sharing their penalties of attainder and forfeiture.

In 1460 Wenlock took part in two raids on Sandwich, and then in the siege of the Tower of London, and early in 1461 he fought for the Yorkist cause at Mortimer's Cross, Ferrybridge, and Towton. At a time when that cause enjoyed limited support from the nobility and gentry, Wenlock's military skills, continental contacts, and diplomatic experience were great assets to Edward IV, and he received rich rewards for his desertion of Henry VI. He was appointed chief butler, chamberlain of the duchy of Lancaster, and steward of the duchy of Cornwall, and elected a knight of the Garter, while on 26 July 1461 he was summoned to parliament as Lord Wenlock. He also received numerous grants of wardships and custodies, and was given many of the estates of Chief Justice Sir John Fortescue. He continued to serve as a diplomat, playing a major part in negotiations that in the early 1460s led to a truce between England and France and the withdrawal of Scottish aid from the Lancastrian exiles. Not surprisingly, a series of deputies had to be appointed to carry out some of Wenlock's duties as butler, since he had 'not leisure to attend to the same' (*CPR*, 1461–7, 332).

Wenlock continued to be associated with Warwick in the embassies of the mid-1460s which treated with France over the question of Edward IV's marriage, and in a letter to the Franco-Burgundian agent Jean de Lannoy he expressed his disgust at the king's secret marriage to Elizabeth Woodville; this reverse, and his developing affiliation to Warwick, may explain his ultimate lapse of judgement in deserting Edward. In 1468 Wenlock's servant John Hawkins seems to have incriminated his master, along with other prominent Yorkists, in dealings with the Lancastrians. Yet Edward continued to show him favour, justifiably, it must have seemed, when in April 1470 Wenlock, as deputy captain of Calais, refused to admit a now rebellious Warwick into the town. Edward rewarded him by making him lieutenant of Calais, but a few months later, during the readeption of Henry VI, Wenlock is said by the Burgundian chronicler Commines to have encouraged Warwick to send several hundred men into the town, whose allegiance was thus swiftly transferred to Lancaster. Remaining in France, Wenlock joined Margaret of Anjou, and with her crossed to England in April 1471, but on 4 May was killed in the battle of Tewkesbury. A local chronicle notes that his body was 'take fro hens to be buryed' (Kingsford, 377).

Wenlock's place of burial is unknown, though he had doubtless intended to be buried in the Wenlock chapel at St Mary's Church, Luton, which he extensively renovated in the 1460s in memory of his first wife, Elizabeth Drayton; the widow of Christopher Preston, she was probably married to Wenlock about 1441. She was dead by March 1466, and in 1468 Wenlock married Agnes Danvers, widow of Sir John Fray, who outlived him, and married Sir John Say of Broxbourne. Wenlock's changes of allegiance seem to have earned him a reputation for shiftiness and time-serving, but the suggestion that he was so widely distrusted that he was seldom called upon to act as a feoffee or executor is hardly borne out by the surviving evidence, which shows him to have been quite frequently employed in those capacities, and it is likely that his political movements were largely responses to changing circumstances, and were no more unprincipled than those of most of his contemporaries. Whatever the motives for his actions, he left little in the way of memorial to them. There were no children of either of his marriages, and his heir, had his possessions not been forfeited, would have been a remote cousin, one Thomas Lawley.

MARGARET LUCILLE KEKEWICH

Sources J. S. Roskell, 'John Wenlock of Someries', *Publications of the Bedfordshire Record Society*, 38 (1958), 12–48 • J. S. Roskell, *The Commons and their speakers in English parliaments, 1376–1523* (1965) • C. Ross, *Edward IV* (1974) • C. L. Scofield, *The life and reign of Edward the Fourth*, 2 vols. (1923) • J. G. Nichols, 'A summary catalogue of monumental art, existing in parish churches, Bedfordshire' [1], *The topographer and genealogist*, ed. J. G. Nichols, 1 (1846), 63–82, esp. 77–8 • C. Rawcliffe, 'Wenlock, William', HoP, *Commons, 1386–1421*, 4.806–7 • R. A. Griffiths, *The reign of King Henry VI: the exercise of royal authority, 1422–1461* (1981) • M. L. Kekewich and others, eds., *The politics of fifteenth-century England: John Vale's book* (1995) • *Memoirs of Phillipe de Commynes: the reign of Louis XI, 1461–83*, trans. M. Jones, pbk edn (1972) • R. Somerville, *History of the duchy of Lancaster, 1265–1603* (1953) • A. C. Reeves, *Lancastrian Englishmen* (1981) • *Chancery records* • H. Cobbe, *Luton church* (1899) • *The Paston letters, 1422–1509 AD*, ed. J. Gairdner, new edn, 1 (1872) • GEC, *Peerage*, new edn, 12/2.479–85 • C. L. Kingsford, *English historical literature in the fifteenth century* (1913) • 'The chronicle of John Harrison', Gon. & Caius Cam., MS 249/277, fol. 133v
Wealth at death property in Shropshire, Bedfordshire, and Hertfordshire, but forfeited to Crown: Roskell, *The Commons*, 371

Wenman [*née* Fermor], **Agnes**, **Lady Wenman** (*d.* 1617), translator, was one of the two eldest of the sixteen children of Sir George Fermor (1550–1612), of Easton Neston,

Northamptonshire, and his wife, Mary Curzon (d. 1628), daughter of Thomas Curzon, of Addington, Buckinghamshire. In 1595 she married Richard *Wenman (1572/3–1640) [see under Wenman, Thomas, second Viscount Wenman], eldest son of Sir Thomas Wenman (d. 1577) of Thame Park, Oxfordshire, and his wife, Jane (fl. 1572–1613), daughter of William West, first Baron De La Warr. He was knighted the following year. They had eight children.

Wenman was suspected of involvement in the Gunpowder Plot of 1605. She came from a Catholic family, and was related to the known recusant Elizabeth Vaux, and, as the result of a misunderstanding over a letter of Vaux's, Wenman was examined twice. Although the charges against her were dropped, it is clear that Wenman had some knowledge of illegal Catholic activities, even if not of the Gunpowder Plot itself. John Morris identifies her as the lady with whom the Jesuit missionary Father John Gerard (1564–1637) was playing cards, disguised as a layman, when they were visited by George Abbot (1562–1633), future archbishop of Canterbury, who had recently published an attack on Gerard; as Gerard reports, Wenman 'could scarce keep her countenance, thinking within herself what he would have said if he had known whom he was answering' (Morris, 347).

Wenman's 'The historyes and chronicles of the world by John Zonaras' (an English rendering of Jean de Maumont's French version of a thirteenth-century Greek text) makes her one of the many early modern women whose writing began to attract attention only towards the end of the twentieth century. It is arguable that evidence of Wenman's choice of text provides additional evidence of her Catholicism. Although De Maumont's preface stresses that the work is one of 'secular and humane learning' (CUL, MS Dd.i.18, fol. 2v), it describes rulers who 'seperated themselves' from 'the sincere and true doctrine of God' (ibid., fol. 9v), and its translation in the late sixteenth or early seventeenth century might well have been regarded as a political act.

The work survives in only two manuscripts, neither of which preserves the full text. The first of these is one of Wenman's own notebooks; the second, a scribal publication in two large folio volumes, whose page layout and title-page imitate those of a printed text. The 'published' version of the 'Historyes' was evidently copied from Wenman's holograph; the scribe's annotations appear in the surviving notebook, and the majority of his more idiomatic renderings of Wenman's engaging but often extremely literal translation are incorporated in the later manuscript. It seems likely, therefore, that this manuscript was produced by a friend or relative, and that the work did not achieve a wide circulation; since the title-page records her as 'deceased', it is possible that the folios were intended as a private memorial. However, both translation and copying would have demanded considerable time and effort, and, in view of the religious climate, should be read as a form of self-identification or an affirmation of faith, even if a private one.

Wenman was buried near other members of her husband's family at Twyford church in Buckinghamshire on 4 July 1617. JANE GRIFFITHS

Sources DNB · G. Anstruther, Vaux of Harrowden: a recusant family (1953) · G. Baker, The history and antiquities of the county of Northampton, 2 (1836–41) · J. Morris, The life of Father John Gerard (1881) · C. H. Cooper, 'Corrections for the genealogy of Wenman', Herald and Genealogist, 2 (1865), 521–3 · CSP dom., 1603–10 · B. Willis, The history and antiquities of the town, hundred, and deanry of Buckingham (1755) · A. Fraser, The Gunpowder Plot: terror and faith in 1605 (1996) · F. G. Lee, History and antiquities of the church of the Blessed Virgin Mary of Thame (1887) · B. Burke, A genealogical history of the dormant, abeyant, forfeited and extinct peerages of the British empire, new edn (1883) · IGI · H. Love, The culture and commerce of texts: scribal publications in seventeenth century England (1998)

Archives CUL, MSS, Dd.i.18, Dd.i.19, and Mm 3, 32

Wenman, Philip, sixth Viscount Wenman (1719–1760), politician, was born on 23 November 1719 and baptized on 13 December at St James's, Westminster, the eldest son of Richard Wenman, fifth Viscount Wenman (1687–1729), and his wife, Susannah Wroughton (d. 1736), of Twyford, Berkshire. He succeeded his father as sixth Viscount Wenman on 28 November 1729. He attended Abingdon School under Thomas Woods, matriculated from Oriel College, Oxford, on 9 June 1737, and was made a DCL on 15 April 1741. On 13 July 1741 he married Sophia Herbert (1715–1787), eldest daughter and coheir of James Herbert of Tythrop House, Buckinghamshire, and in 1749 he succeeded her brother Philip as member of parliament for the city of Oxford.

The Wenman family was closely connected to the high tory interest which dominated Oxfordshire county politics during much of the first half of the eighteenth century. Their opponents damned these tories as Jacobites, but there is no evidence that Wenman ever gave active support to the Pretender, James Stuart, apart from his refusal in 1745 to subscribe to a pro-Hanoverian association. He became prominent when in 1752 his cousin Norreys Bertie, son of the earl of Abingdon, declined the nomination for one of the county parliamentary seats and put him forward instead. The tory candidate for the second seat was another cousin, Wenman's old schoolfellow Sir James Dashwood of Kirtlington, the sitting MP and hero of the Oxfordshire 'old interest'.

The county seats had not been contested since 1710, so the tories were taken by surprise when the whigs put up a fight on this occasion. The initial impetus behind this challenge was the ambition of Sir Edward Turner of Ambrosden, an opportunistic nouveau riche, but the whig interest at large, represented by such county grandees as Charles Spencer, third duke of Marlborough, and George Parker, second earl of Macclesfield, was willing to support an assault on the tory heartland of Oxfordshire and the university, and Macclesfield's son, Viscount Parker, came forward as the second whig candidate. The whig or 'new interest' campaign was well co-ordinated by the whig gentry, in particular Lady Susan Keck. The 1754 Oxfordshire election became a test case for the whigs' ambition to exclude the tories from their remaining bastions of political influence.

None of the contestants was a figure of any particular weight, nor was there any issue of importance—apart from the Bill for the Naturalization of Jews, first passed and then repealed in 1753—to focus the opinion of voters. Wenman and Dashwood, both of whom seemed more resolute in their loyalty to the old interest than far-sighted in their calculations, none the less found themselves committed to an ever-steepening spiral of expenditure before the polls closed on 23 April 1754. The contest was enlivened by plentiful helpings of the vigorous pamphleteering and allegations of scandal which were customary at the time, spiced in this case with malice of a particularly donnish flavour, and gave Hogarth his inspiration for a famous *Election* series of prints. Outright corruption, however, was less significant in influencing the result than either side alleged at the time. Wenman's own personality proved to be too inconspicuous to attract anything out of the ordinary in either praise or blame: he was disparaged as 'one who scarce deserved a thought' ('The poor supporters of the poor old interest', Bodl. Oxf., GA A248.7) and praised for his integrity, 'Like Wenman be modest, like Wenman be true' ('A song in season', Bodl. Oxf., GA A248.13), in more or less conventional terms.

At the declaration, Blackall, the high sheriff, declared Wenman and Dashwood elected with majorities of 114 and 95 respectively over Turner and Parker. The whigs immediately demanded a scrutiny, and Blackall decided to make a double return, thus leaving the decision to the House of Commons. After an interminable examination of witnesses, the Commons eventually voted, on 24 April 1755, in favour of Turner and Parker. R. J. Robson has calculated, on a detailed analysis, that the true result should have been a confirmation of Wenman and Dashwood in their seats.

The two tories paid dearly for their prolonged defence of the old interest. Their expenses were calculated at £20,068 1s. 2d., of which sum £6163 19s. 4d. was initially subscribed by Wenman, followed by a further £5736 5s. 7d. Wenman's estate was seriously embarrassed by this drain. In September 1754 he secured borrowings of £6000; in July 1755 he was obliged to sub-let his London house in Grosvenor Square, and to sell the furniture; in 1761, a year after his death, £20,000 was raised against his estate in a desperate attempt to avert the dissolution which overwhelmed the Wenman inheritance half a century later.

Apart from his disastrous involvement in the election of 1754 Wenman's life offers little of note. In 1745 he amended his country seat, Thame Park, by demolishing some of the old monastic buildings and replacing them with a Palladian range which was probably designed by William Smith, who was working for Dashwood at Kirtlington about the same time. His portrait (now lost), which was at Tythrop until 1933, suggests a personality more stubborn than intelligent and certainly not one over-endowed with political cunning. Wenman died on 16 August 1760, aged forty, and was buried on 23 August in the chapel at Thame Park. He was succeeded by his son Philip.　　　　　　　　　　M. St John Parker

Sources R. J. Robson, *The Oxfordshire election of 1754: a study in the interplay of city, county and university politics* (1949) · *The Oxfordshire election of 1754: an archive teaching unit prepared by a joint working party set up by the Oxfordshire County Record Office and the Oxfordshire Education Committee* (1970) · F. G. Lee, *The history, description and antiquities of the prebendal church of the Blessed Virgin Mary of Thame* (1883) · will, PRO, PROB 11/861, sig. 447 · Wykeham–Musgrave papers, Bodl. Oxf., MS Top. Oxon b. 261, fols. 32–147 · J. Townsend, *The Oxfordshire Dashwoods* (1922) · 'The building of Thame Park', *Country Life* (17 July 1909) · J. Lodge, *The peerage of Ireland*, rev. M. Archdall, rev. edn, 4 (1789), 286–7 · Foster, *Alum. Oxon.*, 1715–1886, 4.1525 · 'The poor supporters of the poor old interest', and 'A song in season for the Oxfordshire election of 1754', Bodl. Oxf., GA fol. A248.7, 13 · parish register, St Mary Thame, Oxfordshire, 13 Dec 1719 [baptism] · 'An account of the Wenman family', Bodl. Oxf., MS Willis 93.127

Likenesses oils, *c.*1748, repro. in Robinson, *Oxfordshire election of 1754*, 5 · G. Kneller, portrait; formerly at Tythrop House, Buckinghamshire, 1883 · G. Kneller, portrait (as a child); formerly at Tythrop House, Buckinghamshire, 1883

Wealth at death estates at Caswell, Thame, Twyford in Oxfordshire, and Sydenham in Buckinghamshire bequeathed to heirs (together with large debts secured on the estates): will, PRO, PROB 11/861, sig. 447; assortment of Wykeham–Musgrave papers, Bodl. Oxf., MS Top. Oxon b. 261, fols. 32–147

Wenman, Richard, first Viscount Wenman (1572/3–1640). *See under* Wenman, Thomas, second Viscount Wenman (1596–1665).

Wenman, Thomas, second Viscount Wenman (1596–1665), politician, was the elder of two surviving sons of **Richard Wenman**, first Viscount Wenman (1572/3–1640), and his first wife, Agnes *Wenman (d. 1617). His father was the eldest son of Sir Thomas Wenman (d. 1577) of Thame Park, Oxfordshire, and his wife, Jane, daughter of William West, first Baron De La Warr (of the second creation). Richard Wenman matriculated at Oxford on 8 December 1587 as a scholar of John Case, formerly fellow at St John's College, but does not seem to have taken a degree. About 1595 he married Agnes, daughter of Sir George Fermor; they had eight children. For his bravery as a volunteer at the taking of Cadiz, Richard Wenman was shortly afterwards knighted by the earl of Essex, on 22 or 27 June 1596. Following Agnes's death in the summer of 1617, on 4 November 1618 at St Bartholomew-the-Great, London, he married Anne, the reputedly rich widow of Robert Chamberlayne, and previously of Thomas Roland. Wenman was returned as one of the MPs for Oxfordshire on 20 December 1620, and again in 1625. In 1627 he acted as sheriff for Oxfordshire, and in the following year, by letters patent dated 30 July 1628, was created Baron Wenman of Kilrainham, co. Meath, and Viscount Wenman of Tuam. Anne having died, he married twice more; his third wife, Elizabeth, was buried at Twyford, Buckinghamshire, on 27 April 1629, and his fourth wife, Mary, daughter and coheir of Thomas Keble of Essex, was buried there on 28 July 1638. He died on 3 April 1640, and was buried at Twyford on 7 April.

Thomas Wenman matriculated from Balliol College, Oxford, on 23 November 1604, aged eight; he entered the Inner Temple as a student in 1614. Shortly before 5 July 1617 he married Margaret, second daughter and later coheir of Edmund Hampden of Wendover, Buckinghamshire, and Margaret Ball. He was knighted on 10 September 1617, and on 11 December 1620 was returned to parliament for Brackley in Northamptonshire, retaining his seat until August 1625. He was returned for Oxfordshire in February 1626 and for Brackley on 3 March 1628. In the 1630s he served in Ireland and on 20 December 1639 King Charles ordered that 'in return for his forwardness in serving the Crown in Ireland, his arrears of creation money be paid up, and the fee paid regularly in future' (*CSP Ire.*, *1633–47*, 229). It appears, however, that Wenman did not own property in Ireland, because in May 1641 his proxy vote conveyed to the earl of Thomond was contested on that basis by the peers sitting in Dublin. Perhaps soon after the death of his father in April 1640 and his succession as second viscount, Wenman had returned to England, where he was returned as MP for Oxfordshire on 28 October 1640.

At the outbreak of the civil war Wenman was a moderate advocate of the parliamentarian cause, but quickly gravitated to the peace party. When Charles advanced on London in late 1642, he was one of the five commissioners who met him at Colnbrook on 11 November, with a petition from parliament proposing negotiations. Wenman and his fellow commissioners proceeded to Oxford on 1 February 1643 with proposals for an accommodation. In 1644 he was appointed a commissioner to carry new peace proposals to the king, attending him at Oxford on 24 November, and was present at the end of the year during the negotiations at Uxbridge. His anxiety for peace may well have been increased by the royalists' seizure of his estates, and on 3 June he obtained from parliament a grant of £4 a week for his maintenance pending their recovery. On 20 August 1646 the allowance was discharged by order of the house. In April 1647 Wenman was nominated to the parliamentary committee appointed to supervise the visitors of Oxford University. In this period he often visited Bulstrode Whitelocke's house and engaged there in discussions with other members of parliament. On 28 December 1647, Whitelocke 'and Mr Pierrpont dining with the Lord Wenman, they had much discourse about the Scotts proceedings in the Treaty of the Isle of Wight, and feared a new war' (*Diary of Bulstrode Whitelocke*, 203). On 1 September 1648 he was once more appointed a peace commissioner, to treat with the king at Newport, and has plausibly been characterized as prepared for a peace on almost any terms. He was one of those who voted that the terms accepted by Charles were sufficient grounds for the house to proceed upon, and for this was secluded at Pride's Purge in December, and imprisoned. On his release in 1649 he retired to Thame, employing as his chaplain there Seth Ward, later bishop of Salisbury, who had been driven from Cambridge for opposing the solemn league and covenant. After the conquest of Ireland, Wenman became one of the adventurers, subscribing £600 and on 23 February 1654 received a grant of 1000 acres in the barony of Garricastle in King's county.

Wenman was returned for Oxfordshire in the Convention Parliament of 1660, and was introduced by proxy to the Irish house of peers on 13 July 1661 in succession to his father. He died on 25 January 1665, and was buried at Twyford two days later. He was succeeded as viscount by his brother Philip (1610–1686). His wife, Margaret, had died on 1 May 1658 and been buried at Twyford. Their son Richard (*b.* 1621/2) died childless in 1646, so Wenman's substantial wealth was divided between his brother and the families of his daughters, Frances, wife of Richard Samwell of Upton, Penelope, wife of Sir Thomas Cave of Stanford in Northamptonshire, Elizabeth, wife of Sir Greville Verney of Compton Verney, Warwickshire, and Mary, wife of her cousin Sir Francis Wenman of Caswell in Oxfordshire, who was named as his father-in-law's executor.

E. I. CARLYLE, rev. STEPHEN WRIGHT

Sources GEC, *Peerage* · *CSP Ire.*, *1633–47* · Foster, *Alum. Oxon.* · Keeler, *Long Parliament* · R. Spalding, *Contemporaries of Bulstrode Whitelocke, 1605–75* (1990) · *The diary of Bulstrode Whitelocke, 1605–1675*, ed. R. Spalding, British Academy, Records of Social and Economic History, new ser., 13 (1990) · D. Underdown, *Pride's Purge: politics in the puritan revolution* (1971) · *JHL*, 7 (1644–5); 10 (1647–8) · will, PRO, PROB 11/316, sigs. 20 and 22

Wealth at death see will, PRO, PROB 11/316, sigs. 20 and 22

Wenman, Thomas Francis (1745–1796), civil lawyer and botanist, was born at Thame Park, Oxfordshire, on 18 November 1745, the second son of Philip *Wenman, sixth Viscount Wenman (1719–1760), politician and landowner, and Sophia (1715–1787), the eldest daughter of James Herbert of Tythrop, Buckinghamshire. He attended Westminster School from 1755 to 1762 and then proceeded to University College, Oxford, whence he matriculated on 22 October 1762. In 1764 he was admitted to the Inner Temple, and in 1770 was called to the bar. From 1765 until his death he was a fellow of All Souls, Oxford; he was awarded the degrees of BCL (1771) and DCL (1780). He stood unsuccessfully for the borough of Wallingford in 1774 but was returned to parliament in October of that year as MP for Westbury, largely through the influence of Lord Abingdon. During his six years as MP he played little part in parliamentary proceedings and made only one speech.

Wenman was elected keeper of Oxford University archives on 15 January 1781 and appointed regius professor of civil law in 1789, posts that he retained until his death. He soon gave up his lectures in civil law 'for want of an audience' (Quiller-Couch, 147) and concentrated instead on his passion for natural history. He was a close friend of John Sibthorpe, professor of botany, who bequeathed to Wenman, for completion, his notes and materials for a 'Flora graeca'. Wenman died, unmarried, a few months later, on 8 April 1796, by drowning in a stretch of the River Cherwell near Water Eaton while seeking botanical specimens for his collection. He was buried in All Souls chapel on 15 April; according to the inscription on his tomb 'the whole university wept when he died'. Many of his writings are preserved among the warden's manuscripts at All Souls, including an unpublished history of the college.

W. P. COURTNEY, rev. M. J. MERCER

Sources J. Brooke, 'Wenman, Hon. Thomas Francis', HoP, *Commons, 1754–90* · *Old Westminsters*, 2.980 · Foster, *Alum. Oxon., 1715–1886*, 4.1525 · GEC, *Peerage* · J. L. Barton, 'Legal studies', *Hist. U. Oxf. 5: 18th-cent. Oxf.*, 593–606, esp. 596 · *GM*, 1st ser., 66 (1796), 357 ·

L. M. Quiller-Couch, ed., *Reminiscences of Oxford by Oxford men, 1559–1850*, OHS, 22 (1892) · *Monumental inscriptions in All Souls College, Oxford*, 2nd edn (1997), 45 · G. V. Cox, *Recollections of Oxford*, 2nd edn (1870), 23–4 · monument, All Souls chapel, Oxford
Archives All Souls Oxf., MSS

Wensleydale. For this title name *see* Parke, James, Baron Wensleydale (1782–1868).

Wentworth. For this title name *see* individual entries under Wentworth; *see also* Noel, Anne Isabella, *suo jure* Baroness Wentworth, and Lady Byron (1792–1860); Blunt, Anne Isabella Noel, *suo jure* Baroness Wentworth (1837–1917).

Wentworth, Anne (1629/30–1693?), religious writer, may have come from a Lincolnshire family, but little else is known of her background except that she was 'of no mean parantage' (A. Wentworth, *Englands Spiritual Pill*, 1679, 48). She married William Wentworth of London, who was possibly a glover, in 1652 or 1653; although the exact date of the union cannot be ascertained she had apparently been married for twenty-three years when her pamphlet *A True Account* was published in 1676. They lived at Kingshead Court, Whitecross Street, London, and had one child, a daughter.

Wentworth was deeply unhappy in her marriage and in 1670, at the age of forty, began to make prophecies expressing her distress. By 1674 she had written openly and critically about her husband. These early writings were lost, and most of the details relating to Anne's life have to be gleaned from her four extant texts: *A True Account of Anne Wentworth* (1676), *A Vindication of A. W.* [Anne Wentworth] (1677), *Englands Spiritual Pill* (1679), and *The Revelation of Jesus Christ* (1679), the last of which was financed for publication by an anonymous 'Friend in love to Souls' (Wentworth, *The Revelation*, title-page). In *Englands Spiritual Pill*, Wentworth explained the origin of her desire to write: during a 'hectick Feaver' God visited her with a command to 'discover my Husbands cruelty to me' (Wentworth, *Spiritual Pill*, 4, 5). The couple were living separately by September 1677, and Wentworth swore never to return unless her husband 'be a new-man, a changed man, a man sensible of the wrong he has done me, with his fierce looks, bitter words, sharp tongue, and cruel usage' (Wentworth, *A Vindication*, 5). Wentworth's castigation of her husband in print probably reveals the emotions of a 'battered wife' (Hobby, 51). William seized some of the earlier versions of Anne's texts, probably to suppress this personal attack on him, turned her out of the family home, and sublet it. Anne managed to reoccupy the house in the summer of 1679.

In addition to their autobiographical content, Wentworth's works are also religio-political critiques of the Baptist community to which she was temporarily aligned. Her criticism of the Baptists for empty formalism was probably one reason for Wentworth's excommunication, which occurred in February 1675. Arguably more important, however, was the fact that William Wentworth gained the support of the Baptist hierarchy, and presumably turned them against Anne. She had therefore to oppose the patriarchal authority of both her husband and the Baptist elders in order to write. Initially Anne had been championed by the prominent London Particular Baptist Hanserd Knollys, who decreed her work to be 'from God, and for the good of Souls' (Wentworth, *Spiritual Pill*, 5). When Knollys and other important Baptists (among them William Dix and Thomas Hicks) turned against her, Wentworth denounced their 'evil dark spirit' and indulged the latent fear of Catholicism in seventeenth-century society by comparing them to 'Papists' (ibid., 32, 14). In the late 1670s anti-Catholic sentiment was running high owing to the many objections against the Catholic James, duke of York, attaining the throne, giving Anne's objections to the Baptists a political dimension. Therefore, as Elspeth Graham observes of Wentworth's work, 'the private both reflects and foreshadows the public' (Graham, 182).

Wentworth's texts took a prophetic form, which involved writing as though at God's command in order to criticize personal or political enemies. This format, pursued in all of her works, was relatively uncommon in the post-Restoration period (the largest outpouring of prophetic writing belonging to the 1650s). Her apocalyptic judgments on the nation, addressed to the king and the lord mayor in July 1677, have been preserved in the *Calendar of State Papers Domestic*, 1677–8. Even though by November 1677 people had begun to 'decline her predictions' (*CSP dom.*, 1677–8, 478), Wentworth continued to write until November 1679, the date of the last of her prophecies in *Englands Spiritual Pill*.

Nothing is known of Wentworth's later life, but she may have been the Anne Wentworth who lived in St John's Court and was buried on 22 May 1693 at St James's Church, Clerkenwell. Although Wentworth lacked the male support essential to becoming successful as a female prophet in the seventeenth century, in her attempt to overcome her oppression she was, one critic maintains, like the 'phoenix who arises from the ashes' (Hinds, 105): a woman who created herself anew in life and in print.

CATIE GILL

Sources *CSP dom.*, 1677–8 · E. Graham and others, eds., *Her own life: autobiographical writings by seventeenth-century Englishwomen* (1992) · H. Hinds, *God's Englishwomen* (1996) · E. Hobby, *Virtue of necessity: English women's writing, 1649–88* (1988) · R. Houenden, ed., *A true register of the christenings, mariages, and burialles in the parish of St James, Clarkenwell*, vol. 5: *Burials, 1666 to 1719*; *Harleian Society Registers*, Harleian Society, vol. 19 (1893) · P. Mack, *Visionary women* (Berkeley, Los Angeles and London: University of California Press, 1994) · V. Taft, 'Anne Wentworth's life and works', chaucer.library. emory.edu/wwrp · Wing, *STC* · W. T. Whitley, *The Baptists of London, 1612–1928* (1928)
Archives Yale U., Beinecke L., commonplace book

Wentworth, Benning (1696–1770), merchant and colonial governor, was born on 24 July 1696 at Portsmouth, New Hampshire, the eldest of the fourteen children of John *Wentworth (1672–1730), merchant and lieutenant-governor of New Hampshire, and his wife, Sarah (1674–1741), daughter of Mark Hunking of Portsmouth.

Wentworth grew up in an insecure frontier environment where wars with the French and Native Americans

Benning Wentworth (1696–1770), by Joseph Blackburn, 1760

and strong demand for New Hampshire timber resources provided abundant opportunities to amass wealth. As the eldest son of a wealthy mast-trading merchant, whose markets were in Spain and England, Benning undoubtedly was groomed to take over the family business. However, he was so wild and undisciplined that after graduating from Harvard College in 1715, where he set a new record in windows broken and fines paid, his father, while building a family dynasty as lieutenant-governor of New Hampshire, kept Benning at arm's length by having him serve an apprenticeship in Boston at his uncle Samuel Wentworth's counting-house and then reside in Boston as a mariner-merchant plying the West Indian and Spanish trade in timber, wines, and brandies throughout the 1720s. Although Benning acquired no property in Boston, on 31 December 1719 he married Abigail (bap. 1699, d. 1755), the daughter of John Ruck, a prominent Boston merchant. The couple had three sons. Only after his father's death in December of 1730 did Wentworth return to Portsmouth to assume his inheritance of £2000, extensive real estate, the family's overseas trade in masts and timber, and his place as head of an extensive family political faction now in opposition to the new governor of Massachusetts and New Hampshire, Jonathan Belcher,

and his kinsman ally, Richard Waldron, the province secretary. These two politicians had just ousted the Wentworth 'clan' from the positions of political authority, and Benning sought retribution.

Upon his arrival in Portsmouth, Wentworth joined Theodore Atkinson to do everything possible to obtain Belcher's removal. In August 1732 he gained election to the colonial assembly and, using the influence of the new lieutenant-governor, David Dunbar, in 1733 both Wentworth and Atkinson were appointed to the New Hampshire council. In both the assembly and the council the two men worked incessantly to embarrass and undermine Belcher and Waldron, who sought to unite New Hampshire to Massachusetts, while the Wentworth faction wanted a complete political separation of the two colonies, with a greatly enlarged New Hampshire and its own royal governor.

After Britain colonized Georgia in 1732, relations with Spain deteriorated, and in 1733 the Spanish government refused to pay Wentworth for an £11,000 shipment of oak timber, which put him at the mercy of Boston creditors. Using his English merchant connections, especially John Thomlinson, a wealthy London merchant, Wentworth borrowed in London to pay off the Bostonians. Now under pressure from London creditors and on the verge of bankruptcy, Wentworth went to London in 1738 to work something out with them. At that point a commission that had been established to determine the boundary lines between New Hampshire and Massachusetts decided, under member Atkinson's influence, to rule in favour of New Hampshire's claims, doubling its territory. In London, Thomlinson thereupon worked out a plan by which for £300 Wentworth would be appointed governor of a separate New Hampshire and later surveyor-general of the king's woods in return for Wentworth's dropping all claims against the British government. His supporters raised the necessary money, and in 1741 the governorship was purchased for him.

Wentworth served as governor of New Hampshire from 1741 to 1767, a longer continuous tenure than any other governor in British colonial American history. He did so primarily because of his connections with John Thomlinson, whose patron was in turn the duke of Newcastle. Thomlinson served the crown as deputy paymaster of troops in North America and as a mast contractor for the Royal Navy. He obtained masts from Benning's brother, Mark Wentworth, and after 1732 from his brother-in-law Theodore Atkinson. Thomlinson was also the agent for the New Hampshire assembly in England and an avid supporter of the Church of England in the colony. His influence proved crucial to Wentworth's success as governor as he thwarted numerous efforts by Wentworth's enemies to remove him from office in the 1740s and 1750s.

Wentworth's political acumen proved almost as important to his long tenure. A shrewd, compromising, and accommodating politician, his general approach was to buy off those who might become opponents by distributing over one hundred justice of the peace and military commissions, granting land in new townships to anyone of local influence, including members of the council and assembly, and placating the all-important timber interests by ignoring the white pine laws and allowing free enterprise in the woods so long as the lumberers kept his brother Mark supplied with masts for the Royal Navy. All the while he kept up a correspondence with the British bureaucracy, portraying himself as a model administrator who enforced all royal policies. In most instances of conflict with the assembly, however, he proved willing to sacrifice royal prerogatives in order to obtain needed policies. For example, though the crown opposed large issues of paper money, during wars Wentworth compromised with the assembly over the use of paper money to pay the militia so that he could obtain a substantial number of troops. Moreover, he allowed the passage of most legislation without suspending clauses that allowed crown review and approval. Yet because of his vindictiveness towards his bitterest political enemies he provoked a constitutional crisis which stopped all legislative activity in the colony from 1748 until 1752, in a successful effort to end his enemies' efforts to remove him. When his enemies obtained a majority in the assembly in 1748, Wentworth unilaterally extended representation to some new towns that he knew were favourable to him and vetoed the assembly's choice of speaker, Richard Waldron. The assembly objected to both actions, but Wentworth obtained additional royal instructions supporting his positions while Thomlinson undermined Waldron's efforts to have Wentworth replaced.

While he was governor Wentworth did everything he could to extend his family's authority and the power of Portsmouth's mast-trading mercantile community. He packed the government bureaucracy, including the council, with his relatives and built roads west to the Connecticut River so that his family and Portsmouth's merchants could retain dominance in the mast trade. After most of his 'clan' converted to the Church of England in the mid-1730s, he joined them and in the early 1740s supported the church's missionary arm (the Society for the Propagation of the Gospel) with frontier land grants. Wentworth's control of patronage and the mast trade along with his numerous land grants to himself and his supporters ensured their dominance until the American War of Independence. With some of the gains he built a fifty-two-room mansion at Little Harbor (outside Portsmouth) in 1750. Yet in the course of the 1750s all three of his sons and his wife died, thwarting his personal ambitions for his children. Obese and suffering from gout, on 15 March 1760 he married his 23-year-old housekeeper, Martha Hilton (1737–1805)—an act that scandalized his family—and began fathering children with her, all of whom were stillborn. Coincidentally he began a new round of township grants west of the Connecticut River in territory under dispute with New York colony, 111 grants in all, giving himself 500 acres in each.

These land grants and Thomlinson's gradual decline in health and in influence at court ultimately led to Wentworth's dismissal as governor. Over the course of his administration Wentworth had granted 124 townships in the disputed territory between the Connecticut and Hudson rivers (now Vermont) at moderate fees, minimal quitrents, and as low a cost as 2 cents an acre. Known as the New Hampshire grants, they attracted large numbers of settlers as well as timber interests tied to Portsmouth. New York's landed and timber interests protested as did its governors, and in 1763 the Board of Trade in Britain held hearings on this boundary dispute. The hearings became a full-scale assault against all of Wentworth's activities. The board reported to the privy council Wentworth's negligence, disobedience, greed, abuse of power, simony, and other derelictions of duty, and recommended that the privy council award the disputed territory to New York. In 1764 the privy council did so, much to the dismay of the local settlers and New Hampshire's élite. Wentworth faced dismissal, but the intervention of his nephew, John Wentworth, who had developed connections with the marquess of Rockingham, then secretary of state, allowed Wentworth quietly to resign his offices in 1766; John assumed these offices in 1767. The creation of an independent state of Vermont was undoubtedly the most important yet unintentional consequence of Wentworth's land policies, as the local settlers in the New Hampshire grants wanted nothing to do with New York's land speculators and legal system.

Over the years Benning Wentworth had gained the reputation of being haughty and arrogant yet shrewd and tenacious. His political enemies referred to him as Don Granada and Don Diego and as a man with 'guts' but no brains; however, they vastly underestimated him. Wentworth was able to maintain a family dynasty and Portsmouth's control of the prosperous mast trade for a generation and perhaps even British America's first political machine, but his greed finally caught up with him. While he amassed a small fortune (over 10,000 guineas and extensive real estate), he had no heirs to reward and was shunned by his extended family for his marriage to a socially inferior woman; as an act of revenge he disinherited all his relatives in his will, leaving everything to Martha. He died in his mansion at Little Harbor on 14 October 1770 and was buried in the Portsmouth Church of England cemetery at Queen's Chapel shortly thereafter.

DAVID E. VAN DEVENTER

Sources J. Daniell, *Experiment in republicanism: New Hampshire politics and the American Revolution, 1741–1794* (1970) · C. K. Shipton, *Sibley's Harvard graduates: biographical sketches of those who attended Harvard College*, 6 (1942), 113–33 · J. Daniell, 'Wentworth, Benning', *ANB* · J. Wentworth, *Wentworth genealogy* (1878) · J. F. Looney, 'The king's representative: Benning Wentworth, colonial governor, 1741–1767', PhD diss., Lehigh University, 1961 · C. E. Clark, *The eastern frontier: the settlement of northern New England, 1610–1763* (1970) · D. E. Van Deventer, *The emergence of provincial New Hampshire, 1623–1741* (1976) · P. W. Wilderson, *Governor John Wentworth and the American Revolution* (1994) · M. A. Bellesiles, *Revolutionary outlaws: Ethan Allen and the struggle for independence on the early American frontier* (1993) · N. Bouton and others, eds., *Provincial and state papers: documents and records relating to the province of New Hampshire*, 40 vols. (1867–1943), vols. 5–7, 10, 18–19 · *Collections of the Massachusetts Historical Society*, 6th ser., 4 (1891) · *Collections of the Massachusetts Historical Society*, 6th ser., 6–7 (1893–4) [*The Belcher papers*, vols. 1–2] · *Collections of the Massachusetts Historical Society*, 6th ser., 9 (1897) [*The*

Bowdoin and Temple papers, vol. 1] • *Collections of the Massachusetts Historical Society*, 6th ser., 10 (1899) [*The Pepperrell papers*] • J. J. Malone, *Pine trees and politics* (1964)

Archives New Hampshire Historical Society, Concord, MSS | L. Cong., New Hampshire misc. MSS

Likenesses J. Blackburn, oils, 1760, New Hampshire Historical Society, Concord [*see illus.*]

Wealth at death over 10,000 guineas in cash: Shipton, ed. *Sibley's Harvard Graduates*

Wentworth, Charles Watson-, second marquess of Rockingham (1730–1782), prime minister, was born on 13 May 1730 at Wentworth Woodhouse, near Rotherham, Yorkshire, the fifth but only surviving son (and eighth but third surviving child) of Thomas Watson-Wentworth, first marquess of Rockingham (1693–1750), politician, and his wife, Mary (1701–1761), the daughter of Daniel *Finch, second earl of Nottingham and seventh earl of Winchilsea, politician, and his second wife, Anne, the daughter of Christopher, first Viscount Hatton. On his father's side he was descended from Edward Watson, second Baron Rockingham (1630–1689), of Rockingham Castle, Northamptonshire, who married Anne, the daughter of the royalist politician Thomas Wentworth, first earl of Strafford, of Wentworth Woodhouse. Their second son, Thomas (1665–1723), assumed the additional name of Wentworth on succeeding to the West Riding estates of his uncle, the second earl of Strafford, in 1695. His only son was Charles Watson-Wentworth's father, who married on 22 September 1716. He was MP for Malton (1715–27) and Yorkshire (1727–8) and lord lieutenant of the West Riding (from 1733); a staunch ally of the court whigs, he was created a knight of the Bath (27 May 1725), Baron Malton (28 May 1728), and earl of Malton (19 November 1734), and, having succeeded his kinsman as sixth Baron Rockingham (26 February 1746), was awarded a marquessate (19 April 1746).

Childhood and Yorkshire inheritance Charles Watson-Wentworth, who entered Westminster School in April 1738, was styled Viscount Higham from 1739 to 1746 and earl of Malton from 1746. In October 1745, aged fifteen, he was appointed colonel of a regiment of volunteers raised against Charles Edward Stuart, the Young Pretender. That winter he slipped away under a false name and, having reached Carlisle, offered his services to the commander-in-chief, William, duke of Cumberland, a gesture for which he received the congratulations of an amused court. From 1746 to 1748 he pursued a desultory course of study under George Quarme in Geneva, and for the next two years he lived in Italy under Major James Forrester; he returned to England, via Austria, Prussia, Hanover, and Brunswick, in 1750. Although he had had several childhood illnesses, it may also have been in Italy, through at least one sexual liaison, that he contracted what was probably a persistent problem in his urogenitary system. His 'old complaint', as he called it, caused him frequently recurring bouts of debilitating sickness and may have made him impotent, though some contemporaries regarded him as a hypochondriac.

Watson-Wentworth was created earl of Malton in the

Charles Watson-Wentworth, second marquess of Rockingham (1730–1782), by Sir Joshua Reynolds, 1766–8

Irish peerage on 17 September 1750, and succeeded his father as second marquess of Rockingham on 14 December that year, becoming one of the wealthiest peers in Britain. In addition to extensive properties in Northamptonshire and co. Wicklow, and a London town house at 4 Grosvenor Square, he inherited the princely estates centred on the palatial family home of Wentworth House (as it was then known). He is estimated to have received an annual income of over £20,000 in 1751, which probably at least doubled over the following thirty years. On 26 February 1752 he married his childhood fiancée, Mary Bright (*bap.* 1735, *d.* 1804) [*see* Wentworth, Mary Watson-], at the house of her stepfather, Sir John Ramsden, third baronet, in Golden Square, St James's, Piccadilly. She was the daughter and heir, with a fortune of £60,000, of Thomas Bright of Badsworth, near Pontefract, the son of John Bright, formerly Liddell, MP for Pontefract (1698–1701), and his wife, Margaret, the daughter of William Norton of Sawley, near Ripon. Rockingham's social prestige was enhanced by the fact that for many years he was the only nobleman to hold the rank of a British marquessate as his principal title, so that, to his friends, he was simply 'the Marquess'.

Offices, electoral patronage, and leisure pursuits Like his father before him, Rockingham was highly esteemed by Thomas Pelham-Holles, duke of Newcastle, the northern secretary of state, and his early political connections were naturally with Henry Pelham's court whig ministry. On 18 July 1751 he was appointed lord lieutenant and *custos rotulorum* of the West Riding of Yorkshire and of the county of the city of York, and *custos rotulorum* of the North Riding, and on the same day he became a lord of the bedchamber to George II. He took his seat in the House of Lords on 21 May 1751, and made his maiden speech on 17 March 1752, in defence of the government's bill to confiscate the lands of Scottish Jacobite rebels, but he declined to move the address in late 1753, and for a long time he was inactive in parliament. He took a close interest in the fortunes of the Yorkshire woollen manufacturers, on which subject a pamphlet was addressed to him in 1752. He largely baulked at the programme of political education prepared for him by his uncle William Murray, later Lord Mansfield, the solicitor-general, and in the early 1750s displayed a youthful naïvety and an occasionally headstrong element—which he never entirely lost—in what was otherwise a placid temperament.

Rockingham made a precipitate attempt to promote the candidacy of his friend Sir George Savile, an archetypal independent country gentleman, for the representation of Yorkshire at a county meeting in York on 16 July 1753, but withdrew without trying his strength. His embarrassment arose from having dared to oppose the two sitting ministerialist whig MPs and at finding that his appeal to the freeholders had raised their hackles against overt aristocratic interference. Nevertheless, although the representation was unchanged at the general election of 1754, Savile was elected unopposed on a vacancy in January 1759, and thereafter Rockingham, who had learned the necessity of endeavouring to lead public opinion by appearing to follow it, had the most important influence in county affairs. At the large freeman borough of York, where in December 1753 the Whig Club was renamed after him, he gained control of one seat in 1754 and of the other by 1768. He was patron of the rotten boroughs of Malton and Higham Ferrers, disposed of a seat at Hull from 1766, when he became its high steward (7 April), and had influence at Beverley, Hedon, and Scarborough. He also had an interest in co. Wicklow elections to the Irish parliament.

Rockingham was elected a fellow of the Royal Society in 1751 and of the Society of Antiquaries in 1752; he became a member of White's, the Jockey Club, and the Society of Dilettanti in the 1750s; and in 1763 he was appointed a trustee of Westminster School and a governor of Charterhouse. He applied himself to the improvement of his estates, which included the encouragement of mining and canal developments, and was praised for his efforts by the agriculturist Arthur Young. He also completed the work begun by his father on Wentworth House, erected several monuments in the grounds, and built a lavish stable block. This reflected his predominating interests in racing and gambling, and he was one of the foremost patrons of the turf, being responsible, for example, for naming the St Leger at Doncaster after his friend Colonel Anthony St Leger. An art collector, one of his commissions was Stubbs's magnificent canvas of his horse Whistlejacket (now in the National Gallery). He was knowledgeable on the coins of the Roman empire.

Early political career, 1756–1765 Rockingham, who was appointed vice-admiral of Yorkshire on 27 February 1755, gained a reputation for acting with initiative and moderation in county matters. He restored peace after the food riots in Sheffield in 1756 without resorting to the use of force, and, despite local disturbances, successfully raised three militia regiments the following year. Remaining loyal to Newcastle, he declined the offer of becoming master of horse to the prince of Wales in late 1756, and showed a determination to resign his household office, which did not in the end prove necessary, during the ministerial crisis in June 1757, when George II had to appoint a court whig ministry led by Newcastle and William Pitt. In recognition of his potential political influence, he was nominated a knight of the Garter on 4 February 1760, and was installed on 6 May. He continued to hold the office of lord of the bedchamber on the accession of George III that year, and assisted at the coronation on 26 September 1761.

Rockingham showed an early distaste for the complexion of the new court and disliked the appointment of the king's favourite, John Stuart, third earl of Bute, as northern secretary of state in March 1761. His aversion was increased by the ministerialist opposition he experienced in Yorkshire at the general election that year and by the growing disrespect with which Newcastle was treated in matters of patronage and policy. He began to believe that the new reign would mark a displacement of the old whig families who had created the Hanoverian settlement, and on 9 May 1762 wrote to Newcastle: 'I must look and ever shall upon you and your connections as the solid foundations on which every good, which has happened to this country since the Revolution, have been erected' (BL, Add. MS 32938, fol. 123). He therefore supported his chief's resignation that month, and, although, like him, he initially eschewed the idea of formal opposition, he was involved in organizing what proved to be a disastrous attack on the popular peace preliminaries at the opening of parliament (9 December 1762). After the king's petulant dismissal of William Cavendish, fourth duke of Devonshire, the lord chamberlain, Rockingham took a lead in resigning from the bedchamber on 3 November, and, punished along with other 'Pelhamite innocents', he was removed from his lord lieutenancies in December 1762.

Not alone in thinking that circumstances would soon provide the opening for humiliating the king into taking back a strengthened court whig ministry, Rockingham divided steadily but silently with the opposition whigs and began to play an increasingly prominent part in their activities over the following three years. He maintained close relations with Newcastle and Devonshire, as well as Cumberland, the king's uncle, who provided a royal focus for the connection. He had an important role in liaising with Pitt, a difficult but almost indispensable ally, so that, while he had no sympathy with the licentiousness of John Wilkes, he supported the campaign against general warrants. To encourage opposition whig MPs, he helped organize their conduct in the Commons, urging them, for example, to attack the cider tax in March 1763 and countenancing the establishment in February 1764 of an opposition club, Wildman's. He bridged the age gap between the enthusiastic 'young friends' of Newcastle and the elderly grandees, but sometimes despaired of achieving power with an unorganized and ineffectual faction. However, by mid-1765 George III was determined to replace George Grenville as prime minister. At a meeting of opposition leaders at Newcastle's house on 30 June, Rockingham concurred in his friends' decision to accept office and voted in the majority of twelve to six to do so without Pitt.

First ministry, 1765–1766 Rockingham, who, during former negotiations, had been suggested as a possible first lord of the Admiralty, lord chamberlain, or lord lieutenant of Ireland, had held no ministerial office of any rank before he was sworn of the privy council (10 July 1765) and became first lord of the Treasury (13 July). The following month he was reappointed to his lord lieutenancies. That he should have been promoted to the nominal headship of the ministry was a reflection of his enhanced status within the recent opposition, but it was also due partly to the absence of other candidates—Devonshire having died in 1764 and Newcastle, who instead became lord privy seal, too old and, in any case, unacceptable to Pitt. Rockingham's administration was a coalition, in which some of the king's former ministers were retained, such as Robert Henley, first earl of Northington, the lord chancellor, and John Perceval, second earl of Egmont, first lord of the Admiralty. Although they could not all be accommodated, several of his and Newcastle's supporters were given junior offices, and Augustus Henry Fitzroy, duke of Grafton, and Henry Seymour Conway were made secretaries of state. The old tory William Dowdeswell was appointed chancellor of the exchequer, and the young Edmund Burke became Rockingham's private secretary. As the administration had been formed under Cumberland's auspices, his death on 31 October further elevated the role of Rockingham, who quickly assumed the authority of prime minister.

The ministry was dominated by the American Stamp Act crisis, and Rockingham, whose initial concern to enforce the act soon gave way to a spirit of compromise, nevertheless always maintained that the imperial parliament had the power to tax the colonies. Since he was closely connected with a number of leading merchants whose affairs were endangered by the American embargo, his was one of the voices in a divided cabinet in favour of repealing the act on the grounds of commercial necessity. He was anxious to restore the peace of mind of the Americans by acting with moderation and integrity, thus to win the grateful obedience of the colonies by the benevolence of the 'mother country'. Although the ministry was plagued by internal instability, the way was paved for the Stamp Act Repeal Bill by Pitt's declaration in its favour, and, partly to please the hardliners, a Declaratory Act was also introduced to assert Britain's parliamentary supremacy. The passage of the repeal bill was, however, disrupted by the opposition of the Bedfords and Grenvilles, and by several of the 'king's friends', office-holders who were not disciplined by the king for their hostile votes. Such misunderstandings diminished Rockingham's limited credit with George III, so that, for example, when Lord Strange announced that the king would prefer modification of the Stamp Act (10 February 1766), Rockingham had to extract an embarrassing reiteration of his former statement supporting repeal.

Among the essentially backward-looking and self-justificatory measures passed by the government, however, were the liberalization of commercial relations with the West Indian colonies, the repeal of the cider tax, and the condemnation of general warrants. But Rockingham showed his administrative inexperience, and his parliamentary management was poor. In the Lords, where he spoke only once or twice, his performance was abysmal, leading Granville Leveson-Gower, second Earl Gower, jokingly to reprove John Montagu, fourth earl of Sandwich: 'how could you worry the poor dumb creature so!' (Walpole, *Memoirs of … George III*, 2.317). Relations with George III, who treated Rockingham honestly, if not loyally, continued to deteriorate, notably over Rockingham's refusal to accept the admission of Buteites to office, the appointment in May 1766 of Charles Lennox, third duke of Richmond, as Grafton's replacement, and his ineptness in failing to make parliamentary provision for the princes. Having decided to turn to Pitt, the king used a disagreement over the government of Canada as a pretext to remove Rockingham, who was surprised, but greatly relieved, to leave office on 30 July 1766.

Formation of the Rockingham whig party, 1766–1770 Rockingham, who was at first supportive of the new ministry, in which many of his friends remained under the earl of Chatham (as Pitt had become), received several congratulatory addresses on returning to Yorkshire in August 1766. His premiership had given him a strong claim to the leadership, and Newcastle complained to William Henry Cavendish Cavendish-Bentinck, third duke of Portland, on 1 October that Rockingham, 'who takes upon himself to be the head of the party, is full as dry, as uncommunicative to me, out of power, as he was, when he was in it' (Portland MS PwF 7516). The dismissal of Lord Edgcumbe, the treasurer of the household, later that year, an alarm which signalled the resignation of a few close supporters, enhanced his role as leader of a small but distinct group in opposition. He co-operated with John Russell, fourth duke of Bedford, and George Grenville in harrying the ministry during the spring and summer of 1767, advocating a more conciliatory policy towards America and defending the chartered rights of the East India Company. He was doubtful about the merits of factious opportunism, as when the Rockinghams, as they were increasingly known, forced a reduction in the land tax in the Commons on 27 February 1767.

Through his private connections and personal charm, Rockingham began to set a tone of moral resolution, consistency, and self-righteousness for his party's conduct, which precluded opposition for its own sake. Rebuffing an approach from another parliamentary group, he recorded on 8 January 1767:

> I acknowledged that I thought the state of us and our friends viewed through political glasses would appear a forlorn hope and that no immediate success could be expected, but that on the other hand we were not in an uncomfortable situation, because every dictate of honour and principle encouraged us to persevere on the same plan which we had done for years.　(Rockingham MS R1-743; Albemarle, 2.32)

He broke up the promising negotiations with the Bedfords on 20 July 1767 over his wish to retain Conway and suspicions that the hardline views on America of Bedford's ally Grenville might come to prevail. He presumably endorsed Dowdeswell's 'memorandum' (Rockingham MS R1-842), which defended the virtuous exclusiveness of his party, and stressed the need for it to take the directing role in any future administration. Though a court whig in origin, he was by temperament much more of a country whig, and he brought to his party such attributes as distrust of the executive and the desire to protect individual liberties.

Rockingham could count on the loyalty of a number of mainly northern magnates and their electoral followings, and on a group of diverse independents, so that, after the general election of 1768, there were about sixty MPs and thirty peers in the Rockingham whig party. Although his following shrank over the next decade and was largely ineffectual in parliament, it remained a distinct element in both houses and claimed the occasional success, as in the passage of the Nullum Tempus Bill in 1769, a response to Portland's recent electoral struggles. It was in defence of the rights of electors, though with no wish to agitate the wider issues of radical participatory politics with which the affair was enmeshed, that Rockingham added his support to the cause of Wilkes, MP for Middlesex, who had been unseated by the Commons. At a *conciliabulum*, or meeting of party leaders, at Wentworth in September 1769, he reluctantly agreed to sanction a Yorkshire county meeting, which he chose not to attend, provided it was confined to addressing the king for a dissolution. In parliament he went further, personally advocating measures of 'economical reform', such as alteration of the civil list in March 1769. In his own thinking, personal resentment of Bute—who was blamed for his friends' dismissals in 1762—had by now been transformed into a coherent, albeit warped, theory of 'secret influence', an ideology encapsulated by Edmund Burke in his party manifesto *The Thoughts on the Cause of the Present Discontents* (1770). Indeed, Burke played a crucial role in the development of Rockingham's political character, for not only was he a capable 'man of business' who constantly cajoled Rockingham into greater activity, but he expounded a generalized

understanding of the political ills of the state and vindicated virtuous party opposition as the instrument for its rehabilitation. Furthermore, no doubt because he was frustrated by his leader's usual lack of urgency, the insistent and compelling tone of his letters had the effect of drawing forth from Rockingham just the sort of innate sense of aristocratic responsibility which Burke most sought to inculcate in him.

Speaking ability, leadership, and the limitations of opposition, 1770–1774 It was nervousness that made Rockingham such a poor public speaker. Of one debate, he reported to Portland on 3 March 1769:

> I was from beginning to end, in a most violent agitation and was obliged to *speak* notwithstanding, *three* times. I got a good draft of Madeira before I went to the House, and had a comfortable breathing of a vein, by Mr Adair's lancet afterwards.　(Portland MS PwF 9016)

He made his first major recorded speech on 22 January 1770, when, moving for an inquiry into the state of the nation, he demonstrated how the 'principle of prerogative' lay behind each incident and issue which had arisen since George III's accession. From then onwards he not only voted frequently, but also spoke often enough and sufficiently well to explain his party's position in parliament.

Prey to illness, idleness, or country distractions, and being a lazy correspondent, Rockingham was not always an active politician, but he made periodic attempts to organize the party. Pamphlets were issued intermittently, and, though little use was made of newspapers, he encouraged the composition and publication of Lords' protests, most of which he signed. He called pre-sessional meetings, compiled lists of party members in both houses, held proxies for friends in the Lords, sometimes attended debates in the Commons, and usually summoned his supporters and informally co-ordinated their parliamentary tactics. The extent and importance of his authority was revealed by the problems experienced in his absence during the winter of 1770–71, with his sick wife at Bath, and of 1772–3, when he was ill himself. As his deputy, Richmond, wrote to him on 16 February 1771:

> the want of you to keep people together, particularly the House of Commons gentlemen, is too apparent. There are many of them who will upon most occasions vote with us, but want to be spoke to … and the thing that influences them is the personal regard they have for you, which will make them do for your speaking what they will not do for another man's.　(Rockingham MS R1-1363)

In 1769 and 1770 Rockingham worked warily with the more radically inclined Chatham in a 'united opposition' that centred on the Middlesex election, about which he introduced a motion of censure on 2 February 1770. On 18 May he made a significant intervention in the Lords in favour of moderation towards America. He used the Falkland Islands crisis to exploit the lack of ministerial preparations on 22 November, and protested against the exclusion of strangers from both houses for bogus reasons of national security on 10 December. He gained credit in the City by ostentatiously visiting in the Tower on 30 March 1771 the magistrates Crosby and Oliver, who had been imprisoned by the Commons for upholding the freedom of the press. In 1772 and 1773 he lent support to measures for extending toleration to dissenters. He spoke against the Royal Marriages Bill on 20 February and 2 March 1772, and in mid-1773 he again defended the East India Company, in which he was a proprietor, in both cases opposing the surreptitious extension of the influence of the crown. In the autumn of 1773 he led a successful non-partisan but self-interested lobby against the imposition of a tax on Irish absentee landowners.

The American War of Independence, 1774–1778 Rockingham, who blamed the North government for provoking American resistance, nevertheless condemned the Boston Tea Party and other outrages, and in this respect did not differ from the rest of the British establishment in his attitude to the colonies. Moreover, he was hampered by his commitment to his own Declaratory Act, and was accused of having worsened the situation by his capitulation to American pressure in 1766, which was said to have taught the colonies to use violence to attain their ends. Yet, influenced by a number of American correspondents, he still believed that moderation and trade concessions, such as abolition of the tea duty, would restore peace and prosperity, and he persisted in leading the Rockinghamite opposition during a period of exceptional difficulty. He presented an American petition against government legislation to reform the administration of Massachusetts (11 May 1774), advocated conciliation (18 May), and opposed the Quebec Bill (17 June). He gave some support to Chatham's imperial proposals on 20 January 1775. On 7 February he rose at the same time as the colonial secretary, William Legge, second earl of Dartmouth, but failed in his attempt to bring up an American merchants' petition before the main business of addressing the king to enforce British legislative authority was considered. He presented other petitions on the dire commercial implications of antagonizing America on 15 March, and the following day pointed out the arbitrary nature of the proposed measures. He moved an amendment to the address of thanks to re-establish peaceful relations on 26 November 1775, and four days later, with widespread support, defeated a bill to indemnify the employment of foreign troops.

At the time of the general election of 1774 Rockingham had expressed his dismay at the state of politics, and although in late 1775 he could write of the 'conscientious satisfaction' (Rockingham MS R1-1610) of maintaining a principled opposition to the popular war with America, he recognized that his position would be hopeless as long as he was seen as appeasing or aiding the enemy's cause. After the poor party showing in early 1776, he supported the idea of a remonstrance against the whole conduct of the government, but this did not materialize. The planned secession of his parliamentary supporters, during the 1776–7 session, failed to make a great impression because it was too often broken, not least by Rockingham himself, who moved an amendment to the address (31 October 1776) and attacked the use of the civil list to promote secret influence (16 April 1777). Beguiled, as he was most

summers, by the pleasures of life away from politics, he was forced by his despair at the eclipse of the nation's guiding constitutional principles to continue his efforts. He wrote to Portland, on 5 November 1777, that he felt:

> most strongly that there is a duty which I perhaps most particularly owe to the *persons* of those, who not only encouraged and incited me, but also, whose principles deserve a better fate, than to be buried in the ruins of their country. I confess I feel a solicitude even for myself, I could wish to have it to say, and I could wish to have it remembered and recorded, that to the last moment *we* struggled in behalf of this poor infatuated country. (Portland MS PwF 9117)

He was active in the united opposition campaign of early 1778, making interventions on 6 February and 23 and 30 March, and he was present at Chatham's last fatal appearance in the Lords on 7 April. Critical of the management of the war, he was by now reluctantly prepared to concede independence to America, especially given the additional security dangers posed by the outbreak of war against France. He made a major speech in condemnation of the peace commissioners on 7 December 1778, declaring that their threat to desolate the colonies was 'repugnant to the principles of Christianity' (Rockingham MS R81-105).

Domestic, colonial, and constitutional affairs, 1778–1782 Rockingham sponsored Savile's Catholic Relief Bill, reporting from the Lords committee on it on 25 May 1778. He was active in the defence of the whig admiral Augustus Keppel, whose court martial at Portsmouth he attended, and after the latter's acquittal he moved a vote of thanks to him in the Lords on 16 February 1779. On 5 May he had an audience with the king to appraise him of the dangerous situation of Ireland, and in parliament, on 11 May, he moved an address for the relief of distress there and the liberalization of trade. He criticized Sandwich's handling of the navy on 25 June, in a speech in which he justified the course of his own career. Later that year Rockingham, who had been reappointed to the office of vice-admiral of Yorkshire in December 1776, acted decisively to defend Hull from the pirate John Paul Jones. He was thanked by the king, though his conduct was a part of the patriotic reaction of the governing élite at a time of national emergency.

Yet, at the same time, Rockingham continued to hope that the delusions of the people would be shattered, and that the declining ministry would be brought down. He called for the dismissal of ministers on 25 November, condemned the lack of measures to pacify Ireland on 1 December, and advocated alteration of the civil list on 7 December. The reduction of public expenditure and the abolition of places and pensions served both financial and constitutional purposes, which were at the heart of his attitude to the crown. However, he objected to the ideas of parliamentary reform which were promoted by Christopher Wyvill's association movement that winter. Although he attended a Yorkshire county meeting on 30 December 1779, he was relieved that the petition avoided such 'crude propositions' as increased county representation or tests for parliamentary candidates. He declined to attend another meeting in 1780, and the only concession he made was to agree with the reduction of the duration of parliament to three years, that being the period fixed after the revolution of 1688. In a detailed speech on the public accounts on 8 February, he linked developments in America, India, and Ireland with the undue weight of monarchical influence, and he criticized ministers on 21 February and 1 and 6 March 1780.

While support was accruing to the opposition, internal divisions were becoming more marked, so that Rockingham's refusal to countenance parliamentary reform risked alienating Chatham's just as independently minded successor, William Petty, second earl of Shelburne. The two men differed, too, in their reactions to the Gordon riots, after which Rockingham attended the privy council to approve measures to restore law and order (7 June 1780). Later that month Rockingham was approached with a proposal to strengthen the ministry, but he set three unacceptable preconditions: that the king would not veto American independence, but would allow certain items of economical reform, and would appoint leading Rockinghamites to office. Caught by surprise at the dissolution of parliament that year, he managed to preserve his electoral influence, saving face in Yorkshire by countenancing the unopposed return, with Savile, of Henry Duncombe, a member of Wyvill's association. In the Lords he objected to the extension of hostilities against the Dutch states (25 January 1781), made a statistical speech against the burdensome nature of the loan (21 March), opposed the address (27 November), and presented a comprehensive account of the calamitous state of the nation (19 December). Although he led the largest portion of the opposition, when, in March 1782, the defeat of the British forces at Yorktown finally destroyed Lord North's administration, it was Shelburne who took the initiative in negotiating for the appointment of a new ministry.

Second ministry and death, 1782 Rockingham returned to the Treasury on 30 March 1782 without the full trust of George III and in such a poor state of health that he had little authority or strength to settle the quarrels over patronage and policy which beset his second ministry. The offices of the two (reduced from three) secretaryships of state were shared between the two sides of the former opposition. Charles James Fox, who was a leading proponent of American independence, became foreign secretary, but disagreed frequently with Shelburne, whose responsibilities covered home and colonial affairs, and who favoured holding back the offer of independence as a bargaining counter. Not only the peace negotiations, but also the demands for parliamentary reform made by Richmond, who went to the Ordnance as master-general, threatened to split the cabinet, which again had the appearance of an uneasy coalition. The lord chancellor, Lord Thurlow, was retained, and the former Chathamites were represented by Lord Camden, the lord president, and Grafton, the privy seal. Of the other Rockinghamites, Keppel (now a viscount) was made first lord of the Admiralty and Lord John Cavendish was appointed chancellor of the exchequer.

The first government to implement in office the programme which it had formulated in opposition, the second Rockingham administration made some striking short-term changes, which, however, were of little long-term significance. The war was brought to an end, but virtually no progress was made in securing what could be salvaged of Britain's imperial possessions and naval supremacy. Portland, the lord lieutenant of Ireland, oversaw the hurried implementation of legislative independence, but the repeal of the Declaratory Act and the modification of Poynings' law failed to resolve the problem of how Ireland was to be governed. Though considerably watered down, unprecedented economical reforms were none the less made, by the exclusion from the Commons of revenue officers (Crewe's Act) and government contractors (Clerke's Act), and by the controls on state expenditure introduced by Burke, the paymaster of the forces, in his Civil Establishment Act. Yet little was done to gain the confidence of the king, who was already secretly negotiating to replace Rockingham, when Rockingham's death, on 1 July 1782 at his home in Wimbledon, Surrey, brought the ministry to an end. Shelburne became prime minister, and a few days later the Rockingham whigs split, with Fox leading a band of supporters back into opposition.

Rockingham, whose death, although attributed to influenza, was almost certainly due to his lifelong illness, was buried in York Minster on 20 July 1782. He and his wife had no children, and all his titles became extinct. By his will, dated 4 September 1764, and several codicils, for which administration was granted in London on 5 June 1784, he made bequests to members of his family, including the children of his sister Henrietta Alicia and her Irish groom, William Sturgeon. Rockingham's affectionate and drily humorous wife, who acted as a political secretary and was a source of moral support, received £5000 and lived at Hillingdon House, near Uxbridge, Middlesex, until her death, on 19 December 1804. The estates, and about half the personalty of £84,400, were inherited by Rockingham's nephew, his sister Anne's son, William Fitzwilliam, second Earl Fitzwilliam (the fourth Earl Fitzwilliam in the Irish peerage). It was Fitzwilliam who, in 1826, as its patron, had the local Swinton pottery works renamed after his uncle, who is therefore commemorated in the china known as Rockingham ware.

Character and posthumous reputation Rockingham, a tall and dignified man, was almost universally admired for his unimpeachable private virtue, his immense personal charm, and his calm and temperate manner. He was most likeable when at ease at Wentworth, and once admitted to Richmond (in June 1769):

> I often think, that I could set down here, attend and watch on the wants and necessities of those who are near to me, be of use and assistance to many, and finally secure to myself the comfort of thinking, that I have done some good. (Rockingham MS R1-1199)

Yet unfulfilled personal ambition, a quietly stubborn streak, and an all-pervading sense of duty to the public ceaselessly drew him back to the unrewarding field of politics. In a sense he personified a form of suffering nobility, and the notion of an aristocratic trusteeship over the true constitutional virtues of Britain, at a time when an ill-advised king presided over a diseased body politic, suffused the whole of his public conduct.

As a statesman, however, Rockingham was wholly inadequate, and it was his rank and fortune alone, combined with luck, that propelled him to prominence. Horace Walpole, a severe critic, was only doing him justice when he wrote, on the day of his death:

> his parts were by no means great; he was nervous, and mere necessity alone made him at all a speaker in Parliament, where, though he spoke good sense, neither flattery nor partiality could admire or applaud. He was rather trifling and dilatory in business than indolent. Virtues and amiability he must have possessed, for his party esteemed him highly, and his friends loved him with an unalterable attachment. In the excess of faction that we have seen, he was never abused, and no man in public life, I believe, had ever fewer enemies. (Walpole, Corr., 25.288)

Rockingham's ministries achieved little, and, at least in national politics, he was rarely successful in the causes he espoused, while to a certain extent his connection itself, like his electoral interest, barely outlived him. His guiding principle, that there was a powerful system of secret influence, controlled first by Bute and later by others, was essentially false. It provided an explanation of failure and a motivation for continued opposition, but was otherwise barren—although it may have had a significance in the contribution it made to the revolutionary American misunderstanding of monarchical tyranny in Britain.

But, if Rockingham was palpably unfitted for the career of a politician, his close friendships, consistently held principles, and steady political stance were the means of binding together the party which bore his name. As he showed from the early 1760s, his personal charm enabled him to mediate between the conflicting personalities and competing opinions of his colleagues and working partners, and by the 1770s his higher public profile and improved organizational abilities ensured that he led what was effectively the only political party in existence. Throughout the period of his leadership he attempted to advance the same principles: at home, the defence of individual liberties, chartered rights, and private property; and abroad, the promotion of commerce, just colonial relations, and peace in Europe. Above all, he sought to restore the purity of the revolution constitution, not only by implementing a programme of economical reform, but by insisting, in the course of several abortive negotiations for entering office, on the creation of a stable and independent government, in which his most trusted friends would hold the dominant positions. Although he did not live long enough to benefit from it, the very emphasis that he placed on virtue, principle, and consistency itself gave a momentum to the fortunes of the Rockingham whig party, whose coherence was in a sense strengthened by its limited size and exclusive nature. His untimely death, therefore, immediately secured him a place in the pantheon of whig heroes, which was confirmed by Fitzwilliam's erection at Wentworth of a classical mausoleum designed by John Carr. Its grandiloquent inscription, written by Burke, commended him for his establishment of a permanent means of safeguarding the constitution:

> for it was his aim through life to convert party connection and personal friendship (which others had rendered subservient only to temporary views and the purposes of ambition) into a lasting depository of his principles, that their energy should not depend upon his life, nor fluctuate with the intrigues of a court, or with the capricious fashions amongst the people. (Albemarle, 2.486–7)

Rockingham was never an unequivocal 'friend of America'. Neither were his principles the foundation of nineteenth-century liberalism or his party the precursor of a system of alternating two-party politics, as whig historians of the Victorian era imagined. Recent scholarship, assisted by the opening of the Wentworth Woodhouse muniments to public access in the 1950s, has rightly delineated the personal and political failings of Rockingham and his friends. Yet he can nevertheless be credited with the leadership of a unique, albeit small and rudimentary, parliamentary party, which in the mid- to late eighteenth century claimed back the label 'whig', and which therefore earned its place in the broad continuum of whiggery from Walpole to Grey. S. M. FARRELL

Sources Rockingham MSS, Sheff. Arch., Wentworth Woodhouse muniments · Fitzwilliam papers, Sheff. Arch., Wentworth Woodhouse muniments · Burke papers, Sheff. Arch., Wentworth Woodhouse muniments · *Wentworth Woodhouse manuscripts handlist and index*, List and Index Society Special Series, 19 (1984) · G. Thomas, earl of Albemarle [G. T. Keppel], *Memoirs of the marquis of Rockingham and his contemporaries*, 2 vols. (1852) · Northants. RO, Fitzwilliam (Milton) papers · BL, Newcastle MSS, Add. MSS 32723–33083 · U. Nott. L., Portland MSS · *The correspondence of Edmund Burke*, ed. T. W. Copeland and others, 10 vols. (1958–78) · E. Burke, *The thoughts on the cause of the present discontents* (1770) · *The correspondence of King George the Third from 1760 to December 1783*, ed. J. Fortescue, 6 vols. (1927–8) · *The Grenville papers: being the correspondence of Richard Grenville … and … George Grenville*, ed. W. J. Smith, 4 vols. (1852–3) · *Correspondence of John, fourth duke of Bedford*, ed. J. Russell, 3 vols. (1842–6) · *Correspondence of William Pitt, earl of Chatham*, ed. W. S. Taylor and J. H. Pringle, 4 vols. (1838–40) · *Memorials and correspondence of Charles James Fox*, ed. J. Russell, 4 vols. (1853–7) · H. Walpole, *Memoirs of King George II*, ed. J. Brooke, 3 vols. (1985) · H. Walpole, *Memoirs of the reign of King George the Third*, ed. G. F. R. Barker, 4 vols. (1894) · Walpole, *Corr.*, vol. 25 · *The historical and the posthumous memoirs of Sir Nathaniel William Wraxall, 1772–1784*, ed. H. B. Wheatley, 5 vols. (1884) · Cobbett, *Parl. hist.*, vols. 16–23 · J. E. T. Rogers, ed., *Protests of the Lords*, 3 vols. (1875) · G. H. Guttridge, *The early career of Lord Rockingham, 1730–1765*, University of California Publications in History, 44 (1952) · C. Collyer, 'The Rockinghams and Yorkshire politics, 1742–61', *The Thoresby Miscellany*, 12, Thoresby Society, 41 (1954), 352–82 · R. J. S. Hoffman, *The marquis: a study of Lord Rockingham, 1730–1782* (1973) · M. Bloy, 'Rockingham and Yorkshire: the political, economic and social role of Charles Watson-Wentworth, the second marquis of Rockingham', PhD diss., University of Sheffield, 1986 · M. Bloy, 'In spite of medical help: the puzzle of an eighteenth-century prime minister's illness', *Medical History*, 34 (1990), 178–84 · F. O'Gorman, *The rise of party in England: the Rockingham whigs, 1760–1782* (1975) · P. Langford, *The first Rockingham administration, 1765–1766* (1973) · J. Brooke, *The Chatham administration, 1766–1768* (1956) · W. M. Elofson, *The Rockingham connection and the second founding of the whig party, 1768–1773* (1996) · S. M. Farrell, 'Divisions, debates and "dis-ease": the Rockingham whig party and the House of Lords, 1760–1785', PhD diss., U. Cam., 1993 · H. Butterfield, *George III and the historians*, rev. edn (1959) · *GM*, 1st ser., 52

(1782), 358 • *Annual Register* (1782) • *Morning Chronicle* (2 July 1782) • *Leeds Mercury* (9 July 1782) • A. Young, *A six months tour through the north of England*, 4 vols. (1770) • R. B. Wragg, 'The Rockingham mausoleum (1784–1793)', *Yorkshire Archaeological Journal*, 52 (1980), 157–66 • R. J. Hopper, 'The second marquis of Rockingham, coin collector', *Antiquaries Journal*, 62 (1982), 316–46 • A. Cox and A. Cox, *Rockingham pottery and porcelain, 1745–1842* (1983) • GEC, *Peerage*

Archives Sheff. Arch., corresp. and papers • W. Yorks. AS, Leeds, corresp.; corresp. and papers | BL, corresp. with James Adair, Add. MSS 53800–53815 • BL, corresp. with Lord Holdernesse • BL, corresp. with duke of Newcastle, Add. MSS 32723–33083 • BL, letters to Charles Yorke, Add. MS 35430 • Chatsworth House, Derbyshire, letters to fourth duke of Devonshire • Durham RO, letters to John Lee • Northants. RO, Fitzwilliam (Milton) MSS, corresp. with Edmund Burke • Notts. Arch., corresp. mainly with Sir George Savile • NRA, priv. coll., corresp. with Lord Hopetoun • NRA, priv. coll., letters to Lord Shelburne • PRO, letters to first earl of Chatham, PRO 30/8 • PRO NIre., letters to earl of Abercorn • Sheff. Arch., Fitzwilliam MSS • Sheff. Arch., Burke MSS • Sheff. Arch., Wentworth Woodhouse muniments • Suffolk RO, Bury St Edmunds, letters to duke of Grafton • U. Nott. L., corresp. with duke of Portland • W. Yorks. AS, Leeds, Ramsden MSS

Likenesses J. Reynolds, double portrait, oils, 1766–8 (with Edmund Burke), FM Cam. • J. Reynolds, oils, 1766–8, St Osyth's Priory, Essex [*see illus.*] • J. Singleton-Copley, group portrait, oils, 1779–81 (*The collapse of the earl of Chatham in the House of Lords, 7 July 1778*), Tate Collection • J. Reynolds, oils, 1781–3 (studio replicas of single portrait, 1766–8), Mansion House, York, Royal Collection • J. Sayers, caricature, etching, pubd 1782, NPG • J. Nollekens, bust, Palace of Westminster • J. Nollekens, marble bust, Althorp House, Northamptonshire • J. Nollekens, marble bust, Goodwood House, West Sussex • J. Nollekens, statue, Rockingham mausoleum, Rotherham, South Yorkshire • after J. Reynolds, oils (after portrait, 1766–8), NPG; repro. in W. M. Ormrod, ed., *The lord lieutenants and high sheriffs of Yorkshire, 1066–2000* (2000), frontispiece • J. Tassie, paste medallion, Scot. NPG • J. Tassie, sculpture, Ickworth House, Suffolk • Wilson, portrait, Royal Collection

Wealth at death £84,400 personal wealth: Northants. RO, Fitzwilliam (Milton) MSS, misc. vol. 83

Wentworth, D'Arcy (1762–1827), medical practitioner and public servant in Australia, was born on 14 February 1762 near Portadown, co. Armagh, Ireland, the sixth of the eight children of D'Arcy Wentworth, an innkeeper, and his wife, Martha Dixon, also of co. Armagh. The Irish family traced its ancient ancestry to Wentworth Woodhouse in Yorkshire and was related to the wealthy and influential Fitzwilliams. The young Wentworth attended a local school and studied medicine under Dr Alexander Patton of Tanderagee. In 1782, with the assistance of his patron Lord Fitzwilliam, he served as an ensign in the 1st provincial battalion of Ulster volunteers. In 1785 he went to England to continue his medical studies. A handsome, tall man with blue eyes and considerable charm, he was invariably popular with all classes and both sexes. He hoped for employment with the East India Company as an assistant surgeon, but seems to have lived beyond his means and kept very doubtful company. At the Old Bailey sessions beginning on 12 December 1787 he was charged three times with highway robbery. Twice he was found not guilty, and in the third instance acquitted for lack of evidence. He again appeared and was again found not guilty at the sessions beginning on 9 December 1789. He then applied successfully to be discharged so that he could

D'Arcy Wentworth (1762–1827), by unknown artist, *c.*1815–20

take up an appointment as an assistant surgeon in the convict colony at Botany Bay.

Wentworth arrived in the fledgeling penal settlement of New South Wales with the Second Fleet on 28 June 1790. He had gained some notoriety for his alleged exploits on Hounslow Heath, but he managed to avoid attention on the voyage. *En route* he formed a liaison with Catherine Crowley (*b.* 1772), a convict who bore him three sons, including the statesman William Charles *Wentworth. In August D'Arcy Wentworth and Catherine sailed to Norfolk Island, where he became an assistant in the hospital. Ceaseless self-advocacy, industry, reliability, and a capacity to please everybody served him well. His income grew steadily, status followed, and, despite his ambiguous record in England, he found respectability and scope for promotion. Affable and discreet in his public career, he rejoiced in a warm although irregular family life. Catherine died in 1800, but he formed other alliances, chiefly with Maria Ainslie and Anne Lawes, by whom he had seven children. Wentworth was to serve in a medical capacity again in Norfolk Island from 1804 to 1806, and in Sydney and Parramatta. Eventually he was appointed principal surgeon in February 1809, to be confirmed by July 1811. For all these and other appointments—and for the attainment and advancement of his commercial, professional, and social goals—he constantly and successfully sought the support of Lord Fitzwilliam.

Wentworth was appointed justice of the peace and magistrate in May 1810, and in December was put in charge of Governor Macquarie's newly reformed police force. He became the chief magistrate in Sydney, one of the first commissioners for the Parramatta turnpike, and treasurer of the Police Fund (which disbursed most of the locally raised revenue).

In 1816 Wentworth was one of the founders of the Bank of New South Wales. He seems to have combined probity with a skill in amassing a considerable fortune, so that he died one of the wealthiest men in the colony. His record made him unacceptable to John Macarthur and the 'exclusive' faction of non-convict settlers, but he managed to keep out of colonial squabbles, staying on good working terms with governors Phillip, Hunter, King (up to a point), and Brisbane. He was Governor Macquarie's personal physician. Governor Bligh referred to him as a 'highwayman' and had him court-martialled in 1808 for alleged misuse of convict labour—although for the most part Wentworth was attached to the 'emancipist' (ex-convict) party socially as well as politically.

Wentworth was an old-established Sydney trader, and in 1810 was one of the main contractors for the building of the 'Rum Hospital' for Macquarie. The contractors received licence to import spirits in return for building the hospital, in a controversial arrangement that was ultimately not very profitable. Wentworth's administration of public health was not universally admired, and he fell out with Judge Bent over the latter's refusal to pay tolls. When J. T. Bigge arrived in New South Wales to conduct his commission of inquiry he heard a good deal of evidence about Wentworth's manifold pursuits, some of it none too complimentary. Indeed his long public career, supervisory role, and daily routine had involved him for better or worse in almost every aspect of colonial life. In his latter years he naturally became involved in his son's turbulent rise. He supported trial by jury and the election of a colonial legislature on the ground of 'no taxation without representation'.

In increasingly poor health, Wentworth was replaced as principal surgeon in October 1819, as superintendent of police in April 1820, and as treasurer of the Police Fund in June, but returned as superintendent from 1821 to 1825. He died at Homebush, Sydney, on 9 July 1827. The funeral service at Parramatta, where he was buried, was conducted by Samuel Marsden and the procession was said to be a mile long. JOHN EDDY

Sources Mitchell L., NSW, Wentworth MSS, A 751 ff · [F. Watson], ed., *Historical records of Australia*, 1st ser., 2–13 (1914–20); 4th ser., 1 (1922) · Sheff. Arch., Wentworth Woodhouse muniments · D. R. Hainsworth, *The Sydney traders* (1981) · A. C. V. Melbourne, *William Charles Wentworth* (1934) · J. Ritchie, *Punishment and profit: the reports of Commissioner John Bigge* (1970) · J. D. Ritchie, *Lachlan Macquarie* (1986) · K. M. Dermody, 'D'Arcy Wentworth, 1762–1827: a second chance', PhD diss., Australian National University, 1990 · J. D. Ritchie, *The Wentworths: father and son* (1997) · D. E. Fifer, 'Man of two worlds: the early career of William Charles Wentworth', *Royal Australian Historical Society Journal and Proceedings*, 70 (1984), 140–70 · C. A. Liston, 'William Charles Wentworth: the formative years', *Royal Australian Historical Society Journal and Proceedings*, 62 (1976–7), 20–34

Archives Mitchell L., NSW · Sheff. Arch., Wentworth Woodhouse muniments

Likenesses silhouette, c.1815–1820, Mitchell L., NSW [*see illus.*]

Wealth at death very wealthy; over 20,000 acres of land in New South Wales: Dermody, 'D'Arcy Wentworth'; *AusDB*

Wentworth, Henrietta Maria, *suo jure* Baroness Wentworth (1660–1686), royal mistress, the only child of Thomas *Wentworth, fifth Baron Wentworth (*bap.* 1613, *d.* 1665), and Philadelphia Carey (*d.* 1696), daughter of Sir Ferdinando Carey, was born on 11 August 1660. She was

the mistress of James *Scott, duke of Monmouth (1649–1685), accompanied him into exile in 1684, and guaranteed the loan which enabled him to launch his ill-fated rebellion in 1685.

Henrietta Wentworth spent her early years at the family manor of Toddington in Bedfordshire, succeeding to the barony of Wentworth after the death of her father in 1665. By 1674 she was at court, taking part in *Calisto*, a masque by Thomas Crowne. One of the 'men that danced' at the performance was the king's by then celebrated (though illegitimate) son James, duke of Monmouth, and it was probably then that she was introduced to him. Married in 1663 at the age of fourteen to Anne Scott, equally young and heiress to a Scottish title, Monmouth had ignored his young wife and gone on to a career as one of the Restoration's more notorious rakes: besides relationships with various actresses and court women, he had fathered several children by Eleanor Needham, daughter of Sir Richard Needham, by the time he met Henrietta Wentworth.

Nothing seems to have come of any introduction immediately: for the next six years Monmouth was increasingly involved in public activity and there is no reference to a connection with Henrietta Wentworth until 1680. Characteristically (for Monmouth) it came in a scandal: in 1680, and within weeks of each other, two women were obliged to leave London in a hurry for the countryside, and Monmouth's name was associated with both. One was the wife of Ford, Lord Grey, a long-time friend and political associate of the duke, and here the quarrel (if such it was) was quickly patched up. But the other case involved Henrietta Wentworth and was more serious. She was being groomed to marry the young earl of Thanet when Monmouth, then at the height of his influence at court, took a hand. When her mother packed Henrietta off to the countryside 'in such haste that it makes a stir' (*Diary of … Sidney*, 1.263), the duke followed her to the family manor at Toddington and moved in to begin a permanent relationship. A later plan of the house names two adjoining rooms as 'the Duke of Monmouth's Parlor' and 'the Lady's parlor'. When implicated in the Rye House plot in 1683, Monmouth retired to Toddington to spend most of that summer in hiding there, writing bad verse on the virtues of a private life, watching the local hunt, and carving Henrietta's name on an oak tree close to the house—a tree thereafter known locally as the Monmouth oak. Restored briefly to favour again in 1684, but finally disgraced for refusing to testify publicly against his whig friends Algernon Sidney and John Hampden, Monmouth revisited Henrietta at Toddington before going into exile in Holland, where she soon joined him.

Henrietta Wentworth was received by William, prince of Orange, as the duke's recognized mistress, and for nearly a year the two lived together in private domesticity, keeping well apart from the other English and Scots exiles and adventurers who thronged the Low Countries. There can be no doubt that the relationship between the two was deep and genuine: certainly Monmouth was a reformed man once his attachment to Henrietta began.

Thomas Bruce, earl of Ailesbury, once in love with Henrietta himself, recorded the depth of the couple's attachment to each other, and their sincere belief that in the eyes of God they were man and wife. Their domestic happiness was one reason why Monmouth at first refused to take any action on the shattering news of his father's death in February 1685. But when he finally gave way to the arguments of his fellow exiles that his honour would be irretrievably compromised if he did nothing to stop the accession of his detested Catholic uncle James II, arguments reinforced by the independent preparations for a rebellion in Scotland by the earl of Argyll, Henrietta gave him her fullest support. Unable to raise any money from potential supporters in England, Monmouth had to borrow some £6000 from a Dutch merchant—but could not do so until Henrietta had pledged her jewellery, cash, and credit as security: enough to hire a small ship and buy arms for a few hundred men. Only this backing made the rebellion possible, for Monmouth and his fellow exiles were nearly penniless, and the Dutch government kept a very prudent distance from the enterprise.

On the scaffold after the rebellion's defeat Monmouth renewed his pledges of devotion to Henrietta. When the two bishops present badgered him over his conduct with her, he broke in angrily that he had been married to his wife when only a child, that Henrietta had reclaimed him from a licentious life and he had been faithful to her, and that she was a 'religious, godly lady' (Clifton, 228). Almost his last act was to ask an attendant to convey a memento of him to her. After the execution she remained in Holland until at least mid-August 1685, when she spoke with James II's envoy Bevil Skelton on the shore near Scheveling. According to his hostile account, she seemed mainly concerned about the £4000 of goods and plate of which she had been cheated by one of Monmouth's merchant creditors, haughtily asking him for his help in getting it back, and appearing indifferent to her lover's death: if true, it is likely to be as much a matter of the demeanour required by her situation and the face to be presented to the emissary of her lover's enemy as of a genuine reflection of her feelings.

Not long after this she returned to England, but did not long survive her lover, dying on 23 April 1686: some said of a broken heart, but the vindictive, from over-painting her face with mercury. She was buried at Toddington church, where her mother erected a monument to her in the north transept. The barony passed to Henrietta's aunt Anne, Lady Lovelace, and on her death to her granddaughter Martha Lovelace. Lady Henrietta's estate at death was said to be some £4000 p.a.: her aunt fought her mother over the validity of her will.   ROBIN CLIFTON

Sources R. Clifton, *The last popular rebellion: the western rising of 1685* (1984) · *DNB* · *Bishop Burnet's History*, vol. 5 · N. Luttrell, *A brief historical relation of state affairs from September 1678 to April 1714*, 6 vols. (1857) · Ford, Lord Grey, *The secret history of the Rye-House plot: and of Monmouth's rebellion* (1754) · Evelyn, *Diary* · *Memoirs of Thomas, earl of Ailesbury*, ed. W. E. Buckley, 2 vols., Roxburghe Club, 122 (1890) · *Diary of the times of Charles the Second by the Honourable Henry Sidney (afterwards earl of Romney)*, ed. R. W. Blencowe, 2 vols. (1843) · GEC, *Peerage* · *CSP dom.*, 1685–7 · *Seventh report*, HMC, 6 (1879)

Archives Bodl. Oxf., Rawl. MSS A 139, D 316 · PRO, Barillon dispatches, 31/3/158
Likenesses R. Williams, mezzotint (after G. Kneller), BM, NPG
Wealth at death see *CSP dom.*

Wentworth, Jane [Anne; *called* the Maid of Ipswich] (*c*.1503–1572?), visionary, was a daughter of Sir Roger Wentworth of Gosfield, Essex, and came of a prominent East Anglian gentry family. Her remarkable story is recorded in a contemporary narrative by Robert, Lord Curzon, and in Thomas More's *Dialogue Concerning Heresies*, published a dozen years later.

From November 1515, aged about twelve—presumably at the onset of puberty—Wentworth began to exhibit hysterical symptoms interpreted as demonic possession, having fits, uttering blasphemies and obscenities, and (according to More) manifesting clairvoyant gifts. These lasted until Lady day (25 March) 1516, when a vision of Our Lady brought relief. In consequence, she made a pilgrimage to the nearby chapel of Our Lady of Grace at Ipswich. There, three weeks later, amid dramatic convulsions and before a large crowd which included numerous local notables (including Lord Curzon and the abbot of Bury St Edmunds), she was cured, and promised to make a second visit of thanksgiving. When her parents sought to postpone her return visit—the first of several indications in Curzon's account that her immediate family were far from sympathetic to her performances—she collapsed again, saying to her parents, 'see here what ye have doon to me and pute me agayne to theese gret paynes be cawsse of brekynge of my promyse' (BL, Harley MS 651, fol. 195*v*).

The return visit was arranged for the following Thursday and culminated in a midnight summons from the young girl to the local worthies, whom she harangued for a couple of hours. There may have been some scepticism expressed by the clergy and her family, for, announcing that 'ye schalle see what goode ye all doo to me with your argumentes for I schalle be by and by in the same casse I was that daye I was holpen by our blyssyde lady' (BL, Harley MS 651, fol. 196*r*), she manifested her symptoms one last time. When her sister and another female relative promptly burst out shrieking protestations of their utter conviction, she recovered once more and forgave them. Her brother John then begged mercy for his previous incredulity, and had to be restrained by four men as he roared and raged, 'Where is that horson my father? Yfe I myght gete hym I wolde kylle hym' (ibid., fol. 196*v*). The whole party made one last trip to the lady chapel, where the young maid healed and reconciled a number of raving relatives, saving her brother until last. The edification of the good people of Ipswich was completed later that day (Sunday) by the Cambridge theologian Dr John Bailey in his capacity as parish priest of St Matthew's, Ipswich (and thus curator of the shrine), who preached a sermon assuring his flock that such miracles as they had witnessed had not been seen in England since the time of its conversion.

Neither of the early accounts gives the girl's name. The name Margaret sometimes given for her has no early authority. The name Anne is first given in the 'Confutation of unwritten verities' compiled from Cranmer's notes by the unidentifiable 'E. P.' about 1556. The name is given in the concluding chapter (added by E. P. himself), which is characterized by inaccuracies and exaggerations that give no strong reason to credit a name apparently unknown to earlier authorities. Thomas More relates that after her cure the girl took the veil and retired to the 'Minories'. It is usually concluded that he meant the London Franciscan convent popularly known by that name. If so, then she had certainly died by 1538, for no Wentworth is found among the nuns at the closure of the house that year. However, the possibility of a confusion between the order, often known as the Minoresses, and the London house known as the Minories, is raised by a record of one Jane Wentworth living at Framlingham in 1554 as a former nun of Bruisyard (a Franciscan convent in Suffolk), described on that occasion as an honest Catholic woman. She is clearly the Jane Wentworth, gentlewoman, of Framlingham, whose will, made in 1565 (and proved in 1572), evinces conservative religious sensibilities in naming the local magnate Sir Robert Wingfield as executor and chief beneficiary, and in requesting that he dispose of her unbequeathed goods in deeds of charity. It would have been at least as likely for her to have joined the Franciscan nuns of Suffolk as those of London, in which case Jane Wentworth may be her true identity.

The whole episode of the Maid of Ipswich exhibits striking parallels with the case of Elizabeth *Barton, the Holy Maid of Kent, who made a dramatic impact on public life in the late 1520s and early 1530s. It is fascinating to note that Elizabeth Barton's spiritual director, Edward Bocking, a monk of Christ Church, Canterbury, no doubt came from Bocking in Essex (a manor and peculiar jurisdiction of the archbishop of Canterbury), which is just 3 miles down the road from Gosfield (though he must have left for the monastic life before the girl was even born). Both cases fit into a broader pattern of female teenage visionaries generally found in Catholic Europe, but not unknown in Lutheran territories, and even found occasionally in post-Reformation England. Occurring shortly after Wolsey's arrival at the height of his power, the case at Ipswich enhanced the prestige of his native town's shrine. The matter certainly attracted Wolsey's attention, as he made a pilgrimage there the following year. Indeed, Wolsey's Ipswich connections may well have smoothed the way for the acceptance of the young girl's experiences as authentic. For in themselves the events recorded do not inspire confidence as to their spiritual character. Lord Curzon's account, despite its author's touching faith in the girl, gives enough hints of a strained family background and an attention-seeking teenager to arouse suspicion. And although Thomas More adduces the case as proof that miracles still happen, neither the cure nor his unspecific claims of second sight defy natural explanation (and his obviously derivative and sanitized account is less circumstantial than Curzon's). But the girl's experiences were legitimated by the power of the abbot of Bury and the knowledge of a Cambridge don, which perhaps delivered

also the assent of the local lay élite. Subsequently, Wolsey sought to include the parish church of St Matthew and its lucrative shrine in his collegiate foundation at Ipswich. This project was resisted by the parish priest, Dr Bailey, but was brought about after his death in 1525, when Wolsey collated his own son, Thomas Winter, to the benefice.

RICHARD REX

Sources BL, Harley MS 651, fols. 194–6 · St Thomas More, *A dialogue concerning heresies*, ed. T. M. C. Lawler and others, 2 vols. (1981), vol. 6 of *The Yale edition of the complete works of St Thomas More*, pt 1, pp. 93–4 · *Miscellaneous writings and letters of Thomas Cranmer*, ed. J. E. Cox, Parker Society, [18] (1846), esp. 65 · G. Baskerville, 'Married clergy and pensioned religious in Norwich diocese, 1555', *EngHR*, 48 (1933), 43–64, 199–228, esp. 219 · will, Suffolk RO, Ipswich, IC/AA1/22/18 · D. MacCulloch, *Suffolk and the Tudors: politics and religion in an English county, 1500–1600* (1986)
Archives BL, account of visions, Harley MS 651, fols. 194–6

Wentworth, John (1672–1730), merchant and politician in America, was born on 16 January 1672 at Great Island (New Castle), New Hampshire, the third of seven children of Samuel Wentworth (1641–1691), tavern-keeper, and his wife, Mary (1648–1725), daughter of Ralph Benning of Boston and London and his wife, Ann. John held the post of lieutenant-governor of New Hampshire from 1717 to 1730, and was the founder of the Wentworth political dynasty that dominated the colony until the American War of Independence.

Wentworth's father established a tavern in Portsmouth in the early 1680s, so young John grew up in a central institution of Portsmouth's commercial and political life, as New Hampshire between 1679 and 1692 moved from Massachusetts's control to royal colony, to part of the dominion of New England, back to Massachusetts's control (after the revolution of 1688), and, finally, to royal colony status. John's father died suddenly of smallpox on 25 March 1691, leaving him a legacy of £80. John then went to sea, probably under the tutelage of Captain Mark Hunking, whose daughter, Sarah (1674–1741), he married on 12 October 1693.

By the late 1690s Wentworth was commanding ships involved in the lucrative mast trade to Spain and England. With wealth and connections gained from his overseas mercantile career he purchased and refurbished the family tavern in 1709 and became a Portsmouth merchant active in New Hampshire politics; he received appointments to the colony's council in 1712 and acted as judge of the court of common pleas in 1713.

Wentworth attained his dominant political position in part because of New Hampshire's peculiar institutional structure. Between 1699 and 1741 the royal governor of Massachusetts also served as royal governor of tiny New Hampshire, but the crown also provided lieutenant-governors for both colonies, who served as the governor's deputies when he was out of that colony. In 1716–17 Wentworth and kinsman Samuel Penhallow engineered a crisis between New Hampshire's lieutenant-governor George Vaughan and the new governor, Samuel Shute, and, through his London mercantile connections, Wentworth obtained Vaughan's post for himself. After 1718 Governor Shute visited New Hampshire only three times, leaving its politics in the hands of Wentworth, Penhallow, and their Portsmouth merchant allies until 1729. Consequently, Wentworth replaced the older dominant Vaughan and Waldron families with most of his own fourteen children and their new relatives in New Hampshire's political offices. He and his Portsmouth allies also codified and standardized New Hampshire's laws, moved all the courts to Portsmouth, appointed only Portsmouth judges, and stacked the colony's council with Portsmouth merchants. Such actions brought serious complaints from the outlying townsmen about unfair courts and the aristocratic and controlling Wentworth 'clan'. In 1728 the assembly tried to prohibit the council from hearing appeals in cases dealing with lands of the outlying towns, and even asked the council to join it in petitioning the crown to be annexed to Massachusetts.

Meanwhile, Wentworth and his Portsmouth-based party sought to extend New Hampshire's boundaries through giving township grants in territory claimed by Massachusetts, in order to gain control of valuable timberlands and to enlarge the colony to the point where it could have a separate governor. However, these plans were set aside briefly when Jonathan Belcher was appointed governor in 1730. As a kinsman to the Vaughans and Waldrons, Belcher cut off Wentworth's salary and replaced as many of his allies as he could, putting Richard Waldron (III) in charge of New Hampshire. Wentworth fell into a lethargy and died on 12 December 1730 in Portsmouth, where he was buried.

However, his 'clan' fought on against Belcher and Waldron throughout the 1730s, and, using its London connections (especially merchant John Thomlinson), obtained in 1740 an advantageous settlement of the boundary dispute, more than doubling the colony's size, and in 1741 a separate royal governor in the person of John's son Benning *Wentworth (1696–1770), who would hold office until 1767. He would be followed by Wentworth's grandson John *Wentworth from 1767 to 1775. Thus, the Wentworth party and its policies prevailed until the American War of Independence.　　　　　DAVID E. VAN DEVENTER

Sources New Hampshire Historical Society, Concord, New Hampshire, Wentworth MSS · J. Wentworth, *Wentworth genealogy*, 1 (1878) · S. Noyes, C. T. Libby, and W. G. Davis, *Genealogical dictionary of Maine and New Hampshire*, 5 vols. (Portland, ME, 1928–39) · J. Belknap, *The history of New-Hampshire* (1831) · C. E. Clark, *The eastern frontier: the settlement of northern New England, 1610–1763* (1970) · J. R. Daniell, *Colonial New Hampshire: a history* (1981) · D. E. Van Deventer, *The emergence of provincial New Hampshire, 1623–1741* (1976) · C. E. Clark, 'Wentworth, John', *ANB* · N. Bouton and others, eds., *Provincial and state papers: documents and records relating to the province of New Hampshire*, 40 vols. (1867–1943), vols. 2–4, 18–19, 32
Archives New Hampshire Historical Society, Concord, MSS
Wealth at death over £14,000: will, Bouton and others, eds., *Provincial and state papers*, vol. 32, pp. 378–81

Wentworth, Sir John, first baronet (1737–1820), colonial governor, was born on 9 August 1737 in Portsmouth, New Hampshire, America, the son of Mark Hunking Wentworth (1710–1785) and his wife, Elizabeth Rindge. He was born into a prominent New Hampshire political family; both his grandfather John *Wentworth and his uncle

Sir John Wentworth, first baronet (1737–1820), by John Singleton Copley, 1769

Benning *Wentworth had served as royal governors of the colony. The foundation of the family's success had been set by **William Wentworth** (*bap.* 1616, *d.* 1697), landowner in America, who was baptized on 15 March 1616 at Alford, Lincolnshire, the eldest son of William Wentworth of Rigsby and Susannah, *née* Carter, widow of Uther Fleming. Wentworth was a close friend of John Wheelwright (1592?–1679), who was then vicar in the neighbouring parish of Bilsby. Both men were committed puritans who became embroiled in religious controversy. In April 1636 Wentworth and Wheelwright travelled to Boston, Massachusetts. Two years later Wentworth once more joined with Wheelwright after his earlier ejection from Boston, again following religious controversy. Together they founded the settlement of Exeter in New Hampshire, before settling in Wells, Maine, in early 1643. After a spell in Dover, Massachusetts, Wentworth finally returned to New Hampshire, where he remained for the rest of his life and became a ruling elder of the Congregational church. He died at Dover on 16 March 1697.

Wealthy and well connected, William's descendant John Wentworth was in a good position to enjoy a profitable and public career. However, John's adult preferences for a sybaritic lifestyle contrasted vividly with the Wentworth family's puritan roots. During the early 1760s Wentworth spent five years in London. This period was particularly revealing because it demonstrated that, in addition to being able to charm fellow colonials at home, Wentworth was equipped to mix effortlessly in English élite society. Indeed, so adept was he in this latter respect that he gained the support and patronage of the whig political leader and prime minister, Charles Watson-Wentworth, marquess of Rockingham. Wentworth was to flatter Rockingham further when, having married his cousin, Frances Deering Wentworth, on 11 November 1769, he named his only child Charles Mary after the Rockinghams, a childless couple.

On his return to New Hampshire, Wentworth was appointed surveyor-general of the king's woods in North America, a position previously held by his uncle. He took his duties—notably the provision of masts for the Royal Navy—particularly seriously as well as enjoying the freedom of the outdoors. On 11 August 1766 he succeeded his uncle to become royal governor of New Hampshire.

As governor Wentworth had to contend against a charge of corruption brought against him by one of his councillors, the disputatious Peter Livius. He managed to overcome this challenge to the Wentworth hierarchy by 1773, though not before incurring considerable legal costs. His disappointment in not benefiting from his uncle's will in 1770 rendered these costs even more burdensome. Yet in terms of the larger picture these occurrences were mere inconveniences compared with the turbulence then being created by the advancing tide of radicalism in the thirteen colonies which finally affected even quiet New Hampshire. Confident of his abilities, Wentworth fled the colony only in 1775. In order to continue the struggle, he then took steps to organize a volunteer corps of loyalists—an effort which was abandoned only after the defeat at Saratoga in October 1777. His return to England found him hardly unique in being both an exile and, having lost his American possessions, in very much reduced circumstances. Wentworth made do by establishing the legitimacy of a loyalist pension and by a habitual effrontery in the face of creditors; though clearly angling for the post of governor of Nova Scotia, he eventually decided in 1783 to accept a resumption of the lesser role of surveyor-general. As before, he pursued his duties with vigour. On the occasions when he did return to Halifax, he was astute enough to remain aloof from the controversies surrounding the governor, John Parr. However, Wentworth's new position was not to the liking of his wife, Frances, who found solace in openly flaunting a relationship with the much younger Prince William Henry during his sojourns in harbour. Wentworth himself was to have one openly acknowledged natural son in addition to another child who was the result of a liaison with a woman of maroon origin from Jamaica in the 1790s. Despite these infidelities, however, John and Frances retained a genuine affection for each other. Fortuitously, they were in London together in 1791 when news arrived that John Parr had died. The resulting situation was ideally suited to Wentworth's lobbying skills. Thus it was that at a salary of £2300, Wentworth proudly set sail for Halifax in March 1792 and was sworn in as lieutenant-governor on 13 May. His record of achievement in the early years of his long term of office did much to efface the reputation of the colony as 'Nova Scarcity'. Helped immeasurably by the onset of increased economic activity resulting from the French Revolutionary Wars, the public debt had been wiped out by 1797. Unlike Parr, Wentworth established a co-operative relationship with the holder of the first colonial bishopric, Charles Inglis. As in New Hampshire, Wentworth again put himself in the forefront of educational change. In a manner consistent with their social pretences, if not with their finances, the Wentworths also entertained lavishly. Wentworth's importuning for a baronetcy was crowned with success on 16 May 1795. His coat of arms brandished his connection with the Rockinghams, a claim which was as politic as it was spurious.

If these years marked the high point in terms of Wentworth's family's social status, they also saw his career beset with an increasing series of problems, that were mainly, if not entirely, of his own making. Faced with the need to balance the claims of earlier settlers and those who like himself had fled the American War of Independence, Wentworth did little to hide his partiality in gubernatorial appointments. Important posts went to his own kind. To this was added a bias in favour of the Haligonian merchants as opposed to agriculturists and outport interests. Wentworth also suffered in these years from his being a civilian governor during wartime. Nevertheless, he did not help his own cause by letting the expense of raising the Royal Nova Scotia regiment (after 1793) get out of control. Another controversial episode in Wentworth's later term of office was the result of his prolonged attempt (1796–1801) to settle a colony of maroons in Nova Scotia. The maroons were descendants of slaves who had escaped to form a community of *de facto* independence in Jamaica; they had subsequently come to Nova Scotia after armed conflicts in 1795–6. Now they showed themselves unwilling to make many concessions to their supporters, who expected them to adopt a segregated, settled, and Christian existence. Undoubtedly Wentworth was prompted to uphold their cause more because he saw them as a means of solving an acute wartime labour shortage rather than from any degree of enlightened attitude on his part towards 'outsiders'. For example, in this regard he displayed only a tincture of concern for the Mi'kmaqs and the Acadians after the prospect of conflict with France became a real one. The débâcle ended when the decision was made to send the unfortunate maroons to Sierra Leone. The whole affair had been an expensive experiment, soon to be exacerbated by the rising costs incurred in the building of a new government house. So unsatisfactory were matters at the turn of the century that it appeared for a time as if Wentworth's term of office might well be terminated.

Aside from the disastrous financial implications of such a change for Wentworth, it might have been better had he been spared the acrimonious and bitter struggle which ensued with a member of the assembly by the name of William Tongue or Tong (1764–1832). The latter was an early settler who portrayed himself as representing 'country' interests against a corrupt and effete 'court' party. Tongue also donned the mantle of 'tribune of the people'—a claim which Wentworth, given his own view of himself as at one with his subjects, was bound to resent. The personal feud became interwoven with constitutional disputes between the assembly and the council with Wentworth at its head. After what he had experienced in New Hampshire, Wentworth was apt to interpret any form of opposition as being potentially rebellious. Hence the lieutenant-governor became increasingly vindictive towards his tormentor. Ultimately, Wentworth did succeed in driving Tongue out of office and from the colony. But it was a pyrrhic victory. The record keepers in the new Colonial Office (1801) could hardly have failed to notice how much of Wentworth's official correspondence was obsessively related to Tongue. The completion of the elegant government house in 1808 at a cost of £30,000 was not enough to save him. The couple returned in 1810 to England, where Frances died on 14 February 1813. Wentworth, even in his dotage, did not escape the indignity of having to run from his creditors once more. He returned in 1812 to Nova Scotia, where an annuity, the salary as surveyor-general, and a few firm friends provided for him until his death there on 8 April 1820; he was buried at St Paul's, Halifax. The baronetcy ceased upon the death of Charles Mary in 1844. JAMES STURGIS

Sources DNB · B. C. Cuthbertson, *The loyalist governor: a biography of Sir John Wentworth* (Halifax, Nova Scotia, 1983) · J. Fingard, 'Wentworth, John', *DCB*, vol. 5 · N. Mackinnon, *This unfriendly soil: the loyalist experience in Nova Scotia, 1783–1791* (1986) · J. Fingard, *The Anglican design in loyalist Nova Scotia, 1783–1816* (1972) · P. J. Marshall, ed., *The Oxford history of British empire*, 2 (1998) · L. S. Mayo, *John Wentworth, governor of New Hampshire, 1767–1775* (1921) · S. B. Elliott, *The legislative assembly of Nova Scotia, 1758–1983: a biographical directory* (Nova Scotia, 1984) · M. B. Norton, *The British Americans: the loyalist exiles in England, 1774–1789* (Boston, 1972) · W. Brown, *The good Americans: the loyalists in the American revolution* (New York, 1969) · K. Stokes, 'Sir John Wentworth, 1737–1820', PhD diss., U. Lond., 1938

Archives Linn. Soc., account of white vegetable earth · Public Archives of Nova Scotia, Halifax, corresp., letter-books, and papers · U. Edin. L., corresp. relating to Nova Scotia | Northants. RO, Fitzwilliam (Milton) papers · PRO, CO 217/36–7, 63–90; CO 218/12–16, 21–4 · Sheff. Arch., letters to Lord Fitzwilliam; letters to Lord and Lady Rockingham · U. Mich., Clements L., corresp. with Thomas Gage · University of New Brunswick, Harriet Irving Library, Winslow papers · W. Yorks. AS, Leeds, corresp. with Lord and Lady Rockingham

Likenesses J. S. Copley, pastel on paper, 1769, Dartmouth College, Hanover, New Hampshire, Hood Museum of Art [*see illus.*] · attrib. R. Field, oils, c.1808, Government House, Halifax, Nova Scotia · J. S. Copley, oils, NYPL

Wealth at death established claim with government of £8864, which was paid to his son after death: Cutherbertson, *Loyalist governor*, 145–6

Wentworth, Mary Watson- [*née* Mary Bright], **marchioness of Rockingham** (*bap.* **1735,** *d.* **1804**), political wife, was baptized on 27 August 1735 at Ackworth, near Pontefract, Yorkshire, the daughter and heir of Thomas Bright (*d.* 1739), son of John Bright (formerly Liddell) of Badsworth, near Pontefract, and Margaret (*d.* 1775), daughter of William Norton of Sawley, near Ripon. Descended from the Hallamshire family of Bright, she brought a fortune of £60,000 and the estates of Badsworth and Ecclesall, near Sheffield, to her husband, Charles Watson-*Wentworth,

Mary Watson-Wentworth, marchioness of Rockingham (*bap.* 1735, *d.* 1804), by Hugh Douglas Hamilton

second marquess of Rockingham (1730–1782), of Wentworth Woodhouse, near Rotherham, whom she married on 26 February 1752 in Golden Square, St James's, Piccadilly, at the house of her stepfather, Sir John Ramsden, third baronet, of Byram, Yorkshire.

An intelligent, quick-witted, and musical woman, Lady Rockingham had eccentric habits and an engaging sense of humour—which some found too frivolous—and enjoyed a happy married life, despite having no children. She had a penchant for obscure or extended metaphors which encouraged similar literary flourishes from her correspondents, one of whom, Edmund Burke, she once insisted on calling 'Mr Boork' because she said that 'Mr Burke' was 'so *pert* she cannot bear it' (Cavendish-Bentinck MSS PwG 55). She was headstrong in her various enthusiasms, which apparently included in 1760, shortly before he ascended the throne as George III, the prince of Wales. In June 1768, when Horace Walpole asked Lord Strafford 'is it true that Lady Rockingham is turned Methodist?' (*Letters*, 7.205), Lady Mary Coke commented:

> I shou'd not be in the least surprised if Ly Rockingham took a religious turn. Some passion she must have, her first was His Majesty, her second politicks, & I shou'd not think her unwise to sacrifice both those to God. Disappointments in life naturally give a turn to devotion. (*Letters and Journals*, 2.283)

Lady Rockingham remained a devout Anglican, but there was evidently some latitude in her religious beliefs; writing to the earl of Chichester in 1801 she recollected the 'Old Times when we *used to say our Prayers together* in John Street Chapel' (BL, Add. MS 33108, fol. 209).

The Yorkshire country gentleman Sir George Savile stated in August 1774 that 'Lady Rockingham knows that I have long plac'd her near the top of my list of politicians' (Wentworth Woodhouse MS R1-1496), and she was undoubtedly a well informed and astute observer of the political scene. She called herself her husband's 'secretary' (BL, Add. MS 33072, fol. 129), and was so referred to by others, and energetically assisted him in his network of correspondence—which he tended to neglect—copying many, especially the more sensitive, of his letters, and skilfully placating awkward associates such as the duke of Newcastle. While she sometimes acted on Rockingham's instructions, she exercised considerable initiative on her own account, and the opposition whigs often directed their political letters to her, judging her to be an almost equal partner in Rockingham's leadership of their party. She contributed to the parliamentary management of the Rockingham whigs; in June 1767, for example, she helped her sick husband to organize the signing of a formal protest in the House of Lords. She was equally active in extra-parliamentary matters, being particularly involved in canvassing support for Admiral Augustus Keppel, whose defence at his court martial in 1779 was taken up as a party issue by her friends. Retiring by nature, she nevertheless influenced events through her personal intervention. On one remarkable occasion, at Bath in 1765, she used the opportunity of 'coquetteries' over the purchase of two coach horses from the politically indispensable, but virtually reclusive, William Pitt to make an overture to him from Rockingham's friends (*Correspondence of Edmund Burke*, 2.52–3).

Although by her illnesses, notably in the winter of 1770–71, Lady Rockingham sometimes distracted her husband from national life, it was her positive influence upon him that was her most significant contribution to politics. She gave him the benefit of her forthright opinions on all subjects, expressing herself, however, with just the right beguiling tone of bantering exhortation, which he usually required if he were to be persuaded into any course of action. On the death of the duke of Cumberland in late 1765, a few months after Rockingham had become prime minister, she wrote him a detailed letter, advising that he consolidate his position by immediately securing the king's undivided confidence. However, after the fall of his first government the following year, she seems to have encouraged him to view coalitions as a snare and the pursuit of office as a delusion, distrust of the executive being one of the country whig attitudes by which she urged him to abide. Thereafter she not only concurred with the policies adopted by the Rockingham whigs, but she also admired their reliance on principle and consistency—even if this doomed them to party exclusiveness and isolation in opposition. This conviction had a specifically religious foundation: on 13 April 1767 she declared to her husband that 'you will allow that a statue will not do without a pedestal, neither will our best moral actions suffice, except they are raised upon the motive of obeying God's commands' (Wentworth Woodhouse MS R168-17). One of her obituarists, who also praised her Christian beliefs, recorded that 'it was her favourite maxim, that truth, honour, and integrity, were the best system of policy, both for

nations and individuals' (*York Herald*, 19 Jan 1805). Comparing his wife, a constant assistant and faithful guide, to the Roman goddess of wisdom, Rockingham called her '*My Minerva* at my elbow' (Chalus, 227).

Having been widowed in July 1782, shortly after Rockingham had resumed the premiership, Lady Rockingham, who was well provided for under his will, settled at Hillingdon House, near Uxbridge, Middlesex, in 1785. There, ever cherishing her husband's memory, she interested herself in gardening and corresponded with Sir James Edward Smith, the first president of the Linnean Society. Although separated from the centre of affairs, she continued to indulge her taste for politics, remaining true to Rockingham's principles so far as to condemn the adherence of his heir Lord Fitzwilliam to Pitt's ministry in 1794. She died at Hillingdon House on 19 December 1804 and left the bulk of her estate, which included personal wealth sworn under £10,000, to her stepsister Elizabeth, widow of William Weddell. On 9 January 1805 she was buried, with her husband, in York Minster. As Burke had written to her after Rockingham's death, 'Your Names indeed ought to go down together; for it is no mean part you have had in the great services which that great and good man has done to his Country' (*Correspondence of Edmund Burke*, 5.46).   S. M. FARRELL

Sources J. Foster, ed., *Pedigrees of the county families of Yorkshire*, 3 vols. (1874) · *The correspondence of Edmund Burke*, ed. T. W. Copeland and others, 10 vols. (1958–78) · R. J. S. Hoffman, *The marquis: a study of Lord Rockingham, 1730–1782* (1973) · Sheffield City Libraries, Wentworth Woodhouse MSS, Rockingham MSS · U. Nott. L., Portland MSS, Cavendish-Bentinck MSS · *Correspondence of Emily, duchess of Leinster (1731–1814)*, ed. B. Fitzgerald, 3 vols., IMC (1949–57) · *The letters and journals of Lady Mary Coke*, ed. J. A. Home, 4 vols. (1889–96) · *The letters of Horace Walpole, fourth earl of Orford*, ed. P. Toynbee, 16 vols. (1903–5) · *Memoirs and correspondence of the late Sir James Edward Smith, M. D.*, ed. Lady Smith, 2 vols. (1832) · E. Chalus, '"My Minerva at my elbow": the political roles of women in eighteenth-century England', *Hanoverian Britain and empire: essays in memory of Philip Lawson*, ed. S. Taylor, R. Connors, and C. Jones (1998), 210–28 · *York Herald* (19 Jan 1805) · *GM*, 1st ser., 74 (1804), 1248–9 · *GM*, 1st ser., 75 (1805), 180–81 · *IGI*

Archives Sheff. Arch., Rockingham MSS, corresp. · W. Yorks. AS, Leeds, corresp. and papers | Barnard Castle, Bowes Museum, Lee MSS, MSS D/Bo/C 143–59 · BL, corresp. with duke of Newcastle, Add. MSS 32886–33072, *passim* · Linn. Soc., letters to Sir James Smith · Sheff. Arch., Fitzwilliam MSS, corresp. with Edmund Burke · U. Nott. L., corresp. with third duke of Portland

Likenesses H. D. Hamilton, pastel, Muncaster Castle, Cumbria [*see illus.*]

Wealth at death under £10,000—personal wealth: will, 1805, PRO, death duty registers, IR 26/96/116, no. 187; Ramsden MSS at W. Yorks. AS, Leeds

Wentworth, Paul (1534–1594), member of parliament, was the third son of Sir Nicholas Wentworth of Lillingstone Lovell, Oxfordshire, and Jane Josselyn. In 1563 he married Helen Tildesley, *née* Agmondesham, of Heston, Middlesex; they had four sons and four daughters. Together with his elder brother Peter *Wentworth, Paul was frequently at odds with Queen Elizabeth over policy and questions of parliamentary privilege. He sat in three parliaments, consisting of five sessions: for Chipping Wycombe (1559), Buckingham (1563), and Liskeard (1572).

Wentworth was identified in 1564 as being earnest in religion, and his puritan leanings came to the fore in the third session of the 1572 parliament when he moved 'for a publique fast to the end that it might please God to blesse us in our actions better then we had beene heretofore, and for a sermon to be had every morning' (Hartley, 1.526). The house debated the matter and Wentworth's motion passed rather narrowly. However, three days later the speaker reported that the queen strongly objected to their decision, because she had prohibited them from discussing religious matters. Vice-chamberlain Sir Christopher Hatton added that although the queen liked fasting, prayer, and sermons, on no account did the Commons have the right to order a public fast; this rested solely in her royal prerogative. Speaker John Popham was rebuked for allowing the house to be divided on the matter, Wentworth having failed to make a legislative proposal. The Commons apologized, pleading that they had not acted out of malice but lack of proper consideration.

Wentworth was not one to mince words in his speeches. During a long debate on Mary, queen of Scots, in 1572, a diarist recorded Wentworth's contribution as follows: 'Wisheth it may be put to the question of the Howse whither wee should call for an axe or an acte' (Hartley, 1.376). However important might be regarded these later contributions to the history of Elizabeth's parliaments, there is no doubt that Wentworth's key intervention came early in his parliamentary career. In 1566, the second session of the 1563 parliament, the Commons was much preoccupied with the related questions of the queen's marriage and the succession. On Saturday 9 November, just over a week into the session, the queen ordered all discussion to cease on the matter. On the following Monday Wentworth rose to ask three questions: first, 'Whether hyr Hyghnes' commawndment, forbyddyng the lower howse to speake or treate any more of the successyon and of any theyre excuesses in that behalffe, be a breache of the lybertie of the free speache of the Howse or not?' Second, whether her ministers, in pronouncing her commandment to the house in her name 'are of awthorytye suffycyent to bynde the Howse to scylence in that behalffe, or to bynde the Howse to acknoledge the same to be a direct and sufficient commawndment or not?' And, last, whether her commandment 'be no breache of the lybertie of the Howse' or sufficient 'to bynde the Howse to take knoledge theroff, then what offence is it for anye of the Howse to err in declaryng his opynyon to be otherwyse?' (Hartley, 1.154). A later reader of the questions endorsed them as concerning 'the liberty of the Hows in freedom of speech for succession' (ibid.), and this is how most historians since have regarded them, most notably Sir John Neale. However, in the 1980s Sir Geoffrey Elton, among others, challenged the importance placed on the questions. Although they were much debated on the day, Elton suggested that, significantly, Wentworth's questions were left unanswered, and MPs quickly let the matter drop in their haste to turn to the major business of a parliament, legislation. Their

interest may well lie, as one of Wentworth's biographers remarked, 'in the context of the centuries-long debate on freedom of speech in the Commons' (HoP, *Commons, 1558–1603*, 3.596) rather than in their significance for the history of the 1566 parliamentary session. Nevertheless, given the number of draft speeches and notes on the subject, there is little doubt that members were gravely concerned with the matter of the succession and the queen's marriage, the substantive issues which gave rise to Wentworth's questions in the first place.

Unlike his brother, none of Wentworth's parliamentary activities seems to have caused the queen to take action against him. In 1569 Thomas Howard, fourth duke of Norfolk, was lodged at Wentworth's manor of Burnham, Buckinghamshire, before entering the Tower. Wentworth had secured the lease of Burnham through his marriage, his wife being widow to a groom of the chamber, William Tildesley, who was the first lessee of Burnham Abbey after its dissolution. In 1589 the queen, noting Wentworth's dutiful service, especially with regards to Norfolk, granted him an extended renewal of his lease. Wentworth was active in searching for Catholics in Oxford and Buckinghamshire and his will, drawn up in September 1593, bears the full flavour of an English puritan. He died on 13 January 1594, leaving his widow as sole executor. He was buried at Burnham, where the inscription in the church declared that he lived 'most Christian-like' and died 'most comfortably strong in faith, steadfast in hope, fervent in love, a zealous professor of the truth, and an earnest detester of all superstition'. DAVID DEAN

Sources HoP, *Commons, 1558–1603* · T. E. Hartley, ed., *Proceedings in the parliaments of Elizabeth I*, 3 vols. (1981–95) · W. L. Rutton, *Three branches of the family of Wentworth* (1891) · S. D'Ewes, ed., *The journals of all the parliaments during the reign of Queen Elizabeth, both of the House of Lords and House of Commons* (1682) · JHC · VCH Buckinghamshire · *Calendar of the manuscripts of the most hon. the marquis of Salisbury*, 24 vols., HMC, 9 (1883–1976) · J. E. Neale, *Elizabeth I and her parliaments*, 2 vols. (1953–7) · G. R. Elton, *The parliament of England, 1559–1581* (1986) · will, PRO, PROB 11/83, sig. 10 · PRO, SP 41/16

Wentworth, Peter (1524–1597), member of parliament, was the first son born to Sir Nicholas Wentworth (*d.* 1553) of Lillingstone Lovell, Oxfordshire, chief porter of Calais, and his wife, Jane, daughter of John Josselyn of Hyde Hall, Sawbridgeworth, Hertfordshire. His early life remains obscure. Both Peter Wentworth and his brother Paul *Wentworth (1534–1594) became famous for their interventions on the issues of parliamentary privilege, freedom of speech, and the succession to the crown. Trained at Lincoln's Inn, Peter entered parliament rather late in life, being selected for the first time in 1571 to represent Barnstaple. He sat for the Cornish borough of Tregony in 1572, and for the town of Northampton in the parliaments of 1586–7, 1589, and 1593. Wentworth owed his seat at Tregony to the influence of the second earl of Bedford, a well-known supporter of radical protestants. His sister Clare had been a Marian exile, and it is likely that Wentworth shared such views. His first wife, Lettice, was a daughter of Sir Ralph Lane of Horton, Northamptonshire, first cousin of Queen Katherine Parr. His second marriage, to Elizabeth Walsingham (*d.* 1596), made the anti-Catholic secretary Sir Francis Walsingham his brother-in-law. In 1579 the privy council investigated a complaint that a puritan minister was administering the sacraments out of Wentworth's house at Lillingstone Lovell, similarly suggestive of radical protestantism.

However, Wentworth was not a central figure in the key religious agitations of the parliaments in which he sat. He was certainly opposed to overbearing episcopal authority. In 1571 Wentworth was a member of a Commons delegation appointed to explain their omission of non-doctrinal articles (such as the reading of homilies and the consecration of bishops) from a bill confirming the articles of religion. Questioned by Archbishop Parker, Wentworth defended the omission on the grounds that the committee had not had the time to compare the articles with the scriptures. Parker insisted that this was a matter best left to the bishops. Wentworth would have none of it. 'Noe, by the faith I beare to God, wee will pass nothing before we understand what it is, for that were but to make yow popes' (Hartley, *Proceedings*, 1.432). Here Wentworth was defending the Commons' right to legislate on religious matters. Indeed, he noted that experienced MPs had informed him that the most important laws governing the protestant religion in England had been initiated in the lower house. This does not make Wentworth a puritan, but it indicates the strength of his commitment to the protestant cause, which was to form the overwhelming concern of his public life.

Like so many MPs Wentworth was engaged with the agitation over Mary, queen of Scots, and Thomas Howard, fourth duke of Norfolk, in the first session of the parliament of 1572. He frequently urged their execution, and was clearly frustrated by the delay in ordering the duke's execution and by the queen's stalling on the fate of Mary Stuart. Her failure to approve the Commons' bill against Mary deeply distressed Wentworth. In his view, by ignoring their advice the queen had abused her people. This was the argument he advanced on the very first day of the new session in 1576. Wentworth must have taken everyone by surprise by offering a premeditated speech with the resounding introductory proposal: 'Sweet indeed is the name of libertye and the thing it selfe a value beyond all inestimable treasure' (Hartley, *Proceedings*, 1.425). Wentworth argued that without the ability to speak freely, parliament would become simply 'a very schoole of flattery and dissimulacion and soe a fitt place to serve the Devil' (ibid., 426). Two particular things prevented free speech. The first were rumours, such as 'the Queen's Majestie liketh not of such a matter' or that she liked a matter and would be offended by any who opposed it. The second impediment was the bringing of messages into the house 'either of commandinge or inhibiting' (ibid., 426, 427). In a speech punctuated with biblical references, Wentworth argued that MPs had to be able to speak freely properly to fulfil their constitutional role of advising the monarch and making laws. By resisting their legislative endeavours, the queen had put herself and the state in danger. At this point Wentworth was stopped in his tracks. On the order of the house he was taken into custody, examined by a committee, and imprisoned in the Tower. There he remained until the queen ordered his return two days before the end of the session.

As its editor has remarked, the speech's most 'theoretically challenging part of the argument was denied the House' (Hartley, *Elizabeth's Parliaments*, 131). Wentworth did not seem to object to Elizabeth's deciding the parliamentary agenda, but rather her curtailing their ability to speak freely once summoned. His speech was no resounding call for the Commons to play a central constitutional role, but it certainly made the claim that, to fulfil their function, MPs had to be able to speak their mind. Indeed, in his closing section Wentworth directed his anger against those MPs who voted against matters for which they had spoken, and at the apparently common custom of waiting to see which way the more prominent members were voting in order to follow suit. The same preoccupation explains his vicious personal attack on Sir Humphrey Gilbert who had criticized Speaker Bell in 1571 for raising the issue of the queen's granting of monopolies.

In 1586–7 Wentworth asked the speaker to put a number of leading questions to the house. Designed to be answered in the affirmative, the questions would have confirmed MPs' freedom of speech, prevented the reporting of words and actions to the queen, and stopped the speaker from interrupting speeches. However, his questions were never answered. Speaker Puckering simply pocketed them and informed the council, with the result that Wentworth found himself once again temporarily in the Tower.

Wentworth's remaining days as a parliament man focused on the issue that lay at the heart of his concerns over religion and the security of England: the succession. Soon after Mary Stuart's execution in 1587, Wentworth drafted *A Pithie Exhortation to her Majestie for Establishing her Successor to the Crowne*. He hoped to offer it in the parliament of 1589, but, having failed in that ambition, Wentworth lobbied for its presentation to the queen and found himself in temporary confinement once again. He was quite incorrigible, and his meeting with several MPs before the parliament of 1593 to discuss how they might pursue the subject in the Commons turned out to be a fateful decision. Wentworth found himself back in the Tower, and there he remained until his death. He never wavered in his belief that it was better to offer his queen a faithful lover's wounds, as he put it in 1576, than dissemble and flatter and offer her 'a detestable Judas his kisse' (Hartley, *Proceedings*, 1.428). Indeed, Wentworth took the opportunity of his imprisonment in the Tower to write against Doleman's tract on the succession. His response, *A Discourse Containing the Author's Opinion of the True and Lawful Successor to her Majesty*, was published alongside *A Pithie Exhortation* a year after his death.

Wentworth and his second wife, Elizabeth, had five daughters and four sons, including Walter and Thomas *Wentworth (1567/8–1628) who both sat in later parliaments. Elizabeth was given permission to live with her husband in the Tower where she died in July 1596. Wentworth himself died there on 10 November 1597. Shortly before his death he composed a poem entitled 'The causes of my longe imprisonmente' in which he quipped:

Syth I have said, and done my best
meekly wth prayer, god grant me rest.
(BL, Egerton MS 3139B)

Although his parliamentary agitations came to little, they led Wentworth to offer theoretical positions of some novelty and importance.   DAVID DEAN

Sources HoP, Commons, 1558–1603 · T. E. Hartley, ed., Proceedings in the parliaments of Elizabeth I, 1 (1981) · P. Wentworth, A pithie exhortation to her majestie for establishing her successor to the crowne (1558) · T. E. Hartley, Elizabeth's parliaments: queen, Lords and Commons, 1557–1601 (1992) · J. E. Neale, 'Peter Wentworth', EngHR, 39 (1924), 36–54, 175–205 · G. R. Elton, The parliament of England, 1559–1581 (1986) · W. Coffie Rutton, Three branches of the family of Wentworth (1891) · will, PRO, PROB 11/39, sig. 19 · J. E. Neale, Elizabeth I and her parliaments, 2 vols. (New York, 1958) · S. D'Ewes, ed., The journals of all the parliaments during the reign of Queen Elizabeth, both of the House of Lords and House of Commons (1682) · C. H. Garrett, The Marian exiles: a study in the origins of Elizabethan puritanism (1938); repr. (1966) · W. P. Baildon, ed., The records of the Honorable Society of Lincoln's Inn: admissions, 1 (1896), 53 · BL, Egerton MS 3139 B
Archives BL, speech to 1587 parliament, Cotton MSS, Stowe, Lansdowne, Add. MSS · Inner Temple, London, Pety MSS, speech to 1576 parliament

Wentworth, Sir Peter (1592–1675), politician, was the son of Nicholas Wentworth of Lillingstone Lovell, Oxfordshire (later Buckinghamshire), and his wife, Susanna, daughter of Roger Wigston of Wolston, Warwickshire. He was grandson of Peter *Wentworth (1524–1597), the vociferous champion of free speech in the Elizabethan parliaments. He matriculated at Magdalen Hall, Oxford, in 1610 and became a student at Lincoln's Inn in 1613. He was made a knight of the Bath at Charles I's coronation and served as a JP in Oxfordshire. As sheriff in 1634–5 he experienced difficulties with the collection of ship money, which led to his being questioned before the privy council. He is the probable author of A pack of puritans, mayntaining the unlawfulness, or inexpediencie or both of pluralities and nonresidency … as also a defence of the authority of princes and parliaments to intermeddle with matters of religion (1641). He was listed as having refused the king's summons to fight against the Scots in the first bishops' war and was elected to the Long Parliament for Tamworth, Staffordshire, in December 1641. He subscribed £100 and three horses for the defence of the realm in June 1642, and signed the solemn league and covenant in September 1643.

Though evidence is sparse for Wentworth's wartime parliamentary activity, he was among the more radical of MPs. As such the 'presbyterians' accused him of self-interested, arbitrary abuse of committees, ordinances, and county influence. Denzil Holles called him one of the 'small Prophets' and attacked him over his involvement in the disputed manor of Wolston. Wentworth's father had purchased Perrie Mill on the estate in 1605, and George Warner of Wolston purchased the majority of the manor in 1612: Warner's failure to compound as a royalist within the three-month period of grace allowed under the conditions given at the surrender of Lichfield saw Wentworth able to purchase Wolston, valued at £6000, for £2038. Warner complained of obstruction from Wentworth, who was aided by the Somerset MP John Ashe, who later chaired the Commonwealth compounding committee. Wentworth was added to the committee on 9 April 1649, and was a trustee for the maintenance of ministers, by which he benefited from the estate of Richard Chamberlain of Temple House and Astley, Warwickshire, and Buriton, Hampshire.

In September 1647 Wentworth joined Henry Marten as teller against a motion to make a further application to the king for a settlement, indicating membership of the minority group willing to settle the kingdom without the king. He was named to the high court of justice to try Charles I, but pleaded that a series of falls and subsequent ill health kept him at home. Although he may have been avoiding controversy, his subsequent Commonwealth career also displays erratic attendance. He was named to the second, fourth, and fifth councils of state, combining long, unbroken stretches in attendance—when he invariably arrived early—with similar periods of total absence. His friendships were typical of a committed republican. He combined an intimacy with John Milton, to whom he would bequeath £100 (referring to Milton's writing against the French monarchist Salmasius), with fellowship with Henry Marten. Marten and Wentworth were named during Cromwell's speech dismissing the Rump on 20 April 1653 for having disgraced the parliamentary process, resorting to alehouses and stews. Wentworth retorted that Cromwell's language to parliament was 'unbecoming', but his 'prating' was silenced (Memoirs of Edmund Ludlow, 1.352–3).

Wentworth withdrew from London during the protectorate but acted against Cromwell in the localities. His prosecution of a tax collector in Warwickshire, following the dissolution of the first protectorate parliament, brought him before the council. He claimed a constant commitment to the principle that 'no money ought to be levied upon the people without their consent in parliament', but then submitted to Cromwell and withdrew his suit, justifying himself to Ludlow that his age and infirmity had sapped his will to fight (Memoirs of Edmund Ludlow, 1.413–4). With the fall of the protectorate he took his seat in the restored Rump, and again sat on the council of state. When the army dismissed the Rump for the second time, in 1659, he managed to break back into the Commons chamber from the Thames-side. The council of state assigned him Whitehall lodgings in January 1660, and he continued to sit when the Long Parliament was briefly reconstituted in February 1660. Having withdrawn from politics at the Restoration he died, unmarried, on 1 December 1675, and was buried in the church at Lillingstone Lovell. His Warwickshire property descended through his grandnephew, Fisher Dilke, on condition that he take the name of Wentworth.   SARAH BARBER

Sources DNB · D. Holles, 'Memoirs of Denzil, Lord Holles', Select tracts relating to the civil wars in England, ed. F. Maseres, 1 (1815) · E. S.

Cope, 'Wentworth, Sir Peter', Greaves & Zaller, *BDBR* • *VCH Warwickshire*, vol. 6 • M. A. E. Green, ed., *Calendar of the proceedings of the committee for compounding … 1643–1660*, 1, PRO (1889) • *CSP dom., 1650* • D. Underdown, *Pride's Purge: politics in the puritan revolution* (1971) • Keeler, *Long Parliament* • S. Barber, *Regicide and republicanism* (1998), 23 • *The memoirs of Edmund Ludlow*, ed. C. H. Firth, 2 vols. (1894)

Wentworth, Thomas, first Baron Wentworth (1501–1551), nobleman, was born at Nettlestead in Suffolk, the eldest son of Sir Richard Wentworth, *de jure* fifth Baron Despenser (*d.* 1528), and his wife, Anne, daughter of Sir James *Tyrell of Gipping, Suffolk, the alleged murderer of the princes in the Tower who was executed in 1502. Originally from Yorkshire, Thomas's family had settled in Suffolk in the mid-fifteenth century. Through his father he was a cousin of Queen Jane Seymour and her brother Edward, later duke of Somerset. About 1520 he married Margaret, elder daughter of Sir Adrian Fortescue and his first wife, Anne Stonor (*d.* 1518), with whom he had a large family, which numbered at least eight sons and nine daughters. The eldest son was Thomas *Wentworth, second Baron Wentworth and *de jure* seventh Baron Le Despenser.

The young Thomas Wentworth participated in the invasion of France in 1523, during which he was knighted by the duke of Suffolk (notwithstanding his associations with the Brandons, he should not be confused with Suffolk's vice-chamberlain, Thomas Wentworth of West Bretton). Wentworth's elevation to the nobility, in 1529, was probably unexpected. For the parliament of 1529 he was elected a knight of the shire for Suffolk, but on 2 December 1529 he joined three other MPs among a group of seven new barons created by Henry VIII, probably in part to bolster lay membership of the Lords in advance of attacks upon the church.

As a peer Wentworth participated in the trials of Queen Anne and Lord Rochford in May 1536, and in those of Baron Montague and the marquess of Exeter in 1538. In 1539 he was absent from the session at which his own father-in-law, Sir Adrian Fortescue, was attainted for treason, but the act of attainder none the less included a clause safeguarding the interests of Wentworth and his wife. Wentworth's family woes continued in 1540, with the death of his wife's sister Frances, Lady Fitzgerald (whose husband had been executed in 1537). As Lady Fitzgerald died while in Wentworth's custody and his wife stood to inherit her estate, he begged Thomas Cromwell to conduct an investigation to dispel rumours of murder.

Outside parliament, Lord Wentworth served the crown faithfully at home and abroad. At court he assisted at the baptism of Prince Edward (whose kinsman he was) on 15 October 1537. As well as a Suffolk JP (from 1531), he was regularly nominated to special commissions in the county, where he was the leading resident nobleman, and where he sometimes showed a domineering temperament in disputes with relations and neighbours. In 1545 he was an oyer and terminer commissioner (eastern circuit), as well as a commissioner to levy the benevolence in

Thomas Wentworth, first Baron Wentworth (1501–1551), attrib. John Bettes the elder, 1549

Suffolk. In the summer of 1543 Wentworth supplied fifty men for service in Flanders, and the following year he served under the duke of Norfolk at the unsuccessful English siege of Montreuil. He also headed the county musters commissioners.

During the 1530s Wentworth actively advanced the cause of religious reform around Ipswich. He energetically investigated Suffolk clergy accused of preaching the papal supremacy, and assisted Archbishop Cranmer in pursuing Hugh Payne, a conservative preacher once curate at Hadleigh. In April 1538 he arranged the removal to London of an image of the Virgin at Ipswich, and that same month claimed possession (as a descendant of the founder) of the Ipswich Greyfriars, denouncing its residents as 'an idell neste of dranes' (Miller, 241). Wentworth was also a zealous promoter of local evangelicals. He intervened with Cromwell on behalf of an Essex man accused of heresy, and in 1538 he appointed the reformer Thomas Becon (who had ties to Nettlestead) to an Ipswich chantry. Most notably, the evangelical writer John Bale, previously prior of the Ipswich Carmelites, credited Wentworth personally with converting him to the reformers' cause. For Wentworth, as a leading figure in Suffolk, the conservative reaction that followed the fall of Cromwell presented difficult dilemmas, as in 1545 when he presided over the Ipswich trial of two men accused of denying transubstantiation. One of the prisoners, John Kirby, publicly accused Wentworth of acting against his conscience in condemning him; the clearly uncomfortable judge could only blush and stammer a lame reply. According to Foxe, during the subsequent executions in Ipswich market place, Wentworth 'did shroud himself behind one of the posts of the gallery, and wept' (Townsend, 5.532). Despite such damaging incidents, Wentworth retained his reputation as being sympathetic to reformers. With the accession of Edward VI the religious climate changed once more, and evangelical works appeared from the presses with Wentworth's support: Richard Argentine dedicated his translation of one of Luther's sermons (printed at Ipswich in 1549) to his former patron, while in the preface to his 1550 edition of the German Lutheran Johann Brenz, Richard Sherry praised Wentworth as a favourer of the scriptures.

Under his cousin Lord Protector Somerset, Wentworth (who had had a grant under Henry VIII's 'unwritten will') was admitted to the privy council, apparently as early as August 1547. As a councillor resident in East Anglia, he played a leading part in pacifying the Suffolk rebels in July 1549, and immediately afterwards in Northampton's disastrous attack on Norwich. Following these troubles, Wentworth profited from Warwick's council coup against the protector. In October 1549 he was named one of six noblemen to attend upon the king in his privy chamber, and on 2 February 1550 he replaced the Catholic Lord Arundel as lord chamberlain of the household. In the previous month he had showed his support for Warwick, who shared his evangelical views, by taking part in the interrogation of Sir Thomas Arundell, a Catholic supporter of Somerset.

In addition to his principal seat at Nettlestead, Wentworth inherited five manors in Suffolk and five in Yorkshire, to which were added lands in Lincolnshire and elsewhere. In 1538 he acquired the Ipswich Greyfriars (although his legal title remained contested), and three years later he and his wife secured some Stonor properties. With the plunder of the bishops' estates by Warwick's regime, in 1550 Wentworth obtained Cheyneygates (the former residence of the abbot of Westminster), together with the Middlesex manors of Hackney and Stepney.

Lord Wentworth last attended the privy council on 14 February 1551, and died on 3 March following. His funeral at Westminster Abbey four days later was a lavish state occasion, and included a sermon preached by the royal chaplain Miles Coverdale, as befitted a prominent protestant nobleman. He was buried in the chapel of St John, but has no memorial. His wife briefly survived him. Wentworth's will, drawn up in 1544, was proved on 27 November 1551 by his son Thomas, who succeeded to the title.

P. R. N. Carter

Sources *LP Henry VIII*, vols. 3–21 · HoP, *Commons, 1509–58*, 3.583–5 · D. MacCulloch, *Suffolk and the Tudors: politics and religion in an English county, 1500–1600* (1986) · H. Miller, *Henry VIII and the English nobility* (1986) · will, PRO, PROB 11/34, sig. 35 · *CPR, 1547–53* · J. N. King, *English Reformation literature: the Tudor origins of the protestant tradition* (1982) · *The acts and monuments of John Foxe*, new edn, ed. G. Townsend, 8 vols. (1843–9); facs. edn (1965), vol. 5, p. 5 · D. E. Hoak, *The king's council in the reign of Edward VI* (1976) · S. J. Gunn, *Charles Brandon, duke of Suffolk, c.1484–1545* (1988) · M. A. R. Graves, *The House of Lords in the parliaments of Edward VI and Mary I* (1981) · *The diary of Henry Machyn, citizen and merchant-taylor of London, from AD 1550 to AD 1563*, ed. J. G. Nichols, CS, 42 (1848) · PRO, exchequer, king's remembrancer, accounts various, E101/76/35 · GEC, *Peerage*, new edn, 12/2.497–9

Likenesses attrib. H. Holbein junior, chalk drawing, before 1543, Royal Collection · attrib. J. Bettes the elder, oils, 1549, NPG [*see illus.*] · Bettes, copy, priv. coll.; repro. in R. Strong, *Tudor and Jacobean portraits*, 1 (1969), 325

Wentworth, Thomas, second Baron Wentworth and *de jure* seventh Baron Le Despenser (1525–1584), soldier and administrator, was the eldest of at least eight sons and the heir of Thomas *Wentworth, first Baron Wentworth (1501–1551), nobleman, and his wife, Margaret (d. 1551), elder daughter and coheir of Sir Adrian *Fortescue and his first wife, Anne. The younger Thomas Wentworth had nine sisters. He was educated at St John's College, Cambridge, but took no degree.

Wentworth was not brought up at court and did not hold a household appointment, despite his father's regular attendance on Henry VIII. He may have served under his father in the campaigns of 1543 and 1544, when Lord Wentworth fought in France. He married his paternal cousin Mary (d. 1554), daughter of Sir John Wentworth of Gosfield, Essex, and his first wife, Anne, at Gosfield on 9 February 1546. This match was designed to consolidate family property and influence. Within a year he had joined the retinue of his second cousin, Edward Seymour, duke of Somerset and lord protector to Edward VI, and followed the army on its invasion of Scotland in 1547, where he distinguished himself at the battle of Pinkie on 10 September. For this service he was rewarded with the rank of banneret by Somerset at Roxburgh on 28 September, having two days previously been elected MP for his native Suffolk. His return to parliament reflected his father's dominant position in the county after the fall of Thomas Howard, third duke of Norfolk.

On 3 March 1551 Wentworth succeeded his father as second Baron Wentworth. He inherited extensive estates in Suffolk, Yorkshire, Oxfordshire, and Lincolnshire worth at least £560 per annum in 1546–7 and increased yet further during 1547–51. Wentworth, like his father, quickly became an adherent of John Dudley, earl of Warwick. He attended on Mary of Guise, dowager queen of Scotland, when she stayed at court in October 1551. He was among the peers who tried and condemned Somerset for felony on 1 December. He benefited from Warwick's patronage as a result, receiving a favourable tax assessment and a licence to retain eighty gentlemen or yeomen in his livery in March 1552. He was appointed lord lieutenant of Suffolk on 16 May, with practical oversight of military organization in the eastern part of the county, while also exercising strong influence over many aspects of civil affairs. He was reappointed on 24 May 1553.

Wentworth witnessed Edward's settlement of the succession on Lady Jane Grey, but did not sign the document formally bastardizing Mary and Elizabeth or the engagement to oversee it because he was not a privy councillor. Geography as much as anything determined his course of action in July 1553. On the 11th he and his cousin Sir

Thomas Wentworth, second Baron Wentworth and *de jure* seventh Baron Le Despenser (1525–1584), by unknown artist, 1568

Thomas Cornwallis, sheriff of Norfolk and Suffolk, proclaimed Jane queen at Ipswich, Suffolk. Only a day or two later Cornwallis defected to Mary and winning over Wentworth became a prime aim of her East Anglian supporters. The legitimacy of her cause appears to have been decisive and on the 14th Wentworth agreed to support her, a decision he made public by joining her at Framlingham, Suffolk, with a sizeable body of men on the 16th. He was rewarded with immediate appointment to her privy council and as lord marshal of her army. After the failure of the coup by the duke of Northumberland (Warwick), Wentworth was among the privy councillors investigating the gentlemen pensioners who had supported it. However, generally his appointment as a privy councillor was honorary and reflected the queen's gratitude towards him for his loyalty.

The next stage of Wentworth's career was determined by the decision in September 1553 to appoint as lord admiral the then lord deputy of Calais, Lord William Howard. On 13 September Wentworth was nominated his successor and he took up his post in December. His wife probably died at Calais in 1554. They appear to have had no surviving children. He married his late wife's cousin Anne or Agnes (*d.* 1574), daughter of Henry Wentworth of Mountnessing, Essex, and his wife, Agnes, by 1556. They had two

sons, Lord William Wentworth (1555/6–1582) and Lord Henry Wentworth (1558–1593), and a daughter.

As early as March 1555 doubts were expressed about Wentworth's relative youth and inexperience as well as his previous protestant leanings, and the choice does seem an odd one. Simon Renard, the imperial ambassador, regarded him as 'rather lightweight' (*CSP Spain, 1554–8*, 144). Political reliability appears to have been the primary reason, for the loyalty of the officers of the garrison was suspect, especially the highly respected William Grey, thirteenth Baron Grey of Wilton, captain of Guînes, the only modernized fortification of the Calais pale. A definite tension can be detected between Wentworth and Grey of Wilton during the following years. It was Wentworth's misfortune to hold the command of Calais when François de Lorraine-Guise, second duc de Guise, invested it in the closing days of 1557. His surrender of the town to Guise at six o'clock in the morning of 7 January 1558 after a siege lasting only seven days sealed his historical reputation. The causes of the fall of Calais were many and various. Mary I's privy council bore a considerable responsibility, especially for its failure to act on Wentworth's requests in December 1557 for naval interception of French convoys of artillery and supplies up the English Channel. However, Wentworth himself was guilty of at least three major misjudgements. He believed that the French intended to attack the imperial town of Hesdin and not Calais—a mistake that neither Grey of Wilton nor Philip II's administration in Brussels made. Second, when the French approached he refused to flood the plains round the town (the key to the defence system) on the grounds that he needed fresh water to brew beer for the garrison, and therefore expected a protracted siege. Third, only on 2 January 1558 did he request reinforcements from Philip, a delay that the latter's ministers later claimed absolved them from any responsibility for the disaster. Not irrelevant was a persistent rumour that Wentworth was personally opposed to allowing Habsburg troops into Calais if he could avoid it because of fear that they would seize the town on behalf of their master. George Ferrers in 1569, Thomas Churchyard in 1579, and others published vivid and full accounts that made the English public aware of the details of the siege and portrayed mid-sixteenth century warfare in all its viciousness.

Wentworth's wife escaped from Calais in December 1557 but was sent to the Fleet prison on charges of a religious nature on 19 August 1558. She was released at the end of the month and sent to her mother's home in Essex. A prisoner of war in France after 7 January 1558, Wentworth was indicted on 2 July of conspiracy to deliver Calais to the French, adhering to Henri II, and failing to call the array for musters or to raise the levies. On 15 July papers were issued sequestering Wentworth's estates and taking an inventory of his goods. He was eager to remain in France.

The accession of Elizabeth I in November altered Wentworth's position and the new government finally accepted his ransom. He returned to England in March

1559. He was arrested on 21 April on a warrant issued the previous day and William Parr, marquess of Northampton, organized his trial in his capacity as lord high steward. The trial took place on the 22nd. Lack of evidence and the unwillingness of the court to reopen questions relating to the Marian regime meant that Wentworth was acquitted: he 'quytt hym-seylff, thanke be God, and clen delevered, and whent in-to Wytyngtun colege, and there he lys' (*The Diary of Henry Machyn, Citizen and Merchant-Tailor of London, from 1550–1563*, ed. J. G. Nichols, *Camden Miscellany*, CS, 1st ser., 42, 1848, 195).

Wentworth did not hold nationally important military office again but remained significant in local affairs, while retaining strong ties with the court. Elizabeth did not retain him as a privy councillor but he, and his family, were still regarded as loyal. Two brothers, James and John Wentworth, were drowned when the queen's ship *Greyhound* was lost carrying reinforcements to Le Havre in April 1563. Wentworth was part of the entourage that received Eric XIV, king of Sweden, on 8 September 1560. Like his wife, he was regarded as protestant and an English version of Heinrich Bullinger's 'Sermons' translated by John Day was dedicated to him in 1561. He was appointed lord lieutenant of Suffolk in 1560–61 and of Norfolk and Suffolk in 1569. This was possibly intended to counter the growing influence of Thomas Howard, fourth duke of Norfolk, whose pre-eminence in East Anglia eclipsed Wentworth's own. Wentworth organized the defence of Suffolk during the crisis years 1569–70. Having first been named JP for Suffolk in 1554, he was promoted of the quorum in 1558–9. He was appointed JP for Middlesex in 1561 and of the quorum in 1577. He used his influence to settle local disputes, maintained order, watching out for the activities of suspected Anabaptists, and regularly attended the Ipswich quarter sessions. Wentworth also busied himself in the early 1560s with the problem of insufficient numbers of ministers to fill vacant Suffolk parishes. He was trier of petitions in the House of Lords on a number of occasions and was a diligent legislator. He frequently served as a muster commissioner for London and sat on a variety of other commissions dealing with his locality. He still benefited from royal patronage, receiving a patent for concealed lands in 1570. Wentworth sat on Norfolk's trial in January 1572 and oversaw elections in Suffolk during the aftermath of the duke's fall. Rather surprisingly, his influence diminished after this. This was perhaps because he spent less time at the family seat of Nettlestead, Suffolk, and more time in Middlesex.

Lady Wentworth died on 2 September 1574 and was buried in Stepney church, Middlesex, the next day. Wentworth's eldest son also predeceased him. Wentworth died intestate at Stepney on 13 January 1584, was probably buried with his wife, and was succeeded by his second son, Lord Henry Wentworth, who received administration of his father's goods on the 18th. Wentworth may have married a third time: the navigator William Borough married a Lady Wentworth in Stepney on 9 September 1589.

BARRY DENTON

Sources *APC, 1552–82* · papiers d'état de l'audience, National State Archives, Brussels, 115–16 · Archivo general de Simancas, Estado 810–811 · HoP, *Commons, 1509–58* · *CPR, 1550–54; 1558–72* · *CSP for., 1553–8* · GEC, *Peerage* · C. S. L. Davies, 'England and the French war, 1557–9', *The mid-Tudor polity, c.1540–1560*, ed. J. Loach and R. Tittler (1980), 159–85 · *CSP Spain, 1554–8* · D. MacCulloch, 'The *Vita Mariae Angliae Reginae* of Robert Wingfield of Brantham', *Camden miscellany, XXVIII*, CS, 4th ser., 29 (1984), 181–301 · D. MacCulloch, *Suffolk and the Tudors: politics and religion in an English county, 1500–1600* (1986) · P. T. J. Morgan, 'The government of Calais, 1485–1558', DPhil diss., U. Oxf., 1966 · DNB · A. F. Pollard, ed., *Tudor tracts, 1532–1588* (1903), 289–330 · D. L. Potter, 'The duc de Guise and the fall of Calais, 1557–1558', *EngHR*, 98 (1983), 481–512 · court of king's bench, crown side, baga de secretis, PRO, KB 8/38 · administration, PRO, PROB 6/3, fol. 91v · W. L. Rutton, *Three branches of the family of Wentworth* (1891) · Venn, *Alum. Cant.*
Archives PRO, SP 69 · Suffolk RO, Ipswich, letters to the Bailiffs of Ipswich
Likenesses portrait, 1568, NPG [*see illus.*]

Wentworth, Thomas (1567/8–1628), lawyer and politician, was the third son of the Elizabethan parliamentarian, Peter *Wentworth (1524–1597) of Lillingstone Lovell, Oxfordshire, and his second wife, Elizabeth Walsingham (*d.* 1596), sister of Sir Francis Walsingham, secretary of state. He married into a puritan family. His wife, Dorothy, mother of their eight children, was the daughter and coheir of Thomas Keble of Newbottle, Northamptonshire.

Wentworth matriculated at University College, Oxford, on 30 October 1584 and a year later entered Lincoln's Inn, where he was appointed Lent reader in 1612 and treasurer in 1621. His legal training is apparent in his parliamentary arguments from statute and precedent: he was called 'an honest lawyer' (*CSP dom.*, 1623–5, 197). His connection with Oxford was never broken and he represented the city in every early Stuart parliament before 1640. In September 1607 he was elected recorder of Oxford but his term of office was not without difficulty. Said to have behaved 'turbulently', he was described as 'a fomenter and author of divers troubles between the University and the city' in their dispute over the night watch (Wood, *Ath. Oxon.*, 3rd edn, 2.414). The scholars called him 'Mr. Wantworth' (*Letters of John Chamberlain*, 1.360). He was 'discommoned' by the university in 1611 but reinstated two years later.

Parliament, puritanism, and the law were central themes throughout Wentworth's life. In these he followed in his father's footsteps, although Sir Henry Wotton when writing to Sir Edmund Bacon in 1614 said that Thomas had 'rather inherited his [father's] fortune than his understanding' (Smith, 2.37). In King James's first parliament Wentworth was on the committee to formulate the apology that presented the Commons' claim of privileges to the crown. Although it was never delivered, the apology stood throughout the early Stuart period as a confirmation of the rights of the lower house. He was often outspoken against crown policy: he opposed the proposed act of union with Scotland on ideological and practical grounds, saying that 'all changes in state are dangerous', and that the house was already full enough with as many members as 'one Speaker can moderate' (*Diary of Robert Bowyer*, 278); in 1610 he sat on the committee to prepare arguments against impositions; and he spoke ardently for a rule of law, saying in November that year that 'If the King have a power over the laws, we cannot have security, therefore we must see if the law can bind the King' (E. R. Foster, 2.393–4). James would have punished Wentworth for his speeches, and went so far as to study Queen Elizabeth's arguments against Wentworth's father, searching for a precedent for imprisonment, but was dissuaded by members of the privy council.

In 1614 Wentworth again argued against impositions but this time was unable to escape the wrath of the crown. For a speech on 21 May regarding the assassination of Henri IV of France he was imprisoned in the Tower, the crown's justification being that he had offended the French ambassador. Throughout his parliamentary career he supported legislation professing the need to rid the kingdom of recusants and Jesuits. Noting in 1614 that 'The root of the powder treason [is] not dead' (Jansson, *Proceedings, 1614*, 60), he said in 1621 that 'these walls (methinks) do yet shake at it' (Notestein and others, 2.489).

In 1621 Wentworth spoke at length on religious grounds against a Spanish marriage, arguing that Catholicism would have its effect for 'wives take up a great part and room in the husband's heart' (Notestein and others, 2.491). A protestant queen would ensure a protestant succession, a subject familiar from his father's experience. Later, in 1626, he admitted that his father had been imprisoned in 1593 'about the matter of succession because he and others had [had] secret conference to move it in parliament' (Bidwell and Jansson, *Proceedings, 1626*, 3.245–6). In 1624 he was adamant against the Spanish marriage treaties on the same grounds regarding succession. In the following year he participated in the debate regarding Arminianism and Richard Mountague, canon of Windsor, reminding the Commons that King Alfred had read the Bible fourteen times over. Wentworth held numerous committee appointments and spoke often in 1626 addressing issues of church and state. In considering the evidence against George Villiers, duke of Buckingham, he drew on his legal expertise for offering an explanation of 'common fame' and 'rumor' (ibid., 3.16, 46). Although he was returned for the parliament that convened in March 1628 it is unclear whether he went to London; there is no indication of his presence in the opening session. During his difficulties as recorder in Oxford he had moved to Henley, where he died in March or April 1628 and where he was buried. Martin Lister was one of his executors and may have been a relative by marriage. The authorship of multiple editions of *The Office and Duty of Executors* is assigned to Wentworth, whose name appears on the title-page of the third printing in 1641. Although it was believed earlier that the work was written by Sir John Doddridge there seems to be no proof to that effect.

MAIJA JANSSON

Sources Wood, *Ath. Oxon.*, new edn, 2.414–15, 429, 625 · *The life and letters of Sir Henry Wotton*, ed. L. P. Smith, 2 (1907), 37 · W. Notestein, *The House of Commons, 1604–1610* (1971) · E. R. Foster, ed., *Proceedings in parliament, 1610*, 2 (1966), 82–3, 108, 273 · W. Notestein, F. H. Relf, and H. Simpson, eds., *Commons debates, 1621*, 2 (1935), 489, 491 · M. Jansson, ed., *Proceedings in parliament, 1614 (House of Commons)* (1988), 60 · W. B. Bidwell and M. Jansson, eds., *Proceedings in parliament, 1626, 3: House of Commons* (1992), 245–6 · M. Jansson and W. B. Bidwell, eds., *Proceedings in parliament, 1625* (1987), 379 · *The parliamentary diary of Robert Bowyer, 1606–1607*, ed. D. H. Willson (1931), 278 · Wing, *STC* · R. E. Ruigh, *The parliament of 1624: politics and foreign policy* (1971), 226 · *CSP dom., 1603–10*, 649; *1623–5*, 197 · *APC* · Foster, *Alum. Oxon.* · W. P. Baildon and R. Roxburgh, eds., *The records of the Honorable Society of Lincoln's Inn: the black books*, 5 vols. (1897–1968) · PRO, PROB 11/156, fols. 372v–373 · J. E. Neale, 'Wentworth, Peter', HoP, *Commons, 1558–1603* · *The letters of John Chamberlain*, ed. N. E. McClure, 1 (1939), 360, 533, 540 · *DNB*

Wentworth, Thomas, earl of Cleveland (1591–1667), royalist army officer, was the elder son of Henry Wentworth, third Baron Wentworth of Nettlestead (1558–1593), and his wife, Anne Hopton (d. 1625). Wentworth matriculated, with his brother Henry, at Trinity College, Oxford, on 12 November 1602, and they appeared before James I at Christ Church on 27 August 1605. Thomas was created a knight of the Bath on 4 June 1610, and in 1611 he married Anne Crofts (d. 1638). Their eldest son was Thomas *Wentworth, fifth Baron Wentworth. On the death of his great-aunt Jane Wentworth, widow of Henry, Lord Cheney, on 16 April 1614, he inherited the estate of Toddington in Bedfordshire, which henceforth became his principal residence. He became *custos rotulorum* for Bedfordshire in 1619, and was admitted to Gray's Inn on 9 March 1620. He was appointed lord lieutenant of Bedfordshire on 5 May 1625, an office that he continued to hold until 1642.

Wentworth regularly attended the Lords throughout the parliaments of the 1620s, although there is no evidence that he was a frequent speaker. He nevertheless secured Buckingham's patronage and this helps to explain his creation as earl of Cleveland on 7 February 1626. The following year he served under Buckingham in the expedition to La Rochelle, and in August 1628 he was present when John Felton assassinated the duke at Portsmouth. As the 1630s progressed, Cleveland's extravagant lifestyle led him deeper and deeper into debt and prompted him to raise loans from various notable figures. For example, in September 1634 he borrowed £10,000 from Anne, Viscountess Dorchester, while the following year he obtained a loan of £2000 from Mary, countess of Home. By 1637 many of his lands in Bedfordshire and Middlesex were heavily encumbered (especially the manors of Stepney and Hackney), while his debts were thought to stand at £19,200. Three years later his total debts were estimated at £60,100. When the Long Parliament met, Cleveland introduced a private bill that would have enabled him to sell some of his lands and use the proceeds to pay off his debts, but a number of individuals submitted petitions against the bill pointing out that by this time the earl leased, rather than owned, many of his lands and was therefore not entitled to sell them.

Cleveland's first wife died on 16 January 1638, and by 25 October that year he had married his second wife, Lucy Wentworth (d. 1651), daughter of Sir John Wentworth, baronet, of Gosfield, Essex. The following year Cleveland joined the king with ten troops in the first bishops' war, and he also was present during the second war. He was friendly with his distant kinsman Thomas Wentworth, earl of Strafford, and in January 1641 was sworn as a defence witness in Strafford's trial. On 10 May 1641 the Lords ordered Cleveland to convey to Strafford the king's consent to his attainder, and two days later he attended the earl to the scaffold. On 5 March 1642 he was among the sixteen peers who entered protestations against the militia ordinance, and at the beginning of the civil war he became captain of the gentlemen pensioners. He may have been at Edgehill, and he was wounded at the first battle of Newbury on 20 September 1643.

Cleveland sat in the Oxford parliament which assembled in January 1644, and during the following summer he emerged as a highly successful cavalry commander. On the night of 29 May 1644 he surprised Abingdon with a party of 150 horse, but he was forced to retreat and lost his prisoners. This was a bold move that prompted Clarendon later to characterize Cleveland as 'a man of signal courage, and an excellent officer upon any bold enterprise' (Clarendon, *Hist. rebellion*, 3.352). At Cropredy Bridge on 29 June Cleveland led a cavalry charge against Sir William Waller, and then, after a second charge, succeeded in driving Waller back over the bridge. He was then sent to Cornwall, where on 30 August near Fowey he made an unsuccessful attempt to prevent the flight of Essex's cavalry after their defeat at Lostwithiel. He helped to relieve Portland Castle on 14 October, and on 27 October he commanded the left wing of the royalist cavalry at the second battle of Newbury. During the charge his horse fell under him and he was captured and imprisoned in the Tower. The houses refused requests for him to be exchanged for a parliamentarian prisoner, although he was periodically granted bail for three or four months at a time. In July 1647 he wrote to Prince Charles pledging his loyalty despite his confinement, and the following year he was in Colchester during the siege. In September 1648—after producing a doctor's certificate stating that he needed fresh air and more exercise—he was granted bail for a further three months. Shortly before that period expired in December he escaped to the continent, and by June 1649 he had joined Charles II at The Hague.

By April 1650 Cleveland was in attendance on Charles II at Beauvais, where it was reported that he threatened to cane or beat anyone who called him a presbyterian. He sailed for Scotland with Charles on 2 June 1650, but he and his son were required to leave Scotland in October for refusing to take the covenant. He commanded a regiment of horse at the battle of Worcester on 3 September 1651, and by a daring charge in the streets of the city gave Charles enough time to escape. Cleveland himself was captured on 13 September at Woodcote in Shropshire and was committed to the Tower. At his trial on 29 October he narrowly escaped the death sentence through the casting vote of Lord Mordaunt. Shortly afterwards Cleveland's second wife died on 23 November and was buried at Toddington. He remained a prisoner until 20 July 1658, although he was granted the liberty of the Tower on 16 February 1652. On his release he may have retired to Lord Lovelace's house at Water Eaton, near Oxford, and in 1659

royalist agents listed him as a possible activist in Booth's rising.

Early in the civil war Cleveland's estates had been sequestrated, and on 17 November 1645 the committee for the advance of money set his fine at £2000. In August 1650 the total debts of him and his son were estimated at £100,000. Proceedings in the committee for compounding with delinquents dragged on until 1655, by which time nearly all his landed property was leased or sold to creditors.

Cleveland re-emerged at the Restoration, and at the king's entry into London on 29 May 1660 he led a regiment of 300 horse from Buckinghamshire and Hertfordshire. On 20 June he was reappointed captain of the gentlemen pensioners, and the following month lord lieutenant of Bedfordshire; he continued to hold both offices until his death. He was appointed colonel of a regiment of horse on 1 September 1662. John Evelyn described a review in Hyde Park on 4 July 1663 in which 'the old Earle of Cleveland trail'd a pike, and led the right-hand file in a foote company, commanded by the Lord Wentworth, his son, a worthy spectacle and example, being both of them old and valiant souldiers' (*The Diary and Correspondence of John Evelyn*, ed. W. Bray, new edn, ed. H. B. Wheatley, 4 vols., 1906, 2.159). In January 1666 Cleveland was instructed to raise a regiment of 500 horse for use in the Second Anglo-Dutch War, but in August the regiment was disbanded without seeing military action.

Cleveland was not permitted to repossess lands that he had sold in order to pay his composition fine, and between 1660 and 1667 three private acts of parliament were passed enabling him to sell certain settled lands for the benefit of his creditors. On 13 March 1667 Lady Wentworth wrote that only a 'litle remnant of Lord Cleveland's estate' was left (Lady Wentworth to [Joseph Williamson], PRO, SP 29/193/109). Less than two weeks later, on 25 March, Cleveland died; he was buried on 4 April at Toddington.

One leading military historian has described Cleveland as 'a much underrated field commander' (Newman, 403), and his relative posthumous obscurity belies the positive impression that he made on a number of contemporaries. Clarendon's favourable assessment has already been quoted, and Sir Philip Warwick similarly regarded Cleveland as 'a nobleman of daring courage, full of industry and activity, as well as firm loyalty, and usually successful in what he attempted' (Warwick, 270).

DAVID L. SMITH

Sources Clarendon, *Hist. rebellion* · state papers domestic, Charles I, PRO, SP 16 · state papers domestic, interregnum, PRO, SP 18 · committee for compounding papers, PRO, SP 23 · council of state papers, PRO, SP 25 · state papers domestic, Charles II, PRO, SP 29 · main papers of the House of Lords, HLRO · *JHL*, 4–10 (1628–48) · GEC, *Peerage*, new edn · P. R. Newman, *Royalist officers in England and Wales, 1642–1660: a biographical dictionary* (1981), 403–4 · P. Warwick, *Memoires of the reigne of King Charles I* (1701) · D. Lloyd, *Memoires of the lives … of those … personages that suffered … for the protestant religion* (1668) · *Diary of the marches of the royal army during the great civil war, kept by Richard Symonds*, ed. C. E. Long, CS, old ser., 74 (1859)

Likenesses oils, 1636? (after A. Van Dyck), priv. coll. • A. Van Dyck, portrait, priv. coll.; in possession of the earl of Verulam, 1866 • A. Van Dyck, portrait, priv. coll.

Wealth at death debts in August 1650 est. at £100,000: *Calendar of the committee for compounding*, 5 vols. (1889–92), 3.2157

Wentworth, Thomas, first earl of Strafford (1593–1641), lord lieutenant of Ireland, was born on Good Friday, 13 April 1593, in a house in Chancery Lane, London, which belonged to his grandfather Robert Atkinson, a barrister of the Inner Temple. He was baptized on 22 April at St Dunstan-in-the-West. He was the second and eldest surviving son of William Wentworth (1562–1614) of Wentworth Woodhouse, a wealthy Yorkshire landowner, whose family had long been settled in the southern part of the West Riding, and Anne (*d.* 1611), daughter and heir of Sir Robert Atkinson of Stowell in Gloucestershire. William Wentworth was made first baronet in 1611. His ancestors included the Nevills of Westmorland and the fifteenth-century judge Sir William Gascoigne of Gawthorpe, and Thomas himself always took great pride in belonging to a house which in wealth and lineage equalled many families raised to the peerage in the sixteenth century.

Early years Wentworth was educated at first by the dean of Ripon, Dr Higgins, in his house at Well. His fellow pupils included Henry, Lord Clifford, eldest son of the earl of Cumberland, and Christopher Wandesford, both close friends in later years. In November 1607 he entered the Inner Temple in London and in Easter term 1609 he matriculated from St John's College, Cambridge, where Richard Senhouse, later bishop of Carlisle, was his tutor. On 22 October 1611 he married Lady Margaret Clifford (*d.* 1622), eldest daughter of Francis Clifford, fourth earl of Cumberland, at Londesborough, her father's seat. In December 1611, having been knighted by the king on 6 December at Royston, Wentworth left England for France to complete his education. He travelled widely and visited among other places Paris, Orléans, Bordeaux, and Saumur. He learned not only French but also—to a lesser extent—Italian and Spanish, and read a number of works fashionable at the time, such as Justus Lipsius's letters. After returning early in 1613 he became the head of his family and inherited the title of baronet through his father's death in September 1614. He now had an annual income of about £4000 at his disposal but was also saddled with the responsibility for the education and career of his eight younger brothers.

Earlier in 1614 Wentworth had been elected one of the knights of the shire for Yorkshire (the other knight was Sir John Savile, soon to become his inveterate enemy) and represented his county in the so-called Addled Parliament in April 1614. Although he hardly raised his voice in the debates of this short-lived parliament two draft speeches among his papers testify to his attempt to reconcile the interests of king and country. In December 1615 Wentworth was appointed *custos rotulorum* (keeper of the records) for the West Riding of Yorkshire. Savile, his predecessor in this office, had been forced to step down after having been ordered to appear before the court of Star Chamber to answer charges of fraud and intimidation.

Thomas Wentworth, first earl of Strafford (1593–1641), by Sir Anthony Van Dyck, *c.*1636

Apparently Savile himself suggested Wentworth as his successor on the assumption that a young man like Wentworth could easily be made to resign once Savile had managed to mend his reputation. Savile had, however, misjudged Wentworth's character. When George Villiers, the earl of Buckingham, with whom Savile had in the meantime successfully managed to ingratiate himself, asked Wentworth to resign as *custos* in September 1617 Wentworth refused, arguing that such a demand was an attack on his honour as a gentleman; 'Itt might justly be taken as the greatest disgrace that could be done unto me', he wrote to Buckingham (Gardiner, *Fortescue Papers*, 26). He even denied knowledge of the fact that Savile had nominated him his successor. Buckingham withdrew his request for Wentworth's resignation, but the latter's relations with the ever more powerful royal favourite never quite recovered from the repercussions of this incident. Moreover, Wentworth now found himself involved in a bitter feud with Savile and his family, which was to last for more than a decade until Savile's death in 1630, and beyond.

Court, county, and parliament in the early 1620s Wentworth was aware that he could prevail against Savile only if he managed to gain influence at court as well as in Yorkshire. At court his principal contacts about 1620 were Sir George Calvert, one of the two secretaries of state, and Sir Arthur Ingram, a London merchant, financier, and customs farmer of dubious reputation who was also a substantial landowner in his native Yorkshire. Wentworth, who now spent long periods of time in London, could also count to some extent on the patronage of the new lord treasurer appointed in September 1621, Lionel Cranfield, contacts with whom had been established by Ingram. In December 1620 Wentworth sought election as knight of the shire for Yorkshire with Calvert as a fellow candidate. In spite of strong opposition by Savile, who stood as a candidate himself, Wentworth and Calvert were elected, although the election was later (unsuccessfully) challenged in the House of Commons; Wentworth and his supporters were, probably not without some justification, alleged to have exerted undue pressure on the voters. In parliament Wentworth tried to mediate between the king and those who saw the crown's policy as a threat to the privileges of parliament and the ancient liberties of the king's subjects. Totally out of sympathy with those who tried to urge the king to pursue a more active anti-Spanish foreign policy, he discouraged the house from debating foreign affairs while at the same time defending the privilege of free speech. It was probably Wentworth who first suggested that the Commons should not only investigate the controversial monopoly patents granted by the crown but instigate proceedings to have the patentees punished by parliamentary judicature. During the spring and summer recess of 1621 Wentworth turned to his voters to explain the stance he had taken in Westminster and to reassure himself of their support. He spoke at Rotherham on 23 April emphasizing the 'harmonious union betwixt the kinge, the nobles and Commons' which he hoped for if the parliament were to achieve its real objective, successful legislation (Cooper, *Wentworth Papers*, 153–5). When parliament met once more in the autumn he implored his fellow knights and burgesses not to enter too deeply into disputes about their privileges and the king's prerogative. Their liberties, he argued in a draft speech of 23 November 1621, would be much safer if they remained 'wrapte up in a sacred and questionable doubtfulnesse' instead of being unravelled by an 'over precise curiosity' (ibid., 164, cf. 166).

After the dissolution of parliament Wentworth tried to strengthen his contacts with the court. In April 1622 Lord Treasurer Cranfield offered him the receivership of crown lands in Yorkshire. He passed this office on, however, to a successor about a year later and it is possible that Wentworth resigned under political pressure. His standing at court was certainly not secure during these years, although the new lord president of the council of the north, Lord Scrope, had nominated him as a member of the council on 10 July 1619. Moreover, there were rumours in 1622 that he would be made comptroller of the household and be raised to the peerage. Nothing came of this; during the years 1622–4 Wentworth was often seriously ill, and was forced to give up his London residence.

The death of his wife, Margaret, on 14 August 1622 marked a crisis in Wentworth's life. His marriage had been childless and it had not been marked at first by great passion, but he was nevertheless deeply afflicted by Margaret's death. During her fatal illness he prayed with her and read the Bible and the Psalms to her, as the detailed account of her death which he subsequently gave testifies; the religious sensibility which he displayed at this moment was clearly influenced by strictly protestant ideals. According to the biographical account by his friend Sir George Radcliffe, at moments of crisis Wentworth was no stranger to the religious self-examination which is often seen as typical for a particularly puritan variety of religious fervour, although he clearly did not share the wider political outlook associated with puritanism. After his wife's death Wentworth led a more withdrawn life than before. When he recovered his health and mental strength in the spring of 1624 the political scene had changed, becoming decidedly more unfavourable to his ambitions. The deterioration of relations with Spain made open war with the house of Habsburg (always rejected by Wentworth as pointless and dangerous) more than likely. At the same time the influence of his patron Cranfield, himself an opponent of war, was rapidly declining: parliament impeached the lord treasurer and forced him to resign in 1624. Wentworth represented the borough of Pontefract in parliament in 1624. He had not contested the election for the county seats of Yorkshire, and Savile and his son took both those seats unopposed. In the Commons Wentworth spoke cautiously and not without reservations in defence of Cranfield and against the contentious impositions. He also voiced his enthusiasm for action against recusants, but in general did not play a very prominent part in the proceedings of the parliament.

Political and personal disappointments, 1625–1626 Although Wentworth did not entirely give up his hope of finding favour at court he was about to enter into a closer alliance with men who were strongly opposed to the king's favourite, the (now) duke of Buckingham, and his policies. As Wentworth's enemy Savile was supported by the duke, it was natural for Wentworth to canvass the support of all those who rejected Buckingham's warlike foreign policy and especially the burdens with which it was likely to saddle the country—all the more so as he genuinely believed this policy foolish. Personal attachments and connections drew Wentworth into the camp of those increasingly critical of official royal policy in the early years of Charles I's reign. After Margaret's death he looked for a new wife, if possible an heiress. Mary, daughter of the City magnate Sir William Craven, Lady Diana Cecil, daughter of the earl of Exeter's heir, and the dowager countess of Dorset were all wooed with varying degrees of intensity, but in the end Wentworth made suit for Lady Arabella Holles (1608/9–1631), daughter of John *Holles, first earl of Clare (d. 1637), one of the richest landowners in Nottinghamshire. Arabella was a strikingly beautiful girl of sixteen and Wentworth seems to have fallen passionately in love with her. They married on 24 February 1625. Wentworth's new father-in-law had strong links with Bishop Williams of Lincoln, the lord keeper, who, however, lost his office shortly after Charles's accession. The earl of Clare, disappointed in his hopes for advancement, came to take an increasingly critical view of royal policy, and became a leader of the opposition to Buckingham in the House of Lords after 1625.

In the elections for Charles I's first parliament in 1625 Wentworth again sought to obtain one of the county seats for Yorkshire, with Sir Thomas Fairfax as his running mate. The elections were hotly contested, as Savile had mobilized the weavers of Leeds and Halifax to defeat Wentworth. At the height of the turmoil on polling day the high sheriff, Sir Richard Cholmondeley, closed the poll and declared Wentworth and Fairfax elected. This decision was questioned in the Commons when parliament met. While the house debated the validity of the election Wentworth took his seat, a breach of the rules of procedure. He thereby provoked the anger of Sir John Eliot, who was speaking at that very moment, although Eliot's later account of this incident in which he claimed that he had denounced Wentworth immediately as a Catilina—the Roman revolutionary defeated by Cicero—is of questionable authenticity. The Commons did indeed declare the election invalid, but Wentworth returned to parliament in early August 1625 having been re-elected by a clear majority of the voters.

Although Wentworth, who still hoped to find favour with the duke, refrained from openly attacking Buckingham in parliament, he felt to some extent 'obliged to be obstructive' because he was aware that too much compliance could lose him credit in his native Yorkshire (Salt, 155–6). He thus opposed the granting of further supply on 12 August until the two subsidies already granted had been fully collected. Nevertheless, he saw the king's decision, taken on Buckingham's advice, to have him appointed sheriff of Yorkshire in November 1625, with the intention of rendering him incapable of sitting in the next parliament, as a mark of disfavour which he had done nothing to provoke. In fact, his association with Bishop Williams and Archbishop Abbot, as well as with the earl of Arundel and to a lesser extent the earl of Pembroke, may have been responsible for Buckingham's desire to keep him out of parliament, as well as Savile's efforts to depict him at court as a dangerous troublemaker. Undeterred, the following spring Wentworth applied for the office of lord president of the north, which he thought would become vacant through the resignation of Lord Scrope. However, Scrope held on to his office, and, even more galling for Wentworth, his enemy Savile was subsequently appointed vice-president. Worse was to come. In July 1626 Wentworth was ordered to relinquish the office of *custos rotulorum*, which he had held since 1615, and was dismissed from the commission of the peace. He was deeply disappointed, as he believed that he had come to an understanding with Buckingham during a visit to Whitehall about Easter 1626 and that he had even contracted a 'friendship' with the favourite (*Strafforde's Letters*, 1.34–5). This disgrace and humiliation affected him even more deeply, as he was notified of his dismissal while presiding over a session of the commission of the peace.

The 'honest patriot', 1627–1628 Although Wentworth tried to remain true to the principle of not contending 'with the prerogative out of Parliament, nor yet to contest with a King but when I am constrained thereunto' (letter to Wandesford, 5 Dec 1625, *Strafforde's Letters*, 1.32), he was inexorably drawn towards a more radical position. The fact that Savile had been appointed comptroller of the household in 1627 and now dominated contacts between

Yorkshire and the court left Wentworth little choice but to ally himself even more openly than before with those opposed to the king's favourite and his policies. In fact many of his closest friends and relations, for example, Wandesford, Radcliffe, and Clare, were among the most outspoken critics of royal policy during these years. When faced with a demand to pay the forced loan raised to finance the war against France in 1626–7 Wentworth refused, although he clearly hesitated to commit himself irrevocably to a conflict with the crown. Summoned to appear before the privy council he pleaded illness. In the end, however, he stood his ground and was committed to the Marshalsea prison in June 1627. Wentworth seems to have shared the concern of many of his friends about the grave constitutional implications of the forced loan, and if he did not want to lose all credit with his fellow Yorkshiremen he probably had little choice but to refuse to pay regardless of his convictions. However, he was careful not to do or say anything that would preclude eventual reconciliation with the king and his advisers. He was transferred from the Marshalsea to Dartford prison six weeks after his imprisonment and was finally released on 27 December, having petitioned the king in November to be allowed out of confinement to attend business.

In 1628 Wentworth was once more elected as a knight of the shire to represent Yorkshire in parliament. His position as an acknowledged martyr for the cause of the liberties of the subject in itself ensured that he played a leading role in the proceedings of this parliament. On 22 March he spoke to the house asking them to vindicate 'our ancient, sober, vital liberties' in a speech that already contained much of the substance of the future petition of right (Johnson, *Proceedings*, 2.60). Wentworth, like others, however, insisted that only a proper law, not a mere petition, could safeguard the king's subjects against any future infringement of their rights, so that 'his Majesty's goodness' in promising to respect his subjects' traditional liberties in future would 'remain to posterity' enshrined in a public act of state (ibid., 2 May 1628, 3.211). Only very reluctantly did Wentworth accept the proposal to proceed by petition. At the same time, however, he continued to advocate the ideal of harmony between the crown and its subjects. He preferred to assume that only misguided advice had led the king to raise the forced loan, and expressed his hope that 'it shall never be stirred here whether the King be above the law or the law above the King' (ibid., 26 April 1628, 3.98). Wentworth was aware that only adequate financial resources would enable the king to govern in accordance with the law and tradition, and that any further refusal to grant him tonnage and poundage—even after a bill or petition of right had been passed—would only force the king to raise revenues by means incompatible with the letter of the law.

There was, therefore, always room for compromise with the political forces dominant at court, in particular as Wentworth, even while in open conflict with official policy, had never adopted the rhetoric of violent anti-popery so popular with other leaders of opposition to an allegedly arbitrary government. Wentworth's moderation, based in part on a much more secular conception of politics than that of many contemporaries, now proved a valuable asset, as Charles I and Buckingham, concentrating on the war effort against France, had decided to seek peace with Spain. Buckingham tried to bring about a reconciliation with a number of influential proponents of a pro-Spanish policy after the parliament of 1628 and as part of this political reshuffle Wentworth was elevated to the peerage as Baron Wentworth of Wentworth Woodhouse and baron of Newmarch and Oversley on 22 July 1628. Sir Richard Weston, the recently appointed lord treasurer, had acted as a mediator between Wentworth and the favourite. However, the fact that Wentworth's old enemy Savile was created Baron Savile of Pomfret on the previous day indicates that the outcome of the contest for favour at court remained open, as long as Buckingham dominated the king's entourage. As Wentworth had played such a prominent part in leading the resistance to the forced loan and in the struggle for the petition of right his apparent change of sides was immediately commented on and seen as controversial. His friend Wandesford testified that in Yorkshire common opinion was now passing him 'under Sir John Savile's character, and that there is a Thomas as well as a John for the king' (Wandesford to Wentworth, 30 July 1628, Cooper, *Wentworth Papers*, 301). However, Wentworth had always with considerable consistency, though not with equal success, tried to act as a mediator between his county and the court: it was, therefore, not altogether surprising that he accepted advancement and office once the most blatant local and national grievances outside the religious sphere, which did not greatly preoccupy him, had to all appearances been redressed.

In office at last: Wentworth as lord president of the north Buckingham's death in August 1628 and Charles I's decision to end the war against France as well as the struggle against Spain removed the last obstacles to Wentworth's advancement. On 13 December 1628 he was created Viscount Wentworth and on 25 December Charles appointed him lord president of the north in Scrope's place. At the same time Savile, accused of having accepted bribes from recusants, was removed from office as vice-president. Finally on 10 November 1629 Wentworth was made a privy councillor. The delay between his appointment as lord president and his entry into the privy council may indicate that the king did not yet entirely trust him. However, later accounts, though uncorroborated by official records, maintain that Wentworth was sworn in as a privy councillor only after he had brought to the king's attention a libellous tract which was in essence a blueprint for arbitrary government by an absolute monarch. The tract had apparently been distributed with the intention of discrediting Charles by creating the impression that he wanted to govern permanently without parliament. Wentworth's father-in-law, Clare, was among those who had read and possibly circulated the tract and now faced prosecution in Star Chamber for conspiracy. Whatever Wentworth's part in this incident, his relations with his in-laws certainly deteriorated at this time. In fact they had already been strained before this incident, as Denzil

Holles, one of Clare's sons, had been involved in the fracas which led to the dissolution of parliament in 1629 and was subsequently imprisoned while his brother-in-law was promoted by the king.

On taking up his office as president, Wentworth, in a speech delivered to the council of the north, had again enunciated his political philosophy, stressing the old theme of harmony between the king and his subjects and condemning those who wanted to create a division between the two. In practice, however, the ruthlessness and vindictiveness which he demonstrated in his new office did little to foster the political harmony which he so often praised as his highest political ideal. By nature a man who believed in the need for strong authority he had, once in office, little sympathy for those who saw royal policy as a threat to long-established legal and constitutional traditions. He had, indeed, shared some of those concerns in the 1620s, but then England had been involved in an apparently futile war fundamentally undermining the country's traditional constitutional framework.

As lord president, Wentworth immediately filled positions in the council and in the commission of the peace with his supporters, including Wandesford, Sir George Radcliffe (who became the king's attorney for the council), Sir John Hotham, Sir William Constable, and Sir Thomas Hoby. Moreover, he used the authority of his office to thwart the interests of his old opponents. Thus a scheme for draining Hatfield Chase promoted by Sir Cornelius Vermuyden and supported by the Savile family was systematically obstructed by Wentworth. In this case concern for the many smallholders who would have lost their land or grazing rights probably motivated Wentworth's action as much as enmity to the Saviles, but for his opponents personal animosities and higher political purpose were difficult to distinguish. As receiver of recusant fines in the north, an office in which he had succeeded Savile in June 1629, Wentworth increased the fiscal pressure on Catholic landowners who did not lack influence and friends in some parts of Yorkshire. In fact, his appointment as lord president had greatly disturbed Catholics in northern England, as the new president was known to be less tolerant than his predecessor—'the Papists already hang down their heads like bulrushes', as his friend Wandesford put it (*Strafforde's Letters*, 1.49). However, as Wentworth was used to living among a sizeable Catholic minority his anti-Catholicism always remained more pragmatic and less fanatical than that of many fervent protestants from a different background.

Even so, opponents who openly challenged Wentworth's authority in Yorkshire were harshly punished and humiliated. Sir Henry Bellasis, the son of Thomas, Lord Fauconberg, was imprisoned by the privy council and had to apologize publicly for not having shown the lord president proper respect during a session of the council of the north. While Wentworth energetically collected the knighthood fines which were to bolster Charles I's revenues, James Maleverer, a Yorkshire puritan, and Sir David Foulis, himself a member of the council of the north, tried to organize local resistance to the scheme. In

1632 Foulis accused Wentworth of having misappropriated the funds which he had collected as lord president. Wentworth was furious and on his insistence Foulis was not only dismissed from the council in 1633, but was heavily fined and imprisoned.

Wentworth was hardly universally popular as lord president but he undoubtedly strengthened the authority of the council, which had declined under his predecessors. He deliberately emphasized the importance of his office by insisting on a great deal of pomp and ceremony when appearing in public in his official capacity and by embarking upon an extensive building programme which, among other projects, transformed the king's manor in York into a residence worthy of the monarch's representative in the north. In March 1633 the king confirmed Wentworth's success by issuing a new commission and instructions for the council which brought its powers into line with those of the Star Chamber in the south.

The years following Wentworth's elevation to the peerage brought him success and prosperity. However, the death of his wife on 5 October 1631 was a major personal setback. While pregnant, Arabella had had a fall which brought on a premature confinement. She did not survive, and Wentworth felt this personal disaster all the more deeply because his wife's family held him responsible for her death as it was he who had asked her to travel in spite of her pregnancy. Rumours even accused him of having struck her, thus causing the accident. Together they had had four children, of whom three survived: William (1626–1695), Ann (b. 1627), and Arabella (b. 1630); a second son, Thomas, died as an infant in 1631. In spite of his grief at Arabella's death Wentworth soon married again, in October 1632. His third wife, Elizabeth (c.1614–1688), daughter of Sir Godfrey Rodes of Great Houghton in Yorkshire, came from a strongly puritan family and was about eighteen at the time of the marriage. The fact that the ceremony took place in secret and that Wentworth did not publicly acknowledge her as his wife until about a year after the wedding may indicate that he feared public reproach for having married again so soon. This marriage resulted in the birth of a daughter, Margaret (d. 1681).

Promotion or banishment? Appointment as lord deputy of Ireland At the time of his third marriage Wentworth was about to take up a new office, the position of lord deputy of Ireland. When his appointment was first debated in the summer of 1631, there was no lack of advice warning him against abandoning England for Ireland. One of Wentworth's friends, Sir Edward Stanhope, pointed out in September 1631 that the deputyship had always been 'a fatall place to pack men of eminancy into … for their overthrowe' (Zagorin, 315). Wentworth would have no clients or friends to rely on in Ireland, in contrast to his native Yorkshire. If he were to tackle the difficult problem of alienated royal rights and titles he would provoke uncontrollable animosity, not least among the influential protestant planters. Thus the problems that awaited a new lord deputy were clearly visible. Moreover, Wentworth was probably aware that Weston, the lord treasurer, and Lord Cottington, the chancellor of the

exchequer, who were primarily responsible for the king's decision to offer him the deputyship in July 1631, though officially his friends, both saw him as a potential rival who could do less harm in Ireland than in England. Nevertheless, Wentworth clearly welcomed what he saw as an important promotion and eagerly accepted the position. Apparently he believed that he could govern Ireland as successfully as northern England, provided he had the king's full support. In fact he laid down a number of conditions, to which he asked the king to agree before he accepted the new office: he should be allowed to return to England and attend the court whenever he saw fit to do so; no grant relating to Ireland was to be made without his knowledge and consent; and the king was not to allow any appeals against his decisions unless a manifest perversion of justice could be demonstrated. Wentworth also expressed a wish to be created an earl before he left for Ireland but this wish, as opposed to his other demands, was denied. However, he was allowed to retain his office as lord president of the north and could delegate the actual functions of the office to his vice-president, Sir Edward Osborne, a wealthy Yorkshire landowner who enjoyed Wentworth's total confidence. Wentworth was appointed lord deputy on 12 January 1632 but did not leave England for Ireland until July 1633. This delay gave him the chance to sort matters out in Dublin through his political allies and agents, while still being able to exert personal influence on decisions in England, a vital precondition for not being outmanoeuvred at court by possible opponents before he had even taken up office.

It was clear from the outset that Wentworth's appointment as lord deputy was intended to be a new start for the government of Ireland. As early as 1623 a royal commission sent to Dublin to examine the problems facing church and state in Ireland had revealed how far the king had been defrauded of income and property by his own office-holders. The commission's report had strongly advised, among other things, the re-endowment of the church because ecclesiastical property had been alienated on a large scale to laymen, mostly New English protestants. None of the commissioners' recommendations could really be implemented in the following years, but when peace with Spain was restored in 1630 the situation was more favourable and Wentworth was determined to make the most of this chance. He clearly mistrusted the class of protestant office-holders and planters (the New English) whom he found in power when he came to Ireland in 1633: 'I find myself in the society of a strange people, their owne privates altogether their study without regard to the publique' (Wentworth to Arundel, 19 Aug 1633, Wentworth Woodhouse muniments, Strafford papers, 8, fol. 11r). Wentworth deliberately antagonized vested interests in Ireland, including those of the protestants, confident that he need not care whom he pleased or displeased as long as he retained the support of the king. The problem of Catholicism was to be seen in a long-term perspective. The Catholic church was to be vanquished not by direct persecution but on one hand by a new series of plantations which would weaken Catholic landowners and bring new English settlers to Ireland, and on the other by a reform and financial re-endowment of the established church which would enable it to pursue its mission in Ireland successfully. To seek religious conformity without such prior internal ecclesiastical reforms would be to act 'as a man going to warfare without munitions or arms' (letter to Laud, 31 Jan 1634, *Strafforde's Letters*, 1.187).

Even before Wentworth left England for Ireland he had prepared the ground for his administration in close co-operation with Francis Annesley, Lord Mountnorris, the Irish vice-treasurer, who had travelled to England to defend himself against accusations of administrative malpractice. In the past Mountnorris, who had many friends at the English court but had remained an outsider among the New English office-holders in Ireland, had often acted as a check on the Dublin administration on behalf of the king and his councillors. In the period between Wentworth's appointment and actual arrival in Dublin, Mountnorris proved a valuable ally for the new deputy.

Prior to Wentworth's arrival the dominant faction in the Irish privy council led by Richard Boyle, first earl of Cork, the richest planter in Ireland and one of the two acting lords justices, tried to tie the new deputy's hands by pursuing a policy of more active persecution against Catholics. The fines for recusancy were to be strictly enforced and were to replace the contribution which the Catholic and protestant landowners alike had agreed to pay in 1628 to finance the army. Had Cork and his allies been able to implement this policy, Wentworth would have found even a limited and temporary co-operation with the Catholic Old English impossible. He would instead have remained dependent on the New English like his immediate predecessors. However, Wentworth entered into negotiations with the Catholic peerage and gentry. Under the threat of renewed persecution the leaders of the Old English agreed in December 1632 to extend for another year the payment of the contribution they had granted in 1628 and which was due to cease at the end of 1632. Later this contribution was further extended until December 1634. This gave Wentworth the necessary breathing-space to find other means (in the form of parliamentary grants and an improved income from the customs) to finance the army and other expenditure.

New foundations: parliament, state, and church When Wentworth finally arrived in Dublin on 23 July 1633 he had already formed a clear opinion of the problems awaiting him, and also to some extent of the men who dominated the Dublin administration. It is therefore not surprising that in his early reports from Ireland he found fault with almost everything he saw: the army, neglected by its absentee officers, ill-trained, insufficiently armed, and incapable of fighting; the church, without resources and with ecclesiastical benefices in the hands of badly paid clergy without a proper education who neglected their flocks; and the crown's finances in disarray, thanks not least to the cavalier attitude or downright corruption of the king's own office-holders. With great energy and determination, which he never failed to present to the king and his councillors in the most favourable light, Wentworth set out to put these matters right. Among his first priorities were the army and navy, the latter essential to protect shipping and trade, the former an indispensable instrument for enforcing his orders against those who sought to resist him. Characteristically Wentworth, ever conscious of his own honour and the dignity of his office, also sought from the outset to transform his own entourage in Dublin into a quasi-royal court.

Most important in Wentworth's eyes, however, was an improvement in the state of the Irish revenues. Only if the income from these revenues produced a substantial and steady surplus could he guard Ireland against intervention from England, as he clearly desired, and realize his own political objectives. The foundations for a sound financial policy were to be laid by a generous grant of parliamentary taxation. Wentworth therefore asked the king in January 1634 for permission to convene the Irish houses of parliament; parliament met on 14 July 1634 and the first session lasted until 2 August of that year. A second session was held between November and December 1634, and a third from January to April 1635. The first session, in which Wentworth deliberately played protestants off against Catholics and vice versa, was a great success. This was made possible not least by the large number of candidates elected to the House of Commons who owed their seats to official patronage. In July parliament granted six subsidies, a very considerable sum by Irish standards. This grant was made all the more valuable as each subsidy was fixed at £40,000. Thus attempts to evade taxes by underassessing one's wealth (a common practice in England) were rendered largely futile. In fact, the richest man in Ireland, the earl of Cork, who had become accustomed to paying no taxes at all, later complained that he paid such a considerable sum in subsidies after 1634 that it would have been sufficient to 'have ransomed me if I had been prisoner with the turkes' (Grosart, 2.4, p. 186).

In the second session of parliament, which first met on 4 November 1634, it became clear that Wentworth was not prepared to have the 'graces' of 1628 confirmed without major modifications. The graces were a catalogue of concessions which the king had made during the war against Spain and France to protestants and Catholics alike. They were, however, of particular importance to the Old English landowners as they gave them security of tenure. Until November, Wentworth had deliberately created the impression that all the graces would eventually be confirmed. Late in November, however, he could no longer conceal the fact that only a limited number would be given force of law by statute, while others would be implemented only at the deputy's discretion, and those confirming titles predating the completion of the Elizabethan conquest not at all. At this stage, however, Wentworth commanded sufficient financial resources for a number of years and no longer needed the co-operation of the Old English. In spite of some minor setbacks he was able to steer most of his legislative programme successfully through parliament with protestant support.

The Irish convocation met at the same time as parliament. With the help of his closest assistant in ecclesiastical affairs, Bishop John Bramhall, who had originally accompanied him as his personal chaplain from Yorkshire to Ireland before being promoted to the see of Derry, the lord deputy managed convocation as successfully as parliament. A set of canons was passed by the assembled clergy which brought the Church of Ireland much more into line with the Church of England and with the peculiar ecclesiastical aspirations of Archbishop Laud. In fact, throughout the 1630s Wentworth and Laud co-operated closely in fighting for a political and ecclesiastical programme in Ireland and England respectively for which they used the catchword 'thorough' as opposed to the laxer approach favoured by Lord Treasurer Portland or the chancellor of the exchequer, Cottington. Wentworth may not have shared Laud's personal religious sentiments—his enthusiasm for the 'beauty of holiness' and his concern for the continuity between the Church of England and the pre-Reformation universal church, let alone his alleged Arminianism—but like Laud he was convinced that secular and ecclesiastical authority stood or fell together. Those who attacked the one committed as much of a crime against God as those who attacked the other. In fact, like Laud, Wentworth was convinced that to rob the established church of her rightful property and to undermine her dignity and authority was tantamount to sacrilege. In their concern for order and discipline and their conviction that the church and the clerical order had to be restored to their pristine splendour Laud and Wentworth were of one mind, different as their personal religious sensibilities and theological convictions may have been. United in their zeal for authoritarian reform, for a policy of 'thorough', Laud and Wentworth became close allies in the 1630s and it was largely due to the archbishop's influence at court that Wentworth could pursue his policy in Ireland successfully. Laud did have his reservations at times about the lord deputy's ruthlessness and his quest for personal profit, but the two men's alliance withstood the test of time, although Wentworth continued to co-operate on occasions with men who had no great love for the archbishop, such as Lord Cottington.

In Ireland, as in England, Laud's ecclesiastical policy, which Wentworth tried to implement, was far from popular. Nevertheless, after some acrimonious debates the deputy persuaded parliament to pass a number of statutes which were designed to address the most pressing problem facing the Church of Ireland: its poverty. All bishops and clergy were forbidden in future to make leases of church lands for longer than twenty-one years to laymen. Another act made void all leases held by a minister or vicar who was absent from his cure for twelve or more weeks in the year. Thus the widespread practice by which lay owners of advowsons nominally appointed a clergyman to several benefices at the same time, while the income from the benefices remained almost totally in their own hands, became illegal. Armed with these statutes Wentworth and Bramhall could exert considerable pressure on laymen who had acquired church property or leased impropriate rectories. Faced with the possibility of a trial in the court of castle chamber, the Irish equivalent of the Star Chamber, many laymen preferred an out-of-court settlement or submitted, however grudgingly, to arbitration. Thus the financial situation of the established church improved markedly, although the success of this campaign for the re-endowment of the church was most clearly visible in the north, in the province of Armagh, where protestantism had been established only after 1603.

Wentworth and the earl of Cork Matters were more difficult in Ireland's other ecclesiastical provinces. Here greater resistance was encountered. One of the most prominent opponents of Wentworth's ecclesiastical policy was Richard Boyle, earl of Cork. Cork had arrived in Ireland in 1588 and acquired a vast fortune as a land speculator, thanks to his position as a minor official in Munster, which had provided him with valuable information about titles likely to be deemed defective by the Dublin administration. Created an earl in 1620 and elevated to the office of lord high treasurer of Ireland in 1631, his position in Ireland seemed secure before Wentworth's arrival. Nevertheless, Cork had offered the deputy the hand of his eldest daughter in marriage after the death of Wentworth's second wife; clearly this was meant to be the foundation of a lasting political alliance. Wentworth had not accepted this offer but had, however, helped to arrange a marriage between Cork's eldest son, Lord Dungarvon, and his own niece, Elizabeth Clifford. Cork included in his son's marriage portion one of his most controversial acquisitions, the lands of the former College of Youghal in Munster, an ecclesiastical corporation rich in estates and impropriate rectories. This provided him with insurance should the way in which he had acquired his enormous fortune come under closer scrutiny.

Nevertheless, relations between Wentworth and Cork deteriorated rapidly after the deputy's arrival in Dublin. Wentworth's portrayal of Cork in his official reports as an avaricious social upstart and a pompous hypocrite may indeed be a caricature, but there can be no doubt that Wentworth's dislike of the successful planter was genuine and went beyond a mere conflict of interests. Cork's social pretensions may have been common enough among the New English but they could easily seem ridiculous from an English perspective. Cork's enormous wealth only confirmed Wentworth in his opinion that men like the earl were to blame for the poverty of the church and crown in Ireland. He therefore decided to humiliate Cork in public by forcing him in 1634 to dismantle the enormous funeral monument which he had built for his family in the choir of St Patrick's, Dublin. The official reason for having the monument taken apart was that it stood where the high altar ought to be. But Cork was soon to undergo an even more painful ordeal. In October 1634 he had to appear before the court of castle chamber to answer charges in connection with his possession of the College of Youghal. Although Cork was eventually allowed to retain the college and its lands he was forced in April 1636 to agree to pay a fine of £15,000, and to cede the rectories belonging to the college with all their revenues to the church. He had to make further concessions in 1637 with regard to the lands of the diocese of Lismore and the episcopal palace which he had acquired under very favourable but also highly questionable terms. Cork left Ireland for England in the following year. Raised to the status of privy councillor, he tried to come to an arrangement with Wentworth and did indeed manage to have his title to the lands of the College of Youghal confirmed. Both men tried to strengthen their contacts with the queen's entourage, now increasingly influential, in the late 1630s, and thus found a basis for limited co-operation. It was only in 1641, when Cork realized that Wentworth's downfall was a foregone conclusion and that the lord lieutenant's attempts to defend himself in his impeachment trial by bringing Cork's shady methods of acquiring property into the open posed a threat to himself, that the earl joined the ranks of Wentworth's enemies.

Confiscations and plantations The campaign for the re-endowment of the church which Wentworth and Bramhall pursued primarily affected protestant landowners. However, Wentworth's plans to confiscate vast tracts of land in areas which had not yet been planted threatened Catholic proprietors, Gaelic and Old English alike, much more than their protestant counterparts. After the parliament of 1634–5 Wentworth hastened the preparations for a new plantation in Connaught. This, contrary to older plans which the earl of Cork and other office-holders had tried to put into practice before Wentworth's arrival in Ireland, was to include co. Galway, an area traditionally dominated by Old English, not Gaelic, proprietors. Overall 4000 quarters of land were to be claimed for the king in Connaught, of which 1000 were actually to be confiscated and settled by planters from England. The original owners would receive a secure title for the rest, provided that they paid the necessary fees and charges to the king.

The inquisitions undertaken in Roscommon, Mayo, and Sligo in the summer of 1635 went smoothly enough and the king's title to the relevant lands in these counties was established at the end of July under Wentworth's personal supervision. Matters were, however, far more difficult in co. Galway. Here the most powerful local magnate, Richard Burke, fourth earl of Clanricarde, was in the forefront of opposition to the plantation. Clanricarde lived in England, where he held the title of earl of St Albans, and where he could mobilize the support of a number of friends and relations, including his stepson, Robert Devereux, third earl of Essex. Clanricarde managed to persuade the king to receive a delegation from the Galway landowners in November 1635, but died soon afterwards. Nevertheless, a member of the delegation, the lawyer Patrick Darcy, remained active in England for some time and tried to shake the king's confidence in Wentworth's financial honesty by supplying him with damaging information about the Irish customs farm. In May 1636 Darcy was finally sent back to Ireland, where he and the other members of the Galway jury which had rejected the evidence presented by the crown's agents were thrown into prison,

convicted, and each fined £4000. It was not until December of that year that the jurors submitted and acknowledged the king's title to the lands claimed for the crown in co. Galway. Even after this victory for the deputy, Ulick Burke, fifth earl of Clanricarde, and heir to his father's vast estates, remained a force to be reckoned with. On good terms with Secretary Windebank and other courtiers, he gradually managed to persuade Charles I by the end of the 1630s that it was unwise to antagonize one of the most powerful Catholic noblemen in Ireland while his own authority was threatened by radical protestants in Scotland. In February 1639 Charles finally confirmed Clanricarde's titles and thereby exempted his estates from any future plantation. It was not until October 1640 that Wentworth acknowledged defeat with ill grace and accepted the king's decision. Clanricarde never forgave Wentworth and rejoiced in the thought that 'when Parliament doth sit, the day will come [he] shall pay for all' (Clanricarde to Windebank, 9 Oct 1640, Yorke, 2.196). The earl of Essex's pronounced hostility towards Wentworth, which played no small part in bringing about the latter's downfall and execution in 1641, may owe something to the resentment Essex felt about the harsh treatment to which his Burke relations had been subjected by the lord deputy.

Even without royal confirmation of Clanricarde's property rights, the plantation in co. Galway and in Connaught in general would probably have faltered. Rumours of an impending military conflict with Spain in 1637, the crisis in Scotland that came to a head in the following year, and also the fact that migration to New England now offered an attractive alternative to settlement in Ireland, made it next to impossible to find enough suitable settlers. Nor did another plantation scheme in co. Tipperary make much headway in the 1630s, although Wentworth had managed to gain the co-operation of the local magnate, the protestant earl of Ormond, one of the few members of the Irish peerage to be closely allied to him. The king's title to the baronies of upper and lower Ormond was confirmed by a jury in Clonmel in August 1637 with the earl's support. Similarly Wentworth relied on the support of Henry O'Brien, the protestant fifth earl of Thomond, for a projected plantation of co. Clare, another largely abortive project.

Public finance, private profit, and English court politics When Wentworth first went to Ireland he had closely co-operated with the Irish vice-treasurer, Lord Mountnorris, but this association soon ended as Mountnorris controlled the considerable cash balances in the Irish exchequer, on which Wentworth himself wanted to lay his hands. Moreover, Mountnorris had a one-eighth share in the Irish customs farm. Wentworth, who considered the vice-treasurer dishonest and unreliable, and who resented the independent stance he had taken during the later sessions of the 1634–5 parliament, wanted to rearrange the customs farm. The covenant which in 1632 the crown had signed with the farmers, including Mountnorris, Sir Arthur Ingram, and Wentworth himself, had proved embarrassingly disadvantageous for the king because revenue from the customs had unexpectedly risen. Previous attempts to persuade Mountnorris to resign and to withdraw from the customs farm failed. However, in the spring of 1635 Mountnorris committed an indiscretion. A kinsman of his had, perhaps deliberately, dropped a stool on Wentworth's gouty foot shortly after Mountnorris's brother, an officer in the Irish army, had been struck with a cane by the deputy during a review because of insubordination. At a dinner given by Lord Chancellor Loftus, Mountnorris declared that the pain his kinsman had inflicted on the deputy had been in revenge for Wentworth's arrogance, and that his brother might take even more drastic revenge for the insult he had received. As Mountnorris himself held a commission as a captain in the Irish army such remarks could theoretically be seen as an offence punishable by a court martial. On 31 July Wentworth received the king's permission to sentence Mountnorris according to martial law at a time of his own choosing. For the time being, however, he merely investigated Mountnorris's malpractices as vice-treasurer. Only when Mountnorris still refused to resign and began to accuse Wentworth in letters sent to the king of making huge profits out of the customs farm at the crown's cost did Wentworth finally decide to convene a court martial and had Mountnorris condemned to death on 12 December 1635. Clearly, Wentworth had only wanted to force Mountnorris to resign; his death was not envisaged and the deputy set him at liberty once his resignation had been obtained. Nevertheless, such extreme measures did nothing to improve Wentworth's reputation in England, all the more so as his administration of the Irish customs increasingly came under scrutiny. At court the earl of Holland and Lord Wilmot supported the attacks on Wentworth. Holland was one of the many courtiers whom Wentworth had managed to antagonize by his arrogance and intemperate remarks. Wilmot was a New English landowner in Ireland who, like many others, had felt the lord deputy's heavy hand.

Matters seemed to come to a head at the beginning of 1636, when there were rumours that the attorney-general would investigate the administration of the Irish customs farm. However, Charles's decision to appoint Bishop Juxon as lord treasurer in March 1636 defused the crisis. Nevertheless, Wentworth, who after Portland's death had denied all rumours that he wanted to become treasurer himself, decided to travel to England in 1636 to justify his proceedings in Ireland. When he arrived at court in June, he managed fully to restore the king's confidence in his actions. The six weeks he spent at court and in London in June and July 1636 have been called 'the most triumphant and unclouded of all his public life' (Wedgwood, 212). The contract for the customs farm was renewed: the lord deputy paid the same rent as before (£15,500); of the additional profit—exceeding the rent—he was to retain one-quarter; one-eighth was to go to his friend, Sir George Radcliffe; and all the rest to the king, as Mountnorris and Sir Arthur Ingram no longer had a share in the farm.

However, Wentworth's actions were severely criticized by some in England. Clare, the father of his second wife, called his proceedings against Mountnorris 'blouddy, and

tyrannicall' and found his behaviour all too 'Prince like in every particular' (Clare to Lord Haughton, 1 Feb 1636, *Letters of John Holles*, 3.477). Clare had no real influence at court but many members of the king's entourage shared his sentiments. In the past English courtiers had considered it as no less than natural that they could benefit from 'cast up in Ireland whereby so many are enriched' (earl of Ancram to Wentworth, 22 Dec 1635, Wentworth Woodhouse muniments, Strafford papers, 8, fol. 365r). But Wentworth was adamant in thwarting the suits of even those nearest to the king when he felt that his own long-term plans, the crown's revenues, or his own profits were threatened. Even the earl of Arundel, the influential earl marshal, had to abandon his plans to claim extensive estates in counties Waterford, Carlow, and Kilkenny, which had allegedly belonged to his and his wife's ancestors. Wentworth roundly rejected his claims, taking the side of the local magnate, the earl of Ormond, whose property in co. Kilkenny was threatened by Arundel's attempts to acquire land. It must, however, have been particularly galling for Arundel that Ormond passed Idough, one of the lordships he had claimed himself, on to the Irish master of the rolls, Christopher Wandesford, in 1636. Wandesford was Wentworth's close friend and a member of the small coterie of Englishmen—often from Yorkshire—who had accompanied him to Ireland, a group which included Wentworth's brother George and Sir George Radcliffe. Arundel did not forget this incident, and during Wentworth's impeachment—over which Arundel presided as lord steward—the use of force against landowners in co. Kilkenny in the course of the new plantation provided the prosecution with valuable material (article 15 of the impeachment). Arundel was not the only English or Scottish courtier who found that Irish grants had become much more difficult to obtain than in the past. Others such as the marquess of Hamilton fared no better. Secretary Coke, the earl of Carlisle, and the duke of Lennox were among the few courtiers who managed to co-operate successfully with the deputy in pursuit of their interests in Ireland.

Perhaps Wentworth's reluctance to oblige courtiers by supporting their suits for grants in Ireland would have made him less unpopular if he had not made such a vast fortune in office himself. At the end of the 1630s he derived a profit of about £8700 per annum from the Irish customs farm alone. His overall income can be estimated at about £23,000, of which £6000 came from his estates in Yorkshire, largely lands he had inherited or bought in the 1620s. A further £5500 was the annual rent of his lands in Ireland, all of which he had acquired after his appointment as lord deputy, exploiting the opportunities his office offered for purchases on favourable terms. Moreover, before the collapse of the personal rule, Wentworth was in a position further to increase his income. In January 1638 a monopoly for the sale of tobacco was created for Ireland (parallel to a similar project for England). Wentworth farmed this monopoly himself for an annual payment of £7000 to the crown; a rival offer by the marquess of Hamilton had been rejected by Charles I, who furthermore allowed Wentworth to use money from the Irish exchequer to the tune of £40,000 to build up a stock of tobacco. It is unlikely that Wentworth derived any profit from this monopoly before the meeting of the Long Parliament, although there were unsubstantiated rumours that he had already made £100,000 from it. Under more favourable circumstances he could have expected an additional annual income of at least £2000 for his share of the farm.

Ireland and the Scottish crisis The years 1636–7 mark the high point of Wentworth's authority and success in Ireland, although later events revealed that the basis of this success was by no means stable. Even in 1637 political decisions taken at court which he was unable to control threatened to undo everything he had achieved. In the early months of 1637 it seemed as if Charles I, in alliance with France, would enter into a war against Spain. For Ireland the consequences of such a decision would have been disastrous as it would have forced Wentworth to make concessions—in particular to the Old English—which were incompatible with his own political objectives. In March in a long memorandum the deputy warned Charles against a warlike policy. He feared that a war could be financed in England only by resorting to extreme measures which would destroy the political consensus he apparently still saw as the ultimate objective. A war would:

> necessarily put the King into all the high ways possible else will he not be able to subsist under the charge of it, and if those fail the next but be the sacrificing those that have been his ministers therein. (Wentworth to Laud, 3 April 1637, *Strafforde's Letters*, 2.66)

This—in retrospect prophetic—remark clearly shows that he was still as strongly opposed to the 'high ways' a war would provoke as ten years earlier, despite the undeniable change in his stance on other issues.

At the same time, however, Wentworth tried to establish closer contacts with members of the anti-Spanish and pro-French faction at court, who were close to the queen, probably realizing that the influence of his principal ally and friend at court, Archbishop Laud, would probably decline should Charles enter into an open alliance with France. Wentworth welcomed the earl of Northumberland's appointment as lord high admiral in February 1638 and also established connections with Northumberland's brother-in-law, the earl of Leicester, who was known to be no great friend of Laud's ecclesiastical policy. Leicester hoped to succeed Wentworth in Ireland, should he return to England. Northumberland's sister Lucy, widow of the earl of Carlisle, one of Wentworth's old allies at court, was among his closest friends, and helped to establish these contacts. Wentworth greatly admired Lady Carlisle for her beauty and charm. A few months before his death he said of her that: 'a nobler nor more intelligent friendship did I never meet with in all my life' (Whitaker, 221). Thus personal affection to some extent formed the basis of a possible political co-operation with members of the pro-French faction at court.

In spite of his attempts to forge new alliances at court

the crisis in Scotland, which assumed ever more menacing dimensions in 1638, threatened to undermine Wentworth's position in Ireland and his support in England. The king's master of the horse, the marquess of Hamilton, one of the few courtiers with any influence in Scotland, now emerged as a key figure at Whitehall. Wentworth mistrusted Hamilton, as he increasingly did almost all Scotsmen, and he and the marquess were also at odds over a number of the latter's projects in Ireland. Having already outmanoeuvred Hamilton over the Irish tobacco monopoly, Wentworth also opposed the marquess's attempt to gain control of the lands of the Londonderry plantation, forfeited in 1635 and surrendered to the crown in 1637. Desperately in need of cash, Charles looked for a syndicate which would farm the plantation at the highest rent possible. One offer for the land came from Randal MacDonnell, earl of Antrim, and his associates, and was backed by Hamilton. Antrim was a grandson of the last earl of Tyrone and a Catholic, but was also married to the duke of Buckingham's widow, Katherine. Hamilton himself had married one of the duke's nieces and closely co-operated with Antrim, who professed himself to be Hamilton's client. Wentworth, who wanted to become the principal farmer for the plantation lands himself, argued that Antrim, as an Irish Catholic, would eject the protestant English settlers living in co. Londonderry and replace them with native Irishmen. Antrim's and Hamilton's intentions are not quite clear, but they certainly considered extending the leases only of the smallholders (of whom many were native Irish) while replacing the more substantial landholders with new tenants. Wentworth also opposed another bid for the plantation lands which came from some of the wealthier existing tenants themselves. These were represented by Sir John Clotworthy, the son of an English soldier–adventurer settled in Ulster, but himself a presbyterian in sympathy with the covenanters and a man who had close connections with Wentworth's enemies in England, in particular the earl of Holland. Clotworthy, who was related by marriage to John Pym, was later to play a considerable part in the impeachment proceedings against Wentworth. For the time being the king rejected all offers made for the plantation lands—including Wentworth's own—and decided to administer the estates for his own account.

However, the future of the Londonderry plantation was not the only problem Wentworth had to confront in 1638. While unrest spread from Scotland to Ulster, where the Scottish settlers, mostly presbyterians, sympathized with the covenanters, the earl of Antrim submitted a proposal to the king in the summer of 1638 to attack the covenanters in Scotland with an army recruited primarily among his own clan in Ulster and Scotland. The MacDonnells or MacDonalds (as they were called in Scotland) still maintained a foothold in the western highlands and in the isles. While Antrim could rely on Hamilton's support at court, Wentworth systematically obstructed and sabotaged the earl's preparations for the campaign in western Scotland. The deputy did not believe that Antrim could realize his ambitious military plans; the earl had in fact almost no ready cash to spend, and it would therefore have been the task of the Irish exchequer to finance and equip his army, a prospect Wentworth did not relish. Moreover, Wentworth pointed out that the very proposal to recruit an army of Irish Catholics in Ulster was politically highly explosive, all the more so as Antrim originally envisaged appointing professional Irish soldiers who had served abroad and fought for Spain as officers, men like his cousins Owen Roe O'Neill and Daniel O'Neill, who were both later to play a considerable role in the Ulster rising of 1641. Nevertheless, Antrim's potential ability to gain support in Scotland may have been greater than Wentworth was prepared to admit. After months of hesitation Charles I finally ordered the deputy to support the earl in April 1639. However, by now it was definitely too late and the MacDonnells were unable to attack before the pacification of Berwick in June 1639.

Wentworth himself had been busy strengthening and enlarging the army in Ireland. The major part of the army was now stationed in Ulster to increase the pressure on the Scots settled there. In May 1639 they were required formally to abjure the covenant. The so-called 'black oath', administered to all adults of Scottish descent in Ulster in 1639, did nothing to endear Wentworth, who had already acquired a reputation as one of their most inveterate enemies, to either the presbyterian Scots in Ireland or their kinsmen in Scotland itself.

The king's chief councillor However, Wentworth's very radicalism, which now became ever more apparent, recommended him to the king as chief councillor when Charles realized that the very foundations of his monarchy were about to crumble in the summer of 1639. At this moment of despair Charles I, who in spite of the support he gave him had never unreservedly trusted Wentworth in the past, turned to the lord deputy and asked him to return to England. Wentworth received Charles's letter, written in his own hand and delivered by the bishop of Raphoe, on 5 August 1639. Wentworth arrived in England late in September and became a member of the important war council in December. Two months earlier the privy council had dismissed an appeal which the Irish chancellor, Lord Loftus, who was involved in a long-standing judicial feud with the lord deputy, had launched against a sentence of the Dublin court of castle chamber. Loftus now lost his office and was replaced by a candidate of Wentworth's choosing, Sir Richard Bolton. In January 1640 Wentworth was elevated to the position of lord lieutenant of Ireland, which allowed him to govern the country during his absence through a deputy, and on 12 January he was created an earl, taking the title of Strafford. He was also created baron of Raby. Raby Castle was owned by Sir Henry Vane, who became Sir John Coke's successor as one of the two secretaries of state in February, so by taking this particular title Strafford insulted one of the most important members of the privy council at the very moment of his greatest personal triumph—a personal slight which Vane never forgave.

Strafford, who had managed parliament in Ireland so successfully in 1634–5, was confident that this success could be repeated and that with parliamentary support he would be able to mobilize an army in Ireland which would considerably strengthen the king's hand in a renewed confrontation with the Scottish covenanters. Moreover, the support Strafford expected to receive from the Irish parliament was to serve as an example for parliament in England, which he advised the king to summon as soon as possible. He clearly underestimated the resentment against the policies of the personal rule and, as someone from the north of England, perhaps still saw the Scots as England's natural enemies, thereby overestimating the popular support for a national war against Scotland. In any case, Strafford's own ability to guide the king's policy during these crucial months was considerably diminished by his failing health. Recurrent attacks of gout, dysentery, and other health problems almost crippled him. Nevertheless he returned to Ireland in March to preside over the session of the Irish parliament which had met on 16 March. The two houses granted four subsidies of £45,000 each, but considerable pressure and intimidation was necessary to achieve this result. The money was to finance a new Irish army of 9000 men, recruited over the coming months and transported from Ulster to Scotland at the end of June. As opposed to the army already in existence, this new force consisted mostly of Catholic soldiers, although the great majority of the officers were protestant. Some among the handful of junior officers who were Catholics, however, played an important part in the rising of 1641. Strafford, who had vehemently rejected the earl of Antrim's plans for a Catholic army in 1638–9, now pursued a very similar policy himself. The new army was not ready for action until the end of July, and even then means of transport were lacking, so it could not intervene in the second bishops' war. Its very existence did, however, greatly increase fears in England that the king might use force against open or passive resistance to his policies— and, even more dramatically, fears that there might be a popish conspiracy against England's liberties and established religion. Strafford did little to deny rumours that the new Catholic army might be employed in England as well as Scotland, although this was clearly not the plan of action in the summer of 1640.

The Irish parliament was prorogued on 31 March and Strafford immediately returned to England, where the Short Parliament assembled on 15 April. Due to his failing health the lord lieutenant did not arrive in London until three days later. When Charles's attempt to persuade parliament to finance a renewed war effort against the covenanters ran into difficulties Strafford advised the king to mobilize the Lords against those who rejected his demands in the Commons. However, he also spoke out in favour of a conciliatory attitude towards the Commons. Apparently he thought it best for the king to abandon ship money without an express demand for adequate financial compensation, on the assumption that the Commons would eventually grant supply once their mood had improved. Strafford's counsel was adopted by the privy council only in modified form, but on his insistence it advised the king to content himself with a grant of eight subsidies by the Commons in exchange for ship money. When Secretary Vane nevertheless insisted in parliament on twelve subsidies, negotiations broke down. In the council meeting early on the morning of 5 May, Strafford, like other members of the council, advised the king to dissolve parliament. When the eight members of the Scottish committee met after the dissolution on the same day, Strafford seems to have taken an even more extreme line, although the reliability of the records for this debate remains controversial. However, he clearly advised the king to pursue an offensive war against Scotland, convinced that Scotland's military strength was a mere façade and that 'the quiet of England will hold out long'. He thought that now parliament had refused supply, Charles was 'absolved from all rules of government', and was entitled to raise money to finance the war by the authority of his prerogative alone (Russell, *Fall*, 126). According to the existing record Strafford also said 'you have an army in Ireland you may employ here to reduce this kingdom' (ibid., 127). The immediate context of the debate makes it more than likely that 'this kingdom' referred to Scotland, all the more so as at this time Strafford clearly did not anticipate any open resistance in England.

The lord lieutenant hoped that Spain could be persuaded to support Charles financially and entered into negotiations with the Spanish ambassadors. But Spanish power and financial solvency had reached its nadir in 1640 and nothing came of this. In July it was still envisaged that Strafford would take command of the Irish army, and on 3 August the king appointed him captain-general of the army which he was to lead into Scotland. Nevertheless, his patent also empowered him to suppress any sedition in Ireland, England, or Wales, should this prove necessary. In Ireland itself the situation was becoming increasingly critical as Strafford's friend Wandesford, who governed the kingdom as lord deputy in his absence, was confronted by an ever stronger and seemingly united opposition of Catholics and protestants. Strafford might have been able to quash this opposition, but he had to abandon his plans to go to Ireland, as Northumberland, the official commander of the king's forces in northern England, had fallen ill. As Northumberland's lieutenant-general, Strafford belatedly tried to create an army out of the scattered, ill-armed, unpaid, and demoralized troops which had been hastily recruited to fight against the Scots. In no condition to command an army, because of his failing health, not to mention his lack of military experience, he arrived in York on 26 August but soon recognized that the situation was utterly desperate. Indeed, he could do nothing to avert the impending catastrophe. After the battle of Newburn his authority declined rapidly and his attempts to steer the deliberations of the great council of peers which met on 24 September were largely futile, in spite of his hopes of renewing the war effort against the Scots. There were signs that he no longer enjoyed the king's wholehearted support. Many peers—both courtiers and lords who had been out of favour with Charles during the 1630s—held him responsible for the disastrous policies the king had pursued after the pacification of Berwick.

Black Tom Tyrant as popular pamphlets called him was to foot the bill not only for these more recent political miscalculations but for all the mistakes and sins Charles I had committed over the past ten years.

Impeachment and attainder When parliament met on 3 November 1640 Strafford preferred to stay with the army in Yorkshire. He was clearly aware that he risked impeachment should he go to London. In spite of the king's defeat and his own political isolation he was not yet seen as a spent force but rather as the only man capable of tipping the scales and regaining the political initiative on the king's behalf. It was assumed, not without justification, that he was prepared to use force against his opponents, relying on the new Irish army still waiting beyond St George's Channel and the remnants of the king's army in Yorkshire. It was known that in the face of defeat his political outlook had become ever more radical and it was expected that he would not hesitate to have those he considered disloyal tried for treason, if given a chance to do so. Such assumptions explain the enormous hostility to him and the fear and hatred which his very name evoked. Moreover the Scottish covenanters, who saw him as their most dangerous enemy, wanted him out of the way. All the same Charles I, who now had few councillors he could rely on, asked Strafford to join him in London. The earl obeyed, very much aware of the danger awaiting him but too proud to reject the challenge to confront his enemies and perhaps also afraid that he would lose the vast fortune he had amassed in the king's service should he flee abroad.

Arriving in London on 10 November Strafford proposed to accuse the members of either house who had invited the Scots into England of high treason. Nevertheless, when he took his seat in the Lords on the 11th he did not raise the issue of the pro-Scottish party in England. He left, having remained silent. His enemies, led by John Pym, alarmed by his presence in London, were therefore able to pre-empt the charges he might bring against them. On the same day a committee of the Commons accused him of high treason and impeached him before the Lords. When Strafford hurriedly returned from Whitehall to the House of Lords he was arrested and committed to the gentleman usher of the black rod. It was not until 25 November, when the Commons had assembled a list of preliminary charges against him, that he was sent to the Tower. The Commons took a considerable time to draw up a complete catalogue of charges, and the trial in the House of Lords did not open until 22 March.

The impeachment obviously raised a number of complicated legal and constitutional issues. The traditional definition of treason enshrined in medieval and Tudor statutes made it difficult to consider treasonable actions which were not crimes against the king's person. Strafford's prosecutors could to some extent circumvent this problem by arguing that a councillor who advised the king to subvert the fundamental laws of the kingdom created a division between the monarch and the people and thereby undermined the very foundations of his rule. Strafford's actions were depicted not so much as actions against an impersonal state but against the legal order on which the king's rule was founded and therefore against his natural person—inseparable from the legal order which constituted his kingship—as well as against his body politic. Whatever the theoretical plausibility of such an argument, in practice it was not easy to sustain against a man who visibly still enjoyed the king's support. Even more serious than these legal problems was the difficulty of actually proving that Strafford had committed crimes which subverted the established legal order. The majority of the more serious charges against him related to his period of office in Ireland. The prosecution had been provided with abundant material by those who had suffered under his government, in particular the New English office-holders and planters. Nevertheless for the charges to stick it had to be assumed that the same legal rules were valid in Ireland as in England, and that the mere thought that Ireland was a 'conquered nation' inferior in status to England (article 3) constituted treason. Such an argument may have been popular with the Dublin parliament but was much less so with the English House of Lords. Although it could be shown that Strafford's rule in Ireland had often been high-handed and arbitrary, he could demonstrate that earlier chief governors had ruled the kingdom with similar methods, admittedly mostly at times more turbulent than the 1630s. However, even the charge that he had used soldiers to collect revenues for the crown, to confiscate property and to enforce his orders in peacetime, thereby 'levying war' against the king's subjects (article 15), lost some of its impact when the frequent use of military force and martial law in Ireland in the past was taken into account. More serious, however, was the charge that he had advised Charles I to use the Irish army against his English subjects on 5 May 1640, the day of the dissolution of the Short Parliament. On the other hand this accusation was supported only by the testimony of a single witness, Sir Henry Vane, the secretary of state. The other members of the Scottish committee of the privy council in which Strafford was said to have given the allegedly treasonable advice either could not remember the relevant sentence, or were convinced that the lord lieutenant had meant Scotland when he had spoken of 'this kingdom' against which the army should be sent.

With enormous skill and great courage Strafford took apart most of the charges raised against him. He demonstrated that he was still the outstanding and charismatic orator who had dominated the House of Commons in 1628. He argued that if his opponents were allowed to create a new, unprecedented kind of treason out of individual actions which in themselves were at most misdemeanours, no man holding office could any longer feel safe. However, with the impeachment proceedings likely to collapse, Strafford's opponents changed their tactics. On 10 April the Commons decided to proceed by bill of attainder. Thus an act of legislation would declare Strafford's behaviour treasonable and at the same time condemn him to death. Clearly the stakes were now so high that it seemed impossible to abandon the attempt to have Strafford condemned. Moreover, less prominent members of

the Commons seem to have feared that their leaders would come to some sort of fudged compromise with the king which would enable Charles to regain the upper hand politically, if Strafford was spared. The Commons passed the bill of attainder on 21 April by a majority of 204 to 59 votes. However, at the time the pressure on Strafford's supporters had already become very intense; the 'Straffordians', whose names were published soon after the division, were threatened by angry crowds, and feared for their lives. Although the Lords, who had come to resent the Commons' behaviour, had at first proceeded with the trial against the earl as if the bill of attainder had not been passed by the lower house, they were now exposed to the same popular pressure which had already intimidated many members of the other house. On 1 May the king appealed in person to the Lords not to condemn his former minister to death, stressing also—much too late—that he would never again employ him in his service. But at the same time he declared that he would never consent to a bill of attainder. He therefore offered an escape route to all peers who did not want to see Strafford executed but who were afraid to vote against the bill, for without the king's consent the bill could not become law. Charles committed a second mistake by sending soldiers to the Tower on 2 May to free Strafford, an attempt which failed. This incident, together with news about a much more wide-ranging plot to bring armed force to bear against parliament, created enormous excitement verging on hysteria in London. Strafford now released the king from his promise given in a letter on 23 April that he would save his servant's life, come what may. Strafford's letter to the king, which showed him willing to sacrifice himself, might have been used for a last appeal to the peers to show him mercy, but Charles failed to exploit this chance. On 7 May the Lords passed the bill in a thinly attended house. In all likelihood the majority in the crucial division was only 26 to 19, although some reports record a majority of 51 to 9 for the ultimate vote, when the matter of fact had already been decided. Fearing for the security of his family and for his crown, the king gave his assent to the bill of attainder on 10 May. When he heard of Charles's decision Strafford, in spite of his earlier willingness to lay down his life for the king, is reported to have remarked, 'put not your trust in princes' (Wedgwood, 380). He was executed by beheading (he was spared the traditional punishment for treason, to be hanged, drawn, and quartered) on the morning of 12 May 1641 on Tower Hill, facing death with great calm and courage. His body was later buried at Wentworth Woodhouse.

Strafford's death was greeted with jubilation by the London crowds, and at the time was probably mourned by only a handful of close friends, including Archbishop Laud who was himself a prisoner in the Tower. Nevertheless, far from solving the political crisis which threatened monarchy and parliament alike, it made any lasting political settlement almost impossible, for the king could never forgive those who had forced him to abandon one of his most faithful servants.

Historical reputation Strafford was a controversial figure in his own lifetime and remained so after his death. A poem, probably written by John Cleveland shortly after Strafford's execution, stated:

> he lived and died here in a mist
> A Papist and a Calvinist
> …
> The people's violent love and hate.
> (*Poems of John Cleveland*, 66)

In Ireland he was almost universally unpopular at the time of his fall. The Catholics were not alone in seeing him as a great oppressor who, shortly after his arrival in Dublin, 'began to play rex' and had behaved like a Turkish 'Bashaw' (Clarke, 'Discourse', 167, 169). In England, on the other hand, royalists naturally considered him a martyr of their cause, although the judgement of his character which *Eikon basilike* gave in the king's name remained ambiguous, depicting Strafford as a man whose overweening self-confidence was likely 'to betray him to great Errors' (*Eikon basilike*, 5–6). Clarendon to some extent shared this assessment of Strafford's personality as flawed, 'a nature too elate and arrogant of itself' (Clarendon, *Hist. rebellion*, 1.341), while David Lloyd, who devoted the first chapter of his *Memoires* to Strafford as the 'Protomartyr for Religion and Allegiance', was less reserved in his praise (Lloyd, 20).

Whereas Nalson's *Impartial Collection* gave an account of Strafford's trial in the Restoration period which was intended to clear him of all charges raised against him, Rushworth documented the arguments of the prosecution as extensively as the lord lieutenant's own defence. The publication of Wentworth's letters by Knowler in the eighteenth century was an important landmark, but was highly selective, as Knowler's patron, the first marquess of Rockingham, Strafford's great-grandson, wanted to restore his ancestor's reputation by the edition. It nevertheless provided the essential foundation for all later historical works on Strafford's political life until the second half of the twentieth century. In his *History of England* David Hume came to the conclusion that Strafford's execution was an act of judicial murder, as his conduct in office was 'innocent, and even laudable' (Hume, 5.312). The prevailing liberal mood of the nineteenth century, however, was not favourable to Strafford's historical reputation. Macaulay called him 'a man of great valour and capacity, but licentious, faithless, corrupt, and cruel' (Macaulay, 1.119), though he was impressed by the force of the personality so vividly captured in Van Dyck's portraits of the lord lieutenant. Strafford's tragic end appealed to the romantic imagination of nineteenth-century authors, even to seemingly sober academic historians like S. R. Gardiner. For Gardiner, Wentworth's real tragedy lay in the fact that his political ideals were remnants of a bygone era: 'he attempted to maintain the Elizabethan constitution, long after it was possible to maintain it, and when the only choice lay between absolute government, and Parliamentarian supremacy' (Gardiner, *History*, 9.370).

In the first half of the twentieth century the decline of classical liberalism as a dominant political force and the increasing sympathy for authoritarian forms of government noticeable even in Britain gave rise to a more positive assessment of Strafford's personality and policies. Hugh O'Grady's *Strafford and Ireland* (1923) offered a very detailed, though clearly partisan, account of his period as lord deputy. He depicted Strafford as a great and high-minded reformer, whose downfall was brought about by narrow-minded proponents of 'particular interests' and the forces of sectarian fanaticism which did much more harm to Irish national interests by appealing to the English parliament against him than Strafford had ever done. The three biographies published in the 1930s by Lady Burghclere (1931), Lord Birkenhead (1938), and C. V. Wedgwood (1935) all showed a great deal of sympathy for Strafford. He emerged as a heroic though not necessarily flawless figure. The most scholarly and influential of the three is that by Wedgwood. It was reissued in a second edition in 1961, when Strafford's unpublished correspondence had finally become accessible, and has in its revised form remained the standard account of his life. However, the period after the Second World War witnessed a much more critical assessment of Strafford's personality. The fact that the Strafford papers could now be consulted, rather than the misleadingly selective edition of his letters by Knowler, revealed the less high-minded side of his character. Both Terence Ranger and Hugh Kearney exposed the ruthlessness and, as they thought, hypocrisy of his actions as lord deputy in Ireland, holding him responsible for the crisis which led to the outbreak of rebellion in 1641, an account which has only recently been qualified or contradicted by other historians.

Conclusion No complete reassessment of Strafford's personality and policies has emerged during the past decades, but historians looking for a politician who in his opinions and actions embodies Charles I's alleged political agenda as an absolutist ruler still see him as the man best qualified to play this role. However, these historians face the same problem as their nineteenth-century predecessors or, indeed, the men who brought Strafford to trial in parliament in 1640–41. Being absent from London, Strafford's influence on the politics of the personal rule in England before the autumn of 1639 was very limited. Although his ruthlessness and autocratic cast of mind were already visible during his period of office as lord president of the north, this was arguably more a matter of political style than of principle. Matters were certainly different in Ireland, but given the traditions of English government there he was no exception in employing ruthless methods, often with scant regard for legal niceties, to achieve his objectives. What distinguished his policy from that of earlier governors was primarily his determination to attack the vested interests of the protestant officeholders and settlers just as radically as those of the Catholic landowners. Although he clearly took great pride in his achievements as lord deputy, there is no real evidence that Strafford really believed that Ireland could serve as a model for England—Scotland was potentially a different matter—unless extraordinary circumstances totally changed the traditional framework of government in

England. Strafford's fate was determined by the fact that he returned from Ireland under exactly such extraordinary circumstances, when Charles I was fighting a war in which his political survival was at stake and which could, it seemed, be won only by desperate means. Strafford was prepared to resolve this crisis with the same ruthlessness which he had shown in Ireland, but it is unlikely that he would have pursued a similar course of action had he returned to England under less extreme circumstances. In fact, until the very end parliament remained a natural part of the political order Strafford tried to uphold. He was indeed convinced that parliaments could and needed to be 'managed', and should not attempt to give direction to government policy, but at least the latter conviction was no more than a traditional view shared by many contemporaries.

Looking at Strafford's correspondence from the 1630s one encounters an autocratic ideal of government and high-sounding denunciations of meddlesome common lawyers, but in the last resort his political apprenticeship in Yorkshire offers a more important key for understanding his personality and political position than the ideal of absolutism to which he allegedly subscribed. He began his political life in the poisonous atmosphere of faction-ridden Yorkshire county politics where to win political battles court connections were exploited just as ruthlessly as opportunities to appeal to popular sentiment against one's opponents. Early on he himself became the victim of public humiliations and attacks. Once in office he remained prone to pursuing personal vendettas against real or suspected enemies, a pattern that persisted in Ireland. Moreover, he was singularly incapable of understanding the convictions of men who did not share his own political outlook, be they Irish Catholics or radical English protestants who saw the pope's hand in every setback they suffered. Rejecting the comprehensive anti-popery so widespread among strict protestants at the time, he saw English puritans or Scottish presbyterians primarily as rebels against the established order in church and state. Being obsessed even more than other members of the early seventeenth-century gentry and peerage with status, honour, and the defence of the traditional social hierarchy, the 'Puritan popular humour' (letter to Radcliffe, 5 Nov 1640, Whitaker, 219) was clearly anathema to him, not so much, it seems, for theological or religious but for political reasons.

Strafford was a man who played many parts in his life, most of them as a truly accomplished actor, who, depending on the stage he was acting on, unreservedly identified himself with his role: 'honest patriot' and defender of the subject's liberties; conscientious office-holder and autocratic governor of a country half-province, half-colony; potential favourite and leading minister relentlessly in search of personal advancement and profit; and, finally, his last role—as the allegedly 'evil councillor' sacrificed to atone for his master's misguided policies and as a man who after defending himself with great courage and skill against his enemies stoically faced the inevitable. Some of these roles he chose and devised himself, others he found

ready-made, or accepted because political circumstances and social conventions forced him to do so. Perhaps the twenty-first century is better qualified to understand such a complex personality than earlier periods of history, which tended to believe in the ideal of the autonomous individual inspired in his actions by a consistent set of values and principles. Yet in the end Strafford's life, in spite of the many roles he played, had a greater consistency than many of his enemies or later critics were prepared to admit.   RONALD G. ASCH

Sources G. Radcliffe, *The earl of Strafforde's letters and dispatches, with an essay towards his life*, ed. W. Knowler, 2 vols. (1739) • C.V. Wedgwood, *Thomas Wentworth, first earl of Strafford, 1593–1641: a revaluation* (1961); repr. (1964) • J. P. Cooper, ed., *Wentworth papers, 1597–1628*, CS, 4th ser., 12 (1973) • *DNB* • J. F. Merritt, ed., *The political world of Thomas Wentworth, earl of Strafford, 1621–1641* (1996) • H. Kearney, *Strafford in Ireland, 1633–41: a study in absolutism*, 2nd edn (1989) • Strafford papers, Sheff. Arch., Wentworth Woodhouse muniments • R. C. Johnson and others, eds., *Proceedings in parliament, 1628*, 6 vols. (1977–83) • J. Watts, 'Thomas Wentworth, earl of Strafford', *Statesmen and politicians of the Stuart age*, ed. T. Eustace (1985), 83–114 • R. G. Asch, *Der Hof Karls I. von England: Politik, Provinz und Patronage, 1625–1640* (1993) • P. J. S. Little, 'Family and faction: the Irish nobility and the English court, 1632–42', MLitt diss., TCD, 1992 • state papers domestic, Charles I, PRO, SP 16 • S. P. Salt, 'Sir Thomas Wentworth and the parliamentary representation of Yorkshire, 1614–1628', *Northern History*, 16 (1980), 130–68 • T. Clavin, 'Court, faction and government in Ireland: the high politics of Wentworth's deputyship of Ireland, c.1631–1636', MA diss., University College Dublin, 1999 • state papers Ireland, Elizabeth I to George III, PRO, SP 63 • J. P. Cooper, 'The fortune of Thomas Wentworth, earl of Strafford', *Land, men and beliefs: studies in early-modern history*, ed. G. E. Aylmer and J. S. Morrill (1983), 148–75 • P. Little, 'The earl of Cork and the fall of Strafford, 1638–41', *HJ*, 39 (1996), 619–35 • HLRO, Braye papers • report of commission on Ireland, 1623, BL, Add. MS 4756 • P. Zagorin, 'Sir Edward Stanhope's advice to Thomas Wentworth', *HJ*, 7 (1964), 298–320 • *The Fortescue papers*, ed. S. R. Gardiner, CS, new ser., 1 (1871) • *The Lismore papers*, ed. A. B. Grosart, 10 vols. in 2 series (privately printed, London, 1886–8) • papers relating to Strafford's impeachment, BL, Harley MS 2233 • M. Jansson and W. B. Bidwell, eds., *Proceedings in parliament, 1625* (1987) • P. Yorke [earl of Hardwicke], ed., *Miscellaneous state papers, 1501–1726*, 2 vols. (1778) • H. O'Grady, *Strafford and Ireland: the history of his vice-royalty with an account of his trial*, 2 vols. (1923) • J. T. Cliffe, *The Yorkshire gentry from the Reformation to the civil war* (1969) • D. Edwards, 'The poisoned chalice: the Ormond inheritance, sectarian division and the emergence of James Butler, 1614–1642', *The dukes of Ormond, 1610–1745*, ed. T. Barnard and J. Fenton (2000), 55–82 • B. Fitzpatrick, *Seventeenth-century Ireland: the war of religions* (1988) • T. W. Moody and others, eds., *A new history of Ireland, 3: Early modern Ireland, 1534–1691* (1976) • *The poems of John Cleveland*, ed. B. Morris and E. Withington (1967) • Clarendon, *Hist. rebellion* • GEC, *Baronetage* • *Letters of John Holles, 1587–1637*, ed. P. R. Seddon, 3 vols., Thoroton Society Record Series, 31, 35–6 (1975–86) • T. B. Macaulay, 'John Hampden', *Critical and historical essays*, 2 vols. (1907), vol. 1, pp. 102–49 • D. Hume, *The history of England from the invasion of Julius Caesar to the revolution in 1688*, new edn, 8 vols. (1778); repr. in 6 vols. (1983–5) • D. Lloyd, *Memoires of the lives ... of those ... personages that suffered ... for the protestant religion* (1668) • S. R. Gardiner, *History of England from the accession of James I to the outbreak of the civil war*, 10 vols. (1883–4) • J. P. Kenyon, ed., *The Stuart constitution: documents and commentary*, 2nd edn (1986) • D. A. Orr, 'Sovereignty, state, and the law of treason in England, 1641–1649', PhD diss., U. Cam., 1997 • F. Pogson, 'Making and maintaining political alliances during the personal rule of Charles I: Wentworth's associations with Laud and Cottington', *History*, new ser., 84 (1999), 52–73 • C. Russell, 'The theory of treason in the trial of Strafford', *EngHR*, 80 (1965), 30–50 •

P. Zagorin, 'Did Strafford change sides?', *EngHR*, 101 (1986), 150–63 · state papers domestic, James I, PRO, SP 14 · Ormonde–Wentworth correspondence, Bodl. Oxf., MS Carte 66; material relating to Wentworth's deputyship, MS Carte 176 · Irish letter-books, PRO, SO 1, signet office · W. Notestein, F. H. Relf, and H. Simpson, eds., *Commons debates, 1621,* 7 vols. (1935) · F. W. F. Smith, earl of Birkenhead, *Strafford* (1938) · T. O. Ranger, 'Strafford in Ireland: a revaluation', *Past and Present,* 19 (1961), 26–47 · W. R. Stacy, 'Matter of fact, matter of law, and the attainder of the earl of Strafford', *American Journal of Legal History,* 29 (1985), 323–47 · J. D. McCafferty, 'John Bramhall and the reconstruction of the Church of Ireland, 1633–1641', PhD diss., U. Cam., 1996 · J. P. Cooper, 'Strafford and the Byrnes' county', *Land, men and beliefs: studies in early-modern history,* ed. G. E. Aylmer and J. S. Morrill (1983), 176–91 · NA Scot., Hamilton papers and Hamilton papers [uncatalogued], GD 406 · *The works of the most reverend father in God, William Laud,* ed. J. Bliss and W. Scott, 7 vols. (1847–60) · A. Clarke, ed., 'A discourse between two councillors of state, the one of England, and the other of Ireland (1642)', *Analecta Hibernica,* 26 (1970), 161–75 · C. Russell, *The fall of the British monarchies, 1637–1642* (1991) · L. J. Reeve, *Charles I and the road to personal rule* (1989) · M. Perceval-Maxwell, 'Strafford, the Ulster Scots and the covenanters', *Irish Historical Studies,* 18 (1972–3), 524–51 · corresp., NL Ire., Ormonde papers, 2304–2306 · miscellanea, Staffs. RO [narration of proceedings against Strafford] · J. Rushworth, *The tryall of Thomas earl of Strafford* (1680) · GEC, *Peerage* · J. H. Timmis, *Thine is the kingdom: the trial for treason of Thomas Wentworth, earl of Strafford* (1974) · A. Clarke, 'Sir Piers Crosby, 1590–1646: Wentworth's "tawney ribbon"', *Irish Historical Studies,* 26 (1988–9), 142–60 · correspondence, N. Yorks. CRO, Milnes family papers (Lady Milnes-Coates) · T. Comber, *Memoirs of the life and death of the lord deputy Wandesforde* (1778) · N. Canny, *The upstart earl: a study of the social and mental world of Richard Boyle, first earl of Cork, 1566–1643* (1982) · A. Clarke, *The Old English in Ireland, 1625–1642* (1966) · M. C. Fissel, *The bishops' wars: Charles I's campaigns against Scotland, 1638–1640* (1994) · A. Fletcher, *The outbreak of the English civil war* (1981) · J. H. Ohlmeyer, *Civil war and Restoration in the three Stuart kingdoms: the career of Randal MacDonnell, marquis of Antrim, 1609–1683* (1993) · M. Perceval-Maxwell, *The outbreak of the Irish rebellion of 1641* (1994) · W. P. Kelly, 'The early career of James Butler, twelfth earl and first duke of Ormond (1610–1688), 1610–1643', PhD diss., U. Cam., 1997 · Cambs. AS, Huntingdon, Montagu papers · Charles I, *Eikon basilike* (1649) · *The autobiography and correspondence of Sir Simonds D'Ewes,* ed. J. O. Halliwell, 2 vols. (1845) · CKS, Foulis papers · T. D. Whitaker, ed., *The life and original correspondence of Sir George Radcliffe* (1810) · W. Gardner, Lady Burghclere, *Strafford* (1931) · N. Canny, *From Reformation to Restoration: Ireland, 1534–1660* (1987)

Archives NRA, priv. coll., letters from him to his wife · Sheff. Arch., corresp., letter-books, and papers | BL, papers relating to his impeachment, Harley MS 2233 · BL, report of commission on Ireland 1623, Add. MS 4756 · Bodl. Oxf., corresp. Ormond–Wentworth, MS Carte 66 · Bodl. Oxf., material relating to Wentworth's deputyship, MS Carte 176 · Cambs. AS, copy of trial proceedings · CKS, papers relating to his trial and his dealings with Foulis family · HLRO, Braye papers, material relating to his impeachment · N. Yorks. CRO, Milnes family papers (Lady Milnes-Coates), corresp. between Wentworth and his wife · NA Scot., Hamilton papers and Hamilton papers, GD 406 · NL Ire., Ormonde papers, corresp., 2304–2306 · PRO, signet office, 'Irish' letter-books, SO 1 · PRO, state papers domestic, Charles I, SP 16 · PRO, state papers domestic, James I, SP 14 · PRO, state papers Ireland, Elizabeth I to George III, SP 63 · Staffs. RO, MS narration of proceedings against Strafford

Likenesses oils, type of *c.*1632–1633 (after A. Van Dyck), Rockingham Castle, Northamptonshire, NPG; version, NPG · A. Van Dyck, double portrait, oils, type of *c.*1636 (with P. Mainwaring), priv. coll. · A. Van Dyck, oils, *c.*1636, Petworth House, Sussex [*see illus.*] · oils, type of *c.*1636 (after A. Van Dyck), Euston Hall, Suffolk · W. Hollar, etching, 1641, BM, NPG · A. Browne, mezzotint, pubd *c.*1684 (after A. Van Dyck), BM, NPG · T. Rawlins, gold medal, BM ·

A. Van Dyck, oils, second version (of portrait, Petworth House), NPG · miniature, NPG

Wealth at death approx. £22,800 p.a. in 1639; financial affairs in disarray in 1641: *Land, men, and beliefs,* ed. Aylmer and Morrill, 171

Wentworth, Thomas, fifth Baron Wentworth (*bap.* **1613,** *d.* **1665**), royalist army officer, was baptized at Toddington, Bedfordshire, on 12 February 1613, the eldest son of Thomas *Wentworth, fourth Baron Wentworth (1591–1667), and his first wife, Anne Crofts (*d.* 1638). He was made a knight of the bath at the coronation of Charles I on 1 February 1626; upon the elevation of his father as earl of Cleveland four days later he was styled Lord Wentworth. In 1631 he was at The Hague, attending the court of Elizabeth of Bohemia. Back in England, in May 1635 he fought a duel with Thomas Weston, son of Lord Treasurer Portland. The following year he fought another duel, with Lord 'Beny'; for this and for intemperate words reported by the lord chamberlain he found himself in the Tower of London briefly in the summer of 1636. He and his father joined the king's army during the first bishops' war in 1639 and accompanied him to Berwick in October of the following year. Notwithstanding he was returned to the Commons in both the Short and Long parliaments, and was formally translated to the upper house on 25 November 1640 in his father's barony of Wentworth.

At the outset of the civil war Wentworth was with George Goring in Portsmouth, but after the fall of that garrison he joined the king's main field army, and as Lord Wentworth raised a company of dragoons. He fought at Marlborough, Wiltshire, in December, and at Cirencester, Gloucestershire, on 2 February 1643 he became major-general of dragoons, in succession to Sir Arthur Aston. In the early part of the civil war dragoons formed a substantial part of the mounted arm, although merely infantry-men set on ponies and other small horses initially regarded as unsuitable for cavalry troopers. As the war progressed, however, standards dropped and with all riding horses, irrespective of size or condition, going to the cavalry, dragoons dwindled in both numbers and importance. All too often they simply discarded their muskets and started calling themselves troopers. Consequently Wentworth followed suit and on 5 February 1644 succeeded Sir Thomas Byron as colonel of the Prince of Wales's regiment of horse. At Cropredy Bridge he commanded a cavalry brigade with such good effect that he was afterwards appointed major-general of horse in succession to Lord Wilmot, when the latter was dismissed before the battle of Lostwithiel. However, on 14 November 1644 he relinquished this post in order to join Lord Goring's army in the west country. After Goring's defeat at Langport and subsequent dismissal Wentworth was appointed major-general of horse under the western army's new commander, Lord Hopton. Unfortunately Hopton, whose reputation owes more to his very readable memoirs than to his overrated abilities, was soon on bad terms with Wentworth and contrived to get himself badly beaten at Torrington on 14 March 1646. As a result the already demoralized western army surrendered soon afterwards, but Wentworth escaped with Prince Charles first to the Isles of Scilly and then to Jersey.

In 1649 Wentworth accompanied Charles to Paris and in the following year both he and his father, the earl of Cleveland, sailed with him to Scotland. Charles was compelled to subscribe to the covenant as a condition of being recognized as king, but many of his followers neglected to do so. Despite the defeat of the Scots army at Dunbar on 3 September 1650 both Wentworth and his father were as non-subscribers accordingly ordered out of the country on 17 October, but like the earl of Forth and other prominent royalists they ignored this edict and subsequently fought at Worcester on 3 September 1651. Although his father was afterwards captured Wentworth got safely away and until the Restoration in 1660 attended Charles II's émigré court. In 1656 he was responsible for organizing and commanding a regiment of foot guards, which served with the Spanish army at the battle of the Dunes in June 1658. There is some doubt as to whether he fought there, but after the Restoration he brought the regiment home to England and it became the 1st foot guards (afterwards the Grenadier Guards). He had married by mid-March 1658 Philadelphia Carey (d. 1696), daughter of Sir Ferdinando Carey; their only child, Henrietta Maria *Wentworth, was born on 11 August 1660. Wentworth died on 1 March 1665 and was buried six days later at Toddington. He predeceased his father by two years. His daughter succeeded to the barony upon the latter's death. STUART REID

Sources GEC, *Peerage* · P. R. Newman, *Royalist officers in England and Wales, 1642–1660: a biographical dictionary* (1981) · S. Reid, *All the king's armies: a military history of the English civil war* (1998) · *DNB*
Likenesses oils, 1640, repro. in F. W. Hamilton, *The origin and history of the first or grenadier guards*, 3 vols. (1874); in possession of H. R. Clifton, Clifton Hall, Nottingham, 1899
Wealth at death estate heavily encumbered; however, widow left legacies totalling more than £12,000 in 1696

Wentworth, Thomas, first earl of Strafford (1672–1739), diplomatist and army officer, the second son and surviving heir of Sir William Wentworth (d. 1692) of Northgate Head, Wakefield, Yorkshire, and the grandnephew of Thomas Wentworth, the minister of Charles I, was born at Stanley Hall, near Wakefield, and baptized on 17 September 1672. His father was the son of William Wentworth of Ashby Puerorum, Lincolnshire, who died at Marston Moor, and his mother, Isabella (c.1653–1733), the daughter of Sir Allen Apsley, the treasurer of the household of James, duke of York. Isabella, who gave birth to four girls and five boys, served as lady of the bedchamber to James II's queen, Mary of Modena.

His mother's position helped secure Wentworth's appointment as page of honour to the queen consort in 1687. The next year he switched allegiances and careers; he followed his brother into the military service of William III and served as cornet (31 December 1688) in the expedition against Lord Dundee. His bravery during the Nine Years' War, particularly at the battles of Steenkerke (1692) and Landen (1693) and at the siege of Namur (1695), secured his appointment as aide-de-camp to the king in

August 1692, promotion to guidon and major in the first troop of Life Guards (4 October 1693), cornet, first major (20 January 1694), groom of the bedchamber (6 May 1695–8 March 1702), and colonel of the Royal regiment of dragoons (30 May 1697 – June 1715). After 1697 he served in the military only intermittently, although he was later promoted brigadier of the horse (7 January 1703), major-general (1 January 1704), and lieutenant-general (1 January 1707). He served under Marlborough in Flanders in 1702, and during one skirmish had his horse shot from under him. In 1706 he narrowly escaped being captured by the French while on a foray near Menin. The loss of three brothers in war did not diminish his enthusiasm; his elder brother, William, died in 1693 from a fever contracted while on guard duty, and his two younger brothers, Paul and Allen, were killed in action respectively at the siege of Namur in 1695 and in the storming of Liège in 1702.

Wentworth was always importuning the court for some honour or promotion. Upon hearing the news of his elder brother's death, he immediately rode to Breda to request his sibling's former position but arrived too late. The need to secure his fortune may partially account for his unabashed self-seeking. On 16 October 1695, on the death of his cousin William, earl of Strafford, Wentworth succeeded to the peerage as fourth baronet and third Baron Raby. Although he inherited the title, the earl had bequeathed most of his estates to his nephew Thomas Watson, the son of Lord Rockingham.

A courageous man, Raby enjoyed the challenge of battle and claimed to have 'often repented the hour I left the army' (Raby to Marlborough, 8 March 1710, BL, Blenheim MSS, M37, Berlin), and later regretted 'being in inaction when all the world is in arms' (Raby to Cadogan, 16 Feb 1709, BL, Add. MS 22196, fol. 181). His physical courage was unquestionable, as illustrated by his having singly attacked a wild boar while hunting which nearly killed him. Although he left the army to embark on a diplomatic career, at least one contemporary thought that he carried that spirit into the antechamber of the court and 'rushed an enterprize like a colonel of dragoons' (Roussel, 1.284).

Raby's diplomatic career began when he accompanied the duke of Portland to Paris in 1698. In March 1701 William III dispatched him to Berlin to convey his congratulations to the elector Frederick III of Brandenburg on the latter's becoming king in Prussia as Frederick I. The success of that mission led to his appointment in 1703 as envoy and in 1706 as ambassador-extraordinary to Brandenburg-Prussia, where he served until April 1711. His suspicions that John Churchill, duke of Marlborough, was circumventing him at Berlin, first through Friedrich Wilhelm von Grumbkow, who served as liaison officer to Marlborough and to Dutch officials during the War of the Spanish Succession (1702–13), and later through special emissaries such as General Francis Palmes, were not unfounded. Raby became increasingly jealous of Marlborough's authority, and relations between the two men deteriorated. Their estrangement undermined Raby's position at court and aggravated the difficulties inherent in his position. Marlborough's remark that Raby was 'both impertinent and insignificant' (Marlborough to F. Godolphin, 31 May 1709, BL, Add. MS 9105, fol. 60) was coloured by that rivalry.

Despite Marlborough's assessment, Raby was shrewd enough to understand the political and personal maze of intrigues at the Berlin court and to exploit them in order to secure Prussian troops for the coalition against France. However, his alliance with the prime minister, Johann Kasimir Kolbe, Graf von Wartenberg, and his liaison with the countess of Wartenberg, the mistress *en titre* of the king, intertwined his fate with that faction. He must also have been a man of some charm, for he won over not only the countess but also Frederick and his queen, Sophie Charlotte. Raby was a tall, well built, good-looking man; both Kneller and D'Agar depicted him with large eyes, an aquiline nose, and full lips in an oval face. Punctilious in most things, he was well suited to the court of Berlin, where Frederick sought to endow his newly established kingship with the magnificence and etiquette found in Paris. Unkindly dubbed 'le singe de Louis XIV', the ape of Louis XIV, Frederick, a weak and indecisive man, was crippled by a sense of fatalism, an ingrained timidity, and a capacity for self-delusion. Enmeshed in the great power rivalry, he often found his options limited. In this environment Raby could play a key role. Certainly a man who sought to guide rather than be guided, he bombarded the secretary of state with long letters. He so fiercely defended Prussian interests that he laid himself open to the criticism that he was a 'Prussian because of the liberty I have several times taken of giving my poor advice of what is to be done' (Raby to Marlborough, 4 Feb 1710, BL, Add. MS 9108, fols. 41–2).

Over time Raby's influence was threatened at court in part because of the king's increasing dissatisfaction with the allies, but also because of the ministerial intrigues, his equivocal relations with the countess of Wartenberg and her own unpopularity, and the enmity of powerful individuals. Raby's friendship with the king saved him from being recalled in 1706 and sent to Vienna as English envoy. This position would have meant a loss of station for Raby, who had been promoted to ambassador at Berlin. A fiscal crisis in Berlin coupled with overwhelming evidence of fraud and embezzlement led to the dismissal of Wartenberg in 1711. Uncomfortable with the changing power alignment at court, Raby welcomed his appointment in March of that year as ambassador-extraordinary and plenipotentiary to the states general of the United Provinces, where he served until 1714. Even St John, the secretary of state, felt constrained to apologize for the choice: 'You will find him to be the best we could at present send you', he confided to his agent John Drummond (*Letters and Correspondence*, 1.52–3). St John acknowledged Raby's weaknesses, especially his 'warmth' but noted that the queen had promised him the appointment (ibid.).

On 6 September 1711 Raby married Anne (*d.* 1754), the only daughter and heir of Sir Henry Johnson of Bradenham, Buckinghamshire, a wealthy shipbuilder with estates in Suffolk and Bedfordshire. She brought with her a substantial fortune, and the marriage produced three

daughters, Anne, Lucy, and Henrietta, and a son, William (1722–1791). In the same year as his marriage Raby was sworn of the privy council (14 June) and created Viscount Wentworth of Wentworth-Woodhouse and of Stainborough and earl of Strafford (29 June). He became elder brother of Trinity House on 3 September 1712 and master thereof on 1 June 1713. He served as first lord of the Admiralty (30 September 1713 until September 1714 for which he received a £2000 bonus on his salary) and as one of the lords justices (1 August until 18 September 1714). On 25 October 1714 he was created a knight of the Garter. Strafford's seemingly unbridled ambition coupled with his hauteur antagonized many. Jonathan Swift described him as having 'some life and spirit; but … infinitely proud and wholly illiterate' (Swift, 2.489). These qualities did not serve him well at The Hague. He was instructed to maintain the illusion of Anglo-Dutch co-operation and at the same time to insist that the Dutch should fulfil their obligations to the coalition. A pretence of co-operation with the Dutch was necessary in order to allow the tories to extract the best possible terms from France and to ensure that the Dutch did not conclude a separate peace. By no means partial to the Dutch, Strafford often angered them by his hectoring and tactlessness. The Dutch in turn reviled him. On occasion his windows were smashed and the tories denounced as disguised papists. Undoubtedly he was not as popular as his predecessor, Charles, Viscount Townshend, because Strafford helped coerce the Dutch into signing a new barrier treaty (1713), which created an artificial military frontier in the Southern Netherlands. This agreement, however, represented a significant reduction from that of 1709. Strafford, who argued that 'We have been the dupes of the Warr and must take great Care that We are not so of the Peace …' (Strafford to St John, 2 June 1711, BL, Add. MS 31135, fol. 388), did not hesitate to threaten that the British would conclude a separate peace.

On 23 December 1711 Strafford was appointed ambassador-extraordinary and second plenipotentiary to the Utrecht peace congress jointly with John Robinson, bishop of Bristol, lord privy seal, the first plenipotentiary. Most of the important issues were handled in London or Paris rather than Utrecht. Strafford was often not told of certain concessions that had already been given; he was not informed of the secret Anglo-French negotiations or of all the details of the London preliminaries. Still, he could intermittently influence the negotiations; he ensured that Tournai was not ceded to France and that Upper Guelders went to Prussia.

In May 1712 Strafford was called back to London, and on his return to The Hague personally delivered the suspension of arms to James Butler, second duke of Ormond, captain-general of the British forces in Flanders. These orders enjoined Ormond not to co-operate in any siege or battle with Prince Eugene, commander of the imperial forces, and meant Britain's abandonment of her allies. Ormond's withdrawal of 12,000 British troops from the allied army left it vulnerable to the manoeuvres of the

French. Although in July 1712 he referred to the allies as 'new enemies' (Herman, 117), Strafford, along with Robinson, ignored orders in March 1713 to sign separately with France. Because he wanted the peace to be a general one he delayed the signing until many of the allies' demands were met.

Although he always contended that he was 'of neither party called wig or Tory' (Strafford to W. Cadogan, 16 Feb 1709, BL, Add. MS 22196, fol. 184), Strafford's participation in the peace earned him the vilification of the whigs. After the death of Queen Anne in August 1714 and the accession of George I, he was criticized for abandoning Britain's allies and formally recalled from The Hague, although he did not leave his post until December. In January 1715 the privy council requested that he turn over his official papers on the Utrecht negotiations. The whig-dominated committee of secrecy examined them and voted to impeach not only Strafford but also Harley, St John, and James Butler, duke of Ormond. Ultimately the six articles of impeachment against Strafford charged that he had been instrumental in promoting 'separate, dishonorable, and destructive negotiations' and that he had 'prostituted the honour of her majesty … and grossly violated her powers and instructions'. Strafford professed his innocence and contended that he had always acted with 'the utmost integrity' and claimed that he was 'totally ignorant of any treacherous correspondence with the emissaries of France' (State trials, 15.1014-44). Although the House of Commons was not convinced by his defence, Strafford was never prosecuted. Still, many shared the view of Lord John Hervey that Strafford 'had the double honour of being a very dirty executor of a very dirty errand' (Herman, 201). He was specifically excluded from the Act of Grace granted by George in 1717 and never held another office.

Strafford then turned to the Jacobites and corresponded with the Pretender, who appointed him commander-in-chief of the Jacobite forces north of the Humber and bestowed on him the title duke of Strafford (5 June 1722). He still spoke in the House of Lords, alternately exasperating and amusing his colleagues. Lord Hervey described him in 1735 as a:

> loquacious, rich, illiterate, cold, tedious, constant haranguer in the House of Lords, who spoke neither sense nor English … in short there was nothing so low as his dialect except his understanding, nor anything so tiresome as his public harangues except his private conversation. (Hervey, 2.148-9)

In 1737 Strafford admitted that he 'was bad with the last ministry, worse with this, and he did not doubt but he should be worse with the next should he ever see another; therefore as an unbiased man, he gave his vote for the king' (DNB). After his retirement from public life Strafford devoted himself to his estates in Yorkshire and his family. His correspondence reveals a deep affection for his family and their myriad pets. He died 'of the stone' at Wentworth Castle on 15 November 1739 and was buried on 2 December in Toddington, Bedfordshire. He was survived by his wife, who died on 19 September 1754. When his son, William, died without an heir, the titles passed by special remainder to Frederick Thomas Wentworth (1732–1799), the second earl's cousin and the grandson of Peter Wentworth (d. 1739), brother of the first earl. When he died without an heir, the earldom was temporarily extinct.

LINDA FREY and MARSHA FREY

Sources The Wentworth papers, 1705-1739, ed. J. J. Cartwright (1883) · L. Frey and M. Frey, Frederick I: the man and his times (1984) · L. Frey, M. Frey, and J. C. Rule, eds., Observations from The Hague and Utrecht: William Harrison's letters to Henry Watkins, 1711-1712 (1979) · L. Frey and M. Frey, eds., The treaties of the War of the Spanish Succession: an historical and critical dictionary (1995) · State trials · 'Committee of secrecy appointed to examine papers relating to the late negotiations of peace and commerce', JHC, 18 (1714-18), 290-94 · DNB · Letters and correspondence, public and private, of the Right Honourable Henry St John, Lord Viscount Bolingbroke, ed. G. Parke, 2 vols. (1798) · W. S. Churchill, Marlborough: his life and times, 6 vols. (New York, 1933-8) · R. Geikie and I. A. Montgomery, The Dutch barrier, 1705-1719 (1930); repr. (1968) · D. Coombs, The conduct of the Dutch: British opinion and the Dutch alliance during the War of the Spanish Succession (1958) · O. Weber, Der Friede von Utrecht (1891) · M. C. Herman, 'Sir Thomas Wentworth, third earl of Strafford, and the treaty of Utrecht', PhD diss., University of South Carolina, 1988 · A. Legrelle, La diplomatie française et la succession d'Espagne (1892) · F. Salomon, Geschichte des letzen Ministeriums Königin Annas von England (1710-1714) und der englischen Thronfolgefrage (1894) · M. R. Roussel, marquis de Courcy, La coalition de 1701 contre France, 2 vols. (1886) · The letters and dispatches of John Churchill, first duke of Marlborough, from 1702 to 1712, ed. G. Murray, 5 vols. (1845) · J. Swift, Journal to Stella, ed. H. Williams, 2 vols. (1948) · GEC, Peerage · J. Hervey, Memoirs of the reign of George the Second, ed. J. W. Croker, 2 vols. (1848)

Archives BL, corresp. and MSS, Add. MSS 22192-22267, 31128-31152 · Sheff. Arch., Vernon-Wentworth muniments and Leader collection · Sheff. Arch., miscellaneous MSS | BL, Blenheim MSS, corresp., M33-M37, C2-C3 [provisionally catalogued] · BL, corresp. with Charles Whitworth, Add. MSS 37350-37381 · BL, corresp. with Lord Orrery, Add. MS 37209 · BL, corresp. with Lord Lexington, Add. MSS 46543-46547 · BL, corresp. with Robert Bruce, Add. MS 63467 · BL, corresp. with Robert Harley, loan 29 · Bodl. Oxf., Rawlinson MSS, MSS relating to the Treaty of Utrecht, A.285 · Bodl. Oxf., corresp. with Adam Cardonnel, MS Eng. lett c. 291 · Central Public Library, Sheffield, Stainborough letters, MSS, and prints, 1700-1770 · CKS, corresp. with Alexander Stanhope · CKS, letters to James Stanhope · Nationaal Archief, The Hague, Archief Staten Generaal · Nationaal Archief, The Hague, Archief Antonie Heinsius · PRO, State Papers, Prussia, 90, vols. 2 and 3 · PRO, Foreign Entry books, SP 104, vols. 51-2, Prussia · W. Sussex RO, letters to Marquess of Huntly · Zentrales Staatsarchiv, Dienstelle, Merseburg, Repertorium 11, England

Likenesses P. C. Leygebe, oils, 1711, Gov. Art Coll. · C. D'Agar, oils, c.1712, Palace of Westminster, London · G. Kneller, oils, 1714, Hunt. L. · G. Vertue, line engraving, 1714 (after G. Kneller), BM, NPG; repro. in W. Knowler, The earl of Strafford's letters and dispatches (1739) · G. Hamilton, group portrait, oils, 1732, National Gallery of Canada, Ottawa · J. M. Rysbrack, terracotta statuette, c.1740, V&A

Wealth at death see will, 22 June 1732, Sheff. Arch.

Wentworth, William (bap. 1616, d. 1697). See under Wentworth, Sir John, first baronet (1737–1820).

Wentworth, William Charles (1790-1872), politician and landowner in Australia, was born on 13 August 1790 on board the Surprize, in harbour at Cascade Bay, Norfolk Island, Pacific Ocean, eldest son of D'Arcy *Wentworth

William Charles Wentworth (1790–1872), by unknown photographer

(1762–1827), a surgeon from Portadown, co. Armagh, and his mistress, Catherine Crowley (1772–1800), a felon.

Early life and education The family went to Sydney in 1796 and thence to Parramatta, where they settled. Catherine Crowley died in 1800. Late in 1802 Wentworth was sent with his brother D'Arcy to England, where they were educated from 1803 at the Revd Mr Midgley's school at Bletchley. From 1805 to 1809 Wentworth attended Dr Alexander Crombie's institution at Greenwich. Having abandoned ideas of becoming a naval midshipman or a cadet in the East India Company, Wentworth embarked for New South Wales in October 1809, rather at a loss as to his future. A familiar figure in Sydney, he was tall and broad, and wore his auburn hair like a mane. He could speak with a brilliance that befitted a scion of the whig aristocracy and seemed something of a Gulliver in Lilliput. And yet his features were coarse, his appearance was untidy, his gait was clumsy, and his language at times resembled that of a convict brat. In October 1811 Governor Lachlan Macquarie appointed him acting provost-marshal and in 1812 Wentworth established his estate, Vermont, on a grant of 1750 acres by the Nepean River. Knowing that a number of the free immigrants (the 'exclusives') wanted to exclude former convicts (the 'emancipists') from positions of trust

and influence in the colony, he set out to become more powerful than those who had slighted his family.

In May 1813 Wentworth accompanied William Lawson and Gregory Blaxland in the first great feat of inland exploration, the crossing of the Blue Mountains. The discovery enabled pastoral expansion, and Wentworth was rewarded with a further 1000 acres. To help his father secure valuable sandalwood from a Pacific island, he joined a schooner as supercargo in 1814. He was nearly killed by natives at Rarotonga while courageously attempting to save a sailor whom they clubbed to death. Wentworth helped to bring the ship safely to Sydney. If much of what he did was stamped with majesty, he could none the less be mean and underhand. In 1816 a scroll of satirical verse was found in the streets of Sydney. It lampooned the lieutenant-governor, Colonel George Molle, not least for being Macquarie's secret enemy. Protracted enquiries revealed that Wentworth had composed the lines before departing for London in March.

To prepare himself to be 'the instrument of procuring a free constitution for my country', Wentworth entered the Middle Temple in February 1817. For a time he was characteristically restless. He petitioned the Colonial Office to allow him to explore Australia, but was told that his services were not required. He spent over a year in Europe, chiefly in Paris, where he roistered by night and squandered his money. In 1819 he published *A Statistical, Historical, and Political Description of the Colony of New South Wales*. His hopes of marrying John Macarthur's daughter Elizabeth came to nothing. Then Henry Grey Bennet MP declared in his *Letter to Lord Sidmouth* (1819) that D'Arcy Wentworth had been sent to Sydney as a convict. Cut to the quick, Wentworth challenged Bennet to a duel and later rebuked Commissioner John Thomas Bigge for repeating the libel in his report on the state of the colony; but his pride had suffered a shock, and he more resolutely identified himself with the emancipists' cause.

Wentworth's book was reissued in revised and enlarged editions in 1820 and 1824. In proposing reforms for New South Wales, he pressed for a nominated legislative council and an assembly elected on a small property franchise; former convicts were to be denied neither membership nor the vote. No taxation should be imposed without parliamentary sanction. There should be trial by jury and free immigration. Yet the book was no tract for democracy. Landed property was 'the only standard', he conceived, 'by which the right either of electing, or being elected, can in any country be properly regulated'. The council bore 'many resemblances to the House of Lords': it formed a 'just equipoise between the democratic and supreme powers of the state', and was 'necessary not less to repress the licentiousness of the one, than to curb the tyranny of the other'.

After being called to the bar in February 1822, Wentworth entered Peterhouse, Cambridge, where he competed for the chancellor's gold medal for a poem on Australasia. His entry, placed second, speedily published and dedicated to Macquarie, ended with the hope that

Australasia, with flag unfurled, would become 'A new Britannia in another world'.

Return to Australia and entry into journalism Wentworth returned to Sydney in 1824, determined 'to hold no situation under government': 'As a mere private person I might lead the colony, but as a servant of the Governor I could only conform to his whims.' He had had some influence on the New South Wales Act of 1823, which instituted a nominated legislative council and permitted trial by jury in civil actions, when demanded by both parties. With Dr Robert Wardell, a lawyer who had edited the London newspaper *The Statesman*, he planned, in journalism and at the bar, to champion the emancipists and smaller free settlers, and to campaign for self-government, a free press, and trial by jury. Meanwhile, disputes and litigation flourished in the unsettled colony, and Wentworth and Wardell built up a lucrative practice.

On 14 October 1824 the first issue of their newspaper, *The Australian*, appeared. They had not sought permission to publish the paper, but Governor Brisbane thought it 'expedient to try the experiment of full latitude of freedom of the Press'. Despite Colonial Office objections, approval continued well into the reign of his successor. The exclusives bitterly prophesied a nation of freebooters and pirates, but could do nothing while *The Australian* retained Government House favour.

Wentworth pilloried the exclusives as the 'yellow snakes of the Colony' and awaited a pretext for attacking autocratic government. In October 1825 he reworded a farewell address to Brisbane, acknowledging his emancipist sympathies, and demanding the 'two fundamental principles of the British constitution': trial by jury and representative government. Then in November 1826—after a soldier, Joseph Sudds, convicted of felony, died after being put in irons and drummed out of his regiment on the orders of Governor Darling—Wentworth seized on the alleged illegality of Darling's act and, with violent invective, demanded his recall.

At a meeting on 26 January 1827, which resulted in a petition calling for an elective assembly of at least 100 members, Wentworth also called for trial by jury and taxation by consent. Convinced that the licentiousness of the press should be restrained by laws, Darling submitted two bills to the legislative council to regulate newspapers and impose a stamp duty. Chief Justice Forbes regarded the licence clauses as being 'repugnant to the laws of England' and refused to certify them. Wentworth vilified Darling, who then prosecuted the 'vulgar ill-bred fellow' for seditious libel. In his defence, Wentworth overwhelmed the lamentably weak crown prosecutors with torrents of invective and masterly arrangement of his facts. Darling wrote that Wentworth and Wardell kept 'the Court and the Bar by their effrontery and talent equally in subjection', but, largely as a result of Wentworth's insistent demands, the 1828 New South Wales Act allowed civilian juries in civil cases, on the application of either party and the approval of the Supreme Court. Wentworth prepared

articles of 'impeachment' against Darling but never followed them up. They did little damage to the governor's reputation at the Colonial Office, but they certainly undermined Wentworth's, so intemperate was their language. None the less, by taking up the fight against autocracy, and by his defence of the emancipists, Wentworth had awakened a political instinct among the people of Sydney and become their hero.

Wentworth and self-government The swelling tide of immigration lowered the proportion of former convicts in the population, and the exclusive–emancipist issue gradually receded into the background of politics. A larger fight remained—to achieve self-government. Changes in Wentworth's status and activities began to cause disillusion among many who only partially understood his aims. Bequests from his father had added substantially to his landholdings. On 26 October 1829, at St Phillip's Church, he married Sarah (1805–1880), the daughter of an emancipist blacksmith, Francis Cox. Their cottage at Vaucluse was rebuilt into a stately mansion. It was adorned with the trappings of the Old World and became a symbol of the new era that was coming to the rich in New South Wales. With his large legal earnings, Vaucluse, his father's estate at Homebush, and up to fifteen sheep- and cattle-stations, Wentworth increasingly considered himself the prototype of a new nobility, a governing class which would re-create in the Antipodes the way of life of the whig aristocracy of eighteenth-century England. His own way of life became spacious, even to the point of lapses from his marriage vows.

With Darling's successor, Richard Bourke, Wentworth had much in common, and in 1835 his name was on Bourke's list of possible legislative councillors. In London there was growing support for Wentworth's policies: the Reform Act and events in Canada fostered a climate of opinion favourable to constitutional change. At the foundation-day meeting in 1833 another petition for self-government was drafted, which Henry Bulwer presented to the House of Commons. In 1835 the Australian Patriotic Association was formed to agitate for an amended constitution. Wentworth was its vice-president; Bulwer and Charles Buller were employed as its agents in the Commons. With help from William Bland, who was his chief local supporter after Wardell's murder in 1834, Wentworth drafted two alternative bills for the consideration of the British government, and the second, considerably modified, formed the basis of the New South Wales Act of 1842 which granted a degree of representative government. In an enlarged legislative council two-thirds of the members would be elected, though the electors' property qualification was high enough to exclude two-thirds of the adult male population. The governor ceased to preside over the council and was replaced by an elected speaker.

As Wentworth's whiggism intensified, he increasingly identified political capacity with property and poverty with ignorance. He had given up his legal practice to concentrate on his landed interests. His wealth increased rapidly. The onset of middle age, his experience of the crowd, and the shift in the balance of population caused by assisted immigration all strengthened his conservatism. Lord John Russell's decision to abolish convict transportation to New South Wales in 1840 and to raise the price of crown land drew the exclusives and leading emancipists into united opposition to any change in the conditions allowing them cheap land and cheap labour. When Wentworth supported the idea of importing 'coolies' from Asia, he alienated many former supporters and was spurned by newly arrived radicals. In January 1842 *The Australian* summed up popular feeling: 'Mr Wentworth … first taught the natives of this colony what liberty was, but he has betrayed them.'

Gipps recommended Wentworth's appointment to the legislative council in April 1839, but was soon at enmity with him. In 1840 Wentworth and some associates bought from seven Maori chieftains, for a pittance, nearly one-third of New Zealand. Aghast, Gipps persuaded the council to block the scheme. It would have made Wentworth the greatest landowner on earth. In his frustration, he swore 'eternal vengeance'. Gipps withdrew his nomination to the council. The enmity between the two was to bedevil almost every issue until the governor left in 1846. Wentworth was elected to the legislative council in 1843 to represent Sydney. With his unrivalled knowledge of parliamentary procedure and colonial affairs, he led the council against Gipps. As an orator, he could marshal arguments brilliantly, but he relied little on subtlety or logic. He created a mood, and stormed rather than seduced the mind. Careless and even slovenly in manners and dress (he now wore corduroys with his badly fitting morning-coat), he knew his power and was unconsciously arrogant.

Wentworth led the squatters in their demands for new land regulations and the surrender to the legislative council of imperial control over crown lands. Seeking security of tenure so that they could improve their runs without fear of displacement, they waged unceasing war against Gipps's policies. They won most of their demands in the Imperial Act of 1846, which gave them security, for varying periods, in the 'settled', 'intermediate', and 'unsettled' districts, and they could thwart most would-be purchasers by buying key points on their runs, such as the land around waterholes. Henceforward the graziers could build spacious homesteads and develop the way of life of a landed, governing class. Because pastoral interests were strong in the partly elected council, Wentworth held a firm position there, but he was never again popular as he had been in 1831. In the 1848 election, despite the public outcry over the renewal of transportation, he again headed the Sydney poll, but in 1851—when his unpopularity stood at its height through his insistence on a preponderance of squatter-controlled rural representation over that of Sydney, and his opposition to a wide franchise and to the 'spirit of democracy abroad'—he came in third.

Wentworth's fury against unintelligent officialdom or military autocracy sprang from the same source as his distrust of mob rule: a hatred of anything which shackled the human spirit. He was no democrat and no leveller. Individuals must be free, but free to rise. The welfare of the community depended on men of substance. Like his father, he was a monopolist at heart. The realities of the Australian economy, combined with his whiggism, taught him that the landed interest was the one to which, as he told them in 1851, the inhabitants of Sydney 'were indebted for all their greatness, all the comforts, all the luxuries, that they possessed'. He told them, too, with no little courage, that he 'agreed with that ancient and venerable constitution which treated those who had no property as infants, or idiots, unfit to have any voice in the management of the State'. The way out of infancy, or idiocy, was through education.

Wentworth played a leading part with Robert Lowe (Viscount Sherbrooke) in establishing in 1848–9 the first real system of state primary education in New South Wales. The colony was on the brink of gaining responsible government, which, he argued, would be workable only through national education. He went on in 1849–50 to lead the movement that resulted in the founding of the first colonial university in the British empire, the University of Sydney. In his view, tertiary education should be open to all, regardless of religious denomination, and would serve two ends: 'to enlighten the mind, to refine the understanding, to elevate the soul of our fellow men'; and to train men to fill 'the high offices of state'. Wentworth helped to endow the university and was a member of its first senate.

When leading the opposition to Gipps in the legislative council, Wentworth had wanted to make ministers responsible to the elected representatives of the people, but he lost enthusiasm for this reform after Gipps's successor, Sir Charles FitzRoy, eased the friction between executive and legislature. Wentworth then turned to demands that the colony should control crown lands, official appointments, colonial revenue, and all local affairs. These demands, expressed in the remonstrances of 1850 and 1851, remained urgent when gold was discovered and the pastoral ascendancy seemed likely to be seriously threatened by 'pure democracy'. Although the Colonial Office finally agreed in 1852 that New South Wales should have responsible government, the council's select committee which drafted the constitution in 1853 provided only a limited form of individual responsibility for some members of the executive. With Wentworth as chairman, it recommended a lower house of fifty members elected on a £10 property franchise, and a nominated upper house consisting of members with hereditary titles. The rural bias of the proposed lower house and the idea of a peerage were vociferously opposed in Sydney, and despite Wentworth's vigorous defence, the bill, as eventually passed, provided for a nominated legislative council (shorn of the hereditary principle) and an elected legislative assembly. With Edward Deas Thomson, Wentworth sailed for England in 1854, and in July 1855 had the satisfaction of seeing the new constitution made law. The General Association for the Australian Colonies—which he formed in London in 1857 to induce the Colonial Office to inaugurate a federal parliament for Australia—died an early death.

Last years His life's work triumphantly achieved, Wentworth spent his remaining years in England, except for a brief return to Sydney in 1861–2, when he was prevailed upon to accept the presidency of the council. He had consolidated his fame more by staying away and being remembered for his great achievements than if he had returned, been drawn into the political fray, and tried to halt the democratic tide. In England he became a member of the Conservative Club and lived at Merly House, near Wimborne, Dorset. There he died on 20 March 1872, survived by his wife, five of their seven daughters, and two of their three sons. His estate was sworn for probate at £96,000 in Sydney and £70,000 in London. As he had wished, his body was taken to Sydney and, following a state funeral on 6 May 1873, was laid to rest in a vault on his estate at Vaucluse.

Wentworth was an heir to the whig tradition and a child of the Romantic movement. The chief intellectual influence upon him was Edmund Burke. Emotionally, however, he was Byronic. The subjection of his proud and romantic nature to the classical restraints of law and politics, though sometimes imperfectly achieved, increased rather than diminished his achievement. In his determination to secure for his own country those free institutions which in eighteenth-century England bore an aristocratic form, he may have regretted that their very freedom would allow them to become democratic, but their freedom meant more to him than their form. His love of Australia was, he confessed, the 'master passion' of his life. It is his chief claim to greatness that he played a significant part in securing in Australia, in one lifetime, that which he and other contemporaries revered as the fundamental liberties of the British constitution.

MICHAEL COLLINS PERSSE and JOHN RITCHIE

Sources Mitchell L., NSW, William Charles Wentworth MSS · Mitchell L., NSW, D'Arcy Wentworth MSS · *Historical records of Australia*, ser. 1, vols. 7–26; ser. 4, vol. 1 · A. C. V. Melbourne, *William Charles Wentworth* (1934) · C. M. H. Clark, *A history of Australia*, 1–4 (1962–78) · J. M. Ward, *James Macarthur* (1981) · C. Liston, *Sarah Wentworth, mistress of Vaucluse* (1988) · AusDB · B. H. Fletcher, *Ralph Darling* (1984)
Archives Mitchell L., NSW | Mitchell L., NSW, Bligh MSS · Mitchell L., NSW, Bourke MSS · Mitchell L., NSW, Brisbane MSS · Mitchell L., NSW, Darling MSS · Mitchell L., NSW, Gipps MSS · Mitchell L., NSW, King MSS · Mitchell L., NSW, Macquarie MSS
Likenesses T. Woolner, bronze medallion, c.1854, NPG · P. Tenerani, marble statue, 1861, University of Sydney, Australia · J. Allan, lithograph, Mitchell L., NSW; copy, Vaucluse House, Sydney, Australia · J. Anderson, oils, Mitchell L., NSW · R. Buckner, oils, Legislative Assembly, Sydney, Australia · oils, Parliament building, Sydney, Australia · photograph, State Library of Victoria, Melbourne, La Trobe picture collection [*see illus.*]
Wealth at death £96,000: probate sworn in Sydney according to AusDB, 2, p. 589, Sydney · under £70,000—in England: probate, 11 May 1872, CGPLA Eng. & Wales

Werburh [St Werburh, Werburgh, Werburga] (*d.* **700×07**), abbess, was the daughter of *Wulfhere, king of Mercia (*r.* 658–75), and of Eormenhild, daughter of *Eorcenberht (*d.* 664), king of Kent, and St *Seaxburh. Her career is the subject of a number of not wholly consistent traditions. According to the Worcester chronicle and to her life, Werburh early showed a disposition towards the religious life and after Wulfhere's death entered the monastery of Ely where her great-aunt Æthelthryth (*d.* 679) was abbess. Later she was recalled to Mercia by her uncle *Æthelred, Wulfhere's brother and successor, and given authority over the nunneries of his kingdom. She performed miracles while living on her father's estate at Weedon, in the later Northamptonshire, and died in her monastery of 'Triccengeham' (almost certainly Threekingham, Lincolnshire). After some dissension she was buried in accordance with her wishes in the monastery of Hanbury, in west Mercia, where nine years later her body was elevated at the command of her cousin, the Mercian King Ceolred (*r.* 709–16), and found to be miraculously uncorrupted. Her relics remained enshrined at Hanbury until the Danish invasions, shortly after which they were removed to Chester. By then the body had crumbled into dust.

A different tradition, first recorded in Old English writings from Kent and elaborated at Ely in the mid-twelfth century, alleges that Werburh succeeded her grandmother and mother as abbess in turn of Seaxburh's Kentish foundation of Sheppey and of Ely. Such a claim, however, is difficult to reconcile with the short space of time that elapsed between the deaths of Seaxburh (after 695) and Werburh herself (700×07). More dubious still are William of Malmesbury's assertion that the saint was a nun at Chester and the story linking her with Wulfhere's supposed sons, venerated at Stone.

Werburh's cult appears to have been promoted by Mercian kings both in their own homelands and in Kent; her origins made it an obvious vehicle for attempts to foster links between the two kingdoms. Later she was venerated at Ely where her maternal relatives were buried and where her life, traditionally attributed to Goscelin, was composed in the late eleventh century. From the tenth century, however, the main focus of her cult was Chester, where her remains were enshrined in the minster later known as St Werburgh's, probably at the command of Æthelflæd (*d.* 918), lady of the Mercians. The cult was especially active in the twelfth century after the refoundation of the minster as a Benedictine monastery in 1093. In addition to the saint's early feast day (3 March), a new commemoration, St Werburh 'in summer', was celebrated there on 21 June. In the earlier fourteenth century the saint was housed in an elegant shrine, and in the early sixteenth a life in English verse, based on local sources since lost, was composed by Henry Bradshaw, a monk of Chester.

Some thirteen medieval parish churches and two chapels were dedicated to the saint. They included several minsters in the Mercian heartlands, one in Kent, and an early church in London, perhaps reflecting the early promotion of the cult at major centres, ecclesiastical and urban, in the Mercian kingdom. Other dedications, such as those at Dublin and Bristol, were probably diffused from the cult centre in Chester.

At the Reformation, St Werburgh's Abbey became the

cathedral of the new see of Chester. The shrine, dismantled by 1635, was reconstructed in 1888 and placed behind the high altar of Chester Cathedral.   ALAN THACKER

Sources 'Vita sancti Werburgi', Acta sanctorum: Februarius, 1 (Antwerp, 1658), 386–90 · John of Worcester, Chron., vol. 2 · E. O. Blake, ed., Liber Eliensis, CS, 3rd ser., 92 (1962) · Willelmi Malmesbiriensis monachi de gestis pontificum Anglorum libri quinque, ed. N. E. S. A. Hamilton, Rolls Series, 52 (1870) · H. Bradshaw, The life of Saint Werburge of Chester, ed. C. Horstmann, EETS, 88 (1887) · D. W. Rollason, The Mildrith legend: a study in early medieval hagiography in England (1982) · A. T. Thacker, The origins and diffusion of a Mercian cult: the case of St Werburg [forthcoming] · VCH Cheshire, vol. 5 · lives of Sts Æthelthryth, Seaxburh, Eormenhild, and Werburh, CCC Cam., MS 393 · lives of Sts Seaxburh, Eormenhild, and Werburh, Trinity Cam., MS 0.2.1 · MS containing lives of Sts Seaxburh and Werburh, lections for feasts of Sts Seaxburh, Eormenhild, and Werburh, BL, Cotton MS Caligula A.viii

Werden, Sir John, first baronet (1640–1716), diplomat and politician, was born on 25 March 1640, the eldest son and heir of Robert *Werden (1621/2–1690), of Burton Hall, Cheshire, and his first wife, Jane Barnham. Werden entered the Middle Temple in 1653 and was called to the bar on 9 February 1660. He became baron of the exchequer for Cheshire in November 1664, but owed his fortunes to his father's close connections with James, duke of York. He joined the earl of Sandwich's flagship in 1665 as a volunteer, recommended by James, and was soon sent to Copenhagen to confirm a diplomatic arrangement. In 1666 he joined Sandwich's entourage on his embassy to Madrid, providing drawings of the approaches to Corunna for later naval use and other sketches of Spain which are preserved in Sandwich's journal. In November Sandwich sent him to Lisbon with unsuccessful proposals for a Portuguese truce with Spain, and he was left at Madrid as chargé d'affaires when Sandwich returned to England in July 1668.

In November 1669 Werden was sent to the Netherlands to instruct Sir William Temple to moderate his zeal for the triple alliance. He became envoy-extraordinary to Sweden in July 1670, and on his return two years later was appointed the duke of York's secretary and secretary to the Admiralty. He passed on the duke's instructions to naval commanders, and received their replies, arousing the ire of Prince Rupert, who preferred his captains to deal directly with James. Werden was granted a baronetcy on 28 November 1672, shortly after his marriage on 22 October to Lucy Osbourne (d. 1679), daughter of a Gloucestershire rector. He relinquished his Admiralty post when his patron had to resign in 1673, but continued as James's secretary and as commissioner for the navy, in which capacity he was admitted freeman of Portsmouth in 1675.

Werden was returned MP for Reigate on 31 January 1673 in the duke of York's interest; the election was declared void but he was immediately re-elected. He was reckoned a court dependent in Danby's lists of 1675 and 1678 and was moderately active, sitting on thirty-seven committees. He was denounced by Shaftesbury and in opposition propaganda as a supporter of popery, but was crucially named to the committee to investigate the Popish Plot,

where on 25 October 1678 he recorded Titus Oates's evidence in shorthand for his fellow MPs.

Werden was defeated at the first election of 1679, and accompanied James to Brussels as his secretary. In May 1681 his prestigious lodgings at the Stone Gallery in Whitehall were burgled. He was appointed a trustee to provide funds for Prince George of Denmark on his marriage to Princess Anne, and himself had a brief second marriage from about 1682 to Mary Osbourne, who died in August 1683. On James's accession he was returned unopposed as MP for Reigate; he also became commissioner for customs and in August 1687 a lieutenant for the City of London. He did not choose to try for parliament in autumn 1688 or oppose the revolution; James excluded him from those he was prepared to pardon.

Werden retained his post at the customs under William III, possibly through Sidney Godolphin's influence, but in June 1694 Somers successfully recommended his replacement in the remodelling of the commission, saying that although Godolphin had claimed 'he had experience, and was uncorrupt' (CSP dom., 1694–5, 179) his own intelligence indicated 'he does show great partiality in preferring officers who are disaffected to the Government'. In 1700 Werden unsuccessfully tried to become a commissioner for Irish forfeitures. He was restored to the customs commission in June 1703, remained in office throughout Anne's reign, and was finally removed in November 1714. He died on 29 October 1716, probably in his house in Pall Mall, and was buried at St Martin-in-the-Fields on 7 November, being succeeded by John, his son from his second marriage. His daughter Lucy married Charles Beauclerk, second duke of St Albans.   TIMOTHY VENNING

Sources GEC, Baronetage, 4.55 · BL, Harleian MS 2040 · Stowe MSS, BL, 200, 201, 210, 211 · CSP dom., 1664–95 · W. A. Shaw, ed., Calendar of treasury books, 7, PRO (1916); 10 (1935); 17–18 (1936–47); 21 (1952); 29 (1958–9) · Private correspondence and miscellaneous papers of Samuel Pepys, 1679–1703, ed. J. R. Tanner, 2 vols. (1926) · Seventh report, HMC, 6 (1879) · The manuscripts of the House of Lords, 4 vols., HMC, 17 (1887–94), vol. 2 · N. Luttrell, A brief historical relation of state affairs from September 1678 to April 1714, 3–5 (1857) · Foster, Alum. Oxon. · H. A. C. Sturgess, ed., Register of admissions to the Honourable Society of the Middle Temple, from the fifteenth century to the year 1944, 1 (1949) · J. L. Chester, ed., The marriage, baptismal, and burial registers of the collegiate church or abbey of St Peter, Westminster, Harleian Society, 10 (1876) · R. Anderson, ed., Third Dutch War, Naval Records Society, 86 (1946) · G. T. Forrest, The parish of St Margaret, Westminster, ed. M. H. Cox, 1, Survey of London, 10 (1926) · M. H. Cox and G. T. Forrest, The parish of St Margaret, Westminster, 3, Survey of London, 14 (1930) · G. Gater and W. Godfrey, The parish of St Martin-in-the-Fields, 2: The Strand, Survey of London, 18 (1937) · The parish of St James, Westminster, 1/2, Survey of London, 30 (1960) · Further correspondence of Samuel Pepys, 1662–1679, ed. J. R. Tanner (1929) · G. Hempson, J. P. Ferris, and B. D. Herring, 'Werden, Robert', HoP, Commons, 1660–90 · R. East, ed., Extracts from records in the possession of the municipal corporation of the borough of Portsmouth (1891) · F. R. Harris, The life of Edward Montagu … first earl of Sandwich, 2 vols. (1912) · R. Ollard, Cromwell's earl: a life of Edward Mountagu, 1st earl of Sandwich (1994) · Impartial Protestant Mercury (23–6 May 1681)

Archives BL, corresp. | BL, Stowe MSS, letters in capacity of duke of York's secretary, 200 (fols. 208, 344); 201 (fols. 268, 365); 210 (fol. 327); 211 (fol. 210) · PRO, other letters to Captain Hartgill, S. P. Dom. Carolus II 335, no. 87

Wealth at death house at Pall Mall, London; estate at 'Cholmeaton', Cheshire, and legacy to daughter (enough to purchase a house in the Strand, London): GEC, *Baronetage*; LCC, *Survey of London*, vol. 30, p. 547; LCC, *Survey of London*, vol. 18, p. 94n.

Werden, Robert (1621/2–1690), army officer, was the son of John Werden (d. 1646), attorney, of Chester, and his wife, Katherine, daughter of Edward Dutton, governor of Barbados. He was aged fifteen when he matriculated from Christ Church, Oxford, in 1637. Roger North described John Werden as 'an incomparable courtier, cavalier, and a most faithful servant in the royal family' (North, 374). Following his father's example, Werden was one of the most active royalists in Cheshire during the early 1640s, serving as colonel of a troop of horse under John Byron, first Baron Byron. He took part in the defence of Chester, but was wounded and taken prisoner at Christleton on 18 January 1645. His father assisted in the negotiations for the surrender of the town, and signed the articles of surrender on 3 February 1646. On 26 March John Werden begged to be permitted to compound for his delinquency. The commissioners for compounding accepted this application, and, although he had not come in within the prescribed terms, they only imposed on him the small fine of £600. When their sentence was confirmed by the House of Commons on 9 July, Robert was included in the composition, causing the Cheshire county committee to protest that Robert had caused 'general astonishment and terror to the whole country' (Green, 1154). Parliament, however, upheld the original decision and he was finally cleared by an ordinance of February 1647, by which time his father was dead. In 1648, however, his estates were again sequestered on the suspicion that he harboured treasonable designs, a fifth being allowed his wife for maintenance. They were discharged for a second time on 27 January 1652.

So far Werden had seemed a steadfast royalist, but there is evidence that from the mid-1650s he was playing a double game. In April 1655, in the aftermath of Penruddock's rising, during which he had been arrested, he told John Thurloe that he had offered the protectoral government his assistance before the rebellion. Later that year he asked for his decimation assessment to be waived in view of unspecified past services (Thurloe, 3.337, 4.315–16). Other members of the royalist underground were suspicious, and their doubts about him became all the stronger when he participated in the ill-fated uprising organized by Sir George Booth in August 1659. Werden was arrested and his estates sequestered for a third time. When, on his release, he joined the court in exile, Roger Whitley denounced him as the traitor who had betrayed their cause, but by March 1660 Charles II had accepted his professions of innocence. After the Restoration he sought a pardon for his erratic loyalties in the 1650s and gained the endorsement of Booth. The claims by Cromwell's spymaster Thomas Scott that Werden had tried to betray the king in 1651 and that he had indeed betrayed Booth in 1659 were ignored.

The doubts about his past loyalty failed to hamper him after 1660. The lands in Pembrokeshire belonging to the regicide Thomas Wogan were granted to him, and by 1661 he had become one of the duke of York's grooms of the bedchamber. This link with York then served to advance his military career. On 4 June 1665 he was appointed a lieutenant in York's regiment of guards. He was later promoted, becoming a major on 29 June 1667 and a lieutenant-colonel on 2 October 1672. On 10 February 1673 he was returned to parliament for Chester, retaining his seat until the dissolution in 1679. He sat again for this constituency in 1685. On 1 May 1678 he received the commission of brigadier of the horse, and in the summer served in Flanders against the Dutch. From 1675 he served as comptroller of York's household.

In 1685, in the reshuffle of his senior servants following his accession, James II rewarded Werden with the office of treasurer and receiver-general to the queen. Other appointments soon followed. On 19 June 1685 he was promoted to become the senior brigadier in the army, and on 31 July was appointed major-general. On 24 October he received the command of a regiment of horse (later the 4th dragoon guards), and on 8 November 1688 attained the rank of lieutenant-general. James's trust in him was well founded—until the king's flight in December 1688 Werden remained loyal to him.

Werden was twice married: first, before 1640, to Jane Barnham; secondly, before 1679, to Margaret Towse. By his first marriage he was the father of Sir John *Werden; Robert, a captain in the Royal Navy, who was killed fighting against the Dutch at Sole Bay on 28 May 1673 while in command of the *Henrietta*; and Katherine, who married Richard Watts of Muchmunden in Hertfordshire. Werden died on 23 January 1690. ANDREW BARCLAY

Sources G. Hampson, J. P. Ferris, and B. D. Henning, 'Werden, Robert', HoP, *Commons, 1660–90* · *CSP dom.*, 1655–88 · M. A. E. Green, ed., *Calendar of the proceedings of the committee for compounding …1643–1660*, 5 vols., PRO (1889–92) · Thurloe, *State papers*, vols. 3–4 · R. North, *The lives of … Francis North … Dudley North … and … John North*, ed. A. Jessopp, 3 (1890) · *Calendar of the Clarendon state papers preserved in the Bodleian Library*, 3: *1655–1657*, ed. W. D. Macray (1876); 4: *1657–1660*, ed. F. J. Routledge (1932); 5: *1660–1726*, ed. F. J. Routledge (1970) · R. H. Morris, *The siege of Chester, 1643–1646*, ed. P. H. Lawson (1924) · D. Underdown, *Royalist conspiracy in England, 1649–1660* (1960) · PRO, LR8/418 · J. Y. Akerman, ed., *Moneys received and paid for secret services of Charles II and James II from 30th March 1679 to 25th December 1688*, CS, 52 (1851) · *The diary of Thomas Cartwright, bishop of Chester*, ed. J. Hunter, CS, 22 (1843) · J. Burke and J. B. Burke, *A genealogical and heraldic history of the extinct and dormant baronetcies of England, Ireland, and Scotland* (1838)
Archives PRO, account as treasurer to Mary of Modena, LR8/418

Werferth [Wærferth] (d. 907x15), bishop of Worcester, was literary assistant to Alfred the Great, at whose instigation he translated the *Dialogues* of Gregory I.

Werferth first appears as bishop of the important and well-endowed see of Worcester in a charter of 872, as the Danish menace was starting to spread into western Mercia. Subsequent diplomas show him zealous in furthering the material interests of his diocese. He seems soon to have become more widely known, and in probably the early 880s was brought into the circle of King Alfred of Wessex. Chapter 77 of Asser's life of Alfred, apparently written in 893, describes Werferth as 'thoroughly learned' (*bene eruditum*) in scripture, and a suitable person for Alfred to turn to as he sought churchmen to translate into English the works he had selected for his 'great books' programme. Werferth was allocated the *Dialogues* of Gregory the Great, a key work in spreading both knowledge of St Benedict's life and miracles and lore about the fate of souls after death which contributed greatly to the evolution of the medieval notion of purgatory. Werferth's work was among the earliest of these translations to have been undertaken; it must have been complete by 893, for it is mentioned by Asser as having been done 'meticulously and stylishly' (*lucubratim et elegantissime*).

Whether or not Werferth made the entire translation single-handed (it is possible that he was assisted by a priest called Werwulf, also mentioned by Asser), it reflects clear Mercian characteristics. Alfred seems to have been pleased, for he supplied the translation with his own (prose) preface; there is an alternative preface in verse by Bishop Wulfsige of Sherborne. As it is known that the other work of Gregory's which Alfred selected (and translated himself), the *Cura pastoralis*, was to have been sent to all the bishops in England (it happens that the best-known extant copy is that sent to Werferth) it is reasonable to suppose that the translation of the *Dialogues* had similarly wide circulation, but no manuscripts of it earlier than 1000 survive whole. In the early eleventh century it was reworked thoroughly to reflect changes in the language; the result is such a drastic alteration of Werferth's original as to be almost an independent translation.

Alfred's respect for Werferth is shown by the benefaction of 100 mancuses made to him (by name, not just as bishop of Worcester) in the king's surviving Old English will. Werferth outlived his royal patron by fifteen years or so; evidence for his activity in the reign of Edward the Elder is confined to charters, which suggest that he died between 907 and 915.   RICHARD W. PFAFF

Sources *Alfred the Great: Asser's Life of King Alfred and other contemporary sources*, ed. and trans. S. Keynes and M. Lapidge (1983) · *Asser's Life of King Alfred: together with the 'Annals of Saint Neots' erroneously ascribed to Asser*, ed. W. H. Stevenson (1904); repr. with a supplementary article by D. Whitelock (1959) · H. Hecht, ed., *Bischof Waerferths von Worcester Übersetzung der Dialoge Gregors des Grossen*, 2 vols. (Leipzig, 1900–07) · D. Yerkes, *The two versions of Waerferth's translation of Gregory's 'Dialogues': an Old English thesaurus* (1979) · C. Plummer, *The life and times of Alfred the Great* (1902) · D. Whitelock, 'The prose of Alfred's reign', *Continuations and beginnings*, ed. E. G. Stanley (1966), 67–103 · J. M. Bately, 'Old English prose before and during the reign of Alfred', *Anglo-Saxon England*, 17 (1988), 93–137 · P. Sims-Williams, *Religion and literature in western England, 600–800* (1990) · M. Godden, 'Waerferth and King Alfred: the fate of the Old English Dialogues', *Alfred the Wise: studies in honour of Janet Bateley*, ed. J. Roberts and J. L. Nelson (1997), 35–51 · *AS chart.*, S 1282, 1837, 1838

Werner [*formerly* Chaima], **Abraham Abel** (1837–1912), rabbi, was born in Tels, a small town in the Kovno (Kaunas) district of Lithuania, then part of the Russian empire. Of his parents little is known, save that they were Orthodox Jews. His father was Yakov Chaima; the surname Werner was adopted by Abraham before he moved to Finland. Lithuania then boasted some of the most vibrant centres of Talmudic scholarship in Europe, and Tels was especially distinguished in this respect. The young Werner studied under the direction of prominent Lithuanian rabbis; at the age of twenty he received the rabbinical diploma, and in 1865, at an astonishingly young age, he was appointed a *dayan*—that is, a member of the Jewish ecclesiastical court—of Tels, a testimony to the reputation of his rabbinical scholarship. In 1854 Werner had married Sima Gittel (1837–1906). There were two sons and a daughter of the marriage. In 1880 he moved to Helsingfors (Helsinki) to become the chief rabbi of Finland. Eleven years later he accepted an invitation to journey to London to become the rabbi of a small but immensely influential community of Orthodox Jews in that city.

In 1891 London Jewry was in the middle of a veritable *Kulturkampf*. That summer Hermann Adler had succeeded his father, Nathan Marcus Adler, as chief rabbi of the British empire, a post which was, in effect, in the gift of the United Synagogue, presided over by the house of Rothschild. The Judaism of the United Synagogue represented a compromise: nominally it was Orthodox, but most of its members did not practise this orthodoxy, and there had developed during the 1880s a bitter rift between the United Synagogue (in effect, the Anglo-Jewish establishment at prayer) and the Jewish refugees from Russia and Poland who flooded into England, and primarily into London, during that decade to escape persecution and to seek economic advancement.

The Yiddish-speaking immigrants had accepted the authority of Nathan Adler, a Talmudic scholar of international repute, but they had much less time for Hermann, whom they regarded as lacking in rabbinical scholarship and weak in commitment to Orthodox Judaism. Moreover, they were outraged at Hermann's determination that he alone should be accorded the status and title of rabbi (indeed, of chief rabbi) within the British empire; in eastern Europe every Jewish town had one or more rabbis, all of whom could exercise ecclesiastical jurisdiction. To fight Hermann's claims an alliance had been formed between two rigidly Orthodox communities, one of German and Austro-Hungarian origin, the other composed of Russian and Polish immigrants. Together, these groups established the Chevra Machzike Hadath ('the society of the upholders of the religion'). And it was from this Chevra that Werner received the invitation to come to London a short time after Hermann had succeeded to his father's position.

Werner lost no time in declaring war on United Synagogue Judaism and on the United Synagogue's rabbinical leadership. He condemned the meat and poultry sold as kosher under Hermann Adler's authority, and established a quite separate facility, under his supervision, for the slaughter and preparation of kosher meat and meat products. He solemnized marriages and authorized divorces without any reference to Hermann Adler, and he established a Talmud Torah (religion school) which taught in Yiddish, a language the Anglo-Jewish establishment despised.

The Machzike Hadath grew in popularity and size, and

in 1898 moved into a former Huguenot chapel at the corner of Brick Lane and Fournier Street, in the heart of the Jewish East End of London. Known as the Spitalfields Great Synagogue, it became the acknowledged centre of immigrant opposition to Adlerian Judaism. Its success inspired other communities of Jewish immigrants in Liverpool and Manchester to rebel also against Hermann Adler's jurisdiction. By the end of the nineteenth century Hermann was faced with a full-scale rebellion on the part of the immigrants, who now comprised the numerical majority of the Jews in Great Britain. What saved his authority, and that of the Anglo-Jewish establishment, was the financial poverty of the Machzike Hadath and of its members. In 1905, in return for financial assistance, the community agreed to recognize Adler's jurisdiction; Werner renounced his right to authorize marriages and divorces, and his separate slaughtering facilities were also brought under Adler's overall authority. Werner was criticized in some quarters for what was seen as a capitulation. A man of great humility, his concern was never for his own status, but rather for the status of Orthodox Judaism; in this respect, the United Synagogue had learned a lesson which it was never to forget: that it had to accommodate the wishes of East End as well as of West End Jews.

Werner also clashed with Adler over Zionism. Hermann, fearful for the status of emancipated Jews in Britain, had condemned Zionism as contrary to Jewish principles. Werner, from a much stronger Talmudic perspective, supported the Zionist movement, and spoke at the famous monster rally which Theodor Herzl addressed at the Great Assembly Hall, Mile End, east London, in October 1898.

In his long black frock coat and flowing beard, Werner was an imposing figure. He wrote little. His strengths lay in his faith, his piety, his Talmudic learning, and in the propagation of the study of the Talmud among British Jews. His death in London at 9 Princelet Street, Spitalfields, on 20 December 1912, provoked one of the largest gatherings of Jews ever seen in Britain, and his funeral, at the Federation Jewish cemetery, Edmonton, the same day, witnessed an outpouring of grief which was certainly without precedent; it merited a report in the *Manchester Guardian* (23 December).   CHIMEN ABRAMSKY

Sources *Jewish Chronicle* (27 Dec 1912) · *Manchester Guardian* (23 Dec 1912) · *Daily Sketch* (23 Dec 1912) · I. Finestein, *Anglo-Jewry in changing times* (1999) · L. P. Gartner, *The Jewish immigrant in England, 1870–1914* (1960) · B. Homa, *A fortress in Anglo-Jewry* (1953) · B. Homa, *Footprints in the sand of time* (1990) · T. Z. Ferber, *Zikaron L'Dor Akhron* [A memoir of the last generation] (1953) · d. cert.

Werner, Alice (1859–1935), teacher of Bantu languages, was born in Trieste, then part of the Austrian empire, on 26 June 1859, one of seven children in the family of Reinhardt Joseph Werner (1817–1874) of Mainz, teacher of languages, and his wife, Harriett (1822–1904), daughter of John Taylor, a baker. The Sinologist Edward Theodore Chalmers Werner (1864–1954) was her younger brother. Alice's father, a naturalized British subject since 1852, indulged his wanderlust during Alice's first fifteen years, and thus she experienced a constant change of scene and sound, living in New Zealand, Mexico, the United States, and Europe, until the family settled in Tonbridge in 1874.

Alice Werner was educated privately, and then attended Newnham College, Cambridge, from 1878 to 1880 as a Goldsmiths' scholar, but left, with no tripos, in order to teach at Truro high school. She also wrote for periodicals and undertook translating. From 1893 to 1895 she visited the Church of Scotland mission in Blantyre, Nyasaland, to do linguistic work and prepare school textbooks, and Pietermaritzburg, Natal, where she acquired Zulu and Afrikaans. Following the outbreak of the Second South African War in 1899 she gave private classes in London in these languages—classes which were transferred to King's College, London, in 1901; in 1910 these were formally recognized by the University of London, the first British university to promote the teaching of Bantu languages (Swahili had been taught in Berlin since 1887). From 1911 to 1913 Alice Werner visited British East Africa on a Mary Anne Ewart travelling scholarship from Newnham. She spent much of her time in Swahili-land, where she met the poet and scholar Muhammad Kijumwa al-Bakry, who provided her with manuscripts and information about the language and literature of the Swahili-speaking people. From 1913 she held a two-year research fellowship at Newnham, while continuing to teach at King's.

After the School of Oriental Studies opened in 1917 Alice Werner was appointed lecturer and subsequently reader in Swahili and other Bantu languages (with her sister Mary as lecturer from 1918 to 1930). In 1919 she completed her London doctoral thesis (submitted in 1929), 'Introductory sketch of the Bantu languages', drawing on her first-hand knowledge of south, central, and east Africa. In 1922 she was promoted professor in Swahili and the Bantu languages, the first such chair in the British Isles; she then established the school's diploma in Swahili studies (1924), the first qualification of this kind in a British university. She was awarded a DLitt in 1928 by London University. When she retired in 1930, having served the school devotedly for its first twelve years, she was appointed CBE, and was awarded the silver medal of the African Society.

Werner's editions of *Utendi wa Ayubu* ('The life of Job'), subsequently reprinted in a Dar es Salaam newspaper, became the first of the Swahili epics to reach a wide public both in Europe and along the east African coast. Her publication of *The Advice of Mwana Kupona* in 1934, a poem from northern Swahililand, was the first literary composition by 'an East African native woman' to be published in Great Britain. *Myths and Legends of the Bantu* (1933) was probably her most popular book.

Werner never met W. E. Taylor, whose obituary she wrote; while not rivalling his mastery of Swahili, she excelled him in her wide command of Bantu languages. Werner died at her home, 74 Parkway, Welwyn Garden City, Hertfordshire, on 9 June 1935. She was unmarried.

P. J. L. FRANKL, *rev.*

Sources *The Times* (11 June 1935) · *Bulletin of the School of Oriental Studies*, 4 (1926–8) · *Bulletin of the School of Oriental Studies*, 8 (1935), 281–2 · *Zeitschrift für Eingeborenen Sprachen*, 19 (1928–9) · *Zeitschrift*

für Eingeborenen Sprachen, 26 (1935–6) · A. J. Lamont Smith, 'Werner, Alice', *DSAB* · b. cert. · d. cert. · m. cert. [Reinhardt, Joseph Werner] · d. certs. [R. J. Werner; Harriett Werner]
Archives SOAS, papers
Wealth at death £74 8s. 6d.: probate, 16 Aug 1935, *CGPLA Eng. & Wales*

Wernher, Sir Julius Charles, first baronet (1850–1912), mining magnate and philanthropist, was born at Darmstadt in the grand duchy of Hesse and by Rhine on 9 April 1850, of an old and reputable protestant family. His grandfather, Wilhelm Wernher, had been privy councillor and president of the court of appeal in his native Hesse. His father, Friedrich August (nicknamed Gustel) Wernher, an eminent railway engineer and friend of Robert Stephenson and Isambard Kingdom Brunel, married Elise Weidenbusch in 1844. Julius was the second child and elder son of a family of two sons and two daughters. His father's duties took him to Mainz and, when the boy was in his ninth year, to Frankfurt am Main. There Julius was educated and, although he was interested in engineering as a profession, decided on a business career.

Early career in banking After a commercial education, Wernher served an apprenticeship in a bank in Frankfurt. An aptitude for languages, including Spanish and French, and his knowledge of banking, secured him an appointment in Paris in 1869 with the bank of Ephrussi Porgès. On the outbreak of the Franco-Prussian War in 1870 he served as a cadet in the dragoons of the 4th cavalry division and in the army of occupation, without being in the least touched, as appears from his letters, by the wave of military and imperial sentiment then sweeping over Germany. After the war he went to London, where he first worked as a bookkeeper in a firm of German druggists and then in a bank. By a great stroke of fortune his employer in Paris, Théodore Porgès, had given him a warm letter of recommendation to Jules Porgès, a diamond merchant of Paris and London, whose firm was reputedly the greatest and wealthiest diamond business in the world at the time of the discovery of diamonds in South Africa. In a letter dated 11 November 1871 Wernher described Porgès to his parents as 'the most charming and beneficent man in the world … I put all my trust in him' (Wernher MSS). Porgès offered young Wernher a two-years engagement as assistant to his partner, Charles Mège, then setting out to buy diamonds in the fields.

The Kimberley diamond mine Mège and Wernher arrived at Port Elizabeth on 4 January 1872. At Du Toit's Pan the newcomers set up their canvas house, opening an office a little later in the neighbouring camp of New Rush, later named Kimberley. Wernher made himself master of the infinitely difficult and delicate business of diamond buying, and by the spring of 1872 was able to write home, 'I am already indispensable to my Frenchman', and again, 'I am proud to say that my voice has its full weight'.

When Mège returned to Paris in the autumn of 1873, Wernher became a partner in the firm of Jules Porgès & Co. and its sole representative in Kimberley. Porgès came to trust him absolutely. Wernher wrote modestly:

Sir Julius Charles Wernher, first baronet (1850–1912), by Sir Hubert von Herkomer, 1910

> I am not one of those people who create new fortunes by genius or new combinations, and lose them again and win them again. I only walk well-known paths, but I walk steadily and only act out of conviction, without, indeed, paying too much attention to my own point of view.

Such a personality was well suited to win its way through the long series of crises caused by over-production, indiscriminate selling, prolonged droughts, wars, and falls of reef, which form the chequered history of the diamond mines of Kimberley. Wernher, a giant in physical strength, living a wise and temperate life, outlasted most of his competitors. Sir David Harris, a contemporary who travelled with Wernher on board RMS *Northam* to South Africa in 1871, described him as 'A tall, lanky German, he had served as a Uhlan in the Franco-German War. In after-life we became friends. Possessed of a charming personality, he was a born diplomat, courteous, affable and considerate' (D. Harris, *Pioneer, Soldier and Politician*, 1931, 7).

By 1876 Wernher had been joined by Charles Rube, and had persuaded Porgès to visit the fields, where he arrived on 12 December. He formed a syndicate to purchase claims in the Kimberley mine, and in April 1877 accompanied Porgès to Paris where all the syndicate's claims were put into a private company called the Griqualand West Diamond Mining Company. Wernher was soon the head of one of the most important diamond producing companies in the fields. 'I have put a little order', he wrote in 1878, 'into the mining board [of which he was a director], and I am teaching them', he added significantly, 'to provide for the time when the mines are worked in common.' In the busy mining camp he was already trusted and acknowledged as a leader, as much for his integrity of character as for his intellectual power. The Kimberley mine, originally divided into surface claims 30 feet square, had gone down into great depths; claims, sometimes subdivided, had crumbled one upon another and the surrounding reef had fallen in upon the whole. The mining board, with little capital or influence, was unequal to the task of control, which ever grew more complicated; Wernher was one of the first to see that consolidation was the only solution. His company, the Compagnie Française des Mines du Cap, formed in Paris in 1880 (usually called the French Company), gradually and constantly enlarged its holdings by making judicious purchases.

Relations with Beit and Rhodes As the work of the mine became more absorbing Wernher was forced to neglect the diamond buying business, hitherto the mainstay of the firm, and arranged with several younger men to operate on joint account, the firm supplying the capital for shipment. Thus in 1884 Alfred Beit became a partner in Jules Porgès & Co. Wernher wrote in 1879 that he was living:

> with Rube and Van Beek and Beit. With the last, the nicest of all, I lived for a long time in Old De Beers. He is a cheery, optimistic fellow of extraordinary goodness of heart and of very great business ability.

Beit, having invested for his own account in the De Beers mine, was brought into intimate contact with Cecil John Rhodes. Thus Rhodes and his friends in De Beers were able to come to a firm understanding with Wernher and the French Company operating in the Kimberley mine as regards amalgamating the various mines. This struggle for supremacy and consolidation led to conflict with Barnett Isaac, known as Barney Barnato. With the aid of Wernher, during a flying visit to Europe in 1887, Rhodes bought the French Company and in so doing forced Barnato to merge all his diamond interests in the Kimberley Central Diamond Mining Company. In the meantime Wernher and Beit had been quietly buying large holdings in Du Toit's Pan and elsewhere with the knowledge of Rhodes. As a result the rival claim holders were ultimately forced to agree to the amalgamation of the chief diamond mines of Kimberley into the De Beers Consolidated Mines (1888).

The London diamond syndicate Meanwhile, in order to stop the wasteful competition and reckless selling of diamonds, Wernher, who had returned to London in 1880, set about the creation of a diamond syndicate there. From 1880 to 1882 he directed the London office of Jules Porgès & Co., while Porgès operated in Paris. Wernher returned to Kimberley in 1883 but in 1884 he was back in London where Alfred Beit joined him in 1889. In 1886 the London Diamond Syndicate was established which stabilized the price of diamonds. After Porgès retired at the end of 1889 the firm was reconstituted, in January 1890, as Wernher, Beit & Co. of London.

Wernher and Beit formed a most successful partnership which was only terminated by Beit's untimely death in 1906. Beit was regarded as the financial genius, a man of flair who would take enormous risks, whereas Wernher was the hard-headed, conservative businessman, somewhat aloof, who kept in the background (so much so that, to his amusement, people often thought Wernher was Beit's Christian name). Interestingly, Wernher is said to have abhorred first names and only once was heard to address Beit as 'Alf'. Taylor, who was their Johannesburg partner, attributed their success to the fact that:

> Beit had all the initiative and creative faculties, whilst Wernher saw to it that all their enterprises were placed on a sound financial basis with adequate reserves. No crises ever found Wernher unprepared. If prices slumped, and the bottom fell out of the market, Wernher took up all the firm's paper under rebates, and sat ready with a huge cash balance, prepared to take advantage of any business that might be offered to him. Beit's judgement about markets might sometimes be at fault, leading him at times to make large purchases of shares at a wrong moment, but Wernher would always come to the rescue with the pluck to sell and cut a loss. To my knowledge this happened more than once.
> (Taylor, 72)

Wernher was one of the pioneers of Kimberley who played a major role in the amalgamation of the diamond mines. In 1898 he was appointed a life governor of De Beers Consolidated Mines.

Goldmining on the Rand The discovery of the Witwatersrand goldfields in 1886 brought the firm into goldmining. Acting on expert advice, Alfred Beit sent Joseph Benjamin Robinson to the Witwatersrand to buy up large and valuable properties for the syndicate that he had formed with Robinson and his partner, Marcus. Meanwhile Jules Porgès had asked Hermann Ludwig Eckstein and James Benjamin Taylor, whom he knew from Kimberley, to open a branch of his firm in Johannesburg. The new company of H. Eckstein (which became known as the Corner House—a pun on Eckstein's name which meant 'corner stone') was established for the purpose of floating companies to develop their properties, and in due course the partners bought out Robinson and Marcus. However, H. Eckstein & Co.'s most important flotation was Rand Mines Ltd, registered in February 1893 and formed for the express purpose of developing Wernher/Beit/ H. Eckstein's deep level properties. By the end of the 1890s Wernher/Beit/H. Eckstein had established a recognized hegemony in the industry and the group's mines accounted for nearly 50 per cent of the value of the Witwatersrand's total gold production.

Although Wernher only visited the Witwatersrand for the first time in 1903 (the year in which the partners moved to their magnificent new building at 1 London Wall), it is said that he so completely mastered the intricacies of goldmining on the Reef from his office in London that he was familiar with the workings of each mine in the group. He played an important role in organizing the industry on a stable and profitable basis, and the formation of Rand Mines justified his faith in the deep levels. However, the pinnacle of Wernher's career as a mining financier was undoubtedly the formation of the Central

Mining and Finance Corporation Ltd Incorporated in London on 9 May 1905 for the purpose of taking over the business of the African Ventures Syndicate, which Wernher had formed in 1903 to buy gold shares 'with a view of steadying the market and regaining the confidence of the Transvaal mines', as well as to attract mainly French capital, Central Mining had a nominal capital of £6 million in 300,000 shares of £20 each. Referred to as 'the £6,000,000 Kaffir Trust' by the London financial papers, it has also been described as 'the biggest trust of its kind the Rand or even London and Paris had ever seen'. The management of the corporation was vested in Wernher, Beit & Co. until such time as the partnerships could be wound up and all the assets transferred to Central Mining. Wernher was the first chairman, a position he held until his death. By 1910 the group annually had control of raw gold worth about £12 million, and in 1912, the year of Wernher's death, the goldmines under the control of his group produced 3.5 million ounces of fine gold and paid no less than £4.25 million— that is, 51 per cent of the profits of the whole of the Witwatersrand.

However, there was a darker side to the business career of the man to whom 'The City of London raised its hat … and henceforth (from the time of the formation of Central Mining) spoke of … with the respect that normally it reserved for the Rothschilds' (Cartwright, 248). First Beit and then Wernher were duped by a Frenchman called Henri Lemoine into believing that he could produce synthetic diamonds of gemstone quality. The affair, which became known as 'L'Affaire Lemoine', started with Beit in 1905 but dragged on until January 1908 when Lemoine was first brought to trial and Wernher was openly ridiculed by the French press and public.

Later life, marriage, and death In 1911 Wernher was awarded the gold medal of the Institution of Mining and Metallurgy for his personal services to the advancement of technological education. In honour of his memory the institution established, thirty-five years after his death, a series of lectures in his name, the objective being to bring to the attention of the public matters of importance to the mining industry. After his second visit to the Witwatersrand in 1909 Wernher had been so appalled by the conditions and health hazards on the mines that he consulted, in February 1911, the British bacteriologist, Sir Almroth Wright, who had won acclaim for his development of the typhoid vaccine and was working on the problem of pneumonia which was rife in the goldmines, particularly among the so-called 'tropical labour'. As a result Wright and his three co-workers came to Johannesburg in October 1911 and conducted mass inoculation experiments between 1914 and 1918.

Although business necessitated Wernher living in London, and he had wanted to become a British citizen in 1879, in deference to his family he refrained from becoming a naturalized British subject until 1898. On 12 June 1888 he had married Alice Sedgwick (known as Birdie; 1862–1945), daughter of James Mankiewicz of London, in Christ Church, Lancaster Gate. Three sons, Derrick Julius (*b.* 1889), Harold Augustus (*b.* 1893), and Alexander Pigott

(*b.* 1897), were born of the marriage. He bought an estate in Bedfordshire, Luton Hoo, in June 1903, and at his London residence, Bath House, 82 Piccadilly, indulged a lifelong taste for art and formed a fine collection of pictures, principally of the Renaissance period. One of the best pictures in his collection, Watteau's *Le gage d'amour*, he left in his will to the National Gallery. He was a man of deep culture and he read widely, even during his Kimberley days.

When Wernher became rich his philanthropy took the form of great and well-considered benefactions. He left an estate of £11.5 million. The King Edward VII's Hospital for Officers was a recipient of his generosity during his lifetime and in his will he left it £25,000 with a share of the residuary estate, estimated to be worth a possible total of £465,000 a year after his death; he left a further £100,000 to be distributed among charities. He was deeply concerned at the backwardness of his adopted country in practical science, and served as a member of Lord Haldane's departmental committee (1904–7) which recommended the establishment by royal charter of the Imperial College of Science and Technology in London; this institution Wernher endowed with £250,000, and in his will with a further sum of £150,000. Like Rhodes and Beit he was deeply interested in education. He gave £250,000 to the Union of South Africa 'to assist in building and if sufficient partly endowing a University at Groote Schuur' (Trevelyan, 253), home of Cecil Rhodes. This became the University of Cape Town. He also made handsome gifts to other educational and research organizations. During the Second South African War his firm equipped the first Johannesburg volunteer regiment, the Imperial light horse. He remained aloof from politics generally, and especially from what he called 'high politics', but supported a programme of reconciliation in the Transvaal after 1907. He declared himself in favour of tariff reform in Britain but never threw himself into the politics of his adopted land or accepted any office of honour in his county. In 1907 the German Kaiser had bestowed the order of the Crown (third class) on him, and in 1911 Buckingham Palace granted permission for him to wear the insignia. His self-effacement amounted almost to a passion; with it went a notable loyalty to old friends and to the people who worked for him; his chief pride lay in the fact that he had made his wealth honestly, and that he had earned the complete and profound trust of the industry which he had done so much to establish. His death marked the end of an era in the history of his firms in London and Johannesburg, and 'leaves a great void and you and I have lost our best friend', wrote Friedie Eckstein (F. Eckstein to L. Phillips, 24 May 1912, Archives of the Central Mining and Investment Corporation Ltd., Sandton, South Africa). He was created a baronet in 1905. He died on 21 May 1912 at his home, Bath House, 82 Piccadilly, London, after a long and painful illness, and was buried on 28 May at East Hyde in Bedfordshire. The eldest of his three sons, Derrick Julius, succeeded to the title.

I. D. COLVIN, *rev.* MARYNA FRASER

Sources R. Trevelyan, *Grand dukes and diamonds* (1991) · M. Fraser, 'Rooted in gold', 1994, Barlow (Rand) Archives, Sandton, South

Africa · L. Phillips, *Some reminiscences*, ed. M. Fraser (1986) · A. P. Cartwright, *The Corner House* (1965) · A. J. Wilson, *The professionals* (1992) · J. B. Taylor, *A pioneer looks back* (1939) · C. Newbury, *The diamond ring: business, politics and precious stones in South Africa, 1867–1947* (1989) · *DSAB* · *CGPLA Eng. & Wales* (1912) · private information (1927) · Luton Hoo, Bedfordshire, Wernher MSS · Barlow (Rand) Archives, Sandton, South Africa, Archives of the Central Mining and Investment Corporation Ltd. · Barlow (Rand) Archives, Sandton, South Africa, Archives of Wernher, Beit & Co.

Archives Luton Hoo, Bedfordshire | Barlow (Rand) Archives, Sandton, South Africa, Archives of Central Mining and Investment Corporation Ltd · Barlow (Rand) Archives, Sandton, South Africa, archives of H. Eckstein & Co. · Barlow (Rand) Archives, Sandton, South Africa, archives of Wernher, Beit & Co.

Likenesses H. von Herkomer, oils, 1910, priv. coll. [*see illus.*] · H. von Herkomer, oils, second version, 1910, Johannesburg Art Gallery · P. T. Cole, watercolour drawing, 1912, Rand Mines Ltd, Johannesburg · N. Jacobson, bronze sculpture, 1982, Rand Mines Ltd, Johannesburg · London Stereoscopic Co., photograph, NPG · P. Montford, bust, ICL

Wealth at death £5,000,000: probate, 10 June 1912, *CGPLA Eng. & Wales*

Wesel, Gerhard von (c.1443–1510), merchant and administrator, was the second of three sons of the Cologne merchant Hermann von Wesel (d. 1484) and his wife, Kathrinchen. Of Gerhard's education it is only known that he matriculated at the University of Cologne while still a minor (not yet fourteen) in 1457. Although Gerhard later spoke and wrote German, Latin, and English, and owned books in German and Latin, he was not marked out for a clerical or academic career, but followed in his father's footsteps. He was married three times: his first wife was Gertrud von Merle, whom he married before 1468; they had a daughter, Gertrud, who married a Cologne merchant, Konrad Rinck. Gertrud died on 8 August 1483. There were no children of either his second marriage, to Elisabeth Glidermann, whom he married late in 1483 and who died on 1 January 1486, or his third, to Adelheid Bischoff, whom he married in February 1489; she died after 27 July 1518. Gerhard von Wesel traded initially in his father's name, later on his own, along the main artery of Cologne's international commerce (Frankfurt–Cologne–Burgundy–London).

Like his father von Wesel was a member of the Cologne town council. Co-opted for the first time on 24 June 1481, he served the usual one-year term eight times between 1487–8 and 1508–9. In this urban context he was to enjoy a distinguished career, serving during the same period, usually more than once, in a wide variety of administrative, judicial, fiscal, and military offices, and being four times chosen mayor of Cologne, for the years 1494–5, 1497–8, 1502–3, and 1507–8. In addition von Wesel represented Cologne at the Reform Diet of Worms (1495), which Maximilian I, the king of the Romans (r. 1493–1519), opened with an urgent request for an emergency loan—to be repaid from the proceeds of an imperial poll tax (*gemeiner pfennig*)—in order to repel the French invasion of Italy. A committee of estates was formed to apportion the loan, and the imperial towns elected von Wesel and the mayor of Augsburg as their representatives. The proposal put forward by the princes on the committee proved explosive: not only the towns, but also the *geselschaften* in the empire,

were to pay up. The phrase was ominous: did the *geselschaften* include mercantile corporations (in which case the towns would be subject doubly), or did the princes only have knights' organizations in mind? Von Wesel and his colleague demanded clarification, and, when their worst fears proved to be correct, persuaded the committee to drop the notion of taxing the *geselschaften* and so reduce the towns' burden. The real issue was not the towns' reluctance to pay an ever-increasing share of imperial expenses (although that was certainly a factor), but rather the need for constitutional reform of the empire, which would reduce the power of the monarchy by establishing and funding independent institutions answerable to the estates.

Von Wesel's role in English history had begun many years earlier. For almost a century Anglo-Hanseatic tension had built up over the issue of reciprocal rights. English merchants, who controlled Anglo-Prussian trade but still lacked a firm legal footing, demanded rights in Prussia equivalent to those enjoyed by the Hanse in England. While these demands were satisfied by the treaty of London (1437), Prussia's refusal to ratify the treaty led to a sustained campaign by the English crown, which twice (in 1442 and 1447) suspended Hanseatic privileges in England. Each time Cologne, whose merchants suffered disproportionately, managed to rescue the situation. Edward IV used different tactics, and only granted the Hanse members the use of their rights for a limited period, making confirmation of their charters dependent upon negotiations on reciprocity. Cologne, whose merchants had much to lose from any disruption of trade with England, led all the Hanseatic diplomatic efforts. In 1468, in a separate incident, the Danish king seized six English ships bound for Danzig as a reprisal for the depredations of English merchants in Iceland. Since the English had no hope of compensation from the Danes, they decided to use the incident for a different purpose. Seizing upon the fact that Danzig ships and seamen had been involved, they petitioned the crown to arrest all Hanseatic merchants in England and sequester their goods.

When this storm broke in late July 1468, Gerhard von Wesel was acting alderman of the Steelyard (the Hanseatic headquarters in London), all the senior members having left for the continent at Easter. It was a terrible responsibility for a young man. While Gerhard led all the delegations to plead the Steelyard's case before the council, and took the lead in preparing its legal defence, he came under increasing pressure from Cologne to avoid entanglement in the difficulties of the eastern Hanse members. Cologne felt—with considerable justification—that since the 1440s its merchants had been made to bear the consequences of the rash actions of Danzig and Lübeck. If these hotheads had picked yet another quarrel with England, then they should resolve the difficulties they had brought upon themselves, without expecting Cologne to follow their lead or foot the bill. Von Wesel was initially loath to accept this view, though he must have been tempted, as the crown clearly favoured Cologne: while Hanse members had been imprisoned in July 1468 and condemned to pay compensation of £20,000 by the council in November 1468, Cologne merchants had been released from custody and acquitted. Nevertheless, von Wesel loyally acted in the interest of the imprisoned Hanse merchants until the spring of 1469, when he came around to the position of his elders in Cologne. On 16 May 1469, shortly after the Hanseatic diet had ordered a complete break with England, a separate Cologne Steelyard was constituted with von Wesel at its head. In that capacity he was instrumental in obtaining privileges for the Cologne merchants, and he continued to preside over the Cologne Steelyard until it became clear that its final act was being played out. Charles the Bold of Burgundy had used his good offices to establish diplomatic contacts between England and the Hanse, and in 1474 the treaty of Utrecht resolved the crisis in Anglo-Hanseatic relations. However, Edward IV was forced to break with Cologne, which—as von Wesel noted bitterly—had loyally supported him. The treaty and a separate note obliged the crown to deny Hanseatic rights to Cologne, which had been expelled from the Hanse in 1471. Despite his bitterness at Edward's breach of faith, von Wesel seriously considered becoming an English subject and a London citizen, should Cologne remain estranged from the Hanse.

In the end events drove Cologne and the Hanse into one another's arms, and Cologne was readmitted in the concord of Bremen of 1476. However, the Steelyard could not bring itself to readmit Gerhard von Wesel, who was hated with particular venom. It required considerable efforts to overcome this enmity, but in the end von Wesel was successful, and in 1479 was allowed back, though he remained wary as late as 1487. Gradually, however, the bitterness faded, and the Hanse came to appreciate his expert knowledge of English affairs and his wide circle of powerful English friends. Until his death he was crucially involved in every round of Anglo-Hanseatic negotiations (at Antwerp in 1491 and 1497 and at Bruges in 1499). Thereafter von Wesel withdrew from international politics, though he remained active in the administration of Cologne. He died there on 4 September 1510 and was buried in the St Vincent Chapel of the Augustinian monastery in Cologne. STUART JENKS

Sources W. Stein, ed., *Hansisches Urkundenbuch*, 9–11 (1903–16) · G. von der Ropp, ed., *Hanserezesse zweite Abteilung: Hanserezesse von 1431 bis 1476*, 6–7 (1890–92) · D. Schäfer, ed., *Hanserezesse dritte Abteilung: Hanserezesse von 1477 bis 1530*, 1–4 (1881–90) · B. Kuske, ed., *Quellen zur Geschichte des Kölner Handels und Verkehrs im Mittelalter*, 4 vols., Publikationen der Gesellschaft für rheinische Geschichtskunde, 33 (1917–34) · *Deutsche Reichstagsakten unter Maximilian I*, 3, ed. E. Block (Göttingen, 1972) · *Deutsche Reichstagsakten unter Maximilian I*, 5, ed. H. Angermeier (Göttingen, 1981) · *Deutsche Reichstagsakten unter Maximilian I*, 6, ed. H. Gollwitzer (Göttingen, 1979) · R. Knipping, ed., *Die Kölner Stadtrechnungen des Mittelalters mit einer Darstellung der Finanzverwaltung*, 2 vols., Publikationen der Gesellschaft für rheinische Geschichtskunde, 15 (1897–8) · W. Stein, ed., *Akten zur Geschichte der Verfassung und Verwaltung der Stadt Köln im 14. und 15. Jahrhundert*, 2 vols., Publikationen der Gesellschaft für rheinische Geschichtskunde, 10 (1893–5) · H. Keussen, ed., *Die Matrikel der Universität Köln*, 1 (Bonn, 1928) · H. von Loesch, ed., *Die Kölner Zunfturkunden nebst anderen Kölner Gewerbeurkunden bis zum Jahre 1500*, 2 vols., Publikationen der Gesellschaft für rheinische Geschichtskunde, 22 (1907) · P. Ullrich,

'Gerhard von Wesel, ein Kölner Kaufherr und Bürgermeister', PhD diss., University of Marburg, 1918 · J. Deeters, 'Gerhard von Wesel—ein Kölner Kaufmann im Londoner Hansekontor', *Norwegen und die Hanse: wirtschaftliche und kulturelle Aspekte im europäischen Vergleich*, ed. V. Henn and A. Nedkvitne (Frankfurt am Main, 1994), 161–76 · G. Hirschfelder, *Die Kölner Handelsbeziehungen im Spätmittelalter*, Veröffentlichungen des Kölnischen Stadtmuseums, 10 (1994) · R. Knipping, 'Das Schuldenwesen der Stadt Köln im 14. und 15. Jahrhundert', *Westdeutsche Zeitschrift für Geschichte und Kunst*, 13 (1894), 340–97 · M. Wensky, *Die Stellung der Frau in der stadtkölnischen Wirtschaft im Spätmittelalter*, Quellen und Darstellungen zur Hansischen Geschichte, new ser., 26 (1980)
Archives Historisches Archiv der Stadt Köln, Cologne
Likenesses stained glass window, St Peter's Church, Cologne
Wealth at death see will, calendared in Kuske, ed., *Quellen zur Geschichte des Kölner Handels*, 3, nos. 270, 357–8

Wesenham, John (*fl.* 1333–1382), merchant, shipowner, and financier, was named after the Norfolk village of Weasenham, 6 miles east of Bishop's Lynn. In the early stages of his career his economic interest clearly centred on shipping and the grain trade, which in East Anglia went hand in hand; hence his earliest recorded venture, in the form of a licence of 20 March 1333 to export corn to Norway in his own ships and return with fish. Intermittently customs collector at Boston between 1335 and 1337, on 3 June 1335 he obtained a lifetime grant of wool tronnage duty in that port, but this was later revoked, since it already belonged to someone else. On 18 April 1337 he was released from the Tower of London pending inquiries into suspected breaches of shipping regulations; he was later cleared of the charges. From 8 June 1337 to 25 March 1338 Wesenham was in personal command of a heavily armed ship from Bishop's Lynn, which served in Gascony, and he continued to be active in naval affairs; on 20 July 1342 he and other men of Bishop's Lynn, then engaged in arraying ships for the king's northern fleet, were respited from an indictment alleging the plunder of a ship called the *Taryte*. There is no evidence that he exported wool before the beginning of the Hundred Years' War, and he played no part in Edward III's attempt to monopolize the nation's wool trade in 1337 by using the prerogative right of purveyance. Not until 1340 did Wesenham, in partnership with Walter Chiriton, contract to buy 600 sacks of Warwickshire wool, part of the tax in kind granted to the king that year; in 1341 he bought 600 sacks in Norfolk. Wool was probably still peripheral to his interests, but the business led to his receiving a personal summons to an assembly of merchants in July 1340. Thereafter he was regularly summoned to other such meetings which distinguish the middle years of Edward III's reign.

In August 1345 Wesenham seized the opportunity to move into the inner circle of royal financiers, when a syndicate of English merchants currently farming the customs duties was unable to meet the king's request for a loan. In partnership with his brother Simon and others Wesenham raised 20,000 florins in Bruges and was awarded the customs farm at the existing rent of £50,000 a year. At Michaelmas 1346 they were outbid by a syndicate led by Walter Chiriton, Wesenham's partner in 1340, but in April 1347 the rivals agreed to co-operate to dispose of a tax of 20,000 sacks of wool. In July 1348 Wesenham paid Chiriton £4000 and in return received a pledge on the king's great crown, then held by the latter. After the collapse of Chiriton's company in April 1349 Wesenham restored the crown to the king without immediate payment, but in June 1350 he was awarded rents in London belonging to members of the company, to be held until the debt was liquidated. Only part of Wesenham's advances to the king in this period came from his personal fortune; the rest was borrowed on Wesenham's own credit from other Englishmen and Hanseatic merchants; reimbursements came from remissions of export duties, assignments of lay subsidies, and the issues of alien benefices in the king's hands. It was a risky business, but it paid off and was the key to further royal favour. From 11 January 1347 to Michaelmas 1350 Wesenham held the office of royal butler and during the general recoinage, beginning at Michaelmas 1350, he served as exchanger of coins.

Wesenham retired from the centre of royal finances after receiving, on 23 April 1352, a generous pardon for any and all offences he may have committed. He remained active in trade; on 28 July 1353 he was licensed to export wool without payment of the alien duty, then also paid by denizens; throughout the decade he received licences to export corn. At this period, like many other successful merchants, he was probably investing in land to create an inheritance for his posterity. The full extent of his estates is not known, but on 14 March 1350 he and his heirs were granted free warren in their demesne lands in Weasenham and eleven other places in Norfolk. He also farmed a number of lands from the crown, including the temporalities of the bishopric of Lincoln, held for 3740 marks a year from 1 February 1357 to 6 October 1360. He married his son, Hugh, to Agnes, daughter of John Bruis, whose wardship he bought from Simon Islip, archbishop of Canterbury (d. 1366), for 500 marks. Hugh and Agnes received her lands in April 1353, but in 1358 had to surrender half to a sister, who earlier had been wrongly described as a nun.

On 30 January 1360 Wesenham again became active in the king's service, undertaking to provide, equip, and man ships in the North Sea, for a lump payment of £4500. He commanded this fleet in person, and on 10 July payment was authorized from the proceeds of a lay subsidy. His last major service was as one of two mayors, heading a company of merchants formed to govern Calais from 1 March 1363. The intention was to stop a drain on the exchequer and make the town and garrison financially self-supporting, largely through duties imposed on wool passing through the staple which was established there. The experiment ended in failure after less than a year. For Wesenham one of the consequences was a spell of imprisonment in the Tower, together with Henry Brisele, master of the Calais mint, presumably for suspected coinage offences. They were released on 22 June 1365. Towards the end of his life Wesenham may have fallen on hard times. On 20 June 1380 he was granted a life annuity of £46 13s. 4d. and 2 tuns of wine, 'in aid of his estate', for good services to Edward III. This was charged against the customs

collectors of Bishop's Lynn and Boston. An order to pay arrears, dated 18 November 1382, is the last known reference to Wesenham.

T. H. LLOYD

Sources *Chancery records* · *CIPM*, vol. 11 · *Calendar of inquisitions miscellaneous (chancery)*, PRO, 2 (1916)

Wesham, Roger of (d. 1257), bishop of Coventry and Lichfield, probably derived his name from Weasenham, Norfolk. A close associate of Grosseteste, Wesham was educated in Oxford and had graduated MA by 1233. In that year he became prebendary of Elstow, Bedfordshire, and may have held this benefice until 1235-6. Still a deacon, he was admitted rector of Walgrave, Northamptonshire, on 21 March 1234, but held this cure only until some time in the following year, presumably because he was pursuing a teaching career in Oxford, where he was third secular lector in theology to the Franciscan convent (1235–40). This would have required the holding of benefices without cure of souls. Probably in May 1237 he became archdeacon of Oxford, an office he held until some time between 17 June and 13 July 1240. On the authority of Le Neve it is said that he was concurrently archdeacon of Rochester (from 1238), but this is unlikely, and probably the consequence of confusion with a man of the same name who was both chancellor of Oxford and archdeacon of Rochester. He held the prebend of Weldland in St Paul's for a time between 1229 and 1248, but this was probably concurrent with his next office, the deanery of Lincoln, to which he had been appointed by Grosseteste following the chapter's refusal to elect a successor to Master William of Thornac', who had resigned and become a Cistercian at Louth Park in 1239–40. Wesham is first recorded as dean on 21 August 1240. In that office he became embroiled in the litigious struggle between his chapter and Grosseteste concerning the latter's right of visitation, a contest that shifted to the papal court at Lyons. The subsequent settlement, almost entirely in Grosseteste's favour, led to charges of Wesham's having betrayed the chapter. However, before this, Wesham had been provided, on Grosseteste's recommendation, to the see of Coventry and Lichfield, following yet another disputed election. Consecration by the pope occurred between 17 May and 4 July 1245, but Wesham did not receive the temporalities until 25 March 1246, which probably reflected the king's anger at his not being consulted.

It is hard to assess Wesham's conduct of diocesan affairs, since neither registers nor rolls were as yet kept at Lichfield. Given Wesham's close links with Grosseteste, who did keep rolls at Lincoln, this is perhaps surprising. What evidence there is suggests his engagement with the affairs of his diocese was real. As might be expected, he gathered learned men around him, for instance the Franciscan Brother Vincent, John of Basingstoke, a noted scholar of Greek, and Ralph of Sempringham, chancellor of Oxford University in the early 1250s. He arbitrated carefully in a dispute between Haughmond and Ranton abbeys concerning jurisdiction in 1247; he was careful about the endowment of Hillmorton, Warwickshire. In 1252 he issued thirty-five visitation articles, touching on every aspect of church discipline. He also prepared the *Instituta*, a document instructing his clergy in dogma and suggesting topics for sermons in the vernacular. At Lichfield he augmented the income of the senior archdeaconry, that of Chester, by annexing to it the prebend of Bolton, as well as founding the prebends of Bubbenhall and Ryton, and endowing a chantry to benefit the bishops of Lincoln and Lichfield and the deans of Lincoln.

By 1253 Wesham was already ill, for on 7 August 1253 he was granted a faculty to appoint a coadjutor by reason of infirmity by Pope Innocent IV (*r.* 1243–54). In 1256 he was stricken with paralysis and sought permission from Alexander IV (*r.* 1254–61) to resign his office. Henry of Lexinton, bishop of Lincoln (*d.* 1258), was appointed to receive his resignation, which he did at the episcopal manor of Brewood, Staffordshire, to which Wesham had retired, on 4 December 1256. He lingered there until Sunday 21 May 1257, when he died. He was buried on the following Tuesday at Lichfield, with Fulk of Sandford (*d.* 1271), archbishop of Dublin, officiating. M. J. FRANKLIN

Sources Emden, *Oxf.* · *Ann. mon.* · H. E. Savage, ed., *The great register of Lichfield Cathedral known as Magnum registrum album*, William Salt Archaeological Society, 3rd ser. (1924, [1926]) · F. N. Davis, ed., *Rotuli Roberti Grosseteste*, Lincoln RS, 11 (1914) · W. P. W. Phillimore and others, eds., *Rotuli Hugonis de Welles*, 3 vols., Lincoln RS, 3, 6, 9 (1912–14) · 'Thomas de Eccleston de adventu fratrum minorum in Angliam', *Monumenta Franciscana*, ed. J. S. Brewer and R. Howlett, 1, Rolls Series, 4 (1858) · *Fasti Angl., 1066–1300*, [Lincoln] · M. Gibbs and J. Lang, *Bishops and reform, 1215–1272* (1934) · C. R. Cheney, *English synodalia of the thirteenth century* (1968) · K. Major, 'The *familia* of Robert Grosseteste', *Robert Grosseteste: scholar and bishop*, ed. D. Callus (1955), 216–41

Wesley, Charles (1707–1788), Church of England clergyman and a founder of Methodism, was born on 18 December 1707 at Epworth rectory, Lincolnshire, the sixteenth or seventeenth child and third surviving son of Samuel *Wesley (*bap.* 1662, *d.* 1735), rector of Epworth, and his wife, Susanna *Wesley (1669–1742), daughter of Samuel *Annesley and his second wife, Mary White. Among his elder siblings was Hetty [*see* Wright, Mehetabel], who later achieved prominence as a poet.

From birth to conversion, 1707–1738 Wesley was born prematurely, wrapped in soft wool, and opened his eyes and cried only at two months. He was subjected to Susanna's strict and methodical child-rearing, based on subduing the child's will to its parents. Charles entered Westminster School in 1716 where he was overseen by his brother Samuel, one of the ushers, who imbued him with his own high-church tory principles. He became king's scholar (1721) and captain of the school (1725), and protected William Murray (the future lord chief justice the earl of Mansfield), who was persecuted for his family's Jacobite associations. Charles also did some acting, and his lively personality sometimes led him into difficulties. The story has often been repeated that during his schooldays Garrett Wesley of Dangan, co. Meath, Ireland (who some accounts claim was a relative), offered to make Charles his heir and supported him financially at school. Charles, however, refused the offer and Garrett adopted his cousin

Charles Wesley (1707–1788), by unknown artist, *c.*1735

Richard Colley, the grandfather of the future duke of Wellington. The claim to a family relationship is almost certainly mistaken. However, the rest of the story first appeared in print in John Whitehead's biography of the Wesleys (1793), citing John Wesley's manuscript biography of Charles, which a letter proves he began in 1788—though it has since disappeared. Charles's daughter Sarah *Wesley claimed that her father told the story to his friend Lord Mornington, father of Wellington, before Mornington's death in 1781. There is therefore probably real substance to the story.

On 13 June 1726 Wesley matriculated and in 1727 was elected a student of Christ Church, Oxford, with a Westminster scholarship of £100 p.a. He graduated BA in 1730 and proceeded MA in March 1733. Freed of family restraints Charles now led a more relaxed life, including excursions to London and emotional entanglements with London actresses. To his brother John *Wesley's attempts to make him more serious he objected: 'What? would you have me to be a saint at once?' (Moore, 1.151).

But by January 1729 Wesley was prepared to reform:

My first year in college I lost in diversion. The next I set myself to study. Diligence led me into serious thinking. I went to the weekly sacrament and persuaded two or three young scholars to accompany me and to resume the method of study prescribed by the statutes of the university. This gained me the harmless nickname of Methodist. (letter to

Dr Chandler, 29 April 1785, Methodist church archives, DDWES/1/38)

Later that year John Wesley 'came to our assistance' (ibid.). It is on the basis of this letter that Charles is sometimes credited with being the first 'Methodist', though this probably overplays the significance of the term. Charles in 1785 wished to claim that Methodism had been an organization loyal to the church until its betrayal by John Wesley's ordinations of 1784. There is no known contemporary reference to 'Methodists' before August 1732, and Charles's informal efforts were systematized by John.

As a student Charles Wesley told John that he was 'very *desirous* of knowledge but can't *bear* the drudgery of coming at it near so well as you could. … My head will by no means keep pace with my heart' (Baker, *Charles Wesley*, 12). Like John, he was attracted by the Kirkham circle, centred on John's close friend Sally Kirkham (Varanese), in Stanton, Oxfordshire, Charles's nickname being Araspes; as late as February 1736 he addressed an emotional, self-critical letter to Kirkham. Serious concerns did not stifle Charles's ebullience or jokes about his poverty. John Gambold was told in 1730 about 'the whimsical Mr Wesley, his preciousness and pious extravagancies'. He found Charles 'a man made for friendship', vivacious but considerate for a friend's needs, though deferential to his brother who 'was always the chief manager' (Tyerman, *Oxford Methodists*, 157). Both brothers were influenced by the nonjurors even, to some extent, after their conversions in 1738.

Wesley was ordained deacon and priest on 5 and 12 October 1735. At this point he 'only thought of spending all my days in Oxford. But my brother, who always had the ascendant over me, persuaded me to accompany him and Mr Oglethorpe to Georgia'. Charles's letter also makes clear that John had been instrumental in pushing his brother towards an ordination which he 'exceedingly dreaded' (letter to Chandler, 29 April 1785, Methodist church archives, DDWES/1/38). In Georgia from 1736, Charles acted as secretary to James Edward Oglethorpe. However, designing women and pastoral naïvety divided the brothers from Oglethorpe by mutual suspicions of misconduct. Despite an emotional reconciliation, Charles was so shattered by physical illness and emotional and spiritual depression that he offered his resignation on 25 July 1736, when Oglethorpe perceptively advised him that, being 'of a social temper', he would find 'in a married state the difficulties of working out your salvation exceedingly lessened, and your helps as much increased' (*Journal*, ed. Jackson, 1.35). Charles left for England and after a difficult voyage landed there on 3 December 1736.

Wesley continued to think that he should return to the colony, though as a minister rather than secretary, but finally resigned his Georgia post on 3 April 1738, swayed by medical advice and by his mother's and brother's opposition to his return. Meanwhile he had visited friends, and from July to November 1737 descanted frequently on 'the new birth' and 'inward change' which affected some of his hearers, reflecting the ideas of the devotional writer William Law. Early in 1738, however, the Moravian Peter Böhler persuaded the Wesleys to accept the idea of justification by grace through faith, experienced through a sudden conversion. It was Charles who first received the gift, on 21 May, in a way at once less clear-cut and more apparently supernatural than did his brother. Inspired by a mysterious voice (in fact that of a Moravian adherent) 'I found myself converted, I knew not how nor when' and 'found myself at peace with God and rejoiced in hope of loving Christ' (*Journal*, ed. Jackson, 1.91–2). John's conversion followed on 24 May, and shortly afterwards Charles's poetic gift was released in his 'conversion hymn' 'When shall my wondering soul begin'.

Travelling evangelist, 1738–1756 Wesley's health and temperament seemed poorly fitted for the hardships of a travelling evangelist. A return to Oxford or parish life appeared more suitable options even to his demanding brother. Yet Charles seemed relieved when a prospective living fell through in February 1739. Instead he spent his time in testifying to his new-found faith to individuals and small groups and in preaching. In July 1738 he began what became a lifelong interest by speaking to condemned prisoners at Newgate gaol and achieved startling results despite initial doubts about deathbed repentances. From then until August 1739 he was also an unlicensed curate to George Stonehouse in Islington, finally being forced out by the bishop and churchwardens. On 25 October he began to preach without notes, which gave him greater freedom and made a greater impact upon his hearers; and on 29 May 1739 he followed George Whitefield and John Wesley by preaching in the open air.

Despite his successes Wesley frequently longed for retirement or even death. He was troubled by converts' convulsions and encounters with the French prophets who claimed divine inspiration and healing powers. Though far from denying supernatural influences, Charles became more sceptical than his brother, for he saw some convulsionaries as exhibitionists and put them aside, after which they quietened down. Soon there were also conflicts with Moravians who taught 'stillness', the notion that people must wait passively for God to convert them. Charles, who was more open to mystical impulses than John, may have briefly wavered on the issue. But on 20 July 1740 John Wesley broke with the Moravians and Charles purged the 'still brethren' in Bristol. In March 1741 a similar break occurred with the predestinarian followers of George Whitefield in Bristol and London, which provoked Charles to write hymns on the universal offer of salvation. He nevertheless often acted as peacemaker and tried to maintain friendly relations with those estranged by his brother.

At first the Wesleys ministered to their followers by shuttling to and fro between London and Bristol. From 1740 the work expanded to Wales, then northern England, Cornwall, Ireland, and finally, in 1751, to Scotland. Except in Cornwall, John usually preceded Charles. It appears that the general plan was for each brother in turn to attend to London and Bristol while the other visited the more remote areas. Lay preachers filled the gaps between the brothers' visits and met in an annual conference from 1744.

The Methodists often faced mob violence, which provided some of the most dramatic passages in the Wesleys' journals. In the edgy mid-1740s they were suspected of being Jacobites, Charles being cited before the magistrates at Wakefield in March 1744 for praying 'that the Lord would call home his [spiritual] banished' (*Journal*, ed. Jackson, 1.361). However, he dissuaded John from issuing a declaration of Methodist loyalty which might identify them as a sect.

On 28 August 1747 Charles Wesley first met Sarah Gwynne [*see below*], the twenty-year-old daughter of Marmaduke Gwynne of Garth, Brecknockshire, a magistrate who supported the Methodists. In September 1748 Charles expressed his love plainly in verse:

Two are better far than one
For counsel or for fight!
How can one be warm alone
Or serve his God aright?
(Baker, *Charles Wesley*, 58)

Fortunately John Wesley supported his brother's suit and was able to satisfy members of the Gwynne family, concerned about Charles's income, by guaranteeing him £100 p.a. from their book profits. Charles had concluded by December that the marriage was indeed God's will for him, and he and Sarah were married on 8 April 1749. 'A stranger that intermeddleth not with our joy said "It looked more like a funeral than a wedding". My brother seemed the happiest person among us' (*Journal*, ed. Jackson, 2.56). It was a love-match of rare harmony and achieved a degree of happiness seldom seen in the marriage of a Wesley.

In that same year, 1749, came the confused and painful attempt by John Wesley to marry Grace Murray (who subsequently married the Methodist preacher John Bennet), followed by his disastrous marriage to Mrs Mary Vazeille in 1751. To both Charles Wesley reacted with alarm and high emotion. The rights and wrongs of the Murray affair remain debatable. Charles believed that John Bennet had the prior claim to Grace Murray, that her union with John Wesley would split Methodism, and that she was socially unsuitable. He therefore hustled Bennet and Murray into marriage. The account handed down by Charles's wife, Sarah, to her daughter depicted Grace Murray as at best an unstable woman torn between love for Bennet and a prestigious marriage to her leader, but this probably exonerates the Wesley brothers, and especially Charles, too easily. John's marriage to Mary Vazeille dismayed Charles, and he and his sister-in-law remained mutually distrustful until she left her husband in 1771. It may well be that the strained relationships between the brothers over the Murray affair and John's marriage continued to aggravate disagreements on policy over the next few years.

Certainly these personal disturbances coincided with tensions within Methodism. John Bennet's decision to break away was followed by the charge of sexual misconduct by the preacher James Wheatley which led the brothers to agree that Charles should from now on investigate preachers' characters and abilities. Although Charles

reluctantly sanctioned lay preachers he doubted their talents and competence. In response to his criticisms in 1751 John Wesley said they needed all the men they could recruit and that 'I prefer grace before gifts' (*Works of John Wesley*, 26.472). Charles wrote on this subject to Selina, countess of Huntingdon, in intemperate terms. The preachers, he insisted, should live by their trades and only occasionally take preaching journeys; in addition new recruits would be thoroughly tested by the Wesleys. In making these comments Charles confided his underlying interest that these measures 'will break his [John's] power, their [preachers] not depending on him for bread' and so 'reduce his authority within due bounds as well as guard against that rashness and credulity of his which has kept me in continual awe and bondage for many years' (Baker, *Charles Wesley*, 84–5).

Wesley was even more alarmed about preachers' lack of loyalty to the Church of England. In the mid-1750s a crisis erupted which recurred periodically for the next thirty years. Some preachers registered under the Toleration Act as a defence against persecution and some pressed for the right to administer sacraments. Both actions appeared to imply separation from the church. In October 1754 a preacher administered communion in London and, according to Charles, John maintained that '"We have in effect ordained already". He urged me to sign the preachers' certificates: was inclined to lay on hands, and to let the preachers administer' (Baker, *Charles Wesley*, 92). Charles was only partly reassured at the conference of 1755 when John issued a statement concluding that, whether or not separation was 'lawful', it was not 'expedient'. Doubting John's resolution, Charles urged his evangelical friends to put pressure on his brother, even sympathizing with suggestions that the lay preachers should become mere assistants to evangelical clergy. John Wesley believed that to curb them in this way risked losing the evangelistic effectiveness of Methodism.

Between September and November 1756 Wesley made his last tour of the midlands and north of England and then ceased to itinerate. Although family responsibilities, recurring ill health, and depression restricted his movements, his daughter Sarah later claimed that his main concern was not to create discord within the Methodist movement. This was a discreet indication that Charles's doubts about the quality of their preachers and fears about separation from the church would lead to conflict with his brother. She may have been correct in this interpretation, for some of the preachers were certainly hostile to him. On the other hand, Charles's retirement from itinerancy did not prevent him from criticizing his brother.

John Wesley deplored his brother's abandonment of itinerancy. In a revealing letter in October 1753 he had already demanded that Charles 'either act really in connexion with me: or never pretend to it'. In reality, he complained, 'Either you move (quite contrary to me) by those impressions which you account divine or which is worse, *pro ratione voluntas* [will instead of reason]'. Charles, he said, had not acted in concert with him 'for ten years last past and upwards' (*Works of John Wesley*, 26.527–8). Though John's complaints were coloured by his desire to control preachers' movements, it does look as though Charles's focus, particularly after his marriage, was more on problem areas (especially where there was disaffection towards the established church) rather than on a co-ordinated approach with his brother. He never visited Scotland, nor Ireland after 1748, nor Cornwall after 1753. While seemingly free to interfere where his prejudices were threatened, Charles appeared unwilling and unable to accept regular responsibilities of leadership.

Ministry in Bristol and London, 1756–1788 Charles Wesley remained in Bristol until 1771, though he frequently visited London as well as, on occasions, friends and relatives elsewhere in the south. During this period he continued to worry over the issue of preachers and possibility of separation from the Church of England. In February 1760 three preachers in Norwich administered communion, but John Wesley proceeded as planned to Ireland, merely asking Charles to look into the matter. Charles reacted violently, going so far as to tell the veteran preacher John Nelson: 'John, I love thee from my heart: yet rather than see thee a dissenting minister, I wish to see thee smiling in thy coffin' (Baker, *Charles Wesley*, 101). While acknowledging that preachers faced uncertain prospects after the Wesleys' deaths, he could only promise (unrealistically) that he would use his 'interest' to obtain Anglican orders for them. His priorities contrasted sharply with his brother's: 'My chief concern upon earth … was the prosperity of the Church of England; my next, that of Methodism, my third that of the preachers'. He would in effect give up the preachers for the good of the Methodists and the Methodists for the good of the church (ibid., 101, 102). During 1760 he was, in addition, at odds with John over the outbreak of claims to Christian perfection and was much distressed by the trial and execution of Lady Huntingdon's homicidal cousin, Lord Ferrers.

Wesley's growing interest in the careers of his precocious musical sons, Charles *Wesley (1757–1834) and Samuel *Wesley (1766–1837), helped to influence his decision to move to the London area in 1771. He was given the remaining lease on a fully furnished house, 1 Chesterfield Street, in Marylebone (including a cellar of wine), by his friend Mrs Gumley, whose sister-in-law was married to the earl of Bath. Despite his misgivings about Methodism, Charles seems to have been content to act as resident minister in Bristol and then in London, and showed no sign of wishing to settle in an Anglican parish despite rumours of offers. He regularly preached and administered communion in church service hours, using the Book of Common Prayer. A diligent pastor and prison visitor, he also enjoyed social relationships with the upper classes more than his brother, partly to further his sons' careers.

Wesley took little direct part in the Calvinistic controversy of the 1770s, though he did provide support for his friend John Fletcher, the main protagonist against the evangelical Calvinists. In 1771–3 and again in 1786 he attempted a reconciliation with the Moravians, hoping to combat Methodist separatism. In June 1777 he was greatly

exercised over the trial and execution of the popular clergyman William Dodd for forgery. Like his brother, he attacked the American revolutionaries and the Wilkite radicals, though in his case in verse rather than prose. In 1780 he witnessed the anti-Roman Catholic Gordon riots, which he vividly described in letters, poems, and hymns. He furthered the careers of his musical sons by concerts in his home to save them from a more worldly environment, though this also brought Methodist disapproval.

Despite his interventions when the interests of the church seemed threatened, Wesley always made it clear that he dreaded taking on full leadership responsibilities himself. The fate of Methodism after John Wesley's death was a recurring problem. Both Wesley brothers had hopes of a clerical successor, John Fletcher of Madeley being the most favoured candidate. However, in 1773 Fletcher not only refused, but even suggested Charles as his brother's successor. In the end John had to turn to the preachers. In 1784 he enrolled a deed of declaration, fixing the composition and powers of the annual Methodist conference as his legal successor. Meanwhile the American War of Independence had temporarily severed ecclesiastical relations with England, and John seized on the opportunity in 1784 to supply the American Methodists with an ordained ministry together with a revised version of the Book of Common Prayer and articles of religion. He ordained two of his preachers, together with his clerical colleague Thomas Coke as a 'superintendent', and Coke was to ordain Francis Asbury as his co-superintendent in America. In the last years of his life John also ordained for Scotland and, finally, three preachers apparently in reserve for England.

Wesley, who had not been consulted, was outraged at what he took to be the final seal on separation, though John denied this. Charles's disgust was expressed partly in letters, partly in verse:

> W— himself and friends betrays,
> By his good sense forsook,
> While suddenly his hands he lays
> On the hot head of C—.

Still more insultingly:

> A Roman emperor 'tis said
> His favourite horse a consul made
> But Coke brings other things to pass,
> He makes a bishop of an ass.
> (*Representative Verse*, 367)

It was in this context that Charles wrote his autobiographical letter to Dr Chandler in April 1785 to portray Methodism as a church movement betrayed by his brother. He quoted Lord Mansfield's assertion that ordination meant separation. The brothers had to agree to differ, Charles leaving John to his own devices. Yet despite their differences he continued his London ministry and summed up his feelings by writing: 'Thus our partnership here is ended but not our friendship. I have taken him for better for worse till death do us part—or rather re-unite in love inseparable' (letter to Chandler, 29 April 1785, Methodist church archives, DDWES/1/38).

In 1788 Wesley's health deteriorated, and despite John's

characteristic optimism that travel and folk-remedies would revive his brother, Charles died at home, aged eighty, of exhaustion on 29 March 1788. It is symptomatic of the brothers' ecclesiastical differences that John was buried behind his City Road Chapel, denying the notion of consecrated ground. Charles, however, was interred in the graveyard of his parish church, St Mary's, Marylebone, on 5 April, his pall borne by eight clergymen of the Church of England. The claim that, ironically, this churchyard was unconsecrated appears to be an error. Charles's family had so little money at the time of his death that his funeral expenses were defrayed by his friends.

Wesley as churchman, theologian, preacher, and hymn writer
John Wesley described himself as 'an high churchman, bred up from my childhood in the highest notions of passive obedience and non-resistance'. He was also a 'tory', meaning 'one that believes God, not the people, to be the origin of all civil power' (*Letters*, ed. Telford, 7.305–6, 6.156). So too was Charles Wesley, yet both violated church order. Likewise, Charles shared John's general view of evangelical theology plus a belief in a form of sacrifice and real presence in the Lord's supper, which he expressed with dramatic physicality in his hymns. But Charles thought Christian perfection scarcely attainable before death. John, operating with a restricted view of sin as 'a voluntary transgression of a known law which it is in our power to obey' (*Works of John Wesley*, 25.289, 318), claimed that the gift could be received at any time, by faith. Charles, by contrast, visualized a gradual and incomplete growth in holiness. He also believed that God used suffering as a purifying agent and might discipline individuals by withholding assurance of salvation, a view which John rejected as unscriptural. These divergences clearly reflected their respective temperaments. Elsewhere, John neatly hit off their differences in preaching style thus: 'In connexion [reasoned argument] I beat you; but in strong pointed *sentences* you beat me' (*Letters*, ed. Telford, 5.16). Charles was liable to open his Bible and select a text at random. Even in old age he sometimes recovered his old fire, and once accidentally knocked the Bible off the pulpit to be fielded by Thomas Coke. Equally, though, he could also fall into long introspective pauses or announce a hymn if he felt faint. Some thought both brothers were liable to offer poor fare in old age, and Charles's monopoly of the City Road pulpit was resented by some lay preachers.

Charles Wesley has long been regarded as the greatest of English hymn writers, yet in range and intention he was really a writer of 'sacred poems' as well. Of his 9000 poems, 'hymns' (depending on definition) form between one- and two-thirds of the total. It is only fairly recently that he has received recognition as a poet because hymns have commonly been regarded as too limited in content, metre, and purpose to be assessed as poetry. Charles habitually expressed his feelings and beliefs on a wide range of religiously orientated private and public concerns in verse, including charming pieces for his children:

> There was by fond mamma supplied
> Six reasons against Sammi's ride. …

Because 'tis wet, because 'tis dry …
Or any other reason why

and on the family cat:

> I sing Grimalkin brave and bold
> Who makes intruders fly …
> (*Unpublished Verse*, 1.280)

Charles's mind was pervasively furnished with material and images from the classics, the Book of Common Prayer, and English poetry, but above all from the Bible. All these materials were adapted to express Christian experience, above all the love of God. The boundary between sacred and secular here was easily crossed— some poems to his future wife were later adapted as hymns. What has been termed his 'physicality', even 'carnality', did undoubtedly cause uneasiness in later minds. However, to early Methodists Wesley showed that body as well as mind and feelings could express religion, a belief which informed some of the dancing metres and rhythms used in his writing. Like Isaac Watts he adapted literary culture to the needs of less educated readers, but with a much more remarkable range of metres and technical poetic skills. Ideas and images were transmuted and compressed into a few compelling words, simplicity being varied with dramatic use of Latinate words to express feelings or theological paradoxes: 'indissolubly joined', 'inextinguishable blaze',

> Our God contracted to a span,
> Incomprehensibly made man.

Methodists unaware of Charles's subtle skills nevertheless unconsciously absorbed a measure of theology and culture as well as expressing their faith and feelings.

Character, reputation, and significance Charles Wesley was short but somewhat stouter in face and figure than John. In college days:

> full of the muse, and being shortsighted, he would sometimes walk right up against his brother's table and, perhaps, overturn it. If the 'fine phrensy' was not quite so high, he would discompose the books and papers in the study, ask some question without always waiting for a reply, repeat some poetry that just then struck him, and at length leave his brother to his regularity. (Moore, 2.368)

In old age he would compose hymns on horseback in shorthand, and on reaching the City Road house rush in 'crying out "Pen and ink! pen and ink!"' and write out the hymn he had composed (ibid.). His handwriting was neat, he kept accounts meticulously, but his wife had to attend to his clothes. He wore full clerical dress, preached in gown and bands even in the open air, but unlike his brother wore a clerical wig.

Temperamentally Wesley was subject both to extreme exaltation (especially after preaching successfully) and extreme despair, expressing a desire for death with regularity throughout his life. Yet he also showed considerable moral and physical courage when confronting mobs critical of Methodism. Though a warm friend and tender consoler to the grieving, John Wesley claimed that Charles 'suspects everybody, and he is continually imposed upon, but I suspect nobody, and I am never imposed upon' (Tyerman, *Wesley*, 3.297). This was an exaggerated response to

Charles's claim that John was too trusting. Charles could be suspicious of those suspected of hostility to the church, and John thought he was liable to be influenced by the person to whom he had last spoken. His sense of public duty conflicted with his modesty and desire for retirement. An affectionate husband and father, he was anxious to imbue his children with the strength of his own evangelical beliefs.

Except as a hymn writer Charles Wesley's reputation has been overshadowed by that of his brother and has been clouded by their disagreements on policy. Unfortunately his journal survives only from 1736 to 1756, with gaps, and the complete text has never been published, though a modern edition is now in preparation. There is no complete or modern edition of his letters or even of his poetry. The fullest biography by Thomas Jackson (1841) is uncritical and, with the exception of Frank Baker (1948) and J. R. Tyson's *Reader* (1989), later biographers have largely tended to recycle published material.

Charles Wesley's overall significance for Methodism and the eighteenth century revival remains difficult to estimate, but he was clearly more than a hymn writer, however distinguished he proved in this field. Liable to be seen as a well-intentioned but misguided drag on his brother's mission, he deserves to be judged as an independent personality and in terms of his own vision of Methodism. His early journeys for evangelism and oversight significantly aided Methodism's take-off, while his role as pastor stabilized the important Bristol and London societies. John Wesley's pragmatic attitude to irregularities was probably necessary for Methodism's dynamism, yet it is arguable that Charles's restraints on his brother's 'rashness' helped to raise preachers' standards and warded off the risk of a premature break with the church in the 1750s which would have narrowed the appeal of the movement at a critical stage. Recent research suggests that his opposition to his brother's ministries was supported by a significant body of leading laymen especially in London.

Charles's wife, **Sarah Wesley** [*née* Gwynne] (1726–1822), Methodist sympathizer, was born on 12 October 1726 at Garth, Brecknockshire, the fifth of the nine children of Marmaduke Gwynne (1691–1769), gentleman, and his wife, Sarah (1695–1769/70), daughter of Daniel Evans and his wife, Mary. She was educated by private masters, and by the age of ten was proficient in music and singing. Her father was a firm Anglican and magistrate, but his conversion by Howell Harris, the Welsh evangelical, led him to support the Methodists. Her mother was one of six heiresses, each reputedly with a portion of £30,000.

Sarah was devout from an early age, receiving communion at fourteen and accompanying her father to hear Harris. She first met Charles Wesley on 28 August 1747 and it appears to have been a case of love at first sight. They were married at Llanllywenfel on 8 April 1749. Sarah had agreed to allow Charles to maintain his vegetarian diet and travels, even to Ireland, against her mother's protests. The journeys recommenced almost at once, though they took a house in Bristol in September 1749. Sarah became a

willing hostess to visiting preachers, saying that these plain men 'were proofs that grace supplied all the felicitous aid of education and good breeding' (Methodist church archives, DDWES 1/59). Her sweet singing sometimes surprised and delighted visitors and Methodist meetings.

At first Sarah Wesley patiently endured the privations of travelling with Charles, including mob violence. Late in 1753 she was struck down with smallpox, having refused vaccination apparently through religious scruples, and was left so disfigured as to be almost unrecognizable. She ironically commented that this 'afforded great satisfaction to her dear husband who was glad to see her look so much older and better suited to be his wife' (S. Wesley, 'Memoir of Mrs Sarah Wesley', 509). Their first child also died of smallpox on 7 January 1754. They had eight children but only three survived to maturity: a daughter, Sarah, and the precocious musicians Charles and Samuel.

Sarah Wesley enjoyed friendship and correspondence with socially prominent people, especially evangelical peeresses. Her circle widened further with the family's move to Marylebone in 1771. Following her husband's death in March 1788, she was left with recurring financial problems. Accounts of the reasons for this vary. It appears that capital equivalent to her husband's £100 p.a. from Methodism was invested for her, but other money was realized and spent, and she received an annuity from William Wilberforce and occasional income from legacies and the Methodists. Her son Samuel's debts also drained her resources.

Despite her own difficulties, Sarah was conspicuous for her care of the poor and pity for evil-doers, since she thought anyone might fall but for divine grace. She had a strong sense of her sins and a recurring fear of death except in her last illness. Sarah's reading was confined to religious books, for she did not relish any others. Her daughter thought her chief faults were excessive hospitality and indulgence of her children. In fact Sarah's life was principally devoted to her husband's welfare and her care probably prolonged his life. She provided a much needed balance to his fluctuating temperament and his brother's demands, while her social contacts aided her sons' careers. Her quiet personality masked a strength of will expressed in her marriage despite family doubts. She insisted that she be allowed to attend George Whitefield and other 'gospel ministers' despite the Wesleys' opposition to their Calvinism. Solicitous of the brothers' reputation she passed on family traditions favourable to them to her daughter and so to later biographers, and her short memoir of Charles prefaced a volume of his sermons (1816). She died on 28 December 1822, weakened by a cold and old age, and was buried with her husband in the churchyard of St Mary's, Marylebone.

HENRY D. RACK

Sources *DNB* · Charles Wesley papers, JRL, Methodist Archives and Research Centre, DDCW 1–10 [calendar by G. Lloyd, 2 vols., 1994] · Wesley family papers, JRL, Methodist Archives and Research Centre, DDWF 1–26, DDWES 1–9 [calendar by G. Lloyd, 3 vols., 1992–3] · *The journal of the Rev. Charles Wesley*, ed. T. Jackson, 2 vols. [1849] · *The journal of the Rev. Charles Wesley, 1736–1739*, ed. J. Telford (1910) · G. Lloyd, *Charles Wesley: a new evaluation of his life and ministry*, PhD diss., U. Lpool, 2002 · T. Jackson, *Life of Charles Wesley*, 2 vols. (1841) · F. Baker, *Charles Wesley as revealed by his letters* (1948) · J. R. Tyson, ed., *Charles Wesley: a reader* (1989) · G. J. Stevenson, *Memorials of the Wesley family* (1876), 427–46 · *The letters of the Rev. John Wesley*, ed. J. Telford, 8 vols. (1931) · *The works of John Wesley*, 25–6, ed. F. Baker and others (1980–82) · F. Baker, *John Wesley and the Church of England* (1970) [repr. 2000] · F. C. Gill, *Charles Wesley: the first Methodist* [1964] · S. Wesley the younger, 'Memoir of Mrs Sarah Wesley', *Wesleyan Methodist Magazine*, 45 (1822), 133, 506–11 · *Representative verse of Charles Wesley*, ed. F. Baker (1964) [introduction rev. and issued sep. as *Charles Wesley's verse: an introduction* (1988)] · J. R. Watson, *The English hymn: a critical and historical study* (1997), 205–64 · D. Davie, *Purity of diction in English verse* (1952), 70–81 · J. E. Rattenbury, *The eucharistic hymns of John and Charles Wesley* (1948) · J. C. Bowmer, *The sacrament of the Lord's supper in early Methodism* (1951) · *Unpublished verse of Charles Wesley*, ed. S. T. Kimbrough and O. A. Beckerlegge, 1 (1988) · [S. Wesley the elder], 'Memoir of Charles Wesley', in C. Wesley, *Sermons* (1816) · C. Evans, 'The ancestry of the Wesleys', *N&Q*, 193 (1948), 255–9 · J. Whitehead, *Life of John … [and] … Charles Wesley*, 1 (1793) · letters of Sarah Wesley the younger, Wesley College, Bristol, D6/1/276–300 · H. Moore, *The life of the Rev. John Wesley*, 2 vols. (1824–5) · J. Telford, *Sayings and portraits of Charles Wesley* (1927) · private information (2004) [P. Forsaith] · F. Baker, 'The birth of Charles Wesley', *Proceedings of the Wesley Historical Society*, 31 (1957–8), 25–6 · L. Tyerman, *The Oxford Methodists* (1873) · W. F. Swift, 'Was Charles Wesley buried in unconsecrated ground?', *Proceedings of the Wesley Historical Society*, 31 (1957–8), 123–4 · L. Tyerman, *The life and times of the Rev. John Wesley*, 2nd edn, 3 (1872), 297 **Archives** JRL, Methodist Archive and Research Centre, corresp., literary MSS, DDCW 1–10 · JRL, Methodist Archive and Research Centre, family MSS, DDWF 1–26; DDWES 1–9 · JRL, Methodist Archive and Research Centre, letters · NL Wales, letters · Wesley College, Bristol, corresp. · Westminster Institute of Education, Oxford, Methodist Studies Centre, letters | JRL, Methodist Archive and Research Centre, corresp. with J. Wesley and others **Likenesses** oils, *c.*1735, Epworth Old Rectory, Lincolnshire [*see illus.*] · J. Russell, oils, 1771, Charles Wesley's House, Bristol · J. Russell, oils, 1771 (Sarah Wesley), Charles Wesley's House, Bristol · J. Spilsbury, stipple, pubd 1786, NPG; example, Epworth Old Rectory, Lincolnshire · W. Gush, oils, 1850–59, Kingswood School, Bristol · attrib. J. Russell, oils (Sarah Wesley; in old age), Wesley's Chapel, City Road, London · oils, Methodist Publishing House, London **Wealth at death** see copy of will, JRL, Methodist Archives and Research Centre, Charles Wesley papers, DDCW/4/66

Wesley, Charles (1757–1834), musician, was born in Bristol, possibly at 19 Charles Street, on 11 December 1757, the son of Charles *Wesley (1707–1788), Methodist preacher, and his wife, Sarah Gwynne (1726–1822). He was the third of eight children and the oldest of three who survived to maturity. It would appear to have been primarily from his mother that Charles and his brother Samuel *Wesley (1766–1837) inherited their musical aptitude; Sarah was an accomplished performer on the guitar and harpsichord and had a particular love of Handel's oratorios, a taste which she passed on to her son. According to his father's account Charles was aged two and three-quarters when he began to display musical precocity, imitating his mother's playing on the harpsichord 'without study or hesitation' (*Journal*, 2.151). John Broderip, organist at Wells Cathedral, heard the boy at an early stage and predicted that he would be a great musician.

At the age of four Charles was taken to London by his father and Broderip's opinion was confirmed by the blind organist John Stanley. John Beard, manager of Covent Garden, offered to procure Charles a place among the choristers of the Chapel Royal, but the boy's father refused as he had no intention of raising his son to be a musician. After his return to the family residence in Charles Street, Bristol, Charles was placed under the tutelage of an organist named Rooke, although in his father's words, Rooke 'sat by, more to observe than control' (*Journal*, 2.152). Charles's parents oversaw other aspects of education, and without other children to interact with Charles and his sister Sarah (Sally) *Wesley, his junior by almost two years, developed an exceptionally close relationship which was never to diminish.

It became clear that Charles and his younger brother Samuel wished to become professional musicians and in furtherance of this aim the family moved in 1771 to 1 Chesterfield Street, Marylebone, Middlesex. Charles received lessons from Joseph Kelway and William Boyce, and from 1779 to 1786 the brothers performed in subscription concerts at the family home. Charles also gave command performances for George III and the prince of Wales. His career did not live up to its early promise. He made his living by giving recitals and more regular employment as organist at several Anglican chapels in the London area, namely Surrey, South Street, Welbeck, Chelsea Hospital, and finally Marylebone parish church.

Wesley's output as a composer was almost negligible. His earliest published works were five string quartets which he wrote about 1778 and six keyboard concertos from the same period. He also wrote organ voluntaries dedicated to the prince regent and a set of variations for the piano dedicated to the Princess Charlotte. His other published compositions include the cantata *Caractacus* and a number of glees and anthems. His work made little impact in his own day and is largely forgotten. His abiding musical characteristic was conservatism and he paid little attention to contemporary developments.

Wesley never married, but lived with his parents and afterwards with his sister Sally in rented lodgings in the capital until her death in 1828. One of his final addresses, in 1830–33, was on Edgware Road in London. He also made regular visits to Bristol and Brighton. He died on 23 May 1834 and was buried alongside his parents at Marylebone parish church.

The life of Charles Wesley is an excellent example of precocious talent which does not live up to expectation. He appears to have lacked ambition and to have been somewhat eccentric. One contemporary described him:

> C Westley is as good natured a soul as ever breathed: brimful of vanity he is nevertheless three times as agreeable as any other person that had so large a share. He possesses quickness of thought and sharpness of apprehension which cultivated in his earlier periods of life would probably have settled into poignancy of wit and inexhaustible memory … he knows no heaven beyond his harpsichord and unemployed with that, he passes his time in dress mimicking ridiculous characters … or recounts the anecdotes of people of fashion.   (JRL, Charles Wesley MSS, DDCW 6/85A)

It is possible that had his parents taken at an earlier stage the opportunity of a musical education in London, he might have progressed, but as it is his musical legacy is insignificant compared with that of his brother, and his nephew Samuel Sebastian Wesley (1810–1876).

GARETH LLOYD

Sources DNB · *The journal of the Rev. Charles Wesley*, ed. T. Jackson, 2 [1849], 140–52 · E. Routley, *The musical Wesleys* (1968) · G. Lloyd, 'The life of Charles Wesley junior', paper presented to the Charles Wesley Society Conference at Drew University, Oct 1998, JRL · JRL, DDCW and DDWF · R. W. Brown, *Charles Wesley: hymn-writer* (1993) · D. M. Lewis, ed., *The Blackwell dictionary of evangelical biography, 1730–1860*, 2 vols. (1995) · F. C. Gill, *Charles Wesley: the first Methodist* [1964]
Archives Dorset RO, diaries and corresp. · JRL, Methodist Archives and Research Centre, corresp. · NRA, diaries | JRL, Methodist Archives and Research Centre, Wesley family MSS · Man. CL, Manchester Archives and Local Studies, letters to Miss Essex Cholmondley

Wesley [Wellesley], **Garrett**, **first earl of Mornington** (**1735–1781**), composer, was born on 19 July 1735, probably at Dangan Castle, co. Meath, the son of Richard *Wesley (or Wellesley, formerly Colley), first baron of Mornington (1690–1758), and Elizabeth Sale (d. 1738). Educated at Trinity College, Dublin, he graduated BA in 1754 and MA in 1757. He sat in the Irish House of Commons for the family borough of Trim, co. Meath, beginning in 1757. On his father's death in 1758 he took his seat in the Irish House of Lords as the second baron. His surname is sometimes given as Wellesley, but though he used this name for the viscountcy he received in 1760, Wesley was his usual surname in his lifetime.

Wesley showed signs of musical talent at an early age. His mother's death when he was three left him in the doting hands of his father and sisters, who fostered his musical interests. By age nine he played the violin with some skill and began training on his father's harpsichord and organ, which had long been a part of the family home, Dangan Castle. According to his godmother, Mrs Delany, he grew up nicely: 'My godson, Master Wesley, is a most extraordinary boy; he was thirteen last month, he is a very good scholar, and whatever study he undertakes he masters it most surprisingly' (*Autobiography … Mrs Delany*, 2.501). In his years at Trinity College and afterwards, Wesley immersed himself in Dublin society and music. He composed glees and church music with great success, and in 1758 he assembled a music academy for philanthropic purposes. The academy attracted well-heeled amateurs who met regularly under Garrett's direction to indulge their love of music and to hold concerts, the proceeds of which went to loans for poor tradesmen. In 1764 Trinity College conferred upon him the degree of doctor of music.

On 6 February 1759 Mornington married Anne Hill (1742–1831), the eldest daughter of a Dublin banker, Arthur Hill, later Lord Dungannon. Anne was a lively, intelligent young woman but, according to Mrs Delany, was wanting in judgement and manners: 'What I think L. M. [Lady Mornington] may be wanting in, is what few people have attained at her age, who have not had some real superiority of understanding and a little experience

of the manners of the world' (*Autobiography … Mrs Delany*, 3.534–7). The following year on 2 October 1760 Wellesley was rewarded for his musical and philanthropic achievements with an elevation in the Irish peerage as first Viscount Wellesley of Dangan and first earl of Mornington.

Lord and Lady Mornington had nine children, seven of whom survived childhood and six of whom lived into adulthood. Richard *Wellesley, the future Marquess Wellesley (1760–1842), came first, followed by the first Arthur (1762–1768?) and William (1763–1845), the future William Wellesley-*Pole, third earl of Mornington. The short-lived Francis came in 1765 and Anne in 1768. Anne (1768–1844) married first the Hon. Henry Fitzroy, and second Charles Culling Smith. These were followed by the second Arthur *Wellesley, the future duke of Wellington (1769–1852), Gerald Valerian (1770–1848), prebendary of Durham, Henry *Wellesley, first Baron Cowley (1773–1847), and Elizabeth (1773–1794). The Morningtons decided to educate their children in England, and the boys attended Eton College. Consequently, the family divided their time between Ireland and London. The practical consequences were significant as increased expenses combined with declining income from the family's estates to dissipate the family fortune. When Lord Mornington died suddenly, in Kensington, London, on 22 May 1781 he left his family in straitened circumstances. He was buried in Grosvenor Chapel, South Audley Street, London, after an elaborate funeral planned by his heir, Richard. Lady Mornington lived into her ninetieth year; constant financial difficulties in those years turned her into a severe and demanding woman largely ignored by her children. She died on 10 September 1831 and was buried with her husband in Grosvenor Chapel.

JOHN K. SEVERN

Sources E. Longford [E. H. Pakenham, countess of Longford], *Wellington, 1: The years of the sword* (1969) · BL, Wellesley MSS, Add. MSS 13914 and 37416 · I. Butler, *The eldest brother: the Marquess Wellesley, the duke of Wellington's eldest brother* (1973) · R. R. Pearce, *Memoirs and correspondence of the most noble Richard Marquess Wellesley*, 3 vols. (1846) · *The Wellesley papers: the life and correspondence of Richard Colley Wellesley, Marquess Wellesley*, ed. [L. S. Benjamin], 2 vols. (1914) · *The autobiography and correspondence of Mary Granville, Mrs Delany*, ed. Lady Llanover, 1st ser., 3 vols. (1861) · P. Guedalla, *The duke* (1931) · U. Southampton, Hartley Library, Wellington MSS · Burke, *Peerage* · GM, 1st ser., 51 (1781), 243 · DNB · R. A. Austen-Leigh, ed., *The Eton College register, 1753–1790* (1921)
Archives BL, Wellesley MSS · PRO, Cowley MSS, FO 519 · Stratfield Saye House, Hampshire · U. Southampton, Hartley Library, Wellington MSS · Wellington Museum, London
Likenesses oils, c.1760, Stratfield Saye House, Hampshire · oils, Stratfield Saye House, Hampshire
Wealth at death nearly bankrupt; estates mortgaged: Longford, *Wellington: years of the sword*; Butler, *The eldest brother*

Wesley [Westley], **John** (**1703–1791**), Church of England clergyman and a founder of Methodism, was born on 17 June 1703 at Epworth rectory, Lincolnshire, the thirteenth or fourteenth child and the second of three sons to reach maturity of Samuel *Wesley (bap. 1662, d. 1735), rector of Epworth, and his wife, Susanna *Wesley (1669–1742), daughter of Samuel *Annesley and his second wife, Mary. He was baptized on 3 July at Epworth church (that he was named John Benjamin at his baptism, as sometimes

John Wesley (1703–1791), by Nathaniel Hone, c.1766

stated, is a nineteenth-century error). Samuel still spelt the family name Westley in 1694 and others occasionally did so later. Both parents, though children of dissenting ministers ejected in 1662, became high-church Anglicans early in life, and puritan influence on John's upbringing is debatable.

Early life, 1703–1720 Though much is known about the Wesley family, little but anecdote survives about John himself in this period. It has often been observed that his cool intelligence and passion for order reflect his mother's character, while his brother Charles *Wesley's mercurial temperament echoed his father's, but John could be hasty too. Both brothers were junior to their precocious and talented sister, Hetty [see Wright, Mehetabel]. Several events in John's early life have commonly been emphasized as significant for his later development. His parents saw as providential the rescue of their children from a rectory fire in 1709. In 1711 Susanna resolved 'to be more particularly careful of the soul of this child that thou hast so mercifully provided for'. Later tradition related this to Wesley's adoption of the motto 'a brand plucked from the burning' to claim that he was seen as singled out early for a special destiny. However, Wesley's sense of a providential calling came much later (Heitzenrater, *Elusive Mr Wesley*, 1.40–43). Tight maternal discipline applied to all the children, though with variable results. Regularity was enforced in eating, sleeping, education, and religion. This was a severe, religiously focused version of John Locke's educational principles, and 'breaking the will' was seen as the foundation of religion and morality. In 1712, during her husband's absence at

convocation, Susanna Wesley conducted informal meetings in the rectory which some have seen as an anticipation of later Methodist practice. In 1716–17 there appeared the Epworth ghost, Old Jeffery, apparently a poltergeist with Jacobite sympathies who knocked loudly when George I was prayed for. The family only gradually concluded that Jeffery was a supernatural visitant, but John Wesley, though absent at the time, believed this from the first, thus signalling a lifelong belief in divine and diabolical intervention. He also seems to have shown early the habit of a reasoned approach as the way to solve even the most personal problems. His father wisely remarked 'you think to carry everything by dint of argument, but you will find how little is ever done in the world by close reasoning'. John, he said, 'would not attend to the most pressing necessities of nature unless he had a reason for it' (Clarke, 2.321).

On 28 January 1714 Wesley became a foundation scholar at the Charterhouse on the nomination of his father's patron, the duke of Buckingham. Little but anecdotal traditions survive from this period. Thus Wesley is said to have justified preferring the company of younger boys with the Miltonic assertion 'Better to rule in hell than serve in heaven' (Tyerman, 1.20), which probably reflects later charges of ambition. His claim in 1738 that he had not sinned away the grace of baptism until he was ten years old may reflect the brutal impact of a contemporary public school, but he acknowledged even so that he was not guilty of outward sins.

Oxford and the Holy Club, 1720–1735 Wesley entered Christ Church, Oxford, on 24 June 1720 with a Charterhouse exhibition of £20 p.a. He matriculated on 18 July, was awarded a scholarship, and proceeded BA in 1724. Until 1725 his letters suggest a cheerful and dutiful son without pressing religious problems, though short of money. Like other undergraduates he wrote poetry and adopted the temperate diet recommended by the physician George Cheyne. His serious pursuit of religious discipline began in 1725 when his father urged him to seek holy orders, and in April he began a private diary as a means of self-examination. Correspondence with his mother shows that he was reading Jeremy Taylor's *Holy Living and Holy Dying* and Thomas à Kempis's *Imitation of Christ*. (It was probably only in 1730–32 that he encountered his contemporary William Law's *Serious Call* and *Christian Perfection*.) Though repelled by some of their severities, Wesley was convinced by these guides of the necessity of inward as well as outward holiness and the possibility of 'Christian perfection', which became his central concern. Though Wesley's diary records ever more elaborate rules and schemes of self-examination, his pursuit of holiness did not exclude playing cards, reading plays, and, as late as July 1733, dancing. He also cultivated a deeply affectionate, though also religious, friendship with Sally Kirkham ('Varanese') of Stanton, Oxfordshire, despite her marriage at the end of 1725. The effect of this relationship on his religious development is a matter for speculation. Between 1730 and 1734 he corresponded with her friend

Mary Pendarves ('Aspasia'), the later Mrs Delany, in a pseudo-classical style.

On 17 September 1725 Wesley was ordained deacon, and with the help of friends and Lincolnshire connections was elected fellow of Lincoln College on 17 March 1726. He proceeded MA on 9 February 1727, and was ordained priest on 22 September 1728. After acting as his father's curate at Wroot (near Doncaster) he was recalled to college for tutorial duties in November 1729.

In the same month Wesley began to organize the so-called Holy Club, initially as a study group. This was not, as traditionally portrayed, a single organization under his leadership but a network of groups in several colleges, members varying in their commitment. Among the nicknames levelled at the club was Methodist (first recorded in August 1732). An old term with varying uses, it was taken up later by Wesley, eventually with some pride. Suspicion over the club's activities deepened following the madness and death of William Morgan in 1732, blamed on Methodist excesses. They were attacked in *Fog's Weekly Journal* (December 1733), though described more sympathetically in *The Oxford Methodists* (1733; often accredited erroneously to William Law). Wesley's defence was circulated privately but published in the preface to the first instalment of his *Journal* in 1740. The club's activities included religious exercises and visiting sick people and prisoners. From 1732 Wesley was much influenced by high-church and nonjuror circles in Manchester through his Oxford friend John Clayton. He taught Wesley advanced notions of primitive Christianity based on early church practices such as fasting twice weekly and triple immersion for baptism, and introduced him to mystical writers. The fruit of this was his first publication, *A Collection of Forms of Prayer* (1733).

Looking back on this period after his conversion in 1738, Wesley dismissed his Oxford disciplines as a vain attempt at salvation by works. He later modified this judgement, concluding that he had had 'the faith of a servant, though not that of a son' (*Journal of John Wesley*, 1 Feb 1738, *Works*, 18.215 n.). By 1734–5 he probably felt in need of a fresh start. He was pressed to succeed his father at Epworth to secure his mother's home but was reluctant to do this, arguing at length that he could be more holy and useful at Oxford. However, in 1735 he responded positively to an invitation to go to Georgia as a missionary to the Native Americans for the Society for the Propagation of the Gospel in Foreign Parts. Significantly, he asserted that his chief hope was to save his own soul by starting primitive Christianity afresh in a spiritual state of nature and an idealized wilderness.

Georgia, 1735–1738 Wesley was accompanied by his brother Charles and his friends Benjamin Ingham and Charles Delamotte, and the published version of his *Journal* begins with the voyage to Georgia. It was to become a major, though partly misleading, source for future biographers, for it was not the simple and objective record that is often assumed. Appearing in three instalments from 1740, often several years after the events recorded, the selection and interpretation of material often reflects Wesley's views at the time of publication, though written up from his private diary and other materials. The first three instalments were designed to defend his conduct in Georgia, towards the Moravians and in his first evangelical work. Thereafter it became a vehicle for presenting his version of the religious revival of which he was a part and for expressing his views on many matters, both religious and secular. It was more a work of high-class propaganda and a travelogue than the diary of a soul.

Georgia was founded with a mixture of humanitarian idealism, a concern to defend an exposed frontier, and hopes of profit. The leading figure was James Oglethorpe, the colony's first governor, who evidently hoped that the Wesleys and their friends would help to discipline and civilize the unruly settlers. Wesley indeed soon turned from the Native Americans to work among the colonists.

As a minister in Georgia, Wesley revived traditional Anglican disciplines with some nonjuror additions; he experimented with small devotional groups and published his first hymnbook, *A Collection of Psalms and Hymns* (1737). Despite some positive response from individuals, he offended more by his austere demands. Then he compounded his offences by an unsuccessful courtship of Sophia Hopkey, the niece of Thomas Causton, a leading figure in the colony. After much vacillation Wesley drew back from a formal proposal, deterred by the opposition of friends, religious scruples, and, perhaps, psychological inhibitions. Tired of his hesitations, Sophia married William Williamson on 12 March 1737. After further attempts to influence her, Wesley concluded that she had been deceitful and excluded her from holy communion. Williamson and Causton then indicted him for ecclesiastical irregularities and excluding Sophia from communion, though Wesley gained supporters among those disaffected against the colony's leaders and Causton himself was suspected of financial irregularities. Wesley left Georgia in December 1737, virtually as a fugitive from justice, arriving in England on 1 February 1738.

While in Georgia, Wesley's religious doubts had been deepened by encounters with Moravian refugees who had accompanied him on the outward voyage. He was impressed by their calm during a storm and their example of primitive Christianity, order, and piety. Soon after landing he was challenged by the Moravian leader A. G. Spangenberg, who asked: '"Do you know Jesus Christ?" ... "I know he is the saviour of the world" ... "True ... but do you know he has saved you?" ... "I hope he has died to save me"' (*Works*, 18.146). Though Spangenberg privately recorded that he thought grace was at work in Wesley, Wesley himself clearly had growing doubts. On the voyage home he recorded on 24 January 1738 how he had been confused by different theological guides, and concluded 'I went to America to convert the Indians, but Oh! who shall convert me?' (ibid., 18.211).

Conversion, 1738 Back in England Wesley was gradually convinced by his Moravian friend Peter Böhler that the 'saving faith' he sought could be received in a sudden experience, and meanwhile he was urged to preach faith until he received it. On 1 May he helped to found a new religious society in Fetter Lane, London, with some Moravian features. Charles Wesley received the gift first on 21 May. On 24 May 1738 John went 'very unwillingly' to a religious society in Aldersgate Street, where 'one was reading Luther's *Preface to the Epistle to the Romans'*.

> About a quarter before nine, while he was describing the change which God works in the heart through faith in Christ, I felt my heart strangely warmed. I felt I did trust in Christ, Christ alone for salvation, and an assurance was given me that he had taken away *my* sins, even *mine*, and saved *me* from the law of sin and death. (*Works*, 18.248–50)

Wesley preceded this account with a review of his previous religious life which he judged a vain attempt at salvation by works; in later editions of the *Journal* he added footnotes modifying this judgement.

The significance of Wesley's conversion for his later life and theology has been subject to conflicting interpretations. Methodists and other evangelicals have generally seen it, like Wesley himself at the time, as completely and permanently reversing his previous beliefs. At the opposite extreme, Roman Catholics, Anglo-Catholics, and others have located his real conversion in the turn to seriousness and search for holiness in 1725, with May 1738 marking a temporary surrender to Moravian ideas or, at most, a psychological stimulus giving him confidence for evangelism.

It is true that Wesley rarely referred to the May experience later, and in his accounts of Methodism often traced it back to the Oxford search for holiness. However, this needs to be set against the fact that he tended to play down Moravian influences on Methodism after he broke with them and that his views of the process of salvation also changed later. Nevertheless, he refused to abandon his belief in justification by faith as a gift of God which could be received in a moment, by grace, while maintaining his belief in the pursuit of holiness. He also retained his high valuation of the sacraments, but dropped his prejudices in favour of apostolic succession in bishops and committed many breaches of Anglican church order.

The event of May 1738 seems at first to have suggested to Wesley that justification, assurance, and perhaps even perfection could be received in a single experience. During the next few years, however, he developed a view of salvation as a process moving from conviction of sin, through repentance, to justification, followed by assurance, and on to the pursuit of holiness culminating in perfection, which may be cultivated but also received in a moment, by faith. In 1746 he wrote: 'Our main doctrines, which include all the rest, are three: that of repentance, of faith and of holiness. The first of these we account, as it were, the porch of religion; the next the door; the third, religion itself' (J. Wesley to T. Church, 17 June 1746, *Letters*, ed. Telford, 2.268). To 'John Smith' he wrote: 'I regard even faith itself not as an *end*, but a *means* only. The end of the commandment is love. ... Let this love be attained, by whatever means, and I am content' (J. Wesley to 'J. Smith', 25 June 1746, *Works*, 26.203).

The long-term significance of the conversion for Wesley's personal experience is less clear. It seems that such moments of intense religious emotion were rare for him, difficult to retain or repeat. Some have suspected that he found his teaching confirmed more by observation of others' emotional experience than by his own.

Methodism emerges, 1738–1743 Wesley was indeed soon troubled by doubts about the completeness and reality of his conversion. Between June and August 1738 he visited the Moravians in Germany and from them found evidence that full assurance of faith could be delayed. On his return in September he busied himself with preaching and visiting societies in a highly charismatic atmosphere, recalling that of apostolic times, complete with conversions, visions, demon possession, and spiritual healing. Yet in the last self-examination published in his *Journal* on 4 January 1739 he still lacked assurance of his own condition. Churches now began to be closed to him, and old friends like John Clayton lamented his irregularities, but Wesley, disclaiming hope of a normal Anglican ministry, proclaimed 'the world is my parish' (J. Wesley to J. Clayton?, 28 March 1739?, *Works*, 25.616).

George Whitefield, the most electrifying orator of the revival, was evangelizing the neglected miners of Kingswood, near Bristol, and urged Wesley to consolidate the results. Still under Moravian tutelage, Wesley drew lots and, with considerable misgivings, arrived in Bristol on 31 March 1739. On 2 April, following Whitefield's example, he 'submitted to "be more vile"' (*Works*, 19.46) by preaching in the open air, a practice he was to continue for the rest of his life. Screaming, fainting, and convulsions affected his audiences here, as they often did in newly evangelized areas. Wesley interpreted cases as variously due to natural, diabolic, and divine causes.

In 1740–41 disputes broke out that divided the emerging revival. In October 1739 a Moravian visitor, Philip Molther, encouraged the Fetter Lane society to accept 'stillness'— that is, to avoid all means of grace and wait passively for God to give justification. Wesley urged active pursuit of salvation and appealed to cases of people being converted while receiving communion. On 20 July 1740 he abandoned Fetter Lane with his followers to occupy the refurbished King's Foundery. He had already in May built the New Room in Bristol for society and preaching meetings. He then fell out with Whitefield over the latter's belief in predestination, which Wesley rejected. In February 1741 Wesley published a sermon on free grace to which Whitefield replied in an open letter. Early in 1741 Wesley purged the societies in Bristol, Kingswood, and London and broke with the predestinarians. Though he was later personally reconciled with Whitefield and occasionally attempting until the 1760s to form a common front with other evangelicals, for the next three years Wesley consolidated his own following.

At the same time orthodox Anglicans were attacking Wesley on three charges which would often be repeated: 'enthusiasm' (claims to special revelations); teaching salvation by faith to the neglect of good works; and breaches of church order. These issues were the substance of a confrontation with Joseph Butler, bishop of Bristol, in August 1739. The irregularities began to include the use of lay preachers, lay converts who moved from private testimonies to public speaking. Early in 1741 Thomas Maxfield offended Wesley in this way but Susanna Wesley is said to have convinced him that 'the Lord owns him as truly as he does you or your brother' (Moore, 2.11).

In October 1739 Wesley first entered Wales, though his influence there was restricted by the prior emergence of Welsh-speaking Calvinistic Methodism from 1735. In the midlands and north of England he had been preceded by Benjamin Ingham and the Moravians, but in May 1742 he reached Newcastle upon Tyne, where he soon created his northern headquarters. From 1743 he began work in Cornwall, which became a strong Methodist area to be visited as an offshoot of his regular annual journeys round the London–Bristol–Newcastle triangle. Ireland was added in 1747 and Scotland in 1751, though his success was limited there. To a significant extent, however, Wesley's connexion grew by absorbing networks created by local evangelists.

Methodism organized and attacked, 1744–1748 'Methodism', in eighteenth-century usage, was applied almost indifferently to Welsh Calvinists, the connexions of Whitefield and Lady Huntingdon, Anglican evangelical clergy, and even clergy appearing 'serious', as well as to Wesley's followers. Wesley's organization, however, was distinctive for its development of a centrally directed national network with common loyalties, in contrast with the localized independence of most English religious bodies of its day.

This organization emerged piecemeal between 1738 and 1748 by a mixture of borrowing and improvisation. Local societies were open to all who 'desired to flee from the wrath to come' and evidenced this in conduct (*Works*, 9.70). Unlike the old Anglican societies they were open to all denominations and, importantly, to women. Within them the more earnest were organized in bands, borrowed from the Moravians, and by December 1740 there were select bands or select societies, which apparently came to contain those claiming perfection. Class meetings, originally a fund-raising device, were added from February 1742. Unlike the more exclusive bands and select bands, they were used to divide the whole society into small pastoral groups.

Until 1744 the scattered societies were held together by the personal supervision of the Wesley brothers. Attempts in 1739 and 1743 to co-ordinate work with other evangelical groups having failed, in June 1744 Wesley summoned a conference of his own assistants: Charles Wesley, four other clergy, and four lay preachers. Doctrine, organization, and discipline were discussed. The conference became an annual event, and evolved from a meeting ostensibly for free discussion into a ruling and regulatory body capable of surviving Wesley's death. Wesley selected its membership, and its decisions, despite disagreements, clearly expressed his will. Proceedings were conducted in question-and-answer form like Wesley's self-examinations at Oxford. Annual minutes began to be published from 1765, but from 1753 a selection of decisions ('*Large Minutes*') were published as the basis for Methodist discipline. From 1746 societies were grouped in large circuits or rounds, which from 1748 began to be governed by a quarterly meeting of leaders. Preaching-houses were run by trustees, who from 1763 were urged to use a model deed securing control of the pulpit to Wesley and his successors, though not all complied. The system was run by full-time travelling preachers, stationed for up to two years and assisted by part-time local preachers. Though not officially recognized, from the 1760s Wesley allowed some women to preach, about forty so doing during his lifetime. This organization was designed not simply for administration, evangelism, and pastoral care, but as a vehicle for members to pursue the desired goal of holiness and Christian perfection.

In the 1740s growing publicity and hostility led to literary attacks on Methodism on the issues already raised by Bishop Butler in 1739. Wesley replied publicly by pamphlet and open letter, notably to Bishop Gibson in 1747; to Bishop Lavington's *Enthusiasm of Methodists and Papists Compared* (1749) in 1750–51; and in private correspondence in 1745–8 to John Smith (often erroneously identified as Thomas Secker). At a lower social level, though sometimes led by local clergy and gentry, Methodism also suffered mob violence. This was provoked by local xenophobia, alarm at the disruptive effects of Methodism on communities and families, and, in 1744–5, by suspicions that they were 'popish' Jacobites. Wesley did not hesitate to appeal to the higher courts against the prejudices of local magistrates.

Love and marriage, 1749–1751 In *A Thought on Marriage and Celibacy* (1743) Wesley expressed a preference for celibacy, and in a letter to Charles on 25 September 1749 he gave a history of his opinions on the subject. At first he thought he would not marry 'Because I should never find such a woman as my father had' (*Works*, 26.380–82). Later, he was deterred by financial reasons; by primitive teachings that the physical taint on marriage excluded perfection; and by fears of hindering his mission. Now, however, the objections had been removed, the purpose of the letter being to defend his proposed marriage to Grace *Murray (1715–1803).

Murray was a widow who became Wesley's housekeeper at Newcastle. Wesley claimed that she agreed to marry him, and in July 1749 formally contracted to do so. But meanwhile she seems to have agreed to marry John Bennet, one of Wesley's leading lay helpers. After meeting them at Epworth on 1 September 1749 Wesley wrote sharply to Bennet asserting his claim. Charles Wesley, believing that Bennet had the prior claim, that Grace was socially unsuitable, and that her marriage to John would disrupt the societies, married Grace to Bennet at Newcastle on 3 October 1749. Wesley's private account of the story minutely justified his conduct and expressed his grief at the débâcle (published by A. Léger as *Wesley's Last Love*, 1910). Yet it is doubtful whether his intentions were as clear to Grace as he claimed, and his tortuous conduct curiously resembled that with Sophia Hopkey years before. By 1752 Bennet had left Wesley and become an Independent minister in Cheshire.

Wesley was probably persuaded by his friend Vincent Perronet, vicar of Shoreham, that marriage would be a wise precaution against scandal, and he chose Mrs Mary (Molly) Vazeille, née Goldhawk (1709/10–1781), the widow of a London merchant. On 9 February 1751 Wesley secured her fortune of £3000 to her use, no doubt to deter suspicions of fortune-hunting. They were married on 18 or 19 February, it is said by Charles Manning, vicar of Hayes, Middlesex, at an unknown location.

Wesley's attitude to marriage was perilously exacting, following his principle that no married preacher should travel less than a bachelor. His wife complied for a time but tired of travel. She has generally been regarded as pathologically jealous and possessive, but she had cause for complaint. She particularly resented Wesley's fondness for female friendships and correspondence. Naïvely innocent though these relationships were, they were indiscreet in his position. Mrs Wesley was particularly hostile to Sarah Ryan (1724–1768), Wesley's housekeeper at Kingswood. Ryan had a bigamous past, despite her impressive spiritual experiences and close friendship with the Methodist saint Mary Bosanquet. By 1755 the Wesley marriage was visibly in trouble. Mrs Wesley opened his letters and, according to John Hampson, once dragged Wesley round by his hair (Hampson, 2.127). Wesley's attempts to placate and control her were eventually marked by more logic than understanding, and on 23 January 1771 she left him. In his published *Journal* Wesley wrote, without naming her: 'non eam reliqui, non dismissi, non revocabat' ('I have not left her, I have not sent her away, I will not recall her'; *Works*, 22.262). Though returning for a time in 1772 she left him finally in 1776, and allegedly tried to publish doctored versions of his letters to damage him. She died on 8 October 1781 leaving him a gold ring 'in token that I die in love and friendship towards him' (*DNB*). Wesley heard of her death only some days later. His preference for celibacy among Methodists was reiterated in *A Thought upon Marriage* (1785), and though most did not agree he often discouraged their marriages.

Methodism and the Church of England, 1752–1760 While Wesley's marriage was being strained he had to face a crisis over Methodist relationships with the Church of England. He always claimed that Methodism was merely an auxiliary to the Church of England and did not separate from it so long as Methodists attended its worship and taught its doctrines, but his irregularities seemed to contradict these claims and many Methodists criticized the church. The 1744 conference defined the Church of England restrictively, following article 19 of the Anglican articles of faith, as 'the congregation of English *believers* in which the *pure word* of God is proclaimed and the sacraments *duly* administered'. This ignored establishment and canon law, and Methodists were to obey bishops only in 'things indifferent'. The 1745 conference sketched a pragmatic account of the origins of different ecclesiastical polities in a way which seemed to justify Wesley's creation of Methodism. In his *Journal* for 20 January 1746 Wesley claimed that Peter King's *Enquiry into the Constitution … of*

the Primitive Church (1691) convinced him that bishops and presbyters were originally of one order, and at some point Edward Stillingfleet's *Irenicum* (1654) convinced him that no church order had divine sanction. The 1747 conference pronounced a 'national church' to be 'a merely political creation'. In the last resort Wesley subordinated church order to the needs of his mission. To John Smith he wrote on 25 June 1746:

> What is the end of all *ecclesiastical order*? Is it not to bring souls from the power of Satan to God? And to build them up in his fear and love? *Order*, then, is so far valuable as it answers these ends; and if it answers them not it is nothing worth. (*Works*, 26.206)

The parish system, he implied, was inferior to his own.

In the early 1750s there were complaints of Wesley's authoritarianism, and purges of unsatisfactory preachers and of those who attacked the church. In October 1754 Charles Wesley complained that Charles Perronet had administered communion without authority and others followed suit. John said 'We have in effect ordained already' and was 'minded to lay on hands and to let the preachers administer [communion]' (Tyerman, 2.202 n.). For the conference of 1755 John prepared a paper 'Ought we to separate from the Church of England?'. He urged that, whether or not it was lawful, separation was not expedient, believing that as a result Methodism would dwindle into an ineffective sect. But in September 1755 he admitted to Samuel Walker, the evangelical curate of Truro, that he could not answer all the preachers' objections against Anglican canon law and the liturgy. He also (unlike Charles Wesley) defended the use of preachers and societies even in evangelical parishes.

From 1756 Charles Wesley virtually ceased to itinerate and settled first in Bristol and then in London as minister to the Methodists in those places. Charles had married in 1749, and though his retreat from itinerancy has often been ascribed to family cares, he had also alienated many of the preachers by his criticisms of them and suggestions that they be subordinated to evangelical parish clergy.

In 1760 Methodist preachers in Norwich once again administered communion. Though still refusing to ordain, John Wesley treated the offenders more calmly than Charles, who also condemned preachers who took licences under the 1689 Toleration Act to defend themselves against attack, while denying that they were dissenters. In 1764–5 a questionable Greek bishop, Erasmus of Arcadia, ordained some Methodist preachers, not all with Wesley's knowledge, and it was rumoured that Wesley had asked to be ordained as a bishop. The scandal this caused forced Wesley to disown those ordained.

The perfectionist controversy, 1760–1770 Much more to Wesley's taste, and more central to his vision of Methodism's mission, was an outbreak of perfectionist experiences late in the 1750s. Perfection had been preached, experienced, and discussed in the 1740s, but Wesley claimed that such cases had ceased for twenty years. Though he always argued for perfection from scripture, in 1759 he went so far as to claim that he would give up the doctrine if there were no living witnesses. The new outbreak apparently began in some places in the middle of 1758. Certain preachers had placed it in an alarming light by claiming that believers are in a state of damnation unless they have achieved it and could perish if they died before obtaining it. This led Wesley to elaborate his paradox that perfection could co-exist with infirmities of various kinds, since its essence is an unbroken relationship of love towards God and one's neighbour.

From 1760 the experiences proliferated, sometimes accompanied by shrieks and groans reminiscent of the early days of the revival. Wesley thought these experiences favourable to the growth of the movement. By 1761 some were speaking of third blessings or of separate experiences of the sanctification of the mind and of the heart by faith. The movement culminated in Thomas Maxfield and George Bell, former guardsman, and their followers claiming that God was to be found only in their meetings, that they were restored to the purity of Adam and Eve, and that they were incapable of falling away. They also claimed gifts of healing, and Bell attempted to cure blind people and raise the dead. Always attracted by perfectionism, Wesley was at first slow to act. But he was hurt when Maxfield left him, and finally repudiated Bell when he prophesied that the world would end on 28 February 1763.

The Maxfield and Bell secession may have numbered only 200 people, but more serious was the legacy of distrust of perfection among Methodists and the sharpened suspicions of Calvinists. The controversy also led Wesley to define his doctrine more and more carefully in *Thoughts on Perfection* (1759), and he reviewed the history of his teaching in his *Plain Account of Christian Perfection* (1767). He continued to teach it, however, and to emphasize more than ever that it could be received in a moment by faith. In 1790 he claimed that it was 'the grand depositum which God has lodged with the people called Methodists, and for the sake of propagating this chiefly he appeared to have raised us up' (J. Wesley to R. Carr Brackenbury, 15 Sept 1790, *Letters*, 8.238).

The Calvinist controversy, 1770–1775 Conflicts, literary and personal, between Calvinistic Methodists and Wesley and his followers had surfaced periodically ever since the breach with Whitefield. In the early 1770s the old dispute erupted violently. Wesley was typical of the Anglicans of his day, though unusual among English evangelicals, in his rejection of Calvinism and especially the doctrine of predestination. Most evangelical Calvinists were moderates, and their Calvinism came more from experience than a detailed knowledge of earlier Western debates of predestination, though A. M. Toplady and some of Lady Huntingdon's followers were more extreme and more informed. Wesley's view of Calvinism was brutally simplistic: predestination makes God appear unjust and unfeeling and it undermines any incentive for morality.

Lady Huntingdon, though now a Calvinist, still aspired to aid all evangelical parties. She used Wesley's preacher Joseph Benson and John Fletcher, vicar of Madeley, to serve her college at Trefeca, founded in 1768—a project which seems to have excited some jealousy in Wesley.

Already on 1 December 1767 he recorded some remarkable reflections in his *Journal* to the effect that people could have the experience and effects of justification without using the correct language; even that they could (like William Law, he said) deny the doctrine and yet possess its reality. 'He that feareth God and worketh righteousness is accepted with him' (*Works*, 22.114). But public controversy broke out over a minute from the 1770 conference which emphasized the goal of holiness, with an enhanced role for good works, while dismissing what Calvinists regarded as essential technical distinctions about merit as mere hair-splitting. Moreover, Whitefield had died in America on 30 September 1770 and in November Wesley preached a memorial sermon for him, emphasizing only the doctrines on which they had agreed.

Lady Huntingdon dismissed Benson from her college and Fletcher resigned. She and her supporters threatened to attend the conference of 1771 to insist on the retraction of the offending minute. Although a revised version appeared to satisfy both parties, Wesley reignited the controversy by publishing a manuscript by Fletcher defending the original offending statement. In the literary battle that followed, Wesley, though replying to pamphlets by Toplady and Richard Hill, left most of the work to other friends and, above all, to Fletcher in his *Six Checks to Antinomianism* (1771–5; the alleged neglect of moral law ascribed to Calvinists). In the course of the controversy Fletcher and Wesley appeared to go as far as to teach a 'second justification' by works as necessary for final salvation. This confirmed Calvinist suspicions that Wesley had abandoned salvation by grace through faith.

Politics and America, 1775–1784 Individual Methodists had evangelized in the West Indies since 1759 and there was talk of an African mission in 1778, but the missionary enthusiast Dr Thomas Coke found little support from Wesley for organizing such projects until 1786. Wesley thought they had sufficient to do at home unless they had a clear call from Providence. But voluntary activity in America from the early 1760s led Wesley to allow ten preachers to travel there to oversee the work between 1769 and 1774.

It was the American War of Independence and reformist agitations at home that provoked Wesley into his most active interventions in politics. Despite early high-church and even Jacobite associations, his advice in 1747 had been to vote for 'one that loves God' or at least one who 'loves King George who has been appointed to reign over us' (*Works*, 11.196–8). Between 1768 and 1778 he took sides more decisively by opposing Wilkite cries for 'liberty' in *Free Thoughts on the Present State of Public Affairs* (1768) and *Thoughts on Liberty* (1772).

On America, in *Free Thoughts*, Wesley conceded that the ministry's actions could not be defended and in 1775 privately warned ministers against coercion and the dangers of war. But in his *Calm Address to our American Colonies* (1775; based largely on Samuel Johnson's *Taxation No Tyranny*, 1775) and in *Some Observations on Liberty* (1776) he condemned the Americans and portrayed them as allied with

English radicals. This volte-face provoked charges of hypocrisy and plagiarism. The French alliance with the Americans aroused in Wesley a fear that this 'popish' power was conspiring with the Americans and radicals to ruin England.

Despite Wesley's remarkable *Letter to a Roman Catholic* (1749), pleading for mutual tolerance on the basis of a few shared basic principles, Wesley more characteristically displayed the traditional English protestant paranoia towards Catholics as people who would become persecuting political subversives if given the opportunity. He was personally tolerant of individuals and the practice of Catholic worship, but resisted the granting of political rights. Hence he opposed the Catholic Relief Act of 1778 and defended Lord George Gordon's Protestant Association which landed him in controversy. He actually signed a petition against the act (Treasury Solicitor's MSS, TS11/389/1212; English, 362 and n. 70).

War and suspicion of loyalism forced all the English Methodist preachers out of America by 1778 except Francis Asbury, who was to become a kind of American Wesley. Independence, however, set Wesley free to plan American Methodism's future, which coincided with new arrangements for England as well.

Securing the future, 1784–1788 Though heartened by signs of fresh local revivals and the more rapid growth of Methodism in the 1780s by evangelism and population changes, Wesley now had to face more urgently the question of what would happen to Methodism after his death. The problem was not new. The 1763 model deed was designed, where used, to secure control of preaching-house pulpits to the Wesley brothers, followed by William Grimshaw, vicar of Haworth, and finally the 'yearly Conference of the people called Methodists'. Grimshaw died that year, and in 1769 Wesley guessed that only a third of the preachers would stay with Methodism after his death. They should be led by a small committee, taking turns to be 'moderator'. In 1773 he proposed that John Fletcher should be his successor but Fletcher refused. In 1775 Joseph Benson proposed purging the preachers and ordaining some of them. Fletcher then proposed that if the bishops refused to ordain preachers, Wesley should ordain some himself, and set up a 'Methodist Church of England' with a revised prayer book and articles, his successors in leadership to be a body of moderators.

Nothing came of these proposals, but by 1784 not only the succession but control of the preaching-houses (nearly 400 of them by now) had become a problem, for it was found that the 'yearly Conference' had never been legally defined. Early in 1784 Wesley enrolled a deed of declaration in chancery defining the conference and its powers. It was to consist of 100 named and self-perpetuating preachers who were to elect an annual president. The hundred included some young preachers but omitted some senior ones. Some of the omitted, including Wesley's first biographer, John Hampson, then left the Methodist movement. Despite the deed, Wesley continued to select and control the conference, though in his last years he sometimes gave way to the majority and used a cabinet of advisers.

The same year Wesley devised a scheme for an independent American Methodist church, complete with a revised Book of Common Prayer and reduced articles of religion. Relying on his old claim that bishops and presbyters were originally of one order, he claimed to be a scriptural 'episkopos' with the right to ordain. On 1 and 2 September 1784, with the help of Thomas Coke and James Creighton, he ordained two preachers for America and then Coke as a superintendent, with a view to his ordaining Asbury as co-superintendent for America. This was evidently designed to secure Wesley's control over American Methodism. The Americans, however, insisted on approving the appointments for themselves and by 1788 had annoyed Wesley by labelling their superintendents 'bishops'.

Wesley argued that he was free to ordain for America since the Church of England no longer exercised jurisdiction there after independence. From 1785 he also ordained for Scotland, where the established church was presbyterian. Those ordained for Scotland were forbidden to administer sacraments in England. Wesley's further plans for England were and are a matter of controversy. Though some alleged that he regretted ordaining at all, others denied this, or claimed that he was pressurized by unscrupulous preachers. In 1788 he ordained three men who remained in England, one of them, Alexander Mather, allegedly as a superintendent. It seems arguable that Wesley was holding these men in reserve in case he needed to concede Methodist sacraments for some places in England.

Despite these actions, Wesley continued to claim that he had not separated from the Church of England, though he was finally forced to define separation as applying only to a formal secession. His apparent inconsistency may best be explained as a policy of limited concessions where pressures for separation were greatest, with a view to keeping Methodism as united as possible, thereby reducing the pressure for a concerted and formal separation. This, in effect, is what he claimed himself, however paradoxically.

Last years and death, 1788–1791 In Wesley's last years he observed, with a mixture of surprise and wry appreciation, that he had become almost respectable. His journeys continued almost to the end, though latterly in a chaise, and became almost triumphal processions with people anxious to catch their last glimpse of an almost legendary figure. H. Crabbe Robinson in October 1790 said that Wesley's voice was barely audible. But 'his reverend countenance, especially his long white hair, formed a picture never to be forgotten … It was for the most part a pantomime, but the pantomime went to the heart' (H. C. Robinson, *Diary*, ed. T. Seddon, 1899, 1.19–20).

Despite many illnesses and in 1753 the conviction that he was about to die of consumption, Wesley marvelled in his *Journal* on his birthday on 28 June 1776 NS that he was 'far abler to preach' than when he was twenty-three. He ascribed the 'natural means God has used' for this as constant exercise and travelling, early rising, ability to sleep at will, and evenness of temper (*Works*, 23.21). In the later 1780s he regularly described his health on his birthday; only on 28 June 1789 did he concede that 'I now find I grow old', and not until the following year did he admit to failing sight and strength. Though he could still be sprightly, observers at his last conference in 1790 noted that he was nearly blind, with his memory much decayed so that Mather conducted the business. Yet he could still intervene sharply if opposed.

In July 1790 Wesley finally gave up keeping his accounts, saying that 'I save all I can and give all I can, that is all I have' (*Journal of John Wesley*, 8.80 n.). In October he preached his last sermon in the open air, and his final sermon on 23 February 1791. On 24 February he wrote his last recorded letter, urging on William Wilberforce in his anti-slave trade campaign. The same day he entered his house in City Road, London, for the last time. His friend Miss Ritchie later wrote a detailed account of these days, unfolding in a series of 'pleasing, awful scenes'. Among his last recorded words were 'The best of all is God is with us' and an attempt to sing Isaac Watts's 'I'll praise my Maker while I've breath' (ibid., 8.131–44). John Wesley died at his home on 2 March 1791 and was buried behind his City Road chapel on 9 March. By his will he ruled that there should be no hearse, no coach, no escutcheon, no pomp except the 'tears of those that love me'; and that 20s. should be paid to each of six poor men to bear his body to the grave. His papers were left to three executors and the management of his books to other trustees. Both provisions led to unseemly wrangles later. The funeral service was read by his assistant Revd John Richardson, who substituted 'father' for 'our dear brother here departed', thus emphasizing the filial relation in which the preachers stood to him (Moore, 2.394). The funeral sermon was preached by his physician John Whitehead, another later biographer.

Doctrine and devotion Wesley's theological position has been variously described. He produced no systematic theology and was highly eclectic in his selective borrowings from patristic writers, Roman Catholics (notably the seventeenth-century French quietists), high-church and puritan Anglicans, as well as Moravians. Following Anglican tradition, he appealed to the combined authority of scripture, early church tradition, and reason, though increasingly also to experience. Though giving scripture primacy, he allowed for some textual criticism in his *Expository Notes* on the Old and New testaments (1761, 1755), based chiefly on J. A. Bengel's *Gnomon* (1742). His use of reason was influenced by John Locke's *Essay Concerning Human Understanding* (1690), though even more by Peter Browne's *Procedure, Extent and Limits of Human Understanding* (1728). He was strongly empiricist in principle, rejecting innate ideas. However, he stretched empiricism to cover 'a new class of senses' 'opened in your souls' by God, 'not depending on the organs of flesh and blood' (*Works*, 8.276). His belief in the supernatural was strong, for he claimed it was justified by scripture and credible witnesses. His debt to the eighteenth-century temper also shows in his impatience with traditional protestant scholastic systems of theology and his toleration of those agreeing with him on fundamentals, though he was not always consistent here in his treatment of Calvinists and Roman Catholics.

Rejecting predestination, Wesley saw salvation as being open to all through prevenient grace, with freedom to accept or reject the offer. Unlike Calvinists, Wesley believed salvation once gained could be lost and had to be pursued actively. Similarly, assurance of salvation is usually obtainable, partly by recognition of a changed life, partly as a direct gift from the Holy Spirit, but there is no guarantee of Calvinist final perseverance.

Despite his acceptance from 1738 of justification by grace through faith as the basis of salvation, Wesley's mature doctrine of salvation shifted away from the Reformation's stress on justification and towards the development of a holy life. Justification begins this process of sanctification, which culminates in the attainment of a 'perfection' characterized by unbroken love to God and humanity. This gift may even be received in a moment, by faith. Thus Wesley seems to have combined the Moravian understanding of an instant gift with the more 'Catholic' notion of the systematic cultivation of holiness. Wesley evaded charges of 'salvation by works' by saying that even the 'perfect' depend every moment on grace and faith. Wesley denied that he taught 'sinless' perfection. This seems to rely on his definition of sin 'properly so called' as being limited to 'a voluntary breach of a known law' (J. Wesley to M. Pendarves, 19 June 1731, *Works*, 25.289).

Wesley retained his high-church beliefs in frequent communion and in a version of the real presence and a kind of sacrifice in the eucharist, expressed in vivid physical terms in his brother Charles's hymns. In matters of worship he was less conservative. While regarding Methodist worship as only supplementary to Anglican services he provided much else for Methodists. Hymns and extempore prayer were freely used. From various sources he adapted the love feast (a kind of folk sacrament with bread and water and religious testimonies); the covenant service, which became an annual act of rededication; and the watch-night, which became a new year counter to secular celebrations. Wesley edited *Hymns for the Use of Methodists* (1780), arranged to follow the pattern of Methodist religious experience, and he claimed for it the 'spirit of poetry' as well as of 'piety' (preface).

Political and social attitudes Wesley's mother was a Jacobite, his father a tory who supported the new Hanoverian dynasty. Though possibly flirting with Jacobitism and certainly criticizing the Walpole administration during his Oxford period, Wesley soon adopted his father's position. In 1775 he said he was 'an high churchman, the son of an high churchman, bred up from my childhood in the highest notions of passive obedience and non-resistance' (J. Wesley to earl of Dartmouth, June 1775, *Letters*, 6.156). In 1785 he claimed that he and his brother Samuel were, like their father, 'Tories' but not Jacobites ('I am no more a Jacobite than I am a Turk'). In a letter to the editor of the

Gentleman's Magazine (24 December 1785) Wesley stated that a tory is 'one that believes God, not the people, to be the origin of all civil power' (ibid., 7.305-6). This was in contradiction of social contract and natural rights ideas, and explains his opposition to John Wilkes and the American revolutionaries in the 1770s. He was influenced by scriptural injunctions to obey the powers that be as ordained by God; by the consideration that the Hanoverian kings upheld religious toleration (important for Methodists); and by his fears in the 1770s of disorder. But the description of his family traditions suggests that, like other tories, he had transferred earlier ideas of divine right to the Hanoverian dynasty.

On social matters Wesley was a philanthropist and an occasional critic of contemporary economic vices and prejudices. His sermon entitled 'The use of money' (1760) expounded the aphorism 'gain all you can, save all you can, give all you can' (*Works*, 2.263). The first point only partially endorsed aggressive capitalism, for it was restricted by prohibitions on speculation and bill broking. The second was directed against conspicuous consumption and elaborated in later sermons against luxury— Wesley was particularly exercised against women's hats. Gaining and saving were only in order to give—sacrificially. In 1744 Wesley had even planned a kind of apostolic community of goods, though this was not achieved. As to his own finances, on marrying in 1751 he lost his fellowship of Lincoln and its income. His allowances from Methodism were not above £30 p.a. and some gifts, but his publications eventually realized an income which enabled him to give away £1000 annually.

Wesley was in his century unusual for his distrust of the rich (who did not respond well to his evangelism) and for his love of the poor, whom he treated with respect. He did not believe their poverty was due to their improvidence. He organized collections in times of distress and in 1747 set up a free dispensary, including electric shock treatment. His *Primitive Physick* (1747, and later editions to at least 1840), though often mocked for its folk remedies, also drew on respectable medical authorities while avoiding their more lethal prescriptions. He also recommended fresh air, cold water, a quiet mind, and prayer.

Wesley was an early supporter of the anti-slave trade campaign, adapting Anthony Benezet's attack in his *Thoughts on Slavery* (1774). In education he supported Methodists' schools and the rising Sunday school movement, as well as founding his own Kingswood School (1748), though he often despaired of making it truly 'Christian'. More negatively, he praised the refounded Society for the Reformation of Manners in a sermon in 1763 and attacked the wasteful luxury of tea drinking and the poison of spirit drinking. (Wesley, however, was not a teetotaller, and among his more curious letters are those describing the debilitating effects of tea but also inveighing against the adulteration of honest English ale by hops.) Given his multifarious activities and the humble status of many of his followers it is not surprising that Wesley, while supporting the efforts of others, did not organize large-scale moral and social campaigns on the lines of the Clapham Sect.

Preacher and author Though inferior to Whitefield as a popular orator, Wesley could often create highly emotional effects in his audiences. He contrasted his own style with his brother's by saying that he excelled in 'connexion' (reasoned argument), Charles in 'strong pointed sentences' (J. Wesley to C. Wesley, June 1766, *Letters*, 5.16). He preached extempore for an hour or more, striving for plain language but rising to controlled rhetoric in his concluding appeals. Horace Walpole in 1766 thought him 'as evidently an actor as Garrick. He spoke his sermon but so fast, and with so little accent, that I am sure he has often uttered it, for it was like a lesson'. Despite 'parts and eloquence' at the end he 'exalted his voice' and 'acted a very ugly enthusiasm' (*Selected Letters of Horace Walpole*, ed. W. S. Lewis, 1973, 119). Sir Walter Scott heard him tell excellent stories, but for some he fell too readily into anecdotage in old age, and Hampson thought he only preached well if he prepared, and too often he did not. He preached too frequently and insisted on doing so 'if he could stand on his legs' (Hampson, 3.169-71).

As an author Wesley was astonishingly prolific on secular as well as religious subjects. He valued conciseness and plain language, and much of his output consisted of extracts from, or condensations of, other men's works, not always acknowledged. His *Christian Library* (1749-55) included condensed versions of devotional classics both Catholic and protestant. *A Survey of the Works of God in Creation* (1775), based on Buddeus of Jena, was a 'natural philosophy' to display what the title suggested, but it also showed his empiricism in his claim 'barely to set down what appears in nature, not the causes of the appearances' (preface); but while he distrusted Sir Isaac Newton's hypotheses he loved to record 'wonders'. Similarly, in *Primitive Physick* he looked only for remedies that allegedly worked, criticizing traditional medical systems. His *History of England* (1776) was based on Goldsmith, Rapin, and Smollett, and he criticized historians for not showing God as the supreme ruler of the world. He wrote history, he said, 'to bring God into it' (J. Wesley to C. Wesley, 13 Jan 1774, *Letters*, 6.67). This was more obvious in his *Ecclesiastical History* (1781), based on Archibald Maclaine's translation of Mosheim. He criticized Mosheim for treating church history like secular history and omitting the role of the Holy Spirit, though he acknowledged that few saints would be found in the history of the church.

Wesley's *Arminian Magazine* (from 1778) was begun as a counter to Calvinist magazines, but included Methodist biographies, travel literature, snippets of science, poetry, and many accounts of witchcraft and providential interventions. In his *Appeals to Men of Reason and Religion* (1743-5) he addressed a cultured audience; in his short *Words* for various moral offenders, a more popular readership.

In controversy Wesley was generally courteous, though he could be unfair, and some complained that he evaded substantive issues by nice logical distinctions. His *Journal*, whatever problems it poses as an objective historical source for his life, is the record of a tireless traveller and observer of a wide range of people and manners. It was also a vehicle, like so much of what he wrote, not only for his confident opinions but also for educating his people and (he no doubt hoped) a wider audience. He never lost the instincts of an Oxford tutor. He was, it may be claimed, a kind of cultural mediator between the educated world and the moderately literate people of Methodism and even beyond them.

Appearance and character Wesley was less of a gift to caricaturists than Whitefield, and satirical attacks on him were most prominent during the political and Calvinist controversies of the 1770s. He was typically portrayed as a hypocrite in sheep's clothing or an aged lecher. More objectively he appears as the austere Methodist of John Williams's portrait (1742), the persuasive preacher of Nathaniel Hone's (c.1766), or the benevolent patriarch of George Romney's (1789). Physically, he was short (5 feet 3 inches), slim, muscular, with piercing blue eyes, a fresh complexion, and hair (until it turned white in old age) variously described as brown or auburn. Though dispensing with a wig (except possibly in later life) his hair was curled at the ends. He had a passion for cleanliness and neatness in his person and surroundings.

Hampson's much quoted description of Wesley in old age emphasized his 'cheerfulness mingled with gravity, a sprightliness which was the natural result of an unusual flow of spirits and was yet combined with … the most serene tranquillity'. 'His manner in private life … was sprightly and pleasant to the last degree', unlike that of Methodists 'who seemed to have ranked laughter among the mortal sins'. (The preacher John Pawson thought Wesley's conversation edifying only if a serious friend kept him to the point.) Wesley dressed in 'a narrow plaited stock, a coat with a small upright collar, no buckles at his knees, no silk or velvet in any part of his apparel' (Hampson, 3.166–8, 178–9). He habitually preached in gown and bands.

In 1776 Wesley wrote: 'I *feel* and *grieve*, but, by the grace of God I *fret* at nothing' (*Works*, 23.21). The younger Wesley was less tranquil. Observers agreed that he had achieved control by discipline over a naturally warm and impetuous temperament which sometimes still erupted in old age. His judgements on people could be hasty and he tended to take them at face value, particularly if they displayed apparent spiritual gifts. Some thought him open to flattery. Judgements of this kind, however, were coloured by dislike of his policies or advisers. There are many testimonies to his wit and charm, but his isolated position as leader of a movement with few members of his own social status hindered close friendships, while his affectionate correspondence with female disciples provoked gossip and scandal, despite its essential innocence. His rigorous timetable, as Samuel Johnson complained, inhibited relaxed conversation. Behind the charm, too, there was an iron will: 'granite in aspic' (V. H. H. Green, *John Wesley*, 127).

The chief charges against Wesley, even by some friends, were that he was obsessed with absolute power and that he was excessively credulous. His authoritarianism and

confidence in his own judgement are undeniable, though they could be defended as necessary to control an ebullient movement and, in his own eyes, as a providential charge. His credulity refers to his keen interest and outspoken belief in the supernatural as evidence of the unseen world and intervention by God or the devil. Reading as he rode on his travels, he made snap judgements on books, pronouncing on the most diverse subjects with the utmost confidence, especially against conventional wisdom. Thus he defended Mary, queen of Scots, and Richard III, but condemned Elizabeth I as a persecutor.

Wesley's spirituality is evidenced by his lifelong disciplines of devotion, though his inner life becomes hard to gauge after 1739. He said he had 'more need of heat than of light' (*Works*, 26.161 n.), and one of his bolder associates told him that he had 'the *knowledge* of all *experience* but not the *experience* of all you *know*' (ibid., 26.415). This and passing remarks of Wesley himself may suggest that he lacked the capacity for the felt spiritual raptures experienced by many of his followers. Despite his enthusiasm for perfection he never claimed the experience for himself, whether from prudence or lack of conviction that he possessed it. Yet his writings give glimpses of considerable spiritual insight and, if he judged himself severely, even non-Methodist obituarists agreed that he had led a life of extraordinary selflessness, discipline, and devotion to religion and the care of the poor.

Significance and legacy For Methodist biographers the standard interpretation of Wesley evolved from the crop of studies up to 1825 by men who had known him, though their judgements were affected by current controversies about Methodism. Henry Moore's *Life of John Wesley* (1824–5) established the consensus that Wesley was a faultless paragon of many-sided abilities whose religious position was settled by his conversion in 1738. Moore rejected or omitted the critical observations of other biographers. An alternative view has recurred since Anglo-Catholic writers in the 1870s claimed 1725 as his 'real' conversion, playing down Wesley's conversionist evangelism. G. C. Cell's *Rediscovery of John Wesley* (1935) was unusual in that, while emphasizing justification by faith and religious experience, he concluded that Wesley achieved 'a necessary synthesis of the Protestant ethic of grace with the Catholic ethic of holiness' (Cell, 361). The accumulation of fresh information and editions of the *Journals* and *Letters* in the first half of the twentieth century inspired numerous studies of special aspects of Wesley's beliefs and activities—as evangelist, sacramentalist, mystic, puritan, and social reformer. Biographers, however, tended to recycle and popularize the traditional material without altering the overall interpretation, though non-Methodists were more critical of him. From the early 1960s use of the Oxford diaries and their more accurate decipherment revived interest in Wesley's early development. Other studies related him more closely to the continental revival. American Methodists have recently attempted to develop a distinctive 'Wesleyan' theology and apply it to present-day religion. The basis of future biographies has been laid by the first critical edition of Wesley's *Works*

(1975–). The latest biographers have re-evaluated the sources and related Wesley more closely to his social and intellectual environment.

On wider issues of interpretation, Wesley has been seen as challenging and reviving the moribund Church of England and ministering to the neglected poor. It has been claimed that Methodism helped to save England from violent revolution and provided a home for people uprooted by the industrial revolution. He has been credited with a role in social reform along with Wilberforce and the Clapham Sect. His doctrine of perfection has been seen as an original contribution to theology.

None of these claims can be readily substantiated. Wesley's long life and voluminous *Journal* have tended to exaggerate his role as initiator and leader of a revival which was part of an international 'awakening'. His organization, with its mixture of formal and informal worship, centralization yet flexibility, was, however, distinctive and a challenge to the localized and static character of most English churches. His perfection doctrine, though also distinctive, survived only within Methodism and as an element in later 'holiness' and Pentecostalist movements. Methodism's counter-revolutionary role is now debatable and some would rather see Methodism as emerging from opposition to whig hegemony.

How far Wesley affected the unchurched poor is unclear. Methodist membership was stronger among skilled than unskilled workers and perhaps appealed to, or helped, the upwardly mobile. Autobiographies also suggest that the committed membership had early concerns about religion. The movement, however, had a diffused effect beyond the membership and did attract people who found no satisfaction in conventional churches. Methodist experience of lay organization arguably helped to influence working-class movements in later times. Despite Wesley's hostility to democracy, Methodism gave much scope to male and female lay activity in contrast to the clergy-dominated churches of the day. The irony is that Wesley's stated aim was 'not to form any new sect but to revive the nation, especially the church [of England]—and to spread scriptural holiness through the land' (*Large Minutes*, 1763, 1789, in *Minutes of the Methodist Conferences*, 446). Yet his most tangible legacy was the later creation of the largest new family of churches to be thrown up by the revival in Britain and in the rest of the English-speaking world.   HENRY D. RACK

Sources *The works of John Wesley*, ed. F. Baker, 2, ed. A. C. Outler (1985); 9, ed. R. E. Davies (1989); 18–23, ed. R. P. Heitzenrater and W. R. Ward (1988–95); 25–6, ed. F. Baker (1980–82) · *The journal of the Rev. John Wesley*, ed. N. Curnock and others, 8 vols. (1909–16) · *The letters of the Rev. John Wesley*, ed. J. Telford, 8 vols. (1931) · J. Wesley, MSS diaries (1725–35), JRL, Colman Collection · *The works of … John Wesley*, 14 vols. (1872) · J. Hampson, *Memoirs of … the Rev. John Wesley*, 3 vols. (1791) · J. Whitehead, ed., *Life of the Rev. John Wesley*, 2 vols. (1793–6) · H. Moore, *The life of the Rev. John Wesley*, 2 vols. (1824–5) · A. Knox, 'Remarks on the life and character of John Wesley', in R. Southey, *The life of Wesley*, ed. R. C. Southey, 3rd edn, 2 vols. (1846), 2.293–360 · A. Clarke, *Memoirs of the Wesley family*, 2nd edn, 2 vols. (1836) · *Minutes of the Methodist conferences, from the first, held in London by the late Rev. John Wesley …*, 20 vols. (1812–79) [1744–98 conferences] · L. Tyerman, *The life and times of the Rev. John Wesley*, 3 vols.

(1870–71) · A. Léger, *Wesley's last love* (1910) · R. P. Heitzenrater, *The elusive Mr Wesley*, 2 vols. (1984) · R. Green, *The works of John and Charles Wesley: a bibliography*, 2nd edn (1906) · V. H. H. Green, *The young Mr Wesley* (1961) · R. P. Heitzenrater, 'John Wesley and the Oxford Methodists, 1725–35', PhD diss., Duke U., 1972 · J. C. English, 'John Wesley and the rights of conscience', *Journal of Church and State*, 37 (1995), 349–63 · V. H. H. Green, *John Wesley* (1964) · R. P. Heitzenrater, *Mirror and memory: reflections on early Methodism* (1989) · M. Schmidt, *John Wesley: a theological biography*, 3 vols. (1962–73) · F. Baker, *John Wesley and the Church of England* (1970) · C. W. Williams, *John Wesley's theology today* (1960) · J. Orcibal, 'The theological orginality of John Wesley and continental spirituality', *History of Methodism in Great Britain*, ed. R. E. Davies and E. G. Rupp, 1 (1965), 81–112 · D. Hempton, *The religion of the people* (1996) · W. R. Ward, *The protestant evangelical awakening* (1992) · J. E. Rattenbury, *The eucharistic hymns of John and Charles Wesley* (1948) · G. C. Cell, *The rediscovery of John Wesley* (1935) · J. Telford, *Sayings and portraits of John Wesley* (1924) · J. Kerslake, *National Portrait Gallery: early Georgian portraits*, 1 (1977), 297–304 · A. M. Lyles, *Methodism mocked* (1960) · J. Walsh, *John Wesley, 1703–1791: a bicentennial tribute* (1994) · private information (2004)

Archives Emory University, Atlanta, Georgia, corresp. and papers · Hunt. L., letters · John Wesley's Chapel, Bristol, letters and registers of the Bristol Society · JRL, Methodist Archives and Research Centre, corresp. · JRL, Methodist Archives and Research Centre, corresp. and papers · JRL, Methodist Archives and Research Centre, corresp., sermons, journals, and papers · JRL, Methodist Archives and Research Centre, letters · JRL, Methodist Archives and Research Centre, scrapbook containing letters and related papers · Lincoln College, Oxford, letters · NL Wales, letters · NRA, priv. coll., letters · Southern Methodist University, Dallas, letters · St John's Theological College, Auckland, letters · University of Georgia, Athens, journal · Wesley College, Bristol, corresp. and sermons incl. shorthand diary · Wesley Cottage Trust, Launceston, letters · Westminster Institute of Education, Oxford, Wesley and Methodist Studies Centre, letters | BL, letters to Ann Tindall, Add. MSS 43695–43696, 43739–43740 · Drew University, Madison, New Jersey, United Methodist Archives and History Center · Duke U., Frank Baker collection · Lincoln College, Oxford, corresp. with James Hervey · NA Scot., letters to Sir Achibald Grant · NRA Scotland, priv. coll., Hog MSS

Likenesses J. M. Williams, oils, 1742, Wesley College, Bristol; version, Lincoln College, Oxford · J. W. Tinney, mezzotint, *c*.1750, NPG · R. Hunter, oils, *c*.1765, Wesley's Chapel, London · N. Hone, oils, *c*.1766, NPG [*see illus.*] · mezzotint, pubd 1770 (after N. Hone), BM, NPG · J. Russell, oils, 1773, Kingswood School, Bristol · T. Horsley, oils, *c*.1784, Richmond College, Surrey · E. Wood, ceramic bust, 1785, Methodist Archives and Research Centre, London · W. N. Gardiner, stipple, pubd 1788 (after S. Harding), NPG · W. Hamilton, oils, 1788, NPG · G. Romney, oils, 1789, Philadelphia Museum of Art; replica, NPG · T. Holloway, line engraving, pubd 1791, BM, NPG · W. Ridley, stipple, pubd 1791, BM · W. Ridley, stipple, pubd 1792 (after H. Edridge), NPG · coade-ware bust, 1793, Methodist Archives and Research Centre, London · Fry, stipple, pubd 1824 (after print by Bland), NPG · H. Bone, pencil and chalk drawing, Scot. NPG · J. Greenwood, mezzotint (after N. Hone), BM, NPG · J. Watson, mezzotint (after J. Williams), BM, NPG · marble bust, NPG · stipple and line engraving (after J. Jackson), NPG

Wealth at death allegedly gave away minimum £1000 p.a. in later years · legacies to be taken from main asset, profits from books (est. at £4827 10s. 3½d., 1788): Tyerman, *Life and times of the Rev. John Wesley*, 3.559–60

Wesley [Wellesley; *formerly* Colley], **Richard, first baron of Mornington (1690–1758)**, landowner, was the youngest son of Henry Colley (*d.* 1700) of Castle Carbury, Kildare, and his first wife, Mary, daughter of Sir William Usher of Dublin. The Colleys were of English origin, having gone to

Ireland like so many Anglo-Irish in the capacity of civil servant or soldier. The first of the Irish Colleys, Robert Colley, served as bailiff of Dublin in 1515 but it was his grandson, Sir Henry Colley, deputy lieutenant and steward of King's county, who firmly established the Colley place in Ireland.

Richard Colley followed a path well worn by the ascendancy Irish. He matriculated at Trinity College, Dublin, where he graduated BA in 1711 and MA in 1714, under the name Cowly. On 23 December 1719 he married Elizabeth (d. 1738), daughter of John Sale, a lawyer, MP for Carysfort and registrar of the diocese of Dublin. The couple had two daughters, Elizabeth and Frances; Elizabeth married Chichester Fortescue in 1743 and in 1750 Frances married William Francis Crosbie. Colley's son and heir, Garrett *Wesley, was born several years later on 19 July 1735. The death of Richard's elder brother, Henry Colley, in 1723 left the family property of Kildare solely in his hands, though the estate was modest owing to the ample provision his father had made for his unmarried daughters. On 23 September 1728 Richard inherited the property of his cousin Garrett Wesley (or Wellesley) of Dangan and Mornington in co. Meath, who died without issue. On 15 November 1728 he took the surname of Wesley, later altered to Wellesley by his grandson.

An amiable and sociable man, Richard Wesley appreciated his good fortune and he enthusiastically adopted an expansive generosity. He was both gentleman farmer and member of the Irish parliament for the borough of Trim (1729–46), but these were only sidelines. His real occupation was entertaining friends and expanding, remodelling, and enhancing Dangan Castle and its extensive grounds. Wesley's obsession with improving his estate reflected the values of ascendancy Ireland. Rising out of the nondescript landscape of co. Meath, Wesley's estate became a showplace. Mary Delany, Wesley's well-connected friend, left behind flattering descriptions of both the house and the park, but she reserved most praise for its owner:

> The more I am acquainted with Mr. Wesley the higher my esteem rises for him. He has certainly more virtues and fewer faults than any man I know. … He values his riches *only* as they are the means of making all about him happy. (*Autobiography … Mrs Delany*, 2.501)

On 17 June 1738 his wife, Elizabeth, died but her loss neither altered nor curtailed Wesley's activities. His daughters served as hostess and surrogate mother until their marriages, and life went on as usual. On 9 July 1746 Wesley was rewarded for his untiring sociability with an Irish peerage, becoming baron of Mornington; he took his seat in the Irish House of Lords on 6 October 1746. He died at his house on Grafton Street, Dublin, on 31 January 1758. Though he had expended enormous sums on Dangan, he still left his son an ample income of £8000 per annum. Garrett Wesley, who later became the first earl of Mornington, was the father of Arthur *Wellesley, duke of Wellington, and Richard *Wellesley, Marquess Wellesley.

JOHN K. SEVERN

Sources *DNB* · E. Longford [E. H. Pakenham, countess of Longford], *Wellington*, 1: *The years of the sword* (1969) · BL, Add. MSS 13914, 37416 · I. Butler, *The eldest brother: the Marquess Wellesley, the duke of Wellington's eldest brother* (1973) · *The autobiography and correspondence of Mary Granville, Mrs Delany*, ed. Lady Llanover, 1st ser., 3 vols. (1861) · Burke, *Peerage* · *GM*, 1st ser., 28 (1758) · R. R. Pearce, *Memoirs and correspondence of the most noble Richard Marquess Wellesley*, 3 vols. (1846)
Archives BL, Wellesley MSS
Likenesses W. Hogarth, group portrait, oils, *c*.1731, Stratfield Saye House, Hampshire · H. P. Bone, miniature, Stratfield Saye House, Hampshire · attrib. J. Latham, oils, Stratfield Saye House, Hampshire · attrib. J. Richardson, oils, Stratfield Saye House, Hampshire · oils, Stratfield Saye House, Hampshire
Wealth at death £8000 p.a. income from estate: Longford, *Wellington: years of the sword*; Butler, *The eldest brother* (1973)

Wesley, Richard. *See* Wellesley, Richard, Marquess Wellesley (1760–1842).

Wesley, Samuel (*bap.* 1662, *d.* 1735), Church of England clergyman and poet, was baptized on 17 December 1662 in Winterborne Whitechurch, Dorset, probably the third of at least four children of the Revd John Westley (1635/6–1671), vicar of Winterborne Whitechurch until his ejection, in 1662, under the Act of Uniformity, and his wife, the daughter of John White (1574–1648) and allegedly the niece of Thomas Fuller, the church historian. His grandfather Bartholomew Westley was also ejected in 1662. The family name was spelt Westley by Samuel as late as 1694 and by others until much later.

Education, marriage, and early clerical career Samuel Wesley was educated at Dorchester grammar school under Henry Dolling and was sent to be prepared for the Independent ministry, under Theophilus Gale, at Newington Green but he reached London on 8 March 1678, after Gale's death. He then attended another grammar school before entering the academies first of Edward Veel (or Veal) in Stepney and after two years that of Charles Morton in Newington Green, where his fellow students included Daniel Defoe. There he wrote lampoons against Thomas Doolittle, head of a rival presbyterian academy.

Dr John Owen, the former vice-chancellor of Oxford University, believing that degrees would soon be open to dissenters, urged Wesley to study at a university. According to his son John *Wesley (1703–1791) it was an attempt to vindicate dissent that led instead to Wesley's move towards the Church of England; apparently he slipped away early one morning to Oxford to avoid opposition from his strongly dissenting family. Though he had mixed feelings about Oxford behaviour he was also disgusted by dissenting ribaldry against the church and the Stuarts, while he admired the latitudinarian John Tillotson. However, he resolved to turn Anglican only after three months in London.

Having paid off some debts with the help of dissenting funds Wesley returned to Oxford, on 22 September 1684, and, as a servitor, entered Exeter College, where he matriculated on 18 November. After three months he found himself destitute and mocked by his fellow undergraduates for his dissenting background. He felt himself

Samuel Wesley (*bap.* 1662, *d.* 1735), by George Vertue, 1735

at risk of moral collapse and, in a letter of 22 August 1692, wrote: 'had not God by providence recall'd me to myself by those kind afflictions, I believe I had grown as ill a man as most in the university' (Beecham, 104). Despite his financial difficulties he told his brother Matthew, in 1731, that he had entered Oxford with £2 5s. od. yet left with £10 15s. od. While at Oxford he published anonymously, through his brother-in-law John Dunton, a volume of verse, entitled *Maggots [Whimsies], or, Poems on Several Subjects Never Before Handled* (1685). He later claimed to have ceased to support James II, over the expulsion of the fellows of Magdalen (16 November 1687), while being unwilling to oppose him actively. But in 1688 he contributed verses to *Strenae natalitatiae Oxoniensae* (1688), in honour of the birth of James's son on 10 June. However, he soon transferred his allegiance to William and Mary, Queen Anne, and George I.

Having graduated BA on 19 June 1688 Wesley reached London on 1 July and was offered a chaplaincy place in Cornwall. He was ordained deacon at Bromley on 7 August 1688 by Thomas Sprat, bishop of Rochester. He then acted as curate of St Botolph, Aldersgate, for about ten months. On 12 November 1688 he married Susanna Annesley (1669–1742) [*see* Wesley, Susanna], youngest daughter of Dr Samuel Annesley, a leading dissenting minister, and his second wife. Susanna had also abandoned dissent for Anglicanism. On 24 February 1689 Wesley was ordained priest by Henry Compton, bishop of London.

Next Wesley had an unhappy six months at sea as a naval chaplain, at £70 per annum, from about June to late November 1689. Then, after some months as a literary hack, he obtained, during the first half of 1690, a curacy at Newington Butts, Surrey, at £30 per annum. His first son, Samuel Wesley the younger [*see below*], was born on 10 February 1690 or 1691 in Spitalfields. Early in the 1690s he wrote a letter which described in critical terms the tone and education of dissenting academies, and which was to be published, with damaging effects, in 1703.

Though offered a post in Virginia, Wesley refused this in favour of the living of South Ormsby, Lincolnshire, which came to him from the Massingberd family, probably through the influence of John Sheffield, marquess of Normanby. He was presented on 25 June 1691 and instituted on 9 July. He returned to London to raise money and first signed the parish register at South Ormsby on 25 August 1691. He had added a nearby curacy, probably Maltby-le-Marsh, by March 1692.

While at South Ormsby Wesley wrote a good deal. With John Dunton he contributed to the *Athenian Gazette* (1691–7) and to the *Young Student's Library* (1692), probably mainly on religious subjects. His heroic poem *The Life of our Blessed Lord and Saviour Jesus Christ* was published in 1693 (and dedicated to Queen Mary in 1694). Lord Normanby made Wesley his chaplain in 1694 and recommended him, unsuccessfully, for an Irish bishopric. Also in 1694 Wesley was incorporated MA at Corpus Christi College, Cambridge. He resigned from South Ormsby following his refusal to allow the mistress of James Saunderson (later earl of Castleton) to visit his own wife.

Preferral to Epworth On 15 March 1695 Wesley was appointed rector of Epworth, Lincolnshire, a crown appointment, probably on account of his political support (Wesley said it was for the dedication of his life of Christ to Queen Mary but she had died before the appointment). He was inducted on 24 April but appears to have acted as curate at South Ormsby until May 1697, so he probably did not move to Epworth until then. According to Wesley, Epworth was a town of 1100 people in 1701, the living being nominally worth £200 per annum, though he did not always receive this amount. There were no 'papists' or presbyterians in the parish but about 40 Quakers, more than 70 Anabaptists, and about 100 of no religion. He complained of the children's ignorance of the Lord's prayer and creed. Already in debt on his arrival, by 1700 he owed £300. Despite efforts to make money, admittedly while supporting his mother, he was a poor manager as well as suffering many misfortunes. His wife remarked that he was 'not so wise in their generation as the children of this world' (Stevenson, 200). He was visited with a series of natural disasters as well as attacks on his property, possibly even arson in the case of the rectory fires of 1702 and 1709. In 1705 he backed tory candidates in a disputed county election, believing that the opposition was being supported by dissenters against the church. As a result, during the election there was 'drumming, shouting and firing of pistols and guns under the window where my wife lay, who had been brought to bed not three weeks'. A clergyman in Lincoln heard them cry 'if they got me in the castle yard they would squeeze my guts out'. At Epworth they threatened to 'turn ye all out of doors a-begging' (Clarke, 104). His enemies engineered Wesley's imprisonment for debt but he was eventually released with the help of a university brief and of government supporters.

The family itself was politically divided. Unlike Samuel, Susanna adhered to the divine right of the exiled Stuarts. Early in 1702 she refused to say 'amen' to her husband's prayer for William III. John Wesley claimed that Samuel flew into a rage and vowed not to cohabit unless she submitted. He left for convocation and threatened to take up a naval chaplaincy but the accession of Anne reconciled them. This account understated Susanna's resolution and her agonies of conscience. She consulted the nonjuror bishop George Hickes and refused mediation. The crisis continued after Anne's accession and was only resolved when Wesley, persuaded by a friend, returned. In 1709 Susanna still maintained that a king by divine right could be judged only by God and not by his subjects.

In 1703 there was published anonymously *A letter from a country divine to his friend in London concerning the education of dissenters in their private acadaemies*. This was the letter written privately by Wesley in the 1690s to a friend, probably Charles Goodall; it was now published by Robert Clavel. Wesley claimed that it was originally provoked by a meeting he attended in 1693, where dissenters expressed scurrilous hostility to the church and to the memory of Charles I. (It was probably not, as is usually claimed, a meeting of the so-called Calve's Head Club, whose reputation in any case may owe much to tory propaganda.) Samuel denied that he had authorized publication, though in a somewhat equivocal fashion. Publication was timed to reinforce the current attacks on dissenters and especially on their academies. A pamphlet war ensued over the next four years, yet in the midst of this, in 1705, Wesley actually proposed to offer to serve as a missionary overseas.

In 1709 the rectory was burnt for the second time and the young John Wesley was rescued, as if by a miracle. In March 1710 came the trial of Dr Henry Sacheverell and, according to John Wesley, Wesley wrote his speech for the defence. There is no other evidence for this, though it is generally believed that Sacheverell did not write it himself. During Wesley's absence at convocation in 1710–12 Susanna held meetings in the rectory for prayer, religious readings, and conversation, upholding her duty to do so, despite opposition from the curate and doubts on Wesley's part. Methodists often saw this as foreshadowing John Wesley's later class meetings. In 1714 John was sent to the Charterhouse on the recommendation of the duke of Buckingham (Wesley's old patron, the former marquess of Normanby) but with the accession of George I this tory nobleman lost influence and with it went Wesley's last hopes of preferment.

In 1716–17 came the remarkable episode of Old Jeffery, the Epworth ghost whose knockings and door slammings would now identify him as a poltergeist but, in this instance, identified him as a Jacobite who knocked loudly when the king was prayed for. The family at first suggested natural explanations but finally settled for a supernatural power. John Wesley, though absent, had no doubt that it was a punishment for his father's rash vow in 1702.

Later career From 1722 Wesley added the rectory of Wroot, at £60 per annum, to Epworth but with little profit, and in 1724 came the unhappy episode of his daughter Mehetabel (Hetty) Wesley [*see* Wright, Mehetabel], later fictionalized by Sir Arthur Quiller-Couch in *Hetty Wesley* (1903). Wesley opposed her proposed marriage and, when she was seduced and pregnant, married her to a drunken plumber, William Wright. Wesley refused to be reconciled with her and John Wesley obliquely criticized him from the pulpit. Hetty lost all her babies, expressing her suffering in poignant verses. Wesley consoled himself for his misfortunes with literary labours in prose and verse, his later years being devoted to a massive volume of dissertations on the Old Testament book of Job. It was published in 1735, after his death, and was dedicated to Queen Caroline, who is said merely to have admired its pretty binding.

In 1731, still apparently in debt, Wesley was taken to task by his brother Matthew, a London physician, who blamed him for his improvidence and for his large family: 'a black account; let the cause be folly, or vanity or ungovernable appetite' (Clarke, 5). To this Samuel replied with a rather jocular but not ineffective account of his years of financial misfortune. Despite his misfortunes and shortcomings Wesley was a dedicated and zealous parish priest, utilizing all the contemporary Anglican initiatives to improve parochial morality and religion. In 1698 he preached in support of the reformation of manners, and from March 1699 he corresponded with the Society for Promoting Christian Knowledge, which supported parish schools and the distribution of religious literature. In 1702 he told the society that he had considered creating a local society for the reformation of manners but instead he formed a religious society on the pattern of those pioneered by Josiah Woodward from 1678, for prayer, religious reading, the reformation of manners, and correspondence with similar societies abroad. He had in mind the continental pietists, the Halle orphan house, and the Danish overseas missions. It is not known what became of this venture but Wesley certainly upheld the more traditional disciplines of the church. His *Pious Communicant Rightly Prepared* (1700) advocated frequent communion and included a discourse on baptism, reproduced by John Wesley as *A Treatise on Baptism*, in 1756, without acknowledgement. In 1701 he initiated a monthly communion, though only twenty people attended, and in 1734 he even offered to pay for a weekly communion for a friend. Initially he catechized all the year round though later, as was customary, only during Lent. He held two services every Sunday with weekday services on Wednesdays, Fridays, and feast days and he imposed public penance for sexual offences. At a mass confirmation at Epworth in 1712 he told Bishop Wake that it would have been more proper 'for my parish to have come by themselves and none to have been confirmed but those whose names had been given in by the minister' (Sykes, 173–4). He expressed his ideals for the clergy in *A Letter to a Curate* (1735). He was a proctor in convocation in 1703 and in 1710, a duty which he took very seriously.

Despite difficulties and differences Wesley was deeply attached to his wife, a woman of exceptional intelligence and of a character very different from his. They had a large family, commonly reckoned at nineteen children though now thought more likely to have been seventeen. Of these, ten (three sons and seven daughters) reached maturity. The daughters were lively and cultured and all but one married, nearly all unhappily, in part through Wesley's interventions. Apart from Mehetabel the most unfortunate case was that of Martha, who married the unstable Revd Westley Hall, once a Methodist but later a practising polygamist. As a widow Martha became a friend of Dr Samuel Johnson.

On 4 June 1731 Wesley was injured by a fall from a wagon and never fully recovered. On his deathbed he is reported to have foretold the coming religious revival. John Wesley claimed, in support of his doctrine of assurance, that his father said 'The inward witness, son, the inward witness, that is the proof, the strongest proof, of Christianity' (*Works of John Wesley*, 26.288–9). Samuel Wesley died at Epworth rectory on 25 April 1735 and was buried three days later in Epworth churchyard. In person he was short, a family characteristic; in character he was learned, zealous, pious, courageous for his principles, affectionate where his prejudices were not aroused, and devoted to his sons' welfare. But he was also obstinate and partisan.

Wesley's literary works were in part a bid for preferment and a consolation for misfortunes, but some were dedicated to improving clerical standards. He is likely always to be remembered mainly as the father of his famous sons. He was only a very minor poet, a mere item in the first edition of Alexander Pope's *Dunciad*, though his hymn 'Behold the saviour of mankind' would not be unworthy of his son Charles *Wesley. His scholarly ambitions were not fulfilled for his volume on Job was largely a monument to misplaced and conservative erudition, though Adam Clarke, who published *Memoirs of the Wesley Family* in 1823, thought its polyglot collations valuable. He nevertheless remains worthy of attention as an example of the best type of clergyman of his time in his attempts to implement the early eighteenth-century high-church movement for parochial renewal, and not without success. The 20 communicants of 1701 had risen to 100 by 1733, and John Wesley allowed that some had been influenced by his father.

Eldest child Samuel Wesley the younger (1690/91–1739), Church of England clergyman and poet, was born in Spitalfields, London, on 10 February 1690 or 1691, the eldest child of Samuel and Susanna Wesley. The uncertainty over his date of birth stems from a letter in which he gave 1690 as his year of birth (Beecham, 84*n*.) but his gravestone says that he was in his forty-ninth year when he died. The fact that he gave his age on matriculation at Oxford as eighteen only adds to the confusion. It is said that he scarcely spoke until he was nearly five, when he

suddenly said, 'Here I am, mother' (Clarke, 363). He became a precocious learner, mastered the alphabet in a few hours, and was able to learn words at first sight. He entered Westminster School in 1704, under Dr Busby, was elected king's scholar in 1707, and became devoted to the classics. He matriculated at Christ Church, Oxford, on 9 June 1711, proceeding BA in 1715 and MA in 1718. He became head usher at Westminster School, probably from 1713, and took orders soon afterwards on the advice of Francis Atterbury, bishop of Rochester. He was also active in founding the first Westminster Infirmary, in 1719, which later became St George's Hospital. He married, about 1715, Ursula Berry, daughter of the Revd John Berry, vicar of Walton, Norfolk. Of their six children, four died in infancy and only a daughter outlived her parents. Ursula fell out with Samuel's brothers and his mother and was still estranged at her death about 1742.

Wesley became friendly with tory politicians and poets such as Robert Harley, earl of Oxford, Alexander Pope, and Jonathan Swift, but the Atterbury connection ensured that he would receive no ecclesiastical preferment. In 1722 Atterbury was arrested for complicity in Jacobite plots and, in 1723, exiled to France. Wesley never wavered in his loyalty to Atterbury and wrote squibs against Sir Robert Walpole. This association branded him a Jacobite though there is no evidence that this went beyond literary opposition. In 1785 John Wesley claimed that he and Samuel, like their father, were tories but not Jacobites, Samuel only differing from him in believing it to be legitimate to oppose the king's ministers.

In 1732–3 (the exact chronology is not entirely clear) Samuel failed to secure the under-mastership at Westminster School through political prejudice, though ostensibly this was because he was married. He was offered the headmastership, apparently unsolicited, of Tiverton grammar school, Devon. The school had kept down the fees for fear of losing pupils but Samuel boldly raised them to £20 per annum. His first year added forty boys to the school and numbers increased in the following years. In February 1733 he refused to follow his father at Epworth to provide a home for his brothers and sisters. John Wesley also refused, with lengthy reasons for remaining in Oxford, to which his brother responded: 'I see your love to yourself but your love to your neighbour I do not see' (*Works of John Wesley*, 25.411).

Wesley took his responsibilities as eldest son and surrogate father with great seriousness. In 1733 his father acknowledged: '[you have been] a father to your brothers and sisters, especially the former, who have cost you great sums in their education' (Stevenson, 136). He kept an eye on John at Charterhouse and, in 1785, Charles recalled that he was 'placed under the care of my eldest brother Samuel, a strict churchman, who brought me up in his own principles' (Baker, *Charles Wesley*, 7). After his father's death he helped to pay his debts and shared in the care of Susanna until she settled in London in 1739. Samuel supported James Oglethorpe's work for the Georgia colony and supplied it with communion plate. But he disapproved of Charles voyaging there, seeing in this John's will rather than God's. He clashed repeatedly with John's conduct and beliefs after the latter's conversion, in 1738, and lamented his mother's countenancing his new ideas. In October 1739 he wrote: 'Is it not enough that I am bereft of both my brothers, but must my mother follow too?' (Longworth, 34).

As a poet Samuel produced satirical and political as well as religious verse. He was a competent, if uninspired, neo-classical poet, unusual only in substituting Christian for pagan personifications. More attractive were his verses on his wife for, unlike most of the Wesley family, he had a happy marriage. Though deserving respect for his political and religious integrity and for his devotion to his family, Samuel was only a very minor poet. His influence shows in the persisting high-churchmanship of his brother Charles, and his early death removed the one person capable of standing up to John Wesley as an affectionate equal. He died at Tiverton grammar school, after a short illness, on 6 November 1739 and was buried in Tiverton churchyard.   HENRY D. RACK

Sources L. Tyerman, *The life and times of the Rev. Samuel Wesley* (1866) · G. J. Stevenson, *Memorials of the Wesley family* (1876), 54–8, 231–57 · A. Clarke, *Memoirs of the Wesley family* (1823), 60–233, 362–455 · J. Priestley, *Original letters of the Rev. John Wesley and his friends* (1791) · H. A. Beecham, 'Samuel Wesley senior: new biographical evidence', *Renaissance and Modern Studies*, 7 (1963), 78–100 · S. Wesley, *A letter from a country divine to his friend in London, concerning the education of the dissenters in their private academies*, 2nd edn (1704) · E. McClure, ed., *A chapter in English church history* (1884), 178–82, 297, 343–5 · R. Walmsley, 'John Wesley's parents: quarrel and reconciliation', *Proceedings of the Wesley Historical Society*, 29 (1953–4), 50–57 · A. Longworth, *Samuel Wesley junior* (1990) · *The works of John Wesley*, 25–6, ed. F. Baker and others (1980–82) · M. L. Edwards, *Family circle* (1949), 1–46, 100–31 · V. H. H. Green, *The young Mr Wesley* (1961), 41–60 · R. E. G. Cole, ed., *Speculum dioeceseos Lincolniensis sub episcopis Gul: Wake et Edm: Gibson, AD 1705–1723*, Lincoln RS, 4 (1913), 157, 175 · H. N. Fairchild, *Religious trends in English poetry* (1939), 1.112–16, 295–302 · N. Sykes, *William Wake, archbishop of Canterbury*, 1 (1957), 173–4 · *The London diaries of William Nicolson, bishop of Carlisle, 1702–1718*, ed. C. Jones and G. Holmes (1985), 321 · *Calamy rev.* · F. Baker, *Charles Wesley as revealed by his letters* (1948) · private information (2004) [F. Baker, S. Himsworth]

Archives Christ Church Oxf., minutes of Convocation of Church of England · JRL, Methodist Archives and Research Centre, corresp., sermons, and notebooks · Wesley College, Bristol, corresp., notebooks, and poems

Likenesses G. Vertue, line engraving, 1735, NPG [*see illus.*] · N. Parr, line engraving, BM, NPG · Ridley, engraving (S. Wesley junior), NPG; repro. in Stevenson, *Memorials* · line engraving, BM, NPG; repro. in S. Wesley, *Maggots* (1685), frontispiece · oils; Christies, 10 Dec 1965, lot 167, now lost

Wesley, Samuel, the younger (1690/91–1739). *See under* Wesley, Samuel (*bap.* 1662, *d.* 1735).

Wesley, Samuel (1766–1837), composer and organist, was born on 24 February 1766 at Charles Street, Bristol, the youngest of the three children to survive infancy of the Methodist hymn writer Charles *Wesley (1707–1788) and his wife, Sarah, *née* Gwynne (1726–1822). He was the grandson of Samuel *Wesley (*bap.* 1662, *d.* 1735), the younger brother of Charles *Wesley (1757–1834), the nephew of John *Wesley, and the father of Samuel Sebastian *Wesley.

Samuel Wesley (1766–1837), by John Jackson, *c.*1815–20

Childhood and adolescence Like his brother Charles, Samuel Wesley was a musical child prodigy. Charles's musical talents attracted the attention of many of the leading musicians of the day, including Samuel Arnold, William Boyce, John Worgan, Thomas Augustine Arne, and Joseph Kelway, many of whom visited the family home, and it was here, by the side of his brother, that Samuel received his first musical experiences. According to his father's account, at just under three he was able to play his first tune, at four had taught himself to read from a copy of Handel's oratorio *Samson*, and at five 'had all the recitatives, and choruses of *Samson* and the *Messiah*: both words and notes by heart' (Winters, 32). When he was six he had some keyboard lessons from David Williams, a Bristol organist, though his father remarked that 'it was hard to say which was the master and which the scholar' (Lightwood, 20). He also had violin and organ lessons, and at the age of seven played a psalm at a service at St James's Church. His first attempts at composition were also from this time. According to his father he had composed the airs for his oratorio *Ruth* before he was six, but was not able to write them down until he was eight. Shortly afterwards, the Wesleys were visited by Boyce, anxious to hear the 'English Mozart'. He looked over the score of *Ruth* and afterwards commented: 'these airs are some of the prettiest I have seen; this boy writes by nature as true a bass as I can by rule and study' (Winters, 35). Wesley's general education was from his father, from whom he gained a good grounding in Latin, Greek, and Hebrew, and a wide knowledge of English literature.

Unlike William Crotch, who spent much of his early childhood on a succession of damaging and demeaning concert tours, Wesley was never commercially exploited as a child prodigy. None the less, his talents made him the object of a good deal of attention and he spent much of his childhood in the company of adults. A major influence at this time was his godfather Martin Madan, chaplain of the Lock Hospital and himself an amateur musician, who took him on many extended visits to family friends, including the painter John Russell (1745–1806), who painted his portrait in 1776, and the scientist James Price, who later left him a house at Epsom and £1000 in his will.

In 1771 Wesley's father accepted the gift of the lease of a house at Chesterfield Street, Marylebone, then a village on the outskirts of London. For a while, the family lived in both Bristol and Marylebone, but in 1776 they moved permanently to Marylebone. There, Charles and Samuel were able to widen their musical experiences and learn with the best teachers. But their father was initially reluctant for them to perform in public, and their appearance at a concert at Hickford's Rooms on 20 May 1777 under the direction of J. C. Bach appears to have been an isolated occurrence. Between 1779 and 1787 they organized a series of private subscription concerts at Chesterfield Street, in which both performed and for which both composed music. The concerts, intended by Charles Wesley to provide opportunities for his sons to develop their musical skills without the risk of being corrupted by worldly influences, involved a small professional instrumental ensemble and attracted fashionable audiences of sometimes more than fifty.

Around 1778 Wesley started to attend Roman Catholic services at one or more of the London embassy chapels. As he was later to admit in his *Reminiscences*, his initial involvement with Roman Catholicism was for musical rather than religious reasons, for it was in the embassy chapels that the most elaborate and sumptuous church music in London was to be heard. He would have been made welcome by Samuel Webbe I, the organist of the Sardinian and Portuguese embassy chapels and the central figure in London Roman Catholic church music at the time, and he would also have met Webbe's son Samuel II, less than two years his junior. By November 1780, doubtless encouraged by Webbe and other Catholic musicians, Wesley was composing Latin church music for use in the embassy chapels.

The attitude of his father to Wesley's involvement with the embassy chapels is not recorded, but it can hardly have been one of equanimity, and it is perhaps an indication of his tolerance that he permitted it to continue at all. By late 1783 Wesley's interest in Roman Catholicism had gone beyond the purely musical, and in May 1784 he converted, marking the event by composing an elaborate setting of the mass which he dedicated to and dispatched to Pope Pius VI. Wesley's conversion caused his father and other members of his family considerable hurt and sorrow, and in the wider Methodist community it was a major scandal which was discussed and agonized over for many years afterwards.

Wesley's whole-hearted commitment to Roman Catholicism appears to have been brief, and it is possible that adolescent rebelliousness may have been involved to a large extent in his conversion. In later life his attitude to Roman Catholicism was deeply ambivalent: he retained his fascination with its music and liturgy while rejecting its doctrines, remarking in a letter of 1809 that 'if the Roman Doctrines were like the Roman *Music* we should have Heaven upon Earth' (*Letters*, ed. Wesley, 36). According to his obituary in *The Times* he later denied ever having been a convert, saying that 'although the Gregorian music had seduced him to their chapels, the tenets of the Romanists never obtained any influence over his mind' (*The Times*, 12 Oct 1837).

If Wesley's conversion to Catholicism was the major cause of concern to his family, other aspects of his behaviour were scarcely less worrying. Family letters of the period contain references to wild behaviour which seems to have gone far beyond normal adolescent rebelliousness and may indicate the onset of the bipolar or manic-depressive illness which affected him for the rest of his life. A particular cause of concern was his relationship with Charlotte Louisa Martin (1761–1845), whom he met in October 1782 and was eventually to marry in 1793. Little is known of her: at the time of their initial meeting she was twenty-one to his sixteen, possibly a schoolteacher, and certainly on the evidence of her few surviving letters a well-educated woman. Their relationship was violently opposed by Wesley's family on the grounds of Martin's supposed unsuitability of character and family background. In one revealing letter of November 1792 to his mother, Wesley sought to correct the prevalent view of Martin as being 'of a careless, prodigal Disposition, and as closely resembling an extravagant Father and a vain Mother', pointing out that for several years she had lived 'decently and out of debt', on an allowance of £30 per year (Wesley, to his mother, 7 Nov 1792, John Rylands University Library of Manchester, DDWF/15/5). Wesley's father demanded that he should break off the liaison, and Wesley's refusal to do so exacerbated already existing family tensions.

Early adulthood Problems arising from Wesley's relationship with Martin continued after the death of his father in 1788. By now the main family preoccupation had moved from attempting to persuade Wesley to break off his relationship with her—for this was clearly impossible—to persuading him to regularize it by marrying her. Under different circumstances this might have been a reasonable request, for Wesley and Martin were passionately committed to each other and at this stage fully intended to spend the remainder of their lives together. But Wesley was implacably opposed to marriage: not to the institution, but to any form of marriage ceremony, whether conducted by the church or by the state. His objections derived from arguments put forward by Madan in his notorious *Thelyphthora* (1780), according to which marriage was established not by any civil or religious ceremony, but by sexual intercourse. On this basis, as Wesley explained to his mother in November 1792 in a letter of perhaps unnecessary frankness, he and Martin were married already and had no need of any official ceremonies to legitimize their union.

During the later 1780s and early 1790s Wesley's public career as a composer and performer was largely in abeyance. He made a living by giving music lessons at one or more girls' schools in London, but he hated teaching and regarded it as 'A B C drudgery'. His disillusionment with the music profession and with life in London at this time appears to have been total, and he seriously considered the advantages for his health of a permanent move to the country. In 1787 Wesley is said to have suffered a serious head injury as a result of falling into a building site when returning home late one night from a visit to a friend. According to his obituary:

> the medical attendants wished to perform the operation of trepanning; but Wesley obstinately refused his consent, and the wound was permitted to heal. This he ever after regretted; for it is supposed that in consequence of some portion of the skull adhering to, or pressing upon, the brain, those periodical states of high nervous irritability originated, which subsequently checked and darkened the splendour of his career.

Although this anecdote seems to have come from Wesley himself, it is uncorroborated by information from any other source. Its appearance for the first time in an obituary notice fifty years later gives grounds for scepticism about the accuracy of all its details, and in particular its explanation of Wesley's mental health problems.

On 17 December 1788 Wesley became a freemason and was admitted to the Lodge of Antiquity. On 13 May 1812 he was created grand organist by the duke of Sussex, but resigned this position in 1818 to Sir George Smart.

In the autumn of 1792 Wesley set up house with Martin in the small village of Ridge, Hertfordshire, some 13 miles from London. At this stage they were still determinedly unmarried, but the discovery of Martin's pregnancy early in 1793 prompted a capitulation to more conventional mores, and they eventually married at Hammersmith parish church on 5 April of that year. Their first child, Charles, was born on 25 September. He was educated at St Paul's School and Christ's College, Cambridge, was ordained in 1821, and later became subdean to the Chapel Royal and chaplain to the royal household at St James's Palace. He died in 1859. A daughter was born in late 1794 and died in December 1797. Meanwhile, Wesley's prophecy to his sister, Sarah *Wesley (1759–1828), in a letter that if forced into marriage with Martin he would 'marry her and hate her tomorrow' (Wesley to Sarah Wesley, 5 June 1791, Fitzwilliam Museum, Cambridge) was proving all too accurate. As early as October 1794, while waiting for his wife's confinement with their second child, he was ruefully confessing to his sister Sarah that she was 'never designed for [his] second self' (Wesley to his sister, 26 Oct 1794, Emory University, Atlanta, Georgia), and family letters of the period show that the marriage was already unhappy.

Musical career, 1793–1816 During his time at Ridge, Wesley continued to teach and carry out other professional engagements in London, staying overnight as necessary at the family home in Chesterfield Street. His one major composition from this period was the *Ode to St Cecilia* for soloists, chorus, and orchestra, on a text by his grandfather Samuel Wesley, which he completed in October 1794. It was first performed on 22 February 1799.

In the summer of 1797 Wesley and Charlotte left Ridge and moved to Finchley, probably as a result of their dissatisfaction with the isolation of country life and Wesley's decision to resume his professional career in London. In the summer of 1799 they moved again, to Highgate; their son John William was born around this time. Wesley's relationship with Charlotte continued to be stormy, with frequent quarrels, incidents of domestic violence, extramarital affairs, temporary separations, and alternating periods of estrangement and reconciliation. A further daughter, Emma Frances, was born in early 1806.

There is little direct information about Wesley's musical activities in the years around the turn of the century, but his numerous compositions from the period indicate that it was a fruitful time. His Latin church music compositions show that he had renewed his involvement with the world of the Roman Catholic embassy chapels, probably with the chapel of the Portuguese embassy in South Street, South Audley Street, where Vincent Novello had recently become organist. A large number of glees, songs, and duets, mostly unpublished, show Wesley's involvement with the glee club and with other forms of informal and convivial music-making. His major work of the period was his large-scale setting for soloists, chorus, and orchestra of Psalm 116, *Confitebor tibi, domine*, which he completed in 1799. As with the *Ode to St Cecilia*, nothing is known about the circumstances of its composition. Its only performance in Wesley's lifetime was on 4 May 1826.

Wesley was also beginning to establish his reputation as the foremost organist of his day, and on 21 April 1800 he appeared as the soloist in one of his own concertos at one of the first London performances of Haydn's *The Creation*. In 1802 he organized a series of subscription concerts at the Tottenham Street Rooms of the Concert of Ancient Music with his brother Charles, and it may have been for this series that he wrote his symphony in B♭. A turning point was reached in Wesley's life and career with his discovery of the music of J. S. Bach and his subsequent involvement in the English Bach movement. Although he had known some examples of Bach's music earlier, and had made a manuscript copy of the forty-eight preludes and fugues in early 1806, the explosive awakening of his interest seems to have occurred early in 1808. By April of that year he was consulting Charles Burney about the best way to promote Bach's music and was planning a programme of activities which included concerts, lectures, and publications. Wesley's role in the English Bach movement is reflected in his well-known letters to Benjamin Jacob, first published in an edition by his daughter Eliza in 1875. His activities in promoting Bach's music also included his collaboration with C. F. Horn in the publication of the first English editions of the organ trio sonatas and the *Forty-Eight Preludes and Fugues* and his participation in a series of celebrated recitals of Bach's music at the Surrey Chapel with Crotch, Jacob, Novello, and the violinist Johann Peter Salomon.

The period inaugurated by the discovery of the music of Bach was the most active, fruitful, and financially profitable of Wesley's career. From 1808 to 1816 he was involved in almost every activity open to a professional musician at the time. He was much in demand as an organist, both as a recitalist and at choral and orchestral concerts. From 1813 he was the regular organist at the Covent Garden oratorio concerts, for which he later remembered that he was paid 6 guineas per concert, or 10 guineas if he played a concerto. He was active in the provinces, directing performances from the organ at a music festival at Tamworth, Staffordshire, in September 1809 and at the Birmingham festival in October 1811; he also gave recitals and played at festivals at Norwich, Great Yarmouth, Ramsgate, Margate, Ipswich, and elsewhere. In 1809, following Crotch and John Wall Callcott, he lectured on music at the Royal Institution. He gave two similar courses at the Surrey Institution in 1809 and 1811. From March 1814 to December 1816 he was the author of the unsigned column of reviews of new musical publications in the *European Magazine*. He also continued to be involved with Novello in the music of the Portuguese embassy chapel. He became a full member of the Philharmonic Society on 1 June 1815 and a director on 22 November of the same year, and was actively involved with the society's affairs in 1815 and 1816. His motet 'Father of light' was performed at the society's concert of 29 April 1816, but this was the only work by him to be performed by the society, and he never himself appeared in or directed a concert.

Meanwhile, Wesley's marriage to Charlotte had irrevocably broken down. The final break appears to have been precipitated by Wesley's affair with the fifteen- or sixteen-year-old Sarah Suter, who was living at the time with the family as a servant or housekeeper. Wesley and Charlotte separated in 1810, no doubt following the discovery of the affair and of Sarah's pregnancy. Wesley and Sarah subsequently set up house together, and their first child, Samuel Sebastian, named after Johann Sebastian Bach, was born on 14 August. They continued to live together unmarried until Wesley's death in what appears to have been a loving and mutually supportive relationship. A large collection of Wesley's letters to Sarah and their children is now in the British Library. Seven of their children survived to adulthood: Samuel Sebastian, Rosalind, Eliza, Matthias Erasmus, John, Thomasine, and Robert Glenn, named after the husband of Rosalind. Two further children died in infancy or early childhood, in 1813 and 1816. Wesley's maintenance commitments to Charlotte, initially set at £130 per annum by a deed of separation of 1812, continued to be a heavy drain on his finances, and non-payment resulted in his being briefly imprisoned for debt on at least one occasion, in May 1825.

Breakdown and recovery, 1816–1830 Wesley's long run of success came to an end with a series of events triggered by his child's death in August 1816. He collapsed later that month while on a journey to Norwich to fulfil a professional engagement, but was able to make a partial recovery and to continue with his professional commitments until late March of the following year. In early May he threw himself out of a window in what appears to have been delirium, and narrowly escaped permanent injury. He was subsequently confined for a time in a private lunatic asylum. Financial and practical help for Wesley and his family at this difficult time appears to have come principally from his masonic friends, including William Linley.

Wesley made a slow and gradual recovery. By early 1819 he was picking up some of his former professional activities and had returned to his position as organist of the Covent Garden oratorios. But he was still in low spirits, unable to compose, and financially hard pressed. His breakdown was a watershed in his career. His enforced absence from musical life for almost two years caused him to lose contacts and opportunities, and as a result he was never able to regain the ground he had lost. None the less, he continued to be in demand as an organist and a lecturer on music through much of the 1820s and he was also able to develop his career in new directions. In 1824 he was appointed organist to the recently built Camden Chapel (All Saints, Camden Street); this appears to have been his first paid church appointment, and followed many unsuccessful earlier applications elsewhere. At the same time he had recovered his self-confidence sufficiently to complete and publish by subscription his Anglican service in F, parts of which he had written as long ago as 1808. Wesley had long been a leading practitioner and a respected authority in church music, and the publication of his service inevitably attracted a good deal of critical attention, including reviews couched in respectful but not entirely favourable terms in the *Harmonicon* and the *Quarterly Musical Review and Register*, the two principal musical periodicals of the time.

In 1826 Wesley obtained permission from the University of Cambridge to transcribe and publish music from the collection of the Fitzwilliam Museum; a similar permission had earlier been granted to Novello. While on a visit to Cambridge later that year he discovered the autograph manuscript of three hymns by Handel, written in the 1740s to words by Wesley's father, which he immediately edited and published. Encouraged by the success of this venture, he later compiled and published in 1828 a volume of tunes to the hymns by his father in current use by Methodist congregations.

Wesley's negotiations with the Methodist connexional editor Thomas Jackson over the publication of the Handel hymns may have been the cause of his partial reconciliation with the Methodist community. In May 1827 he was a warmly received guest at the annual breakfast of the Children of the Methodist Preachers, and he was invited to give the opening recital on the organ of the Brunswick Chapel, Leeds, on 12 September 1828.

Wesley's organ playing and lecturing activities also took him back to Bristol, which he had not visited since 1809. In September and October 1829 he gave a number of organ recitals there, including three at St Mary Redcliffe, when he was joined by his son Samuel Sebastian. The following January he returned and gave a course of lectures at the Bristol Institution. Both of these visits were probably arranged through his friend D. G. Wait, rector of Blagdon, who had also been involved in his activities at the Fitzwilliam Museum in Cambridge.

Final years Following a further attack of depression in 1830 which effectively brought his career to a close, Wesley's last years were spent in retirement and in conditions of financial hardship. A subscription was arranged in 1830 by a group of his musical and masonic friends, led by John Capel, William Linley, and Vincent Novello. On the death of his brother Charles in 1834 the annuity which had been granted to the Wesley family by the Methodist Book Room in respect of the copyright of Charles Wesley senior's hymns descended to him, and these payments helped to alleviate his financial problems in his final years.

Wesley made few public appearances in the 1830s. In August 1834, at a Sacred Harmonic Society concert, he accompanied a performance of his anthem 'All go unto one place', written for the memorial service for his brother Charles.

By 1836, perhaps at the suggestion or with the encouragement of Sarah and his children, Wesley wrote his manuscript *Reminiscences*, in which he recorded all he could remember of his life in music. Although containing much of interest, the *Reminiscences* lack the sardonic humour and outspoken views of Wesley's letters. It is in no sense a finished document, and its laborious handwriting and repetitiousness show that Wesley's physical and mental powers were by this time failing. Also contained in the same manuscript are passages of historical writing, clearly written with publication in mind, and relating to Wesley's last piece of published work, an article entitled 'A sketch of the state of music in England, from the year 1778 up to the present time', which appeared in the first number of the *Musical World* on 18 March 1836.

Wesley's spirits revived shortly before his death. In July 1837 he wrote out from memory the full score of his *Ode to St Cecilia* of 1794, which he believed to have been lost. On 12 September 1837, less than a month before his death, he attended a recital by Mendelssohn at Christ Church Greyfriars and was afterwards persuaded to play. Mendelssohn was generous with his praise, but Wesley could only say, 'Sir, you have not heard me play. You should have heard me 40 years ago' (quoted in Lightwood, 227).

Personality, reputation, and historical significance Wesley was the most original British composer of his time. His compositions, in almost every genre except opera, reflect and are enriched by his deep knowledge of a wide range of music from the sixteenth century to his own time. Much of his most ambitious and characteristic music, lacking the potential for large sales, remained unpublished in his lifetime, and many of the works that were published were unashamed potboilers, written for the amateur market. But his music had wide exposure through repeated performances at his own concerts, and his obituary notices attest to the high regard in which he was held.

Wesley was best known as an organist and was particularly famed for his extempore playing. According to *The Times*, 'his resources were boundless, and if called upon to extemporize for half-a-dozen times during the evening, each fantasia was new, fresh, and perfectly unlike the others' (*The Times*, 12 Oct 1837). There are many contemporary accounts of his playing; Edward Hodges, who heard him play in Bristol in October 1829, described his performance as 'truly astounding … it was the most wonderful I ever heard, more even than I had before been capable of conceiving; the flow of melody, the stream of harmony, was so complete, so unbroken, so easy, and yet so highly wrought that I was altogether knocked off my stilts' (quoted in Lightwood, 215).

Despite his brilliance as a composer and organist, Wesley held no official or church appointments of any importance, and was never quite in the innermost circles of London musical life. His lack of advancement is largely explained by his rebellious character, his famous outspokenness, the scandal of his personal life, and the violent mood swings to which he was subject. According to his obituary:

> His passions were exceedingly strong, and from a habit of always speaking his mind, and his having no idea of management or the *finesse* of human life, he too often by the brilliancy of his wit, or the bitterness of his sarcasm, unthinkingly caused estrangements, if not raised up an enemy. (*The Times*, 12 Oct 1837)

With less need of restraint, Mary Sabilla Novello, the wife of Vincent Novello, commented in a letter of around 1842 to the singer Henry Phillips on the 'opposite extremes of mad fun and excessive depression, to which alternations Wesley always was subject', adding:

> I knew him unfortunately, too well; pious Catholic, raving atheist, mad, reasonable, drunk and sober—the dread of all wives and regular families, a warm friend, a bitter foe, a satirical talker, a flatterer at times of those he cynically traduced at others—a blasphemer at times, a pueling Methodist at others. (Mary Sabilla Novello, fragment of a letter to Henry Phillips, c.1842, Lbl Add. 31764, fol. 34)

Wesley died at his home at 8 King's Row, Pentonville, on 11 October 1837 after a short illness. His funeral service on 17 October was at old St Marylebone parish church. He was buried in an adjoining burial-ground, in the family plot alongside his father, his mother, and his brother Charles.

PHILIP OLLESON

Sources J. T. Lightwood, *Samuel Wesley, musician* (1937) · G. J. Stevenson, *Memorials of the Wesley family* (1876) · *The Times* (12 Oct 1837) · *The Times* (18 Oct 1837) [funeral] · 'Professional memoranda of the late Mr Samuel Wesley's life', *Musical World* (20 Oct 1837), 81–93, 113–18 · 'Memoir of Samuel Wesley, the musician', *Wesley Banner and Revival Record*, 3 (1851), 321–8, 361–70, 401–11, 441–53 · T. Jackson, *The life of the Rev. Charles Wesley, MA* (1841) · D. Barrington, 'Account of Master Samuel Wesley', *Miscellanies* (1781), 291–310 · *Letters of Samuel Wesley to Mr Jacobs*, ed. E. Wesley (1875) · Wesley family letters and papers · S. Wesley, 'Reminiscences', c.1836, BL, Add. MS 27593 · *The letters of Samuel Wesley: professional and social correspondence, 1797-1837*, ed. P. J. Olleson (2000) · T. Jackson, *Recollections of my own life and times*, ed. B. Frankland, new edn (1874), 231–2 · J. Higgs, 'Samuel Wesley: his life, times and influence on music', *Proceedings of the Musical Association*, 20 (1893–4), 125–47 · W. Winters, *An account of the remarkable talents of several members of the Wesley* *family* (1874) · F. G. E. [F. G. Edwards], 'Bach's music in England', *MT*, 37 (1896), 585–7, 652–7, 722–6, 797–800 · F. G. Edwards, 'Samuel Wesley', *MT*, 43 (1902) · P. J. Olleson, 'The Tamworth festival of 1809', *Staffordshire Studies*, 5 (1993), 81–106 · P. J. Olleson, 'Family history sources for British music research', *A handbook of studies in 18th-century music*, ed. M. Burden and I. Cholij, 3 (1993), 1–36 · J. Ogasapian, *English cathedral music in New York: Edward Hodges of Trinity Church* (1994) · C. W. Pearce, *Notes on old London city churches, their organs, organists, and musical associations* (1909) · P. J. Olleson, 'Samuel Wesley and the *European Magazine*', *Notes*, 52 (1996), 1097–1111 · *The Mendelssohns on honeymoon: the 1837 diary of Felix and Cécile Mendelssohn together with letters to their families*, ed. and trans. P. W. Jones (1997), 96, 102–3, 192

Archives BL, corresp. and papers, Add. MSS 27593, 35012–35017, 35019, 35020, 35022, 56228, 56411 · Dorset RO, family corresp. · Emory University, Atlanta, Georgia, family and professional corresp. · FM Cam. · FM Cam., family letters · JRL, Methodist Archives and Research Centre, corresp. and papers · Royal College of Music, London | BL, letters to Sarah Suter, Joseph Street, Vincent Novello, Add. MSS 11729–35012 · Royal College of Music, London, letters to Benjamin Jacob

Likenesses J. Russell, oils, 1777, Royal Academy of Music, London · W. Dickinson, mezzotint, pubd before 1778 (after J. Russell), BM, NPG · J. Jackson, oils, *c*.1815–1820, NPG [*see illus.*] · Gilling, watercolour miniature, BM · J. J. Masquerier, pencil drawing; copy, NPG · pencil drawing (in old age), BM

Wesley, Samuel Sebastian (1810–1876), composer and organist, was born on 14 August 1810, probably at 11 Adam's Row, Hampstead Road, London, the eldest of the seven surviving children of an irregular union between the organist and composer Samuel *Wesley (1766–1837) and his housemaid, Sarah Suter (1793/4–1863). He was named after his father's musical idol, Johann Sebastian Bach. His earliest years were passed under the shadow of extreme family disapproval of his parents' liaison. They were also clouded by his father's constant shortage of money (due in large part to the substantial maintenance payments he was required to pay to his estranged wife) and, from 1816, his father's descent into a prolonged bout of severe depression. Acceptance as a child (chorister) of the Chapel Royal, St James's Palace, in November 1817 provided an escape from the poverty-stricken household and also marked the beginning of his formal musical education. Later declared by William Hawes, the master of the children, to have been the 'best boy he had ever had', Wesley was among those regularly chosen to join the small group who travelled to sing at the Royal Pavilion, Brighton, when the king (George IV) was in residence. Here he was a fellow performer with Rossini at one Saturday evening concert and was also presented with a gold watch by the king.

Early musical career Shortly after leaving the choir in 1826 Wesley was appointed organist of St James's Chapel, Hampstead Road, London, and during the next six years he held similar appointments at St Giles, Camberwell (1829–32), St John's, Waterloo Road (1829–31), and Hampton parish church (1831–2). By now he was becoming known as an organist—and particularly as a pedal player—and was one of the first in England to give a solo performance of one of J. S. Bach's organ fugues when he played the 'St Ann' at a trial for the post of organist at St Stephen's, Coleman Street, in November 1827. He had also

Samuel Sebastian Wesley (1810–1876), by William Keighley Briggs, *c*.1849

continued his association with Hawes and the latter's multifarious musical activities; he acted as pianist and 'conductor of the chorus' at the English Opera House (*c*.1828–32) and as organist at the Lenten oratorio concerts (1830–32). At the former he was responsible for the overture and 'melo-dramatick' music for *The Dilosk Gatherer*, a melodrama by Edward Fitzball produced in July 1832, while his setting of the Benedictus had been given at the latter on 30 March 1832. By now he had also begun to make his mark as a composer of songs and piano and organ music (including a virtuoso set of *Variations on God Save the King*, 1829), and looked to be destined for a promising career in the capital. On 10 July 1832, however, he was elected to the post of organist at Hereford Cathedral (whose recently appointed dean, John Merewether, had formerly been incumbent at Hampton) and shortly thereafter he left London, never to return.

Hereford and Exeter cathedrals Notwithstanding his stated wish to be able to devote himself to the composition of church music, the move was one Wesley was to regret ever afterwards:

> Painful and dangerous is the position of a young musician who, after acquiring great knowledge of his art in the Metropolis, joins a Country Cathedral. At first he can scarcely believe that the mass of error and inferiority in which he has to participate is habitual and irremediable. (Wesley, *Cathedral Music*, 11)

Yet the change of circumstances had a remarkable effect on his development as a composer, and resulted in his early masterpiece, the anthem 'The Wilderness', written to commemorate the opening of the rebuilt cathedral organ and first performed on 10 November 1832. Clearly benefiting from its composer's experience in the theatre and concert hall, it remains a remarkable achievement when viewed against the moribund background of contemporary cathedral music. Its up-to-date idiom, however, was not sufficiently of the church to satisfy the three judges for the Gresham prize medal for which Wesley submitted it in 1833, one of whom (R. J. S. Stevens) dismissed it as 'a clever thing, but not Cathedral Music'. With this disappointment, and Wesley's failure earlier in the year to achieve more than a run-through of an overture by the Philharmonic Society, came the realization that for a young and little-known composer from the provinces to achieve success in London was a near impossible task. The award of prize medals for his glees 'I wish to tune my quiv'ring lyre' (1833) and 'At that Dread Hour' (1834) by the Gentlemen's Glee Club, Manchester, offered some recompense, as did the opportunity to perform his overture in E, Sanctus, and sacred song 'Abraham's Offering' at the Hereford festival in 1834. But nothing could compensate for Hereford's position as a musical backwater and this, frustration with the low musical standards at the cathedral, and his pitifully small salary (£60 per annum) led Wesley to apply for the post of organist and sub-chanter at Exeter Cathedral, to which he was appointed on 15 August 1835. His marriage three months earlier (on 4 May) to Mary Anne, the sister of Dean Merewether—presumably without family approval, as it was by special licence and took place in the nearby village of Ewyas Harold—doubtless provided a further reason to move.

While at Hereford Wesley had completed another of his best-known anthems, 'Blessed be the God and Father' (1834/1835), and it was during his early years at Exeter that he consolidated his position as the foremost and most innovative composer of church music of his generation. Especially notable are the three outstanding large-scale anthems 'O Lord, thou art my God', 'Let us lift up our heart', and 'To my Request and Earnest Cry' (all written c.1836) and that deeply felt miniature 'Wash me throughly from my wickedness' (c.1840). All reflect both Wesley's complete command of a highly coloured and emotionally charged harmonic idiom of great individuality and his consummate handling of contrapuntal writing, yet only one, 'O Lord, thou art my God', received even a single performance at the cathedral. Bearing in mind Wesley's later—apparently autobiographical—comment about cathedrals which 'would not go to the expense of copying the parts out for the Choir', one can make assumptions concerning the fate of these works. Certainly the amicable working relationship Wesley had initially enjoyed with the dean and chapter quickly soured after the elevation of the precentor, Thomas Hill Lowe, to the deanery in 1839. For the remainder of his time in the city he was almost constantly at loggerheads with his clerical superiors. It was this, more than anything else, which convinced him that he should qualify himself for an alternative career as a university professor of music. To this end he matriculated at Magdalen College, Oxford, on 3 June 1839 and took the degrees of BMus and DMus by accumulation on 21 June; his exercise, 'O Lord, thou art my God', was performed in Magdalen Chapel on 20 June. Thus equipped, Wesley was a candidate for the Reid chair of music in the University of Edinburgh in 1841, but was defeated by Henry Bishop. Well before the result was known, however, another opportunity to escape from Exeter had arisen: having played at the opening of the organ in the newly built parish church in Leeds on 18 October, Wesley was (according to his pupil William Spark) 'so much impressed with the wealth of Leeds ... that bearing in mind his disagreement with Dean Lowe ... he forthwith accepted the offer of organist at £200 per annum, guaranteed for ten years' (Spark, *Reminiscences*, 166). With only one daily service and no troublesome dean and chapter with whom to deal, it was an offer he could hardly refuse.

Although Wesley was ultimately desperate to move away, his early years in Exeter had been among his happiest, with the birth of two sons—John Sebastian (*b.* 17 June 1836) and Samuel Annesley (*b.* 28 Dec 1837)—and extensive participation in local music-making. Warmly welcomed on his arrival by the members of the Devon Madrigal Society (whose monthly meetings he regularly chaired), he also organized a series of subscription concerts for the 1836–7 season and attempted to form an orchestral society in 1837 and a choral society a year later. But none of these initiatives was particularly successful, and from thenceforth—with the exception of the birth of another son, Francis Gwynne, on 29 January 1841—he was dogged by misfortune: the death of his two-month-old daughter Mary in February 1840, the destruction by fire of the plates for a collection of anthems in October 1840, and continuing disputes about his attendance and conduct at the cathedral, particularly a notorious unprovoked attack on two choristers in the cathedral song school in September 1840. He received a series of reprimands: had he not chosen to leave of his own accord he could well have suffered the ignominy of being forced to resign. Even his final departure was marred by controversy, as he unilaterally chose to leave Spark to serve out his notice by proxy. This, and subsequent wrangling over money he claimed was owed to him, reveal a less attractive side to his nature; indeed, Wesley was described by the chapter clerk (with whom he had frequently crossed swords) as 'the most to be avoided man I ever met with' (Exeter Cathedral Archives, MS D & C Exeter/7061/Wesley Papers/10).

Leeds and Winchester Wesley's fame had preceded him, and he was much fêted on his arrival in Leeds in February 1842. As at Exeter, the move to new surroundings reinvigorated him, and his first few years in the town were marked by a series of new publications and compositions. Among these were three of his most important keyboard works, the two sets of *Three Pieces for a Chamber Organ* and the *March and Rondo* for piano (all issued in 1842), a printed psalter with chants for the parish church choir (1843), and his *Morning and Evening Cathedral Service* in E (1845). For the publication of the last he was indebted to the generosity of Martin Cawood, who was a wealthy brass-founder and unofficial music adviser to the vicar, Walter Farquhar

Hook, and who had already been instrumental in securing his appointment. After hearing the setting of the Nicene creed (written at Hereford), Cawood had 'proposed to the Author the completion of the entire Service, undertaking to remunerate him for his work, and incur the sole risk and responsibility of its publication' (Wesley, 'Preface', vi–vii). With its independent obbligato organ part, resourceful use of harmonic colour, and sense of scale, Wesley's service forms a landmark in the history of the genre and, despite failing to satisfy the critics, served as an inspiration to his contemporaries and successors. Its publication also gave him the opportunity to precede it with an extended preface, in which he outlined his strongly held views on the need for reform in cathedral music. He had first broached the subject in the preface to the second edition of *A Selection of Psalm Tunes* (1842), and had continued his campaign in two series of lectures on choral music given at the Liverpool Collegiate Institution in 1844 and 1846; its culmination was reached with his lengthy pamphlet *A Few Words on Cathedral Music and the Musical System of the Church, with a Plan of Reform* (1849), to which the *Reply to the Inquiries of the Cathedral Commissioners, Relative to Improvement in the Music of Divine Worship* (1854) forms a postscript. To Wesley the Anglican choral service was an art form uniting music, language, and architecture, and the church musician (in other words, himself) was an artist in the service of God. But such a romantically inspired vision was too personal to command wide support, and the immediate impact of his writings was consequently slight (although much of what he had striven for in the raising of musical standards and the better treatment of musicians was gradually achieved during the next three decades).

Wesley's last two sons, Charles Alexander (*b*. 4 Feb 1843) and William Ken (*b*. 8 July 1845), were both born in Leeds. During this period Wesley was also active in musical life away from the parish church, as player, teacher, and conductor. Foremost among these activities was his involvement in a new Leeds Choral Society, which, after an auspicious start, fell victim to rivalry with the 'old' Leeds Choral Society and was disbanded in 1845. Also worthy of notice was his participation (as pianist) in the first provincial performance of Beethoven's symphony no. 9 at the 1843 annual meeting of the Yorkshire Amateur Musical Society. But it was as an organist that his fame was greatest, and he made two highly praised appearances as solo organist at the Birmingham festivals of 1843 and 1849. Indeed, after the former it was confidently stated by the *Musical World* that 'Dr. Wesley, as an organist, has no rival now living, except Dr. Mendelssohn' (*Musical World*, 18, 1843, 324).

Notwithstanding the promising start he had made at the parish church, it did not take Wesley long to discover that his own and Hook's aims were rarely identical. 'Disappointed as I was with Dr Hook & his powers to either aid his Church Music or me—I soon bitterly repented of leaving Exeter' (letter to Henry Ford, Royal School of Church Music, MS album of letters), he was later to write, and the invitation to open the new organ in Tavistock parish church in June 1846 led him seriously to consider accepting the post of organist. His last three years in Leeds were clouded by regular disagreements with the vicar and also by injury: on the evening of 23 December 1847, while returning from a fishing expedition to the River Rye, he fell and badly fractured his right leg, and for the next six months he was laid up at the Black Swan at Helmsley. With unaccustomed time on his hands he turned again to composition and wrote two anthems, 'Cast me not away from thy presence' and 'The Face of the Lord', and a second sacred song with orchestral accompaniment, 'I have been young and now am old' (first performed at the 1850 Gloucester festival). All three set penitential texts, and both anthems contain autobiographical references to injury and accident: few pages of Wesley's music are more affecting than the harsh discords which accompany the words 'That the bones which thou hast broken shall rejoice' in the first. During his convalescence (and unknown to him), Wesley's name had been put forward for the vacant Heather chair of music in the University of Oxford, but he was again passed over in favour of Sir Henry Bishop. Finally, in August 1849, he was successful in his application for the post of organist at Winchester Cathedral. His departure from Leeds was fortunately marred by none of the personal bitterness which had so soured his leaving Exeter, and in February 1850 he was invited back for a farewell dinner and to be presented with his portrait, painted by the local artist and singer W. K. Briggs.

Something of Wesley's reputation was clearly known in Winchester, and before his appointment was confirmed he was required by the dean and chapter to give a written undertaking to resign should they consider such a step to be advisable. Yet at first such a reassurance must have seemed unnecessary: in the precentor, W. N. Hooper, Wesley found someone willing to defer—in practice if not in theory—to his greater musical expertise. As in the past, new surroundings and a new position provided a stimulus to composition, and within two years he had completed his well-known anthems 'Thou wilt keep him in perfect peace' (*c*.1850) and 'Ascribe unto the Lord' (1851). More importantly, he was also able to achieve his long-cherished ambition to publish a collection of anthems. The first announcements for a volume of six anthems had appeared as long ago as 1836 and printing had begun in 1840. But having lost money when the plates were destroyed (and become disillusioned over the failure of the dean and chapter of Exeter to support his music), Wesley had felt in no hurry to proceed further and did not return to the project until his enforced stay at Helmsley. By the time of its eventual publication in 1853 the collection had doubled in size. It represents Wesley's finest achievement and, arguably, the single most important English church music publication of the century. Despite including 'Ascribe unto the Lord', 'Blessed be the God and Father', 'Cast me not away', 'Let us lift up our heart', 'O Lord, thou art my God', 'The Face of the Lord', 'The Wilderness', 'Thou wilt keep him in perfect peace', and 'Wash me throughly', its publication passed largely unnoticed, and this, together with the critical attacks made after the performance of an orchestrated version of 'The Wilderness' at the Birmingham festival a year earlier, can have done little to encourage him. His best years as a composer were in fact already past, and the lack of public appreciation and recognition began increasingly to take its toll: few of his later anthems (among them 'By the word of the Lord', written for the opening of the new cathedral organ in June 1854, and 'Give the king thy judgements', written to celebrate the marriage of the prince of Wales in March 1863) maintain a uniformly high level of inspiration. Only 'Praise the Lord, o my soul', written for the opening of the organ in Holy Trinity Church, Winchester, in September 1861, approaches the standard of his earlier works.

The mid-1850s were an unhappy period for Wesley, as he was also at the centre of a controversy over the design he had prepared for the organ in St George's Hall, Liverpool. Although not completed by Henry Willis until 1855, it had been conceived a decade earlier, and the delay had magnified its old-fashioned features: for these, and for his insistence on 'G' compass and mean-tone temperament, he was sternly taken to task by the musical press, and a heated public debate ensued. Indeed, in many ways Wesley was becoming a lonely, reactionary figure, unwilling—or unable—to adapt to the changing musical conditions. Even his application in 1856 for the vacant chair of music in the University of Cambridge seems to have been half-heartedly made, and he withdrew before the vote. Never one to court the friendship of his fellow musicians, he had relied for companionship on those of his father's generation, and as death now overtook them he found himself increasingly alone. With the appointment of an over-zealous precentor, Henry Wray, in 1858, life at the cathedral also became considerably less comfortable. Reprimands over the dereliction of his duty became more frequent, and when in February 1865 he was asked to adjudicate between candidates for the post of organist at Gloucester Cathedral he offered to take it himself.

Wesley's stay in Winchester had been the longest of his career, owing, it is said, to his desire to have his sons educated at Winchester College (of which he had been appointed organist in December 1850) and his appreciation of the fishing. His time there also saw his effective withdrawal from most musical activity outside the cathedral, although he maintained his association with the Royal Academy of Music (where he had been appointed the first professor of organ in August 1850) and continued his career as a recitalist. One notable appearance was at the opening of the organ in the Agricultural Hall, Islington, London, on 3 November 1863, when he played his newly written *Andante cantabile*, and he returned to the hall in October 1864 to conduct the only extended choral work of his maturity—a setting for soloists, chorus, and orchestra of W. H. Bellamy's *Ode to Labour*, written for the opening of the North London Working Men's Industrial Exhibition.

Final years Although Wesley had had little to do with orchestral or large-scale choral works since leaving Leeds, within a short time of his arrival in Gloucester he found

himself having to devise programmes for the forthcoming Three Choirs festival which it was the city's turn to host in 1865. Not surprisingly his choice of music was unadventurous—Handel's *Messiah*, Mendelssohn's *Elijah* and *Hymn of Praise*, Mozart's Requiem, and Spohr's *Die letzten Dinge*—although he also orchestrated 'Ascribe unto the Lord' and for the 1871 festival introduced J. S. Bach's St Matthew passion. Notwithstanding his inexperience as a conductor (exacerbated by his nervousness on the podium), his direction of the Gloucester festivals of 1865, 1868, 1871, and 1874 remains his most significant achievement in the city. Indeed, on the evidence of both the music sung and contemporary comments on the state of the choir, he almost gave up the fight to raise musical standards at the cathedral. Composition, too, seems to have lost its attraction, and most of the works from his last decade were either reworkings of earlier material or commissions which lacked the spark of inspiration; one of the few exceptions was the unaccompanied chorus 'The Praise of Music', written in 1872 for Gounod's Royal Albert Hall Choral Society.

Yet Wesley still had one important contribution to make to church music, and in 1872 he published his vast collection of hymn and psalm tunes, *The European Psalmist*. Over twenty years in compilation, it included many of his own compositions as well as the largest number of J. S. Bach's chorale harmonizations yet published in England, but as a separate tune-book it was already obsolescent when issued. By now Wesley was very much a senior figure in the musical establishment and at last receiving the critical and public acknowledgement he had so yearned for in his youth: in 1873 he was offered the choice between a knighthood and a civil-list pension of £100 per annum, and chose the latter. But such recognition, welcome as it must have been, had come too late, and the final years of his life were clouded by ill health and spent (as he wrote in 1870) in an 'objectionable' place where there was 'no great demand for any peculiarly experienced musical ability and I must be content to rank with the low ones' (BL, Add. MS 35019, fol. 168), a sad anticlimax to what had gone before. Only his financial position had improved following the sale in 1868 of most of his copyrights to Novello & Co. for £750. To the end, however, his reforming zeal remained undimmed, and in 1875 he proposed to Joseph Bennett a radical scheme for the abolition of cathedral chapters and their replacement by working clergy. Nothing, needless to say, came of this proposal. Wesley played for his last service on Christmas day 1875, and died from Bright's disease—a malfunctioning of the kidneys—on 19 April 1876; he was buried beside his daughter Mary in the old cemetery, Exeter.

To the world at large Wesley presented an often prickly exterior, but this masked a basic sense of insecurity which made him ever ready to spring to the defensive or imagine a slight where none had been intended—reactions which particularly coloured his relations with professional colleagues and music critics. By those, like his pupils, from whom he felt no professional rivalry he was seen very differently, and one pupil, J. Kendrick Pyne, summed up his character thus: 'He was kind-hearted, manly, and courageous, though somewhat Utopian in his views. He would have become eminent in *any* profession' (Pyne, 'Wesleyana', 380).   PETER HORTON

Sources P. Horton, *Samuel Sebastian Wesley* (2003) · P. Horton, 'The music of Samuel Sebastian Wesley', DPhil diss., U. Oxf., 1983 · F. G. E. [F. G. Edwards], 'Samuel Sebastian Wesley', *MT*, 41 (1900), 297–302, 369–74, 452–6 · W. Spark, *Musical memories*, 2nd edn (1888) · W. Spark, *Musical reminiscences: past and present* (1892) · W. Spark, 'Samuel Sebastian Wesley', *MT*, 17 (1875–6), 490–92 · J. K. Pyne, 'Wesleyana', *MT*, 40 (1899), 376–81 · J. K. Pyne, 'Dr Samuel Sebastian Wesley', *English Church Music*, 5 (1935), 4–8 · G. J. Stevenson, *Memorials of the Wesley family* (1876) · P. Chappell, *Dr S. S. Wesley, 1810–1876: portrait of a Victorian musician* (1977) · letters, BL, Add. MSS 35019, 69435 · S. S. Wesley, *A few words on cathedral music and the musical system of the church* (1849) · S. S. Wesley, 'Preface', *A morning and evening cathedral service* (1845) · W. J. Gatens, *Victorian cathedral music in theory and practice* (1986)
Archives Exeter Cathedral · Henry Watson Music Library, Manchester · JRL, Methodist Archives and Research Centre · Royal College of Music, London | BL, Music Collections, letters to Benjamin Jacob relating to J. S. Bach, Add. MS 62928 · BL, Music Collections, letters to Vincent Novello, Add. MS 11729 · U. Edin. L., letters to R. A. Atkins
Likenesses oils, *c.*1835, Royal College of Music, London · W. K. Briggs, drawing, *c.*1849, unknown collection; copyprint, NPG [*see illus.*] · W. K. Briggs, oils, 1849, Royal College of Music, London · photograph, *c.*1865, priv. coll.
Wealth at death under £3,000: probate, 10 June 1876, *CGPLA Eng. & Wales*

Wesley, Sarah (1726–1822). *See under* Wesley, Charles (1707–1788).

Wesley, Sarah (1759–1828), Methodist writer, was born on 1 April 1759 in Charles Street, Bristol, and baptized on 28 April in St James's Church, Bristol, the fourth child and only surviving daughter of Charles *Wesley (1707–1788) and Sarah *Wesley, *née* Gwynne (1726–1822) [*see under* Wesley, Charles]. She was partly brought up by a beloved Methodist nurse and for a time attended a school in Bristol, but was also taught Latin by her father. She was a silent child with the shyness and love of solitude and books which characterized her throughout life. She was under 5 feet tall, and when young was very handsome until, like her mother, she was disfigured by smallpox. According to her musician brother Charles *Wesley (1757–1834) she had a good ear for music, sang well, and would have been a good instrumentalist but preferred reading to the rigours of practice. She wrote poetry from an early age but was reluctant to show her verses to her critical father.

In contrast to the rest of her family Sarah Wesley did not hold tory principles; nor did she regard Charles I as a martyr, which made her father say that 'the rebel blood of some of her ancestors flows in her veins' (Stevenson, *Memorials*, 475). Though she had an aversion to politics she rejoiced at the destruction of the Bastille while abhorring the treatment of the French royal family during the revolution. She was a favourite of her uncle John *Wesley, but her chief confidante was her aunt Martha Hall, who introduced her to Samuel Johnson. She was not afraid of him, and her brother said 'She used to show him her verses and he would pat her head and say to my aunt "Madam, she will do"' (ibid.).

Sarah's father was dedicated to her well-being and offered to share his knowledge of books and poetry. He thought she had a thirst and capacity for knowledge, but that she would be hindered by her lack of resolution to rise early and study regularly. Above all he was concerned for her religious development but, though he urged her to be grateful to the Methodists, he would not force her into Methodist meetings in case aversion to their company prejudiced her against religion. He thought she would not relish the writings of Thomas à Kempis and William Law, but did allow her to read one of his own favourite works, Edward Young's *Night Thoughts*.

Sarah was evidently not immune from fashion. Charles once suspected she had had a fall through wearing fashionable shoes, and her evangelical friend Hannah More once remarked that she found her 'more wit than Methodist' (Pollock, 155). Like her mother she was often used by donors to distribute charity. She was a member of City Road Chapel and there attended a ladies' working circle which sewed clothes for the poor while discoursing on religious and moral issues. Her circle of friends and correspondents included minor literary figures such as Elizabeth Benger, novelist and biographer, the Methodist artist John Russell (who painted her portrait), and the educationist Elizabeth Hamilton, who thought highly of Sarah's ability and believed that, had she made the effort, she could have earned a living by writing. Certainly Sarah appears to have translated material for George Gregory to use in his periodical articles. However, it seems likely that her retiring nature and modesty inhibited her from pursuing a literary career, though she wrote a good deal of poetry, mostly unpublished. Her principal legacy and chief significance for Methodism was indirect, acting as a repository and transmitter of the Wesley family traditions, partly from her mother. Adam Clarke's *Memoirs of the Wesley Family* (1823) owed much to her manuscripts and recollections. She was particularly anxious to counter unfavourable judgements on the Wesley brothers' actions and characters.

Sarah Wesley never married, though she appears to have received at least two proposals. She spent much of her time in the company of her gentle and rather unworldly brother Charles, and was much troubled by the irregular life of her brother the composer and organist Samuel *Wesley. Though living in London for much of her life (from 1771 at 1 Chesterfield Street, Marylebone), her affections centred on Bristol. During a last visit there she fell ill and died of a throat disorder on 19 September 1828. She was buried in the churchyard of St James's, the church of her baptism.   HENRY D. RACK

Sources JRL, Methodist Archives and Research Centre, Wesley Family papers, DDWF 1–20; DDWES 1–9 [calendared by G. Lloyd, 3 vols., 1992–1993] · JRL, Methodist Archives and Research Centre, Charles Wesley papers, DDCW 1–10 [calendared by G. Lloyd, 2 vols., 1994] · G. J. Stevenson, *Memorials of the Wesley family* (1876) · MS letters of Sarah Wesley, jun., Wesley College, Bristol, D6/1/276–300 · G. J. Stevenson, *City Road Chapel* (1872) · J. Telford, *Sayings and portraits of Charles Wesley* (1927) · J. Pollock, *Wilberforce*, pbk edn (1978)

Archives JRL, family MSS · JRL, family MSS and letters | Wesley College, Bristol, letters of Sarah Wesley, jun.
Likenesses J. Russell, oils, 1770–79, repro. in Telford, *Sayings and portraits*, 183 · M. Claxton, group portrait, oils (*Holy triumph* of John Wesley's deathbed, including Sarah Wesley jun.), Wesley's Chapel, London

Wesley [*née* Annesley], **Susanna** (1669–1742), theological writer and educator, was born on 20 January 1669 in Spital Yard, Bishopsgate, London, the youngest daughter of the Revd Samuel *Annesley (*bap.* 1620, *d.* 1696), nonconformist minister, and his second wife, Mary White (*d.* 1693). Her life story links the three major expressions of early modern English protestantism (puritanism, Anglicanism, and Methodism) and demonstrates how each of these could nourish a woman's independent spirit.

The family heritage was staunchly puritan. Susanna's maternal grandfather sat in the Long Parliament and her father served as chaplain in the parliamentary navy and was placed in the London living of St Giles Cripplegate by Richard Cromwell, only to be ejected at the Restoration. He then gathered his own nonconformist congregation in Spitalfields, preaching a moderate Presbyterian gospel but occasionally suffering penalties under the repressive legislation meant to keep dissenters in check. Known for his 'Greatness of Soul', as his parishioner Daniel Defoe put it in an obituary, Annesley stocked his library with Anglican and Roman Catholic volumes as well as puritan tomes. Amid such books in the house that was her birthplace (and which still survives amid the new office blocks surrounding Liverpool Street Station) the young Susanna Annesley was educated. Though it is likely that her mother played a key role there is little documentation to prove it.

There is early evidence, though, of Susanna Annesley's own methodical mind and independent spirit. Not yet thirteen she elected to separate from nonconformist ranks and join the established church. 'I had drawn up an account of the whole transaction', she later wrote her eldest son, 'under which head I had included the main of the controversy … as far as it had come to my knowledge; and then followed the reasons that determined my judgment to the preference of the Church of England' (*Complete Writings*, 71). The twelve-year-old daughter's principled stand against the family's faith tradition (and in favour of the institution that had caused it such pain) must have stunned her father. To his credit, however, he supported her move, kept in lifelong connection with her, and made her his literary executor at his death.

The young Susanna's conscientious conversion paralleled that of a young man with an equally impeccable puritan pedigree, Dorset-born Samuel *Wesley (*bap.* 1662, *d.* 1735), at that time studying in a dissenting academy in London. Their friendship initially seems to have consisted of theological conversations (Susanna credited her new friend with saving her from the temptations of Socinianism) but it also soon ripened into love. He, too, joined the Church of England, thus opening his way to Oxford, deacon's orders, and a curacy, and allowing the couple to contemplate marriage. They were wed on 12 November 1688 in the parish church of St Marylebone and they remained in London while Samuel was ordained priest, after which he served two curacies and a brief stint as a naval chaplain. Meagre compensation led them to live much of that time in the Annesley home, where their first child, Samuel *Wesley [*see under* Wesley, Samuel], was born in 1690. The following year Wesley obtained his first parish, not in the metropolis, where his literary and ecclesiastical ambitions might have been better nourished, but at South Ormsby in the Lincolnshire wolds, 150 miles to the north. Six years later, forced to resign from that living, he took another parish in the same county, this time in the fen country 30 miles north of Lincoln. There, in Epworth (and occasionally in the neighbouring parish of Wroot), the Wesley family resided from 1697 until the rector's death in 1735.

The forty-six-year marriage probably deserves to be called companionate, despite its difficulties. In any case it presented Susanna Wesley with all the customary role expectations of an early modern English wife, mother, and mistress of a rectory. However, just as she challenged the traditional father–daughter relationship with her precocious ecclesiastical decision so she also contested conventional practice in the way in which she related to husband, children, and the church. As wife Susanna Wesley dutifully followed her husband into the rustic confines of his Lincolnshire parishes, miles from the civilized precincts of her girlhood home. She did not, however, abandon the conscience she had nurtured in puritan London; rather, she employed it now in a high-church Anglican context to resist her husband's theological, political, and marital authority. On one notable occasion, for example, she expressly refused to say 'Amen' to her husband's petition for the king at family prayers in late 1701 or early 1702. Why her scruples in favour of the deposed (and recently deceased) James II came to the fore at that point remains a mystery, as William III had been installed by parliament since 1689 and had been ruling alone since Queen Mary's death in 1694. In any case her nonjuring defiance was duly noted by the rector, who took her aside and told her, 'You and I must part: for if we have two kings, we must have two beds' (Clarke, 83). She refused to budge and he abandoned Epworth for several months to attend the church convocation in London—thereby granting her the only respite from pregnancy that she would enjoy during her childbearing years. Her correspondence with Lady Henrietta Yarborough, a noblewoman residing in the nearby Yorkshire parish of Snaith, and also with the Revd George Hickes, a leading nonjuring cleric, reveals both her profound internal struggle and her resulting determination to follow the dictates of her conscience at whatever cost. The quarrel was finally resolved in early 1702—with important historical consequence. The rector returned home, on hearing that the family had suffered a fire in the rectory, and both found that they could agree on the divine right legitimacy of William's successor, Queen Anne. A signal result of the restored relationship arrived in June of the following year: a baby son, named John [*see* Wesley, John (1703–1791)].

Heretofore the bearing and raising of that one son has led to Susanna Wesley's celebration as a sort of Methodist Madonna; except for his fame there would be little record of her, and without her there would have been no John Wesley and no Methodism. Nevertheless even discounting pious legend her maternal role is still perhaps her greatest claim to fame. Her large family (seven daughters and three sons surviving from eighteen or nineteen births) demanded a methodical approach. With little domestic help, minimal support from a study-bound and financially inept husband, and resultant frequent brushes with poverty, an ordered family life was not only a puritan ideal from her own childhood but also an absolute present necessity. Her legendary regimen may ring harsh in modern ears but her insistence on 'conquering [children's] wills' is not that far from John Locke's contemporary goal of gaining the 'compliance and suppleness of their wills'. And she is no more severe than Locke in reserving a measured place for the rod. Nevertheless there were clear rules and expectations; the children were 'put into a regular method of living … from their birth' (Complete Writings, 368–9). Such discipline, however, was mitigated by the loving personal attention that came with it. When each of her children turned five, for example, she would rearrange the household schedule in order to give that child a day-long first reading lesson, using the book of Genesis as a primer. Later such focused attention would continue as she devoted a weekly individual session to each child.

John Wesley, his elder brother Samuel and his younger brother Charles, co-founder of Methodism and prolific hymn writer [see Wesley, Charles (1707–1788)], all easily moved from their mother's schoolroom to places in London public schools and finally to Oxford. As most of her surviving letters attest Susanna remained their informal theological tutor (both critical and supportive) well into their undergraduate years and beyond. Although John was later a fellow of Lincoln College and a recognized leader of the Methodist movement she still doled out advice and counsel to him. Aware of the effect of his mother's method upon him her most famous and appreciative pupil asked her to write an account of it. She complied, and after her death he published what was to become her most influential writing, her letter 'On educating my family'. Historians have regarded it as the epitome of the 'caring but authoritative discipline' of evangelical child-rearing practice, linking puritan culture to early nineteenth-century evangelical culture (Stone, 293). In the late twentieth century North America homeschooling advocates have embraced her as an early distinguished predecessor.

Near the forefront of contemporary practice Susanna Wesley was particularly concerned with the education of her daughters. One of her most notable house rules addressed the gendered educational disparity of the age, declaring:

that no girl be taught to work till she can read very well …
for the putting children to learn sewing before they can read perfectly is the very reason why so few women can read fit to

be heard, and never to be well understood. (Complete Writings, 373)

Love and a sense of religious duty drove her to provide them with serious instruction in their adolescent years as well. Thus in the wake of a disastrous fire that destroyed the Epworth rectory in 1709 and caused the temporary dispersal of her children she began an ambitious project of catechetical writings, primarily for her daughters. Not published during her lifetime but circulated in the family, these works included an explication of the apostles' creed and the beginnings of a similar reflection on the ten commandments, both written as extended letters to her namesake second daughter, and 'A religious conference between Mother and Emilia', a theological dialogue constructed as a conversation between herself and her eldest daughter. Despite her lack of formal education and society's ambivalence towards women's writing she nevertheless turned out substantial, well-informed essays, fully engaging with the practical theological issues of the day.

Susanna Wesley's children learned by her precept but also by her example. At home they would have seen her steal away three times a day for a period of prayer and meditation, reading, and writing. They may have understood that these times of retreat into 'a room of her own' helped her to maintain a sense of self and cope with family and parish life but they were not likely to be aware of the several notebooks of devotional entries that she filled during those times. They now stand as an important part of her legacy, a window into an eighteenth-century woman's interior life.

Most of the daughters, as well as nine-year-old John, also had the chance to observe the act of marital insubordination and ecclesiastical disobedience that took place in the winter of 1711–12 while the rector attended convocation in London. What started as Sunday evening family prayers in the rectory soon attracted as many as 200 parishioners, who began to absent themselves from the regular Sunday morning ministrations of the curate in the parish church. Writing from London, Samuel rebuked his wife for presiding at this irregular public worship, and Susanna trumped him by demanding his 'positive command' that she stop so that she would not be held guilty at the last judgement for neglecting her neighbours' souls (Complete Writings, 82–3). Her temporary de facto reversion to nonconformity within the church must have impressed John Wesley, who later found himself promoting meetings outside church hours and even allowing women to lead them.

Following her husband's death on 25 April 1735 Susanna Wesley stayed in turn with her daughter Emilia, a schoolmistress in Gainsborough; her eldest son, Samuel, headmaster of Blundell's School in Tiverton, Devon; and her daughter Martha, wife of the minister Westley Hall, in Wootton, Wiltshire, and at Fisherton, near Salisbury. Finally she returned with the Halls to London and in 1739 she joined her son John in his newly acquired headquarters, The Foundery, near City Road, London, and less than half a mile from her birthplace. The woman who had been raised a puritan and lived most of her life as an Anglican spent her last four years as one of the early Methodists. As such she defended her son in a shrewdly written anti-Calvinist pamphlet, *Some Remarks on a Letter from the Reverend Mr. Whitefield* (1741), the only work she published, albeit anonymously, during her lifetime. She died at The Foundery on 30 July 1742 and was buried, appropriately, in the nearby nonconformist cemetery, Bunhill Fields, on 1 August 1742.

In addition to her famous sons at least two of her daughters deserve mention: the poet Mehetabel *Wright (1697–1750), whose marriage brought scandal to the rectory and was dramatized in A. T. Quiller-Couch's 1903 historical novel *Hetty Wesley*, and Martha Hall (1706–1791), who moved to London as a widow and became a member of Dr Johnson's circle. CHARLES WALLACE, JUN.

Sources *Susanna Wesley: the complete writings*, ed. C. I. Wallace (1997) · J. A. Newton, *Susanna Wesley and the puritan tradition in Methodism* (1968) · A. Clarke, *Memoirs of the Wesley family* (1824) · B. I. Young, 'Sources for the Annesley family', *Proceedings of the Wesley Historical Society*, 45 (1985–6), 46–57 · F. Baker, 'Investigating Wesley family traditions', *Methodist History*, 26/3 (1988), 154–62 · F. Baker, 'Susanna Wesley: puritan, parent, pastor, protagonist, pattern', *Women in new worlds: historical perspectives on the Wesleyan tradition*, ed. R. S. Keller, L. L. Queen, and H. F. Thomas, 2 (1982), 112–31 · R. L. Harmon, *Susanna: mother of the Wesleys* (1968) · C. I. Wallace, 'Some stated employment of your mind: reading, writing, and religion in the life of Susanna Wesley', *Church History*, 58 (1989), 354–66 · C. I. Wallace, 'Susanna Wesley's spirituality: the freedom of a Christian woman', *Methodist History*, 22/3 (1984), 158–73 · L. Stone, *The family, sex and marriage in England, 1500–1800*, abridged edition (1979) · J. Todd, ed., *A dictionary of British and American women writers, 1660–1800* (1984) · A. A. Dallimore, *Susanna Wesley: the mother of John and Charles Wesley* (1993) · F. E. Maser, *Seven sisters in search of love: the story of John Wesley's sisters* (1988)
Archives JRL, Methodist Archives and Research Centre · priv. coll. · State Library of Victoria, Melbourne · United Methodist Historical Society, Baltimore · Wesley College, Bristol · Wesley's Chapel, London
Likenesses J. Williams, oils, 1738, Wesley College, Bristol; inaccurately restored, 1891 · engraving, 1860–99, Old Rectory, Epworth; repro. in Wallace, ed., *Susanna Wesley: the complete writings*, cover · engraving (after J. Williams), repro. in J. Kirk, *The mother of the Wesleys*, 6th edn (1876)

Wessex. For this title name *see* Godwine, earl of Wessex (*d.* 1053).

Wessington, John (*c*.1371–1451), prior of Durham Cathedral priory, was a member of the community of St Cuthbert at Durham and held the office of prior there for almost thirty years, from his election on 5 November 1416 until his resignation in June 1446. Probably born in the village of Washington 10 miles north of his future cathedral city, he was related—if somewhat distantly—to the Durham county knightly family of Wessington that included some of the remote ancestors of the first president of the United States of America among its members. John Wessington entered the cathedral monastery at Durham in 1390; and shortly after receiving priest's orders he was sent to Durham College, Oxford. Although Wessington never acquired a university degree, he remained a fellow of his college for the next thirteen years, often serving as one of its two bursars. Apparently never celebrated for scholastic learning himself, Wessington was otherwise a

highly regarded 'university monk' of his period: in 1426 he was to serve as president of the provincial chapter of the English black monks at their assembly in Northampton. Soon after returning from Oxford to Durham in 1407 he became both sacrist and chancellor of his mother house. In the latter office he presided over the reorganization of his convent's archives. His fellow monks were probably even more impressed by the skill with which he exploited those muniments to defend the franchises of his community.

By 1416 Wessington's intense commitment to the preservation of his monastery's privileges against external aggression had already emerged as the most characteristic feature of his career. It was no doubt largely for this reason that in November of that year he was elected prior by the sixty-nine members of his community. Nor is it likely to be a coincidence that Wessington's term of office coincided with a period when the convent's registers, obedientiary account rolls, and other documents were particularly well compiled and conserved. Almost always resident within the county of Durham (he is only known to have visited London three times in thirty years), he made no attempt to perambulate his manors in the fashion of his predecessors. Although Wessington normally spent several weeks every year at his favourite country retreat of Beaurepaire (Bear Park), he was usually to be found in his prior's quarters at Durham itself. It was in this sumptuous set of chambers, largely reconstructed or refurnished by himself, that he spent much of his time entertaining visiting nobles, local clergy, and members of his own convent. Thus between May 1430 and May 1431 the prior invited to dinner at Durham not only Bishop Thomas Langley of Durham but also the bishop of Carlisle, the abbot of Whitby, the prior of Tynemouth, Sir Robert Umfraville, and a large number of local gentlemen and officials. Wessington's continuously cordial relations with Bishop Langley during the latter's long episcopate (1406–37) was indeed crucial to the success of his rule as prior. In return for providing his bishop with valuable written evidence for the defence of his episcopal franchises, notably when the latter were challenged by a powerful group of Durham knights in 1433, Wessington could always rely upon Langley's advice and support on his own economic and political problems.

By contrast Wessington's relationship with Robert Neville (*d.* 1457), who succeeded Langley at Durham in 1438, began with a dispute about the date of the new bishop's enthronement and was never quite so harmonious. Nevertheless Wessington had been remarkably successful in securing the goodwill of the senior members of the Neville family in extremely difficult circumstances. After the death of Ralph Neville, first earl of Westmorland, in October 1425, the prior played an important and much appreciated role as an unofficial peacemaker during the violent conflict that then erupted between the two branches of the family. Of the two arch-rivals in the dispute, Ralph Neville, second earl of Westmorland (*d.* 1484), regularly chose Wessington as one of his arbiters, while Richard Neville, earl of Salisbury (*d.* 1460), invited him to attend the christening of his son George, the future archbishop of York (d. 1476), at Middleham in 1432.

Throughout his priorate John Wessington's authority was accordingly more usually put at risk by the turbulence of the local gentry than by the feuds of the higher aristocracy of northern England. In the delicate political art of cultivating the friendship of influential knights and esquires within the county of Durham, the prior's appointment of his chief lay steward provided him with his most valuable link with the non-religious world. Both of Wessington's chief stewards, Thomas Langton of Winyard (1416–36) and William Hoton of Hardwick Hall (1437–46), worked strenuously on the convent's behalf, as indeed did many of the other members of the county gentry retained by the convent for legal support in times of need. Such assistance was all the more necessary to the prior because lengthy and expensive litigation with local landlords over such issues as rights to common pasture and watermills was a perennial feature of his rule at Durham. Most of these disputes were eventually settled by arbitration out of court; but the possibility of armed attack on the monks of St Cuthbert was certainly always present. In 1419 Thomas Claxton and Thomas Billingham, two of Wessington's discontented tenants, not only ambushed one of the Durham monks on the highway but placed the convent itself in a state of unofficial siege. Despite the prestige of his position Wessington therefore found it difficult to impose his authority in the face of some of the dangerous pressures which inevitably confronted so large a monastery with so many (nine) daughter houses. During the early 1440s he was faced not only with an alarming new challenge to his monastery's control over its cell of Coldingham in Scotland, but also with the totally unexpected withdrawal of obedience by William Partrike, prior of Lytham, Lancashire. After the severe agrarian crisis of the late 1430s Wessington also had to defend his financial administration of the priory from a variety of serious criticisms, made before and after Bishop Robert Neville's visitation of the cathedral in 1442. But by that year Wessington was over seventy years old and increasingly 'wexit with greyt sekenesse' (Dobson, *Durham Priory*, 110–111). He resigned the prior's office on 8 June 1446 and was assigned five attendants, an annual pension of £40, and attractive living accommodation either at Finchale Priory or within his convent's own monastic infirmary. He died at Durham five years later, on 9 April 1451.

John Wessington's most distinctive achievements as prior of Durham undoubtedly lay in his personal contributions to learning within his cloister. If not himself a historian in any modern sense of the word, he was nevertheless one of the most historically minded of all late medieval English Benedictine monks. Besides devoting much time and care to the custody and cataloguing of the thousand or so manuscripts within his monastery's various book collections, Wessington was responsible for the building of an entirely new reference library (completed by 1418 at a total cost of over £90) between the chapter house and the south transept of the cathedral church. The range and quality of his own written work, nearly always

composed 'for the defence of the church of Durham', was famous in his own lifetime (*Historiae Dunelmensis scriptores tres*, cclxviii–cclxxi). As Wessington was never a writer concerned to publicize his personal authorship of the numerous compilations now ascribed to him, it can be difficult to distinguish between what he wrote himself and what he commissioned from other monks. However he was certainly directly responsible for an ambitious, if highly derivative, new history of the church of Durham from its origins at Lindisfarne to at least the year 1356. Among his other major and usually very well-informed enterprises were a series of treatises on the origins and ideals of the Benedictine order. More interesting and voluminous still are the highly miscellaneous smaller *compilationes* (of which between thirty and forty survive), which demonstrate the prior's remarkable ability to use historical sources within the convent's archives as evidence in defence of the church of Durham's rights, possessions, and incomparable legal status. To cite Wessington's own words to Bishop Robert Neville in 1440, 'I haff doon my diligence and shewid in yees maters such evidence and wrytyng as I haff' (registrum parvum, II, fol. 112).   R. B. DOBSON

Sources R. B. Dobson, *Durham Priory, 1400–1450*, Cambridge Studies in Medieval Life and Thought, 3rd ser., 6 (1973) · R. B. Dobson, 'The priory of Durham in the time of John Wessington, prior, 1416–1446', DPhil diss., U. Oxf., 1962 · registrum, III, IV, Durham Cath. CL, dean and chapter muniments · registrum parvum, II, III, Durham Cath. CL, dean and chapter muniments · obedientary account rolls, 1416–46, Durham Cath. CL, dean and chapter muniments · *Historiae Dunelmensis scriptores tres: Gaufridus de Coldingham, Robertus de Graystanes, et Willielmus de Chambre*, ed. J. Raine, SurtS, 9 (1839), 147, ccviii–cccviii · J. T. Fowler, ed., *Extracts from the account rolls of the abbey of Durham*, 3 vols., SurtS, 99–100, 103 (1898–1901), 99, 100, 103 · R. B. Dobson, 'Mynistres of Saynt Cuthbert': the monks of Durham in the fifteenth century (1974) · R. B. Dobson, 'Contrasting chronicles: historical writing at York and Durham at the close of the middle ages', *Church and chronicle in the middle ages: essays presented to John Taylor*, ed. I. Wood and G. A. Loud (1991), 201–18 · R. L. Storey, *Thomas Langley and the bishopric of Durham, 1406–1437* (1961) · Emden, *Oxf.*, 3.2018 · A. Piper, 'The libraries of the monks of Durham', *Medieval scribes, manuscripts and libraries: essays presented to N. R. Ker*, ed. M. B. Parkes and A. G. Watson (1978), 213–49 · S. L. Greenslade, 'John Washington, prior of Durham, 1416–1446', *Historical Magazine of the Protestant Episcopal Church*, 16 (1947), 233–45
Archives Durham Cath. CL, registrum, III, IV · Durham Cath. CL, registrum parvum, II, III

West, Sir Algernon Edward (1832–1921), civil servant, born in London on 4 April 1832, was the third son of Martin John West (1786–1870), recorder of King's Lynn, and his wife, Lady Maria Walpole (d. 1870), third daughter of Horatio, second earl of Orford, of the second creation, and great-granddaughter of the prime minister Sir Robert Walpole. He was sent to Eton College in 1843, where he made his mark as an oar, but experienced 'an almost total neglect of any kind of education beyond a very superficial smattering of Latin and Greek' (West, *Recollections*, 1.50). After two years of travel and study he matriculated in 1850 at Christ Church, Oxford, intending to take orders. The next year, having kept only two terms, he changed his plans and accepted a clerkship in the Inland Revenue, but was transferred to the Admiralty a year later. At the end of

Sir Algernon Edward West (1832–1921), by James Russell & Sons

1854 official business took him to the seat of war in the Crimea, where he was disgusted by the 'gross mismanagement' (ibid., 1.177). On 12 August 1858 he married Mary (d. 1894), daughter of Captain the Hon. George Barrington, granddaughter of Charles, second Earl Grey.

Tall, handsome, and a favourite in society, West earned advancement by tact, ability, and hard work. After service as private secretary in the India Office (1860–66) to Sir Charles Wood (afterwards Viscount Halifax) and the earl of Ripon, his great opportunity came in 1868 when Gladstone, then prime minister, appointed him to be his private secretary. After nearly four years of working closely and on good terms, Gladstone rewarded him with a commissionership of Inland Revenue (1872), a post in which for twenty years he served in succession eight chancellors of the exchequer from Robert Lowe (afterwards Viscount Sherbrooke) to George Goschen. He proved to be a staunchly orthodox Gladstonian in his handling of fiscal questions. His financial capacity endeared him to Gladstone, and the two men became quite close friends. It was on West's suggestion that Gladstone abolished the malt tax in 1880. In 1883 West cruised in the *Pembroke Castle* with Gladstone and Tennyson, and was entrusted with the negotiations which ended in Tennyson's acceptance of a peerage.

West, who had been chairman of the Board of Inland Revenue since 1881, was created KCB in 1886. In 1892 he retired from the civil service and acted as private secretary to Gladstone, who was forming his last administration. His *Private Diaries* (posthumously edited in 1922 by H. G.

Hutchinson) provide a lively account of Gladstone's difficulties with his colleagues. In March 1894 West retired with his chief from party politics and was made a privy councillor. He was promoted GCB in 1902. Almost to the last Algy West was a conspicuous figure in Brooks's Club, on the London county council, and as director of several companies in the City. In retirement he wrote *Recollections* (1899), *Memoir of Sir Henry Keppel* (1905), *One City and Many Men* (1908), and *Contemporary Portraits* (1920). West died at his London house, 14 Manchester Square, on 21 March 1921 and was survived by three sons and one daughter.

F. W. HIRST, *rev.* M. C. CURTHOYS

Sources *The Times* (22 March 1921) · A. E. West, *Recollections, 1832 to 1886*, 2 vols. (1899) · *Private diaries of Sir Algernon West*, ed. H. G. Hutchinson (1922) · private information (1927)
Archives BL, diary, Add. MS 62123 | BL, corresp. with W. E. Gladstone, minutes, etc., Add. MSS 46048–46084 · BL, corresp. with Lord Ripon and his secretary, Add. MSS 43513–43514 · Bodl. Oxf., corresp. with Sir William Harcourt, Lewis Harcourt, and S. E. Spring-Rice · Bodl. Oxf., Ripon MSS · CAC Cam., corresp. with Lord Randolph Churchill · NL Scot., corresp. with Lord Rosebery
Likenesses marchioness of Granby, drawing, *c*.1899, repro. in A. West, *Recollections*, frontispiece · H. von Herkomer, oils, repro. in Hutchinson, ed., *Private diaries of Sir Algernon West*, frontispiece · J. Russell & Sons, photograph, NPG [*see illus.*] · Spy [L. Ward], caricature, watercolour study, NPG; repro. in *VF* (13 Aug 1892)
Wealth at death £55,128 9s. 10d.: probate, 6 May 1921, *CGPLA Eng. & Wales*

West, Benjamin (1738–1820), history painter, was born on 10 October 1738 in Springfield (now Swarthmore), Pennsylvania, the tenth and youngest child of John West (1690–1776), innkeeper, and his second wife, Sarah (1697–1756), daughter of Thomas Pearson of Marple, Pennsylvania. Both parents came from Quaker families. An important source of biographical information on West is John Galt's *The Life, Studies, and Works of Benjamin West, Esq., President of the Royal Academy of London* published in two volumes in 1816 and 1820. Although West himself read and approved the first volume in manuscript form, the two volumes are full of improbable tales that serve to glorify the artist as a self-taught genius. Perhaps the most quoted myth from Galt is that the local Indians showed West how to make his first colours from wild berries and the young artist plucked hairs from his cat's tail to make his first paintbrush. Yet from a young age West seems to have had an unwavering belief in his own ability and a sense that he was predestined for fame. Both his early artistic training and his basic schooling were, however, quite limited and, while he advanced as an artist with his mother's encouragement, he was always, even in old age, awkward in verbal and written expression.

America, 1747–1760 In Philadelphia about 1747, West met the young English artist William Williams (1727–1791), who impressed him with his pictures and lent him his first books on art, by Charles Alphonse Du Fresnoy and Jonathan Richardson. West also received some instruction in painting, as he mentioned years later to the painter and diarist Joseph Farington, from a 'Mr. Hide', a German artist who was probably John Valentine Haidt, a substitute

Benjamin West (1738–1820), self-portrait, c.1776

preacher in Philadelphia in 1754–5 (Farington, *Diary*, 2.88).

Among West's earliest documented works are two oil on panel overmantels, *Storm at Sea* and *Landscape with Cow* (*c.*1752–3; Pennsylvania Hospital, Philadelphia), and a pair of small portraits, *Robert Morris* and *Jane Morris* (both *c.*1752; Chester County Historical Society, West Chester, Pennsylvania). Although the first two, particularly the second, appear to be based on lost engravings, these works as a group are probably influenced by Williams's lost early paintings.

While in Lancaster, Pennsylvania, to paint portraits, West accepted a commission from a gunsmith, William Henry, to create his first history picture, the *Death of Socrates* (priv. coll.). Henry proposed the subject, read the story to West, and urged him to be ambitious enough to attempt a multi-figured composition. Although partly based on the engraved illustration to Henry's text, Charles Rollin's *Ancient History*, West's version of about 1756 is more powerfully expressive than the engraving and sufficiently impressed a Philadelphia visitor, the Revd William Smith, that he offered to give West the rudiments of a classical education tailored for an artist. Thus in summer 1756 West moved to Philadelphia to live with his sister and brother-in-law and become a protégé of Smith, a young Anglican minister, classical scholar, and cultural leader in the position of provost at the new College of Philadelphia (now the University of Pennsylvania). West continued to paint portraits, such as *Thomas Mifflin* (*c.*1758–9; Historical Society of Pennsylvania, Philadelphia), now under the influence of the itinerant English artist John Wollaston, and perhaps under Smith's tutelage, West tried to earn enough money to study in Italy. He spent some time painting portraits for this purpose in New York. Then Provost Smith arranged for him to take passage on a merchant ship bound for Leghorn on 12 April 1760.

Italy, 1760–1763 West's trip to Italy, originally intended to be short, was extended to three years when he was advanced funds by wealthy Philadelphians in exchange for copies after old master works. From Leghorn, West travelled on to Rome and there met the artists and connoisseurs (including Anton Raphael Mengs, Gavin Hamilton, and Cardinal Albani) at the centre of the emerging neo-classical movement. As the first American artist ever to have travelled to Italy, he was welcomed as no less than a phenomenon. The *cognoscenti*, he recalled to Galt, accompanied him to the Vatican to see how he would react to the *Apollo Belvedere* (Vatican Museum, Rome), considered an ancient Greek original and the most perfect male figure in sculpture. At his first sight of it West pleased them all by exclaiming, 'how like it is to a young Mohawk warrior' (Galt, 105). As Mengs advised, he copied antique sculptures and then toured northern Italy, learning by copying old master paintings (especially those of the sixteenth and seventeenth centuries) before beginning a commission for a small history picture. In Venice, in 1762, he had met Richard Dalton, librarian to George III, who was on a buying tour for the king and offered him a royal commission for a painting of the lovers Cymon and Iphigenia (1763). The finished work was much admired in Rome. With the encouragement of Dalton and other English friends in Italy, West decided in 1763 to visit London, via Paris, in hope of further commissions from George III.

England, 1763–1820 Good-natured, well-bred, and capable, West seemed easily to inspire the confidence of others. Portraits of him, such as an early *Self-Portrait* (*c.*1776; Baltimore Museum of Art) reveal that he was a conventionally handsome man, well-built, athletic, 5 feet 8 inches tall, with regular, refined features and piercing eyes. All his life he was unusually blessed with good fortune, and his arrival in August in London was no exception. He evidently expected to spend a short time there and then return to Philadelphia, but he was so well received as a self-taught prodigy who had studied in Italy, with the potential to become a great history painter in the tradition of Raphael (he was called the American Raphael by 1764), that he stayed for the rest of his life. His fiancée, Elizabeth Shewell (1741–1814), the daughter of a Philadelphia merchant, joined him within a year, after crossing the Atlantic with West's father, and they were married in London at St Martin-in-the-Fields on 2 September 1764. Elizabeth's cousin, the painter Matthew Pratt, also accompanied her and became the first of three generations of American artists (including Gilbert Stuart, John Trumbull, and Washington Allston) to study with West in London.

West entered two scenes of fabled lovers, his *Cymon and Iphigenia* (from *The Decameron*) and *Angelica and Medoro* (from *Orlando Furioso*), together with a third picture, *General Robert Monckton* (priv. coll.) as his London début at the exhibition of the Society of Artists in 1764. While the

Angelica and Medoro is an eclectic work that reflects the recent British art historical past in being a typically rococo subject, the military portrait of Monckton, ambitiously full-length, backed by an army, and in a pose recalling the *Apollo Belvedere*, is more indicative, in its combination of realism and neo-classicism, of West's future. The pose is also reminiscent, perhaps flatteringly, of an earlier quotation of the *Apollo* in a portrait of Commodore Keppel by London's leading painter, Joshua Reynolds (1753–4; NMM). Reynolds, who welcomed West, expounded the view that artists could improve themselves by quoting such superior work and embracing the best of the Italian old masters through combination.

History paintings Despite West's remarkable versatility throughout his career in terms of subject matter, it is as a history painter that he became best known. The most prominent artists in London followed the demand chiefly for portraiture so that the city lacked history painters of his potential stature. West's history picture *The Choice of Hercules* (1764; V&A) marks the beginning of a more pronounced neo-classical style. It is strongly influenced by Nicolas Poussin's composition for the same subject (Stourhead, Wiltshire), and therefore quotes, in reverse, the famous antique sculpture *Meleager* (Vatican Museum, Rome). Perhaps because it was so derivative, West did not exhibit it. Instead the archbishop of York Robert Hay Drummond's commission for a history painting led to the picture that established West as a leader of the neo-classical movement. The large *Agrippina Landing at Brundisium with the Ashes of Germanicus* (1768; Yale University Art Gallery, New Haven, Connecticut), showing an example of heroic courage from Tacitus, is arranged in an antique frieze format after the *Ara pacis Augustae* (Altar of the Augustan Peace) which West had copied in Rome. Not only the subject but also the style is classicizing. George III was so pleased with the *Agrippina* that he ordered a similar Roman subject for himself, *The Departure of Regulus from Rome* (1769; Royal Collection), the first of many royal commissions.

In 1768, while at work on *Regulus*, West played an instrumental role with the king in obtaining patronage for a Royal Academy of Arts. He also joined other charter members in helping to elect Reynolds as its first president. Eventually, despite his American origins, West became historical painter to the king in 1772, surveyor of the king's pictures in 1791, and second president of the Royal Academy in 1792, after Reynolds's death.

West's most famous picture, *The Death of General Wolfe* (1770; National Gallery of Canada, Ottawa), in the neo-classical tradition, was conceived as a history painting with the intention of morally uplifting its audience, but it is painted with the movement, drama, and more vivid colour associated with Romanticism. Furthermore, it marks a major departure in depicting a contemporary event as a highly dramatized (and therefore unusually self-conscious) history painting. Modern history painting had been attempted before, most notably by Francis Hayman, but without the impact of this picture. The subject is Major-General James Wolfe's death in 1759, at the

moment when the British announced victory in a decisive battle against the French in Quebec. Reynolds objected strenuously to the use of modern dress, arguing against breeches and in favour of Greek or Roman costume as more appropriate to the content of patriotic self-sacrifice at an exalted level (akin to that of the ancients). Clearly he feared a threat to the status of history painting, within the academy, as the most high-minded form of art. West, however, prevailed, as Reynolds admitted, by producing an electrifyingly inspirational piece, with a Christ-like Wolfe, that was enormously successful when entered in the annual exhibition at the Royal Academy in 1771. Through this precedent, which incorporated portraits with accurate detail and opened up the possibility of contemporary subjects, West introduced a new degree of realism (despite the fictitious grouping) to history painting. The popularity of this picture (purchased by Lord Grosvenor, who eventually owned at least eleven pictures by West) and the engraving that was produced after it by William Woollett in 1766, one of the most commercially successful prints ever produced, served as an inspiration to aspiring history painters for many years. Yet the impression that West's feat could be reproduced by others was largely an illusion. The market for history painting, with a number of exceptions, never really developed beyond commissions from the king, and West was the sole recipient of these.

From 1779 to 1801 West was engaged in decorative schemes at Windsor Castle which were part of a renovation to make Windsor the chief royal residence. He had already supplied six history paintings to hang with *The Departure of Regulus* at Buckingham House (later Palace), and several royal portraits, when the king turned his attention to the improvement of Windsor. In the most ambitious undertaking of his life, West eventually completed eighteen large canvases for the royal chapel at Windsor on the biblical theme of revealed religion. The project came to an abrupt halt, however, with the king's illness in 1801, and the paintings (never installed) were finally returned to West's family. Seven of the group, including the large *Ascension* (*c*.1781–2), were reunited in the War Memorial Chapel at Bob Jones University, Greenville, South Carolina. For the audience chamber at Windsor, West produced eight pictures (1786–9; Royal Collection) from the reign of King Edward III in the fourteenth century, which were remarkable at the time because of their relative accuracy in historical detail. West also provided an altarpiece (Detroit Institute of Arts) and designs for stained glass windows (des.) for St George's Chapel in the lower ward of the castle, and designs for an allegorical ceiling in the Queen's Lodge (des.). Nevertheless, his chief project at Windsor was the royal chapel with its planned works, numbering about thirty-six large pictures.

It is because of the royal chapel and a second commission in 1796 (also never completed) from the writer and art collector William Beckford to provide scenes from the book of Revelation for Fonthill Abbey, Wiltshire, that West became known as the premier painter of religious subjects in England. Indeed he reinforced this reputation by creating and exhibiting three huge biblical compositions in the last decade of his life: *Christ Healing the Sick* (1811; Tate collection), for which he received the record sum of 3000 guineas; *Christ Rejected* (1814; Pennsylvania Academy of the Fine Arts); and *Death on the Pale Horse* (1817; Pennsylvania Academy of the Fine Arts). The preliminary sketch (1796; Detroit Institute of Arts) for the last, an image of the four horsemen of the apocalypse, as a seeming explosion of energy and colour, is the antithesis of his earlier neo-classical style and much more vibrant than the version of 1817. West's late oil sketches were often justifiably preferred to the resultant large-scale works which, especially during the 1790s, were rather strongly outlined for the benefit of engravers. The sketches are more lively, and on a smaller scale West's deficiencies in training are generally less noticeable.

With a diverse output of over 700 known works, West clearly ventured in a number of different directions, such as genre painting, for example, *Drayman Drinking* (1796; priv. coll.), 'historical landscape', as in *Lot and his Daughters Conducted by Two Angels* (1810; Detroit Institute of Arts), or literary painting, as in *The Cave of Despair* (1772; Yale Center for British Art, New Haven), precisely to maintain a show of leadership in the London art world. The latter suicide scene taken from Spenser's *Faerie Queene* is an early effort to evoke the terrible sublime as defined by Edmund Burke. To perpetuate his position West also attempted sequels to his *Death of General Wolfe*, but only one of them, involving collaboration with an engraver, came close to duplicating his earlier success in terms of content. In 1806 he completed a large *Death of Lord Nelson* (Walker Art Gallery, Liverpool), depicting the popular hero's death, several months before, at the moment of his greatest triumph, as the British under his leadership defeated the combined French and Spanish fleets off Cape Trafalgar. Nelson received the fatal bullet on the deck of his flagship and died, several hours later, below deck in the cockpit, but West dramatically enhanced the moment by placing him on deck with a multitude of supporting figures. He later corrected this inaccuracy in his more effective, probably Rembrandt-inspired, lantern-lit *Death of Lord Nelson in the Cockpit of the 'Victory'* (1808; NMM).

Later years West's complacency and even self-puffery offended some of his contemporaries, but these weaknesses were perhaps balanced by an unusual openness, generosity, and kindness particularly towards students. He maintained a friendship with George III that was only occasionally threatened, by, for instance, Queen Charlotte's dislike or his visit to Paris in 1802 and admiration for Napoleon. When offered a knighthood (*c.*1792), he refused it in the mistaken belief that he might gain a hereditary title instead. As president of the Royal Academy he maintained his position with dignity and was re-elected over many years, despite some jealous political manoeuvring that led to his resignation in 1805 and re-election in 1806. West died on 11 March 1820, at his long-term residence, 14 Newman Street, London, and, as its president, lay in state at the Royal Academy before being buried on 29 March with great ceremony in St Paul's Cathedral.

Reputation Angry over West's support of Lord Elgin's seizure of the Elgin marbles, Byron tried to undermine the artist's reputation in his poem *The Curse of Minerva* (1812), by calling him a 'flattering, feeble dotard'. Nine years later, however, the *British Press, or, The Morning Literary Advertiser* had reason to claim that West's 'reign in taste is now perfectly established' (Alberts, 393). West's students, many of whom had assisted him in his larger pictures, were even more effusive after his death. William Dunlap predicted that 'his influence on the art he professed will never cease' (Dunlap, 33). Yet by 1840 if not earlier, West's reputation had gone into a precipitous decline. Recent scholarship, most especially Helmut von Erffa's and Allen Staley's *Paintings of Benjamin West* (1986), with the first *catalogue raisonné*, lent support to the gradual rehabilitation of West during the second half of the twentieth century. This catalogue establishes West as more versatile, in both style and subject, and more influential than most historians had previously acknowledged. His work was important internationally as a developing stimulus to the neo-classical movement. But, in a kind of reversal, his greatest contribution to the development of painting with *The Death of General Wolfe* was through promoting a new kind of picture, the long-lived modern history painting. More than anyone else in Europe he helped to revive an interest in history painting at the end of the eighteenth century, chiefly through the number and extraordinary popularity of engravings that were done after his work. By the time he died, West was one of the most prominent artists in the English-speaking world. He also changed the course of the history of American art by establishing the need for study abroad, particularly in England. As a teacher and fellow artist he led others by his example rather than through his 'Discourses' (of which only a fragment survives in manuscript) along an optimistic path, encouraging ambition and a certain amount of experimentation and always maintaining a high-minded purpose.

The elder of West's two sons, **Raphael Lamar West** (1766–1850), history painter, trained under his father whom he often assisted. He pursued the career of an artist with some success, but lacked his father's industry. He painted *Orlando and Oliver* (1789), from *As You Like It*, for John Boydell's Shakspeare Gallery, and exhibited at the Royal Academy for a decade beginning in 1781 and ceasing when he failed to be elected an associate member. A large painting, *The Battle between Michael and Satan* (stolen, 1982), of which a photograph exists, is possibly the picture exhibited by R. L. West at the Royal Academy in 1782 (von Erffa and Staley, no. 406). Very little of Raphael West's output is known to survive other than some of his drawings, etchings, and lithographs inspired by the work of his father and that of Salvator Rosa. In 1800–02 he tried unsuccessfully to emigrate, with his wife, Maria Siltso to an undeveloped part of the United States of America. He inherited a considerable fortune after his father's death and, with his brother, Benjamin West, erected West's New Gallery, at 14 Newman Street, London, to display his father's pictures in a commercial venture. In his later years, however, he had to apply to the Royal Academy for financial assistance. He died at Bushey Heath, Hertfordshire, on 22 May 1850. DORINDA EVANS

Sources H. von Erffa and A. Staley, *The paintings of Benjamin West* (1986) · R. C. Alberts, *Benjamin West: a biography* (Boston, 1978) · A. Staley, *Benjamin West: American painter at the English court* (1989) [exhibition catalogue, Baltimore Museum of Art, 4 June – 20 Aug 1989] · W. Dunlap, *History of the rise and progress of the arts of design in the United States* (New York, 1834); repr. (1969), vol. 1, pp. 33–97 · J. Galt, *The life, studies, and works of Benjamin West, Esq., president of the Royal Academy of London*, 2 (1820) · Farington, *Diary* · A. U. Abrams, *The valiant hero: Benjamin West and grand-style historical painting* (Washington, DC, 1985) · R. S. Kraemer, *Drawings by Benjamin West and his son Raphael Lamar West* (New York, 1975) · J. Dillenberger, *Benjamin West: the context of his life's work, with particular attention to paintings with religious subject matter* (San Antonio, 1977) · N. L. Pressly, *Revealed religion: Benjamin West's commissions for Windsor Castle and Fonthill Abbey* (San Antonio, 1983) · D. H. Solkin, *Painting for money: the visual arts and the public sphere in eighteenth-century England* (1993) · will, PRO, PROB 11/1634, sig. 504 · R. Strong, *And when did you last see your father?* (1978) · B. West, *A discourse delivered to the students of the Royal Academy, Dec. 10, 1792* (1793)

Archives Fordham University Library, New York, autobiography · Hist. Soc. Penn., MSS · Morgan L., MSS · RA, letters and receipts · Royal Arch., MSS · Swarthmore College, Pennsylvania, Friends Historical Library, MSS | Bodl. Oxf., letters to William Beckford · RA, corresp. with Thomas Lawrence

Likenesses B. West, self-portrait, miniature, c.1758, Yale U. Art Gallery · B. West, self-portrait, watercolour miniature, c.1758–1759, Yale U. Art Gallery · A. Kauffmann, chalk drawing, 1763, NPG · M. Pratt, oils, 1765, Pennsylvania Academy of Fine Arts, Philadelphia · B. West, self-portrait, oils, c.1771, National Gallery of Art, Washington, DC · B. West, group portrait, oils, 1772, Yale U. CBA · B. West, self-portrait, oils, 1773 (*Self-portrait with Raphael West*), Yale U. CBA · B. West, self-portrait, oils, c.1776, Baltimore Museum of Art, Maryland [*see illus.*] · J. Downman, two paintings, oil on copper, 1777, NPG · G. Stuart, oils, c.1785, NPG · G. Stuart, oils, c.1785, Tate collection · B. West, self-portrait, oils, 1793?, RA · T. Holloway, line engraving, pubd 1798 (after B. West), BM, NPG · B. West, self-portrait, oils, c.1806, Pennsylvania Academy of Fine Arts, Philadelphia · F. Chantrey, bust, 1811, New York Historical Society · T. Lawrence, oils, exh. RA 1811, Yale U. CBA · J. Nollekens, marble bust, 1812, Royal Horticultural Society, London · C. Watson, oils, exh. RA 1816, NG Scot. · F. Chantrey, bust, 1818, RA · C. Heath, line engraving, pubd 1818 (after W. J. Newton), BM, NPG · B. West, self-portrait, oils, 1818, Society of the Dilettanti, London · T. Lawrence, oils, 1818–21 (Benjamin West), Wadsworth Athenaeum, Hartford, Connecticut; replica, Tate collection · F. Chantrey, marble bust, 1819, NPG · B. West, self-portrait, oils, 1819, Smithsonian Institution, Washington, DC · W. Wilson, medal, 1866, NPG · G. Dance, pencil drawing, RA · J. Downman, miniature, NPG · C. Muss, pen and ink drawing (after T. Lawrence), NPG · H. Pratt, group portrait, oils (*The American School*, 1765), Metropolitan Museum of Art, New York · H. Singleton, group portrait, oils (*Royal academicians*, 1793), RA · J. Spilsbury, mezzotint (after B. West), BM, NPG · J. Zoffany, group portrait, oils (*Royal academicians*, 1772), Royal Collection · pen, ink, and pencil drawing (after T. Lawrence), NPG

Wealth at death approx. £100,000; £11,000 in debts: will, PRO, PROB 11/1634, sig. 504; Alberts, *Benjamin West*

West, Charles (1816–1898), physician, was born in London on 8 August 1816, the second son of Ebeneezer West (*b.* 1776) and his wife, Jane (1783–1871), daughter of Major Johnson of the Durham fencibles. In 1821 Ebeneezer West became a Baptist minister at Chenies, Buckinghamshire, and opened a school, which he later moved to Amersham. Here West received his early education, followed by attendance at a private school in Totteridge. In 1831 he was

apprenticed to Mr Gray, a local general practitioner who had been apothecary to St George's Hospital. After two years, in which he learned the dispenser's art, he entered St Bartholomew's Hospital as a medical student. In 1835 he went to the University of Bonn where he won a prize for an essay on the female pelvis and its influence on parturition. He then went to Paris and Berlin where he graduated MD in September 1837.

After returning to London, West bought a partnership in a City practice, which failed. In 1838 he studied midwifery at the Rotunda Lying-in Hospital, Dublin, and also served at the Meath Hospital. He then returned to St Bartholomew's as clinical clerk to Dr George Burrows. In 1842 West gained the MRCP and became physician at the Waterloo Road Dispensary for Women and Children. In the summer of 1844 he married Mary Hester, daughter of N. B. Cartwright of Stroud, Gloucester; they had a son and a daughter. In 1845 he was appointed lecturer on midwifery at the Middlesex Hospital, and physician accoucheur in 1846. His lectures on the diseases of children were published in the *Medical Gazette* in 1847 and later as a book which saw seven English editions and was translated into several European languages and Arabic. This work made West famous as the father of British paediatrics. In 1848, now an FRCP, he was appointed joint lecturer on midwifery with Edward Rigby at St Bartholomew's Hospital. When Rigby resigned in 1849 West continued the lectures alone. Based on practical experience and expressed in elegant English, the lectures enhanced his reputation. He was designated honorary physician accoucheur with charge of the lying-in department and a ward of thirteen beds. He also gave a weekly clinical lecture, but his work was unrecognized, his name never appearing in the list of physicians of the hospital, despite more than ten years' service. From 1855 on he petitioned the hospital for recognition; it was repeatedly refused and he resigned in 1861.

In the 1840s West tried unsuccessfully to convert the Waterloo Road Dispensary to a children's hospital. In 1849–50 he investigated the facilities for treating children at other London hospitals and wrote to all the children's hospitals on the continent. He personally visited every London physician to canvass support for a children's hospital. Richard Bright directed him to Henry Bence Jones who lent his house for meetings and used his personal influence to obtain financial support. On 19 March 1851, at a public meeting chaired by Lord Ashley, the Children's Hospital was founded and two weeks later the house at 49 Great Ormond Street, formerly the home of Queen Anne's physician, Richard Mead, was obtained for the hospital. West was its first physician and wrote the early reports. He lectured on children's diseases and wrote a little manual on nursing sick children which was published for the benefit of the hospital.

In 1874 West joined the Roman Catholic church. His first wife died and he remarried. His second wife was Marie Octavie Agatha Clotilde Flon (*d.* 1923); there were no children. In 1875 West resigned as physician to the Great Ormond Street Hospital which he had served since 1852. He was appointed consulting physician and retained his place on the committee of management. He also donated his extensive medical library to the hospital. But in 1877, following a disagreement with the committee, his connection with the hospital came to an end, though he continued to oversee the building of the school of nursing which he had designed. It was opened in 1878. He continued in private practice, but London's fogs troubled him and from 1880 he wintered annually in Nice. In 1885, with improved health, he moved back to London and many former patients returned to him, but he always wished to resume his life's work with children and sought in vain for a post in a children's hospital.

Throughout his life West was a prolific writer on medical subjects; he was also one of the finest public speakers of his generation. At the Royal College of Physicians he was Croonian lecturer in 1854, Lumleian lecturer (1871), and Harveian orator (1874). He regarded the profession of medicine as a sacred duty and his strict moral code made him a demanding colleague. On two notable occasions he argued forcefully to prevent the entry of women to the Royal College of Physicians. In 1865 he was elected a corresponding member of the Académie de Médecine, Paris, and in 1892, *membre étranger*, a rare honour attained by very few Englishmen.

West suffered a severe attack of neuralgia in 1891 from which he never fully recovered. The London fogs had again forced him to winter on the Riviera and in 1897 he went south, although warned that the journey might prove too much. On 20 December in Nice an acute attack of herpes further reduced his strength. He left Cannes for London on 1 March 1898, but at Paris he was forced to break his journey and, after three weeks of increasing weakness, he died peacefully at the Hotel Terminus on 19 March 1898. He was buried at St Mary's Catholic Church, Chislehurst, Kent, on 23 March.   N. G. COLEY

Sources *The Lancet* (2 April 1898), 968–70 · *BMJ* (2 April 1898), 921–3 · Munk, *Roll*, 4.53–4 · Boase, *Mod. Eng. biog.*, 3.1275–6 · *The Times* (23 March 1898), 12 · N. Moore, *The history of St Bartholomew's Hospital*, 2 (1918), 727–9 · F. J. Poynton, *Address upon some incidents in the history of the Hospital for Sick Children, Great Ormond Street* (1939) · J. Kosky, *Mutual friends: Charles Dickens and Great Ormond Street Hospital* (1989) · *Statement by the Committee of Management [of Great Ormond Street Hospital] in reply to a letter addressed by Dr. West, Jan 17, 1878* · I. S. L. Loudon, 'John Bunnell Davis and the Universal Dispensary for Children', *BMJ* (5 May 1979), 1191–4 · H. R. Wiedemann, 'Charles West (1816–1898)', *European Journal of Pediatrics*, 151/3 (1992), 153 · *CGPLA Eng. & Wales* (1898)
Archives Great Ormond Street Children's Hospital, London, West Library · Great Ormond Street Children's Hospital, London, Medical MSS and letters | Bodl. Oxf., corresp. with Lady Byron
Likenesses photograph, *c.*1878, Great Ormond Street Hospital, London · photograph, repro. in *BMJ*, 921
Wealth at death £11,300 6s. 7d.: resworn probate, Aug 1899, *CGPLA Eng. & Wales* (1898)

West, Charles Richard Sackville-, sixth Earl De La Warr (1815–1873), army officer, born on 13 November 1815, in Upper Grosvenor Street, London, was the second but eldest surviving son of George John *West, fifth Earl De La Warr (1791–1869) [*see under* West, John, first Earl De La Warr], and his wife, Lady Elizabeth, later first Baroness Buckhurst (1795–1870), daughter of John Frederick *Sackville, third duke of Dorset. The fifth earl and his sons took the additional name of Sackville on 30 November 1843 by royal licence. After education at Harrow School, Charles obtained the commission of ensign in the 43rd foot on 26 July 1833, and was promoted to a second lieutenancy on 30 August. On 5 June 1835 he became lieutenant in the 15th foot, and on 15 April 1842 captain in the 21st foot. In 1845 and 1846 he served as aide-de-camp and acting military secretary to Sir Hugh Gough during the First Anglo-Sikh War, and was several times mentioned in dispatches. On 3 April 1846 he obtained the brevet rank of major, and in the following year received the Indian medal with three clasps. On 2 August 1850 he attained the brevet rank of lieutenant-colonel, and on 23 April 1852 the regimental rank of major. Following the death of his elder brother, George John Frederick Sackville-West, Viscount Cantelupe, on 25 June 1850, he became heir to the earldom, and from then until his father's death he used the courtesy title Lord West.

Lord West was sent to the Crimea in 1854, was present at the battle of Inkerman in command of a wing of the 21st fusiliers, and initiated the attack on the battery on Shelf Hill which is believed to have led to General Dannenberg's retreat. On 28 November 1854 he was promoted colonel. On 18 June 1855 he commanded the reserve in the unsuccessful assault made against the west flank of the Redan, and after the death of Sir John Campbell (1816–1855) assumed the command of the attack. In the same year he received the Crimean medal with four clasps, and on 27 July was made CB. On 24 July 1856 he obtained the local rank of major-general. On 2 August 1856 he was made an officer of the Légion d'honneur. He also received the Military Medal of Sardinia, and was made a knight of the third class of the Mejidiye on 2 March 1858. On 29 October 1864 he became a major-general. He succeeded his father as sixth Earl De La Warr on 24 February 1869, and on 20 May 1871 was created KCB. He was a Conservative peer, but supported Irish disestablishment in 1869. On 30 September 1871 he was appointed a commissioner to carry out the abolition of purchase in the army. On the morning of 22 April 1873 he left The Bull inn, Cambridge, and drowned himself in the River Granta; the coroner's jury's verdict was 'temporary insanity'. He was unmarried, and was succeeded by his brother Reginald Windsor Sackville-West, seventh earl.   E. I. CARLYLE, *rev.* H. C. G. MATTHEW

Sources *Hart's Army List* · GEC, *Peerage* · A. W. Kinglake, *The invasion of the Crimea*, 8 vols. (1863–87) · *Annual Register* (1873), pt 2, p. 46 · d. cert.
Archives ING Barings, London, corresp. with earl of Northbrook
Likenesses R. & E. Taylor, wood-engraving (after photograph by J. Watkins), NPG; repro. in *ILN* (17 Feb 1872)
Wealth at death under £30,000: probate, 16 June 1873, *CGPLA Eng. & Wales*

West, Charlotte (*fl.* 1787–1821), writer, published *A Ten Years' Residence in France* in 1821, apparently to warn the British against the dangers of revolution. She is apparently not related to the West family whose head was Earl De La Warr, which included Lady Charlotte West (1761–

c.1779) mentioned in Horace Walpole's letters. A moderately educated protestant woman of impoverished means, she describes herself as 'a bodily sufferer under the rigorous measures of a Revolutionary Government' (West, 1). The book was published with the assistance of sixty-three subscribers and printed by George Sams, a freemason. It is not known whether West is using a pseudonym, or how far her exploits are fictionalized.

In order to economize in late 1787, West settled with her husband in Challons-sur-Marne, Champagne, where her family had a summer home, and where she witnessed the 'glorious vintage' of that year (West, 2). In 1788 she saw the future empress Josephine on a number of occasions in the village of Pierre. In 1790 she moved to Rheims, joined the society of freemasons (a feat not uncommon in France, but more difficult for women in England), and attended masonic meetings for two and a half years. She rejoiced at the news of the destruction of the Bastille. On the anniversary of this event two years later, she witnessed wanton destruction by the Marsellois, a group of French youths who accosted her for wearing a black feather (a sign of aristocracy). She remarks how 'Monsieur Chánláire', a king's counsellor, had his nose cut off (though deaf, blind, and almost ninety years old) for mistakenly identifying himself as an aristocrat (West, 18–21).

As these sensational details suggest, West presents herself as a loyal British subject in this self-aggrandizing narrative, faithful to 'England, her king and Constitution' (West, 27). Horrified by the 'licentiousness' of the French revolutionaries, she advises the English nobility, in case of a revolution, not to abandon their king (ibid., 28). The French revolutionaries despised English Jacobins for reviling their own country, she notes. She views the French Revolution as a 'stalking-horse for all designing men' that promised liberty and reform and brought only the reformers' self-interest (ibid.).

West claims to have attended a dinner held for Louis XVI and Marie Antoinette and their family at Maison-de-Lintendance, where she 'sobbed' aloud for their fate; rescued the dauphin from the queen's own arms when she thought he was in danger of being musketed by a belligerent soldier; defended a deserter named Roberts (of a prominent Irish Catholic family in Cork) from a French mob; been present when the Girondin General 'Dumorrier' (Charles-François du Périer Dumouriez; 1739–1823), recently appointed commander-in-chief of the army of the north, ordered the battle of Jemappes (6 November 1792) to be fought, careless of the lives he had been charged with; and, on 21 January 1793, observed the execution of Louis XVI in front of 40,000 men. Temporarily detained while attending a play at the Palais-Royal, she was later arrested (along with many other English men and women) after the failure of the English expedition to Quiberon. At this point she was separated from her husband, and was shuttled between four different convents, which served as 'prisons' or internment camps. She provides an amusing account of the Parisian mayor's undemocratic feasts 'at the expense of the Great Nation' he professed to revere (West, 75). When she sang 'God Save

the King' in prison, an English colonel named Keating informed the authorities and she was almost executed; knowledge of the mayor's secret feasts (her leverage for a bribe) helped her avoid the guillotine. Her husband appears as an inconsequential figure who sometimes reproves her for her reckless bravery.

The book seems to have been written to warn the British against a second wave of enthusiasm for revolutions taking place on the continent in Spain, Italy, and Portugal. Nothing further is known of West's life; she was presumably still alive when the book was published in 1821.

JONATHAN DAVID GROSS

Sources C. West, *A ten years' residence in France, during the severest part of the revolution, from the year 1787 to 1797, containing various anecdotes of some of the most remarkable personages of that period* (1821) · Walpole, *Corr.* · M. C. Jacob, *Living the Enlightenment: freemasonry and politics in eighteenth-century Europe* (1991) · B. Kanner, *Women in context: two hundred years of British women autobiographers, a reference guide and reader* (1997)

West, Sir Edward (*bap.* **1782**, *d.* **1828**), judge and political economist, was baptized on 5 April 1782 at St Marylebone, Middlesex, the son of John Balchen West, the receiver-general for Hertfordshire, and his wife, Elizabeth. His parents died early in his life, and he was brought up by his uncle Sir Martin Brown ffolkes (*d.* 1821), MP for King's Lynn in Norfolk, and his aunt Fanny Turner (*d.* 1813), daughter of Sir John Turner bt of Warham. He was educated at Harrow School and University College, Oxford, where he obtained his BA in 1804. Between 1804 and 1807 he studied classics and mathematics, and was elected a fellow in 1807. He then turned to the law, and was called to the bar at the Inner Temple in 1814. He wrote the *Essay on the Application of Capital to Land* (1815) as a contribution to the early corn law debates, then in 1817 published a legal work, *A Treatise of the Law and Practice of Extents*. This was a reforming work addressed to indemnities against direct or indirect debts to royalty, and their use in the court of chancery. West was appointed recorder of Bombay in 1822, and following customary practice was knighted. He married his first cousin Lucretia G. B. ffolkes at Marylebone church on 26 August 1822, and they left for India six months later. They were never to return to Britain, and both in 1828 fell to the fate of so many aspiring young professionals seeking to make careers in India, that of an early death.

Soon after he arrived in Bombay, West was appointed chief justice of the crown, or one of the king's judges appointed to act as a check on the East India Company and to protect the interests of the Indian people. The role was a difficult one, as most of the European community in Bombay was connected to the East India Company. Despite his isolation he took his position seriously, and set out to check corruption, and to take up in the courts grievances of Indian servants and labourers against their masters. He wrote reports and letters, and made speeches on native legal rights, on the failings of the company magistrates, and on the irregularities of the police magistrates. He died before his reforms could be implemented, and was replaced by a chief justice seen to favour the company.

Lucretia West, an educated woman of the lesser gentry, took great interest in the politics of the day. Before her marriage she canvassed for her brother for the seat of Lynn in Norfolk against Colonel Walpole. Her journals in Bombay recounted her husband's long sessions in court, in the intervals of which he worked on his tracts of political economy, first on *The Price of Corn and Wages of Labour* (1826), then on a treatise which was never completed. She vividly set out the day-to-day lives of the British middle classes in India in her account of their own problems of adaptation. She described their friendships, the social ostracism they encountered during West's reform of legal practice in Bombay, and the almost daily deaths among those they knew. She had a daughter, Fanny Anna, in June 1826 and just over two years later she died in childbirth in Bombay a few months after the death of her husband. Fanny Anna was taken back to Britain after the death of her parents, and on coming of age went to live at her parents' childhood home of Hillington Hall, Lynn.

Sir Edward West is remembered for proposing a theory of differential rent based on diminishing returns in his pamphlet *Essay on the Application of Capital to Land* (1815). This was published just before David Ricardo's *Essay on Profits* (1815) and virtually at the same time as Thomas Malthus's *An Inquiry into the Nature and Progress of Rent* (1815). Ricardo in his *Principles of Political Economy and Taxation* (1817) attributed to both West and Malthus the 'true doctrine of rent'. West's pamphlet was followed by a book in 1826, *The price of corn and wages of labour, with observations upon Dr. Smith's, Mr. Ricardo's and Mr. Malthus's doctrines upon those subjects*. West's contributions to political economy, though on a subject of enduring interest to him, were written in the interstices of a distinguished legal career, practised mainly in Bombay.

West's contributions to political economy were particularly striking for insights which so closely anticipated Ricardo's analysis, and for the intellectual isolation in which he appears to have written them. He argued the case for the principle of diminishing returns in much the same way as Ricardo was to do independently, and developed a theory of the falling rate of profit which might only be postponed by the repeal of the corn laws. West inferred from his theory of diminishing returns that rents would fall, with the result of universal benefit from free trade. Ricardo's *Essay on Profits* (1815), by contrast, argued that rents would fall, with the implication that landlords had a selfish interest in supporting the maintenance of the corn laws. West later changed his argument when he published *The Price of Corn* (1826). He did, however, take the debate on the corn laws to a new stage by arguing that there was no danger in free trade leading to extreme specialization between manufacturing and agricultural countries. Diminishing returns would apply as much to foreign food producers as it had to domestic, and so provide limits to international specialization.

West's *The Price of Corn and Wages of Labour* (1826), though written in India, was remarkably up to date in its deployment of recent accounts of distress in the British manufacturing districts. He used these to provide an alternative to Smithian, Malthusian, and Ricardian price and wage theory. West's was a demand theory, based in turn on the consumption of the manufacturing classes. Manufacturing, he argued, in becoming an increasingly dominant sector, was more subject to international price fluctuation. Those in the manufacturing districts were more subject to alternations of luxury and distress: 'at one time … the wives and daughters of journeymen used the most expensive articles of dress, such as silk stockings, etc; at other times … there were troops of the manufacturers wandering about the country for want of employment, ragged, apparently wasted from want of sufficient food' (*The Price of Corn and Wages of Labour*, 50). The division between luxuries and necessities also affected demand; the demand for necessaries might be tied to the level of wages and incomes; that for luxuries was also dependent on the vagaries of taste. With the international division of labour the price uncertainties experienced in luxury markets now extended to all markets. Yet, just as he argued in *Essay on the Application of Capital to Land* (1815), the adverse impact of this international specialization would be checked, in this case by the proliferation of markets, and reduced dependence on any single market.

West drew on his experience in India. He argued that the low rates of wages in India might entail lower production costs and prices, but not necessarily so. The higher productivity, and especially intensity of labour in Britain yielded even lower production costs (*The Price of Corn and Wages of Labour*, 71). He also drew attention to the uncertainties of international markets from India to South America, predicting, however, greater stability with more international integration (ibid., 141). Writing from the extremities of the empire, West developed a much more global perspective than many contemporary political economists on the determinants of prices and wages. He died at Poona on 18 August 1828, and was buried there. Hindus, Parsis, and Muslims combined to fund a scholarship in West's honour.   MAXINE L. BERG

Sources M. Blaug, 'West, Edward', *The new Palgrave: a dictionary of economics*, ed. J. Eatwell, M. Milgate, and P. Newman, 4 vols. (1987) • F. D. Drewitt, *Bombay in the days of George IV: memoirs of Sir Edward West* (1907) • W. D. Grampp, 'Edward West reconsidered', *History of Political Economy*, 2 (1970), 316–43 • *DNB* • *IGI*
Archives BL OIOC, corresp. and papers of West and his wife, MSS Eur. D 888 | BL OIOC, corresp. with Mountstuart and Elphinstone and papers relating to West, MSS Eur. F 87–89 [copies]

West, Edward Charles Sackville-, fifth Baron Sackville (**1901–1965**), novelist and music critic, was born on 13 November 1901 at 105 Cadogan Gardens, London, the elder child and only son of Major-General Charles John Sackville-West KBE CMG, fourth Baron Sackville of Knole (1870–1962) and his first wife, Maud Cecilia (1873–1920), elder daughter of Matthew Bell of Sandgate. His father was then a major in the King's Royal Rifle Corps, who had served in the Second South African War as aide-de-camp to Sir Redvers Buller. After active service in France during the First World War he became in 1918 British military representative on the supreme war council, and remained in Paris as military attaché from 1920 to 1924. He succeeded his brother as fourth baron in 1928. Edward Sackville-West inherited from his mother, as did his sister Diana (Lady Romilly, later Lady Hall), the debilitating disease telangiectesia, an abnormal dilation of blood capillaries, which in Lord Sackville's case took the form of profuse nosebleeds.

Known for most of his life as Eddy Sackville-West (he held the barony of Sackville for only three years), on his father's accession he became heir to Knole, the great Elizabethan mansion at Sevenoaks, but in 1946 the house was handed over to the National Trust. As a young man, however, Eddy Sackville-West was provided with apartments at Knole by his uncle, third Baron Sackville of Knole, father of the writer and gardener Vita Sackville-West.

Sackville-West was educated at South Lodge preparatory school at Enfield in Middlesex, from which he went on to Eton College and Christ Church, Oxford, although he left Oxford without taking a degree. At Eton he had displayed prodigious gifts as a pianist, and while waiting to go up to university he toyed with ambitions to be a composer. But while at Christ Church he commenced a brief literary career, writing the first of five autobiographical novels, *The Ruin*. This appeared in 1926 as his second novel, for publication was held up when it was realized how easily identified the characters would be. The main protagonist, Marcus Fleming, was Jack McDougal, an undergraduate at New College and later Evelyn Waugh's publisher, with whom Sackville-West had had an affair. Eddy himself appears as Denzil, and *The Ruin*, like all the gothic literary efforts over which Sackville-West took infinite but rather pointless pains, was heavily laced with the mannered style of the late nineteenth-century 'decadent' movement epitomized by Huysmans, with whose work Eddy had unfortunately become enamoured when he was seventeen.

At the time, however, *The Ruin* itself, *Piano Quintet* (1925), *Mandrake over the Water-Carrier* (1928), *Simpson* (1931), awarded the Femina Vie Heureuse prize, and *The Sun in Capricorn* (1934) were generally well received by the critics. Two further novels, *The Eye of the Statue* and *Sinfonia eroica*, remain unpublished. Sackville-West's best works were *A Flame in Sunlight: the Life and Work of Thomas De Quincey* (1936), which won the James Tait Black memorial prize, and *The Rescue: a Melodrama for Broadcasting*, for which Benjamin Britten produced a score. First heard in 1943, and published in 1945 with illustrations by Henry Moore, *The Rescue* has been revived on numerous occasions, and was considered by the BBC producer Val Gielgud to be 'a genuine broadcasting classic'.

On 16 March 1935 Sackville-West contributed his first 'Gramophone notes' to the *New Statesman*, and for the next twenty years he became one of the most widely read and respected music critics of his generation. Very early in Benjamin Britten's career Sackville-West recognized his genius, and was rewarded with the dedication by Britten of his *Serenade* for tenor, horn, and strings (1943). From 1950 to 1955 he was a director of Covent Garden, urging on his fellow trustees a first performance in 1955 of Michael Tippett's *The Midsummer Marriage*. The other artistic field

in which Sackville-West revealed somewhat unexpected gifts was as a wartime producer at the BBC, where he shared an office with Stephen Potter.

In 1945 Sackville-West acquired his first permanent home, Long Crichel House near Wimborne, where with the music critic Desmond Shawe-Taylor, the painter Eardley Knollys, and the literary critic Raymond Mortimer, he established what in effect was a male *salon*, entertaining at the weekends a galaxy of friends from the worlds of books and music. It was at Long Crichel that Sackville-West and Shawe-Taylor compiled their famous *Record Guide*, first published in 1951 and several times revised.

It was also at Long Crichel that Sackville-West sat for his most successful portrait, arguably the finest portrait painted by Graham Sutherland. It hangs today at Knole. He was painted also by Vanessa Bell and by Duncan Grant, with whom he had an affair, and by a succession of lesser artists: E. M. Bennett (when a boy), Aldous Huxley (who had taught him at Eton), Ian Campbell-Gray, and John Banting, with whom he also had an affair, one of many liaisons which ended in disaster. The two most painful were with the sculptor Stephen Tomlin, whose bust of Sackville-West is at Long Crichel House, and with the owner of Herstmonceux Castle, the MP and baronet Sir Paul Latham. While in Germany as a young man Sackville-West underwent a futile and painful form of aversion therapy in an attempt to be 'cured' of his homosexuality, a condition with which he never fully came to terms. In desperation and loneliness he made at least one serious proposal of marriage, but when a young woman with the appropriately romantic name of Jane Eyre fell in love with him he made no attempt to respond. It was Jane Eyre's eventual husband, Ian Phillips, who commissioned the Sutherland portrait.

As a boy, Sackville-West had been a pious Anglo-Catholic. At the age of twenty-three he discarded religion, but in 1949 he was received into the Roman Catholic church, a decision which in part prompted his purchase in 1956 of a property called Cooleville House at Clogheen in co. Tipperary. On his accession as Lord Sackville in 1962 he took his seat in the House of Lords but never spoke. He became a knight of Malta, and he spent the last and the happiest years of his life in Ireland, dying at Cooleville on 4 July 1965 from a seizure caused by an acute asthma attack. He was buried at St Mary's Church, Clogheen, on 9 July. His unsigned *Times* obituary was written by Lord David Cecil, who had been one of his most affectionate friends at Eton. He was succeeded as sixth Baron Sackville of Knole by his cousin Lionel Sackville-West.

MICHAEL DE-LA-NOY

Sources M. De-la-Noy, *Eddy: the life of Edward Sackville-West* (1988) · b. cert. · d. cert. · [D. Cecil], *The Times* (6 July 1965)
Archives BBC WAC · BL, corresp., diaries, papers, and literary papers, Add. MSS 68904–68921 · Ransom HRC, corresp. and literary papers | Tate collection, corresp. with Graham Sutherland and Kathleen Sutherland · U. Sussex, letters to Clive Bell [copies]
Likenesses E. M. Bennett, oils, 1912, priv. coll. · G. Sutherland, black chalk and gouache drawing, 1953, Beaverbrook Foundation Art Gallery, Fredericton, New Brunswick · G. Sutherland, oils,

1954, Knole, Kent · G. Sutherland, oils, 1957, Birmingham Museums and Art Gallery

Wealth at death £180,297: probate, 14 Oct 1965, *CGPLA Eng. & Wales*

West, Edward William (1824–1905), orientalist, born at Pentonville, London, on 2 May 1824, was the eldest of twelve children (six sons and six daughters) of William West and his wife, Margaret Anderson. His ancestors on the paternal side for three generations had been architects and engineers. Owing to ill health he was at first educated at home by his mother, but between the ages of eleven and fifteen he attended a day school at Pentonville. In October 1839 he entered the engineering department of King's College, London, where he won high honours in 1842. A year later, after a severe illness, he spent twelve months in a locomotive shop at Bromsgrove, Worcestershire.

West's parents had lived in India for some years before their marriage, his father at Bombay and his mother in Calcutta. In 1844 West travelled to Bombay, where he arrived on 6 June, to superintend a large establishment of cotton presses. He retained this post for five years. Before leaving England he had studied Hindustani for a few weeks under Professor Duncan Forbes of King's College, London, and had learned to read the Perso-Arabic script as well as the Nagari, in which the classical Sanskrit language of India is commonly written. Otherwise his knowledge of oriental languages was self-taught. His method was to study direct from grammars, dictionaries, texts, and manuscripts, supplemented by occasional conversations with native Indians. He soon interested himself in Indian religions, especially that of the Parsis. A visit to the Indian cave temples at Elephanta, near Bombay, in March 1846, excited his interest in Hindu antiquities. A vacation tour made in March the following year with the Revd John Wilson and a party, including Arthur West, his brother, to the island of Salsette, north of Bombay, enabled him to visit the Kanheri caves, and inspired him with a wish to copy the inscriptions carved there in Pali, the sacred Buddhist language. In January 1850, after resigning his office of superintendent of the cotton presses, West revisited the Kanheri caves; but he spent the next year in England, and it was not until 1852 that he was able to inspect the caves properly. In that year he became civil engineer of the Great Indian Peninsula Railway, which ran through Bombay presidency. He later became the chief engineer of the railway.

Early in 1860 West laid before the Bombay Asiatic Society his copies of the Buddhist cave records of Kanheri, and the results were published in 1861 in the society's journal. He also made copies of the inscriptions in the Nasik caves to the north-east of Bombay, which were published in 1862. Later there followed transcripts of the Kura cave inscriptions and of other Buddhist sculptural records. As early as 1851 West had begun to compile from the Buddhist scriptural text, the Mahavamsa, a glossary of the Pali language in which all the cave records were written; but he afterwards abandoned this lexicographical project and ultimately withdrew from Pali studies, to the development of which he made a significant contribution.

West's lasting reputation rests on his Iranian studies. Almost as soon as he reached India, occasional conversations with the Parsi manager of the cotton presses drew his attention to the Zoroastrian religion. But it was chiefly Martin Haug's *Essays on the Sacred Language, Writings, and Religion of the Parsis* (1862) that stimulated his interest, which was confirmed when he made the personal acquaintance of the author at Poona in 1866. West began work on a copy of the Avesta, using a Gujarati translation and Dhanjibhai Framji's *Pahlavi Grammar* (1855). He read a paper on 10 ton cranes before the Bombay Mechanics' Institute in March 1857. The rest of his life was devoted, in co-operation with Haug, to the study of the Pahlavi language and literature of Sasanian Persia. Both he and Haug returned to Europe in 1866, when Haug was appointed in 1867 to the professorship of Sanskrit and comparative philology at the University of Munich. West went to Munich for six years (1867–73) and spent his time on the publication and translation of Zoroastrian Pahlavi texts. He edited the *Diary of the Late Rajah of Kohlapoor during his Visit to Europe in 1870* (1872) and contributed articles on the history of Kolhapur and the 'Bombay Karnatak' to the *Gazetteer of the Bombay Presidency* and the *Bombay Government Records* (1869–). On 17 June 1871 the University of Munich awarded him the honorary degree of doctor of philosophy. After a year in England (1873–4) West revisited India (1874–6) in order to procure manuscripts of the important Pahlavi books Denkard and Dadistan i Denig; he paid a last visit to the Kanheri caves on 6 February 1875.

In 1876 West resumed residence in Munich, but soon settled finally in England, first at Maidenhead and afterwards at Watford. His main occupation was the translation of a series of Pahlavi texts. Five volumes of translations appeared in Max Müller's Sacred Books of the East and the still valuable monograph, *Pahlavi Literature*, was published as part of Geiger and Kühn's Grundriss der iranischen Philologie (1897).

West's services to oriental scholarship, especially in Pahlavi, were widely recognized. In 1887 the Bavarian Academy of Sciences made him a corresponding member. From 1884 to 1901 he was a member of the Royal Asiatic Society of Great Britain and Ireland; and on 6 July 1901 he was presented with the society's gold medal, personally handed to him with an address by Edward VII. The American Oriental Society also conferred upon him honorary membership (16 April 1899). West was generous with personal aid to scholars who corresponded with him. With characteristic modesty he acknowledged, shortly before his death, that 'although his studies and researches had always been undertaken for the sake of amusement and curiosity, they could hardly be considered as mere waste of time'. In fact his writings and editions, pioneering works for their time, are still referred to a century later in the standard bibliographies of Iranian studies.

West died in his eighty-first year at his home, 10 Westland Road, Watford, on 4 February 1905. He was survived by his wife, Sarah Margaret Barclay, and by an only son, Max, an artist. A. V. W. JACKSON, *rev.* J. B. KATZ

Sources private information (1912) · L. C. Casartelli, *Manchester Guardian* (13 March 1905) · *BL cat.*, [online] · J. D. Pearson, ed., *A bibliography of pre-Islamic Persia* (1975) · M. J. Dresden, 'Survey of the history of Iranian studies', *Handbuch der Orientalistik: der nahe und der mittlere Osten*, ed. B. Spüler and others, 4: *Iranistik* (Leiden, 1968), 172–3 · *CGPLA Eng. & Wales* (1905)

Archives BL OIOC, corresp. and papers relating to railways, MSS Eur D 1184 · BL OIOC, personal corresp., IOR MSS Eur D 1184 · Royal Asiatic Society, London

Wealth at death £5848 5s. 3d.: probate, 2 March 1905, *CGPLA Eng. & Wales*

West, Elisabeth (*fl.* 1690–1709), servant and memoirist, was born in Edinburgh. Details of her parents are not known apart from the fact that her father died on 13 January 1700. She received her early instruction from her mother and an aunt, who took great pains with her education. In the period covered by her memoir she was a servant to a succession of families in and around Edinburgh. An exception occurred in 1708, when for a short period she taught young children as mistress of the Trades Hospital in Edinburgh. She became a communicant of the Church of Scotland in August 1694.

West attended the Tron Kirk in Edinburgh and was under the ministry of William Erskine until his death in May 1692. Erskine was succeeded by George Meldrum, whom West describes as the 'Lord's messenger to me' (West, 6). In 1695 her parish church became Trinity Church, or 'college kirk', a congregation vigorously opposed to episcopacy. The minister was John Moncrieff, who had been denounced in 1682 for holding conventicles. It was at the instigation of the Trinity Church kirk session that in 1709 James Greenshield was summoned to the Edinburgh presbytery for reading the prayers of the Church of England, and ordered to desist. When he refused the Edinburgh magistrates imprisoned him.

Elisabeth West began her 'Memoirs, or, Spiritual exercises' on the advice of Meldrum, who exhorted her to keep a record of the Lord's dealings with her soul. She received similar advice from John Flint, the Church of Scotland minister of Lasswade. Flint was a protégé of the Cameronians and was probably one of the first ministers to influence West towards the stricter covenanting section of the Scottish church. Her memoirs cover the period from 1690 to 1709 and provide important source material for gaining an understanding of the post-revolution Church of Scotland, as well as an insight into the life and thinking of a member of the stricter section of the Scottish Church. She drew up several personal covenants and regularly attended communion seasons, often walking many miles to these gatherings when evangelical ministers were preaching. The memoir abounds with references to her reading volumes of puritan practical divinity.

The years covered by the memoir are those in which William Carstairs guided the affairs of the Scottish church. The stricter Presbyterians were dissatisfied with Carstairs's policy, and a number were on the verge of separation from the established church. Elisabeth West attended meetings of these groups, known as the 'society people', and on at least one occasion went to hear John Hepburn (*d.* 1723), of Urr, whose views were similar to the Cameronians. Her commitment to the distinct viewpoint of the stricter Presbyterians is seen in her opposition to the union of Scotland with non-covenanting episcopal England, her belief that the solemn league and covenant was binding on successive generations, and her outright opposition to episcopacy. Elisabeth West's memoir, which was published in Glasgow in 1766, was read extensively by those converted in the 1742 revival at Cambuslang. The date and place of her death are not known.

ROY MIDDLETON

Sources E. West, *Memoirs, or, Spiritual exercises* (1807) · *Fasti Scot.*, new edn, vol. 1 · A. I. Dunlop, *William Carstairs and the kirk by law established* (1967) · W. McMillan, *John Hepburn and the Hebronites* (1934) · D. Mcfarlan, *The revivals of the eighteenth-century particularly at Cambuslang* [n.d.] · A. Fawcett, *The Cambuslang revival* (1971) · F. Goldie, *A short history of the Episcopal church in Scotland* (1951) · T. Maxwell, 'Presbyterians and episcopalians in 1688', *Records of the Scottish Church History Society*, 13 (1957–9), 25–37 · W. McMillan, 'The covenanters after the revolution of 1688', *Records of the Scottish Church History Society*, 10 (1948–50), 141–53 · E. S. Towill, 'The minutes of the Trades Maiden Hospital', *Book of the Old Edinburgh Club*, 28 (1953), 1–47

West, Francis (1586–1633/4), colonial governor, was born on 28 October 1586, probably at the family seat of Wherwell Abbey, Hampshire, the fourth but second surviving son of Thomas West, second Baron De La Warr (1555/6–1602), nobleman, and Anne, daughter of Sir Francis Knollys. West arrived in Virginia in 1608 with the second expedition under Captain Christopher Newport to provide the colony with supplies. That autumn he accompanied Newport in his fruitless exploration some 30 miles beyond the falls of the James River, and at the end of the year went with Captain John Smith, who had recently become the president of the colony's council, on his successful quest for food supplies from the Powhatans. With twenty men West then went back to the falls, seeking corn but finding only berries and acorns.

In May 1609 the Virginia Company secured a new royal charter which, *inter alia*, replaced the elected president of the council in the colony by a governor (and captain-general) appointed by the company in London. Thomas *West, third Baron De La Warr, West's elder brother, was to be the first governor, and Sir Thomas Gates was sent immediately as his deputy with a fleet of nine ships. In late summer 1609 six of the vessels straggled into the Chesapeake, and almost at once there was trouble. Among those arriving was Gabriel Archer, an old opponent of Captain Smith. The latter gained the support of the mariners, but the gentlemen, egged on by Archer, wanted the young Francis West as Smith's successor and secured his appointment to the Jamestown council. Henceforth he was, if not a leader, at least a figurehead of the gentry who sought autonomy within the colony. Smith, however, was still president of the council, and to avoid the prospect of starvation in the coming winter, just before his departure from the colony that autumn he dispersed the colonists up and down the river, sending West to the falls with more than a hundred men, where West Fort was established. But West was not there long. During the 'starving time' that winter he commanded one of the colony's three vessels and sought food for Jamestown. That done, deserting the colony, he sailed for England at the very time his brother Thomas was *en route* for Virginia.

West soon returned to the colony. In 1612 he succeeded George Percy as commander at Jamestown, and in 1617 was appointed master of the ordnance. By 1614 at the latest he and his younger brothers were in possession of 500 acres at Westover on the north bank of the James near the falls. The exact bounds of the estate were uncertain, and in 1619 there was a dispute with the new governor, Sir George Yeardley, when, according to the Wests, Yeardley assigned part of their holding to the associates of Berkeley hundred. Visiting England in 1620, West joined with other 'ancient planters' who were also there seeking the appointment of a governor of 'Eminence, or Nobillytie' (Kingsbury, 3.231).

Yeardley's successor, Sir Francis Wyatt, was instructed in July 1621 to reappoint West to the Jamestown council despite his absence from the colony. Indeed West may at that time have considered abandoning it altogether, for in November 1622 Sir Ferdinando Gorges appointed him admiral of New England and a member of the council there advising the governor-general. Briefly in Virginia in March 1623, West then spent the summer in New England waters, but, finding 'the fisher men to be stuberne fellows' (*History of Plymouth Plantation*, 1.312), he was back in Virginia by the end of the year.

Participating thereafter in council activity, West married late in 1625 or in 1626 Margaret (*d.* 1627/8), the widow of Edward Blaney. They had a son, Francis, and a daughter, Elizabeth—who was apparently dead by 1629. Margaret herself died in the winter of 1627–8. In 1626 Wyatt had returned to England and Sir George Yeardley became interim governor, but Yeardley too died in little more than a year, whereupon West became governor and on 28 March 1628 married Yeardley's widow, Temperance (*d.* 1628), daughter of Anthony Flowerdew. She died at the year's end, and three months later, perhaps to settle her estate, West left for England, where before the end of the year he had married Jane, daughter of Sir Henry Davye, and had made his will. While there he opposed Lord Baltimore's plan for a colony within Virginia's boundaries. Back in Virginia by the end of 1631, he resumed his seat on the council, where he sat for the last time on 9 February 1633. His widow proved his will in England on 28 April 1634. A family tradition alleges that he had been drowned.

Politically West's career was of minor significance; but socially, following George Percy's departure, he and his brothers were indisputably the first family in Virginia. Perhaps his career is most noteworthy, however, as an example of the frequency with which early Virginians took to the water. In addition to cruising Chesapeake Bay

in search of corn, West crossed the Atlantic seven times in twenty-four years, and made at least one round voyage to New England.   DAVID R. RANSOME

Sources F. S. Drake, *Dictionary of American biography, including men of the time* (1872) · P. L. Barbour, *Three worlds of Captain John Smith* (1964) · P. L. Barbour, ed., *The Jamestown voyages under the first charter, 1606–1609*, 2 vols., Hakluyt Society, 2nd ser., 136–7 (1969) · *The complete works of Captain John Smith (1580–1631)*, ed. P. L. Barbour, 3 vols. (1986) · D. B. Quinn, A. M. Quinn, and S. Hillier, eds., *New American world: a documentary history of North America to 1612*, 5 vols. (1979) · E. Arber, ed., *Travels and works of Captain John Smith*, 2 vols. (1895) · S. M. Kingsbury, *The records of the Virginia Company of London*, 4 vols. (1906–35) · R. Hamor, *A true discourse of the present state of Virginia* (1615) · H. L. Osgood, *The American colonies in the seventeenth century*, 3 vols.; repr. (1957) · W. Bradford, *History of Plymouth plantation, 1620–1647*, ed. W. C. Ford, 2 vols. (1912); repr. (1968) · *CSP col.*, vol. 1 · will, PRO, PROB 11/165, sig. 33 · *IGI* · A. Brown, ed., *The genesis of the United States*, 2 (1890), 1045 · N. M. Nugent, *Cavaliers and pioneers*, 1 (1934)

West, Francis (*d.* 1652), parliamentarian army officer, was born in London, the eldest son of George West of London (probably a silkman) and his wife, Margaret Bradborne, from near Northampton. On 16 May 1626 he married in All Hallows, Bread Street, Margaret Gooding, daughter of John Gooding, a London haberdasher, with whom he had two sons and four daughters. West was a principal inhabitant of Bread Street, where he traded as a silkman, and was described as an esquire in an official listing of 1642. He is not to be confused with his namesake, and fellow parishioner and silkman from the junior branch of the family, **Francis West** (*fl.* 1624–1634), freeman of the Grocers' Company. The latter was the son of Francis West (*d.* 1624) of London, a 'grocer', and his wife, Alice, daughter of John Cheney of St John Walbrook, grocer. He married Ann Carrell, daughter of Blase Carrell of London, merchant, on 22 July 1624. His date of death is unknown.

Francis West of the senior branch became a common councillor for the ward of Bread Street in 1641 and in 1644–5 served on the important City lands committee. By the spring of 1642 he had also become senior captain in the Blue regiment of the London trained bands under its colonel, Alderman Thomas Adams; he subsequently rose to the ranks of sergeant-major and lieutenant-colonel in 1642–3. West demonstrated an early commitment to parliament, subscribing one of the radical petitions of December 1641, acting as a collector and assessor for parliamentarian levies, contributing to the cavalry, and serving on the 1643 subcommittee for new subscriptions. At the same time he joined with other godly zealots in All Hallows, Bread Street, in a petition of September 1642 for the appointment of Lazarus Seaman as their rector. When a presbyterian structure was later erected in the London province, he was appointed one of the lay triers for vetting elders.

A good performance as commander of the Blue regiment (in the absence of their colonel, Adams) at Gloucester and at the first battle of Newbury in September 1643 brought West to the attention and favour of the earl of Essex, who promoted him to the rank of colonel. However, this promotion was made on Essex's own authority and hence enraged the London militia committee, which claimed the right to appoint all officers in its forces. The insistence that Adams remained the legitimate colonel led to clashes with some of West's local supporters within the regiment and an intervention by the committee of both kingdoms in August 1644. Shortly afterwards West became an agent of the committee for compounding employed to extract money from sequestered royalists.

But West finally achieved a pre-eminent London position in May 1645 when he replaced Isaac Penington, forced out by the self-denying ordinance, as lieutenant of the Tower. West was to retain the lieutenancy until the summer of 1647, when his control of the Tower was seen as a vital element in London's attempted counter-revolution. Consequently, when Fairfax occupied the capital in August, West was removed from the lieutenancy in favour of the army's candidate, Robert Tichborne. Yet in May 1648 he was reappointed to the lieutenancy, and he retained the post until his death in the Tower, after a short illness, on 11 August 1652. His funeral was attended by militia from the Blue regiment and Tower Hamlets as the Tower's guns sounded a final salute; he was buried in London some time after 17 August. His eldest son, John West (b. 1628), succeeded to his estate.   KEITH LINDLEY

Sources W. B. Bannerman, ed., *The registers of All Hallows, Bread Street, and of St John the Evangelist, Friday Street, London*, Harleian Society, register section, 43 (1913) · *The visitation of London, anno Domini 1633, 1634, and 1635, made by Sir Henry St George*, 2, ed. J. J. Howard, Harleian Society, 17 (1883), 338 · *CSP dom.*, 1644, 404; 1651–2, 364, 370, 572; 1652–3, 484 · H. A. Dillon, ed., 'On a MS list of officers of the London trained bands in 1643', *Archaeologia*, 52 (1890), 129–44, esp. 137 · BL, Harleian MS 986, fol. 16 · M. A. E. Green, ed., *Calendar of the proceedings of the committee for compounding … 1643–1660*, 1, PRO (1889), 35, 784 · *The names, dignities, and places of all the collonells … of the city of London* (1642) [Thomason tract 669.f.6(10)] · petition of citizens, etc. trading into Ireland, 24 Dec 1641, HLRO, main papers collection · petition of parishioners of All Hallows, Bread Street, 9 Sept 1642, HLRO, main papers collection · C. H. Firth and R. S. Rait, eds., *Acts and ordinances of the interregnum, 1642–1660*, 1 (1911), 796, 928, 1261–2; 2 (1911), 123, 371 · PRO, SP 28/131/pt 3, fol. 7 · PRO, SP 19/1/38; 19/1/89; SP 16/491/47 · vestry minutes, St Augustine, Watling Street, GL, MS 635/1 · *Perfect Account of the Daily Intelligence from the Armies* (11–18 Aug 1652) [Thomason tract E 674(4)] · J. L. Chester and J. Foster, eds., *London marriage licences, 1521–1869* (1887) · *IGI*

Wealth at death £122 owed at death for Tower payments: *CSP dom.*, 1652–53, 484

West, Francis (*fl.* **1624–1634**). *See under* West, Francis (*d.* 1652).

West, Francis Robert (*c.*1749–1809). *See under* West, Robert (*d.* 1770).

West, Frederick Walter Stephen [Fred] (**1941–1995**), murderer, was born on 29 September 1941 at Bickerton Cottage, Much Marcle, Herefordshire, the eldest surviving child of Walter Stephen West (1914–1992), an agricultural worker, and his wife, Daisy Hannah, *née* Hill (1923–1968). He had three younger sisters and three younger brothers. His childhood was brutal and primitive. Walter West was a man of strong sexual appetites and obsessions whose first wife had died mysteriously in 1937. Daisy West probably provided her favourite son's sexual initiation when he reached puberty in 1954.

West was a dirty, scruffy, and deceitful child who never learned to spell at the village school. During the late 1950s he worked as an agricultural labourer and took other ill-paid jobs. In 1961 he was twice convicted and fined for small-scale thieving before being acquitted in November at Herefordshire assizes of incest: his pregnant thirteen-year-old sister refused in court to name the father of her child. He was licentious, predatory, and sly; he liked to boast of his skills as an abortionist. On 17 November 1962 he married Catherine Bernadette (Rena) Costello (1944–1971), a Glasgow prostitute already pregnant by her pimp. In 1962–5 he lived with her in Scotland, mainly driving an ice-cream van, until he ran over and killed a young customer.

A series of Gloucestershire caravan parks provided West's homes in 1966–70. In March 1967 he contributed to the death of a youth who was hanged in a bondage rite. In August 1967 he murdered his girlfriend Ann McFall and, having removed their unborn child from her body, buried them together in Fingerpost Field, Kempley. In January 1968 he probably abducted and murdered a waitress of his acquaintance, Mary Bastholme, aged fifteen. In October 1969 a girl was hired to look after the two children living with West, Charmaine (the pimp's child) and his and Rena's daughter, Anne Marie (*b.* 1964). This hired helper was Rosemary Pauline (Rose) Letts (*b.* 1953), second of three daughters of William Andrew Letts, a schizophrenic who had been a violent parent. At the age of sixteen she was impregnated by West and she gave birth to their daughter Heather in October 1970. In June 1971, shortly after serving seven months' imprisonment for dishonesty and theft, West murdered his stepdaughter Charmaine, and buried her remains beneath the kitchen of his house in Gloucester. Two months later he murdered his wife, and buried her in Letterbox Field, Kempley.

On 29 January 1972 West married Rosemary Letts. They conceived two sons and three daughters between 1970 and 1980. Additionally Rose West had three daughters fathered by other men before being sterilized in 1983. In the period from 1970 West had a succession of jobs including milkman, lorry-driver, fibreglass presser, and jobbing builder. The Wests in September 1972 moved into a small terraced house at 25 Cromwell Street, Gloucester. They took in male lodgers, with whom Rose West had sex singly and jointly. Her husband revelled in watching or hearing her couplings with both men and women. Under his tutelage she became increasingly devoted to sadomasochism. In December 1972 they abducted, beat, and indecently assaulted their former nanny, for which crime they were fined £50 each in January 1973. Shortly afterwards the cellar of their house was converted into a torture dungeon. There, in April 1973, they sexually tortured, mutilated, and murdered Lynda Gough, aged nineteen, whom they had befriended. This crime excited their lust, and in November they similarly tortured and killed Carol Ann Cooper, aged fifteen. The following month, on 20 December, they abducted, abused, and murdered Lucy Partington, an undergraduate aged twenty-one; in April 1974, Thérèse Siegenthaler, a Swiss student aged twenty-one;

and in November 1974 Shirley Hubbard, aged fifteen. Rose West's sadistic ferocity and erotic compulsions came to surpass her husband's; she became the dominating partner, and he worshipped her. Two regular visitors to the house, Juanita Mott, aged eighteen, and Alison Chambers, aged seventeen, were abused and killed in April 1975 and September 1979 respectively. In June 1978 a lodger in Cromwell Street, Shirley Robinson, who was eight and a half months pregnant with West's child, was murdered. The Wests' eldest child, Heather, aged sixteen, was murdered in June 1987. These nine bodies were all buried at 25 Cromwell Street.

In August 1992 West was charged with three counts of rape and one of buggery perpetrated on one of his daughters; Rose West was charged with abetting him. They were acquitted in June 1993 after two child witnesses refused to give evidence against them. Their younger children were taken into care by Gloucester social services, who thus came to hear of Fred West's 'joke' that their sister Heather was 'buried under the patio' (Wansell, 288). On 24 February 1994 the police arrived at 25 Cromwell Street with a warrant to search the garden for the missing girl. West was arrested the following day, and by 2 June had been charged on eleven counts of murder. Subsequently his wife was detained. On 1 January 1995 West hanged himself in his cell at Winson Green prison; on 29 March he was cremated at Canley crematorium, near Coventry. On 21–2 November 1995 his widow was convicted on ten counts of murder and sentenced to life imprisonment.

RICHARD DAVENPORT-HINES

Sources G. Wansell, *An evil love* (1996) · G. Burn, *Happy like murderers* (1998) · B. Masters, *'She must have known'* (1996) · A. O'Hagan, *The missing* (1995) · A. M. West and V. Hill, *Out of the shadows* (1995) · S. West and M. West, *Inside 25 Cromwell St.* (1995) · H. Sounes, *Fred and Rose* (1995) · m. certs. · *CGPLA Eng. & Wales* (1995) · *The Times* (30 March 1995)
Likenesses photographs, repro. in Wansell, *An evil love*
Wealth at death under £125,000: administration, 20 Jan 1995, *CGPLA Eng. & Wales*

West, George John Sackville-, fifth Earl De La Warr (1791–1869). *See under* West, John, first Earl De La Warr (1693–1766).

West, Gilbert (1703–1756), author, was the eldest son of Richard West DD (1671–1716) and his wife, Maria (*d.* 1763), daughter of Sir Richard *Temple (1634–1697), and sister of Richard *Temple, Viscount Cobham. West's father was a fellow of Magdalen College, Oxford, from 1697 to 1708, prebendary of Winchester from 1706, and archdeacon of Berkshire from 1710 until his death on 2 December 1716. He published an edition of Pindar in 1697 and an edition of Theocritus in 1699. West's younger brother was Vice-Admiral Temple *West. His sister Maria married Alexander Hood, later Viscount Bridport. The John West, scholar of Eton and King's College, Cambridge, who was born on 5 February 1713 and died of smallpox in Cambridge in 1732, may have been another brother.

West was educated at Eton College, and Christ Church, Oxford, where he matriculated on 16 March 1721, and graduated BA (1725). He served for some time in the army,

and was afterwards employed under Lord Townshend (1674–1738). About 1729 he married Catherine Bartlett (*d.* 1757), and retired to the village of West Wickham in Kent where he devoted himself, in Johnson's words, 'to learning and to piety'. He had close family connections with George Lyttelton, first Baron Lyttelton (1709–1773), and William Pitt, first earl of Chatham (1708–1788), both of whom visited him frequently. One of the walks in West's garden was known as 'Pitt's walk'. West was a correspondent of Philip Doddridge and a friend of Pope, who left him £5 for a ring and a reversion of £200 at the death of Martha Blount (who outlived West). Fifty-four letters are preserved in the Huntington Library, mostly to Elizabeth Montagu, also a family connection, who became a close friend in the last five years of his life. West had one son, Richard, who matriculated at Merton College, Oxford, on 20 November 1752 and died about December 1754.

West's first poem, addressed to Pope and published anonymously in 1732, described his uncle's gardens at Stowe. He published imitations of Spenser (*A Canto of the Fairy Queen* in 1739 and *Education: a Poem* in 1751), and *The Institution of the Order of the Garter: a Dramatick Poem* in 1742. Though apparently a doubter in earlier years, in 1747 he published *Observations on the History and Evidence of the Resurrection of Jesus Christ*, which earned him the Oxford degree of DCL (30 March 1748), and a reputation as 'the miracle of the moral world, a Christian poet' (Montagu, 1.278). By 1749 the work had gone through four editions and had been translated into French and German. Towards the end of his life he was engaged on a work to prove the authenticity of the New Testament. In 1749 West published his translation of a selection of the odes of Pindar, together with a dissertation on the Olympic games. While the translation itself is conventionally elegant, West's notes mark a breakthrough in the reading of the odes in terms of their historical occasion, and the dissertation, praised by Gibbon, offers a rare eighteenth-century appreciation of the cultural and political significance of sport. West's miscellaneous poetry and his translations were included in Johnson's collection.

On 20 May 1736 West was granted an annual pension of £250, and in 1752 he was given a clerkship of the privy council. On 16 April 1754 he was made paymaster to Chelsea Hospital. He suffered severely from gout (and translated Lucian's 'The triumphs of the gout'). West died of 'a stroke of the palsy' in Chelsea on 26 March 1756 and was buried in West Wickham. His widow was allowed a pension of £200 a year from 5 July 1756; she died in 1757. A memorial tablet to West and other members of the family was placed in St John's Church, West Wickham, by his brother's grandson, Admiral Sir John West, in 1846.

PENELOPE WILSON

Sources DNB · S. Johnson, *The works of the English poets, with prefaces, biographical and critical, by Samuel Johnson*, 70 vols. (1779–81) · E. Montagu, *Correspondence, 1720–1761*, ed. E. J. Climenson (1906) · Nichols, *Lit. anecdotes*, 2.210, 708–10 · *The correspondence of Robert Dodsley, 1733–1764*, ed. J. E. Tierney (1988) · J. Spence, *Observations, anecdotes, and characters, of books and men*, ed. J. M. Osborn, new edn, 2 vols. (1966) · *The correspondence of Alexander Pope*, ed. G. Sherburn, 5 vols. (1956) · R. A. Austen-Leigh, ed., *The Eton College register, 1698–*

1752 (1927) • Foster, *Alum. Oxon.* • Venn, *Alum. Cant.* • GEC, *Baronetage*, 3.31 • *Engraved Brit. ports.*, 6.431

Archives Hunt. L., letters mainly to Elizabeth Montagu

Likenesses E. Smith, line engraving, pubd 1824 (after W. Walker), NPG

West, James (1703–1772), politician and antiquary, was born on 2 May 1703 and baptized on 21 May at St Swithin's, London Stone, the only son of Richard West, of London and Prior's Marston in Warwickshire, and his wife, Mary Russell, of Strensham, Worcestershire. He was educated from 1720 at Balliol College, Oxford, where he graduated BA (1723) and proceeded MA (1726), and from 1721 at the Inner Temple. He was called to the bar in 1728, and on 23 January 1738 was admitted at Lincoln's Inn. He was elected a bencher of the Inner Temple in 1761, reader in 1767, and treasurer in 1768.

From a young age West engaged in the study of antiquities and science. He was elected a fellow of the Royal Society on 23 November 1726, acted as the society's treasurer from 30 November 1736 to 30 November 1768, and served as its president from the latter date until his death. He became FSA on 23 November 1726, and on 19 February 1729 was elected a member of the Spalding Society. As a trustee of Lady Oxford's estates, he completed the sale of the Harleian manuscripts to the British Museum in 1753 for £10,000.

West collected books, manuscripts, pictures, prints, plate, coins, and medals, but lost many items, valued at almost £3000, through a fire in his chambers at the Inner Temple on 4 January 1737. Undaunted, he subsequently gathered around him a marvellous library and curiosities of all kinds at his town house, situated at the west end of the piazza in King Street, Covent Garden. His country seat was at Alscott, Preston-on-Stour, Gloucestershire.

West reputedly revived the 'love of black-letter lore and of Caxtonian typography' (Dibdin, 376–84). He greatly assisted James Granger in his biographical work on portraits, and he subscribed for Hearne's books and gave him a plate for Domerham's *Glastonbury* (1727). He also assisted in Walter Hemingford's *History of Edward I, II, and III* (1731).

On 15 August 1738 West married Sarah (*d.* 1799), the daughter and heir of Sir Thomas Steavens, a timber merchant at Southwark and of Eltham in Kent. Ultimately, the marriage brought him £100,000 to add to the £1000 per annum left to him by his father. The couple had a son, James (*d.* 1795), and two daughters: Sarah (*d.* 1801), who became the wife of Andrew, second and last Lord Archer, and Henrietta (*d.* 1815).

At the general election in 1741 West was returned as MP for St Albans, Hertfordshire, and continued to represent the borough until 1768, when he was elected for Boroughbridge, Yorkshire. Between 5 April 1758 and July 1760 he was recorder of St Albans and from 23 November 1759 its high steward. From 1746 he was also recorder of Poole, Dorset. In December 1743 he was appointed secretary to the chancellor of the exchequer, an office he held until May 1752. He was also joint secretary to the Treasury from May 1746 until November 1756, when he resigned with his

patron, the duke of Newcastle, who secured for him a pension of £2000 per annum. He returned to government as joint secretary in July 1757, and once again resigned with Newcastle in May 1762. When Rockingham began forming an administration in July 1765, Newcastle pressed for the reinstatement of many of his former adherents. West became the unfortunate victim of Rockingham's decision to assert his independence, being turned down for a return to the Treasury as treasurer to the navy, and even for a consolatory groomship of the chamber for his son. All this he bore uncomplainingly, and in January 1768 he was formally reconciled with Rockingham. He continued to send Newcastle frequent and valuable reports of parliamentary proceedings.

West died on 2 July 1772. In the early months of 1773 his extensive collections were all sold. The manuscripts, including many which had belonged to Bishop Kennett, were purchased by Lord Shelburne, and now form part of the Lansdowne manuscripts at the British Library. Horace Walpole considered that the prints went for a 'frantic sum', while the books were 'selling outrageously' (*Letters*, 5.439, 455). The books alone realized £2927 1s. Gough bought many of them, particularly those with Kennett's annotations, and they afterwards went to the Bodleian Library. W. P. COURTNEY, *rev.* PATRICK WOODLAND

Sources HoP, *Commons* • Nichols, *Lit. anecdotes* • Nichols, *Illustrations* • T. F. Dibdin, *Bibliomania, or, Book madness: a bibliographical romance*, new edn (1876) • C. R. Weld, *A history of the Royal Society*, 2 vols. (1848) • *The letters of Horace Walpole, earl of Orford*, ed. P. Cunningham, 9 vols. (1857–9) • *GM*, 1st ser., 1 (1731), 500 • *GM*, 1st ser., 8 (1738), 435 • *GM*, 1st ser., 42 (1772), 343 • *GM*, 1st ser., 69 (1799), 438 • J. Sydenham, *The history of the town and county of Poole* (1839) • E. Brydges, *Restituta, or, Titles, extracts, and characters of old books in English literature*, 4 vols. (1814–16), vol. 1, pp. 65–91 • *Letters between Rev. James Granger … and many of the most eminent literary men of his time*, ed. J. P. Malcom (1805), 33–6 • *N&Q*, 2nd ser., 11 (1861), 101–2, 162 • J. Nichols, *A list of the members of the Society of Antiquaries of London, from their revival in 1717, to June 19 1796* (1798) • IGI • Foster, *Alum. Oxon.* • W. H. Cooke, ed., *Students admitted to the Inner Temple* (1868–77)

Archives BL, commonplace book containing entries on antiquities, statutes, laws, and customs, Lands MS 196 • BL, corresp. and papers incl. some relating to his historical researches, Add. MSS 34727–34747 • BL, MS collections • BL, notes, incl. some of the debates in the Commons and financial papers, Add. MSS 6048, 18248, 30203, 35877–35878 • Bodl. Oxf., corresp. and papers incl. some relating to antiquarian subjects • History of Parliament Trust, London, transcripts of West MSS (Alscott) • Warks. CRO, corresp. and papers | BL, corresp. with duke of Newcastle, Add. MSS 32711–33088, *passim* • Bodl. Oxf., copy of Thomas Tanner's *Notitia Monastica*, with his copious MS notes and additions • Bodl. Oxf., letters to Thomas Hearne • NL Scot., letterbook of corresp. with John Maule

Likenesses T. Hodgetts, mezzotint, pubd 1819, NPG

West [*née* Iliffe], **Jane** (1758–1852), writer and poet, was born on 30 April 1758 in a building which afterwards became St Paul's Coffee House, London, the only child of Jane and John Iliffe. Her parents moved with her when she was eleven to Desborough in Northamptonshire. A useful source for West's early life is her letter of 1800 seeking Bishop Percy's patronage in order to support her 'rising family' which is reprinted along with other biographical and literary information in her obituary (*GM*, 2nd ser., 38.99–101). West states that she was 'self-instructed' and began writing poetry at the age of thirteen, having by the age of twenty a 'formidable' catalogue of compositions: 'I scorned corrections, and never blotted' (ibid., 99). By 1783 she had married Thomas West (*d.* 1823), a yeoman farmer from neighbouring Little Bowden, Leicestershire, members of whose family had been rectors of the parish for a century and a half. Thomas West was related to Vice-Admiral Temple West and to Gilbert West, a minor poet. They had three sons: Thomas (1783–1843), John (*b.* 1787), and Edward (1794–1821). Jane West was to outlive them all (Lloyd). In 1810 she paid a visit to Bishop Percy at Dromore in Ireland. After Percy's death, she continued to write but her popularity seems to have suffered from the loss of her patron and of influential subscribers. West was also a correspondent of Sarah Timmer, the educational and children's writer.

All of West's works are didactic and conservative in their ethical judgements regarding political change and women's role in society. Her first novel, *The Advantages of Education* (1793), written under the pseudonym Prudentia Homespun, aims 'to enstruct rather than entertain' (preface). This was followed by what is now her best-known novel, *A Gossip's Tale* (1796), also published under the facetious pseudonym, and written to expound 'The Advantages of Consistency, Fortitude and Domestic Virtue'. Critics have noted how *A Gossip's Tale* with its anti-sentimental plot line anticipates the themes and judgements of Jane Austen's fiction, particularly the latter's *Sense and Sensibility*. Her third novel, *A Tale of the Times* (1799), addresses her familiar theme of the necessity for young women to make the right marriage choice, but expands on this with its expression of anxieties of the day, particularly fears of revolutionary upheaval. In its anti-Jacobin, tory, and reactionary emphasis *A Tale of the Times* forms a counterpoint to the Jacobin novels of the period.

West's other novels include *The Infidel Father* (1802) which attacks atheism; *The Refusal* (1810); *The Loyalists: an Historical Novel* (1812), credited as a possible influence on Walter Scott's first novel *Waverley*; and *Alicia de Lacey: an Historical Romance* (4 vols., 1814) which is indebted to Scott's historical romances. *Ringrove, or, Old Fashioned Notions* (1827), her last novel, written when West was sixty-nine, broke a silence of over ten years. Pamela Lloyd has also identified a children's story, *The Sorrows of Selfishness* by Prudentia Homespun, as the work of West.

West's conservative views on woman's role are particularly strident in her popular conduct literature: *Letters to a Young Man* (1801), written to her son and dedicated to Percy, went through six editions by 1818. This was followed by *Letters to a Young Lady* (1806), which was dedicated to the Princess Victoria and addressed to Miss Maunsell, who died in 1808. In many respects *Letters to a Young Lady* forms an ideological counterpart to Mary Wollstonecraft's *Vindication of the Rights of Woman* (1792). Where Wollstonecraft advocates 'Rights', West insists on 'Duties'. However both, as feminist critics have pointed out, were involved

in the debate on the 'Woman's question' and foregrounded the necessity of improved education for women, although not for the same ends.

Jane West wrote poetry from a young age, much of it in a didactic vein. Roger Lonsdale, editor of *Eighteenth Century Women's Poetry* (1990), considers her best poetry to be that written in a familiar manner rather than her more polished, consciously literary verse. Her poetic works include *Miscellaneous Poetry, Written at an Early Period of Life* (1786), her least interesting collection; *The Humours of Brighthelmstone: a Poem* (1788); *Miscellaneous Poems and a Tragedy* ['Edmund'] (1791); *An Elegy on the Death of the Right Honourable Edmund Burke* (1797); *Poems and Plays* (vols. 1 and 2, 1799; 3 and 4, 1805); and *The Mother: a Poem in Five Books* (1799). *Miscellaneous Poems, Translations and Imitations* (1780), previously attributed to her, is now known to be the work of Benjamin West. West's poems also appeared in journals and anthologies of the day. She also wrote *Select Translations of the Beauties of Massillan* (1812) and *Scriptural Essays Adapted to the Holy Days of the Church of England* (2 vols., 1816). West's dramatic works have now been largely forgotten. A contemporary commentator attributes her lack of dramatic success to the vogue for German sentimental drama (*GM*, 1st ser., 69.1129). West was herself a contributor for many years to the *Gentleman's Magazine*.

West's reputation in her own day was for the clear didacticism of her texts. It was reported that Queen Victoria purchased her novels, and Bishop Percy, who had praised West's writing and character in the *British Critic* (1801), complained of his delay in obtaining a copy of *A Tale of the Times* from the circulating libraries at Brighton owing to its popularity. Her works were recommended for 'their pure morality, and forcible arguments', and her character described as 'a model of imitation' in her roles as 'a wife, a mother, and a daughter' (*GM*, 1st ser., 69.1128). Her obituarist took great pains to dispel any inference of lowly status associated with the author insisting that her 'gentlewoman' status was concurrent with her literary accomplishments (ibid., 1st ser., 72.99). Little is known of West's actual social status during her lifetime, although Pamela Lloyd has uncovered her will and other papers which reveal that West, as sole beneficiary of her parents, inherited in 1805 property which, when sold in 1812, produced £3000. West's descriptions of herself reinforce a linking of domesticity and morality with female literary authority: she insists that 'My needle always claims the preeminence of my pen. I hate the name "rhyming slattern"' (*GM*, 1st ser., 72.99). However later critics (Lonsdale, 1990, Shattock, 1993) have pointed out that West was not above self-promotion and exploiting the media of the day; about 1800 there seems to have been a conscious campaign to obtain a wider audience for her.

West's life and writing career were long but towards the end of her life she felt herself to be out of kilter with the times. This sense of isolation was increased by her failing sight. She describes herself as 'an old Q. in the corner whom the rest of the world has forgotten' (Lloyd, 470). West died on 25 March 1852 at Little Bowden aged ninety four, having lived most of her adult life there, in a 'retired situation with few connections', as she described her circumstances, and never achieving the wider literary fame that she courted. She was buried at St Nicholas's Church, Little Bowden. Her estate was divided among her six grandchildren; her manuscripts and letters were originally left to her grandson the Revd Edward West, but these have not been traced.   GAIL BAYLIS

Sources P. Lloyd, 'Some new information on Jane West', *N&Q*, 229 (1984), 469–70 · R. Lonsdale, ed., *Eighteenth-century women poets: an Oxford anthology* (1989); pbk edn (1990) · *GM*, 1st ser., 69 (1799), 1128–9 · *GM*, 1st ser., 72 (1802), 7, 99 · *GM*, 2nd ser., 38 (1852), 99–101 · V. Sanders, *Eve's renegades: Victorian anti-feminist women novelists* (1996) · M. Butler, *Jane Austen and the war of ideas* (1975) · J. Spencer, '"Of use to the daughter": maternal authority and early women novelists', *Living by the pen: early British women writers*, ed. D. Spender (1992) · J. Shattock, *The Oxford guide to British women writers* (1993) · J. West, *Letters to a young lady*, [3rd edn] (1811); repr. in *Female education in the age of Enlightenment*, 4–6 (1996) · J. Spencer, *The rise of the woman novelist: from Aphra Behn to Jane Austen* (1980) · R. C. Alston, ed., *A checklist of women writers, 1801–1900: fiction, verse, drama* (1990) · J. R. de J. Jackson, *Romantic poetry by women: a bibliography, 1770–1835* (1993) · Blain, Clements & Grundy, *Feminist comp.* · d. cert.

Archives CUL, account of a tour in Wales and Ireland | Bodl. Oxf., corresp. with Thomas Percy

Wealth at death see Lloyd, 'Some new information'; will, PRO, PROB 11/2154

West, John, first Earl De La Warr (1693–1766), politician and army officer, was born on 4 April 1693, the son of John West, sixth Baron De La Warr (c.1663–1723), and his wife, Margaret (d. 1738), the daughter and heir of John Freeman, a London merchant. He was educated at Eton College and then went on the grand tour, from which he returned in 1712. On 18 August of that year he was appointed clerk-extraordinary of the privy council, a post he held until 1723. He was elected as MP for Grampound in Cornwall on 27 January 1715. A loyal government whig, he voted with the ministry on all but one occasion, and did not stand for re-election in 1722.

West continued to serve in the army, rising to the rank of lieutenant-colonel in December 1717. On 25 May 1721 he married, in secret, Lady Charlotte Maccarthy (d. 1735), the daughter of Donough *Maccarthy or MacCarty, fourth earl of Clancarty, with whom he had two sons and two daughters. On his father's death in May 1723 he became seventh Baron De La Warr. He was made lord of the bedchamber to George I on 3 June 1725, became KCB in the same year, and on being assigned treasurer of the household in 1731 he was sworn of the privy council. In March 1736 he was sent to Saxe-Gotha to accompany Princess Augusta to England, where she was to marry Frederick, prince of Wales. According to Lord Hervey, De La Warr was chosen on account of his unprepossessing figure and awkwardness in company. This, it was hoped, would prove unattractive to the princess and curb the prince's jealousy.

On 2 July of the following year De La Warr was appointed captain-general and governor of New York and New Jersey, though he remained in England, where he continued to play an active role in politics from the Lords. In February 1732 he criticized the reintroduction of Samuel Sandys's Pension Bill. He served as speaker during the absence of Peter, Lord King, in 1733, actively promoted legislation against Edinburgh following the Porteous riots in 1736, and criticized in February 1739 those who petitioned against the recent convention with Spain. In the same month he attempted to have the author and publisher of an anti-government satire, *Manners* (1739), questioned in the Lords. His bid to arrest the author, Paul Whitehead, for non-attendance was at first opposed but then supported in the house.

De La Warr's eclectic but always pro-government political career continued in the 1740s. In June 1742 he spoke against a measure to secure trade and navigation rights for merchants in wartime. He later defended the ministry's Spirituous Liquors Bill and criticized a bill proposing increased trade to the Levant (May 1744) while defending the Turkey Company—of which he was governor—against charges of being a monopoly. He also took an active part in debates over the political responsibilities of the House of Lords. In February 1740 he defended the ministry's decision to request war finances from the Commons alone. This was a position he later came to regret, as a speech on 12 March 1742 makes clear. Later in the same year he introduced several changes to procedures in the Lords, notably on the issue of proxy voting. In December 1747 he was appointed governor of Tilbury, and on 29 April 1752, of Guernsey. In March 1754 he was for a second time elected speaker of the house, during Lord Hardwicke's absence.

On 15 June 1744 De La Warr married his second wife, Anne Nevill, *née* Walker (d. 1748), the widow of George Nevill, thirteenth Baron Abergavenny. In May 1749 he made an appearance at the jubilee masquerade at Ranelagh dressed as Queen Elizabeth's porter, a costume he wore again at a Russian masquerade at Somerset House on 6 February 1755. He also pursued his military career in the 1740s: he commanded a brigade at the battle of Dettingen (1743) and was promoted to the rank of major-general (March 1745), lieutenant-general (September 1747), and general (March 1755). In March 1761 he was created Earl De La Warr and Viscount Cantelupe by George III. He died on 16 March 1766 and was buried on 22 March at St Margaret's, Westminster.

His son, **John West**, second Earl De La Warr (1729–1777), politician and army officer, entered the army in 1746 as an ensign in the 3rd infantry guards and rose to the rank of colonel (May 1758), major-general (8 March 1761), and lieutenant-general (30 April 1770). From 1761 to 1766 he was vice-chamberlain to Queen Charlotte, and served as master of the horse from 1766 to November 1768, when he was named lord chamberlain. He died in Audley Square, London, on 22 November 1777, and was buried on 30 November at St Margaret's, Westminster. He married on 8 August 1756 Mary (d. 1784), the daughter of Lieutenant-General John Wynyard. They had two sons, William Augustus (1757–1783), who became third Earl De La Warr, and John Richard (1758–1795), fourth earl, who married Catherine (d. 1826), the daughter of Henry Lyell and Catherine Allerstree of Bourne, Cambridge.

The fourth earl's son, **George John Sackville-West**,

fifth Earl De La Warr (1791–1869), politician, was born in Savile Row, London, on 26 October 1791. He was educated at Harrow School and Brasenose College, Oxford, and graduated BA in 1812 and MA in 1819. He was appointed a lord of the bedchamber to both George III and George IV and served from July 1813 to March 1828. He was created LLD of Cambridge in 1828, and DLC of Oxford in 1834. On 21 June 1813 he married Elizabeth (1795–1870), the daughter of John Frederick *Sackville, third duke of Dorset, and in November 1843 acquired a royal licence to put his wife's surname of Sackville before his own. In September 1841 he was sworn of the privy council and appointed lord chamberlain by Sir Robert Peel, a post he held until 1846. He held the same office under Lord Derby from February 1858 to June 1859. De La Warr, who met Byron while at Harrow, was the 'Fair Euryalus' of the latter's 'Childish Recollections' and the inspiration behind two further poems. He died at Knole Park, Kent, on 23 February 1869; he was succeeded by his eldest son, Charles Richard Sackville-*West, sixth Earl De La Warr, and was survived by his wife, who in April 1864 had been created Baroness Buckhurst in her own right. She died at 17 Upper Grosvenor Street, London, on 9 January 1870.

M. E. CLAYTON

Sources E. Cruikshank, 'West, Hon. John', HoP, *Commons* · John, Lord Hervey, *Some materials towards memoirs of the reign of King George II*, ed. R. Sedgwick, 3 vols. (1931) · GEC, *Peerage*, new edn, vol. 2 · Cobbett, *Parl. hist.* · H. Walpole, *Memoirs of King George II*, ed. J. Brooke, 3 vols. (1985)
Archives BL, MSS collection · Herts. ALS | BL, corresp. with duke of Newcastle, Add. MSS 32691–32864, *passim* · BL, MSS collection [George John Sackville-West] · CKS [George John Sackville-West] · CKS [John West] · U. Southampton L. [George John Sackville-West] · W. Sussex RO [George John Sackville-West]
Likenesses W. Byron, ink and wash drawing, 1719, BM · S. W. Reynolds, portrait, 1823 (John West; after J. Reynolds), NPG · G. Hayter, group portrait (George John Sackville-West. *The trial of Queen Caroline, 1820*), NPG · W. H. Mote, portrait (George John Sackville-West; after E. D. Smith), NPG · H. Roberts, line engraving (after W. Byron), BM, NPG
Wealth at death under £16,000—George John Sackville-West: probate, 1869

West, John, second Earl De La Warr (1729–1777). *See under* West, John, first Earl De La Warr (1693–1766).

West, Sir John (1774–1862), naval officer, was born at Twickenham, Middlesex on 28 July 1774, the eldest son of Lieutenant-Colonel Temple West (*d.* 1783), of the Grenadier Guards, and his wife, Jane, daughter of Pitt Drake. He was the grandson of Vice-Admiral Temple *West and, through his grandmother, great-grandson of Admiral Sir John Balchen; his father was the second cousin of William Pitt the younger; his grandfather's sister was the first wife of Alexander Hood, Viscount Bridport. West entered the navy in June 1788 on board the *Pomona*, with Captain William Domett, himself a follower of Alexander Hood. He was afterwards in the *Salisbury*, flagship of Vice-Admiral Mark Milbanke, and in the *London*, flagship of Alexander Hood. He was promoted lieutenant on 27 July 1793, and in 1794 was a lieutenant of the *Royal George* in the battles of 1 June 1794 and 23 June 1795. On 7 September 1795 he was

made commander; in December was appointed to the sloop *Diligence* in the West Indies, and on 15 November 1796 was posted to the frigate *Tourterelle* (30 guns). From 1807 to 1809 he commanded the *Excellent* (74 guns), in the Mediterranean, and from 1809 to 1814 the *Sultan* (74 guns), in the Mediterranean and on the home and West Indian stations.

West married, in May 1817, Harriett (*d.* 1858), only daughter of John Adams of Northamptonshire; they had three sons and two daughters. West became a rear-admiral on 12 August 1819, vice-admiral on 22 July 1830, and admiral on 23 November 1841; he was made a KCB on 4 July 1840. From April 1845 to April 1848 he was commander-in-chief at Devonport, with his flag in the *Queen* (110 guns). He was made admiral of the fleet on 25 June 1858, and a GCB on 18 May 1860. He died, at his residence, 99 Eaton Square, London, on 18 April 1862. West's career was made by family connections, and distinguished largely by longevity.

J. K. LAUGHTON, *rev.* ANDREW LAMBERT

Sources D. Syrett and R. L. DiNardo, *The commissioned sea officers of the Royal Navy, 1660–1815*, rev. edn, Occasional Publications of the Navy RS, 1 (1994) · O'Byrne, *Naval biog. dict.* · Boase, *Mod. Eng. biog.* · GM, 3rd ser., 13 (1862), 644–5 · *CGPLA Eng. & Wales* (1862)
Wealth at death under £90,000: probate, 9 May 1862, *CGPLA Eng. & Wales*

West, John (1839–1922), gas engineer, was born at Northampton on 10 August 1839, the eldest son of Joseph West, a gardener, and his wife, Ann, *née* Perkins. He was taken on at an early age as an articled pupil by the manager of the local Northampton gasworks and worked his way up to become a departmental manager. After fourteen years he left Northampton and within two years had become manager and engineer of the Maidstone gasworks. It was while at Maidstone, in 1873, that he took out the first of his many patents—for a machine for stoking gas retorts. He set up a company to manufacture the machines, though sales remained limited.

In 1880 West's growing reputation won him the prestigious job as chief engineer of the Manchester corporation gas department, and while there he set about widening the appeal of his stoking machines by applying power to their operation in the form of compressed air, an idea he first patented in the same year. At first his success was limited because the machines kept breaking down; none the less, in 1884 he felt confident enough to give up his salaried post and devote himself full-time to his business, West's Gas Improvement Co. Ltd. Yet business remained slow until in 1893 he finally perfected the compressed-air machinery which soon became widely adopted in Britain and abroad. These machines, together with those of his great rival, William Foulis, gave Britain a world lead in the field, and West's company began to prosper as it also began the manufacture of coal- and coke-handling equipment. In 1898 the capacity of his works at Miles Platting, Manchester, was doubled and a year later the workforce numbered 300.

In 1905 West joined forces with Samuel Glover to manufacture a vertical retort which charged and discharged coal and coke by gravity in a continuous gas-making process. These Glover–West retorts were widely adopted in Britain and overseas, and when West also set up a company to manufacture refractory materials for gasworks he was in a position to contract for the building of entire gasworks anywhere in the world. Despite his advancing years he maintained a close interest in the firm. He took out a patent in 1920, at the age of eighty, and in the same year made a trip to the United States and opened an office in New York. The company continued to grow, so that by the time of his death in 1922 it employed 1100 workers.

West, whom the *Gas Journal* described on his death as 'an outstanding figure in the gas profession, exceeding the memory of any practising gas engineer', was energetic and inventive but practical. Typical of his generation of engineers in Britain, he had no formal theoretical training but this did not seem to be a barrier to world leadership in his chosen field. He was a strong-minded man, emphatic in his judgements. As an employer he was paternalistic; he treated his workforce to an excursion to Blackpool each year and entertained them to dinner. He led by example. When one of his machines was being installed in London in 1890 the union men refused to work it without higher pay. He replaced them with non-union labour and this provoked a violent confrontation. But he won through and the editor of the *Gas Journal* remembered him 'with his shirt sleeves rolled up and overalls on … with dark faces about him, teaching men how to operate his machine' (ibid.).

West was an active member the Gas Institute (the gas engineers' society); he was its president in 1893–4 and was awarded their highest honour, the Birmingham medal, in 1918. He was also an active freemason and a magistrate in Manchester from 1904; a staunch Anglican and a sidesman in his parish church where he lived in Southport, he was also at one time the Church of England representative on the Manchester school board.

West was married twice but nothing is known of his wives or the dates of his marriages. He and his second wife had two daughters and five sons, three of whom were active in his company. The eldest, Frederick, succeeded as chairman in 1922, built up the firm into an international concern, and was knighted in 1936. John West died at his home, Alton Lodge, 39 Park Crescent, Southport, on 12 January 1922. DEREK MATTHEWS

Sources *Journal of Gas Lighting* (19 Feb 1884) · *Journal of Gas Lighting* (22 May 1890) · *Journal of Gas Lighting* (13 Oct 1891) · *Journal of Gas Lighting* (17 Nov 1891) · *Journal of Gas Lighting* (8 July 1909) · *Gas Journal* (17 Feb 1920) · *Gas Journal* (21 July 1920) · *Gas Journal* (9 Nov 1921) · *Gas Journal* (18 Jan 1922) · *Gas Journal* (18 Nov 1959) · *Gas World* (29 Dec 1894) · *Gas World* (26 Feb 1898) · *Gas World* (15 July 1899) · *Gas World* (19 Nov 1904) · *Gas World* (14–20 Jan 1922) · *Southport Visiter* (14 Jan 1922) · W. T. K. Braunholtz, *The Institution of Gas Engineers: the first hundred years, 1863–1963* (1963) · b. cert. · d. cert. · *CGPLA Eng. & Wales* (1922) · D. Matthews, 'West, John', *DBB*
Likenesses photograph, repro. in Braunholtz, *Institution of Gas Engineers*, 284

Wealth at death £78,510 12s.: probate, 13 June 1922, *CGPLA Eng. & Wales*

West, Joseph (d. **1691**), army officer and colonial governor, was probably born in England, with a possible connection to the West family in Sussex. Little else is known about his early life, except that he was a London merchant before his departure for America. West served in the Royal Navy during the Second Anglo-Dutch War under the command of James Carteret. James was the son of Sir George Carteret, one of the eight proprietors of Carolina. On 27 July 1669 the lords proprietors gave West command of a small fleet and ordered him to sail from England to Port Royal, South Carolina, by way of Ireland and Barbados. This 'first fleet' arrived at its final destination in April 1670, and settled along a waterway named the Ashley River (in honour of proprietor Anthony Ashley Cooper, first Baron Ashley and first earl of Shaftesbury) at a place called Charlestown. The designated governor, William Sayle, then took command of the colony. West established residence in the settlement and soon became the proprietary shopkeeper and a member of the grand council. When Sayle died in March 1671, local leaders gave West the responsibility of governing the fledgeling colony. His wife, known only as Joanna (d. in or before 1681), joined him in Carolina in August 1671.

Historians credit West, through his rational management of material resources and people, with the early survival of the South Carolina colony. However, the proprietors were less pleased with his performance. West routinely ignored directives from London, which typically offered advice ill suited to circumstances in the nascent colony and which demanded that the settlers search for a profitable staple crop. He favoured a more practical plantation programme. As a result, the proprietors replaced West as governor, appointing Sir John Yeamans to the office in April 1672. West then returned to his position as proprietary shopkeeper and he also became the registrar of the colony's land records.

Yeamans quickly proved an unsatisfactory choice; during his administration the settlement did not become self-sufficient. Planters exported locally grown produce to the West Indies, the lords proprietors continued to supply the settlers with foodstuffs, and the governor pocketed the profits. When Yeamans died in office in August 1674, the grand council appointed West as his temporary replacement. The proprietors had already commissioned West as the permanent governor the previous April, but the slow transmission of information across the Atlantic delayed news of his official return to power.

In his second administration West again pursued the physical and economic security of the colony. In 1678 the settlement moved to a more defensible geographic position at Oyster Point. West fostered the deerskin trade and peaceable relations with the neighbouring American Indians, and he promoted agricultural and pastoral farming sufficient to meet the needs of residents and create a surplus for export. In May 1682, again dissatisfied with West's performance (he was accused of failing to suppress both trade with pirates and traffic in American Indian slaves), the proprietors of the colony commissioned a new governor named Joseph Morton. West returned to office briefly in September 1684 as a replacement elected by the council. He was later recommissioned by the proprietors, but persistent political factionalism and increasingly poor health appear to have caused him to resign as governor the following summer.

In an attempt to reverse the course of his illness, West left South Carolina for Massachusetts in late June or early July 1685. He arrived in Boston on 15 September and received visits from many of the colony's leading figures. Diarist Samuel Sewall recorded that the suffering West went to New England 'for cure of Dry Gripes', a common ailment caused by drinking rum distilled through lead pipes. Historians suggest that he may also have contracted malaria, which plagued Charlestown in 1684. The colony's governor, Simon Bradstreet, called on West ten days after his arrival in New England. In January 1686, with his health greatly improved, he dined at the governor's home. The following autumn West returned to South Carolina.

During his tenure in South Carolina West amassed a considerable fortune in land and slaves. As a cassique and landgrave he was entitled theoretically to 60,000 acres of land in the province. Records indicate that West actually owned a house and lot in Charlestown and a 130 acre plantation. He also obtained a grant for 1500 acres along the Cooper River in 1680. A magnificent illumination of the plan and grant of this property survives in the South Carolina Historical Society in Charleston. In 1685 West also owned ten African and two American Indian slaves, as well as the indentures of two male servants. After his return from Massachusetts in late 1686 West sold much of his estate. No evidence remains regarding his activities from the summer of 1687, when he left South Carolina, until his death in New York city in 1691. At this time his estate consisted of £800 of gold and silver, an enslaved girl named Moll, and an enslaved man called Will. Without a surviving wife or children, West designated the Quaker poor of London as his residual heirs.

MEAGHAN N. DUFF

Sources C. H. Lesser, *South Carolina begins: the records of a proprietary colony, 1663–1721* (1995) · C. D. Clowse, 'West, Joseph', *ANB* · St J. R. Childs, 'The naval career of Joseph West', *South Carolina Historical Magazine*, 71 (1970), 109–16 · W. J. Rivers, *A sketch of the history of South Carolina* (1856–) · R. M. Weir, *Colonial South Carolina: a history* (1983) · M. E. Sirmans, *Colonial South Carolina: a political history, 1663–1763* (Chapel Hill, NC, 1966) · L. Cheves, ed., *The Shaftesbury papers and other records relating to Carolina* (1897) · [A. S. Salley and W. N. Sainsbury], eds., *Records in the British Public Record Office relating to South Carolina*, 5 vols. (1928–47) · B. J. Osborn, 'Governor Joseph West, a seventeenth century forgotten man', *New York Genealogical and Biographical Record*, 65 (1934), 204–5

Archives South Carolina Historical Society, Charleston, land grant

Wealth at death owned two slaves at death; gold and silver coin and plate valued at over £800; appears to have sold all his land before death: Lesser, *South Carolina begins*, 416; Osborn, 'Governor Joseph West'

West, Lionel Sackville Sackville-, second Baron Sackville (1827–1908), diplomatist, born at Bourn Hall, Cambridgeshire, on 19 July 1827, was the fifth son of George John Sackville-*West, fifth Earl De La Warr (1791–1869) [*see under* West, John, first Earl De La Warr], and his wife, Lady Elizabeth (1795–1870), daughter and coheir of John Frederick Sackville, third duke of Dorset and Baroness Buckhurst, by creation in 1864. His elder brother Mortimer (1820–1888) was created Baron Sackville in 1876. Privately educated at home, Lionel served as assistant précis writer to the fourth earl of Aberdeen when secretary of state for foreign affairs in 1845, and after further employment in the Foreign Office was appointed attaché to the British legation at Lisbon in July 1847. He was transferred successively to Naples (1848), Stuttgart (1852), Berlin (1853), was promoted to be secretary of legation at Turin 1858, and was transferred to Madrid in 1864. In November 1867 he became secretary of embassy at Berlin, and in June 1868 was transferred to Paris in the same capacity with the titular rank of minister-plenipotentiary. He served under Lord Lyons throughout the exciting incidents of the Franco-Prussian War, following him to Tours when the capital was invested by the German forces, and returning with him to Paris on the conclusion of peace. He was left in charge of the British embassy during the first weeks of the commune, when the ambassador had accompanied the French ministry to Versailles. In September 1872 he was promoted to be British envoy at Buenos Aires, but remained in charge of the embassy at Paris until 7 November and did not arrive at his new post until September 1873. In January 1878 he was transferred to Madrid, where he served for over three years, acting as the plenipotentiary of Great Britain and also of Denmark in the conference which was held in 1880 to define the rights of protection exercised by foreign legations and consulates in Morocco.

In June 1881, shortly after the assassination of President Garfield, West was appointed to succeed Sir Edward Thornton as British envoy at Washington, and then entered upon the most eventful and, as it turned out, the final stage of his diplomatic career. The feeling in the United States towards Great Britain had improved since the settlement of outstanding questions provided for by the treaty of Washington in 1871, and the reception given to West was cordial. But he soon found that the influence in Congress and in the press of the Irish Fenian party formed a serious bar to the satisfactory settlement of important questions. The measures taken by the British government for the protection of life and property in Ireland after the Phoenix Park murders of 1882 caused intense excitement among sympathizers with the Fenian movement in the United States. The publication in the American press of incitements to murder and violence, and the arrests in the United Kingdom of Irish-born naturalized citizens of the United States, on a suspicion of crime, involved West in disagreeable correspondence between the two governments, and when some of those who had taken part in the Phoenix Park murders were traced and convicted, there were veiled threats against

Lionel Sackville Sackville-West, second Baron Sackville (1827–1908), by unknown photographer

the British minister's life at the time of their execution. A trip in the president's yacht was deemed a wise precaution.

The discussion of various questions connected with Canada, especially the seizure by United States cruisers of Canadian vessels engaged in the pelagic seal fishery, and the measures taken by the Canadian government to protect their fishing rights in territorial waters against incursions by United States fishermen, occupied much of West's attention in succeeding years. In June 1885 he was made KCMG. In 1887 he was called upon to discuss in conference with the United States secretary of state and the German minister the questions which had arisen in regard to the status of the Samoan archipelago, but the negotiations did not result in an agreement, and the matter was left to be settled at Berlin in 1889. In October 1887 the British government decided to send out Joseph Chamberlain on a special mission for the purpose of negotiating jointly with West and Sir Charles Tupper (the Canadian high commissioner in Britain) a treaty for the settlement of the questions connected with the fishery rights in the seas adjacent to British North America and Newfoundland. A treaty was concluded on 15 February 1888, but was not ratified by the United States senate. It was however accompanied by a provisional arrangement for a *modus vivendi* under which United States fishing vessels were admitted for two years to fishing privileges in the waters of Canada and Newfoundland on payment of a moderate licence fee; thus the risk of serious friction was for the time removed.

During the seven years of his residence at Washington, West, who was both genial and laconic, had enjoyed unqualified popularity, and had maintained excellent personal relations with the members of the United States government. Yet in the autumn of 1888 his mission was brought to an abrupt and unexpected close. In September of that year, six weeks before the presidential election, he received a letter from California purporting to be written by a British subject naturalized in the United States, expressing doubts whether the writer should vote for the re-election of President Cleveland on account of the hostile policy which the democratic president appeared to be bent on pursuing towards Canada, and asking for advice. West unguardedly answered that any political party which openly favoured Great Britain at that moment would lose in popularity, and that the Democratic Party in power were no doubt fully alive to that fact, but that he had no reason to doubt that President Cleveland if re-elected would maintain a spirit of conciliation. West was the victim of a political trick. The letter sent to him was an imposture, and on 22 October his reply was published in the *New York Tribune*, a republican paper, for the purpose of discrediting the democratic president with the Irish party. For a foreign representative to advise a United States citizen on how to vote was obviously a technical breach of international conventions. West, probably ill-advisedly, gave interviews disclaiming the statements attributed to him in the newspapers, but the United States government held them, in the absence of a published repudiation, to justify the immediate delivery to West of his passports. His mission consequently terminated on 30 October 1888, Lord Salisbury's attempts to exonerate him proving unsuccessful. Benjamin Harrison, the republican candidate, won the election. This unhappy episode ended West's diplomatic career. He formally retired on pension on 2 April 1889. He was made GCMG in September 1890.

West on the death (16 October 1888) of his elder brother Mortimer, first Baron Sackville, had succeeded to the title by special remainder a fortnight before his departure from the United States, and had inherited the historic property of Knole Park, near Sevenoaks. He passed the rest of his life at Knole, and died there on 3 September 1908.

Lord Sackville was not married. While an attaché at Stuttgart in 1852 he had made a liaison with Josefa Durán y Ortega, known as Pepita (daughter of Pedro Durán, a barber in Malaga, and his wife, Catalina Ortega, a Gypsy), whom he met during a visit to Paris; she subsequently left the stage to live with him, but, as she was a strict Catholic and already married to Juan Antonio de la Oliva, who survived her, no divorce was possible. Sackville had with her two sons and three daughters. The daughters joined him at Washington, their mother having died some years previously, in 1871, and were received there and in British society as his family. The two sons were settled on an estate in Natal. The younger, Ernest Henri Jean Baptiste Sackville-West, claimed on his father's death to be the legitimate heir to the peerage and estates, but his action, after long delays in collecting evidence on either side, was finally dismissed by the Probate Division of the High Court in February 1910. The title and entailed property consequently descended to Sackville's nephew Lionel Edward (eldest son of Lieutenant-Colonel the Hon. William Edward Sackville-West), who had married Sackville's eldest daughter, Victoria Josefa; Victoria (Vita) Sackville-*West (1892–1962) was their daughter.

T. H. SANDERSON, rev. H. C. G. MATTHEW

Sources *The Times* (4 Sept 1908) · *FO List* (1909) · L. Sackville-West, *My mission to the United States, 1881–1889* (1895) · V. Sackville-West, *Pepita* (1937) · *The letters of Queen Victoria*, ed. A. C. Benson, Lord Esher [R. B. Brett], and G. E. Buckle, 9 vols. (1907–32)
Likenesses P. A. de Laszlo, pastels, Knole, Kent · photogravure, NPG [*see illus.*]
Wealth at death £8516 8s. 8d.: probate, 3 Dec 1908, *CGPLA Eng. & Wales*

West, Nicholas (d. 1533), bishop of Ely and diplomat, was born at Putney in Surrey. His father, John West, was a baker in that town. Nicholas was educated at Eton between about 1478 and 1483, and was admitted to King's College, Cambridge, as a scholar in the latter year. He incepted as BA in 1487 and MA in 1490, having become a fellow of his college as early as 1486. While he was a scholar he was involved in some disturbance which ended in part of the provost's lodgings being set on fire, but this does not seem to have affected his career adversely. John Fisher was a contemporary on the arts course, and became a lifelong friend. West took his higher degrees in the civil law: his LLD was taken before 1500, possibly from Oxford. Sanuto's Venetian diaries allege that he studied at Bologna as well.

Early advancement The first benefice that West acquired was the rectory of Yelford in Oxfordshire, which he held from 1489 to 1498. It was another decade before decisive evidence of his future career success began to emerge. In 1499 Richard Fox, then bishop of Durham, presented him to the rectory of Egglescliffe, Durham, which he retained until his elevation to Ely. Fox then became his active patron, making him his vicar-general when he moved to the diocese of Winchester in 1501, and launching him on the beginning of his career in royal service. Other benefices rapidly followed: West was vicar of Kingston upon Thames from 1502 to about 1505; rector of Witney, Oxfordshire, from 1502; treasurer of Chichester Cathedral from early 1507; vicar of Merton, Oxfordshire, from 1508; and finally dean of St George's, Windsor, from 1509 to 1515. Like many of his successful ecclesiastical contemporaries he had become a pluralist on the grand scale, mainly in return for services rendered to the regime of Henry VII.

Fox sent West on his first foreign embassy in November 1502, when he became junior colleague to Sir Thomas Brandon on a mission to Emperor Maximilian. Two years later he became a royal councillor: on 26 November 1504 he was one of those sitting in the Star Chamber when a dispute between the merchants of the staple and the merchant adventurers was resolved. In 1505 West was the sole

ambassador negotiating a treaty with Georg, duke of Saxony, at Calais, which aimed to prevent him from protecting the Yorkist claimant Edmund de la Pole, earl of Suffolk; this was ratified at Dresden in December of that year. The following year West was one of the commissioners who negotiated the important commercial treaty with the Low Countries known as the *malus intercursus*. Within a few months he was abroad again, ratifying a treaty at Valladolid for a marriage between Henry VII and Marguerite of Savoy, sister of Philip the Fair of Castile. Although this project failed it must have marked West as a suitable marriage broker: in 1508 he was one of those deputed to assist with marriage negotiations between the Archduke Charles of Austria and Henry VII's younger daughter Mary, the treaty being signed by Henry on 8 December 1508. His final service to his royal master was a visit to France to receive Louis XII's oath to observe the treaty he had agreed in March 1509.

The accession of Henry VIII brought a short respite from the routines of diplomacy, but by November 1511 West was nominated ambassador to James IV of Scotland and travelled to York before his journey was stopped for political reasons. In February 1513 he was appointed with Lord Dacre to settle differences with the Scots: a commission to resolve border problems was established and met in June 1513, but nothing was resolved and the Scots invasion of England followed. West was then pressed into action in France again, appointed in August 1514 with Sir Thomas Docwra to take Louis XII's oath to the 1513 treaty, and to celebrate by proxy the marriage of Henry's sister Mary to Louis XII. He had scarcely returned from this journey to Paris when Louis XII died, and West was again sent, with the duke of Suffolk and Sir Richard Wingfield, to condole François I and organize a defensive alliance. He received François's oath to observe the treaty and his promise to pay the 1 million gold crowns due for the return of Tournai. It was this burst of diplomatic activity that seems to have won Nicholas West the prize of the bishopric of Ely. The temporalities were granted to him from 18 May 1515, and he was consecrated by Warham at Lambeth on 7 October.

Bishop of Ely The grant of Ely enabled West to live in the grand manner. The see was worth approximately £2000 per annum, the fourth wealthiest of the English bishoprics. Robert Steward, last prior of Ely, asserted that he had a hundred servants, and a level of largess that allowed for the feeding of 200 poor with warm meat and drink at his gate. There can, on the other hand, have been only limited evidence that Nicholas West would emerge as a committed pastor to his Ely flock. He had admittedly given some attention to his office as dean of Windsor, residing there at the beginning of Henry VIII's reign, and overseeing the work of completing the vaulting of the chapel. In 1513 he negotiated with the crown for lands granted to the chapel in fulfilment of Lady Margaret Beaufort's will. But, like his old patron Bishop Fox, he must have assumed that he was too necessary to the governmental system to be allowed to reside steadily in his see or make it the prime focus of his attention. Events in the next decade partially confirmed this view. West was on his travels again in May 1516, when he went to Scotland with Lord Dacre and Thomas Magnus, archdeacon of the East Riding, to settle a treaty. Between October 1517 and October 1518 he was deeply involved in ambassadorial work in France, and with Wolsey's spectacular negotiations for a treaty of universal peace, and two years later he was one of the essential attendants at the Field of Cloth of Gold. He was also at Wolsey's side during the Calais negotiations of the summer of 1521 with Charles V and François I. After a brief respite in the early 1520s he was made a principal negotiator of the truce between England and France which ended the second French war, and the final 'Treaty at the More', signed on 30 August 1525, seems to have owed something to his skill.

Despite these heavy commitments West showed from the beginning of his episcopate that he had absorbed lessons in more than diplomacy from Fox. He inherited a see that had been neglected by his aristocratic predecessor, James Stanley, who was noted mainly for his hunting skills and the mistress he kept at the episcopal palace of Somersham. West was resident in his diocese for significant parts of each year from 1516 and 1528, when the bishop's register (which provides most of the relevant information) ceases. Only in 1527 is there a prolonged absence that cannot be explained by diplomatic activity. The bishop conducted his primary visitation in person in 1516, complaining to Wolsey on 4 April about the disorder at Ely Priory that 'if it had not been looked upon betimes I suppose it would not have been able to have continued a monastery four years' (PRO, SP 1/13/396). He usually undertook his own ordinations, either in the diocese or at the London residence, Ely Place; moreover he adjudicated disputes about benefices in person, and his register suggests a certain interest in the learning of his clergy. Two candidates for admission to benefices were required to engage in further study, in one case to gain a better knowledge of scripture. Although no records of his sermons survive, there is the testimony of Fisher that he was a preaching as well as a resident prelate.

Problems at Cambridge West also showed a close interest in the University of Cambridge and its humanist learning. He became visitor of St John's College in the foundation statutes of 1516, and patronized John Siberch, the printer to the university, and Richard Croke, the second holder of the official lectureship in Greek. The latter dedicated his *Orationes duae* (1520) to the bishop, as a favourer of 'good letters'. As the Lutheran threat became more visible, however, West had to turn his attention from such cultural civilities to the maintenance of orthodoxy. When John Fisher offered him the dedication of *Defensio regiae assertionis* (1525), with its defence of Henry VIII's tract against Luther, he observed that West had already seen and discussed drafts of the work two years earlier and had urged him to publish. By the time Fisher finally went public his friend was already assailing heterodoxy among his clergy. In October 1525 George Giles, instituted to the Cambridgeshire parish of Little Eversden, had to take an oath additional to the usual promises of canonical obedience and residence, by which he renounced all heretical

Lutheran teaching and swore that he would neither preach nor maintain it. West's successor, Thomas Goodrich, believed that the new oath was then administered to all those instituted in the diocese, though the evidence of the episcopal registers is that it was offered selectively, probably when there was fear about the candidate's credentials. It was, for example, administered to West's own nephew, Nicholas Hawkins, who was rumoured later to have been made to recant heretical beliefs by his uncle. In 1528 West issued statutes at his diocesan synod which, among other things, forbade the use of Tyndale's translations of the scriptures and tightened control over unlicensed preaching. The latter issue was particularly sensitive for the bishop, who in 1525 had inadvertently licensed that dangerous figure Thomas Bilney to preach in the diocese. Two years later West was present at Bilney's submission before Wolsey, and his registrar duly recorded that the licence was cancelled because of heresy.

West's most noted encounter with Cambridge heterodoxy came when he confronted Hugh Latimer. Though Latimer was licensed to preach by the university, West could claim jurisdictional interest because his preaching was heard by townsmen as well. According to Cranmer's secretary Ralph Morice, he therefore appeared at a Great St Mary's sermon to judge the danger himself. After the sermon, in which Latimer had supposedly changed his theme to address the worldliness of prelates, West tried to persuade him to preach against Luther, only to be checked with the response that he knew nothing about the German's ideas since his works were banned. This elicited the retort 'well, well, Mr. Latimer I perceive that you somewhat smell of the pan, you will repent this gear one day' (BL, Harleian MS 422, fol. 85). Latimer was prohibited from preaching in the diocese, and in the university by the vice-chancellor. Wolsey then created confusion by overturning both these decisions on appeal and giving Latimer a legatine licence, asserting that he could preach on the worldliness of prelates to the bishop of Ely's beard, 'let him say what he will'. West's only resort was to preach against heresy at Barnwell Abbey on the outskirts of Cambridge.

The running sore of Cambridge heterodoxy and university independence deeply disturbed the bishop. In the aftermath of the Latimer incident his official principal, Robert Cliffe, fell foul of the vice-chancellor for attempting to discipline a cleric from Barnard Hostel for conjuring and fornication. The incident may have started as a jurisdictional mistake, but it escalated until West had excommunicated the entire senate for their opposition to his authority and Wolsey and Fisher had become deeply involved. In June 1529 Wolsey even took the extreme step of seeking a papal bull to free both universities from all forms of episcopal control, allegedly so that he could better ensure orthodoxy. Nothing came of this, and in 1531, in the reforming sessions of convocation provoked by the divorce crisis, the tables were turned when it was proposed that the bishops of Ely and Lincoln should be given full powers of visitation in their respective universities in order to root out heresy. Such a challenge to the privileges of Oxford and Cambridge was more than even convocation could stomach, and when its legislation was promulgated in 1532 there was no mention of the issue.

Last years and death Nicholas West was a chaplain to Katherine of Aragon, and the beginnings of the divorce crisis once again caught him up directly into national events. In July 1529 he offered testimony to the legatine court appointed by the papacy to consider the validity of Katherine's marriage to Henry, supporting, with some equivocation, the queen's denial that she had had sexual relations with Prince Arthur, and appealing to Rome as the only proper place for the case to be tried. West remained one of Katherine's key supporters in the next two years, and in the process incurred royal wrath. He was one of the group of eight bishops charged with *praemunire* in 1530, supposedly for their acquiescence in Wolsey's abuse of legatine power, but more significantly for their opposition to royal policy. In September 1530 Fisher, West, and Clerk of Bath and Wells took the bold step of appealing to Rome against the decisions of the 1529 parliament, especially the legislation limiting the number of benefices a cleric might hold. This led to arrest and a brief period of imprisonment for all three, perhaps the issue that broke West's resistance.

During the next eighteen months very little is known of West's movements, though he managed to attend sessions of convocation while complaining of the burden of growing ill health. He was, by curious accident, one of the rump of only three bishops who finally gave assent to the submission of the clergy in May 1532, though his continuing sympathy for Katherine is indicated by the fact that she retired from London to his house at Hatfield in August 1532. He must have felt, however, that he needed to accommodate to the new regime, for his last letters, dated from his manor of Downham in February and March 1533, address Cromwell in tones of loyal devotion previously reserved for his correspondence with Wolsey. He stressed personal connection through shared geographical origins and 'god-brothership' to trade in favours, though it is doubtful whether the new political star would have appreciated the 'token of St. Audrey, whereof you shall be sure for your life' (*LP Henry VIII*, vol. 6, no.218). West died at Downham on 28 April 1533, and was buried in the magnificent chantry chapel that he had constructed in Ely Cathedral. He died rich: the extraordinary inventory of his goods shows over 5000 ounces of silver and silver gilt, more than, for example, either the monasteries of Ely or Ramsey surrendered at the dissolution. The inventory also reveals a cultivated mind: his library consisted of approximately 250 volumes.　　　　　　　　FELICITY HEAL

Sources F. Heal, 'The bishops of Ely and their diocese, c.1515–1600', PhD diss., U. Cam., 1972 · *LP Henry VIII*, vols. 1–6 · R. Rex, *The theology of John Fisher* (1991) · 'Roberti Stewarde, prioris ultimi Eliensis, continuatio historiae Eliensis', *Anglia sacra*, ed. [H. Wharton], 1 (1691), 675–7 · CUL, Ely diocesan records, West register G/1/7 · Emden, *Cam.*, 629 · register of William Warham, LPL · *Letters of Richard Fox, 1486–1527*, ed. P. S. Allen and H. M. Allen (1929) · *CSP Venice, 1202–1509* · J. Fisher, *Defensio regiae assertionis contra Babylonicam captivitatem* (1525) · R. Croke, *Orationes duae* (Paris, 1520) · PRO, State papers domestic, Henry VIII, SP 1/13/396 · BL, Harleian MS 422 · 'Collections', *The life of Cardinal Wolsey*, ed. R. Fiddes, 2 pts in 1 vol. (1724), pt 2, pp. 1–260
Wealth at death £1665 and 5060 oz. plate (silver and silver gilt): *LP Henry VIII*, 6.625

West, Raphael Lamar (1766–1850). *See under* West, Benjamin (1738–1820).

West, Sir Raymond (1832–1912), administrator and judge in India, was born at Ballyloughrane, co. Kerry, on 18 September 1832, the elder son of Frederick Henry West, journalist, and his wife, Frances, daughter of Richard Raymond, of Ballyloughrane, Ballybunnion, co. Kerry. His father's occupation was precarious, and West's education was much neglected; but he was helped by his mother's personality and culture, and won a scholarship to Queen's College, Galway, where he graduated BA with the highest honours in 1855 (MA 1869, honorary LLD of Queen's University 1882). He entered the Bombay civil service of the East India Company as one of the second batch of 'competition-wallahs'. He arrived in India in September 1856, and was posted to the southern Maratha country, where he soon saw active service as civil officer with the force sent against the rebel Sawant clan. His experiences were of lasting value; but he was always conscientiously averse to wearing his mutiny medal in India.

West joined the judicial department in 1860, and in 1863 was appointed registrar of the new high court, where he distinguished himself in building up the judicial service, by his annotated edition of the Bombay code, *Acts and Regulations in Force in the Presidency of Bombay* (1867–8), and by his collaboration with Dr J. G. Bühler in the important *Digest of Hindu Law* (1867–9), a collection of the replies of the *shastris* (Hindu law officers attached to the former Zilla courts) to questions of Hindu law asked by the courts. The *Digest*, with its scholarly introduction and annotation, illuminates the relations of custom and revelation as sources of Hindu law, and it helped the Bombay high court steer a middle course, avoiding the exaggerated deference to revelation and the unnecessary search for 'custom' which prevailed elsewhere in India. As district judge of Kanara (1866) and as judicial commissioner in Sind (1868), West had further opportunities of carrying out his ideas of judicial organization. His tenure of the latter post was broken by two years' furlough necessitated by overwork, a 'rest' spent in omnivorous legal study and in obtaining a call to the Irish bar (King's Inns, Dublin, 1871). From 1873 to 1886 he was a puisne judge of the Bombay high court (where he had already officiated in 1871). His judgments reportedly enjoyed an authority in India not exceeded by that of any other judge, though the conservatism of some of them was criticized by Hindu reformers.

In India a continuing concern of British officials was peasant indebtedness and land loss to moneylenders, and how best to protect peasant cultivators. From the 1860s some officials rejected the *laissez-faire* policies of their predecessors and favoured state intervention. Among them was West, notably with his influential *The Law and the Land in India* (1872). Conservative, West sympathized with traditional landlords and wanted them bolstered. He believed

Sir Raymond West (1832–1912), by Lock & Whitfield, pubd 1889

peasant indebtedness and land transfer repugnant, partly for their moral and social results, including 'a widespread and corroding political demoralisation' (Charlesworth, 119). In *The Law and the Land* he claimed society was much more complex than the economists allowed for, condemned the introduction of *laissez-faire* in land ownership, and argued that, to preserve social stability, the state should have retained customary rights over land disposal. He warned that Deccan peasants were rapidly losing land to alien moneylenders. He justified pro-peasant state intervention with his concept of 'protective ownership of the state in land' (Ambirajan, 141); the state should claim part ownership of the land to protect the peasants. Partly owing to West a climate of opinion in favour of paternalist government intervention was created. Nevertheless he criticized the controversial 1879 Deccan Agriculturists' Relief Act.

West's immense and varied reading, in addition to his judicial duties, had already brought on insomnia, from which he suffered the rest of his Indian service. From 1879 he served on the Indian statute law commission at Simla; he wrote the section of its report on principles of codification, and the whole report owed much to his experience. In 1884 his services were lent to the Egyptian government as *procureur-général* to reform the judiciary, and he produced a voluminous report. The fundamental reorganization he recommended was not liked by Nubar Pasha, the prime minister, and was considered by Sir Evelyn Baring (later Lord Cromer) to make insufficient allowance for temporary political difficulties. West soon left but his proposals, though not considered immediately practicable,

were later partly implemented. Cromer later wrote that West was 'an Indian judge of distinction … of great learning and capacity' (Cromer, 288). In 1887 West became judicial member of the executive council of the governor of Bombay, and was created KCIE in 1888. In the extensive government judicial business he continued to add to his reputation, and it has been suggested that an edition of his judgments and minutes would be of even wider legal interest than his earlier work. In the purely executive work of government he was perhaps hampered by his judicial conservatism. He advocated civilian rather than military officers, claiming the former were less likely to succumb to the blandishments of Indian courts. He was among those concerned at the bad influence of such courts, alleging years of service there 'lower an officer's morale and patriotic tone' (Copland, 194). He retired in 1892.

West deserves to be remembered for his judicial eminence and for his guidance of the subordinate judiciary. English law and justice in India were exotics which required personal explanation and example to render them workable or even intelligible. It was an even greater task to build up a sound tradition, an *esprit de corps*, and, above all, an efficient system of inspection and control. To the progress of Bombay, West also contributed by his long connection with the university, culminating in his vice-chancellorship (1878 and 1886–92). He insisted on a high standard of examinations, and believed in an Indian nationalism open to the best European influences. In conversation with students his slight awkwardness disappeared and he was always ready to fire their imagination with frank talk on great subjects. He was awarded the honorary degrees of LLD by Bombay University and, in 1893, LLD by Edinburgh.

West was twice married: first in 1867 to Clementina Fergusson (d. 1896), only daughter of William Maunsell Chute, of Chute Hall, co. Kerry, with whom he had a son and three daughters; second on 12 June 1901 to Annie Kirkpatrick, eldest daughter of Surgeon-General Henry Cook MD, of Prior's Mesne, Lydney, Gloucestershire.

At Cambridge West was admitted at Downing College, and was university teacher (Indian Civil Service) in Indian law (1895–1907) and reader in Indian and Islamic law (1901–7). He was also vice-president of the Royal Asiatic Society.

West died on 8 September 1912 at his home, Chesterfield, College Road, Upper Norwood, Surrey. He was survived by his second wife.

S. V. FITZ-GERALD, rev. ROGER T. STEARN

Sources *The Times* (9 Sept 1912) · *Times of India* (March–April 1892) · W. Lee-Warher, 'Sir Raymond West', *Journal of the Royal Asiatic Society of Great Britain and Ireland* (1913), 245–50 · private information (1927) · Venn, *Alum. Cant.* · *WWW, 1897–1915* · Burke, *Peerage* (1907) · Kelly, *Handbk* (1891) · S. Ambirajan, *Classical political economy and British policy in India* (1978) · I. Copland, *The British raj and the Indian princes* (1982) · N. Charlesworth, *Peasants and imperial rule: agriculture and agrarian society in the Bombay Presidency 1850–1935* (1985) · W. Menski, *Indian legal systems past and present* (1997) · J. M. Brown, *Modern India: the origins of an Asian democracy*, 2nd edn

(1994) · earl of Cromer [E. Baring], *Modern Egypt*, 2 (1908) · P. Mansfield, *The British in Egypt* (1971)

Likenesses Lock & Whitfield, photograph, pubd 1889, NPG [*see illus.*]

Wealth at death £71,203 19s. 8d.: probate, 23 Nov 1912, *CGPLA Eng. & Wales*

West, Richard (*c.*1569–1645/6), poet, is identified by Venn and Cooper as graduating BA from Pembroke College, Cambridge, in 1588. West was ordained deacon and priest in Lincoln on 24 May 1592 and remained in Lincolnshire to hold ecclesiastical office at Thorpe (1593–1600) and Burgh in the Marsh (1605). In July 1606 *Newes from Bartholmew Fayre* appeared, of which a fragment is preserved at the Bodleian Library, Oxford. The poem is a lively description of the scenes at the fair, of the exporters supplying it, and of the public visiting the stalls and displays. This was followed, in August 1607, by *The Court of Conscience, or, Dick Whippers Sessions*. The text, dedicated to West's friend Francis Moore and to his master William Durdant, was influenced by a contemporary outbreak of satire. The author confesses his own poverty, and proceeds to denounce the profanities, conceits, and sins of his age. Dick Whipper dominates the framework of this exploration, having summoned an exemplary jury 'To be inpannled on the worser sort' (line 70). After illuminating society's major short falls his valedictory gestures are, however, conciliatory:

> But my desire is that we may bee friends,
> And all the world leave their disorder quite,
> If you do so, ile make you all amends,
> Ile breake my corde, and fling away my whip
> (sig. [E4]v)

In 1619 a new edition of Francis Seagar's *School of Vertue*, previously issued in 1557, appeared with a second part by West. The work was intended to regulate the behaviour of children in a variety of social environments. Commonly known as the 'Booke of demeanour' it was reprinted in 1677 and in 1680. In 1868 F. J. Furnivall included its secular precepts, together with 'The babees book' and other similar treatises, in a volume edited for the Early English Text Society. One other work has been attributed to West: *The Wits A.B.C., or, A Centurie of Epigrams*, which was printed, as a first experiment in verse, in April 1608. West died in Lincolnshire in 1645 or 1646.

E. I. CARLYLE, rev. ELIZABETH HARESNAPE

Sources Venn, *Alum. Cant.* · Cooper, *Ath. Cantab.* · *STC, 1475–1640* · Arber, *Regs. Stationers*, 3.326, 358 · R. West, *The court of conscience, or, Dick Whippers sessions* (1607) · T. Corser, *Collectanea Anglo-poetica, or, A … catalogue of a … collection of early English poetry*, 11, Chetham Society, 111 (1883), 377–82 · F. J. Furnivall, ed., *The babees book and other tracts on nurture and manners* (1868)

West, Richard (*c.*1691–1726), lord chancellor of Ireland, was the eldest son of Richard West, a London merchant. Some sources, including O'Flanagan, suggest that he was born in 1670, but a later date is more likely, since he entered the Inner Temple in 1708 and was called to the English bar on 13 June 1714. In April that year he had married Elizabeth (1692–1748), daughter of Gilbert *Burnet, bishop of Salisbury; they had a son, Richard *West, and a daughter, Molly.

In addition to the impeccable whig credentials derived from his marriage, West was clearly a man of remarkable legal ability, being appointed king's counsel after only three years of practice, on 21 October 1717. He was made a bencher of the Inner Temple in the following year, although on the understanding that he was to have neither chambers in the inn nor a claim to the office of treasurer. Also in 1718, he was appointed standing counsel to the Board of Trade. He was the first appointee to this important post, which made him a legal adviser to the government on matters concerning colonial trade.

While at the bar West published some political pamphlets, including *A Discourse Concerning Treasons and Bills of Attainder* (1716) and *An Enquiry into the Origin and Manner of Creating Peers* (1719), in which he argued in support of the 1719 Peerage Bill. These pamphlets 'attracted much notice, and gave him strong claims to Government patronage' (O'Flanagan, 39). Accordingly, West was returned in the whig interest for the Cornish borough of Grampound in a by-election on 13 March 1721, and for the neighbouring borough of Bodmin in the general election of 1722.

West appears to have been fairly active in parliament, speaking on matters as diverse as army increases and elections in the City of London. His most important political role was, however, as one of the managers of the trial of Thomas Parker, first earl of Macclesfield, in 1725. In a 'masterly' speech (Ball, 102), delivered on 11 May, he summed up the case for impeachment with great skill and vigour, and was scathing in his condemnation of the lord chancellor's corruption and avarice (*State trials*, 16.1057–80).

West's legal reputation was in no way dulled by his foray into politics. In 1724 he was considered for both the Irish chief justiceship of the common pleas and the recordership of London. In the end, however, he was appointed lord chancellor of Ireland, receiving his patent on 23 July 1725. Ball considers his appointment fully justified, describing him as 'a man of brilliant talents, of which he had given proof by a phenomenally rapid rise in his profession' (Ball, 102). Burke, on the other hand, says his only qualification for the post was that he was a 'pamphleteering partizan' (Burke, 119), although in the light of his previous legal and political successes this is clearly unfair.

It cannot be denied, however, that West's elevation owed much to his politics and to his friendship with Hugh Boulter, archbishop of Armagh. Boulter was strongly of the view that English dominance in Ireland could be maintained only by appointing men of English birth to the great Irish offices of state. Disconcerted by the recent appointment of Thomas Carter, an Irishman, to the mastership of the rolls, Boulter lobbied strenuously for the placing of an Englishman on the Irish woolsack. As a friend of Thomas Pelham-Holles, duke of Newcastle, and one of the three lords justices of Ireland, he exerted considerable influence on crown appointments, and so it was that West became head of the Irish judiciary.

West's brief tenure of the Irish lord chancellorship was fairly unremarkable, although he apparently acquired a considerable understanding of Ireland and her people, and 'he appears … to have given much satisfaction' in the execution of his office (Burke, 119). It was his duty, as head of the Irish courts of equity, to administer the Irish parliament's penal laws against Catholics. West had previously shown some sympathy with the plight of English Catholics. In 1723, for instance, he had twice spoken against a bill which sought to raise £100,000 from Catholic subjects. This sympathy was also discernible in some of his judgments from the woolsack. Thus he ruled that under the statute 9 William III c. 28 there had to be a conviction before any property could be forfeited, and it was not unknown for him to deprive protestant plaintiffs of their costs where the action, though legally required to succeed, was plainly unfair. None the less, West was by no means a champion of the Catholic cause—had he been, he would hardly have acquired high Irish office—and some of his judgments reflect the protestant zeal prevalent at the time. Thus in *Leymore* v. *Burke* he held that:

> [the] Protestant who marries a Popish wife is a more odious Papist than a real and actual Papist in profession and principle … the Acts against the growth of Popery, expressing *every Papist or person professing the Popish religion*, &c., take in and regard *constructive*, as well as *actual*, Papists. (Howard, 1.261)

West continued his literary endeavours during his chancellorship, and in 1726 he published a tragedy, *The Hecuba*. It was performed at the Theatre Royal in Drury Lane, London, but was not well received, a fact attributed by West to the gods' intimidation of the actresses and audience.

West had been in office for less than a year and a half when he succumbed to 'a fever of the most malignant type' (Burke, 119). It was hoped to the last that he would recover, but after twelve days' illness he died in Dublin on the afternoon of 3 December 1726. Archbishop Boulter wrote that 'his death is very much lamented by all here, but especially by the lawyers, whose good-will and esteem he had entirely gained, by his patience, civility, and great abilities' (ibid.). He was buried in St Anne's, Dublin, on 6 December.

West's death gave rise to some suspicion, and there were rumours to the effect that his wife, having taken West's secretary John Williams as her lover, had poisoned her husband. The rumours were never substantiated, however, and in fact Williams went on to marry West's daughter. On his death, West left 'little more than would answer his debts on both sides of the water' (Cruickshanks), but through the exertions of Boulter and John Carteret, second Baron Carteret, a state pension of £250 per annum was granted to his widow.

NATHAN WELLS

Sources J. R. O'Flanagan, *The lives of the lord chancellors and keepers of the great seals of Ireland*, 2 (1870) · O. J. Burke, *The history of the lord chancellors of Ireland from AD 1186 to AD 1874* (1879) · F. E. Ball, *The judges in Ireland, 1221–1921*, 2 (New York, 1927) · E. Cruickshanks, 'West, Richard', HoP, *Commons, 1715–54* · *DNB* · C. J. Smyth, *Chronicle of the law officers of Ireland* (1839) · F. A. Inderwick and R. A. Roberts, eds., *A calendar of the Inner Temple records*, 3 (1901) · Sainty, *King's counsel* · *Catalogue of the paintings, engravings, serjeant's rings … etc. belonging to the Honourable Society of the Inner Temple* (1915) · Holdsworth, *Eng. law*, vol. 12 · Cobbett, *Parl. hist.*, vol. 8 · J. E. Martin, ed., *Masters of the bench of the Hon. Society of the Inner Temple, 1450–1883, and masters of the Temple, 1540–1883* (1883) · *Report on manuscripts in various collections*, 8 vols., HMC, 55 (1901–14), vol. 6, pp. 55–6 · G. E. Howard, *A treatise on the rules and practice of the equity side of the exchequer in Ireland*, 2 vols. (1760)

Likenesses attrib. J. Richardson, oils, *c.*1725, NPG · oils, Inner Temple, London

Wealth at death hardly enough to cover debts: O'Flanagan, *Lives*; Cruickshanks, 'West, Richard'

West, Richard (1716–1742), poet, was the only son of Richard *West (*c.*1691–1726), lawyer, playwright, and politician, and Elizabeth Burnet (1692–1748), daughter of Gilbert *Burnet. He was educated at Eton College with Thomas Ashton, Thomas Gray, and Horace Walpole, forming a 'quadruple alliance' of friendship, and was known among them as Favonius. In youth he was 'tall and slim, of a pale and meagre look and complexion' (*Works of Thomas Gray*, 1.cv), and he was then reckoned a more brilliant genius than Gray (Mason, 3). The rest of the friends went to Cambridge, but West matriculated from Christ Church, Oxford, on 22 May 1735 at the age of nineteen.

West was from his youth marked out for the profession of the bar, through the influential positions of his father and his uncle, Sir Thomas Burnet, and he was admitted a student at the Inner Temple between November 1732 and November 1733 (*Calendar of Inner Temple Records*). On 21 February 1738 he was at Dartmouth Street, Westminster; by the following April he had left Oxford, and was studying at the Inner Temple. Gray went to London in September 1738 to join him at the bar, but was drawn off into travelling to France and Italy with Horace Walpole. West wearied of legal study, and moved out of lodgings at the Inner Temple in June 1740. West wrote to Gray from Bond Street to inform him of his move (5 June 1740); Gray wrote back from Florence (16 July 1740), encouraging West to persevere with the law (*Correspondence of Thomas Gray*, 1.164, 167–70). West then thought of the army as a profession, but his strength was failing, and in September 1741 Gray found his friend ill and weary in London.

In March 1742 West was at Pope's (or Popes), 2 miles to the west of Hatfield in Hertfordshire, the seat of David Mitchell. He wrote to Gray from Pope's (4 April 1742), enclosing Latin verses he wrote at 4 a.m., being unable to sleep for chronic coughing (*Correspondence of Thomas Gray*, 1.189–91). He died at Pope's of 'a consumption' (Horace Walpole, letter to Sir Horace Mann, 24 June 1742, Walpole, *Corr.*, 17.468–9) on 1 June 1742. He was buried in the chancel of Hatfield church, immediately before the altar-rails, and a gravestone to his memory was placed in the floor. Thomas Ashton wrote an elegy on his death, which was printed in the *London Magazine* in June 1742 (11.305). The elegy was later reprinted in the *European Magazine* in January 1798 (7.45). Before reading of West's death, Gray sent him a letter enclosing his 'Ode on the Spring'. This letter was returned unopened. In response to West's death Gray wrote an English sonnet ('In vain to me the smiling mornings shine') and elegiac verses in Latin with which he abruptly concluded 'De principiis cogitandi', a poem addressed to West.

Most of West's small output of poetry was enclosed in

letters to Gray. 'Ad amicos', an imitation of Tibullus (book 3, elegy 5) was sent from Christ Church, Oxford (4 July 1737). An elegiac epistle in heroic couplets, it describes the poet's isolation and anticipates his early death in obscurity. He expresses the desire only to raise his tomb in the breasts of his friends. Two Latin elegies were sent in later letters, and an 'Ode to May' ('Dear Gray, that always in my heart') on 5 May 1742. The 'Ode to May', which invokes Gray to join West in summoning the 'tardy May' to resume her reign, produced Gray's 'Ode on the Spring' in response. These poems by West were published in Robert Anderson's collection (1795; 10.237–9). West also wrote a 'Monody on the Death of Queen Caroline', which was published in Robert Dodsley's *Collection of Poems by Several Hands* (1748; 2.269–75). Gray and John Mitford both intended to collect and publish West's remains, but did not carry out their projects. West's works are included in section 2 of Duncan C. Tovey's *Gray and his Friends* (1890).

West's letters to Gray were first published in Mason's edition of *The Poems of Mr. Gray* (1775). The standard modern edition is *Correspondence of Thomas Gray*, ed. Paget Toynbee and Leonard Whibley (3 vols., 1935; with corrections and additions by H. W. Starr, 1971, vol. 1). West's letters to Walpole and Ashton, in addition to those to Gray, were published in *The Correspondence of Gray, Walpole, West and Ashton* (ed. Paget Toynbee, 2 vols., 1915). The standard edition of West's letters to and from Walpole is *Horace Walpole's Correspondence* (ed. W. S. Lewis, vol. 13, ed. George L. Lam and Charles H. Bennett, 1948, 90–250). Appendix 6 (14.249–55) of the Lam and Bennett volume also includes extant parts of West's unfinished play *Pausanias*.

West's premature death limited his writings to a small number of poems. But Edmund Gosse commented that they 'are of sufficient merit to permit us to believe that had he lived he might have achieved a reputation among the minor poets of his age' (Gosse, 5). As it is, his name lives in his friend Gray's poetry, and in his letters to the members of the Quadruple Alliance.

W. B. HUTCHINGS

Sources W. Mason, 'Memoirs', *The poems of Mr Gray: to which are prefixed memoirs of his life and writings by W. Mason* (1775) · D. C. Tovey, ed., *Gray and his friends: letters and relics in great part hitherto unpublished* (1890), section 2 · *The correspondence of Gray, Walpole, West and Ashton*, ed. P. Toynbee, 2 vols. (1915) · *Correspondence of Thomas Gray*, ed. P. Toynbee and L. Whibley, 3 vols. (1935) · *The works of Thomas Gray*, another edn, ed. J. Mitford, 2 (1816) · F. A. Inderwick and R. A. Roberts, eds., *A calendar of the Inner Temple records*, 4 (1933), 279 · Walpole, *Corr.*, 13.90–250, 17.468–9 · *The letters of Horace Walpole, earl of Orford*, ed. P. Cunningham, 9 vols. (1861–6) · D. H., *GM*, 1st ser., 72 (1802), 492–3 · E. W. Gosse, *Gray*, English Men of Letters (1882) · Foster, *Alum. Oxon.*

Archives BL, letters to Thomas Ashton, MS 32562 [copies]

West, Robert (*b.* 1649, *d.* in or after **1684**), lawyer and conspirator, was born in December 1649 and baptized on 30 December in Banbury, Oxfordshire, the eldest surviving son of James West (*bap.* 1614, *d.* 1684), mercer and rising townsman of Banbury, and his wife, Bridget Bentley (*bap.* 1616, *d.* 1696). On 1 December 1665, aged fifteen, he matriculated from Magdalen College, Oxford, where he was a demy until 1668. On 27 October that year he was admitted

to Gray's Inn; he was called to the bar in 1674. At an unknown date he married Sarah, daughter of Thomas Cox.

The native of a proverbially puritan town West became keenly active in radical and dissenting politics. According to Bishop Gilbert Burnet he was 'a witty and active man, full of talk, and believed to be a determined atheist' (Burnet, 2.357). A member of the Green Ribbon Club he was probably the Robert West who signed the May 1679 whig petition presented to London's court of aldermen calling for a parliament and a redress of the nation's grievances. In March 1681, amid fears of popish plotting, he was questioned by the authorities for allegedly spreading the rumour that Holborn would be burned and that the streets would run with blood. On 15 June West transferred to the Middle Temple and in August he and fellow whig lawyer Aaron Smith were employed by the earl of Shaftesbury as counsel for the infamous 'Protestant Joiner', Stephen College, during his trial for treason at Oxford. In Oxford West lodged with John Locke at the home of the mathematician John Wallis. In November 1682, like so many radicals, West armed himself by having a sword made by a sword-cutler in Fleet Street.

By the spring of 1683 West had become deeply involved in the radical underground, planning a general insurrection and the capture of the Tower of London. He even hid the duke of Monmouth in his chambers. In June 1683 West was implicated in the Rye House plot to assassinate Charles II and his brother, James, duke of York. He was arrested shortly after Josiah Keeling revealed the plot to authorities on 12 June. He readily gave evidence against his former friends, writing to the earl of Rochester on 22 June that he was resolved to 'unburden my soul to you or the Secretary or Council as I shall be required and to be ingenuous' (*CSP dom.*, *1683*, 334). The duke of Ormond described 'West the lawyer' to the earl of Arran as 'a man of quick wit and fluent tongue' (*Ormonde MSS*, 65). Along with Colonel John Rumsey, West turned king's evidence. During interrogations between 23 and 27 June he told a story of how London whigs had contrived two plans to prevent the accession of the Catholic duke of York and what they believed would be the consequent introduction of popery and arbitrary government. One plan was to raise a general insurrection throughout England and another was to assassinate the king and duke of York in their coaches at Rye House mill as they returned from Newmarket. West was also aware of whig efforts to engage Scottish dissidents gathered around the ninth earl of Argyll. West's main connections were with Robert Ferguson, John Wildman, Richard Goodenough, Richard Rumbold, Nathaniel Wade, Richard Nelthorp, and above all, Colonel Rumsey, who was the godfather of West's son. He claimed little contact with the so-called 'Protestant Lords' concerned in the plotting, who, he understood from Ferguson, were the duke of Monmouth, William, Lord Russell, Lord Grey of Werk, and Lord Howard of Escrick. Burnet believed that Rumsey and West, who were 'perpetually together', forged the story of the Rye House assassination plan and that when they started contradicting each other Rumsey charged West 'with concealing some things'. Thus West was 'laid in irons and was threatened with being hanged. For three days he would eat nothing, and seemed resolved to starve himself, but nature overcame his resolutions and then told all he knew and perhaps more than he knew' (*State trials*, 9.498, 503). It is true that Rumsey accused West of not revealing all that he knew and gave the authorities a list of questions to be put to West. But West confessed few new details, and his story remained similar to others told amid the interrogations and trials. His testimony, along with the testimony of Rumsey and Lord Howard, was later used to convict Captain Thomas Walcott, an associate of the earl of Shaftesbury, on 12 July, and Algernon Sidney, on 21 November, of treason for their participation in the plot. Both were executed. West was pardoned of all treasonable activity on 5 December 1684. Nothing more is known of him: he did not join the Monmouth rebellion in the spring of 1685 nor did he participate in the revolution of 1688–9.

MELINDA ZOOK

Sources J. S. W. Gibson, ed., *Baptism and burial registers of Banbury, Oxfordshire*, pts 1–2, Banbury Historical Society, 7 (1965–6); 9 (1968) • Foster, *Alum. Oxon.* • J. Foster, *Register of admissions to Gray's Inn, 1521–1881* (privately printed, London, 1887), 305 • H. A. C. Sturgess, ed., *Register of admissions to the Honourable Society of the Middle Temple, from the fifteenth century to the year 1944*, 1 (1949), 203 • *State trials*, 9.358–666 • *CSP dom.*, 1679–85 • N. Luttrell, *A brief historical relation of state affairs from September 1678 to April 1714*, 1 (1857), 266–7, 289 • E. M. Thompson, ed., *Correspondence of the family of Hatton*, 2 vols., CS, new ser., 22–3 (1878), vol. 2, p. 24 • *Calendar of the manuscripts of the marquess of Ormonde*, new ser., 8 vols., HMC, 36 (1902–20), vol. 7, pp. 54, 65 • R. L. Greaves, *Secrets of the kingdom: British radicals from the Popish Plot to the revolution of 1688–89* (1992) • R. Greaves, 'Robert West (*fl.* 1680–1685)', Greaves & Zaller, *BDBR* • M. Zook, *Radical whigs and conspiratorial politics in late Stuart England* (Pennsylvania, 1999), 11, 25, 102–3, 105, 110, 200 • R. Ashcraft, *Revolutionary politics and Locke's two treatises of government* (1986), 346–7, 360–70, 379, 391–3, 395–6, 403, 433 • *Bishop Burnet's History*
Archives BL, Bridgman's collection, Lansdowne MSS 1, 152A • BL, Middleton collection, Add. MSS 41809–41821

West, Robert (*d.* 1770), drawing-master, was born in Waterford, Ireland, the son of a city alderman, and studied in Paris with François Boucher and Carle Vanloo. He then started a drawing school in George's Lane, Dublin, and in 1744 was employed by the Dublin Society to teach twelve boys there. When the society established its own drawing school in Shaw's Court, off Dame Street, in 1757, West was appointed the first master. Many of his pupils went on to become well-known artists. He suffered a mental breakdown, and in 1763 was replaced by a former pupil, Jacob Ennis. On Ennis's death in 1770, West was reappointed, but died in Dublin in the same year. His drawing of Lawrence Richardson was engraved in mezzotint by R. Purcell in 1748 and published in Dublin.

His son **Francis Robert West** (*c.*1749–1809), drawing-master, also studied in Paris as a pupil of Vanloo, and worked in the French Academy. On 11 October 1770 he succeeded his father as master of the Dublin School of Design; his pupils included the portrait painter Martin Archer Shee. A talented draughtsman in crayon, Francis

West painted little in oils. Ten plates of moral emblems were engraved after his designs. He died in Dublin on 24 January 1809. The National Gallery of Ireland holds six portraits in charcoal and pastel by F. R. West.

Robert Lucius West (*d.* 1849), drawing-master, was the son of Francis, and acted for some years as his father's assistant. On his father's death he succeeded to the mastership of the school, which he retained for about forty years. He painted portraits and historical subjects, and in 1808 exhibited at the Royal Academy, London, a work inspired by Thomas Gray's *Elegy*. He was a member of the Irish Society of Artists, and on the foundation of the Royal Hibernian Academy in 1823 was one of the original academians. He died in early 1849.

F. M. O'DONOGHUE, *rev.* ANNE PIMLOTT BAKER

Sources W. G. Strickland, *A dictionary of Irish artists*, 2 vols. (1913) • Redgrave, *Artists* • A. Pasquin [J. Williams], *An authentic history of the professors of painting, sculpture, and architecture who have practiced in Ireland … to which are added, Memoirs of the royal academicians* [1796] • Bryan, *Painters* • R. N. James, *Painters and their works*, 3 vols. (1896–7) • A. Le Harivel, ed., *National Gallery of Ireland: illustrated summary catalogue of drawings, watercolours and miniatures* (1983)
Likenesses M. W. Peters, self-portrait, charcoal drawing, 1758 (with Robert West), NPG • F. R. West, portrait; known to have been at the Royal Hibernian Academy, 1913 • R. L. West, portrait (West, Francis Robert); known to be at the Royal Hibernian Academy, 1899 • R. L. West, self-portrait, miniature; known to be NG Ire, 1899

West, Robert Lucius (*d.* 1849). *See under* West, Robert (*d.* 1770).

West [*née* Cooke], **Sarah** (1790x95–1876), actress, the only daughter of Isaac Cooke, a master upholsterer and amateur actor in Bath, and his wife, Martha, was born in Bath either in 1790 or in 1791 (she died aged eighty-five, according to her death certificate) or on 22 March 1795. Her mother was descended from a Gloucestershire family. Her cousin was the actress Harriet Cooke, later Waylett. On 22 May 1810 she appeared, not very successfully, at the Bath Theatre, for the benefit of her actor uncle James, as Miss Hardcastle in *She Stoops to Conquer*. In the next year at the same house she was Emily Tempest in the *Wheel of Fortune*. In the summer of 1812 she played at Cheltenham and Gloucester under Watson. She was seen by Charles and Maria Kemble, who formed a very favourable opinion of her and recommended her to Harris at Covent Garden, where she made her London début on 28 September 1812 as Desdemona. Various roles followed with mixed success, Oxberry saying that 'she somewhat bordered on the mawkish'. Next season she was Fanny Sterling in the *Clandestine Marriage* and the first Georgiana in *Folly as it Flies*. She moved to Edinburgh where she was Juliet on 10 November 1814 for ten nights in succession. The coldness of Scottish criticism was thawed into a tide of approbation. In March 1815 in the English church in Edinburgh she married William West [*see below*], a musician and comic actor who played simple lads and country boys. Stanzas by 'J. M.' on her Edinburgh performances were printed in Oxberry's *Dramatic Biography*. She proceeded to Bath where she remained for two seasons, in a variety of parts, enjoying patronage and many friendships. On 17

Sarah West (1790x95–1876), by Thomas Woolnoth, pubd 1820 (after Thomas Charles Wageman)

September 1818 she made, as Desdemona, her first appearance at Drury Lane with Elliston. Leading parts, mostly tragic, were assigned to her. Sarah Siddons and Elizabeth Kemble publicly expressed high appreciation of her rendering of Belvidera in *Venice Preserv'd*. She supported Kean in many parts. In October 1818 she was Lady Macbeth to his Macbeth, but he remarked that he did not think she would shine in characters of that class although she was excellent in the tender parts. She spoke eloquently on 31 October 1820 at the family benefit for Alexander Rae with whom she and Kean had appeared in *Lear*. From 1820 to 1828 at Drury Lane, with occasional appearances at the Haymarket, she played many different parts, some original. After this time her recorded performances were scanty. In 1835 she was at Covent Garden under Osbaldiston playing only secondary parts. Thereafter she was at minor theatres or in the country. Her last London engagement was at the Marylebone about 1847. She parted early from her husband, with whom she had two sons. She died on 30 December 1876 at 24 St George's Road, Glasgow, the house of her great-nephew Henry Courte Cooke, and was buried at Sighthill cemetery on 2 January 1877.

Sarah West was of average size, had eloquent eyes, a transparent skin, and brown, luxuriant hair. She was said to be the most beautiful woman of whom the stage of the time could boast and a fine tragic actress. She was, however, not at her best in parts which called for passions other than love. Her Lady Macbeth was tame and unreal, and she was accused of 'ranting' in her later career. In comic parts she was refined but only moderately humorous.

William West [*called* the Father of the Stage] (1797/8–1888), actor and composer, lived to be called the Father of the Stage. His father was connected with Drury Lane. After studying music under Thomas Welsh and C. E. Horn he appeared at the Haymarket in 1805 as Tom Thumb. He then at Drury Lane played parts such as Juba in the *Prize* and Boy in *Children in the Wood*. In 1814 he followed Sarah Cooke to Edinburgh, and the next year married her in the teeth of much competition. His first appearance in Edinburgh was on 10 November 1814 as Don Carlos in the *Duenna*. After playing in Bath and Bristol he appeared in London at the East London Theatre, and on 9 May 1822 at Drury Lane played Lord Ogleby in the *Clandestine Marriage*. He also acted at the Olympic and other theatres. He gave in 1842 an entertainment illustrative of the clowns of Shakespeare. For some time he was a teacher of music. He died at 45 Tavistock Crescent, Kensington, London, on 30 January 1888, aged ninety. His most popular songs were 'When love was fresh from her cradle-bed', 'Alice of Fyfe', and 'Love and the Sensitive Plant'. His glees included 'The Ocean King', 'Up Rosalie', 'Oh, Bold Robin Hood', and 'The Haaf Fishers'. He was also responsible for a sonata entitled 'Maid Marian' and *An Ancient English Morris Dance with Variations*. JOSEPH KNIGHT, *rev.* J. GILLILAND

Sources Mrs C. Baron-Wilson, *Our actresses*, 2 vols. (1844) · 'Memoir of Mrs W. West', *Theatrical Inquisitor, and Monthly Mirror*, 13 (1818), 403–4 · *Oxberry's Dramatic Biography*, 2/20 (1825) · *The life and reminiscences of E. L. Blanchard, with notes from the diary of Wm. Blanchard*, ed. C. W. Scott and C. Howard, 2 vols. (1891) · Genest, *Eng. stage* · *The biography of the British stage, being correct narratives of the lives of all the principal actors and actresses* (1824) · [J. Roach], *Authentic memoirs of the green-room* [1814] · W. C. Russell, *Representative actors* (*c*.1875) · Boase, *Mod. Eng. biog.* · *The Era* (7 Jan 1877)

Likenesses C. Baugniet, lithograph, 1843, NPG · H. R. Cook, stipple (after W. Foster, 1813), BM · H. Cooper, stipple (after R. Drummond), BM; repro. in *The Drama* · T. Woolnoth, stipple vignette (after T. C. Wageman), NPG; repro. in *London Magazine*, 1 (1820) [*see illus.*] · engraving, repro. in *Lady's Monthly Museum*, new ser., 14 (1813), 121 · engraving, repro. in *La Belle Assemblée*, new ser., 18 (1818), 243 · portrait, repro. in *Actors by Daylight* (28 April 1883) · portraits, Harvard TC · print, Garr. Club · two portraits, repro. in *Oxberry's Dramatic Biography*

West, Temple (*bap.* 1715, *d.* 1757), naval officer, was baptized at St Martin-in-the-Fields, Westminster, on 27 March 1715. He was the son of Richard West (1687?–1716), archdeacon of Berkshire, and his wife, Maria (*d.* 1763), eldest daughter of the politician Sir Richard Temple and sister of Richard Temple, Viscount Cobham, and Hester, Countess Temple, wife of Richard Grenville, Earl Temple. These links bound him closely to the Grenville 'cousinhood' that was growing in political power at this time. The author and translator Gilbert *West was his elder brother.

West entered the navy in September 1727 as a volunteer per order on board the *Revenge*, with Captain Conningsby Norbury, in the fleet at Gibraltar under Sir Charles Wager. In July 1728 he was moved into the *Canterbury* with Captain Edmund Hook, on the home station and in the Mediterranean, and as volunteer and midshipman continued in her for over three years. In 1733 he was in the *Dursley Galley* with Captain Thomas Smith. He passed his examination on 21 December 1733. Two months later, on 23 February 1734, he was promoted to be third lieutenant of the *Dorsetshire*, from which in May he was moved to the *Norfolk*. On 7

April 1736 he became second lieutenant on the *Gloucester*. On 14 May of the following year he was promoted to be commander of the sloop *Alderney*. On 6 June he married Frances Balchin (1710–1793). In June 1738 West was posted to the frigate *Deal Castle*, which he commanded in the channel or on the coast of Portugal until February 1741, when he was moved to the *Sapphire*, and from her in April to the *Dartmouth*, one of the ships with Rear-Admiral Nicholas Haddock in the Mediterranean.

On 3 June 1743 Haddock's successor, Vice-Admiral Mathews, moved West into the sixty-gun ship *Warwick*, which he commanded in the action off Toulon on 11 February 1744. The *Stirling Castle*, followed by the *Warwick*, formed the head of the British line, and both ships kept aloof from the French, firing on them from a distance. The ships astern did the same, and thus in the van there was no close action. At the time there was no criticism of either West or Captain Cooper of the *Stirling Castle*, but West was called to give evidence to the House of Commons inquiry into the battle on 28 March 1745. Although he was in the van and the main subject of the inquiry was Vice-Admiral Lestock's failure to bring the rear division into close action, he did venture the opinion that all the officers he had spoken to, except Lestock's flag captain, blamed the vice-admiral for failing to intercept the rear of the Franco-Spanish line. A month after Lestock's court martial and acquittal in June 1745, West was dismayed to find that Lestock had charged him and Cooper with disobedience in failing to engage the enemy van closely. Both officers were brought to a court martial. After five days' hearings, West's court martial ended on 13 December 1745. Notwithstanding his defence, like Cooper's, that he had had to keep to windward of the French van to prevent it from tacking around the front of the British line and doubling the leading ships, he was found guilty of not keeping to the line of battle and was cashiered. Although he was certainly in breach of the fighting instructions and article eleven of the articles of war, his actions were probably correct under the circumstances of the battle. This and the powerful political support of the Grenvilles earned West and Cooper a reinstatement by order in council in 1746.

In 1747 West commanded the *Devonshire*, as flag captain to Rear-Admiral Peter Warren in the action off Cape Finisterre on 3 May. In 1748 he was commodore and commander-in-chief at the Nore. During the peace he remained on shore, and was for a short time (January 1753–April 1754) MP for Buckingham, on the accession of his cousin, Richard Grenville, to the peerage as Earl Temple. He did not stand again in the general election of 1754. On 4 February 1755 he was promoted rear-admiral of the red, and during the summer commanded a small squadron in the Bay of Biscay. In the following spring, with his flag in the *Buckingham*, he went out to the Mediterranean as second in command, with Admiral John Byng. In the action near Minorca, on 20 May, he had command of the van, which did engage closely, and, being left unsupported, received a good deal of damage. He was afterwards summarily superseded and recalled to England, but no

blame was attached to him and he was released while Byng was taken into custody to face a court martial.

The Grenville 'cousinhood' were important supporters of William Pitt and when Pitt came to power with the duke of Devonshire on 15 November 1756, West was nominated a member of the Board of Admiralty, of which his cousin, Lord Temple, was the head. On 8 December he was promoted to be vice-admiral of the blue, and shortly afterwards he was appointed to command a squadron on particular service. He hoisted his flag in the *Magnanime*, but despite having given evidence against Byng at the admiral's court martial, he none the less refused to 'serve on terms which subject an officer to the treatment shown Admiral Byng'. He accordingly struck his flag. He was dissuaded by Temple from resigning his seat on the Admiralty board, despite Byng's execution on 14 March 1757, until the Pitt–Devonshire ministry was dismissed in early April 1757. With Pitt's return to power in July he resumed his seat on the Admiralty board, but only for a few weeks, dying on 9 August. He was buried at St John's, West Wickham, Kent, on 15 August 1757. He was survived by his wife, who died on 27 January 1793. His grandson, Sir John *West, had a distinguished naval career, being made admiral of the fleet in 1858.

J. K. LAUGHTON, *rev.* RICHARD HARDING

Sources PRO, Adm 1/2652 (1736–40); Adm 1/2653 (1741–3); Adm 1/2654 (1744) · captains' letters, PRO, Adm 1/2655 (1745) · courts martial reports, PRO, Adm 1/5282 · warrant and commissions books, PRO, Adm 6/13; Adm 6/16 · lieutenants' passing certificates, PRO, Adm 107/3 · admiralty minute book 19/11/1756–16/1/1758, PRO, Adm 3/65 · seniority list, PRO, Adm 6/424 · will, PRO, PROB 11/833, sig. 290 · *Augustus Hervey's journal*, ed. D. Erskine, 2nd edn (1954), 237, 311 · H. Walpole, *Memoirs of King George II*, ed. J. Brooke, 3 vols. (1985) · Philip Yorke's 'Parliamentary Journal', 1743–5, BL, Add. MS 35337 · R. S. Lea, 'West, Temple', HoP, *Commons, 1715–54* · J. V. Beckett, *The rise and fall of the Grenvilles: dukes of Buckingham and Chandos, 1710 to 1921* (1994), 9
Archives Hydrographic Office, Taunton, Admiralty Library, letter-book · Royal Naval Museum, Portsmouth, letter-book
Likenesses bust on monument, Westminster Abbey
Wealth at death see will, PRO, PROB 11/833, sig. 290

West, Thomas, eighth Baron West and ninth Baron de la Warr (1472–1554), soldier and courtier, was the son and heir of Thomas West, seventh Baron West and eighth Baron de la Warr (1448–1525), and his first wife, Elizabeth, daughter of Hugh Mortimer of Mortimer's Hall, Hampshire, where West was probably born. The younger Thomas was made a knight of the Bath on 29 November 1489, the occasion of the creation of Henry VII's son Arthur as prince of Wales, and in 1492 he may have been admitted to Gray's Inn. By August 1494 he had married Elizabeth (*b.* 1474), daughter of Sir John Bonville of Halnaker, Sussex. It was through her that West inherited Halnaker in 1498, which was to be his seat for forty years.

West attended the funeral of Henry VII and was a server at the coronation of Henry VIII, and for the first twenty years of the new reign he fulfilled all the duties of the eldest son of a provincial lord. He undertook administrative duties as a JP in Sussex and Hampshire, and was sheriff of Sussex in 1524–5. He fought in the French wars of 1513–14, where he was knighted, and served again in France in

1522–5. He was present at the wedding of the king's sister Mary to Louis XII of France in August 1514, the Field of Cloth of Gold in 1520, and the meeting with the emperor Charles V in 1522. He was appointed a carver at court in 1521, and witnessed the creation of the king's bastard son Henry Fitzroy as duke of Richmond in June 1525. In October that year his father died, and West inherited the de la Warr barony. Consequently his duties increased, although he was usually able to appoint a proxy for parliament, pleading poverty. He did, though, sit on the panels of peers summoned to condemn Anne Boleyn and her brother in 1536, and lords Darcy and Hussey in 1537. He also carried out ceremonial duties by uncovering the basins for the presiding bishop at Prince Edward's baptism in October 1537, and by carrying the canopy for the funeral of the queen in the following month.

During the 1530s, however, de la Warr became increasingly dissatisfied with the regime. He was close friends with Viscount Lisle, the marquess of Exeter, and Robert Sherburne, bishop of Chichester, all ageing conservatives who were unhappy with the reforms of the 1530s. De la Warr's intimate friend George Crofts, a prebendary of Chichester, said that he had never found de la Warr wavering from his conservative opinions regarding the intercession of the saints, pilgrimages, purgatory, free will, and justification, and Anthony Wayte, Bishop Sherburne's servant, told Lady Lisle that de la Warr was 'the whole stay of our corner of Sussex, for if we lacked him we might well say to have lost the greatest part of wealth and catholics, for he is surely a good lord and just' (*Lisle Letters*, 2.265).

None the less, de la Warr was prepared to conform, and he was made a commissioner of oaths for the royal supremacy in Sussex in 1534. Given his own beliefs, and the friends that he kept, this was undoubtedly an act of policy by the government. When Crofts told his friend that he was planning to flee the kingdom, de la Warr persuaded him to conform, and Crofts, too, took the oath of supremacy.

De la Warr's conservative conformity is best seen in the dissolution of Boxgrove Priory. As owner of Halnaker, de la Warr also inherited the rights of the priory's founder, and in the early 1530s he established a chantry there. However, when the prospect of dissolution arose in 1536, he immediately wrote to Thomas Cromwell in the house's defence. He pleaded for Boxgrove's survival as a priory, but if it were to be dissolved he asked that he might have the farm. He reiterated this request a few months later, asking also if he might buy the ornaments, and that the church of the priory might remain as a parish church. De la Warr can be seen as sincerely wishing to preserve the priory, but eventually conforming, and by doing so making the best of a bad lot, both for himself materially, and spiritually for the locality. Following its dissolution de la Warr was granted a lease of the priory, and the commissioners reported back to Cromwell that 'the King, by the vigilance and diligence of lord Lawarre, has more profit there than in any other house dissolved in Sussex' (*LP Henry VIII*, 12/1, no. 747).

Yet despite his conformity de la Warr nearly came unstuck in 1538 through what has become known as the Courtenay conspiracy. During 1537 and 1538 Henry VIII's cousin Cardinal Pole was trying to raise Catholic Europe in a crusade against schismatic England. Towards the end of 1538 Pole's brothers, mother, and close friends were suddenly arrested, allegedly on the discovery of a plot against the king. It is now generally accepted that no such plot existed, although it is not clear whether Henry was making a pre-emptive strike, or whether it was simply a useful time to remove the last of the Plantagenet line.

Several of de la Warr's intimate friends were arrested, including the marquess of Exeter, Sir Geoffrey Pole, and George Crofts. De la Warr feared that he too would be arrested, shouting up to Bishop Sampson of Chichester from the pavement outside his palace that he must defend him if he were attacked. The bemused bishop carefully responded that if de la Warr was innocent there would be no need. But de la Warr was right to be worried, for throughout October and November 1538 the interrogations of the accused, and depositions of others, show that the regime was becoming increasingly interested in him. Sir Geoffrey Pole told his interrogators that de la Warr had grumbled against the regime throughout the 1530s, discussing a better world with Pole, although he was less interested in Pole's opinions after the king had stayed at Halnaker during his progress through Sussex in 1536. Crofts told them that in his opinion de la Warr had never wavered in his traditional beliefs, and that de la Warr had persuaded him to conform and take the oath of supremacy against his conscience. He also told them that although de la Warr had condemned the Pilgrimage of Grace, he had said that the peers had only been prepared to condemn Lord Darcy because they had been led to believe that he would receive a royal pardon. Most worrying was the evidence of de la Warr's own brother-in-law, Sir Henry Owen, who stated that he had heard de la Warr openly criticizing acts of parliament, and saying that God would punish the dissolution of the monasteries and the reading of new English books.

On 1 December 1538 de la Warr was examined by seven prominent members of the privy council. They wrote to the king saying that they could find no sufficient ground for sending him to the Tower, though they had placed him under house arrest. However, the next day he was transferred to the Tower. It is not clear exactly what accusation was made against de la Warr. His examination took place on the day before the trials of his friends, and in the light of his comments about the trial of Lord Darcy it might be that he refused to serve on the panel of peers trying them. Otherwise, the worst that could be laid against him was that he had known of Crofts's objections to the supremacy and had not reported them. However, de la Warr was not perceived as a threat like Exeter or Montagu, and was a useful magnate in Sussex, so he was released on 21 December, undertaking with a bond of £3000 to appear before the council when summoned. This was not to be his only punishment, however, for early in 1539 the king, who had taken a liking to Halnaker, suggested an exchange of land. De la Warr's forgiveness was clearly dependent on this, and he agreed to exchange his home of forty years for the nunnery of Wherwell in Hampshire. At the same time his bond was discharged. From 1539 de la Warr lived at Offington, Sussex, where his father had lived before him.

De la Warr continued to act as an important provincial lord after his release from the Tower. As early as February 1539 he was being trusted to defend the Sussex coast, suggesting that he had never seriously been suspected of conspiracy, and he was made vice-admiral for Sussex in 1543. He attended the reception of Anne of Cleves in January 1540, and in March 1542 he held the mantle for the creation of John Dudley as Viscount Lisle. The latter had been a ward of de la Warr's brother-in-law, Sir Edward Guildford, and his mother had married de la Warr's friend Arthur Plantagenet, Viscount Lisle. This connection gave the conservative de la Warr protection under Edward VI, and was no doubt influential in gaining him the Garter in December 1549. He continued to be a leading agent for the government in Sussex, serving on the commission to collect church plate from 1552, and as lord lieutenant of Sussex from 1551. Dudley's support must have been particularly helpful in 1549 when de la Warr placed a private bill before parliament to disinherit his nephew **William West**, first Baron De La Warr (c.1519–1595). The latter was the son of the ninth baron's half-brother Sir George West of Warbleton (d. 1538) and his wife, Elizabeth, daughter of Sir Robert Morton of Lechlade, Gloucestershire. His uncle was childless, and had at some time adopted William as his heir. However, West tried to gain the de la Warr estate early by poisoning his uncle. The attempt was unsuccessful and he was in the Tower by October 1548. He was disinherited by an act of parliament in 1550, although he had been reinstated as heir by the time of his uncle's death.

Despite his links with Dudley, de la Warr did not help him in his attempt to place Jane Grey on the throne; indeed, he was given an annuity by Queen Mary for his assistance against the duke. He was admitted to the privy council on 17 August 1553, but seems to have attended only two meetings. He died at home at Offington on 25 September 1554 and was buried on 10 October, with his father in the church at Broadwater, Sussex. Henry Machyn, in reporting his funeral, gave him the epitaph of the 'best howsse-keper in Sussex' (*Diary of Henry Machyn*, 71).

Now reinstated as his uncle's heir, William West was unable to inherit the barony owing to the act of parliament. Some time previously he had married Elizabeth, daughter of Thomas Strange of Chesterton, Gloucestershire; after her death he married Anne, widow of Thomas Oliver and daughter of Henry Swift of Andover, Hampshire, who survived him. Involved in the Dudley conspiracy, West was arraigned in the Guildhall on 30 June 1556. He insisted on answering the charge as William, Lord de la Warr, forcing the heralds to prove that he had no right to the title. He was convicted of treason and sentenced to death. The punishment was not carried out, however, and he was pardoned in 1557, shortly before fighting for the queen at St Quentin. In 1563 he was restored in blood by Elizabeth I, and on 5 February 1570 he was knighted and

created Baron De La Warr. This was regarded as a new creation, and in his lifetime he sat in the House of Lords as junior baron. Like his uncle before him he was the government's agent in Sussex, serving at times as lord lieutenant. Unlike his uncle he was a protestant and was particularly active in the prosecution of recusants. No doubt for that reason he took part in the trials for treason of the duke of Norfolk in 1572 and the earl of Arundel in 1589. He died at Wherwell, Hampshire, on 30 December 1595, and his son Thomas succeeded to the barony, successfully claiming the precedence within the peerage that had belonged to his title before his father forfeited it.

MICHAEL RIORDAN

Sources *LP Henry VIII* · M. H. Dodds and R. Dodds, *The Pilgrimage of Grace, 1536–1537, and the Exeter conspiracy, 1538*, 2 vols. (1915) · M. St C. Byrne, ed., *The Lisle letters*, 6 vols. (1981) · *The diary of Henry Machyn, citizen and merchant-taylor of London, from AD 1550 to AD 1563*, ed. J. G. Nichols, CS, 42 (1848) · C. Wriothesley, *A chronicle of England during the reigns of the Tudors from AD 1485 to 1559*, ed. W. D. Hamilton, 2 vols., CS, new ser., 11, 20 (1875–7) · *VCH Sussex* · *VCH Hampshire and the Isle of Wight* · GEC, *Peerage*, 4.56–60 · *DNB* · J. Foster, *The register of admissions to Gray's Inn, 1521–1889, together with the register of marriages in Gray's Inn chapel, 1695–1754* (privately printed, London, 1889) · W. R. Douthwaite, *Gray's Inn: its history and associations* (1886) · W. B. Bannerman, ed., *The visitations of the county of Sussex ... 1530 ... and 1633–4*, Harleian Society, 53 (1905) · W. H. Rylands, ed., *Pedigrees from the visitation of Hampshire ... 1530 ... 1575 ... 1622 ... 1634*, Harleian Society, 64 (1913)
Archives PRO, Slate MSS
Likenesses follower of H. Holbein junior (called De La Warr), oils, c.1550 (William West), Tate collection

West, Thomas, third Baron De La Warr (1577–1618), colonial governor, was born on 9 July 1577 and baptized at Wherwell, Hampshire, the third child and second son of Thomas West, second Baron De La Warr (c.1550–1602), and Anne, daughter of Sir Francis *Knollys and cousin of Elizabeth I. He matriculated from Queen's College, Oxford, in March 1592, and toured Italy in 1596–7 following the death of his elder brother, Robert, in 1594. On 25 November 1602 he married Cecily or Cecilia (d. 1662), daughter of his godfather Sir Thomas Shirley of Wiston, Sussex, at St Dunstan-in-the-West, London. He served in parliament as member for Lymington, Hampshire, in 1597–8 before campaigning in Ireland and perhaps the Low Countries. West was knighted by the earl of Essex in Dublin on 12 July 1599, and his association with the condemned lord lieutenant resulted in his temporary imprisonment in 1601. Essex's declaration that West was unacquainted with any rebellion cleared him of treason. Soon after his release West enjoyed considerable political influence. He became third Baron De La Warr upon his father's death in March 1602, served as a privy councillor to both Elizabeth I and James I, and was created MA at Oxford in 1605.

De La Warr made his greatest impact as a colonial promoter and administrator. On 20 November 1606 he was named to the fourteen-member king's counsel of Virginia, overseeing American colonial projects between thirty-four and forty-five degrees north latitude. In 1609 the Virginia Company of London appointed him first lord governor and captain-general of Virginia for life (commission dated 28 February 1610). After two years of dissension, desertions, high death rates, and damaging relations with the Powhatan Indians the Jamestown colony needed stronger governance by a respected authority, broad reforms, and military leadership. Given his rank, court connections, and generous support of the company (£500 invested in 1609), De La Warr was an obvious choice to become the first nobleman to govern in English America, replacing the previous leadership of untitled, self-made men such as Captain John Smith.

During De La Warr's governorship Virginia was transformed from an infant colony struggling for life in 1609 to a more mature and populous colony with a profitable tobacco economy by 1618. But De La Warr himself was not personally responsible for most of that progress. Alexander Brown's 1890 assessment that he was the 'one man' who deserved to 'be called the founder of Virginia' greatly exaggerated his contribution (Brown, 2.1049). He only resided in America for ten months, much of which he spent aboard ship, debilitated and bedridden with fevers, diarrhoea, gout, and scurvy. His hasty and embarrassing return to England in March 1611 was so potentially damaging to investors' confidence that the Virginia Company quickly issued *The relation of the right honourable the Lord De-La-Warre, … to the … counsell of Virginea, touching his unexpected returne home, and afterwards delivered to the generall assembly of the said company* (1611). In his long absence from Virginia critical leadership duties fell to a succession of talented deputy governors—Sir Thomas Gates, Sir Thomas Dale, and Captain Samuel Argall. De La Warr contributed more style than substance to the stabilization of the Jamestown colony, and his most significant accomplishment occurred by accident. When Deputy Governor Gates reached Virginia on 23 May 1610, he found only ninety emaciated and terrified colonists who had survived a six-month Powhatan siege of Jamestown (the 'Starving Time', November 1609–May 1610). He evacuated the indefensible settlement on 7 June and set sail for England—only to encounter De La Warr's arriving relief fleet the next day while still in the James River. This providential meeting was made possible by Argall's brilliant navigation of a faster Atlantic crossing—thus preventing a second lost colony and altering American history.

De La Warr formally assumed office with great pomp on 10 June 1610 in an elaborate ceremony with fifty red-cloaked halberdiers in his livery before the pitiful ruins of James Fort. He carried out the orders of company and crown by instituting harsh martial law over the colonists and by launching military offensives against the Indians in the First Anglo-Powhatan War. Between July 1610 and December 1611 Gates and Dale used well-supplied and armour-clad veteran troops to conquer key portions of the James River, from present-day Richmond to Hampton Roads. Although he rarely saw combat himself, De La Warr treated the native 'Canaanites' with Old Testament wrath, ordering an Indian warrior's hand to be sliced off and desiring that a Powhatan mother be burned alive after the English murdered her children. Thanks to Dale and

Argall, diplomacy, not cruelty, finally ended Virginia's first Indian war in April 1614—three years after De La Warr had left the scene.

Lord De La Warr, who contributed more of his purse than his person to Virginia, was en route to quell a new political crisis in the colony when he died at sea, perhaps along the Nova Scotia coast, on 7 June 1618. His mixed and controversial legacy includes receiving credit for the deeds of others and demonstrating all too often that an excellent pedigree does not guarantee excellent performance. He left behind three brothers, Francis, John, and Nathaniel, who settled permanently in Virginia, as well as his name on Delaware Bay, which Argall discovered in 1610. J. FREDERICK FAUSZ

Sources A. Brown, *The genesis of the United States*, 2 vols. (1890) · *The relation of the right honourable the Lord De-La-Warre* (1611) · *A voyage to Virginia in 1609. Two narratives. Strachey's 'True reportory' and Jourdain's 'Discovery of the Bermudas'*, ed. L. B. Wright (1965) · *Adventures of purse and person: Virginia, 1607–1624/5*, rev. V. M. Meyer and J. F. Dorman, 3rd edn (Richmond, Virginia, 1987), 655–61 · J. F. Fausz, 'Argall, Samuel', *DAB* · J. F. Fausz, 'Pocahontus', *DAB* · J. F. Fausz, 'Powhatan', *DAB* · J. F. Fausz, 'An "abundance of blood shed on both sides": England's first Indian war, 1609–1614', *Virginia Magazine of History and Biography*, 98 (1990), 3–56, esp. 27–48 · W. Strachey, *Historie of travell into Virginia Britania* (1612); ser. 2, vol. 103, ed. L. B. Wright and V. Freund, Hakluyt Society (1953), 50 n. · GEC, *Peerage* · *DNB* · A. M. Mimardière, 'West, Thomas II', HoP, *Commons, 1558–1603*, 3.602–3 · R. C. Gabriel, 'West, Thomas III', HoP, *Commons, 1558–1603*, 3.603–4

Likenesses attrib. Hilliard, portrait, pubd 1883, repro. in Brown, *The genesis of the United States*, I.xxxvi, facing p. 1010; priv. coll. · W. L. Shephard, oils (after unknown portrait), Virginia State Library, Richmond

West [*formerly* Daniel], **Thomas** (1720?–1779), antiquary and writer, was born in Inverness, probably on 1 January 1720. The identities of his parents are unknown. He received his early education 'in the public schools in Edinburgh' (*Antiquities*, 409). For some time he was 'a traveller in trade' (Oliver, 39), possibly travelling on the continent. It is uncertain when or why he changed his name to West. About 1749 he began divinity studies at the College of the English Jesuits at St Omer, and in September 1751 he entered the noviciate of the English province of the Jesuits at Watten; subsequently he studied at Liège. In October 1750, when he was apparently living in Deptford, he applied for membership of the Society of Antiquaries: he is described in the minute book as 'well skilled in several curious parts of antiquities' (Holt, 'Father Thomas West', 131). He was elected two years later. West was ordained as a priest on the continent about 1757. After returning to Britain, he may have spent time at Swynnerton, Staffordshire, and Holywell, Flintshire. After a further period on the continent he returned once more in 1765, and was appointed to Dalton in Furness, Lancashire. For about ten years he lived at Titeup Hall near Dalton; later he may have moved to Swarthmoor Hall near Ulverston, and to Ulverston itself. West was on friendly terms with Lord George Cavendish of Holker, to whom he dedicated his *Antiquities of Furness*; he spent much time at Sizergh, near Kendal, the seat of the Catholic Strickland family, and probably lived there in the last months of his life. His correspondents included his fellow Jesuit William Strickland, who lived at Alnwick in Northumberland, as well as other prominent antiquarians such as Thomas Pennant.

West's reputation as an antiquary rests chiefly on his *Antiquities of Furness*, first published in 1774, which is primarily concerned with the history of Furness Abbey. His *Guide to the Lakes*, which first appeared in 1778, was revised and enlarged for the second edition of 1780, with a distinctly patronizing preface by the editor William Cockin; the *Guide* reached its eleventh edition in 1821. Drawing freely on the work of previous writers, notably Thomas Gray, Thomas Pennant, and John Brown, and very much reflecting the contemporary interest in what West himself calls 'landscape studies', the *Guide* is nevertheless a work of considerable individuality, displaying a real sensitivity to the visual qualities of the district. The recommended 'stations' for viewing the landscape were a significant innovation. The author's antiquarian passion and his curiosity about industrial activities are clearly evident. The *Guide* undoubtedly did much to popularize the district. West also published 'An account of a volcanic hill near Inverness', in *Philosophical Transactions*, 67 (1777), 385–7, and 'Antiquities discovered in Lancaster, 1776', in *Archaeologia*, 5 (1779), 98–100.

West died at Sizergh, Westmorland, on 10 July 1779, and was buried close to the Strickland family chapel in Kendal parish church. The editor of his *Antiquities*, William Close, remembered West in disappointingly conventional terms as 'a man revered for his piety, and the benevolence of his disposition, as much as for his learning' (*Antiquities*, 410).

ROBERT INGLESFIELD

Sources papers, Lancs. RO · T. G. Holt, 'Father Thomas West', *Transactions of the Cumberland and Westmorland Antiquarian and Archaeological Society*, [new ser.,] 79 (1979), 131–8 · G. Holt, *The English Jesuits, 1650–1829: a biographical dictionary*, Catholic RS, 70 (1984), 76 · A. C. Parkinson, *A history of Catholicism in the Furness peninsula, 1127–1997* (1998), 42–6 · *The antiquities of Furness … with additions by William Close* (1805), 409–10 · G. Oliver, *Collections towards illustrating the biographies of the Scotch, English and Irish members of the Society of Jesus*, 2nd edn (1845), 39–40
Archives Lancs. RO, corresp. and papers; corresp., papers, and MS collections

West, Victoria Mary [Vita] **Sackville-** (1892–1962), writer and gardener, was born on 9 March 1892 at Knole near Sevenoaks, Kent, the only child of Lionel Edward Sackville-West (1867–1928), and his wife and first cousin, Victoria Josefa Dolores Catalina Sackville-West (1862–1936), society hostess, the illegitimate daughter of Sir Lionel Sackville Sackville-*West, second Baron Sackville (1827–1908), and the Spanish dancer Josefa de la Oliva (*née* Durán y Ortega, known as Pepita). Her father succeeded her grandfather as third Baron Sackville in 1908. She was known throughout her life as Vita. Her upbringing, both privileged and solitary, was shaped above all by the romantic atmosphere and associations of Knole, the sprawling Tudor palace set in a spacious park in Kent, where she spent her childhood. Her literary taste and temperament were created substantially by this aristocratic and historical backcloth and intensified both by the colourful and eccentric personality of her mother and by the

Victoria Mary Sackville-West (1892–1962), by Sir Cecil Beaton, 1958

gradual realization, with which she never entirely came to terms, that as a woman she could never inherit the Knole estate. Until she was thirteen she was educated by governesses at home before moving to Miss Woolff's day school in London, but her voracious reading in literature and history made her essentially an autodidact.

Sackville-West was also exposed to French culture from an early age through her mother's friendship with Sir John Murray Scott, ultimate residuary legatee of the art collector Sir Richard Wallace and owner of the Château de Bagatelle in Paris. Before the First World War she also enjoyed the opportunity to travel to Italy, Russia, Poland, Austria, and Spain. Throughout her life these cosmopolitan early years (which left the residue of fluency in Italian and French) were juxtaposed, and not without tension, with a deep sense of rootedness within the Kent countryside. She began to write at an early age and completed eight historical novels, five plays, and a number of poems before she was eighteen. She privately published a verse drama about the poet Thomas Chatterton in 1909. However, continual shadows played across her youth in both direct and indirect forms. Most publicly there were two lawsuits that threatened the security and reputation of her family: in the first her mother's relatives tried to prevent her father's inheritance of Knole, and in the second, where Vita was one of the major witnesses, the relatives of Sir John Murray Scott tried to overturn his large bequest to Lady Sackville on grounds of undue influence. Both were successfully overcome, but they took their toll on her parents' marriage. These events, combined with her mother's increasingly manipulative and emotionally quixotic behaviour, made the outwardly dominant and self-confident Sackville-West more diffident and uncertain.

On 1 October 1913, despite conducting love affairs with women, Sackville-West married Harold George *Nicolson (1886–1968), son of Sir Arthur *Nicolson (later Lord Carnock), at Knole. Sackville-West retained her maiden name. Nicolson was at this stage in his career a junior diplomat, and they began their married life in Constantinople, where he was currently posted. They returned to Britain in 1914 and their first son, Lionel Benedict *Nicolson, was born in August that year. They lived both in London and at Long Barn, a house near Knole, which served as their country home between 1915 and 1930, where Vita wrote most of her early books and developed her first garden. A second son was stillborn in 1915, and their last child, Nigel, was born in London in 1917. These years were crucial in three respects—for the emergence across a range of genres of her professional literary persona; for the full exploration of her sexual and emotional identity (what she called her dual nature); and perhaps above all for the maturation of an unconventional but harmonious marriage. Sackville-West, who signed all her books V. Sackville-West, published *Poems of East and West* in 1917, a collection of lyric poems composed while she was in Constantinople. In *Heritage* (1919), her first novel, she explored her own history through metaphors of genetic determinism, and in *The Heir* (1922) she vented her feelings about Knole. *Knole and the Sackvilles* (1922), a historical work, found a large audience which continued once public access to stately homes began to increase.

In the years immediately after the First World War Sackville-West became committed to a stormy and nearly self-destructive love affair with her schoolfriend Violet *Trefusis (1894–1972), daughter of Mrs Alice Keppel, mistress of King Edward VII. The lovers travelled around Europe with Sackville-West occasionally cross-dressed as a fictive persona, Julian. They collaborated on a novel, *Challenge* (1923), that was published in America under Sackville-West's name but suppressed in Britain. It is dedicated to Violet and is about their relationship. Sackville-West very nearly left her husband altogether. However, this crisis in fact proved eventually to be the catalyst for Nicolson and Sackville-West to restructure their marriage satisfactorily so that they could both pursue a series of relationships through which they could fulfil their essentially homosexual identity while retaining a secure basis of companionship and affection. Sackville-West's other lovers included the journalist Evelyn *Irons and Hilda *Matheson, head of the BBC talks department, and she was also very close to Virginia *Woolf, whom she met in December 1922. Sackville-West's *Seducers in Ecuador* (1924) was written for Woolf. Woolf returned the favour with her historical-fantasy novel *Orlando* (1928), a public love letter and tribute to Sackville-West. The novel sums up with unique subtlety and perception Vita's own multifaceted and sometimes discordant personality and her androgynous sexual appeal, historical imagination, and love of Knole. Meanwhile Sackville-West's marriage sought to explore the boundaries of friendship. Gradually a pattern

emerged whereby Harold and Vita wrote to each other every other day, spending the weekends together in the country while following separate lives during the week in Kent and London. This framework was reinforced once Nicolson resigned from the diplomatic service in 1929 to follow a new career, first as a journalist and then as a politician.

As a writer Sackville-West enjoyed success in the 1920s as a prolific poet, novelist, and biographer. Her poem *The Land* (1926), dedicated to her lover, the poet Dorothy Wellesley, was an ambitious attempt to write a modern version of Virgil's *Georgics* by celebrating the annual round of the Kentish farming year. It rose above the conventions of Georgian poetry to achieve a personal vision, and proved enduringly popular. The poem received the Hawthornden prize in 1927. Even more successful in the short term was her novel *The Edwardians* (1930), which celebrated the lavish style of country house life that she had observed in her parents' heyday at Knole. Yet much of her best, most uninhibited, and least self-conscious writing was in travel pieces and essays, especially *Twelve Days* (1928), a book of literary sketches of the mountains of Persia, the result of a visit to her husband, who was posted to Tehran in 1925.

In 1930, when both Nicolson and Sackville-West were approaching middle age, they left Long Barn and purchased Sissinghurst Castle, the sketchy remains of a Kentish Elizabethan mansion, which they set about restoring and developing into the setting for a large-scale garden: this was a joint project where the principles of design were contributed by Nicolson and the planting schemes and maintenance by Sackville-West. In many ways it expressed a fusion of their own temperaments in which the effect achieved combined 'the strictest formality of design, with the maximum informality in planting' (Sackville-West, 'The garden at Sissinghurst', 403). The linked but individual sections of the garden were distinguished by predominant colour themes (such as the influential white garden), or by concentration on the flowers of a certain season, and simultaneously evoked characteristic English and Kentish gardens while also assimilating more exotic Mediterranean touches.

The responsibility of managing the garden ensured that Sackville-West lived a more solitary life at Sissinghurst than she had previously done at Long Barn, although there were frequent travels to Europe and a lecture tour in the USA in 1933. After her mother's death in 1936 she enjoyed relative financial security and was able to concentrate on her writing and her gardening plans, although she was also a regular broadcaster in the early days of BBC radio. In the 1930s her most notable works were two novels, *All Passion Spent* (1931), a story of an independent widow, and *Family History* (1932), and two biographical studies, *St Joan of Arc* (1936) and *Pepita* (1937), a memorable evocation of her mother and grandmother in which she tried to come to terms with the most unsettling and uncomfortable aspects of her early life and her dual nationality. During the Second World War, which she spent at Sissinghurst, she completed a novel, *Grand Canyon*, which imagined a German victory, and another long poem, *The Garden* (1946), which tries to sum up her own horticultural aesthetic and is in some respects superior to its predecessor *The Land*. It won the Heinemann award for literature in 1946. Alongside her work for the Kent committee of the Women's Land Army she completed another study of female sainthood, *The Eagle and the Dove: St. Teresa of Ávila, St. Thérèse of Lisieux* (1943). In 1948 she was appointed a Companion of Honour for her services to literature. The garden reached its full maturity in the 1950s, and in 1955 Sackville-West was awarded the gold Veitch medal of the Royal Horticultural Society. The popularity of Sissinghurst with the public, taken together with her highly successful gardening columns written in *The Observer* between 1946 and 1961, brought Sackville-West a kind of fame she had not anticipated, and which has been enhanced since her death by the transfer of the garden into the hands of the National Trust. Indeed, it is the image of Vita dressed as a gardener in gamekeeper's breeches and gaiters that has displaced in public memory the earlier depictions of her tall, strong-featured appearance by society painters such as de Laszlo and Strang. In her last decade she published a further biography, *Daughter of France* (1959), a study of 'La Grande Mademoiselle', the duchesse de Montpensier, and a final novel, *No Signposts in the Sea* (1961), a story of doomed love. In the course of 1961 she became seriously ill with stomach cancer, and she died at Sissinghurst on 2 June 1962. She was cremated and was buried in the Sackville family vault at Withyham, Kent.

Sackville-West's unconventional personal life has provoked much discussion, and a BBC television series in 1989, thanks to her son Nigel's memoir *Portrait of a Marriage* (1973). It was based on a manuscript found in a locked Gladstone bag in the tower at Sissinghurst, written when Vita was twenty-eight. 'It was an autobiography … a confession, an attempt to purge her mind and heart of a love which had possessed her, a love for another woman, Violet Trefusis' (Nicolson, 1–2).

Sackville-West's career was the product of the irreconcilably disparate priorities within her own life, which enabled her to rise above conventional, stock literary forms while inhibiting her from attaining that unified 'central transparency' which Virginia Woolf prized as the mark of the entirely successful literary artist. It is perhaps no surprise in these circumstances that despite the genuine distinction of parts of her longer poems, her travel writing, and some of her biographies it is for the garden at Sissinghurst and her horticultural writing that she will be best remembered; for no other aspect of her creativity better synthesized and embodied the mysterious amalgam of alluringly romantic imagination, risk taking, and intelligent practicality that characterized both her life and the colourful persona which impressed her circle of friends so profoundly. T. J. HOCHSTRASSER

Sources V. Glendinning, *The life of Vita Sackville-West* (1983) · N. Nicolson, *Portrait of a marriage* (1973) · A. Scott-James, *Sissinghurst: the making of a garden* (1975) · V. Sackville-West, *Pepita*, repr. (1986) · V. Sackville-West, 'The garden at Sissinghurst Castle, Cranbrook, Kent', *Journal of the Horticultural Society*, 78 (Nov 1953), 400–08 · S. Raitt, *Vita and Virginia: the work and friendship of V. Sackville-West and Virginia Woolf* (1993) · *Vita and Harold: the letters of Vita Sackville-West and Harold Nicolson*, ed. N. Nicolson (1992) · *The letters of Vita Sackville-West to Virginia Woolf*, ed. L. De Salvo and M. A. Leaska (1984) · *DNB* · P. Jullian and J. Phillips, *Violet Trefusis: a biography* (1976); repr. (1986)
Archives Sissinghurst Castle, Kent | BL, corresp. with Society of Authors, Add. MS 63324 · Bodl. Oxf., corresp. with Sibyl Colefax · King's AC Cam., letters to Clive Bell · Royal Society of Literature, London, letters to the Royal Society of Literature · U. Reading L., letters to the Bodley Head Ltd · U. Reading L., corresp. with the Hogarth Press · U. Sussex, corresp. with Leonard Woolf and Virginia Woolf · UCL, lecture notes for the Lord Northcliffe lectures
Likenesses P. A. de Laszlo, oils, 1910, Sissinghurst Castle, Kent · photographs, *c*.1910–1950, Hult. Arch. · W. Strang, oils, 1918, Glasgow Museum and Art Gallery · H. Coster, photographs, 1931–9, NPG · G. Freund, print, 1939, NPG · J. Bown, photograph, 1950–1959?, repro. in Glendinning, *Life of Vita* · W. Stoneman, photograph, 1957, NPG · C. Beaton, photograph, 1958, NPG [*see illus.*]
Wealth at death £56,398 16s.: probate, 2 Nov 1962, *CGPLA Eng. & Wales*

West, William, first Baron De La Warr (*c*.1519–1595). *See under* West, Thomas, eighth Baron West and ninth Baron de la Warr (1472–1554).

West, William (*c*.1548–1598), legal writer, was the son of Thomas West of Beeston, Nottinghamshire, and his wife, Anne, daughter of William Bradbury of the Peak, Derbyshire. He was descended from the Wests of Aughton near Sheffield, Yorkshire. He may have attended Corpus Christi College, Oxford, and on 25 June 1567 was licensed as a schoolmaster in the diocese of York, having been found sufficiently competent in Latin, Greek, and Hebrew. He was admitted to the Inner Temple in November 1568, then being of Darley, Derbyshire. He was not called to the bar, but practised as an attorney. By 1571 he had married Winifred, daughter of Adam Eyre of Offerton, Derbyshire; she was dead by 1596 at the latest. He subsequently married Audrey Mann, who also predeceased him. With his first wife he had five sons and three daughters. Their eldest son, William, was admitted to the Inner Temple in November 1590. With his second wife West had one son.

From 1580 until 1597 West acted as steward of the court baron and of the manor court of Sheffield to George and Gilbert Talbot, successively earls of Shrewsbury, and is said to have made a fortune in the practice of the law. He was living at Rotherham, Yorkshire, by 1583, playing an important role in the town's administration, and by 1594 had purchased land at Firbeck outside Sheffield where he built Firbeck Hall. In 1590 he published *Symbolaeographia*, dedicated to Sir Edmund Anderson. Incorporating material from Thomas Phaer's *A Newe Boke of Presidentes*, first published in 1543, West's book was the first printed systematic treatise on the writing of legal instruments, including not only precedents in conveyancing but also of indictments and proceedings in chancery. West introduced his precedents with theoretical discussions of the relevant legal principles, drawing upon civilian and continental scholarship. The book, which came to be regarded as a work of authority, was useful and popular, and rapidly revised in two parts. The first part of the new edition (dealing chiefly with covenants, contracts, and wills) appeared in 1592 and was reissued with further corrections eleven times between 1594 and 1647. The second part of the new edition appeared in 1593, and again a further ten times between 1594 and 1641.

Shortly after the appearance of the *Symbolaeographia* West, 'being now minded to cease his practice and employ himself in study' (Davies, 1188), applied to be called to the bar by the Inner Temple. Letters were written on his behalf by Sir Christopher Wray, Sir Edmund Anderson, Sir John Puckering, and Mr Justice Beaumont, but it was resolved in November 1595 that call would not be permitted until he had performed the necessary learning exercises. Beyond the *Symbolaeographia* West produced an edition of Littleton's *Tenures* in 1581, and contributed a table to Richard Crompton's edition of Sir Anthony Fitzherbert's work on justices of the peace. West was ill by December 1597, and despite nursing by Elizabeth Grene, a widow whom he had intended to make his third wife, he died between June and August of the following year at Firbeck, where he was buried.   N. G. JONES

Sources J. C. Davies, ed., *Catalogue of manuscripts in the library of the Honourable Society of the Inner Temple*, 3 vols. (1972) · T. W. Hall, *Incunabula of Sheffield history* (1937) · J. Foster, ed., *The visitation of Yorkshire made in the years 1584/5 … to which is added the subsequent visitation made in 1612* (privately printed, London, 1875) · W. Dugdale, *The visitation of the county of Yorke*, ed. R. Davies and G. J. Armytage, SurtS, 36 (1859) · C. B. Norcliffe, ed., *The visitation of Yorkshire in the years 1563 and 1564 made by William Flower, esq., Norroy king of arms* (1881) · will, PRO, PROB 11/92, sig. 92 · W. H. Cooke, ed., *Students admitted to the Inner Temple, 1547–1660* [1878] · T. W. Hall, ed., *Sheffield, Hallamshire: a descriptive catalogue of Sheffield manorial records from the 8th year of Richard II to the Restoration*, 3 vols. (1926–34) · *STC, 1475–1640* · J. Guest, *Historic notices of Rotherham* (1879) · T. W. Hall, ed., *Sheffield and Rotherham from the 12th to the 18th century: a descriptive catalogue of miscellaneous charters … relating to the districts of Sheffield and Rotherham* (1916) · *Hist. U. Oxf.* 3: *Colleg. univ.* · F. A. Inderwick and R. A. Roberts, eds., *A calendar of the Inner Temple records*, 1 (1896) · E. Poole, 'West's *Symboleography*: an Elizabethan formulary', *Law and social change in British history*, ed. J. Guy and H. Beale (1984), 96–106

West, William (1770–1854), bookseller and antiquary, was born on 23 October 1770 at Whaddon, Surrey, into a family of eleven children. While the identity of his parents remains unknown, it is understood that his father's side of the family had a long heritage of agricultural pursuits with West's great-grandfather owning an estate near Stonehenge before moving to a property in Surrey. To this rural background West, by his own admission, attributed his limited education and as a young boy was undecided in his pursuit of a trade.

According to West it was the death of Samuel Johnson in 1784 which inspired him to move to London and pursue a career in the world of literature and bookselling. In December that year he travelled to London on foot in the company of his elder brother, determined to be bound as an apprentice stationer. In the following January West repeated the journey and found employment with the bookseller Thomas Evans, to whom West's brother had been apprenticed since 1778. Within months he was apprenticed at Stationers' Hall to Robert Colley before being turned over to Evans.

As a young apprentice West was shy and timid but exhibited a thirst for literature and a passion for the bookselling trade, such that in 1788 he was appointed manager of Evans's business. By this time, before the end of his apprenticeship, and unknown to his master and parents, West had settled on marriage, which produced two daughters and one son named Samuel West. For three years following the completion of his apprenticeship West continued to work for Evans's son James, until the latter was declared bankrupt and fled to America in 1795. West then went into business for himself and in 1800 was joined as partner by Thomas Hughes. On 3 October 1801 both were declared bankrupt, but by 1808 West had re-established himself as a bookseller in Cork, where he published *A Picturesque Description of Cork and its Environs* (1808). Although the *Gentleman's Magazine* states that West spent some thirty years residing in Ireland, the dates of his sojourn remain unknown and, given the known chronology of his career, it seems unlikely that he spent so long out of England. It is known that West remained in Cork until 1830, during which time he wrote the anonymous *Tavern anecdotes and reminiscences of the origin of signs, clubs, coffee houses, streets, city companies, wards … by one of the old school* (1825) and the disjointed biographical miscellany *Fifty Years' Recollections of an Old Bookseller* (1830).

In 1830 West moved to Birmingham, there composing two topographical works including his significant *The History, Topography and Directory of Warwickshire* (1830). He wrote two further books, one published in Cork in 1835 and the other published in Leeds in 1839, before taking control as editor of the *Aldine Magazine of Biography, Bibliography, Criticism and the Arts*, which was published in London between December 1838 and June 1839. The *Aldine Magazine*'s 'great object' was 'to be *useful* and *instructive* as well as *amusing*', and such was their belief in the superiority of their product, that the editors challenged 'comparison with the similar articles of any other Miscellany' (preface, *Aldine Magazine*, collected volume, 1839). The magazine contained not only poetry, reviews, and announcements of new books and upcoming events but, perhaps most importantly for book historians, the series 'Letters to my son at Rome'. Written by West, these informal pieces recount 'the experiences and vicissitudes of the "Old Bookseller's" life and acquaintances' (*Aldine Magazine*, 1/1, 1 Dec 1838, 1). They cover such topics as 'Notice of the Rivington family', 'Liberality and illiberality of booksellers', 'Account of the firm of Messrs. Longman and Co.', and 'Pros and cons between authors and booksellers'.

It is likely that West by this time was again living in London; although he did not return to bookselling, he appears to have secured a living as a bookseller's assistant or in a literary occupation. His last years were spent as a pensioner at the Charterhouse, where he died on 17 November 1854 from a condition that caused paralysis. It is not known where he was buried.   MICHAEL T. DAVIS

Sources W. West, *Fifty years' recollections of an old bookseller* (1830) · I. Maxted, *The London book trades, 1775–1800: a preliminary checklist of members* (1977) · *DNB* · *GM*, 2nd ser., 44 (1855), 214–15 · d. cert.

Likenesses S. West, oils, *c.*1830, repro. in West, *Fifty years' recollections* · portrait, *c.*1830 (*The literary laboratory*), repro. in West, *Fifty years' recollections*, 8

West, William (1797/8–1888). *See under* West, Sarah (1790x95–1876).

Westall, Richard (1765–1836), painter and illustrator, was born on 2 January 1765 at Reepham, Norfolk, the eldest son of Benjamin Westall (1736–1794), a brewer, and his first wife, Mary (1739–1770), the daughter of John Ayton of London. He was baptized at All Saints', Norwich, where his father was a churchwarden, on 13 January 1765. The *Dictionary of National Biography* suggested that he was born in Hertford: this error is of some significance, as he was never regarded as a Norwich artist, although one of the Cromes (probably John) purchased his pictures and the Norwich artist, John Thirtle exhibited *Venus and Cupid* (*after Westall*) in 1805. However, the Westalls were an established Norfolk family. The family residence of Kerdistone Manor has been traditionally linked to the Chaucer family, and a connection with Geoffrey Chaucer's grandmother Mary de Westhale—who is believed to have been the model for the Wife of Bath—is possible.

The death of Richard's mother in 1770 left Benjamin Westall with four young children, the youngest of whom was blind; at about the same time his brewery failed and he was made bankrupt. Westall later referred to these difficult times in his poem *A Day in Spring* (1808), describing how a relation of his mother, William Ayton, provided assistance:

> Thou, the parent of my fame,
> Thou, whose warmth preserved the flame,
> Which was dying in my breast,
> By cold penury opprest.

Benjamin Westall soon married again, and, with his second wife, Martha Harbord, went to manage a brewery in Hertford: here Richard's younger brother William *Westall (1781–1850), also an artist, was born on 12 October 1781.

After being placed with an attorney in Norfolk, Westall moved to London, where in 1779 he became apprenticed to John Thompson, a heraldic engraver on silver; he also studied at an evening school run by Thomas Simpson. The Norfolk artist John Alefounder instructed him in the execution of miniatures and advised the young man to become a painter. Accordingly, in 1784 Westall exhibited the first of 384 pictures at the Royal Academy. He was admitted as a student of the Academy Schools in the following year, when he exhibited an illustration of Chaucer's *Wife of Bath's Tale*, became an associate of the academy in 1792, and was made a full academician in 1794—the same year as his close friend Thomas Lawrence, with whose family he lived between 1790 and 1794.

Westall 'soon attracted attention by his large and highly finished drawings in watercolour' (*DNB*), including the noteworthy *Mary Queen of Scots on her Way to Execution* (exh. RA, 1787). Horace Walpole described the figure of Sappho

Richard Westall (1765–1836), by Sir Thomas Lawrence, mid-1790s

in *Sappho Chanting the Hymn of Love* (exh. RA, 1796) as 'beautiful beyond description' and his *Hesiod Instructing the Greeks* (exh. RA, 1796) as 'by far one of the finest compositions ever painted in England' (*Letters*, 15.404). Joseph Farington recorded in his diary that 'the King particularly dwelt on Westall's drawings and said he had never seen anything equal to them' (Farington, *Diary*, 2.527). However, Westall had his critics. John Williams, who wrote under the pseudonym Anthony Pasquin, remarked of the *Hesiod* picture, 'This is such an effort, as no person, possessing taste and knowledge, can regard with satisfaction; yet it involves that trickery and finery which is so captivating to vulgar minds' (A. Pasquin, *A Critical Guide to the Royal Academy*, 1796, 24). Some years later William Hazlitt exclaimed to James Northcote: 'I confess I never liked Westall. It was one of the errors of my youth that I did not think him equal to Raphael and Rubens united, as Payne Knight contended' (W. Hazlitt, *The Round Table*, 1908, 382). A further comment from Pasquin, in his critique of the 1794 exhibition, provides stimulus to thought: 'He [Westall] has been precipitated to the command of the fleet, before he well knows the principles of navigation' (A. Pasquin, *A Liberal Critique on the Present Exhibition of the Royal Academy*, 1794, 25). Richard Payne Knight was Westall's most liberal patron and sympathetic critic. In his *Analytical Enquiry into the Principles of Taste* (1805), he singled out Westall's *Storm in Harvest* (1796) as one of the 'most interesting and affecting pictures that art has ever produced' (p. 304). Indeed, he purchased the picture, along with another, *The*

Grecian Marriage, in which he discerned 'the utmost purity and dignity of heroic character and composition embellished and not impaired by the most rich and splendid harmony of colouring' (*Edinburgh Review*, 23, 1814, 287).

In the 1790s Westall was a contributor to Boydell's Shakspeare Gallery and to Fuseli's Milton Gallery. He went on to illustrate several editions of Sir Walter Scott's novels, the works of Byron (of whom he also painted several portraits, one of which is held by the National Portrait Gallery, London), William Cowper, James Thomson, Robert Burns, George Crabbe, and many leading authors and poets. Byron provided a generous accolade by remarking that Westall's illustrations for *Don Juan* 'are quite beautiful—the drawings are superb—the brush has beat the poetry' (*Byron's Letters and Journals*, ed L. A. Marchand, 1973–82, 7.165, 168). Westall's naval associations were evident from several oils depicting the life of Nelson, shown at the Royal Academy in 1807 and now in the National Maritime Museum at Greenwich. He also negotiated with the Admiralty, through Sir Joseph Banks, over his brother's pictures of Australia.

Westall's career reached its height in 1814, when he staged his own exhibition in Pall Mall of 312 pictures, 240 'never before exhibited'. The names of the proprietors of his paintings and illustrations (listed in the exhibition catalogue) reflect the high contemporary standing of Westall's art. As well as Knight, they included Thomas Hope, the earls of Oxford, Carlisle, and Harrowby, Byron, Samuel Rogers, the prince regent, Isaac D'Israeli, and Westall's brother-in-law and fellow artist William Daniell. Publishers, naturally, were prominent among those who owned his illustrations. The exhibition met with enthusiastic reviews. The critic in the *Repository of Arts* commented:

> That honour which Great Britain has derived from the discovery of the art of painting in transparent water colours, and which most enlightened foreigners have so willingly accorded to us, is in great degree to be ascribed to Mr Westall. His drawings for many years formed the principal feature of attraction at the exhibitions of the Royal Academy. (*Repository of Arts*, 1814, 357–8)

The critic of the *New Monthly* reviewed the exhibition over two issues and remarked that *Dionysius and Damocles*, owned by Hope, was 'one of the most splendid, tasteful and elegant cabinet pictures of any modern master' (*New Monthly*, 1814, 141–2, 248–9). Another painting which attracted interest was *Elijah Raising the Widow's Son*, exhibited at the British Institution in 1813 and then purchased by that body for 450 guineas. *The Times* of 5 February 1813 extravagantly compared it to the works of Titian and Rembrandt. This painting was presented to Egham parish church (St John the Baptist) in 1834 but was badly damaged by fire in 1950. The head of Elijah, however, is still visible. John Nash's only surviving London church, All Souls, Langham Place, has an altarpiece by Westall of *Christ Crowned with Thorns*, presented to that church by George IV at its opening in 1824.

From about 1815 onwards Westall's reputation slowly declined. In addition, he broke his right arm after falling from a horse and the injury took two years to mend. Almost bankrupt, he considered leaving for France. Perhaps the most interesting exhibited paintings of his later years were from Goethe's *Faust*. His *Faust and Lilith, the Young Witch* (exh. RA, 1831) bears comparison with Eugène Delacroix's 1828 lithograph of the same subject. In this instance, it appears that Westall may have been inspired by the French artist's illustration, but Delacroix profited by Westall's works in turn. His painting of *Gulnare rend visite à Conrad en prison* (1822/3) drew on the composition of Westall's drawing of this scene from Byron, engraved by Charles Heath. This was not the only instance of Westall's illustrations influencing the work of foreign artists. Engravings of his works were widely available abroad, particularly in France, and won him an international reputation that outlasted his celebrity at home. William Etty, after a visit to France in the 1820s, mentioned Westall as among those whose work is 'not only admired but imitated' (D. Farr, *William Etty*, 1958, 44, 120). Recent research has shown that the French lithographer Camille Rocqueplan made use of Westall's illustrations of Scott, while Géricault drew on his Byron illustrations, and his *Faust* paintings have been found to have influenced the German artist Theodore Matthias von Holst. Westall was also a major inspiration for the American artist Edward Hicks.

Westall remained a bachelor but was apparently once engaged to a Miss Bennett, the sister of his pupil William James Bennett; he painted a portrait of his intended bride for the 1804 exhibition at the Royal Academy. He died on 4 December 1836 at his home, 4 Russell Place, Fitzroy Square, London. For the last nine years of his life he had been drawing master to Princess Victoria; he visited her twice a week and painted a charming portrait of her (Royal Collection), which was exhibited at the Royal Academy in 1830. Echoing his own poem, the princess sorrowfully recorded that the once popular painter had died 'by cold penury opprest'.

Also saddened by Westall's death was John Constable, who attended his funeral. The link between the two men was not an artistic one. As a representative of another generation of painters, Constable had been critical of 'the School of Westall'; C. R. Leslie, Constable's biographer, no doubt echoed the opinion of his subject when he wrote in 1812 that 'His [Westall's] faults seem to arise from a wish to improve upon nature' (C. R. Leslie, *Autobiographical Recollections*, ed. T. Taylor, 1860, 18–20). Westall had clearly belonged to the neo-classical, romantic, and historical schools of the late eighteenth century, and his reputation declined quickly in the robust atmosphere of the early nineteenth century. Nevertheless, he was a significant and innovative figure in the development of the English watercolour, his elegant and precise book illustrations set new standards in that field, and his portraits and historical and religious paintings have deservedly received more scholarly attention recently than hitherto. He was a leading artist for some twenty years, and fruitful comparisons of his works with those of other better-known contemporaries can and have been made: his portraits have been considered alongside those of Thomas Lawrence, while his more sentimental pieces resemble the pastorals of Francis Wheatley and his illustrations to Milton stand comparison with the works of Henry Fuseli. Examples of Westall's work, including *Milton and his Daughters*, are in Sir John Soane's Museum, London.

RICHARD J. WESTALL

Sources R. J. Westall, 'The Westall brothers', *Turner Studies*, 4/1 (1984), 23–38 · *DNB* · Farington, *Diary* · *Catalogue of an exhibition of a selection of the pictures and drawings of Richard Westall* (1814) [exhibition catalogue, New Gallery, London, 1814] · M. Warner, *Queen Victoria's sketchbook* (1979) · M. Clarke and N. Penny, eds., *The arrogant connoisseur: Richard Payne Knight, 1751–1824* (1982) [exhibition catalogue, Whitworth Art Gallery, Manchester, 1982] · A. Wilton, *British watercolours, 1750–1850* (1977) · *The letters of Horace Walpole, fourth earl of Orford*, ed. P. Toynbee, 16 vols. (1903–5); suppl., 3 vols. (1918–25) · *IGI* · B. S. Wright, 'Scott's historical novels and French historical painting, 1815–1855', *Art Bulletin*, 63 (1981), 268–7 · G. Schiff, 'Theodore Matthias von Holst's "A Scene from Goethe's *Faust*", 1833', *Arts Magazine*, 54 (1980), 146–9 · L. Eitner, *Gericault: his life and works* (1982), 260–61 · A. Ford, *Edward Hicks: painter of the peaceable kingdom* (1952), xii · T. Crombie, 'Salute to Stubbs', *Apollo*, 92 (1970), 477–8 · L. Johnson, 'La collection Charles Cornault', *Bulletin de la Société de l'Histoire de l'Art Français* (1978), 249–62 · A. Peach, 'Portraits of Byron', *Walpole Society*, 62 (2000), 1–144 · *John Constable's correspondence*, ed. R. B. Beckett, 4, Suffolk RS, 10 (1966) · Graves, *RA exhibitors* · A. Ballantyne, 'The most interesting and affecting pictures: Richard Westall and Richard Payne Knight', *Sheffield Art Review* (1995), 5–17 · R. J. Westall, 'Towards a catalogue of Richard Westall prints', *Antiquarian Book Monthly*, 27 (2000), 17–21 · bradonpace.com/westall, 4 March 2002 · S. Keynes, 'The cult of King Alfred the Great', *Anglo-Saxon England*, 28 (1999), 225–356 · www.trin.cam.ac.uk/sdk13/histpaint/imagesAlfred~index.html, 23 Jan 2003

Archives Courtauld Inst., Witt Library, boxes of illustrations | AM Oxf. · RA, corresp. with Thomas Lawrence

Likenesses R. Westall, self-portrait, oils, 1793, RA · T. Lawrence, 1793–7, priv. coll. [*see illus.*] · G. Dance, drawing, 1803, RA · H. Singleton, group portrait, oils (*Royal Academicians, 1793*), RA · charcoal drawing, NPG

Wealth at death in penury: Warner, *Sketchbook*

Westall, William (1781–1850), painter and engraver, was born on 12 October 1781, in Hertford, the son of Benjamin Westall (1736–1794) a brewer, and his second wife, Martha, (1752–1806) daughter of Henry Harbord of Norwich. He was the younger brother of Richard *Westall RA. William attended schools in Sydenham and Hampstead, exhibiting early an artistic talent. His first known drawing, of Kelso church, was made when he was fourteen. He was taught by his elder brother, Richard, until he became a probationer at the Royal Academy in 1799. In that year he was engaged as landscape draughtsman for a voyage to New Holland (Australia) and the south seas under the command of Matthew Flinders. The painter and traveller William Daniell had signed up for the voyage but decided to stay in England to marry Westall's half-sister, Mary.

Under Flinders's command the *Investigator* set sail on 18 July 1801, calling at Madeira and the Cape and arrived off the west coast of Australia on 6 December. Moving along the west and south coasts with occasional stops for visits ashore, the ship spent four weeks in St George's Sound. Westall's oil painting of part of the sound showing two Aborigines making a fire was based on this experience. In February a disaster befell eight members of the crew who

William Westall (1781–1850), by William Daniell, pubd 1854 (after George Dance)

were lost when returning from shore. Westall's sketches later resulted in an oil painting *The Entrance to Port Lincoln from behind Memory Cove* (exh. Royal Academy, 1812) where Flinders had commemorated the lost crew members.

In May 1802 the *Investigator* arrived in Sydney and Westall sketched Government House from Sydney Cove. Leaving in late July, they sailed up the east coast. A painting by Westall of the view from the summit of a mountain named after him by Flinders was exhibited at the Royal Academy in 1810. In August 1802, Flinders discovered Port Bowen, Queensland; Westall's *View of Port Bowen* was exhibited at the Royal Academy in 1812. After carrying out a survey of the Gulf of Carpentaria, where Westall completed sketches on which his *View of Sir Edward Pellew's Group, Gulf of Carpentaria* (exh. Royal Academy, 1812) was based, Flinders called at Timor (of which Westall made at least two drawings) and found that the condition of his vessel made a rapid return to Sydney imperative. They sailed via the west and south coasts, during which journey six deaths occurred due to illness. On reaching Sydney the *Investigator* was deemed unseaworthy.

Westall sailed for England on the *Porpoise*, but the vessel was wrecked on a reef in the Coral Sea on 27 August 1802. Westall's sketches on Wreck Reef resulted in an oil painting now at the National Maritime Museum. He was among those saved by the *Rolla*. Having arranged for his drawings of Australia to be sent without delay to England, Westall travelled to Canton (Guangzhou), arriving on 14 December 1803, and staying until 5 February 1804. During this time he sketched a merchant's garden and later painted the beautiful *Scene in a Mandarin's Garden* (exh. Royal Academy, 1814).

Westall journeyed, on board the *Carron*, to India arriving in Bombay at the end of April for a three and a half month stay. Perhaps the most successful paintings of his career were based on his experiences there. A scene in the Indian mountains appeared in a number of versions, at the Royal Academy in 1817 and 1824 and at the British Institution in 1818 and 1825. A reviewer in the *Literary Gazette* found it 'striking, grand and picturesque' (10 July 1824, 442) and another in the *Repository of Arts* described it as 'peculiarly romantic and well painted' (June 1823, 3rd ser., 355). The *European Magazine*'s reviewer suggested that 'Turner's absence is in great measure compensated by Calcott and W. Westall', the latter's picture exhibiting 'a grand assemblage of Indian Forest scenery' (85, June 1824, 547–8).

William Westall arrived back in England in February 1805. He was elected a fellow of the Linnean Society that December and set out to re-visit Madeira and go on to Jamaica. An exhibition of his foreign views at Brook Street, in 1808, did not succeed. John Landseer maintained that this was due to lack of advertising (*The Athenaeum*, 2 Feb 1850, 136). He exhibited ten foreign views in watercolours at the gallery of the Associated Artists in 1808, and fifteen drawings in 1809. He became an associate of the Society of Painters in Water Colours on 11 June 1810, and a full member on 10 June 1811, and contributed thirteen drawings in 1811 and 1812 to that society's exhibitions. His drawing of Rievaulx Abbey, Yorkshire, 1811, is in the British Museum.

The Admiralty commissioned Westall to paint oils of the Australian voyage and on the basis of two paintings exhibited in 1812 he was elected an associate of the Royal Academy. Matthew Flinders had returned to England in 1810, and his account of his voyage was written and published with an atlas in 1814 as *A Voyage to Terra Australis* with nine engravings after Westall's drawings and twenty-eight coastal views. Bernard Smith suggested that Westall's coastal profiles are 'more elaborate and more skilful than the profiles drawn by Hodges or Webber' (*European Vision and the South Pacific*, 1960, 142).

In 1815 Westall appears to have had a mental breakdown (Farington, *Diary*, 13.4749; 14.4759). Helped by Sir George Beaumont he became a regular visitor to the Lake District and became acquainted with Robert Southey and William Wordsworth. Southey wrote the introduction to Westall's *Views of the Valley and Vale of Keswick*, published in 1820 and regarded him as 'by far the most faithful delineator of the scenery of the Lakes' (*Southey's Correspondence*, 5, 1850, 52). Wordsworth penned three sonnets in 1818 'suggested by Mr W. Westall's views of the caves etc. in Yorkshire' (*Blackwood's Magazine*, January 1819 cited in M. Moorman, *William Wordsworth: a Biography—the Later Years, 1803–1850*, 1968, 372). After Westall's death Wordsworth wrote on 6 March 1850 to the artist's youngest son, Robert: 'His delineations of this country (the Lakes) must always be valued by those who visit it and wish to carry away faithful portraitures of its beautiful scenery' (*The Letters of William and Dorothy Wordsworth*, ed. A. G. Hill, 7, 1988, 916). Works by

William Westall are in Admiralty House, the National Maritime Museum, the Victoria and Albert Museum, and the British Museum, London; the National Library of Australia, Canberra and the Library of New South Wales, Sydney; at Dove Cottage, Grasmere; and the Whitworth Art Gallery, Manchester and the Glasgow Museum and Art Gallery. Others are in private collections. His *View of Fort Cornwallis, Prince of Wales Island, Penang* (1804), made the year before Stanford Raffles arrived in Penang, was included in the exhibition 'The golden sword: Stanford Raffles and the East' at the British Museum in 1999.

Westall married Ann Sedgwick (1789–1862), daughter of the Revd Richard Sedgwick, vicar of Dent, on 22 September 1820. Her brother Adam Sedgwick, became professor of geology at Cambridge University where he taught Charles Darwin. Sara Hutchinson, Wordsworth's sister-in-law, wrote on 12 September 1820 of Mrs Westall that she 'will take good care of her husband a thing very necessary as he is a reckless sort of person' (K. Coburn, ed. *Letters of Sara Hutchinson*, 1954, 209–10). William and Ann Westall had three sons, William, Thomas, and Robert.

As an engraver and lithographer, William Westall was always interested in the mechanics of print work. Michael Twyman noted that 'Westall is of special interest because of his range of skills as a printmaker; there can't have been many draughtsmen of the period that mastered so many different processes' (letter, 14 April 1983, priv. coll.). His lithographs of London and the aquatints for Ackermann of the Thames, the universities, and public schools are highly regarded. The steel-engravings for *Great Britain Illustrated*, first published in parts (1828–29) by Charles Tilt, brought topographical prints to a wide audience. A number of Westall's Indian views appeared as aquatints in Robert Grindlay's *Scenery, Costumes and Architecture Chiefly on the Western Side of India* (2 vols., 1826; 1830), and his work appeared in the new print format patented by George Baxter (for example, *The Pictorial Album, or, Cabinet of Paintings, for the Year*, 1837).

In 1848 Westall exhibited at the Royal Academy *Commencement of the Deluge* (1848; Tate collection), an oil painting which contemporaries compared poorly with John Linnell's *Eve of the Deluge*, although more recently it has been regarded as a painting of considerable merit. In total, William Westall exhibited seventy works at the Royal Academy, thirty paintings and drawings at the British Institution, and seven in the Suffolk Street Gallery. Seven hundred prints after his work have been located.

William Westall died on 22 January 1850, at Northbank, St John's Wood, where he was living, and is said to have left 'a considerable fortune' (A. Story, *James Holmes and John Varley*, 1894, 45). He was buried in Highgate cemetery near John Constable. His son, Robert Westall, wrote an obituary for the *Art Journal* (April 1850, 104–5) with an afterword by Landseer. RICHARD J. WESTALL

Sources DNB · T. Perry and D. Simpson, eds., *Westall's drawings* (1962) · R. J. Westall, 'The Westall brothers', *Turner Studies*, 4/1 (1984), 23–38 · R. J. Westall, 'William Westall in Australia', *Art and Australia*, 20/2 (1982), 252–6 · R. J. Westall, 'William Westall: a catalogue of his book illustrations', *Antiquarian Book Monthly Review*, 13

(1986), 448–55 • R. J. Westall, 'An unrecognised heritage', *Antiquarian Book Monthly*, 22 (1995), 10–15 • R. J. Westall, 'William Westall in India', *Marg Publications*, 47/4 (June 1996), 94–6 • Farington, *Diary* • R. Westall, 'Memoir of William Westall', *Art Journal*, 12 (1850), 104–5 • R. Reinits and T. Reinits, *Early artists in Australia* (1963), 80–123 • B. Smith, *European vision and the south Pacific, 1768–1850* (1960) • M. Flinders, *A voyage to Terra Australis*, 2 vols. (1814) • J. W. Clark and T. M. Hughes, *The life and letters of the Reverend Adam Sedgwick*, 1 (1890), 37–8 • *The Raffles drawings in the India Office Library*, ed. M. Archer and J. Bastin (1978, 1979) • E. Findlay, *Arcadian quest: William Westall's Australian sketches* (Canberra, 1998) • bradonpace.com/westall, 4 March 2002 **Archives** BM • Mitchell L., NSW • NL Aus. • PRO | Courtauld Inst., Witt Library, boxes of illustrations • priv. coll., handwritten manuscript of the original article by Robert Westall, the artist's son, written for the *Art Journal* early in 1850 after his father's death • priv. coll., photographs of the Admiralty paintings by Eileen Tweedy with transparencies • Royal Commonwealth Society, London, drawings **Likenesses** W. Westall, self-portrait, oils, *c*.1811; Sotheby's, 24 Oct. 1990 • J. W. Gear, portrait, exh. RA 1844 • R. Westall, watercolour, 1845, repro. in Perry and Simpson, eds., *Westall's drawings* • E. J. Physick, bust, 1850 • W. Daniell, engraving, pubd 1854 (after G. Dance), NPG [*see illus.*] • G. K. Childs, woodcut (after R. Westall, 1845), repro. in Westall, 'Memoir of William Westall' • lithograph (after unknown artist), NPG **Wealth at death** a considerable fortune: Story, *James Holmes and John Varley* (1894)

Westall, William Bury (1834–1903), novelist and journalist, born on 7 February 1834 at White Ash, near Blackburn, Lancashire, was the eldest son of John Westall, a cotton spinner of White Ash, and his wife Ann, daughter of James Bury Entwistle. Richard *Westall (1765–1836), the painter, belonged to the same family. Educated at Liverpool high school, Westall worked in his father's cotton-spinning business until about 1870, after which he lived much abroad, and devoted himself to journalism. From Dresden he sent articles to *The Times* and *The Spectator*. He moved in 1874 to Geneva, where he acted as foreign correspondent to *The Times* and the *Daily News*, besides editing the *Swiss Times*, of which he became part proprietor.

Westall's first book was *Tales and Traditions of Saxony and Lusatia* (1877) but his earliest success in fiction, *The Old Factory*, a story of Lancashire life with strong local colouring, was published in 1881. His later novel *Her Two Millions* (1897) amusingly depicted the conditions of Anglo-continental journalism in Geneva, where Westall became acquainted with Russian revolutionaries, particularly Prince Kropotkin and S. Stepniak (Sergey Mikhailovich Kravchinsky). He persuaded the latter to settle in London, and collaborated with him in translations of contemporary Russian literature, and of Stepniak's book on the reformers' aims, *Russia under the Czars* (1885). Westall was long a prolific writer of novels, mainly dependent on incident and description, drawing on his experiences in Lancashire, on the continent, and elsewhere. He travelled in North and South America and the West Indies, and finally returned to England, residing at Worthing, Sussex.

Westall was married twice: on 13 March 1855 to Ellen Ann, second daughter of Christopher Wood of Silverdale, Lancashire, with whom he had two sons and one daughter; and at Neuchâtel, Switzerland, on 2 August 1863, to

her elder sister Alicia (marriage to a deceased wife's sister was then not legally possible in England), with whom he had two sons and two daughters. He had just completed his last novel, *Dr. Wynne's Revenge*, when he died at Long View, Heathfield, Sussex, on 9 September 1903; he was buried at Heathfield. His second wife survived him.

E. S. HOOPER, rev. ROGER T. STEARN

Sources *The Times* (12 Sept 1903) • *T. P.'s Weekly* (18 Sept 1903) • *WWW, 1897–1915* • private information (1912) • *CGPLA Eng. & Wales* (1903) **Wealth at death** £978 3s. 9d.: probate, 30 Oct 1903, *CGPLA Eng. & Wales*

Westaway, Katharine Mary (1893–1973), classical scholar and headmistress, was born on 8 February 1893 at School House, 128 Chapel Street, Dalton in Furness, Lancashire, the only child of Frederick William Westaway, headmaster and HM inspector of schools, and his wife, Mary Jane Collar, formerly of Hammersmith, London. Frederick Westaway was a teacher, specializing in mathematics and science, and at the time of Kate Westaway's birth he was a headmaster in Dalton. Her mother was also a teacher before her marriage. The pedagogic tradition was strong on both sides of the family.

By 1902 Frederick Westaway was a schools inspector in Bedford, where his daughter entered the high school, one of the two Harpur Trust girls' schools. As the only child of scholarly parents, Kate Westaway was close to both and the focus of attention particularly of her father, who coached her in mathematics. Fortunately, perhaps, she was an academically able child. Her early achievements included school exhibitions, honours in public examinations, and an open scholarship in classics to Newnham College, Cambridge, in 1912. She was well liked at school and a keen supporter of school societies, although her only attempt at sport was to play tennis and suffer ignominious defeat in her time as head girl of the school. Her own account of this was humorous and self-deprecating and none of her considerable academic success appeared to make her either boastful or the object of envy.

While at Cambridge Westaway studied for both the classical tripos (she was awarded a first in part two in 1915) and a London BA degree (1914, graduating MA in 1917). At Cambridge she entered fully into college life, becoming a well-liked president of the college debating society. Her sense of fun combined with a calm demeanour were to be lifetime characteristics. The war postponed a plan to study at Heidelberg and she began a course at the teacher training college at Cheltenham Ladies' College. She was quickly offered a teaching post in the school but by 1919 had been awarded the Marion Kennedy research fellowship at Newnham. She studied at Leiden and London, writing her thesis, 'The educational theory of Plutarch' (DLitt, London, 1921), which was published in 1922. In 1920 she was appointed lecturer in classics at Royal Holloway College and seemed set for an academic career of teaching and research. Then in 1924 the headship of Bedford high school fell vacant. With the encouragement of her father and Bedford friends she applied and was appointed to the post at the age of thirty-one.

Westaway rapidly established herself with authority among both staff and pupils, despite the fact that some of the former had been her own teachers. Her aspirations as a scholar took second place to the educational, pedagogic, administrative, and social demands made upon the headmistress of a large, successful girls' school. She embarked on a highly successful scheme to provide new buildings for the school and to diversify the curriculum so as to cater for the less academically able girls. She developed facilities for teaching in science, built a new gymnasium and library, encouraged the teaching of domestic science, and introduced secretarial and pre-nursing courses for older girls. Meanwhile the school continued to send girls to Oxford, London, and Cambridge, and to other universities. She dealt firmly with staff, pupils, and governors alike while maintaining good relations and the respect of all. There was rejoicing when she refused appointment as head of Cheltenham Ladies' College in the mid-1930s.

Nationally, Kate Westaway served on the executive committee of the Association of Headmistresses and as a member of the Burnham committee. She decided to retire in 1949 and moved to the Yorkshire dales with her lifelong companion, Eleanor Osborne. In retirement she served a ten-year stint as a Harpur Trust girls' schools governor. She returned to Bedford in the 1960s and died at Clapham Hospital, Clapham, Bedfordshire, on 16 June 1973. Her ashes were buried at Renhold church.

FELICITY HUNT

Sources D. Kitchener, *Kate Westaway, 1893–1973: a memoir* (privately printed, Bedford, 1981) · J. Godber and I. Hutchins, eds., *A century of challenge: Bedford high school, 1882 to 1982* (privately printed, Bedford, 1982) · M. F. Hunt, 'Secondary education for the middle class girl: a study of ideology and educational practice, 1870 to 1940, with special reference to the Harpur Trust Girls' Schools, Bedford', PhD diss., U. Cam., 1984 · b. cert. · d. cert.
Likenesses photograph, repro. in Kitchener, *Kate Westaway*, cover · photograph, repro. in Godber and Hutchins, eds., *Century of challenge*, 432
Wealth at death £3,046: probate, 29 Oct 1973, *CGPLA Eng. & Wales*

Westbourne. For this title name *see* Lyle, (Charles Ernest) Leonard, first Baron Lyle of Westbourne (1882–1954).

Westbury. For this title name *see* Bethell, Richard, first Baron Westbury (1800–1873).

Westcote. For this title name *see* Lyttelton, William Henry, first Baron Lyttelton and first Baron Westcote (1724–1808); Lyttelton, William Henry, third Baron Lyttelton and third Baron Westcote (1782–1837); Lyttelton, George William, fourth Baron Lyttelton and fourth Baron Westcote (1817–1876).

Westcote [Westcott], **Sebastian** (*c.*1515–1582), musician and theatrical entrepreneur, was born at Chulmleigh in Devon, the son of Joan Westcote, Westcote being a common local name. No record survives of his education, musical training, and early employment; however, close by lay the important collegiate church and choral foundation of Crediton, and his having been educated in that town might explain his generous conferment of relief

upon its poor by his will. As a Catholic layman he cannot be equated with the man of this name who was a stipendiary priest of Chulmleigh about 1541, and it appears most unlikely that he can be identified with the Sebastian Westcote who occurs in 1545 among Henry VIII's yeomen of the chamber.

Although still not employed at St Paul's Cathedral, London, in November 1541, Westcote had been engaged as one of the six lay vicars-choral (singing-men) of its choir for a period sufficiently long by 7 October 1547 not only to be named as legatee and sole executor of his eminent colleague John Redford, but to be appointed to succeed Redford (certainly by Christmas 1548) as master of the choristers and almoner. He is likely to have been at least thirty to be considered for such an important post. His duties were to attend daily in the cathedral, directing the eighteen men and ten chorister boys of the choir in executing the music of the services; the training of the boys was his special obligation. Until May 1549, and again from December 1553 until June 1559, the services sung each day were the ten principal observances of the Latin, Catholic rite of Salisbury (Sarum) use; from 1549 to 1553, and after June 1559, these were replaced by the three daily services ordered by the vernacular Book of Common Prayer. Scarcely any appointment in church music outside the Chapel Royal carried greater responsibility, especially in respect of the occasional services of national thanksgiving, celebration, or penitence that were conducted at St Paul's by royal command.

Almost immediately Westcote embarked on supplementary enterprises of his own. The abolition of obits in 1548 and the imposition of a much attenuated liturgy in 1549 simultaneously reduced the choristers' sources of income and visited upon them unwonted volumes of spare time. By nature impresario as well as entrepreneur, Westcote addressed both problems by engaging for profit the boys' natural capacities as performers. As singers and instrumentalists he made them available to entertain livery companies such as the Merchant Taylors at their major feasts and gentlemen such as Sir William Petre at their London homes. More significantly, Westcote revived John Redford's capacity for employing the boys' abilities as actors, and in the festive season of Christmas 1551, with his colleague John Heywood (minor canon of St Paul's, *c.*1530–*c.*1572), he mounted a play before Princess Elizabeth at her residence of Hatfield House.

So began a long-lived and fruitful connection. Even though the restoration both of the lost revenues and of the Catholic service in December 1553 effectively prescribed an end to such extra-curricular activities, Westcote was still able to take the boys on a return visit to Hatfield in April 1557 to entertain the princess with a play; and in August 1559 Elizabeth, now queen, inspired the earl of Arundel to invite the choristers, under Westcote and Heywood, to present a play before her at Nonsuch Palace. Thus established as particular favourites of the queen, and expedited by the cathedral's return in 1559 to the attenuated vernacular service, Westcote and the

'Children of Paul's' were invited to court to entertain Elizabeth with a play at Christmas 1560 and regularly thenceforth, twice or (after 1570) once in each winter festive season right through until Westcote's death in 1582. Although not the only troupe of amateur boy actors so favoured, Paul's boys were by far the most frequent invitees, and between August 1559 and December 1581 mounted at court not fewer than twenty-eight productions. So elevated and so constant a degree of royal favour probably rendered Westcote the leading producer and arbiter of taste in English drama between 1560 and the later 1570s.

Before their presentation at court the plays were rehearsed in the hall of the lodging of the boys and their master; this lay in St Paul's Churchyard adjacent to the cathedral nave's south aisle. At some stage, and for a charge, Westcote began to admit members of the public to watch the final rehearsals; by December 1575 this was becoming a regular business, and the city authorities resolved to invite the chapter in effect to bring Westcote's unregulated enterprise to an end. It appears that the canons ignored the city, and that each year thereafter Westcote presented on his home premises a brief winter season of perhaps one or two plays for public enjoyment; moreover, his testamentary bequests indicate that by 1582 his household was being augmented by five commensals, possibly all former choristers now briefly retained to amplify the amateur acting troupe of ten cathedral boys.

To inaugurate England's earliest semi-permanent indoor theatre constituted Westcote's greatest innovative enterprise. Of his dramatic presentations the titles of eleven are now known, though the texts of only two or three; not known is the number (if any) that were of his own authorship. It has been inferred that his tastes were broad, encompassing old-fashioned interludes as well as modern plays; they extended to moralities, Roman history, tragedies from Greek mythology, and some comedies, all probably well laced with the vocal and instrumental music which was the boys' speciality. Not only broad-minded in his patronage of playwrights, Westcote's creation of a fashionable indoor theatre did much to channel a middle-class public eager to be associated with courtly values towards an enthusiasm for drama. Indeed, it is as inadvertently a seminal figure in the London commercial theatre which within a generation was to produce Marlowe and Shakespeare that Westcote is now most remembered.

Westcote was overtly Catholic, and it was not until 1554, under a Marian chapter, that he was formally appointed master of the choristers at St Paul's. His adherence became evident at Bishop Grindal's visitation of 1561; he declined the protestant communion and refused to subscribe to the royal supremacy, and consequently was ejected from his ecclesiastical benefice of vicar-choral in 1564. Nevertheless, he was well known to enjoy the queen's favour, and, especially following intervention on her behalf through the earl of Leicester, despite his refusal to subscribe to the thirty-eight articles of religion

(as they were between 1563 and 1571), he was left in full enjoyment of his lay appointment as master of the choristers. In 1574, while certain of his friends laboured under suspicion of treason, Elizabeth found it politic to decline to receive the play prepared for Shrovetide, and for eleven weeks at the start of 1578 he was even imprisoned 'for papistry'; however, the queen's favour protected him from inconveniences any more serious than these. More routinely, in 1571 he is found in York recruiting singing-boys for the choir, and at Christ's Hospital, London, in 1580. Irrespective of his purely seasonal theatrical sidelines, day-to-day responsibility for the cathedral's music remained his primary professional concern. Though evidently accomplished, his choristers were never more than intermittent actors, and never did they become transformed from a professional liturgical ensemble to a professional 'theatre company'.

Westcote was particularly eminent as a pedagogue to young musicians. Among his choristers were the future composers Nicholas Carleton, Robert Knight, Thomas Wilkinson, and William Fox, and the hugely accomplished Thomas Morley and Peter Phillips; greatest of all was William Byrd, whose two elder brothers Simon and John were also Westcote's boys. Many of these learned from him not only music, but also, as Grindal feared, Catholic sympathies and belief. Towards the end of his life, however, he taught by deputy, and it was not Westcote but his assistant John Bold (Bolt) whom Morley later remembered with respect as his principal teacher.

Already styled 'gentleman' in 1554, Westcote died sufficiently wealthy to make bequests which exceeded £240 in cash and included much domestic property, some silver and rings, and a valuable chapter lease with stock, goods, and chattels. His bequests to the choristers' house included his chest of violins and viols 'to exercise and learn the children and choristers there'. 'Grieved with sickness', he made his will on 3 April 1582; death was imminent, since probate was granted on 14 April, and his successor was in office by 17 May 1582.

ROGER BOWERS

Sources GL, St Paul's Cathedral MSS · T. Lennam, *Sebastian Westcott, the children of Paul's, and 'The marriage of wit and science'* (1975) · H. N. Hillebrand, *The child actors*, 2 vols. (1926), 1–355 · M. Shapiro, *Children of the revels* (1977), 11–14 · R. Gair, *The Children of Paul's: the story of a theatre company, 1553–1608* (1982) · R. Gair, 'The conditions of appointment for masters of the choristers at Paul's (1553–1612)', *N&Q*, 225 (1980), 116–21 · R. Bowers, 'The playhouse of the choristers of Paul's, *c*.1575–1608', *Theatre Notebook*, 54 (2000), 70–85 · L. P. Austern, *Music in English children's drama of the later Renaissance* (1992) · A. Gurr, *The Shakespearian playing companies* (1996), 218–29 · H. N. Hillebrand, 'Sebastian Westcote, dramatist and master of the children of Paul's', *Journal of English and German Philology*, 14 (1915), 568–84 · M. Shapiro, 'The children of Paul's and their playhouse', *Theatre Notebook*, 36 (1982), 3–13 · A. Brown, 'Three notes on Sebastian Westcott', *Modern Language Review*, 44 (1949), 229–32 · A. Brown, 'A note on Sebastian Westcott and the plays presented by the children of Paul's', *Modern Language Quarterly*, 12 (1951), 134–6 · A. Brown, 'Sebastian Westcott at York', *Modern Language Review*, 47 (1952), 49–50 · E. A. J. Honigmann and S. Brock, eds., *Playhouse wills, 1558–1642: an edition of wills by Shakespeare and his contemporaries* *in the London theatre* (1993), 48–53 • T. Morley, *A plain and easy introduction to practical music*, ed. R. A. Harman (1952) • H. Berry, 'Sebastian Westcott, the children of St Paul's, and Professor Lennam', *Renaissance and Reformation*, 14 (1978), 68–87

Wealth at death £243 in cash; also much domestic property, silver, and jewellery, and the remaining years of a St Paul's chapter lease: will, Hillebrand, *The child actors* Honigmann and Brock, *Playhouse wills*

Westcote, Thomas (*bap.* 1567, *d.* 1637?), topographer, was born at West Raddon, Shobrooke, Devon, and baptized on 17 June 1567 at Shobrooke, the third son of Philip Westcote (*d.* 1600), gentleman, of West Raddon, and his wife, Katherine (*d.* 1614), daughter of George Waltham of Brenton, Exminster, Devon. He fought in Drake's Portuguese expedition of 1589 together with his older brother George who was killed in the assault on Lisbon. After further travels he settled in London, probably at Lincoln's Inn, of which his relative Richard Waltham was a member, although there is no record of his having been admitted there. He retired to Devon and about 1606 married Mary, the daughter of Richard Roberts of Combe Martin, where his son and heir Philip (1607–1647) and the first of his four daughters were born. He may also have lived at West Raddon with his older brother Robert (1560–1637) and in 1627 he held a lease of Thorn Park in the neighbouring parish of Holcombe Burnell.

At the insistence of Edward Bourchier, earl of Bath, Westcote undertook a survey of Devon in the same manner as Richard Carew (1555–1620) had published for Cornwall. The resulting 'View of Devonshire', completed about 1630, is greatly indebted to the manuscript survey of John Hooker (*c.*1525–1601) and he was also acquainted with the topographers Tristram Risdon (*c.*1580–1640) and Sir William Pole (1561–1635). Westcote's survey is arranged by river systems and his style is more literary than that of other contemporary topographers, but he had little sense of history and he has been criticized for his ready acceptance of fanciful ideas. His other compilation 'An account of the pedigrees and matches of most of the antient and eminent gentry of this county, with their coats of arms' traces the descent of some 300 families, not always accurately. A copy of this work was annotated by the historian John Prince (1643–1723) who often compounded his errors. Both works circulated in manuscript until published in 1845, when the editors George Oliver and Pitman Jones corrected many of the errors and extended some of the pedigrees. Westcote probably died at either Holcombe Burnell or West Raddon in 1637, in which year a will proved in the archdeaconry court of Exeter, whose records have since been destroyed, is listed for Thomas Westcott of Holcombe Burnell. By this time he would have been seventy; his wife died in 1666.   IAN MAXTED

Sources G. Oliver and P. Jones, 'Memoir', in T. Westcote, *A view of Devonshire in MDCXXX, with a pedigree of most of its gentry*, ed. G. Oliver and P. Jones (1845) • J. Prince, *Danmonii orientales illustres, or, The worthies of Devon* (1701), 585 • J. L. Vivian, ed., *The visitations of the county of Devon, comprising the herald's visitations of 1531, 1564, and 1620* (privately printed, Exeter, [1895]), 778–9 • J. B. Rowe, 'Presidential address', *Report and Transactions of the Devonshire Association*, 14 (1882), 33–116 [incl. list of MSS], esp. 80–81 • J. Youings, 'Some early topographers of Devon and Cornwall', *Topographical writers in south-*

west England, ed. M. Brayshay (1996), 58–60 • parish register, Shobrooke, Devon, 17 June 1567 [baptism]

Archives BL, pedigrees, Harley MS 2297 • Bodl. Oxf., pedigrees, Topographical MS Devon 14 | Bodl. Oxf., account of Devon, Topographical MS Devon 15 [transcript] • Exeter Central Library, West country studies library, *A view of Devonshire* [two versions; transcripts]

Westcott, Brooke Foss (1825–1901), biblical scholar and bishop of Durham, was born on 12 January 1825 in Birmingham, the only surviving son of Frederick Brooke Westcott, lecturer in botany at Sydenham College medical school, and Sarah, *née* Armitage, the daughter of a local businessman.

Early years and education Westcott's home life was simple, frugal, and solitary, and his only sister was born when he was twelve. It was not an especially religious home and his father's scientific interests were the dominant influence in his upbringing. Among his hobbies were collecting ferns, butterflies, and moths; he also painted and sketched, and the latter became a lifelong interest. One of his childhood memories was seeing the Chartist demonstrations and riots in Birmingham in 1838–9.

From 1837 to 1844 Westcott attended King Edward VI School in the city. He soon came under the influence of James Prince Lee, the headmaster, who inspired in him a concern for accurate scholarship and the precise meaning of words, and introduced him to classical literature and theology. In later years Lee's picture would always be prominent in his study. Westcott became head of school, and showed intellectual promise. Contemporaries remembered a small, shy, intense boy, who had a quick and eager walk and was devoted to work, rarely joining in games. There were signs of a developing religious sensitivity during his last year at school.

In October 1844 Westcott went to Trinity College, Cambridge, where he read for the classical and mathematical tripos. There he established the ascetic lifestyle for which he was later renowned, rising early, eating very little, and working until after midnight. His interests were wide, embracing botany and geology, art and literature, and architecture and history. His circle of friends was wide too, and with some of them he formed an essay-reading club called the Philological Society, or Hermes. He soon distinguished himself academically, winning prizes, scholarships, and medals in Greek and Latin. In January 1848 he gained a first class in the mathematical tripos, and the following month he was placed joint first in the first class in the classical tripos. He also gained the second chancellor's medal for classics.

Westcott's religious awareness was deepening during these undergraduate years. He taught in a local Sunday school, read Keble, Coleridge, and F. D. Maurice, and was conscious of the growing dissension between theological parties within the Church of England. He had more sympathy with the Tractarians than with the evangelicals, but he resolved not to become anyone's disciple. He did have doubts and struggles with his faith—Newman's secession to Rome in 1845 disturbed him deeply—but by his third

Brooke Foss Westcott (1825–1901), by Frederick Sandys, 1885

year at Cambridge he was aware of a vocation to the church.

The teacher: Cambridge and Harrow (1849–1869) In 1849 Westcott was elected to a fellowship at Trinity College, Cambridge. He taught privately and soon gained a reputation as a gifted tutor. Among his pupils were three people who were to become lifelong friends: J. B. Lightfoot and E. W. Benson, who like him had been at King Edward VI School, Birmingham, and F. J. A. Hort, from Rugby School. The friendship with Lightfoot and Hort was deeply to affect the whole pattern of his life and work. In Hort especially he found someone with whom he could share his deepest concerns and convictions.

Outside his teaching one of Westcott's interests was the Ghostlie Guild, a society he formed to investigate alleged supernatural appearances. He eventually concluded that its investigations could not be fruitful. In 1850 he was awarded the Norrisian prize for his essay 'On the alleged historical contradictions of the gospels'; the following year this became his first book, *The Elements of the Gospel Harmony*. It was regarded as a promising début for a young man of twenty-five. On 15 June 1851 he was ordained deacon, and on 21 December priest, in both cases by his former headmaster, James Prince Lee, who was by then bishop of Manchester.

Westcott decided to leave Cambridge, having become engaged to be married some two years previously. In January 1852 he accepted the post of assistant master at Harrow School. On 23 December 1852 he married Sarah Louisa Mary Whithard (1830–1901) in St James's Church, Bristol. They had ten children: seven sons, including George Herbert *Westcott, bishop of Lucknow, and Foss *Westcott, bishop of Calcutta, and three daughters. Westcott's duties at Harrow were to assist the headmaster, Dr Vaughan, with the sixth form, and to be in charge of a small boarding-house. Later he became responsible for a large boarding-house. Westcott was not suited to the work of a schoolmaster. His own secluded and serious childhood had not prepared him for the liveliness and high spirits of the average boy, and he had difficulty in maintaining discipline. As time went on he felt increasingly unhappy, and hoped to return to Cambridge. His influence was perhaps greatest on the more thoughtful and intelligent boys. One of his sermons preached in the school chapel in 1868, titled 'Disciplined life', made a lasting impression on a pupil named Charles Gore, later founder of the Community of the Resurrection.

Westcott's own disciplined use of time made the Harrow years with their school holidays fruitful ones for the pursuit of his studies and writing. He now embarked with Hort and Lightfoot on a number of important projects. Foremost among these was the joint editorship with Hort of a critical edition of the New Testament in Greek. Begun in 1853 this occupied both men for the next twenty-eight years. There was also the ambitious commentary scheme, covering the whole of the New Testament, initiated in 1860 by the publisher Daniel Macmillan in the wake of the *Essays and Reviews* controversy. The three friends agreed to collaborate in a new kind of commentary, which would accept the demands of historical criticism but attest to the unique nature of the New Testament documents. Westcott's part in this was to contribute on the Johannine literature and on the letter to the Hebrews. His *The Gospel According to St John* was published in 1882, *The Epistles of St John* in 1883, and *The Epistle to the Hebrews* in 1889. All three display a wealth of patristic knowledge and a deep theological understanding of the texts. Westcott also contributed numerous articles to Dr Smith's *Dictionary of the Bible* (1860). Among the books he published during this period were an important historical survey, *A General Survey of the History of the Canon of the New Testament* (1855), *Characteristics of the Gospel Miracles* (1859), and his first theological work, *The Gospel of the Resurrection* (1866).

The Harrow period was also the time when, in isolation from the academic world, Westcott worked out his individual and distinctive theological position. In his last years at Harrow he wrote articles for the *Contemporary Review* on Plato, Aeschylus, and Euripides, three classical authors who, along with Origen and Benjamin Whichcote, were crucial for the development of his Christian Platonism. He studied closely the poems of Robert Browning, another important influence, finding in him a striking witness to the incarnation as the key to all life and thought (*Essays in the History of Religious Thought in the West*, 1891, brought together his work on these authors). He also studied the positivist philosophy of Auguste Comte, deriving from him a central conviction about the solidarity of the human race which was to permeate his later preaching and teaching.

The middle years: Peterborough, Cambridge, and Westminster, 1869–1890 At last the church and the academic world recognized Westcott's distinction as a scholar. In 1868 he was invited to become the examining chaplain to William Connor Magee, the newly appointed bishop of Peterborough, and in the following year he was offered a residential canonry. In November 1870 he was appointed regius professor of divinity at Cambridge, which became his permanent home. For the next fourteen years he resided at Peterborough for three months during the long vacation. He took a lively interest in the history and architecture of the cathedral there, and at the same time he wondered how cathedrals might be adapted more successfully to the modern world. He wrote two articles on this subject in *Macmillan's Magazine* in 1870, and an essay in *Essays on Cathedrals* (1872), edited by J. S. Howson, which argued that they should become centres for worship and education for the clergy. He formed a voluntary choir to sing at special services at Peterborough, and published the *Paragraph Psalter* (1879) to make the words of the psalms more comprehensible. He held special services in Lent and Advent, and arranged devotional gatherings of clergy and church workers. Some of his sermons and addresses were later published in *The Christian Life, Manifold and one* (1869), *The Revelation of the Risen Lord* (1881), and *The Historic Faith* (1883). He frequently lectured on St John's gospel at Peterborough, and his deepening love of Johannine theology was another important influence in the shaping of his theology. Among the theological students who came to him for direction was Henry Scott Holland, who later recalled his first view of Westcott lecturing on St John in a side aisle of the cathedral: 'This tiny form, with the thin small voice, delivering itself, with passionate intensity, of the deepest teaching of the mystery of the Incarnation to two timid ladies of the Close' (Holland, 129–30).

Westcott's main work over these two decades, however, was in Cambridge rather than Peterborough. He was now a colleague of Lightfoot, who was Hulsean professor, and in 1872 Hort too returned to Cambridge. In 1870 the three friends had embarked on another joint venture when they joined the New Testament Revision Company. This was a crucial time in the life of the University of Cambridge. The abolition of religious tests for university entrance in 1871 meant that the relationship between the Church of England and the university had to be reconsidered. A series of sermons and papers, published as *On some Points in the Religious Office of the Universities* (1873), argued that the university still had a central religious role in the life of the nation, not primarily to teach the doctrines of the Christian faith, as some thought, but to provide a broad education which embraced history and science, and the old and the new knowledge, and which reconciled the two.

Another urgent requirement was the revision of divinity studies and of regulations for divinity degrees: Westcott was involved in this, and in the attempt to co-ordinate theological studies more satisfactorily. He was the leading figure in establishing a new preliminary examination for those entering the Anglican priesthood in order to raise the standard of the clergy. He became president of a clergy training school in Cambridge, established in 1881, and took an active part in its work; in 1887 a house was purchased to be the home of the school.

At the divinity school Westcott lectured initially on early church history, but from 1874 his main interest was in Christian doctrine. The substance of his lectures on this subject was published in *The Gospel of Life* (1892), the only attempt he made to set out his theology systematically, and one of his most important books. After Lightfoot went to Durham in 1879 Westcott's main concern was the New Testament. Students remembered especially the more informal weekly evening lectures on St John's gospel and the letters of John in which he communicated his special affinity with these writings. Numbers attending his lectures gradually grew until in the 1880s it was common for him to address 300 students. One student later remembered him in the packed lecture room:

> with grey tumbled hair, in silk gown and scarf … He is saying a prayer with intense earnestness, his face flushed and working, and he begins to lecture in a clear voice of great range and with marked and singular emphasis, his eyes downcast and occasionally uplifted, but seldom dwelling on the audience, and every now and then wreathed into a rapt smile. (Benson, 22)

In 1881 Westcott and Hort completed their version of the Greek New Testament, publishing the *Text* on 12 May and the *Introduction and Appendix* on 4 September. The English Revised Version New Testament was published in the same year, on 17 May. Both were major contributions to nineteenth-century biblical scholarship, and both provoked controversy. The Greek text placed the study of the Greek New Testament on what were called 'scientific' principles for the first time and opened a new era in textual studies, though its rejection of the Syrian textual tradition, or *textus receptus*, upset conservative scholars. Hort wrote the famous 'Introduction', but Westcott entirely concurred with its conclusions, and their vast project was a joint work in every respect. The Revised Version was another milestone, a precursor of the many modern translations of the twentieth century. Westcott by most accounts made a major contribution to it, and after publication spoke publicly and wrote articles about it which were collected together in *Some Lessons of the Revised Version of the New Testament* (1897). He then joined Hort and W. F. Moulton in preparing the Wisdom of Solomon and 2 Maccabees for a revised Apocrypha.

Another of Westcott's principal concerns at Cambridge was foreign missions. He reflected deeply on the theology of mission, and on the relationship of Christianity to the other world faiths. It was largely his enthusiasm which led to the founding of the Cambridge mission to Delhi, and four of his sons later served in the church in India. He also founded the Eranus Club, a discussion group which brought together scholars from different disciplines to consider issues of common interest. He supported the university extension movement which planned courses of lectures in industrial areas, and was a member of the university's council of senate from 1872 to 1876 and from 1878 to 1882, the year when he was elected a fellow of King's College, Cambridge. Westcott was now a celebrated figure in the academic world, and he received honorary degrees from the universities of Oxford (1881), Edinburgh (1884), and Dublin (1888).

Westcott's ties with Peterborough were severed abruptly in 1883 when, under pressure from the bishop, he resigned from his office as examining chaplain. Much to his surprise he was then asked to resign his canonry. The bishop apparently believed that he had neglected his duties at Peterborough. Almost immediately, however, Westcott was invited to become examining chaplain to E. W. Benson, the recently appointed archbishop of Canterbury. Then, three months later, W. E. Gladstone offered him a canonry of Westminster. Westcott was installed in the abbey on 2 February 1884, and during the six years of his residence there he preached to large congregations at the Sunday afternoon services and gave weekday lectures. This was a significant move for him: having spent much of his life in the relatively cloistered worlds of Cambridge and Harrow, he now found himself in the heart of the capital city. It was not possible to be at Westminster for long without being affected by its historical and national associations, nor to live in a cathedral precinct surrounded by a large slum parish without being aware of the miseries of urban life.

It is significant that it was at this period that Westcott's interest in social questions was kindled. Social problems and socialism were now being widely debated, and Westcott was forced to consider their significance for the church. In 1889 he became the first president of the newly formed Christian Social Union, and he regarded himself thereafter as a Christian socialist. He became involved in public movements which protested against the massive expenditure of the European nations on armaments, and urged the settling of international differences by arbitration. His central concern was to apply his faith more directly to the social and political issues of the day, a change of emphasis which can be seen in the sermons he preached at Westminster at this time. These were published as *Christus consummator* (1886) and *Social Aspects of Christianity* (1887). At about the same time he discovered his affinity with F. D. Maurice, whose books he had ceased reading many years previously lest he be influenced by them. He considered resigning his professorship to devote himself exclusively to Westminster and, when offered the deaneries of Lincoln (in 1885) and Norwich (in 1889), he declined both. His last year at Westminster was overshadowed by the illness and death, in December 1889, of Lightfoot. The final service Westcott conducted in the abbey was, appropriately, the funeral of Robert Browning.

Final years: bishop of Durham, 1890–1901 Westcott's life took an unexpected turn when, at the age of sixty-five, he was invited to succeed Lightfoot in the northern see. There was some surprise at his appointment: a number thought him too reclusive and impractical for the task. After Westcott's own initial reluctance, he welcomed the opportunity to follow in the footsteps of his friend and to pursue the broader concept of the church's mission which he had gained at Westminster. His consecration took place on 1 May 1890 in Westminster Abbey. In his sermon Hort spoke of a sacred friendship of forty years with Westcott, and of the latter's concern for a social interpretation of the gospel. Westcott's enthronement was held on 15 May in Durham Cathedral.

Under Lightfoot the diocese at Durham had undergone much reorganization. Westcott did not attempt to continue this pattern, nor did he write works of scholarship there as his predecessor had done. He came to the north-east at a time of deteriorating industrial relations in the mining industry, which culminated in a bitter three months' strike in 1892. He invited the miners' representatives and the owners to meet at Auckland Castle on 1 May. Having entertained them to lunch, he addressed them as persuasively as he knew how, and went to and fro between the two parties. Eventually they agreed to return to work on the terms of a 10 per cent reduction in wages (as opposed to the 13.5 per cent decrease which the owners had previously insisted upon) and a joint promise to establish a conciliation board to settle the course of wages in the future. Westcott was widely praised for his intervention, which helped to secure his acceptance by the people of Durham; but the conciliation board was to have limited value for the miners. In 1892 F. J. A. Hort, Westcott's closest friend and colleague, also died. Westcott attended his funeral in Cambridge, conscious that he was now the sole survivor of what had been known as the 'triumvirate'.

One feature of Westcott's episcopate was the bringing together of employers, trade union representatives, and people involved in the life of the community, for conferences at Auckland Castle, at which Westcott would chair discussions on current social and economic problems. Another was his interest in workers' organizations. He gave priority to attending meetings of co-operative societies, temperance organizations, and similar bodies. He supported movements for providing better houses for miners and homes for aged miners. Every year he preached at the service in Durham Cathedral on the Durham miners' gala day. In 1894 he addressed 5000 people at the Northumberland miners' gala in Blyth, the first time a churchman had been invited to do so. A colleague remembered 'the slight, frail and rather weary figure, with the thick masses of hair now turned grey [who] held them spellbound' (Eden, 578–9). Westcott may not have understood fully the industrial and social predicament of working men, but most of them came to believe that he was approachable, kind, and humble, with a genuine concern for their welfare.

Of Westcott's diocesan duties, he particularly enjoyed the work with young ordinands, continuing Lightfoot's

'Auckland brotherhood'. He worked hard to bring before the diocese the challenge of foreign missions. In his time at Durham thirty-six men went to serve in the church overseas. Westcott was convinced that lay people should have a greater voice in the councils of the church, and he supported the Church Reform League in this aim. He frequently welcomed parties of church workers and working people to Auckland Castle. Every year he gave the address at the annual meeting of the Christian Social Union, and he continued to be involved in the movement for international peace and arbitration. When the Second South African War broke out, however, he supported the British cause because of his concern about Boer supremacy in South Africa.

In his spare time Westcott prepared his Cambridge lectures for publication, and worked on his commentary on Ephesians, which was published posthumously. He frequently turned to the writings of Ruskin and to Thomas à Kempis's *Imitation of Christ*. Sermons and addresses from his Durham period were brought together in *The Incarnation and Common Life* (1893), *Christian Aspects of Life* (1897), and *Lessons from Work* (1901). The incarnation remained the cornerstone of his theology, but his preaching and teaching became more practical and less academic than in his Cambridge years, his Christian faith being more related to the social problems of the diocese—poverty, unemployment, class conflict, gambling, drunkenness, and pressures on family life.

By 1897 the strain of Westcott's work had begun to affect his health; further blows were the deaths of his youngest son, in Delhi in August 1900, and of his wife, on 28 May 1901, after a marriage which had lasted half a century. Westcott continued to carry out his diocesan duties for a few months: his last public engagement was a sermon at the annual miners' gala service in Durham Cathedral on 20 July. His strength now failed rapidly, and he died on 27 July 1901 at Auckland Castle, Bishop Auckland. The funeral was held on 2 August in the castle chapel, where he was buried next to his wife.

Westcott, a reserved, intense, and original scholar, was long regarded as the least distinguished of the Cambridge triumvirate, but later he came to be more appreciated. His reputation originally rested largely upon his biblical scholarship—the textual work with Hort, the commentaries, and the contribution to the Revised Version—but he was also a church historian, whose work on the history of the New Testament canon and the Christian Platonists of Alexandria had a lasting significance. His reputation also suffered from criticisms of the obscurity of his theology, as in Liddon's famous observation that whenever there was a dense fog in London it could be 'commonly attributed to Dr. Westcott having opened his study window in Westminster' (Russell, 174). A century later Westcott's distaste for clear-cut theology and his love of paradox were viewed more positively. His presentation of Christ as the 'consecrator' of all human life and the 'consummator' or fulfilment of God's purpose in creation represented one of the most original theological visions of the later nineteenth century. This vision, influenced by

his love of the Alexandrian school, also informed his work in the theology of mission and the relation of Christianity to other world faiths, another aspect of his achievement which received recognition only a century after his death. Finally, Westcott's work as a diocesan bishop and Christian socialist, in which he sought to relate the challenges of contemporary urban life to his incarnational theology, has begun to attract attention. His Christian socialism was often criticized as abstract and idealistic, but he did much to persuade churchmen that 'a gospel that had nothing to say about its social implications was seriously defective' (Vidler, 278). In all this Westcott shared much of the distinctive outlook of F. D. Maurice.

Westcott's name will always be linked with those of Lightfoot and Hort. Like them, he neglected the study of the Old Testament and the synoptic gospels, but the breadth of his achievement and work was no less remarkable than theirs. As a fitting tribute to his memory, the Cambridge training school for the Anglican clergy, of which he had been president, was renamed Westcott House.   GRAHAM A. PATRICK

Sources A. Westcott, *Life and letters of Brooke Foss Westcott*, 2 vols. (1903) · F. Olofsson, *Christus redemptor et consummator: a study in the theology of B. F. Westcott* (1979) · A. C. Benson, *The leaves of the tree: studies in biography* (1911), 21–48 · H. S. Holland, *Personal studies* (1905), 128–38 · *DNB* · G. R. Eden, 'Bishop Westcott', *Great Christians*, ed. R. S. Forman (1933), 577–89 · J. Clayton, *Bishop Westcott* (1906) · C. H. Boutflower, *The adoring student: a recollection of Brooke Foss Westcott* (1924) · A. F. Hort, *Life and letters of Fenton John Anthony Hort*, 2 vols. (1896) · C. K. Barrett, *Westcott as commentator* (1959) · H. Chadwick, *The vindication of Christianity in Westcott's thought* (1961) · O. Chadwick, *Westcott and the university* (1963) · A. R. Vidler, 'Westcott's Christian socialism', *F. D. Maurice and company: nineteenth-century studies* (1966), 259–78 · G. Best, *Bishop Westcott and the miners* (1967) · D. Newsome, *Bishop Westcott and the Platonic tradition* (1969) · D. L. Edwards, 'Lightfoot and Westcott', *Leaders of the Church of England, 1828–1944* (1971) · K. Cracknell, *Justice, courtesy and love: theologians and missionaries encountering world religions, 1846–1914* (1995), 60–71 · G. W. E. Russell, *Dr Liddon* (1905) · D. Newsome, *Two classes of men: Platonism and English Romantic thought* (1974) · W. G. O'Dea, 'Westcott the theologian', MLitt thesis, University of Cambridge, 1972

Archives CUL, corresp., papers, and sermons · Westcott House, Cambridge, corresp., papers, and MSS of published works | BL, corresp. with Macmillans, Add. MS 55092 · CUL, memoir of Archbishop Edward White Benson · CUL, letters to Sir George Stokes · Durham Cath. CL, letters to J. B. Lightfoot · Harrow School, Middlesex, corresp. with H. M. Montagu · LPL, corresp. with E. W. Benson · LPL, corresp. with A. C. Tait · LPL, corresp. with Frederick Temple · NL Scot., letters to Sir Charles Dalrymple

Likenesses F. Sandys, drawing, 1885, Macmillan Trust, London [*see illus.*] · W. B. Richmond, oils, 1889, Westcott House, Cambridge · photograph, 1891, Divinity School, Cambridge · H. A. Olivier, oils, exh. RA 1906, Sherbone School, Dorset · Elliott & Fry, two photographs, NPG · W. E. Miller, oils, Divinity School, Cambridge · photograph, NPG

Westcott, Foss (1863–1949), bishop of Calcutta, was born on 23 October 1863 in Harrow on the Hill, the fifth son of seven sons and three daughters of Brooke Foss *Westcott (1825–1901), Church of England clergyman and future bishop of Durham, and his wife, Sarah Louisa Mary Whithard (1830–1901), the elder daughter of Thomas

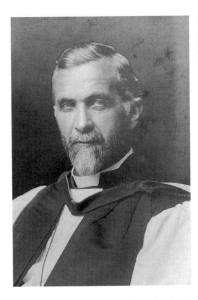

Foss Westcott (1863–1949), by James Russell & Sons, c.1910

Whithard. He had a public-school education at Cheltenham College from 1876 to 1882, before proceeding to Peterhouse, Cambridge, and thereafter reading for his ordination (1887).

Four of the Westcott sons joined the Society for the Propagation of the Gospel as missionaries in India. Foss, with George Herbert *Westcott, his immediate senior, subsequently bishop of Lucknow, was posted to Cawnpore in 1889. There they swiftly inaugurated industrial training for young Indian Christians. As bishop of Chota Nagpur (1905–19) Foss was to develop his concern with education by founding the Bishop Westcott schools for some 400 Anglo-Indian children, while fostering his substantial Christian communities for the Santali and Munda peoples.

In later life he claimed that if he had inherited none of his father's scholarship, he shared his repugnance for controversy. He had absorbed at source the 'social Christianity' taught by his father and family friends such as Bishop Lightfoot, by whom he was ordained priest. This persuasive reading of Christian faith kept divisive doctrinal issues in the background. Public-school education consolidated faith for him, as for many, as an unproblematic ideal of 'service'. To undertake imperial responsibility with manly integrity was in itself to advance Christian civilization.

For many of his class, the norms of arduous sportsmanship embodied the style of this engagement with public life. Westcott, who had played football and cricket for Cambridge, became familiar as a lean, bearded figure striding across the Himalayan foothills. He thought nothing, even in his seventies, of ignoring tea breaks during afternoons of tennis in Calcutta. Westcott never married.

Burdened by routine administration, each of his two bishoprics posed in addition a distinctive challenge to Westcott's eirenic, organicist vision. The first challenge, precipitated by the First World War, was a crisis over German Lutheran missionaries in Chota Nagpur. All fifty or so

had to be interned. The situation was delicate; the Anglicans had benefited from a secession movement in the past, and expatriate opinion was intensely anti-German. Westcott raised funds and substituted staff, refusing all applications to transfer from Lutheran communion to Anglican, lest the Lutherans should some day return. His chivalry was not universally admired. He was translated to Calcutta as metropolitan in 1919. In 1920 Oxford and Cambridge conferred on him honorary degrees of doctor of divinity.

A second challenge transformed his responsibilities as metropolitan. In 1927 parliament freed the church in India from the general superintendence and revision of the archbishop of Canterbury, and it became a self-governing branch of the Anglican communion. This decision entailed laborious administrative implementation, but it also called for progress in the doctrinal integration of distinct denominations, the four southern dioceses of the Anglican church of India, Burma, and Ceylon, the Methodist (originally Wesleyan) church in south India, and the South India United church (Presbyterian, British, and American Congregationalist, and Swiss Evangelical). Westcott initiated this lengthy process with tact and patience. In 1935 he could announce that agreement had been reached in south India on the fact of the historic episcopate, the Nicene and apostles' creeds, and the sacraments of holy communion and holy baptism, and that he fully expected agreement on confirmation to follow.

However, the emergence of Gandhian nationalism and of nationalist sentiment among native clergy and congregations increasingly exposed Westcott's limitations. In correspondence with Gandhi, while solicitous about the mahatma's health and encouraging over social reform, he was bleakly uncompromising on political dissidence and indignant about Gandhi's blackmailing tactic of fasts. He got much the worst of an exchange with Gandhi's Christian associate J. C. Kumarappa. In this Westcott, who had obtained a third-class degree in natural science (1885), referred to the necessarily absolute reliability and fixity of natural law, and insisted that Gandhian civil disobedience violated a corresponding order in social life, invoking St Paul's assertion that 'rulers are not a terror to the good work but to the evil' (Romans 13: 1–3) Kumarappa gratefully printed the complete exchange in Gandhi's *Young India* in June 1930.

Archbishop Cosmo Gordon Lang, who was heavily involved in the work of the parliamentary joint select committee on Sir Samuel Hoare's white paper for the 1935 India Act, grew impatient with Westcott from this period, for losing touch with his responsibilities and for his involvement in the Oxford Group movement. Inspired by the American Lutheran Frank Buchman, this concentrated on inner conversion and self-reformation guided by group interaction. It was particularly active during Westcott's furlough in 1933, when he was allowed extended leave to attend its major meetings. His enthusiasm, justified in a letter to *The Times* (21 September 1933), had less to do with the movement's reactionary political tendencies, however, than with its revitalization of his faith and the supportive collectivism of its adherents. In his later years, he attempted to stimulate public interest in the problems that would face the racially mixed Anglo-Indian community in an independent India. His personal austerities did not prevent him during the war from extending generous hospitality to servicemen passing through Calcutta.

Westcott continued to cycle around Ranchi, India, after retiring there in 1945. He died in Darjeeling on 19 October 1949, and he was buried there.

GERALD STUDDERT-KENNEDY

Sources G. Studdert-Kennedy, *British Christians, Indian nationalists and the raj* (1991), 157–62 • *The Times* (20 Oct 1949) • *The Times* (21 Sept 1933) • *The Times* (17–18 Oct 1933) • *The Times* (1 Nov 1933) • A. Westcott, *Life and letters of Brooke Foss Westcott*, 2 vols. (1903) • Crockford **Archives** LPL, corresp. and papers | BL OIOC, corresp. with F. Brayne, MS Eur. F 152 • Bodl. RH, USPG archive • CUL, corresp. with A. Westcott • LPL, corresp. with Edwin James Palmer **Likenesses** group portrait, 1899 (*Cambridge Mission*), Bodl. RH • J. Russell & Sons, photograph, *c*.1910, NPG [*see illus.*] • group portrait (Westcott with bishops Kennedy and Wood), Bodl. RH • group portrait, Bodl. RH • studio portrait, Bodl. RH

Westcott, George Blagden (*bap.* 1753, *d.* 1798), naval officer, was baptized at Honiton on Otter, Devon, on 24 April 1753, the son of Benjamin Westcott, possibly a baker, at Honiton; his mother, Susanna, whose obituary is given in the *Naval Chronicle* (29.352), died at Honiton in 1813 aged eighty-two. Westcott joined the frigate *Solebay* (28 guns), as master's mate, under the command of Captain Lucius O'Bryen, in 1768. As master's mate, able seaman, and midshipman he continued in the *Solebay* for nearly five years under O'Bryen and George Vandeput. He then served for three years in the *Albion* as midshipman with Samuel Barrington and John Leveson-Gower, and passed his lieutenant's examination on 10 January 1776 when he was described as 'appearing' to be 'more than twenty-two'. On 6 August 1777 he was promoted lieutenant of the *Valiant*, still with Leveson-Gower, and afterwards with Samuel Granston Goodall. In this position he saw action at the battle off Ushant on 27 July 1778, and served in the fleet under Sir Charles Hardy the younger in the summer of 1779, and under Vice-Admiral George Darby at the relief of Gibraltar in April 1781.

In November Westcott was moved into the *Victory*, and he thus carried the flag of Rear-Admiral Richard Kempenfelt in his brilliant attack on the French convoy on 12 December, and of Richard, Lord Howe, in the relief of Gibraltar and the action off Cape Spartel in October 1782. Gaining scarce peacetime employment in the *Medway*, he became, in 1786, first lieutenant of the *Salisbury*, carrying the broad pennant of Commodore John Elliot, the commander-in-chief in Newfoundland, and on 1 December 1787 he was promoted commander. In 1789–90 he commanded the sloop *Fortune*, and from her he was promoted captain on 1 October 1790, during the Nootka Sound crisis with Spain, and he was thereafter appointed to the *London* as flag captain to his old chief Goodall. The *London* was paid off in late 1791, at the conclusion of the Ochakov confrontation with Russia.

Westcott remained on half pay until September 1793,

when he joined the *Impregnable* as flag captain to Rear-Admiral Benjamin Caldwell, with whom he took part in the battle of 1 June 1794. Afterwards he followed Caldwell to the *Majestic*, went with him to the West Indies, and remained there with Sir John Laforey, whom he brought to England in June 1796. As a private ship the *Majestic* then joined the Channel Fleet, was with John Colpoys off Brest in December, and with Lord Bridport during the mutiny at Spithead in April and May 1797. Towards the end of the year she joined the fleet off Cadiz under the earl of St Vincent, and in May 1798 she was one of the ships sent up the Mediterranean to join Sir Horatio Nelson. In the battle of Abu Qir Bay (1 August 1798) her position in the rear of the line made her one of the last to join the action, and in the darkness and smoke she ran afoul of the French *Heureux*, in which position she remained caught for several minutes and suffered heavy loss. At this time Westcott was killed by a musket-ball in the throat. He was buried at sea in Abu Qir Bay on 2 August.

It is as one of the celebrated 'band of brothers' and by his death in the hour of victory that Westcott is best known. Lord Collingwood wrote of him: 'A good officer and a worthy man; but, if it was a part of our condition to choose a day to die on, where could he have found one so memorable, so eminently distinguished among great days?' For Samuel Granston Goodall:

> He sleeps in the bed of honour, and in all probability will be immortalised among the heroes in the Abbey. *Requiescat in pace*. Never could he have died more honourably. I have him to lament among many deserving men whom I have patronised, that have passed away in the prime of their lives. (*Dispatches and Letters of … Nelson*, 3.86–7)

A monument to his memory was erected at the public expense in St Paul's Cathedral. At Honiton also a monument was erected by subscription. However, it must be noted that he had no close links with Nelson, and in fact he was one of five captains never called to Nelson's ship. Samuel Hood remarked uncharitably that his loss was 'not felt' (Lavery, 218).

Westcott was survived by his wife, about whom further details are unknown, and their daughter. In January 1801, while passing through Honiton, Nelson invited them to breakfast, and presented Westcott's widow with his own Nile medal, saying, 'You will not value it less because Nelson has worn it'. On 17 January 1801 he wrote to Lady Hamilton:

> At Honiton I visited Captain Westcott's mother—poor thing, except from the bounty of government and Lloyd's, in very low circumstances. The brother is a tailor, but had they been chimney-sweepers it was my duty to show them respect. (Gamlin, 1.64)

J. K. LAUGHTON, *rev.* P. L. C. WEBB

Sources PRO, ADM 1 [admiralty 'in letters'] • *Naval Chronicle*, 12 (1804), 453 • *Naval Chronicle*, 29 (1813), 352 • B. Lavery, *Nelson and the Nile* (1998) • D. Syrett and R. L. DiNardo, *The commissioned sea officers of the Royal Navy, 1660–1815*, rev. edn, Occasional Publications of the Navy RS, 1 (1994) • *The dispatches and letters of Vice-Admiral Lord Viscount Nelson*, ed. N. H. Nicolas, 7 vols. (1844–6), vol. 3 • H. Gamlin, *Nelson's friendships*, 2 vols. (1899), vol. 1 • *IGI* **Likenesses** R. Smirke, commemorative print, 1798, NMM • Christmas card, 1798, NMM • E. Bell, mezzotint, pubd 1799, BM •

Bartolozzi, Landseer, Ryder, and Stow, group portrait, line engraving, pubd 1803 (*Commemoration of the victory of June 1st 1794*; after *Naval Victories* by R. Smirke), BM, NPG · W. Bromley, J. Landseer, and Leney, group portrait, line engraving, pubd 1803 (after *Victors of the Nile* by R. Smirke), BM, NPG

Westcott, George Herbert (1862–1928), bishop of Lucknow, was born in Harrow on the Hill on 18 April 1862, the fourth son in the family of seven sons and three daughters of the Revd Brooke Foss *Westcott (1825–1901) and his wife, Sarah Louisa Mary Whithard (1830–1901), elder daughter of Thomas Whithard. His father was then a master at Harrow School, but later became bishop of Durham. Westcott enjoyed a dependent relationship with his younger brother Foss *Westcott, ultimately bishop of Calcutta and metropolitan of India, Burma, and Ceylon. Two other brothers also joined the Society for the Propagation of the Gospel (SPG) in India, a field of prime importance to their father. Famous for promoting 'co-operative' industrial relations, particularly in the Durham coalfields, B. F. Westcott's understanding of Christ's incarnation and the social mission of an imperial church profoundly influenced them all.

George went to Marlborough College from 1875 to 1881, returning as assistant master from 1886 to 1889. The norm of an athletic 'Christian' manliness had been established there by successive disciples of Arnold of Rugby. He engaged with this as a boy, but without the distinction achieved by Foss at Cheltenham and Cambridge, where they were contemporaries at Peterhouse. A scholar of the college, he took a second class in the classical tripos in 1885. He was ordained by the bishop of Salisbury in 1887.

In 1889 both men were posted by the SPG to Cawnpore, India. The brotherhood was small, seldom up to strength, financially straitened, and committed already to the expatriate community, to the care of Christian famine orphans and an agricultural settlement, and to teaching in the high school, which Westcott rebuilt in 1892. The brothers started a printing press and industrial workshops, notably a brass foundry, to train orphans, recruiting European instructors, and raising money from grants and deputation work on brief furloughs. By 1916 press and workshops had served their turn and were closed; local factories took on all their employees forthwith, in preference to others and often at improved rates. Christ Church College with its hostels developed from the high school in 1897, and George served on the syndicate of the University of Allahabad to which it was affiliated.

Their fraternal partnership was dissolved reluctantly. Westcott refused the see of Rangoon in 1903, and in 1905 Foss Westcott hesitated before accepting Chota Nagpur, partly on the grounds that his brother 'was far better qualified for Episcopal work than myself' (F. Westcott to Bishop H. H. Montgomery, 23 March 1905, USPG archive). This was probably an accurate assessment at the time as regards the standard burden of diocesan administration, but Westcott was developing less routine inter-faith ambitions. Dr A. Clifford, whom he succeeded as bishop of Lucknow in 1910, informed SPG headquarters in 1909 that

'George Westcott without Foss is not quite the same person' commenting on the mission's loss of 'tone … smoothness and … vigour' (A. Clifford to H. H. Montgomery, 15 July 1909, USPG archive); but he overlooked this significant supplementary distraction.

The brothers' commitment to 'Indianization' and unification of Christian denominations entailed careful defocusing of doctrinal differences, in Foss Westcott's question-begging words on the grounds that 'irregular' sacraments and practices are not invalid but potentially fruitful, where manifestly 'given by God in answer to the sincere faith of the recipients' (F. Westcott to G. H. Westcott, 12 Dec 1917, USPG archive). George Westcott, alarmed by the establishment of religious centres in north India by Muslims, Hindus, and Arya Samaj, sought to apply this simple 'fulfilment theology' in an inter-faith context. From 1908 he eagerly promoted the establishment of a college of study, with accommodation for both Christians and non-Christians, to explore, in constructive, well-grounded confrontation, the gradual fulfilment in Christianity of fundamentally valid non-Christian insights.

He was defeated by 'chronic hardupness' (to quote a sympathetic London Missionary Society missionary), by the war and, he believed, by SPG neglect, but wrote his book, *Kabir and the Kabir Panth* (1907; reprinted 1953). Kabir (*fl.* 1480), had drawn on Sufi and Hindu insights, but particularly from the personal devotionalism of the popular and unorthodox *bhakti* saints and poets, to excoriate exclusivism, ritualism, and caste hierarchy, and to teach a life of Christlike integrity. Characteristically, the principal acknowledgement in Westcott's modest scholarly work was to his own gardener, a *mali* of low caste and a *panthi* or devotee, who had furthered Westcott's enquiries 'with great intelligence' and introduced him to many *mahants* or exponents in Kabir's contemporary following.

As bishop, Westcott cherished the garden he fostered at Allahabad, and against the climatic odds he was notably successful with his roses. Before he could retire to the Nilgiri hills in south India, within reach of his brother, Westcott died, unmarried, at his home, the bishop's house, Allahabad, on 16 January 1928. He was buried in Allahabad. GERALD STUDDERT-KENNEDY

Sources *The Times* (17 Jan 1928) · 'In memoriam: the late bishop of Lucknow. Extract from an Allahabad paper', *The Marlburian* (15 March 1928) · A. Westcott, *Life and letters of Brooke Foss Westcott*, 2 vols. (1903) · G. Studdert-Kennedy, *Providence and the raj: imperial mission and missionary imperialism* (1998) · Bodl. RH, United Society for the Propagation of the Gospel archives · Crockford

Archives Bodl. RH, USPG archive · CUL, Brooke Foss Westcott MSS

Wealth at death £5716 18s. 8d.: administration with will, 3 Nov 1928, *CGPLA Eng. & Wales*

Wester Wemyss. For this title name *see* Wemyss, Rosslyn Erskine, Baron Wester Wemyss (1864–1933).

Westerman, Percy Francis (1876–1959), children's writer and journalist, was born at 41 Kensington Terrace, Portsea, Portsmouth, Hampshire, on 18 May 1876, the son of William Francis Westerman, a master of arms in the Royal

Navy, and his wife, Lavinia Anne Colborne. Educated at Portsmouth grammar school, Westerman was keen to go to sea when he left school at the age of eighteen, but poor eyesight prevented him from being commissioned in the Royal Navy, and he obtained a clerical appointment in Portsmouth Dockyard. He used his leisure time for sailing and travelling, and began to write articles for magazines about his experiences. On 23 April 1900 Westerman married Florence Emily, daughter of John Wager, ship's steward, and a son, John Francis Cyril Westerman, was born in 1901. Westerman continued to combine freelance journalism with his clerical duties, his articles appearing in such periodicals as the *Motor Boat Magazine* and *Yachting Weekly*. As well as proving a useful supplement to his salary, which at the time of his marriage was only £90 a year, Westerman's journalism also provided him with a literary apprenticeship before, almost accidentally, he stumbled into writing more substantially.

According to family legend, Westerman's first book, *A Lad of Grit*, published by Blackie in 1908 (but dated 1909), originated in a 6*d*. bet made by Westerman with his wife that he could write a better boys' story than the 'tosh' he was reading to his small son. On his wife's retort that the book was better than he could manage, the bet was made and in due course *A Lad of Grit*, a tale of Restoration times, appeared. In 1911 Westerman resigned from his Admiralty appointment to devote himself to full-time writing, and other books followed, not only historical fiction, but tales about sea scouts, and contemporary adventure stories, exploiting the emerging technology of submarines, airships, and the wireless. During the First World War Westerman was for a time employed on coastal duties with the Royal Navy, and he later held a commission in the newly formed Royal Flying Corps, these experiences doubtless helping to provide the background for such books as *Rounding up the Raider: a Naval Story of the Great War* (1916) and *Winning his Wings: a Story of the R.A.F.* (1919).

After the war Westerman and his family lived on a houseboat on the River Frome at Wareham, Dorset, and he consolidated his reputation as one of the best adventure-story writers of the day. Although previously his works had appeared under various publishers' imprints, from 1927 his books were published exclusively by Blackie, who contracted Westerman to produce three books a year. Most were written in the evenings in a beautiful longhand which was then typed before submission to the publisher. By the 1930s Westerman's reputation was at its peak. Although he had never settled on any particular locale or group of characters, he had built up a considerable following for his thrilling and well-told tales in a variety of styles, and a new series of books about a recurring hero, Standish of the air police, reinforced his earlier success. He was acclaimed as the most popular boys' author in a referendum run by the *Daily Sketch*, and was the subject of a film made by Pathé Gazette.

During the Second World War Westerman served with the Home Guard in Dorset, and continued writing, *War Cargo* (1941), the story of a transatlantic voyage, being a typical example. Books continued to appear after the war,

but an accident forced Westerman to leave his houseboat in the late forties, and he and Florence moved to lodgings in Wareham. Poor health eventually slowed down his writing, but he still had books published in each of the last four years of his life. A keen sailor and an enthusiastic supporter of the scouting movement, Westerman became a well-known local personality with his nautical figure and peaked yachting cap. By the time he died at St Leonards Hospital, Dorset, on 22 February 1959, he had written over 170 books, which had been translated in half a dozen European languages with total sales of over 1.5 million copies. His son was also a writer of boys' stories.

Although his tales of the sea retain some *aficionados*, Westerman's books remain of interest largely for cultural reasons. His historical novels, such as *A Lad of Grit*, illustrate the survival of the tradition of G. A. Henty into the twentieth century, and tales such as *The Airship 'Golden Hind'* (1920) show how the fascination with aspects of the new technology developed from the onset of the First World War. Westerman's fiction, in general, despite such limitations as a rather pedestrian style, with its emphasis on patriotism, discipline, and tenacity, offers a revealing picture of British character and culture as enjoyed by many in the first half of the twentieth century.

DENNIS BUTTS

Sources D. Brown, 'Percy Westerman pulls it off', *Guardian Weekend* (30 Jan 1982) · D. Butts, 'Percy F. Westerman', *Book Collecting and Library Monthly* (Oct 1968), 186–8 · K. J. Sterck, 'Percy Francis Westerman', *Twentieth-century children's writers* (1978), 1315–20 · *The Times* (25 Feb 1959) · b. cert. · m. cert. · d. cert. · *CGPLA Eng. & Wales* (1959)
Archives priv. coll. · Wareham Pictorial Museum, Dorset
Likenesses P. Clarke, drawing, 1982 (after picture in Wareham Museum), repro. in Brown, 'Percy Westerman pulls it off'
Wealth at death £976 7*s*. 2*d*.: probate, 28 May 1959, *CGPLA Eng. & Wales*

Westermarck, Edvard Alexander [Edward] (1862–1939), anthropologist, sociologist, and philosopher, was born in Helsinki, Finland, on 20 November 1862, the third son and fourth of five children of Constance Gustava Maria Blomqvist (1830–1909) and Nils Christian Westermarck (1826–1904), whose family can be traced to seventeenth-century farmers in Sweden. His parents were of a cultured middle-class university background, his father being bursar of Helsinki University and a former Latin master and his mother the daughter of a professor of the history of ideas. Although not close to his father, Westermarck recorded that his memory of his mother was 'entirely dominated by a feeling of infinite devotion and affection' (*Memories of my Life*, 22). He was similarly attached to his sister Helena, who became a noted artist.

Early years and studies The initial prospects for the young Westermarck were not favourable. Helena recorded that he was a 'delicate and weak' child (H. Westermarck, 17; author's translation). Within a few weeks he developed a malady in his leg that endangered his life and required an operation. The prognosis of lameness proved false, but he continued to be plagued by other ailments, principally asthma. His lifelong propensity for travel and adventure—hiking tours, mountain climbs, and journeys

Edvard Alexander Westermarck (1862–1939), by M. E., 1913

around Morocco—resulted from the need to overcome a fear of immobility inherited from an unhealthy childhood.

As a child in a Swedish-speaking household, Westermarck had an important advantage, since Swedish was the only official language in Finland throughout most of the nineteenth century. When he was eight he was taken by his mother to Böök's Lyceum, and after two years he was moved to the Swedish Normal Lyceum. His eight years at that school were not recalled as a happy time, both because of illnesses and because he was a slow reader with a poor memory that demanded unpleasurable hard work. His favourite subject was essay writing, and even at an early age he chose ambitious topics.

On 23 May 1881 Westermarck passed his matriculation examination with high marks and was enrolled in Helsinki University. He was absorbed in his studies, showing an early interest in aesthetics. Soon he abandoned his Christian beliefs, coming to see religious faith as 'unworthy of a thinking human being' (*Memories of my Life*, 36). The six months he spent writing an honours thesis in history awakened a lifelong devotion to research, with an emphasis on gathering data:

> For the first time in my life I was now able to devote myself to something that might be called creative scientific work of however humble a kind. I had to collect—in great measure from original sources—facts bearing on the subject for the definite purpose of drawing conclusions from them. (ibid., 28)

He then decided to turn to the study of philosophy, with decisive consequences for the whole of his subsequent career, and he wrote a thesis on whether civilization increases the happiness of mankind.

Nineteenth-century Finnish philosophy was heavily influenced by Germans—Kant, Fichte, Schelling, and Hegel—an outlook that Westermarck found anathema. He cited with approval the picture of the typical German philosopher as 'a blind man in a pitch-dark room looking for a black hat that is not there at all', and he later likened

German metaphysics to a shallow river that 'gave the impression of depth simply because it was so muddy' (*Memories of my Life*, 30). In contrast, he was drawn to British empiricism. By 1884 he had read Mill and Spencer in Swedish translation, and he also developed an early enthusiasm for Locke, Hume, and Adam Smith. This initial preference for empiricism remained a fundamental feature of his intellectual outlook. He admired its 'clearness and a sense of reality; and if its hypotheses were not unfailingly true, in every case it seemed possible that they could be corrected by a deeper search into the facts of experience' (ibid., 30). He also encountered the work of Charles Darwin, which implanted in his mind a question about the origin of sexual modesty, the realization that he needed to learn English, and the lesson that 'the greatest danger in science is not to be found in wrong theories but in wrong facts' (ibid., 77). His quest for right facts took him in September 1887 to England, which he described as 'my intellectual fatherland', to do research at the British Museum, for him 'the dwelling of the goddess of thought' (ibid., 79). He chose English as the language for his doctoral dissertation (1889) and almost all his major works, transposing his name to Edward for such publications.

That dissertation was expanded to become, two years later, Westermarck's epochal *The History of Human Marriage*, which with hindsight he called 'the most momentous happening' in his life (*Memories of my Life*, 99). In the book he boldly announced his 'firm conviction that the history of human civilization should be made an object of as scientific a treatment as the history of organic nature' (*History of Human Marriage*, 1). Advancing the claim that the theory of primitive promiscuity held by most anthropologists at that time was hopelessly defective, he appealed to a mass of ethnographical data to maintain the ubiquity of marriage and the evolutionary underpinnings of the institutions of marriage and the family. Indeed, so great was his evidentiary base that one reviewer commended the 29-year-old for the 'earnest labour of the chief part of a lifetime', and Westermarck recounted that he was twice taken for his own son (*Memories of my Life*, 98).

Although this book made Westermarck's name known to an international audience, he did not immediately follow up with other publications aimed at a wide readership. Instead, he wrote articles mostly in Swedish and spent the better part of the 1890s at Helsinki University. He had received his bachelor's degree from that institution on 28 May 1886, his master's on 31 May 1886, his licentiate on 1 February 1890, and his doctorate on 20 September 1890. He had also worked as an assistant at the university library starting as early as September 1882, but his first academic appointment came on 8 August 1890 as lecturer in sociology. From 1894 to 1897 he served as acting professor of philosophy.

Westermarck's most significant activity during the late 1880s and early 1890s was his participation in the Philosophical Society of Helsinki, where he engaged in lively debates with his teacher K. G. T. Rein, Hjalmar Neiglick, Yrjö Hirn, and others. He credited these discussions with the inspiration for his study of the origin and development of the moral ideas, a topic that occupied him for almost twenty years. A plausible timetable would allot the period 1889–93 to his initial conception and exploration of the subject, 1893–8 to the intensive formation of his moral thought, and 1898–1906 to the elaboration and publication of his ideas. What prompted his interest was the stubborn fact of ethical disagreement and whether it resulted from 'defective knowledge or had … a merely sentimental origin' (*Memories of my Life*, 100).

International directions Towards the end of the 1890s Westermarck's activities went in two new directions. In 1897 he received a Rosenberg stipend for the purpose of foreign travel to study, in the first instance, at the British Museum. But his proposal was not limited to armchair study in England; he wrote that he considered it 'desirable to study the problem I have set for myself not only from books but from life, not only to read about the world's multifarious folk but to visit them' (application for Rosenberg stipend, Westermarck Archives, Åbo Akademi, as trans. in Stroup, *Westermarck's Ethics*, 75). His itinerary was ambitious, including the Amazon, Polynesia, Australia, Malaya, and India. In fact, he never got further than Morocco, where he found enough ethnological data to absorb his interest for the rest of his life. As he put it, 'better much about little than a little about much' (*Memories of my Life*, 146).

The second of Westermarck's new directions was towards the movement for Finnish independence. At the time of his birth Helsinki had for more than fifty years been the capital of the Grand Duchy of Finland, a semi-autonomous territory ceded by Sweden in 1809 to Tsar Alexander I of Russia. This colonial relationship troubled Westermarck and desire for an independent Finland prompted him to devote much energy in his middle years to that cause. In 1899 he wrote an article for the *Contemporary Review* entitled 'Finland and the czar', a prelude to his efforts that same year travelling through Italy and Switzerland to obtain signatories to the ultimately unsuccessful 'Pro Finlandia' appeal addressed to the tsar. When the First World War broke out he also travelled to Sweden in the hope of generating moral and financial support for independence. But it was not until September 1918 that, from the deck of a steamer out of Stockholm, he was able 'to behold the great marvel that I had dreamt of but never seen—a free Finland' (*Memories of my Life*, 277).

The first of Westermarck's many trips to Morocco occurred in March 1898. He travelled to Tangier, Tetuan, Marrakesh, and Fez, encountering many hardships. From an intellectual standpoint this visit was unsatisfying because, in the three months allotted, he never had the opportunity to probe adequately into the society. But his stay did teach him a lesson, that 'a journey for ethnological research is a serious undertaking, needing much time and patience' (*Memories of my Life*, 145). He resolved to return, to learn the indigenous languages, and to conduct rigorous anthropological investigations. In 1900 he went back for two continuous years, and altogether he made twenty-one journeys to the country for a combined total

of seven years of fieldwork, although there was a gap in his visits from 1913 to 1923. In Morocco he relied for protection and assistance on his companion for several decades, Sidi Abdsslam al-Baqqali.

Back in England, Westermarck was working through his moral philosophy and participating in meetings of the Sociological Society and the Aristotelian Society, where he encountered such thinkers as Francis Galton, Harald Høffding, James Bryce, Samuel Alexander, Bernard Bosanquet, and Alexander Shand. He also continued his friendship with James Sully, whose acquaintance he had made in the 1880s while walking in Norway. In 1904 he accepted an invitation from the University of London to give a course of public lectures on a sociological subject of his own choice. When the lectures, entitled 'Early custom and morals' and held at the London School of Economics (LSE), were finished he was asked to become an 'appointed teacher of sociology', and he accepted. Thus began an association that continued in at least one term of every academic year until 1930. On 17 December 1907 Westermarck became one of the first two professors of sociology at the LSE, the other being L. T. Hobhouse. The chairs resulted from an endowment by Westermarck's friend Martin White, who was disturbed by the ignorance of sociology among his fellow members of the House of Commons.

Alternating with his teaching in London, Westermarck served as professor at two Finnish institutions: Helsinki University (professor of practical philosophy from 18 August 1906 to 5 November 1918) and the Åbo Akademi (professor of philosophy from 1 September 1918 to 31 December 1932). At the Åbo Akademi he also became the first rector, on 16 September 1918. On the whole, however, he preferred his teaching in England. The English students were 'not so bashful or afraid to display their ignorance', whereas the Finnish students 'sat as mum as mice' (*Memories of my Life*, 199). He also prized the domestic arrangements at the LSE, which encouraged greater closeness among the faculty than he had found at Helsinki University and which gave him a 'much deeper insight into the English character'. The tradition of meeting in the teacher's own room ('mine is one of the largest'; ibid., 201) he found congenial, even noting the freedom shared by men and women to light up cigarettes and pipes. Finally, he was delighted by the international diversity among the LSE students and listed in his memoirs the many countries represented at his lectures and seminars.

The major works Westermarck left no lasting school of students in anthropology, sociology, or philosophy, but he did count among his pupils or those who attended his lectures many notable intellectuals. In England these included Bronisław Malinowski, Morris Ginsberg, E. E. Evans-Pritchard, Raymond Firth, Hortense Powdermaker, Ashley Montagu, and the American Talcott Parsons. Among those in Finland were Gunnar Landtman, Ragnar Numelin, Rafael Karsten, Hilma Granqvist, and Rolf Lagerborg. But Westermarck's most lasting influence has been through his books. His major works were published from 1906 until the end of his life: the two-volume *The Origin and Development of the Moral Ideas* (1906–8), *Marriage Ceremonies in Morocco* (1914), the revised, three-volume *The History of Human Marriage* (1921), the two-volume *Ritual and Belief in Morocco* (1926), *Wit and Wisdom in Morocco* (1930), *Early Beliefs and their Social Influence* (1932), *Ethical Relativity* (1932), *Three Essays on Sex and Marriage* (1934), *The Future of Marriage in Western Civilization* (1936), and *Christianity and Morals* (1939).

The chief focuses of Westermarck's writings were thus morality, marriage, and Morocco. His moral theory was addressed predominantly to the question of whether moral judgements have objective validity. His answer was clearly negative. Against those who held that moral principles are apprehended through acts of intuition or the workings of reason, he maintained that 'there can be no moral truth in the sense in which this term is generally understood' (*The Origin and Development of Moral Ideas*, 1.17), because 'moral judgments are ultimately based, not on the intellect, but on emotions' (*Memories of my Life*, 101), and 'no objectivity can come from an emotion' (*Ethical Relativity*, 60). To support his contention he amassed in *The Origin and Development of the Moral Ideas* a vast compendium of moral practices and beliefs, which enabled him to draw general conclusions about behaviour based on a systematic empirical study. In his later *Ethical Relativity* he coupled this approach with a detailed philosophical analysis of some leading moral philosophers, such as Kant, Mill, and Sidgwick.

Although Westermarck was attacked, notably by G. E. Moore, for reducing moral judgements to expressions or reports of the feelings of the speaker, he emphatically denied doing any such thing. Instead, following Hume, he pointed to a human tendency to turn subjective moral feelings into purportedly objective moral beliefs. This objectivizing he linked to disinterestedness and impartiality as two distinct characteristics of the moral emotions. While all emotions are felt only by the person who has them, he held that some emotions, through social conditioning, come to have reference beyond the mere individual: 'Society is the school in which we learn to distinguish between right and wrong' (*Ethical Relativity*, 50).

Westermarck was concerned lest his view be taken as a form of nihilism, which would have been foreign to all he stood for. He denied that if moral judgements were seen as merely expressive and prescriptive they would cease to have a basis. Morality consists of a development through evolution of patterns of reacting to the natural settings in which people find themselves: 'We approve and disapprove because we cannot do otherwise' (*Ethical Relativity*, 58). Indeed, he thought his view of moral values was ultimately liberating:

> Far above the vulgar idea that the right is a settled something to which everybody has to adjust his opinions, rises the conviction that it has its existence in each individual mind, capable of any expansion, proclaiming its own right to exist, if needs be, venturing to make a stand against the whole world. (*The Origin and Development of Moral Ideas*, 1.20)

Westermarck's writings on marriage were remarkably consistent over a period of more than forty years. He defined marriage as 'a more or less durable connection between male and female, lasting beyond the mere act of propagation till after the birth of the offspring' (*The History of Human Marriage*, 1891, 19–20, 537). He joined a thorough investigation of human sexual practices with a trans-species approach, citing similarities in the behaviour of the higher primates. Thus he practised his belief that 'marriage must primarily be studied in its connection with biological conditions' (*Memories of my Life*, 68). Social institutions develop from social habits; habits can be explained as outgrowths of needs; and needs are biologically determined. Émile Durkheim criticized Westermarck for his appeal to evolutionary theory, which he deemed 'contrary to proper method' (Durkheim, 608; author's translation). But while Westermarck was not an uncritical exponent of Darwinism, he did think that such an approach was generally supported by the evidence and had great explanatory power. Nor was he uncritical of the comparative method, which he practised with scrupulous integrity and an awareness of its limitations, and which he supplemented with his own fieldwork.

The most provocative contention in Westermarck's books on marriage was that exogamy resulted from 'a remarkable absence of erotic feelings between persons living very closely together from childhood' (*The History of Human Marriage*, 5th edn, 1921, 2.192). Indeed, he posited an actual aversion to intercourse between relatives, which in turn accounted for prohibitions against incest. This account was not original with Westermarck; it can be traced back to Francis Hutcheson's *An Inquiry into the Original of our Ideas of Beauty and Virtue* (1725). But Westermarck was definitely challenging the established thought of his time, as recognized by Alfred Russel Wallace, who predicted that the 'hitherto unknown student' would eventually be proved right (Wallace, introduction, *The History of Human Marriage*, 1891, v). Acceptance, however, took a long time in coming. Malinowski wrote that this theory of exogamy 'seems to find favour with no one' (Malinowski, 'Sexual life and marriage among primitive mankind', *Nature*, 109, 22 April 1922, 504), and the roster of opponents was impressive: Durkheim, James Frazer, Havelock Ellis, Robert Briffault, and William McDougall. But Westermarck's most influential critic was Sigmund Freud, who ridiculed 'the most monstrous efforts' to account for prohibitions against incest by early aversion (Freud, *A General Introduction to Psychoanalysis*, trans. G. S. Hall, 1920, 176). Westermarck answered Freud in his *Three Essays on Sex and Marriage*, but only with recent empirical studies, particularly in China, has the 'Westermarck hypothesis' received more widespread adherence.

By contrast, Westermarck has always been recognized as a worthy pioneer for his fieldwork in Morocco. Malinowski exclaimed that 'no better field-work exists ... than that of Westermarck in Morocco. It was done with a greater expenditure of care and time than any other specialised anthropological research' (Malinowski, 867). Westermarck sought to provide a systematic account of beliefs and customs, emphasizing psychological origins.

He studied marriage practices, *baraka* (the quality of blessedness), curses, the evil eye, and other subjects by enquiring of many informants, who became in effect his teachers. He was sensitive to all regions and cultures of the country, and he travelled incessantly in pursuit of knowledge despite real dangers; he wrote of 'living like a nomad in my tent, travelling from tribe to tribe and settling down for weeks or months, now in one, now in another country village where I found useful work could be done' (letter from Westermarck, 21 July 1901, BL, Macmillan Archive, vol. 371). At the time he first ventured to Morocco, much of 'anthropological' enquiry was undertaken by missionaries as a by-product of their proselytizing or by researchers who failed to learn the local language and thus had to rely on interpreters. Westermarck was one of the first to develop modern methods of investigation, and his *Ritual and Belief in Morocco* is still consulted by Moroccanists for its insights.

Westermarck's last work was *Christianity and Morals*, a topic that he had already anticipated in a pamphlet of 1907 published by Prometheus, a Finnish anti-clerical and agnostic society in which he participated. In the book he presents a full-scale treatment of Christian doctrines on such subjects as marriage, divorce, the sacraments, asceticism, and sexual relations. In attempting to arrive at a balanced estimation of Christianity's moral effect, he reached the negative conclusion that it has on the whole been bad. Predictably the book encountered strong opposition from believers, but Westermarck did not live long enough to witness much of this reaction. Less than three months after publication, while on vacation in Lappvik, Finland, he fell violently ill with shortness of breath. Always prone to attacks of asthma, this last onslaught proved too much for him, and he died there on 3 September 1939. He was buried in Helsinki. Thus ended what he had humbly described as 'that infinitesimal ripple on the ocean of eternity which is called my life' (*Memories of my Life*, 307).

Person and scholar In his autobiography, *Minnen ur mitt liv* (1927, published in translation two years later as *Memories of my Life*), Westermarck paraphrased Ovid: *Bene vixit qui bene latuit* ('He lives well who keeps well hidden'; *Memories of my Life*, 307). Perhaps in part this claim of hiddenness was an oblique reference to his own homosexuality and bachelorhood, but others found his complex personality hard to fathom in any absolute way. On the surface, he was described by Ashley Montagu as a 'well-upholstered but not overstuffed' man who 'spoke perfect English with a slight Scandinavian accent', whose 'knowledge was literally encyclopedic', and who always expressed himself with 'the greatest modesty' (A. Montagu, 'Edward Westermark: recollections of an old student in young age', in Stroup, *Edward Westermarck*, 64). Raymond Firth recalled him as 'delightfully witty and humorous' (interview with J. Benthall, 24 Jan 2002). But Westermarck's pupil Gunnar Landtman raised a deeper doubt about the key to Westermarck's character. He recalled that Westermarck was once asked whether anyone knew 'the true

Westermarck'. As described by Landtman, his teacher took the question with great seriousness: 'It was as if it had touched him at a point where wonder can not simply be revoked with a jest, and his head shake indicated a denial of the implications of the question' (Ihanus, 14).

At any rate, Westermarck's public career was anything but hidden. As Claude Lévi-Strauss has observed, he 'performed at the end of the nineteenth century the same role for the social sciences that the Renaissance masters did for modern thought' (Lévi-Strauss, 181).

TIMOTHY STROUP

Sources E. A. Westermarck, *Memories of my life*, trans. A. Barwell (1929) · E. A. Westermarck, *Minnen ur mitt liv* (Helsinki, 1927) [Swedish original of Westermarck's autobiography] · R. Lagerborg, *Om Edvard Westermarck och verkan från hans verkstad under hans tolv sista år 1927–1939* (Helsinki, 1951) · T. Stroup, ed., *Edward Westermarck: essays on his life and works* (Helsinki, 1982), esp. 1–23, 25–61, 63–70 · T. Stroup, *Westermarck's ethics* (Åbo, 1982) · G. Landtman, 'Edv. Westermarck', *Finska Vetenskaps-Societetens Sammanträde* [*Societas Scientiarum Fennica Årsbok* 19C:2] (21 Oct 1940), 3–20 · J. Ihanus, *Multiple origins: Edward Westermarck in search of mankind* (Frankfurt am Main, 1999) · C.-E. Sundman, *Åbo Akademis lärare och tjänstemän, 1918–1968* (Åbo, 1968), 243–4 · H. Westermarck, *Mina levnadsminnen* (Åbo, 1941) · E. Durkheim, 'Review of Westermarck, *The history of human marriage*', *Revue philosophique de la France et de l'étranger*, 5 (1895), 606–23 · S. Freud, *A general introduction to psychoanalysis*, trans. J. Riviere (New York, 1920); repr. (1953) · C. Lévi-Strauss, 'The work of Edward Westermarck', trans. A. Stroup and T. Stroup, *Edward Westermarck: essays on his life and work*, ed. T. Stroup (Helsinki, 1982), 84–100 · B. Malinowski, 'Anthropology of the westernmost Orient', *Nature*, 120 (17 Dec 1927), 867–8 · A. Wolf, *Sexual attraction and childhood association: a Chinese brief for Edward Westermarck* (Stanford, 1995) · K. Suolinna, C. af Hällström, and T. Lahtinen, *Portraying Morocco: Edward Westermarck's fieldwork and photographs* (Åbo, 2000)

Archives Åbo Akademi Library, Åbo (Turku), Finland, Archives Division, documents, clippings, lecture notes, letters, photographs | BL, corresp. with Macmillans, Add. MS 55156 · Keele University Library, LePlay Collection, corresp. and minute book entries as member of Sociological Society committees

Likenesses M. Enckell, oils, 1913, Nylands Students' Union, Helsinki, Finland · M. E., portrait, 1913, London School of Economics [*see illus.*] · H. Backmansson, oils, 1923, Åbo Akademi, Åbo (Turku), Finland · V. Thomé, oils, 1938, Helsinki University, Finland · H. Westermarck, pencil sketch, priv. coll. · photographs, Åbo Akademi library, Åbo (Turku), Finland

Western, Charles Callis, Baron Western (*bap.* **1767**, *d.* **1844**), politician, was the elder son of Charles Western of Rivenhall, Essex, and Frances Shirley, daughter and heir of Frances and William Bollan of Rivenhall (he was agent for the council of Massachusetts), and grandson of Thomas Western (*d.* 1765) and his wife, Anne Callis. He was baptized at Rivenhall on 9 August 1767. His great-grandfather Thomas Western (*d.* 1733) of Rivenhall married Mary, daughter and coheir of Sir Richard Shirley of Preston, Sussex, a near relative of the three famous brothers of Elizabethan fame, Sir Anthony Shirley, Robert Shirley, and Sir Thomas Shirley.

Western was educated at Newcome's school, Hackney, at Eton College, and at Queens' College, Cambridge, but apparently left the university without graduating. From his youth he was a close friend of Thomas Creevey. His father died when he was four years old, and upon attaining his majority he succeeded to the Rivenhall estates, purchasing, two years later, that of Felix Hall, Kelvedon. To this mansion, where he lived, he added a fine classical portico, constructed from a scale drawing of the Roman temple of Fortuna Virilis, given in Desgodetz's *Édifices antiques de Rome* (1682). He filled the house with valuable busts, urns, sarcophagi, and other objects collected during his travels abroad. They are given in a *Descriptive sketch of ancient statues, busts, &c. at Felix Hall … with plates of the most striking objects in the collection* (1833).

Western was elected on 16 June 1790 as MP for Maldon, which borough he represented until 1812, with a break in 1806–7. In these years he was seen as a moderate Foxite. In 1812, he stood successfully for Essex 'upon the old Whig interest', distancing himself from the more radical Burgoyne and receiving some tory support. He represented Essex until 1832. During his forty-two years in parliament he became the mouthpiece of the agricultural interests in the Commons, and boldly attacked, although without any immediate result, the currency question, with which the welfare of agriculture was, he considered, indissolubly bound, for he believed the sinking fund kept stocks artificially high. If not the author, he was one of the leading promoters of the Corn Bill of 1815, and advocated even more protection than it provided. He supported out-and-out protection, being as strongly opposed to the fixed duty of the whigs as to the free-trade doctrines of the Anti-Corn Law League. He became known, inevitably, as 'Squire' Western.

Western was also interested in penal policy. He toured gaols and published *Remarks upon Prison Discipline* (1821) and *Thoughts on Prison Discipline* (1822), which included a design by William Cubitt, the inventor of the treadmill, for a model house of correction to contain 400 prisoners. The earlier tract was highly praised in the *Edinburgh Review* (36, 1821–2, 353), and both were answered by George Holford in a *Vindication of the General Penitentiary at Milbank* (1822).

Despite his pronounced protectionism, Western remained whiggish on Catholic emancipation and parliamentary reform, differing from many Essex men on both. At the first election after the Reform Act he was defeated by thirty-two votes. Melbourne at once created him Baron Western of Rivenhall, Essex. On 21 March 1834 a presentation was made to him at Chelmsford by the county, where he was personally extremely popular. But although he had made his mark in the lower house as a speaker of great ability, he seldom took part in the debates of the Lords, and thenceforth lived in comparative retirement, devoted to practical improvements in farming, and experiments which he invited all agriculturists to examine. He gave his attention particularly to creating improved breeds of sheep; his name was long known and honoured in the colonies for his skilful efforts to 'place Merino wool upon a Leicester carcass'.

Western died at Felix Hall on 4 November 1844, and was buried on the 13th in Rivenhall church with his ancestors. He was unmarried, and the peerage became extinct. The estates devolved upon Western's cousin, Thomas Burch Western, of Tattingstone Park, Suffolk, who was created a baronet on 20 August 1864 and died in 1917.

CHARLOTTE FELL-SMITH, *rev.* H. C. G. MATTHEW

Sources HoP, *Commons* · GEC, *Peerage* · *Chelmsford Chronicle* (8 Nov 1844) · *Chelmsford Chronicle* (15 Nov 1844) · *Essex Herald* (1 Jan 1833) · *The Times* (5 Nov 1844) · *Chelmsford Chronicle* (Nov 1844) · private information (1899) · Burke, *Peerage*
Archives Essex RO, family, legal and estate papers | BL, letters to Arthur Young and others · Northumbd RO, letters to Thomas Creevey · W. Sussex RO, letters to duke of Richmond
Likenesses S. W. Reynolds junior, mezzotint, pubd 1844 (after R. Ansdell), BM · J. S. Copley, double portrait, oils (with his brother, as children), Hunt. L. · J. S. Copley, portrait, Felix Hall, Kelvedon, Essex
Wealth at death under £35,000

Western, Thomas (*bap.* 1624, *d.* 1707), ironmonger and gun-founder, was baptized on 10 October 1624 at St Olave, Hart Street, in the City of London, the son of William Western (*bap.* 1576, *d.* 1640), grocer, and Frances Trott. A member of the Grocers' Company, Western married on 30 September 1651 Martha (*d.* 1699), daughter of Samuel Gott, ironmonger of London. He became an ironmonger himself in the 1650s, and in 1660 leased Brede furnace in Sussex from Samuel Gott, MP, his wife's brother. Afterwards he received orders for guns and shot from the Board of Ordnance, breaking into the monopoly held by the Brownes, the king's gun-founders. By February 1666 he had delivered fifty-four guns and 200 tons of shot, becoming the largest supplier after the Brownes in the second and third Dutch wars. He shared the gun contracts under the Thirty Ships Act with Mary, widow of John Browne, casting over 550 guns in 1678 and 1679.

Western obtained less official business in the 1680s, apart from orders for mortars, beds, and shells. During James II's reign he was said to be 'as much against the King's Government and interest as any, and as hott and violent as the worst' (Woodhead, 174), and was not allowed to hold civic office. Unsurprisingly, he became a supporter of William III. Western's son Samuel, and Peter Gott, his nephew and son-in-law, became whig MPs. Western claimed in 1690 to have supplied since 1689 'several great guns and other provisions of war', and was 'willing further to provide the like at reasonable prices … to a total not exceeding £30,000' (*Calendar of Treasury Books, 1689–1692*, 9.527). Under a second Thirty Ships Act, Western took the largest share, casting almost 1400 guns, worth £48,500, between 1692 and 1699. He was the most important gun-founder under William III.

Western had international interests, buying iron from the Netherlands and Sweden, exporting it to Guinea and the East; and he shipped about £2500 worth of guns, shot, and iron with the East India Company annually in the 1670s. He hired out ballast and guns to merchantmen, and was probably responsible for a series of large iron mortars for the Venetian Republic in 1684. Western cast brass guns for the East India Company and the Board of Ordnance in the 1670s and 1680s in collaboration with William Wightman at the Moorfields foundry. A shareholder in the Royal African Company and the Bank of England, he also invested in land, owning two estates in East Anglia, in addition to property, woods, and ironworks in the Sussex weald. In London he lived at Dyce Key, Billingsgate, and twice served on the common council as well as being deputy lieutenant of London.

At his death Western was one of the most important ironmongers in England. He owned Brede furnace and leased others such as Ashburnham, Robertsbridge, and Waldron as he needed them. He sent iron round the world, both as armament on ships and as cargo. In a business which was notorious for difficulties, Western was said, at his death, 'to be worth 200,000 pounds' (Luttrell, 130). He died on 11 January 1707 at his home, Rivenhall Manor, Essex, at the age of eighty-one, and was buried on 17 January, under an iron slab from his own furnace, in Rivenhall church, Essex; his wife had been buried there on 29 November 1699. Western and his wife had six daughters and five sons, two of whom followed their father's trade; Thomas was active as an ironmonger from 1693 until his death in 1697, after which Maximilian took over, supplying guns to the board and the East India Company until his death in 1720. Western's Gott grandsons owned Conster, Lamberhurst, and other ironworks

RUTH RHYNAS BROWN

Sources R. R. Brown, 'Thomas Western, the great ironmonger', in R. D. Smith, *Cannon technology* [forthcoming] · C. F. Smith, 'The Western family of Rivenhall', *Essex Review*, 10 (1901) · board of ordnance minute books, PRO, WO 47 · board of ordnance bill books, PRO, WO 51 · board of ordnance, Thirty Ships Act bill books, PRO, WO 50 · East India Company, court books and ledgers, BL OIOC · *CSP dom.*, 1650–1703 · W. A. Shaw, ed., *Calendar of treasury books*, 1–9, PRO (1904–31) · N. Luttrell, *A brief historical relation of state affairs from September 1678 to April 1714*, 6 (1857) · J. R. Woodhead, *The rulers of London, 1660–1689* (1965), 174 · H. Cleere and D. Crossley, *The iron industry of the Weald* (1985)
Archives BL OIOC, East India Company MSS · Fort Nelson, Hampshire, Royal Armouries [guns] · PRO, WO MSS
Wealth at death under £200,000: Luttrell, *Brief historical relation*, 130

Westfaling [Westphaling], **Herbert** (1531/2–1602), bishop of Hereford, was born in London, the son of Harbert Westphaling, whose family originated in Westphalia. He entered Christ Church, Oxford, in 1547, aged fifteen, where he graduated BA in 1551 and proceeded MA in 1555. In 1561 he took the degree of BTh, and incepted DTh in 1566. In February 1562 he was ordained priest by Edmund Grindal, bishop of London, and the same year was appointed a canon of Christ Church, Oxford, through the influence of Sir William Cecil. His radical sympathies were apparent early in his career, when in 1560 he was one of a number of petitioners to the earl of Leicester who requested the appointment of Thomas Sampson as dean of Christ Church. At the end of 1562 he was appointed Lady Margaret professor of divinity, a post that he held for little more than a year. In September 1567 he was made treasurer of the diocese of Lincoln, in 1570 was mentioned by Archbishop Parker as a possible bishop of Oxford, and in 1572 was appointed to the living of Brightwell Baldwin in Oxfordshire, which he was licensed to hold in plurality. His preferments continued with his appointment as vice-

Herbert Westfaling (1531/2–1602), by unknown artist [original, 1601]

chancellor of the University of Oxford in June 1576, and the acquisition of a canonry at Windsor the following May.

In 1576 Westfaling was appointed by Grindal, now archbishop of Canterbury, to a commission to investigate complaints against the dean and chapter of Gloucester. This resulted in a report incorporating articles for the better observance of capitular duties. The experience may well have influenced Westfaling's subsequent attitude to his own cathedral chapter after his consecration as bishop of Hereford on 30 January 1586. Since at the beginning of his primacy in autumn 1583 John Whitgift had suggested Westfaling as a possible dean of Windsor if William Day became bishop of London, it seems likely that he owed his elevation to the bench to Whitgift's further efforts and the acquiescence of Lord Burghley. Once installed at Hereford Westfaling, like his predecessor John Scory, experienced the problems of a bishop of somewhat advanced protestant views in a remote diocese with profoundly conservative religious opinions. He had particular difficulties with his own chapter, not least because of the machinations of Bishop Scory's venal and corrupt son Sylvanus, against whom Westfaling conducted a suit for dilapidations. In 1586 he castigated the vicars-choral for their suspect religious views and the use of superstitious images and pictures. Although the cathedral had been granted new statutes in 1583, they left unresolved the vexed question of the rights of the bishop to conduct visitations of the chapter. Although Westfaling insisted that the 'staffe or rodde of discipline God hath undoubtedly given to all trewe bishops' (Hereford Cathedral archives, 7031/2 fols. 123 ff.) his four attempts to visit, in 1586, 1588, 1589, and 1598, all met with defeat. More successful was a survey of the morals and educational qualifications of the diocesan clergy conducted in 1587. This revealed that most possessed no degree, and few of those who were licensed to preach were considered to have attained the status of 'painful' preachers. Although Westfaling was noted for his zeal in converting Roman Catholics, and was regarded by the lords in council as a fit and able person to be employed in conferences with Jesuits and other recusants, he appears to have had little success in Hereford, for his successor Bennett complained that the diocese was full of traditionalists and recusants.

Westfaling was noted for his gravity, and Francis Godwin, a long-time acquaintance, commented that he had scarcely ever seen him laugh. Portraits in the bishop's palace in Hereford and the Bodleian Library, Oxford, are suitably austere in appearance. His effigy in the north transept of Hereford Cathedral, possibly by the sculptor Samuel Baldwin of Stroud, conveys a similar impression. In December 1592 he gave an oration before Queen Elizabeth in the university church, Oxford, during which he was twice ordered by the queen to be brief so that she could herself deliver a speech later in the evening. Westfaling refused to be hurried and the queen was forced to postpone her own speech until the next day.

In 1582 Westfaling published a collection of seven sermons under the title *A Treatise of Reformation in Religion*. He was also the author of a number of manuscript poems in English and Latin, now in the library of Cambridge University (MS Ff.v. 14); but a manuscript translation of 'A discourse of Quintus Cicero to his brother Marcus concerning Suete for the consulship', in the Bodleian Library (MS Rawlinson D. 303) formerly attributed to the bishop, is in fact the work of his son. His personal library contained works by leading reformers of his time, his will mentioning the works of Calvin in folio, which he donated to Christ Church, Oxford, and nine volumes by Wolfgang Musculus, which he bequeathed to Hereford Cathedral Library. Shortly before his death he donated £20 to the Bodleian Library for the purchase of new books.

Westfaling married Anne, daughter of William *Barlow, bishop of Chichester, and widow of Augustine Bradbridge, prebendary of Salisbury and brother of William Bradbridge, bishop of Exeter. Anne Westfaling died at Westminster on 9 December 1597, while her husband was attending parliament. The marriage produced a son and three daughters. Anne, who married William Jeffries, would appear to have remarried, as 'my sonne Jenkes' was named with the bishop's other two sons-in-law as an overseer of his will in 1601. Margaret Westfaling was married to Richard Eedes, dean of Worcester, while her sister Elizabeth married Robert Walwyn of Newland, Worcestershire, from whose father Westfaling purchased an estate at Batch, in Herefordshire; he subsequently bequeathed it to Jesus College, Oxford, to endow two fellowships and scholarships. Significantly, the bequest contained the proviso that 'my kindred shallbe always preferred before anie

others' (PRO, PROB 11/99, sig. 12, fol. 90r). Westfaling also acquired the Herefordshire manor of Mansell Gamage, and in 1591 conveyed it to his son, Herbert, whose heirs possessed it until the late eighteenth century. Westfaling died at Hereford on 1 March 1602, and was buried in the north transept of his cathedral. His will contained generous provision for his servants and for the poor of the city of Hereford and the parish of Whitbourne, as well as bequests of plate to his grandchildren.

MARTIN E. SPEIGHT

Sources G. Aylmerod and J. Tiller, eds., *Hereford Cathedral: a history* (2000) • D. Pearson, 'The libraries of English bishops, 1600–40', *The Library*, 6th ser., 14 (1992), 221–57 • register of Bishop Herbert Westfaling, 1587, Hereford Cathedral archives, HCA 6450/5 • *DNB* • *History from marble, compiled in the reign of Charles II by Thomas Dingley*, ed. J. G. Nichols, 2 vols., CS, 94, 97 (1867–8) • F. O. White, *Lives of the Elizabethan bishops* (1898) • F. Heal, *Of prelates and princes: a study of the economic and social position of the Tudor episcopate* (1980) • will, PRO, PROB 11/90, sig. 12 • Foster, *Alum. Oxon.* • Wood, *Ath. Oxon.*, new edn, 1.719–21

Archives CUL, poems, MS Ff. v. 14

Likenesses oils, 1601, Christ Church Oxf. • engraving (after unknown portrait), Dean's Lodging, Bishop's Palace, Hereford • oils, Bodl. Oxf. • oils, other version (after original, 1601), Jesus College, Oxford • oils, other version (after original, 1601), bishop's palace, Hereford [*see illus.*] • tomb effigy, Hereford Cathedral; repro. in Dingly, *History from marble*, cxxxvii

Wealth at death cash bequests of £13 6s. 8d.; gilt plate; landed estates at Batch and Mansell Gamage, Herefordshire: will, PRO, PROB 11/90, sig. 12

Westfield, Thomas (1573–1644), bishop of Bristol, was born in the parish of St Mary's, Ely, Cambridgeshire, the son of William Westfield. After attending the free school there, in 1589 he matriculated at Jesus College, Cambridge, from where he graduated BA in 1593, proceeded MA in 1596, held a fellowship from 1599 to 1603, and proceeded BD in 1604 (incorporated at Oxford on 9 July 1611). Between 1600 and 1605 he was apparently rector of South Somercote, Lincolnshire, and vicar of Barton, Cambridgeshire, but he spent most of his long clerical career in the diocese of London. After assisting Nicholas Felton at St Mary-le-Bow, he became rector of St Bartholomew-the-Great, Smithfield (18 December 1605) and of Hornsey (28 April 1615), a living he retained until 1637. His patron at St Bartholomew's was Robert, Lord Rich, and Rich's son the earl of Holland also admired him. Westfield received the prebend of Ealdstreet (12 April 1614) in St Paul's Cathedral, which he exchanged for that of Caddington Major (1 March 1615). Thomas Fuller characterized Westfield as a 'contented meek man' because in 1617, having sufficient means for himself, he declined the see of Bristol (Fuller, *Worthies*, 232). At an unknown date he married his first wife, Ann; she was buried at St Bartholomew's on 11 December 1619.

A theological Calvinist, Westfield was from 1631 to 1632 the first president of Sion College, yet he was also William Laud's choice, on 14 November 1631, for the archdeaconry of St Albans. He continued to steer a moderate path, and to enjoy the confidence of those of different viewpoints. In May 1640 he helped lead a protest against the continuation of the convocation after the dissolution of the Short

Parliament, and on 6 August he joined a group of London clergy who signed a petition against the 'etcetera oath'. In March 1641 he was among a varied group of clergy named as assistants to the House of Lords committee on innovations in religion but revealed his essential conformity when, in a sermon at St Paul's on 14 November, he defended episcopacy by praising Morton, Buckeridge, Ussher, Davenant, and other bishops of the Church of England whose books against 'popery' proved they did not deserve trampling by 'the dirty feet of some Sectaries in their scurrilous libels and pamphlets' (T. Westfield, *Eleven Choice Sermons*, 1656, sig. Kk2r). In sermons published much later as *The White Robe* (1660), he asked 'what offence it will be to God' if clergymen 'come to the Lord's Table in their white garments?' (p. 55), and argued that only kings are 'the lord's anointed' (p. 113). John Walker claimed that Westfield suffered abuse in the streets and sequestration that forced him to flee to Oxford. Here, preaching before the king for the first time, he was so overawed that he fainted, although his preaching 'was reckoned powerful and heart-searching', and Bishop John King said 'he was born an Orator' (Lloyd, 303). On 26 April 1642 he was consecrated bishop of Bristol; none the less, he was approved by the Commons as a member of the assembly of divines on 31 May and was back in London in 1643. On 13 May, the Commons committee for sequestrations praised his 'Learning and Merit' and, on the information of the earl of Holland, ordered the tenants on his episcopal lands to cease refusing to pay the rents they owed him. Westfield attended the Westminster assembly's first session on 1 July, the only bishop to do so, but did not return. According to Fuller, 'Dr. Westfield and some few others seemed the only nonconformists amongst them, for their conformity whose gowns and canonical habits differed from all the rest' (Fuller, 6.251).

Westfield died on 28 June 1644 and was buried, as he had wished, in Bristol Cathedral near the tomb of the first bishop of the diocese. He left his estate to his widow and executor, Elisabeth (*d.* 1653), the daughter of Adolphus Meetkerke of Flanders, and sister of Edward *Meetkerke, who was an overseer of his will. They had a son, Edward, who went to Christ Church, Oxford, and a daughter, Elizabeth, who in memory of her father made an anagram of his name: 'Thomas Westfield—I dwell the most safe' (Lloyd, 304).   J. SEARS McGEE

Sources Wood, *Ath. Oxon.*, new edn, vol. 3 · Fuller, *Worthies* · D. Lloyd, *Memoires of the lives … of those … personages that suffered … for the protestant religion* (1668) · Venn, *Alum. Cant.* · T. Fuller, *The church history of Britain*, ed. J. S. Brewer, new edn, 6 vols. (1845) · J. Walker, *An attempt towards recovering an account of the numbers and sufferings of the clergy of the Church of England*, 2 pts in 1 (1714) · *DNB* · *Walker rev.* · R. Newcourt, *Repertorium ecclesiasticum parochiale Londinense*, 1 (1708) · Foster, *Alum. Oxon.* · *Fasti Angl., 1541–1857*, [St Paul's, London] · J. Davies, *The Caroline captivity of the church: Charles I and the remoulding of Anglicanism, 1625–1641* (1992) · C. Russell, *The fall of the British monarchies, 1637–1642* (1991) · W. Reading, *The history of the ancient and present state of Sion College* (1724) · [Chestlin], *Persecutio undecima: the churches eleventh persecution* (1648) · will, PRO, PROB 10/641
Archives St John Cam., sermon notes
Likenesses effigy? on monument, Bristol Cathedral

Westgarth, William (1815–1889), merchant and politician in Australia, was born on 15 June 1815 at Edinburgh, the eldest son of John Westgarth, surveyor-general of customs for Scotland, and his wife, Christian Thomson. The Westgarths were a landed family from Weardale, co. Durham. William attended high schools at Leith and Edinburgh and Dr Bruce's academy at Newcastle upon Tyne. On leaving school he entered the mercantile firm of George Young & Co., Leith.

In July 1840 Westgarth emigrated to Port Phillip district, Australia, and arrived in Melbourne on 13 December. 'The grand bent of all is the making of money', he wrote on Christmas eve to his mother, 'and I do think some is to be made here.' Within two years, however, as an important merchant he was caught in a depression and settled with his creditors. He soon recovered, and formed a prosperous partnership with Alfred Ross in 1845. An 'improver', Westgarth was an unostentatious and indefatigable supporter of good causes such as the Mechanics' Institute and the benevolent society. In 1844 he began his prolific writing career with his first book, *Observations on the present commercial, agricultural and civil condition of the Australian colonies*, published at Leith, and the first of a series of six-monthly commercial and statistical reports on the progress of Port Phillip. In 1846 he reported sympathetically on the 'condition, capabilities, and prospects' of the Aborigines. During a prolonged absence on business in Britain in 1847–9 he persuaded the imperial authorities to subsidize the emigration of German rural workers; the first few arrived in Port Phillip in 1848.

On his return Westgarth soon became one of the two or three most respected men in the infant colony. He was a campaigner for separation from New South Wales, the Melbourne secretary of the League for the Abolition of Transportation, and a leading spokesman for the broad radical front, including many Scottish businessmen, opposing Lieutenant-Governor C. J. La Trobe and the conservative, largely Anglican, official class. He topped the poll for Melbourne at the first election for the Victorian legislative council in 1851, campaigned to unlock the lands, and carried the Convicts Prevention Act (to exclude criminals from Van Diemen's Land). He formed the Melbourne chamber of commerce almost single-handedly, and acted as its first president. He also helped to draw up a straightforward free-trade tariff and proposed a uniform Australian tariff. Soon he became an almost automatic choice to chair important public meetings.

Westgarth was again in Britain in 1853–4 on business and to find a wife; he married Ellison, the daughter of John Macfie, on 6 June 1854 in Edinburgh. It was unfortunate that he was absent for the debates on the Victorian draft constitution. He did not rejoin the legislative council, but chaired the commission of inquiry into the goldfields of Victoria after the Eureka rebellion. The wise report, forced on Governor Sir Charles Hotham by public opinion, recommended an export duty on gold in place of a licence fee, a cheap miner's right which included the vote, and creation of local courts. Affable, modest, urbane, and, above all, tolerant, Westgarth was the complete liberal free-trader for whom Adam Smith was gospel and belief in progress towards the greater happiness of humankind axiomatic. He was also the complete democrat, supporting manhood suffrage, the secret ballot, state education, abolition of state aid to religion—even direct taxation of the wealthy. Yet he was not of the stuff of which popular politicians are made, being a rather tedious speaker, though convivial and a natural peacemaker.

Late twentieth-century Australian historians describe Westgarth as 'the John Stuart Mill of Victoria', 'the outstanding sociological thinker of the colonies', and 'the most perceptive of early Australian historians'. His political-historical writing is a landmark in early Australian intellectual history. Though unpretentious and hurriedly written, his five books on Victoria and his *Australia: its Rise, Progress, and Present Condition* (1861) are distinguished by his probings for explanations of historical change and by generalizations of some profundity about the nature of colonial society.

In 1857 Westgarth left Victoria to establish a sharebroking firm in London, specializing in advice on colonial loans, and carried out innumerable minor diplomatic tasks for colonial governments. A founder of the Colonial Institute in 1869, he gave the first paper to its first ordinary meeting, and many more later, and was the institute's auditor for twenty years. Westgarth was one of the preliminary committee of six which founded the Imperial Federation League in 1884. He frequently presented papers at meetings of the British Association and the Social Science Congress on such matters as bimetallism and land taxation, and was prominent in the foundation of the London chamber of commerce in 1881. He interested himself in economic theory, and in 1887 published a *Sketch of the Nature and Limits of a Science of Economics*. He also became engrossed in the problems of poverty and social inequality.

Westgarth returned to Victoria only once, in 1888 for the centennial celebrations, and met with a great reception. In mid-1889, in declining health, he retired from business. He died on 28 October, when he fell from the attic window of 10 Bolton Gardens, South Kensington, his London home; the inquest recorded accidental death. His funeral took place in Edinburgh. Westgarth had taken £100,000 from his business on retirement and left a considerable estate. He had been a member of the Church of Scotland and held regular morning prayers in his household. His wife and three daughters survived him; the firm of Westgarth & Co. failed in 1890. GEOFFREY SERLE

Sources AusDB · J. A. Ferguson, *Bibliography of Australia*, 7 vols. (1941–69), vols. 3–4, 7 · G. Serle, *The golden age: a history of the colony of Victoria, 1851–1861* (1963) · *The Argus* [Melbourne] (30 Oct 1889) · *The Times* (31 Oct 1889) · C. D. W. Goodwin, *Economic enquiry in Australia* (1966) · CGPLA Eng. & Wales (1889) · m. cert. · private information (2004)

Wealth at death £147,289 4s. 8d.: probate, 10 Dec 1889, CGPLA Eng. & Wales

Westlake, John (1828–1913), jurist, was born at Lostwithiel, Cornwall, on 4 February 1828, the only son of John Westlake (d. 1849), a woolstapler, and his wife, Eleanora (d. 1866), daughter of George Burgess, rector of Atherington, north Devon. In his early years he was taught by his parents, and in 1835 he went to Lostwithiel grammar school. In April 1842 the family moved to Cambridge, where Westlake was privately tutored by, among others, the Revd J. W. Colenso (subsequently bishop of Natal) and Dr W. H. Bateson (who was later appointed master of St John's College, Cambridge).

Westlake went to Trinity College, Cambridge, in Michaelmas term 1846, was scholar in Easter term 1848, and graduated BA in January 1850 as sixth wrangler and sixth classic. He was elected a fellow of his college in October 1851 and took his MA in 1853. He had moved to London in 1852 with his mother and only sister, Mary Elizabeth, his father having died in 1849. There he joined Lincoln's Inn, and he was called to the bar in 1854. In the same year his sister died of cholera, aged twenty-seven. On 13 October 1864 he married Alice, daughter of Thomas *Hare, advocate of proportional representation. Her elder sister, Marion Andrews, was the novelist and historian who wrote under the name Christopher Hare. There were no children of the marriage.

In his early years at the bar, long before he had acquired any sort of standing, Westlake wrote the first edition of the work upon which his later reputation as a jurist was largely and most deservedly to rest—*A Treatise on Private International Law* (1858). At the time the only other treatise on this topic was Joseph Story's, which was considered perfectly satisfactory by the legal fraternity. As A. V. Dicey was to write:

> it is hardly possible to overrate the intellectual originality and boldness of a youthful writer who … took up and worked at the idea of throwing new light on a subject of which Story's work was then supposed in England to be the sole and perfectly adequate exposition. (*Memories of John Westlake*, 25)

Westlake was successful at the bar. He was trained as an equity lawyer, with an emphasis on land law, but his practice consisted largely of cases with an international flavour, and he built up a good practice at the privy council, appearing mostly in Canadian appeals. However, as his obituarist in *The Times* commented, 'Not possessing the mental agility, pliancy, adaptability or temperament of the born advocate, he was unsuitable for the ordinary run of cases' (*The Times*, 15 April 1913), and Westlake was valued more as a drafter of opinion than as an advocate. Nevertheless, some of his most important cases involved court appearances. In 1861 he appeared in *Emperor of Austria* v. *Day and Kossuth*, in which the Austrian government sued in the English court of chancery to prevent Kossuth and his English printers from printing and issuing paper money in the name of the revolutionary government of Hungary. Westlake was the unsuccessful counsel for the defence, but he was certainly on the popular side. Another of his *causes célèbres* was *Brown* v. *Le Curé de Montreal*, a vitally important privy council appeal in which the whole status of the Roman Catholic church in Canada was examined.

In 1874 Westlake was appointed QC and elected a bencher of Lincoln's Inn. Three years later he was made an honorary doctor of laws by Edinburgh University. In 1878 his home town of Lostwithiel elected him its recorder, and in 1880 the second edition of his *Treatise* appeared, having effectively been rewritten since 1858.

In 1885 Westlake was elected Liberal MP for the Romford division of Essex, beating the Conservative candidate by only 64 votes. However, the home-rule crisis which soon followed saw Westlake nail his colours to the Unionist mast, and in July 1886 he stood for re-election as a Liberal Unionist, but lost his seat. Six years later he unsuccessfully contested St Austell as a Unionist.

Westlake gave up practice at the bar in 1888, when he was appointed to the Whewell chair of international law at the University of Cambridge. His connections with international law before the appointment had not been confined to his legal practice and his *Treatise*; among other notable contributions he had, in 1869, co-founded *Le Revue de Droit International et de Legislation Comparée*, the first periodical of international law; and in 1873 he co-founded L'Institut de Droit International, of which he was president in 1895, and permanent honorary president from 1910.

During his time at Cambridge, Westlake published his most important works on public international law: *Chapters on the Principles of International Law* (1894), and *International Law, Part 1: Peace* (1904), and *Part 2: War* (1907). It was also at this time that he sat as one of the British members of the International Court of Arbitration under the Hague Convention, between 1900 and 1906.

Westlake resigned the Whewell chair in 1908, and during his later years he largely withdrew from public life owing to his increasing deafness, though he was by no means a recluse. Besides those honours already mentioned he received many more in recognition of his juristic standing: an honorary DCL degree from the University of Oxford (1908); an honorary doctorate of law from the Free University of Brussels (1909); an honorary fellowship of Trinity College, Cambridge (1910); membership of the Academie Royal of Brussels; the Italian order of the Crown; and the Japanese order of the Rising Sun.

Westlake died on 14 April 1913 at his London residence, the River House, on the Chelsea Embankment. He suffered a stroke, following a heart attack. His ashes were interred at Zennor churchyard in Cornwall, under a celtic cross.

As has been mentioned, much of Westlake's formidable reputation rests on his *Treatise on Private International Law* and his work on the conflict of laws. Before Westlake only Story had considered this subject, but his study lacked the depth and innovation of Westlake's, and he failed to give much coherence to the legal area in question. Westlake, on the other hand, consciously set out to identify the fundamental principles of private international law, not so much by forwarding his own ideas as to what they should be, but rather by arguing that established doctrines accepted by leading continental jurists such as Savigny could and should be applied to solve problems of private international law within the English courts. His skill lay in tailoring these doctrines to fall within the spirit and within the established principles of the law of England, making them not only attractive to, but readily applicable by, an English court. In particular Westlake's work on the law of domicil anticipated many judgments on that topic in the House of Lords.

Many of the doctrines which resulted from Westlake's analysis have been greatly altered over time. His *Treatise* is now wholly outdated, not having been revised since 1925. But his importance lies as much in the effect of his *Treatise* as in its content. It excited discussion, debate, and, most importantly, judicial consideration of previously unconsidered doctrines, and it gave them a coherent form. The resultant case law (which, in the early days, often followed the lines suggested by Westlake) built up into a complex, detailed structure which has now become a free-standing and highly important area of law:

> In 1858, few were the questions as to the conflict of laws which had received a final answer in the English law courts. Before Westlake's death, and greatly owing to the influence exerted by his book, problem after problem of private international law had received in England a decisive solution. (*Memories of John Westlake*, 33–4)

On social and political questions, Westlake was a 'convinced and unflinching liberal' (ibid., 61), with a hatred of all kinds of oppression or injustice, though his strong support for the rights of the individual stemmed perhaps from an idealistically or even naively benevolent view of human nature.

Westlake was a founder in 1854, with F. D. Maurice and others, of the Working Men's College in Great Ormond Street, London, where he taught mathematics. This was a typically selfless gesture by Westlake—in so aiding his fellow human beings he was risking his career at the bar (to which he had only just been called), as Maurice and his associates were at the time popularly viewed as dangerous cranks, infected with the socialism of Louis Blanc, whose activities in the revolutionary year of 1848 were still so repugnant to the English. Westlake was also a strong supporter of the enfranchisement of women, and strongly in favour of proportional representation.

NATHAN WELLS

Sources *Memories of John Westlake* (1914) [chaps. by J. Fischer Williams, A. V. Dicey, and Lord Courtney of Penwith] · *The Times* (15 April 1913) · *CGPLA Eng. & Wales* (1913)
Archives King's AC Cam., letters to Oscar Browning
Likenesses A. Westlake, oils, *c*.1896–1897, NPG · M. Stokes, oils, 1902, NPG · C. H. Shannon, oils, 1910, Trinity Cam. · G. Frampton, marble bust, 1912, Squire Library, Cambridge · G. Jerrard, cabinet photograph, NPG
Wealth at death £8314 15*s*. 5*d*.: probate, 30 May 1913, *CGPLA Eng. & Wales*

Westland, Sir James (1842–1903), administrator in India, eldest of eight children of James Westland, manager of Aberdeen Town and Country Bank, Dundee, and his wife, Agnes Monro, was born in Dundee on 14 November 1842.

The second of his four brothers, William, also had a financial career in India, becoming deputy secretary and treasurer of the Bank of Bengal. James was educated in Aberdeen, and then at Marischal College, Aberdeen, and in Wimbledon, passing first into the Royal Military Academy, Woolwich, in January 1861. In the same year he took the competitive examination for the Indian Civil Service, heading the list of successful applicants.

Westland arrived in Calcutta in October 1862 and held a number of district administrative posts in Bengal, including the collectorships of Nadia and Jessore. In 1870 he was appointed to the finance department of the government of India, and for the next twenty years his mathematical aptitude was rewarded by a series of posts in the finance departments of the government of India and the provincial administrations of Bengal and the Central Provinces, with a brief spell as head of the Egyptian accounts department in 1885. On 23 April 1874 he married Janet Mildred, daughter of Surgeon-Major C. J. Jackson of the Indian Medical Service.

While accountant and comptroller-general to the government of India (1878–85) Westland reorganized and simplified the accountancy practices of the colonial administration. He was subsequently a member of the government of India expenditure commission under Sir Charles Elliott (1886), and was temporary finance member of the executive council from August 1887 to November 1888. He was made CSI in June 1888, and KCSI in January 1895. In July 1889 he was appointed chief commissioner of Assam, but resigned on health grounds the following year to take up sheep farming in New Zealand. In November 1893, however, he returned to Calcutta as finance member of the government of India, in succession to Sir David Barbour.

Westland's term in office as finance member, from 1893 to 1899, was dominated by two of the great economic policy issues that faced the raj in the last quarter of the nineteenth century. In June 1893, at the urging of Barbour and following the report of a currency committee chaired by Lord Herschell, the Indian mints had been closed to the coinage of silver, so that the exchange rate of the rupee against sterling and other European currencies need no longer be governed by the fall in the world price of silver bullion against gold. The government of India was now committed to establishing a new, fixed exchange rate of 15 rupees to the pound, mainly to reduce the amount of taxation needed to meet its fixed costs in London. To Westland fell the task of imposing this policy in practice, and facing the inevitable pressure from business interests as the currency contraction and monetary stringency that accompanied a rising exchange rate depressed exports, cut local demand, and squeezed profit margins. His attempts to mitigate the effects of the stringency by stabilizing the rupee exchange at a lower level and creating a gold coinage in India did not find favour with the London authorities. By the time he left office in 1899 both the 1s. 4d. (6.65p) rupee and the circulation of gold sovereigns as legal tender had been temporarily established, but continued instability meant that currency policy remained a contentious issue in the colonial administration's relations with its subjects for the next half century.

The second controversy in which Westland became embroiled concerned the imposition of tariffs on British trade with India. To bolster the government of India's flagging revenues in 1894, Westland proposed to reimpose the 5 per cent import duties, including those on cotton goods, that had been abolished in 1882. The British government, under political pressure from Lancashire manufacturers, demanded an exemption for cottons, and then imposed a compromise under which Indian-made mill cloth was to be subject to an excise duty at the same level as imports. Despite strong protests from Westland, the viceroy, Lord Elgin, and other members of his executive council, and much evidence that the coarse Bombay cloth did not compete with the finer material made in Lancashire, London's proposals became law in December 1894. In February 1896 both tariff and excise on cotton goods were reduced to 3½ per cent, with an exemption for yarn, but this did not defuse the issue. As a result, nationalist suspicions that Indian fiscal and financial policy would always be manipulated by British manufacturing interests were greatly strengthened, and the charge that Britain imposed free trade on her empire to boost her own economic strength gained wide currency, both at the time and since.

Westland returned to Britain in 1899. He was nominated to the Council of India to advise the secretary of state on Indian finance, but found it hard to settle to the comparative leisure of retirement. He died at the Oatlands Park Hotel, Walton-on-Thames, Surrey, on 9 May 1903, and was buried at Brookwood cemetery. His wife, and four children of the marriage—two sons and two daughters—survived him. F. H. BROWN, rev. B. R. TOMLINSON

Sources P. L. Malhotra, *Administration of Lord Elgin in India, 1894–99* (1979) · *The Times* (16 May 1903) · *Allahabad Pioneer* (29 March 1999) · *Allahabad Pioneer* (31 March 1899) · *CGPLA Eng. & Wales* (1903) · P. Harnetty, 'The Indian cotton duties controversy, 1894–96', *EngHR*, 77 (1962), 684–702 · personal knowledge (1912)
Archives BL OIOC, letters to Arthur Godley, MS Eur. F 102
Wealth at death £21,624 0s. 4d.: resworn probate, Nov 1903, *CGPLA Eng. & Wales*

Westmacott, Charles Molloy (1786/7–1868), journalist and blackmailer, the illegitimate second son of Richard (Dick) Westmacott (d. 1808), sculptor, whose name he took, and of Susannah Molloy, a 'pretty widow' and innkeeper. He was brought up as Westmacott's own son, went to St Paul's School, and trained at the Royal Academy of Arts. On the death of his father, Charles's half-brother, Sir Richard *Westmacott (1775–1856), later professor of sculpture, sent him away penniless, but by his own ability he rose to become proprietor and editor of a scandalous tory journal, the *Spirit of the Age*, with which his name was principally associated.

Westmacott soon acquired a reputation for publishing pseudo-satirical gossip with a view to extortion. Guilty or innocent, the persons he accused would pay either to be kept out of his paper or to have their names cleared. Thus he allegedly extorted £5000 from participants in a single scandalous court intrigue. His notebooks, offered for sale in the catalogue of Thomas Arthur (December 1868), are described as having contained intimate details relating to George IV, Princess Caroline, Beau Brummel, and members of the nobility. By 1834 Westmacott was prosperous and possessed a pretty cottage between Barnes and Richmond, its grounds adorned with sculptures.

Westmacott began his career by publishing the first thirteen numbers of the *Gazette of Fashion* (1822). A regular feature on gambling dens, entitled 'Peep into the pandemonium', exemplifies his blackmailing methods, declaring the existence of 'a list of more than 200 names' to be exposed to 'merited chastisement' and protesting that the aim was 'neither to *extort hush-money*, [n]or point out *individuals* to public execration' (9 February). From 1827 until 1843 Westmacott was the editor and principal writer of the *Spirit of the Age*, which took its title from Hazlitt's essays. He boosted its weekly sales to about 10,000 by publishing sensational news and heaping abuse on well-known political opponents. *Fraser's Magazine* (1834), in its comment on his portrait, mentions as 'the most characteristic touch …, the knowing horsewhip in his hat'. Westmacott's vicious criticism made him feared and hated. One insult that was avenged was his denigration of Fanny Kemble's 'decidedly bad' figure and diction ('a guttural thickness, tainted with very strong provincialisms'): when he attended a performance at Covent Garden in October 1830 her father, Charles Kemble, so *The News* reported, 'administered a discipline with a horsewhip', leaving Westmacott to 'roll about the floor and roar'. Edward Bulwer-Lytton also threatened a flogging for an offensive remark. Westmacott's retaliation came in a letter published in 1833 and referred to in *Fraser's Magazine* as the 'crushing without mercy … [of Bulwer's] volumes … beneath his foot'.

Westmacott's training as an artist shows in two of his publications. *British Galleries of Painting and Sculpture* (1824) is a serious work which claims to describe all the 'Palaces, Mansions, and Galleries … in the Kingdom' (p. vii) and to offer a comprehensive catalogue of all the works of art they contain. *A Descriptive and Critical Catalogue to the Exhibition of the Royal Academy … with a[n] … Account of the Rise and Progress of the Arts of Painting and Sculpture in England* (1823) includes in its preface a threatening attack on 'the Academicians', who had wasted £4000 on 'a splendid banquet'. He also wrote *Points of Misery, or, Fables for Mankind* (1823), with illustrations by Robert Cruikshank, as well as 'a musical farce in two acts', *Nettlewig Hall, or, Ten to One* (1829), in fact a conventional prose play in which an elderly guardian is fooled by his clever nephew.

Whether the following works, published under the pseudonym Bernard Blackmantle, were written wholly by Westmacott (as claimed in biographical accounts shortly after his death) cannot be decided with certainty. *The English spy … satirical and humorous, comprising scenes and sketches in every rank of society* (2 vols., 1825–6; new edn, 1907), with illustrations by Cruikshank, is a gossipy miscellany in the tradition of Egan's *Life in London*, whose author claims that 'from obscurity of birth … he [has risen] into notice by the … exertion of his talents' but, unlike Westmacott, he was

educated at Eton and Oxford (1.14–16). The work was continued as the *St James' Royal Magazine, and Monthly Gazette of Fashion* (1826). *Fitzalleyne of Berkeley: a Romance of the Present Times* (2 vols., 1825) deals with the Berkeley peerage scandal and with illegitimacy, issues which would have attracted Westmacott, in whose *Gazette of Fashion* 'Fitz-Allan' features as an anonymous correspondent signing the Pandemonium columns. *The Punster's Pocket-Book, or, The Art of Punning Enlarged* (1826), illustrated by Cruikshank, refers back to 'The Art of Punning [1719] … ascribed to Dr. Swift … [but] written by Dr. Sheridan' (p. 68). It reprints verbatim, in two parts (pp. 84–5 and 94–6) a fake letter to the editor of the *Gazette of Fashion*, 'On the vice of punning' (9 February 1822).

Wrongly attributed to Westmacott was the Shakespeare burlesque *Othello, the Moor of Fleet Street*, now recognized as the work of Charles Mathews. There is also no evidence that under the pseudonym Abel Funnefello he wrote *The Blue-Coat Boy* (1837).

In the introduction to *Nettlewig Hall*, Westmacott is described as 'a little round man, with a dumpling figure and physiognomy; smart and lively as his farce' (Westmacott, A3). According to *Fraser's Magazine*, he was 'a pluck[y] little fellow' who had 'pushed his way actively in the world' and had 'fought … the battle of the Tories as openmouthedly and as freely as he could'. Notorious and wealthy, he boasted of his talents and his intimacy with the nobility, but never got into society. Eventually he was lost sight of in the press and the London salons and slunk away to Paris, where he died on 24 June 1868.

MANFRED DRAUDT

Sources 'Gallery of literary characters no. XLVIII: Charles Molloy Westmacott, esq.', *Fraser's Magazine*, 9 (1834), 536–7 · 'Obituary: Charles M. Westmacott', *The London Bookseller*, 128 (1 Sept 1868), 642 · Allibone, *Dict.* · W. Maginn, 'XLVIII — Charles Molloy Westmacott', in W. Bates, *The Maclise portrait-gallery of 'illustrious literary characters'* (1883), 235–42 · C. S., 'Thrashing a journalist', *The Theatre*, 4th ser., 10 (1887), 289–99 · D. J. Gray, 'Early Victorian scandalous journalism: Renton Nicholson's *The town*, 1837–42', *The Victorian periodical press: samplings and soundings*, ed. J. Shattock and M. Wolff (1982), 317–48 · D.-G. [G. Daniel], introduction, in C. M. Westmacott, *Nettlewig Hall, or, Ten to one: a musical farce in two acts* (1829), A3 · C. Mathews, *Othello, the Moor of Fleet Street*, ed. M. Draudt (1993) · I. McCalman, *Radical underworld: prophets, revolutionaries, and pornographers in London, 1795–1840* (1988); pbk edn (1993) · 'The Drama…Adelphi', *The Town* [incorporated with *The Sunday Herald*] (3 Feb 1833) [review] · S. J. Kunitz and H. Haycraft, eds., *British authors of the nineteenth century* (1936) · Boase, *Mod. Eng. biog.*
Likenesses A. Croquis [D. Maclise], line engraving, pubd 1834, BM, NPG · engraving, repro. in *Fraser's Magazine*, 537

Westmacott, Sir Richard (1775–1856), sculptor, was born in Grosvenor Square, Westminster, London, on 15 July 1775, the eldest of the thirteen children of the sculptor Richard Westmacott (*bap.* 1746, *d.* 1808) and Sarah Vardy (1750–1826), daughter of the furniture carver Thomas Vardy. The journalist and writer Charles Molloy *Westmacott (1786/7–1868) was his half-brother. The elder Westmacott worked primarily as a sculptor of chimney-pieces and in 1777 published a series of twenty chimney-piece designs. He also executed about fifty-five church monuments, the best-known examples of which are those to

Sir Richard Westmacott (1775–1856), by James Thomson, pubd 1823 (after William Derby, 1822)

Jane and James Dutton (1791, Devizes, Wiltshire) and Mrs Sarah Shrimpton (c.1783, High Wycombe, Buckinghamshire). At the age of fourteen the younger Richard Westmacott was apprenticed to his grandfather Thomas Vardy. He also probably received some training in his father's studio, though he never acknowledged it. In 1792 he travelled to the continent with his tutor, a sculptor from Carrara known only as Casoni, and studied at the Accademia di San Luca in Rome from 1793 to 1795. In the student competition of 1795 he won first prize for his terracotta relief *Joseph Confiding Benjamin to Juda* (Accademia di San Luca, Rome). In Rome Westmacott purchased antiquities for the architect Henry Holland and became acquainted with the well-known neo-classical sculptor Antonio Canova. After he returned to London in 1796, he resided at 24 Mount Street, Mayfair, where he lived until 1818, when he moved to 14 South Audley Street. On 20 February 1798 he married Dorothy Margaret Wilkinson (d. 1834), daughter of a Dr Wilkinson of Jamaica, at St George's, Hanover Square. They had eight children, the eldest of whom, also named Richard *Westmacott (1799–1872), became a successful sculptor.

Westmacott made his début at the Royal Academy in 1797 with two marble busts, including one of Sir William Chambers (Sir John Soane's Museum, London). He was elected an associate member of the academy in 1805 and became a full academician six years later when he submitted his diploma piece, the relief *Ganymede and the Eagle* (Royal Academy of Arts, London). In 1827 he succeeded John Flaxman as professor of sculpture at the Royal Academy, a post he held until his death. During his forty-year

career he created about 275 works and early on distinguished himself as a leading sculptor of civic and national monuments. He obtained eight of the thirty-six commissions for national monuments ordered by the Committee of Taste from 1803 to 1823. The most remarkable of these is the monument to Sir Ralph Abercromby (1803–9, St Paul's Cathedral, London), a dramatic marble group which established his reputation. George IV commissioned one of his most unusual war memorials, the *Waterloo Vase* (1820–27, Royal Collection), which was carved from an 18 foot-high block of Carrara marble on which Napoleon had originally intended to represent scenes of his conquest of Russia.

In 1809 Westmacott gained fame for the monument to Francis Russell, the fifth duke of Bedford (Russell Square, London), one of the first large-scale bronzes created in England in the nineteenth century. He helped revive the craft of bronze casting in Britain with such monuments as those erected to Lord Nelson in Birmingham (1806–9) and Bridgetown, Barbados (1810–13); the duke of Wellington (*Achilles*, 1814–22, Hyde Park, London); George III (1818–22, Liverpool; 1824–31, Windsor Great Park); and the duke of York (1830–34, Carlton House Terrace, London). In addition he produced the colossal bronze group designed by M. C. Wyatt for Lord Nelson in Liverpool (1808–13).

Westmacott's works are generally neo-classical in style, which he sometimes carried to an extreme. His *Achilles* and memorials to George III are only variations of esteemed Graeco-Roman sculptures. The *Achilles* unintentionally became his most sensational monument because the idealized nude male figure was commissioned with funds from British women and because some mistakenly believed it portrayed Wellington himself. In his monuments he sometimes tempered his classicizing inclinations with lifelike portraits and contemporary dress. Many of the figures he made for the galleries of private collectors were initially inspired by antique works but overlaid by rococo sentiment or influenced by Canova, notably the *Cupid* (1823) and *Psyche* (1822, both Woburn Abbey, Bedfordshire) he made for John Russell, the sixth duke of Bedford, and *Cupid Made Prisoner* (1827, Petworth House, Sussex) for George O'Brien Wyndham, the third earl of Egremont. Westmacott received an unprecedented £1050 for *Psyche*, a sum which put him on a par with Canova, who was then considered the greatest sculptor of the day. He departed from classical sources in the series of eight Maltese stone figures (c.1813–18) for the staircase of Ashridge Park, Hertfordshire, which represent the medieval founders and benefactors of a monastery formerly on that site.

Of the 240 marble tomb memorials attributed to Westmacott at least sixty are plain, inscribed, or simply decorated tablets which were largely, if not entirely, executed by studio assistants. Some of his church monuments are among his greatest works. The relief erected to the Hon. John Yorke (c.1801, Wimpole, Cambridgeshire) characterizes his early, short-lived austere style which reflects the impact of John Flaxman's sculpture. Abstract tendencies soften in his mature funerary sculpture. The monument to John William Egerton, the seventh earl of Bridgewater (1825, Little Gaddesden, Hertfordshire) suggests the tender intimacy of Italian Renaissance groups of the Holy Family. Sensual female figures appear in several of his tomb sculptures, notably the graceful entwined angels in the monument to Mrs Elizabeth Eardley-Wilmot (c.1818, Berkswell, Warwickshire) and the charming peasant girl from the monument to Lord and Lady Penryhn (1819, Llandygái, Caernarvonshire). The girl is depicted with a figure of a quarryman, both intended to symbolize the deceased couples' agricultural and industrial improvements on their estate. The monument to Mrs Elizabeth Warren (1824, Westminster Abbey, London) commemorates the wife of the bishop of Bangor as a benefactor of migrant workers. Westmacott portrayed a pathetic group of a destitute young mother and her infant which captivated the public when it was exhibited at the Royal Academy in 1822 under the title *The Houseless Traveller*. The exhibited version was purchased by the marquess of Lansdowne (Bowood, Wiltshire) and the sentimental image was immortalized in poetry, engravings, and Parian ware reproductions. He later created a companion piece for it, *Madonna and Child* (exh. RA, 1825; church of the Transfiguration, New York city), popularly known as 'The Happy Mother', which did not achieve as much popularity.

Throughout his career Westmacott remained a highly respected member of the British art establishment. He was elected to the Society of Antiquaries in 1811 and the Society of Dilettanti in 1817. In 1816 he was one of the experts who testified before the House of Commons in favour of the purchase of the Elgin marbles. From that time on he served as an unofficial adviser to the British Museum and helped in the display of antiquities, and even recommended purchases. He received the honorary degree of DCL from the University of Oxford on 15 June 1836 and was knighted by Queen Victoria on 19 July 1837. He exhibited at the Royal Academy for the last time in 1839, at the age of sixty-four. His son Richard appears to have taken over his business after that time, but he remained active until shortly before his death. In 1843 he served as one of the judges for the parliament fresco competition. Two years later he reported to the government on the condition of the royal tombs in Canterbury Cathedral. In 1849 he supervised the erection of the Nelson's monument in Trafalgar Square in London and acted as commissioner for the Great Exhibition of 1851. In 1855 he served on the committee for English sculpture at the Universal Exhibition in Paris, where he exhibited *The Houseless Traveller* and *Lady Susan Murray* ('Sleeping Infant', 1839, Scone Palace, Perthshire). His last documented work, the pediment group for the British Museum, *The Progress of Civilization*, was installed in 1851. After a brief illness Westmacott died peacefully at his home at 14 South Audley Street, London, on 1 September 1856. He was buried in the churchyard at Chastleton, Oxfordshire, where his son Horatio was rector.

Few details of Westmacott's character and private life are known, in the absence of most of his personal correspondence, contemporary accounts provide only brief glimpses of him. When he applied for family arms in 1829, one of the king of arms is said to have declared, 'You are an industrious fellow—I'll give you a bee' (*Diary*, ed. Pope, 5.390). His arms do in fact feature four bees, appropriate symbols for this vigorous, prolific artist. The diarist Caroline Fox, who visited him in his studio in 1842, described the 67-year-old artist as 'a man of extreme energy and openness of countenance, real enthusiasm for his art, and earnest to direct its aim as high as heaven' (*Memories*, ed. Pym, 2.390). He was a popular member of the Royal Academy and often socialized with other artists, notably Joseph Farington, who mentions him in his *Diary* on several occasions. Westmacott was on friendly terms with most of his aristocratic patrons. His name appears many times in the 'Dinner Books' of Henry Vassal Fox, third Baron Holland, and his wife, Lady Elizabeth Holland. His association with this couple, as well as with Thomas Coke of Norfolk, first earl of Leicester, suggests that he was a whig, as do some of his commissions for John Russell, the sixth duke of Bedford, notably the relief *The Progress of Mankind* (c.1818) on the temple of liberty at Woburn Abbey. Very little is known about Westmacott's family life, or his children other than his son Richard. His unmarried eldest daughters, Dorothy (*b*. 1800) and Eliza (*b*. 1802), cared for him after his wife's death in 1834.

Richard Westmacott's younger brother **Thomas Westmacott** (1776–1798), architect, was born in Grosvenor Square, Westminster, London. He was a pupil of James Wyatt and exhibited four architectural designs at the Royal Academy between 1796 and 1798. He died on 3 December 1798, only three weeks after he had received the silver medal for architecture.   MARIE BUSCO

Sources M. Busco, *Sir Richard Westmacott, sculptor* (1994) · N. B. Penny, 'The sculpture of Sir Richard Westmacott', *Apollo*, 102 (1975), 120–27 · N. Penny, *Church monuments in Romantic England* (1977) · M. Whinney, *Sculpture in Britain, 1530 to 1830*, rev. J. Physick, 2nd edn (1988) · R. Gunnis, *Dictionary of British sculptors, 1660–1851*, new edn (1968) · M. F. Busco, 'The *Achilles* in Hyde Park', *Burlington Magazine*, 130 (1988), 920–24 · A. Yarrington, *The commemoration of the hero, 1800–1864* (1988) · *The diary of Benjamin Robert Haydon*, ed. W. B. Pope, 5 vols. (1960–63), vol. 5, p. 390 · *Memories of old friends, being extracts from the journals and letters of Caroline Fox, from 1835–1871*, ed. H. M. Pym, 2 (1882), 390 · *The Times* (4 Sept 1856) · IGI [Richard Westmacott and Thomas Westmacott] · parish register, St Mary's, Stockport, 1746–54, Ches. & Chester ALSS, P/4/1/9 [baptism] · *GM*, 1st ser., 78 (1808), 274 · *GM*, 2nd ser., 2 (1834), 658 · Boyd's marriage index, 1751–75, Society of Genealogists, 238 · private information (2004) · 'Memoir of Richard Westmacott', *European Magazine and London Review*, 82 (1822), 491–5 · 'Westmacott, Thomas', *DNB* · parish register (marriage), St George's, Hanover Square, London, 20 Feb 1798, Victoria Library, London · F. H. W. Sheppard, ed., *The Grosvenor estate in Mayfair*, 2: *The buildings*, Survey of London, 40 (1980), 295, 317 · grave, churchyard, Chastleton, Oxfordshire

Archives Metropolitan Museum of Art, New York, Thomas J. Watson Library, corresp. | Lpool RO, corresp. on statue of George III (Liverpool) · NRA Scotland, priv. coll., corresp. with William Adam · U. Nott. L., letters to Lord Lincoln relating to restoration of monuments in Canterbury Cathedral · UCL, letters to Society for the Diffusion of Useful Knowledge · Yale U., letters to T. J. Pettigrew

Likenesses C. Benazech, chalk drawing, Oct 1792, NPG · J. Thomson, stipple, pubd 1823 (after W. Derby, 1822), BM, NPG [*see illus.*] ·

W. Brockedon, chalk and pencil drawing, 1844, NPG · C. H. Lear, pencil drawing, c.1845, NPG · L. C. Wyon, medal, 1868 (after R. Westmacott), NPG · J. Thomson, engraving, repro. in *European Magazine and London Review*
Wealth at death see will, PRO, PROB 11/2245

Westmacott, Richard (1799–1872), sculptor, was born in Grosvenor Square, London, the eldest of the eight children of the sculptor Sir Richard *Westmacott (1775–1856) and Dorothy Margaret Wilkinson (d. 1834), the daughter of a Dr Wilkinson of Jamaica. He attended Ealing School, near London, from the age of nine. He originally wanted to become a barrister but yielded to his father's wish that he should enter his studio and be trained as a sculptor, and in 1818 he was admitted to the Royal Academy Schools. In 1820 his father sent him to Italy, where he remained six years, studying ancient sculpture and its history. In Rome he received a few commissions, including a tomb monument for Rosa Bathurst (1824, protestant cemetery, Rome) and a marble figure of Diana for William Morritt (date unknown, Rokeby Park, co. Durham).

On his return to London, Westmacott resided in his father's house, 14 South Audley Street, until 1830, when he moved to 21 Wilton Place. In 1827 he exhibited his first sculpture at the Royal Academy, *Girl with a Bird*. During his career he exhibited eighty-two marble figures, reliefs, and busts at the Royal Academy and four works at the British Institution; most of these sculptures are now lost. In the 1830s he executed several important classicizing figures and reliefs, notably *Venus Carrying off Ascantus* (exh. RA, 1831) and *Venus Instructing Cupid* (exh. RA, 1838) for Francis Egerton, the earl of Ellesmere. His *Cymbal Player* (exh. RA, 1838; Chatsworth, Derbyshire) was purchased by the sixth duke of Devonshire, who commissioned Westmacott to make a chimney-piece (c.1833) for the dining-room at Chatsworth. For Henry Petty, the marquess of Lansdowne, he carved two reliefs, *Mercury Presenting Pandora to Prometheus* (exh. RA, 1837; priv. coll.) and *Paolo and Francesca* (exh. RA, 1838; plaster version ex Sothebys, London, 12 May 1995).

In 1838 Westmacott was elected an ARA and became a full member in 1849, when he presented the relief *Go and Sin No More* as his diploma piece (Royal Academy, London). From 1840 until he retired in 1855 he executed mainly portrait busts and funerary monuments. One of his most accomplished busts portrays John Henry Newman (exh. RA, 1841; Birmingham Oratory), the future cardinal and his childhood friend from Ealing School. His greatest tomb monuments are those raised to Charles Hussey Packe (c.1842, Prestwold, Leicestershire), Philip Yorke, third earl of Hardwicke (c.1845, Wimpole, Cambridgeshire), and Charlotte Egerton (1847, Rostherne, Cheshire). He also made a commemorative memorial to the Arctic explorer Sir John Franklin (1859, Royal Naval College chapel, Greenwich). His only important public work in London was the sculpture in the pediment of the west front of the Royal Exchange, erected 1842–4. On 26 June 1845 he married Caroline Elizabeth, the eldest daughter of Harry Edgell of Cadogan Place, London; the couple had several children.

In 1857 Westmacott succeeded his father as professor of sculpture at the Royal Academy, an office which he held until 1867. He was a fellow of the Royal Society, to which he was elected on 25 May 1837. Well known as a writer and lecturer on art, he contributed articles on sculpture to the *Encyclopaedia metropolitana*, the *English Encyclopaedia*, and the *Penny Cyclopaedia* and published *The Handbook of Ancient and Modern Sculpture* in 1864. In addition, in 1839, he designed eight engraved illustrations and wrote the text to a moral allegory *The Fighte of Freewille*. Richard Westmacott retired from the Royal Academy about a year before his death, which took place at his home at 1 Kensington Gate, Hyde Park, London, on 19 April 1872.

CAMPBELL DODGSON, rev. MARIE BUSCO

Sources W. Sandby, *The history of the Royal Academy of Arts*, 2 (1862), 197–9 · Graves, *RA exhibitors* · R. Gunnis, *Dictionary of British sculptors, 1660–1851*, new edn (1968) · *The Athenaeum* (27 April 1872), 534 · *The Builder*, 30 (1872), 380 · *ILN* (11 May 1872) · *The Times* (22 April 1872) · M. Perry, '"La pauvre Miss Bathurst": memorials to a tragedy in Stendhal's Rome', *The Connoisseur*, 197 (1978), 292–7 · *IGI* · *Morning Post* (5 Sept 1856) · *GM*, 2nd ser., 2 (1834), 658 · *GM*, 2nd ser., 24 (1845), 301 · *The letters and diaries of John Henry Newman*, ed. C. S. Dessain and others, [31 vols.] (1961–), vol. 16, p. 74
Archives Lpool RO, corresp. · Metropolitan Museum of Art, New York, Thomas J. Watson Library, corresp. | NRA, priv. coll., corresp. with William Adam · U. Nott. L., letters to Lord Lincoln · UCL, letters to Society for the Diffusion of Useful Knowledge · Yale U., letters to T. J. Pettigrew
Likenesses J. Partridge, pencil drawing, 1825, NPG · Count D'Orsay, pencil and chalk drawing, 1831, NPG; repro. in *Drawings of men about town* (1832–48) · R. Taylor, engraving, repro. in *ILN* · J. Watkins, photograph, NPG
Wealth at death under £25,000: probate, 18 May 1872, *CGPLA Eng. & Wales*

Westmacott, Thomas (1776–1798). *See under* Westmacott, Sir Richard (1775–1856).

Westmeath. For this title name *see* Nugent, Richard, first earl of Westmeath (1583–1642); Nugent, Richard, second earl of Westmeath (1626–1684); Nugent, Thomas, fourth earl of Westmeath (1668/9–1752); Nugent, John, fifth earl of Westmeath (1671/2–1754).

Westminster. For this title name *see* Murray, Alexander, of Elibank, Jacobite earl of Westminster (1712–1778); Grosvenor, Robert, first marquess of Westminster (1767–1845); Grosvenor, Richard, second marquess of Westminster (1795–1869); Grosvenor, Hugh Lupus, first duke of Westminster (1825–1899).

Westminster, Edward of (d. 1265), administrator, was the son of Odo the Goldsmith, whom he succeeded in 1240 as keeper of the king's works at Westminster, which then chiefly concerned the palace. In the following year he was made responsible for the new shrine that Henry III was beginning for Edward the Confessor. In 1245, when the king began to rebuild the abbey itself, Edward became keeper of the works, along with the master mason and a representative of the abbot and convent. While colleagues came and went, he retained this position until his retirement in 1263/4, thus overseeing the building of the eastern chapels, chancel, transepts, chapter house, and a large part of the choir, virtually the whole of King Henry's achievement.

Westminster's first responsibility was for the receipt and expenditure of the money assigned for the operations, a responsibility discharged through a special exchequer set up in 1246, over which he presided. He was far more, however, than a mere passive conduit for funds. He was actively involved both in obtaining money and materials and in ensuring that work was actually carried out. In November 1252, for example, the king told him both to seek timber for the new roof of the abbey and to see that a great new bell was hung before the feast of St Edward: he was not to leave London until it was done. In June 1259 it was to Westminster and two colleagues that the writ was addressed that ordered the pulling down of 'the old fabric of the church of Westminster … as far as the vestry which is by the king's seat … and to have the same church rebuilt … in such a manner as the new fabric there requires' (CClR, 1256–1259, 390), an order that marked the beginning of work on the choir. In securing money for the abbey Westminster was helped by his position as a baron of the exchequer and keeper from 1248 of the exchequer seal; he is one of the earliest known chancellors of the exchequer.

Aside from his work on the abbey Edward of Westminster was constantly involved in procuring vestments, jewels, and a range of other precious objects for the king. He interpreted Henry's wishes to the craftsmen and saw that tight deadlines were met. That he satisfied so impatient and fastidious a monarch for so long says much for his efficiency and sensitivity. It is clear, moreover, that his counsel was valued on artistic matters. In 1245 the king accepted his advice that it would be more splendid to have the leopards, which were planned to go beside the throne at Westminster, made of bronze rather than of marble. It is not impossible, therefore, that Edward influenced features of the abbey's design. Certainly his skill as an administrator was a vital factor in ensuring that so much was built so quickly and magnificently.

Westminster was presumably a clerk in minor orders, since his rewards for his services included the livings of Benenden, Kent, and Ickworth, Suffolk. He was also able to add substantially to his inherited estate, and in 1258 settled lands in Westminster, Surrey, Middlesex, and Hertfordshire on his mistress, Katherine of Ely, with successive remainders to their three sons, Odo, Nicholas, and Thomas. He died in 1265.   D. A. CARPENTER, rev.

Sources Chancery records · R. Brown, H. M. Colvin, and A. J. Taylor, eds., The history of the king's works, 1 (1963) · R. K. Lancaster, 'Artists, suppliers and clerks: the human factors in the art patronage of King Henry III', Journal of the Warburg and Courtauld Institutes, 35 (1972), 81–107 · P. A. Brand, 'Family and inheritance, women and children', An illustrated history of late medieval England, ed. C. Given-Wilson (1996), 58–81

Westminster, Matthew of (supp. fl. 1300). See under Paris, Matthew (c.1200–1259).

Westmorland. For this title name see Neville, Ralph, first earl of Westmorland (c.1364–1425); Beaufort, Joan, countess of Westmorland (1379?–1440); Neville, Ralph, second earl of Westmorland (b. in or before 1407, d. 1484); Neville, Ralph, fourth earl of Westmorland (1498–1549); Neville, Henry, fifth earl of Westmorland (1524/5–1564) [see under Neville, Ralph, fourth earl of Westmorland (1498–1549)]; Neville, Charles, sixth earl of Westmorland (1542/3–1601); Fane, Francis, first earl of Westmorland (1583/4–1629) [see under Fane, Sir Thomas (d. 1589)]; Fane, Mildmay, second earl of Westmorland (1602–1666); Fane, John, seventh earl of Westmorland (bap. 1686, d. 1762); Fane, John, tenth earl of Westmorland (1759–1841); Fane, John, eleventh earl of Westmorland (1784–1859); Fane, Priscilla Anne, countess of Westmorland (1793–1879); Fane, Francis William Henry, twelfth earl of Westmorland (1825–1891).

Weston, Dame Agnes Elizabeth (1840–1918), philanthropist and temperance activist, was born at 35 Great Coram Street, Bloomsbury, London, on 26 March 1840, the daughter of Charles Henry Weston (1802–1874), barrister, and his wife, Agnes Sarah (c.1810–1895), daughter of Judge Robert Bayly. Several of Agnes Weston's siblings having died young, only she, a sister, and a brother survived to adulthood. The family were comfortably off (Charles Weston's father had been a merchant), and a happy and caring home was provided for the children. The family wealth rendered Agnes Weston independent of both marriage and remunerative work, allowing her to devote her energies to social welfare, particularly among naval seamen.

The Westons moved to Lansdown, Bath, in 1845, where Agnes Weston benefited from a home education unusual in its breadth; she also attended private schools in Bath. An early skill in essay writing was a foundation for the huge amount of letter writing and periodical articles which became a feature of her voluntary work. She participated in her father's interests in astronomy and geology, and was encouraged in riding and swimming. After leaving school she added the unusual skill of organ playing to her accomplishments: after an initial training in Bath, she became a pupil of the famous organist at Gloucester Cathedral, Dr S. S. Wesley (1810–1876), achieving near-concert standard in the instrument. This demonstrated the single-minded drive she brought to bear on any chosen project.

Religion was always important in Agnes Weston's life. She was inspired initially by her parents' faith, but her personal development as a committed evangelical Anglican may be traced to her mid-teens and the influence of the Revd James Fleming (1830–1908). Over the next fifteen years her involvement in religious and social welfare activities developed through Sunday school teaching, youth work, and hospital sick visiting to the provision and organization of recreation rooms and activities for the ordinary ranks from the local army barracks. In effect a soldiers' institute, this was the model for the facilities she was later to develop for naval ratings in Plymouth and Portsmouth. She gained experience in working among and addressing groups of young men, and in fund raising. It was during this period that she embraced the temperance cause and signed the pledge.

Dame Agnes Elizabeth Weston (1840–1918), by unknown artist

Before the 1870s Agnes Weston had no strong naval connections. However, her soldier contacts returning from overseas drew her to Plymouth, where she also had relations. It was there, in 1872, that she met her coadjutor, Sophia Gertrude Wintz (1847–1929), who became her close associate and eventual successor in her naval welfare work. Agnes Weston began her work by launching a correspondence mission, typical of missionary activity among seafarers, and particularly to be compared with the work from 1809 of the Revd George Charles Smith (1782–1863), the founding father of the worldwide seamen's Bethel movement, the earliest organized seamen's missions. Her *Monthly Letters* were eventually circulated to every ship in the fleet, together with the magazine of her movement, *Ashore and Afloat*. In Plymouth small-scale activity by the two ladies among naval ratings quickly led to the development of institute facilities, and then overnight accommodation, for which the title Sailors' Rest (later Royal Sailors' Rest) was chosen. At the same time Agnes Weston was emerging as a leading figure in the temperance movement, serving in the Royal Naval Temperance Society as principal organizer among naval personnel: initially she was allowed to address the boys on the naval training ships, but this soon spread to other naval ships.

From her mid-thirties Agnes Weston devoted herself to naval seafarers. To create and extend her Sailors' Rests she raised large sums nationally, drawing on her extensive network of contacts and attracting numerous supporters to run what became large hotels/clubs with beds for over 600 in the main establishments at Plymouth (opened in 1876) and Portsmouth (1881) on sites close to the dockyards. These buildings became her home, where, as effectively a resident, though unpaid, managing director, she kept close watch on her widening range of activities. As well as her Royal Naval Temperance Society work, she lent support to seamen's families, organizing naval wives' groups and Bands of Hope for seamen's children. When naval ships were lost, she was quick to promote the formation of disaster funds to support seamen's dependants.

Although Agnes Weston's activities were organized on societal lines, such was her central and dominant role during her lifetime that it is hard to distinguish that played by others in the formation, development, and operation of her organization. What she achieved must be balanced by two qualifications. She was not the first to address either the religious or social needs of naval seafarers. The Bethel movement had been active since the 1820s and the sailors' home movement since the 1850s: both continued to be active in naval ports during her lifetime. Secondly, there is some doubt about the extent to which she kept pace with the social and educational development of naval personnel. This had changed considerably by 1900 through popular education and the navy's own training programme, which had been in its infancy in 1876. In particular, her continued use of the image of the improvident, drunken seaman as a fundraising device caused offence among some ratings and petty officers in the years before the First World War, while some supporters resented her frequent calls for their support. Nevertheless, she created what in effect became the navy's welfare arm, working in the early years against a culture that normally excluded women and exploiting the opportunities offered by the naval ports, where there was ample space for a new initiative. Her forceful personality enabled her to supplement significantly previous efforts and to promote her campaigns more widely.

The 'mother figure at the heart of a stable home' was a common fantasy among seafarers, which the public image of Agnes Weston well fitted. The combination of stories about her tea parties for sailors and her rescuing drunks, with the pictures of a mature, rounded face, severe hair style, sober clothes, and fuller figure, served well to foster something of a mother cult. Mother Weston, the Sailors' Friend, was awarded an honorary LLD by Glasgow University in 1901 and made dame (GBE) in 1918. She died following a heart attack on 23 October 1918 at the Royal Sailors' Rest in Devonport. On 26 October she was honoured with a full naval funeral, and was buried, after a memorial service at the Dockyard Chapel, at Weston Mill cemetery, Devonport. ALSTON KENNERLEY

Sources A. Weston, *My life among the bluejackets*, new edn [1919] · D. Gulliver, *Dame Agnes Weston* (1971) · S. G. Wintz, *Our blue jackets: Miss Weston's life and work among our sailors*, new edn (1884) · b. cert. · d. cert. · *CGPLA Eng. & Wales* (1919) · will, proved, London, 16 Jan 1919 · *Western Morning News* (24 Oct 1918) · *Western Morning News* (28 Oct 1918) · Portsmouth City RO, Royal Sailors' Rests records, Acc. 205A · *Royal Sailors' Rests Annual Reports*, 1905–33, City of Plymouth and West Devon RO, Plymouth, Acc. 1188 · R. Kverndal, *Seamen's missions: their origin and early growth* (1986) · A. Kennerley, 'Seamen's missions and sailors' homes: voluntary welfare provision for

British merchant seafarers, 1815–1970', PhD diss., University of Plymouth, 1989 · L. Yexley, *Charity and the navy: a protest against indiscriminate begging on behalf of 'Poor Jack'* (1911)
Archives Portsmouth City RO, Royal Sailors' Rests records
Likenesses photograph, c.1880, repro. in Wintz, *Our blue jackets*, frontispiece · oils, NPG [*see illus.*] · photographs, repro. in Gulliver, *Dame Agnes Weston* · portrait, repro. in Weston, *My life among the bluejackets*, frontispiece
Wealth at death £10,036 14s. 3d.: probate, 16 Jan 1919, CGPLA Eng. & Wales

Weston, Sir Aylmer Gould Hunter- (1864–1940), army officer, was born at Hunterston, West Kilbride, Ayrshire, on 23 September 1864, the elder son of Lieutenant-Colonel Gould Read Hunter-Weston (1823–1904), and his second wife, Jane (1837–1911), daughter and heir of Robert Hunter, twenty-fifth laird of Hunterston. He was educated at Wellington College (1875–82), entered the Royal Military Academy, Woolwich, in 1882, and commissioned lieutenant in the Royal Engineers in 1884. He saw active service on the north-west frontier and in Egypt, being promoted captain in 1892 and brevet major in 1895. In 1898 he entered the Staff College, Camberley, where Hunter-Bunter, as he was nicknamed, did well, and became master of the Staff College draghounds, a much-cherished honour.

During the Second South African War, Hunter-Weston commanded a force of mounted engineers that operated behind Boer lines, destroying enemy road and railway links, most notably cutting the railway near Bloemfontein, and thus preventing the Boers from reinforcing that town. He showed great courage, a level head, and technical skill, and in 1900 he received his brevet lieutenant-colonelcy and was made DSO. Between the end of the Second South African War and 1914 he held various staff positions in Britain, becoming a full colonel in 1908, and assistant director of military training at the War Office (1911–14). His motto as a trainer of troops was 'Teach the trainers how to teach before they try to teach the Tommies' (*The Times*, 19 March 1940). On 5 December 1905 he married Grace (b. 1883/4), daughter of William Strang Steel, of Philipshaugh, Selkirk; they had no children.

In February 1914 Hunter-Weston was given command, as brigadier-general, of the 11th infantry brigade at Colchester. He took the brigade to France on the outbreak of the First World War, and it fought well at Le Cateau and on the Aisne: it was the first British formation to cross the River Aisne, using a damaged bridge. He was made major-general in October 1914, and given command of the 29th ('Incomparable') division, and led it in the landings at Cape Helles at Gallipoli in April 1915. A beachhead was established at the cost of heavy casualties. In May 1915 he was promoted acting lieutenant-general and given charge of 8th corps at Gallipoli. On 3 July John Churchill reported 'The 29th Div is down to small numbers now … These continual frontal attacks are terrible, and I fear the Generals will be called butchers by the troops. H[unter] W[eston] already has that name with the 29th' (Gilbert, 1072–3). In August Hunter-Weston collapsed from sunstroke and was invalided home, where he was knighted.

Hunter-Weston was made acting lieutenant-general

again in March 1916, and given command of 8th corps again, which by this time had been moved to France. At the opening of the battle of the Somme on 1 July 1916, 8th corps was given the task of capturing the heavily fortified hamlets of Beaumont-Hamel, Beaumont-sur-Ancre, and Serre. That day 8th corps suffered 14,581 casualties. No enemy positions were captured, except for a few isolated stretches of front line positions, all of which had to be abandoned within a day of their capture. Hunter-Weston remained a corps commander, but was not given the task of conducting a major offensive again until the closing stages of the war. In October 1916 he was given leave, and stood successfully as a Unionist candidate in the North Ayrshire by-election; his opponent, a clergyman standing as a peace candidate, polled some 1300 votes to Hunter-Weston's 7000. He was elected for Buteshire and North Ayrshire in 1918, and retained the seat until 1935. He was promoted substantive lieutenant-general in 1919 and retired from the army in 1920. He died on 18 March 1940, after falling from a turret at his home in Hunterston. He was survived by his wife.   J. LETHBRIDGE

Sources *The Times* (19 March 1940) · C. F. Aspinall-Oglander, ed., *Military operations: Gallipoli*, 2 vols., History of the Great War (1929–32) · J. E. Edmonds, ed., *Military operations, France and Belgium*, 14 vols., History of the Great War (1922–48) · M. Middlebrook, *The first day on the Somme, 1 July 1916* (1971) · B. H. Liddell Hart, *History of the First World War*, rev. edn (1970) · *Army List* · M. Gilbert, ed., *Winston S. Churchill*, companion vol., 3/2 (1972) · m. cert. · Burke, *Gen. GB* (1937) · CCI (1940) · DNB
Archives BL, diaries and papers, Add. MSS 48355–48368 · NAM, diaries and papers · NRA, priv. coll., papers | CAC Cam., corresp. with Sir E. I. Spears · PRO, letters to Lord Kitchener relating to Dardanelles expedition, PRO 30/57; WO 159 | SOUND IWM SA, oral history
Likenesses E. Patry, 1916 (after P. A. de Laszlo), Royal Engineers HQ mess, Chatham, Kent · F. Dodd, drawing, 1917, IWM · Swaine, print, c.1917–1919, NPG · W. Stoneman, photograph, 1918, NPG
Wealth at death £41,688 11s. 0d.: confirmation, 23 Aug 1940, CCI

Weston, Charles (1731/2–1809), merchant and philanthropist, was born in Calcutta, the son of William Weston, register (chief clerk) of the mayor's court, Calcutta, until the mid-1740s. His mother was possibly Mrs Mary Ballantine, who married a William Weston in October 1731. Weston spent his life in or near Calcutta. As a youth he was apprenticed to the surgeon John Zachariah Holwell (1711–1798), later a member of the council at Fort William, Calcutta, in whose service he was when Siraj ud-Daula attacked the fort in 1756. Weston escaped imprisonment in the Black Hole, since he was on the River Hooghly looking after Holwell's baggage boats when the fort fell. He was listed among the European sufferers who received compensation in 1759 for financial loss.

Holwell helped Weston with capital to start his career, a debt returned when Weston supported Holwell in his old age and left bequests to his grandchildren. Weston built his fortune through commerce, judicious purchase of Calcutta property, and the provision of mortgages. As determined in business as he was compassionate in private life, he pursued his interests through the civil court in the 1760s, and in 1778 foreclosed on the Revd J. Z. Kiernander, the founder of the Old Mission Church, Calcutta, with which Weston and his family had a close association. But, when Kiernander's house was put up for public auction, Weston used his son-in-law, Philip Leal, to buy the house back for himself. In that year Weston was among a group of Calcutta merchants and agents who asked for, and received, naval protection of their trade returning from China and the Malay coast at the start of war with France. By then he owned several Calcutta properties and held mortgages on others. His wealth was much augmented when, also in 1778, he drew the first prize in the Calcutta lottery, Tiretta's Bazar, which stood opposite the site of his childhood home, worth Rs 196,000 with a monthly income of Rs 3500.

As a prominent Calcutta citizen, Weston served, despite his being Eurasian, on the jury which tried the notorious case of Maharaja Nandakumar in 1775. He acted too as parish clerk to St John's, Calcutta. His charitable work among the poor of Calcutta during his lifetime was munificent. He is said to have distributed each month 100 gold *mohurs* (approximately £150 at contemporary value) to the poor, and provided many with pensions. At his death this charitable work was crowned by his trust of Rs 100,000 to be administered by St John's vestry for those whom Weston had supported in his lifetime and for the general relief of poverty.

On 9 November 1758 Weston married Amelia de Rozario (1736?–1774x7), and, after her death, Constantia (*b.* 1735/6, *d.* in or before 1801). Of his nine known children, only his eldest son Charles, who was mentally and physically handicapped, survived him. Portraits of Weston in old age depict him as slender and of medium height, well but simply dressed, dark of hair and countenance, with an air of dignity, sagacity, and kindliness.

When Charles Weston died, at Chinsura on 25 December 1809, he owned four houses and considerable personal effects, including a gold snuff-box which bore a portrait of his patron Holwell. A large library attested to his erudition, and two pianos and scores—bequeathed to granddaughters—to his musical interests. Many legacies, large and small, went to relatives and friends. Rs 230,000 remained in bonds from those to whom he had lent money in his life with little expectation of repayment. He was buried on 25 December at South Park Street cemetery, Calcutta, after a lifetime 'of benevolence and charity, seldom equalled, and never yet exceeded in British India' (*Bengal Obituary*, 94). Weston's personality and generosity with his wealth overcame the prejudice which existed against those of mixed parentage in the European community. He was indeed 'a striking and existing example, that chaste and refined sentiments are not confined to complexion and climate' (ibid.).

CHRISTOPHER HAWES

Sources Bengal proceedings, 1704–1937, BL OIOC, I, (P) · Bengal public consultations, 1759, BL OIOC, P/1/31 · mayor's court proceedings, 1744–51, BL OIOC, P/155/23 · mayor's court proceedings, 1767, BL OIOC, P/155/41 · mayor's court proceedings, 1768–9, BL OIOC, P/155/45 · returns of baptisms, marriages and burials, 1698–1969, BL OIOC, (N) · Bengal returns, 1713–1948, BL OIOC, N/1 · accountant-general's records, c.1601–1974, BL OIOC, L/AG · will, Charles Weston, 1810, BL OIOC, L/AG/34/29/22, 1–12 · inventory, Charles Weston, 1810, BL OIOC, L/AG/34/27/41, 737–54 · 'Leaves from the editor's notebook', *Bengal Past and Present*, 2 (1908), 83–104 · *The Bengal obituary, or, A record to perpetuate the memory of departed worth*, Holmes & Co. (1851) · C. Lushington, *The history, design, and present state of the religious and charitable institutions founded by the British in Calcutta* (1825) · H. E. A. Cotton, *Calcutta old and new: a historical and descriptive handbook to the city*, rev. edn, ed. N. R. Ray (1980) · W. S. Seton-Karr and H. D. Sandeman, eds., *Selections from the Calcutta Gazettes*, 5 vols. (1864–9), vol. 1 · H. E. Busteed, *Echoes from old Calcutta*, 2nd edn (1888) · H. B. Hyde, *The parish of Bengal* (1899) · H. Yule and A. C. Burnell, *Hobson-Jobson*, new edn (1986), 573–4

Likenesses miniature, St John's Church, Calcutta · oils, St John's Church, Calcutta · oils, priv. coll.

Wealth at death Rs 572,931 [approx. £57,000]; incl. Rs 184,431 personal effects; Rs 3500 cash; Rs 385,000 government stock: BL OIOC, inventory of Charles Weston, L/AG/34/27/41, 1810, 737–54

Weston, Edward (1565?–1635), Roman Catholic priest, was the son of William Weston of Lincoln's Inn and Ellen, daughter of the martyr John *Story (*d.* 1571), and was born in London. He matriculated from Lincoln College, Oxford, on 20 March 1579, and was there placed under the private tuition of the Catholic John Case. After five years at Oxford he ended what Wood calls 'his conversations with the Muses' without taking a degree and entered the English College, Rheims, in 1584. From there he proceeded to the English College, Rome, in the spring of 1585, and in 1586 signed a petition of fifty students on behalf of the Jesuit administration against a faction of malcontents. After being ordained priest at the Lateran on 26 March 1589 he was made doctor of theology at the University of Monreale, Turin.

Weston returned to Rheims on 7 June 1592 as lecturer on cases of conscience, but moved to Douai the following year to prepare for the return of the English College to that town. He continued to lecture there until 1602, when he was described by the spy John Fawther as 'a proper man of person and of all sort of knowledge and learning', adding, 'They make the comparison betwixt him and Campion to be equal'. That year he published *De triplici hominis officio* 'against atheists, politiques and sectarians', with particular mention of John Reynolds of Oxford in his preface. He was then sent to labour on the English mission in the Durham district, where he spent some ten years.

On Weston's return to Douai, on 23 September 1612, he was caught up in the controversy on the oath of allegiance, supporting Cardinal Bellarmine against the Benedictine Thomas Preston (alias Roger Widdrington). In reply to the latter Weston drew upon his correspondence with the cardinal for his *Iuris pontificii sanctuarium* (1613). The following year he published a manual of controversies in two parts under the general title of *The Trial of Christian Truth*: the first part treated of faith, in 1614, and the second of hope, in 1615. But he failed to bring out his promised sequel on the further virtues of charity and religion. Instead, he was involved in the political troubles of his college, as he supported his colleague William Singleton in opposition to the president of Douai, Matthew Kellison, on the question of the oath of allegiance. For this he was summoned to the internuncio at Brussels on 6 August 1617 and to Rome on 28 August. Thus it was under a shadow that he departed from Douai and was appointed canon of the collegiate church of St Mary at Bruges.

Some years later Weston again appears on the side of the Jesuits in the controversy between the two Jesuits, John Fisher (or Percy) and John Sweet, and the two protestant ministers, Daniel Featley and Francis White. In 1624 he published a book, *The Repair of Honour*, in the form of a letter to the Jesuits, noting that their dispute had brought about the conversion of two earls to the Catholic church. Weston went on to publish two further books in Latin, *Theatrum vitae civilis ac sacrae* (in 5 vols.) in 1626 and *Iesu domini nostri coruscationum … enarrationes* in 1631. He died at Bruges in 1635. PETER MILWARD

Sources G. Anstruther, *The seminary priests*, 1 (1969), 376–7 · Wood, *Ath. Oxon.*, new edn, 2.573–4 · C. Dodd [H. Tootell], *The church history of England, from the year 1500, to the year 1688*, 3 (1742), 96 · H. Foley, ed., *Records of the English province of the Society of Jesus*, 6 (1880), 508 · P. Milward, *Religious controversies of the Jacobean age* (1978), 103–4, 178, 222 · A. F. Allison, 'The later life and writings of Joseph Cresswell, SJ (1556–1623)', *Recusant History*, 15 (1979–81), 79–144 · Foster, *Alum. Oxon.*

Weston, Edward (1703–1770), government official and author, was born at Eton, Buckinghamshire, on 3 January 1703, the second son of Stephen *Weston (1665–1742), bishop of Exeter, and his wife, Lucy Sleech (*d.* 1742). He was educated at Eton College and at King's College, Cambridge, where he was admitted in 1719 and graduated BA in 1723 and MA in 1727. Early in 1730 he married Penelope (*d.* 1754), the granddaughter of Bishop Patrick and the eldest daughter and coheir of the Revd Symon Patrick, of Dalham, Suffolk, and his wife, Anne, *née* Fountayne, of Melton, Yorkshire.

Upon leaving Cambridge, Weston obtained the post of tutor for the children of Charles, second Viscount Townshend, and in 1729 he was appointed Townshend's secretary when the latter became secretary of state for the north. When Townshend retired in the following year Weston became under-secretary to his successor, Lord Harrington, and he remained in that position until 1746. In November of that year Harrington went to Ireland as lord lieutenant and Weston accompanied him as chief secretary and privy councillor. He stayed in Ireland until 1751 and then, for reasons of health, went into retirement for ten years. He enjoyed a moderate income from several sinecures, including comptroller of the salt office, to which he had been appointed in 1728, and editor of the *London Gazette*, at a salary of £500 per annum. He also acquired by purchase the parish of Somerby and much of the parish of Searby in Lincolnshire. Following the death of his wife, Penelope, in 1754, Weston married two years later Anne, the daughter of John Fountayne of Melton.

At Lord Bute's earnest request, Weston, 'a very able, worthy, good man', returned in March 1761 to his old post in the northern department. He was a diligent secretary, interested in enhancing departmental efficiency, and Bute valued his administrative expertise and relied on his authoritative grasp of European affairs. Following Bute's elevation to the Treasury, Weston served under his successor as northern secretary, George Grenville, and then, in

October 1762, transferred to the southern department, headed by Lord Halifax. Despite intermittent bouts of ill health, he pursued his official functions until August 1763, when he accompanied Halifax upon the latter's move to the northern department. There he again occupied a vital position, drafting and modifying state papers and preparing commissions and warrants, including the general warrant against Wilkes and others connected with the *North Briton* affair. Weston was also a clerk of the signet, and was allowed to perform his duties by deputy. In August 1762 he received a grant for thirty-one years of the office of alnager in Ireland, but resigned it a year later, on receiving a pension of £500 per annum for the same period. On 1 September 1763 he was appointed one of the commissioners to execute the office of privy seal.

Unremitting ill health finally forced Weston to retire in April 1764. A yearly pension of £750 was granted to him for his valuable services. He continued to provide informal advice and guidance on diplomatic matters over the next few years, but he declined to resume office when asked by Grafton in July 1765. He remained in retirement, pursuing classical studies, writing pamphlets and sermons, and contributions to the *London Gazette*. Among the various pamphlets attributed to him, only two can be definitely identified as his: *The Englishman Directed in the Choice of his Religion* (4th edn, 1767) and *Family Discourses by a Country Gentleman* (1768). He also wrote an answer to Bishop Warburton, and the long epitaph in Fulham churchyard on Bishop Sherlock was composed by him. He died at Buxton, Derbyshire, on 15 July 1770, and was buried on 17 July at Somerby, Lincolnshire, where a monument records his memory. KARL WOLFGANG SCHWEIZER

Sources T. Harwood, *Alumni Etonenses, or, A catalogue of the provosts and fellows of Eton College and King's College, Cambridge, from the foundation in 1443 to the year 1797* (1797) · R. A. Austen-Leigh, ed., *The Eton College register, 1698–1752* (1927) · L. Scott, 'Under-secretaries of state, 1755–1775', MA diss., University of Manchester, 1950 · J. C. Sainty, ed., *Officials of the secretaries of state, 1660–1782* (1973) · *Reports on the manuscripts of the earl of Eglinton*, HMC, 10 (1885) · *The Grenville papers: being the correspondence of Richard Grenville … and … George Grenville*, ed. W. J. Smith, 4 vols. (1852–3) · K. W. Schweizer, 'Edward Weston (1703–1770): the papers of an 18th century under-secretary in the Lewis Walpole Library', *Yale University Library Gazette*, 71/1–2 (1996), 43–8 · K. W. Schweizer, 'A handlist to the additional Weston papers', *BIHR*, 51 (1978), 99–102 · *DNB*

Archives BL, corresp., Add. MSS 57305–57308, 57927–57928, 58213 · BL, corresp., Add. MSS 6808–6809, 6823, 6831, 38201–38205 · Derbys. RO, Matlock, corresp. relating to Ireland · priv. coll., corresp. and papers · Yale U., Lewis Walpole Library, diplomatic corresp. and papers | BL, letters to S. Dayrolle, Add. MS 15868 · BL, corresp. with earl of Liverpool, Add. MSS 38201–38202, 38304–38305, 38469 · BL, letters to duke of Newcastle, Add. MSS 32688–32935 · BL, letters to T. Robinson, Add. MSS 23780–23829 · BL, corresp. with Walter Titley, MSS 2683–2693 · BL, letters to T. Villiers, Add. MS 22530 · NRA, priv. coll., letters to first Earl Waldegrave

Weston, Elizabeth Jane (*bap.* 1581?, *d.* 1612), Latin poet, was born in Chipping Norton, Oxfordshire, on 2 November 1582 according to information on her tombstone; but an undated record of her baptism appears in the parish register between records dated 4 March and 31 October 1581, respectively, and a date within this period would accord better with her statement (in a poem on the death of her mother) that she was some six months old when her father died. She was the second of two children of John Weston (identified only as 'clark' in the record of his burial on 6 May 1582) and Jane Cooper (*bap.* 1563). Her mother subsequently married Edward *Kelley, associate of Doctor John Dee, and accompanied him in 1583 to Poland and eventually to Prague, where Kelley was appointed alchemist to the emperor, Rudolph II. Elizabeth and her brother John Francis (1580–1600) apparently remained behind with their grandmothers before joining their mother and new stepfather in Prague a few years later.

Weston was later to thank a John Hammonius, or Hammond, for teaching her Latin (this may be the John Hammond whom John Dee had employed as tutor in Trebon in 1588), but beyond this nothing is known of her formal education, though her brother was schooled locally at the Clementine College and then sent to the University of Ingolstadt in 1598. Kelley prospered at first in Rudolph's service, receiving the title of *eques aureus*; but his fortunes turned for the worse after a duel in 1591 when he killed a member of the court. A series of prison stays ensued, with rumours of attempts at escape and even of a suicide in prison with the assistance of his family.

Kelley's death some time about 1597 left his family destitute, with their properties in the hands of creditors. At this point Weston began to compose the many letters and lyrics (all of them in Latin; no document has survived in any of the modern languages that she was said to have mastered) which she addressed to members of the court and to other learned members of the international republic of neo-Latin letters who might be able to intercede for her with Rudolph.

The pathos of Weston's position—as an orphaned 'Virgo Angla' with widowed mother and sickly brother away at university—awakened enthusiastic responses of chivalric empathy from a wide range of European humanists. That she was able to express her anguish clearly and simply in elegiac distichs that generally avoided straining after arcane allusions suited her maidenly image and led her to be acclaimed as a tenth Muse, a fourth Grace, a new Sappho or Theano. The librarian at Heidelberg, Paul Melissus, sent her a laurel wreath and thereby formally welcomed her into the circle of laureated humanist poets. A Silesian aristocrat, George Martinius von Baldhoven, undertook to edit and collect her writings, first in a two-book volume, *Poëmata* (1602), and subsequently (*c.*1607) in an expanded three-book collection of her poems and letters which he entitled *Parthenica*, or 'Maidenly writings', even though in the meantime (April 1603) she had married the jurist Johannes Leo, an agent of the duke of Brunswick and prince of Anhalt.

Manuscript verses, addressed to the reader and signed 'Elisabetha Joanna, Uxor Joannis Leonis in Aula Imperiali Agentis, ex Familia Westoniorum, Angla' and dated 16 August 1610, appear in two copies of *Parthenica*, one in Prague and the other in the British Library. In them Weston complains that all her writings have been categorized as 'maidenly' even when written after her marriage,

and she hopes that a more accurate edition, purged of the many errors that have crept into this one, may emerge with the passage of time.

Kelley's disgrace at the time of his death presumably accounts for Weston's almost total failure to mention him by name in her writings; references to her nobility have been taken to link her with a noble line of Westons (one of whom presumably, recusant and/or spendthrift, died in Prague), when in fact they must refer to Kelley's Rudolphine title. It was not until Karel Hrdina discovered a unique copy of the pamphlet lamenting the death of her mother and reported it in 1928 that Weston's connection to Kelley became known to readers of Czech; and not until 1990 that J. W. Binns made this information more readily available to readers of English.

Baldhoven's addition of letters to and from Weston in *Parthenica* gives a fuller picture of Weston's position in the humanist world than is seen from the poems alone in the 1602 volume. Poems to influential men in the Rudolphine court usually appear without answering poems or letters, or are sent with a letter to a mutual friend who is asked to intercede on her behalf. Her correspondents outside the court, on the other hand, are typically seen responding to requests (often from Baldhoven himself) for poems to include in the forthcoming volume, and they usually ask for similar poems by her in return, for the same reason. Some of these correspondents are connected to Paracelsian circles and may have been associated with Kelley, such as Oswald Croll who asks for a poem to include in his forthcoming *Basilica chymica* (1609). Weston's possible involvement in her stepfather's alchemical projects is hinted in letters to her brother; and the esotericism of Rudolph's circle may have been part of her appeal to scholars outside Prague, who could also understand her anxious dependence on a patronage that continued to elude her.

In one of her poems Weston develops parallels between her condition and that of Ovid in his *Tristia*, rejected by his emperor and forced to live far from his native land, all because of some mysterious scandal. The conflicting explanations of Ovid's own exile—whether because of his scandalous *Art of Love* or because of his knowledge of some scandal at court—are deftly echoed to hint at Weston's own fate, as a victim of her stepfather's disgrace or perhaps blamed for her own 'art' that speaks out against envious courtiers who begrudge her mother and herself their rightful property. In this way, Weston makes her own position (with its need for prudent suppression of details) expressive of the hopes and frustrations of life at the centre of an imperial court.

Although her correspondents frequently ask Weston to send a portrait of herself, few images of her have been identified. An engraved portrait by Balzer appears in F. Pelcel's biography of her (*Abbildungen Böhmischer und Mährischer Gelehrten*, 1777, 3.77); a more reliable contemporary likeness may be the anonymous portrait bearing her name in the Hessisches Landesmuseum, Darmstadt (inventory number Hz.1696).

Weston died of consumption in Prague on 23 November

1612, having borne seven children, three daughters who survived her and four sons who did not. Her tomb in the church of St Thomas in Prague bears a eulogistic epitaph along with the date of her death and a precise (if mistaken) statement of her age as being thirty years and three weeks.   DONALD CHENEY

Sources *The writings of Elizabeth Jane Weston*, ed. and trans. D. Cheney and B. Hosington (2000) · A. Truhlář and K. Hrdina, eds., *Enchiridon renatae poesis Latinae in Bohemia et Moravia cultae* (1966–82), 5.470–77 [bibliography] · K. Hrdina, 'Dvě práce z dějin českého humanismu', *Listy Filologické*, 55 (1928), 14–19 · J. W. Binns, *Intellectual culture in Elizabethan and Jacobean England: the Latin writings of the age* (1990) · A. Kolář, *Humanistická Básnířka Vestonia* (1926) · parish register, Chipping Norton

Likenesses J. Balzer, engraving, repro. in F. M. Pelcel, *Abbildungen Böhmischer und Mährischer Gelehrten und Künstler*, 3 (1777) · drawing, Hessisches Landesmuseum, Darmstadt, Germany

Weston, Sir Francis (1511–1536), courtier, was the only son of Sir Richard *Weston (*c.*1465–1541) and his wife, Anne Sandys. He followed his father to court, where by 1526 he was a page. A contemporary French account attributes his rise to favour to his skill at games and his good graces and manners. Weston frequently appears in the privy purse accounts as receiving small sums of money from the king. In 1530 he won a total of sixteen angels by winning four times against Henry at tennis, and at other times the king also lost to him at dice, bowls, 'imperiall', and 'pope Julius's game'. His closeness to the king was acknowledged in 1532 when he was made a gentleman of the privy chamber, while in 1533 he was appointed governor of Guernsey jointly with his father. In May 1533, during the festivities of Anne Boleyn's coronation, he was made a knight of the Bath.

Among the games at which Weston excelled were those associated with courtly love. In May 1530 he had married Anne, daughter and heir of Sir Christopher Pickering of Killington, Cumberland. It may be significant, however, that in the 1550s George Cavendish remembered him as one 'That wantonly lyved without feare and dreade … Followyng his fantzy and his wanton lust' (*Life of Wolsey*, 30). On 18 May 1535 Queen Anne took him to task for neglecting his wife, and for flirting with Margaret Shelton, possibly an old flame of the king's who was then being pursued by Henry Norris, the groom of the stool. Weston replied that Norris came to the queen's chamber more for Anne than for his intended bride, and capped this by saying that he himself loved someone in her household better than either his wife or Margaret. When the queen asked him who that was, he replied 'it ys your self, and then she defyed hym'—quelled his impudence (ibid., 452). The role of the courtier who proposes to the great lady who rejects him with scorn was part of the courtly love convention, but in the sexually charged and suspicious atmosphere of Henry VIII's court it was a dangerous one for Weston to play.

How dangerous became clear the following year. On 1 May 1536 Queen Anne was arrested on a charge of adultery, and soon afterwards, in the hearing of Sir William Kingston, the constable of the Tower, she told of Weston's

heavy-handed flirtation of the previous year. Consequently Weston was himself arrested, probably on the 5th, and taken to the Tower. He had links with opponents of Thomas Cromwell, who was probably glad of an excuse to strike at him. On 12 May he and three others were brought to trial in Westminster Hall, where it was claimed that Anne had given money to Weston and the others accused, as she had done to many of the commonly penurious young courtiers, gifts which were now interpreted as tokens of a treasonable contract. Weston pleaded not guilty both to treason and to charges of adultery with Anne at Whitehall and Greenwich in May and June 1534. But despite efforts to save him by his family and by the French ambassador, Jean de Dinteville, he was condemned to death. The sentence of hanging, drawing, and quartering at Tyburn was commuted by royal mercy to beheading on Tower Hill.

Weston was executed on 17 May 1536. That he then failed to protest his innocence was conventional, for royal mercy could be withdrawn and friends and family might suffer. Instead he declared that his fate was a warning to others not to presume on life's continuance, 'for I had thought to have lived in abomination yet this twenty or thirty years and to have made amends' (Ives, 392). He had written a farewell letter to his parents, one which sums up the tragically curtailed life of a rather shallow young man caught out of his depth. He left debts totalling £925 7s. 2d., which he asked his parents to pay—his creditors included his draper, embroiderer, tailor, goldsmith, shoemaker, barber, and saddler. He was buried outside the chapel of St Peter ad Vincula in the Tower. The poet Sir Thomas Wyatt, himself under arrest in the Tower, but released after Anne's execution thanks to Cromwell's protection, wrote a lament in prison over the dead, Weston among them:

> Ah! Weston, Weston, that pleasant was and young,
> In active things who might with thee compare?
> All words accept that thou diddest speak with tongue,
> So well esteemed with each where thou diddest fare.
> And we that now in court doth lead our life
> Most part in mind doth thee lament and moan:
> But that thy faults we daily hear so rife,
> All we should weep that thou are dead and gone.
> (Wyatt, 192)

                JONATHAN HUGHES

Sources *LP Henry VIII*, vols. 4–10 · *Cavendish's life of Wolsey*, ed. S. W. Singer, 2nd edn (1827) [includes Cavendish's *Metrical visions*, separately paginated] · E. W. Ives, *Anne Boleyn* (1986) · N. H. Nicholas, ed., *Privy purse expences of Henry VIII* (1827) · BL, Cotton MS Otho CX, fols. 209v, 222, 223, 224v, 225 · BL, Harley MS 283, fol. 134 · T. Wyatt, *Collected poems*, ed. J. Daalder (1975) · HoP, *Commons, 1509–58*, 3.590–92

Wealth at death debts of £925 7s. 2d.: letter to parents, *LP Henry VIII* 1536, no. 869

Weston, Frank (1871–1924), bishop of Zanzibar, born at Bervie House, Roupell Park, London, on 13 September 1871, was the fourth son and fifth child of Robert William Gibbs Weston (*d.* 1882/3), a tea broker in Mincing Lane, and his wife, Amelia, daughter of Dr Robert Valentine. His father came from a Leicestershire family, but three of his grandparents were Scots, and he was proud of his descent

Frank Weston (1871–1924), by Vandyk

from two seventeenth-century bishops of Brechin. After preparatory school in St Leonards and following his father's death, he was educated as a day boy at Dulwich College, and at Trinity College, Oxford, where he obtained first-class honours in theology in 1893. Turning his back on academic life, he was ordained deacon in 1894 and priest by the bishop of St Albans in 1895. He then took two curacies in London's slums, the first (1894–6) with the Trinity College Mission at St John's, Stratford East, from which he resigned to take another at St Matthew's, Westminster (1896–8).

Weston never married. A fervent Christian socialist, he moved at university in high-church Anglican circles, and committed himself to a celibate vocation as a missionary in response to Bishop Smythies' appeal in Oxford on behalf of the Universities' Mission to Central Africa (UMCA) in 1892. Despite reservations about his health he eventually joined the UMCA in 1898, and for nine years was stationed at Zanzibar. As chaplain (1898–9) and principal (1901–8) of the school at St Andrew's Training College, Kiungani, and in running St Mark's Theological College, which he had established (1899–1901, and again 1906–8), his work was chiefly educational. It was marked throughout by his distaste for the great obstacle to African advancement posed by European race consciousness, by his doubts as to the 'civilizing' impact of European trade on Africa, and by his conviction that missionaries should identify themselves with Africans' own ideals, lifestyles, and traditions. Only education in such a spirit could help develop an African-led church. An intensely energetic

man with too few colleagues, he also functioned as a canon of Christ Church Cathedral and chancellor of the diocese of Zanzibar. He found time to gain a BD degree in 1906, a qualification he felt was demanded by the chancellorship, and published *The one Christ* (1907) to the general approval of theologians such as Bishop Charles Gore, Canon Scott Holland, and his former Oxford tutor, William Sanday.

Notwithstanding his lack of exposure to the varied currents of Anglicanism, his single-mindedness, and his limited ability for compromise Weston was in other respects an obvious successor to Dr E. J. Hine, who resigned as bishop of Zanzibar in 1908. Having declined the bishopric of Mashonaland in 1907, Weston was consecrated in Southwark Cathedral in October 1908. In the fashion of the peripatetic bishops of the UMCA he immediately set about traversing and reorganizing his diocese, spending only about three months of each year in Zanzibar itself. He worried in particular about the 'debased civilisation' (Smith, 96) of the European-run plantations, and the corrupting impact on African family life of the commercial society of coastal towns; these he thought quite as threatening as the omnipresent expansion of Islam and the practices of 'witchcraft'. Zanzibar, he wrote, 'is more and more immoral—Piccadilly, Sodom, and a public bar!' (ibid., 187). Impatient of anthropological findings while insisting on high standards for Africans as for Europeans, he fretted at the fragility of African Christianity in such a setting. Sensitive to the mission's overwhelming dependence on the efforts of African Christians, he struggled endlessly to balance the need for trust in his clergy with the dangers of 'a premature grant of home rule' to local churches (ibid., 88). As a further support to the mission's work Weston drew on his acquaintance with British female orders to establish in 1910 the Community of the Sacred Passion, above all to contact African women in their own homes.

It was, however, Weston's highly critical reaction to the proceedings of the Kikuyu missionary conference of 1913 which made him widely known in British church circles. Kikuyu was the latest of several conferences between the Church Missionary Society and other protestant missionaries. Presided over by the bishops of Mombasa and Uganda, and designed to foster their common cause against Roman Catholicism and Islam, the conference drew up proposals for an ecclesiastical federation and intercommunion under Anglican leadership. This apparent blurring of denominational divisions came at a time when, against the background of modernist criticism, Anglo-Catholics in Britain itself were increasingly fearful for the coherence of the Church of England and its doctrines. Weston denounced the scheme, appealed to the archbishop of Canterbury, and developed his wider views on the nature of the church in *Ecclesia Anglicana: for What does she Stand?* (1913). A great stir ensued, and Weston was summoned home to explain his impulsive, exaggerated claims of heresy and schism. His polemical, passionate, and abstract arguments alienated as many as they enthused, and Archbishop Randall Davidson's skilful diplomacy and published decision of 1915 were together sufficient to calm all parties. However, thinking many of his questions unanswered, Weston thereafter continued to write as a powerful exponent both of the Anglo-Catholic position within the Anglican church and of alternative plans for co-operation and unity.

At the start of the First World War, being still on leave in England, Weston was spared internment with his mainland colleagues in German East Africa. After returning to Zanzibar, where the military campaigns seriously disrupted his diocese, he was appalled at the methods used to compel Africans to assist allied forces. In 1916 he therefore took up the challenge to recruit a carrier corps of his own. Remarkably, as a major commanding some 2500 men, he suffered no casualties, and was appointed OBE. This commitment to the well-being of Africans not only echoed both his missionary concern and his earlier Christian socialism. It also led him into wartime propaganda, with his indictment of German colonial practice in *The Black Slaves of Prussia* (1917), and prompted his vigorous attack after the war on Britain's approach to labour recruitment in the east African colonies, *The Serfs of Great Britain* (1920). 'We regard forced labour', he wrote, 'as in itself immoral; and we hold that forcing Africans to work in the interests of European civilization is a betrayal of the weaker to the financial interests of the stronger race' (Hewitt, 1.165). He played an important role in the successful political campaign by humanitarians and churchmen to change imperial policy.

In 1920 Dr Weston attended the Lambeth conference as well as the first Anglo-Catholic Congress. On this occasion, despite his reputation for uncompromising advocacy, he surprised many present by his warmth and goodwill even to doctrinal foes such as Hensley Henson, and he made a significant contribution to Lambeth's Appeal to all Christian People with its renewed approach to questions of Christian unity. Tall, imposing, a brilliant and gifted speaker equally capable of holding an audience of thousands in the Albert Hall as of fascinating a handful of African children, Weston's presence on this occasion was later represented as an 'extraordinary mixture of generosity and menace' (Bell, 1010). Often naïve, prone to feelings of insecurity, and lacking much practical sense of the evolving history of the church, Weston in Britain was widely seen as unreliable and unpredictable. His last major public appearance in Britain, as president of the Anglo-Catholic Congress of 1923, seemed to bear this out. His telegram of greetings from the congress to the pope prompted widespread disquiet and outrage, scarcely helpful to Anglo-Catholic interests. Archbishop Davidson regretfully wrote of him as 'a source and centre of real danger to the Church at present owing to the unguarded way in which he writes and speaks' (Bell, 1277).

Weston returned to Zanzibar in September 1923, wearied from his exertions rather than fresh from the change of scene. Much admired there for his dedication, sense of service, and fair-mindedness, he immediately resumed the administration of his expanding diocese. A year later,

suffering from blood poisoning from a poorly treated carbuncle, he died at Hegongo, Msalabani, on 2 November, and was buried in Msalabani churchyard that same evening. The appeal for a memorial fund attracted a large sum for the purposes of the Zanzibar diocese, and provided a memorial altar and tablet in St Matthew's, Westminster.

ANDREW PORTER

Sources H. M. Smith, *Frank, bishop of Zanzibar: life of Frank Weston* (1926) · A. G. Blood, *The history of the Universities Mission to Central Africa, 1907–1932* (1957), vol. 2 of *The history of the Universities Mission to Central Africa* · Dulwich College archives, Frank Weston file · S. P. Mews, 'Kikuyu and Edinburgh: the interaction of attitudes to two conferences', *Councils and assemblies*, ed. G. J. Cuming and D. Baker, SCH, 7 (1971), 345–59 · G. K. A. Bell, *Randall Davidson, archbishop of Canterbury*, 3rd edn (1952) · G. White, 'Frank Weston and the Kikuyu crisis', *Bulletin of the Scottish Institute of Missionary Studies*, new ser., 8–9 (1992–3), 48–55 · A. E. M. Anderson-Morshead, *The history of the Universities' Mission to Central Africa, 1859–1909*, 5th edn (1909) · R. Oliver, *The missionary factor in east Africa*, 2nd edn (1965) · T. L. Ormiston, *Dulwich College register, 1619 to 1926* (1926) · *WWW* · G. Hewitt, *The problems of success: a history of the Church Missionary Society, 1910–1942*, 2 vols. (1971–7)
Archives Dulwich College, London, archives, file, incl. newspaper cuttings, esp. obituaries, and the original data from which *Dulwich College register* was compiled | Bodl. RH, corresp., Universities Mission to Central Africa · LPL, Archbishop Davidson papers
Likenesses Vandyk, photograph, NPG [*see illus.*] · photographs, repro. in Smith, *Frank*, frontispiece and pp. 16, 80, 144, 240

Weston, (Willard) Garfield (1898–1978), food manufacturer and industrialist, was born 'in the smell of bread' (*DBB*) at Toronto, Canada, on 26 February 1898, the eldest son of George Weston, baker, and his wife, Emma Maude. He was educated at the Harboard Collegiate Institute, Toronto, his father meanwhile adding biscuit production to his bakery, the largest in the city. During the First World War, Weston served with the Canadian engineers in France from 1914 to 1916, before joining his father's firm on the marketing side. In 1921, the year of his appointment as vice-president of George Weston Ltd, he married Reta Lila Howard (*d.* 1967); they had three sons and six daughters.

On his father's death in 1924, Weston became president of the firm. By 1928 he had quintupled its profits; he then incorporated George Weston Ltd and used the cash from shareholders to begin purchasing bakeries in Canada and the United States. In 1934 he moved to Britain. Having seen during his periods of leave in the war the unprogressive state of the biscuit industry in the UK, he set up extensive plants at Slough and in south Wales to make biscuits at half the price of current quality brands. Within five years his biscuit sales were higher than those of any British rival, and equal to those of the two former leaders, Huntley and Palmers and Peek Frean, combined. By then he had also acquired thirty UK bakeries and introduced wrapped bread to British consumers. He registered Allied Bakeries Ltd in 1935, renamed Associated British Foods twenty-five years later.

After the beginning of the Second World War, Weston took advantage of the party truce to become National Unionist MP for Macclesfield; a largely silent member, he did not stand in the 1945 general election. Interested as he was in the affairs of the older Commonwealth—where some of his companies were to be found—he persistently campaigned against Britain's increasing involvement in Europe. Weston's individual bakeries in the UK were merged in 1949 under the common name Sunblest which gave their loaves a coherent identity in the standard bread market, securing them a position akin to that already achieved by Hovis in the brown bread market (*DBB*).

Having continued to acquire North American bakeries, in the late 1940s Weston began to buy into distribution companies, which by his death were to contribute 70 per cent of his total sales. A critical step was his acquisition of the Canadian Loblaw grocery in 1953. Of minor but symbolic importance was his purchase of the prestige store Fortnum and Mason in London in 1951. Weston took a personal interest in the store, kept it separate from his other businesses, and improved its profitability.

In 1955 Weston moved into supermarket retailing when he acquired the Fine Fare chain in Britain. His attempts to gain a hold over the country's flour-milling industry led to a prolonged contest with his competitors, Spillers and Ranks, and set off a renewed acquisition spree for bakeries. He was no less active overseas, bringing supermarkets to Germany. In Canada he bought into confectionery, fish processing, and paper and box making. In South Africa he acquired the country's largest baking and milling combine, in Australia bakeries and biscuit firms, and in India a paper box manufacturer. Since many purchases were made through nominees, his ownership of them was not known for some time. This secrecy helped to shield him from official anti-trust moves and to permit massive tax avoidance, but hindered the kinds of rationalization measures needed to raise the low returns on capital in many plants.

Weston could not have built up what became one of the twenty largest industrial enterprises in the world without possessing extraordinary energy and single-mindedness. Much of his resolve no doubt sprang from a strict Methodist upbringing. In his personal life, certainly, he was unassuming and a virtual teetotaller. Yet as a corporate predator Weston could be cunning and ruthless. He made his presence felt among managers through fear, and has been described as 'a more modest Howard Hughes' (*DBB*). When his new Toronto head office was being planned, for example, he instructed his architects to install a private elevator strictly for his own use, 'so that he could come and go without being seen' (ibid.). He is said, however, to have been a considerable philanthropist, giving £100,000 in 1940 to build Spitfire and Hurricane aircraft and £10,000 in 1941 for tanks. In 1968 he donated £250,000 to the new University of Ulster. For some years after 1945 he paid for exchange visits by boys between Britain and Canada.

From the later 1960s Weston largely relinquished responsibility for his British and Canadian controlling companies. In 1967 he handed over the chairmanship of the British-based operator, Associated British Foods, to his son Garry, but made himself president. Weston finally gave up the chairmanship of his North American operation George Weston Ltd in 1974, with his youngest son Galen becoming chairman and managing director. He took an active interest in Fortnum and Mason until his death, however, and remained its chairman.

Weston's first wife died in 1967 and five years later he married Marguerita Martin de Montoya, a former victim of the Spanish Civil War; they had no children. Weston died of a heart attack in Toronto, Canada, on 22 October 1978. Long before his death the assets and profits of his business empire had been channelled into a holding company, Wittington Investments Ltd. T. A. B. CORLEY

Sources S. Hunt, 'Weston, Willard Garfield', *DBB* · W. S. Rukemser, 'The $4 billion business Garfield Weston built', *Fortune* (1 June 1967), 117–42 · A. Lumsden, 'Fine Fare's recovery diet', *Management Today* (June 1969), 79–166 · *The Times* (24 Oct 1978) · T. A. B. Corley, *Quaker enterprise in biscuits: Huntley and Palmer of Reading, 1822–1972* (1972) · J. B. Jefferys, *Retail trading in Britain, 1850–1950* (1954) · R. Evely and I. M. D. Little, *Concentration in British industry, 1935–51* (1960) · *WWW* · *CGPLA Eng. & Wales* (1980) · d. cert.

Archives Associated British Foods, archives · HLRO, corresp. with Lord Beaverbrook

Likenesses photograph, *c.*1960, repro. in Lumsden, 'Fine Fare's recovery diet', 80

Wealth at death £93,423—in England and Wales: probate, 20 Nov 1980, *CGPLA Eng. & Wales*

Weston, Hugh (*c.*1510–1558), dean of Windsor, was born at Burton Overy, Leicestershire. He was educated at Balliol College, Oxford, and St Mary Hall, where he was elected exhibitioner on 21 April 1529, vacating by October 1531. He was fellow of Lincoln College from 1532, sub-rector (1538–9), and rector from 8 January 1539, vacating by August 1556. He was admitted BA on 18 July 1530, incepted MA on 17 February 1533, supplicated BM on 30 May 1537, was admitted BTh on 2 May 1539, incepted DTh in July 1540, and incorporated the last degree at Cambridge in 1554–5. He had an exhibition of the crown in 1537, and was senior proctor in 1537–8. From 1542 to about 1551 he was Lady Margaret professor of divinity. Lincoln College presented him to the free chapel of Petsoe, Buckinghamshire, to which he was instituted on 3 February 1541 and which he held until death. He became rector of St Nicholas Olave, London, on 15 September 1541, vacating by December 1548. On 17 October 1545 he was collated to the archdeaconry of Cornwall, retained to August 1554. On 21 March 1546 he was instituted rector of his native parish, and on 1 April 1547 he was dispensed for a further benefice.

In September 1549 Weston was arrested in Leicestershire and committed to the Fleet because of his conservative religious views. He was released into Cranmer's custody in the following autumn, in hope of his being converted, but he remained unreformed, and led opposition in London to the archbishop's forty-two articles in May 1552. It is supposed he lost his Oxford chair at the time of his arrest, but payment of his stipend continued for about two years. Mary made him her chaplain and, on 14 September 1553, dean of Westminster. He was installed on 18 September and assisted at the coronation on 1 October. On 16 October he was elected prolocutor of the lower house of the convocation of Canterbury; his *Oratio coram clero* was printed. In a sermon at Paul's Cross on 22 October he publicized the eucharistic debate which dominated the session of convocation. On 22 January 1554 he was collated to the archdeaconry of Colchester. On 7 February (Ash Wednesday), when Wyatt's rebels entered London, Weston celebrated mass before the queen at Whitehall, when (by his own admission) he wore armour beneath his vestments. He subsequently attended Wyatt and the duke of Suffolk at their executions. On 3 March he arranged his own presentation by the dean and chapter of Westminster to their principal living, the Oxfordshire rectory of Islip, to which he was admitted on 20 April, and retained to death. On 2 April he was presented by the crown to the rectory of Cliffe-at-Hoo, Kent, where he was instituted on 25 October 1555, and where he remained incumbent until his death.

In April 1554 Weston was reappointed prolocutor of the Canterbury clergy, in order to preside at the disputation in Oxford which would convict Cranmer, Ridley, and Latimer of heresy. He opened proceedings with a speech in the church of St Mary the Virgin on 14 April, and chaired the sessions in the divinity school. At times he lost control of the debate, and of his own temper. His conduct earned him much vilification, which subsequent allegations of drunkenness and debauchery appeared to validate. Ridley complained of his not allowing him written submissions as had been promised. Weston pronounced the three bishops excommunicate on 20 April, and returned to London to certify the sentence. Foxe's story that he opened and refused to deliver a letter Cranmer sent with him to the council has been doubted, but it is likely enough that he advocated execution of the adjudged heretics without further process. As a devoted servant of the regime he led public intercessions at the time of the queen's supposed pregnancy; he also composed a prayer to be said by the boys of Westminster School for the occasion (*STC, 1475–1640*, 25291.5). During 1555 he was among the examiners of John Bradford and John Philpot. In the following year he interrogated suspects in the Dudley conspiracy.

In order to make way for the revived monastery at Westminster, Dean Weston and his secular chapter resigned (with some reluctance) on 26 September 1556. But on 8 November the queen appointed him dean of Windsor, and on 5 January 1557 he received the associated office of register of the Order of the Garter. In August 1557 he was deprived of his deanery on a charge of indecency, which he denied. Weston also lost his archdeaconry of Colchester but (apparently at Bonner's instance) retained his parochial livings. He attempted to travel to Rome to appeal against his deprivation, but was arrested and sent to the Tower. On 3 December 1558 Elizabeth released him on medical grounds to the house of William Wynter in Fleet Street, where he died on 8 December and was buried the same day in the Savoy. He made bequests to Oxford University, and to Balliol and Lincoln colleges. The many other beneficiaries included one of the monks of the revived Westminster Abbey, and an old woman of Eton who had brought Weston flowers.   C. S. KNIGHTON

Sources Emden, *Oxf.*, 4.616–17 · *Hist. U. Oxf.* 3: *Colleg. univ.*, 349nn., 351 · Wood, *Ath. Oxon.*, new edn, 1.295–7 · *APC, 1547–50*, 324; *1550–52*, 81; *1558–70*, 6, 11–12 · *CSP dom.*, rev. edn, *1553–8*, nos. 390–91, 432, 442, 442n · *The diary of Henry Machyn, citizen and merchant-taylor of London, from AD 1550 to AD 1563*, ed. J. G. Nichols, CS, 42 (1848), 46, 81, 161, 181 · J. G. Nichols, ed., *The chronicle of Queen Jane, and of two years of Queen Mary*, CS, old ser., 48 (1850), 64, 73 · J. G. Nichols, ed., *Narratives of the days of the Reformation*, CS, old ser., 77 (1859), 287 · *The acts and monuments of John Foxe*, ed. S. R. Cattley, 8 vols. (1837–41), vol. 6, pp. 395–7, 440–520, 533–5, 541, 544–5 · *The works of Nicholas Ridley*, ed. H. Christmas, Parker Society, 1 (1841), 191–2, 305, 375–6 · *The examinations and writings of John Philpot*, ed. R. Eden, Parker Society, 5 (1842), 104–11, 167 · H. Robinson, ed. and trans., *Original letters relative to the English Reformation*, 1, Parker Society, [26] (1846), 305, 373 · *The writings of John Bradford*, ed. A. Townsend, 1 vol. in 2 pts, Parker Society, 31 (1848–53), pt 1, pp. 538–41, 550–53 · C. S. Knighton, ed., *Acts of the dean and chapter of Westminster*, 1 (1997), xxxviii, 77–8, 81, 99 · R. Simms, ed., *Bibliotheca Staffordiensis* (1894), 503–4 · wills, PRO, PROB 11/42B, fols. 55v–56v · S. Gardiner, *De vera obedientia*, trans. M. Wood (1553)
Archives St Margaret's, Westminster
Wealth at death see will, PRO, PROB 11/42B, fols. 55v–56v

Weston, James (1688?–1748?), stenographer, hailed from Edinburgh; nothing is known of his parentage or early life. He was probably employed taking shorthand at trials in London in the 1710s. Established as a shorthand 'professor' by 1722, he claimed to have taught more than 200 pupils by mid-1724, many by post, waging that no Westonian writer could be matched for speed. He courted publicity through a protracted and costly advertising campaign puffing his services and *Stenography Compleated* (1727), the most lavish shorthand book yet printed. A projected engraved shorthand Bible never materialized, but in 1730 he published part of the prayer book in shorthand, and in 1743 a reformulation of his system, as well as crib sheets and copybook materials, some in manuscript. His system's appropriation of Theophilus Metcalfe's 1630s alphabet, its dependence on arbitrary symbols and awkward rules, and its ambiguous, inelegant written results all militated against its lasting success; few Westonian manuscripts survive. 'Warlike' and 'blustering' Weston's significance in shorthand history lies rather in having 'done service by making a noise and raising attention to shorthand' (*Private Journal*, 1.73; 2.327), his 'warm and proud temper' (*British Journal*, 143, 1725, 4) occasioning public spats and competitions with stenographer rivals.

TIMOTHY UNDERHILL

Sources *The private journal and literary remains of John Byrom*, ed. R. Parkinson, 2 vols. in 4 pts, Chetham Society, 32, 34, 40, 44 (1854–7) · *British Journal* (1722–8) · *Daily Journal* (1722–8) · *Daily Post* [London] (1722–8) · *London Journal* (1722–8) · J. Westby-Gibson, *The bibliography of shorthand* (1887) · R. C. Alston, *A bibliography of the English language from the invention of printing to the year 1800*, 8: *Treatises on shorthand* (1966) · W. Musgrave, *Obituary prior to 1800*, ed. G. J. Armytage, 6, Harleian Society, 49 (1901), 242 · E. H. Butler, *The story of British shorthand* (1951)
Archives LUL, Sterling Library, Carlton collection, MSS
Likenesses J. Cole, engraving (after J. Darling), repro. in J. Weston, *Stenography compleated* (1727)

Weston, Jerome, second earl of Portland (1605–1663), politician, was born on 16 December 1605, the eldest son of Richard *Weston, first earl of Portland (*bap.* 1577, *d.* 1635), and his second wife, Frances (*d.* 1645), daughter of

Nicholas Waldegrave of Borley, Essex. He matriculated at Trinity College, Cambridge, at Easter, 1623, graduating MA in 1626. Although he entered the Middle Temple on 11 May 1626, he was never called to the bar. He married, at Roehampton Chapel on 25 June 1632, Frances (1617–1694), third daughter of Esmé *Stuart, third duke of Lennox.

In 1628 Weston entered parliament as member for Gatton, Surrey, being returned with Sir Thomas Lake at the behest of one Copley, a Lincolnshire Catholic who claimed an electoral monopoly in the borough. The election was disputed, however, and on 26 March the indenture of the return was torn off the file by order of the House of Commons; Samuel Owfield and Sir Charles Howard sat instead by the election of all the inhabitants. Weston, however, continued to sit in that parliament, though for what constituency does not appear in the returns, and on 2 March 1629 he defended his father, the lord treasurer, against Sir John Eliot, who had demanded Sir Richard's impeachment. This well-attested intervention makes unlikely the claim that Weston had a hand in the diplomacy which led to the Anglo-French treaty of Susa, signed on 14 April 1629. But in pursuance of his father's foreign policy objectives he certainly was sent as ambassador-extraordinary to Paris and Turin in July 1632 to urge Louis XIII to declare in favour of the restitution of the palatinate. In November Charles I instructed him to protest against the proposed division of the Spanish Netherlands between France and the Dutch. He returned in March 1633 with Richelieu's proposals for a defensive alliance against the house of Austria; he also brought with him unlicensed letters he had intercepted written by Henry Rich, earl of Holland, and the queen of England, both enemies of his father. The opening of these letters provoked Holland to challenge Weston to a duel, but Charles I approved of Jerome's conduct, placed Holland under house arrest, and suspended him from the privy council.

Styled Lord Weston after his father's creation on 17 February 1633 as earl of Portland, Jerome succeeded as second earl on 13 March 1635 whereupon his career in government and politics stepped up a gear. He appears to have succeeded his father as captain-general of the Isle of Wight, and on 28 May 1635 he was made vice-admiral of Hampshire. On 3 June 1641 he was appointed joint lord lieutenant of Hampshire, but his royalist and religious sentiments rendered him suspect to parliament, and on 2 November the House of Commons resolved to deprive him of the government of the Isle of Wight. Upon conference with the House of Lords on the 18th this 'resolution was put off', the lords professing themselves much satisfied with Portland's 'solemn protestation of his resolution to live and die a protestant, as his father did'—a somewhat dubious promise, considering that it had been widely rumoured that his father had died a Roman Catholic (*CSP dom.*, 1641–3, 154, 167). On 8 August 1642, the Lords, acting on the recommendation of the committee of safety, committed Portland to the custody of one of the sheriffs of London on suspicion of complicity in the plot to deliver Portsmouth into the king's hands, and he was sent to the

Tower on 12 August. After a protracted campaign for his release he was granted a conditional discharge on 11 January 1643. According to Clarendon, after his release Portland remained in London 'as a place where he might do the king more service than anywhere else' (Clarendon, *Hist. rebellion*, 3.142). Prominent among the royalist 'peace lords', he was soon accused of having had some share in the plot of his friend Edmund Waller. Waller himself alleged Portland's complicity, and, although the earl denied the charge, he underwent another seven weeks' imprisonment. On 31 July 1643 he was released on bail, for which the earl of Denbigh and Lord Hunsdon stood security. A fortnight later he made use of his liberty to take refuge with the king at Oxford, where he sat in the royalist parliament. Entangled in the factional rivalries which divided the king's court at Oxford, Portland tried unconvincingly to dissemble best wishes towards George Lord Digby and his circle.

On 1 March 1644 the king appointed Portland lord president of Munster, an office coveted by Murrough O'Brien, earl of Inchiquin. Probably as a result of this disappointment the powerful Inchiquin turned parliamentarian, and, as a nominee of the parliament, made himself master of the province. Replaced by Philip Sidney, Viscount Lisle, in 1646, Inchiquin again changed sides, whereupon he received Charles's commission as lord president, so that Portland had no opportunity of taking up his appointment even had he been so inclined. He had surrendered his patent by 8 February 1662 in return for an annual pension of £1000, and the leases in reversion on several properties in Surrey.

Portland was apparently at Oxford until its surrender on 24 June 1646, and then at Wallingford, which held out until 27 July. On 6 October following he compounded for his delinquency on the 'Wallingford articles', and on 10 November he was fined two-thirds of his estate, £9953 10s.; on 14 September 1647 his discharge was ordered after a division of the house, and on 11 June 1650 his fine was reduced to £5297 11s. 8d., possibly at the intercession of his brother, Benjamin, MP for Dover, who had declined to act in the trial of Charles I, yet conformed with the kingless regime after 1649.

Portland lived quietly at Ashley House, Walton-on-Thames, during the Commonwealth and protectorate, and in 1660 took his seat in the Convention Parliament, greatly assisting the accomplishment of unconditional restoration. The resumption of Stuart rule saw Portland attain not inconsiderable influence as a key supporter of the Clarendonian regime in the House of Lords. Although his father had been the object of Clarendon's intense hatred, the second earl was a close personal friend and ally of the lord chancellor, and he shared intimately in the responsibility for delivering the government's legislative programme in the Cavalier Parliament. In spite of his background he had an important hand in strengthening the Act of Uniformity as a bulwark against informal toleration of Catholicism. He also helped turn a reasonably interventionist corporation bill into a measure for the emasculation of municipal self-government. Conversely, he worked to scupper the kind of cavalier measures, such as the earl of Derby's bills for restitution of estate sold in the 1650s, which threatened to undermine the whole basis of the Restoration land settlement.

Never anywhere near as close to the throne as his father had been, none the less Portland was rewarded for his services. He was restored to the posts he held before the war, and received grants of other lands. On 7 November 1660 he was made a councillor for trade and navigation, and on 1 December for the colonies; on 3 April 1662 he was sworn of the privy council. Had he lived longer, he might have attained higher office, at least while Clarendon's star was in the ascendant. He died at Ashley House on 17 March 1663, and was buried on the 22nd in the church at Walton-on-Thames, where there is an inscription to his memory. His wife survived him by thirty-one years; she died in 1694 and was buried in Westminster Abbey on 17 March of that year. The couple had at least two daughters, one of whom was baptized Henrietta Maria, and a son, Charles (1639–1665). He succeeded as third earl of Portland, but was killed during the naval battle with the Dutch off the Texel on 3 June 1665. He died unmarried, and the earldom and barony devolved upon his uncle Thomas Weston. He died in 1688 with no surviving heirs, with which the barony of Weston and earldom of Portland became extinct.

SEAN KELSEY

Sources GEC, *Peerage*, new edn, 10.585–6 · Venn, *Alum. Cant.*, 1/3.373 · H. A. C. Sturgess, ed., *Register of admissions to the Honourable Society of the Middle Temple, from the fifteenth century to the year 1944*, 1 (1949), 117 · *JHL*, 4 (1628–42), 446 · *JHL*, 5 (1642–3), 261–2, 270, 284, 545 · *JHL*, 6 (1643–4), 90, 94, 97, 100–03, 115–18, 124–5, 132–3, 142, 146, 153–4, 159, 161 · *JHL*, 9 (1646–7), 426, 429, 435 · *Members of parliament: return to two orders of the honorable the House of Commons*, House of Commons, 1 (1878), 478 · *JHC*, 1 (1547–1628), 875 · *JHC*, 3 (1642–4), 126, 131, 132–3, 137, 150, 151, 159, 160, 167, 169–70, 185, 187 · *JHC*, 5 (1646–8), 300 · *CSP dom.*, 1633–4, 3, 11–12, 14–15, 326; 1635, 88; 1637, 257; 1641–3, 154, 167; 1644, 234, 562; 1645–7, 48, 72, 140; *addenda, 1625–49*, 453, 454; 1660–61, 327, 491; 1661–2, 46, 270, 302, 419, 562 · J. L. Sanford, *Studies and illustrations of the great rebellion* (1858), 563–4 · R. Lascelles, ed., *Liber munerum publicorum Hiberniae … or, The establishments of Ireland*, 2 vols. [1824–30], vol. 2, p. 185 · M. A. E. Green, ed., *Calendar of the proceedings of the committee for compounding … 1643–1660*, 5 vols., PRO (1889–92), 1539 · *CSP col.*, 1.492 · W. Notestein and F. H. Relf, eds., *Commons debates for 1629* (1921), 242, 262 · Clarendon, *Hist. rebellion*, 2.73, 541; 3.40, 51, 142, 152 · S. R. Gardiner, *History of England from the accession of James I to the outbreak of the civil war*, 7 (1884), 73, 204, 214–18 · S. R. Gardiner, *History of the great civil war, 1642–1649*, new edn, 1 (1893), 145, 156, 158, 199, 333 · M. van Cleave Alexander, *Charles I's lord treasurer: Sir Richard Weston, earl of Portland (1577–1635)* (1975), 32, 133, 143, 166–7, 170 · P. Seaward, *The Cavalier Parliament and the reconstruction of the old regime, 1661–1667* (1988), 93, 135, 153–5, 169, 202 · A. Swatland, *The House of Lords in the reign of Charles II* (1996), 24, 65–6, 105–6, 165, 188, 237, 239–40 · *The earl of Portlands charge delivered to the Lords house by Mr. Pym* (1642) · *The kings resolution … whereunto is annex't the parliaments determination concerning the earle of Portland* (1642) · *DNB* · will, PRO, PROB 11/312, fols. 87v–89v

Archives U. Nott., Portland MSS

Likenesses J. Meyssens, engraving (after portrait of J. Weston? by A. Van Dyck), repro. in A. Van Dyck, *L'Iconographie* (Leipzig, 1877), 134?

Wealth at death limited real estate in Cambridgeshire and Hertfordshire; also 500 acres of fenland within the Great Level: will, PRO, PROB 11/312, fols. 87v–89v

Weston, Jessie Laidlay (1850–1928), Arthurian scholar, was born on 28 December 1850 in New Park, Clapham, Surrey, the eldest of the three daughters of William Weston (d. 1887), tea broker and member of the Salters' Company, and his second wife, Sarah Burton (d. 1856). Following his second wife's death when his daughters were still young children, William Weston married Clara King with whom he had five children. Jessie Weston's early education was at a school in Brighton, the family's home town. Later she studied music in Germany at the Hildesheim conservatory, a setting which inspired her long narrative poem 'The Rose Tree of Hildesheim' and provided the title for her first collection of verse (1896). She also took classes at the Crystal Palace School of Art in London. However, the most important intellectual influence of her youth was Gaston Paris, the French medieval scholar with whom she studied in Paris.

Despite having spent much of the initial forty years of her life being engaged in increasingly serious scholarship, Jessie Weston wrote nothing for publication until after her father's death in 1887. Her first book, a verse translation of Wolfram von Eschenbach's *Parzival*, was published in 1894 when she was forty-three. Like many of her contemporaries she had become an ardent Wagner enthusiast, having first encountered his music as a student in Hildesheim. Bayreuth was developing into a gathering-place, not only for Wagnerites but for medievalists from all over Europe. Weston was attracted to Wagner's music mainly because of his use of medieval heroic narratives. After having attended a performance of *Parsifal* at the 1892 Bayreuth festival with the publisher Alfred Nutt, she deplored the fact that the English public knew so little of the sources on which Wagner's operas were based. With Nutt's encouragement she embarked on a 2400-line annotated verse translation of *Parzival* which she dedicated to the memory of Wagner, 'whose genius has given fresh life to the creation of medieval romance' (Hyman, 509). This work opened the way to further retelling of stories from Wagner and to a collaboration with Nutt which lasted until his death by accidental drowning in 1910.

In the years before he began collaborating with Jessie Weston, Nutt had already been working as an independent scholar. He had been one of the founder members of the Folk-Lore Society in 1878 and became publisher of the society's journal, *Folk-Lore*, in 1890. European scholars had tended to regard the twelfth-century French poet Chrétien de Troyes as the originator of Arthurian romance, but the comparative method involved in the study of folklore was leading Nutt to become interested in the Celtic origins of Arthurian material. Jessie Weston's studies of Arthurian texts led her to side with Nutt and other Celticists against the continental or inventionist school which saw Arthurian romance as deriving from the 'inventive genius' of Chrétien de Troyes. While Weston took issue with the German scholars of the inventionist school, she also diverged from Celticists such as Nutt who argued that the grail legends sprang from Irish sources. She argued for their Welsh provenance and postulated that they originated with a Welsh story-teller, Bleheris, cited by Giraldus Cambrensis, and who pre-dated Chrétien. Her early publications also attempted to reconfigure the existing hierarchy of Arthurian heroes. Her first publication in Nutt's Grimm Library series in 1897, *The Legend of Sir Gawain*, attempts to re-establish Gawain rather than Perceval as the pre-eminent Arthurian hero and to restore his reputation from the damage done by Sir Thomas Malory's treatment which had been reiterated to English nineteenth-century readers by Tennyson in his *Idylls of the King*.

Weston's participation in the controversies about the origins of Arthurian texts led her to a preoccupation with the significance of the grail legends. The interpretation of the grail as the central object of Christian ritual was irreconcilable with the argument that the legends surrounding it predated Christianity. Like many of her generation she was influenced by Sir James Frazer's *The Golden Bough* (1890), which explored the recurrence of themes of sacrifice, death, and rebirth throughout different religious practices and beliefs and traced these themes to ancient rituals. In her most popular work on the subject, *From Ritual to Romance* (1920), she expresses her indebtedness to Frazer for 'the initial inspiration' which set her 'on the road to the Grail castle' (p. vii), appropriately acknowledging the extent of Frazer's influence. However, the notion of Arthur as the personification of a vegetation god had surfaced as early as 1842 in the German scholar Karl Simrock's book *Parzival und Titurel*. Weston first began to formulate her own theory in a paper, 'The grail and the rites of Adonis', which she had delivered to the Folk-Lore Society in 1906 and published the following year in *Folk-Lore*.

Weston's views increasingly led her into disputes with A. E. Waite, especially after the publication of *The Legend of Sir Perceval* in 1906 which emphasized her view of the grail story as deriving from pre-Christian Celtic ritual. Waite, an acknowledged authority on the cabbala, the tarot, and other forms of esoteric knowledge who had broken away both from theosophy and from the order of the Golden Dawn to form his own group based on Christian mysticism, ardently supported the view that the grail legends were Christian in origin. Waite also saw Galahad as the most significant hero of grail literature, whereas Weston believed that grail stories focusing on Galahad were very late developments in grail literature when the grail stories had been 'finally remodelled on the lines of Christian mysticism' (J. L. Weston, 'The quest of the Holy Grail', *The Quest*, 1, 1910, 526). Waite's intemperate and personal attacks on her became increasingly vehement after her death.

Weston's belief that the grail legends represented the written survival of ancient ritual which had later passed into occult practices—'the confused record of a ritual, once popular, later surviving under conditions of strict secrecy' (*Ritual*, 1920, 4)—found its most widely read expression in *From Ritual to Romance*. By 1920 other scholars such as Jane Harrison and Gilbert Murray, who had also been influenced by Frazer, had played a role in generating public interest in an anthropological

approach to comparative religion, and English-speaking readers were also still fascinated with Arthurian lore through the many Victorian popularizations; an audience was ready for the book. While *From Ritual to Romance* can be seen as Weston's final word on grail legends, it differs from her other works in its lack of scholarly apparatus and its odd references to an unnamed informant who was supposedly an initiate of occult rituals. Despite these inconsistencies, it was widely known and influential, particularly after T. S. Eliot, in his notes to *The Waste Land* (1922), acknowledged his debt to her explication of grail legends and the role of the Fisher King.

Weston's belief that German Arthurian scholars were seriously mistaken became more confirmed as her career developed. By 1901 she felt able to declare in her book on Lancelot that German scholars were 'radically unsound' and that her reading of their work had shaken her 'belief in the soundness and reliability of foreign criticism of the Arthurian cycle' (Hyman, 511). This rejection of German scholarship reflected a trend which was occurring in many other scholarly fields where previously unassailable German authority was now being challenged or dismissed. During the First World War her critique of German intellectuals took on political significance when she produced a pamphlet to combat what she saw as the 'undue value' placed on German research findings and charging that German literature could make little claim to cultural uniqueness because so much of it derived from French models. Another pamphlet, *Germany's Crime Against France* (1915), more explicitly polemical, denounced German war atrocities.

For much of her life as an active scholar Weston lived in a fashionable district of Paris, travelling frequently to England to keep up her contacts with British folkloric circles and with such groups as the Quest Society. As did many intellectual and professional women of the period, she maintained a membership at the Lyceum, a club which she had helped found in 1904. In the last years of her life she began to find Paris less congenial and in 1923 returned to England to take up residence in a London flat at 85 Biddulph Mansions, Elgin Avenue, Maida Vale.

Despite failing health, Weston's enthusiasm for controversy remained undimmed in her final years. She wrote an article for publication in *The Quest* attacking the *Church Times* and deploring the way in which she saw the Church of England tending towards an alliance with Catholicism. The more Christocentric approach, with a focus on 'the great Drama of the Passion' which cast Jews as the villain and a neglect of the Old Testment, inevitably led, she warned, to a chronic antisemitism. The editors of *The Quest* did not apparently agree or else found her attack on Anglo-Catholicism too controversial and the article remained unpublished.

Jessie Weston's career is a remarkable one for more than her appetite for controversy. Less than ten years after the publication of her first book she had succeeded in establishing herself as an authoritative translator and interpreter of medieval texts and was soon recognized as the leading English Arthurian scholar. Despite the fact that she published nothing until she was over forty, she was the author of more than twenty books and numerous articles as well as a volume of verse and one of short stories set in the medieval period. The standard reference works of her time, the *Encyclopaedia Britannica* and the *Cambridge Medieval History*, commissioned her to write articles on Arthurian material, thus lending weight to her sometimes disputatious views. Formal institutional recognition was bestowed somewhat more slowly. In 1920 the British Academy awarded her the Rose Mary Crawshay prize of £100—a sum which she invested in cataract surgery. In 1923 the University of Wales awarded her the honorary degree of doctor of letters. At the awarding ceremony Mary Williams, a professor of French literature whose own work had been influenced by Weston, described her mentor's research as being 'prosecuted with that patience, zeal and love of the truth which are characteristic of the great scholar' (Grayson, 43). Weston died, unmarried, on 29 September 1928 at Warrington Lodge, Warrington Crescent, Maida Vale, London.

GILLIAN THOMAS

Sources J. Grayson, 'In quest of Jessie Weston', *Arthurian Literature*, 11 (1992), 1–80 • S. E. Hyman, 'Jessie Weston and the forest of Broceliande', *Centennial Review*, 9 (1965), 509–21 • J. Wood, 'The Celtic tarot and the secret tradition: a study in modern legend making', *Folk-Lore*, 109 (1998), 15–29 • R. M. Dorson, *The British folklorists: a history* (1968) • *The Times* (1 Oct 1928) • b. cert. • d. cert.
Archives NL Wales, research papers | NL Wales, Mary Williams MSS
Wealth at death £14,099 14s. 0d.: resworn probate, 27 Nov 1928, *CGPLA Eng. & Wales*

Weston, Sir Richard (c.1465–1541), courtier, was the eldest son of Sir Edmund Weston (d. before 1509) of Boston, Lincolnshire, and Katherine, daughter of Robert Cammel of Fiddleford, Dorset. By 1502 he had married Anne, daughter of Oliver Sandys of Shere, Surrey; they had a son, Francis *Weston, and two daughters. Sir William *Weston, who was the last prior of the knights of St John of Jerusalem and died on the same day as the dissolution of his order in 1540, was his brother.

Edmund Weston had been a supporter of the Lancastrians and gained favour at the court of Henry VII, to whom he was an esquire of the body. Richard entered the service of Henry's queen, Elizabeth of York, and his wife, Anne, may have been one of Elizabeth's ladies-in-waiting. She later served Katherine of Aragon. Richard began to accumulate profitable positions during the last years of Henry VII's reign: he was a groom of the chamber by 1505, acquired a number of keeperships and stewardships, and became forester of Windsor Forest and lieutenant of Windsor Castle. Further offices followed under Henry VIII. He was named an esquire of the body and also (like his father) governor of Guernsey and neighbouring islands in 1509, a position he held until his death. In 1510 he was granted the manor of Ufton Pole, Berkshire, which had been forfeited by the attainder of Viscount Lovell. He was a JP for Berkshire (from 1510), Kent (1518), and Surrey (from 1524). In 1511 he was a member of the small English contingent sent to aid King Ferdinand of Aragon in a campaign against the Moors. Knighted in 1514, Weston was made a knight of the body in 1516 and a knight of the Bath in 1518. In 1514 he was among those present at the marriage of Henry VIII's sister Mary to the French king Louis XII. He was named keeper of the swans on the Thames (1517), one of the king's cup-bearers (1521), a commissioner for the subsidy (1523), and a commissioner for the tenths of spiritualities (1535).

In 1518 Weston was appointed to join the ageing Sir Thomas Lovell as master of the wards. Under Henry VII the crown's rights of wardship had been exploited with ever increasing thoroughness, a process which continued under Henry VIII. It was in keeping with this development that when Sir Edward Belknap succeeded Lovell in 1520 he and Weston were no longer 'masters' in their patent but 'surveyors, governors, keepers, and sellers of wards and their possessions', with a salary of £100 each (*LP Henry VIII*, vol. 3, pt 1, no. 1121 [10]). They were also licensed to call on members of the council for assistance with legal problems. Belknap died a year later, and Weston remained in control of the office. It does not seem to have brought him much profit, since in 1525 he tried to exchange it for the chancellorship of the duchy of Lancaster.

Weston made his bid for the exchange of offices through Cardinal Wolsey. There is some evidence that he was a follower of Wolsey. In particular, when in spring 1519 the cardinal attempted to control the king's privy chamber by ejecting Henry's young 'minions' and replacing them with courtiers of a more mature and sober stamp, Weston was one of the latter. The minions soon recovered their former places, but Weston was present at many of the great events of Henry's reign: the Field of the Cloth of Gold (1520), the meetings between the king and Emperor Charles V (1520, 1522), the christening of Prince Edward (1537), and the reception of Anne of Cleves (1540). He did not obtain the chancellorship of the duchy, suggesting that his influence with Wolsey was limited, but late in 1525 was made treasurer of Calais, a position he held until 1528. His term there was dogged by financial difficulties and by quarrels with Baron Sandys, the captain of Guînes, but he did at least reinforce the sea defences with a new wharf. On resigning from Calais he was made under-treasurer of the exchequer, and held that office until his death.

In 1521 Weston had been a member of the jury which convicted Edward Stafford, third duke of Buckingham, of treason. Following the duke's execution Weston was granted his manor of Sutton in Surrey. Here he proceeded to build a great country house that ranks with the king's palace of Nonsuch, Baron Sandys's house The Vyne, and Sir William Fitzwilliam's Cowdray as one of the chief monuments of the early Renaissance in England. He himself was probably responsible for much of the architecture; a few years earlier he had visited the French royal château of Blois, then still under construction, and was evidently eager to copy some of its details in his own residence. Built in the shape of a square surrounding a central courtyard, the house has since been altered by the demolition of the entrance front.

Weston sat in the Reformation Parliament which began

in 1529. Possibly through the influence of Charles Brandon, duke of Suffolk, he was returned as a knight of the shire for Berkshire. In 1536 Weston's son, Francis, was implicated in the fall of Anne Boleyn. Convicted of adultery with the queen, he was executed on 17 May, the king having refused to grant him a reprieve. Sir Richard remained one of Henry's confidants and councillors, however, and, when the Lincolnshire rising broke out later in the year, he was summoned to attend the king with 150 men. In 1539 William Fitzwilliam, earl of Southampton, visited Weston to see if he would serve again in the coming parliament, but found him sick in bed, protesting that he was more likely to die than perform any further service. He recovered sufficiently to greet Anne of Cleves in January 1540, but died on 7 August 1541, probably at Sutton. His brief will, drawn up on 16 May, included a traditional preamble leaving his soul to the Virgin Mary and made lavish provision for masses for his soul. He left his lands and possessions, which according to an earlier assessment were worth more than £400 a year, to his wife. After her death, because of his son's execution, they were to pass to his seven-year-old grandson, Henry Weston; should Henry die they were to pass to the children of his daughters Margaret, who had married Sir Walter Denys, and Katherine, who had wed Sir John Rogers. The executors, in addition to Lady Weston, were the earl of Southampton and Sir John Russell, the lord high admiral. Weston requested burial in Holy Trinity Church, Guildford, in a chapel he had built for the purpose. If an imposing tomb marked the site of his interment it no longer exists. STANFORD LEHMBERG

Sources *LP Henry VIII*, vols. 1–16 · HoP, *Commons, 1509–58*, 30590–92 · M. St C. Byrne, ed., *The Lisle letters*, 6 vols. (1981) · *Hall's chronicle*, ed. H. Ellis (1809) · J. J. Scarisbrick, *Henry VIII* (1968) · E. W. Ives, *Anne Boleyn* (1986) · R. M. Warnicke, *The rise and fall of Anne Boleyn* (1989) · *Surrey*, Pevsner (1962) · will, PRO, PROB 11/29, fol. 102v · *DNB* · D. Starkey, *The reign of Henry VIII: personalities and politics* (1985) · P. Gwyn, *The king's cardinal* (1990) · H. M. Colvin and others, eds., *The history of the king's works*, 3 (1975) · J. Hurstfield, *The queen's wards* (1958)

Wealth at death rated at £400 for 1523 subsidy: *Letters and papers of Henry VIII*

Weston, Richard (*d.* 1572), judge, was probably a grandson of William Weston (*d.* 1513/14) of Essex and London, mercer, and lived in Essex until his death. The arms on his monument were the same as William's but differenced by a martlet charged with a molet, indicating that he was the third son of a fourth son. To judge from his standing in the Middle Temple, he was probably admitted in the mid-1530s, in which case he would have been born in the 1510s. That makes it difficult to identify him with the youngest son of Richard Weston of Colchester, Essex, who (together with two elder brothers) was under age at his father's death in 1541–2. Some pedigrees make him the second son of John Weston of Lichfield, Staffordshire, who was the fourth son of John Weston of Rugeley, and whose descendants included two judges in the reign of Charles I. Nothing is known of the lawyer before 1548, when he was counsel to Admiral Seymour. In 1553 he was returned to parliament by Lostwithiel, and he served for three other constituencies in the 1550s. About 1554, the year in which he became a justice of the peace for Essex, he succeeded Anthony Browne (another Essex Middle Templar) as clerk of assize on the home circuit. That was also the year in which he delivered his only reading in the Middle Temple, on a statute of 1539 concerning joint tenants and tenants in common. Now well established in his profession, he purchased in January 1555 the manor of Skreens in Roxwell, near Writtle, Essex, which he made his principal seat. He acquired various other lands in Essex, from Tilbury in the south to Dunmow in the north.

On 20 November 1557 Weston was appointed solicitor-general, an office that ended on the demise of the queen one year later. However, on 26 January 1559 he was created serjeant-at-law at a single call, the first of its kind for a serjeant who was not being appointed a chief justice. It seems that he was already marked to fill the vacancy in the common pleas created by Catlin's promotion on 22 January, but he was made to serve at the bar for most of the year as one of the queen's serjeants before he received his judicial patent in October 1559. He remained a puisne justice of the common pleas until his death on 6 July 1572, when he was buried at Writtle, Essex, near the body of his second wife. There is a tomb chest in the church with three brass shields of arms, but no inscription or effigy, in accordance with his testamentary wish that it should be 'made withoute curiositie'. The impalements on the shields record his three marriages. His first wife was Wyburgh (*d.* 1553), daughter of Anthony Catesby of Whiston, Northamptonshire, and widow of Richard Jenour (*d.* 1548) of Great Dunmow, Essex, clerk of the court of surveyors. Their only son, Jerome, was the father of Richard *Weston, first earl of Portland. They also had a daughter. The judge's second wife was Margaret, daughter of Eustace Burneby and widow of Thomas Addington. They had one son, Nicholas, still under age in 1572, and two daughters. His third wife, whom he married in 1566, was Elizabeth, daughter of Thomas Lovett of Astwell, Northamptonshire, widow of Anthony Cave and of John Newdegate. Elizabeth died in 1577. J. H. BAKER

Sources HoP, *Commons, 1509–58*, 3.589–90 · Baker, *Serjeants*, 171, 543 · will, PRO, PROB 11/54, sig. 26 · C. H. Hopwood, ed., *Middle Temple records*, 1: *1501–1603* (1904) · BL, Harley MS 5156, fols. 38v–40 · W. C. Metcalfe, ed., *The visitations of Essex*, 1, Harleian Society, 13 (1878), 319 · S. Erdeswick, *A survey of Staffordshire*, ed. T. Harwood, new edn (1844), facing p. 164 [pedigree] · *CPR, 1553–4*, 32; *1554–5*, 104 · inquisition post mortem, PRO, C142/160/35 · BL, Harley MS 1137, fol. 60

Weston, Richard, **first earl of Portland** (*bap.* 1577, *d.* 1635), politician, was baptized at Chicheley, Buckinghamshire, on 1 March 1577, the elder son of Jerome (later Sir Jerome) Weston (*d.* 1603) of Skreens in Roxwell, Essex, and his first wife, Mary (*d.* c.1593), daughter and coheir of Anthony Cave of Chicheley; Sir Richard *Weston (*d.* 1572) was his grandfather. His father was a conscientious mid-Essex JP from 1586 and a devoted captain of a trained band company of 600 foot, 'one of the fairest in the shire' in the view of his deputy lieutenants, and one so big that he was excused the shrievalty while he remained in command

Richard Weston, first earl of Portland (*bap.* 1577, *d.* 1635), after Sir Anthony Van Dyck

(PRO, SP 12/254/58). There seems to be no record of Richard's education before he was admitted to Trinity College, Cambridge, where he graduated BA early in 1594, and he entered the Middle Temple on 18 June following. He spent 'some years' studying law, according to the earl of Clarendon, before travelling abroad, probably quite briefly late in the 1590s and possibly for the only time prior to service as an ambassador in 1620 (Clarendon, *Hist. rebellion*, 1.59). About 1597 he married Elizabeth, daughter of William Pinchon of Writtle, Essex, and Rose, daughter of Thomas Reding of Pinner, Middlesex. She died in 1603, and was buried on 15 February at Roxwell, leaving one surviving son and two daughters. About two years later Weston married Frances, daughter of Nicholas Waldegrave of Borley and Catherine, daughter of Weston Browne of Rookwood Hall, Abbess Roding, Essex.

Early public life In 1601 Weston sat for Maldon in Essex in the first of seven consecutive parliaments as a commoner, always for different seats. He was knighted on 23 July 1603, a few months after his father. On Sir Jerome's death late in December 1603 Richard inherited Roxwell and other Essex estates, as well as property at Nayland in Suffolk. He was among the signatories to the indenture for the Essex shire election of 1604, which had much exercised its peers and gentry, but owed his own return to parliament to an early by-election for the Catholic Montagu family's seat at Midhurst in Sussex. By March 1607 he had become an Essex JP, remaining so for the rest of his life. In June 1612 the earl of Sussex nominated him as one of his deputy lieutenants for Essex and kept him in commission until July 1620. He returned in June 1623 but was left out, with the duke of Buckingham's approval, in September 1626, before coming back in January 1628. From 5 February 1629 until his death he served as joint lord lieutenant of Essex, intended as a courtly restraint on his puritanical partner, Robert Rich, second earl of Warwick. While his other interests allowed he contributed what he could to local administration, blending occasional out of sessions work with frequent attendances at quarter sessions and assizes until 1619–20. He became a privy councillor in September 1621, and thereafter matters of state began to claim his whole attention. In the difficult days ahead he was to prove deaf to the urgings of his fellow deputy lieutenants and JPs to 'bee pleased upon all just occations to bee the patron and father of our countie' (4 April 1627; Quintrell, no. 444). Between 1626 and 1629 the Essex deputies, with some difficulty, gained concessions from the council on at least seven occasions, based either on their heavy expenditure during an invasion threat in 1625 or on Elizabethan precedent; but there is no indication that Weston ever provided the help that other councillors sometimes did for counties with which they had an association.

Weston sat for the only time as a knight of the shire for Essex in the parliament of 1614 and, possibly under the influence of Henry Howard, earl of Northampton, pressed for action against the suspected practice of undertaking. Unlike his father he was not content with county life, but was moving into circles in the City and Whitehall where men of business mingled with hopeful courtiers. In 1615 he was busy assisting Sir Arthur Ingram in raising a loan for the lord treasurer, the earl of Suffolk, while in July of the following year he and his unstable eldest son, Richard, were jointly appointed collectors of petty customs in the port of London, with a life grant in February 1618. He paid £1000 for the collectorship of the pretermitted customs in London about 1620 and held it until 1624. Lionel Cranfield's influence secured him a place in the commission for reducing the royal household's expenditure in November 1617, as it did in a more effective commission for the reform of the navy in June 1618. This had similar membership and, under the new lord admiral, the marquess of Buckingham, went on to implement its own recommendations and build ten new warships in the next five years. Weston was one of the commissioners for the East India Company chosen to negotiate with their Dutch counterparts about trading practices in July 1619, and was among those often named in newsletters as hopeful of substantial offices falling vacant in and around the court. As early as 8 January 1620 Chamberlain noted a rumour that he was about to join Fulke Greville, the chancellor of the exchequer, as his assistant and under-treasurer, and in the autumn, after filling the office informally for a month, Weston finally replaced Greville as chancellor of the exchequer on 7 November 1621. Seven years later Archie Armstrong recalled that the earl of Carlisle even then would have preferred him as lord treasurer, but Weston himself was content to serve under his friend Lionel Cranfield, whose elevation to the Lords as Baron Cranfield had recently enabled Weston to be returned to parliament at a by-election for the Howard seat at Arundel.

Chancellor of the exchequer and diplomat, 1621–1628 During a fruitless embassy to Brussels and Prague with Sir Edward Conway in 1620, after James's son-in-law Frederick, the elector palatine, had paid a humiliating penalty for accepting an invitation from rebel noblemen to take the throne of Bohemia, and another embassy to Brussels in 1622 to press for the recovery of the Palatinate from Habsburg forces, Weston provided a shrewd commentary for Cranfield as well as for Buckingham. Unlike John Digby, earl of Bristol, at Madrid, Weston in 1622 was quick to appreciate the limits of Spanish influence and the emptiness of imperial assurances, and was by 1624 treading a characteristically cautious line between the king's continuing preference for peace and the offended sensibilities of a prince denied a Spanish match, who, as men of ambition could not afford to forget, represented a reversionary interest to which James feared Buckingham increasingly subscribed. Whereas in the 1624 parliament Cranfield's aversion to war enabled Buckingham to bring him down, Weston pursued a more subtle line, appreciating that calling off the treaties with Spain would necessitate precautionary funding on a substantial scale.

Weston's position remained a moderate one, by a narrow margin sufficiently acceptable to the king to ensure that at least temporarily he succeeded Cranfield in the treasury. Writing to Buckingham on 24 May, with the sealed patent to hand, Lord Keeper John Williams reported that Prince Charles had hoped his father would not have gone ahead with the appointment, and remained opposed, even though he 'durst not speak to crosse it'; yet Williams also assured Buckingham that he himself did not doubt Weston's loyalty to the duke's interests, and concluded that he knew 'no fitter man in England for the office if he come in as a creature of the Prince and your Grace's; nor unfitter, if he should offer to take it without your likings' (*Cabala*, 94). But although the acting treasurer's busy 'tricking and trimming' of Winchester House, newly leased in August 1624 on his removal from Holborn, prompted speculation about a more secure future, and Conway reported that under his influence the king 'beginnes to instruct his large heart to keep intelligence with his Exchequer', a limit was soon put on his immediate aspirations (*Letters of John Chamberlain*, 1.577; PRO, SP 14/175/48). Weston expected to be at Cambridge for Ambassador Ville-aux-Clerc's first audience, due to take place on 12 December 1624 prior to negotiations over the French marriage treaty, but at a late stage James decided he need not come. On 11 December James Ley, the

elderly but still ambitious judge married to one of Buckingham's young nieces, was sworn in there by the king as the new treasurer and promptly ennobled, as Prince Charles's reservations about Weston as Cranfield's man belatedly took effect. Weston nevertheless remained chancellor of the exchequer and sat in the parliaments of 1624, 1625, and 1626 for Cornish seats where duchy influence was overlaid with Buckingham's interest: at Bossiney in 1624, Callington in 1625, and Bodmin in 1626.

As acting treasurer Weston had proved insistent on maintaining the full authority of his office, punctilious in observing proper administrative process, and unhesitating in suspending pensions and other claims on the exchequer by courtiers lacking what he considered to be adequate warrant. With the inexperienced Ley as treasurer he found it harder to keep his grip on finances, and struggled to accumulate the funds needed for wars with Spain and then also with France. Neither the 1625 nor 1626 parliament provided war supply. At the Oxford meeting in 1625 Weston was among those ministers relatively conversant with foreign affairs whose contribution was overshadowed by the prominence the king allowed Sir John Coke, a leading naval commissioner yet to be made a privy councillor, who performed resolutely in the king's presence at short notice but whose lack of seniority attracted much adverse comment. Nevertheless, in both parliaments Weston stressed the king's financial exigencies without conceding the impracticality of what he was attempting, and from firsthand experience was able to defend the duke's contribution to naval reform. He also exercised a moderating influence where he could, most notably in the case of Sir Thomas Wentworth. Drawing on his association with Cranfield and Ingram he managed to persuade Wentworth that there were sound practical reasons for tempering his criticisms of Charles's war policy, honest and well considered though they might be. In the process Wentworth lost all confidence in Buckingham's assurances of amity, followed as they invariably were by blows to his influence and esteem. Most, however, seem to have been the work of the king; and despite the duke's preference for the Saviles, Wentworth's rivals in Yorkshire, Weston persevered. Just before Buckingham's death in August 1628 he brought Wentworth into the ambit of court favour, and in the 1629 session of parliament Wentworth joined Weston, ennobled on 13 April 1628 as Baron Weston of Nayland, in the upper house. Soon afterwards he also managed formally to reconcile Arundel with the king, at odds since 1626.

Weston's own relationship with Buckingham was still compromised by his association with the fallen Cranfield, whose intermediary he continued to be, leaving him uncertain of the duke's approval. He assured Buckingham that summer that his expeditions had priority over all else, but he had not entirely escaped the sharp criticism which Ley's inadequacies drew from the king, and remained a man who ventured little. Buckingham's own political future, in urgent need as it was of an emphatic military success, had come to depend unduly on a cautious man bent on retrenchment, more concerned with shoring up the royal economy by reducing its expenditure and securing peace than he was with generating new revenues. For all his familiarity with the fevered language of the court the duke must have wondered at Sir Humphrey May's description of Weston in October 1627 as 'not a sparke but a flame of fire in any thinge that concernes you' (PRO, SP 16/80/60). He may have recalled that earlier that year Weston, never neglecting his own interests, had acquired the manor of Mortlake from the crown for a modest outlay, and had thus begun on the lavish development of his Roehampton estate, with intermittent help from Tobie Matthew, a courtier who had turned to Rome in 1606 and who by the mid-1620s was very probably a Jesuit priest.

Lord treasurer, 1628–1635 Ley resigned as treasurer following the appointment on 26 June 1628 of a nine-man committee of councillors to report to the king on his financial obligations. Weston succeeded him on 15 July 1628, and may well have drawn on the committee's deliberations in setting out on 13 August his assessment of the state of the king's finances and proposals for remedial action. He astutely sent the details first to Buckingham so that he could deliver them to Charles and make sure that the king appreciated them. The paper was then to be destroyed, and nothing more done until the duke had set out on his impending expedition. Buckingham thus found himself closely associated with the economical measures the king wanted. Clarendon's speculation, long afterwards, that Buckingham would have had Weston 'cashiered' on his return may reflect what the duke would have liked; but it is more probable that, had Buckingham not been assassinated that August, he would have learned to adapt to what the new lord treasurer hoped would become 'a quiett and settled court' where 'rest and vigilancy' would, in their different ways, remedy current financial failings (Clarendon, *Hist. rebellion*, 1.61; PRO, SP 16/112/75; PRO, SP 16/113/14). In the 1629 session of parliament Sir John Eliot, bitter that Wentworth was now enjoying court favour while he was not, adopted a different perspective in calling for the treasurer's impeachment: in Weston's person, he feared, 'is contracted all the evill that we doe suffer: If we looke either into religion or policye, I finde him building on the grounds layd by the Duke of Buckingham, his great Master' (Notestein and Relf, 259; 2 March 1629). Like William Laud, Weston had no wish for the early recall of parliament in the 1630s. He felt much more comfortable with retrenchment by prerogative means, an approach which had been favoured by Northampton and Cranfield.

Although the absence of parliament was not to keep him from political hostility within the court, in less than seven years in office Weston paid off the bulk of the war debt (£2 million in 1629), and added £50,000 a year to the king's ordinary income, by then in excess of £600,000 a year. As treasurer he served on all five of the council's standing committees and, despite occasional bouts of taciturnity, combined effectively with Sir Francis Cottington, who, as he had hoped, had replaced Edward Barrett as chancellor of the exchequer in March 1629. He worked closely with the customs farmers, restoring three-year

grants of farms in December 1632, and improving customs revenues so that they represented almost one half of that total, and, with Cottington, he encouraged alderman Abraham Dawes, an experienced customer and (according to John Harrison) Weston's 'great creature', to draw up a well-contrived book of rates which, launched in 1636, swelled crown revenues in the later 1630s, although too much remained appropriated (BL, Stowe MS 326, fol. 60r). Unlike his father Charles resorted to the expedient of distraint of knighthood, a levy on those of sufficient substance throughout the country who had failed to take up a knighthood they had not actually been offered at the time of his coronation, and he succeeded in legitimately tapping the wealth of the elusive mercantile and professional classes of London so effectively that overall £174,000 was raised during the early 1630s with little resistance. Weston was less successful in his leadership of one of the two English fishing associations, intended to compete with the Dutch in the North Sea, and, despite his lengthy concern with naval reform and his current role as the most senior of the admiralty commissioners, he played a relatively minor part in introducing a new version of ship money in 1634–5. Despite Weston's participation in recent negotiations with their agent Necolalde, the Spanish had failed to deliver financial support promised for Charles's growing fleet, which was intended to demonstrate his sovereignty of the British seas, partly for their benefit. Weston may not have welcomed an alternative means of funding which held out a distant prospect of direct parliamentary support for the navy, and was certainly agitated at the speed with which Charles insisted on having John Coke present an outline of his 'great business' to the council early in June 1634 (Scrope and Monkhouse, 1.94). To his relief, and perhaps after his intervention, Coke in the event provided little more than a catalogue of obstructions to British trade in continental Europe and beyond, which matching assertiveness in home waters might remedy; no foreign policy or financial implications were raised. The managers of the new levy's introduction were leading courtiers with firmly Calvinist convictions, principally Lord Keeper Thomas Coventry, Lord Privy Seal Henry Montagu, earl of Manchester, and Secretary John Coke, assisted by the attorney-general of the day, William Noy. However, Noy died on 9 August 1634 and his successor, Sir John Bankes, was closer to Weston. The treasurer's hand may also be seen in the number of Catholic-leaning officers in the fleet of 1635, prompting the application of the oaths of supremacy and allegiance to those in command in 1636.

Weston's influence within the court was widely apparent by 1634. Although never a favourite he was firmly established in the king's regard from the early days of personal rule, and enjoyed the goodwill of the earls of Dorset, Carlisle, and especially Arundel. In April 1630 he had been the king's nomination for the chancellorship of Oxford, left vacant by the death of William Herbert, third earl of Pembroke, only for it to transpire that Laud had somehow already been elected. Weston did however succeed Pembroke as steward of Bristol, after accepting a similar office at Exeter in 1629. He was appointed to the Order of the Garter in April 1630, filling the vacancy left by Buckingham, and during the year commissioned from Hubert Le Sueur an equestrian statue of the king for the garden of his house at Roehampton. He leased Wallingford House, London, after the duke's death, and began to hold meetings of the admiralty commissioners there, prompting a rumour in June 1631 that he was about to become lord admiral.

During 1632 Weston sought to strengthen his association with the inner court by ambitious dynastic alliances. In June his heir, Jerome *Weston (1605–1663), married Lady Frances Stuart, the youngest daughter of the late Esmé Stuart, third duke of Lennox, the king's cousin, in a ceremony in the chapel at Roehampton attended by Charles and Henrietta Maria, at which Laud officiated; Arundel's heir had married her sister in 1626. In December Weston's daughter Anne married Basil *Feilding, heir to William Feilding, first earl of Denbigh, whose wife, Susan, was Buckingham's sister and first lady of the queen's bedchamber; James Hamilton, third marquess of Hamilton, another courtier close to Charles, had already married a Feilding daughter. On 17 February 1633 Weston was created earl of Portland, a title reflecting a recent association with the strategically important county of Hampshire, where in February 1631 he had become sole lord lieutenant and captain of the Isle of Wight in succession to Edward Conway, Lord Conway, the former secretary of state. His kinsmen, the Tichbornes, who had never found their Catholicism a serious handicap to county office, had long been established there.

Portland's health had been uncertain since at least 1631, when Sir Edward Stanhope, in advising Wentworth against accepting the deputyship of Ireland, assumed that the treasurer was 'not likely to injoy his place long, his corpulency and corporall infirmityes fitt enoughe to subtract from whatt nature might have allowed him', and became more erratic in 1634 as kidney disease took hold (Zagorin, 304). At much the same time his critics at court made a sustained attempt to undermine his entrenched position. Most prominent were his 'great opposite', Coventry, Archbishop Laud in vexed association with Wentworth, growing testy and untrusting in Ireland, and the earl of Holland, a fading favourite of the queen, upset at his inability to become lord admiral, and smarting at the disappointing outcome of a clash with Jerome Weston over interference with innocent correspondence of Henrietta Maria and himself with France early in 1633 (BL, Add. MS 35332, fol. 29r). A series of threads ran through their complaints. Coventry resented Weston's part in working against an early recall of parliament, looking increasingly improbable by 1632, and, like Sir John Eliot, deeply distrusted his popish connections. Laud allowed himself to be aggravated by Weston's enduring friendship with his old enemy, Bishop John Williams, and, like Wentworth, deplored his handling of business in both state and church, which combined a sluggish but self-righteous approach with an eye to his advantage rather than theirs. Henrietta Maria's favour, on which her husband insisted,

was seldom wholehearted: not only did Weston take it upon himself to urge on her the economies imposed on the household in 1629–30, but he had welcomed Cardinal Richelieu's survival of the 'Day of Dupes', and consistently advised Charles against inviting her exiled but extravagant mother, Marie de Medici, to live in England. He managed, too, to get the king to appoint his friend Sir John Bankes as Noy's successor in preference to her servant Finch. There were many others about the court, like Henry Cary, Viscount Falkland, Walter Aston, Lord Aston, Sir Thomas Roe, and Sir Henry Wotton, who, as either creditors or pensionaries of the crown, found themselves brusquely denied payments due to them. Further pleading served only to aggravate matters. As James I had noted, Weston had a sharp tongue, and continual ill health was not improving his temper. The king's subjects, he believed, had a duty to make sacrifices while he attended to his master's financial well-being. In time, such high-handedness left him so heavily dependent on the support of the king that he became openly fearful of losing it.

Portland was the more vulnerable, as Coventry and Eliot appreciated, because of his inescapable associations with popery and with Spain. His wife, Frances, had been born into one of the leading Essex Catholic families, the Waldegraves of Borley. In 1624 she and her children were held to have attended the Church of England sufficiently often, even if not communicating, to gain exemption for her husband from the list of Catholic office-holders then being drawn up by parliament, but in 1628 Weston had been named, alone among the king's leading ministers, in a mainly provincial list, as one 'vehemently suspected to be ill-affected in religion' because of his household's failings, an assessment supported by his son Jerome's disqualification from the Commons after a double return for Gatton, a seat notoriously susceptible to popish influence (*Portland MSS*, vol. 1). Lady Weston was seen again at church, despite keeping her own priests and being busy during the 1630s among the proselytizing women around the queen. Yet whatever parliament thought, English Catholics did not accept that Weston was among their number. He not only attended church, but helped his household chaplain, Dr James Halsey, to a prebend of Winchester Cathedral in 1631 and, as Laud later claimed, was sufficiently concerned with the church to advance the career of the scholarly bishop, Augustine Lindsell. But godly Calvinists noted that both men were Arminians, thus reinforcing their political reservations about Weston. He had dealt with Spanish and French diplomats at intervals since 1620 and, although not uncritically, was party with Cottington to the treatings in 1629–30 which had sealed the peace with Spain and to the maritime negotiations since then, none of them welcome in godly circles. In February 1632, moreover, he took advantage of the death of Dudley Carleton, Viscount Dorchester, 'for a tyme [to] supplye the service' of secretary of state himself, in order to dash Calvinist hopes of an agreement with the Swedes over recovery of the Lower Palatinate by force (PRO, SP 16/211/74).

The antagonism increased in 1633–4. Coventry, who was

obstructive over recusant forfeitures early in 1633, joined with Laud the following May in attacking the popish soap monopolists, in whom Portland had an interest, and, with Manchester, later refused to draw the proclamation authorizing them to go ahead. In April 1634 Coventry and Laud took up the rumour that Portland had subverted the king's intention of selling just enough royal forest to cover the costs of building two new warships, the *James* and the *Unicorn*, by setting aside more than was needed and, having sold the surplus cheaply by arrangement, subsequently bought it back for himself. Clarendon believed he thus acquired the whole of Chute Forest; but it would have been a clumsy and impractical way of doing so, and there seems no hard evidence that Portland, who was then quite ill, dealt improperly with any part of the royal forest. The duke of Lennox and the duchess of Buckingham interceded on his behalf, and Charles demonstrated his belief in his innocence by inviting him to kiss his hand in open court at Greenwich on 24 May 1634.

A more sweeping attack on Portland, and those thought to be associated with him, came in the summer of 1634 when Holland, as chief justice in eyre south of Trent, conducted a court of justice seat in Dean Forest. Noy was too sick to accompany him, and his place was taken by the queen's attorney-general, Sir John Finch. How much Henrietta Maria knew of what they intended has never become clear; but it seems likely that Holland and Finch believed that their efforts to embarrass Weston, by prosecuting his supposed associates for alleged exploitation of Dean's resources, would be well received, even though the treasurer's standing with the king had been emphasized in May when he had been appointed to the newly constituted queen's court charged with administering the consort's estates. Finch reminded the court of justice seat of the widely held belief that, had the Spanish been defeated in 1588, English Catholics would have destroyed Dean, traditionally the staple source of timber for the royal navy. Not all the prosecutions were well grounded, and some of the fines were eventually reduced, but Portland was fearful enough to shed his friends, including his long-serving secretary, John Gibbons, leaving them to further prosecution, on other grounds, in the law courts at Westminster.

While rumours of his possible successor circulated Portland returned subdued from the waters at Tunbridge Wells, but he recovered his spirits by recalling the king's instruction 'to believe nothing of those things which may seem of importance, and are brought to me, till I speake with him' (PRO, SP 16/273/64, 22 Aug 1634). Within a month he was trying to rout his critics. At the end of a council meeting on 29 September 1634 he asked the king to stay while he laid a complaint. Laud made to defend himself, but Portland indicated that he was aiming at Coventry, who had evidently been reflecting on his fondness for gratuities. Charles refused to hear them out, but ordered Portland to provide him with a list of gifts and payments since July 1628. It amounted to £44,000 and duly met with royal approval on 21 October. Charles himself was responsible for the biggest sum—£10,000 bestowed

'within a while … for his present support'—while Burlamachi, anxious to extricate himself from impending bankruptcy, had, as the king knew, given £9000 (Scrope and Monkhouse, 1.158). The other fourteen contributions were smaller. The list suggests that Portland averaged at least £7000 a year in perquisites, in itself not an unusual sum for a lord treasurer, and acceptable to the king, but it is not likely to have been exhaustive.

Portland again reacted sharply when Sir Anthony Pell's bill, 'of strange coinage' as Laud put it, came before Star Chamber late in 1634 (*Works*, 7.97). The defendants were Sir James Bagg, Sir Richard Tichborne, Gibbons, and another of Portland's secretaries, William Lake, and it cast an oblique shadow over his activities while concentrating on those of his subordinates. He intervened after the defendants, in his absence, had entered a demurrer on 26 November. On 1 December, according to James Howell, Portland 'out of the light of honour and innocencye knowne to himself and beleeved in the accused … wa[i]ved it in court and pressed a proceedinge to proofe'. He readily acknowledged what some privy councillors had said earlier, that his 'Honour could not be vindicated in any Place more properly than in this [court] … Therefore', he added, 'I desire that this Business may be ordered to be heard with all Speed'. Howell thought it risky, for 'if it fayle [it] will like a stone fall heavie on the thrower's head' (PRO, SP 16/278/3; *Earl of Strafford's Letters and Despatches*, 1.377–8); in the event it was Pell who had reason to feel sore. Such was Portland's determination to protect his interests towards the end of his life that in his last two active months, January and February 1635, he was attending routine meetings of the privy council more frequently than he had done for years. Customarily he had been present at one meeting in three; but on the evidence of the council register he managed to attend twelve of the eighteen meetings to 22 February, most of them when the king was present as well as his leading critics.

Death and legacy Portland died on 13 March 1635 at Wallingford House, 'in great pain, entring his bed not above one hour' before, according to the account given to George Garrard by his friend Lord Cottington (*Earl of Strafford's Letters and Despatches*, 1.389). Laud and Bishop Matthew Wren offered to attend him, but Tobie Matthew was at hand, and it was 'whispered and believed he died a Roman Catholick' (ibid.). Charles had briefly visited him shortly after giving him charge of Winchester Castle. Appropriately for the lord lieutenant of Hampshire he was buried, on 24 March, in Winchester Cathedral, where a bronze effigy, thought to be by Francesco Fanelli, was erected in the north-east chapel. Depressed by the state of his own finances Portland had proved reluctant to turn to testamentary matters. There was said to be less than £100 in the house at the time of his death. On 9 March Cottington, 'with much difficulty … brought him … to make his will, asking him, from his wife to his youngest child, what he would bequeath to them', so that Attorney-General Bankes, at the bedside, could get down the details (*Earl of Strafford's Letters and Despatches*, 1.388). Yet, although formally drawn up, and signed and sealed by Portland at the time, the will does not seem ever to have been sent for probate. Cottington's questions had necessarily been direct and specific, concerned with essentials and not attempting to range over the whole of Portland's financial affairs and miscellaneous assets. No mention, for example, was made of his plate, some of which was sold for £1200 to pay for his burial, or of the £12,000 which Charles had given him at Christmas 1634 or, indeed, of the inheritance of Jerome, his eldest son from his second marriage, regarded as his heir even before the death of his first son Richard 'mad and kept at Coventry' in April 1634 (*Earl of Strafford's Letters and Despatches*, 1.243). Garrard reckoned that Portland left land and property worth at best £6600 a year, but charged with debts of at least £25,000. His widow had £1500 p.a. for her jointure and was given the use of Roehampton for life; of their younger children, Thomas got the Roxwell estate (worth £600 p.a., and promptly sold), Nicholas and Benjamin were left annuities of £300, Mary received £4000 and Catherine (who married Richard White of Hutton, Essex) £1000. His daughters from his first marriage, Elizabeth, wife of Sir John *Netterville, and Mary, wife of Walter Aston, second Baron Aston, and two daughters from his second, Anne Feilding (who predeceased him by three days) and Frances, wife of a staunchly Catholic Staffordshire squire, Philip Draycott of Paynesbury, went unnoticed. The sole executor was Jerome, who, his father hoped, would find a suitable place at court and make his seat at Winchester. A report in 1634 that Jerome was about to replace secretary Coke had proved ill-founded, and his father's strenuous efforts in his last days to secure him the mastership of the court of wards came to nothing. Charles was prepared to protect his treasurer but not to promote a ministerial dynasty.

Portland was the first lord treasurer to die in office since Robert Cecil in 1612. That he did so owed much to Charles's determination to support a minister who set out to achieve financial stability without resort to novel ways, and on such terms Portland served his master well. But the king's experiences in the early 1630s, and the tensions within the treasury commission after Portland's death, persuaded him of the almost equally pressing need to establish a quiet and settled court. William Juxon, who was chosen to succeed Portland in 1636, carried little contentious baggage even though he was a senior bishop, and, in Sir Henry Wotton's words, seemed 'the very reverse of his proud predecessor who made a scorn of my poverty and a sport of my modesty' (Smith, 2.375). Without Buckingham as a focal point for court politics Portland had found himself subjected to continual criticism from rival interests on a variety of fronts, and his religious ambivalence and conspicuous expenditure made him an easy target. So did his erratic manner, at times overbearing, at others fearful. The nature and extent of his errors and excesses is by no means entirely clear, however, and it seems unlikely that he profited from office to the degree his enemies believed he did. Nevertheless he felt isolated, and grew notably anxious that those corresponding with the court should not pass him by. Although he was party to many of Charles's more confidential dealings he lacked

the status of a favourite and his patronage, both political and cultural, was circumscribed, primarily directed to procuring from the king those he wanted around him like Cottington, Bankes, and Secretary Sir Francis Windebank. As a creature of the court he had limited time and little inclination to develop local connections, yet he proved unable to build an effective body of support at the centre; even Cottington found himself torn between Portland and Wentworth. Wentworth, whom Portland had once brought into favour but then helped to remove to Ireland, prudently let him know before he left for Dublin that he remained 'the very principall' of his courtly friends, but on Portland's death confessed himself to be 'delivered from the heaviest adversary' he ever had (*Earl of Strafford's Letters and Despatches*, 1.79, 411). Like Wotton, who deeply regretted his misjudgement in sending the treasurer a eulogy 'of the richest materials' as a new year's gift in 1633, he could now lay such conceits aside (Smith, 2.334, 375). Portland had come to depend almost entirely on the king, who knew his value and did not desert him. In a few years he had done much, by imposing economies on others, to stabilize royal finances; but at the last he found it hard to face up to the extravagant confusion in which he was leaving his own.

BRIAN QUINTRELL

Sources PRO, SP 12/254/18; SP 14/175/48, 14/216/6; SP 16/80/60, 16/112/75, 16/113/14, 16/211/74, 16/216/6, 16/273/64, 16/278/3 · BL, Add. MS 35332, fol. 29r · BL, Stowe MS 326, fol. 60r · Strafford papers, Sheff. Arch., Wentworth Woodhouse muniments, 12–14, 24 · CKS, U269/1/OE 778 · *The manuscripts of the Earl Cowper*, 3 vols., HMC, 23 (1888–9) · *The manuscripts of the duke of Beaufort … the earl of Donoughmore*, HMC, 27 (1891) [Sir Richard Hutton's diary] · *The manuscripts of his grace the duke of Portland*, 10 vols., HMC, 29 (1891–1931), vol. 1 · *Cabala* (1654) · J. Hacket, *Scrinia reserata: a memorial offer'd to the great deservings of John Williams*, 2 pts (1693) · G. Radcliffe, *The earl of Strafforde's letters and dispatches, with an essay towards his life*, ed. W. Knowler, 2 vols. (1739) · R. Scrope and T. Monkhouse, eds., *State papers collected by Edward, earl of Clarendon*, 3 vols. (1767–86) · Clarendon, *Hist. rebellion* · *The letters of John Chamberlain*, ed. N. E. McClure, 2 vols. (1939) · *The works of the most reverend father in God, William Laud*, ed. J. Bliss and W. Scott, 7 vols. (1847–60) · J. Oglander, *The Oglander memoirs*, ed. W. H. Long (1888) · W. Notestein and F. H. Relf, eds., *Commons debates for 1629* (1921) · *Letters of John Holles, 1587–1637*, ed. P. R. Seddon, 3 vols. (1975–86) · *The life and letters of Sir Henry Wotton*, ed. L. P. Smith, 2 vols. (1907) · 'A collection of several speeches and treatises of the late lord treasurer Cecil', ed. P. Croft, *Camden miscellany, XXIX*, CS, 4th ser., 34 (1987) · B. W. Quintrell, ed., *Maynard lieutenancy book, 1608–1639*, 2 vols. (1993) · W. C. Metcalfe, ed., *Visitations of Essex, 1552–1634* (1878) · P. Morant, *The history and antiquities of the county of Essex*, 2 vols. (1768) · P. Zagorin, 'Sir Edward Stanhope's advice to Thomas Wentworth', *HJ*, 7 (1964), 298–320 · M. Oppenheim, *A history of the administration of the Royal Navy* (1896) · L. J. Reeve, *Charles I and the road to personal rule* (1989) · A. F. Upton, *Sir Arthur Ingram, c.1565–1642: a study in the origins of an English landed family* (1961) · M. Prestwich, *Cranfield: politics and profit under the early Stuarts: the career of Lionel Cranfield, earl of Middlesex* (1966) · M. Alexander, *Charles I's lord treasurer: Sir Richard Weston* (1975) · F. C. Dietz, *English public finance, 1485–1631*, 2nd edn (1964) · V. Treadwell, *Buckingham and Ireland, 1616–1628: a study in Anglo-Irish politics* (1998) · M. Whinney and O. Millar, *English art, 1625–1714* (1959) · J. F. Merritt, ed., *The political world of Thomas Wentworth, earl of Strafford, 1621–1641* (1996) · *Hist. U. Oxf. 4: 17th-cent. Oxf.* · J. Morrill, P. Slack, and D. Woolf, eds., *Public duty and private conscience in seventeenth-century England* (1993) · T. K. Rabb, *Jacobean gentleman: Sir Edwin Sandys* (1998) · M. F. S. Hervey, *The life … of Thomas Howard, earl of Arundel* (1921) · G. Anstruther, *The seminary* *priests*, 2 (1975) · D. Mathew, *Sir Tobie Mathew* (1950) · R. Lockyer, *Buckingham: the life and political career of George Villiers, first duke of Buckingham, 1592–1628* (1981) · K. Sharpe, *The personal rule of Charles I* (1992) · Venn, *Alum. Cant.* · W. A. Shaw, *The knights of England*, 2 vols. (1906); repr. (1971) · GEC, *Peerage* · will, PRO, PROB 11/104/84 [Jerome Weston]

Archives BL, letters during his embassy to Brussels, to the secretary of state, 16 | Bodl. Oxf., Clarendon MSS · CKS, corresp. with Lionel Cranfield · PRO, State MSS, SP 14, SP 16

Likenesses attrib. D. Mytens, oils, *c.*1633, Woburn Abbey, Bedfordshire · C. Warin, medal, *c.*1633, BM · attrib. H. le Sueur, bronze effigy, *c.*1635, Winchester Cathedral, Hampshire · W. Hollar, etching, 1645 (after A. Van Dyck), BM, NPG; repro. in Van Dyck, *Iconographie* · after A. Van Dyck, oils, Kingston Lacy, Dorset [*see illus.*] · oils (after A. Van Dyck, *c.*1633), Clarendon College; on loan to Council House, Plymouth; version, Gorhambury, Hertfordshire

Weston, Sir Richard (1578/9–1658?), lawyer, was the son of Ralph Weston (*d.* 1605) of Rugeley, Staffordshire, and his wife, Anne, daughter of George Smyth of Appleton, Lancashire. He matriculated from Exeter College, Oxford, on 14 October 1596, aged seventeen, and was admitted to the Inner Temple in 1599. About 1605 he married Anne, daughter of Richard Barbour of Hilderstone; they had three children, Elizabeth, Richard (*b.* 1608/9), and Ralph. Weston was called to the bar in 1607. Six years later he inherited the family estates at Rugeley on the death of his grandfather, Philip Weston.

In 1621 Weston was elected as MP for Lichfield. Like his namesake, the chancellor of the exchequer and future earl of Portland, he was an active member. In June he obtained for himself and his son Richard the office of pretermitted customs in the port of London but in the course of acting as solicitor for alehouse keepers, who were petitioning parliament, was temporarily committed by the house to prison. For many years Weston was a Staffordshire JP. He became a bencher of his inn in 1626 and a judge on the Welsh circuit in 1632. On 19 April 1634 he was created serjeant-at-law and subsequently, on 6 May, became baron of the exchequer in place of his recently deceased kinsman Sir James Weston, probably at the behest of Portland.

Weston suffered from a pronounced lameness in one leg: he remarked at his investiture as serjeant 'that he was himself soe lame of the left leg, but he was upright of the right syde and that he knew he would be soe, his hart was right' (Baker, *Serjeants*, 370). He appears to have been largely confined to the unpopular home circuit throughout his career, although this may have been a concession to his disability which would have made travelling difficult. He was knighted at Whitehall on 7 December 1635. In 1638 he was one of seven judges who, in *Hampden's case*, affirmed the crown's right to collect ship money. His opinion is of some significance. Weston affirmed that the king could act independently of parliament as sole judge of when the kingdom was in imminent danger, and that he himself was convinced that such a danger currently existed from foreign navies. Furthermore, he concluded that the form of the ship money writ was good in law and that ship money extended to the nineteen inland counties

and not just to the thirty-three maritime counties. He justified his opinion not simply with a direct appeal to the equity of 'necessity' of the matter, but also with an appeal to precedent and English history, citing previous 'custom and usage' in the thirteenth and fourteenth centuries (*State trials*, 3.1265–78).

In the two elections of 1640 Richard Weston the younger was elected MP for Stafford; he probably voted against the attainder of Strafford. The following year Weston senior was one of six judges impeached and imprisoned by parliament for their support of ship money, although he was not brought to trial. Both father and son seem to have joined the king in August 1642; the latter was disabled from parliament on 30 October that year, while the former was disabled from the judiciary on 24 October 1645 'as though he was dead'. By this time the family's estates in Staffordshire had been plundered, and on 29 March 1645 the county committee ordered that Lady Weston hold the lands of her husband, described as a delinquent, in return for £104 a year.

The Westons' misfortunes may have been somewhat mitigated by the fact that both their son-in-law Richard Floyer and Lady Weston's nephew Leicester Barbour were committee members, but the family continued to suffer for its royalism. Richard Weston the younger, who had become a colonel, was taken prisoner at Colchester in July 1648 and was killed in the king's service on the Isle of Man in 1652 (a date often erroneously given for his father's death). Weston himself was described as a 'papist' in 1648, and by the time he drew up his will on 18 November 1655 reckoned that 'these late troublesome times have much impoverished me' just as 'the late death of my late dear wife hath much troubled my mind'. The disposition of his remaining goods was left to his executors, his son Ralph and his grandsons Philip (son of Richard the younger and his wife, Catherine Cockayne) and John. Weston probably died on 18 March 1658; Ralph obtained probate of the will on 17 April 1660 and Philip succeeded to the family estates.

D. A. ORR

Sources W. R. Prest, *The rise of the barristers: a social history of the English bar, 1590–1640* (1986), 401 · Foster, *Alum. Oxon.* · W. H. Cooke, ed., *Students admitted to the Inner Temple, 1547–1660* [1878], 243 · Baker, *Serjeants* · *VCH Staffordshire*, 5.156 · W. Notestein, F. H. Relf, and H. Simpson, eds., *Commons debates, 1621*, 7 vols. (1935) · J. C. Wedgwood, 'Staffordshire parliamentary history [2/1]', *Collections for a history of Staffordshire*, William Salt Archaeological Society, 3rd ser. (1920), 25–6 · J. S. Cockburn, *A history of English assizes, 1558–1714* (1972), 262–93 · D. H. Pennington and I. A. Roots, eds., *The committee at Stafford, 1643–1645*, Staffordshire RS, 4th ser., 1 (1957), 31–2, 48, 285, 349, 351 · Keeler, *Long Parliament* · will, PRO, PROB 11/298, fol. 163r · *State trials*, 1265–78 · W. J. Jones, *Politics and the bench: the judges and the origins of the English civil war* (1971) · G. Burgess, *The politics of the ancient constitution: an introduction to English political thought, 1603–1642* (1992)

Weston, Sir Richard (1591–1652), canal builder and agriculturist, was the eldest son of Sir Richard Weston (1564–1613), of Sutton, Surrey, and great-grandson of Sir Francis *Weston. His family was quite distinct from those of the first earl of Portland and of Sir Richard Weston, baron of the exchequer. The agriculturist is said to have been educated in Flanders, or at least to have spent a considerable part of his early life there; but there are phrases in his *Discours* which imply that he was visiting Flanders for the first time in 1644. In 1613, on his father's death, he succeeded to the family estates at Sutton and Clandon. On 27 July 1622 he was knighted at Guildford. He married Grace (*d.* 1669), daughter of John Harper of Cheshunt, and they had seven sons and two daughters.

A promoter of the pound lock as a means of improving navigation on canals and rivers, Sir Richard Weston attempted by this means to make the Wey navigable from Guildford to its junction with the Thames at Weybridge. In 1635 he was appointed one of the royal commissioners for the prosecution of the work. It was perhaps the expenditure necessitated by his canal scheme which forced him in 1641 to sell Temple Court Farm at Merrow, with the mansion at West Clandon, to Sir Richard Onslow, MP for Surrey in the Long Parliament. Shortly after this the river undertaking was interrupted by the civil war. Sir Richard was a royalist and a Catholic. The manor house of Sutton was entirely unsuited for defence, while the neighbouring town of Guildford was in the hands of the parliamentarians; Sir Richard's possessions were sequestrated, and he seems to have been compelled to flee from the country. In 1644 he was at Ghent, Bruges, and Antwerp. It was in the course of his exile that he made those observations on the agricultural methods of the Low Countries which were subsequently embodied in his work, *A Discours of Husbandrie used in Brabant and Flanders* (1650).

In 1649 Weston entered into an agreement with Major James Pitson, commissioner for Surrey under the parliament, that the latter should solicit the discharge of his sequestration and forward his schemes for rendering the Wey navigable. Accordingly a petition was presented in the names of Pitson and the corporation of Guildford. A bill authorizing the works was brought into the House of Commons on 26 December 1650, and passed as an act on 26 June 1651. The capital was £6000, of which Sir Richard was to find half, undertaking at the same time to complete the canal within six months. Sir Richard employed two hundred men at a time, and used timber of his own to the value of £2000. Materials and timber were also taken, by permission of the parliament, from the king's estates of Oatlands and Richmond. Weston died in May 1652, less than a year after the passing of the act, and by then some 10 out of the 14 miles of canal were completed, though at an expenditure much exceeding the original estimate.

The work was continued by Weston's son and Major Pitson, and the canal was opened in November 1653. The completed canal had ten locks, four weirs, and twelve bridges; but, although it produced a large revenue, it involved the family in litigation which, when finally settled in 1671, had more than swallowed up all the profits. At the Restoration an attempt was made by a certain John Radcliffe to gain control of the canal. A committee of the House of Commons which sat to investigate his claims came to the conclusion that 'Sir Richard Weston was the designer of the navigation, and they were satisfied that

Mr. [John] Weston's estate was left to him encumbered by reason of his father undertaking the navigation' (Manning and Bray, 3, appx lvi).

Even more important than Sir Richard Weston's canal schemes were his agricultural improvements. He writes himself that at the time he went out of England he had had 'thirtie years' experience in Husbandrie' and had 'improved my Land as much as anie man in this Kingdom hath done both by water and fire' (Weston, 5). Following Rowland Vaughan, Sir Richard raised rich crops of hay by 'floating' water meadows, and these are referred to by a contemporary writer:

> Because hay is dear in those parts this year, near three pound a load, Sir Richard Weston told me he sold at near that rate one hundred and fifty loads of his extraordinary hay which his meadows watered with his new river did yield. (Speed, 35)

Sir Richard's account of Flemish husbandry was written about 1645, and addressed to his sons from abroad. This was circulated in manuscript, and there is no evidence that it was printed before 1650, when an imperfect copy was published by Samuel Hartlib, with a dedication to the council of state. Hartlib did not at this time know who the author was. The account is the first English description of the use of a farming rotation including turnips and clover to obtain maximum output from heathlands formerly considered of little agricultural value. Although it is not known to what extent Sir Richard emulated on his own estates what he saw in Flanders, he described a farming system that was to become the cornerstone of the English 'agricultural revolution' a century later.

An 'enlargement' of the *Discours* was published in 1651 (Perkins, 61), and on 2 May of that year and again on 10 October Hartlib wrote to Sir Richard, whom he had been 'credibly informed' was the author of the *Discours*, asking him for some further information on the subject of clover cultivation and requesting him to 'make compleat and sufficiently enlarged' for the benefit of all 'his former treatise'. As Sir Richard took no notice, Hartlib published a second edition of the pamphlet in 1652, adding transcripts of his two letters to Sir Richard. Hartlib's *Legacie … of Husbandry* (a collection of anonymous notes on agricultural matters) has sometimes been erroneously attributed to Sir Richard Weston.

Weston died at the age of sixty-one, in May 1652, and was buried in Trinity Chapel, Guildford, on 8 May. His wife died in February 1669, and was buried with her husband. Sir Richard was succeeded by his second son, John.

ERNEST CLARKE, *rev.* MARK OVERTON

Sources F. Harrison, *Annals of an old manor house* (1899) · O. Manning and W. Bray, *The history and antiquities of the county of Surrey*, 3 vols. (1804–14) · [R. Weston], *A discours of husbandrie used in Brabant and Flanders*, ed. S. Hartlib (1650) · S. Hartlib, *His legacie, or, An enlargement of the Discourse of husbandry used in Brabant and Flanders*, 2nd edn (1651) · A. R. Mitchell, 'Sir Richard Weston and the spread of clover cultivation', *Agricultural History Review*, 22 (1974), 160–61 · P. A. L. Vine, *London's lost route to the sea: an historical account of the inland navigations which linked the Thames to the English Channel* (1965) · A. Speed, *Adam out of Eden, or, An abstract of divers excellent experiments touching the advancement of husbandry* (1659) · W. F. Perkins, *British and Irish writers on agriculture*, 3rd edn (1939) · W. C. Metcalfe,

A book of knights banneret, knights of the Bath and knights bachelor (1885)
Archives BM, pedigree of the Westons of Sutton

Weston, Sir Richard (1620–1681), judge and politician, was the son of Edward Weston (*d.* 1645) of Hackney, Middlesex, and his wife, Mary. The Westons were descended from a Sussex family and owned land in the county. Richard Weston was his father's heir and, presumably, his eldest son. Weston matriculated from Corpus Christi College, Cambridge, in 1639, and from Jesus College, Cambridge, in 1641. He took no degree, however, and entered Gray's Inn on 10 August 1642. Weston was called to the bar in 1649. In 1645 his father died and Weston took possession of the family lands. On 30 June 1657 he married Frances Marwood, daughter of Sir George Marwood, baronet, of Little Busby in Yorkshire. No children are mentioned in Weston's will.

After the Restoration, Weston practised law, and his arguments in court were sufficient to gain mention in Sir Thomas Raymond's *Reports of Divers Special Cases*. Weston also had a brief parliamentary career, as the member from Weobley, Herefordshire, in the Convention Parliament of 1660. He served on eight committees, including those which drafted the Indemnity Bill and confirmed parliamentary privileges. His legal expertise probably proved useful to the committee to continue judicial proceedings, and he also served on the committee that examined Oliver Cromwell's counsellor and spymaster, John Thurloe. In his few recorded speeches Weston emerged as a supporter of the episcopal church, and it seems likely that he was already displaying the strong royalist bent for which he later became known. Weston's parliamentary career was cut short on 16 July 1660 when, for unknown reasons, the House of Commons voided the Weobley election.

Weston never re-entered parliament. In 1664, probably due to his wife's Yorkshire connections, he was made a justice of the peace in Cawood, in the West Riding. Weston purchased the Yorkshire estate of Little Cattall in 1669. He served as a commissioner for assessment in the West Riding from 1673 until 1680, and as the recorder of Beverley from 1675 to 1678. As for his legal career, Weston was made reader of Gray's Inn in 1676, serjeant-at-law on 23 October 1677, and king's serjeant on 5 February 1678, whereupon he was knighted. The climax of his career came with his appointment to the bench of the exchequer on 7 February 1680. Weston's ascent seems to have been fuelled by the favour of Thomas Osborne, earl of Danby. He apparently repaid this patronage by drafting Danby's pardon in 1679. This was no doubt unpopular with the House of Commons, which responded by expressly forbidding Weston from acting as Danby's counsel. By this time Weston had become entangled in the factionalism of these tumultuous years, and he was known as a staunch defender of royal prerogative.

As a judge Weston was 'obliging, condescensive, and communicative' (Irving, 114), but he also displayed a hot temper (reportedly exacerbated by gout). Weston caused a stir while presiding over the Kingston assizes in July 1680. When a group of nonconformists was brought before him, Weston's charge to the grand jury included scathing remarks about Calvin and Zwingli. He also declared that 'now they were amusing us with fears, and nothing would serve them but a parliament … for my part I know no representative of the nation but the king; all power centres in him' (Foss, *Judges*, 719). These intemperate remarks would haunt Weston. At the same assizes he made an enemy of George Jeffreys, who appeared before him as an advocate. Weston abruptly rebuked Jeffreys when the latter engaged in an overly hostile examination of a witness. When Jeffreys complained of this treatment, Weston exclaimed 'Ha! Since the King has thrown his favours upon you … you think to run down everybody. If you think you are aggrieved, make your complaint. Here nobody cares for it.' Reports of this exchange soon worked their way to London. Jeffreys may have had a hand in Weston's subsequent troubles before parliament. When the Commons moved to impeach a number of tory judges (including Chief Justice Scroggs) Weston was included for his remarks at the Kingston assizes, which were considered derogatory to the Reformation and tending to raise discord. Undaunted, Weston defied the house by granting a writ of habeas corpus to another of its targets, Thomas Sheridan. But the dissolution of the parliament delayed the impeachment proceedings. In August 1680 Weston presided over the trial of a nonconformist accused of assaulting an Anglican priest, during which he was accused by the defendant of being 'popishly affected' (*CSP dom.*, 22.422). Controversial to the end, Weston died suddenly on 18 March 1681 at his home in Chancery Lane, London, and was buried three days later at Hackney.

JEFFREY R. COLLINS

Sources HoP, *Commons, 1660–90* • Foss, *Judges* • *State trials*, vol. 16 • *CSP dom.*, 1680–81 • *Seventh report*, HMC, 6 (1879) • H. B. Irving, *The life of Judge Jeffreys* (1898) • G. W. Keeton, *Lord Chancellor Jeffreys and the Stuart cause* (1965) • PRO, PROB 11/365, sig. 18 • PRO, PROB 11/368, sig. 152 • *DNB*

Weston, Richard (*bap.* 1732, *d.* 1806), writer on agriculture, was baptized on 13 July 1732 at St Martin, Leicester, the son of Thomas and Elizabeth Weston. He started out in life as a thread-hosier in Leicester. He took a keen interest in agriculture and gardening, and promoted the planting of trees, particularly alongside turnpike roads as an investment for future generations. In 1773 he was living at Kensington Gore, then a rural district, within easy reach of the market gardens of Chelsea, Battersea, and Westminster.

Weston's first important work was his *Tracts on Practical Agriculture and Gardening* with an appended 'Catalogue on English authors who have wrote on husbandry, gardening, botany, and subjects relative thereto' (1769), which he dedicated to the Society of Arts. Weston's mind was of an orderly cast and ran to the making of useful lists and catalogues, among them his *Botanicus universalis et hortulanus* (4 vols., 1770–77), and his *Flora Anglicana, seu, Arborum fruticum, plantarum, et fructuum … catalogus* (2 vols., 1775–80). He contributed many articles to the *Gentleman's Magazine*, and became secretary of the local agricultural society.

From about 1800 Weston devoted himself to the local history and literature of Leicestershire. He collected materials and announced his intention of publishing similar lists and catalogues on this topic, but failed to do so before his death at Leicester on 20 October 1806.

ERNEST CLARKE, *rev.* ANITA MCCONNELL

Sources S. Felton, *On the portraits of English authors on gardening*, 2nd edn (1830), 66–70 · G. E. Fussell, 'Richard Weston, 1733 to 1806', *Gardeners' Chronicle*, 3rd ser., 133 (1953), 221–2 · *GM*, 1st ser., 76 (1806), 1080–81

Weston, Robert (*b.* in or before **1522**, *d.* **1573**), lord chancellor of Ireland, was the third son of John Weston (*d.* after 1525), of Weeford, Staffordshire, and his wife, Cecilia (*d.* after 1525), sister of Ralph *Neville, fourth earl of Westmorland (1498–1549). One brother, James Weston (*c.*1525–1589), was an MP. Robert Weston entered All Souls College, Oxford, where he devoted himself to the study of civil law. He was elected a fellow of the college in 1536 and attained the degrees of BCL on 17 February 1538 and DCL on 20 July 1556. From 1546 to 1549 he was principal of Broadgates Hall, acting during the same time as deputy reader in civil law under Dr John Story and holding the regius professorship in civil law for a few months in 1546. He was sole regius professor from 26 March 1550 to 29 September 1553. He had married Alice (*d.* in or after 1573), daughter of Richard Jenyns of Great Barr, Staffordshire, by 1551/2. They had one son, John Weston (1551/2–1632), and three daughters, including Alice (*d.* after 1585), who married as her second husband Geoffrey *Fenton (*c.*1539–1608) in June 1585.

Weston was vicar general of Exeter, Devon, under Miles Coverdale, bishop of Exeter, from 1551 to 1553 and was returned as MP for Exeter in March 1553 and for Lichfield, Staffordshire, in 1558, and again in 1559. On 12 January 1559 Weston was created dean of the arches and was a commissioner for administering the oaths prescribed to be taken by ecclesiastics according to the Act of Uniformity (1559). He was consulted in regard to Elizabeth I's commission issued on 6 December confirming Matthew Parker as archbishop of Canterbury, and was included in a commission issued on 25 April 1564 and 8 November 1564 to inquire into complaints of piracy committed against the subjects of Philip II. His reputation for learning was deservedly high, and he was considered as a potential English representative at the general council which it was rumoured was to be summoned by Pius IV in 1560.

In April 1566, at the request of the lord deputy of Ireland, Sir Henry Sidney, Weston was nominated as lord chancellor in the place of Hugh Curwen, archbishop of Dublin. More than a year elapsed before letters patent were issued appointing him on 10 June 1567, the queen expressing her confidence in her choice as 'our trusty, well-beloved Doctor Weston, dean of the arches here, a man for his learning and approved integrity thoroughly qualified to receive and possess the same'. To increase his income she also appointed him dean of St Patrick's Cathedral, Dublin, *in commendam*, 'whereof the archbishop of Armagh [Adam Loftus] is now dean, and yet to leave it at our order, as we know he will'. He was advanced £133 6s.

8d. for the expenses of his journey, of which half was to be a gift and the other half to be deducted from his salary (E. P. Shirley, ed., *Original Letters and Papers in Illustration of the History of the Church of Ireland*, 299, 303).

Weston arrived in Dublin in early August 1567 and was sworn into office on the 8th. Shortly afterwards Sidney departed for England, and Weston and Sir William Fitzwilliam, the vice-treasurer, were sworn as lords justices in Christ Church on 14 October. Weston was reluctant to assume the onerous duties of the office, pleaded his ecclesiastical duties as a reason for leaving the hard work to his colleague, and stressed his unworthiness 'wanting, as he does, the courage and skill in martial affairs of Sir H. Sidney' (*CSP Ire.*, *1509–73*, 343, 347). Although he became dean of St Patrick's in 1567 he soon discovered that there was a great difference between his nominal and actual salary. Early in 1568 he persuaded Elizabeth to make him an additional yearly grant of £100. In 1570 she conferred on him the deanery of Wells *in commendam*, which he was to hold, as with the deanery of St Patrick's, as a lay fee to increase his income. In June 1568 Weston was included in a commission to inquire into offences against the Acts of Uniformity and Supremacy in Ireland. His duties as lord justice prevented him from paying as much attention to the chancery as he would have wished, and in August he asked that John Ball, student of civil law at Christ Church, Oxford, be sent over to assist him. His request appears to have been complied with. Nevertheless he established an excellent reputation as chancellor, proving himself, according to John Hooker:

> a man so bent to the execution of justice, and so severe therein, that he by no means would be seduced or averted from the same, and so much good in the end ensued from his upright, diligent, and dutiful service, as that the whole realm found themselves most happy and blessed to have him serve among them. (R. Holinshed and J. Hooker, *Holinshed's Chronicles of England, Scotland, and Ireland*, 6 vols., 1807–8, 6.336)

Perhaps Hooker was biased by the favourable judgment by Weston in the matter of the claim of Sir Peter Carew to the barony of Idrone, co. Carlow. Fitzwilliam, lord deputy, nevertheless praised his integrity, writing to William Cecil, Baron Burghley, the lord treasurer, in 1572 that Weston 'is godly and cannot be corrupted by gifts' (*CSP Ire.*, *1509–73*, 464). Weston was a moderate protestant allied with Hugh Brady, bishop of Meath, and Thomas Lancaster, archbishop of Armagh, in favour of persuasion rather than coercive measures to advance his religion. He supported local reformers in securing the act of 1570 to establish diocesan free schools and supported the establishment of a university, although the latter did not come to fruition until 1592.

In an age when most of his contemporaries actively sought sinecures Weston resisted these being imposed on him by others. Even before his appointment to the deanery of Wells, he expressed his doubts to Burghley as to the propriety of taking the fees of the deanery of St Patrick's and yet neglecting to serve in the post, and in 1572 wrote to him saying that 'even from the first I liked not very well spiritual livings for temporal service' (*CSP Ire.*, *1571–5*, 272).

As to the Irish, who had known Christianity for a thousand years, he shared the general opinion of his compatriots that they remained barbarous and basically pagan in their habits, but he preferred peaceful conversion to military suppression. He recommended the sending to Ireland of protestant ministers to save 'many thousands of souls … that else would perish'. He believed that it 'would work a willing and more perfect obedience in all subjects than any fear of sword or punishment can do' (Canny, 128). Shortly after arriving in Ireland he developed gout, and both on the ground of health and of his moral scruples he pleaded to be recalled, which he continued to do throughout his life. Although he was not included again in the commission for government during the absence of the lord deputy his services were too useful to be dispensed with. Despite holding the deanery of Wells from 1570 his position was difficult, for, on 19 August 1571, Fitzwilliam informed Burghley that Weston had 'broken up his house through want' (*CSP Ire.*, *1571–5*, 104). His increasing illness and his conscientious doubts prevented him from enjoying the benefits of his ecclesiastical livings, and he begged Burghley on 17 June 1572 to obtain permission for him to resign and to return to England.

In March 1573 Weston petitioned the queen herself to be relieved, but it was too late. He died in Dublin on 20 May 1573. His death is touchingly described by Holinshed. With the Irish privy council, friends, and household gathered round and all having taken communion, he exhorted the Irish privy council to be 'virtuous in God's true religion', to be mindful of their duty to Elizabeth and 'the great charge of the government laid upon them', and to be 'valiant, careful and studious' in its performance, 'to the glory of God, honour to the queen, and the benefit to the whole realm'. Having done this 'he bade them farewell, and not long after, he being fervent in his prayers, he died most godlie, virtuously, and Christian like' (O'Flanagan, 1.261–2). He was buried in St Patrick's beneath the altar, 'leaving behind him an excellent character for uprightness, judgment, learning, courtesy, and piety' (H. Cotton, *Fasti ecclesiae Hibernicae*, 5 vols., Dublin, 1845–78, 2.97).

Weston's granddaughter Catherine (*d.* 1630), the daughter of Weston's daughter Alice Fenton, married Richard Boyle, first earl of Cork, on 25 July 1603. Cork's monument in St Patrick's is surmounted by an effigy of Robert Weston in a recumbent position and in his robes of state, under an arch which forms the upper part of the monument, with an inscription recording that he 'was so learned, judicious and upright in the course of judicature, as, in all the time of that employment, he never made order or decree that was questioned or reversed' (Mason, 167–71, appx, liv). There is also a bronze bust by Sir Henry Cheere in All Souls College, Oxford.   ANDREW LYALL

Sources *CSP Ire.*, *1571–5* • Emden, *Oxf.*, 4.618 • J. R. O'Flanagan, *The lives of the lord chancellors and keepers of the great seal of Ireland*, 2 vols. (1870), 1.258–62 • J. G. Crawford, *Anglicizing the government of Ireland: the Irish privy council and the expansion of Tudor rule, 1556–1578* (Dublin, 1993) • S. G. Ellis, *Ireland in the age of the Tudors* (1998) • *CSP Ire.*, *1509–73*, 358, 360–65, 370–74, 400–02, 404, 439, 495; *1563–6*, 505; *1566–9*, 124 • HoP, *Commons*, *1558–1603*, 3.606 • F. E. Ball, *The judges in Ireland, 1221–1921*, 2 vols. (1926); repr. (1993), vol. 1, p. 211 • N. P. Canny, *The Elizabethan conquest of Ireland: a pattern established, 1565–76* (1976) • W. M. Mason, *The history and antiquities of the collegiate and cathedral church of St Patrick's* (1820), 167–71, app, liv • O. J. Burke, *The history of the lord chancellors of Ireland from AD 1186 to AD 1874* (1879) • PRO, PROB 11/55, sig. 25 • *DNB* • Foster, *Alum. Oxon.* • *Hist. U. Oxf.* 3: *Colleg. univ.*, 40, 264, 285–7, 358–60

Likenesses H. Cheere, bronze bust, *c.*1756 (after contemporary portrait), All Souls Oxf. • photograph of bust, repro. in Burke, *History*, facing p. 59 • tomb effigy, St Patrick's Cathedral, Dublin

Weston, Stephen (1665–1742), bishop of Exeter, probably the son of Stephen Weston, a farmer, was born at Farnborough, Berkshire, on 25 December 1665. In 1679 he was admitted to Eton College, and in 1683 he matriculated as a scholar of King's College, Cambridge; he graduated BA in 1687 and proceeded MA in 1690, and BD and DD (Oxon) in 1711. Weston was elected a fellow of King's in 1686, and admitted to Gray's Inn on 20 December 1692. He became an assistant master at Eton in 1690, and lower master or usher in 1693. In 1707 he retired from teaching, apparently on grounds of ill health, and was elected a fellow of Eton. He was vice-provost from 1721 to 1725. Thomas Sherlock reckoned him an able classical scholar, and a hard-working and successful schoolmaster. At Eton his name became associated with the former stable yard because he lived in a house in the yard.

Weston was ordained deacon on 29 September 1707, and priest on 5 October 1707 by the bishop of London. In 1710 he intended to stand for the provostship of King's in opposition to Dr John Adams. To qualify for this he needed to hold a DD degree. As it was suspected that this might be resisted by friends of Adams at Cambridge he incorporated at New College, Oxford, and proceeded BD and DD there. Hearne called Weston 'a good scholar and a good-natured man' (*Remarks*, 3.277–8). Weston married Lucy, daughter of Dr Richard Sleech, assistant master and fellow of Eton, and sister of Dr Stephen Sleech, provost of Eton (1746–65). She died on 4 March 1742, and was buried with her husband. They had three sons and two daughters. Their second son was Edward *Weston, civil servant and author. Weston was a canon of Ely from 1715, and vicar of Mapledurham, Oxfordshire, from 1716. In 1724, through the influence of Sir Robert Walpole, whom he had taught at Eton, he was appointed bishop of Exeter. The bishopric was poorly endowed, and to supplement his income he held *in commendam* the rectories of Calstock in Cornwall and Shobrooke in Devon, the treasurership and a prebendal stall in Exeter Cathedral, and, from 1732, the archdeaconry of Exeter. He was unusual among eighteenth-century bishops in conducting all his ordinations in Exeter, occasionally, in his early years, in the cathedral, but mostly in the palace chapel. He seems to have spent most of his time in Exeter, rarely attending the House of Lords. He undertook an extensive visitation of Devon in 1726 and Cornwall in 1728, in the course of which he visited and confirmed in most of the main local centres in the diocese. An anonymous verse notes

In Honour's Paths in Dubious Times he Trod
Firm to his Prince, as faithful to his God,
By Courts prefer'd yet not to Courts a Slave,
(Good men approved of what grateful Walpole gave)

Humane of Temper, Though his look Severe,
Cautious of Speech, in Promise as Sincere.
(Weston, *Sermons*, vol. 1, Exeter Cathedral Library copy, MS
sheet initialled 'R.W.')

Weston was reputed to be rather too schoolmasterly towards his clergy, 'who were much dissatisfied with him upon that account, as also upon his rough and ill-hewn manner of behaviour' (Hollis, 119). Sherlock noted 'the best Greek and Roman Writers were so familiar to him, that it leads him frequently into their Manner of Construction and Expression, which will require, sometime the Attention of the English Reader' (Weston, *Sermons*, vii).

During his final years at Exeter he was incapacitated by ill health, and unable to travel. He died at the bishop's palace, Exeter, on 8 January 1742, and was buried in the south aisle choir of Exeter Cathedral, where he is commemorated by a mural monument. W. M. JACOB

Sources C. Hollis, *Eton: a history* (1960) · Venn, *Alum. Cant.* · G. Oliver, *Lives of the bishops of Exeter, and a history of the cathedral* (1861) · W. Sterry, ed., *The Eton College register, 1441–1698* (1943) · ordination book, 1701–50, Devon RO, Chanter 52 · visitation book, 1726, Devon RO, Chanter 223 · S. Weston, letter to diocese of Exeter in support of the Devon and Exeter Hospital, Devon RO, Chanter 1572 · *Remarks and collections of Thomas Hearne*, ed. C. E. Doble and others, 11 vols., OHS, 2, 7, 13, 34, 42–3, 48, 50, 65, 67, 72 (1885–1921) · S. Weston, *Sermons on various subjects, moral and theological*, ed. T. Sherlock, 2 vols. (1747)
Likenesses T. Hudson, oils, *c*.1731, Bishop's palace, Exeter · G. White, mezzotint, 1731 (after T. Hudson), BM, NPG · T. Hudson, oils, Eton

Weston, Stephen (1747–1830), antiquary and classical scholar, was born in Exeter, the eldest son of Stephen Weston (*d*. 1750), registrar of Exeter diocese, and Elizabeth Oxenham of South Tawton, Devon. Stephen *Weston (1665–1742), bishop of Exeter, was his grandfather. According to the cathedral register Stephen was baptized in private on 8 June 1747 and received into the church at Exeter Cathedral on 10 July. He attended Blundell's School, Tiverton, and in 1759 entered Eton College, where he remained until 1763. His tutor, Mr Stinton, said, 'after overhawling him, that He found him an admirable Scholar' (*Eglinton MSS*, 406). Weston matriculated from Exeter College, Oxford, on 7 June 1764 and lived in college from 4 July 1764 to 7 July 1768. He graduated BA on 29 January 1768, MA on 14 November 1770, and BD on 2 May 1782, and was a Devonshire fellow from 1768 to 1784.

Weston accompanied Sir Charles Warwick Bampfylde of Devon as his tutor in a long tour of the continent. As a result of this tour he conceived a passion for travel and a particular love for France and, especially, for Paris. He was in Paris during the revolution of 1791 and 1792, but thought it expedient to leave the city rather than take unnecessary risks. His stay in Paris in 1791 and 1792 was marked by two anonymous publications, *Letters from Paris during the Summer of 1791* (1792) and *Letters from Paris during the Summer of 1792* (1793). He returned to Paris in 1802, and this visit too was celebrated by a publication, *The Praise of Paris: a Sketch of the French Capital in 1802* (1803). He began by writing, 'Paris is derived from Par Isis as this city was built

near the famous statue of that goddess near St. Germain des Prés', prompting a contributor to the *Gentleman's Magazine* to write that although 'as an archaeologist he may have had something to learn, his little book is vividly written, and his descriptions as clean cut as a cameo' (*N&Q*, 27). Not content with these, Weston wrote *A Slight Sketch of Paris in its Improved State since 1802: by a Visitor*, published in 1814, evidence of both another visit and a liking for familiar titles. Further indications of his love of the continent are other titles reflecting later visits to France, Belgium, Italy, Germany, and Switzerland. In 1824 he published *The Englishman abroad, part i: Greece, Latium, Persia, and China; part ii: Russia, Germany, Italy, France, Spain, and Portugal*, which was something of a hotchpotch of prose and verse and translations.

On 29 March 1777, thanks to the nomination of Lord Lisburne, Weston was admitted to the rectory of Mamhead in Devon. Seven years later, on 17 January 1784, he obtained the rectory of Little Hempston in the same county, and he gave up his fellowship at Exeter College the same year, having married Penelope (*d*. 1789/90), youngest daughter of James Tierney, a commissioner of accounts, of Cleeve Hill in Mangotsfield parish, Gloucestershire. She died of consumption aged thirty-one at Caen in Normandy late in 1789 or early in 1790 and was embalmed and returned to Bristol, where she was buried in the family vault. Weston's anonymous translation *Turtle Dove*, from the French of Claris de Florian, was published in Caen in 1789. Late in 1790 he gave up the living of Mamhead, but he kept the benefice of Little Hempston until 1823. He lived for some years in London and had a varied acquaintance. He was elected a fellow of the Royal Society on 1 March 1792, and a fellow of the Society of Antiquaries on 18 December 1794.

The first of some fifty published works by Weston, exclusive of those appearing in *Archaeologia*, in the *Gentleman's Magazine*, and in the *Classical Journal*, was according to his obituary in the *Gentleman's Magazine* (1830) *Hermesianax, sive, Conjecturae in Athenaeum* … (1784). He is thought to be the anonymous author of *Viaggiana: Remarks on the Buildings, &c, of Rome* (1776; with another edition in 1790), a work not listed as his in the *British Library Catalogue of Printed Books*. The reviewer for the *Gentleman's Magazine* concluded his remarks on *Hermesianax* by writing, 'We need not add, that a writer like this may justly be added with the Toups and Marklands of the age' (1784). Among Weston's many other works, other than travel literature, are translations from Chinese, Persian, and other languages, classical emendations, poems, biography, theological treatises, philological studies, and pieces on antiquarian subjects. Many of his works are of short compass, making understandable the great number of them. Thus, the reviewer of his *Conquest of the Miao-tsé; an Imperial Poem* … in the *Quarterly Review* could write:

the appearance of the translation of another Chinese work; small, indeed, in point of bulk, and trifling in comparative importance, but more difficult in as much as poetry, in proportion as it becomes more concise and condensed, is more intricate and obscure than plain prose … we do not think that Mr. Weston has exercised much judgment in the choice of a subject for the employment of his talents; or that the results of his labours will prove eminently useful to the general cause of literature.   (QR, 361)

Taking into account his contributions to journals, there was virtually no year in the period of his life from 1783 until 1818 in which Weston did not have something published.

Weston's contributions to Archaeologia began in 1800 and were published almost yearly up to 1818, occasionally to the number of two or more in some years. So, too, with his letters to the Gentleman's Magazine, some twenty in number (there are three uncertain attributions), beginning in 1783 with a 'Query for explication of lines in "Battle of Hastings"', signed 'S. W.' (GM, 53/1, 1783, 123), and ending in 1813 with the anonymous 'The tears of the booksellers' (GM, 1st ser., 83/1, 1813, 160). The 1783 'Query' was answered by Thomas Holt White. Weston's letters are on a variety of subjects, with most dealing with classical literature and most carrying his initials, although he also employed some pseudonyms.

Weston was also a Shakespearian scholar, albeit a minor one. He contributed twenty-four notes on eighteen of Shakespeare's plays to the 1785 Shakespeare edition, edited by Isaac Reed. In the first sentence of his advertisement to his Short Notes on Shakespeare, by Way of Supplement to Johnson, Steevens, Malone, and Douce (1808) Weston states, mistakenly, that he had contributed to Steevens's 1793 Shakespeare. He wrote:

> Mr. Steevens having done me the honour to give a few notes of mine a place under the signature of S. W. among the chosen band of commentators in his very correct edition of Shakespeare, 1793, which I consider the temple of his fame; I venture to add a few more for the purpose of showing, among other things, how the antients and our own poet have thought, and express themselves alike, without imitation on the part of Shakespeare, most certainly, for whom they were not translated, and who had no power of reading the originals.

On 7 July 1797 Steevens had successfully proposed Weston as a candidate for membership in The Club, and it may be that Weston wished, retrospectively, to link his name with Steevens's. There are sixty notes on many of the plays in the canon. Unlike many of his contemporaries, Weston was chary of emendations, both in the 1785 Shakespeare and in his Short Notes. Among other matters, his notes reflect his extensive travel on the continent, his intimate knowledge of the classics, and his eye for detail. Although one modern editor of Shakespeare's plays thought Weston's Short Notes of little value, they throw additional light on the extent of his widespread learning—and on his need to associate himself with some of his better-known contemporaries. Most of Weston's library was sold by Robert Harding Evans of Pall Mall in 1827. Weston died in Edward Street, Portman Square, London, on 8 January 1830.   ARTHUR SHERBO

Sources DNB · Reports on the manuscripts of the earl of Eglinton, HMC, 10 (1885) · N&Q, 7th ser., 9 (1890), 26–7 · GM, 1st ser., 83/1 (1813), 160 · GM, 1st ser., 54 (1784), 276–7 · GM, 1st ser., 100/1 (1830), 370–73 · QR,

4 (1810), 361–72 · private information (2004) [M. Vaulbert de Chantilly]
Archives BL, letters to C. P. Yorke, Add. MS 45038 · BM, MS notes by Weston in G. Uskefield's In Euripides Heccham, 11705. cc. 40 · Bodl. Oxf., corresp. with Isaac D'Israeli · Folger, letters to George Steevens, MS c. b. 10, items 174, 180
Likenesses D. Turner, etching, 1828 · Harding, print · oils, Exeter College, Oxford · print (after bust by Behnes, 1824)

Weston, Thomas (d. 1644×7), merchant and colonial adventurer, played a leading role in supporting and setting out the pilgrims who settled Plymouth plantation in New England during 1620. His earlier trading activities in the Netherlands were halted by the privy council, following complaints from the Merchant Adventurers that he was trading without licence. On 20 February 1620, through the influence of a business associate, John Peirce, he acquired a patent from the Virginia Company enabling him to establish a plantation in the colony. Later in the year he went to Leiden offering to support the leaders of the English congregation, with whom he was previously acquainted, who were then considering emigrating to America with Dutch support. With a group of associates, Weston was prepared to set out the pilgrims, promising that 'they should … neither fear want of shipping nor money' (Bradford, 37). Following the pilgrims' acceptance of Weston's proposals, he returned to London to organize their voyage to America. He hired the Mayflower and acquired a group of additional settlers to accompany the original party of thirty-five from Leiden.

Weston has been criticized for the rigorous conditions he imposed on the pilgrims, but his support for them was primarily commercial. He also had to take account of the interests of his partners: according to John Smith they numbered about seventy merchants, gentlemen, and artisans (Bradford, 37). When the pilgrims' leaders refused to accept a revised set of conditions presented to them in England, Weston was 'much offended and told them they must then look to stand on their own legs' (ibid., 49). After their safe arrival in New England, where they decided to stay instead of sailing on to Virginia, he set out the Fortune with thirty-five new settlers, which arrived at Plymouth in November 1621 with a patent from the recently established Council for New England for the pilgrims' settlement. The ship was laden with a return cargo of clapboards and beaver skins valued at £500. By 1622, however, the London partnership had started to disintegrate. Weston sold his adventure and debts in the venture and advised William Bradford, now governor of Plymouth, to break away from the joint stock.

Later in 1622 Weston set out a small colonizing expedition to establish a plantation near Plymouth, under the leadership of his brother Andrew and his brother-in-law Richard Greene. His aim seems to have been to combine fishing and trade along the coast of New England. Although the pilgrims assisted the fifty or sixty men who arrived at Plymouth in June 1622, they were an unwelcome, if not undesirable, presence in the colony. They went on to establish a small plantation at Wessagusset, but their disorderly behaviour, fed by rumours that one of the chief leaders in the settlement kept Native American women, alarmed Bradford, who later dismissed them as 'heathenish Christians' (Bradford, 375). Wessagusset, however, was also a potential rival for trade with the indigenous people, which the pilgrims were then developing. After a difficult winter, Weston's men apparently quarrelled with the Native Americans, and had to be rescued by an expedition from Plymouth. Most of the survivors subsequently returned to England.

Shortly after the collapse of Wessagusset, Weston arrived at Plymouth, alone and without supplies, having sailed from England with some fishermen 'under another name', disguised as a blacksmith (Bradford, 119). With Bradford's assistance he began to trade along the coast. When Robert Gorges arrived in Plymouth in September 1623, with a commission from the Council for New England to act as governor of the entire region, Weston was summoned to answer charges concerning the illegal export of ordnance from England and the behaviour of his men at Wessagusset. The charges were not pursued, partly through Bradford's mediation, and Weston was allowed to resume his trading activities. Bradford later complained that Weston repaid his help with nothing more than 'reproaches and evil words' (ibid., 120).

In 1624 Weston moved to Virginia where he acquired a plantation and sat in the house of burgesses in 1628. His career in the colony remains shadowy, though he was apparently in trouble with the colonial authorities on several occasions. In 1642 he moved on to neighbouring Maryland where he acquired a grant of 1200 acres for Westbury Manor, and became a freeman and member of the assembly. Thereafter he returned to England and died at Bristol some time between 1644 and 1647. He was survived by one daughter, Elizabeth, who married Roger Conant of Marblehead.

Weston emerges from Bradford's *History of Plymouth Plantation* as an enterprising, if unscrupulous, adventurer, whose religious sympathy for the pilgrims was tempered by commercial considerations. Modern authorities have treated him more leniently; at least one has argued that the history of the pilgrims might have taken a very different course but for his support in 1620 (Andrews, 1.331).

JOHN C. APPLEBY

Sources W. Bradford, *Of Plymouth Plantation, 1620–1647*, ed. S. E. Morison (1952) · E. Winslow, 'Good newes from New England', *Chronicles of the pilgrim fathers of the colony of Plymouth, from 1602 to 1625*, ed. A. Young, 2nd edn (1844) · CSP col., vol. 1 · APC, 1621–3 · W. L. Grant and J. F. Munro, eds., *Acts of the privy council of England: colonial series*, 1: 1613–80 (1908) · DAB · C. M. Andrews, *The colonial period of American history*, 1 (1937) · B. Smith, *Bradford of Plymouth* (1951) · A. Young, ed., *Chronicles of the first planters of the colony of Massachusetts Bay, from 1623 to 1636* (1846) · R. A. Preston, *Gorges of Plymouth Fort: a life of Sir Ferdinando Gorges, captain of Plymouth Fort, governor of New England, and lord of the province of Maine* (1953) · R. G. Usher, *The pilgrims and their history* (1918) · F. Jennings, *The invasion of America: Indians, colonialism, and the cant of conquest* (1975) · N. Salisbury, *Manitou and providence: Indians, Europeans, and the making of New England, 1500–1643* (1982)

Archives PRO, customs accounts · PRO, colonial, state papers

Wealth at death died heavily in debt: Bradford, *History of Plymouth*, ed. Morison, 37n.

Weston, Thomas (1737–1776), actor, was the son of Thomas Weston, a cook to the court of George II. He obtained a position as turn-broach under his father but was dismissed for misbehaviour and sent to sea instead as a midshipman aboard the *Warspite*. Life in the navy proved to be distasteful to him, though, and at the first opportunity he managed to get himself discharged and joined a group of strolling players near London. It is believed that about 1759 he was performing at Bartholomew fair in a booth owned by Shuter and Yates. He made his first appearance on a London stage on 28 September 1759, playing Sir Francis Gripe in Susannah Centlivre's *The Busy Body* at the Haymarket. Shortly after this he married a milliner named Martha, whom he encouraged onto the stage. They parted by mutual consent two years later but were reunited in the 1770s. The marriage produced no children.

Weston was not billed again in London until 28 June 1760, when he appeared at the Haymarket once more as Dick in Samuel Foote's *The Minor*, and in the interim he is likely to have returned to playing the provinces. By the winter he was at Henry Mossop's Smock Alley Theatre in Dublin, where he appeared for the first time on 17 November 1760. In the summer of 1761 he was engaged by Arthur Murphy and Foote, who had rented the Drury Lane Theatre for twenty-three performances. Here he played Dick once more, and took on new roles such as Brush in Murphy's *All in the Wrong* (on 15 June), Dapper in Murphy's *The Citizen* (2 July), and the Doctor in Thomas Bentley's *The Wishes* (27 July). Playing every night over the summer, he caught the attention of David Garrick, who offered him a contract at Drury Lane for the coming season. Here he added to his repertory Jeremy in William Congreve's *Love for Love*, Butler in Joseph Addison's *The Drummer*, Charino in Colley Cibber's *Love Makes a Man*, and Shallow in *The Merry Wives of Windsor*. He also played Polonius to Garrick's Hamlet there on 14 October 1761. For the summer of 1762 he returned to the Haymarket to take on the roles of Papillon in Foote's *The Lyar* and Mr Honeycombe in George Colman's *Polly Honeycombe*.

Weston's name is absent from playbills for the 1762–3 season, and he was probably once more playing in the provinces. He joined Foote again at the Haymarket for the summer season in 1763 to take on the part of the henpecked husband Jerry Sneak in *The Mayor of Garratt*, a role written for him by Foote and in which he enjoyed great success. It was also at this time that he first played Scrub in George Farquhar's *The Beaux' Stratagem*, a part which became his most memorable. By now he had earned himself a respectable reputation as an actor, and he was able to consolidate this during the 1763–4 season at Drury Lane with strong performances as Foresight in *Love for Love*, Sharp in Garrick's *The Lying Valet*, and Abel Drugger in Ben Jonson's *The Alchemist*. He then disappeared from all playbills for two years, perhaps as a result of a need to dodge creditors, and resurfaced in June 1766 once more at the Haymarket, playing three roles in *The Minor*. He joined his

Thomas Weston (1737–1776), by Thomas Parkinson, 1772 [as Billy Button in *The Maid of Bath* by Samuel Foote]

wife at the King's Theatre in August and then returned to Drury Lane as the Sexton in *Much Ado about Nothing* on 23 October.

Between 1766 and 1769 Weston does not seem to have been cast quite so frequently and added relatively few characters to his portfolio. The parts he did take on were not always as significant as he might have wished, and this may have been due, to some degree, to the rivalry for attention he must have had to tolerate from the great comic actor Ned Shuter at both Drury Lane and the Haymarket. During this period Weston adopted the roles of Gripe in Thomas Otway's *The Cheats of Scapin*, Roderigo in *Othello* (both in the summer of 1767), and Dr Last in Foote's comedy *The Devil upon Two Sticks* (30 May 1768). Some of the Haymarket company, Weston included, transferred to a new Edinburgh theatre for the winter season 1770–71. Here he added Paris in Colman's *The Jealous Wife*, Sir Harry Sycamore in Isaac Bickerstaff's *The Maid of the Mill*, and Tom in Richard Steele's *The Funeral* to his repertory. After a brief stint in York he returned to the Haymarket on 5 May 1771 for a heavy summer's schedule of more than sixty performances. He then alternated between Drury Lane and the Haymarket until his death in January 1776.

There is uncertainty surrounding the precise date of Weston's demise. It was first announced in the *Public Advertiser* of 3 January 1776 that he had died on 31 December 1775, but the *Morning Post* of 13 January assigned his death to 12 January, at Newington Butts, London. The *Public Advertiser* of 16 January then agreed with the *Morning Post*. The funeral probably at St James's, Clerkenwell, however, did not take place until 21 January, suggesting an even later date for the death. The cause of death, though, is not disputed and is put down to Weston's excessive drinking.

Drunkenness and illness marked his last years, and his death did not come unexpectedly. In a letter to his brother dated 7 November, Garrick stated that it was clear that 'Weston is dying, & with him goes a good Actor, & a very bad Man' (*Letters*, 3.1046). By December it became clear to Weston that he was unlikely to climb onto the stage again, and though he made plans to spend time at the spa in Bath he was never to make the journey.

A mock will, credited to Weston, the contents of which were as acrimonious as they were witty, was circulated shortly after his death and published in the third volume of *Dramatic Table Talk*. In it Weston was purported to have left Garrick all his money, 'as there is nothing on earth he is so very fond of'; to Foote he bequeathed his consequence, to Reddish a grain of honesty, to Brereton a small portion of modesty, and to Jacobs his shoes 'for which he has long waited' (Holcroft, 2.122–3). This will was refuted by Martha Weston and Richard Hughes in the *Morning Post* of 12 February 1776, where the contents of the genuine will were also printed.

As an actor Weston was an accomplished comedian and excelled in the parts of fools and clowns. Among his contemporaries, only Ned Shuter (who had been bequeathed Weston's example in the mock will) offered him any significant rivalry. Thomas Holcroft, in his *Theatrical Recorder*, recalled his ability to assume a character completely and to perform 'with such a consistent and peculiar humour, it was so entirely distinct from anything we call acting, and so perfect a resemblance of the person whom the pencil of the poet had depicted' (Holcroft, 2.120). It was this skill that caused Davies to couple Weston with Benjamin Johnson as the only men who became 'so truly absorbed in character, that they never lost sight of it' (Davies, 2.106). He also placed his interpretation of Abel Drugger on a par with Garrick's who, though he himself excelled in the role, declared that Weston's work was one of the greatest pieces of comic acting he had ever witnessed. When the two men played opposite one another in *The Beaux' Stratagem*, Garrick, as Archer, could hardly keep a straight face against Weston as Scrub. Weston's friend Francis Gentleman held his acting in great esteem and, in his *Dramatic Censor* (1770), praised his work in a number of roles.

MARK BATTY

Sources T. Holcroft, *The theatrical recorder*, 2 vols. (1805–6), vol. 2 · Genest, *Eng. stage* · T. Davies, *Dramatic miscellanies*, 3 vols. (1784) · W. C. Russell, *Representative actors* [1888] · *The letters of David Garrick*, ed. D. M. Little and G. M. Kahrl, 3 vols. (1963) · Highfill, Burnim & Langhans, *BDA*

Likenesses J. Zoffany, oils, 1769, Castle Howard, North Yorkshire · T. Parkinson, oils, 1772, Garr. Club [*see illus.*] · U.-L. De-Faesch, ink and watercolour drawing, Folger · R. Dighton, ink and watercolour drawing, BM · theatrical prints, BM, NPG

Weston, Walter (1860–1940), mountaineer and missionary, was born on 25 December 1860 at 22 Parker Street, Derby, the sixth son of John Weston, elastic manufacturer, and his wife, Emma Butland. He was educated at

Derby School (1876–1880), where for some years he held the record for the mile run (4 min. 47 sec.), and Clare College, Cambridge, where he graduated BA in 1883, and proceeded MA in 1887. After study at Ridley Hall, Cambridge, he was ordained deacon in 1885 and priest in 1886, and was appointed to the curacy of St John's, Reading, in 1885. He climbed extensively in the Alps in 1886 and 1887. In 1888 he began work for the Church Missionary Society at Kumamoto, Japan, and served as British chaplain in Kobe from 1889 to 1895.

Weston climbed Fuji in 1890 and soon travelled and climbed throughout Japan, which he described in *Mountaineering and Exploration in the Japanese Alps* (1896); this was later translated into Japanese. He worked for a year as assistant chaplain with the missions to seamen at the port of London, and for five years beginning in 1897 was priest in charge at Christ Church, Wimbledon, Surrey. On 3 April 1902 he married Frances Emily (1872–1937), the second daughter of Sir Francis *Fox, civil engineer, of Wimbledon. She also became a well-known climber. They lived in Yokohama from 1902 to 1905 as missionaries for the Society for the Propagation of the Gospel. He then served as vicar of Ewell, Surrey, until 1911, when he returned to Yokohama as British chaplain until 1915.

After resettling in London, Weston was recognized as an authority on Japanese mountaineering. The Royal Geographical Society awarded him the Back grant for his exploration in Japan in 1917. He published *The Playground of the Far East* (1918), *A Wayfarer in Unfamiliar Japan* (1925), and *Japan* (1926). He was Cambridge University extension lecturer and lecturer for the Gilchrist Educational Trust. He also served on the council of the Japan Society. By the end of his life some British climbers referred to him as 'the father of mountaineering in Japan'. While such rhetoric is clearly hyperbole, Weston was widely respected in Japan. He helped found the Japanese Alpine Club in 1906, and was elected its first honorary member. The Japanese emperor conferred on Weston the order of the Sacred Treasure (fourth class) in 1937, the same year that the Japanese Alpine Club erected a bronze tablet in his honour in the Japanese Alps.

Weston was short and stocky, and blind in one eye throughout his life. Contemporaries described his climbing as tenacious and inspired by his religious views, and remembered him as a generous and devoted chaplain. He died at home at 57 Iverna Court, Kensington, London, on 27 March 1940. After a funeral on 30 March at St Jude's, Courtfield Gardens, South Kensington, he was cremated and interred on 1 April at Putney Vale cemetery.

PETER H. HANSEN

Sources T. A. Rumbold and H. S. Bullock, 'In memoriam: Walter Weston', *Alpine Journal*, 52 (1940), 271–5 · E. H., *GJ*, 95 (1940), 478–9 · *The Times* (29 March 1940) · *GJ*, 90 (1937), 288 [obit. of Frances Emily Weston] · *WW* (1940) · W. Weston, diaries, 1894, Alpine Club Library, London · W. Weston, diaries, 1912–14, Alpine Club Library, London · H. Belcher, scrapbook, 1860–1951, Alpine Club Library, London · W. Weston, correspondence, 1892–1930, RGS · *Derby School register, 1570–1901* (1902) · *The Times* (10 March 1937) · *The Times* (24 June 1937) · Venn, *Alum. Cant.* · b. cert. · m. cert. · d. cert. · *CGPLA Eng. & Wales* (1940)

Archives Alpine Club, London, diary · RGS | Alpine Club, London
Likenesses photograph, *c.*1930, repro. in Rumbold and Bullock, 'In memoriam: Walter Weston'
Wealth at death £1220 11*s*. 11*d*.: probate, 26 Oct 1940, *CGPLA Eng. & Wales*

Weston, Sir William (*b.* after 1469, *d.* 1540), prior of the hospital of St John of Jerusalem in England, was the second son of Sir Edmund Weston (*d.* before 1509) of Boston, governor of Guernsey and esquire of the body to Henry VII, and Katharine (or Kathryn) Lempriere, *née* Camell, of Shapwick, Dorset. His elder brother was the courtier Sir Richard *Weston. He was born in the Jersey manor of Rozel, his mother being the widow of its seigneur, Renaud Lempriere. On reaching adulthood William continued the remarkable family tradition of service to the order of St John. Two of his uncles and two of his great-uncles had been hospitallers, his great-uncle William Dawney and uncle John Weston both becoming turcopoliers (coastguard commanders) of Rhodes, and the latter prior of England between 1476 and 1489. Although William Weston perhaps joined the order in his uncle's lifetime, he does not appear in its records until 1498, when he attended a general chapter at Rhodes. By this time he was a preceptor, responsible for one of the order's houses, probably that of Ansty in Wiltshire. In 1504, while he was still in Rhodes, William was granted the Cambridgeshire estate of Sawston by the grand master, Émery d'Amboise. Two years later he was among those praised for providing hospitality to the party of Sir Richard Guildford on its way to the Holy Land. Soon after he was promoted to be preceptor of the Hampshire house of Baddesley, which he returned to England to administer in 1510. He remained there until summoned to attend the general chapter held in Rhodes in 1517, and was in the Aegean for the next five years.

During the Turkish siege of Rhodes in 1522 Weston commanded the post of England, which was the scene of some of the heaviest fighting of the conflict, and lost a finger to an arquebusier's shot on 24 September. He may have been more seriously injured than this would suggest, as charge of the English post was then bestowed elsewhere. By the time of the order's departure from the island, on 1 January 1523, however, he was sufficiently recovered to be given command of the order's great ship, which he conducted to Crete. Elected turcopolier there in February, Weston was soon granted expectancy to the priorate of England and returned home. In the following year he was sent by Henry VIII to Italy to deliver 50,000 écus to the duc de Bourbon. Having had some difficulty discharging this responsibility, he went on to the order's convent, then at Viterbo, and remained there until June 1527, when he was elected prior of England after the death of Sir Thomas Docwra. He returned home and managed to defuse Henry VIII's threats to confiscate the order's lands, or transfer its personnel to Calais, by a discreet bribe of £4000, following which the king ostentatiously granted a similar sum towards the recovery of Rhodes.

During the first years of his priorate Weston was preoccupied with the recovery of Sir Thomas Docwra's effects from the latter's family and servants, and with the handover of the prioral estate of Sandford (Oxfordshire) to Cardinal College, Oxford. Once he had established himself the priory suffered heavily from the legislation of the Reformation Parliament, especially the Act of First Fruits and Tenths (1534), which Weston opposed from the Lords. In non-financial matters, however, he obediently toed the line, signing the Act of Succession of 1534, and agreeing to the letters patent which subjected all English members of the order to royal control in 1538. Despite this he was always regarded as a conservative by the crown, and was employed on less government business than his predecessor had been. In 1539 he suffered a major blow with the execution of his favoured nephew, Sir Thomas *Dingley, for treason, and when the order was dissolved in 1540 he expired, at the priory of St John, Clerkenwell, Middlesex, on 7 May, the day the act passed through the Commons. He was buried in the old nunnery church of St Mary, Clerkenwell, later the church of St James. Although his elaborate marble tomb was largely destroyed during the rebuilding of the church in 1788, an exceptionally fine cadaver figure from it has survived, and is conserved in the hospital's former priory church, now in the hands of the order of St John.

G. J. O'MALLEY

Sources National Library of Malta, archives of the knights [vols. 36, 54, 57, 80–86, 284, 286, 395–417] · *LP Henry VIII* · A. Luders and others, eds., *Statutes of the realm*, 11 vols. in 12, RC (1810–28), vol. 3 · H. P. Scicluna, ed., *The book of deliberations of the venerable tongue of England, 1523–1567* (1949) · G. Bosio, *Dell'istoria della sacra religione e ill.ma militia di San Giovanni Gierosolimitano*, 2nd edn, 3 vols. (1621–84) · G. R. Balleine, *A biographical dictionary of Jersey*, [1] [1948] · W. B. Bannerman, ed., *The visitations of the county of Surrey … 1530 … 1572 … 1623*, Harleian Society, 43 (1899) · *The begynnynge and foundacyon of the holy hospitall & of the ordre of the knyghtes hospytallers of Saynt Johan baptyst of Jerusalem* (1524) · A. Mifsud, *Knights hospitallers of the ven. tongue of England in Malta* (1914) · J. Caley and J. Hunter, eds., *Valor ecclesiasticus temp. Henrici VIII*, 6 vols., RC (1810–34) · special collections Minister's Accounts, PRO, SC 6/Henry VIII/2402 · W. J. Pinks, *The history of Clerkenwell*, ed. E. J. Wood (1865) · *Hall's chronicle*, ed. H. Ellis (1809), 838 · BL, MS Cotton Vesp. E. VI · BL, Lansdowne MS 200 · *DNB*

Likenesses tomb sculpture, Church of St John of Jerusalem, Clerkenwell, London

Wealth at death £2385 19s. 11¾d.—gross annual income: Caley and Hunter, eds., *Valor ecclesiasticus*, 1.403–6, 1535 · £2464 15s. 11½d.—gross annual income: PRO SC 6/Henry VIII/2402 (1539–40), 1540

Weston [*alias* Edmunds, Hunt], **William** (1549/50–1615), Jesuit, was born in Maidstone, Kent. Nothing is known of his family.

Education and noviciate According to most sources, he was educated at Oxford, though there is no clear evidence for this in the university registers. He has been assumed to be the William Weston who was admitted to Christ Church in 1564 and obtained his BA on 17 February 1569. He may have been at Lincoln's Inn in 1570. He was already a Catholic when he moved to Paris in 1571 to continue his studies. At Paris he was invited to come to the newly founded English College at Douai. He went there in 1572 and received minor orders, together with other seminarists, at Brussels the next year. At Douai he crossed the path of Edmund Campion, who then left for Rome to become a Jesuit. In the summer of 1575 Weston made his pilgrimage on foot to Rome, and on 5 November, aged twenty-five, he entered the Jesuit noviciate at Sant' Andrea; Robert Persons and Henry Garnet had also joined that year. The next eight years Weston spent in Spain. He completed his noviciate in Montilla and studied philosophy and theology at Córdoba for three years. After having been ordained priest in 1579, he worked in San Lucar and Cadiz and taught Greek at the English College at Seville from 1582 to 1584.

English mission The first Jesuits, Campion and Persons, arrived in England in 1580 and began their efforts to organize the mission. In 1581, after the publication of *Decem rationes*, Campion was executed at Tyburn and Persons had to flee the country. Despite these early set-backs and the intensified persecution of Catholics in the 1580s, English priests continued to be sent to their home country from the seminaries. In 1583 Weston received a summons to go to Paris from his general, Claudio Acquaviva, but he could leave Seville only after the winter. In Paris in 1584 he learned from Persons that he was to be sent to England as a missionary (on Persons's recommendation). Weston was apprehensive when on 12 June he wrote to Acquaviva accepting his mission, fearing the cruelties of torture and execution. He assumed the alias of Edmunds out of respect for Campion.

After spending about three months with Persons in Paris, Weston left the city on 26 August 1584. On 10 September he landed on the Norfolk coast, accompanied by Ralph Emerson, the Jesuit lay brother who had been Campion's companion. However, within two weeks Emerson was arrested for bringing over Catholic books and committed to the Poultry prison. He was to languish in English prisons for twenty years. Weston's first deeds in England were the conversion to Roman Catholicism of Philip Howard, earl of Arundel, and a brave visit to the Tower to see the Jesuit priest Jasper Heywood, together with Heywood's sister Elizabeth and her son, the subsequently famous poet John Donne: 'So I accompanied her to the Tower, but with a feeling of great trepidation as I saw the vast battlements, and was led by the warder past the gates with their iron fastenings, which were closed behind me' (*Autobiography*, 10–11). Heywood was exiled in 1585 and Weston succeeded him as superior of the Jesuits in England, facing the difficult task of organizing the mission. For some time no other Jesuit was at liberty in England.

In 1585 the act against all priests was passed, making it treason for any priest to be in England and felony punishable by death for anyone who helped or harboured missionaries. Weston later commented:

As far as I was concerned, I thought it would be well to retire myself to some place where I could judge from my own observation the way things were likely to go. I would be able then to see how Catholics thought and felt: whether they would retain their old loyalty to the faith, search out priests, ask them to their houses and maintain them; or whether they would keep them at a distance and agree to be abandoned by them in a time of such peril. Far better, I thought, that they should invite or summon me to them, than that I should thrust myself on them and have them risk their lives and property for my sake. (*Autobiography*, 22–3)

In April he attended a conference of Catholic gentry and seminary priests at Hoxton, near London. It was decided that priests were to stay at inns, and a fund to support them was established by the gentry.

Exorcisms During the years 1585–6 Weston and a group of secular priests were involved in the practice of exorcism. Though it was not popular among the priests of the Counter-Reformation, an interest in demonology was not unusual, and the priests concerned may have been influenced by public exorcisms practised in France. Weston was convinced of the power of God to cure demoniacs through the Catholic church and the priest–exorcist. He felt people wanted such public exorcisms and, as a proselytizer, thought it possible thus to confirm waverers in their faith. The exorcisms have been presented as a conversion campaign, based on the unreliable confessions of Anthony Tyrrell, a priest–exorcist turned informer, who spoke of a total of at least 500 conversions. Weston's exorcisms, however, all took place in recusants' private houses, mostly that of Sir George Peckham of Denham, Buckinghamshire, and were on a considerably smaller scale.

At this time rumours were spread of a connection between the Denham exorcisms conducted by Weston, John Cornelius, Robert Dibdale, and possibly John Ballard, and the Babington plot, an intricate affair involving Walsingham's machinations against Mary, queen of Scots. Ballard (former companion of Tyrrell) was a main conspirator of a group plotting the assassination of Queen Elizabeth, a Spanish invasion, and the installation of Mary as queen of Britain. The affluent gentleman Anthony Babington and his romantic associates hoped to free their beloved queen from prison, at first without any idea of regicide. Babington possibly visited the Denham exorcisms, and his servant Nicholas Marwood was Weston's first demoniac. The government allowed the exorcisms to continue in the hope of implicating a wider circle of Catholics while waiting for the best moment to explode the manipulated plot and damage the reputation and the organization of English Catholicism. In June 1586 the house at Denham was raided and the prisons were prepared for the Babington arrests.

After the Hoxton conference Weston had help from two new arrivals. The Jesuits Henry Garnet and Robert Southwell landed in England on 7 July 1586 and Weston met them in London on 13 July. On the same day or the next morning Babington sought Weston's advice on the difficult situation in which he had landed himself. Weston understood he needed to dissociate himself from the foolhardy Babington and took the newly arrived Jesuits to Harlesford, near Marlow, Buckinghamshire, the home of his friend Richard Bold. Here a conference crucial to the development and organization of the English mission took place from 14 to 23 July. From his first days in England Weston had worked to maintain and build on the network of Catholic gentry contacts, and he compiled a list of private hiding-places for the incoming priests. His work, together with the new instructions from Rome, formed the basis of the continued missionary effort. He spent happy days at Harlesford, where there was time for friendship, prayer and mass in the chapel, and musical performances by members of Bold's household. The composer William Byrd was also among the company.

Imprisonment Soon after the Harlesford meeting, on 3 August 1586, Weston was arrested outside Bishopsgate and imprisoned in a private house near the Clink prison. He had been recognized by Walsingham's spy Nicholas Berden, but his arrest had not been planned. In fact this was the beginning of the round-up of the Babington plot. Ballard was arrested the next day and Weston was locked up in order to avoid alarming Babington, who was arrested on 14 August. Though Walsingham had spread rumours of Weston's complicity, at a later stage he appears to have instructed his agents not to associate influential priests with the plot. Yet the government perhaps hoped that Weston would become involved. After the trials and executions of the conspirators in September Weston was transferred to the Clink prison. His friends the priests John Lowe, John Adams, and Robert Dibdale were executed at Tyburn on 8 October. Weston was left to wonder why his trial was delayed, reflecting every day on his possibly imminent death. Shortly before the execution of Mary, queen of Scots, on 8 February 1587 Weston was interviewed by a clerk of the privy council, mostly about the exorcisms, but he was never brought to trial.

In January 1588 Weston was moved to Wisbech Castle, the prison for notable Catholics in Cambridgeshire, where he was kept in isolation for the first four years. After this period conditions in the prison improved, and the priests could move about and receive visitors. Weston played a considerable part in organizing the priests' common life under the difficult circumstances in prison. Initially, a group of some eighteen secular priests set up rules for the confraternity and wished Weston, the only Jesuit, to be their leader. Garnet, who had succeeded Weston as superior in England, allowed Weston moral leadership but no authority over the priests. Tensions developed between Weston's group and another led by the secular priest Christopher Bagshaw. The situation deteriorated after the death of Cardinal Allen in 1594. A long series of disputes and attempts at reconciliation ensued, but the prison community remained divided. The Wisbech stirs, as these quarrels became known, had at their core an anti-Jesuit impetus which centred on the Jesuit Weston's alleged ambition to domineer over the seculars. They were no isolated event. During the 1580s Jesuit–secular friction had occurred in the English College at Rome and in Flanders. The idea took hold that the Jesuits, who were in charge of most of the seminaries, wanted absolute control over the English mission. Following the appointment of the first arch-priest George Blackwell (with jurisdiction over the secular clergy) next to the Jesuit superior Garnet in 1598 issues of the English mission, such as toleration of

Catholics, political allegiance, and Jesuit presence in England, were debated in the bitter confrontations of the arch-priest controversy. The Wisbech stirs were a prelude to this serious disruption in English Catholic relations.

In December 1598 Weston was taken to the Tower and locked in solitary confinement for five years. He suffered from insomnia, headaches, increasing blindness, loneliness, and quite possibly also mental illness. The reason for this move was not given, but the guards accompanying Weston to the Tower told him:

> that I had meddled in Spanish politics and favoured the Spanish party ... They felt certain that unless I was put out of the way and had my mouth stopped, they would never be able to come to a decision on the matters which they had set in motion. Let that suffice for the affairs of Wisbech.
> (*Autobiography*, 192–4)

In July 1598, before Weston's transfer, a manuscript compilation known as Weston's 'Book of miracles' was discovered. This work came into the hands of the bishop of London, Richard Bancroft, who, with his chaplain Samuel Harsnett, was involved in a campaign against the puritan exorcist John Darrell. Darrell was condemned as a fraud in 1599. As the appellants sought negotiations with the government, Bancroft and the privy council, aiming to divide the Catholics, collected their papers and supported the publications of the appellant polemicists, among them Bagshaw's *True Relation of the Faction Begun at Wisbich* (1601), which incriminated Weston and the Jesuits. In 1602 Bancroft and Harsnett became interested in exposing the exorcisms at Denham as related in the 'Book of miracles', and an inquiry was started sixteen years after they had taken place. Thus Harsnett's satirical *Declaration of Egregious Popish Impostures* (1603), while forming part of a series of attacks on Darrell's practices, cleared the bishop of the charge that he was concerned only with suppressing puritans and revealed not just its anti-Jesuitism, but also Bancroft's interest in manipulating the arch-priest controversy. Harsnett's work, as well as tracts of the arch-priest controversy, were used by Shakespeare, especially in *King Lear*, written in 1604–5, bringing the Denham devils Fliberdigibbet and Frateretto, among others, universal fame.

Exile and death After the accession of James I in 1603 Weston was given a choice between taking the oath of allegiance and exile on the continent. He chose exile and was released from the Tower on 13 May. He probably never saw Harsnett's *Declaration* published that summer. Weston recovered his health somewhat at St Omer. He went to Rome in 1604 and worked for a few months at the English College of St Alban's at Valladolid as spiritual prefect. In 1605, a year before his friend Henry Garnet's execution after the Gunpowder Plot, Weston left for Seville, where he worked as spiritual director of the English College and resumed lecturing on theology, Hebrew, and Greek. Here he met Francisco de Peralta, the college superior and an old friend from his years in Córdoba, who was to write his biography. In 1611 Weston started his autobiography at the request of his general and related his experiences as a missionary in England. Written with

restraint and containing interesting observations, it is a valuable firsthand account of Tudor England. The only complete copy was translated into English by Philip Caraman.

Weston stayed at Seville until 1614, when he was made rector of the English College of St Alban's at Valladolid. Here he died after a brief illness between 14 and 19 April 1615. His reputation suffered considerably and unjustly from the appellant publications which long influenced writers on the Catholic controversies from Charles Dodd to T. G. Law. Testimony of friends, the autobiography, and the few extant letters by Weston naturally create a different, at times also too saintly, impression of the man. Modern commentators (though not always in agreement) have offered a fairer estimate of his character and activities.

THEODOR HARMSEN

Sources *William Weston: the autobiography of an Elizabethan*, trans. P. Caraman (1955) · 'The life of Father William Weston, S.J.', *The troubles of our Catholic forefathers related by themselves*, ed. J. Morris, 2 (1875), 1–284; repr. (1970) · P. Renold, ed., *The Wisbech stirs, 1595–1598*, Catholic RS, 51 (1958) · S. Harsnet, *A declaration of egregious popish impostures ... practised by Edmunds, alias Weston* (1603); repr. in F. W. Brownlow, *Shakespeare, Harsnett and the devils of Denham* (1993) · 'The conclusion of the autobiography of Fr William Weston, SJ, 1589–1603', ed. J. H. Pollen, *Miscellanea, I*, Catholic RS, 1 (1905), 72–85 · F. W. Brownlow, *Shakespeare, Harsnett and the devils of Denham* (1993) · A. Pritchard, *Catholic loyalism in Elizabethan England* (1979), chap. 5 · T. G. Law, ed., *A historical sketch of the conflicts between Jesuits and seculars in the reign of Queen Elizabeth* (1889) · T. M. McCoog, *The Society of Jesus in Ireland, Scotland, and England, 1541–1588* (1996), chap. 4 · B. Basset, *The English Jesuits, from Campion to Martindale* (1967), 102–4 · T. F. Knox and others, eds., *The first and second diaries of the English College, Douay* (1878), 5, 18, 24, 103 · Stonyhurst College, Stonyhurst, Lancashire · Society of Jesus, Rome · T. M. McCoog, *English and Welsh Jesuits, 1555–1650*, 2, Catholic RS, 75 (1995) · APC, *1542–1631* · T. H. B. M. Harmsen, *John Gee's Foot out of the snare* (1624) (1992) · *CSP dom., 1558–1603* · E. Henson, ed., *The registers of the English College at Valladolid, 1589–1862*, Catholic RS, 30 (1930), xxiii–xxiv · *The Elizabethan Jesuits: Historia missionis Anglicanae Societatis Jesu (1660) of Henry More*, ed. and trans. F. Edwards (1981) · H. Foley, ed., *Records of the English province of the Society of Jesus*, 7 (1882–3), 830 · Wood, *Ath. Oxon.*, new edn, 2.576 · M. Murphy, *St Gregory's College, Seville, 1592–1767*, Catholic RS, 73 (1992) · L. Hicks, ed., *Letters and memorials of Father Robert Persons*, Catholic RS, 39 (1942), 252, 265, 271, 335 · P. Milward, *Religious controversies of the Elizabethan age* (1977) · Foster, *Alum. Oxon.* · J. H. Pollen, ed., *Unpublished documents relating to the English martyrs*, 1, Catholic RS, 5 (1908), 308 · J. H. Pollen, ed., 'Official lists of Catholic prisoners during the reign of Queen Elizabeth', *Miscellanea, II*, Catholic RS, 2 (1906), 219–88, esp. 253, 257, 268 · M. E. Williams, *St Alban's College, Valladolid: four centuries of English Catholic presence in Spain* (1986) · T. G. Law, ed., *The archpriest controversy: documents relating to the dissensions of the Roman Catholic clergy, 1597–1602*, 2 vols., CS, new ser., 56, 58 (1896–8) · T. G. Law, 'Devil hunting in Elizabethan England', *Nineteenth Century*, 35 (1894), 397–411 · J. H. Pollen, 'Supposed cases of diabolic possession in 1585–6', *The Month*, 117 (1911), 449–64 · P. Ryan, ed., 'Diocesan returns of recusants for England and Wales, 1577', *Miscellanea, XII*, Catholic RS, 22 (1921), 1–114, esp. 102

Archives Archivum Romanum Societatis Iesu, Rome, autobiography, MS Anglia 30 II, fols. 517–59 [transcript copy] · Archivum Romanum Societatis Iesu, Rome, MS life of Weston, MS Anglia 8, fols. 216–27v · Scottish Catholic Archives, Edinburgh, Relatio · Stonyhurst College, Lancashire, MS autobiography, MS A IV, 5 · Stonyhurst College, Lancashire, a self-styled transcript of late eighteenth/early nineteenth century, MS A V, 48 | Archivum Romanum Societatis Iesu, Rome, related corresp., Fondo Gesuitico,

651 · Archivum Romanum Societatis Iesu, Rome, corresp. with Acquaviva, Fondo Gesuitico, 651/661 · Stonyhurst College, Lancashire, MSS Anglia · Stonyhurst College, Lancashire, Christopher Grene's copies of Catholic corresp., MSS Collectanea P
Likenesses oils, 1620, St Alban's College, Valladolid, Spain · oils, 1620, Sant' Andrea, Rome · C. Weld, drawing (after portrait), Stonyhurst College · skull, British Province of the Society of Jesus, London
Wealth at death personal possessions to Douai Abbey, Woolhampton, Berkshire: Morris, 'Life of Father William Weston', 1.284

Weston, William [*name in religion* John Baptist] (1654/5–1729), Franciscan friar, joined the English Recollect Franciscans in 1672, and was ordained a priest in 1679. He was a zealous missionary in England for many years and was appointed guardian of the Douai friary on two occasions. He participated in the consecration of the St Amand Chapel for the Eyston family at East Hendred, Berkshire, on 24 September 1687. The chapel was open to all comers until 11 December 1688, when it was raided by 'some loose fellows', but Weston, who happened to be in the district, said mass there again on Monday, 24 June 1689, and the chapel continued in use. He is described as a man who liked solitude and was a strict advocate of a well regulated religious mode of life, given to afflicting his body, and was called an example of true Franciscan humility to everyone. Father Thaddeus praised his description of evangelical poverty, stating that it was scarcely possible to describe it more clearly or accurately.

Weston's book, *An abstract of the doctrine of Jesus-Christ, or, The rule of the frier-minors: literally, morally, and spiritually expounded*, was published in 1718. In some copies it is followed by *A supplement to the abstract, being examples of holy men, drawn from the monuments of the order, and apply'd to each text of the rule*, which dates to 1726. In the preface he declared that his one intention was to promote the observance of the rule *ad litteram, sine glossa*, forgetting that his work was a very long gloss indeed and included the glosses of other writers. He used four earlier expositions of the rule by Antonio of Cordoba (1621), Bonaventure Dernoye (1657), Pierre Marchant (1669), and Gaudentius vanden Kerchove (1700). The dissection of the rule into so-called precepts and counsels was then well under way. He quoted abundantly from the Old and New Testaments, and used the *opuscula* and *legenda* of St Francis, together with the chronicle and the annals of the order. The book was popular, to judge from the number of extant copies in friaries.

In the *facultas* (permission) he is named as *custos custodum*. A Franciscan province, such as England, was made up of many guardianates, divided into a few custodies for administrative purposes, with a *custos* in charge of each; one was chosen to represent and to co-ordinate the work of the others, this post being the one held by Weston. He also wrote a commentary, perhaps unpublished, on the Barcelona general statutes of the order, presumably meaning those promulgated in 1621 by the minister general, Benignus of Genoa, rather than those promulgated by the general chapter in Barcelona in 1461. According to his obituary notice Weston died rather suddenly, if not unexpectedly, aged seventy-four, on 11 April 1729 at Douai, in the friary of the Friars Minor Recollects of England, and was buried in the north end of the cloister there.
IGNATIUS FENNESSY

Sources R. Trappes-Lomax, ed., *The English Franciscan nuns, 1619–1821, and the Friars Minor of the same province, 1618–1761*, Catholic RS, 24 (1922) · Father Thaddeus [F. Hermans], *The Franciscans in England, 1600–1850* (1898) · F. Blom and others, *English Catholic books, 1701–1800: a bibliography* (1996)

Westphal, Sir George Augustus (1785–1875), naval officer, son of George Westphal, of Hanoverian descent, whose uncle was tutor to the duke of Kent, and his wife, *née* McGrigor, widow of Captain Bachop RN, was born on 26 July 1785; Admiral Philip *Westphal was his brother. He entered the navy, under the auspices of the duke of Kent, in 1798 on the frigate *Porcupine*, on the North American station. He afterwards served on the home station and in the West Indies, and in March 1803 joined the *Amphion*, which carried Nelson out to the Mediterranean. Off Toulon he was moved into the *Victory*, and, continuing in her, was present at Trafalgar, where he was severely wounded. While Westphal was lying in the cockpit Nelson's coat, hastily rolled up, was put under his head for a pillow. Some of the bullions of one of the epaulettes got entangled with his hair and was stuck to it with dried blood, so that the coat and Westphal could be separated only by cutting off some four or five of the bullions, which Westphal long treasured as memorials of the hero. He afterwards served in the *Ocean*, flagship of Lord Collingwood, and in the *Caledonia*, flagship of Lord St Vincent, off Brest; and on 15 August 1806 was made lieutenant in the sloop *Demerara* in the West Indies. In 1807 he had to be invalided, and was returning to England in a merchant ship when, after a gallant resistance, she was captured by a French privateer and taken to Guadeloupe. Westphal, who had been severely wounded, afterwards escaped, and was picked up at sea by an American schooner, from which he got on board an English privateer and was taken to Antigua, ultimately returning to England in the frigate *Venus*. He was appointed to the *Foudroyant*, from which he was removed to the *Neptune*, and from her to the *Belle-Isle* in the West Indies, and served on shore at the capture of Martinique. The *Belle-Isle*, under Commodore George Cockburn, then returned to England, and in July and August was employed in the Scheldt, Westphal being in command of a division of the gunboats.

Westphal afterwards followed Cockburn to the *Indefatigable*, and in the expedition to Quiberon Bay in March 1810 had command of the boat which landed the agents of the king of Spain. Continuing in the *Indefatigable*, he took part in the defence of Cadiz and in escorting the Spanish ships to Havana. He was again with Cockburn in the *Marlborough*, both at Cadiz and afterwards in the Chesapeake, where, on several occasions, his gallant conduct was praised by Cockburn, and led to his promotion to commander on 8 July 1813. He then was appointed to the sloop *Anaconda* and commanded her in the Gulf of Mexico and in the expedition against New Orleans, where he was landed with the naval brigade. In July 1815 the *Anaconda* was condemned at Jamaica, and Westphal returned to England as a passenger. He married first, on 8 January 1817, Alicia (d. 1847), daughter of Charles Stuart of Worcester and widow of William Chambers; in 1849 he married Mary Anne, daughter of John Racey of Quebec and widow of George Addenbrooke Gore of Barrowmount, Kilkenny: she survived him. On 12 August 1819 he was promoted captain. In May 1822 he was appointed to the *Jupiter* (60 guns), in which he carried out Lord Amherst to India. On his return he was knighted on 7 April 1824—according to Peel, then home secretary, more for his gallant war service than for taking out the governor-general of Bengal. In 1832 he joined the *Vernon* (50 guns), as flag captain to Sir George Cockburn on the North American station, but was compelled to invalid in the spring of 1834.

Westphal had no further service, but was appointed naval aide-de-camp to the queen in November 1846, and was advanced to rear-admiral on 17 August 1851, vice-admiral on 10 September 1857, and admiral on 23 March 1863. For nearly forty years he lived in the same house, 2 Brunswick Square, Hove, Sussex, and died there on 11 January 1875. He was a magistrate of Brighton and Hove, but seldom sat. Westphal was a brave and resourceful junior commander, and continued selection by Cockburn demonstrated his great abilities as a sea officer.

J. K. LAUGHTON, *rev.* ANDREW LAMBERT

Sources D. Syrett and R. L. DiNardo, *The commissioned sea officers of the Royal Navy, 1660–1815*, rev. edn, Occasional Publications of the Navy RS, 1 (1994) · A. J. Pack, *The man who burnt the White House: Admiral Sir George Cockburn, 1772–1853* (1987) · R. Morriss, *Sir George Cockburn* (1997) · O'Byrne, *Naval biog. dict.* · Boase, *Mod. Eng. biog.* · *Dod's Peerage* (1858) · *The Times* (14 Jan 1875) · *CGPLA Eng. & Wales* (1875)
Likenesses engraving, repro. in *The Graphic*, 11 (1875), 137
Wealth at death under £70,000: probate, 27 Feb 1875, *CGPLA Eng. & Wales*

Westphal, Philip (1782–1880), naval officer, was the elder son of George Westphal, of a noble Hanoverian family, whose uncle was tutor to the duke of Kent, and his wife, *née* McGrigor, widow of Captain Bachop RN; Sir George Augustus *Westphal was his younger brother. He entered the navy in 1794 under the patronage of the duke of Kent, on the *Oiseau* on the North American station. In 1796 he was successively in the *Albatross* and the *Shannon* on the home station, and from 1797 to 1800 in the *Asia* on the coast of North America. In 1801 he was in the *Blanche*, one of the frigates with Nelson at Copenhagen on 2 April. For his share in this action Westphal was promoted on 5 April to lieutenant of the *Defiance* (74 guns). In May 1802 he was appointed to the *Amazon* (38 guns; Captain William Parker) with Nelson off Toulon, and in his cruise to the West Indies in the spring of 1805, and in 1806 with Sir John Borlase Warren, when the French frigate *Belle Poule* surrendered to the *Amazon*. The first lieutenant of the *Amazon* having been killed in the action, Warren gave Westphal an acting order as captain of the *Belle Poule*, which he refitted and took to England. The Admiralty refused to confirm the acting order, and Westphal continued lieutenant of the *Amazon* until she was paid off in 1812.

Westphal was then appointed to the *Junon*, a 38-gun frigate, in which he had active service on the coast of North America. In January 1815 he was moved by Sir George Cockburn into his flagship, and on 13 June was at last promoted commander. In November 1828 he was appointed to the *Warspite* (76 guns), again with Sir William Parker; but, as Parker was very shortly afterwards appointed to the royal yacht, Westphal was moved to the *Kent* (78 guns), from which, on 22 July 1830, he was advanced to post rank. In 1847 he was retired on a Greenwich Hospital pension, becoming rear-admiral on 27 September 1855, vice-admiral on 4 October 1862, and admiral on 2 April 1866. He died, the oldest naval officer, on 16 March 1880 at Ryde, Isle of Wight, where he had settled in his retirement.

J. K. LAUGHTON, *rev.* ANDREW LAMBERT

Sources D. Syrett and R. L. DiNardo, *The commissioned sea officers of the Royal Navy, 1660–1815*, rev. edn, Occasional Publications of the Navy RS, 1 (1994) · O'Byrne, *Naval biog. dict.* · Boase, *Mod. Eng. biog.* · *The Times* (19 March 1880) · *Dod's Peerage* (1858) · *CGPLA Eng. & Wales* (1880)
Wealth at death under £3000: resworn probate, June 1880, *CGPLA Eng. & Wales*

Westrup, Sir Jack Allan (1904–1975), music scholar and conductor, was born in Dulwich, London, on 26 July 1904, the second of the three sons (there were no daughters) of George Westrup, insurance clerk, of Dulwich, and his wife, Harriet Sophia Allan. He was educated at Dulwich College, where he was a scholar, and then gained a Nettleship scholarship in music to Balliol College, Oxford. There was no honours degree in music at that time, so he first read classics, gaining a first in moderations (1924) and a second in *literae humaniores* (1926) before proceeding to the BMus degree in 1926. He took an active part in music in the university both as a keyboard and brass player. However, his most important contribution to Oxford music was his part in founding the university opera club while still an undergraduate; he returned to it later as conductor, when elected to the Heather professorship in 1947.

In spite of a research grant on going down from Oxford—when Westrup worked on 'Noëls provençaux' in Avignon—appointments for musical scholars were then so scarce that he went back to his old school and taught classics. Then in 1934 he returned to music as a critic on the *Daily Telegraph* until the war put an end to most concerts in London, whereupon he did another short stint as a schoolmaster. In 1938 he married Solweig Maria (d. 1984), daughter of Per Johan Gustaf Rösell, musical director of an infantry regiment in Linköping, Sweden; they had one daughter and three sons.

Westrup's chance to enter academic life came in 1941 when he was offered, and accepted, a lectureship at King's College, Newcastle upon Tyne, followed by his election to the Peyton and Barber chair of music at Birmingham University in 1944. He flourished at Birmingham, making full use of the excellent facilities offered by the Barber Institute Library, and the opportunities for conducting. Oxford conferred upon him an honorary DMus in 1944, and in 1947 he returned to his old university as Heather professor of music. Much as this pleased him, it was not an easy time for him, as there were some Oxford musicians who did not welcome his election. However, in 1950 the university finally allowed music to become an honours course and Westrup was mainly instrumental in designing a new syllabus which demanded a wider knowledge of musical scholarship than the old BMus. This gave him satisfaction and confidence.

Westrup's energy was remarkable. Not only did he fulfil meticulously his duties as professor, but during his twenty-four years at Oxford he conducted seventeen operas for the university opera club—mostly unfamiliar and including one first performance and one British première. He also edited *Music and Letters* from 1959 and was president of the Royal Musical Association (1958–63), the Incorporated Society of Musicians (1963), and the Royal College of Organists (1964–6).

Westrup was a person with complete self-control and with a presence which alarmed those who did not know him well. He did not suffer fools gladly, and had no patience with the yes man. If one disagreed with him his face would light up and his interest was immediately stimulated. In matters of detail he was most meticulous and expected others to be likewise. But to those who had the fortune to know him well he was a kind and humble man, never too busy to offer help and almost incapable of saying 'no' to the most mundane of requests. Apart from his university degrees he was a fellow of the British Academy (1954), the Royal College of Organists (1942), Trinity College, London (1946), the Royal College of Music (1961), and the Royal School of Church Music (1963). He was also an honorary member of the Royal Academy of Music (1960). For his services to music he was knighted in 1961.

It was to the lasting regret of Westrup's friends and colleagues, and a serious loss to music, that while at Oxford his energies were not directed more towards writing books. It was hoped that he would follow up his outstanding books *Purcell* (1937), *Handel* (1939), and *An Introduction to Musical History* (1955) with works of similar stature. Instead he indulged in much editing (in 1947 he became chairman of the editorial board of *The New Oxford History of Music*), writing articles, compiling lexicons, and lecturing abroad. These, though important, were no substitute for what a man of his talent should have achieved.

Westrup's versatility—as a practical musician and as a musicologist—can best be summed up by two quotations from his Deneke lecture of 1945 (published in 1946):

> Nothing can better aid our endeavours than performance—performance not merely by amateurs, to whose enthusiasm we so often owe a lively acquaintance with the past, but by expert musicians who unite with their skill an understanding of what they are trying to do. (Westrup, 16)

And:

> Perhaps the virtue that we need most of all is humility—not the crawling acquiescence that accepts great reputations and can find no flaw, but the readiness to believe in lesser men until we can prove them to be charlatans. (ibid., 25)

The last paragraph of this lecture might well have been written of him rather than by him: 'The great historians of music are those who have carried musical souls about them, who to industry and scholarship have added vision and found the power to share it with their readers' (ibid., 32). Westrup died at his home, Maycroft, Hurland Lane, Headley, Hampshire, on 21 April 1975.

BERNARD ROSE, *rev.*

Sources S. Abraham, *PBA*, 63 (1977), 471–82 · P. Dennison, 'Westrup, Sir Jack Allan', *New Grove* · A. Westrup, *The meaning of musical history* (1946) · personal knowledge (1986) · private information (1986) · *CGPLA Eng. & Wales* (1975)
Archives SOUND BL NSA, performance recording
Wealth at death £5625: probate, 24 June 1975, *CGPLA Eng. & Wales*

Westwood, John Obadiah (1805–1893), entomologist and palaeographer, was born on 22 December 1805 at Sheffield, the son of John Westwood (1774–1850), a medal designer and die-sinker, and his wife, Mary, daughter of Edward Betts of Sheffield. Westwood was educated at the Society of Friends' school at Sheffield; in 1819 his family moved to Lichfield where he was educated at the grammar school; they later moved to Chelsea.

Westwood was first apprenticed as an engraver, but in the autumn of 1821 he was articled to a firm of solicitors in London, where he was briefly a partner. Of his arrival in London, Westwood declared that 'instead of studying Coke upon Lyttleton, I greedily devoured all the information to be obtained from Samouelle's *Compendium*, Haworth's *Lepidoptera Britannica*, Shaw's *Zoology*, and other similar works' (*Entomologist's Monthly Magazine*, 49). However, by the end of 1828 he had been enrolled as attorney of his majesty's court of king's bench at Westminster, attorney in common pleas, and solicitor in his majesty's high court of chancery.

Westwood began collecting insects from all orders at an early age, acquiring both native and foreign specimens. In later life he toured across Europe and Russia visiting libraries and collections. Having small private means, he preferred to devote himself to entomology and antiquarian pursuits, augmenting his income by writing and drawing and, in time, he became one of the greatest living authorities on Anglo-Saxon and medieval manuscripts. His drawings of insects were masterpieces of correct delineation, and he excelled in reproducing old manuscripts, illuminations, and representations of old ivories and inscribed stones.

In March 1824 Westwood first met the entomologist Frederick William *Hope (1797–1862). Hope, the first president of the Entomological Society, became Westwood's patron, and in August 1834 he engaged Westwood for one day each week to arrange his insect specimens. In 1839 Westwood married Eliza Richardson (*d.* 1882), who accompanied him on all his archaeological tours, and who assisted him in making sketches and rubbings of the inscribed stones for his *Lapidarium Walliae* (1876–9).

About 1849 Hope decided to give his collections to Oxford University by a deed of gift officially accepted by convocation in April 1850. Hope was also keen to establish a new chair of zoology at Oxford, and in 1860 the Hope professorship of zoology was endowed. Hope's collections were transferred from Hammersmith (where Westwood also resided) to Oxford, but by 1855 he was worried about their condition. Thus in 1857 Westwood was appointed conservator of Hope's collections and, on 31 July of the same year, Westwood's own insect collection (having been purchased by Hope) was added to the Hopeian Museum. In January 1861 Westwood was nominated by Hope for the post of first Hope professor of zoology and in due course was appointed. In 1858 he joined Magdalen College, becoming a fellow in 1880.

Westwood was a prolific author. His antiquarian works included *Palaeographia sacra pictoria* (1843–5), *Illuminated Illustrations of the Bible* (1846), *On the distinctive character of the … ornamentation employed by the early British Anglo-Saxon, and Irish artists* (1854), *A Descriptive Catalogue of the Fictile Ivories in the South Kensington Museum* (1876), *Lapidarium Walliae: the Early Inscribed and Sculptured Stones of Wales* (1876–9), and *The Book of Kells: a Lecture* (1887). His most important entomological work was *An Introduction to the Modern Classification of Insects* (2 vols., 1839–40). Other important works in this field included *The Entomologist's Text Book* (1838), *British Butterflies and their Transformations* (2 vols., 1841–55), *The Butterflies of Great Britain* (1855; edn 1887), *Catalogue of Orthopterous Insects in the Collection of the British Museum. Part I. Phasmidae* (1859), and *Thesaurus entomologicus Oxoniensis, or, Illustrations of new, rare, and interesting insects, for the most part contained in the collections presented to the University of Oxford by the Rev. F. W. Hope* (1874). He also contributed to works by other naturalists and published more than 350 papers.

Although Westwood received no formal training as an artist, he produced illustrations for J. F. Stephen's *Illustrations of British Entomology* (1828–46), F. W. Hope's *Coleopterist's Manual* (1837–40), and T. V. Wollaston's *Insecta Maderensia* (1854). He produced new editions, and contributed notes to a number of works, including D. Drury's *Illustrations of Exotic Entomology* (3 vols., 1837) and M. Harris's *The Aurelian: a Natural History of English Moths* (1840). The name *Westwoodia* was bestowed in his honour by Brullé in 1846 on a genus of Hymenoptera, and his name was similarly employed by C. S. Bate in 1857 for Crustacea, and by Kaufs in 1866 and Castelnau in 1873 for Coleoptera.

In his time, Westwood's work 'forged a bridge between entomologists and gardeners' (Clark, 210). He was on the staff of the *Gardeners' Chronicle* for nearly half a century as entomological referee, and in this journal, and the *Agricultural Gazette*, he published a series of articles around 1860, disputing Darwin's theories of evolution and natural selection. Moreover, Westwood, like many of his contemporaries, was unable to accept the doctrine of evolution and remained a staunch anti-Darwinist to the end, although he did live to see the subject taught at his university.

Westwood was elected a fellow of the Linnean Society on 1 May 1827, and was on the honorary list of nearly every entomological society of his period. He had co-operated actively in founding the Entomological Society of London in 1833, and was honorary secretary from 1834 until 1847

(from 1836 to 1843 he also held the post of honorary curator). He was president of the society for three terms (1851–2, 1872–3, 1876–7), and edited the society's *Transactions*. In 1883 he was elected honorary life president. His work *An Introduction to the Modern Classification of Insects* (1838–40) gained him the Royal Society's gold medal in 1855, and although frequently urged to become a candidate for fellowship to the society he declined the offers. He was also made an honorary member of the London Vaccine Institution in 1833, and the emperor of Brazil, Pedro II, made Westwood a knight of the imperial order of the rose.

About 1884, a bad fall caused damage to Westwood's left arm, and prevented the pursuit of his studies. By 1892 he was confined to a bath chair, and on 2 January 1893 he died at his residence, 141 Woodstock Road, Oxford. He was buried at St Sepulchre's cemetery, Jericho, Oxford. In 1893 a vestry was erected at St Andrew's Church, Sandford-on-Thames, in his memory. YOLANDA FOOTE

Sources R. McLachlan, *Entomologist's Monthly Magazine*, 29 (1893), 49–51 · *The Zoologist*, 3rd ser., 17, 99 · *Archaeologia Cambrensis*, 5th ser., 10 (1893), 179 · G. H. C., *Natural Science*, 2 (1893), 151–3 · private information (1899) [niece, Miss Swann] · catalogue [BM] · catalogue, NHM · A. Z. Smith, *A history of the Hope entomological collections in the University Museum, Oxford* (1986) · J. F. M. Clark, 'Science, secularization, and social change: the metamorphosis of entomology in nineteenth century England', PhD thesis, 1994 · R. F. Smith, T. E. Mittler, and C. N. Smith, eds., *History of entomology* (1973) · S. A. Neave, *The centenary history of the Entomological Society of London, 1833–1933* (1933)

Archives AM Oxf., notes and copies of illuminated MSS · BL OIOC, drawings, NHD 5 · Bodl. Oxf., corresp.; collections relating to ecclesiastical antiquities; diary of tour in South Wales · NHM · Oxf. U. Mus. NH, Hope Library, corresp., diaries, notes and papers · Smithsonian Institution, Washington, DC, corresp. and papers · U. Cam., Museum of Zoology, drawings | Linn. Soc., letters to William Swainson · Oxf. U. Mus. NH, letters to J. C. Dale; letters to G. A. J. Rothney · Royal Entomological Society, London, letters to A. H. Haliday · Royal Literary and Scientific Institution, Bath, letters to Leonard Blomefield

Likenesses T. H. Maguire, lithograph, 1851, BM · photograph, 1851, Hope Entomology Library, Oxford · E. Edwards, photograph, 1864, NPG; repro. in L. Reeve, ed., *Portraits of men of eminence*, 2 (1864) · W. Rivière, oils, 1876, Hope Entomology Library, Oxford · oils, before 1876, Oxf. U. Mus. NH · H. von Herkomer, oils, 1890, AM Oxf. · photograph, Hope Entomology Library, Oxford · portrait, repro. in McLachlan, *Entomologist's Monthly Magazine*

Wealth at death £13,774 15s. 3d.: resworn probate, Oct 1893, CGPLA Eng. & Wales

Westwood, Joseph (1884–1948), trade unionist and politician, was born on 11 February 1884 at Wollescote near Stourbridge, Worcestershire, the son of Solomon Westwood, a coal miner, and his wife, Harriet, *née* Sidaway. His father moved north in 1887 to get a job in the fast-expanding Fife coalfield, and Westwood attended Buckhaven higher grade school, Fife. He left school at thirteen, and after a year as a draper's assistant became a miner in the Wemyss collieries, where he worked from 1898 or 1899 to 1916. In 1906 he married Frances Scarlett (*d.* 1948), daughter of James Scarlett and his wife, Frances Harvey; they had three sons and five daughters. The Wemyss collieries, with their model housing, welfare halls, and railway and tramway systems, were a notably paternalist enterprise, and Westwood did not share the militancy for which the western 'little Moscow' part of the Fife coalfield, around Cowdenbeath and Lumphinnans, was noted. (In 1935, as a Kirkcaldy councillor, he defended the celebration of George V's jubilee on the eve of the communist Willie Gallacher's victory in West Fife.) He was also an active member, along with his wife, of the Salvation Army in Kirkcaldy.

In 1916 Westwood left the coalface to become industrial organizer of the Fife Miners' Union under the moderate William Adamson. From 1918 until 1929 he was organizer for the Scottish Miners' Union. Adamson headed the conservative-minded miners' agents who made up nearly half the Scottish Labour members of parliament after 1918. Westwood was also a councillor and JP in Kirkcaldy, and a member of Fife education committee. In March 1921 he was nominated by the union for selection as Labour candidate for Kirkcaldy Burghs at a by-election, but was defeated by Thomas Kennedy, who went on, unexpectedly, to win the seat. In 1922, however, Westwood was elected Labour member for the largely mining constituency of Peebles and South Midlothian. In June 1929 he became parliamentary private secretary to Adamson, who in March 1931 had resumed the position which he had held in the Labour government of 1924 of Scottish secretary (since 1926, secretary of state). On 25 March 1931 Westwood succeeded Tom Johnston as under-secretary for Scotland. In the ensuing general election of August 1931 Westwood, like twenty-nine out of the thirty-six Scottish Labour members elected in 1929, lost his seat. He performed creditably but unsuccessfully for Labour in the chaotic East Fife by-election in 1933, when five candidates stood, including Eric Linklater, who described it in his novel *Magnus Merriman* (1934).

Westwood returned to Westminster in 1935 as member for Stirling and Falkirk Burghs, but despite a modest increase in Scottish Labour members from seven to twenty his mentor Adamson was defeated in West Fife by Gallacher. Westwood held the seat until his death in 1948. The diaries of James Chuter Ede record Westwood as one of the rank and file with whom the Labour leadership liked to keep in touch, but he was not exceptional in any other sense. In the wartime coalition he was one of the two under-secretaries appointed by Churchill to the Scottish Office under Ernest Brown, on 17 May 1940, and he maintained this position under Johnston. In the office, now based at St Andrew's House, Edinburgh, Henry James Scrymgeour-Wedderburn (later eleventh earl of Dundee) took charge of industry and security, and Westwood of health and education. He was in charge of piloting the pendant to R. A. Butler's Education Act, the Education (Scotland) Act (1945), through the House of Commons: a demanding assignment, as Johnston was always reluctant to leave Scotland.

In July 1945 Johnston withdrew from party politics to lead a series of Scottish public bodies, notably the Scottish Tourist Board and the Forestry Commission and, after 1948, the new Hydro-Electric Board. Johnston had toyed with the idea of remaining secretary of state but with a

seat in the House of Lords and resident most of the time in Scotland, but Attlee would not accept this, partly because the general election had not gone particularly well for Labour in Scotland. Westwood, who took office as secretary of state on 4 August 1945 (his under-secretaries were George Buchanan and Tom Fraser), was generally regarded as a weak appointment, in the tradition of the dour and inarticulate Adamson rather than the charismatic Johnston, but he was penalized both by a rigorous time in office before the Labour government was formed and by a debilitating illness which removed him from many cabinet meetings in the early stages of the government. Westwood was unionist 'by personal conviction' (Fry, 195), yet when John MacCormick's Scottish convention pressure group met him in February 1946 they found him 'not unsympathetic' to Scottish self-government.

Nevertheless Westwood's period in office saw the confirmation of Johnston's successes in power-generation politics, with the continuing autonomy of the North of Scotland Hydro-Electric Board won against the opposition of the Ministry of Power, and with the securing of Scottish authority over planning and education. There was also success in setting up new light engineering and consumer goods plants, though the census of production for 1947 showed these yielding only 2.7 per cent of jobs. Scotland's new-won planning powers were particularly significant in the Clyde valley plan of 1946, and in November Westwood designated the pioneer new town of East Kilbride. However he opposed an attempt at further devolution by Lewis Silkin in July 1947 by establishing a Scottish committee of the Central Land Board. Housing was a major problem, with a communist-organized squatting campaign in summer 1946. Westwood's Housing Finance (Scotland) Bill of that year doubled the subsidy on housing, and retrospectively covered those (mainly pre-fabricated) houses built since March 1944, but foul weather and lack of materials meant that his target of 24,000 houses for 1947 was not approached, let alone met.

Westwood had the ill fortune as secretary of state for Scotland to follow the greatest holder of that post, Tom Johnston, and he did not last long. He left office on 7 October 1947 in the ministerial reshuffle, and legend has it that he was the recipient of the most laconic of Attlee's dismissals: asked why, the prime minister replied ''Cos you don't measure up to the job. That's why. Thanks for coming. Secretary will show you out' (Donnachie, Harvie, and Wood, 67–8). Westwood had the difficult task of coping with what George Pottinger has seen as a determined effort by Whitehall to claw back powers which it thought the Johnstonian Scottish Office had filched. The verdict of the usually judicious James Margach in the *Sunday Times* was that Westwood did not stand up for Scotland's rights, while the unionist *Scotsman* greeted his resignation with the judgement that his was one of the weakest teams ever to reign over Scottish affairs. But his successor, Arthur Woodburn, regarded Westwood as having 'a mind like a needle' and his career was one of persistent effort (Donnachie, Harvie, and Wood, 78).

Westwood and his wife were killed in a car accident on

17 July 1948 at Strathmiglo in Fife, and were buried in Dysart cemetery, Kirkcaldy. The funeral service was conducted by the general secretary of the Scottish Salvation Army. CHRISTOPHER HARVIE

Sources DLB · W. Knox, Scottish labour leaders, 1918–1939 (1987) · WWW · WWBMP · The Times (19 July 1948), 4d, 7e · I. Donnachie, C. Harvie, and I. S. Wood, Forward! Labour politics in Scotland, 1888–1988 (1989) · G. Pottinger, The secretaries of state for Scotland, 1926–1976: fifty years of the Scottish office (1979) · M. Fry, Patronage and principle: a political history of modern Scotland (1986) · L. Paterson, The autonomy of modern Scotland (1994) · S. Macintyre, Little Moscows (1980) · D. Milne, The Scottish office and other Scottish government departments (1957) · A. K. Cairncross, ed., The Scottish economy: a statistical account of Scottish life by members of the staff of Glasgow University (1954) · C. Harvie and M. Russell, 1946: the people's story (1986) · Labour and the wartime coalition: from the diaries of James Chuter Ede, 1941–1945, ed. K. Jefferys (1987) · J. Margach, The anatomy of power (1979) · J. Mitchell, Strategies for self-government: the campaign for a Scottish parliament (1996) · G. Walker, Thomas Johnston (1988) · E. Linklater, Magnus Merriman: a novel (1934) · CCI (1948)
Wealth at death £5159 2s. 5d.: confirmation, 20 Dec 1948, CCI

Westwood, Thomas (1814–1888), poet and bibliographer of angling, was born on 26 November 1814 at Westwood Cottage, The Chase, Enfield, the youngest son of Thomas Westwood of Enfield and his wife, Mary. Westwood senior was an unusual character with a hump and reportedly stood 4 feet and 'a nail high' (Works of Charles and Mary Lamb, 833). He was vividly described by Charles Lamb in several letters to William Wordsworth between 1829 and 1830. The Lambs moved in next door to the Westwoods' cottage in September 1827, when Thomas Westwood senior was employed as an agent of the Phoenix Insurance Company. In October 1829 the Lambs were forced to give up their house and became lodgers with the Westwoods. This arrangement lasted until May 1833. Originally complimentary of Westwood senior's company and manners Lamb soon began to tire of his 'one anecdote' (ibid.) and miserly behaviour.

As a youth Thomas Westwood made the acquaintance of Lamb and was deeply impressed by his illustrious neighbour, becoming a regular visitor, though he was not yet thirteen. Not surprisingly he was a shy youth and was somewhat in awe of Lamb but Lamb warmed to him and granted the teenager free access to his library, even flinging presentation copies over the fence into the Westwoods' garden for Thomas to pick up. Mary Lamb also influenced the youngster, teaching him Latin and giving him a taste for popular fiction. Many years later in Notes and Queries Westwood contributed an interesting and personal article on Lamb giving a generous appraisal of his talents, stating that he was 'a seventeenth-century man mislaid' (N&Q, 3rd ser., 10, 222).

Westwood became acquainted with and was greatly influenced by Izaak Walton through reading Lamb's copy of the Compleat Angler. Reading Hawkins's 1760 edition Westwood regarded it, in biblical allegory, as 'my chief treasure, pearl of price' (Lucas, 727).

With the introduction to many of Lamb's literary friends, including the regular visits of William Wordsworth—whom Westwood senior disliked for taking too much sugar in his tea—Westwood developed an interest in writing. A small volume entitled Poems was published in 1840. Critical reviews were favourable, and the reviewer for The Athenaeum in 1841 commented that Westwood had 'a poetical eye, a poetical heart, and a musical ear'. He also published Beads from a Rosary (1843) and Burden of the Bell and other Lyrics (1850), after many of the poems had appeared in the Gentleman's Magazine. His most ambitious work is The Quest of Sancgreall (1868). Westwood produced many poems and published a number of collections but was conscious that they lacked something. In a humorous sonnet entitled 'Small Poets' he wrote 'Oh for a wizard's sleight to turn this swarm of mites into one mighty!'. However, W. S. Landor remarked that he would have liked to have written Westwood's 'Love in the Alpuxaras'.

After working for Lamb's friend Ader the merchant in 1844, Westwood was posted to Belgium, where he became the Brussels director and secretary of the Tournai and Jurbise Railway. Most of his later life was spent in west Flanders. Here he continued with his interest in angling, building up an impressive library on the subject (now partly in the New York Public Library). In 1861 he published, through The Field office, A new bibliotheca piscatoria, or, General catalogue of angling and fishing literature, with bibliographical notes and data. Westwood became the acknowledged authority on the subject and three years later issued his Chronicle of the Compleat Angler. This book was an elaborate bibliography of Izaak Walton's work and was later printed as a supplement to Marston's 1888 edition of The Compleat Angler, with a new preface.

The Bibliotheca piscatoria: a Catalogue of Books on Angling, the Fisheries and Fish-Culture (1883) was a supplement to Westwood's magnum opus of 1861 but was practically rewritten. With the collaboration of Thomas Satchell, Westwood produced a handsome quarto edition containing well over 5000 separate entries. In the same year, with his own expert introduction to accompany it, Westwood reprinted John Denny's 1613 The Secrets of Angling. Twelve Sonnets and an Epilogue (in Memoriam I. Walton) appeared in 1884. Westwood stayed unmarried and died in Belgium on 13 March 1888. THOMAS SECCOMBE, rev. J.-M. ALTER

Sources A. H. Miles, ed., The poets and poetry of the century, 4 (1892) · N&Q, 3rd ser., 10 (22 Sept 1866) · N&Q, 4th ser., 5 (1870) · N&Q, 4th ser., 10 (23 Nov 1872) · The works of Charles and Mary Lamb, ed. E. V. Lucas, new edn, 6 vols. (1912), vol. 2 · E. V. Lucas, The life of Charles Lamb, 2 vols. (1905); repr. (1987), vol. 2 · C. A. Prance, Companion to Charles Lamb: a guide to people and places, 1760–1847 (1983)

Wet, Christiaan Rudolph de (1854–1922), army officer and politician in the Orange Free State, born at Leeuwkop, Smithfield district, in the Orange Free State, on 7 October 1854, was the sixth son of Jacobus Ignatius de Wet, of Dewetsdorp, and Aletta Susanna Margaretha Strijdom; he belonged to the sixth generation of the family settled in the Cape. He was privately educated and in 1865, aged eleven, accompanied his father to the frontier during the Basuto War. In 1873 he married Cornelia Margaretha (1856–1936), daughter of Isaak Johannes Christian Kruger, of Bloemfontein; they had five sons and one daughter.

Strongly opposed to British annexation of the Transvaal republic (1877), de Wet served with the republican forces in the various engagements during the First South African War (1880–81) which culminated in the British disaster on Majuba Hill (27 February 1881). After retrocession of the Transvaal, de Wet farmed there for some years, and in 1885 was elected to represent Lydenburg in the republican Volksraad. Ill-suited to routine, however, he soon resigned, ultimately returning to the Free State.

In 1889 de Wet rode with an armed force to Bloemfontein to protest against the building of a railway line from the coast. His vigorous political methods were noted and approved, and he became a member of the Free State Volksraad until 1898.

In the Second South African War, in October 1899, de Wet was conscripted as an ordinary burgher and sent to the Natal frontier. He gained military distinction, when, as an acting commander with 300 men, he attacked a 1000-strong British force which had left Ladysmith and halted at Nicholson's Nek on 30 October. De Wet captured the whole force, scoring the first important success of the campaign. On 7 December he was promoted to the rank of field general on the western borders of the Free State, where British troops were massing for the relief of Kimberley. There General Piet Cronjé was supreme commander, but, despite de Wet's efforts to guide and later to rescue him, Cronjé made tactical errors which led to his capture by Lord Roberts and surrender at Paardeberg on 27 February 1900. Meanwhile de Wet had further distinguished himself by capturing Roberts's convoy at Waterval on 13 February and was appointed commander-in-chief of the Free State forces. The republican cause and the morale of the commandos had been undermined by surrender and desertion but de Wet, supported by Martinus Steyn, president of the Orange Free State, and by General De la Rey, rallied and reassembled his forces. On 31 March he ambushed Colonel R. G. Broadwood's mounted brigade at Sanna's Post, outside Bloemfontein, and on 4 April defeated a British detachment at Reddersburg.

As the war moved to the Transvaal, de Wet remained behind British lines and re-established the fighting spirit of his men. He and the Boer Transvaal leaders chose guerrilla tactics, of which de Wet became a skilled exponent. With a few thousand followers he kept the field for the next two years against tremendous odds, to the despair and admiration of his opponents. He was still undefeated, his reputation worldwide, when, as acting president of the Orange Free State for one day, he signed the treaty of Vereeniging in 1902, ending the war.

After the war de Wet visited Europe with his fellow Boer generals and peace negotiators, and, responsible government granted to South Africa in 1907, he was elected a member of the first parliament of the Orange River Colony and appointed minister of agriculture. He was a delegate to the Union Convention of 1908–9 and a member of the union defence council under General Louis Botha. He left politics after union in 1910.

In 1911 Botha and General J. B. M. Hertzog disagreed on South Africa's relations with the British empire. De Wet supported Hertzog and the movement towards secession and re-establishment of the republics of the Orange Free State and Transvaal. He resigned from the defence council in 1913. After the outbreak of the First World War in August 1914 Botha announced his intention of invading German South-West African territory with South African troops in alliance with the British. Already hostile to the expedition, de Wet was influenced by his mistaken belief that Botha's government had ordered the death of his fellow wartime commander and friend General De la Rey, shot by accident on 15 September. De Wet and General C. F. Beyers, the leader of the Transvaal rebels, planned armed revolt. On 24 October Beyers raised the standard in the north, and two days later de Wet followed suit in the Free State. Thousands responded. Botha, however, summoned his supporters, took the field in person, and swiftly defeated Beyers (27 October). He then turned upon de Wet, who was in hiding at Mushroom Valley in the central Free State, and dispersed de Wet's forces (12 November). De Wet resorted to his old guerrilla tactics but in the era of the motor vehicle Botha was able to harry and hustle the mounted commandos, giving them and their horses no rest. Within ten days de Wet was fleeing westward, with only a handful of men, to the Kalahari Desert and German territory. However, on 2 December Botha captured de Wet on the farm Waterberg in the Kuruman district. Beyers had died the previous week while trying to cross the Vaal River, and with both its leaders accounted for the uprising was soon stamped out.

Found guilty of high treason at Bloemfontein on 15 June 1915, de Wet was sentenced to six years' imprisonment and fined £2000. After public protest, Botha released him on parole and he was allowed to return to his farm in the Free State. He lived quietly, dying on the farm Klipfontein, Dewetsdorp, on 3 February 1922. He was buried at the Vrouemonument ('women's monument') at Bloemfontein beside his old leader President Steyn. He published an account of his campaigns of 1899–1902; an English edition, entitled *Three Years' War*, appeared in 1902.

LYNN MILNE

Sources M. C. E. van Schoor, 'De Wet, Christiaan Rudolph', *DSAB* · T. R. H. Davenport, *South Africa: a modern history*, 4th edn (1991) · T. Pakenham, *The Boer War* (1979) · J. F. Maurice and M. H. Grant, eds., *History of the war in South Africa, 1899–1902*, 4 vols. (1906–10) · L. S. Amery, ed., *The Times history of the war in South Africa*, 4 (1906); 5 (1907); 6 (1909); 7 (1909) · *DNB*
Likenesses Ebni, chromolithograph caricature, NPG; repro. in *VF* (31 July 1902) · E. Kress, photographs · C. Steynberg, bronze statue, Raadzaal, Bloemfontein, South Africa · Van Wouw, bronze bust, Bloemfontein War Museum and National Museum of Cultural History, Pretoria, South Africa · A. van Welie, portraits, Bloemfontein War Museum and National Museum of Cultural History, Pretoria, South Africa

Wetenhall, Edward (1636–1713), Church of Ireland bishop of Kilmore and Ardagh, was born at Lichfield on 7 October 1636. Educated at Westminster School under Richard Busby, he was admitted king's scholar in 1651, and went to Trinity College, Cambridge, as a foundation scholar in 1655. After graduating BA in 1658 he migrated (1660) to Lincoln College, Oxford, of which he became chaplain, was incorporated BA on 18 June, and graduated MA on 10

Edward Wetenhall (1636-1713), by Isaac Beckett (after Jan van der Vaart)

July 1661. He held the perpetual curacy of Combe, Oxfordshire, and the vicarage of St Stephen's, near St Albans, Hertfordshire; on 11 June 1667 he was collated to a prebend at Exeter, holding with it the mastership of the Blue-Coat School. He graduated BD at Oxford on 26 May 1669, and was incorporated BD at Cambridge in 1670. Michael Boyle the younger, then archbishop of Dublin, took him over to Dublin in 1672 as master of the Blue-Coat School. He was made DD at Trinity College (1674), became curate of St Werburgh's, and afterwards chantor of Christ Church. On the death (22 December 1678) of Edward Synge, bishop of Cork, Cloyne, and Ross, the sees were separated, and Wetenhall was made (3 February 1679) bishop of Cork and Ross, being consecrated on 23 March 1679 in Christ Church, Dublin.

Following the accession of James II, Wetenhall travelled through the diocese preaching on the duty of obedience. In 1686 he published six of these sermons under the title *Hexapla Jacobaea: a Specimen of Loyalty to … James II*. He was one of only seven bishops who remained in Ireland during the crisis of 1688–91, and one of only four who attended James's Irish parliament. According to his own account his opposition to the proceedings there almost led to penalties for contempt, and he was subsequently a prisoner in Cork city during Marlborough's siege (23–8 September 1690). Nevertheless his perceived collaboration exposed him to accusations of Jacobite sympathies. These reportedly led to his being passed over when the vacant see of

Cashel was filled in 1691 (James Bonnell to J. Strype, 21 Feb 1691, Strype correspondence, 1, fol. 87v). *The case of the Irish protestants in relation to recognizing or swearing allegiance to and praying for King William and Queen Mary stated and resolved* (1691), published anonymously but widely recognized as Wetenhall's work, did not wholly rebut these charges. It defended protestant acquiescence in the Revolution, but conspicuously failed to repudiate passive obedience or to declare that James had ceased to be lawful king. Instead the argument was that James had made it impossible for protestants to maintain their vows of allegiance, combined with an appeal to providence: 'God has now put us under the power of the second William the Conqueror' (*The Case*, 6). In 1699 Wetenhall was transferred to the diocese of Kilmore and Ardagh, although he appears to have had some qualms about thus taking the place of the ousted nonjuror William Sheridan.

Wetenhall's attitude to protestant dissent has been characterized as 'moderately ecumenical' (Greaves, 378). *The Protestant Peacemaker* (1682) praised the positive qualities of all protestant religious denominations, while arguing that dissenters were not justified in separating from the established church. The following year Wetenhall was one of those who opposed the government's campaign of repression against conventicles. After the revolution he opposed early calls for the extension to Ireland of the sacramental test, on the grounds that this was a profanation of the sacrament. His own theological orthodoxy was called into question when he intervened in the controversy on the doctrine of the Trinity raised by the publications of William Sherlock DD and John Wallis. His *An Earnest and Compassionate Suit for Forbearance … by a Melancholy Stander-by* (1691) and *The Antapology of the Melancholy Stander-by* (1693) led Archbishop King and others to conclude that his views on the Trinity were unsound. Having attended Thomas Emlyn's trial for heresy, he later visited him in prison. In 1698–9 an initially friendly meeting with William Penn led to an acrimonious exchange of pamphlets, commencing with Wetenhall's *The testimony of the bishop of Cork as to a paper entitled 'Gospel truths' … by the people called Quakers* (1698) and continuing with his *A brief and modest reply to Mr Penn's tedious, scurrilous and unchristian defence against the bishop of Cork* (1699). In 1710 he was a signatory to the memorial submitted to the lord lieutenant, the second duke of Ormond, in support of the attempts of John Richardson, a clergyman in Wetenhall's diocese, to promote missionary work through the Irish language among the Catholic population.

Wetenhall seems generally to have been remembered as a conscientious bishop, who actively promoted pastoral work, courageously and energetically rallied his flock during the crisis years 1688–91, and contributed out of his own resources to the repair of the episcopal residences at Cork and Kilmore and the restoration of the cathedral of Ardagh. Archbishop King, however, reported in 1714 that Kilmore and Ardagh had generally been neglected owing to Wetenhall's absence and poor health. Moreover he had been influenced by others to discontinue the church-building programme commenced by his predecessor and to obstruct the disciplinary proceedings of the latter's chancellor. Later King listed him as one of those bishops who had despoiled their sees for personal gain, instancing the sale of a wood belonging to Kilmore. Wetenhall had a particular interest in religious instruction. His *The Catechism of the Church of England, with Marginal Notes* was published in London in 1678 (apparently one of several pre-1696 editions) and in Dublin in 1696, with a revised version, *A Tried Method of Catechising*, in 1698 (Dublin edition, 1706). Bonnell, a relative by marriage, characterized him as 'a vigorous good man, and very useful to the church', not wholly successful in his printed works 'because he does not exhaust a subject', but excelling in extempore preaching and in 'practical casuisticalness' (Webster, 293–4).

Wetenhall married twice; his second wife was Philippa (*d.* 1717), sixth daughter of Sir William D'Oyly, bt, of Shotticham, Kent. His later years were spent in London, where he died on 12 November 1713; he was buried on 18 November in the south transept of Westminster Abbey, where there is an inscribed gravestone to his memory. In his will he affirmed the Church of England and Ireland to be 'the purest church in the world', though 'there are divers points which might be altered for the better' in 'articles, liturgy, and discipline, but especially in the conditions of clerical communion'. His eldest son with his first wife was Edward Wetenhall MD (buried on 29 August 1733, aged seventy). Another son, John (*c.*1669–1717), followed his father into the church and became archdeacon of Cork in 1697. ALEXANDER GORDON, *rev.* S. J. CONNOLLY

Sources C. A. Webster, *The diocese of Cork* (1920) · Venn, *Alum. Cant.* · Wood, *Ath. Oxon.*, new edn · H. Cotton, *Fasti ecclesiae Hibernicae*, 1–5 (1845–60) · T. W. Moody and others, eds., *A new history of Ireland*, 9: *Maps, genealogies, lists* (1984) · R. Mant, *History of the Church of Ireland*, 2 vols. (1840) · P. Kilroy, *Protestant dissent and controversy in Ireland, 1660–1714* (1994) · I. Green, '"The necessary knowledge of the principles of religion": catechisms and catechizing in Ireland, *c.*1560–1800', *As by law established: the church of Ireland since the Reformation*, ed. A. Ford, J. McGuire, and K. Milne (1995), 69–88 · R. L. Greaves, *God's other children: protestant nonconformists and the emergence of denominational churches in Ireland* (1997) · C. S. King, *A great archbishop of Dublin: William King D.D., 1650–1729* (1906) · Strype correspondence, CUL, Baumgartner MSS · J. L. Chester, ed., *The marriage, baptismal, and burial registers of the collegiate church or abbey of St Peter, Westminster*, Harleian Society, 10 (1876)

Likenesses J. van der Vaart, mezzotint, pubd 1678–99 (after J. van der Vaart), NG Ire.; repro. in Webster, *Diocese of Cork* · R. Dunkarton, mezzotint, pubd 1813 (after J. van der Vaart), NPG · I. Beckett, mezzotint (after J. vander Vaart), BM [*see illus.*]

Wetherall, Sir Edward Robert (1815–1869). *See under* Wetherall, Sir George Augustus (1788–1868).

Wetherall, Sir Frederick Augustus (1754–1842), army officer, was the son of John Wetherall, a government official, of North Great George Street, Dublin. He obtained a commission as ensign in the 17th foot on 23 August 1775, embarked for Boston in September, and became lieutenant on 27 August 1776. During the American War of Independence he served with his regiment in the defence of Boston, and at the actions of Brooklyn, White Plains, Princeton, Brandywine, and Monmouth. In 1780 he was in command of a company serving as marines on HMS *Alfred*

and participated in the victories off capes Finisterre and St Vincent. In 1781 he married Elizabeth Mytton (*d.* 1810). Their son was Sir George Augustus *Wetherall. On 17 May of that same year he was made captain of an independent company which he had raised, and which was embodied in the 104th foot on 2 March 1782.

Wetherall exchanged to the 11th foot on 16 April 1783, served six years with that regiment at Gibraltar, and accompanied the duke of Kent, as a member of his household, to Quebec in 1791. He was aide-de-camp and comptroller of the duke's household during the operations in the West Indies, and received two wounds at the taking of Martinique in March 1794. He had become major in the 11th on 1 March, and on 23 August, when the duke of Kent took command of the troops in Nova Scotia, he was appointed deputy adjutant-general there. On 20 May 1795 he obtained the lieutenant-colonelcy of Keppel's regiment, newly raised for service in the West Indies, and served with it in San Domingo. While on his way with dispatches to Barbados he was wounded and taken prisoner. He was kept in irons at Guadeloupe for nine months before he was exchanged, and suffered such privations that some men of the 32nd, who were also prisoners, raised a subscription for him. He returned to Halifax, Nova Scotia, as adjutant-general, but on 3 August 1796 he was transferred to the lieutenant-colonelcy of the 82nd regiment, which was then in San Domingo.

When the duke of Kent became commander-in-chief in North America in 1799, Wetherall again served on his staff as adjutant-general, but the duke resigned the following year. On 29 April 1802 Wetherall was made brevet colonel, and in 1803 he raised a regiment of Nova Scotia fencibles, and was appointed its colonel from 9 July. In May 1806 he was appointed brigadier in the Caribee Islands, and in October at the Cape of Good Hope. On 25 October 1809 he was promoted major-general and placed on the staff in India. Early in 1810, on his way to Calcutta, he was taken prisoner and held in Mauritius for two months until exchanged. The same year his wife died at the Cape.

In November 1810 Wetherall was appointed second in command, under Sir Samuel Auchmuty, of the expedition to Java. He was thanked in general orders for his share in the battle of Cornelis, on 26 August 1811, and received the thanks of parliament and the gold medal for the conquest of Java. Later, in 1827–8, he made unsuccessful attempts to claim an extra £20,356 in prize money for the campaign, believing that the distribution made in 1815 was unjust. From Java he returned to India, and held command in Mysore until June 1815. He had become lieutenant-general on 4 June 1814, and was equerry, and afterwards executor, to the duke of Kent. In 1817 he married Elizabeth Ann Broad (1778/9–1846), the widow of Major Richard Broad and the daughter of W. Mair of Kensington.

In February 1833 Wetherall received the grand cross of the Royal Guelphic Order; he had petitioned unsuccessfully in 1816 to be created a knight commander of the Bath. On 10 January 1837 he relinquished the governorship of Blackness Castle, which he had held since 1830, when he became both a general and colonel of the 62nd foot. He was transferred to his old regiment, the 17th, on 17 February 1840. He died, aged eighty-eight, at his home in Castlebar Hill, Ealing, on 18 December 1842, and was buried on 24 December in St Mary's churchyard, Ealing, where he has a monument.

E. M. LLOYD, rev. PETER B. BOYDEN

Sources 1783–1842, NAM, Wetherall MSS, ARC 1962-10-72 · 1817–43, Ealing local history library, Wetherall MSS (legal and financial), Acc. 77 · F. B. McCrea, *Tree and services of the Wetherall family* (1912) · *The memorial of Lieutenant-General Wetherall to the … lords commissioners of his majesty's treasury with statement of the military services of Lieutenant-General Wetherall* (1828) · *An exposition of the facts sustaining the claim of Lieut.-General Wetherall … for his proportion of the Java prize money … submitted to … the duke of Wellington* (1828) · J. Philippart, ed., *The royal military calendar*, 3rd edn, 5 vols. (1820) · memorial inscription, Elizabeth Ann Wetherall, 21 June 1846, St Mary's, Ealing · *GM*, 2nd ser., 19 (1843), 318

Archives Ealing Local History Library, London, corresp., bank books, legal papers, and papers relating to execution of will, Acc. 77 · LMA, family estate MSS, Acc. 1028 · NAM, corresp. and papers **Likenesses** portrait, repro. in McCrea, *Tree and services of the Wetherall family*, facing p. 13

Wealth at death £32,179 13s. 7d.—his estate, excl. freehold of Castlebar Hill: Ealing local history library, Wetherall MSS, Acc. 77.167

Wetherall, Sir George Augustus (1788–1868), army officer, was the son of General Sir Frederick Augustus *Wetherall (1754–1842) and his first wife, Elizabeth Mytton (d. 1810). He was educated at Hyde Abbey School, Winchester, and the Army College, Farnham, being already commissioned, aged seven, as lieutenant in the 7th (Royal Fusiliers) on 29 July 1795. In 1798 he was placed on half pay, but on 9 July 1803 began active service, joining the regiment of Nova Scotia fencibles formed by his father. Hitherto his name had been erroneously in the army list as F. Augustus, but the seniority given to him marks his identity. He became captain on 13 May 1805, and exchanged to the 1st (Royals) on 27 November 1806.

Wetherall was brigade major under his father at the Cape in 1809, was taken prisoner with him while sailing to India in 1810 (they were released in an exchange of prisoners after two months), and served as his aide-de-camp in the conquest of Java in 1811. He was made brevet major on 12 August 1819, and regimental major on 30 December. He was military secretary to the commander-in-chief at Madras from 1822 to 1825, and deputy judge-advocate-general in 1826. On 11 December 1824 he was made brevet lieutenant-colonel, and on 7 August 1828 lieutenant-colonel of the Royals. He commanded the 2nd battalion of the regiment at Bangalore, in the Madras presidency, brought it home in 1831, and went with it to Canada in 1836. He was in command of the troops at Montreal when the insurrection broke out in the autumn of 1837. On 25 November, at the head of four companies of the Royals, a detachment of the 66th, and a troop of Montreal cavalry, with two six-pounders, he stormed a stockade held by Thomas Storrow Brown and other insurgents at St Charles who had refused to negotiate. His horse was shot and he lost twenty-one men. On 15 December, at the head of a brigade consisting of the Royals and some colonial troops, he and his son Edward [see below] took part in the action of St

Eustache under Sir John Colborne. He had received the Hanoverian order (KH) in 1833, and was made CB on 13 June 1838, brevet colonel on 28 June, and aide-de-camp to the queen on 29 July 1842.

Wetherall left the Royals on 14 July 1843, being appointed deputy adjutant-general at Montreal. In June 1850 he was given a post at the War Office in London. He was promoted major-general on 11 November 1851, and was appointed adjutant-general on 1 December 1854. From 1860 to 1865 he commanded the northern district of England, and on 21 August 1866 was appointed governor of the Royal Military College, Sandhurst. He had been given the colonelcy of the 84th foot on 15 June 1854, and had become lieutenant-general on 8 September 1857 and general on 23 October 1863. He was made KCB on 5 February 1856, and received the grand cross on 28 March 1865.

Wetherall was an exceptional soldier and one of the few officers who served in North America to proceed to significant posts in the United Kingdom.

He died at the Royal Military College, Sandhurst, on 8 April 1868, aged eighty. In 1812 he had married Frances Diana, daughter of Captain Denton EICS. Their only son, **Sir Edward Robert Wetherall** (1815–1869), army officer, entered the army on 27 June 1834, as ensign in his father's regiment, the 1st (Royals). He became lieutenant on 22 August 1837, and served in the Canadian uprising. He distinguished himself in the attack on St Eustache. Promoted captain on 19 December 1845, he transferred to the Scots Fusilier Guards on 15 July 1854. He served in the Crimea, as assistant quartermaster-general, until the fall of Sevastopol, and was the guide of the cavalry in the flank march to Balaklava. He was made brevet major on 12 December 1854 and brevet lieutenant-colonel on 17 July 1855. He was afterwards deputy quartermaster-general to the Turkish contingent at Kerch, and director-general of land transport (which he reorganized) in the Crimea. He received the medal with four clasps, CB, Légion d'honneur (fifth class), Mejidiye (third class), and Turkish medal. On 11 December 1855 he was made aide-de-camp to the queen, and colonel.

Wetherall was appointed deputy quartermaster-general to the forces in China in 1857, but was employed in India, owing to the outbreak of the mutiny. He was chief of the staff of the central India field force under Sir Hugh Henry Rose, and was present at the storming of Kunch and the battle of Gulauli, 22 May 1858, in which his horse was shot. He afterwards commanded a field force in south Oudh, as brigadier, and on 3 November stormed the fort of Rampur Kussia, taking twenty-three guns. He lost seventy-eight men, and Sir Colin Campbell was 'much put out' that he had not waited for Sir Hope Grant, as had been arranged. Even so, he received the medal and clasp, and was given an unattached lieutenant-colonelcy for his services in central India.

Wetherall was appointed deputy quartermaster-general to the forces in Ireland on 28 January 1859, and was rewarded for distinguished service on 20 December 1861. On 28 April 1865 he was made deputy quartermaster-general at headquarters, and in 1868 he succeeded Sir

Thomas Larcom as under-secretary in Ireland. He was made KCSI on 16 September 1867, and promoted major-general on 8 March 1869. On 26 January 1847 Wetherall married Katherine, daughter of John Durie of Astley Hall, Lancashire. He died suddenly at his home, Ashtown Lodge, Phoenix Park, Dublin, on 11 May 1869, having already won 'the cordial respect of all with whom he had official intercourse' (*The Times*). He was survived by his wife, three sons, and three daughters.

E. M. LLOYD, rev. H. C. G. MATTHEW

Sources GM, 4th ser., 5 (1868), 690 · *Hart's Army List* · *Army List* · *Colburn's United Service Magazine*, 2 (1869), 285 · *DCB*, vol. 9 · J. H. Siddons, *A personal history of the horse-guards, from 1750 to 1872* (1973) · H. S. Thomas, *The story of Sandhurst* (1961) · J. Schull, *Rebellion: the rising in French Canada, 1837* (1971) · R. Cannon, ed., *Historical record of the sixth, or royal first Warwickshire regiment of foot* (1839) · *Annual Register* (1838), 10 · *The Times* (14 May 1869) · Boase, *Mod. Eng. biog.*
Archives NAM, corresp. and papers | NL Scot., letters to Sir George Brown · W. Sussex RO, letters to duke of Richmond
Likenesses portrait, repro. in *ILN* (9 May 1868)
Wealth at death under £3000: probate, 1868 · under £5000—Edward Robert Wetherall: probate, 1869

Wethered, Joyce [*married name* Joyce Heathcoat-Amory, Lady Heathcoat-Amory] (**1901–1997**), golfer and horticulturist, was born on 17 November 1901 at Coombefield, Malden Road, New Malden, Surrey, the only daughter and younger child of (Herbert) Newton Wethered (*b.* 1869), artist and author, and his wife, Marion Emmeline, *née* Lund. She was educated privately at home. Her father was the author of a number of books on golf, and her brother, Roger Henry *Wethered (1899–1983), was one of the outstanding golfers of his era. She first began to play golf as a child in Bude, Cornwall, and at Dornoch in the highlands, where the family took a house overlooking the links. She burst upon the golfing scene in 1920 when she defeated the great Cecil Leitch in the final of the English ladies' championship at Sheringham. She proceeded to win the English ladies' championship another four years in a row. She won the British ladies' amateur championship in 1922, 1924, and 1925. She then retired from competitive golf until 1929 when she won the championship again. After that she did not enter further championships but captained the first British Curtis cup team against the United States in 1932, having represented her country against France the previous year.

In all, Wethered entered twelve national championships and won nine, was runner-up in two, and reached the semi-final in the other. Her competitive career was really for only six years between 1920 and 1925. Bobby Jones described her in 1935 as 'one of the greatest players of either sex' (*The Golfer*, June 1935). Walter Hagen felt that when she was at the top of her game there was not another woman player in her class. Glenna Collett Vare described her as 'the most perfect golfer I have seen' (Collett, 21). Bernard Darwin felt that Bobby Jones and Joyce Wethered were 'in the class of game playing geniuses that only arise once in a very long while' (Darwin, 6). She was renowned for her swing and concentration on the golf course. It was reputed that she did not hear an express train roaring behind her back while putting for the match

Joyce Wethered (1901–1997), by H. N. Wethered, 1923

at her first English championship at Sheringham in 1920. She herself wrote thirteen years later with typical modesty that

the story varies slightly in detail; but the point of it seems to depend on whether I heard the train or not—whether indeed, I was so oblivious of my surroundings that my oblivion became a glorious instance of concentration—and that is a question which for me is still wrapped in mystery. (Wethered, 37–8)

Again at the 1925 ladies' amateur championship in Troon she holed a critical putt with a train snorting on the line behind her, but this time she was fully aware of the locomotive as 'it was puffing smoke in clouds behind the green in a way that could not very well be ignored' (Wethered, 68–9).

After winning the ladies' amateur at Troon, Wethered retired from championship golf because

a less active role has always suited me perfectly. I can enter into the emotions of the game and enjoy them just as I like without having to preserve a state of elaborate calmness as a player over incidents which are in reality causing me acute excitement and probably no little apprehension and alarm. (Wethered, 65)

She wanted to try her hand at other sports such as fishing and tennis, and to get away from the limelight. Her retirement lasted until 1929 when the ladies' amateur championship was to be played at St Andrews. The lure of playing at the home of golf was too great for her. She reached the final, where she met Glenna Collett, the great American player. In a highly dramatic match of fluctuating fortunes Wethered won by 3 and 1 despite being down by five holes up after nine had been played. Wethered did not compete in any more ladies' amateur championships but she continued to make her annual appearance in the Worplesdon mixed foursomes, which she won in 1922, 1923, 1927, 1928, 1931, 1932, 1933, and 1936.

In 1933 Wethered took a job as the golf adviser at Fortnum and Mason's. The following year the definition of an amateur golfer was changed, and on 5 March 1934 the Royal and Ancient ruled that she was not eligible to play as an amateur if she received any 'consideration' in connection with her appointment. She took advantage of her new professional status in 1935 to tour the United States and Canada, representing the John Wannamaker Company. It was reputed that the tour earned her in excess of £4000, having received a guarantee of $300 per match. She played at least fifty-two matches, travelling all over America from May until September, and set thirty-six new records. One of the highlights was when she played in a foursome against Bobby Jones at the East Lake country club in Atlanta. O. B. Keeler, Jones's biographer, felt that the sight of Jones and Wethered playing in the match 'will stand out as the prettiest picture of a lifetime in sport … the greatest match I ever witnessed' (Keeler).

After her return Wethered met her future husband, Sir John Heathcoat-Amory, third baronet (1894–1972), chairman and later president of John Heathcoat & Co., lacemakers, and older brother of Derick Heathcoat-Amory, Viscount Amory, on the first tee at the Royal North Devon golf club as part of a weekend house party. They were married on 6 January 1937 in London. There were no children of the marriage. Sir John's family home was Knightshayes, a Victorian Gothic mansion just outside Tiverton, Devon. William Burges designed the building and some very lavish interiors, only a few of which were completed before he was replaced by John Crace. At the time of their marriage the gardens consisted largely of a few formal terraces, some bedding out, some topiary, a small rose bed, and a large expanse of lawn with woodland. In 1946 the Heathcoat-Amorys began to plan the garden in earnest, and over the next twenty-five years they created an exciting new landscape. Sir John was awarded the Royal Horticultural Society's Victoria medal of honour in 1966 and Lady Heathcoat-Amory received the same award in 1981. Both awards were for developing the Knightshayes gardens. In 1980 she wrote:

> Gardening has been full of excitement for me. Although the joy and adventures I shared in laying out a garden can never fade, I know at heart I am a plantswoman, and in the company with all those who are devoted to horticulture, Knightshayes has been for me, a constant source of delight. (Lees-Milne and Verey, 25)

The Heathcoat-Amorys continued to play social golf together until the 1960s. She was the first president of the English Ladies' Golf Association in 1951 and, rather academically, she was reinstated as an amateur by the Royal and Ancient on 23 May 1954. Sir John died on 22 November 1972 and the house was given to the National Trust the following year. Lady Heathcoat-Amory continued to live in one wing of the house until her death there, of old age, on

18 November 1997. She wrote one book as a sole author, *Golfing Memories and Methods* (1933), and with her brother wrote *Golf from Two Sides* (1922); she contributed three chapters to *The Game of Golf* (1931). She also wrote a chapter in *The Englishwoman's Garden* (1980) as well as the introduction to the National Trust guide to Knightshayes Court (1981).
                         PETER N. LEWIS

Sources J. Wethered, *Golfing memories and methods* (1933) · A. Lees-Milne and R. Verey, eds., *The Englishwoman's garden* (1980) · L. Mair, 'Lady Heathcoat-Amory', *Golf Monthly* (March 1984) · L. Mair, *One hundred years of women's golf* (1992) · B. Darwin, *Golf between two wars* (1944) · G. Collett, *Ladies in the rough* (1929) · H. Meller, *Knightshayes Court, Devon* (1981) · B. Jones, 'On Miss Wethered', *The Golfer* (June 1935) · O. B. Keeler, 'They made a great match', *American Golfer* (Aug 1935) · editorial, 'Chip Shots', *Golfing* (Aug 1935) · *The Times* (21 Nov 1997) · *The Independent* (21 Nov 1997) · minutes of the championship committee, 1934–54, Royal and Ancient Golf Club of St Andrews · *Daily Telegraph* (20 Nov 1997) · *The Guardian* (21 Nov 1997) · Burke, *Peerage* · *WWW* · b. cert. · d. cert.
Likenesses H. N. Wethered, oils, 1923, Knightshayes Court, Devon [*see illus.*] · photographs, 1925–48, Hult. Arch. · W. R. Dick, bronze, Royal and Ancient Golf Club collection · photograph, repro. in *Daily Telegraph* · photograph, repro. in *The Independent* · photograph, repro. in *The Guardian*
Wealth at death £914,778: probate, 13 March 1998, *CGPLA Eng. & Wales*

Wethered, Roger Henry (1899–1983), golfer, was born at Coombefield, Malden Road, New Malden, Surrey, on 3 January 1899, the only son and elder child of Herbert Newton Wethered, artist, and his wife, Marion Emmeline Lund. Owing to poor health in his younger days, he went to school for only a brief period and then was educated by tutors. He was thus introduced to golf earlier than might otherwise have been the case. His father was author and co-author of more than one book on golf, an involvement which almost certainly influenced his son's development as a player. However, Wethered was old enough and fit enough to be commissioned in the Royal Artillery at the end of the First World War (1918) and saw service for a few weeks in France.

On leaving the army Wethered went to Christ Church, Oxford, where, for two years, he played golf in the Oxford side with Cyril Tolley. Together they were described as the first and most conspicuous champions of a new generation. As they were also good friends, it was inevitable that their names were repeatedly bracketed together and their achievements compared. Bernard Darwin, who knew them both well, felt that Tolley was 'always and unquestionably the finer driver but that Wethered was equally and beyond question the better iron player'. Wethered was both powerful and accurate, with a capacity for obtaining the maximum backspin. His driving was less than certain, although its errant ways established his reputation as an exceptional recovery player. When he won the amateur championship at Deal in 1923, he drove magnificently. This feat prompted his sister Joyce to remark 'Why, this is a new Roger.' Joyce *Wethered was the best female golfer of the time and together they stand as the finest brother and sister combination.

Wethered's most notable performance was in tying for the open championship at St Andrews in 1921. This was during his last year at Oxford (he graduated BA in 1921 after the shortened course in English) and followed Tolley's victory in the amateur the previous summer. It was the last time that a British amateur came as close to winning the open; yet Wethered's total of 296 included a penalty stroke in the third round for accidentally treading on his ball. Some assumed it to be logical and incontestable that, if he had not suffered this misfortune, he would have won. It was an unjustifiable assumption but, having been six strokes behind Jock Hutchison, the eventual winner, after the first round, Wethered's final rounds on the last day (72 and 71) were the lowest. The play-off with Hutchison, a Scotsman who became an American citizen, was a disappointment. Wethered, who had planned to be playing cricket in the south, was beaten by nine strokes but, though he never played quite as well again after his victory at Deal two years later, he remained a formidable, popular, and influential figure in the game. He was a man of engaging modesty and charm, described later by an eminent amateur golfer as one of the two most courteous opponents he had ever faced.

Wethered reached the final of the amateur twice again, won the President's Putter five times, and was capped six times for Britain in the Walker cup against America and nine times for England against Scotland. In these later matches he won all his singles and eight out of nine foursomes between 1922 and 1931. As an automatic choice for the Walker cup Wethered developed a long-standing rivalry and friendship with Bobby Jones, an American, who defeated him in the final of the amateur at St Andrews in 1930, the first leg of Jones's unique grand slam. That same year Wethered lost to Jones in the Walker cup singles but his record in that cup did him full justice. Apart from losing his final foursomes in 1934 with his old partner Tolley, he lost only to Jones, whom he first met in 1922.

By the 1930s Wethered was seldom in good practice, a fact that owed much to his having become a hard-working stockbroker in London. He worked on committees at the Royal and Ancient and was elected its captain in 1939, although he did not take office until 1946. He thus had plenty of time to contemplate the ordeal of driving himself in. He continued to play golf and when he was seventy-four went round Wimbledon in a score to match his age; as the senior past captain of the Royal and Ancient he also gave the address at the memorial service for Bobby Jones at St Andrews in 1972. He was a leading stockbroker and chairman of several investment trusts. In 1925 he married Elizabeth, daughter of Lord Charles Cavendish Cavendish-Bentinck, son of the sixth duke of Portland. This marriage was dissolved in 1954 and on 15 August 1957 Wethered married Marjorie Mitford Campbell Stratford (b. 1905/6), daughter of Ernest Stubbs, judge. He had no children by either wife. He died at his home at Garnet House, 31 Camp Road, Wimbledon, on 12 March 1983.

DONALD STEEL, rev.

Sources B. Darwin, Golf between two wars (1944) · The Times (15 March 1983) · b. cert. · m. cert. [Marjorie Stratford] · CGPLA Eng. & Wales (1983)

Likenesses photographs, 1920–32, Hult. Arch.
Wealth at death £271,252: probate, 5 July 1983, CGPLA Eng. & Wales

Wetherell, Sir Charles (1770–1846), politician and lawyer, was born in Oxford, the third son of Nathan Wetherell, dean of Hereford and master of University College, Oxford, and his wife, Ricarda, daughter of Alexander Croke of Studley Priory, Oxfordshire. He went to St Paul's School in 1783, and University College, Oxford, in 1786. From 1788 to 1791 he held a demyship at Magdalen College, Oxford. He graduated BA on 2 June 1790 and MA on 9 July 1793. In accordance with his father's wish he entered the Inner Temple on 15 April 1790 and was called to the bar on 4 July 1794. Under the patronage of Lord Eldon, a friend of his father, he developed an important equity practice, appearing in chancery, and before the privy council, the House of Lords, and parliamentary committees. He was appointed KC in 1816. He became bencher of his inn in 1816 and treasurer in 1825. Piqued that he had not received high legal office and determined to draw attention to his abilities, in 1817 he defended James Watson, charged with high treason after the Spa Fields riots. Wetherell presented an able and vigorous defence and, despite being a tory, denounced the methods used by the tory government in the affair. After Watson was found not guilty, charges against other defendants were dropped, and the episode did nothing to advance Wetherell's career.

Wetherell was MP for Rye from 1812 to 1813, Shaftesbury from 1813 to 1818, Oxford from 1820 to 1826, Hastings in 1826, Plympton Erle in Devon from 1826 to 1830, and Boroughbridge in Yorkshire from 1830 to 1832. He was 'treated by both sides as a whimsical pedant rather than a formidable debater' (GM, 428). He vehemently opposed almost every reform which came before the house, especially Roman Catholic emancipation and parliamentary, municipal, and university reform. He was knighted on 10 March 1824. He finally achieved high office, being appointed solicitor-general on 31 January 1824 and attorney-general in September 1826. He resigned while Canning was in office, but was reappointed in 1828 under the duke of Wellington until his intemperate opposition to Roman Catholic emancipation led to his dismissal. Thereafter he became a bitter opponent of the Wellington and whig administrations.

It was Wetherell's appearance in Bristol which provoked the reform riots there in 1831. As recorder of Bristol he went there on 29 October 1831 to open the assizes, in spite of warnings to stay away. He had been jeered when he came to the city in March 1831 and the recently formed Bristol Political Union publicized his impending arrival in October. He was castigated for his personal opposition to reform and for misrepresenting local opinion, which, despite his assertions in the house, strongly favoured reform. Attempts in late October to enlist the support of Bristol sailors for Wetherell under cover of a declaration of loyalty to the king failed; the sailors declared for the king but resolved not to be 'the cat's paw of the Corporation or its

Sir Charles Wetherell (1770–1846), by Henry Bryan Hall, pubd 1837 (after Moore)

agents' (Harrison, 83). Therein lay the heart of the problem: not only was Wetherell a hated opponent of parliamentary reform, but, as recorder, he was *ex officio* alderman of the common council which was despised by virtually all Bristolians. Despite all this he refused to stay away, perhaps remembering that the corporation had tried unsuccessfully to prevent Bristolians who shared his anti-catholicism turning out to welcome him in April 1829. In 1831 Wetherell simply repeated the warnings to the home secretary and attempted to carry on as normal. On arrival he was jeered and stoned and, after seeking refuge in the mansion house, made an inglorious exit over the roof and in disguise fled the city. The ensuing riot in the city, the worst reform riot in the country, lasted three days and involved spectacular loss of life and destruction of property. In the sacking of the mansion house Wetherell's wig and robe were sought out for destruction and it was even suggested that the authorities burn an effigy of him to assuage the anger of the crowd.

Compared with the treatment which the mayor, Charles Pinney, and the commander of the troops, Thomas Brereton, subsequently received, Wetherell escaped remarkably lightly. He continued as recorder until his death and returned to practice. Wetherell was twice married: first on 28 December 1826 to his cousin, Jane Sarah Elizabeth (*d.* 1831), second daughter of Sir Alexander Croke of Studley Priory; and second on 27 November 1838 to Harriet Elizabeth, second daughter of Colonel Francis Warneford of Warneford Place, Wiltshire. Wetherell died on 17 August 1846 at Preston Hall, Kent, after being injured in a carriage accident on 10 August. He

was buried in Temple Church on 25 August. He had no surviving children from either marriage. With the fortune he had inherited on his father's death in 1807 and that he acquired himself he left more than £200,000 personalty and a considerable amount of land. With fine irony given his role in the Bristol riot, a statue of him was erected at Clifton, Bristol, in 1839.   ELIZABETH BAIGENT

Sources HoP, *Commons* · *GM*, 2nd ser., 26 (1846), 426–30 · *The Times* (19 Aug 1846) · M. Harrison, *Crowds and history* (1988) · S. Thomas, *The Bristol riot* (1974) · *DNB*

Archives Durham RO, letters to Lord Londonderry · Niedersächsisches Hauptstaatsarchiv Hannover, Hanover, corresp. with duke of Cumberland

Likenesses W. Heath, caricature, coloured etching, 1831, V&A · cartoon, 1831, repro. in Harrison, *Crowds and history*, p. 310 · H. B. Hall, stipple, 1837 (after Moore), BM, NPG; repro. in H. T. Ryall, *Portraits of eminent conservatives and statesmen* [in pts, 1836–46] [*see illus.*] · Tyley, statue, 1839, Meridian Place, Clifton, Bristol · J. Doyle, caricature, pencil drawing (*The man wot prefers his character to his place*), BM · J. Smith III, line engraving (after J. K. M.?), NPG · caricature, etching, NPG

Wealth at death £200,000 personalty; mainly in South American stock; a considerable fortune in realty: *DNB*; HoP, *Commons*; *GM*

Wetherell, Nathaniel Thomas (1800–1875), geologist, was born on 6 September 1800 at The Grove, Highgate, Middlesex, the seventh of the eight children of William Roundell Wetherell (1767/8–1821), surgeon, and Anne Maria Gibson. He was educated in private schools and at the Middlesex Hospital. He became a licentiate of the Society of Apothecaries in 1824 and a member of the Royal College of Surgeons of London in 1828.

Wetherell's spare time was given to the study of the geology of north London. He visited railway cuttings, road excavations, and well sections, at Camden Town, Chalk Farm, Hampstead, and Highgate, where the London Clay was temporarily exposed, and amassed an exceptionally fine collection of fossils. He was a founder of the Palaeontographical Society and many of his specimens were illustrated in its monographs. By 1836 he had noticed a vertical change of fauna within the London Clay and proposed lower, middle, and upper divisions of that formation; one of the first English manifestations of the idea that lithological units could be further subdivided by fossils. On 20 March 1837 he married Louisa Mary (*bap.* 1819, *d.* 1900), daughter of William Robert Casson, at St Pancras Old Church.

Wetherell also studied the glacial drift deposits around Finchley and Muswell Hill and formed a collection of interesting specimens, particularly banded flints. He was elected a fellow of the Geological Society in 1832, left in 1856, rejoined in 1863, but finally resigned in December 1869 owing to deafness. His main collection was bought for the British Museum (Natural History) through James Tennant, a dealer, in 1871. This was added to earlier donations making the total number of specimens received from him almost 5000. Other specimens were donated to the Geological Survey's museum and Geological Society.

Wetherell was regarded by contemporaries as a caring, gentle, good, kind, modest, and unassuming Christian. He died, at his lifelong home, The Grove, Highgate, on 22

December 1875 owing to chronic enlargement of the prostate and exhaustion; he was buried on 29 December in the old burial-ground, Highgate. He was survived by his wife, the sole beneficiary of his will dated 3 August 1861, four sons, and three daughters. W. H. GEORGE

Sources J. Evans, *Quarterly Journal of the Geological Society*, 32 (1876), 90 · *Geological Magazine*, new ser., 2nd decade, 3 (1876), 48 · *The history of the collections contained in the natural history departments of the British Museum*, British Museum, 1 (1904), 335–6 · D. T. Moore, J. C. Thackray, and D. L. Morgan, 'A short history of the museum of the Geological Society of London, 1807–1911', *Bulletin of the British Museum (Natural History)* [Historical Series], 19 (1991), 51–160, esp. 144–5 · E. F. Freeman, 'The origins of the Geologists' Association', *Archives of Natural History*, 19 (1992), 1–27 · A. Wrigley, 'Faunal divisions of the London Clay', *Proceedings of the Geologists' Association*, 35 (1924), 245–59 · parish register (baptism), 23 Oct 1800, London, Highgate Chapel · parish register (marriage), 20 March 1837, London, St Pancras Old Church · Highgate Literary and Scientific Institution archives

Archives NHM, fossils | BGS · GS Lond. · Highgate Literary and Scientific Institution

Likenesses two photographs, Highgate Literary and Scientific Institution

Wetheringsett [Wethersett], **Richard of** [Richard of Leicester] (*fl. c.*1200–*c.*1230), churchman and theologian, is recorded as a student under William de Montibus at Lincoln in the years round 1200. The author of the *summa Qui bene presunt* about 1220, he is the earliest identifiable chancellor of Cambridge University (serving some time between 1215 and 1232); he is not to be confused with the later chancellor Richard Leicester, who served in 1349–50.

Wetheringsett's *summa* is a milestone in the history of Christian education in England. It is organized as a guide for preachers, who are first to learn about the most basic elements of 'faith and morals', and then go on to preach about them to the people. He identifies twelve topics for consideration, in a list that, with minor alterations, was to become normative for catechetical preaching during the following centuries. That list begins with the creed and the articles of faith, followed by the Lord's prayer, the gifts of the Holy Spirit, the virtues, the vices, the seven sacraments, the two evangelical precepts, the ten commandments, the rewards of heaven and pains of hell, the errors of the people, the things to be avoided, and the things to be done. Although none of these topics was new in the thirteenth century, their being assembled in a programmatic guide for preachers helped to shape the religious literature of England for centuries to come. Its influence can be seen, for instance, in the syllabus of things to be preached regularly by parish priests that Archbishop John Pecham (*d.* 1292) published in his famous constitution *Ignorantia sacerdotum* of 1281. Still unpublished, the *summa* survives in some sixty manuscript copies.

Much of what is known about Wetheringsett's life derives from his *summa*. It reveals that the author studied under William de Montibus in the cathedral school at Lincoln, some time between 1180 and 1213. However, differences between manuscripts also serve both to obscure his identity and to raise intriguing possibilities about it, referring to him variously as Richard of Leicester, Richard of Wetheringsett, and Richard de Montibus (this last a confusion with Richard's frequently quoted master, William de Montibus). Some manuscripts describe him as rector of the church of Wetheringsett, some as chancellor of the University of Cambridge, and some as chancellor of Lincoln Cathedral (perhaps again a confusion with William de Montibus, also chancellor). One mid-thirteenth-century manuscript neatly reconciles his surnames by identifying him as 'Master Richard of Leicester, rector of the church of Wetheringsett' (Shrewsbury School, MS 7, fol. 109*v*). There is independent corroboration that the earliest known chancellor of Cambridge was named Richard of Leicester; and the wealthy prebend of Wetheringsett, Suffolk, which was in the gift of the bishop of Ely, who had oversight of Cambridge University, would have provided suitable emolument for the latter's chancellor. Richard is depicted lecturing in the initial 'Q' in one copy of *Qui bene presunt*, next to a note describing the text as the 'summa magistri R. Cancellarii de Kantebrug' (CUL, MS Additional 3471, fol. 125*r*).

The evidence that Wetheringsett was also chancellor of Lincoln is less secure, owing to possible confusion with his mentor, William de Montibus. But there is nothing implausible in the notion that, as the author of a highly respected theological *summa*, Richard would have been invited to succeed his master as chancellor and head of the Lincoln Cathedral school. This possibility is perhaps strengthened by independent evidence that the chancellor of Lincoln from 1220 to 1228, Richard le Grant, was known by the cognomen de Wethershed, probably a variant of Wetheringsett. This evidence is far from secure, but it raises the possibility that Richard of Wetheringsett, the author of *Qui bene presunt*, who was rector of Wetheringsett church and an early chancellor of Cambridge University, is also to be identified with Richard *Grant, chancellor of Lincoln Cathedral, and archbishop of Canterbury from 1229 until his premature death in 1231.

JOSEPH GOERING

Sources J. Goering, 'The *summa Qui bene presunt* and its author', *Literature and religion in the later middle ages*, ed. R. G. Newhauser and J. A. Alford (1995), 143–59 · J. Goering, *William de Montibus (c.1140–1213): the schools and the literature of pastoral care*, Pontifical Institute of Medieval Studies: Texts and Studies, 108 (1992) · Emden, *Cam.* · L. E. Boyle, 'Three English pastoral *summae* and a "Magister Galienus"', *Studia Gratiana*, 11 (1967), 134–44 · M. B. Hackett, *The original statutes of Cambridge University* (1970), 48–51 · A. L. Kellogg, 'St Augustine and the "Parson's tale"', *Traditio*, 8 (1952), 424–30

Archives CUL, Add. MS 3471, fol. 125*r* · Shrewsbury School, MS 7, fol. 109*v*

Likenesses manuscript, CUL, Add. MS 3471

Wetwang, Sir Joseph (1622/3–1684), naval officer, was descended from an old freeholder family of Dunstan, Northumberland. Nothing is known of his early life prior to his marriage to Isabel Middleton (*b.* 1628) at All Saints' Church, Newcastle, on 23 December 1648. He was engaged in merchant shipping in Newcastle and the east coast at the time of the First Anglo-Dutch War (1652–4). The loss of his ship to the Dutch caused the mayor of Newcastle to petition the admiralty on his behalf for some employment, and in February 1653 he was appointed to command the *Sparrow*, a small Dutch prize then fitting out at Newcastle. Wetwang spent the rest of the war cruising against Dutch privateers on the east coast, and convoying trade from Newcastle to London and Hamburg. He continued in command of the *Sparrow* after the war's end, plying off Scotland under the orders of General George Monck. His requests to be transferred to a bigger ship were unsuccessful, and he left the navy when the *Sparrow* was withdrawn from service in September 1654.

Wetwang probably returned to merchant service, not re-entering the navy until February 1665 when he was appointed to command the fifth-rate *Norwich*. Wetwang was highly regarded by his superiors at this time, being described by the lord admiral's secretary, Sir William Coventry, as 'a very good man' (Coventry MS 99, fol. 91) and by Monck, now duke of Albemarle, as 'a diligent officer and a good seaman' (NMM, LBK/47). Wetwang moved to the *Tiger* on 10 May 1666, taking part in Sir Robert Holmes's attack on Terschelling, and remained in command of her until November 1667, being regularly employed on convoy and cruising duties in his native waters. He commanded the *Dunkirk* and the *Edgar* briefly in 1668, returning to command the latter in January 1672 at the outbreak of the Third Anglo-Dutch War and fighting in the earl of Sandwich's division of the Blue squadron at the battle of Solebay (28 May 1672). Wetwang was captain of the *Warspite* over the winter of 1672–3 and of the *Henry* from March to June 1673, commanding the latter in Prince Rupert's division of the Red squadron at the two battles of Schooneveld (28 May and 4 June 1673) and earning high praise from Rupert for his conduct. On 1 July 1673 he became second captain of Rupert's flagship, the *Sovereign*, fighting at the battle of the Texel (11 August) and remaining aboard her until the end of October. He then commanded the *Newcastle*, chiefly in the Mediterranean, from November 1673 to February 1676, capturing a valuable Dutch East Indiaman at the very end of the Third Anglo-Dutch War. In the French war scare of 1678 Wetwang commanded the *Monmouth* before serving as second captain of the *Royal James*, the flagship of Admiral Sir Thomas Allin, between March and August. He subsequently went to Flushing and Ostend to organize the re-embarkation of the army which had been sent to Flanders. Wetwang commanded the *Northumberland* briefly in 1679 before taking his last naval command, the *Woolwich*, in which he served (again in the Mediterranean) from October 1679 to May 1681. He was knighted on 20 November 1680.

Wetwang had always maintained his mercantile connections, part owning a number of merchant vessels, attempting in 1676 to get a patent for making all merchant bills in the port of London, and becoming in 1679 water bailiff for the rivers Humber and Trent and their tributaries, in reversion. The fact that by 1682 his half pay was three years in arrears seems to have persuaded him to seek employment outside the navy, and in 1682 he became captain of the new East India Company vessel, the *Royal James*, flagship of the force intended to re-establish trade with Bantam. He died on board his ship at Fort St George, Madras, soon after his arrival, on 12 July 1684. By his will, dated 18 October 1683, Wetwang made bequests to his wife, Isabel, and to his four sons, Robert (b. 1649), John (b. 1651), Samuel (1653–1685), and Joseph. All had held posts in the customs at Newcastle in the 1670s, but Joseph then entered the navy, being dismissed as lieutenant of the *Happy Return* in 1684 for drunkenness and abusing his captain. He was saved from a court martial only by the kindness of Admiral Lord Dartmouth towards his father, but was in prison by 1687 for other 'grand misdemeanours'. Samuel was a factor at Madras at the time of his death on 1 February 1685. Another of Wetwang's sons succeeded him in command of the East Indiaman *Royal James*, dying in command of her in 1689.

J. D. DAVIES

Sources CSP dom., 1652–4; 1678; 1682–3 • W. A. Shaw, ed., *Calendar of treasury books*, 5–9, PRO (1911–31) • *A history of Northumberland*, Northumberland County History Committee, 15 vols. (1893–1940), vol. 2, pp. 189–91 • parish registers, Newcastle, St Andrew's, Northumbd RO, Newcastle upon Tyne • PRO, PROB 11/379, fol. 396 • *The Tangier papers of Samuel Pepys*, ed. E. Chappell, Navy RS, 73 (1935) • B. Capp, *Cromwell's navy: the fleet and the English revolution, 1648–1660* (1989) • N. Luttrell, *A brief historical relation of state affairs from September 1678 to April 1714*, 6 vols. (1857) • statement of services, PRO, ADM MSS, esp. ADM 10/15, 136 • letter-book of George Monck, duke of Albemarle, 1665, NMM, LBK/47 • William Coventry's lists of officers, Longleat House, Wiltshire, Coventry MS 99, fol. 91 • PRO, HCA 13/77 • BL OIOC, G/19/3, pt. 2, 96
Archives PRO, ADM MSS
Wealth at death see will, PRO, PROB 11/379, fol. 396

Wever, R. (*fl.* 1550), playwright, is known solely from the appearance of his name ('quod R. Wever') at the end of two of the three surviving editions of *An Enterlude called Lusty Juventus*, apparently written during the reign of Edward VI, and notable for its strong anti-Catholic tone. A play thus entitled was recorded (without attribution) in the Stationers' register under the year 1560–61, and the successive editions are datable within the subsequent fifteen years. No information has otherwise come to light as to R. Wever's identity, and even his forename (sometimes given as Richard, or Robert) is a matter of conjecture. Attention has been drawn to the existence of a protestant clergyman called Richard Wever, who took a BA degree at Oxford in 1524. He may be the person of that name who became a fellow of St Chad's College, Shrewsbury (in 1546), and then prebendary of Bubbenhall (in 1549) and Hansacre (in 1554) in the diocese of Lichfield. This man was probably the Richard Wever whom Foxe mentions in the *Acts and Monuments* as one of a number of persons examined at Lichfield in 1556. However, nothing is known that would connect him with the composition of *Lusty Juventus*.

RICHARD BEADLE

Sources R. Wever, *Lusty Juventus*, ed. J. M. Nosworthy (1971), xxii–xxiii

Wewitzer, Ralph (1748–1825), actor, was born in Salisbury Street, off the Strand, London, on 17 December 1748, probably the eldest of the five children of Peter and Ann

Wewitzer known to have acted in London in the late eighteenth century. According to the *Hibernian Magazine* (January 1775) their father was Norwegian, though alternative and likelier accounts suggest that he was Swiss.

Russell claimed that Ralph Wewitzer was apprenticed to, and briefly practised as, a jeweller before making his theatrical début at Covent Garden as Ralph in Isaac Bickerstaff's *The Maid of the Mill* on 12 May 1773. The occasion was the benefit of his younger sister Sarah [*see below*], and his success was sufficient to determine his future career. It has been suggested, but cannot be confirmed, that he spent the 1773-4 season acting in Dublin, either to evade or to earn sufficient to pay off his creditors, but he was with the company at Covent Garden from 1774 to 1789 and a regular summer performer at the Haymarket after 1780. In terms of the theatrical categories of his age, Wewitzer was a low comedian who specialized in the roles of foreigners—French, Jewish, Spanish, Dutch, or German. John O'Keeffe generously acknowledged his contribution to the success of his musical spectacular *Omai* (Covent Garden, 1785), in which, as a South Sea warrior addressing Captain Cook, he:

> came out with a kind of grand extempore declaration, as if it was the original language of some of the islands: this had a sham English translation, which was printed in the book of the songs. Wewitzer did this piece of state harangue-pomposo wonderfully well. (O'Keeffe, 2.115)

It was in another piece by O'Keeffe, *The Young Quaker* (1783), that Wewitzer created his most celebrated character, Shadrach the Jew, whose enduring popularity was matched only by his Doctor Caius in *The Merry Wives of Windsor*. He was able to exploit the vogue for lampooning foreigners that was the theatrical reaction to Britain's burgeoning interests overseas, not least because he was himself a speaker and reader of French during the Napoleonic era.

Wewitzer cherished entrepreneurial and literary ambitions almost throughout his long career on the stage, but may well have lost more money than he gained by them. His brief management in 1790 of the Royalty Theatre, Wellclose Square, was unsuccessful, and a scheme to set up business as a fishmonger came to nothing. Three forgotten pantomimes have been ascribed to him, as well as a genealogical *Pedigree of King George III* (1812), a scantily researched reference work called *A Theatrical Pocket Book* (1814), and two posthumously published volumes of anecdotal history, *Green Room Gossip* (c.1826) and *Dramatic Reminiscences* (c.1855). He may, for a while, have acted as financial adviser to the actress Harriet Mellon, by then the widowed duchess of St Albans, but, given her charitable history, it is unlikely, if his advice had been useful, that she would have done nothing to alleviate the poverty of his last years. James Boaden cites the plight of 'poor Wewitzer' in mounting an argument for the establishment of a retirement home for decayed actors (Boaden, 342–3).

Although the details are obscure, Wewitzer seems to have married twice, first at St Peter's, Church Street, Liverpool, to Mary Daniels on 14 September 1776 (who is known to have been still alive in 1783 and with whom he had one daughter) and second to a Miss Brangin, also of Covent Garden Theatre, on 23 December 1787; but at the time of his death, on 1 January 1825, he was living alone, 'under circumstances of peculiar distress' (Russell, 212), in Wild Passage, off Drury Lane. He was buried in Finsbury. He had for several years been dependent on an annual stipend of £65 from the Theatrical Fund of Drury Lane, the theatre with which he had been predominantly associated since 1791.

Sarah Wewitzer (*bap.* 1756, *d.* 1820), actress and singer, baptized at St Paul's, Covent Garden, on 18 July 1756, was the sister of Ralph Wewitzer. She may already have appeared as a singer in London's pleasure gardens before making her theatrical début at Covent Garden on 4 November 1772. Her voice and personality were ideally suited to the musical romances of Isaac Bickerstaff, and most of her early successes were in his work: *Daphne and Amintor* (1772), *The Maid of the Mill* (1773), and *The Padlock* (1773). It was either she or an elder sister who sang with the operatic bass Frederick Reinhold at Marylebone Gardens in the summer of 1774, and it was certainly she who fluttered the hearts of young Dubliners by her appearances at the Smock Alley Theatre during the 1774-5 season. An attractively engraved portrait was featured in the *Hibernian Magazine* of January 1775, capturing her as Rosetta in Bickerstaffe's *Love in a Village* in the act of delivering the song 'Cease, gay deceivers', which she had made the rage of Dublin. Her reputation for virtue further piqued the interest of the city's bachelors—and not only the bachelors. Sarah Wewitzer had made Dublin her home by the time she entered into an adulterous relationship with James Cuffe, member of parliament for co. Mayo. Cuffe's wife had been granted a legal separation not long after their marriage in 1778, and Wewitzer left the stage to set up home with him and bear his children. Cuffe was created Baron Tyrawley of Ballinrobe in 1797, and when his wife died in 1808 Wewitzer adopted the name of Lady Tyrawley. There is no record of a marriage and neither of their sons, James Cuffe, MP for co. Mayo, or Henry Cuffe, succeeded to the peerage. It may be that the couple had separated before Wewitzer's death, at Ballinrobe on 4 October 1820. According to the *Journal of the Society for the Preservation of Memorials in Ireland* (vol. 7, p. 152), she was buried at Ballinrobe as Lady Tyrawley.

PETER THOMSON

Sources Highfill, Burnim & Langhans, *BDA* · D. E. Baker, *Biographia dramatica, or, A companion to the playhouse*, rev. I. Reed, new edn, rev. S. Jones, 3 vols. in 4 (1812) · T. Wilkinson, *The wandering patentee, or, A history of the Yorkshire theatres from 1770 to the present time*, 4 vols. (1795) · J. Boaden, *Memoirs of Mrs Siddons*, another edn (1896) · J. O'Keeffe, *Recollections of the life of John O'Keeffe, written by himself*, 2 vols. (1826) · W. C. Russell, *Representative actors* [1888] · M. Sands, *The 18th-century pleasure gardens of Marylebone* (1987) · IGI
Likenesses J. Warren, oils, 1775 (Sarah Wewitzer as Rosetta) · J. S. Agar, engraving, 1806 · S. De Wilde, pencil and watercolour drawing, 1808, Garr. Club · engraving (Sarah Wewitzer; after J. Warren), repro. in *Hibernian Magazine* (1775)
Wealth at death abject poverty: all sources

Wewitzer, Sarah (*bap.* 1756, *d.* 1820). *See under* Wewitzer, Ralph (1748–1825).

Wex, Bernard Patrick (1922–1990), civil engineer, was born on 24 April 1922 in Acton, Middlesex, the only child of Julius Wex, a lace merchant from Germany, who had gone to England in 1900, taken British nationality in 1911, and in the same year married Gertrude Brady, a fashion saleswoman. His father died of pneumonia two weeks before he was born, and his mother went to live with her mother in Acton. He attended Acton county grammar school, where he showed all-round prowess, matriculating in 1938. On the outbreak of the Second World War his desire to become a Royal Air Force pilot was thwarted by minor astigmatism. After attending Sandhurst, in 1943 he became a tank commander (lieutenant) in the Royal Armoured Corps (23rd hussars). Having suffered pleurisy and pneumonia in 1944, he was transferred to administrative work until demobilization as captain in March 1947. In 1945 he married Sheila Evelyn Lambert, widow of Malcolm Kingsbury Lambert, RAF pilot, and daughter of Peter Thompson, a builder in north-west London; it was a very happy marriage, of which there were two sons. In October 1947 he was accepted by Imperial College, London, to read civil engineering and he graduated in 1950 with first-class honours, being top of his year and winning the Unwin medal.

Wex immediately started work with Freeman Fox & Partners under Gilbert Roberts and, later, Oleg Kerensky. His early work included Auckland harbour bridge (built in 1955–9) and schemes for the 1000 metre Severn and Forth suspension spans. He gained site experience on the 600 megawatt Castle Donington power station. Design work on another power station was followed by six 177 metre span oil pipeline suspension bridges in India, and a further series of bridges to carry high-pressure gas in Pakistan, including the 1770 metre multi-span River Sutlej crossing, which was built entirely in one dry season.

Appointed a partner in Freeman Fox in 1969, Wex oversaw construction of the M5 Avonmouth Bridge and took charge of the newly authorized Humber Bridge project. This had originally been studied by the firm in 1927–8 and proposed as a single 1372 metre span by Sir Ralph Freeman in 1935. Wex directed its final design and construction, adopting 'slip-formed' concrete for the towers, rather than steel, thus making substantial cost savings. He also used novel methods for sinking the south tower and anchorage foundations through 40 metres of water and silt to reach the Kimmeridge clay. The construction period coincided with unprecedented inflation and worsening industrial relations, which caused severe delays and mounting costs. Undaunted, Wex piloted client and contractors through to a supremely successful conclusion. The bridge was opened by Queen Elizabeth II on 17 July 1981. At 1410 metres its main clear span was the world's longest by 110 metres. Wex was appointed OBE in the 1982 new year honours list.

Although the Humber Bridge was Wex's crowning achievement, he packed much else into the decade of the 1970s, including the cable-stayed box-girder Myton swing bridge in Hull and a slender 165 metre concrete arch bridge in South Africa. In 1979 he prepared a design for one of six contractors bidding in competition for the proposed River Foyle Bridge near Londonderry, Northern Ireland. His graceful 234 metre span twin-steel box-girder scheme was judged the winner for appearance by the Royal Fine Arts Commission and was also the lowest priced. The bridge was completed in October 1984.

Wex led the seven-year inquiry into the 1969 collapse of the 381 metre Emley Moor television mast, and served energetically on many technical committees and on the council of the Welding Institute. He contributed much to the work of the International Association for Bridge and Structural Engineering, chairing its British group and technical committees; it made him an honorary member in 1990. He helped to found the Steel Construction Institute in 1986 and remained its chairman until shortly before his final illness. He wrote sixteen papers on six subjects, eleven of them between 1976 and 1984, which were published in ten countries, and he delivered many lectures at home and abroad.

With his lifelong enthusiasm, unquenchable good humour, and first-class brain, Wex became a most proficient and successful creator of bridges, the equal of any of his time. He was a perfectionist in all he attempted, becoming a skilful photographer and cabinet-maker. He was elected a member of the Institution of Civil Engineers (ICE) in 1956 (fellow, 1968), and a fellow of the Welding Institute, where he also took the practical welding course, in 1972. In 1982 he was elected to the Fellowship (later Royal Academy) of Engineering, and awarded the fellowship of the City and Guilds Institute. In 1985 he won the ICE's Telford gold medal and became a fellow of the Institution of Structural Engineers.

Wex was tall, of athletic build, fair-skinned with blond hair (which mostly disappeared in his early twenties), good-looking, and of extrovert personality. Wex died on 31 July 1990 in St Bartholomew's Hospital, London, while undergoing chemotherapy treatment for myeloid leukaemia. He was survived by his wife.

RALPH FREEMAN, *rev.*

Sources *The Independent* (22 Aug 1990) · *The Times* (14 Aug 1990) · Acer Group Ltd archives, Freeman Fox records · personal knowledge (1996) · private information (1996) [S. E. Wex]
Archives Acer Group Ltd, Freeman Fox MSS
Likenesses photograph, repro. in *The Times*
Wealth at death £202,318: probate, 30 Oct 1990, *CGPLA Eng. & Wales*

Wey, William (1405/6–1476), author and pilgrim, originated in the diocese of Salisbury. First recorded in 1430 as a fellow of Exeter College, Oxford, he was ordained acolyte and subdeacon on 7 March 1433 to the title of his fellowship. By 1439 he had proceeded MA, and in the following year was admitted a fellow of Eton College, a position he retained until about 1467. Recorded intermittently as bursar of the college between 1445 and 1465, he also retained links with Exeter, to which he gave two books in 1457. He made a collection of Latin sermons, and gave a copy of it to the Bridgettine abbey of Syon, but is better known for his accounts of his pilgrimages, to Santiago de Compostela in 1456, and to Jerusalem in 1457–8 and again in 1462.

Wey's writings on pilgrimages, which are preserved in Bodl. Oxf., MS Bodley 565, are divided into fifteen sections. Much of the collection is in Latin, but the first three sections are in English. The last of these, 'A Prevysyoun' giving advice in lacklustre verse to the would-be pilgrim to the Holy Land, is based upon the *Provisio pro peregrinis* which occurs later in the collection, but contains additional material and doubtless reflects Wey's wish to instruct. He states of his account of his 1457–8 pilgrimage that he was asked by devout men to write it, and he took his didactic role seriously. His writings contain details of exchange rates of money, useful phrases in Greek and Hebrew, and much practical advice to travellers proposing to follow him to the Levant—about distances, the need to take food and bedding, dealing with the authorities, and precautions against pickpockets and heat. They are also enlivened by much incidental detail; he describes the burial of one doge and the election of another at Venice in 1462, tells how when the pilgrims entered Jerusalem small boys threw stones at them, and in retailing rumours of the bloody exploits against the Turks of the Wallachian 'baro de Flake' was probably the first Englishman to note the existence of the man who would eventually be transmogrified into Dracula.

Wey was not composing a travelogue, however, and his principal motive in writing was devotional. No doubt he expressed his faith in the sermons he records preaching at Jerusalem and Corunna. On the evidence of his writings it was a piety focused primarily upon relics and their associated indulgences. His response to Calvary, for instance, is that

> Ther ys more pardon in that hylle
> Than eny Crystyn man can telle.
> (*Itineraries*, 10)

It was in keeping with this outlook that Wey should himself have collected a number of relics, including stones from the holy sepulchre and the cave of the nativity at Bethlehem, and made exact measurements of some of the principal shrines. His motive for doing so is disclosed by his will. About 1467 he entered the house of the Bonshommes at Edington, Wiltshire, where he died on 30 November 1476, aged seventy, and was presumably buried. He bequeathed his relics to 'the chapel made to the lyknes of the sepulkur of oure Lorde at Jerusalem', a chapel that also contained replicas made in 'bordys' of the chapel at Calvary, the church at Bethlehem, and 'the Mounte of Olyvete and the vale of Josaphath' (ibid., xxviii–xxx). He also left a map of the Holy Land. This was once identified with the map preserved as Bodl. Oxf., MS Douce 389, but the latter was clearly neither made by Wey nor owned by him.

Wey's writings seem to have circulated in or shortly after his lifetime—they were used by the author of the tract issued by Wynkyn de Worde in 1498 as *Informacon for Pylgrymes unto the Holy Londe*. They were published in an excellent edition by George Williams for the Roxburghe

Club in 1857, and have since been a rich source of information about late medieval pilgrims and travellers to Palestine. HENRY SUMMERSON

Sources *The itineraries of William Wey*, ed. G. Williams, Roxburghe Club, 75 (1857) · Emden, *Oxf.*, 3.2028–9 · Bodl. Oxf., MS Bodley 565 · Bodl. Oxf., MS Douce 389 · R. J. Mitchell, *The spring voyage: the Jerusalem pilgrimage in 1458* (1964) · J. Sumption, *Pilgrimage: an image of medieval religion* (1975) · E. G. Duff, ed., *Information for pilgrims unto the Holy Land* (1893) · M. W. Labarge, *Medieval travellers: the rich and restless* (1982)
Archives Bodl. Oxf., MS Bodley 565

Weyer, Deryk Vander (1925–1990), banker, was born on 21 January 1925 at Bridlington, Yorkshire, the second child and only son of Clement Vander Weyer, insurance company manager, and his wife, Harriet. He was educated at Bridlington School and in 1941 joined Barclays Bank. He served in the Indian army during the Second World War, where he reached the rank of major. On his return to Barclays, a company hitherto influenced by members of the families who had combined to form it in 1896, he was able to take advantage of the company's training courses for people from its ordinary intake who showed ability and promise. He married Marguerite Warden in 1950—they had a son, Martin, and a daughter—and began his ascent of the ladder of promotion at Barclays. In 1956 he was made assistant manager in Liverpool, in 1960 manager of Barclays' Chester branch, and in 1965 a local director in Liverpool.

The opportunity to create a distinctive role for himself came in October 1967, when Barclays seconded Weyer for six months to the Oxford Centre for Management Studies (later renamed Templeton College). His dissertation on marketing in banking, written while there, caught the attention of Derek Wilde, Barclays' senior general manager, and John Thomson, its chairman. No British bank then had a marketing department, and touting for business was anathema. Wilde and Thomson brought Weyer to Barclays' London headquarters, authorized him to establish a marketing and planning department, and promoted him to assistant general manager. His requests for facts and figures led to the creation of management accounting within Barclays, and he became a general manager in 1969, with both marketing and planning responsibilities. He approved of Barclays' adoption of 'management by objectives' techniques in its branches and welcomed the freer lending made possible by government acceptance of a 1971 Bank of England report on credit control.

Weyer wrote occasional articles for *The Banker*; they were lucid and forward-looking, and, while much that they contain could not be considered revolutionary, they were of great interest to people in other banks, who saw in them pointers to developments which became obvious only some eighteen months later. The articles enhanced his reputation as the thinking person's banker, and also the reputation of Barclays. Within the bank, the structure of a central bureau presiding over thirty local boards, peopled largely by those with family connections to the 1896 partnerships, seemed inappropriate to Weyer in the

1970s. As general manager of domestic banking in 1972, he orchestrated, with the support of Barclays' main board, a series of useful reforms of local boards. However, the boards were only finally abolished after he left office.

Tall, lean, brisk in thought and manner, Weyer was later described as 'an achiever and by his own admission always ambitious' (*The Times*, 21 June 1990). Much liked by the secretaries and chauffeurs who worked for him and appreciated his kindnesses, he was 'a quiet man with an impish humour but his authority was never in doubt' (ibid.). Inevitably the organizational changes he promoted, and his implicit criticism of those who resisted them, did not endear him to all. Nevertheless, his undoubted ability ensured his progression to senior general manager in 1973, board director in 1974, vice-chairman in 1977, and deputy group chairman in 1980. He was also chairman of Barclays' embryonic merchant bank and chairman of Barclays Bank UK from 1980 to 1983. The latter was intended as a logical counterbalance to Barclays Bank International, but in fact Barclays group board was in real control of Barclays' domestic banking. His task was to end Barclays Bank UK, consolidating authority within the group board (into which Barclays Bank International was also merged in 1985). He was only the third of Barclays' non-'family' general managers to sit on the group board, and the second to be an executive director. However, he was not considered for the chairmanship, a post intended for Sir Timothy Bevan (from one of the founding families) long before. In 1983 Weyer resigned executive positions within Barclays, though he remained a deputy chairman. He became executive deputy chairman of British Telecom (BT), nursing it through privatization and, contrary to his centralizing mission in Barclays, chafing against over-centralization.

As chairman of the chief executive committee of the Committee of London Clearing Bankers (1974–6) Weyer helped rescue fringe banks in the 1973–4 crisis. Valued by the Bank of England, he was made a director in 1986, and in 1987 a member of its new board of banking supervision. Ill health caused him to retire from BT in 1986, and from Barclays and the Bank of England in 1988. He served as a member of the royal commission on the distribution of income and wealth (1977–9), president of the Institute of Bankers (1979–81), and governor of the Museum of London (1978–83), and was made a CBE in June 1986. A lover of music, he was also on the board of the English National Opera.

Weyer was proud of being a Yorkshireman and of his Flemish and Huguenot origins, and was a painter of local scenes in his spare time. He died at his home, Gatefield, High Road, Chipstead, near Coulsdon, Surrey, on 16 June 1990; he was survived by his wife, son, and daughter.

MARGARET ACKRILL

Sources Barclays Bank Archives, Wythenshawe, Manchester · private information (2004) · *WW* (1988) · *Barclay News*, 2/4 (1977), 8 · *The Times* (21 June 1990) · d. cert.
Archives Barclays Bank Archives, Wythenshawe, Manchester, notes, etc.

Likenesses photograph, repro. in *The Independent* (June 1990) · photographs, Barclays Bank Archives, Wythenshawe, Manchester · photographs, Barclays Bank Archives, Wythenshawe, Manchester; repro. in Barclays' annual reports

Weyland, John (1774–1854), writer on the poor laws, was born in Westminster on 4 December 1774, the eldest of three sons and six daughters of John Weyland (1744–1825), of Woodrising, Norfolk, and Wood Eaton, Oxfordshire, and his wife, Elizabeth Joanna (d. 1822), daughter and coheir of John Nourse of Wood Eaton. The family had made money in the City of London and acquired country estates; his father, 'a noted farmer', was high sheriff of Oxfordshire in 1777 (*VCH Oxfordshire*, 5.312). Weyland matriculated from Christ Church, Oxford, as a commoner in 1792, but migrated in 1794 to St Mary Hall (a move usually suggestive of some delinquency). He left the university, of which he later called himself 'an unworthy member' (*Principles of Population*, 1816, vi), without a degree, but was called to the bar by the Inner Temple in 1800. On 12 March 1799 he married Elizabeth, daughter and heiress of Whitstead Keene MP, of Richmond.

Weyland was a justice of the peace for the counties of Oxfordshire, Berkshire, Surrey, and Norfolk, served as an ordinary member of the board of agriculture, and was elected FRS. In 1811, dissatisfied that the two leading periodical reviews, the *Edinburgh* and the *Quarterly*, lacked a definite religious tone, he founded the *British Review* and appointed William Roberts, an evangelical barrister, as its editor. The journal, which took an evangelical, tory line, reviewed secular works 'in a Christian spirit', as Hannah More approvingly noted (Roberts, 65n), until its demise in 1822. In 1813 he urged the court of proprietors of the East India Company to endow an ecclesiastical establishment in India and to sanction missionary endeavour (*Letter to Sir Hugh Inglis Bart on the State of Religion in India*, 1813).

Weyland is now remembered as a critic of Malthusian population theory. He was concerned to uphold the existing social order in the countryside, and was an outspoken defender of the existing system of poor relief, for example in his *A Short Enquiry into the Policy, Humanity and Effect of the Poor Laws* (1807). His major work, *The principles of population and production, as they are affected by the progress of society; with a view to moral and political consequences* (1816; repr., 1994), attacked Malthus's argument on empirical grounds, disputing the belief that the population in England was outstripping the resources for subsistence, and reaffirming the benignity of the providential design. Weyland's principal object was to show that the poor laws were both beneficent and necessary, and were not a cause of pauperism, which he attributed to a lack of moral and religious instruction among the poor. Although his assertion that the population had reached a state of 'non-reproduction' was demonstrably absurd (despite the lack of issue from his own marriage), his advocacy of poor relief for large families where the wage-earner could not provide for all his children interested promoters of family allowances a century later. Malthus responded to Weyland in the fifth edition (1817) of his *Essay on Population*.

On 31 July 1830 Weyland was elected MP for the borough

of Hindon, Wiltshire, whose scale of parochial relief for wage-earners had been held up for criticism by R. A. Slaney's 1828 parliamentary select committee on the poor laws. He continued his defence of the poor laws in parliament. He voted for the second reading of the parliamentary Reform Bill (22 March 1831), which brought about the disfranchisement of Hindon, and the loss of his own seat, in December 1832. On the death of their father, Weyland's younger brother Richard Weyland (1780–1864) succeeded to the Wood Eaton estate, while John Weyland inherited Woodrising Hall, in Norfolk, where he died on 8 May 1854. M. C. CURTHOYS

Sources DNB · Burke, *Gen. GB* · Foster, *Alum. Oxon.* · P. James, *Population Malthus* (1979) · A. Roberts, *The life, letters and opinions of William Roberts* (1850) · B. Hilton, *The age of atonement: the influence of evangelicalism on social and economic thought, 1795–1865* (1988)

Weyland, Sir Thomas (c.1230–1298), justice, was the third son of Herbert Weyland and his wife, Beatrice, one of six daughters and coheirs of Stephen of Witnesham, a minor landholder at Witnesham near Ipswich in Suffolk. His eldest brother, John, was a clerk of the common bench from c.1244 until his death in 1259. A second older brother, William, pursued an administrative and judicial career in both Ireland and England from 1248 onwards which included service as the seneschal of the earl of Norfolk's Irish liberty of Ross, as an itinerant royal justice in Ireland in 1257–8, as escheator of England south of the Trent between 1261 and 1264, as seneschal of the liberty of Kildare (in 1269), and as an itinerant justice and justice of the common bench in England between 1271 and his death in 1274. His younger brother Richard followed an administrative career in East Anglia in the service of various magnates including the earl of Norfolk and John de Burgh and at least two religious houses (Ely Cathedral priory and the abbey of Bury St Edmunds) from c.1265 until his death in 1296 or 1297.

Thomas Weyland first appears in the records in 1251, as the attorney of his eldest brother for the making of final concord. In 1258 he was in a position to pay 100 marks to purchase the Suffolk manor of Chillesford, and in 1259 paid a further 300 marks to purchase a second Suffolk manor at Blaxhall, but it is unclear how he accumulated this money or what career he was then pursuing. There is no evidence that he was a professional lawyer, and it seems unlikely that he had followed his elder brother into clerical service in the courts. Later evidence suggests that he received a clerical tonsure at an early stage in his adult life, but had abandoned it by the time of his first marriage to Anne, the daughter of Richard de Coleville, in or before 1266. By 1270 he had also received knighthood. It is possible that his early career resembled that later followed by his younger brother Richard, but it is only during a brief period immediately preceding his first appointment as an itinerant royal justice at the very end of the reign of Henry III that evidence survives to place him in the service of Roger (IV) Bigod, earl of Norfolk (d. 1306), and in that of the earl's brother-in-law, John Fitzjohn (d. 1275).

Thomas Weyland became a justice of the common bench in Michaelmas term 1274, two terms after the death of his elder brother William. He served as a junior justice until Master Roger of Seaton (d. 1279) retired as chief justice in the summer of 1278. He then held office as chief justice of the court for eleven years, until the end of Trinity term 1289. His period as chief justice is the first for which a substantial quantity of law reports survives. These indicate that Weyland played a major role in determining the litigation of the court, either on his own or with a single colleague, William of Brompton, and that he possessed a clear and sharp legal mind. A rather different light is shed on his period of office by the complaints of misconduct lodged against him and his colleagues after his removal from office. Not all were justified, but some evidently were. In the most egregious instance he can be shown to have corruptly altered his own plea roll in land litigation involving one of his relatives, and to have then been rewarded for his assistance by being granted an interest in the property in dispute. Weyland made substantial property acquisitions while chief justice: seven manors or substantial holdings in his home county of Suffolk, three manors or substantial holdings in Essex, and various other holdings elsewhere. He spent an average of about £150 a year on property acquisitions between 1278 and 1289. These may in part have been financed from the legitimate profits of judicial office. They may also in part have been paid for out of the income from the extensive land holdings in both England and Ireland, worth at least £150 a year, that he possessed when he became chief justice, of which around two-thirds had been inherited from his brother William. His second wife's dower lands also brought in a substantial income. But his evident lack of scruple may have meant that these acquisitions were partly financed out of the proceeds of judicial corruption as well.

It was not, however, judicial misconduct that led to Weyland's removal from office. On 20 July 1289 two of his servants committed a murder at a fair. The victim was an Irish servant of the earl of Norfolk living in Suffolk, variously known as William Carwel, Carewel the Forester, and Carewel the Parker of Framlingham. The killing may have been the unpremeditated outcome of a drunken brawl. It is more likely, however, that it was connected with a bitter factional struggle between the followers of the earl of Norfolk which was taking place at this time. Weyland and his servants may have become involved in these because of Weyland's own close ties with the earl as one of his leading counsellors. There is no suggestion that Weyland had sent his servants to commit the murder, but he became an accessory after the fact when he failed to have them arrested when they returned to his Suffolk manor of Monewden, even though he knew of the murder. The earl's desire to have the killers punished led to the issuing of a special commission of inquiry on 4 September. The special justices had the killers arrested, and they were convicted and hanged at a gaol delivery session at Melton in Suffolk on 14 September. The jurors also indicted the chief justice for harbouring the killers, and orders were given for his capture. A clerk of the sheriff was sent to Witnesham to arrest Weyland, but after his arrest he escaped under cover of darkness and made his way to the Franciscan priory of Babwell, just outside Bury St Edmunds. Here he took the order's habit and resumed clerical tonsure. When his place of refuge became known, Edward I sent Robert Malet to supervise local arrangements for starving him out of the priory. By the middle of January 1290 Weyland had surrendered, probably in return for a safe conduct to the Tower of London. When he reached the Tower he was offered a choice between standing trial, perpetual imprisonment, and exile. He chose exile. At a special gaol delivery session held at the Tower on 20 February he took an oath of abjuration, promising to leave England and not return to it or any other of the king's territories (including Ireland, where until recently he had held lands) without the king's special permission. He was assigned Dover as his port of embarkation, and given nine days to reach it on foot.

Thomas Weyland's family was fortunate. An abjuration normally meant not only the forfeiture of the abjuror's chattels but also the escheat of all of his lands. Edward I was merciful to Weyland's second wife, Margaret, whom he had married by 1276 and whose maiden name was probably Filliol; she was allowed to keep not only her clothes, jewels, and personal possessions but also the goods and chattels in the manors she held in dower from her first husband, John of Moze, even though in strict law these all belonged to her husband. Weyland had retained sole title to at least three of his manors and these did escheat. However, he had taken considerable care to make provision for each of his children and for his widow when he died. His lands were to be divided between the three children of his first marriage (John, William, and Alina) and three of the children of his second (Richard, Elena, and Margaret); the fourth (Thomas) entered the church, and his widow was to retain a life interest in part of the lands. One by-product of the way he had made these arrangements was that he was only the joint tenant for life of almost all his other lands, and thus they were not legally liable to escheat. Although his children and his widow were engaged in long litigation with the lords concerned, they ultimately made good their claim to almost all his lands with the exception of the Gloucestershire manor of Chipping Sodbury, which the earl of Gloucester managed to retain.

By 1292 Thomas Weyland had taken up residence in Paris. When a representative of Edward I canvassed various Parisian experts on the Scottish succession question in that year, he brought back with him an opinion from the exiled chief justice. Eventually (probably in 1297) Edward I pardoned Thomas Weyland and allowed him to return home. It was at his wife's dower manor of Brundon in Essex (now in Suffolk) that he died in January 1298. He may have been buried in the priory church of Woodbridge in Suffolk, of which he had been a benefactor.

PAUL BRAND

Sources P. Brand, 'Chief justice and felon: the career of Thomas Weyland', *The making of the common law* (1992), 113–33
Likenesses caricature (possible), CUL, MS Dd.7.14, fol. 370*v*

Wealth at death moveables to the value of £200 and more, but no lands: PRO, E 368/69, m.120d

Weyman, Stanley John (1855–1928), novelist, was born at 54 Broad Street, Ludlow, on 7 August 1855, the second of the three sons of Thomas Weyman, a Ludlow solicitor, and his wife, Mary Maria, daughter of Samuel Black. Weyman (pronounced 'Wyman') was educated at Ludlow grammar school, at Shrewsbury School, and at Christ Church, Oxford, where he obtained a second class in modern history in 1877. He showed no literary precocity, and wrote nothing save a few minor sketches of university life and character, more than one of them published in *Chambers's Journal*, until overmuch leisure and scanty income compelled more serious efforts. He became history master at the King's School, Chester, where he remained for eighteen months; caving in to family pressure, he left in 1879 to study for the bar. Called to the bar by the Inner Temple in 1881, he practised on the Oxford circuit, with so little material result that he rarely exceeded an annual income of £130.

Weyman had begun to write stories in the style of Anthony Trollope during this period (later collected in *Laid up in Lavender*, 1907). Some were accepted by the *Cornhill Magazine*, and its editor, James Payn, suggested that he work on a larger scale. In the meantime Weyman and his younger brother Arthur, travelling in the south of France in 1885, were arrested on suspicion of being British spies, an incident which necessitated the intervention of the British ambassador. There was a protest in the British press and some notice in parliament. By the time they had been cleared of all charges, Weyman had gained a great deal of publicity and the incident may well have secured his success as a romance writer.

The chance of picking up Henry White's *Massacre of St Bartholomew* led to Weyman's writing *The House of the Wolf* (1890). This ran serially in the *English Illustrated Magazine* from October 1888 to March 1889, and when published as a novel brought him immediate recognition. He gave up his law practice in 1891, the year in which *The New Rector*, a skilled copy of Trollope, was published. But, drawing upon his knowledge of French history, particularly of the reign of Henri IV, it was *A Gentleman of France* (1893) which established Weyman's reputation as a highly popular exponent of romance with an eye for historical accuracy (he travelled widely to research the scenes for his dramas, usually in the company of the novelist Henry Seton Merriman). The novel was thought 'the ideal historical romance' and elicited a dedicatory poem from R. L. Stevenson, and, as Roger Lancelyn Green has suggested, instituted the basic 'triangular' plot involving an apparent hero, a real hero, and the brief appearance of a heroine, which was duplicated with very little innovation throughout his career (Green, 174). At its best Weyman's fiction was suspenseful in an atmosphere of political or religious agitation, with an interesting interpretation of social issues. At its worst his work is staid, sentimental, and prone to archaisms. Oscar Wilde recommended Weyman's novels as first-rate reading for convicts.

Weyman modestly referred to his own work as 'pleasant fables' (Zaidman).

Under the Red Robe (1894), written on a houseboat on the upper Thames, combined these elements to the greatest effect. It is perhaps the book by which Weyman is best remembered, and was staged in London in 1896 and produced as a musical by the Shuberts in New York in 1927. After publishing the French revolutionary tale *The Red Cockade* in 1895, Weyman remained silent for the next three years, during which he married Charlotte Kate Elisa Panting on 1 August 1895 and settled at Plas Llan-rhydd, near Ruthin, Denbighshire. They had no children. He did not return to form with his unsatisfactory romance *Shrewsbury* (1898), but the exhilarating *The Castle Inn* (1898) and *Count Hannibal* (1901) restored his reputation. His treatment of Swiss history in *The Long Night* (1903) won him a testimonial from the citizens of Geneva. *The Abbess of Vlaye* (1904) was a typical historical romance and successful for that, while *Starvecrow Farm* (1905), set in the Lake District, failed to impress. After *Chipping* (1906), a political thriller set during the time of the Great Reform Bill which Weyman considered his best book, and *The Wild Geese* (1908), an unremarkable tale of Jacobite Ireland, Weyman retired from writing; he announced: 'I think I have told all the tales I have to tell' (Green, 176).

Weyman now immersed himself in public and local affairs in Ruthin as chairman of the bench of magistrates and supporter of the Welsh church for the next ten years. When his wife became an invalid in 1916, he came out of retirement, mystifyingly under the pseudonym Jefferson Carter with *Madame Constantia*, a story of the American War of Independence, which consequently disappeared without a trace. *The Great House* (1919), about the anti-corn law movement, serialized in the *Cornhill Magazine* under his own name, was a popular success. *Ovington's Bank* (1922) was his most accomplished literary endeavour; it recalled his early reliance on Trollope and forced comparisons with Alexandre Dumas *père*. *The Lively Peggy*, running as a serial at the time of his death, blended Trollope with historical romance. Weyman died on 10 April 1928 at Plas Llan-rhydd of bronchitis and emphysema following long-standing tuberculosis. He was buried in St Meugan's cemetery, Llan-rhydd. There is a statue of him in Ruthin; his conventional moustache and monocle belied his true calling as an adventure novelist.

Weyman was not only one of the most popular and skilled of the historical romance novelists of the cloak and dagger school (and it is by such novels that he made his living), but was perhaps mistakenly considered by his contemporaries to be among the greatest popularizers of the 'new' romance. Even during his 'retirement' he was kept in the public eye through his inclusion in *The Lock and Key Library* (1910), in which he shared company with Kipling, Wilkie Collins, and R. L. Stevenson. He was widely read in Britain, America, France, and Russia, and by children, and, although he languished in the public memory for some decades following the decline in popularity of historical romances after the First World War, several of his books were reprinted in the 1960s. *Under the Red Robe*

was included in George MacDonald Fraser's *Five Classic Adventure Novels* (1995) with works by Rider Haggard, Arthur Conan Doyle, P. C. Wren, and Anthony Hope; he has also provoked some interest on the internet. It is unlikely, however, that he will ever be restored to the reputation he enjoyed during his own lifetime.

T. E. WELBY, rev. CLARE L. TAYLOR

Sources R. L. Green, *Tellers of tales: children's books and their authors from 1800 to 1968*, rev. edn (1969) • W. F. Naufftus, ed., *British short-fiction writers, 1880–1914: the romantic tradition*, DLitB, 156 (1996) • L. M. Zaidman, ed., *British children's writers, 1880–1914*, DLitB, 141 (1994) • L. Henderson, ed., *Twentieth-century romance and historical writers*, 2nd edn (1990) • S. J. Kunitz and H. Haycraft, eds., *Twentieth century authors: a biographical dictionary of modern literature* (1942) • S. J. Weyman, preface, in S. Weyman, *The house of the wolf: a romance* (1911) • J. A. Salmonson, 'On Stanley Weyman, greatest of the yellow nineties swashbuckling romancers', www.violetbooks.com/weyman.html, 14 Nov 2000 • home.freeuk.net/castlegates/weyman.htm, 'Stanley John Weyman', 14 Nov 2000 • D. D. Rudin, 'Stanley John Weyman: "Prince of Romance"', *Lost Club Journal*, freepages.pavilion.net/users/tartarus/weyman.html, 21 Jan 2003 • b. cert. • m. cert. • d. cert. • private information (1937)

Archives Hunt. L., corresp. and literary MS • NRA, corresp. and literary MSS | NYPL, De Coursey Fales collection, MSS • Richmond Local Studies Library, London, corresp. with Douglas Sladen • U. Leeds, Brotherton L., letters to Clement Shorter

Likenesses London Stereoscopic Co., cabinet photograph, NPG • photographs, Hult. Arch.; repro. in Naufftus, ed., *British short-fiction writers* • statue, Ruthin, Denbighshire

Wealth at death £99,408 13s. 5d.: probate, 26 June 1928, *CGPLA Eng. & Wales*

Weymouth. For this title name *see* Thynne, Thomas, first Viscount Weymouth (*bap.* 1640, *d.* 1714); Thynne, Thomas, third Viscount Weymouth and first marquess of Bath (1734–1796).

Weymouth, George. *See* Waymouth, George (*fl.* 1587–1611).

Weymouth, Richard Francis (1822–1902), philologist and biblical scholar, was born at Plymouth Dock on 26 October 1822, the only son of Commander Richard Weymouth RN and his wife, Ann Sprague, also of a Devon family. After education at a private school he went to France for two years. He matriculated at University College, London, in 1843, and graduated in classics (BA, 1846; MA, 1849). On 18 June 1852 he married Louisa Sarah (1823/4–1891), the daughter of Robert Giles Marten, secretary of the Vauxhall Bridge Company, of Denmark Hill. They were to have three sons and three daughters.

After acting as an assistant to Joseph Payne, the educational expert, at the Mansion House School, Leatherhead, Weymouth ran a successful private school, Portland grammar school, at Plymouth. In 1868 Weymouth was the first to receive the degree of doctor of literature at University College, after a severe examination in Anglo-Saxon, Icelandic, and French and English language and literature. The degree was not conferred again until 1879.

In 1869 Weymouth, who was elected fellow of University College, was appointed headmaster of Mill Hill School, Middlesex, which had been founded by nonconformists and was now first reorganized on the lines of a public school. A zealous Baptist, Weymouth was for a long period a deacon of the George Street Baptist Chapel, Plymouth, and subsequently a member of the committee of the Essex Baptist Union. At Mill Hill he proved a successful teacher (of Greek, Latin, and English), an effective organizer, and a strict disciplinarian. In his seventeen years as headmaster numbers grew from 47 to 180, and academic standards were high. Among his assistants was James A. H. Murray, editor of the *New English Dictionary*. Weymouth retired with a pension in July 1886, when the school showed temporary signs of decline. He then chiefly devoted himself to biblical study. He had joined the Philological Society in 1851 and long sat on its council. In 1864 he edited for the society Bishop Grosseteste's *Castell of Loue*, and he contributed many papers to the society's *Transactions*.

Some of Weymouth's later contributions to philology comprised *Early English Pronunciation, with Especial Reference to Chaucer* (1874), a literal translation of Cynewulf's *Elene* into modern English (1888), and various papers in the *Journal of Classical and Sacred Philology* and the *Cambridge Journal of Philology*. In 1885, as president of the Devonshire Association, Weymouth read an address, 'The Devonshire dialect: a study in comparative grammar', an early attempt to treat English dialect in the light of recent philology. He was awarded a civil service pension of £100 in 1891. His first wife having died in this year, on 26 October 1892 he married Louisa (*b.* 1842/3), the daughter of Samuel Salter of Watford.

On textual criticism of the Greek New Testament, Weymouth spent many years' study. He codified the latest results of critical research in his *Resultant Greek Testament, exhibiting the text in which the majority of modern editors are agreed* (1886). Then followed a tract, *The rendering into English of the Greek aorist and perfect, with appendices on the New Testament use of gar and oun* (1894; new edn, 1901). Weymouth's last work, issued after his death and widely popular, was *The New Testament in Modern Speech* (1902; 2nd edn, 1903; 3rd edn, 1909). Based upon the text of *The Resultant Greek Testament*, it was partly revised by Ernest Hampden-Cook. Weymouth was to be remembered for this work in particular, a forerunner of the numerous twentieth-century translations of the scriptures into modern English.

From 1892 Weymouth lived at Collaton House, Brook Street Hill, near Brentwood. He died there on 27 December 1902, and was buried in the then new cemetery on 1 January 1903. A memorial window was put up in the Mill Hill School chapel.

G. Le G. Norgate, *rev.* John D. Haigh

Sources N. B. James, *The history of Mill Hill School, 1807–1923* (1923), 212–13, 218–22, 257–62, and passim · private information (1912) · *The Times* (30 Dec 1902) · R. F. Weymouth, 'Preface', *The New Testament in modern speech*, 2nd edn (1903), ix–xiv · *CGPLA Eng. & Wales* (1903) · d. cert.

Archives UCL, corresp.

Likenesses S. Paget, portrait, repro. in James, *History of Mill Hill School*

Wealth at death £4586 17s. 10d.: probate, 22 Jan 1903, *CGPLA Eng. & Wales*

Whale, James (1889–1957), theatre and film director, was born on 22 July 1889 at 40 Brewery Street, Dudley, Worcestershire, the sixth of the seven children of William Whale (1855–1936), a blast furnaceman, and his wife, Sarah (1855–1937), a nurse, daughter of James Peters, a coalminer, and his wife, Sarah. In later years Whale took pains to expunge every trace of this working-class background from his speech, dress, and bearing. He was educated at local charity schools until his mid-teens. Too delicate in build to follow his elder brothers into the mines or the mills, he found work with a cobbler, and supplemented his income by drawing signs and price-tags for shops. He used this money to pay for tuition at the Dudley School of Arts and Crafts, where he enrolled as an evening student in 1910. His artistic studies were curtailed by the outbreak of war, and in October 1915 he joined up. Commissioned second lieutenant, he was sent to the Flanders front in the summer of 1916. He survived a year in the trenches before being taken prisoner during an assault on the German lines in August 1917.

Imprisoned at Holzminden, near Hanover, Whale passed the time painting and helping to mount regular theatrical shows, for which he discovered an inborn aptitude. After the armistice he returned to Britain set on a stage career. He made his professional acting début with the Birmingham repertory theatre, but soon moved to London. Over the next ten years he made his living as actor, set designer, stage manager, and occasional stage director, achieving a solid reputation in the profession but no great fame. His breakthrough came in 1928. *Journey's End*, written by an unknown playwright, R. C. Sherriff, based on his own experiences in the trenches, was to be given two performances by the London Stage Society. Three directors had already turned down the underpaid assignment. Whale took it on, though none too keen. The lead role was played by a young actor of promise, Laurence Olivier. Against all expectations the play became the smash hit of the season, and transferred (though without Olivier) to the West End, where it ran for nearly 600 performances. Whale, suddenly famous, was invited to New York to stage the play's Broadway première, and then to Hollywood to direct the film version. He was lucky in his timing. With the advent of sound, Hollywood was eagerly importing stage talent to help with the techniques needed for the new medium. The film version of *Journey's End* (1930) was made by a team of British producers that included Michael Balcon, but shot in Hollywood, where sound equipment was more readily available. The producers were reluctant to let Whale direct, in view of his limited film experience; but Maurice Browne, who had produced the play on stage and held the rights, argued strongly for him. Browne's faith was justified. Though today the film may seem stiff and stagey, it caught the tenor of the time with its fatalistic anti-war mood, and was enthusiastically received by public and critics.

On the strength of its success Whale was offered a contract by Universal Studios. His first assignment was a weepy melodrama, *Waterloo Bridge* (1931), on which he acquitted himself creditably; but it was with his next film

James Whale (1889–1957), by unknown photographer, c.1934

that his name would always remain firmly associated. Universal, who had just enjoyed a box-office hit with *Dracula* (1930), starring Bela Lugosi, were looking for subjects in a similar vein and hit on Mary Shelley's Gothic novel *Frankenstein, or, The New Prometheus*. Robert Florey was initially assigned to direct but was supplanted by Whale, who now ranked as the studio's star director. Colin Clive, who had starred in *Journey's End*, was brought in to play the title role; the all-important part of the monster, originally intended for Lugosi, went to a little-known bit-part player, Boris Karloff.

Whale brought to *Frankenstein* (1931) a playful wit, a sense of pathos, and a visual acuity that lifted it far above the run of horror movies. In its imagery and set design the film was clearly influenced, but not overwhelmed, by the conventions of German expressionism. Drawing on his art school training, Whale himself largely designed the physical appearance of the monster, and crafted a lasting cinematic icon; and under his guidance Karloff gave a performance of touching, inarticulate dignity. Though diverging widely from Shelley's original, the film created a potent myth of its own, and marked the creation of the modern horror film. (The contrast with the previous year's *Dracula*, which now looks creakingly old-fashioned, is startling.) *Frankenstein* scored a major box-office hit, launched Karloff as the best-known of all horror movie stars, and defined Whale's career for good. Though he was to make films in many other genres, it was for this and his three subsequent horror movies that he would be remembered—rather to his irritation.

After a slight if agreeable romantic comedy, *The Impatient Maiden* (1932), Whale directed an adaptation of a J. B. Priestley novel, *The Old Dark House* (1932). This gleefully self-parodistic horror-comedy gave full play to his taste for the tongue-in-cheek and wilfully eccentric. A similar sardonic humour pervaded *The Invisible Man* (1933), taken from H. G. Wells's classic novel. The title role was originally intended for Karloff, but in the event marked the Hollywood sound screen début of Claude Rains, who gave a commanding if—for obvious reasons—largely vocal performance, and the film was notable for its state-of-the-art special effects, devised by John P. Fulton. Here, as in *Frankenstein*, Whale took a sympathetic view of his monster, hunted down by the forces of conventional society—an affinity for outsiders that some have linked to his homosexuality.

Two accomplished but lesser films followed: an elegantly formal farce in the tradition of Ernst Lubitsch, *By Candlelight* (1933), and an adaptation of a John Galsworthy novel, *One More River* (1934), a high-society melodrama set in England and indicting Britain's rigid divorce laws. But Universal were eager for a sequel to *Frankenstein*, Whale's biggest commercial hit to date. At first reluctant, the director was finally talked into it, and made what most critics consider his masterpiece. Besides allowing Karloff to deepen his portrayal of the monster, *The Bride of Frankenstein* (1935) gave Whale more scope for his quirky humour and delight in stylized grotesquerie, which he indulged in the casting of such idiosyncratic actors as Ernest Thesiger (who had appeared in *The Old Dark House*) and Elsa Lanchester. In her *tour de force* double role, as the monster's far from ardent bride and, in the film's prologue, as Mary Shelley herself, Lanchester gave the screen performance of her career.

Bride of Frankenstein found Whale's visual and dramatic skills at their height. In it he achieved a sophisticated balance of extravagant humour and macabre power that few subsequent horror movies have equalled. The film's box-office success outstripped even that of its predecessor. He followed it with a diverting excursion into the then popular genre of screwball comedy, *Remember Last Night?* (1935). In this witty soufflé a group of bright young things, emerging from hung-over sleep to find their host has been murdered, set out rather unsteadily to solve the mystery. The film featured poised playing from Robert Young and Constance Cummings—clearly influenced by William Powell and Myrna Loy in the similar *The Thin Man* (1934), but none the worse for that—a fine turn from Arthur Treacher as a splenetic butler, and stunning art deco sets by Danny Hall.

Now at the summit of his Hollywood career, Whale was assigned one of the studio's most prestigious properties, the seminal Jerome Kern–Oscar Hammerstein musical *Show Boat* (1936). Whale's unease with the material's cornier elements was palpable, but his dramatic instincts stood him in good stead and the film turned out easily the best of the three screen versions so far. (The other two were made in 1929 and 1951.) Paul Robeson and Helen Morgan triumphantly repeated their Broadway roles. *Show Boat* recouped its substantial cost, but not soon enough to save Universal Studios from financial crisis. Carl

Laemmle, who had founded the studio in 1912, stepped down and Universal passed into new hands.

It was Whale's misfortune that the new regime coincided with his first major flop. High expectations were riding on *The Road Back* (1937). It was adapted from a novel by Erich Maria Remarque, a sequel to *All Quiet on the Western Front*, the source of a hugely successful 1930 film. But any hopes of a follow-up hit were scuppered by casting weaknesses and by the interference of the German consul in Los Angeles, Dr Georg Gyssling, who threatened a German boycott if the film was not modified. Whale ignored him, but Universal capitulated: they cut several scenes and brought in another director to shoot extra material, including a clumsy new ending. Not surprisingly, the film did badly. After this Whale's assignments at Universal became steadily less attractive, and though still under contract he began to seek work at other studios. For Warners he made a beguiling theatrical *jeu d'esprit*, *The Great Garrick* (1937), concerning a supposed visit by the famous actor–manager to his colleagues at the Comédie Française. The prevailing air of elegant artifice suited Whale perfectly, and he drew a stylish performance from Brian Aherne in the title role. But the film's humour was too subtle to appeal to the general public.

At MGM, Whale directed *Port of Seven Seas* (1938), a valiant but doomed attempt to cram Marcel Pagnol's Marseilles trilogy (*Marius*, *Fanny*, and *César*) into a single Hollywood film, with Wallace Beery sadly out of his depth in Raimu's old role. Back at Universal, Whale was assigned two films of little account, after which he escaped to United Artists for his last film of any note, a spirited adaptation of Dumas's perennial swashbuckler *The Man in the Iron Mask* (1939). His final film for Universal was a rubbishy jungle melodrama, *Green Hell* (1940). At Columbia he started filming a turgid anti-Nazi drama, *They Dare not Love* (1941), but was fired in mid-shoot by the studio's boss, Harry Cohn. Twelve years after his fêted arrival in Hollywood, Whale's directorial career was effectively over.

Whale had never been able to take Hollywood quite seriously. 'That they should pay such fabulous salaries is beyond ordinary reasoning. Who's worth it? But why not take it?' he told an interviewer. 'And the architecture! And the furnishings! ... All the world's made of plaster of paris!' (*New York Post*, 1 June 1936). This stance of amused detachment no doubt made it easier for him, when his career slumped, simply to walk away rather than resort to directing poverty-row movies like many of his colleagues. Having saved prudently while the going was good, he had no need to work, and retired with dignity to his Hollywood villa, where he lived in relative seclusion and took up painting, occasionally emerging to direct stage productions in Britain or America. His long-term companion from 1929 was David Lewis (*c*.1904–1987), a producer at Warners.

It has been suggested that Whale's sexuality—he was quite openly, though unflamboyantly, gay—may have been a factor in the decline of his status as a director. However, other gay Hollywood film-makers, such as George Cukor, made no secret of their orientation and it did not harm their careers. It seems more likely that Whale's personality did him few favours with the Hollywood hierarchy and left him unsupported when his films stopped ringing bells at the box-office. Fastidious, class-conscious, and always impeccably dressed, he could act with cool English hauteur towards those he considered his intellectual or artistic inferiors—which included most producers and studio executives.

Whale directed only two more films: a half-hour army training film in 1943 and, seven years later, a forty-minute adaptation of a William Saroyan play, *Hello Out There*, intended as one half of a two-part film but not released until many years later. In the end the years of idleness took their toll and the creator of *Frankenstein* felt that he himself had become a monster. 'I looked at myself in the mirror', he told a friend, 'and I suddenly realized what I'd done' (Curtis, 381). In 1956 Whale suffered a stroke; he was put on drugs, and his worsening eyesight made it hard for him to paint. On the morning of 29 May 1957 he was found drowned in his own swimming-pool at 788 S. Amalfi Drive, Pacific Palisades, California. He left behind a note: 'The future is just old age and illness and pain. ... I must have peace and this is the only way' (Curtis, 384). His body was cremated on 3 June at the Wayside Chapel, Westwood, Los Angeles.   PHILIP KEMP

Sources J. Curtis, *James Whale: a new world of gods and monsters* (1998) · M. Gatiss, *James Whale: a biography, or, The would-be gentleman* (1995) · C. Denton, *James Whale, ace director: a career study* (1979) · R. Ellis, *A journey into darkness: the art of James Whale's horror films* (1980) · P. M. Jensen, *The men who made the monsters* (1996) · I. Thirer, 'Director James Whale here en route to Europe', *New York Post* (1 June 1936)
Archives FILM BFI NFTVA
Likenesses photographs, *c*.1930–1935, Hult. Arch. [*see illus.*]
Wealth at death £815 18*s*. 6*d*. in England: administration with will, 25 Feb 1959, *CGPLA Eng. & Wales* · $600,000: Curtis, *James Whale*

Whale, John Seldon (1896–1997), United Reformed church minister and theologian, was born at Mevagissey, Cornwall, on 19 December 1896, the son of the Revd John Whale (1863–1916), who in 1901 ceased to be a hired local preacher among the Free Methodists and entered the Congregational ministry. His mother was Alice Emily Seldon (1861–1948). After schooling at Hoe and Ashburton grammar schools, and at Caterham (1908–14), he served the YMCA, the Friends' Ambulance Unit, and the Serbian Relief Fund as a pacifist during the First World War. He proceeded to St Catherine's Society, Oxford (1919–22), and took a first in modern history. He pursued theological studies and ministerial training at Mansfield College, Oxford (1922–5), and in the latter year was ordained and inducted to the pastorate of Bowdon Downs Congregational Church in Cheshire. On 26 July 1926 he married Mary (*b*. 1904), daughter of the Revd H. C. Carter of Emmanuel Congregational Church, Cambridge. They had three sons and two daughters.

In 1929 Whale succeeded J. Vernon Bartlet in the Mackennal chair of church history at Mansfield College. He continued the practice of lecturing on early church history, but paid particular attention to the traditions flowing from the Reformation. With Bernard, Lord Manning, he drafted a letter 'To the ministers of Christ's holy gospel in the churches of the Congregational order' (1939), which was signed by Mansfield's principal, Nathaniel Micklem, and other Congregational notables. This prompted the formation of the Church Order Group, whose members, in the face of liberal theological tendencies, sought to recall Congregationalism to its roots in Genevan doctrine and church order.

In 1932 Whale became president of Cheshunt College, Cambridge, where he raised the academic profile of the college and presided over the refurbishment of its buildings. In 1936 (in which year he declined a call to London's City Temple), and again in 1948, he was Russell lecturer at Auburn and New York. At the request of the Cambridge board of the faculty of theology he gave a series of lectures during Michaelmas term 1940, which were published under the title *Christian Doctrine* (1941) and which exemplify the depth yet accessibility of his teaching. The Congregational Union, the London Missionary Society, and the government occupied parts of the Cheshunt premises during the Second World War, and by 1943 (during which year, as in 1957, he was select preacher in the University of Cambridge) there was but one theological student left. In 1944 he delivered the Warrack lectures, and in the same year, to the surprise of those who had never envisaged him as a schoolmaster (though his talent with sixth-formers was soon seen to be notable), Whale became the last of ten ordained headmasters of Mill Hill School, then evacuated to St Bees, Cumberland. He presided over the school's return to London, instilled fresh academic vigour into its life, and brought imagination and zeal to its governance. Some of the more traditionalist governors and old boys were made restive by his policy of enrolling able boys from local grammar schools, who were funded by bursaries from Middlesex county council, and by his belief that scholarship should take precedence over sport. Feeling that he had made his contribution, and wishing to concentrate upon teaching and writing, Whale resigned from Mill Hill in 1951, and made Widdecombe in the Moor, Devon, his base. For the next two years he taught at Drew University, New Jersey. During this period and for the next seven years he fulfilled a number of lecturing appointments at North American institutions. In 1952 he was Alden Tuthill lecturer, Chicago, and Greene lecturer, Andover; in the following year he was Currie lecturer at Austin, Texas, and in 1954 he was Hill lecturer at St Olaf College, Minnesota. He was a visiting lecturer at the University of Toronto in 1957, and in 1958 he was a Danforth scholar in the United States and the Sir D. Owen Evans lecturer at Aberystwyth. In 1959 he was a visiting professor at the University of Chicago, and in 1960 senior fellow of the council of humanities, Princeton University. The Whales left Widdecombe for Struan Lodge Nursing Home in Balgreen Road, Edinburgh, in 1995, and there John Whale died on 17 September 1997, survived by his wife. A service

of cremation took place at Warriston crematorium, Edinburgh, on 24 September 1997.

Whether through the spoken or the written word Whale was a force to be reckoned with. To David Lloyd George he was 'a pulpit genius' (*The Times*, 19 Sept 1997). He was a valued lecturer and, from his students' point of view, one whose learning they respected, and by whose high standards of liturgical preparation and of scholarship they were challenged. Students whose ideals were less elevated soon discovered Whale's abomination of sloppiness. If some felt him inclined to 'play God' over their academic or career choices, a number were grateful in retrospect for his interventions. His churchly and scholarly contributions were recognized by his election to the moderatorship of the Free Church Federal Council (1942–3) and by the award of an honorary DD of the University of Glasgow (1938).

In pulpit and in print Whale was a communicator *par excellence*. Whether traversing the thickets of Calvinist–Arminian controversy in the company of specialists or delivering a series of broadcast talks to the masses—such as that entitled *The Christian Answer to the Problem of Evil* (1936), his homework was exemplary and his meaning plain. Serious and urgent, he was not without humour: 'It would be an Irish result if the only discernible mark of the Church were its invisibility' (Whale, *Christian Doctrine*, 134); and he could be pungent against both totalitarian and individualistic conceptions of the church. Steeped in the Christian thought of the ages, Whale had a particular love of Luther, Calvin, and the reformed tradition, as *The Protestant Tradition* (1955) exemplifies. But what the book also brings out is Whale's conviction that genuine protestantism is truly catholic, and is therefore equipped for the ecumenical age. In his 1970 Congregational lectures, published as *Christian Reunion: Historic Divisions Reconsidered* (1971), he raised the possibility that from those very 'acids of modernity' which have prompted the abandonment of specious dogmatic and ecclesiological claims there may flow healing for the church's divisions. Meanwhile in *Victor and Victim* (1960) he had presented an account of Christ's saving work, which led him on to speak of the church as the saved community, the sacraments, and the resurrection hope as necessarily corporate. Through all his writings there runs the theme of the holy God of grace who hates sin—'The divine love is against all that is against love' (*Victor and Victim*, 167)—but who yet justifies the ungodly.

ALAN P. F. SELL

Sources b. cert. · d. cert. · *WW* · C. Binfield, 'A learned and gifted protestant minister: John Seldon Whale, 19 December 1896 – 17 September 1997', *Journal of the United Reformed Church History Society*, 6 (1997–), 97–131 · *Yearbook* [United Reformed church in the UK] (1998) · *The Times* (19 Sept 1997) · private information (2004) [J. Whale (son); Revd R. J. M. Collins and other Cheshunt College alumni] · S. C. Orchard, 'Cheshunt College, 1768–1968', *Cheshunt College* [1968], 4–18 · J. W. Grant, *Free churchmanship in England, 1870–1940* [1955] · E. Kaye, *Mansfield College, Oxford: its origin, history and significance* (1996) · N. Micklem, *The box and the puppets* (1957) · J. S. Whale, *Christian doctrine* (1941) · J. S. Whale, *Victor and victim* (1960) · *Congregational Year Book* (1917), 211f [on Whale's father]
Likenesses P. K. C. Jackson, portrait, Mill Hill School, Leeds · photograph (after P. K. C. Jackson), repro. in *The Times*

Whaley, John (*bap.* **1710**, *d.* **1745**), poet and tutor to Horace Walpole, was baptized at St Andrews, Norwich, on 4 April 1710, the son of Thomas Whalley, a tradesman, and his wife, Mary. His father died when he was young, leaving him in the care of his mother; nothing more is known of his parents. Whaley was on the foundation at Eton College (1724–8) before entering King's College, Cambridge (BA 1731/2, MA 1735), of which he was a fellow (1731–45); he was ordained deacon in 1745. He started writing poetry soon after entering King's College; here, William Cole states, 'he was reckoned a man of genius and a poet', and 'his company was sought after, and he spent his time in a continual scene of jovial amusements and mirthful society' (Cole, 73–5). He gathered around him a circle of bright young men, and may have indulged what Cole terms 'his turn for a dissolute and debauched kind of life' (ibid.). However, Cole's observation that, of all men, Whaley was 'the most abandoned and worthless and the most unfit to be trusted with the Education' of the young, must be treated with caution since it probably hints only at Whaley's homosexuality (BL, Add. MS 5842, fol. 122).

Whaley's first volume, *A Collection of Poems, by John Whaley*, was published by subscription in 1732, and is an accomplished, witty performance in a variety of styles and measures. The poems range from formal panegyrics and imitations of Greek and Latin authors, and versified biblical stories in the manner of Prior, to informal epistles to friends, and fables in Dryden's style. Some of the material reveals Whaley's connection with his home city, for instance a prologue and epilogue for a Norwich school play. A number of poems indicate (or feign) familiarity with Venice and Rome, and an interest in art history, notably the 'Essay on painting' in couplets.

About 1735 Whaley was appointed tutor to Horace Walpole. No letters from Walpole to Whaley survive, but Walpole appears to have held him in fairly high esteem, and may have been influenced by his tutor's interest in art connoisseurship. In his dealings with the Walpoles, Whaley was deferential and often unctuous. In politics he was a staunch Hanoverian whig. His 1732 volume includes a lavishly flattering 'Epistle to the Right Honourable Sir Robert Walpole' and a poem entitled 'Kew Gardens' celebrating Caroline, the queen consort.

In summer 1735, Whaley, his pupil John Dodd, and two other young men undertook a tour of England, covering Kent, the south coast, the west country, and the north as far as Manchester. A number of lively letters to Walpole survive from this journey, along with Cole's transcription of Whaley's journal of this journey, now preserved in the British Library. The journal pays particular attention to architectural sights and paintings, as well as revealing Whaley's interest in the life and economies of cities. Whaley was a socially ambitious man, and his journal also indicates that he was able to gain an entrée into some of the most illustrious houses in England. He never married.

In 1745 Whaley brought out *A Collection of Original Poems and Translations*, dedicated to Horace Walpole and published by Bowyer. This comprises imitations of classical writings, particularly of Horace, Tibullus, and Martial, and a number of occasional shorter poems on informal subjects. John Whaley is named as the principal author, but about two-fifths of the poems are attributed to other hands. Horace Walpole's annotations to his copy of this volume (now in the Dyce collection at the Victoria and Albert Museum) identify the other authors. Many of the contributions are by Whaley's friend the Revd Sneyd Davies, a contemporary of his at Eton and a fellow of King's, who had also contributed to Whaley's 1732 volume. He is said to have given the poems to Whaley as an act of charity to a friend in financial difficulties. Whaley's poem 'A journey to Houghton' was reprinted at the end of Horace Walpole's *Aedes Walpolianae* (1747), a catalogue of the works of art at his father's seat. In a note to his own copy of this work (in the Dyce collection), Walpole states that Whaley died in December 1745.   KAREN O'BRIEN

Sources Walpole, *Corr.* · MSS of William Cole, BL, Add. MS 5957; Add. MS 5842, fols. 122–136; Add. MSS 5814–5817 · *A journal of my journey to Paris in the year 1765, by the Rev. William Cole*, ed. F. G. Stokes (1931) · Venn, *Alum. Cant.* · Nichols, *Lit. anecdotes*, 2.175 · C. H. Cooper and J. W. Cooper, *Annals of Cambridge*, 5 vols. (1842–1908), vol. 4 · *IGI*

Archives BL, journal of European Tour, Add. MSS 5842, 5957 [copy]

Whaley, Thomas (**1766–1800**), politician and gambler, was born in Dublin on 15 December 1766, the eldest surviving son of the seven children of Richard Chapel Whaley (*c.*1700–1769) of Dublin and Whaley Abbey, co. Wicklow, and his second wife, Anne (*b. c.*1741), daughter of the Revd Bernard Ward, who had married in 1759. Whaley's father, who owned considerable property in Ulster and who was MP for co. Wicklow from 1747 to 1760, was nicknamed Burn Chapel Whaley during his lifetime because of the number of Roman Catholic chapels he is said to have destroyed by fire. Whaley was only two years old when his father died and he inherited estates worth £7000 per annum, together with a lump sum of £60,000. He attended school until he was sixteen, after which his mother sent him to France, accompanied by an indifferent tutor, to complete his education. After a series of adventures, which included his losing £14,800 in one drunken gambling session and fathering an illegitimate child, he records that he returned to Dublin, escorted by his stepfather, John Richardson, and was 'treated like the prodigal son' (*Buck Whaley's Memoirs*, 33).

Whaley was elected MP for Newcastle, co. Dublin, in 1785 when he was only eighteen years old, and he represented that constituency until 1790. He made little impact on politics, and only came to notice when he moved an address to the lord lieutenant, the duke of Rutland, on the opening day of the session on 18 January 1787. Indeed, he admits that his early interest in politics soon waned, and that 'the dissipated life into which I afterwards plunged, soon put a period to this and every other serious and laudable application' (*Buck Whaley's Memoirs*, 276). It was at this stage in his career that he accepted a bizarre wager while attending a dinner at the duke of Leinster's town house.

Upon being asked by one of the guests what part of the world he meant to visit next, he replied 'Jerusalem'. Some of those present suggested that there was no such place then existing; others questioned the possibility of his getting there even if it were still in existence. Whaley then 'offered to bet any sum' that he would go to Jerusalem and return to Dublin within two years from his departure. He soon had about £15,000 depending on the outcome of the wager. On 20 September 1788 he set out for Deal, where his companion, Captain Wilson, joined him; they left that port on board the *London* on 7 October 1788. Although ill health soon halted Wilson's progress on the journey, Whaley met another friend, Captain Hugh Moore, who joined the expedition at Gibraltar. They left Smyrna for Acre on 3 February 1789 on board the *Heureuse Marie*, and reached Jerusalem on 28 February. Both returned triumphantly to Dublin in July 1789 amid bonfire celebrations, whereupon Whaley produced to his friends clear proof that he had visited the Holy City, and successfully claimed his reward. His journey to Jerusalem cost him £8000 in expenses, leaving him a profit of £7000; 'the only instance', he records, 'in all my life before, in which any of my projects turned out to my advantage' (*Buck Whaley's Memoirs*, 270). This globe-trotting adventure also earned him the title Jerusalem Whaley, and it was probably about this time that he acquired his alternative nickname, Buck.

After his expedition Whaley spent most of his time gambling and indulging in various acts of bravado, which were distinctive traits of a class of the gentry called 'Bucks'. On one occasion, in Daly's Club, he successfully wagered that he would jump from the drawing-room windows of his mother's house in St Stephen's Green into the first barouche that passed, and kiss its occupant. He remained in Dublin for about two years, and during that time formed an acquaintance with a Miss Courtney (*d. c.*1799), with whom he had two sons, Thomas and Richard, and a daughter, Sophia Isabella. Whaley then resided briefly in London before moving on to Paris, where he witnessed many scenes of the revolution in 1791. However, his stay there was short-lived because the worsening political unrest curtailed his gambling pursuits. A restless inquisitiveness next led him to Switzerland, where he moved comfortably in high society circles meeting, among others, the novelist William Beckford, the historian Edward Gibbon, and the duchess of Devonshire.

Following a short tour of Italy, Whaley returned to Paris to try to recover debts amounting to £25,000. However, he soon found himself nearly penniless as a result of gambling losses and was obliged to flee to Ostend in disguise following a dispute with Count Arthur Dillon. He then made his way to London, only to be imprisoned in a sponging house. However, he was rescued from this predicament by the Irish lord chancellor, John Fitzgibbon, first earl of Clare, who had married his eldest sister, Anne, on 1 July 1786. Desperate to avoid any further embarrassment, Whaley proceeded to Dublin, where he sold all of his remaining estates for the discharge of his personal debts.

He was left with a surplus of about £5000, and he decided to gamble once more and either retrieve himself or complete his ruin. The outcome was disastrous, and he reflected: 'in the course of a few years I dissipated a fortune of near £400,000, and contracted debts … of £30,000 more … without ever purchasing or acquiring contentment or one hour's true happiness' (*Buck Whaley's Memoirs*, 332).

After this calamity Whaley moved to the Isle of Man, where he wrote his *Memoirs* in a spirit of contrition. However, he soon took up gambling again and his winnings were so substantial that he was able to begin building a luxurious mansion near Douglas—Fort Anne—which was near to completion in 1798. In that year he made a return to politics, paying £4000 to secure his election for the borough of Enniscorthy, co. Wexford. Over the following two years he played his part in divisions concerning the parliamentary union with Great Britain. He supported the proposal for a union in 1799, no doubt influenced by his brother-in-law, Lord Clare, but in 1800 he was bribed by the opposition to oppose the measure. However, the opposition could not satisfy his rapacious demands, and he voted for a union once more. The government rewarded him with the office of escheator of Munster. His companion, Miss Courtney, died during his residence on the Isle of Man, and not long after he married Mary Catherine, daughter of Nicholas Lawless, first Baron Cloncurry (1733–1799), and Margaret Browne (1748–1795), in January 1800. However, his married life came to an abrupt end before the year was out. While on his way from Liverpool to London he caught a chill, which developed into rheumatic fever. He died, aged thirty-three, on 2 November 1800 at Knutsford in Cheshire, and was buried in Knutsford churchyard. His widow continued to live at Fort Anne, in charge of his three children, whom she brought up as her own.   DAVID LAMMEY

Sources *Buck Whaley's memoirs*, ed. E. Sullivan (1906) · A. C. Kavanaugh, *John Fitzgibbon, earl of Clare* (1997) · *The journals of the House of Commons of the kingdom of Ireland*, 19 vols. (1796–1800) · *DNB* · J. Porter, P. Byrne, and W. Porter, eds., *The parliamentary register, or, History of the proceedings and debates of the House of Commons of Ireland, 1781–1797*, 17 vols. (1784–1801) · Hobart list of commons and lords, 1788, PRO NIre., T 2627/1/1 · *The Act of Union* (PRO NIre., 1973) [education facs. pack] · *GM*, 1st ser., 70 (1800), 1114, 1209–10
Archives London Library, memoirs
Likenesses portrait (as a boy), repro. in E. Sullivan, ed., *Buck Whaley's memoirs*
Wealth at death left £2000 to each of his 'natural' children; £1000 to Val. Goold; £500 to Hugh Moore; £500 to Thomas Goold; and residue to wife: *Buck Whaley's memoirs*, ed. E. Sullivan

Whall, Christopher Whitworth (1849–1924), stained-glass artist and craftsman, was born on 16 April 1849 at the rectory, Thurning, Huntingdonshire, the third of eight children of the Revd William Whall (1808–1874), rector of Thurning-cum-Little Gidding, and his wife, Mary Elizabeth, *née* Boultbee (1817–1891). Christopher Whall's rural childhood in the hamlet of Thurning was a lifelong inspiration, and his art was rooted in his sympathy with vernacular craftsmanship and a profound love of nature. He was largely educated at home but from 1863 to 1865 attended Rossall School, Lancashire. His ambition, despite parental opposition, was to be an artist. He moved to London, and in 1867 enrolled at the Royal Academy Schools, where he studied painting for the next seven years; Lord Leighton (one of his teachers) and the Pre-Raphaelites were early influences on his work. In the late 1870s he travelled in central and northern Italy for almost three years, studying painting and decorative art, guided by the writings of John Ruskin. At Lucca he felt called to dedicate himself to 'Catholic art' (C. W. Whall, 'Private Journal'). After returning to London in 1879, he became a Roman Catholic and was helped by the Rosminian Order of Charity at St Etheldreda's, Ely Place, who commissioned his first designs for stained glass for the newly restored church. The windows were only a partial success, and further experience of designing for firms such as James Powell & Sons reinforced Whall's growing frustration with the division of labour between artist and executant in the craft.

On 10 November 1884 Whall married Florence Chaplin (1849–1936), a portrait painter, and in the following year they moved to a cottage and smallholding at Stonebridge, near Dorking, Surrey, where their five children were born. Whall's career remained precarious until in 1887, having converted part of his cowshed into a workshop, he determined to learn the technical processes of stained glass—cutting, painting, and glazing—so that no aspect of the craft would be beyond his experience and control. His works shown at the Arts and Crafts Exhibition Society in 1888 were described as among 'the most important' (*The Year's Art*, 1889, 97) and he soon gained commissions from leading architects such as J. D. Sedding and Henry Wilson (lady chapel windows, St Mary's, Stamford, Lincolnshire, 1891–3) and E. S. Prior (east window, Holy Trinity, Bothenhampton, Dorset, 1895).

Identifying with the continuous tradition of English stained glass, not just its medieval triumphs but also the humbler work of eighteenth-century plumber-glaziers, Whall created an innovative, expressive style based on materials and honest craftsmanship. It was a logical development from Morris & Co.'s stained glass, with the added dimension brought by Whall's own constant involvement in workshop practice. His windows are emphatically glassy rather than purely pictorial in character, combining sumptuous colours, thickly textured 'slab' glasses, and bold leading patterns. The beautifully drawn figures, often framed by silvery canopies of foliage and set against backgrounds of patterned quarries, blend the Italianate grace of late Pre-Raphaelitism with a peculiarly English—and Gothic—sensibility. The general effect subtly echoes, without imitating, historic forms.

By the late 1890s Daddy Whall (as he was called by his studio staff) was assisted by a team of young pupil-apprentices, many of whom progressed to distinguished careers of their own. Their collaboration was essential to his most important commission, the glazing of the lady chapel and chapter house at Gloucester Cathedral (1898–1913), which established him as the leading stained-glass artist of the arts and crafts movement. Acclaimed by the American architect Ralph Adams Cram as 'perfectly Medieval and perfectly Modern' (R. A. Cram, *My Life in Architecture*, Boston, 1936, 192), much of the Gloucester work was undertaken for payment which barely covered costs. It led, however, to many subsequent commissions: windows for Canterbury Cathedral (1900–02), for the new cathedrals at Cape Town (1908) and Pretoria (1909–10), and for churches in the USA.

In 1896 Whall and his family had returned to London, where W. R. Lethaby invited him to teach stained glass at the London County Council Central School of Arts and Crafts and, later, at the Royal College of Art. Whall's inspirational teaching, stressing technical mastery alongside design skills, is encapsulated in his book *Stained Glass Work* (1905), still the best manual ever written on the subject. Friends and followers felt that his windows truly expressed the man. He was, like the saints depicted in his glass, 'gentle, friendly, great-hearted' (Connick, 245).

The extent of Whall's influence on British, Irish, and American stained glass in the early twentieth century would be difficult to exaggerate, for almost every major designer-craftworker of the period belongs, in some sense, to his 'school'. It would include, among many others, Louis Davis, Henry Payne, and James Hogan in England, Douglas Strachan in Scotland, Wilhelmina Geddes and Harry Clarke in Ireland, and Charles Connick in the USA. In art education his impact was seminal: he helped set up art courses at Dublin and Birmingham and, throughout the English-speaking world, his *Stained Glass Work* became the standard textbook on the craft. Whall was master of the Art Workers' Guild in 1912 and closely involved in organizing the British arts and crafts exhibitions at Ghent (1913) and Paris (1914) and at the Royal Academy (1916). Although eminent within his profession, he disliked publicity and self-promotion, declining a knighthood as incompatible with his lifestyle as a practising craftsman.

From 1907 Whall's studio-workshop was at 1 Ravenscourt Park, Hammersmith, a short walk from 19 Shaftesbury (later Ravenscourt) Road, where he lived for over twenty years. His daughter, Veronica Whall (1887–1967), began work in the studio while still in her teens and many later commissions were designed and made jointly with her, for example the east window at Leicester Cathedral in 1920. Their collaboration was formalized in 1922 as Whall and Whall Ltd. In 1921 Whall moved to 37 Harvard Road, Gunnersbury, where he died on 23 December 1924. Despite contracting leukaemia, he continued to work almost to the end. Examples of his designs are in the Victoria and Albert Museum and the William Morris Gallery, London, where an exhibition of his work was held in 1999–2000. Nature studies, including *The Oak Tree and its Inhabitants* by Whall and his pupils, are in the British Museum.

PETER CORMACK

Sources V. Whall, 'Notes on the life and work of Christopher Whall, 1849–1924', c.1953, priv. coll. • P. Cormack, *The stained glass work of Christopher Whall, 1849–1924: 'aglow with brave resplendent colour'* (Boston, 1999) • C. J. Connick, 'Christopher Whall, artist-craftsman', *Journal of the American Institute of Architects*, 13 (1925),

245–50 · C. W. Whall, 'Private journal', 1885–91, priv. coll. · C. W. Whall, 'Babblings of green fields', 1913, V&A NAL · C. W. Whall, 'Notes accompanying gift of designs to the Dept. of Prints & Drawings, V&A Museum in 1924', printed catalogue, V&A, department of prints and drawings · P. Cormack, introduction, in C. W. Whall, *Stained glass work: a text-book for students and workers in glass*, new edn (1999), [1]–[16] · *The Times* (30 Dec 1924) · S. Image, letter, *The Times* (6 Jan 1925) · V. Whall, 'Autobiographical notes', *Stained Glass* [Quarterly of the Stained Glass Association of America], 27/3 (autumn 1942), 51–8 · W. B. Whall, *Whall of ye county of Norfolk* (1905) · b. cert. · m. cert. · d. cert. · census returns, 1881, 1901 · *CGPLA Eng. & Wales* (1925)

Archives priv. coll. · V&A NAL, corresp. and papers, incl. autobiography

Likenesses J. Cooke, oils, c.1912, Art Workers' Guild, London · photographs, William Morris Gallery, London

Wealth at death £3963 9s. 1d.: probate, 11 March 1925, *CGPLA Eng. & Wales*

Whalley, Edward, appointed Lord Whalley under the protectorate (*d.* **1674/5**), regicide and major-general, was the second son of Richard Whalley, a landowner of Kirkton and Screveton, Nottinghamshire, and his second wife, Frances Cromwell, daughter of Sir Henry Cromwell of Hinchingbrooke in Huntingdonshire. He was thus a cousin of the future lord protector, Oliver Cromwell. Whalley was admitted a pensioner of Emmanuel College, Cambridge, on 2 July 1614, and graduated BA in 1617 or 1618. In 1619 he was apprenticed in London to Nathaniel Bushere, a member of the Merchant Taylors' Company, and he became a freeman of that company in 1627. He married twice, his first wife being Judith, daughter of John Duffell of Rochester in Kent, and his second Mary Middleton. One of these wives, probably Mary, was seriously ill in July 1656 following a miscarriage. His daughter by his first wife, Frances, married his army colleague and fellow major-general William Goffe. Whalley's younger brother, Henry, was a lawyer who shared his elder sibling's political and religious outlook and during the 1650s served as one of the judges of the Scottish admiralty court and advocate-general of the English army in Scotland.

Civil war At the beginning of the first civil war Edward Whalley took up arms for parliament. He may initially have served as a cornet in the earl of Essex's army, but by 1643 he had been appointed a major in Oliver Cromwell's regiment of horse and he fought alongside his cousin for the remainder of the decade. After the battle of Gainsborough in 1643 Cromwell reported to parliament that Whalley had carried himself 'with all the gallantry becoming a gentleman and a Christian' (*Writings and Speeches*, 1.246). The following year he was raised to the rank of lieutenant-colonel and fought at the battle of Marston Moor. When the New Model Army was formed in 1645 Whalley was given command of one of the two regiments of horse created out of Cromwell's original force. He was present at the battle of Naseby and the siege of Bristol and by the end of the year was active in the Oxford area. In the spring of 1646 he laid siege to Banbury, which surrendered to him in early May. He then commanded the forces laying siege to Worcester, but before the town surrendered in late July he had been replaced by Colonel Thomas Rainborowe.

Whalley's friend Richard Baxter later claimed that he had been removed from the command at Worcester because he was considered too conservative in his religious outlook. Whalley was in fact probably already an Independent and was certainly a member of Thomas Goodwin's congregation in London a few years later in the early 1650s. He was, however, less hostile towards those who favoured a national church structure than most of his fellow separatists, and he had personally invited the presbyterian Baxter to act as chaplain to his New Model regiment. Baxter had found the religious opinions of many of Whalley's troopers far too radical for his taste and had subsequently resigned.

Army politics and regicide Following the parliamentarian victory in the first civil war, Whalley's regiment, which contained a high proportion of religious and political radicals, was fully involved in the army's attempts to resist disbandment, and at the army council meeting at Saffron Walden in May 1647 Whalley requested that the rank and file soldiers be given more time to present their grievances to the high command. After Cornet George Joyce had seized Charles I at Holdenby in June 1647, Whalley and his regiment were given responsibility for guarding the king. They continued to hold him until his escape from army custody at Hampton Court. Throughout this time Whalley appears to have dealt with Charles with courtesy and fairness; for example, he refused to carry out orders from parliament to remove the king's chaplains without authorization from his commander, Thomas Fairfax. When Charles fled from Hampton Court in November 1647 he left Whalley a letter thanking him for the kindness he had shown him. Clarendon, however, claimed that in reality Whalley was 'a man of a rough and brutal temper who had offered great violence to his nature when he appeared to exercise any civility and good manners' (Clarendon, *Hist. rebellion*, 4.262).

During the second civil war Whalley fought at the battle of Maidstone. He was subsequently sent in pursuit of the earl of Norwich and was present at the siege of Colchester. He attended the debates of the army council at Whitehall in December 1648 and in January 1649 was appointed one of the commissioners for the trial of Charles I. He attended every session of the court except one and signed the king's death warrant [*see also* Regicides]. In March 1649, he participated in the discussions of the army officers at Whitehall about how to proceed with the reconquest of Ireland. Adopting a more conciliatory stance towards the Irish than most of his army colleagues, he argued that 'noe ill termes bee impos'd upon him [the enemy], as either to eradicate the Natives, or to divest them of their estates' (Firth, *Clarke Papers*, 2.208). In April 1649 around thirty of Whalley's cavalry troopers, including the prominent Leveller sympathizer Robert Lockyer, mutinied and seized control of The Bull inn in Bishopsgate, London. They refused to respond to Whalley's calls for their surrender, and only submitted on the arrival of Cromwell and Fairfax several days later. Lockyer was subsequently court martialled and shot for his part in the incident. A pro-Lockyer tract which appeared in April 1649 made reference to Whalley's flamboyant taste in dress, reporting that a soldier of his regiment had found him dressed 'in his sky colour satin waistcoat laced with silver and his pantophles [slippers] dawbed with silver lace' (*The Army's Martyr*, 6).

In 1650 Whalley, who had by now been raised to the rank of commissary-general, accompanied Cromwell to Scotland and was wounded at the battle of Dunbar. Later in the year he was stationed at Carlisle, and in early December he took part in the defeat of Ker at Hamilton. In May 1651 he argued with Sir Archibald Johnston of Wariston over the providential meaning to be ascribed to the English army's success: for Whalley it was a clear sign of divine approval. He rejoined Cromwell to pursue Charles Stuart into England and in September fought at the battle of Worcester. In August 1652 he presented the petition from the army which called on the Rump Parliament to proceed more quickly with a programme of constitutional and legal reforms, and after the Rumpers failed to respond he supported their suppression in April 1653 and the establishment of the protectorate at the end of that year.

Whalley purchased a number of crown and royalist lands during the early 1650s. These included the manors of Sibthorpe in Nottinghamshire, bought from the trustees of the earl of Devonshire's estate, and of West Walton in Norfolk which had formerly been owned by Henrietta Maria. The Rump Parliament also made over to him lands in Scotland worth £500 per annum, and in October 1653 he purchased fenland in Cambridgeshire from a private owner.

Major-general Whalley represented his native Nottinghamshire in the first protectorate parliament of 1654–5. In the autumn of 1655 he was appointed one of Cromwell's major-generals and given responsibility for an east midland association made up of the counties of Derbyshire, Leicestershire, Lincolnshire, Nottinghamshire, and Warwickshire. Writing to Cromwell in late January 1656 to thank him for appointing Whalley as their major-general, the Nottinghamshire commissioners for the securing of the peace of the Commonwealth described him as 'our native countryman, of an ancient and honourable family, and of singuler justice, abilitie and piety' (Bodl. Oxf., MS Rawl. A 34, fol. 767).

Whalley was one of the first of the major-generals to be active, starting work in Nottinghamshire at the beginning of November 1655 and spending the remainder of that month touring his counties 'to set the wheeles agoing' (Bodl. Oxf., MS Rawl. A 32, fol. 177). Once he had completed the initial arrangements for the assessing and collection of the decimation tax within his association, he concentrated most of his energies on the attempt to bring about a moral reformation, an aspect of the major-generals' work which he considered to be of the utmost importance. As early as the end of November he informed Cromwell's secretary of state, John Thurloe, that the government's reform aspirations were foundering on the lack of commitment shown by the local magistracy. Complaining that 'what some justices in order to reformation doe,

others undoe', he urged the government to place the major-generals into the commissions of the peace of their areas (ibid., fol. 806). He also made a particular effort to win the backing of the godly clergy of the east midlands for his reform efforts, and in Coventry he assisted the puritan mayor, Robert Beake, in his efforts to combat irreligion and ungodliness in the town.

By early 1656 Whalley believed his efforts were beginning to achieve results. He told Thurloe in early January that he had been very busy ejecting suspect clergymen, arresting vagrants, and closing down unlicensed alehouses 'which were growne to incredible numbers' (Bodl. Oxf., MS Rawl. A 34, fol. 428). A few days later he added: 'You cannot imagine what an awe it hath strucke into the spirits of wicked men what incouragement it is to the godly' (ibid., fol. 563). By late April he was claiming that 'you may ride over all Nottinghamshire and not see a beggar or wandring rogue, and I hope suddenly to have it so in all the counties' (Bodl. Oxf., MS Rawl. A 37. fols. 570–73). He had arrested so many vagrants and beggars that the gaols of his association were full and he repeatedly requested permission from the government to proceed with their transportation.

But if Whalley was fully committed to the goals of moral reformation, he also as major-general displayed the more conciliatory, eirenic side to his character. He allowed the annual horse-race for Lady Grantham's Cup to be run at Lincoln in the spring of 1656, and later told Cromwell that he had assured the earl of Exeter that 'it was not your highnes intention in the suppressing of horse races to abridge gentlemen of that sport' (Bodl. Oxf., MS Rawl. A 36, fol. 371). He also showed more interest than most of his fellow major-generals in social issues. In March 1656 he praised the assize judge Matthew Hale for the great concern he had shown for poor litigants while on circuit in the east midlands, and he subsequently wrote to Thurloe to urge the government to take action to prevent fraudulent practices in markets, profiteering by tradesmen and alehouse keepers, and enclosure which led to depopulation and unemployment. He even commissioned his own survey of the effects of enclosure in Leicestershire, and in December 1656 he tried unsuccessfully to introduce into parliament a bill to prevent further enclosure.

Whalley also continued to display during the 1650s the same tolerant approach towards religious differences that he had shown in the mid-1640s. In December 1655 he expressed his firm support for the re-admission of the Jews into England, informing Thurloe: 'I am glad so godly and prudent a course is taken concerning the Jewes, yet cannot conceave the reason why so great variety of opinion should be amongst men as I heare are called to consult about them'. He added that he believed there were both 'politique and divine reasons' for allowing them to return, the principal of these being the economic benefits to the state and the increased opportunity it would allow to bring about their conversion to Christianity (Bodl. Oxf., MS Rawl. A 33, fols. 355–8).

Whalley was returned to the second protectorate parliament for Nottinghamshire. During the debates on how to proceed against the Quaker James Nayler in December 1656 he declared that he believed Nayler to be guilty of horrid blasphemy but also attempted to cool the passions of his fellow members and to reconcile their different positions, commenting at one point: 'I would have this agreed upon in peace and charity; that those that are for a low punishment might not be censured for coldness, nor those for a higher punishment censured for a preposterous zeal' (*Diary of Thomas Burton*, 1.101–2). He himself favoured the death penalty for Nayler, but suggested that a reprieve should be offered him if he recanted after sentence. Along with his fellow major-generals, Whalley both supported Disbrowe's Militia Bill in December 1656 and January 1657, and opposed the moves to make Cromwell king in the spring of 1657. In early April 1657 he was one of the tellers for the noes when the house voted to renew their offer of the crown after Cromwell's initial rejection. Some contemporaries, however, reported that by the time Cromwell finally rejected the offer of the crown in early May Whalley and two of his fellow major-generals, William Goffe and William Boteler, had become reconciled to a return of the monarchy. Later in 1657 Whalley was appointed to Cromwell's House of Lords.

Restoration and exile After Oliver Cromwell's death Whalley supported his son, Richard, in his political struggle against the army, but he failed to persuade his regiment to follow this line. Following the return of the Rump in 1659 Whalley was relieved of command of his regiment and refused another commission. In November 1659 he and his son-in-law William Goffe were part of a four-man delegation sent to Scotland to outline to Colonel Monck the reasons for the expulsion of the Rump, but their trip failed to bring about a reconciliation between Monck and the New Model regiments stationed in England.

At the Restoration, Whalley and Goffe, who as regicides were both excluded from the Act of Indemnity, fled to New England, Whalley using the name Richardson. They arrived at Boston in July 1660 and lived initially in Cambridge. In 1661 they moved to New Haven, Connecticut, where tradition has it they lived in a cave in the woods outside the town for three years to avoid discovery by the agents sent from England to capture them. In 1664 they moved on to Hadley, Massachusetts, where they remained until their deaths. All efforts to arrest them proved fruitless as the colonists were generally sympathetic to the fugitive regicides and refused to reveal their whereabouts. A report in the Colonial State Papers declares that they were held in 'exceeding great esteem for their piety and parts' and that they 'held meetings where they preached and prayed, and were looked upon as men dropped down from heaven'. Another later report stated that they were feasted in every place they visited and provided with horses and guides (*CSP col.*, 5.54, 345). Details are also in existence of the attempts by Charles II's agents to apprehend them (ibid., 45, 80, 81, 96, 160–2, 1103, 1300).

By 1674 Whalley was in very poor health. Goffe wrote to his wife in August of that year that her father was 'scarce capable of any rational discourse, his understanding memory and speech doth so much fail him and [he] seems

not to take much notice of anything that is either done or said, but patiently bears all things' (*DNB*). 'Your old Friend', Goffe wrote to Whalley's brother-in-law William Hooke, '… saith I desire nothing but to acquaint myselfe with Je: Chr: & that fullnesse that is in him for those that Beleeve and have interest in him. This sentence he uttered with some stopps, yet with more freedom and clearnesse than usuall' ('Letters and papers relating to the regicides', 155–6). Whalley died soon afterwards and was buried at Hadley in an unmarked grave. CHRISTOPHER DURSTON

Sources Thurloe state papers, Bodl. Oxf., MS Rawl. A · C. H. Firth and G. Davies, *The regimental history of Cromwell's army*, 1 (1940), 208–9, 212 · G. Jaggar, 'The fortunes of the Whalley family of Screveton, Nottinghamshire', MPhil. diss., U. Southampton, 1973 · interregnum state papers, PRO, SP 18–28 · *Diary of Thomas Burton*, ed. J. T. Rutt, 4 vols. (1828) · I. Gentles, 'The debentures market and military purchases of crown land, 1649–1660', PhD diss., U. Lond., 1969 · *CSP col.*, vol. 5 · T. Hutchinson, *The history of Massachusetts*, 3rd edn, 2 vols. (Boston, MA, 1795) · 'Letters and papers relating to the regicides', *Collections of the Massachusetts Historical Society*, 4th ser., 8 (1868), 122–225 · *DNB* · *Reliquiae Baxterianae, or, Mr Richard Baxter's narrative of the most memorable passages of his life and times*, ed. M. Sylvester, 1 vol. in 3 pts (1696) · *The writings and speeches of Oliver Cromwell*, ed. W. C. Abbott and C. D. Crane, 4 vols. (1937–47) · G. Jaggar, 'Colonel Edward Whalley: his regimental officers and crown land, 1650 to the Restoration', *Norfolk Archaeology*, 36 (1974–7), 149–66 · *The army's martyr, or, A faithful relation of the barbarous and illegal proceedings of the court-martiall at White-Hall upon Mr Robert Lockier, with his … dying speech … 27 of April, 1649* (1649) [Thomason tract E 552(11)] · *Diary of Sir Archibald Johnston of Wariston*, 2, ed. D. H. Fleming, Scottish History Society, 2nd ser., 18 (1919), 59 · *The Clarke Papers*, ed. C. H. Firth, 2, CS, new ser., 54 (1894), 208 · Clarendon, *Hist. rebellion*

Archives Bodl. Oxf., Thurloe state MSS, Rawlinson MSS, A

Wealth at death estate confiscated for treason

Whalley, George Hammond (1813–1878), politician, was born on 23 January 1813, the eldest son of James Whalley, a merchant and banker of Gloucester, and his wife, Elizabeth, daughter of Richard Morse, of Gurshill, Blakeney, Gloucestershire. He was a descendant of Edward Whalley, the regicide. He was educated at University College, London, where he gained first prizes in rhetoric and metaphysics, and entered Gray's Inn in 1835, being called to the bar in 1839. From 1836 to 1847 he was an assistant tithe commissioner, writing weekly articles on tithe commutation in the *Justice of the Peace* between 1838 and 1842. He published two treatises on the Tithe Acts in 1838 and 1839, which were consolidated and enlarged as *The Tithe Act and the Whole of the Tithe Amendment Acts* (1848, 6th edn 1896).

On 25 January 1846, at Brighton, Whalley married Anne Wakeford, the daughter of Richard Attree of Selborne, Hampshire; they had a son and two daughters. During the Irish famine of 1847 he established fisheries on the west coast of Ireland, exploring in his yacht the location of fishery banks. Resident at Plas Madog, Ruabon, Denbighshire, he was high sheriff of Caernarvonshire in 1852, a deputy lieutenant of Denbighshire, and a captain of the Denbighshire yeomanry.

Whalley's national significance lies in his parliamentary career and in his defence of protestantism. He unsuccessfully contested Leominster in 1845 and Montgomery in 1852, but was returned for Peterborough as a Liberal on

6 December 1852. He was unseated on petition in 1853, but was again returned on 30 April 1859 at the general election, and retained his seat until his death. A low-church Anglican, Whalley accepted in the spring of 1861 an invitation from prominent ultra-protestants to lead the parliamentary campaign against Roman Catholicism, taking up the burden left by the ailing Richard Spooner MP (1788–1864). His particular objective was to abolish the annual state grant to Maynooth College, the Catholic seminary in Ireland. Britain, he argued, was paying for the creation of ultramontane priests whose goal was to transform protestant Britain into a citadel of 'popery'. His motions in 1861, 1862, and 1863 for a committee to consider repeal of the grant were all defeated, and he experienced increasing difficulty in making his anti-Catholic tirades heard amid the vociferous opposition of Irish MPs. In 1866 he claimed to have evidence that Vatican machinations had caused the defeat of British troops in New Zealand, that Cardinal Cullen, the Irish primate, intended to place a Stuart pretender on the throne of England, and that the pope had taken control of the British artillery corps, the police, the telegraph office, and railway companies. In 1871 he feared that the prime minister, Gladstone, had joined the Church of Rome. He became a supporter of the Tichborne claimant, and as a result of a letter which he wrote to the newspapers on the case he was fined £250 by Lord Chief Justice Cockburn for contempt of court (23 January 1874) and imprisoned in Holloway gaol for refusing to pay. The fine was paid by Whalley's sister on the following day.

Whalley died at Trevor Tower, Llangollen, Denbighshire on 8 October 1878. His son, George Hampden Whalley (b. 1851), was MP for Peterborough in 1880–83. A lecture delivered by Whalley at Peterborough about 1860, *Early British History: Ecclesiastical and Secular*, which drew an analogy between St Augustine's mission and the re-establishment in 1850 of the Catholic hierarchy in Britain, with Cardinal Wiseman at its head, was published at Hove in 1922.

FRANK H. WALLIS

Sources Boase, *Mod. Eng. biog.* · T. Nicholas, *Annals and antiquities of the counties and county families of Wales*, 2 vols. (1872) · *Wrexham Advertiser* (12 Oct 1878) · *The Times* (21 Sept 1861) · *The Times* (13 Feb 1867) · *The Times* (9 Oct 1878) · W. Arnstein, *Protestant vs. Catholic in mid-Victorian England* (1982) · F. H. Wallis, *Popular anti-Catholicism in mid-Victorian Britain* (1993) · *The Bulwark*, 13 (1863–4), 70–1 · *The Bulwark*, 11 (1861–2), 315 · *Hansard 3* (1861), 163.548–58; (1867), 185.113–19 · *British Standard* (7 May 1862)

Archives BL, Gladstone MSS · BL, Layard MSS · UCL, corresp. with E. Chadwick

Likenesses W. M. W., woodcut, 1863, repro. in *The Bulwark*, 13, p. 70 · Ape [C. Pelligrini], chromolithograph caricature, NPG; repro. in *VF* (18 Feb 1871) · J. & C. Watkins, carte-de-visite, NPG · carte-de-visite, NPG

Wealth at death under £18,000: probate, 25 Nov 1878, *CGPLA Eng. & Wales* · £9000: administration with will, 29 May 1879, *CGPLA Eng. & Wales*

Whalley, John (1653–1724), astrologer and almanac writer, was born on 20 April 1653. He arrived in Dublin in 1682, where he settled and—with one interruption—remained for the rest of his life. His first address was at the Golden Last on the Upper Comb, and from there, beginning in 1685, he produced an annual astrological almanac, which

brought him increasing fame and notoriety. His almanac for 1685 was entitled *Vox Urani*, and its author named as 'Iatromathematicus'; that for the following year *Syderus nuncius*. These and future editions not only provided the usual information regarding the year's astronomical events and their astrological implications, but advertised Whalley's services in 'physick and mathematicks'—that is, dispensing remedies for various ailments, analysing their course astrologically from the time of onset ('decumbitures'), and providing astrological advice in response to personal enquiries ('horaries'). He soon had a thriving business.

Whalley was a lifelong whig polemicist, whose vitriol against 'popery' stands out even in an age much given to extreme political and religious rhetoric. Using his almanac for this purpose too, he recommended a price of £5 on the heads of priests, and described Catholics as 'God-eating monsters, cannibals true'. Such sentiments naturally made him highly unpopular with the Irish people, and he was attacked in a bitter satire, composed by Ferdaragh O'Daly, of twenty-one stanzas in Irish. The accession of James II left him in a dangerously exposed position, and he was publicly pilloried in Dublin in 1688, after which he retreated to England. While working as a coffee-house keeper, he managed to produce *England's Mercury, or, An Ephemeris* for at least 1688 and 1690–92. In the dedication for the issue of 1690, he took care to emphasize his connections with Daniel Finch, the secretary of state.

Some time about 1692, Whalley returned to Dublin and settled at the sign of the Blew Post, next door to the Wheel of Fortune, on the west side of St Stephen's Green. He recommended his annual almanac, now entitled *Mercurius Hibernicus*, for this year. About 1698 he moved to Nicholas Street, next door to The Fleece tavern.

In 1701 Whalley published *Ptolemy's Quadripartite, or, Four Books Concerning the Influence of the Stars* (2nd edn, 1786), the first English translation of Ptolemy's work, which attracted some notice. In the same year also appeared *An Appendix Concerning [the] Part of Fortune* and *A Treatise of Eclipses*. In descending order of importance, these constitute Whalley's chief contribution to the astrological tradition. But here, too, there is a polemical element. His *Quadripartite* was dedicated to the London astrologer John Partridge (along with a physician in Drogheda, Michael Cudmore), a radical whig and protestant like Whalley, and the acknowledged leader of a correspondingly radical movement in astrology—a campaign to restore, in Whalley's words, the 'Truely Natural and Primitive Purity' of Ptolemaic astrology, with its Aristotelian naturalism and rationalism. Their enemies were the customary magico-divinatory astrology of the common people (exemplified by horary) on the one hand, and on the other the efforts to reform astrology along Baconian lines, led by Anglican and crypto-Catholic astrologers (usually also associated, however loosely, with the Royal Society) like John Gadbury, George Parker, and Henry Coley. In his preface to the *Quadripartite* Whalley lashed the 'Adulterous Innovations [and] Scandalous Ridiculous Falsehoods' of the reformers.

The source of Whalley's *Appendix* was the monk and astrologer Placidus de Titis (1603–1668), who had attempted the same Aristotelian reform of astrology in Italy, led, as he wrote, only by 'Ptolemy and reason'. Partridge's and Whalley's efforts were later taken up by John Worsdale.

In practice, of course, Whalley was often obliged to provide the divinatory services that he decried in theory; for one thing, the birth times required for drawing up a Ptolemaically proper nativity were often not known. One of his several Dublin competitors, John Coats, was quick to point out the hypocrisy of Whalley's claims to sole rectitude in this respect.

In 1703 Whalley moved first to 1 Patrick Street, and then to Arundel Court, near St Nicholas's Gate (between St Nicholas Street and Patrick Street), at the sign of the Blue Ball. While continuing with his almanacs, he also produced, from 1714, a popular non-astrological broadsheet, *Whalley's News-Letter*. Given his talent for scandal and satirical abuse, this too was a success, and inspired many imitators.

Whalley's last almanac was for 1724. Having predicted 'a year of darkness' on account of an eclipse, he died in April. It is only from his will that the existence of his wife and family is known: he named his 'beloved wife Mary' as sole executor, and left to his eldest son his two volumes of *Salmon's Anatomy* and his mathematical books, and to a cousin his three volumes of *Bibliotheca medica chymigica*. His almanac was taken over by Isaac Butler, apparently his favourite apprentice, who continued to produce it until his own death. PATRICK CURRY

Sources E. Evans, *Historical and bibliographical account of almanacks, directories, etc., etc., published in Ireland from the sixteenth century: their rise, progress and decay, with jottings of their compilers and printers* (1897) · P. Curry, *Prophecy and power: astrology in early modern England* (1989) · B. S. Capp, *Astrology and the popular press: English almanacs, 1500–1800* (1979) · A. J. Webb, *A compendium of Irish biography* (1878) · K. T. Hoppen, *The common scientist in the seventeenth century: a study of the Dublin Philosophical Society, 1683–1708* (1970) · DNB

Whalley, Peter (1722–1791), author and literary editor, was born at Rugby, Warwickshire, on 2 September 1722, the second of the seven children of Peter Whalley (*bap.* 1693, *d.* 1772), attorney-at-law, and his first wife, Elizabeth White. His family had been associated with Northamptonshire for at least two centuries. He attended Merchant Taylors' School from 1731 to 1740. In July of that year he entered St John's College, Oxford, became a fellow in 1743, and graduated BA in 1744. He took a BCL in 1768. From 1748 to 1762 Whalley held the vicarage of St Sepulchre's in Northampton; from 1753 to 1766 that of Preston deanery and from 1762 to 1763 the rectory of Ecton, both in Northamptonshire. In 1752 he became master of Courteenhall grammar school in that county. From 1760 to 1776 he was upper grammar master of Christ's Hospital in London in succession to James Townley. In 1766 Whalley was appointed by the corporation of the City of London rector of the united parishes of St Margaret Pattens and St Gabriel Fenchurch. He was made vicar of Horley, Surrey, in 1768 and held both benefices until his death. From 1784 to 1789 he was headmaster of St Olave's Grammar School, Southwark, and a justice of the peace.

Whalley's writings were firmly rooted in the Augustan tradition. His *Essay on the Manner of Writing History* (1746), the first free-standing essay in the eighteenth century on that subject, developed the notion, derived from classical texts, that the purpose of historical writing was instruction and improvement and not literary effect. In *On the Learning of Shakespeare* (1748) Whalley showed by detailed textual analysis that Shakespeare possessed extensive knowledge of classical authors and made considerable use of them, something hitherto unappreciated; at the same time he acknowledged the creative power of Shakespeare's imagination and so pointed the way forward to later developments in Shakespearian criticism. He also published a number of sermons.

As an editor Whalley was responsible for the first critical edition of the works of Ben Jonson (7 vols., 1756). He was one of the last commentators in the eighteenth century to defend Jonson's reputation, remarking favourably on his learning, his skill in characterization, and his imaginative plots, as well as the lyricism of some of his poems. Whalley's textual notes attempted to explain the obscurities of Jonson's language, but his omissions attracted some unfavourable contemporary comment. Whalley prepared a second edition, but publication by Francis Waldron, which began in numbers in 1792, after Whalley's death, did not get beyond the second number. Whalley's edition remained the standard one until replaced by that of William Gifford in 1816.

In 1757 Whalley was chosen by a committee of local gentlemen to continue the process of editing for publication the materials collected by John Bridges for a *History of Northamptonshire*, following the failure of Benjamin Buckler and Richard Gifford to carry out the task. He re-edited and improved that portion of the book which had been brought out by Samuel Jebb in 1739 and, with additions, the first volume of the finished work appeared in 1763. The first part of the second volume came out in 1769, but no further progress was made on the rest of the material for many years because of Whalley's other commitments, financial concerns, and the deaths of the members of the Northamptonshire committee. Whalley eventually completed the project, largely following Bridges' plan, and the book was finally published in the autumn of 1791, shortly after his death. In 1788 Whalley sought subscriptions for a book on the history of the royal hospitals in the City of London, but it never appeared.

Whalley's first wife, Mary, died in 1767. On 16 January 1768 at St Antholin, Budge Row, London, he married Elizabeth (Betsy) Jacobs of List Lane, London, but her extravagance led him into financial difficulties and he was forced to hide in the house of his friend Francis Waldron. When his hiding place was discovered he fled to the Low Countries, and died at Ostend on 12 June 1791. His widow survived until 16 March 1803. A. E. BROWN

Sources GM, 1st ser., 18 (1748), 25–7, 113–14; 22 (1752), 3–4; 46 (1776), 433; 61 (1791), 588, 773; 73 (1803), 293 · T. Brown and G. Foard, *The making of a county history, John Bridges' Northamptonshire*

(1994) • R. M. Serjeantson, *History of the church of St Giles, Northampton* (1911) • B. Vickers, ed., *Shakespeare: the critical heritage*, 3: *1733–1752* (1975) • D. H. Craig, ed., *Ben Jonson: the critical heritage* (1990) • A. Ralli, *A history of Shakespearean criticism*, 1 (1932) • K. Stewart, introduction, in P. Whalley, *An essay on the manner of writing history*, Augustan Reprint Society, 80 (1960) • 'ART, Review of the works of Ben Jonson … by Peter Whalley', *Critical Review*, 1 (1756), 462–72 • E. Blunden, *Christ's Hospital: a retrospect* (1923) • Mrs E. P. Hart, ed., *Merchant Taylors' School register, 1561–1934*, 2 vols. (1936) • *DNB* • *IGI*
Archives BL, Add. MS 5833, fol. 186 • BL, Add. MS 5841, fol. 60
Likenesses W. Ridley, stipple (after drawing by E. Harding), BM, NPG; repro. in E. Harding, *Shakespeare illustrated by an assembly of portraits and views* (1793)

Whalley, Richard (1498/9–1583), administrator, was born into a well-established Nottinghamshire gentry family, the only son of Thomas Whalley (*d.* in or after 1549), landowner of Kirton, and his second wife, Elizabeth, daughter of John Strelley of Woodborough.

Early career At an unknown date Whalley was sent to St John's College, Cambridge, essentially to round out an education hitherto based largely on martial exercise and etiquette. He did not take a degree, and subsequently completed his training in the household of Sir Thomas Lovell, probably thanks to his father, who had been an archer in Lovell's retinue in 1508. Richard Whalley was a gentleman of Lovell's household by 10 December 1522 and served until 25 May 1524. Thomas Cromwell employed a Richard Whalley to investigate Cardinal Wolsey's dissolved monasteries in 1527, but this was probably Richard Whalley (*d.* 1560) of Dalby in Yorkshire, who was attorney to the council of the north from 1536.

Before 1540 Richard Whalley of Kirton had married Laura, daughter of Thomas Brookman of Essex. They had five children, including Richard's heir, Thomas (*d.* 1582). Whalley profited from his work for Cromwell. He advised his son Hugh, also one of Cromwell's servants, to buy former monastic land in Leicestershire in 1536 and himself began purchasing Nottinghamshire properties. These included the Newark and the Welbeck Abbey estates (the latter valued at £249 6*s.* 3*d.* p.a. when he bought it on 26 February 1539), as well as other lands, among them Hardwick, Osberton, and Worksop, in 1540. He petitioned John Gates unsuccessfully in 1542 to further his suit for other property near his estates worth £66 13*s.* 4*d.* p.a. Cromwell was probably behind his appointment as JP for the North Riding in 1538. By 1540 Laura Whalley was dead and her husband had remarried, his second wife being a woman named Ursula; they had thirteen children. Whalley quickly found a patron after Cromwell's fall and was controller of the household of Thomas Manners, first earl of Rutland, from 1540 to 1541. An esquire by no later than May 1542, he also began accumulating profitable royal offices, including the receivership of the court of augmentations for Yorkshire from 1545. On 17 September that year he bought Worksop Priory, along with the advowson of the vicarage. He was named JP for Nottinghamshire in 1546, and was already one of the wealthiest gentlemen in the county when on 25 July he was granted the reversion of the college, wardenry, and chantry of St Mary of Sibthorpe. He took possession when its warden, Thomas

Magnus, died on 28 August 1550. These acquisitions brought local responsibilities, including membership of important commissions in Yorkshire and Nottinghamshire. At court he was an esquire of the body by 1545.

Service to Somerset, 1547–1551 By 1 July 1547 Whalley had been appointed chamberlain of the household of his kinsman by marriage Edward Seymour, duke of Somerset and lord protector. He received no salary, but instead enjoyed lucrative perquisites as one of the ducal council. Whalley was about the same age as Somerset, and like the lord protector he was a committed protestant. During Mary I's reign he entertained the prominent evangelical scholar William Ford at Welbeck Abbey, and he married sons to the daughters of a cousin and servant of Thomas Cranmer. Thomas Fisher, Somerset's secretary, noted that Whalley was a member of the duke's intimate circle by July 1548, though, unlike William Cecil and the principal secretary Sir Thomas Smith, he did not counsel Somerset about matters of state, his role being more practical but no less useful or valued. He was rewarded with more offices. In May 1547 Whalley was added to the quorum of the peace for the North Riding and was appointed JP for the East Riding. He was MP for Scarborough in 1547 and was probably returned to the final session of parliament in January 1552. Whalley disbursed royal money for Boulogne in summer 1549. In April 1549 Somerset procured Mortlake lodge and park for Cecil and wanted Wimbledon parsonage for Whalley. He had found both men invaluable supporters during the fall of his brother Thomas Seymour, Baron Seymour of Sudeley and lord admiral. Initially, Cecil petitioned for Wimbledon but Somerset preferred to have him 'ney unto hyme' at Mortlake because it was closer to his own houses at Syon and Sheen (PRO, SP 10/6/36, M, fol. 82*r*). Whalley got Wimbledon instead. In August Cecil solicited Somerset's steward, Sir John Thynne, for an office on behalf of the receiver of the court of augmentations, John Aylworth. He worried that Whalley might, without the steward's assistance, 'ride before hym' (Longleat, Thynne MS 2, fol. 116*r*). Cecil believed that Whalley would succeed to one of Sir Anthony Denny's offices in the royal household but the October coup that toppled Somerset confounded any expectations that the chamberlain may have had.

Whalley was active on Somerset's behalf during the October coup. He helped organize his master's defence against the London council by conveying coffers to his own house at Wimbledon on 7 October 1549 and may have sheltered his kinswoman the duchess of Somerset there. That Whalley was sent by Somerset to protect the duchess and 'to recomfort her' underlines his closeness to them (PRO, SP 10/9/42, M, fol. 82*r*). Not all of Somerset's people proved so loyal. On 10 October Sir William Paget, chancellor of the duchy of Lancaster, agreed to betray his patron by apprehending Somerset and his leading supporters, including Whalley. The following day most of them were placed under house arrest by Sir Anthony Wingfield, vice-chamberlain and captain of the guard, at Windsor Castle, but Whalley appears to have been still at large, probably at

Beddington with the duchess. Eventually he was apprehended and sent to the Tower of London but on 25 January 1550 was among the first to be released, on a bond of £666 13s. 4d. A few days later he was ordered to pay the wages of the ducal household.

In mid-1550 John Dudley, earl of Warwick, now the effective head of the government, began to forge ties with Cecil through Whalley. Relations within the Somerset household were strained during this time and John Raves, its clerk comptroller, complained that Whalley had embezzled £60 owed to him. Having lost his dignity as lord protector, Somerset felt vulnerable and had difficulty adapting to a new, more circumscribed role. His wife was pushing him to be more assertive, while servants and clients like Whalley solicited practical support by turning to disgruntled members of the privy council and nobility. It was against this background that Whalley wrote to Cecil on 26 June 1550, recounting a discussion with Warwick in which Somerset's arrogant behaviour was criticized sharply. This constituted a blunt warning to members of the ducal household that they should moderate their own counsel towards Somerset because they 'fondlie perswadyde' him to take dangerous courses. Whalley expressed his own loyalty to his patron, despite the difficulty of service in the present circumstances, and asked Cecil to be Somerset's good servant and good counsellor. Warwick acted as Whalley's 'veare [very] goode lorde' and assisted him a few days later in the purchase of crown lands worth £50 p.a., probably on favourable terms (PRO, SP 10/10/9, M, fols. 21v–22r). However, soliciting another patron was common and Whalley was still Somerset's man. Cecil too, remained close to the duke, despite becoming one of Warwick's intimates.

Somerset sent his servants and clients to several leading noblemen and gentlemen to gain their support during late 1550 and early 1551, probably in order to reduce his sense of isolation rather than to seek restoration to the protectorate. This role suited Whalley's intense personality, being 'a busy headed man anxious to be set on work' (HoP, Commons, 1509–58, 3.595). On 16 February 1551 he was interrogated 'for perswading divers nobles of the Realme to make the duke of Somerset protectour at the next parleament'. He denied it but Henry Manners, second earl of Rutland, affirmed it 'manifestly' (BL, MS Cotton Nero C.x, fol. 29v). Whalley was sent to the Fleet prison, and on 18 February the privy council questioned Sir Francis Leke, Rutland's uncle, about his activities. It transpired that Whalley had been sent to talk with Rutland at Belvoir Castle, Leicestershire, and the earl told Leke, 'he [Whalley] hathe been here with me and pratled very muche, whiche I like not' (APC, 1550–52, 217). Whalley was released on a bond of £1000 on 2 April.

Imprisonment and financial difficulties, 1551–1559 On 18 October 1551 Whalley was re-arrested and sent to the Tower, where he was examined several times and pressured into testifying against Somerset at the duke's trial at Westminster Hall on 1 December. He received occasional visits from his wife, who had 'accesse to hym at any convenient tyme, though the sayd Lieutenaunt [Sir John Markham] be not present', and from his half-brother Walter (APC, 1552–4, 31). He remained in prison until 19 June 1552, when he relinquished his position as receiver of the court of augmentations and gave bonds. Edward VI recorded that Whalley confessed:

> how he lent my money upon gaine and lucre … how he bought myne owne land with my money, how in his accomptes he had made many false suggestions, how at the time of the fall of money he borowed divers swomes of money and had allowance for it after, by wich he gained 500 pound at one crieng downe, the hole summe being 2000^li and above. (BL, MS Cotton Nero C.x, fol. 65v)

As a result Whalley was re-arrested and sent to the Tower on 20 September, before being moved to the Marshalsea prison; although his imprisonment was 'ostensibly for peculation, it was probably a political sanction' (HoP, Commons, 1509–58, 3.595). He had not handled large amounts of money, and although his accounts were in arrears there is little evidence of peculation. Probably he speculated on the foreign exchanges using the king's money, but this was commonplace. Interestingly, the privy council protected his estates during his imprisonment. In prison he encouraged Richard Eden's experiments in transmutation, while his financial problems mounted, especially because of complications over manors that he had mortgaged to Sir Maurice Denys, who claimed £3000 by default because Whalley overvalued them.

Released on 6 August 1553 and rehabilitated by Mary, Whalley was restored as JP for Nottinghamshire in 1554, returned as MP for East Grinstead, Sussex, in April 1554 and, perhaps through the patronage of Rutland, with whom he was again on friendly terms, as knight of the shire for Nottinghamshire in November 1554 and 1555. However, on 19 February 1556 the privy council denied his petition for restoration to the office of receiver, perhaps because of the earlier accusations. He did attempt to recover his losses. In 1553 or 1554 he brought an action in the exchequer alleging that his goods to the value of £126 6s. 4d. had been seized when he was 'wrongly imprisoned' in the Tower 'through the cruelty and by the malicious commandment' of Warwick (Bryson, Cases Concerning Equity, 1.72). By 1559 debts amounting to about £4800, mainly due to fines, forced him to consider selling Welbeck Abbey, and he took up residence at Screveton, Nottinghamshire. Although he sold other manors he was able to retain Welbeck, probably through astute land management (he was a leading figure in providing the government with timber from 1559).

Final years, 1559–1583 Whalley's position improved after the accession of Elizabeth I, perhaps due to his protestantism and his old association with Cecil. He was added to the quorum of the peace for Nottinghamshire in 1558–9. On 14 July 1561 he was granted the Nottinghamshire manors of Whatton and Hawksworth and Towton in the West Riding, valued in total at £139 7s. 8d. p.a. Despite the political and financial vicissitudes of his long life, Whalley was able to provide for his many children in his will and left a third of his fortune to his third wife and executor, Barbara (*d.* in or after 1590), the mother of his last seven children. He died on 23 November 1583, aged eighty-four, and was buried in Screveton church. Within a year his widow had raised a fine alabaster tomb to his memory, Italianate in style, with his recumbent effigy in full plate armour, and an epitaph reminiscent of the words Somerset composed on the night before his execution. His head rests on a whale—a rebus which also appeared on his coat-of-arms. He was succeeded by his grandson, Richard Whalley (*c.*1558–*c.*1632), the father of the regicide Edward Whalley.   ALAN BRYSON

Sources *APC*, 1542–54 · C. Brown, *Lives of Nottinghamshire worthies and the celebrated and remarkable men of the county* (1882), 107–08 · A. Bryson, '"The speciall men in every shere": the Edwardian regime, 1547–1553', PhD diss., U. St Andr., 2001 · *CPR*, 1547–9, 1553–4, 1558–66 · J. T. Godfrey, *Notes on the churches of Nottinghamshire: hundred of Bingham* (1907) · HoP, *Commons, 1509–58*, 3.594–6 · HoP, *Commons, 1558–1603*, 3.607 · *DNB* · chancery, patent rolls, PRO, C 66/801, mm. 11*d*–12*d*; C 66/864, m. 5*d* · *Thoroton's history of Nottinghamshire*, ed. J. Throsby, 2nd edn, 3 vols. (1790–96) · state papers domestic, Edward VI, PRO, SP 10 · Longleat House, Wiltshire, Thynne MS 2 · BL, MS Cotton Nero C.x · W. H. Bryson, ed., *Cases concerning equity and the courts of equity, 1550–1660*, 2 vols., SeldS, 117–18 (2001–2)
Archives BL, Egerton MS 2815 · Longleat House, Wiltshire, Seymour MSS 4, 9, 10, 11, 12 · Longleat House, Wiltshire, Thynne MSS 1, 2, 3 · PRO, state papers domestic, Edward VI, SP 10
Likenesses alabaster effigy on monument, 1584, Screveton church, Nottinghamshire

Whalley, Thomas Sedgwick (1746–1828), poet and traveller, was born at Cambridge, the third son of John Whalley DD (*d.* 1748), master of St Peter's College, Cambridge, regius professor of divinity in that university and one of the king's chaplains in ordinary, and his wife, Mary (1706/7–1803), only child of Francis Squire, canon and chancellor of Wells Cathedral. He was educated at Ilminster School, Somerset, and admitted on 27 April 1763 to St John's College, Cambridge, where he graduated BA in 1767 and MA in 1774. He was ordained about 1770. In March 1772 Edmund Keene, bishop of Ely, presented him to the rectory of Hagworthingham, near Spilsby in Lincolnshire, and, in consequence of its unhealthy situation in the fens, made it a condition that he should never enter into residence. This stipulation he readily complied with, and for the long period of more than fifty years the duties were discharged by a curate. About 1825 Whalley built a parsonage house for the benefice. He was appointed on 22 August 1777 to the prebendal stall of Combe (13) in Wells Cathedral, and retained it until 1826.

On 6 January 1774 at St Marylebone, Middlesex, Whalley married Elizabeth (*d.* 1801), only child of Edward Jones of Langford Court in Burrington parish, Somerset, and widow of John Withers Sherwood. The marriage brought Whalley a great fortune and the estate at Langford Court where he resided for many years. About 1776 he purchased the centre house in the Crescent at Bath, and entertained with great hospitality both there and at Langford. He was a conspicuous figure in Lady Miller's circle at Batheaston, and wrote verses for her literary salon. Frances Burney

described him as 'immensely tall, thin and handsome, but affected, delicate, and sentimentally pathetic' (*Diary*, 1.314). In the summer of 1783, under the spur of economy, he and his wife broke up their establishments in England and went to Europe. Langford Court was let for many years and eventually sold in 1804. Whalley spent the spring and winter for a long period in southern France, Italy, Switzerland, and Belgium, and kept journals of his continental experiences.

As a rule Whalley spent the summer at Mendip Lodge, formerly called Langford Cottage, on the Mendip hills, where the grounds were remarkable for their grottoes and terrace walks. Mrs Siddons often visited him there, and Hannah More was a neighbour. Whalley supported Hannah More's action over the school at Blagdon in an anonymous pamphlet, *Animadversions on the Curate of Blagdon's Three Publications* (1802).

Whalley was created an honorary DD of Edinburgh University on 10 July 1808. Next winter he bought a house in Baker Street, London, and for some years lived there in great extravagance. His first wife had died on 8 December 1801, and in May 1803 he married a Miss Heathcote, a lady of good family and property in Wiltshire; she died at Southbroom, near Devizes, on 10 October 1805. On 3 October 1812 he married the widow of General Horneck (probably Charles Horneck who died at Bath on 8 April 1804). He soon discovered that she was heavily in debt, and they agreed to separate. She received from Whalley a comfortable settlement and a large house in Catharine Place, Bath, in which she gave grand parties.

Two volumes of Whalley's *Journals and Correspondence* were edited in 1863 by Revd Hill Wickham, rector of Horsington. Prefixed to the first volume is a print by Joseph Brown of Whalley's portrait by Reynolds. They contain many interesting letters from Hester Lynch Piozzi and Sarah Siddons, but are burdened with huge epistles from Anna Seward. Wilberforce described Whalley in 1813 as 'the true picture of a sensible, well-informed and educated, polished, old, well-beneficed, nobleman's and gentleman's house-frequenting, literary and chess-playing divine'. Whalley was a patron of painting; the celebrated picture of *The Woodman* by Barker of Bath was painted for him, and, at his request, Sir Thomas Lawrence made an admirable crayon drawing of Cecilia Siddons, his goddaughter.

Whalley's writings include: *Edwy and Edilda* (1779), a poetic tale in five parts; *The Castle of Montval* (1781), a tragedy in five acts which was performed at Drury Lane in 1799 and 'tolerably well received' (D. Baker, *Biographica dramatica*, rev. I. Reed and S. Jones, 3 vols., 1812, 2.87); *The Fatal Kiss* (1781); and *Mont Blanc* (1788).

After the peace of 1814 Whalley went to Europe again. On his return in 1818 he purchased the centre house in Portland Place, Bath. In 1825 he bought the lease of a house at Clifton, and in 1828 he left England for the last time. A few weeks after his arrival at La Flèche, France, he died there of old age on 3 September 1828. Although in his will he requested to be buried with his first two wives in a vault in Burrington church, he was buried in a Roman Catholic church in La Flèche, a handsome sarcophagus of dark slate, with a Latin inscription, marking the spot.

W. P. COURTNEY, rev. REBECCA MILLS

Sources will, PRO, PROB 11/1752, sig. 117 · IGI · Venn, Alum. Cant., 2/6.419 · H. R. Luard, ed., Graduati Cantabrigienses, 6th edn (1873), 506 · Journals and correspondence of Thomas Sedgewicke Whalley, ed. H. Wickham, 2 vols. (1863) · J. Collinson, The history and antiquities of the county of Somerset, 1 (1791), 204 · The clerical guide, or, Ecclesiastical directory (1817), 17, 273 · Fasti Angl. (Hardy), 1.210 · GM, 1st ser., 42 (1772), 151 · GM, 1st ser., 98/2 (1828), 474 · [D. Rivers], Literary memoirs of living authors of Great Britain, 2 (1798), 376 · Watt, Bibl. Brit., 2.959 · The thespian dictionary, or, Dramatic biography of the present age, 2nd edn (1805) · D. E. Baker, Biographia dramatica, or, A companion to the playhouse, rev. I. Reed, new edn, rev. S. Jones, 3 vols. in 4 (1812) · [J. Watkins and F. Shoberl], A biographical dictionary of the living authors of Great Britain and Ireland (1816)
Archives JRL, letters to Hester Lynch Piozzi · St John Cam., corresp. with Sophia Weston
Likenesses J. Brown, line engraving, pubd 1863 (after J. Reynolds), NPG
Wealth at death very wealthy; left thousands of pounds to charities, schools, servants, relatives, and friends; fine furniture, art, books, and coin collection to nieces and nephews: will, PRO, PROB 11/1752, sig. 117, fols. 132–44

Wharncliffe. For this title name see Wortley, James Archibald Stuart-, first Baron Wharncliffe (1776–1845); Wortley, John Stuart-, second Baron Wharncliffe (1801–1855) [see under Wortley, James Archibald Stuart-, first Baron Wharncliffe (1776–1845)].

Wharton. For this title name see Wharton, Thomas, first marquess of Wharton, first marquess of Malmesbury, and first marquess of Catherlough (1648–1715).

Wharton [née Lee], **Anne** (1659–1685), poet, was born at Ditchley Park, Oxfordshire, on 20 July 1659. Her father, Sir Henry Lee (1637?–1659), of Ditchley, had died four months earlier; the death within days of her mother, Anne Danvers (1636–1659), daughter of Sir John *Danvers (1584/5–1655), the regicide, left her and her elder sister Eleanor (1657–1691) coparcenary heirs to the vast wealth of Henry *Danvers, earl of Danby (1573–1644), which had been left to his sister by Danby's heir male, his nephew Henry Danvers (1633–1654). Both girls were placed by their mother's will under the guardianship of her mother-in-law, twice widowed Anne, countess of Rochester (1614–1696), mother by her second husband, Henry Wilmot, created earl of Rochester in 1652, of the poet Rochester. In her expert hands both motherless girls thrived, but there is little evidence of any formal education for either. When the countess was appointed groom of the stole to the duchess of York in recompense for her role in the complicated dealings that had left her old friend Edward Hyde, earl of Clarendon, in possession of the principal Danby estate of Cornbury Park, her wards receiving the confiscated estate of Sir John Danvers in exchange, the Lee girls appear to have accompanied their grandmother to the court of St James's. When in the country they lived with their guardian at the Wilmot house at Adderbury which, after having served as a billet for both sides in the civil war, had been left virtually ruinous before the countess

had it rebuilt, and, with the benefit of the Lee girls' money, magnificently refurbished.

A principal source for the biography of the poet is the correspondence of Sir Ralph Verney, who was one of her trustees, and John Cary of Woodstock, who acted as steward of Adderbury. In August 1672 thirteen-year-old Anne Lee spent three months at Bath being treated for a virulent sore throat; in September of the following year, against the wishes of the king, who was promoting a match with the heir of Sir John Arundel of Trerice, she was privately married to Thomas *Wharton (1648–1715), who, contrary to the provisions of the will of his mother, Jane Goodwin, who stipulated that her considerable estate be shared with his brother Goodwin Wharton (1653–1704), was created for the purpose sole heir of his father, Philip, fourth Baron Wharton (1613–1696), leader of the country party in the House of Lords. According to the unreliable autobiography of Goodwin Wharton, besides being debauched when very young by Henry Mordaunt, second earl of Peterborough (1624?–1697), Anne had 'lain a long while by her uncle Rochester' (BL, Add. MS 26006, i, 308). Her elegy on the death of the poet in 1680 is evidence of her deep attachment to him; in it she claims that he taught her to write poetry. The sight of her elegy in manuscript prompted poetic responses from John Grubham Howe and Edmund Waller. In March 1681, after recurrent episodes of acute illness, she was escorted by her husband to Paris for medical treatment. Before it could be completed he required her to return to England; with her she brought her verse paraphrase of the Lamentations of Jeremiah which she showed to the nonconformist divine Samuel Clark, who responded that it would 'afford more comfortable reflections at a dying hour, than conversing with what belongs only to, or is fit for the Theater' (Bodl. Oxf., Rawl. MS, letters 53, fols. 351–2), implying both that her verse play, 'Love's Martyr, or, Wit above Crowns' (BL, Add. MS 28693), was written before this date and that she was not expected to recover.

In July 1682 Mrs Wharton began a correspondence with Gilbert Burnet, who showed her verse paraphrase of Isaiah 53 to Edmund Waller who wrote his two cantos 'Of Divine Poesy' in response. After Burnet's flight to Holland, Mrs Wharton engaged in a poetic correspondence with William Atwood and became involved in the project to stage Rochester's rifacimento of Fletcher's Valentinian which was acted by the United Company at the Theatre Royal on 11 February 1684. In his preface to the printing of the play Robert Wolseley represents himself as acting upon instruction; an exchange of poems between Wolseley and Mrs Wharton reinforces the suspicion that the instruction came from her. By the summer of 1685 she was once more gravely ill and betook herself to Adderbury so that she could drink the waters at nearby Astrop. Her condition worsened; for weeks she lay racked with agonizing seizures. On 29 October she died, and on 12 November she was buried in the Wharton family vault under the chancel of the church of St Mary Magdalen at Winchendon, Buckinghamshire. At the reading of her will it was discovered that she had left her whole fortune, beyond some personal legacies to servants and £3000 to Rochester's daughter by Elizabeth Barry, to her notoriously neglectful and unfaithful husband. Though the countess of Rochester repeatedly besought the earl of Abingdon, since 1672 husband of Mrs Wharton's sister and coheir, and her grandson, Edward Henry Lee, earl of Lichfield, to bring an action to overturn the will, it was never contested. In February 1686 Master William Phillips entered a caveat in the Stationers' register preventing any member of the Stationers' Company from publishing 'a play called Love's Martyr … and other poems written by the Honnoble Mrs Wharton'. Anne Wharton's surviving œuvre consists of twenty-four poems, all but five of which were printed in miscellanies in the years following her death, her play, seven letters to her husband, and one to Sir Ralph Verney.

GERMAINE GREER

Sources *The surviving works of Anne Wharton*, ed. G. Greer and S. Hastings (1997) · Claydon papers and archives, Claydon House, Middle Claydon, Buckinghamshire · PRO · Bodl. Oxf., MSS Rawl. · MSS Rutland, Belvoir Castle · University of Rochester Library, New York, MS D29
Archives Österreichische Nationalbibliothek, Vienna, MS 14090 · BL, Add. MS 38012 · BL, Add. MS 4162 · BL, amateur scribal copy of play, Add. MSS 28, 693 · BL, letters, Add. MSS 4, 162 · Bodl. Oxf., Add. MS D. 40 · Brasenose College, Oxford, archives · Folger, MS X d 383 · PRO · TCD, MS 879 · University of Rochester Library, New York, MS D29 | Belvoir Castle, Leicestershire, Rutland MSS · BL, Egerton MS · BL, Harley MS · BL, Sloane MSS · Bodl. Oxf., MS Aubrey · Bodl. Oxf., MS Carte · Bodl. Oxf., MS Clarendon · Bodl. Oxf., MS Dyce · Bodl. Oxf., MS Firth · Bodl. Oxf., MS Rawl. · Bodl. Oxf., MS Rolls Oxon. · Bodl. Oxf., MS Top. Oxon. · Bodl. Oxf., MS Wharton · Bucks. RLSS, Dillon papers · Bucks. RLSS, Lee papers · Bucks. RLSS, St Mary's parish register, marriages 1598–1695 · Claydon House, Middle Claydon, Buckinghamshire, Claydon papers and archives · Cumbria AS, Carlisle, marquess of Lonsdale papers · Cumbria AS, Carlisle, Lowther MSS, letters · NL Wales, Kemys-Tynte papers · Ohio State University, 'A choyce collection' · Princeton University, Firestone Library, Addison miscellany MS · U. Nott. L., Portland MS · Yale U., Beinecke L., Osborn collection
Likenesses studio of P. Lely, 1682 · J. Boydell, mezzotint, pubd 1776; Sothebys, 24 May 1993, lot 24; formerly at Houghton Hall, Norfolk · R. Ealom, print, pubd 1776 (after P. Lely), BM, NPG · E. Boucquet, stipple, pubd 1806 (after P. Lely), BM, NPG · English school, portrait · studio of P. Lely, portrait, priv. coll.; Sothebys, 11 July 1990, lot 18 · P. Lely, portrait; Commeter, Hamburg, 20 Nov 1937, lot 12 · Walker & Boutall, photogravure (after P. Lely at Claydon House), repro. in *Memoirs of the Verney family*, vol. 4, facing p. 243

Wharton, Arthur (1865–1930), sportsman, was born on 28 October 1865 at Jamestown, Accra, Gold Coast Colony, the eighth child of the Revd Henry Wharton (1819–1873) and his wife, Annie Florence Grant. Henry Wharton, born in Grenada, West Indies, was the first African-Caribbean to be ordained as a Wesleyan Methodist missionary in Africa. He was the progeny of a free-born African-Grenadan woman and a Scottish merchant. Arthur's mother was the daughter of the Scottish trader John C. Grant and Ama Egyiriba, a member of the Fante royal family. Between 1875 and 1879, for an elementary education, Arthur attended Dr Cheyne's school in west London. In 1882 he returned to Britain, having been enrolled at the Wesleyan Methodist Shoal Hill College, at Cannock, Staffordshire; when this closed in 1884 he moved to Cleveland College,

Arthur Wharton (1865–1930), by unknown photographer [detail]

Darlington, which he attended until about 1887 or 1888. The intention was that he should train for the ministry or teaching. However, his athletic talent soon emerged.

In July 1886 the willowy, handsome, light brown six-footer won the Amateur Athletics Association 100 yards title in 10 seconds, later ratified as the first world record. Never had 'even time' been recorded at a major championship. The following year with his upright style, slow start, and lengthy stride, Wharton retained the title. In 1888 he turned professional and won the prestigious September handicap at the Queen's ground, Sheffield, his last major sprinting triumph.

Wharton also played football as a goalkeeper. As an amateur with Preston North End—'The Invincibles'—he played in the semi-final of the FA cup in March 1887. In September 1889 he signed professional forms for Rotherham Town. His other senior clubs were Darlington, Sheffield United, Stalybridge Rovers, Ashton North End, and Stockport County, where he ended his professional career in 1901–2 with six games for the second-division club. He also played for the Newcastle, Northumberland, and Durham representative teams. In February 1895 he became the first African to play in division one of the Football League, for Sheffield United against Sunderland.

Wharton was noted for his idiosyncratic interpretation of the art of goalkeeping. A spectator recalled with incredulity, half a century after the event, his unorthodox gymnastics:

In a match between Rotherham and [Sheffield] Wednesday at Olive Grove I saw Wharton jump, take hold of the cross bar, catch the ball between his legs, and cause three onrushing forwards—Billy Ingham, Clinks Mumford and Micky

Bennett—to fall into the net. I have never seen a similar save since and I have been watching football for over fifty years. (*Telegraph and Independent*)

He also excelled at other sports. He played professional cricket in the Yorkshire and Lancashire leagues. And, riding a tricycle between Blackburn and Preston in August 1887, he set a record of two hours.

Wharton unsuccessfully applied for a position in the Gold Coast colonial administration in 1893. He was told that there were 'many native officers deserving promotion on the West Coast of Africa'; internal comments made by civil servants referred to the 'over-indulgence in alcohol' by his brother and the 'life of ill-repute' led by his sister as making it 'inadvisable' to give him employment (PRO, CO96/238/2044). Ironically, his return to Ghana would not have been as a sporting celebrity. His achievements were not considered worthy of public mention, even though his uncle was proprietor of the *Gold Coast Times*.

Dying in poverty, Wharton left few personal possessions save a Bible and some photos. The little that is known of his character suggests an extrovert, proud man grounded in his blackness. At one athletics meeting he overheard two competitors boasting that 'we can beat a blooming nigger anytime'. The 'nigger' offered to box them. They declined. At another meeting he felt he had won a race. Awarded a salad bowl as second prize, he smashed it and told the organizing committee to make a new one out of the bits. Similarly, in a ball throwing competition his two longest efforts beat all the other competitors—so he demanded first and second prize! He won numerous prizes as an amateur athlete, and along with many of his colleagues was accused of 'shamateurism'—accepting cash for competing. During the 1890s he also earned his living as a publican in Rotherham and Sheffield, and was one of the few players to hold shares in the football industry.

On 21 September 1890, at Masbrough, Rotherham, Wharton married a local plumber's daughter, Emma Lister (1865–1944). They had no children, and on Arthur's death Emma declined to lay a memorial headstone or, on her death, be buried alongside him. That her husband may well have been the father of her sister Martha's two daughters, Minnie and Nora, probably explains this seemingly uncaring behaviour.

Wharton spent the last twenty or so years of his life working as a colliery haulage hand in the pit villages of south Yorkshire. From 1913 he was employed at the Yorkshire Main colliery at Edlington, near Doncaster. He died on 13 December 1930, of facial cancer and syphilis, at his home, 54 Staveley Street, Edlington, Doncaster, and was buried four days later in a third-class grave in Edlington cemetery.

Obituaries appeared in the national and local sporting press, detailing Wharton's finest moments. They tended to concentrate on his triumphs as an athlete. In 1930 his significance as the world's first black professional footballer was not realized. Perhaps his greatest accomplishment on field and track, however, was his practical and symbolic denial of scientific racism, an influential ideology that argued black people were inferior to white. The rediscovery of Wharton's sporting career was begun by Dr Ray Jenkins (*d.* 1993), of Staffordshire University. On 8 May 1997, after a successful campaign to raise money for a gravestone by the Sheffield-based Football Unites—Racism Divides, a memorial ceremony was held at his previously unmarked plot. Fittingly, given Wharton's lifelong concern with issues of personal and social justice, it was the Professional Footballers' Association that funded the greatest proportion of the cost. PHIL VASILI

Sources R. Jenkins, 'Salvation for the fittest? A west African sportsman in Britain in the age of the new imperialism', *International Journal for the History of Sport*, 7 (1990), 23–60 • P. Vasili, *The first black footballer. Arthur Wharton 1865–1930. An absence of memory* (1998) • W. Moister, *Henry Wharton: the story of his life and missionary labours … with a brief account of Wesleyan missions in western Africa* (1875) • *Telegraph and Independent* [Sheffield] (12 Jan 1942) • *Stalybridge Reporter* (27 Dec 1930) • *Doncaster Chronicle* (19 Dec 1930) • *Sheffield Daily Telegraph* (16 Dec 1930) • *Sporting Chronicle* (19 Dec 1930) • *Sheffield Sports Special* (19 Dec 1930) • PRO, CO96/238/2044 • private information (2004) [Sheila Leeson] • d. cert.

Archives priv. coll., Jenkins MSS • PRO, CO 96/238/2044 | FILM BFI NFTVA, *Black Britain*, BBC2, 16 April 1997 • BFI NFTVA, *Tales from the map*, Channel 4, 4 Oct 2000 | SOUND BL NSA, documentary recording • BL NSA, sports footage

Likenesses photograph, repro. in *The Footballer*, 2/4 • photograph, priv. coll. [*see illus.*]

Wharton, Edward Ross (1844–1896), philologist and genealogist, was born at Rhyl, Flintshire, on 4 August 1844, the second son of Henry James Wharton (1798–1859), vicar of Mitcham, whose ancestors had long been settled at Winfarthing in Norfolk. His mother was a daughter of Thomas Peregrine *Courtenay. He was educated as a day boy at Charterhouse, where he was captain of the school, under the headmastership of Richard Elwyn, and elected to a scholarship at Trinity College, Oxford, in 1862, graduating BA in 1868 and MA in 1870. Though never robust in health, and suffering at this time from weak eyesight, he had a distinguished university career. In his second year he won the Ireland scholarship, though for the Hertford and Craven he came out only proxime. He was placed in the first class in classical moderations, and also in the final classical school. In 1868 he was elected to a fellowship at Jesus, which he was obliged to relinquish after his marriage in 1870 to Susanna Maria (*d.* 1899), daughter of Samuel Hicks Withers of Willesden. He was connected almost continuously with the college until his death, as assistant tutor and Latin lecturer, and was re-elected to a fellowship after the change in statutes in 1882. He devoted himself to acquiring a thorough knowledge of both Latin and Greek, to which he added an understanding of the cognate languages.

Wharton's first book was *Etyma Graeca*, an etymological lexicon of classical Greek (1882), which lists with minimal explanation the derivations of about five thousand common words. *Etyma Latina* (1890) was similarly constructed, but included an appendix showing the changes that letters undergo in the cognate languages as well as in Latin. He also contributed several papers to the London Philological Society and to the French Société Linguistique. His other published works were translations of Aristotle's *Poetics* and book i of Horace's *Satires*.

Wharton was a keen walker, especially in the British Isles and the Alps. He met Karl Baedeker in Koblenz, and made numerous suggestions for early editions of his guides. During the last few years of his life much of his interest was transferred to genealogy. The results of his researches, largely among original documents, are contained in six manuscript volumes, which he bequeathed to the Bodleian Library, dealing with all who had borne the name of Wharton or Warton. A short sketch of the baronial family of Wharton of Wharton Hall in Westmorland, which he had finished just before his death, was printed by his widow as a memorial volume. He died at 3 South Parks Road, Oxford, on 4 June 1896, and his remains were cremated at Woking. He had no children.

A younger brother, **Henry Thornton Wharton** (1846–1895), born at Mitcham, was educated at Charterhouse and at Wadham College, Oxford, where he graduated with honours in natural science in 1871. He was best known for a book on Sappho—memoir, text, selected renderings, and a literal translation (1885)—which passed through four editions. He was also one of the joint compilers of the official list of British birds issued by the British Ornithologists' Union (1883), his special task being to supervise and elucidate the Latin nomenclature; and he contributed a chapter on the local flora to a work entitled *Hampstead Hill* (1889). He died on 22 August 1895 at his home, Madresfield, 2 Acol Road, Hampstead, where he had practised for some years as a surgeon (MRCS, 1874). He left a widow, Caroline Wharton, and was buried in the neighbouring Hampstead cemetery in Fortune Green.

J. S. COTTON, *rev.* RICHARD SMAIL

Sources E. R. Wharton, *The Whartons of Wharton Hall* (1898) [incl. memoir by J. S. Cotton repr. from *Academy*, 13 June 1896] · R. L. Arrowsmith, ed., *Charterhouse register, 1769–1872* (1974) · Foster, *Alum. Oxon.* · private information (1899) · Boase, *Mod. Eng. biog.* · *CGPLA Eng. & Wales* (1895) [Henry Thornton Wharton]
Archives Bodl. Oxf.
Likenesses photograph, Jesus College, Oxford
Wealth at death £5541 13s. 5d.: probate, 11 July 1896, *CGPLA Eng. & Wales* · £389 13s. 11d.—Henry Thornton Wharton: probate, 11 Sept 1895, *CGPLA Eng. & Wales*

Wharton, Sir George, first baronet (1617–1681), astrologer and royalist, was born on 4 April 1617 at Strickland, near Kirkby Kendal in Westmorland, the son of George Wharton, a blacksmith and small farmer. He was descended, as Anthony Wood notes, 'from an antient and genteel family' (Wood, *Ath. Oxon.*, 4, col. 6), probably the Whartons of Kirkby Thore. His father died while Wharton was still a small child and he inherited an estate of about £50 a year; he was brought up by two uncles, William and Cuthbert Wharton. He spent some time at Oxford in 1633 studying mathematics and astronomy, but finding logic and philosophy of little appeal returned home without matriculating. By 1641 he had moved to Bishop Auckland, near Durham, where he appears to have had relatives. He published his first almanac for that year, with help from William Milbourne, curate of nearby Brancepeth, and perhaps also from the parson–astrologer John Vaux of St

Sir George Wharton, first baronet (1617–1681), by David Loggan, *c.*1663

Helen Auckland. It appeared under the pseudonym Naworth, which he adopted to prevent the common people accounting him a conjuror.

Wharton's first two almanacs were bland productions, partly because the censors suppressed his prophecies about the Scots. On the outbreak of the civil war he moved to Oxford, where he was appointed a gentleman clerk of the ordnance office. In this capacity he saw action at the battles of Edgehill and Brainford in 1642. In his spare time he pursued his mathematical studies at Queen's College, and according to Wood might have been made MA had he not neglected the opportunity. In 1645 he made the acquaintance of Elias Ashmole, recently appointed to the ordnance office, who was to become a close friend and protector. Other friends included the natural philosopher Richard Rawlinson, fellow of Queen's, the physician Charles Scarburgh, and Edward Sherburne of the ordnance office, and he was clearly on the fringe of the scientific circle then flourishing in Oxford. It may also have been during these years that he married Anne Butler, with whom he had four sons and three daughters.

Wharton quickly emerged as the foremost royalist astrologer, producing polemical almanacs at Oxford with the king's blessing. These drew him into fierce battles with his parliamentarian rivals, John Booker and William Lilly. In the edition for 1644, composed in October 1643, he denied that the recent conjunction of Saturn and Jupiter heralded the overthrow of monarchy and damned Booker for hinting at the fall of the 'man of three letters', which some had interpreted as 'rex', or King Charles. Wharton retorted that 'Pym' fitted equally well, and predicted the parliamentary leader John Pym's speedy death—a prophecy fulfilled even before the almanac appeared in print. Booker replied in *Mercurius Coelicus* (1644), dismissing 'No-worth' as a 'court parasite' with sinister popish and Irish connections. Wharton penned an abusive reply, *Mercurio-Coelico mastix*, within six hours of reading Booker's squib, and published it with an annotated reprint of *Mercurius Coelicus*. For the following year, 1645, he issued two almanacs, one as Naworth, the other under his own name with a fierce assault on the 'impudent and senseless' writings of Lilly, which Lilly later admitted hurt him deeply. In May 1645 Wharton published *An Astrologicall Judgement on his Majesties Present March*, predicting that Charles would be victorious in his new military campaign. Lilly's *Starry Messenger* (1645) gave a diametrically opposite reading and contained a 'Postscript' rebutting Wharton's prediction. Naseby gave the victory to Lilly.

On 8 March 1645 Wharton was commissioned a captain of horse, raising his troop by selling his estate in Westmorland. He fought in a number of actions before sharing in the crushing defeat under Sir Jacob Astley at Stow in March 1646, where he was wounded. There was no almanac for 1646, probably because he was too busy fighting. His credibility had also suffered, and one pamphleteer later claimed he had been driven out of Oxford before its surrender in July 1646. There does seem a personal edge to Wharton's bitter remark in 1647 that every honourable man at court had found himself 'despised … by the Parasiticall Faction' (*No Merline, nor Mercurie but a New Almanacke*, sig. B3). After the fall of Oxford he found refuge with a royalist squire in Yorkshire, before making his way to London later in the year. There he published on his own account a defiant almanac for 1647. It contained an entire section devoted to vitriolic abuse of Lilly, whom he challenged to submit their differences for adjudication by Charles Scarburgh, Jonas Moore, and Vincent Wing. He renewed the attack in *Merlini Anglici errata* (1647), a medley of astrological, political, and personal abuse. Wharton's belligerent royalism was unshaken by the king's defeat. He mocked Booker's *Bloody Irish Almanack* (1646), which predicted the impending devastation of Ireland, by celebrating the Irish Catholics' continuing success. In his remarkable *Bellum Hybernicale*, published in December 1646, he openly justified the rebellion of 1641 on the grounds of the Irish people's long history of repression, and suggested that the English and Scots were at least equally to blame for the massacres. This pamphlet, with his almanac for 1648, prompted the House of Commons on 25 September 1647 to order his arrest, though he evaded capture for a further six months.

Following the civil war Wharton lived on the meagre earnings from his pamphleteering and help from Ashmole and other friends. In the late summer of 1647 he was struck down by plague, and, though he survived, a pseudonymous pamphleteer described finding him poverty-stricken and unkempt, 'all greasy and beastly' (Col. Th.—, 12). On regaining his health he embarked on a precarious new career editing royalist newspapers. *Mercurius Elencticus*, a weekly launched on 5 November 1647, combined cavalier propaganda with attacks on old astrological rivals, and developed to become one of the leading cavalier titles. Wharton used it to attack Independents and levellers, and on the execution of the king he boldly proclaimed his son as Charles II. It survived until November 1649 before falling victim to the fierce new censorship law. During this period Wharton also continued to publish his almanacs. Rather optimistically he agreed to write an uncontroversial almanac for 1648 for the Company of Stationers. Some of them passed a draft to Booker, however, who as licenser decided to suppress it. Wharton, furious, responded by publishing an unauthorized edition in which he abused the company, predicted the king's recovery, and proclaimed Laud a martyr. After months on the run he was at last betrayed, and arrested in bed on 13 March 1648. His books and papers were confiscated, and after being grilled by a parliamentary committee he was left to rot in Newgate, where he remained until contriving an escape on 26 August. Remarkably, he was able to publish a new almanac for 1649, drafted in prison and completed four days after his escape, which he dedicated defiantly to Charles I.

Wharton was deeply shocked by the king's execution in January 1649. He gave an emotional account in his newspaper, while his almanac for 1650 lashed out at the parliamentary leaders as 'the most prodigious Monsters that ever the Earth groaned under' (*Hemeroscopeion*, 1650, 19), and threatened them with execution and hell-fire. This attack led to his rearrest in November 1649. Examined before the council of state on suspicion of treason and committed to the Gatehouse, he expected to be hanged, the fate that John Bradshaw, head of the court established to try leading royalists, apparently intended for him. He owed his life, unexpectedly, to his old enemy Lilly, who at Ashmole's request interceded with the council of state through his friend Sir Bulstrode Whitelocke and secured Wharton's release on 2 February 1650, on Wharton's promise to write no more against the state. His release prompted rumours that he had betrayed his cavalier friends, a charge he vigorously denied. His almanac for 1651, published by the Company of Stationers, supplied his own version of events and acknowledged Lilly's help.

Free but destitute, Wharton was saved when Ashmole generously offered him the use of his house at Bradfield in Berkshire. Wharton helped with estate matters, but spent most of his time pursuing his studies. At Ashmole's suggestion he translated and published a work on chiromancy by Johannes Rothman, claiming it as the first such work ever to appear in England. He embarked too on a translation of Ptolemy's astrological writings, though this was never completed. He continued to publish almanacs, often sailing very close to the wind. He was arrested again briefly in September 1651, when Ashmole stood bail for him. In his almanac for 1653 (published in the autumn of 1652) he boldly predicted that the new republic was sick and about to die. The council of state responded on 1 November 1652 by ordering his arrest once more. Thereafter he dropped political predictions, though he still found other ways to signal his political views.

Wharton's almanac for 1654 caused different problems. He had quarrelled with the Company of Stationers over its refusal to pay a £20 fee still due for his 1653 almanac, so he sold his copy for the 1654 edition privately, flouting the company's monopoly. On 20 September 1653 the company secured a warrant to seize and destroy the whole impression as seditious; it seized 5000 copies and produced its own counterfeit edition. Wharton thereupon sued in the Guildhall for his unpaid fee. His suit was checked when he refused to take the engagement, but on resuming it the company hastily settled out of court. Wharton produced another independent almanac for 1655 and returned to the quarrel in *Apotelesma* (1655), which denounced the greedy 'Monopolizing Stationers'. The later 1650s saw an uneasy truce between Wharton and the company, whose name did not appear on his title-pages. In *Apotelesma* he also hit out at the government once more, predicting the imminent downfall of those 'ruling by Tyranny and Oppression, new Conquerors and Usurpers' (*Apotelesma*, 26). Not surprisingly, he was among the cavaliers rounded up in 1655. Arrested at Bradfield on 16 June he was sent prisoner to Windsor Castle, where he remained until the following spring. He compiled his almanac for 1656 in prison, dubbing it his 'Windsor Recreations'. Wharton continued to smear the regime by innuendo. Sheltering behind the proposal to make Cromwell king he felt free to commend monarchy, using carefully drafted verses undoubtedly meant as Stuart propaganda. He came under suspicion once more over the royalist assassination plot for which Dr John Hewitt was executed in June 1658. After the fall of the protectorate he at once ridiculed the Cromwellians, and he attempted to annex the phrase the 'Good Old Cause' for the cavaliers.

From the early 1650s Wharton gave less prominence to predictions, offering instead essays on historical computation, the nature of comets, and astrological methodology. The 'Chronology' or table of events, always a key feature of his titles, he used to provide a partisan record of events since 1640. From 1657 it became a separate section as 'Gesta Britannorum', extended back to 1600 and explicitly designed to recall the miseries and follies of recent times. Wharton always insisted that he wrote only for educated and loyal readers. In the 1650s many of his almanacs, unusually, carried dedications to friends and patrons, among them John Robinson, later lord mayor and lieutenant of the Tower, his kinsman Thomas Wharton, physician and anatomist, and William Backhouse, both friends of Ashmole with astrological and alchemical interests. Wharton showed his own interest in the occult sciences by transcribing the fifteenth-century alchemist George Ripley's *Cantalena*, at Ashmole's request, and by

his preface to Richard Saunders's work on physiognomy and chiromancy, his notes on Hermes Trismegistus, and an exposition of the 'Cabal of the Twelve Houses Astrologicall', printed in his almanac for 1659 with an admiring comment from William Oughtred. Noah Bridges, an authority on cipher and shorthand, was another friend.

Wharton continued to write almanacs after the Restoration, dedicating his edition for 1661 to the new king. In September 1660 he was also made licenser for almanacs, turning the tables on his former rivals, though the post lapsed under the Licensing Act of 1662. In 1661 his almanac verses were reprinted as *Select and Choice Poems*. His almanacs did not offer astrological predictions, except of the weather, and the 'Gesta' replaced the traditional 'Prognostication'. They remained highly partisan, however, and the final edition (for 1666) contained a jingoistic diatribe against the Dutch.

Wharton's life after the Restoration gradually led him away from journalism. In 1660 he was reappointed as gentleman clerk in the ordnance office, with lodgings in the Tower, and he appears to have been an effective public servant. On the death of William Legg, lieutenant of the ordnance, he was appointed in November 1670 to a newly created post as treasurer and paymaster of the ordnance, with a salary of £400 and funds of £200,000 to cover the ordnance needs of the army and navy. The office brought him considerable wealth. As a reward for his services and sufferings under two kings Wharton was created a baronet on 19 December 1677, an honour first mooted as early as 1663.

Though he published nothing in his later years, Wharton continued to pursue a variety of mathematical interests. His circle included Jonas Moore, Edward Sherburne, Robert Hooke, Richard Towneley, and Lord Brouncker. In 1675 his son and heir, Polycarpus, married Sherburne's niece. In 1680 the tory astrologer John Gadbury, an old acquaintance, begged his help when facing trial for complicity in the Popish Plot and Wharton, though ailing and crippled by gout, promptly wrote to the king on his behalf. Wharton died on 12 August 1681 at his house in Enfield, Middlesex, his family residence since at least the late 1660s. He was buried in the chapel of St Peter ad Vincula, in the Tower, on 25 August. Many of his publications, including sections from the almanacs, were reissued by Gadbury in *The Works of that most Excellent Philosopher and Astronomer, Sir George Wharton*, in 1683. All the evidence confirms Wood's portrait of him as a staunch cavalier, 'a boon companion, a witty droll and waggish poet' (Wood, *Ath. Oxon.*, 4, col. 6). BERNARD CAPP

Sources *Elias Ashmole (1617–1692): his autobiographical and historical notes*, ed. C. H. Josten, 5 vols. (1966 [i.e. 1967]) · Wood, *Ath. Oxon.* · W. Lilly, *Mr William Lilly's history of his life and times: from the year 1602, to 1681*, 2nd edn (1715); repr. with introduction by K. M. Briggs (1974) · B. S. Capp, *Astrology and the popular press: English almanacs, 1500–1800* (1979) · J. Frank, *The beginnings of the English newspaper, 1620–1660* (1961) · I. Roy, ed., *The royalist ordnance papers, 1642–1646*, 2 vols., Oxfordshire RS, 43, 49 (1964–75) · GEC, *Peerage* · CSP dom. · *The journals of the House of Commons, vol. 5, 1646–8* (1803) · Col. Th.—, *The late storie of Mr William Lilly* (1648) · J. Booker, *Mercurius Coelicus*

(1644) · B. Capp, 'George Wharton, *Bellum Hybernicale*, and the cause of Irish freedom', *EngHR*, 112 (1997), 671–7
Archives Bodl. Oxf., Ashmolean MSS
Likenesses D. Loggan, line engraving, *c.*1663, NPG [*see illus.*] · T. Cross, engraving, repro. in *Almanac* (1659–60) · T. Cross, line engraving, BM, NPG; repro. in G. Wharton, *Calendarium ecclesiasticum* (1657) · W. Faithorne, engraving, repro. in *Almanac* (1656) · W. Faithorne, engraving, repro. in G. Wharton, *The works of Sir George Wharton, collected by J. Gadbury* (1683) · W. Faithorne, line engraving, BM, NPG · R. Vaughan, line engraving, BM, NPG; repro. in G. Wharton, *Hemeroscopeion* (1654) · engraving (T. Cross), repro. in *Almanac* (1657)

Wharton, George (1688–1739). *See under* Wharton, Thomas (1614–1673).

Wharton, Goodwin (1653–1704), politician and autobiographer, was born on 8 March 1653, the third and youngest son (there were also four daughters) of Philip *Wharton, fourth Baron Wharton (1613–1696), and his second wife, Jane, daughter of Arthur *Goodwin (*d.* 1643) of Winchendon, Buckinghamshire. His mother died when he was five. After a private education in France, which included a year at the protestant academy in Caen (1663–4), Wharton briefly sat as an MP in the parliament of 1680 as member for East Grinstead, before a hotheaded pro-exclusionist speech forced him to lie low. He became involved in business ventures, such as wreck-salvaging and deep-sea diving, though these proved unprofitable.

On his father's death in 1696 Wharton inherited estates in Buckinghamshire. He had meantime become a JP, serving in that role until his death; he was elected MP in 1690 for Malmesbury and in 1695 for Cockermouth, and subsequently knight of the shire for Buckinghamshire, sitting until his death. Belligerently anti-French and anti-Catholic, he was a vocal supporter of William III, an energetic champion of whig principles, and a ferret of Jacobite plotters. Appointed first a lieutenant-colonel of horse in Lord Macclesfield's regiment, and then a lord commissioner of the Admiralty, he saw active service in the channel during the Nine Years' War before a stroke in 1698 put a premature end to his military career and probably hastened his death. He never married, but had an illegitimate son, Hezekiah Knowles. Though eclipsed by his elder brother, Thomas *Wharton (later first marquess of Wharton), and cutting less of a dash than his two other brothers—William (by his father's third marriage), the wit and gallant, slain in a duel, and Henry, the soldier politician who died young while campaigning in Ireland—Goodwin Wharton nevertheless played no small part in post-1688 whig politics.

If his public life was typical of the whig grandees of his day, Wharton lived a private life (at least in his head) that was bizarre in the extreme. An unpublished autobiographical memoir, kept from 1686 until near his death and running to some half a million words, reveals a florid fantasy life. He records his fury at being treated 'like a slave' and swindled by his family, while enjoying ambiguous sexual relationships with his stepmother, Anne Carr Popham, Lady Wharton, and also with Anne *Wharton, the wife of his brother Thomas. He describes persecution by government agents during the reign of James II. He

relates a lasting erotic liaison with a certain Mary Parish, an astrologer, cunning woman, and medium, with whom he lived in Long Acre, and by whom he claimed to have had progeny numbering 106. His autobiography tells of expeditions to Hounslow Heath, on the advice of Major John Wildman, to dig up buried treasure, of programmes of alchemical experiments, and of meetings with dignitaries from the fairy kingdom of the Lowlanders (whose queen, Penelope, he believed he married). He recounts his illicit amours with Mary of Modena, Queen Mary, and Queen Anne. Absorbing his father's deep piety, he believed himself to be in direct communication with angels and with the Lord himself, who had predestined him to be 'King of Kings and Solar King of the World', sent to repopulate his nation. Wharton's autobiography ranks high in the annals of psychopathology. He died on 26 October 1704.   ROY PORTER, *rev.*

Sources Goodwin Wharton's autobiography, BL, Add. MSS 20006–20007 · Bodl. Oxf., MSS Carte · J. K. Clark, *Goodwin Wharton* (1984) · E. R. Wharton, *The Whartons of Wharton Hall* (1898) · B. Dale, *The good Lord Wharton: his family, life and Bible charity* (1906) · B. M. Crook, E. Cruickshanks, and B. D. Henning, 'Wharton, Hon. Goodwin', HoP, *Commons, 1660–90* · IGI
Archives BL, autobiography, Add. MSS 20006–20007 | Bodl. Oxf., Carte MSS
Wealth at death substantial estates in Buckinghamshire

Wharton, Henry (1664–1695), Church of England clergyman and historian, was born on 9 November 1664 at Worstead, Norfolk, and baptized, probably in the parish, on 20 November, the eldest son of Edmund Wharton (*bap.* 1635, *d.* 1717), vicar of Worstead, rector of adjacent Sloley and later of Saxlingham in the same county, and his wife, Susanna, daughter of John Burr, a wealthy clothier of Dedham, Essex. Henry had a younger brother, Edmund, and a sister, Susan. He was born with two tongues, both of the same size and shape. As an infant, he was examined by natural philosophers. The lower tongue gradually receded until it was no longer an impediment.

When he was six Wharton attended school at North Walsham, Norfolk, for a year; thereafter he was taught at home by his father. The surviving extracts from his autobiography record his teenage achievements in Latin and Greek composition and, according to the posthumous biography of him by his near-contemporary Thomas Green, his father's thorough teaching, especially in the classical languages, ensured that 'at his entrance into the university he had the reputation of an extraordinary young man' (Green, sig. A3*r*). He was admitted pensioner at Gonville and Caius College, Cambridge, on 17 February 1680, matriculated the same year, and was elected scholar of his college in November. He graduated BA in 1684. Wharton was a brilliant student, excelling in classics, philosophy, French and Italian, and mathematics: in the last he was one of 'a select Company' taught by Isaac Newton 'in his private Chamber' (ibid., sig. A4*r*). At Cambridge, his biographer observed, Wharton was 'in all his Conversation exemplary for Sobriety and good Government of himself, and innocent and obliging in his Behaviour, duly observant of College Orders, and constant in frequenting

Henry Wharton (1664–1695), by Robert White, pubd 1698 (after Henry Tilson)

the Prayers and Sacraments in the Chapel' (ibid., sig. A4v).

Career and works However, Wharton was unable to obtain a fellowship, and upon the recommendation of a senior fellow of his college he became the assistant to the church historian William Cave, a position he held from 1686 to 1687. Cave allowed him a salary of £10 a year and access to his library, while Caius allowed him to keep his scholarship until Michaelmas 1687. Wharton collaborated with Cave on his *Scriptorum ecclesiasticorum historia literaria* (1688), an account of European writers from ancient times to the Reformation. Wharton wrote most of the section that dealt with the period after 1300, and felt that his contributions were not properly acknowledged. On 27 February 1687 he was ordained deacon by Thomas White, bishop of Peterborough, and in July proceeded MA, the degree being conferred on him by proxy as at the time he was sick with smallpox.

Wharton worked on medieval manuscripts at Cambridge University and in the royal library at St James's during 1687 and 1688. In the latter year he wrote or edited four books which assailed Roman Catholic doctrines for their lack of scriptural and historical foundation. His patron for these works, which included *A Treatise of the Celibacy of the Church* and *A Treatise Proving Scripture to be the Rule of Faith* (both published in 1688) was Thomas Tenison, vicar of St Martin-in-the-Fields, London, and future archbishop of Canterbury. In *The Enthusiasm of the Church of Rome Demonstrated* (1688) Wharton argued that the 'extraordinary Illuminations' of Catholic saints like Loyola testified to the irrationalism and fanaticism of the Roman church, as opposed to the 'rational piety' of Anglicanism (*Enthusiasm*, 15).

William Sancroft, archbishop of Canterbury, became Wharton's patron in 1688. Much impressed by Sancroft's piety and support of learning, Wharton wrote that he could not 'be otherwise than diligent' in his scholarship (Douglas, 143). He was made one of Sancroft's chaplains, ordained priest by him on 9 November 1688, and was licensed to preach throughout Canterbury. Wharton was nominated by him to the rectory of Minster, Kent, in October 1688 and to the rectory of Chartham in the same county in September 1689, positions which he held for the rest of his life. Many of Wharton's clerical duties were performed by curates, thus allowing him time for his scholarly pursuits. He befriended two of Sancroft's domestic chaplains, John Battely, archdeacon of Canterbury, and Henry Maurice, both of whom were scholars of church history.

Wharton was an amazingly productive scholar. He added to the manuscripts in Lambeth Palace, transcribed the treatises in them, and catalogued the collection, sixteen volumes in all; this catalogue forms the basis of the printed catalogue of Lambeth manuscripts and is thus a valuable resource for scholars. He also edited a new edition of Archbishop James Ussher's *Historia dogmatica* (1689) and wrote *A defence of pluralities or holding two benefices with cure of souls as now practised in the Church of England* (1692). In all his works, Wharton wrote as a champion of the church and defender of its doctrines.

Relations between Wharton and his patron became strained when in 1689 Wharton took the oath of allegiance to William and Mary and publicly prayed in Lambeth chapel for the new sovereigns. Sancroft refused to swear allegiance, and told Wharton not to mention the new sovereigns again in the public prayers. The archbishop was deprived of church office and became the leading nonjuror. He personally scolded Wharton for his breach of faith. During his final illness Sancroft wanted only nonjurors in his company, and Wharton was thus excluded. Nevertheless Wharton remained on friendly terms with Sancroft and with other nonjurors, including George Hickes—sharing their high-church views. In his last days Sancroft turned over to him the diary and manuscripts of the high-church martyr William Laud, which Wharton edited and published in 1695 as *The History of the Troubles and Tryal of … Dr. William Laud*. Wharton called Laud a 'Blessed Martyr' who strove to re-establish 'the Beauty, the Honour, and the Force of religion' (unpaginated preface).

Wharton's association with Sancroft hindered his advancement in the post-revolution church. His prospects for preferment were not helped by a literary attack he launched in 1693 against Bishop Gilbert Burnet, who was well connected in church and state. Wharton, employing the pseudonym Anthony Harmer and a sarcastic tone, wrote *A Specimen of some Errors and Defects in the History of the Reformation ... by Gilbert Burnet* (1693), in which he suggested that as a 'foreigner' the Scottish Burnet was not up to the task of writing about the English Reformation (Wharton, pt 4, 161). This provoked a spirited rejoinder from the bishop who, among other things, accused Wharton of aiding and abetting popery in his *Specimen*.

Relations between Wharton and Burnet were strained even before Wharton's critique. The whiggish Burnet was an adversary of Sancroft and rebuffed Wharton when he approached him after the revolution in hopes of winning his favour. Wharton believed that Burnet blocked his attempt to become one of Queen Mary's chaplains. Burnet, who had criticized Wharton's *Anglia sacra* (discussed below) in 1691, believed it was revenge which motivated Wharton to write the *Specimen*. He complained of the incivility and 'sourness' which Wharton had displayed in the *Specimen* (Burnet, 28).

Not all of Wharton's relations with whig eminences were so contentious. His connection to Thomas Tenison has already been noted. Tenison's predecessor as archbishop, John Tillotson, allowed Wharton continued access to the Lambeth manuscripts. While he was Sancroft's chaplain, Wharton befriended William Lloyd, bishop of St Asaph (1680–89) and of Lichfield and Coventry (1692–9). Lloyd had urged Burnet to write his *History of the Reformation* and offered him valuable assistance on the project. Indeed Burnet's retort to Wharton's *Specimen* was his *Letter ... to the Ld Bishop of Coventry and Litchfield* (1693).

Historian of the medieval church Wharton wrote or edited over twenty books during his short life. His most important work was *Anglia sacra* (1691), written in Latin and published in two folio volumes of over 1500 pages. *Anglia sacra* was a collection of medieval manuscripts that chronicled the history of the English church. The first volume consisted of histories, written by monks, of the monastic cathedrals—Canterbury, Winchester, Rochester, Norwich, Coventry and Lichfield, Bath and Wells, Durham, and Ely. The second volume contained the lives of bishops and the history of their sees. Wharton wrote the concluding sections of the narratives, which continued the chronicles to the Reformation. A letter in 1689 described his research:

> Considering that the history of our church before the Reformation was little known, and that great numbers of the civil antient histories were already published ... I resolved to make a collection of histories purely ecclesiastical, and publish them together ... When I had gained many of these histories and caused them to be transcribed out of several libraries, I found that they were all particular of some one church, relating almost wholly to the affairs of that church of which the writer was a monk or canon. Hence I immediately conceived, that if such histories could be found of every episcopal see, a perfect history of our bishops would then arise ... I have turned over innumerable registers, histories etc., and procured much from other persons. (Douglas, 145–6)

Wharton did not completely realize his vision. He finished his history of the monastic sees, but not of those served by secular canons.

Anglia sacra made a major contribution to the sources of medieval English history. It enabled scholars to canvass and compare a wealth of medieval chronicles. The lives of many English prelates appeared in print for the first time, including John of Salisbury's life of St Anselm, William of Malmesbury's life of Wulfstan, and Eadmer's lives of Bregwim and St Oswald. *Anglia sacra* was used extensively by later scholars. John Lingard and William Stubbs were among the nineteenth-century historians who drew upon it.

Anglia sacra ran counter to the conventional wisdom of Wharton's time which held that the pre-Reformation church, mired in superstition and popery, was not a subject that merited extensive scholarly research. Similarly, his pseudonymous *Specimen of some Errors*, though far less influential than *Anglia sacra*, was an original work of scholarship. In this 200-page book Wharton anticipated modern historians by arguing that the late medieval church showed many signs of spirituality and vitality, and challenged the commonplace view, expressed by Bishop Burnet, that the pre-Reformation church was corrupt and oppressive. Where Burnet saw only ignorance and sloth in the monastaries, Wharton found learning and piety.

Burnet was wrong when he said that suffragan bishops had been abolished in the late medieval church and were only revived with the Reformation. 'If the Historian', wrote Wharton, 'had pleased to acquaint himself with the State of the Church of England before the Reformation, he could not have been Ignorant, that for about 200 years before the Reformation, Suffragan Bishops had been frequent in England' (Jones, 123). And Wharton objected to the anti-clerical, Erastian bias of Burnet's *History*. He took issue with Burnet's view that papal interference increased during the late middle ages. Kings frequently had their way in the appointment of bishops, no more so than in the sixty years before the Reformation.

Wharton disputes Burnet's view that the papacy imposed 'cruel exactions' over kings and parliaments right up to the Reformation. 'Our Ancestors', he wrote, correctly, 'had before the Reformation got the better of the Court of Rome in many points converted between them' (Wharton, 8). He argues, against Burnet, that the Statutes of Provisors and *Praemunire* were effective in limiting papal interference. Throughout the *Specimen* Wharton compared Burnet's transcription of documents with the originals and found them to be faulty: he submitted that 'the Reformation of our Church was begun and carried out with so much piety, wisdom, and fulness of due Authority that a faithful and exact Account is the best Vindication and defence of it' (Wharton, 160).

There is no contradiction between the anti-Catholic works which Wharton undertook for Thomas Tenison and the balanced portrayal of the pre-Reformation church displayed in the *Specimen of some Errors* and *Anglia sacra*. The latter was a major work of scholarship, but its empathetic portrayal of the medieval church also reflected the Laudian, high-church view that the pre-Reformation church, though marked by abuses, was a true Christian church, meriting close study. Wharton's anti-Catholic works were written under the direction of a whig churchman who was campaigning against the widely perceived threat of popery in the reign of James II. The paradox was that many Restoration clerics, like Wharton, decried the errors of Rome, but did not view Roman Catholicism as idolatrous.

Personal traits and death Wharton was of middle height, handsome, strong, with a dark complexion. Devoting his life to scholarship, he never married. In his autobiography he recounted how he resisted the temptations of vice and preserved his virginity. He was very serious, self-assured, and energetic. He worked tirelessly on his scholarship, more than twelve hours a day, standing up as he wrote. He ignored cold weather, writing until his hands and feet were numb. This disregard for his health may have contributed to his early death. He continued to live at Canterbury until 1694, when he moved to his rectory in Chartham. In his final months he was burdened with clerical duties and regretted that his scholarly activity languished. He fell ill during the summer of 1694 and travelled to Bath, Somerset, in hopes that the mineral waters there would cure him. But he died in Chartham on 5 March 1695, probably of tuberculosis, at the age of thirty.

Wharton was buried in Westminster Abbey on 8 March. His funeral was performed by Thomas Sprat, bishop of Rochester and dean of Westminster, and there were many bishops (including Tenison and Lloyd, who had both visited him during his last illness) in attendance, as well as the abbey's prebendaries and the king's scholars. Anthems were written specifically for the occasion by Henry Purcell. The pomp and ceremony of Wharton's funeral indicate that his scholarly achievements were not unrecognized during his lifetime. Posthumous publications included a two-volume collection of the sermons that he had preached at Lambeth prefaced by Green's biography, which went through three editions (1697–8, 1700, and 1728). His autobiography in Latin apparently no longer survives. However, extensive extracts from it were copied by Thomas Birch and were eventually published in 1821 as an appendix to George D'Oyly's biography of Archbishop Sancroft.   LAIRD OKIE

Sources DNB · G. D'Oyly, *The life of William Sancroft, archbishop of Canterbury*, 2 vols. (1821), 2.103–74 · [T. Green], 'The life of Mr Hen. Wharton', in H. Wharton, *Fourteen sermons preach'd in Lambeth Chapel*, 2nd edn, 1 (1700) [2 vol. collection; 2nd vol. entitled *One and twenty sermons preach'd …*] · Venn, *Alum. Cant.* · H. Wharton, *A specimen of some errors and defects in the history of the Reformation of the church of England, wrote by Gilbert Burnet* (1693) · G. Burnet, *A letter writ by the lord bishop of Salisbury to the lord bishop of Cov. and Litchfield* (1693) · D. C. Douglas, *English scholars, 1660–1730*, 2nd edn (1951) · E. Jones, *The English nation: the great myth* (1998) · IGI
Archives LPL, MS collections, MSS 577–595
Likenesses R. White, line engraving (after H. Tilson), BM, NPG; repro. in H. Wharton, *One hundred and twenty sermons preach'd in Lambeth Chapel* (1698) [*see illus.*]

Wharton, Henry Thornton (1846–1895). *See under* Wharton, Edward Ross (1844–1896).

Wharton, Jeremiah (*fl.* 1654), grammarian, is known only through his one publication, *The English-Grammar* (1654). In his discussion of Wharton's phonetic descriptions of, for instance, a 'hard g' in *ringer, longing, hanging, longeth*, etc. and the pronunciation of 'ou' and 'ow' spellings, Dobson suggests he may have been a northerner but admits that 'it is impossible to prove a connexion with the North' (Dobson, 338). A Jeremy Wharton matriculated as a sizar of Trinity College, Cambridge, in 1621, graduated BA in 1625, and proceeded MA in 1633, but nothing further is known about this man; however, Wharton is described on the title page of his grammar as 'Mr of Arts' (Wharton, title page).

The English-Grammar, like all seventeenth-century English grammars, relied heavily on previous grammars for its material, and Wharton's debt to Mulcaster, Coot, Gil, Jonson, and Butler is acknowledged in the margin of the prefatory address. Nevertheless Vorlat dismisses it as 'mere plagiarism of Lily and Butler' (Vorlat, 432). Be that as it may, the work was intended as a textbook to facilitate the transfer to the study of Latin, on the grounds that the rules for any one language 'for the most part may bee applied' to any other (Wharton, sig. A6r). This statement, as Michael observes, is 'the most explicit reference in any grammar before 1660 to the assumption governing the idea of universal grammar' (Michael, 165).

Wharton's thinking may have been advanced, but he showed a degree of realism in his attitude to education when he says

> for *one* that is trained up in the Grammar Schools, to any perfection, fit for the Universitie, or any learned Profession, a hundred are taken away before; of whom the most, very shortly after, wholly in a manner, forget their Latine; so that if they bee not bettered in the knowledg of their Native Language, their labor and cost is to little or no purpose. (Wharton, sig. A4v)

Wharton was also an early advocate for the advancement of the English language because 'the puritee and Elegancie of our own Language is to bee esteemed a chief part of the honor of our Nation' (Wharton, sig. A4r). His confidence in the virtues of his nationality and language is apparently borne out by an advertisement, at the end of the preface, for *The Illuminator of the English Tongue*. It seems that Wharton was about to publish a grammar, entirely devoted to English, where the student would not need Latin. However, no record exists of the book's ever having been published. There is no way of knowing whether the failure was because Wharton himself was impecunious, lacked patronage, or had died.

The English-Grammar was reissued in 1655 under an amended title: *A New English-Grammar*.   R. D. SMITH

Sources J. Wharton, *The English-grammar* (1654); facs. edn (1970) · E. J. Dobson, *English pronunciation, 1500–1700*, 2nd edn, 1 (1968) · Venn, *Alum. Cant.* · I. Michael, *English grammatical categories and the tradition to 1800* (1970) · E. Vorlat, *The development of English grammatical theory, 1586–1737, with special reference to the theory of parts of speech* (1975) · G. A. Padley, *Grammatical theory in western Europe, 1500–1700: trends in vernacular grammar I* (1985)

Wharton, John (*fl.* 1575–1578), religious writer and schoolmaster, appears to have lived in London. He signed the preface to *A misticall devise of the spiritual and godly love betwene Christ the spouse, and the church or congregation* (1575), attributed on the title-page to Jud Smith. In Wharton's opinion, the work, in verse and adapted from the Song of Solomon, was far more edifying than 'olde bables, as I may terme them, or stale tales of Chaucer' ('To the Christian reader'). Henry Hickman was licensed in 1576 to print Wharton's 'novels', while on 26 July the same year his ballad 'Whartons follie' was licensed to John Hunter. Wharton also issued *Whartons dreame: conteyning an invective agaynst certaine abhominable caterpillers as userers, extorcioners, leasmongers and such others* (1578), describing himself on the title-page as a schoolmaster. He claimed that the work had been 'Perused and thought well of for the correcting of vice and terrifying of the wicked: by these following. John Fox, Robert Crowley, William Wager, Thomas Buckmaister, and others' (title-page verso). In a preface to Alexander Nowell, the dean of St Paul's, Wharton presented 'the little talent of my exile and slender learning' and apologized for 'my rusticall and rude sentences'. 'To the Christian reader' complains of the city of London that 'there was never such avarice in Sodom, never such riotousness in Gomorrah, never such pride in Tyre' and predicts 'a day of correction which will be most sharp and horrible'; there then follow verses upon 'Wharton's dream' by Buckmaister, William Vallans, Thomas Smith, and George Rogers. Nothing further is known of Wharton.

E. I. CARLYLE, *rev.* STEPHEN WRIGHT

Sources J. Wharton, ed., *Whartons dreame: conteyninge an invective agaynst certaine abhominable caterpillers as userers, extorcioners, leasmongers and such others* (1578) · ESTC

Wharton, Philip, fourth Baron Wharton (1613–1696), politician, son of Sir Thomas Wharton (*c.*1588–1622) of Easby, Yorkshire, and his wife, Philadelphia (*d.* 1654/5), daughter of Robert Carey, first earl of Monmouth, was born on 8 April 1613.

Education and marriage In 1624 Wharton went to Eton College for a year. His father having died in 1622, on 25 March 1625 Philip succeeded to the barony of his grandfather, also Philip. He matriculated at Exeter College, Oxford, on 3 March 1626. In 1629 he and his brother, Sir Thomas, had licence to travel abroad for three years, and Wharton is said to have served for a time as a volunteer in the army of the prince of Orange. Reputedly he combined militancy in the cause of international protestantism with a love of dancing and a connoisseur's taste in art. His collection of works by Anthony Van Dyck, for whom he sat himself, had found its way to the Hermitage in St Petersburg by 1914. On 23 September 1632 he married Elizabeth, daughter of Sir Rowland Wandesford of Pickhill, Yorkshire. On coming of age in 1634 he inherited an estate estimated to have brought him an annual income of £8000. His wife, Elizabeth, having died, on 7 September 1637 he married Jane (*bap.* 1618, *d.* 1658), daughter and heir of Arthur *Goodwin of Winchendon and Wooburn, Buckinghamshire, MP for

Philip Wharton, fourth Baron Wharton (1613–1696), by Sir Godfrey Kneller, 1685

Buckinghamshire in the Long Parliament. They had six sons of whom three survived and four daughters. In 1638 Wharton was admitted to Lincoln's Inn on the interest of William Lenthall, future speaker of the same assembly.

Parliamentary supporter During the first bishops' war of 1639 Wharton compounded for his attendance on the king at York, paying £500 rather than repair, as ordered, to his northern estates and wait there in arms. He sat in the Short Parliament of May 1640 and voted against the precedence of supply over redress of grievances. The following summer he helped to organize the Yorkshire petitions protesting against the military burdens placed on the county by the preparations to fight the Scots, and other grievances. The king personally rebuked him and Burnet claimed that the earl of Strafford went so far as to threaten to have Wharton shot at the head of the army as a seditious incendiary. It has been plausibly suggested that there was an intimate connection between the Yorkshire petitions and the efforts of those opposition peers colluding at this time with the Scottish covenanters in order to pressurize the king into summoning a new parliament. Wharton was entirely in sympathy with the petition of the twelve peers calling on the king to do just that, presented to Charles at York on 2 September 1640, although his name does not appear on the original, only on subsequent versions. Wharton was one of the peers chosen to negotiate with the Scots at Ripon in September and again at London in November 1640. Robert Baillie remarked on his friendly disposition towards the Scots, and the king evidently distrusted him, including him in the list of witnesses he intended to call in prosecution of the six members in January 1642. Sympathy for the covenanters' cause reflected Wharton's own religious outlook, which was strongly anti-Laudian. In September 1641 he protested when by a slender majority the House of Lords voted to uphold the form of public worship then established in law, rather than countenance the House of Commons' forthright condemnation of religious innovations.

Wharton was immediately to the fore on the parliamentary side at the outbreak of the civil war. He was appointed lord lieutenant of Lancashire by the Long Parliament on 28 February, and of Buckinghamshire on 24 June 1642. That summer he was also appointed to command an army, which in the event never materialized, intended to quell the Catholic rebellion in Ireland. On 30 July Wharton accepted a commission instead to command a regiment of foot in the army of the earl of Essex, to which he recruited men from the Wharton fief of Kirkby Stephen in Westmorland. The honour of his service in the field at Edgehill was disputed. For his part, Lord General Essex did not scruple to dispatch Wharton to Westminster to give parliament an account of the engagement. In a speech given at the Guildhall almost immediately afterwards Wharton did nothing to deny the ignominy of his regiment's flight without a fight, but neither did he say anything which could possibly be construed as confirming the rumour, apparently only current many years later, that he himself had run away and hid in a saw-pit. Wharton did not, however, venture forth in arms again. He was one of the most active parliamentarian peers during the civil wars, serving as speaker of the upper house on numerous occasions, and was appointed to many of the most important executive committees.

Their estates in the north of England having been overrun by the earl of Newcastle's royalist army, Wharton and Lord Howard of Escrick had held preliminary talks with the Scots in spring 1643 which eventually produced the alliance with the covenanters. Wharton was a founding member of the committee of both kingdoms, and also an energetic lay member of the Westminster assembly. But his faith in the Scottish alliance was almost entirely a matter of military convenience. Although he promoted the assembly's directory in the north, at least as a preferable alternative to prayer book worship, Wharton was probably closer to the religious Independents. Certainly his support for the assembly evaporated once he and his war party associates revolted from their pro-Scottish allegiance, and he eventually advocated its dissolution. By the close of 1644, increasingly concerned by the new threat which the Scottish army posed to his northern estates, Wharton was aligning himself with the political Independent cause of English self-sufficiency in arms and the repudiation of Scottish influence over English affairs.

Eager to oust the earl of Essex from his command of the parliamentarian forces, Wharton was one of the keenest supporters in the House of Lords of the self-denying ordinance and the foundation of the New Model Army.

Once the new military arrangements were successfully established in the field Wharton energetically sought ways of terminating the Scottish alliance. His patronage secured the election of Henry Ireton, commissary general of the new army, for the borough of Appleby in Westmorland. Uncharacteristically, and perhaps deceptively, he appears to have played no part in the clash between parliament and army in 1647. His behaviour the following year is equally difficult to interpret. He was identified as one of a cabinet junto of grandees at Derby House undermining the terms of the vote of no addresses by seeking to negotiate a settlement with Charles I in private. Yet in June 1648 he was also accused of concealing a plot to assassinate the king on the Isle of Wight, of which imputation he was cleared by the House of Lords. The following month it was rumoured that he, Lord Saye and Sele, and Oliver Cromwell had met to consider using the army to crush support for a personal treaty with the king in the City. However, in a show of journalistic humility rare for the age, the story was subsequently retracted, and on balance it seems entirely likely that Wharton supported the negotiations with the king conducted in the autumn at Newport on the Isle of Wight. He later claimed to have protested publicly at the purge of the Commons. Certainly he did not sit in the Lords after 7 December 1648, and ignored a summons to attend, so was not present in the upper house on 2 January 1649 when the peers rejected the Commons' ordinance for the trial of the king. Almost certainly he did not agree with the proceedings which ensued and he certainly did not accept their outcome, despite the frequent urgings of his intimate acquaintance, Oliver Cromwell, who implored him that he accept the harsh dealing with the king, and wrote 'be not offended at the manner ... perhaps no other way was left' (Firth, 231–2). Vainly Cromwell summoned to mind Wharton's years of personal sacrifice during the civil wars: 'You were with us in the form of things: why not in the power?' (ibid.).

Although Wharton kept aloof from the regimes which governed England in the years that followed, Cromwell evidently flattered himself to think they remained on sufficiently good terms that a match could be pursued in 1652 between his son Henry and one of Wharton's daughters. It was not just the reluctance of the lady in question which prevented the union, but also the misgivings of her father, which Cromwell frankly acknowledged 'may make the business uneasy' (*Writings and Speeches*, 2.561). In December 1653 Wharton was given to understand that Cromwell had it in mind to have him sit on his council, but evidently nothing came of it. In 1654 Wharton attempted to use what personal influence he still had with Cromwell on behalf of his kinsman Lord Claneboye, an Ulster protestant whose claim to the benefit of articles granted at the surrender of Ormond in April 1650 had been slighted by the commissioners for the government of Ireland. An ordinance indemnifying Claneboye's estate was drawn up, but at the last seems to have come unstuck. Wharton was one of several peers summoned to sit in Cromwell's House of Lords in 1657. Although he 'thought of accepting' (Firth, 250), a robust letter from Lord Saye and Sele, who swore never to divest the nobility of England of their birthright by falling into the tyrant's embrace, emboldened Wharton to refuse.

Restoration politics and disillusionment In spring 1660 Wharton's home was said to have been one of the venues for meetings of the presbyterian junto at Westminster which wanted Charles II seated on his throne conditionally on his acceptance of the terms agreed with his father at the treaty of Newport in 1648, although it was also claimed that Wharton himself favoured unconditional restoration. He was probably one of those former parliamentarians growing increasingly alarmed in the later 1650s at the rise of the most astounding religious heterodoxy. His appointee to the parish of Kirkby Stephen, Francis Higginson, was in the front line of the confrontation with spiritual enthusiasm when it arose in the region in the early 1650s in the persons of George Fox, James Naylor, and others whom Higginson referred to as 'Satan's Seeds-men' (Breay, 167). After taking their seats in the Convention in April 1660 Wharton and his fellow presbyterian peers were instrumental in bringing about the Stuart Restoration, although many of them saw in it little more than a defence against the imminent immolation, as they imagined, of civil society.

Wharton ostentatiously welcomed Charles II on his return to England, although he did so dressed in black for a wife who had died two years earlier. There was some danger of his exemption from the Act of Indemnity in connection with the allegations surrounding the supposed assassination plot of 1648, but it was supposedly averted by the intercession of his son-in-law, Lord Willoughby of Eresby, future earl of Lindsey, and Wharton suffered relatively slightly in his estate, losing lands in Ireland. The duke of York himself was also said to have deflected criticism of Wharton, an indication of the Stuarts' willingness to court their old enemies in order to balance the ardour of their most loyal friends. In 1660 it had seemed likely that Wharton might be persuaded to accept a modified episcopacy, and he chaired the committee of the convention which produced the broadly conciliatory act for confirming and restoring ministers. But the creeping Anglicanism of the Restoration church settlement meant that he found his religious allegiances cast him further and further out into nonconformity. He was to the fore in the organization of the 'presbyterian' caucus in the Cavalier parliament which worked to curb the potentially devastating impact of the church settlement on law-abiding protestants who scrupled to conform, opposing for example, the episcopal reordination of ministers who owed their position to presbyterian examination. On 24 or 26 August 1661 he married Anne (d. 1692), widow of Edward Popham and daughter of William Carr. They had one son.

Initially, far from being an opponent of the new regime,

Wharton probably ought to be seen as acting in the capacity of a manager of the court interest, but the failure to secure any real comprehension for nonconformist protestants seems to have sapped his loyalty, and he began instead to attack the court. He was suspected of involvement in the 1663 armed uprising of political and religious radicals in Yorkshire and Westmorland, and in July supported the earl of Bristol's attempted impeachment of Clarendon (although he remained neutral four years later in the debate on whether to commit the impeached lord chancellor to the Tower). In 1663–5 Wharton attacked the Conventicle and Five Mile Acts, renewing his opposition to the former at the debates on its renewal in 1670. From the mid-1670s Wharton was one of the acknowledged leaders of the country party in the House of Lords. He was prominent in his opposition to Danby's Test Act in 1675, and was arrested the same year while worshipping in the congregation of the dissenting minister Dr Thomas Manton. He was sent to the Tower in 1677 for arguing that the Cavalier Parliament was dissolved by the fifteen-month prorogation. He took little part in the politics of the Popish Plot and subsequent exclusion crisis, his sons Thomas *Wharton, later first marquess of Wharton, and Goodwin *Wharton taking more of a lead in the harrying of Catholics in general and the duke of York in particular.

Revolution and final years Wharton left the country on the accession of James II, and was an enthusiastic advocate of the revolution of 1688. In the council of peers held after the king's flight, when Clarendon urged consideration of the rights of the prince of Wales, Wharton answered 'I did not expect at this time of day to hear anybody mention that child … and I hope we shall hear no more of him' (*DNB*). Wharton became a privy councillor to William and Mary in February 1689. His last action on the political stage was, however, to oppose the 1690 bill for an oath abjuring James II. He died on 4 or 5 February 1696 at Hampstead and was buried at Wooburn on the 12th. He was succeeded by his son Thomas. SEAN KELSEY

Sources Bodl. Oxf., MSS Carte 79, 80, 103 · *The parliamentary or constitutional history of England*, 2nd edn, 24 vols. (1751–62), vol. 14, pp. 44–61 · *DNB* · G. Lipscomb, *The history and antiquities of the county of Buckingham*, 1 (1831), 544–8 · GEC, *Peerage*, new edn, 12/2.602–6 · C. H. Firth, *The House of Lords during the civil war* (1910) · *The writings and speeches of Oliver Cromwell*, ed. W. C. Abbott and C. D. Crane, 4 vols. (1937–47) · G. F. Trevallyn Jones, *Saw-Pit Wharton* (1967) · J. Breay, 'Kirkby Stephen churchwarden's accounts, 1658–1670', *Transactions of the Cumberland and Westmorland Antiquarian and Archaeological Society*, 54 (1955), 165–83 · G. F. Trevallyn Jones, 'The composition and leadership of the presbyterian party in the convention', *EngHR*, 79 (1964), 307–54 · R. Davis, 'The "presbyterian" opposition and the emergence of party in the House of Lords in the reign of Charles II', *Party management in parliament, 1660–1784*, ed. C. Jones (1984), 1–21 · J. S. A. Adamson, 'The peerage in politics, 1645–1649', PhD diss., U. Cam., 1986 · A. Swatland, *The House of Lords in the reign of Charles II* (1996) · D. Scott, '"Hannibal at our gates": loyalists and fifth-columnists during the bishops' wars—the case of Yorkshire', *Historical Research*, 70 (1997), 269–93 · D. Scott, 'The "northern gentlemen", the parliamentary Independents, and Anglo-Scottish relations in the Long Parliament', *HJ*, 42 (1999), 347–75 · will, PRO, PROB 11/430, sig. 23
Archives BL, letters, Add. MSS 18979, 19398 · Bodl. Oxf., corresp. and papers | Bodl. Oxf., MSS Rawl., letters 49–54 · N. Yorks. CRO,

corresp. with Philip Swale · Yale U., Beinecke L., letters to Lord Dartmouth

Likenesses A. Van Dyck, oils, 1632, National Gallery of Art, Washington, DC · G. Kneller, portrait, 1685, Easton Neston, Northamptonshire [see illus.] · W. Hollar, etching, BM, NPG

Wealth at death disposed of extensive real estate seventy years earlier; estate said to have been valued at £8000 p.a.: will, PRO, PROB 11/430, sig. 23; GEC, *Peerage*

Wharton, Philip James, duke of Wharton and Jacobite duke of Northumberland (1698–1731), rake and politician, was born Philip Wharton at either Adderbury or Ditchley, Oxfordshire, probably on 21 December 1698, the only son and heir of Thomas *Wharton, fifth Baron Wharton and later first marquess of Wharton and Malmesbury and first marquess of Catherlough (1648–1715), and his second wife, Lucy, *née* Loftus (d. 1716). His godparents included William III and the future Queen Anne.

Early career Educated privately under his domineering father's supervision, Wharton (known as Viscount Winchendon from 1706 to 1715) was groomed to perpetuate his father's political principles and cultivate similar oratorical prowess. Yet his propensity for disobedience was demonstrated in 1715 when he eloped with Martha Holmes (c.1700–1726), the virtuous but relatively impoverished daughter of Major-General Richard Holmes. Their clandestine marriage on 2 March infuriated and embarrassed Wharton's father. Following the old marquess's death on 12 April 1715, Wharton's substantial estates were placed under the control of his mother and several of his father's whig associates. He then went to France and Switzerland to finish his education, supervised by an austere Swiss Calvinist tutor.

Stifled by his teacher's moralizing, Wharton abandoned him and visited James Francis Edward, the Stuart pretender to the British throne, in Avignon in August 1716, thus initiating a longstanding flirtation with the creed that had been anathema to his father. James created his impressionable visitor duke of Northumberland on 22 December 1716. By 5 December Wharton had returned to England, then proceeding to Ireland where, despite his conduct, he took his seat in the House of Lords as marquess of Catherlough on 27 August 1717, and was sworn of the privy council on 20 September 1717. His speeches and enthusiasm there sparked popular acclaim. He was created duke of Wharton in the British peerage on 28 January 1718, nearly two years shy of his majority, the youngest recipient of a dukedom, excepting close relatives of the monarch, since the fifteenth century. While it is tempting to surmise that the honour had been intended for Wharton's father, the circumstances and the peerage preamble suggest it was actually in recognition of his own merits and a desire to cement his allegiance to George I. He was introduced into the British House of Lords on his majority, 21 December 1719.

Hopes that Wharton would settle down as a member of the whig élite were to be dashed; his reckless behaviour led to financial and personal crises. Prior to 1718 Wharton hardly cohabited with his wife. Following a brief reconciliation his only child, Thomas, was born in 1719, an

Philip James Wharton, duke of Wharton and Jacobite duke of Northumberland (1698–1731), attrib. Joseph Highmore

event which brought him great joy. The child's baptism was attended by George I. Wharton's admonitions that his wife avoid London during a smallpox epidemic were ignored, and Thomas's death from the disease on 1 March 1720 precipitated additional indifference between them. Moreover, a profligacy perhaps unparalleled in Augustan England now began to demonstrate its effects. Wharton had evidently acquired loans from Jacobite bankers as early as 1718. After having sold off a sizeable portion of his Irish estates he returned from Ireland in 1720 with cash to invest in the South Sea Company. He suffered catastrophic losses of over £120,000 in the subsequent crisis, partly prompting his famous diatribe against the ministry on 4 February 1721 which so infuriated James, Earl Stanhope, that it hastened Stanhope's death by stroke.

Wharton's social life seemed driven by a desire to take indulgence to extremes. From 1719 to 1723 he was the recognized founder and chairman of the notorious Hellfire Club, a secret organization open to members of both sexes that scandalized contemporaries with its reputed satanic rituals. Sometimes confused with a similar club later associated with Sir Francis Dashwood, Wharton's group seems to have been primarily concerned with promoting dissolute behaviour and sarcastic parodies of established religion. Wharton also served as grand master of the freemasons in 1722, sparking controversy by singing a strongly pro-Stuart ballad at a ceremony.

Opposition whig, or Jacobite? Wharton's opposition political activities and the origins and extent of his Jacobitism have long been controversial. He lent significant support to a small, determined opposition group in parliament which actively lodged protests from 1720 to 1723, and was reckoned among the group's more effective orators. He was mentored by its leader, the disgruntled whig and former lord chancellor William Cowper, first Earl Cowper. Yet Wharton's support for the opposition was, at best, fickle and inconsistent. In December 1721 he deserted his opposition friends for a bribe, and he supported the ministry in debates over the habeas corpus suspension in late 1722. His return to opposition was confirmed on 15 May 1723 by his remarkable speech defending the Jacobite conspirator Francis Atterbury, bishop of Rochester. Wharton delineated distinguishing features of each side's arguments with remarkable skill. The speech was so persuasive that it permanently established Wharton's oratorical reputation, and was printed and later included among his posthumously published writings. Less well known was Wharton's visit to Walpole the night before his speech, a visit undertaken on the pretext of seeking an overview of evidence suggesting Atterbury's guilt, so that he could speak the next day in support of the ministry's position. Wharton personally accompanied Atterbury to the ship that carried him into exile. His defence of Atterbury was followed by his publication of the *True Briton*. Printed by Samuel Richardson, who later supposedly modelled Loveless, his archetypal villainous rake, after Wharton, the *True Briton* was an influential anti-Walpole political journal published twice weekly until early 1724. Wharton composed many of its more notable essays, and the authorities lamented his public appearance as a leader of the Jacobites in the City of London, and his slanderous attacks on the government.

Wharton's mercurial nature and escalating indebtedness render assessments of the genuine extent of his Jacobitism quite problematic. Several studies argue that his Stuart adherence fluctuated until after 1723, while other historians see Wharton as a committed Jacobite from perhaps 1716 onwards. Whether intermittent professions of old whiggism along his father's lines were intended to sustain political influence and allow for the surreptitious provision of intelligence to the Jacobites, or merely exemplify erratic actions fogged by frequent revelries, remains uncertain. His behaviour after 1725 implies the latter, but Wharton exhibited scant inclination towards adherence to any firm principles. His most exhaustive and sympathetic biographer concludes that Wharton was largely indifferent towards Jacobitism after 1723, and engaged in its doctrines and undertook a Jacobite mission abroad merely because this was a convenient way to avoid creditors while remaining in the international limelight.

By 1725 Wharton was closely associated with Charles Boyle, fourth earl of Orrery, the *de facto* English Jacobite leader following Atterbury's banishment. Wharton and several other diehard ministerial opponents joined Orrery in vain attempts to maintain opposition activities from 1723–5. Wharton verbally attacked the court in 1724, and protested against measures regulating City of London elections the following year. His interest in City politics reflected extensive personal influence and involvement, which was viewed as potentially valuable in a Stuart restoration, since few Jacobite politicians successfully encouraged disgruntled City politicians to oppose Walpole's ministry. Wharton also evinced sincere interest— as his finances allowed—in borough and county elections in areas such as Buckinghamshire and Cumberland where he possessed estates, even while abroad, but the disastrous condition of his personal affairs restricted his influence. He calculated his total debts in 1725 to exceed £70,000. Anxious to flee his unhappy marriage and mounting debts, he therefore eagerly accepted appointment as Stuart plenipotentiary to the imperial court at Vienna in August 1725. Orrery, forced to lend Wharton £500 to enable his departure, was named a trustee of his estates and supervised his affairs, endeavouring to sell off or mortgage estates to stave off his flamboyant friend's bankruptcy.

Jacobite diplomatist Wharton left for the Netherlands *en route* for Vienna in 1725. War in Europe appeared imminent. Although he was confident of success in procuring Habsburg assistance for a Jacobite invasion, his prospects were diminished by British government intelligence and his own personal habits. Prone to over-indulgence and lacking any diplomatic experience whatsoever, he publicly drank the Pretender's health before departing, and his indiscretion prompted Jacobites to fear their incrimination. Walpole's ministry rightly suspected a connection with Orrery's simultaneous trip to Paris, and soon verified the reasons for Wharton's journey. Wharton was advised by the Jacobite agent in Vienna, and eventually secured audiences with Austrian ministers and Austria's military commander, Prince Eugene of Savoy. Initial indications of co-operation in a landing of 4000 Austrian troops in England and James's dispatch to Brussels to reside under imperial protection, however, proved premature. Austrian suspicion about the strength of Jacobite support in Britain, and Wharton's dissolute behaviour, convinced the imperial council to reject his proposals outright in February 1726. Furthermore, the expulsion to Spain of Count Ripperda, an untrustworthy Austrian minister with whom Wharton had negotiated, and continuing negative publicity over the estrangement of James and his wife, hindered efforts abroad. Thus Wharton left Austria, stopping off briefly in Rome, where he received the Order of the Garter from James. He then proceeded to Madrid to confer further with Ripperda about the royal separation. There he was invested with his Jacobite KG by James Butler, second duke of Ormond, and proceeded pompously to display the order publicly.

In 1725 Wharton's own much maligned wife became desperately ill following a miscarriage. Languishing for months, she never fully recovered, finally expiring on 14 April 1726 at her house in Gerrard Street, Soho. The same week Wharton was summoned by privy seal order to return to England; he contemptuously discarded the document into a Madrid gutter. Ripperda subsequently betrayed to British authorities Wharton's elaborate plans for an Austro-Russian alliance with Spain to enthrone the

Pretender, and his betrayal effectively alienated Wharton from other leading Jacobites in Spain. By the time he learned of his wife's death Wharton was already in love with a Spanish maid of honour, Maria Theresa O'Neill O'Beirne (1706?–1777), daughter of a colonel in the Spanish service, Henry O'Beirne, and his wife, Henrietta O'Neill. Only after strenuous efforts could he persuade the Spanish queen to consent to their marriage; evidently a prerequisite was Wharton's conversion to Roman Catholicism. In the afternoon of 23 July 1726 NS, following a long examination by Spanish inquisitors, Wharton married the object of his affections in a simple ceremony that immediately provoked gossip.

Wharton's conversion effectively ruined his remaining significance in Jacobite politics, yet it may have been designed to rally the support of Irish Jacobite exiles in Spain under his leadership. None the less sceptical observers generally interpreted his religious change as irrefutable proof of his untrustworthiness. It was thought that Wharton's conversion to acquire a wife meant he might 'exchange his Loyalty for the Means of Maintaining her for no body thinks that he has any fix'd Principles' (Stuart papers, 95/128). Jacobite leaders often concurred, infuriated by such conversions and anxious about resulting perceptions among British supporters. Although sympathetic, even Atterbury grimly concluded the conversion had irreversibly rendered Wharton a liability. Wharton vainly attempted to defend his conversion as a long contemplated step, but his actions and subsequent comments provide meagre evidence that religious precepts mattered greatly to him. When chided by Atterbury for his conversion Wharton responded that people might just as easily think he had mutated into a Turkish Muslim. Contemporaries believed he had intentionally scorned religion by engaging in clamorous Sabbath-day hunting on his estates. His lifestyle, and the fact that he frequently voiced aspirations such as serving as one of Satan's courtiers, hardly endeared him to religious leaders or popular opinion. He enjoyed flaunting his disdain for any form of authority or ideology; one Jacobite remarked that his 'slighting expressions of the Scriptures' proved that Wharton's politics were as 'unsettl'd as his Principles of Religion' (ibid.).

Decline and death After his marriage and conversion, opinions of Wharton deteriorated to new levels of ridicule. Astonished diplomats relayed how on his wedding night he had become 'drunk early' and had 'produced, in the midst of the Grave Dons and their dames, what (to use his own expression) he told his bride *she was to have that night in her Gutts*' (PRO, State papers foreign, 78/184/230v), dispersing his wedding party in chaos. Jacobites who once esteemed Wharton their most influential adherent now lamented this 'wild, Giddy & unaccountable Man' (Stuart papers, 95/110). If his licentiousness was not sufficiently outrageous, his desperate poverty provoked both humour and disgust. Dishevelled and reclusive, reduced to stealing food from acquaintances, he was now an impoverished, aristocratic pariah rejected by Spaniards and fellow Britons. He and his wife retired to a village to survive frugally and avoid harassment by omnipresent creditors. In defiance, he tried to resign his British dukedom and sold it for a pittance, returning a deed repudiating the title to George I. In 1726 and 1727 Wharton repeatedly requested he be allowed to return to Rome.

Increasingly ignored by his former master, Wharton was inspired by other Jacobite exiles and joined the Spanish army as it engaged the British in the war that erupted in 1727. Wharton was commissioned lieutenant-colonel in the Hainault regiment, composed of Irish exiles, and named aide to the Spanish commander of an expedition besieging Gibraltar. Here in May 1727 Wharton attempted to dispel his widely held reputation for cowardice. Emboldened by brandy, he approached British troops defending the fortress wall and taunted them with obscenities and huzzahs for the Pretender. In an ensuing bombardment a bursting shell partially shattered Wharton's foot. Although he recovered from the wound, he was unable to continue his active military career. More significantly, his actions in taking up arms against British forces prompted his indictment as a traitor, and on 3 April 1729 parliament passed an informal, though arguably not legally binding, resolution that was held to have outlawed him and made his estates and titles forfeit. Although he secured a brief clandestine interview with James at Parma, he was denied hope of further Jacobite employment.

With his trustees now prohibited from dispatching any additional funds, Wharton abruptly sought to reconcile himself to the British government. He travelled to Paris in 1728 and approached the Hanoverian regime via Walpole's brother Horatio, the British resident in France. In several letters and a personal visit, Wharton asked for clemency, insisting he had resigned from the Pretender's service over a year earlier. In exchange, he assured authorities he would reveal detailed Jacobite intelligence, yet only 'as far as was consistent with his honour' (Coxe, 2.633–4). Consistent to his own nature, Wharton proceeded straight from the ambassador's house to dine with the attainted Atterbury. His haughty caveat hardly inspired government leniency. Since Walpole's spies already provided ample reports of Jacobite activities, including Wharton's, and he was judged so universally discredited as to nullify his political influence, the offer was curtly rejected by George II and his secretary of state, the duke of Newcastle.

Ensconced in modest lodgings in Rouen, growing ever more desperate, Wharton was now such an embarrassment to the Jacobites that he was firmly admonished not to journey to Rome. James enforced these warnings with a series of small bribes. By 1729 Wharton and his wife had returned to Spain, forced to subsist off his small regimental salary. In the following year his wife's mother's death terminated a pension from the Spanish court shared with her daughter and wayward son-in-law. At a formal ball he was insulted by the valet of the governor of Barcelona. After administering a fierce caning to the valet, he was briefly imprisoned and then banished from the city. He publicly renounced the Pretender and unsuccessfully requested another pardon in 1730. Years of drunkenness and subsisting largely on brandy rendered him exhausted and malnourished. After a brief recovery he was driven to seek relief at a Franciscan monastery near Poblet, where he died alone among strangers on 31 May 1731, and was buried the following day. He signed his will Philip James, the second forename presumably assumed to indicate his Jacobitism. Wharton's passing nearly went unnoticed among leading Jacobites. Perhaps secretly relieved, James lamented his widow's destitution, supplied her with a small pension, and employed Orrery to help secure her jointure, which was achieved with the proving of Wharton's will in 1736. Maria Theresa settled in London, where she enjoyed a long, modestly comfortable, secluded life until her death in Golden Square, Westminster, on 13 February 1777. She was buried in St Pancras old churchyard. After Wharton's death his titles almost certainly all became extinct, but despite this the barony of Wharton was successfully claimed by a descendant of one of his aunts in 1915. In 1733 Wharton's forfeited estates were settled on trustees for the payment of his debts, the surplus to benefit his sisters, Jane (d. 1761) and Lucy (d. 1739).

Literary activity and reputation Wharton was intermittently involved in various types of literary and journalistic activities. In addition to the *True Briton* he briefly assisted Nathaniel Mist in composing anti-Walpole rhetoric from Rouen in 1728 that proved so effective that Walpole offered Wharton a complete pardon, preservation of his estates, and retention of all his titles, if only he agreed to abstain from such public attacks. Pride, arrogance, and stubbornness prevented his acceptance. After his death Wharton's writings were collected and released in several forms. *Select and Authentick Pieces* was published in France in 1731 and included his speech defending Atterbury and the 1728 attack on Walpole. A somewhat unconvincing argument for Wharton's actions, hinging upon his adoption of Jacobitism in the spirit of liberty and genuine pre-1714 whiggism, was contained in his 1728 essay *Reasons for Leaving his Native Country*, which was also the centrepiece of *The Life and Writings of Philip, Late Duke of Wharton*, published in 1732. A number of brief miscellaneous poems and parodies are also attributed to Wharton. Before his flight from England in 1725 Wharton was the object of numerous play dedications. Supposedly fluent in at least five languages, Wharton's Latin expertise was obtained through an intense friendship with Dr Edward Young, whose character Lorenzo in Young's *Night Thoughts* is thought to be modelled on Wharton, and whose intercession supposedly secured an unpaid £250 bequest to All Souls, Oxford, for which Wharton was promised an inscription and honorary doctorate.

Accounts of Wharton's life generally take one of two approaches. Sympathetic writers strenuously attempt to explain away his groundless beliefs and apparent lack of moral and political principles, insisting that in his case 'strict logic … leads to the most hopeless confusion' (*Life and Writings*, ed. Melville, 142). Others have adopted a more condemnatory tone. Unpredictable and unreliable,

Wharton's juvenile outbursts of spiteful behaviour, his tendency toward inebriated self-denial and incessant protestations of unaccountability for his actions, his cowardice, and his profound deviation from his father's politics, coupled with an excessive perception of self-importance and arrogance, and strong ambition to be a party leader, ultimately cast him as an aristocratic master dissembler, shunned by friend and foe alike. His personality was characterized by audacity and eccentricity, and brief, fleeting glimmers of brilliance and wit, and contemporaries often chastised his fondness for prankish behaviour viewed as beneath his station. Indeed, most of his life lends itself to anecdotal narration, such as his hiring of musicians and a funeral hearse for processions commemorating the death of the South Sea Company.

Although much new information has emerged in the last century about specific aspects of Wharton's various activities, the salient features of his life remain those noticed by earlier biographers: reckless abandon seemingly driven by an utter inability for self-control and contemporary decorum, and a squandering of an undeniable stock of personal talent and an enormous fortune. Erratic political allegiances and intermittent Jacobite support inevitably raise questions of his sincerity for any creed or principles. Pope's 'Epistle to Sir Richard Temple' portrayed Wharton as 'the scorn and wonder of our days', a gifted individual destined for greatness but who, 'wanting nothing but an honest heart', was 'Too rash for thought, for action too refined'. Despite possible mitigating factors for his actions and his personality with its inherent flaws, it is extremely difficult not to conclude as did one Jacobite contemporary, that there were few examples 'of a Man who had so fair a Game in his hands & that play'd it so ill' (Stuart papers, 96/8). LAWRENCE B. SMITH

Sources *The life and writings of Philip, late duke of Wharton*, 2 vols. (1732) · Royal Arch., Stuart papers · *The life and writings of Philip, duke of Wharton*, ed. L. Melville (1913) · *Memoirs of the life of his grace Philip, late duke of Wharton* (1731) [by an impartial hand] · E. Beresford Chancellor, *Col. Charteris and the duke of Wharton* (1925), vol. 3 of *The lives of the rakes* (1924–5) · M. Blackett-Ord, *The hell-fire duke* (1982) · GEC, *Peerage* · *Letters of George Lockhart of Carnwath, 1698–1732*, ed. D. Szechi, Scottish History Society, 5th ser., 2 (1989) · State papers foreign, France, 1725–31, PRO, SP 78/183–98 · *Calendar of the Stuart papers belonging to his majesty the king, preserved at Windsor Castle*, 7 vols., HMC, 56 (1902–23) · letters to William, first Earl Cowper, 1717–21, Herts. ALS · *The poetical works of Philip, late duke of Wharton* (1732) · *GM*, 1st ser., 36 (1766) · *GM*, 1st ser., 37 (1767) · C. Jones, 'The new opposition in the House of Lords, 1720–1723', *HJ*, 36 (1993), 309–29 · E. Cruickshanks, 'Lord Cowper, Lord Orrery, the duke of Wharton, and Jacobitism', *Albion*, 26 (1994), 27–40 · diplomatic correspondence of Charles, Viscount Townshend, Oct 1716–Nov 1727, BL, Add. MS 48981 · W. Coxe, *Memoirs of the life and administration of Sir Robert Walpole, earl of Orford*, 3 vols. (1798) · J. R. Robinson, *Philip, duke of Wharton* (1896) · 'Philip, duke of Wharton's examination by the Spanish Inquisition on renouncing Protestantism, 1726', BL, Spanish Egerton MS 1509, fol. 394 · R. F. Gould, 'Masonic celebrities no. vi: the duke of Wharton, G. M., 1722–23; with which is combined the true history of the Gormogons', *Ars Quatuor Coronatorum*, 8 (1895), 114–55 · [marquis de Argens], *Memoirs of the count du Beauval, including some curious particulars relating to the dukes of Wharton and Ormond, during their exiles* (1756) · *Reports on the manuscripts of the earl of Eglinton*, HMC, 10 (1885) · H. Walpole, *A catalogue of the royal and noble authors of England*, 3rd edn (1759) · A. T. Thomson,

G. Wharton, and P. Wharton, *The wits and beaux of society* [n.d.] • W. Russell, *Eccentric personages*, 2 vols. (1844) • E. Timberland, *The history and proceedings of the House of Lords from the Restoration in 1660 to the present time*, 8 vols. (1742–3) • *The letters of Francis Atterbury, bishop of Rochester, to the chevalier de St. George and some of the adherents of the house of Stuart*, ed. J. H. Glover, 2 vols. (1847) • warrant for recall of the duke of Wharton to England, 1726, BL, Add. MS 36126, fol. 43 • R. Sharp, *The engraved record of the Jacobite movement* (1996) • journal of Mary Caesar, 1729–40, BL, Add. MS 62558 • Cobbett, *Parl. hist.*, vol. 8 • P. Yorke, earl of Hardwicke, ed., *Miscellaneous state papers from 1501 to 1726*, 2 vols. (1778) • P. Stanhope, Lord Mahon, *History of England from the peace of Utrecht, to the peace of Aix-La-Chapelle*, 5 vols. (1737) • *Memoirs and correspondence of Francis Atterbury, D.D., bishop of Rochester*, ed. F. Williams, 2 vols. (1869) • papers of the duke of Newcastle, 1724–6, BL, Add. MS 33199 • *Report on manuscripts in various collections*, 8 vols., HMC, 55 (1901–14), vol. 8 • W. Seward, *Anecdotes of some distinguished persons*, 4 vols. (1795–6) • *A biographical history of England, from the revolution to the end of George I's reign: being a continuation of the Rev. J. Granger's work*, ed. M. Noble, 3 vols. (1806) • Burke, *Peerage* (1999)
Archives N. Yorks. CRO, estate corresp. and papers • Royal Arch., corresp. and related material • U. Nott. L., corresp., Pw2/HY1478–1523; MSS of poems, PwV487–501 | Herts. ALS, letters to first Earl Cowper
Likenesses G. Vertue, engraving, pubd 1732 (after C. Jervas), BM, NPG; repro. in *Life and writings of Philip, late duke of Wharton*, 2 vols. (1732); version, formerly in the possession of A. M. Broadley, 1913; repro. in *Life*, ed. Melville, 160 • R. Carriera, oils, Royal Collection; repro. in Blackett-Ord, *Hell-fire duke* • R. Carriera, pastel drawing, Royal Collection • attrib. J. Highmore, portrait, priv. coll. [*see illus.*] • C. Jervas, oils, repro. in Blackett-Ord, *Hell-fire duke* • J. Simon, mezzotint (after C. Jervas), BM, NPG; repro. in *Life*, ed. Melville, frontispiece • mezzotint (after C. Jervas), repro. in Noble, *Biographical history*, 3.26

Wharton, Thomas, first Baron Wharton (*c*.1495–1568), soldier and administrator, was born at Wharton in Westmorland, the eldest son and heir of Thomas Wharton (*d.* after 1515) of Wharton and Nateby, Lancashire, landowner, and his wife, Agnes, daughter of Reginald Warcop of Smardale, Westmorland, and his wife. The Whartons were a long-established gentry family in Westmorland and Cumberland with a service connection to the Clifford family. Thomas Wharton's great-grandfather was MP for the borough of Appleby, Westmorland, 1436–7, a seat controlled by Thomas Clifford, eighth Lord Clifford, and his family held the manor of Wharton from the Cliffords throughout the fifteenth century. His father, as well as serving the Cliffords, also served the crown, particularly in the Scottish campaign of 1513 under Thomas Howard, earl of Surrey. When his father died, some time after 1515 when he finished his term as escheator in Cumberland and Westmorland, his wardship was given to Henry Clifford, tenth Lord Clifford, who sold it for 200 marks.

Early career and service to the Percy family, 1515–1537 Little is known of Wharton's early life. By 4 July 1518 he had married Eleanor (*d.* 1547×61), third daughter of Sir Brian Stapleton of Wighill, Yorkshire, and his wife, Joan. They had two sons, Thomas *Wharton, second Baron Wharton (1520–1572), and Sir Henry Wharton (*d.* 1550), and two daughters, Joanna and Agnes. More significantly, marriage into the Stapleton family brought him into the affinity of the Percy earls of Northumberland. In April 1522 Wharton served under the captain of Berwick, Sir

Anthony Ughtred, on a raid into Scotland accompanied by Sir Thomas and Sir Ingram Percy, two sons of Henry Percy, fifth earl of Northumberland. Two years later he was appointed JP for Westmorland, perhaps evidence of his rising status with the Percy family and continuing ties with the Clifford family. He was knighted between 1527 and 1530. In 1529 Wharton was returned to the Reformation Parliament for Appleby and this was immediately followed by his being chosen as sheriff of Cumberland (1529–30). Wharton's involvement with parliament continued throughout his career despite his increasing commitments in the north: he may have been chosen for Appleby again in 1536 and 1539 and almost certainly, along with his son Thomas, was returned as knight of the shire for Cumberland in 1542. After his elevation to the peerage in 1544 he was a regular attendee in the House of Lords.

Wharton epitomized the successful servant of a great nobleman, who was then recruited into royal service as a result of his conspicuous abilities. He entered the household of Henry Percy, sixth earl of Northumberland, between 1522 and 1528. In May 1528 he was made comptroller of the earl's household and steward of the lordships of Tadcaster and Healaugh in the West Riding of Yorkshire, as well as receiving an annuity of £20 for life. In October 1530 a series of grants transformed him into the holder of 'traditional Percy authority in Cumberland' (Hoyle, 'The fall of the house of Percy', 189). These appointments were the lieutenancy of the honour of Cockermouth to be held by him and his heirs in perpetuity; the stewardship of the lordships of Eskdale and Wasdale and the constableship of Egremont Castle; the herbage of the park of Cockermouth, and a grant of mills, mines, and six manors in Cumberland at a below market-level rent of £72 to be held by him and his heirs male; and an annuity of £100 payable from the issues of those manors, in effect in lieu of rent. Wharton's place within the earl's affinity was strengthened by the close friendship with other Percy servants such as Sir Raynold Carnaby, gentleman of the chamber, and further favours from the ailing and incompetent earl. In 1534, on the disgrace of William Dacre, third Lord Dacre of Gilsland, Northumberland recommended Wharton for the captainship of Carlisle. This favour, and his continued service to Henry Clifford, fifteenth Lord Clifford and first earl of Cumberland, led to royal grants that reinforced his position within border society: he was appointed JP for Northumberland and the East Riding in 1532. He reinforced his local consequence through a series of marriage negotiations with leading members of the northern gentry; his daughter Agnes married Sir Richard Musgrave in 1534 and his best friend, Sir Thomas *Curwen (*c*.1493–1543) [*see under* Curwen family], married his sister Florence by 1538.

The reasons for Northumberland's favouring Wharton seem straightforward. It was not, as M. E. James supposed, to bolster the failing Percy influence in Cumberland in the face of hostility by the crown and the Cliffords. Rather, as Richard Hoyle has shown, Wharton's rise to prominence was in large part due to Northumberland's ill health and inherited indebtedness, which forced him to rely more and more heavily on men like Wharton and Carnaby. Moreover, Wharton's military prowess made him the ideal candidate for leading the Percy affinity in the defence of the borders. The earl drew attention to Wharton's service against the Scots and his talents were predominantly military.

Service to the king, 1537-1544 Wharton's standing was transformed by the outbreak of the Pilgrimage of Grace in 1536 and Northumberland's death in 1537. During the early stages of the pilgrimage he remained inactive and perhaps even went into hiding but, possibly because of his poor relationship with Dacre or even his reputation as a harsh landlord, he found himself a target of the rebels' hostility. He aided Thomas Howard, third duke of Norfolk, in the suppression of the rebellion and was well placed to benefit from the redistribution of power in the north in its aftermath. Wharton was recommended as warden of the west marches but Norfolk advised against appointing a gentleman rather than a nobleman to the office. Norfolk's point was that he felt only an established nobleman with a long-standing affinity had the necessary stature to carry out the office. Therefore, on 28 June 1537, Wharton was made deputy warden under the discredited Cumberland but effectively carried out the office. He was promoted to full warden on Cumberland's death in 1542. Between 1537 and 1544 Wharton continued to carve a military career for himself. He was appointed captain of Carlisle in October 1541, and in 1542 he presented an audacious plan to raid Scotland and capture James V at Lochmaben, Dumfriesshire. This plan was rejected and he consoled himself with raids north of the border in October and November of that year. On 24 November Wharton achieved the pinnacle of his career: victory over a Scottish army of some 18,000 men with just 3000 borderers at the battle of Solway Moss. He was aided by his kinsmen, Sir William Musgrave and Walter Strickland, in this, and his outstanding military success calls into question Michael Bush's assertion that Henry VIII's attempt to defend the marches without resort to noble power was a failure. As a result, Wharton was created first Baron Wharton by patent on 18 March 1544, with grants of land in co. Durham, Yorkshire, and Westmorland.

Border magnate, 1544–1560 Wharton was reappointed warden of the west marches on 1 February 1544 and held the office until 17 April 1549, when he was replaced by his rival, Dacre, in the shake-up of offices following the fall of Edward Seymour, duke of Somerset and lord protector to Edward VI. He was a member of the king's council in the north from about 1545. He was added to the quorum of the commission of the peace for Westmorland in 1547 and his heir was made JP for Westmorland and Cumberland at the same time. Wharton saw to it that his son was sheriff of Cumberland in 1547–8. His reports on a border raid by the Scots of March 1547 were essential as a pretext for Somerset's invasion. With Matthew Stewart, earl of Lennox, he provided a diversionary raid during the Pinkie campaign by entering south-western Scotland and capturing a series

of castles between 9 and 14 September. Wharton frequently dealt with the Assured Scots, including disseminating English propaganda to them, and had quite an effective network of spies in Scotland. He led frequent raids and had the difficult task of keeping the English garrisons in Scotland supplied during the campaign between 1547 and 1550. Serving the crown, despite conflict with neighbours, brought satisfaction and pride as well as local power and financial reward; Wharton told Somerset 'I have had great comfort many years from the good acceptance of my poor services to the King' (*CSP dom.*, *1601–9*, *addenda*, *1547–65*, 376). He was appointed deputy warden of the three marches on 31 July 1552 under John Dudley, duke of Northumberland, but was replaced in the west march by Sir Thomas Dacre in November.

After Mary I's accession Dacre became again warden of the west march and Wharton was appointed between July and December 1555 as, among other things, warden of the east and middle marches, captain of Berwick, constable of Alnwick Castle (where he appears to have resided), and steward of Rothbury, Northumberland. He was JP for all three ridings from 1554. In August 1557, upon the restoration of Thomas Percy as seventh earl of Northumberland, Wharton was named as joint warden with him. During Elizabeth I's reign he served as a counsellor assistant to Thomas Howard, fourth duke of Norfolk, the lieutenant-general of the north, but the latter's recommendation that he be reappointed captain of Berwick in June 1560 was not followed. Wharton married Anne (*d.* 1585), second daughter of Francis *Talbot, fifth earl of Shrewsbury, and his first wife, Mary, and widow of John Bray, second Baron Bray, on 18 November 1561. They had no children.

Wharton's position in northern society was secured, above all, by service to the crown. His income from the family lands was probably less than £100 a year but his fees from crown office were already 200 marks a year by 1537. By July 1552, as deputy warden under the duke of Northumberland, his annual income from fees was 1000 marks. Moreover, Wharton profited greatly from the dissolution of the monasteries. By March 1545, for example, he was steward of the former lands of Furness Abbey, Lancashire, and M. E. James has estimated that at its height his annual income from fees and wages was some £700. He also received grants of lands to bolster his position. These included former monastic land but also parcels of the lands of the attainted Sir Francis Bigod in 1537. Further acquisitions in the West and North ridings and Cumberland made Wharton an important regional figure. No complete rental for these new lands exists but James has estimated that his annual rental income must have been in the order of £750, some eight times that which he had inherited from his father.

Wharton was clearly a difficult and unpopular man. His unpopularity stems not from the fact that he was a 'new man', erected by Henry as part of a concerted effort to attack the regional power of the northern nobility, but, it appears, from his character itself. In the 1540s and 1550s, despite his family's long association with the Cliffords, he quarrelled openly with Cumberland, causing the intervention of the privy council. Similarly, Wharton had a long-standing feud with the Dacres. In 1551 and 1554 the privy council forced them into public displays of conciliation. This animosity does not seem to have stemmed primarily from their dislike of Wharton as a 'new man'. In 1549 Somerset prevented Henry Wharton from fighting a duel with William Grey, thirteenth Lord Grey of Wilton, warden of the east march, and their lack of co-operation probably foiled a joint invasion of Scotland in February 1548, although betrayal by certain Assured Scots and bad strategic planning were also major factors. The skills that served Wharton so well as a soldier did not endear him to others. His ongoing feud with Robert Maxwell, sixth Lord Maxwell, which originated when Wharton hanged the latter's pledges in February 1548, was instrumental in his not being appointed warden of the west march in 1560. At Carlisle he was constantly at loggerheads with his subordinate officials and feuded with other local gentry, such as the Lampleughs and Musgraves. He was also an unpopular landlord: he was the focus of tenant discontent during the Pilgrimage of Grace and according to the Wharton family history his decision to empark Ravenstonedale in Cumberland led to such hatred towards him among his tenants that he abandoned living on his Westmorland estates for Healaugh in Yorkshire. However, this story seems to be apocryphal because he was being assessed for the subsidy in Cumberland during the 1540s. He maintained a house in Cannon Row, London, too. His unpopularity and the difficulties the Tudors experienced in governing the north of England in the years after 1536 stemmed not so much from the folly of a royal policy aimed at extinguishing the ancient northern nobility but from the failure of the Percy, Clifford, and Dacre families to produce adequate men for the job and the character of the monarch's chosen successors, men like Wharton.

Final years, 1560–1568 That Wharton was no radical, planted by the Tudors to upset the traditional social and political order of the northern shires, is confirmed by his own traditional piety. Wharton's religious beliefs seem to have been governed by that Tudor ideology, obedience to the crown. Despite his involvement in the dissolution of the monasteries and the chantries, in parliament he voted against the acts of 1549 authorizing priests to marry and against images. He was appointed to inquire into offences against the Acts of Uniformity and Supremacy in 1561. The preamble to his will followed a Catholic formula. His grammar school, established at Kirkby Stephen, Westmorland, by the terms of this will, remained doctrinally traditional despite embracing some of the newer, humanist disciplines.

Wharton was less active for the remainder of his life and did not attend parliament in 1559, 1563, or 1566. His heir's behaviour drew suspicion on the family. Wharton made his will on 18 July 1568 and died on 23 August at Healaugh, where he was buried on 22 September; a funeral monument was erected there showing him alongside his two wives. There is also a funeral monument to him at Kirkby Stephen.   DAVID GRUMMITT

Sources M. E. James, *Change and continuity in the Tudor north*, Borthwick Papers, 27 (1965) · M. L. Bush, 'The problem of the far north: a study in the crisis of 1537 and its consequences', *Northern History*, 6 (1971), 40–63 · R. W. Hoyle, 'Henry Percy, sixth earl of Northumberland, and the fall of the house of Percy, 1527–1537', *The Tudor nobility*, ed. G. W. Bernard (1992), 180–211 · M. Bush, *The Pilgrimage of Grace: a study of the rebel armies of October 1536* (1996) · R. W. Hoyle, 'Faction, feud and reconciliation amongst the northern English nobility, 1525–1569', *History*, 84 (1999), 590–613 · J. Nicolson and R. Burn, *The history and antiquities of the counties of Westmorland and Cumberland*, 2 vols. (1777) · GEC, *Peerage* · HoP, *Commons, 1509–58* · M. Merriman, *The rough wooings: Mary queen of Scots, 1542–1551* (2000) · CSP dom., 1601–9, addenda 1547–65 · CSP Scot., 1547–63 · J. Bain, ed., *The Hamilton papers*, 2 vols. (1890–92) [includes letters from Wharton] · *LP Henry VIII* · *State papers published under … Henry VIII*, 11 vols. (1830–52) · M. E. James, 'Two Tudor funerals', *Transactions of the Cumberland and Westmorland Antiquarian and Archaeological Society*, new ser., 66 (1966), 165–78
Archives BL, political corresp., Add. MSS 32646–32656, 32091 · BL, state papers, letters · PRO, State Papers, letters
Likenesses effigy, Healaugh, Yorkshire; repro. in James, *Change and continuity in the Tudor north* · effigy, Kirkby Stephen, Westmorland
Wealth at death land income of approx. £750 p.a.: James, *Change*, 49

Wharton, Thomas, second Baron Wharton (1520–1572), soldier and administrator, was probably born at Kirkby Stephen, Westmorland, the elder of the two sons of Thomas *Wharton, first Baron Wharton (c.1495–1568), soldier and administrator, and his first wife, Eleanor (d. in or after 1547), third daughter of Sir Brian Stapleton of Wighill, Yorkshire, and his wife, Joan. Like his father, Wharton followed a military and administrative career on the Scottish marches. On 17 October 1536 he was captured during the Pilgrimage of Grace by the rebels who had gone to Kirkby Stephen in search of his father. Evidently, however, he did not suffer at their hands or by any association with them. By 8 November 1542 he had entered the service of the master of the horse, Sir Anthony Browne. Over the following three years Wharton carved out a reputation serving in Browne's company during the Scottish wars. He was probably present at the battle of Solway Moss on 24 November 1542, and was prominent in border raids and served his father, who was either deputy warden or warden of the west, middle, or east marches for most of the period 1537 to 1557. Having taken part in the successful expedition into Scotland between 8 and 23 September 1545 of Edward Seymour, earl of Hertford, Wharton was knighted by him on 23 September at Norham Castle, Northumberland.

During Edward VI's reign Wharton's administrative duties also burgeoned. He was appointed JP for Cumberland, Westmorland, and the West Riding of Yorkshire from 26 May 1547 (added to the quorum for Cumberland and Westmorland in 1554); pricked sheriff of Cumberland in November; and was returned as MP for Cumberland in November (having already sat in parliament in 1544 and possibly 1542). His role as an MP saw him acting as a link between the privy council and the administration on the marches. Throughout the late 1540s Wharton also continued his military exploits: in mid-March 1548, for instance, he raided into Annandale and Nithsdale. In May 1547 he married Anne (d. 1561), daughter of Robert Radcliffe, first earl of Sussex, and his second wife, Margaret. The couple had two sons, including Philip Wharton, third Baron Wharton (1555–1625), and two daughters.

Mary I's accession in July 1553 brought a rapid rise in Wharton's fortunes. He declared for her on 12 July, among the first to do so, and attended upon her at Kenninghall, Norfolk, and Framlingham, Suffolk. It is possible that he was already a member of her household. His continued attachment to Mary was partly religious (he remained a committed Catholic) and partly due to his marital connection: his brother-in-law, Henry *Radcliffe, second earl of Sussex (c.1507–1557) [see under Radcliffe, Robert, first earl of Sussex (1482/3–1542)], magnate, was one of the queen's strongest supporters. Wharton was made a privy councillor on or before 21 August and a member of the queen's council of the north in September. He attended the privy council regularly. He also received lands and offices in Yorkshire, including the position of chief steward of the East Riding and steward of Beverley from 20 October. He was appointed master of the queen's henchmen on 26 October. Wharton sat in the parliaments of October 1553 (Cumberland), April (Hedon) and November (Yorkshire) 1554, 1555 (Northumberland), and 1558 (Northumberland or Yorkshire). On 20 July 1554 he was present at Southampton when Philip of Spain was invested with the Order of the Garter and the king acted as godfather to Wharton's son the following year. He was described by a Spanish envoy as 'a good man, harmless; he is retiring' (CSP Spain, July 1554 – November 1558, 374, 455).

The renewal of war with Scotland in 1557 saw Wharton again serving on the borders. In July he took command of 1000 men for the defence of the east and middle marches and was with Thomas Percy, seventh earl of Northumberland, at Berwick in August. He continued to receive lands in the north from Mary, probably to bolster his military resources and to prepare him to succeed to his father's offices, and remained a key figure in the Marian administration, acting as witness to the queen's will on 30 March 1558 and serving at her funeral on 14 December.

Under Elizabeth I, however, his religious sensibilities meant that Wharton soon fell from favour. He was not appointed to her privy council and was removed as master of the henchmen. He was, however, reappointed to the council of the north in December 1558. It is probable that Wharton was less interested in northern society than his father and may even have tried to concentrate his estates in the south. He sold his stewardship of Beverley in 1561. On 3 June 1561, with his wife and other leading former Marians, he was indicted for hearing mass. Found guilty, Wharton and his wife were committed to the Tower of London. He submitted on 16 July and was pardoned but continued to be, in the words of John Best, bishop of Carlisle, 'evil of religion' (HoP, Commons, 1509–58, 3.601). During the northern rising of 1569 Wharton did nothing to check the rebels' progress but was probably saved from suffering their fate when he fell from his horse in early

December, an accident that almost claimed his life. Having succeeded his father on 23 or 24 August 1568, Wharton, once recovered from his riding accident, took his seat in the House of Lords on 2 April 1571. He died intestate on 14 June 1572 at his house on Cannon Row, Westminster. The administration of his estate was given to his son and heir, Philip Wharton, on 28 February 1579. He was buried in Westminster Abbey. DAVID GRUMMITT

Sources CPR, 1547–9; 1553–8; 1560–63; 1566–72 · J. Nicolson and R. Burn, The history and antiquities of the counties of Westmorland and Cumberland, 2 vols. (1777) · GEC, Peerage · HoP, Commons, 1509–58, 3.599–601 · administration, PRO, PROB 6/2, fol. 164v

Wharton, Thomas (1614–1673), physician, only son of John Wharton (d. 1629), and his wife, Elizabeth (d. 1646), daughter of Roger Hodson of Fountains Abbey, Yorkshire, was born at Winston, co. Durham, in 1614 probably in August, and was baptized there on 31 August of that year. Little is known of Wharton's childhood and youth other than that he experienced a self-described 'pestilential fever' in 1633. He matriculated as a sizar at Pembroke College, Cambridge, in 1637. Wharton then migrated to Trinity College, Oxford, where he may have been influenced by followers of William Harvey, some of whom were then members of Trinity. At Trinity he tutored John Scrope, natural son of Emanuel, Lord Scrope of Bolton. From 1642 to 1645 Wharton spent much time with John Scrope at Bolton Castle in the North Riding of Yorkshire, studying chemistry and medicine. In December 1644 Wharton accompanied Mr and Mrs Elias Ashmole to the South Lambeth house of John Tradescant the younger: he subsequently participated in cataloguing part of the Tradescants' collection of scientific curiosities, which was later acquired by Ashmole and became the nucleus of the Ashmolean Museum in Oxford. At Bolton, Wharton also served as a member of the royalist garrison from 1642 to 1645. Subsequently he moved to London to study medicine with the physician John Bathurst, who had Yorkshire connections, and assisted him with his practice.

When John Scrope died in 1646 Wharton returned to Oxford, where he was created DM on 7 May 1647. A candidate of the College of Physicians, London, in 1648, he became a fellow in 1650, incorporated at Cambridge on his doctor's degree in 1652, and served as a censor of the college in 1658, 1661, 1666, 1667, 1668, and 1673. From 1648 he practised medicine in London, and his patients included the Ashmoles, the artist William Faithorne, and the countess of Northampton. On 25 June 1653 he married Jane (d. 1669), daughter of William Ashbridge, of London. They had three sons, Thomas, Charles, and William; the latter two died young. In 1657 Wharton was appointed physician to St Thomas's Hospital, London, a post he held for the rest of his life. During the London plague of 1665 he was one of the few college physicians who remained in the capital, where he treated plague sufferers at St Thomas's Hospital. As a reward he was promised the next available appointment as physician to the king, but the post was given to another, and Wharton received only an augmentation of his paternal coat of arms.

Thomas Wharton (1614–1673), by unknown artist, c.1650

In 1652 or 1653 Wharton delivered the Goulstonian lectures at the College of Physicians on the subject of the glands, a topic assigned to him by the college president, Sir Francis Prujean (1593–1666). These six lectures formed the basis of his only anatomical work, the 287 page Latin text *Adenographia, sive, Glandularum totius corporis descriptio*, first published in London in 1656. Other editions include those published at Amsterdam (1659); Oberwesel (1664, 1671, 1675); and Düsseldorf (1730). Portions of *Adenographia* also appear in LeClerc and Mangot's *Bibliotheca anatomica* (Geneva, 1699, 1.200–03; 2.755–73). An English translation by Stephen Freer, with a historical introduction by Andrew Cunningham and a facsimile of the 1656 edition, was published in 1996.

Adenographia is the first European text devoted entirely to the glands. Previously, anatomists had not considered glands important in understanding the functioning of the body. For example, both Galen and Vesalius noted various glands, but they did not consider them as a separate topic, and their treatment was cursory. A 1559 text by the Italian Realdo Columbus, *De re anatomica*, devoted one of its fifteen books to the glands, but the book consists of just two pages. Wharton's extended presentation of glands as classes of related natural objects changed this; consequently, for several decades after its initial publication, *Adenographia* was considered a basic reference on the subject. In addition to discovering the duct of the submandibular (salivary) gland, Wharton named the thyroid gland (though he was not its discoverer).

Wharton, a self-proclaimed Aristotelian, adopted scholastic modes of reasoning in *Adenographia*. For him, as for his mentor Francis Glisson, various kinds of matter had specific qualities and affinities, not just the properties of

mass, extension, and motion. For them, different bodily fluids ended up in the right places because of an attraction of like for like. Wharton did not use a microscope and disparaged the virtuosi among whom the microscope was popular. In contrast, contemporary mechanist anatomists, such as Marcello Malpighi, used the microscope to discover fine structures, which they then related to the behaviour of particles and substances. By the later seventeenth century mechanical analyses that emphasized structure–function relationships and denied the possibility of special properties were displacing scholastic accounts, and *Adenographia* began to lose influence.

Wharton wrote four English verses, entitled 'Arcanum, or, The grand secret of hermetic philosophy', prefixed to a translation by Elias Ashmole, and published in Ashmole's *Theatrum chemicum Britannicum* (1652). He was also a close friend of Izaak Walton, who acknowledged his integrity and anatomical assistance in *The Compleat Angler*.

The Royal College of Physicians holds five volumes of Wharton's manuscripts numbered SR 640–644. In letter no. 10 in MSS SR 640, which was written in 1673, the year Wharton died, he responded to the query of a Mrs Church as to whether her son should become a physician. Wharton compared unfavourably the professional situation of physicians with those of attorneys and clerics. He also derided the universities for abandoning the 'old and sound Aristotle learning' for 'new-fangled fripperies of Cartes [Descartes], Gassendus, Boyle, Hobbs, and Regius, etc'.

Wharton's outburst against mechanist natural philosophers belies the impression contemporaries had of him as a leader in developing new medical knowledge. For example, in 1657 the prominent physician Walter Charleton, in his *Immortality of the Human Soul, Demonstrated by the Light of Nature*, portrayed the College of Physicians as a veritable 'Solomon's House' of intense collaborative investigation of the structure and function of animal bodies and noted Wharton among the 'Miners of Nature' for his investigations of glands . Wharton's collaborators included Francis Glisson, George Ent, Baldwin Hamey, and John Bathurst, all members of the College of Physicians.

Wharton died in London on 15 November 1673 and was buried next to his wife at the church of St Michael Bassishaw, London, where a monument was erected. The church was demolished in 1897, and the monument moved to St Lawrence Jewry, where it was destroyed by enemy action during the Second World War. Wharton's grandson **George Wharton** (1688–1739), physician, was the eldest son of Thomas Wharton (1652–1714), who followed his own father, Thomas, to Pembroke College and practised medicine; he was buried at Durham in 1714. George's mother was Mary, daughter of John Hall, an alderman of Durham. He was born at Old Park, Durham, on 25 December 1688, and matriculated from Pembroke College, Cambridge, on 6 July 1706, proceeding MB in 1712 and MD in 1719. He was elected a fellow at the Royal College of Physicians on 30 September 1720, and was censor in 1725, 1729, 1732, and 1734. He was treasurer from 1727 until his death. Wharton married Anna Maria, daughter of William Petty. In 1729 George Wharton presented a portrait of his father to the Royal College of Physicians. He died from 'mortification of the bowels' at his home in Fenchurch Street, London, on 21 March 1739. As he died childless, the Old Park estate passed to his younger brother, Robert, mayor of Durham. A number of later descendants, including Christopher Wharton (d. 1990), were physicians and fellows of the Royal College.

ROBERT L. MARTENSEN

Sources DNB · *Thomas Wharton's Adenographia*, trans. S. Freer (1996) · RCP Lond., Wharton MS SR 640–644 · R. G. Frank, *Harvey and the Oxford physiologists* (1980) · H. J. Cook, *The decline of the old medical regime in Stuart London* (1986) · Bodl. Oxf., MSS Ashmole 243, 331, 339, 374 · Venn, *Alum. Cant.* · Munk, *Roll*
Archives RCP Lond., letter-book and case notes
Likenesses oils, c.1650, RCP Lond. [*see illus.*] · Beynon & Co., lithograph, Wellcome L. · G. P. Harding, watercolour (after portrait by unknown artist), BM · W. Worthington, engraving (after portrait by unknown artist), RCP Lond. · portrait, Butlers Marston, Warwickshire

Wharton, Thomas, first marquess of Wharton, first marquess of Malmesbury, and first marquess of Catherlough (1648–1715), politician, was born in late August 1648, the third but eldest surviving son of Philip *Wharton, fourth Baron Wharton (1613–1696), politician, and his second wife, Jane (*bap.* 1618, *d.* 1658), daughter and coheir of Arthur *Goodwin. Young Thomas was born into English politics. His birth elicited a letter from Oliver Cromwell, who congratulated Lord Wharton and the 'dear little lady' on the new heir. Cromwell hoped that Lord Wharton would see the birth of 'the young baron' as a divine mercy and that it would draw him nearer to the despised but victorious saints (Bodl. Oxf., MS Rawl. 49, fol. 25).

A pious education A few months later, when Colonel Pride purged the House of Commons and Charles I was executed, Lord Wharton distanced himself both literally and figuratively from the new regime. He moved from his London house in Clerkenwell and retired to Upper Winchendon, one of his rich estates on the hills of northern Buckinghamshire. This decision meant that young Thomas (Tom to his family and eventually to political England) spent most of the first ten years of his life at Winchendon. He maintained his principal base of operations there even after he inherited many other manors, in Buckinghamshire, Yorkshire, Cumberland, and Westmorland.

The Whartons were notably pious. Lord Wharton, a Calvinist himself, was a patron of presbyterian and Independent ministers. The Wharton children lived among men who took life, the Bible, and God's will very seriously. But if Lord Wharton was a precisian who had scruples against plays and Sunday travel and who feared that kissing the Bible in taking oaths might constitute idolatry, he was also an English aristocrat with an eye for beauty and a feeling for the social graces. His scruples stopped short where music, dance, and poetry were concerned. The Wharton children were not merely permitted, but required, to take music and dancing lessons, and the youngest son, William, became a poet. Like his friend Andrew Marvell, Lord Wharton loved gardens. He also

Thomas Wharton, first marquess of Wharton, first marquess of Malmesbury, and first marquess of Catherlough (1648–1715), by Sir Godfrey Kneller, c.1710–15

loved painting and his collection of Van Dycks rivalled that of Charles I. His son Tom inherited his tastes as well as his gardens and art collections.

The year 1658 began the transformation of the Wharton world. On 21 April Lady Wharton died, leaving her children to be raised by servants; and on 3 September Oliver Cromwell died, leaving the puritan cause to disintegrate. Lord Wharton abandoned Winchendon for Wooburn, in southern Buckinghamshire, and leased a London town house at St Giles-in-the-Fields. the restoration of the monarchy in 1660 and the subsequent re-establishment of the Anglican church brought further changes. In the new order nonconformists were removed from the universities and from church livings. This meant, among many other things, that young Thomas would not be sent to Oxford or Cambridge and that his principal tutors would be unemployed dons. Another major change in the boy's world occurred in August 1661 when Lord Wharton married Anne, widow of Colonel Edward Popham and daughter of William Carr.

Meanwhile Tom Wharton had been undergoing a rigorous course of study, including four hours a day of Greek and Latin, under tutors Abraham Clifford, Thomas Elford, and Philip Romerill. In June 1662 his education was taken over by the scholarly Theophilus Gale, an Independent and a former fellow of Magdalen College, Oxford. Gale, who had agreed to supervise Tom and his brother Goodwin *Wharton during an educational sojourn in France and a tour of Europe, was favourably impressed by his student. The lad, he told Lord Wharton, had 'a quick and apprehensive' mind and was obviously 'fit to take in the more noble parts of humane literature'. He was perhaps 'a little intent' upon sports and somewhat difficult to arouse at five in the morning, but he seemed very tractable, and he would no doubt make great academic progress (Bodl. Oxf., MS Rawl. 49, fols. 44, 48). Gale went to France in 1662 to select a place for the boys' education. Tom and Goodwin did not arrive in Caen, Gale's choice, until 25 June 1663.

The young men stayed in Caen, a Huguenot stronghold, almost two years until April 1665. There Tom, in formal classes for the first time at the age of fifteen, impressed his French masters with his Latin oratory and rhetoric, achieving 'such perfection', according to Gale, that the regent published specimens of his art 'about the town' (Bodl. Oxf., MS Rawlinson 49, fol. 101). Outgoing and personable he was immediately popular with his French classmates. This popularity led in turn to his first recorded revolt. When Gale insisted upon screening the boys he brought home to the pension Tom disputed his authority and then went on to question other strict rules. Robert Bennett, deprived vicar at Winchendon, sent by Lord Wharton to investigate, agreed that Gale, a good man in the wrong place, should be recalled, and in October 1664 Abraham Clifford took over the boys' education in Caen. A puritan like Gale, but much more adroit at handling adolescent youngsters, Clifford had been a fellow at Pembroke College, Cambridge. He quickly noted the intelligence of the young Whartons—their 'quick, lively, and pregnant parts'—and their 'loving and ingenuous' natures (Bodl. Oxf., MS Rawlinson 53, fol. 7), and he soon learned the limits of Tom's complaisance. Now sixteen the young man insisted upon choosing his own companions, and he bristled at the mere suggestion of leaving Caen. Too wise to provoke another battle Clifford let Tom bring his friends, both choice and questionable, to the pension where they could be supervised, and he waited for a direct order from Lord Wharton before setting out for Paris, which they reached on 24 April 1665.

The planned grand tour, however, was disrupted by war and the plague and dwindled to a few weeks of sightseeing in the Spanish Netherlands. On 10 October the young men were back in their Paris lodgings. Before new instructions arrived from Lord Wharton disease and politics intervened again. On 21 November, the day after Lord Holles, the English ambassador, had taken the boys to see Louis XIV, Tom came down with a virulent attack of smallpox. While he was recovering it became clear that France would join the Dutch in their war against England, and Lord Wharton ordered the boys home. It was 1 June 1666 before the young men actually boarded ship at Dieppe and set out for England and Wooburn—three years after they had left.

Wharton's education in France had at least two significant effects upon his political career. From his puritan tutors he received a command of scriptures and religious controversy that, along with a mordant wit, would make him formidable in parliamentary debates on toleration, schism, and occasional conformity and that would help him defend men like Gale and Clifford against Anglicans who wished to silence them. Also important was the young man's saturation in the French language (the language of diplomacy, and sometimes of treason).

Marriage, horse-racing, and politics Lord Wharton had made tentative passes at the problem of finding a rich and virtuous wife for his heir even before Tom had set out for France. In late 1671 began an intricate negotiation that lasted more than a year and sent Tom Wharton on four extended trips to Devon. The projected match involved a wealthy young lady named Elizabeth, daughter and heir of the late Richard Cabell, one-time sheriff of the county. In February and March 1673, however, Tom became involved in his first parliamentary election—a disputed contest at Wendover against Alderman Edward Backwell. He had promised to return to Devon by 1 March, but he remained in London until 19 March, when the House of Commons decided the election in his favour. For Mrs Cabell this choice of politics over love confirmed her doubts as to his suitability. She broke off the match. After the repulse at Devon, Lord Wharton began negotiations for the hand of Anne Lee (1659–1685) [see Wharton, Anne], coheir to the extensive properties of her father, Sir Henry Lee. Anne, who later achieved recognition as a poet, was born on 20 July 1659, four months after the death of her father and a few days before the death of her mother. Her guardian was her paternal grandmother, the dowager countess of Rochester. It was the countess and Sir Ralph Verney, a trustee of Anne's estate and a long-time neighbour of the Whartons, who arranged the match. The settlement gave Wharton £8000 in cash and an annual income of about £2000.

Before the marriage itself took place—at Adderbury on 16 September 1673—Wharton was challenged to a duel by a disappointed rival, John Arundell (son of Lord Arundell of Trerice). Ill with a fever and in danger enough 'if he had gone only to meet the cold air', as one of his friends said (Bodl. Oxf., MS Rawlinson 53, fol. 27), Tom lost the duel. Arundell disarmed him and then in view of his courage granted him his life. (Wharton would win later, bloodless duels—against Lord Haughton in 1687, Lord Cheyne in 1699, and young 'Mr. Dashwood' in 1703—disarming all three opponents.)

For Wharton his marriage with Anne Lee meant independence. With money and property settled upon him, a country house at Winchendon and a town house at Chelsea, with stables and gardens at both places, he was free from his father's supervision and rich enough to pursue his interests in politics and horse-racing.

While Wharton was learning his trade as a politician he was also beginning his career as an owner and, sometimes, rider of racehorses. Wharton's devotion to horses and racing became legendary. The tracks at Brackley, Woodstock, Campfield, Banstead Downs, Datchet, Quainton Meadows (Wharton's home course near Winchendon), and, above all, Newmarket were among Wharton's favourite haunts, and some of his horses—Careless, Snail, Colchester, Chance, and Wharton's Gelding—became famous in turf lore.

One of Wharton's first recorded victories occurred at

Woodstock on 2 September 1676, for a plate worth £50. Next day, however, he lost a match race and a £100 wager to Lord Lovelace. Wharton's most dramatic loss came at Banstead Downs on 15 May 1679, when he was thrown from his horse, knocked unconscious, and 'taken up for dead' (Ormonde MSS, new ser., 5.102). One of his expensive losses, £500, came in a match race at Newmarket on 11 April 1698, when Careless, carrying too much additional weight, was beaten by King William's horse Stiff Dick. Perhaps Wharton's richest victory, also at Newmarket, came in April 1699 when Careless beat a horse backed by the duke of Devonshire for a wager of £1900.

Wharton won his most prestigious race in France on 25 February 1683. On a racecourse near St Germain-en-Laye in an event sponsored by Louis XIV and witnessed by the king, the queen, and many French courtiers, Wharton's Gelding defeated a select field of horses from 'divers nations' and won the king's plate, valued at 1000 pistoles (roughly £850). 'Very much pleased' with the English horse, which had been entered by the duke of Monmouth, Louis offered to buy it for another 1000 pistoles. Wharton, however, declined the offer. He would give Louis the horse as a present, he said, but he would not sell it. Louis, in turn, refused to accept the gift (Oldmixon, Memoirs, 97).

In the parliamentary sessions of 1675–8 Wharton was still primarily a back-bench observer, and he missed the last two months of the summer session of 1678 when he took his wife, Anne, to Wiltshire for her health. He emerged from the political shadows after the 'revelations' of Titus Oates and the furore surrounding the Popish Plot had deranged English politics. On 5 February 1679 he was elected at Aylesbury, along with young John Hampden, as knight of the shire for Buckinghamshire. Though the election was uncontested threats that the court would enter candidates and / or move the election to Buckingham made the Whartons and Hampdens assemble all their friends, including the duke of Buckingham. The entertainment at Aylesbury inns cost each candidate about £800. Wharton would eventually spend (according to Memoirs of the Life, 27) 'above £80,000' on elections.

At the second general election of 1679 Wharton and Hampden again stood for the county. This time Thomas Edgerley, the high sheriff, did move the election from Aylesbury to Buckingham. The last-minute manoeuvre failed. The young whigs, again aided by the duke, led an army of supporters to the enemy town and achieved another victory.

Meanwhile, as an exclusionist, Wharton opposed the duke of York both in and out of parliament. On 26 June 1680 he and a group of other whig notables, including Shaftesbury, met at Westminster Hall to submit to the Middlesex grand jury an information against the duke—a list of reasons for believing what had never been officially admitted, that James was a Catholic. The jury, they hoped, would present James as a recusant before the judges of the king's bench. Even if he were acquitted, they reasoned, the propaganda value of a trial would be immense. The scheme was foiled, however, when the royal judges got wind of the plot and dismissed the grand jury for the term.

The court did not try to unseat Wharton in the county election of 1681, when he stood with Richard Hampden. At the third Exclusion Parliament the king offered a regency plan; but the Commons, with an unassailable whig majority, insisted upon exclusion. Wharton was appointed to the committee that drew up the bill. On 28 March 1681, before the bill could be read a second time in the Commons, the king called the houses together and dissolved the parliament.

Wharton was not named among the suspects in the Rye House Plot of 1683—an alleged conspiracy to assassinate the king and the duke of York—and he took no part in the consults that doomed William, Lord Russell, the earl of Essex, and Algernon Sidney. Nevertheless the king's agents searched Winchendon for arms in the post plot investigations. They found enough weapons and armour to equip about eight cavalrymen, and they deposited the collection at the White Hart inn in Aylesbury. Wharton complained to the earl of Bridgewater, lord lieutenant of the county: 'I must leave it to your Lordship whether such a proportion be not convenient for me and necessary for the security of my family' (Bodl. Oxf., MS Carte 81, fol. 726). To Bridgewater, a wealthy landowner like Wharton, the collection seemed unremarkable.

Scandals One night in June 1682 Wharton and his brother Henry and two or three friends were entertained by a gentleman named Bray in the village of Great Barrington in Gloucestershire. After several hours of drinking the frolicsome group broke into St Mary's parish church. There they rang the bells, cut the bell ropes, broke the cover of the font and the desk of the pulpit, and ripped the church Bible. Then, as the actions (to paraphrase Wharton's later apology) grew worse in the execution than they had been in the design, the revellers relieved themselves in the church. They might have contrived other enormities if the clangour of the bells had not brought out an unamused crowd of villagers, who chased them back to Bray House. Besides committing sacrilege Wharton had perpetrated an indelible political error (which the Memoirs of the Life never mentions). He had made himself a permanent target for tory pamphleteers. In mid-August, before official action was taken, Wharton wisely threw himself upon the mercy of Robert Frampton, bishop of Gloucester. In a letter of 15 August he wrote an abject apology for his drunken escapade. Although he was confident that the faults were not so gross as they appeared in 'the prodigious story' that had grown up since the event he would not deny the truth of any particular allegation. His present concern was to confess how sensible he was of his faults and submit himself entirely to the bishop's judgment. The letter was carried to Frampton by the eminently respectable John Cary, who vouched for its sincerity. Wharton, he explained, was the son of the pious Lord Wharton and was himself 'a man of very great parts [abilities] and estates' (Bodl. Oxf., MS Tanner 35, fol. 73).

On both Christian and prudential grounds Frampton decided that Tom Wharton should not be turned into 'a downright enemy' but allowed to redeem himself with a suitable penance. From the sinners he demanded a formal letter of apology, a public confession, a fine of 50 guineas in commutation of penance, and payment for the damages at Barrington. Wharton duly wrote the required letter, and the brothers appeared before the bishop at Stow on the Wold, where they paid their fine and begged pardon for their offence before three clergymen and three laymen. Pleased with their repentance (and their promptness in advancing money for the repairs at Barrington) Frampton returned to them 10 of the 50 guineas; the other 40 he gave 'in their presence' towards the renovation of Stow church (Bodl. Oxf., MS Tanner 35, fol. 111). He dismissed the pair with 'wholesome admonitions' (ibid.). These he followed with a letter reminding Wharton of his sins, for which Wharton thanked him and again apologized.

Officially the affair was closed after Archbishop Sancroft had reviewed and approved Frampton's follow-up reports of January and February 1683. Unofficially Wharton's punishment had only begun. The story grew more outrageous with retelling. In December 1705 Wharton (then Lord Wharton) was silenced by the story during a debate in the Lords. After baiting the tories on their politic fears that the church was in danger under a low-church government Wharton made the mistake of asking, rhetorically, just who they feared. The duke of Leeds (formerly Danby) gave a quick reply: 'If there were any that had pissed against a communion table or done his other occasions in the pulpit, he should not think himself safe in such hands' (Bishop Burnet's History, 5.242). By January 1711 Jonathan Swift, writing for the tory Examiner, had moved the episode from Barrington to Gloucester Cathedral and raised the fine from 50 guineas to £1000. Wharton's friends, however, were inclined to ignore or shrug off the event. Sir Ralph Verney, for example, found Tom readily forgivable. In explaining why he supported Wharton in the 1685 election for knight of the shire he declared: 'I am confident that he will serve the King and the country faithfully, though he is wild enough in drink and I am troubled at it, but who lives without great faults' (BL, Verney MS M 636/39, 2 March 1685).

While Wharton was scandalizing the social world he and Anne were also having difficulties. From 1680 Anne had been experiencing seizures and in March 1681 she went to France seeking better health. In April, fearing she would not recover, she wrote to Tom, 'Goodbye, my Dear, Best Dear. Pardon me that I say no more, for I am so very ill I can hardly hold the pen or know what I write' (Cumbria AS, Carlisle, Lonsdale MS D/Lons/L1/4, 20 April 1681). In June Wharton went to Paris, but their brief reunion brought an emotional crisis. Anne was conscious of a distance between them and, as she tried to explain later, she found it difficult to express herself. When Tom said at parting that he 'loved nothing so well' as her, she did not quite believe him, and she could not reply (ibid., 2 July 1681).

When Anne returned from France the gulf between the couple widened temporarily because of what Goodwin called their 'mutual jealousies' (BL, Add. MS 20006, 308). Anne probably found herself facing a serious rival—

Wharton's mistress, Jane (b. 1661, d. in or after 1689), daughter of Sir Edward Dering, second baronet; while Wharton found himself competing with his brother Goodwin and his friend John Grobham (Jack) Howe. In early December 1682 Gilbert Burnet, later Bishop Burnet (a friend and political ally of the Whartons), tried to intervene. His enquiries and lectures brought a sharp rebuke from Anne, who told him not to believe gossip and to mind his own business. After this crisis the damage to the Wharton marriage was, for a time, largely repaired. By May 1683 the pair were back at Winchendon, Anne was lending Sir Ralph Verney one of her she-asses to provide milk for his health, and on 21 May Anne and Tom dined with the Verneys at Middle Claydon. They soon moved from Chelsea to one of the residences in the new and fashionable Soho Square.

Changing fortunes, 1685–1688 In late June 1685 Anne became ill again. At first the malady did not seem dangerous—merely another episode in what Sir Ralph Verney called 'the colic'. Attended by Dr Richard Lower and 'two or three doctors from Oxford', she seemed, in Sir Ralph's judgement, to be in more peril from the medicine than from the disease (BL, Verney MS M 636/40, 20 June 1685). About 12 August she went from Winchendon to Adderbury to stay with her grandmother and to drink Astrop waters. Wharton, meanwhile, had gone to Tunbridge Wells some time in July. There he was joined by his mistress, Jane Dering, and his brother Henry. Jane did not live openly as Wharton's mistress but the liaison between the pair was well known. On 16 August John Verney reported their presence at Tunbridge Wells to his father. 'Tom Wharton is here', he wrote, 'and so is Mrs. Dering, though I hear Mrs. Wharton is not yet well' (ibid.).

When Wharton returned from Tunbridge Wells in time for the races at Quainton on 26 August Anne's condition still seemed hopeful, but then she took a sudden turn for the worse. On 2 September John Cary reported from Adderbury that Anne lay 'very weak and ill', attended 'most diligently' by the famous Dr John Radcliffe. On 6 September Sir Ralph wrote that he was much afraid for her: 'Yesterday she lay in great pains and convulsions' (BL, Verney MS M 636/40). Finally, on 29 October, Anne died.

Wharton brought her body home for burial in the church at Winchendon. As a tribute to a beloved lady a great throng turned out for the funeral, held on the evening of 10 November. Anne was buried in silk rather than the woollen required by English law. For this last nicety Wharton paid a fine of 50s., which was distributed among the poor of the parish.

Meanwhile the general election of 1685 had gone badly for the whigs. Wharton's two brothers Henry and William were defeated in normally safe boroughs, and Wharton himself was obliged to stand with the moderate tory John Egerton, Viscount Brackley, rather than his former colleague Richard Hampden—and to expend about £3000. Despite the election being moved to Newport Pagnell, Wharton's supporters turned out in overwhelming force and he was one of the few whigs who survived the tory landslide of that year. Wharton and the handful of other exclusionists in the new House of Commons were too few and too wise to oppose the torrent of court measures.

Wharton was also too wise to take part in Monmouth's rebellion, apparently believing that after the long hysteria of plots and counterplots the nation was much readier for a breathing space than a civil war. In the words of *Memoirs of the Life* (p. 28), 'He [Wharton] looked upon the Duke of Monmouth's attempt as chimerical, and he never had any thoughts of joining it on the foot of his rash invasion'.

In the crucial parliamentary session of November 1685 (the last King James would meet) Wharton's position was drastically altered. Now a leader of the whigs by attrition he found himself in the strange position of supporting tories such as his old enemy Sir Edward Seymour, who opposed the king's attempts to retain the Catholic army officers he had employed and to maintain a sizeable standing army. Wharton agreed with the unspoken fear that a standing army officered by Catholics and perhaps helped by Louis XIV would be fatal to English protestantism.

Wharton spoke three times in the early debates, once to recommend a bill for making the militia more useful and twice to urge drastic cuts in the government's proposals for supply. His most important speech came, however, after the Commons had asked the king, in a tactfully worded address, to dismiss his Catholic officers, whose appointment in defiance of the Test Act, they said, set a dangerous precedent. The address enraged James. He returned a blistering reply, citing his own reputation for uprightness and berating the Commons for their lack of trust. 'But however you may proceed on your part', he concluded, 'I will be steady in all my promises I have made to you and be very just to my word in every one of my speeches' (Cobbett, *Parl. hist.*, 4.1386).

The king's reply stunned the house into silence for a time. Then Wharton, one of the first to recover, coolly 'moved that a day might be appointed to consider of his Majesty's answer to the address of this House, and named Friday next' (BL, Lansdowne MS 253, fol. 58). When the House of Lords took up the argument and appointed a day to examine the king's speech James prorogued parliament and commenced aggressive measures to implement his pro-Catholic policies.

Revolution and the junto, 1688–1696 In 1688 the assembling of troops for summer exercises at Hounslow Heath made it relatively easy for Wharton and his brother Henry (then a lieutenant in the Coldstream Guards and a captain in the duke of Norfolk's regiment of foot) to help assemble a 'Treason Club' at the Rose tavern in Drury Lane—a vital part of the army conspiracy against the king. Wharton's membership in this group and the plot to disintegrate the king's army during the revolution may be his greatest contribution to William's success—even greater than his famous song 'Lilliburlero'.

The song itself resulted from the king's appointment in 1687 of Richard Talbot, the Catholic earl of Tyrconnell, first as commander of the army in Ireland and then as lord deputy, replacing the Anglican Lord Clarendon. These

appointments alarmed all Anglo-Irishmen; and the Whartons, who owned property in co. Carlow and co. Westmeath, had a special reason for concern. Confiscation might be just over the horizon. Thus Wharton was on the alert when the second appointment was announced, and he was inspired to some stanzas of doggerel verse that encapsulated the fears and scorn of the English. Composed from the point of view of an Irish peasant waiting anxiously for his hero, the song began:

> Ho brother Teague, doest hear the decree
> Lilliburlero bullen a-la
> That we shall have a new Debitie
> Lilliburlero bullen a-la

After several verses of comment upon Talbot and the new order, which would bring the Irish 'commissions gillore' and hang the English and their 'Magno Carto', the song ended triumphantly:

> Now, now de heretics all go down
> Lilliburlero bullen a-la
> By Chreish and St. Patrick the nation's our own
> Lilliburlero bullen a-la
> Lero, lero, lero, lero
> Lilliburlero bullen a-la
> Lero, lero, lero, lero
> Lilliburlero bullen a-la
> (Carswell, 354–5)

What the pseudo-Irish refrain lacked in sense it made up for in rhythm. English armies would march to it for years. For the time being, however, Wharton's verses merely smouldered. It was not until autumn 1688, after fears of Irish troops had risen several degrees, that 'Lilliburlero' swept the army and the country (*Bishop Burnet's History*, 3.336). It would help, as Wharton later boasted, to drive King James out of three kingdoms.

Wharton was credited by White Kennett with having written the draft of the invitation to William of Orange, but this is highly unlikely. The conspirators, who included Bishop Compton, the earl of Danby, and the earl of Shrewsbury, needed no help in composing the letter, which is in Henry Sidney's handwriting. That Wharton was in close touch with Danby is very probable. He and his army friends were meeting at the Rose tavern during the period, and in early October he was conferring in Yorkshire with Danby and the earl of Devonshire, who would lead risings in the north. He was also receiving letters from the prince via one Joseph Flight. More important than communications, however, was the success of the Treason Club in persuading four of Colonel Langston's officers to join him in delivering their regiment to the prince of Orange. This operation, described years later by the Jacobite Colonel Ambrose Norton, was completed on 12 November 1688. It was the first major defection from the royal army, and although some of the troops returned it was the first of the shocks that eventually demoralized the king.

Wharton himself and his friend Lord Colchester, accompanied by a number of gentlemen and several life guards of Colchester's troop, were the first aristocrats to join the prince of Orange after his landing at Torbay. After arriving in Exeter on 10 November 1688 they were followed, a few days later, by Sir Edward Seymour and the earl of Abingdon. Henry Wharton, now in Lord Lichfield's regiment, stayed with the royal army at Salisbury until 24 November, when he went over to William, along with Prince George and the duke of Ormond. Goodwin Wharton, delayed by ambiguous revelations, did not join the prince until the army reached Henley.

In the Convention Parliament, Wharton insisted that the throne had become vacant when James fled to France. To the question of whether the king could be deposed Wharton answered that 'whether he may be deposed or deposes himself, he is not our King ... for I believe not myself nor any Protestant in England safe if you admit him' (Grey, 9.11). After the Commons agreed that the throne was vacant Wharton went on the next day (29 January 1689) to nominate William and Mary as joint sovereigns—a measure that after much debate in the Lords, who would have preferred a regency, was ultimately adopted by both houses.

After William and Mary accepted the crown Wharton was made a privy councillor (21 February) and comptroller of the household, a post which gave him apartments in Whitehall and Hampton Court with fees and allowances amounting to about £1200. Lord Wharton was made a privy councillor and a groom of the stole. Henry, now knight of the shire for Westmorland, had been made colonel of his regiment when Lord Lichfield resigned, and Wharton was able to secure the post of cursitor baron in the court of exchequer for his lawyer brother-in-law William Carr.

In spite of these prizes and Wharton's later appointments on treaty and army commissions (10 May and 13 May), the year 1689 was grim for the Whartons. On 26 May Anne Carr, Wharton's older sister, died; and only three weeks later, on 17 June, less than three months after his appointment to the bench, William Carr died also. Most devastating to Wharton was the loss of his brother Henry—Harry to his family and friends—who died of the fever in Ireland. Their sister Mary, who was in London when the bad news arrived, reported to her husband, 'My poor brother [Tom] Wharton stole out of town this morning so melancholy as I never saw anybody' (NL Wales, Kemeys-Tynte MSS, fol. 152).

In December Wharton and his whig friends made difficulties by attacking the tory members of William's coalition government and by attempting to purge the tory MPs who had abetted Charles and James in attacking town charters. Moreover, on 25 December Wharton wrote a letter charging William with ingratitude towards the whigs, who had made him king. William's trimming policy, Wharton said, in effect, paralysed government and discouraged the king's real friends. This letter helps to explain some of Wharton's tactics through the next twenty-five years of partisan warfare.

In William's reign Wharton's conviction that tory ministers should be replaced by whigs accounts for his attack on the earl of Nottingham after the Smyrna fleet disaster and his exploitation of the East India bribery scandal to remove Sir John Trevor as speaker of the House of Commons and to wound the duke of Leeds. The demand for a disciplined, one party ministry also led to the formation of the famous whig junto. When the whigs were in power, the junto, leaders of the court whigs, served as a virtual cabinet—a committee on strategy and tactics. When whigs were out of power the junto became a shadow cabinet, regrouping its forces and waiting for its opponents to make serious mistakes. Wharton was particularly valuable as a notable electioneer, a devoted party man, and, perhaps above all, a tireless worker. The overall impression derived from following Wharton session by session through the journals of the Commons and Lords and the associated batches of documents is that he worked diligently on a great variety of problems—an impression confirmed by Richard Steele, who praised Wharton in a letter of 11 April 1713 for his competence over 'the whole compass of business' (*Correspondence of Richard Steele*, 48). This praise was repeated in a *Spectator* dedicated to Wharton.

During the 1690s two important events in Wharton's personal life expanded his political power. The first of these was his marriage, in July 1692, to the Hon. Lucy (1669/70–1717), daughter and sole heir of Adam Loftus, Viscount Lisburne in the Irish peerage. Lisburne, who had died in the Irish war, on 15 September 1691, left his daughter, then twenty-one, estates worth about £5000 per year. They included Rathfarnham Castle in Ireland. The match between Wharton and Lucy, described by one of Tom's army friends as 'the witty fair one' (Bodl. Oxf., MS Carte 79, fol. 420), seems to have been romantic. Goodwin, who saw the couple dancing together at a ball in Kensington Palace on 6 January 1692, called Lucy Tom's 'new mistress' (BL, Add. MS 20007, fol. 161). Eventually Lucy would be a toast of the whig Kit-Cat Club and the target of tory scandalmongers.

The other dramatic transformation in Wharton's life was the death, on 4 or 5 February 1696, of his father, at the age of eighty-two. Considering his precisianist convictions Lord Wharton had been indulgent with his free-living son. Wharton, in turn, admired his father. To the end of his life he would carry on Lord Wharton's campaign to expand and defend liberties for dissenters, though he later conformed to the Anglican church and explained to the House of Lords that he would 'live and die in the communion of it' (BL, Lansdowne MS 1024, fol. 168).

Lord Wharton, 1696–1710 Lord Wharton's death placed his son, now fifth Baron Wharton, in the House of Lords (on 24 February) and added considerably to his social prestige. 'Lord Wharton' was a great deal more dignified than Tom or Honest Tom (a name derived from Wharton's frequent description of whigs as the honest party, as opposed to the hypocritical tories). The promotion also placed Wharton in the house where the king's ministers ordinarily sat and where final decisions were made on vital measures. Finally, Lord Wharton's death raised his son's income to about £8000 a year, which, along with his new wife's patrimony, enabled him to expand his interest among the electors. In good years for whigs he could win about twenty seats, but in bad years he might be reduced to a handful.

The year 1698 brought a marked shift in the political wind. Wharton was not made secretary of state nor a member of the commission for governing Ireland as he and his friends hoped he might be. William softened the blow by offering him the Spanish embassy, which Wharton declined, and he had to remain satisfied with his appointments (23 April 1697) as lord lieutenant of Oxfordshire and chief justice in eyre and warden of the royal forests south of the Trent. After nine years of war, moreover, the country was tired of taxes, large armies, and foreigners and in the 1698 elections court whigs lost control of the Commons. Wharton himself was able to win only about half of his elections. His candidates were even defeated in Oxfordshire, despite his lord lieutenantcy. Although Wharton retained his own appointments and continued to carry William's messages to the House of Lords, his junto friends were gradually replaced in government positions by tories and country whigs.

On 24 December 1698 Wharton's family, if not his political, fortunes seemed to improve when Lucy had a son, whom they named Philip [see Wharton, Philip] after his grandfather. They later had two daughters, Jane (b. 1706) and Lucy (b. 1710). King William and the duke of Shrewsbury were Philip's godfathers at the baptism on 5 January, and Princess Anne (later Queen Anne) was the boy's godmother. A month later Wharton's favourite sister, Mary Kemeys, saw her brother, her sister-in-law, and the baby in their new residence on Gerrard Street. The boy, Mary reported, was a 'very lusty child' and the lady 'very fond' of him, but, despite now having an heir, her brother, though 'extreme kind', seemed 'melancholy'. Before her visit, he said, he had not been up to the nursery for a week (NL Wales, Kemeys-Tynte MSS, fol. 325). Had Wharton been able to foresee the career of Philip (later the duke of Wharton) he would have suffered something more severe than melancholy.

About this time John Macky, an agent for William, gave a thumbnail sketch of Wharton. At the age of fifty, Macky says, Lord Wharton is of 'middle stature' and 'fair complexion'. He is 'certainly one of the completest gentlemen in England, hath a very clear understanding, and manly expressions, with abundance of wit. He is brave in his person [and] much of a libertine'. King William, Macky wrote, thought him too popular, too much a republican, and too bold in censuring court measures to hold an administrative office (Memoirs of the Secret Services, 91–2).

When Anne took the throne in March 1702 Wharton was dismissed from his post as comptroller, from his other offices, and even from the privy council. Anne, a devoted churchwoman, installed a tory government headed by Lord Treasurer Godolphin and supported by a tory House of Commons. Wharton and his whig friends, now on the defensive, supported the renewed war with France, but they were hard pressed to keep the tories from passing a bill against occasional conformity. With a large

whig presence in the Lords and good organization Wharton's troops managed to defeat the measure twice—once with an amendment and once with a quick vote of rejection. Wharton also involved the houses in a jurisdictional dispute in the famous case of Ashby v. White. He financed the whig voter Ashby, who had been struck off the rolls by the tory officials of Aylesbury, to argue his case that an individual's right to vote was cognizable before the courts and ultimately the Lords, rather than before the Commons, who claimed the sole right of judging elections.

With his ally Lord Somers, Wharton played a major role in producing the Regency Bill, which set up the mechanism for installing the Hanoverian successor and which inspired a letter, in French, from Wharton to the future George I. Wharton also helped to formulate the legislation that led to the union with Scotland. The latter achievement earned him an honorary LLD from Cambridge (16 April 1705), an appointment as a commissioner for the union treaty (10 April 1706), reappointment to the post of chief justice in eyre (9 September 1706), and a promotion in the peerage. He became Viscount Winchendon and earl of Wharton on 23 December 1706.

The election victories in 1705 (said by Memoirs of the Life to have cost Wharton £12,000) and the unflagging support which junto whigs gave to the war on the continent convinced Wharton and his allies that they had earned major offices in the government. The process, aided by another election victory in 1708, was slow and tortuous, but eventually the earl of Sunderland became secretary of state, Lord Somers became lord president, and Wharton, on 4 December 1708, became lord lieutenant of Ireland. He appointed Joseph Addison as his secretary and found safe seats for him at Lostwithiel and later at Malmesbury.

Wharton began his lieutenancy by calming churchmen, who feared he might try to repeal the Irish Test Act. In a series of meetings with Irish MPs and lords he set about reducing tensions and animosities. When he opened the session he promised that the test would not be disturbed. He hoped, however, that the heavily outnumbered protestants could unite in the face of common dangers and that churchmen would find methods of relieving 'the uneasiness' of dissenters (JHC, Ireland, 21 vols., 1763–81, 3.566–7). Military supply bills were passed without difficulty. In the wake of the foiled attack on Scotland by James Francis Edward Stuart (the Pretender) the previous year, Anglo-Irishmen were happy to finance regiments and arsenals. As a further deterrent to the growth of popery, they also passed a bill providing that estates of Irish Catholics should descend to their protestant heirs. They also agreed with Wharton's proposal to settle in Ireland 500 families of protestant refugees from the Palatinate.

Wharton was a hard-working lord lieutenant, as his correspondence with the English government shows. He was also assiduous in filling vacancies with whigs—a policy that would bring heavy fire from the tories. For himself he acquired a regiment of dragoons. His greatest mistake in distributing favours was his failure to select Jonathan Swift, then a whig, as his chaplain. Instead he chose Dr Ralph Lambert, who was shortly appointed dean of Derry.

Had Wharton fastened the great satirist to the whig establishment he might have deprived Robert Harley's government of its finest propagandist and saved himself many lashes.

Wharton's greatest short-term mistake was his active part in the impeachment and trial of Dr Henry Sacheverell, whose attack upon Lord Treasurer Godolphin, toleration, occasional conformity, and (by implication) the revolution brought charges of seditious libel. The affair ended in a famous contest before the House of Lords. Frankly discarding the warming-pan theory, Wharton stoutly defended the whig version of the revolution, as a preservation of the constitution against invasions by arbitrary (and popish) royal power. Widely perceived as a whig attack on the Church of England the crisis brought out London mobs, who sacked meeting-houses and threatened Wharton's town house in Dover Street. In the election of September 1710 the whigs, in spite of Wharton's exertions, lost control of the Commons, helping Wharton's inveterate enemy, Robert Harley, strengthen his hold on the government.

Final years and reputation In October 1710 Wharton was removed as lord lieutenant, and on 11 January 1711 his regiment was disbanded. Meanwhile Swift began an assault on Wharton's character and his administration in Ireland. In the tory *Examiner* of 30 November 1710 and in *A Short Character of His Ex. T. E. of W.* (published anonymously and without imprint in December 1710) Swift pictured Wharton as a hardened, greedy politician, bawdy and profane, whose corrupt addiction to wealth and pleasure had cost Ireland dearly. On its title-page the 1711 edition of the *Short Character* described itself as a forerunner of impeachment.

Swift's anonymous attack brought him an oblique reprimand from Archbishop William King, who (without overtly accusing Swift of authorship) condemned the pamphlet as unchristian and unjust. The threat of impeachment also met opposition and soon evaporated. On 11 January 1711 Addison wrote that he heard 'no more of the impeachment'. He supposed that Swift's 'scurrilous little book' would never have been written if Harley's government had been able to proceed (*Letters*, 253–4). Whatever profits Wharton made during his governorship (in addition to his salary of £12,000 and expense allowances of £3000) they fell within the then recognized rules of the political game. This was also found to be true in 1713 when Wharton was charged with having used his influence to get a place in the English customs for George Hutchinson, who paid him £1000. When the debates revealed that the money had been given to Wharton's needy sister Lady Lockhart and that the event had occurred before the general pardon of 1709 the charges were dropped.

In autumn 1711 Wharton and his friends began a campaign against the government's peace proposals. In preparation for their counter-offensive the Kit-Cat Club planned a demonstration for Queen Elizabeth's birthday on 17 November—a procession and pope-burning in the style of 1680. For the occasion they prepared elaborate effigies of the pope, the Pretender, and the devil. A nervous government forbade the demonstration and confiscated the effigies, triggering a memorable line from Wharton. When asked what had happened to the three bogeymen, he answered, 'merrily', 'Their Disciples came by night and stole them away' (Oldmixon, *History*, 478).

To block the peace Wharton made an agreement with his old opponent the high tory earl of Nottingham. The junto whigs would support a bill against occasional conformity if Nottingham's friends in the Lords would vote against the peace. They would abandon their dissenting clients, at least temporarily, in order to prevent a potentially ruinous agreement with France. Both parties delivered on their promises, and on 8 December a majority of Lords agreed to a 'no peace without Spain' clause in an address to the queen (*JHL*, 19.339).

In a historic manoeuvre the queen thwarted the whig stratagem by creating twelve new peers, introduced in the house on 2 January 1712. The so-called tory dozen evoked another celebrated remark from Wharton, who asked one of the new members 'whether they voted by their foreman' (Boyer, *History*, 533). But Wharton's wit could not alter the new balance of power and in the end the whigs managed to defeat only the commercial clauses of the peace treaty. In the general election of 1713 Wharton was hard pressed to find seats for some of the whig leaders in the Commons, and his candidates lost the county election at Aylesbury, traditionally his home grounds. He and Lady Wharton appeared there with wool in their hats, symbolizing whig devotion to the English wool trade; but Lord Cheyne's nominees, John Fleetwood and John Verney, Viscount Fermanagh, prevailed.

Wharton then appears to have supported a whig proposal to dissolve the union in order to embarrass the government and win Scottish votes, although he was absent when the vote was taken and the measure was defeated. Wharton was defeated also, during the 1714 session, when he attacked the Schism Bill, a tory measure which closed the schools of the dissenters. His final speech, however, as he flayed Harley (now earl of Oxford), who had been raised and educated, like himself, as a dissenter, was perhaps the most incisive of his long career, and his closing reminder to the bishops of the gospel's 'do unto others' was brilliant (Cobbett, *Parl. hist.*, 6.1351–2).

During the 1714 session Wharton hammered away at the succession in danger theme. A formal motion, that the succession was not safe under the present government, was defeated in the Lords by only 12 votes, prompting Wharton to remark 'you carried it by your dozen' (*Wentworth Papers*, 366). When Queen Anne died and the Regency Act went into effect Wharton was not among the regents named by George I—an omission perhaps designed to conciliate tories. He was singled out, however, for special attention when George arrived in Greenwich on 19 September 1714; and on 23 September he was appointed lord privy seal and made a member of the privy council. Of his many activities over the next few months by far the most important was his work on the elections of January and February. In Buckinghamshire Wharton and

Lord Cheyne agreed to return one tory, Fleetwood, and one whig, John Hampden, in the county election, to save the expense of a contest; overall a solid whig majority was returned. On 15 February 1715 Wharton was created marquess of Wharton and of Malmesbury, and on 28 February he was granted a pension of £2000 a year. He was also made baron of Trim, earl of Rathfarnham, and marquess of Catherlough in the Irish peerage, but the patent for this title was not issued until 12 April, too late for Wharton to see.

In early April Wharton became ill. His condition, according to Dr Hans Sloane, who attended him, 'proceeded in a great measure from the attendance he gave to a multiplicity of business he was engaged in'—from 'fatigue' of body and mind (BL, Sloane MS 222, fol. 77). There was an additional complication. On 2 March Wharton's son Philip, then sixteen, had eloped with Martha, daughter of General Richard Holmes. Wharton tried vainly to have the marriage annulled, and his anger may have aggravated his illness. In any event he made his will on 8 April. On 12 April 1715, at his house on Dover Street, he died. On 22 April he was buried in the church at Winchendon. His widow, who died on 5 February 1717, was also buried there.

On the day of Wharton's death the duchess of Marlborough, informed by Dr Samuel Garth that 'Lord Wharton is given over', wrote a short testimony to his political value: 'I should be very sorry for his death, having never in my whole life seen so useful a man as he was in the Parliament, and so constantly right in all things that concerned the true interests of England' (Letters of Sarah, Duchess of Marlborough, 1875, 117–18). This statement might be called the standard whig version of Wharton's career. As a leader in the glorious revolution, a zealous defender of toleration, and a promoter of the protestant succession, he was one of the 'patriots' who had helped save England from popery and arbitrary power and the established church from suicidal high-church doctrines.

In view of Wharton's political rectitude whigs found it easy to ignore or excuse his lapses from strict moral virtue. His sexual adventures the Memoirs of the Life (p. 21) could dismiss as 'youthful sallies' and they could be blamed upon the debauched court of Charles II, where Wharton had once been welcome. Tory charges of political lying and corruption were simply slander, the malice of a desperate party, and tributes to Wharton's effectiveness as a whig leader.

Two days after Wharton's death Thomas Hearne delivered a tory verdict on his career, describing him as 'another great atheistical, knavish, republican, Whiggish Villain' (Remarks and Collections of Thomas Hearne, ed. D. W. Rannie, 1901, 5.45). This view was echoed, with variations, by Ned Ward in The Lord Whiglove's Elegy (1715) and by various tory wits. It received its final expression years later from Jonathan Swift, who dismissed his old enemy as 'the most universal villain I ever knew' (Memoirs of the Secret Services, 92).

Wharton never analysed his own career, and Swift asserted that he was totally indifferent to posthumous fame. It seems obvious, however, that Wharton had good reason to be satisfied. The party he had helped to construct and hold together, in good times and bad, had triumphed. The time, energy, and money he had devoted to the cause had been well spent. He had been damnably mauled by tory pamphleteers, of course, but that was a small price to pay for victory.

J. KENT CLARK

Sources Bodl. Oxf., MSS Rawl. 49–54; MSS Carte 79, 81, 91, 103, 109, 117, 228, 233; MS Tanner 35; MSS Wharton 1–10; Add. MS D 40 [marriage contract between Anne Lee and Thomas Wharton]; MS Rawl. D 148 [Colonel Norton's account]; Calendar of Carte papers · BL, Add. MSS 20006-20007 [autobiography of Goodwin Wharton]; Verney MS M 636, fols. 28–42 [microfilm of Verney letters at Claydon House]; Lansdowne MSS 253, 1024; Stowe MS 222, fols. 406–7; Add. MS 61634; Sloane MS 22, fol. 79 [Wharton to elector of Hanover]; Add. MS 18730 [Anglesey diary]; Add. MS 4107, fol. 28 [Wharton's letter to King William] · Claydon House, Buckinghamshire, Verney papers · Cumbria AS, Barrow, Lonsdale MS D/Lons/L1/4 · NL Wales, Kemeys-Tynte papers [letters of Mary Wharton Kemeys] · PRO, SP 63–366; 67/3 [Wharton's corresp. with government on Ireland]; SP 8/1, pt 2, fols. 224–7 [invitation to William]; C 5/637/73 [Wharton–Abingdon suit over properties]; will, PROB 11/290, fols. 291–2 [Sir Henry Lee]; will, PROB 11/430, fols. 181–2 [Philip, Lord Wharton]; PRO, PRO 31/3, fols. 141–2, 160, French diplomatic corresp.; SP 44/338, p. 238 · parish registers, Winchendon and Wooburn, Bucks. RLSS · Bucks. RLSS, Verney papers · manuscript minutes of Lords' Journal, 1696–1715; proxy books, 1696-1715, House of Lords Archives · J. K. Clark, 'Wharton between revolutions', Hunt. L., Ellesmere MS EL 10706a; HM 60960 · JHC, 9–11 (1667–97) · JHL, 15–20 (1691–1718) · CSP dom. · W. A. Shaw, ed., Calendar of treasury books, [33 vols. in 64], PRO (1904–69) · GEC, Peerage, new edn · DNB · E. Cruickshanks, 'Wharton, Hon. Thomas', HoP, Commons, 1660–90 · Cobbett, Parl. hist., vols. 4–6 · State trials, 7.1294–1599; 9.578–723, 818–915, 1053–1126; 10.1227–1330; 11.1023-1103, 1123–65; 15.1572 · A. Grey, ed., Debates of the House of Commons, from the year 1667 to the year 1694, 10 vols. (1763) · N. Luttrell, A brief historical relation of state affairs from September 1678 to April 1714, 6 vols. (1857) · The parliamentary diary of Narcissus Luttrell, 1691–1693, ed. H. Horwitz (1972) · Bishop Burnet's History · [J. Oldmixon?], Memoirs of the life of the most noble Thomas, late marquess of Wharton (1715) · P. Rogers, 'The memoirs of Wharton and Somers', Bulletin of the New York Public Library, 77 (1974), 224–35 · J. Carswell, The old cause (1953) · C. Robbins, The earl of Wharton and whig party politics, 1679-1715 (1992) · E. R. Wharton, The Whartons of Wharton Hall (1898) · G. F. T. Jones, Saw-Pit Wharton (1967) · J. K. Clark, Goodwin Wharton (1984); repr. (1989) · B. Dale, The good Lord Wharton (1906) · W. S. Sachse, Lord Somers (1975) · M. Blackett-Ord, Hell-fire duke (1982) · T. B. Macaulay, The history of England from the accession of James II, new edn, ed. C. H. Firth, 6 vols. (1913–15) · G. M. Trevelyan, England under Queen Anne, 3 vols. (1930–34) · J. P. Hore, The history of Newmarket and the annals of the turf, 3 vols. (1885–6) · K. H. D. Haley, The first earl of Shaftesbury (1968) · A. Browning, Thomas Osborne, earl of Danby and duke of Leeds, 1632–1712, 3 vols. (1944–51) · S. B. Baxter, William III and the defense of European liberty, 1650–1702 (1966) · J. Childs, The army, James II, and the glorious revolution (1980) · W. A. Speck, Reluctant revolutionaries: Englishmen and the revolution of 1688 (1988) · W. A. Speck, Tory and whig: the struggle in the constituencies, 1701–1715 (1970) · L. Shwoerer, The declaration of right (1981) · Letters illustrative of the reign of William III from 1696 to 1708 addressed to the duke of Shrewsbury by James Vernon, ed. G. P. R. James, 3 vols. (1841) · Memoirs of the secret services of John Macky, ed. A. R. (1733) · The Marlborough–Godolphin correspondence, ed. H. L. Snyder, 3 vols. (1975) · G. S. Holmes, British politics in the age of Anne, rev. edn (1987) · G. S. Holmes, The trial of Doctor Sacheverell (1973) · The letters of Joseph Addison, ed. W. Graham (1941) · The correspondence of Richard Steele, ed. R. Blanchard (1941) · The correspondence of Jonathan Swift, ed. H. Williams, 5 vols. (1963–5) · The prose works of Jonathan Swift, ed. H. Davis and others, 14 vols. (1939-68) · A. Boyer, The history of the reign of Queen Anne, digested into *annals*, 11 vols. (1703–13) · A. Boyer, *The political state of Great Britain*, 60 vols. (1711–40) · J. Oldmixon, *The history of England, during the reigns of King William and Queen Mary, Queen Anne, King George I* (1735) · W. Kennett, *A complete history of England*, 3 vols. (1719) · *A true copy of the last will and testament of the most honourable Thomas late marquess of Wharton* (1715) · J. P. Malcolm, ed., *Letters between the Rev. James Granger, MA, rector of Shiplake, and many of the most eminent literary men of his time* (1805) · *Report on the manuscripts of F. W. Leyborne-Popham*, HMC, 51 (1899), 267–8 · *Calendar of the manuscripts of the marquess of Ormonde*, new ser., 8 vols., HMC, 36 (1902–20) · R. Steele and J. Addison, *The Spectator*, ed. D. Bond, 5 vols. (1965) · *The diaries and papers of Sir Edward Dering, second baronet, 1644 to 1684*, ed. M. F. Bond (1976) · *The Wentworth papers, 1705–1729*, ed. J. J. Cartwright (1883)

Archives BL, autobiography of Goodwin Wharton, Add. MSS 20006–20007 · BL, Add. MS 61634 · BL, Anglesey diary, Add. MS 18730 · BL, letter to King William, Add. MS 4107, fol. 28 · Bodl. Oxf., marriage contract between Anne Lee and Thomas Wharton, Add. MS D 40 · Bodl. Oxf., Norton's account, Calendar of Carte papers, Add. MS D 148 · Bodl. Oxf., corresp. and papers, MSS Carte 79–81 · Bucks. RLSS, Verney MSS · Claydon House, Buckinghamshire, Verney papers · NL Wales, letters of Mary Wharton Kemeys, Kemeys-Tynte MSS · PRO, corresp. on Ireland, SP 63–366; 67/3 · PRO, invitation to William, SP 8/1, pt 2, fols. 224–7 · PRO, Wharton–Abingdon suit over properties, C 5/637/73 · PRO, French diplomatic corresp., SP 44/338. p. 238 · PRO, legal papers, C104/20, 42–43, 63–64, 84–91, 109–111, 135–137, 152–153 | BL, Lansdowne MSS 253, 1024 · BL, Wharton to elector of Hanover, Sloane MS 22, fol. 79 · BL, Stowe MS 222, fol. 406–7 · BL, Verney MS M 636, fols. 28–42 [microfilm of Verney letters at Claydon House] · Bodl. Oxf., MSS Carte 79, 81, 91, 103, 109, 117, 228, 233 · Bodl. Oxf., MSS Rawl. 49–54 · Bodl. Oxf., MS Tanner 35 · Bodl. Oxf., MSS Wharton 1–10 · TCD, corresp. with William King

Likenesses G. Kneller, oils, *c*.1710–1715, NPG [*see illus.*] · J. Faber junior, mezzotint, 1733 (after G. Kneller), BM, NPG · J. Houbraken, line engraving, pubd 1744 (after G. Kneller), BM, NPG · T. Flatman, miniature, Hunt. L. · school of Kneller, oils, NG Ire. · J. Smith, mezzotint (after G. Kneller), BM, NG Ire., NPG · line engraving (after G. Kneller), NG Ire.

Wharton, Sir William James Lloyd (1843–1905), naval officer and hydrographer, born in London on 2 March 1843, was the second son of Robert Wharton, county court judge of York, and his wife, Katherine Mary, daughter of Robert Croft, canon residentiary of York. After receiving his early education at Woodcote, Gloucestershire, and at the Royal Naval Academy, Gosport, Wharton entered the navy in August 1857. On passing his examination in 1865 he was awarded the Beaufort prize for mathematics, astronomy, and navigation. As sub-lieutenant he served in the corvette *Jason*, on the North America and West Indies station, and on 15 March 1865 he received his commission as lieutenant. In July 1865 he was appointed to the sloop *Gannet*, and in her served for another three years on the North American station. In February 1869 Sir James Hope, commander-in-chief at Portsmouth, on the recommendation of Professor Thomas John Main of the Royal Naval College there, offered Wharton the appointment as his flag lieutenant. Wharton was inclined to refuse, wishing to enter the surveying branch, but accepted on the advice of Main, who thought that the three years ashore would be to his advantage. On 2 March 1872 he was promoted commander, and in April was appointed to command the *Shearwater*, in which during the next four years he made

surveys in the Mediterranean, including a detailed examination of the currents in the Bosphorus, and on the east coast of Africa. In May 1876 he was appointed to the *Fawn*, and continued his surveys on the same stations until 1880. He married, on 31 January 1880, Lucy Georgina, daughter of Edward Holland of Dumbleton, Woodcote, Gloucestershire; they had three sons and two daughters.

On 29 January 1880 Wharton was promoted captain, and in February 1882 was appointed to the *Sylvia*, in which he conducted surveys on the coast of South America, and especially in the Strait of Magellan. In 1882 he published his *Hydrographical Surveying: a Description of the Methods Employed in Constructing Marine Charts*, which at once became the standard textbook. In August 1884 he was appointed hydrographer of the navy in succession to Sir Frederick Evans, and held this post until August 1904, becoming the longest serving hydrographer after Sir Francis Beaufort. From the Naval Defence Act of 1889 onwards, the hydrographic service under his control became increasingly concerned with the needs of the navy, and, by the end of his time, with the North Sea. Wharton was a fellow of the Royal Society and of the Royal Astronomical and Royal Geographical societies. He perhaps devoted most time to the last named of these, as a vice-president, and as a member of numerous committees on which he did much important work. He was retired on 2 August 1891, though he continued to be employed as hydrographer, and was promoted rear-admiral on the retired list on 1 January 1895. He was made a CB (civil) in 1895, and was raised to KCB (civil) at the jubilee of 1897. In 1899 he took a prominent part in the work of the joint Antarctic committee of the Royal Society and Royal Geographical Society.

The chief of Wharton's publications were his *Hydrographical Surveying*, already mentioned, of which new editions appeared until it was superseded in 1938; *A Short History of HMS Victory*, written while he was flag lieutenant at Portsmouth, and re-issued in 1888; *Hints to Travellers*, an edition of which he edited for the Royal Geographical Society in 1893; and the *Journal of Captain Cook's First Voyage*, which he edited with notes in 1893.

In July 1905 Wharton went to Cape Town to act as president of the geographical section of the British Association for the Advancement of Science, which was holding its annual meeting in South Africa. He subsequently visited Victoria Falls, where he fell ill with enteric fever. He was taken to the observatory, Cape Town, where he was the guest of Sir David Gill. He died there on 29 September 1905, and was buried with full naval honours in the naval cemetery at Simonstown. After his death the Wharton Testimonial Fund was formed, out of which an addition was made to the value of the Beaufort prize for naval officers, the double award being entitled the Beaufort Testimonial and the Wharton Memorial.

L. G. C. LAUGHTON, *rev.* R. O. MORRIS

Sources A. Day, *The admiralty hydrographic service, 1795–1919* (1967) · G. S. Ritchie, *The Admiralty chart: British naval hydrography in the nineteenth century*, new edn (1995) · *The Times* (30 Sept 1905) · *GJ*, 26 (1905), 684 · *CGPLA Eng. & Wales* (1906)

Archives Hydrographic Office, Taunton · NMM, log | CUL, corresp. with Lord Kelvin · c.CUL, letters to Sir George Stokes
Likenesses photograph, c.1904, Hydrographic Office, Taunton; repro. in Day, *Admiralty hydrographic service* · W. Allen, oils, c.1905 (after photograph), NMM · W. Allen, oils (posthumous; after photograph), NPG
Wealth at death £25,483 18s. 10d.: resworn probate, 1 Jan 1906, *CGPLA Eng. & Wales*

Whateley [*née* Wood; *other married name* Balfour], **Dame Leslie Violet Lucy Evelyn** (1899–1987), director of the Auxiliary Territorial Service, was born on 28 January 1899 at 63 Porchester Terrace, Paddington, London. Her mother was Ada Lilian Wood, formerly Hutton, and her father was Captain (later Colonel in the City of London regiment) Evelyn Michell Fitzgerald Wood, whose active service began with the Asante expedition of 1895. Leslie Wood was educated at convents of the Society of the Holy Child Jesus in St Leonards, Sussex, and in Cavendish Square, London. After leaving school at the age of sixteen she became secretary to her grandfather Sir (Henry) Evelyn *Wood VC, one of the army's legendary nineteenth-century field marshals, at his home near Winchester, where she received a thorough grounding in army admin-istration and methods. She assisted Sir Evelyn during the period when he was writing his book *Winnowed Memories* (1918). Later she worked as a secretary for several district nursing associations. On 8 July 1922 Leslie Wood married William John Balfour (1893/4–1934), a brewer, at the par-ish church, Kensington, London. They had one son, who was born in 1923. Balfour, who had been a cavalry officer during the First World War and from whom Leslie obtained a divorce, died in 1934. Her second marriage, to Squadron Leader Harry Raymond Whateley (b. 1910/11), took place on 21 September 1939.

In September 1938 Leslie Balfour drove to the Territorial Drill Hall at Camberley, Surrey, to join the Auxiliary Terri-torial Service (ATS) in response to a BBC announcement about the formation of the women's army. 'With the Army tradition I had behind me … there was never any doubt as to how I should try to serve my country', she wrote in her book *As Thoughts Survive* (p. 11). She was com-missioned as a 'one-pipper', with the ATS rank title of company assistant, inevitably abbreviated to 'coy ass'; this was equivalent to a second lieutenant. At the outbreak of war a year later she was posted to the War Office where she swiftly won a reputation as an outstanding adminis-trator. She worked closely with Dame Helen Gwynne-Vaughan, the first director of the ATS, whom she described as 'the old battleaxe'. 'We were all terrified of Dame Helen', Leslie Whateley later recalled. 'She didn't think I would be much good when we first met—I enjoy remembering that' (Terry, 126). At the War Office Dame Leslie worked alongside Lord Cavan's stepdaughter, Daphne Mulholland; Lord Gort's daughter, Jacqueline Ver-eker, who became Lady de L'Isle and Dudley; and Lady Trenchard's daughter, Belinda Boyle. 'I was the lowest of the low among Dame Helen's assistants. Dame Helen was a snob and she gathered all kinds of titled people around her' (ibid.), Leslie said. Of all Dame Helen's assistants Les-lie Whateley was undoubtedly the most capable and the

Dame Leslie Violet Lucy Evelyn Whateley (1899–1987), by Henry Lamb, 1943

most efficient. When Dame Helen retired in 1941, she was succeeded as director of the ATS by the stunningly attract-ive Senior Commander (Major) Jean Knox, later to become Lady Swaythling, who at the relatively young age of thirty-three was given the rank of chief controller, equivalent to major-general. Leslie, then forty-two, was appointed Jean Knox's deputy with the rank of senior controller, thus becoming the first ATS officer to attain the equivalent rank of brigadier. Her rise in the ATS had been meteoric. Jean Knox's immediate task was to repair the damage to the ATS, which had suffered severe criticism from the press. Lord Beaverbrook's *Daily Express* had led the attacks by printing exposures of maladministration and inci-dents of irregular conduct that had undermined the authority of Dame Helen. While Jean Knox spent most of her time as director 'absent at conferences, on tour and visiting the women's services of the Dominions and Allies', as the official announcement stated, Leslie Whate-ley effectively ran the ATS. This was one of the most cru-cial and active periods of the ATS, when membership expanded from a mere 40,000 to 204,000 as a result of con-scription of all single women between eighteen and thirty years of age. Reading Leslie Whateley's book *As Thoughts Survive* one is left with the impression that Jean Knox rarely attended the numerous official functions at which the director's presence would normally be required. As a result Leslie had to stand in for her director, even at the official fifth birthday celebrations of the ATS in Septem-ber 1943 when the queen took the salute at Westminster Abbey. The next month, on 31 October, Jean Knox resigned on grounds of ill health and Leslie Whateley was appointed her successor. On the eve of the official announcement of her appointment Leslie Whateley went to a party at Claridges with the Mountbattens, who, she said, 'were absolute angels to me' (Terry, 134). There the press laid siege to her, seeking the background to Jean Knox's resignation. Leslie Whateley was whisked away by General Sir Ronald Weekes, vice-chief Imperial General Staff. All her life Dame Leslie maintained a strict silence over the reasons for Jean Knox's premature resignation.

Leslie Whateley's first task was to address a letter to each of the more than 6,000 officers in the service, an unprecedented step, and her contribution in restoring morale and the image of the ATS was immense. Although she lacked some of the traditional advantages of a military bearing, being of slight build, small in stature and quiet by nature, she ended the war as a capable and efficient head of an army that was larger than many generals have the opportunity to command. As George Ivan Smith wrote in the *Daily Telegraph* obituary:

> Courage ran in her veins. She was a military person with a heart and great human understanding. She faced life with the discipline of a soldier's daughter. Dame Leslie was a splendid rudder guiding the ATS into the great contribution it made in a war in which the work of women was greatly needed, pre-dating the mode of modern feminism

During her time as director from 1943 to 1946 Leslie Whateley worked closely with the princess royal, who was controller-commandant of the ATS, and in 1945 was 'proud and honoured' when the nineteen-year-old Princess Elizabeth elected to join the ATS and underwent her training at the ATS Mechanical Transport Training Centre at Aldershot. The princess, later to become Elizabeth II, was commissioned as Second Subaltern Windsor on 5 March 1945. The achievement of the three wartime directors of the ATS is summed up by a saying in the ATS: Helen Gwynne-Vaughan dug the foundations, so deep that everyone fell in; Jean Knox put up the curtains, before the windows were in; and Leslie Whateley put on the roof, and finished the job.

Leslie Whateley was appointed CBE in 1943, and in 1946, when she retired as director, she was made a DBE. The French made her a chevalier of the Légion d'honneur in recognition of her services in equipping and training French *volontaires feminines* during their stay in Britain. She was also awarded the Croix de Guerre with silver star. The Americans, whom she had advised on the enlargement of their women's services, awarded her the Order of Merit. In 1948 Dame Leslie became one of the first non-royal women to be made an honorary colonel of a regiment when she was appointed colonel of the 668th battalion of the heavy anti-aircraft regiment, Royal Artillery. She received the Territorial Decoration in 1951. Dame Leslie Whateley retired on 3 May 1946, to a farm in Devon where she and her husband set about restoring an almost derelict 500-year-old property. In 1951 she was appointed director of the World Bureau of the World Association of Girl Guides and Girl Scouts. During her thirteen years in this role she travelled the world encouraging the spread of the

Girl Guide movement, especially in Asia. Her courage and indomitable spirit became evident in 1960 when attending in Addis Ababa, Ethiopia, a United Nations seminar on the place of African women in public life. She was in the chair during one session when gunfire from Ethiopian rebels interrupted the proceedings. Dame Leslie managed to keep the conference going smoothly, despite a bullet passing through her skirt. She was unperturbed by the incident, declaring: 'A miss is as good as a mile' (*Daily Telegraph*). In her mid-seventies Dame Leslie was still administering the voluntary services of Queen Mary's Hospital, Roehampton, but found time in 1974 to publish a second book of reminiscences, *Yesterday, Today and Tomorrow*. She died aged eighty-eight on 4 July 1987 in Little Somerford, Wiltshire.   ROY TERRY

Sources J. M. Cowper, *The auxiliary territorial service* (1949) · H. C. I. Gwynne-Vaughan, *Service with the army* [1942] · M. Izzard, *A heroine in her time* (1969) · L. Whateley, *As thoughts survive* (1948) · R. Terry, *Women in khaki* (1988) · *Daily Telegraph* (8 July 1987) · *The Times* (9 July 1987) · personal knowledge (2004) · b. cert. · m. cert. · *WWW* · L. Whateley, *Yesterday, today and tomorrow* (1974)

Likenesses H. Lamb, portrait, 1943, IWM [*see illus.*] · photograph, repro. in Whateley, *As thoughts survive*, p. 48 · photograph, repro. in Terry, *Women in khaki*, p. 129 · photographs, IWM

Wealth at death £5345: probate, 3 Oct 1987, *CGPLA Eng. & Wales*

Whateley [*married name* Darwall], **Mary** (*bap.* 1738, *d.* 1825), poet, was born on her father's farm in Beoley, Worcestershire, the last of nine children of William Whateley (*bap.* 1694, *d.* 1763), gentleman farmer, from Beoley, and his wife, Mary Beach (*b.* 1695), who was from Tanworth. She was baptized at Beoley on 9 February 1738. The Whateleys were well known and influential in Beoley, where John Whateley, Mary's grandfather, had been churchwarden at the parish church of St Leonard's.

Mary Whateley first came to minor prominence by publishing a few poems under the pseudonym of Harriott Airy in the *Gentleman's Magazine* in 1759. One of these she addressed to Mr Copywell, pseudonym of the writer William Woty, who replied in that same magazine. In 1761 William Shenstone, the pastoral poet and landscape gardener, told Thomas Percy, collector of ballads, and his friend Richard Graves, that he had received Mary Whateley's collection of manuscripts of her own poetry, which he edited as well as praised (*Letters*, 588–9). Shenstone described Mary Whateley as:

> neither handsome, nor, I believe, in affluent circumstances; has seen mighty little of the world. On the other hand, she is young, unaffected, and unassuming; and that she has generous and delicate sentiments, as well as ingenuity, may, I think, be fairly concluded from the whole tenor of her Poetry.   (ibid., 158)

His doctor, John Wall, wrote a brief account of her in the *Gentleman's Magazine* (1761), presumably in order to attract a readership for her poetry by demonstrating that she had the little education of 'the meanest of menial servants'. But in 1762, in an attempt to correct the impression he had created of Mary Whateley's servitude, he amended this biography and described her education as 'such as is usually given to the daughter [of] a substantial farmer [who] occupied his own estate'. Mary Whateley was taught reading, writing, and needlework, comprehending most of what is thought necessary. But her genius is not to be confined to such slender limits. She had a great love for literature, and applied herself with great assiduity to the reading of the best authors. (*GM*, 1762)

In 1760 Mary Whateley left Beoley in order to keep house for her brother, an attorney in Walsall, Staffordshire (although, at the death of her father, she returned to Beoley for about three years, in 1763). She published her first volume of poetry, *Original Poems on Several Occasions*, by subscription in 1764. John Langhorne, who wrote the preface to this volume, also praised it in the *Monthly Review* (1764, 445–50). On 4 November 1766 she married a widower, the Revd John Darwall (1732–1789) of Walsall, who had six children from his first marriage. John Darwall wrote music for hymns, as well as poetry and sermons, some of which he published on his own printing press: *A Visitation Sermon* (1775) and *Political Lamentations* (1777). Mary Darwall subsequently had six children of her own: Leicester Yonge (*b.* 1767), Whateley (*b.* 1768), Charles Henry (*b.* 1769), Harriet (*b.* 1771), Frederick (*b.* 1773), and Elizabeth (*b.* 1776). She wrote hymns for her husband's congregation in Walsall as well as epilogues and a play for local theatre. John Darwall died in December 1789 and Mary Darwall then lived for a time in Deritend, near Birmingham, with her stepson John. In 1793 she moved to Newtown, Montgomeryshire, and published by subscription her second work, *Poems on Several Occasions* (2 vols., 1794), which included pastoral and elegiac poems mainly in quatrains with an occasional sonnet. In one of these poems, 'Lines, Occasioned by Seeing a Beautiful Print of the River Clyde' (Whateley, *Poems*, 1.14–18), Mary Darwall allied herself with the work of Robert Burns and Helen Maria Williams:

Can'st thou the glen, or pine-topp'd hill
Like Burns, with strains ecstatic fill?
Or dare to touch thy humble wire,
Where beauteous Helen's sweet-ton'd lyre
Breathes harmony in every gale …

The second volume printed fourteen sonnets by her two daughters. One of these daughters, Harriet Darwall, also published her own work, *The Storm and other Poems* (1810).

Mary Darwall died in Walsall on 5 December 1825. In 1924 and again in 1979 the Gregynog Press, Newtown, reprinted from her *Poems on Several Occasions* her landscape poem, 'Written on Walking in the Woods of Gregynog in Montgomeryshire, the Seat of Arthur Blayney, esq.', dated 1 July 1794, as a limited edition broadsheet. Mary Whateley's poetry has since received attention because of an increase of critical interest in the history of women's poetry generally. In 1989 a few of her poems were reprinted by Roger Lonsdale in *Eighteenth-Century Women Poets: an Oxford Anthology*. JENNIFER BREEN

Sources M. Whateley, *Original poems on several occasions* (1764) • M. Whateley, *Poems on several occasions*, 2 vols. (1794) • A. Messenger, '"Daughter of Shenstone"?: being a brief life of Mary Whateley Darwall', *Bulletin of Research in the Humanities*, 87 (1986–7), 462–81 • *GM*, 1st ser., 29 (1759), 282, 334, 483, 538 • *GM*, 1st ser., 31 (1761), 635–6 • *GM*, 1st ser., 32 (1762), 84 • *GM*, 1st ser., 36 (1766), 188–9 • *London Magazine*, 31 (1762), 46, 81 • *The letters of William Shenstone*, ed. M. Williams (1939) • *Monthly Review*, 30 (1764), 445–50 • M. Williams, *William Shenstone: a chapter in eighteenth-century taste* (1935) • M. Darwall, *Written on walking in the woods of Gregynog in Montgomeryshire* (1794); repr. (1924) [pamphlet] • R. Lonsdale, ed., *Eighteenth-century women poets: an Oxford anthology* (1989), 256–62 • Blain, Clements & Grundy, *Feminist comp.*, 266 • parish register, Beoley, Worcestershire [baptisms, marriage] • A. Messenger, *Woman and poet of the eighteenth century: the life of Mary Whateley Darwall* (1999)

Whately, (Elizabeth) Jane (1822–1893), religious author, was born on 1 June 1822 in Oxford, the eldest child of the Revd Richard *Whately (1787–1863), and Elizabeth Pope (*d.* 1860). She had three sisters and one brother. She spent the first few years of her life in Suffolk, where her father had been presented to the living of Halesworth. The family returned to Oxford in 1825, when her father took up the principalship of St Alban Hall. Her sister described the young Jane (as she was known) as 'earnest and thoughtful'. Her mother, who was herself an author of some religious works, took charge of Jane's education, although Richard Whately saw to it that all of the children had some grounding in Latin. Jane's early interests, however, mirrored her mother's and she showed an early interest in, and aptitude for, music, French, and Italian. On her family's relocation to Dublin in 1831, when her father became archbishop, Jane's education was continued by a governess and 'the best masters Dublin then possessed'; as a bright eldest daughter Jane also pursued subjects 'not then usual for girls' (Wale, 11, 9). Since her governess could not provide this, she shared her brother's lessons with the Revd Blanco White as well as receiving instruction from her father.

Jane benefited from her father's Oxford connections: when in London they stayed with the Nassau Seniors and summer holidays often included a visit to the Arnolds at Rugby. Richard Whately evidently encouraged his children in their pursuits, offering affectionate criticism; *A Selection of English Synonyms* (1851; many later editions) is one result of his interest. With her mother and sisters Jane was active in local philanthropic endeavours; she and her sister Mary *Whately taught for the Irish Church Mission Society. Italians living in Dublin were also a focus of her attention, as was the cause of converting Spain to protestantism. As the eldest daughter of an archbishop Jane had extensive social and domestic responsibilities which increased after the death of her mother in 1860. As her two surviving sisters (the youngest had died in 1859) were living abroad for health reasons, the burden of caring for the ailing Richard Whately as well as her brother's children fell on her.

The death of Archbishop Whately in the autumn of 1863 marked the end of Jane Whately's settled residence in Dublin and the development of her literary and missionary career. Before her father's death Jane had written a few small works based on her own Bible study, co-authored a book on mothers' meetings, and produced a biography of Martin Luther as well as the *Selection of English Synonyms*. After her father's death Jane began work on his biography;

she began in 1864 by publishing a collection of his sermons and *Miscellaneous Remains from the Commonplace Book of Richard Whately*. Her *Life and Correspondence of Richard Whately, D.D.* (1866) was completed with the assistance of her father's pupil and friend Nassau Senior. She later published abridged versions of Richard Whately's *The Kingdom of Christ Delineated* (1877) and *The Errors of Romanism* (1878).

Jane seems to have had stronger evangelical leanings than her father and was ever ready to elucidate the dangers of Roman Catholicism; a substantial portion of her published works deal with this subject, for example: *Maude, or, The Anglican Sister of Mercy* (1869) and *Romanism in the Light of the Gospel* (1882). The bulk of her writings, however, took home and foreign missions as their subject. Indeed, missionary journeys dominated Jane Whately's later life. Until her sister Mary's death in 1889, Jane spent most winters at her sister's mission in Egypt where she established a school for girls. Jane never acquired a facility for Arabic, so the girls were taught in French and English. Summers were spent largely in France or Switzerland with her sister Henrietta and her family. Throughout her life Jane was troubled by asthma and many of her travels (whether to Egypt, Spain, or Italy) were intended to improve her health. These sojourns—when travelling she was known to take tracts with her and speak openly to passers-by. Her health weakening, Jane was advised to winter in Guernsey; she died there, unmarried, at St Peter Port on 19 February 1893 and was buried on the island.

L. E. LAUER

Sources [H. Wale], *Elizabeth Jane Whately: reminiscences of her life and work by her sister* (1894) · Boase, *Mod. Eng. biog.*, 6.837 · F. Hays, *Women of the day: a biographical dictionary of notable contemporaries* (1885), 213–14
Archives U. Birm. L., Church Missionary Society Archive, corresp.
Wealth at death £23,213 14s. 9d.: probate, 27 March 1893, *CGPLA Eng. & Wales*

Whately, Mary Louisa (1824–1889), educationist and missionary, was born on 31 August 1824 at Halesworth in Suffolk, where her father was rector. She was the third child and second daughter of the five children of the scholar Dr Richard *Whately (1787–1863), later archbishop of Dublin, and Elizabeth (*d.* 1860), a charity worker who wrote on religious matters, the daughter of J. C. Pope of Hillingdon Hall, Uxbridge. When Richard Whately became principal of St Alban's Hall in 1825 the family moved to Oxford. In 1831 he was appointed to the see of Dublin: the family lived in Dublin in winter and in the summer at Redesdale, 5 miles from the city. The children were educated at home by their parents; they helped their mother to visit the Irish poor in their homes and taught in the village school built by their father.

In 1849, while accompanying her brother to France and Italy for his health, Mary Whately painted and learned Italian. On her return to Ireland she put much energy into the ragged schools (for children whose parents could not afford fees) and homes of the Irish Church Mission; she also visited poor Italians in Dublin. Through this work she gained first-hand experience of teaching people of different languages and cultures. In 1856–7 Mary Whately travelled to Cairo and the Holy Land with a friend; unfortunately her journals of this visit were lost. However, a fellow traveller described how, faced by Bedouin with flashing weapons, she began to sketch the scene. 'By the life of the Prophet!' exclaimed the chief. 'The Englishwoman is writing us down!' and, with a friendly greeting, wheeled and galloped off (Porter, 229–33).

In 1860, when her mother and her youngest sister had died, Mary Whately returned to Cairo to open the first school in Egypt for poor Muslim girls. She soon had thirty pupils and began to train teachers. She learned Arabic and was joined in her work by a Lebanese missionary to Muslims, Mansoor Shakoor, and his brother, Yousif; they, and later Mansoor's wife, worked with her for over twenty years. After visiting Ireland briefly in 1863 when her father died, Mary returned to Egypt to settle. She and the Shakoors opened a boys' Sunday school and later a ragged school for boys. She recorded her experiences in a lively and anecdotal style in *Ragged Life in Egypt* (1861) and *More about Ragged Life in Egypt* (1863). From time to time she returned to Europe, and in 1866 took with her Mansoor Shakoor and his betrothed wife (whom Mary raised as her adopted daughter and educated).

Mary Whately's work was funded by her own small income and donations. The schools became a regular visit on the itinerary of British travellers in Cairo, and in 1869 she was given a grant of land by the khedive. There, following Shakoor's plans, she built her house, a school, and mission buildings. The number of children in the two schools rose to some 500. The boys followed a full curriculum, covering basic academic and vocational subjects, while the girls (of whom there were about 100 in 1872) learned to read and write in Arabic, to sew, and embroider. A few girls progressed to a full elementary curriculum.

Mary Whately also took her Christian mission to the houses of the Egyptian poor, to the Bedouin camps in the desert, and to the villages along the Nile, working first with Shakoor and, when he died in 1872, with his widow. They told the stories from the Bible and distributed Arabic scriptures. In some villages they were coldly received, but more frequently they were welcomed. Whately wrote of her close relationship with these people in *Among the Huts in Egypt* (1872) and *Stories of Peasant Life on the Nile* (1888). In 1879, with the help of a Syrian doctor who married into the Shakoor family, she opened a medical mission, which was soon caring for some 3000 patients a year. At the dispensary she explained the Bible stories 'in her simple and graphic way in the colloquial Arabic the people understood' (E. J. Whately, 78). The ragged schools flourished and her elder sister, Elizabeth Jane *Whately (1822–1893), joined her and opened a private school for the 'mixed multitude' of foreign residents in Cairo.

In 1881 the 'Arabi rebellion' forced Mary Whately to withdraw from Egypt for a time, but she soon returned. On her visits to Europe she 'eloquently pleaded for Egypt and Islam at meetings and on every occasion that offered' (E. J. Whately, 82). She wrote and illustrated a number of books about everyday life in Egypt, as well as old family stories written in Spain and Switzerland, a memoir of Shakoor, and interesting fictional works 'illustrative of Egyptian manners and customs'.

An intrepid and far-sighted woman, Mary Whately was strongly opposed to slavery and deplored the status of women in Egypt, hoping that one day they would 'come and go as one created to be neither a toy nor a drudge, but a helpmeet to man' (E. J. Whately, 126). Her writing promoted understanding of modern Egypt among her readers.

Mary Whately died in Cairo of a chest infection on 9 March 1889, shortly after one of her mission journeys up the Nile, cared for to the end by Mrs Shakoor. She was buried in Cairo on 9 or 10 March. Her schools did not survive her for long, but the Church Missionary Society, which had supported her work with several annual grants, had heeded her prompting to start a second Egypt mission to evangelize Muslims and had worked in the country from 1882. DEBORAH MANLEY

Sources E. J. Whately, *The life and work of Mary Louisa Whately* (1890) · M. L. Whately, *Ragged life in Egypt*, 2nd edn (1863) · M. L. Whately, *More about ragged life in Egypt*, 2nd edn (1864) · M. L. Whately, *A memoir of Mansoor Shakoor of Lebanon* (1873) · M. L. Whately, *Scenes from life in Cairo* (1883) · F. Hays, *Women of the day: a biographical dictionary of notable contemporaries* (1885) · J. Johnson, *Noble women of our time* (1882) · M. L. Whately, *Stories of peasant life on the Nile* (1888) · M. L. Whately, *Among the huts in Egypt* (1872) · J. L. Porter, *The giant cities of Bashan* (1865) · M. Fowler, *Christian Egypt* (1901) · E. L. Butcher, *The story of the church of Egypt* (1897)
Likenesses engraving, repro. in Whately, *Life and work of Mary Louisa Whately*, frontispiece
Wealth at death £4439 2s. 6d.: probate, 6 Nov 1889, *CGPLA Eng. & Wales*

Whately, (Mary) Monica (1889–1960), campaigner for women's rights and civil liberties, was born on 30 November 1889 at 16 Trebovir Road, Brompton, London, the eldest daughter of Major Reginald Pepys Whately (*b.* 1860), officer with the Royal Sussex regiment, and Maude Isabel, a singer, daughter of Thomas John Davis, Church of England clergyman. She was a great-great-niece of Archbishop Whately, and her parents converted to Catholicism in 1899. She was educated at home and at the London School of Economics, where she studied politics and world affairs. Family wealth made her financially independent, with the time and means to travel extensively throughout her life, gathering information and contacts to promote a wide range of political and humanitarian causes. She was an internationalist in the best sense of that term, and a prodigious worker for the issues she believed in, both at home and abroad.

Monica Whately came of age politically within the militant suffragette movement, where she developed a talent for publicity and public speaking. In 1912, with her mother, she became a founder member of the Catholic Women's Suffrage Society, and honorary treasurer and secretary of its post-1918 successor, the St Joan's Social and Political Union. However, her independent views and strong feminism were more suited to the nascent Six Point Group, an organization of mainly younger activists

such as Vera Brittain and Dorothy Evans, formed in 1921. Its vigorous promotion of equal rights for women was based on a conception of equality that sought to diminish the social consequences of sexual difference. Monica represented the group on the domestic and international fronts over the next four decades. She was its delegate to the World Conference of Women Against War and Fascism in Paris in 1933, and for many years, with other members of the group, lobbied the League of Nations for an equal-rights treaty, which was finally incorporated into the United Nations charter in 1945. Between the wars she campaigned across a number of organizations and issues, and was an active member of the National Union of Societies for Equal Citizenship until the split of 1926–7, when she sided with those on the executive who unsuccessfully opposed the ascendancy of new feminism. She was particularly concerned with women's employment rights and the economic position of married women, which came under attack in the early 1930s and which underpinned the work of the Open Door Council, for which she was honorary treasurer. She organized a well-publicized picket of Austin Motors in 1933 after its chairman called for male workers to replace female as a remedy for unemployment.

It was chiefly Monica Whately's involvement with the Open Door Council and its outspoken resistance to protective legislation for women workers which brought her into conflict with the Labour Party leadership. Politically ambitious, she stood three times for parliament (1929, 1931, 1936), albeit as an Independent Labour Party (ILP) candidate because the national executive committee refused to endorse her. She made common cause with left-wing, mainly ILP feminists within the women's sections, including Frida Laski, Dorothy Jewson, and Dora Russell, refusing to toe the party line and working with other organizations at a time when this was frowned upon. She had more success as a local councillor, standing against Oswald Mosley and winning the London county council (LCC) ward of Limehouse in 1937. In addition to serving on the management committees of schools and hospitals, she campaigned vigorously against the marriage bar: the LCC ban on married midwives was lifted in 1940, largely through her efforts. During the Second World War she worked for the Ministry of Labour, Ministry of Information, and Save the Children. In the 1940s she became involved with the Equal Pay Campaign Committee and Women for Westminster. Her experience of party politics, however, convinced her of the continuing need for autonomous feminist action, and she successfully resisted an attempt to merge the latter with the Six Point Group. She represented the group on both the National Council for Civil Liberties and the National Assembly of Women in the 1950s, and served as its chairwoman until her death.

International work was an important cornerstone of Monica Whately's life. Famine relief effort in the early 1920s in central and eastern Europe led to an involvement with Save the Children. Like many of her generation she was active in peace work, as a member of the Peace Army and the No More War Movement, and as a speaker for the

League of Nations Union. This was coupled with a deep concern to uphold civil liberties and democracy as fascism gathered pace. She worked closely with the British Campaign Against War and Fascism, and a visit to Nazi Germany in 1934 to seek legal redress for women imprisoned without trial alerted her to the evils of the Nazi regime. Throughout the 1930s she spoke and wrote on this subject, and with Jewish and other groups organized a boycott of goods made in Germany. She made several visits to Spain during the civil war and under Franco, and also travelled beyond Europe, developing a deep interest in movements for colonial freedom. In 1931 and 1934 she visited India, met Gandhi, and was a signatory to the India League delegation report which investigated the effects of British imperialism and the causes of Indian nationalism. She journeyed to the USA and to South Africa—the latter being a prelude to her involvement with the South African Committee for Colonial Freedom in the 1930s and anti-apartheid work after the war. One of her last trips was to revolutionary China, where she observed the status of women and conditions of life for working people.

A flamboyant figure, remembered years later for her cropped hair, black clothes, and sweeping black cloak with its red lining, Monica Whately had presence and tremendous energy. Hazel Hunkins Hallinan, who knew her in the Six Point Group, once remarked that she 'splashed her talents around' (Harrison interview). The cross-fertilization that came from working across many campaigns made her a lively maverick and a useful conduit of ideas, albeit one who 'just missed greatness' (ibid.). Her career might seem to epitomize the dissipation of energy which fragmented the inter-war women's movement. But it was precisely because she channelled her feminism into many diverse campaigns and issues that she showed its relevance to all the key movements of the twentieth century. She died on 12 September 1960 at 35 Amherst Road, London. There was no funeral, but characteristically she donated her body to the Middlesex Hospital for medical research and her eyes to Moorfield Hospital.

LINDA WALKER

Sources F. C. Burnand, ed., *The Catholic who's who and yearbook* (1924) · *The Catholic who's who* (1936) · *Annual Reports* [Catholic Women's Suffrage Society] (1912–15) · *Catholic Suffragist* (1912–18) · A. J. R., ed., *The suffrage annual and women's who's who* (1913) · *Hutchinson's women's who's who* (1934) · *Daily Worker* (16 Sept 1960) · *Six Point Group Newsletter* (Oct 1960) · *Six Point Group Newsletter* (Dec 1960) · *The Times* (14 Sept 1960) · *Annual Reports* [Six Point Group] (1931–60) · Six Point Group MSS, Women's Library, London · *Annual Report* [Open Door Council] (1927–30) · B. Harrison, interview with Hazel Hunkins Hallinan, 8 Feb 1975, Women's Library, London · M. Pugh, *Women and the women's movement in Britain, 1914–1959* (1992) · *CGPLA Eng. & Wales* (1960)
Likenesses photograph, repro. in *Daily Herald* (21 June 1933) · photograph, repro. in *Clapham Observer* (24 Aug 1934) · photograph, repro. in *Birmingham Gazette* (21 Oct 1933) · photograph, repro. in *Independent Feminist Weekly* (9 March 1935)
Wealth at death £9046 11s. 2d.: administration, 13 Dec 1960, *CGPLA Eng. & Wales*

Whately, Richard (1787–1863), Church of Ireland archbishop of Dublin and philosopher, was born on 1 February 1787, at Cavendish Square, London, the youngest of nine

Richard Whately (1787–1863), by unknown photographer

children of the Revd Canon Joseph Whately (d. 1797) of Nonsuch Park, Surrey, and his wife, Jane Plumer. It was a well-connected political and professional family of some distinction: his paternal uncle Thomas *Whately (1726–1772) had been George Grenville's private secretary and subsequently secretary to the Treasury in Grenville's administration, attaching himself after Grenville's death to Lord North. Richard Whately's maternal uncle, William Plumer (1736–1822), the MP for Hertfordshire, in whose house he had been born, was a wealthy, dedicated Foxite, who had been preceded as a whig MP by his father, William Plumer (1687–1767). The gentlemanly professions were equally well represented in the family: another paternal uncle had been a banker, and Whately's brother William became a lawyer; his brother Thomas, the poor-law reformer, was an Anglican clergyman.

Early education and Oxford Whately was six years younger than his nearest sibling, an isolated child, slight in build, timid, and retiring in manner. He had few companions, but compensated for this by learning to read and write very early and going on nature rambles. A prodigy at mental arithmetic, he lived in an imaginative world of his own construction: 'I was engaged either in calculation or castle-building' he later commented (*Life and Correspondence*, 1.5). At the age of nine years he was sent to a private school near Bristol with strong West Indian connections run by a Mr Philips. Although he was there drawn out of himself, and grew up tall and strong (looking, it has been said, like a Yorkshire ostler), his school life was not particularly happy: he still went on solitary rambles, observing natural history, and continued his habit of 'visionary speculations' (ibid., 6.6). He became a first-rate shot and fisherman. However, he did lose both his passion and ability for mental arithmetic, which he now learned with difficulty and slowly.

Whately entered Oriel College in 1805, graduating BA (double second class) in 1808 and proceeding MA in 1812. In 1810 he won the English essay prize and in 1811 was elected a fellow of the college. He then settled at Oxford as a private tutor, in which capacity he taught Nassau Senior, the economist, and Samuel Hinds, later bishop of Norwich, who had also attended Philips's school near Bristol. He became a dedicated, if unconventional, teacher (he taught lying on a sofa with one leg over the back), taking particular delight in encouraging diffident characters. He disregarded Oxford conventions: in the early morning he could be seen walking Christ Church meadows, not wearing a cap and gown as required, but a white hat and coat (he was known as the White Bear), accompanied by his white dog which he had trained to climb trees and from there jump into the water. However, his rough-and-ready manners (he once shocked Henry Bathurst, bishop of Norwich, by receiving him with his feet on the table) and eccentricities (he kept herrings in his college rooms to grill on his fire for breakfast) meant that he was never popular. His friendships, which he particularly cherished, were largely confined to the society of Oriel: in addition to Senior and Hinds, he cultivated Edward Hawkins, Thomas Arnold, and (until a few months before his death in 1860) Baden Powell.

Whately and early Noeticism Whately had regarded his tutor at Oriel as 'utterly incompetent' (*Miscellaneous Remains*, 149). The turning point in his intellectual career had been the lectures of Edward Copleston, whose intellectual disciple he became and whose views, in the early phase of his career, he was happy to represent and publicly acknowledge: two of his early works—the *Bampton Lectures* (1822) and *Elements of Logic* (1826)—were expressly dedicated to Copleston. Copleston became godfather to Whately's daughter and in later life Whately edited Copleston's *Remains* (1854).

Copleston was the founder of the Noetic school of Anglican apologetics at Oxford, a group of scholars who sought to provide a defence of Christianity on the ground of its reasonableness against the onslaught of deists and Unitarians. The Noetics also attempted to shore up Anglicanism by ensuring that the ancient universities were educationally capable of producing clergymen competent of defending the Church of England against such intellectual assaults. In the 1810s and early 1820s their approach was seen as a worthy bulwark of the Church of England, and not, as it was to be seen later, by the Tractarians in particular, as the first stage in the dilution of Anglicanism by secularism.

In this sense Whately, spreading the Coplestonian message, operated, if not within the pale, then certainly as an intellectually acceptable ally, of the high-church tradition. Thus he shared with the 'high and dry' Henry John Rose a loathing of German theology and philosophy. He looked down upon the evangelicals of St Edmund Hall, while dismissing eighteenth-century latitudinarianism as 'spurious liberality of sentiment' (R. Whately, *The Use and Abuse of Party Feeling*, 1822, 220). With more irony than accuracy, he described himself as a 'divine right tory' (*Miscellaneous Remains*, 64) on account of his belief in obedience to the secular state, so long as a legal order existed, and his rejection of social contract theory as the basis of politics. (In fact he was an uncontroversial supporter of the revolution of 1688.) Above all, in his early theology, which was praised by the high-church *British Critic*, he sought to demonstrate the truth of Christian evidences (as opposed to natural theology), and to do so not by dogmatic assertion but by the use of modern tools of academic discourse.

Whately's first substantial essay, *Historic Doubts Relative to Napoleon Buonaparte* (1819), was a characteristic production with regard to both intellectual purpose and author. It was a bold, ironic attack on Hume's essay on miracles, in which he sought to weigh the evidence for the existence and exploits of Napoleon in order to demonstrate that proof of the existence of the exceptional can only ever amount to a probability, relying as it does on testimony and not experience. But, he argued, if it were accepted that Napoleon existed, in the absence of any prejudice against religion, there was equally no reason to doubt that Christ had performed the miracles recorded in the Bible. It was intended as a *bouleversement* of the rationalist sceptic position, using Hume's method against himself. It was a popular success, demonstrating a capacity for satire (it included a history of Napoleon in parody of the Bible) which in later life he sought to curb.

Historic Doubts owed something to William Paley and the eighteenth-century bishop of Durham Joseph Butler in its insistence that there was no improbability that testimony could not outweigh. But of the two, Whately's greater debt (as was the Noetics') was to Butler. In part 2 of his famous *Analogy*, Butler had indicated that the difficulties involved in written revelation were similar to those found in experience. Acknowledging this insight, the Noetics sought to develop an inductive theology to study the Bible, just as induction was the basis of the study of the natural world: in the same way that the world of nature was a world of facts, so revelation consisted of scriptural 'facts'. In this enterprise Whately was a leading participant, albeit that this participation was not systematic. Like his mentor, Copleston, Whately's writings tended to be occasional pieces, written for an ephemeral purpose, rather than learned monographs. 'A great work is a thing I have never undertaken', he once wrote (*Life and Correspondence*, 2.173), attributing this on another occasion to a natural indolence which he attempted to overcome. He was partially successful: he was infinitely more prolific than Copleston, but never as academic as his friend and fellow Noetic Renn Dickson Hampden.

The study of the Bible as a collection of facts required that their nature be identified. Whately understood this to be limited. As he explained in his earliest theological essays (his 1921 edition of Archbishop William King's *Discourse on Predestination* and the *Essays on some of the Peculiarities of the Christian Religion*, published in 1825, which for the main part was a collection of sermons delivered at Oxford in 1820), the purpose of the scriptures was to teach man the way to eternal happiness, and not to teach him the nature or essential qualities of things as they are in themselves. But therein also lay their superiority, for they taught lessons that were not discernible by the exercise of man's reason. They were the product of divine revelation.

From this understanding of the Bible four conclusions flowed. The first was that the Bible did not seek to teach all truth: it was not intended as a substitute for natural philosophy. For example, the biblical account of creation was not a geological theory, but simply served the purpose of informing its readers that God created the world. This was scarcely a new approach to biblical study, even within the Anglican church. It had been advocated, for example, by John Hey, the Cambridge theologian, at the beginning of the century (Oriel College Library had purchased a new copy of Hey's Norrissian lectures in the early 1820s on Pusey's recommendation). Second, the Bible taught by analogy. In describing divine qualities in human terms it did not ascribe human qualities to God. Indeed, one of the principal purposes in republishing King's *Discourse* was to bring to public attention an earlier description of man's analogical understanding of God that had been praised by Copleston in his own *Enquiry into the Doctrines of Necessity and Predestination* (1821). Third, the Bible was written so as to produce practical results, and was thus couched in historically relative terms. It was therefore best understood by being acquainted with the historical circumstances, habitual modes of thought, and understanding of the persons who constituted its first audience. Fourth, because scriptural revelation consisted in the teaching of necessary facts, it was not possible to go beyond the realm of facts even where they appeared to be contradictory. That they appeared contradictory did not render them any less 'factual': as Butler taught, many apparently contradictory matters existed in nature and the same difficulties were to be expected in scripture as in nature, since both were collections of facts.

This understanding of the limited, but factual, nature of the Bible was used by Whately for orthodox ends: to attack sceptics, rationalist Unitarians, and Calvinist evangelicals. Thus natural theologians were dismissed on the ground of the superiority of the Bible. According to Whately, 'the study of natural religion ought properly to *follow*, or at least to accompany, and not to precede, that of revelation' (R. Whately, *Essays*, 1825, x–xi). The doctrine of the immortality of the soul, for example, could be discovered only from the Bible. Likewise St Paul was not a Calvinist, but an orthodox Anglican. Whately demonstrated this in his *Essays on some of the Difficulties of the Writings of St Paul* (1828) in which, for example, in relation to the doctrine of election, he argued that its true meaning was to be ascertained by reference to the Old Testament's notion of divine election from which it could be seen that election was conditional on being a faithful follower of the church. Thus he sought to ensure that St Paul's writings were regarded as 'a principal bulwark of the Gospel' (ibid., 46–7) and censured their comparative neglect.

In 1820 Whately met Elizabeth Pope (*d.* 1860), the cousin of his Oriel friend Sherlock Willis and the third daughter of William Pope of Hillingdon Hall, Uxbridge; on 18 July 1821 they were married at Cheltenham, 'for love', as he recorded in his commonplace book. They were to have four daughters and a son. The second of their daughters was the missionary and teacher Mary Louisa *Whately. Marriage necessitated his leaving his Oriel fellowship, and in August 1822 his uncle presented him to the living of Halesworth in Suffolk. He was resident there for less than three years owing to his wife's illness. None the less, he founded an adult school and weekly lecture, and was active in his local poor-law union. He advocated the abolition of relief for the able-bodied poor unless they were employed by parish officers on work of a public nature. This was as much on account of the demoralization that idleness brings as the 'vice' of indolence. In so doing he also identified a 'benefits trap': a labourer had little incentive to seek employment if local wages were no more than the level of local relief. By taking themselves out of the pool of available labour, such persons also kept local wages artificially high in relation to supply.

Whately was summoned back to Oxford in 1825 on his appointment by Lord Grenville, chancellor of Oxford University, as principal of St Alban Hall. This patronage had been secured by Copleston, as part of his design to elevate and improve Oxford teaching. St Alban was one of two halls of residence (the other being St Mary's) that Copleston wished Oriel to acquire: he was successful in neither objective, though Oriel did subsume St Mary Hall in 1902. However, he did succeed in bringing both under Noetic influence (Hampden became principal of St Mary's in 1833). Like St Mary's, St Alban Hall had a low academic reputation; it was known as the 'Botany Bay' of the university. Whately changed this, with the assistance, as vice-principal, first of John Henry Newman—then a Noetic protégé—and from 1827 of his former pupil Hinds.

Whately's concern for Christianity as a reasonable religion led him to ensure that Anglicans were versed in the right methods of reasoning not only through his teaching but also his publications. His most notable achievement in this regard was his textbook *Elements of Logic*, which had first appeared in the *Encyclopaedia metropolitana* (1826). It was written at the suggestion of Copleston and with the assistance of Newman and Nassau Senior. Indeed, as early as 1822 Newman had constructed a rough draft of the article after copying out various Whately manuscripts on logic, and this formed the basis of the work. Its production was typical of the collaborative enterprises in which the Noetics indulged. It is most famous in retrospect as a work of meta-logic—that is, for its distinction between induction as the process of collecting or investigating facts, which was not a process of reasoning, and induction as the right method of inference from the facts collected.

This was the deductive method, its tool was the syllogism and its greatest exponent was Aristotle. But the *Logic* was more than a textbook which dominated reading lists for twenty years until replaced by John Stuart Mill's *System of Logic*. It was also intended as a polemic in two senses. First, it was to promote sound reasoning to counteract religious scepticism. 'The adversaries of our Faith', Whately wrote, 'would, I am convinced, have been … more satisfactorily answered … had a thorough acquaintance with logic been more common than it is' (R. Whately, *Elements of Logic*, 1827, xxviii). Second, it was to serve as an agent of university reform. Whately argued that logic should be made compulsory for candidates at Oxford for academical honours: to this end his preface was separately reprinted and circulated. In the same genre was Whately's less successful, but equally widely circulated, manual *Elements of Rhetoric* (1828), the purpose of which was to describe 'the process of *conveying truth* to others, by reasoning' (R. Whately, *Elements of Rhetoric*, 1828, 23).

Although Whately's Christianity was a religion of reason resting on evidence (thus the fault of evangelicalism and Roman Catholicism was that they were anti-intellectual, the former believing sincerity was enough, the latter sacrificing independent judgement to tradition), it was not dry and rationalist. He was a firm advocate of zeal for the gospel, and he believed that creeds were a necessary component of a church: the laying aside of formularies would be tantamount to putting an end to the society. He was a supporter of foreign missionary work and established the first Irish branch of the Society for the Propagation of the Gospel in Foreign Parts. But he cautioned against partisan zealotry that distorted truth and led to heresy. Indeed, for Whately heresies were the product of false reasoning allied to distorting passions, the product of a common human nature rather than a quality peculiar to heretics. This was the burden of his *Bampton Lectures* in 1822 and of his later work, dedicated to the former Catholic priest Joseph Blanco White, *The Errors of Romanism Traced to their Origin in Human Nature* (1830). Whately held that Wesleyanism was the product of ambition, while Unitarianism was attributable to a love of novelty, and many Calvinists were motivated by an undue love of disputation. He advocated toleration of dissenting views on the ground that their true meaning might be misunderstood by orthodox protestants, or that they might be the product of a lack of education or the seeking of truths from the Bible that it was incapable of supplying. But he valued the Church of England over other churches because it asserted the primacy of the scriptures, which contained God's full and final revelation.

By the mid-1820s Whately had become the Noetics' leading light and it had become the dominant intellectual movement at Oxford. In 1830 a journalist on *John Bull* could salute him as the intellectual leader of Oriel and could refer (wrongly) to Thomas Arnold as Whately's 'bottle holder'. Copleston had become increasingly involved in political affairs outside Oxford and in 1828 left Oxford altogether, having become bishop of Llandaff in 1827; his successor, Edward Hawkins, was never able to match

Whately in intellectual verve or dominance. Meanwhile, a number of Whately's friends succeeded to various Oxford appointments and were thus physically within his sphere of influence: in 1825 Senior became the first Drummond professor of political economy; in 1827 Hinds returned to Oxford as Whately's vice-principal at St Alban Hall; and, in the same year, Baden Powell returned as Savilian professor of geometry. In 1826 Blanco White came to reside at Oxford and obtained common-room rights at Oriel, and in 1829 Whately's former pupil Hampden was appointed to the board of examiners and came to live at Oxford. This was also the year that the Noetics sought a metropolitan voice: Senior and Whately founded the *London Review*, with Blanco White as editor. It was intended as a (short-lived) protest against the sectarian temper of its rivals: the *Quarterly*, *Edinburgh*, and *Westminster* reviews. It folded after only two issues, a premonition of what was to follow, partly because of its academic tone, partly because even the literate classes wanted sectarianism.

Whately and late Noeticism The second half of the 1820s heralded a time of major political change. As the threat of the French Revolution receded, there was increasing clamour for national institutions to be reformed to reflect the growth of dissenting populations in the towns and the strength of the Catholic population in Ireland, which since 1801 had formed part of the Union. Such reform became increasingly likely when, in 1827, the liberal tory George Canning became prime minister. Thus in 1828 the Test and Corporation Acts were repealed and in 1829 Catholic emancipation was achieved. Whately supported both measures. The reform of national political institutions prompted a reconsideration of the role of the Anglican church and Anglican institutions, including the ancient universities, and the emergence of church parties. Indeed, it was Catholic emancipation and the re-election of Sir Robert Peel as MP for Oxford University that precipitated the symbolic split of Newman from Whately. It is in this context that the second phase of Whately's career has to be understood. In the political context of the late 1820s and 1830s his stance on the political questions of the day became increasingly to be associated with whiggery. Although the substantive analysis changed little, and Whately remained loyal to Copleston's Noetic upbringing, the second-order reforms which he advocated placed him firmly on the side of political liberalism even if, by intellectual background, he stood outside the traditional whiggery of the Fox–Holland–Grey school.

In his anonymously published *Letters on the Church by an Episcopalian* (1826), Whately attacked the whig Warburtonian alliance between church and state on the ground that, since Christ's kingdom was not of this world, the interference of the secular power in religious affairs was at variance with Christ's teaching. Indeed, it imparted to the church a coercive power which created the impression that religion was simply a state contrivance for maintaining order. Whately was therefore opposed to the church carrying out secular administrative functions such as maintaining registers of births, marriages, and deaths, and was equally opposed to the royal appointment of bishops, their participation in the House of Lords, and parliament's ultimate control over the Church of England's articles and liturgy. The separation of church and state, however, would not result in the church losing the right to its property, since this was not the state's property but the church's. For example, tithes were not a tax levied by government. None the less, the state did have a right to take away property whenever the inutility or harmfulness of the institution rendered its abolition important to the public welfare.

Whately argued that the church itself was not merely a voluntary organization of believers: it had as legitimate a claim to be acknowledged as of divine origin as did the Jewish theocracy. It had authority in matters of faith, including the authority to declare Christian doctrines and duties and to exclude members who did not conform. Thus, to disregard the authority of the church, in Whately's eyes, was to commit an offence against Christ himself. In this he followed the teaching of his fellow Noetic Hawkins. But this did not mean that what the church declared to be the faith was necessarily the true faith. Although the teaching of doctrine was an office that Christ had bestowed on the church, its lessons were subject to the higher authority of the Bible. In a conflict between church teaching and the scriptures, the scriptures were superior. Moreover, he asserted in later works, because the scriptures consisted simply of facts and were not mathematical propositions from which 'true' equations could be deduced, creeds, liturgies, and catechisms (that is, the 'equations') were only the writings of able and pious men. This was the conclusion that his pupil Hampden was to illustrate with such controversy in the 1830s.

Although this view of church–state relations influenced Newman, as he recorded in his *Apologia pro vita sua*, and thus the Tractarian high-church tradition, it was more than capable of a liberal interpretation. By contemplating the withdrawal of Anglicanism as a state church while allowing that, on limited public interest grounds, governments might interfere with the distribution of church property, Whately recognized the possibility of church reform. Whately never publicly supported disestablishment, but he did support measures which to his mind took the church out of politics. In particular, he became a lifelong advocate of the revival of convocation in exchange for parliament withdrawing its control over spiritual matters such as the prayer book. For a similar reason he advocated Jewish emancipation, since to grant Christians a monopoly of civil rights was a violation of the rule of 'rendering to Caesar the things that are Caesar's'. Likewise, he could contemplate and support payment of Catholic priests out of the consolidated fund because this was not a protestant source of finance, but revenues contributed by both Catholics and protestants, to which the former also had a right to an equitable share. He also supported the grant to the Catholic Maynooth College and advocated the removal of religious tests of entry to national institutions, notably the ancient universities, other than the church itself. He himself succeeded in 1837

in abolishing the religious oath which the members of the Order of St Patrick had to swear.

In 1829 Whately succeeded his former pupil, Senior, as Drummond professor of political economy. This provided him with a further opportunity to Christianize secular teaching and ensure that this branch of knowledge remained in the hands of the advocates of 'social order'. He seized upon the *Introductory Lectures* (1831) as a means of extending Paley's *Natural Theology* to the 'body politic'. This willingness to engage with secularizing thought, unremarkable earlier in the century, now distinguished him from high-churchmen, who increasingly regarded such encounters as a form of contagion rather than inoculation. His strategy was twofold. His first objective was to limit the scope of the science of political economy in order to present it as a neutral professional discipline. Accordingly, his preferred name for the subject was the more technical 'catallactics', or the science of exchanges, since it was not a science of happiness: it could assist a statesman in the decisions he had to take, but was no substitute for them. For the same reason it did not trespass on scriptural territory: the Bible taught religious and moral truths which political economy did not purport to teach, and thus the two areas of instruction were mutually exclusive. Secondly, he sought to show that the study of political economy provided further evidence of 'a wise Providence'. In his account, man emerged from a savage state characterized by indolence and want of forethought as a result of a miraculous revelation. The desire for wealth and emulation, combined with the division of labour (a principle derived from Genesis) and security of property, led to the advancement of civilization. As economic progress occurred, more would be released from mere mechanical toil and knowledge would advance. The division of labour need not lead to a debasement of the mind: it could be counteracted by education. The Malthusian evil of overpopulation, famine, and death would occur only in the absence of the exercise of human reason. In an age of 'dismal' economics, Whately was an optimist.

This optimism was justified by Whately's scientific method, explained in his *Introductory Lectures*, which owed much to Dugald Stewart, the Scottish philosopher and heir to Adam Smith. According to Whately, a science required both a correct ascertainment of the data from which to reason and a correct process of deduction. Because sciences required induction, they were in principle not capable of the certainty that pure deductive reasoning brought; only mathematics was capable of such certainty. This was a further difference between scientific study and the study of the scriptures since scriptural fact was, by virtue of being revealed fact, necessarily true. No scientific fact, dependent on human and thus fallible observation, could possess that degree of certainty. However, political economy, unlike other sciences, depended on few facts and these were in the range of everyone's observation. This being so, assuming the correct deductive process was applied, the conclusions to be drawn from them were akin to mathematical propositions.

Whately, however, was not merely concerned with ensuring that members of the ruling élite were not secularized by the new sciences. He also believed that educating the poor was a means of ensuring the continuity of the social order, and not—as his more conservative contemporaries feared—subverting it. In a sermon preached in aid of the national school at Halesworth in 1830, he argued that the desire for education among the poor was so great that it ought not to be left in the hands of anti-Christians. This accorded with the will of God in that as the Bible was intended for the poor as much as the rich, the poor could become acquainted with it only by learning to read. Whately held that public worship and the teaching of the clergy were insufficient, and he became a prolific popularizing author, writing and compiling school textbooks. In this context his two most famous works were his *Easy Lessons on Money Matters for the Use of Young People* (1833), a simplified version of his lectures on political economy, which was circulated by the Society for Promoting Christian Knowledge, translated into many foreign languages (including Maori and Japanese), and was read by the young Stanley Jevons, and his *Introductory Lessons on Christian Evidences* (1838), which, when circulated in Irish national schools, was to become a focus of controversy.

Archbishop of Dublin: the early years In 1831 Earl Grey, the whig prime minister, offered Whately the archbishopric of Dublin, second in the Anglican hierarchy in Ireland to the archbishopric of Armagh (the former was lord primate of Ireland, whereas the latter was lord primate of all Ireland). It had first been offered to the whig bishop of Norwich, Henry Bathurst, who, at some eighty-seven years old, had declined it. Henry Brougham, the lord chancellor, then suggested either Thomas Arnold or Whately. Grey chose the latter, although he had never heard of him; it was rumoured that Grey had extracted a promise from Whately to support the government's proposed Irish national system of education, but this was not, in fact, the case. For his part Whately received the offer at breakfast while staying at Arnold's house at Rugby. He put it in his pocket without remark, walked the garden for an hour, and then told his family. Why he accepted it is a mystery.

Copleston believed it was from a sense of duty, as Whately regarded it as 'a call to the helm of a crazy ship in a storm' (*Life and Correspondence*, 1.110). It was a task for which he was unsuited: his brusque manner was capable of giving offence at a time when diplomacy was required; he had scarcely any pastoral experience; and he was not a partisan whig who could be relied upon to support the government in the Lords. Above all, doctrinally he was out of kilter with the Church of Ireland, then dominated by a high-church evangelicalism. As the author of a work advocating the separation of church and state and a leading exponent of the Noetic view that sabbatarianism rested not on scriptural authority but merely on the tradition of the church, Whately by 1831 had little in common with either high-churchmanship or evangelicalism. This was particularly unfortunate in Dublin, where his predecessor, William Magee, an evangelical, had been responsible for rekindling ecclesiastical conflict with the Catholics

after a number of years of relative peace. Not surprisingly his appointment was greeted with dismay, and rumours circulated charging him with various heresies and secret membership of the Jesuits.

The most pressing problem facing the Church of Ireland in the 1830s was the refusal of the peasantry to pay tithes, which were then the chief income of the ordinary clergy. However, the most pressing problem facing the government as regards the Irish church was its wealth in relation to its size, which prompted Catholic outrage. In 1834 the Anglican population in Ireland was less than that of the diocese of Durham, but it was governed by four archbishops and twenty-two bishops and had notional revenues of some £800,000, three-quarters of which came from tithes paid by more than 6 million Roman Catholics. Ending clergy distress and achieving church reform went hand in hand. Whately played his role in both, although he took the lead in neither.

As regards tithes, Whately first favoured commutation, but by 1836 he favoured their abolition and replacement by a rent-charge to be collected by the landlords. But this was a second-best option. He would have liked the government to purchase tithes for a capital sum which would have been administered by the Irish ecclesiastical commissioners. (As early as 1831 he wanted all church revenues to be administered by an ecclesiastical board.) The government was against such a proposal and Whately had to settle for the imperfect Tithe Rent-Charge Act of 1838. In the meantime, by way of alleviating the distress of the clergy, he worked closely with the parliamentary draftsmen on the 1833 Million Act, which provided £1 million to be lent to the clergy in the absence of tithe payments; he himself gave the profits of several of his books to the relief of the clergy. Whately also took part in discussions with the government over the Irish Church Temporalities Act of 1834, which suppressed eight Irish bishoprics and established the Irish ecclesiastical commission, although the lead was taken by Archbishop Beresford of Armagh. He was one of only two bishops to be loyal to the primate at the time of the bishops' revolt in March 1833, following the introduction of the bill in February, and he spoke, to the whig government's pleasure, in favour of it in the House of Lords.

Whately's principal public role, however, was as the only Irish episcopal supporter of the whig government's national system of education, by which government-financed grants were given to schools offering combined (that is, non-denominational) moral and literary instruction and separate religious instruction. (By contrast the archbishops of Armagh and Tuam and fifteen other bishops in 1832 had signed a petition against the scheme.) Whately, in the absence of the titular head of the board of commissioners, the duke of Leinster, invariably took the chair, and on the board formed an alliance with his Roman Catholic counterpart, Archbishop Daniel Murray, that extended beyond the education system. He refused, for example, to join the Royal Dublin Society because Archbishop Murray had been blackballed. In 1838 the education commissioners published Whately's *Lessons on the*

Truth of Christianity, a modified edition of his *Introductory Lessons* published in England.

Whately also played his part in the Irish administration, acting as *ex officio* lord justice in the absence of the lord lieutenant. However, he was scathing about the Irish government: he wished to see the Irish Office abolished and the country run from London, since only London could guarantee meritocratic government and ensure that patronage was not abused. He was also in favour of the abolition of the lord lieutenancy: this personage, he held, had no duties 'but to preside at a mock court and make after-dinner speeches' (*Life and Correspondence*, 2.393). Consequently, the office was a cheap source of disaffection. Instead he wished to see the queen reside in Dublin for an annual period. Whately was a strong unionist, but less because he saw Ireland as an outpost of a Greater Britain than because he feared that repeal would lead to civil war: there would be a struggle between Catholics and protestants as the former sought to establish their ascendancy, followed by a struggle between the rich and the poor as the poor realized they would not be made any richer by repeal. Anarchy and mutual slaughter would ensue. Likewise, he was sufficiently clear-sighted to view the Church of Ireland less as a native church than a colonial church, similar to the Anglican communion in India.

The 1830s were the years of Whately's greatest political influence: he advised Lord Melbourne on ecclesiastical appointments and he was consulted by Lord Duncannon on Irish matters. In 1835 his threat to resign from the education board was instrumental in ensuring that its grant did not fluctuate with the fortunes of the Church of Ireland, but was paid out of the consolidated fund. However, his influence should not be exaggerated: following the controversy over the appointment in 1836 of Whately's friend Hampden to the regius chair of divinity at Oxford, Melbourne was deterred from appointing other of his nominees. Although he was appointed in 1833 to chair the royal commission on the Irish poor at the suggestion of his friend Senior, the government ditched its conclusions in support of substantial public works programmes to stimulate employment, opting instead for the (cheaper) introduction of the English workhouse system as recommended by George Nicholls, one of the English poor-law commissioners, after a brief visit to Ireland. This left Whately feeling somewhat bitter: he described Nicholls's consideration of the issues as no more than getting 'one bottle of water out of the Liffey and one out of the Shannon' (McDowell, 227). As a result, according to Lord Holland, he was averse to attending the House of Lords and was, 'some said a little lukewarm on any matter affecting the Ministry' (Kriegel, 359).

Whately remained equally singular in other matters. He did not court Irish popularity. He favoured the promotion of theological learning over evangelical enthusiasm: 'true Christianity is a very quiet and deliberate religion' he wrote (*Life and Correspondence*, 2.379). He revived the rite of confirmation which had not been administered in his diocese for many years. He personally examined ordinands, not leaving the task to his chaplains. He sought to found a

separate theological college for clerical education, a scheme which was finally blocked by the whig government in 1839. Although he was one of the founders of the Society for Protecting the Rights of Conscience in Ireland (1850), which provided financial support for former Catholics, he insisted he did not do so in order to encourage protestant converts but to give protection to those excluded from employment on religious grounds. Indeed, he controversially prevented the militant protestant evangelical Revd Tresham Gregg from preaching in Dublin in 1842. He preached against the evangelical beliefs that the cholera epidemic of 1832 and the Irish famine were divine judgments. This did not prevent him from opposing outdoor relief, though, whatever his public views, in private he gave about £8000 in 1846–9 for relief of the poor. His principal solution, however, was a well-organized and vigorous system of emigration and colonization: for him the Irish problem was excess population.

In intellectual matters Whately maintained his enthusiasms, but did not develop them: if new causes were espoused, this was principally because they reflected old concerns. He supported the (in his case gradual) abolition of the slave trade. In 1832 he founded the chair of political economy at Trinity College, Dublin; he was also a founder of the Dublin Statistical Society in 1847 and a decade later presided over the statistical section at the Dublin meeting of the British Association for the Advancement of Science. His agitation against transportation (his influential 1832 pamphlet *Thoughts on Secondary Punishments* led in part to the House of Commons select committee inquiry) was founded on his belief that punishment and effective colonization were contradictory aims. Indeed he was an ardent penal reformer: although favouring the abolition of the death penalty, he also believed that prisoners should know the real meaning of their sentences and was thus a supporter of certain sentences being irremissible. He became an enthusiastic phrenologist: he had a cast of his head made at Oxford in 1831 and submitted it to three phrenologists in all. This was no doubt because he sympathized with, if he did not entirely endorse, George Combe's view of phrenology as the philosophy of the New Testament. It was another example of the compatibility of Christianity with the new sciences, and in particular a 'scientific' demonstration of man's moral faculty, the existence of which Whately asserted in opposition to Paley's moral utilitarianism.

Archbishop of Dublin: the later years As he himself would have been the first to admit, Whately's was not a profound mind: 'I know nothing thoroughly', he remarked in 1818 (*Miscellaneous Remains*, 54). His intellectual skill was in explaining the theoretical principles of subjects: logic, political economy, rhetoric, theology. 'Elementary studies are most to my taste', he declared, 'I resemble one whose trade is to make instruments for others to work with' (ibid., 55). He had little visual sense. If he did not read widely (though he much exaggerated his own lack of reading), neither did he read deeply. As his opportunities for reading declined outside Oxford, so did his appetite for it.

He increasingly stuck to what he knew, tending to be dismissive of new developments. Of Chambers's *Vestiges of Creation* (1844), he wrote that he 'certainly thought it could be improved by being mended' (*Life and Correspondence*, 2.275). He could not, and did not, read the philosopher of science William Whewell. By the mid-1840s he was, in George Combe's description, 'an old man, tall and thin, and is afflicted with some irritability of nervous fibre ... it [is] impossible for him to sit still' (Gibbon, 1.271). Increasingly he spent his time at Redesdale, the house which he took outside Dublin, surrounded by his books and gardening (he was a keen experimenter in propagating new species). If he did not lose his sense of fun in private (one of his favourite pastimes was using a boomerang), in public he increasingly saw his task, as he noted in 1849, as combating the prevailing tendencies of the age.

The first of these was Tractarianism. When he left Oxford in 1831 Whately was still a supporter of Newman: he suggested him as his second choice to take over St Alban Hall. But the controversy over the Irish Church Temporalities Act of 1834, the admission of dissenters to Oxford (Whately was in favour of their admission to the university, but not to colleges that administered religious tests), and over the appointment of Hampden in 1836 to the regius chair of divinity increasingly isolated him from his former university. In 1838 he paid his last visit of any length. And he turned controversialist, publishing in 1841 *The Kingdom of Christ*. This contained an attack on apostolic tradition as the true foundation of the church, as opposed to the scriptures. Whately asserted that the reformers had been scrupulous to distinguish, and not to blend, scripture and tradition. Those who advocated a notion of authoritative tradition erected a double barrier to the pursuit of religious truth. They demanded that a Christian should not only believe the truths found in the Bible, but also a particular account of them. This doctrine Whately named the doctrine of double-reserve, and he accused its supporters of impiety since it created a barrier between man and God. In private he was less temperate: Tractarians were a 'pestilence' and 'unthinking bigots' (*Life and Correspondence*, 1.460; 2.21). He denied Pusey permission to preach in his archdiocese and in later years declined to receive Newman.

Whately also became increasingly out of sorts in Dublin: the 1850s saw the end of the Anglican–Catholic period of relative harmony that Whately had sought to establish with his Catholic counterpart Archbishop Murray. On the one hand, ultramontanism became increasingly dominant in the Irish Catholic church. This became particularly significant in 1852 when, following the death of Archbishop Murray, the leading ultramontanist Paul Cullen was appointed in his place. On the other, popular protestantism, partly in reaction to ultramontanism, intensified. In England it was epitomized by Lord John Russell's *Letter to the Bishop of Durham* of 1850 attacking the pope's establishment of a Catholic hierarchy in England, a letter which Whately considered 'most absurd' (*Life and Correspondence*, 2.194); in Ireland it was represented by a series of protestant missions.

Whately was caught in this crossfire when in 1852 he sought to ensure that his *Scripture Lessons* and *Lessons on the Truth of Christianity*, which were on the Irish education board's list of approved books, were used in all of its model schools as he had believed them to be: he had visited Clonmel model school and found both to be absent. Archbishop Cullen openly attacked both books, in particular the latter as having been compiled for the purpose of giving a united religious instruction. The board gave way to such pressure: the *Lessons on the Truth of Christianity* was removed from the board's list of approved works and it ruled in relation to *Scripture Lessons* that it was not to be used in ordinary school business where any parent objected. Whately resigned from the board, which thus lost the last leading advocate of the Irish mixed system. The incident revealed him to be both dogmatic and out of touch. He had believed that the use of scripture extracts in mixed lessons was important not because they were a substitute for dogmatic religious instruction, but because they were a rational means of leading Catholics to rational religion (in other words, Anglicanism). However, by the 1850s the national system was in effect a denominational system (less than 5 per cent of its schools were under mixed management and three-quarters were under clerical managers, the vast majority of whom were Catholic).

Whately also became alienated from developments in liberal theology. He departed from his liberal friends when they departed, as they increasingly did, from an evidential defence of Christianity, and particularly of Christ's miracles. In the 1830s he had separated from Blanco White, whom he had taken to Dublin as private tutor to his children, when Blanco White embraced transcendental Unitarianism (he did, however, contribute to his pension). A more significant departure was his 1859 attack in the *Quarterly Review* on the former Noetic Baden Powell's *Order of Nature* (1859). (Until her death in 1844, Baden Powell had been married to Whately's wife's sister.) In this work Powell had argued that miracles were facts of faith, but impossibilities of science. Whately accused Powell of having joined the infidel party. Baden Powell returned to the same theme in his contribution to *Essays and Reviews* (1860), which was published between the death of Whately's youngest daughter in March and that of his wife in April. (Powell himself died less than three months after publication.) There he explicitly attacked Whately's *Historic Doubts* as both anachronistic and wrong. Whately's response was simply to repeat his old argument: 'there are some who seem quite unfit to appreciate the *combined* force of several distinct probabilities' (*Miscellaneous Remains*, 201).

It is difficult to escape the conclusion that by the 1850s Whately was increasingly ill at ease in Victorian intellectual life. As he wistfully noted in his last charge in 1863, in preceding generations those who had denied the truth of the scriptures had also been adverse to Christianity, but in the present generation a large proportion of those who professed themselves Christians 'were far more remote from what is commonly understood by the word than the religion of the Jews or of the Mahometans'. This intellectual displacement was accompanied by physical ill health: in 1856 he suffered creeping paralysis of his left arm and leg and his left hand began to shake. By 1860 he was becoming very infirm and by 1861 the palsy had extended to his right hand; in 1863 he developed an ulcer in his right leg. His devotion to homoeopathy led him to refuse to consult the leading Dublin surgeons: in 1862 the Royal College of Surgeons had prohibited its members from applying homoeopathic cures. The disease made rapid progress and he died at Roebuck Hall, his country house outside Dublin, to which he had moved from Redesdale following his wife's death, at 11 a.m. on 8 October 1863. He was buried in St Patrick's Cathedral and Mozart's Requiem was performed at the service; his devoted black dog, Jet, followed him under the hearse to the cathedral.

Assessment Whately did not found a school. Unlike his contemporaries Newman and Arnold he did not have a deep emotional influence on his pupils. Although as archbishop of Dublin it was often alleged that he surrounded himself with a party of like-minded persons, they were not, in fact, promoted as a party. If two of his chaplains became Irish bishops, neither his clergyman son nor son-in-law obtained high ecclesiastical office. Nor did Whately achieve any influence with the Irish protestant upper classes: as Senior remarked, they hated his politics, disliked his political economy, were not favourably impressed by the total absence of pomp, and dreaded his jokes. To the Tractarians, his tactical concessions to liberal church reformers were a betrayal; of his episcopate, the high-church Thomas Mozley caustically remarked that he aimed at nothing and hit it. To the liberals, his Anglican apologetics became indefensible in the light of the development of scientific knowledge. Consequently Whately has best been remembered as a teacher, principally through his writings, of an eclectic collection of major Victorian thinkers: of Newman and his anti-Erastianism, of John Stuart Mill and his *System of Logic*, of Henry Mansel and his Christian agnosticism, and of Senior and his political economy.

That his memory was kept alive at all was due in no small part to the devotions of his daughter Jane *Whately (1822–1893). During his life she was his assistant, notwithstanding that she was determinedly more evangelical in outlook than he was; after his death she was his memorialist. In 1864 she published his *Miscellaneous Remains*, and in the 1870s she edited abridged versions of his anti-Tractarian *The Kingdom of Christ* and his *Errors of Romanism* from 1830. Above all, with the assistance of Herman Merivale, one of Whately's successors as Drummond professor of political economy, she was his biographer. The *Life and Correspondence of Richard Whately, DD*, first published in 1866 with subsequent editions in 1868 and 1875, is still the best account of Whately. Although it observes Victorian pieties in omitting controversy (it does not acknowledge the anonymous *Letters on the Church by an Episcopalian*,

1826), and at times it reads defensively, it is not blind to Whately's defects and idiosyncrasies.

More than a century after his death Whately has come to be appreciated as a major intellectual figure in his own right: historians have increasingly turned their back on the search for the origins of the great mid-Victorian conflicts between science and religion and of the secular social sciences in order to map out an earlier age when it was believed that it was possible to marshall the sciences as auxiliaries in the greater conflict between Christianity and atheism. Whately is now seen as a major exponent of this earlier position: as a consequence his eclectic teachings can be better appreciated as forming a unity. If the turning of the intellectual tide that he hoped to see in 1863 never happened, leaving him socially successful but intellectually anachronistic, it is at least possible to view him in an earlier age when he was both socially successful and intellectually inventive.   RICHARD BRENT

Sources E. J. Whately, *Life and correspondence of Richard Whately, D.D.*, 2 vols. (1866) · *Miscellaneous remains of Archbishop Whately*, ed. E. J. Whately (1864) · P. Corsi, *Science and religion: Baden Powell and the Anglican debate, 1800–1860* (1988) · A. M. C. Waterman, *Revolution, economics and religion: Christian political economy, 1798–1833* (1991) · D. H. Akenson, *The Irish education experiment: the national system of education in the nineteenth century* (1970) · R. Brent, *Liberal Anglican politics: whiggery, religion, and reform, 1830–1841* (1987) · S. G. Checkland, 'The advent of academic economics in England', *Manchester School of Economic and Social Studies*, 19 (1951), 43–70 · P. Corsi, 'The heritage of Dugald Stewart: Oxford philosophy and the method of political economy, 1809–1832', *Nuncius, Annali di Storia della Scienza* [Istituto e Museo di Storia della Scienza di Firenze], 2/2 (1987), 89–144 · R. Brent, 'God's providence: liberal political economy as natural theology at Oxford, 1825–1862', *Public and private doctrine: essays in British history presented to Maurice Cowling*, ed. M. Bentley (1993), 85–107 · H. C. G. Matthew, 'Noetics, Tractarians and reform of the University of Oxford', *History of Universities*, 9 (1990), 195–225 · D. H. Akenson, *The Church of Ireland: ecclesiastical reform and revolution, 1800–1885* (1971) · D. Bowen, *The protestant crusade in Ireland, 1800–70* (1978) · O. Chadwick, *The Victorian church*, 2nd edn, 2 vols. (1970–72) · I. Ellis, *Seven against Christ: a study of 'Essays and reviews'* (1980) · C. Gibbon, *The life of George Combe: author of 'The constitution of man'*, 2 vols. (1878) · B. Hilton, *The age of atonement: the influence of evangelicalism on social and economic thought, 1795–1865* (1988) · D. A. Kerr, *Peel, priests, and politics: Sir Robert Peel's administration and the Roman Catholic church in Ireland, 1841–1846* (1982) · Lord Holland [H. R. V. Fox] and J. Allen, *The Holland House diaries, 1831–1840*, ed. A. D. Kriegel (1977) · R. B. McDowell, *The Irish administration* (1964) · T. Mozley, *Reminiscences, chiefly of Oriel College and the Oxford Movement*, 2 vols. (1882) · J. H. Newman, *Apologia pro vita sua*, ed. M. J. Svaglic (1967) · M. Pattison, *Memoirs*, ed. Mrs Pattison (1885) · W. A. Phillips, ed., *History of the Church of Ireland*, 3 (1933) · J. Tulloch, *Movements of religious thought in Britain during the nineteenth century* (1885) · *Wellesley index* · J. M. Goldstron, 'Richard Whately and political economy in school books, 1833–1880', *Irish Historical Studies*, 15 (1966–7), 131–46 · R. E. McKerrow, 'Richard Whately on the nature of human knowledge in relation to the ideas of his contemporaries', *Journal of the History of Ideas*, 42 (1981), 439–55 · R. E. McKerrow, 'Whately's earliest rhetoric', *Philosophy and Rhetoric*, 11 (1978), 43–58 · P. Mandler, 'Tories and paupers: Christian political economy and the making of the new poor law', *HJ*, 33 (1990), 81–103 · S. Rashid, 'Richard Whately and Christian political economy at Oxford and Dublin', *Journal of the History of Ideas*, 38 (1977), 147–55 · S. Rashid, 'Dugald Stewart, "Baconian" methodology and political economy', *Journal of the History of Ideas*, 46 (1985), 245–57 · *DNB*

Archives LPL, corresp. and papers · Oriel College, Oxford, corresp. and lecture notes | Auckland Public Library, letters to Sir

George Grey · BL, corresp. with Lord Aberdeen, Add. MSS 43250–43251 · BL, corresp. with Caroline Fox, Add. MS 51965 · BL, letters to Macvey Napier, Add. MSS 34613, 34615, 34616, 34623 · BL, corresp. with Sir Robert Peel, Add. MSS 40399, 40411, 40493, 40499 · BL, corresp. with Lord St Germans, Add. MS 43207 · BL, corresp. with Lord Wellesley, Add. MSS 37306–37307 · Lpool RO, letters to Lord Stanley · NL Scot., letters to Alexander Campbell Fraser; corresp. with George Combe · NL Wales, corresp. with Nassau Senior · Oriel College, Oxford, letters to Renn Dickson Hampden; corresp with Edward Hawkins; letters to J. W. Parker · TCD, corresp. with John George Beresford; corresp. with Sir William Hamilton · U. Durham L., letters to second Earl Grey

Likenesses W. Behnes, plaster bust, 1833, Oriel College, Oxford · F. C. Lewis, stipple, 1836 (after W. Bewnes), NG Ire. · G. Sanders, mezzotint, 1853 (after S. C. Smith senior), NG Ire. · G. & E. Dalziel, wood-engraving, 1866 (after S. L.), NG Ire. · T. Farrell, tomb effigy, St Patrick's Cathedral, Dublin · H. Meyer, stipple (after C. Grey), BM, NPG · S. C. Smith, portrait · etching (after S. C. Smith), repro. in Whately, *Life and correspondence* · oils, Oriel College, Oxford · photograph, NPG [*see illus.*]

Wealth at death under £40,000: probate, 21 Dec 1863, *CGPLA Eng. & Wales*

Whately, Thomas (1726–1772), politician and author, was born in December 1726 near Epsom, Surrey, the eldest son of Thomas Whately (*c.*1685–1765), a merchant and director of the Bank of England, and his wife, Mary, the daughter of Joseph Thompson, a wealthy merchant of Hackney, Middlesex. He was the elder brother of the Revd Joseph Whately of Nonsuch Park, Surrey, and William Whately, a banker of Lombard Street, London. A member of the Church of England, he was the uncle of Richard *Whately (1787–1863), archbishop of Dublin. Through his mother, Whately was a descendant of Major Robert Thompson, one of four puritan brothers from Hertfordshire who rose to great wealth and importance during the Commonwealth. Prominent in the settlement of New England, the family became well connected. Whately's grandfather was a cousin of Lord Haversham, while his mother's brother, also named Joseph Thompson, was a lawyer and a dissenter of substantial wealth. Unmarried, the uncle took a great interest in his nephews and left his estate to them. Through the Thompson connection the Whately family also inherited extensive, if disputed, colonial land claims in Pennsylvania and Massachusetts. Their claims helped to generate a family correspondence with Andrew Oliver of Massachusetts, a distant cousin, and Thomas Hutchinson, Oliver's brother-in-law.

After his graduation from Clare College, Cambridge, in 1745, Whately studied at the Middle Temple, London, and was called to the bar in June 1751. Through a family connection, Sir Peter Thompson, he succeeded James West as the recorder of St Albans in 1760. Sir Peter, with West, had represented St Albans in the Commons, and West, a more prominent politician, who had served as secretary to the Treasury from 1746 to 1756, introduced Whately to Lord Bute. Considered an able and rising young man, Whately was brought into the Commons during the election of 1761 for Ludgershall, Wiltshire, which he represented until 1768. His preferment proved rapid. In May 1762 he became George Grenville's private secretary, and, after

Grenville was made first lord of the Treasury in April 1763, in October 1763 was appointed a secretary to the Treasury, a position he shared with Charles Jenkinson.

Whately was charged with the administration's developing colonial policy, and he played a dominant role in the final framing of the American Revenue Act of 1764 and the controversial American Stamp Act of 1765. He ably defended the administration in two publications, *Remarks on the Budget* and the more important *The Regulations Lately Made Concerning the Colonies*, both published in January 1765. He never deviated from his declared opinions, and consequently many Americans in London came to see him as their arch-foe.

When Grenville was dismissed in July 1765, Whately joined him in opposition. From 1765 to 1770 he acted as Grenville's party manager in the Commons, and the extensive correspondence between the two men illustrates well his devotion to Grenville's interest. He was prominent in the opposition to the repeal of the Stamp Act in March 1766, and in October 1766 published a well-received defence of Grenville's motives and policies, *Considerations on the Trade and Finance of the Kingdom*, which was considered so important by the *Gentleman's Magazine* that it was serialized between October and December 1766. Whately's organizational skills were crucial to the Grenvillite party during these years, but following Grenville's unexpected death in November 1770 he gravitated towards the North administration. Attacked by Junius for possessing all the dubious talents of an attorney, he was clearly influenced by Grenville's close friend Lord Suffolk, in whose interest he had represented Castle Rising, Norfolk, since the election of 1768.

Having been appointed a lord of trade in January 1771, Whately exchanged this position for the sinecure of keeper of the king's roads in June 1771, when Lord Suffolk appointed him his under-secretary of state in the northern department. He did not enjoy his return to office for long, for he died unexpectedly, unmarried and intestate, on 26 May 1772. His younger brother William administered his effects, a duty which led him to fight a duel with John Temple, a distant relative of Grenville, over his brother's stolen correspondence with Oliver and Hutchinson. The letters had been given to Benjamin Franklin, who sent them to Massachusetts for publication, an action which discredited Franklin in London and which clouded Whately's own reputation.

Little can be said regarding Whately himself as the vast majority of his existing correspondence concerns political affairs. He was well known in London literary circles, and left unfinished a study of *Macbeth* and *Richard III*, which his brother Joseph Whately published in 1785 as *Remarks on some of the Characters of Shakespeare*. Considered by some as an important influence on the concept of modern gardening, he had published before his death *Observations on Modern Gardening* (1770). Although some disagreed with his taste, the book went through six editions and was translated into French. Thomas Jefferson purchased a copy, was impressed by it, and consulted it while laying out the grounds of Monticello. Whately's lasting monument in the United States remains, however, in Massachusetts. In 1771 his friend Thomas Hutchinson, then governor, named a new township Whately in his honour.

RORY T. CORNISH

Sources I. R. Christie, 'Thomas Whately, 1685–1765', *N&Q*, 237 (1992), 62–4 · E. J. Whately, *Life and correspondence of Richard Whately, D.D.*, 2 vols. (1866) · *Collections of the Massachusetts Historical Society*, 6th ser., 9 (1897) [*The Bowdoin and Temple papers*, vol. 1] · R. T. Cornish, *George Grenville, 1712–1770: a bibliography* (1992) · F. B. Wickwire, 'King's friends, civil servants or politicians', *American Historical Review*, 71 (1965–6), 18–42 · HoP, *Commons* · Venn, *Alum. Cant.* · *GM*, 1st ser., 42 (1772), 247

Archives BL, corresp., Egerton MS 2670 | BL, corresp. with George Grenville, Add. MSS 42084–42087, 57817 · BL, corresp. and papers of George Grenville and Richard, second Earl Temple, Add. MSS 42086–42088 · Hunt. L., letters to Grenville family · Suffolk RO, Ipswich, corresp. with earl of Albemarle

Whately, William (1583–1639), Church of England clergyman and puritan preacher, was born at Banbury, Oxfordshire, on 21 May 1583, the son of Thomas Whately (1550–1637), mercer, alderman, and twice mayor of the town, and his wife, Joyce Knight (d. 1612). He matriculated from Christ's College, Cambridge, in 1598 and graduated BA in 1601. While at Cambridge he frequented the sermons of two of the most renowned puritan preachers at the university, Laurence Chaderton and William Perkins. On 16 November 1602 he married Martha (d. 1641), the daughter of George Hunt, rector of Collingbourne Ducis, Wiltshire, and granddaughter of John Hunt, who had narrowly escaped martyrdom in Mary's reign. Whately was influenced by his father-in-law to pursue a clerical career and with this intention he was incorporated at Oxford at St Edmund Hall in 1602 and proceeded MA in 1604. In 1605 he was appointed curate and lecturer at Banbury and was instituted as vicar in 1610.

Whately's employment at Banbury allowed him to transmit the moderate scholarly puritanism that he had imbibed at Cambridge to an urban parish, which had already acquired a reputation as a puritan enclave. Members of Whately's immediate family had been actively involved in fostering puritanism in Banbury in their capacities as town governors. Thomas Whately and his brother Richard had been instrumental in getting the town's market cross removed in 1600 and Richard Whately had instigated an earlier campaign against maypoles in the parish. William Whately initially encountered some opposition at Banbury and was presented by a fellow curate in 1607 for administering communion to those who refused to kneel, for preaching against ceremonies, for not praying for the bishops, and not reading divine service or administering the sacrament of baptism. He was, however, supported in his ministry by his two brothers-in-law, Robert *Harris (1580/81–1658), rector of Hanwell, and Henry *Scudder (d. 1652), minister at Drayton, who at this stage in their careers met him on a weekly basis to translate and analyse chapters of the Bible.

Whately soon acquired a widespread reputation as a persuasive preacher and he was renowned for his eloquence and scriptural learning. He was involved in a number of local lectures by combination including that at Stratford upon Avon. Under Whately's aegis Banbury became so strongly associated with puritanism that Ben Jonson satirized the Banbury godly in the hypocritical character of Zeal-of-the-Land Busy in *Bartholomew Fair*, first performed in 1614 and published in 1631. After Whately's death Henry Scudder described him in the pulpit as 'both a terrible *Boanerges*, a sonne of Thunder, and also a *Barnabas*, a sonne of sweet consolation' (H. Scudder, 'The life and death of M. Whately', Whately, *Prototypes*, A2v–A3r). Many of the sermons which Whately preached were published and his works on salvation were eagerly received by his contemporaries. *The Redemption of Time* (1606) was printed six times during Whately's lifetime and *The New-Birth, or, A Treatise of Regeneration* (1618) seven times. The famed dissenter Richard Baxter later recalled that in his youth Whately's works were 'very savoury to me: especially his *New Birth*, his *Care-Cloth* and his sermon of *Redeeming Time*' (Whately, *The Redemption of Time*, 1673, introduction by Baxter, A2v). Whately's sermons demonstrate that he espoused the Calvinist belief in predestination and regarded preaching as the 'chief and principal instrument' to guide the elect into the necessary state of godliness (Whately, *New-Birth*, 130).

Whately was also the author of two popular treatises on marriage, *A Bride-Bush* (1617) and *A Care-Cloth* (1624), which offer insights into early modern clerical assumptions about marriage and gender relations. Whately repudiated the first edition of *A Bride-Bush* of 1617 because it was published from notes without his permission. The second edition, which was printed in 1619, was much expanded and may be regarded as the definitive version of this work. It contradicted the first edition by arguing that it was lawful for a man to beat his wife if she had repeatedly and wilfully disobeyed him, an opinion which was at variance with the majority of English clerical authorities at the time. Whately also argued in both editions that divorce and remarriage were allowable for the innocent party on the grounds of adultery or desertion. This accorded with continental reformed practice, but was not accepted in England, and Whately was forced to recant his views on divorce by the high commission in 1621. The final edition of *A Bride-Bush* (1623) includes Whately's two-page disclaimer, although the offending passages had not been removed, according to Whately because of the carelessness of the printer.

Whately's willingness to recant his opinions illustrates his moderate approach to the theological debates of the time and in general he was careful to avoid controversy in his printed works. Whately was able to avoid direct confrontation with church authorities because Banbury was a peculiar jurisdiction and was exempt from episcopal visitation. Meetings of the peculiar court were held in Banbury and Whately himself sometimes acted as the presiding official.

Whately died at Banbury on 10 May 1639 and was buried

four days later. His will included bequests to his wife, Martha, who was named as his executor and their three sons, William, an apothecary, Thomas, a clergyman, and George. Whately's links with other puritan clergy were marked by bequests to Robert Harris and Henry Scudder, and by the gift of his own ring to the aged John Dod, vicar of Fawsley, who had been deprived of his living at Hanwell some thirty years earlier and had helped to smooth the acceptance of both Whately and Harris by their parishioners. Whately's death was widely mourned by the godly, and Brilliana, Lady Harley, was among those who hoped for his recovery during his final illness.

JACQUELINE EALES

Sources B. J. Blankenfeld, 'Puritans in the provinces: Banbury, Oxfordshire, 1554–1660', PhD diss., Yale U., 1985 · A. Beesley, *The history of Banbury* (1841) · W. Whately, *Prototypes, or, The primarie presidents out of the booke of Genesis* (1640) · J. Eales, 'Gender construction in early modern England and the conduct books of William Whately (1583–1639)', *Gender and Christian religion*, ed. R. N. Swanson, SCH, 34 (1998), 163–74 · W. Whately, *The redemption of time* (1673) · will, PRO, PROB 11/180, fols. 298v–299r · *VCH Oxfordshire*, 10.98 · *Letters of the Lady Brilliana Harley*, ed. T. T. Lewis, CS, 58 (1854), 49 · W. D. [W. Durham], *The life and death of … Robert Harris* (1660) · PRO, SP 14/121/7 · Venn, *Alum. Cant.* · J. S. W. Gibson and E. R. C. Brinkworth, eds., *Banbury corporation records: Tudor and Stuart*, Banbury Historical Society, Records section, 15 (1977), 328
Likenesses line engraving, 1647, BM, NPG; repro. in Whately, *Prototypes*, new edn (1647) · engraving, repro. in Whately, *Prototypes*

Whatman, James (1702–1759), paper maker, was born in Loose, near Maidstone, Kent, and baptized there on 4 October 1702, the only son and the youngest in the family of three children of James Whatman (1656–1725), a tanner, and his second wife, Mary (d. 1726), daughter of George Charlton. The Whatman family had been in Kent since the fifteenth century. Whatman inherited the tanyard in Loose on his mother's death, and although he is described as a tanner until 1740, he became involved in paper making in 1733, when he bought Old Mill, Hollingbourne, the site of an old fulling mill, built a new paper mill, and installed Richard Harris. Harris moved to Turkey Mill, on the River Len, east of Maidstone, in 1736, and bought it in 1738, with capital provided by Whatman. He then pulled down the old mill and rebuilt it. It is likely that Harris, after finishing his apprenticeship, had visited Holland to learn new techniques, and that he began to apply these at Hollingbourne, and then at Turkey Mill, installing new machinery, including the 'Engine' (later called the 'Hollander Beater') which was used for turning linen rags into pulp. When Harris died in November 1739, he left Turkey Mill to his widow, Ann (1708–1789), daughter of Thomas and Sarah Carter of Leeds, Kent, and on 7 August 1740 she married James Whatman. He became joint life tenant with her of Turkey Mill, and moved to Turkey Court. They had one son, James Whatman [see below], and one daughter, and Ann had one daughter from her first marriage.

At Turkey Mill, with the new equipment, Whatman very soon began to make high-quality white paper. The first known Whatman watermark dates from December 1740, in *Select Harmony Fourth Collection*, a set of six concertos published by John Walsh. From 1747 many state papers were written on Whatman paper, and it was increasingly used in aristocratic households. Although at first Whatman's reputation was based on the quality of his writing paper, by the 1750s his paper was being used in printed books, and Horace Walpole's Strawberry Hill press printed 500 copies of Lucan's *Pharsalia* on paper marked 'J. W.' in 1758. More importantly Whatman was the first paper maker in Europe to make wove (or vellum) paper. Made by a different process from laid paper, wove paper was smoother, with a more uniform thickness, and although at first it was intended only for fine printed books, by 1800 it had completely replaced laid paper. In 1796 Whatman's son told the American paper maker Joshua Gilpin that his father first made wove paper in 1756, and the earliest known example is in John Baskerville's edition of Virgil's *Bucolica, georgica et Aeneis*, printed in 1757, which contains some pages of wove paper. After more experiments to improve the quality of the paper, Whatman supplied Baskerville with wove paper for his quarto edition of Milton's *Paradise Regained* in 1759, and J. and R. Tonson printed Edward Capell's *Prolusions: or Select Pieces of Ancient Poetry* (1759) on Whatman's wove paper. Whatman died on 29 June 1759 and was buried in Loose church on the same day.

His son, **James Whatman** (1741–1798), was baptized on 25 August 1741 in Boxley, Kent. In June 1759 he was gazetted a lieutenant in the West Kent militia, formed in the face of the threat of a French invasion and disbanded in December 1762. On 2 October 1762—at St Mary's, St Marylebone Road, Middlesex—Whatman married Sarah (1744–1775), eldest daughter of Edward Stanley, secretary to the commissioners of customs and a member of the Society of Antiquaries.

Four days before the wedding Whatman's mother transferred the business to him, and moved to Devon with her daughter. It was already one of the largest paper-making concerns in Kent, and Whatman soon became a leading figure in the industry. As early as 1764 he was chosen by the paper makers of Great Britain to petition the commissioners of the excise about the duties on paper, and in 1767 he served as high sheriff for Kent. When William Hickey visited Turkey Mill in 1768 he wrote of the 'great paper manufacturer, who entertained us in a princely style', and by 1771 Whatman was claiming to make more paper than any other English manufacturer. Like his father he experimented with new techniques, and in 1772 he made his first sheets of 'antiquarian' paper, the largest paper ever made in England, 52 in. x 31 in., for James Basire's copperengraving of 'The Field of the Cloth of Gold'. This paper was soon much in demand from engravers, and he first exported it to the continent in 1775, a significant moment in the history of English paper making, when for the first time English makers rivalled continental ones. By 1778 Whatman's reputation was such that Edward Hasted, in his *History of Kent*, noted that he made the manufacture of writing paper 'to a degree of perfection superior to most in this kingdom' (vol. 2, 132).

Whatman's wife died in July 1775, and on 3 December

1776 he married Susanna (1753–1814), the eldest of the six children of Jacob Bosanquet, a merchant and banker, and a member of a Huguenot family which had arrived in London from Languedoc in 1686. Her notebook on household management was published in the name of Susanna *Whatman in 1952. Their son, James, was born in 1777. The business continued to prosper. Average annual profits between 1781 and 1787 were £4000, and in 1785 Whatman bought a third mill, Poll Mill. He had bought the adjoining estate of Vinters, with 84 acres, in 1783, and after rebuilding the house and converting the land into a park, he moved there in 1787. In 1797 he employed Humphrey Repton to redesign the park, but Whatman died before the alterations could be carried out.

Whatman did not make much wove paper at first, but after Benjamin Franklin had exhibited wove paper in Paris in 1777, inspiring several French makers to try to make their own, Whatman began to develop it again: he told Gilpin that he had brought it into repute in 1778–9. The government first used wove paper for state papers in 1784, at about the time that other English makers began to produce it, and he began to make antiquarian wove paper. Whatman paper was used for public documents in Washington from 1789. A series of classical texts published by T. and T. Payne, printed on yellow wove, included the works of Sallust (1789), four volumes of Tacitus (1790), and Livy's *Histories* (1794) in eight volumes. William Blake used Whatman paper for his illuminated books, including *Songs of Innocence* (1789) and *The Marriage of Heaven and Hell* (1790). Whatman wove paper was used in several large printing projects, including Boydell's edition of Shakespeare (1791–1804), Thomas Macklin's seven-volume edition of the Bible (from 1790), and Bowyer's edition of Hume's *History of England* (from 1794). At the same time he was installing new iron engines in the mills, and experimenting with bleaching.

Despite all this activity Whatman was making less profit in the early 1790s. He had a severe stroke in February 1790, and his profits fell to £181 in 1791. After the outbreak of war with France in February 1793 a number of banks and businesses failed; this, combined with labour unrest and his poor health, led him in October 1793 to initiate the sale of the business for £20,000 to the Hollingworth brothers of Maidstone. The sale was completed in August 1794. He lent his manager William Balston £5000, which enabled him to buy a partnership in the new firm, but he does not seem to have considered giving any share in the business to his sixteen-year-old son. Whatman allowed the new firm to use the 'JWhatman' watermark, and after the Hollingworths left the firm in 1806, W. and R. Balston, makers of high-quality writing and drawing paper, continued to use the Whatman trademark.

Whatman was ill again in 1796, and had an operation in London in July. He died at his home on 17 March 1798, the day on which he made codicils to his will. The cause of his death was never revealed, but it was probably suicide. He was buried at Boxley church on 26 March 1798. His widow lived on at Vinters, handing it over to her son on his marriage in 1811. ANNE PIMLOTT BAKER

Sources J. N. Balston, *The elder James Whatman: England's greatest papermaker*, 2 vols. (1992) · J. N. Balston, *The Whatmans and wove paper* (1998) · T. Balston, *James Whatman father and son* (1957) · R. L. Hills, *Papermaking in Britain, 1488–1988* (1988), 65–79 · R. Jenkins, 'Papermaking in England, 1495–1788', *Links in the history of engineering and technology from Tudor times: the collected papers of Rhys Jenkins* (1936), 155–92 · D. C. Coleman, *The British paper industry, 1495–1860* (1958), 151–5 · A. H. Shorter, *Studies on the history of papermaking in Britain*, ed. R. L. Hills (1993), 216–17, 239–40 · J. Wardrop, 'Mr Whatman, papermaker', *Signature*, 1st ser., 9 (July 1938), 1–18 · T. Balston, *William Balston* (1954) · *IGI* · parish register, Boxley, CKS
Archives CKS, Whatman and Balston archives
Likenesses portrait, *c*.1740, priv. coll.; repro. in Balston, *The elder James Whatman*, pl. 6 · N. Dance, oils, 1762, repro. in Balston, *James Whatman father and son*, facing p. 20 · J. Smart, miniature, 1778, repro. in Balston, *James Whatman father and son*, facing p. 50

Whatman, James (1741–1798). *See under* Whatman, James (1702–1759).

Whatman [*née* Bosanquet], **Susanna** (1753–1814), writer on household management, was born in Hamburg, Germany, on 23 January 1753, the eldest child of the three sons and three daughters (a fourth died young) of Jacob Bosanquet (1713–1767), a director of the East India Company and also of the Levant Company, and his wife, Elizabeth (1725/6–1799), daughter of John Hanbury of Kelmarsh, Northamptonshire. Her Huguenot grandfather, David Bosanquet, had fled France in 1686 and established himself in England as a Turkey merchant.

Nothing is known of Susanna Bosanquet's education, but in September 1775 a visitor to Albyns, her father's country home, 5 miles north of Romford, Essex, was James *Whatman (1741–1798) [*see under* Whatman, James (1702–1759)], the son of a great Kentish papermaker. Whatman and his father are generally reckoned to be inventors of 'wove' paper. His first wife had died earlier that year, leaving him with two daughters to bring up. Susanna married Whatman on 3 December 1776, and gave birth to a son, also called James, two years later.

As mistress of Turkey Court, an elegant house half a mile from Maidstone, Susanna Whatman gave meticulous attention to the supervision of her domestic staff; she embodied her thoughts on the running of her establishment in a manuscript that she first drew up about 1776. A move in 1787 to Vinters, a nearby manor house, led Susanna to revise her domestic memoranda, so as to be in keeping with the demands of a larger establishment. In it she listed the duties of the individual maids, itemizing the regularity, and also the particular manner, in which the rooms and pieces of furniture were to be cleaned. 'The housemaid must be an early riser', she noted, 'because the ground floor should be ready against the family come down stairs' (*Housekeeping Book*, 1956, 19). The cook's weekly schedule was clearly laid down: 'She should bake Wednesdays and Saturdays, clean her Larder and Pantries Mondays and Fridays, and rise Tuesday to wash her own things' (ibid., 250). Likewise, the schedule for the laundry maid included the stipulation that she was to rise early on Tuesdays to undertake the weekly 'wash'.

Many of the instructions were designed to preserve furniture and other valuable objects. Thus care had to be taken that chairs were not knocked, that the plaster on the walls was not cracked, and that the books were not meddled with. However, the latter could be dusted 'as far as a wing of a goose will go' (*Housekeeping Book*, 1956, 20). In these and other dicta, Whatman exemplified the mistress who 'managed her property like a museum curator administering her collection, for the neatness and order of a house were a quintessential feature of genteel economy' (Vickery, 147).

It is likely that Susanna absorbed much of her knowledge of domestic management from her mother. She subsequently passed on her own writings on the subject, contained in a small quarto notebook, to her daughter-in-law (who in turn bequeathed it to the wife of a son). First published in 1952, it appropriately appeared as a National Trust Classic in 1987.

James Whatman had a stroke in 1790 and this caused him to sell the papermaking business; he died on 17 March 1798. His widow remained as mistress of Vinters until her son's marriage in 1811. She spent her final years either in London or at Northaw Cottage, Hertfordshire. Although troubled by ill health, she remained in good spirits, writing to a friend that: 'My trust in providence is unbounded' (*Housekeeping Book*, 1956, 16). She died at Baker Street, London, on 29 November 1814.   ROBERT BROWN

Sources *Susanna Whatman, her housekeeping book*, ed. T. Balston (1952) · *The housekeeping book of Susanna Whatman, 1776–1800*, ed. T. Balston (1956) · T. Balston, *James Whatman, father and son* (1957) · *The housekeeping book of Susanna Whatman, 1776–1800*, ed. C. Hardyment and T. Balston (1987) · A. Vickery, *The gentleman's daughter: women's lives in Georgian England* (1998) · G. L. Lee, *The story of the Bosanquets* (1966)

Likenesses Romney, oils, 1782 · engraving (after Romney), repro. in Balston, ed., *Susanna Whatman*, frontispiece

Whatton, William Robert (1790–1835), surgeon and antiquary, born at Loughborough, Leicestershire, on 17 February 1790, was the son of Henry Whatton and Elizabeth (*née* Watkinson). Whatton was very proud to belong to a family which could trace its descent back more than 900 years. In 1804 he was apprenticed to a surgeon and apothecary, Bernard Maddock of Nottingham. Soon after qualifying as a member of the Royal College of Surgeons, in London, in March 1810, he left for Portugal, where he served as a surgeon in the Peninsular War. He gained wide experience of the treatment of wounds working at the De Graca Hospital, Lisbon.

Following the end of hostilities in 1815 Whatton moved to Manchester, where he was appointed resident surgeon to the Manchester poorhouse. He resigned in 1817 and entered private practice. Whatton was moderately successful and was remembered by one of his pupils as a well-mannered, rather stout gentleman with a dignified military bearing. In 1822 he joined the Manchester Literary and Philosophical Society. Whatton was interested in local history and published in 1828 *The History of the Manchester Grammar School*. His *History of Chetham's Hospital and Library* appeared in 1833. Together these formed the third volume of S. Hibbert-Ware's series, *Foundations in Manchester*. In 1829 Whatton published two pamphlets suggesting

that a university should be established in Manchester as part of the Royal Institution, which had been founded in 1816. Nothing came of the proposal, though a similar scheme was again put forward in 1836 by Henry Longueville Jones.

Whatton married Harriet Sophia Seddon of Eccles in 1822. Their son, Arundel Blount Whatton (1827–1862), became a clergyman. They also had a daughter. Whatton is best remembered as one of the surgeons who attended the politician William Huskisson after an accident at the opening of the Liverpool and Manchester Railway on 15 September 1830. Huskisson was knocked over by a train near Newton-le-Willows, seriously injuring his leg. While on the journey back to Manchester, his condition worsened and his companions stopped the train at Eccles and sent for Whatton and John Ransome, honorary surgeon to the Manchester Infirmary. Had Huskisson been a younger and more robust patient, the surgeons would have undoubtedly amputated the leg. However, they decided that the 60-year-old politician was too weak to undergo such trauma and, later that evening, Huskisson died. Whatton and Ransome were subsequently criticized for not taking more decisive action to save their patient. Both surgeons defended themselves vigorously. Huskisson's wife, Emily, was entirely satisfied that her husband had received the best possible care; she thanked Whatton warmly and presented him with an engraved gold snuffbox.

Three years later Whatton himself was elected honorary surgeon to the infirmary ahead of Joseph Jordan, one of Manchester's leading medical teachers. While on the infirmary staff he published the papers *Spinal and Spino-Ganglial Irritation*, and *An Address to the Pupils of the Manchester Royal Infirmary*, offering advice on a successful career. He performed a number of operations, including a partial amputation of the foot, which he described to the anatomy section of the British Association.

Whatton died suddenly in Manchester on 5 December 1835, aged forty-five, after contracting meningitis. His colleagues were shocked at losing a surgeon of talent at a relatively early stage in his career.   STELLA BUTLER

Sources W. Brockbank, 'William Whatton, 1790–1835', *The honorary medical staff of the Manchester Royal Infirmary, 1830–1948* (1965), 1–4 · J. S. Whatton, *The family of Whatton* (1930), 56–62 · S. M. Ellis, *William Harrison Ainsworth and his friends* (1911) · *DNB*

Archives Bodl. Oxf., letters to S. P. Rigaud · Chetham's Library, Manchester, collections relating to the history of Chetham Hospital and Library · Man. CL, Manchester Archives and Local Studies, corresp.

Likenesses portrait (after earlier portrait), JRL

Wheare, Diagory [Degory] (1573–1647), historian, was born in Berry Court, Jacobstow, Cornwall. Little is known of his family. In his youth he frequented the Cornish puritan circle of Sir Anthony Rous of Halton St Dominick, with whose fourth son, Francis Rous, he formed a lifelong friendship. After his father's death in 1585, the one-year-old John Pym joined the Rous establishment when his mother became Sir Anthony's second wife. Wheare matriculated with Francis Rous at Broadgates Hall, Oxford (later Pembroke College), on 6 July 1593, graduated BA in 1597 and proceeded MA in 1600. In 1599 Pym became a student at Broadgates, and Wheare acted as his tutor. They remained in close touch, as shown by their correspondence and Wheare's signature on a 1614 deed placing Pym's estates in trust.

From 1602 to 1608 Wheare was a fellow of Exeter College, Oxford, resigning to become travelling companion to Grey Brydges, fifth Baron Chandos, a favourite of James I. After returning with Brydges from the Netherlands in 1610 he remained in Chandos's household at Sudeley Castle until the baron's death in 1621. He then took up residence in Gloucester Hall, Oxford (later incorporated in Worcester College), where he became principal in 1626. The hall flourished under his firm administration, and the students were urged to apply themselves to useful knowledge befitting a gentleman.

Throughout his life at Oxford Wheare was an indefatigable contributor of Latin poems to collections issued by the university to mark special occasions such as the accession of James I in 1603, the return of the future Charles I from Spain in 1623, the birth of the future James II in 1633, and Charles I's return from Scotland in 1641. He published tributes to his patron, the celebrated antiquary William Camden, in *Pietas erga benefactores* (1628) and *Parentatio historica* and an account of Gloucester Hall in 1630.

On 19 November 1621 Wheare's friend at Gloucester Hall, the mathematician Thomas Allen, recommended him to Camden when the latter was in the process of endowing the first chair in history at Oxford. He described Wheare as 'a man who, besides his abilities of learning sufficient for such a place, is known to be of good experience (having sometimes travelled), and of very honest and discreet conversation' (Camden, 315). The benefaction was accepted by the university in May 1622, the donor specifying that he wished Wheare to lecture on the epitome of Roman history by Lucius Annaeus Florus. In a letter dated 6 January 1623 Camden stated that the new professor

> should read a civil history, and therein make such observations as might bee most usefull and profitable for the younger students of the University, to direct and instruct them in the knowledge and use of history, antiquity, and times past. (Jones, 175)

For more than twenty years after he began lecturing in 1623 Wheare obeyed Camden's instructions to develop themes from sections of Florus. He deposited the Latin manuscript of many of his lectures in the Bodleian Library in 1645. Occasionally he drew parallels with modern times, and suggested how Roman examples might be followed by statesmen, but, despite his contact with Rous and Pym, he made no specific allusions to contemporary political troubles in Britain. His reputation rests less upon these lectures than upon his Latin manual on how to read and profit from history, which he composed and published at the beginning of his tenure, and revised and expanded in subsequent editions. Two titles were used: *De ratione et methodo legendi historias dissertatio* (1623, 1625, 1628) and *Relectiones hyemales de ratione et methodo legendi*

utrasque historias civiles et ecclesiasticas (1637, 1662, 1684). The 1662 edition contained many additions by Nicholas Horseman. Further changes and additions were made in an English translation by the tory pamphleteer Edmund Bohun, *The Method and Order of Reading both Civil and Ecclesiastical Histories* (1685, 1694, 1698, 1710). A later incumbent of the Camden chair, Henry Dodwell, added a preface to the 1694 English version entitled 'An invitation to gentlemen to acquaint themselves with ancient history'.

The Method and Order was one of the best and last examples of the Renaissance *ars historica*. This popular genre was based on *obiter dicta* on the nature and purpose of history pronounced in classical antiquity and applied by historians then and since. Its practitioners glossed not only the ancient texts but also each other's remarks about them. History was assumed to have both a practical and a moral application indicated by the phrase attributed to Dionysius of Halicarnassus, 'history is philosophy teaching by examples'. The European authors of *artes historicae* differed as to whether the readers should first study the precepts exemplified by history before approaching the subject matter or whether these precepts should be directly inferred from historical example. It was Wheare's achievement to see both sides of this issue, and to attempt to reconcile them. In so doing he displayed remarkable erudition in both classical and Renaissance historians. He was less informed about medieval historians, but this weakness was compensated for by the additions of Horseman and Bohun.

In 1643 Wheare endeavoured to have his son Charles (*b.* 1613) endorsed as his successor in the Camden chair. He does not seem to have played any part in politics at Oxford during the civil war, and was still Camden professor and principal of Gloucester Hall when he died in Oxford on 1 August 1647, leaving a widow and four sons. He was buried in Exeter College chapel. Charles Wheare ran as a candidate for the chair, but was not elected.

J. H. M. SALMON

Sources W. Camden and others, *Viri clarissimi Gulielmi Camdeni et illustrium virorum ad G. Camdenum epistolae*, ed. T. Smith (1691) · D. Wheare, *The method and order of reading both civil and ecclesiastical histories*, trans. E. Bohun (1694) · 'Lucii Annei Flori: Punica publicis praelectionibus illustrata a Degoreo Whear historiarum professore Camdeniano prima', Bodl. Oxf., MS Auct. F. 2. 21 [Wheare's MS lectures] · Wheare's letter-book, Bodl. Oxf., MS Selden Supra 81 · *Degorei Wheari prael. hist. Camdeniani pietas erga benefactores* (1628) · W. H. Allison, 'The first endowed professorship of history and its first incumbent', *American Historical Review*, 27 (1921–2), 733–7 · H. S. Jones, 'The foundation and history of the Camden chair', *Oxoniensia*, 8–9 (1943–4), 169–92 · J. H. M. Salmon, 'Precept, example and truth: Degory Wheare and the *ars historica*', *The historical imagination in early modern Britain*, ed. D. R. Kelley and D. H. Sacks (1997), 11–36 · Wood, *Ath. Oxon.*, new edn · *DNB*
Archives Bodl. Oxf., MSS

Wheare, Sir Kenneth Clinton (1907–1979), constitutional expert, the elder son (the other died in infancy) of Eustace Leonard Wheare, insurance agent, and his wife, Kathleen Frances Kinahan, was born at Warragul, Victoria, Australia, on 26 March 1907. He had one sister. He was educated at Scotch College, Melbourne, and at the University of Melbourne. Wheare entered Oriel College,

Oxford, as a Rhodes scholar in 1929 and obtained a first class in the honours school of philosophy, politics, and economics in 1932. He rapidly thereafter took a leading place in the university's teaching of colonial history and political institutions as lecturer at Christ Church (1934–9), Beit lecturer in colonial history (1935–44), and tutorial fellow of University College (1939–44). In 1934 he married Helen Mary Allen, with whom he had one son. The marriage was dissolved. In 1943 he married Joan, daughter of Thomas Jones Randell, solicitor; they had two sons and two daughters.

In 1944 Wheare was elected to the Gladstone chair of government and public administration and to a fellowship at All Souls College. He was the first holder of the Gladstone chair to come from academic rather than public life and his tenure witnessed an important extension of the systematic study of his subject in the university. Public service in his case followed upon his appointment. He was constitutional adviser to the National Convention of Newfoundland (1946–7) and to the conferences on central African federation (1951, 1952, 1953). He was also chairman of the departmental committee on children and the cinema (1947–50), and a member of the committee on administrative tribunals and inquiries (1955–7) chaired by Sir Oliver (later Lord) Franks.

Wheare's activities in the university itself were extended through his representation of it on Oxford city council (1940–57), his fellowship of Nuffield College (1944–58), and his membership of the hebdomadal council (1947–67). He was elected rector of Exeter College in 1956 and there presided over an important period of expansion and development, both physical and academic. While not altogether sympathetic to the social trends that culminated after his time in the college becoming mixed, in common with nearly all others at Oxford, his relations with the undergraduates themselves were exceptionally warm and confident, and he and Lady Wheare made their lodgings a centre of hospitality for the whole college and for wider circles in the university at large. He gave himself ungrudgingly to the administrative aspects of the college's affairs and was further burdened during his rectorship by university business, culminating in his vice-chancellorship (1964–6), and by the affairs of the Rhodes Trust, of which he was trustee from 1948 to 1977 and chairman from 1962 to 1969. It was thus not surprising that he decided to relinquish the rectorship in 1972, five years before attaining the statutory age limit, so as to return to the life of scholarship at All Souls College, which elected him to a distinguished fellowship in 1973.

The calls upon Wheare's practical services were not, however, at an end. He had served on the University Grants Committee from 1959 to 1963, was a Nuffield trustee from 1966 to 1975, and a member of the governing body of the University of London's School of Oriental and African Studies. But it was the University of Liverpool which elected him to the high office of chancellor—a rare honour for an academic—in 1972. He retained the post until forced to resign it through failing health not long before his death in 1979. Wheare much enjoyed his new association with this great provincial city and was punctilious in fulfilling the duties of his office, although he found the hierarchical aspects of 'redbrick' university life and his enforced distance from junior staff and students less congenial than the more democratic ways of Oxford. An honour he appreciated, arising from his new connection with the north-west, was that of honorary admiral of the Isle of Man herring fishery fleet (1973–5).

During the whole of his career Wheare continued to study and publish in his chosen fields: British government, the institutions of the evolving commonwealth, and comparative institutions, particularly federalism in its various incarnations. His first book, *The Statute of Westminster, 1931* (1933), was superseded by his *The Statute of Westminster and Dominion Status* (1938), and that in turn by *The Constitutional Structure of the Commonwealth* (1960). His other books were *Federal Government* (1946); *Abraham Lincoln and the United States* (1948); *Modern Constitutions* (1951); *Government by Committee* (1955); *Legislatures* (1963); and *Maladministration and its Remedies* (the Hamlyn lectures, 1973). His published lectures included important contributions on the centenary of the Northcote–Trevelyan report and on Walter Bagehot, a political writer with whom he shared a robust and direct approach to the business of government.

Wheare, who was averse to air travel and believed that the place for Oxford professors was Oxford, was never subjected to the total immersion in American 'political science' common among his juniors, nor were its pretensions much to his taste. His own writings combined three principal strands: a respect for the legal and conventional framework of political action in all democratic systems, an understanding of the historical roots of the different Anglo-Saxon polities and institutions, and, above all, an awareness of how people actually behave in the political and administrative context—an awareness solidly based on his own practical experience in getting things done at many levels. It was this combination that enabled him to write the most original of all his books, *Government by Committee*, and to subtitle it, without compunction, *an Essay on the British Constitution*.

For Wheare style was inseparable from content. He did not go in for massive compilations nor for discursive treatments of his themes; he valued brevity and elegance and worked hard and successfully to achieve them both. While devoid of ideological fervour and without overt party commitment, he was in matters political and academic throughout a reforming conservative. It is not out of character that he was engaged in his last years in studying the life and work of an innovating administrator turned statesman, Sir George Cornewall Lewis.

Wheare's contributions to learning were recognized by election to the British Academy in 1952—he was president from 1967 to 1971—and by the award in 1957 of the Oxford degree of DLitt. Honorary doctorates came his way from Columbia, Cambridge, Exeter, Liverpool, and Manchester universities, and he was elected to honorary fellowships at Oxford colleges Exeter, Nuffield, Oriel, University, and Wolfson. For his public services, he was appointed CMG in

1953, was knighted in 1966, and was awarded the queen's jubilee medal in 1977.

A witty speaker, much in demand, he remained, however, a private rather than a public person, enjoying the affection of a close-knit family and of many friends. Never strong in health, his exercise was limited to the sociable pastime of walking. Wheare was a regular churchgoer and his (Anglican) faith helped him to support uncomplainingly the inroads of sickness in his last years. His university sermon on the annual theme of the 'sin of pride' in 1974 will long be remembered by the crowded congregation. In many ways, and not least in some carefully and humorously cultivated foibles, he represented the model of a true Oxford don, as then understood. Wheare died in Oxford on 7 September 1979, and was buried there.

MAX BELOFF

Sources G. Marshall, 'Kenneth Clinton Wheare, 1907–1979', PBA, 67 (1981), 491–507 · private information (2004) · personal knowledge (2004) · CGPLA Eng. & Wales (1980)
Likenesses W. E. Narraway, oils, 1971, Exeter College, Oxford · Elliott & Fry, photograph, repro. in Marshall, 'Kenneth Clinton Wheare, 1907–1979', facing p. 491 · photograph, All Souls Oxf.
Wealth at death £14,199: probate, 3 April 1980, CGPLA Eng. & Wales

Wheatcroft, George Shorrock Ashcombe (1905–1987), university professor, was born on 29 October 1905 in Derby, the eldest of three children, a son and two daughters, of Hubert Ashcombe Wheatcroft, solicitor, and his wife, Jane Eccles, daughter of a Liverpool cotton broker. He was educated at Rugby School and New College, Oxford, taking a third in mathematical moderations in 1924 and a second in jurisprudence in 1926. He qualified as a solicitor in 1929.

Always known as Ash, Wheatcroft had several successful careers. The first was from 1929 to 1951 as a practising solicitor in his father's firm, Corbin, Greener, and Cook, of 52 Bedford Row, London, with which he had been articled. This was interrupted by war service from 1940 to 1945 with the Royal Army Service Corps, during the north African and Italian campaigns, a period which included the task of running the port of Naples for a year. He was twice mentioned in dispatches and was released with the honorary rank of lieutenant-colonel. On returning to practice he specialized in company law and estate duty.

Wheatcroft's second career, from 1951 to 1959, was as master of the Supreme Court (Chancery Division), where he was widely respected by those who appeared before him. Although this would have been a full-time job for most people, he regarded it as a part-time occupation which left him free to write and build up his reputation in taxation. His first book, The Taxation of Gifts and Settlements (1953), might claim to be the first book on tax planning. In 1956 he founded the first scholarly journal on taxation, the British Tax Review, which he edited until 1971, when he became consulting editor. A significant event, from the point of view of his later life, was his teaching of the first university course in England on taxation, at the London School of Economics (LSE) in 1957. In 1959 he founded a tax discussion and dining society, the Addington Society,

the membership of which was limited to sixty, with roughly equal representation from solicitors, barristers, accountants, and economists. His third career, which naturally followed, was as professor of English law at the LSE from 1959 to 1968, during which he specialized in tax law and built up an international reputation. He played a full part in administering the law department, being its convenor, and during this period he also wrote The Law of Income Tax, Surtax and Profits Tax (1962) and, with A. E. W. Park, Wheatcroft on Capital Gains Taxes (1967). His fourth and final career was as a director and vice-chairman of Hambro Life Assurance, later known as Allied Dunbar Assurance. Outside his work, he was an excellent chess player, representing England at Stockholm in 1937 and serving as president of the British Chess Federation, and bridge player.

Wheatcroft's contribution to taxation law was immense. Not only did he teach the first tax course at London University, but he did the same in Oxford and Cambridge, and such courses spread rapidly. In 1972 a survey showed that tax law was taught in thirty-two of the forty-one institutions offering law degrees, and, by the time of Wheatcroft's death, it would have been a matter of comment if any similar institution failed to offer such a course. Perhaps the previous neglect of tax law as a subject for academic study stemmed from its being a statute-based branch of law compared to the traditional judge-made common law, which is the basis of the study of law at universities. Wheatcroft demonstrated that this statutory basis did not imply any lack of principles, and that, on the contrary, the statutory basis was its virtue, particularly for postgraduates with a thorough grounding in other branches of the law, for whom academic tax study formed an excellent start to subsequent tax practice. Certainly attitudes had changed completely by the time of his death. Among his other innovations was the founding of a course to help economists and lawyers understand each other's views on tax law, a subject they were approaching from different points of view. As a tall and solidly built person he made a commanding lecturer, who delighted in difficult problems. He was appointed honorary fellow of the LSE in 1976 and of University College, Buckingham, in 1978; he received the honorary degree of LLD at Buckingham in 1979.

Wheatcroft's writings, which included standard works on income tax, capital gains tax, and corporation tax, together formed the British Tax Encyclopedia published by Sweet and Maxwell (1962, loose-leaf), and he also wrote books on VAT (value added tax), many of them later updated by succeeding authors. He wrote many articles on all aspects of taxation. He was honorary adviser to customs and excise on the introduction of VAT.

In 1930 Wheatcroft married Mildred Susan (1906–1978), daughter of Canon Walter *Lock DD, formerly warden of Keble College, Oxford. They had two sons and a daughter. His wife had a first-class Oxford degree in philosophy, politics, and economics, and worked on management research, and also on economic intelligence at the British embassy in Washington, where she had taken the family during the war. Wheatcroft died in Berkhamsted on 2 December 1987 and was buried at Aston Tirrold near Didcot in Oxfordshire. J. F. AVERY JONES, *rev.*

Sources personal knowledge (1996) · private information (1996) [John Wheatcroft, son] · *CGPLA Eng. & Wales* (1988)

Wealth at death £1,039,512: probate, 22 March 1988, *CGPLA Eng. & Wales*

Wheatcroft, Harry (1898–1977), rose grower, was born on 24 August 1898 at 23 Handel Street, Sneinton, Nottingham, the younger son of George Alfred Wheatcroft (*b.* 1862/3), a journeyman stonemason and builder, and his wife, Sarah Elizabeth Wood. They were dedicated members of the Independent Labour Party, whose leaders visited the modest family home, and on many occasions the young Harry sat on Keir Hardie's knee. Wheatcroft attended schools in Nottingham and also the École Camille Desmoulins at St Quentin, France, where he became fluent in French. After working in a lace factory and a motor firm he was conscripted in 1916, despite being a registered conscientious objector. He was court-martialled for disobedience and sentenced to two years' imprisonment in Wormwood Scrubs. Diagnosed with tuberculosis, however, he was released after serving one year to convalesce at a Quaker health home.

Wheatcroft considered whether to enter politics or join his brother Alfred as a market gardener. The politician James Maxton guided him into horticulture, saying, 'You'll bring beauty into the world. Politics is a very dirty business' (Wheatcroft, *Root of the Matter*, 12). The horticultural firm of Wheatcroft Brothers was established in 1919, with a bicycle as the only means of transport, and in 1920 roses became a speciality. Alfred managed the business and Harry was the salesman, often away looking for custom and attending horticultural shows. This worked well because the two never got on, Alfred being misanthropic and Harry outgoing. In 1927 they introduced the Princess Elizabeth rose to honour the royal baby; it was the first of many public relations successes. For the rest of his career Wheatcroft sought and won media attention. He grew into a striking figure, tall and slender until he filled out in middle age, with a pleasing gruff voice and a gift for witty repartee. He cultivated flowing hair and whiskers, finding them 'more convenient to grow … than to waste valuable time shaving them off' (ibid., 116).

On 15 June 1929 Wheatcroft married Dorothy, known as Doss (1905–1999), the daughter of John Averill, a wealthy Tamworth farmer. She was a gymnast and dietician. Under her influence Wheatcroft became mainly vegetarian and his health improved. They lived at the nursery in Gedling, Nottingham, in a custom-built Gypsy caravan, arousing curiosity when they took it to the shows. In winter Wheatcroft used a motor cycle when seeking wholesale outlets for unsold plants. He visited breeders in Spain and France, utilizing his linguistic skill, and returned with rose varieties for future introduction. Wheatcroft's marketing of some of those plants might suggest that the firm had originated them, but in truth they had minimal success as rose breeders. In 1935 their launch of Herbert Robinson's Phyllis Gold and Christopher Stone with

Harry Wheatcroft (1898–1977), by Lewis Morley, 1960s

unprecedented publicity surprised the British rose world. Such vigorous salesmanship was something new.

On the outbreak of the Second World War Wheatcrofts had 600,000 roses 'about four feet high and in full flower. It appeared there was only one course we could take, which was to destroy our trees and convert the land for food production' (Wheatcroft, *Root of the Matter*, 109). They became instead successful producers of vegetables and breeders of pigs and cattle. After the war Wheatcroft contacted François Meilland of Lyons, whose rose Peace, the sensation of the time, he introduced to Britain in 1948. In 1952 he secured another coup, by introducing Queen Elizabeth from the USA. In 1953 Wheatcrofts sought to register eleven rose names as trade marks, to give them a monopoly over Meilland's creations. In the Chancery Division, 'With his Dundreary whiskers, his mane of black hair, his suit of black-and-white check … the Nottingham rose king made as picturesque a figure this week as the Law Courts have seen' (*News Chronicle*, 28 Nov 1953). He made the judge laugh, lost the case, but reckoned the publicity well worth the £2000 costs.

Wheatcroft displayed brilliant showmanship with two German roses. Super Star, exhibited in London before the name had been agreed, appeared as 'the Great Unnamed Seedling', and he made Fragrant Cloud the talking point of the National Rose Society's autumn show in 1963 by filling a bowl with its wonderfully scented petals. The acquisition of these varieties, with Peace and Queen Elizabeth, are Wheatcroft's enduring achievements, a tribute to his energy, good rose judgement, and entrepreneurial skills.

In 1962, when long-standing strained relationships with his brother came to a head, Wheatcroft joined his sons in a rival firm which bought out the older company to become the Wheatcroft Organization. With capable young family members running the day-to-day business—never his strong suit—Wheatcroft gave his publicity skills free rein. His whiskers and dress became more bizarre. Out of a huge maroon Rolls Royce would appear his tall, gangling figure, clad in a floral shirt with royal-blue trousers flecked with colour, or perhaps in a suit of dogtooth tweed trimmed with tangerine velvet, against which his horn-rimmed spectacles swung wildly from a string. He captivated photographers, the media, and the gardening public. Show reports carried his picture even when his firm's participation had been minimal. He travelled the world, lectured extensively, and wrote books, and his television appearances included a commercial advertising cheese.

During this period Wheatcroft committed a social indiscretion at the Royal Horticultural Society's Chelsea show by staging roses without a shirt on. It has been recounted that the president, Lord Aberconway, approached: 'A hot day, Harry!' 'Indeed, my lord.' 'Tell you what, Harry, if you'll put a shirt on, I'll take my jacket off!' The society honoured him in 1972 with the Victoria medal of honour, and in 1973 he was awarded the Royal National Rose Society's Dean Hole medal.

Wheatcroft's prosperity and enjoyment of life's good things never blunted his sometimes naïve expression of left-wing views. He offended a Texan audience by declaring that America might not be embroiled in the Vietnam combat if more Americans grew roses. Yet on attending the May day parade in Moscow's Red Square, he admiringly described the militarism on display as awe-inspiring. At home he was a quiet, even subdued family man, happy with his five children though with little time to spend with them, for they attended boarding-school, and summer holidays coincided with shows. His wife, Doss, was infuriated by a string of infidelities; he disarmingly shrugged them off, maintaining that yielding to temptation is 'a natural bent, isn't it?' (Wheatcroft, *Root of the Matter*, 41). In the 1960s he named a red rose for his wife, and an appropriately flamboyant red and yellow rose bore his own name in 1972. After suffering a stroke at home in Nottingham, Wheatcroft died peacefully in Nottingham General Hospital on 8 January 1977.

PETER HARKNESS

Sources H. Wheatcroft, *The root of the matter* (1974) · H. Wheatcroft, *In praise of roses* (1970) · J. Harkness, *Roses* (1978) · D. L. Flexman, 'Round the nurseries', *Rose Annual* (1950), 141–2 · H. Wheatcroft, 'An American journey', *Rose Annual* (1954), 145–50 · H. Wheatcroft, 'Francis Meilland', *Rose Annual* (1959), 128–9 · H. Wheatcroft, 'In Jamaica', *Rose Annual* (1960), 63–4 · H. Wheatcroft, 'To the San Diego rose convention', *Rose Annual* (1962), 116–20 · H. Wheatcroft, 'Roses in Russia', *Rose Annual* (1965), 118–21 · C. W. Gregory, 'Harry Wheatcroft, DHM, VMH', *Rose Annual* (1977), 151–2 · *News Chronicle* (28 Nov 1953) · *Tyler Courier-Times-Telegraph* (16 Oct 1966) · newspaper cuttings in two scrapbooks, priv. coll. [C. Wheatcroft] · personal knowledge (2004) · private information (2004) · b. cert. · m. cert. · d. cert.

Archives FILM priv. coll., 'Man of the month', Fordson Newsreel, Ricochet
Likenesses S. Grimm, oils, exh. RA 1952, Nottingham Castle Art Gallery · L. Morley, photograph, 1960–69 [*see illus.*] · A. Gray, bronze sculpture, 1966, priv. coll. · P. Duncan, oils, *c.*1970, priv. coll. · photograph, *c.*1970 · N. Egon, pastel drawing, *c.*1972 · D. Glass, photograph, repro. in *The Times* (*c.*1956)
Wealth at death £60,163: probate, 16 Feb 1977, *CGPLA Eng. & Wales*

Wheatcroft, Leonard (1627–1707), craftsman and author, was born on 1 May 1627 at Ashover, Derbyshire, the eldest of nine children of Leonard Wheatcroft (*d.* 1648), yeoman, and his wife, Anne Harrison (*c.*1605–1693). He worked as a tailor with his father, and after the latter's death taught this trade to four of his brothers. He later claimed to have been a soldier 'in the days of King and Parliament' ('Autobiography', 90) and probably served in the local militia for eight or nine years from 1653. He was parish clerk of Ashover from 1650 to 1663 and again from 1680, when he also became sexton, until about 1703, when his son Titus succeeded him.

On 20 May 1657 Wheatcroft married, after a courtship lasting over two years, Elizabeth Hawley of Winster (*d.* 1689). They had nine children between 1659 and 1679, all of whom save one survived their father. During the early years of his marriage, Wheatcroft's spending outran his income. In 1667–8 he was three times imprisoned for debt and he had to mortgage and sell his house and land over the next few years. His fortunes subsequently improved, but it was not until 1700 that his eldest son, Leonard, bought this property back. During his career Wheatcroft turned his hand to gardening, orchard planting, malting, ale-house keeping, and carpentry, as well as his inherited craft of tailoring. From 1680 onwards he usually combined schoolteaching with his work as parish clerk. He also took shares in some lead mines and was involved in certain 'water works' ('Autobiography', 91–2), probably mine drainage. Wheatcroft lived away from Ashover only during the years 1664–9, when, probably because of financial difficulties, he resided in Bolsover. He nevertheless walked long distances from his home to do work, see sights, attend fairs or wakes, christenings, marriages, and lawsuits, visit relatives, and help place his children in service or apprenticeship. He went to London at least three times.

Wheatcroft was, for a man of his social position, an exceptionally prolific author. He wrote a concise yet vivid and revealing autobiography and composed a considerable amount of verse. His surviving manuscript verse collection 'The Art of Poetry, or, Come ye Gallants Look and Buy, here is Mirth & Melody' also contains a uniquely detailed and colourful account of Wheatcroft's courtship and marriage. Other writings mentioned in his autobiography are an account of his activities as a soldier, a catechism (completed about 1673), 'The memorys recreation' (begun about 1674), and 'The Bright Starre of Love Appearing to Batchelors', designed 'for the pres' ('Autobiography', 87) though not, it seems, published. Despite his staunch protestantism and his authorship of a catechism, Wheatcroft's surviving works bear no imprint of deep spiritual experience. Loyal to his parish and its neighbourhood, he was a sociable and convivial man who wrote with warm appreciation of bell-ringing, hunting, and horse-racing. His compositions include love poems, personal tributes, many in the form of elegies, and occasional verses commemorating important local events. In Wheatcroft's eyes, his writings were 'things of noate' (ibid., 90). The individuals whose virtues he celebrated ranged from his own wife and son to such leaders of local society as his 'very good freind' the former royalist John Milward MP ('Art of Poetry', pt 2, 81), and the duke of Newcastle. His admiration of men's sterling qualities transcended political differences. In 1696 he was invited to Haddon Hall to give some birthday verses to the earl of Rutland, who was 'no little pleased with them' ('Autobiography', 98). His verse, for the most part borrowed, derivative, or homely, thus brought him some local fame. His success in naming the muses and their attributes in a bibulous ale-house contest with a rival poet organized by some gentlemen at Tupton about 1695 was rewarded with a crown of laurel and the nickname of the Black Poet. Wheatcroft died on 1 January 1707 and was buried on 3 January at Ashover. RALPH HOULBROOKE

Sources 'The autobiography of Leonard Wheatcroft of Ashover, 1627–1706', ed. D. Riden, *A seventeenth-century Scarsdale miscellany*, ed. [J. V. Beckett and others], Derbyshire RS, 20 (1993), 71–117 • L. Wheatcroft, 'The art of poetry, or, Come ye gallants look and buy, here is mirth & melody', Derbys. RO, MS PZ 5/1 • C. Kerry, 'Leonard Wheatcroft, of Ashover', *Journal of the Derbyshire Archaeological and Natural History Society*, 18 (1896), 29–80 • *The courtship narrative of Leonard Wheatcroft: Derbyshire yeoman*, ed. G. Parfitt and R. Houlbrooke (1986)

Wheathill, Anne (*fl.* 1584), writer, is known only as the author of *A Handfull of Holesome (though Homelie) Hearbs*, a collection of forty-nine prayers printed in 1584 by Henry Denham, a major printer of religious books in sixteenth-century England. On the title-page and at the end of her preface, she is styled 'gentlewoman', which is all that is known about her social status.

In her preface, recognizing her presumed limitations as a woman, Wheathill counters by asserting her humility and her zeal and claiming that writing the book shows how well she has used her time in her state of virginity. Although she might be merely using her chastity as other female writers had, to justify writing or publishing a book, it seems very likely that she was unmarried. She never writes with a personal, female voice, nor addresses issues specific to women, such as the needs of wives, mothers, and widows. Furthermore, unlike virtually all other general prayer books of the period, her book contains no prayers for women in childbirth. This is probably because she was addressing a general, not just a female, readership, but again, it may be because she was unmarried.

Wheathill was almost certainly a member of the Church of England since Denham is unlikely to have published a book by someone who was not. Her prayers are full of echoes and quotations from the Bible, illustrating the extensive knowledge of both testaments one would expect of a devout protestant. She believes firmly in predestination, repeatedly using the word 'elect' in the book and asserting that salvation comes only from Christ's purchase by his 'precious blood' (Wheathill). She refers to the sacrament of baptism, but never mentions the eucharist or lord's supper. This is consistent with the Calvinist theology of the English church in 1584, so we cannot label her a puritan.

Wheathill organized the forty-nine numbered prayers in *A Handfull of Holesome (though Homelie) Hearbs* not by the usual occasions (times of the day, going to church, marriage, and so on) but according to a highly sophisticated numerological scheme called the 'week-of-weeks', comprising seven groups of seven, reflecting the seven days of creation. Her knowledge of the hexaemeral tradition suggests that she had access to learned works such as Guillaume du Bartas's *La semaine* (1578) and Pico della Mirandola's *Heptaplus* (1489).

COLIN B. ATKINSON and J. B. ATKINSON

Sources A. Wheathill, *A handfull of holesome (though homelie) hearbs, gathered out of the goodlie garden of Gods most holie word, for the common benefit and comfortable exercise of all such as are devoutlie disposed, collected and dedicated to all religious ladies, gentlewomen, and others, by Anne Wheathill, gentlewoman* (1584) • C. B. Atkinson and J. Atkinson, 'Anne Wheathill's *A handfull of holesome (though homelie) hearbs* (1584): the first English gentlewoman's prayer book', *Sixteenth Century Journal*, 27 (1996), 631–44 • C. B. Atkinson and J. Atkinson, 'Numerical patterning in Anne Wheathill's *A handfull of holesome (though homelie) hearbs* (1584)', *Texas Studies in Literature and Language*, 40/1 (1998), 1–25

Wheatley, Benjamin Robert (1819–1884), bibliographer, born in London on 29 September 1819, was the eldest son of Benjamin Wheatley, an auctioneer in Piccadilly. His half-brother Henry Benjamin *Wheatley was a well-known historian. Wheatley was educated at King's College School, London, and after leaving, at the age of just seventeen, he prepared a catalogue for his father of the twelfth part of the huge library of the bibliophile Richard Heber, which was published in 1841.

Wheatley became a professional cataloguer and indexer, highly productive, accurate, and organized. He was judicious in the classification and arrangement of works, modifying the essentially pragmatic Paris system of classification to suit the character of the library in which he was working: his principles were explained in a paper entitled 'Desultory thoughts on the arrangement of a private library', which appeared in 1878 in the *Library Journal*. In 1843 he catalogued a portion of the library of the Athenaeum, under the supervision of C. J. Stewart, the bookseller. In 1844 he catalogued the library of Charles Shaw-Lefevre (afterwards Viscount Eversley) at Heckfield in Hampshire, and in 1845 the remains of the library at Hafod in Cardiganshire collected by Thomas Johnes, the translator of Froissart. In the same year he catalogued the library of the Geological Society, and in 1846 that of the numismatist Charles Richard Fox in Addison Road, Kensington, and the collection of the Mancunian Jacobite John Byrom at Kersal Cell (published 1848). During his stay at Manchester he made the acquaintance of the lawyer and antiquary James Crossley and of other literary figures.

Between 1847 and 1850 Wheatley catalogued, among others, the libraries of the marquess of Lansdowne at Bowood in Wiltshire, and in Lansdowne House, Berkeley Square, of the Royal College of Physicians, and of the Army and Navy Club.

From 1850 to 1851 Wheatley was engaged in compiling an index of subjects to supplement the catalogue of authors at the Athenaeum library; it was printed in 1851 and served as a model for several subsequent indexes. In 1852 he catalogued the libraries of the Travellers' and the Oxford and Cambridge clubs, and in 1853 that of the United Service Club and the Dugald Stewart collection, bequeathed to the club by his son Colonel Matthew Stewart. In subsequent years Wheatley catalogued various other libraries, including that of the privy council office and that of Lady Charlotte Guest at Canford Manor, Dorset. In 1854 he made an index to the first fifteen volumes of the Statistical Society's *Journal*; he continued to make the indexes of the annual volumes until his death.

In 1855 Wheatley was appointed resident librarian of the Royal Medical and Chirurgical Society, for whom he had worked as early as 1841. From this date he ceased to work on library catalogues, with the exception of one with bibliographical notes which he subsequently prepared for the Royal College of Physicians. In 1857 he completed an index to Thomas Tooke's *History of Prices* (1838–57). He also made two printed catalogues of the Royal Medical and Chirurgical Society's library in 1856 and 1869, and two indexes of subjects in 1860 and 1879; the edition of 1879 was a useful guide to medical literature. In addition, he found time to make a manuscript catalogue of the collection of engraved portraits of medical people in the possession of the society, with short biographies of 900 of the individuals portrayed. He also compiled indexes to the *Transactions* of the Pathological and Clinical societies of London which were published in 1878 and 1880 respectively.

Wheatley was one of the organizing committee of the conference of librarians, and served on the first council. He occasionally acted as vice-president of the Library Association. Its Wheatley medal is awarded annually for the best British index. He also contributed articles on bibliographical subjects to the *Transactions and Proceedings of the Conference of Librarians*, the *Monthly Notes of the Library Association of the United Kingdom*, *The Bibliographer*, and the *Library Journal*. Wheatley was an amateur poet as well as a bibliographer, and printed several of his poems privately, including *Buds of Poesy* (1838). He died in London, unmarried, on 9 January 1884, in his rooms at 53 Berners Street, the premises of the Royal Medical and Chirurgical Society. His sister Maria, herself a spinster, had lived with him for many years. E. I. CARLYLE, *rev.* NILANJANA BANERJI

Sources The Academy (19 Jan 1884), 44–5 · Medical Times and Gazette (19 Jan 1884), 79–80 · The Athenaeum (19 Jan 1884), 88 · H. B. Wheatley, Bibliographical notes on the life of the late Benjamin R. Wheatley (1884) [repr. from The Bibliographer, March 1884] · DNB · CGPLA Eng. & Wales (1884)

Wealth at death £3501 3s. 1d.: probate, 28 Feb 1884, CGPLA Eng. & Wales

Wheatley, Clara Maria. *See* Pope, Clara Maria (*bap.* 1767, *d.* 1838).

Wheatley, Dennis Yates (1897–1977), writer, was born on 8 January 1897 at Brixton, south-west London, the elder child and only son of Albert David Wheatley (*d.* 1927), wine merchant, and his wife, Florence Elizabeth Harriet (*b.* 1874), youngest of the three children of William Yates Baker, ironmaster, of London and his wife, Mary Ann. After an unhappy year at Dulwich College he became a cadet in HMS *Worcester*. At seventeen, after a year learning something of the wine trade in Germany, he worked in his father's shop in the West End of London. During the First World War he was, after determined efforts, commissioned in the Royal Field Artillery and, in spite of ill health, later spent a year on the western front, where he was gassed and invalided home.

For eight years after the war Wheatley played a part in the family business and on 17 June 1922 he married Nancy Madeline Leslie Robinson (*b.* 1898/9), with whom he had a son, Anthony. Wheatley's father died in 1927 and, on inheriting the business, he embarked on a scheme of expansion which led to failure during the 1930 slump. His first marriage also having failed, he married on 7 August 1931 Joan Gwendoline Pelham Burn (*b.* 1895/6), a widow, and the daughter of the Hon. Louis Johnstone; it was she who urged him to take up writing.

The Forbidden Territory (1933) had immediate success, assisted by vigorous promotion on Wheatley's part. Forty years later it had sold a million and a half copies and the quartet of characters he had created, headed by the duke de Richleau, continued their adventures in ten subsequent books. Wheatley's course was now set but he determined from the start to extend his range of characters and type of story. *Black August* (1934) introduced Gregory Sallust, who served him for eleven novels over thirty-four years.

Wheatley's reputation rests with *The Devil Rides Out* (1934), in which he successfully combined two genres which were in decline by the early 1930s: the 'shocker' of the First World War and the supernatural tale of the 1920s. By amalgamating these two, using knowledge of black magic rituals learned from acquaintance with Aleister Crowley, by cashing in on Nazi symbolism (Hitler had just come to power), and by appending an 'infamous' author's note about the dangers of dabbling in the supernatural, Wheatley created a uniquely exciting supernatural thriller. This *œuvre* proved so popular that eight novels were based on it and Wheatley came to be regarded as something of an expert in a field of which he knew little except through reading.

Wheatley's early success as a writer of adventure stories was reinforced by a diversion in 1936–9 in the form of 'crime dossiers' (with J. G. Links). The novelty of these books (reproduced in facsimile over forty years later) not only sold them by the hundred thousand: they made the name of Dennis Wheatley celebrated in many countries. During the first two years of the Second World War Wheatley, now with fourteen novels to his credit, wrote a

Dennis Yates Wheatley (1897–1977), by Paul Joyce, 1975

series of papers on various aspects of the war and current affairs. These were circulated to acquaintances in influential positions and resulted, in 1941, in an invitation to join the planning staff responsible for enemy deception. He was commissioned in the Royal Air Force Volunteer Reserve (his third service) and for four years his fertile imagination was given full rein. He also became privy to a great deal of secret information of which he could make no direct use when he returned to writing. He therefore began, with *The Launching of Roger Brooke* (1947), a series of twelve novels set in the period 1785–1815 and so free from any restraints. Many years later he was able to tell the story of his war years in *The Deception Planners* (1980), which was published posthumously, following three volumes of memoirs.

Although unable to compete with the more violent and erotic thrillers which became fashionable after the Second World War, Wheatley's books found new readers with the mass consumption of paperbacks during the 1960s and early 1970s. In 1968 *The Devil Rides Out* was filmed (Seven Arts–Hammer Films joint production) starring Christopher Lee and Charles Gray, but Wheatley was disappointed with the result. More catastrophically, the reinvention of the supernatural horror thriller by Peter Blatty (*The Exorcist*), Stephen King (*Carrie*), and James Herbert (*The Rats*) and the subsequent films of both Blatty's and King's work relegated Wheatley's thrillers to a world which appeared nostalgic and quaint. By contrast, in recent years Wheatley's relationships with Aleister Crowley, Maxwell Knight, and counter-espionage operations have provided the biographical thrills that the fiction alone can no longer support.

Wheatley wrote seventy-five books in his forty-five years as an author, most of which remained in print throughout his life, published under the same imprint. He aged remarkably little physically, his black hair always parted in the middle as in his youth. It was not until 10 November 1977 that he at long last, to use his own words, 'ran out of steam'; he died at his home, 60 Cadogan Square, Chelsea, London.

J. G. LINKS, *rev.* CLIVE BLOOM

Sources personal knowledge (2004) · D. Wheatley, *The time has come: the memoirs of Dennis Wheatley* (1981) · M. Booth, *A magick life: a biography of Aleister Crowley* (2000), 469 · m. certs. · d. certs.
Archives IWM, diary and papers relating to service in France | U. Leeds, letters to Mr and Mrs John Gardiner
Likenesses G. Argent, photograph, 1970, NPG · P. Joyce, photograph, 1975, NPG [*see illus.*]
Wealth at death £77,267: probate, 13 Dec 1977, *CGPLA Eng. & Wales*

Wheatley, Francis (1747–1801), painter, was born in London, the son of a master tailor of Wild Court, Covent Garden. His father first placed him under a neighbour, Daniel Fournier, a drawing-master, and later moved him to the drawing school run by William Shipley, the founder of the Society of Arts, where he received the only regular instruction of his life.

Early career In 1762 and 1763 Wheatley won prizes awarded by the Society of Arts for youths under sixteen who drew the human figure. Instead of formal instruction he appears to have associated with other young men who were apprenticed to leading artists, but he took up his studies again when admitted as one of the Royal Academy's first students on 13 November 1769, applying also to draw at the academy of the Society of Artists on 14 December. He had exhibited for the first time at the Society of Artists in 1765, sending *Portrait of a Gentleman*, and was elected to the society on 4 September 1770; he continued to exhibit there as required for the next seven years, and became a director on 7 March 1774.

Wheatley derived professional advantage from his friendship with John Hamilton Mortimer, a fellow member of the Society of Artists. By copying his drawings and paintings Wheatley is said by his obituarist in the *Gentleman's Magazine* to have 'acquired a style more pure', evident in his portraiture alone, for Mortimer's wiry line is not reflected in Wheatley's drawing style. The commission to paint the *Cascade* scene at Vauxhall Gardens in 1771 was probably due to the influence of Mortimer, who engaged him that same year to assist in painting the ceiling of the saloon at Brocket Hall, Hertfordshire, for Peniston Lamb, Lord Melbourne. Divided into compartments framed in gilt stucco, the decorations were executed in light, gay colours and symbolized Love, Time, and Fecundity, with intermediate frames containing grotesques and arabesques. Wheatley's last known decorative commission was also for Lord Melbourne, for whom Sir William Chambers built a grand town house in Piccadilly; in the finest room—the saloon on the first floor which was finished by 1775—the elaborate ceiling and alcoves were decorated by Giovanni Battista Cipriani and Biago Rebecca and the walls with large inset panels representing landscapes by Wheatley.

For the next ten years Wheatley painted landscapes in both oil and watercolour, exhibiting them regularly at the Society of Artists in London and Dublin and at the Royal Academy. The earliest known, *The Harvest Waggon* (1774; Nottingham Castle Museum and Art Gallery) reflects Gainsborough as his source of inspiration, but he soon discarded such imaginative scenes of nature in favour of the

Francis Wheatley (1747–1801), by William Hamilton, c.1785

landscape views which were the taste of the day. Dutch landscape painting with its wide open skies emphasizing the horizontal plane and its soft yellowish green and russet-brown tones became notable influences in his compositions, of which *The Medway at Rochester* and *View on the Banks of the Medway* (both 1776; Yale U. CBA) foreshadow his more popular placid renderings of places. The figures enlivening his landscapes are often very generalized, a problem he overcame on occasions by enlisting the collaboration of Mortimer, Sawrey Gilpin, and even P. J. de Loutherbourg.

Wheatley's watercolour landscapes, deriving from studies from nature made during sketching tours in the south of England, the Lake District, and later in Ireland, were worked up in the studio into highly finished drawings in pen and ink, lightly tinted in greys, blues, greens, and browns, as for example *View near Ilfracombe* (1778; V&A). They appear to have been faithful portraits of places, sometimes with trees added to balance the composition, and peopled with small figures going about their everyday activities; a number were made to be sold as pairs.

Early in his career Wheatley exhibited small portraits, mostly in the fashionable medium of crayon, none of which has been identified, and soon branched out into small whole lengths in oils. In 1772 he attempted an ambitious theatrical conversation piece, *The Duel*, from *Twelfth Night* (Manchester City Art Galleries), which was praised for its spirit and good likenesses, 'but upon the whole an Effect is wanted' (J. H. Mortimer and T. Jones, *Candid Observations on the Principal Performances now Exhibiting at the New Rooms of the Society of Artists*, 1772). It was from Mortimer that Wheatley learned to silhouette his sitters against a

background of trees or landscape, and he imitated Mortimer's lustrous renderings of silk and satin to great effect, but Wheatley's handling was richer and more fluid, while his detailed rendering of foliage harks back to Gainsborough. The informal small whole-length portraits of the 1770s in which Wheatley gave his sitters a lively air, painting them in bright colours in a landscape setting, for example *Portrait of a Man with a Dog* (Tate collection), *Thomas Grimston* (priv. coll.), and *Lord Spencer Hamilton* (Royal Collection), soon led to commissions for conversation pieces. With his ability to paint a good likeness and to set his gaily dressed sitters before a composition of trees and distant landscape or in front of a portico, Wheatley's family groups were a fashionable formula that he continued to repeat until the late 1780s: *The Browne Family* (c.1779; Yale U. CBA); *Mr and Mrs Richardson* (c.1777; NG Ire.); *Mrs Ralph Winstanley Wood with her Daughters* (1787; Henry E. Huntington Library and Art Gallery, San Marino, California).

Ireland, 1779–1783 By 1778, when Wheatley first exhibited at the Royal Academy, he had built up a good practice and was praised by the critics, but he fell in with extravagant company and was forced to flee not only his creditors but also an irate husband, the artist John Alexander Gresse. In summer 1779 he was in Dublin with Elizabeth Gresse (d. c.1799), whom he passed off as his wife. There Wheatley quickly took advantage of the political excitement generated by the demands for free trade that gave rise to the volunteer movement and painted a large group, *A View of College Green with a Meeting of the Volunteers* (NG Ire.; engraved 1784), which brought him into prominence with the Irish aristocracy. In *The Irish House of Commons* (1780; Leeds City Art Gallery) Wheatley again captured a moment of political fervour when Henry Grattan made a famous speech on the repeal of Poynings' law before a full house and galleries thronged with fashionable crowds; his composition, for all its bright colouring and recognizable likenesses, is one of reportage. The success of these two pictures led in the early 1780s to many commissions from Irish families for large groups and informal conversation pieces both commemorating events and providing a setting for family portraits: examples include *Lord Aldborough on Pomposo, a Review in Belan Park, County Kildare* (1780–81; Waddesdon Manor), *Review of Troops in Phoenix Park by General Sir John Irwin* (1781; NPG), *The Fifth Earl of Carlisle in Phoenix Park* (1781; priv. coll.). Other commissions were half-length and small whole-length single portraits, including *Henry Grattan* (1780; NPG), *Miss Fridiswede Moore* (1782; exh. Sothebys, New York, 22 May 1992).

Wheatley recorded the Irish landscape, particularly the beauty spots around Dublin which were admired for their picturesque and romantic situations, as in his *Ennischerry* (lost; engraving in British Museum), *The Hill of Howth* (c.1782–1783; Southampton Art Gallery), and his views of Dublin Bay, the waterfalls of the River Dargle, and the Liffey. He also made drawings of houses—for example *Malahide Castle* (1778; priv. coll.)—and noted landscape views for engraving in Thomas Milton's *Collection of Select Views* and the *Copperplate Magazine*. In addition he produced lightly tinted watercolours of mountain, sea, and river, some of which he transposed into subject pictures in oil, for example *Salmon Leap at Leixlip with Nymphs Bathing* (1783; Yale U. CBA). His most immediate, and lasting, success was with the watercolour scenes of Irish rustic life, of fairs with tents and whisky-stills, of peasants, Gypsies, and fisherfolk, scenes that he continued to produce until the end of his life. But in spite of commissions for portraits and the profit from his watercolours, Wheatley again fell into debt, and his imposture in passing off Mrs Gresse as his wife was discovered. Dublin no longer being agreeable, he returned to London towards the end of 1783.

Later career Turning to the printsellers for patronage, Wheatley's future long connection with Alderman John Boydell, the publisher and printseller, began with a commission to paint *The Riot in Broad Street* (des.) for engraving. He was one of the first artists to contribute to the *Shakspeare Gallery*, initiated in 1786 by Boydell to encourage history painting by exhibition and engraving. *The Winter's Tale* (1788; Theatre Royal, Drury Lane, London) is a composition of elegant and graceful figures, as were his contributions to Macklin's Poets' Gallery and Bowyer's History of England, also set up to foster history painting. Only Wheatley's scene from *The Comedy of Errors* (1794; Royal Shakespeare Theatre, Stratford upon Avon) is an essay in historical painting in the grand manner.

While Wheatley continued his practice as a portrait painter of single figures and groups, including *Arthur Philip* (1786; NPG) and *The Return from Shooting* (1788; priv. coll.), and produced a large number of fine landscape watercolours, the making of designs for engraving henceforward became the basis for his success and future reputation. His own attempts at working the copperplate, for example *St. Preux and Julia* (1786; watercolour and engraving, BM), being quickly abandoned in favour of professional engravers, Wheatley produced a wide variety of compositions of allegorical figures, of scenes from literature and contemporary poetry, of bourgeois life, as well as fancy pictures reflecting high-flown sentimental subjects in a pastoral–moral vein. Stemming from the new-found sensibility of Jean-Baptiste Greuze and contemporary French printmakers, Wheatley adapted his rural landscapes and rural figures, which were based on direct observation, into softer prettified and elegant scenes of pastoral life. His work in these genres is significant as a mirror of late eighteenth-century taste and sensitivity— recognized by Wheatley himself when he deposited *A Peasant Boy* as his diploma picture on his election to the Royal Academy in 1791. His series of *The Cries of London*, exhibited at the Royal Academy and engraved and published in pairs from 1793, has proved his most lastingly popular work, and found a ready market on the continent.

Marriage and death Few biographical facts are known about Wheatley's career after his return from Ireland. He continued to lead the pleasure-loving life that brought about his final downfall, and was described as 'a handsome man, of elegant manners, and generally a favourite

in genteel company. He understood his art, and spoke with great taste and precision on every branch of it' (A. Chalmers, *Biographical Dictionary*, 1817). Probably in or before 1787 he married Clara Maria Leigh [*see* Pope, Clara Maria (*bap.* 1767, *d.* 1838)], the daughter of Jared *Leigh (1724–1769), a proctor in Doctors' Commons and landscape painter. Clara, who became well known as a flower painter, taught drawing in order to make money and help provide for their children; after Wheatley's death she married the actor and miniature painter Alexander Pope. Wheatley suffered from gout in the 1790s, becoming severely crippled by the end of the decade; this illness affected both his output and his style and his late productions are weak. His last years are recorded in Joseph Farington's *Diary*. They are a wretched story of continuous ill health and debt from 1796 until his death on 28 June 1801. He was buried in the great cemetery of St Marylebone Church, Middlesex, on 2 July.

Wheatley was a proficient artist technically with a fine sense of colour; he recorded eighteenth-century society in a series of accomplished portraits and conversation pieces, while three of his larger compositions are important visual commemorations of major political events of the years 1779 and 1780. He was one of the most talented designers of fancy and genre subjects, his fluent and graceful art images perfectly idealizing the sentiment of his age, unmoved by any of its deeper currents.

MARY WEBSTER

Sources M. Webster, *Francis Wheatley* (1970) • E. Edwards, *Anecdotes of painters* (1808); facs. edn (1970), 268–9 • R. Dossie, *Memoirs of agriculture, and other oeconomical arts*, 3 (1782), 406, 415 • J. Gandon and T. J. Mulvany, eds., *The life of James Gandon* (1846), 206–9 • *GM*, 1st ser., 71 (1801), 765, 857 • Farington, *Diary* • W. Roberts, *F. Wheatley, R.A.* (1910) • S. C. Hutchison, 'The Royal Academy Schools, 1768–1830', *Walpole Society*, 38 (1960–62), 123–91, esp. 135 • D. Lysons, *The environs of London*, 2nd edn, 2/2 (1811), 546–7, 561 • R. D. Altick, *Paintings from books: art and literature in Britain, 1760–1900* (Columbus, OH, 1985)

Likenesses W. Hamilton, pencil and watercolour drawing, *c.*1785, NPG [*see illus.*] • G. Dance, drawing, 1793, RA • H. Singleton, group portrait, oils, 1795 (*The Royal Academicians*, 1793), RA

Wealth at death died deeply in debt: Farington, *Diary* (1800–01)

Wheatley, Henry Benjamin (1838–1917), bibliographer and editor, was born on 2 May 1838 in London, posthumous son of Benjamin Wheatley, an auctioneer, and his wife, Madalina Rosa Hibernia Burdett, *née* Abercromby. Soon orphaned, he was educated within the family, mainly by his brother Benjamin Robert *Wheatley (1819–1884), a bibliographer, who instructed him in booklore and library management. Although Wheatley contributed to his brother's compilations, his first sole work was the *Catalogue of the Board of Trade Library* (1866). From 1861 to 1879 he was clerk to the Royal Society and *de facto* librarian of that institution, preparing its first catalogue of manuscripts. Privately he had also been preparing an index of anonymous literature, the notes for which he passed to Samuel Halkett. From 1881 to 1884 he edited *The Bibliographer*, and after the journal folded, a series entitled the Book-Lover's Library, which included several works of his own on bibliographical subjects. With his brother he was involved in the foundation of the Library Association (later CILIP, the Chartered Institute of Library and Information Professionals) in 1877; he was a council member in its early years, and wrote several works for the association on library management. He also acted as inspector of the Cambridge University Library from 1877 to about 1882.

Wheatley had a strong interest in language and literature; with F. J. Furnivall he was one of the founders and the first secretary of the Early English Text Society. He served as treasurer from 1872 to 1916, and edited several texts for the society. He also read papers to the Philological Society in the 1860s, and published *Anagrams* (1862) and an edition of Levins's *Manipulus vocabularum* (1867). His lexicographical expertise led to *Chronological Notices of the Dictionaries of the English Language* (1867). Active in the New Shakespere Society and chairman of the council of the Shakespeare Association (1914–16), Wheatley edited several sixteenth-century plays. In addition to these pursuits, he was a keen antiquary and topographer: his early topographical works included *Round about Piccadilly and Pall Mall* (1870). Elected a fellow of the Society of Antiquaries in 1875, he contributed heavily between 1880 and 1886 to *The Antiquary* on subjects as various as the Adelphi, Dr Johnson, Cornwall, and precious stones.

In 1879 a career change took Wheatley to the Society of Arts, where he was assistant secretary until his retirement in 1908. He edited the society's *Journal* and carried out much administrative work with Sir Henry Trueman Wood. The society's policy of keeping fingers in many pies, such as the London blue plaque scheme, was very much suited to Wheatley's own *modus operandi*. From the Society of Arts he co-ordinated the Pepys memorial appeal, which culminated in the monument to Samuel Pepys in St Olave, Hart Street. Pepys was the subject of his private scholarship as well as his public work: in 1880 he published *Samuel Pepys and the World he Lived in*, which was later followed in 1893–9 by the fullest edition of the diary before the Latham one. He was also founder and president of the Samuel Pepys Club from 1903 to 1916. Other literary figures to engage his interest included Johnson and Dryden: he was prior of the Johnson Club in 1906–7, and his Dryden collection is now in the Beinecke Library, USA. Wheatley's broad knowledge of seventeenth- and eighteenth-century literature is reflected in the three chapters which he wrote for the *Cambridge History of English Literature* (1912–13).

Wheatley continued to pursue his topographical interests, publishing (among many works on his native city) *London Past and Present* (3 vols., 1891). Although not a member of the London and Middlesex Archaeological Society, he gave talks to it, and was president of the Hampstead Antiquarian and Historical Society (1906–16) and of London Landmarks; he also founded (in 1880) one component of the London Topographical Society, and served as vice-president from 1900 to 1916. In addition he developed an interest in artistic matters: he served as secretary of the applied arts section of the Society of Arts, edited a series of

Handbooks of Practical Art, and probably wrote the obituary of William Morris for the *Journal*. Several of his publications were on bookbindings, of which he assembled an excellent collection, sold at auction in 1918. Portraits, bookplates, and maps were a further source of interest: in 1879 he edited *The Particular Description of England, 1588*, by William Smith.

Wheatley's bibliographical interests did not flag: he was a member of the bibliographical club the Sette of Odd Volumes and served as its president in 1909, and he was also the president of the Bibliographical Society from 1911 to 1916. In 1877 he founded the Index Society, which was plagued by financial problems. In 1891 it amalgamated with the British Record Society's index library, an institution with rather different aims, and it was not until 1957 that an organization embodying Wheatley's ideals came into existence. Few book indexes can be conclusively attributed to Wheatley, but he certainly wrote *What is an Index?* (1878) and *How to Make an Index* (1902), the latter of which has not been superseded; the essay on indexes in the ninth edition of the *Encyclopaedia Britannica* (1881) was also by him.

Handsome, with abundant dark hair and a moustache, Wheatley was an urbane clubman, cheerful and gregarious in manner. He was the friend of London literati such as Richard Garnett, of historians such as G. L. Gomme, and of bibliographers such as Henry Bradshaw and T. J. Wise. On 4 July 1872 he married Louisa Louise (1846/7–1899), daughter of Dr George Robins; they had two sons and three daughters. Having lived at 53 Berners Street in central London in his younger years, Wheatley later resided at several addresses in Hampstead. He died there, at his home, 96 King Henry's Road, on 30 April 1917, and was buried in Highgate cemetery on 4 May. His library was sold on 8–12 April 1918 by Sotheby, Wilkinson, and Hodge.

Any assessment of Wheatley must take account of his prodigious output, much of it anonymous: it included at least twenty-eight works, ninety-seven articles, and twenty-two editions over five decades of work. Despite his great productivity, his writing was not dashed off and his research was usually thorough. His London topographical work and his connection with Pepys ensured his posthumous reputation, but other commemorations also celebrate his life and work. Wheatley was honoured in his lifetime by a DCL from Durham University in 1913, and later in the naming of the Wheatley manuscript, a Middle English religious poem held by the British Library and edited by the Early English Text Society. In 1962 the Library Association, in conjunction with the Society of Indexers, instituted its annual Wheatley medal for a high-quality index.

J. D. Lee

Sources WWW • P. Norman, 'HBW: an appreciation', *London Topographical Society*, 12 (1920), 103–7 • E. K. Green, 'Henry Benjamin Wheatley, DCL, FSA', *The Indexer*, 4/4 (autumn 1965), 115–17 • E. K. Green, 'Henry Benjamin Wheatley, DCL, FSA', *The Indexer*, 5/1 (spring 1966), 35–7 • H. T. Wood, *Journal of the Royal Society of Arts*, 65 (1916–17), 457–8 • *Catalogue of the magnificent library formed by the late H. B. Wheatley* (1918) [sale catalogue, Sothebys, 8–12 April 1918] • E. L. C. Mullins, 'In memoriam HBW', *The Indexer*, 8/2 (Oct 1972), 94–

7 · K. A. Mallaber, 'An early Wheatley catalogue', *The Indexer*, 7/2 (autumn 1970), 42–5 · M. B. Hall, *The library and archives of the Royal Society, 1630–1990* (1992) · W. A. Munford, *Who was who in British librarianship, 1800–1985* (1987) · J. L. Thornton, *A mirror for librarians* (1948) · D. McKitterick, *Cambridge University Library, a history: the eighteenth and nineteenth centuries* (1986) · RSA · m. cert. · *The Times* (2 May 1917) · *IGI* · J. D. Lee, 'Henry B. Wheatley and the theory of indexing', *Anthology for the millennium* (Society of Indexers, 1999), 30–33 · J. D. Lee, 'The father of British indexing: Henry Benjamin Wheatley', *The Indexer*, 23/2 (Oct 2002), 86–91

Archives Athenaeum, London · Bishopsgate Institute, London · BL · CILIP, London · RS · RSA | CUL, letters to Sir George Stokes · LUL, letters to Austin Dobson · U. Edin. L., corresp. with James Halliwell-Phillipps · Yale U., Dryden MSS

Likenesses photograph, 1882, U. Cam. · J. P. Emslie, drawing, *c*.1889, repro. in *Ex Libris Journal*, 8 (1898), p. 97 · J. R. Edis, photograph, 1913

Wealth at death £17,472 6*s.* 10*d.*; excl. library valued at over £3000: *The Times* (7 Aug 1917), 9

Wheatley, John (1869–1930), politician, was born on 19 May 1869 in Bonmahon, co. Waterford, the eldest child of Thomas Wheatley, a labourer, and his wife, Johanna Ryan. In 1876 the family left for Scotland, and John Wheatley grew up at Bargeddie, near Baillieston in Lanarkshire, where his father found work in the expanding local coalfield. Wheatley often recalled the grinding hardship of a childhood spent with his parents and seven brothers and sisters in a single room miner's cottage without either drainage or its own water supply. He attended St Bridget's Catholic Parish School in Baillieston, where the local church and its priests, notably Peter Terken, were a powerful influence upon him. All his life Catholic beliefs would be a point of reference for his political thinking and activism, first in the United Irish League then in the Independent Labour Party.

At the age of eleven, after showing promise at school, Wheatley joined his father as a miner and worked underground for more than twelve years, a formative experience which he described vividly in *Mines, Miners and Misery* (1908). When he was twenty-four he left the mines and worked as a shop assistant and in a public house. On 9 June 1896 he married Mary Meechan (or Meighan; *b.* 1871/2), a domestic servant, the daughter of Bernard Meechan, an Irish railway foreman, then joined his brother Patrick in running a grocery shop in Shettleston, on the eastern edge of Glasgow. The business closed in 1901 and the following year Wheatley secured work collecting advertising copy for the *Glasgow Observer*, a newspaper with a vigorous circulation among Catholics of Irish descent in west and central Scotland.

In 1908 Wheatley set up his own publishing company, which prospered under the name Hoxton and Walsh. It handled regular Catholic church and Labour Party contracts, as well as moving into local newspaper production. This secured a comfortable income for Wheatley who was able to buy a substantial house for his family and to provide education at fee-paying Catholic schools for his children.

Even when he was working arduous shifts as a miner Wheatley continued his education, reading widely and

John Wheatley (1869–1930), by Walter Stoneman, 1924

attending evening classes in Glasgow. He became a forceful speaker and organizer, initially in local branches of the United Irish League which sought to mobilize the immigrant community in Scotland behind the cause of home rule. His reading and work experience, however, drew him to socialism. He joined the Independent Labour Party in 1906, standing for it unsuccessfully as a local council candidate the next year.

In November 1906 Wheatley formed a Catholic Socialist Society, which worked to win Irish votes over to the labour cause as well as to develop a synthesis between recent Catholic social teaching and Labour policy. His active role in the society led him into some polemical clashes with the local clergy but the archdiocese of Glasgow took no action against him over his political views.

In 1910 Wheatley was narrowly elected to a Shettleston seat on the Lanarkshire county council and he held it for Labour in 1912 when Shettleston was incorporated within Glasgow. He became a very active councillor, specializing in housing and pressing the case for council initiatives to build houses for letting at fair rents to working-class tenants. He had already moved on from the politics of Irish nationalism but was not yet a convert to a centralist belief in the British state as an instrument for social advance. He took the view that effective municipal action by socialists could even make the state's role redundant.

In August 1914 Wheatley was one of just two of Labour's nineteen Glasgow councillors to oppose Britain's declaration of war on Germany and he supported the creation of a Glasgow branch of the Union of Democratic Control, which campaigned for a negotiated peace. Working-class patriotism was something he never mocked but he fought hard to prevent it being exploited by wartime profiteers and landlords. In 1915 he took a major role in a rent strike in Glasgow which influenced the government's decision to bring in rent restriction legislation.

Wheatley also opposed conscription and worked closely with the Clyde Workers' Committee, which represented shop stewards from engineering and munitions plants in the Glasgow area. When some of its most militant members were arrested early in 1916 it was to Wheatley that the committee's funds were entrusted. One of these activists, Willie Gallacher, later paid tribute to Wheatley's support in his 1936 memoirs, *Revolt on the Clyde*. Gallacher and others later recalled Wheatley as a bespectacled, smartly dressed, and increasingly corpulent figure, benevolent in manner but with a sharp forensic mind and an incisive speaking style.

By 1918 Wheatley was the chairman of the Labour group on Glasgow council and also chairman of the Scottish Housing Association. He was present in George Square, Glasgow, on 'Red Friday', 31 January 1919, when striking engineering workers were charged by mounted police, and helped arrange the legal defence for some of those arrested. He failed by only seventy-two votes to enter parliament as Labour MP for the Shettleston constituency in the 1918 general election but won the seat four years later, holding it until his death in 1930. As an MP he was subjected to bitter personal attacks by Conservative opponents which led him to sue two of them unsuccessfully in 1927 for allegations about his business affairs.

After entering parliament Wheatley supported the confrontational tactics of the Clydeside group of Labour members and was suspended from the house in June 1923. His formidable skills in debate ensured him a place in the first minority Labour government which Ramsay MacDonald formed in January 1924. Within weeks of becoming minister of health he was at the centre of a major controversy in which he supported left-wing socialist rebels in Poplar in London's East End who wanted to pay out maximum benefit to the needy through the local board of poor-law guardians. He survived controversy of a different kind, when, though hard pressed by birth control campaigners, he declined to authorize contraceptive advice being given by public health authorities. This was the only instance in his career of Catholic church teaching being the deciding factor in a political decision he made.

Wheatley's Housing (Financial Provisions) Act was the only major legislative achievement of the 1924 Labour government. Until its subsidy provisions were repealed by the National Government in 1934, a substantial proportion of all rented local authority housing in Britain was built under its terms and sixty years later there were still people in Scotland who spoke of Wheatley houses. The act was a complex one, bringing together trade unions, building firms, and local authorities in a scheme to tackle a housing shortage which was guaranteed central government funding provided that building standards set by the act were adhered to. The act did little for actual slum clearance but it hugely enhanced Wheatley's reputation despite the loss of a companion measure, the Building Materials Bill, which would have given central government a wide range of controls over supplies of building materials to local councils operating the Housing Act.

Wheatley was aware of the way his legislation's financial implications had alarmed the orthodox Philip Snowden at the Treasury. Once out of office he moved rapidly to a position of opposition to what he saw as the Labour leadership's infirmity of socialist purpose. He espoused the under consumptionist economics of J. A. Hobson and argued for initiatives to revive consumer demand as a way of tackling unemployment. This earned him the admiration of the young Oswald Mosley, though they disagreed over the case for taxation as an instrument of income redistribution, which Wheatley supported. What he had come to see as a 'British Road to Socialism' demanded a strong state controlling prices, profits, wages, and imports in order to run a rejuvenated economy as a single national workshop.

Wheatley's passionate advocacy of the miner's cause in the 1926 general strike and the subsequent protracted lock-out in the coalfields, as well as his identification with the fiercely anti-capitalist Cook-Maxton manifesto of June 1928 made it inevitable that he would remain on Labour's back benches in parliament. The formation of a second Labour government in 1929 widened further the distance between him and his party leaders. He had made clear his rejection of the idea of another minority government and was not invited to serve in it. By this time his opponents within the Independent Labour Party had built up strong majorities against him on its Scottish divisional council. At the party's Scottish conference in January 1930 Wheatley was strongly criticized for his attacks on the government. Though he still wrote and spoke trenchantly in defence of his views and in criticism of the MacDonald government his influence on events was diminishing, though the Independent Labour Party as a British party still supported his basic left position.

Wheatley's health had been poor for some time and he died from a brain haemorrhage at his home, Braehead House, Sandyhills Road, Shettleston, on 12 May 1930. His burial at Glasgow's Dalbeth cemetery was the biggest political funeral the city had seen since that of the revolutionary Marxist John Maclean in 1924. It took place on 15 May and all the political parties were represented.

Wheatley left a sizeable sum as well as a controlling financial interest in Hoxton and Walsh. He was survived by his wife, and by a son and daughter. The son, John, first studied medicine and then qualified in law before entering the family business. The daughter, Elizabeth, became a doctor and had a successful career in England as a schools medical adviser, first in Burnley, Lancashire, and later in London.

Politically, John Wheatley's career embodies the convergence of immigrant Irish nationalism with the aspirations of a Scottish working class feeling its way towards support for an independent political labour movement.

Initially this was a movement which identified itself with Scottish home rule, which Wheatley also supported until in the final years of his life he became convinced that the best way to socialism was to work within the existing British state. His work as a communicator and propagandist would have made him a significant figure irrespective of the part he played on the Whitehall and Westminster stage. His achievement there was a major one even if he ended his life close to political isolation. While without the charisma of James Maxton or John Maclean, he had qualities which some felt gave him the makings of an alternative leader to MacDonald and his death created a gap on the left of the labour movement which was not easy for anyone else to fill. IAN S. WOOD

Sources I. S. Wood, *John Wheatley* (1990) · W. Knox, ed., *Scottish labour leaders, 1918–39: a biographical dictionary* (1984) · S. Gilley, 'Wheatley, John', *DLB*, vol. 7 · D. Howell, *A lost left: three studies in socialism and nationalism* (1986) · I. McLean, *The legend of red Clydeside* (1983) · A. McKinlay and R. J. Morris, eds., *The ILP on Clydeside, 1893–1932* (1991) · R. K. Middlemas, *The Clydesiders: a left-wing struggle for parliamentary power* (1965) · G. Brown, *Maxton* (1986) · J. Hannan, *The life of John Wheatley* (1988) · W. Gallacher, *Revolt on the Clyde: an autobiography* (1936) · R. E. Dowse, *Left in the centre: the independent labour party, 1893–1940* (1966) · T. Gallagher, *Glasgow, the uneasy peace: religious tension in modern Scotland* (1987) · I. G. C. Hutchison, *A political history of Scotland, 1832–1924* (1986) · I. Donnachie, C. Harvie, and I. S. Wood, *Forward! Labour politics in Scotland, 1888–1988* (1989) · E. Wertheimer, *Portrait of the labour party* (1929) · J. Melling, *Rent strikes: people's struggle for housing in West Scotland, 1890–1916* (1983) · D. Russell, *The tamarisk tree*, 3 vols. (1975–85) · *Glasgow Herald* (15–16 May 1930) · private information (2004) · m. cert. · d. cert. · J. J. Smyth, *Labour in Glasgow, 1896–1936: socialism, suffrage, sectarianism* (2000)

Archives NL Scot., papers | PRO, corresp. with Ramsay MacDonald, PRO 30/69/1/211 | FILM BFI NFTVA, news footage

Likenesses Hutchinson & Russell, photograph, c.1924, NPG · W. Stoneman, photograph, 1924, NPG [*see illus.*] · B. Partridge, ink and watercolour, NPG; repro. in *Punch Almanack* (1 Nov 1926) · A. P. F. Ritchie, cigarette card, NPG · photograph, repro. in Wood, *John Wheatley*

Wealth at death £19,230 8s. 2d.: confirmation, 1930, Scotland

Wheatley, John Thomas, Baron Wheatley (1908–1988), politician and judge, was born on 17 January 1908 at 231 Main Street, Shettleston, Glasgow, the third and youngest child of Patrick Wheatley (1875–1937), sometime miner and later publisher, who was born in co. Waterford, and his wife, Janet (1877–1951), a pupil teacher and daughter of Peter Murphy, a labourer who was born in Belfast. The families of both his parents had come to Scotland from Ireland seeking employment. His father was eventually in business as a newspaper proprietor. Wheatley was educated at St Mark's School, Carntyne, St Aloysius College, Glasgow, and the Jesuit boarding-school Mount St Mary's College, Sheffield. He attended Glasgow University, where he graduated MA (1928) and LLB (1930). He served a legal apprenticeship in Glasgow, and in 1932 passed advocate after devilling to John Cameron.

In Glasgow on 5 August 1935 Wheatley married Agnes Nancy (1906–1995), daughter of Samuel Nichol, a joiner from Selkirk then living in Glasgow. Both families were supporters of the labour movement, and from his earliest

John Thomas Wheatley, Baron Wheatley (1908–1988), by Elliott & Fry

days Wheatley was active in politics. In his autobiography he states that, when aged eight, he was given honorary membership of the Shettleston Independent Labour Party (ILP), to which he had been introduced by his uncle, also John Wheatley, later a member of parliament and minister of health in the first Labour administration in 1924. From his schooldays Wheatley was drawn to the law, and it was his ambition to become an advocate. He had been born into a Catholic family, and so it was that throughout his life, he felt strongly about three things: religion, politics, and the law.

Between 1932 and 1939 Wheatley practised as an advocate at the Scottish bar. His was a general practice covering reparation, divorce, and crime. His reparation work was mainly for pursuers. When war broke out in 1939 Wheatley supported the war, and resigned from the ILP, which was a pacifist organization, to join the Labour Party. In those days appointments of prosecuting counsel (advocates-depute) were made on a political basis by the lord advocate of the day, and when the Churchill government was formed in 1940, Wheatley became sheriff court advocate-depute, so beginning a long connection with the crown office. In 1941 he was called up for army service in the Royal Artillery. It was a tradition during wartime that members of the Faculty of Advocates on leave could appear in court in uniform without wig and gown. Before he was commissioned, and while still a lance-bombardier, Wheatley made history as the first non-commissioned officer to appear in court in uniform without wig and gown. He was very proud of having this distinction. During the latter part of his war service he served in the judge advocate-general's department.

While still in uniform Wheatley was adopted as Labour candidate for North Ayrshire and Bute. He fought in the general election of 1945 but was defeated, and under the Labour government became an advocate-depute. This was a part-time salaried appointment, and he continued his practice in the civil courts. In 1946 he lost the Bridgeton by-election for Labour, but in March 1947 he was appointed solicitor-general for Scotland, and later that year he became lord advocate at the early age of thirty-nine. At the by-election caused by the resignation of George Thomson, the previous lord advocate, who had become lord justice clerk, Wheatley became member of parliament for East Edinburgh, a seat he held until his own elevation to the bench seven years later.

As a member of the government from 1947 to 1951 Wheatley was involved in much of the legislation concerning nationalization and the welfare state. As regards Scotland, he was closely involved in legislation which introduced legal aid and advice, and established the Law Society of Scotland. In 1954, with a Conservative government in power, he was appointed to the bench as a senator of the college of justice at the relatively early age of forty-six. In 1972, with another Conservative government in office, he became lord justice clerk. He continued to hold this office until 1985, by which time he was seventy-seven, having been appointed before the introduction of a compulsory retiring age for judges of seventy.

Although not one of the great judges of the twentieth century, Wheatley was a distinguished judge who served Scotland well. He had a sound knowledge of the law, and a strong desire to do justice. Sitting on his own in the outer house or presiding at a trial, he was not an easy judge to appear before because he tended to have preconceived ideas about any case he was hearing; being a strong character, he consciously or subconsciously tried to impose his own views on counsel in the case. However, he was prepared to change these views when addressed by a counsel who was persistent and persuasive. The judgments he delivered were always clear, if at times somewhat wordy.

It was during his thirteen years as lord justice clerk that Wheatley had his greatest influence on the law of Scotland. Again it must be said that the second division of the Court of Session over which he presided was not always a pleasant court in which to appear as counsel. He and his colleagues were not good listeners and interrupted constantly. In the criminal appeal court Wheatley was not comfortable in delivering extempore judgments on the bench; this had the unfortunate consequence that no reason was given for some decisions on appeals which, through pressure of work, had to be disposed of instantaneously. But the court led by Wheatley issued many important decisions, the fairness and soundness of which were never in doubt. As lord justice clerk he had a special part to play in the criminal field, and his guidelines on granting bail are still followed nearly twenty years after

being promulgated. He also set the tone in sentencing. Other judgments by him are often cited in the courts.

Outside the law Wheatley gave notable service to his community. He was chairman both of an inquiry into teaching in Scotland from 1961 to 1963, and of the royal commission of local government in Scotland from 1966 to 1969. In 1970 he was given a life peerage and became Baron Wheatley of Shettleston. In 1971 he conducted an inquiry into crowd safety at sports grounds. He served on many voluntary organizations, including the NSPCC and Age Concern. He was the first chairman of court of Stirling University. He received honorary degrees from Glasgow and Stirling universities.

Wheatley died from cancer on 28 July 1988 at his home, 3 Greenhill Gardens, Edinburgh. In his latter days he was one of the best-known public figures in Scotland, recognized for his religious faith, for his past service in politics, and as a leading judge who was never slow to speak his mind. He published his autobiography in 1987. He was proud of his four sons, his daughter, and his grandchildren. Off the bench he was unpretentious, and despite being a total abstainer, very convivial. He was also a big-hearted man, and he, more than anyone, would have regretted the fact that by attending the Roman Catholic service at Wheatley's funeral in 1988, Lord Mackay of Clashfern, the lord chancellor, was excommunicated by the Free Presbyterian church. DONALD M. ROSS

Sources J. T. Wheatley, *One man's judgement: an autobiography* (1987) · *WW* (1985) · F. J. Grant, ed., *The Faculty of Advocates in Scotland, 1532–1943*, Scottish RS, 145 (1944) · S. P. Walker, *The Faculty of Advocates, 1800–1986* (1987) · *Scots Law Times: News* (16 Sept 1988), 250–51 · private information (2004) [J. Wheatley QC] · d. cert.
Likenesses D. Dunnett, oils, priv. coll. · Elliott & Fry, photograph, NPG [*see illus.*] · oils, Mount St Mary's College, Sheffield
Wealth at death £241,347.83: confirmation, 7 Dec 1988, *CCI*

Wheatley, Paul (1921–1999), geographer, was born in Bisley Old Road, Stroud, Gloucestershire, on 11 October 1921, the only son of Albert Edward Wheatley and Edith Elsie Gould (1885?–1948?). His father originally worked in a walking-stick and umbrella factory but after he was seriously injured in the First World War the family moved to a community for disabled former servicemen established by Earl Haig at Enham in Hampshire. Here, Paul attended the local primary school and Andover grammar school. After the death of his father, the officers of the community arranged for him to attend the Lees School in Cambridge.

In 1939 Wheatley entered King's College, London, then evacuated to the University of Bristol, to read geography. Given the strong emphasis on surveying and cartography, it was natural that when Wheatley entered the Royal Air Force in 1940, he should train as a navigator. He had already been strongly influenced by *The Seven Pillars of Wisdom*, and his understanding of the Arab world was given a new dimension when he was posted to Palestine and north Africa; he then served with 150 bomber squadron and the pathfinder group 205.

After the war, on 3 October 1945, Wheatley married Thelma Norma Bayly (*b.* 1921) and the following year entered the University of Liverpool to continue his geographical studies. Here he found immediate rapport with the newly appointed John Rankin professor of geography, H. C. (later Sir Clifford) Darby. Following graduation in 1949 with a first-class honours degree, he was appointed to an assistant lectureship at University College, London, where his first task was to undertake a contribution on Staffordshire for Darby's *Domesday Geography of England*. His budding interest in China and south-east Asia was nurtured in a department where area studies were being actively promoted.

In 1952 Wheatley was appointed to a lectureship at the University of Malaya (Singapore), where he had an inspiring influence on his colleagues and wrote an acclaimed monograph, *The Golden Khersonese: Studies in the Historical Geography of the Malay Peninsula before AD 1500* (1961). It was the first of four seminal books that developed his thesis on the city as what he believed to be the style centre of the traditional world, controlling the manner and quality of life in the countryside.

Each monograph bore a title as alluring as if it had come out of a poem by James Elroy Flecker (for whose work Wheatley had a lifelong affection). *The Golden Khersonese* was followed by *The Pivot of the Four Quarters* (1971), for which Wheatley devoted himself to the study of classical Chinese. In it he dealt with the origins and character of the ancient Chinese city and developed a highly original and influential theory to explain the worldwide genesis of cities from ceremonial centres. His *From Court to Capital* (1978) researched into the Japanese urban tradition and his *Nagara and Commandary* (1983) into that of south-east Asia. *Malaka* (1983), a two-volume work on the Malay capital from 1400 to 1980 edited with his friend and colleague Kernial Singh Sandhu, proceeded side by side with the monographs. The manuscript of a fifth book, *The places where men pray together: cities in Islamic lands, seventh through the tenth centuries* (2000) had just been completed at the time of his death.

The monographs were written against a variety of backgrounds. From Singapore, where he transformed the department of geography, Wheatley went to the University of California at Berkeley in 1958. There he greatly invigorated the Berkeley tradition of cultural geography, and his interdisciplinary interests made him an ideal chairman of the committee on south-east Asian studies. In 1966 he returned to a chair at University College, London, where his inaugural lecture, entitled 'City as symbol', had a memorable impact on the college community. Five years later he moved to a chair of geography at the University of Chicago, and shortly afterwards was appointed Irving B. Harris professor of comparative urban studies and chairman of the committee on social thought. Here he found his intellectual home, as well as being much appreciated for the civility with which he handled the deliberations of what he spoke of as a 'committee of prima donnas'. In Chicago, too, everything conspired to the personal harmony that made his final years so fruitful—the body in the Middle West, the mind in the Middle East, both in the midst of a devoted family. His first marriage

had ended in an amicable divorce in 1956 and he remained in close contact with the son from that marriage, Julian Karl. On 25 October 1957 he had married Margaret Elsie Ashworth (*b*. 1921), a teacher known as Margo; they had a son, Jonathan.

Wheatley's prose was ornate and Latinate. He hated intellectual parochialism and was unmoved by the tides of disciplinary fashion. When his contemporaries submitted to the quantitative revolution, he stood aside—or learned another language, sought out another manuscript, or simply polished another paragraph. Life for him was an affair with books, not with the latest technology. 'His computer was in his head', Donald Whitcomb, an American colleague, commented in his memorial address. For some, Wheatley was a workaholic, but for him work was a source of pleasure and, as he himself remarked, 'an anodyne for pain'. Wheatley was happiest in a seminar or a tutorial. Oratory was not for him. He could be forceful without being dogmatic, and proceeded by insinuation and suggestion.

Wheatley's distinction was recognized by his election to the American Academy of Arts and Sciences and as a corresponding fellow of the British Academy. Wheatley died on 30 October 1999 at Porter, Indiana, USA, after suffering from cancer. It was his wish that his ashes should be scattered on Inkpen Beacon in Berkshire on the chalk scarplands that had meant so much to him in his youth.

W. R. MEAD

Sources personal knowledge (2004) · memorial addresses, UCL, Paul Wheatley MSS · *The Independent* (22 Dec 1999) · b. cert. · m. cert.
Archives priv. coll., books, MSS, articles, maps

Wheatley [*married name* Peters], **Phillis** (*c.*1753–1784), poet, was born along the banks of the Gambia River, probably of aristocratic African parentage. The slender facial features, small nose, thin lips, and narrow brow rendered in the woodcut portrait used as the frontispiece to her only printed volume most closely resemble those of Africa's Fulani who inhabited the Gambia region by the mid-eighteenth century. She was seven or eight years old (as suggested by the presence of her adult front teeth), when she was sold on the block 'for a trifle' to John and Susanna Wheatley, who insensitively named her after the slave schooner the *Phillis*, which had brought her from Africa to Boston. At this age she had doubtless already been influenced by a syncretistic amalgam of animism, hierophantic solar worship, and Islam practised in that region of the Gambia at the time of her birth. Despite the efforts of her Christian owners to convert her, elements of these beliefs persist throughout her poetry, and solar imagery constitutes the dominant image pattern of her verse.

Wheatley first came to the attention of the British audience with the London publication of her much celebrated elegy on the death of George Whitefield, friend of the Methodist John Wesley and of his Anglican brother Charles, and privy chaplain to the philanthropic Selina Hastings, countess of Huntingdon. Whitefield had died on 30 September 1770 in Newburyport, Massachusetts, just a week after having preached in Boston where he had probably lodged with the Wheatleys, as Susanna was a correspondent with the countess. Almost certainly crossing the Atlantic with news of this famous evangel's passing, variant forms of this elegy were widely circulated in broadside. Briefer and more accessible to the public than Charles Wesley's 536-line elegy on his friend or Thomas Gibbons's Latin epitaph, it soon came to the admiring eyes of the countess, later to be a pivotal player in the evolution of Wheatley's career.

As a slave and a woman, Wheatley would have acquired only with difficulty the learning necessary to compose the sophisticated poetry of her *Poems on Various Subjects* (1773). John Wheatley, nevertheless, claimed that she could read all parts of the King James Bible within sixteen months of her arrival in Boston and that, since that time, she had acquired expertise in Latin. Her brilliant version of the Niobe episode from book VI of Ovid's *Metamorphoses* ably attests her ability; almost doubling Ovid's Latin Wheatley renders 'Niobe in distress …' as a 212-line epyllion or short epic. The biblical tale of David and Goliath she also transforms into an epyllion of 222 lines, and she demonstrates even more extensive knowledge of Greek and Roman classical forms in her composition of several epic hymns, most of which are, significantly, written in celebration of women.

Little is known about how Phillis Wheatley acquired her great learning, although it is possible that Mary Wheatley, John and Susanna's daughter, who was six years older than Phillis, taught her to read the Bible in English. As none of the Wheatley family appears to have known Latin, she must have gone outside the family for this education. It has been suggested, based on the evidence of pervasive verbal parallels between her verse and the poetry of Mather Byles, that he may have acted as her tutor and poetic adviser. Byles, who lived across the street from the Wheatleys and was Harvard-educated, was a once popular poet who had become the Congregational minister of Boston's Old South Church.

When in early 1772 Wheatley tried to assemble a volume of her poetry in Boston, she met an unreceptive audience. Learning of her difficulty, the countess encouraged her to seek a London publisher. Hence began the series of events which brought her in the summer of 1773 to London where she prepared her book for publication by the London printer and acquaintance of the countess, Archibald Bell. This volume, probably subsidized by the countess, was quite different from that she had proposed to the Boston audience. The earlier volume (which never appeared) was to have contained enough poems favourable to the fomenting colonial rebellion that it could have been called a clarion for the revolution. By contrast, the 1773 volume was more muted, including pieces on such aesthetic topics of the time as memory, imagination, and the religious sublime.

While Wheatley herself claimed that her London trip was undertaken on medical advice, her activities there were hardly those of one affected by ill health. In London for only six weeks from 17 June to 26 July, she used this time most efficiently, almost certainly writing 'To Maecenas', one of her most difficult pieces, as an introduction to the volume, preparing the revised edition of *Poems* for a British audience, and touring Westminster Abbey, the British Museum, and the Royal Observatory, among other sights. Although she was not able to meet the countess, who appears to have been ill at the time, she did meet many notable people, such as the earl of Dartmouth, Thomas Gibbons, and Granville Sharp. By Wheatley's own testimony Sharp befriended her, escorting her on tours of London, and there can be no doubt that he informed her that, although still a slave in Boston, she was technically free because of the famous Somerset decision of 1772 which held that 'as soon as any slave sets foot upon the soil of England he becomes free'. Having returned to the colonies in August, Wheatley announces in a letter of 18 October 1773 her Boston manumission; her legal freedom in Boston was, however, not won generously but only 'at the desire of my friends in England'.

As it was Wheatley's success as a writer which brought her to the notice of her British friends, her pen literally freed her. Following the death of Susanna on 3 March 1774, Phillis Wheatley continued to live in the Wheatley mansion until her marriage on 1 April 1778 to John Peters, a free African American who was a grocer and advocate for black rights before the Massachusetts courts. The years after her own manumission find her struggle for freedom now embracing her black brothers and sisters. For example, in a letter dated 11 February 1774, Wheatley eloquently defines liberty for all human beings: '… in every human Breast, God has implanted a Principle, which we call Love of Freedom; it is impatient of Oppression, and pants for Deliverance.' During the American Revolution, in a poem calling for an American victory, she also dares to demand that freedom from the British crown will also result in freedom for 'Afric's blameless race'. Phillis Wheatley died in poverty on 5 December 1784 in Boston from complications of childbirth; all three of her children had died in infancy.

In her own time, Wheatley received many accolades. Her *Poems* was reviewed favourably in London at least nine times before the end of 1773. Voltaire read her work while he was in residence in England, and commented in a 1774 letter that she was the author of 'très-bon vers anglais'. Such renowned personages as Johann F. Blumenbach, John Stedman, Gilbert Imlay, and Thomas Clarkson, praised and quoted her. During the nineteenth century, Wheatley was celebrated by such abolitionists as Henri Grégoire and Frederick Douglass, the latter of whom twice printed the entirety of the *Poems* in his *North Star*. The 1773 volume of *Poems* was reprinted many times in England and America during the later eighteenth and nineteenth centuries, although it appeared less frequently in America in the years following the civil war.

In the past, when considered at all, Wheatley's work was almost universally applied to some sort of socio-anthropological argument against slavery and/or racism. In the last quarter of the twentieth century, however, a revival of interest in her poetry has resulted in more serious critical comment than in all of the two hundred years since her death. Her poetry has been anthologized in surveys of American and world literature, such as the fourth edition of the *Norton Anthology of Poetry*. Once marginalized as a woman and as a black person, Wheatley now occupies a secure place as one of early America's best poets.

JOHN C. SHIELDS

Sources *The collected works of Phillis Wheatley*, ed. J. C. Shields (1988) · W. H. Robinson, *Phillis Wheatley and her writings* (1984) · J. C. Shields, 'Phillis Wheatley', *African American writers*, ed. V. Smith and others (1991), 473–91 · *Style*, 26 (1993), 167–270 [J. C. Shields, guest ed.] [4 articles on Wheatley] · W. H. Robinson, ed., *Critical essays on Phillis Wheatley* (1982) · S. A. O'Neale, 'A slave's subtle war: Phillis Wheatley's use of biblical myth and symbol', *Early American Literature*, 21 (1986), 144–65 · P. M. Richards, 'Phillis Wheatley and literary Americanization', *American Quarterly*, 44/2 (1992), 163–91 · J. C. Shields, 'Phillis Wheatley's use of classicism', *American Literature*, 52 (1980), 97–111 · J. C. Shields, 'Phillis Wheatley and Mather Byles: a study in literary relationship', *College Language Association Journal*, 23 (1980), 377–90 · P. Bennet, 'Phillis Wheatley's vocation and the paradox of the Afric muse', *PMLA*, 113/1 (1998), 64–76 · M. Watson, 'A classic case: Phillis Wheatley and her poetry', *Early American Literature*, 31 (1996), 103–32 · M. A. Isani, '"Gambia on my soul": Africa and the Africans in the writings of Phillis Wheatley', *MELUS*, 6 (1979), 64–72 · M. M. Oddell, 'Memoir', in P. Wheatley, *Poems on various subjects* (1834)
Archives American Antiquarian Society, Worcester, Massachusetts · Boston PL · CAC Cam. · Dartmouth College, Hanover, New Hampshire · Harvard U., Houghton L. · Mass. Hist. Soc. · NA Scot. · NYPL, Schomburg Center for Research in Black Culture · Westminster College, Cambridge, Cheshunt Foundation
Likenesses S. Moorhead?, woodcut, repro. in P. Wheatley, *Poems on various subjects, religious and moral*, 1st edn (1773), frontispiece
Wealth at death destitute: Oddell, 'Memoir'; Robinson, *Phillis Wheatley*

Wheatley, William (*fl.* 1305–1317), schoolmaster and author, first appears about 1305, when he was authorized by the dean and chapter of York Minster to receive holy orders. He seems to have been related to four men with the same surname, two of whom were clergy and two staff of the king's wardrobe. William was ordained acolyte in 1305 by the bishop of Paris, perhaps having gone to that city to study, and was presented by John Droxford, keeper of the wardrobe, to be rector of Sulham, Berkshire, in 1305. In April 1306 he was described as a subdeacon and granted permission to be ordained deacon; in the following September he was licensed to study at Oxford or another English university for three years. By 1309 he had been appointed master of the grammar school of Stamford, Lincolnshire, resigning Sulham, and was promoted by 1316 to be master of the cathedral grammar school at Lincoln; both appointments belonged to the chancellor of Lincoln Cathedral. As it was usual for Lincoln schoolmasters to be masters of arts, Wheatley is likely to have graduated at this level while at Oxford. In 1317 Master William Wheatley was admitted as rector of Yatesbury, Wiltshire, on the resignation of Hugh Wheatley. William was then described as an acolyte, which conflicts with his earlier designation as subdeacon, and his tenure of the rectory is not fully dated; it is not known

when he died, but the next known rector was admitted in 1331.

Wheatley was the author of commentaries on Boethius' *De consolatione philosophiae* and on the pseudo-Boethian *De disciplina scholarium*. The latter was written at Stamford in 1309, while the former (dedicated to Henry Mamesfield, dean of Lincoln, among others) probably dates from his time at Lincoln. The great English famine of 1315–17 prompted him to write two other short works: a tractate *De signis prognosticis future sterilitatis* ('On the signs foretelling future sterility'), and two hymns in honour of St Hugh of Lincoln for an entertainment on Christmas day 1316. Wheatley declared that he wrote the hymns in a year of great dearth and mortality among men and animals, 'intending to comfort himself and others in their misery'. These works, with a letter to Roger Martival, bishop of Salisbury, are preserved in Oxford, New College, MS 264; there are two other extant manuscripts of *De consolatione* and three (a further three are lost) of *De disciplina*. A further commentary, *De questionibus Cratonis*, survives in BL, Arundel MS 52.

NICHOLAS ORME

Sources Emden, *Oxf.*, 3.2030–31 · R. Sharpe, *A handlist of the Latin writers of Great Britain and Ireland before 1540* (1997) · *Registrum Simonis de Gandavo, diocesis Saresbiriensis, AD 1297–1315*, ed. C. T. Flower and M. C. B. Dawes, 2 vols., CYS, 40–41 (1934) · *VCH Lincolnshire*, vol. 2 · Tout, *Admin. hist.*, 6.30, 35 · New College, Oxford, MS 264
Archives BL, Arundel MS 52 · New College, Oxford, MS 264

Wheatly, Charles (1686–1742), Church of England clergyman and liturgical scholar, the son of John Wheatly, a gentleman of London, and his wife, a descendant of Sir Thomas White, founder of St John's College, Oxford, was born on 6 February 1686 in Paternoster Row, London. He was sent to Merchant Taylors' School in 1699 and in 1705 matriculated at St John's College, Oxford, where he was elected a fellow in 1707, graduating BA in 1710 and proceeding MA in 1713. He incorporated at Cambridge in 1728. His tutor was James Knight (1672–1735), later vicar of St Sepulchre's in London: Wheatly maintained that he continued '… his *pupil* to his dying-day.' (*GM*, 1801, 110). He resigned his fellowship in 1716, on his marriage, on 9 August that year, to Mary (*c*.1676–1724), daughter of William Findall of the Clarendon Press, and after her death in 1724 he married Mary, daughter of Daniel Fogg, rector of All Hallows Staining; she survived him. After holding lectureships in London at St Mildred Poultry and St Swithin with St Mary Bothaw, Wheatly was instituted in 1726 to the combined benefices of Brent and Furneux Pelham in Hertfordshire, where he built a new vicarage house and secured augmentation for the livings from Queen Anne's Bounty.

Arguably the most influential liturgical scholar of his generation, Wheatly is best remembered for *The Church of England Man's Companion, or, A Rational Illustration of … the Book of Common Prayer* (1710; 8th edn, 1759; many other edns). This epitomized earlier studies by Hamon L'Estrange, Anthony Sparrow, Thomas Comber, and William Nicholls, and remained the standard work on its subject for over 100 years. Markedly high-church in emphasis, it drew on deep patristic learning to uphold the Church of England's claims to a spiritual commission independent of any reliance upon the State; to assert the indispensable nature of the apostolic succession in the ministry; and to justify the use of external ceremonies in the conduct of public worship. Much of its teaching, particularly in relation to eucharistic theology, was identical to that of 'usager' nonjurors. However, Wheatly rejected Jacobitism, arguing in the *Rational Illustration* and elsewhere in favour of allegiance to the *de facto* powers.

Wheatly was an active writer and controversialist, who maintained a regular correspondence with both conforming high-churchmen, such as Daniel Waterland, and nonjurors like Thomas Brett and Richard Rawlinson. His Moyer lectures for 1733–4 (published in 1738) defended the Nicene and Athanasian creeds as indispensable statements of orthodox Christian belief. A notable opponent of the spread of Methodism, he used an important opportunity at St Paul's in October 1739 to distinguish between the calm spirit of real devotion and '… those high Raptures and *Feelings* of Joy … to … which some modern Enthusiasts pretend.' (Wheatly, *Fifty Sermons*, 1.217). He died of dropsy and asthma on 13 May 1742 at Furneux Pelham, and was buried in the parish church there, where an inscription was placed in his memory. He left several of his books to St John's College, including important annotated editions of R. Hooker's *Ecclesiastical Polity* and the Book of Common Prayer. A collection entitled *Fifty Sermons on Several Subjects and Occasions*, edited by Wheatly's friend John Berriman, with a short biographical note, was published in three volumes in 1746 and reprinted in 1753.   RICHARD SHARP

Sources C. Wheatly, *Fifty sermons on several subjects and occasions*, 3 vols. (1746) [with biographical *Preface* by John Berriman (vol. 1)] · C. Wheatly, *The Church of England man's companion, or, A rational illustration … of the Book of Common Prayer* (1710) [and later edns] · C. Wheatly, *The Nicene and Athanasian creeds … explained and confirmed…* (1738) · *GM*, 1st ser., 12 (1742), 275 · *GM*, 1st ser., 71 (1801), 109–11 · Clutterbuck, *History … of Hertfordshire* (1827), 3.449, 455, 457 · W. H. Hutton, *History of St. John's College* (1898), 239 · Foster, *Alum. Oxon.* · Venn, *Alum. Cant.* · *Remarks and collections of Thomas Hearne*, ed. C. E. Doble and others, 11 vols., OHS, 2, 7, 13, 34, 42–3, 48, 50, 65, 67, 72 (1885–1921)
Archives Bodl. Oxf., letters to Thomas Brett · Bodl. Oxf., letters to Richard Rawlinson

Wheatstone, Sir Charles (1802–1875), developer of telegraphy, was born on 6 February 1802 at the Manor House, Barnwood, Gloucester, the second of four children of William Wheatstone (1775–1854), shoemaker, and his wife, Beatta. In 1806 the family moved to London, where Wheatstone went to school. At the age of fourteen he was apprenticed to an uncle, also Charles Wheatstone, who had a musical instrument manufacturing business in the Strand. Young Wheatstone did not take to business life, but he was fascinated by the physics of sound, and studied the working of musical instruments. In particular, he wanted to know what distinguished sounds of the same pitch but different timbre, and how sounds were transmitted through solid rods and stretched wires.

On his uncle's death in 1823, Wheatstone, together with his younger brother William, took over the business. In

Sir Charles Wheatstone (1802–1875), by Samuel Laurence, 1868

the same year he contributed a paper to Thomson's *Annals of Philosophy*, describing his early experiments with sound. Other papers followed, including a description of his 'kaleidophone'. This instrument consisted of steel wire of rectangular cross-section fixed to a heavy base and carrying a silver bead at the top. The times of vibration of the bead in two directions at right angles being regulated by the particular rectangular section of the wire, the bead could be made to describe very beautiful curves illustrating the combination of harmonic motions of different periods. In 1825 he constructed a mouth organ with free reeds governed by a small button keyboard; further experiments led to the bellows-blown concertina (patent 10,041 of 1844), an improvement on the German instrument, which was allied to the accordion. One of the few original British musical instrument designs, it is still being played at the present time. His principal contribution to acoustics, a memoir on the so-called Chladni's figures, produced by strewing sand on an elastic plane and throwing it into vibration by means of a violin bow, was presented to the Royal Society and published in their *Transactions* (1833). Wheatstone showed that in square and rectangular plates every figure, however complicated, was the resultant of two or more sets of isochronous parallel vibrations; and by means of simple geometrical relations he carried out the principle of the 'superposition of small motions' without the aid of any profound mathematical analysis, and succeeded in predicting the curves that given modes of vibration should produce.

Wheatstone made several important contributions to

optics. The stereoscope, which, by presenting slightly different pictures to each eye, gives the viewer an apparently solid image, is entirely due to Wheatstone. In 1835 he read a paper on the 'Prismatic analysis of electric light' before the British Association meeting at Dublin. He demonstrated that the spectrum of the electric spark from different metals included rays of definite refrangibility, producing a series of lines differing in position and colour from each other. Thus the presence of a minute portion of any given metal might be determined. 'We have here', he said, 'a mode of discriminating metallic bodies more readily than by chemical examination, and which may hereafter be employed for useful purposes.' This remark is typical of his far-sightedness into the practical utility of any known scientific fact. His 'polar clock' was another instance of this trait. When David Brewster discovered that light from the sky is always polarized in a plane 90° from the sun, Wheatstone devised a clock by which it was possible to tell the hour of the day by the light from the sky even though the sun might be invisible.

This skill in turning knowledge to practical account was used to its full in Wheatstone's telegraph inventions. Although his inventions in other branches of science are as numerous as they are various, the name of Wheatstone has been most closely connected with the electric telegraph. He was not the 'inventor' of this; indeed, no one can lay claim to such a title. But to Wheatstone, with his collaborator William Fothergill Cooke, is due the credit for having been the first to render it available for the public transmission of messages. In 1834, at about the time he was appointed professor of experimental philosophy at King's College, London, Wheatstone began experimenting on the rate of transmission of electricity along wires, using about half a mile of copper wire. He then obtained permission from the college to suspend 4 miles of wire in the vaults under the buildings. Three interruptions of this circuit were made by three pairs of brass knobs with a small interval between them. One of these interruptions was in the middle of the conductor, and the other two were near the ends. A Leyden electrical storage jar was discharged through the wire, and the interval of time between the occurrence of the sparks at the ends and the occurrence of the spark at the middle was observed by noting the displacement of the image of the middle spark in a mirror revolving at a known speed. This experiment yielded a transmission velocity of about 250,000 miles per second—rather more than the true speed of 186,000 miles per second.

From this research Wheatstone passed on to the transmission of messages by electricity, and, in conjunction with Cooke, he devised the five-needle telegraph, and then the two-needle telegraph, the first that came into general use. Wheatstone's fertility of scientific resource led to many new developments, including the letter-showing dial telegraph in 1840, and the type-printing telegraph in 1841. The automatic transmitting and receiving instruments by which messages were sent with great rapidity over the telegraph system in the last third of the

nineteenth century were designed by Wheatstone alone, after the partnership with Cooke had been dissolved. Wheatstone was the first to appreciate the importance of reducing to a minimum the amount of work to be done by the current at the receiving station, by diminishing as far as practicable the mass, and therefore the inertia, of the moving parts; this was beautifully exemplified in that marvel of ingenuity, the 'ABC' letter-showing telegraph, which was much used for private telegraphic communication.

From 1837 Wheatstone devoted a good deal of time to submarine telegraphy, and in 1844 experiments were made in Swansea Bay, with the assistance of J. D. Llewellyn. Wheatstone also had a share in the development of the electric generator. In 1837 he devised a method of combining several armatures on one shaft so as to generate a continuous current, and in 1867 he described to the Royal Society a method of making such machines self-exciting. He used a shunt circuit; the use of a series circuit for the same purpose by Werner Siemens was described at the same meeting. Wheatstone was also inventor of a system of electro-magnetic clocks for indicating time at any number of different places united on a circuit.

Wheatstone had an extraordinary facility in deciphering hieroglyphics and cipher dispatches, and himself invented a cryptograph, or secret dispatch writer, which was used by the British army. His miscellaneous inventions are too numerous to mention in detail but they include electric chronographs, apparatus for making instruments record automatically, and instruments for measuring electricity and electrical resistance, including the rheostat. It was he who called attention to Christy's combination of wires, commonly known as 'Wheatstone's bridge', in which an electric balancing of the currents is obtained, and he worked out its application to electrical measurement. He was one of the first in Britain to appreciate the importance of Ohm's simple law of the relation between electromotive force, resistance of conductors, and resulting current—the law which is the foundation of all electrical engineering. He was elected a fellow of the Royal Society in 1836.

Wheatstone married, on 12 February 1847, Emma (d. 21 Jan 1865), daughter of J. West, and they had a family of two sons and three daughters. He was made a chevalier of the Légion d'honneur in 1855, and a foreign associate of the Académie des Sciences in 1873. On 2 July 1862 he was created DCL by the University of Oxford, and in 1864 LLD by the University of Cambridge. Moreover he possessed some thirty-four distinctions or diplomas conferred upon him by various governments, universities, and learned societies. On 30 January 1868 he was knighted.

Wheatstone bequeathed his collection of books and instruments to King's College, London. Although nominally professor of experimental philosophy there, he seldom lectured after 1840, and indeed was an indifferent teacher because of an almost morbid timidity in the presence of an audience. On a one-to-one basis, however, he was an excellent tutor, and there are testimonies to his eloquence in such circumstances. He died of bronchitis in the Hôtel du Louvre, Paris, on 19 October 1875, and was buried on 27 October in Kensal Green cemetery.

S. P. THOMPSON, rev. BRIAN BOWERS

Sources B. Bowers, *Sir Charles Wheatstone* (1975) · G. Hubbard, *Cooke and Wheatstone and the invention of the electric telegraph* (1965) · *PRS* (1876) · *Extracts from the private letters of the late Sir William Fothergill Cooke*, ed. F. H. Webb (1895) · J. J. Fahie, *History of electric telegraphy* (1884) · *Telegraphic Journal*, 3 (1875), 252 · *Nature*, 13 (1875–6), 501–3 · m. cert. · d. cert. · *CGPLA Eng. & Wales* (1875) · *The Times* (22 Oct 1875) · *The Times* (28 Oct 1875) · G. Romani and I. Beynon, 'Concertina', *New Grove*

Archives King's Lond., corresp. and papers · Royal Institution of Great Britain, London, letters · RS, papers · Sci. Mus., drawings relating to electric telegraph · Sci. Mus., papers and drawings | BL, letters to Charles Babbage, Add. MSS 57191–57201 · Inst. EE, corresp. with Sir Francis Ronalds

Likenesses W. Brockedon, chalk drawing, 1837, NPG · A. Claudet, stereoscopic daguerreotype, c.1851–1852, NPG · S. Laurence, chalk drawing, 1868, NPG [*see illus.*] · C. Martin, oils, exh. RA 1870, RS · London Stereoscopic Co., carte-de-visite, NPG · Mayall, carte-de-visite, NPG · drawing, repro. in *Nature* (1875) · oils, Inst. EE · photograph, King's Lond. · woodcuts and prints (after photographs), BM, NPG

Wealth at death under £70,000: probate, 9 Nov 1875, *CGPLA Eng. & Wales*

Wheeldon [*née* Marshall], **Alice Ann** (1866–1919), revolutionary socialist and anti-war campaigner, was born on 27 January 1866 at 5 Russell Street, Derby, the daughter of William Marshall, an engine tenter, and his wife, Ann, *née* Elliott. On 14 August 1886 she married William Augustus Wheeldon (*b.* 1851/2), a widowed engine fitter fourteen years her senior. They had at least three children—Harriet Ann, Winifred, and William—but in later life Alice Wheeldon seems to have lived apart from her husband. In the years before 1914 she and Harriet had become active members of the militant Women's Social and Political Union, selling *The Suffragette* and other literature, although according to Sylvia Pankhurst they were not involved in 'serious militancy'. By 1915 Alice Wheeldon was proprietor of a second-hand clothes shop at 12 Pear Tree Road, Derby; Harriet was teaching scripture at a school in Ilkeston; Winifred, also a teacher, had married Alfred Mason, a laboratory assistant at Hartley University College, Southampton; and William Wheeldon had been imprisoned as a conscientious objector. All the family were involved in left-wing politics and anti-war campaigning. Harriet was the secretary of the Derby branch of the No-Conscription Fellowship and was engaged to Arthur MacManus, an activist of the Socialist Labour Party who was a member of the Clyde Workers' Committee and seems to have had connections with the anarcho-syndicalist Industrial Workers of the World. By 1916 the Wheeldons were sheltering conscientious objectors at the Pear Tree Road shop, and MacManus was helping them to smuggle the fugitives out to Ireland or the USA.

In December 1916 Alice Wheeldon was approached by a young man calling himself Alex Gordon who claimed to be a conscientious objector on the run looking for a refuge. His real name was Francis W. Vivian and he was a former radical socialist now employed by the intelligence services to infiltrate organizations deemed subversive. While already hiding a conscientious objector, Alexander Macdonald, Alice Wheeldon put up 'Alex Gordon' over the night of 27/28 December. On 29 December he introduced to her a man whom he called Comrade Bert, describing him as an army deserter and Industrial Workers of the World activist. This was actually Herbert Booth, another intelligence operative, who seems to have acted as Vivian's 'control', and the two targeted the Wheeldons as subversives. The Wheeldons were already writing to each other in code, using a chessboard cipher with the key sentence 'We will hang Lloyd George from a sour apple tree.' However, their mail was being intercepted and decoded. On 4 January 1917 Winifred Mason sent Alice Wheeldon four small glass tubes containing the poison curare that her husband, Alfred, had obtained through his work; Alice Wheeldon later claimed that these were to be used to kill guard dogs at concentration camps where conscientious objectors were being held, in order to help them to escape. The interception of this parcel gave the authorities a pretext to act, and on 30 January Alice Wheeldon was arrested in Derby, along with Alexander Macdonald, and Harriet and Winifred at the schools where they taught. They were charged under the Offences Against the Person Act (1861) with conspiring to assassinate the prime minister, David Lloyd George, together with the prominent Labour Party war supporter Arthur Henderson and other unspecified persons, by firing poisoned darts at them.

The trial took place at the beginning of March 1917. The only barrister willing to represent Alice Wheeldon was a Dr Riza, a Persian, while the prosecution was led by the attorney-general, F. E. Smith (later Lord Birkenhead), who had no trouble in convincing the jury of Alice Wheeldon's guilt by association, especially since she admitted under cross-examination that she hated Lloyd George and had referred to him and Henderson as 'buggers'. Although Vivian was not called as a witness his evidence was crucial in securing a conviction. Alice Wheeldon was sentenced to ten years' penal servitude, and Alfred and Winifred Mason to seven and five years respectively; Harriet was acquitted, but lost her job as a teacher through her involvement in the case, as did Winifred.

Alice Wheeldon was imprisoned in Aylesbury gaol, where she resisted the regime to the extent of hunger-striking. In December 1918 she was released on licence (Alfred and Winifred were similarly released at the end of January 1919). By this time her second-hand clothes business had collapsed, and according to Sylvia Pankhurst she was reduced to growing tomatoes with the help of Harriet. She died, aged fifty-three, in the post-war influenza epidemic, on 21 February 1919 at 907 London Road, Derby, where she had been living since her release. She was buried in the Nottingham Road cemetery, Derby, on 26 February, with a ceremony reported as displaying a simplicity devoid of Christian content. An impromptu political graveside address was given by John S. Clark.

Alice Wheeldon was unusual at the time not only for her politics but because (like her son, William) she was a spiritualist. However, in other respects she seems to have been regarded by her neighbours as unexceptional, and most unlikely to have committed the crime for which she was imprisoned. There is apparently a tradition in Derby that her ghost walks the tunnels under the Guildhall, where she was briefly imprisoned before her trial.

DAVID DOUGHAN

Sources S. Rowbotham, *Friends of Alice Wheeldon* (1986) · *Derby Mercury* (9 March 1917) · *Derby Mercury* (16 March 1917) · *Derby Mercury* (31 Jan 1919) · *Derby Mercury* (28 Feb 1919) · *Derby Daily Express* (22 Feb 1919) · *Daily Herald* (27 Dec 1919) · *The Socialist* (6 March 1919) · *The Times* (8–10 March 1917) · *Workers' Dreadnought* (3 Jan 1920) · www.derbycity.com, March 2002 · b. cert. · m. cert. · d. cert.

Archives PRO, file CRIM 1/166

Wealth at death £112 15s. 5d.: administration with will, 10 Oct 1919, *CGPLA Eng. & Wales*

Wheeler [*née* Cowherd], **Agnes** [Ann] (*bap.* 1734, *d.* 1804), writer on dialect, was baptized at Cartmel Priory church, Lancashire, on 3 July 1734. She was the daughter of Edward and Eleanor Cowherd (sometimes spelled Coward) of Church Town, Cartmel. Nothing is known of her education, and details of her life are sparse. At some stage she travelled to London to take up a post as housekeeper to a family, and while she was there she married a Captain Wheeler. After her husband's death she returned to the north and made her home with her brother, William Cowherd, who lived at Arnside Tower in the village of Beetham, Westmorland.

Under the initials A. W., Mrs Wheeler published at Kendal in 1790 *The Westmoreland dialect in three familiar dialogues, in which an attempt is made to illustrate the provincial idiom.* The book not only had a second edition in 1802, with a fourth dialogue added, but was reprinted twice more (in 1821 and 1840), with Ann Wheeler acknowledged as author. Her work also featured in work by the Revd Thomas Clarke and others, *Specimens of the Westmorland Dialect* (1887).

Mrs Wheeler died at home in Beetham and was buried there on 4 November 1804. Her life remains something of a mystery, and her reputation rests on a single, pioneering work, of which the first edition is so rare that not even the British Library possesses a copy. ROY PALMER

Sources private information (2004), Cumbria AS · A. Wheeler, *The Westmoreland dialect in four familiar dialogues* (1840) · A. Sparke, *A bibliography of the dialect literature of Cumberland and Westmorland* (1907) · Cumbria AS, WPR 89/5 [baptism] · Cumbria AS, WPR 43/3 [burial]

Wheeler [*née* Doyle], **Anna** (1785?–1848x50), philosopher, born in co. Tipperary, Ireland, was the daughter of Anna Dunbar and her husband, Nicholas Milley Doyle, a graduate of Trinity College, Dublin, and prebendary of Fennor parish in co. Tipperary. She did not have a formal education but learned French, geography, and skills of repartee from foreign dignitaries visiting her military relatives and gained political insights from her godfather, Henry Grattan. Clever, forthright, and not suffering fools gladly, Anna Doyle was a 'reigning beauty of the Irish countryside' (Sadleir, 71). In 1800, despite her mother's opposition, she married Francis Massy Wheeler (1781–1820), a wealthy squire from Ballywire, co. Limerick. She spent her

Anna Wheeler (1785?–1848x50), by Maxim Gauci, pubd 1825 (after J. Porter)

unhappy marriage reading the works of Diderot, Holbach, Condillac, Mary Wollstonecraft, and Mary Hays. Exhausted by marital acrimony, in 1812 Wheeler decided to leave her alcoholic husband. With her daughters, Henrietta and Rosina, and her spinster sister Bessie, she sailed to the island of Guernsey, where her uncle General Sir John Doyle (1750–1834) was governor.

In Caen in 1816, with followers of Henri Saint-Simon, founder of 'French socialism', Wheeler's philosophical acumen and patronage to young intellectuals titled her the 'Goddess of Reason' (Sadleir, 76) and 'most gifted woman of the age' (ibid., 79). When her estranged husband died in 1820, Wheeler went to London, where she formed close relationships with men of liberal ideas, such as the utilitarian Jeremy Bentham, the charismatic co-operative leader Robert Owen, and William Thompson, the Irish political economist, feminist, and critic of capitalism.

Living in Paris in 1823, Wheeler met Charles Fourier, the French utopian socialist and a frequent visitor to Wheeler's salon; she dedicated herself to disseminating Fourier's ideas among London Owenites. To Fourier most of Owen's disciples seemed like pedants beside the exuberantly eclectic Anna Wheeler; she translated Fourier's writings on human harmony to make his turgid philosophy accessible, while using her diplomatic skills to mediate competitive disputes between Fourier and Owen. Wheeler stayed in France until 1826, and became a supporter of Greek independence in collaboration with Marc

Antoine Jullien, the Pestalozzi educationist and Owenite follower. Wheeler returned to London after her daughter Henrietta died tragically from a 'wasting disease'. She was absent from a public gathering on 6 May 1827 at the Société Philotechnique de Paris, where Marc Antoine Jullien read his eulogy praising the mother–daughter loyalty of Wheeler and Henrietta.

In 1825 collaborative work between Wheeler and William Thompson resulted in the *Appeal of One Half the Human Race*, a challenge to utilitarians who looked for universal happiness but excluded women, half the human race. The *Appeal* is a seminal statement, combining elements of liberal and socialist feminism; it exposes the misogyny in James Mill's invented fiction that women and men share an 'identity of interests', a fiction Mill used to justify the exclusion of women from the suffrage in his *Essay on Government* (1820). Wheeler brought a woman's reasoning and experience to the *Appeal*, a role affectionately acknowledged by Thompson in an introductory 'Letter to Mrs Wheeler'. Only a few pages of the text were written exclusively by Wheeler but Thompson considered the text their 'joint property' (*Appeal*, vii). Intertextual comparisons with Wheeler's other writings indicate the passages written by her pen alone. An example would be the searing critique of marriage so central in the *Appeal*. A graphic portrayal of domestic, economic, and psychic causes of human oppression are balanced against a proposal for an alternative life of co-operative community living where gender justice might be possible.

Wheeler adopted the pseudonym Vlasta when publishing controversial essays in the Co-operative Press on such subjects as women's enslavement to a learned ideology of romantic love, which concentrates their thoughts on pleasing male sensuality. An 1829 lecture at Finsbury Square on 'Rights of women' shows that Wheeler decried the social conditioning of men by corrupt institutions, but she aimed always to promote harmony between the sexes rather than adversarial rancour, to plead the cause of men in advocating the rights of women. Her articles stressed the need for women to act on principles and reason, liberating themselves from a captivity to uncritical social custom and conditioning; such views were encouraged by Wheeler's women friends among Saint-Simonians and Owenites, such as Frances (Fanny) Wright, Desirée Veret, Jeanne Victoire, and Flora Tristan.

In May 1833 Wheeler wrote of her close friendship with the deceased William Thompson in a eulogy signed Vlasta and read to friends of co-operation at Lord Hampden's residence. Hampden admitted that no one knew Thompson better than Anna Wheeler, yet Thompson had determined never to marry within the unequal legal provisions constraining women. Wheeler's friends continued to try to arrange for her return to France before the 1848 revolution, but a crippling neuralgia forced her into seclusion. Wheeler's undocumented death came between 1848 and 1850.

Wheeler's ideas on sexual equality were perpetuated by her daughter Rosina, Lady Bulwer-*Lytton (1802–1882), who had two children, Emily Elizabeth (1828–1848) and

Edward Robert Bulwer-*Lytton, first earl of Lytton (1831–1891). After a publicly acrimonious divorce from Edward Bulwer-Lytton, Rosina wrote *An Appeal to the Justice and Charity of the English Public* (1857), exposing the social ostracism women experience in defending their reputations against false allegations. Anna Wheeler would not have been surprised at this tragic turn of events, having never felt either affection or respect for Bulwer-Lytton. Wheeler's great-granddaughter Lady Constance Lytton (1869–1923), third child of Edward Robert Bulwer-Lytton, continued the line of prominent feminists, and collaborated with Emmeline Pankhurst in the Women's Social and Political Union, a group prepared to face prison to acquire the suffrage. DOLORES DOOLEY

Sources *Letters of the late Edward Bulwer, Lord Lytton, to his wife*, ed. L. Devey (1884) · L. Devey, *Life of Rosina, Lady Lytton* (1887) · A. Doyle, *A hundred years of conflict: some records of the services of six generals of the Doyle family, 1756–1856* (1911) · F. H. C. Doyle, *Reminiscences and opinions* (1886) · M. Sadleir, *Bulwer: a panorama*, 1: *Edward and Rosina, 1803–1836* (1931); new edn as *Bulwer and his wife: a panorama, 1803–1836* (1833) · D. Dooley, *Equality in community: sexual equality in the writings of William Thompson and Anna Doyle Wheeler* (1996) · H. Desroche, 'Images and echoes of Owenism in nineteenth-century France', *Robert Owen, prophet of the poor*, ed. S. Pollard and J. Salt (1971), 239–84 · J. Beecher, *Charles Fourier* (1986) · S. Burke, 'Letter from a pioneer feminist: A. D. Wheeler to Marc Antoine', in J. L. Noyce, *Studies in labour history* (1976), 19–23 · E. Nash, *Unpublished letters of Lady Bulwer Lytton to Alfred Edward Chalon, R. A.* (1914) · St J. D. Seymour, *The succession of parochial clergy in the united diocese of Cashel and Emly* (Dublin, 1908) · E. R. Bulwer-Lytton, first Earl Lytton, *The life, letters and literary remains of Edward Bulwer, Lord Lytton*, 2 (1883) · W. Thompson, *Appeal of one half the human race, women, against the pretensions of the other half, men* (1825) · Burtchaell & Sadleir, *Alum. Dubl.*, 2nd edn · J. M. Morgan, *Hampden in the nineteenth century, or, Colloquies on the errors and improvement of society*, 2 vols. in 1 (1834)
Archives Archives Nationales, Paris, corresp. with Charles Fourier, 10 AS, 25d · Co-operative Union, Holyoake House, Manchester, corresp. with Robert Owen
Likenesses M. Gauci, engraving, pubd 1825 (after J. Porter), NPG [*see illus.*] · photograph, repro. in W. Thompson, *Appeal of one half the human race* (1825) · portrait, UCL, Goldsmiths' Library

Wheeler, Sir Arthur, baronet (1860–1943), stockbroker and corporate financier, was born at Derby Road, Nottingham, on 18 September 1860, the son of Benjamin Wheeler, a heating engineer, and his wife, Mary, *née* Radford. He was educated at Nottingham high school (1871–6) and spent his early business career with Simon, Meyer & Co. (later Simon, May & Co.), a rapidly growing Anglo-German merchant house which exported lace to Russia, Latin America, and other overseas markets. He was quick with figures and rose to be chief clerk. In 1896 he married Mary, the daughter of Frederick Pullman, a Nottingham JP; they had two sons and two daughters.

In 1899 Wheeler, together with Arthur Blake, launched his own business in Leicester as Blake and Wheeler, stockbrokers. The partnership was not a member of the stock exchange and so not subject to its restrictive practices. By doing business as jobbers—then a separate occupation—the partners were able to buy stock and shares and to advertise for business by circulating clients (customers) or potential buyers. The partnership was dissolved in 1910, when Blake became a member of the Nottingham stock exchange (later, as Sir Arthur Blake, he was its chairman). Wheeler continued in Leicester as what was called an outside broker.

Wheeler's success was based on his recognition that in provincial towns such as Leicester, Birmingham, and Nottingham there were many substantial shareholdings from deceased estates languishing on the market. The handful of small local brokers in such places lacked the organization to market them because they were not allowed, by stock exchange rules, to make any kind of approach to potential clients. Very often such shareholdings were in sound local industrial and commercial enterprises that were nevertheless too small to find recognition in the City of London, where stockbrokers were slow to respond to the opportunities offered by smaller companies. Wheeler conceived the idea of mailing advertisement circulars on a selective basis to people who had the specific interest to understand the value of these shares and the means to purchase them. Thus his circulars for shares in drapery stores went to drapers, for breweries to publicans, for shares in hosiery and knitwear companies to people prominent in the midlands textile industry, and so forth. The result of this careful targeting of mailshots was a high response rate, with most of Wheeler's acquisitions being taken up very quickly and few shares left over. Other entrepreneurs imitated Wheeler but the biggest of them did not do one-twentieth of his business, so there was little effective competition for him.

Wheeler steadily built up what would now be called a large database of customers, fed by shareholders' names from the companies registration office. In the early 1920s the list topped a quarter of a million names, and by the end of the decade it had reached three-quarters of a million. With such a rapidly growing clientele, Wheeler was able to circulate prospectuses of new issues and take large shareholdings in them. His marketing strength was such that if he recommended a new share issue a buoyant sale was assured, and several investment institutions sought his imprimatur before taking large lots from the merchant banks responsible for the issue. Beechams' share issue of 1927, to take just one example, could not have been undertaken without Wheeler's backing; in the event it was oversubscribed.

Wheeler's growing familiarity with the needs of small companies and small investors led to further developments in the 1920s. In 1924 he launched a new venture in the City of London, the Gresham Investment Trust, to make small industrial issues, and the following year the Charterhouse Investment Trust Ltd, to undertake larger share issues. The City establishment did not altogether approve of Wheeler, but the two enterprises came to be recognized as pioneers in bridging what later (1931) became known as 'the Macmillan gap'—the absence of financial organizations with the expertise to finance smaller businesses. In this period Wheeler became chairman or a director of a number of companies that he helped to finance, including Beecham Estates and Pills

(then being built up by Philip Hill), Rolls Razor, Low Temperature Carbonization, United Drapery Stores, and the British Hosiery Trust, an attempt to amalgamate Wolsey, Byfords, and several other Leicester firms.

Wheeler was created a baronet in 1920 for his work in selling war bonds, to which he devoted his entire energy during the First World War. He found time in his long working days for public and charitable causes, and was a generous subscriber to numerous local causes. He recruited several managers of outstanding ability, some of whom maintained the momentum of his financial initiatives after 1931; in particular Sir Nutcombe Hume (1893–1967) built up Charterhouse (later Charterhouse Japhet) as a leading investment house, while John Kinross (1904–1989) used his early career experience with Gresham to develop the Industrial and Commercial Finance Corporation Ltd (ICFC), the leading post-war investment bank for small firms, later called Investors for Industry or 3 i.

As Wheeler's business increased, he found it necessary to finance it by bank overdrafts secured by the deposit of stocks and shares. This was easy while shares held their value, but the collapse in prices in 1929 compelled the banks to call for a reduction in overdrafts or increase in collateral, at which point Wheeler became embarrassed for want of working capital. Matters came to a head early in 1931, when he had no funds to pay for a war loan conversion for which he had accepted numerous orders and payments, and he filed his petition for bankruptcy in March. In October he was tried at Leicester assizes for fraudulent conversion and gaoled for twelve months. As an undischarged bankrupt, Wheeler was unable to rebuild his business, and was forced to retire to Norfolk. He died at Home Farm, Holme next the Sea, on 20 May 1943, following a cerebral thrombosis. S. D. CHAPMAN

Sources private information (2004) · J. M. Keyworth, 'Wheeler, Sir Arthur', *DBB* · L. Dennett, *The Charterhouse Group, 1925–1979: a history* (1979) · J. Kinross, *Fifty years in the City: financing small business* (1982) · J. M. Keyworth, *Cabbages and things: the background and story of the Covent Garden property companies to 1970* (privately published, 1990) · b. cert. · d. cert.
Archives priv. coll.

Wheeler, Sir Charles Thomas (1892–1974), sculptor, was born on 14 March 1892, in Church Lane, Codsall, Staffordshire, the second son of the five sons and one daughter born to Samuel Phipps Wheeler (b. c.1860), a freelance journalist who ran a small company, and his wife, Annie Florence, née Crowther (c.1872–c.1930). He grew up happily in Wolverhampton, in a disciplined, impoverished, rather unconventional middle-class family. In this liberal-minded, nonconformist household a love of the arts was encouraged. He attended St Luke's elementary school but, his health weakened by rheumatic fever, was allowed to leave higher grade school at fifteen to enter the Wolverhampton School of Art. Robert Emerson, a dynamic sculpture master appointed in 1910, fired his enthusiasm for sculpture. In 1912 Wheeler won a national exhibition to the Royal College of Art, in London, and was one of the last students taught by Edward Lantéri. Unfit to fight in 1914, he served on the home front casting and moulding prostheses for amputees. Prize-money for medal designs in 1917 and 1918 secured him a studio at 2 Justice Walk, Chelsea, and happiness. On 24 August 1918 he married Muriel Bourne (1888–1979), a painter and sculptor he had met at the Wolverhampton School of Art, the younger daughter of Arthur Ward Bourne of Shrewsbury, Shropshire. They were devoted to each other and to their children, Neil Bourne (Robin) Wheeler (1919–1978) and Carol Rosemary Wheeler (b. 1927).

At the end of the war Wheeler came to the attention of the architect Herbert Baker. The commissioning of a *Madonna and Child* (Portland stone, 1924) for the Winchester College memorial cloister began a close collaboration and friendship which ended only with Baker's death in 1946. It was Wheeler's first direct carving, made *in situ*, a practice he enjoyed and subsequently adopted widely throughout his career. A 'traditional modernist', Wheeler was a prominent figure in British sculpture between the wars, best-known for his architectural and monumental work. He opposed the extremes of modern art, but when young was considered stylistically daring, one of a group of sculptors who combined traditional practice with a notion of 'truth to materials'. His modernity reflected the stylistic influences of Ivan Meštrović and Carl Milles. His election as an ARA in 1934 was noted as a 'tribute to the advanced school' and robustly opposed by the then president, Sir William Llewellyn, who feared that the academy would be lost were it to endorse work of Wheeler's 'revolutionary kind' (Wheeler, 64).

Wheeler's stylized animals adorn the Indian memorial to the missing (Euville stone, 1927) at Neuve-Chapelle, French Flanders, and India House (Portland stone) and South Africa House (gilt-bronze) in London, but the extensive sculptural ensemble for Baker's new Bank of England in London (Portland stone, plaster, marble, and bronze, 1928–37), the largest commission of the era, secured his reputation and finances. In 1930 the Wheelers bought a house at 21 Tregunter Road, Chelsea, and built a large studio at the bottom of the garden, in Cathcart Road. The modern solidity of the figures on the façade of the bank, carved direct, caused controversy in 1931, but a statuette of the baroque gilt-bronze *Ariel* for the sub-treasury dome in London was Wheeler's diploma work when elected RA in 1940 (exh. RA, 1941). He worked with many eminent architects besides Baker; his last pre-war commission was the Jellicoe memorial fountain and bust for Lutyens's Trafalgar Square design, for which William McMillan contributed the Beatty fountain and portrait. Notable among numerous post-war works are splendid Portland stone figures for naval memorials at Chatham, Portsmouth, Plymouth, and Tower Hill, London (c.1950), and the colossal *Earth* and *Water* (both 1952) for the Ministry of Defence, Whitehall, London.

Some of Wheeler's most formally innovative and delicately handled works were shown at the Royal Academy. Of critically acclaimed exhibits in 1926, his limewood *Madonna and Child* is now in the Wolverhampton Art Gallery. *The Infant Christ*, a portrait of his son, Robin (bronze, exh. RA, 1924), *Spring* (bronze, exh. RA, 1930), and *Aphrodite II* (stone, exh. RA, 1944) were purchased for the Chantrey collection (all Tate collection). His many portraits include those of T. E. Lawrence (stone, exh. RA, 1936; National Portrait Gallery, London), Yehudi Menuhin (three bronzes, exh. RA, 1961), and Elizabeth II (three bronzes, exh. RA, 1963 and 1964; marble, exh. RA, 1964, Royal Academy of Arts, London).

Wheeler was president of the Royal Society of British Sculptors from 1944 to 1949, having previously been elected an associate in 1926 and a fellow in 1937, and was awarded the society's gold medal in 1949. He was a trustee of the Tate Gallery from 1942 to 1949 and a member of the Royal Fine Arts Commission from 1946 to 1952. In 1956 he became president of the Royal Academy, a position he held for ten years. Appointed CBE in 1948 and made a KCVO in 1958, Wheeler was an honorary fellow of the Royal Institute of British Architects and a member of the Royal Society of Arts, the Royal Society of Painters in Water Colours, the Royal Institute of Painters in Water Colours, and the Royal Society of Painter–Printmakers. He also received honorary degrees from Oxford University (DCL 1960) and the University of Keele (DLitt 1971).

A small figure, Wheeler was frequently seen wearing a bow-tie, and a smock over his tweeds. He was a passionate, disciplined artist, and a sociable teetotaller regarded as a charming, modest humanist, much liked by his many friends. As president of the Royal Academy he wished to make genuine progress, his liberal attitude aiming to balance the arguments of left and right. During his presidency abstract works were shown at the summer exhibitions. In 1962 he was greatly distressed by the sale of Leonardo's cartoon *Virgin and Child with the Infant St John*, which he had been assured was necessary for the financial independence of the academy. Although the sale incurred much opprobrium, the financial gains were short-lived. Humphrey Brooke, secretary of the academy, in a letter to *The Times* after Wheeler's death, praised him as 'an exceptional President' (*The Times*, 29 Aug 1974).

In 1968 Wheeler's autobiography, *High Relief*, was published. He moved from Weavers, Warwickswold, Merstham, Surrey (purchased in 1948), where he had enjoyed drawing and walking the Pilgrim's Way, to Woodreed Farmhouse, Mayfield, Sussex. He continued to work there, but he suffered a stroke in his studio in the spring of 1974. He died at Woodreed Farmhouse on 22 August and was buried at St Luke's, Codsall, on the 27th. One of his sculptures, an angel, was placed on the grave he shares with his wife, Muriel, who died on 2 November 1979. Memorials to him were erected in St James's Church, Piccadilly, London, and in the crypt of St Paul's Cathedral. A portrait bust of her husband by Muriel Wheeler (lead, 1931) is in the National Portrait Gallery.

SARAH CRELLIN

Sources C. Wheeler, *High relief* (1968) · *DNB* · B. Read and P. Skipwith, *Sculpture in Britain between the wars* (1986) [exhibition catalogue, Fine Art Society, London, 10 June – 12 Aug 1986] · RIBA BAL, Herbert Baker MSS · K. Parkes, *The art of carved sculpture*, 2 vols. (1931) · M. Levy, 'An academic humanist', *The Studio*, 165 (1963), 154–

9 · private information (2004) · H. Brooke, letter, *The Times* (29 Aug 1974) · *The Times* (1 Jan 1958) · Graves, *RA exhibitors*
Archives Henry Moore Institute, Leeds, corresp., papers, and photographs · priv. coll. | Essex RO, letters to T. B. Huxley-Jones · RA, members' file · RIBA, Herbert Baker archive · TCD, corresp. with Thomas Bodkin · V&A NAL, questionnaire completed for Kineton Parkes
Likenesses M. Wheeler, lead bust, 1931, NPG · W. Soukop, relief on memorial plaque, 1976, St Paul's Cathedral, London · photographs, Henry Moore Institute, Leeds
Wealth at death £56,245: probate, 10 March 1975, *CGPLA Eng. & Wales*

Wheeler, Daniel (1771–1840), missionary, son of William Wheeler (*d.* 1778?), of Conduit Street, Hanover Square, London, and Sarah (*d.* 1784?), his wife, was born at home on 27 November 1771. His parents were active members of the Church of England. His father, a wine merchant, died when Daniel was about six; his mother died six years later, by which time he was at a boarding-school in London at Parson's Green, Fulham. A clerical relative managed the estate and the business, until his brother could take it over. A situation was obtained for Wheeler on board a merchant ship trading to Oporto, but after two or three voyages he entered the Royal Navy as a midshipman, being then under fourteen. He was soon promoted to a flagship, but abandoned the sea after six years, and, having squandered all his pay, enlisted as a private soldier in a regiment ordered to Ireland. In a year or two he was drafted into one of the new regiments raised to fight the French, and he sailed for Flanders to join the British army under command of the duke of York. Later, having obtained a commission in a regiment destined for the West Indies, he sailed under Sir Ralph Abercromby, about September 1795.

In 1796 Wheeler left the army and settled at Handsworth Woodhouse, near Sheffield, with his elder sister, Barbara, who had married William Hoyland, a Quaker. In 1797 he was received as a member of the society, and set up as a seed merchant in Sheffield. His life was now lived within the Society of Friends. On 13 June 1800 he married Jane (*d.* 1833), daughter of Thomas and Rachel Brady of Thorne, Yorkshire, a well-established Quaker family. They had four sons: William (*d.* 24 Nov 1836), Joshua (*d.* 29 March 1841), Daniel (*d.* 1848), and Charles (*d.* 6 Feb 1840). His elder daughter, Sarah (*b.* 1807), who afterwards married William Tanner of Bristol, survived him. Of his younger daughter, Jane (*d.* 15 July 1837, at Shoosharry), a short account was published in London and Bristol in 1841.

About 1809 Wheeler and his family moved to a farm in the country, where he began to prepare himself for a life of ministry. He was recognized as a minister in 1816. He had had for several years a sense that he should again go abroad, and after the emperor Alexander I of Russia had in 1814 visited a Friend's farm during a visit to England, and had sought a manager of that persuasion for his establishment at Okhta, Wheeler in 1817 proceeded to St Petersburg. He saw the tsar, and explained to him the leaning he had for two years felt towards Russia as a sphere of missionary labour. He then returned to England, wound up

his affairs, and with his wife, family, and servants—in all twenty persons—along with implements, seeds, and cattle, he left Hull for St Petersburg on 22 June 1818.

Besides the tsar's farm, Wheeler was soon appointed to the management of an estate belonging to the dowager empress, consisting, like the other, chiefly of swamp. This, after being thoroughly drained, was divided into farms of 30–100 acres each, which were let to peasants at moderate rents; a portion of each district was kept as a model farm. More than 3000 acres were in cultivation under Wheeler's own eye. The little Quaker meeting he established was visited by William Allen (1770–1843), Stephen Grellett, and Thomas Shillitoe, with whom Wheeler in 1825 returned to Britain. He stayed for three months, and attended the Dublin and London yearly meetings.

About September 1828 Wheeler moved to Shoosharry, near St Petersburg, where visitors were almost unknown. The land, where he bored in vain for water, was on the edge of a huge bog. Wheeler's son William was now his assistant, and in 1830 Wheeler was able to visit Britain, where he held meetings in Yorkshire, Durham, Devon, Cornwall, Ireland, and the Isles of Scilly. On returning to Shoosharry in July 1831 he found cholera rife in the district, but out of his 500 employees none died. A year later he was allowed by an imperial ukase to resign his post in favour of his son.

To the monthly meeting at Doncaster on 23 September 1832 Wheeler unfolded his mission of gospel visits to the Pacific islands, New South Wales, and Van Diemen's Land. While making his preparations, his wife (who had remained in Russia) died. Accompanied by his son Charles, Wheeler set sail from the Thames on 13 November 1833 in the *Henry Freeling*, a cutter of 101 tons, which had been purchased and provisioned by private members of the Society of Friends. The ship arrived off Hobart Town on 10 September 1834, and left again in December, conveying James Blackhouse and George Washington Walker to Port Jackson and Norfolk Island on the way to Tahiti. During the four or five months spent on that island Wheeler held many services, sometimes on board his ship, with the queen and the chiefs, and with the missionaries, English residents, and crews of vessels in the harbour. Queen Pomare remitted the *Henry Freeling*'s port dues because Wheeler's was 'a visit of love, and not a trading voyage' (*Memoirs*, 351). She again came to his meetings on the island of Eimeo.

Christmas day 1835 was spent in the Sandwich Islands, and the first Quaker meeting was held there, attended by native chiefs, the governor, and the queen. The *Henry Freeling* also stayed some time at Honolulu and at Rarotonga, the Friendly Islands, and New Zealand (Christmas 1836). On reaching Sydney in January 1837, the ship was sold and its company discharged. The ship's course was entirely without pre-arrangement, and was directed from day to day by Wheeler's spiritual intimations. In a letter to a friend Wheeler illustrates his sense of divine protection by saying that he has been ashamed, even in landing in canoes through the broken surf, to use a lifebelt which a friend had given him on leaving.

After leaving Hobart Town, Wheeler reached London on 1 May 1838. On returning his certificates to his quarterly meeting, Wheeler laid before them his wish to visit America. First he visited his surviving children at Shoosharry, and then travelled through Finland and Stockholm; finally he sailed for America from Liverpool in November 1838. He attended a number of the yearly meetings there, visited the place where Mary Dyer and other Quakers were executed, went to Newfoundland and Nova Scotia, and returned to England in October 1839, hastened by the illness of his son Charles, who died at St Germains on his way south in the spring of the following year. Wheeler sailed for New York to complete his mission in May 1840 but caught a severe cold at sea, and died six weeks after landing, on 12 June 1840, in the house of his friend John Clapp. He was buried on 15 June in the Friends' burial-ground, Orchard Street, New York.

Wheeler's journals were edited by his son Charles in four parts (1835–9), and in a consolidated volume (1839). *Memoirs of the Life … of Daniel Wheeler* (1842) was edited by his son Daniel and was popular in several editions and versions. Wheeler's writings provide a vivid and quite candid account of a Quaker missionary's varied activities.

CHARLOTTE FELL-SMITH, *rev.* H. C. G. MATTHEW

Sources *Memoirs of the life and gospel labours of the late Daniel Wheeler* (1842)

Archives RS Friends, Lond., corresp., journals, and papers; letters

Wheeler, (William) Gordon (1910–1998), Roman Catholic bishop of Leeds, was born on 5 May 1910 at Hillcrest in the village of Dobcross, Saddleworth, Yorkshire, the first child of Frederick Wheeler (1880–1971), cloth bleacher and finisher, and his wife, Marjorie (1881–1938), daughter of William Barber Upjohn of Worsley, Lancashire, and his wife, Mary. His only sibling, Marjorie Elizabeth, was born in 1912. Gordon Wheeler (as he was always known to family and friends) was baptized at St Mark's parish church, Worsley, on 3 July 1910, and his family's deep Anglican faith was a formative influence on his early life and career. He was educated at Manchester grammar school (1924–9) and at University College, Oxford (1929–32), from where he graduated with a second in history. He then chose to study for the Anglican priesthood at St Stephen's House, Oxford (1932–3); he was ordained to the diaconate in December 1933 by the bishop of Chichester, George Bell, and in December 1934 he was ordained priest by the bishop of Derby in All Saints' Cathedral, Derby. Between 1933 and 1936 he served as curate at St Bartholomew's, Brighton, and at St Mary and All Saints, Chesterfield, and then at Lancing College, Sussex, as an assistant chaplain and master. From an early age he identified firmly with the Anglo-Catholic wing of the Church of England, and he developed an admiration for Cardinal Newman. At various times he considered whether to become a Roman Catholic; he finally decided to do so in 1936 and was received into that church at Downside Abbey on 18 September of that year. Subsequently he went to Rome and

the Beda College (1936–40) to prepare for his ordination to the Roman Catholic priesthood. This took place at Westminster Cathedral on 31 March 1940 and was performed by the archbishop of Westminster, Cardinal Hinsley. His first appointment in the Westminster diocese was to the parish of St Edmund, Edmonton, as assistant priest. He remained there until 1944, when he joined the staff of Westminster Cathedral with responsibility for editing the *Westminster Cathedral Chronicle*. In 1950 he became the Catholic chaplain to the University of London. Pope Pius XII appointed him a privy chamberlain in 1952.

In 1954 the archbishop of Westminster, Cardinal Bernard Griffin, appointed Wheeler administrator of Westminster Cathedral, a post he held for the next ten years. In 1955 he was created a domestic prelate to Pope Pius XII, and the following year he became a chaplain to the British Association of the Sovereign and Military Order of Malta. From 1991 to 1995 he was the association's principal chaplain.

Wheeler enjoyed a reputation as an able administrator, a fine intellect, and a man of great charm and wit. It was accepted that he was destined to become a bishop, and in 1964 Pope Paul VI appointed him coadjutor bishop of Middlesbrough, to assist the bishop of the diocese, George Brunner. He was consecrated bishop by the apostolic delegate Archbishop Igino Cardinale at St Mary's Cathedral, Middlesbrough, on 19 March 1964. He expected in due course to succeed Bishop Brunner, but in 1966 he was appointed as the seventh bishop of Leeds, following the translation of George Patrick Dwyer to the archdiocese of Birmingham the previous year. He was enthroned as bishop of Leeds in St Anne's Cathedral, Leeds, on 27 June 1966. He retired on 10 September 1985 and was granted the title of bishop emeritus of Leeds.

Although Wheeler's cultural and educational background may have differed from that of most of his fellow bishops in the English Catholic church of the 1960s, he shared with them a common task: implementing at diocesan level the far-reaching decisions taken by the Second Vatican Council of 1962–5. To that end he established the Wood Hall Pastoral and Ecumenical Centre in 1967, the Diocesan Pastoral Council, and the Diocesan Justice and Peace Commission: all important initiatives which placed him at the forefront of post-conciliar reform. In 1971 he became the first English bishop to ordain married men to the diaconate; he also accepted as candidates for the priesthood several married Anglican clergymen who had converted to the Catholic faith, although their ordinations did not take place until after Wheeler retired. In later years, and in hindsight, he tended to regret that his initiatives had not achieved more to disseminate the fruits of the Second Vatican Council, and wondered whether it would have been preferable to concentrate on promoting this aim in the parishes both among priests and lay people.

This self-assessment was rather severe, for Wheeler had achieved much. Undoubtedly he was at heart a theological and liturgical conservative; nevertheless he accepted that the church has always undergone development in these and other areas. Thus he accommodated and, indeed, promoted innovation; it was this, together with his sympathetic approach to troubled individuals and situations, which enabled him to guide his diocese through the upheavals and controversies of the period relatively unscathed, not least through the aftermath of the 1968 encyclical *Humanae vitae*. Wheeler's achievement was an example to the wider English Catholic church and helps to explain why he was seen by some as a potential archbishop of Westminster when Cardinal Heenan died in 1975. In the event it was Gordon Wheeler who promoted the cause of Heenan's eventual successor, the abbot of Ampleforth, Dom Basil Hume.

Having taken part himself in the later sessions of the Second Vatican Council, Wheeler envisaged the spiritual and intellectual renewal of the church through a balanced consideration and implementation of its decrees, in contrast to what he saw, from the viewpoint of a 'progressive traditionalist', as frequently expressed misinterpretations and misrepresentations. In 1969 he published a pamphlet entitled *Let's Get this Straight* in which he argued that the council was not the cause of 'unrest and uncertainty' but was in fact 'God's answer' to the troubles and problems of the age. At the national level he was able to influence some of the most significant changes to emerge from the council, through his membership of the National Liturgical Commission, which he chaired from 1970 to 1975, and of the International Commission on English in the Liturgy. His loyalty to the council was evident in 1980, when he ceded fifty parishes from the Leeds diocese to form the greater part of the new diocese of Hallam, centred on Sheffield; as a consequence his former auxiliary bishop, Gerald Moverley, became the first bishop of Hallam. In this way Wheeler accepted the principle that a modern diocese should, as far as possible, be of a size which enables a single bishop to provide effective administration and pastoral care.

As bishop of Leeds Wheeler lived at Eltofts, near Thorner, on the outskirts of the city in a style characterized by 'warm hospitality, gracious manners [and] the highest standards', in the words of Cardinal Basil Hume (*Diocese of Leeds Directory 1999*, 124). In retirement he went to reside at the College of the Blessed Virgin in Headingley, where he was cared for by the Little Sisters of the Poor. As his successor, Bishop David Konstant, later recalled, Wheeler's retirement was 'everything that such a time should be' (*The Tablet*), and it was during these years that he wrote his memoirs, *In Truth and Love* (1990), and compiled a collection of homilies and essays, *More Truth and Love* (1994). He died on 20 February 1998 at Mount St Joseph's home, Shire Oak Road, Leeds, and his funeral took place at St Anne's Cathedral on 3 March; on the same day he was buried in the crypt of St Edward's Church, Clifford, near Boston Spa in Yorkshire. While some may have regarded Gordon Wheeler as 'the last of the prince-bishops' (*The Guardian*), on its own this would be a superficial judgement; he was a man of strong faith and deep prayer, a holy man who was also 'an urbane and effective diocesan bishop' (*The Times*) at one of the most turbulent periods in the modern history of the Catholic church. ROBERT E. FINNIGAN

Sources W. G. Wheeler, *In truth and love* (1990) · Wheeler Collection, Leeds Diocesan Archives · *Diocese of Leeds directory 1999* (1998) · *The Tablet* (28 Feb 1998) · *The Guardian* (27 Feb 1998) · *The Independent* (7 March 1998) · *Daily Telegraph* (23 Feb 1998) · *The Times* (25 Feb 1998) · G. Scott, *The RCs* (1967) · H. Johnson, *Roy de Maistre: the English years, 1930–1968* (1995) · P. Doyle, *Westminster Cathedral, 1895–1995* (1995) · b. cert. · d. cert. · *CGPLA Eng. & Wales* (1998)
Archives Leeds Diocesan archives
Likenesses R. de Maistre, oils, 1958, St Anne's Cathedral, Leeds · A. Festing, oils, 1990, Diocese of Leeds Pastoral Centre, Hinsley Hall, Leeds
Wealth at death £72,211: probate, 18 June 1998, *CGPLA Eng. & Wales*

Wheeler, Sir Hugh Massy (1789–1857), army officer in the East India Company, was born on 30 June 1789 at Clonbeg, co. Tipperary, Ireland, the son of Captain Hugh Wheeler of the East India Company's service and his wife, Margaret, second daughter of Hugh, first Lord Massy. He was educated at Richmond, Surrey, and at Bath grammar school. Wheeler married Frances Matilda (d. 1857), the Anglo-Indian widow of Thomas Samuel Oliver, at Agra on 6 March 1842, and they had a son and two daughters.

Wheeler was commissioned ensign in the 24th Bengal infantry, in the East India Company's service, in 1803 and the following year served with his regiment during Lord Lake's campaign against Delhi. On 5 April 1805 he was promoted lieutenant, and captain on 1 January 1818. Wheeler was sent on detached duty in December 1824 with two companies, and dealt successfully with the robber Diraj Singh. On 27 June 1835 he was promoted lieutenant-colonel and in December was appointed to command the 48th native infantry. Wheeler led this regiment in Afghanistan in 1838–9, and was present at the assault and capture of Ghazni on 23 July 1839 and the occupation of Kabul on 6 August. For his services during the war he was mentioned in dispatches in October and made a CB on 20 December 1839. Wheeler was also highly commended by Sir Willoughby Cotton and mentioned in dispatches when on 19 August 1840 he dealt with a gathering of hostile Waziri tribesmen near Kaja, 30 miles from Jalalabad, and destroyed several enemy forts. In December 1840 Wheeler accompanied Cotton to India, his regiment forming part of the escort guarding Dost Muhammad, the former shah, who had surrendered. For his services in Afghanistan Wheeler was allowed to accept from the Shuja al-Mulk and wear the order of the Durani empire.

Wheeler was appointed to command the 2nd infantry brigade, composed of the 50th foot, 48th native infantry, and the Sirmur battalion, in the army of the Sutlej on 13 December 1845. At the battle of Mudki on 18 December he was badly wounded, but, although still suffering from his injuries, with his brigade he joined Sir Harry Smith near Ludhiana on 26 January 1846 and took a prominent part in the battle of Aliwal two days later. In his dispatch dated 30 January 1846 Sir Harry Smith observed: 'In Brigadier Wheeler, my second in command, I had a support I could rely on with every confidence, and most gallantly did he head his brigade.' On 17 February Wheeler led his brigade across the Sutlej River and occupied the strong fort at Phillaur, before advancing to the banks of the Beas. For his services he was made aide-de-camp to the queen with the rank of colonel in the army from 3 April 1846.

On 29 April Wheeler was appointed to command the Jullundur Doab as a brigadier-general of the first class. Following the outbreak of the Second Anglo-Sikh War he took the field in September, and on 14 October reduced the strong fortress of Rangal Naga. For this action he was congratulated by Lord Gough, who ascribed the success to 'his soldier-like and judicious arrangements'. Wheeler was appointed to command the 9th brigade of the 4th infantry division of the army of the Punjab on 8 November 1848. Later that month he was mentioned in dispatches by Sir Hugh Gough for his important role in the reduction of Kalawala. While commanding the Punjab division and the Jullundur field force Wheeler was also later mentioned in dispatches for his assault and the capture of the heights of Dallah during his difficult operations against Ram Singh. When the war ended the governor-general commented in general orders on the great skill and success with which Wheeler had carried out the duties assigned to him. For his services Wheeler received the campaign medal, the thanks of both houses of parliament, and the thanks of the directors of the East India Company; on 16 August 1850 he was made a KCB.

Wheeler resumed his command of the Jullundur Doab, and on 20 June 1854 was promoted to be major-general. He was appointed to the command of the Cawnpore division on 30 June 1856. When the Indian mutiny began in May 1857 Wheeler remained surprisingly optimistic when news reached him that the Indian regiments stationed at Meerut and Delhi had mutinied. As a precautionary measure, however, Wheeler selected a defensive position outside the city of Cawnpore, near the sepoy lines, where some half-completed barracks offered suitable accommodation for the European men, women, and children under his command. His small European force was also reinforced by a small detachment from Lucknow, and despite Sir Henry Lawrence's words of warning Wheeler also enlisted the support of the Raja Dundhu Panth of Bithur (afterwards known as Nana Sahib). Three hundred of his men and two guns arrived at Cawnpore on 22 May and took over the custody of the treasury at Nawabganj. The incomplete entrenchment was quickly occupied by the European women, children, and other non-combatants who were joined at the beginning of June by Wheeler. On 1 June Wheeler confidently wrote to Lord Canning informing him that he had sent transport to bring in the European population of Allahabad 'and in a few days—a very few days—I shall consider Cawnpore safe—nay, that I may send aid to Lucknow if needed'. Despite Sir Henry Lawrence's unease about Cawnpore's defences, two officers and fifty men were sent two days later from the city to help defend Lucknow. He had good grounds for concern. In fact, Wheeler's position at Cawnpore was very weak. A combination of over-confidence about the loyalty of the Indian regiments stationed at Cawnpore and his anxiety not to provoke an incident had persuaded Wheeler deliberately to reject occupying the easily defensible magazine, a large walled enclosure near the river that was amply supplied with arms, ammunition, and stores, which could have held out until help arrived. The hastily constructed entrenchment that he had chosen to occupy instead was badly sited, its defences were weak, and inadequate supplies had been collected to withstand a long siege.

During the night of 4 June the 2nd cavalry regiment and 1st native infantry stationed at Cawnpore mutinied, joining with the Nana's troops at Nawabganj. The treasury was looted, public buildings set on fire, and the magazine, with its heavy artillery, ammunition, and stores, was occupied by the rebels. The two unaffected native infantry regiments followed suit the next day and the mutineers, laden with loot, started marching towards Delhi until the Nana persuaded them to return to attack the Europeans—numbering just under 1000—gathered at Cawnpore. On the night of 6 June the bombardment of Wheeler's position commenced, using guns captured at the arsenal. Heavy casualties were inflicted in the exposed entrenchment each day, including Wheeler's already wounded son, Godfrey, who was decapitated by a roundshot. A combination of intense heat, hunger, and thirst caused further intense suffering among the handful of defenders and the large number of non-combatants crowding the position. On 25 June Nana offered the garrison terms of surrender, but although Wheeler wanted to reject them outright he was persuaded by his fellow officers that the safety and well-being of the civilians was paramount. The remnant of the garrison, with the surviving women and children, marched out of the entrenchment under arms after a three-week siege on the morning of 27 June, under a safe conduct from the Nana to proceed downstream by river to Allahabad. While this column embarked on boats at the Satichaura Ghat and started to journey downriver, however, the mutineers and Nana's troops suddenly opened fire, killing and wounding large numbers of the surviving soldiers, women, and children. Wheeler was among those killed, along with his wife and elder daughter, Margaret Frances. His eighteen-year-old daughter, Ulrica, was rescued from the ghat by an Indian cavalryman who later married her. The women and children who survived the massacre were imprisoned in atrocious conditions in the *bibigarh* in Cawnpore, and later murdered.

T. R. MOREMAN

Sources S. N. Sen, *Eighteen fifty-seven* (Delhi, 1958) · *DNB* · P. J. O. Taylor, ed., *A companion to the 'Indian mutiny' of 1857* (1996) · C. Hibbert, *The great mutiny, India, 1857* (1978) · M. Thompson, *The story of Cawnpore* (1859) · P. C. Gupta, *Nana Sahib and the rising at Cawnpore* (1963) · G. O. Trevelyan, *Cawnpore* (1865) · V. C. P. Hodson, *List of officers of the Bengal army, 1758–1834*, 4 (1947)

Archives PRO, letters to Charles Napier, 30/64

Wheeler, James Talboys (1824–1897), historian of India, son of James Luff Wheeler, bookseller (*d.* 1862), and his wife, Anne Ophelia, daughter of David Alphonso *Talboys, was born at Oxford on 22 December 1824. Educated at a private school, he was unsuccessful as a publisher and bookseller but gained some credit as a writer of handbooks for university students and of a more elaborate work on the geography of Herodotus (1848). During the Crimean War he was appointed to a supernumerary clerkship at the War Office. He married, on 15 January 1852 in Cambridge, Emily, daughter of Robert Roe, printseller; they had three surviving sons and one daughter.

In 1858 Wheeler went to India as editor of the *Madras Spectator*, but abandoned journalism on being appointed professor of moral and mental philosophy in the Madras Presidency College in 1858. In May 1860 he was employed by the Madras government to examine its records; the results of his research appeared as *Madras in the Olden Time* (1861). On 26 February 1862 he was appointed assistant secretary to the government of India in the foreign department, and moved to Calcutta, where, among other duties, he had charge of the foreign and, later, of the home offices when the secretaries were at Simla. In Calcutta he compiled under orders of government a series of background memoranda on the history and political relations of a number of countries bordering on India. Early in 1870 he was transferred to Rangoon as secretary to the chief commissioner of British Burma. In November 1870 he visited Mandalay and Bhamo in that capacity, and had an interview with the king of Burma.

In 1873 Wheeler obtained a long leave of absence in England, where he continued his work on an extended *History of India*, the first volume of which had been published in 1867; the last of its four volumes appeared in 1881. After returning to India in 1876, he was employed to report on the records in the home and foreign departments at Calcutta; he compiled two volumes, which he was allowed to publish. He also prepared and published an official *History of the Imperial Assemblage at Delhi* (1877). In 1891 he retired from the service. He died at Ramsgate on 13 January 1897. Wheeler was one of the first historians of British India to rely primarily on documentary sources. Although his perspectives were unequivocally imperialist, his work continues to be consulted for its empirical strengths.

STEPHEN WHEELER, rev. DAVID WASHBROOK

Sources *The Times* (14 Jan 1897) · Allibone, *Dict.* · C. E. Buckland, *Dictionary of Indian biography* (1906) · m. cert.

Wheeler, John (*d.* 1617), secretary of the Company of Merchant Adventurers, is of obscure origins. His supposed connection to Great Yarmouth appears to be solely the result of confusion with John Wheeler (*fl.* 1610), the member of parliament for that town. By 1589 Wheeler had joined the Society of Merchant Adventurers, the controllers of the cloth trade between England and the continent, and was the secretary by 1601. In that year the privy council granted freedom of trade to the two Hanseatic League cities of Hamburg and Stade, and Elizabeth granted a ten-year licence to the earl of Cumberland for the export of 'white' or unfinished cloth. Both these grants threatened to undermine the arrangements made by the society to regulate the cloth trade and to keep in check its German rival, the Hanseatic League. In April 1601 Thomas Milles distributed his tract *The Customer's Apology*,

which attacked the society and its supposed monopolistic practices.

Within two months Wheeler had written and published his 40,000-word reply, a strongly worded defence of the society entitled *A Treatise of commerce wherein are showed the commodities arising by a well ordered and ruled trade such as that of the Society of Merchants Adventurers is proved to be, written principally for the better information of those who doubt the necessities of the said society in the state of the realm of England*. The prefatory dedication was signed by Wheeler on 6 June 1601 in Middelburg in Zeeland, then the society's base on the continent, and it is there that the first edition was printed. The second edition appeared in London later in the month. An eight-page draft of the *Treatise*, possibly in Wheeler's hand, is in the Public Record Office.

Written to persuade the English government and merchants of the value of the society and to convince the friends of the Hanseatics that they would not be reinstated in England, the *Treatise* proved to be a most successful piece of propaganda. Although much of the historical background and even some of the statistics were taken from George Nedham's 1565 'Letter to the earls of East Friesland', in the absence of other records, Wheeler's account of the society's development over the centuries provided such detail that it remains the principal source for the history of the Merchant Adventurers. His draft begins: 'The traffick of this land hath been managed under the government of a companie almost 400 years, first in the staple and wool trade and next in the M. Adventurers and cloth trade' ('John Wheeler's treatise', 167). The stability given to the trade by this management was such 'that the State and Commonwealth hereby reapeth more profit than if men were suffered to run a loose and irregular course without order, command or oversight' (Hotchkiss, 341). The allegation that the society was a monopoly was 'a slander and injurious imputation, maliciously devised by the Hanses', behind whom were the Spanish, whose object was 'through the side of the Merchants Adventurers to hurt and wound the state of England' (ibid., 73).

In 1602 Wheeler was considered the natural successor to George Gilpin in the important diplomatic post of councillor to the council of estate in the Low Countries, but he nevertheless remained in the society's employ. Christopher Hoddeson, the governor of the society, wrote of him:

> The man is wise and honest, hath a sharp sight and quick conceit to prevent any mishap, is of good estimation and long acquainted with the manners of the Netherlanders. He hath their language, Latin and French as perfect as English, with a good taste of Italian and Greek. He is not sparing of his pen, [and] hath good advertisements from Prague, Cologne and other places of far remote matters. (*Salisbury MSS*, 12, 390)

In 1608 Wheeler prepared *The lawes customes and ordinances of the fellowshippe of Merchantes Adventurers of the realm of England collected and digested into order by John Wheeler*. Although the original is now lost, a contemporary copy is in the British Library. In 1609 a new ordinance was added to forbid marriage with foreign-born women, which

Wheeler himself transgressed, and he was disfranchised from the society until February 1612.

Following privileges given to the Merchant Adventurers by the city of Hamburg in 1612, the chief seat of the society moved there. Wheeler, who opposed the move, stayed on in Middelburg, partly because of the threat posed by the interlopers in the Netherlands. The Merchant Adventurers' control of the cloth trade had been weakened because, he wrote, 'Amsterdam, in maintaining the interloperie, sucketh the very heart blood from us' (*Buccleuch MSS*, 122).

In 1614 Alderman William Cokayne, perhaps the wealthiest and most influential of London merchants, threw the cloth trade into crisis. Through his persuasion, the king suspended the society's charter on 2 November 1614, and arranged the grant of a new charter to the King's Merchant Adventurers of the New Trade of London on 29 August 1615. Cokayne's intention was to foster in England the trades of dyeing, dressing, and finishing woollen cloth in England so as to compete with both the Merchant Adventurers in the export of cloth and also the foreign manufacturers of finished cloth. It was an idea that Wheeler had himself tested in 1612 by ordering the export of coloured cloths to Antwerp as an experiment to find out the reaction of authorities there. Although Wheeler was initially unwilling to join the new venture, the crisis deepened and, after holding out for eight or nine months, he joined the King's Merchants. The new project did not prosper against the opposition of the society and the foreign markets, and great damage was done to the cloth trade. On 1 January 1617 the king restored the society, and on 9 January the King's Merchants surrendered their charter. Wheeler was dismissed by the Merchant Adventurers after twenty-seven years' service and died within the year, in 1617. The society contributed £50 towards the upkeep of his orphans.   PIERS WAUCHOPE

Sources G. B. Hotchkiss, *A treatise of commerce by John Wheeler* (1931) · W. E. Lingelbach, *The Merchant Adventurers of England: their lives and ordinances with other documents* (1971) · 'John Wheeler's treatise of commerce 1601', PRO, SP 12/283, fols. 167–71 · G. D. Ramsay, ed., *The politics of a Tudor merchant adventurer: a letter to the earls of East Friesland* (1979) · *Report on the manuscripts of his grace the duke of Buccleuch and Queensberry … preserved at Montagu House*, 3 vols. in 4, HMC, 45 (1899–1926), vol. 1 · *Calendar of the manuscripts of the most hon. the marquis of Salisbury*, 24 vols., HMC, 9 (1883–1976), vols. 12, 21 · *Report on the manuscripts of the marquis of Downshire*, 6 vols. in 7, HMC, 75 (1924–95), vols. 3–5 · C. T. Carr, ed., *Select charters of trading companies, AD 1530–1707*, SeldS, 28 (1913) · A. Friis, *Alderman Cockayne's project and the cloth trade: the commercial policy of England in its main aspects, 1603–1625*, trans. [A. Fausboll] (1927)

Wheeler, Maurice (1647/8–1727), Church of England clergyman, was the son of Maurice Wheeler of St Giles, Dorset. He matriculated from New Inn Hall, Oxford, on 1 April 1664, aged sixteen, and proceeded BA on 17 October 1667. He was ordained deacon on 19 December 1668 at Worcester. He was appointed chaplain of Christ Church, Oxford, in 1670, and on 5 July that year proceeded MA. Also in 1670 he was appointed rector of St Ebbe's, Oxford. In 1673 he became the tutor of William Wake, the future bishop of Lincoln and archbishop of Canterbury. Also in

1673 Wheeler published *The Oxford Almanac for the Year of Our Lord 1673*, more than 30,000 being printed. Such was his success that the Society of Booksellers 'bought off the copy for the future' (Wood, *Ath. Oxon.*, 4.785–6). While rector of St Ebbe's Wheeler married. Both the identity of his bride and the date of the marriage are uncertain, but the most likely possibility is that he married Anne Lowe in Christ Church in 1679. The St Ebbe's parish registers record the burial of twin sons in June 1680. According to his will his son George was the only survivor of eight sons, although he also had a daughter, Susanna, who survived him out of a total of eleven children.

On 4 August 1680 Wheeler was installed as rector of Sibbertoft, Northamptonshire. He stayed four years before being appointed on 11 September 1684 master of the cathedral school in Gloucester, known as College School. In 1684 Wheeler demonstrated his interest in the manufacture of clocks when he published *A letter to Dr. Robert Plot, concerning a movement that measures time after a peculiar manner, with an account of the reasons of the said motion*, and that same year he contributed a section 'Of curiosity' to an English translation of Plutarch's *Moralia*. Thereafter Wheeler concentrated on west country affairs and in particular his school. According to Bonner he 'new modelled it in every respect, both within doors and without' (Bonner, 17–18), even to the extent of designing the school clock. While in Gloucester Wheeler maintained a regular correspondence with William Wake, by now a rising star in the Church of England. In June 1702 he offered Wake the opinion that 'I have more charity for any sort of honest dissenter, than for such kind of church-man among us who of all men seem to me to have the least sense of religion' (Wake MSS, 23/138). It was Wheeler's connection to Wake which saw him installed as a prebendary of Lincoln on 13 March 1708. From about 1708 Wheeler's letters to Wake evinced a yearning to retire. On 3 October 1708 he recorded that he had preached for the first time in 'about 25 years' (Wake MSS, 23/183). On 19 August 1711 Wheeler's wife died after many years of ill health. This allowed Wheeler to leave Gloucester after twenty-eight years as master, following his installation as rector of Wappenham on 17 May 1712. By this date Wheeler suffered from poor eyesight, which made reading difficult. His intention was to retire once his daughter had been provided for, and on 20 May 1714 she married his curate, John Fletcher. Wheeler duly resigned Wappenham to his son-in-law, who was installed on 13 May 1715 'by my interest in the R. R. William Ld Bp of Lincoln' (will, fol. 234*v*).

Wheeler was installed as rector of Thorpe Mandeville, Northamptonshire, on 12 November 1720, which he retained until his death. According to Rudder he died on 6 October 1727, being buried at Wappenham on 9 October 1727. He made his will in his seventy-eighth year in May 1726. He referred to his son George as 'now in a languishing condition' (will, fol. 234*r*); he received just £10 'having formerly in his education and farther encouragement bestowed upon him more than at that time could well be afforded' (ibid.). His daughter Susanna Fletcher received furniture including the desk 'where I have spent many delightfull hours in usefull meditations upon the vanitys of this World' (ibid.). John Fletcher received his books and mathematical, musical, and mechanical instruments. There was also a bequest to Wappenham's rector and churchwardens towards a charity school and workhouse to be formed 'by a friendly combination of the neighbouring parishes' (ibid., fol. 234v), but if no progress had been made after two years the money was to go to the charity school and workhouse at Gloucester with which Wheeler had been much concerned.   STUART HANDLEY

Sources will, PRO, PROB 11/618, fols. 234r–235r • Foster, *Alum. Oxon.* • H. I. Longden, *Northamptonshire and Rutland clergy from 1500*, ed. P. I. King and others, 16 vols. in 6, Northamptonshire RS (1938–52), 15.23, 16.144 • *Fasti Angl., 1541–1857*, [Lincoln] • Wood, *Ath. Oxon.*, new edn, 4.785–6 • *VCH Gloucestershire*, 2.331 • Christ Church Oxf., Wake MSS, Epistle 23, nos. 128–296 • S. Rudder, *A new history of Gloucestershire* (1779), 170–71 • N. Sykes, *William Wake, archbishop of Canterbury, 1657–1737*, 2 vols. (1957) • T. Bonner, *Illustration … consisting of six views of the interior of Gloucester Cathedral* (1806?), 17–18 • *IGI*

Archives Christ Church Oxf., Wake MSS, Epistle 23, nos. 128–296

Wheeler, Sir (Robert Eric) Mortimer (1890–1976), archaeologist and broadcaster, was born on 10 September 1890 in Glasgow, the eldest of the three children and only son of (Robert) Mortimer Wheeler (d. 1936), journalist, and his second wife, Emily Baynes (d. 1951), niece and ward of Thomas Spencer *Baynes of St Andrews University. After several years in Edinburgh the family moved in 1894 to Saltaire near Bradford, and to nearby Shipley in 1899. Bobs (his family nickname—he was later generally known to friends as Rik or Rikki) and his sisters were educated by their parents, father and son becoming particularly close, united in a love of the visual arts, literature, and outdoor pursuits. From 1899 to 1904 he attended Bradford grammar school, where he acquired Latin but shunned ball games. His formal schooling ended in 1904 when the family moved to London. Here, encouraged by his father to educate himself, he spent much time in museums and art galleries, intending to pursue an artistic career.

In 1907 Wheeler won a scholarship to read classics at University College, London, with, from 1909, a special arrangement to attend art classes at the Slade School of Fine Art. He now became aware that his artistic ambitions were unrealistic, but his artistic flair and experience can be seen in his later archaeological record drawings. Taking a BA in 1910 and an MA in 1912, in 1913 he was awarded the Franks studentship in archaeology to study Roman pottery in the Rhineland; this research he later successfully submitted as a doctoral thesis in 1920.

Also in 1913 Wheeler obtained a probational post as junior investigator for the Royal Commission on Historical Monuments (RCHM). In the following year he married Tessa Verney (1893–1936) [see Wheeler, Tessa Verney], a history graduate who became an outstanding field archaeologist in her own right, working closely with her husband; as an archaeological partnership they became known as 'the Wheelers'. Their only child was Michael Mortimer Wheeler QC (1915–1992).

On the outbreak of First World War, Wheeler initially

Sir (Robert Eric) Mortimer Wheeler (1890–1976), by Bassano, 1939

served in Britain as an instructor with the Royal Field Artillery. In October 1917 he was posted as a major to the 76th army brigade, serving briefly in Belgium and Italy before being transferred to the western front in March 1918, where he served with distinction and was awarded the Military Cross. The discipline, hierarchy, and order of military life and the drama and heroicism of military action suited his temperament, bringing out his qualities of leadership. He was described at this time by a contemporary, Jacquetta Hawkes, as 'tall, lean, and handsome, with a mop of wavy hair' (DNB).

After demobilization in 1919 Wheeler returned briefly to his post with the RCHM, but in August 1920 secured appointments as keeper of archaeology at the National Museum of Wales and lecturer in archaeology at the University College of South Wales and Monmouthshire, Cardiff. Approaching the task with vision, he established the National Museum of Wales as the focus of a network of Welsh provincial museums which he encouraged and revived. Appointed director of the National Museum in 1924, he began a lifetime of successful fund-raising from private and public sources, obtaining the critical funds to complete building work on the museum.

Wheeler also encouraged popular interest in the national past, lecturing, publishing *Prehistoric and Roman Wales* (1925) and, with Tessa, excavating key Roman sites, Segontium (1921–2), Gaer near Brecon (1924–5) and Caerleon (1926). On these and subsequent digs he trained many eminent archaeologists of the future in his radical techniques. Almost alone in having adopted the excellent excavation principles of the pioneer, General Pitt-Rivers, he began a crusade to introduce scientific techniques and rigour into the conduct and recording of excavations, notably by applying the principle of true stratification.

Wheeler's rapid publication of his results (*Segontium and the Roman Occupation of Wales*, 1923; *The Roman Fort Near Brecon*, 1926) set a standard that he was thereafter to insist on as a virtue, although his excavations and publications were to be criticized by some of his colleagues for their lack of depth, absence of consideration of social and economic aspects, and precipitate elevation of hypothesis into firm interpretation, and at times for their over-dramatization. He did not hesitate to use any popularizing means available, as at Caerleon where he invoked the popular name for the remains of the Roman amphitheatre, King Arthur's Round Table, to win public support and funding for the excavation. This was his first, successful, exploitation of the media: he obtained sponsorship from the *Daily Mail*, granting it exclusive rights to cover the excavation. This aspect of Wheeler's approach to his work also found disfavour with some of his colleagues.

In July 1926 Wheeler became keeper of the run-down London Museum, giving him the opportunity he had sought to return to the capital, which remained his base for the rest of his life. He and Tessa began work on a project dear to his heart, the establishment of an Institute of Archaeology to provide training in archaeological science, field techniques, and conservation. It was more than a decade before the dream was finally fulfilled, when the institute was officially opened on 29 April 1937. Owing to a substantial legacy from Sir Flinders Petrie, given on condition that it housed his major collection of Levantine antiquities, the institute curiously had two contrasting focuses, the Near East and Britain.

Meanwhile, Wheeler applied his usual vigour to setting the London Museum on its feet, cataloguing and reorganizing the collections, publishing guidebooks, putting on exhibitions, using it as a centre for lectures and concerts, and raising funds from private individuals and the Treasury. He and Tessa undertook increasingly ambitious excavations, of the Romano-British villa and cult centre at Lydney Park in 1928–9 (*Report on the excavations of the prehistoric, Roman and post-Roman site in Lydney Park, Gloucestershire*, 1932), Roman and immediately pre-Roman St Albans in 1930–34 (*Verulamium: a Belgic and Two Roman Cities*, 1936), and the massive hill fort of Maiden Castle in 1934–7 (*Maiden Castle, Dorset*, 1943). At the last, finding the traditional trench layout inadequate, he devised a layout of grid squares separated by baulks, which was to become the hallmark of the Wheeler excavation method: these provided numerous sections in two directions, giving an excellent picture of the stratigraphic development of the excavated area.

In April 1936 Tessa Wheeler died of a pulmonary embolism. In her Wheeler lost not only a valued companion but also a devoted and highly intelligent second in command.

It is probable that overwork to meet his exacting, superhuman standards contributed to her untimely death. Her latter years had been rendered unhappy by his blatant unfaithfulness; and sexual adventures with many women were to remain an important feature of his life. In March 1939 he married Mavis de Vere Cole (*b. c.*1909), an intimate friend of Augustus John, 'as unashamedly libidinous as himself' (Hawkes, 183); this inappropriate match lasted less than three years. Divorced in 1942, they remained, however, on friendly terms until her death in 1970.

During the late 1930s, Wheeler had extended his investigations to the Iron Age hill forts of north-western France, culturally linked with those of Britain. Completion of this work and publication of his findings (*Hillforts of Northern France*, 1957) was delayed by the outbreak of the Second World War. Eager to resume his martial career, Wheeler was frustrated to spend the early war years in Britain, raising and ruthlessly training the 48th light anti-aircraft battery which swelled into the 42nd Royal Artillery regiment. Finally in September 1941 they were posted to north Africa, participating in Alamein. In addition to heroic military action, Wheeler worked to secure official protection for antiquities in the areas the army occupied. Promoted brigadier, he took part in the invasion of Italy in 1943; this meant postponing for some months his acceptance of the post of director-general of the archaeological survey of India, an institution that had greatly declined in the years since Sir John Marshall's retirement.

Returning to England in November 1943, Wheeler proposed marriage to Margaret (Kim) Norfolk (*née* Collingridge), a former student and colleague and a devout Roman Catholic. Wheeler made an insincere conversion to Catholicism while courting her but remained throughout his life a pagan; this disparity in beliefs drove a wedge between them, dooming their marriage, which took place in 1945 in India, at Simla.

Wheeler sailed for India in February 1944, using the journey to draw up plans and sweeping into action immediately on arrival. Within the brief four years of his office he achieved an astonishing amount, reorganizing and revitalizing the archaeological survey, extracting greatly increased funds from the government, and running training excavations in which he initiated a whole generation of Indian archaeologists into the Wheeler method. He founded a journal, *Ancient India*, in which the results of these excavations—at the great city of Taxila in 1944-5, the Roman trading station of Arikamedu in 1945, the Indus city of Harappa in 1946, and the southern megalithic sites of Brahmagiri and Chandravalli in 1947—were rapidly published. His strong interest in military matters led him to misinterpret the flood-defence walls at Harappa and Mohenjo-daro, an example of his lifelong tendency to make confident and somewhat narrow interpretations based on rapidly gathered and insufficient data; but there is no doubting the major contribution that he made to an understanding of the prehistory of the subcontinent. On later visits he was heaped with honours and adulation by former colleagues, from leading scholars down to gardeners.

Wheeler returned to a lesser role in Britain in 1948: a part-time professorship at the Institute of Archaeology in the University of London. For several years, however, he was also archaeological adviser to the newly formed Pakistan archaeological department, running a small training excavation at Mohenjo-daro in 1950 which he failed, uncharacteristically, to publish, although it received considerable coverage in his Cambridge History of India volume, *The Indus Civilization* (1953). He undertook his last major excavation in Britain in the following year, on the hill fort of Stanwick in Yorkshire (*The Stanwick Fortifications*, 1954), and returned to Pakistan in 1956 to fulfil a long-held ambition to excavate Charsada (*Charsada: a Metropolis of the North-West Frontier*, 1962). His final official involvement with the subcontinent came in the 1960s, when he was a key member of the UNESCO team concerned with the preservation and conservation of Mohenjo-daro.

In 1949 Wheeler took part in the movement to reform the British Academy, of which sleepy body he had been a fellow since 1941. Elected in 1949 as its secretary, he showed his customary vigour in obtaining substantial private grants, vastly increased government funding, and a significant widening of its role, the five British schools of archaeology overseas now coming under its aegis. During his long term of office he was able to add a further two schools, in east Africa and Tehran, Iran. By the time that he retired in 1968, he had transformed the British Academy into the major grant-giving body for research in the humanities.

In the last two decades of his life Wheeler wrote prolifically, publishing memoirs (*Still Digging*, 1955; *Alms for Oblivion*, 1966; *My Archaeological Mission to India and Pakistan*, 1976) and a classic exposition of his crusading excavation techniques (*Archaeology from the Earth*, 1955), as well as a good half-dozen scholarly and popular works on a variety of archaeological subjects. He gave a tremendous boost to popular interest in archaeology as an early television broadcaster, appearing with Glyn Daniel in the successful quiz programme *Animal, Vegetable, Mineral?* in which a panel of experts had to identify an object from a museum, and the series *Buried Treasure*, in one programme of which he and Daniel disgustedly shared a reconstruction of Tollund Man's last meal. He was voted television personality of the year in 1954. He also regularly entertained and enlightened a smaller audience as a lecturer on Swan Hellenic cruises. Official and academic honours were heaped upon him, including a knighthood in 1952, the Companionship of Honour in 1967, and in 1968, to his great pleasure, a fellowship of the Royal Society.

A personal gain in Wheeler's association with the British Academy was his fortunate acquisition of Molly Myres as his secretary. Ably assisting his work for the academy, she also became a close personal friend, 'his female looker-after' as she called herself, aiding him in many ways, particularly after his marriage to Kim finally broke down in 1956, and giving him a home in his final years when his health declined. He died at her house in Bothy Downs Lane, Leatherhead, Surrey, on 22 July 1976, having suffered a stroke the previous day. JANE MCINTOSH

Sources J. Hawkes, *Mortimer Wheeler: adventurer in archaeology* (1982) · S. Piggott, *Memoirs FRS*, 23 (1977), 623–42 · M. Wheeler, *Still digging* (1955) · *DNB* · G. Clark, *Sir Mortimer and Indian archaeology* (1979) · D. K. Chakrabarti, *A history of Indian archaeology from the beginning to 1947* (1988) · J. Hawkes, 'Robert Eric Mortimer Wheeler, 1890–1976', *PBA*, 63 (1977), 482–507

Archives Colchester and Essex Museum, Colchester, Camulodunum excavation records · Dorset County Museum, Dorchester, Maiden Castle excavation records · S. Antiquaries, Lond., papers and drawings relating to Iron Age camps in northern France · Verulamium Museum, St Albans, Verulamium excavation records | Bodl. Oxf., letters to O. G. S. Crawford · Rice University, Houston, Texas, Woodson Research Center, corresp. with Sir Julian Huxley · U. Cam., Museum of Archaeology and Anthropology, letters to C. F. Fox · U. Reading L., letters to Sir Frank Stenton and Lady Stenton · W. Sussex RO, corresp. with Oswald Barron | FILM BFI NFTVA

Likenesses photographs, 1930–42, repro. in Wheeler, *Still digging* · photograph, 1932, NPG · E. G. Malindine, photograph, 1934, NPG · Bassano, photograph, 1939, NPG [*see illus.*] · W. Stoneman, photograph, 1951, NPG · H. Coster, photographs, 1956, NPG · C. Ware, photograph, 1956, Hult. Arch. · J. A. Grant, charcoal drawing, 1960, S. Antiquaries, Lond. · W. Bird, photograph, 1961, NPG · G. Argent, photograph, 1970, NPG · Lafayette, photograph, NPG · photograph, repro. in Hawkes, 'Robert Eric Mortimer Wheeler' · photograph, repro. in Piggott, *Memoirs FRS* · photographs, repro. in Hawkes, *Mortimer Wheeler*

Wealth at death £65,842: probate, 18 Oct 1976, *CGPLA Eng. & Wales*

Wheeler, (Thomas) Norman Samuel (1915–1990), army officer and secret operations officer, was born on 16 June 1915 at 89 Victoria Avenue, Worcester, the eldest son of Thomas Henry Wheeler, bandmaster of the 4th Worcestershire regiment, who had served in the 3rd hussars during the Second South African War and later became an officer in the South African police, and his wife, Wilhelmina Abernethy. He was educated at Water Kloof House, South Africa, and St Helen's College, Southsea, Hampshire, before entering the Royal Military College, Sandhurst. Of Irish extraction on his maternal side, he was commissioned into the Royal Ulster Rifles (RUR) in August 1935. A brother, later Air Chief Marshall Sir (Henry) Neil George Wheeler (b. 1917), entered the Royal Air Force College, Cranwell, in the same year.

Wheeler first saw active service during the Arab rising in Palestine, where he received the first of his four mentions in dispatches. In 1939 he married Helen Clifford, younger daughter of F. H. E. Webber of Emsworth, Hampshire. They had one son and one daughter. The outbreak of the Second World War found him in Ulster as adjutant at the RUR depot, which in 1940 moved from Armagh to new barracks at Ballymena. In 1941 he left Ballymena for a spell at Staff College; he subsequently became brigade major of 38th (Irish) brigade and served in several quartermaster posts in the Sudan and Eritrea. In September 1943 he joined the Special Operations Executive (SOE), Britain's secret sabotage organization. Brigadier E. F. ('Trotsky') Davies, also formerly of the RUR, whose subaltern Wheeler had been on coronation day in 1937 when they lined the route at Piccadilly Circus, was organizing an SOE mission to the Albanian partisans and had swept his old regiment for volunteers to go with him. Charged with the duties of administration and quartering officer and promoted lieutenant-colonel, Wheeler parachuted into enemy-occupied Albania in mid-December 1943.

The original plan had called for Wheeler to join Davies's base in the Cermenike mountains north-east of the capital, but bad weather and enemy offensives prevented any link-up before Davies was wounded and captured, whereupon command of all SOE operations in southern Albania devolved upon Wheeler. He carried out this new role with typical energy and skill, more than once leading his joint force of SOE personnel and partisans safely through the mountains to break out of German encircling moves. He was also well placed to witness the remarkable growth in partisan strength during the spring of 1944, a fact which he reported in forceful terms to SOE headquarters and which influenced the development of British policy towards Albania. Major General Colin Gubbins, head of the SOE, remarked in a confidential note of June 1944 on the 'good work' done by Wheeler: 'a loyal, hardworking soldier of great capacity' (private information).

Withdrawn from Albania in late May 1944, Wheeler rejoined the 2nd Royal Ulster Rifles in Normandy in July and fought with them throughout the campaign in northwest Europe, first as support company commander and later as second in command. In 1945 he returned to Palestine, as assistant adjutant and quartermaster general to the 6th airborne division. In the following year he moved to Aldershot and the headquarters of the airborne establishment. In 1949 he became military assistant to General Sir James Steele, adjutant-general to the forces, at the War Office. From 1951 to 1952 Wheeler was on the British services' liaison staff at Melbourne, Australia, after which he returned to the 1st battalion RUR in Hong Kong as adjutant. From 1954 to 1957 he served as a full colonel on the general staff in the northern army group headquarters and the British army of the Rhine headquarters, West Germany.

In 1958, reverting to lieutenant-colonel, Wheeler assumed command of the 1st battalion RUR for operations in Cyprus during the Ethnike Organosis Kypriakou Agonos terrorist campaign, and was appointed OBE. He also received his fourth mention in dispatches, adding to the two he had received during the Second World War. In the following year he took command of 39th infantry brigade at Lisburn in Northern Ireland. From 1962 to 1963 he served as chief of staff at 1st (British) corps, British army of the Rhine, and from 1964 to 1966 as general officer commanding 2nd infantry division, being appointed CBE in 1964. In 1969, after three years as chief of staff of contingencies planning at the supreme headquarters of the allied powers in Europe, he reached the peak of his military career by becoming chief of staff at British army of the Rhine headquarters, a post he held until retiring from the army in 1971. He was appointed CB in 1967.

Wheeler then embarked on a successful business career, becoming a director and secretary of the Independent Stores Association and assisting in its merger with a similar group to create Associated Independent Stores Ltd, of which he became deputy managing director in 1976. From 1980 Wheeler was chairman of J. E. Beale Ltd, of Bournemouth, until finally retiring in 1983. But at heart he remained an RUR man, and he held the presidency of the RUR Association from 1975 until his death.

Wheeler was robust and handsome with a fine military bearing and military moustache, but equally kind, good-humoured, and approachable, with a strong faith and positive attitude and an ability to get along with everyone, civilian and soldier alike. His son followed him into the RUR (which later became part of the Royal Irish Rangers), and as General Sir Roger Neil Wheeler was chief of the general staff at the Ministry of Defence from 1997 until 2000. Norman Wheeler died of heart failure at his home at Glebe House, Liston, Sudbury, Suffolk, on 21 September 1990. His wife survived him.   RODERICK BAILEY

Sources *Daily Telegraph* (2 Oct 1990) · *The Times* (2 Oct 1990) · E. F. Davies, *Illyrian venture: the story of the British military mission to enemy-occupied Albania, 1943–44* (1952) · R. Hibbert, *Albania's national liberation struggle: the bitter victory* (1991) · *The Blackthorn: regimental journal of the royal Irish regiment* (1991) · private information (2004) [sources including special operations executive adviser] · b. cert. · d. cert. · *CGPLA Eng. & Wales* (1990)
Archives King's Lond., Liddell Hart C., papers
Wealth at death £18,124: probate, 23 Nov 1990, *CGPLA Eng. & Wales*

Wheeler, Dame **Olive Annie** (1886–1963), educationist and psychologist, was born on 4 May 1886 at the High Street, Brecon, the younger daughter of Henry Burford Wheeler, a master printer, and his wife, Annie Poole. After secondary education at Brecon County School for Girls, she became an undergraduate at the University College of Wales, Aberystwyth, graduating BSc in 1907 and MSc in 1911. After completing her DSc in psychology at Bedford College, London, in 1916, she studied briefly at the University of Paris before commencing her teaching career in England at Chesterfield high school.

Most of Olive Wheeler's career, however, involved training teachers for secondary schools, beginning at St George's Training College, Edinburgh, and then lecturing in mental and moral science at Cheltenham Ladies' College. In 1918 she was appointed lecturer in education at Manchester University, becoming dean of education from 1923 to 1925, when she moved back to Wales as professor of education at the University College of South Wales and Monmouthshire, Cardiff, remaining there until retirement in 1951. She was dean of the faculty of education at Cardiff from 1948 and professor emeritus of the federal University of Wales from 1951 until her death.

Olive Wheeler's reputation as an educationist was based on her application of psychology to issues of educational policy and practice, as expressed in her published books: *Youth: the psychology of adolescence and its bearing on the reorganisation of adolescent education* (1929, 2nd edn 1933), *The Adventure of Youth* (1937, further editions 1945 and 1950), *The Psychological Basis of Adult Education* (1938), *Nursery School Education* (1939), and *Mental Health and Education* (1961). In addition she published numerous scholarly papers and books on anthropomorphism, Bergson, the intellectual development of children, and on creativity. Her progressive approach to education led her to anticipate later work on 'comprehensive schools', links between schools and industry, and the development of vocational guidance and educational counselling for adolescent pupils and students. She argued strongly for a socially just democracy supported by, and expressed through, the educational system, and wrote that 'it is difficult to see how civilisation can escape disaster if during the formative stage of early adolescence some of the most highly gifted pupils are trained to be technicians, others to be grammarians, and none to be whole "individuals"' (*The Adventure of Youth*, 1945, 21). These progressive views were expressed in lecture tours at home and abroad and in her work for a wide number of national bodies. Her distinction as a scholar was recognized in her fellowship of the British Psychological Society and her election as British delegate to the International Congress of Psychology in Montreal in 1954.

Olive Wheeler was made a DBE in 1949 for services to education in Wales. These services were extremely varied and reflected a lifelong devotion to political and social issues, especially those of women and young people. She had been an active student politician at Aberystwyth where, as president of the students' union, she had chained herself to the promenade railings outside Alexandra Hall for Women Students as a protest against its appalling food and petty restrictions. Contemporary university records describe her as 'a spirited young woman of marked ability' (E. L. Ellis, *Alexandra Hall 1896–1986*, 1986, 11). She was a loyal servant of the University of Wales, serving on its court, the council of the Welsh National School of Medicine, the academic board of the university, the University Guild of Graduates, and the appointments board. She unsuccessfully stood as a Labour parliamentary candidate for the University of Wales in the general election of 1922. As dean of the faculty of education at Cardiff she helped develop closer links between the teacher training colleges and the universities, and established a collegiate centre in Cathedral Road, Cardiff, where local teachers could develop skills for research in schools and classrooms.

Dame Olive Wheeler became vice-president of the British Federation of University Women, and was an executive member of the South Wales Association of Girls' Clubs, a regional adviser to the South Wales Women's Voluntary Service, and chair of Cardiff and District Nursery School Association. She was chair of the south Wales district of the Workers' Educational Association (WEA), a member of the Welsh Joint Education Committee and of the Central Advisory Council for Education (Wales), and chair of the Welsh Advisory Committee for Youth Unemployment. She was also a Welsh representative on the General Advisory Council of the British Broadcasting Corporation.

Dame Olive Wheeler, or the Dame, as some colleagues referred to her, was a charismatic lecturer and teacher who filled lecture halls by power of personality and a strong administrator of considerable drive. Her college principal, Anthony Steel, described her as 'a most distinguished educationist known in many parts of the world by her numerous papers and books—a great personal loss and a loss to Wales' (*Western Mail*, 28 Sept 1963). She enjoyed golf and, as William Boyd (1874–1962), reader in education at Glasgow acknowledged, she was a good hostess: 'The Dame is one of those strong minded managing women whom nobody likes very much, but she and I got on very well. She is retiring this year and once confided in me that anyone who had anything to do with Education in the Welsh Colleges would heave a sigh of relief: But I will say for her that she has a good cook and that she did her duty by me' (W. Boyd, MS journal, 27 May 1951). Dame Olive Wheeler collapsed and died in the Kardomah Café, 38 Queen Street, Cardiff, on 26 September 1963. She never married. Her books and publications in her library of psychology and education were given to University College, Cardiff. She left £500 for an annual prize for the best student or students in her former department of education, and a further £500 divided equally between the South Wales WEA and the Park End Presbyterian Church, Cardiff. JOHN B. THOMAS

Sources Burke, *Peerage* (1963) · *WW* (1963) · Hutchinson and Co., *Hutchinson's woman's who's who* (1934) · private information (2004) · *TLS* (2 March 1946) · *Western Mail* [Cardiff] (28 Sept 1963) · *South Wales Echo* (27 Sept 1963) · D. Allsobrook, 'The department of education' in, *The University College of South Wales and Monmouthshire: a centenary history 1883–1983*, ed. S. B. Chrimes, 1983, U. Wales, Cardiff · private papers of Dr William Boyd, priv. coll. · *The Times* (15 Nov 1963), 16 · b. cert. · d. cert.
Archives NL Wales, letters to Thomas Iorwerth Ellis
Likenesses photograph, repro. in *Western Mail* · photograph, repro. in *South Wales Echo*
Wealth at death £27,434 9s. 0d.: probate, 8 Nov 1963, *CGPLA Eng. & Wales*

Wheeler, Rosina Anne Doyle. *See* Lytton, Rosina Anne Doyle Bulwer (1802–1882).

Wheeler, Tessa Verney [*née* Tessa Verney] (1893–1936), archaeologist, was born in 1893 in Johannesburg, the only child of the union of the shadowy John Verney, doctor, and Annie Kilburn, a native of Bishop Auckland in co. Durham. The latter already had a son, John, from her first marriage to the equally shadowy Mr Mather. Taken to England, Tessa spent a happy childhood in the household of her mother's third partner, Theophilus Morgan Davis, chemist, who encouraged her to take a degree in history at University College, London. There she met (Robert Eric) Mortimer *Wheeler (1890–1976), archaeologist, whom she married in 1914.

When the First World War broke out, Mortimer Wheeler initially served in Britain. Whenever possible, Tessa, with their only child, Michael (*b.* 1915), moved to be near him in his various postings. In 1917 he was posted overseas; Tessa wrote regularly and was tireless in tracking down items which Wheeler requested in his frequent letters. This set the pattern that continued throughout her life: devotion to her husband and unremitting efforts to meet his exacting private and professional demands.

Although latterly she suffered blackouts and constant gastric problems, friends and colleagues found her sympathy, help, and support to be limitless, coupled with high intelligence, great competence and organizational ability, and remarkable diplomacy, 'No one ever saw her out of temper and nothing could induce her to spare herself', observed Sir Frederick Kenyon in her obituary and Lord Bledisloe added that 'she simply radiated inspiration and knowledge, coupled with a cheerfulness and charm which endeared her to all who were brought into contact with her' (*The Times*, 18 April 1936).

In August 1920 Mortimer Wheeler was appointed keeper of archaeology at the National Museum of Wales in Cardiff. Already Tessa was working tirelessly alongside him—they installed beds in the museum so that they could sleep there when working late. In 1921 they began the first of many joint excavations. Mortimer directed and oversaw these excavations and interpreted the results while Tessa was responsible for all the preparations, organization, administration, and day-to-day running. She also dealt with and recorded the finds. Together the Wheelers excavated Segontium (1921–2) and Gaer near Brecon (1924–5), and were about to excavate the amphitheatre at Caerleon in 1926 when their plans were altered by Mortimer Wheeler's appointment as keeper of the London Museum.

The move was a wrench for Tessa. After years of living in rented accommodation, the Wheeler family had recently moved into their own house in Cardiff, which had now to be abandoned for a rented flat in London, coupled with a hefty decrease in income. But Tessa threw herself with her customary zeal and cheerfulness into transferring her family to the capital and excavating Caerleon without Mortimer through the winter of 1926–7. Michael was now at boarding-school, but spent his holidays with his parents on their excavations at Lydney (1928–9), St Albans (1930–34), and Maiden Castle (from 1934). The *Daily Mail* provides a portrait of Tessa at this time: 'A woman with dark wavy hair and smiling brown eyes, dressed in a business-like brown jumper and skirt and brown Wellingtons' (Hawkes, 157). A darker side to Tessa's life had also developed, however, for Wheeler was by now openly unfaithful. Although Tessa endured the situation with patience and fortitude, it caused her great distress and misery.

Caerleon, Lydney, and St Albans were published jointly by the Wheelers ('The Roman amphitheatre at Caerleon', *Archaeologia*, 78, 1928, 111–218; *Report on the excavations of the prehistoric, Roman and post-Roman site in Lydney Park, Gloucestershire*, 1932; *Verulamium: a Belgic and Two Roman Cities*, 1936), a reflection of Tessa's growing status as an archaeologist in her own right. By 1928 she was a part-time lecturer at the London Museum and was elected fellow of the Society of Antiquaries; she later served on its council and was on its research committee. In addition, she worked indefatigably in support of Wheeler's activities, in particular playing a major part in realizing his dream of creating an archaeological institute in London. Highly successful in raising funds to finance its foundation, she was also active in looking after the students and arranging their

teaching when the institute came into being in 1934. At this stage it still lacked a home but largely through Tessa's efforts premises both suitable and affordable were eventually found in St John's Lodge, Regent's Park.

In the spring of 1936 Mortimer Wheeler visited the Levant, and Tessa took this opportunity to have a minor operation. She then became ill with suspected appendicitis, but an exploratory operation found nothing. Visited by Michael after a few days' convalescence, she seemed well on the road to recovery. That same night, however, she suffered a fatal pulmonary embolism, and she died at the National Temperance Hospital, London, on 15 April 1936. The strain of overwork may have played a major part in her untimely death. She was cremated at Golders Green crematorium a few days later.

Tessa Wheeler lived in an age when professional women often worked almost anonymously as extensions of their husbands. It is therefore difficult to disentangle her achievements from those usually credited to Mortimer. However, the Wheelers were viewed as a team by their contemporaries, and many regarded her as the finer archaeologist. When the Institute of Archaeology was officially opened in 1937, a black marble plaque was unveiled as a memorial to Tessa, who had played such a major role in its foundation and whose premature death had robbed archaeology of one of its most distinguished students.

JANE MCINTOSH

Sources J. Hawkes, *Mortimer Wheeler: adventurer in archaeology* (1982) · M. Wheeler, *Still digging* (1955) · C. Peers, obituary, *Antiquary's Journal*, 16 (1936), 327–8 · *The Times* (17 April 1936) · *The Times* (18 April 1936) · M. Diaz-Andreu and M. L. Stig Sørensen, *Excavating women: a history of women in European archaeology* (1998)
Likenesses group portrait, photograph, repro. in Hawkes, *Mortimer Wheeler* · photograph (at time of her marriage), priv. coll.; repro. in Hawkes, *Mortimer Wheeler* · photograph, priv. coll.; repro. in Hawkes, *Mortimer Wheeler*
Wealth at death £681 5s. 8d.: administration with will, 19 June 1936, *CGPLA Eng. & Wales*

Wheeler, Thomas (1754–1847), apothecary and botanist, second son of Thomas Wheeler (*bap.* 1710, *d.* 1769/70), and his wife, Susan Rivington, was born on 24 June 1754 in Basinghall Street, London, where his father practised as an apothecary. Mrs Cibber, the actress, was his father's first cousin. His grandfather, John Wheeler, surgeon to the Bridewell and Bethlem hospitals, died in 1740 during his year of office as master of the Barber–Surgeons' Company. Thomas Wheeler received his elementary education under the Revd David Garrow, the father of Sir William Garrow, at Hadley, Middlesex, and was admitted a pupil at St Paul's School on 25 January 1765, where he became an excellent classical scholar. After leaving St Paul's he was apprenticed to his father on 5 July 1768 for eight years. He gained his freedom of the Society of Apothecaries on 4 July 1775 by patrimony, as his father had died a few years before. On 24 July that year he entered St Thomas's Hospital as a pupil of Mr Whitfield, one of the apothecaries. Wheeler spent a year at St Thomas's, and it is probable that he then worked at the firm of Truesdale and Partridge, royal apothecaries.

From an early age Wheeler showed a great interest in

botany, a taste which was fostered by William Hudson, the botanical demonstrator at the Society of Apothecaries. On 18 March 1778 Wheeler was appointed 'Botanic Demonstrator … at the usual salary and an additional 40s. for the summer excursion', so making a total of £32 a year (Society of Apothecaries, MS 8200/9), at the physic garden at Chelsea, London, in succession to William Curtis. In 1784 Wheeler began a series of lectures on botany in the library of the Apothecaries' Hall, but the poor attendance deterred him from continuing it after 1786. In 1783 he was living in George Street, Foster Lane, when he was appointed assistant apothecary to Joseph Roberts at Christ's Hospital; 'being [a] very sober, diligent and knowing man in his business, and living near the hospital [he] will be ready on any call to attend' (Christ's Hospital, MS 12,806/12, fol. 368). Wheeler held the position until September 1801, when he was made apothecary. He resigned in December 1806 as he had been, 'favor'd with the appointment of Apothecary to St Bartholomews' Hospital' (ibid., MS 12,806/13, fol. 490). His salary as a result had now been increased from £250 a year to £350 with 'a house rent and taxes free' (Church, 26). He resigned in June 1821, when he was succeeded by his second son, Charles West Wheeler; in 1822 his third son, James Lowe Wheeler, succeeded him as botanical demonstrator at the Society of Apothecaries. Wheeler had married Ann Blatch (d. 1800) of Amesbury, at Pancras Old Church, on 24 June 1789, and they had six sons, all of whom were freemen of the Society of Apothecaries and practised medicine.

Wheeler was admitted an assistant of the Society of Apothecaries on 29 June 1815; he served as junior and then senior warden between 1821 and 1823, and he was master in 1823–4. He was also appointed a member on 19 July 1815 of the first court of examiners under the act of that year. On his resignation Wheeler continued to live in London; first with his son Charles in St Bartholomew's, until the latter's resignation in 1835, after which he went to live with his eldest son, Thomas Lowe Wheeler, at 61 Gracechurch Street and then at Newcastle Court, College Hill, Cloak Lane, Queen Street.

Wheeler, a devotee of the doctrines of Linnaeus, was an able botanist, and as a teacher he was eminently successful, the 'herborisings' of the Society of Apothecaries under his guidance becoming famous throughout England. He took part in these excursions until 1834, when he was eighty, clad in an old hat, worn suit, and a pair of leather gaiters, but full of good spirits and agility. A man of simple faith and habits Wheeler was a non-smoker and abstained from alcohol, but he would break the ice in order to bathe in winter. He taught himself Hebrew at the age of seventy-five. Wheeler died at his home in Newcastle Court, Queen Street, London, on 10 August 1847 and was buried at Norwood cemetery.

D'A. POWER, rev. JUANITA BURNBY

Sources Society of Apothecaries, court minutes, GL, MS 8200/6, 8, 9 · L. G. Matthews, *The royal apothecaries* (1967), 150–51, 179–80 · Society of Apothecaries, account books, GL, MS 8202/6 · Christ's Hospital, court minutes, GL, MS 12,806/12 fol. 368; MS 12,806/13 fols. 355, 490 · Christ's Hospital, general accounts, GL, MS 12,819/23, fol. 27 · St Bartholomew's Hospital, minutes of the governors, St Bartholomew's Hospital, London, HA1/16, 200, HA1/17, 578 · *Society of Apothecaries, London, Yearbooks* [membership lists] · *Medical Register* (1779) · *Medical Register* (1780) · *Medical Register* (1783) · D. Power, 'The octocentary of the foundation … Thomas Wheeler', *St Bartholomew's Hospital Journal*, 30 (1922–3), 85–7 · W. S. Church, 'Our hospital pharmacopoeia and apothecary's shop', *St Bartholomew's Hospital Reports*, 22 (1886), 1–55, esp. 26 · D. E. Allen, *The naturalist in Britain: a social history* (1976), 9, 46 · C. L. Feltoe, *Memorials of J. F. South* (1884), 65–7 · *IGI*
Archives Guildhall, London, Christ's Hospital, archives · Society of Apothecaries, Apothecaries' Hall, London, archives
Likenesses G. Richmond, watercolour, 1822; in possession of Mrs Wheeler of Woking in 1899 · H. P. Briggs, oils; presented to the Apothecaries' Society in London in 1843 · P. Rouw, wax vignette
Wealth at death few possessions; furniture and silver plate; money invested in the Apothecaries' Society joint stock; some valuable books: will, proved London, 21 Dec 1847

Wheeler, Sir William Ireland de Courcy (1879–1943), surgeon, was born in Dublin on 8 May 1879. His father, also William Ireland (later de Courcy-) Wheeler, was president of the Royal College of Surgeons in Ireland in 1883–4. His mother was Frances Victoria, daughter of Henry Shaw, of Tullamain, co. Dublin, granddaughter of Bernard Shaw, and thus a cousin of G. B. *Shaw. Wheeler graduated as a junior moderator in natural science at Trinity College, Dublin, in 1899, and took the MD degree in 1902. He was a demonstrator and assistant to the professor of anatomy there, and for his researches into deaths under chloroform the Dublin Biological Association, of which he was later to become president, awarded him its medal in 1903. In 1904 Wheeler joined the staff of Mercer's Hospital and he was also attached to the Rotunda and to the National Children's Hospital. He became FRCS (Ireland) in 1905. While he was still in his twenties his whole career was threatened by an accident which caused the loss of an eye, but he overcame this handicap and in after years few suspected its existence. In 1909 he married Elsie (d. 1951), eldest daughter of Thomas *Shaw (later Baron Craigmyle), and they had a son and a daughter.

During the First World War Wheeler served in France with the rank of lieutenant-colonel; he was mentioned twice in dispatches, and in 1919 he was knighted. He was honorary surgeon to the forces in Ireland, donor and surgeon to the Dublin Hospital for Wounded Officers, and consulting surgeon to the Ministry of Pensions. His work as head of the military surgical centre at Blackrock, near Dublin, led to a close friendship with Sir Robert Jones.

After the war Wheeler became known as a leading surgeon not only in Dublin but throughout Great Britain and America. He was appointed surgeon-in-ordinary to the lord lieutenant (1922), and was president of the Royal College of Surgeons in Ireland (1923–5), of the surgical section of the Royal Academy of Medicine in Ireland, of the Irish Medical Schools and Graduates Association, and of the Leinster branch of the British Medical Association (1925–6). Wheeler was a close friend and visitor of George Washington Crile, the brothers Mayo, and other leading surgeons of the United States. He was an honorary fellow of the American College of Surgeons and president of the Inter-State Post Graduate Medical Assembly of North

America. His versatility and wide contacts made him a valued member of the editorial staffs of the leading surgical journals, both British and American.

In 1932 Wheeler was persuaded by Lord Iveagh to migrate to England and to accept a position on the visiting staff of the newly constructed Southend General Hospital. He also joined in London the staffs of All Saints' Hospital for Genito-Urinary Diseases and the Metropolitan Ear, Nose and Throat Hospital. He took an active part in the medical life of London and frequented the medical societies there; he became chairman of the Marylebone division of the British Medical Association and, a year or two later, president of the metropolitan counties branch. On the outbreak of war in 1939 he was appointed consulting surgeon to the Royal Navy in Scotland, with the rank of surgeon rear-admiral.

Wheeler was the author of *A Handbook of Operative Surgery* (1918); *Injuries and Diseases of Bone* (1928); *Pillars of Surgery* (the John B. Murphy oration, 1933); and a large number of papers and addresses on almost every branch of surgery. Apart from his clinical wisdom and his brilliance as an operating surgeon, Wheeler had a genius for friendship and few surgeons of his time were so well known both at home and abroad. Wheeler died suddenly in Aberdeen on 11 September 1943. His widow died on 3 October 1951.   W. J. BISHOP, *rev.* H. C. G. MATTHEW

Sources *BMJ* (25 Sept 1943), 406–7 · *BMJ* (2 Oct 1943), 437 · *The Lancet* (25 Sept 1943) · *The Times* (14 Sept 1943)
Wealth at death £30,347 19s. 1d.: probate, 9 June 1944, *CGPLA Eng. & Wales*

Wheelhouse, Claudius Galen (1826–1909), surgeon, born in Snaith, Yorkshire, on 29 December 1826, was the second son of James Wheelhouse, surgeon. At seven he left the grammar school in Snaith for Christ's Hospital preparatory school in Hertford, and he entered Christ's Hospital in London in 1836. He was apprenticed at sixteen to R. C. Ward of Ollerton, Newark, and remained a strong advocate of the apprenticeship system. He entered the Leeds school of medicine in October 1846, and was admitted MRCS on 25 March 1849 and a licentiate of the Society of Apothecaries in 1850. He then went to the Mediterranean on a yachting cruise as surgeon to Henry Pelham, afterwards fifth duke of Newcastle and secretary of state for war. The party sailed to Spain, Greece, Turkey, Egypt, Syria, and Palestine, and Wheelhouse took many photographs, using the wax-paper process. Unfortunately all the negatives were destroyed by fire in 1879, though some of his prints survived.

Wheelhouse returned to England in 1851, and entered into partnership with Joseph Prince Garlick of Park Row, Leeds, the senior surgeon to the Leeds Public Dispensary and lecturer on surgery at the Leeds school of medicine. In the same year he was elected surgeon to the public dispensary and demonstrator of anatomy in the medical school, where he was successively lecturer on anatomy, physiology, and surgery. In 1860 he married Agnes Caroline Cowell, daughter of Joseph Cowell, vicar of Todmorden. They had three daughters.

During his career at the Leeds medical school Wheelhouse twice served as president of the school, and when the new University of Leeds was inaugurated in October 1904 he was made honorary DSc. He was surgeon to the Leeds Infirmary from March 1884.

Elected FRCS on 9 June 1864, Wheelhouse served on the college council from 1876 to 1881. He was president of the council of the British Medical Association (1881–4), and presided at the Leeds meeting in 1889. In 1897, when the association held its annual meeting in Montreal, McGill College made him honorary LLD. He also received the gold medal of the BMA.

In 1886, when the Medical Act brought direct representatives of the profession onto the General Medical Council, Wheelhouse headed the poll in England and Wales and he was re-elected in 1891. From 1870 to 1895 he was first secretary and afterwards treasurer of the West Riding Medical Charity.

On retiring from practice at Leeds in 1891 Wheelhouse settled in Filey, where he became active in local affairs. He served on local committees and as a justice of the peace for the East Riding. He died at his home, at Cliff Point, Filey, on 9 April 1909, and was buried at Filey on the 13th.

Wheelhouse was unusual as a general practitioner who made a name in pure surgery. An admirable teacher, he did much to make the Leeds medical school an integral part of the university. In 1876 he advocated a form of external urethrotomy for impermeable strictures, using a grooved lithotomy staff. The operation was known as 'Wheelhouse's operation' and in his day it displaced all rival methods. Wheelhouse described his method in a paper entitled 'Perineal section as performed at Leeds' (*BMJ*, 1, 24 June 1876, 779). He also wrote *The special temptation of early life … to which is appended … a letter from a mother to her son on … his leaving home for school for the first time* (1886).   D'A. POWER, *rev.* KAYE BAGSHAW

Sources *BMJ* (17 April 1909), 983–6 · *The Lancet* (17 April 1909), 1145–7 · R. Pare, ed., *Photography and architecture, 1839–1939* (1982) · V. G. Plarr, *Plarr's Lives of the fellows of the Royal College of Surgeons of England*, rev. D'A. Power, 2 vols. (1930) · *CGPLA Eng. & Wales* (1909)
Likenesses photograph, possibly RCS Eng. · portrait, repro. in *The Lancet*
Wealth at death £18,590 15s. 11d.: probate, 3 June 1909, *CGPLA Eng. & Wales*

Wheelock, Eleazar (1711–1779), Congregationalist minister and educator in America, was born on 22 April 1711 in Windham, Connecticut, the only son of Ralph Wheelock, a prosperous farmer, and his wife, Ruth Huntington. He was the great-grandson of Cambridge-educated Ralph Wheelock, an English puritan clergyman who settled in Dudham, Massachusetts, in 1637. True to his heritage he became a Congregationalist minister. From 1729 to 1735 he attended Yale College, where he received an award for excellence in classical studies. Thereafter he served the Second Congregational Church in Lebanon, Connecticut, for thirty-five years. About 1735 he married Sarah Davenport Maltby, a widow, with whom he had six children. She died in 1746, and in 1747 he married Mary Brinsmeade (*d.* 1783), with whom he had five more children.

An enthusiastic participant in the religious revival known as the great awakening, which swept New England during the late 1730s and early 1740s, Wheelock conducted numerous evangelistic expeditions to nearby towns. His sermons aroused the emotions of his audience, causing them to cry out in fear of God's eternal punishment. Jonathan Edwards and George Whitefield encouraged his itinerancy, though it provoked criticism from some parishioners and ministerial colleagues.

Despite Wheelock's contemporary fame as a New Light evangelist, he is best remembered as an educator and administrator. Partly because his parish failed to pay him the salary to which he thought he was entitled, he began to prepare young men for college. After a Christian Mohegan named Samson Occom enrolled in 1743 and progressed in Wheelock's school, he developed a plan to convert and educate other American Indians who were to become missionaries and teachers among their people. By 1765 thirty-four males, twenty-nine of them American Indians, and ten American Indian females had matriculated. The females were taught to read, write, and become housewives. The curriculum for males included English, Latin, Greek, and arithmetic. Students attended morning and evening worship services at which they were instructed in the Westminster catechism. Ten of the men became teaching missionaries to the Six Nations (Iroquois) and in 1765 had 127 American Indians enrolled in their schools. Wheelock's first American Indian student, Occom, had been ordained by the Suffolk, Long Island, presbytery in 1759 and was assigned to a mission to the Mohawk and Oneida Indians. Wheelock vigorously promoted his project by raising funds from both public and private sources. An early benefactor, Colonel Joshua Moor of nearby Mansfield, provided a house, schoolhouse, and land for the school that was named Moor's Indian Charity School in his honour. The Massachusetts general court sponsored six American Indian children by paying for their education, clothing, and food. The general assembly of New Hampshire also contributed generously. Even people in Britain provided monetary assistance. In 1765 Wheelock sent Occom to Britain where he preached throughout the country to appreciative audiences and raised £12,000. Funds contributed in England were controlled by trustees of whom the earl of Dartmouth was president. The Scottish Society for Propagating Christian Knowledge was in charge of funds collected in Scotland. Occom's tour spread Wheelock's fame. As a result the University of Edinburgh conferred on him the degree of doctor of divinity in 1767.

Nevertheless, Wheelock was disappointed. Out of their normal environment several of his American Indian students became ill and died. Others returned to their traditional lifestyle. Sir William Johnson, British superintendent for Indian affairs in the northern department and supporter of the school, became alienated when he suspected that Wheelock was trying to obtain land from the Six Nations (Iroquois). Consequently Wheelock concluded in the late 1760s that his attempt to educate American Indians to become missionaries and schoolmasters

among their peoples had not fulfilled his hopes. Wheelock then determined to expand his school by adding a college that would train white missionaries, by separating the school for American Indians, by giving up attempts to educate females, and by changing the location. He submitted his plans to the English trustees of the money Occom had raised, who approved them. He named the college after the earl of Dartmouth, a generous benefactor.

Rejecting offers of land and financial support from Massachusetts governor Francis Barnard, from the citizens of Albany, New York, and from others, Wheelock selected a site in western New Hampshire where Governor John Wentworth provided over 24,000 acres and the promise of a charter which was granted in 1769. The citizens of New Hampshire and Vermont provided additional land and funds. In 1770 Wheelock moved Moor's Indian Charity School, its seventy students, and his wife and children to the remote Connecticut river valley town of Hanover. There he organized what became Dartmouth College. The trustees named him president, an office that he held for the rest of his life. He directed the clearing of land, construction of buildings, purchase of supplies, recruitment of students and faculty, and development of the curriculum. In addition he preached to the congregation that he gathered there and served as the town's justice of the peace. In 1772 Wheelock reported a student body of seventy-two. Between 1771 and 1774 fifteen whites were licensed to preach or ordained, and ten American Indians were trained to be schoolmasters. The depletion of English funds and the turmoil of the American War of Independence threatened but did not destroy the young college. After 1775 Wheelock's fragile health declined noticeably. On 6 March 1779 he suffered a series of epileptic seizures and died on 24 March. He was buried in Hanover two days later. His second wife, Mary, and eight of his children survived him. His son John succeeded him as president of Dartmouth College. JOHN B. FRANTZ

Sources D. McClure and E. Parish, *Memoirs of the Rev. Eleazar Wheelock, D.D., founder and president of Dartmouth College and Moor's Charity School* (Newburyport, MA, 1811) · L. B. Richardson, *History of Dartmouth College*, 2 vols. (Hanover, NH, 1932) · J. D. McCullum, *Eleazar Wheelock: founder of Dartmouth College* (1969) · F. B. Dexter, *Biographical sketches of the graduates of Yale College*, 1 (New York, 1885), 493–9 · W. B. Sprague, *Annals of the American pulpit*, 1 (New York, 1859), 397–403

Archives Brown University, Providence, Rhode Island · Dartmouth College, Hanover, New Hampshire · New York Historical Society · New York State Library, Albany

Likenesses A. Reed, engraving (after J. Steward), repro. in McClure and Parish, *Memoirs*, frontispiece

Wheelocke, Abraham (*c.*1593–1653), linguist and librarian, was born in the parish of Whitchurch in Shropshire. He was brought up at Loppington in the same county, and remained deeply attached to Shropshire throughout his life. Wheelocke was always ready to help students from Shropshire, and it appears to have been their common origins that account for his lasting friendship with one of his principal patrons, the merchant Thomas Adams. Wheelocke matriculated as a sizar at Trinity College, Cambridge, at Easter 1611, and graduated BA in 1615 and MA in 1618. In

1619 he was appointed Exeter fellow of Clare College, and in the following year he voted for Thomas Paske as master. He was ordained deacon in London on 19 December 1619 and priest at Peterborough on 22 September 1622. In the same year he was made vicar of the church of Holy Sepulchre in Cambridge, a living which he retained until 1642. In 1623 he was appointed one of the university preachers. In 1625 he proceeded BD but failed to succeed Andrew Downes as professor of Greek. In the following year he became rector of Passenham in Northamptonshire, and he relinquished his appointment in 1627. In 1629 he was nominated public librarian and amanuensis at Cambridge University Library.

Professor of Arabic While he was at Clare College, Wheelocke, already a competent Hebraist, embarked on the study of Arabic. By 1624 he had made considerable progress. He studied with William Bedwell, and in 1631 Bedwell's wife told Thomas Adams he was 'as able as any in the kingdom' (Holt, 40). Wheelocke also learned Persian, Syriac, and Samaritan, and seems to have obtained at least a smattering of other Eastern languages.

Probably late in 1631 Wheelocke proposed to Thomas Adams that a chair of Arabic be set up at Cambridge, financed either by the City of London or by a merchant company. Adams replied that it would be easier to find an individual ready to subsidize the professorship. Soon after, when he was sure of the approval of the university and of Richard Holdsworth, then professor of divinity at Gresham College, Adams himself promised a salary of £40 for a period of three years. By 23 March 1632 Wheelocke had been installed as the first professor of Arabic in England, with the obligation of lecturing twice a week. Adams continued to pay him for as long as he lived.

Wheelocke's motives for studying Arabic are connected with his piety and his interest in the English church. Like so many of his contemporaries he was drawn by Arabic on account of its use for biblical studies. When urging Adams to found a chair he dwelt on the value of the language for the propagation of Christianity in the East, and his work on the Koran was undoubtedly intended as an aid to missionaries. For this purpose he regarded the Arabic-speaking Christians as useful vehicles. But he was also attracted by the Christianity of the East as the source of a pristine Anglo-Saxon Christianity free of the Church of Rome. The investigation of such a tradition, in increasing fashion at the time, was an additional incentive for him to study Old English. Wheelocke justified what he called 'my two-fold imployment', his concern with both Arabic and Anglo-Saxon, in a letter to Sir Simonds D'Ewes in January 1640. He wished, he wrote:

> to compile a body of our Divinity, I say of our doctrine out of the Saxon, & British writers: & to present the papists with these, as a rule to leade them by, if they would be constant to the best Antiquities: most sure it is, that Antiquitie tels us we owe more to the Easterne Church then to Rome: and what of good from Rome, even that we have from the Easterne. (Ellis, 157–9)

Wheelocke was clearly fascinated by Arabic as a language—from 1635 on he followed his signature in the registers of Holy Sepulchre with the Arabic 'hamdullah' ('thanks be to God')—but he seems to have had little interest in Arab culture. In the 1640s he hoped to publish a translation of the Koran into Latin and Greek, together with a refutation, and he dispatched a specimen to Samuel Hartlib. In his letters he revealed a loathing for Islam which went far beyond the frequently rhetorical hostility of his contemporaries. 'Set aside some grosse idolatries of the church of Roome, & their Tyrannicall government,' he wrote, 'the onlie pressure on the bodie of the Church of Christ is Mahomets Alcoran' (Hartlib papers, 33/4/2). He described the Koran as 'full of hipocrisie, falshoode, savage crueltie against the world of mankinde, which it would subdue; & against the sonne of God whom it pretends to advance' (ibid., 33/4/3).

Although such statements are in accordance with Wheelocke's orthodoxy—in 1639 he expressed his horror to D'Ewes that the ideas of those he regarded as the great heretics of the sixteenth century, Castellio, Servetus, and Socinus, should be 'alive againe', and added 'I could wish theire very names were buried' (BL, Harley MS 374, fol. 133v)—they are in contrast with the efforts of two fellow professors of Arabic, Jacobus Golius at Leiden and Edward Pococke at Oxford, to introduce a more objective approach to Islam by way of a deeper investigation of Muslim culture. Wheelocke's prejudices may also account for Hartlib's decision to reject his specimen, possibly prompted by the German Arabist Christian Ravius.

Wheelocke lectured regularly in Arabic. His few pupils included a number of students from King's College (where his son Abraham would study), such as Robert Austin, Richard Hunt, future Gresham professor of rhetoric, and, most distinguished of all, Thomas Hyde, future librarian of the Bodleian and successor to Edward Pococke as Laudian professor of Arabic at Oxford. To both Austin and Hyde, Wheelocke also taught Persian. In the late 1640s Wheelocke did his utmost to set up an oriental press at Cambridge, and tried to obtain a better set of Arabic types than had been bequeathed by William Bedwell.

Professor of Anglo-Saxon Ever since the early 1620s Wheelocke had been particularly helpful to scholars from outside the university who were looking for manuscripts in Cambridge. With his appointment at the university library he had unlimited access to the main Cambridge collection and a limited access, of which he made good use, to the college libraries. He continued to assist his correspondents in locating manuscripts, copying them, or simply checking details. It was thus, in the mid-1630s, that he made the acquaintance of the historian and antiquary Sir Henry Spelman, engaged in his major work, the *Concilia*. Wheelocke served him in his quest for Anglo-Saxon manuscripts and, with Spelman's encouragement, turned to the study of Old English himself. In 1638 Spelman agreed to finance a chair for a lecturer and reader of the Old English language and the history of the early British church. In November he gave Wheelocke the vicarage of Middleton in Norfolk, the proceeds of which were to be regarded as part of his salary, even though it was not until

1640 that the lectureship was actually approved by the university.

With Wheelocke's appointment as professor of Anglo-Saxon the study of the subject shifted to Cambridge. It had previously been centred on the library of Robert Cotton in London, but the library had been closed by the king from 1629 to 1631, the year of Cotton's death, largely because of the political significance assumed by the examination of early texts in connection with legal and constitutional history. With his work on the church councils Spelman placed the study of early English documents in the strictly ecclesiastical sphere it had occupied in the sixteenth century, when the principal purpose of research had been to prove a tradition of independence from Rome, linking the reformed Church of England to its Anglo-Saxon predecessor.

Wheelocke's own contribution to Anglo-Saxon studies was immense. The object of the Cambridge lectureship was to publish Old English sources and to prepare an Old English grammar and dictionary. In 1643 Wheelocke published the *editio princeps* of the Old English translation of Bede's *Historia ecclesiastica* and the Anglo-Saxon Chronicle. He reissued these works a year later, together with an edition of William Lambarde's *Archaionomia* of 1568. He based his text of Bede on three manuscripts, one at Cambridge University Library, one at Corpus Christi College, and one in the Cotton Library. The Anglo-Saxon Chronicle was taken almost entirely from the so-called Winchester text in a manuscript at the Cotton Library; Wheelocke completed it with another codex at Corpus Christi. Because he made no use of the other five surviving manuscripts Wheelocke was severely criticized by Edmund Gibson, who published a further edition of the Anglo-Saxon Chronicle at Oxford in 1692, and Gibson's objections were taken up by many subsequent scholars. It has since been proved, however, that Wheelocke was fully aware of the existence of the other codices, but wished only to provide 'a consciously selective edition of the Winchester text' (Lutz, 63). That the original Cotton manuscript should have been almost completely destroyed by fire in the eighteenth century adds to the importance of Wheelocke's work for modern scholars. Objections to his edition as mutilated and incomplete are unfounded, but he is more open to criticism in his failure to identify Anglo-Saxon verse. Accustomed to prose, he knew nothing of the structure of Old English alliterative poetry, as his own attempts at writing it show. He dismissed those sections of the Anglo-Saxon Chronicle written in verse as obsolete and coarse. At the time of his death he was also preparing an Old English dictionary and grammar.

Librarian and poet Wheelocke's other great achievements were as librarian of Cambridge University Library. When he was appointed in 1629 the library had barely 1000 volumes; when he died in 1653 it had about 12,000. Such an advance was not due to Wheelocke alone, but he took an active part in persuading donors to present their collections, and, above all, in ordering and describing what actually entered the library. He thus assisted the university in obtaining the collection of some eighty-six oriental manuscripts assembled by Thomas Erpenius, the professor of Arabic at Leiden. The collection had been purchased by the duke of Buckingham in 1625, the year after Erpenius's death, and was finally presented to Cambridge by the widowed duchess in June 1632. It contained a wide variety of Eastern manuscripts, mainly Arabic but also Turkish, Persian, Hebrew, Syriac, Coptic, and Javanese, and included five of the oldest Malay manuscripts in existence. The acquisition of the collection meant that Cambridge, which had previously only had a single Arabic manuscript, could briefly compete with Oxford. In 1648 parliament decided to buy and present to the university library the invaluable collection of 167 books and manuscripts imported from Italy by the London bookseller George Thomason. Although the works were mainly in Hebrew, they also included texts in Syriac, Arabic, Armenian, and Slavonic. Wheelocke described and listed them.

In 1632 Wheelocke renounced his fellowship at Clare College, moved to a house near Queen's College, and, against the advice of Adams, married Clemence Goad (*fl.* 1610–1653), a widow. She already had a son, Christopher, and had five more children with Wheelocke: Abraham, Sarah, Clemence, Joan, and Ann. Wheelocke often advanced the necessity of supporting so large a family as a reason for his state of permanent financial distress. He seems, however, to have exaggerated his poverty. It has been estimated that for six years after his marriage he had an annual income of about £60, and that this rose to about £130 in 1638. Besides his fear of not having enough money, Wheelocke was haunted by the terror of losing the favour of his patrons (and consequently his salary). This too proved unfounded. Adams paid him throughout his life, and after Henry Spelman's death in 1641, Wheelocke continued to receive his wages, first from Spelman's son John, and then from his grandson Roger.

By nature Wheelocke was sedentary, retiring, and diffident. In the encomium he delivered at Wheelocke's funeral William Sclater, another student of King's who had known Wheelocke well at Cambridge, said 'that … which I observed remarkable, and worthy of universall imitation in him, was, under his many and exceeding abilities, his humble and exceeding modestie; so that others took more notice of him, than he did of himselfe' (Sclater, sig. E3r). Wheelocke's intellectual accomplishments were appreciated both in England and on the European continent (where his correspondents included Johannes de Laet). John Selden and James Ussher admired him, and John Lightfoot referred to 'the Al-learned Mr. Wheelocke, to whom nothing is too difficult or unattainable' (Lightfoot, sig. b3r).

Wheelocke exhibited his versatility in various poems written on royal occasions: Latin verses lamenting the death of Anne of Denmark in 1619, and celebrating the marriage of the future Charles I to Princess Henrietta Maria of France in 1625; Latin and Greek poems on the births of the future Charles II and his sister Mary in 1631; Greek verses on Charles I's coronation in Scotland and the birth of the future James II in 1633 (and those contributed to James Duport's *Thrinothriambos* in 1637); and verses in Hebrew and Anglo-Saxon on Charles I's return from Scotland in 1641.

Later years and death By 1651 Wheelocke had started to prepare his edition and Latin translation of the gospels in Persian. He was assisted by his former student Robert Austin, then a fellow of King's. In order to conclude his work and see to its publication, Wheelocke took up temporary residence in what he described to Richard Minshull, the vice-chancellor of Cambridge, as 'an obscure and little cell' in London (Todd, 233). The Persian gospels were in fact edited (with Wheelocke's unfinished commentary) by John Pearson, the future bishop of Chester, and published posthumously at Adams's expense in 1657. This other *editio princeps*, however, was not entirely satisfactory. The Bodleian manuscript (MS Laud. Or.2) and the manuscript in Cambridge University Library (MS Gg.5.26), on which the text is mainly based, are of an inferior translation. At a late stage in his labours Wheelocke borrowed a codex belonging to Pococke (Bodl. Oxf., MS Pococke 241) which contained an earlier and better version translated from Syriac. Wheelocke acknowledged its superiority but was reluctant to ask Austin, already on the verge of a nervous breakdown, to start all over again. Wheelocke's edition was thus immediately surpassed by the version, based entirely on Pococke's manuscript, prepared by his pupil Thomas Hyde for the London polyglot Bible, which also came out in 1657.

Wheelocke's combination of piety and interest in languages induced him to join James Ussher, Brian Walton, William Fuller, Herbert Thorndike, and Bruno Ryves in signing the first printed proposals for the polyglot Bible on 1 March 1653. He assisted the editors with the Samaritan text, and is said to have intended to help Edmund Castell correct the Syriac and Arabic versions. In the end, however, Wheelocke's tasks were taken over by Hyde. Wheelocke's health had been declining for some time; he died in London, and was buried at St Botolph, Aldersgate, on 25 September 1653. ALASTAIR HAMILTON

Sources J. C. T. Oates, *Cambridge University Library: a history from the beginnings to the Copyright Act of Queen Anne* (1986) · G. J. Toomer, *Eastern wisedome and learning: the study of Arabic in seventeenth-century England* (1996) · A. Lutz, 'The study of the Anglo-Saxon Chronicle in the seventeenth century and the establishment of Old English studies in the universities', *The recovery of Old English: Anglo-Saxon studies in the sixteenth and seventeenth centuries*, ed. T. Graham (2000), 1–82 · M. Murphy, 'Abraham Wheloc's edition of Bede's *History* in Old English', *Studia Neophilologica*, 39 (1967), 46–59 · F. L. Utley, 'Two seventeenth-century Anglo-Saxon poems', *Modern Language Quarterly*, 3 (1942), 243–61 · H. Ellis, ed., *Original letters of eminent literary men of the sixteenth, seventeenth, and eighteenth centuries*, CS, 23 (1843) · P. M. Holt, *Studies in the history of the Near East* (1973) · M. Murphy and E. Barrett, 'Abraham Whelock, Arabist and Saxonist', *Biography*, 8 (1985), 163–85 · *DNB* · Venn, *Alum. Cant.* · H. J. Todd, *Memoirs of the life and writings of the right Rev. Brian Walton*, 1 (1821) · R. Parr, ed., *The life of the most reverend father in God, James Usher … with a collection of three hundred letters* (1686) · L. Twells, *Life of Dr Edward Pocock, the celebrated orientalist* (1816) · A. Hamilton, *William Bedwell the Arabist, 1563–1632* (1985) · J. R. Wardale, *Clare College* (1899) · R. H. Bremmer, 'The correspondence of Johannes de Laet (1581–1649) as a mirror of his life', *Lias*, 25 (1998), 139–64 · Hartlib papers, Sheffield University, 33/4/2–3 · W. Sclater, *The crowne of righteousness* (1654) · J. Lightfoot, *The harmony, chronicle and order of the Old Testament* (1647) · CUL, MS Mm.1.44 · BL, Harley MS 374

Archives CUL, corresp. | BL, corresp. with Sir Henry Spelman, Add. MSS 34600–34601 · BL, letters to D'Ewes, Harley MS 374

Wealth at death see Oates, *Cambridge University Library*, 183–7 · will, CUL, MS Mm.1.37, fol. 224

Wheelwright, John (1592?–1679), minister in America, was probably born in Saleby, Lincolnshire, in the early part of 1592, the son of Robert Wheelwright (*d. c.*1612) and his wife, Katherine. He graduated BA from Sidney Sussex College, Cambridge, in 1614 and MA in 1618. New England tradition had Oliver Cromwell saying that he had been more afraid of meeting Wheelwright on the football fields of Cambridge than of any army, for Wheelwright would invariably trip him up. Wheelwright was also noted in college for his skill at wrestling. He married his first wife, Marie Storre, daughter of the vicar of Bilsby, Lincolnshire, on 8 November 1621. After his father-in-law's death Wheelwright was inducted as vicar of Bilsby on 9 April 1623. Marie was buried on 18 May 1629 and shortly thereafter he married Mary Hutchinson from Alford, Lincolnshire.

As a minister Wheelwright had a more than local reputation of being good at helping Christians seeking assurance that they were among the saved. Whereas most puritan ministers would encourage those Christians to take heart from signs of their holiness, he claimed that such evidence was only secondary. Instead, he encouraged them to seek a charismatic experience of the Holy Spirit. Wheelwright shared this emphasis with his sister-in-law, Anne Hutchinson, and the prominent puritan minister John Cotton, both of whom were to be involved with him in religious controversy in Massachusetts.

Wheelwright was convicted of simony in 1632 for selling back his living to his patron. He stayed in Lincolnshire until April 1636, when he departed for Massachusetts, arriving there with his wife and five children on 26 May 1636. He joined the Boston church, where Cotton was teacher and Anne Hutchinson a member, on 12 June 1636. Doctrinal tensions over the proper methods of assurance were already mounting in the colony at the beginning of what is often called the antinomian controversy. Hutchinson was propagating her own understanding of Cotton's teaching, and Henry Vane—Boston church member, recent immigrant, son of a member of Charles I's privy council, and newly elected governor—was giving Bostonian doctrine the approval of the colony's highest office. Throughout 1636 there was a growing conviction, at least among the colony's ministers, that Bostonian emphasis on the Holy Spirit, which expressed itself in a variety of ways, was grounded in the heresies of familism and antinomianism and, if not checked, would lead to moral anarchy and the overthrow of the authority of the Bible. However, some of the laity were outspoken in their preference for Wheelwright and Cotton's views, and some, including Hutchinson, were more theologically radical than either.

Wheelwright, being the only minister besides Cotton to

be suspected of heretical leanings, was plunged into the controversy. As ministerial conferences failed to produce consensus, he and Cotton began to suspect that opposition to their doctrines indicated a damnable dependence on salvation through good works rather than faith in Jesus, an opinion that some lay people, including Anne Hutchinson, expressed even more forcefully. A move to make Wheelwright co-teacher with Cotton at Boston was blocked single-handedly by the congregation's most prominent lay person, John Winthrop, on 30 October 1636. Winthrop, together with the pastor, John Wilson, opposed the direction in which his congregation was headed. As tensions in the colony mounted the general court proclaimed a fast day on 19 January 1637. On that day Wheelwright preached an incendiary sermon at Boston in which he denounced his opponents as opponents of Jesus and called for a spiritual combat in the colony, whatever the cost. This sermon led to his conviction for contempt and sedition at the March meeting of the general court. The three-day trial was hard fought, and the hostile intervention of the bulk of the colony's ministers determined its outcome.

Wheelwright's conviction marked the turning point of the antinomian controversy. On 17 May 1637 Vane lost the governorship to Winthrop, and he returned to England at the beginning of August. At a synod held at the end of the summer Cotton worked out a theological compromise with the other ministers, to which Wheelwright refused to assent. Unwilling to acknowledge any impropriety in his sermon and unwilling to leave the colony voluntarily, he was sentenced to banishment at the beginning of November, along with Anne Hutchinson and one member of the general court.

That winter Wheelwright moved to what is now Exeter, New Hampshire, followed by some of the Boston congregation. They set up a church with the approval of the Boston church. After Massachusetts moved to incorporate that region in the early 1640s, Wheelwright followed a few of his congregation to what is now Wells, Maine, in early 1643. Meanwhile he mended fences with the Massachusetts authorities. The general court gave him a safe-conduct to travel to Massachusetts on 10 May 1643, after which he had a successful conference in Boston with some of the ministers, who said they would work for the lifting of his sentence. Wheelwright wrote two very carefully worded letters to John Winthrop, apologizing for his intemperate and incautious language and his support of persons who were more heterodox than he had realized at the time, but never acknowledging that the court sentence against him was just. He may have made that acknowledgement in a letter not surviving, as the court on 29 May 1644 lifted its sentence of banishment, claiming Wheelwright had admitted the justice of its action.

However, the reverberations of the antinomian crisis had not yet died out for Wheelwright. *A Short Story*, the official Massachusetts version of the crisis, which magnified his heterodoxy, was published in London in 1644. Wheelwright or his son wrote an answer, *Mercurious Americanus* (London, 1645), in which the author placed all the

responsibility for the crisis on the Massachusetts authorities. Wheelwright moved to be minister of Hampton, New Hampshire, in 1647, but he continued to brood over the aspersions cast upon his name, repeated in Samuel Rutherford's *The Spiritual Antichrist* (1648). He contemplated returning to England, which prompted his parishioners, on 1 May 1654, to draw up a petition to the general court asking it to clear him; however, on 20 August Wheelwright preached a sermon at the Boston church which was an uncompromising restatement of his doctrines, and that seems to have led to calls for his censure. Even so, the general court issued a tepid endorsement of Wheelwright on 24 August 1654.

Not exactly vindicated, Wheelwright left for England the following summer. He stayed there for several years, enjoying the friendship of Sir Henry Vane and having an audience with Cromwell. He published a further defence of himself and a blistering attack on his opponents in 1658. He returned to New England in the summer of 1662 and was offered the position of pastor at Salisbury, New Hampshire, in time to participate in the last persecution of Quakers. He remained in Salisbury for the rest of his life. Wheelwright died on 15 November 1679.

MICHAEL P. WINSHIP

Sources *The journal of John Winthrop, 1630–1649*, ed. R. S. Dunn, J. Savage, and L. Yeandle (1996) · *John Wheelwright: his writings*, ed. C. H. Bell (Boston, MA, 1876) · S. Bush, '"Revising what we have done amisse": John Cotton and John Wheelwright, 1640', *William and Mary Quarterly*, 45 (1988), 733–50, esp. 741 · S. Groome, *A glass for the people of New-England* (1676), 5–7 · T. Hutchinson, *The history of the colony and province of Massachusetts-Bay*, ed. L. S. Mayo, 1 (1936), 58 · N. B. Shurtleff, ed., *Records of the governor and company of the Massachusetts Bay in New England*, 5 vols. in 6 (1853–4), vol. 1, pp. 189, 196, 200, 205, 207, 211, 236; vol. 2, pp. 32, 37, 50, 67; vol. 3, p. 6; vol. 4/1, p. 157 · J. Wheelwright, *A brief, and plain apology* (1658) · E. M. Wheelwright, 'A frontier family', *Publications of the Colonial Society of Massachusetts*, 1 (1895), 271–303 · D. D. Hall, ed., *The antinomian controversy, 1636–1638: a documentary history*, 2nd edn (Durham, NC, 1990) · J. Mitchel, notes of sermons, 1654–5, 20 June 1654, Mass. Hist. Soc. · S. A. Green, 'Rev. John Wheelwright', *Proceedings of the Massachusetts Historical Society*, 2nd ser., 8 (1892–4), 505–17 · H. Knollys, *The life and death of that old disciple of Jesus Christ and eminent minister of the gospel, Mr Hanserd Knollys*, ed. W. Kiffin (1692), 11–15 · M. P. Winship, '"The most glorious church in the world": the unity of the godly in Boston, Massachusetts, in the 1630s', *Journal of British Studies*, 39 (2000), 71–98

Wealth at death real estate: Bell, ed., *John Wheelwright*, 229–32

Whelan, William Augustine (1935–1958). *See under* Busby Babes (*act.* 1953–1958).

Wheldon, Sir Huw Pyrs (1916–1986), television broadcaster, was born on 7 May 1916 at his grandmother's home in Prestatyn, the eldest in a family of two sons and two daughters of Sir Wynn Powell Wheldon (1876–1961), solicitor and civil servant, and his wife, Margaret (Megan) Edwards. His father worked in David Lloyd George's law practice before the First World War, had a brave military career, and went on to become registrar of the University College of North Wales in Bangor and then permanent secretary to the Welsh department of the Ministry of Education. Huw Wheldon was educated at Friars School, Bangor (he did not speak English until he was seven) and

Sir Huw Pyrs Wheldon (1916–1986), by Bob Collins, 1958

later at the London School of Economics and Political Science where he gained a BSc (Econ.) in 1938. He joined the staff of the Kent education committee, and then war interrupted his career. Enlisting in the East Kent regiment as a private, he was commissioned into the Royal Welch Fusiliers (1940), and volunteered to join the airborne forces. He served in both the 1st and 6th airborne divisions, ending the war as a major in the Royal Ulster Rifles, having won the MC shortly after D-day in 1944.

In 1946 Wheldon became director of the Arts Council in Wales, and in 1949 joined the directorate of the Festival of Britain. He helped to ensure the festival reached all of Britain, and for his work he was appointed OBE in 1952, the year he joined the BBC as publicity officer, television. He wanted to be involved in programmes and first made his mark on the screen as the presenter of the children's programme *All your Own*. He became a national figure when he devised a conkers competition that drew 58,000 conkers from all over Britain. In 1954 he was appointed senior producer, television talks, although he had never directed or produced a programme. His first series was *Men in Battle* with Lieutenant-General Sir Brian Horrocks, and his second *Orson Welles's Sketchbook*.

From 1958 to 1964 Wheldon devised, edited, and presented *Monitor*, the first arts programme on television. In this pioneering fortnightly programme he introduced a growing audience to major artists, in numbers and range remarkable for its time. He built around him a team of talented people including John Schlesinger, Ken Russell, Humphrey Burton, David Jones, Patrick Garland, and Melvyn Bragg. He required of all his programmes fidelity and attention to the subject, to the audience, and to the integrity of the programme maker.

Inevitably Wheldon progressed to the most senior posts in BBC television: he was the first television producer to become controller of programmes (1965–8) and he was the first holder of the new post of managing director (1969–75). This was the time when BBC television was at its best with some remarkable series (*Civilisation* with Sir Kenneth Clark, *The Ascent of Man* with Jacob Bronowski, and Alistair Cooke's *America*), challenging drama, refreshing comedy, and lively current affairs and sports programmes. Despite the restrictions of his office (concerned with the BBC's strategy, standards, and finances), programmes and programme makers were what Wheldon cared about most. In his own phrase, he wished programmes to 'give delight and insight'. Although he was a candidate for the post of director-general when Sir Hugh Greene retired, the BBC governors, led by Baron Hill of Luton, preferred to give the job to someone with a lower profile, Charles Curran. Wheldon served him loyally as his deputy until his own retirement in 1976, the year he was knighted.

Three factors helped to shape Wheldon's life: Wales and the advantages of a close-knit family life, the army and its discipline, and the BBC and its creative ethos. They gave him a reference for language and for institutions and for the need to protect them and keep them alive. Wheldon was a tall man, slightly stooped. It was his face that was remarkable: piercing eyes, a pointed chin, a hawk's nose. He was the most generous and companionable of men, the best and sometimes longest teller of stories, and he had an enormous zest for life.

After he left the BBC, Wheldon returned to programme making and wrote and presented the *Royal Heritage* series (1977) and *Destination D-Day* (1984), on the fortieth anniversary of the allied landings in Normandy. He became an honorary fellow (1973) and chairman of the court of governors of the London School of Economics (1975–85). He was the president of the Royal Television Society (1979–85) and received every honour possible in television. From 1976 he was a trustee of the National Portrait Gallery and from 1983 a trustee of the Royal Botanic Gardens, Kew. He had five honorary doctorates, from Ulster (1975), Wales (1978), London (1984), Loughborough (1985), and the Open University (1980), which he helped to establish.

In 1956 Wheldon married Jacqueline Mary (Jay; *d.* 1993), the daughter of Hugh Clarke, who had a tool-designing business in Chiswick. They had one son and two daughters. Their family house at 120 Richmond Hill, Richmond, Surrey, was an exceptionally happy home and he died there, from cancer, on 14 March 1986. He was cremated at Mortlake crematorium and his ashes were buried in Kew Gardens. A memorial service was held in Westminster Abbey on 7 May 1986, which would have been his seventieth birthday. PAUL FOX, *rev.*

Sources *The Times* (15 March 1986) · M. Bragg, *Sunday Times* (16 March 1986) · N. Podhoretz, *Washington Post* (26 March 1986) · personal knowledge (1996) · private information (1996) [widow] · *CGPLA Eng. & Wales* (1986)

Archives BBC WAC | FILM BBC NFA, interview | SOUND BBC NSA, interview
Likenesses B. Collins, photograph, 1958, NPG [*see illus.*] · P. Joyce, bromide print, 1977, NPG · G. Stuart, oils, 1983 · W. Thomson, portrait, BBC Television Centre, London · photograph, repro. in *Sunday Times*
Wealth at death £465,590: probate, 22 May 1986, *CGPLA Eng. & Wales*

Wheler, Edward (*bap.* 1732, *d.* 1784), chairman of the East India Company and administrator in India, was baptized on 27 April 1732 at Leamington Hastings, Warwickshire, the fourth of the five sons of Sir William Wheler, baronet (*d.* 1763), and his wife, Penelope (*d.* 1740), daughter of Sir Stephen Glynne, baronet, of Bicester, Oxfordshire, and his wife, Sophia. Although boys of the family usually attended Rugby School, Edward Wheler did not, and particulars of his education appear to have gone unrecorded. He started business as a linen draper in Cornhill, although his firm, Wheler, Higginson & Co., later handled government contracts and further diversified into providing financial services to East India Company servants and others in India. He was first elected a director of the East India Company in 1765. For the elections held in April 1773 two rival lists of candidates were presented: a house list expected to continue the policy of the incumbent administration in opposing government interference in company affairs, and a proprietors' list backed by government. Included in the victorious proprietors' list, Wheler was chosen as deputy chairman. Three months later the chairman died, and Wheler was propelled into his place. After the financial crisis of 1772 the company was in dire need of purposeful leadership. This Wheler was temperamentally ill-equipped to provide, and his thoughts turned towards securing a seat in the Bengal supreme council, which was predominantly a legislative body with authority over the East India Company's other presidencies.

In October 1776, when Hastings's resignation by proxy was accepted by the directors, Wheler waited on John Robinson, Lord North's right-hand man, to bid for the consequent vacancy in the Bengal council. The choice lay between Wheler and Justice Chambers of the Calcutta supreme court. The king signalled his support for Wheler as 'most likely to be acceptable to the Court of Directors and as a person who has steadily supported Government' (BL, Add. MS 37833, fol. 87). Wheler was duly appointed. However, when Hastings annulled his resignation Wheler's commission had to be hurriedly altered to allow him to fill the vacancy arising from the death of Colonel George Monson.

Wheler arrived in Calcutta in October 1777. Affable, kindly, and impressionable, he had no very strong views of his own and readily bent to those of stronger-willed individuals around him. His advent critically affected the balance between the two parties in council. Would he follow Hastings or would he join with Philip Francis? No sooner had the *Duke of Portland* entered the Hooghly than Wheler was assiduously courted by emissaries from both factions. A decision had to be made. A genuine enough fever aided and abetted his vacillation but in the end,

unsurprisingly given his past record, he sided with Francis. For the ensuing three years Wheler did his best to satisfy his demanding ally.

Wheler's wife, Harriet Chicheley (1740–1778), the fourth of the twelve children of the Revd James Chicheley Plowden, whom he had married in 1772, accompanied him to Calcutta, but died after only seven months. In 1780 Wheler married Charlotte (*b. c.*1738), the daughter of George Durnford, a Winchester attorney. There were two daughters.

In failing to win over Wheler, Hastings wrote him off as 'a mere cypher and the echo of Francis' (Gleig, 2.186), yet after Francis had returned to England in 1780, and John Macpherson and John Stables had joined the council, Hastings came to count on Wheler's reluctant acquiescence in his policies. In 1784 he wrote:

> Mr Wheler is really a man of business. Yet I cannot convince him of it, nor persuade him to trust to his own superiority. He … will always be [guided] by those who command him, and possess, at the same time, a majority of voices. (ibid., 3.145–6)

G. G. Ducarel stated the case rather more bluntly when he observed that Wheler 'abhors Hastings's measures but has not the strength of mind to resist him' (Ducarel to Francis, 27 July 1782, BL OIOC, MS Eur. E21, item 16). In fact, Wheler claimed that Francis had previously agreed that active opposition to Hastings's measures would 'not only be *useless*, but *dangerous*' (Wheler to Francis, 5 Dec 1782, BL, Add. MS 40763, fols. 136–8), although that did not deter Francis from trying to direct Wheler from a distance by correspondence.

Wheler died of a burst blood vessel at Suksaghur, 35 miles north-east of Calcutta, on 10 October 1784, and was interred in South Park Street burial-ground, Calcutta, next day. He left £40,000 and the residue of his estate to his wife, and £5000 to each of his daughters. Wheler was a thoroughly decent man who rose above his capabilities.

T. H. BOWYER

Sources *Memoirs of the life of the Right Hon. Warren Hastings, first governor-general of Bengal*, ed. G. R. Gleig, 3 vols. (1841), vols. 2–3 · L. S. Sutherland, *The East India Company in eighteenth century politics* (1952) · S. Weitzman, *Warren Hastings and Philip Francis* (1929) · W. K. Firminger, 'Some further letters of Alexander Elliot', *Bengal Past and Present*, 6 (1910), 179–99, esp. 181–2 · *Bengal Past and Present*, 26 (1923), 165 · Burke, *Peerage* (1959) · Burke, *Gen. GB* (1952) · J. Parkes and H. Merivale, *Memoirs of Sir Philip Francis*, 2 vols. (1867), vol. 2 · BL OIOC, Francis MSS, MS Eur. E21, item 16 · BL, Francis MSS, Add. MS 40763, fols. 136–8 · H. E. Busteed, *Echoes from old Calcutta*, 4th edn (1908) · *Memoirs of William Hickey*, ed. A. Spencer, 2–3 (1918–23) · biographical index, BL OIOC · *IGI* · GEC, *Baronetage*, 3.200 · J. G. Parker, 'The directors of the East India Company, 1754–1790', PhD diss., U. Edin., 1977 · will, Family Records Centre, London [microfilm]
Archives BL OIOC, corresp. and papers | BL, letters to David Anderson, Add. MS 45417 · BL, Francis MSS · BL, letters to Warren Hastings and others, Add. MSS 29132–29194 · BL OIOC, letters from Philip Francis, MSS Eur. C8, D18, E12–22, F5–6 · BL OIOC, corresp. with his private secretary R. C. Plowden
Wealth at death £50,000; property in Calcutta: will, PRO, Family Records Centre [microfilm]

Wheler, Sir Francis (*c.*1656–1694), naval officer, was the youngest son of Sir Charles Wheler, second baronet

(c.1620–1683), of Birdingbury, Warwickshire, and his wife, Dorothy (d. 1684), daughter of Sir Francis Bindloss, of Borwick Hall, Lancashire. The Whelers had sold their original Worcestershire estates in the early seventeenth century, and Francis's grandfather became a goldsmith. His father had been a fellow of Trinity College, Cambridge, before service in the royalist army during the civil war led him to court, parliament, and the governorship of the Leeward Islands under Charles II. Francis was himself clearly well educated, to judge from his elegant handwriting. He joined the navy as a 'king's letter' (volunteer) officer thanks to his family's cavalier loyalties: as was usual he was primarily a soldier, but he quickly developed an aptitude for the sea service to which he was repeatedly seconded. On 22 October 1674 he was commissioned ensign in Prince Rupert's company in the garrison at Windsor Castle. His naval promotion was owed chiefly to Admiral Herbert (later Lord Torrington), who on 30 April 1678 appointed him second lieutenant of the *Rupert*. On 5 May 1679 he was promoted first lieutenant in the same ship, and on 6 April 1680 he transferred to the *Bristol* as first lieutenant.

On 11 September 1680 Wheler was given his first command, the *Nonsuch*. While his ship was careening at Gibraltar in February 1681 he wrote to his father asking for assistance in his regimental and naval careers; he looked shortly to 'try [his] fortune with the Argerins' (BL, Add. MS 28054, fol. 208; Davies, 239). Success duly came with the seizure of a corsair on 8 April. On 10 August at Tangier he took possession of the *Kingfisher* by Herbert's commission, and brought her back to Portsmouth in October 1682. On 26 January 1683 he was promoted captain in the army. On 25 August he was appointed to the *Tiger* to assist with the evacuation of Tangier, where he arrived on 29 September. Pepys, who was also present during the last months of the English occupation, met Wheler several times and heard others tell of his notable obsequiousness to Herbert, allegedly performing menial tasks for him, and owing his place to his being so much 'privy to things' that the admiral 'durst not but oblige' him (*Tangier Papers*, 118). Since Pepys also reported what he must have known to be a wholly false complaint that Wheler had been made captain without having served as lieutenant, his other comments invite little respect. Wheler clearly made himself useful to his admiral, but Herbert would not have been impressed by mere servility.

Wheler returned to England, not without mishap, by the end of March 1684, after spending the best part of six years in the Mediterranean. In June 1685, as captain of the *Tiger*, he was active in intercepting Dutch ships running munitions to Monmouth's rebels. On 12 November he married Arabella, daughter of Sir Clifford Clinton. By 3 June 1687 he had been knighted, and on 12 June he was promoted lieutenant-colonel of foot. On 18 September 1688 he was made captain of the *Centurion*. This ship was badly damaged in an accident at sea and needed to return to Chatham, an embarrassment compounded by a large-scale desertion of the crew. The king was reported to be angered by the mishandling of the ship, but Wheler

escaped censure and was transferred to the command of the *Kent* on 16 November. In the course of the revolution immediately following, Wheler's associations with Herbert and the duke of Grafton (now his military commander) aligned him with the Orangists, and his career was secured under the new regime. In April 1689 he was given command of the *Rupert*, and during the summer he successfully intercepted a number of French ships taking arms and dispatches to the Jacobites in Ireland. On 5 January 1690 he was appointed to the *Albemarle* (90 guns), which fought at Beachy Head (30 June). In August he was shortlisted for a flag: this was not yet to be his, but on 20 December he was given the captaincy of Deal Castle.

Meanwhile the English colonies in the West Indies waited anxiously for the strong naval force they required for protection and, if possible, for assault on the French islands. In July 1691 James Kendall, governor of Barbados, had urged that the command be given to 'a gentleman of good sense, well affected, and a seaman', suggesting that Wheler fitted this profile (*CSP col.*, 13.498). The recommendation was accepted, and in October Wheler's instructions were drafted: he was due to go to the Caribbean in April 1692, but only a small squadron under Robert Wrenn could be sent that year. Wheler remained in home waters, and commanded the *Albemarle* at La Hogue in May. In July, still afloat, he submitted a vast twenty-seven-point proposal for revising the instructions for his West Indies command, particularly asking to be independent of the colonial governments, and for a defined share of plunder ashore. The latter was conceded by assigning a detachment of 400 soldiers to his personal command. He also stressed the need for adequate medical facilities, in line with what would be the most positive outcome of the current war. The privy council approved his instructions on 18 October. Attacks were envisaged on Martinique and Hispaniola; to this the king added the extraordinary order that on his way home Wheler should call in and annex Canada. At the same time Wheler was designated rear-admiral of the blue, effective from 6 February 1693. Having made his will on 30 October, with the provision that if his fortune were increased by £500 or more this should go to his younger son, he joined his fleet at Cowes on 21 December.

Wheler sailed on 9 January 1693 aboard the *Resolution*, accompanied by ten other warships, together with supports, and carrying about 1500 soldiers. They reached Barbados on 28 February/1 March, and on 3 March Wheler was sworn of the island council. A message was sent to Christopher Codrington, governor of the Leewards, to rendezvous off Martinique. Wheler left Barbados on 30 March and arrived at Cul de Sac Marine, Martinique, two days later. While reinforcements were awaited some successful raids were made ashore. Codrington arrived on 9 April, and an assault on the fort of St Pierre was begun on 17 April. On the 20th, however, a council of war decided to abandon the attempt, only Wheler and another officer arguing for continued naval bombardment. On 22 April they withdrew to Dominica, where a further council rejected an assault on Guadeloupe. By this time Wheler's forces were severely depleted by an infection caught at Barbados, and he sailed to the healthier climate of St Kitts to recover as best he could. Since leaving England he had already lost almost 700 men. The campaigning season was now virtually over; his orders were to quit the Caribbean before the rains at the end of May, and as soon as he had regrouped he sailed north.

By 12 June Wheler reached Boston, to find that the governor of Massachusetts, Sir William Phips, was wholly unprepared for his arrival; the projected attack on Quebec was therefore abandoned. Wheler was understandably keen to hurt the French somewhere, and Phips suggested that Newfoundland might be the place to do so. But when Wheler actually proposed an attack, Phips discovered a string of constitutional and practical reasons for withholding his own forces. His concern in fact was to prevent what remained of Wheler's men from becoming a burden on his own colony. Wheler therefore sailed homewards on 22 September, and arrived at Portsmouth on 18 October. There was much anger that so carefully prepared an expedition had achieved nothing, but Wheler's leadership was not held accountable. He was immediately re-engaged, being appointed commander in the Mediterranean on 1 November, ranking as rear-admiral of the red. He sailed on 27 December and arrived at Cadiz on 19 January 1694. On 17 February he left to pass through the straits, but on the night of the 18th met a hurricane off Malaga. In the confusion several of his ships ran aground in Gibraltar Bay. Wheler's flagship, the *Sussex*, struck at 5 a.m. on 19 February, with the loss of all but two Turks from the complement of 550. It was consequently never possible to establish the precise circumstances of the accident or of Wheler's death. The disaster seemed to confirm suspicions already voiced about the inherent instability of 80-gun ships with only two decks, such as the *Sussex*, and a third deck would be added for new ships of this armament.

Wheler was survived by his wife, his eldest son, Charles (who died soon afterwards), his younger sons William and Francis, and his daughter Anna Sophia. Among his executors were Sir Cloudesley Shovell and his kinsman William Binckes, dean of Lichfield. Wheler was a gallant and competent officer, and it cannot be reckoned his fault that his career achieved little, and ended in calamity.

C. S. KNIGHTON

Sources J. Charnock, ed., *Biographia navalis*, 2 (1795), 76–87 · J. Burchett, *A complete history of the most remarkable transactions at sea* (1720), 477–80, 490–94 · *The Sergison papers*, ed. R. D. Merriman, Navy RS, 89 (1950), 71, 84–6, 285–6, 295–8 · *The Tangier papers of Samuel Pepys*, ed. E. Chappell, Navy RS, 73 (1935), 53, 117–18, 138, 141, 144, 158, 273, 293–4, 296, 320 · J. D. Davies, *Gentlemen and tarpaulins: the officers and men of the Restoration navy* (1991), 30, 102, 185, 187, 213, 239–40 · G. H. Guttridge, *The colonial policy of William III in America and the West Indies* (1922), 65–8, 74–5, 102 · W. T. Morgan, 'The British West Indies during King William's War (1689–97)', *Journal of Modern History*, 2 (1930), 393–7, 399, 400 · J. Ehrman, *The navy in the war of William III, 1689–1697* (1953), 233, 504–5, 509–10, 539, 609, 648–9 · D. Syrett and R. L. DiNardo, *The commissioned sea officers of the Royal Navy, 1660–1815*, rev. edn, Occasional Publications of the Navy RS, 1 (1994), 466 · J. P. Ferris, 'Wheler, Sir Charles', HoP, *Commons, 1660–90*, 3.702–4 · Burke, *Peerage* (1997), 2997 · *CSP dom.*, 1673– 5, 382; *1684–5*, 132–3; *1685*, 180, 186; *1687–9*, p. 10, no. 2; *1689–90*, 396; *1690–91*, 99, 192, 542–3; *1691–5* · *CSP col.*, vols. 13–14, esp. 13.498 · BL, Add. MS 28054, fol. 208 · Magd. Cam., Pepys Library, MS 2351, fols. 121–4 · *The manuscripts of the earl of Dartmouth*, 3 vols., HMC, 20 (1887–96), vol. 1, pp. 193–206

Archives Magd. Cam., journal as captain of the *Kingfisher*, 2351 | CKS, corresp. with Alexander Stanhope · PRO, CO 5 [*CSP colonial, America and West Indies, 1693–6*, 41–2, 124] · PRO, SP domestic [*CSP dom., 1691–2*, 346–52, 392–3, 447–8, 458–9]

Wealth at death £600 cash plus estate and household effects: will, proved 28 April 1694, PRO, PROB 11/419, fols. 351v–352

Wheler, Sir George (1651–1724), Church of England clergyman and scholar, was born at Breda in the Netherlands on 20 January 1651, the third child and eldest son of Charles Wheler, a colonel in the Life Guards, and his wife, Anne, daughter of John Hutchin of Egerton, Kent, who were royalists living in exile. The family had been originally from Tottenham High Cross, Middlesex, and had changed their name from Bradford to Wheler in order to inherit an estate. They were able to return to a house at Charing, Kent, in 1652. Wheler was educated at schools in Ashford and Wye, of which he retained an unfavourable memory. After the death of Sir William Wheler of Westminster, the family acquired his substantial property, so that a university education for George became feasible, and on 31 January 1668, aged seventeen and helped by a letter of introduction from the son of the rector, he matriculated at Lincoln College, Oxford. Within a week he caught smallpox, but although he had been a frail child, unable to indulge in sports or hunting, his health did not suffer further and in fact improved. While at Oxford he read widely, and took up an interest in heraldry, decorating his rooms with coats of arms. He was a man of many interests and practical skills. As a boy he had amused himself with woodwork, constructing a birdcage and a small harpsichord, and had taken an interest in plants; the latter he maintained in Oxford by frequent visits to the physic garden.

On 4 July 1671 Wheler was admitted to the Middle Temple, at least partly in order to facilitate his father's legal battle over the terms of Sir William Wheler's widow's will, but law did not appeal to him. By the summer of 1673 the lawsuit had reached a successful conclusion and Wheler, now financially secure, set out on a continental tour with George Hickes, one of his former tutors. On his travels he displayed keen curiosity and took the opportunity to collect plant specimens. While at Venice in 1675 he made the acquaintance of Jacques Spon, a doctor from Lyons, with whom he travelled in Greece in 1675–6. Both travellers published an account of their adventures, Spon in 1678 and Wheler in 1682. The latter's *A Journey into Greece* is a large volume with illustrations of inscriptions, coins, plants, and buildings (one of the engravings shows the Parthenon before the fateful explosion of 1687), but much disfigured by misprints (which the author took the trouble to correct in a copy he presented to his college). A French translation appeared in 1689, with a reprint in 1723; in the preface Wheler is complimented for the fact that he had provided a much more accurate map of Greece than had previously been available.

On 3 September 1677 at St Martin-in-the-Fields, Westminster, Wheler married Grace (1662?–1703), daughter of the diplomat Sir Thomas *Higgons (1623/4–1691) and his second wife, Bridget Grenville. The same year he became a fellow of the Royal Society, but he devoted himself mainly to an ecclesiastical career, in which he doubtless owed much to his acquaintance with Nathaniel, Lord Crewe, who had been elected rector of Lincoln College while he was a student there and from 1674 was bishop of Durham. Wheler was knighted on 1 September 1682, was ordained about 1683 (in which year he was created MA of Oxford) and became a canon of Durham in 1684. From 1685 to 1702 he was vicar of Basingstoke, Hampshire.

In 1689 Wheler published a slim volume entitled *An Account of Churches and Places of Assembly of the Primitive Christians*. It is an attempt to use the evidence of Eusebius, combined with the author's own experience of archaeological sites, to reconstruct the plan of certain early churches in Tyre, Jerusalem, and Constantinople, and is illustrated with plans. The book appears to be one of the earliest studies of Christian archaeology. A sign of Wheler's continuing interest in the affairs of Greece is that in 1693 he was involved in an abortive project to endow places for Greek students at Gloucester Hall, Oxford.

In 1702 Wheler became DD by diploma. He subsequently enjoyed additional preferment in Durham, being appointed rector of Winston in 1706 and then of Houghton-le-Spring in 1709. At Houghton he founded a charity school for girls and enlarged the almshouse. He died in Durham on 15 January 1724 and was buried in Durham Cathedral. His will, begun on 3 May 1717 and completed, after several codicils, on 4 September 1723, reveals that he had extensive property in London, including a tenement called Skinners in the parish of St Margaret's, Westminster, 'where I lately lived' (1717). He and his wife had had eighteen children, of whom two sons and six daughters were alive in 1723. The elder son, George, was his father's chief heir; the younger son, Granville *Wheler (1701–1770), 'being intended for the study of divinity', was left his books on theology and by Greek and Latin authors. Substantial and complicated charitable bequests included £100 for the Society for the Propagation of the Gospel, a house for the minister of the new conformist French church at Spitalfields, and endowments for the poor of St Oswald, Houghton, for the school and almshouse there, and for Joanna, Lady Thornhill's poor school at Wye, Kent. He gave to his Oxford college more than thirty Greek manuscripts, acquired mainly in Athens and Constantinople; they included a priceless illuminated typicon, the foundation charter of a convent established in Constantinople about 1300. His plant specimens were given to the Oxford Physic Garden. Wheler occupies a significant position in the history of botany, since he introduced to Britain some plants hitherto unknown, including St John's wort.   N. G. WILSON

Sources autobiography, LPL, MS 3286 · Desmond, *Botanists* · H. M. Clokie, *An account of the herbaria of the department of botany in the University of Oxford* (1964) · A. M. Coats, *The quest for plants* (1969), 15–17 ·

T. Zarch, *Works* (1820), 2.99–218 · Foster, *Alum. Oxon.* · H. A. C. Sturgess, ed., *Register of admissions to the Honourable Society of the Middle Temple, from the fifteenth century to the year 1944*, 1 (1949), 184 · will, PRO, PROB 11/597, sig. 126, fols. 273v–281r · *IGI* · *DNB* · C. Knight, 'The travels of the Rev. Sir George Wheler (1650–1723)', *Georgian Group Journal*, 10 (2000), 21–35 · P. de la Ruffinière du Prey, *Hawksmoor's London churches: architecture and theology* (2000)
Archives BL, collection of ancient inscriptions, Add. MS 35334 · Bodl. Oxf., *hortus siccus* · LPL, autobiography covering his early life · W. Yorks. AS, Leeds, corresp. and papers, LD
Likenesses W. Bromley, line engraving, 1816, BM, NPG; repro. in R. Surtees, *The history and antiquities of the county palatine of Durham* (1816) · oils, Durham Cathedral

Wheler, Granville (1701–1770), experimental philosopher, was born in August 1701 in London, the third son of Sir George *Wheler (1651–1724) and his wife, Grace (*d.* 1703), daughter of Sir Thomas Higgons of Grewel, Hampshire. At the time of his son's birth, Sir George was a canon of Durham Cathedral. Wheler attended school at Durham before being admitted pensioner at Christ's College, Cambridge, in 1717; he graduated BA in 1721, held a fellowship at Christ's in 1722–4, and proceeded MA in 1734. He was ordained deacon and priest at St Margaret's, Westminster, London, and was rector of Leake, Nottinghamshire, from 1737 until his death. His first wife was Lady Catherine Maria (*d.* 1740), daughter of Theophilus *Hastings, seventh earl of Huntingdon; they had seven children. His second marriage, to Mary, daughter of John Dove of London, was childless.

Wheler acquired the estate of Otterden, near Charing, Kent, about 1717, by purchase from the widow of his deceased brother, and in the spacious galleries of Otterden Place he and his friends, among them John Godfrey, Stephen Gray, and Thomas Ruddock, carried out various electrical experiments on the lines of those published by Benjamin Franklin and others. They confirmed Franklin's identification of lightning as an electrical discharge, and sought to discover how to communicate electricity, leading the 'electric virtue' through silk threads running through the building. They tested various substances, identifying those that could receive a charge and those that did not. To Wheler fell the fame of being the first in England to electrify a live animal. He succeeded in leading electricity through the bodies of live chickens, then through the footboy, 'a good stout lad', whom he suspended by a silk rope, touching his hand or foot with a long glass rod, which had been previously rubbed so as to bear a charge, and making another person point to the boy's face or hands, whereupon sparks crackled between the two, and they felt a burning sensation. Wheler was elected to the Royal Society on 27 June 1728, to which he wrote in later years conveying news of his experiments. Wheler died on 12 May 1770, and was buried in Otterden church.   ANITA McCONNELL

Sources T. Ruddock, letter, *GM*, 1st ser., 102/1 (1832), 393–9 · J. Priestley, *The history and present state of electricity*, 3rd edn, 1 (1775); repr. (1966), 37–41, 67–8 · J. L. Heilbron, *Electricity in the 17th and 18th centuries: a study of early modern physics* (1979), 246–7, 249–50, 254–9, 290 · *GM*, 1st ser., 40 (1770), 239

Archives BL, MSS relating to electricity, Add. MSS 4433–4434 · RS, papers | Leics. RO, corresp. with ninth earl and countess of Huntingdon, incl. some letters of his wife, Catherine Hastings

Wheler, Robert Bell (1785–1857), antiquary, was born at Stratford upon Avon on 7 January 1785, the fourth child but only son of Robert Wheler (1742–1819), a solicitor of that town. His mother was Elizabeth Loader (1756–1786) of Quinton, Warwickshire, who died when he was only a year old. His forenames were derived from Robert Bell, who lodged with the Whelers until his death in 1802. He was the brother-in-law of Dionysius Bradley, a Stratford attorney, to whom Robert Wheler had been articled in 1777. Robert Bell Wheler was educated at the town's grammar school and was articled to his father in 1803. He appears scarcely to have left Stratford, except in 1812, when he went to London for a month at the date of his formal admission as a solicitor in the court of king's bench. He practised his profession at Stratford until his death, residing continuously in a house now known as Avoncroft in Old Town.

In youth Wheler joined the Stratford volunteer corps and in 1810 was commissioned as an ensign in the 3rd regiment of Warwickshire militia, stationed at Stratford; he later became lieutenant and quartermaster. But his main interest through life was in Shakespearian research and local topography. At the age of twenty-one he published his first book, *The History and Antiquities of Stratford-upon-Avon* (1806), the research for which had been completed, by his own account, three years earlier. This accurate and careful compilation, illustrated with his own accomplished sketches, though based largely on printed sources, included transcripts of, or reference to, several previously undiscovered documents relating to Shakespeare and his family. This was followed in 1814 by his *Guide to Stratford-upon-Avon*, in some respects an abridged version of his *History*, but incorporating additional discoveries he had since made concerning Shakespeare and other Stratford figures with Shakespearian associations. It also contained a rudimentary history of Shakespeare's birthplace, which was treated more fully in his final published work, *A Historical and Descriptive Account of the Birthplace of Shakespeare* (1824). Wheler also contributed articles, chiefly on Shakespearian subjects, to the *Gentleman's Magazine*. He was secretary to the committee which organized celebrations in Stratford to commemorate, in 1816, the bicentenary of Shakespeare's death, and, from 1820 to 1823, secretary and treasurer to another seeking to erect a 'mausoleum' in the town in memory of the poet. He was a friend of the antiquary John Britton, and intimate with Captain James Saunders of Stratford, in conjunction with whom most of his research was undertaken. On Saunders's death in 1830, 'a great loss' to him, Wheler's antiquarian activities, which had already been curtailed by his father's death in 1819, virtually ceased. He died unmarried on 15 July 1857 at his house, Avoncroft, in Old Town, Stratford and was buried six days later beside his father in the churchyard (Holy Trinity) of his native town.

Wheler left a quarto autograph manuscript volume of 'Collectanea de Stratford', containing personal anecdotes and many transcripts and notes, some from sources since lost, which has become a major source for the history of the town. This, together with his other notes and part of his library, his collection of local deeds and original documents, coins, and other relics local and Shakespearian, were given by his sister Anne Wheler (1783–1870) to the trustees of Shakespeare's birthplace, and are now located in the record office of the Shakespeare Birthplace Trust. Also of great importance is another autograph volume, now in the British Library, largely comprising copies from a lost manuscript history of Warwickshire by the antiquary Simon Archer (1581–1662).

W. S. Brassington, rev. Robert Bearman

Sources S. Schoenbaum, *Shakespeare's lives*, new edn (1991) · R. Bearman, *Shakespeare in the Stratford records* (1994) · R. Bearman, *Captain James Saunders of Stratford-upon-Avon: a local antiquary*, Dugdale Society, 33 (1990) · 'Collectanea de Stratford', Shakespeare Birthplace Trust RO, Stratford upon Avon, ER 1/8 · parish register (baptism), 20 June 1785, Stratford upon Avon, Holy Trinity · parish register (burial), 21 July 1857, Stratford upon Avon, Holy Trinity · affidavits of execution of Articles of Clerkship, PRO, Court of King's Bench, KB 105 · d. cert.
Archives BL, collections relating to Warwickshire, Add. MS 28564 · Boston PL, corresp. · Folger · Shakespeare Birthplace Trust RO, Stratford upon Avon, antiquarian corresp., papers, and collections | Shakespeare Birthplace Trust RO, Stratford upon Avon, letters to J. G. Nichols
Likenesses silhouette (aged thirty), repro. in Bearman, *Shakespeare in the Stratford records*
Wealth at death real estate (£180 p.a.): account of succession duty, DR 42/496

Whelpdale, Roger (d. 1423), bishop of Carlisle, was later said to have been born of a Cumbrian gentry family near Penrith. Educated at Oxford University, he was a fellow of Balliol College before 1400, and then became successively fellow, chamberlain, treasurer, and, in 1404, provost of Queen's College. He was senior proctor of the university in 1403–4. The author of treatises on logic and mathematics, he had proceeded BTh before January 1413. His earliest promotions outside Oxford were in southern England, successively to the rectories of Stockton, Wiltshire, and Burghclere, Hampshire. It is not known to whose patronage he owed these benefices, or through whose agency he became bishop of Carlisle in 1419, following the death of William Strickland on 30 August. Licence to elect was given on 12 October, and Whelpdale was papally provided on 22 December. The temporalities of the see were restored on 17 March 1420, and he was consecrated in London on 21 August in that year, professing obedience to York on the same day.

Whelpdale's episcopate was brief, and all that can be said of it is that, like his predecessor, Whelpdale concerned himself with the protracted restoration of his cathedral, and in January 1422 obtained an indulgence for those contributing to the works. He was clearly not always resident in his diocese, and might, indeed, have been absent from it for some time, since on 22 November 1422 he was appointed to represent the northern province at the church council summoned to Pavia in 1423. Presumably his preparations for attendance account for his having been in London when he made his will, on 25 January

1423, and when he died there on 4 February following. He had requested burial in a church dedicated either to the Virgin, or to St Mary Magdalen, or to St Paul, and was consequently interred in St Paul's Cathedral in London.

Whelpdale's will shows him as concerned for his family, his see, and his *Alma Mater*. It also shows that he was a man of means, able to make bequests whose value amounted to about £530, part of which was to be raised by the sale of property in Beverley, Oxford, and, apparently, north Kent. The beneficiaries of his will included a sister, a nephew, and a niece, and the children of Matthew Whelpdale, presumably also a relation. He left vestments, furnishings, and plate to Carlisle Cathedral, and £200 to found a chantry there for two of his Cumbrian friends. He had brought books from Oxford to his official residence at Rose Castle; these, with other volumes of theology, political theory, and canon law, he now bequeathed to Queen's College, together with vestments, plate, £10 for the repair of the vestry, and 20s. to buy keys to the library for the fellows. A more general bequest gave £20 to be distributed among Oxford scholars. HENRY SUMMERSON

Sources Emden, *Oxf.* · [J. Raine], ed., *Testamenta Eboracensia*, 3, SurtS, 45 (1865), 65–8 · Bodl. Oxf., MSS St Edmund Hall, 7/2, fols. 166–8 · *CEPR letters*, vol. 7 · *Chancery records* · R. G. Davies, 'The episcopate in England and Wales, 1375–1443', PhD diss., University of Manchester, 1974
Wealth at death over £530: Raine, ed., *Testamenta Eboracensia*, 3.65–8

Whetham, William Cecil Dampier. *See* Dampier, Sir William Cecil Dampier (1867–1952).

Whethamstede [Bostock], **John** (*c.*1392–1465), scholar and abbot of St Albans, was probably born at Wheathampstead, Hertfordshire, *c.*1392—in 1442 he was described as being 'in about his fiftieth year' (*CEPR letters*, 9.266). His father, Hugh Bostock (*c.*1360–*c.*1430), was a landowner originally from the west midlands who had settled at Wheathampstead following his marriage to Margaret (*c.*1370–*c.*1420), daughter of Sir Thomas Makery. This and other fortunate marriages seem to have raised the Bostocks from the ranks of the lesser gentry, so that in old age John could claim kinship with local nobles like Elizabeth, Lady Sudeley. John was the eldest child and only son, and as a result he appears to have retained control of the family estates and manors despite his later monastic career.

Early career and promotion According to a family memoir, Whethamstede attended a local grammar school 'at a young age' (*ad annos dociles*), and proved himself a proficient scholar (*multum proficiens*; BL, Harley MS 139 fol. 91r). Before he was sixteen, however, between *c.*1405 and *c.*1408, he had entered St Albans as a novice. His unusually early admission, though probably a testimony to his promise as a scholar, must also have been a product of close family ties with the monastery: his uncle, William Whethamstede, had been a distinguished prior of the St Albans cell at Tynemouth, where his cousin John had also been a monk. Following his profession Whethamstede was sent to study at Gloucester College, the Benedictine *studium* in Oxford. Making rapid progress there, as early as 1414 he served as the college's *prior studentium*, and in

1417, after less than a decade of study, he incepted as doctor of theology.

Whethamstede probably returned to St Albans in the same year or shortly after, and on 2 September 1420 was elected abbot. His election was exceptional for a monk so young, and again reflected his reputation as a man of considerable intellectual capabilities. The expectation that attended his election might explain the fact that within the first months of his administration he was drawn into national ecclesiastical and political affairs. In May 1421 he was selected, together with five other more senior abbots, to represent the Benedictines before the king's commissioners at the Council of Westminster. Henry V had convened the council to examine the case for monastic reform, a case vigorously rejected by the monks. Although the youngest of the negotiators, Whethamstede emerged as his order's most able spokesman, and it was he who compiled and presented the proposals that eventually sealed an agreement between the parties. His compromise recommendations for reform were adopted throughout the English communities and also formed the basis of his own internal reforms which he introduced during visitations at St Albans and its cells in 1422–3.

Whethamstede was again called upon to represent his order in spring 1423, as a delegate at the Council of Pavia. His journey to Italy took him through much of Germany, and he remained for some time at Ulm and Worms. During the council Whethamstede fell into a bitter dispute with Richard Flemming, bishop of Lincoln, from whose episcopal jurisdiction the St Albans monks claimed complete exemption. Flemming appears to have threatened to raise the question of St Albans' status before the pope, but the bishop's health collapsed, and when he did reach Rome some time later he was reconciled to the abbot. Whethamstede followed the council when it removed to Siena, and then travelled to Rome for his own audience with Martin V to secure confirmation of St Albans' most important privileges. Before he could complete his suit he was taken ill with dysentery, and was later said to have survived only through the intercession of St Alban himself, and following a vision in which St Bernard appeared and reassured him that he would live. Following his recovery he successfully concluded an agreement with the pope which provided both recognition of the abbey's existing privileges and also a number of important new dispensations.

The first abbacy Whethamstede returned to St Albans in February 1424. He devoted much of the rest of the 1420s and 1430s to internal reforms, and to reviving the material condition of the community. From 1425 to 1426 he conducted a thorough visitation of the dependent cells. He dissolved the priory at Beadlow entirely, and devised reform constitutions for the communities at Redbourne and Tynemouth. He embarked on an extensive programme of rebuilding, spending £2334 on fabric and furnishings, including £641 on plate and vestments alone. He expended a further £2000 on conventual properties outside the abbey, including a large contribution to the new buildings at Gloucester College. He also reorganized the abbey's financial administration, spending more than £1000 on the acquisition of new properties, and creating a new office of 'master of works' to supervise the distribution of resources. In the later 1420s and 1430s Whethamstede also made renewed efforts through litigation and negotiation to defend the abbey's endowments and extend its exemptions and other privileges. In 1428 he won a case against the abbot of Westminster over claims to certain manors. He also worked to establish new guarantees for the abbey's long-standing claims of independence from episcopal and secular authorities. In 1425 he negotiated royal recognition of the exemptions and privileges recently confirmed by the pope. Between 1431 and 1433 he also successfully challenged efforts by William Alnwick, bishop of Norwich, to subject the cell at Binham, Norfolk, to episcopal visitation. Whethamstede's monks regarded these battles over properties and privileges as among their abbot's most significant achievements: when his portrait was added to the *Liber benefactorum* after his death he was depicted proudly clutching bulls and charters to his chest.

In pursuing these cases Whethamstede benefited from the support of a number of distinguished allies among the senior clergy, the nobility, and the court circle. He appears to have cultivated friendships with such figures as Cardinal Henry Beaufort, Thomas Beckington, dean of the court of arches, Richard Beauchamp, earl of Warwick, and John, duke of Bedford. However, his closest relationship was with the protector, Humphrey, duke of Gloucester. Gloucester was a frequent visitor to St Albans and in 1423 Whethamstede granted him, his wife, and his retinue rights of confraternity. Their friendship seems to have been based on mutual intellectual interests, focused in particular on the work of Italian classical scholars. However there was also a political dimension to the alliance: Gloucester was Beaufort's rival for influence over the king and in the 1430s and 1440s an early focus of opposition towards Henry VI and his advisers. In the 1420s Whethamstede seems to have used his connection with the duke as a defence against Beaufort, who showed some hostility towards St Albans. But when the king declared his majority in 1437 and Gloucester was reduced to an isolated and increasingly suspect figure, Whethamstede became more openly partisan. When the duke died in captivity in 1447 the abbot sued for custody of his remains, and had them interred in the abbey church in a chantry he may have originally prepared for himself.

Resignation and second abbacy By the end of the 1430s Whethamstede's work of reconstruction and reform had placed considerable strain on conventual resources and his continuous disputes had damaged his own public reputation, leaving him physically exhausted, and even allowing dissension to emerge within the community. In November 1440 he resigned the abbacy and retired to his own manor at Wheathampstead. The abbot himself seems to have blamed his difficulties on his external and internal opponents, although he also recognized that his public image had been tarnished, confessing that he found himself increasingly awkward in confrontations

and was 'given to excessive blushing' (*Annales … Amundesham*, 2.234). His monks, however, attributed his failure to his own inflated ambitions, which had led to almost unrestrained prodigality with conventual resources. Whethamstede seems to have left St Albans precipitately, leaving books and other personal items behind which he never recovered. His activities during his retirement remain obscure: it seems likely he spent much of the time pursuing his scholarly interests, although he may have returned to St Albans briefly in 1447 to supervise the burial of Humphrey of Gloucester. Following the death of Abbot John Stoke in January 1452, Whethamstede was persuaded to return to St Albans and on 16 January was re-elected abbot. Stoke's administration had proved disastrous and there seems to have been a small but vocal minority that had been working to secure Whethamstede's return since the late 1440s. Even so, his re-election appears to have been an eleventh-hour decision, coming only after other candidates had withdrawn. The townspeople were said to have rejoiced at Whethamstede's re-election, describing it as a miracle comparable to Saul's transformation on the road to Damascus.

Whethamstede's second administration was undoubtedly more troubled than his first, but none the less he continued to make significant improvements to the fabric and fortunes of the abbey. In an address following his election he outlined a wide-ranging programme for reform, with a particular emphasis on reviving the intellectual activities of the monks: the number of monks attending the universities was to be increased and teachers and preachers were to be provided to direct the studies of the monks in the cloister. He also launched a detailed review of the administration of his obedientiaries: the audit for 1452 had revealed a significant fall in conventual income despite the abundant harvests and rising prices that had prevailed throughout the 1440s. The review revealed serious maladministration on the part of the bursar and official-general, William Wallingford, and further evidence of corruption emerged in 1454. Whethamstede was unable to pursue charges against Wallingford because of the latter's powerful position within the community, but he did succeed in dismissing some corrupt lesser officials, including his own secretary, who was known to be a habitual frequenter of taverns.

Whethamstede also resumed his efforts to defend and extend the abbey's properties and privileges in the face of royal and seigneurial intervention. He initiated litigation against a number of local lords, and entered into a protracted dispute with the royal exchequer over infringements of the abbey's rights during Stoke's rule. He recovered a loan of £600 from Henry VI, and in 1456 successfully petitioned for confirmation and resumption of all gifts and grants made to the abbey since the beginning of the reign, including the significant privilege of a remission of £20 on all clerical tenths levied by the crown. Whethamstede also continued to make improvements to the abbey buildings. He constructed a self-contained library building to provide a new focus for the studies of the monks, he glazed the cloister windows, and rebuilt the parochial chapel of St Andrew.

Last years and death Despite his advancing age, throughout his second administration Whethamstede continued to be drawn into public affairs. In the late 1450s he was involved in discussions over the planned crusade against the Turks: two Hungarian clerics visited St Albans in 1457 to discuss the matter, and in 1459 he also met the papal legate to consider the issue. He also seems to have become involved in the case against Reginald Pecock, bishop of Chichester, whose writings were condemned as heretical in 1459: Whethamstede's register is filled with detailed notes on Pecock's conclusions. In the political struggles between Henry VI and his opponents, Whethamstede seems at first to have strongly opposed the king and his followers, and in the early 1450s he supported parliamentary demands for the posthumous exoneration of Humphrey of Gloucester from accusations of treason. But after military conflict began he became less partisan: following the first battle of St Albans, on 22 May 1455, he demanded that the duke of York make proper provision for the burial of the dead, and himself offered, and subsequently provided, burial places in the abbey church for the bodies of Beaufort, Clifford, and Percy. After two decades of poor relations, he also made new overtures to the king, and as late as 1458 invited Henry VI to spend Easter at St Albans. According to his register, as the political crisis intensified after 1460 Whethamstede became increasingly depressed, and following the second battle of St Albans in February 1461 he recommended that the community be temporarily dispersed, and himself probably withdrew to his family manor, there to pursue the contemplative life.

From the mid-1450s Whethamstede suffered increasing infirmity, and he was forced to delegate daily administration to his officials. Too ill to attend the Coventry parliament in 1459, in 1460 he was forced to cede the direction of a lawsuit against Lord Sudeley to his archdeacon because of his sickness. Shortly afterwards he appears to have retired from active life at St Albans and returned to Wheathampstead: an abbatial document dated 1464 was issued 'from our house of solitary residence at Makery End' (Riley, 2.23). He died, probably at Wheathampstead, on 20 January 1465 and was buried in the abbey church, in the chantry chapel which he himself had constructed, before the 25th. His death does not seem to have been marked with great ceremony at St Albans, an indication perhaps that he had few supporters remaining in the community, and it is significant that within a decade William Wallingford, the monk whose fraud he exposed in the 1450s, was himself elected abbot.

Whethamstede was the leading Benedictine of his time, a defender of traditional monastic interests, but also a champion of monastic reform. In addition to his involvement in the council of 1421 he served three times as president of the Benedictine general chapter, and also organized the Benedictine delegation to the Council of Basel in 1440. He was especially energetic in his promotion of the monastic studia at Oxford and Cambridge, and in his later years became Gloucester College's most important benefactor, funding the construction of both its chapel and library. Through his extensive and lively correspondence he also encouraged other abbots to adopt his devotional and educational reforms in their own communities. These achievements notwithstanding, Whethamstede probably never fulfilled his full potential as a prelate: increasingly his public role was undermined by arrogance, litigiousness, and ill-advised political alliances.

Scholar and man of letters Indeed, Whethamstede's most significant achievements were not as an abbot but as an educationist, a scholar, and writer. Regarding intellectual activities as being at the heart of the monastic life, he devoted considerable effort and expense, during both his administrations, to make better provision for the studies of his monks. He had a large number of new books produced for the conventual library, which he himself described as 'the best in the whole country' (BL, Egerton MS 646 fol. 105r). He also commissioned new works for the use of the monks, including an English life of St Alban and St Amphibalus from John Lydgate, and a St Alban motet from the composer John Dunstaple. His own intellectual interests were very broad: although trained as a theologian he also studied and wrote on astronomy, grammar, history, philosophy, poetry, and politics. His surviving notebooks reveal him to have been an almost compulsive writer, their pages filled with a diverse range of letters, verses, and other scribbles. He was also an accomplished scribe and several of the extant St Albans books are copied in his own hand. Many of his own compositions were intended as aids to his studies, for instance, an analytical index to John of Salisbury's *Policraticus*. He also composed numerous commemorative verses relating to his own life, such as his defeat of his episcopal opponents in the 1420s and 1430s, and the construction of his library in the 1450s, and wrote several epitaphs. In the 1450s he also compiled and edited his own collection of letters.

Whethamstede's principal intellectual interests, however, were in classical scholarship and the new work of the Italian humanists, interests he had developed during his time in Oxford and as a result of his travels in Italy. He collected copies of classical and humanist texts and cultivated the friendship of Italian scholars. He was probably the first English scholar to cite Leonardo Bruni's translation of Aristotle's *Politics* and he also owned early copies of translations of Plato and of the Latin Plutarch. He sustained a brief correspondence with Piero da Monte, and according to Amundsham also met with other unidentified Italian scholars while at Florence in 1423. He also composed his own works in which he developed his interest in poetry and philosophy, ancient history, and mythography. His largest and most important work was the *Granarium* (its title was a deliberate pun on his own name), which combined material on a diverse range of historical and literary topics. Three of its four parts survive (BL, Cotton MSS Nero C.vi; Tiberius D.v; Add. MS 26764). He also compiled a number of collections based on the work of classical and high-medieval writers: three of these, the *Palearium poetarum*, the *Pabularium poetarum*, and the

Manipularium doctorum, survive in incomplete texts, while three more, the *Florarium*, the *Propinarium*, and the *Proverbiarium*, have been lost.

These writings were compilations of extracts rather than self-contained commentaries, and are less important for the insights into the subject that they offer than for the wide range of sources from which they were drawn. Whethamstede demonstrated a remarkably wide knowledge of Latin and Greek classical texts, including Quintilian's *Institutes* and Cicero's *De oratore*, which had only recently been discovered. It would be mistaken, however, to suggest that Whethamstede's own work was comparable to that of the Italians: he cannot be described as a 'humanist'. But he was among the first English scholars to promote the writings and values at the heart of the European classical revival in England, and his own compilations did play an important role in the transmission and reception of classical and humanist texts in English learned communities from the second half of the fifteenth century. Humphrey of Gloucester included a three-volume edition of Whethamstede's *Granarium* among the books he donated to Oxford University in 1437, and even in the early sixteenth century, under the nickname Frumentarius, his work continued to attract a considerable following.   JAMES G. CLARK

Sources Emden, *Oxf.* · D. R. Howlett, 'Studies in the works of John Whethamstede', DPhil diss., U. Oxf., 1975 · *Annales monasterii S. Albani a Johanne Amundesham*, ed. H. T. Riley, 2 vols., pt 5 of *Chronica monasterii S. Albani*, Rolls Series, 28 (1870–71) · H. T. Riley, ed., *Registra quorundam abbatum monasterii S. Albani*, 2 vols., Rolls Series, 28/6 (1872–3) · D. Knowles [M. C. Knowles], *The religious orders in England*, 2 (1955), 193–7 · R. Weiss, *Humanism in England during the fifteenth century* (1941), 30–38 · R. Weiss, 'Leonardo Bruni Aretini and early English humanism', *Modern Language Review*, 36 (1941), 443–8 · R. Weiss, 'Piero del Monte, John Whethamstede and the library of St Albans Abbey', *EngHR*, 60 (1945), 399–406 · M. Harvey, 'John Whethamstede, the pope, and the general council', *The church in pre-Reformation society: essays in honour of F. R. H. Du Boulay*, ed. C. M. Barron and C. Harper-Bill (1985), 108–22 · A. Gransden, *Historical writing in England*, 2 (1982), 371–86 · W. F. Schirmer, *Der englische Frühhumanismus: ein Beitrag zur englischen Literaturgeschichte des 15. Jahrhunderts* (Leipzig, 1931), 82–98, 193–45 · E. F. Jacob, 'Florida verborum venustas, some early examples of euphuism in England', *Bulletin of the John Rylands University Library*, 17 (1933), 264–90 · R. Sharpe and others, eds., *English Benedictine libraries: the shorter catalogues* (1996), 563–81 · R. Sharpe, *A handlist of the Latin writers of Great Britain and Ireland before 1540* (1997), 344–5 · *CEPR letters*, vols. 7–12, esp. vol. 9 · W. A. Pantin, ed., *Documents illustrating the activities of … the English black monks, 1215–1540*, 3 vols., CS, 3rd ser., 45, 47, 54 (1931–7) · K. H. Vickers, *Humphrey duke of Gloucester: a biography* (1907), 338 · BL, MS Harley 139

Archives BL, Add. MS 26764 · BL, Egerton MS 646 · BL, Cotton MS Nero C.vi · BL, Cotton MS Tiberius D.v · Gon. & Caius Cam., commonplace book, MS 230 | BL, Cotton MS Claudius D.i · BL, Cotton MS Otho B.iv · Bodl. Oxf., MS Auct. F inf. 1.1 · Bodl. Oxf., MS Bodley 585 · Coll. Arms, MS Arundel 3

Likenesses portrait, BL, 'Book of Benefactors' of St Albans Abbey, Cotton MS Nero D.vii

Whetnall [*married name* Niven]**, Edith Aileen Maude** (1910–1965), otologist, was born on 6 September 1910 in Hull, Yorkshire, the youngest daughter of the Revd Arthur John Whetnall, Wesleyan minister, and his wife, Eleanor (*née* Stormer). Edith was about to enter King's College, London, as a medical student, when deafness was diagnosed in a three-year-old niece; no doubt influenced by her niece's disability, she decided even before qualifying MB BS in 1938 that she wanted to be an ear, nose, and throat specialist. On 2 September 1939 she married Robert Barrie Niven, a physician.

Throughout the years of the Second World War Edith served in the Emergency Medical Service: first as house surgeon at King's College Hospital, then, from the end of 1940 until September 1945, as assistant in ear, nose, and throat surgery to Victor Negus, at one of the sector hospitals; from 1942 to 1945 she was also registrar to the ear, nose, and throat department at King's College Hospital. Between July 1945 and August 1946 she was assistant to C. S. Hallpike in the aural department of the National Hospital for Nervous Diseases in Queen Square, and in the latter year she was appointed assistant surgeon to the Royal National Throat, Nose, and Ear Hospital. During this same period she became a fellow of the Royal College of Surgeons (1940), and she obtained a mastership in surgery (MS) in 1944.

While Edith was recovering from an injury sustained in a car accident she was visited by one of her chiefs, Terence Cawthorne, distinguished otologist and aural surgeon to the London county council, in which latter capacity he held special clinics for deaf children at County Hall. Edith began to attend his clinics as soon as she had recovered.

In 1947 the Royal National Throat, Nose, and Ear Hospital in London set up a deafness aid clinic, with Edith as its first director. This later became the audiology unit, and subsequently the Nuffield Hearing and Speech Centre. Although this unit dealt with hearing-impaired people of all ages, Edith saw no fewer than fifty-seven deaf children in its first year. She also succeeded Terence Cawthorne as consultant otologist to the London county council. After establishing a close collaboration with Dennis Fry, then reader, later professor of experimental phonetics in the University of London, she published a key paper with him in *The Lancet* in 1954, and later published two books with him, *The Deaf Child* (1964) and (posthumously) *Learning to Hear* (1970).

In the mid-twentieth century it was widely assumed that severely deaf children, especially those born deaf, would be unable to learn to talk; and that if they were to learn to talk at all, they would have to be taught by lipreading. However, Edith Whetnall and Dennis Fry found that several of the children with severe hearing losses attending the unit were holding their own in ordinary schools, and when they began to look for an explanation for these successes, it soon became clear that they all had one thing in common. In the words of Dr Robert Niven, Edith's husband:

> Their mothers had realized … usually in the first or second year, that their children were deaf. They had then done what appeared to them to be the natural thing. They had each drawn their child close to her and spoken into the ear.

In fact, they had given them auditory training. After the inception of the National Health Service in 1948 the

'Medresco' (MEDICAL RESEARCH COUNCIL) hearing aid was produced; its use made possible the training of that residual hearing which is present in the majority of children who are born deaf or have acquired deafness in very early life.

Edith Whetnall recognized that as in hearing children, so in deaf children speech is developed most naturally through hearing. She also emphasized that age is of crucial importance in the learning process, the ability to recognize and interpret sounds being learned to a large extent during the first year or so of life. This she described as the period of 'readiness to listen'. Later experimental evidence supported the concept of critical periods for speech and language development, at an age when the nervous system is most receptive to sensory stimulation. She realized this essential truth in the middle of the twentieth century; by the end of it, it became increasingly accepted that profoundly deaf children who have electrodes (cochlear implants) inserted into their inner ears, to stimulate surviving nerve fibres, can achieve optimal benefit only if the procedure is carried out very early, ideally in the first two years or so of life, and in any event before they are five.

Though somewhat sensitive, Edith was fiercely determined and she preached her message with missionary zeal; but throughout her professional life her work was opposed by a vociferous minority of people who held that deaf children should be allowed to develop non-orally within their own 'deaf culture'. Although this controversy continued for some years, the principles espoused by Edith Whetnall gained widespread support. She died, after a long struggle with the neurological condition of myasthenia gravis, at her residence, 9 Queen Anne Street, Marylebone, London, on 23 October 1965, and was cremated at South London crematorium, Streatham Vale, on the 26th.   JOHN BALLANTYNE

Sources private information (2004) · personal knowledge (2004) · *CGPLA Eng. & Wales* (1966)
Likenesses sepia photograph
Wealth at death £18,857: probate, 26 May 1966, *CGPLA Eng. & Wales*

Whetstone, George (*bap.* 1550, *d.* 1587), writer, was born in London, where he was baptized at St Lawrence, Old Jewry, on 27 July 1550, the third son of Robert Whetstone (*d.* 1557), a wealthy merchant and haberdasher, and Margaret, daughter of Philip Barnard of Suffolk. Whetstone's father had been imprisoned in the Tower in 1554 after acting as foreman of the Guildhall jury which had refused to find Sir Nicholas Throckmorton guilty of treason after his part in Wyatt's rebellion, as reported in Holinshed's *Chronicles*. He was fined £2000 for his conduct, but released from seven months' imprisonment after paying about a tenth of this sum.

Family and early years On their father's death, estates in Essex, Leicestershire, Middlesex, Kent, Suffolk, and Yorkshire were part of the Whetstone children's patrimony: George received from his father's estate London houses in

Cheapside and Gutter Lane later valued at £23 a year. Despite coming of age in 1571, he did not receive his inheritance until 1573, signing the receipt 'Per me Georgium Whetstonn'. Throughout the 1570s there were legal battles over the children's inheritance following Margaret Whetstone's remarriage to Robert Browne of Northamptonshire. Browne was a neighbour of Sir Thomas Cecil, and Cecil's kindness to the family was acknowledged by Whetstone in his dedication to 'The Orchard of Repentance' in *The Rocke of Regarde* (1576):

> righte worshipfull, waying howe deepely bothe my good mother and all her children are bounde unto you for received friendships, among the rest (acknowledging your desire of my well doing) I have sought howe (for suche benefites) to avoyde the vile vice of ingratitude.

After Browne's death in 1572 his widow married Francis Ashby of a Leicestershire family. As a child, Whetstone probably lived in Cheapside with his stepfather and mother, although he may have spent time on Browne's estate at Walcot. He did not, unlike some of his brothers, attend university until his inheritance from his father in 1573, after which he registered to study law at Furnival's Inn. He addresses a poem in *The Rocke of Regarde*, 'written from my lodging in Holborne' to 'my friends and companions at Furnival's Inn'.

Accounts of Whetstone's life at this period have tended, in the absence of much hard evidence, to take for truth a colourful and supposedly autobiographical section of *The Rocke of Regarde*, in which the young hero seeks preferment at court but is unsuccessful and, having spent his inheritance on dissolute living, becomes an officer in the army and serves in the Low Countries. There is, however, nothing to corroborate this account of Whetstone's career, and, indeed, he denies in his later work *The Honorable Reputation of a Soldier* (1586) that he had had any military experience before going to the Netherlands with his older brother Barnard in 1585–6. The autobiographical application of *The Rocke of Regarde* cannot, however, be entirely resisted. At the end of his *A Touchstone for the Time* (1584), Whetstone asserts that the earlier work was indeed true:

> no man was ever assaulted with a more daungerous strategeme of cosonage than my selfe, with which my life & living was hardly beset. No man has more cause to thanke God for a free delivery than my self, nor anie man ever sawe, more suddaine vengeance inflicted upon his adversaries, than I my selfe of mine: as lively appeareth in the ende of my booke intituled *The Rocke of Regarde*.

This allusion is to the legal battle which lasted some three years in the Star Chamber, and its fictionalized counterpart in the section of *The Rocke of Regarde* entitled 'The Invention of P. Plasmos'. From these accounts, it seems that in a complicated fraud, Whetstone was tricked into signing over his property to four acquaintances who then tried to implicate him in violent quarrels so that he would be killed and thus the property would revert to them. Whetstone took the four to court to get redress: the outcome of the lengthy process is not known.

Perhaps this experience stirred the interest in social and legal reform which characterizes much of Whetstone's diverse literary output. His literary career may have received its initial stimulus from the group of writers associated with the inns of court, and many of his early poems are enmeshed in personal networks of friendship and obligation: his first published verse was in commendation of George Gascoigne's *Flowers*, published in 1575, and in 1577 Whetstone was to begin his career as an elegist with a volume of poetry entitled *A Remembraunce of the Wel Imployed Life and Godly End of George Gaskoigne*, claiming to have been an eyewitness to the poet's death while Gascoigne was staying at Whetstone's house in Stamford, Lincolnshire. His further elegies commemorating Sir Nicholas Bacon (1579), Sir James Dyer (1582), Thomas Radcliffe, earl of Sussex (1583), and Francis Russell, earl of Bedford (1585), culminated in his verse life of Sir Philip Sidney in 1587, of whose death at Zutphen he may have heard from Barnard Whetstone, who also provided an account of Sidney's funeral published with the elegy. In his poem, George Whetstone likens himself to a Homer praising an English Alexander, and his apparently carefully researched biography takes Sidney from childhood virtue and education, via his travels in Europe from which he returned untainted by foreign influences, his courtliness, his manly courage in the Netherlands, to his eloquent death speech. Whetstone is little concerned with Sidney as a writer, although he does mention the *Arcadia* as 'unmacht for sweete devise'. Sidney's death predated Whetstone's own by almost a year, but the two events have some curious connections. Whetstone's death was publicly announced by his publisher, Thomas Cadman, in an epistle to the reader of *Sir Phillip Sidney, his Honorable Life, his Valiant Death, and True Virtues*; and it seems likely that the Captain Edmond Uvedall or Udall at whose hand Whetstone met his own death was the same person that he had praised in his elegy on Sidney. It is not clear that Whetstone knew the subjects of his elegies personally, but he was conscious that, as the elegy on Sussex puts it, 'some skill I have on good men's tombs to write' and ever aware of the classical ideas of fame and posterity through verse. In his apparent care to ascertain detailed information about his subjects, he has a claim to be called the first professional biographer.

Promos and Cassandra and other works Whetstone's most famous work, an apparently unperformed two-part play called *Promos and Cassandra* (1578), is his best-known because it is a major source for Shakespeare's *Measure for Measure* (1604). Its title-page suggests the proximity of the two stories: 'In the fyrste parte is showne, the unsufferable abuse, of a lewde Magistrate: the virtuous behaviours of a chaste Ladye: the uncontrowled leawdenes of a favoured Curtisan. And the undeserved estimation of a pernicious Parasyte'. Whetstone's tale of urban low life was dedicated 'to his worshipfull friende and Kinseman William Fleetewoode Esquier, Recorder of London'. This dedication, like the rest of the play, shows his abiding interest in civic life and morals, and his depiction of the underworld urban characters in *Promos and Cassandra* adds a distinctly contemporary feel to his Italian source. Promos is the equivalent of Shakespeare's Angelo,

a deputy left in charge of Julio, a city in Hungary; Cassandra is the Isabella figure who comes to plead for her brother's life. Whetstone's additions and alterations to his source material are taken up by Shakespeare in a number of ways: Whetstone's sense of the urban moral landscape, his stress on the emotional relationships between the characters, and his tempering of the crime of his Claudio, here called Andrugio, from rape to pre-marital but mutual sexual intercourse all reappear in Shakespeare's play. Like Philip Sidney in his *Defence of Poesy*, Whetstone stresses that the function of dramatic literature is didactic: 'the conclusion showes, the confusion of Vice, and the cherising of Vertue'. He decries the fashion for transgressing the dramatic unities, arguing that it is the particular fault of the English playwright that 'he fyrst groundes his worke on impossibilities', and also condemns generic mingling, explaining to Fleetwood that it is 'decorum', derived from the authority of Plato, which has encouraged him to divide the play into two parts so as to separate out its divergent generic trajectories.

The dedication to *Promos and Cassandra* explains that the author has not had time to correct his work, because he has 'resolved to accompane, the adventurous Capraie, Syr Humfrey Gylbert, in his honorable voiadge'. Whetstone travelled on the *Hope* under the command of Gilbert's half-brother Carew Ralegh, on an expedition beset by bad winds and ship defects which seems never to have got beyond the west coast of Ireland. After his return to England, he travelled in Italy during 1580, visiting Rome, Naples, and Ravenna. It seems unlikely, given the tenor of his published opinions, that he was the 'Whetstonn' listed among supposed English Catholics remaining in France in April 1580 (*CSP for.*, 1579–80, 279).

In 1582 Whetstone published the main literary fruits of his Italian tour, his *Heptameron of Civill Discourses*, a series of courtly Italianate romance stories. He dedicated the work to Sir Christopher Hatton and, in his epistle, mentions in veiled terms the Italian nobleman shadowed as Phyloxenus, the originator of the stories. T. W.'s dedicatory poem gives an indication of Whetstone's didactic literary aims, announcing that:

Morall Whetstone, to his Countrey doth impart,
A Worke of worth.

The collection is particularly concerned with the condition of marriage, and different stories illustrate the folly of forced or hasty marriages, ways of maintaining love within marriage, and general precepts for married and unmarried alike. A prose version of *Promos and Cassandra* is included. The *Heptameron* was reprinted under the title *Aurelia, the Paragon of Pleasure and Princely Delights*, in 1593.

In 1584 Whetstone published the moralistic collection *A Mirror for Magistrates*, dedicated to the mayor, aldermen, and recorder of London and expounding the example of the Roman emperor Severus in suppressing urban vices such as insanitary conditions, prostitution, usury, and gambling. This classical precedent was given a more local application in *A Touchstone for the Time* (1584), which comprises a detailed discussion of the London underworld with suggestions for civic reform, including the suppression of prostitution and the closing of taverns and gaming houses. In a similar vein *The English Myrror* was published in 1586. Its detailed title-page gives an indication of its tone and content:

> A regard wherein al estates may behold the Conquests of Envy: containing the ruine of common weales, murther of Princes, causes of heresies, and in all ages, spoile of devine and humane blessings […] publishing the peaceable victories obtained by the Queenes most excellent Majesty, against this mortall enimie of publicke peace and prosperitie.

This compendium of historical narrative, proverbial wisdom, and patriotic encomium combines the moralistic concerns of his earlier works and makes explicit the protestant fervour which had underlined them. Unlike other near contemporaries such as Robert Greene, Thomas Nashe, or Thomas Dekker, Whetstone's anatomization of urban failings does not slip into cynicism, nor does he take an obvious vicarious enjoyment in the vices he describes. By contrast with these other writers, his didacticism is apparently sincerely felt.

The same tone is evident in *The Censure of a Loyall Subject*, published in 1587 with a second edition in quick succession to take account of the execution of Mary, queen of Scots. The book takes the form of a dialogue between three interlocutors about the hanging of those implicated in the Babington conspiracy in 1586. It has been suggested that the character of 'Weston', who has not witnessed the executions, is a figure for the author (Izard, 221). His conduct book for soldiers *Honourable Reputation of a Soldier* was published in London in 1585, and in Leiden the following year with a parallel Dutch translation and vocabulary and pronunciation appendices designed to help Dutch readers learn English. The book is less concerned with military strategy than with personal conduct, stressing the importance of religious preparation as well as courage and mercy in warfare.

Death and reputation In 1587 Whetstone got a fatal taste of warfare. At the instigation of Burghley, to whom he had dedicated *The Censure of a Loyall Subject*, he was appointed 'commissary of musters' (Eccles, 'Whetstone's death', 648) under the mustermaster-general, the mathematician Thomas Digges, in the Low Countries. He was killed in a duel outside the garrison town of Bergen-op-Zoom in September 1587, having accused his adversary Udall of financial abuses. Digges wrote that Whetstone died 'no doubt because he could not be corrupted' (ibid.); the comment draws together Whetstone's life and his work in a way he, as a biographer, would have admired, and suggests that he died by the principles of honesty and uprightness his work had consistently advocated as the proper conduct of rulers, citizens, and nations. Udall was acquitted of his murder by a military court who judged that he had acted in defence of his reputation. Whetstone's wife, Anne, of whom no more is known, was named in letters of administration regarding his will in January 1580.

Whetstone's literary reputation has left some traces. Francis Meres, in his *Palladis tamia* (1598), included him with 'the most passionate among us to bewaile and bemoane the perplexities of love', although it is not clear from his extant work that he is primarily a love-poet. In 1586 William Webbe identified him as one worthy to 'weare the Lawrell wreathe … a man singularly well skyld in his faculty of Poetrie' (E. Arber, ed., *A Discourse of English Poetrie*, 1871, 35). Neither of these comments captures the ceaseless and earnest didacticism about individual and civic behaviour which is so characteristic of Whetstone's writing.
EMMA SMITH

Sources M. Eccles, 'George Whetstone in star chamber', *Review of English Studies*, new ser., 33 (1982), 385–95 • M. Eccles, 'Whetstone's death', *TLS* (27 Aug 1931), 648 • T. Izard, *George Whetstone: mid-Elizabethan man of letters* (New York, 1942) • *CSP for.*, 1579–80

Whetstone, Sir Thomas (1630/31–1668?), naval officer and adventurer, was the eldest son of Roger Whetstone (*d.* before 1656), a professional soldier, and Catherine Cromwell (*bap.* 1597), favourite sister of the protector. Whetstone was born abroad, probably in the Netherlands where his father served, and naturalized by act of parliament in 1656. He owed his rise wholly to the protector's misplaced patronage. He first appears as a volunteer serving on Penn's flagship in the expedition to Hispaniola in 1654, and Penn soon yielded to Cromwell's pressure by promoting him lieutenant. On the homeward voyage in 1655 Whetstone was advanced to command the *Golden Cock*. Despite his lack of experience he was then rapidly advanced to the fourth-rate *Phoenix* in 1656 and the third-rate *Fairfax* in October 1657, and further distinguished by being chosen to carry English diplomats abroad. He joined the fleet under Stokes at Lisbon late in 1657, and after it moved into the Mediterranean in late December Stokes made him commander of a squadron plying between Malta and Candia (Crete). The results were disastrous: Whetstone flouted orders, and sold for his own use a prize carrying grain desperately needed by the fleet. In exasperation Stokes revoked his command, whereupon Whetstone deserted his force and sailed for Algiers. He was still able to rely on his connections at home, however, and when Stokes was directed in May 1658 to assign a squadron to join with French naval forces at Marseilles for a combined operation against Spain, he reluctantly gave its command to Whetstone. Stokes hoped to tie him down by a set of very restrictive instructions, but in the event Whetstone indulged in junketing ashore while quarrelling with his officers and sending bitter complaints to England. The joint operation did not materialize. On receiving news of Cromwell's death in September 1658 Stokes at last found the courage to dismiss Whetstone, and sent him back to England as a prisoner, with the approval of the new protector, Richard. Whetstone was examined by the council of state, and a court martial nominated to try him, though in April 1659 he complained that he was still waiting for a chance to clear his name. In June Whetstone threw in his lot with the royalists, who believed, falsely, that as Cromwell's nephew he would be a valuable tool to win over the fleet. He crossed to Brussels, where Charles II knighted him and dispatched him to Copenhagen in late June with a promissory letter to Mountagu, commanding the English fleet in the sound.

But Whetstone was too well known, and too unpopular, to be able to make direct contact, and his cover was blown when he bumped into Mountagu and the republican commissioner Sidney in the street. Mountagu had him conveyed secretly back to Flanders, and the intrigue ended in farce. Whetstone returned to England at the Restoration, destitute, and was languishing in a debtors' gaol in Marshalsea by 1661. He bombarded the government with petitions for employment, and also begged the estates of his late stepfather, the regicide Colonel John Jones, who had been executed for treason in October 1660. The king eventually agreed to pay him £100 to set him up as a planter in Jamaica, and he sailed in the spring of 1662. Shortly before, in December 1661, he obtained a licence to marry Anne Dehuberlant (b. 1630/31), a widow. Whetstone quickly established himself as a leading figure in Jamaica, with the support of its governor, Sir Thomas Modyford. By 1663 he was commanding a force of thirteen privateers, and he served as speaker of the Jamaica assembly in 1664. In 1666 he led a force which seized the Spanish colony of Providence Island, but the Spaniards recaptured the island in August and Whetstone was sent prisoner to Panama, where he was held in irons for seventeen months. Though eventually released, he was never heard of again, and probably died soon afterwards. A flood of complaints in the late 1650s had characterized Whetstone as insolent, arrogant, greedy, and idle, and his short-lived naval career remains an object-lesson in the dangers and temptations of nepotism. BERNARD CAPP

Sources M. L. Baumber, 'The protector's nephew: an account of the conduct of Captain Thomas Whetstone in the Mediterranean, 1657–1659', Mariner's Mirror, 52 (1966), 233–46 · B. Capp, Cromwell's navy: the fleet and the English revolution, 1648–1660 (1989) · CSP dom., 1655–62 · Calendar of the Clarendon state papers preserved in the Bodleian Library, 4: 1657–1660, ed. F. J. Routledge (1932); 5: 1660–1726, ed. F. J. Routledge (1970) · CSP col., vol. 5 · JHC, 7 (1651–9) · Bodl. Oxf., Clarendon MSS · Bodl. Oxf., MS Rawl. C. 381 · Bodl. Oxf., MS Carte 73 · M. Noble, Memoirs of the protectorate-house of Cromwell, 2 vols. (1784) · J. L. Chester and G. J. Armytage, eds., Allegations for marriage licences issued from the faculty office of the archbishop of Canterbury at London, 1543 to 1869, Harleian Society, 24 (1886)
Archives Bodl. Oxf., corresp., Rawl. MS C381

Whetstone, Sir William (d. 1711), naval officer, was probably the son of John Whetstone, naval officer. He was a member of Bristol corporation and master of the Mary of Bristol, a merchant ship trading with Virginia and Barbados. He carried a wide variety of goods including serges. He seems to have married his first wife, Sarah (d. 1698), before 1677, in which year he took on an apprentice for seven years. He had two sons and two daughters by his first marriage; his eldest daughter, Sarah, married the naval officer Woodes Rogers. Whetstone's first wife was buried in St Nicholas's, Bristol, on 19 October 1698. On 30 July 1689, the date from which he took post, he was appointed captain of the hired ship Europa. For the next two years he served in Ireland convoying victuallers. He served as captain of the Portsmouth from 3 February to 12 August 1691. Admiral Russell described him as 'a good man' but he was unemployed in 1692. In 1693 he was part owner of the Delavall privateer and the same year was

given a commission to command the Norfolk, being built at Southampton, and also to man the ship, launched on 27 March 1693. He was discharged from the Norfolk on 23 May and held a series of brief commands before holding command of the York from 13 July 1693 to 13 June 1695.

Whetstone was appointed to the Dreadnought on 6 July 1696 and served at Newfoundland and in the channel until discharged on 13 July 1699. He was appointed to command the Yarmouth, from 19 May 1700 to 4 June 1701, then the York, with the rank of commodore and the command of the squadron to be sent out to Jamaica. The York was twice forced into Plymouth for repairs and, having sustained more damage on the way to Cork, was there surveyed and pronounced unfit to go to the West Indies. Consequently he moved into the Canterbury on 4 February 1702, on board which he arrived in May, joining Vice-Admiral John Benbow at Port Royal and taking the local rank of rear-admiral. Benbow left him to command at Jamaica while he went to look for a small French squadron expected in the area. When the squadron returned to Port Royal, Whetstone was president of the courts martial which tried the several captains who had shamefully conspired against their admiral. When Benbow died on 4 November 1702 Whetstone succeeded to the command, which he held until the following June, when he was superseded by Vice-Admiral John Graydon. He destroyed a number of privateers off San Domingo but an attempt on the French colony at Placentia was abandoned because of the weather, the island's defences, and sickness in the fleet. When Whetstone and Graydon came to leave Jamaica they were asked by the governor to leave ten ships for defence; Whetstone advised that seven should remain but in the end only four small ships were left. He returned to England in October 1703.

In January 1704 Prince George promoted Whetstone to rear-admiral of the blue, to show that he approved of his conduct while holding acting rank, and at the same time to separate him from charges arising against Graydon. This promotion, over the heads of other captains including Sir James Wishart, caused great offence and Sir George Rooke, with whom Wishart was serving, threatened to resign his commission unless things were put right. The matter was eventually settled by making Wishart rear-admiral of the blue, and senior to Whetstone through antedating his commission. In March 1704 Whetstone commanded a squadron in the channel. On 18 January 1705 he was promoted to rear-admiral of the white and on 17 February was appointed commander-in-chief in the West Indies, being knighted on 22 February. With his flag on board the Montagu he arrived at Jamaica in the middle of May. The smaller vessels under his command took several valuable prizes but his squadron was not strong enough to let him attack any Spanish settlements. To an invitation to declare in favour of King Charles, the governor of Cartagena replied that 'he knew no sovereign but King Philip'. In 1706 Whetstone and Governor Handyside continued to try and persuade the Spanish at Cuba and Cartagena to declare for Charles and join the allied cause. Later that year William Kerr was sent out with a squadron to relieve Whetstone and, with considerable knowledge of how things stood in South America, he returned to England in December 1706.

In May 1707 Whetstone commanded a squadron off Dunkirk, with orders to look out for Forbin, a dangerous corsair. In June he was ordered to convoy nineteen ships of the Muscovy Company as far as the Shetland Islands. He accompanied the convoy well past the Shetlands and then parted company with them; later Forbin fell in with them and captured fifteen ships. Though Whetstone had more than fulfilled his orders, which were clearly insufficient, there was an outcry from the Muscovy Company merchants and he was tried for leaving the ships to be attacked. The Admiralty defended him and declared that the only ships which had been taken were those which had left the regular convoy and that none had been attacked until three weeks after he had left them. However, a victim was needed, and he was dismissed from his command and not employed again. He was buried in St Michael's, Bristol, on 3 April 1711 and on 7 May letters of administration were granted to his widow, Mary (or Maria) Whetstone, with whom he had one daughter, Mary. An inventory dated 30 April 1711, though badly damaged, shows that Whetstone was owed over £2500 by various people.

J. K. Laughton, *rev.* Peter Le Fevre

Sources P. McGrath, ed., *Merchants and merchandise in seventeenth-century Bristol*, Bristol RS, 19 (1955), 12 · Bristol port books, 1684, PRO, E190/1147/2, fol. 30 · volume of passes, 1683, PRO, ADM 7/75, fol. 75 *v* · list of captains, 1688–1715, NMM, Sergison MS SER/136 · E. Russell, 'Characters of captains, Nov. 1691', Folger, Rich MS xd 451 (98) · B. D. G. Little, *Crusoe's captain: being the life of Woodes Rogers, seaman, trader, colonial governor* [1960], 20–40 · R. Bourne, *Queen Anne's navy in the West Indies* (1939), 59, 165 · inventories, PRO, PROB 5/5878, 5/6098 · administration, PRO, PROB 6/67, fol. 52 · B. Rogers, 'Admiral Sir William Whetstone', *Mariner's Mirror*, 15 (1929), 67–8
Archives PRO, Bristol port books
Likenesses M. Dahl, oils, *c.*1707, NMM; repro. in Little, *Crusoe's captain*
Wealth at death over £2500; incl. bonds of various values, clothes, and various goods: inventory, PRO, PROB 5/5878

Whewell, William (1794–1866), college head and writer on the history and philosophy of science, was born on 24 May 1794 at Brock Street, Lancaster, the eldest of seven children of John Whewell, master carpenter, and his wife, Elizabeth Bennison.

Education Whewell at first attended the Blue School in Lancaster. Subsequently, at the suggestion of the Revd Joseph Rowley, the master of Lancaster grammar school, his father agreed to send him there, rather than making him an apprentice carpenter. In 1810 he transferred to Heversham grammar school in order to compete for a scholarship, worth £50 a year, to Trinity College. Before going to Cambridge he was also tutored for some months by John Gough, the blind mathematician of Kendal. Whewell was formally entered at Cambridge in 1811 and began his first term in October 1812 as a sub-sizar.

During his undergraduate years most of Whewell's family died: his mother in 1807, three younger brothers by 1812, and his father in July 1816. Only two sisters—Martha and Ann—remained after the eldest, Elizabeth, died in

William Whewell (1794–1866), by J. Rylands

1821. In his early years Whewell's own health is said to have been poor, and he was described as a delicate boy, but in November 1812 he told his father that 'I have enjoyed very good health since I left Lancaster' (Douglas, 9). From then on, Whewell's tall and powerful physical form was remarked on by his contemporaries, and was seen to match the vigorous style of his intellectual and personal exchanges.

Whewell's letters from Cambridge to his family convey a strong sense of being their chosen representative in a different social world. Announcing a first place in every subject in June 1814 Whewell told his father that 'We have reason to be proud' (26 June 1814, Whewell MSS, Add. MS a. 301). His string of academic successes began with the Latin declamation prize in 1813. In 1814 he won the Chancellor's medal for an English poem on Boadicea (published in 1820), but assured his family that he was not neglecting mathematical studies. These triumphs were unexpectedly interrupted when Whewell graduated as second wrangler in January 1816, beaten by Edward Jacob of Caius College, who was also first Smith's prizeman, with Whewell taking the second prize.

However, Whewell's aim was not just academic glory but a fellowship that would justify the financial support of his father and give him an independent position. His father died in July 1816, before his graduation and election as fellow in October 1817. Of the latter event, Whewell explained to his sisters that it was 'the most substantial benefit at which you ever had to rejoice with me. It secures me a comfortable establishment for life at least so long as my life is a simple one' (1 Oct 1817, Whewell MSS, Add. MS a. 301). He was appointed mathematical lecturer and assistant tutor in 1818, tutor in 1823.

Social elevation and marriage These academic achievements were accompanied by personal trials associated with the passage from Lancaster to Cambridge. For a time Whewell was not only very much alone, but also seen as unusual. His manners and speech were considered rude or rustic. There is a report of Whewell's comment upon a herd of pigs being driven past the college gate soon after his arrival: 'They're a hard thing to drive—very—when there's many of them—is a pig' (*The Athenaeum*, 333). Having visited London for the first time in 1815 Whewell admitted to his sisters that he had only seen the city from 'the outside' because, not knowing anyone there, he could not 'see anything of its society' (14 April 1815, Whewell MSS, Add. MS a. 301). Whewell regarded Trinity College as a second home, so much so that his letters to his family were punctuated with excuses for not making more visits to Lancaster. In April 1815 he explained to his sister that a trip to Lancaster was expensive and that, in spite of the plague in Cambridge, he had decided to stay 'because I can employ my time better here' (ibid.).

Although known for his constant reading Whewell appears to have participated in a wide range of undergraduate social activities; indeed, Isaac Todhunter hinted that some of his early acquaintances were not salubrious, and that he ignored the proper boundaries between town and gown (Todhunter, 1.3). But the summer pursuits Whewell described to Richard Gwatkin in 1815 were harmless: 'shooting swallows, bathing by half dozens, sailing to Chesterton, dancing at country fairs, playing billiards, turning beakers into musical glasses, making rockets, riding out in bodies' (ibid., 2.8). In March 1817 he was president of the union—a society of undergraduates—when the vice-chancellor sent the proctors to disband a meeting. It is not clear why, but at a time when some European countries were monitoring student societies and the Sidmouth Acts in Britain banned large assemblies the prospect of critical political discussion no doubt frightened the leaders of the university. Whewell is reported to have stood his ground, achieving an audience with the vice-chancellor, even though the meeting did then disband.

Whewell was able to make and sustain friendships that gave him intellectual and personal support. Richard Sheepshanks, another student from the north of England with scientific interests, entered Cambridge in the same year as Whewell. From 1819 they made several trips to the continent, after surviving a shipwreck on their first attempt. Whewell also travelled in 1823 with Kenelm Digby to study the architecture of churches and abbeys in Normandy and Picardy. He met John Herschel (senior wrangler in 1813), Charles Babbage, George Peacock, Michael Slegg, and Edward Bromhead as members of the Analytical Society, founded by Babbage and Herschel in 1811 to advocate continental mathematical notation in the use of the calculus, and to introduce formal algebraic analysis into Cambridge teaching. Whewell was at first impressed by their plans, but when in a position to influence the curriculum, through his textbooks, he began to fear that continental analysis, especially Lagrange's treatment of the calculus, did not ensure a proper geometrical grasp of the problems addressed in mechanics and other branches of mixed mathematics. In addition to these mathematical friends the political economist Richard Jones, the astronomer George Biddell Airy, the professor of botany John Henslow, and the classical and theological scholars Julius Hare, Connop Thirlwall, and Hugh James Rose were all colleagues at Cambridge. The geologist Adam Sedgwick, who graduated in 1805, was an older and respected member of the college; with him Whewell took geological field trips to the Lake District, and first met William Wordsworth there in 1821.

By 1817 two of his closest friends, Herschel and Jones, had left Cambridge, and Whewell spoke of the loss he felt. However, he continued a lively correspondence with them, as he did with other early friends such as Hare and Rose, and later with younger men, some of whom he worked with on various projects: John Lubbock, Robert Willis, Augustus De Morgan, William Rowan Hamilton, and James Forbes. Whewell's extensive correspondence reveals him as a candid and sensitive friend, a penetrating critic, and an astute participant in a range of scientific and university debates and activities.

During the 1820s Whewell began to move more easily in the social circles outside the university. In 1823 he met Sir John Malcolm, who lived at Hyde Hall, near Cambridge, and he subsequently enjoyed the friendship of the Malcolm family. There is a definite sense in which this was a surrogate family for Whewell; his correspondence with Lady Malcolm continued after the family moved from the Cambridge area in 1827, and soon after his marriage in 1841 Whewell told her that he remembered this earlier period as 'one of the bright passages of my life' (Douglas, 239). Whewell also met aristocratic graduates of Cambridge such as the third Earl Fitzwilliam (1786–1857) and the second marquess of Northampton (1790–1851), both of whom were involved in the affairs of scientific societies.

From the 1830s Whewell's activities extended beyond Cambridge as he became more involved with the British and European scientific and intellectual communities. He was consulted by William Vernon Harcourt, the first secretary of the British Association for the Advancement of Science (founded in 1831) and suggested the commissioning of annual reports on the state of the various sciences. Whewell's own reports on mineralogy (1832) and electricity and magnetism (1835) were informed by the historical insights later used in his major works. Whewell did not attend the first meeting of the British Association in York, but subsequently served as vice-president in 1832 and 1837, local secretary in 1833 for the Cambridge meeting, and president in 1841.

Whewell's social rise was completed in June 1841 when he was engaged to Cordelia (d. 1855), the daughter of John Marshall, a flax spinner of liberal political sympathies; his eldest daughter, Mary, had married Lord Monteagle. Whewell had been introduced to the Marshalls by the Wordsworth family. On 12 October 1841 Cordelia married Whewell in Cumberland. On the same day Christopher Wordsworth, master of Trinity, wrote to Whewell saying that he intended to resign; by 17 October 1841 Sir Robert Peel, the Conservative prime minister, had written that the queen had accepted his recommendation of Whewell as the next master—a decision that passed over his senior colleague, Sedgwick, who might have been appointed under a whig government.

Early writings Whewell's first book was *An Elementary Treatise on Mechanics* (1819), a textbook that he revised in five later editions; this was supplemented by *A Treatise on Dynamics* (1823). The second work, in particular, introduced calculus to Cambridge undergraduates and praised its use by the French mathematician and astronomer, Pierre Laplace, in his *Mécanique céleste*. But subsequent editions of both these books contained far less calculus and more emphasis on geometrical methods. Whewell's *Essay on Mineralogical Classification and Nomenclature* (1828) sought to offer a revision of Friedrich Moh's system. In 1830 he published, anonymously, *Architectural Notes on German Churches, with Remarks on the Origin of Gothic Architecture*; other editions appeared in 1835 and 1842, both now bearing his name. This discussed the mechanical principles underlying Gothic architecture, a topic pursued in more detail by Whewell's collaborator, Robert Willis. In 1833 his *Astronomy and General Physics*, a volume in the Bridgewater Treatises on Natural Theology, was a clear success, becoming the best-seller of the series and reaching a sixth edition in 1864. This offered a fairly conventional argument from design: Whewell suggested that the position of the earth in the solar system and its orientation to the sun were clearly and benevolently adapted to the needs of living things, including human beings. But he also included a discussion of inductive and deductive thinking, noting the tendency of the latter to dilute appreciation of design in nature. Two major works followed: *History of the Inductive Sciences* (3 vols.) in 1837 and *The Philosophy of the Inductive Sciences* (2 vols.) in 1840. During this period Whewell also wrote reviews for some of the major quarterly journals, scientific papers on mineralogy and chemistry (both on nomenclature), a pamphlet on mathematical education, a book *On the Principles of English University Education* (1837), *Sermons, Preached in the Chapel of Trinity College* (1847), reports for the British Association for the Advancement of Science, and (with others) a translation of Goethe's *Hermann und Dorothea* (1837).

Master of Trinity By 1841 Whewell had made his scholarly mark and completed an extraordinary feat of social elevation. The conventional markers of this rise were his university posts and his writings. He was assistant mathematics tutor in 1818, head tutor at Trinity in 1823, ordained deacon in 1825 and priest in 1826, professor of mineralogy in 1828, Knightbridge professor of moral philosophy (formerly moral theology) in 1838, and master of Trinity from 1841. Whewell took formal possession of the master's lodge on 16 November 1841. This position allowed a continuation of his association with Trinity—the college, as he often reflected, of Bacon and Newton. As master he allowed a statue of another past resident—Lord Byron—to be rescued from a London vault and installed in the college library in 1843; he also commissioned a copy (by Henry Weekes) of the statue of Francis Bacon at St Albans for the ante-chapel. Whewell revised the college statutes in 1844, sought to limit the system of private tuition and placed more emphasis on professorial lectures. As master of the largest college in the university he was well positioned to influence academic policy, which he did in the role of vice-chancellor in 1842–3 and again in 1855. Whewell initiated the installation of Prince Albert as chancellor in 1847 and seems to have had his support for broadening the Cambridge curriculum—as achieved with Whewell's introduction of the moral sciences and natural sciences triposes in 1848. When the royal commission into Cambridge reported in August 1852 Whewell replied to its queries but resisted its intrusion, partly because he wanted reform to be internally directed rather than externally imposed, but also because he did not wish to weaken the autonomy of the colleges in favour of the central power of the university. He defended the practice of election as the mode of entry to fellowships, rejecting open competition on the ground that this might weaken the obligation of fellows to the colleges. Whewell was also reluctant to abandon the tradition by which the master and eight senior fellows governed the college.

In his early years as master Whewell acquired a reputation for imperiousness and formality. Not all of this was new behaviour, because his dominating physical presence, fierce debating, and hard horse riding were well known. Airy remembered a section of Cornwall as the place 'where Whewell overturned me in a gig' (Airy, 84). Hare's advice to Whewell in December 1840 not to think of taking up a college living was informed by a judgement that he was better suited as a doctor, not a pastor, of the church. Hare mentioned the possibility of the mastership, but when it came to Whewell a year later this new office elicited a stiffness and formality that had not been so evident. Whewell's admonition of Sedgwick is often cited. Whewell wrote to his older colleague in 1845 saying that 'your frequent appearance in the College courts accompanied by a dog [his pet] is inconsistent with ... Rules [of the College] and with the Statutes cap.xx' (Clark and Hughes, 2.97–8). But even Whewell's harshest critics agreed that he was the most prestigious master of Trinity since Richard Bentley.

Scientific interests and achievements As second wrangler in 1816 Whewell had the credentials for major participation in science, and might have been expected to use the security of his fellowship as a basis for such activity. This was the path to a scientific vocation pursued by colleagues such as Sedgwick in geology and Airy in astronomy, although it differed from that followed by Herschel, Charles Lyell, and Charles Darwin, whose independent incomes allowed full-time devotion to scientific research.

Whewell's practical scientific work indicates his considerable presence in a number of fields. While his mechanics textbooks reflected pedagogic rather than research interests, he was involved in geological expeditions with Sedgwick from 1821 and sought the most advanced instruction in mineralogy and crystallography in Berlin, Freiburg, and Vienna in 1825. Commenting on a paper by Whewell about mathematical aspects of crystallography, Herschel affirmed that it was 'fit for the transactions of any Society in the world' (Herschel to Whewell, 15 Oct 1823, RS, Herschel MSS, vol. 18, no. 164). This paper appeared in the *Philosophical Transactions of the Royal Society of London* in 1824; he also contributed four papers on related topics to the *Cambridge Philosophical Transactions* between 1821 and 1827. In May 1826 Whewell set off to Cornwall with Airy to spend several weeks in a mine shaft experimenting on the mean density of the earth. They planned to compare the effect of gravity on invariable pendulums at the surface and at a depth of 1200 feet. Whewell wrote letters to Herschel and Lady Malcolm describing himself as a correspondent 'sitting in a small cavern deep in the recesses of the earth' (Todhunter, 2.65–7; Douglas, 103–4). The experiment was not successful and they made another attempt two years later, accompanied this time by Sheepshanks. A description of their efforts was published as *Account of Experiments Made at Dolcoath Mine, in Cornwall* (1828). In that year Whewell became professor of mineralogy, nominating for the position on the platform of applying mathematics to crystallography and improving classification in mineralogy. He had already published five papers in the area. In 1834 he began to develop a self-registering anemometer to measure the velocity of the wind; by 1837 he had devised such an instrument. These scientific activities supported Whewell's election to the Royal Society in 1820, admission to the Geological Society in 1827 and nomination for its presidency in 1837, a position he occupied until 1839.

Whewell's most significant scientific work was his study of tides—or 'tidology', as he called it—recorded in fourteen papers presented to the Royal Society of London from 1833 to 1850. With John Lubbock (his former student) he began a quest to chart the movements of the world's oceans, aiming to produce a map of co-tidal lines showing the points throughout the globe where high water occurs at the same time. This research was substantially funded by the British Association, and, although he was not fully satisfied with the results, Whewell was rewarded in 1837 with a royal prize medal from the Royal Society. In spite of these achievements Whewell did not consider himself a major scientific discoverer. His contributions in mineralogy and tidology were important, but neither met his own criteria for truly significant advances in science. By 1840 Whewell was devaluing his scientific achievements, saying that 'there is nothing of such a stamp, in what I have attempted, as entitles me to be considered an eminent man of science' (Todhunter, 2.286).

Whewell as omniscient Leslie Stephen remarked that the sheer mass of Whewell's publications evinced his 'extraordinary powers of accumulating knowledge' (*DNB*). But Stephen also identified a puzzle: 'Whewell began as a man of science' but then 'scarcely became a philosopher' (ibid.). From a late Victorian perspective this made Whewell's reputation an indeterminate one. Francis Galton offered a similar diagnosis in 1869. Noting that fame in science was heavily influenced by the association of an individual's name with some striking discovery, he cited Whewell as an example of one who, in spite of being among the most able of his generation, was destined to be forgotten.

Sydney Smith's quip—that science was Whewell's forte but omniscience his foible—has influenced most responses to the man and his work. It is not surprising that Whewell has commonly been approached as a polymath, an individual who, on his own early confession, aspired to 'universal knowledge' or omniscience (Whewell to George Morland, 15 Dec 1815, Todhunter, 2.10). By any measure, the range of his writings and accomplishments was remarkable: mathematics, mechanics, architecture, mineralogy, tidology, moral philosophy, political economy, educational theory, natural theology, translations of Greek philosophy and German poetry, and the history and philosophy of the physical sciences. This breadth and productivity were extraordinary, especially by the standards of a Cambridge don at a time when research was not a required duty of academic life. When Lyell told a friend that he had taken Whewell's last work to read while travelling on the continent he was asked to clarify to which of the three works—published within a year—he was referring (*Life, Letters, and Journals*, 2.38). Herschel doubted whether any other individual had gathered a 'more wonderful variety and amount of knowledge in almost every department of human inquiry ... in the same interval of time' (Herschel, liii).

Thus Whewell was seen as a phenomenon—the equal of other polymaths of the period like Macaulay, Brougham, and Coleridge—but different in that science was his forte, even though he did not make a major discovery. On the other hand, members of the scientific community appreciated the synthetic overview his works provided. Critical reflection on the nature and value of science was not peculiar to Whewell—other men of science such as Herschel, Lyell, and David Brewster also made such pronouncements. But, in admitting that research and discovery were not his main concerns, Whewell was seen to be different. In 1836 Lyell said that he used to regret that Whewell had not concentrated on one or two sciences, but now he believed that by being a universalist rather than a specialist he was assisting the progress of science. Lyell told

Whewell that this was his proper calling (Todhunter, 1.112). In the same year Whewell told Herschel that 'In a year of two I expect to be a philosopher and nothing else' (Todhunter, 2.235). How did Whewell pursue this vocation?

Critic and reviewer of science Even before his two major works Whewell offered critical commentaries on the nature of science. He did this in his address to the British Association in 1833, in two reports to that body on the state of particular sciences and, for a wider audience, in reviews of scientific works in periodical journals. His review of Herschel's *Preliminary Discourse on the Study of Natural Philosophy* (1830) in the *Quarterly Review* for July 1831 was his first appearance in public (albeit under the convention of anonymity) as a philosophical writer. In the same year he reviewed two other major works: the first volume of Lyell's *Principles of Geology* (1830) and the *Essay on the Distribution of Wealth, and on the Sources of Taxation* (1831) by his friend, Richard Jones—both in the *British Critic*. These three works allowed him to discuss Baconian methodology and comment on the new sciences of geology and political economy in relation to the mature disciplines of astronomy, mechanics, and optics. Whewell explained that the mature sciences had reached the stage of being able to deduce consequences from general laws. On the other hand, some political economists were being prematurely deductive, without having the necessary empirical data, such as that contributed by Jones about different kinds of rent. Geologists, however, now had a good store of observations. In reviewing, at Lyell's request, the second volume of *Principles of Geology* for the *Quarterly Review* in March 1832, Whewell coined 'Uniformitarian' and 'Catastrophist'—terms that were adopted as labels for the opposing doctrines in the geological debates of the day. Later, Whewell described disciplines such as geology, archaeology, and philology as 'palaetiology'—studies of historical causation—and supplied Lyell with Eocene, Miocene, and Pliocene as names for geological periods.

Whewell also first introduced the term 'scientist' in a review article on Mary Somerville's *On the Connexion of the Physical Sciences* (1834) in the *Quarterly Review* (51, 1834, 59). He had made this suggestion—by way of analogy with 'artist'—at a meeting of the British Association in 1833. He used the context of this review to offer this word as a means of noting the common enterprise of those who studied the natural world, even if the various scientific disciplines were becoming more specialized and less unified than Somerville thought. Whewell confirmed this neologism in the *Philosophy*, saying that 'as an Artist is a Musician, Painter, or Poet, a Scientist is a Mathematician, Physicist [also his word], or Naturalist' (*The Philosophy of the Inductive Sciences*, 1847, 2.560). One of his other significant contributions to scientific terminology came in the course of discussions with Michael Faraday about appropriate terms to describe opposing directions of electric currents. In 1834, and again in subsequent letters, after rejecting some of Faraday's suggestions, Whewell recommended

'anode' and 'cathode' (Whewell MSS, O.15.147–8; Todhunter, 2.179–81).

Historian and philosopher of science Whewell's two major works, *History of the Inductive Sciences* (3 vols., 1837) and *The Philosophy of the Inductive Sciences* (2 vols., 1840; 2nd edn 1847), were appreciated as considerable achievements when they appeared. Even his critics drew upon the *History*, but the *Philosophy* was seen by some as too close to Immanuel Kant's idealist epistemology. Herschel and Jones, for example, regarded this as inconsistent with the empirical character of scientific inquiry and a threat to its claim to offer true descriptions of the natural world. Today, however, Whewell's work is seen as posing some of the central issues of the philosophy of science—the relationship between theory and observation, the role of imagination and hypotheses, and the concept of theoretical revolutions, all supported by appeals to the historical record.

Whewell saw these two works as parts of a single inquiry into the philosophy of knowledge, focusing on the nature of 'the most certain and stable portions of knowledge which we already possess' (*The Philosophy of the Inductive Sciences*, 1847, 1.1). It was commonly accepted, he contended, that these were the sciences concerned with knowledge of the material world. In the *History*, Whewell abandoned the orthodox Baconian account of induction assumed in his earlier notebooks, and defended the speculative guesses of Johann Kepler as the more usual path to great discoveries. In using the term 'induction' he referred to the general process by which laws and theories were attained; but he stressed that this was more than a mere generalization from the facts because it involved the addition of a conception from the mind of the scientist. When a number of facts were brought together under some conception Whewell called this the 'Colligation of Facts' (ibid., 1.ix). He made this point directly in *The Mechanical Euclid*, published in 1837: 'Some notion is *superinduced* upon the observed facts. In each inductive process, there is some general idea introduced, which is given, not by the phenomena, but by the mind' (*Mechanical Euclid*, 1837, 178). Whewell suggested that once this had been accomplished previously detached observations assumed a unity that now required an imaginative effort to dissolve: 'The pearls once strung, they seem to form a chain by their nature' (*Philosophy*, 2.52).

In the *History*, Whewell began with this assumption:

> the present generation finds itself the heir of a vast patrimony of science; and it must needs concern us to know the steps by which these possessions were acquired, and the documents by which they are secured to us and our heirs for ever. (*History of the Inductive Sciences*, 1.4)

He outlined a three-stage pattern in the progress of particular sciences, especially in astronomy, his 'pattern science'. In this tripartite scheme, the crucial period of discovery—the 'inductive epoch'—was marked by a convergence of distinct facts and clear, appropriate ideas in the minds of great discoverers. This was preceded by a 'Prelude' in which these facts and ideas were gradually clarified. The inductive epoch was succeeded by a 'Sequel' in which the discovery was accepted and consolidated by the scientific community. Although progress was the motif of the drama that Whewell unfolded he was not dismissive of failures, arguing that they often revealed clues about the nature of scientific discovery. One implication was that present theories, especially in new scientific disciplines, may not be permanent ones.

Whewell's historical vision of the inductive sciences combined moments of dramatic, theoretical change—he used the term 'revolution'—with periods of gradual progress and consolidation. On this view, each science built on its past, incorporating aspects of older doctrines in most recent developments. This idea of a balance between progress and continuity was also a feature of Whewell's political outlook, one that resonated with Peel's Conservatism. In a letter to James Marshall (his brother-in-law) Whewell professed his belief in 'our National Constitution and in our National Religion', and argued that both needed to be invigorated by 'a formative spirit which makes *reform* unnecessary' (Douglas, 282).

In the *Philosophy* Whewell elaborated the epistemological doctrine underlying his view of the intimate connection between facts and ideas in the formation of scientific theories. He called this the 'Fundamental Antithesis' of philosophy. Whewell contended that all knowledge depended on the practical union of sensations and ideas, facts and theories; equally, philosophy required their analytical separation. Thus while not denying such distinctions, he argued that the distinction between 'Fact and Theory' was not a simple one. There was, he declared, 'a mask of theory over the whole face of nature', so that a fact from one perspective was a theory under another (*Philosophy*, 1.42).

Whewell believed that inadequate views about the nature of scientific and other knowledge could in part be attributed to John Locke's view of the mind as a passive receiver of knowledge from the world. For Whewell the mind was active: ideas were not simply transformed sensations; they were the active element that gave form to sensations. 'We cannot,' he explained, 'see one object without the idea of space; we cannot see two without the idea of resemblance or difference'. These and other 'Fundamental Ideas' (as he called them) such as time, number, cause, substance, likeness, and polarity supplied 'Ideal Conceptions' appropriate to the various sciences: for example, that of the ellipse in Kepler's astronomy, or force in dynamics. Whewell claimed that these, and other ideas, regulated the active operations of the mind and were the grounds of the necessary truths which certain branches of science had so far established (*Philosophy*, 1.66). Over time other fundamental ideas would be progressively revealed as the basis of necessary truths in other branches of science (*On the Philosophy of Discovery*, 1860, 354–75). Because different branches of science were grounded in distinctive fundamental ideas, there was, in Whewell's philosophy, a limit to synthetic notions of the unity of sciences.

In Whewell's account of science the mind was dynamic and creative; great discoverers were imaginative and speculative in their quest for knowledge of nature. There was no simple art or method of discovery, but Whewell sought a philosophical understanding of how knowledge advanced. This included some reference to what later became known as the logic of proof and verification. Thus Whewell's notion of the 'Consilience of Inductions' suggested a way of identifying powerful hypotheses: for example, 'cases in which inductions from classes of facts altogether different have thus *jumped together*, belong only to the best established theories which the history of science contains' (*Philosophy*, 2.65).

In noting the anti-Lockean disposition of the *Philosophy*, Leslie Stephen judged that Whewell's work had not been very influential: even towards the end of Whewell's mastership John Stuart Mill was the authority in Cambridge. This assessment made the conflict between idealist and empiricist epistemology crucial for the estimation of Whewell's achievement—a consideration that has since affected his reputation, placing him on the losing side. Stephen said that his philosophy of scientific knowledge was 'scarcely coherent' (*DNB*) and did not gain acceptance. Nevertheless, Henry Sidgwick and Mark Pattison both admired Whewell's work for the way it kept the natural sciences in contact with philosophical thought. Sidgwick remarked that 'it is to Whewell more than to any other single man that the revival of Philosophy in Cambridge is to be attributed' (Sidgwick, 241–2). James Clerk Maxwell endorsed Whewell's search for the philosophical assumptions behind particular experimental inquiries, and soon regarded himself as more metaphysical than Whewell (Maxwell, 206–7). Another commentator, looking back on the *History* and *Philosophy* suggested that at the time Whewell was 'probably the only Englishman who was capable of conceiving the work, or of carrying out the conception' (Carlisle, 144).

Whewell answered philosophical criticism of his position, especially in a short book, *Of Induction* (1849), which replied to J. S. Mill's *System of Logic* (1843). Here Whewell marshalled his superior knowledge of the historical record. In a letter to Herschel, Whewell insisted that the role of fundamental ideas did not compromise the empirical content of science: 'Our real knowledge is knowledge because it involves ideas, real, because it involves facts' (*On the Philosophy of Discovery*, 1860, 488). But he was concerned about an unfavourable reception from practising men of science, and acknowledged that criticism of the section on physiology in the *History* indicated a more general issue:

> Those who have well studied that subject, feel a persuasion, a very natural and just one, that nothing less than a life professionally devoted to the science, can entitle a person to decide the still controverted questions which it involves; and hence they look, with a reasonable jealousy, upon attempts to discuss such questions, made by a *lay* speculator. (*Philosophy*, 1840 edn, 1.xii)

Educational writings Whewell published three contributions to the debate on university education. The first of these—*Thoughts on the Study of Mathematics as a Part of a Liberal Education* (1835)—assumed that mathematics provided an invaluable mental training. Whewell did not think this needed a defence, although he was happy to argue the claims of mathematics against those of logic (philosophy)—as put by Sir William Hamilton in a review of this pamphlet in the *Edinburgh Review* in 1836. Whewell's main concern was with the appropriate kind of mathematics for undergraduates. On this question (as mentioned earlier), he was convinced that analysis, as practised on the continent, was not suitable, and he stressed the importance of solid geometrical reasoning in any elementary curriculum. He recommended the inclusion of Newtonian mechanics and hydrostatics in the undergraduate programme, and edited book 1 of Newton's *Principia* (1846). His two larger books—*On the Principles of English University Education* (1837) and *Of a liberal education in general; and with particular reference to the leading studies of the University of Cambridge* (1845–52)—considered the ideal of liberal education, again emphasizing the foundational character of geometry and classical languages. Both works proposed a distinction between 'permanent' and 'progressive' studies that allowed only the most advanced (and stable) physical sciences to be included among the permanent elements of the curriculum. Lyell complained to Whewell that this was a recipe for the exclusion of most of the modern sciences for perhaps a century, or until their degree of theoretical consensus matched that of Newtonian mechanics. Thus although Whewell was able to introduce a natural sciences tripos in 1848, his views on the priority of geometry and classics were seen as unhelpful to the campaign aimed at raising the status of science in Victorian society.

In his major writings Whewell did not comment in any detail on the triumphs of what is now seen as the industrial revolution. While acknowledging that the practical and mechanical arts (or technology) sometimes produced phenomena subsequently explained by science, he firmly distinguished technical applications from the theoretical understanding sought by science. However, in a lecture of 26 November 1851 on *The General Bearing of the Great Exhibition on the Progress of Art and Science* (published in 1852), Whewell praised the display of objects and machinery and accepted that modern technological developments—such as the electric telegraph and chemical industry—were more closely dependent on scientific discoveries.

Final years Whewell's major writings on science and education were published by 1845. In the latter part of his career he produced new editions of the *History* (1847 and 1857) and *Philosophy* (1847); the latter was also rearranged (with some additions) under new titles: *Novum organon renovatum* (1858), *The History of Scientific Ideas* (2 vols., 1858), and *On the Philosophy of Discovery* (1860). His response to the anonymous *Vestiges of the Natural History of Creation* (by Robert Chambers) was a selection of chapters from his two major works, published as *Indications of the Creator* (1845). He also published two books on moral philosophy—*The Elements of Morality, Including Polity* (2 vols., 1845) and *Lectures on Systematic Morality* (1846), neither of which were well received, being seen as ponderous and conservative, especially by J. S. Mill and other utilitarian ethical

thinkers. However, Whewell viewed them as important for his views on the analogies between the development of moral and physical knowledge. His *Lectures on the History of Moral Philosophy in England* (1852) derived from his teaching as professor of moral philosophy.

Whewell's most engaging and controversial work in the latter part of his life was the anonymous *Of the Plurality of Worlds: an Essay* (1853), followed by *A Dialogue on the Plurality of Worlds* (1854), a short supplement to the original essay. The book (well known to be by Whewell) reached a seventh edition by 1859—an indication of the reaction to his iconoclastic rejection of the commonly held belief in the probable existence of intelligent life on other planets. Whewell dismissed the analogies by which this belief was sustained, arguing for the uniqueness of rational life and human history on earth. In the course of his discussion Whewell also rejected a version of the principle of plenitude—as maintained by critics such as David Brewster—that God had filled all possible space with life. To this Whewell asked rhetorically 'whether Mount Blanc would be more sublime, if millions of frogs were known to live in the crevasses of its glaciers' (W. Whewell, *A Dialogue on the Plurality of Worlds*, 1854, 366). The prospect of Whewell (with his reputation for arrogance) choosing this topic stimulated Stephen to observe that the book was meant to prove that 'through all infinity, there was nothing so great as the master of Trinity' (*DNB*).

Whewell also edited other writings—explaining their significance in careful prefaces. James Mackintosh's *Dissertation on the Progress of Ethical Philosophy* (1836) and Butler's *Three Sermons on Human Nature* (1848) were relevant to his quest for a non-utilitarian ethics; the edition of *Literary remains, consisting of lectures and tracts on political economy, of the late Rev. Richard Jones* (1859) derived from Whewell's respect for Jones and his own interest in political economy. Whewell published three papers in the *Transactions of the Cambridge Philosophical Society* (1830, 1831, and 1850) on the political economy of, respectively, Thomas Perronet Thompson, David Ricardo, and J. S. Mill. In each case Whewell gave a mathematical exposition of the deductive reasoning of these writers, clarifying their premises, and then leaving open the suggestion that these were not grounded in empirical observation—of the kind Jones provided with respect to rents. In returning to this topic in 1850, at the time of his dispute with Mill over philosophy of science, Whewell indicated that Mill's inadequate grasp of induction in physical science was also revealed in his political economy. Between 1859 and 1861 Whewell produced *Platonic Dialogues for English Readers*; in 1857 he reviewed James Spedding's edition of the complete works of Francis Bacon for the *Edinburgh Review*; in 1860 he edited *The Mathematical Works of Isaac Barrow*; in 1862 he wrote two reviews of English translations of *The Iliad* for *Macmillan's Magazine*, and one of George Grote's edition of Plato, which was published posthumously in *Fraser's Magazine* in April 1866. His essay on 'Comte and positivism' for *Macmillan's Magazine* (1866) appeared in the month of his death.

The last ten years of Whewell's life were marked by personal losses. His wife, Cordelia, died after a long illness on 18 December 1855. He married Everina Frances, widow of Sir Gilbert Affleck, on 1 July 1858. She died on 1 April 1865. Whewell preached his last sermon in Trinity College chapel on 11 February 1866, returning to themes that had appeared both in earlier sermons and in his writings on science. Noting that geology and astronomy imagined 'vast cycles of change succeeding each other' he warned that this did not remove the religious conviction that there was a beginning, and that there will be an end, to the world. The manner of this event lay outside the common history of the world, but Whewell reminded his audience that the scriptures spoke of it as 'an event which is to be sudden, violent, and overwhelming' (Todhunter, 1.343–4). On 24 February he went riding outside Cambridge and fell from his horse; the injuries were severe and Whewell died at Trinity College on 6 March 1866. He was buried in the ante-chapel on 10 March 1866.

Reputation At the time of his death Whewell was known as a great master of Trinity and a man of enormous intellectual power and learning. Within the scientific community throughout Europe he was recognized for his research on the tides, his contributions to conceptual debates and terminology, and for his unrivalled knowledge of the history of the sciences. Although some aspects of his philosophy of science were criticized, Whewell's work set an example for the critical study of the nature of science and, since the 1970s, the historical inquiry on which he claimed to base his philosophy of science has been more warmly appreciated. He combined this study of the physical sciences with publications on education, moral philosophy, and other subjects in a manner that astonished his contemporaries. He did this at a time when intellectual activity was becoming more specialized—a phenomenon that Whewell recognized in his own philosophy of knowledge. Today we are able to see that his achievement was one of the last of its kind.

RICHARD YEO

Sources I. Todhunter, *William Whewell: an account of his writings, with selections from his literary and scientific correspondence*, 2 vols. (1876) • J. S. Douglas, *The life and selections from the correspondence of William Whewell DD* (1881) • J. F. W. H. [J. F. W. Herschel], *PRS*, 16 (1867–8), li–lxi • *DNB* • H. Carlisle, 'William Whewell', *Macmillan's Magazine*, 45 (1881–2), 138–44 • R. Yeo, *Defining science: William Whewell, natural knowledge and public debate in early Victorian Britain* (1993) • M. Fisch and S. Schaffer, eds., *William Whewell: a composite portrait* (1991) • W. F. Cannon, 'William Whewell, FRS: contributions to science and learning', *Notes and Records of the Royal Society*, 19 (1964), 176–91 • H. W. Becher, 'William Whewell's odyssey: from mathematics to moral philosophy', *William Whewell: a composite portrait*, ed. M. Fisch and S. Schaffer (1991), 1–29 • J. Morrell and A. Thackray, *Gentlemen of science: early years of the British Association for the Advancement of Science* (1981) • R. Robson, 'William Whewell, FRS: academic life', *Notes and Records of the Royal Society*, 19 (1964), 168–76 • H. Sidgwick, 'Philosophy at Cambridge', *Mind*, 1 (1876), 235–46 • J. C. Maxwell, 'Whewell's writings and correspondence', *Nature*, 14 (1876), 206–8 • *Life, letters, and journals of Sir Charles Lyell*, ed. Mrs Lyell, 2 vols. (1881) • *Romilly's Cambridge diary, 1832–42: selected passages from the diary of the Rev. Joseph Romilly*, ed. J. P. T. Bury (1967) • J. W. Clark and T. M. Hughes, *The life and letters of the Reverend Adam Sedgwick*, 2 vols. (1890) • G. B. Airy, *Autobiography of Sir George Biddell Airy*, ed. W. Airy (1896) • D. A. Winstanley, *Early Victorian Cambridge* (1940) • M. Fisch, *William Whewell: philosopher of science* (1991) • *The Athenaeum* (10 March 1866), 333–4 • W. G. Rimmer, *Marshalls of Leeds, flax-spinners, 1788–1886* (1960) • F. Galton, *Hereditary genius: an inquiry into its laws and consequences*, 2nd edn (1892) • H. Becher, 'William Whewell and Cambridge mathematics', *Historical Studies in the Physical Sciences*, 11 (1980–81), 1–48 • J. H. Brooke, 'Natural theology and the plurality of worlds: observations on the Brewster–Whewell debate', *Annals of Science*, 34 (1977), 221–86 • R. Yeo, 'The principle of plenitude and natural theology in nineteenth-century Britain', *British Journal for the History of Science*, 19 (1986), 263–82 • B. Hilton, *The age of atonement: the influence of evangelicalism on social and economic thought, 1795–1865* (1988) • W. Whewell, *History of the inductive sciences*, 3 vols. (1837) • W. Whewell, *The philosophy of the inductive sciences*, 2 vols. (1840); new edn (1847) • d. cert. • Trinity Cam., Whewell MSS • RS, Herschel papers

Archives Harvard U., Houghton L., corresp. • RS, letters and papers • Sci. Mus., letters • Trinity Cam., corresp. and papers; family corresp. | BL, letters to Charles Babbage, Add. MSS 37182–37201, *passim* • Bodl. Oxf., letters to William Somerville and Mary Somerville • CUL, corresp. with Sir George Airy • CUL, letters and accounts relating to Cambridge University • Durham Cath. CL, letters to J. B. Lightfoot • GS Lond., letters to Roderick Impey Murchison • LPL, corresp. with Christopher Wordsworth • NL Ire., corresp. with Lord Monteagle • Oriel College, Oxford, corresp. with Edward Hawkins • Ransom HRC, letters to Sir John Herschel • Royal Library of Belgium, Brussels, letters to Adolphe Quetelet • RS, corresp. with Sir John Herschel; letters to Sir John Lubbock • U. St Andr. L., corresp. with James David Forbes

Likenesses J. Lonsdale, oils, 1825, Trinity Cam. • E. U. Eddis, lithograph, pubd 1835 (after W. Drummond), BM, NPG • G. F. Joseph, oils, 1836, Trinity Cam. • M. Carpenter, miniature, 1842, Trinity Cam. • S. Laurence, oils, 1845, Trinity Cam. • E. H. Bailey, marble bust, 1851, Trinity Cam.; plaster cast, NPG • T. Woolner, marble statue, 1872, Trinity Cam. • E. Edwards, photograph, NPG; repro. in L. Reeve, ed., *Portraits of men of eminence* (1863) • J. Rylands, carte-de-visite, NPG [*see illus.*] • plaster death mask, Trinity Cam.

Wealth at death under £70,000: probate, 3 May 1866, *CGPLA Eng. & Wales*

Whibley, Charles (1859–1930), journalist and author, was born at Sittingbourne, Kent, on 9 December 1859, the eldest son of Ambrose Whibley, merchant, and his second wife, Mary Jean Davy. Whibley was educated at Bristol grammar school and Jesus College, Cambridge, where he took a first in classics in 1883. He was elected an honorary fellow there in 1912. His brother Leonard *Whibley (1863–1941) had a similar career at Pembroke College, Cambridge.

After three years in the editorial department of the publishers Cassell & Co., Whibley became an independent author and journalist. In 1889 he published *In Cap and Gown: Three Centuries of Cambridge Wit*, an anthology whose introduction he wrote. He became friendly with W. E. Henley, whom he assisted in editing the *Scots Observer* (later the *National Observer*) and he wrote several of the introductions for Henley's *The Tudor Translations* (in 1924 he himself edited a second series). His article for the *Scots Observer* (31 October 1891) on Degas was one of the first in English. When Henley left the *National Observer*, Whibley worked with H. J. C. Cust, editor of the tory evening paper, the *Pall Mall Gazette*. In 1894 he became its Paris correspondent, a post that suited his artistic and literary tastes; he moved in the symbolist circle of Stéphane Mallarmé, Marcel Schwob (the authority on François Villon), and Paul

Valéry. In Paris, in 1896, he married Ethel Birnie Philip (1862–1920), daughter of J. B. *Philip and secretary, model, and sister-in-law of the artist J. M. Whistler, who called her 'Bunnie' and Whibley 'Wobbles'.

Whibley returned to Britain to write for *Blackwood's Magazine*, contributing anonymously (but with known authorship) 'Musings without Methods' to it for more than twenty-five years, which gave ample scope for his ventilation of often acerbic high-tory commentary. His more considered opinions were published in *William Pitt* (1906), *Political Portraits* (1917 and 1923), and *Lord John Manners and his Friends* (1925). He responded vigorously to the war with *A Call to Arms* (1914) and with *Letters to an Englishman* (1915), reprinted from his column of that name in the *Daily Mail*: he had become a crony of Lord Northcliffe, visiting the United States with him in 1907 and subsequently writing *American Sketches* (1908). As well as a steady stream of literary publications, largely introductions to reprints, Whibley was a reader for the publishing house of Macmillan and a friend of Sir Frederick Macmillan. He was Leslie Stephen lecturer (on Swift) at Cambridge in 1917. He was a friend of Lady Cynthia Asquith and through her aided D. H. Lawrence financially. Whibley was able to build Broomhill House, at Great Brickhill, near Bletchley, Buckinghamshire, a country house with a large library which he built to house his large collection of first editions. A widower from 1920, he married, in 1927, his goddaughter Philippa, daughter of Sir Walter *Raleigh, the literary critic and professor; there were no children by either of his marriages. He suffered in later years from acute neuralgia and died at La Maisonette Costebelle, Hyères, France, on 4 March 1930, and was buried at Great Brickhill. He was a tory belletrist, who preserved Victorian literary traditions into the twentieth century.   H. C. G. MATTHEW

Sources *The Times* (5 March 1930) · *DNB* · R. Dorment and M. F. Macdonald, *James McNeill Whistler* (1994) · *Lady Cynthia Asquith: diaries, 1915–1918* (1968) · Venn, *Alum. Cant.*
Archives BL, corresp. with Macmillans, Add. MSS 55024–55025 · BL, corresp. with Lord Northcliffe, Add. MS 62281 · U. Leeds, Brotherton L., letters to Edmund Gosse
Likenesses G. Kelly, oils, exh. RA 1926, Jesus College, Cambridge · P. Evans, pen-and-ink drawing, 1929, NPG

Whibley, Leonard (1863–1941), classical scholar, was born at Gravesend on 20 April 1863, the second son of Ambrose Whibley, linen draper, of Gravesend and Bristol, and his second wife, Mary Jean, daughter of the late John Davy, iron merchant. He was educated at Bristol grammar school and entered Pembroke College, Cambridge, as a scholar in 1882. In 1885 he was classed with A. E. Brooke and R. S. Conway in the first division of the first class of the classical tripos, part one, and in the following year gained a distinguished first in part two. In 1888 he was the first winner of the recently established Prince Consort prize for historical studies, his subject being 'Political parties in Athens during the Peloponnesian War', and in 1889 he was elected to a fellowship at Pembroke.

Whibley did not immediately settle into the academic groove. For a time he was associated with the publishing firm of Methuen and shared a house at Fernhurst with his

brother Charles *Whibley, W. E. Henley, and G. W. Steevens; he was also for a short period assistant secretary of the university press, but decided to be a teacher and a historian rather than a publisher. In 1893 he won the Hare prize with an essay on Greek oligarchies, which was published in book form three years later. From 1899 to 1910 he was university lecturer in ancient history and in 1905 edited the *Companion to Greek Studies* for the university press, of which body he was a syndic for some years. The *Companion* was recognized as a standard book of reference for students and was revised more than once during its editor's lifetime. In college Whibley served as classical lecturer, assistant tutor, and domestic bursar. He had a shrewd business sense and a fine, though not extravagant, taste in food and wine. To the friends and pupils whom he entertained in his rooms he seemed to embody all the qualities of the bachelor don. But in 1920, after serving for a time in the Foreign Office, he quietly astonished his colleagues by announcing his forthcoming marriage (17 February 1920) to Henriette Leiningen (Rhita), daughter of Major-General William Brown Barwell and Elise, countess of Leiningen-Westerburg. There were no children from this marriage.

After his marriage Whibley went to live first at Wrecclesham and afterwards at Frensham, Surrey; but he remained senior fellow of Pembroke and kept in close touch with the college. He also developed a keen interest in eighteenth-century literature and especially in Thomas Gray. From 1925 he collaborated with Paget Toynbee in the preparation of a new edition of Gray's letters and on Toynbee's death in 1932 he revised the whole work, sparing no pains to secure textual accuracy and factual comment. The three volumes, published in 1935, are a model of editorial scholarship.

Whibley was a good clubman. With A. D. Godley he was a co-founder, in 1900, of the Arcades, an Oxford and Cambridge dining club, and he was happy also in his membership of the Johnson Club. To undergraduates he was friend as well as teacher. His literary discipline was strict and he would prick any bubble of pretentiousness with a dry economy of wit; but, once he believed in a pupil, he would take infinite trouble on his behalf. As a young man Whibley had leaned towards radicalism, in an era when there was real heat in Cambridge University politics, but in later life he became a tory stalwart and an active pamphlet-distributor of the right. In 1939 he took great pleasure in celebrating the jubilee of his Pembroke fellowship and on 8 November 1941 he died at his home, the Dial House, Frensham.

SYDNEY C. ROBERTS, *rev.* MARK POTTLE

Sources personal knowledge (1959) · *The Times* (10 Nov 1941) · *Cambridge Review* (15 Nov 1941), 86–7 · Venn, *Alum. Cant.*
Archives Bodl. Oxf., corresp. with J. L. Myers · Notts. Arch., corresp. with H. M. Leman
Likenesses D. Hawksley, pencil drawing, Pembroke Cam.
Wealth at death £43,350 4s. 8d.: probate, 6 Jan 1942, *CGPLA Eng. & Wales*

Whichcord, John (1823–1885), architect, was born on 11 November 1823 at Maidstone, Kent, the son of John

Whichcord (1790–1860), an architect who designed two churches (St Philip and Holy Trinity), the corn exchange, and the Kent fire office in Maidstone, and various churches, parsonages, and institutions elsewhere in Kent. His father was also surveyor to the county of Kent and to the Medway Navigation Company, for whom he executed extensive hydraulic works, some tidal locks, and a number of bridges.

Whichcord was educated at Maidstone and at King's College, London. He was married twice, the first time to an Italian woman. He had seven children. In 1840 he became an assistant to his father, and in 1844 a student at the Royal Academy. In 1848 he was elected a fellow of the Society of Antiquaries. After extensive travel in Italy, Greece, Asiatic Turkey, Syria, Egypt, and the Holy Land (1846–50), and a tour of France, Italy, Germany, and Denmark (1850), he entered into a partnership (until 1858) with Arthur Ashpitel. Together they carried out additions to Lord Abergavenny's house, Birling, Kent (1852), and built fourteen houses on the Mount Elliott estate at Lee, also in Kent (1858). Subsequently most of his output was concentrated upon the design of offices in the City of London; he was responsible for 9 Mincing Lane, 24 Lombard Street, 8 Old Jewry, Mansion House Chambers, the New Zealand Bank, and the National Safe Deposit, all in Queen Victoria Street, and Brown Janson & Co.'s bank, Abchurch Lane. He built the Grand Hotel at Brighton (1862–4) and the Clarence Hotel at Dover, as well as St Mary's Church and parsonage at Shortlands, near Bromley, Kent. One of Whichcord's best-known works is the St Stephen's Club (1874), a classical building with boldly corbelled projections which faces Westminster Bridge. He designed the internal fittings for the house of parliament at Cape Town. He was often employed as an arbitrator of disputes connected with government contracts, and was one of the surveyors to the railway department of the Board of Trade.

From 1854 Whichcord held the post of district surveyor for Deptford, and from 1879 to 1881 was president of the Royal Institute of British Architects (RIBA), where he delivered various addresses and papers. The *Transactions* of the RIBA (1845–80) record his instrumental role in the establishment of the examination system. Whichcord's publications include *The History and Antiquities of the Collegiate Church of All Saints, Maidstone* (1845); *Observations on the sanitary condition of Maidstone, with a view to the introduction of the act for promoting public health* (1849); and, with A. Ashpitel, *Observations on Baths and Wash-Houses* (2nd edn, 1851) and *Town dwellings: an essay on the erection of fireproof houses in flats; a modification of the Scottish and continental systems* (1855).

In 1865 Whichcord unsuccessfully stood as a Conservative candidate for the Barnstaple constituency. He also served with the Kent yeomanry and in 1869 became a captain in the 1st Middlesex artillery volunteers, where he formed a battery composed mainly of young architects and lawyers. He died at his home, 23 Inverness Terrace, London, on 9 January 1885, and was buried at Kensal Green cemetery, London. His second wife, Marian Emma, survived him.   PAUL WATERHOUSE, *rev.* JOHN ELLIOTT

Sources *The Builder*, 48 (1885), 98 · E. Christian, *Journal of Proceedings of the Royal Institute of British Architects*, new ser., 1 (1884–5), 92–5 · biographical file, RIBA BAL · *CGPLA Eng. & Wales* (1885) · Colvin, *Archs.* · *Dir. Brit. archs.* · Pevsner
Archives RIBA, nomination papers · RIBA BAL, biography file
Likenesses L. Alma-Tadema, oils, exh. RA 1882, RIBA · portrait, repro. in *Architects' and Builders' Journal* (30 Dec 1913) · portrait, RIBA, Photographic Collection
Wealth at death £20,479 6s. 9d.: probate, 14 Feb 1885, *CGPLA Eng. & Wales*

Whichcote, Benjamin (1609–1683), theologian and moral philosopher, was born in Stoke, Shropshire, in March 1609, the sixth son of at least seven children of Christopher Whichcote of Whichcote Hall and his wife, Elizabeth (*née* Fox). In 1626 he entered Emmanuel College, Cambridge, where his tutors were first Anthony Tuckney and subsequently Thomas Hill. He graduated BA in 1629, proceeded MA and became a fellow in 1633, and was ordained deacon by Bishop John Williams in 1636. At Emmanuel his pupils included Samuel Cradock, John Wallis, Jeremiah Horrocks, John Smith, and John Worthington but a constellation of younger men came under his wider influence. Notable among them were the so-called Cambridge Platonists—Worthington, Ralph Cudworth, Peter Sterry, and Nathaniel Culverwell. Their circle also took in other members of Whichcote's family—his niece Mary (the daughter of his brother Christopher) who married Worthington, his sister Elizabeth *Foxcroft (1600–1679) (at one time the companion of Anne Conway), her husband, George Foxcroft, and their son Ezekiel Foxcroft.

Having proceeded BD in 1640 Whichcote was, on 26 October 1641, a candidate for the professorship of divinity at Gresham College, but he lost the election to Thomas Horton. From 1643 he lectured at Trinity Church, Cambridge, on Sunday and Wednesday afternoons. That year he married Rebecca Cradock, widow of Matthew Cradock (*d.* 1641), first governor of the Massachusetts Bay Company, and was also presented to the living of North Cadbury, Somerset. He did not resign his fellowship until the following year, and a dispute over the right of presentation prevented him from taking up his preferment until 1645. On 19 March 1645 he was appointed provost of King's College by parliament in place of Samuel Collins, ejected by the earl of Manchester. Whichcote did not himself subscribe to the covenant, possibly because he was absent from Cambridge at the time. In 1649 he became DD by mandate. In 1650 he was appointed vice-chancellor of the University of Cambridge. The sermon that he preached on this occasion resulted, in 1651, in an exchange of letters with Anthony Tuckney, who expressed alarm at Whichcote's subordination of faith to reason. In reply Whichcote defended the role of reason in religious matters and his advocacy of ecumenism, which was based on an agreed minimum set of beliefs. The theological liberalism that he enunciated in response to Tuckney's doctrinaire Calvinism characterizes the Cambridge Platonists and their latitudinarian successors. On 20 September 1651 Whichcote was presented to the living of Milton, near Cambridge. In 1654 he contributed a poem to the collection *Oliva pacis* celebrating Oliver Cromwell's peace

Benjamin Whichcote (1609–1683), by Mary Beale, 1682

with the Netherlands. In 1655 he was one of sixteen divines on the committee set up to advise Cromwell on the readmission of the Jews to England. In 1659, along with Edward Stillingfleet and John Tillotson, he backed Matthew Poole's scheme for supporting able students at university. He was a friend of Samuel Hartlib, and encouraged Thomas Gouge's educational project in Wales.

As provost of King's, Whichcote was an able administrator who steered his college through difficult times, and won the respect of fellows for his considerate treatment of his predecessor, Samuel Collins, and for winning exemption for fellows of King's from subscribing to the covenant. In 1660 Whichcote's academic career came to an abrupt end when he was supplanted in the provostship of King's by James Fleetwood on 26 June. With support from Lord Lauderdale, Whichcote attempted to oppose the appointment of Fleetwood. The vice-provost of King's, Matthew Barlow, and twenty-one fellows supported his petition, commending his 'peaceable and prudent management' during his time as provost (CSP dom., July 1660, petition 94.II). In spite of the fact that his deprived predecessor had died, he was forced to resign in favour of the royal nominee, Fleetwood, who successfully argued that Whichcote could not hold the provostship because college statutes required that the provost be elected from among the fellows of King's. Whichcote was permitted to retain the living of Milton, after resigning it in November 1661 in order that it might be re-presented to him a few days later.

Although he complied with the Act of Uniformity, Whichcote did not obtain another university appointment after his ejection from King's College. Instead, he found employment as a clergyman. On 8 November 1662 he was appointed curate of St Ann Blackfriars. After the fire of London he retired to his living at Milton. In December 1668, with the help of the outgoing incumbent, his friend John Wilkins, he obtained the living of St Lawrence Jewry in London, where he preached twice weekly and where John Locke attended his sermons. While the church was being rebuilt he was permitted to preach at the Guildhall. In 1670, acting as the executor of John Larkin, he founded fellowships and scholarships at Emmanuel College, funded by a bequest of £1000 13s. 4d. In 1673 he preached before parliament. He died in May 1683 in Cambridge at the house of his friend Ralph Cudworth, and was buried on 24 May at St Lawrence Jewry. His funeral sermon was preached by John Tillotson, future archbishop of Canterbury. In his will he bequeathed land to finance poor relief and education in Milton. He had no children. His nephew, Benjamin Whichcote of Bishopsgate, one of his executors, passed his papers to John Jeffrey for publication, though some were still in the hands of his great-nephew, Francis Whichcote, bt, in 1753.

Whichcote impressed those who met him with his mild and courteous disposition. He was, according to Gilbert Burnet, 'a man of rare temper'. During the strife-riven years of the civil war and its aftermath Whichcote was an important eirenic presence in the University of Cambridge. In religion Whichcote placed emphasis on interior spirituality rather than the externals of religion, and on Christian practice rather than on the institutions of the church. For him the core of Christianity was its moral content. He published nothing in his lifetime: his writings consist of posthumously published collections of his sermons and works derived from these. A teacher rather than a systematizer, his most important published legacy comprised the moral and religious aphorisms derived from his sermons. These amount to a consistent body of ethical teachings in which he asserted the permanence of moral distinctions and the rational nature of moral understanding. By reason he meant practical reason, the end of which is the exercise of virtue. Although he never denied the role of revelation he regarded religion as intrinsically rational: reason is the means by which the truth of religion is communicated to men. Indeed, he believed that it was possible to arrive at the truth by reason without scripture. He was, accordingly, optimistic in his view of human nature. He believed, nevertheless, that human beings are fallible, and that therefore it behoved them to be charitable, and therefore tolerant, towards the religious convictions of others.

Whichcote's tolerant, optimistic, and rational theology, with its emphasis on practical ethics, shaped the theology of the Cambridge Platonists, through whom his theological legacy extends to the latitudinarian movement of the latter half of the seventeenth century. His philosophical admirers included his friends Ralph Cudworth and John Locke, Samuel Clarke, who published a volume of his sermons in 1707, and Anthony Ashley Cooper, third earl of Shaftesbury, who edited another volume of his sermons in 1698. He was also held in esteem by John Ray and

William Whiston and continued to attract a readership throughout the eighteenth century, when several collections of his writings were published, including a four-volume collection of his sermons which was published by Samuel Salter in 1753. In the nineteenth century he was highly esteemed by the Anglican scholars J. B. Lightfoot, B. F. Westcott, and H. J. A. Hort, and, in the twentieth century, by W. R. Inge. SARAH HUTTON

Sources *The diary and correspondence of Dr John Worthington*, ed. J. Crossley and R. C. Christie, 2 vols. in 3, Chetham Society, 13, 36, 114 (1847–86) • J. Tillotson, *A sermon preached at the funeral of the Reverend Benjamin Whichcot, DD and minister of S. Lawrence Jewry, London, May 24th 1683* (1683) • J. D. Roberts, *From puritanism to Platonism in seventeenth-century England* (The Hague, 1968) • A. Allen, 'Skeleton Collegii Regalis Cantab.', King's Cam., fol. 3 • 'Eight letters of Dr Antony Tuckney and Dr Benjamin Whichcote', *Moral and religious aphorisms*, ed. J. Jeffrey (1753) [preface] • B. F. Westcott, 'Benjamin Whichcote', in A. Barry, *Masters in English theology* (1877) • W. C. de Pauley, *The candle of the Lord* (1937) • Venn, *Alum. Cant.* • J. B. Schneewind, *The invention of autonomy* (1998), 196–9 • A. A. Cooper, preface, in B. Whichcote, *Select sermons*, ed. A. A. Cooper (1698) • A. A. Cooper, preface, in B. Whichcote, *Twelve sermons*, 2nd edn (1721)
Archives BL, Lansdowne MSS, 998, fols. 18ff and 23 • BL, letters, MSS 426, fols. 188–189; 23314, fol. 9; 34601, fol. 6 • BL, Sloane MSS, 2716; 2903.25, fols 6–16, 41–65, 98–129, 132–4 • CUL, MSS Dd12, 24 and Add. MS 73 • Emmanuel College, Cambridge • King's Cam. | BL, corresp. with Anthony Tackney, Sloane MSS 1710, fols. 309–353; 2903, fols. 88–101 • CUL, Baker MSS, letters [copies]
Likenesses M. Beale, oils, 1682, Emmanuel College, Cambridge [*see illus.*] • C. J. Heaton, stained-glass window, 1884, Emmanuel College, Cambridge • M. Beale, oils, second version, LPL • attrib. Soest, oils, BL, Add. MS 6391, fol. 107, no. 17 • R. White, line engraving, BM, NPG; repro. in *Discourses* (1701) • oils (after M. Beale?), King's Cam.
Wealth at death 'had a plentifull Estate': Allen, 'Skeleton Collegii Regalis Cantab' • £1000 13s. 4d. to Emmanuel College, Cambridge, to fund fellowships and scholarships; 7 acres of land to parish of Milton for support of the poor and to pay for children of parish to learn to read and write; £100 to King's College, Cambridge; £100 to Dr John Collins; £20 to Emmanuel College, Cambridge

Whichcote, George (1794–1891), army officer, born on 21 December 1794, was the fourth son of Sir Thomas Whichcote, fifth baronet (1763–1824), of Aswarby Park, Lincolnshire, and his wife, Diana (*d.* 1826), third daughter of Edmund Turnor of Panton and Stoke Rochford. In 1803 he entered Rugby School, where he fagged for William Charles Macready, the actor. In December 1810, on leaving Rugby, he joined the 52nd foot as a volunteer, and received a commission as ensign on 10 January 1811. That year he joined the British army in the Spanish peninsula, where his regiment, with the 43rd and the 95th, formed the famous light division. He took part in the battle of Sabugal on 3 April, and in the combat of El Bodon on 25 September, though his regiment was not engaged. He assisted in the storming of Ciudad Rodrigo on 19 January 1812, and of Badajoz on 6 April. On 8 July 1812 he became lieutenant, and was present at the battle of Salamanca on 22 July and at that of Vitoria on 21 June 1813, where the 52nd carried the village of Magarita with an impetuous charge. He took part with his regiment in the combats in the Pyrenees in July and August, the combat of Vera on 3 October, and the battle of the Nivelle on 10 November, of the Nive on 10–13

December, of Orthez on 27 February 1814, of Tarbes on 12 March, and of Toulouse on 12 April. He was the first man in the British army to enter Toulouse. While in command of an advanced picket he observed the French retreat, and, boldly pushing on, took possession of the town. At the close of the war the regiment was placed in garrison at Castelsarrasin on the Garonne, and afterwards was sent to Ireland. Whichcote took part in the battle of Waterloo, where the 52nd completed the rout of the imperial guard. He was quartered in Paris during the occupation by the allies, and on his return home received the Waterloo medal and the silver war medal with nine clasps, before he had attained his majority. When his regiment was sent to Australia, Whichcote transferred into the Buffs.

On 22 January 1818 Whichcote obtained his captaincy, and in 1822 transferred to the 4th dragoon guards. He was made major on 29 October 1825, lieutenant-colonel on 28 June 1838, and colonel on 11 November 1851. In 1825 he was placed on half pay, and on 4 June 1857 attained the rank of major-general; he was promoted lieutenant-general on 31 January 1864, and became a full general on 5 December 1871. In 1842 he married Charlotte Sophia (*d.* 1880), daughter of Philip Monckton; they had no children. Whichcote died on 26 August 1891 at Meriden, near Coventry, where he had lived since retiring from active service, and was buried there on 31 August. At his death he was well known as almost the last surviving British officer who had fought at Waterloo.

E. I. CARLYLE, *rev.* H. C. G. MATTHEW

Sources *The Times* (27 Aug 1891) • *Coventry Standard* (28 Aug 1891) • Burke, *Peerage* • *Hart's Army List* • *Army List*
Wealth at death £22,502 14s. 10d.: probate, 12 Nov 1891, *CGPLA Eng. & Wales*

Whichelo, C. John Mayle (1784–1865), watercolour painter, is believed to have been a pupil of John Varley, and of Joshua Cristall, whose style his work more closely resembles. He was chiefly a marine painter who made studies of the channel coasts in England, and to a lesser extent the Netherlands and Belgium, as well as of the harbours and dockyards of his native land. But he was also a landscapist and an art teacher, and he spent his early career as a topographer in London. He was first known as the illustrator of *Select Views of London and its Environs* (2 vols., 1804–5). Some of his drawings were engraved for Robert Wilkinson's *Londina illustrata* (1819) and three plates, after drawings by 'Whichelo', appear in E. W. Brayley's *Beauties of England and Wales* (18 vols., 1801–15). He is also said to have produced topographical drawings to illustrate copies of *Pennant's Tours*, at 5s. each. At this time he lived centrally but in 1823 he moved further out, to Chalk Cottage, Brixton, and later Norwood. From 1834 until his death he again lived in the city.

Whichelo hailed from a family of painters: his son, John (*d.* 1867), became a drawing master, and it is probable that Henry Mayle Whichelo (1800–1884), who exhibited at the Royal Academy from 1818 to 1848, was his brother. Henry was probably the father of Henry Mayle Whichelo junior

(1825/6–1867), who died in Lambeth. Other probable members of the family were Harry Whichelo, who died at Wallingford in 1849, and William J. Whichelo of Brixton, who was active as a landscape painter in the 1860s and 1870s. Further, the potential for confusion in attributing works is made greater by Whichelo's 'proved trick of shedding prefixes', so that exhibition catalogues 'show some looseness in recording his name' (Roget, 1.525). He is listed in the catalogues of the Society of Painters in Water Colours as 'J. Whichelo' (1823–9), 'J. M. Whichelo' (1830–34), and 'John Whichelo' (after 1835). He first appears in the catalogues of the Royal Academy as 'C. J. M. Whichelo' in 1810, when he exhibited *View on Brighton Beach*. In the following year his large *Battle of Trafalgar* was exhibited at the British Institution. In 1812 he sent *Portsmouth Beach* to the Royal Academy. By this date he was described as 'Marine and Landscape Painter to His R. H. the Prince Regent'. After 1818 there is no further mention of his position at court. He exhibited at the academy in 1816–17, and again in 1819—on the latter occasion he sent *A Scene from Roderick the Last of the Goths* which illustrates lines from Robert Southey. Although the subject matter is untypical of his work, the painting, attributed to 'John Whichelo', is assumed to be his. He sent a total of fifteen works to the academy and thirteen to the British Institution.

On 10 February 1823 Whichelo was one of three landscape painters to be elected an associate of the Society of Painters in Water Colours, which was seeking to secure its future by augmenting its numerical strength. Whichelo contributed four sea pieces to the exhibition at the society's new gallery in Pall Mall East in 1823 and remained an associate to his death. He generally sent three or four drawings to the summer exhibitions, besides having some fifty 'sketches and studies' in the first four winter shows. In all he sent over 200 works, the majority of them marine paintings such as *Portsmouth Naval Arsenal* (1827) and *Rotterdam Boats Passing Dort in a Fresh Breeze* (1831). He painted four naval scenes, two of which depicted events of his own time, namely *The Bombardment of St Jean d'Acre* (1841) and *The British Fleet, under Sir Charles Napier, Entering the Baltic* (1854).

Whichelo's last works were chiefly English landscapes, mostly views from Surrey and the New Forest. He painted 'elaborate tree subjects with small figures, in which the foliage, though rather stiff and mannered, was not ill executed' (Roget, 2.202). He also produced some river views from the Rhine and the Scheldt, and landscapes from Switzerland. One or two works on the coast of Sicily were most probably from sketches made by other hands. Whichelo is described by a friend who knew him when he lived in Haymarket (1838–46) as 'a gentlemanlike man, and tall in stature' (ibid., 2.203). He died at his home, Shaftesbury Lodge, Shaftesbury Road, Hammersmith, on 2 August 1865. His drawings and art property were sold at Christies on 10 April 1866. MARK POTTLE

Sources J. L. Roget, *A history of the 'Old Water-Colour' Society*, 2 vols. (1891) • *DNB* • Redgrave, *Artists* • Mallalieu, *Watercolour artists*, vol. 1 • A. Wilson, *A dictionary of British marine painters* (1967) • Wood, *Vic. painters*, 2nd edn • private information (2004) • S. W. Fisher, *A dictionary of watercolour painters, 1750–1900* (1972) • Bryan, *Painters* (1903–5) • S. Houfe, *The dictionary of 19th century British book illustrators and caricaturists*, rev. edn (1996) • Graves, *Artists* • d. cert.

Wealth at death under £1000: probate, 6 Nov 1865, *CGPLA Eng. & Wales*

Whidbey, Joseph (1754/5–1833), hydrographer and marine engineer, details of whose parentage and upbringing are unknown, was made a master in the Royal Navy in 1779 at the age of twenty-four. Although his name appears in Steel's navy list for that year his certification is missing from the Admiralty records. He must have soon gained recognition for, in the reduced peacetime navy of 1786, he was appointed master of the *Europa*, the flagship of the American squadron based at Kingston, Jamaica. There during 1787 and 1788 he collaborated with George Vancouver in a hydrographic survey of the seaward approaches to Kingston. The resulting charts were published later under the joint authorship of Vancouver and Whidbey.

Having been chosen master of the *Discovery* by Captain Francis Roberts, Vancouver's predecessor as commander of the Nootka Sound expedition, Whidbey fitted out the ship for an arduous survey of the north-west coast of America. Vancouver, on succeeding to the command in November 1790, confirmed his friend as master, senior warrant officer, and navigator. Vancouver made him his trusted confidant during over four years of stressful voyaging, mainly in uncharted waters. Whidbey was entrusted with the majority of the arduous boat surveys of that fractured coastline. In the first year he surveyed the area north of the present city of Seattle, in recognition of which Vancouver gave a large island the name Whidbey Island, a name it still bears. Responsible for finding safe passages and sheltered anchorages where the *Discovery* could withstand gales, he contributed greatly to the success of the expedition.

Whidbey told Vancouver of his wish to terminate his sea-service and become a master attendant of a naval dockyard. His first appointment as such was at Sheerness in 1799. His skill in salvaging the Dutch frigate *Ambuscade* from a depth of 32 feet on the Nore bank was widely applauded, and Sir Joseph Banks read his account of the feat at a meeting of the Royal Society on 28 April 1803. His election as a fellow of the Royal Society followed in November 1805. A close friendship with another fellow, John Rennie, then developed.

The lack of a safe harbour for the Channel Fleet impelled the Admiralty to send Rennie and Whidbey to survey Plymouth Sound. In 1806 the plan of Rennie, Whidbey, and James Hemmans for a detached breakwater across the rocky shoals in the centre of the sound was accepted in principle but postponed for financial reasons. Eventually, in 1811, orders were given for the commencement and in 1812 Whidbey was appointed superintending engineer at a salary of £1000 p.a. During the project Whidbey lived at Bovisand Lodge opposite the breakwater. In 1814 he was made a freeman of the borough of Plymouth. Whidbey had many friends and, as Samuel Smiles said of him: 'His varied experience had produced rich fruits in a mind naturally robust and vigorous. ..... He was greatly beloved and respected by all who knew him' (Smiles, 2.275–6). He retired in 1830 to Taunton and lived at St James House where he died on 9 October 1833. He never married and he was looked after both at Plymouth and Taunton by Henry and Catherine Oglan. His stone tomb is in St James's churchyard, Taunton, and he is also commemorated by a plaque in St James's Church hall.

JOHN M. NAISH

Sources J. Naish, 'Joseph Whidbey and the building of the Plymouth breakwater', *Mariner's Mirror*, 78 (1992), 37–56 · J. M. Naish, *The interwoven lives of George Vancouver, Archibald Menzies, Joseph Whidbey and Peter Puget* (1996), 65–69, 379–401 · G. Vancouver, *A voyage of discovery to the north Pacific Ocean and round the world, 1791–1795*, ed. W. Kaye Lamb, 4 vols., Hakluyt Society (1984) · J. T. Walbran, *British Columbia coast names* (1971), 527–30 · S. Smiles, *Lives of the engineers*, 2 (1861), 275–6 · J. Whidbey, 'An account of the sinking of the Dutch frigate *Ambuscade*', *PTRS*, 93 (1803), 321–4 · grave inscription, St James's Church, Taunton, Somerset
Archives NL Scot., Rennie archives, boxes 19798–19799
Likenesses J. Ponsford, oils, Inst. CE
Wealth at death over £20,000 residue invested in 3% government stock for great-niece: will, PRO, PROB 11/1828/127

Whiddington, Richard (1885–1970), physicist, was born on 25 November 1885 in London, the eldest of the three children and the only son of Richard Whiddington, schoolteacher, and his wife, Ada Ann, daughter of Richard Fitzgerald of Swords, near Dublin. His mother, who had left Ireland in her teens, had been appointed headmistress of a girls' school in north London before she was twenty. He attended the William Ellis School at Highgate and entered St John's College, Cambridge, as a scholar in 1905. He was placed in the first class in part one of the natural sciences tripos in 1907, and also in part two (physics) in June 1908. By then he had also completed a London (external) BSc. Whiddington started research in the Cavendish Laboratory in September 1908 and in the following year was awarded the Hutchinson studentship by his college. In 1910 he gained an Allen scholarship, and in 1911 a fellowship at St John's and the degree of DSc of London University. He remained in Cambridge, involved in teaching and research, until the outbreak of the First World War.

In September 1914 Whiddington moved to the Royal Flying Corps establishment at Farnborough, where he remained throughout the war as a member of a group which had been given the task of applying the principles of wireless telegraphy to problems of practical communication in the field of battle. Originally gazetted as captain, Royal Flying Corps, Whiddington finished the war as major, Royal Air Force. He married, in London on 9 April 1919, (Laura) Katherine, daughter of Alexander Reoch Grant, a London-based company director. She had served in France with the Women's Auxiliary Army Corps during the last year of the war and had been mentioned in dispatches. They had one son and one daughter.

Whiddington returned to his college fellowship at the end of hostilities and was appointed university lecturer in experimental physics in 1919. But he had no sooner been appointed than he resigned to take up the Cavendish chair of physics in the University of Leeds in October 1919. He was elected FRS in 1925. By that time he had managed to enlarge and improve his small departmental staff, and in 1932 a new building, in the detailed planning of which he had been fully involved, was finally opened.

From Cambridge, during the period 1909–14, Whiddington published sixteen papers describing his researches on the properties of X-rays and electrons. The most important of these established the relation between the velocity of cathode rays and the capacity of the primary X-rays which they produced to excite characteristic X-rays in various radiators. He also established the relation between the cathode ray velocity and the range of those rays in solid absorbers. For a time he continued this general line of research at Leeds, but in 1926, by which time his own department was providing a steady stream of research students, he took up a new field of electron studies seeking correlations with optical rather than with X-radiation. Some thirty papers, published during the period 1926–39, described the results of this difficult and high-quality work, though it is less often noticed in surveys of twentieth-century physics than his earlier work in Cambridge.

Whiddington spent the whole of the Second World War on government service. He was briefly a member of a Royal Air Force officers' selection board, then of the Admiralty scientific research department dealing with the development of radar for the Royal Navy; finally, he was deputy director of scientific research in the Ministry of Supply. For this service he was created CBE in 1946. Shortly before the war ended he had been invited, on behalf of the scientific advisory committee to the cabinet, to become scientific archivist, but when the war ended he decided he must return to his university post. *Science at War* (1947), which he wrote with J. G. Crowther, reflects his activities during his short spell as archivist.

Meanwhile his wife, Katherine, trained with the Auxiliary Territorial Service before the beginning of the Second World War and was senior commander at the York headquarters at the outbreak of hostilities. She was then sent as commandant to Catterick Camp. In 1941 she was appointed MBE. She remained in the service until late in 1945 as controller, and was deputy director, northern command, at the time of her return to civilian life. During the academic sessions 1949–51 Whiddington served as pro-vice-chancellor of Leeds University. He had, indeed, for many years taken a wide and effective part in university affairs generally. After retiring in 1951 he was president of the Physical Society (1952–4) and scientific adviser to the Central Treaty Organization (1959–63). He lived at The Rookery, Holme-next-the-Sea, on the Norfolk coast, from the summer of 1951 until his death. He died at Holme on 7 June 1970. His wife and children survived him.

NORMAN FEATHER, *rev.* ISOBEL FALCONER

Sources N. Feather, *Memoirs FRS*, 17 (1971), 741–56 · *CGPLA Eng. & Wales* (1970)
Archives U. Leeds, Brotherton L., notes and papers | Nuffield Oxf., corresp. with Lord Cherwell · PRO, corresp. with Sir Henry Dale, CAB 127/228 · U. Leeds, Brotherton L., corresp. with E. C. Stoner

Likenesses A. R. Middleton Todd, oils, 1951; known to be at U. Leeds, 1981 · W. Stoneman, photograph, RS; repro. in *Memoirs FRS*, 17 (1971), facing p. 741

Wealth at death £36,584: probate, 6 Oct 1970, *CGPLA Eng. & Wales*

Whiddon, Jacob (d. 1595), sea captain, whose origins are obscure, was by 1578 the master of the *Hope of Greenway* on the influentially supported but unsuccessful colonizing expedition to Newfoundland headed by Sir Humphrey Gilbert. On 30 January 1584 Sir George Carey, governor of the Isle of Wight, told Sir Francis Walsingham that Whiddon reported great preparation in Lisbon for the fitting out of a large fleet and the collecting of ships in other parts of Portugal and Spain 'for the making of the hugest army by sea that ever was set forth by Spain' for the subversion of religion in England (PRO, SP 12/167, no. 53). He was captain of Sir Walter Ralegh's ship *Roebuck* in the fleet commanded by Sir Richard Grenville which sailed from Plymouth on 9 April 1585, but not before privateering a French ship in the channel. Thomas Harriot (c.1560–1621) had tutored Ralegh's sea captains at Durham House in mathematics and navigation and went on this voyage, recording the findings memorably in *A Brief and True Report of the New Found Land* (1588). In June 1586 Ralegh sent out from Plymouth two privateers, the *Serpent* and the *Mary Sparke*, under Whiddon's command and they took prizes including three Portuguese ships.

Famously, Whiddon took the *Roebuck* against the Armada and was used by Drake to escort into Torbay his prize, the *Nuestra Señora del Rosario*, the crippled flagship of Don Pedro de Valdés. The lords lieutenant of Devon took all the shot and powder out of Valdés's ship and sent it to the navy, as well as a piece of ordnance; Whiddon appears to have rustled out of the galleon nine or ten other pieces of ordnance, a quantity of muskets and calivers, and fourteen or fifteen coffers containing cloth of gold and other rich furniture. In 1589 the States complained that the *Roebuck* had taken from a ship of Holland bound for London four butts of sack, and in March it took into Plymouth the *Angel Gabriel* of Holland returning from Spain; goods worth over £1000 were seized. About the same time, the *Roebuck* took goods belonging to merchants of the United Provinces from a Hamburg ship.

In 1590 Whiddon was captain of the *Pilgrim* which took a prize of £500. In 1591 he served gallantly in the assault by Spanish ships on the *Revenge* off the Azores and stayed all night to help Grenville, escaping in the morning when he was being 'hunted like a hare amongst many ravenous hounds' (Hakluyt, 7.44). In 1594, when Whiddon was arrested at the suit of Dutch merchants, Sir Robert Cecil wrote to the judges of the admiralty court requesting his prompt release, 'for I assure you it concerns Sir Walter Ralegh very near' (BL, Lansdowne MS 158, fol. 395). For Ralegh was sending Whiddon to explore the River Orinoco and its tributaries in Guiana in the search for El Dorado. In preparation, Thomas Harriot had provided Ralegh's ships with new tables from observations of the pole star and sun and laid down rules for the use of the improved instruments of his devising (BL, Add. MS 6788,

fols. 468–492). Whiddon's journey had no very promising outcome. After receiving him with apparent amity, the governor of Trinidad treacherously ambushed eight of his men when Whiddon left temporarily to see a sister ship, the *Edward Bonaventure*. Meeting many other unexpected impediments, Whiddon returned home.

Nevertheless Ralegh sailed for Guiana early in 1595. Arriving at Trinidad on 22 March, he sent Whiddon to speak with the Spaniards who kept guard at Port of Spain and gather information about Guiana. Ralegh secured his base on the island by firing the Spanish settlement at San Josef and capturing the governor, Antonio de Berreo. He put to death all the Spaniards he caught, but spared Berreo and his second in command for the intelligence which they might provide. Once in Guiana, Whiddon and the ship's surgeon went to discover what they could by land when floods prevented Ralegh entering the River Caroli by water; they brought him stones like sapphires, and upon his return to England in August 1595 he declared the empire of Guiana would afford queen and country 'no less quantities of treasure, than the King of Spain hath in all the Indies, east or west' (Hakluyt, 10.351). Whiddon, however, had died in Trinidad on the journey home; Ralegh declared him 'a man most honest and valiant' (ibid.).

G. R. BATHO

Sources W. Ralegh, *The discovery of Guiana* (1928) · *CSP for.*, 1588–9 · D. B. Quinn, ed., *The voyages and colonising enterprises of Sir Humphrey Gilbert*, 2 vols., Hakluyt Society, 2nd ser., 83–4 (1940) · D. B. Quinn, ed., *The Roanoke voyages, 1584–1590: documents to illustrate the English voyages to North America under the patent granted to Walter Raleigh in 1584*, 2 vols., Hakluyt Society, 2nd ser., 104, 105 (1955) · J. K. Laughton, ed., *State papers relating to the defeat of the Spanish Armada, anno 1588*, 2 vols., Navy RS, 1–2 (1894); facs. edn (1987) · R. C. Anderson, ed., *The book of examinations, 1601–1602*, Southampton RS, 26 (1926) · K. R. Andrews, *Elizabethan privateering: English privateering during the Spanish war, 1585–1603* (1964) · K. R. Andrews, *Trade, plunder and settlement: maritime enterprise and the genesis of the British empire, 1480–1630* (1984) · E. Edwards, *The life of Sir Walter Ralegh … together with his letters*, 2 vols. (1868) · R. Hakluyt, *The principal navigations, voyages, traffiques and discoveries of the English nation*, 2nd edn, 3 vols. (1598–1600); repr. 12 vols., Hakluyt Society, extra ser., 1–12 (1903–5) · *The letters of Sir Walter Ralegh*, ed. A. Latham and J. Youings (1999) · G. Mattingly, *The defeat of the Spanish Armada* (1959) · N. L. Williams, *Sir Walter Ralegh* (1965) · BL, Lansdowne MS 158, fol. 395

Whiddon, Sir John (d. 1576), judge, was the eldest son of John Whiddon of Chagford, Devon, where his family had long been established. His mother, whose maiden name was Rugg, was also a native of Chagford. He was admitted to the Inner Temple, probably between 1510 and 1515, though his presence is not recorded before 1519, when he was fined for a moot-fail and was then put out of commons for misbehaviour. Already by 1520 he is mentioned as an attorney in the court of requests, and in the poll-tax assessment of 1523 he was reckoned to be worth £40 in goods, the same as Thomas Audley and Nicholas Hare. He was elected autumn reader in 1528, but the reading was postponed until Lent 1529; it was well attended by future legal dignitaries, including Audley, Hare, and John Baldwin. From 1530 he was a justice of the peace for Devon.

Whiddon was twice married. His first wife was Anne, daughter of Sir William Hollis; they had a daughter. His second was Elizabeth, daughter and heir of William Shilston; they had a large family of six sons and seven daughters. Whiddon gave a second reading in 1536, and served as treasurer of his inn from 1538 to 1539. He was the most senior of the last general call of serjeants projected by Henry VIII; the writs abated on the demise of the crown, but Whiddon and the others were duly created in February 1547. In 1551, on the death of fellow Devonian John Harris, he was made one of the king's serjeants; and on 4 October 1553 he was appointed a justice of the queen's bench. In 1555 he became the secondary justice, and he was knighted the same year. He is reputed to have been the first judge to ride to Westminster Hall on a horse rather than a mule, as was the previous custom. His judicial appointment was renewed by Elizabeth I, and he remained in office until his death on 27 January 1576, which probably occurred at Chagford where he was buried and where there is a monumental inscription. His estates included several tin-workings in the Devon stannaries.   J. H. BAKER

Sources Foss, *Judges* · F. A. Inderwick and R. A. Roberts, eds., *A calendar of the Inner Temple records*, 1 (1896) · Baker, *Serjeants*, 169, 543 · Sainty, *Judges*, 29 · PRO, REQ 1/104, fol. 26*v* · BL, Harley MS 1691, fol. 56 · will, PRO, PROB 11/57, sig. 57 · PRO, C 142/173/26, 45 · monument, Chagford church, Devon

Whiffen, Thomas (1819–1904), manufacturer of fine chemicals, was born in London on 28 July 1819, the son of a cabinet-maker, William Whiffen (1790–1858), and his wife, Mary Ann. Nothing is known of Whiffen's education and early days; as a young man he worked as a clerk to a coal merchant for some time before training as a pharmacist. Once qualified it seems likely that he was employed in the business of a chemist and druggist, of whom there were many. On 29 July 1845 he married Faith, daughter of George White of Penzance; there were three sons of the marriage, Thomas Joseph (1850–1931), William George (1852–1934), and Alfred Herbert (1855–1893).

In 1854 Whiffen joined a small fine chemicals manufacturing business, owned and managed by Edward Herring and Jacob Hulle and located in Battersea, then an industrial area of London much favoured for its proximity to the river. Four years later Herring withdrew, selling his share of the business to his partners, and in 1868 Hulle retired so that the business became wholly that of Whiffen. Although he had a scientific training, Whiffen's strength in business lay rather with his commercial sense and his ability to see and seize opportunities in the marketplace, both at home and abroad, than with research and innovation. It was not until 1884 that Whiffen established a permanent laboratory and even then its work was limited to testing and quality control.

In the second half of the nineteenth century Whiffens was one of the five fine chemical businesses which together came to represent what was described by William Baker (of May and Baker) as 'the backbone of the London chemical trade' (*Chemist and Druggist*, 11 Nov 1893, 699). All were chiefly concerned with the processing and purification of raw materials, both vegetable and mineral, and many of them imported. The products were then supplied in bulk to chemists, druggists, and the medical profession to make up their own pharmaceutical preparations and remedies. After 1864 when the first *British Pharmacopoeia*, setting common standards for medicines and their compounds, was published, meeting the specifications set (noted as BP) became of increasing importance.

Through the 1850s and 1860s Whiffen's product range included quinine and other extracts of bark, nux vomica, strychnine (the trade in which Whiffen claimed a pioneering role), medicinal and aromatic oils, acids, alkalis, and epsom salts. The business also built up a large export trade, particularly with the British colonies. Success at international exhibitions—Whiffens won awards for its alkaloids and salts at Paris in 1879, Sydney in 1879–80, and Melbourne in 1880, and for its cinchona, strychnine, brucin, and salicin in Calcutta in 1883—enhanced the reputation of Whiffens' products. Salicin, discovered in 1876 to be an effective treatment for acute rheumatism, is a good example of Whiffen's commercial perspicacity; when a source of the willow containing salicin was discovered in Belgium, Whiffen moved quickly to secure access to it, joining with the Belgians to create the St Amand Manufacturing Company, which, after extracting the salicin, sold the willows to the local basket-making industry.

As they grew to adulthood, Whiffen's sons joined him in the business. The youngest, Alfred, was sent to Australia to develop the market; he died there in 1893. The two elder sons, Thomas, who had studied at the Royal College of Chemistry, and William, both became partners in 1887. At the same time the Aldersgate Chemical Works was acquired and the manufacturing business moved from Battersea to Aldersgate's site at Southall. Also acquired in 1887 was the chemical business of George Atkinson, established some two hundred years earlier and with a fine reputation for drug grinding, oil pressing, and saltpetre refining.

By the 1890s Whiffens had become one of the leading fine chemical refiners and dealers and Whiffen himself a much respected figure, with a reputation for honesty and fair dealing combined with shrewdness and commercial acumen. Competitive conditions in the industry in the late nineteenth century led to the creation of cartel arrangements covering many of its products and in these Whiffen played an important role. By 1900 the firm was a significant signatory to agreements establishing prices and quotas for salicin, bromine, caffeine, camphor, iodine preparations, and strychnine.

Whiffen died at his home, Cerris House, West Hill, Wandsworth, on 27 March 1904. Eight years later his two sons, Thomas and William, converted the business into a company. It continued to manufacture and trade independently until 1947 when it was acquired by Fisons.

JUDY SLINN

Sources J. Liebenau, 'Whiffen, Thomas', *DBB* · *Chemist and Druggist* (2 April 1904) · *Pharmaceutical Journal*, 18 (1904), 487 · P. J. T.

Morris and C. A. Russell, *Archives of the British chemical industry, 1750–1914: a handlist* (1988), 203–7 · d. cert. · m. cert.
Archives LMA · NRA, papers · Wellcome L.
Likenesses photograph, priv. coll.
Wealth at death £335,309 0s. 3d.: resworn probate, 8 Aug 1904, *CGPLA Eng. & Wales*

Whillans, Donald Desbrow (1933–1985), mountaineer, was born on 18 May 1933 at St Mary's Hospital, Salford, the first of two children of Thomas Whillans (1906–1986), a grocer, and his wife, Mary Burrows (1909–1985). He attended state schools in Salford and served his apprenticeship as a plumber, studying for but not completing City and Guilds Institute examinations. His early involvement in hiking began while he was at Broughton modern school. He joined the Boy Scouts, but also began a series of extended solo hikes in the Peak District. The hikes continued during his apprenticeship and he did his first rock climb in 1950, untutored and with completely inappropriate equipment, at Shining Clough in Derbyshire.

Whillans became a very good climber very quickly, at a time when the sport was primarily a middle- and upper middle-class activity characterized by protracted apprenticeships. He first met Joe Brown (*b.* 1930), another plumber, climbing at the Roaches (near Leek, Staffordshire) in 1951. The two went on to form through most of the 1950s a partnership, though not a close or lasting friendship, which had a revolutionary effect on British climbing. Climbing together, and with others, they created a series of British rock climbs that were of the highest quality and difficulty, especially given the equipment and technique available at the time.

Later in 1951 Whillans, Brown, and ten others, mostly working-class climbers from Manchester, came together to form the élite Rock and Ice Club. The reputation of the club, and its members, lasted well into the 1960s and influenced several subsequent generations of climbers. These were the 'hard men' who made first ascents of climbs with reputations that terrorized other climbers, and who also knew how to look after themselves in a fight (Whillans's nickname, the Villain, derives from the latter). And Whillans was the 'hardest' of them all—'the 'ard little man in the flat 'at'. The short stature and stocky build of both Whillans and Brown led to some bizarre physiological theories regarding the physique necessary for climbing at the highest level.

Whillans made his first trip to the Alps in 1952, and in the following years he was involved in a number of major first ascents and first British ascents. In 1953 he became a founding member of the élite Alpine Climbing Group, dedicated to raising the standard of British alpinism. On his first Himalayan expedition, to Masherbrum in 1957, he turned back just 300 feet from the summit after some extremely difficult climbing. On an expedition to Trivor in 1960 he suffered from a mild attack of poliomyelitis. But his account of his return trip ('Solo by motorcycle from Rawalpindi to Lancashire') is a small gem of adventure travel literature. The writing is understood and full of good humour, anticipating his subsequent lecture style,

Donald Desbrow Whillans (1933–1985), by Doug Scott

and leaving the reader wishing that he had written more. His autobiography (*Don Whillans: Portrait of a Mountaineer*, 1971) was compiled with Alick Ormerod from a series of interviews.

Between these two expeditions Whillans married Audrey Whittall on 24 May 1958. She was a cutter in a clothing factory, did some climbing with Don, and was invariably tolerant of some of the excesses of his social life. In 1960 they moved to Crawshawbooth in Rossendale, Lancashire, where Whillans had been evacuated for six months during the Second World War; and in 1976 they opened a guest house at Penmaen-mawr in Caernarvonshire.

After the early 1960s Whillans did little serious rock climbing in Britain and focused on expeditions—Aiguille Poincenot (1962) and the central tower of Paine (1963), both in Patagonia, and Gauri Sankar in the Himalayas (1964). The latter involved Whillans in some very difficult face climbing at high altitude, but he turned back before the summit because of avalanche risk and his partner's risk of frostbite. By the late 1960s he had visited the Andes (Huandoy) and Yosemite, California, worked as an instructor in Switzerland, was a popular lecturer, and had begun to design equipment (for example, the Whillans harness for climbing, and the Whillans box for camping in extreme weather).

Whillans's greatest mountaineering success came in 1970, when he and Dougal Haston climbed the south face of Annapurna, the first major face climb on an 8000 metre peak. The following year he and Haston reached the highest point (27,500 feet) on the south-west face of Everest, but failed to reach even that height in bad weather on their return in 1972. He was involved in the ascents of Roraima (H. McInnes, *Climb to the Lost World*, 1974), and Torre Egger, and in attempts on Tirich Mir (1975), Shivling (1981), and both Cerro Torre and Broad Peak in 1983. It should be noted that all of Whillans's climbs were accomplished in spite of the fact that he suffered from vertigo.

Whillans's achievements were honoured by his being given the freedom of the city of Salford on 29 July 1971. He was presented with a commemorative plate by the mayor of Rawtenstall on 23 September 1970, to celebrate the success on Annapurna. The British Mountaineering Council appointed him as a vice-president (1973–6), and subsequently put his name forward to be considered for a queen's honour. Dennis Gray, general secretary of the council from 1974 to 1989, suggests that Whillans was 'perhaps the greatest British mountaineer of his or any other generation'. However, Gray notes that his name was withdrawn from consideration by the prime minister's office after a drunken incident involving a fight with the police resulted in a large fine.

Whillans's occasional bouts of misbehaviour, in part a result of drinking and a feisty nature, but also a consequence of his frequently being challenged because of his small size and large reputation, stand in stark contrast to his enormous good sense and competence as a climber and the great affection in which he was held, and is remembered. The repeated stories about Whillans reached mythical proportions. Mike Thompson's article 'Out with the boys again', on the successful Everest southwest face expedition in 1975 (an expedition to which Whillans was, perhaps unfairly, not invited) describes 'Whillans jokes':

> Happy hours were passed recounting those epics in which Whillans would gradually unfold an account of his rectitude and forbearance in the face of seemingly unbearable chicanery and provocation. Like some Greek tragedy the sequence of events would move inexorably to the inevitable, fateful conclusion. All such tales led to the same final and literal punch-line: 'So I 'it 'im'.

Examples of typical 'Whillans jokes' can be found in Tom Patey's 'A short walk with Whillans' (1963), Jim Curran's 'Whillans!' (1985), and Dennis Gray's 'Simply Whillanesque' (1993). But there are also many stories about aspects of Whillans's character and climbing ability that commanded enormous respect, such as the ones where he risked his own life in attempts to rescue others—Brian Nally on the north face of the Eiger in 1962, Harish Bahuguna on Everest in 1971, and Mick Coffey on Torre Egger in 1974; and where he took care not to place others at risk by pushing for the summit when they were fatigued (for example Masherbrum, 1957).

Don Whillans died of a heart attack while sleeping at a friend's house at 30 Bagley Wood Road, Kennington, Oxfordshire, on 4 August 1985. He had just returned from the Dolomites after another epic motor cycle journey, riding in rain from Paris to the channel. He was cremated at Bangor crematorium, north Wales. His wife, Audrey, scattered his ashes on Snowdon—within sight of Clogwyn du'r Arddu, where he had made a number of his most significant rock climbs. The British Mountaineering Council started a Don Whillans memorial fund later that year—including a 'Buy a pint for Don' appeal—and purchased Rockall Cottage below the Roaches. Audrey Whillans, who first met Don at the Roaches, opened the climbing hut in his name in January 1993.   PETER DONNELLY

Sources D. Whillans and A. Ormerod, *Don Whillans: portrait of a mountaineer* (1971) • private information (2004) • J. Perrin, *The villain: a life of Don Whillans* (2001) • *Mountain*, 105 (1985), 16–17 • D. Whillans, 'Solo by motorcycle from Rawalpindi to Lancashire', in W. Noyce, *To the unknown mountain* (1962), appx A, 157–71 [repr. as 'Rawalpindi to Rawtenstall', in J. Perrin, ed., *Mirrors in the cliffs*

(1983), 308–18] • D. Whillans, 'Interview', *Mountain*, 20 (1972), 24–8 • D. Gray, 'Simply Whillanesque', *Tight rope! The fun of climbing* (1993), 63–102 • J. Curran, 'Whillans ! An appreciation', *Mountain*, 106 (1985), 30–33 • D. Walker, 'Into the nineties', *The first fifty years of the British Mountaineering Council*, ed. G. Milburn, D. Walker, and K. Wilson (1997), 76–96 • D. Gray, 'The eighties', *The first fifty years of the British Mountaineering Council*, ed. G. Milburn, D. Walker, and K. Wilson (1997), 66–75 • T. Patey, 'A short walk with Whillans', *One man's mountains: essays and verses* (1971), 183–92 • M. Thompson, 'Out with the boys again', *Mountain*, 50 (1976), 32–3 • J. Brown, *The hard years* (1967) • C. Bonington, *Annapurna south face* (1971) • C. Bonington, *Everest south west face* (1973) • W. Unsworth, *Encyclopaedia of mountaineering*, 2nd edn (1992) • K. Wilson and M. Pearson, 'Everest: post-mortem of an international expedition', *Mountain*, 17 (1971), 10–29 • D. Scott, 'To rest is not to conquer', *Mountain*, 23 (1972), 10–18 • b. cert. • d. cert.

Archives FILM BFI NFTVA, documentary footage

Likenesses D. Scott, photograph, Alpine Club, London [*see illus.*]

Wealth at death under £40,000: administration, 15 Jan 1987, *CGPLA Eng. & Wales*

Whincop, Thomas (1697–1730), playwright and literary biographer, was the only son of Dr Thomas Whincop (*d.* 1713), rector of St Mary Abchurch, and Judith Hastings (*fl.* 1694–1712), of Shadwell in Middlesex. He was born in London on 2 June 1697, and baptized three days later in his father's church. Among his relatives may be numbered Dr John Whincop (*d.* 1653), rector of St Martin-in-the-Fields between 1642 and 1643, and Samuel Whincop (*d.* 1660), vicar of Cheshunt. Between 1706 and 1709 Whincop attended Merchant Taylors' School in London. He then moved to a school in Bishop's Stortford, before gaining admission to Corpus Christi, Cambridge. In 1713 Whincop's father died, leaving instructions that the family inheritance, invested 'upon Mortgages or upon East-India Bonds or any other new Securities', should be held in trust until his son's twenty-fourth birthday. After graduating BA in 1719, Whincop had every expectation of inheriting this estate. However, before the funds could be released, the entire fortune disappeared in the South Sea stock crash of 1720–21. At an unknown date he married a woman named Martha (*d.* 1782).

Little is known of the final years of Whincop's life. He died at home in Totteridge, Hertfordshire, on 1 September 1730, having spent his final months as a lodger in the house of a Mr Porter. The parish register of St Andrew's Church, Totteridge, where he was buried, describes Whincop as a 'Poet', yet his only known drama, *Scanderbeg, or, Love and Liberty*, remained unpublished until 1747. The tragedy, which dramatizes the struggle of George Castriot to defend Albania from Turkish conquest, takes as its source the 1721 English translation of *Scanderbeg the Great* by Anne de La Roche-Guilhem. In the light of the patriot whig opposition to Walpole, Whincop's dramatic portrait of the Albanian hero whose 'conqu'ring sword / Oppos'd the torrent of the tyrant's power' (*Scanderbeg*, 16) may well have been intended as a propaganda piece. However, Whincop's play was never performed, John Rich telling Whincop's widow that 'it will by no means do for the Stage' (ibid., preface).

More than a decade after its rejection by Rich, Martha Whincop finally succeeded in publishing her husband's play by subscription. Appended to the printed edition of 1747 is 'A compleat list of all the English dramatic poets, and of all the plays ever printed in the English language', illustrated with a series of small medallion engravings by Nathaniel Parr. This 'List', which contains details of over 1500 plays and 350 authors, draws heavily upon Gerard Langbaine's *Account of the English Dramatic Poets* (1691), and Giles Jacob's *Poetical Register* (1720–21). However, as Whincop died in 1730, the extent of his involvement in its compilation is uncertain. Internal evidence suggests that the 'List' was revised and expanded by John Mottley, the entry on Mottley himself being full of personal anecdote.

Following the publication of *Scanderbeg* in 1747, Martha Whincop found work in London as a linen draper. She died on 21 March 1782 and was buried near her husband in the north-east corner of the churchyard at Totteridge.

CHARLES BRAYNE

Sources [J. Mottley], *A compleat list of all the English dramatic poets*, pubd with T. Whincop, *Scanderbeg* (1747) · PRO, PROB 11/547, sig. 167 [Dr Thomas Whincop, father] · Venn, *Alum. Cant.* · S. G. Barratt, *A short history of Totteridge in the county of Hertford* (1934) · J. E. Cussons, *History of Hertfordshire*, 3 vols. (1870–81); facs. repr. (1972) · W. H. Challen, *St Mary Abchurch, London: transcription of marriages* (1558–1736) (privately printed, 1927) · C. J. Robinson, ed., *A register of the scholars admitted into Merchant Taylors' School, from AD 1562 to 1874*, 2 (1883) · Mrs E. P. Hart, ed., *Merchant Taylors' School register, 1561–1934*, 2 vols. (1936) · R. Masters, *The history of the College of Corpus Christi and the B. Virgin Mary … in the University of Cambridge* (1753) · G. J. Armytage, ed., *Allegations for marriage licences issued by the vicar-general of the archbishop of Canterbury, July 1687 to June 1694*, Harleian Society, 31 (1890)

Wealth at death fortune destroyed by South Sea stock crash: Whincop, prologue; Barratt, *Short history*

Whinfield, John Rex (1901–1966), textile chemist, was born on 16 February 1901 at Brambletye, Cavendish Road, Sutton, Surrey, the son of John Henry Richard Whinfield, mechanical engineer, and his wife, Edith Matthews. He was educated at Merchant Taylors' School and Gonville and Caius College, Cambridge, where he received a third class in part one of the natural sciences tripos (1921) and a second in part two in 1922 (chemistry). In the latter year, on 1 November, he married Mayo Elva (*d.* 1946), daughter of the Revd Frederick William Walker.

At Cambridge, Whinfield had studied the chemistry of man-made fibres, and on leaving university spent a year working, without pay, in the London laboratory of C. F. Cross and E. J. Bevan, who had first made viscose rayon in 1892. In 1923 he joined the Calico Printers' Association as a research chemist, at a time when the search was on in many laboratories for new synthetic fibres.

In the late 1930s, with Wallace H. Carothers's nylon nearing manufacture, Whinfield looked for other classes of polymer which might yield a textile fibre. Assisted by James Dickson, he discovered how to condense terephthalic acid and ethylene glycol to yield a substance which could be drawn into a fibre. (Carothers had thought of investigating this route but had eventually concentrated on his polyamides.) The Whinfield–Dickson patent was filed in July 1941, but was suppressed for wartime reasons until 1946. It was then examined for commercial potential by both ICI (who eventually marketed it under the name

Terylene) and DuPont (who called it Dacron). World manufacturing rights eventually fell to ICI.

During the Second World War Whinfield served as an assistant director of chemical research in the Ministry of Supply. He joined ICI in 1947, first in its plastics division and then in the fibres division, a position which involved worldwide travel.

Despite the importance of Terylene and its universal use as a textile fibre, Whinfield received little public honour for his discovery, his appointment as CBE (1954) seeming hardly adequate for his achievement. Possibly he might have published more, and not been content with the record of work provided by patents. His colleagues honoured him, however, by honorary fellowship of the Textile Institute (1955), and the Perkin medal of the Society of Dyers and Colourists (1956). The University of York gave his name to its chemical library and created some Whinfield travelling fellowships. Following the death of his first wife Whinfield married, on 31 July 1947, Nora Eileen Dawes (*b.* 1906/7), former wife of Reginald John Dawes, and daughter of Eric Hodder, architect. She survived Whinfield, who died at his home, 2 Castle Gardens, Dorking, Surrey, on 6 July 1966.

FRANK GREENAWAY, *rev.*

Sources *The Times* (7 July 1966) · P. C. Allen, 'John Rex Whinfield, 1901–1966', *Chemistry in Britain*, 3 (1967), 26 · b. cert. · d. cert. · m. certs. [1922, 1947]

Wealth at death £43,677: probate, 7 Sept 1966, *CGPLA Eng. & Wales*

Whinney, Frederick (1829–1916), accountant, was born on 6 October 1829 in London, the son of Thomas Whinney (1793–1853), a licensed victualler turned livery stable keeper, and his wife, Sarah, *née* Friberg, of German parentage. Little is known of his early life except that he appears to have assisted with the preparation of the stable's accounts during the 1850s, while an entry in a London trade directory for 1856 recorded a Frederick Whinney who advertised as a ship and insurance broker—a possible connection which may have arisen from the fact that his grandfather had been a shipbroker in South Shields and his uncle continued in this business.

From December 1849 Whinney was employed as a clerk by Harding and Pullein, a City firm of accountants founded in 1848 by Robert Palmer Harding and Edmund Pullein. In November 1857 Whinney, then the senior clerk, was admitted to the partnership, and two years later the style was altered to include his name, as Harding, Pullein, Whinney, and Gibbons. When in 1883 Harding left the practice to take the post of chief official receiver, Whinney became the senior partner. At this time there were four partners (the other three being William Hurlbatt, John Smith, and Stanley Harding) and a possible amalgamation with Quilter, Ball & Co. was discussed in December 1883, partly to prevent the latter from merging with their rivals, Turquand, Youngs & Co., although in the event no union materialized.

'Joining the profession at a very favourable time, Mr Whinney soon made a great reputation both as a liquidator and an auditor, and his practice was certainly one of the largest in his day' (*The Accountant*, 582). As a liquidator, Whinney could boast thirty appointments in 1866, and when Harding retired he completed the winding-up of Overend, Gurney & Co., a task not completed until 1893. Unlike the pioneers of the accountancy profession, who prospered almost exclusively as insolvency experts, Whinney found that he was increasingly called upon to perform audit work. The Birmingham and Midland Bank (1885), Equitable Life Assurance Society (1894), Union of London and Smith's Bank (both 1883), and the Union Bank of Australia (1880) were among Whinney's audit clients. The fee income of his firm did not fluctuate greatly during the period of his senior partnership (rising from £12,470 in 1883 to £15,015 in 1900 and £16,864 in 1904), as the era of great insolvency assignments was largely at an end and regular audit fees had come to constitute a higher proportion of earnings, increasing from 20 per cent in 1884 to 53 per cent by 1900.

It was common at this time for leading accountants to be appointed to the boards of major companies, and Whinney became a director of the London, Tilbury and Southend Railway (the firm acted as its auditors from 1892). He was deputed by the English Institute of Chartered Accountants in 1898 to give evidence for the Companies Bill then in committee with the House of Lords. In 1877 he had served on the parliamentary commission to inquire into the parlous state of Oxford University's finances, which prompted the invitation to audit the accounts of All Souls College, followed by those of the Oxford University Fund, the Randolph Hotel, and the Oxford Electric Lighting Company.

Whinney was involved in the efforts to establish accountancy as a recognized profession and became a leading member of the Institute of Accountants in London. William Turquand proposed him for its council in April 1877 as part of a more forceful policy designed to counter the rival Society of Accountants in England. In the event, the two bodies combined their campaign and were granted a royal charter in May 1880. Whinney followed Arthur Cooper as the third president in 1884 and held that office for four years. In 1896 he proposed that the institute sponsor a bill to create a monopoly for the profession. Under its terms, the right to practise as an accountant was to be limited to members of the Institute of Chartered Accountants and the Society of Accountants and Auditors, together with all those at the time of the legislation who had been in business for three years. The scheme was defeated by 1046 to 433 votes.

For three years Whinney acted as treasurer of the London chamber of commerce; he also served as an officer in the 3rd volunteer battalion of the Middlesex regiment, and rose to the rank of major. Ernest Cooper recalled him as a man of strong character and dignified bearing: 'he showed me much kindness … He was, I think, proud of the commanding position his services to our profession had brought him. There was in him a touch of hauteur derived perhaps from his military service' (Cooper, 48).

Whinney was twice married. His first wife, whom he married in 1854, was Sarah Elizabeth Saltmarsh; they had four children before her death from cholera in 1860. His second marriage was to Emma Sophia Morley (*d.* 1891); of their ten children, Arthur (1861–1927) and Frank Toller both entered the firm, and the former became its senior partner. Frederick Whinney died, aged eighty-six, on 15 May 1916 at his home, 85 Avenue Road, Regent's Park, London. EDGAR JONES

Sources E. Jones, *Accountancy and the British economy, 1840–1980: the evolution of Ernst & Whinney* (1981) · E. Jones, 'Whinney, Frederick', *DBB* · *The Accountant* (20 May 1916), 582 · H. Howitt and others, eds., *The history of the Institute of Chartered Accountants in England and Wales, 1880–1965, and of its founder accountancy bodies, 1870–1880* (1966) · E. Cooper, 'Fifty-seven years in an accountant's office', *Proceedings of the Autumnal Meeting* [Institute of Chartered Accountants in England and Wales] (1921), 49 · d. cert.
Archives Institute of Chartered Accountants in England and Wales, London · NRA, papers
Likenesses W. Llewellyn, oils, Ernst & Young, London
Wealth at death £98,434 4s. 3d.: probate, 6 July 1916, *CGPLA Eng. & Wales*

Whinyates, Sir Edward Charles (1782–1865), army officer, born on 6 May 1782, was the third son of Major Thomas Whinyates (1755–1806) of Abbotsleigh, Devon, and Catherine, daughter of Sir Thomas Frankland, bt, of Thirkleby Park, Yorkshire. He was educated at Mr Newcombe's school, Hackney, and at the Royal Military Academy, Woolwich, which he entered as a cadet on 16 May 1796. He was commissioned as second lieutenant in the Royal Artillery on 1 March 1798, and became lieutenant on 2 October 1799. He served in the expedition of that year to The Helder, and in the expedition to Madeira in 1801. When Madeira was evacuated at the peace of Amiens, he went with his company to Jamaica, and was made adjutant. On 8 July 1805 he was promoted second captain, and came home. He served as adjutant to the artillery in the attack on Copenhagen in 1807. In the following year he was posted to D troop of the horse artillery.

In February 1810 Whinyates embarked with his troop for the Peninsula, but the *Camilla* transport, on which he was sailing, nearly foundered, and had to put back. Owing to this, D troop did not take the field as a unit until 1811, but Whinyates was present at Busaco on 27 September 1810, and acted as adjutant to the officer commanding the artillery. He was at Albuera on 16 May 1811 with four guns, and there are letters of his describing this and subsequent actions. He and his troop took part in the cavalry affair at Usagre on 25 May, and in the actions at Fuentes-Guinaldo and Aldea de Ponte on 25 and 27 September.

In 1812 the troop was with Hill's corps on the Tagus; at Ribera, on 24 July, Whinyates made such good use of two guns that the French commander Lallemand enquired his name, and sent him a message: 'Tell that brave man that if it had not been for him, I should have beaten your cavalry' (F. T. Whinyates, 63). The captain of D troop died at Madrid on 22 October, and for the next four months Whinyates was in command of it. It distinguished itself at San Muñoz on 17 November, at the close of the retreat from Burgos, five out of its six guns being injured. General Long, who commanded the cavalry to which it was attached, afterwards wrote of the troop that he had never witnessed 'more exemplary conduct in quarters, nor more distinguished zeal and gallantry in the field'.

On 24 January 1813 Whinyates became captain, and consequently left the Peninsula in March. His service there won him no promotion, as brevet rank was not given at that time to second captains. In 1814 he was appointed to the 2nd rocket troop, and he commanded it at Waterloo. Wellington, who did not believe in rockets, ordered that they should be left behind; when he was told that this would break Whinyates's heart, he replied: 'Damn his heart; let my orders be obeyed.' However, Whinyates eventually obtained leave to bring them into the field, together with his six guns. When Ponsonby's brigade charged D'Erlon's corps, he followed it with his rocket sections, and fired several volleys of ground rockets with good effect against the French cavalry. In the course of the day he had three horses shot under him, was struck on the leg, and severely wounded in the left arm. He received a brevet majority and the Waterloo medal, and afterwards the Peninsular silver medal with clasps for Busaco and Albuera.

At the end of 1815 the rocket troop went to England to be reduced, and Whinyates was appointed to a troop of drivers in the army of occupation, with which he remained until 1818. He commanded H troop of horse artillery from 1823 to 22 July 1830, when he became regimental lieutenant-colonel. He was knighted in 1823 and made CB in 1831. He had command of the horse artillery at Woolwich from November 1834 to May 1840, and of the artillery in the northern district for eleven years afterwards, having become regimental colonel on 23 November 1841.

On 1 April 1852 Whinyates was appointed director-general of artillery, and on 19 August commandant at Woolwich, where he remained until 1 June 1856. He had been promoted major-general on 20 June 1854, and became lieutenant-general on 7 June 1856 and general on 10 December 1864. He was made KCB on 18 May 1860. He had become colonel-commandant of a battalion on 1 April 1855, and was transferred to the horse artillery on 22 July 1864. He was 'an officer whose ability, zeal, and services have hardly been surpassed in the regiment' (Duncan, 2.37).

In 1827 Whinyates had married Elizabeth, only daughter of Samuel Compton of Wood End, North Riding, Yorkshire. They had no children. He died at Dorset Villa, Cheltenham, on 25 December 1865. Whinyates had five brothers, of whom four served with distinction in the army and navy.

The eldest, **Thomas Whinyates** (1778–1857), naval officer, born on 7 September 1778, entered the navy as first-class volunteer on 24 May 1793. He commanded a boat in the attack and capture of Martinique in March 1794, and assisted in boarding the French frigate *Bienvenue*. He was also present at the capture of St Lucia and Guadeloupe. He was in Lord Bridport's action of 23 June 1795, and in that of Sir John Warren on 12 October 1798. He was commissioned as lieutenant on 7 September 1799, and as commander on 16 May 1805. In April 1807 he was appointed to the *Frolic*, an eighteen-gun brig of 384 tons. He took

her out to the West Indies, and spent five years there, being present at the recapture of Martinique on 24 February 1809 and of Guadeloupe on 5 February 1810.

Whinyates was made post captain on 12 August 1812, and on his way home, in charge of convoy, he was attacked on 18 October by the United States sloop *Wasp* of 434 tons. The *Frolic* had been much damaged in a gale, and after an action of fifty minutes, in which more than half her crew were killed or wounded, including her commander, she was boarded and taken. She was recovered, and the *Wasp* was taken by the *Poictiers* the same day. The court martial which tried Whinyates for the loss of his ship acquitted him most honourably, as having done all that could be done. In 1815 he was appointed to a corvette, but she was paid off at the peace. He was promoted rear-admiral on 1 October 1846, and died unmarried at Cheltenham on 15 March 1857. He received the silver war medal with five clasps.

The fourth son of Thomas Whinyates, **George Barrington Whinyates** (1783–1808), naval officer, born on 31 August 1783, entered the navy as first-class volunteer in 1797, and saw much active service, chiefly in the Mediterranean. In 1805, as lieutenant in the *Spencer*, seventy-four guns, he served under Nelson in the blockade of Toulon, the voyage to the West Indies, and the blockade of Cadiz, but his ship, which formed part of the inshore squadron, was sent to Gibraltar for provisions three days before Trafalgar. He was in Duckworth's action off St Domingo on 6 February 1806. In 1807 he commanded the *Bergère* sloop in the Mediterranean and the channel. He died of consumption, brought on by hardship and exposure, on 5 August 1808.

The fifth son, **Frederick William Whinyates** (1793–1881), army officer in the East India Company, born on 29 August 1793, was commissioned as second lieutenant in the Royal Engineers on 14 December 1811, and became lieutenant on 1 July 1812. He was present at the bombardment of Algiers on 27 August 1816, being in command of a detachment of sappers and miners on the *Impregnable*. He left a graphic account of the bombardment (*Royal Engineers' Journal*, 11.26). He received the medal. He served with the army of occupation in France, and made reports on some of the French fortresses (later acquired by the Royal Engineers' Institute, Chatham). He was commanding royal engineer with the field force in New Brunswick when the disputed territory was invaded by the state of Maine in 1839. He was promoted lieutenant-colonel on 9 November 1846, and colonel on 16 December 1854. He retired as major-general on 13 January 1855. He married, on 25 January 1830, Sarah Marianne, second daughter of Charles Whalley of Stow on the Wold, Gloucestershire, and had six children, four of whom became officers of the army. He died at Cheltenham on 9 January 1881.

The sixth son, **Francis Frankland Whinyates** (1796–1887), army officer in the East India company, born on 30 June 1796, entered the East India Company's service at the age of sixteen, and was gazetted as lieutenant-fireworker in the Madras artillery in July 1813. After serving in Ceylon and against the Pindaris, he took part in the Anglo-

Maratha War of 1817–19 as a subaltern in A troop horse artillery, and received the medal with clasp for Mehidpur (21 December 1817). Promoted captain on 24 October 1824, he served at the siege of Kittur at the end of that year. He was principal commissary of ordnance from 1845 to 1850, and then had command of the horse artillery, and of the Madras artillery as brigadier. He left India in 1854, having 'filled, with the highest credit to himself, every appointment and command connected with his corps' (General Order, 10 Feb 1854). He became major-general on 28 November 1854, lieutenant-general on 14 July 1867, and general on 21 January 1872. On 7 August 1826 he had married Elizabeth, daughter of John Campbell of Ormidale, Argyllshire; they had no children. Whinyates died at 94 Sydney Place, Bath, on 22 January 1887.

E. M. LLOYD, rev. H. C. G. MATTHEW

Sources F. T. Whinyates, *Whinyates family records*, 3 vols. (1894) · F. A. Whinyates, *From Coruña to Sevastopol* (1884) · F. Duncan, ed., *History of the royal regiment of artillery*, 3rd edn, 2 vols. (1879) · O'Byrne, *Naval biog. dict.* · private information (1900) · *Army List* · *Navy List* · *CGPLA Eng. & Wales* (1887) [Francis Frankland Whinyates]

Likenesses portraits, repro. in Whinyates, *Whinyates family records*

Wealth at death under £35,000: probate, 21 Jan 1866, *CGPLA Eng. & Wales* · £26,054 1s. 1d.—Francis Frankland Whinyates: probate, 19 March 1887, *CGPLA Eng. & Wales* · under £12,000—Frederick W. Whinyates: probate, 17 Feb 1881, *CGPLA Eng. & Wales*

Whinyates, Francis Frankland (1796–1887). *See under* Whinyates, Sir Edward Charles (1782–1865).

Whinyates, Frederick William (1793–1881). *See under* Whinyates, Sir Edward Charles (1782–1865).

Whinyates, George Barrington (1783–1808). *See under* Whinyates, Sir Edward Charles (1782–1865).

Whinyates, Thomas (1778–1857). *See under* Whinyates, Sir Edward Charles (1782–1865).

Whipple [*née* Stirrup], **Dorothy** (1893–1966), novelist, was born on 26 February 1893 at 9 Edgeware Road, Blackburn, Lancashire. She was the second of eight children (two of whom died, leaving ten years between the older and younger siblings) of Walter Stirrup (1865–1955), architect and land agent, and his wife, Ada, *née* Cunliffe (1868–1942), who had come from 'an old-fashioned sort of family: nine children living with their parents in a comfortable house'—as her daughter would write in her memoir of her own idyllic childhood (Whipple, *The Other Day*, 15). In 1900 the Stirrups moved from the 'steep terrace' (ibid., 39) where Dorothy was born to Elmbank, 52 St Silas's Road; to Hillside, East Park Road, in 1903; to The Hawthorns, 41 Dukes Brow, in 1906; and also at this time began to spend summers (previously spent on the Isle of Man) at Mylah Cottage, Rimington, in the West Riding of Yorkshire, 25 miles from Blackburn. From 1905 to 1910 Dorothy Stirrup contributed more than forty short stories (mostly about fairies, that were first tried out on her younger siblings) to the *Blackburn Weekly Telegraph's* 'Children's corner'. She went to Miss Barrett's school in nearby Shear Bank Road, then from 1903 to 1905 attended Blackburn high school

(which she disliked because she was unsporty and her writing was dismissed as plagiarism), and from 1905 to 1911 the convent of Notre Dame, after which she spent a year in France at a convent at Sens-sur-Yonne. On her return she started work as secretary to the director of education for Blackburn.

In the first week of the war her friend George Owen was killed; she never forgot him, remaining close to his sister Gwen for the rest of her life. Briefly, she tried to be a Red Cross nurse; however, she 'fainted at operations, cried when the patients cried' (*Time* magazine, 21 Nov 1932). On 1 August 1917 at Gisburne parish church near Rimington, she married her employer, (Alfred) Henry Whipple (1869–1958), a widower with a first from Cambridge whose career in the education service had begun in the year his second wife was born. The couple lived at Glenesk, 8 Merlin Road, Blackburn. In 1925, when Henry Whipple became director of education there, they moved to 35 Ebers Road, Nottingham, later spending weekends at nearby South Lodge, Newstead Abbey, Linby.

Despite her early work it seemed not to have occurred to Dorothy to write more than the occasional short story (and at first she must have hoped to have children) until, a decade after her marriage, she completed a novel. *Young Anne* (1927) suffered only one rejection before being taken by Jonathan Cape ('I'm not lost any more. I know what I have to do with my life. I have to write'; Whipple, *Random Commentary*, 11) but they rejected *High Wages* (1930), saying it would not be a commercial success (it has rarely been out of print since), so that John Murray became her British publisher for all her books except two volumes of nonfiction and a final volume of short stories. (Whipple was a great success in America, was translated into many languages, and was published by Tauchnitz.) Her novels are domestic, have 'a kind of North-Country Jane Austen quality' (J. B. Priestley, *The Times*, 21 Sept 1966) and in all of them 'her characters struggle sturdily towards individual salvation. Though she is perfectly aware that too high a price may be paid for security, she realises that without it dignified living is impossible' (*Cornhill Magazine*, February 1937). Hugh Walpole described *Greenbanks* (1932), a Book Society choice, as:

> a picture of a quite ordinary English family … with some of the best creation of living men and women that we have had for a number of years in the English novel … in Mrs Whipple we have a new novelist who will in all probability be of true importance. (*Book Society News*, September 1932)

Six more novels appeared between 1934 and 1953—*The Priory* (1939), which was partly based on Newstead, was also a Book Society choice—and three volumes of short stories in 1935, 1941, and 1961. *They Knew Mr Knight* (1934) and *They were Sisters* (1943) were made into successful films in 1944 and 1945.

In 1939, upon Henry Whipple's retirement, he and Dorothy moved to Barton End, 1 Ridgeway Road, Barton Seagrave, near Kettering, partly in order to be near her sister. *Someone at a Distance* (1953), the only novel not set in or around Blackburn or Nottingham, can now be seen as

Whipple's most important book—yet it received no major reviews and was the first of her novels since *Young Anne* not to be a Book Society choice or recommendation. A reply from the publisher to his depressed author gave a partial explanation: 'editors have gone mad about action and passion' (Whipple MSS, John Murray archive); and she may have remembered St John Ervine's remarks fifteen years before when he dubbed her 'one of the best story-tellers we have … but [he implies "which is why"] the editor of *Who's Who* seems not to have heard of her' (*Good Housekeeping*, January 1937). She was to be passed over for another ten years. Whipple also had the disappointment of seeing her last volume of short stories—eventually dubbed 'illuminating and startling' by Anthony Burgess (*Yorkshire Post*, 6 April 1961)— rejected by Murray and not finding a publisher for several years. Towards the end of her life she wrote three successful children's books, as well as *Random Commentary* (1966), an autobiography compiled from her working notebooks 1925–45.

Upon her husband's death in 1958 Dorothy Whipple immediately returned to Blackburn, to 3 Whinfield Place, but lived there for only seven years before dying from a stroke on 14 September 1966 at the Royal Infirmary, Blackburn. She was cremated at Pleasington on 16 September.

NICOLA BEAUMAN

Sources priv. coll., Whipple MSS · Blackburn Public Library, Blackburn · D. Whipple, *The other day* (1936) · D. Whipple, *Random commentary* (1966) · John Murray, London, archives, Whipple MSS · b. cert. · d. cert.
Archives Blackburn Public Library | John Murray, London, archives
Likenesses portrait, priv. coll.
Wealth at death £43,364: probate, 7 Nov 1966, *CGPLA Eng. & Wales*

Whipple, George Mathews (1842–1893), physicist, was born on 15 September 1842 at Teddington, Middlesex, the son of George Whipple, master of the public school. He was educated at the grammar school, Kingston upon Thames, at Dr Williams's school at Richmond, Surrey, and at King's College, London, taking the degree of BSc of the University of London as a mature student in 1871. Whipple joined the staff of Kew observatory in January 1858, becoming magnetic assistant in 1862, chief assistant in November 1863, and superintendent in 1876. He drew the plates for Warren de la Rue's 'Researches in solar physics', 1865–6, improved the Kew magnetic instruments, and invented, besides other optical apparatus, a device for testing the dark shades of sextants. On 30 June 1870 he married Elizabeth Martha, daughter of Robert Beckley, machinist at the observatory. Their eldest son was the manufacturer and collector of scientific instruments Robert Stewart *Whipple.

Between 1873 and 1888 Whipple undertook a series of pendulum experiments to determine the constant of gravitation. Wind pressure and velocity were his lifelong study; he carried out at the Crystal Palace in 1874 a reinvestigation of the cup anemometer invented by Thomas Romney Robinson, and with General Richard Strachey in

1890 experimented with cloud photography for the meteorological council, communicating the results to the Royal Society on 23 April 1891.

Whipple contributed freely to scientific collections, especially to the *Quarterly Journal of the Meteorological Society*. He joined the Meteorological Society (later the Royal Meteorological Society) on 18 April 1874. He served on its council (1876–87), and acted as its foreign secretary (1884–5). He sat also for many years on the council of the Physical Society of London, and was elected a fellow of the Royal Astronomical Society on 12 April 1872. He was assistant examiner in natural philosophy to the University of London (1876–81), and in the Department of Science and Art, South Kensington (1879–82 and 1884–9). The magnetic section of the *Report on the Eruption of Krakatoa*, published by the Royal Society in 1888, was compiled by him. He died at his home, Oak Villa, Jocelyn Road, Richmond, Surrey, on 8 February 1893. He was survived by his wife.

A. M. CLERKE, *rev.* ANITA MCCONNELL

Sources *Quarterly Journal of the Royal Meteorological Society*, 20 (1894), 113 · *Nature*, 47 (1892–3), 372 · *The Times* (9 Feb 1893) · *Men and women of the time* (1891) · *Symons's Meteorological Magazine*, 28 (1894), 1 · *The Observatory*, 16 (1893), 141–2 · R. H. Scott, 'History of the Kew Observatory', *PRS*, 39 (1885), 37–86 · *CGPLA Eng. & Wales* (1893)
Archives CUL, letters to Sir George Stokes · PRO, corresp. as superintendent of Kew Observatory · RAS, letters to Royal Astronomical Society
Wealth at death £948 1s. 4d.: administration, 12 April 1893, *CGPLA Eng. & Wales*

Whipple, Robert Stewart (1871–1953), manufacturer of scientific instruments and collector, was born on 1 August 1871 in Richmond, Surrey. He was the eldest son of George Mathews *Whipple, scientist and later superintendent of the Royal Observatory, Kew, and his wife, Elizabeth Martha, who formerly assisted with experiments at Kew and was the daughter of Robert Beckley, chief instrument mechanic there. Whipple was educated at King's College School, Wimbledon. He entered Kew observatory as an assistant under Charles Chree in 1888, leaving eight years later to become assistant manager at the instrument makers L. P. Casella. The Whipple connection with Kew continued later when Francis John Welsh Whipple, Robert's younger brother, succeeded Chree as superintendent.

In 1898 Whipple was appointed private assistant to Horace Darwin, who had founded the Cambridge Scientific Instrument Company, of which Whipple became manager and secretary at the end of the year. In 1899 he matriculated at Trinity College, Cambridge, but did not proceed to a degree. He married Helen Muir, daughter of a Glasgow master plumber, Allan Muir, on 8 June 1903 in Glasgow. They had two daughters and a son, George Allan Whipple, who later followed his father into the instrument industry.

In 1909 Whipple became a joint managing director of the company with C. C. Mason, a post he held until his retirement from active management in 1935, after which he became company chairman until 1949. He had a great influence on the introduction of new instruments and in their design and development for laboratory and industrial use. He was closely associated with W. Duddell in the design of his bifilar oscillograph and was responsible for redesigning Einthoven's string galvanometer from a large, water-cooled machine into a portable instrument for cardiography. He was instrumental in the commercial design of H. L. Calendar's temperature recorder and E. H. Griffiths's improvement to it, and in the introduction into this country of C. Féry's radiation pyrometer. Temperature measurement occupied his interest over many years and he patented one accurate instrument with a 17.5 metre spiral scale. In all instrument designs, in common with his colleagues Darwin, Mason, and later Keith Lucas, he followed the geometric design principles established by J. C. Maxwell. During the First World War Whipple helped the Ministry of Munitions to organize the supply of optical instruments and fuse mechanisms, and in the Second World War he was called from retirement to assist with instrument production. Between the wars, he helped the government to set up the British Optical Instrument Research Association, which later became the British Scientific Research Association.

Whipple's enthusiasm for scientific instruments was reflected in his active membership of many institutions. He was a fellow of the Physical Society from 1898, its vice-president from 1914 to 1916 and 1936 to 1939 and treasurer from 1925 to 1935. He was a founder fellow of the Institute of Physics and on its board for twenty-one years between 1920 and 1945. He was a fellow of the Optical Society, over which he presided in 1920 to 1922, and he served the Royal Institution as visitor and manager. He was a member of the Institution of Electrical Engineers, serving on its council from 1929 to 1932, and published a number of papers in its journal, two of which dealt with the medical application of instruments, and earned for him the Ayrton premium in 1919. He gave the institution's 1937 Faraday lecture entitled 'Electricity in the hospital'. He was president of the British Optical Instrument Manufacturers' Association in 1926–8, and again between 1932 and 1937, by which time it had become the Scientific Instrument Manufacturers' Association. In 1939 he presided over the mathematics and physics section of the British Association's Dundee meeting. In 1937 he was elected president of the Highgate Literary and Scientific Institution, founded in north London in 1839, and he was re-elected annually until his death. The institution's continued existence was largely due to his leadership and generosity over seventeen years, and it benefited from a trust, bearing his name, for the promotion of arts and science in north London.

Whipple was intensely interested in the history and development of scientific instruments and he amassed an important and valuable collection of instruments and books dating from the sixteenth century. He presented these collections, together with a sum of money, to the University of Cambridge in 1944, where they form part of the Whipple Museum for the History of Science. He was also a founder member of the British Society for the History of Science in 1947, and its vice-president for 1953–4.

Whipple was kindly and generous in supporting, often anonymously, the causes in which he believed, and many young scientists and engineers owed much to his gentle help and encouragement. He died of cancer on 13 December 1953, aged eighty-two, at 6 the Old Hall, South Grove, Highgate, and after a memorial service at St Michael's Church, Highgate, was cremated at Golders Green.

H. R. LANG, *rev.* JOHN K. BRADLEY

Sources *Engineering* (25 Dec 1953), 820 · *The Engineer* (18 Dec 1953), 811 · *Journal of Electrical Engineers* (1954), 94 · *Proceedings of the Physical Society*, 67 (1954), 1129–30 · [V. Crane], ed., *Heart of a London village: the Highgate Literary and Scientific Institution, 1839–1990* (privately printed, London, 1991) · J. A. Bennett, 'Museums and the establishment of the history of science at Oxford and Cambridge', *British Journal for the History of Science*, 30 (1997), 29–46 · 'The Whipple collection of instruments and books', *Engineering* (2 March 1945), 161–3; (23 March 1945), 223–4 · R. S. Clay, 'The Whipple Museum at Cambridge', *Journal of Scientific Instruments* (28 Sept 1951), 286–7 · M. J. G. Cattermole and A. F. Wolfe, *Horace Darwin's shop: a history of the Cambridge Scientific Instrument Company, 1878–1968* (1987) · '50 years of scientific instrument manufacture', *Engineering* [Cambridge Scientific Instrument Company] (11 May 1945); (25 May 1945); (15 June 1945); (29 June 1945) · R. S. Whipple, 'Tribute to Horace Darwin', *Journal of Scientific Instruments*, 6 (1929) · R. S. Whipple, 'Reminiscences of an instrument maker', *Journal of Scientific Instruments*, 19 (Dec 1942), 178–83 · m. cert. · d. cert.
Archives Whipple Museum for the History of Science, Cambridge, collection of scientific books and instruments
Likenesses M. Gillick?, bronze bas-relief, Whipple Museum, Cambridge · M. Marriot?, oils, Whipple Museum, Cambridge · photograph, repro. in *Proceedings of the Physical Society*, facing p. 1117 · photograph, repro. in V. Crane, ed., *Heart of a London village*, p. 69
Wealth at death £88,169 17s. 3d.: probate, 20 Feb 1954, *CGPLA Eng. & Wales*

Whish, Sir William Sampson (1787–1853), army officer in the East India Company, was the son of Richard Whish (*d.* 1810), rector of West Walton, Norfolk, and vicar of Wickford, Essex, and his wife, Philippa, daughter of William Sandys. He was born at Northwold, Norfolk, on 27 February 1787. He received a commission as lieutenant in the Bengal artillery on 21 August 1804, and arrived in India in December. He was promoted captain on 13 May 1807, and commanded the rocket troop of horse artillery of the centre division of the grand army under the marquess of Hastings in the Pindari and Anglo-Maratha wars at the end of 1817 and beginning of 1818. He afterwards took the troop to Meerut, where, on 26 July 1820, he was appointed to act as brigade major. He was promoted major on 19 July 1821.

Whish married, in 1809, a daughter of George Dixon, and his eldest son, G. Palmer Whish, general of the Bengal staff corps, served with his father at Gujrat. Another son, Henry Edward Whish, major-general of the Bengal staff corps, served with his father at the siege of Multan, and was in the Indian mutiny campaign.

Whish commanded the 1st brigade of horse artillery in the army assembled at Agra, under Lord Combermere, in December 1825, for the siege of Bharatpur. The place was captured by assault on 18 January 1826, and Whish was mentioned in dispatches and promoted lieutenant-colonel for distinguished service in the field from 19 January. On 23 December 1826 he was appointed to command the Karnal and Sirhind division of artillery. He received the CB, military division, in 1838; was appointed a colonel commandant of artillery, with rank of brigadier-general and with a seat on the military board, on 21 December; and in February 1839 he succeeded Major-General Faithful in command of the presidency division of artillery at Dum-Dum. He was promoted major-general on 23 November 1841, and went on furlough to England until the end of 1847.

Whish was appointed to the command at Lahore of the Punjab division on 23 January 1848. In August he was given the command of the Multan field force, 8000 strong, to operate against Mulraj, the Muslim governor of Multan province, and towards the end of the month took up a position in front of Multan. The siege commenced on 7 September, but, owing to the defection of Sher Singh a week later, Whish withdrew his forces to Tibi, and a period of inaction followed, which enabled Mulraj to improve his defences and to increase his garrison in Multan. At the beginning of November Mulraj prepared batteries which threatened Whish's camp, and on 7 November a successful action resulted in the destruction of Mulraj's advanced batteries and the capture of five guns. On 21 December Whish was reinforced by a column from Bombay, and on Christmas day was able to occupy his old position before Multan. On 27 December the enemy were driven from the suburbs, and the siege recommenced on 28 December. The city was captured on 2 January 1849, and the siege of the citadel pressed forward. On 22 January Mulraj surrendered the citadel rather than face an assault.

Leaving a strong garrison in Multan, Whish marched to join Lord Gough, capturing the fort of Chiniot on 9 February, on which day the advanced portion of his force reached Ramnagar. Anticipating Lord Gough's orders, Whish secured the fords of the Chenab at Wazirabad, and on 21 February commanded the 1st division of Lord Gough's army at the battle of Gujrat. He received the thanks of the governor-general, of the court of directors of the East India Company, and of both houses of parliament. He was made KCB, military division, and was transferred to the command of the Bengal division of the army in March. In October 1851 he was appointed to the Cis-Jhelum division, but before assuming command went on furlough, 'driven home by extreme ill health' (GM, 437). He was promoted lieutenant-general on 11 November 1851. Having come from Cheltenham for medical treatment, he died at Claridge's Hotel, Brook Street, London, on 25 February 1853.   R. H. VETCH, rev. JAMES FALKNER

Sources East-India Register · The Times (1 March 1853) · GM, 2nd ser., 39 (1853) · LondG (23 March 1849) · LondG (19 April 1849) · LondG (6 June 1849) · J. Lawrence-Archer, The Punjab campaign, 1848/49 (1878) · J. Dunlop, Mooltan, during and after the siege (1859) · Boase, Mod. Eng. biog. · Venn, Alum. Cant.

Whistler, Anthony (1713/14–1754), poet, was born in Whitchurch, Oxfordshire, and baptized there on 15 November 1714, the eldest of the four sons of Anthony Whistler (1670–1719), Church of England clergyman, and Anne (d. 1753). He was educated at Eton College before going to Pembroke College, Oxford, matriculating on 21 October 1732. There he began a lively lifelong friendship

with William Shenstone and Richard Graves, who shared similar interests in literature. He drafted a tragedy about Dido, and his heroi-comical poem, The Shuttlecock, was published in 1736 by Leonard Lichfield, who published a volume of Shenstone's poetry the following year. He contributed to the riddles controversy in the Gentleman's Magazine in 1739.

Whistler remained in Oxford until 1740, without taking a degree, and then retired to Whitchurch, set up in a small house by his stepfather, the Revd Samuel Walker (1690–1768). He was buried in Whitchurch on 17 May 1754 at the age of forty. Shenstone expressed his sadness to Graves on the end of the 'triumvirate' (Letters, 398) and had Whistler's poems 'Flowers', 'Horace and Lydia', and 'Song' included in Robert Dodsley's Collection of Poems, by Several Hands in editions of 1755 and 1758. Whistler's letters to Shenstone are in the Osborn Collection, Yale University. Shenstone's letters to Whistler were destroyed by John Whistler, Anthony's brother, at the time of his death, much to Shenstone's annoyance.   F. D. A. BURNS

Sources Whitchurch parish register, Oxfordshire Archives · R. Graves, Recollections of some particulars in the life of William Shenstone, ed. J. Dodsley (1788) · Select letters between the late duchess of Somerset … and others, ed. T. Hull, 2 vols. (1778), vol. 1, pp. 160–63; vol. 2, pp. 22–60 · The letters of William Shenstone, ed. M. Williams (1939) · C. Tracy, A portrait of Richard Graves (1987) · Foster, Alum. Oxon., 1715–1886, 4.1536, 1611
Archives Yale U., Osborn collection, letters to Shenstone

Whistler [née Philip; other married name Godwin], **Beatrice** (1857–1896), artist and designer, was born in Chelsea, London, on 12 May 1857, the second of ten children of the Scottish sculptor John Birnie *Philip (1824–1875) and his wife, Frances Black (1825/6–1917). She studied art in her father's Chelsea studio and with the architect Edward William *Godwin (1833–1886), a leading figure in the aesthetic movement. After her father died Beatrice Philip married Godwin on 4 January 1876; the couple had one son, Edward. She worked in Godwin's studio workshop and collaborated on furniture and house designs, such as decorative brick panels for a house designed by Godwin on the Tite Street corner of Chelsea Embankment. Godwin's lost 'Beatrice cabinet' bore her panels of the seasons. Similar panels, and designs for tiles, panels and wallpaper, survive, and some were sold to manufacturers, including Minton's and William Watt & Co.

In the 1880s Beatrice Godwin posed to James Abbott McNeill *Whistler (1834–1903) for her portrait, Harmony in Red: Lamplight (Hunterian Museum and Art Gallery, Glasgow). She joined his pupils, including his mistress, Maud Franklin, and Walter Sickert, and they exhibited in London at the Society of British Artists. Beatrice signed her work with a monogram or trefoil, BP, then BG, but she exhibited as Rix Birnie to avoid being identified as a female or amateur artist. Except for two lovely oil studies, The Novel and The Muslin Gown (priv. coll.), her exhibits have disappeared. Her small oils are sometimes mistaken for Whistler's. Peach Blossom (National Gallery of Art, Washington, DC) was labelled by Whistler, 'Mrs J McN Whistler': with the 's' of 'Mrs' rubbed out, it was bought as a

Whistler. Her subjects are mainly flowers and women, and her curving brush strokes differ from Whistler's narrower, smoother strokes. The drawings of Phil May and Japanese woodcuts influenced her style. Her circle included May, the Pre-Raphaelite painter Frederick Sandys, and Oscar Wilde. *A Caricature of Oscar Wilde* (Hunterian Museum and Art Gallery), drawn with strong, simple lines, shows her sharp humour. This drawing was long attributed to Whistler: distinguishing her work from her partner's is a primary problem in discussing her *œuvre*. Louise Jopling, who exhibited with Beatrice Godwin at the St Stephen's Art Club, Bridge Street, London, in 1881, recalled that 'she was very handsome, and looked very French. She had a delightful devil-may-care look in her eyes, which was very fascinating' (MacDonald, *Beatrice Whistler*, 8).

After Godwin's death Whistler circulated an appeal to help Beatrice Godwin retrain. He also joined a group including the poet laureate, Lord Tennyson, who petitioned successfully for her to receive a pension from the civil list. She apparently studied in Paris. Just before her marriage to Whistler on 11 August 1888 she was described as 'a remarkably clever artist and decorative draughtswoman. Since she has been under the influence of the great James McNeill it can be readily imagined that her undoubted artistic talents have been considerably matured' ('The fate of an "Impressionist"'). After her marriage she used the form Beatrix for her first name, though to her family she was always known as Trixie. It was a happy and productive marriage: 'I look around', Whistler wrote to her, 'and see no others as happy as we two are in each other' ([Feb 1892], MacDonald, *Beatrice Whistler*, 15). He taught Beatrice to etch, and together they etched a view of Loches in France. Beatrice organized the studio and promoted his printmaking. She managed the domestic and business side of Whistler's life, as she had Godwin's, and worked independently, developing a distinct style. A servant described their Tite Street house: 'On the top floor was … Mrs Whistler's studio (she painted beautifully)' (E. B., *The Times*, 17 July 1934). Family and professional models (including her sisters Ethel and Rosalind, and the Pettigrew sisters) posed for both Whistlers. Her drawings of women are vivid and sympathetic, her paintings intimate, with soft, subtle colour harmonies.

J. A. M. Whistler celebrated their marriage by adding a trefoil to his butterfly signature, and Beatrice Whistler designed glassware engraved with this butterfly. Her jewellery designs in the National Gallery of Art, Washington, DC, and Hunterian Museum and Art Gallery, include an enamelled love-bird ring. She also designed stained glass—including, in 1891, a beautiful memorial window to Jane Mary Wilson Holme, executed by Campbell Smith & Co. in Orton parish church, Westmorland. She supervised the decoration of their house at 110 rue du Bac in Paris, designing austerely simple furniture with chequered designs for both house and garden. The illustrator and writer Joseph Pennell recalled that 'there was a trellis over the door designed by Mrs. Whistler, and there were flowers everywhere' (MacDonald, *Beatrice Whistler*, 15).

In 1894 Beatrice Whistler developed cancer. She wrote to her husband, 'I do suffer—I never thought it would be like this, but you know, I was too happy, I am given some aches to remind me that this world is not quite a paradise' ([Nov 1895], MacDonald, *Beatrice Whistler*, 17). His most moving portraits of her, *The Siesta* and *By the Balcony* (lithographs in Freer Gallery of Art, Smithsonian Institution, Washington, DC), were drawn as she lay dying. She died at their home, St Jude's Cottage, Hampstead Heath, London, on 10 May 1896, and was buried in Chiswick cemetery, Middlesex. The Beatrix Whistler collection, the Whistler collection and the Philip Birnie gift and bequest, all in the Hunterian Art Gallery, University of Glasgow, form the major collection of her work and include oils, etchings, watercolours, and pastels.

MARGARET F. MACDONALD

Sources M. F. MacDonald, *Beatrice Whistler, artist and designer* (1997) [exhibition catalogue, Hunterian Museum and Art Gallery, Glasgow, 6 Sept – 1 Nov 1997] · 'The marriage of Mr Whistler and Mrs Godwin', *Pall Mall Gazette* (11 Aug 1888) · 'Parlour furniture', *Building News*, 36 (31 Oct 1879), 522 · *The Times* (7 June 1881) · *The Times* (14 Oct 1886) · exhibition catalogues (1885–7) [Society of British Artists] · 'The fate of an "Impressionist"', *Illustrated Bits* (21 July 1888) · M. F. MacDonald, 'Love and fashion: the Birnie Philips', in M. F. MacDonald and others, *Whistler, women and fashion* (2003)
Archives L. Cong., Pennell–Whistler collection, corresp. · Smithsonian Institution, Washington, DC, Freer Gallery of Art, corresp. of C. L. Freer · U. Glas. L., corresp., press cuttings, and photographs [subject and J. A. M. Whistler and the Birnie Philip family] · V&A, Archives of Art and Design, sketchbooks, corresp., and diaries of E. W. Godwin
Likenesses W. Sickert, etching, 1885–6 (*Beatrice Godwin posing for 'Harmony in red: lamplight'*), priv. coll. · J. A. M. Whistler, oils, 1885–6 (*Harmony in red: lamplight*), Hunterian Museum and Art Gallery, Glasgow · etching, 1888–94 (*Head of 'Rix Birnie' (Beatrice Whistler)*), Hunterian Museum and Art Gallery, Glasgow · photograph (*Beatrice Godwin*), Hunterian Museum and Art Gallery, Glasgow · portraits, repro. in MacDonald, *Beatrice Whistler*

Whistler, Daniel (1618/19–1684), physician, son of William Whistler, gentleman of Elvington, Goring, Oxfordshire, was born at Walthamstow, Essex. He was educated at the free school of Thame, Oxfordshire, and matriculated at Trinity College, Oxford, on 12 June 1635, aged sixteen. He graduated BA in 1639, became a fellow of Merton College in 1640, and on 8 August 1642 began studying medicine at Leiden. He returned to Oxford to take his MA in 1644, in which year he became a member of Gray's Inn, London, and spent time with William Harvey (1578–1657), then warden of Merton, before returning to Leiden, where he graduated MD on 19 October 1645. He incorporated his Leiden MD at Oxford on 20 May 1647, decamped soon after for London, and was elected professor of geometry at Gresham College on 13 June 1648. He became superior Linacre reader at Oxford about the time of his Gresham appointment, though he did not deliver the lectures. He was elected a fellow of the College of Physicians on 13 December 1649. During 1653–4 he and an Oxford colleague, Ralph Bathurst (d. 1704), cared for seamen, wounded in the Dutch war, at Ipswich, Harwich, and possibly London.

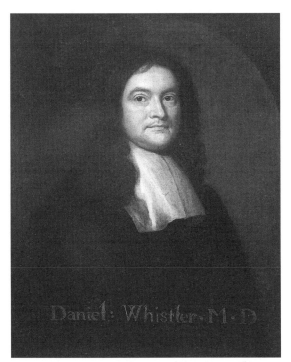

Daniel Whistler (1618/19–1684), by unknown artist, c.1660–70

In 1653 Whistler served as physician to Bulstrode White-locke's embassy to Sweden, which he commemorated with Latin verses on the abdication of Queen Kristina that were printed in the *Journal of the Swedish Ambassy*. In July 1654 he returned to London and developed a lucrative practice. He may have been the Daniel Whistler who, on 7 April 1656, married Elizabeth Lowther at Little Ilford, Essex, at which time he resigned his Gresham professorship. At the College of Physicians he delivered the Harveian oration in 1659 and served twelve terms as censor between 1657 and 1680; he also served as college registrar in 1674–82, elect from 1676, treasurer in 1682, and president in 1683. He was elected a fellow of the Royal Society in 1663.

Whistler completed his major intellectual project, *De morbo puerili Anglorum, quem patrio idiomate indigenae vocant 'The rickets'* (1645) at the age of twenty-six as a thesis for his Leiden MD. During the 1640s the disease of rickets, which may have accounted for as many as 3 per cent of English deaths (bills of mortality for 1659: 476 of 15,000 burials; cited in Walter Langdon-Brown, *Some Chapters in Cambridge Medical History*, 1946, 35), aroused the interest of several English physicians and natural philosophers, including an informal study group of seven from the College of Physicians. Whistler's text is the first printed book devoted to rickets, but it is highly theoretical, contains little original material, and did not influence contemporaries. In contrast, the college project which culminated in Francis Glisson's influential 1650 publication *Tractatus de rachitide* of 416 pages was soon republished in several Latin and English editions.

Whistler seems to have been a man of charming manners and considerable talent, but he died facing imminent disgrace. While Pepys, who dined with him several times, wrote that he was 'good company, and a very ingenious man' and John Evelyn found him exceedingly pleasant in manner, Whistler performed negligently as registrar of the College of Physicians. At the time of his death in London from fever and pneumonia on 11 May 1684 he was living at the college, then in Warwick Lane. He was buried in the north aisle of Christ Church Greyfriars, London. Shortly after his death, Whistler's former colleagues in the college became convinced that he had defrauded it of substantial sums. Wood observed that although Whistler earned £1000 per year from his medical practice and was married to a rich widow, 'yet he died very much in debt'. In 1704 Mr Boulter gave a portrait of him to the college, a gesture its nineteenth-century chronicler believed placed Whistler 'in company too good for his deserts' (Munk, 251).   ROBERT L. MARTENSEN

Sources *DNB* · Munk, *Roll* · R. G. Frank, *Harvey and the Oxford physiologists* (1980) · *The diary of Samuel Pepys*, ed. Lord Braybrooke [R. N. G Braybrooke] and J. Smith, 2 vols. (1925) · *The diary of John Evelyn*, ed. E. S. De Beer (1959) · Wood, *Ath. Oxon.* · A. Wood, *Historia et antiquitates universitatis Oxoniensis*, trans. R. Peers and R. Reeve, 2 vols. (1674) · Foster, *Alum. Oxon.* · *CSP dom.*, 1653, 104, 507 · B. Whitelocke, *A journal of the Swedish embassy*, ed. C. Morton, rev. H. Reeve, new edn, 2 vols. (1855) · will, PRO, PROB 11/376, sig. 96
Archives RCP Lond., papers, incl. commonplace books, cash book, pharmacopoeia, medical aphorisms
Likenesses oils, *c.*1660–1670, RCP Lond. [*see illus.*] · D. Loggan, engraving, 1677 (*Royal College of Physicians with lettering identifying the various doors*; after D. Loggan), Wellcome L. · G. P. Harding, pencil drawing, NPG
Wealth at death died in debt: Wood, *Ath. Oxon.*

Whistler, James Abbott McNeill (1834–1903), painter and printmaker, was born on 11 July 1834 in Worthen Street, Lowell, Massachusetts, the first of five children, all sons (of whom only Whistler and his brother William survived infancy), of Major George Washington Whistler (1800–1849), United States army and railroad engineer, and his second wife, Anna Matilda (1804–1881), second child of Dr Daniel McNeill (1757/8–1827), also known as Charles Donald, who was born in Bladen county, North Carolina. The McNeill family probably came from Taynish, south of the Crinan Canal in Knapdale, near Castle Swene, and emigrated from Scotland in 1746; in 1786 Dr McNeill was temporarily banished from North Carolina for joining the British. Major Whistler's father, John (1758–1829), also served in the British army in the American revolutionary wars; and afterwards as a captain in the American army. The family's descent was probably from English settlers in Ulster; but neither Whistler's belief that his was one of the first families of Virginia, nor the early ancestors claimed by his first biographers, have any reliable foundation in fact.

Early life and education, 1834–1859 Whistler lived his early years where his father worked as an engineer, first in Lowell, then Stonington, Connecticut, and afterwards Springfield, Massachusetts, before the family moved to Russia in 1843 on Major Whistler's appointment as engineer of the

James Abbott McNeill Whistler (1834–1903), self-portrait, *c.*1872
[*Arrangement in Grey: Portrait of the Painter*]

railroad between Moscow and St Petersburg. In 1844 the family received a visit from the painter Sir William Allan, who praised the ten-year-old boy's drawing, after which Whistler received his first formal instruction in drawing at the Imperial Academy of Fine Arts, St Petersburg. Although his early intention was to follow a military career, by graduating from the United States Military Academy, West Point, like his father, who hoped he would become an architect or engineer, Whistler's education in Russia and Britain encouraged him to become an artist. The Whistlers maintained strong links with Britain, in particular Derby and Lancashire, the home of Anna Whistler's stepsisters, where the family stayed on their journeys to and from America; there Whistler met members of Lancashire's industrial and manufacturing society who later became his patrons. In Preston in October 1847 Whistler was groomsman at the wedding of his half-sister Deborah to the English surgeon Francis Seymour Haden, whose aunt Anne was the widow of the Lowell founder Kirk Boott, in whose locomotive machine shops Whistler's father had worked. Haden had taken up etching and encouraged his new brother-in-law's interest in art when Whistler lived with them in London in 1849. That year Whistler visited the Royal Academy to see his portrait by Sir William Boxall (Hunterian Museum and Art Gallery, Glasgow), who also took him to Hampton Court. Through the Hadens, Whistler met members of South Kensington's artistic and scientific society, including Sir Henry Cole, whose family remained lifelong friends.

After the death of Whistler's father from cholera in April, the family returned to America in financially reduced circumstances, and lived in Pomfret, Connecticut, where Whistler and his brother went to school for two years. In July 1851 Whistler entered West Point as a cadet-at-large under Commander Robert E. Lee, and at this time added his mother's family name, McNeill, to his own. He studied drawing under Robert W. Weir, and in 1852 his first work was published, the lithographed title-page to *United States Military Academy: Song of the Graduates.* Although he excelled at drawing by making caricatures of student life and narrative scenes and watercolours after writers including Dickens and Sir Walter Scott, he was discharged two years later from West Point for deficiency in chemistry. After working briefly in the Baltimore locomotive works of Ross Winans, Whistler was appointed in November 1854 to a post in the drawing division of the US coast and geodetic survey, Washington, DC, where he etched topographical plates and maps until his resignation the following February. During this period Whistler painted oil portraits for Ross Winans's son Thomas, whose sister was married to Whistler's half-brother George, who became his guardian. In September 1855 Thomas Winans financed Whistler to study art in Paris, and with George continued to support him by buying his etchings and pictures.

In Paris, after attending classes at the École Impériale et Spéciale de Dessin (1855–6), Whistler entered the studio of Charles Gleyre, whose practice of arranging the colours on the palette before a picture was begun, and treating ivory black as the 'basis of tones', became a lasting influence. During his four years in the quartier Latin, Whistler's English friends included the illustrator George Du Maurier, whose serialized novel *Trilby* (1894) includes a thinly disguised portrait of Whistler as 'Joe Sibley the Idle Apprentice'; the artists Thomas Armstrong and Edward Poynter, and Alexander (Aleco; 1840–1898), and Luke Ionides, whose family bought pictures from him after he moved to London. Reminiscences by these and others suggest that Whistler based his bohemian life on Henry Murger's *Scènes de la vie Bohème* (1851), which was influential when old Paris was being demolished to make way for the new. Accordingly, Whistler sought out subjects for his art, such as in the portrait *La mère Gérard* (1858–9; priv. coll.), an old flower seller at the bal Bullier who had once run a lending library, which reflected the rapidly changing urban scene. This and subjects like it were represented in the resolutely realist style of Gustave Courbet, whose art was the most significant influence on Whistler during his early years in Europe, but which ten years later he disavowed. In 1858 Whistler made a tour of the Rhine and etched *Douze eaux fortes d'après nature*, a series of rural and peasant subjects known as the French Set, printed by Auguste Delâtre, whose 'artistic printing' exerted a strong influence on Whistler's future practice; two of the etchings were exhibited at the Salon of 1859. The set was published from the London home of Francis Seymour Haden whose collection of etchings by Rembrandt and others Whistler studied. Whistler also met the French painters

Alphonse Legros and Henri Fantin-Latour with whom he remained on close terms for a decade. Whistler left Paris for London in 1859, but maintained a strong association with French art and artists by exhibiting at the Salon and regularly visiting Paris in the 1860s.

Early career in London, 1859–1877 In London between 1859 and 1861 Whistler made a series of etchings of the Thames which depicted the riverside activity of wharves and shipping, for which he was awarded the gold medal for etching at The Hague in 1863. Also praised by Baudelaire, sixteen of the etchings, known as the Thames Set, were published in 1871, but Whistler's reputation as an etcher grew slowly because of the pre-eminence which English and French critics accorded to the etchings of Francis Seymour Haden. In 1861 Whistler visited Brittany, and the following year made a prolonged stay in the Biarritz region of the Basses-Pyrénées to paint seascapes. Between 1860 and 1865 he exhibited genre and figure subjects at the Royal Academy, some influenced by Japanese art and the fashion for Chinese 'blue and white' porcelain, as well as marine and London subjects painted in a vigorous realist style. In 1862 his *The White Girl*, which he later called *Symphony in White No. 1* (National Gallery of Art, Washington, DC), a boldly painted full-length representation of a young girl with an enigmatic gaze, for which the model was his mistress Johanna Hiffernan (*b. c.*1843), was rejected by the academy, but a private gallery exhibited it as *The Woman in White*, whereupon the critic of *The Athenaeum* complained of its lack of resemblance to the heroine of Wilkie Collins's popular novel of that name. To this Whistler replied, in his first letter to the press, that it 'simply represents a girl dressed in white standing in front of a white curtain' (*The Athenaeum*, 23). In 1862 Whistler met the poet Algernon Charles Swinburne, with whom he became intimate, and whose theory of 'art for art's sake', developed principally in his book *William Blake: a Critical Essay* (1868), profoundly influenced Whistler; for the artist's *The Little White Girl* (Tate collection), exhibited at the academy in 1865, Swinburne wrote the verses 'Before the Mirror'. In 1863 *The White Girl* was a focus of critical attention when it was exhibited in Paris at the Salon des Refusés; and at the Salon of 1864 Fantin-Latour gave Whistler a prominent place, opposite Manet and other French painters and writers, including Baudelaire, in his group portrait *Hommage à Delacroix* (Musée d'Orsay, Paris). In 1863 Whistler leased a house in Lindsey Row, Chelsea, where his mother joined him from America to live. At this time Whistler was also close to Dante Gabriel Rossetti who introduced him to buyers for his art, including the shipping line owner F. R. Leyland of Liverpool. In the autumn of 1865 Whistler painted seascapes with Courbet in Trouville. In 1866 he undertook a well-paid mission to deliver torpedoes to Chile in its dispute with Spain; several seascapes he painted in Valparaiso show warships anchored in the bay.

Between 1865 and 1870 Whistler revised the role of realism in his art; in a letter of 1867 to his friend Fantin-Latour (letter, Pennell collection, Library of Congress), he regretted Courbet's influence and said that he wished he had been a pupil of Ingres. Whistler re-examined the relationship between colour and line, by fusing the decorative principles of Japanese prints with the expressive potential of neoclassical drawing, which culminated in the oil sketches known as the Six Projects (1868; Freer Gallery of Art, Washington, DC) intended as a decorative scheme for F. R. Leyland and described by Swinburne in 'Notes on some pictures of 1868' (*Essays and Studies*, 358–80). In 1867 Whistler exhibited his recent work at the Salon and the Universal Exhibition in Paris; at the Royal Academy that year he showed a picture of two girls on a sofa dressed in white called *Symphony in White No. III* (Barber Institute of Fine Arts, Birmingham), a title suggestive of the synaesthetic principle advocated by Baudelaire, which had been given controversial expression in English verse by Swinburne in *Poems and Ballads* (1866). Whistler's work met with varying degrees of critical success, but it was insufficient to gain him election as an associate of the Royal Academy. Whistler's deteriorating relationship with his brother-in-law Francis Seymour Haden, who in 1867 contrived his expulsion from the Burlington Fine Arts Club by assembling evidence of physical assaults Whistler made on Legros, himself, and others, caused a permanent division in Whistler's family, and damaged his professional reputation.

In June 1870 Louisa Hanson, a parlourmaid, gave birth to a son by Whistler who was named James Whistler Hanson, and who later acted as his secretary. During the 1870s Whistler extended his practice of giving paintings synaesthetic titles, 'Symphony', 'Arrangement', and 'Harmony' for portraits and figures, and 'Nocturne' for his Thames subjects, in which landmarks of London's riverside were indistinctly viewed through a veil of mist or fog. Whistler intended that a work such as *Nocturne in Blue and Green* (1871; Tate collection) inscribed with a signature in the form of a butterfly which became his trademark, should be understood, not for its topographical accuracy, but for the effect of its colour combination on the viewer. By painting designs derived from Japanese prints on the frames of the Nocturnes, Whistler narrowed the distinction between easel painting and decoration which William Morris's arts and crafts movement also promoted. Whistler therefore designed appropriate room settings and wall decorations for buyers of his work, such as W. C. Alexander, who in 1872 commissioned Whistler to paint portraits of his daughters for the drawing room of his London home. Whistler also designed mosaics for the South Kensington Museum which were commissioned by Sir Henry Cole but never installed.

In 1872 Whistler exhibited at the Royal Academy the celebrated portrait of his mother, *Arrangement in Grey and Black* (1871–2; Musée d'Orsay, Paris), which reputedly was hung only after Sir William Boxall intervened by threatening to resign if it was refused; henceforth Whistler sent his work to private galleries, such as the Society of French Artists in New Bond Street and the Dudley Gallery, where the Nocturnes were exhibited between 1871 and 1875 and regularly found buyers. Early in 1874 Whistler took a year's lease on a gallery at 148 Pall Mall, where he carried out a decorative scheme, by painting the walls in a colour scheme of pink and grey and installing turkey rugs, modern furniture, and flowers, in order to showcase an exhibition of his recent work which opened in June and included the portraits of his mother, of Thomas Carlyle known as *Arrangement in Grey and Black, No. 2* (1872–3; Glasgow Museum and Art Gallery), and of F. R. Leyland (1870–3; Freer Gallery of Art, Washington, DC) and Leyland's wife, Florence (1870–73; Frick Collection, New York), who also commissioned Whistler to paint portraits of his family. The exhibition was well received, and as a portrait painter Whistler was compared to Velázquez, to which Whistler rejoined, 'Why drag in Velasquez?' (Whistler, *Gentle Art*, 47–8). Early in 1876 Whistler worked on decorations for the stairway of 49 Princes Gate, the London home of Leyland, who also commissioned him to make minor modifications to the walls of the dining-room in conjunction with the architect Thomas Jeckyll who had designed furniture and fretwork shelving in the Japanese style, which displayed Leyland's collection of blue and white china, and Whistler's picture *La princesse du pays de la porcelaine* (1863–4; Freer Gallery of Art, Washington, DC) above the fireplace. By the following year Whistler had exceeded the commission, by repainting the walls, ceiling, shelving, and window shutters with an elaborate colour scheme based on a peacock's tail feathers which he called *Harmony in Blue and Gold* (1876–7; Freer Gallery of Art, Washington, DC). Leyland paid Whistler less than half of what he asked for the 'peacock room', and sent him a cheque in pounds sterling rather than guineas, a difference represented by the silver shillings strewn at the feet of one of two peacocks which Whistler painted on the south wall, and described to Leyland in a letter as symbolic of 'L'Art et L'Argent' (letter, Pennell collection, Library of Congress, Washington, DC).

Whistler versus Ruskin, 1877–1879 In 1877 Whistler exhibited at Sir Coutts Lindsay's newly opened Grosvenor Gallery a painting of fireworks against a night sky entitled *Nocturne in Black and Gold: the Falling Rocket* (1875; Detroit Institute of Arts), about which John Ruskin wrote in his pamphlet *Fors Clavigera* addressed to the 'Workmen and labourers of Great Britain':

> For Mr Whistler's sake, no less than for the protection of the purchaser, Sir Coutts Lindsay ought not to have admitted works into the gallery in which the ill-educated conceit of the artist so nearly approached the aspect of wilful imposture. I have seen, and heard, much of Cockney impudence before now; but never expected to hear a coxcomb ask two hundred guineas for flinging a pot of paint in the public's face.   (*Works*, 29.146–69)

Whistler sued Ruskin for libel, claiming £1000 in damages and the cost of the action. In May 1878, in *The World*, Whistler described how friends had tried to persuade him to give the title 'Trotty Veck', a character in Dickens, instead of *Harmony in Grey and Gold* to a picture of a snow scene with a single black figure and a lighted tavern (1876; Fogg Art Museum, Harvard University, Cambridge, Massachusetts), because it could then be sold 'for a round harmony of golden guineas'. Such a practice Whistler

regarded as 'vulgar and meretricious', when the picture 'should have its own merit, and not depend upon dramatic, or legendary, or local interest' (Whistler, *Gentle Art*, 126–8). Whistler argued that:

> As music is the poetry of sound, so is painting the poetry of sight, and the subject-matter has nothing to do with harmony of sound or of colour ... Art should be independent of all clap-trap—should stand alone, and appeal to the artistic sense of eye or ear, without confounding this with emotions entirely foreign to it, as devotion, pity, love, patriotism and the like.   (ibid.)

Whistler defended his art in similar terms when his case against Ruskin came to court in November 1878. For the plaintiff, Whistler, the art critic William Michael Rossetti, the artist Albert Moore, and the playwright William Gorman Wills testified; for the defendant, Ruskin (who was not present), the artists Edward Burne-Jones and W. P. Frith, and the *Times* critic Tom Taylor appeared. The case for Whistler, who claimed that only the professional practitioner of art, not the writer, was qualified to pass judgement on painting rested on Ruskin's libellous damage to his reputation and the traditional right of the artist to ask what he liked for his work. In attempting to justify Ruskin's criticism as privileged, his counsel and witnesses took every opportunity to ridicule the fashionable audience for Whistler's art, and expose what they considered to be its shortcomings. Both sides tried to establish standards by which painting in general, and Whistler's in particular, should be judged, and how the price of a picture should be a fair reflection of the time and labour expended in its production. This issue prompted the attorney-general, Sir John Holker, in his cross-examination of Whistler, to question whether he asked 200 guineas for the labour of two days, to which Whistler gave the famous reply, received with applause in the courtroom: 'No;—I ask it for the knowledge of a lifetime' (Whistler, *Gentle Art*, 2–18).

While definitions of presumed artistic skill and what constituted 'finish' in painting conflicted, the claims made for and against Whistler's art were in essence no different from those which still divided popular opinion about Turner's, on which Ruskin had first staked his reputation as a writer thirty-five years before. Moreover, the language Whistler used to defend his painting was unexceptional to anyone familiar with theories of either Romanticism or modern French art, or even some of the more formalist utterances of Ruskin's own art criticism. For liberal opinion such matters were less important than the powerful reputation of Ruskin, whose radical pronouncements on economics and society were commonly regarded as far more controversial than his influence as an art critic. The verdict, which the jury gave to Whistler, with damages of only 1 farthing, turned less on definitions of art or the labour theory of value, than on 'marginal utility', which recognized that price alone dictated the cost of goods, a principle of the modern *laissez-faire* economy which Ruskin totally opposed but which he was powerless to stem. In his first brown paper pamphlet, *Art and Art Critics: Whistler versus Ruskin*, dedicated to Albert Moore and published within a month of the trial, Whistler characterized his action against Ruskin as one 'between the brush and the pen', a 'war' which he continued to wage against art critics (Whistler, *Gentle Art*, 21–34).

Shortly after bringing suit against Ruskin in 1877, Whistler commissioned his friend the architect E. W. Godwin to design a house for him in Tite Street, to include a studio to accommodate his growing practice as a portrait painter, and a living space suitable for entertaining clients and friends at his Sunday 'breakfasts', which had become a feature of London's artistic society. He also collaborated with Godwin over the design of furniture which was shown at the 1878 Paris Universal Exhibition. That year Whistler made illustrations for the catalogue of Sir Henry Thompson's collection of blue and white Nankin porcelain, and began lithography with the printer Thomas Way. To improve his worsening financial situation Whistler turned to the 'art agent' Charles Augustus Howell, who encouraged him to make mezzotints after the portraits of his mother and Carlyle. But this and other schemes for reproducing work met with little success, and Whistler was obliged to sell his art for substantially less than he had before, in order to pay for the White House, where he lived for only a year until May 1879 when he was made bankrupt with debts of £4500. At an auction of his art and household effects Oscar Wilde was a successful bidder; a further sale was held at Sothebys in February 1880. During this period Whistler destroyed a number of his canvases in order to prevent his creditors acquiring them, in particular F. R. Leyland, whom he blamed for his insolvency and the loss of the White House, which was sold to the critic Harry Quilter. In February 1879 Maud Franklin (1857–1941?), who became Whistler's model in 1872 and sat for numerous portrait studies and etchings, gave birth to Maud McNeill Whistler Franklin, but the baby may not have survived infancy; however, Whistler fathered at least one surviving child by her, Ióne, who was probably born in 1877.

The artist as critic 1879–1884 In September 1879 Whistler left London for Venice with a commission from the Fine Art Society for twelve etchings of the city, where he lived for over a year, making more than fifty etchings and one hundred pastels. In Venice, Whistler became a focus for visiting American artists, such as Otto Bacher, who later published a book of reminiscences, *With Whistler in Venice* (1908). The architectural subjects of Renaissance palaces which Whistler drew and etched, many in intricate detail, the tourist views and lesser-known commercial waterways, were a visual answer to Ruskin's criticism of Whistler's art. Ruskin's campaign to preserve Venice's past from the commerce of modernism identified him with the city; similarly, the pastels Whistler made of Venice are strongly suggestive of Turner, and comparisons with Ruskin and Turner were inevitably made by critics when his Venice work was exhibited in London. The first exhibition of Whistler's Venice etchings, which he printed himself, at the Fine Art Society in December 1880, was not a critical or financial success. For the exhibition of Venice pastels held there in February the following year Whistler

designed a catalogue with brown paper covers as well as a colour scheme for the gallery, in an arrangement of brown, gold, and Venetian red.

After his return to London, Whistler adopted in earnest the role of critic, and took every opportunity to expose the inconsistencies, inaccuracies, and pretensions of art critics. Foremost of his targets were P. G. Hamerton and Frederick Wedmore, both of whom had written patronizingly about Whistler's etchings, as well as Sidney Colvin and Harry Quilter, whom Whistler referred to as ''Arry'. For the second exhibition of Venice etchings in 1883, he decorated the gallery of the Fine Art Society in yellow, including the livery of the attendant; the guests at the private view, which the prince and princess of Wales attended, wore yellow butterflies. For the exhibition he published a catalogue, *Caviar to the Critics*, in which he quoted, and in the case of Wedmore, misquoted, critics' words, in order to make them appear platitudinous and ridiculous. By this device, and by parodying the artistic aspirations of the bourgeoisie, Whistler attracted its patronage, which included members of the *nouveaux riches* and aristocracy, such as Lady Meux (wife of the brewer) and Lady Archibald Campbell, both of whose portraits he painted in 1881–2.

Whistler's cultivation of Oscar Wilde was an extension of this strategy. Their relationship was given public expression in a humorous exchange of telegrams in *The World* in 1883, in which Wilde, in answer to a report of their conversation in *Punch*, wrote that 'When you and I are together we never talk about anything but ourselves'; to which Whistler replied, 'No, no, Oscar, you forget—when you and I are together, we never talk about anything except me' (Whistler, *Gentle Art*, 66). Although Whistler at first accepted Wilde as his disciple, he grew resentful of what he considered to be Wilde's indiscriminate use of his ideas to further his career as spokesman for the aesthetic movement in England and America. Whistler continued to exhibit each year at the Grosvenor Gallery, and at the 1882 Paris Salon, where he had not exhibited since 1867, he showed a full-length portrait of Lady Meux (1881; Academy of Fine Arts, Honolulu, Hawaii); at the Salon of 1883 the portrait of his mother *Arrangement in Grey and Black* (1871–2; Musée d'Orsay, Paris) was awarded a third-class medal and enthusiastically reviewed by the French critic Théodore Duret, whose portrait Whistler painted and exhibited at the Salon of 1885 (1883–4; Metropolitan Museum of Art, New York), together with that of Lady Archibald Campbell (1882; Philadelphia Museum of Art). In 1884 he also exhibited Nocturnes and a self-portrait at the Galerie Georges Petit in Paris, and four paintings in the first exhibition of La Société des XX in Brussels.

By 1883 a younger generation of artists in London, who looked to contemporary French rather than English art for inspiration, had come to regard Whistler as the leader of modern painting. Dedicated to Whistler as assistants and pupils and calling themselves his 'followers', they included Walter Sickert and Mortimer Menpes, who described Whistler at this time in his book *Whistler as I Knew him* (1904):

In appearance Whistler was slight, small-boned, and extremely dainty. He seemed always to have a sparkling air about him. His complexion was always very bright and fresh; his eyes were keen and brilliant; and his hair, when I knew him, was, save for one snowy lock, of a glossy raven-black. His dress was quaint, and a little different from that of other men, and his whole appearance, even his deportment, was studied from the artistic standpoint. (Menpes, 86)

In January 1884 Sickert and Menpes accompanied Whistler to St Ives, Cornwall, and there painted seascapes in an impressionist manner out of doors, on small wooden panels the size of cigar box lids, a way of painting which Whistler had begun to practise in Holland, and in London, where his subjects included children and the shopfronts of old Chelsea. By adopting these methods, and exhibiting independently of the Royal Academy, his art became identified in England with impressionism. At this time he also began to work in watercolour, the results of which were first shown in the exhibition 'Notes—Harmonies—Nocturnes' at Dowdeswell Galleries, London, in May 1884; the catalogue contained the statement:

Industry in art is a necessity—not a virtue—and any evidence of the same, in the production, is a blemish, not a quality; a proof, not of achievement, but of absolutely insufficient work, for work alone will efface the footsteps of work. (Whistler, *Gentle Art*, 115–16)

In November Whistler was elected a member of the Society of British Artists, and began to show his work regularly at their summer and winter exhibitions.

Whistler's 'Ten o'clock' lecture, 1885 On 20 February 1885, at 10 p.m., in the Prince's Hall, London, Whistler delivered the 'Ten o'clock' lecture; which he repeated at Cambridge on 24 March, and at Oxford on 30 April. Whistler's reason for giving the lecture was largely to reclaim his authority as a professional artist, which he felt had been undermined by the populist abrogation of art by critics of the aesthetic movement, in particular Wilde, who though not named was indicted by Whistler in his satire on the dilettantism of dress reformers. In the introduction Whistler distanced himself from the fashion for 'home improvement':

The people have been harrassed with Art in every guise, and vexed with many methods as to its endurance. They have been told how they shall love Art, and live with it. Their homes have been invaded, their walls covered with paper, their very dress taken to task.

Whistler argued that great artists of the past, such as Rembrandt and Velázquez, sought and found 'the beautiful in all conditions and in all times … No reformers were these great men—no improvers of the way of others'. By asserting that 'There never was an artistic period', and that art was sublimely indifferent to social or political change—'False again, the fabled link between the grandeur of Art and the glories and virtues of the State'—Whistler also indicted Ruskin as 'The Preacher "appointed"!', whose advocacy of a fully contextualized art had influenced Wilde as well as William Morris, who was also one of Whistler's targets. In the lecture, notable for its

Swinburnian syntax and Old Testament language, Whistler assumed that 'art for art's sake' implicitly served the purpose of social criticism, for, like Swinburne, he inherited from Poe and Baudelaire a detestation of the philosophy of progress: 'And Birmingham and Manchester arose in their might—and Art was relegated to the curiosity shop'. He also used Baudelaire's 'heresy of didacticism' to condemn art which had a moral agenda: 'Beauty is confounded with virtue, and, before a work of Art, it is asked: "What good shall it do?"' (Whistler, *Gentle Art*, 135–59). Yet the general tenor of the lecture, which assumed an elusive and hermetic art for a bourgeois élite rather than a popular one for the masses, ran counter to much progressive social thinking in 1885. Wilde recognized this, and in his review in the *Pall Mall Gazette* could not accept Whistler's claim that an artist was 'an isolated fact, he is the resultant of a certain millieu' [sic] (*Pall Mall Gazette*, 1–2). Wilde's strongest criticism was a stinging attack on Whistler's dictum 'that only a painter is a judge of painting. I say that only an artist is a judge of art; there is a wide difference … the poet is the supreme artist' (Ellmann, *Artist as Critic*, 13–16). While this became the subject of a sarcastic exchange between them in *The World*, Wilde was the first to recognize the 'passage of singular beauty' in Whistler's lecture, by which it is since remembered:

And when the evening mist clothes the riverside with poetry, as with a veil, and the poor buildings lose themselves in the dim sky, and the tall chimneys become campanili, and the warehouses are palaces in the night, and the whole city hangs in the heavens, and fairy-land is before us—. (Whistler, *Gentle Art*, 135–59)

The growth of Whistler's reputation in Britain and abroad, 1885–1892 In 1885 Whistler and the American artist William Merrit Chase painted each other's portrait, and in August they visited Antwerp, Haarlem, and the International Exhibition in Amsterdam together. In May 1886 Whistler exhibited at Dowdeswell Galleries 'Notes—Harmonies—Nocturnes: Second Series', and published a set of twenty-six etchings of Venice, accompanied by a text consisting of eleven 'propositions' which criticized the fashion for wide margins in etching. Whistler trimmed his own etchings up to the plate mark, leaving only a protruding tab for his butterfly signature, and exhibited them in plain white wood frames. In 1886 Whistler also began a portrait of Lady Colin Campbell (des.) whose divorce case that summer was a *cause célèbre*; at the Paris Salon and in Brussels, he exhibited his portrait of the violinist Pablo de Sarasate (1884; Carnegie Institute, Pittsburgh). In June Whistler was elected president of the Society of British Artists, and set out to reform it by reducing the number of paintings in the exhibitions, redecorating the rooms, and encouraging artists of a more modern persuasion to show their work—a policy which immediately caused some resignations, but which Whistler defended by asking 'whether empty space be preferable to poor pictures—whether, in short, it be their duty to cover walls, merely that walls may be covered—no matter with what quality of work' (Whistler, *Gentle Art*, 189–91). Basing his concept on continental practice, particularly the well-appointed rooms of Georges Petit in Paris, with the intention of creating an 'art centre' rather than a 'shop', Whistler presided over the private views wearing evening dress without a tie. As well as his 'followers', and foreign artists, exhibitors included women artists such as Maud Franklin, who exhibited under the name Clifton Lin, and Beatrice Godwin, the daughter of the sculptor John Birnie Philip and wife of the architect, who exhibited as Rix Birnie; both described themselves as 'Pupils of Whistler'.

In May 1887 Whistler exhibited fifty small oil paintings, pastels, and watercolours at the Exposition Universelle de Peinture, Galerie Georges Petit, Paris, and invited Claude Monet, another exhibitor, to show with the Society of British Artists later that year. In June, *Notes*, his set of six lithographs, was published by Boussod, Valadon, et Cie. During the summer of 1887, jubilee year, Whistler designed an illuminated address and made twelve etchings of the naval review at Spithead which he presented in a bound volume to Queen Victoria; the Society of British Artists subsequently received a royal charter. In the autumn he visited Holland and Belgium with his brother and sister-in-law. In February 1888 he exhibited oils and pastels at the Société des XX, Brussels; and in May, Nocturnes, etchings, and drawings at the Galerie Durand-Ruel, Paris. Whistler's efforts to improve the quality of exhibitions at the Royal Society of British Artists, which included the design of a velarium to soften the light, and a lion and butterfly logo, were insufficient to slow the increasing deficit from the sale of work, and by June he was obliged to resign, together with Menpes, Sickert, Alfred Stevens, Theodore Roussel, and others, who supported him. 'The "Artists" have come out', Whistler explained to a journalist, 'and the "British" remain' (Whistler, *Gentle Art*, 205–10).

Earlier in 1888 the 'Ten o'clock' lecture had been published, which after Whistler asked him to, Swinburne reviewed, with devastating savagery, in the June issue of the *Fortnightly Review*, thus ending their friendship of a quarter of a century. That summer in Paris, Monet introduced Whistler to Stéphane Mallarmé, who translated the 'Ten o'clock' into French, and became an intimate friend. The French critics J. K. Huysmans and Gustave Geffroy also began to write about Whistler's art. In July he sent a large selection of his work to the third Internationale Kunst-Austellung in Munich, and was awarded a second-class medal; in November he was elected an honorary member of the Royal Academy of Fine Arts, Munich. On 11 August 1888 Whistler married the artist Beatrice Godwin (1857–1896) [*see* Whistler, Beatrice], and the couple travelled in France, down the Eure and Loire, to Tours and Loches, where Whistler made etchings of Renaissance architecture. On their return to London they lived in the Tower House, Tite Street, with Oscar Wilde as a neighbour, by which time Whistler's relationship with him had become acrimonious.

In March 1889 a large exhibition of Whistler's work was held at H. Wunderlich & Co., New York; and in April he was awarded a first-class medal at Munich, and the award of the cross of St Michael of Bavaria; banquets were held

in his honour in London and Paris. In May Sickert organized a large exhibition of his work at the College for Working Men and Women, London; and at the Paris Universal Exhibition he was awarded a gold medal. In September Whistler and his wife spent two months in Amsterdam where he made a set of ten etchings, as well as paintings and watercolours, and was awarded a gold medal for his portraits at the International Exhibition. He was also made chevalier of the Légion d'honneur that year. In January 1890, in *Truth*, Whistler ended his association with Wilde by accusing him of plagiarism, and the next month the Whistlers moved to 21 Cheyne Row. With Whistler's informal agreement, the American journalist Sheridan Ford edited a selection of Whistler's correspondence, *The Gentle Art of Making Enemies*, which was printed in Ghent in February 1890. Resisting Ford's additional entreaties to contract for a lecture tour and make etchings in America, Whistler designed the book himself, which was published with the same title by William Heinemann in June; after a lawsuit in Brussels, Whistler had Ford's version suppressed. In March 1890 C. L. Freer of Detroit visited Whistler and began to buy his work. At the Paris Salon that year Whistler exhibited two Nocturnes, and several paintings at the Salon in Brussels. In April 1891 the corporation of Glasgow was persuaded by local artists to buy the portrait of Carlyle, for 1000 guineas, the first of Whistler's works to enter a public collection. Whistler visited Paris with increasing frequency, and in the summer began a portrait of the symbolist poet Comte Robert de Montesquiou-Fezensac (1891–2; Frick Collection, New York); he stopped exhibiting at the Salon, and instead sent two paintings to the new Société Nationale des Beaux-Arts. In August he served on the hanging committee of the autumn exhibition at the Walker Art Gallery, Liverpool; and in November the portrait of his mother was bought for the Musée du Luxembourg for 4000 francs. In 1891 Whistler received a commission for painted panels in Bates Hall, Boston Public Library; $15,000 was made available for the project in 1894, but withdrawn the following year.

Late years, 1892–1903 In January 1892 Whistler was made officer of the Légion d'honneur; and in March a retrospective exhibition of his work, 'Nocturnes, Marines & Chevalet Pieces', was held at the Goupil Gallery in London, for which Whistler selected past criticisms for the catalogue entitled *The Voice of a People*. The exhibition was a critical success and marked a turning point in Whistler's reputation. Many works were sold for two and three times what Whistler had originally received for them, and thereafter Whistler entered into partnerships with Scottish dealers such as Alexander Reid and D. C. Thomson, and E. G. Kennedy of Wunderlichs, to benefit from the resale of his work, mostly abroad, to their mutual advantage. In the spring Whistler moved to Paris to live, buying a house at 110 rue du Bac and acquiring a studio at 186 rue Notre-Dame-des-Champs; he continued to work in pastel and lithography. For the frontispiece of Mallarmé's *Vers et prose* (1893) he drew a portrait of the poet. At the World's Columbian Exhibition in Chicago he exhibited six works and was awarded a gold medal; and five Nocturnes and a portrait of Lady Meux at the Société Nationale des Beaux-Arts. At the sixth Internationale Kunst-Ausstellung, Munich, in June, he was awarded a first-class gold medal. In the summer of 1893 Whistler and his wife visited Vitré, Lanmion, and Paimpol in Brittany, and Perros-Guirec, Côtes-du-Nord, and made etchings and seascapes. At the sixty-third exhibition of the Pennsylvania Academy of the Fine Arts in December 1893, Whistler's portrait of Lady Archibald Campbell, *La dame au brodequin jaune*, valued at $15,000 by the Glasgow dealer Alexander Reid, was bought for the Wilstach collection, the first of Whistler's works to enter an American public collection (1882; Philadelphia Museum of Art).

Early in 1894 Whistler painted a small portrait of Lady Eden (Hunterian Museum and Art Gallery, Glasgow), and her husband, Sir William Eden, sent £100 for it, which Whistler banked. Whistler exhibited the picture in Paris but refused to deliver it, and Eden instituted legal proceedings; whereupon Whistler returned the money but scraped out the figure, substituting that of an American sitter in its place, so that if he lost the case the portrait could not be recovered. At the civil tribune in March 1895 Whistler was ordered to hand over the portrait and pay damages; but after two appeals, in 1897 and 1900, Whistler was finally granted the picture and Eden was ordered to pay expenses. In *Eden versus Whistler: the Baronet and the Butterfly* (1899) Whistler published his account of the case, which entered French law by establishing that artists do not enter into ordinary commercial contracts of sale with their patrons.

In December 1894 Whistler was awarded the Temple gold medal at the sixty-fourth annual exhibition of the Pennsylvania Academy of the Fine Arts; and in 1895 a gold medal at Antwerp. During 1895 and 1896 he spent more time in England, as the health of his wife deteriorated. In the autumn of 1895 he worked for nearly two months in Lyme Regis; and in December an exhibition of his lithographs was held at the Fine Art Society, London. For the first three months of 1896 he stayed with his wife at the Savoy Hotel and worked in lithography on portraits and views of the Thames. In May, Beatrice Whistler died of cancer. For a while Whistler made his home with William Heinemann, and over the next five years stayed frequently at Garlant's Hotel, and with his wife's family. Her younger sister, Rosalind Birnie Philip, acted as his secretary, and became his ward and executor. He frequently visited northern France to work. In April 1897 Whistler formed the Company of the Butterfly, with premises in Manchester Square, London, to market his art. That month he testified for Joseph Pennell the printmaker, and his future biographer, in the successful action he brought against Sickert, who had written that Pennell's drawing on transfer paper instead of stone was not true lithography. In May, George W. Vanderbilt commissioned Whistler to paint his portrait (National Gallery, Washington, DC), and he also worked on portraits of the Birnie Philip sisters (Hunterian Museum and Art Gallery, Glasgow) and others in London and Paris, in pastels and oils, to

which he gave mythological and biblical titles. In April 1898 he was elected president of the International Society of Sculptors, Painters and Gravers, the aims of which included the non-recognition of nationality in art; Whistler took an active part in its organization and exhibitions. In October he became patron of the Académie Carmen in Paris, opened by his model Carmen Rossi at 6 passage Stanislas, which until its closure in 1901 was a mecca for students of all nationalities, particularly Americans, who hoped to learn Whistler's methods. Whistler made sporadic visits, and in 1899 he articled Inez Bate as his legal apprentice to act under his command; thereafter his visits became less frequent. In January 1899 Whistler exhibited at the first World of Art Exhibition, in St Petersburg.

In 1900 Whistler was elected an academician of the Academy of St Luke, Rome; and at the Universal Exhibition in Paris, where he exhibited *The Little White Girl*, a self-portrait, and a portrait of his sister-in-law, he was awarded a grand prix for paintings and another for etchings. In August he visited Holland, and then joined the Birnie Philip family near Dublin. In December, to recuperate from illness, he visited Gibraltar, Algiers, Tangier, Marseilles, and then Corsica, where he stayed until the following May. In 1901 he was awarded gold medals in Buffalo and Dresden, and in Paris elected honorary member of the Académie des Beaux-Arts. In October, Whistler closed his Paris studio and sold his house; he spent the winter months convalescing in Bath. In January 1902 he was awarded the gold medal of honor at the Pennsylvania Academy of the Fine Arts. In April he leased 74 Cheyne Walk from its architect, C. R. Ashbee, and lived there with the Birnie Philips. On holiday with C. L. Freer in The Hague in July, Whistler became seriously ill, but visited Scheveningen, the Mauritshuis, and galleries at Haarlem. In April 1903 he was awarded an honorary degree of doctor of laws by Glasgow University, but was too ill to attend the ceremony. On 17 July of that year Whistler died of heart failure. After a funeral service at Chelsea Old Church on 23 July, where his pallbearers were Théodore Duret, Sir James Guthrie, John Lavery, Edwin A. Abbey, G. Vanderbilt, and C. L. Freer, Whistler was interred in Chiswick cemetery; a catafalque designed by his stepson Edward Godwin was later erected over his grave and that of his wife.

Memorials, influence, and posthumous reputation Three retrospective memorial exhibitions of Whistler's work were held: the first was organized by the Copley Society, Boston, in 1904; the second by the International Society in London, in 1905; the third at the École des Beaux-Arts, Paris, also in 1905. The International Society commissioned a memorial to Whistler from Rodin, who succeeded Whistler as president of the International Society; but casts of the sculpture, which were intended for England, France, and America, were never installed. However, two permanent memorials to Whistler exist in the form of the comprehensive collection of his work C. L. Freer bequeathed to the Smithsonian Institution (Freer Gallery of Art, Washington, DC), opened in 1923, and the extensive collections of Whistler's art and memorabilia Rosalind Birnie Philip gifted and bequeathed to Glasgow University in 1935 and 1958, and which now form part of the Hunterian Museum and Art Gallery, Glasgow.

By showing, like the poet Stéphane Mallarmé, that significant expression could be achieved with minimal means, in his graphics as well as his paintings Whistler pushed the conventions of representation in visual art to their limit. In his campaign to emancipate painting from literature, Whistler swept away many accepted values of Victorian art, at the same time that his impressionist contemporaries were contesting the status of academic painting in France. Yet Whistler's art was strongly marked by the European tradition, and over his formal full-length portraits he laboured long and intensively, often fruitlessly, to achieve notions of parity with its canon. Whistler could never satisfactorily account theoretically for the eclectic mix of art and decoration in his own painting, as Swinburne noted, and which Whistler denied to practitioners in the applied arts; an inconsistency stemming from his fear of the democratization of art, that Wilde accepted, but which also became the dilemma of the modernist artist: to be a part of society but remain apart from it. In the last two decades of his life Whistler's influence was considerable. His elusive colours had an immediate appeal for the symbolist generation of the 1890s. In England and Scotland younger artists readily responded to Whistler's art and ideas. His influence on American impressionism was formative and pervasive; and in Germany, Scandinavia, Spain, as well as Russia, though less so in France, Whistler's quintessential modernity made a strong impact, until the values it represented were fragmented by abstract and iconoclastic art which erupted at the onset of the First World War. Whistler's excessive cult of the artist was inimical to modernism's search for art's universal values, and it is significant that, although influenced by him, when Clive Bell published *Art* in 1914, he turned, not to Whistler, but to Cézanne, Gauguin, Matisse, and Picasso, to make his case.　　　ROBIN SPENCER

Sources J. M. Whistler, *The gentle art of making enemies* (1892) · E. Robins Pennell and J. Pennell, *The life of James McNeill Whistler*, 2 vols. (1908) · E. R. Pennell and J. Pennell, *The Whistler journal* (1921) · A. M. Young, M. F. MacDonald, and R. Spencer, *The paintings of James McNeill Whistler*, 2 vols. (1980) · M. F. MacDonald, *James McNeill Whistler: drawings, pastels, watercolours: a catalogue raisonné* (1994) · E. G. Kennedy, *The etched work of Whistler* (1910) · H. K. Stratis and M. Tedeschi, *The lithographs of James McNeill Whistler*, 2 vols. (1998) · R. H. Getscher and P. G. Marks, *James McNeill Whistler and John Singer Sargent: two annotated bibliographies* (1986) · L. Cong., manuscript division, Pennell collection, Whistler MSS · U. Glas., Birnie Philip collection of Whistler MSS · R. Spencer, 'Whistler's early relations with Britain and the significance of industry and commerce for his art: Parts I and II', *Burlington Magazine*, 136 (1994), 212–24, 664–74 · M. F. MacDonald, 'Maud Franklin', *Studies in the History of Art*, 19 (1987), 13–26 · A. C. Swinburne, *William Blake: a critical essay*, 2nd edn (1868) · A. C. Swinburne, *Essays and studies* (1875) · A. C. Swinburne, 'Mr Whistler's lecture on art', *Fortnightly Review*, 49 (1888), 250–62 · R. Spencer, 'Whistler, Swinburne and art for art's sake', *After the Pre-Raphaelites: art and aestheticism in Victorian England*, ed. E. Prettejohn (1999), 59–99 · L. Merrill, *A pot of paint: aesthetics on trial in Whistler v. Ruskin* (1992) · *The works of John Ruskin*, ed. E. T. Cook and

A. Wedderburn, library edn, 39 vols. (1903–12) · O. Bacher, *With Whistler in Venice* (1908) · M. Menpes, *Whistler as I knew him* (1904) · R. Ellmann, ed., *The artist as critic: critical writings of Oscar Wilde* (1970) · R. Ellmann, *Oscar Wilde* (1987) · J. M. Whistler, *The gentle art of making enemies*, ed. S. Ford (1890) · A. Elsen, 'The artist's oldest right?', *Art History*, 11 (1988), 217–30 · J. M. Whistler, *Eden versus Whistler: the baronet and the butterfly: a valentine with a verdict* (1899) · C. Bell, *Art* (1914) · G. Du Maurier, 'Trilby', *Harper's New Monthly Magazine*, 88 (1893–4), 567–87 · R. Spencer, ed., *Whistler: a retrospective* (1989) · R. Dorment, *James McNeill Whistler* (c.1994) · L. Merrill, *The peacock room: a cultural biography* (1998) · R. Spencer, *Whistler* (1993) · private information (2004) · *The Athenaeum* (5 July 1862), 23 · *Pall Mall Gazette* (21 Feb 1885), 1–2 · m. cert. · d. cert. · M. F. MacDonald, ed., *Whistler's mother: an American icon* [forthcoming] · www.whistler2003.com/correspondence [on-line edn of Whistler's correspondence; forthcoming]

Archives Hunt. L., letters · L. Cong., corresp. and papers · NYPL, corresp. and papers · U. Glas. L., corresp. and papers

Likenesses J. A. M. Whistler, self-portrait, oils, 1857–8, Smithsonian Institution, Washington, DC, Freer Gallery of Art · J. A. M. Whistler, self-portrait, etching, 1859, Art Institute of Chicago · photograph, c.1860, Smithsonian Institution, Washington, DC, Freer Gallery of Art · Carjat?, carte-de-visite, c.1864, U. Glas. · J. A. M. Whistler, self-portrait, oils, 1867–8, Art Institute of Chicago · J. A. M. Whistler, self-portrait, oils, 1870–75, Smithsonian Institution, Washington, DC, Freer Gallery of Art · J. E. Boehm, terracotta bust, 1872, NPG · J. A. M. Whistler, self-portrait, oils, c.1872, Detroit Institute of Arts [*see illus.*] · P. Thomas, etching, 1874 (after J. A. M. Whistler), NPG · W. Greaves, oils, 1877, Museum of Art, Toledo, Ohio · London Stereoscopic Co., photograph, 1878, L. Cong. · London Stereoscopic Co., photograph, 1879, U. Glas. · C. A. Corwin, print, 1880, Metropolitan Museum of Art, New York · W. M. Chase, oils, 1885, Metropolitan Museum of Art, New York · photograph, 1885, NPG · H. S. Mendelssohn, photograph, c.1885–1886, U. Glas. · Dornac, photograph, 1890–99, U. Glas. · J. A. M. Whistler, self-portrait, oils, 1893–4, Harvard U. · J. A. M. Whistler, three self-portraits, oils, 1895–1900, U. Glas. · J. A. M. Whistler, self-portrait, oils, 1896–8, National Gallery of Art, Washington, DC · G. Boldini, oils, 1897, Brooklyn Museum · G. Boldini, print, 1897, Museo Boldini, Ferrara · A. P. Barney, pastel drawing, 1898, Smithsonian Institution, Washington, DC · W. Nicholson, coloured woodcut, 1899, NPG · R. P. Staples, chalk drawing, 1901, NPG · M. Beerbohm, caricatures, U. Glas. · M. Beerbohm, caricatures, Birmingham Museum and Art Gallery · M. Beerbohm, caricatures, Harvard U. · W. Boxall, oils, U. Glas. · H. Furniss, two pen-and-ink caricatures, NPG · W. Greaves, oils, NPG · W. Greaves, wash drawing, V&A · E. Haskell, caricature drawing, Cleveland Museum of Art, Ohio · E. Haskell, caricature, etching, V&A · P. Helleu, drypoint print, Louvre, Paris, Cabinet des Estampes · W. Hole, print (after J. A. M. Whistler), NPG · Kyd [J. C. Clarke], watercolour caricature, V&A · London Stereoscopic Co., photograph, NPG · H. D. Martin, pencil drawing, Princeton University, New Jersey · F. Mason, pen and watercolour caricature, V&A · N. Menpes, drypoint print, Cleveland Museum of Art, Ohio · W. Nicholson, lithograph, NPG · B. Partridge, watercolour caricature, NPG · J. Reich, etching, University of Missouri · Spy [L. Ward], watercolour caricature (study), NPG; repro. in *VF* (12 Jan 1878) · J. A. M. Whistler, self-portrait, pen drawing, L. Cong. · pencil drawing, V&A

Wealth at death £11,020 6s. 0d.: resworn probate, Jan 1904, *CGPLA Eng. & Wales* (1903)

Whistler, Sir (Alan Charles) Laurence (1912–2000), glass engraver, writer, and architectural historian, was born at Bryer, Court Road, Eltham, Kent, on 21 January 1912, the youngest child of Henry Whistler (1866–1940), builder and estate agent, and his wife, Helen Frances Mary (1870–1963), daughter of the Revd Charles Slegg Ward, vicar of Wootton St Lawrence, Basingstoke. His maternal great-great-grandfather was the silversmith Paul Storr. He was educated at Stowe School and at Balliol College, Oxford. His ambition to be a poet was encouraged early on when he was awarded the first king's gold medal for poetry, in 1935, and later by the friendship of poets including Walter de la Mare. He published twelve books of poems, his two principal collections being *The World's Room* (1949) and *Enter* (1987), but received little further acclaim in this field. His poems are consciously, even elaborately, crafted. Some are light-hearted celebrations, others love poems, but most record a very private journey through personal tragedy.

Stowe kindled Whistler's passion for classical architecture—he made scale-drawings of its temples for pleasure—and this developed in the 1930s with a commission to write *Sir John Vanbrugh: Architect and Dramatist* (1938), the first biography of its subject. Later he wrote *The Imagination of Vanbrugh and his Fellow Artists* (1954); fine buildings, great and small, remained of absorbing interest to him. His feeling for history and love of occasion, secular or religious, led to a book on traditional celebrations: *The English Festivals* (1947).

Whistler's artistic education came mainly from his elder brother and closest friend, Reginald John (Rex) *Whistler (1905–1944), a precociously talented draughtsman, prolific and successful in many fields, whose work played a major role in Laurence's life—as a powerful influence and a precious legacy. After Rex's death in action, in Normandy in 1944, Laurence devotedly catalogued and promoted his work, publishing (with Ronald Fuller) *The Work of Rex Whistler* (1960) and a biography, *The Laughter and the Urn* (1985).

On 12 September 1939, as war broke out, Whistler married Barbara Dolignon (known as Jill) Furse (1915–1944), elder daughter of Sir Ralph Furse (1887–1973) and Celia, *née* Newbolt. Jill was a young actress of beauty, sensitivity, and talent. Their intensely happy relationship—conducted by letter while Whistler was serving as a signals officer in the rifle brigade, and in brief interludes in a remote cottage in north Devon—coloured the rest of his life. Two children were born to them: Simon in 1940 and Caroline (known as Robin) in 1944. Jill, however, suffered from a recurring blood disorder, and died suddenly on 27 November 1944, soon after Robin's birth (and only four months after Rex's death). Much of Whistler's work as a writer, and later as an engraver, was driven by his need to come to terms with such loss and to create enduring epitaphs to the happiness that he and Jill had shared. *The Initials in the Heart* (1964), perhaps his best-known work, is an account of this marriage.

Meanwhile, encouraged by Rex, Whistler had discovered his own medium—point-engraving on glass—and in so doing pioneered the revival of an art that had languished for 200 years. Starting with verses scratched on a window pane he rapidly taught himself the delicate techniques of stipple and line, developed the tools, and embarked on a stream of commemorative pieces, usually on blown glassware, featuring house portraits, personal emblems, and occasional verse, all embellished with the

rococo decoration and lavish eighteenth-century-style lettering beloved by both brothers.

By the 1960s Whistler was moving on to less ornate work: landscapes, real and imaginary, drawing on the Wessex countryside that he loved. His mastery of stipple technique now allowed for more subtle effects of light, as seen in the *Seasons* centrepiece commissioned by the Goldsmiths' Company in 1967. Architecture remained a favourite theme, buildings of personal significance featuring frequently, along with more fanciful architectural ideas, such as *The Grass Cathedral* (1972); he was also now using his own distinctive alphabets for inscriptions (see the sunrise roundel in Thornham Parva church, Suffolk). He explored Escher-like visual conceits in, for example, *An Overflowing Landscape* (1975), in which a landscape on a bedroom wall escapes its frame to take over the room. He experimented with the three-dimensional effects of engraving more than one surface (in *The Apollo Landing*, 1978, the dramatic moonscape with lunar module is engraved on the inside of the bowl, while half-lit earth floats behind it on the outer side). At his most original, however, he used the qualities of his medium—light drawn on darkness (unengraved glass)—to explore a sense of mysterious symbolism in the visual world. Darkness here becomes as potent as light—to intense poetic effect. Symbols of joy, death, and the journeying soul, in powerful juxtaposition, reveal his deep (though not narrowly orthodox) Christian belief.

On 15 August 1950 Whistler married Jill's younger sister Theresa Thomasin Dolignon Furse (b. 1927), a writer, with whom he had two children, Daniel (b. 1954) and Frances (b. 1957). They lived in Lyme Regis, Dorset. From 1955 he undertook much larger commissions, for memorial church windows. Among the finest are those in Moreton church, Dorset, where over thirty years he designed all twelve windows (a controversial thirteenth piece—on the subject of Judas—remains uninstalled).

Whistler mounted fourteen exhibitions—in London, Oxford, New York, and elsewhere—and published five books of photographs of his work, among them *The Image on the Glass* (1975), as well as a short history, *Point Engraving on Glass* (1992). His work may be seen in the Victoria and Albert Museum, London; the Ashmolean Museum, Oxford; the Fitzwilliam Museum, Cambridge; the Cecil Higgins Museum, Bedford; and the Corning Museum, New York; in several Oxford colleges; and in numerous churches, including Salisbury Cathedral. He was elected founder president of the Guild of Glass Engravers in 1975.

Whistler's second marriage was dissolved on 15 October 1985, by which time he had moved to Alton Barnes, Wiltshire. His third marriage, to Carol Anne Dawson, *née* Groves (b. 1948), began on 24 March 1987 and ended in divorce on 11 October 1991. His last home was in Watlington, near Oxford. After a disabling stroke in 1998 he lived in an Oxford nursing home, his mind still active on ideas for poems, books, and glass. He died in St Luke's Hospital, Headington, Oxford, of a brief fever, on 19 December

2000, shortly after receiving his knighthood, and was cremated in Oxford on 29 December.

Whistler was a very attractive man—widely read, especially in English poetry and philosophical thought, with a gift for conversation and a rich sense of humour. (He delighted in puns, visual and verbal, and misquotation.) But he was also a private person—unconfident even— who felt overshadowed by his brother's brilliant fluency, though his own work was both more original and more profound. ROBIN RAVILIOUS

Sources L. Whistler, *The laughter and the urn* (1985) · L. Whistler, *The initials in the heart* (1964) · L. Whistler, *The image on the glass* (1975) · family papers, priv. coll. · personal knowledge (2004) · b. cert.
Archives priv. coll., MSS | SOUND BL NSA, *Craft lives* series · BL NSA, tapes made 1999–2000 for National Life Story Collection
Likenesses photographs, priv. coll.

Whistler, Reginald John [Rex] (1905–1944), artist, was born at Eltham, Kent, on 24 June 1905, the second of three sons of Henry Whistler (1866–1940), architect and estate agent, and his wife, Helen Frances Mary (1870–1963), daughter of the Revd Charles Slegg Ward, vicar of Wootton St Lawrence, Basingstoke. His maternal great-great-grandfather was Paul Storr, the silversmith. He was educated at Haileybury College, Hertfordshire, and although he made little formal progress there he was already known as a wit, and he continued to pour out sketches and drawings, on which he had been engaged since early childhood. Between 1912 and 1923 he won a prize every year at the exhibition of the Royal Drawing Society. He left Haileybury in 1922 and went to the Royal Academy Schools but stayed there only one term, being considered 'unpromising' by Charles Sims. At the Slade School of Fine Art, to which he then applied, he was at once accepted by Henry Tonks, who in later years told Sir Osbert Sitwell that in the whole course of his own career as artist and teacher he had only met three or four people with a natural gift for drawing, and that Rex Whistler was one of these.

Tonks perceived that Whistler's talent lay in imaginative decoration and he encouraged him to follow this bent. Whistler began to paint seriously in oils. In 1924, with Mary Adshead (later Mrs Stephen Bone), Whistler decorated the walls of the Highways Club, Shadwell, London. When, in 1926, Sir Joseph Duveen offered a new refreshment room to the Tate Gallery, Tonks recommended Whistler as mural decorator. The room was opened in November 1927 and the young artist's murals, on the fanciful theme *The Pursuit of Rare Meats*, were at once acclaimed by critics and public alike for their decorative skill, their wit, and their resourcefulness.

From that moment, at the early age of twenty-two, Whistler was launched on a promising career. His style was quite out of key with the rather rash experimentalism of the 1920s—having more than a touch of the rococo and finding its inspiration in the seventeenth and eighteenth centuries, and, later, the nineteenth century—but

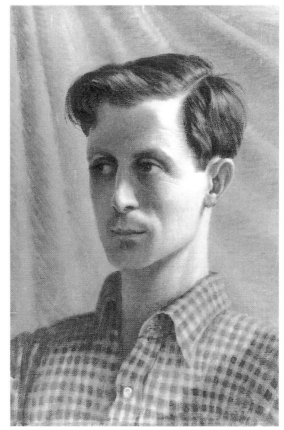

Reginald John [Rex] Whistler (1905–1944), self-portrait, *c.*1934

it made an instant appeal to the taste of the day. Connoisseurs like Captain David Euan Wallace and Sir Philip Sassoon were quick to commission murals from Whistler, but his most impressive wall decorations were done in 1937, for the marquess of Anglesey, at Plas Newydd, Anglesey, and for Lady Louis Mountbatten (later Countess Mountbatten of Burma) at Brook House, Park Lane, London.

While still at school Whistler had begun to discover the delights of poetry, and in his first year at the Slade he had compiled his own private anthology, profusely illustrated in the margins. The decade following the First World War saw a healthy and brilliant revival of British book production, and in this movement Whistler naturally enough took part. Some of his most delightful work was done in the ephemeral medium of the dustwrapper; fortunately some examples have been reproduced for posterity in the biography *Rex Whistler, 1905–1944: his Life and his Drawings* (1948) by his younger brother, (Alan Charles) Laurence *Whistler (1912–2000). More enduring by their very nature are his book illustrations, which virtually began with Edith Olivier's *Mildred* (1926). Among his finest productions were illustrations for a limited edition of Swift's *Gulliver's Travels* in two volumes (1930), Hans Andersen's *Fairy Tales and Legends* (1935), and a series for A. E. W. Mason's *Königsmark*, done in 1940–41 and published in 1952;

the originals of the last are in the Tate collection. A favourite method was to construct a highly decorative rococo marginal frame, in which the illustration was set; in this, as in so much else, Whistler showed the influence of the seventeenth and eighteenth centuries.

The stage also proved a fruitful field for Whistler's high imagination and decorative talent. Work in this kind included scenery and costume for ballets such as *The Rake's Progress* (1935) and *Le spectre de la rose* (1944), both for Sadler's Wells; for plays, including Laurence Housman's *Victoria regina*, in New York (1935) and London (1937), and Oscar Wilde's *An Ideal Husband* (1943); scenery for the operas *Fidelio* and *The Marriage of Figaro* (both 1934), and contributions to half a dozen of C. B. Cochran's revues.

Apart from these three main lines of work Whistler showed astonishing versatility and adaptability in such varied fields as designs for textiles, china, carpets, bookplates, letter-headings, and even luggage labels for Imperial Airways. Although he took a commission in the Welsh Guards in the winter of 1939 he still kept up a vigorous flow of work until he went overseas, with the guards armoured division, to Arromanches, Normandy, at the end of June 1944. He left on the walls of the officers' mess at Brighton a mural painting which is now in the town's art gallery. He could easily have sought employment in camouflage or as an official war artist but he preferred to carry out the infinitely more dangerous task of an active tank troop leader. In an attack across the Orne, east of Caen, on 18 July 1944 he was killed by a shellburst near the village of Le Mesnil, during his first hours in action. He was buried at the Banneville-la-Campagne war cemetery in Calvados, France.

In spite of the echoes from Patinir, Watteau, Canaletto, Boucher, and others, which appear in his work, Whistler had a freshness, a graceful wit, and a linear resource which were all his own. That he should have made his way so instantly and so certainly in a period devoted in such large measure to 'the cube, the cone, and the cylinder' is a tribute not only to his artistic personality but to the percipience of the connoisseurs, publishers, and theatre managers who employed him.

There was no trace of the intellectual in Whistler yet he has been described as one of the most sensitively cultured and intelligent of men. Well built and of medium height, agile in such pursuits as dancing, skating, and skiing, he also won quick popularity by his warmth, his wit, his enthusiastic and persuasive conversation, his charm of manner, and the modest distinction of his bearing. He was not married but children took to him instantly, and he loved them wholeheartedly, spending hours making drawings for their entertainment.

H. B. GRIMSDITCH, rev.

Sources *The Times* (28 July 1944) · *The Times* (31 July 1944) · *The Times* (7 Aug 1944) · *The Times* (23 Sept 1944) · L. Whistler, *Rex Whistler, 1905–1944: his life and his drawings* (1948) · *CGPLA Eng. & Wales* (1944)
Likenesses R. Whistler, self-portrait, oils, *c.*1934, NPG [*see illus.*] · photograph, 1937, Hult. Arch. · R. Whistler, self-portrait, mural,

Plâs Newydd, Anglesey · R. Whistler, self-portrait, oils, Tate collection · R. Whistler, self-portraits, priv. coll.
Wealth at death £4627 17s. 5d.: probate, 21 Nov 1944, *CGPLA Eng. & Wales*

Whiston, James (*bap.* 1641?, *d.* 1706), broker and writer on trade, was probably baptized on 14 June 1641 at St Swithin London Stone, London, the son of James and Ann Whiston. From 1680 probably until his death Whiston produced a weekly commodity price current in London. Initially published in 1680 under the title the *Merchants Remembrancer*, it was later renamed *Whiston's Merchants Weekly Remembrancer, of the Present-Money-Prices of their Goods Ashoar in London*; during most of the 1680s and 1690s a French edition, *Le Memorial des Marchands*, was published. As well as insurance rates, exchange rates, and the prices of commodities, including gold and silver, Whiston listed some stock prices and increasingly incorporated financial and commercial news. Although publication of the price current was continued by Francis Robinson, Whiston's name appeared in its title until 1707.

The imprint on the price current describes Whiston as a broker 'to be heard of at his house in Water-lane, near the Custom-house'. Some of his trading activities can be traced; he bought goods, for example, at auctions held in the 1670s and 1680s by the Royal African Company. In 1680 he applied, in conjunction with William Crouch, for a fourteen-year patent 'for their invention of making black pepper white and merchantable' (*CSP dom.*, 1680–81, 36).

Treasury papers contain a number of references to Whiston's recommendations and proposals concerning customs duties on imported goods, particularly wine and spirits. In 1684 he was rewarded with £100 'for his present encouragement' having insisted that duties on brandy be paid *ad valorem*, rather than as aqua vitae, which proved to be 'to the advantage of the King's revenue' (Shaw, 7/2.1451). Similarly in 1699, Whiston petitioned that because of the underestimation of the capacity of pipes in which wine was imported the king was defrauded of revenue. He claimed that the coming year promised a high wine yield and 'If these wines were honestly gauged in the other ports it would add to the revenue 70,000l. *per ann.*' (Redington, 325). The following year, in the presence of the commissioners of customs, Whiston proposed to the lords of the Treasury how the fraudulent importation of French wine, and the exportation of coin, might be prevented. He proposed the registration and marking of Spanish silver bars, and that the silver held by goldsmiths be melted down at Goldsmiths' Hall. Because of suspicions that wine imported from St Sebastian was French, Whiston suggested that customs should be paid as if it were from France. For these proposals, and some more minor suggestions, the Lords commended 'his zeal' and directed the commissioners 'to order their officers to be civil to him' (Shaw, 15.46).

Whiston developed a number of other proposals concerning trade in published pamphlets. In 1693 he drew up a scheme to form a committee of merchants to sit 'fully Authoriz'd and Impower'd to Inquire and Examine into all Matters Relating to Trade' (Whiston, *Discourse*, 5). For, he argued, 'If Sick, we consult a physitian: So when the Trade of a Nation is to be Secured or Advanced, the Merchants and Tradesmans Advice is questionless best able to accomplish the same' (ibid., 4). Merchants were to elect representatives in each county and members were also to be drawn from particular trading companies. Most pertinent at this time, argued Whiston, were the committee's particular responsibilities in relation to the war with France:

> by Their Care of Securing our Navigation from the French Rapine, &c. They will likewise be able so far to Improve our present Trade, That our Additional Advantages thereby Gain'd to the Nation, shall more than pay for the War to the Easing of the greatest part of our Burthen.

He went on to ask his readers:

> Can we pretend to have English Blood in our Veins, and suffer the Insulting Monsieur to Ravish our Darling Mistress under our very Noses! To Commit a Rape upon our Trade in our own Channel, and on our own Coast? (ibid., 8)

This pamphlet was reworked and republished in subsequent years. Likewise Whiston's writings against the sale of public offices in London as 'dishonourable and of very ill consequence' were published under a number of different titles after initial publication in the early 1680s (Whiston, *Serious Advice*, 1).

Tax assessments gathered for the poll tax in 1692 and the 1693 4s. in the pound tax indicate that Whiston lived with a servant in Dolphin Precinct, in the parish of St Dunstan-in-the-East. The annual rent for his property was assessed at £25 per annum and his stock at £100, but both assessments are probably underestimates. In records relating to further tax assessments in 1695, he is listed as a widower. In 1704 Whiston thought it was 'a fair Request' to ask his readers:

> that they will not be Critical and Scrupulous in examining the wording of his thoughts, being writ by one so infirm a Constitution (by reason of a continued Astma) that his illness wil seldom permit him to digest his thoughts clearly into writing. (Whiston, *Distempers*, 32)

He died in November 1706 and was buried at St Dunstan's on 30 November. From the grant of administration in the records of the prerogative court of chancery it is known that he had a son, James Whiston.

NATASHA GLAISYER

Sources J. J. McCusker and C. Gravesteijn, *The beginnings of commercial and financial journalism: the commodity price currents, exchange rate currents, and money currents of early modern Europe* (1991) • J. Whiston, *A discourse of the decay of trade, the necessity of recovering* (1693) • J. Whiston, *England's state-distempers, trac'd from their originals with proper remedies and means to make her vertuous and prosperous* (1704) • J. Whiston, *Serious advice, presented to the common council of the City of London* (1681?) • D. V. Glass, introduction, *London inhabitants within the walls, 1695*, ed. D. V. Glass, London RS, 2 (1966) • *CSP dom.*, 1680–81 • W. A. Shaw, ed., *Calendar of treasury books*, 7/2, PRO (1916); 15 (1933) • J. Redington, ed., *Calendar of Treasury papers*, 2, PRO (1871) • private information (2004) [J. Sewell, CLRO] • PRO, PROB 6/83, fol. 241r • parish register, St Swithin London Stone, 14 June 1641 [baptism] • parish register, Stepney, St Dunstan-in-the-East, 30 Nov 1706 [burial]

Whiston, John (1711–1780), bookseller, was born in London on 30 July 1711, son of William *Whiston (1667–1752), theologian, and his wife, Ruth Antrobus (1671–1751).

Whiston's early years remain vague, though it is known that he was apprenticed to Fletcher Gyles, a bookseller in Holborn, before being made free of the Merchant Taylors' Company on 6 February 1733; he entered the livery of that company on 19 December 1746. Within a year of completing his apprenticeship, Whiston had established a bookshop in Fleet Street, London, under the sign of Mr Boyle's Head in honour of Robert Boyle and in recognition of his father's position in 1707 as the Boyle lecturer at Oxford. The shop reputedly became the rendezvous for distinguished literati and clergymen.

Whiston's earliest distinctions were as one of the printers of the votes of the House of Commons and as one of the original publishers of priced catalogues. In 1735 he bought and catalogued the entire library of Edward Chishull and in 1747 he catalogued the library of Bishop Moore at Cambridge University which had been bequeathed to George I in 1715. Whiston was also called upon to assist with the disposal of Nicholas Mann's library at Eton College following Mann's death in 1753. Some twelve years later Whiston purchased, seemingly for his own collection, the books which had been in the possession of Adam Anderson (1692?–1765).

Whiston seems to have published numerous books though nothing of any real distinction. His father's writings were a primary concern and it was in 1749 that he issued the *Memoirs of the Life and Writings of Mr William Whiston*; he issued a corrected version in the year after his father's death. During 1761–2, he was actively involved in promoting the *New and General Biographical Dictionary*, which was printed in twelve volumes; a copy of it in the British Library contains extensive marginalia in his hand. He was also noted by John Nichols in *Literary Anecdotes* as the source of much biographical information. It is believed that at one point his elder brother, George Whiston, was associated with Whiston's business, although this cannot be substantiated. However, between 1749 and 1765 Whiston was, in fact, in partnership with Benjamin *White, a former apprentice. It was during this time that Whiston most likely married and his daughters, Sarah and Sophia, were born. On 3 July 1759 Nathaniel Conant was turned over to Whiston to complete his apprenticeship; he later married Whiston's daughter Sarah.

About 1767 Whiston's business moved to premises at 64 Fleet Street following the dissolution of his partnership with White, who opened his own bookshop next door. By most accounts, though, Whiston had not taken an active role in conducting his business since 1759 when he was apparently forced to retire by a nervous breakdown, reputedly, though implausibly, brought on by shock occasioned by a practical joke. It is said that he spent some time in an asylum and that the bookselling business was carried on by Conant in his absence. On 20 November 1766 Whiston drew up a lengthy, complicated, and at times anguished will over which the experience of his breakdown loomed very large. He began by imploring God to 'supply my want of faith and hope both [of] which by a fatal accident I have for more than seven years been deprived of' and concluded with the request that he be buried at Lyndon, Rutland, near the graves of his parents, with a 'plain stone' carrying an inscription that 'A most unhappy [matter?] in May 1759 caused him to pass the remainder of his days in great misery of Mind and Body' (PRO, PROB 11/1066, fols. 71v, 73r). The bookseller Lockyer Davis is cited as one of the executors. However, despite his morbid thoughts of late 1766, Whiston did not die until 3 May 1780 and his will, several lines of which he had crossed out in the meantime, was proved on 22 May.

MICHAEL T. DAVIS

Sources D. F. McKenzie, ed., *Stationers' Company apprentices*, [3]: *1701–1800* (1978) · H. R. Plomer and others, *A dictionary of the printers and booksellers who were at work in England, Scotland, and Ireland from 1726 to 1775* (1932) · I. Maxted, *The London book trades, 1775–1800: a preliminary checklist of members* (1977) · will, PRO, PROB 11/1066, sig. 297 · *DNB*

Whiston, William (1667–1752), natural philosopher and theologian, was born on 9 December 1667 at the rectory, Norton-juxta-Twycross, Leicestershire, the fourth of the nine children of Josiah Whiston (1622–1685), rector at Norton, and his wife, Katherine (1639–1701), daughter of Gabriel Rosse, the previous incumbent at Norton, and his first wife, Elizabeth. Josiah Whiston, a presbyterian, retained his living at the Restoration and, though blind in his later years, served his parish diligently until his death.

Early years and education Whiston was educated at home by his father, for whom he also acted as amanuensis, and attended grammar school at Tamworth between 1684 and 1686. As second surviving son he inherited the family library and provision for university 'that he may be an able minister of the New Testament' (Farrell, 6). He entered Clare College, Cambridge, as a sizar in September 1686.

Whiston excelled as a student. He took a keen interest in mathematics, and appeared on the honours list in 1689–90. He graduated BA in 1689, was elected to the Exeter fellowship in July 1691, and was promoted to probationary senior fellow of the college in February 1693, in which year he received his degree of MA. He established himself as a tutor at Clare, counting among his students the nephew of Archbishop Tillotson. He was ordained a deacon in September 1693 by the latitudinarian William Lloyd (1627–1717), bishop of Lichfield and prophetic exegete, from whom he may have begun to derive his interest in biblical prophecy.

In 1694, claiming ill health, Whiston resigned his tutorship to Richard Laughton, whom he replaced as chaplain to fellow Clare graduate John Moore (1646–1714), bishop of Norwich. During his chaplaincy Whiston divided his time between Norwich, London, and Cambridge—after his ordination he had returned to Clare to study 'particularly the mathematicks, and the *Cartesian* philosophy' (Whiston, *Memoirs*, 35–6). He set out to master Isaac Newton's recently published *Principia mathematica* (1687), encouraged by a paper of the early Newtonian David Gregory (1659–1708). As an undergraduate Whiston had attended only 'one or two' of Newton's lectures, finding them incomprehensible at the time, as he later conceded

William Whiston (1667–1752), after Sarah Hoadly, *c.*1720

(ibid., 36). He first met Newton in 1694, and a friendship began that was to last until their estrangement two decades later.

Newtonian cosmographer, 1696–1702 Whiston's swift conversion to Newton's natural philosophy soon bore fruit in his first publication, *A New Theory of the Earth* (1696). He had shown this millenarian cosmogony in manuscript to Richard Bentley (1662–1742), Christopher Wren (1632–1723), and Newton himself, whom Whiston claims 'well approved of it' (Whiston, *Memoirs*, 43) and to whom the book was dedicated. Whiston's *New Theory* applied the physics of Newton and the geology of John Woodward (d. 1728) to demonstrate that the scriptural accounts of creation, the flood, and the final conflagration were 'perfectly agreeable to Reason and Phylosophy' (ibid.). He also sought to correct Thomas Burnet's Cartesian and deistically tinged *Sacred Theory of the Earth* (1681, 1684), which Whiston had defended for his BA degree. Whiston prefaced his earth theory with an essay on the style of Genesis and, like Newton, argued for a more literal hermeneutic. He drew from Newton's work on comets, and posited that the planetary system had solidified from comets attracted by the sun's gravitation. He used a catastrophist cometography to explain the flood, suggesting that the near approach of a divinely guided comet had initiated the diurnal rotation of the earth, transformed its orbit from circular to elliptical, and caused the deluge through the condensation of vapours from the comet's tail. He also identified stratified sedimentary rock and marine fossils found in continental areas as vestiges of the flood.

The *New Theory* proved popular and after the initial run of 1500 copies went through five further editions (1708–55), was translated into German (1713), epitomized in French (1718), and summarized by the comte de Buffon (1707–1788) in 1749. The latter wrote ostensibly to refute the *New Theory*, but was nevertheless indebted to some of Whiston's ideas, as were other earth theorists. Praised by John Locke (1632–1704) for its novel hypotheses, the *New Theory* was the first full-length popularization of Newtonianism and the most direct cause of Whiston's meteoric rise.

In 1698 Bishop Moore secured the living of Lowestoft-cum-Kessingland, Suffolk, for Whiston, and there the latter regularly delivered sermons, held catechetical lectures, and had 2000 parishioners under his care. Samuel Clarke (1675–1729), with whom Whiston had come into contact in 1697 through their common interest in Newtonianism, replaced him as chaplain at Norwich. Whiston resigned his fellowship at Clare in June 1699 on his marriage to Ruth Antrobus (1671–1751), daughter of George Antrobus, Whiston's headmaster at Tamworth. In 1701, as part of the marriage settlement, Whiston received from his father-in-law farm land near Dullingham, Cambridgeshire, with an annual revenue of £30–£40. Shortly after Whiston's marriage, Newton called him to Cambridge to lecture as his deputy with the full income of his post (Newton had become warden of the Royal Mint in 1696). Whiston began lecturing by February 1701. In December that year Newton resigned and ensured Whiston's election as the third Lucasian professor of mathematics in May 1702.

Lucasian professor, 1702–1710 During his tenure as professor, Whiston published several works on mathematics, physics, and astronomy. In 1703 he produced an edition of Euclid's *Elements* 'for the Use of young Students in the University' (Whiston, *Memoirs*, 131). This text was published in six Latin editions (1703–95), ten in English (1714–72), and one in Greek (1805), with printings in Cambridge, London, Dublin, Amsterdam, Venice, and Vienna. In 1707, with Newton's acquiescence, Whiston published some of the former's lectures on algebra (*Arithmetica universalis*). Later the same year Whiston published his own astronomical lectures (*Praelectiones astronomicae*), which appeared subsequently in English (*Astronomical Lectures*, 1715, 1728). His *Praelectiones physico-mathematicae* appeared in 1710 and was later printed as *Sir Isaac Newton's Mathematick Philosophy More Easily Demonstrated* (1716). Whiston was always far more willing to publish than Newton, and the latter two works, originally composed as undergraduate lectures, offered more accessible treatments of Newtonian astronomy, physics, and mathematics than was available in the abstruse *Principia*. From May 1707 Whiston and the Plumian professor, Roger Cotes (1682–1716), were the first to deliver lectures on experimental philosophy at Cambridge, presenting experiments elucidating the natural philosophy of both Newton and Robert Boyle (1627–1691).

Whiston devoted much time to prophetic researches in this period, publishing his *Essay on the Revelation* in 1706, the first of several works on biblical prophecy. He was also called on to deliver the Boyle lectures for 1707, and chose as his theme the evidence of fulfilled prophecy (*The Accomplishment of Scripture Prophecies*, 1708). Finally, Whiston led an initiative to establish charity schools for the education of poor children in Cambridge, and preached the inauguration sermon at Trinity Church in 1705.

From his achievements as a student and his *New Theory*, through his succession to the Lucasian chair, appointment as Boyle lecturer, and emergence as one of the first leading Newtonians, Whiston accomplished much in these early years. In 1710, however, there came a turning point. By 1706 or 1707, almost certainly as a result of his contact with Newton and Clarke, Whiston embraced an anti-trinitarian theology similar to Arianism, which he often characterized as 'Eusebian'. While the initial impulse to unorthodoxy likely came from Newton, Whiston differed in details—as well as level of caution—from his mentor. He became convinced of the canonicity of the pseudepigraphal and Arian *Apostolic Constitutions*, and in 1708 unsuccessfully attempted to persuade the vice-chancellor of Cambridge to license a treatise he had written on this document. Whiston next wrote to the archbishops of Canterbury and York requesting a review of the *Constitutions*. Spurning advice from friends and superiors, he grew bolder and published a heretical work in 1709 (*Sermons and Essays*). Unwilling to back down, he was brought before the heads of the Cambridge colleges, charged under an Elizabethan university heresy statute, and on 30 October 1710 expelled from his professorship and the university.

London experimental lecturer, 1711–1731 Now a disestablished figure, Whiston began a new phase of his life. Experienced in teaching mathematics, astronomy, physics, and experimental philosophy in an academic setting, he moved to London and became an entrepreneur of natural philosophy, delivering public lectures, publishing popular texts, and successfully seeking patronage from royalty and the nobility for his various schemes. By the summer of 1711 he was living in Hatton Garden and advertising himself as a tutor in mathematics. The following summer he became involved in a public experimental lecture course with Humphrey Ditton (1675–1715), Francis Hauksbee the elder (c.1666–1713), and Francis Hauksbee the younger (1687–1763).

By March 1713 Whiston formed a lecturing partnership with the younger Hauksbee, and a survey of newspaper advertisements reveals that this experimental lecture course was scheduled biannually into the early 1730s. The course syllabus was originally quadripartite, covering mechanics, hydrostatics, pneumatics, and optics; a section on magnetics was added by 1725. In 1714 the partners produced an illustrated course manual, which was reprinted several times into the late 1720s and also used for an experimental course delivered at Oxford by John Whiteside and James Bradley (1693–1762). From the late 1710s to the mid-1720s, Whiston and Hauksbee jointly ran a course of astronomy as well. Both courses were held next door to the Royal Society at Hauksbee's instrument shop in Crane Court, with Whiston delivering the lectures and Hauksbee demonstrating. Whiston also lectured alone on experimental philosophy in Bath and Bristol in the 1720s and into the 1740s on mathematics, astronomy, and longitude in various London coffee shops. Furthermore, he delivered lectures during or after displays of astronomical phenomena, such as eclipses and the aurora borealis, and sold popular charts of the solar system and the solar eclipses of 1715 and 1724. His income was supplemented from 1727 by a £50 annuity from Queen Caroline and King George, and from 1738 by a £20 annuity left by Sir Joseph Jekyll, master of the rolls and one of Whiston's long-time patrons. To these were added various other benefactions and payments of patronage. As he grew older and accumulated more income from patronage, Whiston lectured less frequently.

Longitude projects Whiston also played an important role in early eighteenth-century attempts to determine longitude at sea, having been interested in this problem from his days as Lucasian professor and convinced that a reliable method would benefit both safety and trade. Whiston and Ditton petitioned parliament in 1714 suggesting a reward be offered for a method accurate to one degree at sea. After the intervention of Newton, Clarke, Cotes, and Edmond Halley (1656–1742), and the circulation of a broadsheet printed by Whiston and Ditton, the Longitude Act was passed the same year. The act and its reward triggered a plethora of hopeful solutions, with Whiston himself presenting several methods.

The first of these was Whiston's and Ditton's *New Method for Discovering the Longitude both at Sea and Land* (1714), which proposed that ships anchored at precise intervals across the Atlantic fire star shells to 6440 feet at set times, thus allowing navigators to determine their longitude by calculating the time between the flash and sound of the shell. Whiston also carried out experiments in southern England on the use of star shells for survey work. Second, from 1718 to 1723 Whiston experimented with dipping needles: he presented his findings at the Royal Society and sent the instruments on ocean voyages to various parts of the globe. As part of this work he produced maps of the English Channel, perhaps the first to show isogonic lines (*The Longitude and Latitude Found by the Inclinatory or Dipping Needle*, 1721). A subscription raised in 1721 for his longitude work raised just over £470 from royalty, the nobility, and politicians. In 1724 he outlined a method using solar eclipses. A fourth method involved the observation of the eclipses of Jupiter's satellites (*The Longitude Discovered by the Eclipses, Occultations, and Conjunctions of Jupiter's Planets*, 1738), for which he attempted to improve the design of reflecting telescopes. Finally, supported by £175 from various patrons (including Sir Charles Wager, first commissioner of the Admiralty) and a £500 grant from the board of longitude, Whiston carried out a coastal survey of southern England, and in 1743 published the results in a new map of the English Channel.

Prophecy and biblical studies Whiston's prophetic work figures large as well. Believing that the design argument

was insufficient on its own to convince deists and other unbelievers of the truth of the Bible, he emphasized the argument from prophecy. In his Boyle lectures he claimed that biblical prophecy is 'the most plain and unquestionable evidence that has been produced for the Christian Religion' (Whiston, *Accomplishment*, 2). As in experimental philosophy, he held that the multiplication of proofs increased the probability of the truth of prophecy. He thus presented no fewer than 300 prophetic fulfilments in the lectures. It was probably his quantitative approach to prophecy that encouraged him to expand the prophetic corpus beyond the protestant Bible to defend in print the authority of such pseudepigraphal works as the Sibylline oracles. He also wanted to establish an exact method of prophetic hermeneutics, and with respect to Messianic prophecies rejected allegorical interpretations and multiple fulfilments of the same prophecy. For him, there was only one fulfilment: a literal one, uniquely accomplished in the person of Christ. This claim helped bring him into controversy with the freethinker Anthony Collins (1676–1729), who argued that only the first, historical fulfilment was literal, while Messianic applications were based on strained, allegorical interpretations.

In his desire to secure literal and exact interpretations, Whiston also employed textual criticism to correct corruptions in the Hebrew text putatively introduced by Jewish copyists (*Essay towards Restoring the True Text of the Old Testament*, 1722). This work was the primary target of Collins's *Discourse on the Grounds and Reasons of the Christian Religion* (1724), which declared that the result of such an endeavour would be 'a mere WHISTONIAN BIBLE' (Collins, 225). The *Discourse* elicited three replies from Whiston, including two works that bolstered further his inductive programme by listing page after page of prophetic fulfilments.

Throughout the last three decades of his life, Whiston proclaimed in publications, lectures, and private conversations his belief that by 1766 the temple would be rebuilt, the Jews restored to their land, and the millennium established. This effort included the construction in 1726 of what he contended was 'an exacter model' of the Jerusalem temple (Whiston, *Description*). He lectured on this model in London and the resort towns of Bristol, Bath, and Tunbridge Wells, and presented it at the court of Queen Caroline. Revealing his twofold interest in anomalous celestial and terrestrial phenomena, Whiston held that such were prophetic signs of the coming end. This belief is exemplified by his public lectures during and after the London earthquakes of 1750, in which he proclaimed divine judgement on the wicked city of London.

In the wake of his expulsion from Cambridge and during further heresy proceedings against him, Whiston published a manifesto of his faith (*Primitive Christianity Reviv'd*, 1711–12), a series of commentaries on, and translations of, early Christian writings. Along with Clarke he was at the centre of the trinitarian controversies of the 1710s and 1720s. In 1715 he founded the Society for Promoting Primitive Christianity, which met for two years in his home. Discussions focused on early Christian texts, beliefs, and practices; members included John Gale (1680–1721), Thomas Emlyn (1663–1741), and Arthur Onslow (1691–1768). By the 1720s Whiston also organized a dissenting conventicle of Unitarians, and there is evidence that some dissenters and early Unitarians looked to him as a role model.

During the period of tory ascendancy from 1710 to 1714, Whiston became something of a *cause célèbre* among the whigs, just as Henry Sacheverell was seen by many tories and high-churchmen as a martyr. While heresy proceedings against Whiston were dropped at the death of Queen Anne, and though he was never defrocked, he continued to face opposition, particularly from the high church. In 1721 he was ejected from St Andrew's Church in Holborn by its rector, none other than Sacheverell himself, after which Whiston moved from this parish to Great Russell Street in Bloomsbury. Most of the opposition, however, manifested itself in a steady torrent of critical publications. Objecting to the inclusion in liturgy of the Athanasian creed, with its anathemas against those who denied the Trinity, Whiston was often able to persuade clergy to omit it while he was in attendance. However, when a priest began to read it again at the church in Lyndon in 1747, Whiston walked out and thereafter attended the meetings of the General Baptists.

Whiston produced many publications on theology, church history, chronology, liturgy, ecclesiastical polity, demonology, and miracles. In 1717 he first published his *Astronomical Principles of Religion*, a work highlighting the design argument but also replete with valuable astronomical data and engravings. His translation of the Jewish historian Josephus can be seen as part of these efforts as well. This most successful of Whiston's works, published in 1737 with maps of the Holy Land and engravings of the temple, was long the standard English translation and was in continuous reprint throughout the nineteenth and twentieth centuries. Whiston also published a translation of the New Testament from Beza's text in 1745. His beliefs bore remarkable similarities to those of Newton, not only in his subordinationist Christology, rejection of the Trinity, and antipathy towards Athanasius, but also in his Christian primitivism, eirenicism, acceptance of believers' baptism, and movement away from the eternity of hell.

Although he lived well into his eighty-fifth year, Whiston complained of a weak disposition, which he claimed improved somewhat in later life. In 1710 the German traveller Uffenbach said he '[is] a man of very quick and ardent spirit, tall and spare, with a pointed chin and wears his own hair. In look, he greatly resembles Calvin. He is very fond of speaking and argues with great vehemence' (Mayor, 179). Portraits confirm Whiston's austere appearance; he is said to have gone grey as a young man. Although not a practising minister after 1710, he seems to have retained his clerical garb throughout his life. His writings and actions reveal a headstrong nature and a pronounced martyr complex, along with an attempt to position himself as a religious reformer and latter-day prophet. Nevertheless, he was a principled man whose career clearly suffered for his unwavering commitment to his beliefs.

William and Ruth Whiston had eight children, of whom Sarah, William, George, and John *Whiston survived to adulthood. In 1717 Sarah married the Hebraist Samuel Barker, whose manor, Lyndon Hall, Rutland, became the summer residence for his wife's parents. Her brothers William and George studied at Clare College, though as dissenters they did not take degrees. With their father's involvement the two published a Latin translation of the Armenian historian Mosis Khorenaci (1736). John became a prominent Fleet Street bookseller, who published most of his father's later works and whose home came to serve as his parents' London residence from the 1730s. Thomas Barker (1722–1809), Whiston's grandson through his daughter, published *An Account of the Discoveries Concerning Comets* (1757), along with meteorological reports in the Royal Society's *Philosophical Transactions* and controversial works on baptism, prophecy, and demonology. Whiston died at Lyndon Hall, after a week's illness, on 22 August 1752, and was buried in Lyndon churchyard. At his death he was in possession of farm land valued at over £1300; this was left to his children.

Natural philosopher and theologian A tireless and prolific writer, Whiston published over 120 separate books, pamphlets, and charts, many of which appeared in later editions. His range was considerable, extending from geology, mathematics, astronomy, and longitude, to prophecy, doctrine, chronology, and textual criticism, along with translations of biblical, apocryphal, pseudepigraphal, and historical texts. Near the end of his life, he published an *apologia pro vita sua* (*Memoirs*, 1749–50; 2nd edn, 1753), an uneven but invaluable account of his life.

In natural philosophy Whiston's greatest significance lies not in any important innovations, but in his early and varied efforts at popularizing Newtonianism, along with his role in stimulating the founding of the board of longitude. He was at the forefront of British philosophers that made the transition from Cartesianism to Newtonianism, and one of his most important contributions as Lucasian professor was his teaching of the latter to a new generation. Along with Clarke, Whiston both played a leading role in promoting unitarian theology in England and helped make some of Newton's private theological opinions public. Whiston's commentary on Revelation was cited by eighteenth- and nineteenth-century prophetic exegetes, and his translation of Josephus proved an enduring legacy, finding a place in many Anglo-American homes well into the late twentieth century.

While Whiston's heterodox theology, prophetic views, longitude schemes, and impetuous nature attracted much criticism and ridicule, he was not without supporters, including royal, noble, and whig patrons, along with fellow dissenters. A vigorous opponent of both deism and unbelief on the one hand and high-church orthodoxy on the other, Whiston sought a middle course between what were to him two extremes. There was a unity in his natural philosophical, prophetic, and religious endeavours, and he fervently believed that both

Newton's discoveries in natural philosophy and his own advances in furthering 'primitive Christianity' were preludes to the millennium.   STEPHEN D. SNOBELEN

Sources W. Whiston, *Memoirs of the life and writings of Mr William Whiston: containing memoirs of several of his friends also*, 2nd edn, 2 vols. (1753) · M. Farrell, *William Whiston* (1981) · J. E. Force, *William Whiston: honest Newtonian* (1985) · W. Whiston, *The accomplishment of scripture prophecies* (1708) · A. Collins, *A discourse of the grounds and reasons of the Christian religion* (1724) · Leics. RO, Conant papers, DG11/1018; DG11/DE.730/2 · *The genuine works of Flavius Josephus … illustrated with new plans and descriptions of the tabernacle of Moses and of the temples of Solomon, Zorobabel, Herod, and Ezekiel*, ed. and trans. W. Whiston (1737) · J. E. B. Mayor, *Cambridge under Queen Anne* (1911) · *Daily Courant* (1702–35) · *Daily Post* [London] (1719–45) · guard book, CUL, Lucasian professorship MSS, CUR 39.8 · University of Cambridge matriculation lists, CUL, Graduati 3; Matr. 2
Archives BL, letters and MSS, Add. MSS 4276, 4433, 6727, 23820, 24197, 28104, 32718, 45511, 61619, Harley MS 7032, Lansdowne MS DCCCXXX.2, Sloane MS 1926, Stowe MSS 490, 597 · Bodl. Oxf., commonplace book, MS Eng. misc. d. 297 · Bodl. Oxf., MS vols compiled by Whiston and letters, MSS 42304, 45292–45301 · Bodl. Oxf., sermons, notebooks, and minute book of Society for Promoting Primitive Christianity · Clare College, Cambridge, letters and other MSS, Phillipps MS 25369 · Clare College, Cambridge, papers · CUL, MSS and letters, Guard Book C. U. R. 39.8, 39.12, MS 6.49, MS Dd.2.55(2), D. XI, D. XII · Glos. RO, papers relating to controversy · RS, journal books, record books, letter-books, classified papers, vol. 20, fol. 4.28 (entries, abstract, and letter) · Trinity Cam., letters, MS R.4.42 | BL, letters to Lord Egmont, Add. MS 47150 · Clare College, Cambridge, fellows accounts; college letter-book; extracts from Cotes's and Whiston's lectures · Leics. RO, Conant MSS, letters, DG11/DE.730/2
Likenesses oils, *c.*1690–1699, Clare College, Cambridge · oils, *c.*1700–1710, Lyndon Hall, Leicestershire · S. Hoadly?, oils, before 1720, Lyndon Hall, Leicestershire · G. Vertue, line engraving, 1720 (after S. Hoadly, before 1720), BM, NPG; repro. in L. Stewart, *The rise of public science: rhetoric, technology, and natural philosophy in Newtonian Britain, 1660–1750* (1992), 86 · oils, *c.*1720 (after S. Hoadly), NPG [*see illus.*] · B. Wilson, etching, 1753, BM, NPG; repro. in Whiston, *Memoirs*, frontispiece · carved wooden head, NPG
Wealth at death over £1300—value of property near Dullingham, Leicester: Leics. RO, Conant MSS, DG11/1018

Whitaker. *See also* Whitaker.

Whitaker, Alexander (1585–1617), clergyman and colonist in America, was the son of William *Whitaker (1547/8–1595), regius professor of divinity at Cambridge University and master of St John's College, and his wife, Susan Culverwell, daughter of the prosperous London puritan merchant Nicholas *Culverwell [*see under* Culverwell family]. Through his Culverwell relatives Whitaker was related to Sir Thomas Smith, treasurer of the Virginia Company, and the puritan leaders Arthur Dent, William Gouge, and Laurence Chaderton.

Whitaker went to Eton College at the age of thirteen in 1598, his status as a foundation scholar indicating the modest circumstances in which his family lived after his father's death three years earlier. He entered Trinity College, Cambridge, in 1602, where he was a contemporary of future New England colonists John Cotton and John Winthrop, and graduated MA in 1608. He was ordained in the Church of England in 1609.

Whitaker went to Jamestown, Virginia, in the spring of 1611. He became the minister at Henrico, a new settlement up the James River named in honour of Prince Henry; he

also preached at nearby Bermuda Hundred. Whitaker wrote about his Virginia experiences in letters, two of which were published at the time. One was published as *Good Newes from Virginia* (1613) with a preface by Revd William Crashaw, who had studied under William Whitaker in the 1590s and wrote about Alexander Whitaker's personal call to preach the gospel in Virginia. Crashaw explained that Whitaker had not written for publication; if he had he would have 'written it in Latine or in Greeke, and so to have decked it for phrase and stile, and other ornaments of learning and language' as to show his attainments. But the Virginia Company decided to publish it none the less 'so the naked and plaine truth may give a just affront to the cunning and coloured falshoods devised by the enimies of the Plantation'.

Whitaker studied the religion of the neighbouring Powhatan Indians he hoped to convert, and wrote about it in *Good Newes from Virginia*. His study led him to conclude that the American natives had had knowledge of the Judaeo-Christian God in the past and retained 'many footsteps of Gods image'. Whitaker described the great supernatural powers of the native priests, 'a generation of vipers even of Sathans owne brood', that made them such formidable adversaries, and argued that the Powhatan Indians 'acknowledge that there is a great good God, but know him not, having the eyes of their understanding as yet blinded; wherefore they serve the divell for feare'. He also recognized that these priests worked for their people's benefit. He sent 'one image of their god to the Counsell in England which is painted upon one side of a toad-stoole, much like unto a deformed monster'.

Whitaker's great success in Virginia was the conversion and baptism of Pocahontas, who 'openly renounced her countrey Idolatry, confessed the faith of Jesus Christ, and was baptized' in 1614. The letter to 'my verie deere and loving Cosen M. G.' in which he announced her conversion was published in Ralph Hamor's *True Discourse of the Present Estate of Virginia* (1615). In the same letter he argued strongly that the new colony was a work of God, and remarked on the failure of English ministers 'that were so hot against the Surplis and subscription [to] come hither where neither is spoken of'. He asked if they 'keepe themselves at home for feare of loosing a few pleasures?' He wrote that he was determined to stay until he received a lawful call home, but his career was cut short. Alexander Whitaker drowned while crossing a creek in Virginia in 1617.   KAREN ORDAHL KUPPERMAN

Sources A. Brown, ed., *The genesis of the United States*, 2 vols. (1890) · N. Canny, 'England's New World and Old, 1480s–1630s', *The Oxford history of the British empire*, 1: *The origins of empire*, ed. W. R. Louis (1998), 148–69 · K. O. Kupperman, *Indians and English: facing off in early America* (2000) · H. C. Porter, 'Alexander Whitaker: Cambridge apostle to Virginia', *William and Mary Quarterly*, 14 (1957), 317–43

Whitaker, Sir (Frederick) Arthur (1893–1968), maritime civil engineer, was born in Ladysmith, Natal, on 17 July 1893, the second son of William Henry Whitaker, civil engineer, and his wife, Georgina Primrose Foggo. His father emigrated to South Africa in 1890, but in 1898, after their mother's death, Arthur and his elder brother,

Ambler, went to England and were brought up in Liverpool by their uncle, Frederick Whitaker, a schoolmaster.

Family life, though happy, was strict and disciplined and Arthur had to work hard at school and university: he never forgot these early lessons, which he applied throughout his life. He went to Liverpool Institute High School and Liverpool University, where he gained first-class honours in engineering (1914), research scholarship, and nomination for an 1851 Exhibition industrial bursary. However, war broke out and, in April 1915, he was sent to Rosyth as a 'temporary draughtsman improver' with the Admiralty—at 4s. per day. Undeterred, he continued his studies and, in 1917, obtained an MEng degree at Liverpool University, which conferred on him the honorary degree of DEng in 1960. He married, in 1923, Florence (d. 1978), daughter of John Woods Overend, manager of a marine engineering business in Liverpool. They had one son and two daughters.

The extent and variety of civil engineering work in the Admiralty provided ideal training for a young engineer. After five years at Rosyth on construction of the naval dockyard and the destroyer base at Port Edgar, Whitaker was sent to Jamaica in 1920 to build an oil fuel installation and found himself acting as naval agent and a member of the Jamaica marine board. The 1920s were lean years for the services and promotion was slow, but Whitaker was broadening his experience and building up his reputation and by 1930 had served at Devonport, the Admiralty, Malta, and Portsmouth, and had been engaged in oil installations, jetties, dredging, and many types of harbour works. Early in 1933 he received accelerated promotion to superintending civil engineer, in charge of the construction of the Singapore naval base, which comprised a dockyard, with a 1000 foot dry dock, wharves, naval, armament, victualling, and fuel depots, barracks, and a small township for expatriate personnel. Work had commenced in 1928 and was in full flight when he arrived. However, in 1934, T. B. Hunter, the civil engineer-in-chief, Admiralty, retired and Whitaker was summoned home for further accelerated promotion to deputy civil engineer-in-chief. In January 1940 he succeeded Sir Athol Anderson as civil engineer-in-chief.

The country was again at war and Whitaker himself was now responsible for the wide-ranging programmes of naval works at home and overseas. At home, dockyards, naval bases, all types of storage and fuel depots, wireless telegraphy stations, airfields, and training establishments were expanded and modernized and many new ones built. Much of the storage was underground and many novel requirements had to be met. Overseas, the emphasis was on operational and repair bases, storage, and airfields—scattered all over the world, from Iceland to South Africa and from the West Indies to Australia. For the invasion of Europe special bases and some fifty embarkation yards were built and the department was involved in the design of the Mulberry harbours.

With such a large programme under his control it is difficult to identify any particular project with Whitaker himself, with one exception—the Orkney causeways. The

submarine that sank the *Royal Oak* in October 1939 had entered Scapa Flow through one of the four eastern sounds. Having ordered the immediate sinking of additional blockships, Winston Churchill asked Whitaker whether all four sounds could be permanently closed by causeways. In that remote area, with depths of about 60 feet and currents up to 12 knots at high tide, this was a daunting task. But Whitaker said the project was possible, directed it personally, got work started in May 1940, and had the sounds effectively blocked by 1942. Completion to road level came in 1945.

Whitaker tackled the biggest construction programme ever undertaken by the Admiralty with energy and determination. By his engineering ability, sense of purpose, and speed of decision, he won the respect and loyalty of all his permanent and wartime temporary staff and welded them into an efficient and close-knit team. Although essentially shy and unostentatious, he was a dominant leader, who drove them to their limits: they responded to his challenge and established a reputation for the department which survived long after his death.

After the war, Whitaker chaired the British organizing committee for the nineteenth congress of the Permanent International Association of Navigation Congresses in London in 1957 and was a member of the Commission Consultative des Travaux of the Suez Canal Company and, for fourteen years, of the Dover Harbour Board. He was created CB in 1941 and KCB in 1945 and in 1947 was made a commander of the Légion d'honneur. He retired from the Admiralty in 1954 and then, for eight years, engaged on harbour and dredging work overseas (mainly in South America) as a partner in Livesey and Henderson, consulting engineers.

Apart from his Admiralty department, Whitaker's one abiding interest, to which he gave devoted service, was the Institution of Civil Engineers, of which he was a member for forty-nine years and president in 1957–8. He believed that its role was fundamental to the development of the science and practice of civil engineering and he constantly exhorted his own engineers actively to support it. He delivered the 1946–7 Vernon Harcourt lecture, entitled 'Civil Engineering Aspects of Naval Harbours and Bases'. Whitaker died in Northwood, London, on 13 June 1968.   WILLIAM HARRIS, *rev.*

Sources *The Times* (14 June 1968) · private information (1981) · personal knowledge (1981) · *WWW* · *CGPLA Eng. & Wales* (1968)
Likenesses W. Stoneman, photograph, 1945, NPG · J. and M. Codner, oils, *c*.1958, Inst. CE
Wealth at death £45,826: probate, 25 Oct 1968, *CGPLA Eng. & Wales*

Whitaker, Sir Edward (1660?–1735), naval officer, was appointed lieutenant of the *Swallow*, then commanded by Matthew Aylmer, on 16 October 1688. In 1689 he was in the *Mary*, in 1690 (again with Aylmer) in the *Royal Katherine*, and on 15 May 1690 he was promoted captain of the *Dover* (44 guns), in which, during the following three years, he took several rich prizes and captured many French privateers. On 27 September 1692 he married Ann Stephens (d. 1705) of Leigh, Essex. In the same year he was noted as a client of Edward Russell (later earl of Orford), as well as continuing to enjoy the patronage of Aylmer, under whom he was flag-captain in the *Royal Sovereign* in 1693–4. Between 1695 and 1696 he commanded the *Elizabeth*, *Monck*, and *St Andrew*, and was flag-captain to Sir Cloudesley Shovell in the *Victory*. In the 1690s he was living at Leigh in Essex.

In May 1699 Whitaker was appointed to the *Portland*, and on 13 January 1702 to the *Ranelagh*, one of fifty ships commissioned on the same day. A month later, on 16 February, he was appointed master-attendant at Woolwich; he held that office throughout the year. In January 1703 he took command of the *Dorsetshire*, one of the fleet which went with Sir George Rooke to the Mediterranean in 1704. In the capture of Gibraltar, Whitaker acted as aide-de-camp to Sir George Byng, commanded the boats in the attack, rallied the men when they were panic-stricken by the explosion of a magazine, and hoisted the English colours on the bastion. In the battle of Malaga (August 1704) the *Dorsetshire* was one of the Red squadron, and was closely engaged throughout. Whitaker was knighted soon afterwards, and in 1705 he commanded the *Barfleur*. Early in 1706 he was promoted rear-admiral of the blue and appointed to command a squadron off Dunkirk; in April he convoyed the duke of Marlborough to Holland.

In 1708, with his flag in the *Northumberland*, Whitaker went out to the Mediterranean with Sir John Leake, and in August he commanded the detachment which co-operated in the capture of Minorca. When Leake returned to England, Whitaker remained in command, and on 21 December was promoted vice-admiral of the blue. A commission of 20 December to admiral of the blue seems to have been cancelled, and on 14 November 1709 he was made vice-admiral of the white. In January 1709 he was relieved from the position of commander-in-chief in the Mediterranean by Sir George Byng, with whom he remained as second in command, ferrying imperial troops and taking part in the failed attempt to lift the siege of Alicante. He succeeded to the chief command again when Byng returned to England in September 1709. In the summer of 1710 Whitaker also returned to England, and on 26 June he married Cecil (*d.* 1726), his first wife, Ann, having died on 17 June 1705. He was commanding in the downs, cruising in the channel in 1710–12, and played a major part in the occupation of Dunkirk in July 1712. After declining the post of second in command in the Baltic in 1716 he lived in retirement at Carshalton, Surrey. Whitaker died there on 12 November 1735. His will was proved on 3 December by his niece, Mary Whitaker, sole executrix, his second wife having died on 14 February 1726. The will also mentioned first, a nephew, Samuel Whitaker, captain of a ship at Gibraltar and Malaga, and therefore often confused with his uncle; and, second, a granddaughter Ann, daughter of his son, Edward (*d.* 1729).

J. K. LAUGHTON, rev. J. D. DAVIES

Sources J. Charnock, ed., *Biographia navalis*, 2 (1795), 366–74 · H. W. King, 'A brief memoir of Admiral Sir Edward Whitaker', *Surrey Archaeological Collection*, 8 (1883), 211–18 · *Memoirs relating to the Lord Torrington*, ed. J. K. Laughton, CS, new ser., 46 (1889), 140–

43, 192–5 · *The Byng papers: selected from the letters and papers of Admiral Sir George Byng, first Viscount Torrington, and of his son, Admiral the Hon. John Byng*, ed. B. Tunstall, 2, Navy RS, 68 (1931), 325–31 · S. Martin-Leake, *The life of Sir John Leake*, ed. G. Callender, 2, Navy RS, 53 (1920), 245, 248, 283–4, 358, 364, 381, 390 · W. L. Clowes, *The Royal Navy: a history from the earliest times to the present*, 7 vols. (1897–1903); repr. (1996–7), vol. 2, pp. 394–5, 413–14, 472 · letters of 1715 and 1716, PRO, ADM MSS, ADM/1/577 · D. Syrett and R. L. DiNardo, *The commissioned sea officers of the Royal Navy, 1660–1815*, rev. edn, Occasional Publications of the Navy RS, 1 (1994) · list of recommendations, 1692, PRO, ADM/8/2

Archives CKS, corresp. with James Stanhope · PRO

Whitaker, Edward William (*bap.* 1752, *d.* 1818), Church of England clergyman and charity administrator, was baptized on 26 January 1752 at St Martin Outwich, London, the son of William Whitaker of London and of Sandgates, Chertsey, Surrey, serjeant-at-law, and his wife, Isabella Rebecca North. He spent some of his early life in the household of a dissenter; nevertheless he matriculated at Christ Church, Oxford, on 2 April 1773 as a gentleman commoner, and graduated BA on 4 February 1777.

Following ordination Whitaker's main income originated from his livings. He was instituted to the rectory of St John the Baptist, Clerkenwell, in 1778 and afterwards held the rectory of St Mildred, Bread Street, in the City of London. From 1783 he was rector of St Mary de Castro and All Saints', Canterbury, a living which he held until his death. For many years he lived at Thorpe, near Egham, Surrey, where he kept a school. Other energies went into charitable good works. In the early years of the nineteenth century he established a charity to provide an 'Asylum for Male and Female Outcasts' (*GM*, 76/1.424), later renamed the Refuge for the Destitute. The institution began by providing out-relief, and then 'a place of refuge for persons discharged from prisons, or the hulks, unfortunate and deserted females, and others, who from loss of character, or extreme indigence' (*A Short Account*, 2) could not support themselves. A building on Cuper's Bridge, Lambeth, was acquired and the first two inmates admitted on 12 November 1806. A pamphlet, probably published in 1807, named Prince Frederick, duke of York, as president, with Whitaker as joint treasurer, and stated that of 275 applicants 119 had been admitted, 67 relieved out of house, and 89 rejected, and 64 were at present in the refuge.

Whitaker was also a productive and varied author. He joined in the polemical warfare against Joseph Priestley's Unitarianism with his *Four dialogues on the doctrine of the Holy Trinity, taught throughout the scriptures, and on other points which have of late been subjects of … discussion* (1786) and followed it with *A letter to the Reverend Dr Priestley, on his appeal to the ecclesiastical writers of the first centuries*, which contained trinitarian references drawn from the apostles and the fathers. The *Sermons on Education* (1788) were prompted by his intention of taking pupils; they insisted that each boy must receive a thorough grounding in the principles of Christianity. Whitaker had an incurable interest in prophetic literature. His *A general and connected view of the prophecies relating to the times of the gentiles, delivered by our blessed saviour, the prophet David, and the apostles Paul and John; with a brief account of their accomplishment to the present age* (1795) offers proof of real learning. It was, Whitaker unblushingly admitted, inspired by reading Edward Gibbon on the predictions of the book of Revelation. *The Manual of Prophecy* (1808) was a collection of 'predictions relating to that restitution of all things, which God hath spoken by the mouth of all His holy Prophets since the world began' (p. 3). Whitaker was always strongly anti-Romanist, insisting against other commentators that the Antichrist appeared exclusively in papal guise. His most substantial book was *An Abridgement of Universal History* (1817), in four volumes; the author proceeded on the basis that 'the moral government of the world is sufficiently evinced by the facts of history' (p. v) and included a remarkable amount of non-European material. Whitaker died, unmarried, at Bread Street Hill, London, on 14 October 1818.   NIGEL ASTON

Sources GM, 1st ser., 76 (1806), 424–5, 429, 1070 · GM, 1st ser., 88/2 (1818), 474 · J. Haydn, *The book of dignities: containing lists of the official personages of the British empire*, ed. H. Ockerby, 3rd edn (1894), 412 · F. Turner, *Egham, Surrey: a history of the parish under church and crown* (1926), 232 · Foster, *Alum. Oxon.*, 1715–1886, 4.1536 · G. Hennessy, *Novum repertorium ecclesiasticum parochiale Londinense, or, London diocesan clergy succession from the earliest time to the year 1898* (1898), 245, 251 · *The clerical guide, or, Ecclesiastical directory* (1817), 274 · [J. Watkins and F. Shoberl], *A biographical dictionary of the living authors of Great Britain and Ireland* (1816), 382 · E. W. Whitaker, *A sermon on the thirtieth of January, and three other tracts* (1787) · private information (2004) [J. Curthoys] · *A short account of the refuge for the destitute, Cuper's Bridge, Lambeth* [n.d.] · IGI · archives, Christ Church Oxf.

Whitaker, Sir Frederick (1812–1891), entrepreneur and premier of New Zealand, the eldest son of Frederick Whitaker, deputy lieutenant of Oxfordshire, and his wife, Susanna Humfrey, was born on 23 April 1812 at Manor House, Bampton, Oxfordshire. In 1839, soon after he had qualified as a solicitor, he emigrated to Australia and settled in Sydney. He went on to New Zealand in March 1840 and began to practise at Kororareka, then the seat of government, and moved with the government to Auckland, the new capital, the following year. In 1842 he was appointed a county court judge; in 1844, however, these courts were abolished, and he once more returned to the practice of his profession, and also began investing in mines. On 4 March 1843 he married Jane Augusta Griffith (*d.* 1884), the stepdaughter of Alexander Shepherd, colonial treasurer of New Zealand; they had four sons and three daughters who survived childhood.

In 1845 Whitaker was appointed an unofficial member of the legislative council. A superb legal draftsman, he there began an enduring association with the attorney-general, William Swainson, and the chief justice, William Martin; over the years they framed a new code of statutes. Under the new constitution of 1852 Whitaker was elected a member of the Auckland provincial council; he later became provincial law officer and a member of the superintendent's executive. In 1853 he was nominated a member of the legislative council of the colony, and in 1854 took his seat as such in the first general assembly. In 1855 he was appointed attorney-general in succession to Swainson, and later in the year he became speaker of the legislative council. In June 1856, shortly after the grant of responsible government, Whitaker became attorney-general under Edward William Stafford, and acted as leader of the government in the legislative council. This stable ministry lasted until it was defeated over native affairs on 12 July 1861; this had become an explosively divisive issue with the opening of the New Zealand wars in 1860.

Shortly afterwards, Whitaker entered into a legal partnership with Thomas Russell, a dashing speculator and already a founder of financial institutions. Together they set up one of the most lucrative practices in the colony. Whitaker became attorney-general to the Domett ministry on 1 June 1863. When Domett resigned in October, Whitaker himself became premier, and his partner Russell was appointed minister of defence. Together they represented the 'war party' of Auckland, standing for a military reckoning with 'rebel' Maori and for a sweeping confiscation of their lands. Outraged at the extent of the confiscations envisaged by Whitaker, the governor, Sir George Grey, contrived to topple this ministry in November 1864. In 1865 Whitaker was elected superintendent of Auckland, and in the same year was member for Parnell in the house of representatives. He led the opposition to the change of the seat of government from Auckland to Wellington. His scheme for the administration of the land fund was one of the chief items of his policy.

In March 1867 Whitaker retired from the assembly and the post of superintendent, and devoted himself once more to his profession and his business interests, which had suffered because of his preoccupation with politics. Between 1867 and 1871 he invested heavily, and generally successfully, in provincial gold mining companies. In the 1870s, invariably in association with his partner Russell, he extended his investment in timber, banking, coal, and companies. But above all else Whitaker and Russell were land speculators. Some of their land claims, such as the Piako swamp, came before the legislature and were the subject of acrimonious debate.

In 1876 Whitaker once more returned to politics, and was elected for Waikato to the house of representatives; in September 1876 he entered Atkinson's government as attorney-general, a post he held on seven occasions during his political career. On 15 October 1877 the government was defeated, and in the general election which followed Whitaker lost his seat. But the incoming ministry was relatively short-lived, and when Sir John Hall formed his administration in October 1879 Whitaker became once again attorney-general with a seat in the legislative council. On 21 April 1882, on Hall's resignation, he became premier, albeit reluctantly, and reconstructed the ministry, but on 25 September 1883 he resigned to attend to private affairs, now threatened by a deepening colonial depression. He was created KCMG in January 1884. Again, in October 1887, Whitaker resumed his old position of attorney-general, under Sir Henry Atkinson, and sat in the council until his health began to fail in 1890; in December of that year the ministry resigned, and Whitaker retired from public life. He was broken in health and distraught over heavy business losses: he who had once been wealthy was on the brink of poverty. He died at his office desk, in Symonds Street, Auckland, on 4 December 1891, and was buried on 6 December in St Stephen's cemetery, Parnell, Auckland, with masonic honours and much sign of public mourning.

Whitaker was described by a fellow politician as 'probably the most remarkable public man in New Zealand' (Gisborne, 71). Yet he avoided the limelight, preferring to exercise his influence behind the scenes. There, by the 1880s, his mastery was absolute. Within the legislative council he was said to be 'a Triton among minnows'. As a counsel on political matters he was without peer; his skill in drafting bills in clear, unambiguous language was a byword. Twentieth-century research and better understanding of the Maori people, however, have much diminished the reputation of one so anxious to amalgamate indigenous people with Western society regardless of consequences. Nevertheless, he could be liberal in other causes concerned with colonial democracy, and in such was much ahead of his time.

C. A. HARRIS, rev. R. C. J. STONE

Sources *New Zealand Herald* (25 June 1883) · R. C. J. Stone, 'Whitaker, Frederick', *DNZB*, vol. 1, pp. 492–4 · G. H. Scholefield, 'Whitaker, Sir Frederick', *DNZB*, vol. 1 · R. C. J. Stone, *Makers of fortune* (1973) · J. Millen, *The story of Bell Gully Buddle Weir, 1840–1990* (1990) · W. Gisborne, *New Zealand rulers and statesmen, 1840–1885* (1886) · *Brett's Auckland almanac* (1878), 7, 8, 137 · G. W. Rusden, *History of New Zealand* (1883) · R. C. J. Stone, 'Auckland party politics in the early years of the provincial system, 1853–58', *New Zealand Journal of History*, 14 (1980), 153–78 · J. Belich, *The New Zealand wars and the Victorian interpretation of racial conflict* (1986) · J. Rutherford, *Sir George Grey, KCB, 1812–1898: a study in colonial government* (1961) · *New Zealand Herald* (5 Dec 1891)
Archives Bell Gully Buddle Weir, Auckland, New Zealand, legal firm archives
Likenesses photograph, Parliament buildings, Wellington, New Zealand
Wealth at death virtually penniless: numerous contemporary reports

Whitaker, Jeremiah (1599–1654), Church of England clergyman, was born at Wakefield, Yorkshire; nothing is known about his parents. He was educated at Wakefield grammar school and Sidney Sussex College, Cambridge, where he graduated BA in 1619 and proceeded MA in 1623. He was ordained priest at Peterborough on 25 March 1623.

Whitaker's friend and godly hagiographer, Simeon Ashe, claimed his favourite saying was 'I had rather be a Preacher of the Gospel than an Emperor' (Ashe, 53), and this evangelical mission does seem to have been the main impetus of Whitaker's life. After university he was appointed master of Oakham School, Rutland, founded by the puritan Robert Johnson, who in 1625 promoted him to governor. His energetic extra-curricular activity included reading a weekly lecture in the town and preaching in neighbouring parishes and he quickly established influential puritan contacts. In 1620 he married Chephtzi-bah, daughter of William Peachy, the puritan incumbent at Oakham; they had two sons, Jeremiah and William *Whitaker (d. 1672), both eventually clergymen. More exalted socially were the Cecil family of Burghley, earls of

Exeter, Whitaker's lifelong patrons. He witnessed the will of David, the third earl, and his own funeral sermon was to be dedicated to David's widow. On 17 April 1627 the puritans Sir John Pickering and Robert Horsman appointed Whitaker the rector of nearby Stretton. He continued to read the Oakham lecture, preached at Stretton 'twice every Sabbath', was a 'principal prop to hold up Lectures in the neighbourhood', and attended private godly prayer meetings (Ashe, 56). He even preached at the archdeacon of Northampton's visitation at Uppingham in 1628, but fell foul of the church courts in the same year for conspiring with a parishioner to omit the sign of the cross in baptism.

Ashe claimed that Whitaker played a prominent role in resisting royal policy in the 1630s by refusing to read the anti-sabbatarian Book of Sports (1633), conscientiously objecting to paying the clerical contribution to fund the bishops' wars (1639), and preaching on Sundays not only in the morning but also in the afternoon, which the Caroline church discouraged. Extant church court records contain no account of this intransigence: Ashe conceded that a sympathetic neighbour paid the contribution for Whitaker against his wishes. In August 1640, however, Whitaker was indeed one of the leaders of a conference of puritan ministers meeting at Kettering, which declared the 'etcetera oath' (legitimizing the new Laudian canons) illegal and endorsed the invasion of the Scottish army as a means of attaining a common redress of grievances.

The Long Parliament was regarded as an instrument of godly reformation, and in 1641 Whitaker subscribed to a petition calling for a missionary effort to convert Native Americans. However, the embryonic process of reform was jeopardized by the outbreak of civil war, as Whitaker made clear in a sermon (later printed as *Eirenopoios*) delivered at the parliamentary fast on 25 January 1643 prior to the abortive Oxford negotiations with Charles I. He called for unity among those desiring reformation and reinforced this by signing a plea for an end to the foundation of separatist churches, *Certaine Considerations* (1643). The same year he was chosen as a member of the Westminster assembly of divines, convened to produce a new religious settlement, and served on one of the crucial standing committees. Now a high-profile presbyterian, he made influential contributions on several subjects, most notably condemning ordination by parish congregations. He preached at a further eight parliamentary fasts (1646–8) but the only other sermons to be published were *The Christian's Hope Triumphing*, preached on 28 May 1645, and *The Danger of Greatnesse*, delivered on 14 January 1646. In the latter he attributed the violent deaths of successive kings of Judah to their preference for arbitrary government. He replaced London ministers ejected by parliament during the civil wars at St Stephen, Coleman Street (May to July 1645), and St Mary Magdalen, Bermondsey Street (1644–54). He participated in the presbyterian classis founded by London ministers, and refused to swear allegiance to the republic after Charles I's execution, although he seems to have been on good terms with the subsequent regime of

Lord Protector Cromwell, to whom he wrote with the gift of a book.

Whitaker died at Bermondsey on 1 June 1654 and was buried on 6 June in the chancel of the church. Ashe's funeral oration was the basis of the biography in Samuel Clarke's *Lives*. At a memorial service tributes were delivered by Matthew Newcomen, among others. Ashe said Christ's own comment would have been: 'Our friend Whitaker sleepeth' (Ashe, 68).

J. FIELDING

Sources S. Ashe, *Living loves betwixt Christ and dying Christians preached at St Mary Magdalene in Southwark June 6 1654 at the funeral of Jeremiah Whitaker pastor there* (1654), 50–82 · A. J. Fielding, 'Conformists, puritans and the church courts: the diocese of Peterborough, 1603–1642', PhD diss., U. Birm., 1989, 18, 29–32, 155, 183, 210, 220, 248, 256 · H. I. Longden, *Northamptonshire and Rutland clergy from 1500*, ed. P. I. King and others, 16 vols. in 6, Northamptonshire RS (1938–52), vol. 15, p. 27 · will, PRO, PROB 11/193, sig. 62 [David, earl of Exeter] · will, PRO, PROB 11/245, sig. 109 · BL, Sloane MS 4159 · *DNB* · *Certaine considerations to diswade men from further gathering of churches in this present juncture of time* (1643), 1 · R. Jeffs, ed., *The English Revolution: fast sermons to parliament*, 34 vols. (1970–71), 5.132–99, 20.304–54 · R. S. Paul, *The assembly of the Lord: politics and religion in the Westminster assembly and the 'Grand debate'* (1985), 137, 351, 374, 424, 496, 556 · Tai Liu, *Puritan London: a study of religion and society in the City parishes* (1986), 85, 115, 124 · W. A. Shaw, *A history of the English church during the civil wars and under the Commonwealth, 1640–1660*, 2 vols. (1900), vol. 1, pp. 360, 378; vol. 2, pp. 312, 403, 537 · Northants. RO, Peterborough diocesan records, correction book A47, fol. 25v

Whitaker, John (1735–1808), historian, son of James Whitaker, innkeeper, was born in Manchester on 27 April 1735. He attended Manchester grammar school from January 1745 until 1752, when he entered Brasenose College, Oxford, with a school exhibition. On 2 March 1753 he was elected a Lancashire scholar of Corpus Christi College and became a fellow on 21 January 1763. He graduated BA on 24 October 1755, MA on 27 February 1759, and BD on 1 July 1767. He was ordained at Oxford in 1760 and acted as curate successively at Newton Heath chapel, near Manchester (1760–61), and at Bray in Berkshire. He was elected FSA on 10 January 1771, and in the same year published the first volume of *The History of Manchester*, in quarto, covering the British and Roman periods. A second edition was published in octavo in 1773 with a quarto volume of the 'principal corrections' to the original. The second volume, which extended as far as the Saxon period, was published in 1775 in quarto. A copy of Whitaker's manuscript of the continuation to the fifteenth century is in Chetham's Library, Manchester.

Whitaker deliberately took a very broad approach to the history of his native town—he was a stout critic of the limitations and parochialism inherent in the 'private and dull annals' of local history (J. Whitaker, *The History of Manchester*, 2nd edn, 4 vols., 1773, 1.ix) and instead placed the history of Manchester within the much broader context of the early history of the British people in general. The history received a mixed reception—some readers welcomed the wide range and accessible prose and recognized the substantial amount of erudition behind it; others cavilled at his extravagant generalizations, his unsubstantiated assertions, contrived reasoning, and the strongly tory flavour of his views. Francis Douce's view of

John Whitaker (1735–1808), by G. F. Storm, pubd 1849 (after Henry Bone)

Whitaker, noted on his annotated copy of the *History*, now in the British Library, was that he was a 'bully, brute and blockhead' (ibid., 2.1, BL, C. 28.1.6, 7). John Collier (Tim Bobbin) satirized the history in two tracts published in 1771 and 1773.

Whitaker's next publication responded to the current fashionable interest in the early inhabitants of the British Isles that had been fuelled by the Ossian controversy. *The Genuine History of the Ancient History of the Britons Asserted* (1772) was written in refutation of James Macpherson's *History of Great Britain and Ireland*. This work confirmed Whitaker's reputation as a controversial and provocative polemicist and his penchant for merciless *ad hominem* attacks on those from whose opinions he differed. From November 1773 to February 1774 he held the morning preachership at Berkeley Chapel, London, but left it following a dispute, concerning which he published a typically intemperate *State of the Case*, leading to the threat of a libel suit. While in London he made the acquaintance of Dr Johnson and Edward Gibbon, with whom he continued to correspond after he left London. Gibbon allowed him to read the first volume of *Decline and Fall* in manuscript, which Whitaker greeted with great enthusiasm. Gibbon had, however, withheld the chapter on Christianity, which Whitaker later read with high indignation.

From London, Whitaker moved back in 1774 to Manchester, where he became involved in disputes over the proposed improvement of the town; this gave rise to another ill-tempered paper war over the improvement bill in 1776. He endeavoured to persuade Gibbon, at that time MP for Liskeard, to use his influence to secure restraining clauses in the bill. Meanwhile he remained true to his tory principles, composing an ode to promote the formation of the Manchester regiment intended to reduce the American rebels.

On 22 August 1777 Whitaker was presented by Corpus

Christi College to the rectory of Ruan Lanyhorn, Cornwall. Soon afterwards he married Jane (*bap.* 1742, *d.* 1828), daughter of the Revd John Tregenna, rector of Mawgan in Pyder, Cornwall, and his wife, Elizabeth; they had three daughters. He was an active parish priest and JP, and a forceful figure within the local community. The first ten years of his rectorship were blighted by disputes with his parishioners, who failed to see eye to eye with him on the divine right of tithes. At length he was victorious, and commented that he had his parish in a better state of subjection and amity towards him than any of his neighbours. For many years Whitaker hankered after the wardenship of Manchester collegiate church—a position in which he believed he would be able to employ his talents to the full, and counteract the spread of heretical dissent and radical opinions in Manchester. Despite endless lobbying of political patrons, including Pitt, his ambitions were never realized. He also struck up a friendship with the bishop of Derry, from whom he similarly had high hopes of preferment in Ireland for a time. He blamed his failure to secure preferment in his native town upon the poor reception which his history of Manchester had received there, but the inhabitants had some cause at least to be grateful to him when, in 1787, he published *The Charter of Manchester Translated, with Explanations and Remarks* at the request of a committee engaged in vindicating the rights of the town against the lord of the manor (in return for which he was presented with a silver cup). In the same year he threw himself into historical controversy with his *Mary Queen of Scots Vindicated*, in which he denied the authenticity of the casket letters, championed the cause of Mary, and incriminated her enemies, particularly Elizabeth. A second edition was published in 1790. Throughout the rest of his life he compiled material for a 'Private life of Mary queen of Scots', originally begun as commentary to accompany engravings which he had collected of the queen, but it remained unpublished until George Chalmers, a long-time friend and correspondent, used the material (much of which had in any case originally been supplied by him) in his own life of the queen, published in 1818.

Whitaker reacted strongly to the turn of events in France during the 1790s. In 1791 he published the *Origin of Arianism Disclosed*, in which he warned his readers against the spread of inflammatory ideas of liberty, and attributed the origins of the Arian heresy to the Jews. Appalled by the course of the riots in Birmingham and in Manchester, which he attributed solely to the spread of libertarian ideas and heresy, he proposed to write a history of the disorders, but found himself pre-empted. There was more in a similar vein in *The Real Origin of Government* (1795), originally written as a sermon against the French Revolution. His hopes that this overtly authoritarian pamphlet would secure him preferment from Pitt's government were disappointed. By this time Gibbon's anti-Christian stance had come to seem ever more inimical to Whitaker's extremely orthodox sensibilities, and in 1791 his comments were published in a compilation of reviews from

ten issues of the *English Review*. As with so much of Whitaker's *œuvre*, some legitimate criticisms were overshadowed by absurd generalizations and vicious personal invective. On the historical side he made an early attempt at interdisciplinary history, combining a study of history and geography, published as *The Course of Hannibal over the Alps Ascertained* (1794). Despite his aversion to the limitations of local history and his low opinion of antiquarian studies in general, in 1804 he issued *The Ancient Cathedral of Cornwall*. While purporting to be a study of the church of St Germans, it was, more controversially, a polemic on the history of early Christianity and druidism (with many a criticism hurled at Cornwall's previous historian, William Borlase) and the history of Gothic architecture. Whitaker's views on early British society were idiosyncratic: in both this and the *History of Manchester*, he argued that the ancient Britons had already established a feudal system, and under the Romans had been entirely converted to Christianity. The *Life of St Neots*, published posthumously in 1809, was similarly intended to challenge traditional orthodoxies in the form of the extant saint's lives. He also published a number of sermons, poems, and articles for Richard Polwhele's *History of Cornwall*. He was a prolific reviewer for the *English Review*, *British Critic*, and *Anti-Jacobin Review*, finding this an important means of supplementing his income and paying for the books necessary for his studies. In addition to his published works he had planned or contemplated a number of other projects: a parochial history of Cornwall, a military history of the Romans in Britain, a history of Oxford, one of London, notes on Shakespeare, and illustrations to the Bible. He was a man of fiery temperament and extreme views, and a fervent belief in all the tenets of 'orthodox' Christianity. He was able to inspire considerable friendship and loyalty from those who knew him best. His close friend Richard Polwhele described him as being of a tall, muscular frame, dark featured, and with light greenish eyes. He reputedly had a squint and wore false teeth made of ebony. He died at his rectory on 30 October 1808 and was buried in the parish; his widow, who had long suffered ill health, lived on until 30 December 1828.

R. H. SWEET

Sources J. E. Bailey, 'John Whitaker, the historian of Manchester', *Papers of the Manchester Literary Club*, 3 (1877) · R. Polwhele, 'Memoir', *GM*, 1st ser., 78 (1808), 1035 · R. Polwhele, *Biographical sketches in Cornwall*, 3 vols. (1831) · R. Polwhele, *Reminiscences in prose and verse*, 3 vols. (1836), 1.83; 2.185 · R. Polwhele, *Traditions and recollections; domestic, clerical and literary*, 1 (1826), 152 · J. Britton, *Reminiscences of literary London from 1779 to 1853* (1896) · J. Britton, *The autobiography of John Britton*, 3 vols. in 2 (privately printed, London, 1849–50), vol. 2 · Nichols, *Illustrations*, 8.563 · J. F. Smith, ed., *The admission register of the Manchester School, with some notices of the more distinguished scholars*, 1, Chetham Society, 69 (1866) · C. Kidd, *British identities before nationalism* (1999) · *DNB* · *IGI*

Archives BL, corresp. and papers, Add. MSS 29763, 34886, 38310, 38448, 39311–39312, 39316 · Chetham's Library, Manchester, commentaries on history of preceding three centuries and notes on 1773 census of Manchester · Chetham's Library, Manchester, MS continuation of 'History of Manchester' [transcript by H. Turner] · V&A NAL, MS life of Mary, queen of Scots | Chetham's Library, Manchester, corresp., incl. letters to George Chalmers · W. Yorks. AS, Leeds, letters to John Watson

Likenesses G. F. Storm, stipple, pubd 1849 (after H. Bone), BM, NPG; repro. in Britton, *Autobiography* [*see illus.*]
Wealth at death put income tax assessment at £1000, 1803: Chetham's Library, Manchester, Chalmers correspondence

Whitaker, John (1776?–1847), composer, was a teacher of music, and organist at the church of St Clement, Eastcheap, in London. He also became a partner in the music-publishing firm of Button and Whitaker at St Paul's Churchyard in the City. In 1818 Whitaker collected and published two volumes of sacred music for four voices entitled *The Seraph*, which included many original pieces. However, he made his name chiefly through the composition of numerous popular dramatic pieces and occasional songs introduced in musical plays at the principal London theatres between 1807 and 1825. He wrote music with William Reeve for *Who's to Have Her?* (1813) and joined Henry Bishop in contributing some songs to a stage version of Scott's *Guy Mannering* (1816), including a number that were favourites in their day: 'Oh, slumber, my darling', 'Dog Tray', and 'O say not woman's heart is bought'. He also composed the music for several pantomines, including *The Weird Sisters, or, The Thane and the Throne*, based on Shakespeare's *Macbeth*. This was produced at Sadler's Wells Theatre on Easter Monday, 12 April 1819, and contained the then famous clown's song 'Hot Codlins', written for Joseph Grimaldi. Other songs that were popular were 'Fly away, dove', sung by Miss Cawse on her début in *The Hebrew Family*, 'Go, rover, go', 'Remember me', 'The Little Farmer's Daughter', and 'The Lily that Blooms'. Comic songs, such as 'Darby Kelly' and 'Paddy Carey', adapted from Irish airs, helped to broaden Whitaker's appeal. Additional works include the glee 'Winds, Gently Whisper', some anthems, music for English versions of the odes of Anacreon and of Aesop's fables, and *Twelve Pedal Exercises* for organ. Whitaker died at his home, Thavies Inn, Holborn, London, on 4 December 1847.

DAVID J. GOLBY

Sources W. H. Husk, 'Whitaker, John', Grove, *Dict. mus.* (1954) · *Quarterly Musical Magazine and Review*, 7 (1825), 258–9 · *GM*, 2nd ser., 29 (1848), 105
Archives GL, corresp. and papers
Likenesses N. Hanhart, lithograph (after F. Y. Hurlstone), BM, NPG

Whitaker, Joseph (1820–1895), publisher, was born in London on 4 May 1820, the son of a silversmith. At the age of fourteen he was apprenticed to Mr Barritt, bookseller, of Fleet Street, London. Nine years later he joined the firm of John William Parker in the Strand. He then became the London agent for the Oxford booksellers J. H. and J. Parker, opening a branch in the Strand.

In 1849 Whitaker started the *Penny Post*, the first penny monthly church magazine, which long continued in its original form, and edited an edition of the *Morning and Evening Church Services*. In 1850 he projected and published for four years the *Educational Register* and *Whitaker's Clergyman's Diary*. He then started his own business as a theological publisher in Pall Mall. In 1855 he moved to the Strand, where he published, with the assistance of Thomas Delph, *The Artist*, a fine-art review. Between 1856

and 1859 he edited the *Gentleman's Magazine*. In January 1858 Whitaker started *The Bookseller*, intended primarily as an organ for booksellers and publishers, but also for book buyers generally. The new monthly journal was very successful, and was well received by the bookselling and publishing trade; in 1860 *Bent's Literary Advertiser* was merged with it. His most significant publication was *Whitaker's Almanack*, of which he was founding editor. This began in 1868: 36,000 copies of the first issue were subscribed before publication. For a long time the *Almanack*, like *The Bookseller*, changed little except in the direction of natural expansion.

Along with other British publishers, Whitaker had a large share in the organization of a relief fund, which ultimately reached £2000, for Paris booksellers and their assistants who had suffered during the Prussian siege of the city in the winter of 1870–71. As a distributor of the fund he was one of the first Englishmen to enter Paris after the siege.

In 1874 Whitaker produced the *Reference Catalogue of Current Literature*, which consisted of a collection of catalogues of books on sale by English publishers, with an elaborate index. This went through many editions until 1898. He published a few devotional works, including *The Daily Round* and Ridley's *Holy Communion*. Whitaker was always a keen and judicious defender of the interests of the bookselling trade, and was recognized as an authority on copyright. In 1875 he was elected a fellow of the Society of Antiquaries. He died at his home, White Lodge, Enfield, Middlesex, on 15 May 1895.

Whitaker had a family of fifteen children, of whom the eldest was **Joseph Vernon Whitaker** (1845–1895). He was born on 3 February 1845, and was educated at Bloxham School. He preferred a life of adventure to business, and, after a voyage to the East Indies, enlisted in the army, and became a sergeant at the age of twenty-one. Having purchased his discharge, he entered the office of *The Bookseller* for a year or two. At the invitation of George William Childs of Philadelphia he went to the United States; he was editor of the *American Literary Gazette*, and then acted as sub-editor of the *Public Ledger* for three years. He returned to England in 1875 to resume his connection with *The Bookseller*, and ultimately became editor of both it and the *Reference Catalogue*. In 1880 he started the *Stationery Trades' Journal* with his father. He took an active interest in all trade questions, especially those of a social and charitable character. He and his American wife, whom he married in 1875, had two children. He died on 15 January 1895, at Redcliffe Gardens, South Kensington, London. He was survived by his father by a few months and by one of his children.

H. R. TEDDER, rev. JOSEPH COOHILL

Sources *The Times* (16 Jan 1895) · *The Times* (18 Jan 1895) · J. Whitaker and C. Whitaker, eds., *Whitaker's Almanack* (1868–96) · *The Bookseller* (6 Feb 1895) · *The Bookseller* (8 June 1895) · *Publishers' Circular* (19 Jan 1895) · *Publishers' Circular* (18 May 1895) · *Publishers' Circular* (25 May 1895) · *The Athenaeum* (19 Jan 1895) · *The Athenaeum* (18 May 1895) · *CGPLA Eng. & Wales* (1895)
Likenesses portrait, repro. in *The Bookseller* (6 Feb 1895) · portrait, repro. in *Publishers' Circular* (25 May 1895) · portrait, repro. in *The Bookseller* (8 June 1895)

Wealth at death £16,934 0s. 9d.: probate, 22 June 1895, *CGPLA Eng. & Wales* · £1138 16s. 6d.—Joseph Vernon Whitaker: probate, 19 Feb 1895, *CGPLA Eng. & Wales*

Whitaker, Joseph Vernon (1845–1895). *See under* Whitaker, Joseph (1820–1895).

Whitaker, Laurence (1577/8–1654), politician, was, according to Anthony Wood, 'a Somersetshire man born' (Wood, 1.300), but he bore arms associated with the Whitakers of Lancashire. He may have been the son of Lawrence Whitaker and his wife, Cicely, widow of Robert Beale of Peterborough, Northamptonshire. He matriculated from St John's College, Cambridge, in 1593, graduated BA in 1597 and MA in 1600, and was incorporated at Oxford in 1603. He wrote verses for *Crudities* and *Crambe* (1611), by Thomas Coryate, and was associated with the Mermaid literary club. By 1611 he was secretary to Sir Edward Phelips, master of the rolls, who appointed him a clerk of the petty bag, a post he held until Phelips's death in 1614. He entered the Middle Temple in 1614 and went into the service of the earl of Somerset in the same year. His new patron was disgraced in 1615 and Whitaker may have suffered by association. From 1619 he was again in favour, securing a grant from James I of fee-farm rents in sixteen counties (1619–24) and then an appointment as clerk extraordinary to the privy council in 1624; he remained in office until *c.*1642. Whitaker married, after 1613, Margaret (1577–1636), daughter of Sir John Egerton of Egerton, Cheshire, and widow of Thomas Hall of London. They had no children.

Elected as MP for Peterborough in 1624, 1625, 1626, and 1628, Whitaker resided in Drury Lane (becoming a JP for Middlesex and Westminster) and Turnham Green, Chiswick, from 1624. In 1635 he missed out on promotion to the post of clerk to the privy council in ordinary, but a variety of commissions from the king and council provided many opportunities for him to pry into economic activities, maintain monopolies, and exact fees. Although a court agent, a consistent thread of his parliamentary career was his abiding anti-Catholicism and puritanism. Whitaker was a vestryman of St Giles-in-the-Fields from 1622 and supported a fund for building a new church. The threat from Catholics was constantly raised by him in parliamentary debate. In a speech on 25 June 1625 he linked the failures of foreign policies with the activities of domestic papists. On 6 June 1628 he raised the bogey of their 'flocking' in the suburbs, claiming that in his neighbourhood of Covent Garden they outnumbered protestants by three to one and had set up an autonomous community (Keeler, Cole, and Bidwell, 151). Again on 17 February 1629 he declaimed against this 'colony of papists' that was 'too strong' for 'we the ministers of justice' to 'cast out' (Notestein and Relf, 219–20). He opposed the Arminians and gave evidence (1628–9) to the Lords as one who had heard the notorious sermon at St Giles by the king's chaplain, Roger Maynwaring. His zeal earned him the nickname Holy Lawrence. Yet on more overtly political issues he was moderate.

Whitaker's first wife having died on 1 February 1636, he married, by a licence of 6 February 1638, Dorothy (*d.* 1671), daughter of Charles Hoskins of Holborn, Middlesex. In January 1641 he was returned as MP for Okehampton. The king thought he was as big a monopolist as those later expelled from the Long Parliament, but despite his earlier favour at court his puritan sympathies probably inclined him towards the parliamentary side and he soon turned away from the court. He signed the protestation in May, but was sent to the Tower for a week in July when his seizure of the papers of Sir John Eliot thirteen years earlier was brought up. Forgiven and rapidly advanced by the Commons' managers, he joined the important recess committee in September and chaired the inquisitorial information committee in January 1642. He continued to serve on commissions and committees, notably helping to draft the New Model Army ordinance in 1645, chairing the committee on church government in 1645–6, and agreeing to try the king, although he did not sit on the trial commission in 1648. An MP who fled to the army in August 1647, a member of the Rump Parliament, and a dissentient from the crucial vote for further negotiations with the king in 1648–9, he served the regime continuously in Middlesex and Westminster, supervising money raising and defence from 1643 to 1652 and 'judging scandal' (*DNB*) in Suffolk in 1647. Whitaker kept a diary of proceedings in the house, mainly giving the sense of the Commons from 1642 to 1647, now in BL, Add. MS 31116.

Whitaker died on 15 April 1654 aged seventy-six and was buried in St Giles, where memorials to him and his first wife were erected. He left a modest fortune, chiefly property and rents, to his wife. VALERIE PEARL, *rev.*

Sources V. C. D. M., 'Whitaker, Laurence', HoP, *Commons, 1604–29* [draft] · Wood, *Ath. Oxon.: Fasti*, vol. 1 · Keeler, *Long Parliament* · W. Notestein and F. H. Relf, eds., *Commons debates for 1629* (1921) · R. C. Johnson and others, eds., *Commons debates, 1628*, 6 vols. (1977–83), vol. 4 · M. Jansson and W. B. Bidwell, eds., *Proceedings in parliament, 1625* (1987) · BL, Add. MSS 18779–18780, 31116 · BL, Harley MSS 162–165 · BL, Lansdowne MS 878 · Bodl. Oxf., MS Rawl. D. 715, 17–21 · will, PRO, PROB 11/233, sig. 44 · G. Ormerod, *The history of the county palatine and city of Chester*, 2nd edn, ed. T. Helsby, 2 (1882), 629

Whitaker [*née* Taylor], **Marjorie Olive** [*pseud.* Malachi Whitaker] (1895–1976), writer, was born on 23 September 1895 at 9 Clara Road, Bolton, near Bradford, the eighth of the eleven children of James Taylor (*d. c.*1938), bookbinder and Annie Hey. Her father's profession gave her access to a store of knowledge, and she began writing from an early age. For her first poem she was rewarded with a sixpence by her father, but when she gave him her second, inferior to its predecessor, he said: 'You're too late, lass. Shakespeare said this first, and much better' (Whitaker, *Crystal Fountain*, 10). She had a distant relationship with her father, who she felt never 'exerted himself in any way for the good of humanity', and for a long while she tore up everything that she wrote, fearing that it had been said before (Whitaker, *And So Did I*, 119). She remembered her mother as a good woman who had an eccentric way with words. Marjorie read voraciously, particularly from the

Bible, looking for words 'like hell and devil' (Whitaker, *Crystal Fountain*, 10). At her first school she won every available scripture prize, but at her second she performed badly in examinations and was 'so miserable that I was forced to make a world of my own to get along at all' (ibid.). She explored the Yorkshire countryside that became the canvas for her later writing: 'There was so much to see, so much to do and think about. One of my favourite pursuits was following streams. If they went underground, so did I' (ibid.). Aged fifteen she wrote stories in the style of Jack London and Bret Harte, which were published in an amateur magazine that was bound by her father's firm.

During the First World War Marjorie Taylor, still resolved on being a poet, 'made up a set of windy martial verses', and sold them to a firm manufacturing Christmas cards for a small sum. At this time she was also working twelve hours a day, possibly for her father, whose business fell into financial trouble after the war. Aged twenty she wrote her autobiography, which remained unpublished in that form: she later remarked that 'All I was not I put in that autobiography' (Whitaker, *Crystal Fountain*, 11). On 8 December 1917 she married Leonard Whitaker (*b.* 1892/3), then serving in the army, and lived in Rouen for a while where her husband was involved in business, and she wrote a 'business novel'. Like much of her early work it is lost; it fell overboard from a channel steamer. For the next six or seven years she wrote nothing. When they returned from France she got a job in the share department of a large company, and they lived in various temporary homes including a tent pitched in the corner of a field. In 1926, however, the Whitakers built a house on top of a hill in Yorkshire (she also kept a *pied-à-terre* in London), and adopted two children because they could not have any of their own: with customary frankness she said that the 'only physical result of our union was that I was left with the itch' (Whitaker, *And So Did I*, 70).

Settled in her new home, Marjorie Whitaker swapped her gramophone for a typewriter and swiftly wrote the short story 'Sultan Jekker', and found her own voice. In this starkly narrated tale two women fight for the affections of a brutal navvy. Using the pen-name Malachi Whitaker, she nervously sent it to John Middleton Murry at *The Adelphi* because she admired D. H. Lawrence, another contributor to that magazine. Meanwhile she unleashed a number of stories, one of which was published in *Outlook*. *The Adelphi* published 'Sultan Jekker' and at least four other stories within eighteen months. Edward Garnett accepted *Frost in April* (1929), her first collection, for Jonathan Cape. The *Sunday Observer*'s critic commented that one of the stories was 'like a piece of fog cut out and preserved'. Vita Sackville-West judged her to be a 'born writer' (Whitaker, *Crystal Fountain*, 7), and the collection was warmly praised by Arnold Bennett in the *Evening Standard*. Many of the stories are rooted in spiritual or financial deprivation, but they are shot through with desire or a momentary vision. In 'Old Abraham' a proud man is humiliated and abused by a new wife. But in 'The

Music Box' a mother and child long for music in their joyless lives and achieve it for a brief moment. The neglected child in 'The Enchanted Morning', possibly modelled on Whitaker herself, becomes a goddess for a split second in a 'shock of vision'.

In Whitaker's second collection, *No Luggage?* (1930), she honed her style, stripping the story down to its smallest component: a mother giving instructions to her daughter before going out into a howling gale, a boy jumping out of bed at the sound of his mother's call. Like 'The Wife', in which a woman dreads separation from her husband, the stories are pervaded by a vague and often unexplained sense of anxiety. In her next collection, *Five for Silver* (1932), the critic in the *Times Literary Supplement* thought this quality had been intensified into an insistence 'on grotesque details, on ugly occupations, on repulsive physical characteristics, on the mean behaviour of young men to girls and the hostility that dwells in homes' (*TLS*, 10 Nov 1932). In these stories a man visits a cemetery and remembers a tragedy; another falls from a building; and a young woman hopes that her baby will be born with a hare-lip. *Honeymoon* (1934), her fourth collection, contains 'X', one of her most unusual and disturbing stories, which economically interweaves madness, incest, vampirism, and fratricide.

For three or four years following *Honeymoon* Malachi Whitaker wrote very little, but in 1939 she brought out the extraordinary *And So Did I*. The title is from *The Rime of the Ancient Mariner* at the moment when the mariner recognizes his fate:

And a thousand thousand slimy things
Lived on; and so did I.

It was described rather portentously by Whitaker as her 'record of her search for God and the Truth', but by the end of the book she says she is no nearer to the end of her quest: 'God has not turned up. … But I do say that life has been perfect in parts' (p. 147). This, as a reviewer points out, is the keystone of her philosophy and work (*TLS*, 14 Jan 1939). Narrated in her crisp and conversational style, it is a frank if fragmented account of life just before the outbreak of the Second World War. Like her short stories it is poised on a knife edge.

Apart from two editions of selected stories in 1946 and 1949, *And So Did I* was Malachi Whitaker's final statement to the world. Vita Sackville-West had compared her to Katherine Mansfield, and she had also been called the 'Bradford Chekhov', but in spite of this, or maybe because of it, she announced in 1939 that she had nothing more to say. She remained silent until her death on 7 January 1976 at Skipton General Hospital, Skipton, her husband having predeceased her. *The Crystal Fountain* (1984), the first new edition of her work for almost forty years, signalled renewed interest in her work. She left a frustratingly enigmatic portrait of herself: 'I have two eyes, a nose, and a mouth, and a skin without any spots, but the whole effect is just a face' (Whitaker, *And So Did I*, 38).

Clare L. Taylor

Sources M. Whitaker, *And So Did I* (1939); repr. (1990) · M. Whitaker, *The crystal fountain and other stories*, ed. J. Hart (1984) · P. Parker and F. Kermode, eds., *The reader's companion to twentieth-century writers* (1995) · *TLS* (28 Nov 1929) · *TLS* (11 Dec 1930) · *TLS* (10 Nov 1932) · *TLS* (18 Oct 1934) · *TLS* (14 Jan 1939)

Whitaker, Thomas Dunham (1759–1821), topographer and antiquary, was born on 8 June 1759 at the rectory, East Raynham, Norfolk, son of William Whitaker (1730–1782) and his wife, Lucy (*d.* 1788), daughter of Robert Dunham and widow of Ambrose Allen. His father had been curate of East and West Raynham from 1756, but in 1760 he succeeded to his family's ancestral estate at Holme in Cliviger, between Burnley and Todmorden in Lancashire. In November 1766 Whitaker was sent to board at Rochdale grammar school, then run by the Revd John Shaw, and he remained there until November 1774. After a brief period of private tuition with the Revd William Sheepshanks of Grassington in the West Riding, he was in October 1775 admitted to St John's College, Cambridge. In November 1781 he took the degree of LLB and seemed destined for a legal career, but the untimely death of his father in June 1782 put paid to that ambition, although in 1801 he received his LLD. On 13 January 1783 at Leeds parish church he married Lucy Thoresby (1759–1837), daughter of Thomas Thoresby, a relative of the Yorkshire antiquary Ralph Thoresby. They had six children. He returned to Cliviger and assumed the mantle of a country squire. His passion for the ancestral property and the neighbouring countryside was a driving force for the rest of his life. He determined to enter the church, but with no ambition beyond that of ruling in the locality. Although ordained in 1785 he sought no living, but in the same year paid £400 to obtain the right of presentation to the chapel at Cliviger. In 1788 he had the old chapel demolished and, at a cost to himself of £870, a new one was built and consecrated in 1794.

The first part of Whitaker's strategy was concluded in 1797, when, as patron of the living, he licensed himself to the perpetual curacy of Holme in Cliviger on the death of the curate, William Halliwell. It is clear, however, that for some years he had been, *de facto*, in control of the chapel and all its affairs. In 1809 he fulfilled his next great ambition, when he became vicar of the great parish of Whalley, which covered much of east Lancashire and was the second largest (and one of the most populous) in England. In November 1818 his already very considerable local position and status were greatly augmented when he became, in plurality, vicar of Blackburn. In the interim, from 1813 to 1819, he had also been rector of Heysham, near Lancaster.

All this might imply that Whitaker was interested merely in aggrandizement, financial and social, but that was not the case. He was an assiduous and meticulous pastor, and proudly claimed that he preached at least once a year in each of the churches and chapels of his great personal empire. In 1799 he was appointed a county magistrate for Lancashire and in 1800 for the West Riding, and from 1815 to 1821 presided over the Cliviger select vestry. His great personal authority was employed in 1820, when, as vicar and the leading local magistrate, he drove into Burnley during a bloody strike by local miners and, rather than order the military out (with the likelihood of further bloodshed) addressed the strikers and persuaded them to return home. He was known as a severe and demanding man, possessed of abundant energies and intolerant of the failings or weaknesses of others, reactionary in his views of class and social status, perhaps respected rather than loved. His attention to detail, and to intellectual curiosity, is exemplified by the registers of Holme in Cliviger, which he wrote in person from 1791 until 1815. The pre-1812 register contains remarkable detail, of great interest to social and economic historians, giving the age, residence, occupation, and cause of death of almost all those buried, and the occupation of the father in all baptism entries. For 1795 and 1805–12 it also includes tabular statistical analyses of age at death. His love of the Lancashire and Yorkshire Pennines is emphasized by his landscape 'improvements' in the Cliviger area. He undertook large-scale schemes for planting and beautifying the wild moorland and impressive gorge, according to the most fashionable taste—he planted about half a million trees between 1785 and 1815, and his work is still the prevailing influence upon the scenery in the valley.

For posterity these many legacies are eclipsed by the results of Whitaker's other great love—topography and antiquarian studies. In the early 1790s, influenced by his friend and patron Charles Towneley of Towneley Hall, 2 miles from Holme, he began work on a monumental history of the parish of Whalley, a project which fuelled his growing ambition to become vicar of that parish and which was researched extensively from original sources. The history was published, as a subscription work, in 1801 and was an immediate success: a second edition appeared in 1806 and a third in 1818. Whitaker's *Whalley* is among the most important and valuable topographical-cum-antiquarian histories of the early nineteenth century, and its interest is greatly enhanced by the author's employment of the young J. M. W. Turner to illustrate the book. Turner was introduced to Whitaker through their mutual friend Charles Towneley, and he visited the Whalley area to paint a number of watercolours from which the published engravings were made. The success of *Whalley* encouraged Whitaker to extend his geographical scope. In 1805 he published his *History of Craven*, which went into a second edition in 1812; in 1816 came *Loidis and Elmete*, a history of the area around Leeds, including lower Wharfedale and Airedale; and in 1823, posthumously, *The History of Richmondshire*, the first and only part of a projected history of Yorkshire. The last two were also illustrated by Turner, their value today being associated more with the artist than the author. Whitaker also published a number of other minor works, including twenty-eight articles in the *Quarterly Review*, but it is the topographical histories which remain his monument.

Whitaker died at the vicarage in Blackburn on 18 December 1821 and was buried at Holme in Cliviger chapel on 24 December in a coffin made from one of the larch trees which he had planted on the estate thirty-five years before. One of his sons, Robert Nowell Whitaker, succeeded him as perpetual curate of Holme in Cliviger in 1830. ALAN G. CROSBY

Sources J. G. Nichols, 'Biographical memoir of Thomas Dunham Whitaker', in T. D. Whitaker, *An history of the original parish of Whalley*, rev. J. G. Nichols and P. A. Lyons, 4th edn, 1 (1872), xiii–lvi · T. Thornber, *A Pennine parish: the history of Cliviger* (1987), 78–84 · J. L. O. Holden, ed., *The register of the parochial chapelry of St John the Divine (formerly St John the Evangelist), Holme in Cliviger (or Holmes Chapel), 1742–1841*, Lancashire Parish Register Society, 124 (1985) · *VCH Lancashire*, 6.482 · will, Lancs. RO, WCW 1821 · S. Daniel, 'The implications of industry: Turner's Leeds', *Reading landscape*, ed. S. Pugh (1996) · H. R. Rigg, *Turner and Dr Whitaker* (1982) · parish register (baptism), East Raynham, 8 June 1759 · Venn, *Alum. Cant.* · *DNB*
Archives BL, papers, Add. MSS 22651, 29703, 36527 · Chetham's Library, Manchester, notebook of commentaries on the New Testament and legal notes · Suffolk RO | W. Yorks. AS, Leeds, Yorkshire Archaeological Society, letters to William Radcliffe relating to Whitaker's history of Leeds
Likenesses W. Maddocks, stipple, pubd 1805 (after portrait by W. D. Fryer), NPG · P. Audinet, line engraving (after portrait by J. Northcote), BM, NPG; repro. in Nichols, *Illustrations*, vol. 4 · C. R. Smith, effigy on monument, Whalley?, Yorkshire
Wealth at death under £3000: will, Lancs. RO, WCW 1821

Whitaker, Tobias (*bap.* 1601?, *d.* 1664), physician, may have been the Tobias Whitaker, son of Francis Whitaker, who was baptized on 1 May 1601 at St Dunstan and All Saints, Stepney, Middlesex. In the preface to his first published work, *A Discourse of Water* (1634), he describes himself as 'Doctor of Physicke, of Norwich', but moved to London some time before 1638. In that year he brought out his principal work, *The tree of humane life, or the blood of the grape, proving the possibilitie of maintaining humane life from infancy to extreame old age without sickness, by the use of wine*, which was republished several times and translated into Latin (Frankfurt, 1655; The Hague, 1660, 1663). The purpose of this work, as stated in the introduction to the 1654 edition, was as 'an addition to our medicinal faculty, and more exactly to declare, how, and after what manner the juice of the Grape may be conducible to humane bodyes, both for Aliment and Medicament'. Whitaker seems to have encountered some criticism of his recommendation of wine as a universal prophylactic and remedy, for he declares that his book is 'for the acquaintance of more reasonable creatures' rather than the 'Tred of Dunghill-Cocks' who oppose him. The work describes wine in terms of temperature and dryness, and parallels symptoms of various illnesses to these two conditions before indicating which can be used to treat each ailment, and concludes rousingly that 'other Herculian braines' should take wine 'plentifull in substance and measure, by which every sense shall be refreshed, every capacity filled, and every intellect really delighted'.

In September 1660 Whitaker was appointed physician-in-ordinary to the royal household with a salary of £50 per year, although the position had first been offered to him by Charles II when in exile in 1649. In 1661 Whitaker published *An elenchus of opinions concerning the cure of the small pox. Together with problematical questions concerning the French pest*, prefixed to which was a portrait engraved by John Chantrey. Whitaker died in 1664. His widow received his pay, in arrears, in 1668.

Both Wood and Munk ascribe the writing of *The Tree of Humane Life* to William Whitaker, admitted a candidate of the College of Physicians in 1654, who died in the parish of St Clement Danes in January 1671. JO PAYNE

Sources *DNB* · T. Whitaker, *The tree of humane life* (1654) · *CSP dom.*, 1660–61; 1665–6; 1664–5 · Wood, *Ath. Oxon.: Fasti*, new edn · Munk, *Roll* · Watt, *Bibl. Brit.*, vol. 2
Likenesses M. Nickson, pen drawing, 1809/10 (after J. Chantrey), Wellcome L. · J. Chantrey?, etching, NPG; repro. in T. Whitaker, *An elenchus of opinions concerning the cure of the small pox* (1661) · oils, Wellcome L.

Whitaker, William (1547/8–1595), theologian and college head, was possibly born in the first year of Edward VI's reign. He was the third son of Thomas Whitaker of Holme, near Burnley, Lancashire, the head of a gentry family established there since the fourteenth century. Thomas had in 1530 or possibly 1531 married Elizabeth, daughter of John Nowell from Read, 10 miles away; William was consequently nephew to three distinguished brothers: Alexander *Nowell (*c.*1516/17–1602), dean of St Paul's, Laurence *Nowell (*c.*1516–1576) [*see under* Nowell, Laurence (1530–*c.*1570)], dean of Lichfield, and Robert Nowell, attorney of the court of wards.

Education and early career Whitaker first attended a private school at Burnley run by William Hatgrave. At the age of twelve or thirteen he was extracted from Lancashire and the Catholic sympathies of his parents by Alexander Nowell, who entered him at St Paul's School, London, then under the high mastership of John Cook. On 4 October 1564 Whitaker was admitted pensioner of Trinity College, Cambridge, where his tutor was Robert West. In 1565 he was admitted scholar. Nowell continued to support his education with a reversionary lease of a St Paul's Cathedral property (5 August 1566). He graduated BA in March 1568. In 1569 he published *Liber precum publicarum*, a Latin rendering of the daily offices, collects, and other matter from the Book of Common Prayer; this he dedicated to Alexander Nowell (23 May). On 6 September that year he became a minor fellow of Trinity. On 25 March 1571 he was advanced to a major fellowship, and five days later he proceeded MA. In this year he published some Greek verses appended to Nicholas Carr's *Demosthenis Olynthicæ orationes tres & Philippicæ quatuor*. In 1573 he provided the Greek version of Nowell's larger catechism, issued with the Latin original. He did likewise for the shorter (1574) and 'middle' (1575) polyglot versions. His work was dedicated to Sir William Cecil with whom the Nowells had long connections, and whom he was evidently now cultivating. His talents had already been recognized by the master of Trinity, John Whitgift. While still a junior figure, he had the assurance to advise Whitgift against responding to Thomas Cartwright's *Second replye* (1575), which he derided as 'loose … childish … unworthy to be refuted by any man of learning' (Paule, 15).

Time of hope On 31 July 1576 Whitaker was presented by the crown to the rectory of St Florence, Pembrokeshire; the appointment seems not to have taken effect, since another presentation was made to the same vacancy in the following year, but on 21 December he was ordained deacon and priest in London. On 25 October 1577 the queen presented him to a canonry of Norwich Cathedral, where he was installed by proxy on 23 February 1578. Shortly afterwards he gave his first university sermon by way of supplicating BTh, as which he was admitted on 14 June. On 14 July he incorporated his degree at Oxford. On 27 September 1578 Nowell had asked William Cecil, Lord Burghley, to obtain for his nephew the living of Withington, Gloucestershire, should John Bullingham be made bishop of Chester, none of which happened. On 3 November there appeared the first of Whitaker's anti-Catholic works, a translation of John Jewel's book against Thomas Harding which he dedicated to archbishops Edmund Grindal and Edwin Sandys, bishops John Aylmer, John Whitgift, and Edmund Freake, and Nowell—a stupendous feat of self-promotion which his disclaimer merely highlighted, but which served its purpose. The elevation of William Chaderton, regius professor of divinity at Cambridge, to the bishopric of Chester was Whitaker's opening. The chair was first offered to and declined by William Fulke; by 4 October 1579 Whitaker was regarded in Cambridge as the only remaining candidate, and he was appointed in the following year. He at once found himself at odds with the Lady Margaret professor, Peter Baro, whose lectures on the book of Jonah had questioned the Calvinist orthodoxy on salvation and election to which Whitaker resolutely adhered. This debate dominated Cambridge theology for fifteen years, and intermittently erupted on to the wider world. On 23 September 1580 Whitaker became chancellor of St Paul's Cathedral by royal grant, though obviously on the recommendation of Dean Nowell. In 1581 Whitaker brought out *Ad rationes decem Edmundi Campiani jesuitæ responsio*. By thus taking on the most gifted of the English Catholic missioners, he built up his reputation as 'David … against the popish Goliath' (*An Answere to … Downame*, 19). The mass of anti-Catholic propaganda which he published ensured him a respected place within the church which may (as in the case of John Reynolds at Oxford) have amounted to a kind of protected status. While adhering firmly to the establishment, he had a continuing sympathy with those protestants who were uncomfortable within it. In the summer of 1583, following the death of Grindal, he feared for puritan ministers under the next régime at Lambeth, and was among those who urged that only those of the Thirty-Nine Articles which concerned doctrine should be enforced by subscription. He joined the puritans who encouraged Cartwright to respond to the Rheims translation of the Bible. Whitaker himself published *Ad Nicolai Sanderi … responsio* in that year. The appointment of Whitgift to Canterbury (August 1583) cannot have entirely gladdened him, though it meant his friends were now in the highest places. He continued to court Burghley's patronage, and submitted to him his answers to Campion's *Quæstiones*. In 1585 he dedicated to him *An Aunswere to … W. Rainoldes*.

By this time Whitaker had acquired another wide and interrelated set of connections in the city of London, in colonial investment, and in religious radicalism. Perhaps early in 1580 he married Susan, widow of Cuthbert Fuller, a London merchant who died late in 1579, and daughter of the haberdasher Nicholas *Culverwell (*d.* 1569) [*see under* Culverwell family]. The couple had three daughters, Susan, Elizabeth, and Mary (all named in the 1589 will of their grandmother Elizabeth Culverwell), and two sons, Alexander *Whitaker (1585–1617) and Samuel (1587–1617). Susan Whitaker predeceased her mother, Mistress Culverwell, but a notable family connection persisted. Susan's sister Cecilia had married in 1577 or 1578 Laurence Chaderton, who became in 1584 the founding master of Emmanuel College, Cambridge. For a time Whitaker and Chaderton had set up house together; they remained closer friends than Whitaker sometimes cared to admit as he advanced his career.

The new master In 1585 Whitaker was being run by Burghley and Whitgift as a candidate for the mastership of St John's College, Cambridge (Burghley's old college), which should have been vacated by Richard Howland's consecration to the see of Peterborough that February. However, most of the fellows were against Whitaker's appointment; some objected simply because he was an outsider, but there were also suspicions of his in-laws and other puritan connections. It was rumoured that Whitaker had withdrawn an application to supplicate DTh before reaching the statutory age because he had developed puritan qualms about taking the title 'doctor'. Less than a quarter of the fellows openly supported his candidacy. He felt obliged to set before Burghley his qualifications for the post, promising to rule the college without partiality. Meanwhile Howland was kept in office, and did his best to promote Whitaker's cause. Only on 17 February 1587 were the college's acting visitors (including Burghley and Whitgift) able to proceed, authorizing an election before the full fellowship could be assembled. Even so, the fellows appear to have chosen another candidate; yet Whitaker was admitted to office by the vice-chancellor in Trinity on 25 February. On 27 May he proceeded DTh. By 29 June he had resigned the chancellorship at St Paul's. On 30 June he was admitted fellow of Eton College.

New statutes (1580) had given the master of St John's increased powers, and Whitaker was determined from the outset to exercise them. His first move was to expel Everard Digby, whom he identified as the leader of opposition among the fellows. Whitaker's real objection to him was his eclectic and relatively liberal theology; but knowing that this alone could not justify dismissal, he concocted a ragbag of disciplinary and financial charges. Digby managed a few hits by way of exchange (quoting Nowell against Calvin; and, having himself been accused of non-residence, mischievously noting that the master spent his nights in town with his wife). Digby was expelled and appealed to Whitgift; both he and Burghley felt that Whitaker had exceeded his powers, and in April 1588 ordered Digby's return. Neither party, however, was looking for a compromise. Digby provocatively boasted of his readeption, while Whitaker raised his game by appealing to the earls of Essex, Leicester, and Warwick. Whitgift continued to regret the 'violence of præcisenesse' with which he saw his protégé acting, and told Leicester that the affair had degenerated into 'private revenge' (BL, Lansdowne MS 57, nos. 70, 72). Leicester intervened decisively by arranging for Digby to have a few months' grace and then, in effect, to be paid off. Whitaker seems to have had no connection with Leicester before this case, which therefore demonstrates the social address and political competence he already commanded.

Love of the brethren Whitaker now embarked on a wholesale revision of the college statutes, designed to ensure the dominance of the divines over those of other faculties, and to curb gambling and other recreations. This was partly the customary purge of a new régime, but in sum it attempted to restructure St John's on the lines of the puritan academy founded at Emmanuel under Chaderton's mastership. The opposition at St John's drafted a counterproposal of forty-three 'flatt breaches of statute' which Whitaker had committed since his appointment, such as pushing through his own, unsuitable, nominations for college posts at inquorate meetings (CUL, CUR 6.1, no. 35). But the fellows could not hope to remove the master under the existing statutes, and he would obviously not consent to changes making this possible; the controversy therefore subsided into deadlock. Meanwhile Whitaker's polemical output continued with *Disputatio ad sacra scriptura*, issued on 2 May 1588, in which he attacked Cardinal Bellarmine.

Further puritan agitation at Cambridge in 1589–90 made Whitaker fear that a new visitation might 'pull up moe good plants than weedes', and he was worried even for his own tenure (BL, Lansdowne MS 62, no. 41). Hostilities in St John's were resumed when it was revealed that in September 1589 a national presbyterian synod had been held in the college. Some said this took place in Whitaker's own lodging while he was away in Lancashire. The issue was raised in a letter of 20 October 1590 from Eleazar (son of John) Knox, one of the conservative fellows. Whitaker was at once summoned to London to explain. That the synod, the last of its kind, took place at St John's, is not in doubt; Chaderton and Cartwright attended, and the host was Henry Alvey, Whitaker's favourite and a noted radical activist. The question exercising the government was what the master knew, and when he knew it. In a carefully worded response, conveyed in a letter to Burghley on 26 October, Whitaker avoided all reference to the specific meeting of the national synod; instead he solemnly swore ignorance of a continuing presbyterian cell within the college—something much harder to define and detect, and in any case not the issue. Whitaker's absence was genuine enough, but it is difficult to believe that on his return he really was surprised to find his lodge appropriated for such a meeting. He was not the last Cambridge head to give covert assistance to a radical cause he was unable openly to endorse. Significantly, his regard for Alvey was undimmed, and in December 1591 he secured him as president (vice-master) against the wishes of the majority of the electors. He used the textbook tactic of provoking the conservatives to withdraw, and voting through his appointees in their absence. He added the delightful touch of naming some of the absentees to minor offices, so demonstrating his magisterial impartiality.

That the remaining years of Whitaker's mastership were uneventful is witness to the success with which he had packed the college with men of his own stamp. He gazed, however, on the lusher pasture next door. In April 1591 Nowell had recommended him for the mastership of Trinity should John Still be made a bishop. Whitaker jeopardized his prospects of any further crown appointment when, that month, he married Joan, widow of Dudley *Fenner (c.1558–1587), puritan minister of Cranbrook, Kent. She brought with her two daughters, More Fruit (d. in or after 1602) and Faint Not (d. in or after 1604). Whitaker would not have given his own children such ostentatiously puritan names, but his sympathies were again expressed in February 1593 in deploring the execution of separatists, which he contrasted with leniency shown to many Catholics.

All sound learning Whitaker's final major publication, *Adversus Thomae Stapletoni* (1594), was a refutation of another leading Catholic apologist. The last year of his life was dominated by the controversy over predestination, simmering at Cambridge throughout his professorship, which he now moved into the public domain. On 27 February 1595, preaching before a congregation including eight peers and many gentry, he condemned the doctrine of universal grace as taught by Peter Baro. In response on 29 April a junior fellow of Gonville and Caius College, William Barrett, preached a university sermon which shocked the establishment with its outright rejection of the Calvinist dogma of assured salvation for the self-recognized elect, and which included personal attacks on Calvin, Pietro Martire Vermigli (known as Peter Martyr), and other leading reformers. Whitaker, as regius professor, took a lead in prosecuting Barrett before the university's consistory court and beyond. Whitgift at first thought Barrett had been harshly treated for what seemed a fair point of academic debate. Whitaker and his colleagues eventually persuaded the archbishop and Burghley (as chancellor) that the emerging anti-Calvinist party, for whom Barrett was obviously a stalking horse, was a threat to the university's *magisterium* and privilege. If such offensive novelties were tolerated, 'greate difference in poyntes of religion will breake furthe' (Trinity College, Cambridge, MS B.14.9, p. 47). Whitgift proposed a conference at Lambeth between Barrett and his principal opponents. The archbishop's continuing confidence in Whitaker is shown by his appointment on 10 May to a canonry in Canterbury Cathedral.

Though further debate at Cambridge was meanwhile forbidden, on 9 October Whitaker set out in a Latin sermon his own uncompromising supralapsarian position. As he left for Lambeth he promised Chaderton he would 'stand to Gods cause against the Lutherans' (*Two Elizabethan Puritan Diaries*, 125). He took with him nine propositions in which his doctrine was hammered home from different angles: salvation and reprobation were determined for eternity; saving grace could never be forfeit. Though minor changes were agreed at the meeting on 20 November, perhaps by way of according Whitgift a share in the drafting, the Lambeth articles remain Whitaker's composition. Whitgift circumspectly commended them as 'private judgments' in settlement of the Cambridge controversy (*Salisbury MSS*, 5.465). Others would have had them tacked to the established articles of religion; this was sought at the Hampton Court conference in 1604, and in 1613 they were formally adopted by the Church of Ireland. In England, though Calvinism remained the orthodoxy for a generation more, the Lambeth articles were the high water mark of Calvinist doctrine. By the time Whitaker was on the way back to Cambridge, the queen had expressed outrage and had ordered the articles to be abrogated. Their particular theological definition, though misliked by her, was less the issue than the attempt by an unofficial assembly to ordain narrow confessionalism in place of settled imprecision. Whitaker had forgotten whose church he served. His usual self-confidence seems to have been ebbing before the Lambeth meeting. On 19 November, in an uncharacteristically whingeing letter to Burghley, he begged for a more lucrative position, with greater freedom for the further writing he planned. As he rode home on 29 November he was taken ill at Trumpington; on arriving at St John's he went straight to bed with a hot ague, and died in the master's lodge on 4 December, trusting 'shortly to see God face to face' (*Two Elizabethan Puritan Diaries*, 125). The whole university mustered for his funeral on the 9th; the vice-chancellor (Roger Goad) preached in Great St Mary's, and John Bois spoke at the interment in St John's on the same day.

Two days after his death Whitaker's widow had a son, whom she called Jabez. She subsequently married Josias *Nicholls (*c*.1553–1639/40), puritan minister and religious controversialist. Whitaker's will does not survive, but he is known to have left means to his eldest son, Alexander. Whitaker had at least eight children. Samuel became a fellow of King's, while Richard was a prominent bookseller and publisher in Paul's Churchyard from 1618 to his death in 1648; in the 1630s he dedicated works to Charles I and Archbishop William Laud, but among his last publications was a work of Calvin. Jabez followed Alexander to Virginia and as a missionary to the Indians; he died in 1624.

The conscience of the rich Despite his many sinecures, Whitaker complained of poverty; no doubt his children and two stepchildren were a hefty expense. He also collected a library which the queen is said to have coveted, though Nowell said it had small resale value. Whitaker may have mismanaged his finances, but the claim that he was a 'contemner of money' (Fuller, 115) is a pious fiction. There is a wider contradiction, since it was axiomatic of Whitaker's anti-Roman polemic to discount the visible church, whose material benefits he nevertheless so obviously enjoyed, and in whose political machinations he excelled. Even his friends sensed this dilemma; Samuel

Ward was thankful that Whitaker had died before becoming (as was expected) provost of Eton, and so being 'overcome with the world' (*Two Elizabethan Puritan Diaries*, 125). Whitaker's reputation was also oddly distorted by the wish of the conservative fellows of St John's to acquire a new master more to their liking; being now in a minority they could not risk a free election, but instead asked Burghley to nominate a successor to Whitaker, whom they could not overtly criticize. They therefore described their late master as a gentle and retiring scholar, whose unrelenting studies had prevented him from noticing the infiltration of the college by radicals. The plentiful encomiums of his friends were less devious but scarcely more plausible; chief among these was a life by Abdias Ashton, fellow of St John's, published in 1599 and reprinted in the 1610 Geneva edition of Whitaker's collected works.

The Whitaker who finally emerges is, by contrast, a formidable but believable figure, as sharp-minded and decisive in his administrative role as he was in theological argument. Yet even there is a paradox. Determined to eliminate mere philosophy from scriptural exegesis, asserting that reason alone was 'no lawful weapon in the Lords warfare' (*An Aunswere to … W. Rainoldes*, 187), he deployed a rarefied system of logic proceeding from his own considerable intellect. In debate he maintained a civil tone (except to Stapleton), and was generally respected by his opponents: it is said that Bellarmine placed his picture above his desk, rather as Montgomery was to keep an eye on Rommel. In appearance Whitaker was darkhaired, with a red face which nobody seems to have attributed to drink. He enjoyed chess and archery and, like his uncle Alexander, was an angler whose skill is recalled by Isaak Walton. When the new chapel was built at St John's in 1869, his memorial was replaced in a position of honour at the centre of the west wall.   C. S. KNIGHTON

Sources BL, Harley MS 7039, fols. 157–157v, 160–64; Lansdowne MS 57, nos. 70–72, 78, 80, 87; Lansdowne MS 62, no. 41; Lansdowne MS 63, nos. 86, 91–3, 95; Lansdowne MS 79, nos. 61, 68–9; Lansdowne MS 80, no. 10 · CUL, CUR 6.1, nos. 35–7; CUR 93, nos. 6, 8; Lett 10, no. 6; Misc. Collect. 5, fols. 75–6 · CUL, MS Mm.1.38, pp. 76–84; MS Mm.2.25, fol. 162 · St John Cam., MS W.1 · Trinity Cam., MS B.14.9, pp. 5–82 · PRO, PROB 6/5, fol. 154; SP 12/125, no. 74; 12/132, no. 24; 12/162, no. 6 · W. Whitaker, *Opera theologica*, 2 vols. (1610) [incl. life by Abdias Ashton, vol. 1, pp. 698–704] · *The works of John Whitgift*, ed. J. Ayre, 3 vols., Parker Society (1851–3), vol. 3, pp. 611–17 · *An answere to a sermon preached the 17 of April anno D. 1608, by George Downame* (1609), 19 · T. Cartwright, *A confutation of the Rhemists translation* (1618), sigs. A3–A3v [Lat. text], A3v–A4 [Eng. text] · J. Heywood and T. Wright, eds., *Cambridge University transactions during the puritan controversies of the 16th and 17th centuries*, 2 vols. (1854), vol. 1, pp. 390–91, 503–4, 506–23, 532–3; vol. 2., pp. 3–5, 12–19, 62–5, 75–8 · H. Ellis, ed., *Original letters of eminent literary men of the sixteenth, seventeenth, and eighteenth centuries*, CS, 23 (1843), 86–7 · C. Hardwick, ed., *A history of the articles of religion* (1851), 332–7 · *CSP dom.*, 1547–80, 600, 634; 1581–90, 117; 1591–4, 149 · *CPR*, 1575–8, 212 (no. 1442), 148 (no. 1084), 483 (no. 3306); 1578–80, 183 (no. 1476) · *Calendar of the manuscripts of the most hon. the marquis of Salisbury*, 5, HMC, 9 (1894), 114, 268, 465 · *Report on the manuscripts of Lord De L'Isle and Dudley*, 2, HMC, 77 (1933), 203 · Venn, *Alum. Cant.* · Cooper, *Ath. Cantab.*, 2.196–200 · W. W. Rouse Ball and J. A. Venn, eds., *Admissions to Trinity College, Cambridge*, 2 (1913), 58 · J. Venn, ed., *Grace book Δ* (1910), 211, 245, 311, 413 · W. Sterry, ed., *The Eton College register, 1441–1698* (1943), p. xxxi · *Fasti Angl.*, 1541–1857, [St Paul's, London],

19 · *Fasti Angl., 1541–1857*, [Canterbury], 27 · *Fasti Angl., 1541–1857*, [Ely], 60 · T. Baker, *History of the college of St John the Evangelist, Cambridge*, ed. J. E. B. Mayor, 2 vols. (1869), vol. 1, pp. 180–89; vol. 2, pp. 597–607 · T. D. Whitaker, *History of the original parish of Whalley and honor of Clithero, in the counties of Lancaster and York*, 3rd edn (1818), 493–7, and table facing p. 264 · R. Churton, *The life of Alexander Nowell* (1809), 325–31 · G. Paule, *The life of … John Whitgift, lord archbishop of Canterbury* (1612), 5, 15 · J. Strype, *The life and acts of John Whitgift*, new edn, 3 vols. (1822), vol. 1, pp. 453–9; vol. 2, pp. 227–319; vol. 3, pp. 337–9 · J. Strype, *Annals of the Reformation and establishment of religion … during Queen Elizabeth's happy reign*, new edn, 3/1 (1824), 642–5 · P. Heylyn, *Historia quinqu-articularis* (1660), pt 3, chaps. 20–21 · T. Fuller, *Abel redivivus*, ed. W. Nichols, 2 vols. (1867), vol. 2, pp. 109–17 · F. Procter and W. H. Frere, *A new history of the Book of Common Prayer* (1901), 124 · A. F. Scott Pearson, *Thomas Cartwright and Elizabethan puritanism, 1535–1603* (1925), 145, 201, 263, 269, 354 · *Two Elizabethan puritan diaries, by Richard Rogers and Samuel Ward*, ed. M. M. Knappen, SCH, 2 [1933], 125 · M. M. Knappen, *Tudor puritanism* (1939), 369–70 · P. M. Dawley, *John Whitgift and the Reformation* (1955), 209–20 · H. C. Porter, 'Alexander Whitaker: Cambridge apostle to Virginia', *William and Mary Quarterly*, 3rd ser., 14 (1957), 317–43 · H. C. Porter, *Reformation and reaction in Tudor Cambridge* (1958), 183–203, 344–75, and *passim* · P. Collinson, *The Elizabethan puritan movement* (1967), 235–7, 400–01, 428 · W. H. Lamont, *Godly rule: politics and religion in England, 1603–60* (1969), 45 · S. Bendall, C. Brooke, and P. Collinson, *A history of Emmanuel College, Cambridge* (1999), 34 · P. Lake, 'The dilemma of the establishment puritan: the Cambridge heads and the case of Francis Johnson and Cuthbert Bainbrigg', *Journal of Ecclesiastical History*, 29 (1978), 25–35, esp. 31–3 · P. G. Lake, *Moderate puritans and the Elizabethan church* (1982), 58–65, 93–115, 169–226, and *passim* · N. Tyacke, *Anti-Calvinists: the rise of English Arminianism, c.1590–1640* (1987), 30–01, 117 n. 57 · H. R. Plomer and others, *A dictionary of the booksellers and printers who were at work in England, Scotland, and Ireland from 1641 to 1667* (1907), 192 · N. Canny, 'England's new world and the old, 1480s–1630s', *Oxford History of the British Empire*, ed. Canny, 1: *The origins of empire* (1998), 155–6, 159, 161, 162, 164 · I. Walton, *The compleat angler*, Folio Society (1949), 33 **Archives** BL, letters, Lansdowne MSS 57, nos. 78, 80, 87; 62, no. 41; 63, nos. 86, 93; 80, no. 10 · BL, letters, Harley MS 7039, fols. 157–157v, 160–64 · Bodl. Oxf., MSS Bodl. 59, 156; MS Crynes 837; MS Rawl. E. 68 · CUL, responses to articles against him, CUR 6.1, no. 36; CUR 93, no. 8 · Gon. & Caius Cam., MS 73/40, no. 64 · PRO, letters, SP 12/162, no. 6 · St John Cam., letters, MS W. 1 · Trinity Cam., letters, MS B.14.9, pp. 21–2, 47–9, 65–9 **Likenesses** two portraits, oils, 1587, St John Cam. · J. Payne, line engraving, 1620, BM · Passe, line engraving, BM, NPG; repro. in H. Holland, *Heröologia* (1620)

Whitaker, William (*d.* 1672), clergyman and ejected minister, was born at Oakham, Rutland, the son of the schoolmaster Jeremiah *Whitaker (1599–1654) and Chephtzibah, daughter of the vicar of Oakham, William Peachy. At Easter 1639 he matriculated as a sizar of Emmanuel College, Cambridge; he graduated BA in 1643. Having become a fellow of Queens' College in 1644, he proceeded MA in 1646. Like his father, Whitaker earned a reputation for his skill as a classical and oriental linguist. According to Samuel Annesley, Richard Holdsworth, master of the college, gave him the keys of the college library and set him the task of translating Eustathius upon Homer, which he performed very creditably. Having resigned his fellowship in 1647, on 2 October 1648 he was appointed by the visitors of the university as vicar of the parish of Hornchurch, Essex, an appropriated rectory of New College, Oxford. It seems that at about this time Whitaker married, for on 1 April

1652 the visitors appointed him a chaplain of New College, but found it necessary to dispense with the regulations against both marriage and non-residence; nothing is known of his wife. Following the death on 1 June 1654 of their rector, Jeremiah Whitaker, the parishioners of St Mary Magdalen, Bermondsey, unanimously elected his son to replace him. On 4 July they petitioned Cromwell to this end, and William Whitaker was admitted on 20 November 1654. He was himself succeeded at Hornchurch the following year by John Johnson.

Following the Restoration, Whitaker was ejected from Bermondsey, where his successor was instituted on 7 November 1662. He then gathered a congregation at Long Walk, Bermondsey, and the authorities were informed that he was preaching there in 1670. Whitaker also preached at the London house of Elizabeth Cecil, dowager countess of Exeter, and was friendly with her chaplain, Thomas Jacombe. For many years his house was full of candidates in divinity, and he had many foreign divines under his care. He was licensed to preach as a presbyterian at Court Yard, Bermondsey, on 2 April 1672, but died later that year. His funeral sermon was preached by Samuel Annesley, who published two of Whitaker's sermons in later editions of his *Morning Exercises*. In 1674 Whitaker's widow published his *Eighteen Sermons Preached on Several Texts of Scripture*. The preface, dedicated to Elizabeth Cecil, thanked her for kindnesses both to William Whitaker and to his father; Jacombe contributed a tribute to his colleague.   STEPHEN WRIGHT

Sources *Calamy rev.*, 524 · M. Burrows, ed., *The register of the visitors of the University of Oxford, from AD 1647 to AD 1658*, CS, new ser., 29 (1881) · T. W. Davids, *Annals of evangelical nonconformity in Essex* (1863) · J. T. Cliffe, *The puritan gentry besieged, 1650–1700* (1993) · Venn, *Alum. Cant.* · S. Annesley, *A sermon preached at the funeral of Reverend Mr Will. Whitaker, late minister of Magdalen Bermondsey, Southwark* (1673)

Whitaker, William (1836–1925), geologist, was born on 4 May 1836 at 69 Hatton Garden, London, the only child of William Whitaker (*d.* 1893), perfumerer and wine merchant, and Margaret Burgess Michie (*bap.* 1806, *d.* 1894), both Londoners. He was educated at a school in St John's Wood and at St Albans grammar school, and took a BA in chemistry from University College, London, in 1855.

Following a short period at the Geological Society, Whitaker joined the geological survey as an assistant geologist in 1857, being promoted to geologist in 1863. On 25 August 1869 he married Mary (1846–1916), daughter of Thomas Keogh, publisher, at the consul's office, Calais. They later had three children, but had separated by 1891. By this time Whitaker had, in 1882, been promoted to district surveyor, despite a superior's report in 1880 which described him as lazy, obstinate, obstructive, controversial, mutinous, and stubborn.

Most of Whitaker's time at the survey was taken up with applied geology in surveying, mapping, and writing of district memoirs and water supply papers that confirmed and greatly expanded the pioneering work of Professor Joseph Prestwich. However, his 1867 publication on subaerial denudation, which finally ended the belief that escarpments were formed by marine erosion, was more theoretical, original, and closely researched; it was highly praised by Charles Darwin. As early as 1889 Whitaker correctly predicted the occurrence of workable coal deposits in the south-east of England. Although he personally surveyed the major part of Essex, Suffolk, parts of Norfolk, and Cambridgeshire, his most important work was centred on London and the Thames valley, resulting in the publication of two major works in 1872 and 1889. Aubrey Strahan (1852–1928) described the latter, *The Geology of London and of Part of the Thames Valley*, as probably the most detailed account of the geology of any region that had ever been published.

In addition to his fieldwork Whitaker meticulously compiled bibliographies on the geology of English counties and carefully collected details of wells and borings which then appeared as appendices to official publications. He has been described as the father of English hydrogeology. On his official retirement in 1896 he moved to 3 Campden Road, Croydon, Surrey, and worked as a water engineer. His knowledge of every deep well and boring from Hertfordshire to the English Channel ensured there was no better opinion on the site for any building, housing development, or sewer. Even in retirement he found time to write or assist in the production of fifteen major official water supply publications.

Whitaker made a great contribution to many national societies. He was elected a fellow of the Geological Society in 1859, was awarded its Murchison medal (1886), Prestwich medal (1906), and Wollaston medal (1923), and served as president (1898–1900). He was elected FRS in 1887 and served on the Royal Society's council (1907–9). He became an honorary member of the Geologists' Association in 1875, served two terms as president (1900–02 and 1920–22), and led fifty-two excursions. For two weeks in 1900 he was president of the Geological Society and the Geologists' Association, a unique achievement. In addition he was at one time delegate to the yearly meetings of the British Association, an associate of the Institution of Civil Engineers, and a fellow of the Royal Sanitary Institute, and in 1890 received a silver medal from the Society of Arts. He was president of several local societies including the South Eastern Union of Scientific Societies in 1899, the Croydon Natural History Society in 1899, 1900, and 1911, and the Essex Field Club in 1911–14. Whitaker was a member of the Belgian, Liverpool, Manchester, Norwich, and Yorkshire geological societies, the Hampshire Literary and Philosophical Society, Hampshire Field Club, and Hertfordshire Natural History Society. For twenty years he was co-opted vice-chairman of Croydon libraries committee. He was a staunch liberal and a member of the National Liberal Club and Croydon Liberal Association.

In his later years Whitaker's appearance was dominated by his long white hair and beard. He was regarded as a kind, good-tempered, unaffected, and honest gentleman. Strahan, who knew Whitaker for more than fifty years, never heard him utter an unkind word, and did not believe he ever had an unkind thought, stated: 'Probably no one has rendered better service to his fellow men than Whitaker in the applications of geology to the needs of civilised life' (Strahan, *PRS*, xi). Whitaker died of cancer at his home in Wellesley Court, Croydon, on 15 January 1925 and was buried in Croydon cemetery, Mitcham Road, on 19 January. He was survived by his son Harry Lynn Whitaker and a daughter, Mary de Fraine Skeats, who was living in Australia. W. H. GEORGE

Sources 'Eminent living geologists: William Whitaker', *Geological Magazine*, new ser., 5th decade, 4 (1907), 50–58 · A. S. [A. Strahan], *PRS*, 97B (1924–5), ix–xii · H. E. Wilson, *Down to earth: one hundred and fifty years of the British geological survey* (1985) · A. Strahan, *Nature*, 115 (1925), 129–30 · *The Times* (23 Jan 1925) · *Croydon Advertiser* (24 Jan 1925) · G. M. Davies, *Proceedings of the Croydon Natural History Society*, 9 (1925), xxxix · J. S. Flett, *The first hundred years of the geological survey of Great Britain* (1937) · E. B. Bailey, *Geological survey of Great Britain* (1952) · H. Dewey, *Proceedings of the Geologists' Association*, 37 (1926), 231–5 · J. W. Evans, *Quarterly Journal of the Geological Society*, 81 (1925), lxi–lxii · W. W. Topley, *Readers' Index*, 27 (1925), 28–9 · P. Thompson, *Essex Naturalist*, 21 (1925), 93–6 · census returns, 1891, PRO, RG 12/914, fol. 25v · parish register, St Andrew's, Holborn, 30 May 1836 [baptism] · d. cert. · cemetery register
Archives BGS, notebooks and papers · Croydon Local Studies Library | BGS, letters to Alan C. G. Cameron
Likenesses photograph, repro. in 'Eminent living geologists: William Whitaker', pl. 3 · photograph, repro. in Strahan, *PRS*, 97 B (1925), 8 · photograph, repro. in Davies, *Proceedings of the Croydon Natural History Society* · photograph, repro. in Dewey, *Proceedings of the Geologists' Association* · photograph, repro. in *Transactions—Institution of Water Engineers*, 29 (1925), 152
Wealth at death £9854 13s. 6d.: probate, 4 March 1925, *CGPLA Eng. & Wales*

Whitbourne, Sir Richard (1561–1635), seaman and publicist for Newfoundland, was born and baptized on 11 June 1561 at Bishopsteignton near Newton Abbot in Devon, the son of John Whitbourne, yeoman, and his wife, Agnes. Serving as an apprentice between 1575 and 1583, probably to John Crooke, merchant adventurer of Southampton, he had voyaged to much of western Europe before sailing to Newfoundland in 1579 in search of whales and trade with the natives. For the next forty years he was a frequent visitor, witnessing Sir Humphrey Gilbert's formal annexation of the island in St John's harbour in 1583, and Sir Bernard Drake's capture of Portuguese fishing ships there in 1585. He was commended by the lord high admiral Lord Howard of Effingham for his services in commanding his own ship and three others against the Armada in 1588. In 1612 he was captured by 'that famous Arch-Pirate' Peter Easton, who was freely impressing fishermen and appropriating their supplies and catches (Cell, *Newfoundland*, 113). Yet once home he supported Easton's elusive search for a pardon. In 1614 he observed the depredations of the privateer-turned-pirate Henry Mainwaring.

In response to these losses, and perhaps upon the representations of the London and Bristol Company (1610), which was promoting settled plantations in Newfoundland, Whitbourne was commissioned by the court of admiralty in 1615 to inquire into alleged abuses in the fishery. That summer, at his own expense, he equipped a ship and crew of eleven, and convened courts of vice-admiralty in the harbours between Trinity Bay and Ferryland. His judicial circuit was the first attempt to institute formal courts in Newfoundland. He adjudicated disputes and received presentments from 170 of the 250 English captains who were fishing there. This documentation and his report, which have not survived, are summarized in his *Discourse and Discovery of New-Found-Land*, which went into 3 editions in 1620–23. The abuses he reported reflected the views of his witnesses: non-observance of the sabbath; the indiscriminate dumping of ballast in the harbours; theft of supplies left to overwinter: boats, salt, casks, fishing stages, drying flakes, bait, and even the catch, predominantly cod and cod oil; the appropriation of overly large fishing rooms (waterlots); the use, contrary to statute, of foreign bottoms in the trade; the destruction of timber; and lazy seamen. Like the complaints regulated by John Guy, as governor of the colony of Cupids in Conception Bay in 1611, Whitbourne's efforts were ignored by the visiting fishermen, their west country employers, and the government.

His experience in 1615 helped to turn Whitbourne, despite his continuing participation in the fishery, into an advocate of colonization. Anthony Parkhurst in the 1570s and Sir Humphrey Gilbert and Edward Hayes in the 1580s had tried to make the case for settlement, but none had Whitbourne's unique combination of experience and practicality. In 1618 he sailed to Renews, south of Ferryland, as governor of the colony established the previous year by William Vaughan, the first independent entrepreneur to purchase land from the London and Bristol Company. Finding the settlers living in temporary shelters and in hopeless disarray, he reorganized the colony. However, it did not long survive his departure the following spring. Three years later he was advising Henry Cary, Viscount Falkland, on his plans for a colony, visiting the subsequent settlement at Renews at least twice before 1626. He was knighted by Falkland (in his capacity as lord deputy of Ireland) in 1625. The next year he sought the patronage of the duke of Buckingham. In 1627 he was serving as lieutenant on the warship *Bonaventure*, but drowned at sea in 1635. His wife, Joanne, whom he married about 1585, had predeceased him in 1620 and was buried in Littleham, Devon. The couple had two daughters, Joan and Katherine.

Whitbourne's historical significance rests on his *Discourse*. To the second edition in 1622 he added 'A loving invitation … to all adventurers … for the advancement of his majesties most hopeful plantation in the new-foundland'. Unlike most contemporaries, who saw a contradiction between the seasonal migratory fishery and settlement, he argued that they were complementary imperial resources. The fishery was a cheap source of protein, a staple which could be exchanged for expensive Mediterranean goods, a 'seminary for fishers' and sailors for the Royal Navy, and a generator of industrial and agricultural supplies and employment at home. Settlement would extend the fishing season, permit the more efficient use of manpower, and lower costs. The island would yield up foodstuffs and minerals, especially iron. It offered an outlet for overpopulation at home and a strategic way station to Virginia. The result would be wealth and glory for the crown, entrepreneurs, and the nation.

The *Discourse* is a lively and practical guide to the climate, topography, vegetation, Native Americans, wildlife, and resources of the island. Detailed recommendations for extending and rationalizing the trade are supplemented by an analysis of costs and prospective profits, and an inventory for equipping a fishing vessel of 100 tons and forty planters. In a few cases Whitbourne was too optimistic. Newfoundland's climate was not benign, and it had a short growing season. Pervasive fog was not to be eliminated by burning off damp underbrush, and tobacco was unlikely to thrive. But these are minor miscalculations in a manual informed by experience, evidence, and enthusiasm; and by humour, as he notes the benefits of mosquitoes (black flies) in encouraging idle men to work, and his sighting of a mermaid in St John's harbour in 1610.

State officials who were increasingly interested in imperial expansion took note. Whitbourne was granted permanent copyright over the *Discourse*. In 1621 the privy council requested that each parish have a copy and take up a collection to recognize his services and help defray his expenses, estimated by him for his books alone at £240. Parishioners might even be canvassed in their homes. Described by the nationalist historian Prowse in 1895 as 'this sturdy old sailor [for whom] every Newfoundlander should feel a deep affection' (Prowse, 118), he is commemorated by the town of Whitbourne, 50 miles west of St John's. CHRISTOPHER ENGLISH

Sources R. Whitbourne, *A discourse and discovery of Newfoundland*, 3 edns (1620–23) · G. T. Cell, ed., *Newfoundland discovered: English attempts at colonisation, 1610–1630*, Hakluyt Society, new ser., 160 (1982) · G. T. Cell, 'Whitbourne, Sir Richard', *DCB*, vol. 1 · D. W. Prowse, *A history of Newfoundland from the English, colonial, and foreign records* (1895) · parish registers and bishop's transcripts, Bishopsteignton, Devon RO · parish registers and bishop's transcripts, Littleham, Devon RO · *CSP col.*, 4.82 · private information (2004) [Richard Whitborne]
Archives BL, 'A discourse and discovery of Newfoundland', Add. MS 22564
Likenesses W. Newton?, miniature portrait, oils, c.1811, priv. coll. · portrait, watercolour, priv. coll.

Whitbread, James William (1847–1916), theatre manager and playwright, was born in Portsmouth on 20 October 1847. Little is known of his early years or parentage, except that the family moved to Scarborough during Whitbread's infancy. His obituary in *Era* (21 June 1916) refers to his touring as a young actor 'with the companies of Joseph Eldred' throughout the north of England and to Dublin, and he appears never to have risen above the rank of respected supporting actor. He married his wife, Rachel, on 8 October 1872. According to the obituary in the *Scarborough Evening News* (12 June 1916) Whitbread became manager for Joseph Elaria, then for Wybert Reeve first at the Royal Edinburgh Theatre and from July 1876 at the Theatre Royal, Scarborough. The first record of his involvement with the Queen's Theatre, Dublin, relates to his producing *Dick Wittington and his Immortal Thomas (the Cat)*, a Christmas pantomime, in 1882. Whitbread, as lessee, took on the management of that theatre in August 1884 and according to an interview published in the *Irish*

Times (1 April 1893) 'by main energy, patience, wisdom and expenditure of money' transformed a lacklustre, impoverished institution into a decent, popular venue.

From 1886 and the staging of his melodrama *Shoulder to Shoulder* Whitbread composed regularly for the Queen's, notably *The Nationalist* (1891), *The Irishman* (1892), and *The Spectre of the Past, or, Homeless in the Streets of Dublin* (1893). As the titles suggest, these early works owed a considerable debt of influence to Boucicault, but Whitbread found an original voice with *Lord Edward Fitzgerald* in 1894. While respecting melodramatic conventions, he foregrounded, as his subject allowed, a distinctly revolutionary politics. A series of patriotic, nationalist dramas followed, beginning with Whitbread's celebrated *Theobald Wolfe Tone* (1898), designed to coincide with the celebrations commemorating the uprisings of 1798. Other dramas focusing on the heroes and martyrs of that period included: *The Ulster Hero* (1902) about Henry Joy McCracken; *The Insurgent Chief* (1902) about Michael Dwyer; and *The Sham Squire* (1903) about Francis Higgins, who plotted Lord Edward Fitzgerald's destruction. Whitbread's detractors, including W. B. Yeats, often assumed that the playwright merely deployed popular myth about these historical figures but there is evidence that Whitbread did read sources carefully. The typescript of *Lord Edward Fitzgerald* submitted for licensing by the lord chamberlain (most of Whitbread's plays toured to English provincial theatres) carries a note on the title-page admitting that a crucial influence had been W. J. Fitzpatrick's *Secret Service under Pitt* (1892). Aspects of the play support the claim. With *Sarsfield, or, The Siege of Limerick* (1905) Whitbread turned to an earlier period of political unrest surrounding the collapse of the Stuart (Jacobite) cause in 1691, but again the play courted fervent nationalist sympathies in its audiences. The same is true of a number of less overtly political dramas that Whitbread penned: *Shadowed*, *Rory O'More*, *The Irish Dragoon*, *The French Hussar*, *The Soldier Priest*.

Joseph Holloway, an inveterate Dublin theatregoer, wrote in his diary that a performance of *Theobald Wolfe Tone* pleased him for its difference from conventional melodramatic fare, notably 'the entire absence of buffoonery in the comic interludes'. There was no doubting Whitbread's seriousness of purpose in attempting to devise a drama that was 'a cut above the usual sensational play'. The patriotic, revolutionary subject matter gave a freshness and energy to rhetorical displays in the dialogue, more conventionally deployed to expose an evil consciousness or to define romantic ardour. The plays include romantic interest but the greater love in the heroes is for Ireland and independence, to which private feeling must give way. Whitbread's agenda is both educational (to teach audiences about their inherited past, free of colonial English interpretation), and inspirational (to instil in them nationalist commitment). Even the climactic episodes have to be interpreted in the light of this intent and not as sensational. *Theobald Wolfe Tone*, for example, ends with stirring military bands accompanying the embarkation of the French troops at Brest rather than

with the collapse of Tone's enterprise with his subsequent arrest in Loch Swilly. The dominant mood is exhilarating, not defeatist. Similarly where a play ends with the revolutionary hero's execution at the hands of the English forces, that death is portrayed through a series of tableaux, where the emphasis is not on the grimly morbid but on the disciplined stoicism which is to be interpreted as martyrdom for the nationalist cause. The irony in all this is that Whitbread was English. What motivated his ideological stance can only be conjectured. The *Era* obituary supposes that Whitbread 'took up the writing of Irish plays because they were the goods to suit his customers'. But such a mercenary interpretation would most likely lead to shoddy hack work, whereas the plays are carefully finished, expertly paced and structured. Moreover they attracted many fine contemporary Irish performers, such as Tyrone Power and Frank Breen, to work consistently at the Queen's, which run-of-the-mill drama would not have done. As well as being performed successfully for Irish communities throughout Britain, America, and Australia, Whitbread's plays were maintained in the Queen's repertory significantly until 1923 and the creating of the Irish Free State, when their ideological strategies were rendered redundant by political circumstance. Their subsequent neglect is unfortunate, since Whitbread's work afforded a necessary development in the evolution of the Irish historical play, manipulating the devices of melodrama to show the past as shaped by conflicting political ideologies. The plays had an admitted influence on Sean O'Casey.

An illustrated 'Address of Appreciation' from the company at the Queen's Theatre, Dublin, commemorating James and Rachel Whitbread's silver wedding anniversary carries cameo portraits of the manager, his wife, and two daughters (Florence and Isabel Louise). His image depicts a broad forehead, wavy hair, well-set eyes, and a flourishing moustache, suggesting a man who carried a handsome, youthful presence into middle age. Whitbread left the Queen's Theatre in 1907 when his lease expired, retiring to Scarborough, where he died of cirrhotic Bright's disease and a cerebral haemorrhage at his home at 38 Londesborough Road on 9 June 1916. He was buried three days later at All Saints' Church. He was survived by his wife; his younger daughter died on the day of the funeral.

RICHARD ALLEN CAVE

Sources collection of Séamus de Búrca relating to Queen's Theatre, Dublin, Dublin Civic Museum · *Era* (21 June 1916), 8 · *Scarborough Post* (13 June 1916), 4 · *Scarborough Weekly Post* (16 June 1916), 7 · *Scarborough Mercury* (16 June 1916), 3 · C. Herr, ed., *For the land they loved: Irish political melodramas, 1890–1925* (1991) · S. Watt, 'Boucicault and Whitbread: the Dublin stage at the end of the nineteenth century', *Eire–Ireland*, 18 (autumn 1983), 23–53 · chromolithographic compositions to advertise performances of *Wolfe Tone* and *Lord Edward* created by David Allen for the Queen's Theatre, Dublin Civic Museum
Archives Dublin Civic Museum, Séamus de Búrca collection
Likenesses cameo portrait, Dublin Civic Museum, Séamus de Búrca collection
Wealth at death £3087 5s. 11d.: probate, 5 Sept 1916, *CGPLA Eng. & Wales*

Whitbread, Samuel (1720–1796), brewer and landowner, was born on 30 August 1720 at Cardington, near Bedford, the seventh of eight children and the youngest of five sons of Henry Whitbread (*d*. 1727) and his second wife, Elizabeth Read. The Whitbread family were of prosperous nonconformist yeoman stock, farming their own land and closely associated with leading Bedfordshire puritans. Whitbread's father was receiver of the land tax for Bedfordshire, and his first wife was the daughter of John Ive, a London merchant. This gave Whitbread the advantage, through a half-brother, of a connection in the City when his widowed mother apprenticed him at the age of sixteen to John Wightman of Gilport Street, a leading London brewer, for the large fee of £300. He set up in business himself in December 1742 with two partners, Godfrey and Thomas Shewell, buying a small brewery at the junction of Old Street and Upper Whitecross Street and another brewhouse for pale and amber beers in Brick Lane, Spitalfields. Whitbread brought an inheritance of £2000 to the firm, plus the proceeds of a small family holding in Gloucestershire, and loans from friends and kinsmen in Bedfordshire. He became free of the Brewers' Company on 8 July 1743. The partnership was valued at £14,016, owning the leases of 14 public houses, with further loans to publicans, and deployed 18 horses and almost 18,000 casks. However, this was the prelude to a dramatic new venture.

Godfrey Shewell withdrew from the partnership as Thomas Shewell and Samuel Whitbread borrowed more to buy the large site of the derelict King's Head brewery in Chiswell Street in 1750. The new brewery was specifically for the single product porter, the basis for the vast brewing enterprises then being developed in London by Henry Thrale and Sir Benjamin Truman. It was named the Hind's Head brewery after the Whitbread family coat of arms. From the outset Whitbread was the leading partner financially, solely responsible for management, and Shewell withdrew completely in 1761, Whitbread buying out his share for £30,000. Great expansion ensued, with such notable innovations as vast underground cisterns containing 12,000 barrels of porter, designed by John Smeaton, and benefiting from installation of only the second Boulton and Watt steam engine in London (Henry Goodwyn, also a brewer, had beaten him by a matter of months). Public renown came on 27 May 1787 with a royal visit to Chiswell Street—by the king and queen, three princesses, and an assembly of aristocrats in train—with James Watt on hand to explain the mysteries of his engine. In the year of Whitbread's death, 1796, the brewery produced an unprecedented total of 202,000 barrels (that is, almost 30 million quart pots of porter).

Great investment in the brewery did not preclude Whitbread's amassing a personal fortune and large estates. On his marriage in July 1757 to Harriet, daughter of William Hayton of Ivinghoe, Buckinghamshire, a leading London attorney, Whitbread began buying land in Cardington, the locality of his birth. His wife died in 1764, leaving him with an only son, Samuel *Whitbread (the couple also had

Samuel Whitbread (1720–1796), by Henry Bone, 1796 (after Sir William Beechey)

two daughters). Whitbread went on to buy the Bedwell Park estate in Hertfordshire in 1765, and he also owned London houses, first at St Alban's Street, Westminster, and then at Portman Square (from 1778), together with a large house in Chiswell Street by the brewery. In 1795 shortly before his death he bought Lord Torrington's Southill Park estate in Bedfordshire and immediately engaged the architect Henry Holland to rebuild the existing house. Whitbread had by this time accumulated a landed estate worth some £400,000.

Affluence brought higher social status and also Whitbread's second marriage on 18 August 1769 to Lady Mary Cornwallis, younger daughter of Earl Cornwallis; but she died in 1770, giving birth to a daughter, Mary *Grey (1770–1858). Whitbread became MP for Bedford in 1768, mainly, but certainly not always, supporting the tory interest until his son took over the seat in 1790. He was regarded as completely independent of the administration and spoke mainly on matters pertaining to the brewing industry, save that he was a firm advocate of the abolition of the slave trade.

Whitbread died on 11 June 1796 at Bedwell Park. He appointed his three senior clerks as his executors because his son was 'a perfect stranger to the whole' (Mathias, 309). Whitbread not only had his own portrait painted by Sir Joshua Reynolds, but he also commissioned Thomas Gainsborough, Gainsborough Dupont, and George Romney to paint portraits to hang in the library at Southill of all nine of his senior clerks and brewers, in recognition of their importance in managing the business. Unfortunately, in their very rich gilt frames the pictures had to observe the dissipation of the great fortune by the younger Samuel Whitbread as he pursued a costly social and parliamentary career, neglecting the brewery which had been the source of the family's wealth and prestige.

PETER MATHIAS

Sources P. Mathias, *The brewing industry in England, 1700–1830* (1959), 59–61, 90–95, 260–63, 277–87, 309 · 'Whitbread, Samuel', HoP, *Commons* · J. A. G. Harley, 'Samuel Whitbread's first enterprise', *Guildhall Miscellany*, 1/9 (1958), 3–26 · S. Whitbread, 'Introduction', *Southill: a Regency house* (1951) · *The story of Whitbread* (1992) · *Whitbread's brewery* (1951) · *The parish of Clerkenwell*, Survey of London, 47–8 [forthcoming]
Archives Beds. & Luton ARS, diaries; letters to his solicitor | NRA, priv. coll., corresp. with John Howard and Samuel Whitbread jun. · Whitbread Archives, The Brewery, Chiswell Street, London
Likenesses J. Reynolds, oils, 1786–7, priv. coll. · W. Beechey, oils, 1790–93, priv. coll. · H. Bone, enamel on copper, 1796 (after W. Beechey), NPG [*see illus.*] · W. Ward, mezzotint, pubd 1797 (after W. Beechey), BM, NPG · J. Bacon sen., marble monument, 1799, St Mary's Church, Cardington, Bedfordshire · S. W. Reynolds, mezzotint, pubd 1803 (after J. Reynolds), BM · H. P. Bone, pencil drawing (after W. Beechey)
Wealth at death supposedly £400,000, plus brewing estate value £200,000

Whitbread, Samuel (1764–1815), politician, was born on 18 January 1764 at Cardington, Bedfordshire, the only son and third child of Samuel *Whitbread (1720–1796), brewer and politician, and his first wife, Harriet, daughter of William Hayton, attorney, of Ivinghoe, Buckinghamshire. She died three months later, and Whitbread senior took as his second wife in 1769 Lady Mary Cornwallis, daughter of Charles, first Earl Cornwallis. She died the following year, after giving birth to a daughter, Mary [*see* Grey, Mary (1770–1858)].

A background in brewing The Whitbreads were minor Bedfordshire gentry by the mid-seventeenth century. Samuel Whitbread senior, a youngest son, was apprenticed into the London brewing trade in 1736. He subsequently went into business on his own account, and at Chiswell Street developed the largest and most technically advanced porter brewery in the country. By 1790 his capital in it was over £271,000. He invested heavily in landed property in Bedfordshire, Hertfordshire, and six other counties. By the end of his life he owned 12,300 acres, of which 10,500 were in Bedfordshire, where he ranked second in acreage only to the dukes of Bedford. The former Torrington estates at Southill, bought in 1795, later became the family home. He was MP for Bedford on his own interest during 1768–74 and 1775–90. A forbidding, deeply devout man, who had abandoned the family's dissenting tradition for Anglicanism, he was a staunch supporter of Pitt.

Education, marriage, and early political career The younger Whitbread's upbringing was largely joyless, and great care was lavished on his education by his well-meaning but overbearing father. At Eton College from 1775, he was befriended there by Charles Grey and William Henry Lambton, youthful disciples of Fox. He entered Christ Church, Oxford, in 1780, but was removed to St John's College, Cambridge, where he resumed his acquaintance

Samuel Whitbread (1764–1815), by John Opie, c.1803

with Grey and Lambton, in 1782. He graduated BA in 1785. On his return from a European tour in 1786 he was introduced by Grey to the salons of high whig society. He fell in love with Grey's sister Elizabeth, but his father initially vetoed a marriage and sent him abroad again in the summer of 1787 for a period of reflection. After a surly penance he got his way, marrying Elizabeth Grey on 26 January 1788.

At the general election of 1790 Whitbread, after thinking better of an attempt on the county (which proved a step too far for the family until 1892), exploited his father's indecision and supplanted him at Bedford, where he was secure for his lifetime. His father, shocked and hurt, found a berth at Steyning in 1792, when his son was already established as one of the leading figures of the Foxite whig opposition in the Commons. Whitbread, who joined Brooks's in 1791 and the Whig Club in 1793, did well in the Ochakov debates of April and June 1791, and particularly distinguished himself on the same subject on 29 February 1792. He supported abolition of the slave trade and religious toleration, causes that he warmly espoused throughout his life. A leading spirit, with Grey, of the Society of the Friends of the People, on 25 May 1792 he advocated parliamentary reform. He supported Fox's calls for peace negotiations in December, and condemned the outbreak of war, on 1 February 1793. For the rest of that parliament he used his powerful if crude oratory to denounce allied war aims and attack coercive legislation. Although his rather superficial measure of 1796 to empower magistrates to fix a minimum wage was unsuccessful, it revealed the humanitarianism in which his liberalism was rooted, and which set him above many of his political associates.

Brewing and wealth On the death of his millionaire father in 1796 Whitbread inherited the brewery, some London property, and estates in seven counties. He later consolidated and increased his Bedfordshire estates to about 12,000 acres and sold most of the outlying lands. He carried on the brewery business alone for two years, but took in three partners in 1798 and three more in 1800: by these arrangements he was freed from the necessity of personal attendance, while remaining individually responsible for the brewery's finances. His net income from land (about £12,600 a year) almost always exceeded brewery profits (about £8000), but the business offered a far more lucrative return on capital. This alone probably explains why he never succumbed to strong political and social pressures to dispose of it. It was, however, a potentially unstable element in his wealth, which forced him into extensive borrowing and was a source of worry, especially from about 1808, when his finances evidently began to run into difficulties.

An uncertain political career Whitbread, who supported parliamentary reform in May 1797, participated in the Foxite secession. After resuming regular attendance in 1801, he acted with the Foxite opposition to Addington, but abstained from the division on the peace settlement on 14 May 1802. He supported Grey's protest against the renewal of war on 24 May 1803, and was active in the combined attack on Addington in 1804, when Fox named him, Grey, and Lord Lauderdale as his most effective political allies. Whitbread took the centre of the national political stage in 1805 with his remorseless attempt to bring Lord Melville to justice for alleged financial malpractice during his tenure of the treasurership of the navy in Pitt's first administration. Although he made some tactical blunders during the parliamentary campaign, which ended in a vote to impeach Melville on 25 June 1805, Whitbread gained much credit for the tenacity with which he conducted it. Its initial success helped to stimulate a revival of radicalism in the country, as well as fatally weakening Pitt's feeble second ministry. Whitbread regarded it as a considerable personal triumph, though Melville's acquittal in June 1806 and the ridicule excited by lapses of taste and judgement in his own concluding speech of 16 May detracted from it.

Whitbread's failure to secure office when the Foxites came to power in Lord Grenville's coalition ministry early in 1806 marked the turning point of his political career. The sketchy evidence suggests that his inferiority complex over his origins and involvement in trade, which made him fear rejection by the aristocratic order represented by Fox and Grey, prevented him from staking a forthright claim in his preliminary discussions with them. Grey, who never understood Whitbread and was an inveterate snob, appears to have taken literally his diffident observation that he did not wish to be considered if his inclusion would create problems. Fox, greatly harassed by the many claims pressing on him, was not disposed to quibble. In any case, Whitbread, in considering himself entitled, as it emerged, to office of cabinet or, at least, important departmental rank, overrated his pretensions. When the intensity of his mortification became clear, Grey—whose earlier throwaway remark that he might sell the brewery, ownership of which disqualified him from the exchequer, had rankled—sought to propitiate him. Whitbread now claimed the offer of the first suitable vacancy. In the reshuffle following Fox's death in September 1806 Grey, with Grenville's approval, offered him the secretaryship at war as soon as the incumbent, Richard Fitzpatrick, Fox's oldest political crony, could be accommodated elsewhere. He convinced Whitbread of the folly of his initial peevish rejection of the proposal because it did not entail cabinet rank; but he further soured their relationship by doing nothing to accelerate Fitzpatrick's removal and by trying to fob off the impatient Whitbread with a peerage, which he indignantly refused. Nothing had been done when the ministry fell in March 1807.

By then Whitbread had put himself at odds with Grey and the other whig leaders on an important political issue, by pointedly opposing on 5 January 1807 the address on the ministry's abortive peace negotiations of the summer, which he denounced as inflexible and unimaginative. In thus revealing himself as an irresponsible extremist and potential political liability, he not only annoyed Grey but also alarmed Grenville and the conservatives. His scheme for reform of the poor laws, which he outlined on 19 February 1807, fell foul of fanatics of various persuasions. He subsequently embodied its most radical proposal, for the establishment of a national system of education, in a separate bill, which, after being amended to make it optional, passed the Commons but was rejected by the Lords.

Whitbread had no realistic claim to the opposition leadership in the Commons when Grey succeeded to the peerage late in 1807. While Grey, who had long been grooming his wife's uncle George Ponsonby for the position, could not be criticized for passing Whitbread over, he was at fault in failing to try to reach a clear understanding with him. His pathetic attempt to mollify his brother-in-law at second hand through George Tierney, who was shocked by his discovery of the intensity of Whitbread's bitterness and resentment, made matters worse. Whitbread, who believed sincerely, if fatuously, in the feasibility of a negotiated peace, lost his temper with Grey on the subject in Grenville's company in January 1808, and soon afterwards gave notice of three resolutions calling for negotiations. A subterfuge initiated by Lauderdale seemed to have succeeded in persuading him to accept a more moderate address; but at the party meeting on the eve of the debate Ponsonby lost control of the warmongers, whose hostility prompted Whitbread to revert to his own resolutions. On 29 February 1808 Ponsonby moved the previous question on the third and last of these, which was lost by 211 votes to 58.

Erratic extremism in politics Although Whitbread was now irrevocably set on a course of erratic extremism, he and the whigs did not actually part company until 1812. He established himself as the most frequent and powerful speaker on the opposition side. His enthusiasm for the Spanish cause was short-lived and, although he was talked out of moving an amendment to the address in 1809, he criticized British involvement in the Peninsula on 19 January, and on 31 January went out on a limb by proposing a peace amendment on the address on the Erfurt overtures. Increasingly influenced and flattered by Thomas Creevey, he enthusiastically took up the cause of economical reform, setting a lead and example for the radical whigs of the 'Mountain', who were seeking to encourage the revival of radicalism inspired by the acquittal of the duke of York on charges of involvement in the corrupt disposal of army patronage in March 1809. Whitbread's call at the Westminster meeting of 29 March for a national campaign for parliamentary reform further shocked the party hierarchy. Yet his relations with the extra-parliamentary reform movement were uneasy: he was never entirely trusted by its leaders, and, indeed, was not prepared to go to their extremes. He did, however, help to perpetuate and sustain the Foxite reforming tradition in unpropitious times.

Attempts by the whig leaders, scenting office, to re-establish a practical relationship with Whitbread in the winter of 1809–10, when Grey again left the dirty work largely to Tierney, failed in so far as he refused to acknowledge Ponsonby's titular leadership. At the same time, he was personally amiable towards Grey and Grenville, and not inclined to be provocative. The 1810 session passed without an open breach, though he showed considerable independence. His bid on 25 January to commit the house to economical reform was defeated by 95 votes to 54. He was included in opposition discussions of their plans for the attack on the Scheldt fiasco, and took a leading and effective part in the debates on it. His guarded support for Burdett in his conflict with parliament, and his advocacy of reform agitation at the London livery dinner on 19 April 1810, earned him a written rebuke from Grenville, but he was politely unrepentant.

Had the whigs come to power on the establishment of the Regency in February 1811, Whitbread, whose ambition for office was still strong, would have become first lord of the Admiralty. Grey and Lord Holland overcame Grenville's resistance but, characteristically, Whitbread himself almost wrecked the arrangement by raising objections to serving under Grenville if he retained his auditorship of the exchequer. He was eventually mollified by Grenville's grudging agreement to forgo the salary, but it was the regent who finally dashed his hopes. He was less active than recently in the 1811 session, when he refused to countenance Cartwright's plan for an alliance between whig reformers and radicals. In 1812 Whitbread went increasingly his own way, and put himself beyond the pale as far as the opposition leaders were concerned. His call on 7 January for peace with and exoneration of Napoleon set the tone, while his motion for information on deteriorating relations with America, on 13 February, secured only twenty-three votes. In May 1812 Grenville, though acknowledging that Whitbread had acted without personal malice in supporting Creevey's attack on the

sinecure tellership of the exchequer held by his brother the marquess of Buckingham, renounced all future political co-operation with him. Grey's was the only dissenting voice when the whig hierarchy excluded Whitbread from consideration for office in the early negotiations for a new administration following Perceval's assassination. Whitbread's ambition and poor judgement betrayed him into supporting Lord Moira's abortive and half-hearted scheme to set up a reforming government. His wild denunciation of Grey and Grenville for insisting on changing the household, which he blamed for its failure, caused great offence.

A political outcast For the rest of his life Whitbread was an outcast from the main body of opposition. He kept up his obsessive demands for peace negotiations and sought, to a limited extent, to promote economic and parliamentary reform. His involvement in 1813 in the campaign on behalf of the princess of Wales, in which he acted as Henry Brougham's lieutenant, was a waste of his talents. After early successes he made a mistake by accusing the commissioners of the inquiry of 1806, Grenville and lords Spencer, Erskine, and Ellenborough, of deliberately misrepresenting evidence. His churlish withdrawal of the charge did him little good. He renewed his efforts in Caroline's cause in 1814, but only succeeded in playing into the hands of ministers and exasperating Brougham. Desperate for peace, he expressed confidence on 20 December 1813 in the ministry's wish to effect it. On 29 June 1814 he concurred in the address on the treaty of Paris and praised Lord Castlereagh, but objected to the notion that the end of the war justified the way in which it had been waged.

On 8 November 1814 Whitbread attacked the government over the war with America. In the following months, when the barely controlled vehemence of his parliamentary speeches raised eyebrows, he voiced his concern at the repression of liberalism in Europe. In March 1815 he protested against a renewal of hostilities, and on 7 April he got thirty-seven votes for an amendment deploring war for the purpose of determining who should rule France. His address of protest on 28 April against a war to destroy Napoleon was rejected by 273 votes to 72. There was a strain of hysteria in many of Whitbread's pronouncements on the situation in Europe, though he denied being an unreserved apologist for the French emperor.

Decline and suicide The decline in Whitbread's health, noticeable for about six years and marked by excessive increase in weight and susceptibility to debilitating headaches, accelerated in June 1815. Worn out, but unable to sleep, he oscillated between extremes of agitation and despair. On receipt of the news of Waterloo and Napoleon's abdication, he caused surprise on 23 June by praising the duke of Wellington and the ministry, albeit in qualified terms. His last speech in the house, on 4 July, was on a motion thanking the duke of York for his work as commander-in-chief, in which, after a brief show of his old defiance, he tamely acquiesced. He spent the evening of the following day in frenzied talks with his attorney on the tangled finances of the Drury Lane Theatre, which had taken up much of his time since he had become chairman of the committee to promote its rebuilding after the fire of 1809. On the morning of 6 July 1815 he killed himself by cutting his throat at his London house at 35 Dover Street, Piccadilly.

The evidence strongly suggests that the mental disturbance prevailing when Whitbread committed suicide had its basis in an organic disorder, possibly Cushing's syndrome, a disease of the endocrine glands. It is idle to speculate whether he was driven to the final act by worry and guilt over the problems of the theatre, or by a paranoiac belief that the defeat of Napoleon symbolized his own political failure. With his wife, who died on 28 November 1848, he had two sons and two daughters: William Henry (1795–1867), MP for Bedford 1818–34; Samuel Charles (1796–1879), MP for Middlesex 1820–30; Elizabeth (1791–1843), who married William, eighth Earl Waldegrave; and Emma Laura (1798–1857), who married Charles Shaw Lefevre, first Viscount Eversley.

Assessment Whitbread's political career was one of honest endeavour rather than achievement, though he was among the half-dozen dominant figures of the House of Commons in the years following the deaths of Pitt and Fox. His waywardness was more a symptom than a cause of whig disarray in the period. While he brought many of his difficulties on himself through deficiencies of temperament and judgement, he was to some extent the victim of aristocratic prejudice against his involvement in trade, and he deserved more sympathetic handling than he received from Grey. Sir Robert Heron wrote of him:

> Though his harsh and overbearing manners had, for a long time, been obnoxious to many of all ranks, and particularly to the poor, even whilst they received benefits from him; yet, the experience of his honesty, his enlightened benevolence, and his indefatigable exertions in almost every department of town and country business had, at length, procured for him universal respect, and, out of Parliament, almost universal acquiescence in his measures; and, probably, few men have been so extensively useful to the country … In Parliament, his bad taste and, what is perhaps the same thing, want of judgment, above all, his impractical disposition, diminished greatly the advantages which might otherwise have been derived from his great ability as an orator, his experience, and his incorruptible firmness. (Heron, *Notes*, 1851, 58–9)

Sir Samuel Romilly commented that 'the only faults he had proceeded from an excess of his virtues' (S. Romilly, *Memoirs*, 1840, 3.191). D. R. FISHER

Sources HoP, *Commons, 1790–1820*, 5.528–45 · D. Rapp, *Samuel Whitbread: a social and political study* (1987) · D. Rapp, 'Social mobility in the eighteenth century: the Whitbreads of Bedfordshire, 1720–1815', *Economic History Review*, 2nd ser., 27 (1974), 380–94 · R. Fulford, *Samuel Whitbread: a study in opposition* (1967) · parish register (birth), 18 Jan 1764, Cardington, Bedfordshire
Archives Beds. & Luton ARS, travel journals, estate corresp. · Derbys. RO, cash books · NRA, priv. coll., corresp. and papers | Beds. & Luton ARS, corresp. with William Lee Antonie · Beds. & Luton ARS, corresp. and papers, incl. some relating to Lord Melville's trial · BL, letters to Grenville, Add. MS 58977 · BL, corresp. with Lord Holland, Add. MS 51576 · Hants. RO, corresp. with George Tierney · N. Yorks. CRO, corresp. with Christopher Wyvill · Northumbd RO, Newcastle upon Tyne, letters to Thomas Creevey · U. Durham L., corresp. mainly with second Earl Grey

Likenesses G. Romney, oils, 1781, Eton · J. Opie, portrait, *c*.1803, priv. coll. [*see illus.*] · S. W. Reynolds, mezzotint, pubd 1804 (after J. Opie), BM, NPG · J. Sayers, caricature, aquatint, pubd 1805, NPG · S. W. Reynolds, mezzotint, pubd 1806 (after J. Opie), BM, NPG · J. Nollekens, marble bust, 1814, Drury Lane Theatre, London · W. Day, lithograph, pubd 1831 (after J. Northcote), BM · T. Gainsborough, portrait · caricatures, BM
Wealth at death under £200,000: PRO, death duty registers, IR 26/692/102; *The Times*, 8 March 1816

Whitbread [*alias* Harcourt], **Thomas** (*c*.1618–1679), Jesuit, was the son of John Whitbread (d. 1625/6) and Anne, *née* Allen (d. 1654) of Fristling Hall, near Writtle, Essex. Educated from 1630 at the English College at St Omer in the Southern Netherlands, in 1635 he entered the Society of Jesus's noviciate at Watten, following the steps of Jesuit formation, during the course of which he was ordained priest in 1645 and finally professed on 8 December 1652. From 1642 he had been teaching at the college at St Omer and in 1647 was sent to work in England. In due course he was twice elected superior of the Jesuit College of the Holy Apostles, in which Jesuits working in Norfolk, Suffolk, Essex, and Cambridgeshire were organized and supported in their often solitary work. He was also for a short period superior of the College of St Hugh, covering Lincolnshire. During the thirty-two years of his work in East Anglia he was based, if not always resident, at Fithlers near Writtle, a property of the influential Roman Catholic Lord Petre, with whom his family had long-established and close connections. In addition to this personal link, Lord Petre contributed largely to the financial stability of the College of the Holy Apostles.

In 1677 Whitbread was elected provincial of the Jesuits' English province and returned to the Southern Netherlands to carry out a visitation of the English colleges there. During this visit he encountered Titus Oates who, having been already expelled from the Jesuit colleges at Valladolid and St Omer, sought his permission to enter the noviciate of the Society of Jesus. Following the inevitable rebuff Oates swore that he would become either a Jesuit or a Judas. Disappointed in his first objective, Oates spent the next year in contriving forged papers and false evidence that would justify his claim to the latter epithet. When Whitbread returned to England following his visitation, he took up residence in the diplomatically exempt house of the Spanish ambassador. For three months he was seriously ill and remained in the embassy. On 24 April 1678 the triennial conference of the English province was convened at the duke of York's residence in St James's Palace, causing considerable anti-papal public alarm in London, and rumours of a Jesuit conspiracy began to circulate. This generally excited sense of general foreboding made possible the arrest of Whitbread from within the boundaries of the Spanish embassy; he was arrested and closely confined in Newgate. On 17 December 1678 with four other Jesuits he was indicted on a charge of high treason. Brought again to trial at the Old Bailey on 13 June 1679 the evidence against the accused was found to be inadmissible and a fresh indictment was drawn up. Among other charges, including one of conspiracy to murder the king,

Whitbread was further charged with financing a projected Roman Catholic rising in Ireland. The counterfeited and perjured evidence of Oates and his companions, Bedloe and Dugdale, underpinned the charges. Whitbread questioned the legality of the proceedings on the ground of double jeopardy, in view of the earlier trial of December 1678. Nevertheless the five accused were found guilty and condemned to the traitor's death by hanging, drawing, and quartering. A petition was made to Charles II for clemency, denying any treasonable activity or intention. This was rejected and Whitbread and his companions were executed at Tyburn on 20 or 30 June 1679 and buried in the churchyard of St Giles-in-the-Fields. Two poems by Whitbread, 'To his Soul' and 'To Death', and a devotional tract, 'The devout elevation of the mind to God', were printed in *A Remonstrance of Piety and Innocence* (1683), commemorating the deaths of Whitbread and his companions. JOY ROWE

Sources J. S. Bennett, 'Who was Fr Thomas Whitbread?', *Recusant History*, 16 (1982–3), 91–8 · T. M. McCoog, *English and Welsh Jesuits, 1555–1650*, 2, Catholic RS, 75 (1995), 201 · G. Holt, *St Omers and Bruges colleges, 1593–1773: a biographical dictionary*, Catholic RS, 69 (1979), 284 · H. Foley, ed., *Records of the English province of the Society of Jesus*, 5 (1879); 7 (1882–3) · M. Tanner, *Brevis relatio felicis agonis* (1683) · G. Oliver, *Collections towards illustrating the biographies of the Scotch, English and Irish members of the Society of Jesus*, 2nd edn (1845), 87
Archives Archives of the British Province of the Society of Jesus, London | Essex RO, Chelmsford
Likenesses M. Bouche, line engraving, NPG; repro. in M. Tanner, *Brevis relatio felicis agonis* (1683)

Whitburgh. For this title name *see* Hay, Alexander, Lord Whitburgh (*d.* 1616) [*see under* Hay, Alexander, of Easter Kennet, Lord Easter Kennet (*d.* 1594)].

Whitby, Daniel (1637/8–1726), Church of England clergyman and author, was born at Rushden, Northamptonshire (on 24 March 1638 according to the *Dictionary of National Biography*, a date which has not been substantiated). His father, Thomas Whitby (*fl.* 1620–1638), was rector of the parish but moved soon after his son's birth to Barrow-on-Humber, Lincolnshire. His uncle and namesake was rector of Theydon Mount, Essex, but was ejected during the civil war, and became a canon of Chichester at the Restoration. Daniel matriculated as a commoner at Trinity College, Oxford, on 23 July 1653, was elected scholar on 13 June 1655, aged seventeen, graduated BA on 20 April 1657 and MA on 14 April 1660, and was elected fellow of Trinity in 1664. He then found favour with the bishop of Salisbury and former president of Trinity, Seth Ward, who made him his chaplain in 1668 and preferred him lavishly in his Salisbury diocese. On top of a valuable prebend and the rectory of St Edmund's, Whitby became precentor in September 1672—a dignity he held until his death—and a canon residentiary in June 1676. He accumulated BD and DD on 13 September 1672.

Whitby's first publications (three anti-Roman works in 1664, 1666, and 1674, and an apological treatise in 1671 to withstand 'the encrease of Atheism and Irreligion';

Daniel Whitby (1637/8–1726), by Michael Vandergucht, pubd 1700 (after Eloas Knight)

D. Whitby, *Logos tēs pisteōs, or, An Endeavour to Evince the Certainty of Christian Faith*, 1671, 2) were fully consonant with orthodox Oxford divinity. Whitby was well read in the fathers, especially the Greek ones, provided some assistance for the preparation of John Fell's Cyprian, and was for years a great admirer of Henry Dodwell, with whom he 'had once the honour of an intimate acquaintance' (Bodl. Oxf., MS Cherry 23, 259). His first deviation was his *Discourse concerning the laws ecclesiastical and civil made against hereticks by popes, emperors and kings* (1682), to show what protestants might expect to suffer under a popish prince. The book was published anonymously and Whitby managed to hide his authorship until 1726, when he claimed it for himself in his last collection of sermons. Although he avoided advocating exclusion explicitly, such was clearly the conclusion that the reader was invited to draw for himself, all the more so as Whitby insisted that no resistance was allowed once a prince had lawfully come to power. He was certainly sincere but this was also a subtle move to turn tory theology against the tories.

Whitby made fuller use of this tactic in his *Protestant reconciler, humbly pleading for condescention to dissenting brethren, in things indifferent and unnecessary for the sake of peace, and shewing how unreasonable it is to make such things the necessary conditions of communion*, also published anonymously (with the imprint of 1683 but actually issued in November 1682), arguing that the very heinousness of schism, as represented by Church of England writers, made it incumbent upon ecclesiastical authorities to cease to impose indifferent ceremonies 'which do occasion the Schism, and consequently the destruction of so many precious and immortal Souls' (D. Whitby, *Protestant Reconciler*, 1683, 30–31). Although Whitby stated that dissenters were guilty too, the *Protestant Reconciler* caused an outcry in ecclesiastical circles and its author, who was soon identified, was subjected to much abuse. He vainly tried to defuse the crisis by hastening to issue, in June 1683, a second part to exhort dissenters to conformity. Nicknamed Whigby, he was even accused of having encouraged the Rye House plot. Two propositions extracted from the *Reconciler* were condemned by the Oxford decree of 21 July 1683, and the book was among those subsequently burnt in the schools quadrangle. Whitby had to make a public submission in Salisbury at the bishop's consistory on 9 October 1683, declaring himself 'truly and heartily sorry' for his book, professing to 'revoke and renounce all irreverent and unmeet Expressions contained therein' and engaging never to print anything hereafter without episcopal approbation (Sykes, vi–vii; Bodl. Oxf., MS Tanner 34, fol. 182r). Whitby protested later that this had not been a recantation:

> That very Morning that I was to make my Submission to the then present Chancellor, I declared, that if any such Thing was required of me, I would rather lose all, be imprisoned and die, than I would do it. (D. Whitby, *A Full Answer to the Arguments of the Reverend Dr. Jonathan Edwards*, 1712, vii)

However, his declaration certainly went under that title, being first circulated in manuscript and then printed in L'Estrange's *Observator*. The Latin manual of ethics which he published in 1684 and which later became a favourite of the Oxford curriculum underwent censure on these questions.

Whitby was not at the end of his troubles, as his case became part of the fierce conflict at Salisbury Cathedral between Ward and Dean Thomas Pierce. The latter's party declared Whitby's submission unsatisfactory and, in the aftermath of Monmouth's rebellion, tried to have him presented at the assizes in September 1685. Whitby was only saved by a certificate 'from the bishop, Chapter and severall Loyall Justices of the Peace, that hee had behaved himself very loyally' since 1683 (Bodl. Oxf., MS Tanner 143, fol. 117r). To justify himself further he published three ultra-tory sermons, in which he taught passive obedience, confuted Samuel Johnson's *Julian*, and even flirted with the patriarchal scheme. The whole affair must have been traumatic for Whitby and may explain his readiness, later in his life, to side with 'heretics' against the tide of clerical feeling.

The politics of James II brought Whitby in line again with dominant Anglican opinion. He contributed his patristic learning to the anti-Roman campaign, offering expert advice and writing himself against image worship, divine service in Latin, and traditions. After the revolution of 1688–9 he had serious scruples about taking the oaths to William and Mary, and almost resolved at one point to become a non-juror, though less because of 'the supposed unlawfuness of complyance' than of 'the scandal it is like

to minister' (Bodl. Oxf., MS Ballard 34, fol. 16r). He managed to satisfy himself, however, and then characteristically rushed into print with four pamphlets to demonstrate that allegiance is due to a king *de facto*.

Whitby was close to Gilbert Burnet, his new bishop, who chose him as godfather of his son, Gilbert junior, and promoted him in April 1696 to the prebend of Teynton Regis, the richest of the diocese. He now spent most of his time on his *Paraphrase and Commentary on the New Testament*. The epistles came out first in 1700 (with a dedication to Burnet who is thanked for having perused and approved the work), and the whole was published in 1703 in two folio volumes. It was regularly reprinted and considered a classic in the eighteenth century. The commentary on Romans 13 shows Whitby fully converted to whig theories of contract and resistance. His extreme Arminianism, which led him to deny any imputation of Adam's sin to his posterity, engaged him in a violent controversy with both John and Jonathan Edwards. According to his own account Whitby, having been 'bred up Seven Years in the University under Men of the Calvinistical Persuasion', had 'once firmly entertained all their Doctrines' but went on to abandon them as contrary 'to the common Reason of Mankind' and conducive to disbelief and deism (D. Whitby, *A Discourse Concerning, 1: The True Import of the Words Election and Reprobation*, 1710, iii–v). He may have struggled for some time to reconcile his new views with the articles and the liturgy, and is said to have declined the deanery of Salisbury to avoid a new subscription. However, he held eventually that it was lawful to subscribe 'in any Sense, of which the words are fairly, and *Grammatically* capable' (D. Whitby, 'An answer to a pamphlet', *Reflections on some Assertions and Opinions of Mr Dodwell*, 1707, 10).

When preparing his New Testament, Whitby had failed to obtain communication of John Mill's then unpublished work and clearly resented the rebuke. This partly accounts for his most famous piece, the *Examen variantium lectionum Millii* (1710), in which he argued that such a huge collection of variants was undermining the certainty of scripture and played into the hands of papists and atheists. Whitby's reaction was thoroughly theological; indeed, according to Hearne he 'hardly knows what a manuscript is' (*Remarks*, 2.112). Freethinkers, starting with Anthony Collins, seized upon it gleefully and it was therefore mercilessly ridiculed by Richard Bentley in his *Remarks upon a Late Discourse of Free-Thinking* (1713, pp. 63–9).

Whitby's anti-Romanism remained fierce to the last and he was increasingly worried by what he perceived as the Romanizing tendencies of the high-church party: hence his furious attack against William Beveridge's posthumous writings in 1711. He had long been an orthodox trinitarian and had published in 1691 a Latin treatise on Christ's divinity which was heavily indebted to George Bull's *Defensio*, but he was won over to Samuel Clarke's *Scripture Doctrine of the Trinity* and entered into a correspondence with the author, putting at his disposal the extended knowledge of the ante-Nicene fathers which was his forte ('for the reasons are much beyond me'; BL,

Add. MS 4370, fol. 8r). He first entered the debate anonymously, but afterwards published under his name an attack against Bull (*Disquisitiones modestae in clarissimi Bulli defensionem fidei Nicaenae*, 1718) and defended it against Daniel Waterland in 1720 and 1721. In his profession of faith, which he arranged to be published after his death by his young friend Arthur Ashley Sykes, he retracted what he had written in his New Testament when he had been following 'the common beaten Road of other reputed Orthodox divines' (Sykes, sig. A2r). His final position has occasionally been labelled unitarian but should more properly be described as Arianism. It explains, together with his dislike of high-churchmanship, his *Dissertatio de S. scripturarum interpretatione secundum patrum commentarios* (1714), in which he turned his patristic learning against the fathers, collecting their mistakes in order to show that they were neither adequate interpreters of scripture nor sufficient authorities to settle the debate on the Trinity. He repeated the same principles in the Bangorian controversy of 1718, in which he sided with Benjamin Hoadly.

According to Wood, Whitby 'hath been all along so wholly devoted to his severer studies, that he hath scarce ever allowed himself leisure to mind' anything else (Wood, *Ath. Oxon.*, 671). He never married and seems to have lived with his sister. His life is very much the story of his books (he published nearly fifty, including pamphlets and sermons). In his old age he had to employ an amanuensis because his sight was failing, but he retained his tenacious memory. He was short and very thin, and his features in his engraved portrait are rather severe; a portrait 'seems to have been presented' to Trinity in 1844 but 'is now nowhere to be found' (Pool, 146). His minute examination of Mill's variants would alone bear witness to his industry. On the other hand, he wrote bad Latin—according to Hearne this was 'school Boy Jargon' (*Remarks*, 3.21)—and his English style was not better; there is some truth in John Edwards's cruel description: 'he is a great Painstaker, and may be said to slave at the Work of Book-Making: But the Labour consists chiefly in Transcribing and in Repetitions' (Edwards, xii). Whitby certainly relished long quotations and was adept at reusing his own works in his later writings. He also unavoidably contradicted himself several times, the most blatant instance, as his orthodox opponents were eager to point out, being his notion of the Trinity.

Whitby could hardly be considered an original thinker and, anyway, the majority of his books were meant to expose and confute the errors of others rather than to expound a personal position. They were none the less influential, and the Latin ones were much read and commented upon on the continent (they were all put on the Roman index in 1757). Whitby was consistently driven by the dread of popery, the tendency to reduce religion to plain morality, and the dislike of subtleties, be they those of theological speculation, of sacramentalism, or of textual criticism. Throughout his long career, from Restoration orthodoxy to the age of reason, he remained a latitudinarian, for whom Chillingworth's *Religion of Protestants*

and Taylor's *Liberty of Prophesying* provided essential references.

Whitby died in Salisbury on 21 March 1726. He had been very well and at church the day before, but 'returning Home was seiz'd with a Fainting, and died the Night following', aged eighty-eight (Sykes, ii).

JEAN-LOUIS QUANTIN

Sources A. A. Sykes, 'A short account of Dr Whitby. To which is added, a catalogue of his works', in *Hysterai phrontides, or, The last thoughts of Dr Whitby, containing his correction of several passages in his commentary on the New Testament, the second edition*, 2nd edn (1728) [preface] · Wood, *Ath. Oxon.*, new edn, 4.671–7 · E. A. O. Whiteman, 'The episcopate of Dr Seth Ward, bishop of Exeter (1662–1667) and Salisbury (1667–1688/9), with special reference to the ecclesiastical problems of his time', DPhil diss., U. Oxf., 1951 · D. Whitby, letters to Arthur Charlett, Bodl. Oxf., MS Ballard 34, fols. 12r–17r · D. Whitby, letters to Samuel Clarke, Bodl. Oxf., MS Add. 4370, fols. 8r–11v · Wood, *Ath. Oxon.*: *Fasti* (1820), 198, 223, 332–3 · *Fasti Angl., 1541–1857*, [Salisbury] · Foster, *Alum. Oxon.* · D. Whitby, letters to Thomas Smith, Bodl. Oxf., MS Smith 54, fols. 127–9 · D. Whitby, letter to Henry Dodwell, Bodl. Oxf., MS Cherry 23, 259 · D. Whitby, *Ethices compendium, in usum academicae juventutis* (1684) [Bod. copy, 8° Rawl. 234, with MS note on suppressed passages] · *Remarks and collections of Thomas Hearne*, ed. C. E. Doble and others, 2, OHS, 7 (1886), 112 · *Remarks and collections of Thomas Hearne*, ed. C. E. Doble and others, 3, OHS, 13 (1889), 21, 65 · *Remarks and collections of Thomas Hearne*, ed. C. E. Doble and others, 9, OHS, 65 (1914), 107 · J. Peirce, *Vindiciae fratrum dissidentium* (1710), 196–7 · Bodl. Oxf., MS Wood F. 45, fol. 101r · J. Edwards, *The Arminian doctrines condemn'd* (1711) · Mrs R. Lane Poole, ed., *Catalogue of portraits in the possession of the university, colleges, city and county of Oxford*, 3, OHS, 82 (1926), 146
Archives BL, Birch collection, corresp. of Samuel Clarke · Bodl. Oxf., MSS Ballard, corresp. of Arthur Charlett · Bodl. Oxf., MSS Tanner, Archbishop Sancroft MSS
Likenesses M. Vandergucht, line engraving, pubd 1700 (after E. Knight), BM, NPG [*see illus.*]

Whitby, Edward (c.1578–1639), politician and lawyer, was born in Chester, the second son of Robert Whitby (d. 1631) and his wife, Anne, daughter of Thomas Wall or Kinge of Helesby, Cheshire. Whitby's father rose to prominence in Chester in the late sixteenth century and was appointed clerk of the pentice (town clerk) in 1602. After his education at Brasenose College, Oxford, where he graduated BA in 1599, Whitby followed in his father's footsteps and entered the Inner Temple in 1600, being called to the bar ten years later. Through the influence of his family in Chester he was granted the recordership of the city in 1613 and shortly afterwards he married Alice, née Bavand (d. after 1639), the widow of his predecessor as recorder, Thomas Gamull. For the next twenty-five years he was involved in a bitter quarrel with other members of the Gamull family, although it appears that this concerned the Whitby family's engrossment of offices in Chester rather than his marriage to Alice. Through Gamull influence within the corporation, and the support of Sir Randle Mainwaring who wished his son-in-law, Robert Brerewood, to succeed to the office, Whitby's father and brother were dismissed as joint clerks of the pentice in 1617. Two years later Whitby narrowly avoided the loss of the recordership and only maintained his position through the intervention of the earl of Derby and two leading members of the Cheshire gentry, Sir Peter Warburton and Sir Thomas Savage. The quarrel between Mainwaring, the Gamulls, and Whitby continued throughout the 1620s before in 1627 he finally succeeded in having Brerewood charged with corruption and removed and his father and brother reappointed clerks. This dispute spilled over into the electoral arena the following year when Whitby and his puritan ally, the beer-brewer John Ratcliffe, were opposed at the elections for the 1628 parliament by Mainwaring and Sir Thomas Smith; the contest was easily won by Whitby and Ratcliffe.

Whitby had served Chester as an MP in every parliament subsequent to his appointment as recorder in 1613. The city customarily elected its recorder as the senior member in order to protect its interests in parliament and Whitby sat in 1614, 1621, 1624, 1625, 1626, and 1628. In 1614 he was returned without incident but during the discussion of candidates by Chester corporation for the 1621 parliament, in the assembly meeting he duplicitously supported the privy councillor, Sir Thomas Edmondes, the preferred candidate of the corporation. At the actual election, however, much to the chagrin of his fellow officials and in particular the Gamulls, he denounced Edmondes and successfully implored the freemen to elect his friend Ratcliffe. During the parliament he gave active encouragement and support to his old friend Clement Coke and his father, Sir Edward; Whitby had undertaken much of the complex legal work on the land settlements concerning Clement's marriage to Sarah Redich and Sir Edward had declared himself beholden to him. In the parliament Clement Coke took offence at Sir Charles Morrison's slur on judges (and thus by implication his father) and physically assaulted him on the stairs of the Commons' vestibule. The house took a dim view of this action and confined Coke to the Tower. Whitby steadfastly defended his friend and eventually informed the house that Coke had realized the error of his ways and that he was ready to be released and reconciled with Morrison. He also supported Sir Edward Coke when Sir Francis Lepton, a notorious patentee of the monopolistic dispensing of apprenticeships grant, submitted to the house a damning written attack on Coke, who had prosecuted him for misuse of the patent. Overall, however, in 1621, 1624, and 1625 Whitby made little impact on the recorded proceedings of the Commons and mainly concerned himself with matters of interest to Chester.

In the two subsequent Caroline parliaments, 1626 and 1628, Whitby played an influential role in the Commons. His long service in the house, legal training, and support for the liberties of the Commons clearly influenced his appointment in 1626 as chair of the grievances committee. He kept notes of the proceedings while he was in the chair. Written in law French in his appalling hand, they nevertheless provide an invaluable record of the activities of the committee. In St Stephen's Chapel he also stoutly defended the actions of the Commons, declaring his dissatisfaction with the tone of the opening speeches by the king and Lord Keeper Coventry, which he felt, left 'many things yet unexplained which touch our liberties' (Bidwell

and Jansson, 1626, 2.419). He was also involved in the attempted impeachment of George Villiers, duke of Buckingham, and he was placed in charge of investigating the duke's sale of honours and offices. Due to illness he was forced to delegate most of this task to his deputy, Christopher Sherland, but this did not save him from being summoned before the attorney-general, Sir Robert Heath, at the end of the parliament to hear the king's displeasure with those who had taken a leading role in the impeachment proceedings. In the 1628 parliament Whitby was chosen by John Selden as his assistant to investigate the ancient liberties of the subject and he was appointed to the committee which drafted the reasons as to why the petition of right should proceed. He was also named to a joint conference with the Lords on the liberty of the subject and to committees concerned with drafting the remonstrance to Charles.

Whitby continued as recorder of Chester until his death on 18 April 1639 and his surviving papers in the Public Record Office and at Chester City Archives reveal his diligence in that position. He was buried a week later in St Mary's Church, Chester, in the vault of Thomas Gamull, his predecessor as recorder and his wife's first husband. The marriage had been childless and his property descended to his cousin, Robert Whitby.   CHRIS R. KYLE

Sources G. J. Armytage and J. P. Rylands, eds., *Pedigrees made at the visitation of Cheshire, 1623*, Lancashire and Cheshire RS, 58 (1909) · BL, Harleian MS 2180, fol. 105v · BL, Stowe MS 812 · PRO, Whitby MSS, CHES 38/48 · W. B. Bidwell and M. Jansson, eds., *Proceedings in parliament, 1626*, 4 vols. (1991–6) · assembly book 1, Ches. & Chester ALSS · M. J. Groombridge, ed., *Calendar of Chester city council minutes, 1603–1642*, Lancashire and Cheshire RS, 106 (1956) · *JHC*, 1 (1547–1628) · R. C. Johnson and others, eds., *Proceedings in parliament, 1628*, 6 vols. (1977–83) · HoP, *Commons* [draft] · J. K. Gruenfelder, 'The parliamentary election at Chester, 1621', *Transactions of the Historic Society of Lancashire and Cheshire*, 120 (1968), 35–44 · J. P. Rylands, ed., *Cheshire and Lancashire funeral certificates, AD 1600 to 1678*, Lancashire and Cheshire RS, 6 (1882) · Foster, *Alum. Oxon.*
Archives BL, Whitby MSS, Stowe MS 812 · PRO, CHES 38/48

Whitby, Sir Lionel Ernest Howard (1895–1956), haematologist, was born in Yeovil on 8 May 1895, the second of the three sons of Benjamin Whitby, glove maker, and his wife, Jane Elizabeth Milborne. He was educated at King's College, Taunton, and Bromsgrove School (of which he later became a governor), and won a senior open scholarship for Downing College, Cambridge. The First World War broke out soon after he had won the scholarship and Whitby served with distinction as a machine-gunner in the Royal West Kent regiment in Serbia, Gallipoli, and France. A severe wound in March 1918 resulted in the amputation of a leg, and he ended his time in service as a very young major with the MC but with a lifelong disability.

Undeterred by this misfortune Whitby went up to Cambridge in October of the same year to study medicine, and he completed his training at the Middlesex Hospital in London as a Freeman scholar and a Hudson and Hetley prizeman. He graduated MB BCh, Cambridge (1923), took the diploma of public health (1924), and qualified MD, Cambridge, and MRCP (1927). In 1922 Whitby married

Ethel, daughter of James Murgatroyd, leather merchant, of Shelf, Yorkshire. She was a fellow undergraduate and qualified in medicine; later she served under him in the army blood transfusion service with the rank of major in the Royal Army Medical Corps. Highly intellectual and artistic, she gave her husband invaluable help. They had a daughter and three sons, two of whom followed their father with distinction into the more scientific branches of medicine.

In 1923 Whitby was appointed assistant pathologist in the Bland-Sutton Institute at the Middlesex Hospital, where he began to develop the wide range of expert knowledge in pathology, bacteriology, and haematology which was eventually embodied in three books: *The Laboratory in Surgical Practice* (1931, with Charles Dodds), *Medical Bacteriology* (1928; 6th edn, 1956), and *Disorders of the Blood* (with C. J. C. Britton, 1935; 7th edn, 1953). These books, like his lectures, showed a most effective combination of erudition, clarity, and common sense.

Whitby sprang into prominence when he was invited to join the team of doctors attending George V in his illness of 1928–9. He was appointed CVO. During the next ten years he busied himself with medical research, becoming increasingly interested in haematology, the study of blood and its diseases, and with a growing practice in clinical pathology. He also undertook experimental studies on the new sulphonamide drugs, first discovered by the German chemist Gerhard Domagk in 1935. In collaboration with Arthur Ewins from the pharmaceutical company May and Baker, Whitby tested a wide range of sulphanilamide derivatives synthesized by Ewins and his colleagues, and selected 'M & B 693' for clinical trial. This drug, later known as sulphapyridine, led to a vast improvement in the treatment of pneumococcal pneumonia. The work was summed up in Whitby's Bradshaw lecture in 1938 to the Royal College of Physicians and in 1939 won him the John Hunter medal and prize from the Royal College of Surgeons.

On the outbreak of war in 1939 Whitby, who had stayed with the Territorial Army, held the rank of colonel. He was appointed the first officer in charge of the army blood-transfusion service. Understanding of the complexity of the blood groups was still rudimentary, so that both basic research and improvements of technique were urgently required. Whitby's imperturbable and friendly competence lightened the exacting teamwork of his assistants in spite of the severe bombing of Bristol, where he was stationed at the army blood supply depot and was responsible for the collection, processing, and supply of blood to armies in the field. He also established a school for training transfusion units to work with the army at home and in other countries. By the end of the war his service had become a model for future peacetime services in the larger medical centres, and he had been promoted a brigadier. The development of blood transfusion for the wounded saved innumerable lives and continued to be one of the major medical and surgical advances of the twentieth century.

During the war, Whitby travelled overseas and all over Great Britain, and he was called into consultation in 1943 and again in 1944 when Winston Churchill was ill. Called the 'M & B man' by Clementine Churchill and 'the Vampire' by her husband, because of his blood transfusion work, Whitby was asked by Lord Moran, Churchill's doctor, to advise on the therapeutic management of the prime minister's fevers. In 1944 Whitby travelled with Churchill to the Quebec conference, his presence and that of the accompanying nurse being kept secret at the time. Whitby was knighted in 1945.

In the same year Whitby was appointed to the regius chair of physic at Cambridge, thus moving out of medical practice at the time of the formation of the National Health Service, with which Whitby was not in complete agreement. In post-war Cambridge it was necessary to replan the entire medical course. Allocated a small hut in the grounds of Downing College, he hung the sign 'Medical School HQ' on the door, and set to the task with considerable enthusiasm. Whitby helped the medical school to develop several important new features, such as the organization of postgraduate studies, the health service for undergraduates, a statistical service, and a department of human ecology. These years also proved Whitby to be an ideal chairman of large medical conferences. Able at a moment's notice to compose a pithy introductory speech and to extract the essence from a medley of opinions, he acted as a most successful president of the British Medical Association in 1948–9 and chairman of the association's educational committee; and in 1953 he was equally effective as president of the first World Conference on Medical Education. He was also president of the International Society of Haematology, in 1950, the Association of Clinical Haematologists, the Association of Clinical Pathologists, and in 1951 of the first international congress in that subject.

Whitby's election in 1947 to the mastership of his old college, Downing, added further responsibilities. The college was enriched with a new chapel, a spacious court, and a hall restored and freshly adorned; and all branches of study found stimulation in his wide intellectual interests. Meanwhile his own research continued; he built up a haematology unit where he ensured close collaboration between clinic and laboratory, and his books needed periodic revision. As chairman of the medical committee of Addenbrooke's Hospital he played a leading part in planning improvements, in easing the take-over of the hospital by the health service, and in organizing the clinical instruction of medical graduates. In 1951–3 Whitby reached the peak of his academic career when he served as vice-chancellor of the university. His quickness of thought and steadiness of judgement, combined with a sympathetic understanding of diverse characters, ensured a distinguished term of office. His duties tied him closely to Cambridge, but before and after this period he travelled widely on medical and academic missions. He gave the Cutter lecture when he was visiting professor at Harvard in 1946; and he was the Sims Commonwealth travelling professor in 1956.

Whitby was elected FRCP in 1933; he received the gold

medal of the Royal Society of Medicine in 1945 and of the Society of Apothecaries in 1948. He was a commander of the American Legion of Merit and a chevalier of the Légion d'honneur; an honorary member of the American Association of Physicians and of the New York Academy of Medicine; an honorary fellow of Lincoln College, Oxford; and he received honorary degrees from Glasgow, Toronto, and Louvain.

Whitby died at the Middlesex Hospital, London, on 24 November 1956 following an operation. He had just returned from a lecture tour of Australia and New Zealand as Sims travelling professor. He was survived by his wife.

A. D. GARDNER, rev. E. M. TANSEY

Sources *BMJ* (1 Dec 1956), 1306–9 · *BMJ* (15 Dec 1956), 1434 · R. E. Barnsley, *BMJ*, 2 (22 Dec 1956), 1493 · *The Lancet* (1 Dec 1956), 1165–7 · *Nature*, 179 (1957), 16–17 · Munk, *Roll* · M. Gilbert, *Winston S. Churchill, 7: Road to victory, 1941–1945* (1986), 938–9, 950, 972 · R. Lovell, *Churchill's doctor: a biography of Lord Moran* (1992), 246 · *WWW* · personal knowledge (1971) · J. Slinn, *A history of May & Baker, 1834–1984* (1984), 124 · private information (1971) · *CGPLA Eng. & Wales* (1957) · *WW*

Archives IWM, papers relating to service with Royal Army Medical Corps

Likenesses W. Stoneman, two photographs, 1945–55, NPG · W. West, oils, Bromsgrove School, Worcestershire; copy, Downing College, Cambridge · photograph, repro. in *The Lancet* · photograph, repro. in *BMJ*, 2 (1 Dec 1956), pp. 1306–9 · photograph, repro. in *BMJ*, 2 (15 Dec 1956), p. 1434 · photograph, repro. in Barnsley, *BMJ*, 2

Wealth at death £25,281 11s. 2d.: probate, 31 Jan 1957, *CGPLA Eng. & Wales*

Whitby, Stephen of (d. 1112?), abbot of Whitby and of St Mary's, York, was one of the leading figures in the revival of monastic life in the north after the Norman conquest. Almost all that is known of him derives from a narrative account which allegedly came from his own hand. The authenticity of this has been much debated, but scholarly opinion now tends to favour acceptance of the narrative as the genuine tradition preserved at St Mary's. Stephen was probably of noble birth, but his first recorded appearance was as a monk at the newly revived monastery at Whitby (c.1078), and shortly afterwards he was elected abbot, taking control of the community from the hermit Reinfrid. However, within a few years hostility from Whitby's lay patron, William de Percy (d. 1096), forced Stephen and a section of the community to move to the former monastery at Lastingham, granted by William I at Stephen's request as a secure retreat from pirate attacks. By 1086 they had moved again, to the outskirts of the city of York. Stephen had taken the advice of Count Alan, of Brittany and Richmond—a man who had been well known to him before his conversion—that an urban location would be advantageous for attracting endowments, and had accepted his offer of the church of St Olave in Marygate. Domesday Book records the abbot of York, unnamed, as a Yorkshire landholder. Two years later, in 1088 or 1089, Stephen secured an even greater success when William II took the community into royal patronage, and provided a larger site adjacent to St Olave's, where the king himself is said to have cut the first turf in preparation for the building of St Mary's Abbey.

The creation of a powerful monastic corporation close to the city brought Stephen into conflict with Archbishop Thomas (I) of York (d. 1100), and William II stepped in to resolve the dispute and compensate the archbishop for losses that he claimed to have sustained as a result of the foundation of St Mary's. Other sources attest a close relationship between Stephen and his royal patron. William entrusted Stephen with the task of arresting Abbot Benedict of Selby, and during the primacy dispute with Canterbury Archbishop Thomas (II) (d. 1114) requested Stephen to use his influence with Henry I to favour York's cause. Stephen took a leading role in ecclesiastical affairs, and with Abbot Hugh of Selby and other prominent churchmen attended the translation of the relics of St Cuthbert at Durham in 1104. Stephen probably died in 1112, and was certainly dead by 1113, when he had been succeeded by Abbot Richard.

A key figure in the formative years of what was to become the premier religious house in the north, during his lifetime Stephen was described by Simeon of Durham as an energetic and efficient abbot of his monastery. He maintained excellent relations with successive kings, and charter evidence attests to the success which St Mary's enjoyed during his abbacy in attracting endowments from all the major barons of the region.

JANET BURTON

Sources BL, Add. MS 38816, fols. 29v –34v [narrative of Abbot Stephen] · A. H. Thompson, 'The monastic settlement at Hackness and its relation to the abbey of Whitby', *Yorkshire Archaeological Journal*, 27 (1923–4), 388–405 · W. Farrer and others, eds., *Early Yorkshire charters*, 12 vols. (1914–65) [vols. 1–3] · D. Knowles, *The monastic order in England*, 2nd edn (1963) · D. Bethell, 'The foundation of Fountains Abbey and the state of St Mary's York in 1132', *Journal of Ecclesiastical History*, 17 (1966), 11–27 · J. Burton, 'The monastic revival in Yorkshire: Whitby and St Mary's, York', *Anglo-Norman Durham*, ed. D. Rollason, M. Harvey, and M. Prestwich (1994), 41–51 · D. Knowles, C. N. L. Brooke, and V. C. M. London, eds., *The heads of religious houses, England and Wales, 1: 940–1216* (1972), 77, 84 · C. Norton, 'The buildings of St Mary's Abbey, York and their destruction', *Antiquaries Journal*, 74 (1994), 256–88, esp. 280–82 · Dugdale, *Monasticon*, 3.529–73 · *Hugh the Chanter: the history of the church of York, 1066–1127*, ed. and trans. C. Johnson (1961)

Archives BL, Add. MS 38816, fols. 29v–34v · CCC Cam., MS 139

Likenesses manuscript (with the monks of St Mary's Abbey at the beginning of the chronicle of Abbot Simon de Warwick, 1258–1296), Bodl. Oxf., Bodley MS, 39

Whitchester, Roger of (d. 1258), clerk and justice, was the son of Robert of Whitchester and his wife, Isabel, who were tenants at Whitchester in Northumberland of the Crauden family, of which Isabel was probably a member; they held the manor of Whitchester from the Bolbec barony. Robert served as sheriff of Northumberland from 1221 to 1223, and was also a commissioner of assize and gaol delivery in that county from 1229 to 1238; he held land in Benwell and Heddon on the Wall as well as Whitchester. Roger inherited from his father between October 1243 and April 1244. He clearly had no wish to become a knight, being unsuccessfully distrained to do so in 1244, and in 1253 secured life exemption from all the local duties for which knights were liable; he retained his minor clerical orders until his death. In 1226 he became rector of Elsdon, but had ceased to be so by 1245; he became rector of Ovingdean, Sussex, about 1248. His main career was as a clerk—and later a justice—of the bench at Westminster, where he was at first in the service of the justice William of York, probably by 1230, certainly by 1236; he also served as an attorney there.

On 28 May 1246 Whitchester was granted an annual salary of £10 as keeper of the writs and rolls of the bench, the first man known to have held such an office. He also received an annual robe as a member of the royal household. In 1247 he went on eyre circuit with Henry of Bath, as keeper of the writs and rolls, returning to the bench in 1249 and remaining there as keeper until Trinity term 1254. It seems likely that he was involved in administrative changes which brought about improvements in the arrangement of the eyre rolls, with the development of special sections for foreign pleas and the appointment of attorneys, and a tendency for the bench rolls to become the impersonal record of the court, rather than the personal records of the justices for whom they were produced. From 1251 onwards he received frequent appointments as an assize commissioner, after 1252 invariably alone. The great majority of them were for cases in Essex and Kent, where he had acquired property. One such commission, involving a dispute at St Albans in Hertfordshire, seems to have earned him the animosity of Matthew Paris. None of his assize rolls has survived, however. Early in Michaelmas term 1254 Whitchester sat for a few days as a bench justice, and then went on eyre circuit as a justice with Gilbert of Preston, returning to Westminster to sit as a bench justice for the whole of Easter term 1255, before continuing as an eyre justice until the spring of 1258, after which he seems to have carried out assize commissions until his death later that year.

Whitchester's career as a royal servant provided him with the means of acquiring landed wealth in a number of counties in southern England from about 1235 onwards, including Oxfordshire, Buckinghamshire, and Hertfordshire in addition to those already mentioned. He continued to acquire interests in Northumberland, some of which he gave as benefactions to the nuns of St Bartholomew's Priory at Newcastle between 1253 and 1257, when he was preparing for death. He had brothers, Robert and Master Nicholas, and sisters, Mabel and Joan, all but the last predeceasing him. He died about September 1258, Matthew Paris describing him in his obituary as a king's clerk and special counsellor, who in bearing the burden of judicial office strove wholly to please the royal will.

DAVID CROOK

Sources C. A. F. Meekings, 'Roger of Whitchester (†1258)', *Archaeologia Aeliana*, 4th ser., 35 (1957), 100–28 · Paris, *Chron.*, 5.716, 6.268 · PRO · *Chancery records*

Whitchurch, Edward (d. 1562), printer and bookseller, was a member of the Haberdashers' Company in London in the 1530s, working from the sign of the Well and Two Buckets in St Martin Outwich. In 1537 he and Richard *Grafton became involved in Thomas Cromwell's project to produce an official English translation of the Bible. In that year the so-called Matthew Bible, translated by John

Rogers, was printed in Antwerp by Matthias Crom; Grafton and Whitchurch acted as publishers, under Cromwell's authority but at their own expense. However, the marginalia in the Matthew text continued to alarm Henry VIII, and in 1538 Cromwell ordered that a revised translation be printed, without marginal notes. Grafton and Whitchurch remained at the heart of the project, due to their experience and their comparatively deep pockets. The printing of what was to become known as the Great Bible was again entrusted to a skilled foreign printer, this time the Parisian François Regnault. However, although the project was undertaken with the permission of the French king, the University of Paris viewed it as heretical. In December 1538 the inquisitor-general seized the sheets that had already been printed; Cromwell was unwilling to intervene, despite Whitchurch's pleas, and the two publishers were forced to return to England. Edmund Bonner, the English resident in Paris who had been supervising the project, was able only to secure the transportation of the equipment, paper and workmen back to England. As a result, Grafton and Whitchurch were forced—apparently contrary to their original intentions—to act as the printers themselves, with some assistance from the king's printer, Thomas Berthelet. They published the first edition of the Great Bible in April 1539.

For Whitchurch this was the beginning of an illustrious career in evangelical publishing. His partnership with Grafton was to prove enduring; they printed at least six editions of the Great Bible in 1539–41, along with various New testaments and English primers. In 1541 they obtained a joint patent for printing service books, which was renewed in 1543 and 1546, and they were given exclusive rights to the official king's primer of 1545. With the accession of Edward VI, they were granted a new seven-year privilege to print service books; and they were responsible for the first editions of the 1549 Book of Common Prayer.

Whitchurch's interest in biblical and liturgical publication went beyond the professional; he was a consistent advocate of evangelical reform. In July 1540 he and Grafton were seized during a general round-up of London evangelicals, accused of failing to attend confession; however, like all the others arrested in this purge, they were quickly released without charge. On 8 April 1543 they were arrested along with six other leading figures in the London book trade for printing heretical books, and imprisoned for three and a half weeks. Whitchurch's approach to such troubles appears to have been pragmatic; in 1541 he counselled the evangelical preacher Robert Wisdom to recant rather than force a confrontation with his old collaborator Bishop Bonner. His greatest contribution to the cause was, of course, as a printer and publisher. Between 1539 and 1543 he published a range of works by moderate evangelicals including Lancelot Ridley, Richard Taverner, and Richard Tracy. After his imprisonment in the latter year, his output became less controversial for the remainder of Henry VIII's reign, but he continued to produce innovative works, such as Roger Ascham's *Toxophilus* in 1545, and *Yny lhyvyr hwnn y traethir*, a primer which was the first book to be printed in Welsh, in 1546. With Edward VI's accession, he was able to produce openly evangelical material once again. He published at least ninety imprints during the six years of Edward's reign, including such key texts as Katherine Parr's *Lamentacion of a Sinner*, Erasmus's *Paraphrases*, and the metrical psalter of Sternhold and Hopkins.

Little is known about Whitchurch's personal life. His first marriage or marriages are unrecorded; at his death he had a son, Edward, and three adult daughters, of whom only two, Helen and Elizabeth, can be named. Likewise, the location of Whitchurch's establishment in the early 1540s is not clear. It is possible he was at the sign of the Bible in St Paul's Churchyard in 1540; in 1544 he was based at the south side of St Mary Aldermanbury Church, but he can be placed in the Old Jewry at roughly the same time. In 1545 Whitchurch moved to John Byddell's old establishment at the sign of the Sun in Fleet Street (which had formerly belonged to Wynkyn de Worde), where he remained until 1553. After Mary's accession, however, Whitchurch's position became uncomfortable once again: he was exempted by name from the coronation pardons of 1553 and 1554. It is likely that he fled to Germany. However, all that is known of his activities during these years is that, at some point after Archbishop Cranmer's execution in 1555, Whitchurch married Cranmer's German widow, Margaret *Cranmer. The archbishop's children became part of his household; Whitchurch negotiated his stepdaughter Margaret's marriage to Thomas Norton before 1561, and was probably instrumental in having Norton appointed as counsel to the Stationers' Company in 1562. Perhaps owing to failing health, Whitchurch's own attempt to resume printing after Mary's death was perfunctory; only two imprints of his are known from this period. In 1562 he retired to a house he had leased in Camberwell. He died within a week of making his will on 25 November 1562.

It has been suggested that a bookseller's account book from 1545 that survives in the Houghton Library at Harvard may have been Whitchurch's. ALEC RYRIE

Sources will, PRO, PROB 11/45, fol. 227r–v • *LP Henry VIII* • *STC, 1475–1640* • E. G. Duff, *A century of the English book trade* (1905) • C. Clair, *A history of printing in Britain* (1965) • J. Foxe, *The first volume of the ecclesiasticall history contayning the actes and monumentes of thynges passed*, new edn (1570) • *APC, 1542–7* • D. MacCulloch, *Thomas Cranmer: a life* (1996) • P. L. Hughes and J. F. Larkin, eds., *Tudor royal proclamations*, 3 vols. (1964–9) • Emmanuel College, Cambridge, MS 261, fols. 92v–93r • S. Brigden, *London and the Reformation* (1989) • *CPR, 1547–8*, 100 • L. M. Oliver, 'A bookseller's account book, 1545', *Harvard Library Bulletin*, 16 (1968), 139–55
Wealth at death 100 marks to one daughter; if standard London procedure followed, perhaps approx. one twelfth of estate: will, PRO, PROB 11/45, fol. 227r–v

White. *See also* Whyte.

White family (*per.* **1795–1846**), shipowners and merchants of Sunderland, first came to prominence through **John White** (1764–1833), who was born at Monkwearmouth, co. Durham, and began his working life as a cooper in the 1780s. During the French wars White diversified his business activities into shipowning to take advantage of boom conditions in this sector, and by 1814 he had accumulated a fleet of 1300 tons with the high value of £2300. In spite of the prolonged post-war economic downturn and the depreciation of shipping values, White's fleet made profits in all but one year during the period 1818–32. This was achieved through the diverse deployment of his fleet in a range of different trades. In addition he made good use of his strategic position in the coal trade, where he also had mining and fitting interests which enabled him to obtain rapid turn-round for his vessels. On 27 May 1788 White married Jane (1769–1826), daughter of Andrew Young, a local ship's chandler; eight children of the marriage survived into adulthood.

By the time of his death on 5 July 1833 at Bishopwearmouth, White had become one of Sunderland's most eminent merchants and shipowners. His death occurred in the middle of a major commercial depression, at which time his sworn effects were valued at only £18,000. The business was carried on by two of his sons, **Andrew White** (1792–1856) and **Richard White** (*b.* 1804?), under whose direction it continued to expand and diversify throughout the 1830s. In June 1814 Andrew White married Ophelia, daughter of a local shipowner, Hugh Dixon. Richard White married Mary, daughter of Stephen Watson, a draper, in August 1827.

The influence of the Whites also extended into local social and political life. John White was renowned for his philanthropy and his support of the Methodist movement. He championed such causes as the building of schools, the abolition of church rates, and winter charity for the poor. Andrew White continued his father's social work and was associated with almost every local charity and benevolent institution, supporting religious nonconformity, temperance, and improvements in education. The family's highly active role in local politics can be seen from the fact that Andrew was closely involved in reviving the ancient corporation of the borough under the Municipal Corporations Amendment Act and was elected the first mayor of the new corporation in 1836. He went on to hold the position two more times. Richard White, too, was mayor on one occasion. Andrew's other local responsibilities included being chief magistrate of the borough, justice of the peace, and deputy lieutenant for the county of Durham. He was also MP for Sunderland between 1837 and 1841. Although he remained on the back benches he spoke up in favour of reform on several occasions. However, reformist principles could still take second place to self-interest; in a debate on the navigation laws in 1840 a fellow MP accused him of abandoning his free-trade beliefs when it came to protection for the shipping industry.

As devout Christians sincerely concerned about corruption in the Church of England, the Whites reflected their wide reformist outlook in their religious work. Andrew White was involved with various religious groups in Sunderland and, during his time as an MP, with various causes in London, including the Presbyterian Mission, the London Missionary Society, the Religious Tract Society, and the Zion Chapel. He defended his interdenominationalism in a short tract recommending mutual forbearance among religious groups. His reformist beliefs were at odds, however, with the more conservative-minded national Wesleyan leadership, and in 1836 he was one of the leading figures among Sunderland Methodists to break away from the official Methodists to join the Wesleyan Methodist Association.

In addition to both their philanthropic activities and their own private business interests, the White family were also actively involved in company promotion during the joint-stock boom of the mid-1830s. They played a leading role in the flotation of many local companies, in industries as diverse as railways, banking, soap manufacture, and insurance. Like many contemporary entrepreneurs, they had private and corporate interests which overlapped in a manner that was sometimes mutually beneficial but that on other occasions resulted in a conflict of interest and, frequently, corruption. The collapse of the Sunderland Joint Stock Bank in 1851 led to allegations that the brothers and their associates had used the bank's funds extensively for personal loans without the necessary degree of scrutiny. By the early 1840s the family business was beginning to weaken under the pressure of adverse economic conditions and an over-commitment to social and political activities. In 1846 the firm collapsed and the two brothers were declared bankrupt. Although Andrew White continued in employment as secretary of the Wear and Durham district coal trade committee, his fortunes never recovered significantly from the bankruptcy; when he died a decade later, on 1 October 1856 at Bishopwearmouth, his effects were valued at only £800. The year of Richard White's death is not known.

The Whites were one of Sunderland's leading business families during the first half of the nineteenth century, and they also played an influential role in local political and religious affairs. Before the collapse of their business Andrew and Richard White had interests stretching across the principal sectors of the local economy, and were involved in banking, shipowning, and the coal and timber trades, as well as metallurgy and engineering.

SIMON VILLE

Sources S. Ville, 'The expansion and development of a private business: an application of vertical integration theory', *Business History*, 33/4 (1991), 19–42 • S. Ville, 'Shipping in the port of Sunderland, 1815–45: a counter-cyclical trend', *Business History*, 32/1 (1990), 32–51 • G. E. Milburn, 'Wesleyanism in Sunderland in the later eighteenth and early nineteenth centuries', *Antiquities of Sunderland*, 26 (1974–6) • *The diary of John Young*, ed. G. E. Milburn (1983) • W. Brockie, *Sunderland notables* (1894) • M. A. Richardson, ed., *The local historian's table book … legendary division*, 3 vols. (1843–6) • WWBMP • M. Phillips, *A history of banks, bankers and banking in Northumberland, Durham, and North Yorkshire* (1894) • Hansard • Boase, *Mod. Eng. biog.* • Newcastle Central Library, Stamfordham baptisms, marriages [John White] • index of baptisms, marriages, and burials, Newcastle Central Library • Durham RO, EP/BIW 46, p. 578 [John White] • U. Durham L., archives and special collections, Durham probate records, 1833 [John White] • U. Durham L., archives and special collections, Durham probate records, 1856 [Andrew White]

Archives Tyne and Wear Archives Service, Newcastle upon Tyne, notebooks and diaries [Andrew White] | Tyne and Wear Archives Service, Newcastle upon Tyne, poor rate books • Tyne and Wear

Archives Service, Newcastle upon Tyne, River Wear commission • Tyne and Wear Archives Service, Newcastle upon Tyne, Sunderland Borough Council • Tyne and Wear Archives Service, Newcastle upon Tyne, Sunderland shipping registers

Wealth at death £18,000—John White: sworn effects, Durham probate records, U. Durham L., archives and special collections, 1833 • £800—Andrew White: sworn effects, Durham probate records, U. Durham L., archives and special collections, 1856

White, Adam (1817–1878), naturalist, was born in Edinburgh on 29 April 1817, the son of Thomas White, a banker's clerk, and his wife, Mary Ann Gellatly. He was baptized in Kirkurd, Peebles, on 2 August 1818. He was educated at the high school in Edinburgh. When he was eighteen he went to London with a letter of introduction to John Edward Gray (1800–1875) of the British Museum and obtained employment in the zoological branch of the department of natural history in December 1835. To begin with his work was directed by the keeper, John George Children. On Children's retirement in 1840, supervision passed to Gray, his energetic successor. Once Gray had established a simple method for the systematic registration of specimens in the zoological department, he made preparations to publish catalogues of them. White was one of four assistants charged with carrying out these tasks. Some of his early work on the arthropod group was hindered by George Samouelle, a fellow assistant who had taken to drink and spited White by removing the registration numbers on many specimens. However, Samouelle was sacked in 1841 and, following the appointment of Edward Doubleday in 1842, White was able to concentrate uninterrupted on the Coleoptera and on Crustacea. On 27 January 1844 he married Helen Bolden (*b.* 1808/9, *d.* in or before 1861), daughter of William Bolden, a bookbinder. The couple had one daughter.

At the museum, White produced a *List of the Specimens of Crustacea in the Collection of the British Museum* (1847), wrote most parts of *Nomenclature of Coleopterous Insects in the Collection of the British Museum* (9 parts, 1847–55), and contributed to the *List of Specimens of British Animals in the Collection of the British Museum* (1850–55). He also published a number of other books, including *A Popular History of Mammalia* (1850), *A Popular History of Birds* (1855), *The Instructive Picture Book* (with R. M. Stark, 1857), and *Heads and Tails* (1870). He contributed two works to the Society for Promoting Christian Knowledge's Diagrams of Natural History series (*c.*1860), and between 1839 and 1867 wrote more than sixty scientific papers. Although known for his work on arthropods, he was also a keen botanist and was the first to apply the suffix '-idea' to designate the family names of insects.

White was elected a fellow of the Linnean Society in 1846. He was a member of the Entomological Society of London from 1839 to 1863, and a member of the Botanical Society of London. Visitors to the museum remembered White's readiness to assist and his scientific knowledge earned him their respect. Unfortunately, he was not always on such good terms with Gray, and never rose above the assistant grade. Nevertheless, employment at the British Museum provided him with first-hand knowledge of the advantages enjoyed by a national museum and, using the pseudonym Arachnophilus, he wrote to

Scottish newspapers advocating the establishment of a national museum for Scotland. The letters were also published separately as *Four Short Letters* (n.d. [1850]).

White's wife, Helen, died in or before 1861, and grief caused him to have a nervous breakdown. He was for a time committed to an asylum in Scotland and retired from the museum on a small pension in 1863. On 28 July 1862 he married his second wife, Margaret Watson, daughter of Alexander Watson, farmer, and his wife, Helen. The couple's first son was born in 1863; by 1874 they had at least two more. However, White's new-found happiness was marred by financial worries and he died intestate at 111 St Andrews Road, Pollokshields, on 30 December 1878.

ANN DATTA

Sources DNB · R. W. Ingle, 'Carcinology in the Natural History Museum, London; the brachyuran crab collections and their curation from 1813–1904 (Leach to Calman)', *Bulletin of the British Museum (Natural History)* [Historical Series], 19 (1991), 161–224 · R. McLachlan, 'Adam White', *Entomologist's Monthly Magazine*, 15 (1879), 210–11 · W. T. Stearn, *The Natural History Museum at South Kensington: a history of the British Museum (Natural History), 1753–1980* (1981) · C. D. Waterston, *Collections in context: the Museum of the Royal Society of Edinburgh and the inception of a national museum for Scotland* (1997) · R. Cowtan, *Memories of the British Museum* (1872) · J. W. Dunning, 'Mr Adam White', *Proceedings of the Entomological Society of London*, 1879 (1879), lxiv · G. D. R. Bridson, V. C. Phillips, and A. P. Harvey, *Natural history manuscript resources in the British Isles* (1980) · B. B. Woodward and others, eds., *Catalogue of the books, manuscripts, maps, and drawings in the British Museum (Natural History)*, 8 vols. (1903–40) · *Catalogue of scientific papers*, Royal Society, 19 vols. (1867–1925) · Desmond, *Botanists*, rev. edn · A. Musgrave, *Bibliography of Australian entomology, 1775–1930* (1932) · R. B. Freeman, *British natural history books, 1495–1900: a handlist* (1980) · Adam White, letters from Edinburgh and various in reference to Adam White, NHM, department of zoology, archives, W. Carruthers correspondence, DF404/8/23 · P. Clark, The crustacean publications of Adam White: genera, species, dates, references, authorities [forthcoming] · Boase, *Mod. Eng. biog.*, 3.1308 · m. certs.
Archives National Museums of Scotland, scrapbook of corresp., cuttings, and notes · NHM · NHM, plant specimens · NL Scot., corresp. · NL Scot., corresp. and papers relating to Lake District and English nature poets · U. Aberdeen, plants · U. Edin., plants · University of Toronto, Thomas Fisher Rare Book Library, school notebook | Elgin Museum, letters to George Gordon · NL Scot., letters to Thomas Carlyle · Norwich Castle Museum, Norwich, T. Brightwell collection
Likenesses J. R. Jackson, mezzotint, 1849 (after J. P. Knight), NPG · photograph, 1859, BM · E. W. Dallas, group photograph, 1865, NHM, Zoology Library; repro. in A. White, *A popular history of Mammalia* (1850), (glued on to the front flyleaf) · photograph, BM; repro. in Waterston, *Collections in context* · photograph (A. White as an old man), BM
Wealth at death £559 17s. 10d.: confirmation, 3 March 1879, CCI

White, Alan Richard (1922–1992), philosopher, was born on 9 October 1922 in Toronto, Canada, the elder of the two children of George Albert White (1888–1940), estate agent, and his wife, Jean Gabriel, *née* Kingston (1888–1957), a children's buyer. His father, a protestant from Strabane, Ireland, and his mother, a Catholic from Cork, had emigrated to Canada. When the marriage broke up in the early 1930s Alan and his brother, Jack, accompanied their mother to Cork, where she worked in the drapery trade. They were educated as protestants, boarding at Midleton

College, co. Cork, until the sixth form, when White transferred to Presentation College, Cork, to prepare for entrance to Trinity College, Dublin. He entered in 1941 with a junior exhibition and a sizarship in classics, and graduated in 1945 with firsts in both classics and mental and moral science. He obtained many prizes including that for Hegelian philosophy, was president of the University Philosophical Society, and achieved a boxing pink as a flyweight.

After a further year at Trinity as university student in classics and lecturer in logic White was, in 1946, recruited to an assistant lectureship in the department of philosophy and psychology at the University College of Hull by its head, T. E. Jessop. Between them the two taught all philosophy courses required for London University external degrees, while White himself continued to teach psychology as well as philosophy students long after the departments of philosophy and psychology were separated and expanded, when the college acquired university status in 1954. It was during this time that White, by now a keen atheist, married, on 12 August 1948, Eileen Anne Jarvis (*b.* 1927), of Hull, a clerk; they had two daughters and a son. Tuberculosis ended his athletic activities, but his research career was just beginning and was soon to produce a prodigious output of publications.

Jessop was an authority on the Irish idealist philosopher Bishop Berkeley, the subject of some of White's first papers. This interest, acquired at Trinity under the guidance of Jessop's collaborator, A. A. Luce, continued through to White's penultimate book, *The Language of Imagination* (1990), with its discussion of Berkeley's supposedly unimaginable unperceived tree. In his early years at Hull, however, White was turning away from the historical, expository approach to develop the techniques of linguistic analysis which typified his life's work. Philosophy, he held, was concerned with concepts, with ways of thinking about things, and since concepts are expressed in language the best way to study them was to examine the uses of language. In 'A linguistic approach to Berkeley's philosophy' in *Philosophy and Phenomenological Research*, 16 (1955), he claimed that Berkeley himself prefigured this method, exemplified by White in his second publication, 'Mr Hartnack on experience' in *Analysis*, 14 (1953), 26. Here he disposes of Hartnack's view that we see facts not things by remarking 'we do not say "I see the *fact* that …"'—a type of move of which White became the acknowledged master.

In the early 1950s White initiated the project, never completed, of providing a comprehensive survey of twentieth-century analytic philosophy, centred upon the nature of conceptual analysis. From this he developed the material that simultaneously became his London University PhD thesis, supervised by A. J. Ayer, 'The method of analysis in the philosophy of G. E. Moore', and the book, *G. E. Moore: a Critical Exposition* (1958), which established his philosophical reputation. Moore's work, if suitably sanitized, provided White not only with a method of analysis but also with one of his principal subject matters, epistemology. From a mass of articles he distilled *Truth* (1970), *Modal Thinking* (1975), and *The Nature of Knowledge* (1982).

At first White's other main concern, under the influence of Gilbert Ryle, was philosophical psychology. His clarificatory studies *Attention* (1964) and *The Philosophy of Mind* (1967), with its discussion of motives, led him to examine the treatment of psychological concepts in the law. Many subsequent papers in law journals resulted in *Rights* (1984), *Grounds of Liability* (1985), and *Misleading Cases* (1991). In these books he aimed to correct the conceptual mistakes which, he believed, had entered the law of the land to its lasting detriment. It was such beliefs that led White to continue the practice of conceptual analysis after its general abandonment in Britain in the 1970s.

The contribution that White made to philosophy has been obscured by this philosophical shift. None the less, so resourceful and meticulous was he in assembling examples of the uses of related concepts, and so skilful in discerning subtle differences between them, that many of his analyses are likely to prove definitive. White's confidence that philosophy could become a cumulative discipline through the collective production and refinement of such analyses, eventually resulting in the dissolution of philosophical problems, may prove misplaced. He was on stronger ground in his conviction that, in the words of Bertrand Russell which he liked to quote, 'all sound philosophy should begin with an analysis of propositions'. White was contemptuous of the muddled thinking that resulted from neglecting it. Serious students of consciousness, for example, should heed the complex relations between being and becoming conscious of, attending to, noticing, and so on, of which White makes the reader aware in *Attention*.

In other areas, too, White extended work initiated by Ryle to reach more reliable conclusions and to dispose of faulty accounts, often those of Ryle himself. Thus, in his lecture *Explaining Human Behaviour* (1962) White attacks Ryle's identification of motives with dispositions, arguing that the former—like reasons—are a *kind* of explanation while the latter—like desires or intentions—furnish possible *factors* in explanation. In *The Nature of Knowledge* White upsets Ryle's famous claim that knowing how and knowing that are two fundamentally different kinds of knowledge by demonstrating that they are, instead, knowledge of two different kinds of thing. Similarly, in *The Language of Imagination* he identifies and refutes numerous Rylean assimilations: of visualizing to seeming to see or to imagining oneself seeing, and of imagining to supposing or to pretending.

Despite the impression White's writing can give, then, of an intellectually detached taxonomizing of his linguistic data he was, like Moore, principally provoked by the assertions of other philosophers. He thereby became part of the tradition of classically educated researchers, centred on Oxford, whose scepticism of larger claims was what provided the prime motivation for their programme of patient and rigorous analysis. Its rationale was, after all, suspiciously theoretical.

At Hull, White's work was rewarded with promotion, and he succeeded Jessop to the Ferens chair of philosophy in 1961, building up a large department which taught philosophy to students of many subjects. His own teaching method followed his professional practice of circulating and discussing his own analyses, supporting them with a wealth of examples, and bearing down opposition with pugnacious irony. A small, sprightly man with a ginger beard, glinting eyes, and a ready wit, he became a familiar figure on the philosophical scene. He moved from secretary of the Mind Association (1960–69) to its president (1972) and Aristotelian Society president (1979–80), and held visiting chairs at several American universities. He was dean of arts at Hull (1969–71) and pro-vice-chancellor (1976–9). His first marriage ended in divorce on 27 November 1977, and on 12 December 1979 he married Enid Elizabeth Alderson (*b*. 1932), deputy principal of a sixth-form college. Taking early retirement in 1985 he moved to live with her in Nottingham where, from 1986, he was special professor at the university, while retaining close connections with Hull. Heart trouble, which had affected him in later years, led to his death at his home, 77 Newfield Road, Sherwood, Nottingham, on 23 February 1992. He was cremated at a secular ceremony at Thoresby crematorium chapel, Mansfield, on 28 February.

PAUL GILBERT

Sources *WW* (1992) · *The Guardian* (27 Feb 1992) · *The Independent* (28 Feb 1992) · *The Times* (7 March 1992) · U. Hull, Brynmor Jones L., A. R. White papers, DAW · private information (2004) · personal knowledge (2004) · *CGPLA Eng. & Wales* (1992)
Archives U. Hull, Brynmor Jones L., papers, DAW
Likenesses photograph, 1973, Brynmor Jones L., Hull
Wealth at death £174,453: probate, 12 June 1992, *CGPLA Eng. & Wales*

White [*née* Smith], **Alice Mary Meadows** (1839–1884), composer, was born at 1 Sidmouth Place, London, on 19 May 1839, the daughter of Richard Smith, a lace merchant, and his wife, Elizabeth, *née* Lumley. She studied with William Sterndale Bennett and George Alexander Macfarren, and first came to notice at the age of twenty-one, when her first piano quartet was performed in 1861 at a trial of new compositions held by the London Musical Society. The same society later performed her first string quartet (1862), symphony (1863), and other orchestral works.

On 2 January 1867 Alice Smith married Frederick Meadows White (*c*.1830–1898) QC, who was later recorder of Canterbury and a county court judge, but not, as is sometimes stated, director of the Royal Academy of Music. In November 1867 she was elected a female professional associate of the Philharmonic Society, and in 1884, Hon. RAM. She composed many large- and small-scale works, and was held in high esteem for much of her creative life. Her clarinet concerto was performed at the Norwich festival in 1872 and her setting of Collins's ode *The Passions* at the Hereford festival in 1882. She also set Keats's *Ode to the North-East Wind* (1880) and Kingsley's *Song of the Little Baltung* (1883). Of the many piano pieces, songs, and duets which she composed, the duet for soprano and tenor 'Maying' was the most popular; the copyright of the piece was sold in 1883 for £663. With few exceptions, her style demonstrated a closer relationship to 'the classic rather than … the romantic school' (*The Athenaeum*, 13 Dec 1884).

Alice White died from typhoid fever at 42 Sussex Gardens, Kensington, on 4 December 1884.

J. C. HADDEN, rev. DAVID J. GOLBY

Sources N. Burton, 'Smith (Meadows White), Alice Mary', *The new Grove dictionary of women composers*, ed. J. A. Sadie and R. Samuel (1994) · *The Athenaeum* (13 Dec 1884), 779 · *The Athenaeum* (20 Dec 1884), 814 [correction] · *MT*, 26 (1885), 24 · b. cert. · m. cert. · d. cert.

White, Amber Blanco [*née* Amber Reeves] (**1887–1981**), writer and civil servant, was born in Christchurch, New Zealand, on 1 July 1887, the eldest of three children of Maud Pember Reeves (*née* Robison; 1865–1953) [*see* Reeves, Magdalen Stuart], suffragist Fabian, and William Pember *Reeves (1857–1932), politician. The family travelled to England in 1897, where her father became New Zealand's agent-general. Her widowed aunt, cousins, 'and attendants' joined the household in Cornwall Gardens, Kensington. 'London was hateful after New Zealand', she said. 'No freedom. No seashore. Streets, streets, streets. Houses, houses' (Harrison and White, 10267). Educated at Kensington high school and Newnham College, Cambridge (1905–8), Amber achieved a first in both parts of the moral science tripos. Her childhood was overcrowded with cousins, squabbling nursemaids, and parents too much preoccupied with work to pay the children much attention. Her mother, whom she admired, thought her 'impertinent' and her father's generosity with books an 'extravagance'. 'When I complained once that I hardly ever saw her, that I didn't love her at all, she boxed my ears. She was doing more important things, she was too busy to look after a child who ought to be doing her lessons'. Left alone 'with a room of her own and piles of books', she would retreat to her father's study, where she crept under the sofa to read. 'I cared more for books than for clothes'. One day, walking down the Charing Cross Road, she opened a book by Kant, 'and read the destruction of Roman Catholicism by reason' (personal knowledge). From then on she determined to go to Cambridge to study philosophy. Her encounter with Freud was similarly random, the result of a mistaken identity in Harley Street in the twenties. From then on she read Freud, Freud, Freud.

When Amber left Cambridge (which she 'adored') in 1908 her tutors—who included 'old Dr Keynes', father of Maynard, who had taught her logic and for whom she never made a single mistake—provided references which described her as a 'clear and vigorous thinker [who] can express herself with admirable force and directness' (J. N. Keynes, Blanco White MSS). However, her intellectual career was interrupted by a passionate love affair with H. G. Wells [*see* Wells, Herbert George]. Wells's advocacy of free love, or communal marriages, enjoyed a notoriety among the intellectual young, and Amber became his Newnham propagandist. Wells described Amber as 'a girl of brilliant and precocious promise … [with] a sharp, bright, Levantine face under a shock of very fine abundant black hair, a slender nimble body very much live and a quick greedy

mind' (G. P. Wells, 68). Country walks and austere conversations about social philosophy soon gave way to love-making in Soho and Pimlico while she began her research into 'Why and how Men are Citizens' at the London School of Economics. Soon a 'trickle of whispered talk' (ibid., 72) began to undermine their unstable union. (George) Rivers Blanco White (1883–1966), a young lawyer and fellow Fabian, resolved to marry her.

Amber meanwhile became pregnant (seized, to Wells's consternation, with 'philo-progenitiveness'), and left with Wells for Le Touquet (and more talk and lovemaking). She returned to London and marriage, at Kensington register office on 7 May 1909, to Blanco White. Wells's novels *Ann Veronica* (1909) and *The Research Magnificent* (1915) tell parts of this story. Their daughter, Anna-Jane, was born in December 1909. Amber collaborated with Wells in writing *The Work, Wealth and Happiness of Mankind* (1932). In August 1939 she wrote to Wells that their love and their daughter 'have never for a moment felt that they were not worth the price' (G. P. Wells, 81).

Their love affair figured vividly in the contemporary imagination and helped to pioneer changed attitudes towards sexual relations. Beatrice Webb, who judged Amber brilliant, vain, heathen, and selfish, as well as shy and sweet, wrote in melodramatic language of the havoc and distress their affair provoked, yet it prompted her—a puritan—to reconsider sexual ethics. Bernard Shaw's heroine in *Misalliance* (1909) was Amber, according to Webb, who disliked Shaw's return to the 'rabbit-warren part of human life' (*Diary*, 133). Reeves wrote three novels between 1910 and 1914 which examined love, marriage, work, and 'progressive' women. Two more children, Justin and Thomas, were born in 1912 and 1914. The Blanco Whites lived in London at Downshire Hill, Hampstead, and in Sussex for most of their married lives.

During the First World War, with Rivers away and short of money, Amber worked first for the Admiralty, when she earned £2 a week, and later—at Winston Churchill's request—in the Ministry of Munitions on women's wages for £2 10s. 'The average woman takes to welding as readily as knitting', she wrote. In 1919 she was appointed to the National Whitley Council for the civil service, but was pushed out, like many other women, in 1921. The children, whom she 'never saw', were looked after by a 'faithful old nurse' who refused to take a salary; she walked to work and breakfasted with cabbies for 3*d*. Amber claimed credit for raising munitions workers' wages from 12*s*. to 28*s*. She did not like Mary Macarthur who, she acknowledged, had an 'impossible job—women don't organize very well by themselves—they'll join the men's trade unions … they grudge the subscription and don't see what they get out of it' (Walker and White, 10297). Her fourth novel, *Give and Take* (1924), was about life in a government department. Sir Matthew *Nathan (1862–1939), imperial administrator and close—sometimes intimate—friend through the twenties, admired the depiction of the strike committee.

Rivers Blanco White stood unsuccessfully as a Labour candidate for Lincolnshire (Holland with Boston) in the general election of 1924; together they edited the *Woman's Leader*. Amber edited *The Townswoman* for the Townswomen's Guild, leaving it when the local people were able to take over. She stood twice as the Labour candidate for Hendon (1931, 1935) because it was a 'hopeless' seat and she wanted to signal her opposition to Ramsay MacDonald, leader of the National Government. As a Fabian she had believed that 'if you gave people better housing and better food and higher wages and better schools they would work harder and more ardently than they would for private employers'. Describing her pre-war suffragism she said that 'living in those days, life was so hopeful—you felt that if you would only work hard enough things would get better and better' (Walker and White, 10293, 10294). Later, 'when I got into the Labour meetings in the slums, among the costers and the railwaymen and the women in tenth-hand velvet hats, when I saw their poor pinched grey and yellow faces in those steamy halls', she wrote to a friend in 1924, 'I knew all of a sudden that they were my people' (Fry, 87). The snobbery and condescension evident in her observations was about education and intelligence as much as birth. Disillusion with the progress of human nature, and disagreement with the Labour Party's colonial policy after 1945, led to the Blanco Whites' resignation.

From 1928 Amber Blanco White lectured for Morley College, in philosophy and psychology. Eva Hubback, the principal, was a friend from Newnham; Amber replaced her as acting head for nearly two years after Eva's unexpected death in 1946. Lecturing was supplemented by research on banking and money for the *New Statesman* which culminated in a book, *The Nationalisation of Banking* (1934). *The New Propaganda* followed in 1939, and *Worry in Women* in 1941. But the book which summed up her thought, she said, was *Ethics for Unbelievers* (1949). In *Ethics* she argues that the origins of moral sense come from the child's conscience. Terrified by fierce passions within and violence without, the child internalizes his severe and powerful parents. Efficient, sensible, encouraging, 'above all reasonable' parents will breed happiness and good citizens. Hers is a reasoning Freud. Psychology blends with economics and evolution. Savages and primitives give way to enlightened reason: 'until order was imposed and education provided by the English, [the Maoris of New Zealand] were cannibals and among the most war-like, formidable and blood-thirsty of the savage races' (Blanco White, 77). Civilization was measured in part by the emancipation of women—'every woman must always desire children, a home and a father for them and the love which seems to make these things secure' (ibid., 210)—and the rights of children; states of mind were less important than actions and behaviour, and moral good must be judged by the kinds of people it produced. Good men and women—the aim of a scientific humanitarianism—were the outcome of good homes; education should include the encouragement of marriage between equals, the wiser handling of children.

Amber nursed her husband after his stroke in the 1960s, and was looked after herself by her cook–housekeeper, a maid, and her daughter-in-law Anne until her own death at the Hospital of St John and St Elizabeth, St John's Wood, London, on 26 December 1981.   SALLY ALEXANDER

Sources personal knowledge (2004) · R. Fry, *Maud and Amber: a New Zealand mother and daughter, and the women's cause, 1865–1981* (Christchurch, New Zealand, 1992) · Blanco White MSS, priv. coll. · *The diary of Beatrice Webb*, ed. N. MacKenzie and J. MacKenzie, 4 vols. (1982–5), vol. 3 · G. P. Wells, ed., *H. G. Wells in love* (1984) · R. Brimley Johnson, *Some contemporary novelists (women)* (1920) · A. Blanco White, *Ethics for unbelievers* (1949) · J. Lewis, 'Intimate relations between men and women', *History Workshop Journal*, 37 (spring 1994) · H. G. Wells, *Ann Veronica* (1909) · H. G. Wells, *The work, wealth and happiness of mankind* (1932) · private information (2004) [Anne Blanco White, daughter-in-law; B. Weber] · B. Harrison, *Prudent revolutionaries: portraits of British feminists between the wars* (1987), chap. 10 · m. cert. · d. cert. · B. Harrison and A. Blanco White, interview, 11 Feb 1977, Women's Library, London · L. Walker and A. Blanco White, interview, 15 Aug 1975, Women's Library, London
Archives priv. coll., papers | University of Illinois, letters to H. G. Wells | SOUND BL NSA, performance recording · London, Women's Library, interviews with Brian Harrison and Linda Walker
Likenesses photograph, priv. coll.
Wealth at death £189,519: probate, 17 March 1982, *CGPLA Eng. & Wales*

White, Andrew (1579–1656), Jesuit and missionary in America, was born of Catholic parents in London. Two brothers, whose identities are not known, became priests. In April 1593 White matriculated at the English College at Douai and during the academic year 1594–5 he studied at the English Jesuit college at St Omer. On 1 November 1595 he was received at the English College at Valladolid and he transferred in 1596 to the English College at Seville, where he completed his theological studies. Ordained most likely in 1604, White arrived in Douai on 4 June after visiting his two brothers in Lorraine. He crossed to England where he worked for two years, but returned to Douai on 24 July 1606, one of forty-nine Catholics expelled as a result of the Gunpowder Plot. On 1 February 1607 he joined the Society of Jesus at the recently opened English novitiate in Louvain. Shortly after his first vows on 2 February 1609, he returned to Valladolid; in 1611 he was assigned to Seville, where he remained for four years.

White was professor of theology or of sacred scripture (perhaps both), at the English Jesuit school of theology in Louvain from 1617 until 1619, but before 13 June 1619 he returned to London, where he pronounced his final vows. In 1622 he resumed his position as professor in Louvain, moving with the theologate to Liège in 1624. In spite of his being a prominent theologian and a lauded professor, well-versed in the humanities and in Hebrew, White's academic career ended in 1629 because of his rigorously conservative adherence to Thomas Aquinas. According to a Jesuit catalogue for that year, White had an excellent intellect and good judgement, but mediocre prudence. In the summer of 1629 he returned to England, where he worked first in London and then in Hampshire in 1630–32.

In early 1629, before his departure from Liège, White had volunteered for the North American missions, in which, despite his melancholic temperament, he was most competent to teach and to work. In November 1633 he was appointed superior of the three Jesuits sent to found the Maryland mission. In three extant works, 'Relatio itineris in Marylandiam', addressed to the Jesuit superior-general in April/May of 1634, 'A briefe relation of the voyage unto Maryland', and 'Declaratio coloniae' (in E. A. Dalrymple, ed., *Relatio itineris in Marylandiam*, 1874, 10–43), White described the journey and the colony both for his religious superior and for future colonists. White studied the native languages of the American Indians, and received the king of the Piscateway and his family into the Roman church. Unfortunately his dictionary, grammar, and catechism in the Timuquana language are no longer extant, but a few pages of prayers and commandments translated into Conoy, the language of the Piscateway, are preserved in the archives of the Maryland province of the Society of Jesus at Georgetown University, Washington, DC. White remained superior of the mission until 1638 and ministered both to the indigenous peoples and the settlers until he and Philip Fisher (alias Copley) were captured by English soldiers in early 1644 and sent back to England in chains. Charged with high treason because they were in England in violation of an Elizabethan statute (27 Eliz. c. 2), they pleaded that they were forcibly carried into the realm and held against their wills.

After his acquittal White was expelled and went to Antwerp where he arrived in March 1648. Either before or immediately after his arrival, he was involved in the controversy surrounding the 'three propositions', a Roman Catholic attempt to win toleration from the Independents in 1647–8. White sided with the Catholic party negotiating with the Independents and wrote in their defence. Rome declared the propositions unacceptable and repudiated the agreement. After a very brief stay in Antwerp, White returned to England and is listed as working in Derbyshire in 1648 and London in 1649. By 1651 he worked in the Residence of St Thomas of Canterbury, Hampshire, where he remained for the rest of his life; he died, probably in Hampshire, on 6 January 1656.

THOMPSON COOPER, rev. THOMAS M. MCCOOG

Sources T. Hughes, *History of the Society of Jesus in North America*, 4 vols. (1907–17) · G. Holt, *St Omers and Bruges colleges, 1593–1773: a biographical dictionary*, Catholic RS, 69 (1979) · M. Murphy, *St Gregory's College, Seville, 1592–1767*, Catholic RS, 73 (1992) · T. M. McCoog, ed., *Monumenta Angliae*, 1–2 (1992) · T. M. McCoog, *English and Welsh Jesuits, 1555–1650*, 2 vols., Catholic RS, 74–5 (1994–5) · H. Foley, ed., *Records of the English province of the Society of Jesus*, 7 vols. in 8 (1875–83) · G. Anstruther, *The seminary priests*, 2 (1975) · T. H. Clancy, 'The Jesuits and the Independents', *Archivum Historicum Societatis Iesu*, 40 (1971), 67–90 · T. F. Knox and others, eds., *The first and second diaries of the English College, Douay* (1878) · *Letters of William Allen and Richard Barret, 1572–1598*, ed. P. Renold, Catholic RS, 58 (1967) · E. Henson, ed., *The registers of the English College at Valladolid, 1589–1862*, Catholic RS, 30 (1930) · E. H. Burton and T. L. Williams, eds., *The Douay College diaries, third, fourth and fifth, 1598–1654*, 1–2, Catholic RS, 10–11 (1911) · B. Lawatsch-Boomgarden, ed., *Voyage to Maryland* (1633) (1995) · A. White, 'A briefe relation of the voyage unto Maryland', *The Calvert papers*, 3 (1899), 26–45 · A. White, 'Declaratio coloniae', *Relatio itineris in Marylandiam*, ed. E. A. Dalrymple (1874), 10–43

Archives Archivum Romanum Societatis Iesu, Rome · Maryland Historical Society, Baltimore, Archives of the Maryland Province of the Society of Jesus · Stonyhurst College, Lancashire

White, Andrew (1792–1856). *See under* White family (*per.* 1795–1846).

White, Anthony (1781–1849), surgeon, was born on 16 December 1781 at Norton in co. Durham, the son of Robert and Isabella White. He was educated near Bishop Auckland, at Witton-le-Wear grammar school, and from 1799 at Cambridge, where he graduated MB from Emmanuel College in 1804. He was also the pupil in London of the able and eccentric surgeon Sir Anthony Carlisle, and he was admitted a member of the Royal College of Surgeons on 2 September 1803.

White now settled in London, where at the Westminster Hospital he was elected assistant surgeon on 24 July 1806, and surgeon on 24 April 1823. He also possessed a very extensive private practice. He was active as a surgeon for twenty-three years until, his hands being so affected by repeated attacks of gout that he could no longer operate, in 1846 he resigned; the governors of the hospital immediately appointed him consulting surgeon. At the Royal College of Surgeons White was elected a member of the council on 6 September 1827, and two years later, on 10 September 1829, he became a member of the court of examiners in succession to William Wadd. In 1831 he delivered the Hunterian oration, and he was vice-president of the college in 1832 and 1840, and served as president in 1834 and 1842. A great lover of the arts, particularly painting and music, he also filled the office of surgeon to the Royal Society of Musicians.

As a surgeon White was celebrated for his dexterity and success. Among his most remarkable work was the first operation to excise the head of the femur for disease of the hip joint, an operation then considered to be so dangerous that Sir Anthony Carlisle and Sir William Blizard not only tried to dissuade him but threatened to report him to the Royal College of Surgeons. White performed the operation with complete success, and sent the patient to call upon his opponents. White's besetting sins were indolence and unpunctuality, and he often completely forgot his appointments. White 'is said to have been the laziest man in his profession. He was habitually unpunctual, yet he was so good a surgeon that he soon obtained a large and lucrative practice' (Plarr, 512). As a result he published little and made few notes or records of his practice. His only publications were a *Treatise on the Plague* (1846) and an inquiry entitled *Proximate Cause of Gout, and its Rational Treatment* (1848).

White himself suffered severely from gout in his later years, and he died in London at his house at 5 Parliament Street on 9 March 1849.

D'A. POWER, rev. PATRICK WALLIS

Sources Venn, *Alum. Cant.* · V. G. Plarr, *Plarr's Lives of the fellows of the Royal College of Surgeons of England*, rev. D'A. Power, 2 vols. (1930) · *The Lancet* (24 March 1849) · *GM*, 2nd ser., 31 (1849), 431 · d. cert. · *IGI*

Likenesses oils, *c.*1815, Westminster Hospital, London · T. F. Dicksee, 1843, RCS Eng. · Simpson, Westminster Hospital, London · W. Walker, mezzotint (after T. F. Dicksee, 1843), Wellcome L.

White, Antonia. *See* Hopkinson, Eirene Adeline (1899–1980).

White, Arnold Henry (1848–1925), journalist and publicist, was born in Hereford on 1 February 1848; he was probably the son of Edward White (1819–1898), a Congregational minister in Hereford and then Camden Town. As a young man he was employed by the P. & O. shipping company; he then became a coffee planter in Ceylon. In the late 1870s this venture failed, and White returned to London, taking up residence in Hampstead. For a while he served as manager of the Edison Electric Light Company, only to find himself unemployed when Edison merged with the rival Swan Company. Heavily in debt, White was obliged to seek another career: he opted for the life of a political agitator.

From 1884 onwards White helped to organize a number of colonizing schemes, in the course of which he visited South Africa, Canada, Australia, and the United States of America. He also began 'exploring' the East End of London to study the social question. This gave him the material for his first book, *The Problems of a Great City* (1886), and led to an invitation to fight the Mile End constituency in the Liberal interest, which he did unsuccessfully in the 1886 general election. Eighteen months later White broke with the Liberals in protest over Gladstone's refusal to condemn the Irish Plan of Campaign. He then stood as the Liberal Unionist candidate for Tyneside in 1892 and 1895, suffering defeat on both occasions.

Frustrated in his parliamentary ambitions, White enjoyed some success as a polemical journalist. His articles were soon appearing in a variety of newspapers and periodicals. Many of them dealt with the question of alien immigration, for White was an ardent 'restrictionist', anxious to check the entry into the United Kingdom of 'destitute' Jews from eastern Europe, a subject on which he gave evidence before several official inquiries. During the 1890s, acting as the agent of the Baron de Hirsch, he also paid a number of visits to Russia in the hope of persuading the tsar's government to establish a colony in Argentina for poor Russian Jews. From the mid-1890s White increasingly turned his attention to the state of the British navy. He served for several years on the executive council of the Navy League and probably drafted some of its more inflammatory manifestos. During the summer of 1900 White visited the Mediterranean Fleet, as the guest of Admiral Charles Beresford, and in June of the following year achieved notoriety when he sent the *Daily Mail* a private letter of Beresford's, complaining about the fleet's deficiencies. Meanwhile, White was forming a firm friendship with the man who shortly emerged as Beresford's bitterest enemy within the service, Admiral Sir John Fisher. Both men were obsessed with the danger posed by the recently founded German high fleet. Indeed, White favoured the sudden and unheralded destruction of the German warships in harbour before they could seriously threaten Britain's naval hegemony. An article to this effect, written in late 1904, annoyed the prime minister, Arthur Balfour, and the Kaiser was so angered by it that, when a party of English journalists visited Germany on a goodwill mission in April 1907, he insisted on White's exclusion.

White landed himself in another scrape in the course of his campaign to bring the crooked company promoter Whitaker Wright to justice; in August 1903 an outspoken article in *The Sun*, while the case was *sub judice*, resulted in his committal to Brixton Prison for contempt of court. This episode reveals White in his favourite role, that of 'tribune of the people' crusading against 'decadence' in high places—a role that he had recently performed with *brio* in *Efficiency and Empire* (1901), the book by which he is perhaps best remembered. White was also a fearless critic of all forms of political ineptitude and misconduct, from whichever party they emanated.

During the 1906 general election White made his final attempt to get into parliament, unavailingly contesting Londonderry North as an independent. From 1907 onwards he supplied a regular column to the popular weekly *The Referee* under the pseudonym Vanoc. White had always taken an interest in eugenics and sat for a while on the council of the Eugenics Education Society. He was also a zealous supporter of compulsory military service, a cause which brought him into contact with the duke of Bedford, who thereafter acted as his patron.

White's political convictions were those commonly found among the Edwardian radical right: he sang the praises of empire and national defence, and fiercely lambasted Irish home rule, socialism, cosmopolitan pacifism, and the corruption engendered by the secret party funds. Many of his contemporaries thought him foolish and hot-tempered, but few questioned his honesty or his patriotism. During the First World War, White's Germanophobia became even more extreme; his pamphlet *The Hidden Hand* (1917) purported to uncover a sinister, long-standing conspiracy to 'Germanize' all aspects of British life. These xenophobic views drew him into an association with the demagogue Noel Pemberton Billing. But military victory, when it came, did not bring White peace of mind; he spent his final years raging impotently against Bolsheviks, Germans, Sinn Féiners, and international Jewry.

In private life White took an interest in climbing, travel, shooting, golf, chess, and gardening. In 1879 he married Helen Constance (*d.* 1918), only daughter of Lowell Price of Farnham Royal, Buckinghamshire; they had one son. White died, a widower, at his home at Farnham Common, Buckinghamshire, on 5 February 1925, aged seventy-seven. In his will he asked to be commemorated by a simple wooden cross, inscribed only with his name, the date of his death, and the words, 'for England'.

G. R. SEARLE

Sources *The Times* (6 Feb 1925) · *Morning Post* (6 Feb 1925) · NMM, Arnold White MSS · G. R. Searle, introduction, in A. White, *Efficiency and empire*, new edn (1973) · *Fear God and dread nought: the correspondence of Admiral of the Fleet Lord Fisher of Kilverstone*, ed. A. J.

Marder, 1–2 (1952–6) • B. Gainer, *The alien invasion: the origins of the Aliens Act of 1905* (1972) • G. R. Searle, 'Critics of Edwardian society: the case of the radical right', *The Edwardian age: conflict and stability, 1900–1914*, ed. A. O'Day (1979) • C. Holmes, *Anti-Semitism in British society, 1876–1939* (1979) • F. Coetzee, *For party or country: nationalism and the dilemmas of popular conservatism in Edwardian England* (1990) • G. S. Jones, *Outcast London: a study in the relationship between classes in Victorian society* (1971) • G. R. Searle, *Corruption in British politics, 1895–1930* (1987) • G. R. Searle, *Eugenics and politics in Britain, 1900–1914* (1976) • *WWW* • census returns, 1881
Archives NMM, corresp. and naval papers | CAC Cam., corresp. with Lord Fisher • Harvester Press Ltd, White-Bray MSS • HLRO, letters to R. D. Blumenfeld • Kilverstone Hall, Norfolk, Admiral Sir John Fisher MSS
Wealth at death £2534 13s. 10d.: probate, 23 April 1925, *CGPLA Eng. & Wales*

White, Beatrice Mary Irene (1902–1986), literary scholar, was born on 6 July 1902 at 20 Staff Houses, Ely, Cambridgeshire, the youngest of the three children of Robert Joseph White (1867–1951) and Beatrice Mary Louisa Barnard (1872–1949). At the time of her birth her father was a sergeant-major serving with the 4th Suffolk regiment, and the family was living in army accommodation.

Beatrice White entered King's College, London, in 1919 and was awarded a BA in English with first-class honours in 1923. She remained at King's College and in 1926 gained her MA (with distinction) for a thesis entitled 'A study of the *Eclogues*, life, and literary activities of Alexander Barclay'. This research was conducted under the supervision of Professor A. W. Reed, to whom Beatrice dedicated her subsequent edition of Barclay's *Eclogues* (1928). She spent 1929–31 in America, having been awarded a fellowship from the Commonwealth Fund to study at Stanford University and at the Henry E. Huntington Library in California.

On her return to London, White undertook editorial work for the Early English Text Society and the Shakespeare Association. In this early part of her scholarly career she published a number of works which established her reputation in the field of early Renaissance literature. For the Early English Text Society she edited Barclay's *Eclogues* (1928) and prepared *The vulgaria of John Stanbridge and the vulgaria of Robert Whittinton* (1932), an edition of two of the numerous school books which preceded Lily's Latin grammar. She also completed Florence Warren's edition of Lydgate's *The Dance of Death* (1931), work which had been disrupted by the First World War and Warren's death in 1917. In addition to these editorial achievements Beatrice White produced a study entitled *Mary Tudor* (1935), which sympathetically situated the queen's tragedy in the context of Mary's fidelity to outmoded loyalties. This attempt to correct the warped historical judgement of 'Bloody' Mary was underpinned by an examination of contemporary documents and state papers, an approach which also characterized her slightly earlier volume *Royal Nonesuch: a Tudor Tapestry* (1933). These were White's principal publications, but she also wrote many articles on a range of medieval and early modern topics, and reviewed extensively in this area for journals such as *Modern Language Review* and *Review of English Studies*. She described herself as

a Tudor specialist who had been drawn into medieval literature by the obligation to teach it, but this modest self-assessment significantly downplays her contribution to medieval studies.

In 1936 White became a recognized teacher of the University of London, and in the same year she was appointed as a lecturer in English language and literature at Queen Mary College. In 1939 she took up a lectureship in the same subject at Westfield College, London, and it was here that she spent the rest of her professional career. Her appointment coincided with the college's temporary removal from London during the war (it was billeted at St Peter's, Oxford). Her links with the English Association also seem to have originated during this time. From 1940 to 1943 she covered the chapter on Restoration literature for *The Year's Work in English Studies* after the previous contributor was called away to a government post. Subsequently she took responsibility for the sections on nineteenth-century literature and (briefly) the chapter on Chaucer, before pressure of other work made her relinquish these contributions.

White was acting head of the English department at Westfield from 1944 to 1946, and in 1945 she was promoted to a readership. Other academic distinctions include the award of a DLitt from the University of London in 1947 on the strength of her publications, and election to fellowships of the Royal Society of Literature (1945), the Royal Historical Society (1947), and the Society of Antiquaries of London (1952). Her service to her discipline extended far beyond her own department. She was a member of several learned societies, including the Philological Society, the Viking Society, and the Folklore Society. She was president of the Medieval Society of the University of London from 1950 to 1954, and was chair of the board of examiners for the BA in English for the university from 1953 to 1956. She gave public lectures at universities in England and Germany, and at the conference of university professors of English in Paris in 1953. Most prestigiously, in 1956 she was the first woman to lecture to the Medieval Academy of America at Harvard University. She also served as external examiner for several British universities, and in 1956–7 was visiting professor at Connecticut College for Women (USA). From 1961 to 1964 she was vice-principal of Westfield College, and in 1967 she became professor of English language and literature by conferment of title. She became emeritus professor following her retirement in 1969, and in 1976 was appointed an honorary fellow of the college.

In terms of research, the early modern court remained a source of fascination to White, as may be seen from her book *Cast of Ravens: the Strange Case of Sir Thomas Overbury* (1965), which reconstructed the events of an early seventeenth-century scandal at the court of James I, involving Overbury's death, apparently by poisoning, and the subsequent trial of the earl and countess of Somerset for his murder. Beatrice White also enjoyed a long career in the English Association. Most significantly she was the co-editor for four years, and the editor for ten, of its major annual bibliography, *The Year's Work in English Studies*. She became co-editor with Frederick S. Boas in 1952 (responsible for volumes 31–4 for 1950–53), and from 1956 she was its sole editor (volumes 35–44 for 1954–63), though benefiting from the assistance of T. S. Dorsch, who succeeded her as editor. In the preface to the 1964 volume Dorsch wrote of the expansion of *The Year's Work in English Studies* that occurred under White's editorship, and her response to its growth in size and scope: 'Dr White's scholarship has been equal to all the exacting demands made on it, and all who have worked with her have felt the benefit of her wise and benevolent guidance'. She was also the collector of two issues of *Essays and Studies* (1962 and 1983), and a contributor to five other volumes; her own Festschrift, edited by T. S. Dorsch, appeared as part of this series in 1972. In addition she served on the association's executive council and on its publications committee, and was a trustee from about 1970.

Beatrice White never married, but surrounded herself with friends of all ages and from many different parts of the world. As a teacher she took a personal interest in her students, concerning herself with both their academic and their social welfare. She delighted in entertaining students and colleagues as well as friends, and enjoyed a reputation as a generous and vivacious hostess during her tenure at Westfield. After her retirement she made her home in Eastbourne, Sussex, occupying herself with interests which included reading, music, and painting; she also remained active as a scholar, continuing to publish academic essays until the mid-1980s. She died at 4 Abbotsrood, 1 Milnthorpe Road, Eastbourne, on 30 March 1986 after a long struggle with cancer and was buried in Hailsham, Sussex, on Monday 7 April.

After White's death the next published volume of *The Year's Work in English Studies* (actually no. 65 for 1984, published 1987), was dedicated to her. The English Association further honoured her memory by instituting an annual prize in her name, awarded for work in the field of English literature written before 1590. White's encouragement of more junior colleagues informed the remit of the prize as 'outstanding articles by, whenever possible, younger scholars'. MARGARET CONNOLLY

Sources T. S. Dorsch, ed., *Essays and Studies by Members of the English Association*, new ser., 25 (1972) [in honour of Beatrice White] · J. Sondheimer, '*Castle Adamant in Hampstead': a history of Westfield College, 1882–1982* (1983) · T. S. Dorsch, ed., *The Year's Work in English Studies*, 45 (1964) · T. S. Dorsch, ed., *The Year's Work in English Studies*, 65 (1984) · T. S. Dorsch, ed., *The Year's Work in English Studies*, 67 (1986)
Likenesses photograph, repro. in Dorsch, ed., *Essays and studies*, frontispiece
Wealth at death £182,121: probate, 2 June 1986, *CGPLA Eng. & Wales*

White, Benjamin (1672–1758). *See* Petre, Benjamin, *under* Petre family (*per.* 1633–1801).

White, Benjamin (*c.*1725–1794), publisher, was the son of John White (1688–1758), barrister, and his wife, Anne (*née* Holt; 1693–1739). He was a younger brother of Gilbert *White (1720–1793), author of the celebrated *Natural History of Selborne* (1789). Ben, as he was known, introduced

Gilbert to Thomas Pennant and Daines Barrington to whom the book's component letters were written, and he edited and published the book. During their lifetimes Ben was much better known than his brother. White was raised with his six brothers and four sisters at The Wakes, Selborne, the family house which Gilbert, who was the eldest brother, later took over. Their father was not rich. One brother and two sisters died young. With his brother Thomas Holt *White (1724–1797), he attended school at Bishop's Waltham, Hampshire. Unlike their brothers the two pursued business careers in London, Thomas as an ironmonger, Ben as a publisher, and became the wealthiest of them; this enabled the family later to refurbish and extend The Wakes. By October 1745 White was working for John *Whiston (1711–1780), a respected publisher and bookseller at Horace's Head, at the junction of Fleet Street and the Strand. Whiston was related to Thomas Barker, of Rutland, who was Gilbert White's brother-in-law. Ben White was made a partner in 1756, and in 1765 he took the firm over. His valuable assistant, Henry Payne, became linked with White's name: about 1773 'White and Payne' offered £100 for the 2000 volume library of the deceased theologian Dr Matthew Horbery. Soon after, however, Payne set up a rival firm in Pall Mall on borrowed credit, became bankrupt, and died.

White produced a wide range of titles, some of great beauty. Horace's Head became a meeting place for naturalists, and, as was customary, was used as a poste restante, in 1775 by Gilbert White's correspondent Thomas Pennant, whose books White published, and by others. White's range of titles is indicated in his advertisement at the end of J. Ellis and D. C. Solander's *Natural History of the Zoophytes* (1786), which he published. They included Mark Catesby's *Natural History of Carolina* in two volumes, which perhaps inspired Audubon; an edition of Philip Miller's *Gardener's Dictionary*; the Revd John Lightfoot's *Flora Scotica* (2 vols.); and eight books by Pennant. White's brother John (1727–1781), named after their father, became chaplain to the forces in Gibraltar. His book on the local fauna was rejected by White, partly on Gilbert's advice, as not commercially viable, and most of the manuscript is lost.

White married Ann Yaldeen, daughter of the vicar of Newton Valence, next to Selborne, and the couple had a home in South Lambeth, as did Thomas White. The family remained close and Gilbert stayed with one or both of the brothers in London most springs for a month or so: on 26 June 1791 fifteen Whites and several others dined at White's home. On 12 July that year White commenced razing and rebuilding Horace's Head, but the following year he retired permanently to Mareland House, near Bentley, in north-east Hampshire.

By 1785 White's son, also Benjamin, was prominent in the business, and he handled the final stages of production of *Selborne*. The firm was renamed Benjamin White & Son, and under that name published Ellis and Solander's *Zoophytes*. By the time White finally retired in 1792 his other son, another John, had also joined the firm. The partnership continued to sell second-hand books and in 1813 the firm, by then White, Cochrane & Co., published with others probably the finest and most complete edition of *Selborne*: in 1993 a facsimile of it commemorated the bicentenary of Gilbert White's death.

Ben White died a wealthy man on 9 March 1794 at Mareland; his name was passed to both his son and his grandson. White never knew the irony that, from about 1810, among all his firm's memorable titles the sparsely illustrated, much edited, rambling diary of his own brother would be its best-seller, and that it would remain in print throughout the twentieth century.

PAUL F. S. CORNELIUS

Sources W. Noblett, 'Pennant and his publisher: Benjamin White, Thomas Pennant and *Of London*', *Archives of Natural History*, 11 (1982–4), 61–8 • P. F. S. Cornelius, 'Benjamin White (1725–1794), his older brother Gilbert, and notes on the hibernation of swallows', *Archives of Natural History*, 21 (1994), 231–6 • *GM*, 1st ser., 64 (1794), 284 • Nichols, *Lit. anecdotes*
Wealth at death 'plentiful': Nichols, *Lit. anecdotes*, 3 (1812), 127

White, Sir (Cyril) Brudenell Bingham (1876–1940), army officer, was born at St Arnaud, Victoria, Australia, on 23 September 1876, seventh child of John Warren White, a stock agent, and his wife, Maria (*née* Gibton), both Irish protestant immigrants. The family moved to Queensland, where Brudenell attended Brisbane normal school (1885–90) and Eton preparatory school, Nundah (1890–91), before becoming a bank clerk in 1892. Having been commissioned in the permanent forces as an artilleryman in 1899, he went briefly to the Second South African War with the Australian commonwealth horse in 1902, but he saw no fighting. Eighteen months later he was made aide-de-camp to Major-General Sir Edward Hutton, commander of Australia's new Federal army, a force White soon knew intimately. On 15 November 1905 he married Ethel Davidson at Christ Church, South Yarra, in Melbourne, daughter of Walter Davidson, a grazier from Elphinstone, Victoria. They were to have two sons and two daughters.

Courteous, intelligent, and efficient, White was in 1906 the first Australian military forces officer to attend the British army Staff College at Camberley. After a brief spell back in Australia he was posted to the War Office (1908–11). Like Hutton and Colonel William Bridges, White believed implicitly in the doctrine that Australian and imperial defence were mutually interdependent and best served by subordinating all military forces to the newly formed Imperial General Staff in London.

In 1912 Major White was appointed director of military operations to develop plans for the efficient mobilization for war of Australia's citizen army. After talks with the New Zealand commander, plans were made for a composite division to be dispatched overseas within six weeks of an order being given. That this was almost achieved in 1914 owed much to White's meticulous planning, and he was named chief of staff in General Bridges' Australian Imperial Force (AIF).

White planned with Bridges the landing at Gaba Tepe on Gallipoli in April 1915, though he wanted a larger force than the one assigned. He made many front-line inspections in the next weeks and was present when Bridges was killed by a sniper in May. In June he was made DSO and in

October he became brigadier-general general staff, in General Sir William Birdwood's Australian and New Zealand Army Corps (Anzac). His partnership with Birdwood was to last until the war's end, with Birdwood supplying the personal leadership and White the detailed orders and workable plans.

White's planning of the evacuation of the Anzac beachhead in December 1915 was a model of its kind. A series of ruses convinced the Turks that the Australians were preparing their trenches for winter, while in eleven nights 35,445 men were evacuated without a casualty. White now masterminded the expansion of the AIF from two divisions to four, was made CB (1916), and then accompanied 1st Anzac corps to France.

White was in his bureaucratic element. Once, in July 1916, Field Marshal Haig criticized a poor Anzac performance—'you are not fighting Bashi Bazouks now!'—whereupon White refuted him in detail and won his point. In May 1917, with the Australian troops exhausted after the battles of Bullecourt, White learned that Haig had not been informed of their need for a rest and threatened that he would never recommend the sending of an Australian force overseas again without guaranteed direct access to the commander-in-chief. Next White prepared for the winter of 1917–18 by building the 'Anzac light railway', which stretched right into the trench-lines, and nissen huts to keep the forward troops warm and dry.

White might have commanded a division and was even offered the corps by Haig in July 1917, but he chose to remain in his staff role. When friends plotted to have him made corps commander next May he demurred and Sir John Monash was given the post. Having been promoted major-general and made CMG (1918), White went with Birdwood to the general staff of the Fifth Army instead.

When hostilities ceased White's first task was to plan the AIF's demobilization as he had its initial mobilization four years earlier. Appointed KCMG in 1919 and an aide-de-camp to the king, he returned to Australia to organize the peacetime army. He left the active list in 1923 to become chairman of the Commonwealth Public Service Board (1923–8), but when the government moved to Canberra he retired to his pastoral property, Woodnaggerak, near Buangor, Victoria, and some business directorships.

Lieutenant-General White (who was appointed KCVO in 1920 and KCB in 1927) was recalled as chief of general staff in 1939 to mobilize the 2nd AIF and was instrumental in drafting the charter which guaranteed that force's integrity. He was promoted full general in March 1940. Brudenell White died tragically on 13 August 1940 in an aircrash at Canberra airport and was buried at Buangor cemetery, Victoria; he was survived by his wife. Elegant and wiry, with piercing blue eyes and a beaky nose, he combined loyalty, balance, and quiet charm with the steel and ability always to get things done. Ever the faithful lieutenant, White was a general staff officer of the very first rank.

CARL BRIDGE

Sources J. Grey, 'White, Sir Cyril Brudenell Bingham', *AusDB*, 12.460 • J. Grey, *A military history of Australia* (1990) • C. E. W. Bean, *Two men I knew* (1957) • G. Verney, 'White', *The commanders*, ed.

D. Horner (1984) · G. Serle, *John Monash: a biography* (1982) · E. M. Andrews, *The Anzac illusion: Anglo-Australian relations during World War I* (1993) · *The Australian encyclopedia*
Archives Australian War Memorial, Canberra, MSS · NL Aus., MSS · priv. coll., MSS | NL Aus., corresp. with Viscount Novar | FILM IWM FVA, actuality footage
Likenesses J. Longstaff, oils, Australian War Memorial, Canberra · photographs, Australian War Memorial, Canberra, collections
Wealth at death A£20,699: Australian probate records

White, Century. *See* White, John (1590–1645).

White, Charles (1728–1813), surgeon and man-midwife, only son of Thomas White (1696–1776), surgeon and man-midwife, and his wife, Rosamond, *née* Bower, was born at Manchester on 4 October 1728 and educated there by the Revd Radcliffe Russell. About 1742 he was apprenticed to his father and subsequently studied medicine in London at the school of William Hunter, who was then establishing a reputation in obstetrics. There White became close friends with William's brother, John, who was also studying at the school. White completed his studies in Edinburgh, before returning to Manchester, where he joined his father's practice as a surgeon and man-midwife.

In 1752 White was instrumental, along with Joseph Bancroft, a local merchant, in founding the Manchester Infirmary. This charity, funded by subscriptions of the wealthy, provided medical advice and treatment for the poor. White served as honorary surgeon from 1752 until 1790.

From the 1750s White began to establish a reputation as an innovative surgeon. He carried out a wide range of procedures, including lithotomy, amputations, and the removal of tumours. In 1760, in a paper before the Royal Society, he described a successful operation on a fractured arm, which brought together and united the two ends of the broken bone. Two years later he presented a further paper describing the use of sponges to stop haemorrhaging. He became a fellow of the Royal Society on 18 February 1762, and a member of the Company of Surgeons in the same year.

White was also concerned to develop the midwifery side of his father's practice. Following the principles established already by his father, he advocated 'rational methods' and became highly regarded. In his well-known and influential book, *Treatise on the Management of Pregnant and Lying-in Women* (1773), he advised that women should give birth 'naturally'. Delivery should not be assisted until the shoulders of the baby were expelled by the force of the mother's labour pains. He advised mothers to get out of bed as soon after delivery as possible and stressed the importance of cleanliness and ventilation. He recognized the analogy between puerperal and surgical fevers. This book, dedicated to his former teacher, William Hunter, was translated into both French and German and was also published in North America.

In 1757 White married Ann, daughter of John Bradshaw, one-time high sheriff for the county of Lancaster. They had eight children—four sons and four daughters. Their second son, Thomas White (*b.* 1763), became physician to

Charles White (1728–1813), by Joseph Allen

the Manchester Infirmary and a man-midwife. He died in 1793 following a fall from his horse. John Bradshaw White, their fourth son, also joined his father's practice but died in 1797.

White played a prominent social role in Manchester, then rapidly developing into an industrial city. He was a founding member of the Manchester Literary and Philosophical Society in 1781. In 1783, along with the physicians Thomas Percival and Thomas Henry, he helped to establish the short lived College of Arts and Science, where he and his son Thomas lectured on anatomy.

In 1790, after a dispute over the enlargement of the Manchester Infirmary, White resigned. Almost immediately he set up another hospital, the Lying-in Charity. This was, at first, a domiciliary service. In 1795 a modest in-patient facility was added. From its foundation the charity's aims were broad. A register of wet-nurses was kept and lecture courses were offered for both apothecaries and female midwives. In 1793 White himself gave a series of talks. White acted as man-midwife extraordinary to the charity until 1811. In 1854 the charity became known as St Mary's Hospital, the title it retains today.

From about 1795 White became interested in the relationships between different human races and between species of plants and animals. He read a number of papers to the Literary and Philosophical Society on the subject, which were published in 1799 as *An Account of the Regular Gradation in Man, Animals and Vegetables*. He concluded that there is general gradation from one species to another, suggesting relationships between species and races. However, he rejected the idea that one species may have developed from another.

In 1803 White had an attack of epidemic ophthalmia, which resulted in blindness in 1812. He died at his country house, The Priory, Sale, Ashton-on-Mersey, Cheshire, on 20 February 1813. In the church of Ashton-on-Mersey a monument to him and several members of his family was later erected. STELLA BUTLER

Sources C. J. Cullingworth, *Charles White, FRS, a great provincial surgeon and obstetrician of the eighteenth century* (1904) · T. Henry, 'Memoirs of the late Charles White FRS with reference to his professional life and writings', *Memoirs of the Literary and Philosophical Society of Manchester*, 2nd ser., 3 (1819), 33–51 · D. Sheehan, 'Charles White, eighteenth-century surgeon', *Annals of Medical History*, 3rd ser., 4 (1942), 132–46 · E. M. Brockbank, *Sketches of the lives and work of the honorary medical staff of the Manchester Infirmary: from its foundation in 1752 to 1830* (1904), 27–65 · J. G. Adami, 'Charles White of Manchester, 1728–1813', *Medical Library and History Journal*, 5 (1907), 1–18 · *DNB* · *The record of the Royal Society of London*, 4th edn (1940)
Likenesses W. Ward, mezzotint, pubd 1809 (after J. Allen), BM, Wellcome L. · bust, 1886; known to be at the Manchester Infirmary in 1900 · J. Allen, oils, Man. City Gall. [*see illus.*] · W. Tate, portrait; known to be at the Manchester Infirmary in 1900 · double portrait (with his father), repro. in Gregson, *Fragments of Lancashire* (1824) · photograph, Wellcome L.

White, Christopher (*c.*1650–1695?), chemist and laboratory technician, was probably born in Oxford, though his origins remain obscure. He is, however, known to be the boy 'Kitt' who in 1663, with his (unnamed) father, assisted in the experimental chemistry courses given privately at Oxford by the German alchemist Peter Stahl, under the patronage of Robert Boyle. He remained a trainee assistant to Stahl for about three years, and then served as Boyle's assistant for ten years, moving to London with him in 1668.

Having returned to Oxford, White became on 21 April 1676 a privileged (tradesman) member of the university, championed by the mathematician John Wallis. His business was (and remained) making chemical medicines, but he was soon designated to run the university chemical laboratory projected as part of the Ashmolean Museum. Begun in 1679, the new institution was opened on 21 May 1683. White himself chose, and perhaps helped to design, some of its apparatus and furnaces.

As 'operator', or university chemist, White's main duty was to demonstrate experiments and techniques in extension of lectures by the professor of chemistry—Robert Plot until 1689, and then Edward Hannes. The first course began in September 1683. In addition, White was authorized to run a public dispensary from the laboratory, where he maintained a storeroom of chemical preparations. He was also in charge of a small library, to which he presented his copy of Joannes Zwelfer's *Pharmacopoeia* (1653).

In 1686 White was one of the stewards of the Oxford and Oxfordshire feast, and when the university went in ceremonial procession to meet James II the following year he deputized for the superior bedel of arts. From at least 1688 he was an acquaintance of John Aubrey, who lodged with him whenever he visited Oxford. Among references to White in Aubrey's letters, mentions of 'a rare medicine that he hath for the stone' (1689) and in 1694 of 'a good lusty vomit' (Powell, 209, 232) offer some insight into the nature of his pharmaceutical practice.

From an early age White had been moulded into a new kind of professional chemist, combining the skills of the alchemist, the apothecary, and the 'philosophical' experimenter. This is reflected in his use of the new occupational title 'chemist'. He inspired the creation of Oxford's earliest ancillary scientific post, becoming in effect the first professional laboratory technician. A contemporary account describes him as 'skilful and industrious'. He did well financially, through the sale of medicines, yet there must have been disappointment, even before his untimely death, at the lack of real academic achievement in his laboratory.

With his wife, Elizabeth (*d.* 1724), White had two sons and two daughters. He trained both sons as chemist apothecaries, the older, Christopher, succeeding to his university post. No record of White's death or burial has survived. When he made his will in Oxford on 27 August 1695 he was already seriously ill, and he probably died shortly after. He was buried at St Cross Church, Oxford.

A. V. SIMCOCK, *rev.*

Sources Oxf. UA, SP/E/144 · chancellor's court wills, Oxf. UA · *The life and times of Anthony Wood*, ed. A. Clark, 3, OHS, 26 (1894), 55, 111, 227; 4, OHS, 30 (1895), 79 · A. Powell, *John Aubrey and his friends*, rev. edn (1988) · A. V. Simcock, *The Ashmolean Museum and Oxford science, 1683–1983* (1984), 8, 17
Archives U. Glas. L., notes on chemistry

White, Claude Grahame- (1879–1959), aviator and aircraft manufacturer, was born at Bursledon Towers, Bursledon, Hampshire, on 21 August 1879, the second son and the youngest of the three children of John White, a man of independent means and a keen yachtsman who later assumed the name Grahame-White, and his wife, Ada Beatrice, the daughter of Frederick Chinnock, a property agent, of London and Dinorbin Court, Hampshire. He was educated at Crondall House School, Farnham, and Bedford grammar school and was afterwards apprenticed to an engineering firm in the town. Later he began work with an uncle, Francis Willey, later the second Lord Barnby, a Yorkshire wool magnate, and it was the engineering side of the business that interested him. He persuaded his uncle to replace the firm's horse-drawn vans with motor lorries, and his first independent venture was to start a motor vehicle service at Bradford, in competition with the steam trams. Having spent three years as the steward of a large Sussex estate, he then made a lengthy visit to South Africa, during which he hunted big game. On his return to London he set up a motor-engineering business in Albemarle Street.

Inspired by Louis Blériot's cross-channel flight in 1909 Grahame-White travelled to France to learn to fly. He met Blériot at a flying meeting at Rheims and spent two valuable months in his Paris factory, watching the construction of a machine for his own use. On 4 January 1910 he became the first Englishman to hold an aviator's certificate, issued by the Aero Club de France, and he later started a British flying school at Pau. He gained fame in England in April 1910 when he raced the French instructor Louis Paulhan for the £10,000 prize offered by the *Daily Mail* for the first London to Manchester flight in under 24 hours. Paulhan won, but Grahame-White's gallant efforts, which included making the first authentic night flight, captured public imagination. He went on to win valuable prizes in air races at Wolverhampton and Bournemouth before travelling to the United States, where he dominated the Boston aviation meeting in September. In October 1910 he won the Gordon Bennett cup, the top prize at the aviation tournament at Belmont Park, Long Island. He also flew to Washington to see President Taft, executing a perfect landing in his Farman III before a large crowd on Executive Avenue. For his exploits in America he was honoured with a special gold medal by the Aerial League of the British Empire.

Grahame-White returned to England in December and used his substantial American winnings to purchase a 207 acre site at Hendon, which early in 1911 opened as the London Aerodrome. Under Grahame-White's dynamic management Hendon became a centre of British aviation. It included in its precincts the Grahame-White Aviation company and flying school, Blériot and Farman agencies, and week-end race meetings. From 1912 weekday night-flying displays were added to the Hendon programme, and an estimated 120,000 spectators attended the four days of flying at Easter 1914. As *The Times* observed: 'Hendon has acquired a wonderful hold on the public' (*The Times*, 14 April 1914).

After a second successful tour of America in August 1911 Grahame-White returned to England, where he organized the first official air-mail delivery, from Hendon to Windsor. In June 1912 he staged the first aerial derby around London: Lord Northcliffe's *Daily Mail* put up a gold cup for the winner. That summer he also launched, jointly with Lord Northcliffe, the 'Wake up, England!' tour to alert the country 'to the realities of the Aeroplane Age' (Wallace, 171). Accompanied by a corps of pilots, Grahame-White flew to the major towns and seaside resorts, spreading the gospel of 'air mindedness'. A young man full of enthusiasm, he flew by Farman to his wedding on 27 June 1912, when he married the wealthy socialite Dorothy Taylor, the daughter of Bertrand Le Roy Taylor, of New York. The marriage was dissolved in 1916 and in December of that year Grahame-White married the revue star Ethel (Grace) Levey, a friend of his former wife, with whom he had fallen in love after difficulties entered into his first marriage.

Grahame-White realized early on the military potential of aviation and in May 1911 gave a display at Hendon to the parliamentary aerial defence committee. On the outbreak of war in 1914 he was commissioned as a flight commander in the Royal Naval Air Service, and on 5 September he made the first night patrol over London, in search of a Zeppelin reported crossing the Essex coast. He hankered after action and on 12 February 1915 was involved in an ill-fated attack on Cuxhaven. The raid began in appalling weather and Grahame-White was forced to ditch in the sea 5 miles from the Belgian coast; he was fortunate to be rescued by a French minesweeper. Ever an individualist, he was irked by military discipline, and in August 1915 he resigned his

commission to concentrate for the remainder of the war on government aircraft construction contracts.

Before the war Grahame-White Aviation manufactured a variety of models at Hendon, including the Aero-bus, designed by J. D. North, 'the most outstanding weight carrier of its day' (Penrose, *Great War*, 141). In October 1913 the Aero-bus set a world record by carrying nine passengers aloft. The company also produced the 1912 Box-kite biplane, a useful trainer which in its ultimate form in 1916 (type 1600) was widely used by both the Royal Naval Air Service and the Royal Flying Corps. Overall, though, Grahame-White Aviation designs were not very successful, and during the war the company's principal role was to manufacture the proven designs of others. One of its staples was the workmanlike Avro 504 biplane; the company accounted for 600 of the 8430 built during the war. In January 1917 the government placed a major contract for 700 DH-6 two-seater biplanes to be used as trainers to facilitate the expansion of the Royal Flying Corps. The plane was built to a rugged design and should have been easy to manufacture: it was said that its square-cut wings were 'made by the mile and cut off by the yard' (Wallace, 209). Instead it became the cause of an 'increasingly bitter controversy' (Penrose, *Great War*, 222) between Grahame-White and the Air Board. In spite of Grahame-White's urgent warnings, problems over the supply of suitable wood for the construction resulted in delays and even the manufacture of unusable planes. Having borrowed heavily from both his uncle and the Admiralty to fund wartime expansion, Grahame-White faced mounting debts as his factory stood idle. In December 1917 he suffered a nervous breakdown and was hospitalized for six weeks.

Matters were made worse by the cancellation, at short notice, of a series of government contracts in summer 1918. This was followed by a complete cessation of orders after the armistice. Facing bankruptcy, Grahame-White diversified into furniture and car manufacture, and he discovered a lucrative business in refurbishing war-surplus Rolls-Royce Silver Ghost chassis. He had some success with post-war plane designs, notably the Bantam single-seater biplane, but his efforts to take a lead in the development of civil aviation were frustrated by the legacy of the wartime DH-6 fiasco and the Air Ministry's refusal to return Hendon aerodrome, which the Admiralty had requisitioned in 1914. When in 1924 the Treasury appointed a receiver to the Grahame-White Aviation company to recover debts, Grahame-White countered with a legal action intended to recover his own wartime losses, as well as the purchase price for Hendon. Although he eventually won this, the Treasury would not settle until Grahame-White threatened to expose the facts in Lord Northcliffe's *Daily Mail*. Disillusioned by the controversy, he gave up any active interest in flying and applied his capital to real estate in Britain and America, where several well-judged deals made him a fortune. In one transaction he bought the site of the Victoria coach terminal in London for £90,000 and sold it shortly afterwards for several times that figure.

In 1927–8 Grahame-White toured the Mediterranean in

his 485-ton yacht *Ethleen*. He also wrote numerous books on aviation, many with his friend Harry Harper, air correspondent of the *Daily Mail*. Some were popular works for boys but others, such as *Flying: an Epitome and a Forecast* (1930), were serious works on the subject. Grahame-White's marriage to Ethel Levey ended with separation in 1934 and divorce in 1939, in November of which year he married Phoebe Lee, of New York. There were no children from any of his marriages. With his third wife he spent the Second World War at Cowes and later Rossmore Court, a Grahame-White development next to Regent's Park. Although he made efforts to re-enter the aviation industry, he played no greater role than that of a fire-watcher during the air raids. He died at 33 avenue Maeterlinck, Nice, France, on 19 August 1959, after a three-week bout of heart trouble. By then he was largely unknown to the contemporary aviation world, except for a few members of the Royal Aero Club, of which he was a founder member. In spite of his seminal contribution to the early years of British aviation he received no public honours.

H. B. GRIMSDITCH, *rev.* ROBIN HIGHAM

Sources G. Wallace, *Claude Grahame-White* (1960) · *Flight* (28 Aug 1959) · *The Aeroplane* (28 Aug 1959), 48 · *Journal of the Royal Aeronautical Society*, 64 (1960) · *The Times* (14 April 1914) · *The Times* (20 Aug 1959) · C. Grahame-White, *Flying: an epitome and a forecast* (1930) · H. Penrose, *British aviation: the pioneer years, 1903–1914* (1967) · H. Penrose, *British aviation: the Great War and armistice, 1915–1919* (1969) · W. Raleigh and H. A. Jones, *The war in the air*, 6 vols. (1922–37); repr. (1969), vol. 1 · C. Chant, *Aviation: an illustrated history* (1978) · J. A. Mollison, ed., *The book of famous flyers* (1934) · PRO, MUN4/6293

Archives FILM BFI NFTVA, 'The great London to Manchester aerial race', 1910 · BFI NFTVA, documentary footage

Likenesses A. Pan, oils, 1951, Royal Aero Club; on loan to RAF Museum · Tec, Hentschel-colourtype caricature, NPG; repro. in *VF* (10 May 1911) · bronze sculpture, RAF Museum · photograph, NPG; repro. in *Reign of George V: representative subjects of the king*, 1 (1913)

Wealth at death £248,708 17s. 6d.: probate, 4 Jan 1960, *CGPLA Eng. & Wales*

White, Sir Dick Goldsmith (1906–1993), intelligence officer, was born on 20 December 1906 at 119 High Street, Tonbridge, Kent, the youngest of three children of Percy Hall White, an ironmonger and agricultural engineer, and his wife, Gertrude (*née* Farthing), of Edenbridge. White's early childhood was comfortable, but his father was over-ambitious in business and careless with money, and in 1913 the family endured a financial crash. White never forgot the shock of the sudden collapse into near penury. In 1917 he was sent to Bishop's Stortford College. Although he was initially seen as a rather quiet and self-contained schoolboy, his potential gradually became clear, and in his final year he was captain of cricket, rugby, and athletics, at the last of which he excelled. In 1925, having applied unsuccessfully to join the Royal Navy, he went to Christ Church, Oxford, to read history. There he came under the influence of the history don J. C. Masterman, who was to be a mentor, friend, and wartime colleague. White, tall, slim, fair-haired, and blue-eyed, made his mark on college and university life as a man at once unassuming and accomplished. A good though not outstanding student, congenial rather than gregarious, he won a blue as a

Sir Dick Goldsmith White (1906–1993), by unknown photographer, 1928

middle-distance runner. Although he narrowly missed a first in his finals, he secured a two-year Commonwealth Fund fellowship to study American history in the United States. White enrolled at the University of Michigan, a useful choice outside the Ivy League which brought him into America's heartland. During his two years in America he travelled widely and for a time studied in California, although without completing any substantial piece of work. He returned home in 1930 uncertain what he should do with his life, although he hankered after the world of letters. He sought an opening in journalism, spent some weeks in Florence learning Italian, and briefly took up and then abandoned a postgraduate exhibition at Christ Church. After an inconsequential and unsettled year he drifted into teaching, initially by supervising a group of public schoolboys visiting Australia and New Zealand under a Dominions Office travel scheme. Early in 1932 he was appointed a schoolmaster at Whitgift School in Croydon. There, it appeared, White had finally found his niche. He quickly made his mark both in the classroom and on the playing field as a gifted and compassionate teacher and an inspiring coach, and he seemed set fair for a career in education; his lifelong friend Denis Greenhill believed that, had he remained in teaching, he would have become 'a great headmaster'.

Recruited to MI5 That White swapped Whitgift for Whitehall was completely a matter of chance. In April 1935 he led a group of Whitgift boys on a cruise of the Mediterranean. He struck up an acquaintance with a fellow passenger, Lieutenant-Colonel Malcolm Cumming of MI5. Cumming was impressed by White, and recommended him to his MI5 superiors for appointment. A few months later White was approached by Guy Liddell of MI5 and was invited to join the service. The decision to accept cannot have been easy for White: he enjoyed teaching, and the job he was being offered in a small and shadowy Whitehall agency staffed mainly by superannuated army officers promised neither a decent salary nor eventual public rank and esteem. But he thought that a war was coming and he could see the value of the work to be done, so after consulting Masterman and deliberating for a time he took the plunge in January 1936.

White was the first recruit to join the Security Service as a graduate, and almost its first without previous military or police experience. His first role was appropriate to someone of his academic background and experience: he was sent in the guise of an advanced student on a nine-month tour of Germany. His task was to observe and to learn rather than to recruit agents or to spy. He perfected his German, and he obtained a valuable insight into the nature of the Nazi regime, while also experiencing the vicissitudes of operating under cover.

On his return to London, White was assigned to counter-espionage, concentrating on the activities of German diplomats in Britain. Modest, willing to learn from others, and incisive, he quickly won acceptance in a service which, despite its hidebound image—particularly as afterwards portrayed by academic imports into wartime Whitehall—had by 1937 succeeded in penetrating the German embassy as well as making contacts with other anti-Nazi Germans, and White dealt with some of these ideologically motivated sources. By the time war was declared, MI5 had enjoyed some success against individual German intelligence operations, although it did not then have a clear view of the overall threat. Officers were successfully running the important double agent Snow, and through him and other sources had obtained a good deal of information on German plans for espionage and sabotage in the United Kingdom and Ireland. Careful management of Snow and of other spies caught in 1939–40 saw the elaboration of the practice whereby captured agents were induced to feed back false and misleading information to Germany and to claim that they had built up networks of sub-agents and informers. In January 1941 an inter-services group, the Twenty (or double-cross) Committee, was established to identify genuine material which could safely be provided for these controlled agents to send back to Germany. This was the genesis of the double-cross system. It soon became clear that almost all enemy agents operating in the United Kingdom were already under British control, a conclusion supported by intercepted German intelligence radio traffic. Within MI5 White, along with other officers including the highly experienced T. A. (Tar) Robertson, played a crucial role in the subtle development of double-cross from a highly successful counter-intelligence operation into an instrument of strategic deception under the overall direction of the chiefs of staff. This work brought White into an interdepartmental milieu for which he was well suited: in partnership with Masterman, who was one of a number of academics and lawyers brought into MI5 during the war and who became secretary of the Twenty Committee, he was able to represent MI5's viewpoint firmly but without creating friction.

White brought to the management of double agents an insight into character, a sureness of touch, and an ability to command the confidence of those with whom he dealt. These were attributes also to characterize his post-war career: even in the poisonous and sometimes paranoid world of secret intelligence, people who met him respected and trusted him. His ability to inspire confidence and to bring people along with him was reflected not only in his standing within the service. In 1943 White was drawn into the planning of counter-intelligence organization and operations in support of the invasion of France, and from then until 1945 he was largely occupied with European security affairs. He worked closely with Eisenhower's staff, including Walter Beddell Smith, a future head of the Central Intelligence Agency. At the very end of the war, by then holding the military rank of brigadier, he was involved in the inter-allied investigation which concluded that Hitler had indeed died in his Berlin bunker. In 1945 he was honoured with the award of the French Croix de Guerre and appointment to the American Legion of Merit. On 28 November that year he married Kathleen (Kate) Somers Tomkinson, née Bellamy (b. 1911/12), who already had a daughter by a previous marriage; they had two sons. White's family life was close-knit, and he was never happier than when at home.

The evolution of double-cross saw a parallel—though not commensurate—rise in MI5's standing within Whitehall. By 1945 there were hopes that its success in developing and managing double-cross, in the face of difficulties which sometimes lay as much in Whitehall as in Berlin, would secure the service a central role in strategic deception in any future military conflict. In the event, the advent of the cold war brought such a weight of security problems, in addition to those arising from pressures for decolonization throughout the empire, that this planned dimension of MI5's post-war activities never took shape.

In 1945–6 White toured the Commonwealth and colonies, both to review and advise on local intelligence and security arrangements and to trawl for talent for MI5. This experience gave him an insight into the range of overseas problems which Britain was to face over the next twenty years as decolonization gathered pace and as the pressures of the cold war grew in Asia and Africa. Within the service he was already seen as a future chief, though he wore the mantle of the coming man lightly and he avoided office intrigues.

Post-war activities In 1945 the director-general of MI5, Sir David Petrie, retired, and Percy Sillitoe, a former chief constable, was appointed to succeed him. This was not a happy choice: Sillitoe brought to MI5 the outlook and management style of a tough provincial policeman, and he had no experience of intelligence affairs. Furthermore, he was unable to adapt to the ways of Whitehall, and this was to cost MI5 dearly when the first post-war security crises broke. White and other senior officers, while uneasy with Sillitoe, kept the show on the road, and the service prospered modestly as a result of its wartime successes. It recruited able and experienced officers from the armed services and from colonial administrations, and it maintained a network of former officers, friends, and contacts within Whitehall and the academic and legal worlds. Furthermore, the very close intelligence and security links with the United States built up during the war were assiduously developed. Here White's personal standing was crucial: his friend Denis Greenhill wrote that 'Dick was not one of those Englishmen who thought that the fact that our secret service could trace its ancestry back to Queen Elizabeth I assured its superiority for all time', and even in the darkest days of the interlinked crises of Guy Burgess and Donald Maclean, and of Kim Philby, the Americans never lost confidence in him personally. The security services of other friendly states inside and outside the Commonwealth held him in equally high regard: in 1981 an ailing former director of Irish military intelligence particularly asked a mutual acquaintance to tell White that 'he's a great man'.

The decade after 1945 saw the revelation, through a series of spy scandals centred first on the Anglo-American atomic weapons programme and second on the Foreign Office and the Secret Intelligence Service (SIS), of considerable long-term Soviet penetration of the British establishment. Although the machinations of the Comintern and the activities of the Communist Party of Great Britain had been among MI5's principal inter-war concerns until the mid-1930s, in contrast to its first pre-war successes against German espionage, which had helped to lay the foundations for its spectacular wartime achievements, its surveillance of known communist groups and front organizations had left it completely unaware of the parallel but more sophisticated subversive activities of Soviet agents operating independently to recruit Englishmen as long-term agents. The result was that during the war a coterie of very able traitors had worked their way into key positions, including Donald Maclean in the Foreign Office, Anthony Blunt in MI5, and especially Kim Philby in SIS. Even when the reality of Soviet penetration of the atomic bomb project was brought to light with the detection of the scientist traitors Alan Nunn May and Klaus Fuchs, and despite warnings from Soviet defectors, Whitehall and in particular the Foreign Office failed to appreciate that the same techniques of ideological seduction could well have been used against other officials.

In the public furore and the Whitehall storm that followed the disappearance of Burgess and Maclean, MI5 emerged in an unfavourable light. Sillitoe was out of his depth, and it fell to White and other senior officers to defend the service externally, to initiate a thorough trawl for other Soviet agents, and to begin to repair relations with the American intelligence agencies. This work was greatly complicated by the fact that within Whitehall opinion was bitterly divided about Philby, under suspicion as a result of the tip-off to Maclean. Investigation and interrogation of this most able of dissimulators proved inconclusive, although White and other MI5 officers concluded that he was a traitor. But many in SIS thought Philby innocent, and after his career officially ended in

1951 he was publicly exonerated by the foreign secretary in 1955.

In 1953 Sillitoe retired from MI5, to the great relief of the service. White was selected to succeed him. This was widely welcomed within MI5 on account of his record, his personality, his high standing with the Americans, his good relations with Commonwealth intelligence services, and his understanding of Whitehall. He brought calm where there had been chaos, he secured the service's flank against attack from other departments, he was incisive and persuasive on paper and in person, and he commanded the confidence of ministers. He instituted a radical reorganization of MI5, including the creation of a separate personnel and recruitment division. He also secured Treasury approval for the long-overdue introduction of a proper career structure along civil-service lines. This enabled the service systematically to recruit and to retain good personnel. White's greatest difficulties during his years as director-general of MI5 arose not in managing internal change or in coping with external criticism of the service's failure to detect Soviet penetration, but in overseeing the necessary post mortems and in supervising the hunt for other Soviet agents within the establishment. In retrospect it is clear that more might have been done earlier to ascertain the extent and persistence of infection; at the time, however, MI5 had to strike a delicate balance between prudence and paranoia.

In SIS and Cabinet Office After three years at the helm in MI5 White was abruptly transplanted to the very different world of SIS. This unexpected move was a consequence of the Commander Crabbe imbroglio, a freelance SIS operation against a Soviet cruiser visiting Portsmouth which went disastrously and publicly wrong. The head of SIS, Sir John Sinclair, was pushed out, and White was offered his post. He accepted out of duty, not ambition: he liked running MI5, and must have been apprehensive about the reaction he would encounter in the rather different world of 54 Broadway. In truth his appointment came more as a relief than a joy to SIS. While he was well known and generally liked, like his reviled predecessor Sinclair he came from outside the service. He had no personal experience of foreign intelligence gathering—he once ruefully remarked to a subordinate that he wished that he had run agents in the field, as he felt that he would then have had a better grasp of the human pressures under which SIS officers worked—but he had vast knowledge of counter-intelligence, he understood Whitehall, he had excellent international contacts, and he could manage. As head of SIS his approach, once he had imposed a necessary reorganization, was to concentrate on the service's external relations with Whitehall and the wider world and to let his directors get on with their jobs, a style which contributed to a perception among some field officers that he was aloof and out of touch.

White's achievements as head of SIS are hard to estimate. He undoubtedly succeeded in restoring morale and in improving relations with the Foreign Office and the Cabinet Office. But secret intelligence operations of their nature are not intended to become public knowledge for a very long time, if ever, and it is uncertain what the organization did or failed to do under White's direction in cold war and other spheres of activity. The biggest known success was the recruitment of the Soviet agent Oleg Penkovsky, who provided an astonishing stream of technical intelligence on Soviet missile technology, crucial during the Cuban missile crisis, until his arrest and execution in 1963; the greatest public disaster was the treachery of the SIS officer George Blake. Philby's betrayal still cast a long shadow, but the Penkovsky success, together with White's presence as head of SIS, went far towards repairing Britain's standing with the American intelligence community.

When the time came for White to retire in 1968, the selection of a successor proved difficult. In the event White was succeeded not by the outstanding internal candidate Maurice Oldfield but by Sir John Rennie, widely regarded as a Foreign Office cast-off beset by serious family problems. His performance was to vindicate his critics. Some felt that White should have tried to prevent that appointment, but the outgoing head of a department has no right of veto on his successor and to oppose the Foreign Office might have been to make enduring trouble for SIS.

On his retirement from SIS, White was appointed to the newly created post of co-ordinator of intelligence in the Cabinet Office. This innovation was seen as the brainchild of the cabinet secretary, his one-time Whitgift pupil Sir Burke Trend, who took a keen interest in intelligence matters and who particularly valued White's unrivalled experience of the secret world and his advice on international and security affairs. The appointment of White to this novel position was not without its critics, and it is fair to say that only a man of his standing, tact, and judgement could have made a success of it without provoking monumental rows. White eschewed any temptation to turn the post into an overlordship of the various intelligence agencies or otherwise to throw his weight around, and instead concentrated on giving advice when asked. Some argue that this approach was tantamount to doing nothing at all, but there is no doubt that White's personal contribution was valued in the Cabinet Office. His influence was crucial in securing government approval for the preparation under F. H. Hinsley of the multi-volume official history, *British Intelligence in the Second World War: its Influence on Strategy and Operations*, an enterprise that demonstrated the extent of MI5's wartime successes both in counter-espionage and in strategic deception as well as the achievements of Britain's code-breakers. In 1972, feeling rather worn out, he retired from Whitehall for good.

In retirement White spent most of his time gardening and reading—his literary streak remained strong, and some of his poetry was circulated among former colleagues. In 1981 he was elected an honorary student of Christ Church, a distinction of which he was very proud. He became as accessible to researchers and journalists as a man could safely be who knew so many state and private secrets, and in 1981 he wrote to *The Times* to deprecate the

claim that Roger Hollis had been a traitor. Some in Whitehall faulted his judgement in retirement in making himself so accessible, arguing that he was ignoring rules and procedures which he had enjoined on others when in office. He was on particularly close terms with the journalist Andrew Boyle, whose book *The Climate of Treason* (1979) led to the exposure of Anthony Blunt; he later granted interviews to the BBC producer Tom Bower, whose rather inappropriately titled *The Perfect English Spy: Sir Dick White and the Secret War, 1935–90* appeared in 1995. Dick White was not a spy at all, but an able, patriotic, and humane leader of men who, exceptionally for one who headed successively the two most secret arms of government, commanded enduring trust across Whitehall and Westminster. White was appointed OBE in 1942, CBE in 1950, KBE in 1955, and KCMG in 1960. He died after a long illness at his home, The Leat, Burpham, near Arundel, Sussex, on 21 February 1993; his wife, Kate, survived him.

EUNAN O'HALPIN

Sources *The security service, 1908–45: the official history* (2000) · T. Bower, *The perfect English spy: Sir Dick White and the secret war, 1935–90* (1995) · F. H. Hinsley and C. A. G. Simkins, *British intelligence in the Second World War, 4: Security and counter-intelligence* (1990) · *The Times* (23 Feb 1993) · *The Independent* (23 Feb 1993) · *The Independent* (5 March 1993) · *WWW* · b. cert. · m. cert. · d. cert. · private information (2004)
Likenesses photograph, 1928, News International Syndication, London [*see illus.*] · photograph, 1945, repro. in *The Independent* (23 Feb 1993) · photograph, 1945, repro. in *The Independent* (5 March 1993) · photographs, repro. in Bower, *Perfect English spy*

White, Dorothy (d. 1686?), religious writer, about whose life and parentage very few details are known, was the second most prolific Quaker woman writer in the seventeenth century; yet there are few Quaker figures as unknown. The standard biographical sources, usually quite comprehensive, merely confirm her obscurity; the major source for White's life is her own work.

White was probably resident in Weymouth, Dorset, in the 1650s, and in London following the Restoration. Of the texts relating to her Weymouth connection—*A Diligent Search* (1659) and *An Alarm* (1660)—the first also describes a brief imprisonment that occurred after White interrupted the service of a local priest. Her association with London emerges in her 'sufferings' writing: *The Voice of the Lord* (1662) and *To All those that Worship* (1664) both indicate that she was imprisoned there. Moreover, in *Upon the 22nd Day* (1659), White explains that she was compelled to 'leave my own countrey in obedience to the Lord' (p. 7), confirming that her residence was not ordinarily London. In the cases of persecution both in Weymouth and London, however, White's text is the only surviving record of the assaults on her as there is no corroborative evidence— unusual given the Quakers' meticulous attitude to recording sufferings.

This absence may just possibly be accounted for by the highly speculative idea that White was in (self-imposed?) exile from Quakerism between 1664 and 1684. The undated *Universal Love* describes, in language that is feminized and domestic, a prodigal returning home to the fold. The prodigal is an outcast, and the postscript to another text may indicate that White had been excluded from the movement: *A Visitation of Love* (1684) contains an endorsement of White's good character, which is arguably unnecessary had there been no dispute over her godliness. Neither of these texts was sanctioned by the Quakers' own publications committee, perhaps further indicating White's marginality.

Equally speculative is the theory that White married John Fincham (d. 1711), a rich Norfolk Quaker who died in Suffolk. Quaker records do no more than identify Fincham's wife as a Dorothy White of Thetford, Norfolk, dating the union to 12 March 1681. Apparently a son, Benjamin (d. 1727), became a banker. However if this marriage was Dorothy's, she later wrote under her unmarried name.

Dorothy White was an authoritative writer, often fashioning a role for herself as a spokesperson for the Quaker cause. When she described the fraught events at the end of the Commonwealth and the beginning of the Restoration as acts of God, her writing aimed to fortify the Quakers' resistance to tyrannical worldly powers. Whereas one would expect less radicalism in the 1680s texts, White's later work shows an interest in prophecy that is consistent with the earlier, more enthusiastic, period of Quakerism. Moreover, her texts seem to evidence considerable erudition: she is exceptionally skilful at writing biblically derivative prose (the 'ranterish' source text, the Song of Solomon, being a favourite). White's poetry, though, is less obviously accomplished. Possibly her spirituality was rather mystical; she certainly says little on the more material issues that commonly concerned Quakers, such as tithes.

Given the difficulty over identification, it is impossible to substantiate the belief that White died of a fever in St Giles Street, Cripplegate, London, on 6 February 1686 (Dictionary of Quaker biography). However, no woman under the name either of White or Fincham died in Dorset, Suffolk, or Norfolk at that time. Despite the almost total lack of information relating to White's position within the Quaker movement, and the fact that George Fox makes no reference to her, her own words perhaps best express her sense of community with Friends: 'my soul doth swim within the sea of love' (*An Epistle of Love*, 1661, 8–9).

CATIE GILL

Sources 'Fincham of Norfolk and Suffolk', *Journal of the Friends' Historical Society*, 21 (1924), 11–12 • W. Blyth, *Historical notices and records of the village and parish of Fincham, in the county of Norfolk* (1863) • 'Dictionary of Quaker biography', RS Friends, Lond. [card index] • Quaker register of births, marriages, and burials, RS Friends, Lond. • P. Mack, *Visionary women: ecstatic prophesy in seventeenth-century England*, new edn (Berkeley, CA, 1994) • J. Smith, *A descriptive catalogue of Friends' books*, 2 vols. (1867)
Archives RS Friends, Lond., MSS

White [*née* Jones], **Eirene Lloyd**, **Baroness White** (1909–1999), politician, was born on 7 November 1909 at Anwylfan, St Johns Avenue, Belfast, the only daughter and eldest of the three children of Thomas *Jones (1870–1955), professor of political economy and civil servant, and his wife, Eirene Theodora Lloyd (1875–1935). In 1916 Lloyd George

brought her father into the cabinet secretariat as an assistant secretary. Subsequently, as deputy secretary to the cabinet, he served four prime ministers until he retired in 1930. His daughter was brought up therefore in daily contact with discussion of public policy and with access to his extraordinary range of contacts. Her twenty-first birthday was celebrated at Cliveden with a party arranged by Nancy Astor.

Educated at elementary schools in Barry and Upper Norwood, Eirene Jones entered St Paul's Girls' School in 1920 and subsequently won a scholarship to Somerville College, Oxford, which she entered in 1929 to read philosophy, politics, and economics, gaining a second-class degree in 1932. After graduating she travelled in Europe and spent the year 1932–3 in the United States as an unpaid readers' adviser in the New York Public Library. For the rest of the 1930s she was largely involved in social work with the unemployed, particularly with young women from Wales seeking work in London, and was also engaged in occasional journalism. She worked in the early years of the Second World War for the Women's Voluntary Service in Cardiff and then from 1941 as a Ministry of Labour welfare officer in south Wales.

In 1944 Eirene Jones resigned from the civil service to enter politics, and in the general election of 1945 she stood for Labour in the safe Conservative seat of Flintshire, considerably reducing the sitting member's majority. She was keen to fight again but had to wait for the next general election. Meanwhile she became political correspondent of the *Manchester Evening News*, and with the backing of three cabinet ministers she was the first provincial journalist allowed access to the parliamentary lobby. It was at a Downing Street briefing that she met John Cameron White (1911/12–1968), son of Alfred Thomas White and a fellow member of the lobby; they married on 2 January 1948. They had no children.

In the general election of February 1950 Eirene White won the new East Flintshire seat for Labour with a comfortable majority. In March 1951 she introduced her Matrimonial Causes Bill, which would have permitted divorce after seven years' desertion. It received a second reading, but she withdrew it when the government undertook to set up a royal commission on marriage and divorce. The subsequent legislation reflected many of her ideas. In 1947 she caused a surprise by winning a seat on the Labour Party's national executive, which she retained until 1953. Her desire to be a moderating influence in the bitter struggles between left and right in the early 1950s angered the right-wing union leaders, who largely determined election to the executive. In protest against intolerance she did not seek re-election in 1953, jumping before she was pushed. She returned to the executive in 1958, however, serving until 1970, and was party chairman in 1968. She was chairman of the Fabian Society in 1958–9. A frequent platform speaker at party conferences, she caused no surprise when after the general election of 1959 she became an opposition front-bench speaker on education.

When Labour returned to power in October 1964 Eirene

White was appointed under-secretary of state at the Colonial Office, and two years later she became the first woman to hold the rank of minister of state at the Foreign Office, where she was much involved in the crisis over Rhodesia. Then in 1967 she returned to Wales as minister of state at the Welsh Office. In 1968, after two years of illness, throughout which despite ministerial duties she nursed him, her husband died from lung cancer. It had been a happy marriage.

Eirene White retired from the Commons in 1970 but was nominated by Harold Wilson for a life peerage, as Baroness White of Rhymni. She immediately became an active member of the Lords, serving on the select committee on the European Communities, chairing it (1979–82), and serving as deputy speaker (1979–89). She also held a number of government appointments, serving as chairman of the Land Authority for Wales (1976–80), deputy chairman of the Metrication Board (1972–6), member of the British Waterways Board (1974–80), and member of the royal commission on environmental pollution (1974–81). In addition, she was president of the University of Wales Institute of Science and Technology (1987–8) and of the Council for the Protection of Rural Wales (1973–89).

Blessed with intellectual confidence, an unmistakable efficiency, and an acerbic way with doubters and opponents, Eirene White was among the most industrious of parliamentarians. Tact was not her strong suit, and her manner could be imperious. But behind that façade was a sympathetic and generous person with a love of music, the countryside and history of Wales, and of Coleg Harlech, the adult residential college founded by her father, which she chaired (1973–84). She died on 23 December 1999 at Trebencyn Park Nursing Home, Abergavenny, of hypostatic pneumonia, and was cremated on 30 December at Croesyceiliog crematorium, Cwmbrân.

JOE ENGLAND

Sources T. Jones, *A diary with letters, 1931–1950* (1954) · D. Lewis Jones, *Eirene: a tribute* (2001) · E. L. Ellis, *T. J. A life of Dr Thomas Jones, CH* (1992) · T. N. Shane, 'The Rt. Hon. Tom Williams, MP', *The British labour party: its history, growth, policy, and leaders*, ed. H. Treacy, 3 (1948), 78–9 · *The Times* (24 Dec 1999) · *Daily Telegraph* (24 Dec 1999) · *The Guardian* (27 Dec 1999) · *The Independent* (5 Jan 2000) · Burke, *Peerage* · *WWW* · private information (2004) · personal knowledge (2004) · b. cert. · m. cert. · d. cert.
Archives Ches. & Chester ALSS, corresp. on colonial issues · NL Wales, personal and political papers | NL Wales, Thomas Jones archive · NL Wales, letters to Thomas Iowerth Ellis · PRO, corresp. with colonial secretary, CO 967, 959
Likenesses photograph, 1982, repro. in *Daily Telegraph* · photograph, 1989, repro. in *The Times* · J. Toler, oils, 1992, Coleg Harlech · J. Toler, oils, 1992, U. Wales, Cardiff · N. Howell, double portrait, oils (with Ann Carlton), priv. coll. · photograph, repro. in *The Guardian* · photograph, repro. in *The Independent*
Wealth at death £325,448—net: probate, 4 Aug 2000, CGPLA Eng. & Wales

White, Elizabeth. *See* Hartley, Elizabeth (1750/51–1824).

White, Eric Milner- (1884–1963), dean of York, was born on 23 April 1884 at Langholm, The Avenue, Southampton, the eldest son and first child of Henry Milner-White, barrister and chairman of Edwin Jones & Co. of Southhampton, and his wife, Kathleen Lucy Meeres. From Harrow School, Milner-White went up to King's College, Cambridge, in 1903 to read history, and was awarded first-class honours in both parts of the historical tripos in 1905 and 1907. In 1906 he was the university's Lightfoot scholar. Following a year at Ripon Clergy College in 1907 Milner-White was ordained deacon in 1908 and priest in 1909 at Southwark. He served as curate at St Paul's, Newington, from 1908 to 1909 and as rector of St Mary Magdalene, Woolwich, from 1909 to 1912, when he was appointed chaplain of King's College, Cambridge, and lecturer in history at Corpus Christi College, Cambridge.

During the First World War Milner-White was chaplain to the forces at the western front and in Italy and was awarded the DSO for his service as senior chaplain and combatant officer in the 7th division in 1917. As army chaplain he contributed an essay, 'Worship and services', to *The Church in the Furnace* (1918); this reflected his belief that the ministry of army chaplains provided by the established church did not meet the needs of the troops in the trenches. In 1918 he was appointed fellow and dean of King's College, Cambridge. Milner-White enjoyed the freedom to experiment in order to find liturgical forms suitable for the particular context of King's College. In memory of those who had fallen in the war, and of his own delivery from death when under fire as an army chaplain, Milner-White transformed one of the side chapels of King's College chapel into a memorial chapel. In 1918 he instituted the annual service of nine lessons and carols, building on a form devised by G. H. S. Walpole in 1880 at Truro Cathedral, and this was first broadcast by the BBC in 1928. The service has been transmitted annually by the BBC (with the exception of 1930) ever since, and rapidly became a major national event. By the early 1930s the BBC was also broadcasting the service on overseas programmes. In 1934 Milner-White introduced the processional Advent carol service at King's College chapel. He was a founder member of the Oratory of the Good Shepherd and its superior from 1923 to 1938; from 1936 to 1941 he was a canon of Lincoln Cathedral. In 1937 he published a novel, *The Book of Hugh and Nancy*, originating in his experiences at summer camps with King's College choristers.

In 1941 the archbishop of York, William Temple, installed Milner-White as dean of York. He took a great interest in education and in Anglo-Catholic public schools in particular. In 1945 he became provost of the northern division of the Woodard Corporation. He was a patron of the arts with a strong interest in restoring and preserving the stained glass both in King's College chapel and in York Minster. Milner-White regarded stained glass as one of the chief media of teaching for the church. In 1948 he was made an honorary member of the Worshipful Company of Glaziers with freedom of the City of London. From 1944 to 1959 Milner-White was a member of the advisory council of the Victoria and Albert Museum. He was one of two vice-chairmen of the Advisory Council for the Care of Churches. He owned a large collection of modern ceramics, much of which he donated to Southampton Art Gallery, the City of York Art Gallery, and the Fitzwilliam

Museum in Cambridge. As dean of York, Milner-White established the Borthwick Institute of Historical Research and the York Institute of Architectural Study. He enlarged the minster library and created a library endowment to ensure that it kept up with new publications. From 1948 to 1962 he was on the literary panel of the committee that produced the New English Bible. Milner-White was awarded a Lambeth DD in 1952 and made an honorary doctor of letters by the University of Leeds in 1962. In 1952 he was also awarded a CBE. A founder member of York Civic Trust, Milner-White was also involved with the founding of the University of York.

As dean Milner-White devised a number of services for special occasions in York Minster, such as an improved service for the enthronement of new archbishops and the wedding of the duke of Kent. He was a member of the liturgical commission of the Church of England from 1955 to 1962 and chairman of the commission on the recognition of saints. He published several liturgical source books, building on his experience of creating liturgies for regular and special occasions. These include *Memorials upon Several Occasions: Prayers and Thanksgivings for Use in Public Worship* (1933) and *My God, my Glory: Aspirations, Acts and Prayers on the Desire for God* (1954). The aim of liturgy, he wrote:

> is not to evoke the interest of the passer-by, but to achieve a common prayer before God of which the worshipping Church cannot tire … Thus gradually, inevitably the quality of prayer rises; its range widens; and liturgy continues to make its silent and immense contribution to the fullest worship of God, and thereby to the movement, along the deepest channels of all, to Christian unity. (Milner-White, 760–62)

Eric Milner-White died of cancer on 15 June 1963 at the deanery, York, and was cremated. His ashes were interred in York Minster. He never married.

NATALIE K. WATSON

Sources P. Pare and D. Harris, *Eric Milner-White, 1884–1963: a memorial* (1965) · R. T. Holtby, ed., *Eric Milner Milner-White: a memorial* (1991) · P. Wilkinson, *Eric Milner-White, 1884–1963* (1963) · *WWW* · *The Times* (16 June 1963) · b. cert. · d. cert. · E. Milner-White, 'Modern prayers and their writers', *Liturgy and worship: a companion to the prayer-books of the Anglican communion* (New York, 1932), 760–62
Archives King's AC Cam., corresp. and papers · York Minster Library, York Minster Archives, corresp. and papers; papers | King's AC Cam., letters to Oscar Browning
Likenesses H. A. Freeth, drawing, 1954, King's Cam. · W. Garrod, drawing, King's Cam.

White, Errol Ivor (1901–1985), palaeontologist, was born on 30 June 1901 in Woodberry Down, Middlesex, the younger son of Felix Ernest White, Borough Market merchant, and his second wife, Lilian Emma Daniels, daughter of a wealthy Spitalfields merchant. (There were also a son and a daughter from the first marriage.) He was educated at Highgate School and entered King's College, London, in October 1918 to read chemistry, but transferred to the school of honours geology, obtaining a second-class BSc in 1921.

In November 1922 White was appointed to the staff of the British Museum (Natural History), working in the fossil fish section. The first of his 102 publications, which subsequently covered all major groups of fossil fishes, was published in 1925. In 1929–30 he participated in a museum expedition to Madagascar, where in difficult conditions he made major collections of Triassic fishes and Pleistocene birds. From 1932 his principal interest centred on the taxonomy, ecology, and stratigraphy of the primitive fish faunas from the Devonian system.

In 1933 White married Barbara Gladwyn Christian (*d.* 1969). The marriage, which was childless, was dissolved in 1940 and in 1944 White married Margaret Clare ('Jane'), daughter of Thomas Craven Fawcett of Bolton Abbey, Yorkshire. They had one son. In 1938 White was appointed deputy keeper at the museum, and the following year he was a member of a joint Anglo-Norwegian-Swedish expedition into Spitsbergen, to collect from the Old Red Sandstone deposits. However, the deteriorating international situation curtailed the expedition, and White arrived back in England the day before war was declared.

From 1940 to 1945 White was seconded to the Ministry of Health in Reading, where he was responsible for co-ordinating local government emergency administration in southern England. Returning to the museum in April 1945 he was much occupied with restoring the collections and the building, but was happiest in resuming his research. A small collection of Australian Devonian fishes from New South Wales, sent to the museum just before the war, came to White's attention. The specimens occurred in limestone and the department had just devised a technique for etching such fossils from the surrounding matrix (an advance that was to revolutionize vertebrate palaeontology). White continued research on these samples, together with others from New South Wales and north-western Australia, until long after his retirement in 1966, his work being facilitated by his appointment as a visiting research geologist at Reading University.

During his career White received many honours. He was elected a fellow of the Royal Society in 1956. He was awarded his DSc by the University of London in 1936, having gained a PhD in 1927, and he was made a fellow of King's College, London, in 1958. In 1962 he was awarded the Murchison medal of the Geological Society of London, and in 1970 the gold medal of the Linnean Society. He was made a CBE in 1960.

In 1955 White was appointed keeper of geology (changed to palaeontology in 1956), and he presided over a considerable expansion of his department between 1955 and 1966. Tall, well-built, and well-dressed, he was in his younger days something of a thorn in the side of the establishment, with a reputation for pugnacity. Yet he was a private and rather shy man, and this often manifested itself as an apparent brusqueness and peremptoriness. In later life he continued to be forthright and outspoken, but by then he had matured into the epitome of an English gentleman. He had a literary bent: his papers were immaculately phrased and constructed.

Although much preoccupied with his official duties,

White contributed to the running of learned societies. As secretary he played a major role in revivifying the Ray Society in the years following the war, and he served as president from 1956 to 1959, when he was made vice-president for life. He served on the councils of the Geological Society (1949–53, 1956–60; vice-president, 1957–60), the Zoological Society (1959–63), and the Linnean Society (1956–9); and he was chairman of the Systematics Association (1955–8). He also served as president of the Linnean Society from 1964 to 1967, and he was greatly moved to be the recipient of the society's first Festschrift in 1967. White died in the Wallingford Community Hospital, Wallingford, Oxfordshire, on 11 January 1985.

HAROLD W. BALL, rev.

Sources J. Stubblefield, *Memoirs FRS*, 31 (1985), 633–51 • W. T. Stearn, *The Natural History Museum at South Kensington: a history of the British Museum (Natural History), 1753–1980* (1981)
Archives NHM, photograph albums incl. NHM, London Zoo, expedition to Madagascar
Likenesses photograph, repro. in Stubblefield, *Memoirs FRS*, 634
Wealth at death under £40,000: probate, 18 April 1985, *CGPLA Eng. & Wales*

White, Florence Louisa (1863–1940), writer on cookery, was born on 20 June 1863 at York Terrace, Peckham, London, the fifth and youngest child of Richard White, a lace buyer for a firm in the City of London, and his second wife, Harriet Jane Thirkell (d. 1869). Richard White came originally from the seaside hamlet of Worthing, Sussex, where his maternal grandfather, and later his father, had been innkeepers in the 1790s and 1830s. Florence remembered, from the 1860s, a regular Sunday dinner of beef spit-roasted in front of the kitchen fire, with the gravy absorbed by a Sussex 'bolster' suet pudding. The Thirkells came from near Cranbrook in the weald of Kent.

In her autobiography, *A Fire in the Kitchen* (1938), Florence recorded how her happy early childhood ended abruptly with her mother's death when she was six. A few months later Florence lost the sight of one eye in an accident with a spinning-top. This resulted in temporary blindness followed by a lifetime's frail health, with persistent neuralgic headaches and a chronically weak heart. Although she hoped during much of her girlhood to go to Girton College, Cambridge, she was removed from school in 1878, when her father's business suffered in the depression. Her job was to shop economically for food (since the family was by then poor), to wait on her uncongenial stepmother, and to teach the three small children of her father's third marriage. During the next two years, Florence and her elder sister expanded this teaching arrangement into a small, fee-paying school. At eighteen, however, she was sent to Fareham, Hampshire, to nurse her father's two elderly sisters, formerly proprietors of the Lion Hotel and Assembly Rooms. From them, as she later described in her autobiography, she learned that 'good epicurean country-house cookery which had been handed down the family from mother to daughter since the days of Queen Elizabeth' (White, *Fire*, 338). Her return to Fareham towards the end of her life, when she opened a cookery school there, was directly inspired by her memories of

learning traditional English cooking techniques, an accomplishment of which she never ceased to be proud.

Between 1884 and 1922, Florence reckoned, she held twenty-eight different types of job, including 'high-school mistress, governess in a private family, journalist, waitress, shopkeeper … matron, club organizer, settlement worker, visiting companion to a professor, newspaper reporter, fashion editor, sculptor's model, [domestic servants'] registry-office keeper, and matron of a governess's home' (White, *Fire*, 258). She was invariably short of money and ready to undertake almost any new job, although by the age of thirty she found herself too frail to continue either as a schoolteacher or as a governess. Her first book, *Easy Dressmaking*, which she persuaded the Singer Sewing Machine Company to publish in 1891, sold 110,000 copies in eight years. Several decades passed, however, before she brought out her next book, *Good Things in England* (1932), a collection of traditional, regional recipes which represented her most abiding, lifelong interest, and its successor *Flowers as Food* (1934).

By the outbreak of the First World War, Florence had been employed in women's journalism in London and Edinburgh; social work in Hoxton; teaching English to private pupils in Paris; running a Girls' Friendly Society lodge in the Scottish countryside; and, in 1899, accompanying two children to India and Burma, where her elder brother had made his career. Despite an independent, almost liberated, lifestyle, she was most fulfilled (she later declared) when 'mothering' somebody, and felt confirmed in her increasingly spiritualized belief that woman's natural place was at the kitchen stove when she entered domestic service in her early fifties. During and after the First World War she looked after a succession of Roman Catholic priests, and in 1921–2 she was cook–housekeeper in a women students' hall of residence in Kensington.

Only in her sixties, living in frugal semi-retirement in a Chelsea basement room, supported by freelance journalism and help from her family, did Florence begin research into the history of her lifelong passion, good, traditional English food. In 1928 she founded the English Folk Cookery Association, and in 1932, as well as producing *Good Things in England*, she edited the first of the association's *Good Food Registers*, which contained information, mainly passed on by contributors who had responded to her advertisements in the press, about towns, villages, hotels, restaurants, or even humble guest houses in which good English cooking or foodstuffs could be found.

Although sketchy by the standard of later cookery writing, these works have a certain pioneering charm, intensified by Florence's determination to rescue true English cooking from the fashionable trend towards everything French. Further editions appeared in 1935 and 1936, the latter entitled *Where Shall We Eat or Put Up?* In a note in this, entitled 'What is real English cookery?', Florence wrote evocatively of

a roast pheasant with Celery Sauce and English Salad Sauce; a boiled pheasant with celery sauce. The correct way of making a Lancashire Hot Pot with oysters and serving it with home-made pickled red cabbage. The stuffing of grouse with red whortleberries. The jugging of hare and serving with redcurrant jelly. The making and frying of sausages. The frying of fish, in which our girls and women who live on the coast excel.   (White, *Where Shall We Eat*, 173)

In 1936, at Fareham, Florence opened her domestic training school or House of Studies, which was intended to be a place where women of all ages and social classes could mingle. English cooking, she announced triumphantly in her autobiography in 1938, was now fashionable and popular, and no longer to be despised as dull or unimaginative. By that time, however, she was almost blind and crippled by various illnesses. She died at 52 Wickham Road, Fareham, Hampshire, on 12 March 1940.

BRIGID ALLEN

Sources F. White, *A fire in the kitchen: the autobiography of a cook* (1938) · F. White, *Where shall we eat or put up?* (1936) · F. White, *Good things in England* (1932) · *CGPLA Eng. & Wales* (1940)
Wealth at death £96 15s. 2d.: probate, 24 Aug 1940, *CGPLA Eng. & Wales*

White, Francis (1563/4–1638), bishop of Ely, was born at Eaton Socon, Bedfordshire, the son of Peter White, who was first the curate and then vicar there. Nothing is known about his mother, but he had four brothers, who all became clergymen, including John *White (1570–1615). He attended the grammar school at St Neots, Huntingdonshire, and in 1579, at the age of fifteen, was admitted a pensioner at Gonville and Caius College, Cambridge, where he graduated BA in 1583 and proceeded MA in 1586. He was ordained to the priesthood by the bishop of London on 17 May 1588. Early in his career White was rector of Broughton-Astley, Leicestershire, and it may have been during this period that he married; his wife's name is unknown. They had several daughters and at least one son, who may have been the Francis White baptized at Barrow upon Soar, Leicestershire, on 18 November 1612.

White subsequently became a lecturer at St Paul's, London, and from about 1617, thanks to his association with his patron, Richard Neile, bishop of Durham, and his growing reputation as an anti-Catholic polemicist, he began to rise rapidly in the church. He acknowledged Neile's patronage in *The Orthodoxe Faith and Way to the True Church*, essentially a defence of his brother John in the latter's controversy with the Catholic controversialist, and former president of Douai, Thomas Worthington. In May 1622, shortly after he was appointed dean of Carlisle, White was called upon by George Villiers, marquess of Buckingham, to help persuade the duke's mother, Mary, countess of Buckingham, against converting to Catholicism. The countess had been under the influence of John Percy, better known as Fisher the Jesuit, who was secretly functioning as her chaplain at the court. White was asked to take the protestant side on the first day of three private debates with Percy organized by the marquess and King James and held in the presence of the Villiers family; the king and William Laud, bishop of St David's, took that role on the second and third days. When, against the king's wishes, Percy spread details of the debates in his *An Answere to a Pamphlet* (1623), White responded by publishing a formal attack on the Jesuit, entitled *A Replie to Jesuit*

Francis White (1563/4–1638), by Thomas Cockson, 1624

Fishers Answere (1624). In the meantime he had received his reward: on 27 September 1622 he was instituted rector of St Peter Cornhill, London.

White's publications surrounding the Percy conflict marked him as a principal spokesman for the growing group of so-called Arminians, whose views were often linked with the Dutch remonstrance theology of Jacobus Arminius (1560–1609). Following the accession of Charles I many of these clerics rose to power in association with Neile, Villiers, who had become duke of Buckingham, and the future archbishop of Canterbury, William Laud. They all upheld the Roman church as a true, though errant, institution, questioned Calvinist opinions about predestination and the pope as the biblically predicted Anti-Christ, and gave greater place to the sacraments and ceremonies than to preaching in the worship service. White was usually one of the least contentious of this group, and his focus tended to be on separating essential matters of theology from those things he considered indifferent. He was most concerned to promote unity and conformity to the national church, and often railed against theological discord, claiming that when it rises, it 'overspreadeth the greene pastures of sacred truth'. Nevertheless White demonstrated his commitment to the 'Laudian–Arminian' party when early in 1625 he helped license for publication

Richard Montague's *Appello Caesarem*, which was openly anti-Calvinist and launched the biggest theological controversy of the late Jacobean period. In endorsing it, White went even further, 'associating Calvin with the most extreme exponents of absolute reprobation' (Milton, 428), a significant move away from his earlier, more moderate, stance, which required some mental gymnastics. With John Cosin, chaplain to Bishop Neile, White formally defended Montague's orthodoxy at the York House conference of February 1626. Here his critical stance on the canons issued by the Synod of Dort and his apparent shift from previously expressed positions earned him a sometimes uncomfortable ride.

White was rewarded, however, with further appointments in the church. Having become senior dean of Sion College, London, in 1625, he was consecrated bishop of Carlisle at Durham House on 3 December 1626 by bishops Neile, John Buckeridge, Theophilus Field, and William Murry. Cosin preached the consecration sermon to a crowd of over 500 people, including Buckingham's sister. For his episcopal visitation of 1627 White used articles previously prepared by Bishop John Overall for Norwich, 'which elevated the sacramental ministry of the priesthood, and enquired minutely into breaches of ceremony by the clergy and the reverence displayed by the laity during divine service' (Fincham, *Visitation Articles*, 1.xx). Following his election as bishop of Norwich in January 1629 he used a similar set for a visitation in 1631. Translated to Ely on 15 November that year, he did not, like bishops in neighbouring dioceses, enforce the railed altar, but his visitation of 1635 sought to establish uniformity of practice in catechizing and to curtail over-long sermons which resulted in the omission of parts of the liturgy. After Charles I reissued the controversial Book of Sports in 1633 White was called upon to defend the crown on the issue of sabbatarianism and responded with *A Treatise of the Sabbath Day* (1635), dedicated to the new archbishop, William Laud.

White died at Ely House, Holborn, in February 1638 and was buried in St Paul's Cathedral. By his more Calvinist-inclined detractors White was considered someone who paid for his positions by renouncing orthodoxy. A note in Archbishop James Ussher's correspondence indicates that White 'sold his orthodoxe bookes and bought Jesuits' (*DNB*). But up to his death White remained committed to a moderate form of protestantism rooted in a distaste for conflict and a concern to promote church unity by an emphasis on church ceremony and the physical 'beauty of holiness'. TIMOTHY WADKINS

Sources Venn, *Alum. Cant.* • P. Milward, *Religious controversies of the Jacobean age* (1978) • T. H. Wadkins, 'Theological polemic and religious culture in early Stuart England', PhD diss., Graduate Theological Union, 1988 • T. Wadkins, 'The Percy–"Fisher" controversies and the ecclesiastical politics of Jacobean anti-Catholicism, 1422–1625', *Church History*, 57 (1988), 153–69 • A. Milton, *Catholic and Reformed: the Roman and protestant churches in English protestant thought, 1600–1640* (1995) • K. Fincham, ed., *The early Stuart church, 1603–1642* (1993) • G. Hennessy, *Novum repertorium ecclesiasticum parochiale Londinense, or, London diocesan clergy succession from the earliest time to the year 1898* (1898) • K. Fincham, ed., *Visitation articles and injunctions of the early Stuart church*, 2 vols. (1994–8) • N. Tyacke, *Anti-Calvinists: the rise of English Arminianism, c.1590–1640* (1987) • J. Davies, *The Caroline captivity of the church: Charles I and the remoulding of Anglicanism, 1625–1641* (1992) • Ely diocesan records, CUL, B/2/47a, fol. 14v

Likenesses T. Cockson, line engraving, 1624, BM, NPG, V&A; repro. in F. White, *Reply to Jesuit Fishers answere* (1624) [see illus.] • G. Mountin, line engraving, BM, NPG • portrait, repro. in J. Percy, *The answere unto the nine points*, 379 (1626)

White, Francis (d. 1657), parliamentarian army officer, is of uncertain origins. He can first certainly be identified when, as a captain in Sir Thomas Fairfax's regiment of foot, he presented the grievances of his regiment at Saffron Walden on 15 May 1647 to the parliamentary commissioners who were overseeing the disbandment of the New Model Army. He continued to act as representative of his regiment, and was cited by his superiors as an agitator who 'issues out orders as if he were the lieutenant colonel' (Firth and Davies, 1.324). In the reorganization of the regiment in June which followed the casting out of officers who would not side with the men against their disbandment, White was promoted major.

White represented his regiment on a committee of the council of the army, where his outspokenness continued unabated. He opposed the proposal to give control of the army to parliament for ten years, contending that the dominant presbyterian faction, with their Scots allies, intended to keep the people in 'servill bondage' (White, *Copy*, 3). In the condition the kingdom now found itself, he affirmed, there was 'no visible authority … but the power and force of the Sword' (*Two Declarations*, 6). He was expelled from the council on 9 September, conceding that his words had given 'distast' (White, *Copy*, 1). He defended his conduct in an open letter to Fairfax dated 23 September, including his opposition to giving a tribunician vote to Fairfax in the army's proposed settlement, *The Heads of the Proposals*, and declared that his only interest was in the restoration to the kingdom of its ancient liberties as they had existed before the Norman conquest.

These sentiments aligned White with the Levellers, and he was among the agitators who participated with them in the Putney debates in October 1647. He continued to affirm that the army was the only legitimate power in the realm, and to warn Fairfax of the folly of attempting to deal with the king. According to a royalist newswriter, at a rendezvous of Fairfax's regiment of foot on 11 November he tried to persuade the men that England should now abandon monarchy: unavailingly, as the men threw their hats in the air, shouting 'A king! A king!' and 'This king! This king!' Nevertheless White was readmitted to the army council's deliberations on 21 December in a general attempt at reconciliation.

White spoke out against treating with the king once more in an open letter to Oliver Cromwell in April 1648, and urged the adoption of the Levellers' *Agreement of the People*. In the summer he evidently served with his regiment in the campaign in the north which culminated in the battle of Preston. He joined the Leveller petition of 11

September 1648, prompting Fairfax to suspend his commission temporarily, and was one of six 'gentleman independent' representatives at the meetings at the Nag's Head tavern with the Levellers in November 1648, at which he supported the army's right to depose Charles I and return power to the people, 'its originall fountain next under God'. White opposed the execution of the king, however, arguing that no court could judge him capitally. He contended that Charles could not be tried legally under any monarchical authority, and that until a new popular authority was constituted as set forth by the *Agreement of the People*, the army should 'use the sword with as much tenderness as may be to preserve the lives of men, and especially the life of the King' (White, *Copies*, 4). He added that the death of Charles I would not of itself avail the people, 'For it is not so much the person that can hurt us, as the power that is made up in the kingly office by this corrupt constitution' (ibid.).

The Levellers praised White in *The Second Part of Englands New-Chains Discovered* (1649) and complained about his failure to secure promotion. His connection with them made him a logical intermediary in the authorities' response to the Leveller-inspired mutiny of May 1649. Fairfax sent him to negotiate with the rebellious cavalry regiments of Adrian Scrope and Henry Ireton. White pleaded with the rebels not to divide the army and, after hearing their grievances and reformulating their demands for a general council, he led them unwittingly into a trap at Burford, Oxfordshire, where they were set upon by 2000 dragoons. As White related the episode he rushed into the night in his slippers to find Fairfax and avert bloodshed. The Levellers accused him of betraying the troops in *The Levellers (Falsly so called) Vindicated*. White replied by asserting his good faith in *A True Relation of the Proceedings in the Businesse of Burford* (17 September), declaring that his 'heart was overwhelmed with sorrow and ready to break' at the bloody denouement (White, *True Relation*, 8).

When Fairfax declined to take part in the invasion of Scotland in 1650 command of his regiment passed to Oliver Cromwell. At Dunbar in September White won Cromwell's praise for his courage, as the regiment led by him and by its lieutenant-colonel, William Goffe, 'at the push of pike, did repel the stoutest regiment the enemy had there' (Firth and Davies, 1.330). Cromwell chose White to carry the news of the victory and the captured enemy colours to parliament, for which he was awarded £300 and promoted lieutenant-colonel. In December 1650 he was a commissioner to treat for the surrender of Edinburgh Castle, and in January 1651 he was in joint command of the unsuccessful attempt to capture Burntisland, Fife, with John Mason. On 12 December 1653 White disbursed the remnants of Barebone's Parliament with Goffe. In 1656 he became MP for Tewkesbury in the first protectorate parliament, where he advocated the imposition of the death penalty on the Quaker James Nayler for his perceived blasphemy. In October 1657 White was sent to Flanders as governor of Mardyke Fort. He drowned in a shipwreck in the North Sea when returning to England in December. He was survived by his wife, Mary, and by three daughters, all minors. In April 1658 the council of state ordered the payment of £600 in trust for the three daughters to be disbursed upon their marriage or their reaching their majority; meanwhile their mother was to receive £36 per annum for their upkeep. ROBERT ZALLER

Sources *The writings and speeches of Oliver Cromwell*, ed. W. C. Abbott and C. D. Crane, 4 vols. (1937–47) · Thurloe, *State papers* · H. N. Brailsford, *The Levellers and the English revolution*, ed. C. Hill (1961) · *The Clarke papers*, ed. C. H. Firth, 4 vols., CS, new ser., 49, 54, 61–2 (1891–1901) · C. H. Firth and G. Davies, *The regimental history of Cromwell's army*, 2 vols. (1940) · F. White, *The copy of a letter sent to … Sir Thomas Fairfax* [11 Nov 1647, Thomason tract, E 413/17] · F. White, *The copies of severall letters* (1649) [20 March 1648/49, Thomason tract, E 548/6] · F. White, *A true relation of the proceedings in the businesse of Burford* (1649) [17 Sept 1649, Thomason tract, E 574/26] · R. Gardiner, *History of the Commonwealth and protectorate*, rev. edn, 4 vols. (1893) · A. Woolrych, *Soldiers and statesmen: the general council of the army and its debates, 1647–1648* (1987) · *Diary of Thomas Burton*, ed. J. T. Rutt, 4 vols. (1828), vol. 1 · *CSP dom.*, 1657–8 · *Two declarations from … Sir Thomas Fairfax, and the general councell of his army* [Thomason tract, E 407/1, 14 Sept 1647]

White, Francis (*d.* 1711), chocolate-house keeper, was an Italian immigrant; in his will he left legacies to his sister and her husband, Angela Maria and Tomaso Casanova, and to his aunt Nicoletta Tomasi, all of Genoa. His name, it has been presumed, may well have been a straight translation from the Italian: Francesco Bianco or Bianchi, perhaps. It has not been possible to trace White in the records of naturalization and denization.

White was the original proprietor of White's Chocolate House, which he set up in a house on the east side of St James's Street, Westminster. In 1697 White moved premises to a higher-rental building on the west side of St James's Street, later no. 69, where it remained until a fire destroyed the premises in 1733. In 1702 White leased an adjoining house to the north of his chocolate house, and soon after he employed the services of John Arthur to assist and later manage the business.

From its inception, White's became associated with both whig politics and élite fashionability. The chocolate house cultivated an air of greater distinction than did the much more demotic coffee houses. The charge for entrance at White's was 6d., while the charge at most coffee houses was only 1d. White's catered to the social rounds of London's male leisured class, although the discourse which took place there was not entirely devoted to the light-hearted matters of 'gallantry and pleasure' which Richard Steele thought most characteristic of the place and which William Congreve epitomized in the first act of *The Way of the World* (1700; *Tatler*, 1, 12 April 1709, Bond, 1.16). It was at White's Chocolate House that James Brydges, the future duke of Chandos and paymaster-general of the army, engaged in debates concerning the popular origins of government; he also discussed more topical matters, such as, in the 1690s, the prospects for a peace and the question of the Spanish succession. Brydges polished his virtuoso credentials there by discussing the contents of the earl of Sunderland's library with Lord Derwentwater and the son of John Lake, the nonjuring bishop of Chichester (Brydges's journal).

But it was gambling and gaming for which White's was

both famous and notorious. Neither the whiggish flavour of its company nor its fashionability endeared White's to tory-inclined critics such as Robert Harley, earl of Oxford, who, according to Jonathan Swift, 'never passed by White's Chocolate-House (the common rendez-vous of infamous sharpers, and noble cullies) without bestowing a curse upon that famous academy, as the bane of half the English nobility' (*Prose Writings of Jonathan Swift*, 12.50). Swift himself occasionally visited White's, although he complained of finding there 'drunken whiggish lords like … Lord Santry who come into the chocolate house and rail aloud at the Tories, and have challenges sent them, and the next morning come and beg pardon' (Swift, *Journal to Stella*, 485).

At the time that he made his will in 1708, in which he left legacies worth £2500, White had a wife, Elizabeth (*d.* 1729?), and four children, all minors. White died in February 1711 and was buried in St James's, Piccadilly. His widow continued to run the chocolate house after her husband's death, and began to promote the sales of tickets to operas, masquerades, and ridottos. She remarried, her next husband being Major George Skene (or Skreen) of Chelsea, who died in 1724; she probably died in 1729. Soon thereafter, the property passed out of the hands of the White family and the business was taken over by White's long-time servant, John Arthur, and his son, Robert (Lillywhite, 640–41). By this point, the society at White's had grown even more exclusive and was dominated by its famous club, the first list of rules and members for which date from 1736, making it the West End club with the longest continuous history. In 1755 Robert Arthur purchased a freehold for the great house in St James's Street, to which White's Club was relocated, and the chocolate house was finally closed.   BRIAN COWAN

Sources J. Ashton, *Social life in the reign of Queen Anne*, 2 vols. (1882), 1.221 • [W. B. Boulton], *The history of White's*, 2 vols. (1892) • P. Colson, *White's, 1693–1950* (1951) • J. Brydges, London journal, 2 vols., 1697–1702, Hunt. L., Stowe MS 26 • B. Lillywhite, *London coffee houses* (1963) • *DNB* • J. Swift, *Journal to Stella*, ed. H. Williams, 2 vols. (1948) • *The prose writings of Jonathan Swift*, ed. H. Davis and others, 14 vols. (1939–68) • D. F. Bond, ed., *The Tatler*, 3 vols. (1987) • J. Timbs, *Clubs and club life in London: with anecdotes of its famous coffee houses, hostelries, and taverns, from the seventeenth century to the present time*, new edn (1908), 92–103 • H. B. Wheatley and P. Cunningham, *London past and present*, 3 vols. (1891), vol. 3, pp. 491–6 • *The parish of St James, Westminster*, 1/2, Survey of London, 30 (1960), 463–4
Archives Hunt. L.

White, Francis Buchanan White (1842–1894), botanist and entomologist, was born at Perth on 20 March 1842, the eldest son of Francis Isaiah White, a well-known Perth physician active in the botanical societies of Edinburgh and London, and his wife, Lilias Anne Bartlet Buchanan. Francis Buchanan White (as he was known) was educated in Perth, first at the school attached to St Ninian's episcopal cathedral and later by a private tutor. He is said to have attended St Ninian's Cathedral as his church throughout his life, despite being a 'thorough-going evolutionist' believing 'that, after all, evolution is but creation under a new name' (Coates).

In 1860 White entered the University of Edinburgh, whence he graduated MD in 1864, his thesis on the relations, analogies, and similitudes of insects and plants giving an indication of his early interest in botany. During his residence as a student in Edinburgh he met Margaret Juliet Corrie, daughter of Thomas Corrie (*d.* 1859), an Edinburgh banker. By the time of her marriage to White on 2 February 1866, both of Margaret's parents were dead, and she had received a substantial legacy. As a result, the couple spent nearly a year in Europe on their honeymoon, before returning to settle in Perth in December 1866. Free from the constraints of professional work, and possessed of 'a considerable competency' (Carrington), Buchanan White proceeded to devote his time entirely to the study of natural science. Although based at their home in Perth (Annat Lodge, purchased for the couple by White's father), almost every year the Whites spent several months in some other part of Scotland, the natural history of which White wished to study.

Throughout his life White was devoted to the study of the Lepidoptera, his contributions to the *Entomologist's Weekly Intelligencer* beginning as early as 1857. From 1869 onwards he also made a special study of the Hemiptera, acquiring specimens from all parts of the world. In botany he devoted much attention to local distribution, and to 'critical' groups, such as the willows; it was his desire for extreme accuracy which delayed the publication of his *Flora of Perthshire* until after his death.

In 1867 White was the moving spirit in founding the Perthshire Society of Natural Science, of which he was the first president, from 1867 to 1872; until his death in 1894 White was always one of the society's officers—president, secretary, or editor. His communications to the society, many of which appeared in its *Proceedings and Transactions*, number over a hundred, and the society's museum was developed along the lines expounded in his presidential addresses. In 1871 he induced the society to establish the *Scottish Naturalist*, a journal which soon achieved an independent existence. White himself edited it from 1871 until 1882.

White, who had great powers of endurance as a mountaineer and was very fond of alpine plants, also initiated the Perthshire Mountain Club as an offshoot from the Society of Natural Science, and in 1874 he was one of the founders of the Cryptogamic Society of Scotland, of which he acted as secretary. He was one of the first to recognize the need for co-operation among local natural history societies, and, acting on this conviction, he brought about the East of Scotland Union of Naturalists' Societies, over which he presided at its first meeting, which was held at Dundee in 1884. One of White's most distinguished achievements was his pioneer description in 1872 of the natural divisions of Scotland, the 'faunal areas', later taken up by Harvie-Brown in his well-known series of Scottish Vertebrate Faunas (1887–1906) and which have remained the basis for all really critical work on Scottish natural history ever since.

White's wider writings included articles on cockroaches, earwigs, ants, bees, locusts, and grasshoppers in *Science for All* (vols. 3–5), the 'Report on pelagic Hemiptera' collected by HMS *Challenger* (*Reports* of the *Challenger* expedition, vol. 7, 1883) and a revision of the British willows in the *Journal of the Linnean Society* for 1890. His separate publications were *Fauna Perthensis-Lepidoptera* (1871), a small quarto monograph intended as the first of a series, but not continued, and *The Flora of Perthshire* (1898), edited after his death by his friend Professor Trail. White joined the Entomological Society of London in 1868 and the Linnean Society in 1873, and was a member of several other scientific societies both at home and abroad.

White died at Annat Lodge on 3 December 1894, survived by his wife, two sons and seven daughters. His various obituaries used words such as amiable, genial, entertaining, patient, gentle, courteous, modest, and retiring, but according to at least one writer he was capable of 'bitter sarcasm' when roused. 'His stalwart figure in his accustomed grey kilt, was one of great power and endurance, little short of perfect physical training enabling one to keep pace with him in those long mountain rambles' (Carrington). In all he was very much an outdoor man, who attended and led over a hundred field outings organized by the Perthshire Society; he was also skip of Scone and Perth Curling Club. He was buried in Wellshill cemetery, Perth. A bronze mural memorial to him was erected in Perth Museum and a stained-glass window in his honour was installed in St Ninian's Cathedral. In 1994, the centenary of his death, a two-day international conference was held in Perth Museum to commemorate the achievements of one of Scotland's foremost pioneer naturalists. White's greatest memorial, however, lies in his establishment of the national journal, the much-loved and highly respected *Scottish Naturalist*, which is still thriving some 130 years later.   J. A. GIBSON

Sources J. W. H. Trail, *Annals of Scottish Natural History* (1895), 73–91 · H. Coates, *Transactions and Proceedings of the Perthshire Society of Natural Science*, 2 (1895), xlv–xlvii, lv–lxvi · M. A. Taylor, 'Francis Buchanan White, 1842–1894, and Scottish botany', *Scottish Naturalist*, 98 (1986), 157–73 · J. W. H. Trail, ed., 'The flora of Perthshire' by *Francis Buchanan W. White* (1898) · J. T. Carrington, *Science Gossip*, new ser., 1 (1894), 241–2 · *DNB*
Archives NHM, notebooks
Wealth at death £7656 6s. 9d.: Scottish probate sealed in London, 23 Feb 1895, *CGPLA Eng. & Wales*

White, George (*fl. c.*1665–1702). *See under* White, Samuel (*c.*1650–1689).

White, George (*c.*1684–1732). *See under* White, Robert (1645–1703).

White, Sir George (1840–1912), shoe manufacturer and politician, was born on 13 March 1840 at Bourne in Lincolnshire, the son of Thomas White, bootmaker, and his wife, Mary. Educated at Bourne grammar school, at the age of sixteen he moved to Norwich as a boot manufacturer's clerk; he continued his education at night-school, and soon became involved in the concerns that were to dominate his adult life—St Mary's Baptist Chapel, the Liberal Party, education, and temperance. In 1863 he married Ann

(1836–1898), daughter of Henry Ransome of Norwich. The couple had one son and seven daughters.

In 1875, following ten years managing the boot department, White became a partner in the firm, then known as Howlett and White. Plant and production expanded rapidly, and by 1909 the company could boast Britain's largest shoe factory under one roof, employing 1200 workers to produce 150,000–200,000 pairs mostly of women's and children's shoes—many for export to the British empire, South Africa, and western Europe. In 1899 the firm converted to a limited liability company, with White as chairman and joint managing director, and though he did relinquish some direct control after entering parliament he continued to hold both positions until just before his death. White's management was vital to the growth of the firm and the Norwich industry as a whole. A modernizer, he successfully led the employers in a number of lengthy disputes which resulted in the introduction of new technology and work practices and helped eradicate outworking for business and moral reasons.

Baptized in 1857, White was a deacon of St Mary's from 1883 to 1912, president of the Sunday School Union in 1905, and in 1903 he became only the third layman to hold the presidency of the Baptist Union. His commitment to temperance linked his business, religious, and political beliefs. He saw drink as the root of many of society's problems, and temperance as an opportunity to create a more efficient workforce, increase the spending power of the working class, get more people into church, and attack the power and privilege of the Conservative Party. President of the Baptist Total Abstinence Society from 1903 to 1912 and vice-president of the United Kingdom Alliance, he was a passionate opponent of state ownership, and advocate of local option combined with the provision of alternative leisure pursuits.

In 1900, following a successful civic career, White was elected MP for North-West Norfolk, which he represented until 1912. A radical Liberal who supported the promotion of working-class representation, municipal socialism, and the welfare provisions of the Asquith government, he was brought to national prominence through his opposition to the 1902 Education Act. Chairman of Norwich's education authority for twenty-five years and an advocate of secondary and technical education, he firmly believed that state education should be Christian but nondenominational. This led him to encourage respectable nonconformists into passive resistance and to use his position as president of the Baptist Union to mobilize dissenters against the government. White was knighted in 1907 and elected chairman of the nonconformist committee at Westminster in 1908. However, free church hopes that the man the *British Weekly* called the leader of nonconformity might become education minister were unfulfilled.

It was said of White that he saw every issue through the windows of a Baptist meeting-house, yet it is apparent that his beliefs were determined as much by modernity as morality. Temperance, education, industrial relations, and municipalization were all to be utilized to modernize industry, the labour force, and the urban environment. Although his 1903 presidential address to the Baptist Union was a reaffirmation of traditional dissenting Liberalism, it was not the sum total of his political ideology, which in fact embraced many of the collectivist elements of the new Liberalism and placed him nearer Lloyd George than Gladstone.

White published a number of pamphlets and magazine articles, many of which were based on his speeches. A strong, imposing figure, he remained a fit and tireless worker into his seventies; although he took up golf on entering parliament, he held that a change of work was as good as leisure. In November 1911 he was diagnosed as having lung cancer, and died at his home, The Grange, Unthank's Road, Eaton, Norwich, on 11 May 1912. Three thousand people attended his interment at the Rosary cemetery on 15 May. BARRY M. DOYLE

Sources *Eastern Daily Press* (13 May 1912) • *Eastern Daily Press* (16 May 1912) • *The Times* (13 May 1912) • *The Times* (16 May 1912) • *British Weekly* (16 May 1912) • 'The funeral of Sir George White', *Eastern Daily Press* (16 May 1912) • The Listener, 'Church and fireside: Sir George White MP', *British Weekly* (14 Nov 1907) • A. B. Cooper, 'Sir George White of Norwich', *The Sunday at Home* (May 1909), 481–8 • D. Jones, '"Business tact and thoroughness": a history of the Norvic Shoe Company', *Journal of the Norfolk Industrial Archaeology Society*, 4/1 (1986), 18–26 • F. W. Wheldon, *A Norvic century and the men who made it, 1846–1946* (1946) • B. M. Doyle, 'Middle class realignment and party politics in Norwich, 1900–1932', PhD diss., University of East Anglia, 1990 • C. B. Jewson, *The Baptists in Norfolk* (1957) • D. W. Bebbington, *The nonconformist conscience: chapel and politics, 1870–1914* (1982) • W. L. Sparkes, *The story of shoemaking in Norwich* (1948) • G. White, *The nonconformist conscience in its relation to our national life* (1903) [presidential address to the Baptist Union] • R. Higham and P. Masefield, 'White, Sir George', *DBB*

Archives Norfolk RO, Howlett & White business records
Likenesses photographs, English Counties Newspapers, Rouen Road, Norwich
Wealth at death £35,340 0s. 7d.: resworn probate, 18 June 1912, *CGPLA Eng. & Wales*

White, Sir George, first baronet (1854–1916), businessman and stockbroker, was born on 28 March 1854 at Kingsdown, Bristol, the second son of Henry White, a painter and decorator, and his wife, Eliza, *née* Tippetts, a domestic servant before her marriage. After attending St Michael's Boys' School in Bristol, he joined a legal firm in the city, Stanley and Wasborough, in 1869, as a junior clerk. He soon impressed by his dedication and grasp of detail. Following the passage of the 1870 Tramways Act, he played a major part in the promotion of the Bristol Tramways Company (1874) by Stanley and Wasborough on behalf of a group of local businessmen. He married Caroline Rosena Thomas (*d.* 1915) in 1876; they had two children.

In 1875 White left the law, and was appointed secretary of the Bristol Tramway Company, later serving as managing director and chairman. During his career, he was also involved in running tramway companies in Bath, Dublin, Middlesbrough, Reading, and York. In west London, White's London United Tramways, established in 1894, created a major suburban network along the main roads radiating from its Hammersmith terminus. In the

Sir George White, first baronet (1854–1916), by unknown photographer

later 1890s he was a pioneer of electric tramways, demonstrating that electrification, though very capital intensive, offered improved services for the general public and attractive returns for investors. His creation of major transport systems in Bristol and west London was among his greatest achievements. White's career was not confined to tramways, but encompassed all forms of mechanized transport. Under his leadership, the Bristol Tramways and Carriage Company began operating motor buses and taxis, entering vehicle production in 1908. By 1914 it was among the biggest employers in Bristol, with a workforce of over 2000.

White managed many of his interests through his stockbroking firm, George White & Co. (established in 1875). His business was strongly regional in nature and very profitable. As well as dealing on behalf of clients, he often acquired an interest in ailing companies that were ripe for restructuring, or could profitably be sold to rivals. His many contacts with leading Bristol businessmen ensured that he had no difficulty raising capital for his ventures. Bristol companies in which he had a major interest included the Great Western Steamship Company, the Bristol Port and Channel Dock Company (which had built Avonmouth docks), and the Bristol and North Somerset Railway. In 1882–3 he played a leading role in the abortive scheme to provide Bristol with an alternative to the Great Western Railway's link with London. Like many Bristolians, he had strong ties with south Wales. He was chairman of the Main Colliery Company, and chaired the shareholders' committee of the Taff Vale Railway, in which he had a large shareholding. In 1891, when the Taff Vale's profits slumped, he removed the entire board of directors, replacing them with his own nominees.

The crowning achievement of White's career was the establishment of the British and Colonial Aeroplane Company in 1910, and also of its sales arm, the Bristol Aeroplane Co. Ltd. The firm subsequently became better known by the latter name. Unlike other pioneers of aviation, who were engaged in developing and testing experimental models, or producing a few planes for rich private customers, White set out from the first to produce aircraft on a commercial scale. The Bristol Boxkite firmly established British and Colonial as a major manufacturer. White was well aware of the importance of publicity, participating in the competitions sponsored by Northcliffe's *Daily Mail* and putting on flying demonstrations for overseas governments and the general public. Flying schools were set up to create a market, and by 1914 nearly half Britain's pilots had been trained on Bristol aircraft. The company went on to play a major role in the war effort. The Bristol Fighter, possibly the best allied aircraft of the First World War, went into production shortly before White's death, and more than 3500 were eventually produced.

Handsome and impeccably dressed, and of an engaging personality, White was widely respected for his business acumen and integrity. He served as president of the Bristol stock exchange for many years. However, his hostility to municipalization of transport utilities and his manipulation of railway shares won him many critics, and he engaged in fierce struggles with the trade unions, insisting that he alone bore responsibility for employees' welfare. Away from business he was a major benefactor of the Bristol Royal Infirmary, the Red Cross, and other charities, and was made a baronet for his public service in 1904. A staunch Conservative, he served as a local councillor and JP but refused to stand for parliament, remarking that a seat on the back benches would be insufficient to interest him. Sir George White died suddenly of a heart attack on 22 November 1916, at his home, Old Sneed Park, Stoke Bishop, Bristol.　　　　　　　　　　　　　JON PRESS

Sources C. Harvey and J. Press, *Sir George White of Bristol, 1854–1916* (1989) · C. Harvey and J. Press, 'Sir George White: a career in transport, 1874–1916', *Journal of Transport History*, 3rd ser., 9 (1988), 170–89 · A. Bradley and J. Press, *Catalogue of the George White papers* (1989) · Bristol RO, George White MSS, 35810 · R. Higham and P. Masefield, 'White, Sir George', *DBB* · *Bristol Times and Mirror* (23 Nov 1916), 5 · A. B. Freeman, *Bristol worthies and notable residents in the district* (1909) · 'Eminent Bristol men', *Clifton Society* (16 July 1903), 51–2 · T. C. Barker and M. Robbins, *A history of London Transport*, 2 vols. (1963–74) · C. H. Barnes, *Bristol aircraft since 1910* (1964) · *CGPLA Eng. & Wales* (1917) · *WWW*, 1916–28 · pedigree of Sir George White, 1904, Coll. Arms

Archives Bristol RO, business and personal corresp. and papers | Bristol RO, Bristol Council Tramways Committee MSS, 28787

Likenesses photograph, 1912, repro. in Harvey and Press, *Sir George White of Bristol*, cover · photograph, Royal Aeronautical Society, London [*see illus.*]

Wealth at death £185,578 15s. 10d.: probate, 28 Sept 1917, *CGPLA Eng. & Wales*

White, George Henry (1817–1889), banking official, was born on 19 August 1817 at Tolleshunt d'Arcy, Essex, the second of three sons and one daughter of William White, a farmer, and his wife, Anne. He moved to London and in 1834 joined Barings, leading merchant bankers, as a junior clerk. By 1844 one of his brothers, who also became a clerk at Barings, and his sister had joined him. White's formal education was probably modest but he acquired detailed knowledge of the classics, poetry, and lexicology, and also became an accomplished watercolourist. In the early 1840s he lived at King's Cross, but he moved to Peckham in 1845 and to Clapham Park by the early 1860s. He never married.

White started at Barings as a fourth-class clerk, was promoted to third class about 1840, to second class in 1841, and to first class about 1850. By 1864 he was the second most senior clerk but poor health forced his retirement prematurely in 1872. His salary rose steadily from £40 in 1834, to £450 in 1850, and to £700 in 1872; by then, the sum was supplemented with a £100 bonus. In 1845 he dealt with stock enquiries, as a 'correspondence clerk', but by 1850 he was assisting the senior partner, Thomas Baring, in arranging bond issues, the firm's most intellectually demanding work.

White emerged as the bank's troubleshooter, and he was sent abroad to solve issues of major importance. In 1852 he assisted the emissary sent by Barings to Buenos Aires to negotiate the settlement of government debts, due to London bondholders since 1828, on bonds issued by Barings. The mission failed but White made his mark.

In 1856 White negotiated the settlement of payments overdue from the French government and shortly afterwards he proceeded to Buenos Aires to resume previous negotiations. Barings left matters to White, telling him, 'exercise your discretion in urging … such improvements in the original proposals … without endangering the chance of a definite conclusion'. By October White had achieved terms 'which certainly ought to satisfy all parties … The government was certainly pleased that the improvement of the terms should … take the form of a graceful concession rather than of a constrained compliance with demands from the bondholders' (Baring archives, HC4.1.34). Having negotiated the first significant rescheduling of a country's external debt, he returned a hero and was rewarded with a bonus of £1000.

In 1862 the Spanish bondholders' leader, David Robertson, hoped that White's 'so very modest and unassuming' manner would not prevent his appointment as 'English commissionaire in Mexico … for the statement of British claims' (Baring archives, HC4.1.29). In March 1862 he arrived at Vera Cruz, Mexico, accompanying the military expedition of France, Britain, and Spain, which ultimately resulted in French influence being established under the emperor, Maximilian. White's brief was to protect the interests of British bondholders, through negotiation with the Mexican government or with the allies, and to obtain settlement of debts long due by the Mexican government to its bondholders. He obtained modest repayment but was largely unsuccessful, and he returned in

1863. White lived in appalling conditions while in Mexico and was attacked on two occasions, which permanently damaged his health.

In 1866 White travelled to Italy to investigate a firm of merchants at Leghorn, which owed large sums to Barings. He initiated a liquidation of their business and was still dealing with this on his retirement in 1872. Robertson petitioned Barings to allow 'my poor friend … of whom I have such a high opinion' to retire 'with his salary for life', a worthy gesture for 'his having accomplished the great and good work at Buenos Aires and done what he could in Mexico' (Baring archives, HC4.1.29).

White retired to St Marychurch, near Torquay, in Devon, to enjoy a full life as a leader of the Torquay Natural History Society, to which he lectured on lexicology, as a founder of a free library, and as a committee member of the local government school of art. Although retired, he gave evidence to the select committee on loans to foreign states in 1875. He died on 15 May 1889 at St Marychurch, bequeathing his library to the Torquay Natural History Society. A portfolio of his watercolours of Mexico has survived in the Baring archives.

At Barings, White performed a junior partner's role; yet he remained a clerk, presumably for want of capital and connections. Otherwise, he would have compensated for the serious lack of judgement among Barings' junior partners, a fact acknowledged by Joshua Bates, who had sought to make him a partner.　JOHN ORBELL

Sir George Stuart White (1835–1912), by Window & Grove, c.1893

Sources P. Ziegler, *The sixth great power: Barings, 1762–1929* (1988) · ING Barings, London, Barings archives, HC4.1.29, HC4.1.34 · d. cert. · *CGPLA Eng. & Wales* (1889) · J. Orbell, 'George Henry White', *European traveler-artists in nineteenth century Mexico* (Mexico City, 1996) · parish register, 1817, Tolleshunt d'Arcy, St Nicholas

Archives ING Barings, London · Torquay Natural History Society | ING Barings, London, HC4.1.29 · NA Canada, Baring MSS · National Library of Canada, Baring MSS

Wealth at death £19,772: resworn probate, Aug 1889, *CGPLA Eng. & Wales*

White, Sir George Stuart (1835–1912), army officer, was born on 6 July 1835 at Rock Castle, Port Stewart, northern Ireland, the second son of James Robert White, of Whitehall, co. Antrim, and his wife, Frances, daughter of George Stuart. He was educated briefly at Bromsgrove, at home, and from 1847 to 1850 at King William's College, Isle of Man, and from 1850 to 1853 at Sandhurst. On 4 November 1853 he was commissioned ensign in the 27th foot (Inniskilling fusiliers), in which he served throughout the Indian mutiny on the north-west frontier, exchanging some years later into the 92nd (Gordon) Highlanders. In 1874 he married Amelia Maria (Amy; d. 1935), only daughter of Joseph Baly, archdeacon of Calcutta, and they had one son, James Robert *White (1879–1946), and four daughters. She survived her husband.

In the Second Anglo-Afghan War, during the advance of Major-General Roberts from Charasia to Kabul, Major White, in command of some 200 of the 92nd highlanders, managed by skill and courage to outflank the Afghans in the Sang Nawishta Gorge (6 October 1879), on the road from Jalalabad to Kabul, and so was largely instrumental in clearing the way for the rest of the force. Roberts wrote

that much of the success of the operations was due to White 'and at one supreme moment, to his extreme personal gallantry' (Roberts, 2.223).

White was fortunate in attracting Roberts's patronage during the Anglo-Afghan War. It was largely responsible for his rise to the highest rank after nearly thirty years of largely humdrum regimental duty. Thenceforward White's advancement was as rapid and remarkable as it had previously been slow. He received the VC for his feats at Charasia and at Kandahar, and was made a CB and brevet lieutenant-colonel. In 1880 he was military secretary to the viceroy. After a short period at home commanding the 92nd, he went on active service to Egypt as assistant quartermaster-general (1884–5). In 1885 a British-Indian army under General Harry Prendergast invaded Upper Burma, and White commanded the 3rd brigade. Mandalay was speedily captured, and Upper Burma was annexed in 1886. There followed a long guerrilla war with bands of dacoits, aggravated by the frontier peoples attempting revenge against the Burmese. In defeating this guerrilla warfare and in pacifying Upper Burma, White, who commanded there from March 1886, played a leading part and established his reputation both as a general and as an administrator. He was made KCB in 1886, and promoted major-general in 1889.

In 1889 White was transferred from Burma to command at Quetta, where he faced the problems of the north-west frontier. The controversy between those wanting to make the Indus the administrative frontier and those wanting to extend it to the borders of Afghanistan was at its height; but the 'forward' school, supported by the commander-in-chief, Sir Frederick Roberts, and by the viceroy, Lord Lansdowne, was in the ascendant, and White, an enthusiastic supporter of Roberts's views, became an instrument of that policy. In the autumn of 1889 he commanded the Zhob valley expedition. The operations, against a people which had long made their almost inaccessible mountain home a base for raids into British territory, were well planned and executed. White, having scaled the heights of the Maramazh, surrounded the principal village of the people, who surrendered. In the following years, with Sir Robert Groves Sandeman, he was occupied with the pacification of Baluchistan, one of the lasting achievements of the 'forward' policy. He showed considerable political and diplomatic skill, and worked harmoniously with his civilian colleagues: in 1893 he was made GCIE.

In 1893 White was chosen over seniors to be commander-in-chief in India. His term saw the greatest development of the 'forward' policy. Encouraged by his success in Baluchistan he supported the policy of opening up communications beyond the Indus and subjugating the unruly Pathan people. This policy brought about a succession of frontier campaigns. The gradual approach of Russia to the northern frontier of Afghanistan, and the threat of a Russian attack upon India, were then the principal military concern, and the chief argument of the advocates of the 'forward' policy was the necessity, in view of this menace, of obtaining better control of the peoples of the north-west frontier, and thereby exerting more influence in Afghanistan. White's command began with a small expedition in 1894 against the Abor people on the north-eastern frontier. This was followed in 1895 by the more considerable Chitral campaign. The relief expedition which was so successful had more than local importance in view of Russian approaches to the Pamirs. The Chitral campaign was followed in 1897 by a succession of outbreaks along the frontier, which caused the expeditions into the Tochi and Swat valleys and against the Mohmands, and before these were ended the most warlike and important frontier peoples, the Afridis and Orakzais, rose and burnt the British forts in the Khyber Pass. There followed the Tirah campaign, the largest in India since the mutiny. While responsibility for the policy of these expeditions was with the viceroy, the earl of Elgin, who had followed the tradition established by Lansdowne, White was responsible for their planning and organization. All were successful in gaining their immediate objectives, but the permanent gains were small. White probably hoped that large-scale operations would finally solve the problem. In that he was not successful.

White implemented the abolition of the military presidency system, and continued Roberts's policies of improving musketry, and encouraging temperance among British other ranks. He also improved mountain warfare training, particularly of the British troops. He was made GCB, and at the end of 1897 was appointed quartermaster-general at the War Office.

In September 1899, before the outbreak of the Second South African War, White was sent, aged sixty-four and inadequately briefed, to command in Natal, to defend it against invasion. His predecessor in command there, Sir William Penn Symons, had advanced to Dundee at the frontier, and though White wanted to concentrate his whole field army in the Ladysmith area, he allowed himself to be overruled by the dashing Symons, and the campaign in Natal began with the British forces divided. The British underestimated the invading Boers and the advantages of their mobility. After a successful action at Talana (20 October), in which Symons was killed, the exposed Dundee column retreated to Ladysmith. The next day the Boers were defeated by Major-General French at Elandslaagte, but by then the invasion had extended far into Natal. A disastrous night operation at Nicholson's Nek ruined White's plan for engaging the enemy at Lombard's Kop (30 October), and his entire army was shut up in Ladysmith (2 November).

White could have retreated south across the Tugela, though this would have been risky and entailed abandoning much ammunition and stores, and might have harmed British morale. He claimed that by attracting the Boers to Ladysmith he preserved the rest of Natal from invasion.

Buller believed that White's blunder in letting his field army be confined in Ladysmith wrecked the entire strategy of the war. White's decision not to withdraw across the Tugela to join the main British force was, and continued to be, controversial. It rendered his field force immobilized and ineffective in Ladysmith, where it deteriorated and many died of typhoid. Moreover, he probably should at least have sent out his mounted troops—four regular cavalry regiments and five colonial regiments. Useless in the siege, they would have been valuable elsewhere: their horses ended as 'chevril', steaks and soup. His command was ineffective and uninspiring. Despondent and indecisive, he seldom left his headquarters, and was nicknamed 'invisible White'. Despite the urging of Colonel Sir Henry Rawlinson and other officers, the defence was essentially unenterprising and passive—he only belatedly and reluctantly agreed to limited counter-attacks. However, he rejected Buller's heliographed suggestion, on 16 December after Colenso, that he make terms with the Boers. After a siege of 118 days, Ladysmith was finally relieved on 28 February 1900 by Buller's Natal field force. Addressing the garrison, White said, 'Thank God we kept the flag flying' (Pakenham, 366).

Roberts, whose protégé and friend White had been, refused to employ him in any responsible position because of his strategic blunder. However, White's health was broken as a result of the siege, and he was invalided back to England. Although to Roberts, Buller, and other officers White was discredited, to the British public he was 'the hero of Ladysmith'. He was welcomed by large crowds and royal and civic honours.

From 1900 to 1904 White was governor of Gibraltar. In

1903 he defended his wartime decisions at the royal commission on the war in South Africa (the Elgin commission). Later in 1903 he was promoted field marshal. Although the king was advised that White 'lacked great abilities, military or otherwise' (Lee, 2.100), in 1905 he was awarded the Order of Merit. He was one of the most decorated officers in the army, and also had honorary degrees from Oxford, Cambridge, Edinburgh, and Dublin. From 1904 he was governor of the Royal Hospital, Chelsea. He made public speeches urging patriotism and military preparedness, though not any specific programme. In 1910 he suffered two heart attacks, and in 1911 aphasia. He died at the Royal Hospital on 24 June 1912 and was buried with his ancestors at Broughshane, co. Antrim.

F. B. MAURICE, *rev.* JAMES LUNT

Sources Lord Roberts [F. S. Roberts], *Forty-one years in India*, 2 vols. (1897) · B. Robson, *The road to Kabul: the Second Afghan War, 1878–1881* (1986) · H. Hensman, *The Afghan war of 1879–80* (1881) · A. Durand, *The making of a frontier* (1889) · L. James, *The Indian frontier war* (1898) · J. F. Maurice and M. H. Grant, eds., *History of the war in South Africa, 1899–1902*, 4 vols. (1906–10) · *The Times* (25 June 1912) · *The Times* (29 June 1912) · A. Farrar-Hockley, *Goughie (the life of General Sir Hubert Gough)* (1975) · *Roberts in India: the military papers of Field Marshal Lord Roberts, 1876–1893*, ed. B. Robson (1993) · W. S. Churchill, 'London to Ladysmith', 'Frontiers and wars': his four early books … edited into one volume (1962) · O. Caroe, *The Pathans* (1965) · T. Pakenham, *The Boer War* (1979) · S. Lee, *King Edward VII*, 2 (1927) · WWW, 1897–1915 · A. T. Q. Stewart, *The pagoda war: Lord Dufferin and the fall of the kingdom of Ava* (1972) · M. Durand, *The life of Sir George White, V.C.*, 2 vols. (1915)

Archives BL OIOC, corresp., diaries, and papers · PRO NIre., papers | King's Lond., Liddell Hart C., Sir Ian Hamilton MS · NAM, letters to Earl Roberts · NRA, priv. coll., corresp. with Sir John Ewart | FILM BFI NFTVA, news footage · NAM, department of film and sound, newsreel footage

Likenesses Window & Grove, photograph, *c.*1893, NPG [*see illus.*] · Cowell, photograph, 1894, NAM · P. A. de Laszlo, oils, *c.*1905, Royal Collection · J. Tweed, bronze equestrian statue, 1922, Portland Place, London · Spy [L. Ward], chromolithograph caricature, NPG; repro. in *VF* (14 June 1900) · Spy [L. Ward], chromolithograph caricature (*A general group*), NPG; repro. in *VF* (29 Nov 1900) · deathmask, probably priv. coll. · photograph (with his daughter), repro. in *Soldiers of the Queen*, 50 (Sept 1987) · photograph, repro. in Durand, *Life of Sir George White, V.C.*

Wealth at death £49,865 2s. 9d.—in England: Irish probate sealed in England, 12 Oct 1912, CGPLA Eng. & Wales

White, Gilbert (1720–1793), naturalist, was born on 18 July 1720 at the vicarage, Selborne, Hampshire, the eldest son of John White (1688–1758), JP and barrister, and Anne (1693–1739), daughter of Thomas Holt (*d.* 1710), rector of Streatham, Surrey. White's grandfather, the Revd Gilbert White (1650–1728), fourth son of Sampson White (1607–1684), twice mayor of Oxford and knighted in 1660 by Charles II for loyalty to the crown, was vicar at Selborne from 1681 until his death in 1728, having previously been a fellow at Magdalen College, Oxford, in whose gift the living at Selborne lay. Shortly after his arrival at Selborne, he had married Rebecca Luckin (1654–1755), daughter of a yeoman farmer on Nore Hill, Newton Valence, a parish adjacent to Selborne, and from this combination of Oxford learning and local knowledge White derived the main influences that determined the principal features of his life and career.

White's father had been called to the bar in 1713 and obtained at the Middle Temple a life interest in chambers (which he retained until his death), but on his marriage in 1719 he retired from practice and devoted himself to country pursuits. Living first at Compton, near Guildford, and briefly at East Harting, near Petersfield, he and his wife, together with their growing family (eleven children were born within thirteen years) soon established themselves permanently at Selborne. The Wakes, a village house on the west side of The Street, as Selborne's main thoroughfare was known, fell vacant and in 1728 John White and family, joined by his now widowed mother from the vicarage, made it the family home for the remainder of the century and beyond. In character John White was quiet and unassuming—he played the harpsichord, observed the weather, and liked nothing better than to take his horse and 'amble along by Hedges under the wind' (*Letters to Gilbert White*, 19)—but he honoured the charitable bequests to the parish instituted by his father, and later (in 1741) laid out the 7 acres of the estate at The Wakes in walks and hedges. These features of his life, linked to his 'christian Temper' (*Letters to Gilbert White*, 136), inspired in his eldest son a gentle filial regard, and during his final illness and decline White planted 'bunches of single snow-drops in bloom under [his] Father's window' (White, *Garden Kalendar*, March 1758).

Childhood and education Familial devotion to parochial concerns, a disposition demonstrated to White not only through the interests of his father and grandfather but also through the country sympathies and country certainties of his paternal grandmother, had a profound effect on the future naturalist. After a childhood immersed in the wisdom of hanger, beech, and stream, including a notable occasion when he planted in the garden an oak and an ash to celebrate his tenth birthday, he went to school, first at Farnham and then to the grammar school at Basingstoke. At the latter he was under the tuition of Thomas Warton (*d.* 1745) and made acquaintance with the Warton brothers, Joseph, a future headmaster of Winchester, and Thomas, who was to become professor of poetry at Oxford University and poet laureate. An extant pocket book of White's shows that he 'carryed to Basingstoke [on] January 17, 1739' (Holt-White, 31) over thirty books for study. Most of the volumes were essential classics (for example, Xenophon, Homer, Horace, Virgil, Caesar, Tacitus, 'Tully' or Cicero), but amid the Greek and the Latin were *The Whole Duty of Man* (anonymous, 1758), and John Wilkins's *Of the Principles and Duties of Natural Religion* (1675); there was also a copy of James Thomson's *The Seasons* (1730) and it seems that it was at Basingstoke that White learned to delight in literature and first tried his hand at making verses in English.

Extensive as this learning was, White retained a growing pleasure in the outdoor life and during his schooldays he began the exploration of southern and central England that in later life was to earn him the sobriquet the Hussar Parson (*Letters to Gilbert White*, 166); he was also adept with the gun. The first record of his observations of nature occur in a notebook belonging to a future brother-in-law,

Thomas Barker (1722–1809) of Lyndon Hall, and were made on the occasion of a visit White made in 1736 to stay with an aunt at Whitwell, Rutland. Proceeding to Oriel College, Oxford, in April 1740 (he had been admitted a commoner on 17 December 1739, but the death of his mother on that day from an attack of measles delayed his entrance), he embraced the life of an undergraduate. From his account books it is known that he played chess, attended concerts and the coffee house, won and lost at cards, visited great houses and gardens (Burghley, Windsor, Stowe, Wilton, for example), and drank, buying wine by the gallon, cider by the hogshead, and tea in variety—green, hyson, balm, congo, and bohea are all mentioned. In addition, he read modern (English) literature, and hunted.

A close companion in the first of these activities was John Mulso (1721–1791) who was to become an enduring friend and a regular informant of events in the church and in literary circles. An uncle of Mulso, John Thomas, was successively bishop of Peterborough, Salisbury, and Winchester, the family often met a leading novelist of the age, Samuel Richardson, and a sister, Hester, was to become, on marriage, Hester Chapone. Mulso corresponded with White from 1744 to 1790; he also visited Selborne on a number of occasions and in 1747 White addressed to him the first version of his most sustained poetic effort, 'An Invitation to Selborne', a work that he later revised and used again. From Mulso's extant letters much can be learned about White's character and pursuits; this source reveals that his reading extended not only to the main figures of the literary tradition—Spenser, Shakespeare, Donne, Milton, Dryden—but also included many contemporaries: Swift, Pope, Fielding, and Richardson are referred to. This delight in literature, both classical and English, was to contribute much to White's education, and later in life, throughout his letters and journals, aspects of this period of his reading figure prominently even when the subject matter is the natural world.

If it was a delight in literature that gave White his literary clothes, it was to his second pursuit, hunting, that can be traced his sense of the natural world as an encounter full of mystery and beauty, waiting to be observed and recorded. Expenses noted in the account books from his Oxford days show that the outlay was considerable. In addition to costs associated with the gun—powder, shot, papers, flints, and repairs to his weapon are all mentioned—there were other expenses since a boy had to be hired, boots paid for, and dogs bought, fed, and attended to; a notable sequence of costs centred on the dog Fairey, who went 'strolling' during a journey one Christmas from Oxford to Selborne, for entries refer to 'Advertising, & crying Fairey', a 'Reward to Bernard Bailey [to whom she had] strolled', and payment to a 'News-man for bringing her to Selborn' (G. White, account books). The persistence of payments of this kind suggests a regular, even relentless, pursuit of avian game, confirmation of which is given by Mulso who, writing in later life about this period, commented: 'at that time You used to practise with your Gun in Summer to steady your Hand for Winter, & inhospitably fetch down our Visitants, the Birds of Passage' (*Letters to Gilbert White*, 293). However, during the routine of 'field-diversions' White experienced an event that was to shape his future and eventually lead to the single work for which he is so well known, *The Natural History and Antiquities of Selborne* (1789). The occasion can be dated precisely to 21 September 1741: up early, and out hunting for partridge, White 'found the stubbles and clover-grounds matted all over with [such] a thick coat of cobweb' that his dogs were 'so blinded and hoodwinked that they could not proceed'; and further, the 'perfect flakes or rags' (of gossamer—for that is what White describes in *Selborne*, Barrington, letter 23) 'hung in the trees and hedges so thick, that a diligent person … might have gathered baskets full'. The immediate outcome of this singular experience was a forced return home, during which he mused on 'the oddness of the occurrence'. But a deeper magic was at work and White's devotion to hunting received a considerable shock. Gratuitous killing (even for sport), he came to realize, was alien to the purposes of Providence, and although he continued to shoot for the table and, later, to provide specimens for identification and dissection, the thrill of the chase and the deceit of the stalk were to be replaced in his maturity by a spirit of enquiry and the outcomes of scientific curiosity.

White's immediate concern, however, was completion of his studies at university, and in June 1743 he graduated bachelor of arts. Award of the degree took place on 30 June and led to a notable memorial. The guest at the ceremony was Alexander Pope and he presented to White a copy of his own translation of Homer's *Iliad*, in six volumes which are now in the British Library and contain the sole authentic likenesses of White; two sketches, in volumes 3 and 5, were 'penned by T:C:', most probably Thomas Chapman of Trinity College, Oxford, with whom White played chess and later shared proctorial office in the university. In the following year, on 30 April, White was elected to a fellowship of his college. In 1746 he spent several months at Thorney, Isle of Ely, attending to the estate of Thomas Holt, a distant relative on his mother's side who bequeathed a small inheritance to each of the White brothers and entailed his estate (conditional on the adoption of his surname) to White's brother Thomas Holt *White (1724–1797), and in the October was awarded his degree of master of arts; this and his fellowship were not the last honours he was to receive from either Oriel or the university, but the prospect of employment beckoned and he now sought to earn a living.

Clerical and academic career From the mid-1740s for a period of nearly fifteen years White pursued a future that might have led to a career at Oxford. Beginning by joining the Anglican church (he was made a deacon on 27 April 1747 at Christ Church Cathedral, Oxford, by the bishop, Thomas Secker), he was appointed curate at a small country parish, Swarraton, Hampshire, held, together with Bradley, by the Revd Charles White, husband to his father's youngest sister, Elizabeth. Although detained that same year at Oxford for much of the autumn by a severe attack of smallpox, through which he was nursed by 'Goody Marshall' who came from Selborne solely for that purpose, on his recovery White soon recommenced a hectic series of tours and visits. At one moment he was in Gloucestershire seeing a college friend, then he visited Sunbury-on-Thames (where Mulso was the incumbent) and Ringmer, near Lewes in Sussex; there he saw a great-aunt, Rebecca Snooke, from whom in March 1780 he was to inherit a tortoise, Timothy, on which he was later to conduct several experiments. (Timothy proved on death to be female; her shell is now in the Natural History Museum, London.) In late summer 1750 he travelled to Wiltshire and on into Devon (where he stayed in the South Hams with an Oriel contemporary, Nathan Wells, and from where he returned with a specimen of sea-kale, *Crambe maritima*, which he was to grow at The Wakes for several years). In the following year, 1751, he was off again in July and August to make a wide, sweeping tour up to the west midlands and on east into Rutland to visit his youngest sister, Anne, who had married Thomas Barker of Lyndon Hall on 6 January that year at Selborne. The date of the marriage is significant as Barker was already a considerable observer of the natural scene (principally meteorology, and he had already submitted the first of more than thirty papers to the Royal Society, to which he was later elected as a fellow), for on the day following the wedding White made the first entry in a new record book that he termed (for that year) 'The Garden-Kalendar for the Year 1751'.

In some form or other White was to keep a near daily record of his activities in the garden and of natural phenomena for more than forty years, until shortly before his death in 1793. Alongside this appetite for observation he continued his clerical duties, becoming in October 1751 curate-in-charge at Selborne (an office he was to hold again in 1756 and in 1758 and, for a fourth time, in 1784 right through to his death); he also maintained the social round, visiting Portsmouth, Winchester, and Midhurst (Cowdray Park), as well as fulfilling the necessary duties as fellow at Oriel. This commitment was to serve him well, for in 1752 the office of junior proctor in the University of Oxford fell to his college and White was elected for a twelvemonth from 8 April. Combining these duties with those of dean in his own college reinforced an interest in an academic future, and in 1757—after a sequence of short curacies, mostly for relatives in the Selborne area but including a period at West Dean in Wiltshire, and social visits in 1753 and 1755 to Bristol Hot-Well—he offered himself for election as provost of his college. Associated as he was with the country scene, and with little academic or other public achievement to his credit, his election was always unlikely and the office went to Chardin Musgrave. White's merits, however, were recognized through preferment as perpetual curate at Moreton Pinkney, Northamptonshire, and, as he was able to hold the parish without residence, he accepted the office. As senior fellow of Oriel he was to receive in later years the offer of a number of wealthy parishes, but although he made numerous visits to inspect each opportunity as it came, he was never

to accept further preferment, for it would have required residence away from Selborne.

With no further prospects available to him, White turned his eyes back to his native village. His paternal grandmother, Rebecca Luckin, had died in 1755, and with the death of his father in September 1758 responsibility for The Wakes (the inheritance of which passed to him in 1763 on the death of the Revd Charles White of Bradley) was to fall to him. In November 1759 he began a tour that extended over six months, the longest absence from Selborne he was ever to make. After calling *en route* at Sunbury to see the Mulsos, he first stayed in London with his brother Thomas (now partner in a wholesale merchant's business in Thames Street), and then set off for Rutland to visit his sister Anne and Thomas Barker at Lyndon Hall; he returned in mid-May 1760 and immediately noted in the 'Kalendar' for 17 May that his garden was 'in very good order ... The Cucumbers in full bearing ... The Cantaleupe-melons in good Condition [and all] the kitchen-crops ... in good plight'. It was a situation in which he felt most at home and which also provided the seeds of his future acclaim.

Beginnings of the naturalist Concurrently with his clerical career and his plans for an academic future, White became interested in the formal study of the garden at The Wakes. His serious interest had been indicated by the purchase in 1743 of the standard text of the day, Philip Miller's *The Gardeners Dictionary*. He planted more trees (elm, fir, and beech in 1750–51) and, most importantly, began, on Monday 7 January 1751, a journal record of work in the garden. This journal, named the 'Garden kalendar', contains much more than its title suggests. As well as being a record of garden operations, details are given about the weather, with annual summaries; about how best to ventilate a hotbed; and about seed-trials—planting potatoes, for example, in 'peat-dust' instead of 'old-thatch' for 'experiment sake'. Further, across the whole journal from 1751 until 1767 occur instances of White's gift for homely measurement: succade melons 'come by heaps' (that is, in abundance); a cucumber in April is 'about as big as the top of one's finger'; snow is 'deeper than a horse's belly'; and after ploughing, the clods stand 'as high as one's knees'. In addition, in 1758 White entered the first explicit references to natural history: 'Saw two swallows' (9 April), and in November the much longer: 'Saw a very unusual sight; a large flock of House-Martens playing about between our fields, and the Hanger'. The location for this observation, the ground behind The Wakes, is significant for it was to the garden that White now looked for his main satisfactions and to which he chiefly directed his energies, particularly as his clerical income was now secure, for he accepted in 1761 the curacy at Faringdon, a parish adjacent to Selborne and an office he was to hold for over twenty years since it could be easily served from The Wakes.

Throughout the 1750s and on into the early 1760s construction work in the garden, aided by the purchase of part of a neighbour's orchard, was unending. It included brick walks leading from the house to an arbour that he used for observation; a grassed terrace, on which a sundial was erected; a turfed mount; a zig-zag path up the slope of the Hanger (the steep slope of Selborne Hill to the west of The Wakes, clothed with beech); a ha-ha (a large ditch at the boundary, effective as a fence to keep livestock out of the garden but also offering an unrestricted view of the surrounding countryside); vistas that looked to huge oil-jars erected on pedestals; and on the Hanger itself a statue of Hercules, and also a hermitage, a mock hermit's cell roofed with thatch. In good weather, this last became a centre of social activity: Henry (1733–1788), White's youngest brother, rector and schoolmaster at Fyfield, near Andover, played the hermit, guests were entertained, and the fruits of White's exertions in the garden were enjoyed at cantaloupe feasts.

In White's records for 1764–5, however, a new note is struck: he began to extend his library. In addition to some travel literature, Hill's *Herbal* (1756) and Jan Swammerdam's *Book of Nature* (1758), he obtained the two texts that launched him on a serious study of nature—Benjamin Stillingfleet's *Miscellaneous Tracts* (1759), and William Hudson's *Flora Anglica* (1762). From Stillingfleet's *Tracts*, and especially from the 'Calendar of flora' that was added to the second edition (1762), White learned about the natural calendar, about the dream that natural phenomena, especially the migration of birds and the growth of plants, would provide, through the determination of dates for sowing and reaping, a prognostic for the labours of the husbandman such that reliable harvests would be secured to the benefit of all. In order to keep the necessary records for such a project accurate identification of natural forms was necessary. Previously he had used John Ray's publications as the authority for naming and identification, especially of native fauna, but there was much he had to learn about flora and it was from Hudson that he obtained the Linnaean nomenclature so necessary if he was to acquire the knowledge that the venture required.

The first fruits of this new, eager stage in White's growth of understanding occurred in the 'Kalendar' for summer 1765 but they were to reach maturity in 'Flora Selborniensis', 1766. This volume, to which he gave the subtitle 'with some co-incidences of the coming, & departure of birds of passage, & insects; & the appearing of Reptiles', was not edited and published until 1911 (by Wilfred Mark Webb, under the title *A Nature Calendar*), but it convincingly demonstrates one of White's principal strengths as a naturalist—an openness to enquiry. Although most of the entries are on vegetation, and although the items included embrace those properly contained in both a *hortus siccus* and a flora, the main focus of the record is on stages of growth. In order to indicate the beginnings of growth White deploys a somewhat elastic vocabulary (plants 'spring', 'sprout', 'shoot', 'emerge', 'peep-out') but when he comes to record flowering, the key stage for the botanist, as for the plantsman and the apothecary, he becomes more precise and establishes a terminology that divides the process into five—'buds for bloom', 'begins to blow', 'blows', 'in high bloom', 'going out of bloom'. Use of this finely graded differentiation

enabled White to make comparisons across species and sites, and (because of necessary variation consequent on differing soils and aspects) prompted some scepticism about the venture. Nevertheless, although White records phenomena within a territory he had known since childhood, and one no larger than a parish, his observations avoid the dullness of familiarity; on the contrary, there is a freshness of phrase, an edge of enthusiasm, that conveys a continual delight in the natural world. This delight, accumulated in the garden at The Wakes and in the fields and meadows of his native place, was later tested in London by conversation and correspondence with the leading naturalists of the time. White's survival of the procedure was a triumphant vindication of the wisdom to be learned within a parochial territory, and was to lead directly to his principal accomplishment, *The Natural History and Antiquities of Selborne* (1789).

Maturity as a naturalist Excited by the formal knowledge he now possessed of the Selborne flora and fauna, White travelled to London in April 1767 to make a customary annual visit to see two of his brothers—Thomas, the general merchant and future fellow of the Royal Society (1777), and Benjamin *White (c.1725–1794), bookseller and principal of the premier shop in London for volumes on natural history. During this visit he made the acquaintance in May of Joseph Banks and Daniel Solander, who were to leave England the following year with Cook on the 1768–72 circumnavigation, and of Thomas Pennant (fellow of the Royal Society, 1767) who was then working on the second edition of his *British Zoology* (1st edn, 1761–6). White greatly admired Banks's fortitude and as he followed details of the voyage in the press he derived much enlightenment from sensing, for the first time, the deprivation that men were prepared to endure in the cause of furthering scientific enquiry; however, it was from meeting Pennant that two important consequences flowed for his own development.

Preparation of a British natural history necessarily required numerous informants, and judging White to be a reliable observer in a part of the country about which he had little personal knowledge (his own home was in Flintshire, north Wales), Pennant invited him to correspond. White took time to weigh this idea but wrote to Pennant on 10 August 1767; this letter, edited and dated 4 August and prefaced by nine specially written putative letters, appeared more than twenty years later as the first 'real' letter in *Selborne* (1789). If the first consequence of meeting Pennant led to White's discovering he had knowledge to communicate to a specialist in natural history, albeit in private correspondence, the second was to lead directly to public recognition.

Late in this same year there arrived at Selborne, as a gift from the author (but prompted by Pennant whose perception of White as a useful contributor to the cause of natural history was to be fully vindicated), a copy of a published design for a naturalist's annual notebook entitled the *Naturalist's Journal* (1767). This journal, devised by Daines Barrington (1727–1800), fellow of the Royal Society (1767), was designed to facilitate at different seasons and across Britain the correlation between meteorological phenomena and the behaviour of flora and fauna. Set within the tradition advocated by Benjamin Stillingfleet of discovering—to the benefit of husbandry and agriculture—the natural calendar, this focus on observation and record appealed to White and harnessed his particular skills to a general purpose. Putting to one side the 'Kalendar' that had served him so well for the preceding thirteen years, but which now seemed essentially a private document, he made the first entry in his new journal for Friday 1 January 1768, and thus initiated a pattern of record-keeping that he was to sustain almost daily for over twenty-five years.

The format of Barrington's design devoted a large, landscape page to each week. After requiring completion of year, location, and soil, columns were available for observation of the weather conditions: thermometer and barometer readings were required, as well as wind direction, measurement of rainfall, and a verbal description of conditions. With these contextual data in place, the observer was then provided with five columns: four of these invited record of trees and fungi, of plants and mosses, of birds and insects, and of fish and other creatures, and the fifth gave opportunity for varied memoranda. For each column there was insistence on precision; for example, the meteorological columns required observations four times daily, and the record of plants and creatures emphasized appearance and disappearance, both concepts being of vital relevance to the purpose of the whole venture.

Although White rarely completed every requirement of the format, especially over the reiterated instrumental data, he warmed to the purpose and acknowledged the rewards that flowed from keeping such meticulous, incremental records. A typical page of data, particularly in the summer, often includes nearly 100 items, but White soon found the columnar structure of Barrington's design insufficient for his purposes, and within a few years he arranged to have his annual volumes of the *Naturalist's Journal* interleaved with blank pages. On these pages, in particular from May 1776, he began to record extended comments and descriptions of his observations, many of which were to appear in *Selborne* (1789) as part of the putative (undated) letters to Barrington. More significantly, and in parallel with the beginning of this process of journal compilation, White began a correspondence with Barrington. After writing to thank Barrington for the gift of the *Journal*, and meeting him in London, first in 1768 but then, for almost a decade, usually annually, White began the sequence of letters that carried his observations of the natural world beyond the confines of his parish and into the rooms of the Royal Society of London and, in later years, to the enduring benefit of posterity, onto the shelves of enthusiasts for the natural scene throughout the world. In large measure this outcome must be ascribed to Barrington's influence on White; his disinterest (professionally he was a judge) and, to use White's terms, his 'candour' and 'affability' appealed strongly, and White responded in kind. Comparison of White's letters to Pennant alongside those to Barrington shows that the

former are descriptive, with a focus on information, which was exactly what Pennant could incorporate in his own volumes of natural history; in contrast, the letters to Barrington are relaxed and speculative, and so varied in content that they convey the interests of an author not only at one with the world of his enquiries but also at one with his own nature.

Both sets of correspondence, however, furthered White's studies. Pennant's absorption in new information led White to reveal that he had a brother John (1727–1780) living in Gibraltar, where he was chaplain, and with Pennant's prompting White encouraged his brother to take up the study of natural history. This the latter did most ably, tutored (and for White's development this was a significant fact) by White himself. It was a new role for White. Previously he had been a student of Miller's gardening knowledge, of Gibson's knowledge of fauna in North America (James Gibson, a contemporary of White's at Oxford, was a naval chaplain at Quebec in 1759), of Stillingfleet's dream of discovering the natural calendar, and of Hudson's *Flora Anglica*, but now he was to become a teacher. He prompted, cajoled, directed, and guided to such good purpose that John White not only initiated a correspondence with Linnaeus but also amassed sufficient materials to prepare, on his return to England in 1772 and during his subsequent office as vicar at Blackburn, Lancashire, a volume on the fauna of Gibraltar. White's enthusiasm for his brother's progress is strikingly indicated by the cargoes of specimens that his brother sent to England. Identification of their many items presented White with some difficulties, but he enlisted assistance from several specialists, William Sheffield and Richard Skinner from Oxford (both of whom visited Selborne), Dru Drury, Lee of Hammersmith, and Pennant himself, and presented some items to the Royal Society (and elsewhere) in the belief that important specimens 'should belong to places where they will be set in natural attitudes and much admired; rather than … be laid up in a box in my study where they will seldom be seen' (Foster, 'Gibraltar correspondence', 499–500).

And yet, if it is to Pennant's curiosity that credit should be assigned for White's knowledge of a fauna and flora in a countryside so different from Selborne, it is to Barrington that acknowledgement must be given for the impetus and opportunity that were to haul White into the public arena. The keys to this encouragement were two suggestions made by Barrington in 1769 and 1770. The first, to write about the birds of the parish, brought White to a new understanding of his powers and to an articulation of his comprehensive knowledge of Selborne ornithology (letters 1 and 2 in the Barrington sequence in *Selborne*). The second, to prepare an account of the animals in his neighbourhood, faced the Selborne naturalist for the first time with the idea of publication. For White the idea of pursuing these unsolicited suggestions was daunting and he was able to contemplate a response only with hesitation. Friends (particularly Mulso) and relatives encouraged him, however, and letter by letter with painstaking care he wrote himself into history, literary as well as scientific.

Certain key stages in his growing confidence can be noted: a decision to publish, if at all, alone and not in concert with Barrington, who had hoped White would collaborate with him on a joint publication; a commitment to local natural history, much emphasized by reading Giovanni Scopoli whose monograph (1769) on the birds of Carniola encouraged him in his belief that the 'more confined y^r sphere of observation … the more perfect will be y^r remarks' (Foster, 'Gibraltar correspondence', 491); the successful completion, at Barrington's invitation, of monographs for the Royal Society on the house martin (*Delichon urbica*), swallow (*Hirundo rustica*), swift (*Apus apus*), and bank martin (*Hirundo riparia*); detailed discussion with Barrington on the completed volumes of the *Naturalist's Journal* for 1774 and 1775; the commissioning in 1776 of Samuel Hieronymus Grimm as illustrator for the projected volume (he painted twelve different watercolours of Selborne in twenty-four days); a decision to broaden an account of the creatures of the parish into a volume that would accommodate the antiquities of the parish; and lastly, the arrival at Selborne in 1781 of Mrs John White, widow of White's brother, who accepted on her husband's death White's invitation to live at The Wakes and assume responsibility for domestic matters. The decision to include antiquities extended the time required for the preparation of *Selborne* by a decade, despite instruction from John Loveday (1711–1789), of Caversham, Reading, in aspects of medieval church history and a considerable contribution made by Richard Chandler (1738–1810) who, as a fellow of Magdalen College, had access to the college records concerning the parish antiquities.

Mrs White's arrival was significant: The Wakes was the family home and White saw it as such. Encouraged by his sister-in-law he not only recorded in his journal a new appreciation of garden produce and culinary satisfaction, but throughout the 1780s (and later) welcomed to the Hampshire village an increasing number of nephews and nieces, that at his last count in January 1793, totalled sixty-two, including spouses. It was with detailed help from two of them, Mary and Benjamin White (the married elder children respectively of his brothers Thomas and Benjamin, who were active participants in 1785 in Benjamin White's Fleet Street shop for natural history books) that *Selborne* was printed, and published, on 1 November 1788 (but with 1789 on the title-page, as volumes available in the final months of the year were permitted to carry the date of the following year).

Final years, publications, and present standing With his major, one might even say his life's, work published, White now devoted himself to new activities. *Selborne*, reviewed in the *Gentleman's Magazine* by his brother Thomas (who frequently shared White's enthusiasms as a plantsman and observer, and who had already contributed to that journal a sequence of articles on trees, as well as for much of the 1780s a series of monthly meteorological diaries), and in *The Topographer*, brought acclaim and, as well as prompting many gifts from local people of

unusual specimens, encouraged new correspondents. Among the latter the most important were George Montagu (1751–1815), author of the *Ornithological Dictionary* (1802), and Thomas Marsham (1708–1797) of Norfolk with whom White pursued an intense correspondence, chiefly on trees, throughout his remaining years. White also enjoyed reflecting on the relation of natural history to the literary tradition (the *Naturalist's Journal* in its concluding phase is much fuller than at earlier periods with reference to literary evocations of the natural scene), and began to prepare a further avian monograph, on the nightjar, *Caprimulgus Europaeus*. Before he could find a sponsor for this new work at the Royal Society, however, he made his last entry in the *Naturalist's Journal* on Saturday 15 June 1793 (and also wrote his last letter, to Marsham); he died quietly at The Wakes eleven days later, on Wednesday 26 June. His funeral, conducted by the non-resident vicar of Selborne, Christopher Taylor, took place on 1 July, and he was buried in Selborne churchyard, at his own wish out of the heat of the sun, near the north wall of the chancel; his grave is marked by a simple stone cut to read 'G. W. 26th June 1793'.

Except for a number of short items (an account of the poet William Collins; a few brief poems; and contributions to the monthly 'Meteorological diary'), all of which are in the *Gentleman's Magazine* above the pseudonym V., White's sole publications in his lifetime were the monographs on the 'hirundines', each of which offered something new and original in observation and which appeared in the *Philosophical Transactions of the Royal Society* (vols. 64 and 65), and *The natural history and antiquities of Selborne, in the county of Southampton, with engravings, and an appendix* (1789), printed in London by T. Bensley for B. White & Son, at Horace's Head, Fleet Street, London. Extending, together with its index, the preparation of which White claimed to be 'an occupation full as entertaining as that of darning socks, tho' by no means so advantageous to society' (Foster, *Gilbert White*, 146), to nearly 500 pages, the quarto volume contains nine plates, all from Grimm's drawings.

Purporting to comprise three sequences of letters—those addressed to Pennant and to Barrington forming the natural history portion of the volume, the remainder, unaddressed (although White considered Chandler an appropriate recipient) forming an account of parish antiquities—*Selborne* needs to be read with discrimination. In contrast to White's observations of the natural world, notably in the 'Garden kalender', in 'Flora Selborniensis', and in the *Naturalist's Journal* across its many annual volumes, all of which offer a scrupulously documented historical record, *Selborne* is a literary work. In preparing it White became conscious that he was freed from the perceptible rhythms and occasions of the natural world, and the outcome is a volume beset by the vagaries of correspondence, by the sensibilities of social discourse, and by the chances of art. Although the core of the natural history portion of the volume remained the letters White exchanged with Pennant and Barrington, when he came to edit those letters he discovered the need both to modify and to extend his material. Features of this process include the omission from the real letters of much personal detail; the changing of actual dates of writing to imagined dates; the admission into the letters of new observations and incidents taken from his journals; and the adaptation of letters to members of his family, and their deployment, as if the originals were to either Pennant or Barrington. In addition, and in order to make an acceptable volume in both design and length, White not only prepared an introductory sequence of letters, which are given as the first nine letters addressed to Pennant, but also raided his journals for new topics and gathered the results together in many of the later letters in the published sequence to Barrington.

In choosing to present his observations in the form of letters, White was following the accepted practice of his time. For decades the exchange of letters between scientists had formed the primary vehicle for reporting new observations and for communicating results, just as in literature the epistolary novel was a dominant form in the years of White's maturity and in an earlier age Defoe had shown how to incorporate in a single volume real alongside fabricated letters. To mediate an understanding of the world by means of letters, whether fabricated or real, invited the reader to participate in the writer's own journey of exploration, to share the very motions of his mind, its doubts alongside its certainties, its astonishment in discovery, and, most important of all, the satisfactions obtained from investigative activity itself.

On White's death his literary papers were passed by his relatives to John Aikin MD (1747–1822), whose first response was to extract previously unpublished material from the journals and issue it as *A Naturalist's Calendar, with Observations in Various Branches of Natural History* (1795). He then advised publication of White's collected writings in natural history, and this was accomplished in *Selborne* (1802). This volume, comprising first the republication of *Selborne* (1789) without the letters on the antiquities, and *A Naturalist's Calendar* (1795), and second a calendar of natural occurrences and memoranda, parallel to Aikin's 1795 publication, but prepared by W. Markwick of Catisfield, Sussex, was prefaced by a brief memoir of White written by John White, son of Benjamin White, the bookseller. There followed in 1813 the first comprehensive edition of White's published works: letters on the parish antiquities were restored, White's known poems were added, and the first notes on his work, by the Revd John Mitford of Benhall, Suffolk, were included. These notes marked a change in the perception of White's work. At the time of his first communications with Pennant and Barrington, and for a decade or so after first publication of *Selborne*, White's observations, as may readily be confirmed by inspection of Pennant's *British Zoology* (1776–7), Barrington's *Miscellanies* (1781), and, for example, W. Bingley's *Animal Biography* (1805), were valued for their new contributions to natural history. With the assimilation of this knowledge into the scientific literature (a process marked by corrections and additions to published work), one might have expected White's volume to lapse into obscurity. This did

not occur: on the contrary, an interest which had initially been focused on factual knowledge was replaced by an interest best described as inspirational.

Throughout the Victorian period and on through the twentieth century, publisher after publisher issued a distinctive addition to White studies. Full bibliographic detail for these many editions of *Selborne*, almost always of the natural history letters alone, are given in E. A. Martin's *Bibliography* (1970), but two broad comments can be made. First, the styles of these many editions bear witness to the concerns of the period of publication; this is especially noticeable in the heavily annotated editions of the mid-Victorian period and, in the twentieth century, in the changing style of the illustrations used to accompany the text. Second, as White's work became better known it was elevated into a classic and found a place in any series that claimed to publish the 'best' books, not only in English literature but in world literature as well. This recognition was the culmination of a process initiated by the 1813 edition: as the nineteenth century neared its end the Victorians, under pressure from the urban excesses of economic and industrial achievement and from the implications of Darwinism, increasingly sought solace in the beacons of the past and *Selborne*, in its gentle, quiet, yet elegant and gracious fashion, reassured many.

Such acknowledgement was in accord with White's own experience as recorded in his 'Advertisement' to *Selborne*. After specifying a three-fold aim in preparing the volume, he averred that if none of his aims was achieved there was:

> consolation ... [that] his pursuits, by keeping the body and mind employed [had], under Providence, contributed to much health and cheerfulness of spirits, even to old age: and [also had] led him to the knowledge of a circle of gentlemen [who] afforded him much pleasing information.

That White's studies granted him both 'pleasing information' as well as cheerful employment is an outcome aspired to by many, but it was an outcome additional to White's declared aims. Of these, the first, to throw 'light upon ancient customs and manners ... especially on those that were monastic', met the purpose of many earlier parish histories. What White attempted, however, in *Selborne* was a new understanding of a history of a parish which, he thought, ought to include the study of natural productions as well as antiquities. It is to this new understanding that White's two further aims relate. The wish to induce 'a more ready attention to wonders of the Creation', was, in fact, his main aim and will be commented on below; another was the wish to 'have lent a helping hand [through his researches] towards the enlargement of the boundaries of historical and topographical knowledge'. At first sight it might be thought this aim was outside the scope of modern natural history, yet it contains, from a scientific perspective, the essence of White's endeavour.

Sceptical of the accuracy of general natural histories and finding support in Scopoli whose *Annus primus* (1769) had led White to claim that writers who 'undertake only one district are much more likely to advance natural knowledge than those that grasp at more than they can possibly be acquainted with' (*Selborne*, Barrington, letter 7), White placed his focus on the importance of local natural history. Even within a territory as narrow as his own parish and with near a lifetime of observation, he was to reach two conclusions: that 'all nature is so full, that that district produces the greatest variety which is the most examined'; and that 'investigations (where a man endeavours to be sure of his facts) can make but slow progress; and all that one [can] collect in many years would go into a very narrow compass' (*Selborne*, Barrington, letter 5). It was with this same belief that he had guided his brother John, at Gibraltar, writing in 1771: 'True naturalists will thank you more for the life & conversation of a few animals well studied & investigated; than for a long barren list of half the Fauna of the globe. Monographers are the best Nat: Historians' (Foster, 'Gibraltar correspondence', 492–3). While true in behavioural and ecological terms, this applies less to species. White's outright discoveries in terms of the identification of species amount to little, the usual citations being: differentiation of the three English species of leaf warbler, identification of the lesser whitethroat, and discovery of the harvest mouse and the noctule bat.

But White aimed at 'life and conversation' and it is satisfaction of that aim that illuminates his wish to enlarge 'the boundaries [the understanding] of historical and topographical knowledge' within (and this needs stressing) his native parish. From this perspective White made a contribution at a general level as well as at a particular. In the former category one might adduce the hermaphrodite nature of earthworms, ideas about coloration and sexual selection in birds, notions of territoriality, the comparison of local soils and climates and the effects on husbandry, ideas of microclimates, experimentation with different soils for growing (especially potatoes), bird identification by flight behaviour, and so on; and in the latter category, for his journals and *Selborne* are delightedly enriched with observations made in his native place of particular occurrences, the first known sighting of an otter, or the itinerant habits of ring ouzel, the felling of a shrew-ash (despite superstitious protests from village believers in its curative powers over cattle), or the discovery of the *centrum phonicum* for a fine natural echo in the parish.

This attention on the local ran counter to the spirit of leading contemporaries, many of whom sought the generalization of knowledge, Samuel Johnson, for example, in a vivid floristic image, claiming that the main business of the philosopher was 'to examine, not the individual, but the species [for] he does not number the streaks of the tulip, or describe the different shades in the verdure of the forest' (*Rasselas*, 1759). It was precisely White's resistance to generalization, together with his unending flow of rich particularity, that enabled him to fulfil his main aim, that of encouraging his readers to give 'a more ready attention' to the flora and fauna of their daily world. 'Ordinary' observers are much more ready to respond to what is happening in the back garden than to entertain large ideas about general theory, and it is this focus of White's on the everyday, on what is accessible to the curious observer in any age, that is a principal reason for the continuing life of *Selborne*.

And yet, although he has had many imitators (Knapp, *Journal of a Naturalist*, 1829, based in Gloucestershire, being one of the closest), nobody has managed to rival the grace and ease of White's writing. In a measure this success must be attributed to his style and personality. Central to this last is a modest acceptance that some aspects of the natural scene are beyond understanding. Such 'fear before God' has delighted readers for more than two centuries, and unites the cabinet (of specimens), the laboratory, and the study, not only with the open field and the leafy canopy of a wooded valley but also with the bare roof ledge outside the window, where pigeons coo, sparrows squabble, or the local robin taps for food.

White's *Natural History of Selborne* is open to everyone, for everyone has observed much of what it describes. Writer and reader each share the inheritance of the natural world, and delight in what is given, so that *Selborne* becomes an expression of universal thanksgiving, treasured by all. PAUL FOSTER

Sources G. White, *A nature calendar*, ed. W. M. Webb (1911) [Calendar of flora; Flora Selborniensis, facs.] · G. White, *The antiquities of Selborne*, ed. W. S. Scott (1950) · G. White, *Garden kalendar, 1751–1771: reproduced in facsimile from the manuscript in the British Library*, ed. J. Clegg (1975) · *The journals of Gilbert White, 1751–1793*, ed. F. Greenoak, 3 vols. (1986–9) · G. White, *The natural history of Selborne*, ed. P. Foster, pbk edn (1993) · *The letters to Gilbert White of Selborne from … John Mulso*, ed. R. Holt-White [1907] · E. A. Martin, *A bibliography of Gilbert White*, rev. edn (1970) · B. Stillingfleet, *Miscellaneous tracts relating to natural history, husbandry, and physick*, 2nd edn (1762) · G. A. Scopoli, *Annus I historico-naturalis* (1769) · D. Barrington, *Miscellanies* (1781) · T. Pennant, *British zoology*, 4th edn, 4 vols. (1776–7) · W. Bingley, *Animal biography, or, Authentic anecdotes of the lives, manners and economy of the animal creation*, 2nd edn, 3 vols. (1805) · R. Holt-White, *The life and letters of Gilbert White of Selborne*, 2 vols. (1901) · P. Foster, *Gilbert White and his records: a scientific biography* (1988) · P. Foster, 'The Gibraltar correspondence of Gilbert White', *N&Q*, 230 (1985), 227–36, 315–28, 489–500 · 'William Sheffield: four letters to Gilbert White', ed. P. Foster, *Archives of Natural History*, 12 (1985), 1–21 · P. Foster, 'The Hon. Daines Barrington FRS—annotations on two journals compiled by Gilbert White', *Notes and Records of the Royal Society*, 41 (1986–7), 77–93 · P. Foster, 'Quebec 1759: James Gibson, naval chaplain, writes to the naturalist, Gilbert White', *Journal of the Society for Army Historical Research*, 64 (1986), 218–23 · P. Foster and S. Markham, 'Gilbert White begins work on the antiquities of Selborne: two letters', *Proceedings of the Hampshire Field Club and Archaeological Society*, 45 (1989), 157–66 · J. E. Chatfield, 'Likenesses of the Reverend Gilbert White', *Proceedings of the Hampshire Field Club and Archaeological Society*, 43 (1987), 207–17 · W. S. Scott, *White of Selborne and his times* (1946) · P. Foster, 'Gilbert White: the natural history writing of a year [1770]', PhD diss., U. Southampton, 1984 · *Philosophical letters: between the late learned Mr Ray and several of his ingenious correspondents*, ed. W. Derham (1718) · T. White, 'Remarks on oaks', *GM*, 1st ser., 55 (1785), 109–12 · T. White, 'Natural history and antiquities of Selborne', *GM*, 1st ser., 59 (1789), 60–63, 144–6 [review] · J. Aikin, *An essay on the application of natural history to poetry* (1777) · W. Johnson, *Gilbert White: pioneer, poet, stylist* (1928) · gravestone, Selborne churchyard, Hampshire

Archives BL, garden calendar and naturalist's journal, annotated copy of T. Pennant's *British zoology*, Add. MSS 31846–31851, 35138–35139, 46472 · Gilbert White Museum, Selborne, Hampshire, Oates Memorial Library, corresp. and papers · Hants. RO, corresp. accounts, and sermons · Harvard U., Houghton L., corresp., accounts, and papers · Harvard U., Houghton L., Henshaw collection, autographs · JRL, corresp. and papers · JRL, letters to his family · Linn. Soc. · NRA, priv. coll., sermon and papers · NYPL, Berg collection, autographs · Oriel College, Oxford, accounts and sermons · RS, papers · RS, autographs | BL, letters to Daines Barrington, Add. MS 35852 · BL, letters to Thomas Pennant, Add. MS 35139 · Bodl. Oxf., letters to Ralph Churton · FM Cam., letters to Mary White · Hampshire County RO, Winchester, parish records · Wilts. & Swindon RO, parish records

Likenesses T. Chapman, pen-and-ink sketch, BL · pen drawing, BL · two sketches, BL

Wealth at death pecuniary gifts of almost £1500 in total (to Oriel College, Oxford, members of his family, and his personal servant); apportioned personal estate (bonds, government stock) into four equal parts for various nephews and nieces (eighteen such being named); bequeathed freeholds in four Sussex parishes (Trotton, Chithurst, Iping, and in East Harting) in three parcels to relatives, and residence in Selborne, The Wakes, and its grounds (which was copyhold) to brother; household goods given to sister-in-law; library given to two nephews; Tanner's *Notitia monastica* given to Ralph Churton of Brasenose College, Oxford

White, Gilbert (1859–1933), missionary and writer, was born on 9 June 1859 at Rondebosch, Cape Colony, southern Africa, son of Francis Gilbert White, clergyman, and his wife, Lucy, *née* Gilderdale; he was named after his great-uncle, the naturalist Gilbert *White (1720–1793). His parents returned to the United Kingdom in 1861 and Gilbert was educated at Fettes College, Edinburgh, and Oriel College, Oxford (BA, 1881; MA, 1885; honorary DD, 1908), where he was a contemporary of Cecil Rhodes. Ordained deacon in 1883 and priest in 1884 by the bishop of Truro, he was advised to emigrate because of a lung condition. He arrived at Townsville, north Queensland, in September 1885 and served on the Herbert River, at Charters Towers (1886); on the Atherton Tablelands (1888); at Ravenswood (1891); and as archdeacon of Townsville and incumbent of Hughenden (1892). On 24 August 1900, to mark the golden jubilee of the Australian Board of Missions, he was consecrated in Sydney the first bishop of Carpentaria and enthroned on Thursday Island in November.

While a bishop, White came to know the Australian inland and its Aboriginal inhabitants as well any living European. His diary—he kept one daily most of his life—of his journey across Australia from Port Darwin to Adelaide in winter 1901 was published first in Brisbane and twice reprinted. In 1904 he established a mission to Aborigines on the Mitchell River, funded by the Australian Board of Missions; in 1908 he helped found a second Aboriginal mission on the Roper River and a station on Moa Island for Aboriginals and south sea islanders from mainland Queensland. He preached lucidly and published widely, in Australia and the United Kingdom, on missionary topics. From July 1915 until September 1925 he was founding bishop of Willochra, a sparsely settled diocese in outback South Australia. His spirited private correspondence with Archbishop Randall Davidson and Bishop H. H. Montgomery reveals a perception of church politics and national and international issues rare among Australian prelates, even in metropolitan sees. While he supported the conscription referendums of 1917 and 1918 and embraced the ANZAC spirit engendered by the war, his outspoken views on social issues such as birth control

('race suicide') and the 'White Australia' policy ('race hatred') prevented his translation to any important Australian see.

A shy and scholarly man, fluent in classical Greek and Latin, French, German, Italian, and Spanish, between 1893 and 1910 White published three volumes of poetry, which show his mastery of the sonnet and his appreciation of the natural world. His prophetic poems 'Australia: 1913' and 'Australia: 1917' appeared first in the *Sydney Morning Herald*. *Poems* (1919), with an introduction by Sir Herbert Warren, contained early work and translations, while extracts and *The Later Poems of Gilbert White* (1930) appeared as *Selected Poems* in 1932. He also published two collections of sermons for the use of lay readers in 1922 and 1926, but he was best-known for his travelogues, *Across Australia* (1909), *Round about the Torres Straits* (1917), and *Thirty Years in Tropical Australia* (1918). He also contributed extensively as author and editor to Anglican church journals in Australia.

In July 1920 White helped draft the 'Appeal to all Christian people', the landmark paper on Christian unity produced by the Lambeth conference of that year. The following August he attended the preliminary world conference on faith and order in Geneva, and in 1925 was Australian delegate at the Stockholm ecumenical conference. His ecumenical endeavours in Australia were little appreciated, however. In 1926 he retired to Epping in Sydney, where he served on the boards of the *Church Standard* and the Australian board of missions, being editor of its *Review* until November 1932. Gilbert White died at his home, Selbourne, Pembroke Street, Epping, Sydney, on 1 April 1933. He never married: successive maiden sisters had kept his house. Many of his poems are dedicated to his sister Margaret. RUTH FRAPPELL

Sources J. W. C. Wand, *White of Carpentaria* [1949] · J. O. Feetham and W. V. Rymer, eds., *North Queensland jubilee book, 1878–1928* (1929) · *Australian Board of Missions Review* (1 May 1933) · *Church Standard* [Sydney] (7 April 1933) · R. Frappell and others, eds., *Anglicans in the Antipodes: an indexed calendar of the papers and correspondence of the archbishops of Canterbury, 1788–1961, relating to Australia, New Zealand and the Pacific* (1999) · D. M. Taylor, 'Bishop Gilbert White and councils of churches: a chapter of inter-church relations in Australia', *Journal of Religious History*, 2/3 (1962–3), 234–49

Archives LPL, Davidson MSS, incl. corresp. with H. H. Montgomery

Likenesses photograph, repro. in Wand, *White of Carpentaria*, frontispiece · photograph, repro. in *Australian Board of Missions Review* · photograph, repro. in *Church Standard*

White, Gordon Henry [*name in religion* Victor White] (1902–1960), Dominican friar, theologian, and psychotherapist, was born on 21 October 1902 at 39 Avondale Road, Croydon, Surrey, the second of the three sons of John Henry White (1866/7–1950), vicar of St Augustine's Church, and his wife, Beatrice Mary Phillips. He was educated at Bloxham School, near Banbury, Oxfordshire, 1916–19. In March 1921 he was received into the Roman Catholic church at St Charles House, Begbroke, Oxford, and was accepted for ordination in the Plymouth diocese.

While pursuing theological studies in Spain at the English College, Valladolid (1921–3), he became increasingly interested in the religious life of the order of Preachers (Dominicans) and joined their noviciate at Woodchester, Gloucestershire, in September 1923, taking the name Victor. Following studies at Hawkesyard Priory, Staffordshire, he was ordained in June 1928.

White was one of a remarkable generation of English Dominicans formed in the period of the charismatic provincialship (1916–32) of Bede Jarrett. In 1929 Blackfriars, Oxford, opened and became the house of studies of the English province and White was lector in theology from then until 1954. He made extensive lecture tours in the USA in 1947–8 and 1954–5. From 1954 he was based at the Dominican priory in Cambridge.

In the 1920s and 1930s White identified with the hopes of a new Christendom focused on land and craft-based family settlements associated with the ideas of the Dominican Vincent McNabb and the sculptor Eric Gill. But his was far too astute an intellect and sensibility to fall into line with any simple traditionalism. He was a regular contributor to the Dominican journal *Blackfriars* which was almost alone in Catholic circles in its refusal to be uncritically identified with the Franco forces in the Spanish Civil War. He was also among the few English Catholic theologians to debate the morality of modern warfare.

The outbreak of the Second World War coincided with a period of doubts about his Dominican vocation. A frequent writer on ecumenism—some of these contributions, with others in philosophy and theology, were collected in *The Unknown God* (1956)—White was interested in joining a planned Catholic and Orthodox community. In this period of turmoil he engaged in an intense analysis with John Layard and thus began that immersion in the work of C. G. Jung that preoccupied him until his death. White sent some of his publications to Jung in October 1945. They met with an enthusiastic response and in August 1946 he made the first of his visits to Jung's retreat at Bollingen on Lake Zürich, and in 1947 White was invited to be a founder member of the C. G. Jung Institute in Zürich. In the days before systematic training of analysts became the norm Jung's own recommendation was sufficient qualification, and White developed his therapeutic skills in work with religious communities and with the More Clinic in London. The intellectual acumen, innovative approach, and striking title of White's *God and the Unconscious* (1952), with a foreword by Jung, led to several translations and reprints. The Vatican authorities unsuccessfully requested the withdrawal of copies of the book in 1959.

Jung found in White a possible bridge to the Catholic world and someone with whom he could discuss on equal terms matters of vital importance to him. Their correspondence shows a sharing of both intellectual and personal concerns, discussing dreams and fantasies as well as points of philosophy and theology. To his cost White was one of the very few of Jung's inner circle at that time to stand his own ground on what he saw as the limitations of Jung's wider neo-gnostic vision. Modest, determined, taciturn, humorous, White's resilience was painfully tested in his years on the borderlands of psychology and theology.

White's arguments for making the 'psyche' of analytic discourse the contemporary equivalent of the theological term 'soul' caused some Catholic dissent, while some of the analysts reacted to his theological stance. Taking up ancient claims for an *anima naturaliter christiana* ('naturally Christian soul') White saw analytical psychology as an experiential and scientific resource for recasting natural theology in the modern age. Correlation of material from the Christian tradition, from the history of religions, and from the findings of analytical psychology was the kind of collaboration Jung desired. White's appeals to Thomistic philosophy for a point of vantage outside the psychological data to supplement and go beyond the comparative method was, however, something Jung was not disposed to permit. For White, 'no particularized science can establish its own first principles, but must accept them from a higher and more generalized science' (White, 213). In seeking in traditional philosophy a rational justification of what for the post-Kantian Jung could never be more than a questionable postulate, White sought an epistemological basis for analytical psychology.

It is in this longer perspective that the polemic over evil that ran from their first to their last contact is to be situated. The conflict of experiential opposites and their possible integration was a key feature of Jung's thinking, and this included the experience of good and evil, with obvious implications for the nature of God. White took the classic Christian philosophical position, confirmed by his own experience of Jungian analysis, that evil can exist only as the privation or distortion of a good and can be finally subsumed in an ultimate good. That is, for him, while good and evil are undoubtedly opposites they are not equivalent contraries. This Jung could never accept. White's initial enthusiasm for Jung's *Answer to Job* (1952) turned to caustic criticism two years later with controversy over its English publication and his exposed position as a supporter of Jung in the Catholic world. The rupture between the two was never satisfactorily healed.

White gave the 1958–9 Edward Cadbury lectures at the University of Birmingham. Published as *Soul and Psyche* (1960), they represent the summation of nearly twenty years engagement with Jungian psychology. Following several months of terminal intestinal cancer he died of a heart attack on 22 May 1960 at 5 Harrowby Court, London, while in the care of the Fabyc community in Kensington. He was buried in the Dominican cemetery at Woodchester, Gloucestershire.   ADRIAN CUNNINGHAM

Sources V. White, 'St Thomas Aquinas and Jung's psychology', *Blackfriars* (June 1944), 209–19 · *C. G. Jung: letters*, ed. G. Adler, 1 (1973) · Blackfriars, 25 George Square, Edinburgh, archives of the English Province of the Order of Preachers · b. cert. · *The Times* (23 May 1960) · A. C. Lammers, *In God's shadow: the collaboration of Victor White and C. G. Jung* (1994) · private information (2004) · bap. cert. **Archives** Blackfriars, 25 George Square, Edinburgh, archives of the English Province of the Order of Preachers

Likenesses double portrait, photograph (with Jung), repro. in G. Adler, ed., *C. G. Jung: letters* · portrait, Blackfriars, 25 George Square, Edinburgh

White, (Vincent) Gordon Lindsay [Gordy], **Baron White of Hull** (1923–1995), industrialist and financier, was born on 11 May 1923 at 124 College Grove, Drypool, Kingston upon Hull, Yorkshire, the son of Charles Victor White, a commercial traveller selling sweets, and his wife, Lily May, *née* Wilson. His father later ran a small printing company specializing in racecards and sporting brochures. Gordy White was educated at De Aston School, Lincolnshire, but was expelled at the age of sixteen after setting fire to school premises. Against his father's wishes he became an office boy with a Hull timber company but left after being refused an increase in his salary of 8s. a week. Shortly afterwards the Second World War was declared and he was able to join the RAF training corps after lying about his age. He then persuaded the army to enlist him and was posted to India, where the Special Operations Executive (SOE) recruited him. As a member of SOE's force 136 he served on flying duties in the destruction of bridges, railways, and shipping as part of the war against the Japanese. He had been a defiant, headstrong adolescent. The SOE disciplined and developed his powers: he lost none of his audacity but gained in self-control. In 1946 he was demobilized with the rank of captain.

After demobilization White returned to work for his father's printing company, Welbecson Press Ltd (of which he was chairman from 1947 until 1965). After his friend the Olympic showjumper Bill Hanson died in 1954, a steadfast bond developed between White and Hanson's older brother James. The two men went into business together importing humorous greeting cards into Britain, and although this venture was not strikingly successful, they sold it profitably and sought other opportunities. Their deep mutual sympathy ultimately yielded outstanding business success. On several occasions during the 1950s they together visited Hollywood, where White flirted with film stars, including Ava Gardner and Grace Kelly (Princess Rainier of Monaco). He had a playboy's keen eye for beautiful women, fast cars, and sleek horses. On 1 December 1958, with Hanson as his best man, he married (Ann) Elizabeth Kalén (b. 1935/6), daughter of Karl Gustaf Kalén, a Swedish diplomat. They had two daughters.

In 1964 Hanson and White sold their truck and van distribution company, Oswald Tillotson Ltd, to the Wiles group, which manufactured fertilizers and sacks. They then took over Wiles, reorganized the company, shed its surplus management, and sold off the fertilizer business. The next acquisition in their continuing diversification programme was a company that shifted muck and debris, Scottish Land Development. Having sold their greetings card firm, Hanson and White, they were unable to use their preferred name of Hanson–White for their new industrial investment company. Eventually, in 1965, they consolidated their interests in the newly formed Hanson Trust, which continued acquiring companies manufacturing sacks, bricks, paints, and fertilizers. The two men at its head were careful to avoid high-risk businesses, technologically advanced industries, or any commitment involving long-term investment. Supported by a small headquarters staff, they stripped the acquired companies down to essentials, pared them of inefficient management, and sold off extraneous parts (sometimes for as much as they had paid for the entirety). White, who was deputy chairman of Hanson Trust from 1965 until 1973, was a deal-maker of intimidating acumen and ruthlessness; he had no aptitude for management, which he left to Hanson.

During the early 1970s White became dismayed by business opportunities in Britain, where the Heath government had retreated from its commitment to economic deregulation and was mired in confrontations with trade unions. He was restless, adventurous, and, believing in himself, felt he was not getting enough action as a director of Hanson Trust. 'For him', Hanson recalled, 'board spelt B-O-R-E-D. His eyes would glaze over and he would not wake up until you started talking about money' (*Sunday Times*, 27 Aug 1995). In 1973 he left Hanson Trust's board and moved to New York. He was promised a stake of 10 per cent in any Hanson business conducted in the US; later this arrangement was exchanged for shares in the parent company. He became the first chairman of Hanson International Management Services, which was formed in 1974 to develop Hanson Trust's overseas opportunities.

Exchange controls prevented White from taking more than £3000 with him, but he ensconced himself in the Pierre Hotel in New York, and began working the telephones. For the rest of their lives, when separated by the Atlantic, Hanson and White spoke by telephone several times daily. White formed an American company, Hanson Industries, and began buying businesses in familiar sectors, notably fertilizers, animal feeds, and garden tools. The first acquisition—J. Howard Smith, a New Jersey family company making fishmeal—cost $32 million and had been rejected previously by more than forty other potential investors. His purchase coincided with a sharp rise in OPEC prices in 1973, and the profits in fish processing rose accordingly. This was typical of his canniness. Although outwardly he was a lavish spending and flamboyant buccaneer, he never gambled on bad risks in business. He was a market tactician who understood investors and covered the downside. Accordingly Hanson Industries made steady progress and (with White as its chairman from 1983) became one of the largest 100 companies in the US. This was an outstanding achievement at a time when few British entrepreneurs had either the daring or the ability to take on American business risks. New York during the Reagan presidency was where White thrived best. He had a notable coup in 1986 when, after a bitterly contested struggle, Hanson Industries paid $926 million for SCM, a company based on the old Smith-Corona typewriter business. Within a few months, White had sold off a third of the business and recouped the entire purchase price. SCM was his last fully hostile take-over. White's principal concern was always the return on capital employed. He relished his reputation as a corporate predator, who was feared in the board-rooms of the United States, but resented being called an asset stripper. Though he travelled incessantly, he never visited factories under his control. Indeed they held little interest for him except as assets. He was heedless of the human or social repercussions of his business decisions.

His first marriage having ended in divorce in 1968, in 1974 White married the actress Virginia North (real name Virginia Anne Northrup), daughter of Allen Northrup. They had a son, Lucas (b. 1974). The marriage was dissolved in 1979. In 1985 White began a relationship with Victoria Ann Tucker (b. 1963), a model from California. They married in 1992. He continued to live in New York even after Hanson Industries relocated its headquarters in New Jersey. He also had homes in Bel Air, Bermuda, and London.

In Britain, Hanson Trust acquired several large businesses, including United Drapery Stores (1983), the London Brick Company (1984), Imperial Tobacco group (1986), and Consolidated Goldfields, for which the trust paid £3.3 billion in 1989. White was crucial in these take-overs, which confirmed the reputation of Hanson Trust for buying low, selling high, and operating its companies with ruthless efficiency. On average nearly one-third of the cost of a Hanson acquisition was recouped through disposal in the first six months. By the start of the 1990s Hanson Trust was Britain's sixth biggest company. The value of its shares rose by 31,077 per cent between 1965 and 1991.

The economic policies and enterprise culture imposed by the Thatcher government were crucial to this phenomenal success, and both White and Hanson tried to show their gratitude. In 1986, during the crisis resulting in the cabinet resignations of Michael Heseltine and Leon Brittan, they supported Margaret Thatcher's wishes by buying a stake of almost 15 per cent in Westland Aircraft and voting for its co-operation with Sikorsky-Fiat. They were keen to help privatize Britain's nationalized industries, though their interest in Hanson Trust's taking over the whole of British Coal and the state-owned electricity generating company PowerGen came to nothing. White and Hanson jointly received the Aims of Industry free enterprise award (1985).

White served on the board of British Airways (1989–93), a company which he and Hanson at one time considered as a take-over target. Both men were friends of British Airways chairman, Lord King of Wartnaby. Their relations with Sir Denys Henderson, chairman of ICI, however, deteriorated after Hanson Trust in May 1991 made a raid on the shares of ICI, buying a 2.8 per cent stake. A rough tussle with the ICI board ensued; Hanson Trust did not bid for ICI, and later sold its ICI shares at a profit of £40 million. Nevertheless the failure of their ICI manoeuvres dented the reputation for infallibility of White and Hanson, and in 1992 both men announced their intention to retire five years later, in 1997.

In the first honours list of the Thatcher administration, in 1979, White was created KBE for services to British commercial and community interests in the USA. Hanson having received a life peerage in 1983, the Thatcher resignation honours of 1990 promoted White to the same level. His title was gazetted in January 1991 as Baron White of Hull, county Humberside. White and Hanson were archetypal capitalists of the Thatcher years, and it was fitting that White should be honoured at the start and close of her long premiership. In the United States he was the first British citizen to receive a national voluntary award (1984), and chaired the international committee of congressional awards (1984–92). His academic honours included an honorary fellowship of St Peter's College, Oxford (1984), and an honorary doctorate in economics from the University of Hull (1985).

The turf was a passion of White's. He started buying point-to-pointers and hunters before spending many millions of pounds on bloodstock. He was never as successful as his outlay deserved, although he was quarter-owner of the 1987 Derby winner, Reference Point. It was at his instigation that a Hanson Trust acquisition, the Ever Ready Batteries company, provided sponsorship in 1984 which ensured the survival of the Derby, the Oaks, and the Coronation Cup at a cost of £600,000 a year. He repeatedly urged that both bookmakers and the government should give greater financial support to horse-racing. In 1989 he and Hanson lunched with the chairman of the Horserace Totalisator Board (Tote), Lord Wyatt of Weeford, who described them as 'an engaging couple who have made vast fortunes'. They offered to invest £100 million in the Tote in exchange for 90 per cent of the shares, but this privatization did not occur. Wyatt noted afterwards of White, 'he is tall and lean and keen' (Wyatt, 6–7, 76). There was controversy when it was revealed in 1991 that Hanson Trust had lost about £7.7 million running three bloodstock syndicates, Cheval 1, 2, and 3; but White was never abashed at revelations of his high-handed methods.

White was 6 feet 5 inches in height, debonair, and had a licence to pilot a helicopter. He lived with gusto, had strong animal spirits, and was phenomenally tough in mind and body. His habits were opulent and restless. He once established a 'desk to desk' record of 4 hours, 20 minutes and 30 seconds from his London office in Knightsbridge to his New York headquarters on Park Avenue by synchronization of Rolls Royce car, Concorde aircraft, and helicopter. His accent evolved into a highly characteristic drawl amalgamating east Yorkshire with Manhattan. He was associated with many glamorous women: Sir David Frost joked at his memorial service in St Paul's, Knightsbridge, on 11 October 1995, that the slimmest book in the world would have been *In Praise of Older Women* by Gordy White.

Despite a hernia operation in 1990 and being diagnosed with pulmonary disease, White never relented in his punishing schedule of work and travel. After helping to finalize Hanson Trust's £2.5 billion bid for Eastern Electricity, he experienced breathing difficulties while flying home to Bel Air, and was admitted to a Los Angeles hospital, where he died on 23 August 1995. He was probably buried in Bermuda where he had bought a burial plot. He was survived by his third wife, Victoria, and by the three children of his previous marriages.

RICHARD DAVENPORT-HINES

Sources *The Times* (28 Aug 1995) · *The Independent* (28 Aug 1995) · *Sunday Times* (27 Aug 1995) · *The journals of Woodrow Wyatt*, ed. S. Curtis, 3 vols. (1998–2000), vol. 2 · *Debrett's Peerage* · *WWW*, 1991–5 · b. cert. · m. cert. [Ann Elizabeth Kalén]
Likenesses S. Morgan, photograph, repro. in *The Independent* · double portrait, photograph (with Grace Kelly), repro. in *The Independent* · photograph, repro. in *Sunday Times* · photograph, repro. in *The Times*
Wealth at death £2,583,092: administration, 3 June 1996, *CGPLA Eng. & Wales*

White, (William) Hale [*pseud.* Mark Rutherford] (1831–1913), writer and civil servant, was born on 22 December 1831 in High Street, Bedford, the eldest son of William *White (1807–1882), radical nonconformist bookseller and pamphleteer, later principal door-keeper of the House of Commons, and his wife, Mary Anne Chignell, a baker's daughter from Colchester. His father was a pillar of the Old (Bunyan) Meeting-House, Mill Lane, in Bedford, the heartland of classic provincial dissent, while his mother's family composed the complexly intermarried core of Colchester's Lion Walk Congregational church. The east midlands tradition of Congregationalist independency animated Hale White's lifelong liberal and democratic outlook, even though from early on he veered away from being the orthodox member his mother in particular wanted. He was educated at a little school for 'young ladies' before entering at the age of ten the English School, Angel Street, Bedford, which was the 'modern school' favoured by local dissenters, Bedford's ancient grammar school having strong Anglican connections. In order to enter the Congregationalist ministry, for which his family designed him, he had to become a full member of the Bunyan Meeting. This involved public testimony, puritan Calvinist fashion, to Christian conversion before the congregation; but as Hale White never ceased to explain, he made his confession without any genuine spiritual experience to support it. Aged seventeen he entered the Countess of Huntingdon's College at Cheshunt, on his road to the ministry: he later called this move 'the great blunder of his life'. He obtained a London University BA, and towards the end of 1851 transferred to the Independent churches' New College in St John's Wood, London. He was beginning to be influenced by the literary and theological ferments of his time. His preferred reading was Carlyle, Ruskin, Tennyson, and Wordsworth. Very soon he and two other students were up before a kind of kangaroo court charged with unsafe views on the inerrancy of the Bible, and they were expelled early in 1852. The case achieved notoriety in the nonconformist and national press, and led to Hale White's father seceding from the Bedford meeting for failing to stand by his son (he published a protesting pamphlet, *To Think or Not to Think*, 1852).

Casting about for employment Hale White took up a schoolmastering post in Stoke Newington, where he

(William) Hale White (1831–1913), by Arthur Hughes, 1887

lasted only a few hours, fleeing for his sanity after a terrible night of vastation, a kind of spiritual urban angst, bouts of which recurred all his life (nervous breakdowns in effect). John Chapman, 'editor' of the radical *Westminster Review* gave him work as a subscription tout and put him up in his raffish ménage at 142 The Strand. A momentous fellow lodger was the woman who actually ran the paper, Marian Evans, not yet the novelist known as George Eliot. Ever after Hale White remembered her kindness, regretted that he allowed her acquaintance to drop, and made her the type of all the sparky out-of-reach females who haunt the men of his stories. In February 1854 Hale White left Chapman for a junior clerkship in the registrar general's office at Somerset House, and moved to the Admiralty accounts department in the same building in 1858. He rose steadily through the civil service ranks. When he retired in March 1892 he was assistant director of naval contracts.

Like many another pious Victorian marooned on the shores of lost faith, Hale White cast about seriously for an ethic of his own to live by. He remained haunted by his native nonconformity. He attended the preaching of renowned London dissenting ministers, Caleb Morris of Fetter Lane and Thomas Binney of the King's Weigh House Chapel. He 'supplied' the Unitarian pulpit at Ditchling, Sussex, for a year (1856–7), preached occasionally for Morris, and at Unitarian chapels in Ipswich and London. In 1859 he and friends rented a room in Little Portland Street, London, for people in need of Sunday rest and home-made pious reflection (he was greatly shocked by the needs of the slum residents he observed).

On his twenty-fifth birthday in 1856 at Kentish Town Congregational Church Hale White married Harriet Arthur, his landlady's half-sister, reputedly a Pre-

Raphaelite beauty, who had studied piano with Sir Arthur Hallé; they had five sons and a daughter. Money was short, and Hale White started supplementing his income by writing for provincial papers of a Liberal nonconformist cast, such as the *Norfolk News* and the *Rochdale Observer*. For many years from 1860 he reported House of Commons proceedings for the *Birmingham Daily Post*, a taxing business indeed (in the house after Admiralty hours, up at 4 a.m., scribbling his pieces in the train coming up from Carshalton, where his family settled).

Hale White never gave up writing for the papers. He even ended up as a sort of doyen of the *British Weekly*, the nonconformist newspaper. But amid all the busy hacking, his literary ambitions were always more high-minded. He assiduously cultivated the acquaintance of notable aesthetic persons: Carlyle, Browning, Ruskin, William Morris, Rossetti, and Swinburne. (He enlisted Ruskin's over the house Philip Webb designed for him at Carshalton; his third son, Jack, married a daughter of the minor Pre-Raphaelite painter Arthur Hughes.) And his grander aesthetic plans fruited publicly when in 1881 *The Autobiography of Mark Rutherford*, fictitiously 'edited by his friend Reuben Shapcott', appeared: White's first book at the age of fifty. *Mark Rutherford's Deliverance* followed in 1885, also edited by 'Reuben Shapcott'. Behind this double pseudonymous hedge—which remained in place for all Hale White's fictional outings—he carefully spilt the beans about the chapel life and the narrow dissenting pietisms of his youth, and vented his satirical fury over what he perceived as the decline of the old nonconformist radicalisms into modern shallowness and hypocrisy. Such are the targets of his most ambitious historical novel, *The Revolution in Tanner's Lane* (1887), as well, more or less, as of the less potent *Miriam's Schooling* (1891), and his retirement novels *Catharine Furze* (1893) and *Clara Hopgood* (1896). In all these books—which he never liked owning up to in public—he showed a compelling aptitude for confessionalism, for serious truth-telling testimony in classic plain-style puritan mode. He tends to overdo the stylistic precision and plainness, perhaps in compensation for that less than truthful confession of faith in his youth. His moral rectitude is a keynote. He was naggingly obsessed with 'purity of life'. The Bible obsessed him. *Mark Rutherford's Deliverance*, for instance, characteristically incorporates his 'Notes on the Book of Job' and an essay, 'Principles'. Protestant writers such as D. H. Lawrence, André Gide, and Donald Davie enthused over what they recognized as a very fine exponent of veracious protestant imagining.

In his own name William Hale White published translations of Spinoza in 1883 and 1905 (Spinoza's *Ethics* was a lifelong inspiration), and *A Description of the Wordsworth and Coleridge MSS in the Possession of Mr T Norton Longman* (1897), *An Estimation of the Charge of Apostasy Against Wordsworth* (1898), and his long meditated *John Bunyan* (1907). As Mark Rutherford he brought out many stories and longer essays in *Pages from a Journal* (1900) and *More Pages from a Journal* (1910). After many years of increasing illness (disseminated sclerosis leading to almost total paralysis), and

of apparent marital estrangement (regretted marriages, unhappy husbands, men desiring lively women not their wives people White's stories extravagantly), Harriet White died on 1 June 1890 in the invalid apartments in the Ashtead house to which the couple's peregrinations across southern England had finally brought them. White the widower, always on the move in search of the ideal abode, was greatly attracted to literary women in his several localities. One of these many admirers, Dorothy Vernon Horace Smith, a novelist in her early thirties, sister of the headmaster of Sherborne School, sister-in-law of Humphrey Milford, the 'printer' to the Oxford University Press, a devout Anglican who worked for a church mission in Beckenham, became his companion and, after cancer set in, his nurse. On 8 April 1911 they married in the church at Groombridge, she thirty-four, he almost eighty. He made her abandon her Sunday Bible class for young men, but not her devoted church attendance. He died on 14 March 1913 at The Cottage, Groombridge; he was cremated and his ashes were buried in Groombridge parish churchyard.

Dorothy White loyally garnered his papers, making copies of his letters and notebooks. She got her brother-in-law's Oxford University Press to publish the *Last Pages from a Journal* (1915), which she edited, *The Early Life of Mark Rutherford, by himself* (1913)—yet one more plain-dealing run around the experiences up to his first marriage—and also the volume *Letters to Three Friends* (1924). Humphrey Milford also published Dorothy White's *Groombridge Diary* (1924), a loving celebration of the husband whose final years she shared—it includes his letters and some photographs. In 1924 W. Robertson Nicoll of the *British Weekly* brought out his memories of Mark Rutherford, deeply intimate with White's position within nonconformity. Dorothy White's nephew the bibliophile Simon Nowell-Smith not only guarded her White papers after her death but produced his *Mark Rutherford: A Short Bibliography of First Editions* (1930) and wrote a family insider's introduction to an edition in 1971 of *The Revolution in Tanner's Lane*. The standard life by Catherine Macdonald Maclean appeared in 1955.

VALENTINE CUNNINGHAM

Sources W. H. White [Mark Rutherford], *The early life of Mark Rutherford, by himself* (1913) · S. Nowell-Smith, *Mark Rutherford: a short bibliography of the first editions* (1930) · W. H. Stone, *The religion and art of William Hale White (Mark Rutherford)* (1954) · I. Stock, *William Hale White (Mark Rutherford): a critical study* (1956) · C. Macdonald Maclean, *Mark Rutherford: a biography* (1955) · S. Nowell-Smith, 'The case of Arthur Craven', *Malahat Review*, 13 (Jan 1970), 47–54 · S. Nowell-Smith, Introduction, *The revolution in Tanner's Lane* (1971) · V. Cunningham, *Everywhere spoken against: dissent in the Victorian novel* (1975) · D. Davie, *A gathered church: the literature of the English dissenting interest, 1700–1930* (1978) · H. Klinke, *William Hale White (Mark Rutherford): Versuch einer Biographie* (1930) · m. cert. [Harriet Arthur] · m. cert. [Dorothy Smith] · d. cert. · *CGPLA Eng. & Wales* (1913)

Archives Bedford Central Library, corresp. and papers · BL, autobiographical notes, Add. MS 44891 · Bodl. Oxf., letters and notes [typescript copies] · NRA, corresp. and literary papers · U. Reading L., letters · University of British Columbia Library, corresp., literary MSS, and papers | BL, corresp. with Sir Sydney Cockerell, Add. MS 52768 · BL, corresp. with Gladys Easdale, Add. MS 47779 ·

Bodl. Oxf., letters to Bertram Dobell · U. Sussex, letters to Erica Storr, SxMs 6
Likenesses A. Foord Hughes, portrait, 1855, probably Bedford Town Council · A. Hughes, drawing, 1887, Cecil Higgins Art Gallery and Museum, Bedford [see illus.] · A. Hughes, portrait, priv. coll. · photographs, repro. in Maclean, *Mark Rutherford* · portraits, repro. in Maclean, *Mark Rutherford*
Wealth at death £5468 18s. 3d.: probate, 8 May 1913, *CGPLA Eng. & Wales*

White, Henrietta Margaret (1856–1936), educationist and college head, was born on 13 July 1856 at Charleville, Roscrea, Queen's county, Ireland, into a protestant Anglo-Irish gentry family, the second of the four children of Henry White, JP and deputy lieutenant, and his wife, Elizabeth Russell. Known to her friends as Hennie, she was educated privately and then at Alexandra College, Dublin, from 1873, and at Newnham College, Cambridge, 1882–5. Her appointment as lady principal of Alexandra College in 1890 came under some initial criticism on account of her lack of scholastic achievements, for she had taken no university examinations at Cambridge, but she soon proved by her vision and qualities of leadership that the choice had fallen on the right person.

Alexandra College had reached a critical stage in its development, with no endowment and large debts totalling almost £10,000, and in need of new buildings. Within a period of ten years the college finances had been placed on a sound footing, and a rebuilding programme begun, due largely to Miss White's energy and initiative. She had a tremendous capacity for friendship and she made Alexandra College a cultural centre around which she gathered a wide circle of friends and patrons, including many influential members of the Anglo-Irish aristocracy. Alexandra College became the first women's college to have an art lectureship attached, the Hermione art lectures, endowed by Hermione, duchess of Leinster, in 1896. Lady Ardilaun of the Guinness family endowed the Ardilaun lectures in history in 1921.

In May 1897 Henrietta White founded the Alexandra College Guild, which brought together old students in active social service work. They formed the Alexandra Guild Tenement Company Ltd, managed entirely by women, in 1898. Its five tenement houses in Dublin were run on the same lines as those managed by Octavia Hill in London. The Social Service Union, which grew out of the guild in March 1901, provided bursaries for 'ladies of gentle birth and education' unable to support themselves. Other guild initiatives included a club for factory girls started at the Greenmount Spinning Factory, Harold's Cross, in 1903; the Alexandra children's holiday fund in 1908; and a hostel for working girls from the country opened in Castlewood House, Rathmines, in 1912. In 1914 the Pembroke Garden Village of twenty-two cottages, the first attempt to create a garden village in Dublin, was handed over to Miss White to administer on behalf of the guild.

Miss White made an important contribution to the intermediate education inquiry commission in 1899. She

rebutted the arguments put forward by those intermediate education board members who were making a last-ditch effort to get through a separate examination programme for girls. Her contribution to women's university education was less successful. As vice-president of the Central Association of Irish Schoolmistresses she warmly supported the successful public campaign to admit women to the degrees of the University of Dublin (Trinity College), but failed to secure state endowment for separate women's colleges. Despite the establishment of a number of specialized departments in Alexandra College, notably the teacher training department, student numbers gradually dwindled away. In 1905 Trinity College, Dublin, conferred an honorary LLD degree on her in recognition of her signal services to women's higher education in Ireland.

Miss White became an early supporter of the women's suffrage movement through her friendship with Mrs Millicent Fawcett, although she never openly campaigned for the vote. As a committed unionist, she did everything possible to involve Alexandra College in various branches of war work. A house for Belgian refugees 'of the better class' was opened in October 1914, in Northbrook Road, Dublin; a guild workroom in Westland Row also opened in 1914, where women knitted socks for the war effort, and a war club for the wives of soldiers and sailors was opened in D'Olier Street in 1915. She was a member of the first Teachers' Registration Council in 1914 and retained this position under the Free State government until 1930. Miss White was also a member of the vice-regal committee on teachers' salaries set up in 1919, and was president of the Irish branch of the International Federation of University Women between 1925 and 1929.

A keen gardener and a noted collector of sweetly scented pelargoniums, Miss White corresponded with the leading horticulturists of the day, including William Robinson, G. H. Engleheart, Maria Theresa Earle, and William E. Gumbleton. She helped promote horticultural education for girls in Ireland by persuading Sir Frederick Moore, then keeper of the Royal Botanic Gardens, Glasnevin, to start the first training course in Ireland for lady gardeners in 1898. After forty-two years as lady principal of Alexandra College, Henrietta White retired in 1932. She died at her home, Coolevin, 65 Ailesbury Road, Ballsbridge, Dublin, on 16 July 1936, and was buried at Charleville. A. V. O'CONNOR

Sources *Irish Times* (17 July 1936) · *Irish Times* (18 July 1936) · *Irish Times* (22 July 1936) · *Irish Times* (24 July 1936) · *Alexandra College Magazine*, 83 (Dec 1932), 1–12 · Lady Moore, *Gardening Illustrated* (25 July 1936) · Alexandra College, Dublin · *Newnham College Roll Letter* (1937), 71–2 · 'Commissioners on intermediate education', *Parl. papers* (1899), 23.178–200, C. 9512 [Ireland] · 'Appendix to the first report: minutes of evidence', *Parl. papers* (1901), 31.245–50, Cd 826 [commission on university education, Ireland] · 'Final report: appendix', *Parl. papers* (1907), 41.263–6, Cd 3312 [royal commission on Trinity College, Dublin] · Burke, *Gen. GB* · parish records (baptism), Roscrea, Queen's county, Ireland, 20 Aug 1856 · d. cert.
Archives Alexandra College, Milltown, Dublin, incl. speeches to students, speeches at the National Union of Women Workers conferences, speech at the National Women's Employment Bureau for Glasgow annual meeting (1908), and corresp.

Likenesses J. E. Bliss, photograph, c.1882–1885 · P. A. de Laszlo, 1901, Alexandra College, Dublin · group photograph, c.1903, Alexandra College, Dublin · W. Orpen, portrait, 1930, Alexandra College, Dublin

Wealth at death £8820 6s. 11d.: probate, 9 Sept 1936, CGPLA Eng. & Wales · £9410 4s. 2d.: will

White, Henry (1784–1851). See under Bewick, Thomas, apprentices (act. 1777–1828).

White, Henry (1812–1880), historian, born at Reading on 23 November 1812, was the son of Charles White. He was educated at Reading grammar school under Richard Valpy and went up to Trinity College, Cambridge, in 1828. He also studied at the University of Heidelberg, where he obtained the degree of PhD. He married in 1837 Elizabeth King of Boulogne. In the earlier part of his career, after working at Geneva with Merle d'Aubigné for some time, he was chiefly occupied with scholastic work, and published several historical textbooks, including Elements of Universal History (1843), History of Great Britain and Ireland (1849), History of France (1850), and Outlines of Universal History (1853). He also translated Merle d'Aubigné's History of the Reformation between 1843 and 1853. In 1858 he was appointed to superintend the compilation of the Catalogue of Scientific Papers published by the Royal Society, and was engaged in this work until his death. He became a fellow of the Society of Antiquaries on 24 May 1860. For some years he also acted as literary critic to the Atlas during the editorship of Henry James Slack.

In 1867 White published his most significant book, The massacre of St Bartholomew, preceded by a history of the religious wars in the reign of Charles IX. This was the first English work to argue that the massacre was the result of a sudden decision, and not of a long-prepared conspiracy. Subsequently, in conjunction with Thomas W. Newton he prepared the Catalogue of the Library of the Museum of Practical Geology, published in 1878. White died suddenly on 4 January 1880 while on duty in the library of the Royal Society in Burlington House, Piccadilly, London. He was survived by his wife and several children.

E. I. CARLYLE, rev. NILANJANA BANERJI

Sources Venn, Alum. Cant. · Allibone, Dict. · The Athenaeum (10 Jan 1880), 58 · Boase, Mod. Eng. biog. · Trubner's American, European and Oriental literary record (1880), 12 · private information (1900) · CGPLA Eng. & Wales (1880)

Wealth at death under £100: administration, 28 Aug 1880, CGPLA Eng. & Wales

White, Henry Julian (1859–1934), biblical scholar and dean of Christ Church, Oxford, was born at Islington in London on 27 August 1859, the younger son of Henry John White, a merchant seaman and later a bank clerk, and his wife, Susannah Wadeson. Educated privately and at the Islington proprietary school, White matriculated in 1878 at Christ Church, Oxford, where, after graduating in classics, he was awarded a first-class degree in theology in 1883. He obtained the Denyer and Johnson theological scholarship in 1884 and the senior Greek testament prize in 1885. He was ordained deacon in 1885 and priest in 1886. One of White's examiners in theology, John Wordsworth, appointed him in 1884 as an assistant in the great critical

edition of the Vulgate New Testament, which Wordsworth had begun six years before. This partnership was to be a significant one.

In 1885 Wordsworth was consecrated to the see of Salisbury. In 1886, after a year as curate at Oxted, Surrey, White followed him in order to become his chaplain and (in 1887) vice-principal at Sarum Theological College, Salisbury. White remained at Salisbury until he became theological lecturer and chaplain at Merton College, Oxford, in 1895. During these years not only did he make his main contributions to the series Old Latin biblical texts, but the first tangible results of the partnership—the 'Wordsworth and White' Vulgate gospels—began to emerge; this work was published in separate parts from 1889 and was finally completed in 1954. The Acts did not appear until 1905, the year in which White left his fellowship at Merton College, which he had held for eight years; he then became professor of New Testament exegesis at King's College, London, a post which he was to hold for fifteen years. On 7 September 1909 he married Clara Miller Warden, widow, daughter of George Berkeley White.

In 1911 White published a convenient minor edition of the Latin New Testament. Nearly all of his spare time was devoted to the Vulgate, but as the Latin and patristic evidence for inclusion grew, so the workload increased; it was made more onerous after Wordsworth's death in 1911. After he became dean of Christ Church, Oxford, in 1920, progress became even slower. White's spare time was now severely limited, and publication of his work had advanced only as far as Ephesians when he died at the deanery, Christ Church, Oxford on 16 July 1934.

White was 'neither a great ecclesiastic nor an exceptional administrator' (DNB). His colleagues at Christ Church were impressed mainly by his personal qualities. But his scholarship was recognized: he received the honorary degree of DD from the universities of St Andrews (1910) and Dublin (1927), and he was elected a fellow of the British Academy in 1932 and an honorary fellow of Merton College in 1921.

JOANNA HAWKE

Sources S. C. E. Legg, 'Henry Julian White, 1859–1934', PBA, 22 (1936), 408–17 · E. W. Watson, Life of Bishop John Wordsworth (1915) · The Times (17 July 1934) · Oxford Magazine (25 Oct 1934) · Journal of Theological Studies, 36 (1935), 11–13 · Allibone, Dict. · DNB · m. cert.

Archives Christ Church Oxf., corresp. and papers; notes on biblical texts | LPL, corresp. and papers relating to Anglo-Continental Society

Likenesses E. Moore, oils, 1928, Christ Church Oxf. · Elliott & Fry, photograph, NPG · E. Moore, oils, Christ Church Oxf.

Wealth at death £13,794 14s. 9d.: probate, 13 Aug 1934, CGPLA Eng. & Wales

White, Henry Kirke (1785–1806), poet and essayist, was born on 21 March 1785 at a house in Exchange Alley, Nottingham, the third of the six children of John White (b. 1750/51), a butcher, and his wife, Mary, née Neville (b. 1755). John White's occupation was an established one in his family, running back to the beginning of the century. Mary White, who became a teacher in 1798 or 1799 when she opened a girls' school, was the daughter of a framework-knitter who had come from Staffordshire to Nottingham to be apprenticed in the trade in 1728, but the

Neville family had been yeoman farmers in Staffordshire from the sixteenth century. At an early age Henry Kirke White was sent to a local school run by a Mrs Garrington, who quickly recognized and nurtured his reading ability and other capacities. From here he went to the Revd John Blanchard's school, reputedly the best in Nottingham. Blanchard further reinforced the view that he was a child of exceptional talent. White's schooling was interrupted by his father's need for assistance in his business, which led to a family dispute finally resolved by his eventual removal to yet another local school. When he was fourteen he found employment in the local textiles trade, working at a stocking-loom for about a year, before he found a place to train in the law, at the offices of Coldham and Enfield, town clerks and attorneys. There he began to learn Latin and Greek, which he worked at in the evenings, and extended his studies to include Italian, Spanish, and Portuguese as well as science. He also joined a local literary society at which he practised his skills in oratory.

White's first literary success is marked by his winning of two prizes in the Monthly Preceptor, for a translation of Horace in 1800, and an imaginary tour from London to Edinburgh in 1801. Further prizes followed, and thus encouraged White became a regular correspondent for the Monthly Mirror, through which he became acquainted with Capel Lofft, and the magazine's owner, Thomas Hill. Lofft and Hill were both known for their work in supporting the notion of a specifically English canon of poetry, and their influence can be seen in White's early productions for the Mirror, under the title of 'Remarks on the English poets'. While there is no evidence to suggest that White was unhappy with his employment, a preference for a career in the church was evident by 1802. Such a move required study at one of the universities, and in order to raise some of the necessary funds, White began work on a small volume of poems that was published in 1803 under the title Clifton Grove, a Sketch in Verse, with other Poems. The volume was dedicated to the duchess of Devonshire, and unluckily described in the dedication as the 'trifling effusions of a very youthful muse', this deference being further reinforced in the preface where White compounded his vulnerability by stating his motive to fund his studies. Such gestures were relatively common at the time, and they invited an equally common response from the critics in the form of ridicule or censure. White was no exception: in the Monthly Review of February 1804, his volume was commended for its effort but damned for its evident failure in 'the difficult art of writing good poetry'. More cutting for White perhaps was the reviewer's exposure of his impecunity and scholarly ambition which also provided the platform for the assertion that should White ever gain the benefits of study 'he will, doubtless, produce better sense and better rhymes'. This volume nevertheless attracted more favourable notice too, most notably from Robert Southey, whose interest in White resulted in some correspondence.

Having failed to make money out of his poetry, White did not give up his plans to enter university. In fact his determination was strengthened by a deepening of his religious conviction, which had been disturbed for a while around 1801 by an interest in deism. By June 1803, however, White had committed himself to the evangelical movement in the Anglican church, and encouraged by his employers and his acquaintance with local clergy, he received an introduction to Charles Simeon, the famous evangelical at King's College, Cambridge. Simeon secured for White a sizarship at St John's, for which he was advised to prepare by studying for a year with the Revd Lorenzo Grainger, curate at Winteringham in Lincolnshire. In 1805 White progressed to Cambridge and competed for a vacant scholarship in his first term. In order to prepare for the examination White read widely and voraciously, neglecting his health in the process, but he was successful, and in his short time at Cambridge, he became a highly regarded scholar. However, White had been ill for some time with consumption, and the punishing regime he set himself for study exacerbated his illness. He died, unmarried, on 19 October 1806 in his rooms at college, and he was buried in All Saints' churchyard, Cambridge.

After his death a large quantity of verse and prose was found among White's papers, and this material was given by his family to Robert Southey, who duly compiled The Remains of Henry Kirke White ... with an Account of his Life (2 vols., 1807). By 1818 The Remains was in its tenth edition, including two American editions, and White's reputation as a promising poet who had died tragically young was firmly established. This volume formed the basis of White's reputation in the nineteenth century, and contains a range of poetry, including sonnets, odes, ballads, and descriptive verse, some religious, and some secular. Byron (a contemporary of White at Cambridge, although they never met) included a portrait of him in English Bards and Scotch Reviewers (1809) as a young genius of great potential, killed in part by his own excessive talent. Later, Keats's friend Richard Woodhouse believed that Kirke White was one of the 'lone spirits who could proudly sing/ Their youth away, and die' alluded to in Keats's Sleep and Poetry (1817). Although there is little evidence to show that White had any influence of note on the poets of the time, there is no doubt about the fact that the success of Southey's edition ensured that his poetry was widely read.

The few attempts that have been made in the twentieth century to revive White's reputation have been unsuccessful. White is rarely represented in anthologies or in accounts of Romanticism, despite the considerable merit of his work, and the potential for its recognition as a prime example of provincial writing in the period. Part of the reason for this rests with the still prevalent view that the significance of late eighteenth- and early nineteenth-century writing must inhere in its innovative qualities, and thus those writers who are working largely within the polite conventions of the period are not granted the attention so freely given to the Romantics. White's works are characterized by a contemplative mode: his sonnets, odes, and longer descriptive and meditative poems commonly feature the solitary condition and pensive mind, and in this respect they belong to the tradition that runs from Milton through Gray to Wordsworth and Coleridge. What little attention White receives tends to highlight his early promise in the accomplished *Clifton Grove*, but his lyrics, sonnets, and odes also repay interest. Most neglected of all is the limited collection of prose pieces, and the series known as *Melancholy Hours*.   PHILIP W. MARTIN

Sources R. Southey, 'Memoir of Henry Kirke White', in *The poetical works and remains of Henry Kirke White* (1858) · R. T. Beckwith, *Poems, hymns and prose writings: Henry Kirke White* (1985) · R. T. Beckwith, 'The ancestry and family relationships of Henry Kirke White', *Transactions of the Thoroton Society*, 97 (1993), 150–53 · *DNB*
Archives U. Nott. L., family corresp., literary MSS, commonplace books, and papers
Likenesses paper silhouette, before 1806, priv. coll. · T. Barber, oils, 1807, priv. coll. · S. Freeman, stipple, pubd 1808 (after T. Barber), BM, NPG · F. Chantry, medallion, 1819, NPG · T. Barber, oils, Castle Art Gallery, Nottingham · F. C. Cooper, oils, Castle Art Gallery, Nottingham · J. Hoppner, oils, Castle Art Gallery, Nottingham · Hoppner, oils, NPG · S. Redgate, oils (after unknown artist), NPG · miniature, V&A · pencil drawing, NPG

White, James (1759–1799), historical novelist, was born in Dublin. He became a scholar of Trinity College, Dublin, in 1778 and graduated BA in 1780. Nothing is known about his family, or the reasons that brought him to England where he spent the rest of his life.

White was an accomplished translator, poet, and novelist. The first signs of his enduring interest in public affairs are already evident in his translation *The Orations of Marcus Tullius Cicero Against Caius Cornelius Verres* (1787), which coincided with the impeachment of 'another provincial governor', Warren Hastings of the East India Company, in which White became involved (Tompkins, 147). This work was followed by a pamphlet entitled *Hints for a specific plan for an abolition of the slave trade and for the relief of the negroes in the British West Indies* (1788). In this spirited abolitionist tract, White manages to combine his polemical spirit with hard-headed arguments and a wry sense of humour in the vein of Jonathan Swift: if skin colour and facial features are valid criteria for designating human beings as 'a species of traffic' such as 'elephant teeth, wax and leather', he argues, why not have laws 'authorizing all *dunces* to be exported from time to time and sold in the West Indies? ... The kingdom would be disburthened of many able-bodied blockheads, and the duty of exportation would advantage the revenue' (*Hints*, 7). White bases his abolitionist thesis on his impressive knowledge of the relevant classical, contemporary, and legal literature. In a coherent and structured way he refutes the main arguments for slave trade one by one, appealing to both the humanity and the common sense of his readers. Fully aware of how hard it would be to convince a 'commercial people', such as the British, to espouse his cause, he took pains to tabulate the costs of importing and maintaining slaves, as compared to converting them into paid workers, and advocated the phasing out of slavery in conjunction with setting up a welfare programme for the benefit of black workers in the British Caribbean (*Hints*, 12–27). Some of his proposals spring from a keen sense of patriotism, often bordering on nationalism, and are in line with colonial aims. Nevertheless, his indignation at the savage practice of human

trafficking is genuine: 'British brutality has become proverbial', he laments, unafraid to be critical of the laws and institutions that sanctioned it (*Hints*, 12).

White's next two works, *Conway Castle* (a poem and the only of White's works to have received unfavourable reviews) and *Earl Strongbow*, a Gothic novel, were published in 1789—a year that shook France and sent a shiver through Pitt's government in Britain. Both *Earl Strongbow* and the novels that followed it—*The Adventures of John of Gaunt* (1790) and *The Adventures of King Richard, Coeur-de-Lion* (1791)—attracted only moderate attention, though *Earl Strongbow* was hailed by at least one reviewer as a work in which 'the reflections are ingenious and just, not a few of them deep and severe' (*GM*, 1790). All three novels bear White's trademark penchant for satire and strong engagement with political issues. While their plots abound with labyrinthine castles, loquacious spirits, and 'very mouldy and mouse-eaten' manuscripts (*The Adventures of John of Gaunt*, iv), these novels often read like whimsical parodies of their Walpolian and Radcliffean prototypes. Drollery notwithstanding, White's comments on contemporary political and social issues are hard to miss, and Tompkins suggests that the character of Strongbow is a direct reference to Lord Temple, former lord lieutenant of Ireland (Tompkins, 151).

In 1792 White published two translations: the *Speeches of M. de Mirabeau* and *The History of the Revolution of France*, from the work by Rabaut de Saint-Étienne. In his preface to the latter White is overtly critical of the state of affairs in Britain. Though he takes care to emphasize that, unlike France, Britain does not need a revolution, he clearly believes that the French example should be the inspiration for political and social reform at home.

The bulk of White's works appeared at a time when the surge of violence in France led to widespread fear of insurrection in England, and when Jacobin sympathies, even as moderate as White's, were likely to arouse suspicion. Indeed, among the critics of Pitt's government several became the target of state-employed spies and suffered for their vociferousness. Suspicion, tension, and rumours of conspiracy theories were rife among both Jacobins and anti-Jacobins. In this context it is tempting to ask whether the 'freakish personality' (Tompkins, 146) that White developed towards the end of his life—the main manifestation of which was the delusion that he was the victim of conspiracies—might not have had some basis in reality.

It seems that White's mental decline was triggered by the double blow of financial hardship (for which he blamed London booksellers) and frustrated love for a nameless lady: he hardly ate, and was often seen wandering the streets of Bath (where he had, apparently, some relations) looking increasingly haggard and deranged. In between bouts of insanity, White appears to have written a series of (as yet untraced) 'Letters to Lord Camden on the state of Ireland' which were praised for 'the elegance and strength of the language, the shrewdness of his remarks, and the perspicuity of his arguments' (*GM*, 1799, 443)— further proof of White's lifelong commitment to public affairs. It appears that at some point a small collection was raised for his relief, which White (by all accounts a proud man) accepted only reluctantly. He used the money to retire to the Carpenter's Arms in Wick, Gloucestershire, where he lay himself down in his bed, refusing all food. He lasted only a few days: the coroner's inquest is dated 15 March 1799. His obituaries stated that he was unmarried.

ARTEMIS GAUSE-STAMBOULOPOULOU

Sources J. M. S. Tompkins, 'James White, Esq.: a forgotten humourist', *Review of English Studies*, 3 (1927), 146–56 • J. Watt, *Contesting the Gothic* (1999) • *GM*, 1st ser., 60 (1790), 550–51 • *GM*, 1st ser., 69 (1799), 442–3 • A. M. Brady and B. Cleeve, eds., *A biographical dictionary of Irish writers*, rev. edn (1985) • J. S. Crone, *A concise dictionary of Irish biography* (1928) • J. Gorton, *A general biographical dictionary*, new edn, 4 (1841) • [J. H. Todd], ed., *A catalogue of graduates who have proceeded to degrees in the University of Dublin, from the earliest recorded commencements to ... December 16, 1868* (1869) • D. J. O'Donoghue, *The poets of Ireland: a biographical and bibliographical dictionary* (1912); repr. (1970) • Watt, *Bibl. Brit.* • Allibone, *Dict.*
Wealth at death penniless

White, James (*bap.* 1775, *d.* 1820), author and advertising agent, was baptized on 17 April 1775 in Worcester, the third son of Samuel White of Bewdley, Worcestershire, and his wife, Mary, *née* Willes. He spent 'many of the earliest days of [his] youth' 'in the Neighbourhood' of the Malvern Hills (White, fol. 6). On 19 September 1783 he was admitted to Christ's Hospital on the presentation of Thomas Coventry. At school he seemed something of a dandy: Leigh Hunt recalled 'admir[ing] his handsome appearance, and unimprovable manner of wearing his new clothes' (Hunt, 2.122). White left the school on 30 April 1790, but continued at Christ's Hospital, working as a clerk in the treasurer's office. A friendship with Charles Lamb, begun in their student days, now ripened. By the mid-1790s White was Lamb's 'most familiar friend' (*Life and Correspondence of Robert Southey*, 6.286).

Lamb introduced White to Shakespeare's *Henry IV* and White, a natural humorist, developed a powerful imaginative identification with Falstaff. He would 'talk you nothing but pure *Falstaff* the long evenings through' (*Works of Charles and Mary Lamb*, 1.229) and occasionally dressed up as Shakespeare's comic hero. He was even known among his friends as Sir John. This fascination with Falstaff culminated in *Original Letters, &c. of Sir John Falstaff and his Friends ... from Genuine Manuscripts* (1796), written with Lamb's assistance. The volume was designed pleasantly to ridicule William Henry Ireland's recent 'discovery' (forgery) of Shakespeare's manuscripts, though Lamb later liked to emphasize the purely literary value of the *Letters*, deriving, he said, 'from the fullness of a young soul, newly kindling at the Shakspearian flame, and bursting to be delivered of a rich exuberance of conceits' (ibid.). *Letters* was not a success on its first publication (there were, however, several posthumous editions) and appears to have been White's only attempt at authorship. In 1800 he founded an advertising agency in Warwick Square which moved to 33 Fleet Street about 1808. This was, arguably, the first such agency to introduce the idea of writing copy for clients' advertisements.

White had romantic ideas about the feasting practised

in 'Old' England and took over Elizabeth Montagu's role as patron of May day feasts for London's chimney sweepers. He served sausages instead of beef and pudding, acting as head waiter himself: Lamb gives an unforgettable account of these occasions in his essay 'The praise of chimney-sweepers'. White married Margaret Faulder (1792–1864), daughter of Robert Faulder, a bookseller, in 1811, and they had six children. He died at his house in Burton Crescent, London, on 13 March 1820, leaving a sizeable fortune, and was buried in Paddington churchyard. Friends remembered him as a man of unmatched good humour and drollness. In 1822 Lamb wrote: 'He [White] carried away with him half the fun of the world when he died—of my world at least' (*Works of Charles and Mary Lamb*, 2.130). White's advertising agency, subsequently R. F. White & Son Ltd, remained in the hands of his family until the death of his great-grandson, Gilbert White, in 1962.

DAVID CHANDLER

Sources The History of Advertising Trust, R. F. White & Son Ltd archive • private information (2004) [family] • *Falstaff's letters ... now reprinted ... with notices of the author collected from Charles Lamb, Leigh Hunt, and other cotemporaries* (1877) • *The works of Charles and Mary Lamb*, ed. E. V. Lucas, new edn, 6 vols. (1912) • J. White, 'August 1805 picturesque excursion into south Wales', 1805/1937, BL, Add. MS 44991 • administration, March 1820, PRO, PROB 6/196, fol. 230 • IGI • L. Hunt, *The indicator*, 2 (1822) • *The life and correspondence of Robert Southey*, ed. C. C. Southey, 6 vols. (1849–50), vol. 6 • T. W. Craik, 'Jem White and *Falstaff's letters*', *Charles Lamb Bulletin*, new ser., 91 (1995), 118–29
Archives BL, account of visit to Wales, Add. MS 44991
Likenesses attrib. W. Newton, miniature, 1811, repro. in BL, Add. MS 44991; priv. coll. • print (after unknown portrait), BL, Add. MS 44991 • watercolour, repro. in T. R. Nevett, *Advertising in Britain: a history* (1982), facing p. 19; priv. coll.
Wealth at death £12,000: administration, 1820, PRO, PROB 6/196, fol. 230

White, James (1803–1862), writer, born in Midlothian in March 1803, was the younger son of John White of Dunmore in Stirlingshire, and his wife, Elizabeth, daughter of John Logan of Howden in Midlothian. After studying at Glasgow University he matriculated from Pembroke College, Oxford, on 15 December 1823, graduating BA in 1827. He served as curate of Hartest-cum-Boxsted in Suffolk, and on 27 March 1833 he was instituted vicar of Loxley in Warwickshire.

In April 1829 White married Rosa (1805–1882), only daughter of Colonel Charles Fitzmaurice Hill. They had two sons and five daughters. On her father's death in 1811 Rosa inherited two farms in Bonchurch on the Isle of Wight. A clause in the will prevented the land from being developed. In 1836 James White had this clause revoked by a private act of parliament, thus enabling him to sell off much of the land for building purposes. He resigned his living in 1839 and retired to the Isle of Wight to write.

White had already written some essays, and between 1845 and 1847 he produced a succession of Scottish historical tragedies, works of some merit, though only moderately successful. Among them were *The Earl of Gowrie* (1845) and *Feudal Times* (1847). Another tragedy, *John Savile of*

Haysted (1847), was acted at Sadler's Wells Theatre, London, in 1847. At a later time he brought out several historical sketches of a popular character, written with considerable power of generalization. The best known is *The Eighteen Christian Centuries* (1858), which reached a fourth edition in 1864.

White possessed a charming style, and interested his readers by his clearness of thought and his ability in selecting and arranging detail. He was a friend of Charles Dickens, whom he met about 1845 and who thought *The Earl of Gowrie* 'a work of remarkable genius' (*Letters of Charles Dickens* to White, 24 Feb 1846, in *Letters of Charles Dickens*, 4.505). In 1849 Dickens rented a house at Bonchurch for some months on James White's recommendation to be near him. *John Savile of Haysted* was dedicated to Dickens. White also translated some of Schiller's works, and wrote a joint biography of Burns and Scott (1858), and various other works. White died in Bonchurch on 26 March 1862, his wife surviving him, and was buried in the churchyard of Bonchurch parish church on 31 March 1862.   E. I. CARLYLE, *rev.* JANET TEDMAN

Sources DNB · Bonchurch parish records, Bonchurch, Isle of Wight · census returns for Bonchurch, 1851 · Burke, *Gen. GB* (1914) [White of Kellerstain] · Allibone, *Dict.* · Foster, *Alum. Oxon.* · J. Forster, *The life of Charles Dickens*, 3 vols. (1872–4) · *The letters of Charles Dickens*, ed. M. House, G. Storey, and others, 12 vols. (1965–2002) · *CGPLA Eng. & Wales* (1862)

Archives Isle of Wight RO, Newport, Bonchurch parish records · NL Scot., corresp. with Blackwoods

Likenesses R. S. Lauder, 1850

Wealth at death under £4000: probate, 17 July 1862, *CGPLA Eng. & Wales*

White, James (*bap.* **1824**, *d.* **1884**), maker of scientific instruments, was baptized on 23 November 1824 in the parish of Kildalton in Islay, Argyll, the son of William White and his wife, Margaret Adam. His father subsequently moved to Glasgow, where he traded as a yarn merchant. The young White was apprenticed about 1839 to Gardner & Co., mathematical, optical, and philosophical instrument makers. He probably worked for the firm as a journeyman until he was about twenty-five, when he set up on his own with £160, partly borrowed from friends, at 14 Renfield Street, Glasgow, in March 1850.

White received early encouragement from William Thomson, professor of natural philosophy at Glasgow University, for whose laboratory he supplied materials and experimental teaching apparatus from 1854 onwards. Sometimes Thomson's scientific curiosity made unusual demands of the instrument maker. One day in 1868 he hurried White to a hairdresser's shop near his workshop in Buchanan Street to see a rubber drive-belt which was used for a rotatory hairbrush. He requested White to get one put up in the classroom immediately, and used it to demonstrate to students and colleagues the principle of kinetic rigidity by forcing it into kinks by hitting it with a stick. White helped to equip Thomson's pioneering new laboratory at Gilmorehill in 1870, and was appointed optician and philosophical instrument maker to the university. Although the two men formed a close relationship as instrument maker and inventor, they were not business partners; only after White's death did Thomson become a partner in the firm.

White's earliest known partner was John Haddin Barr, with whom he traded as White and Barr from 1857 until the dissolution of their partnership in the autumn of 1859, apparently because of Barr's emigration to New Zealand. Within two years a deficit of over £1600 forced White to petition for sequestration, in August 1861. He attributed his losses to 'various unprofitable contracts' and a patent connected with an improved sextant. His business as revealed by the bankruptcy papers was a broadly based retailing operation, involving the purchase of instruments and other items from many of the leading British wholesalers and manufacturers. His stock, by then including photographic apparatus, was thus similar to that of other contemporary instrument firms. After satisfying his creditors by December 1861, he resumed business, and later entered into partnership with Robert McCracken, a dentist; this was dissolved in December 1876.

White's business first became distinguished because of his crucial part in the development of Thomson's pioneering electrical instruments, particularly electrometers and electrical balances, from 1854. Thomson designed, and in 1858 patented, the mirror galvanometer for the Atlantic telegraph project, crediting White with the innovative substitution of lightweight silvered microscope glass for the usual metal mirror. Thomson's attachment to White as a maker was later attributed to the galvanometer's success in enabling the first transatlantic telegraphic contact. The firm also manufactured considerable numbers of the siphon recorder, which followed the galvanometer in 1867, and of other electrical instruments stemming from Thomson's twenty-four patents relating to electrical circuits. White also made specially commissioned instruments such as the portable electrometers which were constructed to Thomson's design for the German scientist J. F. G. Dellman in 1862–3, and those for Lieutenant Alfred Parr and Lieutenant William May's Arctic expedition to measure atmospheric electricity in 1875.

White was an elder of St Matthew's Free Church, Glasgow, and was elected a member of the Glasgow Philosophical Society in 1876. On 5 September 1877 he married Jane Reid, sister of David Hay Reid, muslin manufacturer. There were no surviving children. By 1885 electrical apparatus accounted for less than one third of his company's sales income, which mostly derived from the production of Thomson's patented compasses after 1876, and to a lesser extent from his other marine instruments, including sounding machines. As well as entrusting White with the sole manufacture of almost all his instruments, Thomson relied on his craftsmanship and patience during the demanding stages of design as they refined successive versions of an instrument, from what often began as a rough sketch. Thomson closely supervised production, latterly helped by one of the earliest telephone lines in Britain, which linked his classroom to the workshop. He held the instrument maker in high esteem; after he allowed his tide predictor to be made by Légé in 1872–3, he regretted he had not used White, with 'his genius to help' (Wilson, *Correspondence*, 2.454). According to one of Thomson's pupils, while White was 'no doubt a most skilful mechanic, he had further a singular aptitude in grasping Thomson's ideas and giving them practical shape'. In his lecture room Thomson 'often spoke of and praised the excellence and exactness of White's work' (Murray, 137).

Before an expansion into larger workshops in 1883 White had taken as partners his assistants Mathew Edwards and David Reid (unrelated to his wife). They continued the firm after White's death at 20 Hamilton Drive, Glasgow, on 15 August 1884. The death certificate described the cause as a 'softening of the brain', from which he had suffered since 1880. White left £5244 to his widow as his share of a successful business. In describing him as Sir William Thomson's 'highly-skilled coadjutor', his obituarist (*Engineering*) caught the essence of his talent and achievement as a scientific instrument maker.

TRISTRAM CLARKE

Sources T. N. Clarke, A. D. Morrison-Low, and A. D. C. Simpson, *Brass and glass: scientific instrument making workshops in Scotland* (1989), 252–66 · register of deaths (Glasgow, Partick), General Register Office for Scotland, Edinburgh, 646/3, no. 500, 15 Aug 1884 · register of marriages (Glasgow, Kelvin), General Register Office for Scotland, Edinburgh, 644/9, no. 455, 5 Sept 1877 · register of baptisms (Kildalton parish, Argyll), General Register Office for Scotland, Edinburgh, 541/2, 23 Nov 1824 · census returns of Govan, Glasgow, 1861, General Register Office for Scotland, Edinburgh, 644/9/75, 8; of Barony, Glasgow, 644/6/47, 8; of Partick, Glasgow, 646/2/33, 56 · *Engineering* (12 Sept 1884), 245 · D. Murray, *Memories of the old college of Glasgow: some chapters in the history of the university* (1927), 136–7 · D. Wilson, *William Thomson, Lord Kelvin: his way of teaching natural philosophy* (1910) · D. B. Wilson, *The correspondence between Sir George Gabriel Stokes and Sir William Thomson, Baron Kelvin of Largs*, 2 vols. (1990), vol. 1, p.306; vol. 2, pp. 405, 407, 454–5 · J. A. Ewing, 'Lord Kelvin: a centenary address', *Proceedings of the Royal Philosophical Society of Glasgow*, 53 (1924–5), 1–21, esp. 3 · S. P. Thompson, *Life of Lord Kelvin* (1910), 741–2 · commission rolls of St Matthew's F.C., 1868–83, Mitchell L., Glas., Strathclyde regional archives, CH3/971

Archives NA Scot., sequestration papers, 1861, CS 318/6/362 · NA Scot., inventory of estate, 1884, SC/36/48/108, pp.142–66 · NA Scot., transdisposition and settlement, 1884, SC/36/51/89, pp. 573–6 · U. Glas., department of natural philosophy, Sir William Thomson collection, laboratory records, and scientific instruments · U. Glas., Kelvin collection, business records · U. Glas. L., Kelvin MSS

Likenesses photograph, repro. in Clarke, Morrison-Low, and Simpson, *Brass and glass*, 253

White, James (1877–1927), property developer and speculator, was born on 17 May 1877 at 16A Sun Place, Rochdale, the son of Thomas White, bricklayer, and his wife, Catherine Mullroy. He was educated at St John's Roman Catholic School, Rochdale. At the age of ten he began working half-time in a cotton mill, and at nineteen he allegedly bought a Rochdale circus, disposing of it after two years for a theatre in Matlock. In 1899, at the age of twenty-one, he married Annie Fetton, a woollen operative, daughter of Edward Fetton, a bricklayer. White also described himself as a bricklayer at this time. In 1900 he emigrated to become a navvy on the South African railways, but was

home within a year. He became a speculative builder and later an estate agent and mortgage broker; in 1908 he went bankrupt, but eventually repaid his creditors in full. It is not known when his wife Annie died, but White appears to have married a second wife, Doris, with whom he had a son and three daughters.

Having moved to London, White gained notoriety when in 1911 a boxing match he had organized at Earls Court was banned by the authorities, fearful of disorder as one of the contestants was black. This and other boxing promotions brought White to the attention of the business community. White possessed the kind of charisma that disarmed critics. With deep-blue eyes, an engaging smile, and a Lancastrian breeziness, he impressed those willing to fall under his spell. All sorts of people, from politicians and newspaper proprietors to sporting types, passed through his office in the Grand Hotel, Trafalgar Square, or repaid his hospitality after work with useful commercial information.

An early client was the pill magnate Sir Joseph Beecham. In 1914 White persuaded him to underwrite the purchase of the Covent Garden estate and market in London. Beecham had to bear the entire financial responsibility when the First World War broke out in 1914 and public share issues for non-essential purposes were prohibited. In the autumn of 1916 White produced an interim arrangement, which collapsed when Beecham died suddenly before its signature. The conductor Sir Thomas Beecham was the dead man's elder son, and he became directly involved in the affair. Beecham later recalled that White was bold and dashing in the opening moves of a financial venture, but liable to panic when things started to go wrong. White lacked the tenacity to see through the problems of the Beecham estate to a successful resolution, and it led to a complex chancery case. Others, notably the financier Philip Ernest Hill, finally untangled the estate. However, White remained chairman of the Beecham Trust Ltd, a private Beecham family estate company; and he continued to benefit from his association with the family name.

White was acquainted with Sir Arthur Du Cros, the managing director of the Dunlop Rubber Company, and in 1913 he was appointed the company's financial adviser. Having obtained control of the firm, he subsequently attempted to establish a manufacturing subsidiary in the United States and to extend some affiliates at home. Both projects disintegrated when the post-war recession began in 1920; later White narrowly avoided being sued for his financial miscalculations in Dunlop. His bids to exploit the short-lived cotton boom in Lancashire after 1918 failed to benefit the industry.

White was more successful with his property deals. He bought, for rapid resale, a large urban site in Shaftesbury in Dorset, and prime sites in London's Strand, Bloomsbury, and St Martin's-le-Grand, as well as Selfridge's store in Oxford Street. He also bought a controlling interest in Daly's Theatre, Soho, but had to lease it out after a succession of flops. White sank much money in racing, from his stables at Foxhill, Wanborough, near Swindon, and had some successful horses, especially those ridden by Stephen Donoghue. However, he failed to win admission to the royal enclosure at Ascot.

In 1927 White began to purchase the shares of British Controlled Oilfields, planning to unload them in the United States at a handsome profit. Unfortunately, on the stock exchange's account day, he lacked a considerable sum to pay for shares he was committed to buy. To compound his problems, he was expected within days to find £300,000 for the Wembley exhibition centre, which he was also purchasing. His balance of mind disturbed, no doubt because of these financial embarrassments, White poisoned himself with prussic acid and chloroform at his home, King Edward's Place, Foxhill, Wanborough, on 29 June 1927. He was buried in Wanborough churchyard on 4 July.

White's life was, it was said, 'a glorious speculation, his death the gambler's price of failure' (Meredith, 296). To Sir Thomas Beecham he seemed to be 'one of the group of financial wizards who appeared and vanished like comets in the sky of the business world during the period' (Beecham, 197). Friends from every walk of life regretted his passing. Yet White's recklessness blighted the lives of many, including his wife, Doris, and their son and daughters, about whom nothing further is publicly known.

T. A. B. CORLEY

Sources T. A. B. Corley, 'White, James', *DBB* · H. A. Meredith, *The drama of money making* (1931), 289–96 · M. Seth-Smith, *Steve: the life and times of Steve Donoghue* (1974), 91–102 · J. Cole, *Rochdale Observer* (6 Aug 1983) · *Evening Advertiser and Evening North Wilts. Herald* (30 June 1927) · *Evening Advertiser and Evening North Wilts. Herald* (1 July 1927) · *Evening Advertiser and Evening North Wilts. Herald* (2 July 1927) · *Evening Advertiser and Evening North Wilts. Herald* (4 July 1927) · *Rochdale Observer* (2 July 1927) · *The Times* (30 June 1927) · *The Times* (1 July 1927) · *The Times* (2 July 1927) · *The Times* (5 July 1927) · *The Times* (4 Aug 1927) · T. Beecham, *A mingled chime* (1944), 197 · G. Jones, 'The multinational expansion of Dunlop, 1890–1939', *British multinationals: origins, management and performance*, ed. G. Jones (1986), 24–42 · b. cert. · m. cert. · d. cert. · *North Wiltshire Herald* (8 July 1927)
Likenesses photograph, repro. in Corley, 'White, James' · photograph, repro. in Jones, 'Multinational expansion of Dunlop', 31
Wealth at death £83,003: *The Times*

White, James Robert [Jack] (**1879–1946**), army officer and revolutionary socialist, was born at Cleveland, Montague Place, Richmond, Surrey, on 22 May 1879, the only son of Field Marshal Sir George Stuart *White (1835–1912), famed as the defender of Ladysmith in the first South African War, and his wife, Amelia Maria (Amy), *née* Baly (*d.* 1935). Although the family's permanent residence was at Whitehall, Broughshane, co. Antrim, Ireland, White was educated in England, attending Winchester College and Sandhurst. After growing to a full-framed man of 6 feet 2 inches tall, he was commissioned in the Gordon Highlanders and served in combat in the Second South African War, being appointed DSO (which he attributed to his father's position rather than to his own exploits) and rising to the rank of captain. Following the war he served as aide-de-camp to his father while the latter was governor of Gibraltar. There he met his first wife, Maria de las Mercedes Ana

Luisa Carmen Dolores (Dolly) Mosley (*b.* 1882/3); they married in Chelsea on 24 April 1907. After 1905 he was stationed in India and for a brief period was attached to his regiment in Scotland. Heavily influenced by the ideas of Tolstoy, he resigned his commission in 1908 and began a peripatetic life that continued until his last years. He received a small allowance from his father and after the field marshal's death in 1912 became heir to the Whitehall property.

White first became a language tutor at a school in Bohemia and then set off for a two-year stint in Canada, working in a variety of casual jobs. He then returned to Ireland where his significant work began. In 1912 he joined a small band of Ulster protestants, including Roger Casement, who supported Irish home rule. Visits to Dublin drew him into involvement with the militant labour movement led by James Larkin. Viewing the horrific living conditions of the Dublin proletariat, White related, 'The sands of my gentility had run out' (White, *Misfit*, 219). During the 1913 lock-out, or strike, White proposed the formation of a workers' militia, to strengthen morale and to prevent police assaults on the participants. When the Irish citizens' army, as it was known, was reorganized in the spring of 1914 White became its president or commander and conducted drills at the Irish Transport Union's grounds at Croyden Park. In March 1914 he was arrested for striking two policemen while leading a march of workers through Dublin. His casual conduct of purchases and efforts to build links with the nationalist Irish Volunteers led to conflict with Sean O'Casey, the army secretary (and later playwright), and White resigned in May 1914. O'Casey later commented that 'Captain White was a noble fellow, but a nuisance' (O'Casey, 2.580).

White became an organizer of the Irish Volunteers in Derry and then in Tyrone—although, characteristically, his involvement was short-lived and ended in his acrimonious departure. Upon the outbreak of the First World War White became casually and briefly attached to an Australian ambulance unit in Flanders, and then drifted off to Paris. In his view, war was an evil to be cured by the emancipation of women. Following the Dublin Easter rising of 1916, White agitated for a strike of south Wales coalminers in protest against the death sentence pronounced on James Connolly, one of his labour associates of 1913–14. For this he served three months in prison. Banned from returning to Ireland, he wrote a series of articles, reproduced as pamphlets, which denounced the war and capitalism, and coupled advocacy of socialism with praise for the Russian Revolution. He became involved in the vacant land movement in England, and urged the leaders of the Irish labour movement in December 1916 to launch a campaign for total land usage and employment, partly to deflect the threat of conscription.

White observed the rise of Sinn Féin from the fringes and published a pamphlet in 1919 supporting an alliance between Irish labour and militant nationalism and arguing that 'Ireland cannot be independent until Capitalism is overthrown' (White, *The Significance of Sinn Féin*, 30); he envisioned its replacement by co-operative production in agriculture and industry. By this time his standpoint was socialist, anti-imperialist, and, surprisingly, Christian. In an article of 1920 he voiced an optimistic view that Irish labour was 'the sledge hammer with which the wedge of political independence is being driven home, and which gives more and more a Labour complexion to the sympathies and policy of Sinn Féin' (Red Hand Magazine [Belfast], Sept 1920). In the same year he financed the trip of two Irish delegates to the formative meeting of the Communist International in Moscow. He served further prison terms for agitation in Dublin and Edinburgh during 1920 and 1921, yet, in withdrawing his candidacy for Donegal at the free state election of 1922, he seemed to commit himself only to 'moral force' in the pursuit of socialist aims. A supporter of the returned James Larkin, he headed the London branch of the Irish Workers' League in 1923. He was involved too in the workers' party of Ireland and, in the later 1920s, in abortive efforts to form revolutionary labour organizations in Dublin.

In the early 1930s White centred his activities on Belfast, where he was active in the Revolutionary Workers' Party. In an account of his early life entitled Misfit (1930), he was critical of nobody except himself: he allowed that he was an ineffective crank, but observed that 'an ineffective crank need not be fundamentally a fool'. Involvement in an unemployed workers' demonstration of 1932 in Belfast led to another month in prison and a subsequent exclusion order that severely restricted his movements within Northern Ireland. A civil servant advised the Northern Ireland minister for home affairs that White was 'a stormy petrel and cannot resist the impulse to join any fight that is going' (McGarry, 61). Back in Dublin in 1934 he became leader of a branch of the republican congress made up from former British soldiers. At the beginning of the Spanish Civil War, White went to Spain as part of a British Red Cross unit and soon joined in the struggle. Appalled by communist machinations on the republican side, he joined forces with the anarchists, and his later pamphleteering reflects his increasing identification with anarchism. In 1937 he worked with the American anarchist Emma Goldman in propaganda activities from London, while also assisting in gun-smuggling to Spanish opponents of Franco. In London, too, he met his second wife (his first marriage having ended in divorce). She was Noreen Margaret Shanahan (b. 1903/4), twenty-five years his junior, whom he married in Hampstead on 24 November 1938. They had three sons.

At the beginning of the Second World War White supported Irish neutrality as well as joining forces with General Hugh Gough, of the 1914 Curragh mutiny episode, to urge all-Ireland co-operation in the defence of the country. What White advocated precisely was the formation of an 'Irish People's Army of Home Defence'. His offer to serve in the Home Guard was refused. In the general election of 1945 White put up as a Socialist Republican candidate in Antrim but did not go to the poll. He died of cancer on 2 February 1946 in the Musgrave Clinic, Belfast, and was buried two days later at Broughshane burying-ground, co. Antrim. He once declared that although not a

Catholic, he had committed two mortal sins in his life by marrying two Catholic women; neither union had been happy. His second wife, Noreen, survived him. A latter-day friend of his, T. J. McElligott, said of White, 'He was a twentieth century Don Quixote, ever tilting at the windmills of imperialism and sectarianism' (McElligott, 75).

ARTHUR MITCHELL

Sources J. R. White, Misfit: an autobiography (1930) · J. R. White, 'The meaning of anarchism' [n.d., 1937?] · A. Boyd, Jack White (1870–1946): first commander, Irish citizen army, 2001, Donaldson Archive · J. R. White, The significance of Sinn Féin (1919) [pamphlet] · J. R. White, The Irish question as the key to the labour problem of the world (1916) · S. O Cathasaigh, The story of the Irish citizen army (1919) · 'Under the plough and the stars', S. O'Casey, Autobiographies, vol. 2 · S. O'Casey, Letters, 1942–1954 (New York, 1980) · R. M. Fox, History of the Irish citizen army (Dublin, 1944) · F. McGarry, Irish politics and the Spanish Civil War (Cork, 1999) · G. Burns, 'Capt. Jack White: a forgotten figure in history', Irish Times (15 Sept 1978) · T. J. McElligott, This teaching life: a memoir of schooldays in Ireland (1986) · b. cert. · m. certs. · K. Doyle, 'Captain Jack White (1879–1946)', flag.blackened. net/revolt/anarchists/jackwhite/bio.html, 20 Dec 2002 · Burke, Gen. Ire. (1904) · WWW, 1916–28 · Irish News [Belfast] (4 Feb 1946) · Irish News (5 Feb 1946)

Archives Dublin History Archive, Irish Labour, C. O'Shannon papers, MS 147 · NL Ire., G. Berkeley papers, letters, MS 7879 · NL Ire., T. J. McElligott papers, letters, MS 10419

Likenesses photograph, c.1930, repro. in flag.blackened.net/ revolt/anarchists/jackwhite/bio.html [accessed 20 Dec 2002]

Wealth at death £81 19s. 5d.—in England: administration, 15 May 1946, CGPLA Eng. & Wales

White, Jeremiah (1629–1707), nonconformist minister, is of unknown parents and background. He matriculated as a sizar from Trinity College, Cambridge, in April 1646, graduated BA in 1650, and proceeded MA in 1653. White claimed in his works that he was a fellow of Trinity, but there is no corroborating evidence of this claim. Upon leaving university he became one of the preachers to the council of state and the chaplain to Oliver Cromwell's household. His position with the Cromwells allowed him to befriend Peter Sterry, another of Cromwell's chaplains, and he later wrote a preface to Sterry's The Rise, Race, and Royalty of the Kingdom of God in the Soul of Man (1683).

White appears to have been something of a romantic regarding women, and this seems to have caused him more than a degree of trouble. A tale is told that while he was chaplain to the Cromwell household he became smitten by Oliver's daughter, Frances. The feeling was mutual and White sought to obtain Frances's hand in marriage. Cromwell was too wily for White and caught White kissing his daughter's hand. In order to save face, White claimed that he was pleading with Frances to intervene for him for the hand of her maid, Katherine. Cromwell, however, was one step ahead of the game and had White and the maid married. Whether this story is true is unverifiable, but love letters in the British Library sent by White to Elizabeth Rogerson of Tunbridge Wells (where he holidayed) in 1686–7 show him to be a hopeless romantic.

After the Restoration White remained faithful to his former employers, and it was alleged that he was the chaplain to a republican secret society known as the Calves Head Club. The club, if it existed, met annually on 30 January, the anniversary of the execution of Charles I, between 1693 and 1699. Its aim was to revive the memory of the English republic and to celebrate the liberation from Stuart tyranny. Tory propagandists contended that the club would meet in the dining-room of a London tavern and would place an executioner's axe above the door as a symbol that it was in session. The members would eat a meal consisting of calves' heads, which represented the executed Charles I, and pike, which symbolized tyranny. After the meal a copy of *Eikon basilike* (which was purportedly written by Charles I) would be burnt while the members sang an anti-monarchist anthem holding John Milton's republican *Defensio populi Anglicani*. The meeting would end with White offering a toast to the former republic from the skull of a calf, the wine symbolizing the blood of King Charles. Although these allegations are probably too fantastic to be true, they do show that tory propaganda singled out White as a republican troublemaker.

As White had only been a chaplain, he was not ejected from the Church of England in 1662, but he dissented none the less. By 1666 he and his wife, Katherine, had moved to St Albans, where he reputedly lived as the beneficiary of a trust set up by Elizabeth Cromwell, Oliver's recently deceased wife. In 1669 he was noted as preaching in the Hertfordshire town of Elstree and also occasionally at Meeting House Alley, off Queen Street in Rotherhithe. He was acutely aware of the plight of the dissenters and was among the first to compile an account of the sufferings of the nonconformists under the Anglican-Cavalier regime. Calamy contends that some agents of James II offered him a considerable remuneration if he would publish the account as part of James's attempt to undermine the Anglican establishment; White refused these offers, fearing that he would strengthen the Roman Catholic plans of the king.

Theologically, White was a believer in Origen's doctrine of universal salvation and wrote a posthumously published treatise entitled *The Restoration of All Things* on the subject. This tract was held in high regard and was reprinted in the mid-nineteenth century by Victorian universalists. He also held to the doctrine of universal toleration, and his *A Perswasive to Moderation and Forbearance in Love among the Divided Forms of Christians*, originally delivered as a union lecture in London, was published posthumously. It argued that the departure from the simple message of the Bible 'into the multiplicity or confusion of carnal and worldly wisdom' (p. xi) was to blame for the tyranny of one sect over another. White counselled forbearance and moderation as the steps to union.

After the revolution of 1688 and the Toleration Act, White resumed his calling as a public preacher. In November 1701 he delivered a sermon on 2 Thessalonians 4: 14 to the mourners at the funeral of the nonconformist minister Francis Fuller. He was also the assistant to the congregational leader Robert Bragge in the ministry of the gathered church at Pewterer's Hall. He died in 1707 aged seventy-eight.   E. C. VERNON

Sources Calamy rev. · Venn, *Alum. Cant.* · [J. White], *The restoration of all things* (1712) · *The secret history of the Calves Head Club* (1703) · *DNB* · J. White, *A funeral sermon … upon the death of the Reverend F. Fuller* (1702) · J. White, *A perswasive to moderation and forbearance in love among the divided forms of Christians*, ed. [R. Roach], 2nd edn (1710) · Bodl. Oxf., MS Rawl. D. 992

Likenesses line engraving, 1708, BM, NPG; repro. in J. White, *Perswasive*, ed. [R. Roach]

White, John (1509/10–1560), bishop of Winchester, was born in Farnham, Surrey, the son of Robert White, a tenant of the see of Winchester. He was the brother of Dr Henry White and of Agnes, who married their cousin Sir Thomas White of South Warnborough. The latter had a sister, Sibill, who was married to a John White thought by some (including the diarist Henry Machyn) to have been another brother of the bishop. While this cannot be ruled out, it is made more unlikely by Bishop John's standing as godfather in 1559 to the son (yet another John White) of John and Sibill; if the two older Johns were brothers then it would have been thought inappropriate for godfather and godson to enter into the spiritual relationship which baptism created when they were already so closely related by blood.

In 1521, aged eleven, White was admitted to Winchester College as a scholar. He passed on to New College, Oxford, where he was admitted as a scholar on 3 December 1525, and became a fellow in 1527 (his fellowship was vacated in March 1535). During that time he took his BA (admitted 13 December 1529, determined 1531) and MA (23 March 1534). In 1537 he was appointed headmaster of his old school, Winchester College. At Winchester he was noted for his skill in poetry and oratory. He was ordained priest for the diocese of Winchester on 16 April 1541, a few days after his ordination as subdeacon and deacon, but in keeping with the times this had not prevented him already holding certain benefices; he was collated rector of Chilcombe, Dorset, on 14 November 1537, and was admitted canon and twelfth prebendary of Winchester on 28 March 1541, a few days before receiving major orders. He held the latter *in commendam* with several other benefices and canonries (rector of Cheriton, Hampshire, July 1543; canon of Chichester and prebendary of Ipthorne, 28 March 1550; canon of Lichfield and prebendary of Eccleshall, 4 May 1552), surrendering them only on appointment as bishop. He appears also to have been vicar of Keevil in Wiltshire, though this he had vacated by July 1550. In addition White vacated the headmastership of Winchester College when he was elected its warden in February 1542, a position he vacated about October 1554, several months after his episcopal consecration. At some time during this period he proceeded to the degree of BTh (later incorporated as DTh on 1 October 1555). It was also about 1542 that White became a chaplain to Stephen Gardiner, then bishop of Winchester.

Through the changes of religion wrought first by Henry VIII then by Edward VI, White seems to have been fairly content to comply quietly, at least up to a point. By his own admission, while headmaster of Winchester College he composed certain verses extolling the king's supremacy, and against the bishop of Rome (with the encouragement of Gardiner), which he taught to his scholars. It would appear that by 1551, about the time of Gardiner's trial, his conservative tendencies were becoming noticeable, to the extent that White was excommunicated by archdeacon John Philpot 'for preaching naughty doctrine' (*Examinations and Writings of John Philpot*, 82). About this time also he entered into a controversy with Peter Martyr; White's contribution, a treatise (in verse) on the true presence of the body and blood of Christ in the eucharist, was published as *Diacosiomartyrion. Id est ducentorum virorum testimonium, de veritate corporis, et sanguinis Christi, in eucharistia, adversus Petrum Martyrem* (1553; STC 25388).

White's relationship with Gardiner (he had clearly put himself on his bishop's side at the latter's trial) and his known conservatism made him a candidate for early preferment to the episcopal office after the accession of Queen Mary, and he was a member of several commissions for the deprivation and restoration of bishops. On 1 April 1554 White was consecrated bishop of Lincoln by Edmund Bonner, bishop of London, assisted by Cuthbert Tunstall and Stephen Gardiner at the church of the bishop of Winchester, St Saviour's, Southwark. Five other new bishops were consecrated at the same time. He was enthroned by proxy on 28 April, and again in person over 12–13 October. In the following year, on 28 September, he was appointed a commissioner for the trial of Nicholas Ridley and Hugh Latimer. Foxe reports his courtesy and gentleness towards the two reformers, acknowledged in their words to the bishop in the course of their trial. His dealings with other heretics brought before him may not have been so gentle, judging from Foxe's report of the trial of Stephen Gratwick, where he acted more harshly, an approach which comes through in accounts of other later trials in which he had a part. On one occasion Foxe describes White as showing 'gross ignorance and barbarous cruelty' (*Acts and Monuments*, 8.374), while at the examination of Richard Gibson in 1557 he is recorded as saying that 'it was no pity to burn a heretic' (ibid., 440). This demonstrates, if nothing else, that White was one of the minority of Marian bishops who took an active and personal interest in heresy trials. It also suggests that he may have had more patience in his dealings with senior churchmen, whom he would have seen as his equals in learning and in ecclesiastical standing, than with the increasing number of lay protestants who were being brought for heresy trials in the reign of Mary.

It was as a preacher, rather than as a persecutor of heretics, however, that White came to greatest prominence in the Marian period. Soon after Mary's accession White was preaching in London in support of the restoration of processions. He contributed to a set of verses composed by scholars of Winchester College for the marriage of Philip and Mary at Winchester on 25 July 1554, and a number of important sermons followed. He was at Paul's Cross on 18 November, and preached at the opening of parliament on 21 October 1555. Within a month his former bishop and mentor, Stephen Gardiner, was dead, and White preached at the requiem mass sung for him by Edmund Bonner, bishop of London, on 15 November. When Gardiner's body was taken for burial from Southwark to Winchester

on 24 February following, it was White who conducted the funeral rites. Along with other bishops he received Reginald Pole at the church of St Mary-le-Bow in London on 25 March 1556, where the cardinal was to be invested with the pallium after his consecration as archbishop of Canterbury. White's election to succeed his mentor Gardiner at Winchester on 15 April probably caused little surprise. Though he received custody of the temporalities of his see as bishop nominate on 16 May, it was a whole year before the appropriate bulls of papal provision were obtained from Rome, and he took full possession of his temporalities only on 19 May 1557. Although he appears to have spent little time active in his diocese, his persecution of heretics (conducted, as with his predecessor, largely from his base at Southwark) continued alongside his preaching career. On at least one occasion he combined the two, on 23 May 1557, according to the diarist Henry Machyn, directing a sermon in St Saviour's, Southwark, against an unnamed heretic who was present in the church. It was in that year that he carried out a visitation of his diocese, acting under a commission of Cardinal Pole. He was at Paul's Cross again on 30 January following.

The last months of 1558 saw a number of significant and important deaths; not only the queen and her archbishop of Canterbury (both on 17 November) but also several other bishops died around that time. Maurice Griffith, bishop of Rochester, died on 20 November and was buried on 30th; White preached the sermon at his funeral in the church of St Magnus the Martyr, just the other side of London Bridge from his own Southwark church of St Saviour. It was not for that funeral sermon, though, but for the one he gave at the queen's funeral on 14 December that he is best remembered. In the course of his sermon he made either the biggest *faux pas* of his career, or was subject to the most unfortunate misunderstanding. The main theme of his sermon was to warn against change, and in a passage which probably referred to the preachers of the day he quoted from Ecclesiastes 9: 4, 'better a live dog than a dead lion'. This was taken, perhaps unjustly, as a comparison between the new queen Elizabeth and her recently departed half-sister, and as a result White was placed under house arrest. John Jewel, later bishop of Salisbury, described the sermon (preserved in BL, Sloane MS 1578) as mad and very seditious.

White was called before the council on 19 January 1559, admonished, and set free. On 31 March he took part in the abortive conference at Westminster Abbey between certain bishops and prelates and a number of protestant divines, and for his opposition to reform was committed to the Tower on 3 April. He is alleged in a number of sources to have threatened to excommunicate the queen, but J. H. Pollen argues that this is not found in any contemporary source but derives from a misunderstanding of the situation by William Allen. On 25 May he was allowed to stand as godfather to his namesake John White in the church of St Bartholomew by the Exchange beside St Anthony's. On 26 June he was deprived of his bishopric after refusing to take the oath of supremacy. On account of his ill health he was released from the Tower into the custody of the keeper of the broad seal on 6 July, and thence the next day to Sir Thomas White, the husband of his sister Agnes. He died of an ague at Sir Thomas's house at South Warnborough on 12 January 1560, and was buried three days later in Winchester Cathedral. KENNETH CARLETON

Sources Emden, *Oxf.*, 4.620–22 · Cooper, *Ath. Cantab.*, vol. 1 · *The diary of Henry Machyn, citizen and merchant-taylor of London, from AD 1550 to AD 1563*, ed. J. G. Nichols, CS, 42 (1848) · W. M. Brady, *The episcopal succession in England, Scotland, and Ireland, AD 1400 to 1875*, 2 (1876) · W. Stubbs, *Registrum sacrum Anglicanum*, 2nd edn (1897) · *Fasti Angl., 1541–1857*, [Canterbury] · *Fasti Angl., 1541–1857*, [Lincoln] · C. Wriothesley, *A chronicle of England during the reigns of the Tudors from AD 1485 to 1559*, ed. W. D. Hamilton, 2, CS, new ser., 20 (1877) · *The acts and monuments of John Foxe*, ed. S. R. Cattley, 8 vols. (1837–41), vols. 6–8 · APC, 1558–70 · J. H. Pollen, *The English Catholics in the reign of Queen Elizabeth* (1920) · HoP, *Commons, 1558–1603*, 3.611–12 · *The examinations and writings of John Philpot*, ed. R. Eden, Parker Society, 5 (1842) · episcopal register, Lincs. Arch., 28 · *Registrum Johannis Whyte, episcopi Wintoniensis, AD MDLVI–MDLIX*, ed. W. H. Frere, CYS, 16 (1914) · BL, Sloane MS 1578

White, John (*fl.* 1577–1593), colonist and painter, was apparently of modest Cornish gentry origins. His early and later life remain obscure, owing largely to the commonness of his name. He rose to prominence on the basis of his artistic talent and zeal for American colonization. His watercolour images of Native Americans in the late sixteenth century were exceptional for his era and unsurpassed as a visual record of south-eastern tribal life until the advent of photography.

White's first voyage to America was probably with Martin Frobisher's expedition of 1577, during which it is believed he produced a drawing of a skirmish between the English and the Thule Inuit at Baffin Island. He is probably the same John White listed as a member of the Painter-Stainers' Company in 1580.

In 1585 White set out for America as part of the expedition headed by Richard Grenville and Ralph Lane and promoted by Walter Ralegh. He was paired with Thomas Harriot to collect information about the people, plants, and animals of America for the benefit of subsequent colonization efforts. The sympathetic and lively drawings White produced of Carolina Algonquian life, documenting aboriginal settlement patterns, technology, clothing, body decoration, ceremonial life, and subsistence practices, are among the earliest extant images of Native Americans. These images circulated widely as engravings in the first volume of Theodor de Bry's *America* (1590). Although de Bry's engravings were less naturalistic and accurate than White's originals, the images became ingrained in the European imagination and helped stimulate the colonial enterprise. They also influenced European pictorial representations of Native Americans for centuries to come.

After White's return from the 1585 voyage his involvement in the promotion of the Virginia colony grew. His stalwart faith in American colonization resulted in Ralegh placing him at the head of a company dedicated to planting a permanent settlement. Ralegh named him governor of the colony, and White took a leading role in raising money and recruiting settlers. With the prospective colonists he set out from Portsmouth in April 1587, but he proved an ineffectual leader and was dominated by the ship's Portuguese pilot, Simão Fernandes, whose real interest lay in privateering. Fernandes left White and the colonists, somewhat against their will, at Roanoke (in present-day North Carolina) instead of at their intended destination on Chesapeake Bay.

White's brief leadership on land was also beset with difficulties. Although the colony aspired to peaceful coexistence with the native population, prior mistreatment of the latter by Lane's colonists placed relations on a tenuous footing. White's decision to make a show of strength after the murder of one of his settlers backfired when his men inadvertently attacked a party of friendly Croatoans.

Amid concern over provisions, White's charges convinced him to return to England to lobby for relief, and he was back in Southampton by November 1587. His prompt return to Virginia was thwarted by a variety of circumstances. First, the threat of Spain's armada resulted in the requisitioning of the ships he had intended to take back to Virginia. When White finally set out, in April 1588, he did so with two vessels that were not only smaller than he had hoped but which were dedicated to privateering. The ships were attacked in the course of their activities and forced to return to England.

It was not until 1590 that White could again raise ships and supplies. After reaching Roanoke in that year he found the colony disappeared and his possessions ransacked. Although evidence suggested the colonists had taken shelter among the nearby Croatoans, bad weather and sailing mishaps forced White to abort his search and return to England. Among the missing colonists were his daughter, Ellinor, and his granddaughter, Virginia Dare, the first child born to English parents in America.

White settled in Ireland, and wrote Richard Hakluyt a letter in 1593 from his house in Ballynoe, co. Cork. While the details of his later life have bedevilled researchers, a strong case has been put forward that he lived on Ralegh's estate and produced farm surveys for him as late as 1598. A will for a John White, 'late of parts beyond the seas', was proved in 1606, but whether this was the same John White remains uncertain. KARIM M. TIRO

Sources P. Hulton and D. B. Quinn, *The American drawings of John White, 1577–1590*, 2 vols. (1964) · P. Hulton, *America, 1585: the complete drawings of John White* (1984) · D. B. Quinn, *Set fair for Roanoke: voyages and colonies, 1584–1606* (1985) · D. B. Quinn, ed., *The Roanoke voyages, 1584–1590: documents to illustrate the English voyages to North America under the patent granted to Walter Ralegh in 1584*, 2 vols., Hakluyt Society, 2nd ser., 104, 105 (1955) · W. A. Wallace, *John White, Thomas Harriot and Walter Ralegh in Ireland* (1985)
Archives BM, MSS

White, John (1570–1615), Church of England clergyman and polemicist, was born at Eaton Socon, Bedfordshire, the son of Peter White, vicar of St Neots, Huntingdonshire, and the neighbouring parish of Eaton Socon, and younger brother of Francis *White (1563/4–1638), later successively bishop of Carlisle, Norwich, and Ely; three other brothers also became clergymen. White was educated at St Neots grammar school and then admitted a

En micat ut vultus Johannis gratior Aeui
Inuida vel rumpas ilia Liuor Ferox
Quem modo Coelator cum sculpserit arte supremā,
Ut referat uitam mortua imago Viri :
Forma tamen mentis quo plus diumor oris,
Doctius hoc Scriptis pingitur Ipse sui.
R.B.

John White (1570–1615), by unknown engraver, pubd 1624

sizar of Gonville and Caius College, Cambridge, on 15 February 1586. He was a scholar from Lady day 1588 to Michaelmas 1592, graduated BA in 1590, and proceeded MA in 1593. By 1595 White had married but although his wife survived him her name is unknown. The couple had seven children, the eldest of whom, John, entered Gonville and Caius College in 1611, aged sixteen, and later became vicar of his grandfather's old parish of Eaton Socon; another son is mentioned by Thomas Fuller as having become a druggist in Lombard Street, London.

White was appointed vicar of Eccles, Lancashire, and fellow of the collegiate church, Manchester, in 1606, but resigned these in 1609 after being presented by Sir John Crofts to the rectory of Barsham, Suffolk. In 1612 he proceeded DD. A sermon originally delivered at Paul's Cross, *Anniversary Commemoration of the Kings most Happy Succession to the Crowne of England*, was published in 1615, and early that year White was made a chaplain-in-ordinary to James I.

White was highly regarded as a polemicist against the Church of Rome. He indicated that his writings were pastoral endeavours to 'help the seduced out of their [Catholic] errors and confirm Protestants in the truth' (*Way to the True Church*, preface *3). Against the 1605 publication of

The Treatise of Faith, written by the celebrated Jesuit John Percy (1569–1641), better known by his alias Fisher the Jesuit, White brought out his *Way to the true church wherin the principal motives persuading to Romanisme are familiarly disputed* (1608). Further editions of this Calvinist defence of the reformed faith were issued in 1610, 1612, and 1616. After subsequent replies by Percy in 1612 and 1614, White again took up his pen against the Jesuit with his *Defense of the Way to the True Church* (1614). This treatise occasioned William Wright SJ (1563–1639) to publish *A discovery of certain notorious shifts, evasions, and untruths uttered by M. John White, minister* (1614), and two years later his larger *Treatise of the Church* (1616). The former president of Douai, Thomas Worthington (1549–1622), also entered the fray in *Whyte Died Black* (1615).

In his will White hints at financial 'distresses' suffered at Eccles, 'which I was never able to look through to this day'. This seems to indicate that he was in poverty when he died in Lombard Street, London. He was buried on 28 May 1615 at St Mary Woolnoth in the City. In 1624 his brother Francis White published *The Workes of that Learned and Reverend Divine, John White*, containing the polemics, two sermons and an anti-papal work of his own.

TIMOTHY WADKINS

Sources Fuller, *Worthies* (1662) · PRO, PROB 11/135, fols. 137–8 · F. White, *The workes of that learned and reverend divine, John White* (1624) · P. Milward, *Religious controversies of the Jacobean age* (1978) · T. Wadkins, 'Theological polemic and religious culture in early Stuart England: the Percy/"Fisher" controversies, 1605–1641', PhD diss., Graduate Theological Union, 1988 · *DNB*

Likenesses line engraving, BM, NPG; repro. in White, *Workes* [see illus.]

Wealth at death in poverty: will, PRO, PROB 11/135, fols. 137–8

White, John (1575–1648), clergyman and promoter of colonization, was born on 6 January 1575 in the manor house of Stanton St John, Oxfordshire, the second son of John White (*d.* 1618), yeoman, and Isabel, daughter of John Bawle of Lichfield, Staffordshire. He had four sisters and two brothers, the eldest of whom was Josiah White (1573–1622), rector of Hornchurch, Essex, from 1611 to 1622. The family leased the manor of Stanton St John from New College, Oxford, through the favour of an uncle, Dr Thomas White (*d.* 1588), the warden of New College. Following family tradition, John was educated at Winchester College from 1587 to 1593 and at New College, Oxford. Elected a fellow in 1595 he graduated BA in 1597, and proceeded MA in 1601. Remaining in residence he took holy orders and was appointed rector of Holy Trinity, Dorchester, Dorset, a parish which also incorporated St Peter's, in November 1605. In the following year he married Ann Burges of Peterborough. White was associated with Dorchester for over forty years and if his remaining sermons display a distinct Calvinistic streak he none the less remained a conforming minister of the Church of England, holding traditional views on the nature of divinely appointed authority. Even though he attempted to conduct his religious services within the letter of the law and continued to wear a surplice into the 1640s White became an important figure in the puritan transatlantic network which opposed the religious reforms of Archbishop Laud. His successful attempt to reform Dorchester, a sleepy backwater with something of an unsavoury reputation, eventually won him the title of the Patriarch of Dorchester.

Following the disastrous fire of 1613, which destroyed more than 170 dwellings, White admonished his Dorchester parishioners to transform their ways, reject mere material success, and help the poor. Supported by the local corporation and consistent voluntary financial contributions from his flock he remodelled the town into a well-ordered, godly commonwealth. At the centre of his plans was the creation of a workhouse, a vocational institution which both educated and put the youth of the town to work producing cloth. From its profits the town created a public brewhouse, completed in 1622, which not only regulated the town's drink trade, but also helped finance future reforms; a free school (of which White became a supervisor); the distribution of charity at Christmas; the repair of public streets; and in 1631 the creation of a town library. Indeed, the practical benefits of White's reforms were particularly evident in 1623 when Dorchester suffered another fire, following which the homeless received speedy relief. On the whole a popular minister he regularly visited his parishioners in their homes, lectured three times a week, and on Fridays publicly worked his way methodically through the Bible. This took him six years, after which he started over again. His programme also transcended the walls of Dorchester itself for in March 1624 he presided over the inception of the unincorporated Dorchester Company, an enterprise aimed at creating a godly colony in America.

Between 1621 and 1623 the number of fishing ships leaving west country ports for New England increased fourfold and White's scheme suggested planting a fishing station in America to both facilitate the trade as well as spread the Word to Native Americans. Consequently, in 1622, Richard Bushrod, a wealthy Dorchester merchant, obtained in his name and for his associates, a fishing licence from the Council for New England. In 1623 another White associate, Sir William Erle, a member of the Virginia Company, obtained a patent for a plantation and ships were sent over in 1624 and 1625. By 1626, however, it was clear that the Dorchester Company, like many similar ventures, was failing. Despite setbacks a permanent settlement was established at Cape Ann, and some colonists stayed on and eventually moved with their governor, Richard Conant, to Naumkeag, renamed Salem in 1629.

Together with a few other members of the Dorchester Company, White kept the colonists supplied and looked to his puritan brethren in London for support. By the time of the creation of the New England Company in March 1628 he had become more interested in piety than profit, viewing a future, successful Massachusetts colony as a safe haven for the increasingly persecuted puritan clergy. When the Gorges family challenged the legality of the New England Company's patent another John White (1590–1645), the London lawyer for the Winthrop family, undertook the complex legal business which transformed the New England Company into the Massachusetts Bay Company by royal charter on 4 March 1629. Continuing to play a conspicuous role in the success of Massachusetts, the Patriarch helped finance individual immigration and recruited the west country conforming puritans who left England in the *Mary and John* in March 1630. On the eve of the more famous Winthrop migration, in April 1630, White signed with other puritan leaders the humble request, a conciliatory document which proclaimed their loyalty to the mother church. It was published in May 1630 and incorporated by White in his model promotional tract *The Planter's Plea of the Grounds for Plantations Examined*. During the famine of 1631 he managed to keep the fledgeling colony supplied with grain and if his role in this project has often been underrated his activities had not escaped the attention of Archbishop Laud.

Under White's leadership Dorchester became a leading centre in the resistance to the high-church religious policies of Charles I. White often organized special prayer meetings, petitions, and the collection of funds to support the cause of international protestantism and he was especially prominent in collecting for the Feoffees for Impropriations, a London-based puritan corporation which hoped to transform the Church of England from within by a preaching ministry. Laud viewed all such activities as undermining both church and royal authority and during his campaign to purge the puritan clergy from the pulpit White was increasingly watched after 1630. His opposition to Arminianism, the new ceremonies, and especially to the reading of the Book of Sports (which advocated leisure pastimes on Sundays) in church led to White's papers being seized, his finances being investigated, and in 1635 to his prosecution by the high commission. Although the charges against him were dropped his activities, especially after Dorchester's vocal opposition to the collection of ship money in 1637, were increasingly scrutinized.

During the final crisis which led to the outbreak of civil war Dorchester became increasingly puritan, its militia refusing to muster in support of Charles's campaign against the presbyterian Scots. When hostilities between the king and parliament finally broke out in August 1642 the town collected £200 to support parliament. Spurred on by White's sermons Dorchester raised forces in its defence and the corporation pledged support for the parliamentary cause. Yet in August 1643 Dorchester ignominiously surrendered without a fight to royalist forces under Lord Caernarvon. White, who had compounded his notoriety in royalist eyes by his election to the assembly of divines, had fled and his study and papers were pillaged by cavalry under Prince Maurice. In a later royalist occupation the brewhouse itself was destroyed by troops under Lord Goring.

The assembly of divines first met under the chairmanship of William Twisse in July 1643, and during its first week of deliberation White was elected one of two assessors to assist the prolocutor. Charged by parliament to work out a practical religious settlement under the solemn league and covenant with its Scots presbyterian allies, as well as establishing a new form of church government on the basis of scriptural evidence alone, White came to play a leading role in its deliberations. An upholder of the notions of a truly national church he served on two of the assembly's important committees and was appointed minister to St Mary Savoy. He was later appointed rector of Lambeth in April 1645. Although sympathetic to suggested Calvinistic reforms he remained a voice for conservatism within the assembly and usually allied himself with the presbyterians against the growing, more radical independents. On 26 November 1645 he delivered a sermon in Westminster Abbey on the text of Daniel 9: 15 which called for the creation of a fund from church lands to support exhibitions for needy university students, later published as *The Troubles of Jerusalems Restauration* (1646). In increasing ill health he petitioned parliament to relieve him of his duties in May 1646, and having declined the candidature of the vacant wardenship of New College, Oxford, returned to Dorchester in November that year.

In the aftermath of the first civil war White no longer commanded the respect within Dorchester he had once enjoyed and his conservatism often brought him into conflict with religious radicals. In a sermon at St Peter's attended by the whole town in March 1647 he warned his parishioners against what he perceived to be the rising tide of heresy, and he later published a tract which instructed them how to continue in a moral, godly life, *The Way to the Tree of Life* (1647). Up until his death on 21 July 1648 at Dorchester he worked upon his reflections on Genesis, later published by his son John as *A Commentary upon the First Three Chapters of the First Book of Moses called Genesis* (1656). In his will he left the bulk of his small estate to his youngest son, Nathaniel, who served as a captain in the parliamentary cavalry during the civil war. His marriage also produced two further sons and two daughters. He was buried under the south porch of St Peter's on 24 July, and a monument was finally erected to White's memory in 1902. A modest, pleasant man who largely accepted the teachings of the established church, he played an important role, without ever setting foot there, in the successful settlement of puritan Massachusetts.

RORY T. CORNISH

Sources D. Underdown, *Fire from heaven: life in an English town in the seventeenth century* (1992) · J. White, *The planter's plea* (1630); *Tracts and other papers relating principally to the origin, settlement, and progress of the colonies in North America*, ed. P. Force (1963) · F. Rose-Troup, *John White, the patriarch of Dorchester* (1930) · F. J. Bremer, *Congregational communion: clerical friendship in the Anglo-American puritan community, 1610–1692* (1994) · C. Bridenbaugh, *Vexed and troubled Englishmen, 1590–1642* (1968) · S. E. Morison, *Builders of the Bay Colony* (Boston, 1958) · R. S. Paul, *The assembly of the Lord: politics and religion in the Westminster assembly and the 'Grand debate'* (1985) · F. Rose-Troup, *The Massachusetts Company and its predecessors* (New Haven, 1930)
Archives Mass. Hist. Soc., letters to John Winthrop
Wealth at death see Rose-Troup, *John White*, 413–14

White, John [*called* Century White] (**1590–1645**), politician and lawyer, was born on 29 June 1590, the second son of Henry White of Rhoscrowther, Pembrokeshire, and Jane, daughter of Richard Fletcher of Bangor. He was descended from a family of wealthy merchants associated with the town of Tenby, and both his father and grandfather served

as sheriffs of Pembrokeshire. On 20 November 1607 White matriculated with his elder brother Griffith from Jesus College, Oxford. In 1610 he entered the Middle Temple, where he was called to the bar in 1618. Griffith was sheriff of Pembrokeshire in 1626.

Probably by this time White had married Katherine, daughter of Edward Barfoot of Lambourne Hall, Essex; they had one surviving daughter, Winifred, who later married Richard Blackwell of Bushey, Hertfordshire. Katherine Barfoot was a kinswoman of the Winthrops, and White himself was associated with a number of puritan colonizing ventures and had interests in the Virginia Company, the Dorchester Company, and also the Massachusetts Bay Company, whose charter he has been credited with drawing up. He acted as counsel for William Coryton when charges were drawn against him for his conduct in the 1629 session of parliament. On 30 August 1631, as a widower, White was licensed to marry Mary, eldest daughter of Thomas Stiles or Style of Little Missenden, Buckinghamshire; the wedding took place on 1 September at St Stephen, Coleman Street, London, a church with a strong puritan reputation. A long-term critic of Arminianism and episcopacy, White was described by the earl of Clarendon as 'a grave lawyer, but notoriously disaffected to the Church' (Clarendon, *Hist. rebellion*, 1.264). He was one of the founding members of the feoffees for impropriations, formed with the intention of buying impropriate tithes in order to make better provision for a preaching ministry. Testifying in 1644 at the trial of Archbishop William Laud, White claimed that Laud, while bishop of London, had for these activities attacked him as 'an enemy of the Church, an underminer of religion' (Prynne, 386–7). He had then replied that the feoffees intended only the better maintenance of preachers and that they took pains to ensure the clerics they supported were conformists; he had also offered to remove any of the feoffees and replace them with men approved by Laud. This had been to no avail. In 1632 Attorney-General William Noy filed an information against the group in the court of exchequer, and on 11 February 1633 the court decreed the dissolution of the feoffees and the confiscation of their funds and patronage to the use of the king.

In the autumn of 1640 White was returned to parliament as the junior member for Southwark with his Middle Temple associate Edward Bagshaw; he is not to be confused with his namesake John White (*c.*1599–1655), MP for Rye. He took the protestation in 1641. As MP for Southwark, White was among the delegation sent on 4 February 1642 to thank local women for their petition for church reform, although 'there was no precedent for a petition from women' (Coates, Young, and Snow, 277). He also chaired a number of important committees including the committee for scandalous ministers and, after Sir Edward Dering was disabled from sitting in the Commons, the committee for printing. White actively supported church reforms and opposed the canons of 1640 as 'utterlie against law', arguing that the so-called 'etc oath' attached to the canons was 'verie dangerous and enacted uniustlie, in which he shewed many particulars' (*Journal*, ed. Notestein, 71). In June 1641, during the debate on the first Bishops Exclusion Bill, White advocated that bishops should be excluded from parliament, because all their powers, over and above their ministerial authority, were by *jure humano* and not by divine right. He insisted that the 'Spirituall Monarchy' of the bishops was inclined to return to 'Popery, and the Religion of Antichrist', which he detected in the altar policy of the 1630s, the restraint on preaching about predestination and against Arminian tenets, and the condition of the parish clergy. Eight out of ten ministers, White argued, were 'Idoll, idle or scandalous'. He desired that the powers of the bishops should be reformed and reduced to a 'condition and state agreeable to the word of God' (*A Speech of John White*, 1641). On 31 December White was named to the committee to consider treason charges against twelve bishops. In the ensuing debate he accused the bishops and their adherents as 'the greatest and chiefest authors of our miseries … favourers of the Romish and Arminian faction', who had tyrannized the consciences of 'free subjects' in the exercise of their religion and had orchestrated division between 'the Prince and his people, [and] between the Prince and his Parliaments'. He depicted the bishops as agents of the devil and urged the Commons to reduce their powers and to bring the bishops speedily to trial.

In 1643 White took the covenant and developed the themes of his speeches in his major publication *The First Century of Scandalous, Malignant Priests* (1643). The work, which earned him the nickname 'Century White', detailed the complaints against negligent, immoral, and 'ceremonious' clergy, which were used by parliament to eject them from their livings. Many of the allegedly 'malignant' priests were also accused of preaching or speaking out against parliament. In the introduction White characterized the sequestered ministers as 'priests of Baal, of Bacchus, of Priapus', who promoted the 'errours of Popery and Arminianism' and were given to 'cursing, swearing, drunkennesse, whoredome [and] sodomie'. He justified the sequestrations because they provided parliament with the opportunity to replace 'scandalous' ministers with 'godly, learned, orthodox Divines', who were 'diligent preachers of the word of God' (sig. A2–4). White reiterated his demands for church reform and declared that the will of God was manifest in the calling of parliament to effect reformation. The first of the ensuing 100 sequestrations from areas under parliamentarian control, especially Essex, Suffolk, and Kent, concerned a case of bestiality from Sussex, and the last concerned the efforts of an Essex vicar to compromise the chastity of the widows in his parish. Sandwiched in between were ninety-eight assorted instances of negligent, alcoholic, Laudian, and royalist ministers. White had single-handedly invented the popular press concept of the 'naughty vicar' and, according to Anthony Wood, his intention to publish a subsequent volume was never realized, because White was persuaded that it would bring scandal to the whole body of the clergy (Wood, *Ath. Oxon.*, 3.144).

On 10 June 1642 White had offered £100 to the parliamentarian war effort. That year he was appointed as a lay member of the Westminster assembly of divines. He chaired the committee to consider the assembly's proposals on ordination in September 1644 and introduced the bill for introducing the *Directory for the Publique Worship of God* to replace the Book of Common Prayer. White was also a member of various committees set up to combat idolatry, including the committee chaired by Sir Robert Harley, which drew up the ordinances of 1643 and 1644 for the demolishing of 'monuments of idolatry and superstition'. He was also actively involved in the trial of William Laud and was a member of the committee appointed to manage evidence against the archbishop. In addition to his evidence at the trial about the dissolution of the feoffees, he related the circumstances surrounding the removal of Edward Bagshaw in 1640 as reader at the Middle Temple following a lecture attacking the temporal powers of the clergy. White's final activities in the Commons were as a manager and reporter at the conference on the peace propositions on 8 November 1644.

White died on 29 January 1645, survived by his second wife, four of their sons, and four of their daughters. He was buried on 1 February at the Temple Church, London, near the altar, his funeral being attended by members of the House of Commons. According to Wood, his memorial inscription contained the following lines: 'Here lyeth a John, a burning shining light, His name, life, actions were all White' (Wood, *Ath. Oxon.*, 3.146).

JACQUELINE EALES

Sources Keeler, *Long Parliament* · Wood, *Ath. Oxon.*, new edn, vol. 3 · *N&Q*, 160 (1931), 437–8 · *JHC*, 2–3 (1640–44) · I. M. Calder, *Activities of the puritan faction of the Church of England, 1625–33* (1957) · Foster, *Alum. Oxon.* · Clarendon, *Hist. rebellion*, 1.264 · W. H. Coates, A. Steele Young, and V. F. Snow, eds., *The private journals of the Long Parliament, 1: 3 January to 5 March 1642* (1982) · *The journal of Sir Simonds D'Ewes from the beginning of the Long Parliament to the opening of the trial of the earl of Strafford*, ed. W. Notestein (1923) · W. Prynne, *Canterburies doome*, 1646 · HoP, *Commons*, 1640–60 [draft]

White, John (1764–1833). *See under* White family (*per.* 1795–1846).

White, John (1826–1891), ethnographer and public servant in New Zealand, one of the eight children of Francis White, a blacksmith, and his wife, Jane, *née* Angus, was born in Cockfield, co. Durham, on 3 January 1826, and emigrated to New Zealand with his family in 1834. They settled first at the Hokianga, North Island, and in 1851 moved to Auckland. On 13 March 1854 White married Mary Elizabeth Bagnall, with whom he had eight children. His early and continuing interest in the Maori and their customs led to his employment by the government in positions where he came into frequent contact with Maori. His career centred around appointments as official interpreter and agent for the purchase of native lands, and in this latter capacity he was instrumental in purchasing Maori land in Auckland. From 1852 he was gold commissioner at Coromandel, North Island, and between 1862 and 1865 he was resident magistrate at Wanganui.

White's reputation as an ethnographer and writer of

both scholarly and fictional works based on Maori traditions led to his employment from 1879 by the government of New Zealand to compile a complete history of such traditions. These he collected at times by monetary payment and at others by trading European mythology and legends. He died suddenly *en route* for Whakatane, on the Bay of Plenty, North Island, on 13 January 1891. He had completed six volumes of *The Ancient History of the Maori*, the production of which was helped by neither government cost-cutting nor White's own variable powers of organization. It, and his other ethnographical work, was well received by contemporary scholars. Later commentators have drawn attention to his lack of scholarly vigour, but, as an early commentator on the Maori who based his remarks in large part on first-hand knowledge, helped by fluency in the language, he is undoubtedly important, and his achievements were remarkable.

C. A. HARRIS, *rev.* JANE TUCKER

Sources P. J. Reilly, 'White, John', *DNZB*, vol. 1 · P. Mennell, *The dictionary of Australasian biography* (1892) · A. H. McLintock, ed., *An encyclopaedia of New Zealand*, 3 vols. (1966) · M. Reilly, 'A book's progress', *Turnbull Record*, 24 (1991) · *Auckland Weekly News* (24 Jan 1891)
Archives NL NZ, Turnbull L.
Likenesses group photograph, NL NZ · photograph, NL NZ

White, John (1867–1951), Church of Scotland minister, was born on 16 December 1867 in the Barony parish, Glasgow, the fifth of seven children of Matthew White (1831–1882), grain merchant at Kilwinning, and his wife, Marion (1832–1920), daughter of James Kennedy, farmer. John was educated at Irvine Royal Academy, and then at Glasgow University from 1883 to 1891, taking his MA degree with honours in mental philosophy and training for the ministry of the Church of Scotland. He had a distinguished student career, and was a protégé of the philosopher Edward Caird, later master of Balliol College, Oxford. After serving briefly as assistant minister in New Kilpatrick, White was ordained Church of Scotland minister of Shettleston, near Glasgow, on 14 March 1893. That same year, on 5 September, he married Margaret Gardner (d. 1942), a vivacious daughter of a provisions merchant, and they had three sons and two daughters.

White was a powerfully built man and a keen sportsman, outspoken, with a forceful personality. He was a dedicated pastor, who embraced the social gospel ethos of the 1890s and was committed to restoring the social influence of the national Church of Scotland. His sharp intellect, organizational skills, and pastoral commitment soon attracted notice. In 1904 he was translated to the urban parish of South Leith, and in 1911 he was translated to the Barony parish in central Glasgow. During the First World War he served as a chaplain with the Cameronians for over a year on the western front. Returning to Scotland in September 1916 he took a leading role on the general assembly's commission on the war and helped to create the standing church and nation committee in 1919, with the aim of giving Christian leadership to post-war reconstruction.

White's major achievement was in the area of church union. In 1909 the two largest Presbyterian denominations in Scotland, the Church of Scotland and the United Free Church, began negotiations for union. White was appointed secretary of the Church of Scotland negotiating committee, and soon emerged as the dominant figure in the union movement. The negotiations proved long and arduous, and required parliamentary legislation to give the Church of Scotland, an established church, the spiritual independence that the United Free Church insisted upon as a prerequisite for union. In 1925 White's service to the church was recognized when he was elected to the year-long office of moderator of the general assembly of the Church of Scotland. Four years later, in 1929, the church union was finally completed, bringing the large majority of Scottish Presbyterians together in a free, national Church of Scotland. Recognized as the main architect of the union, White was elected the first moderator of the general assembly of the reunited church.

Following the union White organized the Forward Movement, which aimed to revive the social influence of the restored national church in a Scotland suffering acute economic distress. A Forward Congress convened in October 1931 in Glasgow, and was followed by ten regional 'missions of the kingdom'—though in the event the movement had only a limited impact. In 1933 White launched a church extension campaign, which erected churches and church halls in the new housing areas being developed on the peripheries of older urban areas. There was, however, also a darker side to White's social activism. He embraced a racial nationalism, organizing a Scottish churches campaign between 1923 and 1938 to persuade the state to halt Irish migration into Scotland and to deport many Irish-born residents. One purpose of the national church, he argued, should be to protect the racial purity of the nation. By the later 1930s his ascendancy over the Church of Scotland was fading, as younger, more liberal church leaders emerged. Nevertheless, he received a notable honour in 1935, becoming a CH. His wife, Margaret, died in September 1942, and on 24 April 1945 he married Anne May Calderwood, a Church of Scotland secretary, and the only daughter of David Woodside, a Presbyterian minister. A formidable character to the end, White died unexpectedly in his sleep on 20 August 1951 in his Glasgow home, Barony parish manse, Sunnybank, 61 Partickhill Road. He was buried at Hillfoot cemetery, Glasgow, three days later; he was survived by his second wife.

STEWART J. BROWN

Sources A. Muir, *John White C.H., D.D., LL.D* (1958) · A. Gammie, *Dr. John White* (1929) · *Fasti Scot.*, new edn, 8.289–90 · U. Edin., New Coll. L., John White MSS · *The Times* (22 Aug 1951) · *CCI* (1951) · *Glasgow Herald* (24 Aug 1951)
Archives U. Edin., New College, corresp. and papers · U. Glas. L., sermons, etc.
Likenesses J. Langry, oils, 1925, General Assembly of the Church of Scotland Hall, Edinburgh · J. Mortimer, sculpture, plaque, 1953, Barony church, Glasgow, John White Chapel · photographs, repro. in Muir, *John White*
Wealth at death £13,308 7s. 0d.: confirmation, 3 Oct 1951, *CCI*

White, John Campbell, Baron Overtoun (1843–1908), philanthropist and chemical manufacturer, was born at Hayfield, near Rutherglen, on 21 November 1843, the middle child of seven and only son of James White (1812–1884) and his wife, Fanny Campbell (d. 1891). James White had trained as a lawyer before entering the family firm of John and James White, whose Shawfield chemical works at Rutherglen was the largest chrome producer in the world. He and his wife laid down the pattern of religious and philanthropic concern that their son followed so closely. After education at Glasgow Academy, Campbell White entered Glasgow University, and graduated MA in 1865 with prizes in logic and natural philosophy. He gained business experience in several Glasgow offices before entering his father's firm, where he became a partner in 1867. He married, on 18 September 1867, Grace Eliza (d. 1931), daughter of James H. McClure, a Glasgow solicitor; she fully shared his religious and philanthropic goals. There were no children from the marriage.

Campbell White was greatly influenced by the visit of the American evangelists Moody and Sankey in 1874. One result of their visit was the creation of the United Evangelistic Association, a non-denominational organization conducting mission and charitable work among Glasgow's poor, of which he became president. His liberality and support were evidenced in the buildings in Bothwell Street, Glasgow, which housed the Christian Institute, the Bible Training Institute, and the Young Men's Christian Association. He personally conducted a Bible class in Dumbarton on Sunday evenings, which had about 500 members. At his death he was president or vice-president of a score of religious societies or hospital boards. A staunch supporter of the Free Church of Scotland like his father, he succeeded him as convener of its Livingstonia Mission. In his lifetime Campbell White was estimated to have contributed £50,000 to the central Africa mission, although he declined the opportunity to visit its stations. A promoter of the union between the Free and the United Presbyterian churches, he was swift to pledge £10,000 when the House of Lords judgment of 1904 temporarily deprived the United Free Church of its property.

Campbell White was a county councillor for Dunbartonshire from 1890 and was latterly county convener. He became lord lieutenant of the county in 1907, having been deputy lieutenant since 1884. The burghs of Dumbarton, Clydebank, and Rutherglen were all beneficiaries of his giving, and he received the freedom of Rutherglen in 1905. Raised to the peerage by Gladstone in 1893, on the strength of his philanthropic work rather than his support for the Liberal Party, his title, Baron Overtoun, was taken from the estate which his father had bought in 1859, and where he had built a mansion in the Scottish baronial style. He died at Overtoun House on 15 February 1908 after a short illness, and was buried in the family vault in Dumbarton cemetery on 20 February.

A man of middle height, with small grey eyes, a square jaw and well-chiselled features, Lord Overtoun was always impeccable in appearance and grooming, but was without vanity. He would be remembered solely for his peerless philanthropy and Christian zeal were it not for the fact that the source of his wealth was a chemical works where the wages and working conditions were scandalous. In 1899 Keir Hardie exposed conditions at Overtoun's works in the *Labour Leader*; the allegations were also circulated in pamphlets. There was no effective rebuttal of the charges and Overtoun stood accused of hypocrisy, not least because his passionate sabbatarianism did not extend to closing his chemical works on Sundays. While Overtoun was somewhat distanced from the daily running of the Rutherglen works, it was impossible for him to escape some of the odium for conditions in a third-generation family firm of which he was sole proprietor. It was with these criticisms in mind that one tribute affirmed 'Nothing could be farther from the truth than to picture him as a purse-proud millionaire or a haughty, heartless employer of labour. He was a humble Christian gentleman' (*Scottish Review*, 20 Feb 1908).

LIONEL ALEXANDER RITCHIE

Sources *Lennox Herald* (22 Feb 1908) · *Glasgow Herald* (17 Feb 1908) · *The Scotsman* (17 Feb 1908) · *The Times* (17 Feb 1908) · *Scottish Review* (20 Feb 1908) · *Missionary Record of the United Free Church of Scotland* (April 1908) · D. Carswell, *Brother Scots* (1927), 191–211 · S. Checkland, 'White, John Campbell (Lord Overtoun)', *DSBB* · *The Bailie* (27 April 1887) · *The Bailie* (21 June 1899) · *Glasgow contemporaries at the dawn of the XXth century* (1901), 100–01 · P. C. Simpson, *The life of Principal Rainy*, 2 vols. (1909) · J. MacLehose, ed., *Memoirs and portraits of one hundred Glasgow men who have died during the last thirty years*, 2 (1886), 335–8 · GEC, *Peerage* · Burke, *Peerage* (1910) · *WWW*, 1897–1915 · *DNB* · W. I. Addison, *A roll of graduates of the University of Glasgow from 31st December 1727 to 31st December 1897* (1898)
Archives Mitchell L., Glas., Glasgow City Archives, Christian Institute records, letter-books as secretary to the Christian Institute committee · Mitchell L., Glas., business records of John White and James White
Likenesses G. F. Watt, oils, 1909, Assembly Buildings, Edinburgh · drawings, repro. in *The Baillie*, no. 758 · drawings, repro. in *The Baillie*, no. 1392 · photograph, repro. in *Glasgow contemporaries at the dawn of the XXth century* (1901)
Wealth at death £689,022 12s. 1d.: confirmation, 25 May 1908, *CCI*

White, John Meadows (1799/1800–1863), lawyer, was born at Halesworth, Suffolk, the younger son of Robert Gostling White (d. 1828), a solicitor, and his second wife, Elizabeth Meadows (d. 1831); Robert Meadows *White, Anglo-Saxonist, was his elder brother. On 17 September 1825 he married, at Halesworth, Anne, daughter of Robert Crabtree, an attorney there; they had many children. White was a partner of his father in Halesworth; he then moved to London, becoming partner of T. Barett in Great St Helen's Street. He was later senior partner of Borrett, White, and Borrett, in Lincoln's Inn.

White established a considerable reputation and practice as a parliamentary solicitor, specializing in poor-law, tithe, and copyhold business, on which subjects he published pamphlets, notably those of 1829, 1834, and 1835 on poor-law reform, and of 1841 on copyhold enfranchisement. From 1842 until his death he (acting for his firm) was solicitor to the ecclesiastical commission, in which office he was succeeded by his son, Robert Holmes White. He practised in London from 1835 until 1851 in Lincoln's Inn, and from 1851 in Whitehall Place. White died at Weymouth in Dorset on 19 March 1863.

H. C. G. MATTHEW

Sources Law List · Boase, Mod. Eng. biog. · 'White, Robert Meadows', DNB · CGPLA Eng. & Wales (1863) · Gladstone, Diaries
Archives Suffolk RO, Ipswich, corresp. and papers | UCL, letters to Edwin Chadwick
Wealth at death under £25,000: resworn probate, 15 Sept 1863, CGPLA Eng. & Wales

White, John Tahourdin (1809–1893), classical scholar, born in Selborne, Hampshire, was the second son of John White. He matriculated from Corpus Christi College, Oxford, on 28 January 1830, was elected an exhibitioner in the same year, and graduated BA in 1834; he proceeded MA in 1839, and BD and DD in 1866. He was ordained deacon in 1834 as curate at Swinnerton in Staffordshire, and was appointed reader at St Stephen Walbrook, London, in 1836. He was an assistant master at Christ's Hospital from 1836 to 1869. He became curate at St Ann Blackfriars in 1837, was ordained priest in 1839, and married on 21 April 1840 Anna Grives, youngest daughter of the Revd William Harrison DD. In 1841 he was appointed curate at St Martin Ludgate, where he served until November 1868, when he was instituted rector by the bishop of London. He resigned the living in November 1890 and died at 25 Cambridge Road, Brighton, on 17 December 1893. His wife survived him.

White was an able classical scholar, and published many books for use in schools. He was best-known perhaps for his Grammar School Texts, a series of editions of Latin and Greek authors. In conjunction with Joseph Esmond Riddle he brought out in 1862 A Latin-English Dictionary (7th edn, 1880), founded on Ethan Allen Andrews's translation of Wilhelm Freund's Wörterbuch der lateinischen Sprache. Freund's Wörterbuch was published at Leipzig between 1834 and 1845, and Andrews's translation at New York in 1852. White and Riddle's dictionary, of which there were various abridgements and adaptations, was largely superseded by that of Charlton T. Lewis and Charles Short in 1879.

E. I. CARLYLE, rev. M. C. CURTHOYS

Sources The Times (21 Dec 1893) · Foster, Alum. Oxon. · Boase, Mod. Eng. biog. · Allibone, Dict. · R. Simms, ed., Bibliotheca Staffordiensis (1894) · CGPLA Eng. & Wales (1894) · GM, 2nd ser., 13 (1840), 646
Wealth at death £5232 18s. 1d.: probate, 9 April 1894, CGPLA Eng. & Wales

White, Joseph (bap. 1746, d. 1814), orientalist and theologian, was born at Ruscombe, Gloucestershire, and baptized at Stroud on 19 February 1746, the eldest son of Thomas White (1724–1804), a journeyman broadloom weaver, and Elizabeth Harmer (1723–1772). He received his earliest education from his father and in one of the Gloucestershire charity schools. He started his working life in his father's employment; his talents and attainments, however, attracted the notice of Joseph Ellis, a wealthy neighbour, who, together with the Stroud physician Dr

Joseph White (bap. 1746, d. 1814), by James Thomson, pubd 1796 (after Matthew William Peters)

Samuel Jones, paid for him to pursue his studies at Ruscombe, and afterwards at a school in Gloucester. Their generosity and the liberality of John Moore, a future archbishop of Canterbury, enabled White to enter Wadham College, Oxford, as a commoner on 6 June 1765. In September of that year he was made a scholar of his college and from 1766 to 1773 he held the Hody exhibition for Hebrew. He graduated BA (1769), MA (1773), BD (1779), and DD (1787), and from 1773 he was a fellow of Wadham. At Moore's request he devoted himself to the study of Syriac, Arabic, and Persian, and in 1774 he was elected unanimously to the Laudian chair of Arabic. His command of these languages was clearly demonstrated in his edition of the Syriac Philoxenian version of the gospels, published as Sacrorum evangeliorum versio Syriaca Philoxeniana (2 vols., 1778). This scholarly and accurate work was based on four manuscripts acquired from Mesopotamia by Glocester Ridley, fellow of New College.

On 17 November 1779 White preached before the university an elegant sermon afterwards published as A Revisal of the English Translation of the Old Testament Recommended, and about the same time he was appointed one of the preachers at the Whitehall chapel. From 1780 to 1783 he was occupied in preparing an edition of the Persian text of the 'Institutes of Timur', which was published at the expense of the East India Company in 1783 as Institutes Political and Military … by the Great Timour. The text was accompanied by a translation into English by Major William Davy, then Persian secretary to the governor-general of Bengal.

In 1783 White was chosen to preach the Bampton lectures the following year and he took as his subject a comparison of Islam and Christianity. He called upon the assistance of Samuel Badcock and Samuel Parr but failed to acknowledge his obligation when the lectures were published in 1784. The lectures, which contained a courteous answer to Gibbon as well as a reply to Hume, met with general approbation in academic and literary circles and established White's reputation as 'one of the ablest vindicators of the Christian doctrines modern times has witnessed' (*GM*, 84/1, 627). Largely as a result of this success White was appointed rector of Melton in Suffolk in 1787, whereupon he resigned his fellowship. In 1788 he was presented to a prebend in Gloucester Cathedral, an appointment 'which at once placed him in easy and independent circumstances' (Nichols, *Illustrations*, 4.861). It was not until after Badcock's death in 1788 that the assistance that White had received in the writing of the sermons came to light. Eventually, in 1790, he was obliged to publish a statement of his literary debt to Badcock and Parr; his scholarly reputation was somewhat tarnished but it was generally accepted that White had been responsible for the greater part of the work.

On 31 October 1791 at Prestbury, near Cheltenham, White married Mary (*d*. 1811), daughter of a prosperous grocer, John Turner of Gloucester, and sister of Samuel *Turner (1759–1802). He published little over the few years until 1800, when his edition of ʿAbd al-Latif's manuscript description of Egypt at the close of the twelfth century appeared under the title *Abdollatiphi historiae Aegypti compendium*. He had printed the text sixteen years previously but, not being satisfied with it, had presented the copies to Paulus of Jena, who issued the work in Germany. White's edition embodied a translation begun by the younger Edward Pococke but completed by White himself. He planned to follow this with a comprehensive history of Egypt but this proved unsuccessful and his *Observations on Certain Antiquities of Egypt* (1804) soon became out of date once the modern study of Egyptology began.

The rest of White's literary work was concentrated on the textual study of the Old and New testaments and earned him in 1804 the regius professorship of Hebrew at Oxford, carrying with it a canonry of Christ Church. Besides various pamphlets, in which he advocated a retranslation of the Bible, and proposed a new edition of the Septuagint, to be based on the Hexplar–Syriac manuscript then recently discovered in Milan, he published in 1800 a *Diatessaron, or, Harmony of the Gospels*. In his edition of the New Testament in Greek (1808; often reprinted) he endeavoured to simplify and popularize Griesbach's *Critical Studies*, and his last work, *Criseos Griesbachianiae in Novum Testamentum synopsis* (1811), contains a summary of the more important results.

White was an accomplished and versatile scholar who ranks alongside Humphrey Hody, Robert Lowth, and Benjamin Kennicott as one of 'the major Hebraists of the century' (Patterson, 539). In his private life 'he united a degree of roughness with great simplicity of manners' (Nichols, *Illustrations*, 4.865). He never recovered from the death of

his wife on 25 August 1811 and died, as a result of a paralytic stroke, at his residence in Christ Church on 23 May 1814. He was buried in Christ Church, where there is a monument to his memory.

D. S. MARGOLIOUTH, *rev.* M. J. MERCER

Sources Nichols, *Illustrations*, 4.858–65 · J. Stratford, *Good and great men of Gloucestershire* (1867) · Foster, *Alum. Oxon.* · D. Patterson, 'Hebrew studies', *Hist. U. Oxf.* 5: *18th-cent. Oxf.*, 535–50 · P. J. Marshall, 'Oriental studies', *Hist. U. Oxf.* 5: *18th-cent. Oxf.*, 550–63, esp. 554–60 · Allibone, *Dict.* · *GM*, 1st ser., 81/2 (1811), 287 · *GM*, 1st ser., 84/1 (1814), 626–8 · *IGI*
Likenesses J. Thomson, stipple (after M. W. Peters), BM, NPG; repro. in *European Magazine* (1796) [*see illus.*]

White, Joseph Blanco [*formerly* José María Blanco y Crespo] **(1775–1841)**, author, was born on 11 July 1775 in the calle Jamerdana, Seville, the eldest of the four children of Guillermo Blanco y Morrogh (1745–1815), a merchant, and his wife, María Gertrudis Crespo y Neve (*d.* 1819). He had two sisters and a brother.

Background and early life His paternal grandfather, William White, emigrated from Waterford to Andalusia at the beginning of the eighteenth century and established an import–export business in Seville. His father, also William White, adopted the Spanish form of his name, Guillermo Blanco, and married into the lesser nobility: María's uncle, Felipe de la Neve, was governor of California and founder (in 1781) of Los Angeles. The family firm went bankrupt in 1769 and though reconstituted was much reduced in scale.

Blanco grew up isolated from other children, 'with deeply inculcated ideas of gentility'. He inherited his mother's ardent and mercurial temperament and 'a sensibility beyond description'. His father, a reserved and selfless man dedicated to works of practical charity, set his son to work in the office alongside the Irish clerks, but allowed him private lessons in Latin and music. The music master lent him *Don Quixote*, which he 'devoured' in secret, and later in his aunt's library he discovered the works of the enlightened Benedictine Benito Feijoo, which he regarded as having first awakened his critical faculties. Youthful piety, the desire to please his mother, and an eagerness to exchange the drudgery of the counting-house for the pleasures of literary study prompted him to declare his vocation for the priesthood; after some opposition by his Irish relatives he was sent in 1789 to the Dominican college of Santo Tomás. Henceforth he was to be a Spanish clerical gentleman.

In 1790 Blanco entered the University of Seville, but he learned less from the scholastic course there than from two older students, Manuel María del Mármol and Manuel María de Arjona, who supervised his philosophical and literary formation. In 1794 he joined a private literary academy founded by his close friends Alberto Lista and Felix-José Reinoso for self-education and mutual encouragement in poetry and rhetoric. Under the patronage of the enlightened lawyer J. P. Forner they cultivated an idealistic Christian humanism which was at odds with the anti-intellectual tone of clerical society. The Spanish Jansenist

Joseph Blanco White (1775–1841), by Joseph? Slater, 1812

movement, to which they were drawn and which advocated the reform and purification of the church, put down few roots in Seville.

Although a visit to the more worldly milieu of Cadiz and the first symptoms of 'an amorous temperament' prompted thoughts of escape, Blanco proceeded to ordination as subdeacon in 1796 and priest in 1798. In 1801 he won in open competition the prestigious post of *capellán magistral* in the Royal Chapel of St Ferdinand. In the following year he underwent a profound crisis of faith brought on not only by intellectual doubts and tensions but also by emotional revulsion from a hierocracy that he now regarded as the enemy of self-fulfilment and social progress. One of his sisters died in her convent that year, and the other, under the influence of her confessor, now entered a penitential order, 'misled from the path of practical usefulness into a wilderness of visionary perfection' (quoted in Murphy, 26). His inner conflict is evident in a sermon preached in the Royal Chapel in 1802, in which the conventional warnings against intellectual pride were less convincing than the objections which, as devil's advocate, he voiced against a spirituality of self-annihilation.

After three more years in Seville, outwardly conforming to the church while inwardly rejecting it, Blanco obtained leave in 1805 to reside at Madrid. There he abandoned the practice of the priesthood and sought escape in anonymity, in 'the growing persuasion that the world was not under the direction of an intelligent moral agent' ('Examination of Blanco by White', 35). During this period he formed a liaison with Magdalena Ezquaya, who, after his departure from Madrid, bore him a son. On obtaining the

sinecure of catechist to the recently established Pestalozzian school, he came under the patronage of its protector Manuel Godoy, the 'Prince of the Peace', whom he eulogized in a celebratory ode (1808). After witnessing the riots that led to Godoy's fall, the entry into the city of Murat's troops, and the rising of 2 May 1808, he escaped to Seville in June to join the patriotic resistance. He was there appointed co-editor of the *Semanario Patriótico*, the semi-official organ of the newly constituted central junta. He took an independent and radical line, urging that resistance to the French should be accompanied by internal reform, and when the junta pressed him to moderate his criticisms he resigned. As the French advanced on Seville in January 1810 he joined the loyal exodus to Cadiz, but there seized the opportunity to extricate himself from his personal impasse by taking ship for England.

England, 1810–1832 In London, White enjoyed the patronage of Lord Holland, whom he had already met in Seville, and the friendship of the family of Sir John Moore, whose military reputation he had defended (see Thom, 177–8). Within four months he set up a Spanish-language political journal, *El Español*, which the Foreign Office encouraged at a discreet distance. In the first number of May 1810 he shocked his friends in Cadiz by attacking the now defunct central junta and calling for revolutionary reform. Under the influence of Lord Holland he subsequently moderated his tone, but his endorsement of the revolution in Caracas later that year, and of the right of the Spanish-American dominions to limited self-rule, provoked the regency government at Cadiz to proscribe his journal and to condemn him as a traitor. He continued to edit and write *El Español* single-handed for four years, arguing for the transformation of the Spanish empire into a free commonwealth of self-governing, though not fully independent, nations united by allegiance to the crown. His proposals for constitutional reform included the establishment of a bicameral Cortes on the British parliamentary model. When the constitution of Cadiz was published in 1812, his sarcastic strictures on its doctrinaire utopianism further alienated him from his former colleagues. After the return of Ferdinand VII to Madrid in May 1814 he concluded the journal in a mood of despair at the polarization of Spain between the forces of reaction and revolution. Eloquent, acute, and prophetic, *El Español* exercised a seminal influence in Spanish America. Its articles were reprinted in Mexico, Lima, Caracas, and Buenos Aires, thereby contributing to the development of a common purpose, and it moved Bolívar's political thought in a Burkean direction.

In 1812 the Foreign Office had granted White an annual pension of £250, paid (to his chagrin) out of the secret service fund, as a remuneration for his reports on South American affairs. In 1814 the African Association commissioned him to write a pamphlet in Spanish on the slave trade, containing new evidence on the traffic organized from Havana, and this was distributed in Spain in an attempt to move its government towards abolition. His pension helped him to support his natural son Ferdinand, whom he had brought to London in 1813, though it was some time before he publicly acknowledged his paternity.

Under the influence of evangelical friends, notably the auctioneer James Christie the younger, he joined the Anglican communion in 1812. Two years later his orders were revalidated by the bishop of London and he took lodgings at Oxford in order to prepare himself for his new role as a clergyman by the study of Anglican theology and Greek. In 1815 he returned to Holland House as tutor to Henry Fox, but the strain of reconciling his evangelical piety with the sceptical ethos which prevailed there, and the agitation induced by Lady Holland's caprices, prompted his resignation in 1817. His theological studies over the next four years brought him to the verge of a breakdown as he struggled with his renascent heterodoxy. He found the unitarian case unanswerable, but could not face the social ostracism which a break with orthodoxy would entail. Seeking escape from his theological impasse in renewed literary activity, in 1821 he accepted Thomas Campbell's invitation to write a series of 'Letters from Spain' for the *New Monthly Magazine*, adopting the punning pseudonym Don Leucadio Doblado ('double white'). With their delicacy of style and colourful subject matter, the works, published in book form in 1822, caught the tide of literary taste and made White's reputation as an English man of letters. He himself attached most importance to the third letter, 'A few facts connected with the formation of the intellectual and moral character of a Spanish clergyman', a bitter denunciation of Catholic priestcraft, which lent itself to exploitation by the opponents of emancipation. The same anti-clerical vehemence is evident in the historical novel *Vargas: a Tale of Spain*, showing the influence of Scott, which he published, and then suppressed, in 1822.

In 1823 White returned to the Spanish literary arena as editor of *Variedades*, a magazine published in London by Rudolph Ackermann for the Spanish-American market. Besides earning him an annual salary of £300, which helped to pay for his son's education, the work satisfied his sense of mission. Believing that political stability was contingent on the development of enlightened public opinion, he set out to improve the taste and educate the mind of a new Spain which would avoid the errors of the old. Along with translations of Scott and Shakespeare, and sketches of English life, he included extracts from old Spanish chronicles and articles of literary criticism in which he argued that the true golden age of Spanish literature preceded the imposition of a monolithic theocracy by the Catholic kings. It was his most successful attempt to free himself from the strait-jacket of rationalism and to develop a romantic aesthetic based on figurative, rather than literal, truth. The roles of English clergyman and Spanish journalist finally proved to be incompatible and he resigned the editorship in 1825 after a valedictory warning to the Spanish Americans on the dangers of religious intolerance. In the same year he made his début as an English poet, his sonnet 'Night and Death' being hailed by Coleridge, the dedicatee, as 'the finest and most grandly conceived' in the language (Thom, 1.439).

In 1825 White was persuaded by Southey that it was his 'duty' to warn the British public of the dangers of granting toleration to Roman Catholics, and to this end he wrote *Practical and Internal Evidence Against Catholicism* (1825), a portrait of the writer as victim, in which he exposed his own life as a cautionary lesson. At the suggestion of J. D. Coleridge he also wrote a simplified version, *The Poor Man's Preservative Against Popery* (1825), in the form of 'conversations' with a representative of the working class. These productions dismayed Holland House, while providing the anti-emancipationists with ammunition. In April 1826 he was rewarded when, on the initiative of Edward Copleston, the University of Oxford conferred on him the degree of MA by diploma. He took up residence at Oxford in October 1826 as an honorary member of Oriel College.

Although Oxford seemed to offer White at last the status and repose he desired, his years there (1826–32) were uneasy and creatively fallow. The university failed to give him useful employment and he came to resent his marginalization. Intellectually he found himself at home in the company of Richard Whately and his fellow Noetics Baden Powell, Edward Hawkins, R. D. Hampden, and Nassau Senior. His friendship with the young J. H. Newman, with whom he shared 'grand and beautiful visions', was of a different order: a meeting of hearts rather than minds. They played the violin together and shared a passion for Beethoven. Under the influence of Whately and Senior, he now modified his political stance, and at the Oxford University by-election in 1829 came out in support of Peel and Catholic emancipation on the grounds of expediency, thereby alienating his former patrons. He was taken aback by Newman's militancy on behalf of the anti-Peel party, and by the discovery that Oxford was not immune from *odium theologicum*. Increasingly he spent more time in London, first as editor of the short-lived *London Review* (in which he published Newman's first literary article, on poetry) and then as tutor to Senior's son. Soon after Whately's appointment as archbishop of Dublin in 1832 he accepted an invitation to join him there.

Final years, 1832–1841 In Ireland, White led a retired life, tutoring Whately's son and translating Clairaut's *Éléments de géométrie* for use in the Irish national schools, 'in the hope of contributing to the great object of the education of the poor'. In *The Law of Anti-Religious Libel Reconsidered* (1834) he gave incisive expression to his belief that the law had no place in the defence of religious truth. At Whately's request he re-entered the field of controversy as the anonymous author of *Second Travels of an Irish Gentleman* (1833), an apologia for protestantism in novelistic form, written as a riposte to Thomas Moore. Privately he was now in fact moving away from protestant orthodoxy towards a non-denominational Christianity. When Whately, fearful of being compromised, sounded a warning note, White left his household rather than sacrifice his 'mental independence'. In January 1835 he moved to Liverpool, where his friend Clemente de Zulueta offered him hospitality.

White's new spiritual home was within the Unitarian community presided over by James Martineau, though he was personally closer to J. H. Thom, minister at the Renshaw Street Chapel, whom he chose to replace Whately as his literary executor. In 1835 he published what was intended to be his last theological testament, *Observations on Heresy and Orthodoxy*, in which he finally cut loose from church and dogma. It provoked a rift with Newman, whose campaign against Hampden he saw 'in a lurid and hellish light' as a species of inquisition. In a review for the *British Critic* (January 1836, 204–25), R. H. Froude adopted the deliberate tactic of treating the work as the logical outcome of liberal protestantism in order to cast doubt, by association, on the orthodoxy of Whately and Hampden.

Whately continued to support White with an annual subsidy of £100, and in 1838 helped to secure for him a queen's bounty of £300. In September 1839 White was visited by his cousin Luke Beck, now in charge of the family firm in Seville, who provided the £1100 needed for the purchase of a captaincy in the 40th regiment of foot for Ferdinand White, then serving in India. The sympathetic company of Beck's young daughter, Maria Ana, moved him to write again in Spanish. Discarding the English persona which he had so long assumed, he wrote some of his finest verse with a new-found freedom and simplicity of style, as well as an unfinished novel, *Luisa de Bustamante*, in which he satirized the pretensions of the English middle class. Scorning the *via media*, he had come to regard moderation as a symptom of the English 'fear of going too far'. Within the Unitarian community he lent his support to the establishment of the Liverpool Domestic Mission, whose programme of non-proselytizing philanthropy commended itself to his idealism. His health, always bad, rapidly deteriorated. In February 1841 he was moved from his cottage in Toxteth Park to William Rathbone's house at Greenbank, where he died on 20 May. His disciple Thom recorded his theological testimony: 'God to me is Jesus, and Jesus God—of course, not in the sense of divines.' He was interred in the cemetery adjoining the Renshaw Street Chapel.

Reputation and influence White wrote many versions of his autobiography, but the only one that was confessional rather than apologetic, the 'Examination of Blanco by White' (1818), remained unfinished and unpublished. In 1845 Thom published a three-volume *Life*—an edition of two different autobiographical memoirs together with extracts from correspondence and journals, heavily weighted towards the subject's later life and theology. It had a catalytic effect, helping to impel some—notably Newman and W. G. Ward—over the Roman brink, while moving others, such as A. H. Clough, in a unitarian direction. But the impact was short-lived, and only the sonnet 'Night and Death' survived the eclipse of his fame in England. In Spain the ultra-orthodox polymath Marcelino Menéndez y Pelayo included White in his gallery of *heterodoxos* (*Historia de los heterodoxos españoles*, 2, 1881), praising the style of *Letters from Spain* (which was not translated into Spanish until 1972) but branding the author as an archetypal apostate and *déraciné*. In the 1970s White was rehabilitated by the emigré scholar Vicente Llorens and the novelist Juan Goytisolo as a precursor of modern Spanish dissidence.

White spoke English with only the faintest trace of a foreign accent and, according to Dean Milman, was 'peculiarly prepossessing' in conversation. His many close friendships survived his changes of religious allegiance. F. W. Newman described his head as being:

> of a very remarkable shape, like that which is ascribed to South American Indians, very narrow on the level of the eyes, but very lofty above them, and in appearance sloping up, almost like the gable of a house; but the aspect of his eyes was far more Spanish than Irish. (Quoted in Murphy, 231)

Leigh Hunt noted the 'high sensitiveness and intelligence of his expression' (*Autobiography*, 1949, 228) and his gentleness of manner, interrupted by sudden outbursts of vehemence. Although White attached most importance to his religious witness, his poetry, criticism, and journalism have outlasted his theology. His most enduring legacy has proved to be his life, read as a paradigm of the struggle to reconcile faith with doubt and reason with imagination.

G. MARTIN MURPHY

Sources J. H. Thom, ed., *The life of the Rev. Joseph Blanco White*, 3 vols. (1845) • M. Murphy, *Blanco White: self-banished Spaniard* (1989) • M. Méndez Bejarano, *Vida y obras de D. José María Blanco y Crespo* (1920) • A. Pons, *Blanco White et la crise du monde hispanique, 1808–14* (1990) • J. B. White, *Autobiografía de Blanco White*, ed. and trans. A. Garnica (1988) • J. B. White, 'Examination of Blanco by White', autograph MS, Sydney James Library, Liverpool, 3.56

Archives Harris Man. Oxf., corresp., diaries, notebooks, and other papers • Princeton University, New Jersey • U. Lpool, corresp.; corresp. and papers | Birmingham Oratory, letters to John Henry Newman • BL, corresp. with John Allen, Add. MSS 52174, 52193–52196 • BL, corresp. with Lady Holland, Add. MS 51645 • BL, corresp. with Lord Holland, Add. MS 51645 • Bodl. Oxf., corresp. with John Henry Newman; letters to Robert Southey • LPL, corresp. with Richard Whately and Elizabeth Whately • Oriel College, Oxford, letters to Edward Hawkins

Likenesses portrait, *c*.1808, University of Seville • J.? Slater, pencil and wash drawing, 1812, NPG [*see illus.*] • D. Solly?, oils, 1826, Ullet Road Unitarian Church, Liverpool • A. Edouart, silhouette, 1828, Bodl. Oxf. • F. C. Lewis, stipple, pubd 1836 (after W. Behnes), BM, NPG • marble relief bust, Ullet Road Unitarian Church, Liverpool

Wealth at death £308 8s. 7d.: will, Harris Man. Oxf.

White, Leonard Charles (1897–1955), trade unionist, was born at Cromer, Norfolk, on 12 November 1897, the son of Charles Harold White, a postal clerk, and his wife, Lelita Beatrice Clayton. Len White had part of his education at Paston grammar school, North Walsham. Having entered the Post Office as a learner in 1914, the following year he became a sorting clerk and telegraphist at Northampton. There he showed early interest in trade union affairs.

In 1916 White enlisted in the Royal Naval divisional engineers as a sapper, but he was invalided out in 1917 and returned to his job in the Post Office. Finding that avenues of promotion from 'minor and manipulative' grades to the clerical class were closed for the duration, White threw up his permanent position in the Post Office to become a temporary clerk in the Admiralty. He was successful in a limited competition for clerical posts and was appointed to the Admiralty naval ordnance in 1920.

In the thick of union work again, White was in turn elected secretary of the local branch, assistant secretary of the wider Admiralty section of the Civil Service Clerical Association (CSCA), a member of the Admiralty departmental Whitley Council, and, more significant still, to the national executive committee of the CSCA, all within the four years to 1924. This rapid advance to the forefront of the association was remarked by the general secretary, W. J. Brown, who noted that in the Admiralty he had a branch secretary of unusually high standard.

When strengthening the headquarters' staff in 1925, Brown urged White to apply for a post of clerical assistant. This was obviously an apprenticeship. It was followed by elevation to assistant secretary in 1928, to assistant general secretary in 1936, and to general secretary in 1942 on Brown's election to parliament. Although Brown became parliamentary general secretary and continued until 1949, White assumed full command of administration and negotiation, and had complete authority as leader of the CSCA from 1942. He was associated with Brown as adviser to the Prison Officers' Association; he always felt that prison officers were never fully appreciated and that their crucial and difficult role in society did not receive the reward that was due. He also acted as secretary of the Civil Service Alliance (of the four clerical unions) for seventeen years.

The repeal of the Trade Disputes Act of 1927 by the Labour government in 1946 enabled the CSCA, along with other civil service organizations, to resume affiliation to the Trades Union Congress. At the 1950 congress he led the CSCA's opposition to a continuation of the Attlee government's pay freeze. His contribution at the congress played a significant role in determining the vote to abandon support for the government wages policy, which he regarded as unjust and unequal in its operation. Two attempts to secure White's election to the TUC general council failed. His first defeat in 1946 by the general secretary of the Union of Post Office Workers was not surprising. By the time a second seat on the general council came to be allotted to the civil service associations in 1951, there was no doubt that White had become unacceptable to the powerful men on the general council because of his known communist sympathies and his membership of the board of the *Daily Worker*. They mobilized their large card votes against him and elected Douglas Houghton MP of the Inland Revenue Staff Federation by a six to one majority. But White was a good loser: neither in this defeat nor in other disappointments did he show any personal feeling of resentment. As a platform speaker he was rational, moderate, and convincing. In committee he was businesslike and spoke to the point. In negotiation he was well informed, ably marshalled his facts, and presented his case in a persuasive manner and without overstatement or sabre-rattling.

He had a puckish spirit, full of gentle humour, which somehow manifested itself in his wide, smiling face. Stockily built, but nimble, his whole style and approach encapsulated a quiet authority. He dressed according to his trade—almost typically civil service but always allowing for a touch of informality in the looseness of his tie. He was also a wonderful social companion, full of splendid

stories for any journalistic ear—at least for those he could trust, which meant most of his friends, since they inevitably fell under the spell of his charm, sincerity, and integrity. He was, in short, an immensely civilized man, whose capacity for conveying warmth and care won him enduring friendships. He was twice married: his first marriage, to Ellen Ellis, was dissolved; his second, in 1945, was to Roma Iris Clara, daughter of Harold Larmer, a civil servant, with whom he had one son.

Len White's great and lasting contribution to civil service staff unionism was his resolve to build up a strong central governing body in the national staff side of the civil service Whitley Council. He always condemned sectional attempts at 'leap-frogging' in pay claims, which was a common practice in the early post-war days of wage bargaining. To him the authority of the national staff side was of crucial importance. And in this respect he made his own union, the CSCA, subordinate to the collective group, and called on other civil service unions to do likewise. His far-sighted vision was always fixed on a united civil service force in a more rationalized trade union movement. His ambition was to weld together the competing elements into a more positive, co-operative partnership—a vision he never realized in his lifetime but which has now (1998) largely come to pass.

In his last years White was also keen to curb intemperate policies and militant postures without ever sacrificing his radical instincts. He stood for honouring agreements and for infusing qualities of statesmanship into the governance of his union and the wider field of civil service affairs. His aim, his strength, and his achievements all lay in the opposite direction to those of his predecessor, W. J. Brown. When he became general secretary of the CSCA White inherited a legacy of militancy and unilateral action, and a considerable degree of indiscipline within the union's ranks. Immediately pre-war the civil service staff side had been seriously weakened, and White recognized that he needed to repair the damage. He did so with such success that, in 1955, when the national staff side sought a successor to Sir Albert Day, the overall staff side secretary, the choice fell unanimously on White, a remarkable tribute to his ability and integrity, especially in view of his political leanings. He would have made the move, but he died at his home, 24 Tilehurst Road, Reading, on 11 May 1955 before the appointment could be confirmed.

DOUGLAS HOUGHTON, *rev.* GEOFFREY GOODMAN

Sources private information (1971) · personal knowledge (1971) · *The Times* (12 May 1955) · B. Newman, *Yours for action: the story of the Civil Service Clerical Association, 1903–1953* (1953) · *CGPLA Eng. & Wales* (1956)
Likenesses photograph, repro. in Newman, *Yours for action*
Wealth at death £6741 0s. 7d.: probate, 21 March 1956, *CGPLA Eng. & Wales*

White, Lucy Anna (1848–1923), folk-singer, was born on 4 September 1848 at Puckington, Somerset, the daughter of Sarah Bridge (1823–1892) who in 1855 married William England (1822–1897), a shoemaker, later an agricultural labourer. Her half-sister was **Louisa** [Louie] **Hooper** [*née*

England] (1860–1946), folk-singer. They grew up in a family of six children at Puckington. Lucy may have received some education, but Louie was lame and unable to walk to school, so she spent her childhood among older women employed in glove-making and shirt-making. She herself was a 'collar worker' at the age of ten.

In 1875 Lucy married Jonathan White (1848–1917), an agricultural labourer, and bore him six children in addition to two who were probably illegitimate. Louie married George Hooper in 1884: he died almost immediately, but she bore three children at dates down to 1892. When her parents died during the 1890s, she appears to have moved next door to Lucy and Jonathan White who were by then living at Westport, a hamlet at the southern edge of Hambridge parish.

To Hambridge in 1893 had come the Revd Charles Marson, an enthusiastic, unconventional Anglican priest who was a blend of high-church ritualist and Christian socialist. Marson had an unusual sympathy with his parishioners and, besides trying to get their material conditions improved, he was keenly aware of their potentialities. One of Marson's close friends was Cecil *Sharp, then a London music teacher. In 1903 Sharp came to Hambridge and began his work of collecting English folk music, initially in collaboration with Marson.

It was Sharp's extraordinary good fortune to meet Lucy White and Louie Hooper at the very beginning of his collecting career. The sisters were excellent instinctive musicians and had an enormous repertory of over a hundred traditional songs. Folk song collectors of those days had little idea of what they were looking for and found it difficult to convey to singers the kinds of song in which they were interested. Lucy White and Louie Hooper gave Sharp the knowledge and experience which enabled him to penetrate traditional culture more quickly and more thoroughly than any other collector. Sharp and Marson published twenty-one of the sisters' songs in Folk Songs from Somerset (5 vols., 1904–9), including such favourites as 'Seventeen Come Sunday', 'Henry Martin', and 'The Sign of the Bonny Blue Bell'. Folk Songs from Somerset had a tremendous impact on Edwardian culture, partly because of the excellent quality of the material and partly because it came so much more directly from the sources than previous collections had done. Its success did much to launch the folk music revival which effectively began in 1904.

Lucy White and Louie Hooper got the basis of their repertory from their mother, a renowned singer to whom Sharp traced many of the best songs of the district. They added to that repertory through participation in glove-making and shirt-making, which during their childhood were communal occupations carried on by women meeting in one household and singing at their work. Louie was the more musical of the sisters and the more intense in feeling about the songs. Maud Karpeles wrote of her in an obituary that the songs 'were an essential part of her life's experience, and the stories they told were as real to her as the happenings in her own hamlet' (Karpeles, 57). She had a particular love of instrumental music, and as a child had tried to fashion instruments from household utensils.

Cecil Sharp gave her a concertina which she delighted in playing.

Lucy White died on 17 February 1923 at Westport, Somerset, and was buried at Hambridge, Somerset, on 24 February. Louie Hooper lived on to become the grand old lady of Somerset folk song and to be visited by the pilgrims who began to travel in Sharp's footsteps in the 1930s. In 1941–2 the radio producer Douglas Cleverdon visited her several times and recorded an interview and more than twenty of her songs for the BBC, five or six of which were selected for permanent preservation. Her death on Ash Wednesday (6 March) 1946 marked the end of an epoch, for, so far as is known, she was the last survivor of the Somerset men and women whose songs launched the modern folk music revival. C. J. BEARMAN

Sources private information (2004) [David Sutcliffe] · W. Adams and E. Clarke, interview, 15 Sept 1973, Cecil Sharp House, London, David Bland MSS · D. Cleverdon and L. Hooper, interview, BL NSA, BBC sound archive [sound recording], no. 4039 (BBC 6935) · M. Karpeles, English Dance and Song, 10/5 (1946), 57 · D. Cleverdon, 'Adventures in recording', English Dance and Song, 8/4 (1944), 27–8 · W. A. Newall, 'In the footsteps of Cecil Sharp', English Dance and Song, 7/4 (1943), 27–8 · Langport and Somerton Herald (24 Feb 1923); (3 March 1923) · b. cert. [Lucy White] · d. cert. [Lucy White]
Archives SOUND BBC WAC
Likenesses C. Sharp, double portraits, photographs (with Louisa Hooper), Vaughan Williams Memorial Library, London · photograph (Louisa Hooper in old age), repro. in Karpeles, English Dance and Song

White, Matthew (d. 1641). See under White, Robert (c.1530×32–1574).

White, Maude Valérie (1855–1937), composer, was born on 23 June 1855 near Dieppe, France, sixth of the eight children of merchant Edmund Luscombe White, who died while she was still a child, and his wife, a Miss Harrington (d. 1881). She was educated privately in England and Germany and at schools in Wolverhampton and Paris. In 1876 she entered the Royal Academy of Music in London, after opposition from her mother, who felt that a professional, public life was not suitable for a woman. White studied composition with George Macfarren and in 1879 became the first woman to be awarded the coveted Mendelssohn scholarship for composition. The following year baritone Charles Santley brought her songs 'Absent yet Present' and 'Montrose's Love Song' to widespread attention by performing them at the prestigious Monday Popular Concerts. After her mother's death in 1881 White left the academy and spent several months in South America.

On her return to England in 1882 White moved into rooms of her own in London. In her memoirs she marks this point in her life, after a further period of study with Robert Fuchs in Vienna, as the time at which she became a professional musician, publishing her songs, teaching the piano to children, and performing as accompanist at private and public concerts, including those which she organized herself. The friendship and support of society music lovers and other professional musicians, such as the singer and composer Liza Lehmann, were always of central importance to White's career. By the 1890s she was at the height of her fame. Her setting of words from Shelley's *Prometheus Unbound*, 'My Soul is an Enchanted Boat' (1882), was described in Grove's *Dictionary of Music and Musicians* (1889) as 'one of the best in our language'. This and other songs were performed all over Britain and Europe by the best-known singers of the day, including Raymond von zur Muhlen, Nellie Melba, and Clara Butt.

White never married or settled in one place, living at various addresses while in England, travelling endlessly throughout Europe, Russia, South America, and north Africa, and spending much of the later part of her life based in Italy. She described herself as an 'out-and-out cosmopolitan' (White, *Friends and Memories*, 172), and the music that she heard on her travels often echoes in her own work.

Despite her ballet *The Enchanted Heart* (1913), an unfinished opera *Smaranda*, and a set of orchestral *Serbian Dances* performed during the First World War under Henry Wood, White's reputation rests entirely on her songwriting. She was fluent in many European languages, and set poetry in German, French, Italian, Spanish, and Swedish, as well as English. Contemporary reviewers always praised the quality of her texts, the authors of which ranged from Heine, Goethe, Suckling, and Herrick to Hugo, Verlaine, Tennyson, and the Brownings. A direct communication of the emotions that she read into her text is central to her work, producing songs that are always beautifully crafted, with simple but deeply expressive vocal lines and perfectly judged piano accompaniments. These songs, such as her Byron setting 'So we'll go no more a'roving' (1888) or her d'Annunzio setting 'Isaotta Blanzesmano' (1906), had an important influence over a later generation of British songwriters, such as Roger Quilter and Ralph Vaughan Williams.

Towards the end of her life White's music was falling out of fashion, and she turned to translating books and plays as well as to writing her second volume of memoirs, *My Indian Summer* (1932), following *Friends and Memories* (1914). She died at 40 Pelham Court, Chelsea, London, on 2 November 1937, and was buried at the Roman Catholic church of St Edward the Confessor at Sutton Park in Guildford, after a requiem mass had been held at the Brompton Oratory in London. SOPHIE FULLER

Sources M. V. White, *Friends and memories* (1914) · M. V. White, *My Indian summer* (1932) · S. Fuller, *The Pandora guide to women composers: Britain and the United States, 1629 – present* (1994), 330–34 · G. Bush, 'Songs', *Music in Britain: the romantic age, 1800–1914*, ed. N. Temperley (1981), 266–87 · Ronald, 'Some lady song writers', *Lady's Realm* (1901), 474–80 · *The Times* (4 Nov 1937) · d. cert.
Archives BL, letters to Roger Quilter, Add. MS 70604
Likenesses Barraud, photograph, Royal College of Music, London · Upton, oils, Royal College of Music, London
Wealth at death £352 18s. 5d.: probate, 8 April 1938, *CGPLA Eng. & Wales*

White, Sir Michael (1791–1868), army officer, born at St Michael's Mount, Cornwall, was the third son of Robert White, major in the 27th dragoons, and his wife, Anne, daughter of Sir John St Aubyn, fourth baronet (1726–1772), of St Michael's Mount. He was educated at Westminster School, and obtained a cornetcy in the 24th light dragoons

on 15 August 1804. On 14 May 1805 he was promoted lieutenant. He went to India, and was engaged in active service in 1809 in the campaigns along the Sutlej. On 7 November 1815 he attained his captaincy, and in 1816 he married Mary, daughter of Major Mylne of the 24th light dragoons. In 1817 he was present at the capture of Hathras. He served through the Maratha campaign of 1817–18, and at the siege and capture of Bharatpur in 1825–6. He was promoted major on 10 January 1837, and lieutenant-colonel on 13 December 1839. He commanded the cavalry throughout the Afghan campaign of 1842, accompanying the army under General Sir George Pollock which forced the Khyber Pass, stormed the heights at Jagdalak, defeated the enemy at Tezin, captured the fortified position at Haft Kotal in the pass, and occupied Kabul. After the campaign, on 29 December 1842, he was nominated CB. He served in the First Anglo-Sikh War in 1845–6, under Sir Hugh Gough. He commanded the cavalry at the battle of Mudki on 18 December 1845, when his horse was wounded. At the battle of Ferozeshahr on 21 December, where he commanded a brigade, he was wounded and had his horse killed under him, and at Sobraon he behaved with such bravery that he was nominated aide-de-camp to the queen. He became colonel on 1 April 1846.

In 1848 the Second Anglo-Sikh War began, and White commanded the 1st brigade of cavalry throughout the campaign. At Ramnagar on 22 November he wisely avoided the Sikh trap which caused the deaths of General Charles Cureton and Lieutenant-Colonel William Havelock. On 13 January 1849 he was present at the expensive victory of Chilianwala, where he protected the left of the infantry, and on 21 February 1849 he took part in the victory at Gujrat. On 20 June 1854 he received the rank of major-general, and on 26 August 1858 was appointed colonel of the 7th light dragoons (hussars). On 31 August 1860 he attained the rank of lieutenant-general, and on 10 November 1862 was nominated KCB. He died at 15 Pembridge Crescent, Bayswater, London, on 27 January 1868.

E. I. CARLYLE, *rev.* JAMES FALKNER

Sources *Army List* · *Colburn's United Service Magazine*, 1 (1868), 446 · E. J. Thackwell, *Narrative of the Second Seikh War, in 1848–49* (1851) · *GM*, 5th ser., 1 (1868), 400 · G. Bruce, *Six battles for India: the Anglo-Sikh wars, 1845–6, 1848–9* (1969) · Boase, *Mod. Eng. biog.* · *CGPLA Eng. & Wales* (1868)
Wealth at death under £300: probate, 18 March 1868, *CGPLA Eng. & Wales*

White, Sir Nicholas (c.1532–1592), lawyer and administrator, was descended from a notable family of the English pale. His father, James White, steward of James Butler, earl of Ormond, had been poisoned while in London with the earl in 1546. Nicholas owed his early advancement to Ormond's influence: in recognition of James's loyalty, the earl left £10 for the boy's education at the inns of court. A cadet branch of the family was led by another James White, recorder of Waterford, who joined Walter Cowley in a survey of religious houses in 1541 and was granted monastic property in Kilkenny. Nicholas White married twice. Nothing is known of his first wife except her surname, Sherlocke. His second wife was the daughter of Arthur Brereton of Killyon, Meath.

Education and early career In 1552 White entered Lincoln's Inn, and he was called to the bar in 1558. His contemporaries at the inn were James Dowdall, later chief justice of queen's bench, the rivals Nicholas Nugent and Robert Dillon, who became in succession chief justices of common pleas, and his younger ally and protégé from Waterford, Nicholas Walsh, the last native-born chief justice of common pleas. Nicholas White returned to Ireland and was elected knight of the shire for co. Kilkenny in 1559. On 17 August 1559 he was sent as commissioner by the Irish privy council, along with Francis Cosby, Nicholas Heron, Luke Neterville, and others, to hear a controversy between the lord of upper Ossory and Edward Butler in Kilkenny. He was justice of the peace for co. Kilkenny in 1563 and in the following year was named recorder of Waterford. The original instructions in 1566 for the inchoate lord president and council in Munster named White as one of the resident members of the first council. Along with other leading lawyers, he was named in the lease of Dominican property in 1567 which became King's Inns in Dublin. On 13 June 1569 he became constable of Wexford Castle, a position which had formerly been occupied by a kinsman of his second wife. White established his estate at White's Hall, near Knocktopher, co. Kilkenny.

White earned the favour of successive chief governors, and in 1568 he was given the right to travel to England, where he met the queen and her principal secretary, Sir William Cecil, later Lord Burghley. From that time forward he became a key confidant of Cecil and an important commentator on Irish affairs. He had a notable interview with Mary, queen of Scots, at Tutbury in February 1569, details of which he sent to Cecil on his return to Ireland. On 4 November 1568 Elizabeth appointed him seneschal of Wexford and constable of Leighlin and Ferns, replacing the disgraced adventurer Thomas Stukeley. He retained the office until 1572, concluding his tenure with the pursuit of the rebels who murdered his son-in-law Robert Browne. On 18 January 1569 White was granted reversion of the lands of Dunbrody Abbey, co. Wexford, and other leases, to which he added a grant of St Catherine's Priory at Leixlip, which became his Dublin residence, on 28 May. Although he suffered losses to his property during the wars of the Butlers in 1569, he strengthened his estate by acquisitions in Wexford and he successfully controlled the restless Kavanaghs in that county.

Master of the rolls in Ireland In September 1571 White once again returned to England, with licence to be absent for six months. On the recommendation of the lord deputy, Fitzwilliam, White succeeded Sir Henry Draycott as master of the rolls in Ireland on 14 July 1572, and the lord chancellor was directed to accept a surrender of his lands in exchange for a regrant of them in fee simple. Despite these marks of royal favour, White was viewed by fellow privy councillors in Ireland as suspiciously partisan. Unlike his pliant contemporary Sir Lucas Dillon, White

took independent positions in opposition to the dominant English-born faction on the council. The ambitious lord keeper and archbishop of Dublin, Adam Loftus, demanded custody of the great seal upon the death of Lord Chancellor Robert Weston in 1572 and vied with White on several occasions. When Lord Deputy Fitzwilliam chided Sir Edward Fitton for his arbitrary conduct as councillor in 1573, White was Fitton's lone defender. When the dispute over cess arose in 1577 between Lord Deputy Sidney and the gentlemen of the pale, White was almost alone among Irish councillors who took the part of the Old English élite. He wrote to Burghley on 13 June 1577 that he had no intention to impugn the queen's prerogative, and later warned the queen's principal adviser that Sidney had forfeited the support of the pale over their legitimate constitutional claims. Sidney distrusted him as a client of Ormond, and the new lord chancellor, Sir William Gerard, accused White of excessive partiality as a judge in 1578, saying he was 'greatly allyed in the pale by his mariages ... a depe dissembler, greatly corrupt and wilfully affected with oute regard of troth or equitye' (LPL, Carew MS 628, fol. 311v).

At the height of the cess controversy in April 1578 White was charged by the attorney-general, Thomas Snagge, with misfeasance in office, and suspended as master of the rolls for failing to certify the writs, patents, and licences from the court of chancery to the exchequer. He forfeited the fees of his office, and the locks to his desk were broken open so the rolls could be inventoried in May 1578. The danger passed when Lord Deputy Sidney was himself recalled, Gerard was forced to explain his manoeuvring in relation to the pale gentry, and White was allowed to plead his case in England before Burghley himself in September, after which he was restored to office.

Desmond rebellion The crisis of the cess was unresolved when the perilous rebellion in Munster commenced in 1579 and White worked closely with the successive lords justices Sir William Drury and Sir William Pelham as a veteran official with long experience in the province. None the less, he was now under suspicion as one who consistently favoured the interests of the Old English, and Sir Henry Wallop, the new vice-treasurer in Ireland, blamed him for supporting the cause of the disgraced chief justice Nicholas Nugent, who was precipitately tried and hanged for treason in 1582. Wallop protested against a *concordatum* sent to Ireland awarding White 1000 marks for his work in chancery after his 1580 trip to England, and he blamed White for failing to apprehend the rebels in Wicklow during the rebellion.

In February 1581 White demonstrated his independence in council, refusing to sign a letter to the queen regarding Malby's actions in the Munster rebellion since he was away in England during the deliberations of the meeting. Again, on 28 August 1582 White was accused of withholding his signature to conciliar deliberations on the actions of the deputy during the pale rebellion. However, he continued to demonstrate his valuable insights to Burghley in regular correspondence throughout the period, including letters of December 1581 on the miseries of war, the need for temperate government, and his fear that the wild Irish were glad to see the weakness of English blood in Ireland. In a missive of 13 September 1582 White complained of the unfriendly dealings of Lucas Dillon, his erstwhile companion and fellow Irish-born councillor, stating they had been for a long time of 'contrary minds' (PRO, SP 63/95/95). In spite of his sympathies for the native Irish he was apparently the author of an extraordinary trial by combat in September 1583 in which Teig MacGilpatrick O'Connor and Conor MacCormac O'Connor lost their lives. His usefulness as an Irish speaker and a nominal protestant made White an essential privy councillor for two decades.

Later career On the arrival of the ambitious new lord deputy, Sir John Perrot, White was granted a knighthood in Christ Church, Dublin, on 21 June 1584. White worked with Perrot to establish the effectiveness of common law rule, though forty-eight of the 181 prisoners in the Leinster circuit were executed in autumn of 1584 in an example of rough justice. In December he went into Connaught to investigate charges of corruption against the former lord president, Sir Nicholas Malby, and on 15 July 1585 he was named a commissioner for the cess in that province. White and Dillon attended the lord deputy in September 1586 to Connaught, a sojourn which the combative new lord president, Sir Richard Bingham, much resented. On 29 November 1586 White wrote to Burghley describing the continual bickering in council between the chief governor and the lord chancellor, Loftus, adding that the newly revived court of castle chamber was busy with accusations against the tyrannical government of Bingham and his lieutenants in Connaught. Chief Justice Robert Gardener complained to Burghley in December that Perrot governed with the aid of a minority of Irish councillors such as White, trampling the rights of council and ignoring the need for consensus, hearing many private causes without recourse to law. In May 1587 the temperamental chief governor quarrelled with the aged marshal Sir Nicholas Bagnal at the council board and struck him. White, who reported the incident thoroughly to Burghley, had recommended a full council hearing for Bagnal's agent from which the beleaguered chief governor would be excluded. By the end of Perrot's regime White was viewed as a minion of the lord deputy who was primarily responsible for a policy of favouritism toward Irish-born servitors. The return of his former adversary Sir William Fitzwilliam as lord deputy in 1588 allowed White's enemies on the council to triumph over him.

Arrest and death In 1589 White was included on a commission for pacification of the Burkes, who had rebelled against the arbitrary conduct of the lord president, Bingham. The latter suspected the intentions of the commission, but White reported to Burghley that Bingham was not wholly to blame. Within a few months the career of Sir John Perrot was placed in jeopardy by the allegations of treason levied against him in England by an Irish priest, Denis O'Roughan. White was implicated in these charges and Lord Deputy Fitzwilliam moved swiftly to place him

under arrest in June 1590, sending him to England two months later despite his illness. He was examined on the charges and committed to the Marshalsea prison prior to his testimony before the court of Star Chamber, at a time when his health was in grave danger. Placed in the Tower of London in March 1591, White appealed to the privy council for a servant to attend him, owing to his age and infirmity. White's inquisition before the high court in 1592 affirmed that Perrot had complained of the queen's reluctance to support his government. His earlier support of the deputy compromised his position and he died in the Tower in the same year as his patron.

Both Nicholas White and Lucas Dillon died in 1592, and both Irish-born councillors were replaced by English officials, Sir Anthony St Leger becoming master of the rolls. White's views on government were systematically and forcefully pressed on the queen's advisers and may be summed up in his letter of 1574 to Burghley: 'I wish the country were more governed by law than by discretion' (Brady, 280). In a controversy with John Long, archbishop of Armagh, White counselled tolerance in the matter of oaths and religion during the July 1586 session of parliament, noting the preference of the lord deputy for moderation toward the gentlemen of the pale.

White and his second wife had two sons. Thomas, the elder, was educated at Cambridge University and died in November 1586, while the younger son, Andrew, succeeded to White's estates after completing his education at Cambridge. White also had two daughters, one of whom married Robert Browne of Mulcranan, co. Wexford, leading to White's strong efforts in 1572 to prosecute the rebels who had assassinated his son-in-law. Despite his role as councillor, the Irish privy council in 1573 refused to allow White's writ of appeal for the pardon of Fiagh McHugh O'Byrne and others accused of murdering Browne, declaring 'the graunting of that writ wold renue a blooddie rebellion which withe great travell we have appaysed' (Bodl. Oxf., MS Carte 56, fol. 65v). His ongoing attentions to the Dunbrody property led to the intervention of the privy council in England in October 1587 when White was accused of dispossessing William Browne of the profits of the barony. White's other daughter married into the Old English family of Christopher D'Arcy (or Darcy) of Platten, near Duleek, Meath.

White was closely associated with the career of Sir Nicholas Walsh of Waterford, who followed White to Lincoln's Inn and succeeded him as recorder of Waterford, later becoming chief justice of common pleas (1597). White also kept as wards the sons of leading Munster gentry such as the dispossessed Charles McCarty who sued before the English privy council in April 1590 to regain his property. On 12 February 1593 the privy council authorized White's son to bring his body back to Ireland for burial. After his death the privy council in England remanded a complaint by John Itchingham against the heirs of White (James and Andrew) regarding title to White's property of Dunbrody to common law proceedings in Ireland.

JON G. CRAWFORD

Sources *CSP Ire.*, 1574–85, 285, 304; 1586–8, 101, 206–7, 353; 1588–92, 263, 343; 1592–6, 107 • *APC*, 1578–80, 119; 1591, 13, 39, 46; 1592–3, 125; 1598–9, 226 • J. L. J. Hughes, ed., *Patentee officers in Ireland, 1173–1826, including high sheriffs, 1661–1684 and 1761–1816*, IMC (1960) • Bodl. Oxf., MS Carte 56, fol. 65v • PRO, SP 63/95/95; SP 63/80/147 • LPL, Carew MS 628, fol. 311v • D. B. Quinn, ed., 'Calendar of the Irish council book for 1581–86', *Analecta Hibernica*, 24 (1967), 93–180 • C. Brady, *The chief governors: the rise and fall of reform government in Tudor Ireland, 1536–1588* (1994) • J. G. Crawford, *Anglicizing the government of Ireland: the Irish privy council and the expansion of Tudor rule, 1556–1578* (1993) • A. Vicars, ed., *Index to the prerogative wills of Ireland, 1536–1810* (1897), 487 • C. Kenny, *King's Inns and the kingdom of Ireland* (1992) • F. E. Ball, *The judges in Ireland, 1221–1921*, 2 (1926)

White, Patrick Victor Martindale (1912–1990), novelist and playwright, was born on 28 May 1912 at 17 Wellington Court, Knightsbridge, London, the only son and eldest child of wealthy Australian parents, Victor Martindale (Dick) White (1868–1937), landowner and farmer, and his wife, Ruth Withycombe (1877–1963), a society hostess. Victor and Ruth were second cousins, and both their families were originally farmers from Somerset. White took pleasure in the unsubstantiated family legend that a Withycombe was Edward II's fool. In October 1912 the Whites returned to Sydney to live at Lulworth, a large house at the back of King's Cross, overlooking Rushcutters Bay. White's only sibling, Suzanne, was born in 1915. In the following year White experienced his first asthma attack; the illness, which often left him prostrate and helpless, plagued him throughout his life.

After attending a variety of private schools in Sydney, White returned to Britain to be educated from 1925 to 1929 at Cheltenham College, where he was profoundly unhappy. He went back to Australia and spent two years working as a 'jackaroo' (farm-hand), during which time he began to write novels (which were not published). In 1932 he attended King's College, Cambridge, where he read modern languages and graduated with an upper second in 1935. He was now firmly committed to the life of a writer, and attempted to make his living first as a playwright: indeed his friend Ronald Waters believed that White 'wanted to write one great play, more than all the novels' (Marr, 385). He had several sketches performed in revue, and in the late 1930s he wrote two plays: *Return to Abyssinia* (eventually staged in London in 1947) and *The Ham Funeral*.

White's father settled an allowance on him, which enabled him to survive without having to find paid work, and from 1935 to 1938 he wrote in his small room in Chelsea. Early in 1938 he shared a house with the Australian painter Roy de Maistre, one of his most influential mentors. Here White and the painter Francis Bacon became friends, and Bacon designed for White a superb writing desk. *Happy Valley* (1939), his first novel to be published, received respectable reviews, and won the gold medal of the Australian Literature Society in 1941. Encouraged, he hurriedly wrote a second, *The Living and the Dead* (1941), but in 1940 he was commissioned as an air force intelligence officer, and spent the entirety of the Second World War working in the Middle East, spending his off-duty hours writing. In Alexandria in 1941 White met Manoly Lascaris

(b. 1912), a 'small Greek of immense moral strength' (White, *Flaws*, 100), and the man with whom White spent the rest of his life.

After demobilization White wrote *The Aunt's Story* (1948), but now disenchanted with Britain he and Lascaris left for Australia in 1948. They bought Dogwoods, a 6 acre farm at Castle Hill outside Sydney, and began to farm the land: 'We plough, milk, wash, iron, weed, cook, make the butter and attempt to control the dogs all between 6am and 11pm. I have never felt happier than confined to this small piece of land' (Marr, 261). Happy, after his own fashion, in his new life, but also deeply wounded by the hostile Australian reviews of *The Aunt's Story*, White wrote nothing for several years. For most of his life White's relationship with Australia was ambivalent: he loved and hated the country in equal measure, and a great many Australians, including several influential literary critics, intensely disliked his persistent refusal to portray the country as paradisaical.

However, writing was a compulsion, and in 1952 White began *The Tree of Man* (1955), which he claimed 'had no plot, except the only one of living and dying' (Marr, 282). Set in Australia, stark, and powerfully expressed, it was enthusiastically reviewed everywhere but Australia for its intensity, simplicity, and compassion. White followed it with *Voss* (1957), a fictional account of the epic journey of Ludwig Leichardt, who died in the Australian desert in 1848. It was internationally acclaimed and won the inaugural Miles Franklin award; the book invoked comparisons with Tolstoy and made White famous. In November 1961 White's early play *The Ham Funeral* received its première in November at the Adelaide festival to great critical and public acclaim. White continued, with varying degrees of success, to write for the stage for the rest of his life. Virtually all his dramatic work generated controversy because of its uncompromising subject matter and his bleak vision, which many felt was 'un-Australian'. However, many critics and audiences saw White as a vital, invigorating presence in the formation of a uniquely Australian theatre.

Almost despite himself, however, White was primarily a novelist and in 1961 he published *Riders in the Chariot*, which took as its central subject the Holocaust, and used its 'riders', particularly the Orthodox Jewish refugee Mordecai Himmelfarb and the Aboriginal painter Alf Dubbo, to suggest that all forms of faith, including the work of the artist, are one. In *The Vivisector* (1970) White explored through the protagonist, the painter Hurtle Duffield, the cruelty and obsession which drive the artist. This much praised novel was followed in 1973 by *The Eye of the Storm*, which obviously drew on White's complex relationship with his mother, portraying the life of a powerful and formidable matriarch and her impact on a huge range of characters, including her children. This time White chose an actor to examine the instinctive impulses of the artist. *A Fringe of Leaves* (1976), like *Voss*, was based on an actual event in Australian history. White was fascinated by the true story of Eliza Fraser, who was shipwrecked off the

Queensland coast in 1836 and kept as a slave by Aboriginals until she was rescued by an escaped convict. This fictionalized treatment of her ordeal was seen as a masterly blend of historical details and imaginative reconstruction. *The Twyborn Affair* (1979) placed a homosexual character at the forefront of his fiction for the first time, and anticipated the disclosures in his autobiography. Throughout his novels White demonstrated a striking range of diversity. White's writing is characterized by its compelling blend of epically simple plots and imaginatively bold, sensuous language. His style ranges from the savagely plain linear prose of the earlier novels to the splintered chronology and dazzlingly inventive imagery of the later fiction.

While White was not himself denominationally Christian, most of his fiction depicts the central characters striving for religious enlightenment not only at the expense of their material well-being, but usually at the expense of their own lives. With a painter's eye for detail White drew attention to Australia's unique colours, vegetation, and light, and central to his work was the portrayal of Australia not as a forsaken colony, but as a continent of awesome size and incalculable age, and one which suggested a brooding immensity and mystery.

White was tall, gaunt for most of his life, and fierce-looking for all of it. He cared little for fashion and often appeared in public very shabbily dressed. Emotionally he was cold, but he could fly into fearsome rages, speaking then with a brutality and a savagery which left the recipients of his wrath devastated. Few of his friendships lasted—he was too quarrelsome and vituperative—and he would nurse a grievance for decades. However, many people, from all walks of life, were invited to dinner parties at Dogwoods, and White, an excellent cook, could also be a generous and captivating host, very fond of whisky, laughter, and gossip. Both White and Lascaris were passionate about dogs, particularly schnauzers. White also loved music: in the 1950s and 1960s he was enthusiastic about Mahler, while later he enjoyed Berlioz, Mozart, Berg, and Bartók. He was even more ardent about painting. Above his writing desk in Australia, a copy of the one designed for him by Bacon, he hung de Maistre's *Descent from the Cross*, and the walls of his homes were covered in original Australian and European art work. He was extremely supportive of Australian art and, somewhat to his own surprise, liked the paintings of Brett Whitely, who painted his portrait. Above all he admired Sidney Nolan, who designed several of his book covers and to whom *The Vivisector* is dedicated.

In 1981 White published his autobiography, *Flaws in the Glass*. It was ruthlessly honest, not least in his self-criticism, and it became the best-selling book of his career. It was frank about his homosexuality, his irascibility, and his ambivalent relationship with Australia. White always insisted that he disliked writing, but at the time of his death he had published twelve novels, two volumes of poetry, three collections of short stories, seven plays, and three volumes of non-fiction. He was awarded the Nobel prize for literature in 1973, although he had become increasingly reluctant to accept literary prizes. He also turned down honorary doctorates and fellowships offered throughout his career. He insisted that he was not a public figure but, when his conscience was stirred, he would make public appearances, as he did to protest against Australia's involvement in the Vietnam War and its treatment of Aborigines, and to muster support for environmental causes. White was a philanthropist who gave generously to Aboriginal schools, and donated a large collection of works by Australian painters to the Art Gallery of New South Wales. With money from his Nobel prize he established and endowed the Patrick White literary award.

Having left Dogwoods in 1964, White and Lascaris lived in a Sydney suburb, Centennial Park, until White's death from a bronchial collapse at home in the early hours of 30 September 1990. Lascaris was with him when he died. His body was cremated on 2 October, and in accordance with his will no one was present. The following morning, Lascaris and White's agent, Barbara Mobbs, scattered his ashes on the water near the park bench on which he had often sat to rest. KEVIN MCCARRON

Sources D. Marr, *Patrick White: a life* (1991) · P. White, *Flaws in the glass: a self-portrait* (1981) · *Letters*, ed. D. Marr (1994) · b. cert.
Archives Mitchell L., NSW, letters · NL Aus., letters | U. Reading L., Jonathan Cape papers, letters
Likenesses L. Kahan, oil and enamel on hardboard, 1962, Art Gallery of New South Wales · P. Schipperheyn, bronze bust, 1962, National Australia Day Council · B. Whitely, portrait

White, Peter (*fl.* **1551–***c.***1570**), Church of Ireland dean of Waterford, was born in Waterford city at an unknown date. He was elected a fellow of Oriel College, Oxford, in 1551, and was admitted MA in 1555. After his return to Ireland he became a schoolteacher in Kilkenny, where he ran the grammar school which had been established in the churchyard of St Canice's Cathedral by the earl of Ossory and Ormond, Piers Butler, and his wife, Margaret. On 22 June 1566 he was appointed dean of Waterford by the crown on the resignation of the bishop of the diocese, Patrick Walshe, from the office on 15 June. In recommending White as his successor, Walshe explained to Lord Deputy Sir Henry Sidney that White was a man 'very well learned', and 'of virtuous sober conversation, by whose industry and travail a great part both of the youth of the country and of Dublin have greatly profited in learning and virtuous education' (Morrin, 494). However, White turned out to be a Roman Catholic. He was ousted from the deanery of Waterford about 1570 because of his recusancy and he is said to have returned to teaching in Waterford.

White's reputation as pedagogue is mainly based on the fulsome tributes in three separate printed works by one of his most outstanding pupils, Richard Stanihurst, who referred to White as the 'lucky schoolmaster of Munster' (Stanihurst, 'Description of Ireland', 111). He studied at the academy in Kilkenny for six years, from 1557 to 1563, and attributed his scholarly success to White's talents as a teacher. These lay in his bringing the best out of each pupil:

> by framing the education to the scholars vaine. If he found him free, he would bridle him like a wise Isocrates from his

> booke; if he perceived him to be dull, he would spur him forward; if he understood that he were the worse from beating, he woulde win him with rewardes. (ibid., 59–60)

White may also have compiled his writings for teaching purposes. These included synopses of works by Erasmus and Cicero, and manuals of rhetorical and epigrammatic skills.

Stanihurst mentioned the names of families who sent their offspring to the Kilkenny School: Whites, Comerfords, Walshes, Waddings, Dormers, Shees, Garveys, Butlers, Archers, Strongs, and Lombards. Most of these were from the south-east region of Ireland, but some came from Dublin and the pale. Among the more famous products of White's schooling were: Peter Lombard, Roman Catholic archbishop of Armagh; Thomas White SJ, rector of the Irish college at Salamanca; and the Waterford scholar and missioner Nicholas Comerford SJ. It is not known when White died, but Ware put the date towards the latter end of Elizabeth's reign.

Richard Stanihurst pointed to Peter White as an example of the kind of humanist-teacher needed to foster the reform of Irish society and culture. There is no doubt that White's role was extremely significant in bringing on a generation of talented scholars who made their way in universities in England and on the continent. Many espoused the cause of the Counter-Reformation, but more importantly all were responsible for contributing in some way to an Irish intellectual flowering in the later Renaissance period. White was the midwife of that movement.

COLM LENNON

Richard White (1539–1611), by Lodovico Leoni, 1568

Sources R. Stanihurst, *Harmonia, seu catena dialectica in Porphyrianos institutiones* (1570), a2r · R. Stanihurst, 'The description of Ireland', *Holinshed's Irish chronicle: the historie of Irelande from the first inhabitation thereof unto the year 1509*, ed. L. Miller and E. Power (1979), 59–60, 103, 111 · R. Stanihurst, *De rebus in Hibernia gestis* (1584), 9 · J. Morrin, ed., *Calendar of the patent and close rolls of chancery in Ireland, of the reigns of Henry VIII, Edward VI, Mary, and Elizabeth*, 1 (1861), 494, 495 · Wood, *Ath. Oxon.*, new edn, 1.575 · H. Cotton, *Fasti ecclesiae Hibernicae*, 1 (1845), 18–19 · E. Hogan, *Distinguished Irishmen of the sixteenth century* (1894), 53, 72 · *The whole works of Sir James Ware concerning Ireland*, ed. and trans. W. Harris, 3 (1746), 95–6

White, Richard (1539–1611), antiquary and jurist, was born in Basingstoke in 1539, the son of Henry White, who died at the siege of Boulogne in 1544, and of his wife, Agnes, daughter of Richard Capelin of Southampton. In 1553 White entered Winchester College, and he proceeded to New College, Oxford, in 1555, where he was elected a perpetual fellow, a post declared void through his absence in 1564. He took the BA degree on 30 May 1559. A Roman Catholic, White left England in 1560 and moved to Louvain, where he delivered two orations, 'De circulo artium et philosophiae' and 'De eloquentia et Cicerone'. These were subsequently published in London in 1565 under the title *Orationes duae*, with an introduction by Christopher Jonson, headmaster of Winchester College, testifying that White delivered these two lectures to a large audience in the law school at Louvain. White matriculated at Louvain in September 1559.

In 1563 White went to the University of Padua and delivered further orations; in August 1563 the 'Pro divitiis regum', and, at Pavia on 11 November 1566 an oration 'Pro doctoratu', containing many details of his education and teachers at both Winchester and Oxford, mentioning his Winchester headmaster, Christopher Jonson, his Oxford teacher Thomas Butler, and his teachers at Padua, who included the famous jurist Guido Panciroli. These four orations, with the addition of a fifth, 'De studiorum finibus', were printed as *Orationes quinque* in Arras in 1596, edited by his son Thomas White. This edition was reprinted at Douai in 1604 with the addition of two further orations. In 1572 White was appointed regius professor of law at Douai, a post he retained for the next twenty years. He became a rector of Douai, and was appointed a count palatine of the Holy Roman empire. White was married twice, first to a lady whose surname was Bonvicta, whose fathers and brothers were senators of Douai. The name of his second wife is not recorded. His works contain references to several children, among them Richard, Thomas, Adrian, Peter, and Mary.

White is remembered chiefly for his legal and antiquarian writings. An early work, *Aelia Laelia Crispis antiquum epitaphium* (Padua, 1568; reprinted Dordrecht, 1618), discusses an inscription found in the territory of Bologna. A lengthy volume, *Ad leges decemvirorum libri in duodecim tabulis notae, institutiones juris civilis in quattuor libris, primam partem digestorum in quattuor libris* (Arras, 1597), is dedicated to Philip II of Spain. The aim of the work is to discuss and comment on the texts that were studied in the first year of a seven-year law degree. The *Brevis explicatio privilegiorum iuris, et consuetudinis, circa venerabile sacramentum eucharistiae* (Douai, 1609) was written in 1583, and discusses a canon of Pope Clement V concerning relics and the veneration of saints. The books of the *Historia Britanniae*, which appeared in sections in eleven books at Arras and Douai between 1597 and 1607, books one to nine being reprinted together at Douai in 1602, represent White's masterwork. This is a learned, though of course misguided, attempt to justify the truth of the 'British history' as set out originally by Geoffrey of Monmouth, tracing the story of Britain from the time of Brutus the Trojan. There are certain details of the story with which White disagrees, but essentially he was at one with such scholars as John Leland, Sir John Price, and Humphrey Llwyd in accepting the essential validity of the 'British history'. John Selden, too, quotes him as an authority in his notes to Michael Drayton's *Poly-Olbion* (London, 1612). White assembles an impressive collection of written, antiquarian, and philological arguments to justify his beliefs, and cites numerous highly obscure sources. He was encouraged in his work by Cardinal Baronius, to whom book two of the *Historia* is independently dedicated. The *Brevis explicatio martyrii Sanctae Ursulae et undecim millium virginum Britannarum* (Douai, 1610) is reprinted from book six of his *Historia Britanniae*, and discusses the famous legend of St Ursula and the 11,000 virgins. White's scholarly works are a notable instance of the use, unusual at this time, of detailed endnotes to support the arguments in the main body of his text. He died in 1611 and was buried in the church of St Jacques at Douai. J. W. BINNS

Sources D. E. Rhodes, 'Richard White of Basingstoke: the erudite exile', *Across the narrow seas: studies in the history and bibliography of Britain and the Low Countries*, ed. S. Roach (1991), 23–30 • J. Woolfson, *Padua and the Tudors: English students in Italy, 1485–1603* (1998), 282–3 • Wood, *Ath. Oxon.*, new edn, 2.118–20 • Foster, *Alum. Oxon.* • T. F. Kirby, *Winchester scholars: a list of the wardens, fellows, and scholars of … Winchester College* (1888), 131 • J. W. Binns, *Intellectual culture in Elizabethan and Jacobean England: the Latin writings of the age* (1990), 183–5 • J. W. Binns, 'Richard White of Basingstoke and the defence of Tudor myth', *Cahiers Élisabéthains*, 11 (1977), 17–29 • A. Grafton, *The footnote: a curious history* (1997), 128–31 • A. F. Allison and D. M. Rogers, eds., *The contemporary printed literature of the English Counter-Reformation between 1558 and 1640*, 1 (1989), 180–81 • M. A. Shaaber, *Check-list of works of British authors printed abroad, in languages other than English, to 1641* (1975) • R. White, *Historiae Britanniae libri* (1597–1607) • R. White, *Orationes quinque* (1596)

Likenesses L. Leoni, bronze medal, 1568, BM [*see illus.*] • woodcut, repro. in R. White, *Historiae Britanniae libri* (1602)

White [*alias* Johnson], **Richard** (1604–1687), Roman Catholic priest, was born in the diocese of Winchester of poor Roman Catholic parents; his father's name was Mark White. He entered the English College at Douai on 13 August 1621 and adopted the alias of Johnson, which he retained for the rest of his life. He graduated in philosophy in 1625 and taught grammar in the college in the following academic year, while commencing his study of theology. On 13 September 1629 he was the main speaker in a public disputation held in honour of Viscount Montagu's visit. He was ordained priest on 23 February 1630 and exactly one month later he was sent from Douai to assist Stephen Barnes as confessor of the English Augustinian canonesses of St Monica's at Louvain, where he arrived on 26 May. He acted in that capacity for twenty years, and for thirty-six years after Barnes's death he was principal confessor to the community. In 1633 he was absent in England on business for a short time, and in 1635, when the town was besieged by the French and Dutch armies, he led most of the community into refuge, first at Ghent and then at Bruges, returning after the siege was lifted. For the last

decade of his life he was assisted by George Lynde. In his final few years he was disabled by palsy, and he died in the convent on 12 January 1687. He was buried there.

Johnson left in manuscript over 100 catechetical discourses, 300 sermons, and numerous treatises, most of which were lost at the time of the French Revolution. One of them, a treatise on the sequence of Pentecost ('Veni sancte spiritus') which survives in several manuscript copies, was printed in 1878 and in a different edition in 1913.

THOMPSON COOPER, *rev.* PAUL ARBLASTER

Sources E. H. Burton and T. L. Williams, eds., *The Douay College diaries, third, fourth and fifth, 1598–1654*, 1–2, Catholic RS, 10–11 (1911) • R. Johnson, *The suppliant of the Holy Ghost: a paraphrase of the Veni Sancte Spiritus*, ed. T. E. Bridgett (1878), vii–xii • A. Hamilton, ed., *The chronicle of the English Augustinian canonesses regular of the Lateran*, 2 (1906) • G. Anstruther, *The seminary priests*, 2 (1975), 349

White, Richard (*b.* 1804?). *See under* White family (*per.* 1795–1846).

White, Robert (*c.*1530×32–1574), church musician and composer, was the son of Robert White (*d.* in or after 1574). By 1572 Robert White the elder was styled gentleman and had inherited or acquired the estate of Swallowfield, near Mannings Heath, Sussex. Nevertheless, he and his family appear to have been established in the London parish of St Andrew, Holborn, in whose church stood an especially fine organ donated apparently by the composer's grandfather and preserved from mid-Tudor iconoclasm by his father.

Of the younger Robert White's education and upbringing nothing is known, though a training as a chorister in some great London church appears probable. Between 29 September 1555 and Easter 1559 he was appointed a lay clerk of the choir of Trinity College, Cambridge. (The boy named White who was a chorister there during 1554–5 cannot be identified with the composer.) The function of this choir, founded in 1554 under the auspices of Mary I and intended eventually to consist of eighteen singing-men and twelve boys and their master (who was also organist), was to sing in chapel the full round of the Latin Catholic service—daily high mass and Lady mass and the eight hours services of the office—plus the commemorative obits of the founders. Because certain of his Latin compositions were to texts stipulated in the college statutes of 1554, it appears certain that White's employment there had begun during Mary's reign.

In June 1559 White was promoted to the office of master of the choristers, and his accomplishments as a composer were recognized when on 13 December 1560 he was granted the degree of MusB by Cambridge University, conditional upon his composing a communion service to be sung in the university church on the day of conferment; this was duly accomplished. In support of his supplication White submitted his ten years of experience in the study of music; probably he was now approaching the age of thirty.

However, the Trinity College choir was still incomplete, consisting of but seven men (supplemented by a handful of musically competent fellows and former choristers) and eight boys. Further, by the restoration of the Book of

Common Prayer in June 1559, whereby observance was reduced to just three services a day, and also by new statutes devolved on the college in March 1560, the practice of music in the chapel was greatly attenuated. Finally, the appointment in August 1561 of the austerely protestant Robert Beaumont as master of Trinity College effectively spelt the end of elevated music-making in its chapel. On 29 September 1562 White departed to succeed the prominent composer Christopher *Tye (c.1505–1571×3) as organist and master of the choristers of Ely Cathedral. This was a relatively conservative and well-endowed institution with a choir of (at this time) sixteen men and eight boys. Moreover, White was married to Ellen, daughter of Tye and his wife, Katherine (d. 1574), though whether the marriage took place before or after he entered employment at Ely is not known. Of White's career there nothing is known other than that he had left by 29 September 1566 for appointment (at least by Christmas 1566) to the corresponding office at Chester Cathedral.

Though remote and poorly endowed, this cathedral maintained a choir of fourteen men and eight boys and their master, and in 1566 the chapter made a determined effort to enhance its provision for music, suppressing two choristerships to make available for the master of the choristers a much inflated annual stipend of £16 13s. 4d. There survive no details of White's exercise of his cathedral duties. However, its musicians were invited to contribute to the annual performance of the celebrated cycle of mystery plays mounted each Whitsuntide by the city guilds; and in 1567 and 1568 White was paid 4s. by the smiths and cutlers, apparently for his supply of singers, though perhaps also for his personal musical participation, while for their annual feast on 11 November 1569 the cordwainers paid him 4d. 'for our songs'.

At Christmas 1569 White took up the prestigious office of organist and master of the choristers of Westminster Abbey, thus establishing himself as director of a prominent metropolitan choir of twenty-six men and ten boys, at an annual stipend of £17 13s. 4d. His indenture of appointment was agreed and sealed on 3 February 1570. By 1572 his father, evidently by now a widower, had come to live with the family in Almonry Yard; Robert senior made over apparently the totality of his property to his son in return for his keep.

During November–December 1572 there was obtained for White's use in the abbey church the organ from St Andrew's, Holborn, originally donated to that church by his grandfather and probably by now disused in its parish location. In 1584 the parish churchwarden could only lament how the organs, that 'excellent instrument', now stood in Westminster Abbey, where 'they cannot be bought for any monye so highly they are estemed of for their goodness' (London, Guildhall Library, MS 4249, fol. 232r). Except for this episode, nothing is known of White's management and direction of the abbey's choir and music, though it was there that he spent the rest of his short life.

White was the most conspicuous among the generation of composers immediately preceding William Byrd, who reached maturity contemporaneously with the liturgical reformation and thus had barely completed their apprenticeship as composers for the traditional rite before encountering the obligation to work in a church converted to the ethic and aesthetic of protestantism. To this constraint White's response was to serve in the employment of the reformed church, but to compose music of religious character primarily for the novelty of private performance within the domestic context of the traditionalist home.

While much less varied in style, White's surviving music almost equals that of Thomas Tallis in quantity, and much of it falls little short in quality. Across a relatively brief creative life barely exceeding twenty years, the development of his compositional approach onward from the style of his earlier *cantus firmus* works exemplified strongly the contemporary process of evolution towards the high renaissance ideal of fully integrated imitation. However, his early death denied him the opportunity to engage this in the fully mature manner achieved by Byrd. His possession of an elegant combination of suppleness and strictness in contrapuntal technique was his strongest point, compensating for a prevailing severity in his invention of imitative points and for a certain blandness in terms of rhythmic vitality and harmonic fluidity. Moreover, the aesthetic of his period did not yet aspire to that intimate marriage of word and music that would emerge only after his death.

Most of White's surviving music consists of settings for unaccompanied voices in Latin. A few items are early pieces for the liturgy of the Catholic restoration under Mary. The text of the Marian votive antiphon *Regina celi letare* was specifically prescribed by the 1554 statutes of Trinity College, Cambridge, for performance as a grace following dinner in hall in Eastertide; *Libera nos domine* (a responsory from matins of the dead) was suitable for the three obits of special solemnity observed annually in chapel for founders and benefactors; and the psalm *Deus misereatur* was prescribed for extra-liturgical performance in chapel following the morrow mass on non-festal days under the Latin rite, and following early morning prayers after 1559. *Regina celi* and White's setting of the liturgical Magnificat are conspicuous for their confident and extrovert celebration of contemporary polyphonic styles based on *cantus firmus*.

Although no recusant, White's sympathies lay most probably with the old faith, and in his treatise *A Plaine and Easie Introduction to Practicall Musicke* of 1597 Thomas Morley included him in a list of composers whose skill in composition he surreptitiously associated with their preservation of Catholic values. White's mature works consist mostly of settings of Latin psalms and of the Lamentations of Jeremiah. For these no place could be found in any service of the Book of Common Prayer, and clearly they were conceived for performance in the home, for use as recreation and edification in the households of educated adherents to the values of the old faith. At the time of his death White was owed the considerable sum of £1 10s. 8d.

by Edward Paston, a notable recusant and dedicated collector and preserver of music. It is entirely possible that this sum represented money owed by Paston for White's composition of music created in response to specific requests and commissions.

White's twelve settings of psalms and his settings from the Lamentations exhibit a consistent mastery of polyphonic technique. A disciplined vigour permeates and characterizes such pieces as the third setting of Psalm 15, *Domine quis habitabit*. Meanwhile, in the Lamentations and the more penitential of the psalms (for example, Psalm 50, *Miserere mei deus*) an underlying cogency and coherence of construction is combined throughout lengthy compositions with an arresting poignancy and true expressiveness of mood, sometimes dramatically heightened by the calculated interposition of passages exhibiting a homophonic character with chordal orientation.

Little music by White to vernacular texts has been preserved. For the liturgy of the 1559 prayer book nothing whatever is extant, while as anthems for use following morning or evening prayer only some three or four items survive, of which two have conflicting ascriptions and none is of great distinction. The dozen or so surviving instrumental works, originally for viols and mostly in the form of fantasia or In nomine, are likewise entirely competent though not particularly remarkable.

Morley twice commended White among those whom he considered to be excellent composers, and also listed him among those practitioners whose works he had perused for the authoritative treatment of certain technical points. However, perhaps White's most enduring achievement was his creation of a striking and extensive repertory of vocal music of elevated character for domestic performance. This served as a channel for the transmission of this thitherto predominantly courtly and clerical pastime into the educated gentry and burgess household, so both perpetuating a practice of secular cultivation of art music stretching back to the fifteenth-century carol and preparing and nurturing the ground for the later reception of the madrigal.

An epidemic of plague struck Westminster during autumn 1574, by which White's family was all but extinguished. On 7 November White, 'sicke in bodye', made his will and on 11 November he was buried in St Margaret's churchyard. Ellen White made her will on 21 November, and letters of administration for both wills were issued on 8 December. Of at least five children, the couple were survived by only two daughters. White's work was often attributed in seventeenth-century manuscripts to **Matthew White** (*d.* 1641). Matthew White was a church musician. Of his parentage, education, and musical training nothing is known. He was admitted a vicar-choral of Wells Cathedral on 30 January 1611 and, already an ordained priest, held in plurality the office of gospeller in the Chapel Royal of James I, singing bass, from 2 November 1613 to 24 September 1614. Thereafter he occurs again as vicar-choral of Wells, and on 18 July 1629, in rare recognition of his superior accomplishments as a composer, he was admitted to the degrees of Mus.Bac. and Mus.Doc. of Oxford University. By 22 September 1635 he had become a vicar-choral of Hereford Cathedral, and by the time of his death held also the office of succentor. By 1640 he had been collated in plurality to the vicarage of the parish of St Nicholas, Hereford. He died before 16 October 1641, when a successor was appointed to the succentorship of Hereford Cathedral, vacant by his death.

It is unlikely that either he or William White [*see below*] is to be identified with the Mr White who was the composer of some lightweight catches published by John Hilton and John Playford from 1652 onwards. Indeed, of surviving compositions that are certainly his there remains nothing but two anthems, neither now complete. However, it is a tribute to his contemporary reputation that copyists mistakenly attributed to him music actually by composers of the standing of Robert Parsons, William Mundy, and Robert White.

William White (*bap.* 1571, *d.* 1634), composer, was baptized at St Nicholas, Durham on 17 May 1571, the son of Miles White. Probably he is to be identified with the boy named White who sang as chorister of the choir of Durham Cathedral from 1580 to 1587, and until 1590 continued his education at the King's School. By 28 April 1603 he was a lay clerk of the choir of Westminster Abbey, but at least by the early 1630s had returned to Durham. In London he was a friend of the composer Thomas Tomkins, whose dedication to him of the madrigal 'Adieu, ye city-prisoning towers' in 1622 may perhaps have marked White's return to the north. At the end of the seventeenth century a local historian recollected him as 'a celebrated doctor' resident in Elvet, Durham. White died probably in Durham, and was buried on 11 February 1634.

Of William White's composition of sacred music there survive one incomplete verse anthem and three full anthems, including the popular 'O praise God in his holiness' once attributed to Robert White. Fourteen pieces for consort of viols, mostly written in free contrapuntal fantasia form but including also two pavans, were copied into numerous early seventeenth-century manuscript sources. These items owed such high regard to their fluency and idiomatic skill, especially in composition in five and six parts.

ROGER BOWERS

Sources Trinity Cam. · CUL, Ely Cathedral archive · archive of Chester Cathedral, Ches. & Chester ALSS · archive, Westminster Abbey · *Robert White, 1: five-part Latin psalms*; *Robert White, 2: six-part Latin psalms and votive antiphons*; *Robert White, 3: ritual music and lamentations*, ed. D. Mateer, Early English Church Music, 28–9, 32 (1983–6) · P. C. Buck and others, eds., *Tudor church music*, 5 (1926) · I. Spector, *Robert White: instrumental music*, Recent Researches in the Music of the Renaissance, 12 (1972) · F. Hudson, 'Robert White and his contemporaries: early Elizabethan music and drama', *Festschrift für Ernst Hermann Meyer*, ed. G. Knepler (Leipzig, 1976), 163–87 · H. Benham, *Latin church music in England, c.1460–1575* (1977), 212–16 · D. Wulstan, *Tudor music* (1985), 301–5 · D. Mateer, 'Further light on Preston and Whyte', *MT*, 115 (1974), 1074–7 · J. Blezzard, 'A note on Robert Whyte', *MT*, 115 (1974), 977–9 · L. M. Clapper, ed., *Records of early English drama: Chester* (Toronto, 1979), 78, 86, 89 · *VCH Cambridgeshire and the Isle of Ely*, vol. 3 · Dotted Crotchet, 'St Andrew's Church, Holborn: London churches, 3', *MT*, 46 (1905), 153–63 · A. M. Burke, ed., *Memorials of St Margaret's Church, Westminster* (1914), 30, 32 · *VCH Sussex*, vol. 6/3 · *New Grove* · will, PRO, PROB 11/11 Carew · *IGI*

Wealth at death owned small landed estate in parish of Nuthurst, Sussex: will, PRO

White, Robert (*fl.* 1617), masque writer, remains intriguing in his obscurity. Nothing is known of his origins or personal life; however, he was perhaps the same Robert White (Whyte) who received his BA from Merton College, Oxford, on 4 November 1608. Some time before May 1617 White wrote a masque entitled *Cupid's Banishment* for performance by the 'younge Gentlewomen of the Ladies Hall in Deptford at Greennwich'. The masquers included daughters of court officials and two of Queen Anne's goddaughters. This, coupled with the presentation of the masque to the queen as a token of the girls' esteem, suggests that Ladies' Hall was a school for gentlewomen (Dews, 176–9). Robert White was probably the master of Ladies' Hall (Bentley, 5.1257–8).

White's introduction to *Cupid's Banishment* thanks Lucy, countess of Bedford—the queen's attendant and herself a masquer—for her 'honourable furtherance and noble encouragement' in bringing his masque to performance. Nevertheless, little is known about the actual occasion. The masque was played on 4 May 1617, at a time when King James was on progress in Scotland and Queen Anne was in Greenwich. In the tradition of the masque as celebration and offering the young ladies presented the queen with needlework gifts, on which her initials were emblazoned. The author performed the role of Occasion, who introduces the masque; men from the King's Musick played minor parts.

Among the masquers in *Cupid's Banishment* was Master Richard Browne, who later became the diplomat Sir Richard Browne of Sayes Court, Deptford. It was Browne who preserved the only extant manuscript of *Cupid's Banishment*. Eventually this passed to his daughter and her husband, the celebrated diarist John Evelyn, who added it to his personal library. Evelyn's writing exists on the outside cover of the manuscript and also on the page opposite the title; it identifies Richard Browne as being twelve years of age when he acted before the queen. Some also believe that it is Evelyn's autograph on the cover (McGee, 235).

The manuscript of *Cupid's Banishment* (MS MA 1296) currently resides in the Pierpont Morgan Library. It is beautifully set forth in the hand of a professional scribe. Historians have speculated that it was either a presentation copy given to White in commemoration of the masque's performance or perhaps a fair copy prepared in anticipation of publication (McGee, 228). Nevertheless the text of the masque was not finally published until it was transcribed by John Nichols in 1828. The music to the song 'Bacchus at thy call' was first printed by Andrew Sabol (1978).

Cupid's Banishment is thoroughly conventional in its dramatic elements and its theme—the superiority of chaste love. Yet, as McGee has noted, it is unconventional in blending the 'customary revels of the school with the lavish display of the court masque' (McGee, 231). The masque's reception remains a mystery. As Peter Walls has noted Ben Jonson clearly knew about *Cupid's Banishment* and accommodated ideas from it in *Pleasure Reconciled to Virtue* (Walls, 80–81). With characteristic enthusiasm John

Payne Collier was certain that White's masque was received 'very gratiously' (Collier, 1.389). But Robert Evans posits that Jonson felt threatened by White's masque writing and that *Pleasure Reconciled* is a parody of White's masque. Whatever the case White never received royal or aristocratic patronage after he presented *Cupid's Banishment*, nor does he seem to have produced other literary work.

Robert White should not be confused with the earlier musician–composer of the same name (1540?–1574) or with the man listed among the 'singing men of Westminster' in 1625 (de Lafontaine, 58). Similarly he seems not to have been related to the two other musician–composers who were his contemporaries—Matthew White (*fl.* 1610–1630) and William White (*fl.* 1620). More recently Diana Poulton has identified another Robert White, from a family or patrons associated with John Dowland, but there is no provable connection with the masque writer (Poulton, 433–4). S. P. Cerasano

Sources R. White, 'Cupid's banishment', 1617, Morgan L., MA 1296 · C. E. McGee, ed., 'Cupid's banishment: a masque presented to her majesty by the young gentlewomen of the Ladies Hall, May 4, 1617', *Renaissance Drama*, 19 (1988), 227–38 · J. Nichols, *The progresses, processions, and magnificent festivities of King James I, his royal consort, family and court*, 4 vols. (1828) · G. E. Bentley, *The Jacobean and Caroline stage*, 7 vols. (1941–68) · P. Walls, 'Jonson's borrowing', *Theatre Notebook*, 28 (1974), 80–81 · R. C. Evans, '"Other men's provision": Ben Jonson's parody of Robert White in *Pleasure reconciled to virtue*', *Comparative Drama*, 24 (1990), 55–77 · *CSP dom.*, 1611–18 · J. P. Collier, *The history of English dramatic poetry*, 2nd edn, 3 vols. (1879) · A. J. Sabol, *Four hundred songs and dances from the Stuart masque* (1978) · *DNB* · Foster, *Alum. Oxon.* · N. Dews, *The history of Deptford*, 2nd edn (1884) · H. C. de Lafontaine, ed., *The King's musick: a transcript of records relating to music and musicians, 1460–1700* [1909]; repr. (New York, 1973) · D. Poulton, *John Dowland* (1972)

White, Robert (1645–1703), draughtsman and engraver, was born in London and was apprenticed to David Loggan, whose position as the leading line engraver for the print trade he was to inherit. His earliest print was made in 1666 and his last in 1702. His output was huge, and has never been fully documented; George Vertue's list has several hundred plates, to which more should be added to complete the catalogue.

White's principal activity was as a portrait engraver. He usually engraved these from his own drawings, made from life in black lead on vellum. Many of them survive: thirteen are in the British Museum, and more are in the Huntington Library, California. Among those in the British Museum is a self-portrait made when White was sixteen, which establishes the date of his birth. The drawings are of remarkable quality, and Vertue was particularly impressed by his ability to capture a likeness:

> He ought to be remembered as a singular artist in his way, having so vast a genius in drawing and engraving a face, and make the picture so like the original … that perhaps he has not left his equal in Europe behind him. (Vertue, 6.183–4)

White also engraved frontispieces, book-plates (one was for Samuel Pepys), almanacs, architectural views, processions, and the occasional semi-popular piece to catch public interest in a topical story. Most of the portraits served as frontispieces for books, and were made on commission from publishers: this explains the number of heads of divines in his output. A small number he published himself at his house in Bloomsbury Market, and these could be large and splendid. Among the finest are a dozen plates, mostly large, made after paintings by Godfrey Kneller. Vertue records that White charged about £4 for a small plate, but up to £30 for a large one, but also says that he died poor. It is difficult to understand how this could have happened as he was obviously very successful. However, White's engraving business must have been affected by the rise of mezzotint, and for a brief period from about 1680 to 1683 he took up mezzotint publishing himself. John Chaloner Smith lists nine such plates, one of which (the countess of Arundel) White scraped himself. He was buried on 26 October 1703 at St Giles-in-the-Fields, and his plates were acquired by the publisher John King. The writing engraver John Sturt (1658–1730) was apprenticed to White in 1674.

George White (c.1684–1732), engraver, was Robert's son and worked with his father until the latter's death. He was an engraver for some years before, about 1712, taking up mezzotint with much greater success. Vertue (who knew him well and gives much information about him) records that he was able to command 15 or 20 guineas a plate, almost double what anyone had earned before, but was extremely dilatory in finishing them. Smith lists fifty-nine mezzotints by him, many of which he published himself. In later years he worked for Samuel Sympson in the Strand, who took over many plates after White's death.

White introduced a method of etching the plate before mezzotinting it and frequently finished his plates with the burin, which gives them an unusual sharpness of focus. He also made portrait drawings: the early ones were in black lead (six are in the British Museum), the later ones in crayon. Like his father, White lived in Bloomsbury, where he died on 27 May 1732, aged about forty-eight.

ANTONY GRIFFITHS

Sources Vertue, Note books, 3.6, 54–5, 59–61; 4.108; 6.183–4 · E. Croft-Murray and P. H. Hulton, eds., Catalogue of British drawings, 1 (1960), 539–40 · C. F. Bell and R. L. Poole, 'English seventeenth-century portrait drawings in Oxford collections, pt 2', Walpole Society, 14 (1925–6), 49–80, esp. 64–71 · J. C. Smith, British mezzotinto portraits, 4/1 (1882), 1591–3
Likenesses R. White, self-portrait, drawing, c.1661, BM · A. Bannerman, line engraving, 1763, NPG; repro. in Walpole, Catalogue of engravers (1763)
Wealth at death poor at death: Vertue, Note books

White, Robert (1802–1874), antiquary, son of James White, a border farmer, was born on 17 September 1802 at the Clock Mill, near Yetholm in Roxburghshire, the son of James White and Mary, née Laidlaw (d. 1829). While he was a boy his father moved to Otterburn in Redesdale, where he herded his father's cattle, and attended local schools. He managed to acquire a knowledge of books, with the encouragement of his father's landlord, James Ellis, a former solicitor in Newcastle upon Tyne, then of Otterburn Hall, a friend and correspondent of Sir Walter Scott. He was sent briefly to Jedburgh as trainee millwright, making bobbins for the weaving trade, but returned to work on the farm. In 1825 he found employment in Newcastle in the counting-house of Robert Watson, a plumber, brassfounder, and millwright, at the High Bridge, where he remained until Watson died forty years later.

At Newcastle, White found time for study and by abstemious living amassed some savings, but his father and brother needed financial help in their farming ventures, leaving little for the purchase of books. His holidays were usually spent rambling on the border with his friend James Telfer the Saughtrees poet, steeping himself in border minstrelsy and gathering knowledge of border life. His first poem, 'The Tynemouth Nun', was written in 1829, and at the suggestion of the antiquary John Adamson (1787–1855) it was printed the same year for the Typographical Society of Newcastle, and enjoyed considerable local popularity. After this he devoted himself to the preservation and reproduction of local legend and song, contributing to many local publications. He was an informant of F. J. Child during the preparation of the latter's work.

In 1852 White became a member of the Newcastle Society of Antiquaries, to which he contributed a paper on the battle of Nevilles Cross (Archaeologia Aeliana, 2nd ser., 1.271–303). Encouraged by its reception, he published a volume on the History of the Battle of Otterburn (1857), adding memoirs of the warriors engaged. This was followed in 1858 by a paper read to the Newcastle society on the battle of Flodden (ibid., 3.197–236), and in 1871 by a History of the Battle of Bannockburn. These monographs were rendered valuable by White's intimate acquaintance with local legend, and by his topographical knowledge. He died, unmarried, at his house at 11 Claremont Place, Newcastle, on 20 February 1874.

In addition to his antiquarian papers, White wrote Poems, Including Tales, Ballads, and Songs (1867), and edited the Poems and Ballads of John Leyden (1858), with a memoir supplementing that by Sir Walter Scott. Several of his songs are to be found in the Whistle Binkie series and in Alexander Whitelaw's Book of Scottish Song (1844). His library of 4400 volumes, rich in the history and topography of Northumberland and the borders, ballads, and chapbooks, was dispersed among his sisters after his death, but in 1942 his great-nephew Professor Sir George White Pickering (1904–1980), regius professor of medicine at Oxford (1956–68), with family help, reassembled the library and presented it to King's College, where it remains in the Robinson Library of the University of Newcastle upon Tyne. E. I. CARLYLE, rev. C. M. FRASER

Sources R. Welford, Men of mark 'twixt Tyne and Tweed, 3 vols. (1895) · L. Gordon, Guide to the special collection in the Robinson Library of the University of Newcastle upon Tyne (1994), 8, 16 · R. White, Autobiographical notes, ed. [F. Thompson] (privately printed, Newcastle upon Tyne, 1966) · Newcastle Weekly Chronicle (1 Oct 1892) · Hawick Advertiser (25 Sept 1869) · parish register
Archives U. Newcastle, Robinson L., corresp., antiquarian, literary, and personal papers | U. Edin. L., letters to David Laing
Likenesses lithograph, repro. in White, Autobiographical notes · portrait, repro. in R. White, Poems, including tales, ballads, and songs, 8 vols. (1867)
Wealth at death under £35,000: probate, 19 March 1874, CGPLA Eng. & Wales

White, Robert Meadows (1798–1865), university teacher, was born on 8 January 1798 at Halesworth, Suffolk, the eldest son of Robert Gostling White (d. 1828), a solicitor in that town, and his second wife, Elizabeth Meadows (d. 1831). His younger brother was the solicitor John Meadows *White. Robert's early schooling was at Bungay under Robert Page, his godfather (1805–1808?), and at Dedham, Essex, under the Revd Haggitts (1808–1813?), and in 1813 he was placed under John Valpy at Norwich, where John Lindley, the botanist, and Raja Sir James Brooke were his fellow pupils. On 26 July 1815 he matriculated from Magdalen College, Oxford, and in the same year was elected a demy; he graduated BA on 14 December 1819, MA on 28 February 1822, BD on 21 November 1833, and DD on 23 November 1843. He was ordained deacon in 1821 and priest in 1822. In 1824 he was elected a fellow of Magdalen College, and retained his fellowship until 1847. From 1832 to 1840 he acted as a college tutor. On 15 March 1831 he became proctor, and on 23 April 1834 he was chosen Rawlinson professor of Anglo-Saxon, which post he held for the statutable period of five years.

Anglo-Saxon professors at that time were sometimes defined as 'persons willing to learn Anglo-Saxon'. White, however, was known as a scholar before he was elected to the chair. He had already planned the publication of a Saxon and English vocabulary, and abandoned the project only because it appeared likely to clash with the *Anglo-Saxon Dictionary* then being prepared by Joseph Bosworth. On giving up this design he turned his attention about 1832 to editing the *Ormulum*, a harmonized narrative of the gospels in verse, preserved in a unique manuscript in the Bodleian Library. This task, owing to other demands on his time, occupied nearly twenty years. In the course of his researches he visited Denmark in 1837, and extended his travels to Moscow, where he was arrested and suffered a short detention for visiting the Kremlin without an official order. His edition of the *Ormulum* was published in 1852 by the university press, and in the following year an elaborate criticism of it was published in English by Dr Monicke, a German professor.

In 1839, at the end of his term of office, White was presented to the vicarage of Woolley, near Wakefield, by Godfrey Wentworth of that parish, to whose son William he had acted as tutor. After Wentworth's death White left Woolley, and went to Lord Yarborough at Brocklesby Park in Lincolnshire, where he acted as tutor to the baron's grandsons. In 1842 he was presented to the rectory of Little and Great Glemham in Suffolk by the Hon. Mrs North, Lord Yarborough's sister, and on 29 October 1846 he was presented by Magdalen College to the rectory of Slimbridge in Gloucestershire, which he retained until his death. He died unmarried at Cheltenham on 31 January 1865, and was buried at Slimbridge churchyard, near the chancel south wall.   E. I. CARLYLE, rev. JOHN D. HAIGH

Sources *GM*, 3rd ser., 14 (1863), 667 · *GM*, 3rd ser., 19 (1865), 111–13 · Allibone, *Dict.* · Foster, *Alum. Oxon.* · G. V. Cox, *Recollections of Oxford* (1868), 246–7 · J. R. Bloxam, *A register of the presidents, fellows … of Saint Mary Magdalen College*, 8 vols. (1853–85), vol. 7, pp. 265–9 · BL, Add. MSS 19155, fol. 92; 19168, fol. 211

Archives Suffolk RO, Ipswich, corresp. and papers, incl. annotated proof copy of *Ormulum*
Wealth at death under £5000: administration, 21 March 1865, *CGPLA Eng. & Wales*

White, Samuel [*called* Siamese White] (c.1650–1689), official in the Siamese service and pirate, was probably born in the west of England and was probably a member of a Bristol merchant family. He was the younger brother of **George White** (*fl.* c.1665–1702), who entered the service of the East India Company as a young man and in the 1660s travelled to India accompanied by Constant Phaulkon, an adventurer from Cephalonia who at first acted as the older White's assistant. George White detached himself from the East India Company and worked as an independent trader. He was not strictly an 'interloper' as he did not encroach on the company's monopoly of trade with Europe, but sold his goods at ports from the Persian Gulf to Indochina and established a good reputation in Siam.

Samuel White sailed for India in 1675 to join his brother. On board ship he met Mary Povey (d. 1682), who was travelling to Fort St George, Madras, to join her fiancé, Mr Jearsey; following their arrival in Fort St George in early 1676 Mary Povey married White instead. They had two daughters, Susan (b. 1676) and Mary (1678–1692?). In Madras, White joined the establishment of the East India Company as a pilot on a salary of £10 a year, with the opportunity for private trade. This employment was safe but limited, and in late 1677 White accepted an appointment in the service of King Narai of Siam, arranged by George White and Phaulkon. Narai seems to have wanted the English East India Company to establish itself in Siam to help counter the Dutch dominance of Siamese trade. The king was also happy to encourage the company's members to enter the Siamese service and strengthen the trading networks under direct royal control.

White's first command was of a royal ship plying between Mergui (a Siamese port on the Indian Ocean, in the province of Tenasserim, later part of Burma) and Masulipatam in India; he was engaged in the exotic traffic of importing elephants for Narai, but was also trading on his own account. White moved his family to Mergui, where his wife died in 1682. George White left Siam in 1681, but Phaulkon remained as an adviser on trade to the king. White benefited from Phaulkon's trade policy, adopted by Narai, by which Siam would seek an alliance with France in order to reduce the influence of the Dutch and also that of the Muslim families of Indian descent who dominated administration on Siam's Indian Ocean seaboard. In autumn 1683, following the departure of his daughters for England, White visited the Siamese capital, Ayutthaya, where he was created a mandarin of the third rank and *shabandar* (harbourmaster) of Mergui. His responsibilities included collecting and managing royal revenues in the province of Tenasserim and the supervision of Siamese maritime interests in the Bay of Bengal. He was also expected to fortify Mergui and assemble a fleet of armed merchant ships, which, with French help, could dominate trade in the Bay of Bengal. Not only did this set Samuel White at odds with his former employers, the East India Company, but it also placed him in a potentially treasonable relationship to England. White did not care which European power was dominant in the area, if his private fortune was assured.

In this aim White achieved a spectacular beginning. Having assembled his fleet and installed English captains on each, he began an undeclared war against the trade of Burma and the Indian kingdom of Golconda (Hyderabad). Narai had at first encouraged an aggressive policy but was persuaded to moderate his stance by advisers sympathetic to Golconda; White ignored orders to avoid confrontation, and encouraged his captains to seize independent, Golcondan, or Burmese vessels alike. He seems to have wished to avoid challenging the East India Company directly, but some of his captains did seize ships belonging to company officials. All vessels belonging to the two selected states plying the Bay of Bengal were at risk, and over a period of two years many were captured. The prize ships were sent to neutral ports under White's influence, and their cargoes were sold as White's private property, realizing about £30,000, of which he sent half back to England, retaining the balance as working capital. Not contenting himself with using his post at Mergui to underpin his operations as a pirate, White also embezzled the funds provided by King Narai for the fortifications of Mergui and drew the wages for an entirely fictitious garrison of soldiers. He was investigated by the Siamese authorities in 1686, but had Phaulkon's support at Ayutthaya and was cleared of wrongdoing.

By this time the Siamese alliance with France and White's piratical activities were causing serious concern to the East India Company, which accordingly asked James II to issue a proclamation against Englishmen sailing under foreign flags. James's proclamation recalled all Englishmen in the king of Siam's service; armed with this authority Elihu Yale, the company's president of Madras, dispatched a small force to Mergui, commanded by Captain Anthony Weltden on the *Curtana*, to seize White's ships by way of reparations and to demand the surrender of all the English inhabitants. Weltden arrived off Mergui in June 1687.

White was aware that foreigners had become unpopular in Siam, and was already planning his escape. He took the precaution of providing himself with a forged pass from the Siamese court, as a protection against prosecution for piracy, and put up only a token resistance to Weltden, sacrificing a Siamese ship before surrendering. Within a month he and Weltden were on excellent terms, spending many evenings drinking together and amusing themselves with thunderous gun salutes while awaiting favourable winds for the voyage to Madras. The sleepless nights helped exhaust the patience of Mergui's inhabitants with White's self-interest; on the night of 14 July 1687 they opened fire with the shore batteries, sinking one of Weltden's ships, then combed Mergui for foreigners and slaughtered every European they could find. The charmed White escaped injury, while Weltden survived a blow to the head only thanks to the thick hat he was wearing. Taking two ships White and Weltden withdrew to Burma; following Weltden's display of incompetence, neither was anxious for an early encounter with the company's officials in India. The ships arrived off Madras in December 1687, but Weltden allowed White to land 30 miles north of Madras to avoid being arrested by the company. White hurried back to England, arriving there before news of the massacre at Mergui, for which he expected to be blamed. He was alleged to have told the Siamese that Weltden had come to seize the town on the company's behalf. In escaping he avoided the fate of Phaulkon, who was executed in April 1688.

White managed to bring the bulk of his wealth home with him, and in the changed political climate following the flight of James II initiated a lawsuit against the East India Company, claiming £40,000 in damages. He argued that he had ruled from Mergui in the company's interest but had been ordered by Narai to attack Golconda. He also claimed that he had been about to leave for England as Narai's ambassador when Weltden arrived. This was obviously a pre-emptive ploy to counter any charges which the company might prefer against him, but before what would surely have been a fascinating case could be brought to court, Samuel White died suddenly in April 1689. He was buried at Bath Abbey on 27 April 1689. His brother George took up his case, but the company, using the evidence of White's colleague Francis Davenport, showed that White's account did not bear scrutiny.

George White's name has been linked with the Dowgate Adventurers (or Dowgate Association, named for their meeting place in the City), a group who sought to challenge the East India Company's monopoly by legitimate means. In this they had some success, leading to the establishment of a new East India Company, and eventually its merger with the old to provide a broad-based company with more shareholders. George White was still active in 1702, when he corresponded with Thomas Pitt. However, ultimately the White brothers' activities in Siam proved disastrous for British and indeed European interests. The East India Company directors noted in 1691 that 'Syam never did nor will bring the Company two pence advantage, but many thousands of pounds of loss' (Keay, 204). The policies followed by Narai and Phaulkon had led to conflict with the East India Company and the Dutch, but left Siam open to exploitation by France as well as by adventurers such as the Whites. Narai's death in 1688 was followed by a period of Siamese isolation from interaction with European powers, which would last for over a century.

STUART RANKIN

Sources M. Collis, *Siamese White*, rev. edn (1965) · J. Anderson, *English intercourse with Siam in the seventeenth century* (1890) · R. Mukherjee, *The rise and fall of the East India Company* (1974), 79–83 · J. Keay, *The honourable company: a history of the English East India Company* (1991), 200–204 · P. Griffiths, *A licence to trade* (1974), 90–92 · A. Farrington, *A biographical index of East India Company maritime service officers, 1600–1834* (1999), 838 · D. K. Wyatt, *Thailand, a short history* (1984) · A. Reid, *Southeast Asia in the age of commerce, 1450–1680*, 2: *Expansion and crisis* (1993), 306–8

White, Stephen (b. c.1574, d. in or after 1646), scholar and theologian, was born in Clonmel, Ireland. Although the details of his parentage are unknown it appears that he belonged to the mercantile élite which also produced the Jesuit Thomas White, rector of the Irish College at Salamanca, and Peter White, sometime dean of Waterford, who was famed for his grammar school teaching at Kilkenny. Stephen White may have been a pupil at this academy and it was possibly he who was one of the three foundation scholars named in the charter of the newly established Trinity College, Dublin, in 1592. If so he quickly left for the continent, studying first at Lisbon about 1594 and then at Salamanca the following year. There, having attained the degree of BA, he joined the Society of Jesus in 1596. He graduated to teaching philosophy and theology at the college. While on the staff he helped William Bathe, spiritual director of the college, in the compilation of the famous *Janua linguarum*, a highly successful manual of linguistics, first published in 1606.

In 1606 White moved to Germany to become professor of scholastic theology, first at Ingolstadt (until 1609) and then at Dillingen, where he taught for fourteen years. As a doctor of divinity he lectured a generation of students, including many Irishmen, and supervised a number of doctoral dissertations. His reputation as a theologian burgeoned within the society, and among scholars in Ireland and on the continent.

The other strand in commentators' admiring assessments emanated from White's achievement as an antiquary and ecclesiastical historian which was to earn him the sobriquet polyhistor. According to his own account he began about 1611 serious study of the history of Ireland, and within a few years produced 'Apologia pro Hibernia adversus Cambri calumnias'. In this work (which remained in manuscript until edited and published in 1849) White aimed to refute the views of the twelfth-century historian Gerald of Wales (Giraldus Cambrensis) in his works *Expugnatio Hibernica* and *Topographia Hiberniae*. He displayed therein an impressive knowledge of medieval and contemporary sources for Irish history, especially those which pertained to the Irish church and its saints.

Evident in the 'Apologia' are signs of the painstaking work of transcription of saints' lives which forms White's main literary monument. Having access to the libraries of many German and Swiss monasteries he made copies of several important manuscripts. Among these were Adamnan's life of St Columba which he made available to the hagiographer John Colgan and Archbishop James Ussher, the Church of Ireland primate. Also transcribed were lives of St Brigid, St Colman, St Patrick, St Erhard, and St Columbanus, copies of which White sent to a number of scholars who were engaged in publishing works on early Irish ecclesiastical history. Although none of his own scholarly research was published his selfless work of furnishing vital sources for other writers was fulsomely acknowledged by them. Ussher paid tribute to White's erudition on a number of occasions, and Colgan praised him handsomely in the preface to his *Acta sanctorum Hiberniae*.

When in his mid-fifties White was sent back to Ireland, about 1629, to take up an academic post in the short-lived Jesuit university in Back Lane, Dublin. After the closure of that institution by the authorities in 1630 White spent some years in Jesuit residences in Dublin and Waterford. During his stay in the former he visited Ussher, who gave him access to his library, and he corresponded with Colgan. He devoted himself to teaching and adjudicating on cases of conscience. By late 1641 he had moved to Galway. The proposed publication of the ailing scholar's work was considered by his superiors in the Society of Jesus but they were cautious about approving the printing of such ideologically engaged work in the highly charged politico-religious climate of the 1640s.

Stephen White died in or after January 1646, and the bulk of his scholarship was lost.   COLM LENNON

Sources E. Hogan, 'Worthies of Waterford and Tipperary: life of Father Stephen White, S.J., theologian and polyhistor', *Journal of the Waterford and South-East of Ireland Archaeological Society*, 3 (1897), 55–71, 119–34 · S. White, *Apologia pro Hibernia adversus Cambri calumnias*, ed. M. Kelly (1849) · W. Reeves, 'Memoir of Stephen White', *Proceedings of the Royal Irish Academy*, 8 (1861–4), 29–38 · T. Corcoran, 'Early Irish Jesuit educators', *Studies: an Irish Quarterly Review*, 30 (1941), 59–74 · E. Hogan, ed., *Ibernia Ignatiana, seu, Ibernorum Societatis Jesu patrum monumenta* (1880) · DNB

White, Terence Hanbury (1906–1964), novelist, was born on 29 May 1906 in Bombay, the only child of Garrick Hanbury White, a district superintendent of police in the Indian police service, and his wife, Constance Edith Southcote Aston, the daughter of a judge on the Indian circuit. His parents later divorced, and at the age of five White was sent to England to be brought up by his maternal grandparents in St Leonards, Sussex. In 1920 he went to Cheltenham College, where the terrifying beatings had a permanent effect on his sexual development. In 1925 he went up to Queens' College, Cambridge, to read English. He obtained a second class (division two) in part one of the English tripos (1927) and a first class with distinction in part two (1929).

After contracting tuberculosis White spent a year in Italy thanks to a fund raised by his tutor and lifelong friend, L. J. Potts, and he began to write a satirical novel, later published as *They Winter Abroad* (1932), under the pseudonym James Aston. He returned to Cambridge and completed his degree course in 1929, submitting a thesis on Malory's *Morte d' Arthur*. In the same year he published *Loved Helen, and other Poems*, started in 1926. For two years he taught at St David's, a preparatory school in Reigate, before being appointed head of the English department at Stowe School in 1932 by the school's headmaster, J. F. Roxburgh. White excelled in this role and for the rest of his life retained many of the attributes of the old-fashioned schoolmaster. He was a bachelor with sadistic fantasies, melancholy and prone to drinking bouts, but with an enormous capacity for new interests and enthusiasms. ('The best thing for being sad', Merlyn says in *The Sword in the Stone*, 1938, 'is to learn something.') It was during his

Stowe years (1932–6) that White took flying lessons and acquired his passion for hunting, shooting, and fishing. Two early novels (*Earth Stopped*, 1934, and *Gone to ground*, 1935), the satirical *Burke's Steerage* (1938), and *England have my Bones* (1936) all have hunting and shooting themes. When he resigned from Stowe in 1936 in order to become a full-time writer, White spent two years in a cottage near the school at Stowe Ridings where he fell in love with a young girl, and experimented with falconry, describing the latter episode in his most successful book, *The Goshawk* (1951).

In 1938 White published *The Sword in the Stone*, selected by the American Book of the Month Club, the first instalment of what was to become an Arthurian tetralogy entitled *The Once and Future King* (1958). It was a brilliantly imaginative, and in parts satirical, account of the boyhood of King Arthur, loosely based on the work of Sir Thomas Malory. White put himself into the character of Merlyn, passing on to the young king his knowledge of wildlife and hunting. He wrote the second instalment, *The Witch in the Wood* (1940), in Ireland, where he spent a fishing holiday at the beginning of 1939, invited by the novelist David Garnett, his mentor and friend. In the event he stayed there for six years, immersing himself in the special atmosphere of rural Ireland, which he found greatly sympathetic. At one time he half-seriously intended to become a Catholic. White's Irish impressions are to be found in *The Godstone and the Blackymor* (1959), illustrated by Edward Ardizzone, and *The Elephant and the Kangaroo* (1948), a fantasy about a second flood, with White as Noah.

White agonized about helping the war effort and in 1941 applied to join the Royal Air Force Volunteer Reserve but his attempts failed, thereby exacerbating his sense of guilt and isolation. It was then that he decided to turn his Arthurian series into a satirical pamphlet attempting to establish the bases for a peaceful society: 'I have suddenly discovered that the central theme of *Morte d'Arthur* is to find an antidote to war' (letter to L. J. Potts, Gallix, *Letters*, 117). Calling himself a 'Nostalgic Tory', he abhorred the post-war labour government and in 1947, after a surprise windfall of £15,000 when his children's book *Mistress Masham's Repose* (1946) was chosen as the book of the month in the USA, exiled himself in Alderney, one of the Channel Islands.

White completed two books of historical essays, *The Age of Scandal* (1950) and *The Scandalmonger* (1952), a translation of a medieval bestiary (*The Book of Beasts*, 1954), on which he had laboured for seventeen years, and his 'Stevenson book for children', *The Master*, in 1957. In 1959 *The Once and Future King* was adapted for the stage as a musical called *Camelot*, by Alan Jay Lerner and Frederick Loewe. Starring Richard Burton and Julie Andrews, it opened in New York on Broadway and was an immediate hit. It was followed by Walt Disney's successful cartoon *The Sword in the Stone* (1963). This sudden acquisition of wealth finally put an end to White's writing career and he became more and more morose. In 1962, he published a limited edition of 100 copies of *Verses* (privately printed). Following a highly

successful three-month lecture tour of America in 1962, described in *America at Last* (1965), he was found dead in his cabin on 17 January 1964 at the port of Piraeus while crossing the Mediterranean. He was buried in the protestant cemetery in Athens on 20 January. He was unmarried.

White was a tall, distinguished, bearded figure, 'looking like one of the Sikhs at Queen Victoria's funeral' (his own description). As the child of a drunkard father and a hysterical over-possessive mother he suffered all his life from sadistic impulses, guilt, and irrational fears. He was a natural recluse who found most human relationships difficult, and was deeply attached to his dogs. However, until his final period, he rose triumphantly above his handicaps. He was a master stylist, a sharp, satirical observer of the social scene with an unfailing capacity for taking up a variety of interests, and the ability to persuade his readers to share his enthusiasms, however out-of-the-way. The great success of the posthumous publication of *The Book of Merlyn* (1977)—which was on the *New York Times* bestseller list for twenty-four weeks—marks the beginning of a fairer appreciation of his novels in which intertextuality plays a very important part.

RICHARD INGRAMS, *rev.* FRANÇOIS GALLIX

Sources F. Gallix, *T. H. White: an annotated bibliography* (1986) · S. T. Warner, *T. H. White: a biography* (1967) · D. Garnett, ed., *The White/Garnett letters* (1968) · F. Gallix, ed., *Letters to a friend: the correspondence between T. H. White and L. J. Potts* (1984) · E. Brewer, *T. H. White 'The Once and Future King'* (1993) · F. Gallix, 'T. H. White and the legend of King Arthur: from animal fantasy to political morality', *King Arthur: a casebook*, ed. E. D. Kennedy (1996) · A. Hadfield, 'T. H. White, pacifism, and violence: the once and future nation', *Connotations* (1996–7)
Archives Ransom HRC, corresp. and literary papers; personal documents | U. Reading L., corresp. with Jonathan Cape Ltd |SOUND BBC, sound archives, personal tapes
Likenesses R. Avedon, photograph, 1960, priv. coll.

White, Sir Thomas (1495?–1567), founder of St John's College, Oxford, was in all likelihood born in 1495 to William White (*d.* 1523), a clothier of Rickmansworth, Hertfordshire, and his wife, Mary, daughter of John Kebblewhite of South Fawley, Buckinghamshire. His birthplace has been disputed, but was probably Reading (rather than Rickmansworth), where it is possible that he attended the grammar school in his early years. In 1504 he was apprenticed to Hugh Acton, a prominent member of the Merchant Taylors' Company in London. Acton provided the capital upon which White's own trading ventures were initially founded, and his own later efforts to help worthy young men establish themselves with loans (not dissimilar to a fund for apprentices set up by Acton) were possibly an acknowledgement of his own debt to Acton's charity. With a bequest of £100 from his late master, combined with a portion from his father, he was able to set up his own business in the cloth trade in 1523, after which his fortunes and status grew rapidly. In 1530 he became the first renter warden of the Merchant Taylors'; in 1533 he was senior warden; and he was probably master of the company in 1535, when he was assessed for the subsidy at £1000. As a resident of the parish of St Michael Cornhill, he was elected alderman in 1544, a burdensome office which he initially refused, and it was only after a period of imprisonment in Newgate (during which the mayor ordered his shop to be shut up) that he relented. Shortly afterwards he was one of the aldermen who raised a loan for the war with Scotland, to which he contributed £300.

White's large-scale charitable provision began in July 1542 with a gift of £1400 to the corporation of Coventry which enabled the purchase of old priory lands. In 1551 the income from this land was secured in the form of interest-free loans for honest and thrifty apprentices from Coventry for forty years after White's death, after which the funds were to be made available in similar loans on a rotating basis to young men from Northampton, Leicester, Nottingham, and Warwick as well as Coventry. In 1545 he similarly bestowed Bristol with a gift of £2000 for the purchase of land, the income from which was likewise directed by a trust established in 1566 which stipulated that sums of £25 should be lent without interest for ten years to young men (preferably clothiers) of twenty-four different cities. It is likely that the cities selected were those involved in the cloth trade, with Bristol being favoured perhaps because of its guild of tailors in honour of St John the Baptist, the patron saint of the Merchant Taylors' Company, and to whom White dedicated the college he later founded. In the meantime he had expanded the scope of his business interests considerably as one of the London merchants responsible for opening up trade with Russia in 1553, and consequently as one of the promoters of the Muscovy Company of merchant adventurers which was granted a royal charter in 1555.

Having served as sheriff in London in 1547, White was elected lord mayor in August 1553, assumed office amid lavish pageantry in October, and was subsequently knighted. He proved a loyal supporter to Queen Mary, both as a financier and in his capacity as lord mayor. In July 1553 he had been one of those who had met the queen at Newhall, presenting her with a gift of 500 half sovereigns to indicate the good will of the corporation of London. During his mayoralty he sat on the commission for the trial of state prisoners—notably including Lady Jane Grey and Thomas Cranmer; he received the Spanish envoys concerned with Mary's marriage treaty; he was instrumental in the suppression of Wyatt's rebellion, both through defending the city from the rebels at Southwark Bridge and subsequently through overseeing the commission for their trial as traitors; and he was in office for the eventual reception of Philip II of Spain. After Wyatt's execution he became caught up in Gardiner's measures to dispel rumours that the council had attempted to implicate Princess Elizabeth in the rebellion, and was summoned before Star Chamber for allowing rumour-mongers in the city to remain unpunished. Further mishap was narrowly averted when a bullet landed next to him while he was listening to a sermon at St Paul's, although this was probably a careless gunman's misadventure rather than an assassination attempt as has been alleged. Finally, his mayoralty was characterized by his efforts to reform the excesses of his fellow citizens

with sumptuary legislation and proclamations against bowling alleys, morris dancing, games, and interludes.

On 26 February 1558 White's first wife, Avicia, was buried in the parish of St Mary Aldermary. Very little is known about her: she was a widow with three children when she married White towards the end of Henry VIII's reign, and it is possible that she was related to the Roper family. On 25 November 1558 he married Joan, widow of Sir Ralph Warren, whose two children White remembered in his will.

Perhaps it was because White never had any children of his own that his benefactions to others were so extensive. The most ambitious of these entailed his foundation of St John's College in Oxford. According to legend his idea to found a college came to him in a dream, which vision directed him to select the former Cistercian college, St Bernard's, as a site. A further source of inspiration may well have been the foundation of Trinity College, Oxford, by his good friend Sir Thomas Pope in March 1554. In May 1555 he obtained a royal licence to found a college comprising a president and thirty scholars. In March 1557 he obtained a new charter, and gave further endowments in this year and again in November 1560. In 1559 he had purchased Gloucester Hall which was intended to house 100 scholars, and in February 1567 he sought to ensure that forty-three scholars would be admitted from London, with preference given to pupils chosen by the master and wardens of the Merchant Taylors'. Despite his bequest of real estate valued at £3634, with his overall outlay estimated at £13,285, the college experienced severe privation in its early years. Suffering diminishing returns from the declining cloth trade, White had been unable to endow the college sufficiently to support his desired quota of scholars, and the college was initially dependent on admitting fee-paying commoners instead of the 'poore Scholars' he had wanted to favour. The stability of the college was further threatened by Elizabeth I's religious policy which resulted in the removal of its first two presidents by 1567 for maintaining papal authority, and the deprivation of twelve fellows between 1567 and 1574. It is likely that White shared their Catholic sympathies up until his death, although this had not precluded his involvement in the establishment of the Merchant Taylors' School (in association with the puritan Richard Hills) in 1561, which had a decidedly reforming emphasis. Troubled by the differences emerging within the fellowship, one of the last letters he wrote to his college exhorted its members to 'love one another as brethren' and to cease strife (Stevenson and Salter, 427).

Thomas White died on 12 February 1567 at his house in Size Lane, London. As requested in his will, he was buried on 24 or 25 February in St John's College chapel, with a funeral oration by Edmund Campion. His intended gifts to St John's and his wife's jointure remained partly unpaid as a result of his dwindling income, leaving the college dependent on the judicious intervention of his executor, Sir William Cordell, and his widow dependent on the good will of the Merchant Taylors' Company for survival. She died on 8 February 1573.

Despite the ultimate disparity between his means and his intentions, White's name has been associated with charity for centuries after his death. He was celebrated as one of London's 'nine worthies' by Richard Johnson in 1592, and characterized as the epitome of benevolence in John Webster's *Monuments of Honour* of 1624. Portraits of him survive in at least seventeen of the cities which benefited from his gifts, although only one (at the Merchant Taylors' in London) was painted in his lifetime. The inscription on a Jacobean portrait at Leicester commemorated him for his 'White name, White gifts, White soul', commending him as a 'White saint in heaven'.

ALEXANDRA SHEPARD

Sources C. M. Clode, *The early history of the Guild of Merchant Taylors of the fraternity of St John the Baptist, London*, 2 (1888) · W. H. Stevenson and H. E. Salter, *The early history of St John's College, Oxford*, OHS, new ser., 1 (1939) · A. Daly Briscoe, 'A Marian lord mayor: Sir Thomas White', *East Anglian Magazine*, 41 (1982) · *Hist. U. Oxf.* 3: *Colleg. univ.* · F. W. M. Draper, *Four centuries of Merchant Taylors' School, 1561–1961* (1962) · W. K. Jordan, *The charities of London, 1480–1660: the aspirations and achievements of the urban society* (1960) · F. F. Foster, *The politics of stability: a portrait of the rulers in Elizabethan London*, Royal Historical Society Studies in History, 1 (1977) · *The diary of Henry Machyn, citizen and merchant-taylor of London, from AD 1550 to AD 1563*, ed. J. G. Nichols, CS, 42 (1848) · R. Johnson, *The nine worthies of London* (1592) · J. Webster, *The monuments of honour* (1624) · T. Fuller, *The worthies of England*, ed. J. Freeman, abridged edn (1952), 236 · J. Stow, *A survay of London*, rev. edn (1603); repr. with introduction by C. L. Kingsford as *A survey of London*, 2 vols. (1908); repr. with addns (1971) · J. Knowles, 'The spectacle of the realm: civic consciousness, rhetoric, and ritual in early modern London', *Theatre and government under the early Stuarts*, ed. J. R. Mulryne and M. Shewring (1993) · R. Tittler, 'Sir Thomas White of London: civic philanthropy and the making of the merchant-hero', *Townspeople and nation: English urban experiences, 1540–1640* (2001)
Archives St John's College, Oxford, papers | Coventry Archives, letters to mayor and justices of Coventry
Likenesses J. Faber senior, mezzotint, 1712, BM, NPG · statue, *c.*1874, Merchant Taylors' School · bust, St John's College, Oxford · portrait, Merchant Taylors' Company, London; version, St John's College, Oxford · portraits, Merchant Taylors' Company, London · statue, clock tower, Leicester
Wealth at death left real estate worth £3634: Clode, *The early history of the Guild*, 2.194; Stevenson and Salter, *The early history*

White, Thomas (1550–1624), benefactor of Sion College, London, was born in the parish of Temple, Bristol, the son of John White, a merchant of that city. It has often been asserted that he was descended from the Whites of Eaton Socon, Bedfordshire. He attended Oxford University and graduated BA from Magdalen Hall on 25 June 1570, MA on 1 July 1573. Shortly afterwards, on 23 November 1575, he was appointed vicar of St Dunstan-in-the-West, London, where his preaching was well received. He appears to have been associated with St Paul's School, attending its yearly 'apposition' as an examiner in February 1577. On 3 November 1577 at Paul's Cross, during a visitation of the plague, White preached against usury and covetousness, especially such excessive indulgence as the use of down beds and the payment of cooks to produce elaborate meals. The plague, he declared, was a judgment: 'London builds apace, beware of blood and iniquity … God shall reckon with you in his rage and give you a taste of his anger, as an earnest penny in this life, of everlasting pains in the life to come' (White, *A Sermon Preached at Pawles Crosse on Sunday the thirde of November, 1577*, 1578, 56–7).

White received the degree of BTh on 11 December 1581 and proceeded to the doctorate on 8 March 1585; briefly, between 1588 and 1591, he acted as vicar of St Gregory by Paul. A sermon given in this period, just after the defeat of the Armada, shows how his zealous patriotic protestantism could lead to criticism, even of the queen's government: 'Our gracious sovereign did suffer long, and too long, almost before she took the sword in hand, and stood to her defence in the cause of the gospel' (White, *A Sermon Preached at Pawles Crosse the 17 of November, 1589*, 1589, 59). But the conflict came anyway: 'hold you not your peace, but tell it in Spain, and in the islands there about … that as Elizabeth of England lived by the Grace of God … He that is mighty hath magnified her, and holy is his name' (ibid., 62).

White married twice, but of his first wife only her family name, Fortune, is known. His second wife, Elizabeth, daughter of William Bovey, a barber–surgeon and citizen of London, died before her husband. Both women were buried in the chancel of St Dunstan's. There were no surviving children. White must not be confused with Thomas White (d. 1588), warden of New College, Oxford, from 1553 to 1573, archdeacon of Berkshire from 1557 to 1588, and chancellor of Salisbury Cathedral from 1571 to 1588—especially since Thomas White of Bristol also attained high position in the dioceses of Salisbury and Oxford. On 21 April 1590 White was instituted by Archbishop Whitgift to the treasurership of Salisbury (with its annexed prebend of Calne). On 26 April 1587 he was awarded by the queen presentation to the next vacant canonry in Oxford diocese; he was installed in 1592 as canon of the eighth prebend.

White's many and lucrative benefices and his later status as a single and childless man combined to make him a wealthy individual. Already in 1613 he had built a hospital in his native Temple parish in Bristol and endowed it with £92 per annum. At his death his circumstances made possible generous provision for several causes. His will, drawn up and signed on 20 February 1623, provided for five exhibitions of £8 per year to scholars of Magdalen Hall, and £4 to the principal, to be paid from the revenues of the manor of Langdon Hills in Essex. White provided for a lectureship at St Paul's in London, bequeathed his folio and Latin books to St George's Chapel, Windsor, and donated to the city of Bristol money for the improvement of roads and other municipal purposes. His will is also of interest for the light it throws on White's attitudes to crime. He financed a yearly lecture for:

> the poor prisoners of Newgate [who] may be manacled and sparred in iron chains hand to hand, men by themselves and women by themselves in long iron chains made for that purpose and so by some of their under officers to be brought there the lower way next Newgate … their sight for example to the people and youth their shame to be seen … And for their chains of iron and one docket to be made I give forty pounds.

He states that concerning their execution:

I would have two ancient honest women to be chosen yearly by the sheriffs of London who together with the executioner only shall strip their body to the end their shame may be covered with such sorry linen as they have ... to hide from the people their secrets ... for it is a sin and a shame for the multitude to stand at such times to feed their eyes with such woeful sights and this will breed remorse in others to leave thieving. (Sampson, 20–22)

White also founded a professorship of moral philosophy at Oxford, with a stipend of £100 per annum to be paid to the university from the revenues of his manor of Langdon Hills. The lectures thus inaugurated were to be aimed chiefly at undergraduates. In providing for the new foundation, White had offered little guidance as to the content of the course to be offered; accordingly, despite Laudian attempts to impose the teaching of Aristotle, many professors gave sermons, which did little for the reputation of the lecture.

Much the largest of White's bequests was the £3000 which he provided for Sion College and for an almshouse, to be built close by. White was clearly very anxious that his college should be under the firm control of the bishop of London, and provided for a governing body which included two deans and four assistants under the bishop's presidency. It was on this basis that on 7 March 1626 Sion College received its original charter. Ironically, however, 'Someone at court, possibly Laud himself ... seems to have objected that it was derogatory to the Bishop's prestige that he should sit as even the perpetual primus of co-equal presbyters' (Huelin, 63). It appears that this was so unthinkable that the charter was revised to provide for the president's election from the fellows; the bishop would act as visitor. The amended charter was given the royal assent on 6 July 1626, and the college was built on a site acquired in April 1627 at the junction of Aldermanbury, London Wall, and Philip Lane. Its fine library attained a wide reputation.

White died on 1 March 1624 and was buried in the chancel of St Dunstan-in-the-West. His funeral sermon was given by William Price, first reader of the lecture in moral philosophy. The text, to which other academics added verses, was published in *Schola moralis philosophiae Oxon in funere Whiti* (1624). A portrait of White, for long in the possession of the Bristol almshouse, was copied and sent in May 1832 to Sion College in London; in 1957 this portrait was restored and hung in the college dining hall.

STEPHEN WRIGHT

Sources W. Sampson, *The life of the Rev Thomas White, DD* (1912) · E. Pearce, *Sion College and library* (1913) · G. Huelin, *Sion College and library, 1912–1990* (1992) · G. Hennessy, *Novum repertorium ecclesiasticum parochiale Londinense, or, London diocesan clergy succession from the earliest time to the year 1898* (1898) · *Fasti Angl., 1541–1857*, [Salisbury] · *Fasti Angl., 1541–1857*, [Bristol] · M. MacLure, *The Paul's Cross sermons, 1534–1642* (1958) · *Hist. U. Oxf.* 4: 17th-cent. Oxf. · M. McDonnell, *The annals of St Paul's School* (privately printed, Cambridge, 1959) · W. H. Jones, *Fasti ecclesiae Sarisberiensis, or, A calendar ... of the cathedral body at Salisbury* (1879) · Wood, *Ath. Oxon.* · will, PRO, PROB 11/143, sig. 22

Likenesses oils, Sion College, London; version, Bodl. Oxf.

Wealth at death approx. £5000, incl. £3000 to Sion College: Sampson, *Life of Rev Thomas White*

White, Thomas (1576x8–1606x11), separatist leader, may have been the Londoner who matriculated from St John's College, Oxford, on 16 April 1594, aged seventeen, graduated BA on 21 October 1596, and proceeded MA on 2 June 1600. Circumstantial evidence in his later life links this man to the curate at Slaughterford, Wiltshire, on a clergy list dated 21 January 1602. About March 1603 White 'left the publique profession of his ministery' and began holding conventicles (examination of William Hore, Wilts. & Swindon RO). White and his adherents believed that the Church of England's episcopacy, ministry, worship, and congregations were anti-Christian, and they soon moved toward communion with the separatist 'church in the west parts of England', apparently a loose association of groups and individuals primarily drawn from the eastern border of Somerset and western boundaries of Gloucestershire and Wiltshire (Johnson, 'To the Christian reader'). These people professed the same faith as Francis Johnson's 'Ancient' separatist church of Amsterdam, and there were substantial ties between the two groups. In fact 'one Johnson', who was 'lately come over from Amsterdame', preached before White's group, probably in late 1603 or early 1604 (examination of William Hore, Wilts. & Swindon RO).

Also during this time White and Thomas Powell, a licensed preacher, engaged in heated controversies with the Wiltshire clergy, including John Awdley, vicar of Melksham, and John Jessop, rector of Manningford Bruce. Participants debated several issues, such as the scriptural validity of non-preaching clergymen as true ministers of Christ and the proper interpretation of Matthew 18: 17 as it related to excommunication. According to White, when Awdley could not prevail in disputation he procured a warrant for Powell's arrest. Powell then openly declared his conversion to separatism and joined the church on 26 February 1604 NS. Fearing arrest, White, Powell, and twelve or thirteen others fled to Amsterdam, where they sought refuge with the Ancient church. White lived with Johnson for nine or ten weeks, and his brethren participated in the church's services. On 10 April 1604, when he stated that he was aged twenty-six, White married Rose Philips (*née* Grempre) of London, a member of the Ancient church.

Differences between White's and Johnson's congregations soon developed, and White's group left to form its own church. However, Rose, who had borne a child, maintained her former membership. She was soon in a difficult position because White forbade her to let the Johnsonians baptize the baby. Consequently, the Ancient church disciplined her. Later she was also cited for committing 'apostasy' by permitting White to entertain the Ancient church's excommunicated elder Matthew Slade in their home. Ultimately she was excommunicated.

Disillusioned with separatism, White travelled to England, where he made his peace with the established church. With the authorities' approval he published *A Discoverie of Brownisme* (1605). This short work was filled with examples of supposed 'debate, malice, adulteries, cousonages and such other like enormities', as well as 'abhominations and unfruitefull workes of darknes' (T. White, 1, 2). In a letter White alleged that 'There is no Sect in Amsterdam (though manie) in such contempt for filthie life' (Lawne and others, 27). Johnson and his followers responded with a lawsuit accusing both Whites of slander. In late 1605 or early 1606 White returned to Amsterdam and appeared before the city magistrates, who were trying the case. According to a partisan account the Johnsonians were absent and the Whites won by default. Municipal records showed that White was discharged on 24 February 1606 NS and his wife was released the next day.

Johnson did not remain silent. He published *An Inquirie and Answer of Thomas White* (1606), in which he claimed that the Ancient church was a true visible church of Christ and that any errors of individual members could not be imputed to the whole congregation. Then he refuted White's accusations point by point, denying, explaining, and qualifying each charge as he thought appropriate. That year White went to the city of Brielle, where he preached. Slade and others, who were organizing the Dutch-affiliated English Reformed church of Amsterdam, considered White as a possible pastoral candidate; but John Paget was chosen. Later that year White moved to London. There he reportedly received a benefice and died some time before 1612. If the report is true, then he was almost certainly the St John's man who was presented by James I to the rectory of St Mary Woolnoth in the city on 14 November 1609. The rector died in 1611 and was buried in his church on 20 November.   MICHAEL E. MOODY

Sources T. White, *A discoverie of Brownisme* (1605) · F. Johnson, *An inquirie and answer of Thomas White* (1606) · C. Lawne and others, *Prophane schisme of the Brownists* (1612), 26–29 · examinations of W. Hore, S. Butler and J. Harford, 6 March 1604, Wilts. & Swindon RO, Wiltshire quarter session great rolls, Easter 1604, A1/110, fol. 148r–v · 'Liber curiarum', May 1601–March 1605, Wilts. & Swindon RO, archdeaconry of Wiltshire act books, D3/4/1 fol. 46v · H. Cotton, bishop's register, 1598–1615, Wilts. & Swindon RO, D1/2/19, fols. 1v, 8r · J. Scheffer, *History of the free churchmen*, ed. W. Griffis [1922], 187 · R. Clyfton, *Advertisement* (1612), 16 · K. Sprunger, *Dutch puritanism* (1981), 62–3, 70, 92 · M. Reeves, 'Protestant nonconformity', *VCH Wiltshire*, 3.99–100 · C. Burrage, *Early English dissenters*, 2 vols. (1912), 1.185–7 · B. White, *The English separatist tradition* (1971), 106–7 · M. Ingram, *Church courts, sex and marriage in England, 1570–1640* (1987), 91 · Foster, *Alum. Oxon.* · G. Hennessy, *Novum repertorium ecclesiasticum parochiale Londinense, or, London diocesan clergy succession from the earliest time to the year 1898* (1898), 315

White [alias Blacklo], **Thomas** (1592/3–1676), Roman Catholic priest and philosopher, was born into a landowning recusant family as the second son of Richard White (*d.* 1634) of Hutton, Essex, and Mary, daughter of the eminent Elizabethan lawyer Edmund *Plowden. His sister Mary married Phillip Waldegrave of Borley, and his elder brother Richard became a proficient mathematician and a fellow of the Royal Society. One younger brother, Jerome, became a Catholic priest; the other, William, left few traces other than a will in which he distanced himself from Thomas's political views. A lifelong Catholic who never saw any reason to renounce 'the religion of our

THOMAS ALBIUS Anglus.
Natus Anno 1588. Obijt 1680. Ætatis suæ 92.
Ascendit ex adverso, opposuit murum pro Domo Israel, et stetit in prælio in Die Domini. Ezech. cap. 13. ver 5.

Thomas White [Blacklo] (1592/3–1676), by George Vertue, 1713

birth and education' (T. White, *Apology for Rushworth's 'Dialogues'*, 1654, 117), White became a secular priest, notorious as leader of the Blackloist faction or cabal of the English chapter, as well as 'a most noted philosopher of his time' (Wood, *Ath. Oxon.*, 3.1247). Author of some forty works on theology, politics, and natural philosophy, he achieved the rare distinction of incurring suspicion and disapproval both from his own church, which consigned all his writings to the Index, and from the English parliament, which suspected him (together with Hobbes) of tending 'to Atheism, Blasphemy, or Profaneness' (Southgate, 32). An engraving by Vertue indicates that White was a serious man with a commanding and possibly pugnacious presence, and an eighteenth-century biographical sketch describes him as being of unblemished morals and 'of a middle size; agreeable in conversation, unbyassed in the controversies of life; and affecting a freedom of opinion, which seldom happens without danger' (Dodd, 3.285). This last comment understates the extent to which White was constantly embroiled in controversies: his personal and published writings reveal a man whose greatest pleasure lay in vigorous debates with friends and enemies.

White's Catholic education and career necessitated extensive European travels and also involved contacts with a succession of continental English colleges. His recusant credentials having been established with a brief incarceration for his faith aged ten, he reached the Jesuit college at St Omer in the Spanish Netherlands by autumn 1605; after graduating in humanities he proceeded in autumn 1609 to Valladolid, Spain, aged sixteen, and then in 1612 to Seville. In August 1614 he went on via Madrid to Flanders, and he completed his theology course at Louvain before arriving at the mother English College at Douai in July 1616. White was ordained as priest at Arras in 1617 and took his degree one year later at Douai. He continued to teach philosophy and theology at Douai until 1623, the year in which he retrieved from England a rib of the recently martyred Thomas Maxfield to serve as a sacred relic at the college. His long-standing, though intermittent, association with Douai was later marked by his appointment as vice-president of the college there in 1650. Meanwhile, in 1625 White was sent as official Catholic agent to Rome, where for four years he maintained lines of communication between the beleaguered English clergy and the pope. In 1630 he reluctantly became the second president of the English College at Lisbon, Portugal, where he established a traditional scholastic curriculum, but, having failed to recruit appropriate theology students from England, he resigned in 1633. That year his name was submitted to Rome as a possible bishop, and ten years later he was proposed as vicar-general. By the early 1640s, however, he was established in Paris as a respected member of the Mersenne circle, and in that cosmopolitan environment he published two major works of natural philosophy: *De mundo* (1642) and *Institutiones peripateticae* (1646) (translated as *Peripateticall Institutions*, 1657) which shows reciprocal influences with his friend Kenelm Digby's *Two Treatises* (1644). These essentially synthesizing works incorporated ideas from the current new philosophy within a traditional Aristotelian framework, and with his remarkable accommodation of Copernican heliocentric cosmology and newly revived atomic theory, White was later identified by Leibniz as one who had contrived to 'reconcile Aristotle with modern philosophy' (Southgate, 9). Favourable assessments of *De mundo* were made by contemporaries including Descartes, and a lengthy critique by Thomas Hobbes, rediscovered and published in 1976, did much to restore interest in White himself.

During the later 1640s and early 1650s there is evidence for White's presence in London, Lyons, Rome, Douai, various parts of Holland, and Paris, where he was described by John Evelyn as 'a learned priest and famous philosopher' (Southgate, 7). In London again by 1655, he became established as leader of the Blackloist group of Catholic chaptermen, including Kenelm Digby, Henry Holden, Peter Fitton, and John Sergeant. Notorious for their willingness to sacrifice Jesuits and any papal temporal powers in return for religious toleration, these 'Papists of the new Modell' (M. Poole, *Nullity of the Romish Faith*, 1666, 39), denied papal infallibility and repudiated conventional and lucrative beliefs about purgatory. Unsurprisingly, White's doctrines, as expressed in such theological works as *De medio animarum statu* (1653; translated as *The Middle State of Souls*), were held in Rome 'in so great a detestation

… that neither that of Luther or Calvin was ever in a greater' (Westminster Diocesan Archives, Old Brotherhood archives, 2.67). Nevertheless, the Blackloists continued to dominate the English chapter for many years: White's disciple John Sergeant was installed as secretary from 1655 until he was ousted in 1667 by Rome's replacement, John Leyburn.

Approached for political advice after Cromwell's assumption of power, White published *The Grounds of Obedience and Government* (1655). Supposedly a theoretical treatise, this had obvious practical implications at the time: with its provocatively emblazoned republican motto of 'salus populi' and its evident recommendation to accept Cromwell's *de facto* position, the book was widely regarded as anti-monarchical, and after the Restoration White was repudiated by protestants and Catholics alike. Under attack from all quarters, he was induced to defend himself in an extensive 'Apology', which survives in manuscript (Westminster Diocesan Archives, Old Brotherhood archives, 2.130), but nothing could save him from contemporary distancing or from subsequent historical neglect.

White's extraordinary intellectual energy in later life is indicated also by his attention to other aspects of philosophy and theology. During the 1650s he enjoyed contacts with men who were to become founding fellows of the Royal Society. Centred on the puritan reformer John Hall, this group included John Wallis, Seth Ward, John Wilkins, Lord Brouncker, Ralph Bathurst, Isaac Barrow, and Pierre Fermat. White acted as a linkman to whom they professed themselves deeply indebted. Stimulated by such company, he published further scientific and mathematical works, including *Euclides physicus* (1657), claimed as an influence on Leibniz, and *Exercitatio geometrica* (1658), in which he fails in attempts to square the circle. Theological works include *Apology for Rushworth's 'Dialogues'*, in which he clarifies his detestation of sceptical uncertainty and affirms oral tradition as the ground of Catholic faith; and *Religion and Reason* (1660) and *Devotion and Reason* (1661), where he reiterates his lifelong belief in the compatibility of Christianity with the rationality of science.

White's work in London was interrupted by the imminent restoration of the monarchy. With his life at risk as a result of his political notoriety, he withdrew to Holland in 1659, explaining later that he had heard 'that his majesty's settled resolution was to hang mee if I came into England' (Westminster Diocesan Archives, Old Brotherhood archives, 2.130). Far from lying low, however, he released further theological broadsides. *Monumetham excantatus* and *Statera morum* (1660), which contained arguments that even the greatest sinners might be redeemed, provoked a moral outcry even from friends. His longstanding enemy George Leyburn described him at this time as a 'wicked old man … known sufficiently and more than that to the Pope and the whole Roman court' (Burton and Williams, 2.547), a view confirmed by official condemnations in 1655, 1657, 1661, and 1663. Indeed, it was agreed by friends and enemies that White might well have encountered even more opposition had not his convoluted style prevented ready comprehension. By 1662 White was back in London, where he published in 1663 a critique of Torricelli's work on the vacuum, and entered a significant debate on scepticism with Joseph Glanvill. The younger man's promotion (in his *Vanity of Dogmatizing*, 1661) of the fashionable Pyrrhonian philosophy provoked White's *Sciri, sive, Scepticis* (1663; translated as *An Exclusion of Scepticks* (1665), where he insisted on the possibility of humans attaining absolutely certain truth; their continuing debate highlighted essential incompatibilities between their respectively 'modern' and 'ancient' positions. Until his own death in Drury Lane on 6 July 1676 White persisted, too, in heated philosophical debates with Thomas Hobbes. White was buried on 8 July in the old St Martin-in-the-Fields, and his will confirms earlier claims that he never had social aspirations or saved money: he left £10, together with any 'wearing apparel and other goods in their house at my death', to John and Mary Gregson, with whom he had been lodging in Drury Lane, 'for the care they have had of me while I lived with them' (Berks. RO, Barrett/Belson MS Q26/2). The residue consisted of arrears from an annuity bequeathed by Kenelm Digby: that was to be held in trust for John Sergeant, who would keep Blackloism alive until his own death in 1707.   BEVERLEY SOUTHGATE

Sources B. C. Southgate, *'Covetous of truth': the life and work of Thomas White, 1593–1676* (1993) · G. Anstruther, *The seminary priests*, 2 (1975) · C. Dodd [H. Tootell], *The church history of England, from the year 1500, to the year 1688*, 3 (1742) · E. H. Burton and T. L. Williams, eds., *The Douay College diaries, third, fourth and fifth, 1598–1654*, 1–2, Catholic RS, 10–11 (1911) · Westm. DA, vols. 19–34 · Westm. DA, Old Brotherhood archives, vol. 2 · Berks. RO, Barrett/Belson MSS · Wood, *Ath. Oxon.*, new edn, vol. 3 · R. Pugh, *Blacklo's cabal* (1680) · J. Wallis, *Commercium epistolicum* (1658) · T. White, *Muscarium ad immissos* (1661) · E. Henson, ed., *The registers of the English College at Valladolid, 1589–1862*, Catholic RS, 30 (1930) · T. Hobbes, *Thomas White's 'De mundo' examined*, ed. H. W. Jones (1976)
Archives Bodl. Oxf., letters and papers | Berks. RO, Barrett/Belson MSS · Westm. DA, Old Brotherhood archives · Westm. DA, Westminster archives
Likenesses G. Vertue, line engraving, 1713, BM, NPG [*see illus.*]
Wealth at death £10 plus wearing apparel and other goods; possible arrears of £60 from annuity of about £300: will and codicil, 26 June 1676, Berks. RO, Barrett/Belson MSS, Q 26/2, Q 26/3

White, Thomas (1628–1698), bishop of Peterborough and nonjuror, was born at Allington, Kent, the son of Peter White, who died shortly after Thomas's birth. Records of his university career record the family as of 'plebeian' rank; his mother may have been a kinswoman of a local gentry family, the Brockmans of Beachborough, and may have gone to live with them after her husband's death. White was educated for three years at Wye School under the mastership of Mr Surety-on-high (or Suretonhie) Nicholls. He was then admitted sizar at St John's College, Cambridge, at the age of fourteen, on 29 October 1642, graduating BA in 1647. His life during the interregnum remains obscure. Despite the confusion caused by so common a name, it is clear that he was neither the lecturer of St Andrew's, Holborn, who wrote an account of the conversion of a Muslim in 1658 (*d.* 1672), nor the rector of St

Thomas White (1628–1698), by unknown artist, 1685–91

Mary-at-Hill, London (*d.* 1682), who both shared his name. However, he appears for certain at the Restoration, when his successful petition of 6 July 1660 to the king for presentation to the vicarage of Newark-on-Trent, occupied by an 'intruder', won the support of no less a person than Gilbert Sheldon. He held the Newark living until 1666, when he assumed the rectorship of All-Hallows-at-Fenn, London, which he kept until 1679, when he took up the rectory of Bottesford in Leicestershire, which he held until 1685; he also became rector of Stepney in 1681.

The elevation of White's career profile from the parochial to the diocesan level was signalled with his promotion as archdeacon of Nottingham (1683–5). In the year that he took up the archdeaconry, and typifying his closeness to the high tory reversionary interest around James, duke of York, he was created DD of Oxford on 4 June 1683—even though he was primarily a preacher—a 'very eloquent' one, according to Evelyn (*Diary of John Evelyn*, 383)—and a diocesan administrator rather than a scholar. However, White was chaplain to York's protestant daughter, the Lady Anne, and the conferment, fully supported by the tory grandee Ormond, took place amid a triumphalist tour of the York family to tory Oxford. White's next move upwards was made when the tory cast of ecclesiastical and episcopal appointments devised as a deliberate strategy during the tory reaction was continued and capped by his consecration as bishop of Peterborough on 25 October 1685. Typifying his energy and reformist drive, in 1686 he carried out for Archbishop Sancroft a metropolitical visitation of the Lincoln diocese belonging to the allegedly negligent Bishop Thomas Barlow, finding the clergy of that diocese immoral and negligent and the lay linchpins of the parochial system, the churchwardens, 'hardened in their foolish obstinacy' (Spurr, 193).

Dedicated churchman and committed tory royalist as he was, White was soon to be confronted with the fatal dilemma presented to such as him by James's adoption, markedly from 1687, of toleration: he 'could not but remember how vehemently the King had declared against toleration and said he would never by any counsel be tempted to suffer it' (Western, 186–7); he took particular umbrage at the threat to the church from indulgence to the dissenters, for he saw little danger from 'popery' (ibid., 230) and had, indeed, taken part in the administration of the London diocese of Bishop Henry Compton, suspended in 1686 for his refusal to suppress Catholic preaching in the city. It was James II's second declaration of indulgence, offering civil and religious rights to non-Anglicans, but required to be read from the pulpits of the very Church of England whose specially protected status it endangered, that impelled White to lead other prominent Anglican malcontents—and above all those of the high tory Yorkist grouping around Sancroft—in resistance to the declaration, beginning with a meeting of leading clerics at the Temple in London on 12 May 1688. White's prominence in the campaign was flanked by the role of Bishop Francis Turner of Ely who, with White, was co-ordinating information between 12 and 18 May on the overwhelming clerical refusals of the reading order and also of rejection of it by nonconformist chiefs; he was also supported by the enthusiasm for the resistance of his dean at Peterborough, Simon Patrick, who, on 17 May, drew up a list of ministers who would not read the declaration, which schedule White took to Sancroft. The following day the recalcitrants drew up a final version of a petition to the king and, in the evening, the seven episcopal leaders of opposition took it to James, who was astonished at the disobedience of his commands by the Anglican clerics whose protestations of total obedience to royal authority he had taken at face value.

On 27 May in a summons to appear before the king in council the names of White and Turner, along with that of Sancroft, were highlighted among those of the other presenters of the offending petition. The examination was followed by imprisonment in the Tower on 8 June and trial on a charge of seditious libel on 29 June, leading to acquittal on the 30th.

On 24 September, in what was, no doubt, an attempt at a placatory strategy on James's part, White, with Sancroft and seven other bishops, was invited by the earl of Sunderland to confer with the king. Following Orange's landing he and William Lloyd (1627–1717) of St Asaph were involved with the tory politicians Rochester and Clarendon in plans to petition the king for a parliament intended to prevent bloodshed, and on 17 November White signed such a petition; remaining at the central steerage of events, he was one of a small group who managed—initially, at least—to persuade Sancroft to join a meeting of peers held in London so as to manage the situation in December 1688, and in January of the new year he was at the archbishop's in discussion of 'the present state of the

publique' (*Diary of John Evelyn*, 896). He is said, somewhat improbably, to have authored—but certainly did not take—the new oath of allegiance to William and Mary, yet despite his refusal he continued to be allowed early in the new year to speak in committees of the Lords. In March his political campaign in defence of the interest of his church took a new tack when he promoted comprehension of protestants within a broad national establishment of religion. However, his status as a leading nonjuror resulted in his displacement from his episcopate, which Evelyn reported on 16 April 1691.

In the remainder of the 1690s White played a part in the attempted creation of a nonjuror Church of England, hosting a consecration of a new nonjuring bishop (nominated by the exiled James II) in February 1694. He was also rumoured to have composed a statement made by the Jacobite conspirator Fenwick protesting his loyalty to James along with his refusal to countenance violence against William. Following White's death in London on 29 May 1698 his funeral and burial at St Paul's on 4 June provided an opportunity for nonjuring Anglicans to commemorate a martyr both to divine right principles and to defence of the church against a king. He was a generous benefactor of Newark and of the poor of Peterborough.

MICHAEL MULLETT

Sources Venn, *Alum. Cant.* · Foster, *Alum. Oxon.* · Wood, *Ath. Oxon.*: *Fasti*, new edn · G. V. Bennett, 'The seven bishops: a reconsideration', *Religious motivation: biographical and sociological problems for the church historian*, ed. D. Baker, SCH, 15 (1978), 267–87 · *The diary of John Evelyn*, ed. E. S. De Beer (1959) · J. R. Western, *Monarchy and revolution: the English state in the 1680s* (1972) · J. Spurr, *The Restoration Church of England, 1646–1689* (1991) · *Bishop Burnet's History*, vol. 4 · R. Thomas, 'The seven bishops and their petition, 18 May 1688', *Journal of Ecclesiastical History*, 12 (1961), 56–70 · N. Sykes, *From Sheldon to Secker: aspects of English church history, 1660–1768* (1959) · *CSP dom.*, 1660–61; 1685–8 · Wing, *STC* · G. V. Bennett, *The tory crisis in church and state: the career of Francis Atterbury, bishop of Rochester* (1975) · R. A. Beddard, 'Tory Oxford', *Hist. U. Oxf.* 4: *17th-cent. Oxf.*, 863–906 · J. E. B. Mayor, ed., *Admissions to the College of St John the Evangelist in the University of Cambridge*, 1: *Jan 1629/30 – July 1665* (1882) · *Calendar of the correspondence of Richard Baxter*, ed. N. H. Keeble and G. F. Nuttall, 1 (1991), 101 · *DNB*

Archives BM, letters to Lord Hatton

Likenesses oils, 1685–91, Bishop's Palace, Peterborough [*see illus.*] · G. Bower, silver medal, 1688, NPG · group portrait, oils (*The seven bishops committed to the Tower in 1688*), NPG · oils, Magd. Oxf.

Wealth at death over £280: *DNB*

White, Thomas (*d.* 1813), astrologer, was the author of *The Beauties of Occult Science Investigated, or, The Celestial Intelligencer* (1810), published in London and Bath, where he may have lived. Little else is known of his life. One of the relatively rare textbooks of astrology published in this period, *The Beauties* was reprinted in 1811. *A Set of Astronomical Tables* for 1780–83 also appeared, in 1811. The title of White's main work assumes that judicial astrology is the essence of occult science. Although strongly criticized by one of the few other astrologers then in print, John Worsdale, it was a reasonably comprehensive introduction to that subject which, together with an ephemeris, would have enabled its practice. It shows signs of the continuing ascendancy of natural philosophy, defining astrology as 'the effects derived from the amazing powers of mutual attraction of the different parts and masses (great or small) of matter' (White, 9).

White is chiefly remembered, however, for his end. In 1813 he was living and working as an astrologer in the Isle of Wight. He was approached by a police informer posing as a client, who asked for and received a reading of his nativity, and paid with marked money. White was then arrested and charged under the Vagrancy Act for 'pretending and professing to tell Fortunes'. He was convicted, and his books and papers seized. He died in 1813 after three months in Winchester gaol. This use of the act against non-vagrant astrologers alarmed many of them. It seems to have set a precedent, and such prosecutions continued sporadically until 1917; the clause was quietly repealed after examination by parliamentary committee in 1989.

PATRICK CURRY

Sources T. White, *The beauties of occult science investigated, or, The celestial intelligencer* (1810) · C. Cooke, *Curiosities of occult literature* (1863), 19 · *Zadkiel's almanac* (1853), 57–8

White, Thomas (1830–1888), journalist and politician in Canada, was born in Montreal on 7 August 1830, the son of Thomas White, a leather merchant, and Dorothea Smeaton. His father came from co. Westmeath in 1826, his mother from Edinburgh. He was educated at Montreal high school, began his working life in his father's business, and ended up in journalism, joining the staff of the official *Quebec Gazette* in 1852. In 1853 he married Esther Vine, of Quebec City; they had seven daughters and three sons. That same year the couple moved to Peterborough, Canada West, where, with his brother Richard, White conducted the *Peterborough Review*. After studying law for four years he returned to journalism in 1864, and with his brother took over the Hamilton *Spectator*, founded eighteen years before. In 1870 they bought control of the Montreal *Gazette*, the leading Conservative newspaper in Canada. Well-written and vigorous, it became the basis of White's growing importance in the ranks of the Conservative Party. An example of the *Gazette's* style is its comment on Edward Blake (17 April 1880), just before Blake became leader of the Liberal Party: 'Mr Blake differs with everybody but Mr Blake and he does not always agree with him'.

In January 1874 White stood for an Ontario seat in the Canadian House of Commons but was defeated by six votes; the same ill luck dogged him in two Quebec by-elections in 1874 and 1875, but finally in 1878 he was elected for Cardwell, an Ontario constituency. The Conservative government of Sir John A. Macdonald had made a mess of the administration of the north-west, which led to the north-west rebellion of 1885; after it was over White was appointed minister of the interior to tidy things up.

White was remarkable. The pity is he had not been given the portfolio years before. He worked like a Trojan to understand and to remedy. One western MP said, 'We trusted him, for he had no purpose to serve save that of the country'. That could well be his epitaph. After three strenuous years of work and travel across the Canadian west, he succumbed to pneumonia in Ottawa on 21 April 1888. His death stunned parliament. He had been like a son to Sir John Macdonald. Sara Jeanette Duncan said in the Toronto *Week* (26 April 1888), 'men turn over the memories of his kindly deeds, his painstaking service, his upright behaviour …'. There are upright men in politics. Thomas White was one. P. B. WAITE

Sources P. B. Waite, 'White, Thomas', *DCB*, vol. 11 · NA Canada, Sir John A. Macdonald collection, political papers, MG26-A, vol. 296 · files of Montreal *Gazette*, NA Canada · *Hansard 3* (1888) **Archives** NA Canada, Macdonald MSS

White, Thomas Holt [T. H. W.] (1724–1797), naturalist and literary critic, was born Thomas White at Compton, Surrey, on 13 October 1724, the second son of John White (1688–1758), barrister, and Anne Holt (1693–1739). He was one of seven brothers and four sisters, the best-known of the brothers being the naturalist Gilbert *White (1720–1793). He received his education at the hands of James Hampton the elder, at Bishop's Waltham, Hampshire, and then entered into business with William Yalden, a wholesale merchant. By 1753 he was a member of the Society of Apothecaries, London. Following the death of Yalden, he married Yalden's childless widow, Mary, *née* Leach (d. 1763), in 1758. They had three children: a daughter, Mary, was born in December 1759, and twin sons, Thomas and Henry, in October 1763, but his wife died a fortnight later.

In 1776 White came into full possession of a large estate bequeathed to him by Thomas Holt, his maternal great-uncle. He added Holt to his name, retired soon after from his business, moved to South Lambeth, Surrey, and devoted himself to gardening and scholarship. He was elected fellow of the Royal Society in 1777 and, with his brother-in-law Thomas Parker, he contributed a number of papers to the society's *Proceedings* on the subject of Parker's annual register of rain, barometric pressure, and temperature in Rutland in the years 1779–95. In 1784 he engaged in a polite controversy concerning trees with Thomas Martyn, exchanging seven letters with him in the pages of the *Gentleman's Magazine*. Between 1768 and 1790 Holt White wrote a total of sixty-five letters, signed T. H. W., that were published in the *Gentleman's Magazine*. Among these were sixteen letters on the trees of England; remarks on Shakespeare, Milton, Virgil, Drayton, Prior, Thomas Warton, 'Pierce Plowman', and Samuel Johnson's life of Milton; and contributions on a variety of aspects of natural history. He also contributed a number of notes to various editions of Shakespeare; namely, Edmond Malone's *Supplement to the Edition of Shakespeare's Plays Published in 1778* (1780), the Johnson–Steevens edition of 1785, and George Steevens's edition of 1793. John Nichols, in his *Literary Anecdotes of the Eighteenth Century* (1812–15), attributed the edition of a reprint of John Evelyn's *Fumifugium* to Holt White. He read some proofs for Gilbert White's *Natural History of Selborne*, published by their brother Benjamin *White (c.1725–1794). Holt White reviewed this work, which he had encouraged his brother to publish, in a two-part review in the *Gentleman's Magazine* for January and February 1789.

Holt White was of considerable assistance to William Curtis (1746–1799) in the latter's endeavours to establish a botanic garden and in the preparation of his *Catalogue of the British, medicinal, culinary and agricultural plants cultivated in the London botanic garden* (1783) and his *Flora Londinensis* (1787). Curtis thanked Holt White and the naturalist Daines Barrington for 'the generosity and public spirit' to which 'the garden in great degree owes its existence' (*GM*, 69/2, 1799, 636). According to an appendix to Curtis's *Practical Observations on the British Grasses* (1790), Holt White had procured from Hampshire and Sussex specimens of turf to be planted in the garden.

Holt White died on 12 February 1797 and was buried at Harlow, Essex. He should be remembered not simply as Gilbert White's 'Brother Thomas' but as a naturalist in his own right, and as a scholar and literary critic.

ARTHUR SHERBO

Sources *GM*, 1st ser., 38–60 (1768–90) · *PTRS*, 69–[85] (1779–95) · R. Holt-White, *The life and letters of Gilbert White of Selborne*, 2 vols. (1901) · *The letters to Gilbert White of Selborne from … John Mulso*, ed. R. Holt-White [1907] · *DNB* · A. Sherbo, 'Thomas Holt White, retired ironmonger', *Shakespeare's midwives: some neglected Shakespearians* (1992) · A. Sherbo, 'Thomas Holt White, brother of Gilbert White', *Letters to Mr Urban of the Gentleman's Magazine* (1997) **Archives** Gilbert White Museum, Selborne, Hampshire, commonplace book · Hants. RO, family MSS · Harvard U., family MSS **Likenesses** T. Robinson, engraving, repro. in Holt-White, *Life and letters of Gilbert White*

White, Walter (1811–1893), librarian and writer, was born at Reading on 23 April 1811, the eldest son in the numerous family of John White (1779–1863), upholsterer and cabinet-maker. He was educated at two local private schools, one of which was kept by Joseph Huntly, father of the founder of Huntly and Palmer's biscuit manufactory. At fourteen White left school to work alongside his father, spending much of his leisure in reading and in the study of French, German, and Latin. In 1830 he went to Derbyshire and Staffordshire, where he married Maria Hamilton; they raised a daughter and three sons. The family settled briefly at Reading, but in hopes of a better life sailed for the United States in April 1834. White plied his trade in New York and Poughkeepsie but without improving his circumstances, finding the cold winters hard to endure. His daughter died during this time. His account of the emigrant's life, 'A working man's recollections of America', was published in the first volume of *Knight's Penny Magazine* in 1846.

The family returned to Reading in May 1839 where White rejoined his father's business, but in October 1842, still tempted by prospects of a better life elsewhere, he left his family in Reading and went to London. He took employment as secretary to Joseph Mainzer, a music teacher, and accompanied Mainzer to Edinburgh when the latter was a candidate for the chair of music at the university. While in Edinburgh he met a variety of learned and self-educated men, visited libraries and attended lectures, including those delivered to the working classes by James Simpson. Simpson wrote him a glowing letter of introduction to Charles Weld, assistant secretary to the Royal Society, then located at Somerset House, Westminster, who offered him the post of attendant in the society's library.

White started work there on 19 April 1844 at an annual salary of £80, his first task being to check the library shelves, which revealed many missing books. From there he became involved in the process of cataloguing and in 1858 he directed the boys hired to compile a catalogue of contents of all natural science periodicals in the library. This volume was published in 1867, the first of the series which eventually covered the century from 1800 to 1900. The boys employed on this lengthy task included Henry White (d. 1880), a distant relative, and one of White's own sons, Alfred Hastings White. When Weld resigned in 1861 White was promoted to assistant secretary at a salary of £300 and entitled to lodgings at Somerset House. He was increasingly employed to service and take minutes for the society's various committees, and became acquainted with the many eminent men who attended and who lectured at the society.

At the end of 1845 White's wife left him and he was obliged to dispose of the family house in the Old Kent Road. Only his eldest son remained with him; another son, Henry, became a sailor. During this time White wrote extensively for *Chambers's Edinburgh Journal*—some 200 articles between 1844 and 1849—and for other serials. In 1850 he began the holiday walks which furnished new material: the narrative of his first month's excursion in Holland was published as 'Notes from the Netherlands' (*Chambers's Edinburgh Journal*, 15, 1858), but later expeditions, to Mont Blanc, the Tyrol, eastern Germany, and Bohemia, and, closer to home, Northumberland, Yorkshire, Shropshire, and London, were published as books. Age and ill health obliged him to resign at the end of 1884. In gratitude for his long continued and valuable service he was granted a life pension of £350, equivalent to his current salary. He lived at 18 Grove Road, Lambeth, London, until his death there on 21 July 1893.

ANITA MCCONNELL

Sources *The journals of Walter White* (1898) · *The Athenaeum* (29 July 1893), 160 · private information (2004) · M. B. Hall, *The library and archives of the Royal Society, 1630–1990* (1992) · council minutes, 1878–92, RS · *Men of the time* (1862), 787–8 · *DNB* · d. cert. **Archives** RS, corresp. | CUL, Gosse MSS · CUL, letters to Sir George Stokes · NHM, letters to A. Gunther relating to Royal Society expedition **Likenesses** photograph, repro. in *Journals* (1898), frontispiece

White, Wilfrid Hyde (1903–1991), actor, was born on 12 May 1903 at the rectory in Bourton on the Water, Gloucestershire, the son of William Edward White, canon of Gloucester Cathedral, and his wife, Ethel Adelaide Drought. He was educated at Marlborough College, where he decided on an acting career—his uncle was the actor J. Fisher White. He studied at the Royal Academy of Dramatic Art and made his stage début as Maitland in the Evans-Valentine hit comedy *Tons of Money* (1922) at Ryde, Isle of Wight, and his London début as a juror in *Beggar on Horseback* (1925) at the Queen's. On 17 December 1927 he married Blanche Hope Aitken (b. 1896/7), who used the stage name Blanche Glynne; they had one son. For a decade he was a busy stage actor, although with no successes of particular note, in the provinces and in London, touring in South Africa in 1932, and briefly as part of Tom

Walls's company at the Aldwych. He made his film début in *Josser on the Farm* (1934) and there soon followed many minor, but often telling, film roles. He appeared exclusively on screen from 1936 to 1940, sometimes billed as Hyde White, in such films as *Rembrandt* (1936); *The Scarab Murder Case* (1936), a rare lead role as an unlikely Philo Vance; *Elephant Boy* (1937) as the commissioner; and *Poison Pen* (1939) as the postman. Through the 1940s he was equally occupied on stage and in films, being well-established in West End drama and comedy and with screen roles becoming larger. He made his New York début in 1947 as Sir Alec Dunne in *Under the Counter* at the Shubert. But it was Carol Reed's film *The Third Man* (1949), from Graham Greene's novella, which first got him noticed by a large audience; he played Crabbit, a bemused British cultural official in post-war Vienna.

White's debonair, often roguish charm was instantly recognizable; 'his unfailing imperturbability and unruffled acceptance of every eventuality made him an ideal choice for light comedy of the drawing room school' (*The Times*, 8 May 1991). He did, though, win further acting spurs in Olivier's Festival of Britain (1951) productions, *Caesar and Cleopatra* and *Antony and Cleopatra*, both at the St James's and the Ziegfeld, New York. And there were other stage successes, such as *Affairs of State* (1952) at the Cambridge, *Hippo Dancing* (1954) at the Lyric with lifetime friend Robert Morley, and, particularly, *The Reluctant Debutante* (1955), also at the Cambridge which, the following year in New York, earned him a Tony award nomination. He took over the part of the Marquess of Candover in *The Jockey Club Stakes* (1972) which, when repeated at the Cort, New York, early the following year, won him a second Tony nomination.

White was increasingly busy on screen, usually as lords, gentlemen, or conmen, often 'smallish roles which he somehow succeeded in making appear bigger' (*The Times*, 8 May 1991), such as *The Browning Version* (1951) as the headmaster, and in his own favourite role, as the bogus Reverend Fowler (alias 'Soapy' Stevens) in *Two Way Stretch* (1960). In that year he was in Hollywood for *Let's Make Love* with Marilyn Monroe, and many films in the film capital followed. In particular he co-starred in *My Fair Lady* (1964) from the Lerner and Loewe musical as Colonel Pickering, the avuncular companion of Rex Harrison's Professor Higgins. It was a role which brought him international recognition.

After the death of his wife, in 1957 White married the American actress Ethel Korenman (stage name Ethel Drew). They had a son, the actor Alex Hyde White, and a daughter. From the mid-1960s, they lived in California. There were some final stage appearances, including *The Prodigal Daughter* (1973) in Washington and then on a UK tour, *An Ideal Husband* (1976) at the Yvonne Arnaud Theatre, Guildford, *Rolls-Royce* (1977) at the Shaftesbury, and, finally, in *Lady Windermere's Fan* again (1978), also at the Arnaud. But it was television movies and guest appearances which were to keep him busy from the late 1960s to the early 1980s. Very few were of particular note, but he

invariably radiated droll good humour with an impeccable style. That style, supplemented by conversation punctuated with many a 'ho-ho', and 'dear fellow', and a tapping of the nose with the forefinger, had been expensive to maintain in real life, exemplified by Rolls-Royces, racehorses, and mistresses, which led to his being declared bankrupt in London in 1979. His wife left him and, chastened by the experience, he managed to give up his inveterate gambling on horses for a year, becoming even busier on television. His career was somewhat revived by the television series *The Associates* (1979), in which he played the senior partner of a New York law firm. His last film appearance was in the British/West German co-production *Fanny Hill* (1983).

In 1985 White became a resident of the Motion Picture and Television Hospital in Woodland Hills, Los Angeles, California, for his last few years being almost bedridden. He died on 6 May 1991 in Woodland Hills of congestive heart failure. ROBERT SHARP

Sources *The Times* (8 May 1991) · *The Independent* (8 May 1991) · *The Guardian* (8 May 1991) · *Daily Telegraph* (7 May 1991) · *WWW* · I. Herbert, ed., *Who's who in the theatre*, 1 (1981) · www.uk.imdb.com, 18 Sept 2001 · b. cert. · m. cert. [Blanche Aitken]
Likenesses photographs, 1947–79, Hult. Arch. · photograph (in old age), repro. in *The Times* · photograph (in old age), repro. in *The Independent*

White, William (*d.* 1428), priest and Lollard heretic, was of unknown origins. There is no indication of the date of his birth, and no clear evidence that he studied at a university. On 6 July 1422, described as a chaplain, he was brought before the convocation of Canterbury province at the summons of Archbishop Henry Chichele (*d.* 1443), accused of being strongly suspected of heresy, and of preaching in the parish church of Tenterden, Kent, without a licence. The proceedings revealed that he had already been imprisoned by the archbishop for the unlicensed preaching, and had been absolved by him from the excommunication incurred. He admitted the suspicion of heresy and abjured his errors. At some date he was allowed to return to Tenterden, as parish chaplain. His dissenting activities continued, principally in this same area of Kent, where he was a member, probably the leading figure, of a wide circle of Lollards. His activities were taken very seriously by Chichele. There are suggestions of a proposed Lollard uprising in the area in 1428 and White may have been one of the leaders, though this is hard to square with his subsequent profession of opposition to warfare. By 1426 at the latest he had also established himself as a Lollard evangelist in East Anglia. It would seem that he moved regularly between the two regions. He took as his wife a woman called Joan.

Lollardy was probably established to a limited extent in East Anglia before White's arrival there. However, he and others working together, including several from Kent, much reinforced and probably enlarged heresy in the region, mainly in an area around the Waveney valley along the Norfolk–Suffolk boundary. He was a leading member of the group, possibly its dominant figure. As an itinerant teacher and evangelist he travelled round the houses of known Lollards, giving instruction and probably holding liturgical services in them. These 'schools and conventicles' were conducted in English and contributed to the development of a Lollard vocabulary. The home in Loddon of Thomas Mone, a well-to-do shoemaker, and his vigorous wife, Hawise, provided one base for his operations, neighbouring Bergh Apton another. 'A great saint in heaven and a most holy doctor ordained and sent by God' was how Margery *Baxter of Martham [see under Lollard women (act. c.1390–c.1520)], another provider of hospitality, described him (Tanner, 47). He wrote various books and tracts, though none of them survives.

When Archbishop Chichele sought to arrest suspected heretics in his diocese in the summer of 1428, White was among those who eluded his grasp, with the help of supporters like Baxter. Shortly afterwards, however, he was captured and brought to trial by the bishop of Norwich, William Alnwick (d. 1449). The trial, which took place in the chapel of the bishop's palace in Norwich on 13 September, was something of a show-piece, with numerous clerics in attendance, and it attests to his reputation. Thomas Netter (d. 1430), prior provincial of the English Carmelites, who was one of those present, described him as a 'great satrap' and 'vassal' of John Wyclif (d. 1384), a 'doctor' and 'great satellite' of the Wycliffites (Netter, Doctrinale, 3, cols. 412, 630, and 795–6). He defended himself with honesty and subtlety, admitting some charges, denying some, and in other cases drawing distinctions. His beliefs lay on the more radical wing of Wycliffism and there is a force and originality of his own. He was forthright in his insistence on the right, indeed the advisability, of priests to marry. Regarding the eucharist, he denied transubstantiation and was accused of substituting for the mass a memorial service of Christ's passion presided over by a layman, a charge he denied. Notable too is the social content of his doctrine: he rejected capital punishment and the lawfulness of war.

The charges admitted by White were sufficient to secure his condemnation. As a relapsed heretic he was handed over to the civic authorities of Norwich for punishment. Accordingly, shortly afterwards, he was executed in the city by being burnt at the stake, together with his Lollard colleagues Hugh Pye, formerly chaplain of Loddon, and the layman John (or William) Waddon, who had been condemned in separate trials somewhat earlier. Margery Baxter, who was present at his execution, said that he tried to preach to the people as he was about to be put to death, but one of the bishop's officials struck him on the mouth to prevent this.

White was a major figure in early fifteenth-century Lollardy. His influence may have spread wider than Kent and East Anglia, though there is no clear evidence to this effect. Links with the west country, for example, were quite possibly made through a priest called Thomas Bikenore and his written works may have had a wide circulation. In East Anglia his impact was striking, though his teachings lost some of their refinement when received

by less educated people. To what extent it persisted after the prosecutions conducted by Bishop Alnwick in the diocese of Norwich between 1428 and 1431 is unclear. In the Tenterden area of Kent, too, his influence was marked. In this case, however, current knowledge of well-established Lollard communities in the same area in the early sixteenth century provides stronger evidence that his memory endured. NORMAN P. TANNER

Sources [T. Netter], *Fasciculi zizaniorum magistri Johannis Wyclif cum tritico*, ed. W. W. Shirley, Rolls Series, 5 (1858) • M. Aston, 'William White's Lollard followers', *Catholic Historical Review*, 68 (1982), 469–97; repr. in M. Aston, *Lollards and reformers: images and literacy in late medieval religion* (1984), 71–100 • N. P. Tanner, ed., *Heresy trials in the diocese of Norwich, 1428–31*, CS, 4th ser., 20 (1977) • *The acts and monuments of John Foxe*, ed. J. Pratt, [new edn], 8 vols. (1877) • *Thomæ Waldensis … doctrinale antiquitatum fidei Catholicæ ecclesiæ*, ed. B. Blanciotti, 3 vols. (Venice, 1757–9) • A. Hudson, *The premature reformation: Wycliffite texts and Lollard history* (1988) • Bale, *Cat.* • J. A. F. Thomson, *The later Lollards, 1414–1520* (1965) • C. Kightly, 'The early Lollards: a survey of popular Lollard activity in England, 1382–1428', DPhil diss., University of York, 1975 • A. E. Nichols, *Seeable signs: the iconography of the seven sacraments, 1350–1544* (1994)

White, William (*bap.* **1571**, *d.* **1634**). *See under* White, Robert (*c.*1530x32–1574).

White, William (*bap.* **1604**, *d.* **1678**), Church of England clergyman, was baptized on 21 June 1604 at Witney, Oxfordshire, the fifth child of Henry White (d. 1631), who was possibly a fuller. He entered Wadham College, Oxford, matriculating on 13 July 1621, graduated BA on 25 February 1625, and proceeded MA on 25 June 1628. He became master of Magdalen College School in 1632, and vicar of Wargrave, Berkshire, thanks to Archbishop Laud, in 1637. At Magdalen School he taught Greek well and 'framed Latine sentences in the belly of each other, as he phrased it' (Stanier, 103). In 1648 the parliamentary commissioners ejected him, but Bishop Brian Duppa of Salisbury procured him the rectorship of Pusey, Berkshire, which he kept 'by the favour of his Friends, and the smallness of its Profits' (Wood, *Ath. Oxon.*, 2.618). In 1662 his former pupil Thomas Pierce, now president of Magdalen, made him also rector of Appleton, Berkshire.

As Guilielmus Phalerius, White wrote a brief teaching manual, *Ad grammaticen ordinarium supplementa* (1648), and a tract urging church unity, *Via ad pacem ecclesiasticam*, (1660). A third small book, on doctrine *Paraphrasis … catechismi Anglicani* (1674), is ascribed to him by his pupil and biographer William Fulman. White died at Pusey, 'a little after midnight before Saturdaie Jun. 1. 1678' (Fulman); he was buried there on 5 June. His punctiliousness appears in his will, dated 26 October 1677: his daughter and heir Elizabeth Pusey, wife of Robert Pusey, was instructed to give Cornelius Yates, vicar of St Mary's, Marlborough, Wiltshire, and Yates's successors £5 annually so long as they catechized their parishioners and advocated the order of family prayers White specified. The dean of Salisbury was to ratify this. White left the vicars his books and papers on condition that his marginalia be favourably construed and that his diaries, kept since 1628, all be burnt. The Marlborough Vicars' Library, which includes books given to White by Henry Hammond, is now in the Bodleian Library, Oxford. Nothing is known of his wife.

HUGH DE QUEHEN

Sources Wood, *Ath. Oxon.*, 2nd edn • W. Fulman, 'William White', *c*.1680, CCC Oxf., MS 307, fol. 111v • R. S. Stanier, *Magdalen School: a history of Magdalen College School, Oxford*, OHS, new ser., 3 (1940); repr. (1958) • F. Madan, *Oxford books: a bibliography of printed works*, 2–3 (1912–31) • Foster, *Alum. Oxon.* • M. Burrows, ed., *The register of the visitors of the University of Oxford, from AD 1647 to AD 1658*, CS, new ser., 29 (1881) • parish register (baptism), Witney, Oxfordshire, 21 June 1604 • *CSP dom.*, 1637–8, 288 • will, 1 July 1678, PRO, PROB 11/357, sig. 80
Archives Bodl. Oxf., Marlborough Vicars' Library | DWL, corresp. with Richard Baker

White, William (1748–1836), Protestant Episcopal bishop of Pennsylvania, was born on 4 April 1748 at Market Street (between 4th and 5th streets), Philadelphia, the first of two children of Colonel Thomas White (1704–1779), a large landholder, and his second wife, Esther (*bap.* 1719, *d.* 1790), daughter of Abraham and Mary Hewlings. Mary (1749–1827), his sister, married Robert Morris, known as the financier of the American War of Independence. White attended the College of Philadelphia (later the University of Pennsylvania), receiving the AB degree in 1765, and pursued further study with the Revd Richard Peters and the Revd Jacob Duché, successive rectors of Christ Church and St Peter's, Philadelphia. In October 1770 he sailed for England, where he was ordained deacon on 23 December 1770 and priest on 25 April 1772. Upon returning to Philadelphia (13 September 1772), White became assistant minister of Christ Church and St Peter's. He married Mary Harrison (1750–1797) on 11 February 1773, and they had eight children. After Duché, a loyalist, departed in 1779, White was chosen as rector of the united churches, a position he held for life. The University of the State of Pennsylvania awarded him a DD degree in 1782.

In 1782, before the treaty of Paris (3 September 1783), which ended the War of Independence, White issued *The Case of the Episcopal Churches in the United States Considered*. He argued that the need to organize the churches was urgent and the prospect of securing an episcopate remote. In the absence of a bishop, it was necessary to construct a federal system built upon parishes within states that would exercise collective authority; the clergy of this body would be able to ordain until a bishop was procured. Lay delegates were to be included at each level of church government. This publication and the reactions to it placed White at the centre of an unofficial committee of correspondence on the affairs of the episcopal churches. White's ideas were generally accepted, except by the Connecticut clergy, who held that a bishop must first be obtained. In a series of conventions, state and general, between 1784 and 1789, clerical and lay delegates reorganized the episcopal churches in America into a republican ecclesiastical system, resupplied their clerical ranks, and secured the episcopate.

The actions of the episcopal clergy and laity in the middle and southern states prompted the Connecticut clergy secretly to select Samuel Seabury to go to England in order to seek episcopal consecration. If unsuccessful in England, he was to revert to the nonjuring bishops in Scotland, where on 14 November 1784 he was consecrated. Bishop Seabury's return to Connecticut made it clear that state conventions needed to elect bishops and secure their consecrations. Pennsylvania elected White, New York elected Samuel Provoost, and Virginia elected David Griffith. Richard H. Lee, the president of congress, John Jay, secretary of foreign affairs, and John Adams, minister to Great Britain, advised the British government of the appropriateness of these consecrations. Parliament enacted a bill on 16 June 1786 authorizing consecrations without the oath of allegiance to the king, and on 4 February 1787 both White and Provoost were consecrated in Lambeth Palace chapel. It was not until 1790 that James Madison of Virginia, who replaced Griffith, was consecrated, thus securing the canonical number of bishops in the English line to perform episcopal consecrations. In 1792 the four episcopal bishops, Seabury included, coalesced in the consecration of Thomas J. Claggett of Maryland.

During the conventions, White, with the help of William Smith, first provost of the College Philadelphia, modelled the American version of the Book of Common Prayer after the English book. He advocated the adoption of the Thirty-Nine Articles and moderated hostility towards Seabury because of his ardent toryism during the war. White was of the tradition of Archbishop John Tillotson (1630–1694) and Bishop Gilbert Burnet (1643–1715), moderate, judicious, and desirous of forming a comprehensive church without compromising essentials. He was an avid reader, well versed in theology and patristics. Active in civic affairs, he served as trustee from 1774 to 1836 of the institutions that became the University of Pennsylvania. His patriotism was evident in his role as chaplain to the congress, beginning in 1777, where he associated with leaders of the republic, such as George Washington.

A lifelong member of the American Philosophical Society, founder of the Philadelphia dispensary, and active in several charitable organizations, White was a first citizen of Philadelphia. Beyond his contributions in church and civic affairs, this venerable man was noted for graciousness, lack of self-consciousness, hospitality, and good humour. White enjoyed robust health throughout his life and was active until a few days before his death at his home, 89 Walnut Street (above 3rd Street), Philadelphia, on Sunday 17 July 1836. Three days later he was interred in the family vault at Christ Church, Philadelphia.

FREDERICK V. MILLS, SR.

Sources B. Wilson, *Memoir of the life of the Right Reverend William White* (Philadelphia, PA, 1839) • W. H. Stowe, *The life and letters of Bishop William White* (NY, 1937) • *Account of the meeting of the descendants of Colonel Thomas White …* (Philadelphia PA, 1879) • W. W. Manross, *A history of the American Episcopal Church* (NY, 1959) • F. V. Mills, *Bishops by ballot: an eighteenth-century ecclesiastical revolution* (1978) • W. B. Sprague, *Annals of the American pulpit*, 3 (1859) • W. W. Manross, *William White* (1934) • J. H. Ward, *The life and times of Bishop White* (NY, 1892) • J. N. Norton, *The life of the Rt. Rev. William White* (NY, 1860) • records, Christ Church, Philadelphia, USA

Archives Christ Church, Philadelphia, collections · Episcopal Archives, Austin, Texas, collections · Hist. Soc. Penn., papers · Maryland Diocesan Library, papers · New York Historical Society, papers
Likenesses H. Inman, General Theological Seminary, New York · B. Otis, Valley Forge Memorial Chapel, Pennsylvania · G. W. Peale, miniature, Christ Church, Philadelphia · G. Stuart, Academy of Fine Arts, Philadelphia · portraits, repro. in Stowe, *Life and letters*
Wealth at death approx. $36,000 all left to family in shares

White, William (1807–1882), printer, and door-keeper of the House of Commons, was born of East Anglian nonconformist stock, probably in Bedford, and educated at Bedford grammar school. His grandmother's maiden name was Hale, suggesting a connection (unproven) with the seventeenth-century chief justice Sir Matthew Hale. White established himself around 1830 as a bookseller and printer in Bedford, and married Mary Anne Chignell of Colchester. He was a strict Calvinist Congregationalist and a political radical, regarded as one of Bedford's best public speakers. As a member of Lord John Russell's election committee in 1832 he was besieged by a mob and had the windows of his house broken. In 1843 he defeated almost single-handed a move to impose a requirement that all schoolteachers under the Bedford Charity should be Anglicans. His newspaper letters on this affair were reprinted in a pamphlet *Bedford Charity not Sectarian*. Influenced by Carlyle he became disenchanted with Calvinist orthodoxy. When in 1852 his son (William) Hale *White, later well known as a writer under the pseudonym Mark Rutherford, was expelled from a Calvinist seminary for questioning the unique inspiration of the Bible, he came to his aid in a pamphlet *To Think or Not to Think*. Hale White claimed that his literary style owed much to his father.

White's political activities ruined his business and he ran into debt. Lord Charles Russell, stepbrother of Lord John and serjeant-at-arms, appointed him assistant, later principal, door-keeper of the House of Commons. He used his ringside seat to gather material for sketches of parliamentary life for the popular weekly *Illustrated Times*. These sketches draw a vivid picture of many notable parliamentary personalities and events of the period from the Crimean War to White's retirement in 1875. A selection of them was published in 1897 by Justin McCarthy, the Irish nationalist MP, under the title *The Inner Life of the House of Commons*. White died at Carshalton, Surrey, on 11 February 1882. E. J. FEUCHTWANGER

Sources W. H. White, *The early life of Mark Rutherford* (1913) · W. White, *The inner life of the House of Commons*, ed. J. McCarthy, 2 vols. (1897); facs. edn in 1 vol. (1973) · W. H. White, *The autobiography of Mark Rutherford*, ed. R. Shapcott, 2nd edn (1888) · I. Stock, *William Hale White (Mark Rutherford)* (1956) · *The Times* (6 March 1882) · Boase, *Mod. Eng. biog.*
Likenesses photograph (Mark Rutherford, aged about 12, with his father), repro. in White, *Early life of Mark Rutherford*, frontispiece

White, William (1825–1900), architect, was born on 12 April 1825, the third son of the Revd Francis Henry White (1781/2–1864), who was a nephew of the naturalist Gilbert White, and his wife, Elizabeth Master (b. 1788). In 1840 White was apprenticed to Daniel Goodman Squirhill, an architect and surveyor of Leamington Spa, and in 1845 he left to join the firm of George Gilbert Scott, a family friend, in London, where he remained for two years before establishing his own practice in Truro. His early works included the rectory at St Columb Major, Cornwall, the success of which brought him the commission for All Saints' Church, Notting Hill, for which he returned to London. On 7 June 1855 he married Ellen Floyer (b. 1826/7) of Salcombe Regis, Devon, daughter of the Revd George Cornish; they had five daughters before her death in 1866.

By 1859 White's practice was at 30A Wimpole Street, an office which he shared for a few years with George Frederick Bodley, and which remained his professional address for the rest of his life. Apart from Humewood Castle, co. Wicklow (1866–70), the bulk of White's work consisted of modest commissions for churches, rectories, and schools throughout Britain, the success of which reflected his belief in functionalism as well as his attention to detail, however modest the project. He also designed cathedrals for Madagascar (1889) and Pretoria (c.1890). White's best-known work is probably the church of St Michael and All Angels, Lyndhurst, Hampshire (1858–67), a vigorous and eclectic composition of red brick with prominent dormer windows.

The Ecclesiological Society, of which White became a member in 1849, published most of his early writings, mainly on principles of design. White's later articles on topics ranging from polychromy, which he consistently advocated, to tight clothing, which he abhorred, appeared in journals such as the *British Architect*, *The Builder*, and *Building News*. Although he produced no books, he wrote pamphlets, including *The Tourist's Knapsack and its Contents*, based on his experiences as a member of the Alpine Club. White became a fellow of the Institute of British Architects in 1859; in 1864 he was elected a fellow of the Society of Antiquaries (thereafter he always styled himself FSA), and was president of the Architectural Association in 1868–9.

By 1869 White had established his family home at Lyndon Lodge, Hanwell, and in 1877 he married Jane Bateson, daughter of Charles Cook of Clay Hall, Middlesex, with whom he had a son and two daughters. He died from influenza at 24 Gayton Road, Hampstead, London, on 22 January 1900 and was buried on 26 January in Hampstead cemetery. White's luxuriant beard and straightforward manner of speaking contrasted with a romantic and caring nature. His surviving buildings express these complexities of his character through his idiosyncratic interpretation of the Gothic revival style. GILL HUNTER

Sources T. H. Watson, 'The late William White', *RIBA Journal*, 7 (1899–1900), 145–6 · P. Thompson, 'The writings of William White', *Concerning architecture*, ed. J. Summerson (1968), 226–37 · 'Our architects and their works', *British Architect* (16 Sept 1881), 464–6 · 'Contemporary British architects', *Building News*, 58 (1890), 168–9 [incl. photograph] · *Dir. Brit. archs.* · *CGPLA Eng. & Wales* (1900) · register of burials, Hampstead cemetery · d. cert. · Alpine Club register · m. cert. [Ellen Floyer Cornish] · baptismal records, Blakesley, Northants. RO

Archives LPL, plans, records of Incorporated Church Building Society · RIBA, drawings collection
Likenesses photograph, before 1890, RIBA; repro. in 'Contemporary British architects', 168
Wealth at death £4244 17s. 10d.: probate, 15 Dec 1900, CGPLA Eng. & Wales

White, Sir William Arthur (1824–1891), diplomatist, the son of Arthur White, who was in the British consular service, and Eliza Lila, daughter of Lieutenant-General William Gardiner Neville, was born in February 1824 in Poland; both his parents were Irish. He was educated at King William's College, Isle of Man, and at Trinity College, Cambridge, where his staunch Roman Catholicism prevented him from taking a degree. He entered the consular service unusually late, already aged thirty-three, on 9 March 1857 as clerk to the consul-general at Warsaw. He frequently acted as consul-general, and on 9 January 1861 he became vice-consul, again acting as consul-general for the greater part of 1862 and 1863. Here, with strong Polish sympathies, he nevertheless managed to avoid offending Russia during the Polish revolution of 1863. On 9 November 1864 he was appointed consul at Danzig, where he also acted for six months in 1866 as Belgian consul, and during the war of 1870 took charge of French interests. While at Danzig he married, in 1867, Katherine, daughter of Lewis Kendzior of Danzig; they left an only daughter, Lila Lucy Catherine Mary (later Lady Abinger). White's wife was 'a lovely and genial lady who for twenty-five years never faltered at his side' (Edwards, 265).

On 27 February 1875 White was transferred to Serbia as British agent and consul-general. This post at last gave him some scope for employing the knowledge which for many years past he had been acquiring, and laid the foundation of his great influence in dealing with Eastern nationalities. Within a few months of his arrival in Serbia the Eastern question entered an acute phase, and in June 1876 the Serbians, following the lead of Herzegovina, declared war against Turkey. Their defeat was followed by the conference at Constantinople in December 1876. There Lord Salisbury was assisted by White, and was deeply impressed by his knowledge and ability. This link with Salisbury enabled him to move from the consular to the diplomatic service.

In 1877 White returned to Serbia; he was transferred to Bucharest in July 1878 and appointed envoy-extraordinary and minister-plenipotentiary on 3 March 1879, though he did not present his credentials until Britain recognized Romania in February 1880. On 18 April 1885 he was nominated envoy-extraordinary at Constantinople, and was at once brought face to face with a question of first importance—the legality of the annexation of Eastern Roumelia to Bulgaria in defiance of the treaty of Berlin of 1878. Russia took the ground that the treaty must be upheld at all costs. White's obstructive diplomatic tactics contributed directly to the consolidation of Bulgarian nationality, and the Bulgarians were not slow to recognize this. Early in 1886 he was specially thanked by the government for his action. He was created CB on 21 March 1878, KCMG on 16 March 1883, GCMG on 28 January 1886, GCB on 2 June

1888, and sworn of the privy council on 29 June 1888; he was made an honorary LLD of Cambridge University on 17 June 1886.

On coming into office in 1886, Lord Salisbury appointed White to the embassy at Constantinople; on 11 October he was confirmed as special ambassador-extraordinary and plenipotentiary, and was the first Roman Catholic to achieve this rank in the British diplomatic service since the Reformation. White's years as ambassador were of unusual importance, for it was from his diplomatic conversations that the first and second Mediterranean agreements of March and December 1887 may be said to have derived. Defence of the straits and partnership with Germany and the triple alliance were the bases of White's approach to the Eastern question. His memorandum of 25 July 1887 set out Britain's cautious support for Turkish railway expansion into Asia Minor under British control, though his efforts to build a railway through the Kaulla concession led to financial disaster (Smith, 112–31). White welcomed German involvement in this railway building, and was subsequently much criticized for allowing the growth of German influence in the Ottoman empire. By the time of his retirement in 1891 his close links with Salisbury had weakened, for the latter had begun to abandon the policy of propping up the Porte.

White left Constantinople on 24 December 1891 and, returning via Berlin, caught a chill and died at the Kaiserhof Hotel there on 28 December. He was buried in the Roman Catholic church of St Hedwig, Berlin, on 31 December. His wife survived him. White was a hard worker with none of the usual relaxations of the diplomatist (sport, food, and cards) (Edwards, 260–61). He had what his biographer called 'a certain superficial roughness which his enemies sometimes mistook for asperity of character' (Edwards, 264).

C. A. Harris, *rev.* H. C. G. Matthew

Sources FO List (1891) · *The Times* (29 Dec 1891) · *The Times* (30 Dec 1891) · *The Times* (1 Jan 1892) · *The Times* (2 Jan 1892) · TLS (12 Jan 1928), 27 · private information (1923) · H. S. Edwards, *Sir William White* (1902) · C. L. Smith, *The embassy of Sir William White at Constantinople, 1886–1891* (1957) · W. N. M., 'The Dictionary of National Biography: Sir W. A. White', BIHR, 5 (1927–8), 58–9
Archives PRO, corresp. and papers, FO 364/1–11 | Balliol Oxf., Layard MSS; Morris MSS, corresp. with Sir Robert Morier · BL, corresp. with Sir Austen Layard, Add. MSS 38939, 39130–39134 · BL, corresp. with Sir Augustus Paget, Add. MS 51231 · CUL, letters to Charles Hardinge · NL Scot., letters to Sir Henry Elliot · PRO, letters to Sir Arthur Nicolson, PRO 30/81 · PRO, Ampthill MSS, PRO 918 · PRO, letters to Lord Odo Russell, FO 918
Likenesses J. Johnstone, carte-de-visite, c.1863, NPG
Wealth at death £14,819 14s. 7d.: resworn probate, April 1892, CGPLA Eng. & Wales

White, Sir William Hale- (1857–1949), physician, was born at 19 Marylebone Road, London, on 7 November 1857, the eldest son of (William) Hale *White (1831–1913), better known as the novelist Mark Rutherford, and his first wife, Harriet Arthur (d. 1890). Educated at the City of London School and at Framlingham College, Suffolk, he entered Guy's Hospital, London, as a medical student in 1875 and graduated MB from London University in 1879. He made many friends at Guy's and seems to have been exceptionally happy from the start. He was demonstrator of anatomy there from 1881 to 1885, and then assistant physician and lecturer on materia medica, pharmacology, and therapeutics. It was not long before his practice grew and in 1890 he was appointed full physician at the unusually early age of thirty-three. On 30 December 1886 he married Edith Jane Spencer Fripp (d. 1945), sister of his friend and future colleague Alfred Downing Fripp, and daughter of Alfred Downing Fripp (1822–1895), painter in watercolours.

Hale-White (the hyphen was adopted at about the time of his father's death) was a consistent worker and a prolific writer; his case reports in the *Transactions* of the Pathological Society covered almost all branches of medicine. His laboratory work, particularly on the methods by which the heat of the body is maintained, led to work on hibernating animals. The textbook which made his name familiar to generations of students was his *Materia medica, Pharmacology and Therapeutics* (1892), affectionately known as 'Hale-White'; it reached its twenty-eighth edition by the time of his death.

In 1896 Hale-White was found to have tuberculosis of the lungs. He spent the winter in Switzerland but did not become much better; he was advised to give up work completely, but family responsibilities made this impossible and he worked for most of each year, taking two months' holiday in the winter in the Channel Islands or Cornwall. Throughout this difficult time he continued his hospital work and practice and gradually, as his health recovered, resumed his full activity. He developed a large consulting practice, was fond of speaking at medical societies and in later years often found himself their president, and held many examinerships in materia medica and in medicine.

Hale-White was one of the editors of *Guy's Hospital Reports* from 1886 to 1893 and contributed many of its papers. He was one of the founders in 1907 of the Association of Physicians of Great Britain and Ireland. He became its treasurer, and he was for twenty years an editor of its *Quarterly Journal of Medicine*.

In the First World War, Hale-White acted as consulting physician to various war hospitals with the rank of colonel and served as chairman of Queen Mary's Royal Naval Hospital, Southend. In 1919 he retired from Guy's and was appointed KBE. He received honorary degrees of MD from Dublin (1909) and LLD from Edinburgh (1927). Although he was soon back at his consulting and other work he had more leisure: he lost his worn-out look and his old buoyancy and enthusiasm returned.

Hale-White finally gave up his practice in 1927 and devoted more of his time to the study of medical history. At Guy's he had a great affection for Keats, and in 1925 he published in the *Guy's Hospital Reports* an account of Keats as a medical student. He prepared photographic copies of Keats's student anatomical and physiological notebook, and published it in 1934, and he also wrote *Keats as Doctor and Patient* (1938). In addition he produced many medical biographies, combining scholarly accuracy with a fluency of style, most of which were published in *Guy's Hospital*

Reports. His *Great Doctors of the Nineteenth Century* (1935) included many people from Guy's. During the Second World War, although he was over eighty, he acted as chairman of the Queen's Institute of District Nursing and became chairman of the council of Bedford College, London, of which he was elected a fellow in 1947.

Hale-White was probably one of the last physicians to cover such a wide range of medicine. There were few branches on which he had not written, and his knowledge was based on a wide experience of clinical medicine and pathology. He was a great teacher through both the spoken and printed word, and doctors and students found him readily approachable, partly because he treated everyone as an equal and at once put them at their ease. Besides his enjoyment of writing he was fond of travelling and had ventured off the beaten track in Palestine, Syria, Greece, Spain, and India. He had many interests including golf, bridge, and photography, and he drove his own car fast and badly until the age of seventy-five. Even as he grew older he always found it easy to fill his time.

Hale-White was a small dapper figure and until his war service had a large black beard. During nearly sixty years of marriage, his home was a happy centre for many friends, though there were sad family losses, for their second son was drowned at sea in the *Natal* in 1915 and their eldest son died in 1939 after a distinguished career as a civil engineer in India. Their third son, Reginald Hale-White, also a doctor, survived him. Hale-White died at 24 Warnborough Road, Oxford, on 26 February 1949.

MAURICE CAMPBELL, rev. ANITA MCCONNELL

Sources M. Campbell, 'Sir William Hale-White', *Guy's Hospital Reports*, 4th ser., 28 (1949), 1–17 · private information (1959) · personal knowledge (1959) · Munk, *Roll* · *The Lancet* (5 March 1949), 421 · *BMJ* (5 March 1949), 414–15; (12 March 1949), 458 · b. cert. · m. cert. · d. cert. · *CGPLA Eng. & Wales* (1949)
Archives Bedford Central Library, corresp. relating to his father
Likenesses W. Stoneman, photograph, 1931, NPG · W. Rothenstein, sanguine and white drawing, NPG
Wealth at death £63,466 18s. 10d.: probate, 3 May 1949, *CGPLA Eng. & Wales*

White, Sir William Henry (1845–1913), naval architect, born at Devonport on 2 February 1845, was the youngest child of Richard White, a currier, of Devonport, and his wife, Jane, daughter of W. Matthews, of Lostwithiel, Cornwall. He was educated at a private school at Devonport and apprenticed as a shipwright in the royal dockyard there. In 1864 he and seven fellow apprentices were sent by the Admiralty to the then newly founded Royal School of Naval Architecture and Marine Engineering at South Kensington for training in naval architecture, higher mathematics, physics, and chemistry; and in 1867 he passed out from this school, obtaining its highest honours. He and five others were at once appointed to the Admiralty staff by Sir Edward James Reed, the chief constructor of the navy, White being engaged as a professional secretary to Sir Edward. Many warships with iron hulls were then building, in private yards as well as in the royal dockyards, in succession to vessels with wooden hulls. New methods of construction were therefore being

Sir William Henry White (1845–1913), by William Logsdail, 1906

devised, and numerous structural features were under discussion. White was largely responsible for collating these technical matters, published in Reed's *Shipbuilding in Iron and Steel* (1869), and for contributing to Reed's *Our Iron Clad Ships* (1869), and his paper 'On the stresses of ships' contributed to the *Philosophical Transactions of the Royal Society* (1871). In 1870 Reed retired from the position of chief constructor of the navy, and the office was devolved into a council of construction with Nathaniel Barnaby as president. This council appointed White as its secretary (1872).

Shortly after Reed's retirement, HMS *Captain*, a fully-rigged, low-freeboard turret ship, designed by Captain Cowper Phipps Coles and built by a private firm, capsized, most of her crew being drowned. Among the ships then building from Reed's designs were the 'all big gun' battleships *Devastation* and *Thunderer*, of comparatively low freeboard, but with no sail. The loss of the *Captain* drew special attention to these vessels, and a committee was appointed to report on their safety. The council of construction proposed certain alterations, which were finally approved by the committee and adopted by the Admiralty, largely through White's advocacy. The first important design approved by the council of construction (Barnaby being the responsible designer) was that of the 'all big gun' *Inflexible* of 1876. She carried four muzzle-loading 16 inch 80 ton guns, mounted *en échelon*, two in each of two turrets on a central citadel. The side armour was limited to the central part of the vessel, and the ends, which had thin side plating, were fitted with high and thick cork belts and strong underwater decks. The design was attacked by Reed and was referred for report by the Admiralty to a

naval and scientific committee. The committee was convinced of its merit by the defence, which was left largely to White. The *Inflexible* and four other vessels, of the same type but somewhat smaller, were built and passed into the fleet.

The breech-loading gun was now so far developed as to be adopted in the *Collingwood*, a vessel of Barnaby's design, laid down in 1880. Turrets were abandoned, and the main armament, of four 12 inch guns in pairs in two barbettes, was mounted on the middle line, one pair towards each end of the vessel. The weights of the revolving material and of the power to actuate it were much reduced, and a secondary armament of six 6 inch guns was carried between the barbettes of the main armament. The cost then considered permissible for a battleship, about £650,000, made it necessary to accept a comparatively narrow belt of armour of about half the length of the ship, leaving the sides at the ends unprotected with armour as in previous vessels. The lower portions of the ends were protected by strong underwater decks, but cork buoyancy was not provided. This design also was very adversely criticized by Reed, and by many naval officers, and others. The defence was again left largely to White; the Admiralty eventually accepted the design, and built the *Collingwood* and five similar vessels with somewhat more powerful armament—*Rodney, Howe, Anson, Camperdown*, and *Benbow*.

White gave much consideration to the design of cruisers, and particularly to that of the *Iris*, laid down in 1875—the first steel vessel built for the navy. He was also one of Barnaby's principal assistants in designing the cruisers *Mersey, Severn, Thames*, and *Forth*, commenced in 1883. These were by far the most powerful of the smaller cruisers then in the navy; they had a speed of 17 knots, a powerful armament, and were protected for their whole length by a strong deck, rising above the water at the middle line of the ship from well below water at the sides. For many years this remained the accepted type of Admiralty cruiser, culminating in 1894 (after White had become director of naval construction) in the *Powerful* and *Terrible*.

In 1883 White left the Admiralty to become designer and manager to Armstrong & Co. at their warship yard, then being constructed at Elswick-on-Tyne. There he did much good work, assisting in laying out the yard and organizing the staff, and designing and building several of the earlier Elswick vessels. He left Armstrongs in 1885 when, on Sir Nathaniel Barnaby's retirement, he was appointed director of naval construction. On his return to the Admiralty as the head of the construction department (1885) he made various improvements in each class of vessel, embodying advances made in machinery, gunnery, and quality of materials. He designed the *Barfleur* and *Centurion*, of 11,000 tons, for service in eastern waters. Step by step he progressed through the eight vessels of the Royal Sovereign class of 1889, and thirty-five additional battleships, to the King Edward VII class, the building of which began in 1902. This class was of 16,500 tons, with an armament of four 12 inch guns, four 9.2 inch guns, and ten 6 inch guns, and a speed of 18½ knots. The cost had risen from £650,000 in the *Collingwood* to £1,500,000 in the *King Edward VII*. Several of these vessels were employed in service during the First World War. Much improvement was made in the large cruisers. In the 'protected' class (without side armour) these ranged from the *Crescent* of 7700 tons and a speed of 19½ knots to the *Powerful* and *Terrible* of 14,200 tons and a speed of 22 knots. In all, twenty 'protected' cruisers were built for the Royal Navy to White's designs. Owing to improvements in the quality of armour the next design for large cruisers—that for the six vessels of the Cressy class—provided for 6 inch side armour, 12,000 tons displacement, and a speed of 21½ knots. A bigger design was that for the four vessels of the Drake class of 14,100 tons and a speed of 23½ knots. Twenty-eight large armoured cruisers, many smaller cruisers, torpedo boat destroyers, and miscellaneous vessels, were designed by White and built for the Royal Navy. In 1902 White retired on account of ill health. During his seventeen years' service as director of naval construction the fleet had grown more than in any preceding period of the same length.

In the early days (1870–73) of his career White was appointed lecturer on naval design at the Royal School, South Kensington, and he continued (until 1881) to act in this capacity on the transfer of the school to the Royal Naval College at Greenwich, where he formulated a scheme of instruction in naval architecture for the executive officers of the Royal Navy. In association with Sir Nathaniel Barnaby, Admiral Sir Houston Stewart, and Sir Thomas Brassey he devised the organization of the Royal Corps of Naval Constructors, dating from 1883. During his year of office as master of the Worshipful Company of Shipwrights, he, with the assistance of the first Lord Norton, founded the educational trust fund, which assisted hundreds of young naval architects to obtain a technical education. He was for some years on the governing body of the National Physical Laboratory, during which time he took much interest in the installation of the William Froude tank. He had considerable literary ability: his *Manual of Naval Architecture* (1877) is a model of clear, popular exposition of a difficult subject; it is enriched by many data that reached the Admiralty during his period of service, especially results of original scientific investigations obtained by William Froude. He contributed twenty papers, all of great merit, to the *Transactions* of the Institution of Naval Architects. He also wrote many important articles for leading magazines, and several pamphlets on special subjects connected with naval architecture.

Many honours were awarded White, among them his appointment in 1885 as assistant controller of the navy; he was created KCB in 1895. He was of genial personality, much liked by his fellows, a ready debater, lucid in his statements and convincing to his opponents. He was a welcome guest at the dinners of many City companies, at which he frequently exercised his influence to obtain donations for assistance in educational matters.

White, who left three sons and one daughter, was twice married: first, in 1875 to Alice (*d.* 1886), daughter of F. Martin, of Pembroke, chief constructor, RN; and second, in 1890 to Annie (who survived him), daughter of F. C. Marshall JP, of Tynemouth. White died suddenly, in the Westminster Hospital, Westminster, London, on 27 February 1913, leaving behind him a brilliant record of work and an example to the corps which he did much to inaugurate. During his lifetime the 'wooden walls of old England', wooden ships carrying what are now regarded as feeble armaments, were replaced by iron and steel armoured vessels carrying guns of very great power. In this revolution Sir William White played an important part.

PHILIP WATTS, *rev.* ANITA MCCONNELL

Sources admiralty records · P. W., *PRS*, 89A (1913–14), xiv–xix · *Transactions of the Institution of Naval Architects* · personal knowledge (1927) · *CGPLA Eng. & Wales* (1913)
Likenesses oils, *c.*1902–1903, NMM · W. Logsdail, portrait, 1906, Inst. CE [*see illus.*]
Wealth at death £38,257 15s. 2d.: resworn probate, 26 March 1913, *CGPLA Eng. & Wales*

Whiteacre, Nigel. *See* Canterbury, Nigel of (*c.*1135–1198?).

White Conduit cricket club (*act. c.***1785–1788**) had its origin in the gatherings of eighteenth-century aristocrats and gentry who frequented the Star and Garter tavern at 100 Pall Mall, London. They played cricket on public land beside the pleasure park in Islington known as the White Conduit Fields, where the game had been played since at least 1718. It is difficult to establish a date when matches first took place under the name White Conduit because two major fires—one at Lord's cricket ground in 1825 and one at Burley House in 1908—destroyed many records. In 1744 some noblemen and gentry had established 'the Articles of the game of cricket at the Star and Garter' (*Reading Mercury*, 24 Feb 1784). Their successors, a generation later, are spoken of as belonging to the 'Grand Old Club' (*Morning Post*, 5 Oct 1778), while 1785 provides the first surviving evidence of a match played by the White Conduit club. This game, and four others recorded in Arthur Haygarth's *Scores and Biographies* (vol. 1, 1862), list some thirty players who appeared for the club.

The need for privacy led some members to invite the Yorkshire-born businessman Thomas *Lord to find a new enclosed ground. This he did on the Portman estate in Marylebone, which gave rise both to a venue bearing his own name and a club named after the district. Thus by 1787 membership of the White Conduit club was becoming merged with that of the new Marylebone Cricket Club although the first recorded match of MCC was one between the newcomer and its predecessor at Lord's in June 1788. Most of the players on each side could have played for the other and the game seems to have been a tangible expression of the transition of nomenclature and domicile which had taken place.

In the forefront of the membership of the White Conduit club must go its treasurer, **George Finch**, ninth earl of Winchilsea (1752–1826), army officer and cricket promoter, who was both a former president of the *Hambledon Cricket Club in Hampshire and the prime instigator in the formation of MCC. He was born on 4 November 1752 and baptized a month later at St James's, Westminster, the son of William Finch, courtier, and his second wife, Lady Charlotte Fermor, daughter of the first earl of Pomfret. He was educated at Eton College and Christ Church, Oxford, where he matriculated in 1767 and graduated MA in 1771. Aged twenty-four he raised a regiment which served for four years (1776–80) in the American War of Independence. Thereafter he played cricket regularly for Hambledon, White Conduit, MCC, and his own elevens until 1800. Winchilsea's decision to play for MCC at Lord's on 16 May 1791 rather than attend a Hambledon committee meeting made clear his weakening loyalties to rural sport and his belief that the immediate future of cricket for himself and his own associates lay in the burgeoning London rather than in Hampshire. As befitted his rank he opened the batting. Despite many modest scores he made three half-centuries and in 1791 scored 345 runs for an average of 15.00. More important to posterity is Winchilsea's undoubted title as the founder of MCC, in whose first recorded match he faced the opening ball. It was he who had undertaken the prime initiative in supporting Thomas Lord in the purchase of a private ground in 1786.

In three of the White Conduit matches for which scores survive the club was strengthened by 'given men' whom Winchilsea had secured from the ranks of the Hambledon players and who were paid to play. An example of this was in the match against Kent at Bishopsbourne in 1786 when the club had two such players, Thomas Walker and **Thomas Taylor** (1753–1806), each of whom made centuries. Taylor, who came from Alresford, Hampshire, where he was publican of The Globe inn, was a high-scoring batsman for Hambledon, averaging 32.00 in his three recorded appearances for White Conduit club. In 1784 he was appointed a gamekeeper to the duke of Bolton at Itchen Stoke.

In addition to his cricket Winchilsea took his public duties seriously, serving as a justice of the peace in Rutland, where he had his country seat at Birley. His concern for the needs of his tenantry won praise from the agricultural writer Arthur Young. Subsequently Winchilsea served as a tory lord of the bedchamber (1777–1812) and was appointed a knight of the Garter in 1805. Variously described as a 'man of elegant and accomplished manners' and a 'nobleman of the old school, and a high-bred gentleman in his manners to all', Winchilsea died, unmarried, on 2 August 1826 at 32 South Street, Park Lane, London (Harris and Ashley-Cooper, 24; Thomas Raikes, *Journal*, 4 vols., 1831–47, 3.51).

A fellow White Conduit club committee member was **Peter Burrell**, first Baron Gwydir (1754–1820), politician, who was born on 16 July 1754 in Upper Grosvenor Street, Hanover Square, London, the first son of Peter Burrell of Langley Park, commissioner of excise, and Elizabeth, *née* Lewis. After an education at Eton College (1761–70) and St John's College, Cambridge (MA, 1775), he was elected MP for Haslemere, which he represented between 1776 and 1780, and thereafter Boston (1782–96) for which he sat as a determined independent country gentleman. On 23 February 1779 he married, at Berkeley Square, London, Lady Priscilla Barbara Elizabeth Bertie (1761–1828), daughter of Peregrine, third duke of Ancaster, and (from July 1779) Baroness Willoughby in her own right. Knighted in 1781, he succeeded his great-uncle as second baronet in 1787 and completed his impressive and then much-discussed social elevation with ennoblement in June 1796 as the first Baron Gwydir.

Burrell's contributions to the White Conduit's fortunes include his 97 which helped the club (with no 'given men') to a victory by 304 runs against the Gentlemen of Kent in June 1785 (Haygarth, 1.62). He died at Brighton from gout on 29 June 1820 and was buried at Edenham, Lincolnshire, on 13 July. However, it had been the batting not of Burrell but of his half-sister Elizabeth Burrell [**Elizabeth Hamilton**, duchess of Hamilton (1757–1837)], which had won the heart of another club member, Douglas, eighth duke of Hamilton (1756–1799). Hamilton fell in love with Elizabeth who 'when she took bat in hand … [her] Diana-like air communicated an irresistible impression' (*Morning Post*, 22 Jan 1778). They were married on 5 April 1778. The attractions of the duchess's sporting prowess appear to have diminished in time; the couple were divorced in 1794 and Elizabeth later married Henry Cecil, first marquess of Exeter (1754–1804). She died at Privy Gardens, Whitehall, on 17 January 1837.

Apart from the duke of Hamilton, other noble members of the White Conduit club included John *Montagu, fourth earl of Sandwich, whose playing days were over long before the 1780s. He had left a match in 1766 when he was unable to move in the field, paid his betting debts and gone home. Another player was **Charles Bennett**, fourth earl of Tankerville (1743–1822), cricket patron and landowner, who was born at St James's Square, Westminster, on 15 November 1743, the first son of Charles Bennett, third earl of Tankerville (1716–1767) and Alicia, *née* Astley (1716–1791). As a player Tankerville was associated with Hambledon (as a given man), for whom he played his last game in 1781. He was a man who laid huge wagers on matches, gave employment to cricketers at his Surrey country seat of Walton-on-Thames, and raised elevens, such as those of England and Surrey, for specific occasions. Married on 7 October 1771 to Emma (1752–1836), daughter of Sir James Colebrooke, Tankerville spent his later life amassing a collection of shells before his death at Walton-on-Thames on 10 December 1822. The diplomatist John Frederick *Sackville, third duke of Dorset, the army officer Charles *Lennox, fourth duke of Richmond, and the politician and cricket promoter Sir Horatio *Mann (1744–1814) were other members of high social standing. Of these Richmond (then Colonel Charles Lennox) was the best player.

Of the remaining twenty or so active members of the club little is known. They are identified either by rank or the suffix 'Esquire' in the score-sheets. Among them were George Boult, a Berkshire man, who was able to raise from his immediate family an entire eleven, which beat the club at Bray in 1783, and Edward Hussey, 'a Kentish bowman, a bold and excellent rider, as well as a good cricketer'

(Haygarth, 1.217). That final match against MCC in which so many members played for one side or the other may be seen as the swansong of the White Conduit club, though to the men concerned it probably represented no more than the acceptance of a new title under which to play in a more acceptable environment. Lord's cricket ground would henceforth come to be identified as the headquarters of cricket. GERALD M. D. HOWAT

Sources A. Haygarth, ed., *Scores and biographies*, 1 (1862) · G. R. C. Harris, Baron Harris and F. S. Ashley-Cooper, *Lord's and the MCC: a cricket chronicle of 137 years* (1920) · D. Underdown, *Start of play: cricket and culture in eighteenth-century England* (2000) · F. S. Ashley-Cooper, *Hambledon cricket chronicle, 1772–1796* (1924) · GEC, *Peerage*
Likenesses J. Highmore, portrait, 1740, NPG · G. Knapton, portrait, 1745, Brooks's Club, London · J. Sayers, drawing, *c*.1782, NPG · T. Gainsborough, portrait, 1783, NMM · E. Conway (Peter Burrell), priv. coll. · J. Copley, group portrait, oils (*The collapse of the earl of Chatham in the House of Lords, 7 July 1778*), Tate collection · J. Liotard, portrait, Gov. Art Coll. · G. Townsend, pencil drawing, NPG · Woodforde, portrait (George Finch, ninth earl of Winchilsea), priv. coll.; repro. in Lord Harris and Ashley-Cooper, *Lord's and the MCC* · medallions, BM · portrait (after Zoffany; Lord Sandwich), NPG

White Eyes [Koguetagechton] (*d.* **1778**), leader of the Delaware Indians, details of whose birth and childhood are unknown, first appears in European records in 1758, when he lived on Beaver Creek in present-day western Pennsylvania. Thenceforth, he was a leading figure among the Delaware: after 1763 he migrated with them to villages westward to the Tuscarawas River, he was named chief of the Delaware grand council in 1774, and by 1776 he became their principal spokesman.

Euro-American documents suggest two related themes in his diplomacy. First, he defended Delawares' political independence, along with their lands north-west of the Ohio River, not only against British colonists but also against the Iroquois, who denied the autonomy of Delawares—whom they derided as 'women'—and who pretended ownership of their territory. While fiercely resisting Iroquois hegemony, White Eyes pursued accommodation with Euro-Americans, particularly welcoming educational and economic assistance from Moravian missionaries; the relationship, however, was more political than spiritual. His accommodationism clashed occasionally with more militant Delawares and frequently with the Shawnees, among whom his people had lived for a generation. In 1774, when the Shawnees fought expansionist Virginians during Dunmore's War, White Eyes kept his Delawares out of the conflict. With the outbreak of the American War of Independence he similarly held most of his people aloof for a time. As most Shawnees, Iroquois, and other nations allied themselves with the crown and interracial violence wracked the frontier, however, neutrality became unsupportable. Continuing to resist Iroquois influence, White Eyes was driven into an alliance with the United States, formalized by the treaty of Pittsburgh in September 1778. In exchange for what the Delaware signatories understood merely as free passage to troops who would build a fort to defend the Tuscarawas

villages, United States negotiators cynically proposed that the Delawares might ultimately join the union as a fourteenth state. As recorded on paper, however, the treaty committed the Delawares to take up arms against their Native American neighbours, and the United States general Lachlan McIntosh clearly intended the Tuscarawas post as a base for offensive operations.

Commissioned a colonel, White Eyes accompanied McIntosh's army into American Indian country in early November 1778, but did not return alive. Although officials claimed he died of smallpox, he was almost certainly shot by a trigger-happy Virginia militiaman. The Pittsburgh treaty—and the intercultural accommodation White Eyes had pursued—did not long outlive him; by 1780 nearly all Delawares had joined the British, and United States troops had destroyed the Tuscarawas towns. Details of his wife or wives are unknown, though he was survived by a son, George White Eyes, who died at Beaver Creek, Pennsylvania, in 1798. DANIEL K. RICHTER

Sources C. H Sipe, *The Indian chiefs of Pennsylvania* (1927), 410–18 · L. P. Kellogg, ed., *Frontier advance on the upper Ohio, 1778–1779* (1916) · C. G. Calloway, 'White Eyes', *ANB* · R. C. Downes, *Council fires on the upper Ohio: a narrative of Indian affairs in the upper Ohio valley until 1795* (1940) · G. E. Dowd, *A spirited resistance: the North American Indian struggle for unity, 1745–1815* (1992) · P. A. W. Wallace, ed., *The travels of John Heckewelder in frontier America* (1958) · H. H. Tanner, ed., *Atlas of Great Lakes Indian history* (1987)
Wealth at death see inventory, Kellogg, ed., *Frontier advance on the upper Ohio*, 168–9

Whitefield, George (1714–1770), Calvinistic Methodist leader, was born on 16 December 1714 at The Bell inn, Southgate Street, Gloucester, the youngest of the six sons and one daughter of Thomas Whitefield (*bap.* 1681, *d.* 1716), proprietor of the inn, and his wife, Elizabeth (1681?–1751), daughter of Richard Edwards and his wife, Mary, both of Bristol.

Early years and education George Whitefield (pronounced Whitfield) was baptized at the church of St Mary de Crypt, Gloucester, on 25 December 1714. When he was aged two his father died, and in 1722 his mother married Capel Longden, 'an unhappy match' (*George Whitefield's Journals*, 39). Whitefield was enrolled in Gloucester Cathedral school, aged eleven. A year later he entered St Mary de Crypt School, priding himself on his elocution, memory, and speech making. Devoted to reading plays and to acting, he often dressed and performed the part of a woman. Through his stepfather's mismanagement The Bell fell into hard times, and after a year or so Whitefield left school to assist with menial tasks. By the late 1720s his mother had separated from Longden and moved from The Bell. At about the age of four Whitefield had contracted measles, the cause of his lifelong squint. Mercilessly teased, on one occasion he repeated the words of the psalm: 'But in the Name of the Lord will I destroy them.' He liked 'to imitate the ministers reading prayers' and even composed sermons (ibid., 38). He re-entered St Mary de Crypt School, and received his first communion on 25 December 1731.

George Whitefield (1714–1770), by John Wollaston, c.1742

On 7 November 1732 Whitefield matriculated at Pembroke College, Oxford. As a servitor, the lowest rank of undergraduates, he performed servile tasks, which continued throughout his Oxford years. Through Charles Wesley, in the summer of 1733 he joined a group practising self-denial, lengthy devotions, and meticulous self-examination. This 'Holy Club' of 'despised Methodists' was led by John Wesley (*George Whitefield's Journals*, 46). 'Whole days and weeks' were 'spent in lying prostrate on the ground', and Whitefield ate 'the worst sort of food' (ibid., 52–3), neglected his appearance, and became obsessed with the devil. Seriously ill following a severe 1735 Lenten fast (when he experienced his inner conversion), Whitefield recuperated in Gloucester. He returned to Oxford in March 1736 and assumed the leadership of the Holy Club, the Wesleys having departed for Georgia. He faced his examination on 14 May and received his BA two months later.

Early ministry 'Fully persuaded it is His will that I should take Orders' (Whitefield, diary, BL, Add. MS 34068), Whitefield was ordained deacon on 20 June 1736 in Gloucester Cathedral by Bishop Martin Benson. The following Sunday he preached his first sermon, in St Mary de Crypt. The next month he covered pastoral duties at the Tower of London and walked through the streets in his gown and cassock, with people crying out, 'There's a boy parson' (*George Whitefield's Journals*, 77). His first London sermon was at St Botolph without Bishopsgate, on 8 August, and for two months he preached at the Tower on the theme of the new birth. By this Whitefield meant a total change of heart, an inner regeneration wrought solely by the action of the Holy Spirit. This experience, in no way dependent upon traditional religious observance, would result in a faith vitally felt. During November and December he officiated at Dummer, Hampshire. He had corresponded with the Wesleys and late in 1736 determined to follow them to Georgia. In the spring he deputized for the vicar of Stonehouse, Gloucestershire. Most of 1737 was devoted to preaching charity sermons for Georgia, especially in Bristol and Bath, then in London for four months from late August; Whitefield generally preached nine times a week and wrote that he was forced from foot to coach in order 'to avoid the hosannas of the multitude' (ibid., 89). During this period he collected £1000 for English charity schools and £300 for Georgia. The effectiveness of these collections induced most parish clergymen 'to open their pulpits to him, which otherwise they were unwilling to do' (Hutton, 183). However, these sermons were not charitable towards them. In his first publication—his subsequently most widely distributed sermon, *The Nature and Necessity of our New Birth in Christ Jesus, in Order to Salvation* (1737)—he castigated fellow clerics for presenting only 'the shell and shadow of religion' (Tyerman, 1.81). He unequivocally maintained that anyone who did not accept the necessity of a new birth would be 'thrust down into Hell' (Thomas, 26.384). This theme remained central.

Whitefield sailed for Georgia in February 1738. On stopping at Gibraltar, he preached frequently and attended a Roman Catholic service, which he considered 'wholly given to idolatry' (*George Whitefield's Journals*, 128). Amply supported by the colony's trustees, who had authorized him to minister, he arrived in Georgia on 7 May 1738. Inspired by the Halle Orphanage in Germany, he laid plans for a similar institution, returning to England after four months. He energetically solicited moneys and secured the trustees' approval for the orphanage. With their support he was ordained priest by Bishop Benson at Christ Church, Oxford, on 14 January 1739. However, Whitefield's outspoken criticisms of clergymen increased. At St Margaret's, Westminster, supporters physically obstructed the appointed preacher and installed Whitefield in the pulpit. He arrived in Bristol in February, where negative reports from London caused most churches to be closed to him. Two months earlier he had initiated correspondence with Howell Harris, whose example in Wales of open-air preaching perhaps inspired Whitefield now to follow suit. He began by preaching on Kingswood Hill, near Bristol, on 17 February. First hearers were colliery miners, but soon massive crowds came from surrounding areas. Raising money for the orphanage, he also solicited collections for a school for Kingswood miners' children, and laid its foundation-stone on 2 April.

Early theological disputes In March 1739 Whitefield wrote to John Wesley that he 'must come and water what God has enabled me to plant' (3 March 1739, *Works of John Wesley*, 25.605). Wesley followed Whitefield's example by preaching in the fields and agreed to assume the Kingswood work. After Whitefield's departure Wesley preached against predestination, stating that believing it 'made God worse than a devil' (Thomas, 27.300). A Calvinistic orientation, not evident in Whitefield's early ministry, had now become central to his thinking. His adherence to predestination set him directly at odds with Wesley, who immediately published his sermon *Free Grace*, condemning it. The theological divide publicly opened was never bridged and, especially in this formative period of Methodism, seriously damaged their personal relationship. Whitefield was in London from May to August. Finding churches closed to him, he preached in the open air, regularly on Kennington Common and at Moorfields, taking collections for the Georgia orphanage and frequently preaching for two hours. He claimed attendances as large as 80,000. However many attended, they were numerous and at least curious. John Byrom wrote in June that 'Mr Whitefield is the chief topic of conversation' (J. Byrom, *Private Journal … of John Byrom*, ed. R. Parkinson, 2 vols., 1857, 2(3).246).

By 1739 writing was central to Whitefield's strategy, and before he was twenty-five he had published forty-six sermons. To promote and finance his work he also began publishing journals of his ministry, and seven volumes appeared from 1737 to 1741. Together with two more describing his earlier life, their self-assurance was remarkable. Beginning with the observation that he, like Christ, had been born in an inn, they stated that 'God has set His seal to my ministry' (*George Whitefield's Journals*, 207). 'The account of my infant years was wrote by the will of God' (Whitefield to J. Wesley, 8 Nov 1739, *Works of John Wesley*, 25.699). Regarding a 1737 London sermon, his *Journals* recorded that 'thousands and thousands of prayers were put up for me. They would run and stop me in the alleys, hug me in their arms, and follow me with wishful looks' (*George Whitefield's Journals*, 92). This confidence he also announced to correspondents. 'I am sure I have received angelic blessings. … The inhabitants are vastly affectionate towards me and are ready to pull out their eyes to give me' (Thomas, 26.382).

In return, followers assured Whitefield that he was a 'faiverite of heaven' or that it would be 'no crime to fall down & worship you' (Library of Congress, Whitefield MSS 2.30, 2.38). One 'used to follow him as he walked the streets, and could scarce refrain from kissing the very prints of his feet' (Jackson, 2.58). However, what to Whitefield's followers was evidence of his God-inspired ministry, to detractors appeared an ego of wide girth. He already had kindled a fierce flame of opposition. His *Journals* prompted a sermon in St Paul's Cathedral, where it was wondered if there had ever been 'such a medley of vanity, and nonsense, and blasphemy jumbled together?' (Tyerman, 1.288). He heard himself strongly attacked in a sermon by Joseph Trapp, which precipitated a prolonged and bitter exchange in the press. Trapp called the *Journals* blasphemous and Whitefield himself besotted either with pride or madness. Whitefield preached and published against Trapp, 'my poor peevish adversary' (*Works*, 5.157), stating that he was no Christian but a servant of Satan. Of the 200 anti-Methodist publications appearing in England during 1739–40, 154 were aimed at Whitefield, triggered

by his open-air ministry, his condemnation of the preaching and theology of parish clergymen, and his denouncing Oxford as a 'harlot' (ibid., 1.80).

Whitefield had previously received some support from bishops, yet by 1739 they were revising their opinions. Benson wrote six months after ordaining him priest to caution against acting contrary to that ordination's purpose: settled service in a Georgia parish. Whitefield replied that if bishops rejected him and fellow Methodists, God would furnish their authority. When the bishop of London, Edmund Gibson, published a pamphlet criticizing his claims of divine guidance and his judging of others, Whitefield responded in print, labelling Anglican clerics as lazy, non-spiritual, and pleasure seeking. Rejecting any ecclesiastical authority controlling his actions, he had concluded six weeks after his ordination as priest that 'the whole world is now my parish' (Thomas, 27.91), apparently antedating by a month Wesley's similar statement.

America's Great Awakening Accompanying Whitefield to America in 1739 was a wealthy layman, William Seward, acting as fund-raiser, business co-ordinator, and publicist. He had orchestrated a barrage of printed support in England, including paid newspaper advertisements purporting to be news articles. On Whitefield's first American preaching mission, Seward now furnished newspapers and booksellers there and in Britain with constant material, including copies of Whitefield's writings. All this firmly focused the image of an exuberant trans-Atlantic revival. Seward sent a poem to colonial newspapers, the first stanza of which ran:

Whitefield, the great the pleasing Name,
Has all my soul possest,
For sure some Seraph from above
Inspires his Godlike Breast.
(Trefeca MS 3174)

Whitefield, also, sent publicity to printers. Of himself, he wrote: 'Great and visible effects followed his preaching, almost wheresoever he went. … There was never such a general awakening, and concern for things of God known in *America* before' (*Works*, 1.179).

For fifteen months Whitefield preached from New England to Georgia. As in England, he aimed attacks primarily at Anglican clergymen, publicly portraying them as God's persecutors. He told Americans that Bishop Gibson knew 'no … more of Christianity, than *Mahaomet*, or an Infidel' (Stephens, 2.307) and advised them 'since the Gospel was not preached in the church, to go and hear it in the meeting-houses' (*George Whitefield's Journals*, 444). In Charles Town, South Carolina, the bishop of London's commissary, Alexander Garden, who had been highly supportive in 1738, now wrote to Gibson of his determination to put a stop to 'the fascinating Gibberish of Young Geo' (Kenney, 85). When he suspended him from the Anglican ministry, Whitefield rejected Garden's authority and joined in publishing a letter denouncing all South Carolina's Anglican clergy, for which he was arrested and granted bail. He challenged Commissary Archibald Cummings to a public debate in the press, after Cummings had announced Pennsylvania's Anglican churches henceforth closed to his preaching. His Philadelphia admirers then, in 1740, erected a building for his preaching. Publicly denouncing ministers sent by the Society for the Propagation of the Gospel in Foreign Parts, to colonial Anglican clerics he became 'the Noisie Mr. Whitefield' (Hall, 36). He fell to traducing divines long dead, publishing in 1740 against the works of two of Anglicanism's revered seventeenth-century authors. Whitefield wrote that John Tillotson, archbishop of Canterbury, had no more been a true Christian than had Muhammad. In a separate publication he attacked Richard Allestree's *The Whole Duty of Man*, one of Anglicanism's most popular spiritual tracts, which on at least one occasion Whitefield had his followers cast 'into the Fire, with great Detestation' (Stephens, 2.320). He published these attacks widely in America and in England, and the Society for Promoting Christian Knowledge, which had furnished him religious books for America, ended its support. Whitefield was ironically a godsend to colonial non-Anglicans. Facing increasing opposition from English bishops, he turned the ecclesiastical tables, attacking colonial Anglicans and cutting his clerical cloth to suit America's predominant Calvinist dissenting ethos. He claimed it likely that he would 'be set at nought by the Rabbies of our Church, and perhaps at last be killed by them' (Seward, 71).

Whitefield's arrival coincided with several local American awakenings. By the time he left, his itinerating had provided the sharpest spur in creating a general Great Awakening. In Pennsylvania he supported the revivalist Presbyterian ministers William and Gilbert Tennent, and his preaching caused a major split in that denomination. In the autumn of 1740 he made his first visit to New England, where five people were trampled to death in a Boston Congregational church in the crush to hear him. Crowds followed him everywhere and, as in England, he was the chief topic of conversation. At the invitation of the Congregational minister Jonathan Edwards he preached at Northampton. Although struck with the power of his sermons, Edwards was deeply disturbed by his unqualified appeals to emotion, his openly judging those he considered unconverted, and his demand for instant conversions. Edwards addressed him forcefully in private, but Whitefield refused a discussion. Shortly after Whitefield's departure, Edwards delivered a series of sermons containing but thinly veiled critiques of his preaching techniques, warning against over-dependence upon a preacher's eloquence and fervency.

Whitefield's presence throughout mainland America from 1739 to 1741, and the hearty acclaim and opposition it produced, contributed directly to the expansion of colonial printing. Before arriving in America, Whitefield had published well over 100 imprints in England. The number of American publications nearly doubled from 1738 to 1741, the majority attributable to his presence, and each year from 1739 to 1745 American publishers produced more works by Whitefield than by any other writer on any subject. He struck up a business relationship with Benjamin Franklin. Serving as his main American publisher, Franklin reaped highly lucrative rewards, and many other colonial printers profited. According to a supporter, Whitefield had 'made *Sermons*, once a *Drug*, a *vendible Commodity*' (J. Smith, *Character, Preaching, &c. of … Whitefield*, 1740, 16).

Whitefield's plan for a Georgia orphanage was central to his preaching, and on 25 March 1740 he laid the first brick for what he called Bethesda, 10 miles from Savannah. Although appointed as its parish minister, he did not reach Savannah until January 1740, over fourteen months after arriving in America. He at once informed the trustees that he was giving up the post, though it had been the basis of their support. When they revoked his authority to serve as minister, he insisted on sole control of the orphanage. During 1740 he even kidnapped children and laid claim to their personal possessions. This brought him into sharp conflict with Georgia's founder, James Oglethorpe, who had them removed from Bethesda. When the trustees asked Whitefield to submit financial accounts, he replied that he would never feel obliged to do so. Meanwhile, with Seward's substantial financial contribution he purchased 5000 acres in Pennsylvania, ostensibly to establish a school for black people but also as a bolt-hole for English Methodists if they faced persecution. This project, to be called either Nazareth or English Town, never materialized. On departing for England in 1741, he left Bethesda's supervision with James Habersham, who had accompanied him to Georgia in 1738 and had remained in the colony. Whitefield took an energetic line with children. During the 1738 crossing he beat a four-year-old boy until he recited the Lord's prayer and tied up another until he repeated a psalm. One of the trustees' objections to his control of Bethesda was that 'a wrong Method' was taken with the children, who 'are often kept praying and crying all the Night' (Coleman, 271).

England and Scotland, 1741–1744 Whitefield had become the most famous person in America but faced serious difficulties upon his return to England in March 1741. He was more than £1000 in debt for Bethesda. Seward, having given a staggering £10,000 for Whitefield's projects, was dead and had left no legacy but a substantial debt, for which Whitefield was under threat of arrest. His assault on Tillotson and *The Whole Duty of Man* had lost him the support of many followers and had resulted in a huge number of hostile publications. Moreover, his London open-air preaching now attracted decidedly fewer hearers. He had left England as the leader of the new-birth movement, but Wesley now assumed that role. Whitefield wrote bitterly, accusing him of undermining his work and proceeded to preach against him, claiming that Wesley's attacks on predestination had alienated 'very many of my spiritual children', some of whom sent 'threatening letters, that God will speedily destroy me' (*Works*, 1.256–7). During his absence in America their theological conflict had taken on a cutting edge, reflected in their sharp exchange of transatlantic letters. Whitefield had printed in both America and England *A Letter to … John Wesley: in Answer to his Sermon Entituled, Free-Grace* (1741), which Wesley considered a 'treacherous' action whereby Whitefield had made himself 'odious and contemptible' (Wesley to

Whitefield, 27 April 1741; *Works of John Wesley*, 26.60–61). Whitefield's remaining London followers in the spring built at Moorfields a large wooden 'tabernacle', close to Wesley's chapel. Wesley travelled widely to counter Whitefield's preaching, publicly shredded a copy of Whitefield's *Letter*, and published extensively against predestination. Whitefield took a leading role in the production of *Weekly History*, the first Methodist magazine. A mouthpiece for Calvinism, it was also a commercial venture, including advertising from evangelical tradesmen. For Whitefield, 'the devotion and business of a Methodist go hand in hand' (Whitefield, *Sermons*, 654).

Whitefield re-established his relationship with Howell Harris, securing his service at the Tabernacle. Harris stood in awe of Whitefield—'I am not worthy indeed to wipe his feet' (Trefeca MS 618)—an attitude material in securing Whitefield a wife. While in America, Whitefield proposed marriage by letter to Elizabeth Delamore of Kent, and her refusal dealt him a severe blow. Intent on finding a wife, he focused on a widow, Mrs Elizabeth James, *née* Burnell (c.1704–1768), already affianced to Harris. At her Abergavenny home she told Whitefield of her love for Harris. Whitefield, replying that he would not be jealous, persisted. A broken-hearted Harris assured the protesting bride that she would be a support to Whitefield's work and officially gave her away when she and Whitefield married on 14 November 1741 in Capel Martin, Caerphilly. Whitefield rejoiced that his wife, about ten years his senior, 'would not, I think, attempt to hinder me in [God's] work for the world' (*Works*, 1.363).

Before he married Whitefield had made his first tour in Scotland, from July to October 1741, the first of fourteen visits. Ralph and Ebenezer Erskine, leaders of the breakaway Associate Presbytery, had constantly urged him to come, but upon arrival he discovered that this sect claimed a Christian monopoly and insisted he preach only in their churches. When he refused, they fell upon him mercilessly, branding him a sorcerer, 'a poor, vainglorious, self-seeking, puffed-up creature', 'a limb of Antichrist; a boar, and a wild beast' (Tyerman, 2.11). He returned to Scotland in the spring of 1742, and during five months his most notable appearances were at Cambuslang and Kilsyth, where revivals had been initiated. He preached three times on his first day at Cambuslang, writing that the physical outcryings 'far out-did all that I ever saw in *America*' (*Works*, 1.405) and that people 'are carryd out by Scores as Dead people out of the fi[e]ld' (Trefeca MS 571). Here, as in America, Whitefield participated in conducting communion services after Presbyterian and Congregationalist forms. While in Scotland he took collections to help pay Bethesda debts. That, and the hysteria of many of his open-air preachings, induced the publication in Edinburgh and Glasgow of seven bitter attacks.

In addition, Whitefield frequently preached in south Wales, usually accompanied by Harris. In 1743 he was appointed at Watford moderator of Calvinistic Methodists in Wales and England. In the autumn Philip Doddridge, holding mixed opinions of Whitefield—'a very honest tho a very weak Man' who 'certainly does much

good & I am afraid some Harm' (Nuttall, 705)—preached at the Tabernacle and invited Whitefield to preach at his Northampton Academy. Doddridge received criticism from fellow dissenters, including Isaac Watts. On 4 October 1743 Whitefield's wife gave birth to a son in London. He baptized him at the Tabernacle and announced that God destined John as a noted preacher. Four months later she and the baby stopped at Gloucester. At the inn where Whitefield had been born his son died; he was buried on 8 February 1744 in the church where Whitefield had been baptized.

American preaching tour, 1744–1748 After publishing several further controversial pamphlets, Whitefield, with his wife, departed in the summer of 1744 for what proved his most lengthy American visit. In Boston he faced considerable opposition. Soon after his arrival thirteen pamphlets were published, ten of them highly critical. Two were by the officials of Harvard and Yale. Despite friendly treatment and invitations to preach in 1740, when he published his *Journal* in 1741 Whitefield had criticized both their education and Christian commitment, lamenting the lack of zeal of New England's Congregational ministers. Faced with their opposition—'how different from what once they were' (*Works*, 2.72)—he claimed that a conspiracy had been mounted. When he left Boston in 1740 Whitefield had induced Gilbert Tennent 'to blow up the divine fire' he had 'lately kindled there'; 'Surely our Lord intends to set *America* in a flame' (ibid., 1.220–21). Tennent and another of Whitefield's clerical followers, James Davenport, had done just that, with New England experiencing fearful religious and social turmoil, necessitating the intervention of civil authority. Many claimed that what Whitefield set in motion had led directly to the break-up of New England's orderly parish system, communities, and even families, and most ministers were determined to prevent a fresh burst of disruption. One group proclaimed that 'religion is now in a far worse state than it was' before his preaching (*Declaration of the Association of the County of New Haven*, 1745, 6).

A leading Pennsylvania Presbyterian minister, George Gillespie, a former supporter, now issued *Remarks upon Mr George Whitefield, Proving him a Man under Delusion*. Revivalist activity generally had subsided significantly, and Whitefield bemoaned the fact that 'nobody goes out scarcely but myself' (*Works*, 2.103). Sobered by the level of opposition, he published *A Letter to the … President and Professors … of Harvard* (1745), which admitted that some of his earlier actions and words had been immature and extreme. However, he saw no reason to implicate himself in the course of events: his 'fire' had been pure, he wrote; it had been corrupted by the 'wild-fire' of others (ibid., 2.73). Attempting to re-establish his reputation in New England, he preached in April 1745 to Massachusetts troops before their campaign against the French at Louisburg, opining that 'Canada is to be given us' (Christie, 267). When news of the Jacobite defeat at Culloden arrived the following year he preached and published *Britain's*

Mercies, and Britain's Duty. Printed both in America and Britain—as were nearly all his productions—this stated Methodist loyalty to the crown.

Still finding that 'many ministers and the heads of the people' in New England 'would not bear' his ministry (*Works*, 2.93), Whitefield focused on southern plantation provinces (in South Carolina, Alexander Garden again announced his dismissal from the Anglican priesthood). Whitefield's base was the home of the extremely wealthy Baynard family at Bohemia Manor, Maryland. He wrote that 'favour is given me in the sight of the rich and great … [I] sometimes think I shall never return to *England*' (ibid., 2.83). Still deeply in debt for Bethesda, he increased efforts to secure donations from well-to-do supporters. James Habersham having departed Bethesda in 1744, Whitefield often left Elizabeth there to supervise its fabric, copy letters, and serve as press agent. Zeal for Bethesda led to a fateful course of action. Whitefield published in 1740 a criticism of slaves' treatment in the southern colonies and occasionally preached to slaves. However, as early as 1738 he had desired an ending of the trustees' prohibition of slavery in Georgia, and the abortive 'school' for black people in Pennsylvania was actually planned as a slave institution. In 1747 his local supporters Hugh and Jonathan Bryan purchased for him in the neighbouring slavery stronghold, South Carolina, Providence Plantation, stocked with slaves as income for Bethesda. He now wooed leading planters, who contributed nearly £300 for the purchase of further slaves. In 1750 the trustees sanctioned slavery, and Whitefield developed a fulsome defence of the institution, claiming its full scriptural justification. 'As for the lawfulness of keeping slaves, I have no doubt' (ibid., 2.404). Over the coming years he added to his stock of slaves, with preaching tours focused on raising money for that purpose. 'Blessed be God for the increase of the negroes' (ibid., 3.211). Whitefield had emerged as perhaps the most energetic, and conspicuous, evangelical defender and practitioner of slavery.

The middle period in England, 1748–1763 Despite stating that he might remain in America, by 1748 Whitefield had returned to England, attracted by the countess of Huntingdon's desire that he become her personal chaplain. The day of his London arrival, 5 July, 'fearing to offend the Countess' (T. Beynon, 201), he presented himself; on 1 September she made the appointment official. Before he left America it was observed that he had 'become exceeding stately, relishing only the Company of the greatest' (Candler, 52). After he began preaching at the countess's London salon services, a supporter noted that he 'preaches more Considered among persons of a Superior Rank who frequent your Ladyship's Lodgings' (Huntingdon MS B46). 'The prospect of catching some of the rich in the gospel net is very promising', wrote Whitefield. When he and the countess were in London he preached twice a week at such gatherings. He was deferential to a fault, telling her that her conduct was 'truly god-like'. 'Tears trickle from my eyes, whilst I am thinking of your Ladyship's condescending to patronize such a dead dog as I am' (*Works*, 2.220, 238; 3.120). He added his position as her chaplain to his title in subsequent publications and refashioned aspects of his ministry to meet her approval. Admitting that many of his English converts had been guilty of 'real madness and ranticism' (T. Beynon, 208), he became far more circumspect towards clerical opponents. He had told others 'of all the scriptures, promises, dreams and providence that have been given him as to his being made Bishop' (ibid., 41) and now, probably encouraged by her, considered this remarkable notion a near certainty. When a bishop accused him of perjury, Whitefield's restrained reply stated that 'the relation in which I stand to the Right Honourable the Countess of H—' made him 'desirous to clear myself from such an imputation' (*Works*, 2.271). He said that he highly esteemed bishops of the Church of England because of their sacred character. When also in 1749 he was severely attacked in print by another bishop, the disarming subtitle of Whitefield's rejoinder was: 'Wherein several Mistakes in some Parts of his [Whitefield's] past Writings and Conduct are acknowledged'. To a correspondent he wrote: 'Alas! alas! In how many things have I judged and acted wrong … I have been too bitter in my zeal' (ibid., 2.144). His level of publishing subsided dramatically. During the first fourteen years of his ministry English and American publishers issued his works at an average rate of about twenty-five a year, but from 1750 the annual output declined to about three. Revising his *Journals*, he removed what he considered offending passages. However, he stated that the changes should not be considered 'express retractions' (Huntingdon MS B46) and did not publish the revision until 1756. When asked if it were 'true that Whitfield has recanted?' Lady Townshend replied: 'No, Sir, he has only canted' (H. Walpole to Horace Mann, 3 May 1749, Walpole, *Corr.*, 20.52).

Before his 1748 return Whitefield spent three months in Bermuda, preaching frequently and collecting £100, some of which he sent for the personal support of Elizabeth, whom he had left in America. Her return to England over a year later coincided with growing hostility between Harris and Whitefield. She and Harris also fell into bitter confrontation. The complicated relationship between the three contributed to Whitefield's dismissal of Harris from the Tabernacle. Harris said that Whitefield's 'preaching hurts christians' and that he 'is now against our Saviour' (T. Beynon, 259, 277). The breach was never healed. Lady Huntingdon's immediate purpose being their conversion, Whitefield initiated correspondence with several members of the aristocracy. He boasted of his new position, not least to Wesley. Since the early 1740s, they made occasional valiant efforts to patch their torn relationship for the sake of Methodist unity; however, they remained deeply divided theologically, and the fabric was beyond repair. Wesley could not forget Whitefield's published claim that 'Infidels of all Kinds are on your Side of the Question' (*Letter to Wesley*, 22). Even though at Whitefield's request Wesley preached his London funeral sermon, he in the end concluded that Whitefield had constantly ill-treated him and that the division had been caused by 'Mr. Whitefield himself' (Wesley to Thomas Maxfield, 14 Feb 1778, Wesley, *Letters*, 6.304).

Chaplain to the countess of Huntingdon, Whitefield gave up his nominal leadership of the Calvinistic Methodists, intending to keep 'myself free from societies' (*Works*, 2.172). However, he was not free of his London Tabernacle, the affairs of which were at a low state. During his American absence vast numbers of members, and several preachers, had left to join the Moravians. Early in his ministry he was influenced by this church and had often used Moravian terminology in his preaching, such as 'the Bleeding God, Agonizing God, Dying God' (T. Beynon, 13). Now he condemned them and in 1753 published a pamphlet attacking their leader, Count Nicholas Zinzendorf, together with their worship practices, and accused them of obtaining vast sums of money dishonestly. Previous close supporters, Moravian leaders were now livid. James Hutton, his former London printer, called Whitefield 'a Mahomet, a Caesar, an imposter, a Don Quixote, a devil, the beast, the man of sin, the Antichrist' (Benham, 579–80). John Syms threatened to make public Whitefield's most secret affairs. Six months after his return in 1748 he observed that where before 20,000 people would come to hear him in the open air, now there were not more than a hundred. He redoubled his efforts and during 1750 pursued a punishing regime in London and many areas of England and Scotland, ending the year confined to bed. 'My continual vomitings almost kill me, and yet the pulpit is my cure' (*Works*, 2.345). Largely through Lady Huntingdon's generosity a new Tabernacle was erected on the spot of the old and opened on 10 June 1753. Also that year he opened a chapel in Bristol, again with Lady Huntingdon's financial backing. She also provided substantial sums for his personal use, and in London he lived in some comfort.

After a brief journey to Georgia and South Carolina from October 1751 to April 1752 to extend his land and slave holdings, two years later Whitefield returned to America, taking twenty-two English children to Bethesda. Most of the ten months of this visit were again spent in the south, although he also visited New England and the middle colonies. During the summer of 1754 he received an honorary MA from the College of New Jersey, which he used in publications in a manner suggesting that it was an Oxford degree. On returning to England in the spring of 1755, he published vivid accounts depicting Holy Week processions in Lisbon, where he had spent a month on his outward journey.

Whitefield had long desired to position himself in London's West End, close to its theatres, and late in 1755 he was offered the use of the dissenters' Long Acre Chapel. The incumbent of the parish, St Martin-in-the-Fields, attempted to put a stop to Whitefield's services there. Frequent disturbances were made outside the chapel, and in April 1756 he received three anonymous letters threatening his life. These commotions persuaded him of the need for his own building in the area, and in November he opened his second London chapel, in Tottenham Court Road, designed for a higher class of auditor than the Tabernacle. Three years later, much extended, Tottenham was the largest nonconformist church building in Britain

and probably in the world. Although a similar residence was built, he and Elizabeth continued to live at the Tabernacle house. During the Long Acre unrest, Whitefield published *A Short Address to Persons of All Denominations, Occasioned by the Alarm of an Intended Invasion* (1756). Violently anti-French, it stated that 'British arms were never more formidable, than when our soldiers went forth in the strength of the Lord; and, with a Bible in one hand, and a sword in the other, cheerfully fought under His banner' (Tyerman, 2.370). The usually hostile London *Monthly Review* found that Whitefield 'here makes good use of the influence he has acquired over the common people' (ibid., 2.371, n.). It also was a diatribe against Roman Catholicism. Certain that they had sent the threatening Long Acre letters, he railed against papists who, he said, had 'massacred, in cold blood', 'tens of thousands of innocent, unprovoking Irish Protestants' a century earlier. Now 'popish priests' were again planning to murder protestants (ibid., 2.371). He carried this message to Scotland in the autumn. The following summer, 1757, again preaching there, Whitefield attended the general assembly of the Church of Scotland, which he highly commended, and then proceeded to Ireland, which he had visited in 1738 and 1751. Now, in the open air in Dublin, he spoke out against Roman Catholicism and was attacked by 'hundreds and hundreds of papists' who wounded him severely and smashed his portable pulpit. Taking refuge in a coach, he rode 'in gospel triumph through the oaths, curses, and imprecations of whole streets of papists' (*Works*, 3.208). It was his final visit to Ireland.

Throughout his ministry Whitefield was especially vigorous in condemning public amusements of all kinds: musical concerts, dances, card playing, and the theatre. On one occasion he upbraided an eminent dissenting minister for singing in a London tavern a song in praise of old English beef. Towards the end of 1759 Whitefield preached a sermon threatening London theatregoers with damnation. This was reciprocated with a vengeance by numerous satirical productions, based on the premise that Whitefield was himself a consummate actor. As early as 1746 he was introduced as the adulterous Doctor Preach Field in the production of Charles Macklin's *A Will and No Will*. Now in 1760 he was treated by the leading theatrical satirist, Samuel Foote. In *The Minor* Whitefield was called Squintum, occasioned by the severe squint in his left eye. Squintum was thenceforward the satirist's usual appellation suggesting that Whitefield focused on the carnal while gazing heavenward. By September *The Minor* had graced stages as far afield as Newcastle and later crossed the Atlantic. *The Spiritual Minor* (1763) and *The Hypocrite* (1768) followed, and Whitefield was the target of most of the satirical writing directed against the Methodist movement. He was harshly handled by novelists in Fielding's *Joseph Andrews* (1742) and *Tom Jones* (1749), and in Smollett's *Humphry Clinker* (1771). Richard Graves, who had graduated with Whitefield from Pembroke College, portrayed him in *The Spiritual Quixote* (1772), where the preacher Wildgoose uttered quotations from Whitefield's publications.

A satirical print by Hogarth, *Credulity, Superstition and Fanaticism* (1762), sold widely.

Whitefield was of average height, with fair complexion and small, dark-blue eyes. As a young man slender, by the late 1750s he had become decidedly corpulent (a change vividly portrayed in his portraits). In 1761 and 1762 he was severely ill and sought medical advice in Bath, Edinburgh, and the Netherlands. 'I am weary', he wrote, 'of the world, of the church, and of myself', and believed that 'a voyage would brace me up' (*Works*, 3.283, 271). In all, he spent perhaps two years of his life at sea and was, in his own words, 'an amphibious itinerant' (JRL, PLP 113.1.20). In 1763, after over eight years' absence, Whitefield was anxious to visit America. Added to distress at satirical attacks was weariness with overseeing his two London chapels. Their management he left to laymen, with instructions not to 'consult me in any thing, unless absolutely necessary', adding that he could not 'bear the[ir] cares' even when in London (*Works*, 3.290, 326).

The final years Most of Whitefield's American visit from 1763 to 1765 was spent in Philadelphia, New York, and Boston, where he received thanks for collecting funds in England after a Boston fire in 1760. A further mending of fences was indicated by an invitation to preach at Yale. After reaching America in September 1763, it was sixteen months before he arrived at Bethesda. In 1757 he had instructed his agents to send away most of the orphans. 'I pity them, but they must blame their parents … I am determined to take in no more than the plantation will maintain, till I can buy more negroes' (*Works*, 3.211). It became clear that he had all along viewed Bethesda as a prospective college; at the end of 1764 he petitioned Georgia's authorities to that effect. He also produced accounts of his financial stewardship, similar to those frequently published over the years.

Back in England, on 6 October 1765 Whitefield preached at the opening of Lady Huntingdon's Bath chapel. During his final decade the bulk of his publications were devotional, including prefaces to a new edition of Samuel Clarke's annotated Bible (1759) and to Bunyan's collected works (1767). There were two exceptions. In 1763 he issued a rebuttal to a publication against Methodism, though in it he repeated contrition for much contained in his *Journals*. The other was his final pamphlet. When six students at St Edmund Hall, Oxford—with whom he had been closely involved—were expelled in 1768 for Methodistic practices, he published *A Letter to the Reverend Dr Durell, Vice-Chancellor*, disingenuously denying connection with the students but protesting at their treatment. That summer he made his last journey to Scotland, reporting that he was 'in danger of being hugged to death' (*Works*, 3.371). He raised collections for Indian education in New England. His wife died of a fever on 9 August 1768 and was buried in a vault at the Tottenham chapel. After their 1744–8 stay in America, where she suffered four miscarriages, she never accompanied him on his travels, remaining at the Tabernacle house. Whitefield reported that 'none in America could bear her' (T. Beynon, 16), while she said that she had been 'but a load & burden' to him (Trefeca MS

1535). It was observed after their 1748 return that she was refusing to submit to him, and that his treatment of her left much to be desired. She concluded that she was 'altogether unfit & unworthy' to be his wife (JRL, PLP 113.2.2). Cornelius Winter, who latterly lived with them, reported that Whitefield 'was not happy in his wife', though he 'did not intentionally make his wife unhappy'. However, 'her death set his mind much at liberty'. Winter also reported that in general personal relationships Whitefield 'was impatient of contradiction'. Once, when his sharpness drove to tears someone trying to please him, he 'burst into tears, saying, "I shall live to be a poor peevish old man, and every body will be tired of me"' (Jay, 81).

Whitefield preached at the opening of the countess of Huntingdon's Trevecca College in Wales on 24 August 1768, as he did at the opening of her Tunbridge Wells chapel on 23 July 1769. He abruptly left for America in September 1769, arriving at Bethesda in December. In spite of objections from ministerial colleagues, who said that since all his collections had been solicited for an orphanage he was not free to transform Bethesda, Whitefield had pursued his plans for a college. Unsuccessful in securing a royal charter, he received a more favourable response from the governor and council of Georgia. He left Georgia in April 1770, preaching in Philadelphia, New York, and New England, there making outspoken common cause with American patriots. As early as 1764 he announced in Boston: 'O poor New England! There is a deep laid plot against both your civil and religious liberties' (C. Bridenbaugh, *Mitre and Sceptre*, 1962, 244). Critical of the 1765 Stamp Act, the following year he wrote: 'Stamp Act repealed, *Gloria Deo*' (Gillies, 248). He notified New Englanders that he would 'serve our civil as well as religious Interests' (S. Adams, *Writings of Samuel Adams*, ed. H. Cushing, 4 vols., 1904–8, 1.26). He attended the House of Commons in 1766 to hear Benjamin Franklin's presentation of colonial grievances and wrote a letter, published in America, praising his performance. (However, their relationship ended in 1769 on a sour note, when Franklin made clear his rejection of Whitefield's religious prescriptions.) In a farewell sermon to his London chapels, setting out on his seventh and final journey to America, Whitefield seemed to burn his British bridges: he denounced 'the great mischiefs the poor pious [Boston] people suffered lately through the town's being disturbed by the [British] soldiers' (Whitefield, *Sermons*, 712).

Although there were frequent references to vomitings during the 1740s and 1750s, probably during 1760–61 his 'constitution … received its material shock' (Jay, 36). He was described, at the age of fifty, as 'an old, old man' (*Journal of John Wesley*, 5.150). Cornelius Winter said that, following each time of preaching, as soon as 'he was seated in his chair, nature demanded relief, and gained it by a vast discharge from the stomach, usually with a considerable quantity of blood', before he could speak (Jay, 26). Wesley described him early in 1769 as sinking towards death. Whitefield often expressed the desire to die in the pulpit and after arriving in New England in August 1770 preached almost daily for the next two months. Following a two-hour open-air sermon he died at the age of fifty-five at 6 a.m. on Sunday 30 September 1770, in the house of the Presbyterian minister of Newburyport, Massachusetts, apparently from angina pectoris. The funeral was in the Newburyport church on 2 October, and he was buried beneath the pulpit. His death cemented his relationship with America. To New Englanders he had been a 'real patriot' (N. Whitaker, *Funeral Sermon*, 1771, 34). Another put it in verse:

When his Americans were burden'd sore
… Unrival'd friendship in his breast now strove:
The fruit thereof was charity and love
Towards America.
(P. Wheatley, *An Elegiac Poem*, 1770, 6)

Five years later several American patriot soldiers entered Whitefield's crypt, cut off small pieces of his garments, and carried them as amulets into battle against British troops. Whitefield, who spent nine of his ministry's thirty-four years there, had become an American icon.

Whitefield bequeathed sums to friends and family members totalling nearly £1500. Questions concerning the source of his personal wealth dogged his memory. His will stated that all this money had lately been left him 'in a most unexpected way and unthought of means' (JRL, PLP 113.1.23). However, much earlier he had lodged £1000 for his wife if predeceasing her and had personally contributed £3300 to Bethesda. He willed everything in Georgia to the countess of Huntingdon, including 4000 acres of land and fifty slaves, commissioning her to pursue his college plan. However, at his death Bethesda still bore a debt of £1235, and soon it lay in ruins. Despite the enormous total of £16,000 expended, only 180 children had at various sporadic times been resident since its founding. Whitefield's most faithful London lay supporter was astonished at the accounts and concluded 'that Mr Whitefield was not directed from above' with Bethesda, 'as no good ever came from it either in spiritual or temporal' (Huntingdon MS A1/8/5).

Whitefield as preacher Franklin attended one of Whitefield's open-air preachings, determined not to contribute to the orphanage, yet found himself turning out his pockets owing to the eloquence of the appeal. Whitefield, denouncing the theatre, was a consummate actor, bringing drama and novelty to countless people. He preached on perhaps 18,000 occasions, and many sermons were perfected by constant repetition. Preaching without note or sermon plan, never stumbling at a word, with constant anecdotes (at which he excelled), and even humour, he utilized his arresting voice and oratorical skills, set off with gestures and vivid part-playing. Towards the close of a sermon he occasionally donned a black cap after the manner of a condemning judge, proclaiming, 'sinner, I must do it; I must pronounce sentence upon you'. He would then, 'in a tremendous strain of eloquence, recite our Lord's words, "Go ye cursed," not without a very powerful description of the nature of the curse' (Jay, 24). When describing Peter's bitter weeping, Whitefield would catch a fold of his gown to wipe away tears. One ardent attender at Tottenham Court Road was 'agreeably entertained with his manner of preaching' but could not 'discern any difference between Mr. Whitefield's preaching and seeing a good tragedy' (Jackson, 5.225). Another observed that he 'could play well on an instrument. … But I did not understand him, though I might hear him twenty times' (ibid., 1.13). In Pennsylvania a German woman who understood no English was blessed merely by his gestures, looks, and voice. Franklin praised his voice and dramatic timing, so 'that without being interested in the Subject, one could not help being pleas'd with the Discourse' (B. Franklin, *Autobiography*, ed. L. W. Labaree, 1964, 180). Men such as Lord Chesterfield held similar views.

A further aspect of Whitefield's preaching was tears, a homiletic hallmark. He also expected them from hearers, since tears were his litmus test for judging effect. Wesley commented that often when preaching Whitefield's '*head [was] as waters*, and his *eyes as a fountain of tears*' (Tyerman, 2.617). Winter said that 'I hardly ever knew him to go through a sermon without weeping … sometimes he exceedingly wept, stamped loudly and passionately, and was frequently so overcome, that, for a few seconds, you would suspect he never could recover' (Jay, 27–8). The former slave Olaudah Equiano observed that he 'sweat[ed] as much as I ever did while in slavery' (P. Edwards, ed., *Equiano's Travels*, 1989, 92). Samuel Johnson believed that Whitefield 'would be followed by crowds were he to wear a night-cap in the pulpit, or were he to preach from a tree' (Boswell, *Life*, 2.79). However, though frequently veering from dramatic bathos to condemnation, he was at times capable of careful and compelling antithesis.

Historical perspective 'I never in my life knew any person so much idolized by some, and railed at by others' (*Calendar*, ed. Nuttall, 4.265). This contemporary observation crisply poses the problem for historical evaluation. The first biography, John Gillies's *Memoirs* (which contains Whitefield's account of his Bermuda visit and portions of the now lost manuscript journal of his later years), appeared less than two years after Whitefield's death, specifically to spike continuing negative images of his ministry, not least concerning financial affairs. Gillies simultaneously published his *Works*, the first three volumes containing 1465 of Whitefield's letters, to which, as editor, he made alterations of substance and style. That the originals of only a few have survived, together with a limited number of others, has presented historians with severe difficulties. Recent writing has focused on specific aspects of his career, such as his 'acting' or his contribution to an expanding consumer economy. Those attempting biographies, from Gillies on, have done so from a non-Anglican viewpoint and have painted with a hagiographic brush. While sometimes admitting his frequent lack of judgement, they have exonerated him by emphasizing his genius as a preacher. However, there is no adequate corpus of printed sermons (a total of seventy-nine, of which fifty-seven were published by Whitefield), and their general quality has always disappointed even his most ardent admirers. Moreover, it is accepted that without his 'voice and motion' his printed sermons convey 'but a very faint idea' (Jay, 30). While it is impossible to gauge the lasting impact of his sermonic power upon the multitudes who heard him, a number of ministers were in no doubt that by it they had received their own experiences of conversion, and many were induced to attempt to emulate his preaching. In many ways a puritan redivivus, George Whitefield re-energized the Calvinist message. Throughout his ministry, and since, the debate over his character and his contribution to Christianity has continued; yet for more than a generation his robust ministry and compelling passionate proclamation of the necessity of a new birth made him the eighteenth century's most sensational preacher in Great Britain and America.

BOYD STANLEY SCHLENTHER

Sources L. Tyerman, *The life of the Rev. George Whitefield*, 2 vols. (1876–7) · *George Whitefield's journals*, new edn (1960) · *The works of the Reverend George Whitefield*, 6 vols. (1771–2) · W. Jay, *Memoirs of the life and character of the late Rev. Cornelius Winter*, rev. edn (1809) · J. Christie, ed., 'Newly discovered letters of George Whitefield, 1745–46', *Journal of the Presbyterian Historical Society*, 32 (1954), 69–90, 159–86, 241–70 · G. Thomas, ed., 'George Whitefield and friends: the correspondence of some early Methodists', *National Library of Wales Journal*, 26 (1989–90), 251–80, 367–96; 27 (1991–2), 65–96, 175–203, 289–318, 431–52 · F. Lambert, *'Pedlar in divinity': George Whitefield and the transatlantic revivals* (1994) · J. Gillies, *Memoirs of the life of the Reverend George Whitefield* (1772) · A. Dallimore, *George Whitefield*, 2 vols. (1970–80) · H. Stout, *The divine dramatist: George Whitefield and the rise of modern evangelicalism* (1991) · R. Roberts, *Whitefield in print, a bibliographic record of works by, for, and against George Whitefield* (1988) · J. Downey, *The eighteenth century pulpit* (1969) · Trefeca papers, NL Wales, Calvinist Methodist archive · L. Cong., manuscript division, George Whitefield MSS · *The works of John Wesley*, 25–6, ed. F. Baker and others (1980–82) · H. D. Rack, *Reasonable enthusiast: John Wesley and the rise of Methodism* (1989) · G. Whitefield, *Sermons on important subjects* (1825) · Whitefield letters, JRL, English MSS, PLP 113 · W. Kenney, 'George Whitefield, dissenter priest of the great awakening', *William and Mary Quarterly*, 26 (1969), 75–93 · A. Chamberlain, 'The grand sower of the seed: Jonathan Edwards's critique of George Whitefield', *New England Quarterly*, 70 (1997), 368–85 · D. Poole, 'Bethesda: an investigation of the Georgia orphan house, 1738–1772', PhD diss., Georgia State University, 1978 · A. Gallay, *The formation of a planter elite* (1989) · T. Hall, *Contested boundaries: itinerancy and the reshaping of the colonial American religious world* (1994) · W. R. Ward, *The protestant evangelical awakening* (1992) · T. Beynon, ed., *Howell Harris's visits to London* (1960) · D. Benham, *Memoirs of James Hutton* (1856) · J. Hutton, 'The beginning of the Lord's work in England to 1741', *Proceedings of the Wesley Historical Society*, 15 (1926), 178–89 · W. Stephens, *A journal of the proceedings in Georgia*, 2 vols. (1742) · C. Huddleston, 'George Whitefield's ancestry', *Transactions of the Bristol and Gloucestershire Archaeological Society*, 59 (1937), 221–42 · G. Whitefield, *A letter to the Reverend Mr. John Wesley: in answer to his sermon entituled, Free-grace* (1741) · T. Jackson, ed., *The lives of early Methodist preachers, chiefly written by themselves*, 3rd edn, 6 vols. (1865–6) · Walpole, *Corr.* · C. Miller, *Benjamin Franklin's Philadelphia printing, 1728–1766* (1974) · B. S. Schlenther, *Queen of the Methodists: the countess of Huntingdon and the eighteenth-century crisis of faith and society* (1997) · W. Seward, *Journal of a voyage from Savannah to Philadelphia, and from Philadelphia to England* (1740) · A. D. Candler and others, eds., *The colonial records of the state of Georgia*, 30: *Trustees' letter book, 1738–45*, ed. K. Coleman (1985) · A. D. Candler, K. Coleman, and M. Ready, eds., *The colonial records of the state of Georgia*, 25 (1915) · Westminster College, Cambridge, Cheshunt Foundation, Huntingdon MSS, A series · Drew University Library, Madison, Huntingdon MSS, B series · *The journal of the Rev. John Wesley*, ed. N. Curnock and others, 8 vols. (1909–16) · *The letters of the Rev. John Wesley*, ed. J. Telford, 8 vols. (1931) ·

G. Whitefield, diary, 1736, BL, Add. MS 34068 · *Calendar of the correspondence of Philip Doddridge*, ed. G. F. Nuttall, HMC, JP 26 (1979) · *The correspondence and diary of Philip Doddridge*, ed. J. D. Humphreys, 5 vols. (1829–31) · E. Welch, ed., *Two Calvinistic Methodist chapels*, London RS, 11 (1975) · parish register, St Mary de Crypt, 25 Dec 1714, Glos. RO [baptism] · R. Austin, 'George Whitefield's schooldays', *Gloucestershire Notes and Queries*, 8 (1913), 384–5 · E. Beynon, 'Mrs James, Abergavenny', *Transactions of the Calvinistic Methodist Historical Society*, 28 (1943), 10–22

Archives BL, diary, Add. MS 34068 · Bodl. Oxf., corresp. · Evangelical Library, Chiltern Street, London, corresp. · JRL, Methodist Archives and Research Centre, letters · L. Cong., corresp. and papers · U. Birm., letter-book | Dartmouth College, Hanover, New Hampshire, Wheelock MSS · DWL, Congregational Library MSS · JRL, Methodist Archives and Research Centre, letters to John Wesley · JRL, Methodist MSS, corresp.

Likenesses J. Cochran, engraving, 1739, repro. in Tyerman, *Life of the Rev. George Whitefield*, frontispiece · J. Wollaston, oils, *c*.1742, NPG [see illus.] · J. Russell, oils, *c*.1768, NPG · J. Greenwood, mezzotint, pubd 1769 (after N. Hone), BM, NPG · J. Watson, mezzotint, pubd 1772 (after J. Russell), BM · J. E. Haid, mezzotint, 1783 (after M. Jenkin), BM, NPG · attrib. J. Badger, oils, Harvard U. · J. Faber jun., mezzotint (after F. Kyte, 1743), BM · J. Faber jun., mezzotint (after G. Beard), BM, NPG · J. Faber junior, mezzotint (after J. Wollaston), BM, NPG · attrib. E. Wood, pottery bust, Potteries Museum Art Gallery, Stoke-on-Trent · line and stipple engraving (after unknown artist), NPG · mezzotint (after M. Jenkin), NPG · mezzotint (after N. Hone), NPG · oils, Pembroke College, Oxford · oils, Whitefield Memorial Church, London

Wealth at death approx. £1500 in bequests to family and friends; *c*.4000 acres of land, fifty black slaves, and all buildings at Bethesda, Georgia: will, 1770, JRL, English MSS, PLP 113

Whitefoord, Caleb (1734–1810), wine merchant and diplomatist, was born in Edinburgh, the natural son of Charles *Whitefoord (d. 1753), an army officer descended from a titled Ayrshire family. He was educated at John Mundell's school in Edinburgh, showing great skill in classics, and at Edinburgh University, where he matriculated on 3 March 1748. His father wanted him to become a minister in the Church of Scotland, but Caleb disliked this idea, and in 1750 he was taken instead to London and apprenticed to Archibald Stewart, an eminent wine merchant in Buckingham Street. He travelled on business to Portugal and France and acquired a love for the London theatre and for the company of men of letters. An inheritance from his father enabled him to set up a partnership in the wine trade in 1754 with Thomas Brown, a young merchant who shared his convivial tastes, at 38 Craven Street, where Benjamin Franklin would become their neighbour and friend. The firm prospered and Whitefoord found time to engage in humorous and political journalism. His *New Method of Reading Newspapers* (1766) greatly amused the usually critical Horace Walpole and also found favour with Oliver Goldsmith and Samuel Johnson. The government hoped he might write a pamphlet on the Falkland Islands question in 1771, and it was Whitefoord who recommended Johnson for the task.

On Franklin's proposal Whitefoord became a member of the Society for the Encouragement of Arts, Manufactures, and Commerce in 1762 and was active in its proceedings for the remainder of his life, serving as a committee chairman and a vice-president. Through his friendship with Joshua Reynolds he became involved in the affairs of the Royal Academy after its foundation in 1768. He collected pictures by old and modern masters and was himself an amateur artist, whose portrait of Franklin was admired by its subject.

Whitefoord's friendship with Franklin earned him both historical importance and contemporary fame. When an end was sought to the war with the American colonies in 1782, Whitefoord was chosen by Lord Shelburne to go with Richard Oswald to France and act as an intermediary between Franklin and the British government. He served for a year as secretary to the commission that concluded peace with the United States and though Oswald had promised to lobby on his behalf for some financial recompense he received no payment until 1793, when he was granted a pension of £200 a year.

In 1790 Whitefoord moved to the Adelphi, first to John Street and then to James Street, where his friend Isaac Disraeli, who he proposed as a member of the nearby Society of Antiquaries, also had an apartment. He was elected a fellow of the Royal Society in 1784 and of the Society of Antiquaries in 1791. He spent much time at Hanworth with Mary Sidday (1775–1852), with whom he had a son, Charles, in 1797 and whom he married on 21 January 1800. Five more children followed: Maria (b. 1802), Caleb (b. 1805), who became rector of Burford, Oxfordshire, twins Charles and Harriet (b. 1807), and John (1809–1892), who became a magistrate in Tasmania. In 1805 he purchased a large house in Argyll Street (no. 28), a turning off Oxford Street, and in the same year he helped to found the British Institution.

Whitefoord was described by J. T. Smith as 'a slight built man and much addicted when in conversation to shrug up his shoulders. He had a thin face, with little eyes' (Smith, Book, 114). His dandified and old-fashioned style of dress noted by Smith was recorded in Wilkie's painting, The Letter of Introduction. His death on 4 February 1810 at his Argyll Street home was caused by a sudden illness that took only two days to prove mortal. He was buried on 9 February in the churchyard of St Mary's, Paddington. His widow remarried on 25 July 1812; her second husband was John Lee. She died on 18 May 1852.

A memoir in the European Magazine described Whitefoord as one of those men of 'easy, good natured, social disposition, that … have always seemed necessary links of the great chain that binds Society together' (European Magazine, 163). His one weakness was a failure to apply himself to any one sphere of creative endeavour. He preferred to work behind the scenes and his significance lies not merely in his famous flurry into international diplomacy, but in his long years of voluntary work, both institutionally and personally, in promoting the arts and letters of his country.   D. G. C. ALLAN

Sources W. A. S. Hewins, ed., The Whitefoord papers (1898) · BL, Add. MSS 36593–36596 · 'Memoir of Caleb Whitefoord esq.', European Magazine (March 1810), 164 · Public characters, 10 vols. (1799–1809) · D. G. C. Allan, 'Caleb Whitefoord FRS, FSA, 1734–1810', The virtuoso tribe of arts and sciences, ed. D. G. C. Allan and J. L. Abbott (1992), 25–85, 381 · C. C. Sellars, Benjamin Franklin in portraiture

(1962), 408–9, 420 · Burke, Gen. GB (1972), 948–9 · J. T. Smith, Nollekens and his times (1949) · J. T. Smith, A book for a rainy day, or, Recollections of the events of the years 1766–1833, ed. W. Whitten (1905) · Transactions of the Society of Arts, 29 (1811), iv · DNB · 'Whitefoord, John', Dictionary of Australian biography, 2.595

Archives BL, corresp., literary MSS, and papers, Add. MSS 36593–36596 | RSA, corresp. and minutes

Likenesses studio of J. Reynolds, oils, 1772–4, NPG · G. Stuart, oils, 1782, Montclair Art Museum, New Jersey · S. W. Reynolds, mezzotint, pubd 1795 (after J. Reynolds), BM, NPG · oils, c.1800, RS · P. Condé, stipple, 1810 (after R. Cosway), BM, NPG, V&A; repro. in 'Memoir of Caleb Whitefoord esq.', European Magazine · W. Daniell, etching, 1810 (after G. Dance, 1795), BM · J. Edgar, group portrait, wash drawing, c.1854 (Robert Burns at an evening party of Lord Monboddo's, 1786), Scot. NPG · J. Gillray, two caricatures, V&A · W. S. Watson, group portrait, oils (The inauguration of Robert Burns as poet laureate of the lodge Canongate, Kilwinning, 1787), Scot. NPG · J. Zoffany, oils, priv. coll.

Wealth at death house in Argyll Street sold for £2782 10s.; total estate sufficient to raise annuity of £400 for widow: will, PRO, PROB 11/1508, sig. 109; Hewins, ed., Whitefoord papers, xxix

Whitefoord, Charles (d. 1753), army officer, was the third son of Sir Adam Whitefoord, first baronet (d. 1727), and his wife, Margaret (d. 1742), only daughter of Alan, seventh Lord Cathcart, and Elizabeth Dalrymple, daughter of James Dalrymple, first Viscount Stair. He entered the Royal Navy in 1718, but despite passing his lieutenant's examination he could not gain a commission. His cousin, John Dalrymple, second earl of Stair, seems to have been responsible for his education at the French academy of Angers and also for his entry into the army in 1720, possibly as a quartermaster in the Inniskilling dragoons.

In 1728 Whitefoord purchased an ensign's commission in the 31st foot commanded by his uncle, Charles Cathcart, later eighth Lord Cathcart. In 1729 he was appointed adjutant to Colonel William Blakeney commanding the regiment in Cathcart's absence. In 1733 he was promoted lieutenant and in 1737 captain. On 13 July 1738 he transferred to the Royal Irish regiment of foot stationed in Minorca. Here he became fat on 'three meals a day and no exercise', and 'I am become an Assembly man, play at quadrille with the ladies, go to Church on Sundays, but then I swear most intolerably the rest of the week' (Whitefoord Papers, 11). War with Spain saw him commissioned a captain in a marine regiment on 14 January 1740 and then on 4 April a major in the American regiment. In July 1740 he was made aide-de-camp to his uncle, now Lord Cathcart, the commander of all the British forces in America, who died in December 1740. Whitefoord joined the expedition against Carthagena in March and April 1741. He was promoted on 27 April 1741 to lieutenant-colonel of the 5th marines. Between July and November 1741 he served in Cuba. Upon his return to England he was stationed in Chatham, where by 1743 he had rented a house.

Whitefoord was in Edinburgh when the 1745 Jacobite rising broke out and immediately offered his services to Sir John Cope, spending much of his time trying to secure adequate supplies for the troops. At the battle of Prestonpans on 21 September 1745 Whitefoord gallantly maintained his position with the artillery after his gunners had fled, and was saved from death by Alexander Stewart of Invernahyle, a Jacobite officer. Whitefoord was sent as a prisoner to Perth and subsequently paroled. After Culloden he repaid the compliment to Stewart by appealing to the duke of Cumberland to spare the fugitive Stewart, who was eventually pardoned by an act of indemnity.

Whitefoord was a key defence witness at Cope's court martial over the débâcle at Prestonpans, which led to the general's acquittal. Following disbandment in November 1748, he was appointed lieutenant-colonel of the 5th fusiliers in September 1751, stationed in Ireland. In November he succeeded as colonel of the regiment, but he died at Galway on 2 January 1753. He left a son, the diplomat Caleb *Whitefoord, and a daughter, Charlotte, both described in his will as his 'natural' children (BL, Add. MS 36596, fol. 345), which suggests that he never married. Caleb was left all his bonds, bills, and debts in order to pay legacies which included £200 to Charlotte and £500 to his 'worthy friend', Charles Schaw Cathcart, ninth Lord Cathcart. STUART HANDLEY

Sources C. Dalton, *George the First's army, 1714–1727*, 1 (1910), 65–74 · *The Whitefoord papers*, ed. W. A. S. Hewins (1898) · BL, Add. MS 36592 · BL, Add. MS 36596, fols. 344–5 · *N&Q*, 12th ser., 10 (1922), 108 · S. S., 'The family of Whitefoord', *The Genealogist*, 4 (1880), 141–4, esp. 142 · *London Magazine*, 22 (1753), 43
Archives BL, corresp. and papers, Add. MS 36592
Likenesses oils (in possession of C. Whiteford, Whitton Paddocks, Ludlow, 1900) · portrait, repro. in Dalton, *George the First's army*, vol. 1, p. 64

Whitehall, Robert (*bap.* 1624, *d.* 1685), poet, was baptized on 18 March 1624 at Amersham parish church, Buckinghamshire. He was the only son of Robert Whitehall (1584–1658), a clergyman who held in plurality the benefices of St Mary Magdalen, Oxford (January 1616 to January or February 1629), and Addington, Buckinghamshire (September 1616 onwards), and his first wife, Bridget Watkins (*bap.* 1603), of Amersham, whom he married there on 12 June 1623. Whitehall's mother died soon after childbirth, and was buried at Amersham on 28 July 1624. Her husband remarried and had seven further children; he was buried at Addington on 1 October 1658.

A king's scholar at Westminster School under Richard Busby, Whitehall became a member of Christ Church, Oxford, in 1643, gaining his BA on 2 November 1647. On 10 May 1648 he refused to submit to the parliamentary visitation with the words, 'As I am summoned a Student of Christ Church, my name itself speaks for me, that I can acknowledge no Visitation but K. Charles', rendered into the couplet

My name's Whitehall, God bless the Poet,
If I submit, the King shall know it.
(Gutch, *History*, 2/2, 583)

He was expelled on 7 July 1648, and probably retired to his father's rectory. He subsequently submitted to the authority of the parliamentary visitors, and with the support of Richard Ingoldsby, the regicide and MP for Buckingham, was appointed to a fellowship at Merton College in 1650. He was awarded his MA on 18 November 1652, appointed *terrae filius* in 1655, and qualified as MB on 5 September 1657 (a licence dated 21 June 1665 allowed him to practise). In response to a letter from Henry Cromwell dated 22 June

1657, the college authorities gave permission for Whitehall 'to give instruction in the University of Dublin' (Brodrick, 94), but there is no record that he did so. On 19 October 1670, probably with reference to the presbyterian-royalist plot led by Sir George Booth in August 1659 to restore the monarchy, he wrote to Joseph Williamson MP, the keeper of state papers and secretary to Lord Arlington, to seek compensation for having been 'worsted in spirituals of 250*l.* a year, and in nearly 1,000*l.* by the Cheshire misadventure' (*CSP dom.*, 1670). In 1671 Whitehall was sub-warden of Merton College.

Whitehall's contemporary at Merton, the unamiable Anthony Wood, dismisses him as a 'pot poet' and 'no better than a meer Poetaster and time-serving-Poet' (Gutch, *History*, 2/2, 583; Wood, *Ath. Oxon.*, 2.596). Much of the surviving *œuvre* consists of well-crafted verse addresses in Latin or English to figures as varied as Oliver Cromwell (1654), Richard Cromwell (1657), Prince Henry, Edward Hyde (1660), the king (1660, 1679), the queen mother (1661), and Catherine of Braganza (1662). These were printed either separately or within the volumes of loyal verses produced by members of Oxford University, where, reflecting his local repute, they were generally accorded by the university printer, Leonard Lichfield, a prestigious position at the end of the collections. Four substantial, if overblown, poems justify the accolade of minor poet: 'The Marriage of Armes and Arts, July 12. 1651' and 'Urania' (1669) are crammed with learned references, and 'The Coronation' (1661) and 'The English Rechabite' (1680) are well paced and engagingly boisterous. Whitehall's exchanges with the artist Mary More, though, reveal a less deft touch (BL, Harley MS 3918): both in 'The woman's right proved false' (his prose rebuttal to her polished essay challenging male authority) and in his verses (separately printed in 1674) following her gift to the university of her 'drawing' of Thomas More (actually Thomas Cromwell), his tone is patronizing and misjudged. His lines generated not only a spirited reply from the donor, in which she cast aspersion on the sexual preferences of the 'Fellow and Batchelour', but also, anonymously, 'A Reproof to R. W.' (Portland MS PwV, 504). Whitehall's only full-length work is his appealing *Hexastichon hieron* (1677), a book of 258 emblems on biblical subjects accompanied by verses. Twelve copies only were printed by Lichfield and then 'richly bound' for presentation, probably to attract patronage; recipients included the king and the young son of John Wilmot, second earl of Rochester, for whom it may have been 'chiefly composed' (Wood, *Ath. Oxon.*, 2.597).

Whitehall provides a unique glimpse of Rochester as an undergraduate at Wadham College between 1660 and 1661; the don 'absolutely doted' on him and 'pretended to instruct the Count … in the art of Poetry' (Wood, *Ath. Oxon.*, 2.490). On 1 January 1667 the genial Whitehall sent him with his portrait a Hudibrastic verse epistle; this describes the author's florid appearance, incidentally supporting Wood's comment, 'following the trade of drinking as he was wont, [he] gained to himself a red face' (Wood, *Modius salium*, 25), and reveals his practice of lending Rochester, for 'night rambles … as protection from proctorial interference', his own academic gown; this the undergraduate

daggled through this towne
To keepe vp discipline, and tell vs
Next morning where you found good=fellows.
(Needham, vi, 44)

Whitehall and Rochester contributed to the volumes of university verses addressed to the king and queen mother in the early 1660s. Although Wood alleges that Whitehall penned Rochester's three poems, they differ significantly in tone; while Whitehall, and even another contributor, Walter Blandford, the warden of Wadham, may have added polish, there is 'nothing in them that might not have been composed by a clever boy of thirteen' (Pinto, 9) and the case for Whitehall's authorship is further weakened by the attack on physicians in Rochester's poem to the queen. The poems were 'unquestionably printed as Rochester's with his knowledge and consent' (*Complete Poems of John Wilmot*, 155) and appeared posthumously in the 'authorized' 1691 edition of Rochester's poems.

Whitehall died a bachelor on 8 July 1685 and was 'buried the next day in the south part or Isle' of his college chapel (Wood, *Ath. Oxon.*, 2.597); there is a commemorative stone in the ante-chapel floor.   NICHOLAS FISHER

Sources Wood, *Ath. Oxon.*, 1st edn, 2.490, 595–7 · A. Wood, *Modius salium* (1674) · J. Welch, *A list of scholars of St Peter's College, Westminster* (1788) · M. Burrows, ed., *The register of the visitors of the University of Oxford, from AD 1647 to AD 1658*, CS, new ser., 29 (1881), 68, 144 · A. Wood, *The history and antiquities of the University of Oxford*, ed. J. Gutch, 2 (1796), pt 2, pp. 583, 598 · A. Wood, *The history and antiquities of the colleges and halls in the University of Oxford*, ed. J. Gutch, appx (1790), 213 · G. C. Brodrick, *Memorials of Merton College*, OHS, 4 (1885), 106, 292 · Foster, *Alum. Oxon.*, *1500–1714*, 4.1619 · CSP dom., 1670 · *Old Westminsters*, 2.988 · F. Needham, *A collection of poems by several hands* (1934), vi, 44–5 · V. de S. Pinto, *Enthusiast in wit: a portrait of John Wilmot, earl of Rochester, 1647–1680* (1962), 7–10, 24–5, 45–6 · *The complete poems of John Wilmot, earl of Rochester*, ed. D. M. Vieth (1968) · *The works of John Wilmot earl of Rochester*, ed. H. Love (1999) · M. J. M. Ezell, *The patriarch's wife: literary evidence and the history of the family* (1987) · G. Manning, 'Hexastichon hieron', *Emblematica*, 6/2 (1992), 307–22 · parish register, Addington, Buckinghamshire · parish register, Amersham, Buckinghamshire · W. J. Oldfield, 'Clerus: index to the clergy in the diocese of Oxford, 1542–1908', 1915, Oxon. RO · *The life and times of Anthony Wood*, ed. A. Clark, 5 vols., OHS, 19, 21, 26, 30, 40 (1891–1900) · parish register, Ipstones, Staffordshire · H. S. Grazebrook, ed., 'The heraldic visitations of Staffordshire … in 1614 and … 1663 and 1664', *Collections for a history of Staffordshire*, William Salt Archaeological Society, 5/2 (1884) · *Collections for a history of Staffordshire*, William Salt Archaeological Society, 5 (1884–5), pt 2 · G. Lipscomb, *The history and antiquities of the county of Buckingham*, 4 vols. (1831–47) · H. Walpole, *Anecdotes of painting in England … collected by the late George Vertue, and now digested and published*, 3 (1763) · Mrs R. Lane Poole, ed., *Catalogue of portraits in the possession of the university, colleges, city and county of Oxford*, 3 vols. (1912–25) · M. Beloff, *Public order and popular disturbance, 1660–1714* (1938) · J. Heywood, ed., *Oxford University statutes*, trans. G. R. M. Ward, 2 vols. (1845–51)

Whitehead, Alfred North (1861–1947), mathematician and philosopher, was born at Ramsgate on 15 February 1861, the last of the four children of the Revd Alfred Whitehead (1827–1898), at that time headmaster of a private school in Ramsgate, and later vicar of St Peter's, Isle

Alfred North Whitehead (1861–1947), by Walter Stoneman, 1917

of Thanet, and honorary canon of Canterbury, and his wife, Maria Sarah (1832–1924), daughter of William Buckmaster, a prosperous military tailor. An elder brother, Henry *Whitehead, became ultimately bishop of Madras; his only child, Alfred's nephew, was John Henry Constantine Whitehead FRS (1904–1960), Waynflete professor of pure mathematics in Oxford University.

At Sherborne School, Whitehead won the Digby prize for mathematics and science three years in succession and in his last year was head of the school and captain of football and cricket. He proceeded in 1880 to Trinity College, Cambridge, where he was a scholar, and where he remained for the next thirty years. In the mathematical tripos of 1883 he was bracketed fourth wrangler, the next year he was elected a fellow of his college, and a few months afterwards was put on the staff as an assistant lecturer. He was also elected to the Apostles that year, but resigned three years later. On 16 December 1890 he married Evelyn Ada Maud Rice (1865–1950), daughter of Captain Arthur Robert Willoughby-Wade of the Seaforth Highlanders and niece of the Chinese scholar and diplomat Sir T. F. Wade. They had a daughter, Jessie, and two sons, North and Eric. Evelyn Whitehead formed a close but chaste friendship with Bertrand *Russell, especially in 1900–01.

Systems of symbolic logic Whitehead's first considerable work was published in 1898 under the title of *A Treatise on Universal Algebra, with Applications*. Its purpose was to investigate systems of symbolic reasoning allied to ordinary algebra, such as Hermann Grassmann's calculus of extension (the main influence on him), the quaternions of Sir W. R. Hamilton, and symbolic logic; the latter subject was treated very fully, the system described being based largely upon that devised by George Boole in 1854. The book was highly original, and gave Whitehead a reputation which led to his election as FRS in 1903.

One of Whitehead's pupils at Trinity, Bertrand Russell, became a specially attached disciple. In 1900 Whitehead and Russell went together to Paris to attend the international congress on philosophy, where they heard lectures by Giuseppe Peano of Turin and his followers, who had recently developed a new ideography for use in symbolic logic. Boole had used only the ordinary algebraic symbols, but Peano introduced symbols to represent logical notions such as 'is contained in', 'the set of all x's such that', 'there exists', 'is a', and 'the only'. Peano's ideograms represent constitutive elements of all the other notions in logic, just as the chemical atoms are the constitutive elements of all substances in chemistry, and they provide the basis of a formal language. Whitehead and Russell immediately recognized the superiority of this ideography and resolved to devote themselves to its development, and in particular to attempt thereby to settle the vexed question of the foundations of mathematics. They arrived at the 'logicist' position, that mathematics is a part of logic, so that a separate philosophy of mathematics does not exist, a view contradicting the Kantian doctrine that mathematical proofs depend on a priori forms of intuition. The investigation was published in the three colossal volumes of Principia mathematica which appeared in 1910–13, and which formed the greatest single contribution to symbolic logic for the time. The revisions and additions of the second edition of 1925–7 were produced solely by Russell, as Whitehead reported rather testily in Mind. There was to have been a fourth volume of the Principia, written by Whitehead and treating of geometries. He had made considerable progress with it; but the death in action of his son Eric in 1918 during the First World War seems to have destroyed his will to complete work of this kind.

In any case, logicism occupied only an (important) intermediate position in Whitehead's conception of mathematics in general, broader than that encompassed by logicism in admitting enquiry into creative and imaginative aspects and applications to the physical world. By contrast, for Russell logicism was the final philosophical position sought for mathematics. While Principia mathematica was Whitehead's main occupation during the 1900s, he wrote a remarkable paper, 'Mathematical concepts of the material world', published in the Philosophical Transactions of the Royal Society (1906). In this he was feeling his way to a general philosophy of nature: as the ultimate existents, he rejected particles of matter and points of space (thereby severing himself completely from classical physics), and in their stead postulated what he called linear objective reals. Some of the principles of his later philosophy first appear here.

In 1910 Whitehead resigned from his senior lectureship in mathematics at Trinity College (though not from his fellowship) and moved to London. This action was partly in protest against Trinity's acceptance of the resignation of the mathematician Andrew Forsyth who had eloped with a married woman, but it also reflected his desire to move into a fresh arena where his fairly progressive views on education might find expression. Later, in 1929 he published The Aims of Education and other Essays, in which he discusses such issues as the roles of classical and technical education, the mathematical curriculum, and the function of the universities. At first, having no teaching appointment, he wrote the short Introduction to Mathematics (1911). From that year to 1914 he was on the staff of University College, London, and from 1914 to 1924 he held a chair of applied mathematics at the Imperial College of Science and Technology.

Epistemology and metaphysics From this time onwards Whitehead became more and more involved in questions which really belonged to epistemology and metaphysics. The discovery of the special theory of relativity in 1904 had opened up new prospects in the philosophy of nature. In 1915–17 he published several papers of a philosophical character, which were followed by two books, An Enquiry Concerning the Principles of Natural Knowledge (1919) and The Concept of Nature (1920). He now developed his own version of process philosophies associated with the names of H. L. Bergson, Samuel Alexander, and C. L. Morgan, and put forward the doctrine that the ultimate components of reality are events. An event is never instantaneous, it always lasts over a certain (although perhaps very short) duration of time: the notions of an 'instant' of time and a 'point' of space were not, in his scheme, accepted as primitive, but were obtained by a limiting process which he called the 'method of extensive abstraction'.

While Whitehead was engaged in his development of process metaphysics in 1914–19, the theory of general relativity was announced, in which the physical phenomenon of gravitation was expressed by a curvature of space-time, varying according to the physical situation from point to point over the whole universe. Whitehead criticized it, and devised an alternative theory which he set forth in a book, The Principle of Relativity, in 1922; his work did not, however, win general acceptance.

Philosophy at Harvard In 1924 Whitehead resigned his chair at the Imperial College in order to accept a professorship in the department of philosophy of Harvard University, which he occupied until his final retirement in 1937. One of Whitehead's first public acts was to deliver the Lowell lectures at Boston in 1925; the expanded printed version came out later that year as Science and the Modern World, and sold very widely. Here he wedded his emerging philosophy of science to a historical survey of the development of the physical sciences.

In the session 1927–8 Whitehead returned to Britain in order to deliver the Gifford lectures at Edinburgh University. These, which were published in 1929 under the title Process and Reality, an Essay in Cosmology, may be regarded as the definitive exposition of his mature philosophy, to which he gave the name 'philosophy of organism' but which is commonly referred to as 'process philosophy'. Process philosophy contrasts with the tradition of substance philosophy which began with Descartes and which, characterized by the dualism of mind and matter, made knowledge problematic and thus brought epistemology to the centre of philosophical discussion. Whitehead challenges this centrality when he says that problems which are apparently epistemological have their origin in the Cartesian metaphysics of substance which, influenced as it was by the physics of its day, needs to be reassessed in the light of twentieth-century scientific thought. In *Process and Reality*, as in his earlier works, the beginning is made with events. Those events which are 'the final real things of which the world is made up' were now called 'actual entities'. Thus the category of 'actual entities' plays the same fundamental part in the philosophy of organism as the category of 'substance' plays in many older philosophies; but whereas the term 'substance' is associated with the notion of something that endures, an 'actual entity' according to Whitehead has no permanence. In order to emphasize the difference between his philosophy and the philosophies of substance, Whitehead described an actual entity not as a 'subject' but as a 'superject', a term designed to suggest its emergence from antecedent entities to itself. He accounted for the permanence that is discovered amid the flux of events by postulating what he called 'eternal objects', which have some resemblance to the 'forms' or 'ideas' of Plato; they have a potentiality of ingression into the becoming of actual entities, thereby contributing definiteness of character to them.

Whitehead also introduced a concept which he called 'creativity', corresponding more or less to Plato's *chōra*, or Aristotle's *prōtē hylē* or to the 'neutral stuff' of the 'neutral monists'. It is an ultimate, behind all forms, without a character of its own; particular eternal objects can, however, infuse their own character into it, thereby constituting actual entities. Thus it is by creativity that the actual world has its character of passage into novelty. Order is another essential notion, since for him the world is layered in various kinds of ordering.

It will be seen that Whitehead's writing abounded in new words, and new senses of old words; he had indeed the conviction that ordinary speech, which, as he had shown in *Principia mathematica*, is inadequate for the purposes of logic, is still more inadequate for the purposes of metaphysics. A new term 'prehension' signified that one actual entity grasps other actual entities into a unity. This word made it possible to express the nature of an actual entity very simply: 'The essence of an actual entity consists solely in the fact that it is a prehending thing.' The word 'concretion' or 'concrescence' is another novelty: it means that togetherness or unity that comes to exist as a result of the prehension. Every event originates as a unity of concrescent prehensions: the process of concrescence is Being. He pursued some educational corollaries in the collection of essays entitled *The Aims of Education* (1929),

and the metaphysical and metaphorical elements of this approach in *Adventures of Ideas* (1933). These aspects of Whitehead's philosophy have made perhaps the greatest impact, as a major constituent of process philosophy, which is practised with most vigour in the USA.

Metaphysical principles, in Whitehead's view, are truths about the nature of God. His God, however, is not omnipotent, and cannot be identified with the God of the Christian religion: he is a non-temporal 'actual entity'. This philosophical theism, which is developed further in *Religion in the Making* (1926), replaced an earlier agnosticism which had itself been the successor to a brief involvement with Roman Catholicism in the 1890s and an Anglican upbringing. It has been the aspect of his thought which has attracted the most interest in the decades following his death. Even before his retirement in 1937 many philosophers at Harvard turned towards logical positivism and the philosophy of Wittgenstein, and among British philosophers Whitehead's later thought has never been popular. But theologians, as well as the philosopher Charles Hartshorne, have developed a 'process theology' which, centred in southern California, has given rise to numerous publications, by Anglicans, Catholics, Methodists, and those of other denominations.

Recognition and death In his later years Whitehead was acknowledged as one of the greatest living philosophers, and was the recipient of many distinctions. In 1922 he was the first recipient of the James Scott prize of the Royal Society of Edinburgh; in 1925 he received the Sylvester medal of the Royal Society; and in 1930 the Butler medal of Columbia University. In 1931 he attained the honour of combining his fellowship of the British Academy with fellowship of the Royal Society, and in 1945 he was appointed to the Order of Merit. He died at Cambridge, Massachusetts, on 30 December 1947. He was cremated and his ashes scattered in Harvard Memorial Church on 6 January 1948. His widow destroyed all his manuscripts, as he had expressly desired.

E. T. WHITTAKER, *rev.* I. GRATTAN-GUINNESS

Sources V. Lowe, *Alfred North Whitehead: the man and his work*, 2 vols. (1985–90) • P. A. Schlipp, ed., *The philosophy of Alfred North Whitehead*, 2nd edn (1951) • R. M. Palter, *Whitehead's philosophy of science* (1960) • G. L. Kleine, ed., *Alfred North Whitehead: essays on his philosophy* (1959); repr. (1963) • M. Code, *Order and organism* (1985) • I. Grattan-Guinness, 'Review of V. Lowe, Alfred North Whitehead, vol. 1', *Transactions of the C. S. Peirce Society*, 22 (1986), 61–8 • D. W. Sherburne, 'Whitehead, Alfred North', *The Cambridge dictionary of philosophy*, ed. R. Audi (1995) • personal knowledge (1959) • private information (1959) • I. Grattan-Guinness, 'Algebras, projective geometry, mathematical logic, and constructing the world: intersections in the philosophy of mathematics of A. N. Whitehead', *Historia Mathematica*, 29 (2002), 427–62

Archives CUL, Turnbull MSS, letters to G. E. Moore • McMaster University, Ontario, Hamilton, corresp. with Bertrand Russell

Likenesses W. Stoneman, photograph, 1917, NPG [*see illus.*] • P. Drury, pencil drawing, 1928, Trinity Cam.

Whitehead [*née* Downer; *other married name* Greenwell], **Anne** (*c.*1624–1686), Quaker organizer and writer, was born in Charlbury, Oxfordshire, the daughter of the vicar,

Thomas Downer, and sister to Elizabeth and Ann-Mary; of her mother, nothing is known.

Anne converted to Quakerism in the early 1650s, a decision earning her the respect of co-religionists, but resulting in her ostracization from her natural family. About 1654 Anne moved to London, where she was one of the first in that city to publicize the Quaker message. Anne was a reliable and practical person, as shown in her decision to offer her services to the imprisoned Quaker leader George Fox, and her subsequent position as his secretary and administrator during his time in Launceston prison, Cornwall. As her time with Fox had shown, Anne's skills could be best employed in practical roles, and there was plenty of scope for administrators in post-Restoration Quakerism. She was a leading figure in the London six weeks' meeting from its inception, and in the London women's meetings.

Anne was to feel the effects personally of the post-Restoration clampdown on sectarians. The Quaker Benjamin Greenwell (d. 1665), whom Anne had married on 24 March 1663, died in Newgate prison on 5 February 1665 under a sentence of banishment; the marriage had been brief and childless.

Anne's post-Restoration profile comes through most clearly in her public identification of herself with the causes and tasks of the women's meetings. Broadly speaking, the duties undertaken by the women's meetings extended the female domestic role, giving women the responsibility of managing charity and overseeing marriages. As a central London figure, Anne was clearly a committed member of the women's meetings, even when opposition to them was voiced during the so-called Wilkinson–Story schism. Anne responded to the criticisms in several published tracts, writing either singly or with other women. What emerges in texts such as *An Epistle for True Love* and *A Tender and Christian Testimony to Young People* is a strong sense of female duty and unity. Such public-spiritedness was evident, moreover, in the anti-persecution tract *For the King and both Houses of Parliament*, written in 1670 by a female collective, including Anne.

On 13 May 1670 Anne married the prominent Quaker George *Whitehead (1637–1724), grocer; they apparently had no children. She died, aged about sixty-three, on 28 July 1686 at South Street, Middlesex, from an unidentifiable illness, and was buried the following day. *Piety Promoted* (1686), a volume commemorating her, was written after her death, in which she was remembered as one of the venerable 'Mothers in *Israel*' (p. 36). It contains testimonies by close friends and family, in addition to a wide cross-section of the London Quaker community. Among these is the account written by her husband, George, who remembered her fondly both here and in his own autobiography, *The Christian Progress* (1725). Looking back on the marriage, George explained that though there were 'divers years' between them, she was 'like a Tender Mother to him' (Whitehead, *Christian Progress*, 321–2).

By the time of her death Anne had become a central figure in southern Quakerism. A redoubtable defender of the women's meetings and a solidly reliable pillar of London Quakerism, she was justly remembered by others as a 'mother in Israel'.   CATIE GILL

Sources 'Dictionary of Quaker biography', RS Friends, Lond. [card index] · *Quaker digest registers of births, marriages and burials for England and Wales, c.1650–1837*, Society of Friends (1992), reel 4 [microfilm] · J. Besse, *A collection of the sufferings of the people called Quakers*, 2 vols. (1753) · W. C. Braithwaite, *The second period of Quakerism*, ed. H. J. Cadbury, 2nd edn (1961); repr. (1979) · R. Foxton, '*Hear the word of the Lord': a bibliographical study of Quaker women's writing, 1650–1700* (Melbourne, 1994) · M. Sturge Henderson, *Three centuries in north Oxfordshire* (1902) · P. Mack, *Visionary women: ecstatic prophesy in seventeenth-century England*, new edn (Berkeley, CA, 1994) · G. Whitehead, *The Christian progress* (1725) · *Piety promoted by faithfulness manifested by several testimonies concerning that true servant of God, Ann Whitehead* (1686) [incl. contribution by G. Whitehead]

Whitehead, Charles (1804–1862), writer, was born in London on 4 September 1804, the eldest of the seven children of a City wine merchant, possibly the Joseph Whitehead listed in contemporary trade directories as the proprietor of wine and brandy vaults in Tottenham Court Road. The details of his early life are exceptionally obscure, and nothing is known of his education. After some time as a clerk in a commercial house he embarked on the hazardous career of a professional author. In 1831 he published *The Solitary*, a lengthy meditative poem whose implacable melancholy was partly occasioned by the drowning of one of his three brothers. This first work attracted favourable notice but few purchasers.

Whitehead married Mary Ann Loomes on 29 October 1833. During the 1830s he contributed widely to magazines (among them *The Monthly*, *The Court*, and *Bentley's Miscellany*) and to such annuals as *Friendship's Offering* and *Amaranth*. He was also, for some eight years, a reader for Bentley and, from 1836, editor of Chapman and Hall's Library of Fiction. Of his more substantial works from this decade, *The Lives and Exploits of English Highwaymen, Pirates and Robbers* (1834) is essentially an updated revision of earlier compilations by other hands, but *The Autobiography of Jack Ketch* (1834) adroitly parodies the vogue for 'Newgate' fiction while simultaneously generating its own macabre comedy. A blank verse historical play, *The Cavalier*, was produced at the Haymarket Theatre, London, in September 1836 and was revived in 1840, 1850, 1856, and 1868.

By the end of the 1830s, then, Whitehead had established himself on the London literary scene (among other affiliations, he was a member of Jerrold and Blanchard's Mulberry Club) and in 1841–2 he produced his masterpiece, *Richard Savage*, a novel based on the career of Samuel Johnson's early friend. The eponymous narrator, vain and unreliable, presents a disturbing study in obsession, and Whitehead skilfully contextualizes his protagonist's deepening paranoia in a credible reconstruction of eighteenth-century Grub Street. *Richard Savage* is a major achievement, but it had no real successor. *The Earl of Essex*, an impenetrably stilted historical romance, enjoyed only moderate sales on its first appearance in 1843, and of the magazine pieces collected in *Smiles and Tears* (1847) only a few dark confessional tales (such as the Poe-like 'Narrative of John Ward Gibson') rise above the level of hack work.

The Life and Times of Sir Walter Raleigh (1854) owes more to scissors and paste than to scholarship.

Whitehead's work was neither prolific nor popular enough to ensure a regular income and as early as 1836 he was petitioning the Literary Fund for relief, an application repeated in 1837, 1843, 1852, and 1854. Constantly in debt and in fear of bailiffs (in 1843 he was being housed and supported by his sisters), his mental and physical health deteriorated, and in 1852 he confessed that 'now-a-days I am a bad hand at writing against time, being excited and highly nervous' (Hodder, 357). Finally, on 13 November 1856, he and his wife left England to start a new life in Australia, arriving in Melbourne on 17 March 1857.

Whitehead rapidly became a contributor to various colonial journals, including *The Examiner* and the *Melbourne Punch*. He may, briefly, have edited the journal *My Note Book*, which began, in 1858, to serialize his new novel *Emma Latham*, but he was, once again, unable to write himself out of poverty. His mentally-ill wife died at Yarra Bend Asylum on 21 August 1860. Whitehead himself drifted into chronic alcoholism (a tendency which perhaps began in England) and, after appearing in a police court 'charged with lunacy, caused through drink' (Turnbull, 20), he was eventually admitted to the Immigrants' Home for the destitute. He died of hepatitis and bronchitis at the Melbourne Hospital on 5 July 1862 and was buried in a pauper's grave.

Whitehead is remembered chiefly as the author invited by Chapman and Hall to write the letterpress for a series of illustrations by Robert Seymour, and who suggested that they approach Dickens instead (a suggestion which resulted in *The Pickwick Papers*). There appears to be no solid evidence for this story, and Whitehead, with characteristic misfortune, has thus survived only as the subject of an apocryphal anecdote. He deserves a better fate, for he was able to harness his brooding, depressive imagination (suicide is a recurrent motif in his work) to produce, in *Richard Savage*, a novel of compelling power.

ROBERT DINGLEY

Sources C. Turnbull, *Australian lives* (1965) · K. J. Fielding, 'Charles Whitehead and Charles Dickens', *Review of English Studies*, new ser., 3 (1952), 141–54 · J. Crump, 'Charles Whitehead: his life and work', *The Dickensian*, 48 (1952), 120–26 · H. T. M. Bell, *Charles Whitehead: a forgotten genius*, 2nd edn (1894) · G. Hodder, *Memories of my time* (1870) · A. Lohrli, ed., *Household Words: a weekly journal conducted by Charles Dickens* (1973)

Archives BL, business papers, Add. MSS 46613–46614, 46649–46652 | BL, corresp. with Richard Bentley, Add. MSS 46613–46614, 46649–46652 · Herts. ALS

Whitehead, David (c.1492–1571), evangelical preacher, is said by Anthony Wood to have been a native of Hampshire, where the Whiteheads had some landed property. The same source reports that he is also said to have been educated at Brasenose or All Souls, Oxford, and, though his name does not appear in the defective registers of the period, there is evidence to suggest that during the early years of Henry VIII's reign he spent some time in Oxford, where he may also have been an Augustinian friar. Sir Henry Billingsley, then a student and later a collaborator with Whitehead in literary ventures, is reported to have

developed his taste for mathematics from studying with Whitehead at Oxford. Whatever the truth of this, it is clear that during Henry's reign Whitehead became increasingly associated with a group of scholars and clerics sympathetic to the gospel. He is said to have been a chaplain to Anne Boleyn; later he was tutor to the young Charles Brandon, second duke of Suffolk. As a member of the party of reform in London he was peripherally involved in the affair of Anne Askew. After Anne's arrest in March 1546 she was examined by Bishop Edmund Bonner, who offered to summon men she esteemed as learned and of good judgement: Edward Crome, David Whitehead, and John Huntingdon. After Anne's destruction on 16 July some sixty protestants fled the city, Whitehead among them.

With the accession of Edward VI, Whitehead's close association with the evangelical party was turned from a liability into an asset. With the death of Charles Brandon in 1551 he retained his place in the household as chaplain to the duchess of Suffolk, a staunch supporter of the regime. He was also marked out for special service by a protestant leadership increasingly admiring of his talents. In 1549 he was one of three divines (with Thomas Leaver and Roger Hutchinson) delegated by Cranmer to the difficult task of effecting the conversion of the protestant radical Joan Bocher. Bocher proved obstinate and was ultimately burnt, one of only two to suffer this fate during the reign. In November 1551 Whitehead was one of a number of protestant divines called to take part in a formal debate on the doctrine of transubstantiation at the house of William Cecil. His presence, alongside Robert Horne and Edmund Grindal, among the young reformers ranged against the conservative champions, John Feckenham, John Young, and Thomas Watson, is an indication of his place in the Edwardian inner circle. The following year Whitehead was first on a list of those whom Cranmer named in a letter to William Cecil as suitable for raising to the episcopal bench as archbishop of Armagh: 'I take Mr. Whitehead for his good knowledge, special honesty, fervent zeal and politic wisdom to be most meet' (Strype, 2.670). Whitehead shared the general reluctance to serve in Ireland and on this occasion refused the promotion; but the reign of Edward VI drew to a close with Whitehead on the verge of episcopal office, having been nominated to the see of Rochester.

Soon after Mary's accession Whitehead fled to the continent; he was one of 175 who sailed with John à Lasco from Gravesend on 17 September 1553. Whitehead was in the smaller vessel which reached Copenhagen on 3 November; the exiles were soon expelled by order of the king on refusing to subscribe to the Lutheran confession. They then made their way to Rostock, where Whitehead pleaded their cause before the magistrates, whose Lutheran requirements they failed to satisfy, and they were compelled to leave in January. A similar fate befell them at Wismar, Lübeck, and Hamburg, but they found a refuge at Emden in March. Here a separate English congregation was established, but Whitehead seems quickly to have decided not to settle in the northern town. He was not named as one of the leaders of the congregation, as his seniority and closeness to John à Lasco would otherwise have made almost certain; and he was not among the thirty or more Englishmen who took up the invitation to enrol as citizens of Emden. Meanwhile an attempt was being made to found a church of English exiles at Frankfurt, and on 2 August 1554 an invitation was sent to Whitehead and other exiles to join the church there: 'on 24 October came Maister Whitehead to Franckford, and at the requeste of the congregation he took the charge for a time and preached upon the epistle to the Romans' (*Works of John Knox*, 4.12).

Whitehead was one of those who wished to retain the use of the English prayer book of 1552, and in the famous 'troubles' at Frankfurt took the side of Richard Cox against John Knox. After the expulsion of Knox (26 March 1555) Whitehead was chosen pastor of the congregation. On 20 September he and his colleagues wrote a letter to Calvin to justify their proceedings against Knox, and repudiating the charge of too rigorous adherence to the prayer book and using 'lights and crosses'; their ceremonies, they pleaded, were really very few, and they went on to attack Knox's 'Admonition' as an 'outrageous pamphlet' which had added 'much oil to the flame of persecution in England' (Robinson, *Original Letters*, 755 ff.). In February 1556 Whitehead resigned his pastorate, being succeeded on 1 March by Robert Horne; the cause is said to have been his disappointment at not being made lecturer in divinity in succession to Bartholomew Traheron. He remained, however, at Frankfurt, signing a letter to Heinrich Bullinger on 27 September 1557.

On Elizabeth's accession Whitehead returned to England, preaching before the queen on 15 February 1559, taking part in the disputation with the Roman Catholic bishops on 3 April, and serving as a visitor of Oxford University, and on the commission for revising the liturgy. As a senior figure among the returning exiles, a former nominated bishop, and, furthermore, one who had championed the prayer book abroad, Whitehead could have relied on nomination to one of the most senior posts in the new church, and indeed he figures on every one of the lists drawn up by William Cecil of possible bishops. There is a persistent tradition that he was offered first the most senior position of all, as archbishop of Canterbury, though given Matthew Parker's closeness to the queen this seems unlikely. Instead he was marked out at one point for Salisbury; on Cecil's first list of bishops, dated June or July 1559, Whitehead appears third behind only William Bill and Parker.

Cecil's plans, however, now ran into an unexpected obstacle: the refusal of many of the nominated bishops to take positions if their incomes were to be further ravaged by the depredations anticipated under action expected to follow the 1559 Act of Exchanges. Whitehead's objections were of a different order: he steadfastly refused all office, including the plum post of the mastership of the Savoy, preferring instead the life of the roving preacher. On 17 September 1561 he wrote to Cecil acknowledging his obligations to him, but lamenting the necessity he was under

of refusing the living he offered. 'So that whether he had any spiritualities of note conferr'd on him is yet doubtful, he being much delighted in travelling to and fro to preach the word of God in those parts where he thought it was wanting' (Wood, *Ath. Oxon.*, 1.396). Whitehead's pursuit of personal purity was not widely admired among his fellow church leaders and after his death the puritan leader John Field would write of him 'as a man that would have all well first, and then he would labour that all should be well' (Collinson, 46). His friends among the foreign exiles, however, remained faithful. In August 1562 Whitehead was one of three English divines, along with fellow exiles Robert Crowley and Miles Coverdale, consulted by the Dutch church in London over the problems caused by Adriaan van Haemstede. He is reported by Whitgift to have frequently deplored the excesses of some ministers, but his own leanings were puritan, and on 24 March 1564 he was sequestered for refusing to subscribe. Francis Bacon, who calls Whitehead a 'grave divine ... of a blunt stoical nature', and says he was 'much esteemed by Queen Elizabeth, but not preferred because he was against the government of bishops', also relates that the queen once said to him 'I like thee better because thou livest unmarried', to which Whitehead replied: 'In troth, madame, I like you the worse for the same cause' (*Works of Francis Bacon*, 7.163). Richard Hilles, however, in announcing Whitehead's death in June 1571, stated that 'he lived about seven years a widower ... but very lately, before the middle of this year, he married a young widow when he was himself about eighty' (Robinson, *Zurich Letters*, 1.242). An engraved portrait by Crispijn de Passe is given in Henry Holland's *Herōologia* of 1620 (173).

Fuller mentions Whitehead's 'many books still extant' (Fuller, *Worthies*, 1.411), but with the exception of some discourses printed in Whittingham's *Brieff Discours of Troubles at Frankfort* (1575) they have not been traced either in print or in manuscript. In 1568 there appeared an edition of Peter Martyr Vermigli's *Most Learned and Fruitfull Commentaries upon the Epistle to the Romanes*, translated by H. Billingsley, which is described as having been 'perused' by David Whitehead (STC 24672). The ascription to Whitehead of the translation of George Ripley's *Medulla alchymiae* contained in Bodl. Oxf., MS Ashmole 1480/3, fols. 9–15*v*, remains uncertain. ANDREW PETTEGREE

Sources C. H. Garrett, *The Marian exiles: a study in the origins of Elizabethan puritanism* (1938) · *Kerkeraads-protocollen der Nederduitsche vluchtelingenkerk to Londen, 1560–1563*, ed. A. A. van Schleven, Historisch Genootschap te Utrecht, 3rd ser., 43 (1921), 343 · S. Brigden, *London and the Reformation* (1989), 372, 376 · B. Usher, 'Sitting on the "old School" bench: the episcopal appointments of 1559–1562 and the failure of William Cecil' [unpubd MS] · P. Collinson, *The Elizabethan puritan movement* (1967), 46 · STC, 1475–1640, 24672 · *The works of John Knox*, ed. D. Laing, 6 vols., Bannatyne Club, 112 (1846–64), vol. 4 · *CSP dom.*, 1547–80 · Wood, *Ath. Oxon.*, new edn, 1.396–7, 761–2 · J. Strype, *Memorials of the most reverend father in God Thomas Cranmer*, 3 vols. in 4 (1848–54), vol. 2 · H. Robinson, ed. and trans., *The Zurich letters, comprising the correspondence of several English bishops and others with some of the Helvetian reformers, during the early part of the reign of Queen Elizabeth*, 2 vols., Parker Society, 7–8 (1842–5) · Fuller, *Worthies* (1811), 1.411 · H. Robinson, ed. and trans., *Original letters relative to the English Reformation*, 1 vol. in 2, Parker Society, [26]

(1846–7) · [W. Whittingham?], *A brief discourse of the troubles at Frankfort*, ed. E. Arber (privately printed, London, 1907) · *CIPM, Henry VII* · *The works of Francis Bacon*, ed. J. Spedding, R. L. Ellis, and D. D. Heath, 14 vols. (1857–74), vol. 7 · *DNB*

Likenesses Passe, line engraving, BM, NPG; repro. in H. Holland, *Heröologia* (1620), 173

Whitehead, David (1790–1865), cotton manufacturer, was born on 11 December 1790 at Meadowhead in the Forest of Rossendale, Lancashire, the fourth of the eight children of John Whitehead (*c*.1732–1802), a yeoman, and his second wife, Ann (1760–1849), the daughter of Lionel Blakey of Marsden and his second wife, Mary. Whitehead's father, a widower, had six surviving children from his first marriage; seven survived from his second. Both parents converted to Methodism after hearing John Wesley preach in Burnley. On the death of her husband, Ann and her seven children moved to a cottage at Brockclough, where she took up hand-loom weaving.

Whitehead's childhood interest in constructing such devices as miniature water-wheels led him to consider becoming a joiner or a mechanic. His formative years, however, encompassed many different jobs, for, as he admitted, he quickly became bored with a task once he had mastered it. Yet as most jobs were textile oriented, he gained valuable insights into diverse aspects of that industry. During this time he also devoted much attention to improving his education. He was largely self-taught, and his keenness to study often caused his work to suffer; however, he considered education a springboard for later advancement.

Whitehead exercised shrewd calculation in his approach to life, even volunteering for the part-time local militia (*c*.1808) rather than risking the ballot for full-time service in the regular militia, which could take him anywhere in Britain. His decision minimized time away from home and work, and helped to augment his income. He usually balanced the cost and benefit of any action that he contemplated. With this foresight, coupled with strength of will, firmness of decision, and a certain charm, he courted, and often won, people's generosity.

Although the beginnings of his textile manufacturing business were marked by several false starts, Whitehead learned the value of informal social contacts with potential investors. About 1811 he entered into partnership with his brothers Thomas and Peter to commence cotton manufacturing, while at the same time working as a warper for another employer. There he invented a more efficient method of warping, boosting his production to the envy of fellow workers. In 1817 the brothers invested in an established spinning mill on Balladen Brook, near Rawtenstall, in partnership with William Clegg, whom they later bought out.

About this time Whitehead converted to Wesleyan Methodism. Following a formal though not unromantic courtship, on 7 July 1818 he married Elizabeth, the daughter of Jonathan Wood, a farmer of Dovesyke, West Bradford. Wood, not convinced of the long-term viability of Lancashire's industrial acceleration, insisted that, before marrying Elizabeth, Whitehead should buy a farm as a financial safeguard, which he did. The marriage produced eleven children, nine of whom survived to maturity.

Whitehead's cotton enterprise continued to expand, and in 1822 he purchased land in Rawtenstall to construct Higher Mill. However, the 1826 hand-loom weavers' protest against power-looms saw the Whiteheads' equipment smashed, along with those of other local manufacturers. East Lancashire came under military control, and many mills were supplied with arms and ammunition. Soldiers disguised as civilian workers were posted in Whitehead's mill after the military learned from spies of a plan to burn it down and assassinate him. Although the plot was abandoned, Whitehead stayed silent on possible reasons for his proposed demise. This is curious, as his brothers were not likewise threatened. Grievances generated in the community, along with envy at his success, may have played a part. Perhaps too a certain annoying smug self-righteousness may be attributed to him, though, while strong in his faith, he was no zealot. A letter reveals the ease with which he dovetailed religion and business: 'Trade and commerce I still pursue with delight … I am quite convinced I am in the way providence designed for me' (Whitehead, *Memoir*, 139–40).

Whitehead's largest project, the construction of two new cotton mills at Holly Mount, Rawtenstall, began in 1833. He and his brother Peter surveyed the site and designed the buildings. 800 power-looms were envisaged. Houses for the workforce, and a school to educate them and their children, were also constructed. In 1836 Whitehead founded a savings bank for employees and encouraged the Temperance Society (he himself became teetotal). Ever the paternalist, he was 'anxious to give the best possible education to the working class, and particularly to our own workpeople' (Whitehead, *Memoir*, 150). While young scholars paid for their education, the revenue was placed in a provident trust, deposited in Whitehead's bank, and returned with interest once the child reached the age of twenty-one. William Cooke Taylor commented on such benevolence in 1842. However, while Whitehead highlighted benefits provided for his workforce, he played down advantages to himself. For instance, he saw technological advance as an opportunity for workers to earn more, while simultaneously reducing piece-rates.

A staunch believer in free trade, Whitehead was a vociferous member of the Manchester Anti-Corn Law Association (later the Anti-Corn Law League) with his friend Richard Cobden. While campaigning for the repeal of the laws he even inflicted lectures upon fellow rail travellers. Keen to help the working class 'understand their political rights' (Whitehead, *Memoir*, 183), he advocated saving to become 40 *s*. freeholders, thereby qualifying to send representatives to parliament. In 1846 he bluffed his way into the House of Lords to witness the repeal of the corn laws. He established the Rawtenstall branch of the Peace Society (1848), and as a delegate attended the Brussels and Paris peace congresses. In 1851 he was appointed a county magistrate. A commentator of his times, Whitehead was often closely involved in the activities he observed. At once a paternalist yet a radical, he was a humanitarian and advocate of working-class political involvement. By 1855 the Whitehead brothers' business had become unwieldy and was divided between them. At the time of his death, on 28 January 1865, at his home, Holly Mount, Rawtenstall, Whitehead and his sons had built a thriving manufacturing concern in their own right. Whitehead, who was survived by his wife, was buried at Longholme Wesleyan Chapel, Rawtenstall.   ANTHONY HART

Sources D. Whitehead, unpublished memoir and correspondence, Rawtenstall Public Library, Lancashire · W. C. Taylor, *Notes of a tour in the manufacturing districts of Lancashire* (1842); 3rd edn (1968) · parish records, Lancashire, Lancs. RO · *Bacup and Rossendale News* (4–18 Feb 1865) · H. Whitehead, *David Whitehead and Sons Limited, 1815–1909* (1909) · D. Bythell, *The handloom weavers: a study in the English cotton industry during the industrial revolution* (1969) · W. Turner, *Riot! The story of east Lancashire loom breakers in 1826* (1992) · J. Elliott, ed., *David Whitehead of Rossendale, 1790–1860* (1973) · A. J. Hart, 'Rural factory settlements in Lancashire, 1780–1835', MA diss., University of Lancaster, 1993 · H. I. Hunt, 'A transcript from the manuscript of the first David Whitehead', 1956, Rawtenstall Public Library, Lancashire · d. cert.
Archives Rawtenstall Public Library, Lancashire, Rossendale collection, diaries, RC 921 WHI
Likenesses photograph, repro. in Whitehead, *David Whitehead and Sons Limited* · portrait, Rossendale Museum, Whitaker Park, Rawtenstall
Wealth at death under £10,000: resworn probate, Jan 1867, *CGPLA Eng. & Wales* (1865)

Whitehead, Sir Edgar Cuthbert Fremantle (1905–1971), prime minister of Rhodesia, was born on 8 February 1905 in Berlin, the third son in the family of five sons and two daughters of Sir James Beethom Whitehead (1858–1928), head of chancery in the British embassy in Berlin, and his wife, Marian Cecilia Brodrick (*d.* 1932). His mother was the youngest daughter of the eighth Viscount Midleton, and sister of (William) St John Fremantle *Brodrick, earl of Midleton, sometime parliamentary under-secretary at the Colonial Office, secretary of state for war, and for India, and leader of southern Irish unionism. Whitehead was educated at Shrewsbury School and University College, Oxford, obtaining a second class degree in history in 1926.

In 1928, on doctor's advice, Whitehead emigrated to Southern Rhodesia, becoming a civil servant in Gwelo district court. He took up farming in the Vumba district and became a leading member of local agricultural organizations which provided a springboard into parliament. In 1939 he was elected to the legislative assembly as member for Umtali North for the United Party led by Sir Godfrey Huggins. On the outbreak of war, despite his poor eyesight, Whitehead returned to England to join the Royal Army Service Corps and was appointed military OBE in 1944 for service in west Africa. After retiring with the rank of lieutenant-colonel, he became acting Southern Rhodesian high commissioner in London in 1945–6. He was re-elected to the legislative assembly in 1946, and served until 1953 as minister of finance and of posts and telegraphs. During these years he sought to maximize white immigration, which he believed would make the white minority more capable of liberalizing its policies towards

Sir Edgar Cuthbert Fremantle Whitehead (1905–1971), by Howard Coster, 1944

Africans. He led the tough negotiations which brought Rhodesia Railways into state ownership, and his interventionist approach to the economy gained him a reputation for 'socialistic tendencies', which he disclaimed. He supported the creation of the Federation of Rhodesia and Nyasaland, hoping for a larger market for Southern Rhodesian industries and agriculture which might form a bastion of British loyalism against an increasingly republican-minded Afrikaner Nationalist government in the Union of South Africa. He championed the cause of multiracial higher education, serving on the council of the University College in Salisbury from 1955 to 1958.

In 1953 Whitehead was forced to retire from politics because of ill health. He was appointed CMG in 1952 and KCMG in 1954. In 1957, however, he accepted appointment as the federation's first diplomatic representative in Washington, attached to the British embassy with the rank of minister, where he witnessed at first hand developments in American civil rights and race relations and the strength of anti-colonial opinion at the United Nations general assembly. In 1958 he was elected leader of the United Federal Party (UFP), succeeding Garfield Todd, prime minister since 1953, a reputed liberal. His first attempt to win a by-election was unsuccessful, triggering a general election in which he was returned for Salisbury North, a wealthy and comparatively liberal constituency. Ominously, the right-wing Dominion Party polled more first-preference votes than the UFP, which only retained power on the basis of second-preference votes. This rightward trend reinforced Whitehead's cautious belief that the broad support of the white electorate would have to be retained in order to avoid a destructive battle between white segregationism and African nationalism.

Whitehead became prime minister and minister of native affairs (1958–60). He marked a change in style from the handsome, charismatic Todd. Half-deaf, thickly spectacled, and a confirmed bachelor, he showed a diffidence and patrician eccentricity unsuited to the intimacy of the small settler electorate. Once, on hearing an account of the American evangelical preacher Billy Graham, he remarked that he wished he too 'had a personality' (Stumbles, 94). Whitehead had come to recognize that African advancement was inevitable, but he believed that he could manage the pace of reform. In 1959 he declared a state of emergency to contain nationalist unrest and intimidation, and suppressed the African National Congress. In 1960 he introduced the draconian Law and Order Maintenance Act and the Emergency Powers Act. These authoritarian measures were accompanied by unprecedented reforms, however, with the appointment of several commissions of inquiry into discriminatory legislation against Africans, as a result of which Africans were admitted to the higher grades of the civil service, to trade unions, hotels, and public swimming pools. Gambling and liquor restrictions were also repealed.

Wider developments did not favour Whitehead's gradualist counter-revolutionary policies. In 1960 the Monckton report on the future of the federation suggested that its constituent territories be permitted to secede, encouraging the expectations of African nationalists and white segregationists alike. Whitehead still believed that a multiracial state could be created in Southern Rhodesia, based on the broad support of moderate Africans and white liberals. In 1961 he negotiated a new constitution with the British government, increasing the assembly to sixty-five seats, of which fifteen would represent a predominately African electorate. Under an immensely complex franchise weighted in favour of educated property owners, he foresaw that growing numbers of Africans would enter parliament and achieve a majority in the assembly by 1976. The British government agreed to give up its reserved powers over Southern Rhodesia, and the constitution was approved in a referendum by a majority of over two to one. The electorate's approval reflected a growing desire for independence from Whitehall rather than residual liberalism, however. White insecurity was intensified by the arrival of Belgian refugees from Congo and the deteriorating economy of the crumbling federation. Moreover, encouraged by nationalist success in the other federal territories, the African nationalists of the National Democratic Party repudiated their initial agreement to the new constitution. Whitehead's 'Build-a-Nation' campaign to register African voters proved a singular failure. He believed nevertheless that an orderly multiracial society could be preserved only if the Land Apportionment Act was repealed, which would create

new classes of modernizing, politically conservative African landowners, educated professionals, and skilled urban artisans. The Land Apportionment Act, however, had long been the cornerstone of white supremacy. In the general election of 1962 Whitehead was decisively defeated by the hardline Rhodesian Front. As leader of the opposition he was unable to prevent Rhodesia's unilateral declaration of independence (UDI) in 1965. He later retired to England, where he died in a nursing home in Newbury, Berkshire, on 22 September 1971.

UDI marked the ultimate failure of Whitehead's policies. Like the wider Anglo-Rhodesian establishment he depended on continuing metropolitan support to enable him to control the pace of change. A keen monarchist, he campaigned unsuccessfully in 1953 for the federation to be known as the kingdom of Rhodesia and Nyasaland, which he believed would bolster loyal sentiment among white and black people alike. The combined strength of metropolitan disengagement, African nationalist determination, and white supremacy proved too strong, however. His suggestion, after his fall from power, that Southern Rhodesia become a self-governing part of the United Kingdom on the same terms as Northern Ireland, so that African rights could be granted by a white majority, demonstrated how far he had lost touch with British as well as Rhodesian opinion.

DONAL LOWRY

Sources *The Times* (24 Sept 1971) · 'Sir Edgar's police state', *New Statesman* (16 Aug 1962) · *WWW* · *The Southern Rhodesia (constitution) order in council, 1961* (1961) · *Debates of the Legislative Assembly* [Southern Rhodesia] (1946–53); (1958–65) · J. Barber, *Rhodesia: the road to rebellion* (1967) · N. Bhebe, 'The nationalist struggle, 1957–1962', *Turmoil and tenacity: Zimbabwe, 1890–1980*, ed. C. Banana (1989) · R. Blake, *A history of Rhodesia* (New York, 1978) · T. Bull, ed., *Rhodesian perspective* (1967) · Baron Butler of Saffron Walden [R. A. Butler], *The art of the possible: the memoirs of Lord Butler* (1971) · E. M. Clegg, *Race and politics: partnership in the Federation of Rhodesia and Nyasaland* (1960) · F. Clements, *Rhodesia: the course to collision* (1969) · T. Creighton, *Southern Rhodesia and the Central African Federation: the anatomy of partnership* (1960) · J. Darwin, 'The central African emergency, 1959', *Journal of Imperial and Commonwealth History*, 21 (1993), 217–34 [special issue] · J. Day, 'Southern Rhodesian African nationalists and the 1961 Constitution', *Journal of Modern African Studies*, 7 (1969), 221–47 · C. Frantz and C. A. Rogers, 'Length of residence and race attitudes of Europeans in Southern Rhodesia', *Race*, 3/2 (1962), 46–54 · *DNB* · L. H. Gann and M. Gelfand, *Huggins of Rhodesia: the man and his country* (1964) · J. Greenfield, *Testimony of a Rhodesian federal* (1977) · R. Gray, *The two nations: aspects of the development of race relations in the Federation of the Rhodesias and Nyasaland* (1960) · I. Hancock, *White liberals, moderates and radicals in Rhodesia, 1953–1980* (1984) · I. Hancock, 'The Capricorn Africa Society in Southern Rhodesia', *Rhodesian History*, 9 (1978), 41–62 · I. Hancock, 'Sane and pragmatic liberalism: the action group in Bulawayo, 1955–1965', *Rhodesian History*, 9 (1978), 65–83 · R. Hodder-Williams, *White farmers in Rhodesia, 1890–1965: a history of the Marandellas district* (1983) · H. Holderness, *Lost chance: Southern Rhodesia, 1945–58* (1985) · F. S. Joelson, ed., *Rhodesia and east Africa* (1957) · P. Keatley, *The politics of partnership: the federation of Rhodesia and Nyasaland* (1963) · A. King, 'The *Central African Examiner*, 1957–1965', *Zambezia*, 23 (1966), 133–55 · A. King, 'The "Build-a-Nation" campaign', 1995, priv. coll. · A. Leys, *European politics in Southern Rhodesia* (1959) · D. Lowry, '"Shame upon 'little England' while 'greater England' stands!": Southern Rhodesia and the imperial idea', *The round table, the empire/commonwealth and British foreign policy*, ed. A. Bosco and A. May (1997) · J. W. Mann and P. L. van den Bergh, 'A Rhodesian

white minority under threat', *Journal of Social Psychology*, 57 (1962), 315–38 • P. Mason, *Year of decision* (1960) • L. J. McFarlane, 'Justifying rebellion: black and white nationalism in Rhodesia', *Journal of Commonwealth Political Studies*, 6 (1968), 54–79 • E. Mlambo, *Rhodesia, the struggle for a birthright* (1967) • P. Murphy, *Party politics and decolonization: the conservative party and British colonial policy in tropical Africa, 1951–1964* (1995) • R. Palmer, *Land and racial domination in Rhodesia* (1977) • M. Perham, 'The Rhodesian crisis: the background', *International Affairs*, 42/1 (1966), 1–13, 86 • C. Palley, *The constitutional history and law of Southern Rhodesia, 1888–1965* (1966) • C. A. Rogeres and C. Frantz, *Racial themes in Southern Rhodesia: the attitudes and behaviour of the white population* (1962) • C. G. Rosberg, 'Turning point in Southern Rhodesia?', *African Special Report* (July 1958) • C. W. Sherwell, 'Sir Edgar Whitehead: a Rhodesian premier's approach to the question of African advancement, 1958–1962', BPhil diss., U. Oxf., 1973 • N. Sithole, *African nationalism* (1959) • N. Shamuyarira, *Crisis in Rhodesia* (1965) • A. R. W. Stumbles, *Some recollections of a Rhodesian speaker* (1980) • R. Tredgold, *The Rhodesia that was my life* (1968) • L. Vambe, *From Rhodesia to Zimbabwe* (1976) • E. Wason, *Banned: the story of the "Africa Daily News", Southern Rhodesia, 1964* (1976) • J. R. T. Wood, *The Welensky papers: a history of the Federation of Rhodesia and Nyasaland* (1983) • Burke, *Peerage* (2000) • *CGPLA Eng. & Wales* (1971) • *Principles and policies*, United federal party (1958) • United federal party, *Our political principles: our achievements and our intentions* (1958) • United federal party, *A policy today for your tomorrow* (1958) • United federal party, *The repeal of the Land Apportionment Act* (1962)
Archives Bodl. RH, papers • Bodl. RH, papers, corresp. and unpublished autobiography | Bodl. RH, papers of Sir Robert Tredgold • Bodl. RH, papers of Sir Roy Welensky
Likenesses H. Coster, photograph, 1944, NPG [*see illus.*]
Wealth at death £14,784: probate, 25 Nov 1971, *CGPLA Eng. & Wales*

Whitehead, George (1637–1724), Quaker leader and writer, was born at Sunbiggin in the parish of Orton, Westmorland, in 1637, the son of poor farmers. He attended the free school at Blencoe, Cumberland, and when he was fourteen rejected the presbyterianism of his parents. At some point during the next eighteen months he was converted to Quakerism by George Fox, whom he first heard preaching at Henry Ward's house at Sunny Bank, Grayrigg, about 8 miles to the south-west of Sunbiggin. Whitehead was active as a Quaker proselyte in disputes with the local clergy until 1654. He then moved south and evangelized through Yorkshire and Lincolnshire into East Anglia and Kent, principally with the Quaker Richard Hubberthorne, but also at times with Fox, John Stubbs, John Rous, and Alexander Parker. Despite his youth, Whitehead was notable as a leader in clashes with clergymen, claiming that God enabled him to identify false syllogisms.

In December 1654 Whitehead endured the first of many periods of imprisonment for the sake of his faith. Having spoken against a sermon at St Peter's Church, Norwich, he was examined and imprisoned for eight weeks; this was followed by a further spell of three weeks in prison in March 1655 when he visited Quakers imprisoned in Norwich Castle. In July he was committed for trial at Bury St Edmunds after defending a paper affixed to the church door of Bures, Suffolk, by another Quaker, Richard Clayton; he was held for three months. On refusing to pay a fine, Whitehead was imprisoned and was released in October 1656 only following direct appeals to Oliver Cromwell, including one by Mary Saunders, a servant of

the Cromwell family. Over the following months Whitehead endured harsh physical punishment: he was set in the stocks in Saffron Walden and was publicly whipped at Nayland.

Whitehead's first two works, *Davids Enemies Discovered* and *Cain's Generation Discover'd*, both attacks on Jonathan Clapham's defence of psalm singing, were published in 1655. These marked the beginning of a redoubtable publishing career: by the time of Whitehead's death, over 100 separate printed items had appeared. Most were controversial works, but some were spiritual testimonies, epistles, and printed sermons. (Sermons of his were also included in the Quaker collections of sermons *Harmony of Divine and Heavenly Doctrines* of 1696 and *The Concurrence and Unanimity; of the People called Quakers* of 1711.)

In 1657 Whitehead made a visit home to Westmorland, by way of the west of England, and was reconciled with his parents (his mother and sister eventually became Quakers); he is also said to have met the Quaker schismatic James Nayler at Great Strickland, although the latter's imprisonment from 1656 to 1659 casts doubt on this. While in the north Whitehead also made successful proselytizing journeys into Northumberland, visiting Newcastle, Berwick, Alnwick, and Holy Island. On his return south he was imprisoned for more than four months at Ipswich on the evidence of a clergyman with whom he had talked on the road south; while imprisoned, he wrote an open letter, 'To the inhabitants of Ipswich, both teachers and people', which does not seem to have been published. His repeated encounters with the law from the mid-1650s onwards helped him amass a vast legal knowledge, which proved especially helpful in defending himself against charges of vagrancy and disturbing religious services. At Ipswich, for example, he caused a sensation in court by pointing out the illegality of the accusation he faced; however, on this occasion he was returned to gaol and freed only following the death of Cromwell in September 1658. Notwithstanding such setbacks, it was to Whitehead that the responsibility fell for showing Friends how to assert their rights in law, something readily observable in the relish with which Whitehead produced many protracted published accounts of his legal battles.

Whitehead later remarked that although there was much 'Pulpit-Noise against us' the Friends 'had some Respite and Ease from open Persecution … after *Richard Cromwel* was set up for *Protector*' (Whitehead, 144). During the hiatus between the collapse of Richard Cromwell's regime and the return of Charles II, Whitehead held public disputes on 29 August 1659 with the Cambridge divine Thomas Smith (who argued that he was a heretic) and on 15 September with the universalists Thomas Moor and John Horn at King's Lynn; both encounters were recorded in pamphlet publications. Similar disputes took place at Fulham and Bluntisford. In the first month of the Restoration, Whitehead had to be protected from a mob in Peterborough by some of John Lambert's soldiers quartered in the town. Charles's proclamation against conventicles led to Whitehead's imprisonment for sixteen weeks in Norwich Castle, where in March 1661 he almost died of ague and fever. Later in the same year he appeared before parliamentary committees and the bar of the House of Commons, with Hubberthorne and Edward Burrough, to protest against anti-Quaker legislation then being drafted by parliament. The three were imprisoned in Newgate; only Whitehead survived the incarceration.

Whitehead spent most of the next decade in prison. On his release from Norwich Castle in 1661 he was again immediately active, this time leading protests against oaths (especially the oath of allegiance). In July 1664 he was arrested for preaching at a Quaker meeting in Surrey and imprisoned at Southwark; while incarcerated he was also accused of involvement in the Westmorland Kipper-Rigg plot of 1663–4. In October he was one of forty-five arrested at a meeting at the Bull and Mouth, London, and was imprisoned in Newgate. When not in prison he lodged with the Quaker Rebecca Travers in London and was active in the city, holding meetings on transport ships at Gravesend and visiting prisoners during the great plague.

The summer of 1670 was an eventful time for Whitehead. On 13 May 1670 he married at the Peel meeting of Quakers in Clerkenwell; his wife, Anne *Whitehead (c.1624–1686), was the daughter of Thomas Downer, vicar of Charlbury, and the widow of Benjamin Greenwell (who had died in Newgate in 1665). An early convert to Quakerism and a prominent preacher, Anne was considerably older than George, who later described her as 'like a Tender Mother' to him (Whitehead, 322). They apparently had no children. In June and July 1670 the city authorities seem to have mounted a sustained campaign against the Quaker meeting in Gracechurch Street. Whitehead was arrested and examined several times; on each occasion he protested that the actions of the meeting had not been illegal under the terms of the Conventicle Act. 'I desire you would not go about to ensnare us, for the Law was not made to make Men Transgressors, but to punish them where it finds such', he warned one of the judges (Besse, 1.414). In spring 1672 he and Thomas Moor negotiated with Charles II a royal indulgence for the release of almost 500 prisoners, not all of them Quakers and many of them dissenters who were in fact enemies of the Friends. This was the first of Whitehead's many interviews with Charles II; in 1673, for example, he pleaded with the king for Fox's liberation from Worcester gaol.

Although Whitehead still toured the countryside preaching and attending meetings—he preached at Erith, Huntingdonshire, in April 1676—the 1670s saw him otherwise settled in the capital, working as a grocer in Houndsditch. When he was arrested with Thomas Burr at a meeting at Norwich in March 1680 and imprisoned, a certificate, signed by two London common councilmen, two churchwardens, and a constable among others, was issued testifying that Whitehead had been a resident of the parish of St Botolph without Bishopgate in London for about ten years; he was 'in Good Repute, and is esteemed a man of a Competent Estate' and 'hath demeaned himself

peaceably in his Conversation' (Whitehead, 417). The certificate was never read at the ensuing trial but both men were nevertheless discharged in July. Whitehead's relative youth, his presence in the Quaker movement since the earliest days, and the death of most of the prominent founding Friends by the 1670s meant that he was effectively the most important Friend in the capital by this date. He helped arbitrate in the so-called Wilkinson–Story controversy that threatened the movement in the 1670s, and was also a key figure in the weekly meeting for sufferings which was established by London Quakers in 1676 and eventually became the 'executive committee' for the movement as a whole (Ingle, 257). Although undoubtedly a resolute follower and close associate of Fox (he had attended Fox's marriage to Margaret Fell in October 1669), Whitehead possessed a patient temperament which was highly effective in dealing with internal dissent and acted as a useful counterbalance to Fox's singular approach.

Whitehead continued to meet Charles II: in January 1680 he presented evidence to the king about how the Friends were confused with Roman Catholics. The following year he was part of a group that attempted unsuccessfully to persuade Charles to free Quakers imprisoned at Bristol. Undaunted, he kept the king informed of the sufferings of Friends in the provinces at meetings in February 1682 and February 1683, defended Quaker language and dress policy in April 1683, and denied Quaker complicity in the Rye House plot in August. The succession of James II in 1685 did not impede Whitehead's access to the monarch: he was impressing on James the extent of Quaker imprisonments and distraints at meetings with the king in early 1686. By June that year Whitehead had helped secure from James warrants for the release of Quaker prisoners and relaxations of the economic and other judicial penalties and prejudices against Quakers. The following April, James issued a declaration of indulgence (granting liberty of conscience) after a further series of interviews in which Whitehead played a major role. Whitehead's conferences with the crown, however, did not mean he was not still subject to arrests and imprisonments for his activities. In 1682–3 he had goods seized to the value of £40 following non-payment of fines for breaching the Conventicles Act; in August 1683 he was arrested for preaching at Westminster; and in August 1684 alone he had £32 worth of goods seized, was arrested for preaching at Southwark, and was convicted following an arrest at a meeting in White Hart Lane, resulting in imprisonment in Newgate for ten days.

The death of his wife, Anne, on 28 July 1686 prompted Whitehead to publish a collection of personal testimonies to her memory, *Piety Promoted by Faithfulness* (1686). Two years later he married Ann Goddard, a shopkeeper in Whitechapel and the daughter of Captain Richard Goddard, a clothier; the ceremony took place at Devonshire House on 19 July 1688. Whitehead later described her as 'an ingenious and careful Wife' (Whitehead, 323). They had only one child, who died at birth. The change of monarch at the end of 1688 presented further opportunities for Whitehead's skills as a lobbyist, allowing him to secure the passing of the Toleration Act in 1689. However, further petitioning was needed in order to gain legal recognition of the fact that, since Quakers refused to take oaths, they were exempt from most of the benefits of the act: namely, rights to take legal action, prove or administer wills, and take up freedoms in cities and corporations, and, in some places, electoral rights. Following the deaths of Fox in 1691 (at whose funeral Whitehead was one of five Quakers who testified) and another leading Quaker, Stephen Crisp, in 1692, Whitehead became the acknowledged leader of the Quaker movement. He continued his campaign for toleration, with his comparison of the Quakers to the tolerated Dutch Mennonites moving William III to such an extent that the king ordered the release of another wave of Quakers from prison. Whitehead was also principally responsible for the Affirmation Act of 1696, a compromise over the issue of oath-taking that in itself offended many Friends, who then implicitly directed much of their criticism at Whitehead. (The issue was not resolved until twenty years later, when parliament finally legislated an acceptable form of affirmation.) Whitehead also succeeded in having the Friends exempted from an act requiring that every dissenting preacher buy a licence for 20s. a quarter.

In addition to his lobbying activities, Whitehead promoted the Quakers in print. In a series of tracts between 1699 and 1712 he defended the principles of the Friends several times, usually against hostile attacks. His health began to fail in 1711 but he continued to address successive monarchs on behalf of the Friends: Queen Anne, George I, and even the future George II. Whitehead died on 8 March 1724 and was buried in the Quaker burial-ground at Bunhill Fields on 13 March. His monthly meeting issued a testimony celebrating him as an 'Elder worthy of double honour' (Beck, 120). Whitehead's own account of his life up to 1711 (the bulk of which concerned his activities before 1689) was published posthumously in 1725 as *The Christian Progress of that Ancient Servant and Minister of Jesus Christ, George Whitehead*. The early twentieth-century Quaker historian William Braithwaite was unimpressed by Whitehead's leadership, describing him as 'cautious and pedestrian … the embodiment of worthy and drab respectability, devoid of genius, and of little humour' (Braithwaite, 177–8). However, as a legal expert and someone who was evidently skilled at gaining, maintaining, and exploiting effectively access to no fewer than seven monarchs, Whitehead was crucial to the development, establishment, and recognition of the Quaker movement.

John Whitehead (*c*.1630–1696), a Quaker preacher and writer from Yorkshire, does not seem to have been a relation.   NIGEL SMITH

Sources G. Whitehead, *The Christian progress of that ancient servant and minister of Jesus Christ, George Whitehead* (1725) • W. C. Braithwaite, *The beginnings of Quakerism*, ed. H. J. Cadbury, 2nd edn (1955) • W. C. Braithwaite, *The second period of Quakerism*, ed. H. J. Cadbury, 2nd edn (1961) • J. F. McGregor, 'Whitehead, George', Greaves & Zaller, *BDBR*, 314–15 • W. Beck, 'Valiant for the truth': George Whitehead, his work and service (1901) • J. Besse, *A collection of the sufferings of the people called Quakers*, 2 vols. (1753) • W. Sewel, *The history of the rise, increase and progress of the Christian people called Quakers*, 3rd edn

(1774) • *The journal of George Fox*, ed. N. Penney, 2 vols. (1911) • *The short journal and itinerary journals of George Fox*, ed. N. Penney (1925) • *DNB* • H. L. Ingle, *First among Friends: George Fox and the creation of Quakerism* (1994)

Whitehead, Henry (1853–1947), bishop of Madras, was born on 19 December 1853, the second of the four children of Alfred Whitehead (1827–1898), headmaster of Chatham House School in Ramsgate, Kent, and later vicar of St Peter's, Isle of Thanet, and his wife, Maria Sarah, *née* Buckmaster (1832–1924). Whitehead's parents strongly encouraged his intellectual gifts and those of his younger brother, Alfred North *Whitehead (1861–1947), who later became a mathematician and philosopher. Educated at Sherborne School (1870–73), Whitehead received a scholarship to Trinity College, Oxford, where he took a first class in both classical examinations, moderations (1874) and *literae humaniores* (1877). He graduated BA and was named fellow in 1877 (MA in 1880), and after ordination as deacon in 1879 (priest in 1880) became preacher at St Nicholas, Abingdon. In 1883 he was appointed principal of Bishop's College, Calcutta, assuming additional duties as superior of the Oxford mission to Calcutta in 1890.

The Anglo-Catholic Oxford mission was isolated in both theology and ritual from other Christian bodies in India, but Whitehead gradually worked out a broader approach to co-operation with them and showed greater sympathy toward the aspirations of Indian Christians for ecclesiastical self-government. After his consecration as bishop of Madras in 1899, he spoke out against the elitism of Anglican missions in India and welcomed the mass movements of untouchables into the churches. He developed a close friendship with V. S. Azariah, a founder of the indigenous Indian Missionary Society, who at the International Missionary Conference in Edinburgh in 1910 delivered a provocative speech appealing for friendship across the barriers of race and empire. Whitehead nominated him as bishop of Dornakal, a new diocese, and in 1912 Azariah was consecrated the first Indian bishop of the Anglican church. In 1911 the movement that in 1947 finally unified the major protestant denominations in the church of south India was initiated at a meeting in Whitehead's house in Madras. Whitehead wrote a study of popular Hinduism, *The Village Gods of South India* (1916), which was still being consulted by scholars sixty years after its publication. Despite his revulsion from aspects of Hinduism, Whitehead detected in south Indian popular religion a universal yearning for God.

On 12 August 1903 Whitehead married Isobel Frances Duncan (1872–1953), who had been one of the first undergraduates to study mathematics at Lady Margaret Hall, Oxford. On 11 November 1904 she gave birth to their only child, John Henry Constantine *Whitehead, who became a mathematician. Isobel Whitehead served as head of women's services in furlough and convalescence camps in India between 1914 and 1918, for which she was made CBE in 1919.

In 1920 the Whiteheads moved to Pincent's Hill, Calcot, near Reading. Whitehead resigned his see in 1922, though he continued to serve as commissary to Madras and Dornakal. He published *Indian Problems in Religion, Education, Politics* (1924), and served as a member of the Lindsay commission on Indian Christian colleges (1931–2). He died at Pincent's Hill, at the age of ninety-three, on 14 April 1947.

JEFFREY COX

Sources *The Times* (17 April 1947) · Crockford (1930) · V. Lowe, *Alfred North Whitehead: the man and his work*, 2 vols. (1985–90), vol. 1 · *The Times* (1 Feb 1907) [obit. of Canon John Duncan] · *The Times* (9 May 1960) [obit. of John Henry Constantine Whitehead] · Burke, *Peerage* (1921) · *New York Times* (31 Dec 1947) · A. Lawrence, ed., *Who's who among living authors of older nations* (1931) · B. Sundkler, *Church of South India: the movement towards union, 1900–1947* (1954) · M. E. Gibbs, *The Anglican church in India, 1600–1970* (1972) · L. Price, ed., *Dialogues of Alfred North Whitehead* (1954) · A. N. Whitehead, 'England and the high seas', *Atlantic Monthly*, 138 (1927), 791–8 · G. Longridge, *A history of the Oxford mission to Calcutta* (1900) · S. B. Harper, *In the shadow of the Mahatma: Bishop V. S. Azariah and the travails of Christianity in British India* (2000)

Archives LPL, corresp. and papers | Johns Hopkins University, Baltimore, Alfred North Whitehead MSS

Likenesses group photograph, repro. in Lowe, *Alfred North Whitehead*, following p. 179 · photographs, repro. in Longridge, *History of the Oxford mission to Calcutta*, facing pp. 45 and 183

Wealth at death £75 5s. 8d.: probate, 21 July 1949, CGPLA Eng. & Wales

Whitehead, Hugh (d. 1551), prior then dean of Durham, was a Benedictine monk of Durham Cathedral priory by 30 March 1499, when he was ordained deacon. He was made priest on 18 December 1501. From that year he was a student at Durham College, Oxford. After seven years' study counted there and two elsewhere (doubtless in his own cloister) he supplicated BTh on 15 January 1509, being admitted on 14 March. He proceeded DTh on 4 July 1513. He was proxy for the prior of Durham Cathedral at the provincial chapter of the black monks on 2 July 1509. He became the prior's chaplain in 1511, and from then until 1515 he was warden of the Oxford cell. He held the major obediences of terrar and hostillar in the priory from 1515 to 1520, and was elected prior on 3 January 1520. He was an enterprising administrator, having licence from the absentee Bishop Wolsey to exploit the mineral wealth of Weardale. During the final years of the priory the monks were generous in grants of leases and advowsons, and co-operated in the surrender of their cells (subordinate houses). Whitehead was nevertheless bold enough to refuse Henry VIII a lease for a client in 1538. He is said to have been present as the shrine of St Cuthbert was destroyed in 1539. The house surrendered on 31 December that year; Whitehead was named dean of the successor secular chapter in the charter of foundation, of 12 May 1541. Over half his former monastic colleagues were accommodated in the new cathedral body; while their interest predominated, life in the close at Durham was uneventful.

In the last year of his life Whitehead was caught up in treason charges intended to unseat the conservative Bishop Tunstall. The privy council had in August 1550 investigated a report that 'great quantitie of treasure' had been taken to the dean's house (*APC*, 3.102). In May 1551 Whitehead was summoned to London and examined by a committee of councillors. On 3 November he was bound in 200 marks to appear before them again on the first day of the following term; but by 8 November he had died in London. He was buried in the church of Holy Trinity Minories, London. His kinsmen Thomas and Hugh received what goods he left in London. Whitehead owned a number of books which survive (including an old breviary, BL, Harleian MS 4664), some of which he gave to his fellow monks.

C. S. KNIGHTON

Sources Emden, *Oxf.*, 4.624–5 · P. Mussett, *Lists of deans and major canons of Durham 1541–1900* (1974), 1 · J. T. Fowler, ed., *Extracts from the account rolls of the abbey of Durham*, 3, SurtS, 103 (1901), 480, 657, 719, 727 · J. Raine, ed., *A description … of all the ancient monuments, rites and customes … within the monastical church of Durham*, SurtS, 15 (1842), 46 · W. A. Pantin, ed., *Documents illustrating the activities of … the English black monks, 1215–1540*, 3 vols., CS, 3rd ser., 45, 47, 54 (1931–7), vol. 3, p. 218 · *LP Henry VIII*, 14/2, no. 772 · *CSP dom.*, rev. edn, 1547–53, nos. 515, 594 (*ter*) · *APC*, 1550–52, 102, 277, 314, 326, 381, 406, 410, 468 · C. Sturge, *Cuthbert Tunstal* (1938), 260, 287, 289 · R. W. Dixon, *History of the Church of England*, 3rd edn, 2 (1895), 149 · D. Marcombe, ed., *The last principality* (1987), 15, 80 · D. Marcombe, 'The Durham dean and chapter: old abbey writ large?', *Continuity and change: personnel and administration of the Church of England, 1500–1642*, ed. R. O'Day and F. Heal (1976), 125–44, esp. 127, 140

Whitehead, James (1812–1885), physician, was born at Oldham, the son of John Whitehead and his wife, Betty, whose surname may have been Bradbury. John Whitehead had a wide reputation in the district as a herbalist and dealer in simples, and it was his great ambition that his son should take up medicine as a profession; thus after working as a boy in a cotton mill Whitehead attended the Marsden Street school of medicine in Manchester, and was afterwards apprenticed first to Mr Clough of Lever Street, Manchester, and subsequently to Mr Lambert of Thirsk. On 11 September 1834 he became LSA and on 15 December 1835 he took his MRCS. He was admitted a fellow of the Royal College of Surgeons after examination on 14 August 1845, and he graduated MD at the University of St Andrews in 1850. In 1859 he became MRCP (London).

In 1836 Whitehead visited France and Germany; he remained in Paris for two years, learning French and visiting the hospitals of that city. On his return to England in 1838 he began to practise as a general practitioner at 123 Oxford Street, Manchester, and in 1842 he was appointed demonstrator of anatomy at the Marsden Street school of medicine. In the same year he moved to 133 Oxford Street and married Elizabeth (b. 1820), daughter of Thomas Hayward Radcliffe of Bank House, Clitheroe. Her untimely death, of puerperal peritonitis, at twenty-four, on 20 September 1844, was a terrible blow to him, and influenced the future course of his career. Because of the nature of his wife's death Whitehead determined to devote his attention to the diseases of women and children; in order to further this aim, in conjunction with Dr A. Schoepf Merei, a Hungarian refugee, he took a house in Stevenson Square and opened the Clinical Hospital and Dispensary for Children. The hospital rapidly grew into the Manchester Clinical Hospital for Women and Children, which opened in 1856 with fifty-six beds and an attached convalescent home. As well as giving much of his time to this hospital Whitehead was lecturer on obstetrics at the Royal School of Medicine, and for fifteen years he acted as surgeon to St Mary's Hospital for Women and Children. In 1851 he moved to 87 Mosley Street, Manchester, where he conducted an extensive and lucrative practice until his retirement in 1881.

One of the most distinguishing features of Whitehead's career was his success in cases of sterility, a problem which he discussed in the monograph *On the Causes and Treatment of Abortion and Sterility* (1847; published in America, 1848). Other published works include *On the Transmission from Parent to Offspring of some Forms of Disease* (1851) and *Notes on the Rates of Mortality in Manchester* (1863). Jointly with Merei he published the first *Report of the Clinical Hospital, Manchester* (1856), and, under the pseudonym of Philothalos, *The Wife's Domain* (1860). He also contributed many excellent papers to various medical journals.

When he retired from practice Whitehead left Manchester to live at Fairlands, an estate he had purchased in Sutton, Surrey. He died there on 3 April 1885 of oesophageal cancer, and was buried in Ardwick cemetery, Manchester, in the vault which contained the remains of his wife.

ORNELLA MOSCUCCI

Sources *DNB* · *BMJ* (25 April 1885), 870–71 · private information (1900) · Boase, *Mod. Eng. biog.* · W. E. A. Axon, ed., *The annals of Manchester: a chronological record from the earliest times to the end of 1885* (1886), 415 · d. cert. [Elizabeth Whitehead] · d. cert.
Wealth at death £47,280 14s. 0d.: resworn probate, Oct 1885, *CGPLA Eng. & Wales*

Whitehead, John (c.1630–1696), Quaker minister and preacher, was born in the Holderness district of Yorkshire. About 1648 he joined the army and was subsequently stationed at Scarborough Castle. Influenced by his parents, he was attracted to puritan ministers and often had 'secret breathings and longings after God', but he eventually concluded that he lacked 'living faith' (*Life and Writings*, 3). When William Dewsbury came to Scarborough about 1652 he convinced Whitehead to become a Quaker. A man of modest education, Whitehead believed that God's 'secrets were with me; for the Spirit as a key opened his treasure and shewed me that which was from the beginning' (J. Whitehead, *A Small Treatise*, 1661, 5). He accompanied Dewsbury to Malton, Yorkshire, and began preaching in December 1652. After leaving the army the following summer, he and Thomas Thompson preached on the Yorkshire moors. At Stokesley he challenged the Baptist William Kaye to demonstrate whether he had an unmediated calling from Christ, whether ministers had received tithes in gospel times, and whether he could disprove Quaker tenets. Kaye published an account of the dispute in *A Plain Answer to the Eighteen Quaeries* (1654). With Dewsbury, George Fox, and James Nayler, Whitehead contributed to *Several Letters Written to the Saints* the same year.

Undaunted by confrontation, Whitehead preached in Lincoln Cathedral in November 1654 and had to be rescued from irate worshippers by soldiers. While incarcerated in Northampton in 1655 he wrote *The Enmitie between the Two Seeds* (1655) as well as epistles exhorting Friends to withstand persecution and suffer patiently. Following his

release he preached in Northamptonshire and Buckinghamshire, and then went to east Yorkshire, where he addressed *A Reproof from the Lord* (1656) to professing Christians in the Hull and Beverley area, accusing them of pursuing earthly wisdom. With George Whitehead and George Fox the younger he refuted the views of John Horne and Thomas Moore in *A Brief Discovery of the Dangerous Principles* (1659).

As hostility against Quakers intensified, Whitehead was physically attacked at York in January 1660. With thirty-five others he signed *This to the King and his Councel* (1660), protesting the disruption of Quaker meetings in Northamptonshire. For refusing to take the oath of allegiance he was incarcerated at Aylesbury in January 1661, and in May he published *A Small Treatise*, denouncing compulsory worship; it included a postscript by his fellow prisoner Isaac Penington.

On 24 April 1662 Whitehead finished *A Manifestation of Truth* (1662), in which he defended Quaker principles from Viscount Saye and Sele's attack in *Folly and Madnesse Made Manifest* (1659). Arrested on 8 July on suspicion of holding a conventicle near Lincoln, Whitehead, then of Owstwick, Yorkshire, refused to take an oath and was recommitted to Lincoln Castle. In *For the Vineyard of the Lord of Hosts* (1662) he defended Quakers from charges of sedition and implored God to 'break' the adversaries' 'teeth … that thy Flock may not be meat for them' (p. 6). In *An Expostulation with the Bishops in England* (1662) he urged prelates to reform their own church. Quakers who had lapsed in the face of persecution were admonished to return in *The Case of such Professors* (1662).

On his return to Yorkshire, following his release in April 1663, Whitehead was briefly detained and his books and letters were seized at Hull in July. By November 1664 he was in gaol at Spalding, Lincolnshire, from where he wrote an epistle encouraging Friends to adhere to their ideal of simplicity, later printed in *A Tender Visitation* (1664). With George Whitehead and others he signed an epistle by Farnsworth in May 1666 warning Friends not to distribute scandalous or divisive books, and in August he and Ellis Hookes, working through the master of requests, persuaded Charles II to release Fox from Scarborough Castle.

As sectarian controversy continued Whitehead contributed a postscript to Thomas Rudyard's *The Anabaptists Lying Wonder* (1672), and when Baptists attacked him in *The Quakers Subterfuge* (c.1672) he responded in a postscript to Robert Ruckhill's *The Quakers Refuge* (1673). Ruckhill and Whitehead were assailed in Thomas Grantham's *The Baptist Against the Quaker* (c.1673), and Grantham recounted his debate with Whitehead at Sleaford, Lincolnshire, which dealt with the sacraments and Christ's post-resurrection body, in *Christianismus primitivus* (1678). William Penn included Whitehead's declaration against the Quaker dissident John Perrot in *Judas and the Jews* (1673). In 1675 Whitehead and John Hall drafted an account of the persecution of Yorkshire Friends for submission to Charles and parliament, and the same year Whitehead wrote an epistle to *Balm from Gilead*, a collection of Quaker testimonies.

When the Popish Plot was under investigation, Whitehead and Thompson asked the assize judges at York on 24 March 1679 which Quakers had been accused of being Jesuits.

At some point before 1682 Whitehead married Elizabeth, with whom he apparently had two sons and a daughter. As a trustee for charitable property, he left for London in May 1682 to deal with a suit in chancery involving a legacy of £200. Stopping to preach at Sutton, Lincolnshire, he was arrested, accused of being a Jesuit, and imprisoned. At the assizes on 31 July he produced certificates attesting to his good behaviour, including one from the vicar and churchwardens at Swine, Yorkshire, where he had moved in 1669. Because he refused to take the oath of allegiance, the grand jury indicted him and he was returned to prison. There he wrote *A General Epistle* (1682), warning Anglicans to beware of an accommodation with Catholics. At his trial on 7 March 1683 he was found guilty of *praemunire*. His family moved to Fiskerton, near Lincoln, in 1683, perhaps to be closer to him. He enjoyed limited freedom, for he was at a Quaker meeting in July 1684 when JPs fined those in attendance. Some time after October 1684 he was discharged, but he and nine others were apprehended at a meeting in Devonshire House, London, on 11 February 1686. He was fined 13s. 4d., but refused to pay and remained in Newgate until 2 June.

During the last decade of his life Whitehead served as clerk of the Lincolnshire quarterly meeting and continued to travel as a public Friend (minister). In 1691 he was one of thirteen Friends Fox designated to supervise the publication of his journal and other writings. After two or three years of poor health Whitehead died at Fiskerton on 29 September 1696 and was buried at Lincoln on 1 October. A short, thick-set man, he was praised by George Whitehead (to whom he was unrelated) as 'a man of a solid and sound judgment' (*Life and Writings*, 279). Lincolnshire Friends described him as 'a nursing father, tender and affectionate, apt to teach' (ibid., 281). His stature in early Quaker history was attested to by Penn in the preface to Whitehead's *The Written Gospel-Labours* (1704).

RICHARD L. GREAVES

Sources *The life and writings of John Whitehead*, ed. T. Chalk (1852) · *The journal of George Fox*, ed. N. Penney, 2 vols. (1911) · J. Besse, *A collection of the sufferings of the people called Quakers*, 2 vols. (1753), vol. 1, pp. 75–6, 331, 347–9, 355, 357, 479, 482, 523–5, 528; vol. 2, pp. 98, 107, 139, 143 · RS Friends, Lond., Penington MS 4.19–22, 116–18 · H. J. Cadbury, ed., *Letters to William Dewsbury and others* (1948) · *The short journal and itinerary journals of George Fox*, ed. N. Penney (1925), 353 · W. C. Braithwaite, *The second period of Quakerism*, ed. H. J. Cadbury, 2nd edn (1961) · A. R. Barclay, ed., *Letters, &c., of early Friends* (1841) · G. F. Nuttall, ed., *Early Quaker letters from the Swarthmore MSS to 1660* (1952) · N. Penney, ed., 'The first publishers of truth': being early records, now first printed, of the introduction of Quakerism into the counties of England and Wales* (1907) · M. L. Schwarz, 'Viscount Saye and Sele and the Quakers', *Quaker History*, 62 (1973), 14–34, esp. 16, 33–4

Archives RS Friends, Lond., Barclay MSS 129 · RS Friends, Lond., Penington MSS · RS Friends, Lond., Swarthmore MSS

Whitehead, John (1739/40–1804), physician and biographer, was born, apparently in Dukinfield, Cheshire, one of at least three sons of 'humble' and allegedly Methodist parents, though they appear to have belonged originally to the dissenting chapel in Dukinfield until joining the Moravians in 1738. Whitehead was brought up as a weaver but received a classical education, probably at the Moravian school in Dukinfield. He was converted in the early 1760s by Matthew Mayer, a leading Methodist local preacher. He became a local preacher and did some teaching, but from 1764 to 1769 he was an itinerant Methodist preacher. With Wesley's encouragement he spent some of his time at Wesley's Kingswood School to improve his Latin and Greek and had hopes of becoming a master there.

After marrying Ann Smith, Wesley's housekeeper at Bristol New Room Chapel, on 25 July 1769 he ceased to be a travelling preacher because of his wife's health. He then set up business on credit in Bristol, first in the tobacco trade, then as a linen draper, but was unsuccessful and had to compound with his creditors. Methodist friends subscribed to send him to Staines, near London, as a schoolmaster where he joined the Society of Friends under his wife's influence. With Quaker support he set up a successful boarding-school in Wandsworth. The leading Quaker physician, John Coakley Lettsom, advised him to study medicine, and the Quaker brewer David Barclay paid him a life annuity of £100 to travel with his son on the continent. He entered as a medical student at Leiden on 16 September 1779 and graduated MD on 4 February 1780. On 19 January 1781 he became a physician at Lettsom's London dispensary. He was admitted LRCP on 25 March 1782 but in 1784 failed on a technicality to secure election as physician to the London Hospital, despite Quaker support. He acquired a post at the Bethlem Hospital but also had a private practice, probably chiefly among the Methodists. He was Wesley's physician and attended his deathbed, and Wesley thought highly of his skill.

In 1784 Whitehead rejoined the Methodists as a local preacher, though it is said that in 1790 he offered to resume itinerating if Wesley would ordain him as a superintending minister, but the offer was ignored. In 1791 he preached Wesley's funeral sermon, sales of which raised £200 for Methodist funds.

Wesley left his papers to Thomas Coke, Henry Moore, and Whitehead, to deal with as they thought fit. As a response to John Hampson's controversial life of Wesley (1791), Whitehead was commissioned to write what was advertised in a broadsheet entitled *Proposals* (6 July 1791) as 'a full accurate and impartial life' of Wesley. Very soon, however, Whitehead fell out with Coke and Moore and other preachers, and an acrimonious verbal and pamphlet warfare ensued. The main disputes were over three issues. First, what should be paid to Whitehead for the work, and what to the Methodist fund for preachers' pensions. Second, who should own the copyright—for (at least in Whitehead's view) connexional possession of copyright would allow for censorship of his work. Third, since Whitehead insisted on keeping Wesley's papers until he had completed the biography, his fellow executors complained that this prevented them from fulfilling Wesley's will that they should decide jointly on disposal of the papers. Whitehead contended that his main concern was to secure copyright to avoid censorship. It was a fear that may well have been justified, despite his critics' claim that they merely wished to keep the copyright to increase the benefits for the charity. In addition, Whitehead also expected to be paid for his work, and the terms he demanded certainly increased in the course of the controversy. His detractors claimed that they had assumed Whitehead was working for the benefit of the preachers' fund, though they soon offered a fee. The dispute over copyright went to law, but the proceedings were stayed and the London Society paid costs of over £2000. Meanwhile, Whitehead was removed from the list of preachers and lost his membership of the society, though he was restored in 1797.

The dispute was complicated and aggravated by the fact that it became part of wider and deeper disputes within Methodism. These included power struggles between the conference, made up of travelling preachers, and chapel trustees and local preachers, as well as between the conference and the trustees of Wesley's publications—an important source of Methodist finance. Methodism was also divided on ordinations and sacraments, and Whitehead blamed Wesley's ordinations on pressure from ambitious preachers. He was supported by laymen opposed to the conference.

To damage the prospects (and profits) of Whitehead's book, the preachers hastily commissioned an official biography of Wesley by Coke and Moore (1792) and circulated the Methodists vigorously to buy it. Whitehead's biography appeared in two volumes (1793, 1796) and included a life of Charles Wesley. The book was not commercially very successful, being reprinted only once (1806). Yet, despite its prejudices, it is superior to most nineteenth-century biographies of Wesley. It is noteworthy that Moore in his *Life of Wesley* (1824–5), despite criticizing Whitehead, frequently quotes him without acknowledgement, and both drew on Hampson. Hampson's and Whitehead's critical appraisals of Wesley's character remain valuable.

Apart from the Wesley biography and controversial pamphlets about it, Whitehead published two medical works, as well as attacks on A. M. Toplady's Calvinism (1775) and on Joseph Priestley's materialism (1778). Evidence is lacking for a clear view of Whitehead's character, but consciousness of his humble origins may have sharpened his evident pride in his status as a literary and professional man and his disdain for what he saw as the inferior culture of the Methodist preachers. No record of his appearance seems to have been preserved. He appears to have been twice married: certainly to Ann Smith, already noted; but his will of 1804 names his wife as Mary, and mentions a son who had predeceased him. He died at his residence, Fountain Court, Old Bethlem, London, on 7 March 1804 and was buried in Wesley's tomb behind City Road Chapel, London, on 14 March 1804.

HENRY D. RACK

Sources J. Pawson, biography of J. Whitehead, JRL, Methodist archives, Tyerman MS 3 [fols. 43–72] · H. Moore, 'A plain account of the conduct of Dr Whitehead', *'Faithful unto death': last years and legacy of John Wesley*, ed. R. P. Heitzenrater (1991), 83–125 · J. Whitehead, *A true narrative of the differences* (1792) · J. Whitehead, *Defence of a 'true narrative'*, 1792 (1792) · *Remarks on a pamphlet entitled 'A true narrative' etc.* (1792) · *Reply to a handbill … by Dr Whitehead* (1792) · *The letters of John Pawson*, ed. J. C. Bowmer and J. A. Vickers, 3 vols. (1994–5) · G. J. Stevenson, *City Road Magazine* (1872) · will, PRO, PROB 11/1406, no. 222, fols. 421v–424v · parish register, St James's, Bristol, 25 July 1769, Bristol RO [marriage] · *Methodist Magazine*, 27 (1804), 271–2 · *Methodist Magazine*, 39 (1816), 7 · *GM*, 1st ser., 74 (1804), 283
Archives JRL, Tyerman MSS, MS biography
Wealth at death £50 annuity for wife, plus £10: will, PRO, PROB 11/1406, no. 222, fols. 421v–424v

Whitehead, John (1860–1899), ornithologist, was born at Colney Hatch Lane, Muswell Hill, Middlesex, on 30 June 1860, the second son of Jeffrey Whitehead, stockbroker, of Newstead, Wimbledon, Surrey, and his wife, Jane Ashton Tinker. He was educated at Elstree, Hertfordshire, and at the Edinburgh Institution, where he developed an interest in natural history. He developed a weakness of the lungs, and was compelled to winter in the Engadine in 1881–2, and in Corsica in 1882 and 1883, when he began collecting, and discovered a bird new to science. On his return to England he prepared for a collecting trip to Mount Kina Balu, North Borneo, which lasted from October 1884 to August 1888. He brought back examples of many new animals, including forty-five new species of birds. The results of this trip are fully set forth in his *Exploration of Mount Kina Balu* (1893).

In December 1893 Whitehead set out for the Philippines. He made nine different trips in those islands, and discovered on Mount Data the first known indigenous mammalian fauna, returning to England in 1896. In January 1899 he started for the Philippines again, intending to complete his researches there; but the war between the United States and Spain put an end to the plan, and, after waiting a few weeks at Manila, he sailed for Hong Kong, and thence set out to explore the island of Hainan. The expedition was, however, attacked by fever. Whitehead struggled back with difficulty to the coast, and died at the port of Hoihow (Haikou) on 2 June 1899.

B. B. WOODWARD, rev. V. M. QUIRKE

Sources *Country Life*, 5 (1899), 804 · 'Pioneer naturalists', *The Spectator* (1 July 1899), 10–11 · private information (1900)

Whitehead, John Henry Constantine (1904–1960), mathematician, was born in Madras on 11 November 1904, the only child of Henry Whitehead, bishop of Madras and sometime fellow of Trinity College, Oxford, and his wife, Isobel Frances (1872–1953), daughter of the Revd John Duncan, vicar of Calne, and an early mathematical student of Lady Margaret Hall. A. N. Whitehead was his uncle. He was educated at Eton College (1918–23), where he was a member of the Pop society, and at Balliol College, Oxford, where he was first a Williams exhibitioner, and then an honorary scholar and where he obtained first classes in mathematical moderations (1924) and in the final honour school (1926), his work much influenced by H. O. Newboult of Merton. Whitehead played billiards and boxed for the university and was elected to the Authentics. He shared a passion for cricket with another mathematician, G. H. Hardy, whom he met at this time.

After eighteen months in the City under the guidance of O. T. Falk of Buckmaster and Moore, stockbrokers, Whitehead returned to Balliol in 1928 for further work in mathematics and in the following year went with a Commonwealth Fund fellowship to Princeton to study under Oswald Veblen. Much of his work was done in differential geometry and in 1932, with Veblen, he published the classic Cambridge Tract in Mathematics and Mathematical Physics, *The Foundations of Differential Geometry*.

In 1932 Whitehead became lecturer in mathematics, and in 1933 fellow and tutor, at Balliol in succession to J. W. Nicholson. In 1934 he married a concert pianist, Barbara Sheila, daughter of Lieutenant-Colonel W. Carew Smyth RE; they had two sons. During the Second World War he served in the Admiralty and the Foreign Office. Returning to Oxford he became Waynflete professor of pure mathematics in 1947 and thus migrated to Magdalen. Towards the end of his time at Princeton he had turned to the study of topology in which most of his remaining work was done and in which his contribution was both massive and fundamental. Some of his most original work was completed in the years before the war although its importance was not fully recognized until later. After the war he produced a large volume of work in combinatorial topology and then in the algebraic side of homotopy theory, returning in the last few years of his life to a more geometrical kind of topology. His reputation was international and research students came from many countries to work enjoyably with him. He was largely responsible for establishing the Mathematical Institute at Oxford, where the library was named after him, was a committee member of the British Mathematical Colloquium, and in 1953–5 presided over the London Mathematical Society. He was elected FRS in 1944.

A sociable and inspiring teacher, Whitehead threw himself with rotund zest into college and university life. He was a keen player of village, and especially Barnacles, cricket, and delighted in discussing sporting controversies. He was a learned devotee of the works of P. G. Wodehouse and of poker, the enjoyment of which he claimed to have learned at his mother's knee. He valued friendships which were wide in both range and age group:

> It was in long mathematical conversations in which every detail had to be hammered out till he had it quite correct and secure that he most delighted and it is by these conversations, gay and informal, in which he contrived to make everyone his own equal

that his fellow mathematicians have recalled him most gratefully. Approachable to everyone, towards women he had an old-fashioned courtesy uniquely his own. His marriage was very happy and the Whiteheads excelled in informal hospitality, first in north Oxford, then at their farm at Noke on Otmoor, where they kept with great success the well-bred herd of cattle which Whitehead had inherited from his mother.

An affectionate and lovable character, Henry Whitehead was a seminal mathematician and an ingenious and humane man. He died on 8 May 1960 while on sabbatical leave at the Institute for Advanced Study at Princeton. He was survived by his wife.

E. T. WILLIAMS, *rev.* JOHN BOSNELL

Sources M. H. A. Newman, *Memoirs FRS*, 7 (1961), 349–63 · *Nature*, 186 (1960), 932 · *Journal of the London Mathematical Society*, 37 (1962) · 'Biographical note', *The mathematical works of J. H. C. Whitehead*, ed. I. M. James, 1 (1962) · personal knowledge (1971) · private information (1971) · *The Times* (10–12 May 1960) · *CGPLA Eng. & Wales* (1960)
Likenesses G. Spencer, oils, Mathematical Institute, Oxford
Wealth at death £31,676 16s. 5d.: probate, 6 July 1960, *CGPLA Eng. & Wales*

Whitehead, Paul (1710–1774), satirist, was born on St Paul's day, 6 February 1710, in Castle Yard, Holborn, London, and baptized on 17 February at St Andrew's, Holborn, the youngest son of Edmund Whitehead, a prosperous tailor, and his wife, Elizabeth. According to early biographers Paul was educated under a clergyman in Hitchin, Hertfordshire, then apprenticed to a mercer in the City, but, not liking that trade, studied law at the Temple while writing occasional political squibs. His name cannot now be traced in the records of any of the inns of court, nor can any early squibs be identified, but he was apprenticed in 1724 to John Wheatly, a painter–stainer.

Whitehead's first notable satire, *The State Dunces* (June 1733), in heroic couplets, was inscribed to Pope and indebted to *The Dunciad* (1728–9), but in so far as Whitehead raises his sights to take in bishops, politicians, and, above all, Walpole, he anticipates Pope's *New Dunciad* (1742). Robert Dodsley bought the copyright for 10 guineas, prompting Johnson, who had a low opinion of Whitehead, to insist on no less for his *London* (1738). *The State Dunces Part II* (1733) is probably not by Whitehead, whose next anti-Walpole satire was *Manners* (February 1739), which attacks the government and praises Frederick, prince of Wales, and opposition politicians around him. The House of Lords decreed that *Manners* was scandalous and ordered the author and publisher (Robert Dodsley) into custody. Whitehead decamped and Dodsley was not further prosecuted: 'the whole process was probably intended rather to intimidate Pope than to punish Whitehead' (Johnson, 3.180–81). Whitehead's politics and stance of proud, honest independence were close enough to Pope's for the two men to be attacked together in the anonymous *Characters: an Epistle to Alexander Pope Esq. and Mr Whitehead* (March 1739), perhaps by Thomas Odell (1691–1749). Whitehead achieved more public notice when, on 9 March 1741, he and Esquire Carey, surgeon to the prince of Wales, organized a mock Masonic procession along the Strand. The joke was repeated in the following year and in both years was the subject of satirical prints.

In 1735 Whitehead had married Anna (d. 1768), only surviving child of Sir Swinnerton Dyer (1688–1736), of Spains Hall, Finchingfield, Essex. Edward Thompson states that she brought him £10,000, but, if this is so, Whitehead did not see the money for some years because it seems that he was imprisoned for debt in the mid-1740s. He befriended the improvident theatrical manager Charles Fleetwood (d.

Paul Whitehead (1710–1774), attrib. Louis François Roubiliac, in or before 1762

1747) and not only wrote a pamphlet on his side during the manager's dispute with the Drury Lane actors in 1743, but co-signed Fleetwood's bond for £3000. Fleetwood defaulted and retired to France; Whitehead could not or would not pay and was imprisoned in the Fleet. The date and length of his incarceration are not known, though Thompson writes of 'many years' (*Poems*, vi–vii).

Whitehead extended his Popeian vein of poetry with *The Gymnasiad, or, Boxing Match* (June 1744), a brief mock epic dedicated to the pugilist John Broughton (1705–1789) and tricked out with an introduction and copious notes by 'Scriblerus Tertius'. Whitehead returned to political verse satire with *Honour* (June 1747), directed against the former patriots, once praised by Pope, who supplanted Walpole and then proved no less corrupt than he was. Two later verse satires attack physicians: *The Battiad* (September 1750), on Dr William Battie (1704–1776), written in collaboration with Moses Mendes and Dr Isaac Schomberg, and an *Epistle* (November 1755) to Whitehead's friend Dr Thomas Thompson which abuses the many doctors who disagreed with Thompson's treatment of the prince of Wales in his last illness. This poem is redeemed only by some relaxed self-reflexive passages reminiscent of Pope's *Imitations of Horace*.

Whitehead's verse became less political but he remained a spokesman for the opposition under the patronage of George Bubb Dodington (*d*. 1762). At the Westminster election in May 1750, one of the most fiercely contested of the century, he wrote songs, handbills, and other electioneering material for the prince of Wales's candidate, Sir George Vandeput. When Alexander Murray, another supporter of Vandeput, was imprisoned for contempt of parliament in 1751, Whitehead wrote a fierce pamphlet on his behalf. His last opposition writings were

two pamphlets supporting Admiral Byng in October 1756 and *Ministerial Influence Unconstitutional* (April 1761). Less creditably, it is alleged, he edited in 1748 the blackmailing memoirs of a courtesan and was paid 'in kind' ('Phillips, Teresia Constantia', *DNB*).

It seems that by the 1750s Whitehead had come into his wife's fortune for they now lived at Colne Lodge on the north side of Twickenham Common, a cottage improved into 'an elegant dwelling' by his friend the architect Isaac Ware (Hawkins, 336). Whitehead's other artistic friends included the painters George Lambert and Francis Hayman, and the actors John Beard, for whom he wrote songs, and William Havard (*d*. 1778), whose tombstone was carved with verses by Whitehead. Presumably it was at this prosperous period that Whitehead's portrait was painted by Gainsborough; the painting is lost, but it was engraved by J. Collyer for Whitehead's *Poems and Miscellaneous Compositions* (1777). It conveys an alert humorous expression and portrays the long nose that gave Whitehead some resemblance to Frederick the Great of Prussia. Sir John Hawkins, who was Whitehead's neighbour from 1759, recalled that he was friendly and kind-hearted but his conversation was 'desultory, vociferous, and profane'; he retained to the end of his life his youthful habit of swearing, he did not go to church, and was suspected of atheism. Hawkins said that Anna Whitehead was 'homely in her person, and little better than an idiot' but her husband treated her with tenderness, 'hiding, as well as he was able, those defects in her understanding, which are oftner the subjects of ridicule than of compassion' (ibid., 335–6).

From the 1750s, perhaps as a relief from his homely wife, Whitehead was one of the scandalous Hell Fire Club under their mock prior Sir Francis Dashwood (1708–1781). He became steward and secretary of this famously lewd and blasphemous society, and in Charles Churchill's *The Candidate* (1764) was denounced as 'Paul, the aged', a brothel door-keeper who chalks the score 'behind a door' (l. 698). Churchill attacked Whitehead also in *The Ghost*, 3 (1762), *The Conference* (1763), and *Independence* (1764), provoked, not by prudery of course (in view of Churchill's own tastes and associates), but by hatred of a political turncoat who had accepted government places. Through Dashwood's patronage Whitehead was appointed secretary to the treasurer of the chamber at £800 p.a. in July 1761, and obtained another sinecure as deputy wardrobe keeper to the king in May 1763; Dashwood also gave him an annuity. Churchill's further *casus belli* was that Whitehead was a long-standing friend of William Hogarth: he had praised Hogarth in *Honour* (1747) and was probably the author of *Pug's Reply to Parson Bruin* (July, 1763), an answer to Churchill's savage *Epistle to William Hogarth*.

Whitehead wrote very little during the last twenty years of his life. His last pamphlet, in 1768, was on the feud between the four men who had recently bought the patent of Covent Garden theatre from his friend John Beard. Anna Whitehead died childless in 1768. Suffering a long painful illness that his doctors could not diagnose, Whitehead made his will on 20 October 1774. Most of his estate, worth about £3000, was divided between his widowed sister Sarah Hutchings (executrix), a nephew and three nieces, and his wife's cousin Elizabeth Dyer. (His elder brother Charles, born in 1705, was dead.) Whitehead's last bequest was his heart to his patron Dashwood, now Lord Le Despencer, with £50 for a marble urn in which it could be placed in Dashwood's mausoleum at West Wycombe. In his last days he burnt many papers: perhaps acts and epistles of the Hell Fire fraternity. He died at his lodgings in Henrietta Street, Covent Garden, at 7 a.m. on 30 December 1774. His will was proved on 4 January 1775, the day most of his corpse was buried beside his wife at Teddington, Middlesex. The urn containing the heart was ceremoniously deposited in the mausoleum at West Wycombe on 16 August 1775 and was stolen by a tourist in the following century. JAMES SAMBROOK

Sources *The poems and miscellaneous compositions of Paul Whitehead* (1777) [incl. 'Life' by E. Thompson] · W. Kenrick, 'Anecdotes of the late Paul Whitehead', *Westminster Magazine* (1775), 397–401 · *Annual Register* (1774), 176 · *Annual Register* (1775), 54–61 · *Annual Register* (1777), 201 · *Annual Register* (1780), 235 · *The works of Samuel Johnson, together with his life*, ed. J. Hawkins, 11 vols. (1787), vol. 1, pp. 330-39 · *GM*, 1st ser., 31 (1761), 335 · *GM*, 1st ser., 33 (1763), 258 · P. Whitehead, *Satires* (1748); repr. with an introduction by V. Carretta (1984) · Walpole, *Corr.*, 17.211, 252; 35.234; 42.477 (facing map), 486 · F. G. Stephens and M. D. George, eds., *Catalogue of prints and drawings in the British Museum, division 1: political and personal satires*, 3 (1877), 387-9 · Boswell, *Life*, 1.124-5; 5.116 · S. Johnson, *Lives of the English poets*, ed. G. B. Hill, [new edn], 3 (1905), 180–81 · R. S. Cobbett, *Memorials of Twickenham* (1872) · S. Johnson, *Political writings*, ed. D. Greene (1977), 218, 241 · *The political journal of George Bubb Dodington*, ed. J. Carswell and L. A. Dralle (1965), 67n., 80, 407-8, 421n. · D. F. Foxon, ed., *English verse, 1701-1750: a catalogue of separately printed poems with notes on contemporary collected editions*, 2 vols. (1975) · Nichols, *Lit. anecdotes*, 2.93; 4.606 · *The correspondence of the late John Wilkes*, ed. J. Almon, 5 vols. (1805) · R. Straus, *Robert Dodsley* (1910) · *IGI*

Archives BL, letters, Add. MS 47013A, fol. 107; Add. MS 30867, fol. 152 | Bodl. Oxf., letters to Lord Le Despencer, MS DD Dashwood B 11/4

Likenesses attrib. L. F. Roubiliac, bust, in or before 1762, priv. coll. [*see illus.*] · J. Collyer, line engraving, 1777 (after T. Gainsborough), BM; repro. in *Poems and miscellaneous compositions* · engraving, repro. in Kendrick, 'Anecdotes of the late Paul Whitehead', 397 · print, repro. in J. Kerslake, *Early Georgian portraits*, 2 (1977), pl. 882

Wealth at death approx. £3000—over £2000 in securities and money; freehold estate with rental of £40 p.a.; diamond ring, gold watch, etc.; testator's heart with £50 for urn: will

Whitehead, Robert (1823-1905), engineer and inventor, born at Mount Pleasant, Bolton-le-Moors, Lancashire, on 3 January 1823, was one of a family of four sons and four daughters of James Whitehead (1788-1872), the owner of a cotton bleaching business at Bolton-le-Moors, and his wife, Ellen, daughter of William Swift of Bolton. Having been educated mainly at Bolton grammar school, Whitehead was apprenticed, when fourteen, to Richard Ormond & Son, engineers, Aytoun Street, Manchester. His uncle, William Smith, was manager of the works, where Whitehead was thoroughly grounded in practical engineering. He also acquired unusual skill as a draughtsman by attending evening classes of the Mechanics' Institute, Cooper Street, Manchester. Meanwhile his uncle became

Robert Whitehead (1823-1905), by unknown photographer

manager of the works of Philip Taylor & Sons, Marseilles, and in 1844 Whitehead, on the conclusion of his apprenticeship, joined him. In 1845 he married Frances Maria (d. 1883), daughter of James Johnson of Darlington, and they had three sons and two daughters.

In 1847 Whitehead began his own business at Milan, where he made improvements to silk weaving machinery, and also designed machinery for the drainage of some of the Lombardy marshes. His patents, however, as granted by the Austrian government, were annulled by the Italian revolutionary government of 1848. Whitehead then went to Trieste, where he served the Austrian Lloyd Company for two years; from 1850 to 1856 he was manager there of the Stabilimento Tecnico Triestino, owned by Wilhelm Strudthoff. In 1856, using local capital, he started the Stabilimento Tecnico Fiumano at the neighbouring naval port of Fiume.

At Fiume, Whitehead designed and built engines for several Austrian warships, and the quality of his work led to his being invited in 1864 to co-operate in perfecting a 'fireship' or floating torpedo designed by Captain Luppis of the Austrian navy. The officer's proposals were dismissed by Whitehead as too crude for further development. At the same time, however, he carried out, with the utmost secrecy, in company with his son John (aged twelve) and one mechanic, a series of original experiments which culminated in 1866 in the invention of the Whitehead torpedo.

The superiority of the new torpedo over all predecessors was quickly established. But it lacked precision; its utmost speed and range were 7 knots for 200 yards, and a further 100 yards at reduced speed. Moreover there was difficulty in maintaining it at a uniform depth when once in motion. The last defect Whitehead remedied in 1868 by an ingenious yet simple contrivance called the 'balance chamber', the mechanism of which was long guarded as 'the Secret'. In the same year, after trials from the gunboat *Gemse*, the right, though not exclusive right, of construction was bought by the Austrian government; a similar right, as the result of trials off Sheerness in 1870, was bought by the British government in 1871. France followed suit in 1872, Germany and Italy in 1873, and by 1900 the right of construction had been acquired by almost every country in Europe, the United States, China, Japan, and some South American republics. Meanwhile Whitehead in 1872 had in conjunction with his son-in-law, Count Georg Hoyos, bought the Stabilimento Tecnico Fiumano, which was renamed Silurificio Whitehead; the works were devoted solely to the construction of torpedoes and accessory appliances. Whitehead's son John subsequently became a third partner. In 1890 a branch was established at Portland harbour, under Captain Payne-Gallwey, a former naval officer, and in 1898 the original works at Fiume were rebuilt on a larger scale.

Repeated improvements were made upon the original invention, many of them by Robert and John Whitehead. In 1876 by his invention of the 'servo-motor', an air-operated slave motor which amplified the motion of the pendulum and balance chamber, and was attached to the steering gear, a truer path through the water was obtained. In the same year he designed torpedoes with a speed of 18 knots for 600 yards, while further changes gave a speed in 1884 of 24 knots, and in 1889 29 knots for 1000 yards. Means were also devised by which the torpedo could be fired from either above or below the surface of the water and with accuracy from the fastest ships, no matter what the speed or bearing of the enemy. Each individual torpedo, however, continued to show idiosyncrasies which required constant watching and correction, and absolute confidence in the weapon was not established until the invention in 1895 by Mr Obry, at one time of the Austrian navy, of a gyroscope, which acted on the servo-motor by means of a pair of vertical rudders and steered a deflected torpedo back to its original course. The invention, which disarmed the torpedo's severest critics, was acquired and considerably improved over the next decade by Whitehead and others.

The first use by the Royal Navy of a Whitehead torpedo was in August 1876 when the frigate *Shah* attempted, unsuccessfully, to torpedo the Peruvian ironclad *Huascar*. The first successful attack was during the Chilean Civil War, when the ironclad *Blanco Encalada* was sunk by the torpedo gunboat *Almirante Lynch* in 1891. Torpedoes had few successes in the Russo-Japanese War (1904–5); of some 350 fired by the Japanese three hit moving targets and a few more were used to sink disabled ships. Even in the First World War successes against warships were few, though the terrible destruction of merchant ships brought the United Kingdom to the verge of defeat.

Whitehead received many marks of favour and decorations from various courts. He was presented by the Austrian emperor with a diamond and enamel ring for having designed and built the engines of the ironclad *Ferdinand Max*, which rammed the *Rè d'Italia* at the battle of Lissa (20 July 1866). On 4 May 1868 he was decorated with the Austrian order of Francis Joseph in recognition of his engineering exhibits at the 1867 Paris Exhibition. He also received orders from Prussia, Denmark, Portugal, Italy, Greece, France (Légion d'Honneur, 30 July 1884), and Turkey. He did not apply for Queen Victoria's permission to wear his foreign decorations.

Whitehead for some years owned a large estate at Worth, Sussex, where he farmed on a large scale. He died at his home, Beckett, Shrivenham, Berkshire, on 14 November 1905, and was buried at Worth. His eldest son, John (d. 1902), was perhaps best known for assisting him at Fiume and making valuable improvements to the torpedo. His second son, Sir James Beethom (1858–1928), was British envoy to Serbia (1906–10); and his third son, Robert, became a successful solicitor. Whitehead's second daughter, Alice (b. 1851), married in 1869 Count Georg Hoyos. Their youngest daughter, Frances, was in 1912 invited to launch a submarine for the Austrian navy; she fell in love with the captain, Georg von Trapp, and married him. Later their children became famous through the film *The Sound of Music* as the von Trapp singers.

S. E. FRYER, rev. DAVID K. BROWN

Sources G. E. Armstrong, *Torpedoes and torpedo vessels* (1901) · G. E. Armstrong, 'The Whitehead torpedo', *Cornhill Magazine*, [3rd] ser., 16 (1904), 490–99 · *The Times* (15 Nov 1905) · Burke, *Peerage* · *Engineering* (20 Sept 1901) · *The Engineer* (18 Nov 1905) · P. Bethell, *The development of torpedo engineering* (1945–6) · G. J. Kirby, 'A history of the torpedo', *Journal of the Royal Naval Scientific Service*, 27, 1– 2 · D. K. Brown, 'The Russo-Japanese War', *Warship* (1996) · D. K. Brown, 'Torpedoes at Jutland', *Warship World*, 5.2 · private information (1912) · *WWW* · *CGPLA Eng. & Wales* (1906) · M. Briggs, 'Innovation and the mid-Victorian Royal Navy: the case of the Whitehead torpedo', *Mariner's Mirror*, 88 (2002), 447–55
Likenesses C. Kirchmayr, oils; in possession of J. Whitehead, 1912 · photograph, priv. coll. [*see illus.*]
Wealth at death £454,760 5s. 10d.: probate, 31 March 1906, *CGPLA Eng. & Wales*

Whitehead, William (*bap.* **1715**, *d.* **1785**), poet and playwright, was baptized on 12 February 1715 at St Botolph's Church, Cambridge, younger son of Richard Whitehead (*bap.* 1673, *d.* 1730), baker, of Cambridge and his wife, Mary (*d.* 1742). His father had aspirations beyond his means, including a good education for William, and with the patronage of Henry Bromley, Cambridgeshire MP (later Lord Montfort), William entered Winchester College in 1728. This was the first of several acts of patronage to benefit Whitehead, who inherited his father's social aspirations without his incapacity to manage his finances. His father died in debt before William had completed two years at Winchester. It was only through his mother's determination to sustain the bakery business that he was able to continue his education.

At Winchester, Whitehead demonstrated an early interest in theatre and poetry. He acted in school productions,

William Whitehead (*bap.* 1715, *d.* 1785), by Benjamin Wilson, 1758–9

started writing verse, and in 1733 won a prize of 1 guinea from Lord Peterborough, for a poem on Peterborough himself, the subject set by Peterborough's friend Pope when they visited Winchester together. Pope was sufficiently impressed to employ Whitehead to translate the first epistle of *Essay on Man* into Latin verse. It seems likely that Whitehead's admiration of Pope was enhanced, greatly influencing his own poetic style, which favoured the polished couplet and wit. By mid-century, when he was poet laureate, this dependence on the style of the past made Whitehead seem old-fashioned.

Whitehead hoped to gain a place at New Hall, Oxford. When he failed to do so, he returned to Cambridge in 1735, and successfully applied for a Pyke scholarship to Clare College. This was a scholarship founded by Thomas Pyke (a baker) in 1720, funding orphan sons of Cambridge bakers for two places at Clare. Whitehead entered the college with a reputation as a poet and social skills well beyond his humble origins. He readily made friends with members of noble families, such as Charles Townshend (1728–1810), and contributed verse to university publications, including the congratulatory verses printed in 1736 on the prince of Wales's marriage. He graduated BA in 1739 and was made a fellow in July 1742, taking his MA in the following year. Whitehead's first independent publication was *The Danger of Writing Verse* (1741), reportedly 'highly approved by Mr Pope' (*Poems*, 3.34). The piece reflects something of Whitehead's philosophy, which allowed him to accept patronage very readily:

Say, can the bard attempt what's truly great,
Who pants in secret for his future fate?
Him serious toils, and humble arts engage,

To make youth easy and provide for age;
While lost in silence hangs his useless lyre,
And though from Heav'n came, fast dies the sacred fire.
(ibid., *Poems*, 2.57)

During his fellowship Whitehead published *An Essay on Ridicule*; *Ann Boleyn to Henry VIII* (1743); *Atys and Adrastus*; and 'On Nobility' (1744). Already his dependence on classical and other literary sources is evident, and always acknowledged by Whitehead. *Ann Boleyn* was based on her letters to Henry published in *The Spectator* (no. 397); *Atys and Adrastus* was modelled on a story from Herodotus' *History*. Whitehead was studying at this time for the church, following the example of his elder brother John, when in 1745 he was recommended to the earl of Jersey as tutor to his son, George Bussy Villiers (1735–1805). Whitehead accepted the post, which involved also teaching a young friend of the family, Humphry Stephens, and moved to the earl's London home. By the following year he decided against the church, and thus had to resign his fellowship at Clare, which required him to become a clergyman.

Once settled in London, Whitehead started writing plays. His first major piece was *The Roman Father*, a tragedy based on Corneille's *Horace*, performed at the Theatre Royal, Drury Lane, on 24 February 1750. The play was a tremendous commercial success: it was reprinted frequently after its first publication in 1750, adapted by Whitehead for revival in 1767, and even translated into French; and it brought Whitehead into contact with Garrick (though he had already written a flattering poem to the actor on his appointment as patentee at Drury Lane), who played the leading role. This was the beginning of an association lasting over twenty years. Most commentators have, however, preferred Whitehead's second tragedy, *Creusa* (1754), dedicated to George Bussy Villiers, although it was less popular on stage. This play was based on the *Ion* of Euripides. Horace Walpole claimed: 'it is the only new tragedy that I ever saw and really liked' (Walpole, *Corr.*, 35.79). Again Garrick took a leading role, and Robert Dodsley, who published all Whitehead's earlier work, on the strength of *The Roman Father*'s success paid him 100 guineas for sole rights. In 1754 Whitehead published *Poems on Several Occasions*, in which he included *The Roman Father* and an interesting blank verse piece, 'The Sweepers', which reflects a concern for the socially dispossessed who sweep the streets of London.

In the summer of 1754 Whitehead was required to accompany his pupil and a friend (George Harcourt, Viscount Nuneham) on a tour of Germany and Italy. He returned to England in 1756, and published *Epistles* (1757), inspired by his travels. The continental tour had been his last office as tutor to Lord Jersey's son, but the family wished to ensure his continued comfort. Lady Jersey had used her influence while Whitehead was abroad to gain for him in 1755 the salaried positions of secretary and registrar to the Order of the Bath. Whitehead was also invited to live with the Jerseys as a companion. He accepted this offer, feeling he served a useful role looking after Lady Jersey whose health was failing. She died in 1762, the earl seven years later, at which point Whitehead insisted on moving to lodgings in London, remaining a constant visitor to both Middleton (the family's country seat in Oxfordshire) and Nuneham (the country home of Lord Harcourt), as well as a welcome guest on a daily basis in the Jerseys' London home.

In 1757 Whitehead, rather by default, was appointed poet laureate. On the death of Cibber the position was offered as a sinecure to Thomas Gray, who declined it, believing it to be a demeaning role. Whitehead's terms of employment required two odes annually, one for the new year and one for the king's birthday. He was paid £100, a significant sum, but, when set beside the £200 paid to the composer who set them to music, a reflection of the inferior status accorded the laureate. In a contemporary judgement William Rider asserted that: 'with regard to the *Birthday Odes* … it seems probable that they will never reach posterity' (Rider, 23). They did not. However, Whitehead does shine by contrast with his immediate predecessors and he was not without admirers among his contemporaries, including Mason, Gray, and Horace Walpole. Whitehead brought to the odes a genuinely patriotic spirit rather than a sycophantic attitude. He loved his nation and respected the king as a symbol of that nation. His verses are seldom banal, usually dignified, and often written with assurance. They reflect the national desire for peace in the face of strife in Europe and rebellion in the American colonies.

In 1758 Whitehead published *Verses to the People of England*, in his laureate vein, seeing the role of the poet to 'wake with verse the hardy deed'. His next major piece for the theatre was to move in a different direction: romantic comedy. *The School for Lovers* was produced at the Theatre Royal on 11 February 1762. Again Whitehead is derivative, drawing on a prose work by De Fontanelle. He Anglicizes the setting and characters, and obviously had to accept some suggestions of Garrick, as the play was published with Whitehead's prologue 'as it was intended' in which he comments that 'He shifts no scenes to dazzle and surprise' (*Poems*, 1.207), alongside the prologue 'as spoken by Mr Garrick':

Change you shall have; so set your hearts at ease;
Write as he will, we'll act it as you please.
(ibid., 1.209)

Although this might suggest tensions between them, Garrick and Whitehead remained on the best of terms. Garrick's opinion of the play was 'Humbug for Nine Nights'— a comment made in a letter written on the ninth night of the performance while he was offstage between the prologue and act II (*Letters of David Garrick*, 1.355). However, he recognized Whitehead's dramatic potential, and trusted his judgement enough to make him his reader of new plays. Garrick was also to come to Whitehead's defence when he was attacked by Charles Churchill: 'still I cannot get it into my Mind that Your Attack upon *him*, is a justifiable one' (ibid., 2.366). Churchill had been bitterly satirical at Whitehead's expense in *The Ghost*, book 3:

Dullness and *Method* still are one,
And *Whitehead* is their darling Son

and in later pieces. This was in reaction to Whitehead's *A*

Charge to the Poets (1762), in which he pompously speaks to his fellow poets 'As bishops to their clergy give their charge' (*Poems*, 2.292), urging them to avoid contention among themselves; to write only when inspired, not for profit; and to remain immune to extremes of criticism or praise. In 'A Pathetic Apology for All Laureats', written for private circulation and published posthumously by Mason, Whitehead allows a little of his well-controlled irritation to become apparent:

Each evening post and magazine,
Gratis adopts the lay *serene*.
On their frail barks his praise or blame
Floats for an hour and sinks with them;
Sure without envy you might see
Such floundering immortality.
(ibid., 3.97)

Although Garrick defended Whitehead, he was wary of the publicity, and Whitehead's last major play, *A Trip to Scotland* (1770), was dedicated to Garrick (who did not take a part) and published anonymously. Whitehead describes the work very aptly as a 'whimsical trifle' (*Poems*, 2.3). In 1774 Whitehead acknowledged authorship when he published *Plays and Poems* in two volumes. This collection did not reproduce all of Whitehead's laureate pieces, several of which were added in a third volume (1788) containing Mason's memoir, which forms half of this volume. Whitehead continued to produce his laureate odes each year until his death, and he also published anonymously two separate moralistic fables, *Variety* (1776), 'a tale for married people', and *The Goat's Beard* (1777). Both went through several editions. His last ode, in response to the recent peace treaty with America, was to offer a 'prophetic truth':

Trust the Muse: her eye commands
Distant times and distant lands:
Through bursting clouds, in opening skies,
Sees from discord union rise;
And friendship bind unwilling foes
In firmer ties than duty knows.
(ibid., 3.110)

Whitehead never married. In this matter he demonstrated his characteristic practicality, admitting in a letter to Lord Nuneham in 1763 that, although he desired marriage, 'a moderate precarious income has but little allurement … it would be madness to think of raising a family without a prospect of at least a tolerable provision' (Harcourt, 7.240). Whitehead had used the profits from his plays to discharge his father's debts. He lived instead for the families he had given his life to serving, as mentor and friend. He died at his home in Charles Street, off Berkeley Square, London, on 14 April 1785 after a short illness brought on by a cold. In his will he left his books to one former pupil, Lord Jersey, and the rest of his estate to his executor, the other pupil, Humphry Stephens (later General Stephens). He was buried in South Audley Street Chapel on 20 April.

Whitehead is essentially of minor status as a writer, but he is marked out from many of his fellows for his moderation and good taste, his easy humour, and his common sense. He rose considerably in society, but never forgot his origins:

My education rose above my birth,
Thanks to those parent shades, on whose cold clay
Fall fast my tears, and lightly lie the earth.
(*Poems*, 2.172)

ROSEMARY SCOTT

Sources W. Whitehead, *Plays and poems*, 2 vols. (1774) · *Poems by William Whitehead, with a memoir by W. Mason*, 3 vols. (1788) · E. W. Harcourt, ed., *The Harcourt papers*, 14 vols. (privately printed, London, [1880–1905]), vol. 7 · E. K. Broadus, *The laureateship* (1921) · A. Bitter, *William Whitehead: poeta laureatus* (1933) [incl. bibliography] · R. Straus, *Robert Dodsley: poet, publisher and playwright* (1910) · Walpole, *Corr.* · *The letters of David Garrick*, ed. D. M. Little and G. M. Kahrl, 3 vols. (1963) · parish register, St Botolph, Cambridge, Cambs. AS, 12 Feb 1715 [baptism] · *Correspondence of Thomas Gray*, ed. P. Toynbee and L. Whibley, 3 vols. (1935); repr. with additions by H. W. Starr (1971) · *Collected letters of Oliver Goldsmith*, ed. K. C. Balderston (1928) · J. R. Wardale, *Clare College* (1899) · [W. Rider], *An historical and critical account of the lives and writings of the living authors of Great Britain* (1762); repr. (Los Angeles, 1974) · Venn, *Alum. Cant.* · will · *European Magazine and London Review*, 7 (1785), 311
Likenesses B. Wilson, oils, 1758–9, NPG [*see illus.*] · W. Doughty, oils, 1776, V&A · Collyer, engraving (after W. Doughty, 1776), repro. in Whitehead, *Poems*

Whitehorne [Whithorne], **Peter** (*fl.* 1549–1563), soldier and translator, described himself on the title-pages of his books as both a student and 'fellow' of Gray's Inn, and was probably the P. Whytame who was admitted to that institution in 1543. Like many men of his generation he was drawn to Italy. In 1549 he travelled to Siena where he met the English diplomat Sir Thomas Hoby. The two men shared an interest in the achievements of the Roman empire, and when they visited that ancient city together they 'searched out such antiquities as was here to bee seene' (Hoby, 25). In 1550 they went on to explore Naples and Florence. Whitehorne then commenced his military career and for the next ten years campaigned with imperial forces in north Africa. He also spent a brief period in Constantinople, where he studied the military organization of the Ottoman empire. However, he continued to be influenced primarily by both contemporary Italian thought and classical authorities.

During his years as a soldier Whitehorne made the first translation into English of Machiavelli's *Arte della guerra*, which was published in London in 1560 as *The Arte of Warre*. He also published in the same year his own treatise, *Certain Waies for the Orderyng of Souldiers in Battelray*, as a supplement to this translation. In this well-regarded study he covered themes not dealt with by Machiavelli, such as fortification, the manufacture of gunpowder, the use of incendiary devices, and signalling. Furthermore, where Machiavelli had been dismissive of artillery, Whitehorne offered a more measured assessment of the utility of cannon. Thus, although a debt to classical authors such as Polybius is evident in the section on signalling, the treatise was an original work of military theory. Its main shortcoming was its brevity; it lacked the detail and copious illustrations that were characteristic of many contemporary continental books. Nevertheless, at the time of its publication, there was no other work in English that offered such insights into the latest developments in siege-craft and military architecture. For this reason Whitehorne can be justly regarded as a pioneer in his field.

Two further editions of these works were published in 1573 and 1588, an indicator of their popularity and influence. Fabio Cotta's Italian translation of the Greek Onosander's *Strategicus* had also attracted Whitehorne's attention, and he published an English version, *Of the Generall Captaine and of his Office*, in 1563. Considering the martial education of his countrymen a patriotic duty, so that England should be 'kept from outrageous cruelty, and ravenous spoil of the enemies' (Webb, 7), Whitehorne was a significant figure in the development of Elizabethan military theory; he helped establish the agenda for the protracted debates on the nation's defence that dominated the last two decades of the sixteenth century.

GERVASE PHILLIPS

Sources N. Machiavelli, *The arte of warre*, trans. P. Whitehorne (1560) · P. Whitehorne, *Certain waies for the orderyng of souldiers in battelray* (1560) · T. Hoby, 'The travels and life of Sir Thomas Hoby', ed. E. Powell, *Camden miscellany, X*, CS, 3rd ser., 4 (1902) · M. J. D. Cockle, *A bibliography of English military books up to 1642 and of contemporary foreign works* (1900) · H. J. Webb, *Elizabethan military science: the books and the practice* (1965) · D. Eltis, *The military revolution in sixteenth century Europe* (1995) · *DNB*

Whitehouse, John Howard (1873–1955), educational reformer and Ruskinian, was born on 8 June 1873 at 81 Albion Street, Ladywood, Birmingham, the second son of George Whitehouse (1846–1925), electroplate worker, and his wife, Jane Enston (1845–1927). He was educated at St Mark's Church of England School, Ladywood, Birmingham, and at a school in Edgbaston. Leaving school at fourteen he successfully attended evening classes at Mason's College and at Birmingham Midland Institute, where he was introduced by Howard S. Pearson to the writings of John Ruskin.

In 1894 Whitehouse joined Cadbury Brothers, the firm of Birmingham chocolate manufacturers. His activities there ultimately led to the establishment of their youth club, works magazine, library, and pensions scheme. He was a founder in 1896 of the Ruskin Society of Birmingham, for which he acted as secretary, editor, and finally publisher of its journal *St George*. On Ruskin's eightieth birthday in 1899 Whitehouse took a congratulatory address to Ruskin, attending his funeral at Coniston in the following year.

In 1903 Whitehouse left Birmingham to become the first secretary of the Carnegie Dunfermline Trust, moving in 1905 to the secretaryship of Toynbee Hall, working alongside William Beveridge and T. Edmund Harvey. The latter became one of his few lifelong friends. Whitehouse founded the National League of Workers with Boys and arranged summer camps for many years, eventually buying a site at Bembridge on the Isle of Wight as a permanent base. It was planned that Baden Powell's new scouting movement should be placed in the hands of the National League, with Whitehouse editing *The Scout*, but the plan fell through. Between 1906 and 1908 he was a manager of east London schools.

John Howard Whitehouse (1873–1955), by Howard Coster, 1937

Following a period as warden of the University Settlement at Ancoats, Manchester (1909–10), Whitehouse entered parliament in 1910 as the Liberal member for Mid-Lanark. A promising career developed, with him as parliamentary private secretary to C. F. G. Masterman at the Home Office under Churchill, and later to Lloyd George at the exchequer. In 1909 he was a member of the Home Office committee on the employment of children and was subsequently on the committee on wage-earning children (1910), the departmental committee on reformatory schools (1912), and the executive committee of the State Children's Association (1914), an independent organization established 'to inform the public mind about State supported children'. The association opposed workhouses and cottage homes, and recommended 'boarding out and scattered homes', and, for certain children, emigration or trade training schools.

Whitehouse at this period was a dedicated campaigner for the reform of the lot of boys. In Birmingham, east London and Ancoats he had seen the problems which beset underprivileged children, and in a steady stream of books, *The Boy's Club* (1905), *Enquiry into Working Boys' Homes in London* (1908), *Problems of Boy Life* (1911), *Camping for Boys* (1911), he strove to improve their lives.

Whitehouse disapproved of Lloyd George's introduction of conscription (1916) and he joined with C. E. H. Hobhouse, Percy Alden, and others to oppose it. Although not himself a conscientious objector, he did much work in parliament on their behalf and of families suffering hardship as a result of conscription. He visited the Balkans

(1911) and Belgium (1914) on fact-finding missions, becoming a commissioner for Balkan relief, and for Belgian refugees—while also finding time to edit and write for *The Champion*. In 1916 and 1917 he held discussions in New York with Colonel House, President Wilson's adviser, to explore the possibility of a negotiated peace. The missions failed, but convinced Whitehouse of the future importance of mutual understanding between the New and Old Worlds. He became a governor of the Sulgrave Institution in 1922. His presentation of an exhibition illustrating English education to New York University led to a fellowship.

Whitehouse's support for women's suffrage, and his opposition to conscription, ruined his political career. Mid-Lanark, and his seat, disappeared with the election of 1919. In that year he had edited *The English Public School: a Symposium*, a volume which arose out of the publication of Alec Waugh's *Loom of Youth*. Here Whitehouse criticized the excessive time devoted to classics at the expense of other subjects; he advocated giving more time to civics and to modern history. He stressed the importance of craftsmanship, the need for the reform of Sundays to give more freedom, and the freeing of schools from the military aspect which surrounded so many of them. Many of these reforms he was to introduce when his interest in education and youth led him to found a boarding-school for boys at Bembridge, on the Isle of Wight. There he wished to combine the best of the old with new ideas, at the same time putting into practice some of Ruskin's and some of his own educational theories—notably the importance of creative education. Art, woodwork, printing, music—with American history, civics, and current history—took their places on the timetable alongside the more academic subjects. He ran Bembridge successfully, caring for the academic and pastoral needs in the 1930s of many refugees from Hitler's Europe. In 1932 he was president of the Froebel Society. At the age of sixty-seven he evacuated his school to Coniston for the war years, returning to Bembridge in 1945. He continued to lead his school almost until his death at the age of eighty-two, seeing it grow into a small village in some 70 acres. His books *Creative Education at an English School* (1928) and *The School Base* (1943) advocating the later comprehensive system, were pioneering works. He ran a happy school and was much respected by his pupils who left Bembridge with a remarkably broad education, general knowledge, and an appreciation of the finer things of life.

In 1928 admiration for the polar explorer Fridtjof Nansen took him on a school journey to Oslo. He found Nansen's vessel the *Fram* rotting, and he established a committee for its preservation. This led the Norwegians to take up the cause, the ship was preserved and a national maritime museum established in Norway. He dedicated a tract of downland in the Isle of Wight to the perpetual memory of Nansen. In 1932 Whitehouse was appointed a knight of the order of St Olav.

On 8 April 1931 Whitehouse married Margaret Vera (*b.* 1907, *d. c.*1985), sister of Old Bembridgian Lewis Chubb. As a calligrapher she studied under Graily Hewitt and she produced a number of manuscripts as gifts for Whitehouse. Particularly fine is the Bembridge School prayer book. The couple separated in the early 1940s.

Ruskin was the great passion of Whitehouse's life. He was a companion of the Guild of St George from 1902 and a trustee from 1918. Ruskin's teaching influenced his entire career, and his life was devoted to furthering Ruskin's work throughout a period when few were interested. In 1919 he arranged the Ruskin Centenary Exhibition at the Royal Academy, and attendant celebrations. He had already begun collecting Ruskin's books, letters, manuscripts, and drawings, and over fifty years he brought together the world's leading collection. At Bembridge he built two galleries to house his collection. They were a civilizing influence in the school, and remembered with pleasure by the scholars who worked there.

Whitehouse founded the Ruskin Society (1932) and the Friends of Brantwood (1935) and wrote or edited many books relating to Ruskin, notably *Ruskin the Prophet* (1920), *Ruskin and Brantwood* (1937), *Ruskin the Painter* (1938), and *Vindication of Ruskin* (1950). Curiosity, coupled with a wish that Ruskin's drawings should be represented in Italian collections, took him in 1932 to Rome personally to present examples to Mussolini and Pope Pius XI.

In 1932 Whitehouse bought Brantwood, Ruskin's home at Coniston, and opened it to the public as an international memorial. Part of his collection was returned to the house, and to ensure its continued permanence in 1944 Whitehouse presented Brantwood to Oxford University. However the university had second thoughts; after three years the gift was returned to Whitehouse's foundation which continued to run the house and estate. In 1947 Whitehouse received an honorary MA from the university. An accident with a cricket ball while umpiring a match at Bembridge began the decline in Whitehouse's health and he died at Bembridge School on 28 September 1955; his ashes were buried in the school chapel which he had built.

Of middle height, Whitehouse had a twinkling eye; he had the knack of creating occasions with himself at their centre. His resounding English will be remembered by all who heard him speak publicly. He was an innovator of great ability. He wished everyone to benefit from and join in his enthusiasms. His educational experiments were pioneering and long-lived, while he kept alive Ruskin's name and teaching. JAMES S. DEARDEN

Sources Isle of Wight RO, Newport, Isle of Wight, Whitehouse MSS · personal knowledge (2004) · private information (2004) [including correspondence with friends of Whitehouse, *c*.1957] · J. S. Dearden, *Ruskin, Bembridge and Brantwood* (1994) · Whitehouse Trustees, 66 Church Road, London, Additional MSS · *The Times* (30 Sept 1955) · *Manchester Guardian* (30 Sept 1955) · *Daily Telegraph* (30 Sept 1955) · *Birmingham Post* (30 Sept 1955) · *Isle of Wight* (1 Oct 1955) · b. cert. · d. cert.

Archives Isle of Wight RO, Newport, corresp. relating to educational issues, politics, and literature, letters to the explorer Nansen · University of Lancaster, Ruskin Library | JRL, *Manchester Guardian* archives, letters to *Manchester Guardian* · NL Scot., corresp. with Sir Patrick Geddes | FILM Hants. RO, Hampshire film archive

Likenesses C. Morton, oils, 1933, University of Lancaster · H. Coster, photograph, 1937, NPG [*see illus.*] · A. C. Davidson-Houston, oils, *c*.1966, Ryde School, Hillway, Bembridge, Isle of Wight · photographs, Isle of Wight RO, Newport, Isle of Wight

Wealth at death £47,175 15s. 5d.: probate, 6 April 1956, CGPLA *Eng. & Wales*

Whitehouse, (Edward Orange) Wildman (1816–1890), surgeon and electrician, was born in Liverpool, the youngest child of a merchant. He had several brothers and at least four sisters. Although best known for his work on the first Atlantic telegraph of 1858 he was trained as a surgeon, qualifying as a member of the Royal College of Surgeons in 1840 and later establishing a successful practice at Brighton.

In the early 1850s Whitehouse turned his attention to electric telegraphy. Encouraged by John Watkins Brett, one of the pioneers of the submarine cable industry, he began to investigate the troubling phenomenon of retardation. Telegraphers had found that initially distinct signals blurred together as they passed along underground lines or submarine cables, limiting the rate at which readable signals could be sent. Moreover, such retardation grew worse on longer cables, threatening to make transoceanic telegraphy unprofitably slow. In his first scientific paper, presented to the British Association for the Advancement of Science in 1855, Whitehouse reported that experiments on a cable Brett had lent him showed retardation to be less of a problem than had been feared. At the same meeting, however, William Thomson showed theoretically that retardation on a cable would increase with the square of its length. Whitehouse fired back in 1856, declaring Thomson's 'law of squares' to be no more than 'a fiction of the schools' (Whitehouse, 'The law of squares'). A heated exchange of letters in *The Athenaeum* settled little but showed Whitehouse to have a facile pen and little concern with theoretical niceties.

The American entrepreneur Cyrus Field, joined by Brett and the young English engineer Charles Bright, was then making ambitious plans to lay a cable from Ireland to Newfoundland. Attracted by Whitehouse's spirited defence of the practicability of transoceanic signalling, in October 1856 Field made him electrician projector of the new Atlantic Telegraph Company. Thomson was elected a director of the company in December and soon patched up his differences with Whitehouse. Bolstered by Whitehouse's assurances that his patented relays and induction coils would virtually eliminate problems with retardation, Field pushed the work ahead. Ill health kept Whitehouse from accompanying the abortive first attempts to lay the cable in August 1857 or the renewed efforts the following summer, his place on board being taken by Thomson. After a series of reverses that almost scuttled the project, the cable was finally completed from Valentia in Ireland to Trinity Bay in Newfoundland on 5 August 1858.

The Atlantic cable was immediately hailed as the wonder of the age; Bright was quickly knighted and Field was heaped with praise. Meanwhile Whitehouse remained closeted at Valentia, adjusting his apparatus. Queen Victoria and President Buchanan exchanged telegraphic greetings, but few other messages came through. Far from eliminating retardation Whitehouse's heavy instruments seemed to make it worse; even brief messages took hours to transmit. Desperate, Whitehouse began to use Thomson's sensitive mirror galvanometer as a receiver, though he claimed publicly that all messages were handled on his own instruments. Exasperated by Whitehouse's delays and evasions, the board of the Atlantic Telegraph Company dismissed him on 17 August and put Thomson in charge. But the cable had already been badly damaged by huge jolts of current from Whitehouse's 5 foot induction coils, and, despite Thomson's best efforts, it soon fell silent. Whitehouse refused to go quietly, filling the newspapers with long letters defending his actions and attacking the perfidy of company officials. But while Field, Bright, and many others certainly shared responsibility for the failure, Whitehouse could not disguise the fact that he deserved much of the blame himself. As a joint committee of the Atlantic Telegraph Company and the British Board of Trade concluded in 1861, while hasty manufacture and rough handling had weakened the cable it was Whitehouse's inappropriate apparatus that finally killed it.

After the 1858 debacle Whitehouse largely disappeared from public view. He consulted on an 1861 Mediterranean cable but played no role in the successful Atlantic cables of 1865–6 or the subsequent growth of a global cable network. He later invented several meteorological instruments, and in 1871 helped found the Society of Telegraph Engineers (later the Institution of Electrical Engineers); he was chairman of its first organizing meeting and served on the council of the fledgeling society. He presented no papers at its meetings, however, and ceased active participation after a few years.

Whitehouse and his wife, Hannah Statham, had two daughters and one son, Arthur Wildman Whitehouse (1865–1944), who was later principal of Glasgow Veterinary College. Although he had retired from practice Whitehouse was elected a fellow of the Royal College of Surgeons in 1876. After living in Greenwich, Hampstead, and rural Hampshire, he returned to Brighton in the 1880s. By then both the fame he had enjoyed in 1858 and the ignominy that had so quickly followed it had largely been forgotten. Whitehouse died at Brighton on 26 January 1890 and was buried in the town's extramural cemetery.

BRUCE J. HUNT

Sources *Brighton Society* (1 Feb 1890), 6 · *The Electrician* (31 Jan 1890), 319 · *The Times* (29 Jan 1890), 1 · *Daily Telegraph* (30 Jan 1890), 1 · *The Lancet* (1 Feb 1890), 277 · *Brighton Guardian* (5 Feb 1890), 8 · *Brighton Observer* (31 Jan 1890), 4 · B. J. Hunt, 'Scientists, engineers and Wildman Whitehouse: measurement and credibility in early cable telegraphy', *British Journal for the History of Science*, 29 (1996), 155–69 · E. O. W. Whitehouse, 'The law of squares: is it applicable or not to the transmission of signals in submarine circuits?', *The Athenaeum* (30 Jan 1856), 1092 · Society of Telegraph Engineers, minutes of council meetings, vol. 1, 1871–6, Inst. EE · C. Smith and M. N. Wise, *Energy and empire: a biographical study of Lord Kelvin* (1989) · C. Bright, *Submarine telegraphs: their history, construction, and working* (1898) · S. P. Thompson, *The life of William Thomson, Baron Kelvin of Largs*, 2 vols. (1910) · 'Board of trade committee to inquire into … submarine telegraph cables', *Parl. papers* (1860), 52.591, no. 2744 · W. Whitehouse, *Report on a series of experimental observations* (1855) · E. O. W. Whitehouse, *The Atlantic telegraph: the rise, progress, and development of its electrical department* (1858) · D. de Cogan, 'Dr E. O. W. Whitehouse and the 1858 transatlantic cable', *History of Technology*, 10 (1985), 1–15 · *Men of the time* (1865), 824–5 · *WWW*, 1941–50, 1229 · *Report of the British Association for the Advancement of Science* (1855–90)

Archives Inst. EE | CUL, Kelvin collection

Wealth at death £1287 7s. 2d.: probate, 24 March 1890, *CGPLA Eng. & Wales*

Whitehurst, John (1713–1788), maker of clocks and scientific instruments, and geologist, was born on 10 April 1713 at Congleton, Cheshire, the eldest child of John Whitehurst (b. 1687), maker of watches and clocks, and his wife, Mary. He had an enquiring mind and encouraged by his father he developed an early interest in local geology. After a rudimentary education he was apprenticed to his father. Upon completing his apprenticeship he travelled to Ireland to extend his knowledge but found it unsatisfactory for one determined to become eminent in his business, so returned to England and settled in Derby, possibly as early as 1735. Initially Whitehurst was unable to trade in the town as he was not a freeman, but following the construction and donation of a turret clock for the new guildhall he was made a burgess in 1737. By 1745 he was sufficiently well established to marry, on 9 January, Elizabeth, the elder daughter of the Revd George Gretton and his wife, Mary, and she was able to assist her husband by correcting his writing. Their only child died at birth.

At his premises at 24 Irongate, Whitehurst established a sound reputation as a clockmaker with a series of well-made but unremarkable domestic clocks and more innovative turret clocks. Some of his turret clocks were fitted with deadbeat escapements and temperature-compensated pendulums (of the Ellicott type) which were unusual features on turret clocks of that period. The temperature compensation depended on the differential expansion of different metals with changes in temperature and it was probably to obtain this information that Whitehurst constructed a pyrometer in 1749. By 1758 he had met and become a member of the influential group of philosophers and entrepreneurs who formed the Lunar Society, to their mutual benefit. Whitehurst supplied one of the members, Matthew Boulton, with clock movements, which were mounted in Boulton's ormolu cases. In 1771 he supplied Boulton with two more elaborate astronomical clocks, the dials of which had been designed by James Ferguson (1710–1776) whom Whitehurst had met when he was lecturing in Derby. He also made a tidal clock for another friend and member of the Lunar Society, Benjamin Franklin.

Whitehurst was consulted widely on mechanical and hydraulic problems and in 1772 he installed what appears to be the first hydraulic ram for raising water, at Oulton Park in Cheshire. His consultancies involved much travelling which enabled him to extend his geological studies over a wider area, partly with a view to finding useful minerals but also to satisfy his curiosity about the formation of the earth. By this time Whitehurst had extended his range of products to include scientific instruments, many of which evolved from those which he originally made to carry out his own experiments. He is known particularly for his barometers, and for scales and weights. Whitehurst supplied assay balances and weights for Matthew Boulton's laboratory at Soho and when the latter was finally successful in his parliamentary petition for the establishment of an assay office in Birmingham the balances and weights are believed to have been supplied by Whitehurst. This may have been one of the factors which influenced the duke of Newcastle to secure Whitehurst's appointment in the following year to the newly established office of stamper of money weights to the mint. The duke was already conversant with Whitehurst's other work as he had constructed two turret clocks and a complete plumbing and heating system for the duke's seat at Clumber Park. As the stamper of money weights Whitehurst received a salary of £200 per annum with an additional £20 for the expenses of an office, which he established at his friend Ferguson's house in 4 Bolt Court, off Fleet Street in London.

Initially Whitehurst divided his time between Derby and London but by 1779 he was almost permanently resident in the capital, occupying the house of the deceased Ferguson. From that time his business in Derby was run by his wife's cousin, James Wright, and then by his nephew John, the son of his brother James. In 1778 he published the results of his geological researches in *An Inquiry into the Original State and Formation of the Earth*, although the work had been substantially completed some years earlier. This book led to his election to the Royal Society in the following year. The importance of this work lies in the 'Appendix on the strata in Derbyshire' rather than his fanciful speculation on the formation of the earth; in the appendix he identifies the volcanic origin of the basalts and also hints at the orderly sequence of strata, one of the great geological generalizations. Both topics are alluded to in the portrait which Wright of Derby painted four years later. William Hutton met him in 1785 and in his *History of Derby* (1791) described Whitehurst as 'near six feet high, straight, thin, and wore his own dark-grey bushy hair; he was plain in his dress, and had much the appearance of a respectable farmer' (W. Hutton, 294).

In addition to attending the meetings of the Royal Society, Whitehurst played an active part in the scientific life of London which centred on the taverns and coffee houses. In particular he attended the meetings convened by Smeaton at the Queen's Head tavern which were the precursor to the Institution of Civil Engineers. In 1774 when the Society for the Encouragement of Arts, Manufactures, and Commerce offered an award for the best solution to the problem of producing a natural standard of length (one which depended on a law of nature) Whitehurst was one of the judges. The award was given for an ingenious but flawed method of measuring the effective length of a pendulum beating seconds. When the contestant failed to develop his idea Whitehurst proceeded to do so, disregarding the advice of William Nicholson who in his *Journal of Natural Philosophy* later described him as 'an ingenious mechanic and worthy man but possessed of

very little science' (Nicholson, 31). Whitehurst published his results in 1787 as *An Attempt towards Obtaining Invariable Measures of Length*. Whitehurst was also involved in the ventilation of the wards at St Thomas's Hospital about 1784 and his *Observations on the Ventilation of Rooms on the Construction of Chimneys and on Garden Stoves* was published posthumously in 1794.

Whitehurst's wife died in 1784 and Whitehurst himself died at 4 Bolt Court on 18 February 1788, possibly from cancer of the colon. He was interred seven days later at St Andrew's burial-ground, Gray's Inn Lane, London. In his will he left his premises at Derby to his nephew John, who was succeeded in turn by his son John. The Whitehurst business ceased with the latter's death in 1855, although it continues in spirit as John Smith & Son, a firm formed by Whitehurst apprentices.   DENYS VAUGHAN

Sources C. Hutton, ed., *The works of John Whitehurst FRS, with memoirs of his life & writings* (1792) · M. Craven, *John Whitehurst of Derby: clockmaker and scientist, 1713–88* (1996) · R. E. Schofield, *The Lunar Society of Birmingham* (1963) · A. E. Musson and E. Robinson, *Science and technology in the industrial revolution* (1969) · J. R. Millburn, *Wheelwright of the heavens: the life and work of James Ferguson* (1988) · N. Goodison, *English barometers, 1680–1860*, rev. edn (1977) · J. Egerton, *Wright of Derby* (1990) [exhibition catalogue, London; Grand Palais, Paris; and Metropolitan Museum of Art, New York, 7 Feb – 2 Dec 1990] · G. R. P. Dyer, 'The office of stamper of money weights, 1774–1870', *Libra*, 5 (1966), 20–21, 29 · W. N. [W. Nicholson], 'A popular account of the experiments which have been made or attempted for the purpose of obtaining an invariable measure of length …', *Journal of Natural Philosophy, Chemistry, and the Arts*, 3 (1799–1800), 29–35 · W. Hutton, *The history of Derby* (1791) · T. D. Ford, 'John Whitehurst FRS, 1713–1788', *Peak District Mines Historical Society*, 5 (1974), 363–9 · W. D. White, 'Derbyshire clockmakers before 1850: the Whitehurst family', *Antiquarian Horology and the Proceedings of the Antiquarian Horological Society*, 4 (1962–5), 240–44
Archives Birm. CA, corresp. with Matthew Boulton · Wedgwood Museum, Stoke-on-Trent, Wedgwood collection
Likenesses J. Wright, oils, 1782, John Smith & Sons, Derby · J. Hall, line engraving, pubd 1786 (after J. Wright, 1782), BM; repro. in Hutton, ed., *The works of John Whitehurst FRS* · A. Smith, engraving, pubd 1788 (after J. Wright, 1782), repro. in *Universal Magazine*, 2 (1788), 225 · M. V. Sears, etching, repro. in S. Glover, *History of Derbyshire* (1829)
Wealth at death greatest part of his property and small estate in Congleton to nephew

Whiteing, Richard (1840–1928), journalist and novelist, was born in London on 27 July 1840, the only child of William Whiteing, a clerk in the stamp office, and his wife, Mary Lander, who died when her son was an infant. Whiteing was brought up by his father at their home in Norfolk Street, the Strand, London, until he was nearly eight years old, when he was sent to school at the old palace, Bromley by Bow. He then went to live with foster parents in St John's Wood, where he was taught by a French émigré. He was subsequently apprenticed for seven years to Benjamin Wyon, medallist and engraver of seals. In the evenings he attended art classes, first at the Department of Science and Art at Marlborough House, London, then at Leigh's Art School in Newman Street, and, for a short time, at the Working Men's College in Great Ormond Street, where he came into contact with F. D. Maurice and

John Ruskin, and also got to know F. J. Furnivall, whose rowing club for working-class girls was to figure in Whiteing's novel *Ring in the New* (1906).

At the end of his apprenticeship Whiteing first set himself up as an engraver, and then, about 1866, acted as secretary of an Anglo-French working-class exhibition held in Paris. In the same year he also began his career in journalism, writing a series of satirical articles on political and social subjects for the *Evening Star*, which were republished in 1867 as *Mr Sprouts—his Opinions*, the ostensible author of the articles being a costermonger named Sprouts, who rose to eminence as an MP and whose pragmatism and shrewd common sense put his social betters to shame. As a member of the staff of the *Morning Star* under the editorship of Justin M'Carthy, Whiteing covered the Paris Exhibition of 1867 and then became the Paris correspondent for both the London and the New York branches of the newspaper *The World*. Based in Paris, he travelled to Geneva to cover the *Alabama* arbitration (1871–2), and also went on assignments to Spain (1873), Vienna, Berlin, Russia, and Rome. In 1876 and 1878 he visited the United States of America. In 1869 he married Helen, niece of Townsend Harris, the first American minister to Japan.

From January 1874 to May 1875 Whiteing served on the staff of the *Manchester Guardian* at the head office, but was soon sent to Paris, where he acted as French correspondent to the newspaper until 1880. In 1886 he left Paris in order to join the *Daily News* team in London, where he remained until 1899. As Alb he published, in 1886, *Living in Paris and France* and, in 1900, *The Life of Paris*. He had already published his first novel, *The Democracy*, in 1876, under the pseudonym of Whyte Thorn. This was followed after twelve years by *The Island* (1888), which in turn was succeeded after another eleven years by *No. 5 John Street*. A keen political insight coupled with the art of satire made this last novel Whiteing's most successful publication and his greatest claim to fame.

Three other novels and one book of essays followed after his retirement from journalism at the age of fifty-nine: *The Yellow Van* (1903), *Ring in the New* (1906), *All Moonshine* (1907), and *Little People* (essays on 'the world's nobodies and failures', 1908). He also wrote an introduction to Emerson's *Essays*, first series, in 1903, and in 1915 published an entertaining volume of autobiography, *My Harvest*, in which, however, he mentions neither his marriage nor, apart from mere passing allusions to two of them, any of his novels.

Whiteing was granted a civil-list pension in 1910. He died at Burford Close, 35A High Street, Hampstead, London, on 29 June 1928, in his eighty-eighth year. Both his wife and son predeceased him by many years, the latter having died in the First World War, in which he served with distinction. Whiteing was buried in the old parish church at Hampstead on 3 July 1928.

Nilanjana Banerji

Sources *The Times* (30 June 1928) · R. Whiteing, *My harvest* (1915)

Archives Hunt. L., letters · NRA, corresp. | BLPES, letters to Fabian Society
Likenesses J. Russell & Sons, photograph, NPG
Wealth at death £1194 12s. 9d.: probate, 20 Aug 1928, *CGPLA Eng. & Wales*

Whitelaw, Annie Watt (1875–1966), headmistress and educationist, was born on 17 August 1875 at 37 Dundas Street, Edinburgh, one of the twelve children of George Whitelaw (*c*.1837–1888), accountant and treasurer of the synod of the United Presbyterian church, and his wife, Grace Hutton (*c*.1844–*c*.1926). Both her parents came originally from Perth, but lived in Glasgow until her father decided to emigrate to New Zealand in 1878. Annie, her mother, and two of her siblings joined him in Auckland the following February, while the rest of her family arrived shortly afterwards. A sensitive, thoughtful child with an insatiable appetite for reading, Annie Whitelaw grew up in a large family home in the Auckland suburb of Ponsonby, where she enjoyed a happy childhood, despite the premature death of her father and two sisters. After receiving her primary education at the local school, she attended the Auckland Girls' High School before transferring to Auckland Girls' Grammar School in September 1888. There she was a senior district scholar in 1890 and passed the medical preliminary before leaving to further her studies overseas in April 1893.

A talented musician, Whitelaw initially thought of studying piano in Germany but eventually chose to study mathematics at Girton College, Cambridge, which she entered in 1894. She obtained second-class honours in part one of the mathematical tripos in 1897, and joined the staff of Wycombe Abbey School in Buckinghamshire as a mathematics teacher. There she enjoyed the companionship of several Girton friends and came under the care of the headmistress, Jane Frances Dove, who recognized her leadership qualities and made her a house tutor in 1899. Whitelaw developed a close friendship with her headmistress and the two Old Girtonians travelled to Dublin together to receive their MA degrees *ad eundem* from Trinity College in July 1905.

Whitelaw, or A. W. as she was known, remained at Wycombe Abbey until 1906, when she was appointed headmistress of Auckland Girls' Grammar School. A forceful, dynamic young woman with 'bright blue eyes, wavy ash-blond hair and an engaging smile' ('Tribute', 8), she returned to her old school determined to establish a routine of work and play which would equip her pupils for the 'responsible part' they were 'expected to take in the development of a great Dominion' (Auckland Girls' grammar school, 21). However, a two-year delay in completing the school's new facilities meant that she had little more than a year in which to set the changes in motion before she was called back to England.

After returning to Wycombe Abbey as headmistress in September 1910, A. W. developed a strong relationship with her staff, who supported her 'questing spirit' as she set about shaping the school into a 'closely knit community … where talents and gifts of all kinds could find their meaning in the service of something worthwhile' ('Tribute', 24). As an 'old friend' of the school (ibid., 25), she also enjoyed the backing of its council, who financed her building projects and supported her campaign for the establishment of a school chapel.

A deeply religious woman, who had been confirmed as an Anglican while at Wycombe, Whitelaw regarded worship 'as the most important, vital, the happiest and biggest thing in life' and became convinced that the school needed its own chapel ('Tribute', 25). An entertaining and imaginative scripture teacher, she inaugurated daily intercession services in 'Big School' during the war and launched a successful chapel appeal fund in 1921. Outside the school she took an active interest in social and religious work and encouraged her pupils to do likewise. As a result, she established a Seniors Social Service Committee and supported the London mission work of Father George Potter through her involvement with the Union of Girls' Schools for Social Service in Camberwell. During her fifteen years as headmistress, she also took a keen interest in educational developments and was the founder and first president of the Association of Head Mistresses of Boarding-Schools.

Whitelaw resigned her post at Wycombe in 1925 to devote herself to social and religious work; she was appointed to a Colonial Office committee on native education and spent six months inspecting schools and colleges in south and central Africa in 1926. On her return to England she became the director of women's education at the Selly Oak Missionary Colleges near Birmingham and lectured there for three years before resigning and moving to London. There she was appointed warden of the Talbot Settlement, an Anglican women's mission dedicated to work in certain parishes in Camberwell, and found scope for her administrative talents; she employed her charm and charisma to fill the house with residents and raise funds to rid the settlement of its debts.

After returning to live with her sisters in Auckland in 1938, Whitelaw renewed contact with her old school and joined the congregation of St Mark's Church, Remuera. Although she missed her friends in England, she kept herself busy by supporting the work of the New Zealand Federation of University Women as a vice-president of its Auckland branch in 1938, 1939, and 1944, while in 1941 she was a member of a commission which examined Maori educational work under the Anglican church. Between 1941 and 1945 she also served on the board of directors of the YWCA, chairing a committee which was responsible for establishing a library for service personnel.

After making two extended visits to England in 1948 and 1953, Whitelaw settled back in Auckland and spent her last years living alone in her home, where she was cared for by her extended family and many devoted friends. After recovering from a stroke, she died at her home, 57 Arney Road, Remuera, Auckland, on 11 August 1966 from pulmonary oedema. Her funeral was held at St Mark's Church and her ashes were interred at Purewa cemetery, Meadowbank, Auckland. Memorial services were held for her in two countries—the first attended by the staff and

1100 pupils of Auckland Girls' Grammar School at St Matthew's Church in Auckland and the second in the chapel at Wycombe Abbey, where her name lives on in the Whitelaw Memorial Library. MARGARET A. E. HAMMER

Sources 'A tribute to the memory of Anne Watt Whitelaw, 1875–1966: a great head mistress', *Wycombe Abbey School Gazette* (July 1967) [suppl.] · K. T. Butler and H. I. McMorran, eds., *Girton College register, 1869–1946* (1948) · memorial book of the New Zealand Federation of University Women (Auckland branch), University of Auckland, Auckland, New Zealand · d. cert. · b. cert. · *New Zealand Herald* (13 Aug 1966) · *The Times* (20 Aug 1966) · *School List* [Auckland girls' grammar school] (1907), 21
Likenesses E. Gabain, oils?, Wycombe Abbey School, England; repro. in 'A tribute' · oils?, Auckland girls' grammar school, New Zealand

Whitelaw, Archibald (1415/16–1498), ecclesiastic and administrator, was born in the second decade of the fifteenth century: in a supplication to the papacy of 5 July 1475 he described himself as in his sixtieth year of age. He entered the University of St Andrews in the 1430s and emerged as a licentiate in arts in 1439; having subsequently reappeared in Cologne as a teacher—an influential one, for among his students was Duncan Bunch, later vice-chancellor of Glasgow University—he returned to teach at his alma mater in the 1450s. Whitelaw's presence on the faculty of arts at St Andrews in the early 1450s may have provided him with the opportunity to come to the notice of James II, whose eldest son, the future James III, was born in St Andrews Castle (late May 1452). By 1459 Whitelaw was certainly in royal service, employed as a diplomat, to conclude a treaty with Richard, duke of York, and as tutor to the heir to the throne.

Whitelaw's blossoming career continued apace after James II's early death (3 August 1460). Under the regency government of the king's widow, Mary of Gueldres, he was clerk register during 1461–2, and by August 1462 he was already acting as royal secretary, a post which he was to retain for an astonishing thirty-one years. During that time he was regular in attending council meetings and in witnessing royal charters. He also carried on his work as a diplomat, and in 1474 was one of the commissioners who negotiated a treaty with England. Not surprisingly, from the late 1460s onwards he held important ecclesiastical livings: the archdeaconry of Moray (1463–7), the archdeaconry of Lothian (1470–98), and the subdeanery of Glasgow (1482–98).

Whitelaw was one of fifteenth-century Scotland's most notable humanists, and the surviving evidence reveals many facets of his classical scholarship—as a teacher at Cologne and St Andrews; as the collector of a fine library, including volumes by Lucan, Horace, Appianus, Sallust, Asconius, and Albertus Magnus; perhaps above all as the senior diplomat on the Scottish embassy to meet Richard III at Nottingham in September 1484, when Whitelaw delivered an elegant Latin oration at the outset of negotiations for an Anglo-Scottish truce. This *Oratio*, which praises Richard III for his martial exploits in spite of his small stature, is liberally endowed with cleverly phrased references to Cicero, Statius, Virgil, Seneca, Sallust, and Livy, and has long been admired as the work of a Christian humanist. Behind the elegant rhetoric, however, lies the tough diplomatic message that the beleaguered English king needed peace more than the Scots; and, as Dunbar and Berwick were still in English hands, there may be an implied rebuke to King Richard in the statement that every prince should be content within the bounds of his own kingdom.

Whitelaw resigned from the secretaryship shortly before Christmas 1493, when he was already in his late seventies. In his time he had been the survivor of more political crises than any other royal servant, remaining in office both when James III was placed under constraint by his subjects in 1482–3 and after that king was overthrown in 1488. He had served three kings, and he may eventually have found the rude transition from James III's static kingship in Edinburgh to the young James IV's hectic itineraries, embracing sea voyages to Dunstaffnage and pilgrimages to Whithorn and Tain, too much for him. He died, possibly at Glasgow, on 23 October 1498.

Whitelaw's reputation as a classical scholar and diplomat is secure, though it would probably be going much too far, on the strength of the 1484 *Oratio* alone, to suggest that he was the forerunner of those sixteenth-century writers, beginning with John Mair in 1521, who preached the virtues of Anglo-Scottish union. As a politician and a person, he remains something of an enigma. His tuition of the young James III does not seem to have made him a close familiar of the adult king; nor, so far as is known, did he exercise the influence over the king as royal secretary that Patrick Paniter was to achieve with James IV. Whitelaw was, perhaps, essentially the indispensable civil servant, at home with any administration. In any event he appears to have failed to pass on the secrets of effective royal government to his pupil James III.

NORMAN MACDOUGALL

Sources D. E. R. Watt, ed., *Fasti ecclesiae Scoticanae medii aevi ad annum 1638*, [2nd edn], Scottish RS, new ser., 1 (1969) · J. M. Thomson and others, eds., *Registrum magni sigilli regum Scotorum / The register of the great seal of Scotland*, 11 vols. (1882–1914), vol. 2 · J. Kirk, R. J. Tanner, and A. I. Dunlop, eds., *Calendar of Scottish supplications to Rome*, 5: *1447–1471* (1997) · A. Whytelaw, 'Oratio Scotorum ad regum Ricardum tertium', *The Bannatyne miscellany*, 2, Bannatyne Club, 19a (1836), 41–8 · A. Whitelaw, 'Address to King Richard III, advocating the strengthening of peaceful ties between the English and the Scots', trans. D. Shotter, *The north of England in the age of Richard III*, ed. A. J. Pollard (1996), 193–9 · A. Grant, 'Richard III and Scotland', *The north of England in the age of Richard III*, ed. A. J. Pollard (1996), 115–48 · J. Durkan and A. Ross, 'Early Scottish libraries', *Innes Review*, 9 (1958), 5–167, esp. 159 · N. Macdougall, *James III: a political study* (1982) · N. Macdougall, *James IV* (1989); repr. (1997) · J. Durkan, *William Turnbull, bishop of Glasgow* (1951) · J. MacQueen, 'The literature of fifteenth-century Scotland', *Scottish society in the fifteenth century*, ed. J. M. Brown (1977), 184–208 · A. I. Dunlop, *The life and times of James Kennedy, bishop of St Andrews*, St Andrews University Publications, 46 (1950) · J. MacQueen, *Robert Henryson: a study of the major narrative poems* (1967), 12–15 · L. J. Macfarlane, *William Elphinstone and the kingdom of Scotland, 1431–1514: the struggle for order* (1985) · C. Innes, ed., *Registrum episcopatus Glasguensis*, 2 vols., Bannatyne Club, 75 (1843); also pubd as 2 vols., Maitland Club, 61 (1843) · A. I. Dunlop, ed., *Acta facultatis artium universitatis Sanctiandree, 1413–1588*, 2 vols., Scottish History Society, 3rd ser., 54–5 (1964)

Whitelaw, James (1749–1813), benefactor and writer, was born in co. Leitrim and educated at Trinity College, Dublin, which he entered in July 1766, becoming a scholar in 1769 and graduating BA in 1771. He studied for the church, and after his ordination became tutor to the earl of Meath, who presented him with the living of St James's, Dublin. Soon after he obtained the more remunerative living of the city's St Catherine's parish. Whitelaw was deeply interested in the condition of the poor who lived in his immediate neighbourhood. His response was the establishment of several charitable institutions, the most useful of which was the Meath charitable loan, founded in 1808, which proved of considerable service to the weavers of the Coombe district during periods of hardship. Due in large part to Whitelaw's efforts, in 1804 the trustees of the Erasmus Smith Fund allocated £2000 for the foundation of a school in the Coombe, at which poor children were given free education. He was subsequently appointed one of the governors of the charter schools of Ireland.

Whitelaw was also an active writer on Dublin life and its history. In 1798 he undertook a census of the city, the results of which he published in his *Essay on the Population of Dublin in 1798* (1805). Epidemic diseases were then frequent in Dublin, but, undeterred by the fear of infection, he personally inspected every house in the city and questioned nearly every inhabitant. Hitherto the extent of the population had been a matter of conjecture, with calculations clearly underestimating the level of overcrowding in many dwellings. In one house alone, for example, Whitelaw discovered 108 people. The government ordered the results of his inquiry to be printed, while the original papers were deposited in Dublin Castle. In 1805 he was made one of the members of the commission to examine the conduct of the paving board of Dublin. He received from John Law, bishop of Elphin, the valuable living of Castlereagh, which he was allowed to hold jointly with that of St Catherine's.

Whitelaw's second major publication was the two-volume *History of the City of Dublin* (1818), written in collaboration with John Warburton, keeper of the records in Dublin Castle. Both men died before the work was finished, and it was completed by the antiquary Robert Walsh. Whitelaw's other studies are *Parental Solicitude* (1800?); *A System of Geography*, of which the maps only (engraved by himself) were published; and *An Essay on the Best Method of Ascertaining Areas of Countries of any Considerable Extent*, published in the sixth volume of *Transactions of the Royal Irish Academy*. Whitelaw died in Dublin on 4 February 1813 from a fever contracted while visiting impoverished parishioners. His widow, about whom no further details are known, subsequently received a government pension of £200 p.a.

D. J. O'DONOGHUE, rev. PHILIP CARTER

Sources R. Walsh, *Sketch of the life of James Whitelaw* (1813) · Burtchaell & Sadleir, *Alum. Dubl.* · Allibone, *Dict.* · A. J. Webb, *A compendium of Irish biography* (1878) · J. T. Gilbert, *History of Dublin* (1903)

Whitelaw, William Stephen Ian, Viscount Whitelaw (1918–1999), politician, was born on 28 June 1918 at 15 Belgrave Crescent, Edinburgh, the son of William Alexander

William Stephen Ian Whitelaw, Viscount Whitelaw (1918–1999), by Humphrey Ocean, 1992

Whitelaw (1892–1919) and his wife, (Helen) Winifred Alice Cumine, née Russell (d. 1978). Both parents came from distinguished Scottish political families. Whitelaw's paternal great-grandfather, Alexander Whitelaw (1823–1879), had earned a fortune as a partner in the great mining and steel making firm Baird & Co. He had been a Conservative MP, as was his own third son, another William (1868–1946), who was Whitelaw's paternal grandfather. Winifred Whitelaw was the great-granddaughter of Henry Baillie (1804–1885), a founder member of the Young England movement and a close friend of Benjamin Disraeli.

Education, war service, and marriage Whitelaw's father (a lieutenant in the Argyll and Sutherland Highlanders) survived a serious gas attack in the First World War, but died of pneumonia before his son's first birthday. The boy, an only child, was brought up by his mother in Nairn, in comfortable circumstances. His generous paternal grandfather had given up politics and eventually became chairman of the London and North-Eastern Railway. In 1938 he inherited the main Whitelaw estate, Gartshore (near Glasgow), on the death of his childless eldest brother, Alexander (the claim of his second brother, Graeme, having been bought out after a family dispute). The value of the extensive property was enhanced by mining royalties.

Winifred Whitelaw was a loving (if slightly formidable) mother, but William was a shy, lonely child, too unhappy at his preparatory schools in Nairn and Berkshire to show much academic promise. It was a surprise to all when he passed the examination for Winchester College. He was more interested in golf than in books. This preference remained during his subsequent career at Trinity College,

Cambridge (1936–9), where he was soon awarded a golfing blue and would have become university captain had war not intervened. Yet he did apply himself sufficiently to achieve a degree, taking a second in history and a third in law.

On leaving Cambridge, and just before the outbreak of the Second World War, Whitelaw joined the Scots Guards. His education had been geared towards the life of a country gentleman who would make himself available for public service, in keeping with the family tradition, if he survived the conflict. More important than his formal academic qualifications was his character, which wartime experience enriched but did not radically change. He was a genial young man, whose consideration towards others inspired confidence, respect, and loyalty. Always ready to laugh (not least at himself), he was also very shrewd, even cunning. In war he proved capable of decisive action, outwardly calm even in an emergency.

Attached to what became the 6th guards tank brigade, Whitelaw spent most of the war in training for an invasion of mainland Europe. At the battle of Caumont (on 30 July 1944) his squadron was subjected to a surprise attack by superior German vehicles. Three tanks were destroyed and their occupants killed. Thanks to Whitelaw's cool leadership under fire the unit regrouped, but he always felt (wrongly) that he could have done more to evade the ambush. He was awarded the MC for his efforts and became second in command of his battalion. The remainder of his advance across Europe was far less dramatic. Yet his years in the Scots Guards produced the most valued friendships of his life. Among his fellow officers was Robert Runcie, later archbishop of Canterbury, who also won an MC. After VE-day Whitelaw served in Palestine, where he was mentioned in dispatches. On the death of his grandfather, however, he resigned from the army.

Following his father's example, Whitelaw had married during wartime (on 6 February 1943, at St Giles's Cathedral, Edinburgh). His wife, Cecilia Doriel (Celia) Sprot, the daughter of Major Mark Sprot, an officer in the Royal Scots Greys, was then serving as a junior commander in the Auxiliary Territorial Service, and also came from a distinguished Scottish family. They had known each other as children, and had fallen in love when they met again during training in the south-west of England. Their first child, Susan, was born in November 1944. Three more daughters followed: Carol (b. 1946), Mary (b. 1947), and Pamela (b. 1951). Celia Whitelaw shared her husband's outlook and supported him in everything he did; theirs was regarded as one of the most successful parliamentary marriages of the time.

Early political career Whitelaw's credentials for public life were recognized in 1952, when he was appointed deputy lieutenant for Dunbartonshire. But by then he had decided that he would try to emulate so many of his forebears and stand for parliament. He had shown little interest in doing so as a young man, apparently on the advice of his disillusioned grandfather. In 1949, however, he spoke at the annual Scottish Unionist conference, in favour of the *Industrial Charter* (1947)—the document which marked the Conservative Party's acceptance of the broad post-war political consensus. The consensual approach was ideally suited to Whitelaw, whose temperament and outlook were alien to the individualism associated with pre-war Conservatism.

In 1950 Whitelaw allowed his name to go forward as his party's candidate for the constituency of East Dunbartonshire. It was never likely that he would win, since his Labour opponent was the popular left-wing MP Davie Kirkwood, and the constituency included the traditional socialist stronghold of Clydebank. Despite his inexperience Whitelaw performed creditably, fending off constant heckling and winning the respect of his opponent. In 1951, after Kirkwood's retirement, he made another unsuccessful attempt, although his party won an overall majority at that election.

After waiting in vain for a more winnable Scottish seat to fall vacant, Whitelaw was asked in 1954 to try a different constituency, Penrith and the Border, where the Conservative MP was standing down. This was one of the safest (and largest) English seats; Whitelaw soon established himself in an area more congenial to him than Gartshore (where the mansion built by his great-uncle had proved impossible to maintain). At the general election of 1955 he was returned with a record majority of 13,672. He continued to represent the constituency until his elevation to the peerage in 1983.

Whitelaw soon adapted to the House of Commons, where he already had friends and quickly acquired new ones. His first government appointment came within a year of his election, in February 1956. The long-serving president of the Board of Trade, Peter Thorneycroft, was looking for a new parliamentary private secretary. Not the least of Whitelaw's qualifications for the vacancy was the fact that he was Thorneycroft's second cousin. When Thorneycroft became chancellor of the exchequer in January 1957 Whitelaw served him in the same capacity; and when Thorneycroft resigned over spending cuts after a year in office Whitelaw departed with him. He had gained valuable insights into the workings of government at the highest level. Perhaps his most important experience was witnessing, from within the administration, the handling of the Suez crisis of 1956–7 by the chief whip, Edward Heath. As a man who valued loyalty above all else, Whitelaw was dismayed by the bitter Conservative divisions of that time, but Heath's patient tolerance towards the rebels on both sides formed the basis of a lasting admiration.

After Thorneycroft's resignation Whitelaw continued to build his parliamentary profile, becoming joint secretary of the back-bench 1922 committee, and taking similar positions on the specialist party committees dealing with horticulture and transport. But his short spell in government had not gone unnoticed. In January 1959 Heath asked him to join the whips' office. The club-like atmosphere of 12 Downing Street was most congenial to him, and he was very popular both with his colleagues in the whips' office and with his parliamentary charges. His social background enabled him to mix easily with the remaining country gentlemen in his party, but his wartime experience and his natural bonhomie allowed him to establish a rapport with the new breed of tory MP, from the middle class or (like Heath) from even humbler homes. At times of stress he was capable of sudden eruptions of rage, but these always subsided just as quickly. For the most part he offered good-natured encouragement to tory MPs, rather than resorting to the strong-arm tactics often associated with the office.

When Whitelaw moved to the Ministry of Labour as parliamentary secretary to the minister, John Hare, in July 1962, he quickly built a reputation for consideration towards officials; and he was generally liked by shadow ministers. He was responsible for piloting several government bills through committees; it helped his general popularity that these were all measures which enjoyed cross-party support, such as the Offices and Shops Act of 1963, which improved working conditions. The government (now led by Harold Macmillan) enjoyed a comfortable majority, but Whitelaw had few rivals in his understanding of parliamentary tactics, which would stand him in good stead when his party returned to opposition.

Chief whip, 1964–1970 In October 1963 Macmillan was replaced as prime minister by Alec Douglas-Home. Whitelaw was surprised by the result; he had expressed a preference for R. A. Butler. But he admired Home, who came from a background similar to his own. When the Conservatives lost the general election of 1964, Home asked Whitelaw to rejoin the whips' office. For a month he acted as deputy to Martin Redmayne, but in November he became chief whip himself. It was a difficult period for the parliamentary party as it readjusted to opposition after thirteen years of uninterrupted rule. The Labour government of Harold Wilson had a slender majority, and Whitelaw came under pressure to organize the kind of unthinking, all-out opposition which he despised. He kept his troops happy by orchestrating one major parliamentary ambush, but tory MPs were demanding leadership more vigorous than Home could offer. In July 1965 Whitelaw told Home that it would be best to stand down. The advice was accepted, and if anything the friendship between the two men deepened as a result; but Whitelaw could never escape the feeling that he had somehow betrayed his leader.

After Heath succeeded Home there was no doubt that Whitelaw would retain his accepted position as right-hand man to the party leader. But his responsibilities remained very taxing, as the party was heavily defeated in the general election of 1966; furthermore, divisive issues such as Rhodesian sanctions, which induced a three-way split in December 1967, stretched even Whitelaw's conciliatory powers. Another role he took upon himself was to complement the qualities of the new leader. He realized that Heath seemed distant, even to Conservative MPs who saw him daily. Whitelaw, by contrast, was always approachable and an invaluable channel of communication between the leader and the other ranks. Heath always appreciated his advice, on tactics and on appointments. Perhaps the key incident of 1966–70 was the sacking of

Enoch Powell from the shadow cabinet in April 1968. A shared love of country pursuits was the only thing that Whitelaw and Powell had in common, and the former offered full support when Heath decided that his dissenting colleague had to go.

The Heath government, 1970–1974 In charge of his party's communications, Whitelaw played a key role in securing the unexpected Conservative victory at the general election of 1970. He was appointed lord president of the council, chaired numerous cabinet committees, and led for the government in the House of Commons. It was not a happy period for him, although success in the role depended on the same negotiating skills which he had deployed as chief whip. The government passed its bills, including the controversial Industrial Relations Act (1971), but there was an ideological edge to Labour's opposition (and to some right-wing rebels in his own party) which Whitelaw instinctively disliked. Whereas a chief whip is mute in the Commons, Whitelaw was now called upon to speak in the most heated debates. Since he wanted to be loved to a degree which was unusual even in a politician, he found these occasions particularly uncomfortable. His usual response to barracking from the opposition benches was a retreat into exaggerated self-deprecation. At the same time, his reputation for administrative competence and conciliatory skill was such that he was often mentioned as a likely successor to Heath. It was only a matter of time before the prime minister entrusted him with full departmental responsibilities.

In March 1972 Heath suspended Stormont, the parliament of Northern Ireland, and Whitelaw was appointed first secretary of state. The rule of law had been breaking down in the province since the late 1960s, when civil-rights demonstrators were subjected to regular attacks by members of the majority (Unionist, generally protestant) population. Feeling unprotected by the largely Unionist police force, the Royal Ulster Constabulary, the minority (Catholic) population increasingly looked to the Irish Republican Army and (after its formation in early 1970) the splinter Provisional IRA for protection. The unrest led to the deployment of British troops, and culminated on 30 January 1972 in the killing by paratroopers of thirteen people in Derry. Reginald Maudling as home secretary was responsible for Northern Ireland; he would not have been equipped to deal with the problem even if he had been able to give it his exclusive attention. Whitelaw was the obvious man to take on the job.

Thus began the most demanding period of Whitelaw's ministerial career. It was also largely thankless; most of his colleagues (let alone the population on the mainland of Britain) were ignorant of the situation, and merely hoped that it would go away of its own accord. Yet the Ulster Unionist Party, which dominated the parliamentary representation of the province, was allied to the Conservatives; and several tory MPs (notably Enoch Powell) held strong views which allowed no room for compromise with the Catholic minority. Whitelaw knew that British troops would be tied up in Northern Ireland for an indefinite period unless he could forge a workable agreement between moderates from both sides of the community. On paper he was something like a viceroy in Northern Ireland; yet at times he felt utterly powerless.

By the time he left Northern Ireland in December 1973 Whitelaw was one of the best-known—and most widely respected—of British politicians. It seemed at the time that he had performed a near miracle, thrashing out an agreement which would entail the sharing of power between the Ulster Unionists and the mainly Catholic Social Democratic and Labour Party. Understandably, he had made mistakes—notably when he held a secret meeting with the Provisional IRA in July 1972. At first he was very patient, trying to establish trust with as many groups as possible, and when he received hints that the Provisional IRA was prepared to strike a compromise which fell far short of its demand for a united Ireland, he jumped at the chance. The meeting was wholly unproductive, and when it was publicized by the Provisional IRA Whitelaw offered to resign. The 'Troubles' reached new depths when Provisional IRA bombs in Belfast on 21 July 1972 killed nine people and left more than 100 injured. Whitelaw's response was to authorize operation Motorman, when thousands of British troops removed barricades from Catholic areas of Derry.

Motorman made it easier for the security forces to apprehend terrorist suspects, who were tried in special (Diplock) courts introduced by Whitelaw in the face of persistent intimidation of juries. Nevertheless, Provisional IRA activity continued, and Whitelaw returned to his original strategy, which envisaged a clear separation between politicians and the men of violence. On the protestant side the distinction was less clear, and although he was prepared to listen to arguments from every quarter Whitelaw found it impossible to negotiate with Dr Ian Paisley, the leader of the hardline Democratic Unionist Party. He concentrated on wringing concessions from the former Unionist prime minister, Brian Faulkner. After prolonged negotiations Faulkner agreed to the power-sharing executive in which his own party would still hold a majority and he would be chief executive. The Social Democratic and Labour Party also agreed, having moved from a position in which the Catholics had enjoyed only token representation in government to one in which they held several key posts.

In December 1973 Whitelaw was recalled to London, where he faced another crisis as secretary of state for employment. The National Union of Mineworkers had imposed an overtime ban in support of a wage claim outside the terms of the government's statutory incomes policy. Its position had been greatly strengthened by the oil embargo imposed by Middle Eastern oil producers; yet many of Whitelaw's colleagues were determined to resist the full wage claim. Whitelaw, who recognized that a generous settlement was unavoidable, was unable to persuade the cabinet to strike a deal. He tried to resist demands for an early general election, which cabinet hardliners favoured as the only way to face down the miners. When the union held a ballot which resulted in an overwhelming majority for an all-out strike, even Whitelaw had to admit defeat. Heath called an election for 28 February 1974; the result was inconclusive, but after unsuccessful attempts to form a coalition Heath resigned in favour of Harold Wilson, whose party had won four more seats than the Conservatives.

Whitelaw had been exhausted even before he tried to resolve the miners' dispute, and the result of the February 1974 election was almost as serious a blow to him as it was to his leader. The election had endangered the power-sharing experiment; in Ulster it was treated as a referendum on a compromise deal which had been given no time to prove its value, and not one of Faulkner's remaining supporters within the Unionist Party was returned to Westminster. Power-sharing was finally extinguished in the early summer of 1974, in the face of a strike which paralysed the province. For the rest of his life Whitelaw was haunted by the possibility that, had he not been recalled, he might have defused the situation. His feeling of disenchantment with Heath was increased by some confusion about his precise role during the miners' dispute; he felt that he had been brought back too soon to produce a lasting settlement in Ulster, and too late to come to satisfactory terms with the National Union of Mineworkers.

Opposition, 1974–1979 While Heath was prime minister Whitelaw was often named as his most likely successor, and speculation increased after the February election. Whitelaw was appointed party chairman, which made it unthinkable for him to press his claims even in private; in any case, he was too loyal to encourage his supporters within the party. A new general election was expected at any time, so his job at Conservative central office was difficult enough already. When Wilson went to the country in October 1974 the tories lost again, and Heath's position now seemed untenable. Had he stood down Whitelaw would almost certainly have been elected in his place; but this second poll of 1974 had also been relatively close, with the tories only forty-two seats behind Labour. With the economy in serious trouble Heath believed that there might be another new election, or even a government of national unity. He decided to stay on.

After a change in the party rules allowed an annual challenge to the leader, Heath offered himself for re-election in January 1975. Having made so many supportive statements in the press Whitelaw could not be a candidate, but the rules allowed new challengers to step in should the first ballot prove inconclusive. As a result, when told that Margaret Thatcher, Heath's main rival, was not attracting enough backers to force a second poll, some of Whitelaw's supporters voted for her rather than abstaining. Since Heath lost by eleven votes, their decision undoubtedly proved decisive. Whitelaw still announced his candidacy for the second round, but three other MPs (James Prior, Sir Geoffrey Howe, and John Peyton) joined the contest. The direct damage to Whitelaw was serious enough, since the clear majority of their supporters

would otherwise have voted for him; and their interventions gave the impression that, contrary to previous expectation, Whitelaw was not running strongly enough to win. The result of the second ballot on 11 February 1975 apparently proved the point, since Thatcher won an overall majority of the votes, beating Whitelaw by 146 to 79. Her campaign certainly gathered momentum after she beat Heath in the first round, but if Whitelaw had engaged in a straight fight against her the result might well have been different.

After his defeat Whitelaw was named as deputy leader of the Conservative Party. At first, relations with Thatcher were strained. Before the leadership election Whitelaw had recognized her abilities, but like most of Heath's allies at this time he had no faith in her political judgement. The nature of her challenge to Heath, after service in a united cabinet, obviously increased his misgivings. For her part Thatcher suspected Whitelaw's motives. Although she endorsed his vice-presidency of the all-party 'Britain in Europe' organization, which campaigned for a 'yes' vote in the referendum of June 1975 on membership of the EEC, the episode only underlined their differences. Given Thatcher's antagonism to what she perceived as a complacent post-war consensus between senior politicians, the direct co-operation between Whitelaw and figures such as Labour's Roy Jenkins and the Liberal leader Jeremy Thorpe was highly unwelcome to her. The issue itself was a further source of tension. Whitelaw's wartime experience had convinced him of the need for closer ties with Europe, but Thatcher was already troubled by the prospect of further dilutions of British sovereignty. In the campaign itself Whitelaw's reassuring speeches undoubtedly helped to shore up support among Conservative voters who might otherwise have been persuaded by the oratory of Enoch Powell; Jenkins warmly acknowledged his contribution to the campaign, in which the pro-Europeans secured more than two-thirds of the popular vote. To the end of his life, Whitelaw lent his name to statements of pro-European sentiment. Yet the European issue was no exception to Whitelaw's instinctive scepticism about ambitious political blueprints. Only the increasing polarization of the debate prevented him from voicing an attitude towards the EU which (in a form of words typical of so many celebrated 'Willie-isms') he might have described as one of sympathetic ambivalence.

Never an ideologue, Whitelaw deplored Thatcher's dogmatic outlook, and (along with his cousin Thorneycroft, the new party chairman) he tried his best to restrain it. In the opposition period there were several rows. One of these, in January 1978, after Thatcher had deviated from party policy on immigration in a television interview, provoked an offer of resignation from Whitelaw. But the deepening economic crisis, and a feeling that stern measures would have to be taken against the trade unions, meant that by the time of the next general election (May 1979) there was much shared policy ground between Thatcher and her deputy. Although Whitelaw would not have chosen Thatcher as a friend, he admired her stamina and application. Most importantly, his defeat in the leadership election of 1975 convinced him that he was best suited to the work of a deputy leader; and, as with Heath, he felt that he could complement Thatcher's own strengths (or compensate for her weaknesses). The underlying differences remained, but a solid working relationship had been established by May 1979.

Home secretary, 1979–1983 Whitelaw had become shadow home secretary in January 1976, and when the Conservatives won the election of 1979 he accepted that position in the cabinet. This was his happiest spell in government, although there were occasional crises. Within a single fortnight, in July 1982, Whitelaw had to deal with two bombs in London, the resignation of one of the queen's senior security men after a sexual scandal, and a break-in at Buckingham Palace. The last event came close to forcing Whitelaw's resignation; only Thatcher's support, and a typical demonstration of charming bluster before the Conservative home affairs committee, saved his career.

Thatcher knew how much she depended on Whitelaw's loyalty, which he had demonstrated by discouraging her opponents (or 'wets') who held a cabinet majority in her early years. Their partnership was cemented when Whitelaw was a key adviser during the Falklands War of 1982; despite his friendship with the foreign secretary, Francis Pym, who wanted to explore every possibility for a peaceful resolution to the dispute, he sided with Thatcher against US-backed negotiations. His popularity with the police, and his firm handling of the Iranian embassy siege (in 1980) and inner-city rioting (mainly during the summer of 1981), would have convinced a normal prime minister that Willie was anything but woolly. Yet Whitelaw shared none of Thatcher's enthusiasm for capital punishment, and at the party conference of October 1981 he again threatened resignation after the prime minister publicly undermined him by applauding a speaker who had called for the reintroduction of hanging. Although Whitelaw had to make some concessions to tory hardliners, his regime at the Home Office was humane. He attempted to reduce the prison population, and although immigration rules were tightened he resisted Thatcher's demands to put a stop to it entirely. He also pushed through the necessary legislation to establish Channel 4 television, and was widely recognized as a well-informed and staunch ally of broadcasters in general.

Leader of the House of Lords, 1983–1987 Whitelaw fought the general election of 1983 but was sent to the Lords immediately afterwards, causing ill feeling in his constituency which he deeply regretted. He was given a hereditary title, as Viscount Whitelaw of Penrith—the first award of its kind since 1964. Although this breach of recent precedent seemed a fitting acknowledgement of Thatcher's debt, the award was in effect a life peerage; Whitelaw had no male heir, and the title would lapse at his death. In any case, to the media and the general public he continued to be known as Willie. For a second time he was made lord president of the council, and he also became leader of the

House of Lords. Suspicions that he would change the culture of an institution whose members valued their distinctiveness from MPs were soon allayed; it was felt that few members of the house had ever adapted so quickly. It was a period of highly controversial legislation, notably the Community Charge Bill and the bill to abolish the Greater London council. Whitelaw always ensured that the principles of key legislation remained unchanged, but he felt that the occasional defeat for the government was necessary to uphold the independence of the Lords.

Whitelaw also provided invaluable service to the prime minister as chairman of several committees, notably the so-called Star Chamber, which adjudicated between the treasury and spending ministers. Unless he sensed serious political problems ahead, he invariably sided with the treasury, feeling that no government could survive if a chancellor's policy was thwarted. This was purely a product of his political instinct; he knew next to nothing about economics. His skills made him an obvious choice as the government's 'minister for banana skins', although even he found it difficult to anticipate or to explain away mishaps such as the Westland crisis of 1986.

Retirement When Whitelaw resigned from the government, after suffering a mild stroke in December 1987, it was felt that the cabinet had lost its linchpin. Although he remained active in the Lords, Thatcher rarely sought his advice, and some colleagues even traced the prime minister's downfall to the absence of a figure who enjoyed trust among all but the die-hard wets and dries within the party. Certainly Whitelaw had played a crucial role in preventing ideological divisions within his party from erupting into a civil war. Former colleagues found it difficult to identify specific instances of Thatcher changing her mind under the direct influence of Whitelaw's cautionary interventions, but it seems that his presence alone was often sufficient to activate her own (insufficiently recognized) pragmatism. Furthermore, Nigel Lawson later testified to his unmatched ability to resolve disputes even before they came to the attention of the prime minister. Yet he had supported the poll tax, which provided the main incentive for MPs to vote against Thatcher in the leadership election of November 1990—a contest which he deplored, although he did advise his old colleague to stand aside, rather than suffer humiliation, when she failed to secure a sufficient majority in the first ballot.

Whitelaw's underlying unease with Conservative policy was registered in public only after John Major succeeded as prime minister. Whitelaw could claim some of the credit for having spotted Major's talents at an early stage; the latter had first held office as a parliamentary private secretary to a junior Home Office minister when Whitelaw was secretary of state. But Whitelaw no longer felt constrained by a personal bond of loyalty, even though Major's political instincts were far closer to his own than Thatcher's had ever been. He spoke out against plans to privatize the Post Office, attacked the government's policy on broadcasting, and expressed strong misgivings over proposed reforms to the police and the army. On the last subject he felt so strongly that in August 1991 he resigned his honorary post of Conservative deputy leader. Typically, though, the timing and presentation of this decision were calculated to prevent his colleagues from guessing his real motives.

The last few years of Whitelaw's life were darkened by illness. He suffered repeated strokes after the mid-1990s, and had to give up his beloved golf, although he continued to support a considerable number of charities. In his final months he was unaware of the chaos into which his party had descended, and he died at his home, Ennim, Blencowe, near Penrith, on 1 July 1999. He was buried on 4 July in the parish churchyard at Dacre, near Penrith. Fittingly, his memorial service was held in the Guards' Chapel, London. He was survived by his wife and their four daughters. The viscountcy lapsed on his death.

Assessment For the sake of his posthumous reputation Whitelaw had served both Heath and Thatcher too well, and perhaps unwisely. His refusal to strike down Heath made him seem insufficiently ruthless, and his support for Thatcher when she was most vulnerable, before the Falklands War, suggested to his critics that he preferred his place in cabinet to the defence of 'one nation' principles. His misfortune was to play a prominent political role at a time when most of his peers were driven by ideology, personal ambition, or an unsavoury mixture of both. While his pose of a bluff, anti-intellectual country gentleman who had stumbled into politics by accident was well suited to defusing tension between colleagues, it left him vulnerable to enthusiasts on both sides of the wet/dry divide, who alleged that he was too ready to take the part of the last person who had spoken to him. As Nigel Lawson remarked, the pose concealed a sharp, calculating mind; but once colleagues had recognized that Whitelaw was much shrewder than he appeared, they were likely to distrust him even more. Yet even when sorely tried by both Heath and Thatcher, Whitelaw never carried his doubts to the length of outright duplicity. He had his own general principles, and (despite his own disclaimers) he did recognize his own leadership qualities, which had been proved at Caumont in 1944 and in Northern Ireland in 1972–3. But he differed from his colleagues in the ordering of his priorities, where principles held a subordinate place to loyalty—to the Conservative Party, and to its successive leaders.

As a departmental minister Whitelaw's legacy of constructive and lasting achievement was fairly thin. Few British politicians have earned more justified praise than he received in Northern Ireland, but his settlement was almost stillborn. At the Home Office he never saw himself as a reforming minister in the mould of R. A. Butler. Yet he would have liked to be remembered for constructive achievements, and he was bitterly frustrated when events (and the intolerant climate of opinion within his party) forced him to spend most of his time on the defensive. When he was 'pushed upstairs' in 1983 it seemed that he had delayed for only a few years the introduction of a harsher line under a prime minister who disagreed with

him on almost every subject covered by his old department. But by his own standards his career in front-line politics was a success. He had devoted himself to his party, and he was a crucial force for unity while he held office.

MARK GARNETT

Sources W. Whitelaw, *The Whitelaw memoirs* (1989) · *The Times* (2 July 1999) · *Daily Telegraph* (2 July 1999) · *The Guardian* (2 July 1999) · *The Independent* (2 July 1999) · *The Scotsman* (2 July 1999) · Burke, *Peerage* · WWW · personal knowledge (2004) · private information (2004) · b. cert. · m. cert. · d. cert. · R. Jenkins, *A life at the centre* (1991) · N. Lawson, *The view from no. 11* (1992) · M. Garnett and I. Aitken, *'Splendid! Splendid!': the authorised biography of Willie Whitelaw* (2002)
Archives priv. coll., papers
Likenesses photographs, 1959–85, Hult. Arch. · photograph, 1989, repro. in *The Times* · H. Ocean, oils, 1992, NPG [*see illus.*] · S. Adler, photograph, repro. in *The Guardian* · G. Griffiths, photograph, repro. in *The Independent* · photograph, repro. in *Daily Telegraph* · photograph, repro. in *The Scotsman*

Whitelegge, Sir (Benjamin) Arthur (1852–1933), factory inspector, was born on 17 October 1852 in Manchester, the son of Henry Whitelegge, gentleman, of Tideswell, Derbyshire, and his wife, Ann Mason Carrington, of Carrington Hall, Cheshire. He was educated at Tideswell grammar school and from 1870 at University College, London. He took the London University BSc in 1874, and qualified MRCS in 1876. There followed a series of clinical appointments: as house surgeon to the Manchester Hospital for Children, then medical officer to the St Pancras Smallpox Sanitarium, and finally medical officer to the Sheffield Fever Hospital.

Meanwhile Whitelegge continued to study, proceeding MB in 1878 and MD in 1881. He was particularly interested in infectious diseases and public health, and in 1881 he took the Cambridge University diploma in public health. In 1884 he was appointed medical officer of health for Nottingham. In 1889 he became county medical officer of health for the West Riding of Yorkshire, a post he combined from 1894 with the position of chief sanitary officer to the West Riding Rivers Board. In 1885 he married Fanny Marian, daughter of the painter John Callcott *Horsley RA. They had two sons.

In 1886 the Local Government Board appointed a commission to investigate Louis Pasteur's claims to have found a cure for rabies. Whitelegge's brother-in-law Victor Horsley served on the commission, and Whitelegge supplied him with pathological specimens from rabid dogs caught around Nottingham. He subsequently gave evidence to a House of Lords committee on muzzling dogs, which he had found effective in controlling the Nottingham outbreak. He went on to conduct epidemiological studies of the transmission and variation of several other epidemic diseases, which established his reputation as an authority in this area. In 1890 the first edition of his *Manual of Hygiene and Public Health* appeared, and in 1891 he was appointed lecturer on hygiene and public health at Charing Cross Hospital medical school. He delivered the 1893 Milroy lectures to the Royal College of Physicians on changes of type in epidemic disease, and he

Sir (Benjamin) Arthur Whitelegge (1852–1933), by William Strang, 1912

served as examiner in state medicine to the University of London from 1895 to 1897.

Whitelegge's knowledge of epidemiology, and his experience of public health administration in industrial districts, recommended him at this time to the Home Office, which was being pressed to reorganize its industrial health work. From 1893 he served on a departmental committee to review the collection and publication of factory statistics, and from 1895 on a committee of inquiry into anthrax among wool sorters. In 1896 he was appointed chief inspector of factories and workshops, the first medical man to hold this position. Under his guidance the factory inspectorate was greatly expanded and systematically reorganized, and the districts assigned to inspectors were redrawn to encourage closer co-operation with local authority health services. He served on the royal commission on arsenical poisoning in beer (1901), and on the Home Office committee on the lighting of factories (1913). In 1902, when the annual meeting of the British Medical Association first ran a section of industrial hygiene and diseases of occupation, Whitelegge presided over that section, and in 1913 he was elected a vice-president of the Royal Sanitary Institute. Whitelegge was appointed FRCP in 1898, CB in 1902, and KCB in 1911.

By the time he retired in 1917, Whitelegge had proved himself a hard-working administrator. Punctilious and at times pedantic, he could appear abrupt and unfriendly. He was not physically robust and his main recreation was playing bridge and parlour games. He died on 25 April 1933 at Westminster Hospital, London, and was buried three days later. STEVE STURDY

Sources *BMJ* (6 May 1933), 806; (20 May 1933), 897–8 · *The Lancet* (6 May 1933), 990–91 · *The Times* (27 April 1933) · *The Times* (29 April 1933) · *The Times* (2 May 1933) · general register, pt 3, 31 March 1900, U. Lond. · m. cert. · d. cert. · *WW*

Likenesses W. Strang, charcoal and watercolour drawing, 1912, priv. coll. [*see illus.*]

Wealth at death £8354 0s. 6d.: probate, 9 June 1933, *CGPLA Eng. & Wales*

Whiteley, Martha Annie (1866–1956), chemist, was born on 11 November 1866 at 7a Queens Road west, Chelsea, London, the second daughter of William Sedgewick Whiteley, house agent's clerk, and his wife, Hannah (*née* Bargh). She was educated at Kensington Girls' School, then Royal Holloway College, Egham, gaining a University of London BSc in 1890. She passed the Oxford honours mathematical moderations in 1891, the year in which she became a teacher at Wimbledon high school.

In 1900 Martha Whiteley became science lecturer at St Gabriel's Training College, Camberwell. In 1902 she obtained her London doctorate, for which she had been studying part-time at the Royal College of Science (RCS) since 1898. She was appointed lecturer on the physical chemistry honours course at Royal Holloway College in 1903, but after gaining her associateship of the Royal College of Science was invited to join the staff of the RCS (which from 1907 was part of Imperial College) as a teaching scholar in the chemistry department in 1904; she became an assistant in 1905, demonstrator in 1908, lecturer in 1914, and assistant professor (equivalent of reader) in 1920. Between 1912 and 1916 she held one of five fellowships awarded by the British Federation of University Women. She retired in 1934. During her career, she apparently refused to accept higher positions at Imperial, preferring to continue her chemical research work. (It was the consensus among her colleagues that she was capable of fulfilling duties at full professorial level.) It was typical of her, too, that she would not always allow her name to be added to collaborative published papers.

In her research work Martha Whiteley worked with some of the great names in chemistry, including Sir Jocelyn Field Thorpe. Her doctoral studies had focused on the organic chemistry of barbituric compounds, and she continued working with this class of chemicals until 1914. Then, with the advent of the First World War, she and many other academic chemists became involved in the war effort—work for which she was officially recorded as a volunteer. The college was involved in the synthesis of compounds for drugs and improved methods of producing them. These included hydrochloride and lactate for β-eucaine, and diethylaminoethanol for novocaine, which were later put into commercial production. She was also involved in the production of sugars and allied

Martha Annie Whiteley (1866–1956), by Edward Cahen, 1907

and signatures of those staff and students who had known her at the college. In the years that followed she continued her work on the *Dictionary of Applied Chemistry* at Imperial College, and edited the fourth edition, published in 1941. During the Second World War, when she was bombed out of her London home, she was offered facilities at Cambridge University, and temporarily transferred her work there. Martha Whiteley died of heart failure, shortly before her ninetieth birthday, at her home, Flat 2, 4 Roland Gardens, South Kensington, on 24 May 1956. She had been associated with the RCS and Imperial College for more than fifty years, latterly through her honorary fellowship of Imperial, awarded in 1946, her work with the Imperial College Women's Association, which she founded in 1912, and her continuing friendships with devoted colleagues. Little is known of her private life other than that she was deeply religious; her funeral service was held at St Augustine's Church, Queen's Gate, on 29 May 1956.   ANNE BARRETT

Sources ICL, Whiteley MSS, B/Whiteley · 'History of Imperial College chemistry department', ICL, KC/1/1 · Royal Society, Royal Society war committee MSS (First World War), CMB 28 (chemistry sub-committee), MS 500–02 · *The supply of munitions part 1: Trench warfare supplies* (c.1921), vol. 11 of Ministry of Munitions, *History of the Ministry of Munitions* (1918–22) · L. F. Haber, *The poisonous cloud: chemical warfare in the First World War* (1986) · *The Times* (30 May 1956)

Archives ICL, lecture notebooks, etc. · U. Sussex Library, papers | RS, Royal Society war committee (First World War), sectional chemistry committee

Likenesses E. Cahen, photograph, 1907, ICL, E. Cahen photograph album, 1907 [*see illus.*] · group photograph, 1912, ICL, Women's Association · group photographs, c.1920–1929, ICL, department of chemistry · group photograph, 1925, ICL, Women's Association · E. M. Hinchley, print, 1937, ICL · P. C. Bull, photograph, c.1940–1949, ICL

Wealth at death £8840 14s.: probate, 23 Aug 1956, *CGPLA Eng. & Wales*

substances. Whiteley developed the lachrymatory gas known as SK (ethyl odoacetate) and the incendiary mixture DW (Dr Whiteley). For these services she was appointed officer in the Order of the British Empire in 1920. Following the war she made contributions to the second and third editions of *Thorpe's Dictionary of Applied Chemistry* and co-authored *A Student's Manual of Organic Chemical Analysis* (1925).

Martha Whiteley also played an important pastoral role in college, particularly towards women. She took an interest in all her students' academic work and in their recreation, instituting the Whiteley cup for squash. In 1913 Sir Alfred Keogh, then rector at Imperial, remarked:

> No one who knows her can doubt that she is one of the most remarkable personalities either amongst men or women in the country. She has an extraordinary power of expression which in some way enables her to obtain a very remarkable influence in the College, and a charm of manner particularly desirable in a teacher. … here you have no ordinary woman. I know of no one more likely to inspire women students to great things in science than Miss Whiteley.

There were few women students in the chemistry department at that time, and Whiteley's influence and 'power of engendering enthusiasm amongst the women students' (Whiteley MSS) extended to all college departments.

Martha Whiteley deplored the fact that there were so few women science students, and also so few trained scientific women in the country able to fill positions vacated by men during the First World War. She was a member of the Chemical Society, and in 1904 she signed a petition with eighteen women chemists requesting the admittance of women to fellowship of the society. Although it was rejected, she continued in the battle, which was finally won in 1920, and was the first woman to be elected a member of the council of the Chemical Society, on which she served from 1928 to 1931. In 1918 she had been elected a fellow of the Royal Institute of Chemistry.

On her retirement in 1934 Martha Whiteley was presented with a book in which was an illuminated address

Whiteley, William (1831–1907), department store owner, was born on 29 September 1831 at Agbrigg, near Wakefield, the youngest of four sons of William Whiteley, corn merchant, and his wife, Elizabeth Rowland. After leaving the village school at fourteen, he spent two years working on his uncle's farm before becoming apprenticed in 1848 as a draper's assistant to Harnew and Glover of Wakefield.

Whiteley's perspective on retailing was transformed in 1851 when he visited the Great Exhibition in London. The displays of goods in the vast galleries of Crystal Palace fired Whiteley's imagination with the idea of developing a large retail emporium. After serving his apprenticeship Whiteley moved to London in 1855 with just £10 to achieve his goal. He set about mastering every detail of the London drapery trade. He began with a position in the traditional store of Willey & Co., Ludgate, where he stayed for fifteen months before moving to the Fore Street Warehouse, an important wholesale business. Finally, he worked with the haberdashers, Leat & Sons, to learn the ribbon trade. All the time he lived frugally, saving his money.

In 1863, having saved £700, Whiteley established a shop

in the then unfashionable suburb of Westbourne Grove, selling ribbons and fancy goods. He started with just two assistants, one of whom, Harriet Sarah Hill, he married in 1867; they had two sons and two daughters. The business expanded rapidly as a result both of Whiteley's own skill and of the opening-up of the nearby Bayswater Station by the Metropolitan railway. By 1867 Whiteley had added greatly to his store which then consisted of seventeen different retail departments. It continued to grow and by the 1880s consisted of eighteen adjoining shop premises. Whiteley undertook to provide every type of goods, adopting the insignia of the two hemispheres and the style of 'Universal Provider'. Asked to supply an elephant, Whiteley apparently responded immediately and obtained one the same day for the customer, which enabled him to advertise that he could supply 'Everything from a pin to an elephant' (DBB, 791). The store was discovered by Queen Victoria, and the royal family became regular clients. The issue of diaries and almanacs was a form of publicity that Whiteley pioneered and used to keep his store in the public eye.

Whiteley's success and business practices attracted considerable hostility from local shopkeepers and he became known as the most hated man in Bayswater. Between 1882 and 1887 Whiteley's department store was plagued by large fires. In 1887 Whiteley offered a £3000 reward for the discovery of the culprits, who were never found. After each fire, however, his business rose more splendidly from the flames. Although courteous to rich customers, Whiteley was a stern employer. Staff who broke the rules were heavily fined, and were often dismissed at short notice. Apt to indulge in Smilesian aphorisms about business, Whiteley wrote an article (undated) entitled 'How to succeed as a shopkeeper' (DBB, 791).

Not content with running his store, Whiteley expanded into farming to provide foodstuffs for his business. In 1891 he bought 200 acres of land at Hanworth, south west of London, and established factories on the site for food processing. In 1894 Whiteley also purchased an additional 34 acre estate which he laid out as a model farm, including model dwellings for estate workers. At his instigation a detailed account was written by Alfred Barnard of the Hanworth estate under the title Orchards and Gardens (1895). By 1899 the store had a turnover of £1 million and was converted into a limited company. The bulk of the shares nevertheless continued to be held by the family, with Whiteley's two sons William and Frank sitting on the board of directors. It was not until 1909 that the shares were publicly subscribed.

Whiteley was a short, stocky man with bright grey eyes, fashionable side whiskers, and a clear complexion, and was possessed of remarkable vitality. As he prospered he developed an increasingly large ego but nevertheless continued to live in close proximity to his store at 31 Porchester Terrace, Hyde Park.

Whiteley's personal life, meanwhile, was in some disarray. He and a financier friend, George Rayner, had liaisons in the late 1870s with two sisters in Brighton, Louisa and Emily Turner. The latter gave birth to a son, and subsequently went to live with Rayner, but the child's paternity was disputed, and Horace George Rayner was brought up to believe Whiteley was his father. In 1881 Whiteley was legally separated from his wife, and he subsequently bought a house for Louisa in Kilburn. They had an illegitimate son in 1885.

In his later years, attired in frock coat and top hat, Whiteley continued to make his presence felt in his daily inspections of his department store. It was on one such visit on 24 January 1907 that the seventy-five-year-old Whiteley was confronted by Horace Rayner, who asked for financial help on the grounds of being his son. Whiteley treated him as a blackmailer and was about to summon the police when Rayner shot him dead. Whiteley was buried at Kensal Green on 30 January 1907. Rayner was sentenced to death for his murder; but this was later commuted to life imprisonment because of the extenuating circumstances. He was released in 1919.

Whiteley was one of the most prominent department store owners of his day. On his death certificate he was styled as 'The Universal Provider of 31 Porchester Terrace'. His estate was valued at almost £1.5 million, and his bequests included provision of £1 million for the construction and maintenance of homes for retired store workers on a 225 acre estate at Burhill, Surrey, which became known as the Whiteley village. Whiteley's department store was acquired by Harry Gordon Selfridge in 1927, and since the Second World War has been owned by a variety of companies.   GARETH SHAW

Sources Ephemerides, *Whiteley's diary, almanac and handbook of useful information for 1877* (1876) · *The Times* (25 Jan 1907) · *The Times* (26 Jan 1907) · *The Times* (28 Jan 1907) · *The Times* (29 Jan 1907) · *The Times* (31 Jan 1907) · *The Times* (1 Feb 1907) · *The Times* (20 Feb 1907) · *The Times* (27 Feb 1907) · *The Times* (26 March 1907) · *The Times* (29 March 1907) · R. Lambert, *The universal provider: a study of William Whiteley and the rise of the London department store* (1938) · J. W. Ferry, *A history of the department store* (1960) · A. Adburgham, *Shops and shopping, 1800–1914: where, and in what manner the well-dressed Englishwoman bought her clothes*, 2nd edn (1981) · *CGPLA Eng. & Wales* (1907) · d. cert. · W. Philpott, 'Whiteley, William', *DBB* · B. Lancaster, *The department store: a social history* (1995) · *DNB*
Likenesses H. Williams, oils, 1889; in possession of his sons, 1912 · Adams-Acton, bust; in possession of his sons, 1912
Wealth at death £1,452,825 5s. 4d.: probate, 16 April 1907, *CGPLA Eng. & Wales*

Whiteley, William (1881–1955), politician and trade unionist, was born on 3 October 1881 in the village of Littleburn near Durham. He was the fourth son of Samuel Whiteley (d. 1921) and his wife, Ellen, née Bragan. Samuel Whiteley had begun work in the mines at the age of seven and was an active member of the Durham Miners' Association (DMA). For many years he was secretary of the Brandon miners' lodge and also a Methodist local preacher.

William Whiteley was educated at the Brandon colliery school and entered the coal mining industry at the age of twelve. But three years later he became a clerk in the DMA offices at Durham, and he continued his education at night school. In 1901 he married Elizabeth Swordy, the daughter of James Urwin Jackson, a blacksmith at Littleburn colliery; they had a son and a daughter.

Although Whiteley lacked the pit experience typical of

miners' leaders, he gained a thorough knowledge of the industry and of the organization of the DMA. In 1912 he was elected a DMA agent, just a year before the union's rules were altered to require all officials to have had five years' experience in the industry. As an agent he was responsible for insurance questions within the DMA; in 1917 he became financial secretary and joint committee secretary. On three occasions—1915, 1918, and 1920—he was a Durham representative on the executive of the Miners' Federation of Great Britain (MFGB).

When Whiteley first became an employee of the DMA the union was identified thoroughly with Lib–Lab politics. The general secretary, John Wilson, was strongly anti-socialist and opposed the affiliation of the DMA to the MFGB. Whiteley seems initially to have shared some aspects of this culture. He was an active Methodist and politically a Liberal. However, in the decade after 1900 the politics of the Durham coalfield began to shift. DMA members voted to affiliate to the MFGB at the end of 1907, and then, despite Wilson's opposition, the DMA backed firmly the MFGB policy of affiliation to the Labour Party. Whiteley shared in this transition; as branches of the Independent Labour Party emerged across the coalfield, along with other activists of his generation, he changed his political allegiance, joining the Labour Party in 1906. The ideological shift was not great, and Whiteley remained a pragmatic and solidaristic trade unionist; he also remained an active Methodist.

By 1918 Whiteley was on the panel of DMA prospective parliamentary candidates and was involved in the organization of the Durham divisional Labour Party. In that year's election he unsuccessfully contested Blaydon. The shift to Labour among DMA officials and activists was not yet matched among the bulk of miners, and only in November 1922 did Whiteley enter the Commons, after winning the Blaydon seat at the general election. This moment was decisive for his subsequent career. Unlike some miners' unions, the DMA required members of parliament to relinquish their trade union posts, and Whiteley committed himself to a political career, backed by the resources and prestige of his trade union.

As a back-bencher Whiteley was a lucid and knowledgeable speaker; his subjects usually related to mining. He became a junior whip in 1927 and a junior lord of the Treasury in the Labour government of 1929. However, in the general election of 1931 Labour fared worse in Durham and Northumberland than in almost any other coalfield. Whiteley was among the defeated DMA candidates. Like several other defeated Labour candidates, he experienced some unemployment, and his application to the DMA for a maintenance grant of £150 a year was turned down. He subsequently found work in the public assistance department of the Durham county council, and taught evening classes.

Decisively returned for Blaydon in 1935, Whiteley resumed work as a whip. He visited Spain during the civil war. With the formation of Churchill's coalition government in May 1940 he became comptroller of the household. Two years later he became Labour chief whip (joint parliamentary secretary to the Treasury), and the following year he was made a privy councillor. He performed effectively in the challenging context of the coalition. His gift for conciliation was evident, and in general the Parliamentary Labour Party maintained its unity.

Within Attlee's post-war Labour government, Whiteley was the government chief whip (the parliamentary secretary to the Treasury). His position within the Parliamentary Labour Party was extremely powerful. He discussed major strategic issues with the prime minister, including ministerial appointments, and he worked closely and effectively with Herbert Morrison (the leader of the house) in the organization of parliamentary business. Although rarely heard in public, he was at the heart of the Attlee government. His reputation as a great chief whip was founded in this period. Since the government's majority was secure until February 1950, his achievement (in recognition of which he was made a CH in 1948) was not that of securing ministerial survival in an uncertain situation. Early revolts over foreign affairs dwindled as the cold war intensified; the government's promised domestic legislation was delivered with little dissent within the party. Whiteley in his style epitomized this sense of shared purpose and eventual achievement. His blend of firmness and conciliation worked its magic on the diverse Parliamentary Labour Party. Hugh Dalton reflected that 'he had done a wonderful job in fitting all our new members, some very temperamental, into useful places in the parliamentary machine, and in talking to them like a wise and kindly father when the need arose' (Dalton, *High Tide*, 3.421). In contrast, from February 1950 the government's small majority and increasing disagreements made survival a priority. Yet to the end of that short parliament, the government was not defeated on a major issue.

After Labour's electoral defeat in October 1951, Whiteley was re-elected as chief whip with acclamation. The years in opposition did not enhance his reputation. Like several of his senior party colleagues he was tired. He had sided strongly with Hugh Gaitskell in the budget crisis of April 1951; in opposition he lacked sympathy with Bevan and Bevanism. When fifty-seven Labour members broke party discipline in March 1952 and voted against the Conservative government's defence estimates, Whiteley favoured withdrawing the whip from all the rebels. Apart from being a disproportionate response, such a draconian measure was not feasible, given the political balance within the party. Whiteley's personal views had always been those of the loyalist right; in his last years they ceased to be tempered with sensitivity towards the diversity of viewpoint within the party. His last significant political intervention was in support of withdrawal of the whip from Bevan in March 1955. The failure of this initiative epitomized the Labour Party's disarray. After the subsequent election defeat in May 1955 Whiteley reluctantly stood down as chief whip. Already ill, he died at the county hospital in Durham, on 3 November 1955. His wife survived him.

Throughout his parliamentary career, Whiteley

remained embedded in Durham society. Active in his union, his chapel, and the Workers' Educational Association, he was a deputy lieutenant of the county and a member of the county education committee and the county insurance committee, and was president for over thirty years of the Durham Aged Miners' Homes Association. As a young man, he had been a talented soccer player and cricketer. His political skills were complemented by a powerful physical presence: 'tall, good looking, always immaculately dressed … he might have passed for a bishop in mufti' (The Times, 4 Nov 1955).

Whiteley represented the Durham miners, typically seen as loyal supporters of the Labour Party leadership, at the party's highest level. His own political formation came at a transitional moment between the Lib–Lab chapel-based character of the DMA in its early years and the secularized union machine of later generations. As a back-bencher he had responded angrily in the last stages of the 1926 lock-out to the behaviour of police imported into the Durham coalfield: 'we are citizens of this country and entitled to treatment as citizens' (Hansard 5C, 18 Nov 1926, 199, col. 2073). His political career can be understood as an attempt to realize that objective.

DAVID HOWELL

Sources H. Beynon and T. Austrin, Masters and servants: class and patronage in the making of a labour organisation (1994) · H. Dalton, High tide and after: memoirs, 1945–1960 (1962) · The political diary of Hugh Dalton, 1918–1940, 1945–1960, ed. B. Pimlott (1986) · The Second World War diary of Hugh Dalton, 1940–1945, ed. B. Pimlott (1986) · DLB · The Times (4 Nov 1955) · M. Webb, The Times (8 Nov 1955) · DNB · CGPLA Eng. & Wales (1956)

Archives NRA, papers | Durham RO, Durham Miners' Association records · National Union of Miners (North Eastern Area), Redhills, Durham, Durham Miners' Association records · People's History Museum, Manchester, parliamentary labour party minutes

Likenesses W. Stoneman, photographs, 1930–45, NPG · W. Stoneman, photograph, NPG

Wealth at death £7449 12s. 5d.: probate, 27 Feb 1956, CGPLA Eng. & Wales

Whitelock, Dorothy (1901–1982), historian, was born on 11 November 1901 at 4 Cliff Mount, Leeds, the youngest of the six children of Edward Whitelock (d. 1903), accountant, and his second wife, Emmeline, née Dawson (d. 1950). She was educated at Leeds Girls' High School, and in 1921 went to Newnham College, Cambridge, where she read English. Section A of the tripos was essentially English literature. Section B offered a very different combination of examination papers, reflecting the wide interests and interdisciplinary approach of Hector Munro Chadwick, Elrington and Bosworth professor of Anglo-Saxon at Cambridge from 1912 to 1941. The choice extended from Old English and Old Norse language and literature to Anglo-Saxon history, the viking age, the Teutonic peoples, and early Britain, drawing students into language, literature, history, and archaeology, and taking them in this process from England into the Celtic world and across the seas to Scandinavia. Section B suited Whitelock very well, and under the tutelage of Chadwick, Bruce Dickins, F. L. Attenborough, and others, she gained first-class honours, with 'special distinction', in 1923. She seems to have been less

well suited to the study of more modern English literature, and gained only second-class honours in section A, in 1924.

Whitelock had been worried as an undergraduate that before she could get going there would be nothing left for her to do. None the less, she embarked on research in 1924, initially at Newnham College (1924–6), then at the University of Uppsala (1927–9), and latterly back at Cambridge (1929–30). For some time Professor Chadwick had been setting his students to work on re-editing the corpus of Anglo-Saxon law-codes and vernacular charters. Florence Harmer's edition of select vernacular documents of the ninth and tenth centuries had been published in 1914, followed by F. L. Attenborough's edition of the earliest Anglo-Saxon law-codes (1922) and A. J. Robertson's edition of the later laws (1925). At Chadwick's suggestion Whitelock began work on the corpus of Anglo-Saxon wills, leading to her edition, with translation and commentary, published in 1930. It was a work of exemplary scholarship, and made readily available a set of texts which are central to any perception of Anglo-Saxon society in the tenth and eleventh centuries.

In 1930 Whitelock moved from Cambridge to Oxford, on her appointment as lecturer in English at St Hilda's College. She became a tutor in 1936, a fellow in 1937, and served as vice-principal from 1950 to 1957. In the 1930s she was evidently preoccupied with teaching and other college duties, and published little, though it is apparent that she was beginning to develop an interest in the career and writings of Wulfstan, bishop of London (996–1002) and archbishop of York (1002–23). Her edition of Wulfstan's Sermo ad Anglos was published in 1939, and was followed in the 1940s by a series of important papers on his legislation. Yet it was the publication of F. M. Stenton's Anglo-Saxon England, in 1943, that must have had the greatest impact on her outlook at this time. Whitelock told Stenton that the book 'solves all problems & seems to make all further discussion redundant' (Whitelock to Stenton, 14 Nov 1943, priv. coll.); and when, two years later, she embarked upon the task of producing a collection of primary sources in modern English translation, she seems to have conceived it as a companion to Stenton's work. It was also in the mid-1940s that she was commissioned to write The Beginnings of English Society for the Pelican History of England. A related aspect of her output in the late 1940s and early 1950s is represented by a flurry of publications on Old English poetry, including a series of lectures, The Audience of Beowulf (1951), in which she advanced a compelling case for the poem's origin in the eighth century, at the court of Offa, king of the Mercians. She reconstructed the historical contexts in which Old English poetry was composed, and which in her view were essential to its proper understanding; she also showed how a sensitive reading of the poetry could contribute so much to a historian's perception of what might otherwise be taken for granted.

It was not easy in the 1930s and 1940s for a woman to make a successful career as an academic, and it was some time before Whitelock achieved the advancement that she so richly deserved. At St Hilda's she was frustrated by the statutory limitations on the power of the fellows to run their own college, and within the university it was frustrating for her to have no formal place in decisions affecting the teaching and examination of her subject. In 1944 she applied for a chair at Liverpool, but was unsuccessful. From October 1944 to April 1945 Whitelock took leave of absence from her duties at St Hilda's, in order to look after her ailing mother, and in these circumstances began to wonder whether she should abandon her academic career. Stenton urged her to persevere, insisting that her resignation would be 'a serious injury to the interests of women in academic life' (Stenton to Whitelock, 19 March 1945, priv. coll.), and Whitelock acknowledged that his letter had strengthened her determination to persevere (Whitelock to Stenton, 21 March 1945, priv. coll.). In 1945 J. R. R. Tolkien was translated from the Rawlinson and Bosworth professorship of Anglo-Saxon to the Merton chair of English literature. Whitelock applied for the vacant post, and was strongly supported on the committee by Stenton and Kenneth Sisam; but in the event the Rawlinson and Bosworth chair went to C. L. Wrenn, of the University of London. It was a bitter disappointment, and was seen as further evidence of 'the inestimable privilege of masculinity' (Lady Stenton to Whitelock, 16 April 1946, priv. coll.). Yet there was no stopping her progress. *The Beginnings of English Society*, written while she was caring for her mother, was published in 1952, followed by a facsimile edition of the Peterborough manuscript of the Anglo-Saxon Chronicle in 1954, and by the massive *English Historical Documents, c.500–1042* in 1955. Whitelock's distinction as a scholar was finally recognized, in Oxford, by her appointment in 1955 as lecturer in Old English, and, nationally, by her election in 1956 as a fellow of the British Academy.

In October 1957 Whitelock returned to Cambridge, upon her appointment as Elrington and Bosworth professor of Anglo-Saxon, in succession to Bruce Dickins, and resumed her direct association with Newnham College, as a professorial fellow (1957–69). She sought and received detailed advice from Stenton about the substance of her inaugural lecture, and was strongly encouraged by him to promote a coherent view of Anglo-Saxon studies, without the distraction of what he regarded as Chadwick's wilder imaginings. The lecture itself, delivered on 21 February 1958, showed how knowledge of Anglo-Saxon England had been greatly extended on such a wide front, yet does seem in certain respects to represent a retreat from the Chadwickian vision. Later that year Whitelock accepted an invitation from David Douglas to write a full-scale biography of King Alfred the Great, and thenceforth devoted ever more attention in her lectures and published papers to matters Alfredian.

Whitelock's principal administrative achievement, as head of department, was symbolic of the vision of her subject which she had propounded under Stenton's influence in her inaugural lecture. The distinctive combination of papers which in its basic form had materialized in 1919 out of the modern and medieval languages tripos, to take its place as section B of the English tripos, had been transferred by Chadwick in 1927 to the archaeological and anthropological tripos. Early in 1957, some time before Whitelock took up her post, the now extended range of these papers was accorded the dignity of its own identity as the Anglo-Saxon tripos; and although the committee recommending change had advocated the institution of a new faculty, it had been decided for administrative convenience that the department of Anglo-Saxon and kindred studies (as it was then called) should remain for the time being within the faculty of archaeology and anthropology. The association had made good sense under Chadwick, yet it was felt by many to separate Old English from medieval English language and literature; so in 1967 Whitelock effected the transfer of her department into the faculty of English, where she, her colleagues, and many others thought that it properly belonged. Two years later the tripos itself was renamed the Anglo-Saxon, Norse, and Celtic tripos.

Whitelock was appointed CBE in 1964. She retired from her chair in 1969, and from then until the onset of illness, in late 1980, she was busily engaged in three major academic projects. The first was the preparation of a second edition of *English Historical Documents*, published in 1979. The second was her (pre-conquest) share in the two-volume collaborative edition of texts bearing on the history of the church from 871 to 1204, first planned by Stenton and others in the 1930s, and published as *Councils and Synods with other Documents Relating to the English Church: A.D. 871–1066* (1981). The third was her biography of King Alfred the Great, for which she had been preparing the ground since the early 1960s, but which she did not start to write in earnest until the late 1970s. The book is a carefully controlled statement of the view of Alfred arising from her own mastery of all the relevant disciplines (literary and documentary sources, archaeology, numismatics, and the corpus of Alfredian prose), never straying far from the evidence or drifting into the realms of analogy and speculation. Sadly, it was left unfinished at her death, but the typescript is preserved among her papers.

Though always conscious of her Yorkshire roots (and a regular visitor to Robin Hood's Bay, near Whitby), Whitelock continued after her retirement to live in Cambridge, with her widowed sister, Phyllis Priestley. She died on 14 August 1982 at a nursing home in Cambridge. Her affection for the Anglo-Saxons had perhaps been fostered by a northerner's disdain for the Normans, as much as by her love of the language and literature of this early period. Her distinction as an Anglo-Saxonist stemmed more directly from the training she received from Chadwick in the 1920s, though her attention thereafter was always more closely focused on the elucidation of the primary sources which form the basis for our knowledge of Anglo-Saxon literature and history. Her concern, quite simply, was to establish the text, to work out its meaning, and then to assess its significance for historical purposes. In this respect she was as much influenced by Stenton as she had been trained by Chadwick; and it was a powerful combination. SIMON KEYNES

Sources Dorothy Whitelock's letters and papers, priv. coll. · *Cambridge University Reporter* (22 March 1967) · P. Clemoes and K. Hughes, eds., *England before the conquest: studies in primary sources presented to Dorothy Whitelock* (1971) [with list of DW's publications, 1930–70, pp. 1–4] · H. Gardner, 'Dorothy Whitelock', *St Hilda's College Report and Chronicle* (1981–2), 12–6 · H. Loyn, 'Dorothy Whitelock, 1901–1982', *PBA*, 70 (1984), 543–54 · H. Loyn, 'Dorothy Whitelock (1901–1982)', *Medieval scholarship: biographical studies on the formation of a discipline*, ed. H. Damico and J. B. Zavadil, 1 (1995), 289–300 · J. Schulman, 'An Anglo-Saxonist at Oxford and Cambridge: Dorothy Whitelock (1901–82)', *Women medievalists in the academy*, ed. J. Chance (2003) · C. Sisam, 'Dorothy Whitelock, 1901–1982', *Medieval English Studies Newsletter*, 8 (July 1983), 1–3 · interview with Dorothy Whitelock, 'Waiting for Alfred', *The Guardian* (18 Aug 1978), 9 · b. cert.
Archives priv. coll., corresp. and papers
Likenesses Elliott & Fry, photograph, repro. in Loyn, 'Dorothy Whitelock', facing p. 543
Wealth at death £147,029: probate, 15 Nov 1982, *CGPLA Eng. & Wales*

Whitelocke, Bulstrode, appointed Lord Whitelocke under the protectorate (1605–1675), lawyer and politician, was the eldest son of Sir James *Whitelocke (1570–1632), judge, and his wife, Elizabeth (1575–1631), daughter of Edward and Cecily Bulstrode of Hedgerly Bulstrode. He was born in Fleet Street, London, on 6 August 1605, at the home of his mother's uncle, Sir George Croke. The second of seven children, only he and two sisters survived childhood.

Early life Much of what is known about Whitelocke is drawn from his own writings; he kept a diary, which begins autobiographically with a record of his birth and early years, before turning into yearly, then daily records of his public and private life. He gave another version of events up to 1660, in 'Annales of his own life dedicated to his children'. At Whitelocke's baptism, at St Dunstan-in-the-West on 19 August, his unpredictable uncle and godfather, Edmund Whitelocke, announced that the baby's name was Bulstrode; offering Elizabeth when asked for an alternative, he said he was resolved the boy should have one of his mother's names. Taught by his mother, Whitelocke was reading by the age of four and at seven was sent to boarding-school during his father's brief imprisonment. About 1614 he was sent to Eton College, but about 1615 transferred to Merchant Taylors' School. He led a gang of boys in street-fighting against boys from St Paul's School and 'many a blacke eye and bloudy nose was had among them' before the twelve-year-old Whitelocke acted as 'ambassador' in an 'Ambassy for peace' arranged by the masters (a foretaste of the future) and gave them an oration, in Latin, on the miseries of civil war and the benefits of peace. In 1619 he went to St John's College, Oxford, and was taught philosophy and logic by the president, William Laud, and by his tutor, Philip Parsons, but was prevented from taking his degree by an accident. Unable to afford a horse for hunting, he followed on foot; on one occasion he injured his leg and lay in a meadow near Islip for about two hours until taken by coach, in 'unspeakable torment', to his parents' home at Fawley Court near Henley-on-Thames.

Bulstrode Whitelocke, appointed Lord Whitelocke under the protectorate (1605–1675), by unknown artist, 1634

In 1622 Whitelocke entered the Middle Temple. He developed an ambition to go on the grand tour but his father persuaded him to explore his own country first and he followed the judges' circuits, being handsomely entertained, studying legal cases, and visiting places of interest. Through his father's influence, he was returned an MP for both Stafford and Boroughbridge in 1626, choosing to represent the former. The following year he was called to the bar and undertook another tour, of the west country and Wales, including visits to Stonehenge, Old Sarum, Maiden Castle, Sandfoot Castle, Penzance, Land's End, Glastonbury, and Wookey Hole by candle-light. At twenty-three, he was chosen master of the revels at the Middle Temple by his colleagues. When the formal revels began, attended by courtiers and others, he entertained lavishly and by Christmas was deeply in debt. He dared not tell his father and his only escape was to earn money as a barrister. He made £152 16s. in one year on the Oxfordshire circuit and, by 1632, was appointed recorder of Abingdon and counsel for the corporation of Henley. That year his legal fees brought in £310 11s. and, with an allowance from his father of £400, he cleared his debts. In 1630 his marriage had been arranged to the charming but unstable Rebecca Benet (Bennet; 1609–1634), daughter of alderman Thomas Benet, sheriff of London. Their only child, James, was born in 1631. Whitelocke's mother died the same year and his father the next and, in obedience to a clause in his father's will, he had an impressive monument to them erected in Fawley church. His inheritance left him well off, and he lived at Fawley Court with his family. He was put in charge of the music for a royal masque, *The Triumph of Peace*, to be presented by the inns of court in the banqueting hall, Whitehall, for Candlemas 1634. He composed a coranto in collaboration with Simon Ive; Queen Henrietta Maria said she could not believe such a lively tune was by an Englishman, and Whitelocke claimed that it remained popular for the next thirty years.

Early in 1634 Rebecca Whitelocke's condition deteriorated; she became violent and was placed in the care of a doctor who claimed he could cure her, provided no one visited her for about six months. Greatly distressed, Whitelocke left for France with a friend. Two innkeepers' wives showed concern for the sad young Englishman; he was guarded in his record as to what this implied, but wrote to a discreet friend in England, asking him to send 72 yards of coloured ribbon 'for a lady to whom I am much ingaged' (Longleat, Whitelocke MSS, vi, fol. 93). Friends in England kept in touch, including his close friend at the time, Edward Hyde. Dr Bartlett wrote that Rebecca's condition improved until her mother insisted on seeing her and talking to her in private, after which Rebecca stopped eating. She died on 9 May. Mrs Benet announced that she would petition for custody of her grandchild and for profits from Whitelocke's estate to be paid to her, until it was known whether he was still alive. He immediately returned to England, shrewdly defeating a plot by French sailors to throw him and his companion overboard and keep their luggage.

Whitelocke wrote that he was now a new beginner in the world. He was twenty-nine, a single father, and owner of a large estate. William Cooke, a tenant farmer, told his young landlord bluntly that he was entertaining too lavishly, his belongings were being sold in Henley market, and the house needed a good wife to look after it. He mentioned Frances Willoughby (1614–1649), daughter of William, third Lord Willoughby of Parham, and niece of the dowager countess of Sunderland, who was staying with her aunt at Hambleden. Whitelocke found a pretext for calling on the countess. He claimed he was so far from thoughts of wooing that he went in shabby clothes with untrimmed hair and beard, but when Frances Willoughby appeared it was love at first sight. The courtship developed with the countess's approval, and that of three-year-old James, who called Frances his lady. Soon Whitelocke was summoned to London, charged by the council with being 'disaffected to the church' because of his refusal, as recorder of Abingdon, to take action against nonconformists. Back in Fawley he called on Frances but during his absence her uncle and trustee, George Manners, earl of Rutland, had announced that his niece could not marry a commoner. The couple exchanged secret notes, and arranged an elopement. They were married in Fawley Court chapel, then were driven to The Ship in Fleet Street for their honeymoon. London society rallied round, eventually Frances's family became reconciled, and from 1 August 1635 the couple actually stayed with Rutland at Belvoir Castle. At first they delighted in the grandeur, but they soon grew weary of great feasting and ceremony and went home. They enjoyed fourteen years of happiness together and brought up six daughters and three sons.

Whitelocke later expressed amazement that, with no political training, Frances could give such wise advice, and he claimed that there was never a cross word between them.

Civil war Whitelocke began to be recognized at the Berkshire, Buckinghamshire, and Oxfordshire assizes. As chairman of the quarter sessions in Oxford, he spoke in support of the temporal courts against the encroachments of ecclesiastical jurisdiction, and gained local popularity by resisting the extension of Wychwood Forest and supporting John Hampden's opposition to the second ship-money writ of 1635. In 1640 he was elected to the Long Parliament for Marlow. Reluctantly he accepted chairmanship of the select committee to prepare the impeachment of Thomas Wentworth, earl of Strafford. He drafted the bill ensuring that the Long Parliament could not be adjourned or dissolved without consent of both houses and joined in proceedings against illegal decrees by convocation. He spent some time with Frances and their children at Fawley Court, and at Abingdon quarter sessions. Early in 1642 he was appointed a deputy lieutenant of Buckinghamshire and of Oxfordshire but accepted military posts with misgivings. In the Commons he favoured the joint authority of king and parliament over the militia and spoke against raising an army, stressing the miseries of civil war. He urged parliament to send propositions of peace to the king. In the summer of 1642 he found people around Fawley terrified at the prospect of parliament raising an army. They were arming themselves and he did so too. In August he and others wrote to the speaker, warning of plans to implement the king's commission of array at Watlington to secure recruits for the royal army. He and a troop of horsemen attacked, capturing some royalists. He advised Lord Saye to garrison Oxford before the king's army did so, but his advice was ignored and in due course royalists seized the city. Other royalist troops under Sir John Byron captured Fawley Court and despite orders not to plunder they ravaged the house, breaking open chests, burning books, and lighting their pipes on Whitelocke's manuscripts. Yet Whitelocke refused to see either party as wholly in the right or in the wrong and worked continuously to promote peace. He was appointed governor of Henley garrison; later, in 1644, he declined the command of the forces of the associated counties of Berkshire, Buckinghamshire, and Oxfordshire. In 1643 he was chosen as one of parliament's commissioners to carry propositions of peace to the king in Oxford. In his account of their stay in the city and of the negotiations, he recorded that he thought Charles showed ability and judgement, but trusted other people's judgement more than his own, causing him to change his mind overnight. Attending parliament again, Whitelocke moved with his family to Highgate. He was there when he heard that his property, The Bell inn, Henley, had been set on fire, and that parliament's soldiers, garrisoned at Phyllis Court, another estate of his near Henley, had plundered the place although he was a parliament man, 'butt bruitish soldiers make no distinctions'. In the Commons he often wore a long coat like a cassock, causing MPs to call 'in Drollery … Mr Deane, Mr Deane'; Cromwell called him that 'in mirth'. By September 1644, with no rents from his plundered estates and earning no legal fees, Whitelocke had to sell his coach and horses.

In November 1644 Whitelocke was once again sent to the king by parliament, to arrange for fresh peace talks. After waiting four hours in the cold, apparently on Headington Hill, the commissioners were allowed to enter Oxford. Dirt and stones were thrown at their coaches; they were abused as rogues, traitors, and rebels, and were lodged in a squalid inn. Despite the commissioners' safe conduct their servants were attacked by two royalist officers, whom Whitelocke and Denzil Holles managed to disarm; the governor duly imprisoned the offenders and placed a guard at the door. The commissioners read parliament's propositions to the king, who said he would consider them. Next day, casually encountering Whitelocke and Holles, the king asked them to write down, unofficially, what they thought he should answer. Embarrassed, they wrote (in an assumed hand) that he should go to parliament immediately, but instead, he wrote expressing his desire for peace. In December 1644, at Westminster, Whitelocke and Maynard were summoned by the earl of Essex to a private meeting, attended by the Scottish commissioners and others wishing 'to rid Cromwell out of the way' as a contentious 'incendiary'. The two lawyers firmly opposed bringing this charge unless adequate proof were available. Late in January 1645 he joined in the attempt to negotiate a treaty at Uxbridge, where accommodation was even worse than in Oxford. He was sent to parliament on 17 February to report on the difficult negotiations but with parliament unable to find any solutions to avert an impasse the talks broke down. In July Whitelocke and Holles were accused by Thomas Savile, earl of Sussex, of high treason because of their private dealings with the king in Oxford. Both were cleared of the charge and told that they could, if they wished, prosecute Savile (by then in the Tower) for damages. By May 1646 Whitelocke was on very good terms with Cromwell. A year later he spoke against parliament's plans to disband the New Model Army, arguing that a victorious army, unemployed, was liable to assume power over its leaders. In this he opposed Holles, against whom the army once more brought accusations relating to the 1644 contacts with the king, in which Whitelocke had also been involved. In the meantime, having recovered his Fawley estate, Whitelocke moved his ever-growing family to Phyllis Court, attending more to his legal business than to parliament. He had been appointed attorney to the duchy of Lancaster and in March 1648 the Commons voted him a keeper of the great seal, for one year, at a salary of £1000.

The king's execution and the protectorate Whitelocke kept busy in his judicial post during the army's seizure of power at the end of 1648, though in late December he and his colleague Sir Thomas Widdrington did discuss with Cromwell the future of the nation, and worked on plans for a compromise settlement between army and parliament. On 23 December he was appointed to a committee of thirty-eight to prepare charges against King Charles. He never attended it: he had spoken in the Commons against

the trial and 'resolved to hazard all, rather then to goe contrary to his conscience'. On 30 January 1649, the day of Charles's execution, he 'stayed all day att home, troubled att the death of the King this day, & praying to God to keep his judgements from us'. On 14 February he was appointed to the new council of state, but avoided giving approval of recent events, which was at first required of members. He opposed the abolition of the House of Lords but was compelled to draft the bill enacting it. He tried to refuse appointment as a commissioner of the great seal of the Commonwealth; the Commons rejected his excuses and he defended his decision to continue on grounds of 'necessity' and the need to preserve the course of the law.

On 16 May 1649 Whitelocke's wife Frances died; he was distraught. After he returned to work, sometimes in tears, he was put in charge of the late king's rare books and medals in St James's Library. In November 1649 he denounced proposals to expel lawyers from parliament, and took part in law reform (including the conduct of legal proceedings in English). He was a constant defender of the common law and his profession. By 1650 friends had begun to introduce him to eligible widows, but he would only consider marrying somebody who would be kind to his ten children. Within days of the February funeral of Rowland Wilson MP, friends suggested Whitelocke should approach his childless widow, Mary (d. 1684), daughter of Bigley Carleton, a London grocer, but he thought it too soon. In April 1650 her chaplain, the Independent minister George Cokayn, brought them together in London and in June the couple met at the home of Cokayn's parents at Cotton End, Bedfordshire, and the courtship began. Mary said she liked Whitelocke's honesty in saying that his money and estates must go to his ten children, while if he and Mary had children she must support them from the fortune left to her by Wilson. On 5 August they rode to Bromham church and were married secretly and on 5 September they were married again, in Hackney church, the speaker and other MPs attending the ceremony. Mary was as tender towards her ten stepchildren as if they were her own, but was in some ways more indulgent than an 'own Mother'. Her first child, Samuel (for whom she later wrote 'Advice to her son Samuel'), was born on 30 May 1651; four more sons and two daughters followed.

In September 1651 parliament sent Whitelocke and three others to congratulate Cromwell on his victory at Worcester against the future Charles II. In November, when Cromwell asked him to support a relative's case in chancery, Whitelocke said he could only follow his conscience and heard later that Cromwell had expected more compliance. The same thing occurred when Cromwell consulted him about the settlement of the nation, as a republic or a modified monarchy; Whitelocke favoured mixed monarchy. In June 1652 he was offered the profitable post of commissioner for the government of Ireland but refused it, believing Cromwell and others wanted him out of the way. Walking in St James's Park in November Whitelocke chanced to meet Cromwell, who respectfully asked his opinion on the state of the country. Whitelocke said that the army was too powerful while many MPs were corrupt, with nobody to control them. Suddenly Cromwell asked 'What if a man should take uppon him to be King?' Whitelocke rejected the idea, saying that Cromwell had as much power as a king, without the title, but that if there were to be a monarch Charles Stuart, king of the Scots, was now so weak that he would accept any terms. Cromwell's manner changed. In April 1653 Whitelocke opposed plans to dissolve the Rump Parliament. In Cromwell's speech at the forced dissolution he was reported as 'looking sometimes and pointing upon particular persons' including Whitelocke, 'to whom he gave very sharp language, though he named them not' (R. Blencave, ed., *Sydney Papers*, 1825, 140). In August 1653 Whitelocke was named as ambassador-extraordinary to Queen Kristina of Sweden. Mary, who was pregnant, begged him not to go, interpreting the appointment as a punishment for having confronted Cromwell, for refusing to judge the king, and for championing the law and the people's rights. His mission was to secure a treaty of amity and the freedom of the Sound. In November he sailed for Sweden with six ships, some ninety-seven men, three laundry-women, and a coach and horses. They landed in Göteborg and on 30 November, with local saddle-horses and wagons, the convoy set off for Uppsala, to be greeted ceremoniously on 20 December. Whitelocke's charm and diplomacy worked well with the young queen. He recorded their conversations in direct speech, including Kristina's confiding in him her decision to abdicate, and his attempt to dissuade her. They became friendly enough to joke and tease each other. Whitelocke negotiated a treaty of amity, which has never been revoked, and was knighted by Kristina. Other matters were postponed for future negotiation. Cromwell, meanwhile, was proclaimed lord protector. Whitelocke and his retinue left Uppsala in May 1654, travelling home via Germany. At a party in Hamburg he was taken very ill. His doctor suspected poison. After nearly being shipwrecked Whitelocke's vessel anchored near Gravesend on 30 June. He disembarked the next day and joined his family in Chelsea, to an emotional welcome, after eight months' absence.

Cromwell welcomed his return and, two days later, greeted Whitelocke in Whitehall with a show of affection. On 14 July Whitelocke took the oath as a commissioner of the new great seal. He was elected for Buckinghamshire in the first protectorate parliament, which met on 3 September 1654. He reported to the house on his embassy, and was voted £2000 to cover arrears. After Cromwell summarily dissolved parliament on 22 January 1655 Whitelocke was approached by the Leveller John Wildman, inviting him to join in a conspiracy against Cromwell, but although he thought the conspirators' declaration on liberty and justice was sound he refused to take part. Cromwell instructed the keepers of the great seal to endorse an ordinance to reform chancery, which he and his council had prepared. Whitelocke and Widdrington objected, claiming that only parliament had authority to alter matters of law. They were dismissed on 8 June, losing a substantial part of their income. Conscious that they had

exercised liberty of conscience, Cromwell recompensed them, on 2 July, by renewing their appointments as commissioners of the treasury, at £1000 a year each. Later that month Whitelocke was appointed, with two others, to welcome the Swedish ambassador, who came to negotiate a trade agreement, which was duly concluded. A member of the committee for trade and navigation, Whitelocke was consulted by Cromwell on foreign affairs. In the second protectorate parliament, which assembled on 17 September 1656, he was again returned for Buckinghamshire. On 27 January 1657 Speaker Widdrington was too ill to take the chair and the house appointed Whitelocke to take his place. He described it as the most difficult, troublesome employment he had ever experienced. Friends said he kept them to the point in debates and dispatched more business than in all previous weeks. He was cordially thanked by the house, and paid £500. Ironically, in view of his earlier advice, Whitelocke was appointed chairman of the committee presenting 'The humble petition and advice', asking the protector to take the title of king. Cromwell refused. At a second attempt he appeared to be amenable, then changed his mind since it might cause mutiny in the army. About this time he often consulted Whitelocke and others behind closed doors. After three or four hours they would relax, and he and Whitelocke would smoke their pipes. Whitelocke welcomed the freedom conferred by the adjournment of parliament from 26 June 1657, but started suffering from kidney stones. On 10 December he received a writ of summons to the protector's new upper house as Lord Whitelocke, and he reported his refusal of Cromwell's offer of a viscountcy. Whitelocke had protested in vain at the suppression of Christmas worship by soldiers, arguing that this was contrary to liberty of conscience.

Cromwell died on 3 September 1658, his son Richard succeeding as lord protector. Whitelocke was often consulted by Richard Cromwell (whom he refers to by his first name) and wrote of Richard's behaving discreetly and better than was expected. At the old protector's funeral, on 23 November, Whitelocke was one of twelve pall-bearers. Unsolicited, Richard reappointed him a keeper of the great seal. By May 1659 the regime had collapsed and army officers took it on themselves to invite back members of the Rump of the Long Parliament, without a king, a single person, or House of Lords. Whitelocke was elected a member of the new council of state, but lost his commissionership of the great seal, and refused the post of a commissioner to mediate peace between Sweden and Denmark, at their negotiations over the Sound. Thomas Scott, the regicide, hinted falsely that Whitelocke was corresponding with Charles II or one of his ministers. In July and August, as president of the council, Whitelocke received reports of insurrections, including that of Sir George Booth, in Lancashire and Cheshire, which was suppressed; he received a letter begging him to spare the rebel's life, which he did. On 13 October the discontented army expelled parliament and Whitelocke was sent for by the council of state to face the officers. To avoid bloodshed, it was agreed that parliament would not sit, the general council of officers would provide for preservation of peace, and a new form of government would be devised. The officers chose Whitelocke, with twenty-two others, to govern under the title the committee of safety. He consented, believing this was better than to have soldiers governing with the sword. He was chosen, with five others, to plan a form of commonwealth government, and was appointed keeper of the great seal. By the end of November he sensed that George Monck intended to restore the king; he wanted Monck checked but was ignored. Instructed by the council of officers, he sealed a proclamation, in December, summoning a parliament for 4 January, without a king or House of Lords, but when the officers tried to stipulate election methods and MPs' qualifications, he insisted it would be contrary to his oath to seal such writs.

Restoration and later career Restoration being inevitable, Whitelocke was asked to urge Fleetwood to send someone trustworthy to the king to negotiate reasonable terms, rather than allow Monck to arrange an unconditional restoration. Charles Fleetwood, the commander-in-chief, asked Whitelocke whether he would go and Whitelocke agreed, but shortly afterwards Vane and Desborough made Fleetwood change his mind. The Rump Parliament reassembled yet again on 26 December, with Monck's support. Whitelocke knew he would meet with hostility, having served on the committee of safety, and stayed away. A note from Speaker Lenthall reminded him of his duty to attend but when he did so he found some former friends were very reserved. There was talk of sending him to the Tower. Disguised in a long coat, on the snowy evening of 30 December he rode out of London with a servant of Samuel Wilson (Mary's brother-in-law). Soon Whitelocke pulled off the road to put on a periwig, as further disguise, and they made their way to Hunsdon House, Hertfordshire, home of William Willoughby, where he arrived without warning but was welcomed and protected. On Whitelocke's instructions, Mary returned the great seal to the speaker, who commended the action. She wrote to her husband through Willoughby, reporting, on 10 January 1660, that parliament was planning to consider the case of MPs who had served on the committee of safety. He returned to London but decided it was too dangerous to appear in parliament. Mary brought him news of events, and on 24 January he was summoned to attend the house in a week's time, or be fined £20. He was undaunted, but hoped Monck's expected arrival might alter parliament's plans, which it did. On 18 February Monck indicated that he favoured the readmission of MPs excluded in 1648. Despite this, Whitelocke expected to be arrested.

On 1 May 1660 Charles II's declaration of Breda was brought to parliament, granting free pardon to all who applied within forty days, apart from any whom parliament might except. The king entered London ceremoniously on 29 May 1660. In June Whitelocke wrote an impressive defence of his political record—he was in jeopardy from people he had opposed in court or parliament, who now wanted revenge. Monck, a former friend whom

he had helped, asserted (with others) that, under the second exception of the Act of Pardon and Oblivion, Whitelocke should be disabled from ever again holding office. Whitelocke visited Monck, who acknowledged that they had been friends but said that Whitelocke's telling the common council that he, Monck, was planning the Restoration might have ruined the whole enterprise. Whitelocke obtained a certificate, addressed to the Commons and signed by several royalists, confirming acts of kindness he had done for them when they were in trouble and he in power. But there were demands for money: the earl of Berkshire, whose daughter had been imprisoned by order of the committee of safety, demanded £500; if the money was not forthcoming, he would persuade the Lords to have Whitelocke excepted. Thomas Napper, Whitelocke's former clerk and later a royalist colonel, fulfilled his promise to help Whitelocke in return for past kindnesses and arranged an interview with the king in June 1660. This went well; Whitelocke restored the treasures from the royal library, telling the king he could have sold the fifth-century Codex Alexandrinus for £4000 overseas, but saved it for his majesty. This valuable introduction appeared to be a friendly gesture, but the following year Napper came for his reward, expecting at least £500. Whitelocke paid £250, which was accepted disdainfully. In parliament Whitelocke's pardon was carried by fifty voices in June 1660; he wished to have this confirmed under the great seal but had to send the chancellor (former friend Ned Hyde) a 'present' of £250, plus 'fees' totalling £37 18s. 8d.

In July 1660 Whitelocke and his family moved to a house in Coleman Street, returning sometimes to Fawley Court. He was in the country in January 1661 when news came of the Coleman Street riot, led by the Fifth Monarchist Thomas Venner. Soldiers raided his Coleman Street house and enemies told the king, falsely, that Whitelocke lived in Coleman Street to advise the 'fanatics'. Some days later, Charles announced that Whitelocke was unfit to serve as a governor of Sutton Hospital. In due course Whitelocke moved to Chancery Lane, closer to his Middle Temple chambers; he also purchased Chilton Lodge, near Hungerford, with Mary's money. Unsolicited, he had decided to write a treatise for King Charles, entitled 'Whitelockes notes upon the kings writt for choosing members of parliament' (published posthumously in 1766). He handed the work, one volume at a time, to the chancellor who told him, on receiving the second of three volumes in April 1661, that the king was very pleased with the first. In March 1663 the king sent a message asking Whitelocke to write his opinion on the royal prerogative in matters ecclesiastical (following parliament's rejection of his first declaration of indulgence). There was no suggestion of payment, but Whitelocke had welcomed Charles's promise, at Breda, to allow freedom of conscience. By 25 March he finished 'The kings right to graunt indulgence in matters of religion'. Although his monthly earnings were small, in December 1663 he sealed the lease on a large house in Fleet Street, giving up the one in Chancery Lane.

Whitelocke's diary entries grow shorter from this time,

with references to family illnesses and discontent. Although suffering from kidney stones, dropsy, and piles, he continued his legal work. Prince Rupert consulted him in June 1671 on his rights as constable of Windsor Castle, saying that an opinion in Whitelocke's hand would satisfy the king. Fees from clients are noted monthly in the diary, ranging from 5 shillings for a servant, to £20 on one occasion, but usually 10 shillings or £1. In June 1675, ill though he was, he earned £5. In July, the month in which he died, he entered two fees of 10 shillings. In the last ten years of his life, with a restricted income from rents and fees, and with some of his children at home young enough to be grandchildren, he still spent money improving his land. Active as ever with his writing, besides his diary, which he continued until a week before he died, he wrote fair copies of sermons he preached to the family. He sometimes attended the local church before conducting a conventicle at Chilton Lodge, which was open house to outsiders wishing to attend; the church sometimes sent a spy. He often preached, as did the popular Independent minister, George Cokayn. A young client, the Quaker William Penn, sometimes came to hear Whitelocke, sometimes to preach himself. Years later Penn published *Quench not the Spirit* (1711), a selection of Whitelocke's sermons, describing him as 'one of the most accomplished Men of the Age' and quoting his definition of religion as 'the Work of the Spirit of God in the Hearts and Souls of Men'. Whitelocke died on 28 July 1675, a few days before his seventieth birthday, and was buried, as he wished, unostentatiously in Fawley church on 6 August. The pleasures and concerns of family life weave in and out of his public life, in his diary and 'Annales', but were expunged by the editor of 'Annales', Arthur Annesley, earl of Anglesey, when publishing them as *Memorials of the English Affairs* in 1682. An edition of *The Diary of Bulstrode Whitelocke, 1605–1675* was published in 1990.

Assessments of the man A 'trimmer', who swam with the tide, or a man who spoke up for law and freedom of conscience? Whitelocke was despised by some historians down to the late twentieth century. Thomas Carlyle labelled him 'Dryasdust', 'our Pedant friend' who showed 'occasional friskiness; most unexpected, as if the hippopotamus should show a tendency to dance'. Charles Morton, editing the first edition of Whitelocke's *Journal of the Swedish Ambassy* (1772), described him as 'a man of sense, learning, integrity, spirit, temper … and knowledge of the world'. Sir Charles Firth in the *Dictionary of National Biography* considered his work was 'greatly overestimated by Whig writers'. Whitelocke emerges from his own records as highly intelligent, musical, flamboyant, with a good opinion of himself, very loving, refusing to toe a party line if he thought it was wrong, and consistently a staunch defender of freedom.   RUTH SPALDING

Sources B. Whitelocke, 'Annales of his own life dedicated to his children', BL, Add. MSS 53726, 37341–37345, 4992 · *The diary of Bulstrode Whitelocke, 1605–1675*, ed. R. Spalding, British Academy, Records of Social and Economic History, new ser., 13 (1990); repr. (1991) [incl. list of Whitelocke's principal MSS and pubd works] · *Liber famelicus of Sir James Whitelocke, a judge of the court of king's bench in the reigns of James I and Charles I*, ed. J. Bruce, CS, old ser., 70 (1858) · R. Spalding, *Contemporaries of Bulstrode Whitelocke, 1605–1675* (1990) · *DNB* · B. Whitelocke, *Memorials of the English affairs* (1709) · B. Whitelocke, *Quench not the spirit*, ed. W. Penn (1711) · B. Whitelocke, *Notes uppon the king's writt for choosing members of parlement*, ed. C. Morton, 2 vols. (1766) · R. Spalding, *The improbable puritan* (1975) · B. Whitelocke, *A journal of the Swedish ambassy*, ed. [C. Morton], 2 vols. (1772) · A. Woolrych, *Commonwealth to protectorate* (1982) · P. Crawford, *Denzil Holles* (1979) · Longleat House, Wiltshire, Whitelocke MSS · parish register, Fawley, Buckinghamshire, Bucks. RLSS, 6 Aug 1675 [burial]
Archives BL, corresp., diaries, and papers, Add. MSS 4211, 4749–4754, 4902, 4991–4995, 21099, 31984, 32093, 36792, 37341–37347, 53725–53728, 59780, 64867; Egerton MS 997 · Bucks. RLSS, estate MSS · CUL, parliamentary diary, 1626 · Longleat House, Wiltshire, personal and collected papers incl. diary · Royal Arch., governors' book · U. Reading, MSS · University of Lund, Sweden, phrase book | Bodl. Oxf., MSS Rawl., letters to Thurloe and Cromwell
Likenesses oils, 1634, NPG [*see illus.*] · oils, 1636–49, St John's College, Oxford · portrait, *c*.1650, NPG · A. and T. Simon, silver medal, 1653, BM · W. Faithorne, line engraving, 1656, BM, NPG · W. J. Alais, statue (after contemporary print by Faithorne), repro. in R. H. Whitelocke, *Memoirs biographical and historical of Bulstrode Whitelocke* (1860)
Wealth at death £50 or £20 p.a. legacies to some of children; rings (each valued at 20s.) to all children, grandchildren, trustees, and certain friends and relatives

Whitelocke, Edmund (1565–1608), courtier, was born on 10 February 1565, in the parish of St Gabriel Fenchurch Street, London, the son of a merchant, Richard Whitelocke (*c*.1533–1570), and his wife, possibly named Joan (*c*.1528–1607), daughter of John Colte and widow of another merchant, named Brockhurst, who had left her a 'competent estate'. The eldest of four boys, the youngest being the future judge Sir James *Whitelocke (1570–1632), Edmund was aged five when his father died of pleurisy in Bordeaux. His mother preserved and invested the legacy left by his father for their sons' education, despite her third marriage, to another merchant, Thomas Price, 'a notable unthrift'. Her sons learned Latin, Greek, Hebrew, French, music, dancing, 'and to write fair' (*Liber famelicus*, 6). Edmund Whitelocke was sent to Merchant Taylors' School, then in 1581 to Christ's College, Cambridge, where he graduated BA. He was admitted about 1585 to Lincoln's Inn, where he 'spent his time among to[o] good cumpanions', and in 1587 'betoke himself to travail into foreyne kingdoms … to redeem his mispent time', visiting numerous universities and learning languages (*Liber famelicus*, 8). The governor of Provence made him captain of a troop of infantrymen stationed in Marseilles, then in Grenoble. Whitelocke failed to keep in touch with his family for nearly twelve years.

After his return to England, Whitelocke's wit and sophistication ensured that 'he grew into great goodliking of many Englishe noblemen' (*Liber famelicus*, 8) and he spent the rest of his life at their expense, notably with Roger Manners, earl of Rutland, who frequently housed him. In 1601 he was arrested and charged with high treason for involvement in the earl of Essex's plot. His account of events was set out in a long letter dated 11 February sent to Robert Cecil, secretary of state. He claimed that on 8 February he had gone in search of Rutland, finding him with a party of gentlemen at Essex House, where 'he willed me to attend him ... presuming, as the ... rumour of the whole company was, that they went for the ending of some private quarrel, I went with him' (*Salisbury MSS*, 11.40–1). Learning that this was not the case, Whitelocke abruptly left the conspirators and hid in the house of a 'citizen of good repute' (ibid.). In spite of this he was arrested, imprisoned, and charged, but as no evidence was found against him he was committed to the custody of his brother James and soon afterwards was discharged.

Whitelocke's next misadventure occurred as a result of his friendship with Henry Percy, ninth earl of Northumberland, whom he supported in a quarrel with Sir Francis Vere in 1602. On 4 November 1605, the eve of the Gunpowder Plot, Whitelocke chanced to dine at Syon House with Northumberland and the earl's distant cousin, Thomas Percy, 'the principal agent in that treason'. Imprisoned once more, he was again released with no evidence against him. For the rest of his life he lived 'with most dependancye upon the erl', who awarded him £40 per annum, later increased to £60. He had permission to visit Northumberland, imprisoned in the Tower until 1621, 'and so passed his time in mirthe and good companye' (*Liber famelicus*, 9). At some point he also became the confidant of Robert Radcliffe, fifth earl of Sussex, and stayed in his house, New Hall, in Essex. In 1602 it was reported that the earl, who was living with one of the countess's former gentlewomen, 'hyres Capt Whitlocke, with monie and ... suites' to tell the Countess 'howe he buyes his wench a wastcote of 10£, and puts hir in hir velvet gowne ... It is conjectured that Capt Whitlocke ... hath incited the E[arl] to followe this sensuall humour ... as he did the E[arl] of Rutland' and that as 'a shuttlecock' he 'flyes up and downe from one nobleman to an other; good for nothing but to ... help them to loose tyme' (*Diary of John Manningham*). Whitelocke died at New Hall from a stomach disorder about 24 August 1608 and was honoured by burial in the Sussex family vault at St Andrew's Church, Boreham, Essex, on 5 September. In a letter of 20 September Dudley Carleton wrote that 'capt. Whitlock, ... is so lamented by all bo[o]n companions as yf the world had not bin worthy of him'. RUTH SPALDING

Sources *Liber famelicus of Sir James Whitelocke, a judge of the court of king's bench in the reigns of James I and Charles I*, ed. J. Bruce, CS, old ser., 70 (1858), iv–v, 4–11, 16 · GEC, *Peerage* · *The manuscripts of his grace the duke of Rutland*, 4 vols., HMC, 24 (1888–1905), vol. 4 · *Calendar of the manuscripts of the most hon. the marquis of Salisbury*, 24 vols., HMC, 9 (1883–1976), vols. 11–12, 14, 17–18 · Cooper, *Ath. Cantab.*, 2.494–5 · *Diary of John Manningham ..., 1602–1603*, ed. R. P. Sorlien (1976), 97, 130 · *CSP dom.*, 1598–1601, 548, 596 · parish register, St Andrew, Boreham, 5 Sept 1608 [burial] · R. Spalding, *Contemporaries of Bulstrode Whitelocke* (1990), 415–18
Archives BL, Add. MS 53725

Whitelocke, Sir James (1570–1632), judge, was born on 28 November 1570, a twin and the youngest of four sons of Richard Whitelocke (*c*.1533–1570), a London merchant, and his wife, possibly called Joan (*c*.1528–1607), previously

Sir James Whitelocke (1570–1632), by unknown artist, *c*.1632

widow of one Brockhurst and daughter of John Colte of Little Munden, Herefordshire. His eldest brother was Edmund *Whitelocke (1565–1608). Their father died trading in France three weeks before the twins' birth. While his brothers pursued adventurous lives (William was killed serving with Sir Francis Drake, while Richard travelled abroad as a merchant), James undertook an ambitious study regime in the face of family financial difficulties and his mother's remarriage on 5 November 1571 to Thomas Price, which proved unhappy. Rich detail of his early life and his career is contained in his 'Liber famelicus' or family book, which also offers unusually candid insights into early Stuart law and politics.

Admitted to Merchant Taylors' School in 1575, Whitelocke won a scholarship to St John's College, Oxford, from where he matriculated in July 1588 and where he later became a fellow. His recollections of Oxford suggest the importance of lay, humanist ideals for his education. His college tutor, Rowland Searchfield, subsequently bishop of Bristol, stressed the study of 'logique and the artes, but above all of historye' (*Liber famelicus*, 13). Yet he also developed friendships at Oxford with men who were later at the forefront of an Arminian design for the church, including William Laud and John Buckeridge, then fellows at St John's. Having embarked on study for the degree of bachelor of civil laws, its lacklustre formal curriculum led Whitelocke to exploit provision for absences from college in order concurrently to study common law. He entered New Inn in 1590 and progressed to the Middle Temple in March 1593, but gained the BCL on 1 July 1594 and remained a fellow at St John's until 1598. As a student in Oxford and London he struggled financially and undertook work for St John's and as a solicitor to make ends meet. His studious character and an active role in the educational life of the inns presaged his call to the bar on 24 October 1600.

On 10 September 1602 Whitelocke contracted what was to be a long and happy marriage to Elizabeth (1575–1631), daughter of Edward Bulstrode of Hedgerly Bulstrode, Buckinghamshire, and his wife, Cecily Croke. They had seven children, of whom four—Mary, Joan, Dorothy and James—died in infancy; Elizabeth, Cecilia, and Bulstrode *Whitelocke (1605–1675) survived. The marriage also provided a house in Fleet Street, a point of entry into the Buckinghamshire and Oxfordshire gentry, and valuable professional connections in the bride's uncles John Croke, then judge in Wales and recorder of London, and George Croke, then a bencher at the Inner Temple. In 1606 Whitelocke became recorder of Woodstock, a few miles north of Oxford. Associations developed in the university led to legal work as steward of St John's, Eton College (from 1610), Westminster School (also from 1610), and the court preserving the liberties of St Martin's-le-Grand in the City, and to annual retainers from bishops John Buckeridge, Richard Neile, and John Howson. In London, Whitelocke gained the patronage of Sir Francis Bacon, Sir Julius Caesar, and Sir Lionel Cranfield, moving between the courts of king's bench, chancery, requests, wards, Star Chamber, and constable. This, coupled with assize work centred on Oxford and assisted by the patronage of Sir David Williams and Sir George Croke, ensured that Whitelocke's income grew steadily. From 1607 he purchased properties near Whitechurch and Witney, Oxfordshire, while renting Clewer House near Windsor. Between 1616 and 1620 he strained his resources to buy £9000 worth of property, most notably the manor of Fawley Court, Berkshire, on the Thames 40 miles west of London.

While in London, Whitelocke extended his intellectual interests through involvement with the Society of Antiquaries, preparing papers on topics such as 'Antiquity, use and cermony of lawful combats in England' and other matters of native custom. The collapse of the society in 1607 mirrored Whitelocke's own uneasy negotiation of common and civil law jurisdictional rivalries. He was elected MP for Woodstock in 1610, and served on a variety of parliamentary committees deploying his legal knowledge. He assumed a highly visible role in the debates on impositions prompted by *Bate's Case* (1606), providing a famous declaration of parliamentary rights which, it has been argued, cut to the heart of constitutional tensions between royal and parliamentary power. Seeking consensus over general principles of taxation, Whitelocke's claim that 'the power of the King in Parliament is greater than his power out of Parliament, and doth rule and control it' (*State trials*, 2.482) was never intended to be controversial, but unwittingly contributed to a new language of politics that emerged after his death, in part through its publication in *A Learned and Necessary Argument to Prove that each Subject hath a Propriety in his Goods* (1641). In separate

legal briefs challenging the jurisdiction of a royal commission into navy corruption (1609) and the jurisdiction of the court of earl marshal (1613), Whitelocke drew himself into a collision course with the Howard family and the lord chancellor, Lord Ellesmere, drawing censure and imprisonment from the crown. On the order of the privy council he was imprisoned from 18 May to 13 June 1613, obtaining release through a personal petition to the king for clemency. Outside parliament, for the four years until his death Ellesmere stymied Whitelocke's political ambitions, earning the latter's criticism that he was 'the greatest enemye to the common law that did ever bear office of state in this kingdome' (*Liber famelicus*, 53). Whitelocke was not cowed but continued his opposition to impositions as MP for Woodstock in 1614: his notes challenging the crown over this issue were burned by the king's order following parliament's 'addled' and abrupt dissolution.

Throughout his career Whitelocke monitored factional influence on legal appointments, privately criticizing—but ultimately accepting—the growing influence of George Villiers. In 1616 he resigned from a lucrative clerkship of enrolments in the court of king's bench as the now Viscount Villiers wrested control of the office. In 1618 Whitelocke was promoted in a contested election for the recordership of London, backed by a merchant faction, but was rejected by the king in favour of Robert Heath, preferred candidate of Villiers the new marquess of Buckingham. Buckingham appears to have borne no grudge against Whitelocke, appointing him to commissions of the peace for Buckinghamshire and Oxfordshire in 1617 and 1618.

In 1619 Whitelocke was made a bencher of the Middle Temple and autumn reader. Choosing the thirteenth chapter of Henry VIII's statute on benefices, he addressed the contentious issues of patronage, non-residence, and plurality, mounting a moderate appeal for the rights of crown and clergy. The reading was widely copied. The following year he was created serjeant-at-law, and on 29 October 1620 he was knighted. He sat again in the 1621 parliament as MP for Woodstock, but was largely absent, concentrating instead on judicial duties. With Buckingham's support, in June 1620 Whitelocke had been appointed chief justice of Chester. Over four years he administered justice in the county palatine of Chester and those border counties within the jurisdiction of the council of the marches of Wales. While financially lucrative (yielding over £1000 per annum), Whitelocke's relations with William Compton, earl of Northampton, president of the council, were poor and led in October 1624 to his removal from Chester to a puisne judgeship in the court of king's bench. He rode the Oxford circuit in 1625, the midland circuit in 1625, the northern in 1627 and 1628, and returned to the Oxford circuit from 1629 until the year of his death. His relations with the crown were strained when Charles I, seeking revenue to fight in Europe, revoked and reduced his circuit fees from 1625 to 1628, to Whitelocke's considerable unhappiness. In this period Whitelocke was also drawn into constitutional test cases which damaged his legal reputation. In the *Five knights' case* (1627) Whitelocke supported the crown's right to imprison subjects without providing explicit cause, but also asserted the subject's right to legal redress through writ of habeas corpus. In *Eliot's case* (1629) Whitelocke initially resisted crown attempts to impose conditions for bail, but then acquiesced in royal demands for security of good behaviour. Stressing the 'supereminent' power of the crown, Whitelocke dismissed John Eliot's claim for parliamentary privilege from prosecution, accusing him of 'sowing sedition to the destruction of the commonwealth' (*State trials*, 3.308). Only a spirited defence of these actions by his son, Bulstrode, prevented parliament from posthumously denouncing and fining Whitelocke.

While his wife was regarded a puritan, Whitelocke adopted a more moderate Calvinist stance, wherever possible avoiding judgment of those high-church clerics who supported him throughout his career. The Arminian vision of his friends put this approach under strain in the 1620s, as Buckeridge and Laud gathered multiple livings to themselves, leading Whitelocke to defend Buckeridge's pluralism to posterity in the 'Liber famelicus', but to challenge Laud's retention of a college parsonage on behalf of St John's in 1621. In 1628 Whitelocke upheld Bishop Neile's expulsion of Peter Smart from Durham Cathedral for preaching against high-church ceremonial. In 1629 he avoided the king's order to the judges of king's bench to release Jesuits arrested at Clerkenwell College, pleading absence from court during crucial parts of the hearing. In 1631 Whitelocke was openly criticized by junior Arminian clerics at the consecration of his private chapel; Bulstrode Whitelocke later suggested that his father privately thought William Laud 'too full of fire, though a just and good man', and worried that his 'want of experience in state matters, and his too much zeal for the Church, and heat, if he proceeded in the ways he was then in, would set this nation on fire' (BL, Add. MS 37343, fol. 201v).

Whitelocke's life was dominated by his ambition to leave a tangible legacy to his family through professional achievement. Despite a 'grave' concern for his children, it is clear that he found time to 'sport' and sing with them; Bishop John Williams remarked that 'no subject in Christendom had better musicke then Judge Whitelocke had in his house' (*Diary of Bulstrode Whitelocke*, 44–5, 51, 65). His son remembered him as a man 'full of witt and pleasantness especially att meales, and as there was occasion his discourse was mixed with excellent learning' (ibid., 66). Predicting his own passing upon the death of his wife on 28 May 1631, Whitelocke retired from public life to settle the details of his estate, leaving Fawley Court and £4500 as well as plate and household goods to his son, £2500 for Cecilia's marriage portion, £10 a quarter to his married daughter Elizabeth, and £100 to build a monument to his wife and himself (which survives) in the south transept of Fawley church. He died on 22 June 1632.

D. X. POWELL

Sources *Liber famelicus of Sir James Whitelocke, a judge of the court of king's bench in the reigns of James I and Charles I*, ed. J. Bruce, CS, old ser., 70 (1858) · D. X. Powell, *Sir James Whitelocke's 'Liber famelicus', 1570–1632: law and politics in early Stuart England* (Bern, 2000) · D. X.

Powell, 'James Whitelocke, chief justice of Cheshire, 1620–1624', *Transactions of the Historic Society of Lancashire and Cheshire*, 143 (1993), 1–34 · W. R. Prest, *The rise of the barristers: a social history of the English bar, 1590–1640* (1986) · *The diary of Bulstrode Whitelocke, 1605–1675*, ed. R. Spalding, British Academy, Records of Social and Economic History, new ser., 13 (1990) · R. Spalding, ed., *Contemporaries of Bulstrode Whitelocke, 1605–1675: biographies, illustrated by letters and other documents* (1990), 425–9 · Greaves & Zaller, *BDBR*, 318–19 · D. X. Powell, 'Sir James Whitelocke's extra-judicial advice to the crown in 1627', *HJ*, 39 (1996), 737–42 · D. X. Powell, 'Why did James Whitelocke go to jail in 1613?' 'Principle' and political dissent in Jacobean England', *Australian Journal of Law and Society*, 11 (1995), 169–90 · *State trials*, 2.479–520; 3.305–8 · G. Tyack, *Fawley Buckinghamshire: a short history of the church and parish* (1986) · B. Whitelocke, *Memorials of the English affairs*, new edn (1732) · will, PRO, PROB 11/62, sig. 113 · Foster, *Alum. Oxon.* · *IGI* [parish register of Beaconsfield]

Archives Longleat House, Wiltshire, corresp. and MSS, vols. 1–5, 21, 24, 26, parcel 9 | BL, letter to R. Cotton, Cotton Julius C.3, fol. 54 · BL, reading on benefices, Hargrave MS 198 · BL, 'Liber famelicus', Add. MS 53725 · Bodl. Oxf., letter to R. Cotton, MS Smith 71, fol. 59 · Bodl. Oxf., transcript of 'Liber famelicus' belonging to John Whitelocke, MS Dep. d804 · CUL, autograph academic commonplace book, MS Dd. 9. 20 · CUL, autograph law commonplace book, MS Dd. 3. 69 · Inner Temple, London, record of Eliot's case and judgment, MS Miscellaneous 19, fols. 241–266v, fols. 265–266v · Inner Temple, London, records examined and noted in the case of impositions, MS Petyt 537. 14, fols. 187v–213v · PRO, Chester crown book of judges' legal memoranda and notes, CHES 21/3, 15 James I–1 Charles I, fols. 49–107 · PRO, MSS relating to landholdings, C 142/481/36

Likenesses oils, *c.*1632, NPG [*see illus.*] · alabaster tomb effigy (with his wife), St Mary's Church, Fawley Court, Buckinghamshire; repro. in Tyack, *Fawley Buckinghamshire*

Wealth at death will dispenses with around £7100 in cash as well as annual allowances of £70, plate and household goods, Manor of Fawley Court (purchased for £9000) and other properties and assets in London and Buckinghamshire valued at over £2000: will, PRO, PROB 11/62, sig. 113

Whitelocke, John (1757–1833), army officer, was the son of John Whitelocke, steward to John, fourth earl of Ailesbury, and his wife, Sarah Liddiard (*d.* 7 June 1809). He was educated at Marlborough grammar school and Lewis Lochée's military academy in Chelsea, London, sponsored by Lord Ailesbury. He joined the 14th foot as ensign on 14 December 1778, by the influence of Viscount Barrington, recently secretary at war, and was soon appointed adjutant, and promoted to lieutenant on 28 April 1780. In 1782 the regiment went to Jamaica, and there about 1783 he married the daughter of William Lewis, a planter, of Cornwall, Jamaica. Her brother, Matthew Lewis, was office keeper at the Colonial Office.

Whitelocke's promotions came through influence more than military expertise. Yet he had real administrative abilities; it was very unusual for an ensign to be made adjutant in his first year of service, but he was successful. His early aristocratic sponsorship was complemented by useful connections in the political and administrative system of the army, but he was also an able administrator. Jamaica's diseases provided plenty of opportunities for advancement for the survivors, and, with influence, this ensured promotion. Whitelocke moved to the 36th foot as captain in 1784, and as major to a new battalion of the 60th four years later. Back in the West Indies he was appointed lieutenant-colonel in the 13th foot in 1791.

John Whitelocke (1757–1833), by James Hopwood the elder, pubd 1808 (after Hastings)

Whitelocke first saw action in September 1793 when, with the local rank of colonel, he was sent to St Domingue (Haiti) with his own regiment reinforced by other troops. He had only 700 soldiers, but succeeded in seizing Jeremie, and advanced along the southern peninsula of the island towards the capital, Port-au-Prince. It was a complex campaign, for the French planters were divided over their response to the revolution in France, the black slaves were rebellious, and yellow fever attacked Whitelocke's men. He was reinforced in February 1794, and at the second attempt captured Tiburon and directed the storm of Fort l'Acul, which opened the way to Port-au-Prince. Superseded in overall command, he led the attacking column which took the capital in June.

He was sent home with dispatches, and on 1 September 1795 was promoted colonel of the 6th West India regiment; he returned, as a local brigadier-general, to the West Indies, where he was employed on administrative duties in Jamaica. He returned to Britain in 1798 to be brigadier-general in Guernsey, was promoted major-general in June 1798, and was appointed lieutenant-governor of Portsmouth in May 1799.

This was a remarkable rise (ensign to general in twenty years). At Portsmouth he again had administrative duties, but for those of a more martial nature he had no aptitude: he was remembered in one exercise directing regiments into collisions and swamps, then leaving subordinates to sort things out. Yet he also successfully administered a recruitment drive for the fencibles, and calmed disputes between touchy officers. It was thus reasonable that he

should be made inspector-general of recruiting in November 1804. He rose to lieutenant-general in October 1805.

Whitelocke's career, rapid promotion, and post as inspector-general were all the result of adhesion to the Pitt regime, and the fall of Pitt's government in 1806 rendered him vulnerable. The new prime minister, Lord Grenville, was keen on retrenchment, and the new secretary of state, William Windham, had his own ideas about recruiting. The news of the capture by an unauthorized British force of Buenos Aires, and then of its recapture by the Spaniards, was therefore seen as an opportunity to remove both Whitelocke and his office.

Several reinforcing expeditions were sent to the River Plate, of which one, commanded by Brigadier-General Sir Samuel Auchmuty, captured Montevideo. Whitelocke was appointed to command all forces, and to act as governor of the province that he was expected to conquer, on 24 February 1807. He reached Montevideo on 10 May 1807 and had to wait for a month before the final reinforcement arrived. He used the time to organize an administration, among other things starting a dual-language newspaper as a vehicle for the new government.

Whitelocke's chief of staff, Major-General John Leveson Gower, had even less experience of combat than Whitelocke, but he devised a plan for the conquest of Buenos Aires which Whitelocke adopted. Gower, of the family of the marquesses of Stafford, was socially much above Whitelocke, and, closeted with him on the voyage south in the frigate Thisbe, he persuaded Whitelocke to accept the plan. The other commanders under Whitelocke were fighting men: generals Robert Craufurd and Samuel Auchmuty and admirals George Murray and Charles Stirling had between them fought in most continents and many battles; as a group they emphasized Whitelocke's martial deficiencies. He was not unimaginative, and he could see the difficulties in attacking Buenos Aires: a population of 70,000 and a grid layout of streets, where each block of buildings was a solidly built minor fort. He walked round Montevideo one day with Craufurd, pointing out such buildings and commenting on their strength. And yet he kept to Gower's plan, which ignored all this, and asked no one else for advice.

One small reinforcement from England failed to arrive, but Admiral Murray contributed 220 seamen, and British merchants were enrolled as a militia to help defend Montevideo. Whitelocke concentrated all available troops into the assault force, landing at Ensenada de Barragon, 32 miles from Buenos Aires, with 8500 men, on 28 June. Whitelocke divided his force into three, and these forces marched on the city, but lost touch with each other. Colonel Mahon's group was left east of the city; the division under Gower and Craufurd drove off a defending force at the outskirts of the city; the third, under Whitelocke, arrived a day later. Whitelocke's behaviour was foul-mouthed and hectoring, and alienated many; he was clearly nervous and uncertain.

The approach march took five days, and used up most of the soldiers' supplies. After a day's rest, Whitelocke revealed his (that is Gower's) plan: each regiment would advance along one or two of the parallel streets as far as the waterfront, at which point it was assumed that the assault would be successful. None of the more experienced soldiers raised objections. Some soldiers were ordered to advance with unloaded muskets, and in one case Gower even ordered them to remove their flints; two corporals with axes accompanied each column. These measures were copied from Auchmuty's successful assault on Montevideo, and were intended to facilitate the reduction of strong points, but the circumstances were now different.

The assault began at first light on 5 July, with thirteen columns advancing simultaneously. The outermost columns, two regiments under Auchmuty on the west and half the 45th under Major Jasper Nichols on the east, established themselves at strong points, respectively the plaza de Toros and the Residencia. In the centre a weak column of dismounted dragoons made no progress at all. Between these, however, there was much fighting and a series of comprehensive British defeats. Craufurd with the light brigade was driven to take refuge in the church of San Domingo, where, surrounded and attacked by sharpshooters and artillery, he was compelled to surrender. Half of the 45th under Colonel Guard suffered a similar fate, even more quickly. Both columns of the 88th had to surrender before reaching the waterfront. The 36th had to retreat out of the city to join up with Auchmuty; he also took command of the 5th, which did reach its objectives. In all, the resistance was much fiercer than the British had expected—better supplied, better armed, and more persistent. Many Spaniards in the houses were bypassed by the marching columns, and then emerged to attack the columns in the rear. A well-served and numerous artillery blocked the streets behind barricades.

Whitelocke knew nothing of this, for he remained all that day at his headquarters. He neither sought nor was given information until next day, when he received a demand for surrender from the Spanish commander, Santiago Liniers. He then went to Auchmuty's post and discovered the bad news. Of his force about 1200 were casualties or missing, and the Spaniards held 1800 prisoners. Whitelocke had about 5400 men available, divided into four widely separated groups. A proposal to bombard the city into surrender, using guns from the fleet, was made, but Whitelocke rejected it: he feared it would endanger the prisoners, but it was also clear that it would have failed—landing anything from the ships was extremely difficult, and it would have been impossible to keep men and guns supplied. Sheer distaste for the idea was another element.

The only alternative was to give up the attack. Once that was decided—with the concurrence of Auchmuty, Gower, and Murray—the whole British position in the Plate area unravelled. Montevideo was untenable alone, and the Spaniards held the prisoners, both those in Buenos Aires and the 71st foot from the previous year, as hostages. Whitelocke had the moral courage to agree to the complete evacuation of the Plate in exchange for the prisoners and supplies for the voyage home. The organization of the

forces for evacuation then brought out Whitelocke's administrative skills, and the troops were recovered and dispatched on time.

Whitelocke returned to England on 7 November 1807, and in January 1808 he was court-martialled at Chelsea. The government had changed again, and his former friends were back in power, but it had been the opposition's expedition. The court martial took seven weeks, and Whitelocke faced four charges covering poor diplomacy, military incompetence, and negotiation of a shameful surrender, each barely relevant to what had happened. He was found guilty and was cashiered. His fault lay in taking on a task beyond his capacity, for which those who appointed him should have shared the blame. It was also a task, in all probability, beyond the capacity of the British forces. All of those who recorded their impressions remarked that holding the Plate area against the wishes of the inhabitants was impossible: they wanted either Spanish rule or independence; a British conquest would have been extremely unpleasant, and ultimately a costly failure. Whitelocke's surrender and evacuation permitted the army to be returned to Britain to fight the real enemy, Napoleon. Many of Whitelocke's regiments went to fight in Spain later in 1808. Nevertheless he had shown himself incompetent.

Whitelocke made no further effort to justify himself. He lived latterly at Clifton, near Bristol, and died, aged seventy-six, on 23 October 1833, at Hall Barn Park, Beaconsfield, Buckinghamshire, the seat of his son-in-law, Sir Gore Ouseley, who had married his eldest daughter. He was buried in the west aisle of Bristol Cathedral.

JOHN D. GRAINGER

Sources *The Georgian era* (1833), 2.475 · Fortescue, *Brit. army*, vol. 5 · PRO, WO 1/1/161–162 · *DNB* · *Whitelocke's court martial* (1808) · B. Edwards, *History of the British West Indies* (1793–1801), 3.155–60 · *Annual Register* (1794), 174–5 · NA Scot., 9021, Cunningham of Thornton MSS 519, 544, 549 · *A memoir of the services of Lieutenant-General Sir Samuel Ford Whittingham*, ed. F. Whittingham, new edn (1868), chap. 2 · *A narrative of the expedition to and the storming of Buenos Ayres by the British army commanded by Lt-Gen Whitelocke* (1801) · L. Holland, diary, UCL · I. Fletcher, *The waters of oblivion: the British invasion of the Rio de la Plata, 1806–1807* (1991) · *GM*, 1st ser., 79 (1809), 589 · *GM*, 1st ser., 103/2 (1833), 475 · *N&Q*, 8 (1853), 521 · *N&Q*, 9 (1854), 87, 201–2 · *N&Q*, 10 (1854), 54

Likenesses J. Hopwood senior, stipple, pubd 1808 (after Hastings), BM, NPG [*see illus.*] · etching (Whitelocke at his trial), BM · stipple, BM

Whitelocke [Whitlock], **William** (c.1520–1584), historian, was born at Wokingham, Berkshire, the eldest son of Richard Whitelocke, holder of the manor of Beaches in Wokingham; his mother was said to be a member of the Grove family from Fingest, Buckinghamshire. After attending Eton College, he was admitted to King's College, Cambridge, in 1537 and graduated BA in 1542, proceeding MA in 1545 and BTh in 1553. He was a fellow of the college between 1540 and 1560, and, as vice-provost, was presented in December 1558 to the vicarage of Prescot in Lancashire; in July 1560 he was admitted to the rectory of Greenford, Middlesex, on the presentation of Sir Edward Thornton. He was collated in March 1561 by Bishop

Thomas Bentham to the prebend of Curborough in Lichfield Cathedral, 'in which church', according to his uncle Sir James Whitelocke, 'he lived for the latter part of his time altogeather' (Bruce, 3).

One of the few clergymen of the period to make a significant contribution to antiquarian studies, Whitelocke completed the first draft of a history of the cathedral church of Lichfield in 1569. His 'Chronicon Lichefeldensis ecclesie', which was compiled at the request of a fellow canon who was curious about the history of the cathedral, went through several drafts. It was mainly a condensed version of the final section, on the bishops of Lichfield, of the Lichfield chronicle written by Alan Ashbourne between 1323 and 1334. Whitelocke made several additions to Ashbourne's account of the holders of the see, and added a further series of brief biographies of the bishops, concluding with the consecration of Bishop Bentham in 1560. To compile his history he used material in the cathedral library, including another chronicle written by John Aston, a contemporary of Ashbourne. The new material which he added on Lichfield traditions, such as the site of a Mercian burial-ground, reflects Whitelocke's antiquarian interests. His episcopal biographies also contain material from the registers of the archbishops of Canterbury, which he might have owed to his friendship with his fellow antiquarian John Twyne, to whom Whitelocke was said to have given information about the dispersal of John Bale's library.

Whitelocke took the extracts from Ashbourne's chronicle from the copy presented to the cathedral by Thomas Chesterfield in the mid-fifteenth century. Henry Wharton, who published several accounts of the history of the cathedral in his Anglia sacra (1691), not only wrongly ascribed extracts from the original Lichfield chronicle to Thomas Chesterfield, but also incorrectly ascribed to Whitelocke another compendium, the 'Historia ecclesiae Lichfeldensis' written in 1575 by an anonymous author, who was possibly Lawrence Nowell, dean of Lichfield between 1560 and 1576. Four versions of Whitelocke's 'Chronicon' survive, all of them dedicated to his fellow canons; in December 1583 he presented an abridgement of the first draft to another antiquarian friend, the lawyer Francis Thynne. Whitelocke died in Lichfield, unmarried, early in 1584. ANN J. KETTLE

Sources M. W. Greenslade, The Staffordshire historians, Staffordshire RS, 4th ser., 11 (1982), 8–9 · H. E. Savage, Lichfield Cathedral: the Lichfield chronicles, an address (privately printed, Lichfield, 1915), 4, 10–12, 16 · Liber famelicus of Sir James Whitelocke, a judge of the court of king's bench in the reigns of James I and Charles I, ed. J. Bruce, CS, old ser., 70 (1858), ii, 3 · Venn, Alum. Cant., 1/4 · W. Sterry, ed., The Eton College register, 1441–1698 (1943) · [H. Wharton], ed., Anglia sacra, 1 (1691), xxxiv–xxxvi, 444–8 · 'Eiusdem authoris continuatio historiae Lichfeldensis ab anno MCCCLIX ad annum MDLIX', Anglia sacra, ed. [H. Wharton], 1 (1691), 448–59, esp. 448 · 'Additamenta ad historiam veterem Lichfeldensem, ex historia Lichfeldensi recentionis cuiusdam scripta circa annum MDLXXV', Anglia sacra, ed. [H. Wharton], 1 (1691), 444–7 · VCH Berkshire, 3.229–30 · H. E. Savage, Lichfield Cathedral: the cathedral under the Elizabethan settlement (1930), 17 · Fasti Angl. (Hardy), 1.594 · T. Harwood, The history and antiquities of the church and city of Lichfield (1806), 223 · M. McKisack, Medieval history in the Tudor age (1971), 63, 127

Archives BL, version of 'Chronicon', Cotton MS Cleopatra C.iii, fols. 240–65 (1583) · BL, version of 'Chronicon', Cotton MS Vespasian E.xvi, fols. 26–37 (1575) · BL, version of 'Chronicon', Harley MS 3839 (1569) · Bodl. Oxf., version of 'Chronicon', MS Ashmole 770, fols. 1–50 (1583)

Whitely, George. See Chandler, (Arthur) Bertram (1912–1984).

Whiter, Walter (1758–1832), philologist and literary scholar, born at Birmingham on 30 October 1758, was at King Henry VIII Grammar School, Coventry, for ten years, under Dr Edwards, where Robert Bree MD was a fellow pupil. He was admitted to Clare College, Cambridge, on 19 June 1776 as sizar, and graduated BA (1781) and MA (1784). On 4 April 1782 he was elected a fellow of Clare, probably on account of his reputation for classical and philological knowledge. He lived in his rooms in college from 1782 to 1797. Richard Porson was one of his close friends, and often wrote notes on the margin of Whiter's books. Porson in 1786 added some notes of his own and of Whiter to an edition by Hutchinson of Xenophon's Anabasis. These were issued separately from Valpy's press in 1810, and George Townsend added them to his edition of 1823.

Whiter was ordained priest in 1783, and was presented by his college in 1797 to the rectory of Hardingham in Norfolk; he held the benefice until his death. His clerical role did not inhibit his lively spirits. Baron Merian, in a letter to Dr Samuel Butler of Shrewsbury School, writes: 'I pity Whiter. A great etymologist, perhaps the greatest that ever lived. A genius certainly, but it seems, like most eminent artists, dissolute' (S. Butler, Life and Letters, 1896, 1.186). Every year on 23 April, the day of St George (titular saint of Hardingham church), it was his harmless practice to collect his friends at a picnic under a beech on a hillock called St George's Mount, and to claim from each of them an appropriate poem in Latin or English. A specimen of his verses on one of these occasions is in the Gentleman's Magazine (86/1, 1816, 542–3).

Whiter's first published work was A Specimen of a Commentary on Shakspeare (1794), containing notes on As You Like It and 'an attempt to explain and illustrate various passages on a new principle of criticism derived from Mr Locke's doctrine of the association of ideas'. Its contemporary reception was limited and critical. 'Such reviews as do exist, while agreeing on the commendation of Whiter's extreme learning, find his views too eccentric and his claims too inflated to make his book of any permanent value' (Whiter, Specimen of a Commentary, xxxi). It therefore went unnoticed by Coleridge, Hazlitt, and the Victorian critics. Only in the twentieth century was Whiter's perceptive treatment of trains of ideas and image clusters given its due, and seen to anticipate the work of such Shakespearian critics as Caroline Spurgeon and W. H. Clemens.

Whiter's other works include the first part of Etymologicon Magnum (1800), a universal etymological dictionary on a new plan, in the preface to which he enlarged on the value of the Romani language. These views and his word-speculations interested George Borrow, who made his acquaintance and introduced him, as understanding some twenty languages, into *Lavengro* (1851). Jeffrey wrote two articles on the *Etymologicon Magnum* in the *Monthly Review* (June and July 1802), assigning to Whiter 'much labour and shrewdness, with a considerable share of credulity'. Whiter also produced the *Etymologicon universale, or, Universal Etymological Dictionary on a New Plan* (vols. 1 and 2, 1822; vol. 3, 1825). These three large quarto volumes were printed partly at the cost of Cambridge University Press. The first volume was originally issued in 1811, and the preface to the first volume in the collected edition of 1822–5 retained the date 15 May 1811. In this work Whiter set out that 'consonants are alone to be regarded in discovering the affinities of words, and that the vowels are to be wholly rejected; that languages contain the same fundamental idea, and that they are derived from the earth'. Baron Merian styled it 'splendid, a very fine book indeed' (S. Butler, *Life and Letters*, 1896, 1.185) but modern lexicographers have found the etymologies unpersuasive. In *A Dissertation on the Disorder of Death, or that State called Suspended Animation* (1819), Whiter tried to show how the apparently dead should be treated with a view to their restoration to life. In the advertisement at the end he announced a series of essays to be called *Nova tentamina mythologica, or, Attempts to unfold various portions of mythology by a new principle*, but these were never printed and are now, with other manuscripts of Whiter, in the Cambridge University Library (*CUL Cat. of MSS*, 4.521, 543–4). Whiter died at Hardingham rectory on 23 July 1832, and was buried in the churchyard on 30 July, a large railed-in tomb being erected to his memory. A bust of him was placed in the library at Clare College but is now lost without trace.

W. P. COURTNEY, *rev.* JOHN D. HAIGH

Sources *GM*, 1st ser., 64 (1794), 928–30 · *GM*, 1st ser., 86/1 (1816), 542–3 · *GM*, 1st ser., 102/2 (1832), 185 · letters from Whiter to Dr Samuel Butler, BL, Add. MSS 34585, fols. 200, 205 · letter from Whiter to Dr Samuel Butler, BL, Add. MSS 34587, fol. 195 · private information (1900) [Clare College, Hardingham church] · Venn, *Alum. Cant.*, 2/6 · W. Whiter, *A specimen of a commentary on Shakespeare: being the text of the first (1794) edition, revised by the author and never previously published*, ed. A. Over and M. Bell, 2nd edn (1967), lxxxi, 233 [notes and intro.] · J. S. Watson, *The life of Richard Porson* (1861), 31–2, 347–50 · K. Muir, 'Shakespeare's imagery—then and now', *Shakespeare Survey*, 18 (1965), 46–57 · Allibone, *Dict.* · *Critical Review*, 32 (1771), 369 · review, *QR*, 81 (1849), 500–25, esp. 502 · *Monthly Review*, 38, 113, 276 · *British Critic*, 5 (1795), 280–90 · *N&Q*, 3rd ser., 6 (1864), 370 · J. Green, *Chasing the sun: dictionary-makers and the dictionaries they made* (1996), 291–2
Archives CUL, etymological collections and notes on Shakespeare; further etymological collections and notes on mythology
Likenesses lithograph (after bust), Norwich Castle Museum; repro. in Whiter, *Specimen of a commentary on Shakespeare*, ed. A. Over (1947), facing p. 6
Wealth at death under £1500; £300 bequeathed to Elizabeth Gibbons (presumably a housekeeper); remainder *in toto* to the Revd Charles Walter White, nephew: will, 1832, *Specimen*, ed. Over, xxix, n.i

Whiteside, James (1804–1876), judge and politician, was born on 12 August 1804 at Delgany, co. Wicklow, the second son of the Revd William Whiteside and Anne, *née* Robinson. Shortly after Whiteside's birth his father moved to Rathmines, near Dublin, where he died in 1806. Mrs Whiteside was left in narrow circumstances, but she

James Whiteside (1804–1876), by John Butler Yeats, 1866

was devoted to her children, and James was indebted to her for much of his early education. He entered Trinity College, Dublin, in 1822, and graduated BA; he proceeded MA in 1832. He had entered Gray's Inn in London in Hilary term 1828, but the following year he entered as a law student at the Inner Temple. He was called to the Irish bar in Easter term 1830. Whiteside spent his first year studying law in the chambers of Joseph Chitty, and on commencing legal practice he joined the north-east circuit. He married, in July 1833, Rosetta, daughter of William Napier of Belfast, and sister of Sir Joseph Napier, sometime lord chancellor of Ireland.

From 1831 Whiteside's progress at his profession was rapid, and he was made a queen's counsel in 1842. He rapidly gained a reputation for forensic advocacy, and his speech in defence of Daniel O'Connell (in the 1843 state trials of the principal members of the repeal movement) placed him in front of all his contemporaries at the Irish bar. Shortly after the O'Connell trials Whiteside's health obliged him temporarily to relinquish his profession. He visited Italy, and was later to publish a three-volume work, *Italy in the Nineteenth Century* (1848), as well as a translation of Luigi Canina's *Indicazione topografica di Roma antica* as *Vicissitudes of the Eternal City* (1849).

After returning to active work, Whiteside acted as leading counsel for the defence of the Young Ireland leader, William Smith O'Brien, and his fellow prisoners in the state trials at Clonmel in 1848, O'Brien having been arrested in the wake of a failed peasant uprising in Ballingarry. Three years later, in 1851, he entered parliament as Conservative member for Enniskillen. In 1859 he was chosen as one of the representatives of Dublin University, and held this position until his elevation to the bench. Whiteside's striking talent as a speaker made him a valuable accession to his party in the House of Commons, and it is said that when there was battle expected in the house, Lord Derby would say to him 'Now Whiteside, where's your shillelagh?' (Hogan and Osborough, 212). On the formation of Derby's first administration in 1852 he was appointed solicitor-general for Ireland, his brother-in-law Joseph Napier being attorney-general. He was in the same year elected a bencher of King's Inns. Whiteside himself was to fill the office of attorney-general from 1858 to 1859, in Derby's second government, and in 1858 he was sworn of the Irish privy council.

During the Liberal administration (1859–66) Whiteside was in opposition; but, despite the claims of his profession, he was able to devote much of his time to his parliamentary duties and took an eminent part in the counsels of the Conservative opposition. He attained a high position in the House of Commons, where his eloquence, wit, and geniality made him popular with all parties. In 1861, on his return to London after the marvellous speech in the celebrated Yelverton case—when he represented Maria Theresa Longworth, in the most famous of all his forensic efforts—Whiteside received a remarkable compliment, being greeted with general cheers as he entered the House of Commons for the first time after the conclusion of the trial.

Having proceeded DL at Dublin University in 1859, Whiteside received from Oxford University the honorary degree of DCL in 1863.

On the return of Lord Derby to office in 1866 Whiteside was again appointed attorney-general. Shortly afterwards he accepted the office of chief justice of the queen's bench in Ireland, on the retirement of Thomas Langlois Lefroy, though it seems that he felt slighted at not having been offered the Irish lord chancellorship. The latter office was generally considered rightfully to be his, but his association with the extreme tory and protestant wing of the Conservative Party would not allow Derby thus to elevate him, since the prime minister wished to form a broad-based Irish executive. Whiteside served as lord chief justice for ten years, but the last of these were clouded by ill health. He died at Brighton on 25 November 1876 and was buried at Mount Jerome cemetery, Dublin.

Whiteside's talents were rhetorical and forensic rather than judicial. Although he brought to his high position great personal dignity and the charm of a singularly attractive personality, he was not very successful as a judge because he was not strong in law. This deficit was countered by a strong reliance on Mr Justice James O'Brien, a quiet, unpresuming man, deeply learned in the law. Indeed, Whiteside was once heard saying to a colleague, 'Yours is, my dear friend, a most gentlemanly judgment, but O'Brien says it's not good law, and we can't risk it' (Ross).

Whiteside is thus best remembered for his advocacy, rather than for his judicial pronouncement. He was unapproached in point of eloquence by any of his contemporaries, and his powerful personality, at once winning and commanding, gave him an almost unexampled pre-eminence. His forensic style has been described as 'impetuously burying facts and law under a golden avalanche of discursive eloquence'; and his parliamentary

oratory was thus praised by Lord Lytton in his poem, 'St Stephen's':

Still Whiteside's genius charms both foes and friends,
So headlong force with sparkling fancy blends,
As torrents flash the more their rush depends.

Whiteside was of course a most influential political figure, but his reputation was really forged through legal advocacy, and his remains one of the most brilliant names in the annals of the Irish bar. NATHAN WELLS

Sources F. E. Ball, *The judges in Ireland, 1221–1921*, 2 (1926) · *The Times* (27 Nov 1876) · D. Hogan and W. N. Osborough, eds., *Brehons, serjeants, and attorneys: studies in the history of the Irish legal profession* (1990) · J. R. O'Flanagan, *The Irish bar*, 2nd edn (1879) · E. Keane, P. Beryl Phair, and T. U. Sadleir, eds., *King's Inns admission papers, 1607–1867*, IMC (1982) · *Reminiscences of John Adye Curran KC* (1915) · J. Ross, *The years of my pilgrimage* (1924) · Boase, *Mod. Eng. biog.* · *Law Magazine*, 4th ser., 2 (1876–7), 334–62 · *CGPLA Ire.* (1877)
Archives Bodl. Oxf., letters to Benjamin Disraeli · Herts. ALS, letters to Lord Lytton · Lpool RO, letters to fourteenth earl of Derby · PRO NIre., letters to Sir J. E. Tennent · Som. ARS, letters to Sir William Joliffe
Likenesses A. B. Joy, marble statue, exh. RA 1800, St Patrick's Cathedral, Dublin · attrib. P. Macdowell, marble bust, exh. RA 1861?, TCD · J. B. Yeats, pen drawing, 1866, NG Ire. [*see illus.*] · T. Woolner, statue, 1880, Four Courts, Dublin · C. Grey, pencil drawing, NG Ire. · D. J. Pound, stipple and line engraving (after photograph by Mayall), BM, NPG; repro. in *Illustrated News of the World* · A. Scott, oils?, King's Inns, Dublin · etching (after C. Grey), repro. in *Dublin University Magazine*, 33 (1849), 326 · portrait, repro. in C. A. Read, ed., *The cabinet of Irish literature*, 4 (1880) · portrait, repro. in *ILN*, 32 (27 March 1858), 313 · portrait, repro. in *ILN*, 21 (6 Nov 1852), 377–8 · portrait, repro. in *ILN*, 13 (7 Oct 1848), 221 · portrait, repro. in *ILN*, 69 (2 Dec 1876), 543 · woodcuts, NPG
Wealth at death under £35,000: probate, 13 Jan 1877, *CGPLA Ire.*

Whiteside, John (*bap.* **1679**, *d.* **1729**), museum curator and experimental philosopher, was born in Kirkham, Lancashire, and baptized on 2 November 1679, the son of George Whiteside, glazier, of Kirkham, and his wife, Margaret. He entered Brasenose College, Oxford, on 16 May 1696, and graduated BA in 1700 and MA in 1704. He took holy orders, and was subsequently chaplain of Christ Church, Oxford (from 1713), and absentee vicar of King's Walden, Hertfordshire.

On 14 December 1714 Whiteside was elected keeper of the Ashmolean Museum, Oxford. His dedication to his duties, and his cultivation of friends and benefactors, helped to consolidate the museum's reputation, both antiquarian and scientific. He restored its administrative and accounting systems and revived (though not thoroughly) the documentation of its collections, all of which his predecessor had neglected. He took special interest in the numismatic collection, rehung the museum's pictures, and made the library more useful and accessible to scholars.

In the museum's lecture room about 1715 Whiteside began to hold courses of experimental philosophy, similar to those recently pioneered by John Keill in Oxford and William Whiston in London. For this purpose he built up at his own expense a large collection of apparatus, which by 1723 he valued at £400. In that year he extended his syllabus by adding architecture, magnetics, and astronomy to the standard topics of mechanics, hydrostatics, pneumatics, and optics. He was a keen astronomer, and two of his observations were communicated to the Royal Society by Edmond Halley. On at least one occasion, in 1720, he also taught a chemistry course.

Whiteside was elected FRS on 3 July 1718. In 1721 he was an unsuccessful candidate for the chair of astronomy at Oxford. He was highly esteemed as an experimental philosopher: his courses had considerable influence, and were continued after his death by James Bradley. He was thus the founder of physics teaching at Oxford University.

Whiteside moderated his obvious industriousness with a love of convivial drinking, gossip, and good humour. From 1715 he was a close friend of the diarist Thomas Hearne, who recorded various insights into his character. He never married, notwithstanding his 'great Affection' for Deborah Wrench. He died in Oxford on 22 October 1729, as a result of gangrene following a fall from his horse during a visit to his Hertfordshire parish, though he blamed his illness on 'drinking a pretty deal of bad small beer'. He was buried in Christ Church Cathedral.

A. V. SIMCOCK, rev.

Sources *Remarks and collections of Thomas Hearne*, ed. C. E. Doble and others, 11 vols., OHS, 2, 7, 13, 34, 42–3, 48, 50, 65, 67, 72 (1885–1921), vols. 5–10 · R. F. Ovenell, *The Ashmolean Museum, 1683–1894* (1986) · AM Oxf. · Bodl. Oxf., MS Ashmole 1820a; MS Bradley 48 · J. Whiteside, syllabus, Bodl. Oxf. [see also MHS Oxf.]

Whiteway, William (1599–1635), diarist, may have been born in Devon. He was the son of William Whiteway (1570–1640), a wealthy Dorchester merchant, and Mary (1579–1655), daughter of John Mounsell, and lived at Dorchester, Dorset, from infancy. He attended Dorchester Free School but did not go on to university, possibly because of ill health: he had visited Oxford in the company of his schoolmaster, Robert Cheeke, in 1614. In 1620 he married Elinor (b. 1601), daughter of John Parkins, another member of the Dorchester élite; there were seven children of the marriage, but all died in infancy except a son (also named William) who lived until 1646, and a posthumous daughter. Whiteway held most of the civic offices in Dorchester that followed naturally from his family's wealth and position in the town: he was elected a capital burgess in 1624, was governor of the Freemen's Company in the same year, and twice bailiff, in 1629 and 1633. He was elected to the 1626 parliament after the death of Dorchester's previous MP, Michael Humphreys, though there is no evidence that he ever attended the house.

Whiteway grew up in Dorchester during a period of remarkable civic improvement, much of it inspired by the formidable rector of Trinity parish, John White. The diary which Whiteway began in 1618, printed in *William Whiteway of Dorchester: his Diary, 1618 to 1635* (1991), records the various projects which transformed Dorchester into one of the most puritan towns in England: a better endowed ministry, a 'hospital' for poor children, a new elementary school, and an expanded system of poor relief financed by the profits of a municipal brewery. The diary also contains much information about county, national, and international affairs, and shows that Whiteway was a keen

observer of the political and religious controversies of his time. Almost the first entry records the appearance of the comet of 1618, which obviously presaged great events. He closely watched developments in the Thirty Years' War, his entries revealing strong support for the protestant side. He also frequently notes events in France, partly because of his sympathy for the Huguenots but also because of his family's trading interests there. He visited France in 1616 and possibly on a later occasion. His comments on English affairs are prudently restrained, but they suggest that he was a moderate puritan, a conforming member of the Church of England, but hostile to Arminian innovations, and although a loyal subject of both James I and Charles I, suspicious of Catholic influence at court.

Whiteway read widely on theological subjects and also dabbled in geography and astronomy. He owned books on travel, logic, mathematics, and medicine, and was interested in architecture and painting. He assembled papers dealing with Dorchester affairs: lists of office-holders and town properties, and an account of the local charitable institutions. However, his greatest intellectual preoccupation was history; his commonplace book (CUL, MS Dd.xi. 73) contains extensive notes on both classical and modern historians. He may have contemplated writing his own history of England since 1603, but does not seem to have made any progress beyond the notes he took on his reading. In February 1635, while running up a steep hill, he suffered either a heart attack or a pneumothorax—'a shortness of breath, with extreme soreness of the brest'; he died in Dorchester on 21 June and was buried there. His diary and his unpublished papers together provide a valuable impression of the mental world of a well-educated, moderately puritan, seventeenth-century provincial townsman.

DAVID UNDERDOWN

Sources *William Whiteway of Dorchester: his diary, 1618 to 1635*, Dorset RS, 12 (1991) · W. Whiteway, commonplace book, CUL, MS Dd.xi. 73 · D. Underdown, *Fire from heaven: the life of an English town in the seventeenth century* (1992) · W. Whiteway, 'Dorchester book', Dorset RO, D1/J8 [copy in D1/10448] · C. H. Mayo, ed., *Municipal records of the borough of Dorchester, Dorset* (1908) · Dorchester, corporation minutes, 1618–39, Dorset RO, B2/16/1, 2 · Dorchester, Freemen's Company, day book, 1621–35, Dorset RO, B2/13/1

Archives CUL, MSS, MS.Dd.xi. 73 · Dorset RO, MSS, D1/J8

Wealth at death considerable wealth: will, *William Whiteway of Dorchester*

Whiteway, Sir William Vallance (1828–1908), politician in Newfoundland, was born on 1 April 1828 at Buckyett House, near Totnes, Devon, the youngest son of Thomas Whiteway, a farmer, and Elizabeth Vallance. Educated privately and at Totnes grammar school, he went to St John's, Newfoundland, in 1843. Having chosen the law over a career in commerce, he was called to the bar in 1852 and developed a successful and prosperous practice. In 1862 he married Mary Lightbourne of Bermuda. They had one daughter before her death in 1868.

In 1859 Whiteway entered the house of assembly as a member for Twillingate and Fogo, and rapidly achieved prominence in the Conservative Party. In 1865 he was made QC and was elected speaker. He openly supported

Newfoundland's joining the dominion of Canada, the central issue in the 1869 election, but in the election he and most other confederates were defeated. He returned to the assembly in 1873 as a member for Trinity Bay, and the following year became solicitor-general in Frederic B. T. Carter's administration.

Whiteway's major responsibility was the presentation of the colony's case before the Halifax tribunal, which was to decide on the monetary compensation to be paid by the United States to Canada and Newfoundland under the fisheries clauses of the treaty of Washington (1871). He handled this matter effectively, and Newfoundland was awarded $1 million. Part of Whiteway's reward was a KCMG in 1880. In 1872 he married Catherine Anne Davies of Pictou, Nova Scotia. They had six children.

By this time Whiteway had taken over as premier and attorney-general, and in 1878 had won his first election as Conservative leader. He had ambitious plans. If Newfoundland's economic potential was to be realized, then a railway had to be built across the island in order to open up the resources of the interior, and the colony had to be able fully to exploit the potential of the so-called French Shore—the island's west coast, where France held fishing rights deriving from the treaty of Utrecht, which significantly curtailed the colony's jurisdiction. He also wanted to develop St John's into a major port, and advocated the building of a large dry dock. These were the main elements of Whiteway's 'policy of progress'.

The imperial government was unwilling to antagonize France, and, while allowing extensions of colonial jurisdiction on the French Shore, refused at first to allow a railway there. Whiteway therefore fell back on a scheme for a narrow-gauge east-coast line from St John's to Hall's Bay. Amid considerable controversy, a contract was made with an American syndicate, and construction began in 1881. Whiteway was also involved in the negotiation of an ultimately abortive compromise agreement with France over fishing rights. These issues created new political alignments. Those favouring railway building, economic diversification, and a deal with France followed Whiteway. Those who differed, fearing the financial implications of railway building, unwilling to compromise with France, and resenting alleged governmental neglect of the fisheries, formed a new party which, though defeated in the 1882 election, remained politically active.

Taking advantage of tensions caused by economic depression and by a serious Orange–Catholic riot in December 1883, Whiteway's opponents managed to oust him from office in 1885 and form a government. He remained outside the legislature until the 1889 election, when, with a rebuilt party, which he styled the Liberal Party, he swept back into power with an unchanged programme.

Whiteway was less dominant in this than in his previous administrations. Though railway building, suspended for some years as a result of the bankruptcy of the original contractors, was resumed in 1890 by Robert G. Reid, Whiteway found himself unable to pursue compromise on the French issue, and was drawn by Robert Bond into an attempt to negotiate a trade agreement with the United States. In 1891 he addressed the House of Lords on the French question, in an effort to prevent imperial legislation to enforce the hated treaties being imposed on the colony. He succeeded, but the compromise agreement he negotiated was later rejected in Newfoundland, a major humiliation.

The Whiteway government was returned in the 1893 election, but was subsequently ousted by the tory opposition, which successfully filed petitions alleging corrupt electoral practice against seventeen government members, including Whiteway. He did not behave well in this crisis, on one occasion leading a mob to attack a warehouse on the waterfront in St John's. These upheavals precipitated the crash of the two local banks in December 1894, in which Whiteway lost a considerable amount of money. The crash also marked the end of the tory government, however, and by February 1895 Whiteway was once again premier, but ill and exhausted. That the situation was stabilized fairly rapidly was due largely to the efforts of Robert Bond.

In 1897 the government was defeated, and Whiteway lost his seat. Two years later he was replaced as party leader. He did not retire gracefully, but returned to active politics in 1904 in opposition to Bond. It was only after his overwhelming personal defeat that year that he finally withdrew from public life. His personal life was saddened by the loss of four children between 1899 and 1908. Whiteway himself died in St John's on 24 June 1908, and was buried there.

Whiteway's monument as Newfoundland's longest serving premier was the transinsular railway. Without his determination, and his vision of what the colony might become, it would never have been built. He also deserves credit for his firm but reasoned attitude towards the French fisheries question. But beyond that, Whiteway failed to achieve perhaps exaggerated ambitions both for himself and for the colony. Hence the contrast between an increasingly contentious public life, and a private, family life where he was liked and respected for his humour and geniality and for his long service to the masonic order and the Anglican church.

JAMES K. HILLER

Sources J. K. Hiller, 'Whiteway, Sir William Vallance', *DCB*, vol. 13 · J. K. Hiller, 'A history of Newfoundland, 1874–1901', PhD diss., U. Cam., 1971 · F. F. Thompson, *The French Shore problem in Newfoundland: an imperial study* (1961) · St John's (Newfoundland), *Evening Telegram* (1879–1908) · St John's (Newfoundland), *Newfoundlander* (1860–84)
Archives Memorial University, Newfoundland, Centre for Newfoundland Studies · Provincial Archives of Newfoundland and Labrador, St John's
Wealth at death $76,000—in Newfoundland: probate, Newfoundland · £140 8s.: administration with will, 3 July 1909, *CGPLA Eng. & Wales*

Whitfeld, Henry. *See* Whitfield, Henry (1590/91–1657).

Whitfeld, John Clarke- (1770–1836), organist and composer, son of John Clarke (d. 17 Sept 1802) of Malmesbury, Wiltshire, was born on 13 December 1770 at Gloucester, and adopted by letters patent in 1814 the family name of his mother, Amphillis (d. 10 Nov 1813), daughter of Henry Whitfeld of The Bury, Rickmansworth, Hertfordshire.

After a musical training at Oxford under Philip Hayes, in 1789 Clarke obtained the post of organist in the parish church of Ludlow, and the following year he married. In 1793 he took the BMus degree at Oxford, and in 1794 he succeeded Richard Langton as organist and master of the choristers at Armagh Cathedral for three years. In 1795 he was awarded the honorary degree of MusD at Dublin University, and in March 1798 he was appointed choirmaster of St Patrick's Cathedral and Christ Church, Dublin. His earliest glees and sonatas were written and partly published in Ireland; but the unsettled condition of the country at length induced him to resign his posts, and after returning to England, he settled at Cambridge, where he became the organist and choirmaster of Trinity and St John's colleges from 1799 to 1820. He dedicated his three volumes of Services and Anthems (1800–05) to the masters and fellows of the two colleges.

In 1799 Clarke was granted the degree MusD Cambridge ad eundem from Dublin, and in 1810 he was incorporated DMus at Oxford. In 1821, on the death of Charles Hague, Clarke-Whitfeld, as he had become, was appointed professor of music at the University of Cambridge, a post which he held until his death. To allow more opportunity for composition he retired to the nearby village of Chesterton, where he set to music many of Sir Walter Scott's verses. He also worked equally industriously on the poems of Byron and Joanna Baillie, and set their words to music in some hundred songs and partsongs. About 1814 he published two volumes of Twelve Vocal Pieces, for which original material was contributed by these and other poets.

From 1820 to 1832 Clarke-Whitfeld was organist and choirmaster of Hereford Cathedral, and in this capacity he was frequently asked to conduct or to play the piano at the Three Choirs festivals. At the Hereford festival of 1822 he produced his oratorio The Crucifixion, and at that of 1825 its continuation, The Resurrection (published in 1835). He resigned in 1832 after an attack of paralysis and died at Holmer, near Hereford, on 22 February 1836. A mural tablet recorded his burial in the bishop's cloisters, Hereford Cathedral. He was survived by his wife, Susannah, who died on 18 April 1845, aged seventy-two.

Clarke-Whitfeld's work was well adapted to his times and popular. He did valuable pioneering work in editing the scores of Purcell, Arne, and Handel, and his collections of Favourite Anthems (1805) and Single and Double Chants (1810) were compiled with good judgement.

L. M. MIDDLETON, rev. NILANJANA BANERJI

Sources Grove, Dict. mus. (1954) · New Grove · J. E. West, Cathedral organists past and present (1899) · Venn, Alum. Cant. · Brown & Stratton, Brit. mus. · Foster, Alum. Oxon. · D. Baptie, A handbook of musical biography (1883) · F. T. Havergal, Monumental inscriptions in the cathedral church of Hereford (1881) · C. F. A. Williams, Degrees in music (1894) · J. Clarke, Anthems, 2 [preface] · D. Lysons and J. Arnott, Origin and progress of the meeting of the three choirs of Gloucester, Worcester and Hereford (1865), 106 · Annual Biography and Obituary, 21 (1837), 139 · R. Clutterbuck, ed., The history and antiquities of the county of Hertford, 1 (1815), 150

Archives Herefs. RO, Bulmer MSS

Whitfield, David (1926–1980), singer, was born on 2 February 1926 in Kingston upon Hull, Yorkshire. He was the third of eight children of James and Lillian Whitfield of Albert Terrace, East Street, in the dockland district of Drypool. James Whitfield was at that time employed by his father as a carter. David Whitfield attended St Peter's School, Drypool, where he sang in concerts, and became head chorister at St Peter's Church. He left school at fourteen and began work as a delivery boy for a Jewish baker. Influenced by the Austrian-born tenor Richard Tauber, Whitfield began to perform professionally: his first paid engagement was at the Perth Street Club in Hull in 1942.

Whitfield served in the Royal Navy between 1943 and 1949. While stationed in Hong Kong he performed in clubs and broadcast over Radio Hong Kong, where he met the comedian Kenneth Williams. On returning to Southampton in 1949 he won first prize in the Radio Luxemburg talent contest Opportunity Knocks, singing 'Goodbye' from the 1930s' musical show White Horse Inn. He then toured the United Kingdom with the Opportunity Knocks variety show, compered by Hughie Green. Following the tour Whitfield returned to Hull, where he took a job as a labourer and returned to performing in local clubs. In June 1952 he married Sheila Priestman. Their first child, Lance, was born in the following year; a second son, Shane, in 1957; and a daughter, Amanda Jane, in 1959.

Whitfield's show business career was rekindled when he was invited to perform in cabaret at the Washington Hotel in London early in 1953. As a result of this engagement he made his first recordings when the impresario Bunny Lewis signed him to the Decca label. His first commercial success came in 1954 with his recording of 'Answer me'. It sold 700,000 copies and reached number one in the hit parade despite the fact that the BBC refused to broadcast the song because of its allegedly sacrilegious lyrics. This was followed by the million-selling 'Cara mia', which was recorded with the orchestra of its composer, Mantovani, and became the first top-ten hit in America by a British male singer. His later hit records included popular ballads such as 'Everywhere' (1955), written by Tolchard Evans, 'Cry my heart' (1958), and 'On the street where you live' (1959).

Over the next decade Whitfield became one of the most popular entertainers in Britain. Managed by Lew and Leslie Grade, he played summer seasons at Blackpool, Southsea, and Bournemouth, appeared in pantomime at the London Palladium, and sang at the royal variety performance in 1954. He made frequent television appearances and starred in his own series for ATV in 1960. Over 2000 people attended his fan club convention in Blackpool in 1955. In 1957 Whitfield began to introduce arias from light opera into his programme and in 1960 he starred in a revival of the 1925 operetta Rose Marie London, which opened in London and toured for nine months. This was followed by the starring role of the Red Shadow in The Desert Song.

David Whitfield (1926–1980), by unknown photographer

Throat problems led to an operation to remove Whitfield's tonsils at the London Clinic in 1958 but this failed to provide a cure. Signs of excessive drinking first appeared in 1960, when it was reported that he kept a bottle of vodka in his dressing-room, and by 1965 his career was in decline. He was reduced to playing the northern cabaret club circuit, and made headlines after a jealous husband assaulted him. The following year he was convicted on a charge of indecent exposure to an eleven-year-old girl.

In his final years Whitfield performed almost exclusively in Australia, New Zealand, and Canada. He died of a cerebral haemorrhage at the North Shore Hospital, Sydney, on 15 February 1980, following his thirteenth Australian tour. He was cremated at the northern suburbs crematorium in Sydney; his ashes were taken home and scattered in the North Sea in a naval burial, some 5 miles south-east of Spurn Point. Rose gardens were laid out in his memory in Portsmouth and in Hull, and a new rose was named after him. There are memorial plaques in numerous theatres, including the London Palladium.

DAVE LAING

Sources A. Britton, *Cara mia: the David Whitfield story* (1993) · P. Hardy and D. Laing, *Faber companion to 20th century popular music* (1995) · B. Henson and C. Morgan, *First hits: the book of sheet music* (1981) · 'David Whitfield', www.orwin.karoo.net/people/dead/People/Whitfield.html · private information (2004) [Vernon Brand]

Likenesses photograph, priv. coll. [*see illus.*]

Wealth at death £23,870: administration, 2 July 1980, *CGPLA Eng. & Wales*

Whitfield, Ernest Albert, first Baron Kenswood (1887–1963), violinist and economist, was born on 15 September 1887 in London, the younger son of John Henry Christopher Whitfield of London and his wife, Louisa, daughter of Michael Farren of Copenhagen. He was educated at Archbishop Tenison's School and University College School, London, the University of Vienna, and London University. A brilliant pupil at school, Whitfield was forced by economic necessity to accept a commercial appointment in Vienna in 1907 and rose to departmental manager while still in his early twenties. His sight began to deteriorate, however, and after struggling with failing vision for two and a half years he had to consider a new profession.

From an early age Whitfield had shown outstanding ability as a violinist and he was induced reluctantly to adopt his musical talent as a way to earn a livelihood. For some time he pursued his business duties while preparing for a professional musical career, assiduously memorizing as much music as was possible with his remaining sight; in 1912 he was awarded the Austrian state diploma for teaching music. The following year he made his début as a soloist and his success seemed assured, but with the outbreak of the First World War he was obliged to return to London after an absence of eight years, and with barely any vision he endeavoured to establish himself as a concert artist.

Through a chance meeting with Sir Arthur Pearson, Whitfield was introduced to the Braille system and he joined the St Dunstan's Blind Musicians' Concert Party, but relinquished the position owing to the stress of constant travelling. In 1917, without revealing that his vision was impaired, he succeeded in gaining a post as leader of the orchestra at Wyndham's Theatre in London. For the first week he memorized all the programme details before admitting his visual handicap, proving that an adequately trained blind musician can fulfil orchestral duties. He remained at Wyndham's for almost two years. He made his first appearance as a soloist in London at the Queen's Hall Promenade Concerts in 1918, and in 1920 he formed the Guild of Singers and Players.

On 13 December 1920 Whitfield married Sophie Madeline, the highly accomplished only child of Ernest Walter Howard of London and Hill Head, Hampshire. From 1921 to 1923 Whitfield won international acclaim for his musical virtuosity and for introducing many new British works, but ill health restricted his concert engagements. He embarked on a deeper study of economics, political science, and philosophy, and, while still perfecting his technique as a violinist, graduated BSc at London University in 1926. His only daughter was born in 1928 and that year he was made a PhD in London for a dissertation on Gabriel Bonnot de Mably, a French pre-Revolutionary philosopher. He reappeared on the concert platform and achieved renown for the mastery of his art.

Ernest Albert Whitfield, first Baron Kenswood (1887–1963), by Walter Stoneman, 1951

In 1928 Whitfield was elected to the executive council of the National Institute for the Blind, later becoming honorary joint treasurer; subsequently he was a British delegate to the World Conference on Work for the Blind in New York in 1931, and other overseas conferences on blind welfare. His son and heir, John Michael Howard, was born on 6 April 1930. Whitfield stood unsuccessfully as a Labour candidate for Marylebone, London, in 1931 and for South Buckinghamshire in 1935, and was a co-opted member of the education committee of the London county council from 1934 to 1939. In 1935 a damaged hand forced him to abandon his musical career.

Whitfield was in France at the outbreak of the Second World War and in 1941, being unable to return to Britain, he moved to the United States. There he undertook musical research for the New York Institute for the Blind. Later he continued this activity in Toronto, in conjunction with rehabilitation programmes for ex-servicemen at the Canadian National Institute for the Blind. On his return to England he became a governor of the BBC from 1946 to 1950. He was created Baron Kenswood on 27 June 1951, during which year he was elected to the presidency of the National Federation of the Blind of the United Kingdom, which he held until 1955. He also became vice-president of the Pembrokeshire Community Council, and in addition he was a member of the Pembrokeshire Old People's Welfare Committee. He served on the committees of several hospitals in the London area and also of schools for deaf and blind children. He contributed to the *Columbia Encyclopaedia of Political Science* and to various periodicals on blind welfare.

A good-looking man of medium height, Kenswood was a keen walker and enthusiastic swimmer. His puckish sense of humour and persuasive delivery made him a popular and effective after-dinner speaker. His deep passion for music, lifelong interest in political life and current affairs, love of country life, and compassion for the less fortunate combined with his personal fortitude to make him a well-liked and fascinating personality.

Kenswood's first wife died on 25 August 1961 at her Pembrokeshire home, Roch Castle, and on 26 July 1962 he married Catherine, widow of Charles Chilver-Stainer and daughter of Frank Luxton. Kenswood died at the Hospital of St John and St Elizabeth, Marylebone, London, on 21 April 1963. He was survived by his wife. Kenswood was succeeded in the barony by his son, John Michael Howard Whitfield. E. T. BOULTER, *rev.* KENNETH R. WHITTON

Sources *The Times* (23 April 1963) · private information (2004) · personal knowledge (2004) · *CGPLA Eng. & Wales* (1963)
Likenesses W. Stoneman, photograph, 1951, NPG [*see illus.*] · F. J. Kornis, plaster bust, 1954, priv. coll.
Wealth at death £1341 15*s.*: probate, 9 Dec 1963, *CGPLA Eng. & Wales*

Whitfield, Frances. *See* Peyronnet, Frances de, Viscountess de Peyronnet in the French nobility (1815–1895).

Whitfield [Whitfeld], **Henry** (1590/91–1657), minister in America, was the son of Thomas Whitfield, an attorney and owner of the manor of East Sheen and West Hall, Mortlake, Surrey, and of his wife Mildred (*née* Manning). He matriculated from New College, Oxford, on 6 June 1610, aged nineteen, but there is no record of his having received a degree; nor is there any evidence for Cotton Mather's assertion that he studied at the inns of court after leaving Oxford. He was ordained and inducted as rector of St Margaret's, Ockley, Surrey, in 1618 and ministered there until 1638.

Whitfield was noted for his charity and hospitality, and was a supporter of protestant unity. In 1631 he was one of the signatories of a testimonial given to John Dury in support of his efforts for reconciliation of protestant churches. He may have been the Henry Whitfield who proceeded BD from Cambridge early in 1632: such a degree would certainly fit with his evident learning and his standing in scholarly and clerical circles. In the spring of 1633 he hosted a conference called to persuade John Cotton and Thomas Hooker to compromise their objections to church practice so that their ministry would not be lost to the English church. Among those joining Whitfield, Cotton, and Hooker were Thomas Goodwin, Philip Nye, John Davenport, and William Twisse. Philip Nye's manuscript account of the meeting does not survive, but the gist of it can be reconstructed from manuscripts in the Hartlib papers. The tables were turned during the debates, with Cotton and Hooker persuading their friends, or some of them, of the idolatrous nature of some of the disputed church ceremonies and that under the changed circumstances of the day conformity was no longer an option.

Goodwin, Nye, and Davenport quickly demonstrated their nonconformity. Whitfield retained his parish responsibilities for a time, but found it increasingly difficult. In the mid-1630s letters seized in the studies of John White and John Stoughton seemed to implicate Whitfield in what the government suspected was a clerical underground seeking to undermine the church. He was author of *Some Help to Stir up to Christian Duties* (1636).

Whitfield resigned his living, sold his estate, and migrated to New England in 1639, taking a number of parish families with him at his own expense. His was the first ship to sail directly from England to the new colony of New Haven. While crossing the Atlantic Whitfield and a group of his fellow emigrants drew up a covenant which became the foundation of their new town. Whitfield, who had substantial means, purchased land on behalf of the township from the local Native Americans. Initially identified by its Indian name, Menumkatuck, the town was renamed Guilford in 1643. Whitfield served as the pastor of the Guilford church for eleven years without pay. In 1643 the Guilford congregation formally gathered itself in the New England fashion and officially chose Whitfield as pastor and John Higginson as teacher. Cotton Mather reported that Whitfield's preaching style was very much like that of Richard Sibbes, and that 'there was a marvelous majesty and sanctity observable in it', and that he frequently visited 'the particular families of his flock, with profitable discourses on the great concerns of their interior state' (Mather, 1.593). Whitfield's own family reportedly included ten children, but nothing is known of his wife.

In 1650 Whitfield, discouraged by the New England wilderness and encouraged by letters from English friends, left Guilford and returned to England, where he resumed his ministry at a parish in Winchester, Hampshire. He retained an interest in New England affairs, however, and particularly in the mission to the Indians. Whitfield knew of John Eliot and his missionary efforts, and on his return to England Whitfield's ship had been forced to put in at Martha's Vineyard; there he had observed and been impressed with the missionary work of Thomas Mayhew jun., listening both to Mayhew and to the tales of Indian converts, and in England he became a member of the Society for the Propagation of the Gospel in New England. Mayhew urged him to tell the story of the missions in England and in 1651 Whitfield published *The Light Appearing More and More towards the Perfect Day*, which related in great detail the work of Mayhew on the islands off the Massachusetts coast. The work also included letters of John Eliot describing his efforts. It was dedicated to parliament in a preface signed by John Owen, Philip Nye, Thomas Goodwin, and other congregationalists. Whitfield encouraged his successor in Guilford, John Higginson, to learn the local native dialect and to preach to and catechize the tribes. He continued his support for the Society for the Propagation of the Gospel and was involved in the publication of *Strength out of Weakness* (1652) and further reports in 1655. He died at Winchester in September 1657.

FRANCIS J. BREMER

Sources C. Mather, *Magnalia Christi Americana*, 3rd edn, 7 bks in 2 vols. (1853–5) · *The Hartlib papers*, ed. J. Crawford and others (1995) [CD-ROM] · T. Webster, *Godly clergy in early Stuart England: the Caroline puritan movement, c.1620–1643* (1997) · F. J. Bremer, *Shaping New Englands: puritan clergymen in seventeenth-century England and New England* (1994) · S. E. Morison, *The founding of Harvard College* (Cambridge, MA, 1935) · J. Savage, *A genealogical dictionary of the first settlers of New England*, 4 vols. (1860–62) · I. M. Calder, *The New Haven colony* (1934) · A. T. Vaughan, *New England frontier: puritans and Indians*, 3rd edn (1995) · Venn, *Alum. Cant.* · Foster, *Alum. Oxon.*
Archives Cambs. AS, letters to Richard Cromwell and Dorothy Cromwell

Whitford, Adam (1623/4–1647). *See under* Whitford, Walter (*d.* 1647).

Whitford, David (1626–1674), army officer and scholar, was the fourth son of Walter *Whitford (*d.* 1647), bishop of Brechin, and Anne (*d.* in or after 1660), daughter of Sir John Carmichael and great niece of the regent, James Douglas, fourth earl of Morton. John *Whitford and Adam *Whitford [*see under* Whitford, Walter (*d.* 1647)] and Walter *Whitford (*b. c.*1617, *d.* in or after 1691) were his elder brothers. He was educated at Westminster School, where he was elected a queen's scholar on a royal warrant dated 21 March 1640. Two years later, aged sixteen, he matriculated from Christ Church, Oxford; he graduated BA on 30 March 1647. On the outbreak of the civil wars he espoused the king's cause and took up arms as a member of the garrison at Oxford. It is said that in consequence he was deprived of his studentship by the parliamentary visitors in 1648, and returned to his native land, although his name does not appear in the published edition of the visitors' register. He became an officer in Charles II's army which invaded England in 1651, and fought at the battle of Worcester. He was wounded, taken prisoner, carried to Oxford, and then conveyed to London, where his friends' importunity obtained his release.

Edward Bysshe, abstentionist MP for Bletchingley in Surrey and intruded garter and clarenceux king of arms, relieved Whitford from straitened circumstances following his imprisonment. The Scot was found employment as an usher teaching Greek at the school in Whitefriars, near Fleet Street, run by the Catholic poet James Shirley. Some complimentary verses penned by Whitford prefaced Francis Goldsmith's *Hugo Grotius his Sophompaneas* in 1652. In 1654 he published Latin translations of three works by Bysshe on the work of various armorial scholars. In 1655 he published *Musaei, Moschi et Bionis*, selections from Theocritus's *Eidyllia* in Latin and Greek dedicated to Bysshe, and republished in 1659. In November 1658 a David Whitford of Ashton, Northamptonshire, gentleman, was entered as a student of the Inner Temple, and although it seems unlikely to have been the Scot, there is no way of knowing for sure. Whitford wrote, possibly as early as 1652, an appendix, entitled *Montrose Redivivus*, which appeared in George Wishart's *Compleat History of the Wars in Scotland*, published in 1660.

On the restoration of Charles II Whitford was reinstated to his Oxford studentship by the visitors, but, finding himself disabled from holding it by the college statutes, he petitioned the king in December 1660 to grant him a dispensation. He was created MA on 14 January 1661. In 1666 he was commissioned chaplain in the regiment of foot under the command of Lord George Douglas. Afterwards he was chaplain to John Maitland, duke of Lauderdale, and in 1672 he officiated as minister to the Scottish regiment in France. In 1673 he was appointed rector of Middleton Tyas in Yorkshire. He died suddenly in his chambers at Christ Church on 26 October 1674, and was buried on the following day in the south transept of the cathedral, near his brother Adam. E. I. CARLYLE, rev. SEAN KELSEY

Sources DNB · Foster, Alum. Oxon. · CSP dom., 1639–40, 567; 1651–2,11; 1660–61, 432; 1665–6, 540 · M. Burrows, ed., The register of the visitors of the University of Oxford, from AD 1647 to AD 1658, CS, new ser., 29 (1881) · J. Griffiths, An index to wills proved in the court of the chancellor of the University of Oxford (1862)

Wealth at death see administration and inventory, Griffiths, Index to wills

Whitford, Helena. See Wells, Helena (1761?–1824).

Whitford, John (d. 1667). See under Whitford, Walter (d. 1647).

Whitford, Richard (d. 1543?), Bridgettine monk and author, probably came from near Whitford in Flintshire. According to his will (previously attributed to an uncle of the same name) made in 1511 before he entered Syon Abbey, he had lands in Flintshire and in Lancashire which he left to his sister's son, John Edwards. Nothing else is known about his parentage, family, early life, or education until he is recorded as a questionist at Cambridge University in 1496–7. From 1498 to 1504 he was a fellow of Queens' College, Cambridge. In 1498 he was granted leave of absence to accompany William Blount, fourth Lord Mountjoy (d. 1534), to study abroad and that same year Whitford was admitted BA by Paris University and proceeded MA in 1499. While in Paris Whitford and Mountjoy became friendly with Erasmus who accompanied them back to England that summer. Whitford returned to Queens', was incorporated MA at Cambridge and became dean of chapel, junior bursar (1500–01) and senior bursar (1501–2) of his college. The only hint about his life between leaving Queens' and entering Syon Abbey, probably about 1511, comes from William Roper's life of Sir Thomas More, repeated by Nicholas Harpsfield (Roper, 8; cf. Harpsfield, 16). They told how More went to see Richard Fox, bishop of Winchester, and then fell into conversation 'with Master Whitford, his familiar friend, then Chapleine to that bishoppe, and after a Father of Syon', but no documentary evidence has been found to confirm that Whitford was Foxe's chaplain.

The next glimpse of Whitford comes from Thomas Bedyll, one of Thomas Cromwell's agents, charged with securing the submission of the brethren of Syon to the Acts of Succession and Supremacy. On 21 July 1534 he reported:

I handled Whitford ... in the garden bothe with faire wordes and with foule, and shewed him that throughe his obstinacy he shuld be brought to the greate shame of the world for his irreligious life, and for his using bawdy wordes to diverse ladys at the tymes of their confession, whereby (I sayed) he

myght be the occasion that shrift shalbe layed downe throughe England: but he hath a brasyn forehed, whiche shameth at nothing. (Wright, 49)

Again, on 28 August Bedyll reported from Syon that 'one Whitford preached—one of the most wilful—and said nothing of the King's title', declaring that he had little learning and was a great railer (LP Henry VIII, 7, no. 1090). However, Whitford remained at Syon until its suppression in 1539 and received one of the higher pensions of £8 a year. There is no evidence as to where he spent the last years of his life; tradition places him in the Mountjoy household. According to the Syon martyrology (BL, Add. MS 22285, fol. 55v) he died on 16 September, almost certainly in the year 1543 since his pension ceased to be paid on 3 October 1543.

Whitford's donation to the brothers' library at Syon, was comprehensive but commonplace: classical authors predominated, especially Cicero, scholastic works by Lombard and Lyre, sermon collections by Bromyard and Gisland, and two spiritual compendia, Busti's Mariale and the Rosetum exercitionum spiritualium; less predictable was Petrus Crescentius's De agricultura and the only trace of humanist interest was the Cornucopia by the fifteenth-century Italian scholar and papal secretary Nicolaus Perottus. Yet his scholarship and critical acumen were approved by two of the most learned men of his day, for Erasmus asked Whitford to judge between his and Thomas More's responses to Lucian's Pro tyrannicida (printed in Paris, in 1506, and dedicated to Whitford).

Whitford was sensitive to English style, making new translations of St Augustine's rule and St Bernard's Golden Epistle which had been brought to him 'in englysshe of an olde translacyon, rugh and rude'. He also pointed out that works might be attributed to men like St Bernard to enhance their authority. Much of his published work was translation: Augustine's rule with Hugh of St Victor's commentary (1525, 1527), the Syon version of the Sarum martyrology (1526), and works attributed to saints Bernard and Bonaventure, Isidore, Chrysostom, and Bernard Sylvester; lengthy quotations from scripture, the fathers, and classical authors were also embedded in his works. Although he has been credited with the popular sixteenth-century translation of Thomas à Kempis's Folowynge of Chryste, that attribution seems to be the consequence of the inclusion by the printer, Robert Redman, of a different version of The Golden Epistle 'nat of the translation nor edicion of this auctor' in his Werke of Preparacion ... unto Comunion (1531?) accompanied by the statement 'it is in some bokes imprynted in the later ende of the boke called in latyn Imitatio Christi that is to say in Englisshe the folowyng of Christe' (Whitford, A Werke of Preparacion, sig. G2v). Nor is it likely that Whitford was the translator responsible for A Looking Glace for the Religious, because its author, Ludovicus Blosius (d. 1566), was considerably younger than him.

Whitford was well aware of the benefits of print. He was repeatedly asked to copy A Dayly Exercyse and Experyence of Dethe, but found the task 'very tedyouse: I thought better to put it in print' (Whitford, A Dayly Exercyse, sig. A1v). He had his works printed in the same format so that they could easily be bound together. But writing at a time when Lutheran texts in English were beginning to circulate and finding one included among his works displacing his own, he repeatedly warned his readers to beware anonymous publications. He added his name to his works not out of pride but for accountability, and the references to his sources that pepper the margins of his works were probably included for the same reason. Because he wrote in English and had his works printed they travelled far beyond the confines of Syon, into other cloisters and into lay households.

Most of Whitford's subjects were quite traditional, but written with a keen appreciation of the dangers and needs of the church on the eve of the Reformation. His substantial treatise on the religious life, *The Pype or Tonne of the Lyfe of Perfection* (1532), also provided a strong defence of that life against Lutheran detractors. His *Dayly Exercyse and Experyence of Dethe* (1534?, 1537, 1538?) was better structured, more practical, and more positive than traditional *ars moriendi* books. But it was his *Werke for Housholders* (1530?, 1530, 1531?, 1531, 1533, and twice in 1537) and related *Werke of Preparacion or of Ordinaunce unto Comunion or Howselyng* (1531?, 1537, 1537?) that broke new ground and established him as the devotional best-seller of the 1530s. Here he turned his attention to the needs of devout lay people and placed the onus for religious instruction, good behaviour, and daily prayer with the householder, as later protestant writers such as Thomas Becon (d. 1567) and the recusant *Manual of Prayers* were to do. Although Whitford's expectations of lay piety were perhaps rather unrealistic he did recognize some of the practical problems of crowded household conditions and sought to make his instructions and meditations adaptable to various needs. Although doctrinally conservative, Whitford's works suggest the way in which the English church was adapting to the changing world of the sixteenth century before it was overtaken by the Reformation.

J. T. RHODES

Sources J. Hogg, 'Richard Whytford's *The pype or tonne of the lyfe of perfection* with an introductory study on Whytford's works', *Elizabethan and Renaissance Studies*, 1, pts 1 and 2, 89 (1979–89) · M. B. Tait, 'The Brigittine monastery of Syon (Middlesex) with special reference to its monastic usages', DPhil diss., U. Oxf., 1975 · V. J. Lawrence, 'The life and writings of Richard Whitford', PhD diss., U. St Andr., 1987 · G. Williams, 'Two neglected London-Welsh clerics: Richard Whitford and Richard Gwent', *Transactions of the Honourable Society of Cymmrodorion* (1961), 23–44 [pt 1] · G. J. Aungier, *The history and antiquities of Syon Monastery, the parish of Isleworth, and the chapelry of Hounslow* (1840) · M. Bateson, ed., *Catalogue of the library of Syon Monastery, Isleworth* (1898) · P. G. Caraman, 'An English monastic reformer of the sixteenth century', *Clergy Review*, new ser., 28/1 (July 1947), 1–16 · W. A. M. Peters, 'Richard Whitford and St. Ignatius' visit to England', *Archivum Historiae Societatis Jesu*, 25 (1956), 328–50 · J. T. Rhodes, 'Syon Abbey and its religious publications in the sixteenth century', *Journal of Ecclesiastical History*, 44 (1993), 11–25 · R. Whitford, *A werke of preparacion or of ordinaunce unto comunion or howselyng. The werke for housholders with the golden pistle and alphabete or a crosrowe called an A.B.C.* (1531?) · T. Wright, ed., *Three chapters of letters relating to the suppression of monasteries*, CS, 26 (1843) · W. Roper, *The lyfe of Sir Thomas Moore, knighte*, ed. E. V. Hitchcock, EETS, 197 (1935) · N. Harpsfield, *The life and death of Sr Thomas Moore, knight*, ed. E. V. Hitchcock, EETS, original ser., 186 (1932) · Syon martyrology, BL, Add. MS 22285 · R. Whitford, *A dayly exercyse and experyence of dethe* (1537)

Whitford, Walter (d. 1647), bishop of Brechin and Church of England clergyman, was the son of Adam Whitford of Milntown (latterly Milton Lockhart), and his wife, Mary, daughter of Sir James Somerville of Cambusnethan, Lanarkshire. His father had been accused of involvement in January 1576 in a conspiracy against the regent, James Douglas, fourth earl of Morton. Walter was educated at Glasgow University, where he graduated MA in 1601, and afterwards acted as regent. On 10 May 1604 he was licensed to preach by the presbytery of Paisley, and on 3 December 1608 he was presented by James VI to the parish of Kilmarnock, Ayrshire. In 1610 he was translated to Moffat, Dumfriesshire, where he was admitted before 8 June. In 1613 he was nominated to the commission of the peace for Annandale, and was involved in several of the family feuds with which the county abounded. Some time in the earlier 1610s he married Anne (d. in or after 1660), fourth daughter of Sir John *Carmichael of that ilk (c.1542–1600), and great-niece of Morton. They had five sons, John [see below], Walter *Whitford (b. c.1617, d. in or after 1691), Adam [see below], David *Whitford (1626–1674), and James, and two daughters.

On 27 June 1617 Whitford signed the protestation to parliament in support of the liberties of the kirk. However, on 15 June 1619 he was nominated a member of the court of high commission, and on 30 August following became a pluralist when he was constituted minister of Failford in Ayrshire by the king. In March 1620 he received the degree of DD from Glasgow University, and on 4 August 1621 he was confirmed in his ministry by act of parliament. In 1623 his commission as justice of the peace was renewed, and he was appointed convener of the stewartry of Annandale. In the same year James proposed to translate him to Liberton in Edinburghshire, but failed to carry out his intention. On 25 October 1627 Whitford was appointed one of the commissioners nominated by the king for taking measures against papists, which on 21 October 1634 was expanded into a high commission to cite and punish all persons dwelling in Scotland concerning whom there were unfavourable reports. On 9 December 1628 he was presented by Charles I to the subdeanery of Glasgow; a dispute as to the crown's right of patronage prevented his taking possession until 1630. On 21 October 1634 he was nominated to the commission for the maintenance of church discipline.

On 15 September 1635 Whitford was consecrated as bishop of Brechin as successor to Thomas Sydserff, apparently on the recommendation of the earl of Stirling. The see was not rich, and it was proposed at one time that it be joined with the abbacy of Arbroath—a matter with which Archbishop William Laud was charged at his trial as an instance of his meddling in the property rights of the laity. Whitford continued to hold the Glasgow subdeanery *in commendam* until 1639, when he conveyed his titles to James Hamilton, third marquess (afterwards first duke) of Hamilton. On 16 April 1635 he was created a burgess of

Arbroath. Whitford used his episcopal authority to support the liturgical changes which Charles I had introduced. The new service book was very unpopular, and in 1637, when Whitford announced his intention of reading it, he was threatened with violence. Undeterred he ascended the pulpit, holding a brace of pistols, his family and servants attending him in arms, and read the service behind closed doors. On his return he was attacked by an enraged mob, and escaped with difficulty.

In February 1638 Whitford was one of the Scottish privy councillors who upheld the royal proclamation declaring opposition to the new prayer book treasonable. His obstinate imposition of the novel liturgy within his diocese and the kingdom at large roused intense feeling against him, and towards the close of the year, after his palace had been plundered, he was compelled to fly to England, and was harried all the way. In October 1638 Sir Archibald Johnston of Warriston had been advised to see to it that, when Whitford was at Edinburgh, 'in some private way, some course may be taken for his terror and disgrace if he offer to shew himself publicly' (Stevenson, 114). On 13 December 1638 he was deposed and excommunicated by the Glasgow assembly, whose authority, in common with the other Scottish bishops, he had refused to recognize. He was accused before the assembly of moral turpitude and closet papistry. On 23 August 1639 he and his fellow prelates drew up a protest against their exclusion from parliament.

On 28 December 1640 Whitford was living in London in great poverty, but on 20 February 1642, as a recompense for his sufferings, Charles presented him to the rectory of Walgrave, Northamptonshire, where he was instituted. In 1645 he was brought before the committee for plundered ministers and sequestered for having demonstrated 'great disaffection to the parliament and the proceedings thereof', both in private and in public, as well as discouraging his parishioners from giving their assistance to the Westminster regime 'in this defensive war' (Walker rev., 286). The compounding committee was subsequently instructed to see to his ejection from the town and parish. In spite of his sufferings at the hands of the Long Parliament, it is notable that, when he died in 1647, he was buried with honour on 16 June in the middle aisle of the chancel of St Margaret's, Westminster.

In 1660 Bishop Whitford's widow petitioned for a yearly allowance out of the rents of the bishopric of Brechin in consideration of the sufferings of her family in the royal cause. Their eldest son, **John Whitford** (d. 1667), Church of England clergyman, was a graduate of Glasgow University. Having been ordained deacon in London on 30 January 1641, through the influence of Archbishop Laud he was instituted on 10 February to the rectory of Northamptonshire. On 31 May 1642 at Blisworth he married Judith (c.1626–1707), daughter of John and May Marriott of Ashton. In 1645 he was ejected, and took refuge with his father. He was reinstated at the Restoration, and on 5 July 1661 received a grant of £100 in compensation for the loss of his books and other property. He died at Ashton on 9 October 1667 and was buried there; his widow died on 5

March 1707. His brother **Adam Whitford** (1623/4–1647), student and soldier, matriculated from Christ Church, Oxford, on 10 December 1641, aged seventeen. Caught up in the civil war, and apparently serving as a soldier, he did not graduate BA until 4 August 1646, after the surrender of the Oxford royalist garrison. He died in the city on 10 February 1647 and was buried the same day in Christ Church Cathedral. His brother James survived to be commissioned ensign in the earl of Chesterfield's regiment of foot in 1667. Rachel Whitford married James Johnstone, laird of Corehead, and Christian Whitford married William Bennett of Bains.

E. I. CARLYLE, rev. SEAN KELSEY

Sources Fasti Scot., 2.216, 3.104, 273 · H. I. Longden, Northamptonshire and Rutland clergy from 1500, ed. P. I. King and others, 16 vols. in 6, Northamptonshire RS (1938–52), 47 · Walker rev., 28617 · D. Stevenson, The Scottish revolution, 1637–1644: the triumph of the covenanters (1973) · Wood, Ath. Oxon., new edn, 3.1016 · Foster, Alum. Oxon. · The letters and journals of Robert Baillie, ed. D. Laing, 3 vols. (1841–2) · R. Douglas, The peerage of Scotland, 2nd edn, ed. J. P. Wood, 1 (1813), 753 · Ninth report, 2, HMC, 8 (1884), 254 · C. Dalton, ed., English army lists and commission registers, 1661–1714, 1 (1892), 79 · R. Keith, J. P. Lawson, and C. J. Lyon, History of the affairs of church and state in Scotland from the beginning of the Reformation to the year 1568, 3 vols., Spottiswoode Society (1844–50), vol. 1, p. 44 · D. Calderwood, The history of the Kirk of Scotland, ed. T. Thomson and D. Laing, 8 vols., Wodrow Society, 7 (1842–9) · The works of the most reverend father in God, William Laud, ed. J. Bliss and W. Scott, 7 vols. (1847–60), vol. 3, pp. 313; vol. 6, pp. 434–5, 438, 590; vol. 7, p. 427

Whitford, Walter (b. c.1617, d. in or after 1691), royalist army officer, was the second son of Walter *Whitford (d. 1647), bishop of Brechin, and his wife, Anne (d. in or after 1660), daughter of Sir John Carmichael. Described by one contemporary as 'tall, corpulent, full-faced, with long brownish black hair' (Pepys MSS, 266), Whitford fought as a colonel on the side of the king in the civil war. He was briefly held prisoner after the battle of Naseby in 1645, and on the overthrow of Charles I took refuge in Holland. In 1649 Isaac Dorislaus, who had taken an active part in the trial of the king, was appointed English envoy in Holland and reached The Hague on 29 April. Among the royalist exiles and followers of Montrose a scheme was laid to murder the new envoy, with the knowledge of the Portuguese ambassador and the blessing of his English confessor. On the evening of 12 May, as Dorislaus was sitting down to supper at the Witte Zwaan, six men burst into his rooms, and while some of them secured his servants, Whitford, after slashing him over the head, passed a sword through his body, and said, 'Thus dies one of the king's judges' (Wood, Ath. Oxon., 3.667). Many royalists received the news of the murder with satisfaction, and even the cautious Sir Edward Nicholas described the assassination as 'the deserved execution' of 'the bloody villain' (Carte). The murderers made their escape with the assistance of the Portuguese ambassador, and Whitford successfully reached safety in Brussels. He rejoined Montrose to serve on his last Scottish expedition of 1650. With the surrender of his garrison at Dunbeath after Montrose's defeat at Carbisdale (27 April) Whitford was sentenced to be beheaded on 8 June with Sir John Urry, Sir Francis Hay, and other royalist officers. While being led to execution he exclaimed that he was to die for his part in killing Dorislaus. The authorities were anxious not to be seen to defend Dorislaus's deeds by executing Whitford on such a pretext and, having obtained confirmation of his part in the assassination, 'the council thought fit to avoid the reproach, and so preserved the gentleman' (Clarendon, *Hist. rebellion*, 5.121). He was issued with a pass to leave the country on 25 June. Whitford was then protected by the earl of Derby, and was sheltered on the Isle of Man, where he avoided the attentions of the parliamentarian governor, who had been ordered to arrest him. By August 1656 he was at the court of Charles II and two years later was back at The Hague with the intention of killing another English diplomat, George Downing. Downing later complained to John Thurloe of the difficulty in securing Whitford's arrest and that he eventually departed for Muscovy 'in a ship loaded with ammunition' (Thurloe, *State papers*, 7.429). Whitford was forced to enter Russian service, though his family was awarded a small pension in 1662, and their coat of arms was altered on the king's orders. He had returned to England in 1663, when he petitioned for money to enable him to rejoin his wife in Russia, as part of the embassy of the earl of Carlisle. He was in England again by July 1666, when he petitioned for the post of town-major of Hull, and subsequently petitioned in 1670 for a pension to prevent his family from starving, stating on both occasions that he was disabled from active military service by his many wounds received in the royalist cause. He served as a lieutenant in the Scots foot guards under the earl of Linlithgow but was dismissed as a papist in 1673. In 1685 he was awarded a pension by James II and continued to be regarded with suspicion in Scotland, where he became a target for the anti-Catholic mob the following year. Bishop Burnet claimed that he died in 1686 following a deathbed rejection of Catholicism, and a recantation for his part in massacres committed in the service of the duke of Savoy in the 1650s (Burnet, 3.115), but Wood correctly noted that he was still living in Edinburgh in 1691 (Wood, *Ath. Oxon.*, 3.1018), from where, destitute and infirm, he had issued one last petition to the Scottish privy council in 1690, pleading for support. His son Charles was principal of the Scots College at Paris in 1714.   J. T. PEACEY

Sources *CSP dom.*, 1645–90 · *The manuscripts of his grace the duke of Portland*, 10 vols., HMC, 29 (1891–1931), vol. 1, pp. 591–2 · *A collection of original letters and papers, concerning the affairs of England from the year 1641 to 1660. Found among the duke of Ormonde's papers*, ed. T. Carte, 1 (1739), 291–2 · Wood, *Ath. Oxon.*, new edn, 3.667, 1018 · P. R. Newman, *Royalist officers in England and Wales, 1642–1660: a biographical dictionary* (1981), 408 · Thurloe, *State papers*, 5.315, 334, 429 · G. Wishart, *The memoirs of James, marquis of Montrose, 1639–1650*, ed. and trans. A. D. Murdoch and H. F. M. Simpson (1893), 298, 496 · *APS*, 1648–60, 575, 580, 588, 594 · Clarendon, *Hist. rebellion*, 5.121 · *Reg. PCS*, 3rd ser. · *Report on the Pepys manuscripts*, HMC, 70 (1911), 266 · *Bishop Burnet's History*, 3.115

Whitgift, John (1530/31?–1604), archbishop of Canterbury, was the eldest son of Henry Whitgift of Great Grimsby, Lincolnshire, and his wife, Anne Dynewell. Uncertainty surrounds the date of his birth, some sources quoting 1533, but as he himself recorded that he had

John Whitgift (1530/31?–1604), by unknown artist

reached his sixtieth year in 1590, 1530 or 1531 seem likelier dates. The Whitgift family held land in the township of that name on the Yorkshire–Lincolnshire border, and a number of them achieved local distinction; John's father became a prosperous merchant in his adopted town and an uncle, Robert, became abbot of the Augustinian house at Wellow, Lincolnshire.

Education and early career It was this uncle who is said to have been an important influence on the young John, taking responsibility for his education at Wellow before sending him to the celebrated St Anthony's School in London, where he lodged with an aunt, the wife of a verger at St Paul's. There is a tradition that, while there, John fell out with his aunt and the canons of St Paul's for refusing to attend mass, and he was returned to the family home in Grimsby. Thereafter John, on the advice of his uncle, by this time dispossessed of the dissolved monastery at Wellow, was sent to Queens' College, Cambridge, but his evangelical leanings led him to migrate to Pembroke where Nicholas Ridley was master. Whitgift matriculated from Pembroke in May 1550 as a pensioner, and was tutored by John Bradford who, like Ridley, was later to suffer martyrdom under Mary. Whitgift was made scholar and Bible clerk before graduating BA early in 1554.

Whitgift's scholarly accomplishments secured election to a fellowship at Peterhouse on 31 May 1555 and, despite his adherence to protestantism, he remained there throughout Mary's reign, proceeding MA in 1557 and quietly fulfilling college duties with the support of the master, Andrew Perne, who dissuaded Whitgift from following his fellow protestants into exile. During the royal visitation of the university by Cardinal Reginald Pole in 1557 Perne, as vice-chancellor, protected his protégé from scrutiny and thereafter the two men established a friendship which lasted until Perne's death in the archiepiscopal palace at Lambeth on 26 April 1589.

Following the accession of Elizabeth I, Whitgift was ordained deacon at Ely on 7 July 1560 and priest later that year; he soon established a reputation as a preacher after a sermon at Great St Mary's, Cambridge, in which he denounced the pope as Antichrist, a subject to which he was frequently to return. The returned exile Richard Cox, now bishop of Ely, made Whitgift one of his chaplains in 1560 and, in the same year, collated him to the rectory of Teversham, Cambridgeshire. Whitgift remained at Peterhouse and proceeded BTh in 1563, when he was also appointed Lady Margaret professor of divinity. In his first lecture he once again identified the pope as Antichrist. This appointment placed Whitgift in an influential position both within the university and the fledgeling church, and his lectures and strong anti-papal stance commended him to some of the more radical young protestants in the colleges, but he opposed them and sided with the college heads in the dispute over the electoral procedures for the vice-chancellorship in 1564. In the following year, however, he revealed his sympathy with the churchmanship of the more radical dons by adding his name to that of the vice-chancellor and others, including his mentor Matthew Hutton, under a letter to the chancellor, William Cecil, on 26 November asking that the order for the wearing of surplices in college chapels be withdrawn. Whitgift had already been named as one of those who had kept the surplice out of Peterhouse chapel and belonged to a moderate group who considered that enforcement of the vestments would deprive the university of many able young scholars.

The letter to Cecil was not well received, and the order was upheld, but the following months seem to represent a watershed in Whitgift's career. Despite his initial objections, Whitgift was soon persuaded of the rightness of government policy and preached in defence of the surplice, thereby establishing early in his career that high regard for hierarchical authority in matters of church order which throughout was to set him at odds with his more radical fellow Calvinists. This shift in position brought him to the notice of Cecil, and preferment followed; he was made a university preacher on 10 June 1566 and on 5 July following his salary as Lady Margaret professor was increased from 20 marks to £20 in recognition of the esteem he was held in by the university for his preaching, which had also begun to attract royal notice. Whitgift proceeded DTh in 1567, taking as his subject once again the proposition 'That the pope is Antichrist'; later that year he was made regius professor of divinity. Already, in April, being by then senior fellow at Peterhouse, he had been elected master of his old college, Pembroke College, in succession to Matthew Hutton, but he only remained there for three months before transferring on 4 July to the

much better endowed mastership of the royal foundation of Trinity College.

Master of Trinity Trinity had a radical fellowship, and when Whitgift arrived his own commitment to the defence of royal policy was still questioned in some quarters. Within three years conflicts with those fellows, and in particular with Thomas Cartwright, were to prove a defining moment in the post-Reformation English church. More immediately, however, college and university business occupied his energies. The college statutes were revised so that the chapel readers were no longer required to attend in the midsummer vacation, and the number of scholars to be admitted annually from Westminster School was restricted to two in order to allow the master and fellows greater discretion in the support of other worthy scholars. Whitgift was soon active within university affairs, intervening unsuccessfully on behalf of Roger Kelk for the mastership of St John's in 1569 and, in the same year, serving on a commission of inquiry into the activities of the religiously conservative provost of King's, Philip Baker. His talents and energy were beginning to be noticed further afield; his preaching had attracted the attention of the queen, who called him her 'White-Gift', and he was part of a commission of inquiry into a dispute between the citizens of Leicester and their preacher in 1567. Whitgift was rewarded by appointment to the third prebendal stall at Ely on 5 December 1568.

This preferment may have influenced Whitgift's decision to resign his professorship in October 1569. He was succeeded by William Chaderton, Lady Margaret professor, but it was the appointment of Thomas Cartwright to this chair that sparked off controversy. In spring 1570 Cartwright delivered lectures on the first two chapters of Acts in the course of which he set out a broadly presbyterian form of church government as the only model authorized by scripture and the primitive church. This amounted to a call for the abolition of episcopal government and received significant support among the younger Cambridge scholars, drawn by Cartwright's learning and rhetorical skills. No public response to these views was produced at this time, but a complaint against Cartwright was made to Cecil by Chaderton on 11 June. The university's fierce divisions on the issue during the summer were characterized in a famous meeting of senate on 29 June in which the supporters of Cartwright vetoed every name proposed for election to its headship, and the vice-chancellor, John May, responded by vetoing the grace required for the award of Cartwright's DTh.

Petitions and counter-petitions landed on Cecil's desk throughout July and he offered Cartwright a conference in Michaelmas term. Whitgift wrote to Cecil on 19 August objecting to this and, following the disturbances of the summer, stressing the need for a new set of statutes for the university. Subsequently drawn up by Whitgift with the help of a few others, including his old friend Perne, these reduced the role of the regents and produced a more oligarchic structure, which effectively placed the government of the university more firmly in the hands of the vice-chancellor and the heads of houses. The statutes quickly received the royal assent on 25 September, and Whitgift's leading role in this matter is perhaps best demonstrated by his election to succeed May as vice-chancellor in early November. By that date the conferences with Cartwright had taken place, but no agreement had been reached, and Whitgift used his new authority to proceed more vigorously against him. On 11 December Cartwright was summoned to the vice-chancellor's consistory court, which met in the master's lodge at Trinity, presented with a list of articles based on his lectures and, under the terms of the new statutes, ordered to recant his opinions: this he refused to do and was deprived of his chair and forbidden to preach in the university. Cartwright withdrew to Geneva, probably in the company of Walter Travers, who was removed from his fellowship at Trinity about this time, and thereafter the points at issue between him and Whitgift moved beyond the confines of Cambridge. Whitgift remained busy within the university for another seven years; Trinity grew in numbers and distinction under his assiduous care so that it rivalled St John's, but it was a care which, in the eyes of opponents such as Giles Wigginton, seemed overbearing and oppressive. Whitgift was a regular attender at hall, sharing commons with the students, and was a conscientious teacher and preacher.

That preaching now also took place at Lincoln, where Whitgift had been elected dean on 19 June 1571, and where he spent time each summer, receiving a faculty from Archbishop Matthew Parker in October permitting him to hold both posts, and any other benefices, in plurality. The Lincoln appointment may have been in anticipation of a move from Cambridge where the continuing battle with Cartwright's supporters was proving divisive. Cartwright's return to Cambridge in 1572 disturbed the college once more and in September Whitgift removed Cartwright from his fellowship on the formal, if tendentious, grounds of the latter's failure to take priests' orders, a decision that brought protests from some members of the college, and provoked in turn a threat of resignation from the master. On 28 September six of his fellow heads of house appealed to Cecil, now Lord Burghley, on Whitgift's behalf, asking the chancellor for some public acknowledgement of his contribution to the governance and intellectual life of the university.

In the same year Whitgift began to play a more public role in the church. He acquired the prebendal stall of Nassington at Lincoln and another at Lichfield Cathedral, exchanged the living of Teversham for a Lincolnshire one at Laceby, and was returned as a representative of the diocese in the lower house of convocation, where he was chosen prolocutor (that is, president). At this time the church was convulsed by the storm that broke over the *Admonition to the Parliament*, and its polemical consequences were to occupy much of Whitgift's time, and that of his old adversary Cartwright, in the following years. The university continued to make heavy claims on him: he served another term as vice-chancellor in 1573 and was one of the commissioners appointed to visit St John's in 1576, when he also wrote to Burghley requesting that

effective steps be taken to prevent the sale of fellowships and scholarships. By that date his public defence of the religious settlement had made it clear that he was going to be a key figure in the future of the English church and that episcopal preferment beckoned; unsuccessfully recommended by Parker for Norwich in 1575, he was nominated to Worcester on 24 March 1577 and enthroned by proxy on 12 May, resigning the mastership of Trinity in June. This promotion owed much to Whitgift's successful, if troubled, mastership, which left the college in good shape financially and intellectually—a fact acknowledged by his successor John Still and one that has been lost to sight in more general histories beneath the disputes with Cartwright and the highly coloured account of Trinity under Whitgift provided by Giles Wigginton in 1584. Yet it was the dispute with Cartwright that thrust Whitgift into national prominence more quickly than would have otherwise been the case, and which was to have far reaching consequences for the English church.

The *Admonition* controversy With the calling of parliament in April 1571 the debate about further reform of the church had moved from Cambridge back to the capital, but the introduction of a bill to remove 'popish abuses' from the prayer book led to a breakdown of relations between the bishops and the puritans, and an episcopal preaching campaign was launched from Paul's Cross against the proposals in the bill. Parliament was dissolved and the bishops demanded from some of the leading radical clergy subscription to the articles of religion, recently given statutory force in parliament. A new parliament was called for May 1572, by which time Cartwright had returned from Geneva. Two London ministers, John Field and Thomas Wilcox, prepared a pamphlet addressed to parliament setting out the desirability of establishing a fully reformed presbyterian church order and adding a list of popish abuses remaining in the English church, which represented a satirical and vituperative attack on the bishops. The tract, incorporating both elements, was considered inflammatory by some radicals and was not published until June. By that time the queen had confiscated a bill 'concerning rites and ceremonies' and, effectively stifling further parliamentary debate, ordered that no matters of religion should be discussed by parliament before they had been approved by the bishops and the lower house of convocation, of which Whitgift was president.

The *Admonition to the Parliament*, an appeal to the public in the guise of a letter to parliament, was the most outspoken protestant criticism of the Elizabethan settlement to appear by that date, and divided the puritans themselves. Its pithy, scurrilous style gave it notoriety and made an immediate impact, drawing a reply from Paul's Cross by Thomas Cooper, bishop of Lincoln, as early as 27 June, and it reached its third edition by August. At about this time Whitgift was entrusted with the task of replying to the *Admonition*, which he took on with some urgency. In a letter of September informing Archbishop Parker of Cartwright's removal from his fellowship, Whitgift declared that he had completed his refutation and had most of it in fair copy, sending the full text to the archbishop in the following month. By that date the authors of the *Admonition* had been identified and imprisoned. Yet before Whitgift's work could be published *A Second Admonition to the Parliament* appeared, penned by his Cambridge adversary Cartwright, in which a fuller account of the presbyterian discipline was set out. Whitgift's *Answer* to the *Admonition* was published, probably in November 1572, and an augmented edition, containing a section addressing Cartwright's *Second Admonition*, appeared in February 1573.

The frenetic rate of publication was continued by Cartwright, whose *Replye to an Answere of Dr Whitgifte* appeared in April 1573. This full exposition of the Reformed position reinvigorated radical support but brought strong reaction from the government. A proclamation ordering the surrender of the *Admonition* and other books was issued. Bishops were required by the privy council to act more firmly against nonconformist clergy and, in December, a warrant was issued for Cartwright's arrest, forcing him into exile once again. Encouraged by Parker, Whitgift devoted much of this year to an extensive response to Cartwright, answering him point by point in his *Defense of the Aunswere to the Admonition Against the Replie of T.C.* which appeared in 1574. On 26 March 1574 he preached the new year sermon before the queen at Greenwich, setting out his defence of episcopal government; it was published later that year. Other supporters of Cartwright entered the debate with Whitgift at this time, but the major response came from the exiled Cartwright himself, in 1575 and again in 1577, to neither of which Whitgift replied.

These years between 1570 and 1575 were crucial to the developing character of the Elizabethan church, and Whitgift's views were to prevail with the queen and with authority; the points at issue between him and his opponents at this time therefore need some consideration. Behind the polemical tone of the controversy it is worth locating points of agreement: both Whitgift and his opponents shared a Calvinist theology and, in matters of ecclesiology, they each recognized the importance of theological scholarship and the central role of scripture in defining the nature of the church. In the climate of the early 1570s they each sought to locate their position between what they saw as the corruptions of the Roman church on the one hand and the excesses of Anabaptism on the other, both of which evils they identified among the views of their opponents. Behind these common protestant assumptions what was at stake was the true nature of the English church and, in the course of the debate, two conflicting views emerged of the Christian community and of its relations with social and political power. For Whitgift the importance of maintaining the distinction between the visible and the invisible church was crucial and it was wrong to try to conflate the two: the invisible spiritual government of the church belonged to God, but 'The visible and external government is that which is executed by man and consisteth of external discipline and visible ceremonies practised in that church that containeth in it both good and evil' (*Works*, 1.183). This

important passage illustrates two key elements in Whitgift's position: first he envisioned the church as comprising both good and evil, thereby differing from Cartwright, who postulated a closer relationship between the visible church, the godly, and the invisible, the elect, and was of the view that the ungodly were not full members of the church and should be firmly excluded from the sacraments. Whitgift's more inclusive definition led on naturally to his second point, for it was precisely because the church contained both good and evil that external discipline was necessary. That discipline was to be provided by the Christian magistrate and therefore 'must be according to the kind and form of government used in the commonwealth' (ibid., 2.263). This moved the earlier debate between the bishops and the puritans on to rather different ground; the dispute over whether ceremonies and church discipline were things indifferent, adiaphora, or scripturally ordained remained central but, whereas earlier defenders of the establishment had generally defended the prayer book and episcopacy on essentially pragmatic grounds, Whitgift now postulated a view of church–state relations that removed any distinction between the church of Christ and the Christian commonwealth, in which the queen, as supreme governor, should 'govern the church in ecclesiastical affairs as she doth the commonwealth in civil' (ibid., 2.264). The settlement of 1559 and the royal supremacy were thus inextricably linked, and this became the cornerstone of subsequent defences of the establishment against criticism from the puritans. It was an argument, however, written in a defensive mode, and Whitgift's lengthy tract lacked the emotional appeal of Cartwright's work; particularly on the question of the church's role in edification, which the puritans described as the building of Christ's kingdom in the community but which Whitgift saw as the growth of understanding in the individual. Thus, while Whitgift laid the foundation for the later theoretical work of Richard Hooker, the style and emphasis of the *Defense* did little to win over his opponents. It did, however, receive the endorsement of the queen and of most of the privy council.

Bishop of Worcester The new bishop was enthroned by proxy on 12 May 1577 and left Cambridge the following month. The diocese to which Whitgift was preferred was a known centre of Catholic activity, and almost immediately he was required to report, with his fellow bishops, on the state of his diocese and the surrounding area, describing it as 'much warped towards popery' (Strype, *Whitgift*, 1–166), with seminary priests active in gentry households. In all thirty-nine Catholics were listed in his report on Worcester, including members of well-established families such as the Throckmortons, Blounts, Talbots, and Heaths. The political clout of these families was considerable and the county continued to cause problems to the bishop, who engaged in public conference with prominent Catholics in 1582 and also sought to gain control over the right of nomination to the county bench. His concern with recusancy stretched beyond the diocese itself for he was almost immediately appointed vice-president of the council in the marches of Wales and, in the absence in Ireland of the president, Sir Henry Sidney, he was the crown's principal official in the region. In this capacity Whitgift fulfilled a number of responsibilities, dealing with musters, investigating charges of treason, and handling factions within the council itself. Recusancy, however, remained his chief concern. In the first eighteen months of his vice-presidency the council carried out a vigorous campaign against Catholics and in particular against the group of well-connected gentry attending mass at Plasnewydd, the home of John Edwards, and those attending pilgrimage at the celebrated shrine at St Winifred's Well. Edwards was imprisoned early in 1579 and in June the council was given a general commission to inquire into the state of the Welsh dioceses and to pursue recusants. Whitgift sought a commission for himself and the Welsh bishops, as he did not trust the local magistrates to act against their Catholic neighbours, but on the return of Sidney in 1580 his policy was modified.

One of the principal weapons of the reformed clergy against Catholicism was preaching, and this was a responsibility that Whitgift took seriously. His first biographer and comptroller of his household, Sir George Paule, portrayed Whitgift at Worcester as the ideal protestant bishop who 'never failed to preach upon every Sabbath-day: many times riding five or six miles to a parish church, and after sermon come home to dinner', a practice which he continued at Canterbury where 'No Sunday escaped him in Kent, as the gentlemen there can well witness' (Paule, 57). According to Paule, Whitgift's style was grave, comely, and plain, virtues also regarded highly among the puritans and, notwithstanding the literary conventions behind this account, Whitgift's preaching activity placed him in a tradition of pastoral episcopacy which his views on episcopal authority have tended to obscure. Whitgift also sought to secure a preaching ministry in his cathedral and diocese and in 1578 was granted by the queen the right of appointment to vacant cathedral posts. This proved of only modest value, but he did appoint two of his former colleagues at Trinity, Godfrey Goldsborough and Gilbert Backhouse, to canonries, and Goldsborough as archdeacon of Worcester. Within the diocese Whitgift was a strong defender of episcopal rights, in particular with regard to his estates. After protracted negotiation, he was granted relief from first fruits for the bishopric, and by careful management he reduced the arrears of his tenants; he returned the rent-corn of two valuable manors, at Hallow and Grimley, to the see, paying £300 to protect the rights of his successors, and he also secured the title to his residence at Hartlebury Castle, though this continued to be a source of dispute for some time. This careful management had important consequences for the social and political authority of the church in the region, enabling Whitgift to provide hospitality in a way that his role in local politics required but which his predecessors had failed to do. Outside Worcester he was called upon to intervene in neighbouring dioceses, drawing up new statutes for Hereford Cathedral and heading a commission inquiring into disputes between William Overton,

recently appointed bishop of Coventry and Lichfield, and the dean and chapter and citizens of Lichfield. In both cases the cathedrals established lectureships as a result of Whitgift's actions. Both these commissions date from 1583, by which time it was clear that Whitgift was the preferred successor to the suspended archbishop of Canterbury, Edmund Grindal. Indeed, one of those commissions was issued in Grindal's name, as provincial, and Whitgift had already been active on the national scene, particularly during the parliament of 1581, when his central role in drawing up the bishops' response to the articles for reform of abuses in the church presented by Sir Walter Mildmay suggests that his advancement to Canterbury was widely anticipated. By 1583 the vacuum in the leadership of the church caused by Grindal's suspension meant that the question of resignation was raised once again, but before the archbishop, now blind and frail, could complete the formalities he died, on 6 July 1583. On 14 August Whitgift was nominated his successor and on 23 October he was enthroned as primate.

Archbishop of Canterbury, 1583–1587: parliamentary opposition The prospect of Whitgift's elevation had already aroused concern in puritan circles and among their sympathizers in the privy council, and they were not to be disappointed. Before his enthronement Whitgift, with other bishops, including John Piers of Salisbury and John Aylmer of London, had prepared a schedule of articles 'touching preachers and other orders for the Church', which received royal approval and were issued to the dioceses on 29 October. These orders amounted to a comprehensive platform of reform, including stricter proceedings against Catholics and non-attenders at church, a survey of the qualifications of the parochial ministry, and closer scrutiny of the quality of candidates for ordination; this programme would have commanded the support of most protestants, but a further clause demanding that all clergy subscribe to three articles aroused opposition. Two of these articles, one endorsing the royal supremacy and another stating that the Thirty-Nine Articles were agreeable to the word of God, were unexceptional to all but the tenderest of consciences, but the second article, which stated that the Book of Common Prayer and the orders of bishops, priests, and deacons contained nothing contrary to the word of God, and that clergy should use the prayer book and no other in public worship, reopened all those points of difference between the puritans and the bishops that had been largely overlooked in the previous six years. The demand for widespread subscription to such a comprehensive endorsement of the prayer book, made public in Whitgift's Paul's Cross sermon on 17 November, in which he inveighed against the disobedience of papists, Anabaptists, and 'our wayward and conceited persons', was bound to alienate not only the radicals but many moderate nonconforming clergy in the provinces.

Whitgift was the prime mover in this policy, and enjoyed the unwavering support of the queen, if not of many of her ministers. The imposition of the 'three articles', as they came to be known, met with resistance throughout the province. The clergy of the Chichester diocese were the first to be asked to subscribe and twenty-four ministers were suspended for refusing: similar responses were received throughout the first half of 1584; some sixty ministers each from the puritan strongholds of Norfolk and Suffolk, seventeen in Kent, twenty-three in Lincolnshire after discussion with the bishop, and in Leicestershire over 300 were recorded as making a limited subscription, suggesting some sort of accommodation. Accommodation there had to be, for Whitgift's articles had revived the dormant organizational powers of the radicals, and in particular those of John Field: meetings of clergy were held in the counties and petitions sent to the privy council, other petitions came from town corporations and from sympathetic gentry in the shires, while prominent protestant scholars, including the venerable John Foxe, argued against rigid subscription when the Catholic threat was increasing. Eventually, in June, Whitgift bowed to the advice of Burghley and of Sir Francis Walsingham and was persuaded to accept conditional subscription from those clergy who did not seek to disturb the peace of the church. In the end only nine ministers, including Field, suffered deprivation for refusing to subscribe. The price, however, was a renewed sense of solidarity among the puritan clergy which created an organization prepared to confront Whitgift on his own terms, as they did in 1584–5 by producing their own surveys of the condition of the provincial clergy in response to the official one.

Thwarted in his attempt at a comprehensive discipline of the church, Whitgift sought to separate the moderates from the radicals by proceeding against the recalcitrant: the weapon chosen for this strategy was the ecclesiastical commission, which had been renewed in December 1583. In May 1584 Whitgift produced a list of twenty-four articles, encompassing the three articles objected to earlier and directed specifically against puritans, which the accused had to answer under the oath *ex officio mero*. This was a procedure in civil law previously used against recusants, the legality of which was vigorously contested by common lawyers. The use of this oath, which required defendants to promise to answer questions before knowing what those questions were, provoked further petitions to Whitgift and led to a widening rift between the archbishop and his erstwhile supporters in the privy council, most notably Burghley, who objected to the 'Romish style' of the new articles. On 20 September a majority of the council wrote to Whitgift and Aylmer complaining of irregularities in proceedings against the godly ministers in Essex.

This troubled year ended with Whitgift writing a lengthy account to the queen in defence of his actions, and with the calling of parliament, which quickly informed Whitgift and the government of the depth of resentment that his policies had caused in the country. Events abroad, the assassination of William of Orange in Delft and the episcopal reaction in Scotland which saw many Scottish presbyterians withdraw to England, fuelled that resentment with insecurity. Conferences of ministers took place in the provinces and sent delegates to

London where Field's organizational powers kept up the pressure, lobbying at parliament was backed by masses of paperwork and by prayer and fasting in the country. Successive bills for reform of the ministry were presented immediately parliament met, but it was on 14 December that the puritan campaign began in earnest when, despite the queen's prohibition on debate about religion, further bills were introduced, including a bill in the Commons requesting the adoption of the Geneva prayer book, recently published in translation by Robert Waldegrave, and the implementation of a presbyterian system of discipline. This was presented to the Lords a week later but, although sympathetic to some of the complaints, they reminded the lower house of the royal prohibition and deferred their answer. This decision was delayed until 22 February, after the Christmas recess, when Burghley answered on behalf of the government reiterating the queen's desire to refer all matters of religion to the bishops and convocation rather than to parliament. Whitgift followed Burghley, answering the Commons' bill point by point at great length and (at least according to Robert Beale, clerk of the privy council) in intemperate language. Whitgift's uncompromising words in defence of episcopacy and the rights of the church angered the Commons, who were preparing a reply when, on 27 February, the queen made her support of the bishops absolutely clear at an audience where Whitgift and representatives of the two houses of convocation came to offer her the clerical subsidy. Wherever the blame for the shortcomings of the church lay, the queen was determined that the remedy lay with the bishops and renewed her prohibition on parliament discussing religion. Despite this the Commons introduced another bill which occasioned a confrontation between Whitgift and the earl of Leicester in the Lords before the session ended on 29 March.

The eighteen months since his nomination had proved a bruising time for the new archbishop who, although he could count on the support of Elizabeth, found his relations with erstwhile supporters on the council severely strained. Throughout these months Whitgift recognized that the issues at stake were essentially the same as those in the earlier conflict with Cartwright, but Cartwright's name, despite the latter's continued exile at Middelburg, came to encapsulate in Whitgift's mind the character of the opposition he faced to a degree that rendered his arguments the more uncompromising and suggested that, for him, there was something more than a matter of principle at stake. Indeed, one contentious issue at this time involved another of Whitgift's former adversaries at Trinity, Walter Travers. Despite not having episcopal orders, Travers was reader at the Temple Church in 1584 when the mastership fell vacant. His candidature was supported by Burghley and some of the benchers, but Whitgift opposed the appointment and in 1585 secured the post for Richard Hooker. The benchers responded by making Travers the afternoon lecturer so that, according to one contemporary, each Sunday the pulpit proclaimed Canterbury in the morning and Geneva in the afternoon. Whitgift was called upon to adjudicate this debate, which he did in March

1586 by revoking Travers's preaching licence. By then Cartwright had returned from exile and Whitgift had on 2 February become a member of the privy council.

Whitgift's elevation to the council was secured during the absence of his chief opponent, Leicester, in the Low Countries. This was a significant appointment, and testimony to Whitgift's standing with Elizabeth, who did not give any other archbishop such a promotion. Its immediate effect was to increase the archbishop's authority, in a formal sense at least. Having seen the effect of clandestine presses in the puritan campaigns of 1584–5, he secured an order from Star Chamber in June 1586 placing control of printing and the press in his hands and those of Bishop Aylmer. This order empowered them to fix the number of printers and, through the Stationers' Company and the ecclesiastical commission, to determine what could be published, adding the punitive sanctions of confiscation and destruction if any illicit presses were discovered.

Meanwhile Leicester's disastrous campaign in the Netherlands, and the implication of Mary, queen of Scots, in the Babington plot in the summer of 1586, diverted attention temporarily from the problem of nonconformity to the international Catholic threat. A new parliament was summoned to deal with the queen's safety, and at its opening in October, Whitgift was one of three commissioners appointed to deputize for Elizabeth while parliament discussed the fate of her cousin. The issue was not resolved until the execution of Mary on 8 February 1587. Discussion then centred on the financing of Leicester's campaign until, on 27 February, Antony Cope rose to present a 'bill and book' for reformation of religion, a programme that represented the culmination of a carefully planned operation. For the previous two years Walter Travers had been editing the Book of Discipline, a comprehensive statement of the ideal form of reformed worship and church government along Genevan lines adapted to the needs of a national church. Manuscript copies of the work had been circulated to conferences of ministers in the provinces for approval and comment, and this was the book to which Cope's bill referred. Cope and other radical MPs were imprisoned in the Tower by the time the government gave its response on 4 March. That response, given by three ministers, included a speech from Whitgift's ally at court, Sir Christopher Hatton, which revealed the close co-operation that had emerged between these two and Hatton's chaplain, Richard Bancroft, in combating puritan claims, an alliance that signalled that the establishment was about to move on to the offensive in its engagement with the puritans. Convocation attacked the bill and book, but parliamentary attempts to curb Whitgift's use of the *ex officio* oath against puritan clergy were stopped only by the queen's veto, perhaps procured by Whitgift, which was couched in terms that brooked no compromise. Henceforth redress in matters of religion was to be strictly limited to the clergy.

Archbishop of Canterbury, 1588–1593: *Marprelate* and the prerogative courts Whitgift's victory in parliament only served to shift the arena of conflict: from parliament to the printing press, from the press to the provinces, and from the provinces to the courts. None of these shifts enhanced Whitgift's reputation, then or thereafter. That there was widespread, organized, puritan activity in some counties commanding the support of significant sectors of the local gentry had become clear during the parliamentary debates, but the failure to bring about reform by statute and the deaths of Leicester and other key figures in 1588 left a mood of angry frustration which spilled over into extremism. This became apparent in October 1588 with the publication of *The Epistle of Martin Marprelate*, the opening salvo in a scurrilous press campaign from the underground press of Robert Waldegrave. The appearance of this satire, which began with a criticism of Whitgift for failing to answer Thomas Cartwright's volumes of 1575 and 1577, was soon followed by others as the press moved around the country, and the archbishop, 'that miserable, and desperate caytiffe wicked John Whitgift, the Pope of Lambehith' (*Theses Martinianae*, 1589, epilogue), was one of the chief targets of Marprelate's pen, in company with bishops Aylmer of London and Cooper of Winchester. Lampooned as 'the Canterbury Caiaphas' in reference to his use of the high commission against godly ministers, Whitgift took on direction of the search for the offending press, endorsed Bancroft's plan for a literary response in kind to the satires, and pursued the offending authors and printers, once found, through the high commission and Star Chamber.

Meanwhile parliament met once again on 4 February 1589, and with Hatton now lord chancellor and moderate puritans uncertain of the wisdom of Marprelate's campaign, Whitgift and his chaplain Bancroft moved on to the attack. Bancroft's sermon at Paul's Cross on 9 February, published the following month, set out a confident defence of episcopacy *per se*, distinguishing the English church from other protestant churches, and in particular the Scottish church, and dismissing the puritans as false prophets, likening them to earlier sectaries. An attempt in the Commons to challenge Whitgift's proceedings in the high commission as contrary to common law got nowhere, and the only debate allowed concerned an abortive bill for the removal of clerical pluralism and nonresidence, in which Burghley and the archbishop found themselves in opposition. The furore caused by the *Marprelate* tracts gave Whitgift the opportunity to pick off those whom he considered to represent the radical presbyterian leadership, especially after the discovery of the press in August 1589 revealed information about the clandestine clerical classis meetings in the midlands. As a result of the evidence he now had, Whitgift pressed home a case against his old foe Cartwright and eight other ministers, first in the high commission and then in Star Chamber. Scores of clergy were hauled before the commissioners in the winter of 1589–90, but the balance of power in the council and in the country had shifted so much that these events and the subsequent trials aroused less opposition than the subscription campaign of 1584. What Whitgift sought was evidence of seditious conspiracy on the part of the accused, but all nine—four from Warwickshire, including Cartwright, three from Northamptonshire, one from Staffordshire, and a roving Devon preacher—refused the *ex officio* oath, effectively blocking proceedings in the high commission. All except Cartwright were therefore deprived of their livings, degraded from orders, and imprisoned in the summer and autumn of 1590, Cartwright joining them at the end of October.

While this case was progressing another presbyterian, John Udall, was also tried, for his authorship of the *Demonstration of Discipline*, which the commissioners deemed a felony, committing the case to the assizes. In July the case was heard, the assizes being held at Whitgift's manor of Croydon, and at a later trial at Southwark in February 1591 Udall was sentenced to death, subsequently commuted to exile, but he died before the sentence could be carried out. In October 1590 Whitgift's personal involvement in the campaign brought a rebuke from Burghley, who advised him not to join the tribunal interrogating Cartwright in order to avoid any suspicion of personal rancour. During the winter of 1590–91 the imprisoned leaders kept in contact with their supporters, who organized petitions on their behalf, and in the spring it was decided, allegedly by Whitgift and Hatton, to transfer the case to Star Chamber. The trial began on 11 May, but the evidence for conspiracy remained difficult to uncover and the ministers put up a stout defence. The Hacket conspiracy of July changed matters, providing circumstantial evidence of contacts between the imprisoned ministers, especially Cartwright, and the lurid events that ended in William Hacket's execution for treason.

The death of Hatton in November removed Whitgift's greatest ally, but by this date his position in the council was so secure that he was able to ensure the succession of Sir John Puckering, the prosecutor in Star Chamber, as lord chancellor. The charge of conspiracy remained unproven but the spirit of the opposition was broken and by the end of the year a way out of the impasse was being sought. In January five of the prisoners were granted bail on signing a submission admitting that their meetings had been offensive to the queen and the council, but Whitgift still proved intransigent, especially in the matter of Cartwright, and at the end of February required another humiliating submission which the prisoners refused to sign. In April a new set of interrogatories were presented by the council which offered a way forward. The replies to these were sufficiently accommodating to permit partial relief by way of house arrest, and over the summer many of the prisoners returned to their homes, though under strict conditions. Cartwright was required to appear before the judges at any time within twenty days' warning being given.

There is no doubt that the puritans saw Whitgift as the chief protagonist in the cases made against them and it is clear both from correspondence with Burghley and his actions in early 1592 that he was intransigent in his opposition. The depth of that opposition was to be revealed in the parliament of 1593. Whitgift preached the sermon at its opening on 19 February, and he and his supporters so dominated proceedings that a Commons bill designed to combat Catholic recusants was transformed into an act, which (exceptionally in Elizabeth's reign) was directed at protestant sectaries, making them liable to banishment. This did not happen without an acrimonious struggle. In the contest between the Commons and Whitgift the separatists Henry Barrow and John Greenwood, who had been under arrest since 1588, were tried under the act against Catholics of 1581 and condemned to death for printing seditious works. Despite Burghley's remonstrations with Whitgift on their behalf, they were executed on 6 April, contemporary reports blaming the malice that the bishops had towards the Commons. Shortly afterwards John Penry, active in the *Marprelate* campaign, followed them to the scaffold. Whitgift's policy had begun as an attempt to remove the puritans from influence in the church through the normal processes of ecclesiastical administration; when this proved impossible he shifted his tactics, attempting to break the presbyterians by a rigorous prosecution of the leaders through the prerogative courts. By the summer of 1593 he had broken their organization and driven them underground, but in so doing he had made few friends.

Archbishop of Canterbury, 1593–1597: theological controversies Whitgift was a convinced Calvinist in matters of doctrine, and his early career had been made expounding that characteristically Calvinist identification of the pope with Antichrist. The disputes of the 1570s and 1580s centred not on doctrine but on matters of worship and discipline, but the boundaries between these categories were porous. This became evident in 1587 in the dispute between William Whitaker, the strongly Calvinist master of St John's College, Cambridge, whose election had been forced through by Whitgift and Burghley in the face of determined opposition from some of the fellows. One of their number, Everard Digby, was a Neoplatonist whose view of human capabilities was directly at odds with the world view of Calvinists like Whitaker, who denounced him as a papist and sought to remove him from his fellowship. The charge of popery was not supported by Whitgift, but Whitaker prosecuted Digby for several breaches of college statutes. Notwithstanding Digby's wilful defiance of the master and Whitgift's earlier support for Whitaker, the archbishop urged a compromise which involved the temporary reinstatement of Digby to his fellowship. What was essentially a matter of doctrine to a Calvinist like Whitaker was a 'thing disputable' to a Calvinist like Whitgift. Yet, when central doctrines, such as predestination and assurance, were openly discussed in Cambridge, as they were between 1595 and 1597, the gap between these positions narrowed considerably, without closing entirely.

On 29 April 1595 a sermon preached in the university church by William Barrett, fellow of Caius, denied the possibility of assurance of salvation to the ordinary believer, and asserted that human sinfulness, not God's will, was the source of reprobation. Thereby advocating a sublapsarian rather than a supralapsarian position on predestination, Barrett was mounting a direct attack on the form of Calvinism dominant in the university and associated with Whitaker and others. Such views were not new, and were similar to those of the Lady Margaret professor of divinity, Peter Baro, but the sermon marked a raising of the stakes. Whether this showed the anti-Calvinists taking the offensive, or whether the sermon was a defensive response to a sermon on atonement delivered from the same pulpit by Whitaker two months earlier, is unclear; but as an offensive tactic, it was ill-judged. Barrett was forced to recant by the heads of houses, and a petition signed by fifty-six dons demanded further action against him. Barrett appealed to Whitgift, presenting himself as the victim of a puritan plot, but the heads countered in a letter accusing Barrett of popery and stressing the encouragement that would be given to papists if he went unpunished. This letter set out the stark choice between popery and reformed purity as one that transcended national concerns, and contained no acknowledgement of the autonomous traditions of the English church which had recently been given theoretical justification by Richard Hooker. Whitgift accused the heads of disregarding his authority, as archbishop, in such matters, and criticized their appeal to the authority of Calvin over that of the Thirty-Nine Articles in determining the doctrine of the English church. Faced with Whitgift's anger the heads appealed to Burghley, and then used the good offices that existed between Whitaker and the archbishop to explain their actions. Although he might disagree about the grounds on which action should be taken against Barrett, the heads were confident that, doctrinally, Whitgift was on their side and, having seen Barrett's answers to articles posed by him in September, the archbishop admitted that he agreed with them on all points except one, that concerning the granting of assurance to all the elect. The archbishop made it clear, however, that it was his authority that counted in these matters, and that orthodoxy was enshrined in the Thirty-Nine Articles before, in the end, he issued a general condemnation of Barrett's views, requiring him to retract.

Whitgift's reconciliation to the heads owed much to the intervention of his old mentor Matthew Hutton, now archbishop of York, whom Whitgift regarded as representing an older generation of English Calvinists who did not seek the more rigid applications of discipline and doctrine associated with Théodore Beza. Hutton was asked to comment on the nine articles which had been submitted to Whitgift by Whitaker and which, after some modifications by the archbishop which toned down but did not change their Calvinist orientation, were issued as the Lambeth articles on 20 November. These articles set out the Calvinist view of election and predestination as a fundamental doctrine of the English church, and Whitgift's position, following Hutton's intervention, seems to have moved closer to that of Whitaker and the heads on the central issue of justifying faith and the individual's assurance of salvation. The status of the articles was unclear and the queen disapproved, ordering them to be withheld on 5 December. In consequence they were never published and Whitgift wished them to be considered a private matter between him and the university authorities. Nevertheless, in addition to their acceptance at Cambridge, they were incorporated into the Oxford University Acts of 1596 and 1597. The puritans continued to view the articles as a vindication of their doctrinal position: at the Hampton Court conference in 1604, they sought unsuccessfully to have doctrinal status conferred on them, and the articles were subsequently adopted by the Irish church in 1615.

Despite their uncertain status the articles, in effect, set out to define in a series of numbered theses the doctrine of the English church, which had previously been a matter of tacit assumption based on the Thirty-Nine Articles. As such the articles represented a departure from Whitgift's usual position on these matters, which acknowledged a legitimate space for adiaphora or things disputable. The anti-Calvinists recognized this shift and, given the absence of royal support, a challenge to the articles was expected; it emerged on 12 January 1596 from the hitherto non-polemical Peter Baro. He claimed that the articles did not impugn his position that man, not God, was the author of sin, exploiting the ambiguity in article 4, which permitted a sublapsarian as well as a supralapsarian interpretation of predestination, and claiming that this view had a respectable pedigree in the English church going back to John Hooper and to the Thirty-Nine Articles. This aroused the opposition of the Cambridge heads, but Baro anticipated support at court and wrote directly to Whitgift on 27 January. Whitgift did not intervene on Baro's behalf but played for time, letting matters take their course. This they did and Baro, recognizing the weakness of his position within Cambridge, did not seek re-election to his chair. The events of 1595–6 represented a victory of sorts for the Calvinists, both Barrett and Baro withdrew from Cambridge, and Whitgift, encouraged by the heads, had issued an unequivocally Calvinist set of doctrinal articles, but these articles had manifestly failed to achieve doctrinal authority and had fallen foul of the queen. As such, the articles attest both to the strength of the Calvinist consensus that existed in the church, and to its limits. Whitgift and the Cambridge Calvinists might have agreed on essentials when it came to doctrine, but the degree to which those essentials should be enforced, and by whom that should be done, remained a source of contention. Two years after these events the archbishop was to be found forcing the election of the anti-Calvinist John Overall to the mastership of St Catharine's College in opposition to the Calvinist heads.

Primate and pastor Alongside these political and theological concerns Whitgift faced the normal responsibilities of an Elizabethan prelate. While at Worcester he had proved himself a doughty defender of ecclesiastical rights and property against the laity, and he continued in this vein at Canterbury. He was a firm opponent of puritan schemes for buying up impropriations in order to augment the stipends of the poorer clergy, since this would undermine the financial position of the hierarchy and of the universities. He was fortunate in his early years at Canterbury for several leases fell due in 1584 and 1585, enabling him to derive an income of over £1000 in each of those years beyond his normal rental income. Whitgift proved an astute manager of his estate, protecting its long-term interests before his personal profit. No lengthy leases were granted, a careful husbandry of the timber on his estates maintained its value, and he preserved the demesne lands at his manors of Lambeth, Croydon, and Bekesbourne. At a period of high inflation Whitgift protected his interests, and those of the church, by making extensive use of rents in kind, which in his early years amounted to 204 fat wethers, 190 quarters of wheat, and 20 loads of hay annually, most of which was consumed within the household.

As archbishop, and with residences close to the capital, Whitgift was particularly prone to visitation by Elizabeth, who stayed with him most years. The political benefits of this relationship—it was after one successful visit that Elizabeth gave him the famous sobriquet 'her little black husband'—had to be set against the financial cost of maintaining a large household and the criticisms that brought from puritan clergy and laity alike. Whitgift trod this narrow line adroitly. He kept a substantial household, as Martin Marprelate caustically observed, of over 100 liveried servants, including some trained captains, which he used to impress the Kentish gentry on his lavish journeys there but which he also placed at the disposal of the crown. On news of rebellion by the earl of Essex breaking in January 1601 it was Whitgift's household captains, at the head of a force of forty horsemen and forty footmen, who secured the arrest of his former pupil, taking him to Lambeth before escorting him to the Tower. His household was clearly at the service of the state and part of his public duty, but that duty went further.

The archbishop's hospitality was not confined to the rich and powerful, but also encompassed the scholarly and the poor. Paule described Whitgift's household as 'a little academy' (Paule, 98) for the lectures and ecclesiastical exercises he saw performed there, including a weekly sermon on Thursdays during term, and the archbishop provided regular support to scholars both within his houses and at the universities. His patronage extended to these younger friends; five fellows of Trinity during his time there were promoted to the episcopal bench, as were seven of his household chaplains, including Richard Bancroft, his successor at Canterbury. Other scholars, such as Lancelot Andrewes, Matthew Sutcliffe, Hugh Broughton, and Hadrian Saravia, also enjoyed his domestic patronage, as did John Stow. This mode of hospitality was easier for Whitgift, as a bachelor, than for many of his colleagues, but was significant even so. He regularly offered financial support from his own resources to Beza and the Genevan church, maintaining a correspondence into the 1590s despite his difficulties with the puritans at home and his own theological differences, and he used his rents from rectory estates to augment poor livings in his diocese. His commitment to a learned clergy is regularly attested in his visitation articles. His learning was exhibited in a personal library of over 4000 volumes, many later acquired by Bancroft, and he had books dedicated to him by scholars from across the theological spectrum, including Baro and Whitaker. In this Whitgift was the model reformed bishop, but the most arresting picture of his household is Paule's description of Christmas when archbishop and household sat down to eat with the poor. The shortages of the 1590s made the plight of the poor particularly acute and it is to this decade that Whitgift's major charitable benefaction can be traced. On 14 November 1595 he bought the site of the Checquer Inn at Croydon for £200, adding further properties soon afterwards. On 22 November he was granted a licence to found an almshouse, dedicated to the Holy Trinity, for up to forty men and women, and the first seven inmates, all former household servants, were admitted. Provision for a school followed the purchase of another site on 6 October 1596, and in 1599 building work was completed at a cost of over £2718. On 10 July 1599 the chapel was consecrated by Bancroft, and on 25 June 1600 the deed of foundation for both school and hospital, which were endowed with lands bringing an annual income of over £185, was signed and the first schoolmaster appointed. During these years the poor beyond Croydon also commanded the archbishop's attention, as it did that of government. In 1596, faced with national food shortages, Whitgift added his voice to that of the queen in asking the clergy of the province to preach in support of measures designed to ensure cheap corn, and urging the bishops to remind them and the wealthy of their duty of hospitality towards the poor.

Final years By 1598 Whitgift, like the queen whose confidence he continued to enjoy, had become something of a survivor of a bygone stage in the English Reformation, and those looking ahead were waiting on the deaths of these old dinosaurs before returning to the unresolved conflicts in the church and its relations with the state. Whitgift could still act forcefully, as he did in the matter of Overall's appointment to St Catharine's, and decisively, as he did over the Essex rebellion, but despite his careful promotion of loyal protégés, he no longer dominated the episcopal bench to the extent he had previously. His main activity in these years was in embedding in the church those administrative reforms for which he had fought. He resisted parliamentary attempts to meddle in marriage law and in ecclesiastical fees in the parliament of 1597, treating them in convocation, and in 1601 he and Elizabeth combined to stop further debate on a bill to restrict pluralism in the church. He continued to defend the independence of the ecclesiastical courts from encroachments by the secular courts, particularly the courts of equity, and in 1600 protested about the increasing use of prohibitions in those courts to suspend proceedings in the church courts. Clerical learning remained a high priority in his various enquiries, though he was more optimistic about this than his critics, and he set up a standard table of ecclesiastical fees and tried to curb non-residence among the clergy in the canons of 1597, which were extended to the northern province as well as Canterbury.

In his official capacity, and from personal friendship, Whitgift played a key role in the events surrounding the illness and death of the queen, and was at her bedside when she died on 23 March 1603. He was chief mourner at her funeral in Westminster Abbey, receiving the offertory and the banners. He was at the council that proclaimed James VI of Scotland king, sending the dean of Canterbury to Edinburgh immediately. At James's request, he sent the new king a report on the state of the church giving details of the learning of the clergy and the state of pastoral provision, and on 25 July presided at the coronation. When James called the Hampton Court conference between the puritans and the bishops on 16 January 1604, Whitgift attended but leadership of the bishops' delegation was assumed by his former chaplain Bancroft, by now bishop of London. That James took the view of the bishops on the key issues would have been a relief to this champion of orthodoxy, but in the following month he caught cold while travelling by barge from his palace at Lambeth to visit Bancroft at Fulham about church business. A few days later he suffered a stroke while dining at Whitehall and he died at Lambeth on 29 February 1604.

Whitgift's body was carried to Croydon where on 27 March his funeral was solemnized, his former pupil at Trinity, Gervase Babington, by now the occupant of Whitgift's old see of Worcester, preaching the sermon. A recumbent effigy, showing the archbishop with his hands in prayer, marked his grave in the chapel of St Nicholas within the church, where the poor and the scholars of his foundation sat during divine service. Thomas Churchyard published a poem on his death called 'Churchyard's good will', but the controversies that dominated his life soon followed him in death through a lampoon circulated by the puritan Lewis Pickering, who quickly found himself before the Star Chamber. By his will Whitgift confirmed to his hospital and school all those lands purchased by him on their behalf; he made substantial bequests to the poor of Canterbury, Lambeth, and Croydon; he left his parchment books to Trinity College, with any duplicates they had going to Peterhouse; he gave Pembroke College his Complutensian Bible and the works of Thomas Aquinas, and left Bancroft, who was an executor, his paper books and writings, which now form part of Lambeth Palace Library; the residue of his estate he divided equally between his surviving brother and the families of three nephews and nieces.

Reputation Whitgift's reputation has been dominated by those controversies that dominated his life. To a conservative like Stow he was a 'man born for the benefit of his country and the good of his church', but to the author of the *Marprelate* tracts he was 'the pope of Lambehith'. From John Strype to Thomas Babington Macaulay, and down to the present, judgements on Whitgift are not far removed from their authors' position on the current state of the established church, or established religion in general. He commanded the support of the queen but was mistrusted by more internationally minded protestants on the council like Leicester and Walsingham; his uncompromising stance often exasperated Burghley, even when he shared

his aims. Whitgift's conscience was difficult to deal with, and he was capable of pursuing his opponents to the utmost. Yet he had made his reputation as a preacher against the papacy in terms that many of the earlier puritans shared, and, despite his differences with them over discipline and the autonomy of the English church, he continued to share with them a concern for a learned ministry and a commitment to Calvinism. He also established one of the most munificent charitable foundations of the late sixteenth century, paying for it in his lifetime and not, like so many others, in his will. He was capable of great loyalty to some and clearly inspired affection from his chaplains and protégés, but where the rights of the church were concerned personal loyalties were ignored and compromise, even in the pursuit of peace and charity, rejected. The portraits which exist at Croydon, Lambeth, in Cambridge, and in the National Portrait Gallery reveal a dark, thin-faced individual with the severity of the administrator rather than the austerity of the scholar, so it is a surprise to discover that music seems to have played an important part in his life. His written works show a defensive cast of mind, thorough but not creative, which nevertheless laid the foundations for a theory of church–state relations that proved enduring, if not universally accepted. After the promise and hopes of the early Elizabethan church it was Whitgift's task, and perhaps his misfortune, to have to steer a path for that church through the conflicts and inconsistencies that earlier generations could ignore in pursuit of the common enemy. In that task he could not always depend on the full support of his episcopal colleagues, many of whom had more sympathy for puritans than he had, but that lack of support also owed something to his character. His personality and temperament were ill-suited to the open debate that had characterized earlier disagreements within the Reformed camp, and indeed such a strategy may not have been welcomed by his sovereign and supreme governor of the church. He fell back, therefore, on the narrow basis of the law, sometimes, as in the case of Penry and in his pursuit of Cartwright, with a vehemence that more moderate figures considered damaging to the cause he was defending. In so doing his inclusive view of the church as comprising all, and his liberal view of 'things disputable' in matters of theology, were gradually submerged beneath his authoritarian insistence on matters of ceremony and church discipline, but it is worth remembering that, in that controversy, it was his opponents who began by claiming that such things were non-negotiable.

WILLIAM JOSEPH SHEILS

Sources G. Paule, *The life of Dr John Whitgift* (1612) · J. Strype, *The life and acts of John Whitgift*, new edn, 3 vols. (1822) · *The works of John Whitgift*, ed. J. Ayre, 3 vols., Parker Society (1851–3) · P. Lake, *Moderate puritans and the Elizabethan church* (1982) · P. Lake, *Anglicans and puritans? Presbyterianism and English conformist thought from Whitgift to Hooker* (1988) · P. Collinson, *The Elizabethan puritan movement* (1967) · J. E. Neale, *Elizabeth I and her parliaments*, 2 vols. (1953–7) · H. C. Porter, *Reformation and reaction in Tudor Cambridge* (1958) · V. J. K. Brook, *Whitgift and the English church* (1958) · P. M. Dawley, *John Whitgift and the English Reformation* (1954) · will, PRO, PROB 11/103, sig. 45 · E. Gilliam and W. J. Tighe, 'To "run with the time":

Whitgift and the Lambeth articles, and the politics of religious controversy in late 16th century England', *Sixteenth Century Journal*, 23 (1992), 325–40 · L. H. Carlson, 'Archbishop Whitgift: his supporters and opponents', *Anglican and Episcopal History*, 57 (1987), 285–301 · F. H. G. Perry, *The history of Whitgift School* (1976) · F. Heal, *Of prelates and princes: a study of the economic and social position of the Tudor episcopate* (1980) · W. M. Garrow, *The history and antiquities of Croydon … to which is added a sketch of the life of John Whitgift* (1818) · P. Collinson, *Godly people: essays on English protestantism and puritanism* (1983) · P. Collinson, *Elizabethan essays* (1994) · P. Collinson, *Archbishop Grindal, 1519–1583: the struggle for a reformed church* (1979) · N. Tyacke, *Anti-Calvinists: the rise of English Arminianism, c.1590–1640* (1987) · A. F. Scott-Pearson, *Thomas Cartwright and Elizabethan puritanism* (1926) · J. S. Coolidge, *The Pauline renaissance in England* (1970) · J. F. New, *Anglican and puritan: the basis of their opposition, 1558–1640* (1964) · S. J. Knox, *Walter Travers, paragon of Elizabethan puritanism* (1962) · M. C. Cross, *The royal supremacy in the Elizabethan church* (1969) · P. Williams, *The council in the marches of Wales under Elizabeth I* (1958) · A. Peel, ed., *The seconde parte of a register*, 2 vols. (1915) · G. Bray, ed., *The Anglican canons, 1529–1947* (1998) · J. Mullinger, *A history of Cambridge University* (1888) · W. P. M. Kennedy, *Elizabethan episcopal administration*, 3 vols. (1924) · G. Donaldson, 'The attitude of Whitgift and Bancroft to the Scottish church', *TRHS*, 4th ser., 24 (1942), 95–115 · *APC*, vols. 14–32 · F. M. Heal, *Hospitality in early modern England* (1990) · *CSP dom.*, 1558–1603 · K. C. Fincham, 'Clerical conformity from Whitgift to Laud', *Conformity and orthodoxy in the English church, c. 1560–1660*, ed. P. Lake and M. Questier (2000), 125–58 · C. Hill, *Economic problems of the church: from Archbishop Whitgift to the Long Parliament* (1956) · Venn, *Alum. Cant.* · *DNB*

Archives BL, corresp. and papers, Harley MSS · Bodl. Oxf., letters and memoranda · Croydon Central Library, letters · Croydon Central Library, letters and indenture · CUL, corresp. and papers · Inner Temple, London, papers · LPL, private accounts; corresp. and papers, MSS 807, 3470–3533, 2003–2019 · NL Scot., corresp. relating to Scotland [copies]

Likenesses oils, *c.*1598, CUL; copy, NPG · woodcut, pubd 1612 (after unknown artist), BM, NPG · J. Fittler, engraving · T. Trotter, engraving · G. Vertue, engraving, repro. in J. Strype, *The life and acts of John Whitfgift*, 3 (1822) · R. White, engraving · alabaster tomb effigy, St John the Baptist Church, Croydon, Surrey · oils, LPL [*see illus.*] · oils (after oils, LPL), Trinity Cam. · portrait, Peterhouse, Cambridge

Wealth at death see will, PRO, PROB 11/103, sig. 45

Whithorne, Peter. *See* Whitehorne, Peter (*fl.* 1549–1563).

Whithorne, Thomas (*c.*1528–1596), composer and autobiographer, was a son of John Whithorne and his wife, Joan, daughter of William Cabell, of Ilminster, Somerset. He was born in Somerset, probably in Ilminster, where the previous three generations of his family were settled; his sisters Joan, Margaret, and Agnes married Ilminster men. He was said to be aged sixteen in 1544 and forty in 1568, but sixty-two in 1596.

Whithorne's life and works to 1575 are recorded in 'A book of songs and sonnets, with long discourses set with them …' (Bodl. Oxf., MS Eng. misc. c. 330) written about 1576, in phonetic spelling, for an unknown friend. It is the earliest known continuous English autobiography. Some of its omitted names and places have been identified. It is the tale of unfortunate patrons and amorous women, and contains numerous verses (but no music), including a bawdy poem in broad Gloucestershire dialect, jests, and proverbs.

Whithorne studied in Oxford, at Magdalen College School (1538–44) and at Magdalen College itself, as a demy

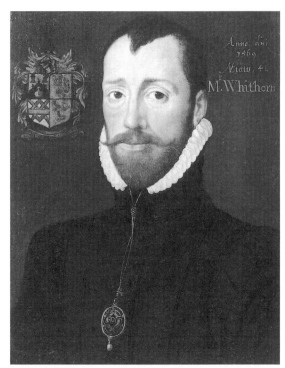

Thomas Whithorne (*c.*1528–1596), by unknown artist, 1569

(1545), but left without a degree. He moved to London to be employed as John Heywood's 'servant and scholar' (Whithorne, 1962, 6) for three years, and there learned to play the virginals and lute and to write poetry. On leaving Heywood, Whithorne hoped to teach music in London but found no openings in the metropolis (where he learned to play the cittern and gittern), so had to live in with country families. He taught one of the duchess of Northumberland's daughters until the family's fall (1553). Thereafter he toured the continent to observe foreign customs.

Back home, Whithorne was in Lord Ambrose Dudley's service by 1557 and remained there until household economies forced him out. In 1560–62 he was private tutor to William Bromfield's son William, who was then at Trinity College, Cambridge. On William's graduation, he and Whithorne went to London. Bromfield senior, having appointed Whithorne to manage his business affairs in London, left for Le Havre but died soon afterwards. Whithorne's health was poor, so again he took a country post. To further his career, he prepared earlier pieces for publication, and *Songes for Three, Fower, and Five Voyces* appeared in 1571. This collection consisted of secular songs for a wide range of abilities: these were, in effect, early madrigals. By about 1576 he had improved some verses and tunes.

Whithorne was appointed chapel master to Archbishop Matthew Parker, for whom he arranged two metrical psalms for four voices; he was in this post at the time of Parker's death in 1575. By 1577 Whithorne was living in the parish of St Alfege, London Wall. On 5 May of that year he married Elizabeth Stoughton in her parish church, St

Martin-in-the-Fields, Westminster. In 1582 he was assessed for the subsidy on a mere £3, in St Mary Abchurch parish, where he finally settled.

Whithorne's *Duos, or, Songs for Two Voices*—which in fact contains some pieces for voices and/or instruments—was published in 1590. The verses of twenty of the fifty-two pieces had appeared in the autobiography, though they may have been written long before. Tipped into the autobiography was a scrap of paper listing early Tudor musicians (for example Robert Fayrfax, John Taverner) on one side, and later ones (including William Byrd, Giles Farnaby, and John Dowland) on the reverse.

Whithorne declared his nuncupative will on or about 5 July 1596: he bequeathed all his goods (unspecified) to his wife, Elizabeth, having no one else. He died quite soon afterwards, and was buried at St Mary Abchurch, on 2 August. In the event, his will was set aside, and administration was granted on 25 August of that year to his widow, who married Robert Souch at St Mary Abchurch on 18 October 1596.

Whithorne's autobiography makes interesting reading, though one could wish that he had been more expansive in certain particulars, as when castigating minstrels as 'the rascal and off-scum' of the profession; mentioning the 'pretty, merry' Neapolitan music; and stating that:

> I join th'English with the stranger, t'agree in music's trade,
> So I the flats and sharps do set …
> (Whithorne, 1962, 203, 145, 146)

Those of Whithorne's pieces which began as solo songs are suitably elaborate, whereas the music he composed for his own poems is very staid. His longer works are less restrained, though on occasion the contrapuntal aspects are overstretched, bringing imbalance. However, his 'songs' were the first English secular partbooks in print, while the 'duos' were the earliest published duets; together they provide a pleasant introduction to Elizabethan middle-class music and song.   JOHN BENNELL

Sources *The autobiography of Thomas Whythorne*, ed. J. M. Osborn (1961); another edn (1962) · J. M. Osborn, 'Whythorne, Thomas', *New Grove* · R. Cooke, *Visitation of London, 1568*, ed. H. Stanford London and S. W. Rawlins, [new edn], 2 vols. in one, Harleian Society, 109–10 (1963), 88 · J. Caldwell, *Oxford history of music*, 1 (1991) · administration of Thomas Whithorne, 1596, GL, MS 9051/5, fol. 50 · archdeaconry court of London, act book, 1596, GL, MS 9050/3, fol. 42 · J. Strype, *The life and acts of Matthew Parker*, new edn, 3 vols. (1821), vol. 2, pp. 433–4 [Whitheare is plainly a misreading of Whithorne] · parish register, London, St Mary Abchurch, 1558–1737, GL, MS 7666 [burial] · J. L. Chester and G. J. Armytage, eds., *Allegations for marriage licences issued by the bishop of London*, 1, Harleian Society, 25 (1887), 75 · T. Mason, ed., *Registers, St Martin-in-the-Fields*, 1 (1898), 68 · R. G. Lang, ed., *Two Tudor subsidy assessment rolls for the city of London, 1541 and 1581*, London RS, 29 (1993), no. 241
Likenesses woodcut, 1568? (aged forty), repro. in T. Whythorne, *Songes* (1571) · oils, 1569; Christies, 19 Nov 1965, lot 41 [*see illus.*] · woodcut, 1590, BM, NPG; repro. in T. Whythorne, *Duos, or, Songs for two voices* (1590)

Whiting, John (1656–1722), Quaker bibliographer and writer, was born at Nailsea near Bristol. His parents were John Whiting (*d.* 1658), a yeoman of Nailsea, and his wife, Mary (*d.* 1666), daughter of John Evans. Whiting recalled that his parents 'came of honest parents, and of good report in the country', where his ancestors had long owned an estate (Whiting, *Persecution*, introduction). They were converted to Quakerism in 1654 by John Audland and John Camm, and the first meetings in Somerset were held in their home. His father died in 1658, leaving the tuition of Whiting and his sister Mary (1654–1676) to their mother, who educated them 'according to truth' (ibid.). In December 1660 his mother was sent with 200 others to Ilchester gaol for refusing the oath of allegiance to the new king, so that he and his sister lived for a time with their grandfather. His mother was released at the spring assizes at Chard, and later in 1661 married Moses Bryant of Nailsea, with whom she had three sons before her death in November 1666.

Educated at a grammar school, but brought up as a Quaker, Whiting noted that 'the wild nature was apt to appear in me, till truth took hold of me and opened in my understanding' (Whiting, *Persecution*, introduction). At the age of twelve he was 'taken off' from 'sports and pastimes' and 'became more sober and religiously inclined' (ibid.). He was taught hat honour—doffing the hat to social superiors—but rejected the practice, regarding it as 'evil' (ibid.). Afterwards he was taught by a Friend, under whom he 'profited most every way'. He evidently found Quaker social customs difficult, however, for:

> the plain language also cost me very dear, it was so hard to take up, so that I could have gone miles about rather than having met some of my relations to speak to them; which how small a thing soever some may count it, I could have no peace till I gave up and took up the cross in that respect, and then it was made easie to me, and I had peace therein.
> (ibid.)

In 1670 Whiting discovered a testimony in his heart against 'hireling priests' and tithe-taking; as he later wrote: 'I could discern a difference between them and Friends, as plain as between the whitest and brownest bread in my father's house' (ibid.).

On the death of his stepfather in June 1672 Whiting went to live with his new guardian, Edmond Beaks, at Portishead, near Bristol, for about three years; there he met the Quakers Charles Marshall and George Cole who, he recalled, 'were as fathers in the truth to me' (Whiting, *Persecution*, introduction). Whiting's sister Mary had become a Quaker preacher and in August 1675 set out on a journey towards London. Whiting joined her in Buckinghamshire in November and they visited Quakers in Reading gaol, after which he returned home and his sister continued her mission northwards. On 1 April 1676 he met her again at Norton, co. Durham, where she was taken ill. Her death a week later, on 8 April, at the age of twenty-two was 'a great exercise' for Whiting. Her youthful piety had an intense effect on her brother, and four years later while in prison he wrote a testimony to her, published in 1681 as *Early Piety Exemplified in the Life and Death of Mary Whiting*.

Whiting returned to Nailsea after his sister's death:

> being then in the 20th year of my age; and having some of my estate in my hands, I manur'd part of it, and sow'd it with corn the latter end of this year, and the next spring some more of it, of which I had a small crop of about ten acres the summer following. (Whiting, *Persecution*, 10)

He was cited to appear in the bishop's court for non-payment of tithes on 28 May 1678. The following year he was appointed overseer of the poor for his parish; he suffered no further persecution until 28 January 1679, when he was arrested and sent to Ilchester gaol. He was committed at first to the sheriff's ward, or Old Nunnery; after some time he was moved to the Old Friary and allowed to take walks outside and occasionally visit Nailsea. Many other Quakers were also prisoners, and on Sundays they held meetings, attended by outsiders, in the great hall or the walled orchard of the gaol. Whiting was in frequent correspondence with London friends who sent him books. He wrote much, and read the works of Jakob Boehme, Sir Walter Ralegh, and others. In 1681 he was moved to the common gaol in Ilchester and put in 'a dark nasty hole, called Doctors Commons', where he lay on damp straw (ibid., 56). About this time he wrote the testimony of his sister and soon afterwards, he records, 'I began to write my own memoirs … chiefly for a memorial to myself of the dealings of the Lord with me from my childhood' (ibid., 57). In 1684 he was allowed to take a room at the home of another Quaker, Widow Scott, which was 'the best prison (except the Friary) that ever I had', and where the men's monthly meetings were held (ibid., 105).

In 1685, on James II's accession, Whiting vainly tried to obtain his release: 'it became a proverb', he recalled, 'that liberty of conscience was in the press, it was so long a coming out' (Whiting, Persecution, 140). He was free by the time Monmouth's army was marching through the west country and he saw Monmouth in Taunton, where he spoke a few words to the duke in the street and noted his thoughtful and dejected appearance. After the rebellion was smashed, and having himself seen the ruthless behaviour of King James's troops, Whiting thought it safer to surrender himself at Ilchester, where he was thrust into irons among Monmouth's men and spent almost six weeks chained to John Hipsley, another Quaker, for refusing to pay the keeper his fees:

> Nor could we put off our clothes at night, but from one arm, and let them hang on the other, so that we could not turn, but lay mostly on one side (being link'd together) which was very tedious in the heat of the summer. (ibid., 146)

He was allowed to go to his own room after thirteen weeks and was an eyewitness to some of the atrocities of Judge Jefferys at the 'bloody assizes', remaining a close prisoner until the king's proclamation of March 1686.

On his release Whiting married Sarah Hurd on 20 May 1686; the couple settled at Long Sutton, where she kept on her trade of linen-draper, and afterwards moved to a shop at Wrington. Whiting and his wife do not appear to have had any children of their own, but his testimony to Sarah Scott, his niece, reveals that when her father Francis Scott died 'her uncle and aunt Whiting took her, to breed up as their own, and educated her in the way of truth' (Whiting, A Memorial, 3) until her death on 27 September 1703 in London at the age of almost thirteen. Whiting set up meetings in the town, and William Penn often visited him and held meetings in the surrounding areas.

Whiting's autobiography ends in 1696. In 1699 he moved to London, and the remainder of his life was spent travelling in various counties in the south and attending to Friends' business in London. In 1700 he was at the second day morning meeting where one of his manuscripts was read, and at another time was asked to look at George Bishop's book of New England's Friends' sufferings, for reprinting purposes. In 1707 the yearly meeting requested that he gather details of ancient Friends' books from the bookseller Thomas Raylton and report these to the meeting for sufferings, a project which eventually led to his *Catalogue of Friends' Books* (1708), the first attempt at Quaker bibliography, two copies of which were sent to each monthly meeting in England and Wales and later to other nations.

As well as *Persecution Expos'd* and the aforementioned works, Whiting wrote numerous tracts such as *An Abstract of the Lives, Precepts, and Sayings of the Ancient Fathers* (1684), together with many defences of Quakerism, for example, *Judas, and the Chief Priests* (1701), an answer to the Quaker separatist George Keith, whom Whiting accused of attempting 'to expose his old Friends to the contempt of the world, and rage of their adversaries', by among other issues charging them with failing to preach 'Christ without' and undervaluing the historic, incarnate Jesus (pp. 1, 4). Other defences included *Truth and Innocency Defended* (1702) in answer to Cotton Mather, *Truth the Strongest of All* (1706), another reply to Keith, and *Christ Jesus Owned as he is God and Man* (1709), a defence of Quaker Christology in answer to Edward Cockson.

Whiting died in the parish of St Andrew, Holborn, London, on 12 November 1722 of a 'fever and inward wasting' (Smith, 922); he was taken from the Bull and Mouth meeting-house on 16 November and interred on the same day at the Quaker burial-ground near Hanover Street, Long Acre. His will shows that he retained property in Somerset, at Congresbury. His wife, who was his executor and main beneficiary, survived him. His bequests were otherwise directed to his cousinage and servants, and to the Quaker poor of his former Somerset and present Strand meetings and the parish poor of Nailsea and St Andrew's, Holborn. He was particularly concerned with the preservation of 'all my originall printed books published by the people called Quakers either bound or unbound except the reprinted collections of their works', left in trust for use by members of the London Friday and Monday meetings.   CAROLINE L. LEACHMAN

Sources J. Whiting, *Persecution expos'd* (1715) · J. Besse, *A collection of the sufferings of the people called Quakers*, 2 vols. (1753), vol. 1 · J. Smith, ed., *A descriptive catalogue of Friends' books*, 2 (1867) · will, PRO, PROB 11/588, sig. 248, fols. 332v–334r · J. Whiting, *Early piety exemplified in the life and death of Mary Whiting* (1681) · J. Whiting, *A memorial concerning Sarah Scott* (1703)
Archives RS Friends, Lond., Bristol MSS, testimony against Northern Separatists, 1679, I, 32 · RS Friends, Lond., Gibson MSS, vols. 1–3

Whiting, John Robert (1917–1963), playwright, was born on 15 November 1917 in Salisbury, the first of the two children of Frederick Charles Whiting (1884–1945), army

John Robert Whiting (1917–1963), by Mark Gerson, 1961

officer and (later) solicitor, and his wife, Dorothy, *née* Herring (1892–1975). After a rather perfunctory education—kindergarten, private preparatory school, minor public school (Taunton)—he enrolled in 1935 for training as an actor at the Royal Academy of Dramatic Art. His subsequent career as a small-part actor was brief and undistinguished. In November 1940 he married Asthorne Lloyd (Jackie; *b.* 1917). There were four children of the marriage: Jonathan (*b.* 1945), Mark (*b.* 1947), Tessa (*b.* 1951), and Catherine (*b.* 1957).

At the outbreak of war in 1939 Whiting at first registered as a conscientious objector but recanted and was conscripted into the artillery in 1940, serving mainly in anti-aircraft batteries. He was commissioned in 1942 and invalided out of the army because of 'illness and nervous debility' in 1944. During the last few months of his army service he began to write a short (and very strange) novel called 'Not a foot of land' (which by the beginning of the twenty-first century was still unpublished). He finished it in 1945 while he was a member of the White Rose Players in Harrogate and, while fulfilling similar engagements at various other provincial theatres, wrote several short stories and one-act plays for radio, some of which were accepted and broadcast by the BBC during the years 1949–50. From 1946 onwards he began seriously to consider writing for the stage.

Whiting's first two plays, both written in 1946, were not staged until after his death: *The Conditions of Agreement* in 1965 and *No More a-Roving* in 1987. His third play, *Saint's Day*, which won the Arts Theatre Festival of Britain competition in 1951, was produced in September of that year but had been preceded on the London stage by *A Penny for a*

Song. Marching Song followed in 1954, *The Gates of Summer* in 1956, and *The Devils* (a dramatization of Aldous Huxley's *The Devils of Loudun*) in 1960. At his death Whiting left half-finished a play called 'Noman', which he had started in 1958. With the exception of *A Penny for a Song*, which is a gentle, sunny, deliciously zany comedy about the expected invasion of England by Napoleon in 1804, the main themes of his writing recur, in one form or another, in all Whiting's plays. The inevitable besmirching of innocence is seen in the doomed figure of Procathren, the cultivated and civilized young poet who suddenly joins forces with three soldier–deserters and commits acts of appalling violence, in *Saint's Day*; the hopeless longing for an absolute perfection displayed by Grandier, the seventeenth-century priest in *The Devils*, overtaken by the crazed sexual jealousy of the abbess, or John and Caroline and Cristos in *The Gates of Summer*; and the inevitability of disillusion, as seen in the case of Forster, the deposed army commander, in *Marching Song*, who discovers that the peasant song which sustained him as he heard it distantly from his prison cell was not the song of idealized love he had imagined, but something grossly coarse and vulgar. The plays are haunted by the sense of a half-hidden, inexplicable terror just behind the mundane, everyday occurrence, symbolized by what Stella, in *Saint's Day*, calls 'the voice from the other room' and visually represented by empty, deserted houses, disused rooms, unfinished paintings, and the like. Children, especially, are almost always seen either as helpless and unwitting victims (like the small boy who hangs himself at the end of the one-act play *No Why*) or, in a Jamesian echo, as spontaneous incarnations of a natural and unreflective evil.

It was a critical truism before and immediately after his death to say that Whiting was *sui generis*, isolated, not part of the mainstream of British play writing, even self-indulgent. A more considered view, appraising the evidence from a broader and less partisan perspective, would probably dissent from this hasty contemporary judgement. Whiting's elegantly muscular prose goes back to Shaw, while his melancholy but steady contemplation of the intrinsic and inevitable chaos at the heart of things prophetically anticipates the work of such writers as Arden, Beckett, and Pinter. Whiting's writing, moreover, represents a positive and recognizable stage in the modern English-speaking theatre's conscious and continuing endeavour throughout the twentieth century to forge a new public speech that is at once free from the preciosity and pretentiousness of the verse dramatists of the first half of the century and the banality and triviality of much of the naturalistic writing of the second half. Whiting, for all the slender quantity of his output, begins to look—so far as twentieth-century British theatre is concerned—like the linchpin in this developing of a resonant, resilient, truly poetic theatrical modern speech form.

In the last three years of his life Whiting wrote theatre criticism for the *London Magazine*. It is often sound, sometimes brilliant, but always unsteady. It does, however, carry some indications that, had he been vouchsafed more time, he might well have settled down into being a major critic as well as a major playwright. (All his *London Magazine* criticism is collected in *John Whiting on Theatre* (1966) and more of his critical writings are included in *The Art of the Dramatist* (1970).) His views on the proper function of the theatre, always trenchant, often crystallized into quite brilliant aphorisms: 'The purpose of art is to raise doubt', he wrote in one of his *London Magazine* articles, 'the purpose of entertainment is to reassure.' This dichotomy was one of which he was always painfully aware, not only in his critical thinking but also in his own practice. In a lecture called 'The art of the dramatist', given at the Old Vic Theatre in 1957, he said:

> A work of art is the statement of one man. It has nothing to do with an audience or a wish to please. It does not necessarily entertain, instruct or enlighten. It can do any or all of those things, but that it should is not the artist's concern. The thing is there: an audience taking from it what it can. It is not the artist's job to simplify the means of communication.

As well as his plays he also wrote a number of film scripts and translated from the French two plays by Anouilh and one each by Salacrou, Obey, and Giraudoux.

Whiting's full potential was never realized and his too-early death seemed almost designed to illustrate the accuracy of his own melancholy view of life. The theatre critic Kenneth Tynan, reporting in *The Observer* on Whiting's 1957 lecture, said: 'I felt I was in the presence of a condemned man. There was resignation in the very set of his gentle, scolded face and the expression in his large, dark eyes seemed to anticipate, even to embrace, defeat' (Tynan). Whiting was thirty-nine at the time. He died six years later of cancer, at the Royal Marsden Hospital, Chelsea, London, on 16 June 1963, and was buried at Fairwarp, Sussex, on the 20th. ERIC SALMON

Sources E. Salmon, *The dark journey: John Whiting as dramatist* (1979) · private information (2004) [family] · b. cert. · C. Fry, 'John Whiting's world', *The Listener*, 72 (1964) · R. Hayman, *John Whiting* (1969) · S. Trussler, *The plays of John Whiting* (1972) · K. Tynan, 'Out of touch', *The Observer* (6 Oct 1957) · *The collected plays of John Whiting*, ed. R. Hayman, 2 vols. (1969) · d. cert.
Archives Theatre Museum, London, unpublished works · University of Indiana, Bloomington, Lilly Library, corresp. and literary MSS
Likenesses photograph, 1944, repro. in Salmon, *Dark journey* · H. Rogers, photograph, 1954, repro. in Salmon, *Dark journey* · M. Gerson, photograph, 1961, NPG [*see illus.*] · F. Topolski, charcoal drawing, 1961, repro. in Salmon, *Dark journey* · pen-and-ink caricature, priv. coll.; repro. in *The Spectator* (31 March 1973)
Wealth at death £19,289 14s. 2d.: administration, 24 Sept 1963, *CGPLA Eng. & Wales*

Whiting, Nathaniel (1611/12–1682), satirist and nonconformist minister, was the son of Nathaniel Whiting, of Horspool Grange, near Desford, Leicestershire, gentleman, and his first wife, Elizabeth, *née* Heath. He was born in Etton rectory, Northamptonshire, the home of his grandfather Giles Whiting (1550–1627), a puritan minister, and was baptized there on 17 September 1612; he was aged seven in 1619. He was admitted to Queens' College, Cambridge, on 1 July 1628 as a pensioner and matriculated on 30 March 1629; he was a scholar from 1630 to 1634, and

graduated BA in 1631 and MA in 1635. At Cambridge and later his generous patron was Sir William Fleetwood (1603–1674) of Aldwincle, Northamptonshire.

Whiting contributed Latin and Greek verse to a Cambridge collection commemorating the birth of the future James II in 1633, and wrote a verse appreciation of poets (including notably Donne) in *Il insonio insonado, or, A Sleeping-Waking Dreame*, published with his most ambitious poem, *Le hore di recreatione, or, The Pleasant Historie of Albino and Bellama* (1637). This last is a farcical, ribald, anti-Roman Catholic burlesque romance, employing a far-fetched, archaic, would-be 'metaphysical', and obscure vocabulary. George Saintsbury, who reprinted it in 1921, allowed it to be a heroic poem, albeit 'graceless and slatternly', and linked it with the prehistory of the novel (Saintsbury, 424–5).

Whiting was ordained priest at Peterborough on 9 June 1639. His first cure is untraced, but in July 1645 he was intruded as rector of Lowick, Northamptonshire (value £300), the previous rector, a royalist, having been ejected by parliamentary ordinance. Thanks to Fleetwood, Whiting was next instituted as (intruded) rector of All Saints, Aldwincle, on 20 March 1652, though he had first signed the accounts as 'minister' on 4 May 1650. He was also master of Aldwincle grammar school. His contentious puritan prose treatise *Old Jacob's Altar Newly Repaired* (1659), on the sufferings and providential escapes of modern saints, was dedicated to Fleetwood and his two soldier brothers; it was reissued, without the dedication, as *The Art of Divine Improvement* (1662). Whiting was ejected from Aldwincle rectory under the 1662 Act of Uniformity (his successor was instituted on 20 February 1663); he was also ejected from the school. He retired to Cranford St Andrew, near Kettering, where he gathered a congregation, and, by the declaration of indulgence, was licensed on 11 April 1672 to preach in his own house and the house of Lady Pickering at Titchmarsh.

At an unknown date Whiting married a woman named Judith, from Over, Cambridgeshire. No children of theirs have been traced. Whiting died of 'a violent fit of the wind' (Calamy, *Abridgement*, 2.496) in 1682: his will, leaving his entire estate of more than £1000 to his widow, was proved on 27 November 1682. Judith did not long survive him: her will, embodying his instructions for disposal of his estate, was proved on 23 January 1684.

JAMES SAMBROOK

Sources A. J. Shirren, 'The Whitings of Etton and Aldwincle', *N&Q*, 198 (1953), 139–45, 192–8 · *Calamy rev.* · E. Calamy, ed., *An abridgement of Mr. Baxter's history of his life and times, with an account of the ministers, &c., who were ejected after the Restauration of King Charles II*, 2nd edn, 2 vols. (1713), vol. 2, pp. 495–6 · E. Calamy, *A continuation of the account of the ministers … who were ejected and silenced after the Restoration in 1660*, 2 vols. (1727), vol. 2, p. 640 · W. Camden, *The visitation of the county of Leicester in the year 1619*, ed. J. Fetherston, Harleian Society, 2 (1870), 92 · N. Whiting, *Old Jacob's altar newly repaired* (1659), dedication · G. Saintsbury, *Minor poets of the Caroline period* (1921), 3.424–38 · J. R. S. Whiting, 'A 17th century Northamptonshire Poet Parson', *Northamptonshire Past and Present*, 4 (1966–71), 223–32 · will, Northants. RO [Judith Whiting]

Wealth at death over £1000: will of Judith Whiting, Northants. RO

Whiting, Richard (d. 1539), abbot of Glastonbury, is of unknown origins (a statement that he was a son of one of the abbey's tenants at nearby Wrington cannot be substantiated). He became a Benedictine monk at Glastonbury, where he may have studied as a child during the abbacy of Richard Bere (1493–1525). He was ordained acolyte in 1498, subdeacon in 1499, deacon in 1500, and priest in March 1501. Having some time held the position of chamberlain at Glastonbury, on Bere's death in February 1525 he was appointed abbot by Wolsey, probably on the suggestion of John Islip, abbot of Westminster; by this time he is thought to have been approaching the age of sixty.

Whiting appears to have lived the typical life of a late medieval abbot of a great house (Glastonbury had the highest net income of any English monastery in 1535). He was fond of hunting, entertained on a grand scale, attended parliament, and presented Christmas gifts to the king. He continued the intensive building work begun under Bere, including the completion of St Edgar's Chapel at the east end of the abbey church. As late as 1539 he was concerning himself with having his own arms set up on new buildings at Glastonbury. He also maintained the tradition of hospitality to all, with the abbey feeding the poor of the neighbourhood twice weekly. His abbacy coincided with a period of general decline for the Benedictines, yet at Glastonbury the number of monks rose from forty-six to fifty-four. During the 1530s, moreover, there was an increase in the number of monks who went from Glastonbury to Gloucester College at Oxford, even though Whiting himself seems to have been more interested in music than scholarship, making arrangements in 1534 for the instruction of the choirboys. A visitation in 1538 suggests that there were divisions among the monks, especially between the older and younger ones, and that the abbot had his favourites in the community. Whiting was also apt to reside away from the monastery, especially at his manors of Sturminster Newton in Dorset and Ashbury in Berkshire. Some of his apparent shortcomings were probably due to ill health, however, and he appears to have had few critics before the events of 1539, being described by John Leland, whom he entertained generously, as 'homo sane candidissimus, et amicus meus singularis' ('a most upright man and my particular friend'; *De rebus Britannicis collectanea*, 6.70).

Early investigations into the management of the abbey and the conduct of its monks found little to complain of (the oath of royal supremacy had been taken by Whiting and his brethren in June 1534), and as late as September 1539 the king's commissioner Richard Layton was severely rebuked by Cromwell for offering a positive appraisal of Whiting's character, a judgement he was quick to retract. By now, however, despite Whiting's efforts to maintain a good relationship with Cromwell, on whom he had bestowed several gifts (notably the advowson of Monkton church) and who as recently as March 1538 had reassured the abbot against 'fear of suppression

or change of life' (*LP Henry VIII*, 13/1, no. 573), the writing was clearly on the wall. Following cross-examination on 19 September at his manor house of Sharpham near Glastonbury by Layton, Thomas Moyle, and Richard Pollard, who found the aged abbot's answers evidence of 'his cankered and traitorous heart', Whiting, 'being but a very weak man and sickly', was dispatched to the Tower of London (ibid., 14/2, no. 206). Even now proof of the treasonable behaviour Cromwell wished to establish in order to suppress the abbey was hard to find, and, although by the beginning of October Layton and his colleagues had secured depositions from discontented monks at Glastonbury alleging such behaviour, the only specific accusations laid against Whiting were possession of a book found at the abbey condemning the royal divorce and his having hidden a number of precious objects from the despoilers.

Whiting's trial before a compliant jury took place at Wells on 14 November, the main charge against him being simply that 'of robbyng of Glastonburye churche' (Wright, 260). Sentenced to death by John, Lord Russell, the abbot was the following day dragged on a hurdle through the town of Glastonbury up to Tor Hill to be hanged, drawn, and quartered, 'att whych tyme he askyd god mercye and the kyng for hys great offensys towardes hys hyghenes … and thereapon toke hys deathe very pacyently' (ibid., 261) alongside two of his monks, John Thorne and Roger James.

Whiting was regarded as a martyr in the late nineteenth century both by the Catholic historian Francis Gasquet and by the agnostic anti-Catholic James Froude, and even the most detached assessment of his last days suggests a man of principle and moral courage, prepared to die for what he believed in. He was beatified in 1896.

NICHOLAS DOGGETT

Sources *VCH Somerset*, 2.94–6 · D. Knowles [M. C. Knowles], *The religious orders in England*, 3 (1959), 379–82, 483–91 · *LP Henry VIII*, 9, no. 313; 13/1, no. 573; 14/1, nos. 271, 716; 14/2, nos. 185, 206, 232, 272, 399, 530–31 · A. Watkin, 'Glastonbury, 1538–9, as shown by its account rolls', *Downside Review*, 67 (1949), 437–50 · *Joannis Lelandi antiquarii de rebus Britannicis collectanea*, ed. T. Hearne, 6 vols. (1715), vol. 6, p. 70 · T. Hearne and C. Eyston, *The history and antiquities of Glastonbury* (1722), 50–52, 97–9 · F. A. Gasquet, *The last abbot of Glastonbury* (1895) · J. A. Froude, *History of England*, 3rd edn, 12 vols. (1862–70), vol. 3, p. 436 · T. Wright, ed., *Three chapters of letters relating to the suppression of monasteries*, CS, 26 (1843) · J. H. Bettey, *The suppression of the monasteries in the west country* (1989) · K. W. Dunning, 'Revival at Glastonbury, 1530–9', *Renaissance and renewal in Christian history*, ed. D. Baker, SCH, 14 (1977), 213–22
Archives Som. ARS, letter

Whitla, Sir William (1851–1933), physician, was born at The Diamond, Monaghan, co. Monaghan, Ireland, on 15 September 1851, the fourth son of Robert Whitla, a woollen draper and pawnbroker, and his wife, Anne, daughter of Alexander Williams of Dublin. Educated at the town's model school, he was articled at fifteen to his brother James, a local pharmacist, completing his apprenticeship with Wheeler and Whitaker, Belfast's leading pharmaceutical firm. Proceeding to study medicine at Queen's College, Belfast, Whitla took the LAH, Dublin, and the

LRCP and LRCS of Edinburgh in 1873. Equipped with these diplomas he obtained a post as resident medical officer at the Belfast General Hospital. He next spent some time in London, possibly at St Thomas's Hospital, for it was there he met his future wife, Ada Bourne (1845/6–1932), daughter of George Bourne, a prominent Staffordshire farmer. She was a ward sister and friend of Florence Nightingale, and a member of the Salvation Army. They married in 1876, setting up house at 41 Great Victoria Street, Belfast, where Whitla established a successful general medical practice, many of Belfast's leading families seeking his advice. He was awarded the MD of the Queen's University of Ireland in 1877, with first-class honours, gold medal, and commendation.

Energetic and enthusiastic, Whitla was appointed physician to the Belfast Royal Hospital (as the General Hospital was then styled) in 1882, a post he held there and in the Royal Victoria Hospital, of which it was the forerunner, until his retirement in 1918. The Whitlas' move in 1884 to 8 College Square North, was an indication of a success by no means near its zenith. He succeeded Seaton Reid as professor of materia medica at the Queen's College in 1890; he was twice president of the Ulster Medical Society (1886–7, 1901–2), and was knighted for distinction in medicine in 1902.

Sir William and Lady Whitla moved again in 1906, settling at Lennoxvale, a commodious suburban mansion, and retaining the professional house in College Square. Once more further distinctions lay ahead. He served the British Medical Association as president (presenting each member who attended the annual meeting held in Belfast in 1909 with a copy of his most recent book, *The Theory and Practice of Medicine*, and entertaining them at Lennoxvale). A strong unionist, he was elected to parliament in 1918, serving until 1923 as representative of the Queen's University at Westminster. He was appointed honorary physician to the king in Ireland in 1919 and was subsequently university pro-chancellor.

Whitla was an exemplary practitioner, both as family doctor and hospital consultant, then an acceptable combination. As a teacher, unlike Professor Cuming, 'the high priest of philosophic doubt', he was 'absolute, almost infallible, epigrammatic, paradoxical, sometimes oracular' (Kidd, 108). It is tempting to seek the roots of his remarkable success in his apprenticeship to a high street chemist, learning at an early age to be endlessly genial, never at a loss for an answer, assured, emollient. He did not engage in clinical research but instead made his knowledge of pharmacy a foundation stone on which his reputation rested. He was familiar with the niceties of compounding medicines at a time when most doctors were accustomed to preparing and dispensing their own mixtures, ointments, pills, and powders. His *Elements of Pharmacy, Materia Medica and Treatment* (1882) and *A Dictionary of Treatment* (1892) went into many editions. Envious colleagues may have been relieved when *A Manual of the Practice and Theory of Medicine* (1908) was a flop.

Raised in a Presbyterian family, Whitla and his wife were both attracted to Methodism early in their marriage.

She was intensely religious, and retained her allegiance to the Salvation Army. When they attended a garden party at Buckingham Palace on the occasion of his knighthood she wore her uniform, a silent admonition perhaps to the racy monarch, Edward VII.

Sir William and Lady Whitla were childless, and they were wealthy. His extensive practice was remunerative; his books brought rewarding royalties. He had, too, a flair for making wise investments, buying oil shares to his great financial advantage. Physically impressive, he was 5 feet 8 inches in height, stoutly built and bearded; because of an arthritic hip he walked with a limp, and he was invariably attired in the frock coat which with a top hat were then *de rigueur* for leading doctors. Many found his manner simple and kindly, while others (inevitably) thought him pompous.

The Whitlas travelled widely, visiting Russia, Canada, and many Mediterranean cities. They kept a good table at Lennoxvale and, though disapproving of alcohol and tobacco in his professional capacity, Whitla enjoyed wine and his pipe. They both were ardent and knowledgeable Shakespearians. Sir Frank and Lady Benson stayed with them when visiting Belfast. General Booth was another welcome guest.

When retirement from the wards (1918), and his chair (1919), reduced his commitments Whitla resumed the biblical studies that had always attracted him. He contributed an introductory study of the nature and the cause of unbelief, of miracles, and prophecy to an edition of Sir Isaac Newton's *Daniel and the Apocalypse* published by John Murray in 1922. As the decade progressed his public appearances were fewer, and after a stroke in 1929 he was confined to his room. Lady Whitla died in 1932; he died at Lennoxvale on 11 December 1933, and was given a civic funeral two days later; he was buried at Belfast city cemetery.

During Whitla's lifetime his gifts to his profession included the Good Samaritan stained glass window (commemorating the heroic behaviour of two Ulster doctors) erected in the Royal Hospital, and a building to house the Ulster Medical Society. At his death Lennoxvale was bequeathed to Queen's University as a residence for the vice-chancellor. The university also was his residuary legatee, and acted on his suggestion that the available funds should provide an assembly hall. The Sir William Whitla Hall was opened in 1949. J. B. LYONS

Sources *DNB* · C. W. Kidd, 'Sir William Whitla: profile of a benefactor', *Ulster Medical Journal*, 31 (1962), 105–16 · R. G. Shanks, 'The legacies of Sir William Whitla', *Ulster Medical Journal*, 63 (1994), 52–75 · R. Clarke, *The Royal Victoria Hospital, Belfast: a history, 1797–1997* (1997) · *The Times* (12 Dec 1933) · *BMJ* (23 Dec 1933), 1193 · *The Lancet* (23 Dec 1933), 1451 · *CGPLA Eng. & Wales* (1934)

Likenesses W. Stoneman, photograph, 1921, NPG · F. McKelvey, Ulster Medical Society; repro. in *BMJ* (1933) · Spy [L. Ward], caricature

Wealth at death £58,405 9s. 6d. in England: Northern Irish probate sealed in England, 15 March 1934, *CGPLA Eng. & Wales* · £26,385 10s. 8d.: probate, 8 March 1934, *CGPLA NIre.*

Whitley, John Henry (1866–1935), speaker of the House of Commons, was born at Halifax on 8 February 1866, the

John Henry Whitley (1866–1935), by George Charles Beresford, 1903

eldest son of Nathan Whitley (d. 1889), of Halifax, and his wife, Sarah Rinder. He was educated at Clifton College, Bristol, to which he always remained devoted, and London University (BA, 1885), before joining his father in the family business of S. Whitley & Co., cotton spinners, of Halifax. On 29 June 1892 he married Marguerita Virginia (d. 1925), daughter of Giulio Marchetti, one of Garibaldi's officers, who settled in Halifax and became manager of Crossley's carpet works. They had two sons, one of whom was Percival Nathan *Whitley (1893–1956), and two daughters.

Whitley took a close interest in social work in Halifax, especially on behalf of youth: this latter interest developed as he grew older and continued throughout his life and in 1921 he became president of the National Council of Social Service. He was a member of the Halifax town council from 1893 to 1900. In 1916 he gave money to be spent in premiums to architects for plans to guide public building and town planning.

Whitley was elected Liberal member of parliament for Halifax in 1900 and represented that constituency until 1928. As a private member, in opposition from 1900 to 1906, Whitley made many contributions to the Commons debates, particularly during the long and controversial discussions on the Education Bill of 1902, the details of which he had mastered with great thoroughness. His careful, closely reasoned speeches, based upon exact knowledge, compelled the attention of the house and influenced the final form of the bill. In this way, and through

his work as a Liberal whip from 1907 to 1910, Whitley acquired a parliamentary reputation, which was recognized by his selection as deputy chairman of ways and means in 1910, and as chairman in 1911, when he was also elected deputy speaker. He was sworn of the privy council in 1911.

In 1916 Whitley was appointed chairman of the committee on relations between employers and employed set up by the government in response to the shop stewards' movement. It became a subcommittee of the government's reconstruction committee. The first report, agreed in March 1917 and published in June, proposed the creation of joint industrial councils to bring together employers and trade union representatives to deal with problems in each industry. Readjustment of labour conditions after the war was clearly likely to be a difficult process, and the recommendations in the Whitley reports were designed to secure regular consultation, co-operation, and conciliation between the two sides in industry. Joint machinery of varying types was recommended, commonly known as Whitley councils, adapted to suit the different degrees of organization in the various trades: as well as national joint councils there were district councils and works committees. The proposals were based on the unproven assumption that in each industry there existed a 'common interest' between the employers and the employed, which needed 'a special organization to express itself', and which would be strengthened by having the opportunity for such expression (Lowe, 92–3). In fact, as Lloyd George recognized early on, the contentions between the two sides in industry, and their mutual suspicion of one another, vitiated the proposed joint consultative machinery. This was in any case meant to be voluntary, and since it received equivocal support from government, employers' federations, and trade unions, the impact of Whitley's high-minded proposals was limited.

When in 1921 James Lowther retired as speaker of the House of Commons, it was obvious that Whitley had strong claims to succeed to the chair. His knowledge of the rules, usages, and traditions of the House of Commons was profound and he knew the tempers of members generally and their idiosyncrasies. There was some questioning of his selection on the part of the Conservatives, who contended that the chairmanship of committees should not be regarded as a stepping-stone to the speakership. The opposition went so far as to select Sir Frederick Banbury as its nominee, but before the day of election the opposition died down and Whitley was unanimously elected.

Whitley's occupancy of the chair—there were five administrations in the seven years—was a disturbed and anxious one. This was the era of the general strike, of miners' unrest, wage disputes, and unemployment. Many of the subjects discussed excited strong feelings and the customary calm of the House of Commons was frequently disturbed: the speaker was obliged to order the withdrawal or suspension of members and even on occasion to suspend the sitting. Throughout, Whitley maintained an unruffled demeanour, calling unruly members to order in quiet, measured tones. Ramsay MacDonald paid tribute to his parliamentary skill at the time of his retirement in 1928, observing:

> You have shown us in a most remarkable way how to be patient and courteous without being lax, how to be strict and severe without being mechanical and formal; and you have also demonstrated to us ... how gentleness can rule and how persuasiveness can subdue. (*Hansard 5C*, 218.1597)

Despite the unprecedented scenes of disorder, Whitley fully maintained the traditions of the chair. If some members considered that he should have shown greater firmness, others—and they represented the more general view—thought that the speaker had been wise in allowing very full play to the strong emotions of members, many of whom were new to the House of Commons, felt deeply about the matters in dispute, and were unaccustomed to the niceties and time-honoured traditions of parliamentary procedure. He showed his firmness, though, during the general strike, when he arranged for parliamentary votes and proceedings to be produced by emergency means. In reply to a threat to withdraw workmen from the houses of parliament he declared that he would not allow the work of the House of Commons to be interfered with, and would, if necessary, conduct the business of the house without printing and by candlelight. Whitley was keenly interested in the Palace of Westminster, its fabric, and its decoration, and he did much to promote knowledge and appreciation of it. He supported enthusiastically the Empire Parliamentary Association, and devoted much time to the entertainment of visiting members of dominion legislatures.

On his retirement from the speakership in June 1928 Whitley was allowed to decline the customary peerage. Following the death of his first wife, he married, in 1928, Helen, daughter of John Albert Clarke, of Hunstanton and Fransham, Norfolk.

From 1929 to 1931 Whitley served as chairman of the royal commission on labour in India. In the conduct of the commission's inquiry, and in the framing of the report, he showed characteristic thoroughness: he displayed, just as characteristically, sympathetic understanding of the viewpoints of Indian employers and employed. The publication of the report was followed by the introduction of ameliorative legislation into the Indian assembly. In 1932 he was awarded the kaisar-i-Hind medal (first class) for his services to India, having asked permission to decline the KCSI. In 1930 Whitley was appointed by Ramsay MacDonald chairman of the board of governors of the British Broadcasting Corporation, a post to which his impartiality and imperturbability of outlook suited him. He held this office until his death; he died at 31 Queen's Gate, London, on 3 February 1935.

H. J. WILSON, *rev.* MARK POTTLE

Sources *The Times* (4 Feb 1935) · personal knowledge (1949) · R. Lowe, *Adjusting to democracy: the role of the ministry of labour in British politics, 1916–1939* (1986) · C. J. Wrigley, *David Lloyd George and the British labour movement: peace and war* (1976) · *A liberal chronicle: journals and papers of J. A. Pease*, ed. C. Hazlehurst and C. Woodland (1994) · *WWBMP* · Walford, *County families* (1919) · H. A. Clegg, A. Fox, and A. F. Thompson, *A history of British trade unions since 1889*, 2 (1985)

Likenesses G. C. Beresford, two photographs, 1903, NPG [*see illus.*] · W. Stoneman, photograph, 1917, NPG · W. Rothenstein, sanguine and crayon drawing, 1924, NPG · G. Philpot, oils, 1929, Speaker's House, Westminster

Wealth at death £44,666 10s. 3d.: probate, 27 March 1935, *CGPLA Eng. & Wales*

Whitley, Percival Nathan (1893–1956), cotton spinner and educationist, was born on 1 October 1893 at Brantwood, Stafford Road, Halifax, the eldest of the four children of John Henry (Harry) *Whitley (1866–1935), cotton spinner and politician, and his first wife, Marguerita Virginia (Margaret; 1872–1925), daughter of Giulio Marchetti of Halifax and his wife, Anne. His maternal grandfather had fought with Garibaldi before settling in Halifax and marrying the daughter of the Halifax carpet manufacturer and philanthropist John Crossley. His paternal grandfather, Nathan Whitley, had acquired the cotton spinning firm of S. Whitley & Co., Hanson Lane Mills, Halifax, in 1881, and twice served as mayor of Halifax. His father in turn became managing director of S. Whitley & Co., served as Liberal (later Coalition Liberal) MP for Halifax from 1900 to 1928, and was speaker of the House of Commons from 1921 to 1928. He subsequently served as chairman of the board of governors of the BBC from 1931 until his death in 1935.

Whitley was educated at Rugby School and New College, Oxford, where he graduated with a pass degree before entering the family cotton spinning firm on the eve of the outbreak of the First World War. He had been introduced at an early age during school and college vacations to the pioneering youth work initiated by his father in Halifax, and after his father's death assumed responsibility for the management of the recreational gymnasium and annual summer camp at Filey for socially deprived Halifax boys (and later girls), which his father had founded. In 1914 he suffered considerable personal abuse and narrowly avoided imprisonment as a conscientious objector, but was twice mentioned in dispatches during the First World War for his distinguished voluntary service with the YMCA. He travelled to France with the British expeditionary force in April 1915 and then to Salonika, where he remained until June 1919, apart from a period of convalescence from malaria in Halifax.

After the war, Whitley returned to the family business and resumed his voluntary social work in Halifax. In 1921 he commenced a long period of office with the Boy Scout movement, ultimately serving as district commissioner from 1931 to 1943. He was also elected as a Liberal to the Halifax town council, following in his father's footsteps, and served on the borough's education committee for thirty years, becoming its youngest chairman in 1932. He shared both his father's preference for local rather than national politics and his unconventional disregard for the honours system. Indeed, his father's declining for personal reasons in 1928 of the hereditary viscountcy traditionally conferred on retiring speakers of the House of

Commons was widely thought to have been out of sensitivity to his son's commitment to youth work in Halifax. Questioned by the press about how he felt about his father's unprecedented action, Whitley declared that he had 'never been more proud of his father than then' (Whitley, 10). As chairman of the Halifax education committee, he initiated a major school and college building programme following the recommendations of the Hadow Report and as a result of the need to provide new schools for the council estates created as a result of slum clearance schemes, and he was also responsible for the reorganization of secondary education under the 1944 Education Act. He became a magistrate in 1933, an alderman in 1934, and mayor of Halifax in 1941–2. During his mayoral year he wrote over a thousand letters to servicemen and servicewomen, and often used the civic car to ferry teams of young footballers across the town on Saturday afternoons. He also publicized the need to provide air raid precautions by plunging suitably attired into freezing cold water at the inauguration of a new static water tank as an emergency fire fighting resource in April 1942. After the Second World War he led a party of young Halifax apprentices to Aachen to help repair bomb damage to the German city, laying the foundation for a highly successful programme of cultural exchanges between the twinned towns.

Whitley had a lifelong association with Park Congregational Church, Halifax, becoming a member at the age of eighteen and later serving as a deacon. He never married, and combined his extensive public service with his role as managing director of the family business. Although often pressed to stand as a parliamentary candidate, he always declined because of his business responsibilities and his commitment to voluntary work in Halifax. Apart from his penchant for pipe tobacco, which ultimately had disastrous consequences for his health, he had an ascetic lifestyle. Fair-haired, with a neatly trimmed moustache, he displayed in photographs a kindly, relaxed countenance and a slim, athletic build, which prompted Mary Trevelyan, the daughter of the historian George Macaulay Trevelyan, to remark that he had 'much of the look of a mediaeval saint' (Mary Trevelyan to P. N. Whitley, 5 Jan 1955, Whitley family MSS). Despite an innate shyness, he displayed a ready wit in dealing with hecklers at political meetings and a great sense of fun within his family circle. After contracting cancer of the tongue and enduring uncomfortable radium treatment, he confided to a family friend shortly before his death that he 'still went to the mill and Town Hall' to reassure himself that he was 'still a little use to somebody' (Nora Dickin to Phyllis Bowman, 4 April 1956, Whitley family MSS). He died at his home, Brantwood, Rawson Avenue, Halifax, on 26 March 1956. Following a private cremation Eric Treacy, the archdeacon and vicar of Halifax, at a memorial service at Park Congregational Church, Halifax, on 29 March 1956, paid tribute to Whitley's 'gentle', good-humoured disposition, his 'outstanding ability', his 'strong convictions', and his decision 'to give himself without stint to the life of Halifax and to remain therefore comparatively unknown in the

wider sphere' (Whitley, 11). His distinguished public service within the locality was recognized by his appointment as OBE, an honour which he was reluctantly persuaded to accept in the year before he died, and by the naming of extensions to the town's college of further education after him in 1957 and the construction of a new sports hall in his memory in 1959.

JOHN A. HARGREAVES

Sources O. J. Whitley, 'Percival Whitley and his forebears', 1st Percival Whitley memorial lecture, Calderdale College, Halifax, 1988 · R. Bretton, 'The Whitleys of Halifax', *Transactions of the Halifax Antiquarian Society* (1963), 68–70 · E. Treacy, 'Percival Nathan Whitley', memorial service address, 1956 · W. Austin Davies, *Biographical memoir of the Rt. Hon. J. H. Whitley* (1953) · *Halifax Courier* (26 March 1956) · *Evening Courier* [Halifax] (2 Feb 1999) · *The Times* (27 March 1956) · private information (2004) [J. P. Whitley; H. W. Harwood] · b. cert. · d. cert.
Archives Calderdale College, Halifax · priv. coll.
Likenesses double portrait, *c.*1898 (with Phyllis Whitley), priv. coll. · photograph, *c.*1903 · F. E. Jackson, photograph, *c.*1916 · Greaves, photograph, *c.*1920 · Vernon Studio, photograph, *c.*1935 · photographs, 1941–1942?, priv. coll.; repro. in Whitley, 'The Percival Whitley story' (presented by Calderdale College to the Whitley family, 23 June 1988) · photograph, 18 April 1942 · photograph, *c.*1950
Wealth at death £69,647 19s. 7d.: probate, 10 Oct 1956, *CGPLA Eng. & Wales*

Whitley, Roger (1618–1697), royalist army officer and politician, was the son of Thomas Whitley (d. 1651) of Hawarden in Flintshire and his second wife, Elizabeth (d. 1668), the daughter of Roger Brereton of Haughton, Flintshire. He entered Christ Church, Oxford, on 29 November 1633 before going to Gray's Inn in 1637. In 1642 he joined the king's forces, serving under his brother-in-law Charles Gerard, later the earl of Macclesfield; by late 1644 he was a colonel and governor of Aberystwyth, which he was forced to surrender in April 1646.

Whitley's two brothers died in the king's cause, but he fought on, joining an abortive Welsh rising and other plots until he was imprisoned briefly in March 1650. He fought at Worcester in 1651 and then spent the 1650s as an enthusiastic royalist conspirator. He had married Charlotte Gerard by 1653 and he worked with his Gerard family connections outside the orbit of the Sealed Knot, the body created to oversee royalist plotting. He played a prominent part in the failed Ship tavern conspiracy, an effort to spark a general rising in early 1654. Within weeks he was plotting again, now leading an attempt to assassinate Cromwell. He continued such work throughout the 1650s—moving constantly between England, Ireland, Wales, the Channel Islands, and the continent. Over time he entered more closely into royal counsels, and by 1657 was a gentleman of the privy chamber. His notebooks from this period reveal a keen interest in contemporary politics, military management, and the techniques of conspiracy, including how one may hide incriminating writings in the body without risking discovery. In 1658, now expert in plotting, he drew up a detailed if unrealistic scheme for organizing royalist forces in England. His chance for insurrection came in August 1659, when he garrisoned Hawarden Castle and led a troop of horse in

Booth's rising. After the rising's collapse Whitley gathered more forces and maintained constant contact with the king's advisers, to whom he counselled another rising, until the Restoration in May 1660. He sat for the Flintshire boroughs in the Convention and in each parliament thereafter through 1679, after which he represented Chester.

Whitley now profited from his loyalty, receiving the mastership of a Chester hospital and becoming receiver of royal aids, receiver of the hearth tax, and excise farmer for north Wales; he was also made a gentleman usher of the privy chamber. He lived largely in London in this period. His wife, Charlotte Gerard, died there in 1662 and was buried in Westminster Abbey, before which time she had borne three sons and six daughters. In 1668 Whitley became knight harbinger, the person who managed the king's travels, and from 1672 to 1677 served as deputy postmaster, using his position to improve the post's efficiency. With the income from these offices he began purchasing East India stock in 1671, becoming a company freeman in 1674. But increasingly his cash went into land, especially from 1679 to 1682, when he acquired extensive properties in north Wales and Cheshire. He also bought Peele Hall, outside Chester, where he cultivated a regional political interest.

Whitley was now prominent among supporters of the duke of York's exclusion from the succession. In 1682 he was one of those Chester leaders who entertained the duke of Monmouth during his politically provocative visit there. Whitley's foes alleged that he flirted with sedition in Monmouth's interest; boisterous Chester crowds shouted Whitley's and Monmouth's names together. Whitley enjoyed great popularity, and that autumn was prevented from becoming Chester's mayor only by a voting process that gave final choice to the twenty-four aldermen. Once famously loyal, he was now suspect at court and had lost all preferment there. The final blow came late in 1684 when he was sued for £30,000 that he had not forwarded to royal accounts while postmaster, of which he was later ordered to pay nearly £20,000. Next came an attack on his political base, Chester, where he and his allies lost their offices when local tories, led by Sir Thomas Grosvenor, won a new charter in February 1685 that installed themselves in power in Chester.

When the duke of Monmouth launched his rebellion that summer Whitley dismissed it as 'foolish and mad' (Bodl. Oxf., MS Eng. hist. c. 711, Whitley diary, fol. 36v). A committed Anglican, he was ambivalent about King James's promotion of non-Anglicans to prominence. Along with others Whitley refused to serve when reappointed to Chester's corporation by another new charter in September 1688, though he resumed his alderman's place when the pre-1685 charter was restored the following month. Civil war memories made him doubt the wisdom of the prince of Orange's intended invasion. But he readily accepted the revolution once it occurred and sat in the convention of 1689, having easily beaten Grosvenor for one of Chester's seats. In 1690 Grosvenor defeated Whitley by a handful of votes, though only after Grosvenor's supporters allegedly employed illegal tactics. His petition against the election ended in the Commons deciding by a majority of one to seat Grosvenor instead.

Whitley now set about restoring his political foundations in Chester. At mayoral elections in 1690 and in 1691 he achieved a great majority among the freemen in the early rounds, but lost each time before the aldermen, whose votes concluded the process. In 1692 he at last prevailed. Thus began Whitley's extraordinary efforts to transform the city's constitution to maintain his authority by boosting the power of the freemen, changes he made with the advice of his ally, the city's recorder, Sir William Williams. By these means he held the mayor's chair for four successive years. In 1695, he regained his seat at Westminster by abandoning Williams on the hustings, and joining instead with his old foe, Grosvenor.

In 1696 Whitley gave up the mayoralty, perhaps because of increasing health problems; he attended no more corporation meetings thereafter, though he continued struggles to control the construction of a new city hall, a project begun during his mayoralty. He made the last entry in his diary on 15 July 1697, two days before he died at either Chester or Peele Hall. He was buried at Hawarden church. At the time of his death Whitley and his Chester allies had a petition before the privy council attacking the new mayor for reversing Whitley's popular constitutional changes. He left a large entailed estate principally to his daughter Lady Elizabeth Mainwaring, his son Roger, and their heirs.

Whitley's papers, largely in the Bodleian Library, include numerous notebooks and commonplace books revealing a meticulous and wide-ranging mind. His diary provides a fascinating account of a regional political network by one of its chief members, and suggests a sociable personality, even with those outside his partisan circle. Whitley rarely figured prominently in parliamentary debates and never achieved high office or a knighthood, despite his enormous energy in the royal cause before 1660. But his loyalty helped him obtain a number of lucrative posts, the income from which funded the regional political influence he developed so successfully in later decades.

PAUL D. HALLIDAY

Sources R. Whitley, diary, 1684–97, Bodl. Oxf., MS Eng. hist. c. 711 · R. Whitley, commonplace and notebooks, Bodl. Oxf., MS Eng. hist. c. 712, e. 308–14, g. 22 · T. Mainwaring, diary, 1648–88, Bodl. Oxf., MS Film 53 · Chester Corporation papers, Ches. & Chester ALSS [assembly books and files, AB and AF; mayors' letters and files, ML and MF; diary of Roger Comberbach, CR 99] · Ches. & Chester ALSS, Shakerley papers · papers of the third baronet, Eaton Hall, Cheshire, Grosvenor MSS · N. R. F. Tucker, 'Colonel Roger Whitley', *Flintshire Historical Society Publications*, 22 (1965–6), 9–24 · G. Hampson, J. P. Ferris, and B. D. Henning, 'Whitley, Roger', HoP, *Commons, 1660–90*, 3.709–11 · R. Stewart-Brown, 'Whitley family of Aston Hall and elsewhere', *Cheshire Sheaf*, 3rd ser., 25 (1928), 63–5 · *CSP dom.*, 1645–7; 1650; 1655–65; 1669; 1671–6; 1682–5; 1687–9 · J. Y. W. Lloyd, *The history of the princes, the lords marcher, and the ancient nobility of Powys Fadog*, 6 vols. (1881–7) · Foster, *Alum. Oxon.* · W. A. Shaw, ed., *Calendar of treasury books*, [33 vols. in 64], PRO (1904–69) · H. Robinson, *Britain's Post Office* (1953) · J. R. Jones, 'Booth's rising of 1659', *Bulletin of the John Rylands University Library*, 39 (1956–7), 416–33 · E. B. Sainsbury, ed., *A calendar of the court minutes … of the East India Company*, 11 vols. (1907–38), vols. 9–10 · *The diary of Thomas*

Cartwright, bishop of Chester, ed. J. Hunter, CS, 22 (1843) · W. D. Christie, ed., *Letters addressed from London to Sir Joseph Williamson*, 2 vols., CS, new ser., 8–9 (1874) · N. Luttrell, *A brief historical relation of state affairs from September 1678 to April 1714*, 6 vols. (1857)
Archives Bodl. Oxf., diary and papers · JRL, corresp. and papers · NL Wales, corresp. and papers · Royal Mail Heritage, London, letter-books and accounts | Ches. & Chester ALSS, Chester Corporation records
Wealth at death large estate in land, largely in Cheshire and north Wales: Stewart-Brown, 'Whitley family', 70–73; will, 1697

Whitley, William Thomas (1858–1942),

art historian, was born on 27 January 1858 at Stormont House, Kensington, London, son of William Whitley, dyer and cleaner, and his wife, Mary, daughter of Patrick Gilday, labourer, of Marylebone, London. He was educated privately, and reluctantly entered his father's business; he wanted to be a painter, and as a young man, between 1887 and 1900, he exhibited nine landscapes and figure subjects at the Royal Academy. On 30 August 1888 he married Mary (1854/5–1931), a journalist, daughter of William Alford; they had one son.

Whitley later turned to research on British art and artists. He wrote the articles on art and artists which appeared twice a week in the *Morning Post*, and also contributed to most of the leading art periodicals, including the *Burlington Magazine*, *The Connoisseur*, and *The Studio*, and to the annual publications of the Walpole Society. In addition, for many years he wrote the articles on contemporary art for the *Annual Register* and *Whitaker's Almanack*. The publication of *Thomas Gainsborough* (1915), still a classic in the field of Gainsborough scholarship, established his reputation as an art historian. It was followed by *Artists and their Friends in England, 1700–1799* (2 vols., 1928), which included passages from newspapers of the period, and gossip and anecdotes about the painters. He also wrote *Art in England, 1800–1820* (1928), *Art in England, 1821–1837* (1930), *Gilbert Stuart* (1932), and *Thomas Heaphy* (1933). Whitley was awarded a civil-list pension in 1931 for his services to art history. He died in the county hospital at Farnborough, Kent, on 17 November 1942.

MARY WOODALL, *rev.* ANNE PIMLOTT BAKER

Sources *The Times* (21 Nov 1942) · *WWW* · Graves, *RA exhibitors* · private information (1959) · personal knowledge (1959) · b. cert. · m. cert. · d. cert.
Wealth at death £307 10s. 4d.: probate, 16 Dec 1942, *CGPLA Eng. & Wales*

Whitlock [née Kemble], Elizabeth (1761–1836),

actress, was the third daughter and fifth child of the provincial actors Roger *Kemble (1722–1802) and his wife, Sarah Ward (1737–1807), and was born at Warrington, Lancashire, on 2 April 1761. Although she was apprenticed to a mantua-maker she acquired some theatrical experience in the provinces, and appeared at Drury Lane on 22 February 1783 as Portia in *The Merchant of Venice*, a part she repeated on 1 March. She subsequently played at York, where Tate Wilkinson, in *The Wandering Patentee*, described her as 'possessed of marks of merit, but wild as a colt untamed'.

Elizabeth Kemble returned to Drury Lane for two seasons, playing, through the influence of her elder sister

Elizabeth Whitlock (1761–1836), by Samuel De Wilde [as Margaret in *The Earl of Warwick* by Thomas Francklin]

Sarah *Siddons, Margaret in Philip Massinger's *A New Way to Pay Old Debts*, Leonora in Edward Young's *The Revenge*, and Elvira in *Love Makes a Man*. Critical comment, however, remained ambivalent about her talents; she returned to York, and on 21 June 1785 married Charles Edward Whitlock (d. 1822). He was manager of the Newcastle, Sunderland, Lancaster, and Chester theatres, and from 1785 to 1791 she was one of the chief actresses of his circuit. The couple had three sons, the eldest of whom, Henry Edward Whitlock (1787–1806), later appeared with them in America. After performing in Edinburgh in 1793, the Whitlocks were engaged in the USA, where they spent the following fourteen years, playing in Annapolis, Philadelphia, Charleston, Boston, and New York, and gaining a solid reputation. Her roles were primarily in tragedy: Belvidera in *Venice Preserv'd*, Imogen in *Cymbeline*, Lady Macbeth, and Lady Randolph in John Home's *Douglas*. Although not as talented as her older sister, Sarah, to whom she was inevitably compared, Elizabeth Whitlock evidently had the more beautiful voice, and was the more vivacious in company. John Bernard, who knew her in America, commented that, despite her heavy figure, she 'could kindle the sympathies and blind the spectator to every deficiency'.

On 6 October 1807 Elizabeth Whitlock reappeared at Drury Lane, acting the part of Elwina in Hannah More's *Percy*. She seems not to have performed again, and she and her husband returned to America for the years 1812–14, before settling at Addlestone, near Chertsey, in Surrey. He died on 3 March 1822, and she some years later, at Addlestone, on 27 February 1836. K. A. CROUCH

Sources Highfill, Burnim & Langhans, *BDA* · C. B. Hogan, ed., *The London stage, 1660–1800*, pt 5: *1776–1800* (1968) · J. Bernard, *Retrospections of America, 1797–1811*, ed. B. Bernard (1887) · T. Wilkinson, *The wandering patentee, or, A history of the Yorkshire theatres from 1770 to the present time*, 4 vols. (1795) · Genest, *Eng. stage* · *GM*, 2nd ser., 5 (1836) · *Monthly Mirror* (1807) · *The thespian dictionary, or, Dramatic biography of the present age*, 2nd edn (1805) · T. Gilliland, *The dramatic mirror, containing the history of the stage from the earliest period, to the present time*, 2 vols. (1808)
Archives NL Scot., untitled MS of verse
Likenesses P. Audinet, line engraving (after S. De Wilde), BM; repro. in J. Bell, *British theatre* (1792) · attrib. T. Beach, oils?, Garr. Club · S. De Wilde, oils (as Margaret in *The earl of Warwick*), Garr. Club [*see illus.*] · W. Dunlap (as Lady Tenzle in *School for scandal*), Harvard TC · J. Opie, portrait · engraving (as Imogen in *Cymbeline*), Harvard TC
Wealth at death £2100; also copyhold of house: will, 1836

Whitlock, Hector Harold (1903–1985), athlete, was born on 16 December 1903 at 33 York Road, Hendon, Middlesex, the son of Charles Robert Octavius Whitlock, a Post Office porter, and his wife, Esmeralda Beatrice, *née* Stevens. He was educated at Hendon county school. Whitlock came to prominence as a race walker in the early 1930s and dominated British walking for the greater part of the decade. 'Tall, dark and comparatively thin', he possessed a 'perfectly fair' walking action, which he combined with 'great courage … and limitless determination' (Webster, 122). A member of the Metropolitan Walking Club, he won the Road Walking Association (RWA) 50 kilometre walk in 1933 and 1935–9, and the London–Brighton race in 1934–7.

In 1933 Whitlock devised a plan of training and competition which was to culminate in an attempt on the 50 kilometre title at the Berlin Olympics. The beneficial effects of this regime were seen in 1935, when he set a world record for the 30 mile walk and became the first man to break the 8 hour barrier for the London–Brighton race, which he won by more than 18 minutes. His record of 7 hr 53 min. 50 sec. stood for twenty-two years. Victory in the 1936 RWA 50 kilometre race, in a time of 4 hr 30 min. 38 sec., established him as one of the favourites for Berlin, notwithstanding the likelihood of a strong threat from countries such as Latvia, Czechoslovakia, and Italy, as well as from his own team-mates T. Lloyd Johnson and J. Hopkins.

In the Olympic contest Whitlock was the last of the thirty-one competitors to leave the stadium, but with well-judged pacing and good discipline he moved through the field to lead at the 35 kilometre mark. Disaster struck soon afterwards when he was overcome by a bout of severe sickness. Johnson and Hopkins had been similarly afflicted at 10 kilometres, at which point they had been well up with the leaders, and the sickness was attributed to a meal that all three had eaten beforehand. Whitlock's obvious difficulties gave the second- and third-placed walkers encouragement and they moved to within 30 seconds of him at the 40 kilometre mark. But he bravely hung on to his lead and on the long slope approaching the stadium 'piled on the pace, yard after yard' to win in 4 hr

30 min. 41.4 sec. (Webster, 124). It was Britain's only individual track gold medal of the Berlin games. The race emphasized the growing popularity of race walking in Europe and established Whitlock as the sport's leading exponent. In September 1938 he completed a double by winning the European title in Paris.

Whitlock competed only intermittently after the Second World War but staged a comeback in 1952, when he came third in the RWA 50 kilometre race and was selected for the Helsinki Olympics. He was over forty-eight when he competed, thus becoming Britain's oldest ever international athlete, and he finished in a creditable eleventh place, behind his younger brother Rex, who came fourth. After his competitive career was over Whitlock became a highly respected race judge and coach, and he officiated at the 1960 Rome Olympics, where his protégé Don Thompson won the 50 kilometre title. He also wrote *Race Walking* (1957), which set out the basic principles of the sport and encouraged the development of many world-class walkers. As a competitor, coach, writer, and administrator Whitlock 'profoundly influenced the development and popularity' of his sport (Lovesey, 139). He played an important part in the introduction of a 20 kilometre event in the international programme, and was involved, too, in the development of the Lugano cup competition, regarded as the world championships of race walking. In 1966 he was appointed MBE for his services to athletics. He maintained his fitness late in life and took part in a 1 hour walk at an open meeting in London on 22 September 1979. Aged seventy-five, he covered just under 6 miles in the allotted time.

Whitlock, who was married with a daughter, worked as a mechanical engineer. He died of a chest infection on 27 December 1985 at 15 High Street, Wicklewood, Norwich.

MARK POTTLE

Sources I. Buchanan, *British Olympians: a hundred years of gold medallists* (1991) · P. Lovesey, *The official centenary history of the Amateur Athletics Association* (1979) · F. A. M. Webster, *Great moments in athletics* (1947) · *The Times* (2 Feb 1943) · *The Times* (31 Dec 1985) · J. Arlott, ed., *The Oxford companion to sports and games* (1975) · *Sunday Telegraph* (16 Sept 1979), 2h · *Sunday Telegraph* (23 Sept 1979), 37a · b. cert. · d. cert.
Wealth at death under £40,000: administration, 4 March 1986, *CGPLA Eng. & Wales*

Whitlock, John (*bap.* 1624, *d.* 1708), presbyterian minister, was baptized on 23 January 1624 at St Peter-le-Poer, London, the third son of Richard Whitlock, merchant, of London, and his wife, Catherine (1596–1649), daughter of David Burdet of Wye in Kent. On 23 June 1642 he was admitted as a pensioner to Emmanuel College, Cambridge; he graduated BA in 1646 and proceeded MA in 1649. During his years at Cambridge he established a lifelong friendship with William *Reynolds (1625–1698), with whom he shared future ministries. Appointed to the living of Leighton Buzzard, Bedfordshire, in November 1646, he was joined by Reynolds in the following month. Together they also supplied the pulpit at Wokingham in Berkshire in 1647 and Aylesbury in Buckinghamshire in

1649. Both men refused to take the engagement in 1649, which led to their being deprived of their posts.

Whitlock's unwillingness to associate with the republican authorities created a favourable impression with the more conservative members of Nottingham's ruling body. In 1651 the marquess of Dorchester presented him to the living of St Mary's, Nottingham. Reynolds was appointed as his assistant, serving as lecturer. They were instructed to establish a 'Presbytery in the town as soon as they could prove and clear the way' (Carpenter, 22). In October 1651 both men were ordained according to the presbyterian discipline at St Andrew Undershaft in London. Not until 1655, with the establishment of John Barret at St Peter's Church, was a classis established within Nottingham. Whitlock attended all but one of the classis meetings over the next four years and served on several occasions as secretary. This 'three-fold cord' of Barret, Reynolds, and Whitlock was to be prominent in the establishment and consolidation of presbyterianism within Nottingham. Whitlock enjoyed considerable links with presbyterians across the country. On 25 March 1652 he married Mary, daughter of the minister Anthony *Tuckney.

At the Restoration Whitlock was indicted for not reading common prayer and on 6 July 1662 his living was sequestered, a full month before the Act of Uniformity took effect. Making his farewell sermon to his congregation he declared he would begin a policy of 'preaching by silence', that is to refrain from public preaching. Although he continued to teach privately at conventicles over the proceeding years, it was not until the declaration of indulgence of 1672 that he took out public preaching licences as a presbyterian for Mansfield and Nottingham. After his ejection Sir John Musters offered Whitlock and Reynolds accommodation and a degree of protection at Colwick Hall. There Whitlock ministered to a conventicle of over 200 persons, according to a report given to the county lieutenant on 6 September 1663. In the same year he published *England's Remembrancer*, a collection of farewell sermons by Nottingham's ejected clergy. In 1665 he and Reynolds were imprisoned for twelve weeks in the Black Moor's Head in Nottingham for preaching. As a consequence of the Five Mile Act of the same year the two men and their families moved to Shirebrook in Derbyshire, and in 1668 to Mansfield in Nottinghamshire. As the town was not a corporate borough, it proved to be a safe haven, and Whitlock enjoyed the friendship of Lord Wharton who often stayed with him on his journeys to the north.

Although Whitlock and Reynolds were imprisoned for five months in 1685 after entering the borough town of Newark, the declaration of indulgence two years later enabled the men to return to Nottingham. There they served as joint ministers of the town's presbyterian congregation until Reynolds's death in 1698. Whitlock published *A Short Account of the Life of the Reverend Mr William Reynolds* (1698) in memory of his great friend and continued to minister at the High Pavement chapel until within two years of his own death. He died at Nottingham on 4 December 1708 and was buried in the chancel of St Mary's on 8 December. His will showed him to own several properties and substantial sums of money were bequeathed to friends, family, and charitable use. Whitlock had two children, a daughter who died in infancy, and a son, John (1661–1723), who succeeded him to the pastorate at High Pavement. STUART B. JENNINGS

Sources 'Will of John Whitlock', *A Nottinghamshire miscellany*, Thoroton Society Record Series, 21 (1962), 28–30 · S. B. Jennings, 'The gathering of the elect: the development, nature and social-economic structures of protestant religious dissent in seventeenth century Nottinghamshire', PhD diss., Nottingham Trent University, 1999 · B. Carpenter, *Account of the original introduction of presbyterianism in Nottingham and its neighbourhood* (1862) · S. Jones, 'Works by three Nottingham worthies: John Barret, John Whitlock and William Reynolds', *Transactions of the Congregational Historical Society* (1913–15), 117–23 · J. Whitlock, *A short account of the life of the Reverend Mr W. Reynolds* (1698) · *Calamy rev.* · Venn, *Alum. Cant.* · original church book belonging to the Society of Presbyterians, Nottingham, U. Nott., Hi 2Mi · *DNB* · E. Calamy, ed., *An abridgement of Mr. Baxter's history of his life and times, with an account of the ministers, &c., who were ejected after the Restauration of King Charles II*, 2nd edn, 2 vols. (1713) · Nottinghamshire lieutenancy book of William, marquis of Newcastle, 1660–77, Notts. Arch., DDP 37/3 · J. H. White, *The story of the old meeting house, Mansfield* (1959) · C. G. Bolam and others, *The English presbyterians: from Elizabethan puritanism to modern Unitarianism* (1968) · *IGI* · parish register, Nottingham, St Mary's, 8 Dec 1708, Notts. Arch. [burial]
Wealth at death property at Basford in Nottinghamshire, Wokingham in Berkshire, and Sutterton in Lincolnshire: 'Will of John Whitlock'

Whitlock, Percy William (1903–1946), organist and composer, was born on 1 June 1903 at 171 Luton Road, Chatham, Kent, the only child of William Thomas Whitlock (1874–1935), a miller's clerk, and his wife, Annie Jemima (1873–1946), a tailor, daughter of John Reeves of Northampton. Having determined that Percy should have an interest in music, his parents enrolled him as a probationer chorister in Rochester Cathedral choir in 1911. He came under the influence of the organist, Bertram Luard-Selby, and his assistant (and Whitlock's first piano teacher) Hector Shallcross. Luard-Selby was succeeded in 1916 by Charles Hylton Stewart (1884–1932), 'a man of flawless integrity', wrote Whitlock, who regarded Stewart as his 'musical father'. In addition to his education at the cathedral choir school, Whitlock travelled to the Guildhall School of Music in London. An 'unhappy' year at King's School, Rochester (in 1917–18), was alleviated by the award of a Kent county scholarship to the Royal College of Music from 1920 to 1924, during which time Whitlock studied composition with Charles Stanford and Ralph Vaughan Williams and the organ with Henry Ley. He had early success with the choral and orchestral piece *The Island* (composed in 1919), solo songs, and chamber music. Of his sacred choral music there are two fine early motets, 'Glorious in heaven' (1925) and 'Jesu, grant me this I pray' (c.1927).

On leaving the Royal College of Music Whitlock remained in Rochester as assistant cathedral organist (from 1921) and as organist of St Mary's Church, Chatham (from 1924 to 1929). In 1928 his health failed, and he spent time in Midhurst Sanatorium recovering from tuberculosis. He resigned from St Mary's and took on the less arduous post at St Matthew's, Borstal. He completed a four-movement piano quintet (1929–30) and his most celebrated work, the *Five Short Pieces* for organ (1929).

In 1930 Hylton Stewart announced his departure for Chester Cathedral. Disappointed at being passed over, Whitlock moved to Bournemouth as director of music at St Stephen's Church. Here he built up the choir and devoted himself to composition, particularly organ music. Whitlock produced a number of notable works at this time, including *Two Fantasie Chorals* (1931; rev., 1933), *Four Extemporisations* (1932–3), *Seven Sketches on Verses from the Psalms* (1934), and, most substantial of all, the sonata in C minor (1935–6).

On 27 January 1931 Whitlock married the soprano Edna May Kingdon (1901–1993), a fellow student at the Royal College of Music, and in the following year he succeeded Philip Dore (on a part-time basis) as Bournemouth's municipal organist, presiding over the Pavilion Theatre's dual-purpose four-manual Compton organ. His work there brought regular contact with the municipal orchestra and its founding conductor, Sir Dan Godfrey. Whitlock was taken up by the BBC and gave over sixty broadcasts as a solo organist between 1933 and 1946. He also appeared in the London recitals promoted by the Organ Music Society.

Dissatisfied with the political pressures of the church, Whitlock left St Stephen's in December 1935 to become full-time borough organist. He composed much orchestral music in the later 1930s, including *Carillon* (1932), the concert overture *The Feast of St Benedict* (1934), the symphony in G minor for organ and orchestra (1936–7), *Poem* (1937), and *Prelude, Air and Fugue* (1939). For his lighter music (such as the *Wessex Suite* and *Holiday Suite*) and for his journalistic work, Whitlock adopted (in 1936) the *nom de plume* Kenneth Lark.

From the outbreak of the Second World War Whitlock spent two years in Bournemouth's food control office. In 1942 he composed a rousing march for HMS *Phoebe*, a light cruiser adopted by Bournemouth. The following month he appeared at the BBC Promenade Concerts as soloist in Handel's 'Hallelujah' concerto, conducted by his friend Sir Henry Wood.

In 1945 Whitlock's health began to deteriorate owing to high blood pressure. His sight failed, and his last weeks were spent in blindness. He died at his home, Brinklea Cottage, Wimborne Road, Bournemouth, on 1 May 1946. The causes of death were stated as cardiac failure, arterial hypertension, and cerebral oedema. His funeral was held on 4 May and was followed on the same day by cremation at Bournemouth north cemetery. In 1983 a charitable trust was set up in Whitlock's name with the intention of restoring to print the larger organ works, to establish a Whitlock archive, and to finance a biography and study of his music.   MALCOLM RILEY

Sources M. Riley, *Percy Whitlock: organist and composer* (1998) · *Radio Times* (1930–46) · *Bournemouth Daily Echo* (1930–46) · *Chatham, Rochester and Gillingham Observer* (1920–46) · personal diaries of Percy Whitlock, 1930–46, Percy Whitlock Trust, Staplehurst, Kent · b. cert. · d. cert. · archives, Rochester Cathedral choir school, Kent · archives, King's School, Rochester, Kent · archives, Royal College of Music, London

Archives Bournemouth Symphony Orchestra, Poole, Dorset, library · Percy Whitlock Trust, Staplehurst, Kent, diaries | BBC WAC · Oxford University Press · priv. coll. | FILM Huntley Film Archives, London · Pathé Film Archives, Pinewood | SOUND EMI Music Archives, Hayes, Middlesex, Central Research Laboratories · Percy Whitlock Trust, Staplehurst, Kent

Likenesses two photographs, *c*.1931–1938, Percy Whitlock Trust Archive · G. Jessup, photograph, 1932, Percy Whitlock Trust Archive · pencil sketch, 1945, Percy Whitlock Trust Archive

Wealth at death £3560 16*s*. 4*d*.: probate, 15 Aug 1946, *CGPLA Eng. & Wales*

Whitlock, William. *See* Whitelocke, William (*c*.1520–1584).

Whitman, Alfred Charles (1860–1910), writer on engravings, was born at Hammersmith, London, on 12 October 1860, the youngest son of Edwin Whitman, a grocer, and his wife, Fanny. He was educated at St Mark's College School, Chelsea, after which he was employed by the firm of Henry Dawson & Sons, a typo-etching company of Farringdon Street and Chiswick. On 12 August 1885 he married, at Hammersmith, Helena Mary Bing. Later that same year, on 21 December, Whitman was appointed an attendant in the department of prints and drawings in the British Museum. For some years he served in his spare time as amanuensis to the translator Lady Charlotte Schreiber, and helped her to arrange and catalogue her collections of fans and playing cards. He was promoted to the office of departmental clerk in the print department on 20 May 1903. His tact, patience, and courtesy, combined with an exceptional knowledge of the English prints in the collection, made his aid invaluable to the museum's visitors, and he acquired, in particular, a well-deserved reputation as an authority on British mezzotint engraving.

Whitman's earlier books, *The Masters of Mezzotint* (1898) and *The Print Collector's Handbook* (1901; new and enlarged edn, 1912), which were aimed at the amateur collector, were popular in character and have less permanent value than his catalogues of eminent engravers' works, which were the outcome of notes methodically compiled during many years, not only in the British Museum, but in private collections and salerooms. *Valentine Green*, published in 1902 as part of a series, *British Mezzotinters*, to which other writers contributed under his direction, is less satisfactory than *Samuel William Reynolds*, published in 1903 as the first volume in a series entitled Nineteenth Century Mezzotinters. It was followed by *Samuel Cousins* (1904) and *Charles Turner* (1907). These two books rank among the best catalogues of an engraver's work produced in England during this period.

Whitman's health began to fail in the autumn of 1908, and he died in London after a long illness, on 2 February 1910; he was survived by his wife. His annotated copy of J. C. Smith's *British Mezzotinto Portraits* was sold at Christies on 6 June 1910 for a considerable sum.

CAMPBELL DODGSON, *rev.* MARK POTTLE

Sources *The Times* (4 Feb 1910) · *The Athenaeum* (12 Feb 1910) · private information (1912) · *CGPLA Eng. & Wales* (1910)
Wealth at death £1514 17s. 2d.: resworn probate, 26 Feb 1910, *CGPLA Eng. & Wales*

Whitmore, Sir George (*b.* after **1572**, *d.* **1654**), merchant and local politician, was born in London, the third son of William Whitmore (*d.* 1593), a London merchant, and his wife, Anne (*d.* 1615), daughter of Sir William Bond, a London haberdasher and alderman, and granddaughter of Sir George Bond, lord mayor of London in 1587–8. George Whitmore's elder brother, Sir William Whitmore (1572–1648), was a lawyer and a member of the Haberdashers' Company and of the Merchant Adventurers; he sat as MP for Bridgnorth in 1621, 1624, and 1625, a constituency held by his son, Thomas (1612–1653) in the Long Parliament, until his expulsion as a royalist in 1644. George Whitmore's sister, Elizabeth, married Sir William Craven, lord mayor of London (1610 and 1618), and was perhaps the richest woman in England when her estate passed to her son at her death in 1624.

Whitmore was apprenticed with his older brother as a haberdasher and later served two terms as master of the Haberdashers' Company (1621–2, 1631–2). He became a member of the Virginia Company in 1609, and owned substantial stock in the East India Company. He and his wife, Mary (1616–1657), daughter of Richard Daniell (*d.* 1630), burgess of Truro, Cornwall, and owner of the former crown manor of Alverton, had at least three sons and four daughters. In 1631 he rebuilt, in the Italianate style, his residence at Balmes (Baumes) House, Hoxton, in the parish of St Leonard, Shoreditch, where he lived until his death.

Whitmore's political career began with his election as sheriff for 1621–2, followed by service as alderman for Farringdon Within (1621–6) and Langbourne (1626–43), and then as lord mayor of London in 1631–2. He was knighted on 27 May 1632 and served as president of Bethlem and Bridewell hospitals in 1632–42. As a wealthy alderman and an undersharer of the customs, in June 1639 he was asked to support a city loan to the crown of £100,000, and later in the month, when the aldermen as a body showed themselves unfavourable to the loan, he was one of the seven who agreed to it. With the loan's failure, the customs farmers secured £250,000 for the king, including loans from Whitmore and five other aldermen. Upon Charles I's return from Scotland in November 1641, he welcomed the king at Balmes in an elaborate ceremony, and had a road cut through his estate to smooth the royal journey.

On 3 December 1641 Whitmore was one of the aldermen who presented a petition to Charles urging him to remain near the capital and condemning recent disorders in the London area. With other wealthy supporters of Charles I he allegedly offered to raise 10,000 troops to protect the king in London at the time of the royal departure in January 1642. In February–March 1642 he was one of the aldermen who signed a petition protesting at parliament's vesting of the London trained bands in the hands of a committee of safety, and acted to defend the claims of the lord mayor and aldermen to control of the city militia.

With the outbreak of the civil war Whitmore was, in December 1642, a supporter of what parliament considered a royalist-backed petitioning campaign in the City, urging the need for an immediate peace. Meanwhile, his refusal to contribute to loans requested by parliament and its committees had been followed by refusal to pay an assessment of £1500 set by the committee for the advance of money, which led to his arrest and imprisonment in Crosby House, London. With six other aldermen he was transferred to prison at Yarmouth, and later moved to Winchester House and thence to Lambeth Palace in 1644; the committee began seizing his assets, including rents from properties in Essex and East India Company stock. Meanwhile the court of aldermen removed Whitmore from his seat on 2 May 1643. He eventually received a discharge for his sequestered estates from the committee for compounding in 1651. He died at Balmes on 12 December 1654 and was buried at St Mary Magdalen, Milk Street, London, on 6 January 1655. The estates he left to his sons included not only Balmes, but also properties in Yorkshire, Northumberland, Berkshire, Somerset, Dorset, and Essex.　　　　　　　　　　DANIEL WEBSTER HOLLIS, III

Sources V. Pearl, *London and the outbreak of the puritan revolution: city government and national politics, 1625–1643* (1961) · M. A. E. Green, ed., *Calendar of the proceedings of the committee for advance of money, 1642–1656*, 3 vols., PRO (1888) · Burke, *Gen. GB* · *CSP dom.*, 1625–6; 1637 · A. B. Beaven, ed., *The aldermen of the City of London, temp. Henry III–[1912]*, 2 vols. (1908–13) · R. R. Sharpe, *London and the kingdom*, 2 (1894) · K. B. Sommers, 'Court, country, and parliament: electoral influences in five English counties, 1586–1640', PhD diss., Yale U., 1978 · Pepys, *Diary* · D. Lysons, *The environs of London*, 2 (1795) · Burke, *Peerage* (1967) · K. Lindley, *Popular politics and religion in civil war London* (1997) · *DNB*
Archives Bodl. Oxf., papers
Likenesses oils, Haberdashers' Company, London
Wealth at death exact wealth unknown, but considerable

Whitmore, Sir George Stoddart (1829–1903), army officer and police officer in New Zealand, was born in Malta on 30 May 1829, the son of Lieutenant (later Major) George St Vincent Whitmore RE and his wife, Isabella Maxwell, the daughter of Sir John Stoddart, chief justice of Malta. He was educated at Edinburgh Academy and destined for a conventional military career, but instead joined the Cape mounted rifles as an ensign in January 1847.

Whitmore flourished in irregular colonial warfare. In South Africa he distinguished himself in the Cape frontier wars of 1847 and 1850–53, and participated in the 1848 defeat of the Boers at Boomplaats, the town where he married Eliza McGlocking about 1851. She died in the early 1860s after they had had three children. In May 1850 Whitmore was promoted lieutenant, and on return to England in 1854 was made captain in the 62nd (Wiltshire) regiment of foot that July. During service in the Crimea and elsewhere from 1855 (during which he was promoted brevet major in 1856, and earned the fourth class of the Turkish order of the Mejidiye) his courage was reconfirmed and his organizational skills finely honed. In 1858 and 1860 (interrupted by a spell as aide-de-camp to the commander

Sir George Stoddart Whitmore (1829–1903), by Herman John Schmidt, c.1890–1900

of forces in Canada) he attended the staff college at Aldershot and passed with top marks.

In 1861 Whitmore became military secretary to Lieutenant-General Duncan Cameron, the newly appointed commander of the imperial forces in New Zealand. But, tiring of the prevailing truce with 'rebel' Maori, he resigned in 1862 to improve a sheep and cattle run he now co-owned at Rissington, near Napier. Soon a JP, he combined a ruthless but efficient run-holding operation with many political, military, and bureaucratic positions in the colonial state, and was also a volunteer on Cameron's staff when war against Maori broke out again in 1863. That year alone he became civil commissioner for his region, a legislative councillor, in command of the local militia, and chief inspector and then commandant in the colonial defence force. On a visit to England on 11 March 1865 he married Isabella, the daughter of William Smith of Roxeth; they had no children.

As head of the local militia, Whitmore made his mark by decisively crushing a small invasion of 'rebels' at Omarunui on 12 October 1866. In March 1868 he was appointed commandant of the armed constabulary, a militarized police body founded to 'pacify' the supposedly defeated Maori. But with renewed 'rebellion' from the forces of Te Kooti Rikirangi and Titokowaru, on the eastern and western seaboards of the North Island respectively, he was given the task of transforming the armed constables into soldiers, and reforming all colonial military forces.

Whitmore now led the campaigns for which he became famous, switching from side to side of the island in pursuit of the 'rebel' chiefs. In effect commander-in-chief of the forces, he was elevated to full colonel on 21 October 1868, and created CMG in 1869. Despite losing key battles against Te Kooti (Ruakituri, 8 August 1868) and Titokowaru (Moturoa, 7 November 1868), he redeemed himself by defeating the former's forces at Ngatapa (5 January 1869) and penetrating his mountain sanctuary that May, and, in between, by pursuing the remnants of Titokowaru's forces after they abandoned their fortress at Tauranga-ika. Although there were further incidents of rebellion, the backbone of resistance to the state had been broken. However, in mid-1869 the inability of the colonial forces to capture the two 'rebel' chiefs led to the fall of the 'war policy' ministry. The new premier, William Fox, sought quickly to demilitarize the armed constabulary, since the colonial military had largely secured peace in the countryside. At the end of July 1869 command of the armed constabulary was stripped from Whitmore (ostensibly on grounds of ill health) and given to a career policeman.

During his arduous campaigning, Whitmore had sat in the Hawke's Bay provincial council (1867–9), and he remained involved in politics, notably as a legislative councillor, as well as farming for the rest of his life. On 18 October 1877 he became colonial secretary in Sir George Grey's Liberal administration, and on 1 January 1878 he was also appointed commissioner of the recently formed New Zealand constabulary force, which combined the colony's policing and military functions. He sought to improve the colony's external defences against the supposed foe, Russia, including by ordering heavy harbour-defence guns. Internally, the job of control and surveillance of both Maori and Europeans gave him considerable authority. That the commissioner was also a minister made him even more powerful. But it also meant that he lost both positions as a result of Grey's fall on 8 October 1879. He was created KCMG in 1882.

In August 1884 Whitmore entered the twelve-day Stout–Vogel ministry as minister without portfolio, and, some time after Stout and Vogel returned to power, he was appointed commander of the forces on 27 April 1885. In November of that year he was again gazetted commissioner of the New Zealand constabulary force (as well as under-secretary for defence). His major job in the Stout–Vogel ministry was to restructure the colony's coercive forces, to reflect both the state of internal tranquillity and further fears of Russian intentions. On 1 September 1886, when separate policing and military organizations were established, Whitmore added to his duties as the most senior military officer and military bureaucrat in New Zealand that of the founding commissioner of the New Zealand police force. He was commissioner only long enough to place the force on a firm footing before resigning on 31 December 1886; meanwhile, on 4 December, his position as linchpin of the colonial forces was recognized when he became the first New Zealander to attain the rank of major-general.

In January 1888 Whitmore resigned from his military positions to return to politics, having abandoned his earlier association with radical politicians. In 1902, while on his way to England to publish *The Last Maori War in New Zealand under the Self-Reliant Policy*, a stroke partially paralysed him. On 16 March 1903, shortly after his return to New Zealand, he died at the Blue Cottage, Napier, Hawke's Bay; he was buried in the local cemetery.

Whitmore combined courage in the field with considerable organizational capacity. He fell out with most people, subordinates and superiors, European and Maori, but dominated the New Zealand politico-military/policing scene for two decades because of his superior abilities.

RICHARD S. HILL

Sources J. Belich, 'Whitmore, George Stoddart', *DNZB*, vol. 1 · R. S. Hill, *The colonial frontier tamed: New Zealand policing in transition, 1867–1886* (1989) · J. Belich, *The New Zealand wars and the Victorian interpretation of racial conflict* (1986) · R. S. Hill, *Policing the colonial frontier: the theory and practice of coercive social and racial control in New Zealand, 1767–1867* (1986) · J. Belich, *I shall not die: Titokowaru's war, New Zealand, 1868–1869* (1989) · R. S. Hill, *The iron hand in the velvet glove: the modernisation of policing in New Zealand, 1886–1917* (1995) · NL NZ, Turnbull L., G. S. Whitmore MSS, MS Papers 161 · *New Zealand Gazette* (1863) · *New Zealand Gazette* (1865) · *New Zealand Gazette* (1878) · *Police Gazette* [New Zealand] (1878) · *Police Gazette* [New Zealand] (1885) · G. Whitmore, *The last Maori war in New Zealand under the self-reliant policy* (1902) · J. Cowan, *The New Zealand wars: a history of the Maori campaigns and the pioneering period*, 2 vols. (1922–3) · W. Gisborne, *New Zealand rulers and statesmen, 1840–1885* (1886)
Archives Archives New Zealand, Wellington · Hawkes Bay Museum, Napier, corresp. and papers · NL Aus., papers · NL NZ, Turnbull L., corresp.
Likenesses H. J. Schmidt, photograph, *c.*1890–1900, National Library of New Zealand, Alexander Turnbull Library [*see illus.*] · photograph, repro. in Whitmore, *Last Maori war in New Zealand* · photograph, repro. in Gisborne, *New Zealand rulers and statesmen* · photograph, repro. in Hill, *Colonial frontier tamed* · photograph, repro. in Cowan, *New Zealand wars* · photograph, repro. in Belich, *I shall not die*

Whitney, Dorothy Payne. *See* Elmhirst, Dorothy Payne (1887–1968).

Whitney, Geoffrey (1548?–1600/01), author, the son of Geoffrey Whitney, was most probably born in 1548, though 1552 has been suggested as an alternative (Borris, 336), near Nantwich, Cheshire, or possibly in London. His family, of minor gentry status descended from the Whitneys of Whitney, Herefordshire, had held a manor at Coole Pilate, near Nantwich, since 1388. His parents held a tenancy at nearby Combermere, where Whitney was probably brought up. He had at least one brother and four sisters, one of whom may have been the poet Isabella *Whitney. Geoffrey Whitney attended Audlem School, near Nantwich, and then studied briefly at Oxford, and for a longer period at Magdalene College, Cambridge, where his tutor was Stephen Limbert, later master of Norwich School. He appears not to have taken a degree. Between 1570 and 1574 he probably studied law at Thavies' Inn or Furnivall's Inn in London, though he was not called to the bar.

From 1580 (and possibly earlier) to 1586, Whitney was under-bailiff of Great Yarmouth. On 2 August 1580 he made a visit to Scratby Island, off Great Yarmouth, and wrote an account in Latin of the journey. About this time, if not earlier, Whitney increasingly sought and attained

the patronage of Robert Dudley, earl of Leicester, who was high steward of Great Yarmouth. In 1584 Whitney became acting under-steward of Great Yarmouth, and Leicester supported his application for official tenure of the office. However, Whitney's application was unsuccessful, and he was forced to resign the acting under-stewardship in 1586 in favour of John Stubbes, author of *A Gaping Gulfe*. Whitney responded with legal proceedings against the corporation of Great Yarmouth; in 1587, with Leicester's support, he received £45 in compensation on condition that he make no further claim for an office. In late November or early December of 1585 Whitney presented to Leicester a manuscript version of an emblem book, just before the earl's departure to the Low Countries as governor-general. Whitney seems to have come into contact with Dutch intellectuals during his sojourn in Norfolk. In 1586 he contributed verses in commendation of Jan Dousa the elder's *Odae Britannicae*. In the early months of 1586 he visited Leiden as a supernumerary in the party of Dousa, taking lodgings from 12 January 1586 for a few nights. On 1 March 1586 he became a student at the new University of Leiden. His period in the Netherlands thus coincided with Leicester's campaign, and Whitney doubtlessly sought to continue his association with the earl, possibly offering himself as a guide to the intellectual culture of Leiden (Manning, 160).

In the Netherlands, Whitney was persuaded by Leicester and Dousa to publish the emblem book presented in manuscript in the previous year to the earl. Whitney's most famous work, *A Choice of Emblemes and other Devises*, was printed at the Plantin press by François Raphelengius in Leiden in 1586 and dedicated to Leicester. It contains 248 emblems, consisting of illustrations, mottos, and explicating verses generally drawing a moral lesson; the work is a considerable expansion and revision of the manuscript version (Tung). It draws upon continental emblematists and is preceded in English by the manuscript emblem book of Thomas Palmer as well as comparable works such as Van der Noot's *A Theatre for Voluptuous Worldlings* (1569). Nevertheless, Whitney became the pre-eminent emblematist of the Elizabethan period, as recognized by Frances Meres in *Palladis tamia* (1598, 285). Whitney's *Emblemes* arguably supports Leicester's militant expansionist protestantism, though the work has also been interpreted as more broadly moralistic and politically cautious. The dedication to Leicester, dated from London on 28 November 1585, praises the earl as 'a zelous favorer of the Gospell, and of the godlie Preachers thereof' (sig. *3); the first emblem celebrates Elizabeth's restoration of reformed religion. Most emblems carry a dedication, such as those on pages 193–5 to the leaders of Leicester's forces in the Netherlands and a number to Whitney's relations and friends.

At some stage Whitney returned to England and apparently to the neighbourhood of his upbringing. He made his will at Royals Green, near Combermere Abbey, on 11 September 1600, and the will was proved on 28 May 1601. He appears to have died unmarried.

ANDREW KING

Sources G. Whitney, *A choice of emblemes and other devises* (Leiden, 1586) · H. Manship, *The history of Great Yarmouth*, ed. C. J. Palmer (1854), 106 · Wood, *Ath. Oxon.*, new edn, 1.527 · Cooper, *Ath. Cantab.*, 2.23–4 · H. Green, *On the emblems of Geffrey Whitney, of Nantwich, in the sixteenth century: a paper read before the Architectural, Archaeological, and Historic Society of Chester* (1865) · K. Borris, 'Geoffrey Whitney', *Sixteenth-century British nondramatic writers: second series*, ed. D. A. Richardson, DLitB, 136 (1994), 336–40 · J. F. Leisher, *Geoffrey Whitney's 'A choice of emblemes' and its relation to the emblematic vogue in Tudor England* (New York, 1987) · J. Manning, 'Whitney's *Choice of emblemes*: a reassessment', *Renaissance Studies*, 4 (1990), 155–200 · J. A. van Dorsten, *Poets, patrons, and professors: Sir Philip Sidney, Daniel Rogers, and the Leiden humanists* (Leiden and London, 1962), 123–7, 131–8 · K. Borris and M. Morgan Holmes, 'Whitney's *Choice of emblemes*: Anglo-Dutch politics and the order of ideal repatriation', *Emblematica*, 8 (1994), 81–132 · M. Tung, 'Whitney's *A choice of emblemes* revisited: a comparative study of the manuscript and the printed versions', *Studies in Bibliography*, 29 (1976), 32–101 · E. Rosenberg, *Leicester: patron of letters* (New York, 1955), 307–11

Whitney, Isabella (*fl.* **1566–1573**), poet, is assumed to be the daughter of Geoffrey Whitney of Coole Pilate, Cheshire, and the sister of Geoffrey *Whitney (1548?–1600/01), author of a minor emblem book, *A Choice of Emblemes* (1586), on the basis of correspondences between persons named in the younger Geoffrey's will and in his volume of emblems, with persons named in *A Sweet Nosgay*, Isabella's second volume of verses. It is possible that references in *Nosgay* to Geoffrey Whitney refer to two other, more distantly connected, contemporary Geoffrey Whitneys; Isabella's own statement was that she was 'bred' in London. If she was the sister of the author Geoffrey Whitney, she was either estranged from Geoffrey, or married (the 'Sister Eldershae' he names), or dead by September 1600, when Geoffrey omitted mention of an Isabella in his will. Her mother's surname may have been Cartwright. Whatever her origins, Isabella Whitney enjoys the distinction of being the first woman under whose name, or initials, a complete, printed volume of original, secular poetry appeared in English.

The Copy of a Letter (1566–7), the first of Whitney's two known miscellanies, survives in only one known exemplar housed at the Bodleian Library. In addition to a prefatory poem by Richard Jones, the printer, the volume contains four jaunty love complaints, two in female and two in male voice. Although some critics have argued that Whitney was author of only two of the poems, 'I.W. To her Unconstant Lover' and 'The Admonition by the Auctor', others—Marquis and Krontiris, most notably—claim that the juxtaposed poems privilege a female complaint about the misuse of women over a male complaint about rebellious women. There have been unreliable editions of *Copy* by J. P. Collier (*Illustrations of Early English Popular Literature*, 1863) and E. Arber (*An English Garner*, 1896); a portion was reproduced by Travitsky in 1980, and a facsimile of the whole was published (with an introduction by Panofsky) in 1982.

A Sweet Nosgay (1573), Whitney's second, more complex miscellany, is extant in an imperfect exemplar held at the British Library. The title poem reworks some of the adages of Hugh Plat's *Floures of Philosophie* (1572), particularly those on love and friendship, flavouring some of the verses with added point of a type that might be called proto-feminist. Like *Copy*, *Nosgay* can be read as focusing on a single motif, in this case the suffering and illness (mitigated somewhat by the love and friendship of family and friends) which eventually caused the author to leave 'good London'. Poetic epistles and other verses to family and friends describe both the addressees and Whitney's situation, thereby relaying to us seemingly autobiographical titbits that state or suggest that she is from a large family; that two of her younger sisters, to whom she proffers advice, are in service; that she is single and therefore free to write verses; that she is of gentle—though not exalted—rank; and that although she has been in service to a woman she admires, she is luckless: she has been ill, has lost her position, and is financially hard-pressed. In the final, most original, and most important poem in the volume, the mock 'Wyll and Testament' Whitney addresses to London before her departure (and her anticipated, mock-serious demise), Whitney describes the city in vivid detail reminiscent of the character sketches of 'Cock Lorell's Boat', of the rogue tracts and cony-catching pamphlets, and of the later city comedies. 'Wyll', though similar to earlier mock testaments, is unusual in being fitted into a narrative frame; Gascoigne may have written his 'Last Will and Testament of Dan Bartholomew of Bath' in imitation. In addition to Panofsky's facsimile of the entire *Nosgay* (1982), parts of the volume were published in the twentieth century.

Both volumes mark Whitney as a very unconventional woman. Earlier Englishwomen who put works in print were noble or associated with court circles, and their pious productions (usually translated) were both inherently blameless and a plausible excuse for their breach of convention. In contrast, there is no evidence to suggest that Whitney was well connected, and her poems give what Beilin has termed 'public' voice to breezily expressed secular concerns. Her jocose tone, in fact, lends credence to the suggestion that she is writing imaginary, rather than heartfelt, laments (as her publisher suggests in his prefatory poem to *Copy*). Whitney was certainly *au courant* with London literary trends; in fact, she can be viewed as a trend-setter for her composition both of rhymed epistles and of a mock testament. The ballad measure which she used frequently was very popular; her use of familiar allusions (including many of her titles) and of exaggerated complaints are consonant with 'the native plain style of poetry' of her time; she is indeed similar—in all but gender—to contemporaries like Gascoigne, Googe, and Turberville. As a woman writer of such verses, however, she is absolutely unique in the mid-sixteenth century: the 'Judith Shakespeare' whom Virginia Woolf posited as an impossibility.

Both of Whitney's complete volumes were printed by Richard Jones, who specialized in popular ephemera. Fehrenbach speculates that 'The Complaint of a Woman Lover', printed by Jones in *A Handefull of Pleasant Delites* (1566?), may have been Whitney's and that Jones may have printed two other poems by Whitney, 'The Lady Beloved Exclaymeth of the Great Untruth of her Lover' and 'The

Lamentacion of a Gentilwoman upon the Death of her Late Deceased Frend William Gruffith Gent.' in *A Gorgious Gallery, of Gallant Inventions* (1578). Green suggested that Whitney might also have been author of 'Another by I.W.', a prefatory poem in Thomas Morley's *A Plaine and Easie Introduction to Practicall Musicke* (1597), although this work was not printed by Jones. There is, however, nothing concrete to tie any of these poems to Whitney.

BETTY S. TRAVITSKY

Sources M. D. Felker, 'The poems of Isabella Whitney: a critical edition', PhD diss., Texas Tech University, 1990 · H. Green, *On the emblems of Geffrey Whitney, of Nantwich, in the sixteenth century: a paper read before the Architectural, Archaeological, and Historic Society of Chester* (1865) · R. J. Panofsky, ed., *The floures of philosophie by Sir Hugh Plat, and A sweet nosgay and The copy of a letter by Isabella Whitney* (1982) · R. J. Fehrenbach, 'Isabella Whitney (*fl.* 1565–75) and the popular miscellanies of Richard Jones', *Cahiers Elisabethains*, 19 (1981), 85–7 · R. J. Fehrenbach, 'Isabella Whitney, Sir Hugh Plat, Geoffrey Whitney, and "Sister Eldershae"', *English Language Notes*, 21/1 (1983), 7–11 · E. V. Beilin, 'Writing public poetry: humanism and the woman writer', *Modern Language Quarterly*, 51/2 (1990), 249–71 · T. Krontiris, *Oppositional voices: women as writers and translators of literature in the English Renaissance* (1992) · P. A. Marquis, 'Oppositional ideologies of gender in Isabella Whitney's *Copy of a letter*', *Modern Language Review*, 90 (1995), 314–24 · B. Travitsky, '"The lady doth protest": protest in the popular writings of Renaissance Englishwomen', *English Literary Renaissance*, 14 (1984), 255–83 · B. Travitsky, '"The wyll and testament" of Isabella Whitney', *English Literary Renaissance*, 10 (1980), 76–95 · B. S. Travitsky, 'Isabella Whitney', *The early modern Englishwoman: a facsimile library of essential works*, ed. S. Woods, B. S. Travitsky, and P. Cullen, 10: *The poets, I* (2001), ix–xi · W. Wall, 'Isabella Whitney and the female legacy', *ELH: a Journal of English Literary History*, 58 (1991), 76–94

Whitney, James (d. 1693), highwayman, earned himself the nickname of the Jacobite robber, and was a reputed participant in a plot to assassinate William III. Of 'mean contemptible parentage' (*Jacobite Robber*, 2), he was apprenticed to a butcher. By late 1692 he had become notorious for his Jacobite sympathies as well as his robberies on the roads outside London. Seeking a pardon he offered to the king his services and those of, variously, thirty to eighty mounted men under his command, plus money. Emissaries were sent to discuss this offer. On 31 December, recognized in a London street, he was run down by a mob, captured, and committed to Newgate, the mob then cheering him on the way to prison. Awaiting trial, wearing 40 lb of leg irons, he commissioned his tailor to make him 'a rich embroidered suit with perug and hatt, worth 100*l*.' (Luttrell, 3.5). He also offered to betray his comrades for a pardon. Tried and convicted on 19 January 1693, he was taken to Tyburn on 27 January to be hanged.

Reprieved at the last minute, Whitney was brought back to Newgate with the rope around his neck. The butchers of Smithfield greeted this news with 'over insolent rejoycings' (*Life*, 30), but there was also more widespread sentiment in his favour, 'so divided were the Affections of the People' (ibid., 28). According to rumour Whitney was going to identify his accomplices, particularly who was behind the frequent robberies of the mails; the truth, however, was more extravagant. The morning he was to be hanged he had sent a letter to Lord Capell, who took it to Chief Justice Holt; in the letter he claimed to have been involved with eleven other men in an abortive plot to kill William III as he hunted in Windsor Forest. The conspiracy, he claimed, was still active. Examined that night at Whitehall, Whitney held out for a pardon before saying anything more; his letter was dismissed as a desperate ruse.

Finally hanged on 1 February near Smithfield bars as a particular lesson to overweening butcher boys and all their sympathizers, Whitney may claim a wider significance. *The Jacobite Robber* and *The Life of Captain James Whitney* (both 1693) offer fanciful and satirical accounts of his exploits, charged with immediate political implications, along with a minimum of actual biographical details. Included in Alexander Smith's *Lives of the Highwaymen* (1713–14), Whitney would become one of the most famous highwaymen of his era, along with James Hind, Claude Duval, and the Golden Farmer. The pro- and anti-Jacobite elements in the earlier texts vanish in Smith's often reprinted account, however, as does almost all residual fact. Whitney stands also as one of many indices to the insecurity of William's regime, bedevilled as it was by plots and rumours of plots. Not since Hind, executed for treason in 1652 for services rendered to the future Charles II, and not for robbery, had the politics of a common criminal been taken so seriously by the state authorities; no other such cases exist during the 'long' eighteenth century.

LINCOLN B. FALLER

Sources N. Luttrell, *A brief historical relation of state affairs from September 1678 to April 1714*, 2–3 (1857) · *A full and true account of the apprehending James Whitney* [1693] · *The Jacobite robber: an account of the famous life, and memorable actions of Capt. Jam. Whitney* (1693) · *The life of Captain James Whitney* (1693) · [S. Grascombe?], *New court contrivances, or, More sham-plots still, against true-hearted Englishmen* (1693) · A. Smith, *A complete history of the lives and robberies of the most notorious highwaymen*, ed. A. L. Hayward, 5th edn (1719); repr. (1926) · L. Faller, 'King William, "K.J.", and James Whitney: the several lives and affiliations of a Jacobite robber', *Eighteenth-Century Life*, 12 (1988), 88–104

Whitney, James Pounder (1857–1939), ecclesiastical historian, was born at Marsden, near Huddersfield, Yorkshire, on 30 November 1857, the only son of Thomas Whitney, perpetual curate of Marsden, and his wife, Ann Jane, daughter of James Morice. Both parents were of south Welsh extraction. A precocious boy, he showed an early interest in academic history. He was educated at King James's Grammar School, Almondbury, near Huddersfield, and was a student at Owens College, Manchester (1874–7), under Sir A. W. Ward, who remained his mentor and friend. As a foundation scholar of King's College, Cambridge (1877), he was a wrangler in the mathematical tripos of 1881 and was also bracketed senior in the first class in the historical tripos of that year. In 1882 he won the Lightfoot scholarship for ecclesiastical history and the Whewell scholarship for international law.

Ordained deacon in 1883 and priest in 1885, Whitney became, after holding three curacies, the rector of Hempstead-with-Lessingham, Norfolk (1890), and then rector of Milton, near Cambridge (1895). He continued to study ecclesiastical history, and was assistant lecturer in history at Owens College from 1882 to 1887. In 1900 he was appointed principal of Bishop's College, Lennoxville, Quebec, Canada, and held the office, along with a canonry of Quebec Cathedral, for five years. He returned to Cambridge in 1906 as chaplain of St Edward's Church (1906–8). In 1906 he was also Hulsean lecturer. From 1908 to 1918 he was professor of ecclesiastical history at King's College, London, and after a brief tenure of the rectory of Wicken Bonhunt, Essex, in 1918–19, was elected Dixie professor of ecclesiastical history and fellow of Emmanuel College at Cambridge in 1919. He held both these posts until his death, which took place at 6 St Peter's Terrace, Cambridge, on 17 June 1939.

Whitney was an inspiring teacher, exerting considerable personal influence over his pupils and generously recognizing younger scholars. He was a man of attractive character and in early years notably handsome. His scholarship was wide and deep, but discursive. He was a joint-editor of the Cambridge Medieval History from 1907 to 1922; he contributed some excellent chapters; but as an editor he was unbusinesslike, and his colleague C. W. Previté-Orton's generous tribute to him in the *Dictionary of National Biography* has to be revised in the light of Peter Linehan's study of the History. Whitney's own works, which included *The Reformation* (1907, revised 1940) and *Hildebrandine Essays* (1932), reveal a judicious and widely read historian. But he published little; the *coup d'œil*, exact, luminous, and instructive, was his forte. He was remembered for his conversational *obiter dicta*; he could be caustic, but he was without rancour. Himself a devout Anglican, he had friends in other denominations. He married on 29 April 1891 Roberta Frances Anne (*b.* 1866/7), daughter of Robert Champley, of Scarborough; there were no children of the marriage. After his death, his widow gave his valuable collection of books to the Seeley Historical Library at Cambridge.

C. W. PREVITÉ-ORTON, *rev.* C. N. L. BROOKE

Sources R. E. Balfour, 'Memoir of Dr Whitney', in J. P. Whitney, *The history of the Reformation*, new edn (1940), vii–xii · J. R. Tanner, ed., *The historical register of the University of Cambridge*, 161, 273–4, 540, 897 · N. Sykes and E. Welbourne, 'James Pounder Whitney', *Emmanuel College Magazine*, 33 (1950–51), 71–3 · Crockford (1938), 1437 · O. Chadwick, 'Dr Samuel Johnson and the Dixie professorship of ecclesiastical history', *Journal of Ecclesiastical History*, 35 (1984), 583–96 · P. A. Linehan, 'The making of the *Cambridge Medieval History*', *Speculum*, 57 (1982), 463–94 · *CGPLA Eng. & Wales* (1939) · m. cert. · *DNB*

Likenesses photograph, 1906?–1908, Emmanuel College, Cambridge

Wealth at death £3102 13s. 8d.: probate, 16 Dec 1939, *CGPLA Eng. & Wales*

Whitrow, Gerald James (1912–2000), mathematician, historian, and philosopher of science, was born on 9 June 1912 at Kimmeridge, Dorset, the eldest son of George William Whitrow (1875–1953), a farmer, and his wife, Emily, formerly Watkins (1872–1955). In 1916 the family moved to Clapham, London. His father became a clerk in Harrods and Whitrow attended Wix's Lane School. He was a very clever child, and at the age of six preferred reading books to playing games. He won a London county council scholarship to Christ's Hospital, Horsham, which he attended from 1923 to 1930. He so impressed one of the school's examiners, Theodore William Chaundy (1889–1966), a fellow of Christ Church, Oxford, that he was offered a scholarship there. He went up in 1930, and took a double first degree in 1933 (MA 1937).

At Oxford Whitrow came under the influence of the astrophysicist E. A. Milne (1896–1950), the first Rouse Ball professor of mathematics, with whom he worked on kinematic relativity theory as a senior university student between 1933 and 1935. Milne and Whitrow developed the idea of functional square roots, and collaborated closely until Milne's death. In 1936 Whitrow was appointed a research lecturer at Christ Church with a glowing testimonial from Milne, who ranked him 'as a first-class investigator'. He took his DPhil in 1938. His interest in the history and philosophy of science began while he was an undergraduate. In 1931 he attended the second International Congress of the History of Science in London, at which the Soviet delegation made a great impact with its view about the nature of science. In 1938 he published his first historical paper on the natural philosopher Robert Hooke (1635–1703), himself a former member of Christ Church.

During the Second World War Whitrow worked on ballistics for the Ministry of Supply, armaments research department. In 1945 he was appointed assistant lecturer in mathematics at Imperial College, London. In the following year he became a full lecturer and on 17 August married Annie Magda Mostel, a librarian and bibliographer. They had no children and enjoyed a remarkably happy marriage, living first in Battersea and from 1967 in Wimbledon. Appointed reader in applied mathematics (1951), he eventually became professor of the history and applications of mathematics (1972). After his retirement in 1979 he remained at the college as a senior research fellow for a number of years. He was an excellent lecturer, his clear intonation matched by the clarity of his exposition. Furthermore, he took part in the running of the college and university and served as college orator from 1972 to 1974.

At Imperial Whitrow fulfilled his early promise with more than a hundred papers and ten books. He was most appreciated by his research students, many of whom went on to distinguished careers in mathematics and science. During his career he made a considerable impact on the philosophy and mathematics of time, associating with such notable scholars as Karl Popper and the Indian astrophysicist and Nobel laureate Subrahmanyan Chandrasekhar.

Whitrow believed that science should have a broad audience and thus ensured that much of his work was accessible to non-specialists; to this end he gave school talks on the radio, worked on Open University programmes, and talked to undergraduate societies. He published in astrophysics, cosmology, and the history and philosophy of time. His first book was *The Structure of the*

Universe (1949), and his last was *Time in History* (1988). With H. Bondi, W. B. Bonnor, and R. A. Lyttelton he wrote *Rival Theories of Cosmology* (1960), which formed part of the debate between the steady-state and big-bang theorists of the universe. Whitrow tended to support the latter theory. His *Einstein: the Man and his Achievement* (1967) was based on a series of radio talks; another such series, 'The nature of time', was published as *What is Time?* (1972). However, *The Natural Philosophy of Time* (1960) was his major contribution to the subject. In this he examined time from every aspect—mathematical, cosmological, historical, biological, and psychological.

Whitrow was active in a number of societies. He was elected a fellow of the Royal Astronomical Society in 1940 and was vice-president from 1965 to 1967. His most important contribution to the society was to reorganize its important library and archives while chairman of the library committee in the 1960s and 1970s, and for many years he was the leading light of the society's dining club. He was an early member of the British Society for the History of Science, serving as president from 1968 to 1970; he was president of the British Society for the Philosophy of Science from 1955 to 1957, and was the founding president of the British Society for the History of Mathematics in 1971. He also played important roles in the Athenaeum and the Wimbledon Literary and Scientific Society.

A kind and polite man with very high personal standards, Whitrow died after a long illness at Queen's Court Nursing Home, 32–4 Queens Road, Wimbledon, on 2 June 2000, survived by his wife. His ashes were scattered on Christ Church Meadow on 12 June.

FRANK A. J. L. JAMES

Sources F. A. J. L. James, 'Gerald James Whitrow', *Astronomy and Geophysics*, 42/2 (2001), 35–6 · *Daily Telegraph* (18 June 2000) · *The Times* (23 June 2000) · personal knowledge (2004) · private information (2004) [family] · b. cert. · m. cert. · d. cert.
Archives ICL, papers | Athenaeum, London · Bodl. Oxf., Milne papers · CAC Cam., Bondi papers · London School of Economics, Popper papers · RAS · Sci. Mus., British Society for the History of Science papers | FILM Open University archives | SOUND BBC talks archives
Likenesses photographs, priv. coll. · photographs, ICL
Wealth at death £210,000: probate, 16 Nov 2000, *CGPLA Eng. & Wales*

Whitrowe, Joan (*fl.* 1665–1697), religious writer, was the wife of Robert Whitrowe (*d.* in or before 1689) and the mother of **Susannah Whitrowe** (*c.*1662–1677) and Jason Whitrowe (*c.*1671–1677). Nothing is known about her parents, childhood, or education, though in a work of 1692 she cited Marcus Aurelius on the virtues of retirement, suggesting that she was then quite advanced in age as well as that she had a degree of familiarity with classical texts. She was called to prophesy in Bristol and London shortly before the plague arrived in London in 1665. She presented herself as a sign of repentance, by fasting, wearing sackcloth, and giving aid and counsel to plague victims. She was initially allied with the Quakers, but she later declared that she was not a member of any sect or 'gathered

people' (*Humble Address*, 1689, 13). Neither her name nor that of her daughter appears in a manuscript list of Quakers active in the period held by the Friends' Historical Library in London.

In the 1670s, Whitrowe and her family were living in Covent Garden, London, and it was there in 1677 that both Jason and Susannah died. Jason, aged about six and a half, had been a student at the Latin school and had announced shortly before his death that he would preach a sermon in a tavern against pride and drunkenness. However, it was the death of Susannah, aged about fifteen, that prompted Whitrowe to write what became her most widely read work, *The work of God in a dying maid, being a short account of the dealings of the Lord with one Susanna Whitrow* (1677). This biography detailed Susannah's utterances against corruption, her initial but mistaken aversion to the Quakers because they were generally socially despised and allowed women to preach, her praise of her mother's spiritual integrity, and her desire to be buried alongside Quakers rather than near a church. In particular, it provides eyewitness accounts of her final illness as she fought 'the tempter', with her mother and the prominent Quaker minister Rebecca Travers at her bedside; after four days of spiritual struggle, she began a period of ecstasy and continuous prayer in anticipation of her own death, which came several days later (Mack, 394). Her final words were 'I am ready, I am ready' (Mack, 395). *The Work of God* went through a number of not always wholly accurate editions through to the 1690s.

Whitrowe blamed her husband's evil life for the deaths of her children—she had, according to Susannah, repeatedly rebuked Robert for offences against God—but she interpreted their deaths as both an offering to God and a commission to forsake domestic life for that of a prophet. From 1682 she wore sackcloth until the death of Charles II. By 1689 she had become a widow, and in the 1690s she was living in Putney, Surrey. Between 1689 and 1697 she wrote a number of prophetic tracts addressed to King William as well as works directed to Queen Mary and to Christians in general. In these publications she recounted her visionary experiences, several of which described a heavenly woman travailing in childbirth, and the transformation of Whitrowe's body and spirit into a state of angelic perfection and mystical union with God. The tracts also contained warnings to king and people to repent in preparation for God's impending judgment. Whitrowe criticized the king's predilection for hunting at a time when the people, corrupted by covetousness, were wallowing in the sins of swearing, drunkenness, and idolatry. She also insisted that her readers repudiate their own personal ambitions and attainments, particularly their obsession with fashion, and renew their dedication to piety, humility, and obedience to God and king.

Whitrowe's writings—which she was adamant that she wrote herself and not with the help of 'some Man' as some had suggested (*Widow Whiterows Humble Thanksgiving*, 1694)—are of historical importance as striking examples of the mystical visionary literature that circulated in the period after the Restoration, and may be said to have culminated in the activities of the Philadelphians during the 1690s and the arrival of the French prophets who were active in London in the early eighteenth century. However, Whitrowe's prophetic writings were more politically assertive than those of other late seventeenth-century prophets, and in her criticism of social and economic injustice she resembles the early Quakers more than the mystical Philadelphians. Thus she criticized cultural and class hierarchies that oppressed the truly humble:

> the Superior by his Craft and Subtilty gets the Estate of the Inferior to himself, by his Oppression and Extortion, and so constraineth the poor silly Souls to labour hard, to maintain the Pride and Luxury of the Rich ... when, at the same time, the Rich Man's Dogs fares [sic] better than the Needy Soul, and all this must be counted Equal, Just, and Right. (Faithful Warnings, 1697, preface)

Whitrowe's works are also interesting as an example of a woman's perception of sacred literature and its relation to her own experience, both as a mother and as prophet 'giving birth' to divine messages: 'I cannot compare [giving myself up to God] with any thing in this World, but a Woman in the strongest Travail and greatest Pain, that ever was known, to bring forth a Child into the World' (Faithfull Warnings, 79).

Nothing is known about Whitrowe's later life and death.   PHYLLIS MACK

Sources J. Whitrowe, *The work of God in a dying maid* (1677) · P. Mack, *Visionary women: ecstatic prophecy in seventeenth-century England* (1992)
Archives RS Friends, Lond., testimony, MSS vol. S.462

Whitrowe, Susannah (*c.*1662–1677). *See under* Whitrowe, Joan (*fl.* 1665–1697).

Whitshed, Sir **James Hawkins**, **first baronet** (1762–1849), naval officer, was born in 1762, third son of James Hawkins (1713–1805), bishop of Raphoe, and his wife, Catherine, *née* Keene. The family fortune came from William *Whitshed. In 1773 he was entered on the books of the sloop *Ranger*, then on the Irish station, and was afterwards on the books of the *Kent*, guardship at Plymouth. He first went afloat in the *Aldborough*, serving on the Newfoundland and North American stations, until on 4 September 1778 he was promoted lieutenant. During 1779 he was in the *Amazon*, on the home station, and in December he joined the *Sandwich*, flagship of Sir George Brydges Rodney, with whom he was present in the action off Cape St Vincent on 16 January 1780. At Gibraltar he was made commander in the sloop *San Vincente*, and, going out to the West Indies with Rodney, was present in the action of 17 April 1780; the next day, 18 April, he was posted to the *Deal Castle*, which, in a hurricane the following October, was blown from her anchorage at St Lucia and wrecked on the coast of Puerto Rico. The crew escaped to the shore, and Hawkins, after recovering from a dangerous fever brought on by exposure, was honourably acquitted by a court martial, and was sent to England with dispatches. In July 1781 he was appointed to the frigate *Ceres*, in which,

the following spring, he took out Sir Guy Carleton to New York, and brought him back to England in December 1783. For the next three years Hawkins commanded the frigate *Rose* at Leith and on the east coast of Scotland. He then studied for three years at Oxford, attending lectures on astronomy, and travelled on the continent, mainly in Denmark and in Russia. In 1791 he assumed the name of Whitshed, that of his maternal grandmother, in accordance with a cousin's will.

Whitshed married, on 11 December 1791, Sophia Henrietta (*d.* 20 Jan 1852), daughter of Captain John Albert Bentinck RN (*d.* 1775), grandson of the first earl of Portland. They had two sons and four daughters. The eldest son was killed in 1813, when a midshipman of the *Berwick*. In 1793 Whitshed was appointed to the *Arrogant* (74 guns), one of the squadron under Rear-Admiral George Montagu in May and June 1794. In 1795 he was moved into the *Namur*, one of the ships which in January 1797 was detached from the Channel Fleet with Rear-Admiral William Parker (1743–1802) to reinforce Sir John Jervis at Lisbon, and to take part in the battle of Cape St Vincent, for which Whitshed, with the other captains engaged, received the gold medal and the thanks of both houses of parliament. He afterwards commanded successively the *Ajax* (74 guns), and the *Formidable* (98 guns), in the Channel Fleet, and on 14 February 1799 was promoted rear-admiral. In April, with his flag in the *Queen Charlotte* (100 guns), he commanded a squadron of four ships of the line which was sent as a reinforcement to the Mediterranean Fleet, on the news of the French fleet's having escaped from Brest. In the pursuit he returned off Brest with Lord Keith. He continued in the channel, with his flag in the *Téméraire* (98 guns), until 1801, and in 1803, on the renewal of the war, was appointed naval adviser to the lord lieutenant of Ireland, to superintend the arrangements for the defence of the Irish coast and to organize the sea fencibles. He became vice-admiral on 23 April 1804, and in the spring of 1807 was appointed commander-in-chief at Cork, where he remained for three years. On 31 July 1810 he was promoted admiral.

Whitshed was made a KCB on 2 January 1815, was commander-in-chief at Portsmouth from January 1821 to April 1824, was made a GCB on 17 November 1830, a baronet on 16 May 1834, baron of the kingdom of Hanover in 1843, and admiral of the fleet on 8 January 1844. He died at his house in Cavendish Square, London, on 28 October 1849. Whitshed's second son, St Vincent Keene (1801–1870), succeeded to the baronetcy; on the death of his only surviving son in 1871 the baronetcy became extinct. The third baronet's only child and heir was Elizabeth Alice Frances Hawkins Whitshed, who married Frederick Burnaby, and was later Mrs Aubrey Le Blond [see Le Blond, Elizabeth Alice Frances].

J. K. LAUGHTON, *rev.* ANDREW LAMBERT

Sources D. Syrett and R. L. DiNardo, *The commissioned sea officers of the Royal Navy, 1660–1815*, rev. edn, Occasional Publications of the Navy RS, 1 (1994) · *Letters of ... the earl of St Vincent, whilst the first lord of the admiralty, 1801–1804*, ed. D. B. Smith, 2 vols., Navy RS, 55, 61 (1922–7) · O'Byrne, *Naval biog. dict.* · *GM*, 2nd ser., 33 (1850), 85 ·

Dod's Peerage (1858) • J. Marshall, *Royal naval biography*, 1/1 (1823), 120–22 • Burke, *Peerage*
Archives NL Ire., letter-books, logbook, and papers • NMM, letter-book, corresp., and papers • Rice University, Houston, Texas, Woodson Research Center, sketchbook and minute book
Likenesses H. P. Bone, pencil drawing, 1799 (after J. Northcote), NPG • Worthington and Parker, line engraving, pubd 1803 (after *Commemoration of a naval victory, 14th February, 1797* by R. Smirke), BM, NPG • F. Cruikshank, portrait, NMM • portrait, repro. in *Naval Chronicle*, 22

Whitshed, William (1679–1727), judge and politician, was the eldest son of Thomas Whitshed MP (1645–1697) and his wife, Mary Quin. He probably never married since his property was inherited by the Hawkins family, who changed their name to Whitshed; Admiral Sir James Hawkins *Whitshed was perhaps the most prominent member of that family. He entered the Middle Temple on 16 June 1694. He was returned for co. Wicklow in the first parliament of Queen Anne. Like many politicians of this period he tried to have a bet both ways; he was considered a whig until October 1707 when he began to waver. However, he returned to the fold after 1709 and was appointed solicitor-general on 5 January 1710, during the whig administration of Lord Lieutenant Wharton, only to be dismissed the following year by the tory Lord Lieutenant Ormond. Whitshed was one of the leaders of the whig party in 1713 and was again returned for Wicklow at the general election of that year. He was a member of the 1713 Commons committee appointed to report on the 'misconduct' of Sir Constantine Phipps. The 1713 parliament was brief and was subsequently dissolved by the queen's death on 1 August 1714. Following the Hanoverian succession Whitshed was appointed, on 14 October 1714, lord chief justice of the king's bench. He was sworn of the privy council on 11 November 1714.

On 7 July 1719 Whitshed was one of those summoned by the lord lieutenant on the eve of parliament to consider how far the relief of dissenters should be pressed (the penal laws of Queen Anne's reign also affected dissenters). Whitshed and Jonathan Swift were enemies. Whitshed pronounced Swift's tract in favour of Irish manufactures a seditious publication but was himself the butt of Swift's cruel lampooning. Whitshed had gained the inheritance of an estate worth some £1000 from the Quin family of High Street, Dublin, by proving the illegitimacy of a son, James. Swift fastened on the 'chicanery' which the Whitsheds were reputed to have used in excluding James Quin from his inheritance to satirize their family motto:

> Libertas et Natale Solum:
> Fine words! I wonder where you stole 'em.
> (Woolley, 181, n. 52)

But perhaps the most interesting event of Whitshed's judicial career was that which occurred on 16 June 1721:

> During the trial [in the court of king's bench] a neighbouring chimney took fire, blew the smoke into the court and gave a panick to all the people who crowded to get out. Many were actually killed on the spot, and many desperately wounded. Among the first Mr John Ormsby, Member of Parliament and a wealthy man of above £1,800 p.a., was killed. Judge

Caulfield got half in and half out of a window, but could not pass through, lost his wig and at last was forced back. Lord Chief Justice Whitshed kept his place and temper till at last the truth was known. (BL, Add. MS 34778, fol. 51)

On 20 December 1726, following the resignation of Lord Chancellor Broderick and the appointment of Chief Justice Wyndham as his successor, Primate Boulter wrote to the duke of Newcastle:

> my Lord Chief Justice *Whitshed* has been with me, to desire that he may be recommended to succeed Lord Chief Justice *Wyndham* in the Common Pleas. He complains that he finds the business of his present station very fatiguing as he advances in life, and says the two stations are about the same value; but the Common Pleas is a place of less trouble: he represents that he has with great zeal and fidelity served his Majesty, and made himself many enemies by so doing, and would hope for this favour as a reward for his services. I must do him the justice to say, that he has certainly served his Majesty with great zeal and affection, and has drawn upon himself the anger of the Jacobites by so doing, and the malice of other discontented persons here, by discountenancing seditious writings in the affair of the halfpence: and if we may have another person of worth from *England* to succeed him, I think he may deserve the favour he desires. (*Boulter Letters*, 1.89–90)

Whitshed had supported the government over Wood's halfpence and had generally behaved in a quiet and loyal fashion; he was duly appointed lord chief justice of the common pleas on 10 February 1727. He died six months later, on 19 August 1727, at Mary Street, Dublin, and was buried in St Michael's Church, Dublin.

E. M. JOHNSTON-LIIK

Sources E. M. Johnston-Liik, *History of the Irish parliament, 1692–1800*, 6 vols. (2002) • *Boulter letters*, 2 vols. (1769–70), 1.89–90 • J. T. Gilbert, *History of the city of Dublin*, 3 vols. (1861), 1.212, 220–22 • J. L. J. Hughes, ed., *Patentee officers in Ireland, 1173–1826, including high sheriffs, 1661–1684 and 1761–1816*, IMC (1960) • *Index to privy counsellors, 1711–1910 (and partially from 1660)* [n.d.] • E. Keane, P. Beryl Phair, and T. U. Sadleir, eds., *King's Inns admission papers, 1607–1867*, IMC (1982) • F. E. Ball, *The judges in Ireland, 1221–1921*, 2 vols. (1926) • H. A. C. Sturgess, ed., *Register of admissions to the Honourable Society of the Middle Temple, from the fifteenth century to the year 1944*, 1 (1949), 234 • *Dublin Gazette* (26 Feb 1715) • *Whalley's Newsletter* (16 July 1715) • *Whalley's Newsletter* (1 March 1720) • *Whalley's Newsletter* (7 July 1722) • *Pue's Occurrences* (18 Feb 1718) • *Pue's Occurrences* (5 July 1718) • *Harding's Dublin Impartial Newsletter* (11 July 1719) • *Harding's Dublin Impartial Newsletter* (20 Feb 1722) • *Harding's Weekly Impartial Newsletter* (9 July 1723) • *Dublin Intelligencer* (19 Feb 1724) • *Dublin Intelligencer* (27 June 1724) • *Dublin Intelligencer* (19 Feb 1726) • *Dublin Intelligencer* (9 July 1726) • *Dublin Intelligencer* (4 July 1727) • *Dublin Weekly Journal* (26 June 1725) • J. Woolley, ed., *Jonathan Swift and Thomas Sheridan: 'The Intelligencer'* (1992) • BL, Add. MS 34778, fol. 51
Archives BL, Add. MS 34778, fol. 51 • PRO NIre., Blenheim MSS, T.3411 • PRO NIre., Burke, extract pedigrees, T.559, vol. 19, p. 249 • PRO NIre., Castle Ward MSS, D.2092/1/7/11 • PRO NIre., transcripts of state papers relating to Ireland, T.519, p. 165 • TCD, corresp. with William King
Wealth at death Mary Street, Dublin; Killencarrig, co. Wicklow; Stormanstown, co. Dublin; income est. at £1500 in 1713

Whitson, John (1553×5?–1629), merchant, was born at Clearwell in the parish of Newland, Gloucestershire. Described by his godson John Aubrey as 'a handsome young fellow' and an early riser who transacted all business before noon, he was a keen falconer (*Brief Lives*, 317). In 1570 he was apprenticed to the wealthy Bristol vintner Nicholas Cutt, whose young widow, Bridget, he later allegedly seduced in a wine cellar; he married her on 12 April 1585. Admitted a freeman of Bristol in that same year, Whitson soon became an important merchant, trading mainly to France, Spain, and the Mediterranean, principally in lead, cloth, and leather in return for wine, currants, and alum. During the 1590s he was a member of a syndicate which fitted out two privateers, apparently donating the proceeds from his share of two enemy prizes to various Bristol almshouses. He was accused of customs fraud in 1600, and in 1623 was found guilty by the exchequer of failing to pay prisage on wine. In 1603 he provided much of the financial backing for Martin Pring's voyage to North America. Along with other Bristol merchants he seceded from the newly revived Spanish Company in December 1605 in order to resuscitate the town's Society of Merchant Venturers, which he served as warden in 1605–6 and master in 1606–7 and 1611–12. Between 1611 and 1622 he also acted as a deputy's deputy in the farm of the wine customs, but confusion over the payment of his annual rent of £1400 led to a lengthy exchequer suit.

According to Aubrey, Whitson 'lived nobly; kept a plentiful table; and was the most popular magistrate' in Bristol (*Brief Lives*, 317); his house in St Nicholas Street allegedly boasted 'the stateliest dining room in the city'. Sheriff of Bristol in 1589–90, he was elected alderman of All Saints' ward in 1600, and served as mayor in 1603–4 and 1615–16, an auditor in 1628, constable of the staple on six occasions, and colonel of the local militia. During his first term as mayor, he was prosecuted by the collector of sums paid to compound for purveyance in Bristol, but escaped punishment by the board of greencloth because his presence in Bristol during time of plague could not be spared. In November 1605 he was returned to parliament for Bristol at a by-election, subsequently representing the town in the assemblies of 1614, 1621, 1625, and 1626, but playing a minor role in proceedings.

Following the death of his first wife, Bridget, in 1608, Whitson married on 21 April 1609 Magdalen Hynde, the beautiful but near penniless widow of a London salter, William Hynde; she died in 1615. He married his third wife, Rachel Aubrey (*d.* 1654), on 18 May 1617. The widow of a Herefordshire gentleman, John Aubrey, her dowry is said to have amounted to £2000. In November 1626 Whitson was stabbed by a litigant while dispensing justice in Bristol, leaving a scar on his cheek. He subsequently wrote *The Aged Christian's Final Farewell to the World*, first published in 1829, in which he condemned the amassing of wealth as 'the idols of earthly minds'. He died in Bristol on 27 February 1629, after falling from his horse, 'his head pitching on a nail that stood on its head by a smith's shop', and was buried with full military honours at a cost of £377 on 9 March in St Nicholas's, Bristol. He left no direct heirs; his three daughters from his first marriage had all predeceased him, and his second and third marriages had proved childless. He therefore left a considerable part of his estate for charitable purposes, which included the foundation of the Red Maids' School in Bristol. After discounting debts amounting to £3000, an inventory made on 1 June 1629 valued his estate at more than £5400, though subsequent litigation demonstrated that a number of properties had not been included in this valuation.

ANDREW THRUSH

Sources 'Whitstone, John', HoP, *Commons* · P. McGrath, *John Whitson and the merchant community of Bristol* (1970) · P. McGrath, ed., *Merchants and merchandise in seventeenth-century Bristol*, Bristol RS, 19 (1955) · P. McGrath, ed., *Records relating to the Society of Merchant Venturers of the city of Bristol in the seventeenth century*, Bristol RS, 17 (1951) · J. Latimer, *History of the Society of Merchant Venturers of Bristol* (1903) · A. B. Beaven, ed., *Bristol lists: municipal and miscellaneous* (1899) · *Aubrey's Brief lives*, ed. O. L. Dick (1949); pbk edn (1992) · P. Croft, *The Spanish Company*, 9 (London Record Society, 1973) · D. M. Livock, ed., *City chamberlain accounts*, 24 (Bristol Record Society, 1966) · W. Leighton, 'The manor and parish of Burnett, Somerset', *Transactions of the Bristol and Gloucestershire Archaeological Society*, 59 (1937), 243–85 · D. B. Quinn and A. M. Quinn, *The English New England voyages, 1602–1608*, Hakluyt Society, 2nd ser., 161 (1983) · *JHC*, 1 (1547–1628), 185b · J. Vanes, ed., *Documents illustrating the overseas trade of Bristol in the sixteenth century*, Bristol RS, 31 (1979) · PRO, STAC 8/292/10, C 142/537/68, C 21/B17/2, C 2/Jas.I/W30/21, C 2/Chas.I/M32/24, C 2/Chas.I/S52/49, C 2/Chas.I/S108/32, E 133/135/14, E 126/2, fol. 288, E 126/3, fols. 41v–43v, E 190/1131/12, E 190/1132/8, E 112/119/416, E 112/119/420, E 112/119/423, PROB 11/156, sig. 71, sentence, PROB 11/156, sig. 107, SP 46/22, fols. 135–137v
Likenesses E. McInnes, mezzotint, NPG · oils, trustees of the Bristol Municipal Charities · tomb effigy, St Nicholas's Church, Bristol
Wealth at death over £5400: McGrath, ed. *Merchants and merchandise*; will, PRO, PROB 11/156, sig. 107

Whittaker, Sir Edmund Taylor (1873–1956), mathematician and astronomer, was born at 7 Virginia Street, Southport, on 24 October 1873, the only son of John Whittaker, gentleman, and his wife, Selina Septima, daughter of Edmund Taylor, who practised as a physician at Middleton, near Manchester. Whittaker was taught by his mother up to the age of eleven, when he entered Manchester grammar school on the classical side, but on promotion to the upper school he gladly escaped to specialize in mathematics. In 1892 a scholarship took him to Trinity College, Cambridge, where in 1895 he was bracketed second wrangler; he obtained a first class in part two of the tripos, and the Tyson medal, was elected a fellow of Trinity (1896), and was awarded the first Smith's prize (1897). In 1901 he married Mary Ferguson McNaghten, daughter of the Revd Thomas Boyd, of Cambridge, Scottish secretary of the Religious Tract Society; and granddaughter of Sir Thomas Jamieson Boyd. They had three sons and two daughters. Their second son, John McNaghten Whittaker (Jack), was professor of pure mathematics at Liverpool (1933–52) and vice-chancellor of the University of Sheffield (1952–65).

Astronomy professorships In 1906 Whittaker was appointed professor of astronomy in the University of Dublin, with the title of royal astronomer of Ireland. The observatory at Dunsink was poorly equipped, and it was tacitly understood that the chief function of the professor was to

Sir Edmund Taylor Whittaker (1873–1956), by Trevor Haddon, 1933

strengthen the school of mathematical physics in the university, where Whittaker gave courses of advanced lectures. Some of his pupils were members of other academic foundations, among them Éamon de Valera, later prime minister and president of Ireland.

In 1912 Whittaker was elected to the professorship of mathematics at Edinburgh where he taught until his retirement in 1946. His personal achievements included the institution in 1914 of what was probably the first university mathematical laboratory in Britain, the establishment of a flourishing research school, and the development of the Edinburgh Mathematical Society.

Whittaker made numerous and important contributions to mathematics and theoretical physics which had a profound effect by reason of their great range, depth, and fertility; but these were rivalled, if not surpassed, in interest, importance, and influence by his scientific books and monographs. In addition he wrote numerous philosophical and historical papers and books, which all bear the marks of his learning, literary powers, and critical judgement.

Whittaker's contributions to pure mathematics were mainly to the theories of interpolation, of automorphic functions, of potential theory, and of special functions. His interest in the theory of interpolation arose from his association with the actuaries engaged in life assurance in Edinburgh, especially G. J. Lidstone. He succeeded in solving two fundamental questions and thus provided a

logical basis for the Newton–Gauss formula and for the method of the graduation or adjustment of observations. In the theory of automorphic functions he solved the problem of the uniformization of algebraic functions of any genus by considering a special discontinuous subgroup of elliptic transformations each of period 2.

Contributions to mathematical physics The most significant section of Whittaker's researches, however, relates to the special functions of mathematical physics regarded as constituents of potential functions. He obtained a general solution of Laplace's equation which brought a new unity into potential theory by exhibiting all the usual special functions in the form of a 'Whittaker' integral, and he also introduced the important confluent hypergeometric functions. In theoretical physics he made substantial contributions to dynamics, to relativity and electromagnetic theory, and to quantum theory. In dynamics his discovery of the 'adelphic' integral provided the solution of the difficulties indicated by Poincaré's celebrated theorem relative to the convergence of the series solutions of celestial mechanics. In electromagnetic theory he gave a general solution of Maxwell's equations in terms of two real scalar wave functions, and gave a relativistic generalization of Faraday's theory of tubes of force. In general relativity he investigated the problem of giving an invariant definition of distance which should correspond to the actual procedure adopted by astronomers, and he obtained a generalization of Gauss's theorem on the Newtonian potential. In his researches on quantum theory he generalized Hamilton's 'principal functions', expressing them in terms of non-commuting variables, and thus obtained a new foundation for Schrödinger's wave equation.

In 1905 Whittaker co-founded the series of Cambridge Tracts in Mathematics and Mathematical Physics, an influential series of short volumes designed to introduce the principal elements of specific modern developments. His own contribution was *The Theory of Optical Instruments* (1907), which was later translated into German. Three of Whittaker's scientific books have had a great influence. *A Course of Modern Analysis*, published in 1902, and in many subsequent editions with the collaboration of G. N. Watson, remained in print throughout the century. It was the first, and for many years almost the only, book in English to provide students with an account of methods in mathematical analysis and mathematical physics. The *Treatise on the Analytical Dynamics of Particles and Rigid Bodies* (1904) remains the standard work on this subject. *The Calculus of Observations* (1924, with G. Robinson; 4th edn, 1944) brought together many techniques in numerical analytical analysis, together with the practical work effected in his laboratory.

Whittaker's monumental *History of the Theories of Aether and Electricity* was first published in one volume in 1910 and subsequently in a greatly enlarged edition of which Whittaker lived to complete only two volumes (1951–3). The *History* provides a systematic and critical account of the development of the physical theories of electromagnetism, atomic structure, and of the quantum theory from the seventeenth century to 1926. It will remain an outstanding achievement by reason of its clarity, comprehensiveness, and penetration, which give it the force and authority of an original investigation, although Whittaker was criticized for attributing special relativity theory to Henri Poincaré and Hendrik Lorentz rather than to Albert Einstein.

Whittaker also wrote historical articles of various kinds—for example, several fine obituaries for the Royal Society, and uncommonly good centenary articles on the appropriate occasion for major figures of the past such as W. R. Hamilton and Laplace. In 1899 he brought the British Association for the Advancement of Science nicely up to date on the three-body problem in celestial mechanics, and in 1912 he wrote the article on the theory of planetary perturbations for the great German *Enzyklopädie der mathematischen Wissenschaften*.

Scientific honours Whittaker, who was knighted in 1945, was elected FRS in 1905, served on the council in 1911–12 and 1933–5 (vice-president 1934–5), and was awarded the Sylvester medal in 1931 and the Copley medal in 1954. With the Royal Society of Edinburgh he had continuous contact, being Gunning prizeman in 1929 and president in 1939–44. He was president of the Mathematical Association (1920–21), of the mathematical and physical section of the British Association (1927), and of the London Mathematical Society (1928–9), being awarded its De Morgan medal in 1935. An honorary member of a number of foreign learned societies, he received honorary degrees from several universities, and was an honorary fellow of Trinity College, Cambridge (1949).

At Cambridge in his Tarner lectures (1947) Whittaker lucidly traced the development of natural philosophy from Euclid to Eddington, and in 1951 he gave the Eddington memorial lecture, 'Eddington's principle in the philosophy of science'. At Oxford he gave the Herbert Spencer lecture (1948), 'The modern approach to Descartes's problem'. He figured as a natural theologian in his Riddell memorial lectures (Durham, 1942) on 'The beginning and end of the world' and in the Donnellan lectures (Dublin, 1946) on 'Space and spirit' in which he restated the classical scholastic arguments for the existence of God in the light of current theories of scientific cosmogony.

Whittaker was received into the Roman Catholic church in 1930. He served as honorary president of the Newman Association (1943–5), was awarded the cross Pro Ecclesia et Pontifice in 1935, and was appointed a member of the Pontifical Academy of Sciences in 1936. He died at his home, 48 George Square, Edinburgh, on 24 March 1956.

Whittaker's death marked the end of an epoch, for he was conversant with a range of mathematics which no other Briton has encompassed. His pervasive influence in mathematics is seen in his peculiar facility for coining names for analytical concepts and entities, many of which have obtained a wide currency in the language of mathematics. That influence was mainly the effect of his amazing intellectual powers but it was reinforced by his never-

failing kindness to his students, the hospitality offered in his Edinburgh home, his slightly mischievous humour, and the devotion and support of his wife.

G. TEMPLE, *rev.* I. GRATTAN-GUINNESS

Sources G. Temple, *Memoirs FRS*, 2 (1956), 299–325 · W. H. McCrea, *Journal of the London Mathematical Society*, 32 (1957), 234–56 · 'Memorial issue', *Proceedings of the Edinburgh Mathematical Society*, 11 (1958–9), 1–70 · *The Times* (26 March 1956), 14c · *Biographical register of old Mancunians* (1965), 80 · b. cert. · *CGPLA Eng. & Wales* (1956) · personal knowledge (1971) · private information (1971)
Archives RS, corresp. and papers | ICL, corresp. with Herbert Dingle · L. Cong., corresp. with O. Veblen · NRA, priv. coll., corresp. with J. M. Whittaker · Nuffield Oxf., corresp. with Viscount Cherwell · RAS, letters to Royal Astronomical Society
Likenesses T. Haddon, oils, 1933, NPG [*see illus.*] · W. Stoneman, photograph, 1933, NPG · B. Schotz, bronze head, *c.*1944, Royal Society of Edinburgh · photograph, repro. in *The Times*
Wealth at death £20,023 6s. 11d.: probate, 2 July 1956, *CGPLA Eng. & Wales*

Whittaker, George Byrom (1793–1847), publisher and bookseller, was born on 6 February 1793 at New Alresford, Hampshire, the eldest of five children of George Whittaker (1761–1833), Church of England clergyman and headmaster, and his wife, Sarah, *née* Budd (1769/70–1827). Whittaker's father was well remunerated from 1795 as headmaster of Southampton grammar school, and he was the author of several popular educational works, amassing sufficient wealth to advance several thousand pounds to his son. In 1807 Whittaker was apprenticed to Charles Law, a long-established and prosperous wholesale bookseller and publisher of 13 Ave Maria Lane, London, and on obtaining his freedom in 1814 he acquired the business, trading under the name Law and Whittaker until 1818. The concern was greatly enlarged under Whittaker's vigorous management, and he became one of the three leading wholesalers serving the country trade. Within a decade he had also expanded the publishing side of the business to such an extent that Thomas Frognall Dibdin bracketed it together with Longman & Co. as one of 'the two greatest Publishers in England' (Dibdin, xii), an accolade supported by evidence that Whittaker was second only to Longmans in the numbers of new titles listed in the *English Catalogue of Books* for this period.

Part of the reason for this success was capital investment, and in 1826 it was estimated that Whittaker possessed copyrights which had originally cost him £160,000, and which were still worth at least £63,000. Much of the capital came from his brother, William Budd Whittaker, who was a partner in the firm from 1818 to 1824, but other members of the family also invested heavily in the business, and in 1826 their total holding was valued at £53,534. In addition, Whittaker had a reputation as a kindly and approachable man, who established relationships of considerable trust with his authors, and it is also evident that he made some inspired business decisions. About 1821, for instance, he acquired for a price estimated to be in excess of £30,000 the copyrights of the hapless William Pinnock's sixty-four educational catechisms, which continued to sell in extraordinary numbers throughout

Whittaker's lifetime, the more so since many were carefully and extensively edited by his own, often celebrated, authors. He also possessed a third share (estimated to be worth £5600) in the copyrights of another failed publisher and educational author, Sir Richard Phillips. These purchases indicate Whittaker's particular strength in educational publishing, a speciality inherited from Law; in addition to elementary and school books (including some of his father's), he published numerous works intended for university students. These were generally published in partnership with the university booksellers, especially J. and J. J. Deighton in Cambridge, and included both mathematical and classical works. However, Whittaker's publishing business was general in nature, and included numerous literary works. One of his earliest literary discoveries was Mary Russell Mitford, whose immensely successful first novel, *Our Village*, he began to publish in 1824.

Whittaker's commercial standing was such that he was elected sheriff of London and Middlesex on 24 June 1823, when only thirty years old. His personal wealth was considerable, and he reportedly possessed seven hunters. However, in the autumn of 1825 he was defrauded by an American-born writer, William Grenville Graham, who had forged bills in Whittaker's name. When the forgery was discovered, Whittaker's bankers demanded a list of his acceptances, and discovered that he had ventured an extensive and unsuccessful speculation in hops. Although the business was still fundamentally sound, the state of financial panic then prevailing resulted in his being denied the usual amount of discount, and as a result he had to stop payment. His debts and liabilities were estimated at over £270,000, but the creditors agreed to leave the management of Whittaker's affairs in the hands of trustees (Self & Co.), in preference to a commission of bankruptcy. Whittaker continued to trade, with financial assistance from the printer Richard Gilbert, who had married his sister Anne in 1823, and was even able to persist with the publication of his splendid edition of Georges Cuvier's *Animal Kingdom* (16 vols., 1827–35), for which the translation and the engraving of the plates alone cost £7000. The trustees administered his affairs well, soon restoring him to his old position in the trade, and at the end of 1828 he was released by his creditors, although they had not received the full debt.

Whittaker was allowed to purchase the remainder of his copyrights, and resumed business in partnership with David Gale Arnot (until 1835) and Joseph Skipper Treacher (until 1838), soon also being joined by William Cumber Hood. The new firm flourished, and in 1830 supplanted Simpkin and Marshall as Robert Cadell's London partner in the publication of the collected edition of Sir Walter Scott's Waverley novels (48 vols., 1829–33). It also continued to attract new literary authors, among them Frances Trollope, whose *Domestic Manners of the Americans* (2 vols., 1832) passed through four editions in a year. The later years of Whittaker's life were reportedly not characterized by the activity of his youth, but he did continue to cultivate some larger projects, including John Payne Collier's new edition of Shakespeare's works (9 vols., 1844).

He died of cholera on 13 December 1847 at his home, 20 Upper Phillimore Place, Kensington, London, and was interred in the catacombs at Kensal Green cemetery. Whittaker never married, and most of his property passed at his death to Anne and Richard Gilbert, the business being continued by his nephew Robert Gilbert, in partnership with William Cumber Hood.

JONATHAN R. TOPHAM

Sources GM, 2nd ser., 29 (1848), 95–6 · *The Times* (3 Feb 1826) · *The Times* (20 Nov 1828) · C. F. Russell, *A history of King Edward VI School, Southampton* (privately printed, Cambridge, 1940) · will of George Whittaker, PRO, PROB 11/1840 · C. Knight, *Passages of a working life during half a century*, 3 vols. (1864–5) · *LondG* (28 July 1818) · *LondG* (26 March 1825) · *LondG* (1 Jan 1836) · *LondG* (6 March 1838) · T. F. Dibdin, *The library companion*, 2nd edn (1825) · Nichols, *Illustrations* · T. Rees, *Reminiscences of literary London from 1779 to 1853* (1896) · E. Bell, *George Bell, publisher: a brief memoir* (1924) · *The life of Mary Russell Mitford, related in a selection from her letters to her friends*, ed. A. G. K. L'Estrange, [2nd edn], 3 vols. (1870) · apprentice memorandum books, Stationers' Company, London · parish register (baptism), New Alresford, Hampshire
Archives BL, Houlston MSS
Wealth at death £60,000: PRO, death duty registers, IR 26

Whittaker, James William (1828–1876), watercolour painter, was born in Manchester on 24 August 1828, one of the two sons of John (sometimes referred to as James) Whittaker, a warehouseman. As a young man he was apprenticed as an engraver to Joseph Heyes, a calico printer in Manchester; this work led him to etching and subsequently to watercolour painting. Sarah, Heyes's daughter, became his wife. By 1858 he had sufficient money to enable him to move to Wales to work full-time as an artist: for £10 a year he rented Frith Cottage on the road between Betws-y-coed and Llanrwst, Denbighshire, from where he drew pictures of Welsh scenery. Initially he sold his pictures to a Manchester dealer for a price between merely £2 and £4, but a meeting in Wales with the artist Francis William Topham encouraged him to stand for election to the Society of Painters in Water Colours. He was elected to the Old Watercolour Society as an associate in 1862 and a full member two years later.

Although he is recorded as having exhibited both continental landscapes and Northumberland coastal scenes, Whittaker is best-known for his meticulous and atmospheric evocations of Welsh scenery, such as *Mountain Scene in North Wales, with Stream and Cattle* and *Road between Capel Curig and Llyn Ogwen* (both Victoria and Albert Museum, London). In all, 177 of his drawings were exhibited by the Old Watercolour Society at its gallery in Pall Mall, London, and another 14 sketches in its winter exhibition of 1876–7, after his death. He was able to command good prices for his work, the highest recorded being £262 10s. for *Flood on the River Conway* at the show of 1864. He also exhibited three pictures at the Royal Academy. His usual signature was J. W. Whittaker.

Photographs of Whittaker portray him as a tall, rather heavily built man with a round face and full beard, evidently well-dressed and prosperous. Success had enabled him to rebuild his cottage as a substantial house which he called Frith Castle, but towards the end of his life he was drinking heavily and the quality of his work deteriorated. He died on 6 September 1876 after falling into the River Llugwy, above Betws-y-coed. His body was washed downstream where he was found drowned with, according to the coroner's inquest, a couple of empty spirit bottles on his person. His wife had predeceased him and he left four children. The agent to the surrounding Voelas estate commented, 'there is not much of any value as he has sold everything he could convert into money' (Lord, 76–7).

SIMON FENWICK

Sources J. L. Roget, *A history of the 'Old Water-Colour' Society*, 2 vols. (1891) • P. Lord, *Clarence Whaite and the Welsh art world: the Betws-y-Coed artists' colony, 1844–1914* (1998) • Bankside Gallery, London, RWS MSS • *DNB* • *The Telegraph* (11 Sept 1876) • S. Fenwick and G. Smith, eds., *The business of watercolour: a guide to the archives of the Royal Watercolour Society* (1997) • Bénézit, *Dict.*
Archives Bankside Gallery, London, Royal Watercolour Society MSS
Likenesses J. Lancaster, photograph, *c.*1863, Bankside Gallery, London • J. Watkins, photograph, *c.*1870, Bankside Gallery, London
Wealth at death under £300: administration, 21 Sept 1876, *CGPLA Eng. & Wales*

Whittaker, John William (*c.*1790–1854), Church of England clergyman, the son of William Whittaker, gentleman, of Bradford, Yorkshire, and his wife, Sarah Buck, was born at Manchester and educated at Bradford grammar school and St John's College, Cambridge, where he was admitted a pensioner on 31 March 1810. He was thirteenth wrangler and graduated BA in 1814, when he took up a Beresford fellowship at his college. He proceeded MA in 1817, BD in 1824, and DD in 1830.

Whittaker published on the Hebrew scriptures in 1819 (with a supplement in 1820) a work which gained him some prominence, and the admiration of Charles Manners-Sutton, archbishop of Canterbury, whose examining chaplain he became. In 1819 he failed to be appointed to the chair of Arabic in Cambridge, and in February 1822 the archbishop presented him to the important vicarage of Blackburn, Lancashire. He was nominated honorary canon of Manchester in 1852. During his time in Blackburn the parish church was rebuilt and twelve new churches in various parts of the old parish were erected.

Whittaker published *Justification by Faith* (1825), *The Catholic Church* (1836), a reply to Nicholas Wiseman (2 vols., 1836–7), and various other works, including a sermon to the Chartists preached in Blackburn in 1839. His learning was wide, and he kept up to the end his reading in philology and geology, and in astronomy, an interest which led him to assist in the formation of the Royal Astronomical Society. One of his unfulfilled projects was a work on the nebular hypothesis and geological time.

On 20 June 1825 Whittaker married Mary Haughton (*d.* 1871), eldest daughter of Sir William Feilden, baronet (1769?–1859), and his wife, Mary Haughton, *née* Jackson; they had nine surviving children. Whittaker died at Blackburn vicarage on 23 August 1854.

C. W. SUTTON, *rev.* H. C. G. MATTHEW

Sources Venn, *Alum. Cant.* • *GM*, 2nd ser., 42 (1854), 3996 • *Monthly Notices of the Royal Astronomical Society*, 15 (1854–5), 119–20 • Burke, *Peerage* • W. H. Burnett, *Blackburn parish church: an historical sketch* (1906), 73
Archives Blackburn Central Library, corresp. • Derbys. RO, family corresp. • Man. CL, Manchester Archives and Local Studies, family letters • St John Cam., papers | Trinity Cam., letters to William Whewell
Likenesses portrait, repro. in Burnett, *Blackburn parish church*, 72

Whittaker, Thomas (1813–1899), temperance reformer, was born on 22 August 1813 near Grindleton, Yorkshire, one of nine children of a tenant farmer. He spent his early years at Clitheroe, where the hell-fire preaching at the Wesleyan chapel made a vivid impression on his imagination, and at the age of six he was sent to work in a local cotton factory. A few years later the family moved to Blackburn and then to Preston, where Whittaker received a little formal education at a night school run by Joseph Livesey (1794–1884), a founder of the teetotal movement. When he was fourteen a drinking incident spoiled Whittaker's prospects in Preston, precipitating a move to Bolton and then to Glossop. At Glossop, aged nineteen, he married, and soon after established his own home.

A few years later, in 1835, Whittaker was involved in a drunken brawl, and he returned to Blackburn, unemployed and temporarily unemployable on account of a shoulder injury. The death of his first child at this point triggered an emotional crisis which formed the background to his signing a pledge of total abstinence at a teetotal meeting the same year. He subsequently renewed his religious commitment, undertook a programme of self-education, and became involved with neighbourhood temperance work. He was invited by Livesey to become a full-time temperance missionary, and, during 1835–6, itinerated throughout Lancashire, Westmorland, Cumberland, Northumberland, and Durham as an agent of the British Association for the Promotion of Temperance. At Holme in Cumberland he acquired what was to become his trademark: a rattle which he used to attract attention when making announcements of teetotal meetings.

In 1837 Whittaker visited London, where, following addresses at Kennington and at Exeter Hall on 20 and 21 May, he was engaged as an agent by the New British and Foreign Society for the Suppression of Intemperance (a London-based national organization which changed its name the following year to the New British and Foreign Temperance Society), a post he held until 1849. During this period he promoted the cause of total abstinence in the capital, the eastern counties, and the west of England. In London Whittaker became a member of the Spitalfields chapel of the Revd Robert Aitkin, the maverick Anglican millenarian preacher who was associated with Methodism in the 1830s. There he met Louisa (1810–1875), the daughter of James Palmer, a coachman, whom he married on 6 August 1838 (his first wife had died in 1837).

In 1849 Whittaker and his wife moved to Scarborough, where he became involved in local politics and journalism. He was often on the Liberal Party's platform, but he failed to gain election to the town council until 1867. He was defeated in the 1873 election, but at a by-election in 1876 he regained a seat which he held until his retirement in November 1884. He was mayor of Scarborough during 1880–81, and was made a JP while in office. His connection with the press began with the establishment of *The Express* in 1865, and in 1868 he founded *The Watchman*. In 1877 he acquired an interest in the *Scarborough Mercury*, to which he contributed comments on local affairs for many years.

Whittaker remained committed to the cause of temperance. He was present at the inaugural meeting of the prohibitionist United Kingdom Alliance in 1853, and he attended all its annual meetings except in 1875, when he visited the United States. In the 1880s, the age of 'gospel temperance', Whittaker was concerned to refute charges that the pioneers of teetotalism had been irreligious.

Louisa Whittaker died on 9 January 1875, having borne six children, three of whom died in infancy. Whittaker remarried in 1880; this marriage produced three children. His third wife died in 1898, and Whittaker himself died at his home, at 1 Belgrave Terrace, Scarborough, on 20 November 1899, following a bout of bronchitis. A funeral service held on 23 November at Westborough Wesleyan church was attended by representatives of temperance organizations from all over the country. Whittaker was buried in Scarborough cemetery.

Whittaker published two autobiographical works, *Life's Battles in Temperance Armour* (1884) and *Brighter England and the Way to it* (1891), the title of which was a word play on William Booth's *In Darkest England* (1890). His life has been characterized by Brian Harrison as epitomizing the temperance movement's 'resolute encouragement of working-class self-respect and self-realization' (Harrison, 27). Whittaker was markedly influenced by Benjamin Franklin's autobiography and George Combe's *Constitution of Man* (1828). He placed great emphasis on the laws of nature, which he believed governed both the physical and the moral aspects of life. He was a very popular orator, and his broad dialect and successful blend of wit and common sense appealed especially to working-class audiences.

MARK CLEMENT

Sources T. Whittaker, *Life's battles in temperance armour* (1884) · *Scarborough Mercury* (24 Nov 1899) · B. Harrison, *Drink and the Victorians: the temperance question in England, 1815–1872*, 2nd edn (1994) · T. Whittaker, *Brighter England and the way to it* (1891) · P. T. Winskill, *The temperance movement and its workers*, 4 vols. (1891–2) · m. cert. [Louisa Palmer]
Likenesses photograph, repro. in Whittaker, *Life's battles*
Wealth at death £11,632 6s. 4d.: probate, 22 Dec 1899, CGPLA Eng. & Wales

Whittaker, William Gillies (1876–1944), composer and university professor, was born on 23 July 1876 in Newcastle upon Tyne, the only son of John Whittaker, a railway clerk for the North Eastern Railway Company, and his wife, Mary Jane Gillies (c.1854–1932), daughter of a Hexham tobacconist. He was educated initially at Rutherford grammar school and won an exhibition scholarship in 1892 to read science at Armstrong College in Newcastle, but abandoned these studies in 1894 without completing the degree in order to pursue a career as a professional musician.

Whittaker was a tall man of over 6 feet 4 inches with ginger hair and a moustache; he became a vegetarian and abstainer from alcohol after 1900. He taught music privately in Newcastle and played the organ in Presbyterian churches. He spent the years about the turn of the century gathering professional qualifications, including the University of Durham BMus in 1901 and FRCO diploma in 1902. He conducted various choral and orchestral societies within the college and in the region at large while studying music history in more depth, concentrating particularly on J. S. Bach.

As a composer Whittaker won a Carnegie award in 1921 for his first mature composition, *Among the Northumbrian Hills* (1918), and another in 1924 for an orchestral piece, *A Lyke Wake Dirge* (1921). He wrote settings for solo voices and for choirs of poems by John Masefield, Walter de la Mare, and P. B. Shelley as well as many settings of the Northumbrian poet W. W. Gibson. Most of his compositions after 1930, when he moved to Glasgow, were never published, including some fine chamber music such as the sonata for violin and piano in G minor and the wind quintet. He composed a handful of orchestral pieces and anthems as well as hundreds of arrangements of Northumbrian folksongs. His original compositions and many of his arrangements anticipated the musical languages of composers like Frank Bridge and Benjamin Britten and, to an extent, Michael Tippett: their unusual admixtures of frequently opposing musical styles were woven into an idiom more subtle than the reception of Whittaker's works would suggest.

Whittaker founded the Newcastle upon Tyne Bach Choir in 1915. He set new standards for his performances, being the first Bach conductor in Britain to give consideration to performance with period instruments. The St John passion, St Matthew passion, and B minor mass were performed regularly in the north-east, and a policy of performing the music of new British composers was also adopted, leading to early performances of works including Gustav Holst's *Cloud Messenger* and Ralph Vaughan Williams's G minor mass. A three-day Bach festival in London in 1922 was critically acclaimed, and in 1924 Whittaker's choir gave the first modern performance of the 'great' service by William Byrd. The choir also travelled to the International Society for Contemporary Music festival in Frankfurt am Main in 1927. Whittaker and his choir were the only British participants in the festival and established Whittaker's reputation on a European level.

Having turned down the chair of music at Cornell University in 1929, Whittaker was appointed the first Gardiner professor of music at the University of Glasgow and the first principal of the Scottish National Academy of Music in January 1930. He raised the standing of music within the university to that of a full degree subject. He also published editions of sonatas by William Young and an arrangement of Henry Purcell's *Chacony* in G minor. Whittaker produced a number of highly regarded journal articles, but his academic efforts are best exemplified in

The Cantatas of J. S. Bach: Sacred and Secular, published by Oxford University Press in 1959. His standing as a Bach scholar was confirmed by the reissuing of this book in paperback in 1979, which showed it to be still a significant piece of Bach scholarship more than half a century after its completion.

Whittaker was made an officier d'académie by the French government in 1919 and was awarded the Durham DMus without examination in 1921 and an honorary DMus by Edinburgh University in 1930. Having conducted a concert of military bands and choirs, he died in his sleep on 5 July 1944 at Stromness in the Orkney Islands, Scotland. He never married.   MICHAEL BROWN

Sources W. G. Whittaker, autobiography, 2 vols., Scottish Music Information Centre, Glasgow · M. Brown, 'William Gillies Whittaker: a provincial musician', MA diss., U. Birm. · *MT*, 85 (1944), 255 · P. Lovell, 'The musicians', *The Literary and Philosophical Society of Newcastle upon Tyne bicentenary lectures, 1993*, ed. [J. Philipson] (1994) · J. Pollitzer, 'Whittaker centenary retrospect', *British Music Society Journal*, 2 (1980), 40–42 · M. Whittaker, 'The Viking pioneer', *British Music Society Journal*, 2 (1980), 42–7 · M. C. Colles and others, 'Whittaker, William G(illies)', *New Grove* · *CGPLA Eng. & Wales* (1944)
Archives Scottish Music Information Centre, Glasgow, autobiography, letters, copies of journals, diaries, MSS · U. Newcastle, Robinson L., papers relating to his north country songs | U. St Andr., letters to Cedric Thorpe Davie | SOUND BL NSA, *Music weekly*, 1986, B972/2 · BL NSA, performance recording · Scottish Music Information Centre, Glasgow, original compositions
Likenesses Stuart, photograph, *c*.1927, U. Newcastle · Epstein, bronze bust, U. Newcastle
Wealth at death £5218 15s. 10d.: probate, 12 Sept 1944, *CGPLA Eng. & Wales*

Whittard, Walter Frederick (1902–1966), geologist, was born on 26 October 1902, in Battersea, London, the youngest of four children of Thomas Walter Whittard, a successful grocer of Clapham, and his wife, Sarah Cotterell.

Whittard attended the county secondary school at Battersea where he was a founder member of the school natural history society. While still at school, he was introduced to T. Eastwood of the Geological Survey who inspired in Whittard an interest in geology and advised him to attend evening classes in geology at Chelsea Polytechnic. There began a lifelong friendship with geologists Oliver Bulman and C. J. Stubblefield. In 1920 he began full-time study at Chelsea Polytechnic. In 1922 he became a student in the geology department of Imperial College under Professor William Watts and obtained in 1924 first-class honours in geology and zoology in the ARCS examinations and also in geology in his external London BSc. Attendance while an undergraduate at David Watson's lectures (at University College, London) enlarged his interest in palaeontology and this remained with him throughout his life, leading to a succession of papers which included important contributions to the study of trilobites.

With the award in 1924 of a Department of Scientific and Industrial Research (DSIR) scholarship, Whittard began his researches on the Valentian rocks of Shropshire under the supervision of Watts, while also pursuing part-time research under Watson on fossil Amphibia. Whittard's investigations of the Lower Palaeozoic rocks of Shropshire continued throughout his life. In two years he gained his London PhD and in 1926 he entered Sidney Sussex College, Cambridge, with a senior DSIR award. Here he joined in the social life with vigour and rowed for his college with distinction. Nevertheless, he completed his work for a Cambridge PhD within two years, and published the first of his major papers on the Valentian rocks of Shropshire (1928). He visited east Greenland as chief geologist to the 1929 Cambridge expedition under J. M. Wordie. This was an experience he greatly valued and he subsequently encouraged his staff and students to join expeditions to Greenland. The same year he was awarded an 1851 senior studentship at Imperial College to continue his Shropshire work and in 1930 he received the Daniel Pidgeon award of the Geological Society. It was in 1930 that he married Caroline Margaret (*d*. 1978), daughter of Albert William Sheppard, an engineer. They later had one son.

In 1931 Whittard was appointed assistant lecturer in geology at Imperial College and in 1935 to a lectureship. In 1937, at the early age of thirty-four, he accepted the chair of geology at Bristol University, made vacant by the move of Arthur E. Trueman to the University of Glasgow. He remained at Bristol for the rest of his life.

Until 1960 Whittard returned regularly to Shropshire to continue mapping and collecting and he became the recognized expert on the geology of the area. His work on the extraordinarily rich harvest of fossils collected over four decades reached its acme with the monograph on the Shelve trilobites, published in eight parts between 1955 and 1966 and effectively complete when he died, although a synthesis of the geology was never finished.

During the Second World War, Whittard was geological adviser to the south-west region of England dealing with problems ranging from the cutting of quartz oscillator plates to water supply. From the mid-1950s he became increasingly involved in marine geology, mapping the geology of the English Channel. The results of this work, which partly appeared in published maps in 1962 and 1965, formed the basis of the subsequent joint Anglo-French map of the English Channel.

Whittard was a most efficient administrator. He built up and ran well a happy department, enlarged threefold during his leadership, served on numerous committees, and executed the move of the department of geology from its old and cramped accommodation into the well-designed Queen's Building in 1958. He simultaneously pursued his research, and was able so to do largely because of his natural energy, the long hours he worked, and his remarkable ability to switch his mind back to research from administrative detail almost immediately. His main recreation was gardening and he lovingly supervised the university gardens. He was a shrewd but kindly man.

Whittard was elected a fellow of the Royal Society in 1957 and in 1965 received the Murchison medal of the

Geological Society. After visiting Canada in 1965 he was taken ill and died of heart failure at his home, Coombe Farm House, Westbury-on-Trym, Bristol, on 2 March 1966. He was cremated at Canford crematorium, Bristol.

BERNARD ELGEY LEAKE

Sources O. M. B. Bulman, *Memoirs FRS*, 12 (1966), 531–42 · F. W. Shotton, *Proceedings of the Geological Society of London*, 1625 (1964–5), 130–31 · O. M. B. Bulman, *Proceedings of the Geological Society of London*, 1636 (1965–6), 214–15 · personal knowledge (2004) · *CGPLA Eng. & Wales* (1966)
Likenesses photograph, 1958?, repro. in Bulman, *Memoirs FRS*, p. 530
Wealth at death £14,601: probate, 20 May 1966, *CGPLA Eng. & Wales*

Whitteridge, David (1912–1994), physiologist, was born on 22 June 1912 at 63 Grange Road, south Norwood, London, the younger son and second of three children of Walter Randall Whitteridge (1879–1955), woollen agent and later civil servant, and his wife, Jeanne Hortense, *née* Carouge (1879–1979). It was from his mother that he learned to speak in unaccented and idiomatic French. He was educated at All Saints' School, north Norwood, the Whitgift School in Croydon (1922–31), and Magdalen College, Oxford (where he was a demy). After graduating with first-class honours in physiology in 1934 he was appointed demonstrator in physiology by Professor Sir Charles Sherrington, and began to do experimental work with John Eccles, who was then a fellow of Magdalen. After completing clinical study at King's College Hospital in London in 1937 he worked for a year as sole resident medical officer at Finchley Memorial Hospital before returning to Oxford in 1938 to continue his scientific work at the invitation of Professor John Mellanby. In the same year he married Gweneth Hutchings (1910–1993), a lecturer at the University of Wales, Bangor, who was to become archivist at St Bartholomew's Hospital in London and a distinguished medical historian. They had three daughters: Nicolette, Janet, and Elizabeth.

Whitteridge ('D.W.' to his friends) began his experimental work at Oxford studying the role of pulmonary afferent fibres in mediating autonomic reflexes. When war casualties began to arrive at local hospitals he installed and operated some of the first electroencephalographs for the diagnosis and localization of brain injuries. In the course of that work he met Sir Ludwig Guttmann, a refugee who had been a pupil of the eminent neurosurgeon Otfrid Förster in Germany. Whitteridge joined Guttmann's unit at the Stoke Mandeville Hospital, studying temperature and blood-pressure regulation in men with severe spinal cord injuries. Their studies formed an important part of the efforts of that group, whose work led to a revolution in the treatment of spinal injuries.

Whitteridge returned to Oxford after the war to take up his duties as a fellow of Magdalen College and to pursue an active research programme in physiology. Best-known was his work in collaboration with Peter Daniel on a systematic study of the representation of the visual fields on the surface of the primate brain. In humans and the

David Whitteridge (1912–1994), by Walter Stoneman

higher primates far more of the cortical surface is devoted to representation of the centre than the periphery of the visual fields. In a characteristically brief and elegant paper Daniel and Whitteridge gave a pictorial and mathematical description of the way that the fields are represented on the cerebral cortex. The differences in area allocated to different regions of the visual fields and the complex folding of the primate occipital lobe were represented on a simple two-dimensional surface. When appropriately folded the map that they produced mirrored precisely the representation of the visual fields on the cerebral cortex. In this work Daniel and Whitteridge pioneered the development of methods for representing the functional organization of the complexly folded surface of the cerebral cortex on a flat and readily interpretable surface map.

Stereoscopic depth perception and its brain mechanism were other phenomena that Whitteridge explored both electrophysiologically and through study of his own depth vision. Once he came to a friend's office in an agitated state. He had with him a copy of an English translation of Helmholtz's textbook on physiological optics. In reference to one of Helmholtz's statements about stereopsis he said, 'but I have done that observation and I don't see that!' They went to the library to consult the original German volume to find that the translator had failed to notice the 'nicht' at the end of the sentence describing the experiment. A typical smile spread over his face. He loved being right, and usually was.

In 1950 Whitteridge was appointed professor of physiology at Edinburgh, where he remained for eighteen years. He returned to Oxford as Waynflete professor of physiology and a professorial fellow of his old college, Magdalen, in 1968. Both in Edinburgh and in Oxford he championed the importance of teaching basic science to medical students. In both universities he served as teacher and mentor to many younger colleagues who went on to distinguished careers in physiology and medicine. He was an active member of the Physiological Society, serving as its secretary from 1947 to 1951, and later as foreign secretary from 1980 to 1986. He received many honours in his life. He was elected fellow of the Royal Society of Edinburgh in 1951, of the Royal Society in 1953, and of the Royal College of Physicians in 1966. He received an honorary degree from the University of Edinburgh in 1993.

Physically Whitteridge was an imposing man. Tall and self-assured, he often terrified medical students and junior colleagues. He had an acid and mordant wit. It was reported to have been said of him that he had the highest IQ and the lowest pH in the Physiological Society. Beneath this often imposing professorial mask he was a pure delight: a loyal friend, and a kind guide to those who worked with him. His genuine enthusiasm and love for his field became clearest after he retired from his official duties as chairman of the physiology department. He continued to do research, first in the psychology department, and later in pharmacology. With his younger colleague Kevan Martin he entered a new and highly productive phase in his research career. In his eightieth year he would still work in the laboratory past midnight recording intracellularly from cortical neurons to help understand how their visual response properties were constructed.

Throughout his adult life Whitteridge was interested in the people, architecture, and scientific work of India. In 1967 and 1973 he was Leverhulme visiting professor at the University of Delhi, where he worked with his former student Autar Paintal on respiratory reflexes. They later helped to elucidate the mechanisms of respiratory failure caused by phosgene gas that had been emitted in the Bhopal disaster. This work was based in good part on Whitteridge's earliest research on the reflex functions of pulmonary afferent fibres. Whitteridge was honoured as a foreign member of the Indian National Science Academy and he was awarded the Mahalanobi medal in 1985.

In their later years at Oxford, Whitteridge and his wife occupied a big house with a large garden in Boars Hill, where he could exercise his passion for cultivating rhododendrons. He loved to recall that when he once said to the then new professor of botany that he felt it to be a minor miracle that a small cutting from a bush could take root and grow into a new plant, he was told that it was not a minor miracle, but a major one. He loved sailing with friends and family on the west coast of Scotland, and on occasion in France or the United States. When in France he was the official food buyer for the boat, amazing the local greengrocers with his accent-free French.

Gweneth Whitteridge died after a long illness in 1993. During her illness Whitteridge took over many of the household chores, shopping and looking after her. When he was diagnosed with cancer his intellect and spirit remained buoyant; he told a friend, 'I have just had a bit of good news; tumours grow half as fast when you are eighty as when you are forty. I've got months to live, not weeks. I'm going on holiday to Australia.' He eventually died at his home, Winterslow, Lincombe Lane, Boars Hill, Oxford, on 15 June 1994. He was survived by his three daughters.

MITCHELL GLICKSTEIN

Sources private information (2004) [Janet Whitteridge; G. Gordon] · K. Martin, *Cerebral Cortex*, 6 (1994), 573–5 · G. Gordon and A. Iggo, *Memoirs FRS*, 42 (1996), 523–38 · K. Martin, *Trends in Neurosciences*, 17 (1994), 446–8 · *The Times* (24 June 1994) · *The Independent* (23 June 1994) · *The Guardian* (1 July 1994) · WWW
Likenesses photograph, *c.*1979, repro. in Gordon and Iggo, *Memoirs FRS*, 524 · photograph, before 1979, repro. in *The Times* · W. Stoneman, photograph, RS [*see illus.*]
Wealth at death £394,708: probate, 5 Aug 1994, *CGPLA Eng. & Wales*

Whittingham, Charles (1767–1840), printer, was born on 16 June 1767 at Stoke Farm, Caludon or Calledon, near Coventry, Warwickshire, the seventh child of Charles Whittingham, farmer, and his wife, Mary. On 25 March 1779 he was apprenticed to Richard Bird, printer and bookseller of Coventry; having completed his apprenticeship in the spring of 1786 he worked for a time in Birmingham before moving to London, where by 1789 he had set up on his own at 10 Dean Street, off Fetter Lane. Whittingham obtained his freedom of the Stationers' Company by redemption on 14 April 1795, and the freedom of the City of London on 6 October of the same year. Over the next few years he occupied various premises in the area of Fetter Lane, and in 1803 established a workshop at 10 Union Buildings, off Leather Lane. It was here that he installed several of the earliest iron Stanhope hand-presses, invented about 1800 and characterized by a large platen allowing an entire sheet to be printed at one impression. For about eight years his business used the imprint the Stanhope Press.

After a further move in 1807 to Goswell Street in Clerkenwell, Whittingham formed a partnership with Thomas Potts and Robert Bishop, capitalizing on Potts's patent for removing tar from old ropes and processing them into pulp for paper making. Premises for this operation were found in 1809 at Chiswick, 7 or 8 miles west of Whittingham's London printing office; within a year he had leased High House on the Chiswick Mall and moved his residence and part of his printing business to Chiswick as well. He left the London shop in the hands of his foreman Robert Rowland, taking him into partnership in 1810, but the London business was gradually given up, and the partnership terminated in 1819. Whittingham also entered into a partnership with the stationer and bookseller John Arliss from 1813 to 1817, and may have been the Whittingham of the ink-making firm of Whittingham and Scarlet, operating in Carnaby Street during the years 1804–10.

By 1811, when Whittingham began on occasion to use the imprint the Chiswick Press, he had already built up a thriving business. His surviving account books, now in the British Library, show a steady progress after the first jobbing entries of 1792, which gradually give way to commissions for type specimen books for the Caslon foundry (1794–6), almanacs and religious tracts printed by the thousands, and even a short-lived anti-Jacobin newspaper (*The Tomahawk! or, Censor General*, 1795–6). In 1799 Whittingham produced on his own account an elegant *Poems* of Thomas Gray, immediately selling the whole edition to two booksellers and going on to print an entire series of neat, compact editions of such standard works as Oliver Goldsmith's *Vicar of Wakefield* (1800), John Gay's *Fables* (1801), and James Thomson's *Seasons* (1802). In 1803 he formed an association with the bookseller John Sharpe, and the two men jointly undertook the publication of several series: the British Classics, Sharpe's British Theatre, and the British Poets. Later, in 1822, Whittingham issued his own British Poets series in one hundred royal 18mo volumes; other of his series include Whittingham's Pocket Novels, Whittingham's French Classics, and Whittingham's Cabinet Library.

In his mature years, Whittingham acquired a considerable reputation as a printer of illustrated books. Samuel Jackson Pratt's *Pity's Gift* (1797) was his first book to feature wood-engraved illustrations, but it was not until he was established at Chiswick that his work began consistently to exhibit the sharpness and evenness of impression associated with his finest illustrated books: the two series of Northcote's *Fables* (1829 and 1833), *The Tower Menagerie* (1829), *The Gardens and Menagerie of the Zoological Society* (1830–31), and *Puckle's Club* (1834). Whittingham has been credited with the innovation of using overlays, pieces of paper or thin card pasted to the tympan for the delicate regulation of the amount of pressure applied to various parts of a wood-engraving, but it is doubtful that he was the first to use this technique. Such technical improvements as the iron Stanhope press, the composition inking roller, and smooth, machine-made paper also contributed to the success of Whittingham's woodblock printing, and he is reputed to have manufactured his own printing ink.

Family tradition represents Whittingham as a charitable if severe man, a strict sabbatarian and a strong-willed disciplinarian. Although he married a Mary Mead, who predeceased him, no children (if there were any) survived to adulthood. In 1810 he took Charles *Whittingham (1795–1876), his older brother's son, into his business, first as an apprentice and later as a journeyman, and then as a partner from 1824 until 1828, when the younger man moved to London and set up his own printing shop. The Whittingham residence and business was moved about 1818 to the river-front College House at the corner of Chiswick Mall and Chiswick Lane; Whittingham the elder remained there after the departure of his nephew, continuing to print until his health failed in early 1838. On 24 July 1839 he entered into an agreement with his nephew, where, in return for the guarantee of an annuity of £358, Whittingham the elder agreed to hand over the goodwill, types, presses, and fixtures to his nephew, provided that

the latter secured a bond of £1000 against possible bankruptcy. On 5 January 1840 Charles Whittingham the elder died at his Chiswick home, leaving his business to his nephew and bequeathing substantial sums to the Stationers' Company, the Printers' Pension Society (which founded special pensions bearing his name), and the poor of Chiswick. He was buried at Chiswick.

JANET ING FREEMAN

Sources A. Warren, *The Charles Whittinghams: printers* (1896) · I. Bain, *John Sharpe: publisher and bookseller, Piccadilly* (1960) · A. J. Flavell, 'The printing office of Charles Whittingham, the younger, during the period 1828 to 1833', MA diss., UCL, 1973 · J. Ing, 'Charles Whittingham the younger and the Chiswick Press, 1852–59', PhD diss., U. Cal., Berkeley, 1985 · [H. Stevens], 'The Chiswick Press', *The Athenaeum* (19 Aug 1876) · 'The Charles Whittinghams' benefactions', *Publishers' Circular and Booksellers' Record*, 124 (1926), 143 · J. Mosley, 'The Stanhope press', in H. Hart, *Charles Earl Stanhope and the Oxford University Press*, ed. J. Mosley (1966), xix–xxxiii **Archives** BL, corresp. and papers, incl. records of the Chiswick Press, Add. MSS 41867–41960, 43975–43989, 50910–50950; Add. Ch. 70986–71003 · Chiswick Public Library | Bodl. Oxf., John Johnson collection, Chiswick Press MSS · NYPL, Chiswick Press MSS and C. T. Jacobi MSS · V&A NAL, C. T. Jacobi MSS **Likenesses** T. Williams, oils, Stationers' Hall, London **Wealth at death** bequests of business to nephew, and substantial sums to charities

Whittingham, Charles (1795–1876), printer, was born on 30 October 1795 at Mitcham, Surrey, the son of Samuel Whittingham, nurseryman. At the instigation—and most likely at the expense—of his father's younger brother in London, the printer Charles *Whittingham (1767–1840), he attended the Islington academy of the Revd John Evans, and on 2 October 1810 was bound apprentice to his uncle, who had recently taken premises at Chiswick. He became free of the Stationers' Company on 4 November 1817, and in 1818 was made a liveryman of the company. He remained in his uncle's printing office for the next ten years, and in 1824 the two men entered into an informal partnership; this was dissolved in August 1828, when the younger Whittingham left Chiswick to set up his own printing shop at 21 Tooks Court, off Chancery Lane in Holborn.

The elder Whittingham provided his breakaway nephew with two secondhand iron presses and about 1200 pounds of well-used type; he also lent him nearly £1500, charging interest at the rate of 5 per cent. Young Charles paid his first wages bill on 23 August 1828, and within two years the new business was employing a dozen men and showing a profit. At a time when rival establishments such as Spottiswoodes and Clowes were filling vast press rooms with steam-powered printing machines, Whittingham chose instead to follow his uncle in retaining the iron hand-press and concentrating on the production of small editions distinguished for their tasteful design and excellent presswork. Throughout his career he relied on a small number of customers, many of them publishers and individuals or societies who shared his aesthetic concerns; other clients, including the Religious Tract Society and a half-dozen almanac publishers, were taken over from his uncle and provided a steady and undemanding source of income.

Soon after his move to Tooks Court, Whittingham made the acquaintance of the bookseller and publisher William Pickering (1796–1854), who became his most important customer as well as his close friend. From about 1830 Pickering began sending most of his work to Whittingham, and was soon providing over half the business that entered the Tooks Court shop. In large part, the books that he printed for Pickering have served to confirm Whittingham's reputation as the finest English commercial printer of the nineteenth century. Much of the credit for the typographic design of the books may belong to Pickering, but it was Whittingham's craftsmanship, particularly in the area of presswork, that ensured the success of such projects as Pickering's 1833 *Dance of Death* and his 1844 folio blackletter reprints of the Book of Common Prayer from six early editions. For these and other books Whittingham commissioned initials and headpieces from the wood-engraver Mary Byfield (1795–1871), suggesting as models alphabets and ornaments employed by sixteenth-century English and continental printers.

With Pickering, Whittingham also began in the late 1830s the typographic experiments that led to the revival of the old face roman types of William Caslon, which had been superseded in the early years of the century by the more fashionable 'modern' faces. The reintroduced Caslon type was used first in 1840 for five Pickering title-pages, and in 1843 Whittingham began work on two books employing Caslon as the principal text type, Hannah Mary Rathbone's *Diary of Lady Willoughby*, published by Longmans in 1844, and an edition in 1845 of Juvenal's *Satires*, an Eton prize book overseen by Pickering. Later, Whittingham commissioned three types for the private use of his printing office: a recutting of one of William Caxton's types (1847); the Basel roman, based on sixteenth-century designs (1850); and a less historically accurate Aldine italic and roman (1856). A distinctive house style, combining proprietary and carefully chosen foundry types with Whittingham's unique stock of borders and initials, was fully evolved by the 1850s, and may be seen to full advantage in such works as the 1853 Queen Elizabeth Book of Common Prayer printed for Pickering, William Calvert's *The Wife's Manual* (Longmans, 1854), and a second Book of Common Prayer employing borders based on the designs of Geoffroy Tory (Longmans, 1864). Unsurpassed in colour printing from woodblocks, Whittingham produced several books for Henry Shaw, including his 1842 *Encyclopedia of Ornament*, as well as a number of colour-printed gift books and the eccentric but dazzling 1847 *Elements of Euclid*, in which Oliver Byrne attempted to expedite the teaching of geometry through the use of colour diagrams.

In 1826 Whittingham married Eleanor Hulley (d. 1854) of Nottingham; two sons and three daughters were born between 1827 and 1840. Both sons were eventually apprenticed to their father, and the two eldest daughters, Charlotte and Elizabeth Eleanor, for many years participated in

the design and engraving of the press's ornamental woodblocks. On his uncle's retirement in 1839 Whittingham took over the management of the Chiswick shop, inheriting the successful business outright a year later and adopting its Chiswick Press imprint for his own books. He maintained two shops until 1848, when his London lease expired and he was forced to concentrate the business at the Chiswick premises, which he abandoned in January 1852 after purchasing the freehold of the Tooks Court buildings. In 1847 Whittingham was elected a member of the Society of Arts, and in 1851 served as a member of the jury for the section on paper, stationery, printing, and bookbinding of the Great Exhibition of the Works of Industry of All Nations; he was the co-author, with Ambroise-Firmin Didot, of the jury's official *Report* (1852).

Throughout this period Pickering continued to be Whittingham's major client, although from 1845 the publisher was unable to keep current with his payments, and in May 1853 declared bankruptcy. Less than a year later he died, owing Whittingham just under £7500; the printer—whose own wife had died just a few weeks earlier—served as executor and arranged for Pickering's burial in the Whittingham plot at Kensal Green cemetery. Pickering's debts to Whittingham were not cleared until 1859, but by October 1853 Whittingham was already making substantial cash advances to another occasional client, the antiquarian bookseller Henry Stevens 'of Vermont' (1819–1886). Stevens's debt, incurred principally through his bookselling activity, reached a high of £6600 in 1859, and was not finally settled until 1881, five years after the printer's death. From 1855 Whittingham also silently took a two-thirds interest in a number of books issued by the publishers Bell and Daldy, possibly viewing the enterprise both as a means of providing work for his skilled personnel and as a way of advertising the special qualities of his printing office and materials.

Whittingham was throughout his career a shrewd businessman, and much of his success must be credited to his ability to combine fiscal good sense with an unusual concern for the quality of the books printed in his shop. In *The Charles Whittinghams: Printers* (1896), Arthur Warren described the younger Whittingham as 'hot-tempered' as a boy and 'brusque and severe' as an adult (Warren, 96); Warren's drafts, based in part on the recollections of the printer's surviving children, are more explicit, calling Whittingham a 'somewhat rough and blunt' man who 'showed little or no affection for any one' (BL, Add. MS 43986, fol. 81). He is said to have softened, personally, after 1860, when he took his manager John Wilkins into partnership and retired from an active role in the press. On Wilkins's death nine years later a new partnership was formed between Whittingham, Wilkins's son John Charles, and Benjamin Franklin Stevens, brother of Henry and husband of Whittingham's daughter Charlotte. In 1872 the Chiswick Press acquired its first steam presses.

On 21 April 1876 Charles Whittingham died at his home in Surbiton, Surrey, and on 27 April was buried at Kensal Green cemetery, London, alongside his friend Pickering.

His considerable property was shared among his four surviving children, and following the death of the last the residuary estates, then totalling £63,784, were transferred to the Printers' Pension, Almshouse and Orphan Asylum Corporation. The Chiswick Press itself was purchased in 1880 by the publisher George Bell, and was merged with the firm of William Griggs & Sons, lithographers, in 1919. In 1937 the business resumed the old Chiswick Press name; in 1944 it was purchased by Eyre and Spottiswoode, and in 1962 it was finally closed down.

JANET ING FREEMAN

Sources A. Warren, *The Charles Whittinghams: printers* (1896) · J. Ing, 'Charles Whittingham the younger and the Chiswick Press, 1852–59', PhD diss., U. Cal., Berkeley, 1985 · A. J. Flavell, 'The printing office of Charles Whittingham, the younger, during the period 1828 to 1833', MA diss., UCL, 1973 · J. I. Freeman, 'Founders' type and private founts at the Chiswick Press in the 1850s', *Journal of the Printing Historical Society*, 19–20 (1984–6), 63–102 · J. M. McDonnell, 'William Pickering (1796–1854): antiquarian bookseller, publisher, and book designer', PhD diss., Polytechnic of North London, 1983 · R. McLean, *Victorian book design and colour printing*, rev. edn (1972) · [H. Stevens], 'The Chiswick Press', *The Athenaeum* (19 Aug 1876) · 'The Charles Whittinghams' benefactions', *Publishers' Circular and Booksellers' Record*, 124 (1926), 143 · IGI

Archives BL, corresp. and papers, incl. records of the Chiswick Press, Add. MSS 41867–41960, 43975–43989, 50910–50950; Add. Ch. 70986–71003 · Chiswick Public Library | Bodl. Oxf., John Johnson collection, Chiswick Press MSS · NYPL, corresp. and papers relating to the Chiswick Press · V&A NAL, C. T. Jacobi MSS

Likenesses photograph, repro. in Warren, *Charles Whittinghams, printers*

Wealth at death under £40,000: probate, 1 June 1876, *CGPLA Eng. & Wales*

Whittingham, Sir Robert (*d.* 1452), merchant and financier, was perhaps the eldest of the four children of Alan Whittingham, who may have been a Londoner; more certainly, he was the nephew of Robert Whittingham, a rich London tailor, and the brother of Thomas, another tailor. Whittingham was established in London as a draper by 1407 and inherited city property from his uncle in 1413. He rose through trade in woad and pepper as well as wool, through links with Italians and deals with city magnates. By 1419 he could afford to pledge £20, the second largest amount, for the new Drapers' Hall. Elected MP for London and warden of his livery in 1416, he was alderman of Bishopsgate ward (1417–22) and of Walbrook ward (1422–38). He served as auditor of London in 1418–19 and 1424–5, and was sheriff in 1419–20, but never became mayor. In the 1420s Whittingham's service with John, duke of Bedford, brother of Henry V and regent of France, took him away from city politics and onto the national stage.

By 1420 Whittingham had married Agnes, daughter of Richard and Joan Buckland. Buckland was treasurer and victualler of Calais (1421–36) and a councillor of Bedford. This connection no doubt led to Whittingham's appointment as Bedford's receiver-general in England by December 1426. He oversaw Bedford's great English estates and profits of office as admiral of England. He also shipped supplies, weapons, victuals, and wine, to the regent in France. His adherence to Bedford, and to the regent's uncle, Cardinal Henry Beaufort, was probably the cause of the reported anger of Humphrey, duke of Gloucester, Bedford's younger brother and political opponent, following a meeting of the court of aldermen in May 1427.

In 1432 Bedford granted Whittingham a substantial annuity (£26 13s. 4d.) on the manor of Salden, Buckinghamshire, and also the advowson of St Stephen Walbrook, Whittingham's London parish church. From 1433 to 1439 Whittingham was receiver-general of the duchy of Cornwall, another key source of Bedford's income. On his deathbed in 1435 Bedford appointed Whittingham an executor. Although he closed accounts as receiver-general of Bedford's former lands in England, Calais, and the Channel Islands in 1438, Whittingham was involved in Bedford's complicated estate for the rest of his life. From 1438, under Beaufort's direction, he collected tallies and paid creditors, recording his efficient administration in a 'boke of declaracion', which survives. Whittingham was trustee of the estates of other magnates, such as Beaufort, Henry, Lord Bourchier (*d.* 1483), and John Holland, duke of Exeter (*d.* 1446), for whom he also served as executor, and acted as banker to such veterans of the French wars as Bedford's chamberlain, Sir Andrew Ogard. According to William Worcester, Ogard left with Whittingham a chest with about 7000 marks in 'French gold'.

In 1436 Whittingham succeeded Richard Buckland as treasurer of Calais and master of the Calais mint. At this critical time for Calais he embarked on a series of loans to the crown, none exceeding £133 6s. 8d., which were repaid in full by 1446. A seasoned wool exporter, he arbitrated in at least one dispute between the mayor and merchants of the Calais staple. By 1439 he was himself mayor of the staple and was present in the Star Chamber when a fellow draper was convicted of concealing wool exports. His Calais responsibilities led to his appointment as ambassador to Flanders and Brabant, Holland and Zeeland, Burgundy and France, on a series of missions in 1438–41. He attended the Anglo-French peace negotiations in 1439, and in 1440–41 the negotiations surrounding the release of the duke of Orléans. Whittingham seems to have represented the mercantile interest, and to have worked for the resumption of Anglo-Flemish trade. He was treasurer of Calais until late December 1441, when a scandal erupted over the town's buildings and defences; Whittingham and his father-in-law were accused of neglect and of misappropriating bricks and timber. Whittingham was threatened with a suit in the exchequer court, but it was deferred from term to term.

Whittingham had acquired his main London house in Walbrook in 1418. With purchases in 1437 and 1447 he came to own most of the east side of Walbrook, backed by a large garden. Besides investing in London property in at least three other London parishes, Whittingham became a country gentleman with five or more manors and other lands and reversions in Hertfordshire, Buckinghamshire, and Berkshire. He served on many commissions, and was sheriff of Essex and Hertfordshire in 1433–4 and 1438–9. It is not known when he bought his main manor of Pendley in Hertfordshire, but it was probably before 1432, when he sat as MP for the county. Whittingham enclosed a park of

200 acres at Pendley in 1440 and built a chapel there by 1442. The date he acquired the neighbouring manor of Maudeleyns in Northchurch, where his uncle had established a chantry in 1413, is also unknown. Whittingham obtained two-thirds of Bedford's former manor of Salden in 1439 through the good offices of Cardinal Beaufort; he recovered it swiftly after the Act of Resumption of 1450. Other properties he owned in Buckinghamshire included the manor of Moulsoe. He bequeathed Donnington manor in Berkshire to his eldest son.

At Whittingham's death on 4 or 5 November 1452 he left life interests in his house in Walbrook and in Salden to his widow, along with the lion's share of his chattels, including all those at Pendley, and divided his other manors, lands, and chattels among his four sons. He elected to be buried at Ashridge Priory, Hertfordshire, which had a special connection with the duchy of Cornwall. Obits were kept for him and for his widow, who died in 1456. In 1575–6 his Verney descendants moved the Whittingham double tomb to the Pendley chapel in the church of St John the Baptist, Aldbury, Hertfordshire, where it survives. A drawing of c.1600 shows the lost armorial glass in the south choir window of St Stephen Walbrook, where Whittingham had laid the third foundation stone of the new building in 1429. It depicts Whittingham's arms: party per fess argent and or a fess vert, overall a lion rampant gules, combined with the arms of Bedford, his principal patron, the ostrich plumes of Lancaster, the arms of England, and the Buckland arms of his wife. His eldest son, another Sir Robert, killed at the battle of Tewkesbury in 1471, has often been confused with his father.

JENNY STRATFORD

Sir Samuel Ford Whittingham (1772–1841), by unknown artist

Sources J. Stratford, *The Bedford inventories: the worldly goods of John, duke of Bedford, regent of France, 1389–1435* (1993) · C. Rawcliffe, 'Whittingham, Robert', HoP, *Commons, 1386–1421,* 4.841–4 [see also Barton, John II, 2.140–43] · J. Stratford, 'Joan Buckland (*d.* 1462)', *Medieval London widows, 1300–1500,* ed. C. M. Barron and A. F. Sutton (1994), 113–28 · Hunt. L., Ellesmere MS 9H15, fols. 27, 87 · LPL, Reg. Kemp, fols. 269–270v

Likenesses Whittingham double tomb, repro. in Stratford, *Bedford inventories,* pl. 68

Wealth at death substantial London property; also at least five manors; chattels

Whittingham, Sir Samuel Ford (1772–1841), army officer, elder son and second child of William Whittingham of Bristol, was born at Bristol on 29 January 1772. His Christian names were contracted by himself and his friends into Samford.

Early life, 1772–1806 Whittingham was educated at Bristol and was intended for the law. Determined to be a soldier, but unwilling to oppose his father's wishes during his lifetime, he entered temporarily his brother-in-law's merchant firm, and travelled for it in Spain. In 1797 at Bristol he joined the mounted volunteers, an anti-invasion force of the wealthier citizens. His father died on 12 September 1801 (aged sixty), at Earl's Mead, Bristol, and Samford, who was in Spain, became independent. He returned to England and was gazetted ensign on 20 January 1803; he bought a lieutenancy on 25 February, and was brought into the 1st Life Guards on 10 March. Whittingham went to

the Royal Military College at High Wycombe, and joined his regiment in London towards the end of 1804. He was introduced by Thomas Murdoch, an influential merchant, to William Pitt, the prime minister, as an officer whose knowledge of Spanish would be useful, and as a result was sent by Pitt at the end of 1804 on a secret mission to the Peninsula; on 14 February 1805, during his absence, he was promoted captain in the 20th foot. On his return he was complimented by Pitt, and on 13 June 1805 he was transferred to the command of a troop in the 13th light dragoons.

Argentina, 1807 On 12 November 1806 Whittingham sailed from Portsmouth as deputy assistant quartermaster-general of the force, under Brigadier-General Robert Craufurd, intended for Lima; but on arrival at the Cape of Good Hope on 15 March 1807 its destination was changed, and on 13 June it reached Montevideo, recently captured by Sir Samuel Auchmuty. General John Whitelocke had arrived to command the combined forces, and as Whittingham's staff appointment ceased on the amalgamation of the forces, Whitelocke made him an extra aide-de-camp to himself. He took part in the disastrous attack on Buenos Aires and in the surrender on 6 July, and sailed for England on 30 July. He gave evidence before the general court martial, by which Whitelocke was tried in London in February and March 1808. Owing to his having served on Whitelocke's personal staff, Whittingham's position was a delicate one; but he acquitted himself with discretion.

Spain, 1808–1819 Whittingham was immediately afterwards appointed deputy assistant quartermaster-general on the staff of the army in Sicily. On arrival at Gibraltar, however, he acted temporarily as assistant military secretary to Lieutenant-General Sir Hew Dalrymple, the governor, and, hearing of a projected campaign of the Spaniards under Don Xavier Castaños against the French, obtained leave to join Castaños as a volunteer, with instructions to report in detail to Dalrymple. This special duty was approved from London on 2 July 1808, and on 18 July Whittingham was appointed a deputy assistant quartermaster-general to the force under Sir Arthur Wellesley, but was ordered to remain with Castaños. He took part under Manuel La Peña on 18 July 1808 in the victorious battle of Bailén, being almost the only British officer present, and for his services he was made a colonel of cavalry in the Spanish army on 20 July.

On his recovery from a severe attack of rheumatic fever, Whittingham was sent to Seville on a mission from the duke of Infantado, and in February 1809 joined the army corps of the duke of Albuquerque in La Mancha, where he took part in several cavalry actions with such distinction that he was promoted brigadier-general in the Spanish army, an appointment dated 2 March 1809. He was present at the battle of Medellin on 28 March, when the Spanish general Cuesta was defeated by the French general Victor. On this occasion Whittingham re-formed the routed cavalry and led them against the enemy. He reported constantly throughout these campaigns to the British minister in Spain, John Hookham Frere, as to the state and operations of the Spanish army.

Shortly before Wellesley's advance into Spain, Whittingham joined the British headquarters on the frontier of Portugal, and became the medium of communication with the Spanish general Cuesta. On 28 July 1809 at Talavera he was severely wounded when gallantly bringing up two Spanish battalions to the attack; he was mentioned in Wellesley's dispatch a day later. He went to Seville to recover, and lived with the British minister, Lord Wellesley; during his convalescence he translated Dundas's *Cavalry Movements* into Spanish. He was promoted major-general in the Spanish army on 12 August.

Whittingham married at Gibraltar, in January 1810, Magdalena, the elder of twin daughters of Don Pedro de Creus y Jiménez, intendant of the Spanish royal armies, and they had a large family, several of their sons serving in the Spanish army.

During his stay at the British embassy in Seville, Whittingham proposed the idea that was to form the basis of his participation in most of the rest of the war. Convinced that Spaniards would make splendid soldiers if commanded by British officers, he suggested to Henry Wellesley that he form a model division of 10,000 troops in the security of Majorca. Armed and clothed by the British and with at least two British officers per battalion, they could then threaten the French armies in eastern Spain (British command of the sea would enable them to be a powerful raiding force on the Mediterranean coast); meanwhile they might also act as a model for reform in the rest of the army. Though Wellesley eagerly took up the idea, such was Spanish suspicion of the British that Whittingham's proposals met a frosty reception when he presented them at the new capital, Cadiz, in August 1810. However, through the patronage of General Castaños, one of the original members of the collective regency established to govern Spain following the fall of the provisional government (the Junta Central) in January 1810, Whittingham was appointed to command the cavalry of the Spanish army based in Cadiz, in which he succeeded in effecting some improvement. In this capacity in March 1811 he took part in an attempt to raise the siege of Cadiz by landing a substantial force of British and Spanish troops behind the lines of the French forces blockading the city. However, owing to the lack of initiative of the Spanish commander, La Peña, the operation failed, while Whittingham's own part in it was limited to containing a few squadrons of enemy cavalry in the action at Barrosa on 5 March.

Immediately after the Barrosa campaign Whittingham left Cadiz for Palma de Mallorca, the regency having at last been persuaded to adopt his plans for the establishment of a new mobile division under his command. Even then, because of obstruction from the Spanish authorities, and especially the captain general of Majorca, Gregorio García de la Cuesta, the new force—known as the división de Mallorca and composed of six battalions of infantry and four squadrons of cavalry—was not ready until the middle of 1812. By then, however, the situation was much changed, and Whittingham's division was incorporated into the expeditionary army sent to Spain from the British base in Sicily. Initially the intention was to besiege the French-held fortress of Tarragona, but this plan was abandoned, and the entire force disembarked at the Spanish-held base of Alicante on 7 August.

Whittingham's troops remained cantoned in the Alicante area through the winter of 1812–13, and suffered extreme privation for want of supplies. The front in this region remained quiet, but in March 1813 the new British commander at Alicante, Sir John Murray, launched an offensive, Whittingham's division being involved in skirmishes at Jijona and Concentaina on 6 and 15 March. In the latter action Whittingham was shot in the cheek, but his wound was apparently not serious enough to force him to relinquish command. Notwithstanding its initial success the offensive soon halted, and in the first week of April a French counter-offensive quickly regained much of the lost ground. By 12 April Murray's entire force was concentrated at Castalla, and on the following day it was attacked by the French forces of Marshal Suchet. Posted on the extreme left of the allied line, Whittingham's division received the full force of the French attack, but managed to beat it off despite a muddle in its orders that led to the English general being caught in the midst of a major change of position. For this action Whittingham deserved great credit: the hard fight by his men vindicated his efforts, and he displayed considerable tactical skill.

Following the battle of Castalla the Alicante front was quiet. Whittingham's next action was Murray's expedition to Tarragona in June 1813. This was a humiliating fiasco; Murray panicked and hastily re-embarked his men in most discreditable circumstances—and the army returned once again to Alicante, being placed under the command of Lord William Bentinck. However, on 21 June Wellington won the decisive victory of Vitoria, which forced the French to evacuate much territory, including the province of Valencia. Whittingham assisted in its reoccupation, then was soon on the Ebro, invading Catalonia on 26 July. Within three weeks, however, a French counter-offensive had sent the army back across the Ebro, the last stages of the retreat being covered by Whittingham, who had to fight a fierce rearguard action at Amposta on 19 August. In the following month Bentinck crossed the Ebro again, but was unable to advance any further than Tarragona due to want of transport and supplies. With the French few in numbers and largely tied up in garrison duty, there was little fighting; Whittingham's division, being left in reserve, did none.

When Ferdinand VII returned to Spain from his French imprisonment in March 1814 Whittingham was in garrison at Valencia, well placed to intervene in the military coup that overthrew the 1812 constitution and restored absolutism. With little love lost between himself and the liberal regime—throughout 1812 and 1813 his long series of disputes with the authorities had become so acrimonious that he had offered his resignation—Whittingham immediately declared his support for the rebellion. To the annoyance of Henry Wellesley, who advocated British neutrality, he headed the march on Madrid, where on the night of 10–11 May 1814 his troops arrested most of the liberal leaders. According to Whittingham, he advised Ferdinand to grant a new constitution more in line with Spanish tradition, but there is no evidence that he ever pressed his views further—he always retained the favour of the king, who in June 1814 presented him with a mosaic snuffbox and made him a lieutenant general, and on the escape of Napoleon from Elba obtained permission from the British government to appoint him to the command of a division in the army that had hastily to be mobilized in the Pyrenees. For his services on this occasion, he received the grand cross of the order of San Fernando. He continued to enjoy the favour of the court, and from 1815 to 1819 remained in Spain. However, his family was increasing, his private means had been much reduced by losses, and no support was available from the Spanish government. So he was delighted, in July 1819, to accept the governorship of the newly acquired British colony of Dominica.

West Indies and India, 1819–1841 Whittingham's period in Dominica was apparently popular; the island's 'plantocracy' marked his departure with the presentation of a sword of honour, and a cross of the order of San Fernando set in diamonds. Moreover, despite his involvement in the 1814 coup he had never fallen from favour in England. In 1814 he received the rank of colonel in the British army and was appointed an aide-de-camp to the prince regent; and having received praise for his discretion at the court martial of Sir John Murray for his Tarragona failure, Whittingham was knighted and created CB on 3 May 1815. The Dominican appointment was only the

first in his distinguished career in British service. In October 1821 he was made a KCH and appointed quartermaster-general—effectively chief-of-staff—of the British forces in India.

Whittingham reached Calcutta on 2 November 1822. He was busy in 1824 with the preparations for the expedition to Ava, and in November with the Barrackpore mutiny. On 27 May 1825 he was promoted major-general; he retained his appointment as quartermaster-general until a command became vacant. He took part in the siege of Bharatpur, was slightly wounded on 13 January 1826, but was present at the capture on 18 January. For his services in this action he was made KCB (military division), on 26 December, and received the thanks of the House of Commons. In February 1827 he was appointed to command the Cawnpore division. On 1 November 1830 he was transferred to the Meerut command, on exchange with Sir Jasper Nicholl. His tenure of command came to an end in August 1833, and he then acted temporarily as military secretary to his old commander, Lord William Bentinck, the governor-general, with whom he returned to England in 1835.

On arrival in England in July he almost fought a duel with Sir William Napier, on account of the slur which he considered Napier had cast on the Spanish troops in his *History of the War in the Peninsula*, but the matter was arranged by Sir Rufane Donkin. In October 1836 Whittingham was appointed to command the forces in the Windward and Leeward islands. He sailed for Barbados on 22 December, with the local rank of lieutenant-general (exchanged in a few months for the substantive). In September 1839 he was given the command of the Madras army; he arrived at Madras on 1 August 1840, and died there suddenly on 19 January 1841, at Fort George, where he was buried with military honours on the following day. A memorial tablet was placed in the garrison church, Madras. He had written several published and unpublished military works.

R. H. VETCH, *rev.* CHARLES ESDAILE

Sources *A memoir of the services of Lieutenant-General Sir Samuel Ford Whittingham*, ed. F. Whittingham, new edn (1868) · C. W. C. Oman, *A history of the Peninsular War*, 7 vols. (1902–30) · *GM*, 2nd ser., 15 (1841), 1 · PRO, War Office records · R. Cannon, ed., *Historical record of the seventy-first regiment, highland light infantry* (1852)
Archives BL, corresp. with Sir James Willoughby Gordon, Add. MS 49490, *passim* · Royal Military College, Sandhurst, letters to Le Marchant · U. Nott. L., letters to Lord William Bentinck, JF 2182–2314 · U. Southampton L., Wellington MSS
Likenesses H. Adlard, portrait (after miniature), repro. in Whittingham, ed., *Memoir* · watercolour miniature; Christies, 7 Nov 1988, lot 90 [*see illus.*]

Whittingham, William (*d.* **1579**), dean of Durham, was the son of William Whittingham, a Chester gentleman, and his wife, a member of the Haughton family of Haughton Tower, Lancashire. About 1540 he entered Brasenose College, Oxford, where he graduated BA in 1545. In the same year he became a fellow of All Souls and in 1547 a senior student of Cardinal College (later Christ Church) and proceeded MA.

Exile, scholarship, and publication Nothing is known about Whittingham's conversion to protestantism, though in later years he gave thanks that he had been 'called from the blindness of idolatry and superstition' (Greenwell, 15). At some point during the reign of Edward VI he travelled on the continent to extend his education in the universities of France, Germany, and Geneva. A skilled linguist (he spoke French and German), he acted for a while as interpreter to Sir John Mason, English ambassador to France. He returned briefly to England soon before the accession of Mary, but his protestant convictions soon forced him to travel overseas again. On 27 June 1554 he arrived at Frankfurt am Main where he became involved in the bitter disputes among the English protestant exiles over the issue of the prayer book of 1552. Whittingham aligned himself with John Knox and the 'democratic', Calvinist party, but the arrival of Richard Cox in March 1555 tilted the balance in favour of the prayer book faction and Knox and Whittingham were compelled to secede to Geneva where their views were more readily acceptable.

Whittingham arrived in Geneva in September 1555 and in December he became a senior of the English congregation. On 15 November 1556 he married Katherine (d. 1590), daughter of Louis Jaqueman, a native of Orléans, she being about ten years his junior. Their first two children, Zachary and Susanna, were born in 1557 and 1558, but both died young. Most of his time at Geneva appears to have been spent in scholarship, the results of which constituted his most lasting achievement: he acted in effect as midwife to the word of God in what was to become protestant England, participating in the preparation of the texts that, with the prayer book, were fundamental to the well-being of the reformed church. He translated the New Testament and assisted with the English version of the Geneva Bible, which went through more than seventy editions between 1560 and 1640 and which maintained its popularity among puritans even after the appearance of the Authorized Version in 1611. He helped produce Thomas Sternhold's and John Hopkins's edition of the Psalms and the Genevan *Form of Prayers*, and translated a book on predestination by Théodore Beza. He also found time to write a preface to Nicholas Ridley's *Brief Declaration of the Lord's Supper* and a controversial introduction to Christopher Goodman's *How Superior Powers Ought to be Obeyed*. Whittingham's involvement with the latter work, directed as it was against rule by the 'regiment of women', caused Elizabeth to be gravely suspicious of his loyalties. When Knox and Goodman returned to England in 1558, Whittingham stayed on to complete his literary projects and, since the congregation was left without a minister, Jean Calvin suggested he should take on that role. Whittingham was reluctant, but in 1558 he became deacon to the depleted congregation and served it in that role, or as minister, for the remainder of his time in Geneva. Certainly there is no record of his appointment as minister in the *Livre des Anglois* and Whittingham's precise clerical status at Geneva was to become an issue later in his career.

Chaplaincy in France and promotion Whittingham returned to England in May 1560, but the events of 1558

had cast a doubt on the way in which his career might develop. In January 1561 he accompanied the earl of Bedford on an embassy to France to express the queen's condolences on the death of François II and in May 1562 Bedford, Lord Robert Dudley, and the ecclesiastical commissioner Richard Goodrich made an unsuccessful attempt to secure for him the rectory of Loughborough, Leicestershire. It was probably about this time that Whittingham became chaplain to Ambrose Dudley, earl of Warwick, and his diverse talents were drawn together in October 1562 when, at the request of Warwick, he joined the English expeditionary force at Le Havre as a fighting chaplain. In this post he showed outstanding courage and ability, often preaching in his armour so that 'when any alarum came … he would be on the town walls as soon almost as any man' (Green, 11). Secretary of State William Cecil was concerned about some of his doctrinal pronouncements, but Whittingham justified these by the circumstances of the war and the need to maintain harmonious relations with the French Huguenots.

In June 1563 Whittingham returned to England followed by a letter from Warwick requesting that the vacant deanery of Durham be bestowed on him. The deanery was already 'half promised' to Thomas Wilson, master of requests, but Warwick's suit prevailed and Whittingham was appointed in July, preaching before the queen at Windsor on 2 September before he made his way north. Whittingham does not appear to have had ambitions to rise beyond the deanery despite offers made to him after 1563. In 1572 his name was put forward as a candidate to succeed Cecil, now Lord Burghley, as secretary and in 1575 Sir Henry Killigrew suggested him as a possible ambassador to Scotland because his 'ableness in all manner of ways cannot be denied by any that have skill' (Marcombe, 'Dean and chapter', 33). During the vacancy of the sees of York and Durham in 1576 he was invited by Leicester to come to court 'and he should not fail to have one of those places' and as late as 1579 it was suggested that he should be sent to France as ambassador. The fact that none of these proposals materialized illustrates that Whittingham was not a careerist—indeed, he professed himself too old, too infirm, and 'very unfit' for the see of Durham or York (Green, 26). It also indicates that he was content with the preferment he had, and that, possibly, the queen still nurtured suspicions about him.

Vestiarian controversy and the issue of conformity The deanery of Durham was a lucrative preferment which actually suited Whittingham's personality and abilities well. Owing to the patronage of Bishop James Pilkington there was already a growing band of protestant prebendaries at Durham, although some conservative elements still lingered in the cathedral, limiting the dean's freedom of action. In 1563 the new dean wrote to Cecil informing him of the good order that had been established: regular services, morning and afternoon sermons on Sundays, and 'a general fast with prayers and preaching of God's word' on Wednesdays and Fridays (BL, Lansdowne MS 7, fol. 24). Moreover, the dean was teaching in the cathedral grammar school on a daily basis and because he was 'skillfull in music' he was 'very careful to provide the best songs and anthems that could be got out of the Queen's chapel to furnish the choir with all' (Green, 23). The idyllic picture was dented somewhat by the storm over vestments which was brewing in the mid-1560s. This was an issue on which Whittingham felt strongly and in October 1565 he wrote to Leicester 'God forbid that we by wearing the Pope's attire as a thing but indifferent should seem thereby to consent to their blasphemies and heresies'. In March 1565 he joined in a plea to Matthew Parker, archbishop of Canterbury, asking to be excused conformity but, despite the support of Bishop Pilkington, in August 1566 he was summoned before the ecclesiastical commissioners at York with Robert Swift, diocesan chancellor, and John Pilkington, archdeacon of Durham. The accusation against Whittingham was that he had celebrated communion in the cathedral in 1563 without cope or surplice and that he usually wore a black gown and round cap. These accusations were not denied and though he was ordered to wear the correct apparel he prevaricated for a full year before he certified his conformity.

The incident was an important watershed for Whittingham because thereafter his conformity does not seem to have been in serious doubt. In 1571 he subscribed to Parker's articles and when three years later Thomas Wood was collecting information for *A Brief Discourse of the Troubles Begun at Frankfurt* (traditionally believed to have been the work of the dean), Whittingham was reluctant to be involved and Wood scolded him for his lack of zeal. Although the *Rites of Durham* maintain that the dean engaged in some acts of iconoclasm in the cathedral, 'for he could not abide any ancient monuments nor nothing that appertained to any godly religiousness or monastical life', this perspective seems to have been highly selective (J. T. Fowler, ed., *The Rites of Durham*, SurtS, 107, 1902, 60). The evidence for widespread puritan radicalism in the cathedral is therefore slight, with growing religious conservatism on the part of the dean after 1567.

Reforming the chapter Whittingham was especially active in administrative matters and initiated important changes which he believed to be in the best interests of the survival of the protestant establishment. He also had a comparatively large family to provide for. He prosecuted determined suits against Captain William Reed for certain lucrative tithes in Norhamshire and Islandshire; and against Walter Jobson for the rectory of Brantingham, Yorkshire. In 1565 he suspended an annual fee to Charles Neville, earl of Westmorland, and caused further dismay by claiming twenty years' arrears of rent from him. Certainly, special efforts were being made in the 1560s and 1570s to follow up rent arrears and in 1568–9 a new exchequer was built over the gatehouse as an improved accounting centre. Although like those of other ecclesiastical estates Durham Cathedral rents remained essentially static, Whittingham made efforts in the 1560s to revive customary services and payments in some chapter manors. But the most fundamental changes concerned tenure on the dean and chapter estates and encompassed the issues of corpes lands and tenant right.

Corpes lands were cathedral estates set aside for the maintenance of the dean and prebendaries. The problem was that in the 1560s most of these were in lease to the families and friends of former prebendaries, thus depriving the protestant chapter of any advantage from them. Finding a flaw in the old leases, Whittingham commenced a series of suits before the council of the north in 1565 to recover the corpes lands and was broadly successful, although he received criticism for leasing out the same land again without a proviso for the prebendary to vacate it when he left his stall. The issue of tenant right was even more intractable. The chapter was attempting to replace customary tenure on the bulk of its estates with 21-year renewable leaseholds, but not all of the tenants were happy to comply with this innovation. Consequently, Whittingham organized a series of 'lotteries' in which leases were divided up among members of the chapter. They were then in a position to sell the lease to the sitting tenant or to evict the tenant and take occupation of the property themselves. This latter approach was especially controversial, and in 1574 and 1576 the chapter tenants banded together to make complaints to the queen and privy council. Though their claim that they held by tenant right (a form of border military service) was not upheld, the privy council was anxious to preserve stability and in 1577 an order was made by Huntingdon to regulate future leasing.

This abrasive policy was not without its consequences. The Nevilles felt particularly wounded by the perceived slights of the 1560s and they were readily supported by other chapter tenants who felt similarly aggrieved. In 1568 Christopher Neville, uncle of the earl of Westmorland, wrote to Cecil saying he was 'sore offended' by the dealings of the Durham chapter and that 'their greedy covetousness is such that ten times so much as they have may not suffice themselves' (Marcombe, 'Rude and heady people', 129). During the northern uprising of 1569, which was motivated partly by such grievances, Whittingham acquitted himself well, using the military experience he had obtained at Le Havre. Before the outbreak he urged Bishop Pilkington to assemble the tenants of the bishopric and dean and chapter, armed, at Durham Castle 'which would be a means to awe the collecting rebels and be a stay and refuge for many gentlemen of the country to resort unto' (Green, 24). When this advice was ignored by the bishop he rode to Newcastle upon Tyne and warned the corporation of the danger of a surprise attack, instructing them how to put their defences in order. He finally left Durham on 10 November 1569, four days before the earls entered the city, 'secret intelligence being brought unto him if he went not away that night he could not pass southward for the bridges would be taken up the next night' (ibid., 25). By 15 November he was at York giving advice to the earl of Sussex and on 28 November he was seeking out intelligence around the Yorkshire borders. Finally he joined the royal army under the earl of Warwick and Lord Clinton and entered Durham with them in mid-December, only to discover that his house and books had been looted by the rebels.

Once the uprising had been finally quelled, underlying issues remained unresolved. In the early 1570s it was alleged that the dean and certain favoured prebendaries had made substantial profits from maladministration of the cathedral estates and Ralph Lever, a dissatisfied protestant prebendary, emerged as the leader of a group who felt themselves excluded, complaining against 'deceitful dealings' (BL, Lansdowne MS 902, fol. 329) and other matters 'tending to the discredit of our society' (Durham University Library, York book, fol. 41). Moreover, in 1574 Thomas Wood warned Whittingham that he had heard Warwick 'once or twice complain of your ingratitude', a veiled reference to the dean's refusal to reward courtiers with grants of church lands (Green, 25). The atmosphere of complaint and counter-complaint thus engendered brought the cathedral and its dean increasingly under the scrutiny of the queen and privy council.

Controversy and death Whittingham had successfully manipulated the chapter because of his good relationship with Bishop Pilkington and the support of three key prebendaries, Robert Swift and the bishop's brothers, John and Leonard Pilkington. In 1576, however, Bishop Pilkington died, precipitating a series of events that were to lead to the dean's downfall. Jurisdictional rivalry between York and Durham had been an issue since the middle ages, and following Pilkington's death a dispute developed between the chapters of York and Durham, both sees being vacant. Although the issue was taken before the court of delegates, it was abandoned when Edwin Sandys was elected to York and Richard Barnes to Durham in 1577.

Sandys, who suspected abuses in Durham Cathedral, persuaded Barnes to act as his surrogate during his first metropolitan visitation. Because this was at variance with traditional practice, which held that the diocese of Durham was exempt from visitation from York, Whittingham opposed the move and when Bishop Barnes arrived to visit the cathedral on 8 August 1577 the dean turned him away at the chapter house door 'taking hold of his gown, and so the business was concluded' (Green, 27). Once more the matter was taken before the court of delegates, but the case moved on slowly and was increasingly costly to maintain. More serious, the second dispute earned for Whittingham the unbending enmity of Sandys and Barnes. The dean's biographer alleged that a 'plot' was hatched in 1577 involving Sandys and Barnes, whose visitation had been frustrated; Ralph Lever, who had inner knowledge of chapter politics and deeply held grievances; and Sir Thomas Wilson, recently appointed secretary of state, whose hopes of the deanery of Durham had been thwarted by Whittingham in 1562. If Wilson could become dean he could work with Barnes and Lever to reform the cathedral and unlock the grants of church land that Pilkington and Whittingham had blocked.

On 10 April 1578 Barnes undertook an unopposed visitation of the cathedral in his position as bishop of Durham and declared himself to Burghley to be dissatisfied with what he found, referring to 'that Augiae Stabulum, the church of Durham …, whose stink is grievous in the nose

of God and of men and which to purge far passeth Hercules' labours' (BL, Lansdowne MS 25, fols. 161–2). Consequently, a commission to undertake a royal visitation of the cathedral was issued on 14 May 1578 with the instruction that it was to investigate all spiritual and temporal offences and letters of orders. The fact that the commission included Sandys and Barnes alongside the earl of Huntingdon, president of the council of the north, and Matthew Hutton, dean of York, did not augur well, since these two factions brought with them long-standing and bitter rivalries.

The commission met for a first session at Durham (23–6 October) and a second session at York (25–8 November) and considered thirty-five articles submitted by Ralph Lever. Though the bulk of these dealt with allegations of immorality, corruption, and mismanagement, virtually all of the discussion centred on the question of the dean's ordination—whether he was properly ordained by Genevan standards and whether Geneva orders were acceptable in the Church of England. Although Whittingham produced certificates from surviving members of the Geneva congregation, Sandys refused to be convinced that he was properly ordained according to the Geneva rite and this appears to have been the main issue at stake. The matter raised high emotions, not least between Sandys and Hutton, and it particularly dismayed Lever, who had hoped for an examination of the more general issues and was not himself dissatisfied with the dean's orders. When the last session broke up in disarray, Whittingham, sensing his advantage, travelled to London to try to get the commission revoked, only to encounter further disagreement on the privy council between Burghley and Wilson.

The long years of acrimony had taken their toll on the dean's health. After returning to Durham, he took to his bed, where he languished for nine weeks. Calling his servants before him, 'which were many', he exhorted them in the fear of God, summoning them one by one and telling them the faults he suspected them of 'and did admonish them to leave them' (BL, Add. MS 33207, fols. 5–8). He made his will on 18 April 1579, leaving legacies to his family, friends, servants, the cathedral staff, and the poor. He died at Durham on 10 June, and was buried in the cathedral. During his time as dean he had bought the manor of Balk, north Yorkshire, and part of the rectory of Mitford, Northumberland, and his personal property (reflected in the will of his widow, who died in 1590) included virginals and a quantity of armour. He was survived by six children: Timothy, Sarah, Deborah, Judith, Elizabeth, and Daniel (b. 1571). Timothy, knighted in 1604 and MP for Thirsk in 1604 and 1611, purchased the Durham manor of Holmside, where he established a landed family which endured for a hundred years.

Whittingham's biography, written by an anonymous author about 1603, paints a picture of a man who was very much a part of the European scene of his day and who brought the ideals of Calvinism and the Renaissance to the far north of England. Less committed sources complained consistently about his favouritism and dubious financial dealings. The fact that he encountered considerable opposition as dean was partly due to the conservatism of the region and partly to Whittingham's unbending conviction of his righteousness, which caused him to press on when more circumspect men might have compromised. DAVID MARCOMBE

Sources Foster, *Alum. Oxon.* · C. H. Garrett, *The Marian exiles: a study in the origins of Elizabethan puritanism* (1938) · A. M. E. Green, ed., 'Life of Mr William Whittingham, dean of Durham', *Camden miscellany, VI*, CS, 104 (1871) · S. L. Greenslade, 'William Whittingham, dean of Durham, 1524–1579', *Durham University Journal*, 39 (Dec 1946) · D. Marcombe, 'The dean and chapter of Durham, 1558–1603', PhD diss., U. Durham, 1973 · D. Marcombe, 'A rude and heady people: the local community and the rebellion of the northern earls', *The last principality: politics, religion and society in the bishopric of Durham, 1494–1660*, ed. D. Marcombe (1987) · [W. Greenwell], ed., *Wills and inventories from the registry at Durham*, 2, SurtS, 38 (1860) · *APC, 1571–5, 1577–8* · York book; dean and chapter registers A, B, and C, U. Durham L. · *CSP for., 1562–3* · high commission act books, 3, 4, Borth. Inst. · P. Collinson, *Letters of Thomas Wood, Puritan*, Institute of Historical Research, special supplement, 5 (1960) · J. Strype, *The life and acts of Matthew Parker*, new edn, 3 vols. (1821), vol. 3, pp. 76–84 · *CPR, 1560–63*, 493 · J. Strype, *Annals of the Reformation and establishment of religion … during Queen Elizabeth's happy reign*, new edn, 1/2 (1824) · P. Collinson, 'The authorship of "A brieff discours off the troubles begonne at Franckford"', *Journal of Ecclesiastical History*, 9 (1958), 188–208 · PRO, SP 12/48/58

Whittingham, William (1740/41–1797), bookseller and printer, details of whose family and upbringing are unknown, married in 1759 the widow of Joseph Lee, bookseller, and succeeded to his business in the High Street, King's Lynn (*Norwich Mercury*, 14 Feb 1761). In 1766 Whittingham purchased the library of the antiquary Charles Parkin, including Parkin's manuscript continuation of Francis Blomefield's *History of Norfolk*. He was persuaded to publish this work by the antiquary Thomas Martin; John Fenn and Antony Norris helped prepare it for the press. Whittingham acquired printing equipment and issued proposals in February 1768, envisaging 200 folio pages to complete Blomefield's third volume, and a further 1000-page volume, for 2 guineas. The first part was published in November 1769, with the remainder appearing over the next six years. However, due to inexperience he had underestimated the size of Parkin's manuscript, and in 1773 was forced to ask subscribers for an additional guinea for a fifth volume. Also, the manuscript for Great Yarmouth was missing and Whittingham therefore included an abridged version of Swinden's *History of Great Yarmouth* (without acknowledgement). This resulted in a retaliatory piracy of Blomefield's and Parkin's *History*, by Swinden's printer John Crouse and the Norwich bookseller Martin Booth, which was published from 1777 to 1781. Whittingham responded by advertising a new history of Norfolk in 1778, but abandoned it after the first volume (covering Norwich) due to a lack of public interest.

Between 1769 and 1795 Whittingham issued a number of sale catalogues of libraries and printed that of Thomas Martin's collections in 1772, but was not involved in their sale. He also published those parts of the Norfolk history for Freebridge (King's Lynn) and Great Yarmouth as separate works in 1772 and 1776, and began reprinting county

histories from the previous century, beginning in October 1775 with Philipot's *Villare Cantianum*. Burton's *Description of Leicestershire* was published in 1777, claiming to be enlarged and corrected, 'but the editorial work was performed in a very slovenly manner' ('Burton, William', *DNB*). An attempt in November 1777 to reprint Thoroton's *Antiquities of Nottinghamshire* was aborted due to local competition. In 1783 Whittingham reissued the unsold sheets of the first volume of his aborted history of Norfolk, as Parkin's *History of Norwich*, although this author had had no part in it.

Whittingham died in King's Lynn on 29 April 1797, aged fifty-six, having printed more than forty works, including poetry, plays, and reports by engineers regarding the draining of the fens. He was also a property owner in the town. A sale of his effects including two presses was advertised in the *Norfolk Chronicle* (27 May 1797), but the business was continued by his son William and grandson Charles until the mid-nineteenth century. Although described as 'an eminent printer and bookseller' (Chambers, 461), Whittingham is noteworthy neither for the number nor quality of his publications. He was, however, one of the first English provincial publishers to develop an identifiable specialization—the printing of topographical histories. Yet his policy of reprinting existing works did not please some contemporary historians. According to Richard Gough, they were 'paltry re-publications' (Nichols, *Lit. anecdotes*, 6.284) and 'to the impediment … or reproach of those who have it in their power to give the world much better and newer ones' (Gough). DAVID STOKER

Sources D. Stoker, 'Mr Parkin's magpie, the other Mr Whittingham, and the fate of Great Yarmouth', *The Library*, 6th ser., 12 (1990), 121–31 · D. Stoker, 'The early booksellers and printers of King's Lynn', *Studies in the provincial book trade of England, Scotland, and Wales before 1900*, papers presented to the British Book Trade Index Seventh Annual Seminar (1989) · R. G. [R. Gough], *British topography*, [new edn], 1 (1780), x · [J. Chambers], *A general history of the county of Norfolk*, 2 vols. (1829), 1157 · D. Stoker, 'The ill-gotten library of "Honest Tom" Martin', *Property of a gentleman: the formation, organisation and dispersal of the private library, 1620–1920*, St Paul's Bibliographies (1991), 90–112 · Nichols, *Lit. anecdotes*, 3.689; 6.284 · H. R. Plomer and others, *A dictionary of the printers and booksellers who were at work in England, Scotland, and Ireland from 1726 to 1775* (1932); repr. (1968), 20 · J. Feather, *The provincial book trade in eighteenth-century England* (1985), 91 · M. W. Barley and K. S. S. Train, 'Robert Thoroton', *English county historians*, ed. J. Simmons (1978), 22–43 · *Norwich Mercury* (14 Feb 1761)
Archives Norfolk RO, Frere and Norfolk and Norwich Archaeological Society deposits, letters, prospectuses, etc.
Wealth at death comfortable: will, PRO, PROB 11/1293/460

Whittington, Richard [Dick] (*c*.1350–1423), merchant and mayor of London, was born at Pauntley, Gloucestershire, the third son of Sir William Whittington (*d*. 1358), a lesser landowner of Gloucestershire, and his wife, Joan Maunsell. He was apprenticed to a London mercer and was sufficiently established in London by 1379 to contribute 5 marks towards a civic gift to the nobles of the realm. At this date a mercer of London dealt in silk, linen, fustian, worsted, and luxury small goods, and the wealthiest of the trade expected to participate in the export of English wool, woollen cloth, and worsted, and to import the other merceries.

As a mercer Whittington's fortune was based in the first place on his skills as a mercer. He had become a major supplier of mercery to the royal court before 1388, when he sold goods worth nearly £2000 to Robert de Vere, favourite of Richard II; other customers included John of Gaunt, the earl of Derby (the future Henry IV), and the Staffords; from at least 1389 he was supplying Richard II, sales of nearly £3500 being made between 1392 and 1394. It is likely that Richard II and his uncle, Thomas of Woodstock, another lover of the luxuries of rank, were Whittington's most diligent and appreciative customers and 'promoters', as they were described in the foundation statutes of Whittington's college. This pattern continued under the succeeding dynasty: he supplied mercery to Henry IV's great wardrobe and for the marriages of Henry IV's daughters, Blanche and Philippa. In the last decade of Whittington's life such sales were less, and he took fewer apprentices, but he continued to import linens and deal in mercery.

Profits in London on imported mercery could be high but it is probable, although there is no precise evidence, that Whittington also engaged in trade with Italy and in the rapidly expanding export of English woollen cloth; he is known to have had close connections with Coventry and these may have derived from the cloth trade. His involvement in the wool trade seems to have occurred only after the accession of Henry IV, when he had to recoup royal debts from the wool subsidies. He was a large, if not remarkable, exporter between 1404 and 1416, and served as a collector of the wool subsidies in London from 1401 to 1403 and from 1407 to 1410. He also acted as mayor of the staple of Westminster from 3 July 1405 until his death (although it is not certain whether he was in office continuously) and of the Calais staple from at least 1406 to 1413.

As a moneylender Whittington's wealth from trade, and his contacts with the great who were his customers, were the basis of his moneylending career. From 1388 he is known to have made nearly sixty loans to the crown, major loans occurring from 1397; his loans to Henry IV and Henry V were larger than any made to Richard II, and several were made in conjunction with others, such as the grocer, Thomas Knolles (1402), or a group of Calais merchants (1406–7); he also lent to private individuals like Sir Simon Burley and John Beaufort, earl of Somerset. His capacity to lend substantial sums consistently over a long period, especially from 1400 to 1423, shows his willingness to use his capital rather than tie it up in land; this willingness may have resulted from his lack of children, from a dislike of excessive personal display, or from a love of the mechanics of such loans and of the society of the often very highly placed persons who sought money from him. His gains would have come in the form of financial profits, together with access to the royal ear and a position of influence. He is unlikely ever to have engaged in usury in the sense deplored by the church; Whittington himself sat as judge in usury trials in London in 1421, a sure sign

that he was regarded as above suspicion. This capacity to avoid almost all criticism suggests a character of austere correctness coupled with an ability to inspire trust. His position as a royal financier was at times of great service to the city as well as to his own purse and the crown.

Civic career Whittington's civic career followed the usual pattern: he had become a common councilman for Coleman Street ward by 31 July 1384, and held this office intermittently until 12 March 1393 when he was elected alderman of Broad Street ward; he moved to the ward of Lime Street in June or July 1397 and remained there until his death. In June 1392 he was one of the twenty-four citizens 'of the second rank of wealth in the city' (*Chronicon Henrici Knighton*, 2.319) summoned to Nottingham by the king to answer charges, with the mayor and aldermen, of misgovernment—an inquiry which allowed the king to seize the city into his own lands. On 21 September 1393 Whittington was elected sheriff, and at midsummer 1395 he was elected a warden of the Mercers' Company for the first time. Meanwhile he was selling mercery to Richard II and acquiring the king's trust. This trust showed itself when the mayor, Adam Bamme, died in office on 6 June 1397 and Whittington was appointed to the vacancy two days later by Richard II at his most high-handed. Within days Whittington had negotiated that the city might purchase its full liberties from the king for £10,000; his fellow citizens showed their gratitude when they elected him mayor on the following 13 October for a complete term. Despite his good relations with Richard II, Whittington was in April 1398 one of those who had to seal blank charters placing themselves and their goods at the king's pleasure. His role during the usurpation of Henry IV is unknown: however personally loyal to Richard he may have been, he acquiesced in the change, and his wealth and status ensured that the new king had as much need of him as had his predecessor; a close associate and fellow mercer, John Shadworth, had suffered imprisonment at Richard's hands and probably took a more active part in the usurpation. Significantly both men sat on the first council of Henry IV from 1 November 1399 to 18 July 1400.

The other details of Whittington's civic career hardly match the anxieties and political manoeuvring of the 1390s. He was warden of the Mercers' Company again in 1401–2 and 1408–9. His first mayoralty had seen the organization of Blackwell Hall as the sole place where non-citizens and aliens could buy and sell cloth. His second full term as mayor, from 13 October 1406, was distinguished by the decision to make customary the mass that had been held before his election. He served for the only time as MP for the city in 1416, a year when the city was quiet and when he made no loan to the crown. On 13 October 1419, when he was certainly in his sixties, he was elected mayor for the third time by his fellow citizens. His attempt to regulate the price of ale and standardize its measures during this term provoked an acrimonious dispute with the Brewers' Company which continued for several years, Whittington winning his point against more temperate advice. Later the brewers were placated by the diplomacy of John Carpenter, common clerk of the city and Whittington's executor. The dispute reveals not only how greatly the old man was respected but also how severe, even embarrassing, his rectitude could be in matters of trade. Only for the last years of his civic career can some assessment be made of his day-to-day involvement: between 1416 and his death in 1423 he attended 50 per cent of meetings of the court of aldermen and all but two of its meetings during his mayoralty year of 1419–20.

Concomitants of Whittington's success and ability were his appointments to commissions and other civic duties: he had been a custodian of the goods of the politically exiled mercer, John More, in 1384; in 1397 as mayor and escheator he had the task of seizing the forfeited goods of Thomas of Woodstock, duke of Gloucester, his old 'promoter', in London; he sat on fifteen commissions of oyer and terminer between 1401 and 1418; he was appointed to supervise the collection of papal revenues in England in 1409; he and Thomas Knolles drew up the list of London citizens liable to pay a subsidy in 1412; between 1413 and 1421 he was one of the supervisors and accountants of the renewed work on the nave of Westminster Abbey begun by Richard II, to which he himself had contributed in 1401/2; and in 1414 and 1418 he was on commissions to seek out Lollards and their goods.

Marriage and estate Whittington's preference for liquid capital, borne out by his failure to acquire a large landed estate, may have been connected with the fact that he had no children. He married Alice, daughter of Sir Ivo Fitzwarin (d. 1412), a Dorset landowner, possibly as late as 1402. Alice was seriously ill by October 1410, when Whittington was licensed to have a Jewish doctor attend her, and she probably died the following 30 or 31 July (the date of her obit). At his death Whittington had few holdings outside the city. The manor of Over Lypiatt, Gloucestershire, was acquired from his maternal uncle, Philip Maunsell, in 1395, in lieu of a debt of £500; it was successfully claimed by his brother, Robert, as a deathbed bequest. He also held lands in Dorset during the life of his father-in-law, possibly in repayment of loans. His most notable purchase in the city was his great house in the Royal, next to the church of St Michael Paternoster Royal, made in February 1402, the possible date of his marriage. His rebuilding of this church was begun in 1409 to provide a suitable resting place for himself and his wife; he undoubtedly planned to make the church collegiate and establish an almshouse there, projects completed by his executors. This almshouse still survives as Whittington College, administered by the Mercers' Company.

Philanthropy Whittington gave to good works throughout his life and a few details are known: a library at the London Greyfriars; Rochester Bridge; a longhouse at St Martin Vintry (public lavatories and almshouse); and a refuge for unmarried mothers at St Thomas's Hospital, Southwark. By 5 September 1421, when he drew up his will, he had decided to leave his entire fortune to charity. His will was largely impersonal, making bequests to the standard charities, and was designed to control his executors but not trammel them. Its substance was that all the estate was to be realized in cash and spent on good works, a sum estimated as in the region of £7000. Until his death on 23 or 24 March 1423 (the date of his obit) major projects must have been discussed with his executors: completing the college of priests and almshouse at St Michael Paternoster Royal; rebuilding Newgate prison, to which money was also left in his will for distribution among the prisoners; rebuilding the south gate of St Bartholomew's Hospital; establishing a library at Guildhall; and installing public fountains in the city.

Whittington's personal interests and friends are difficult to identify. His patronage of two libraries and the known interest of John Carpenter, his chief executor, in education, as well as the association of John Colop, one of those who distributed Whittington's estate in alms, with the dissemination of pious books now known as 'common profit books', argue that Whittington, too, wished to foster the religious knowledge of both clergy and laity. Other important friends were John White, the master of St Bartholomew's Hospital and before that rector of St Michael Paternoster Royal, and John Coventry, mercer, both his executors; Richard Clifford, keeper of the great wardrobe during the period of Whittington's large sales to Richard II, and later bishop of London (1407–21), one of the few men for whom Whittington acted as executor and another promoter of clerical education; and the unknown Roger, once rector of St Margaret, Lothbury, for whom Whittington arranged prayers in his will. Most enigmatic are his relationships with Richard II and Thomas of Woodstock, who with their wives, Anne of Bohemia and Eleanor de Bohun, were to be prayed for at Whittington's foundations in perpetuity.

The legend of Dick Whittington It is one of the curiosities of history that this austerely noble figure should have become the subject of nursery rhymes and Christmas pantomimes. By the early seventeenth century the story was being circulated how Whittington, an orphan from the west country, had travelled to London, where he became a scullion in the kitchen of the wealthy merchant Hugh Fitzwarren (a figure unrepresented in fifteenth-century records); there his master's daughter, Alice, befriended him against an overbearing cook. Like all Fitzwarren's servants he was allowed to contribute to the freight of his master's trading ship, the Unicorn, but the only thing he could offer was his cat, for which he had paid just 1d. When the vessel touched on the coast of north Africa, the king there, driven to distraction by the rats and mice which had overrun his palace, bought the cat for ten times more than the price of the whole of the rest of the ship's cargo. Back in London Whittington had meanwhile despaired of fame and fortune, and set out to leave the city, only to be recalled by the chime of Bow bells, which seemed to be pealing to the words 'Turn again, Whittington, lord mayor of London.' He duly turned, and the return of the Unicorn, bearing the money from the sale of his cat, allowed Whittington to marry his master's daughter and rise to be lord mayor. The elements of folklore discernible in this story—common in north and south Europe and even in Persia—may have flourished all the more strongly because its hero's own personality had been obscured by all the factual evidence for his benefactions. The impression of the historical Whittington as a remote, rather isolated, figure may indeed be overstated by the lack of personal records. What has survived, to be cherished and turned into a legend after his death, is the sense of civic and humanitarian duty which made him leave his personal fortune to the poor.

ANNE F. SUTTON

Sources C. M. Barron, 'Richard Whittington: the man behind the myth', *Studies in London history presented to Philip Edmund Jones*, ed. A. E. J. Hollaender and W. Kellaway (1969), 197–248 • J. Imray, *The charity of Richard Whittington: a history of the trust administered by the Mercers' Company, 1424–1966* (1968), chaps. 1–2, appx 1 • E. F. Jacob, ed., *The register of Henry Chichele, archbishop of Canterbury, 1414–1443*, 2, CYS, 42 (1937), 240–44 • HoP, *Commons, 1386–1421* • M. Sargent, 'Walter Hilton's *Scale of perfection*: the London manuscript group reconsidered', *Medium Aevum*, 52 (1983), 189–216, esp. 205–6 • P. E. Jones, 'Whittington's longhouse', *London Topographical Record*, 23 (1974), 27–34 • C. M. Barron, 'The quarrel of Richard II with London, 1392–7', *The reign of Richard II: essays in honour of May McKisack*, ed. F. R. H. Du Boulay and C. M. Barron (1971), 173–201 • C. M. Barron, 'The tyranny of Richard II', *BIHR*, 41 (1968), 1–18, esp. 5–6, 10–14 • A. Goodman, 'The character of Thomas Woodstock', *The loyal conspiracy: the lords appellant under Richard II* (1971), 74–86 • A. F. Sutton, *The Mercers' Company's first charter, 1394* (1994) • W. Scase, 'Reginald Pecock, John Carpenter and John Colop's "common-profit" books: aspects of book ownership and circulation in fifteenth-century London', *Medium Aevum*, 61 (1992), 261–74 • *Chronicon Henrici Knighton, vel Cnitthon, monachi Leycestrensis*, ed. J. R. Lumby, 2 vols., Rolls Series, 92 (1889–95) • W. A. Clouston, *Popular tales and fictions* (1887)

Archives Mercers' Hall, estate papers, property deeds, almshouse ordinances

Likenesses W. Abell, grisaille painting, *c.*1445–1450, Mercers' Company, London, Whittington estate archives, almshouse ordinances • R. Elstrack, line engraving (after unknown artist), BM, NPG

Wealth at death approx. £7000: Imray, *The charity*, 23–4

Whittington, Robert (*c.*1480–1553?), schoolmaster and grammarian, described himself as a man of Lichfield, Staffordshire, and was probably born in or near the city; his surname is that of an adjoining village. He was a pupil of the grammarian John Stanbridge, perhaps at Lichfield Cathedral school, and is plausibly identical with the Robert Whittington ordained acolyte in Lichfield Cathedral in 1496, and subdeacon there in 1503, to an ordination title provided by Ranton Priory, Staffordshire. He probably became a priest in 1504. Meanwhile, about 1499 he began to study rhetoric and in 1501 to teach as a schoolmaster. These facts emerged when, in 1513, he petitioned the University of Oxford to allow him to be laureated as a rhetorician and to wear silk in his hood, a request granted on condition that he composed one hundred verses of poetry. As Whittington adduced only his rhetorical study and teaching to support his application, it looks as if he had not undertaken significant studies at a university, and there are no grounds for Anthony Wood's assertion that he was taught by Stanbridge at Magdalen College School, Oxford, in the early 1490s.

During the 1510s Whittington appears to have taught in London, while striving to gain the attention of important

people. About 1519 he presented Cardinal Wolsey with a manuscript (Bodl. Oxf., MS Bodley 523) containing a treatise in verse, 'De difficultate justiciae servandae in reipublicae administratione', and a prose 'Panegyricus de quattuor virtutibus cardineis', with a dedication requesting Wolsey's patronage. In the same year he published *Libellus epigrammaton*, an anthology of poems addressed to Henry VIII, Wolsey, Thomas More, and John Skelton. His *Vulgaria*, published in 1520, pays compliments to the late king, Henry VII, to Thomas Linacre, and to More himself, who is famously referred to as 'a man for all seasons'. Whittington's efforts succeeded by 1523, at the latest, when he enjoyed the favour of Henry VIII. It is likely that he succeeded Francis Philip in that year as schoolmaster to the henchmen, the noble youths of the royal household, and he certainly held this appointment from Michaelmas 1528 until Christmas 1538. He also occupied a succession of benefices, including the vicarage of Mancetter, Warwickshire, from 1514 until about the 1520s; the rectory of Bedhampton, Hampshire, from an unknown date to 1523; and the rectory of Drayton Parslow, Buckinghamshire, from 1523. The latter two were both in the gift of the king. He was a canon and prebendary of the collegiate church of Warwick from at least 1535 until its dissolution in 1544, and in 1538 Henry VIII presented him to the valuable rectory of Stoke-on-Trent, enabling him to relinquish his household post. His career was a prosperous one by the standards of most early Tudor schoolmasters. In the 1520s his annual gross income was over £30, including £20 as schoolmaster of the henchmen, and this rose to more than £60 after 1538, Stoke-on-Trent being worth some £40.

Whittington was famous in his day as the author of elementary Latin school books. The list (with first known dates of printing) includes *De nominum generibus* (1511), *Declinationes nominum* (*c.*1511), *De heteroclitis nominibus* (*c.*1511), *Syntaxis* (2nd edn, 1512), *De syllabarum quantitate* (2nd edn, *c.*1512), *De octo partibus orationis* (*c.*1514), *De synonymis* together with *De magistratibus veterum Romanorum* (1515), *Vulgaria* (English and Latin sentences for translation, 1520), and *Verborum preterita et supina* (1521). He also edited John Stanbridge's *Accidence* (*c.*1515). The earliest of these works seems to go back to at least 1510, since *Syntaxis* includes a dedication to Stanbridge (who died in that year) and a complimentary Latin poem by him. Each title dealt with a different aspect of grammar, and they could be bought individually and cheaply; as such they were widely sold and frequently republished up to the early 1530s. Their author seems to have had a high opinion of his own abilities. When William Horman published another large *Vulgaria* in 1519, with commendatory verses by his friend William Lily, high master of St Paul's School, London, Whittington posted verses on the door of Lily's school, ridiculing the size and price of Horman's volume and Lily's judgement in endorsing it. This led to the so-called 'grammarians' war', in which Lily and Horman published a two-part attack on Whittington, called *Antibossicon* (1521), so named because it identified him with the bear-shaped water-tap in Billingsgate, London, built by his namesake Sir Richard Whittington. They criticized Whittington's abilities as a poet and grammarian, and mocked his descriptions of himself, in his books, as 'of Lichfield, master of grammar, and chief poet of England (*prothovates Anglie*), laureated in the most flourishing academy of Oxford'. Whittington rejoined with a tract of his own against Lily, called *Antilycon* ('Against the wolf'), and the 1521 edition of his *De nominum generibus* contains further attacks and a motto promising that 'he will humiliate the slanderer'.

Whittington's grammars continued to be printed during the 1520s, usually by Wynkyn de Worde but briefly also by Richard Pynson. About 1529, however, Whittington seems to have moved his custom to Peter Treveris, who issued his works for the next two years. This arrangement was not satisfactory, and by 1533 Whittington had returned to Worde, his school books now including Latin verses attacking Treveris. Worde, however, ceased to issue Whittington's works after 1534, because of difficulty with the author or falling demand, and Whittington turned his attention to translation from Latin into English. He brought out versions of Erasmus's *De civilitate morum puerilium* (1532), three works by Cicero (*De officinis*, 1534; *Paradoxa*, c.1534; and *De senectute*, c.1535), and three allegedly by Seneca (*The Forme and Rule of Honest Lyvynge*, 1546; *The Myrrour or Glasse of Maners*, 1547; and *De remediis fortuitorum*, 1547), the *Forme* and *Myrrour* being correctly by Martin of Braga. His two remaining benefices of Drayton Parslow and Stoke-on-Trent were both filled by new incumbents in the autumn of 1553, and, though the appointments do not mention his previous tenure, it is likely that he died in possession of them in the summer of that year. NICHOLAS ORME

Sources Emden, *Oxf.*, vol. 3 · STC, 1475–1640, nos. 25443.2–579 · *The Vulgaria of John Stanbridge and the Vulgaria of Robert Whittinton*, ed. B. White, EETS, old ser., 187 (1932) · Bodl. Oxf., MS Bodley 523 · *The register of John Morton, archbishop of Canterbury, 1486–1500*, ed. C. Harper-Bill, 2, CYS, 78 (1991), 116 · Lichfield RO, B/A/1/14ii, reg. Blyth, fol. 1v

Whittle, Anne (c.1532–1612). *See under* Pendle witches (*act.* 1612).

Whittle, Edward [Ned] (1822/3–1871), trade unionist, who was probably born in Blackburn, is a figure about whose origins and early life nothing is known. However, he was unusually literate (and numerate) for a working man of his generation. The first record of Whittle's activities dates from October 1853, at an early stage in the great Preston strike, when he was described at a mass meeting of cotton operatives as the author of the price list which set piece-rates for the weavers of Blackburn. These lists, invariably drawn up after negotiations between representatives of trade unions and employers' associations, regulated the payment of power-loom weavers in the Lancashire cotton industry for most of the next hundred years. Informed outside observers like Sidney and Beatrice Webb depicted them as enormously detailed and incredibly complicated, requiring administrators of great arithmetical ability and immense (if extremely narrow) specialized knowledge, along with a firm commitment to

'mature' industrial relations and the peaceful resolution of conflict.

Whittle was the first in a long line of trade union 'civil servants' in this mould, although the unions with which he was involved in the 1850s were sporadic and short-lived; by the time stable organizations began to emerge, Whittle's trade union activities were over. He was noted as a 'sound, profound and wonderfully proficient mathematician, who contributed frequently to periodicals and magazines and in their pages proposed the solution of many difficult and interesting problems' (Turner, 132).

Unlike the fiery orator Mortimer Grimshaw, Whittle acted in the 1853–4 Preston strike as a conciliator, who did his best to calm passions and avoid public disorder. He resisted the involvement in the strike of outside activists from the Chartist movement, steadfastly opposing Ernest Jones and his short-lived Labour parliament and affirming from the chair of at least one public meeting his hope that peace and concord would soon bind together all the classes. Whittle was a prominent member of the workers' deputation to Lord Palmerston in March 1854 which unsuccessfully sought the home secretary's mediation in the strike. At the end of the Preston dispute, two months later, Whittle used his influence to discourage further strikes among the Blackburn weavers, whose union secretary he had become.

Over the next few years the Blackburn Standard Wage List, for which Whittle was chiefly responsible, became the envy of weavers in other towns. Controversy surrounded his part in a wage dispute at Great Harwood in 1858. Described as 'a bit of a character, [who] liked his drink and had even wrestled with a couple of employers involved in the struggle' (Bullen, 6), Whittle settled the strike without reference to the membership and on terms unacceptable to many of them. A split ensued, with Whittle retaining control of the Blackburn organization and weavers in other towns forming a breakaway union.

Details of Whittle's later years are sparse. He became a schoolmaster for a while and then a mill manager, possibly for the well-known Blackburn manufacturer William Hornby, whose tory politics Whittle had publicly endorsed while still a union official. By the time of his death, at the age of only forty-eight, in Blackburn on 10 September 1871, he was no longer active in the affairs of the labour movement. On his death certificate Whittle was described as a schoolmaster. J. E. KING

Sources H. I. Dutton and J. E. King, *Ten per cent and no surrender* (1981) · A. Bullen, *The Lancashire Weavers Union* (1984) · H. A. Turner, *Trade union growth, structure, and policy: a comparative study of the cotton unions* (1962) · E. Hopwood, *History of the Lancashire cotton industry and the Amalgamated Weavers Association* (1969) · *Blackburn Times* (16 Sept 1871) · d. cert.

Whittle, Sir Frank (1907–1996), aeronautical engineer and inventor of the jet engine, was born on 1 June 1907 at 72 Newcombe Road, Earlsdon, Coventry, the eldest of the three children of Moses Whittle (1882–1965), engineer and inventor, and his wife, Sara Alice, *née* Garlick (1882–1976). Both his parents had working-class backgrounds in the cotton industry of Lancashire, but his father had moved to

Sir Frank Whittle (1907–1996), by Edward Irvine Halliday, 1960

Coventry where he expected to find greater scope for his inventive gifts. In 1916 Moses Whittle bought a small engineering business in Leamington Spa, and the young Frank learned the rudiments of engineering manufacture by working in the factory when he was ten years old. At eleven he won a scholarship to Leamington College. After a bad start he won another scholarship. Rather than doing homework he pored over texts on the theory of flight and practical flying in the public library. At the third attempt he was accepted by the Royal Air Force, and in September 1923 entered the apprentice wing of the RAF College, Cranwell. So outstanding was his ability that he was selected as one of the 1 per cent promoted to the officer training course. For his obligatory thesis at the end of the course, Whittle chose 'Future developments in aircraft design', concluding that for high speed and long range it would be necessary to fly very high. He was thinking of 500 m.p.h., when the top speed of RAF fighters was only about 150 m.p.h. He concluded that a new type of power plant would be required and examined rocket propulsion and a gas turbine driving a propeller, but the scheme of a gas turbine providing jet propulsion directly occurred to him only later.

Whittle passed out second from Cranwell in July 1928 and was posted to 111 fighter squadron at Hornchurch. The following year he was attached to the Central Flying School at Wittering, as a pupil on the flying instructor's course. There he had the idea of a gas turbine producing a propelling jet directly, which was far superior to any of his earlier proposals. One of the Central Flying School instructors, Flying Officer W. E. P. (Pat) Johnson, had trained as a patent agent and helped Whittle to draft a patent, for which the provisional specification was published on 16 January 1930. The Air Ministry showed no interest in this, and it was not placed on the secret list. With a view to exploiting his invention Whittle visited the British Thomson-Houston (BT-H) turbine factory, Armstrong Siddeley, and the engine division of the Bristol Aeroplane Company. On grounds of cost and the absence of suitable materials, all three companies declined to have any part in the development of Whittle's ideas, so he continued his service career, which included test-pilot duties and stunt-flying demonstrations at the RAF's annual Hendon air displays.

In 1932 Whittle was posted to the RAF officers' engineering course at Henlow, where he obtained outstanding results. This led him to apply to the Air Ministry to be sent to Cambridge University to take the mechanical sciences tripos. He was successful and was posted to Cambridge in July 1934. He rented a small house in Trumpington where he established his family, which now consisted of his wife, Dorothy Mary, *née* Lee (1904–1996), an artist, whom he had married in 1930, and two small sons. He kept up his flying through the Cambridge University air squadron, and it was there that he received a letter from Rolf Dudley-Williams, who had been a fellow cadet at Cranwell and had retained his interest in Whittle's turbo jet idea. Williams said that he and his partner, J. C. B. Tinling, thought that they might have a source of funding for developing Whittle's jet engine. When they met at Whittle's Trumpington house, it transpired that the proposed backer was the investment bank O. T. Falk & Partners, who had enlisted M. L. Bramson as a consultant. After meetings with Whittle, Bramson wrote a report which fully vindicated Whittle's proposals. Falk & Partners agreed to advance £2000 for the setting up of a company to be called Power Jets Ltd, to develop the Whittle jet engine. Without waiting for the incorporation of the company, Falks placed a contract with the BT-H Company in Rugby for the design drawings of an experimental engine to Whittle's requirements. The engine was to power a small 500 m.p.h. mailplane and was to consist of a single-stage centrifugal compressor driven by a single-stage turbine at up to 17,750 r.p.m. This concept was far in advance of anything that had been proposed previously.

A tentative assembly drawing of the engine was produced by BT-H in March 1936. Whittle was very dissatisfied with this, but by the end of the month he had completed a revised drawing which he sent to BT-H, where work on the detailed drawings of the prototype engine started in April 1936. Meanwhile, in Cambridge, Whittle's tripos examinations were looming very near. Work on the engine had seriously interfered with his studies, but for five weeks he concentrated entirely on preparation for the tripos, leaving Bramson to deputize for him. Rather to his surprise, he obtained first-class honours. This led his tutor to bring Whittle's achievement to the notice of the director of education of the Air Ministry, who obtained permission for

Whittle to do a postgraduate year on research work, so that he was able to devote the greater part of his time to work on the engine.

The first test run of Whittle's prototype engine took place in the gallery of the BT-H turbine factory on 12 April 1937, with Whittle at the controls. After a normal light-up of the combustion chamber, there was a sudden acceleration from 2500 r.p.m. to about 8000 r.p.m., after which the speed began to drop. The following day a second run-away took place and the cause was identified as fuel leakage from the main burner whenever the fuel pump was run. The fault was rectified, but the BT-H management decided that Whittle's operations could not continue in the main turbine shop. Instead they offered him their disused foundry at Ladywood works, Lutterworth, some 7 miles from Rugby. The site had lain empty for some time and contained a vacant plot on which test houses and engine assembly bays were subsequently built.

Power Jets faced a financial crisis in the summer of 1937. The chairman of the Aeronautical Research Committee had commented favourably on Whittle's work, leading the Air Ministry to propose a contract worth £10,000 for further development. This was reduced to £5000 by officials and was signed only the following March. BT-H also invested £2500 in January 1938. Meanwhile Whittle's postgraduate year at Cambridge expired in the summer of 1937, but he was then transferred to the special duty list of the RAF to continue work on the engine full time. He moved his family to Rugby early in October, which made his life very much easier owing to the great reduction in travelling time. In December 1937 he was promoted to squadron leader, notwithstanding his transfer to the special duty list. Running of the engine at Lutterworth was resumed on 29 April 1938 and on 6 May a run of 1 hr 45 min. was achieved, although it was terminated by a disastrous turbine failure at 13,000 r.p.m. Thrust readings showed that 480 lb was being developed at 13,000 r.p.m. compared with an expected 550 lb. The engine was rebuilt with ten separate combustion chambers instead of the single chamber hitherto used, and was ready for test running in the autumn of 1938.

A critical stage in the development was reached on 30 June 1939 when the director of scientific research of the Air Ministry visited Lutterworth and witnessed a test run of 28 minutes' duration up to a maximum speed of 16,000 r.p.m. Confidence in the development had increased to the point where, two weeks later, Power Jets received a contract for a flight engine and BT-H accepted a subcontract for its manufacture. Simultaneously a contract for an experimental aeroplane, the E28/39, was placed with the Gloster Aircraft Company. The design of the flight engine was carried out by BT-H and was based on the ten combustion chamber layout. Initially a vaporizer combustion system was used, but this proved to be temperamental and was replaced by a pressure-jet system proposed by I. Lubbock of the Shell Petroleum Company. The final design was developed at Power Jets by the team of young engineers recruited by Whittle.

During the manufacture of the W1 engine a number of non-airworthy components had been produced and it was decided to assemble these into a second engine known as the W1X. Much valuable test running was done on this engine in the new test houses at Lutterworth, and at the end of March 1941 the engine was dispatched to the Gloster Aircraft Company for installation in the E28/39 airframe for taxiing trials. Installation was completed on 7 April 1941 and the engine was given its first run in the aircraft. Whittle made some taxiing runs, reaching a speed of about 60 m.p.h. The Gloster chief test pilot, P. E. G. Sayer, then took the controls and after some preliminary runs took the aircraft to the downwind end of the airfield, and on the run back the aircraft was airborne for a short time. Sayer repeated the performance twice more, the final 'hop' being very smooth.

The first flight of the E28/39 aircraft took place on the evening of 15 May 1941 at RAF Cranwell. The ten hours' flight trials were completed rapidly without any problems developing in either the engine or the airframe, which was a great tribute to the ability of all concerned. Interest in jet propulsion developed rapidly in Britain, and under an agreement at the highest government level the W1X engine, a complete set of drawings, and a team of three from Power Jets went to the General Electric Company's turbine factory at Lynn, Massachusetts, in the latter half of 1941. From this start, the development of jet propulsion proceeded apace in the USA.

As a development of the successful W1 flight engine, Whittle had conceived his W2 series which would have higher thrust and lower frontal area. The Ministry of Aircraft Production had been established in 1940 and involved both the Rover Company and BT-H in the manufacture of W2 engines. The first engine was delivered by Rover for testing by Power Jets in May 1941 but its performance was very poor. A complete revision of the design, known as the W2B, was instituted, and this was developed into the Welland engine after Rolls-Royce had taken over Rover's jet-engine activities in January 1943. By intensive development the performance was raised to an acceptable level, and the first Meteor I aircraft were delivered to the RAF in May 1944, and saw service against the German V-1 flying bomb. Meanwhile Power Jets had continued with engine development, producing the W2/500 and W2/700 designs, which showed greatly improved performance. The aerodynamic design of the W2/700 was adopted by Rolls-Royce for their very successful Derwent V engine, which won a world airspeed record of 606 m.p.h. in a Meteor in 1945.

At Power Jets, Whittle had ambitious plans for new engines, including a fan jet, based upon axial flow compressors, together with a supersonic aircraft project with the Miles Aircraft Company. In April 1944 the government nationalized Power Jets, the private shareholders accepting the sum of £135,563 10s. for the company's assets. A new company, Power Jets (Research and Development) Ltd, was established, the gas turbine division of the Royal Aircraft Establishment being amalgamated with it. The engine and supersonic aircraft projects were cancelled, and the key members of the Power Jets team resigned and were snapped up by industry. The remaining Power Jets offices and workshops became part of the National Gas Turbine establishment, and Whittle was no longer connected with them. He became increasingly involved in a taxing programme of lectures in both Britain and the United States. He retired from the RAF on 26 August 1948 with the substantive rank of air commodore; he had been made a KBE in the birthday honours list, had received a £100,000 award from the Royal Commission on Awards to Inventors, and had been elected to the fellowship of the Royal Society.

For the next thirty years Whittle continued to receive national, industrial, and academic awards, culminating in the Charles Stark Draper prize of $375,000, which he shared with Dr Hans von Ohain, the pioneer of jet propulsion in Germany. From 1948 to 1952 he was honorary technical adviser to the British Overseas Airways Corporation and travelled extensively. In the intervals between his travels he worked on the text of *Jet—the Story of a Pioneer*, which was published in 1953. This aroused great interest and was subsequently reprinted in paperback. He had an assignment as technical adviser to Shell Research, which led to his conceiving a novel type of oil-well drill. This was developed in conjunction with Bristol Siddeley Engines (later Rolls-Royce Bristol engine division) but had to be shelved in 1970 owing to the financial crisis at Rolls-Royce. From 1963 until 1976 he lived at Chagford in Devon, where he was looked after by his devoted secretary, Margaret Lawrence.

In 1976 Whittle was divorced from his first wife, from whom he had been separated since 1952. He emigrated to the USA and in the same year married Hazel S. Hall, a nurse and air hostess. They made their home in Columbia, Maryland, and Whittle held a research appointment at the US Naval Academy at Annapolis. His second book, *Gas Turbine Aero-Thermodynamics, with Special Reference to Aircraft Propulsion* (1981), was based upon his lectures there. He was awarded the Order of Merit in 1986 and in his last years was actively developing schemes for large supersonic passenger aircraft. He died of lung cancer at his home, Apartment 707, 10001 Windstream Drive, Columbia, Maryland, on 9 August 1996. He was survived by his second wife, and by the two sons of his first marriage. His ashes were interred at the RAF College, Cranwell, on 10 September 1998.   G. B. R. FEILDEN

Sources personal knowledge (2004) · private information (2004) [family; M. Lawrence] · F. Whittle, *Jet—the story of a pioneer* (1953) · papers, CAC Cam. · G. Jones, *The jet pioneers* (1989) · J. Golley, *Whittle—the true story* (1987) · S. Hooker, *Not much of an engineer* (1984) · D. S. Brooks, *Vikings at Waterloo: the wartime work on the Whittle jet engine by the Rover Company* (1997) · G. B. R. Feilden and W. Hawthorne, *Memoirs FRS*, 44 (1998), 433–52 · *WWW* [forthcoming] · *The Times* (10 Aug 1996) · *Daily Telegraph* (10 Aug 1996)
Archives CAC Cam., personal and research papers · PRO, official corresp. and papers, AIR 62 · Royal Air Force Museum, Hendon, letters and papers, AC 96/S4 · RS | FILM VHS tapes of broadcasts | SOUND VHS tapes of broadcasts · tapes of sound broadcasts
Likenesses photographs, 1948–70, Hult. Arch. · E. I. Halliday, oils, 1960, RAF Cranwell, Lincolnshire [*see illus.*] · W. Stoneman, photograph, *c.*1970 · D. Buckland, cibachrome print, 1987, NPG · drawing, repro. in *The Times*

Wealth at death $673,193: orphans court, Howard county, Maryland, USA, 25 June 1997

Whittle, Peter Armstrong [*pseud.* Marmaduke Tulket] (**1789–1866**), antiquary, was born at Inglewhite in the parish of Goosnargh, Lancashire, on 9 July 1789, and was educated at the grammar schools of Goosnargh, Walton-le-Dale, and Preston. He began business as a bookseller and printer at Preston in 1810, and became an active contributor to various journals. He was intelligent but poorly educated, and consequently his works contain many errors. Although he styled himself FSA, he was not a fellow of the Society of Antiquaries. In October 1827 he married Matilda Henrietta Armstrong; they had two sons: Robert Claudius, author of *The Wayfarer in Lancashire*, and Henry Armstrong.

Whittle was the author of many topographical and historical accounts of local towns and historic sites, including: Preston (1821); Southport, Lytham, and Blackpool (1831); Houghton Tower (1845); St Marie's Chapel, Fernyhalgh (1851); Blackburn (1852); and Bolton-le-Moors (1855). He also prepared for the press (but apparently never published) many works, including a compendium of botany, a history of Wigan, and some lectures on poetry. After giving up his business in 1851, Whittle lived in Bolton for some years before moving to Mount Vernon, Liverpool. In 1858 the prime minister, Lord Derby, gave him a civil-list pension of £50 a year for his services to literature. Whittle, who was a Roman Catholic, died on 7 January 1866 at Liverpool.   C. W. SUTTON, *rev.* NILANJANA BANERJI

Sources P. Whittle, *The history of the borough of Preston*, 2 (1837), 336 · *Men of the time* (1865) · H. Fishwick, *The Lancashire library: a bibliographical account of … literature relating to the county palatine* (1875) · Allibone, *Dict.* · Boase, *Mod. Eng. biog.* · T. B. Johnstone, *The religious history of Bolton*, 2 vols. (1887), 177

Whittlesey, William. *See* Wittleseye, William (d. 1374).

Whitty, Edward Michael (1827–1860), political journalist, was born in London in 1827, the son of Michael James *Whitty (1795–1873), a journalist, and his wife, *née* Neill. Educated at Liverpool Institute and at Hanover, he began his journalistic career early, working on the provincial press from 1844. In 1846 he became a shorthand gallery reporter in the House of Commons, writing the parliamentary summary for *The Times* until 1849. During the same period he was the London correspondent for the *Liverpool Journal*. He worked for the *Daily News* from 1849 until 1852, when he became an editor at *The Leader*, working with George Henry Lewes and E. F. S. Pigott. While at *The Leader* he developed his best-known work—parliamentary sketch writing. These columns began on 14 August 1852, and ran under the byline 'The stranger in parliament' from 13 November 1852. His highly accurate character sketches, written in an 'habitually irreverent' tone, with a certain 'pungency of expression', were received with delight or disgust, depending on the personality and sensibilities of the reader. Their style and tone were generally acknowledged to have been a strong influence on later parliamentary sketch writers, notably Grenville Murray. The early and mid-1850s were the high point of

Whitty's career, and selections of his sketches were published as *History of the Session, 1852–3* (1854; reprinted as *St Stephen's in the Fifties*, 1886), *The Derbyites and the Coalition* (1854), and *The Governing Classes of Great Britain: Political Portraits* (1854; expanded and reprinted 1859). The phrase 'governing classes' was often attributed to him, although Carlyle had used it earlier. His sketches of party leaders in *The Governing Classes* were especially ascerbic. Of Palmerston (who was fifty-six at the time) he wrote, 'Youth, in all its virtues, as well as with all its vices, is the principle characteristic of Lord Palmerston' (*Governing Classes*, 129). He berated Gladstone for his seriousness and what he saw as his blinkered attention to his scholarly work. Of Disraeli's vanity he wrote, 'He does not care for abuse:—let us then abuse him' (ibid., rev. edn, 1859, 208).

In 1857 Whitty argued with Lewes and Pigott and left *The Leader* to become editor of the *Northern Whig* in Belfast. He satirized the other *Leader* editors and their circle in his novel *Friends of Bohemia, or, Phases of London Life* (1857), which was first seen as a critique of literary dandyism, but later as a bitter and unnecessary attack on old friends. He left the *Northern Whig* and returned to London in 1858. His wife and two children died in 1859. Whitty was already a heavy drinker by the late 1850s, and this tragedy seems to have worsened this behaviour. Some of his friends became so fearful for his health that they convinced him to accept their offer of passage on a temperance ship to Melbourne, where Whitty would be able to get work on the newspaper *The Argus*. He left England in late 1859. While on the passage to Australia, Whitty drank some of the ship's doctor's medicinal alcohol. It nearly killed him immediately, but he survived to land in Melbourne. The effects of this poisoning were the most likely cause of his death at the house of a relative, soon after arriving, on 21 February 1860. A few years later, a monument to him was raised in Melbourne.   JOSEPH COOHILL

Sources T. H. S. Escott, *Masters of English journalism* (1911) · [J. Hannay], 'Bohemians and bohemianism', *Cornhill Magazine*, 11 (1865), 241–55 · F. Espinasse, *Literary recollections and sketches* (1893) · M. Macdonagh, *The reporters' gallery* (1913) · *The Athenaeum* (12 May 1860), 651 · S. E. Koss, *The rise and fall of the political press in Britain*, 1 (1981) · Allibone, *Dict.* · *Dublin Review* (July 1857) · J. C. Jeaffreson, *Novels and novelists*, 2 (1858) · private information (1900)
Likenesses memorial, 1862–4, Melbourne

Whitty, Dame May (1865–1948). *See under* Webster, Benjamin (1864–1947).

Whitty, Michael James (1795–1873), newspaper editor and proprietor, born in Enniscorthy, Wexford, was the son of a corn merchant and owner of some vessels trading from that port. Whitty was intended for the priesthood, but did not complete his studies. In 1821 he commenced his literary career in London, and among his earliest friends were Sir James Bacon and George Cruikshank. He was appointed editor of the *London and Dublin Magazine* in 1823, and in its first volume appeared the substance of a work which he later revised and published about 1870 as *Robert Emmet*, with a prefatory note signed M. J. W. He remained editor of the magazine until 1827. From 1823 to 1829 he contributed largely to Irish periodical literature, and was an ardent advocate for Catholic emancipation. He published anonymously in 1824 two volumes of *Tales of Irish Life*, with illustrations by Cruikshank. These stories depicted the customs and condition of the people of his homeland, and were a great success, being reprinted in America and also translated into French and German.

Whitty began his connection with Liverpool in January 1830, when he accepted the post of editor of the *Liverpool Journal*. He vacated this position in February 1836 on his appointment as chief constable of the borough. He had previously been superintendent of the nightly watch. During his twelve years' tenure of the office he perfected the organization of the police force and formed an efficient fire brigade. On his retirement he was presented by the town council with the sum of £1000 in recognition of his services.

Whitty's connection with the *Liverpool Journal* had not been wholly severed during this period of his life, and in 1848 he bought the paper and resumed his literary work. For many years he acted as the Liverpool correspondent and agent of the *Daily News*. In 1851 he was a witness before the parliamentary commission appointed to inquire into the Newspaper Stamp Act, and he vigorously advocated the abolition of the stamp act, the advertisement duty, and the duty on paper. On the removal of these taxes he issued in 1855 the *Daily Post*, the first penny daily paper published in the United Kingdom. *Whitty's Guide to Liverpool* was also published from that office in 1868.

Whitty sold both his newspapers in 1869, and the last few years of his life were spent in retirement at Windermere Terrace, Prince's Park, Liverpool. He died there on 10 June 1873, and was buried at Anfield beside his wife, who was the sister of E. B. Neill, London correspondent of the *Liverpool Albion*. He was survived by his daughter, Anna Whitty, and his son, Edward Michael *Whitty.

W. P. COURTNEY, *rev.* NILANJANA BANERJI

Sources *The Athenaeum* (14 June 1873), 763 · Allibone, *Dict.* · private information (1900) · D. J. O'Donoghue, *The poets of Ireland: a biographical and bibliographical dictionary* (1912) · Boase, *Mod. Eng. biog.*
Wealth at death under £40,000: probate, 27 June 1873, *CGPLA Eng. & Wales*

Whitty, Thomas (*bap.* 1713, *d.* 1792), carpet manufacturer, was baptized in the Independent Chapel, Chard Street, Axminster, on 14 May 1713, the son of Thomas Whitty (1693/4–1756), a tanner, and his wife, Sarah (1689/90–1741), the daughter of William Braddock, a mercer of Lyme Regis, Dorset. Their other seven surviving children were daughters. In 1732 Thomas was apprenticed to Samuel Ramson, a clothier of Axminster, whose daughter Sarah (1716–1787) he married on 26 November 1739. Of their twelve children only six reached maturity. For their eldest son, also named Thomas, Whitty wrote in 1790 *A Retrospective View*, which describes his change of trade from clothmaking—unequal in 1754 'to the expenses of my growing family'—to weaving the hand-knotted pile carpets that brought fame to Axminster. Having become intrigued by the seamless structure of Turkish carpets, after experimenting unsuccessfully on his broadlooms Whitty visited a short-lived carpet manufactory in Fulham, where he saw hand-knotting on perpendicular looms. On midsummer day 1755 'I began the first carpet I ever made, taking my children … for my first workers' (Whitty, 24).

Three competitions for English carpets made like those of Turkey were opportunely promoted by the Society for the Encouragement of Arts, Manufactures, and Commerce between 1756 and 1759. Whitty, the only manufacturer to enter more than once, was twice equal first with Thomas Moore and Claude Passavant, then outright winner. Besides premiums, Whitty gained wide publicity, a London agent (William Crompton), and encouragement to produce finer, more expensive carpets than his highly praised Turkish imitations. The 'rich and elegant Patterns' later mentioned by his trade card alluded to sophisticated neo-classical designs, such as those of Robert Adam for Axminster carpets at Saltram, Devon, and Newby Hall and Harewood House, Yorkshire. Royal approval resulted in an order for several pieces following a visit to the manufactory by George III and Queen Charlotte in 1789. By the end of Whitty's life, Edward Daniel Clarke, visiting the manufactory on his tour of 1791, described Axminster as famous all over the world and mentioned a carpet planned for the empress of Russia.

Visitors who toured Whitty's manufactory described him as ingenious and obliging, and as a dissenter. His *Retrospective View* began and ended with strongly devout sentiments. Two of his daughters married ministers. He died in Axminster on 13 August 1792 and was buried there on 17 August. His will, dated 7 August 1792, revealed little personal wealth: he left £2800 between three daughters, his son Samuel, and a widower son-in-law. His son Thomas (1740–1799), in partnership with him since the 1770s, seems already to have owned workshops, stock, and business assets, not mentioned in the will. Two grandsons, Thomas Whitty (1775–1810) and Samuel Ramson Whitty (1784–1855), in turn inherited the flourishing manufactory, which was destroyed by fire in 1828. Whitty's enterprise eventually closed, bankrupt, in 1836; but from its domestic beginnings it had succeeded longer than any other English manufactory of its kind. 'Axminster' became a generic term for hand-knotted carpet in England and also in America, where William Peter Sprague, who had learned the trade from Whitty and married his niece, established in Whitty's lifetime manufactories advertised as 'after the Axminster mode'.

WENDY HEFFORD

Sources B. Jacobs, *Axminster carpets (hand-made), 1755–1957* (1970) · T. Whitty, *A retrospective view of the origin and progress of the Axminster carpet manufactory* (1790); repr. in B. Jacobs, *Axminster carpets (hand-made), 1755–1957* (1970), 20–29, esp. 20–26 · W. H. Wilkin, 'Some Axminster worthies, part 2', *Report and Transactions of the Devonshire Association*, 66 (1934), 248–51 · will of Thomas Whitty, PRO, PROB 11/1237 · apprentice records, PRO, IR 1/13, fol. 44 · *IGI* · Sun insurance policies, GL, MSS 4936, 4937 · S. Sherrill, *Carpets and rugs of Europe and America* (1996) · E. D. Clarke, *A tour through the south of England, Wales and part of Ireland … summer 1791* (1793) · *The journal of Samuel Curwen, loyalist*, ed. A. Oliver (1972) · G. P. R. Pulman, *The book of the Axe*, 3rd edn (1853) · *London Chronicle* (15–18 Aug 1789) · J. Davidson, *The history of Axminster church* (1835)
Archives RSA, letters to the president and secretary
Likenesses silhouette, priv. coll.; repro. in Jacobs, *Axminster carpets*, fig. 1
Wealth at death £2800 in bequests; £850—insurance valuation of two houses and three tenements in Axminster: Sun insurance policies, GL, MS 11936/385, MS 11937/27, 1792; will, PRO, PROB 11/1237

Whitworth, Charles, Baron Whitworth (*bap.* 1675, *d.* 1725), diplomatist, was possibly born at Blore Pike, near Eccleshall, Staffordshire, and was baptized on 14 October 1675 in his maternal grandfather's church at Wilmslow, Cheshire. He was the eldest of the six sons of Richard Whitworth (*d.* 1718) of Blore Pike, and his wife, Anne, the daughter of the Revd Francis Moseley. He spent his childhood at the family home of Batchacre Park, Adbaston, Staffordshire. After Westminster School (queen's scholar, 1690) he entered Trinity College, Cambridge, in 1694 (BA 1699, fellow 1700). On graduation he became secretary to George Stepney, envoy at Berlin, who had attended the same foundations and who was at that time the best-informed Englishman in the affairs of the Holy Roman empire. In this expertise Whitworth was Stepney's successor, and already in November 1701 was 'fitly qualified' to act as British aide to Cardinal Lamberg, the Holy Roman emperor's chief commissary at the Congress of Regensburg. In February 1702 Whitworth's warrant was signed, but that 'these credentials [were] ready sooner than his money' was, as for all contemporary British diplomats, Whitworth's plight now and throughout his career (BL, Add. MS 37353, fols. 1–3).

Whitworth stood in for Stepney at Vienna when the latter was absent from his ambassadorial duties there, until in September 1704 he was appointed envoy-extraordinary to Russia, where, so Tsar Peter I commented to Whitworth in May 1705, 'for some considerable time no Englishman had appeared with a public character'. Whitworth on his journey from Vienna had been able to meet high incidental expenses only by drawing heavily on his father, expenses exacerbated by time spent discovering the tsar's whereabouts. His initial commission was to attempt regularization in Anglo-Russian commercial relations by remedying the Russia Company's mismanagement of its award (1698) of the tobacco monopoly in Russia. A commercial treaty with Russia was not achieved in Whitworth's lifetime, but that the tobacco monopoly business was resolved between 1707 and 1711 owed much to his assiduity and resource. In 1708 he had to handle Russian sensibilities over an arrest for debt in London of the tsar's emissary, Matveyev, who had been sent to Queen Anne in 1707 to seek British mediation in the Great Northern War between Tsar Peter and Charles XII of Sweden, when the power of the latter was increasingly threatening the very survival of Petrine Russia. But the triumph of Russian arms over Sweden at Poltava in July 1709 transformed the scene in eastern Europe, and recognition of this change was signalled in London by Whitworth's elevation to ambassadorial status in February 1710.

While Whitworth remained formally accredited to Russia until November 1712, the course of events in northern and eastern Europe necessitated commissions for him in Berlin, Vienna, the Palatinate, and The Hague. Augustus of Saxony-Poland, with electoral responsibilities newly accorded by the new emperor, Charles VI, was himself a participant in the Great Northern War, with consequent prejudice to British commercial interests in Danzig; Tsar Peter's peripatetic activity in Brandenburg and Bohemia following his Turkish peace of July 1711 and Russian resentment at the Western powers' apparent disregard of Russia's Balkan vulnerability furnished Whitworth with sufficiently demanding briefs between May and October 1711. Already in 1710 the elector of Hanover, statutorily designated successor to the ailing Queen Anne, and the future George I, had entered into a friendship treaty with Russia with an eye to territorial gains from Sweden in Germany. However, in the face of Russian importunacy Whitworth always upheld the primacy for Britain of her friendship with Sweden, and on 15 April 1711 he wrote to Henry St John with a summary of the current Russian temper: 'on one side their vanity and insatiate desire for new conquests, on the other the fear of losing what is already gained, hang on them like an ague' (*Sbornik*, 61.177). His *Account of Russia as it was in the Year 1710*, though not published until 1758, was soon available in manuscript to the ministry at home. Succinct and perceptive, it was a survey of Petrine Russia which held its readership through to the century's end and beyond. Though a whig by affiliation, Whitworth afforded unimpeachable counsel to the tory government on his return home in 1713 as to how a beleaguered Sweden might be cajoled into an accommodation with her Western allies.

In April 1714 Whitworth was posted to Augsburg to observe the Franco-imperial peace negotiations at Baden that summer, and in the autumn he returned to Regensburg as British minister to the imperial diet. This accreditation lasted until August 1716, when he was appointed envoy at Berlin. In May 1717 he was seconded to The Hague on account of the stubborn refusal of the Dutch to respect the British trade embargo with Sweden and their obdurate adherence to neutrality in international affairs following the costly war with France. Whitworth was also instructed, along with Admiral Sir John Norris, to undertake a mission to the tsar while he was in the United Provinces, its purpose being to further a commercial treaty without a political commitment, and to steer the tsar away from blandishing France and opening his own channel of communication with Charles XII. Whitworth from the outset was sceptical about the mission, which indeed yielded no result; but from then until his return to Berlin in May 1719 he remained in the United Provinces, endeavouring through the thickets of Dutch internal politics to implicate the republic with its formal allies Britain and France (the triple alliance) in plans to serve the interests of the emperor, Charles VI, not only in the contentious Southern Netherlands but against Spain in the Mediterranean (the projected Quadruple Alliance). In November 1717 Whitworth was frustratedly to observe 'this state jogs

along like a resty jade, a whip and a spur make him advance a step or two, but 'ere you are aware he stops short again and your trouble is to begin' (C. Whitworth to G. Tilson, 8 Nov 1717, PRO, State Papers Holland 258).

Whitworth's return to Berlin in 1719 was occasioned by Lord Stanhope's success in London in finally overcoming Hanoverian antagonisms towards Prussia. In 1720 he married the comtesse de Vaulgremont (*d.* 1734), the daughter of a government official in French-speaking Flanders; the marriage was childless. He was raised to the Irish peerage as Baron Whitworth of Galway in January 1721 and entered parliament in 1722 as a member for Newport, Isle of Wight. Whitworth had remained at Berlin until June 1722, opining that 'as for the Czar himself, all England has to wish is only a common intercourse of civility and trade. All further engagements are unnecessary and may be dangerous' (C. Whitworth to C. Townshend, 14 Oct 1721, PRO, State Papers Prussia 90/15). Though a sick man, he served at the Congress of Cambrai (1723–5), an attempt to resolve imperial issues outstanding since the formation of the Quadruple Alliance. This was rendered abortive by the Madrid–Vienna axis of 1725. He died at his house in Gerard Street, London, on 23 October 1725 and was buried on 6 November in the south aisle of Westminster Abbey. His barony lapsed on his death. His friendships suggest an engaging and sagacious man, but Whitworth was firstly a most accomplished diplomat and an unsurpassed interpreter of the Russia of his day. D. D. ALDRIDGE

Sources J. M. Price, *The tobacco adventure to Russia: enterprise, politics, and diplomacy in the quest for a northern market for English colonial tobacco, 1676–1722* (1961) · D. Reading, *The Anglo-Russian commercial treaty of 1734* (1938) · *Sbornik Imperatorskago Russkago Istoricheskago Obshchestva*, 39 (1884); 50 (1886); 61 (1888) · R. Wittram, *Peter I: Czar und Kaiser*, 2 vols. (1964) · J. F. Chance, *George I and the Northern War* (1909) [this work is so intractable that it is easier to use Chance's ser. of articles (with generalized titles, in *EHR* 17–22), which constitute its bulk] · HoP, *Commons* · R. M. Hatton, *Diplomatic relations between Great Britain and the Dutch republic, 1714–1721* (1950) · W. Mediger, *Mecklenburg, Russland und England-Hannover, 1706–1721*, 2 vols. (1967) · L. N. Nikiforov, *Russische-englische Beziehungen unter Peter I* (1954) · J. Rosén, *Det engelska anbudet om fredsmedling 1713* (1946) · P. Barber, *Diplomacy* (1979) · K. H. Ruffmann, 'England und der russische Zaren- und Kaisertitel', *Jahrbücher für Geschichte Osteuropas* (1955)
Archives BL, diplomatic corresp., Add. MSS 37341–37397 · CKS, diplomatic and family corresp. · NYPL, letters | BL, letters to John Ellis, Add. MSS 28902–28916 · BL, letters to Sir John Norris, Add. MS 28155 · CKS, letters to Alexander Stanhope · NA Scot., corresp. with Lord Polwarth, GD 157 · U. Nott. L., letters to Robert Harley
Likenesses J. Ellys, oils, *c.*1722, Knole, Kent · G. Birochon, pastel drawing, *c.*1724, NPG · L. F. Roubiliac, marble bust, 1757, Trinity Cam. · engraving, BL

Whitworth, Sir Charles (*c.*1721–1778), politician and writer, was the only son of Francis Whitworth MP (1684–1742) of Leybourne, Kent, and Joan Windham of Clarewell, Gloucestershire. He was the nephew of Charles Whitworth, Baron Whitworth. He was educated at Westminster School (1730–38) and proceeded to Lincoln's Inn in 1738. On his father's death in 1742 he inherited the family estate at Leybourne, and in 1747 he was returned as MP for Minehead, the constituency his father had also represented. On 1 June 1749 he married Martha (*d.* 1786), eldest daughter of Richard Shelley, commissioner of the stamp office, and niece by marriage of the duke of Newcastle. They had seven children who survived childhood: Catharine (*b.* 1750), Charles *Whitworth, later Earl Whitworth (1752–1825), Mary (*b.* 1753), Francis (1754–1805), later a lieutenant-colonel in the Royal Artillery, Richard (*b.* 1755), who was a captain of the Royal Navy and was lost at sea, Priscilla (*b.* 1760), and Anna Barbara (*b.* 1763).

Whitworth hoped that his connection with the duke of Newcastle would lead to some favour and he continually pressed the duke for appointment to a government office. His persistence was rewarded when he was awarded a secret service pension of £400 p.a. in February 1755. In August 1758 he persuaded Newcastle to appoint him lieutenant-governor of Gravesend and Tilbury Fort in lieu of his pension. At the general election in 1761, under pressure from Newcastle, he stood down as MP for Minehead in favour of Lord Egremont's candidature and stood successfully for Bletchingley instead. He was returned once more at Minehead in 1768 and represented the constituency until 1774.

As an MP, Whitworth played little part in debate and spoke only on practical matters such as the payment of militia officers, with which he was personally concerned, having served as a major in the West Kent militia since 1759. In May 1768 he secured a post for which he had previously stood in 1765, when he was elected chairman of the twin committees of supply and ways and means, to which 'money chair' was attached a secret service pension of £500 p.a. This was a position for which he was well qualified, having published in 1763 *A Collection of the Supplies and Ways and Means from the Revolution to the Present Time*. He was knighted on 19 August 1768. He had found his niche in politics, and was a very competent finance chairman for the decade until his death. To accommodate government wishes he continued to be shuffled from one parliamentary seat to another. At the general election in 1774 he was dissuaded by Lord North from standing again at Minehead and was instead returned for East Looe, but in January 1775 he moved to Saltash.

Whitworth wrote a number of political and historical works of reference. In 1764 he published a directory of members of successive parliaments from 1660 to 1761. This was followed by a *List of English, Scots and Irish Nobility* (1765) and a historical account of the price of wheat in 1768. He demonstrated his grasp of public finance in his *Public Accounts of Services and Grants, 1721–1771* (1771). He also contributed to the 1766 edition of David Lloyd's *State Worthies* the 'Characters of the kings and queens of England', and added improvements to the third edition of Timothy Cunningham's *History of the Customs, Aids and Subsidies of England* (1778). Chosen one of the vice-presidents of the Society for the Encouragement of Arts, Manufactures, and Commerce, at its meeting on 28 February 1755, he supported the society for the rest of his life. Whitworth died at Bath on 22 August 1778.

W. R. WILLIAMS, *rev.* M. J. MERCER

Sources S. R. Matthews, 'Whitworth, Charles', HoP, *Commons, 1715–54* · L. B. Namier, 'Whitworth, Charles', HoP, *Commons, 1754–* 90 · B. Burke, *A genealogical history of the dormant, abeyant, forfeited and extinct peerages of the British empire*, new edn (1883), 582–3 · F. Townsend, *Calendar of knights … from 1760 to the present time* (1828), 62 · GEC, *Peerage* · Allibone, *Dict.*

Archives BL, letters to Thomas Birch, Add. MS 4321, fols. 254–63 · BL, letters to the duke of Newcastle, Add. MSS 32720–32914 · Devon RO, corresp. and papers re his trusteeship of the Acland estate

Whitworth, Charles, Earl Whitworth (1752–1825), diplomatist and politician, was born at Leybourne Grange, Kent, on 19 May 1752, and baptized there on 29 May, the eldest of the three sons (there were also four daughters) of Sir Charles *Whitworth (c.1721–1778), MP, and his wife, Martha (*d.* 1786), the daughter of Richard Shelley of Conduit Street, London, latterly commissioner of the stamp office, and the niece of Sir John Shelley, fourth baronet. After education at Tonbridge School from 1761 to 1765, Whitworth, like his father, initially chose an army career, and on 30 March 1772 he became an ensign in the 1st foot guards. He served in North America in 1776–7. On 22 May 1781 he became a captain, and on 8 April 1783, by exchange, was promoted lieutenant-colonel of the 104th regiment. Later in that year the duke of Dorset was appointed ambassador at Paris and Whitworth, who ventured there, impressed Queen Marie-Antoinette by his handsome figure and insinuating manners. She and Dorset are credited by the memoirist Sir Nathaniel Wraxall with obtaining for him his first diplomatic posting.

Diplomatic career: Poland, Russia, and Denmark Whitworth left England as envoy-extraordinary to Poland in December 1785, pausing at Hanover with a letter of introduction from George, prince of Wales, who assured his brother Frederick that he and Whitworth were convivial intimates and that 'a more gentlemanlike, liberal-minded man never existed' (*Correspondence of George, Prince of Wales*, 1.151). He reached Warsaw on 21 January 1786, and spent two years there during the uneasy reign of Stanislas Poniatowski. Having been ordered to investigate any moves to carve up Poland or Turkey, he obtained little information, though he was sent to Kiev in April 1787 to observe Poniatowski's meeting with the empress of Russia. There he met Catherine, who declined political discussion: he had been authorized to suggest an Anglo-Russian alliance.

In November 1788 Whitworth was transferred to Russia in the same capacity with this objective. He was at first amiably received by the empress. In 1790, however, Russian successes in war against the Turks alarmed Pitt's ministry, which, following Whitworth's advice that Russia was vulnerable, proposed sending an armada to the Baltic to force Catherine to give up the Black Sea port of Ochakov. The empress was defiant, and Whitworth now warned his government of the uncertain prospects of success. He was nevertheless ordered on 27 March 1791 to present Catherine with an ultimatum, only to have it countermanded when Pitt encountered strong opposition in parliament. In June 1791 Whitworth applied to succeed to the Istanbul embassy, which was offered to him in March 1793, whereupon he declined. His impact on the

Charles Whitworth, Earl Whitworth (1752–1825), by Charles Turner, pubd 1814 (after Sir Thomas Lawrence, 1806–7?)

Russo-Turkish peace treaty of Jassy in January 1792 was limited—he had in any case been assisted in negotiations by William Augustus Fawkener. Nevertheless, he was nominated a knight of the Bath on 17 September 1793 and was invested by the empress on 17 November.

The empress's espousal of the counter-revolutionary alliance against France improved Whitworth's position, though his attempts to halt the second partition of Poland in 1793 failed; furthermore, Lord Grenville, the foreign secretary, disliked Catherine's insisting on the restoration of the Bourbon royal family in France. In February 1795 Whitworth negotiated an Anglo-Russian treaty of alliance whereby Russia fielded 65,000 troops in exchange for a British subsidy. Catherine died before its implementation, and the emperor Paul, her successor in 1796, was at first hostile to the alliance, despite professing the contrary to Whitworth. By July 1798 French aggression in Malta had caused the emperor to change his mind, and Whitworth resumed negotiations successfully. In December a provisional alliance, to be joined by Prussia and Austria, was achieved. This was snagged by Prussian aloofness and by subsidy arrangements for Austria, and in March 1799 Whitworth was officially rebuked for his unauthorized negotiations with the Austrian Count Cobenzl, which were supposed in London to have culminated in a signed agreement for a new loan to Austria. This nearly cost him his post, which was offered to Lord Bathurst. He was saved by the intercession of Count Vorontsov, Russian ambassador in London, who perceived that Paul's

resentment of Austrian interference might wreck the alliance.

The treaty with Russia was approved by Grenville, and in April, Russian troops were dispatched to the west. Whitworth was rewarded by the emperor with the order of Malta and in July 1799 an Irish peerage was earmarked for him. Later in that year Paul, irritated by British interference in Malta, changed sides again. By 4 April 1800, when he became Baron Whitworth of Newport Pratt, co. Galway, Whitworth was under orders to leave Russia, where Paul snubbed him. Relations between the two countries were in suspense for a year. Whitworth left St Petersburg on 8 June and travelled via Stockholm. On his return to London he presented a modest memorandum on the state of Russia to Grenville, denouncing the unreliability of Paul, contrasted with Catherine. He found employment, in August, as envoy to Denmark, which as a party, like Russia, to the armed neutrality of the north, was resisting British searches of its vessels. He had not succeeded, while in Russia, in deterring the neutrality's threat to British interests, but he was now accompanied by a naval squadron under Vice-Admiral Dickson, which waited in Elsinore (Helsingor) Roads to reinforce his mission. The Danes gave way on 29 August. After returning to England on 27 September 1800, Whitworth was, as promised the previous year, sworn of the privy council on 5 November.

Marriage On 7 April 1801 Whitworth married, by special licence at Dorset House, Westminster, Arabella Diana Sackville, the dowager duchess of Dorset (1767–1825), the daughter and coheir of Sir Charles Cope, second baronet, of Brewerne, Oxfordshire, and the widow of his old acquaintance John Frederick, third duke of Dorset. Her mother, Catherine Jenkinson, *née* Bishopp (1744–1827), was the second wife of the first earl of Liverpool. They had no children. Thanks to his wife's ample resources, Whitworth's financial future was secured. He had brought home debts from Russia, and further embarrassment in the shape of the Russian Countess Gerbetzov (elsewhere rendered Gerebstov), who claimed to have supported him financially in Russia. She set off for London with her husband, too late to impede the marriage, but not too late, according to Wraxall, to accept £10,000 from the bride for quiet possession of Whitworth, although no surviving evidence corroborates this. Whitworth now had hopes of a peace-making embassy to France, though this was awarded in October 1801 to Lord Cornwallis, with the understanding that Whitworth should proceed to Paris once peace was achieved. He became a deputy lieutenant of Kent on 20 January 1802.

Mission to Paris Following the treaty of Amiens, Whitworth was duly posted to Paris on 10 September 1802. Arriving on 16 November in receipt of revised and sterner instructions, he was presented on 7 December to the first consul, Napoleon Bonaparte, whose royal pretensions were already rumoured, and his wife to Josephine Bonaparte at St Cloud on the 11th. From January 1803 the British government under Addington was increasingly uneasy about Bonaparte's aggressive foreign policy. After getting nowhere with Talleyrand, the French foreign minister, whom Bonaparte had instructed to be haughty to him, Whitworth was further disappointed in a lengthy interview with Bonaparte on 18 February. Bonaparte accused Britain of breach of treaty for failing, as yet, to evacuate Malta or Egypt. This alleged perfidy spoiled the prospects Bonaparte hinted at of France and Britain carving up the world between them, and was the basis of further criticism by Bonaparte at a public levee on 13 March 1803. Whitworth was not given a chance to make any substantial counter-allegations, though he replied diplomatically, refusing to be browbeaten. British visitors among the 200 persons present were addressed by Bonaparte in between barbs directed at Whitworth, and gave him credit for his patience. Bonaparte, who according to one British witness did not raise his voice, afterwards tried to discredit exaggerated reports of the occasion. Despite an attempt to patch up a settlement over Malta through Joseph Bonaparte and Talleyrand, there was no question of conciliating Napoleon, whose politeness to Whitworth amid the diplomatic corps on 4 April followed his own very unpunctual appearance. It was generally supposed that he wished to delay a complete rupture until his intended invasion of Britain was better prepared. Whitworth was ordered to present a British ultimatum, the terms of which he later criticized. He was prevented by indisposition from meeting Bonaparte again on 1 May and, after several delays in the granting of his passport, left Paris on 12 May, six days before hostilities were resumed by the pre-emptive British declaration of war.

At home, 1803–1813 Although Whitworth hankered after further employment, he was placed at a disadvantage. He had no seat in either house of parliament, though his wife was patron of East Grinstead borough. In 1801 his only political attachment had been to his chief Grenville, and his friends, but in the meantime Grenville, who was unconvinced of Whitworth's abilities, and his cousin Pitt, both out of office, had drifted apart. On 9 May 1804, when Pitt returned to power without Grenville, Whitworth wrote unsuccessfully to the premier seeking employment, if only as joint postmaster-general, asking no salary beyond his current pension. In July 1803 he had, as a local figurehead of resistance to Bonaparte, become lieutenant-colonel of the Holmsdale battalion of 600 infantry volunteers, based on Maidstone. Having settled at Knole since their marriage, he and his duchess, both described by the diarist Joseph Farington as having plain and easy manners, were popular in Kent, and were commended for their charity, notably in providing employment for the elderly poor. In 1805 there was some talk of Whitworth's taking the prince of Wales's livery, but the first indication of advancement came, not during Grenville's ministry of 1806, but from the duke of Portland's, which on 15 April 1807 appointed him a lord at the Board of Trade. As such, he complained to Thomas Lawrence, while sitting for his portrait, about the excessive granting of licences to trade with Napoleonic Europe. He had declined the offer by the

foreign secretary, George Canning, of a diplomatic mission to Denmark in September 1807 for private reasons, which gossip confined to distaste for Canning. His prospects changed in 1812 when Lord Liverpool, his mother-in-law's stepson, became premier. On 2 March 1813 he was made a lord of the bedchamber to the king (£1000 a year), and on 3 June 1813 he became viceroy of Ireland (£30,000 a year). This had been declined by the duke of Beaufort and Lord Yarmouth: the former was present when the prince regent ostentatiously toasted Whitworth for his public-spirited acceptance of office. On 14 June he was created a British peer, as Viscount Whitworth of Adbaston, Staffordshire, his ancestral county.

Viceroy of Ireland, 1813–1817 Whitworth was ceremonially installed at Dublin on 26 August 1813 and was created LLD (Dublin) on 23 September. His tenure was made easier by the continuation in office of his predecessor's chief secretary, Robert Peel, and the civil secretary, William Gregory, both of whom found him congenial: Peel, who wished to return to England in 1814, was persuaded by him to remain. In patronage matters he leaned on their experience and insistence on straight dealing, and apart from pensions worth £700 a year for an impoverished sister of his and a nephew's widow, both approved by Peel, he dispensed no personal patronage. Captain Francis Beaufort informed Joseph Farington in 1817 that the viceroy gave 'satisfaction to all and [was] popular from the prudence and justice of his administration without the aid of feastings and other such means of acquiring popularity. The Duchess is likewise much liked from her easy and cheerful manner' (Farington, *Diary*, 14.5001). He succeeded in dissolving the Catholic board, at a time when it had become unpopular, in 1814, and in the same year he saw through the renewal of the Insurrection Act, followed by the Peace Preservation Act, which introduced a constabulary.

The unfortunate death of the duchess's only son, George, the fourth duke of Dorset, on 14 February 1815, after a fall from his horse during a visit to Dublin, led to a leave of absence, during which the three lords justices deputizing for Whitworth were unable to prevent the transfer of 5000 troops from Ireland to Flanders. On his return on 12 May 1815, the deficit was made good by embodying the militia. He was created GCB on 2 June 1815, and on 25 November 1815 was made Baron Adbaston and Earl Whitworth. He had meant to depart after three years, and had threatened to do so in 1816 if an Irish peerage were granted to George Canning, but he agreed to remain until summer 1817 so that arrangements to consolidate the English and Irish treasuries could be concluded. As it was, he was faced with an ominous Irish famine before he left. He regarded the Irish family connections of his successor, Lord Talbot, as a disadvantage to a viceroy, and was relieved when Peel again agreed to extend his stay. He handed over to Talbot on 9 October 1817.

Later years Although he had no taste for further public office, or for the House of Lords, Whitworth remained open to suggestion. In April 1819 he paid an unofficial but stately visit to Paris with the duchess, visiting the restored Bourbons, and was there again in October, *en route* for Naples, both capitals being political hotspots at the time. He had been high steward of Stratford upon Avon in place of his stepson since 26 January 1816 and became FSA on 18 November 1819. On 19 July 1821 he was assistant lord sewer at George IV's coronation, and later that year, ineffectually, was shortlisted by Lord Liverpool to recommend to the king for the lord chamberlainship. Thereafter he spent most of his time at Knole, which he had embellished and planted, and where he died after three days' illness on 13 May 1825. He was buried at St Nicholas's, Sevenoaks, which he had rebuilt. The duchess was his heir to an estate valued at under £70,000. She died on 1 August the same year, making special provision for the preservation of Knole, where a portrait of Whitworth by Hoppner, a drawing by Edridge, and a bust by Kirk are preserved. A bust by Carew adorns his monumental inscription in St Nicholas's, Sevenoaks. Lawrence's portrait of him is in Paris, at the Louvre.

Reputation Whitworth was praised in an obituary as 'one of the best examples of an English nobleman' (*GM*, 95/2, 1825, 82). There is no doubt that he looked the part, and that he sought to act it. This obituary remarked on similarities between him and his kinsman the first Baron Whitworth, whose papers he deposited at Knole. The latter certainly excelled as a diplomatist, and, while both served in Russia, the first baron wrote a notable account of his experiences there, later published, while Charles junior, whose father had been an author, sent a few pages, coloured by disappointment, to Lord Grenville. His long stay in Russia was fraught with difficulties in dealing with its autocratic rulers, especially with the vacillating Paul, who alternately fawned on him or spurned him, eventually dismissing him with a sense of failure. What nearly led to dismissal by his own government in 1799 was a misjudgement of his own, though its gravity was exaggerated by the slowness of communications between St Petersburg and London, sometimes taking six weeks, and resulting in prior information being received from nearer sources. He was, professionally, dutiful and dogged and, if astute, was at that time not particularly perspicacious.

The rebuke by Bonaparte on 13 March 1803 was the most widely reported event in Whitworth's career, and of course Bonaparte stole a show he had himself devised. In these circumstances, the dignified demeanour of the diplomatist taken off his guard was so frequently acknowledged as to earn him retrospective credit. In 1922 the *Cambridge History of British Foreign Policy* opined that no important negotiations had ever been so mismanaged as those with Bonaparte dictated by Addington and Hawkesbury in 1802–3, but from this censure exempted Whitworth, 'who, throughout, tempered firmness with discretion, manliness with extreme forbearance' (Ward and Gooch, 1.325). Even so, judgements of Whitworth's diplomatic acumen are various. His subsequent progression from an Irish barony to a British earldom excited envy among his peers; yet unlike some of them he could point to public services, both diplomatic and viceregal, which

justified it. He could also have pointed to the difficulty caused him by his relative poverty in a farflung diplomatic posting previous to his marriage, when his personal morality was suddenly impugned. The sting was taken out of Countess Gerbetzov's case against him by his wife's resolute backing, but other ladies were less convinced. Mrs Fitzherbert, who had been secretly married to the prince of Wales, told Thomas Creevey in 1805 that Whitworth was a monster, albeit a remorseful one, and hinted darkly that she could tell him far more to make him think so. Lady Bessborough also thought he had treated the Russian countess very badly. If it were true that she, a married woman unhappy with her husband, had spent considerable sums of money on Whitworth in Russia, with a promise of eventual marriage, there would be a case to answer, but doubts were thrown on this story in an article in the *Quarterly Review* for December 1836, which dubs the lady in question Gerepzov. As the sister of the Empress Catherine's last favourite, Prince Platon Zubov, she might be credited with a role in restoring the humiliated Whitworth to Catherine's favourable attention after the Ochakov crisis, and possibly with obtaining political information for him, perhaps at some expense, but the rest has become unattested speculation.   ROLAND THORNE

Sources *GM*, 1st ser., 95/2 (1825), 79–82, 647 · *Annual Biography and Obituary* (1826), vol. 2, pp. 97–120 · C. J. Phillips, *History of the Sackville family*, 2 vols. [1929], 277–302 · D. B. Horn, ed., *British diplomatic representatives, 1689–1789* (1932), 94, 119 · S. T. Bindoff, *British diplomatic representatives, 1789–1852* (1934), 108–9 · *The manuscripts of J. B. Fortescue*, 10 vols., HMC, 30 (1892–1927), vols. 7, 10 · *The historical and the posthumous memoirs of Sir Nathaniel William Wraxall, 1772–1784*, ed. H. B. Wheatley, 5 vols. (1884), vol. 4, pp. 31–6 · P. J. Jupp, *Lord Grenville, 1759–1834* (1985) · *DNB* · Farington, *Diary*, 4.1566; 5.1994; 6.2034, 2111; 9.3279; 14.5001; 16.5712 · *The later correspondence of George III*, ed. A. Aspinall, 5 vols. (1962–70), vol. 3, pp. 1908, 1987, 2209, 2230; vol. 4, pp. 3063, 3537 · *The correspondence of George, prince of Wales, 1770–1812*, ed. A. Aspinall, 1: *1770–1789* (1963) · N. Gash, *Mr Secretary Peel: the life of Sir Robert Peel to 1830* (1961) · A. W. Ward, *The Cambridge history of British foreign policy, 1783–1919*, ed. A. W. Ward and G. P. Gooch, 3 vols. (1922–3), vol. 1, pp. 179, 204–5, 231, 286, 300, 312, 325 · *England and Napoleon in 1803*, ed. O. Browning (1887) · *N&Q*, 5 (1852), 313 · *The diary of Philipp von Neumann, 1819–1850*, ed. E. Beresford Chancellor, 2 vols. (1928), vol. 1, p. 141; vol. 2, pp. 202–3 · *The Creevey papers*, ed. H. Maxwell, 1 (1903), vol. 1, pp. 10, 13, 14 · *Lord Granville Leveson Gower: private correspondence, 1781–1821*, ed. Castalia, Countess Granville [C. R. Leveson-Gower], 2nd edn, 1 (1916), 418 · Duke of Buckingham, *Memoirs of the court and cabinets of George III* (1855), vol. 3, pp. 212–62 · *Diaries and correspondence of James Harris, first earl of Malmesbury* [J. H. Harris], 4 (1844), 207–10 · *The diary of Henry Hobhouse, 1820–1827*, ed. A. Aspinall (1947), 78 · GEC, *Peerage*, new edn, 12/2.618–19

Archives CKS, corresp. and papers · PRO, corresp. and papers, FO 800 | BL, letters to Lord Auckland, diplomatic corresp., Add. MSS 34430–34451 · BL, Bentham MSS, diplomatic corresp., Add. MS 33450, fols. 430–32 · BL, letters to Francis Drake, Add. MSS 46822, 46833 · BL, Fortescue (Dropmore) MSS · BL, corresp. with Lord Grenville, Add. MS 59024 · BL, Grenville MSS, diplomatic corresp., Add. MSS 34437–34452 · BL, Hardwicke MSS, Add. MSS 35536–35541 · BL, letters to Lord Hawkesbury, p-5 · BL, Leeds MSS, diplomatic corresp., Add. MSS 28062–28066 · BL, corresp. with earls of Liverpool, Add. MSS 38235–38323, 38473, 38572–38573 · BL, letters to earl of Liverpool, Loan 72 · BL, corresp. with Sir Arthur Paget, Add. MS 48400 · BL, letters to Sir Robert Peel, Add. MSS 40187–40194 · Hants. RO, corresp. with William Wickham · Hunt. L., letters to Grenville family · NA Ire., viceregal papers · NL Scot., corresp. with Robert Liston · NL Scot., letters to first earl of Minto · NRA Scotland, priv. coll., corresp. with Joseph Ewart · PRO, Foreign Office records, diplomatic corresp., FO 65/22–42; xcvii.341 · PRO, corresp. with Francis Jackson, FO 353 · RA, corresp. with Ozias Humphry · Royal Arch., Royal Library MSS, viceregal papers

Likenesses E. Dayes, group portrait, watercolour drawing, 1791 (*Plenipotentiaries signing the treaty, 1791*), NPG · J. Hoppner, oils, *c*.1800, Knole, Kent · H. Edridge, drawing, 1801, Knole, Kent · T. Lawrence, oils, *c*.1807, Louvre, Paris · T. Smyth, bust, 1814; exh. Dublin, 1819 · C. Turner, mezzotint, pubd 1814 (after T. Lawrence, 1806–1807?), NG Ire., NPG [*see illus.*] · T. Kirk, marble bust, *c*.1817, Knole, Kent · G. Hayter, group portrait, 1820 (*The trial of Queen Caroline*), NPG · H. Robinson, mezzotint, 1830 (after T. Lawrence) · J. Carew, marble bust (funerary monument), St Nicholas's Church, Sevenoaks, Kent · R. Laurie, mezzotint (after A. Graff), BM

Wealth at death under £70,000: *CP*, XII/2, p. 619 · will, PRO, PROB 12/90, 30 June 1825

Whitworth, Geoffrey Arundel (1883–1951), founder of the British Drama League, was born in Kensington, London, on 7 April 1883, the youngest child of William Whitworth, barrister, and his wife, Phyllis Mary Draper; he had two brothers and two sisters. Owing to early developed spinal trouble—which prevented him from going to school and which he met courageously—he was educated privately until he went up to New College, Oxford, where he obtained a third class in modern history in 1906. He joined the staff of the *Burlington Magazine*, edited by Charles Holmes; then, from the autumn of 1907, he worked for Chatto and Windus, the publishing firm. There, in building up a list of contemporary books, he was a colleague of Frank Swinnerton, the novelist, who noticed his 'eager adventurousness' and his 'indomitable good temper, a part of his nature and his faith'. Whitworth knew many writers, established and new; through him the firm attracted works by such authors as G. K. Chesterton, Lytton Strachey, and Clive Bell.

In 1910 Whitworth married Phyllis Grace (*d.* 1964), fifth daughter and ninth of the ten children of the Revd George Edward Bell, vicar of Henley in Arden, Warwickshire, from 1876 to 1914. They had a son and a daughter. During the first two years of their marriage Phyllis Whitworth did the secretarial work for a monthly literary magazine, the *Open Window*, which her husband published from their Chelsea home with Vivian Locke Ellis.

Whitworth's main love was the theatre. He enjoyed going to plays, and occasionally writing them; he had frequented the Court Theatre and was devoted to George Bernard Shaw. But his first enthusiasm at that time was for the project of a national theatre, to be regarded as a Shakespeare memorial and (it was hoped) opened in time for the tercentenary in 1916 of Shakespeare's death. With all his preoccupations in publishing, and his own writing—for example, *A Book of Whimsies* (with Keith Henderson, 1909) and *The Art of Nijinsky* (1913)—Whitworth never ceased to think of the national theatre.

With the coming of war in 1914 these plans were shattered, but Whitworth became in 1919 the honorary secretary of his own organization, the British Drama League,

Geoffrey Arundel Whitworth (1883–1951), by Roger Fry, 1934

founded 'to assist the development of the art of the Theatre and to promote a right relation between Drama and the life of the community'. In the previous autumn he had been much impressed by an amateur rendering, half-reading, half-performance, of a one-act play in a hut attached to a factory at Crayford in Kent—something undertaken, he said, 'in the spirit of community enterprise … which had endowed the performance with a peculiar dignity' (G. Whitworth, 14). He held that this dignity must be the mark of a national theatre, and that the theatre itself, 'for all its costly elaboration, for all its perfection or professional technique', must be 'nothing more and nothing less than a Community Theatre writ large' (ibid., 14–15). For him the drama was '*par excellence* the art of the people, and the theatre everybody's business'.

Hence the conception of the British Drama League, devoted to the 'encouragement of senior amateur actors throughout the land' (*The Times*, 11 Sept 1951). Lord Howard de Walden served as president, Harley Granville-Barker as chairman of council, and Whitworth as honorary secretary. It held its first annual conference in the summer of 1919 at Stratford upon Avon, where one resolution pledged members to help the development of 'acting, the drama, and of the Theatre as forces in the life of the nation', and another called for 'a National Theatre policy adequate to the needs of the people'. These phrases might speak for Whitworth's career: his constant and ardent advocacy of the theatre as a power in life. Rapidly the Drama League burgeoned. In 1928 Whitworth at last left publishing to give his whole time to the league, as a practical achievement, and to the national theatre, as a hoped-for vision. He was able to see in the league's growth—with its many affiliated societies, its 100,000 actors and playgoers, its training department, its National Festival of Community Drama, and its library (eventually the largest in the world devoted solely to the theatre)—a 'new and extraordinary outbreak of dramatic energy'. His steady insistence on the value of drama in education prepared the way for the appointment of full-time professional county drama advisers.

No man was better fitted than Whitworth, selfless, persuasive, and much loved, to battle for causes he admired. As director of the league and as honorary secretary of the Shakespeare Memorial National Theatre Committee (1930–51), he used his talents as speaker and organizer. Before giving his entire time to these tasks, he acted as drama critic of *John O'London's Weekly* (1922) and the *Christian Science Monitor* (1923); and in 1924–5 he organized the theatre section of the British Empire Exhibition at Wembley. From 1919 until 1948 he edited the league's magazine, *Drama*.

At a public tribute to him in 1934, the year before the league's move from Adelphi Terrace to Fitzroy Square, Shaw described Whitworth as 'one of the most important people in the theatre today'. When war again intervened, Whitworth did not cease from crusading. It was owing to his persistence and vision that the league's civic theatre scheme—first suggested in 1942—was approved, and that in 1948 the insertion of a clause (132) in the Local Government Act enabled municipal authorities to spend up to the value of a 6d. rate on providing all kinds of entertainment, including the theatre. Whitworth had a final reward when the queen laid the foundation stone (later moved) of the National Theatre upon the South Bank site, London, in July 1951: it was just two months before his death at the Acland Nursing Home, Oxford, on 9 September 1951. He had retired from the directorship of the Drama League during 1948, a retirement he described as 'a sort of minor death', and had become instead chairman of its council.

Whitworth, a fellow of the Royal Society of Literature, translated *The Legend of Tyl Ulenspiegel* (1918); and wrote a novel, *The Bells of Paradise* (1918), and two notable plays, *Father Noah* (1918) and *Haunted Houses* (1934). He was also the author of works on his special subject, *The Theatre of my Heart* (1930; revised 1938) and *The Making of a National Theatre* (1951), as well as *The Civic Theatre Scheme* (1942). He served on the executive committee of governors of the Shakespeare Memorial Theatre and the committee of the Carnegie United Kingdom Trust. In 1947 he was appointed CBE.

Whitworth was survived by his wife, Phyllis Whitworth, who died in 1964. A tireless worker on behalf of the league, she also directed, and managed, between 1924 and 1931, the Three Hundred Club for staging plays of merit likely at first to have a limited public.

J. C. TREWIN, rev. MARK POTTLE

Sources *The Times* (11 Sept 1951) · *Drama* (winter 1951) · G. Whitworth, *The theatre of my heart*, rev. edn (1938) · R. Whitworth and C. Tennyson, 'A mystic of the theatre', MS biography [location unknown] · F. Swinnerton, *Swinnerton: an autobiography* (1937) · personal knowledge (1971) · *WWW* · *CGPLA Eng. & Wales* (1951)
Likenesses R. Fry, oils, 1934, Theatre Museum, London [*see illus.*] · J. Butler, bronze bust, Theatre Museum, London · O. Nemon, bronze head, Theatre Museum, London
Wealth at death £14,337 5s. 3d.: probate, 19 Dec 1951, *CGPLA Eng. & Wales*

Whitworth, Sir Joseph, baronet (1803–1887), mechanical engineer and machine tool manufacturer, was born at Stockport on 21 December 1803, the son of Charles Whitworth (1782–1870) and Sarah (1780–1814), daughter of Joseph Hulse. His father was a loom framemaker in the textile industry who, when his wife died in 1814, put his three young children in the care of foster parents and took advantage of an offer to train for the Congregationalist ministry. Joseph, who was eleven at the time, seems never to have spoken to his father again.

Education, early career, and marriage Whitworth's childhood was extremely hard, but he appears early to have shown aptitude in working with machinery. He formed the conviction that he would be best able to develop this skill in Manchester, and took the first opportunity to move there in search of engineering employment. There in 1821 he was employed by Crighton & Co., a leading firm of textile machine-makers, as a working mechanic. His first ambition was to be a good workman, and he often in later years said that the happiest day he ever had was when he first earned journeyman's wages.

In February 1825 Whitworth married Fanny Ankers (1800–1870), the daughter of a bargemaster of Tarvin in Cheshire, and shortly afterwards entered the workshop of Maudslay and Field in the Westminster Bridge Road, London. Henry *Maudslay recognized his exceptional talent, and placed him next to one of his most capable mechanics, John Hampson, a Yorkshireman. It was while working for Maudslay that, after intensive effort, Whitworth discovered the means of creating a truly plane surface, by means of which for all kinds of sliding tools frictional resistance might be reduced to a minimum.

The most accurate planes, which were essential in the manufacture of steam engine valves, printing press tables, and in lathes and planing machines, had hitherto been obtained by first planing and then grinding the surface. 'My first step', Whitworth said,

was to abandon grinding for scraping. Taking two surfaces as accurate as the planing tool could make them, I coated one of them thinly with colouring matter and rubbed the other over it. Had the two surfaces been true the colouring matter would have spread itself uniformly over the upper one. It never did so, but appeared in spots and patches. These marked the eminences, which I removed with a scraping tool till the surfaces became gradually more coincident. But the coincidence of two surfaces would not prove them to be planes. If the one were concave and the other convex they might still coincide. I got over this difficulty by taking a third surface and adjusting it to both of the others. Were one of the latter concave and the other convex, the third plane could not coincide with both of them. By a series of comparisons and adjustments I made all three surfaces coincide, and then, and not before, knew that I had true planes.

This account gave less credit than was due to Maudslay, who had previously insisted on his workmen using good plane surfaces. But the importance of Whitworth's improvement can hardly be overestimated, for it laid the foundation of an entirely new standard of accuracy in mechanical construction.

On leaving Maudslay's Whitworth worked at Holtzapffel's, and afterwards at the workshop of Joseph Clement, where Whitworth's aptitude for accurate mechanical work was put to good use in the construction of Charles Babbage's calculating machine. In 1833 he returned to Manchester, where he rented a room with steam power in Chorlton Street, and put up a sign, 'Joseph Whitworth, tool-maker, from London', thus founding a workshop which soon became a model of a mechanical manufacturing establishment. The next twenty years were devoted mainly to the improvement of machine tools, including the duplex lathe, the hollow-box structure, and the quick-return motion and reversing tool in planing machines. These were all displayed and highly commended at the Great Exhibition of 1851. Between 1839 and 1849 he took out fifteen patents for machine tools.

Whitworth's measuring machine and other inventions A natural sequel to the discovery of the true plane was the introduction of a system of measurement of ideal exactness. This was effected between 1840 and 1850 by the conception and development of Whitworth's famous measuring machine. A system of planes was so arranged that of two parallel surfaces the one could be moved nearer to or further from the other by means of a screw, the turns of which measured the distance over which the moving plane advanced or retired. Experience showed that a steel bar held between the two planes would fall if the distance between the surfaces were increased by an extremely small amount. For moving the planes Whitworth used a screw with twenty threads to an inch, forming the axle of a large wheel divided along its circumference into five hundred parts. By this means if the wheel were turned one division, the movable surface was advanced or retired 1/500 of a turn of the screw—that is by 1/10,000 of an inch. This slight difference was found successfully to make the difference between the steel bar being firmly held and dropping. A more delicate machine, made in 1859, made perceptible a difference of one two-millionth of an inch.

As this device was gradually perfected, Whitworth was able to elaborate a system of standard measures and gauges, which soon proved of such enormous utility to engineers and opened the way for the production of standardized parts in tools and machinery. But of all the standards introduced by Whitworth, that of the greatest immediate practical utility was his uniform system of screw threads. He explained this system in a paper read to the Institution of Civil Engineers in 1841, entitled 'On a uniform system of screw threads'. Hitherto the screws used in fitting machinery had been manufactured upon no recognized principle or system: each workshop had a type of its own. By collecting an extensive assortment of screw bolts from the different English workshops, Whitworth deduced as a compromise an average pitch of thread for different diameters, and also a mean angle of 55°, which he adopted all through the scale of sizes. The advantages of uniformity could not be resisted, and by 1860 the Whitworth system was in general use. The efficacy of Whitworth's innovations was first generally recognized at the exhibition of 1851, where his exhibit of patented tools and inventions gained him the reputation of being the leading mechanical constructor of the time. He also won praise for his invention of a street cleaning machine, which was widely adopted in British towns.

Public life In 1853 Whitworth was appointed a member of the royal commission to the New York Industrial Exhibition. The incomplete state of the machinery department prevented his reporting upon it, but he made a journey through the industrial districts of the United States, and published upon his return, in conjunction with George Wallis, *The Industry of the United States in Machinery, Manufactures, and Useful and Ornamental Arts* (1854). In this he drew special attention to the suitability of the machinery which he had seen at the state armoury, Springfield, Massachusetts, for the production of firearms.

In 1856 Whitworth was president of the Institution of Mechanical Engineers, and at the Glasgow meeting delivered an address in which his favourite projects were ably set forth. He deplored the tendency to excessive size and weight in the moving parts of machines and the national loss by over-multiplication of sizes and patterns. He contemplated the advantage that might be derived from decimalizing weights and measures, and this concern led in 1857 to his paper 'On a standard decimal measure of length for engineering work', delivered at the institution. His papers, five in number, each one of which represented a revolution in its subject, were collected in 1858 as a thin volume, *Miscellaneous Papers on Mechanical Subjects, by Joseph Whitworth, F.R.S.*. Whitworth had been elected to the Royal Society in 1857; he was created LLD of Trinity College, Dublin, in 1863, and DCL Oxford on 17 June 1868.

Armaments and further inventions Meanwhile, the course of Whitworth's career had been changed by the Crimean War. In 1854 he had been requested by the Board of Ordnance to design and give an estimate for a complete set of machinery for manufacturing rifled muskets. This Whitworth declined to do, as he considered that experiments were required in order to determine what caused the difference between good and bad rifles, what was the proper diameter of the bore, what was the best form of bore, and what the best mode of rifling, before any adequate machinery could be made. Ultimately the government were induced to erect a shooting gallery for Whitworth's use near his home at Fallowfield, Manchester, and experiments began there in March 1855. These showed that the recently adopted Enfield rifle was untrue in almost every particular. In April 1857 Whitworth submitted to official trial a rifle with a hexagonal barrel and .45 inch bore, which in accuracy of fire, in penetration, and in range, 'excelled the Enfield to a degree which hardly leaves room for comparison' (*The Times*, 23 April 1857). Whitworth's rifle was not only far superior to any small arm then existing, but it also embodied the principles upon which subsequent improvements were based, namely, reduction of bore (to .45 inch calibre), an elongated projectile, more rapid twist, and extreme accuracy of manufacture. This rifle, after distancing all others in competition, was rejected by a War Office committee as being of too small calibre for a military weapon. Yet in 1869 a similar committee recommended the .45 inch bore as most suitable for military use.

The inventor found some consolation for the procrastinations of official procedure in the fact that at the open competition promoted by the National Rifle Association in 1860 the Whitworth rifle was adopted as the best-known, and on 2 July 1860 the queen opened the first Wimbledon meeting by firing a Whitworth rifle from a mechanical rest at a range of 400 yards and hitting the bull's-eye. The new rifle was adopted by the French government, and was generally used for target-shooting until the introduction of the Martini-Henry, a rifle in which several of Whitworth's principles were embodied.

In the construction of cannon Whitworth was equally successful, but again failed to secure their adoption by the British military authorities. In 1862 he made a rifled gun of high power (a 6 mile range with a 250 lb shell). But this gun, despite its unrivalled ballistic power, was rejected by the Ordnance board in 1865. It seems likely that the keen rivalry between Whitworth and Sir William (later Lord) Armstrong in the manufacture of artillery, and the ambivalent attitude of the War Office towards both, substantially retarded the progress of British artillery for nearly twenty years.

It was after the termination of this 'battle of the guns' that Whitworth made the greatest of his later discoveries. Experience had taught him that hard steel guns were unsafe, and that the safeguard consisted in employing ductile steel. A gun of hard steel, in case of unsoundness, explodes, whereas a gun of ductile steel indicates wear by losing its shape, but does not fly to pieces. When ductile steel, however, is cast into an ingot, its liability to 'honey-comb' or form air-cells is so great as almost to neutralize its superiority. Whitworth now found that the difficulty of obtaining a large and sound casting of ductile steel might be successfully overcome by applying extreme pressure to the fluid metal, while he further discovered that such pressure could best be applied, not by the steam hammer but by means of a hydraulic press. Whitworth steel, as it was styled, was produced in this manner from about 1870, and the virtue of its special application in the manufacture of guns was soon exploited. In 1883 the gun-foundry board of the United States, after paying a visit to Whitworth's large works at Openshaw, near Manchester, gave it as their opinion that the system carried on there surpassed all other methods of forging.

At the Paris Exhibition of 1867 Whitworth was awarded one of the five 'grands prix' allotted to Great Britain. In September 1868, after witnessing the performance of one of the Whitworth field-guns at Châlons, Napoleon III made him a member of the Légion d'honneur, and about the same time he received the Albert medal of the Society of Arts for his instruments of measurement and uniform standards.

Whitworth's interest in artillery did not flag, and he continued to make new experiments. He was the first to penetrate armour-plating upwards of 4 inches in thickness, and the first to demonstrate the possibility of exploding shells without using any kind of fuse. In 1873 he gave to the world his own version of the points at issue with the Ordnance department in *Miscellaneous Papers on Practical Subjects: Guns and Steel*. The unfortunate treatment to which he was subjected was due in part, no doubt, to his plain and inflexible determination. Whitworth always refused to modify a model which he knew to be right out of deference to committees whom he regarded as incomparably his inferiors in technical knowledge.

Whitworth appears to have become increasingly irascible and domineering as he grew older, but he was always attentive to the welfare of his own workers. In 1874 he converted his extensive works at Manchester into a limited liability company. Whitworth, his foremen, and others in the concern, twenty-three in number, held 92 per cent of the shares, and had practical control; no goodwill was charged, and the plant was taken at a low valuation. At the same time the clerks, draughtsmen, and workmen were encouraged and assisted to take shares of £25 each. Ironically, ten years after his death, on 1 January 1897, the firm was united with that of his great rival Sir William Armstrong at Elswick, with an authorized capital of upwards of £4,000,000.

Recreation, death, and assessment As early as 18 March 1868 Whitworth wrote to Disraeli, offering to found thirty scholarships of the annual value of £100 each, to be competed for upon a basis of proficiency in the theory and practice of mechanics. In the following year his generous action and his merits as an inventor were publicly recognized by his being created a baronet. Whitworth's first wife, from whom he appears to have become estranged, died in October 1870, and on 12 April 1871 he married Mary Louisa (1829–1896), daughter of Daniel Broadhurst, and widow of Alfred Orrell of Cheadle. Shortly before his second marriage (though still retaining The Firs, Fallowfield, as his Manchester residence) he purchased an estate at Stancliffe, near Matlock. There, upon an unpromising site, amid a number of quarries, he constructed a wonderful park, and he acquired much local celebrity for his gardens, his trotting horses, and his herd of shorthorns. His iron billiard table (remarkable for its true surface), his lawns, cattle pens, and stables were all 'models'. As he advanced in age Whitworth formed the habit of wintering in the Riviera; but he was not fond of going abroad, and in 1885 he made for himself at Stancliffe a large winter-garden, hoping to spend the winters at home. He passed one winter successfully in Derbyshire, but in October 1886 he went out to Monte Carlo, and there he died on 22 January 1887. Lady Whitworth survived her husband, dying on 26 May 1896 and, there being no children from either marriage, the baronetcy became extinct. The second Lady

Whitworth was buried beside her husband in a vault in Darley Dale churchyard.

For many years before his death Whitworth made no secret of his intention to devote the bulk of his fortune to public and especially educational purposes. But when he died he left the apportionment of his considerable fortune to his wife and trustees. After paying £100,000 to the Department of Science and Art in fulfilment of Whitworth's intention expressed in 1868 of permanently endowing thirty scholarships, the legatees, during the twelve years that elapsed after the testator's death, devoted various sums, amounting in all to £594,416, to educational and charitable purposes. A number of bodies in Manchester benefited especially, including the Whitworth Park and Institute as well as Owens College and the Manchester Technical School.

Whitworth was a pioneer of modern production engineering, outstanding for his refinement and systemization of engineering methods. His mind was that of an experimentalist. A man of few words, he encountered each problem in mechanics by the remark 'Let us try.' His pioneering experiments with rifles were a striking example of this. While drawing heavily upon the earlier achievements of others in the development of precision engineering, 'he did more than anyone else to bring these standards of accuracy into general engineering practice' (Musson, 'Whitworth and the growth of mass-production engineering', 126).

THOMAS SECCOMBE, rev. R. ANGUS BUCHANAN

Sources S. Smiles, *Industrial biography: iron-workers and tool-makers*, another edn (1879), chap. 14 · *PICE*, 91 (1887–8), 429–46 · *Institution of Mechanical Engineers: Proceedings* (1887), 152–6 · J. E. Tennent, *Story of the guns* (1864) · A. E. Musson, 'Joseph Whitworth: toolmaker and manufacturer', *Engineering heritage: highlights from the history of mechanical engineering*, 1 (1963), 124–9 · L. T. C. Rolt, *Tools for the job: a short history of machine tools* (1965) · T. Kilburn, *Joseph Whitworth, toolmaker* (1987) · J. Whitworth, 'On a uniform system of screw threads', *PICE*, 1 (1841), 157–60 · *The Times* (23 April 1857) · A. E. Musson, 'Joseph Whitworth and the growth of mass-production engineering', *Business History*, 17 (1975), 109–49 · H. Coles and G. Tweedale, 'Whitworth, Sir Joseph', *DBB* · N. Atkinson, *Sir Joseph Whitworth: 'the world's best mechanician'* (1996)

Archives JRL, biographical material | BL, corresp. with Charles Babbage, Add. MSS 37193–37197 · UCL, corresp. with Edwin Chadwick

Likenesses group photograph, 1850, Man. CL · P. Park, marble bust, 1855, Gawsworth Hall, Cheshire · Dalziel, woodcut, BM · L. Desanges, oils, Whitworth Institute, Darley Dale · C. A. Duval & Co., carte-de-visite, NPG · attrib. E. J. Poynter, oils, Sci. Mus. · J. E. Whinfield, oils, Institution of Mechanical Engineers, London · obelisk, Whitworth Institute, Darley Dale · photographs, Inst. CE · photographs, Institution of Mechanical Engineers, London · portrait?, repro. in *ILN* (16 May 1868) · portrait?, repro. in *ILN* (5 Feb 1887) · prints, NPG

Wealth at death £462,928 8s. 10d.: resworn probate, April 1888, *CGPLA Eng. & Wales* (1887)

Whitworth, William Allen (1840–1905), mathematician and Church of England clergyman, was born at Bank House, Runcorn, on 1 February 1840, the eldest son in the family of four sons and two daughters of William Whitworth, at one time schoolmaster at Runcorn and incumbent of Little Leigh, Cheshire, and of Widnes, Lancashire,

and his wife, Susanna, daughter of George Coyne of Kilbeggan, co. Westmeath, and first cousin to Joseph Stirling Coyne.

After education at Sandicroft School, Northwich (1851–7), Whitworth proceeded to St John's College, Cambridge, in October 1858, and in 1861 was elected a scholar. In 1862 he graduated BA as sixteenth wrangler, proceeding MA in 1865, and he was fellow of his college from 1867 to 1884. He was successively chief mathematics master at Portarlington School and Rossall School and professor of mathematics at Queen's College, Liverpool.

From early youth Whitworth showed a mathematical promise and originality to which his place in the tripos scarcely did justice. While an undergraduate he was principal editor with Charles Taylor and others of the *Oxford, Cambridge, and Dublin Messenger of Mathematics*, started at Cambridge in November 1861; Whitworth remained one of the editors until 1880, and was a frequent contributor. His earliest article, 'The equiangular spiral, its chief properties proved geometrically' (*Messenger*, 1, 1861, 5–13), was translated into French in the *Nouvelles Annales de Mathématiques* (1869). An important treatise, *Trilinear Co-ordinates and other Methods of Modern Analytical Geometry of Two Dimensions*, was issued at Cambridge in 1866. Whitworth's best-known mathematical work, *Choice and Chance, an Elementary Treatise on Permutations, Combinations and Probability* (1867, 5th edn, 1901), was elaborated from lectures delivered to women at Queen's College, Liverpool, in 1866. A model of clear and simple exposition, it presented a very ample collection of problems on probability and kindred subjects, solutions to which were provided in *DCC Exercises* (1897).

Whitworth was ordained deacon in 1865 and priest in 1866, and won high repute in his clerical career. He was curate at St Anne's, Birkenhead (1865), and of St Luke's, Liverpool (1866–70), and perpetual curate of Christ Church, Liverpool (1870–75). His success with parochial missions in Liverpool led to preferments in London. He was vicar of St John the Evangelist, Hammersmith (1875–86), and from November 1886 until his death, vicar of All Saints, Margaret Street, Marylebone, one of the early strongholds of the Tractarian movement. He also held from 1885 a sinecure college living in the diocese of Bangor, and was in 1891–2 commissary of the South African diocese of Bloemfontein. Whitworth was select preacher at Cambridge five times and Hulsean lecturer there in 1903–4, and was made a prebendary of St Paul's Cathedral in 1900. On 10 June 1885 he married Sarah Louisa, only daughter of Timms Hervey Elwes; the couple had four sons, all graduates of Trinity College, Cambridge.

Whitworth, though he had been brought up an evangelical, was influenced at Cambridge by the scholarship of J. B. Lightfoot and B. F. Westcott, and he studied later the German rationalizing school of theology. He was considered a 'vigorous and original preacher' (*The Times*, 9). His sympathies lay mainly with the high-church party, and in 1875 he joined the English Church Union. In the ritual controversy of 1898–9 he took a moderate position, differing from the union over its opposition to the archbishops' condemnation of the use of incense. He contended that the obsolete canon law should not be allowed 'to supersede the canonical utterance of the living voice of the Church of England'. His ecclesiastical publications included an almanac of dates of Easter (1882), a description of All Saints Church, Margaret Street (1891); *Worship in the Christian Church* (1899), and two posthumous volumes of sermons (1906, 1908).

Whitworth died on 12 March 1905 at Home Hospital, 16 Fitzroy Square, after a serious operation on 28 February and was buried at Brookwood, on 16 March, in ground belonging to St Alban the Martyr, Holborn. His wife survived him. There is a slab to his memory in the floor of All Saints Church, Margaret Street.

D. J. OWEN, rev. ALAN YOSHIOKA

Sources *The Times* (13 March 1905) · *The Eagle*, 26 (1905), 396–9 · *The Guardian* (15 March 1905) · *The Guardian* (22 March 1905) · *Church Times* (17 March 1905) · private information (1912) · Venn, *Alum. Cant.* · *CGPLA Eng. & Wales* (1905)

Archives LPL, corresp. with Frederick Temple, bishop of London

Wealth at death £5060 11s. 2d.: probate, 7 April 1905, *CGPLA Eng. & Wales*

Whitworth, Sir **William Jock** (1884–1973), naval officer, was born on 29 June 1884, at 6 Cambridge Terrace, Chatham, Kent, the first of three children of Major Augustus William Whitworth, Royal Warwickshire regiment, of Earls Barton, Northamptonshire, and his wife, Isabel, daughter of Matthew Dysart Hunter of Antons Hill, Berwickshire.

Whitworth entered the Royal Navy after Wimborne grammar school, via the traditional route of two years at the Royal Naval College, Dartmouth, in September 1899 and rapidly displayed ability. Early experience in command of a torpedo boat destroyer instilled in him a love of the small boats of the Royal Navy, though two spells as a flag lieutenant gave him a wider view of naval affairs. On 15 September 1910 he married Marguerite (generally known as Daisy) Ethel Augusta (1884–1970), daughter of Lieutenant-Colonel Alan Henry Maclean, in Wimborne Minster. They had twin sons and two daughters, of whom one son and one daughter predeceased him. In 1914 he was in command of *Cockatrice*, in the fourteenth destroyer flotilla, attached to the battle cruisers. At the time of Jutland she was in dockyard hands. Shortly afterwards he commissioned *Orestes* in which he remained for most of the rest of the war, being gazetted DSO on 8 March 1918.

After the armistice Whitworth served in the naval intelligence division and was promoted captain (31 December 1925). He was appointed captain of the School of Physical and Recreational Training, and then assumed the appointment of captain (D) of the second destroyer flotilla, in the Mediterranean Fleet (1928–31), then serving at the Admiralty, as director of physical training and sports, and head of the naval personnel committee. The Invergordon mutiny caused a reshaping of the personnel and welfare organizations within the Admiralty, and Whitworth became the deputy director of personnel services. Only those with a sure touch in man management were

assigned to such a position. His reward after two years was the appointment to command the flagship of the Mediterranean Fleet, *Queen Elizabeth*. Unusually he then commanded *Rodney*, the flagship of the commander-in-chief, Home Fleet, for six months, before being promoted to rear-admiral (20 July 1936), and serving for two years as naval secretary to the first lord, Duff Cooper, and then Earl Stanhope. Here his principal job was to arrange senior officers' appointments. He was appointed CB in 1938.

In June 1939 Whitworth was appointed rear-admiral commanding the battle-cruiser squadron. On 1 January 1940 he was promoted to vice-admiral. When the Germans invaded Norway, Whitworth was in *Renown* covering a mine-laying operation off Narvik. The German battle cruisers *Scharnhorst* and *Gneisenau* were spotted early in the morning of 9 April, and a running fight ensued in appalling conditions with heavy seas and snow squalls. Nevertheless *Renown* succeeded in badly damaging *Gneisenau*. Whitworth gave chase but the Germans' superior speed allowed them to escape. The official historian wrote that this success was 'due to Admiral Whitworth's immediate engagement and vigorous pursuit under most difficult conditions' (Roskill, *War at Sea*, 1.166–7). An attempt to drive the Germans from Narvik was beaten off on 10 April, for which Whitworth blamed himself for not disobeying Admiralty orders. However, on 14 April he was ordered to destroy the German forces at Narvik. Transferring his flag to *Warspite*, and with nine destroyers, Whitworth took his force up to Narvik, destroying all eight German destroyers and one U-boat without significant damage to his squadron. A brother officer, quoted in Whitworth's obituary in the *Daily Telegraph*, said of him: 'He has applied destroyer tactics to the battleship, and we who served in destroyers are particularly proud of him' (26 Oct 1973). After the Norwegian campaign Whitworth remained in *Hood*, taking part in operations designed to prevent German raiders breaking out into the Atlantic.

On 8 May 1941 Whitworth left *Hood*, two weeks before she was sunk, and became second sea lord and chief of naval personnel. His job was to cope with the vast expansion of the navy as it grew from its pre-war strength of 129,000 to 863,500 by the middle of 1944. Of these 72,000 were in the Women's Royal Naval Service. His duty was to ensure that all the fleets had sufficient manpower to carry out their roles, and he oversaw this in his usual imperturbable style, never allowing himself to become bogged down in red tape. In 1941 he was advanced to KBE, and on 31 December 1943 he was promoted admiral. In February 1944 he took over as commander-in-chief, Rosyth, where his principal roles were to support the invasion of France, and the liberation of Norway. For this latter, and for his performance at Narvik, he was awarded the grand cross of the royal order of St Olav. He retired on 15 September 1946, the forty-seventh anniversary of his entry into the Royal Navy, and lived most of the rest of his life quietly in the hamlet of Stoughton, near Chichester. In appearance Whitworth was of solid build, with the wide shoulders of an athlete. Those who served under him considered him something of a martinet, but there was a much softer side to him for those who got to know him. He was said to fill those who served under him with awe. A member of the Church of England, he addressed the general assembly of the Church of Scotland when commander-in-chief, Rosyth, on the importance of the role of naval chaplains, receiving prolonged applause. Whitworth's wife predeceased him in 1970, and he died on 25 October 1973 at home, Cherington, 15 Stocker Road, Bognor Regis, of a duodenal ulcer, bronchopneumonia, and old age.

ROBIN BRODHURST

Sources S. W. Roskill, *The war at sea, 1939–1945*, 1 (1954) • C. Barnett, *Engage the enemy more closely: the Royal Navy in the Second World War* (1991) • A. Coles and T. Briggs, *Flagship Hood* (1985) • S. W. Roskill, *H.M.S. Warspite* (1957) • *The Times* (26 Oct 1973) • *Daily Telegraph* (26 Oct 1973) • b. cert. • m. cert. • d. cert. • service record of W. J. Whitworth, PRO, ADM 196/49, fol. 47
Archives IWM, corresp. and MSS
Likenesses group photograph, 1940 (with King George VI and Queen Elizabeth), IWM
Wealth at death £132,323: probate, 14 Dec 1973, *CGPLA Eng. & Wales*

Whood, Isaac (1688/9–1752), portrait painter, practised for many years as a portrait painter and professional copyist in Lincoln's Inn Fields, and was a skilful imitator of the style of Sir Godfrey Kneller. He was especially patronized in the 1730s by the duke of Bedford, for whom he painted numerous portraits of members of the Spencer and Russell families to hang at Woburn Abbey, Bedfordshire; some of these were copied by Whood from other painters.

There is a good portrait of Archbishop Wake by Whood at Lambeth Palace, painted in 1736. At Cambridge there are portraits by Whood at Trinity College, including Roger Gale (1738), and Trinity Hall. His portraits of ladies were some of the best of that date. These include, in 1735, *Anne, Third Duchess of Bedford* and, in 1737, *Lady Georgina Spencer* (both Woburn Abbey), of which Sir George Scharf commented 'spiritedly painted, with much breadth of treatment' (Scharf, 127). Some of his portraits were engraved in mezzotint, notably one of Laurent Delvaux the sculptor (1734), engraved by Alexander van Haecken (1735), who assisted Whood 'to dress and adorn his pictures with silks satins velvets embroideryes' (Vertue, *Note books*, 125) and finished a portrait of J. M. Rysbrack after Whood's death, and several by John Faber junior in the 1740s. Whood's drawings in chalk or black lead on vellum are of interest, particularly those now known of Dean Swift (NG Ire.) and William Stukeley (1725; Society of Antiquaries, London; 1727; Bodl. Oxf.), and Vertue wrote that he had 'much advanc'd his knowledge & pencil with more freedom and correctnes abundantly' (ibid., 58). In 1743 he executed a series of designs to illustrate Samuel Butler's *Hudibras*.

As a portraitist Whood was 'as eminent a figure in that Art, as any of that Profession' and 'a most humorous and agreeable companion' (*Daily Advertiser*, 3 March 1752, in Vertue, *Note books*, 160). He was a member of the Spalding Gentlemen's Society (1721) and the Society of Antiquaries (*c*.1751). His finances in later years were severely restricted

as a result of a lawsuit over an estate. He died in Bloomsbury Square, London, on 24 or 26 February 1752, aged sixty-three; the duke of Bedford paid his funeral expenses. L. H. CUST, *rev.* ARIANNE BURNETTE

Sources Vertue, *Note books*, vols. 2–4 • C. H. Collins Baker, notes on artists, NPG, archive • Waterhouse, *18c painters* • J. C. Smith, *British mezzotinto portraits*, 4 vols. in 5 (1878–84) • E. Edwards, *Anecdotes of painters* (1808); facs. edn (1970) • G. Scharf, *A descriptive and historical catalogue of the collection of pictures at Woburn Abbey* (1877) • G. S. Thomson, *Letters of a grandmother* (1943) • J. Evans, *A history of the Society of Antiquaries* (1956) • *The Gentlemen's Society at Spalding: its origin and progress* (1851) • H. Walpole, *Anecdotes of painting in England: with some account of the principal artists*, ed. R. N. Wornum, new edn, 2 (1849); repr. (1862) • Redgrave, *Artists*

Whorwood [*née* Rider], **Jane** (1614/15–1684), royalist sympathizer, was the daughter of one Rider (Ryder or Ryther) of Kingston, Surrey, sometime surveyor of the stables to James I. Her family had well-established connections with the royal court. Her mother had married James Maxwell, one of Charles I's bedchamber, by September 1634, when, by a licence dated 22 September, Jane, aged nineteen, married Brome Whorwood (*bap.* 1615, *d.* 1684), eldest son of Sir Thomas Whorwood of Holton, Oxfordshire.

In 1647 and 1648, when the king was in captivity, Jane Whorwood signalized herself by her efforts to communicate with him and to arrange his escape. She conveyed money to him from loyalists in London when he was at Hampton Court in autumn 1647, and consulted William Lilly the astrologer about where Charles could best hide himself after his intended flight. Lilly recommended Essex, but the advice came too late to be acted upon. Jane consulted Lilly again in 1648 on how to enable the king to escape from Carisbrooke, and obtained from a locksmith whom he recommended files and aquafortis to be used on the window bars of the king's chamber, but through various accidents the design failed. She also helped to provide a ship, and on 4 May 1648 Colonel Hammond, the governor of the Isle of Wight, was warned that a ship had sailed from the Thames, and was waiting about Queenborough to carry the king to the Netherlands. 'Mrs. Whorwood', adds the letter, 'is aboard the ship, a tall, well-fashioned, and well-languaged gentlewoman, with a round visage and pockholes in her face' (*DNB*). Anthony Wood, who had often seen her, added to this description that she was red-haired.

After the frustration of this scheme Jane continued to convey letters to and from the king during autumn 1648, and to hatch fresh schemes. She is often referred to in the king's letters under the cipher 'N.' or '715'. 'I cannot be more confident of any', says the king in one of his letters, and in another speaks of the 'long, wise discourse' she had sent him. Wood identifies Jane with the unnamed lady to whom the king had entrusted a cabinet of jewels which he sent for shortly before his execution, in order that he might give them to his children. But a note in Sir Thomas Herbert's own narrative states that the lady in question was the wife of Sir William Wheeler.

Jane and her husband had at least two children. Their son, Brome, baptized on 29 October 1635, was drowned in September 1657 and buried at Holton. Their daughter,

Diana, married in 1677 Edward Masters LLD, chancellor of the diocese of Exeter. Subsequently the Whorwoods' marriage broke down, Jane obtaining a decree of alimony in June 1659. Her husband's attempts to reverse the decree led to protracted litigation. His reputation was not enhanced, and he was said to have had an illegitimate son. He also represented the city of Oxford in four successive parliaments (1661–81), but, becoming a violent whig, was put out of the commission of the peace in January 1680. He died in Old Palace Yard, Westminster, on 12 April 1684, and was buried at Holton on 24 April. Jane died on 24 September 1684, letters for administration of her estate being granted to creditors in November of that year.

C. H. FIRTH, *rev.* SEAN KELSEY

Sources R. Hammond, *Letters between Colonel Robert Hammond, governor of the Isle of Wight, and the committee of Lords and Commons at Derby-House, General Fairfax, Lieut. General Cromwell, Commissary General Ireton, &c.* (1764) · J. L. Chester and J. Foster, eds., *London marriage licences, 1521–1869* (1887), 1460 · L. Naylor and G. Jaggar, 'Whorwood, Brome', HoP, *Commons, 1660–90*, 3.714–16 · *IGI* · administration, PRO, PROB 6/59, fol. 171 · *Parochial collections made by Anthony à Wood and Richard Rawlinson*, ed. F. N. Davis, 3 vols., Oxfordshire RS, 2, 4, 11 (1920–29)
Archives BL, letters to H. Firebrace, Egerton MS 1788
Wealth at death see administration, PRO, PROB 6/59, fol. 171

Whymper, Edward (1840–1911), mountaineer and wood-engraver, was born on 27 April 1840 at Lambeth Terrace, Kennington Road, London, the second of the eleven children of Josiah Wood *Whymper (1813–1903), wood-engraver, and his first wife, Elizabeth Whitworth Claridge (1819–1859). He was educated at Clarendon House School until the age of fourteen, when he was apprenticed as a draughtsman engraver in his father's firm. His diary from 1855 to 1859 records his avid interest in public affairs and his frequent attendance at Baptist chapel and cricket matches at the Oval. After an early desire to go to sea or become an engineer Whymper developed an intense but unfocused ambition: 'I had ideas floating in my head that I should one day turn out some great person, be *the* great person of *my* day, perhaps Prime Minister, or at least a millionaire' (Smythe, 50). In 1859 the family moved to Town House, Haslemere, Surrey.

In 1860 the publisher William Longman commissioned Whymper to make illustrations of the Alps, for which he visited Saas Fee, Zermatt, Chamonix, and the Dauphiné. Whymper later claimed that he had first gone to the Alps 'to acquire such a knowledge of snow and ice as might perhaps procure me a post upon some future English Arctic Expedition' (*Alpine Journal*, 6, 1873, 161). In 1861 he climbed Mont Pelvoux and was elected to the Alpine Club. Over the following summers he made a series of brilliant climbs and many first ascents, including the Barre des Écrins in the Dauphiné, the Aiguille Verte, and the Matterhorn.

Whymper centred his climbing ambitions on the Matterhorn, and from 1861 to 1865 he made seven attempts from the Italian side, sometimes in partnership with his rivals John Tyndall and Jean-Antoine Carrel, a guide from Val Tournanche. On 14 July 1865 he climbed the Matterhorn from Zermatt with Lord Francis Douglas, brother and heir presumptive to the marquess of Queensberry,

Edward Whymper (1840–1911), by Lance Calkin, exh. RA 1894

Charles Hudson, vicar of Skillington in Lincolnshire, Douglas Hadow, a former student of Hudson's, Michel Croz, a Chamonix guide, and two Zermatt guides named Peter Taugwalder, a father and son. On the descent Hadow, an inexperienced climber, slipped and fell, knocking over Croz and dragging Hudson and Douglas off their feet. Whymper and the Taugwalders braced themselves and the rope tying them to the others broke, plunging the other four climbers 4000 feet to the glacier below. An inquest determined that the rope that broke was a spare piece of inferior quality, which had been improperly used.

Although Whymper was the subject of much personal criticism, his account of the accident helped to quell an acrimonious debate about mountaineering in 1865 and became the dramatic climax of his *Scrambles amongst the Alps in the Years 1860–69* (1871), one of the most popular mountaineering books ever written. 'The book is entirely personal, all ego', Whymper told a friend in 1869. 'It will have a hundred illustrations—the best your humble servant knows how to produce, and they will contain enough sensations for half a dozen volumes' (Smythe, 225). The book is written with simplicity, directness, and verve, and is profusely illustrated with his woodcuts.

Whymper opened an office for his engraving business on the Strand, London, in 1865 and contributed illustrations to numerous books of travel, such as Samuel Manning's *Swiss Pictures Drawn with Pen and Pencil* (1866), and to journals, such as the *Sunday Magazine*, *Leisure Hour*, and the *Illustrated London News*. He also drew many portraits, examples of which appeared in *British Heroes and Worthies*

(1871). With his father he contributed many engravings to Joseph Wolf's *Wild Animals* (1873–4). He eventually took over his father's business, which maintained offices in both Lambeth Road and Ludgate Hill in the 1890s. In the face of competition from cheap photographic reproductions, however, the business closed in 1900.

Whymper occasionally interrupted his work as an engraver to continue his interests in Arctic and mountain exploration. In 1867 and 1872 he explored the interior of Greenland and returned with large collections of fossils and botanical specimens. From 1872 to 1874 he served as vice-president of the Alpine Club, and also in 1872 the king of Italy conferred on him the order of St Maurice and St Lazarus. Prevented by political difficulties from climbing in the Himalayas, however, he travelled in 1879–80 to Ecuador with his former Matterhorn rival J. A. Carrel and the latter's cousin Louis Carrel, to test the physiological effects of low pressure at high altitudes and the phenomenon of 'mountain sickness'. They twice climbed Chimborazo (20,498 feet), the highest mountain in Ecuador, and other peaks including Cotopaxi (19,613 feet), an active volcano. Whymper also surveyed the area and collected over 8000 zoological and botanical specimens. Often considered his *magnum opus*, *Travels among the Great Andes of the Equator* (1891–2) combines a popular account of his ascents with his detailed scientific observations. He also published a pamphlet: *How to Use an Aneroid Barometer* (1891). In 1892 Whymper received the patron's medal of the Royal Geographical Society. He also designed a new tent for his Ecuador journey that was widely used by mountaineers for many years.

Whymper returned frequently to the Alps and spent several years in painstaking and thorough research for his guidebooks on Chamonix (1896) and Zermatt (1897), both of which enjoyed considerable commercial success as a result of his skill as a writer and salesman: he travelled literally from hotel to hotel and from bookshop to bookshop through the Alps selling advertising and collecting royalties for the books. From 1896 to 1901 he spent his summers revising his books and his winters lecturing on the Alps and the Andes.

In 1900 Whymper made a lecture tour of the United States and Canada, and from 1901 to 1909 he returned to the Canadian Rockies periodically to promote tourism on behalf of the Canadian Pacific Railway. With his guides he made ascents and identified walking trails near the route of the railway in the Rockies. In 1905, however, he was injured in a train crash in Canada after which he began to experience memory loss, failing eyesight, and fainting spells. Whymper dropped his aitches throughout his life, but only appears to have been worried about this habit between 1905 and 1908, when he asked a nephew to correct it during his lectures.

Whymper was involved in a brief love affair with Charlotte *Hanbury [see under Hanbury, Elizabeth] that ended with her death in 1900. On 25 April 1906 he married Edith Mary Lewin, forty-five years his junior, the daughter of W. Lewin of Forest Gate, London. They had one daughter, Ethel, before they were divorced in December 1910.

Although Whymper achieved his early ambition in the ascent of the Matterhorn, the bitter-sweet triumph and personal obloquy he endured after the accident permanently embittered him. An 1865 photograph shows the intense gaze of the powerful and confident climber with arms akimbo in a relaxed and resolute pose. An oil portrait by Lance Calkin, exhibited at the Royal Academy in 1894, again depicts Whymper in his climbing gear, but his crossed arms, receding hairline, furrowed brow, downturned lips, granite jaw, and steely eyes darkened by circles from years of insomnia all suggest the forbidding, taciturn, and often morose demeanour for which he was known in his later years.

While on a visit to the Alps Whymper died at Chamonix on 16 September 1911; he was buried in the churchyard of the English church in Chamonix four days later. In 1925 a bronze plaque with a likeness of Whymper was unveiled on the façade of the Monte Rosa Hotel in Zermatt.

PETER H. HANSEN

Sources F. S. Smythe, *Edward Whymper* (1940) · A. L. Mumm, *The Alpine Club register*, 1 (1923) · *Alpine Journal*, 26 (1912), 54–61 · *GJ*, 38 (1911), 439–41 · *The Times* (18 Sept 1911) · Scott Polar RI, Whymper MSS · BL, Whymper MSS · Alpine Club archives, Whymper MSS · P. H. Hansen, 'British mountaineering, 1850–1914', PhD diss., Harvard U., 1991 · R. K. Engen, *Dictionary of Victorian wood engravers* (1985)

Archives Alpine Club, London, letters · BL, corresp., Add. MSS 63084, 63090, 63112 · NHM, papers, incl. notebooks relating to Greenland expedition · Scott Polar RI | BL, Blakeney collection · RGS, letters to RGS · Sheff. Arch., letters to Sheffield Literary and Philosophical Society · Zentralbibliothek, Zürich, Coolidge MSS

Likenesses photograph, 1864, repro. in *Alpine Journal*, 32, 220 · Boissonaz, photograph, 1865, repro. in Smythe, *Edward Whymper*, 117 · Boissonaz, photograph, 1865, repro. in *Alpine Journal* (1911), 55 · photograph, 1871, repro. in Smythe, *Edward Whymper*, 220 · L. Calkin, oils, exh. RA 1894, repro. in Smythe, *Edward Whymper*, frontispiece [*see illus.*] · Wiltmann, photograph, 1910, repro. in *Alpine Journal*, 58 · photograph, 1910, repro. in Smythe, *Edward Whymper*, 316 · O. Hanck, woodcut (after C. Whymper), BM · wood-engraving, NPG; repro. in *ILN* (28 May 1881)

Wealth at death £5308 16s. 4d.: probate, 15 May 1912, *CGPLA Eng. & Wales*

Whymper, Josiah Wood (1813–1903), wood-engraver and watercolour painter, was born on 24 April 1813 at Stoke Green, Ipswich, the second son of Nathaniel Whimper, a brewer and town councillor in Ipswich, and his wife, Elizabeth Orris. The Whimper family was a well-established aristocratic family in Suffolk. After 1840 Josiah adopted what he considered the original spelling of his name, Whymper. His early works are signed 'Whimper Sc', or JW Whimper; later works are signed JW Whymper. He was educated at private schools in Ipswich and then apprenticed to a stonemason because he wished to become a sculptor; a near-fatal accident in the mason's yard terminated his apprenticeship before he was sixteen. When his mother died in 1829 he went to London hoping to join a sculptor's studio, but was dissuaded from this profession by John C. F. Rossi RA. He taught himself to draw and from 1829 studied watercolour painting with W. Collingwood Smith. He and his brother Ebenezzar Whymper set up a wood-engraving business, working in London from premises at 31 Paradise Road, Lambeth.

Josiah Wood Whymper (1813–1903), by John & Charles Watkins

Work on orders for shop notices led to commissions from Charles Knight for *Arabian Nights' Entertainments* (1839), *Pictorial Shakespeare*, and *Penny Magazine*. Josiah Whymper established himself as an illustrator with an etching of New London Bridge on the occasion of its opening (1831), which made £30 profit. Finding that his brother was too irresponsible to share in the running of the business, he moved to new premises at 20 Canterbury Place, Lambeth, about 1842. In 1837 he married Elizabeth Whitworth Claridge (1819–1859), and they had nine sons and two daughters. He intended his sons to continue his business. 'But shall we finally keep to this—I think, in fact I *know* we shall not', he wrote in his diary (Engen, 286). The sons who followed his plan most successfully were Alfred, who was sent to train with the Edinburgh printer R. Clark in 1857, and Frederick, Charles, and Edward *Whymper, who were trained by Josiah as draughtsmen on wood. Edward eventually took over the business. Josiah was also master to an impressive succession of apprentices who were to become some of the most prominent draughtsmen of the 'Sixties school': Frederick Walker, Charles Keene, J. W. North, Charles Green, and G. J. Pinwell. His wood-engraving business became one of the most thriving in London, taking on most of the work for John Murray the publishers, for the Religious Tract Society, and the Society for Promoting Christian Knowledge. Fine examples of his book illustrations are those in Scott's *Poetical Works* (Black, 1857); *Picturesque Europe* (Cassell,

1876–9); some of Murray's editions of Byron's *Childe Harold* and Schliemann's *Works*; 190 engravings after Joseph Wolf for C. A. John's *British Birds in their Haunts* (1862); and twenty engravings after Wolf for *Life and Habits of Wild Animals* (1873–4), produced with his son Edward. Whymper also engraved for periodicals such as *Illustrated London News* (1855) and *Sunday at Home* (1869). He engraved a large number of illustrations by Sir John Gilbert, his friend and constant travelling companion for watercolour sketching: *Lady of the Lake* (1853) and *Lay of the Last Minstrel* (1854) are two of the finest examples. Whymper was also a competent draughtsman illustrator, often engraving his own natural history illustrations. These appeared in C. R. Conder's *Child's History of Jerusalem* (1874), L. J. Jenning's *Field Paths and Green Lanes* (1877), and C. R. Conder's *Tent Work in Palestine* (1878). Although his engraving work did not allow him much time to pursue watercolour painting, he exhibited frequently at the New Watercolour Society from 1844, where he was elected associate in 1854 and member in 1857; and also at the Society of British Artists, the Royal Academy, and the Royal Institute of Painters in Oil-Colours. His wife, Elizabeth, died in 1859, and in 1866 he married Emily Hepburn (*d.* 1886), a talented watercolour painter, who exhibited watercolour landscapes at the Royal Academy in 1877–8 and the Royal Institute in 1883–5. She was also a draughtsman illustrator and illustrated *Beauty in Common Things* (1874). By 1882 Whymper's engraving business at 43 and 45 Lambeth Road was jointly managed with his son Edward and appeared in the directories as J. W. and Edward Whymper, draughtsmen and engravers on wood. From 1859 he had a country house at Haslemere, Surrey, but did not finally retire from his work in London until 1884, when Edward took over the firm, continuing to run it throughout the 1890s. During Josiah's career the Whymper name had established an excellent reputation for high-quality wood-engraving. He died at his home, Town House, Haslemere, on 7 April 1903, and was buried in Haslemere churchyard. Collections of his work are held at the British Museum, the Bodleian Library, Oxford, and the Victoria and Albert Museum, London.

LOIS OLIVER

Sources R. K. Engen, *Dictionary of Victorian wood engravers* (1985) · *DNB* · S. Houfe, *The dictionary of British book illustrators and caricaturists, 1800–1914*, rev. edn (1981) · E. Kilmurray, *Dictionary of British portraiture*, 3 (1981) · Graves, *Artists* · IGI · CGPLA Eng. & Wales (1903) · d. cert.
Likenesses L. Calkin, portrait, exh. RA 1889 · J. & C. Watkins, photograph, NPG [*see illus.*]
Wealth at death £9645 13s. 4d.: probate, 5 May 1903, CGPLA Eng. & Wales

Whytbroke, William (*c.*1500–1569), church musician and composer, is of unknown parentage and upbringing. In 1525, at Lichfield Cathedral where he was a vicar-choral, he took all three major orders up to the priesthood. During 1529–30 he occurs as a priest-chaplain of the choir of Cardinal College, Oxford, then directed by the composer John Taverner. This institution was about to be dissolved, and by 1531 Whytbroke had become a minor canon of St

Paul's Cathedral, London. Apparently he possessed outstanding qualities, and by 1534 had been appointed subdean (senior minor canon) in preference to several colleagues of greater seniority. He filled this office through all the upheavals in religion of the mid-century, and during the 1550s his knowledge of Lichfield and Oxford musicians seems to have contributed substantially to the repertory preserved in the Gyffard partbooks (BL, Add. MSS 17802–17805), which appear likely to represent the St Paul's repertory of four-part polyphony sung in the reign of Mary I. He proved able to accommodate himself to the Edwardian Reformation to the extent of marrying, and of composing to vernacular texts from the 1549 Book of Common Prayer. However, in 1563 he found himself unable to subscribe to the uncompromising protestantism of the thirty-eight articles of religion, and in February 1564 he was ejected from his employment at the cathedral. Nevertheless, he remained on good terms with his former colleagues, and lived in the close or its vicinity until his death.

At Cardinal College, Taverner and Whytbroke appear to have worked in close association. Whytbroke composed an additional part to Taverner's responsory *Audivi vocem*, and his In nomine for four viols likewise takes inspiration from an original Taverner work. His expertise in cantus firmus composition is further exhibited by the mass 'Upon the Square', each movement of which employs one of the pre-existent tunes known as 'squares'; he engaged with assurance the sonorous and elaborately decorative style of the 1520s. His setting of the Jesus antiphon *Sancte Deus* may be contemporary, since the daily performance of this text was stipulated by the Cardinal College statutes. With its more imitative idiom Whytbroke was less at ease, and numerous technical limitations rather compromise the quality of his achievement. For the reformed services of the 1549 prayer book he composed two settings of the vernacular Magnificat and an anthem, 'Let your light so shine'. All adopt the severely plain and chordal style, emphasizing the audibility of the words, that was all that such reformers as William May, the Edwardian dean of St Paul's, were prepared to tolerate.

In his will (made on 14 March 1569, proved on 2 April 1569), which discloses that he died a wealthy man, owning a tavern, shops, and houses in the vicinity of St Paul's, Whytbroke requested burial in the cathedral cloister close to the grave of John Redford. To another former colleague he left 'all my books and songs' yet remaining in the minor canons' lodging, while another beneficiary was the amateur musician Henry Blower, a London wax chandler, who with Whytbroke and the composers Philip ap Rhys and Edmund Strowger had formed a group of music-loving friends in St Paul's Churchyard, a generation earlier than Nicholas Yonge's famous reference to social music-making there. ROGER BOWERS

Sources GL, St Paul's Cathedral, London, archives · H. Baillie, 'Squares', *Acta Musicologica*, 32 (1960), 178–93 · M. Bent, 'Square', *New Grove*, 8.29–30 · F. L. Harrison, *Music in medieval Britain* (1958); 2nd edn [1963] · R. W. Bray, 'British Museum Add. MSS 17802–5 (the Gyffard part-books): an index and commentary', *Royal Musical Association Research Chronicle*, 7 (1969), 31–50 · D. Mateer, 'The "Gyffard" partbooks: composers, owners, date and provenance', *Royal Musical Association Research Chronicle*, 28 (1995), 21–50 · W. Whytbroke, *Sancte deus, sancte fortis*, ed. N. Sandon, Antico Edition, RCM, 117 (1997) · W. Whytbroke, 'Let your light so shine before men', ed. W. H. Cope, *A collection of anthems for parish choirs* (1847) · W. Whytbroke, 'Magnificat [1]', *The Wanley manuscripts*, ed. J. Wrightson, *Recent Researches in the Music of the Renaissance*, 99–101 (1995), 3.95–102 · W. Whytbroke, 'Magnificat [2]', *The Wanley manuscripts*, ed. J. Wrightson, *Recent Researches in the Music of the Renaissance*, 99–101 (1995), 3.113–18, 242–6 · D. Chadd and R. Bowers, 'Whytbroke, William', *New Grove*, 2nd edn · D. Scott, *The music of Saint Paul's Cathedral* (1973) · will, PRO, PROB 11/51, 55*v* · episcopal register, Lichfield, Staffs. RO

Wealth at death considerable, but not quantifiable in terms of cash value since mostly in form of property owned: will, PRO, PROB 11/51, fol. 55*v*

Whyte, Alexander (1836–1921), United Free Church of Scotland minister, was born at Kirriemuir, Forfarshire, on 13 January 1836. His parents were John Whyte (1812–1871) and Janet Thomson (*d.* 1882); they never married. His father left Kirriemuir and Alexander was brought up by his mother, who earned her living as a weaver and harvester; the boy owed much to her influence, and to that of two local ministers and several keenly intelligent artisans. Abandoning the shoemaking trade, to which he had served his apprenticeship, Whyte taught for four years in village schools. At the age of twenty-two (1858) he matriculated in King's College, Aberdeen, and, supporting himself mainly by teaching evening classes, succeeded in graduating as MA with second-class honours in mental philosophy in 1862. Sir William Duguid Geddes and Alexander Bain were the professors who made the deepest impression on him. During this period he became acquainted with the writings of Thomas Goodwin the elder, and Goodwin's influence persisted to the end of his life.

Whyte decided to enter the ministry of the Free Church of Scotland, and four years (1862–6) devoted to the study of theology at New College, Edinburgh, enabled him to become a licentiate. After serving as colleague at St John's Free Church, Glasgow (1866–70), he became colleague to Robert Smith Candlish at St George's Free Church, Edinburgh; on Candlish's death in 1873 he became sole minister of the congregation. Alone for the next twenty-two years, and subsequently with the assistance of a colleague, Whyte held this charge until 1916, when he resigned. He married on 9 September 1881 Jane Elizabeth, daughter of George Freeland Barbour, of Bonskeid, Perthshire. His wife was a cultivated person who shared his intellectual interests, such as corresponding with J. H. Newman. They had three sons and three daughters, and a son who died in infancy. In 1898 he was elected moderator of the general assembly, and in 1909 principal of New College, Edinburgh, a position which he held until 1918; he left an interesting record of the content of the classes he taught (Barbour, 647). The freedom of the city of Edinburgh was presented to him in 1910. The union of 1900, whereby the Free Church and the United Presbyterian

Church of Scotland were merged into one communion, was warmly advocated and welcomed by him. The movement, which began some years later, for the union of the Church of Scotland and the United Free Church also won his enthusiastic support. He was a strong Liberal—an admirer of W. E. Gladstone and, later, a friend of Lloyd George.

A traditionalist himself, Whyte championed the cause of liberty in biblical criticism; a Calvinist in theology, he was catholic in his sympathies with exponents of the devotional life. His preaching was famous even in an age of famous preachers. It was distinguished by a rich imagination, with a streak of humour, genial or grim, running through it; by a passion for righteousness which betrayed him at times into exaggerated confessions and attributions of evil motives; and by a mysticism which expressed itself in rapturous and moving eloquence.

For twenty years Whyte's evening sermons were published in the *British Weekly*, and he wrote many volumes on biblical subjects, including *A Commentary on the Shorter Catechism* (1882) and *Bible Characters* (6 vols., 1896–1902). Between 1892 and 1908 he published books on J. H. Newman, James Fraser, Samuel Rutherford, St Teresa of Avila, Lancelot Andrewes, William Law, Father John of the Greek church, Thomas Shepard, and Thomas Goodwin. He also published *Bunyan Characters* (4 vols., 1893–1908).

In 1919 the Whytes moved to 22 Church Row, Hampstead, London, to be near their children. Whyte died there on 6 January 1921 and was buried on 11 January in the Dean cemetery, Edinburgh, his wife surviving him.

The Whytes' eldest son was **Sir (Alexander) Frederick Whyte** (1883–1970), who, having attended Edinburgh Academy and read modern languages at Jena University and at Edinburgh University (graduating with a first class), was warden of the Edinburgh University settlement in 1907–8. He was Liberal MP for Perth City in 1910–18, being parliamentary private secretary to Winston Churchill in 1910–15. In 1912 he married Margaret Emily, *née* Fairweather; they had one son and two daughters. Whyte edited *The New Europe* from May 1917. He was president of the legislative assembly in India, 1920–25, and was knighted in 1922. In 1929–32 he was political adviser to the national government of China. He was involved in the Round Table and became director-general of the English Speaking Union in 1938. In 1939–40 he was head of the American division of the Ministry of Information. Whyte published several books on world politics, including *Asia in the Twentieth Century* (1926) and *China and Foreign Powers* (1927). He died on 30 July 1970.

A. B. MACAULAY, rev. H. C. G. MATTHEW

Sources G. F. Barbour, *The life of Alexander Whyte, D.D.* (1923) · *DSCHT* · *Dod's Parliamentary Companion* · *WWW*
Archives New College, Edinburgh, sermons, lectures, and papers
Likenesses P. Wissaert, two bronze medallions, 1915, Scot. NPG · J. Guthrie, oils, New College, Edinburgh · J. Guthrie, oils, Scot. NPG
Wealth at death £5001 16s.: probate, 5 March 1921, *CGPLA Eng. & Wales*

Whyte, Sir (Alexander) Frederick (1883–1970). *See under* Whyte, Alexander (1836–1921).

Whyte, Samuel (1734–1811), schoolmaster and poet, was born aboard ship on a voyage between Dublin and Liverpool. His mother, whose name has not been discovered, died soon after giving birth. He was once thought to be the natural son of Solomon Whyte, a very extensive landowner from Banbridge, co. Down, but it now seems much more likely that his father was Solomon's younger brother, Richard Whyte (d. c.1744), who was deputy governor of the Tower of London, probably a sinecure not requiring much attendance. Samuel enjoyed a happy childhood in Liverpool, near St Peter's Church, in the home of foster parents, but his fortunes were to change when he returned to Dublin and was reluctantly taken in tow by relations. The only one with a kind word to say to him was his first cousin, Frances Chamberlaine, nine or ten years his senior, who later married the actor and educationist Thomas Sheridan. No doubt to get him out of the way, Samuel was packed off as a boarder to Samuel Edwards's academy in Golden Lane, Dublin, where he obtained a sound education, although there is no information as to how long he remained there.

Towards the end of 1754 Whyte crossed to Liverpool where he revisited the scenes of his childhood. Having lost nearly all his money in that city, he undertook the journey to London on foot with only 9 shillings in his pocket. He appears to have spent a year or so in London where he may have met the woman who was to be his wife, the Therania, apparently, of several of his poems. However, Mrs Whyte never became reconciled to living in Ireland: she missed her friends and, following the birth of three children, her health deteriorated. It is not therefore surprising that the couple separated, although Whyte was exceedingly bitter about the breakup in the poem *The Retrospect*, written in 1759.

In April 1758 Whyte set up in Grafton Street, Dublin, a seminary for the instruction of youth, which he also described as an English grammar school. Thomas and Frances Sheridan were to prove a source of great encouragement and support in this project, both by sending their own children to the school and by encouraging some friends and relations to do likewise. Having thus got off to a good start, Whyte's academy soon acquired a great reputation, attracting pupils not only from Dublin but from the provinces as well. It was to number among its pupils the writers Richard Brinsley Sheridan and Thomas Moore, and the duke of Wellington is believed to have spent a short period there before proceeding to Eton College. Catering for boys and girls, Catholics and protestants, its co-educational, interdenominational ethos was, in Ireland at least, two centuries before its time. A hands-on headmaster, Whyte was on visiting terms with the parents of many of his pupils, whom, outside the normal curriculum, he encouraged to take part in private theatricals, to write verse and to socialize at balls, plays, and other entertainments.

Whyte's academy continued to be popular and successful up to the end of the century. It went out of favour after the Act of Union 1801, when the absence of a parliament in Dublin was to result in the decline of that city as a centre of fashion, culture, and the arts. The school lingered on for some years after Whyte's death in 1811 under the direction of his son, Edward Athenry, who had been his father's partner for some years. As well as being a headmaster, Whyte had pretensions to being an educationist. His first work in that sphere was his *Treatise on the English Language*, which, though printed in 1761, was published in 1800. His edition of James Burgh's *The Art of Speaking* (2nd edn, 1763) proved popular and reached a seventh edition in 1787; Whyte also published 'An introductory tract on education' that was prefixed to his *Beauties of History* (2nd edn, 1775). In 1772 he published a collection of verse entitled *The Shamrock, or, Hibernian Cresses*, a quarto volume of over 500 pages of which thirty-five were devoted to his 'Thoughts on the prevailing system of school education' and the rest to verse. However, Whyte conceded that only two thirds of the verse in this bulky tome was his own, the rest being in the main the work of his students. Since this leaves the reader in the predicament of not knowing precisely which are Whyte's poems and which are not, any assessment of Whyte's work as contained in this volume is rendered impossible.

In 1792 Whyte's son Edward Athenry collected his father's work in a 400-page volume entitled *Poems on Various Subjects*, of which 280 pages are devoted to verse and the rest to explanatory notes, remarks on Boswell's life of Johnson, and forty pages of what are called 'extracts'. It ran to several editions. Again, some of the poems are by other hands, but such poems are duly credited. In this volume Whyte emerges as a fluent versifier for whom, however, no great claims can be made as a poet. There are occasional pieces, such as 'A Familiar Epistle to J. H., Esq.' (in reality a description of Dublin in 1758), which, apart from being competent verse, are of interest to the social historian as depictions of life in the Dublin of his time.

In 1801 Whyte and his son Edward Athenry published *Miscellanea nova*, a hotchpotch of 280 pages of which only forty are devoted to verse and the rest to letters from various members of the Sheridan family together with Whyte's successful petition to the Irish parliament in the early 1760s to have Thomas Sheridan, then a bankrupt skulking in France, released from his debts. Samuel Whyte died in Grafton Street in September 1811 and was buried in St Anne's churchyard, Dawson Street, Dublin, on 29 September.

PATRICK FAGAN

Sources J. T. Gilbert, *History of the city of Dublin* (1854–9), 3.199–210 · C. Lefanu, *Memoirs of the life and writings of Mrs Frances Sheridan* (1824), 84 · S. Whyte, *Poems on various subjects*, 3rd edn (1795), 333, 335 · S. Whyte and E. A. Whyte, *Miscellanea nova* (1801), 90 · DNB · P. Fagan, ed., *A Georgian celebration: Irish poets of the eighteenth century* (1989) · P. B. Eustace, *Abstracts of wills in Registry of Deeds, Dublin* (1956) · Betham's abstracts of wills, NA Ire. · parish register, St Anne's, Dawson Street, Dublin, 29 Sept 1811 [burial] · *GM*, 1st ser., 81/2 (1811), 486

Likenesses H. Brocas senior, stipple (after pastel by H. Hamilton), BM; repro. in Whyte, *Poems on various subjects*, frontispiece

Whytehead, Thomas (1815–1843), poet and missionary, was born on 30 November 1815 at Thormanby, Yorkshire, the youngest son of Henry Robert Whytehead (1772–1818), curate of Thormanby and rector of Goxhill, and his wife, Hannah Diana (d. 1844), daughter of Thomas Bowman, rector of Crayke, co. Durham. When his father died, on 20 August 1818, Whytehead's mother moved with her five girls and four boys to York. At the age of eight, Thomas Whytehead went to Beverley grammar school; he left at fifteen. Thomas's brother Robert (1808–1863), an undergraduate at St John's College, Cambridge, in 1830, then prepared Thomas for entry to Cambridge. When Robert took a curacy in Swineshead, Lincolnshire, in 1833, Thomas went to visit him, and was initiated into parish life, actively assisting his brother.

In October 1833 Whytehead became a pensioner at St John's College, Cambridge, where a distinguished academic record followed: a Bell scholarship (1834); two chancellor's English medals, with poems entitled 'The death of HRH the duke of Gloucester' (1835) and 'The empire of the sea' (1836); the 1835 Hulsean prize for his essay entitled 'The resemblance between Christ and Moses'; and Sir William Browne's gold medal for Latin and Greek epigrams (1836). In the classical tripos Whytehead came second in February 1837, and he used a copy of the class list to communicate the news to his sister Anne. Whytehead's letters to Anne reflect his love of home ('college may be animating, but it is not *home*', June 1834) and his loneliness ('I have just got a little bird in a cage to make some sort of companion for me, as I often feel as if I w^d give anything for something alive like myself to keep me company', February 1834). In March 1837 he became senior classical medallist and was elected to a fellowship at St John's College. He graduated BA in 1837, MA in 1840, and in 1838 he held a classical lectureship at Clare College; he was admitted *ad eundem* at Oxford in 1841. He was ordained deacon in 1839 and accepted the curacy of Freshwater, Isle of Wight, where his former college tutor I. F. Isaacson was clergyman; he was ordained priest in December 1840. Whytehead's dedication to the religious life is apparent throughout his letters and verse, and his work *College Life* (1845, 2nd edn 1856) presents a view of Oxford and Cambridge primarily as sites of spiritual and moral development. In 1835 Whytehead had volunteered himself to the Church Missionary Society, and he finally agreed to become chaplain to the newly appointed bishop of New Zealand, George Augustus Selwyn. Whytehead's health had never been strong: in particular, a recurring eye problem had dogged his studies. After sailing for Australia on 26 December 1841 he was taken ill in Sydney with a ruptured blood vessel, the precursor of a collapsed lung. He spent months there before being able to progress to New Zealand. He taught himself Maori in this time, translating two hymns, one of them Bishop Ken's evening hymn. He faced his death, as he had lived, with Christian conviction. He died on 19 March 1843 at Waimate, Bay of Islands, and was buried beside the new Waimate church building two days later.

Whytehead made little impression on the literary

world. He was commissioned to write an ode for the installation of the duke of Northumberland in 1842 as chancellor of Cambridge University, performed to music by T. A. Walmisley. His *Poems* (1842) was sufficiently well received to prompt a second edition, published as *Poetical Remains* (1877), edited by Thomas Bowman Whytehead, who appended a memoir based on his uncle's letters. This appeared eight years after the new chapel at St John's, Cambridge, was consecrated, with its full-length painting of Whytehead on the choir roof as one of the nineteenth century's representative figures. In a minor way he was such a representative: a highly-educated clergyman poet whose writing reflected his unswerving faith.

ROSEMARY SCOTT

Sources T. B. Whytehead, 'Memoir', *Whytehead's poetical remains and letters* (1877) · T. F. K. [T. F. Knox], 'Editor's preface', in T. Whytehead, *College life* (1845) · St John Cam., Whytehead MSS, U 23 · J. Julian, ed., *A dictionary of hymnology* (1892) · *Mission Life* (July 1873), 375–90 · Burke, *Gen. GB* · *English Churchman* (17 Aug 1843), 518 · *English Churchman* (7 Sept 1843), 570
Archives St John Cam., corresp. and literary MSS, U 23 | Bodl. Oxf., corresp. with W. C. Cotton
Likenesses G. G. Scott, portrait, St John Cam.
Wealth at death left £681 to the Society for the Propagation of the Gospel, and his library to St John's College, Cambridge: Whytehead, 'Memoir'

Whytt, Robert (1714–1766), physician and natural philosopher, was born in Edinburgh on 6 September 1714. He was the second son of Robert Whytt (*d.* 1714) of Bennochy, an advocate whose family was traceable to the late fifteenth century and had intermarried with the better-known families of Balfour and Melville, and who died six months before Robert was born. His mother, Jean, daughter of Anthony Murray of Woodend in Perthshire, died about 1720. Whytt was educated first at the public school of Kirkcaldy, where his widowed mother had moved. There is little evidence for the common assumption that about 1727 he followed his elder brother, George (*d.* 1728), to the University of St Andrews, which George had left abruptly on the death of their mother. It is much more likely that he was the Robert Whyt recorded as matriculating in arts in Edinburgh in 1729, the year after George died. Certainly Whytt was studying medicine there in the following year under Alexander Monro *primus*, in whose class-list he appears also in 1732 and 1734.

Later in 1734 Whytt left for London to study under the great lithotomist William Cheselden. From the wards of the London hospitals he went to those of Paris and attended the lectures of Jacques Benigne Winslow. After this he studied at the foremost medical school of the time, Leiden, and with the 'teacher of all Europe', the ageing Herman Boerhaave. Whytt took his MD (like many contemporary Scottish physicians) at Rheims, on 2 April 1736. After returning home he took the career steps of taking an equivalent degree from St Andrews, on 31 October 1737, and becoming a licentiate of the Royal College of Physicians of Edinburgh, on 21 June 1738; he was elected a fellow on 27 November and began his practice. His first wife was Helen Robertson, sister of General Robertson, governor of New York. The two children of this marriage died

Robert Whytt (1714–1766), by unknown artist, 1863 (after Bellucci, 1738)

in infancy and Helen died in 1741. On 24 April 1743 he married Louisa Balfour (*d.* 1764), the White Rose of Pilrig. They had fourteen children, of whom eight had died by the age of five.

Whytt's contemporary reputation rested in the first instance on his use of lime water and soap in cases of the stone of the bladder, about which he published his 'Essay on the virtues of lime-water and soap in the cure of the stone' in *Observations and Essays in Medicine by a Society in Edinburgh* (vol. 2, pt 2, 1743). Whytt considered that lime water and soap were the active principle of a secret remedy of Joanna Stephens which had been made public at great cost by parliament. Interest had been heightened by the controversy over the death of Sir Robert Walpole, in which was implicated a medicine containing lime. Whytt's paper went through several editions and was translated into French and German. Soap, when dissolved in lime water, remained popular as a lithontriptic until the second half of the nineteenth century.

By 1739 Whytt had begun to question the received views on the nature of the vital motions, and thus to begin his most important enterprise. The Boerhaavian orthodoxy was that the body was a machine composed ultimately of particles, some with chemical properties. No part was played by the soul as a source of motion in the body, as in the traditional systems of Galen and Aristotle, ultimately because Descartes, the greatest proponent of physiological mechanism, had denied it. Descartes had also espoused a modified form of Harvey's doctrine of the circulation of the blood, leaving a residual problem of whether a wholly mechanical heart could account for the circulation of the whole mass of blood, even through the capillaries. Whytt believed that no mere machine could perform vital actions and held that the living body contained a 'sentient principle' that could perceive and react to stimuli in an unconscious way. Unconscious perception was unintelligible to mechanists, for whom the soul, as the organ of perception and rationality, was entirely distinct from matter. In place of the discredited Galen and Aristotle, Whytt could draw support from Hippocrates, who had divided the bodily parts into 'containing', 'contained', and the *impetum faciens*, the vital spark that provided motion.

Whytt outlined these ideas in a paper read before the Philosophical Society in Edinburgh in 1745 or 1746, which no doubt helped to bring the 'lime-water' doctor more into the public eye. He was teaching in the 'Town's College' in the latter year and was elected professor of the practice of medicine in the Edinburgh medical faculty in the place of Andrew Sinclair, on 26 August 1747. He was also appointed as the professor of the institutes of medicine. Whytt was associated with Alexander Monro *primus* and William Cullen at Edinburgh Royal Infirmary, where he gave clinical lectures in 1760.

Whytt's major work was his *Essay on the Vital and other Involuntary Motions of Animals* of 1751. In it he elaborated his doctrine of the sentient principle: it was the soul, distributed all over the body and acting in a limited way in the organs and tissues it occupied. It carried impressions in the sensory nerves and initiated motion in the muscles. It was not limited to the brain, for a frog survived the loss of its head. Moreover, the headless frog still retained the power to move its foot away from a pricking needle: clearly the frog retained the power of sentience and motion, which combined to generate a beneficial action. This power, now known as reflex action, lay in the spinal cord, as Whytt showed by destroying it. Whytt's work also drew him into the European arena, where he conducted a controversy with the great Albrecht von Haller on 'sensibility and irritability'—the sentient and motive powers of the parts of the body still generally regarded as a machine. Haller and the mechanists represented Whytt as a follower of the religious enthusiasm of Stahl, the pietist of Halle, who argued for the physiological actions in the body of an autonomous, freely acting, and even wilful soul. But Whytt believed that the soul was bound by the laws of the parts of the body it occupied; this was recognized by a number of practitioners who from the 1740s began to react against the mechanism of Boerhaave. One of them was François Boissier de Sauvages, who corresponded with Whytt and taught animist doctrines in Montpellier. A principal argument of Whytt and the animists was that if the body was a hydraulic machine, in the Newtonian manner, then there must be a non-mechanical source of motion that moved it.

Whytt's interest in the sensibility and co-ordination of the nerves led to a major work on nervous diseases in 1764. It has been suggested that this work helped to make 'nervous disease' a fashionable term, replacing 'the vapours'—a remnant of humoral pathology. Whytt's doctrine was that the part of the soul resident in the sensory nerves was so bound by the laws of union of body and soul that it

allowed each nerve to transmit only its own kind of stimulus to the brain and spinal cord. Here the soul, acting as a kind of common sensory agent, redirected the stimulus to appropriate motor nerves. This accounted for the 'sympathy' of the parts of the body, many of them later recognized to be under the control of the sympathetic nervous system. In disease these sensibilities and sympathies became distorted. Whytt's general pathology also rested on the principles of unconscious sentience and response, and his lectures, which remain unpublished, drew on the *Institutiones pathologia* (1750) of Hieronymus David Gaubius, who had been teaching in Leiden since 1744 and who was a follower of Boerhaave.

Whytt's context was the Scottish Enlightenment of Edinburgh and the city's new medical school, and the connections of both with continental and colonial-American medicine. Whytt corresponded with a number of doctors in these places and his works were translated into French and German. His work was recognized by the society of which he was part: he was elected to a fellowship of the Royal Society (16 April 1752) and to the presidency of the Royal College of Physicians of Edinburgh (1 December 1763). His position as physician to the king in Scotland is said to have been created for him. There was a pugnacious side to his writing, and he took part in controversies not only with Haller, but with his Edinburgh colleague Alston (on the topic of lime water).

Whytt died in Edinburgh on 15 April 1766. His medical attendants did not name the disease that killed him, and the post mortem revealed fluid in the thorax, a red spot on the stomach wall, and concretions in the pancreas. He was buried in Old Greyfriars Church, where there is a monument to his memory. Whytt's collected works were published by his son in 1768. ROGER FRENCH

Sources R. K. French, *Robert Whytt, the soul, and medicine* (1969) · W. Seller, 'Memoir of the life and writings of Robert Whytt, MD, professor of medicine in the University of Edinburgh, 1714–1766', *Transactions of the Royal Society of Edinburgh*, 23 (1864), 99 · R. M. Barclay, 'The life and work of Robert Whytt: a preliminary survey', part of an MD diss., Edinburgh, 1922 · A. Bower, *The history of the University of Edinburgh*, 3 vols. (1817–30) · A. Grant, *The story of the University of Edinburgh during its first three hundred years*, 2 vols. (1884) · J. Rurhäh, 'Robert Whytt, M.D., professor of medicine in the University of Edinburgh', *Journal of the Alumni Association of the College of Physicians and Surgeons* (1911) · J. D. Comrie, 'An eighteenth-century neurologist', *Edinburgh Medical Journal*, 3rd ser., 32 (1925), 755 · E. M. W. Balfour Melville MSS, priv. coll. · A. von Haller, *Ad Roberti Whytii nuperum scriptum apologia* (1764) · A. von Haller, *Bibliotheca anatomica*, 2 vols. (Zürich, 1774–7) · *DSB*
Archives Royal College of Physicians of Edinburgh, corresp., casebook, and lecture notes · U. Edin. L., corresp. and lecture notes · Wellcome L., papers incl. unpublished lectures, case reports, and prescriptions | NRA, priv. coll., letters to J. Oswald
Likenesses oils, 1863 (after Bellucci, 1738), Royal College of Physicians of Edinburgh [*see illus.*] · Bellucci?, oils, priv. coll.
Wealth at death 'landed' family

Wiburn, Percival (1533/4–1606), Church of England clergyman, was perhaps from Kent. He was admitted scholar on Cardinal Morton's foundation at St John's College, Cambridge, on 11 November 1546, became a fellow on 8 April 1552, and proceeded BA in that academic year. In

Mary's reign he joined the exile, arriving at Geneva on 8 May 1557 and being formally admitted resident there on 14 October. He returned to Cambridge by summer 1559, when he proceeded MA, and on 24 July became junior dean and philosophy lecturer at St John's. He was ordained deacon in London on 25 January 1560 and priest on 27 March following. By June he was chaplain to Lord Keeper Bacon, and in this capacity promoted many candidates for livings during the next fifteen years. On 23 October 1560 he was himself presented to a canonry of Norwich, which he resigned by January 1562. On 7 February 1561 he was presented to a canonry of Rochester, and on 16 November that year to the like dignity in Westminster Abbey; both stalls he held for life. He became senior fellow of St John's on 6 April 1561, and college preacher that Michaelmas.

About October 1561 Wiburn married and was licensed to preach. In the convocation of 1563 he was proctor for the Rochester chapter. About this time he was recommended to Lord Robert Dudley as 'godlie' (Pepys MSS, 2, misdated), and in 1563 Dudley's brother, the earl of Warwick, hoped to have Wiburn as a chaplain in the Le Havre expedition. On 25 April 1563 Wiburn was presented by the crown to the vicarage of Holy Sepulchre, Holborn, to which he was instituted on 8 March 1564. Wiburn became prominent among the agitators for further reform. He was one of those who on 20 March 1565 petitioned the ecclesiastical commissioners to tolerate some measure of nonconformity. When Archbishop Parker finally summoned the London clergy to Lambeth on 26 March 1566 and required instant assent to the prescribed costume and other requirements, Wiburn must have been among the thirty-seven who refused and were sequestered, with deprivation following automatically after three months. Wiburn's London benefice was lost to him by October, but he retained his canonries.

Meanwhile the puritans looked abroad for support, and in summer 1566 Wiburn led an unofficial delegation to Switzerland. At Geneva, Beza received him amiably, but he had a cool reception from Bullinger in Zürich. The Swiss were reluctant to antagonize the English bishops, which is precisely what Wiburn's mission achieved. He drew up a 'State of the church' describing conditions in England, but was subsequently obliged to deny that he had suggested that many Catholic practices were still countenanced. It is said that Wiburn had to support himself for a time, but he most likely returned to Cambridge, since it was from there that he moved to Northampton. He was invited by local gentry to preach in the latter town, and by May 1570 had established himself as de facto superintendent of the local clergy; he introduced the meetings known as 'exercises' or 'prophesyings', at first with the support of Bishop Edmund Scambler of Peterborough. A more radical scheme involving the civic leadership in a Genevan-style regime for the whole community was drafted on 5 June 1571, still ostensibly with the bishop's support. But just as this 'order of Northampton' was devised, Wiburn (who had been satirized in a ballad distributed by his opponents as 'alias tiburne [Tyburn] tyke')

was summoned to London to be interrogated by Parker. By February 1572 Scambler acted to end Wiburn's whole ministry in Northampton, despite pleas from the earl of Leicester. Wiburn removed himself to the neighbouring village of Whiston, where, under the protection of the lady of the manor, Isabel Catesby, he continued to draw a large congregation. In July 1573 he was again examined in London, this time before Star Chamber, in connection with the dissemination of Cartwright's Replye.

On 9 June 1575 Wiburn was licensed to be absent from his canonries to preach the gospel in the Channel Islands; he was active in Jersey and Guernsey for two years, and with Arthur Wake drafted the islands' first church order. Back at Rochester in 1581 he was appointed the cathedral's divinity lecturer. In the same year, having been authorized to dispute with Catholics, he published a reply to Robert Persons. Despite these official employments he was again suspended from preaching for several years from 1583/4. His dogged refusal to wear the surplice eventually marked him out as an old campaigner. By 1599 his Rochester colleagues acknowledged it would be 'a myracle' if he now changed his ways (Knighton, 'The reformed chapter', 72). At Westminster he latterly occupied the judicial post of archdeacon, and conducted an amiable house-swap with Lancelot Andrewes. In his final years he preached at Battersea, and enjoyed the patronage and society of Ann, Lady Bacon, at Gorhambury.

Wiburn died between 23 April and 16 May 1606. He asked to be buried in Whiston churchyard. He left sons John, Nathaniel (both in orders), and Joseph, and a daughter, Mary (married to William Striddle). He left money to the prisoners in the gaols of Northampton, Rochester, and Westminster Gatehouse, and directed that his Hebrew, Latin, and Greek books be shared among his sons. His wife had clearly predeceased him; her identity is unknown.

C. S. KNIGHTON

Sources C. H. Garrett, The Marian exiles: a study in the origins of Elizabethan puritanism (1938), 331 · A. Peel, ed., The seconde parte of a register, 2 vols. (1915), vol. 1, pp. 13, 30, 82; vol. 2, p. 262 · Calendar of the manuscripts of the marquis of Bath preserved at Longleat, Wiltshire, 5 vols., HMC, 58 (1904–80), vol. 5, p. 185 · Report on the Pepys manuscripts, HMC, 70 (1911), 2–3, 177–8 · Calendar of the manuscripts of the most hon. the marquis of Salisbury, 13, HMC, 9 (1915), 145 · D. J. Crankshaw, 'Peers as patrons: the religious patronage of the peerage in the later English reformation; with particular reference to the Catholic peerage', PhD diss., U. Cam. [in preparation] · Correspondence of Matthew Parker, ed. J. Bruce and T. T. Perowne, Parker Society, 42 (1853), 382 · H. Robinson, ed. and trans., The Zurich letters, comprising the correspondence of several of the English bishops and others with some of the Helvetian reformers, during the early part of the reign of Queen Elizabeth, 1, Parker Society, 7 (1842), 178, 187–91, 363; 2, Parker Society, 8 (1845), 128, 142, 358–62 · P. Collinson, The Elizabethan puritan movement (1967), 51–2, 74, 79–80, 82, 118, 141–3, 148, 151, 266, 369, 439 · W. J. Sheils, The puritans in the diocese of Peterborough, 1558–1610, Northamptonshire RS, 30 (1979), 23–6, 28, 120–21, 127 · V. J. K. Brook, A life of Archbishop Parker (1962), 274 · C. Cross, The royal supremacy in the Elizabethan church (1969), 98–9, 105–6, 213–15 · C. S. Knighton, 'The reformed chapter, 1540–1660', Faith and fabric: a history of Rochester Cathedral, 604–1994, ed. W. N. Yates and P. A. Welsby (1996) [64, 66, 70, 72] · C. S. Knighton, ed., Acts of the dean and chapter of Westminster, 2 (1999), 150, 178, 199, 201 · Fasti Angl., 1541–1857, [Canterbury], 60 n.4, 62; [Ely], 56, 73 · M. R. O'Day, 'The ecclesiastical patronage of the lord keeper, 1558–1642', TRHS, 5th ser., 23

(1973), 101–2 · will, PRO, PROB 11/107, fols. 274r–274v · GL, MS 9535/1., fol. 85 · act book, Medway Archives and Local Studies Centre, Rochester, Kent, Rochester dean and chapter archives, MS DRc/Ac 1, 15

Archives PRO, 'Orders and dealings in the church of Northampton', 5 June 1571, SP 12/78, no. 38

Wealth at death leased property at Cooling, Frindsbury, and Marden, Kent, from dean and chapter of Rochester, which he vested in and bequeathed to sons: Medway Archives and Local Studies Centre, Rochester, Kent, act book of the dean and chapter of Rochester, MS DRc/Ac 1, 15; will, PRO, PROB 11/107, fols. 274r–274v

Wiche, John (1718–1794), General Baptist minister, was born at Taunton, Somerset, on 24 April 1718. His parents were members of Mary Street Baptist Church whose pastor, Joseph Jefferies senior (d. 1746), had rejected Calvinism. Jefferies, who baptized the sixteen-year-old Wiche in the meeting-house on 25 June 1734, and Thomas Lucas, Baptist minister at Trowbridge, Wiltshire, from 1721 to 1743, provided his early education. Joseph Burroughs and James Foster, Socinian pastors of London's non-aligned Paul's Alley/Barbican Baptist Church found assistance from the General Baptist Fund in 1726 for Wiche to study successively at the liberal dissenting academies at Taunton, Kendal (1738–9), and Findern (1740).

In 1743 Wiche went to assist a Mr Phillips, an aged Baptist minister at Salisbury, who soon died leaving Wiche as pastor. Here he met and corresponded with the deist writer Thomas Chubb who lived nearby. In addition, Chubb's sermon *Englishmen Urged to Loyalty by their Sense and Love of Liberty*, about the 1745 Jacobite uprising, foreshadowed Wiche's future concerns for civil and religious liberty. In 1746 Burroughs and Foster introduced him to a small General Baptist church meeting at Rose Yard, Maidstone, and Tovil in Kent. Here he remained as elder for the rest of his life. As a means of livelihood he established a school. In 1755 he married Elizabeth Pine (1735/6–1766) of the leading family in the church. Of their six children, Thomas (d. 11 July 1821, aged sixty-three) became a London bookseller; Sarah married the banker Sampson Kingsford (d. 1821), General Baptist elder and messenger from Canterbury; and Mary married John Evans (1767–1827), pastor of the General Baptist church meeting in Worship Street, London.

When, in 1759, Nathaniel Lardner published his *Letter on the Logos* (written 1730) postulating 'that Jesus Christ is a man with a reasonable soul and a human body' (Wilbur, 2.265), Wiche read it and became a Unitarian. He also began a correspondence with Lardner which lasted until Lardner's death. Lardner's *Letter* also converted Joseph Priestley to Unitarian beliefs, and later, under the pseudonym Nazaraeus, Wiche contributed 'Observations favouring the miraculous conception' to Priestley's *Theological Repository* (5, 1786). Later, after the 1791 Birmingham riots had driven Priestley from his home, Wiche personally approached Henry Dundas on Priestley's behalf. Another of Wiche's correspondents was the Anglican theologian Francis Blackburne. When Wiche publicly supported Blackburne's *Confessional*, which called for an end to subscription to the Thirty-Nine Articles, the two men entered

John Wiche (1718–1794), by unknown engraver, pubd 1797

into another extended correspondence. Until the American war, Wiche had loyally responded to every public fast. The war caused him to re-examine this practice, and henceforth he rejected public fasts as dependent on human authority. Likewise, he rejected Christmas day worship as based on the human authority of the papacy. Scripture alone was the only permitted authority. Eventually he abandoned sermons for scriptural exposition, and regarded public prayers that used the 'we' form as presumptive and unscriptural.

A frugal person, Wiche's only extravagance was to buy books, and he amassed a considerable library. 'Let all descriptions of men write and publish what they please, and every thing that is false can be refuted' (*Protestant Dissenter's Magazine*, April 1797, 128) was his firmly held belief. After he died, on 7 April 1794 at Maidstone, his General Baptist church amalgamated with the Presbyterian/Unitarian congregation in Earle Street, Maidstone, where another friend, William Hazlitt senior (1737–1817), was once minister. Wiche was buried at the General Baptist burial-ground in Tovil, near Maidstone. Quiet and retiring, he valued personal honesty and truthful searching more than popular appeal in ministry. George Wiche (1767–1799), Unitarian minister at Monton, Eccles, Lancashire, from 1788 to 1795, was his nephew.

ALEXANDER GORDON, rev. ANDREW M. HILL

Sources J. Toulmin, 'A sketch of the character of the late Rev. John Wiche', *Protestant Dissenter's Magazine*, 4 (1797), 121–32 · 'Correspondence between Archdeacon Blackburne and Rev. J. Wiche', *Christian Reformer, or, Unitarian Magazine and Review*, 3 (1836), 517–20 · *Life and correspondence of Joseph Priestley*, ed. J. T. Rutt, 1 (1831), 69, 93, 99, 365 · *The General Baptist church meeting at Maidstone, Kent: historical notes*, General Baptist Assembly Occasional Paper, 26 (Oct 1999) · G. E. Evans, *Record of the provincial assembly of Lancashire and Cheshire* (1896), 133 · E. M. Wilbur, *A history of Unitarianism: Socinianism and its antecedents* (1946)

Archives DWL, corresp. with Francis Blackburne · DWL, corresp. with Nathaniel Lardner

Likenesses engraving, NPG; repro. in Toulmin, 'Sketch of the character of the late Rev. John Wiche', facing p. 121 [*see illus.*]

Wickens, Sir John (1815–1873), judge, was born on 13 June 1815, the second son of James Stephen Wickens, solicitor, of Chandos Street, Cavendish Square, London, and his wife, Anne, daughter of John Hayter of Winterbourne Stoke, Wiltshire. Educated under Dr Keate at Eton College (1829–32), where he won the Newcastle scholarship, he went on to win an open scholarship to Balliol College, Oxford, and matriculated there on 30 November 1832. He graduated BA in Michaelmas term 1836 with a double first in classics and mathematics (though, despite statements to the contrary, he did not win the Newdigate prize), and took his MA in 1839. He was unsuccessful as a candidate for a Balliol fellowship, however, and this was variously attributed to an ill-timed display of his wit and to his smoking having annoyed the master.

Wickens was admitted to Lincoln's Inn on 27 April 1837, and was called to the bar in May 1840. His practice grew slowly, but he gained a reputation as a conveyancer, a draftsman of equity pleadings, and an opinion writer. When in 1852 a number of leading juniors took silk as a result of procedural reform in the court of chancery, Wickens became one of the most distinguished juniors at the chancery bar. He was retained in most of the heavy chancery suits of the day, and appeared frequently before the House of Lords and the privy council. He was not a fluent speaker, but had a trenchant and concise way of arguing a point. From January 1843 until his appointment to the bench he was junior equity counsel to the Treasury. His own modesty apart, this appointment prevented him applying to become queen's counsel, and disqualified him from being a parliamentary candidate. In 1845 Wickens married Harriet Frances, daughter of William Davey of Cowley House, Gloucestershire. Their daughter Mary married George Farwell, who became a lord justice of appeal.

In 1868 Wickens became vice-chancellor of the county palatine of Lancaster in succession to Sir William James who became a vice-chancellor. In 1871 Wickens was elected a bencher of his inn, and on 18 April of the same year was appointed to the bench as a vice-chancellor in succession to Sir John Stuart. He was knighted on 29 June 1871. It was said that as a judge he went too slowly and was too much under the influence of precedent, following co-ordinate precedents even if he thought them wrong. But, as his obituary in the *Solicitors' Journal* noted, 'he understood law', and brought to his work a conscientious thoroughness and an intimate knowledge of practice. His judgments contained lucid statements of principle, and masterly applications of principle to new cases. His decisions, rarely appealed from, were even more rarely reversed; an appellate position would have made his ability more conspicuous. Apart from the law, he was known for his wit and humour, his general learning, and the brilliancy and interest of his conversation.

Wickens died at his home at Chilgrove, Westdean, near Chichester, in Sussex, on 23 October 1873.

J. B. ATLAY, rev. N. G. JONES

Sources *Solicitors' Journal*, 18 (1873–4), 20–21 • *The Times* (27 Oct 1873) • *Law Times* (1 Nov 1873), 11 • R. Palmer, first earl of Selborne, *Memorials. Part I: family and personal, 1766–1865*, ed. S. M. Palmer, 1 (1896), 134–5 • Foster, *Alum. Oxon.* • H. E. C. Stapylton, *The Eton school lists, from 1791 to 1850*, 2nd edn (1864) • *CGPLA Eng. & Wales* (1873) • d. cert.

Likenesses M. Carpenter, oils, Eton • wood-engraving (after photograph by J. Watkins), NPG; repro. in *ILN* (6 May 1871), 457
Wealth at death under £35,000: probate, 15 Dec 1873, *CGPLA Eng. & Wales*

Wickes, George (*bap.* 1698, *d.* 1761), goldsmith, was born in Bury St Edmunds, Suffolk, and baptized there on 7 July 1698, the fifth of the six sons and the eighth of ten children of James Wickes, upholsterer, of Bury St Edmunds, and his wife, Dorothy Burton. No record exists of his education: he may have attended the grammar school at Bury St Edmunds or a charity school in nearby Hawstead maintained by a kinsman, Sir Dudley Cullum, who became his brother-in-law in 1710.

Wickes was apprenticed on 2 December 1712 to Samuel Wastell, a London goldsmith, and made free of the Goldsmiths' Company by service on 16 June 1720. By 3 February 1722, when he registered his first maker's marks at Goldsmiths' Hall, he had set up in Threadneedle Street, a move made possible by his marriage on 9 January 1722 to Alder (*d.* 1774), wealthy daughter of Samuel Phelpes, gentleman merchant, and his wife, Mary Aldworth, descendant of merchant princes linked with the East India Company and the Society of Merchant Adventurers of Bristol.

In the early 1730s Wickes joined John Craig, jeweller, in Norris Street, Haymarket. The partnership was dissolved in June 1735 when he was appointed goldsmith to Frederick Louis, prince of Wales, and moved to Panton Street. He was made a liveryman of the Goldsmiths' Company on 13 March 1740. His ledgers, housed in the Victoria and Albert Museum, the only eighteenth-century working goldsmith's ledgers extant, date from 1735. They record purchases by clients, among them Sir Robert Walpole and Robert Butts, bishop of Ely, first cousin to Wickes's mother. This prodigious output engendered a network of subcontractors.

Wickes's own *oeuvre*, lacking perhaps the soaring inspiration of Paul De Lamerie or Paul Crespin, nevertheless places him in the first rank. His Bristol ewer and basin of 1736 are two of the most original and historically important pieces of early English rococo silver. The great Leinster dinner service of 1747 was his swansong: no silver bearing his mark appears thereafter. That year he was joined by Edward Wakelin, who took charge of the workshop. He did not take Wakelin into partnership with him: that the childless Wickes reserved for his protégé, Samuel Netherton, in 1750. The death of the prince of Wales in March 1751 dashed their hopes of royal preferment.

Wickes retired on 11 October 1760 and was succeeded by his former apprentice John Parker in partnership with Edward Wakelin. Accompanied by his wife and Netherton, he moved to Thurston, Suffolk, where he died on 31 August 1761. He was buried in St Peter's Church, Thurston, where a memorial stone was erected. His firm continued to flourish. Robert Garrard joined it in 1780, followed by three sons: it became known as Garrard, the crown jewellers.

ELAINE BARR, rev.

Sources E. Barr, *George Wickes: royal goldsmith, 1698–1761* (1980) • A. G. Grimwade, *London goldsmiths, 1697–1837: their marks and lives*, 3rd edn (1990)

Likenesses portrait, priv. coll.

Wickham, Edward Charles (1834–1910), dean of Lincoln, eldest son of Edward Wickham (1801–1862), at one time vicar of Preston Candover, Hampshire, and his second wife, Christiana St Barbe, daughter of C. H. White, rector of Shalden, Hampshire, was born on 7 December 1834 at Eagle House, Brook Green, Hammersmith, Middlesex, where his father then kept a private school of high reputation. Here he received his early education, entering Winchester College as a commoner in January 1848. On 8 July 1850 he was admitted to a place in college, was senior in school in November 1851, and in January 1852 he succeeded to a fellowship at New College, Oxford, beginning his undergraduate career at the age of seventeen. In December 1854 he took a first class in classical moderations, and a second class in *literae humaniores* in July 1856, winning the chancellor's prize for Latin verse in the same year, and the Latin essay in 1857. He graduated BA in 1857 and proceeded to the degrees of MA in 1859, and of BD and DD in 1894.

Wickham was ordained deacon in 1857 and priest in 1858, and after two years' experience in teaching sixth book at Winchester he was recalled to Oxford, where he still retained his fellowship, by the offer of a tutorship. Here he took a leading part in the series of reforms which threw New College open to scholars and commoners who had not been educated at Winchester, and he helped to amend the statutes so as to allow tutors and other college officers to retain their fellowships after marriage. In conjunction with his friend Edwin Palmer of Balliol he initiated the system of intercollegiate lectures. Wickham's fine scholarship, his influence with the undergraduates, and his power of preaching made him one of the most successful tutors of his time, and it was largely owing to him that New College was transformed into one of the leading colleges.

In September 1873 Wickham succeeded Edward White Benson as headmaster of Wellington College, and shortly afterwards, on 27 December 1873, he married Agnes (1842–1931), eldest daughter of William Ewart *Gladstone. Wickham's twenty years' tenure of the headmastership attracted differing judgements. His cold manner and unimpressive physique (the duke of Wellington, one of the governors, thought him lacking in height and girth) stood in the way of anything like general popularity among boys or masters, and he was subjected to many personal attacks. A series of crises not of his making, notably two epidemics (1883 and 1891) attributed to defective sanitation, and the appointment of a royal commission (1879–80) in response to complaints from army officers that the school's endowment was not being applied to their benefit, effectively ruined his ambitious schemes for expansion. Although in the shadow of a predecessor of almost legendary reputation, he succeeded in leaving the school better equipped and organized than he found it. A fine classical scholar, he devoted his leisure to an elaborate edition of Horace (2 vols., 1874, 1893).

In politics Wickham was a strong supporter of the Liberal Party, following his father-in-law with absolute faith and devotion. After Wickham resigned from Wellington in the summer of 1893, Gladstone, ignoring charges of nepotism, appointed him dean of Lincoln in succession to William John Butler in January 1894. He showed great administrative skill in both cathedral and city affairs. His sermons, exquisitely delivered and given in fastidiously chosen language, had been widely appreciated both at New College and Wellington, and he was chosen select preacher before the University of Oxford for four different years. Wickham also took a prominent share in the debates of convocation and was a member of the committee on prayer book revision. He was active in the organization of primary and secondary education in the diocese of Lincoln, and was vice-chairman of the city education committee. Although he defended the Anglican position in the controversies following the 1902 Education Act, he was conciliatory towards nonconformists, acting as one of the leading spirits on the education settlement committee formed in 1907 to bring nonconformists and churchmen together.

Wickham died on 18 August 1910 at Sierre in Switzerland, where he had gone with his family for a holiday. He was buried there, Dr Randall Davidson, archbishop of Canterbury, performing the service. He was survived by his wife and two sons and three daughters.

J. B. ATLAY, *rev.* M. C. CURTHOYS

Sources L. Ragg, *A memoir of Edward Charles Wickham* (1911) · *The Times* (19 Aug 1910) · *The Spectator* (30 Dec 1911), 1157 · private information (1912) · A. Ryan, 'Transformation, 1850–1914', *New College, Oxford, 1379–1979*, ed. J. Buxton and P. Williams (1979) · D. Newsome, *A history of Wellington College, 1859–1959* [1959] · D. M. Thompson, 'Historical survey, 1750–1949', *A history of Lincoln Minster*, ed. D. Owen (1994), 210–318 · Gladstone, *Diaries* · *CGPLA Eng. & Wales* (1910)

Archives Wellington College, Berkshire | St Deiniol's Library, Hawarden, Glynne–Gladstone MSS, corresp. with Gladstone family

Likenesses group portrait, photograph, 1876, repro. in Ragg, *Memoir of Edward Charles Wickham*, 176 · R. de L'Hôpital, oils, Wellington College, Berkshire · G. Radley, photograph, repro. in Ragg, *Memoir of Edward Charles Wickham*, frontispiece · W. B. Richmond, oils, New College, Oxford · photograph, repro. in Newsome, *History of Wellington College*, 196 · stone bust, Lincoln Cathedral

Wealth at death £43,582 15s. 2d.: probate, 5 Oct 1910, *CGPLA Eng. & Wales*

Wickham, Edward Ralph [Ted] (1911–1994), Church of England clergyman, was born on 3 November 1911 in Walthamstow, London, the fourth child in the family of three sons and three daughters of Edward Wickham (1870–1935), a bilingual employee of the Bank of England, who worked much in France, and his wife, Minnie Florence, *née* Wanty (1883–1921), who was of Huguenot descent. His mother's death when he was still young was a great and lasting blow to him. He was educated at Downhills Central School, Tottenham, leaving at fifteen to join Parker Pipes (a subsidiary of Dunhills) as a clerk, and then Insulators Ltd as a progress chaser. He was early attracted to the Anglo-Catholic parish of St Philip, Tottenham, and this, together with his own high intelligence and energy, enabled him to begin his career in the Church of England. By private study and evening classes he was able to take a BD extramurally at King's College, London, and go to St Stephen's House, Oxford, the Anglo-Catholic theological college, in 1938. He was ordained deacon in 1938 and priest in 1939 by the bishop of Newcastle, and served as curate to the parish of Christ Church, Shieldfield, Newcastle upon Tyne, from 1938 to 1941. In 1941 he was appointed as chaplain to the large Royal Ordnance factory at Swynnerton. There he met his future wife, (Dorothy) Helen Neville Moss (b. 1919), daughter of Kenneth Neville Moss, professor of mining engineering. She was at that time working at the Royal Ordnance factory as a labour officer. They married on 10 June 1944. They had three surviving children, one son and two daughters; unfortunately three other children died in infancy.

In 1944 Wickham was appointed by the bishop of Sheffield to the experimental post of diocesan missioner to industry, a post he held until 1959. His success in that field was such that he was made a residentiary canon of Sheffield Cathedral in 1951. Leslie Hunter had been appointed bishop of Sheffield in 1939. He already knew that the working people of the great industrial cities were largely alienated from the Church of England, except for rites of passage. In particular, the labour and trade union movements were convinced that the church was of no relevance or use to them. The work instituted by Hunter and Wickham was unique in that a direct appeal was first made to both trade unions and management in the large labour-intensive heavy steel industry in Sheffield, and later to the cutlery firms. Not until the goodwill of both sides of industry had been gained did the actual work of visiting begin. The organization of the heavy steel industry at that time was particularly favourable to Wickham's approach. Much of the work was carried on in large shops by comparatively small groups of men, and there were many necessary breaks in the process of steel making. This gave him the opportunity to talk informally with the groups and in the canteens, a task in which he excelled, for he had a cockney accent, a friendly and racy approach, and a quick wit. Above all he had the art of talking theology in understandable terms.

Theological and sociological thinking were leading passions throughout Wickham's career. In discussion he would often quote or cite thinkers, especially the German protestant theologians from Luther onwards and the early sociologists of the nineteenth and twentieth centuries. Unlike many Anglicans he early made contact with the church in Europe, and he was perhaps better known in the later 1940s among the leaders of the infant World Council of Churches than he was in his own country. He was also in close touch with two French Roman Catholic radical movements analogous to his own, the Mission de France and the Mission de Paris.

The success of the Sheffield industrial mission, and the appointment of assistant missioners, gave Wickham the opportunity to apply for and obtain the Stephenson research fellowship at Sheffield University, which he held from 1955 to 1957. This enabled him to support by detailed

research into the history of the church in Sheffield his thesis that the Church of England had not lost the working classes, but had never had them—though Methodism had helped to mould some early labour leaders. In spite of the great nineteenth-century burst of church building in the cities, these large edifices remained largely empty except for small, lower middle-class congregations. The fruit of Wickham's research was *Church and People in an Industrial City* (1957), which also carried his main thesis: that the church should make its appeal, not first to individual men and women, but to the great institutions of organized labour, and then to groups at places of work. The book had a wide influence, but from then on there was a perceptible hardening in the opposition of many Anglican establishment figures to Wickham's work. From the start many parish clergy thought he by-passed the parish churches: 'He didn't get people into the churches', was their complaint; his answer was that the gap between most working people and most parish churches was too wide. Wickham, who had in addition to his great gifts a very considerable personal ambition, would perhaps have liked to be head of the whole developing work of industrial mission in England, but this was denied him. He could be an abrasive talker as well as thinker, and this did not always go down well in the smoother circles of the establishment.

A solution to the problem of the next stage in his career was found. He was nominated in 1959 by the prime minister, with the goodwill of the bishop of Manchester, to the suffragan see of Middleton. He accepted this office with some reluctance, saying to friends, 'I have been blackballed into the episcopacy' (private information). He held this office until his retirement in 1982, then becoming an assistant bishop in the diocese of Manchester. It must be questioned whether this was the best use that the church could have made of Wickham's gifts, for he now found himself translated from the frontiers of the church's mission to a post at the heart of the organization. The work of a bishop-suffragan was still, in those years, essentially that of assistant to the diocesan bishop, and involved a round of confirmations, institutions, ordinations, and committees, and, though he loyally worked at these, they did not make the best use of his abilities. He chaired the diocesan board of social responsibility, an attempt to bring together all the various social and charitable enterprises started by the diocese at various times. He continued to write interestingly on social and industrial topics, publishing, along with numerous essays and articles, *Encounter with Modern Society* (1964), *Growth and Inflation* (1975), and *Growth, Justice and Work* (1985), but these works did not have an impact comparable to that of his earlier book on Sheffield. He put a great deal of energy into creating and running a night shelter for down-and-outs in Manchester, which grew into a network of houses for the homeless. Perhaps his greatest satisfaction came from his work with the newly formed Salford University, of which he became chairman of the council and pro-chancellor (1975–83), and which bestowed on him an honorary doctorate in 1973. He was always at his best outside the walls of the established church and working with other sources of power and influence.

Wickham was a bold and adventurous mountaineer and involved many steel workers in this passion. He was also a keen fly-fisherman. These pursuits reflected his individual energy, skill, and insight. Throughout his ministry he had loyal support from his able and gifted wife, Helen, who gave a great deal of time and energy in hospitality to the numerous visitors, foreign and British, who beat a path to their door in search of inspiration and guidance. She was also involved in much voluntary work in the community.

Wickham died on 29 September 1994 at Hope Hospital, Salford, Manchester, of cancer; his ashes were interred in November 1994 in the churchyard of the Climbers' Chapel, Wasdale Head, Cumberland. He was survived by his wife, son, and two daughters. Although he achieved much as bishop-suffragan of Middleton, the Sheffield industrial mission and his book about Sheffield remained his principal achievements. ALFRED JOWETT

Sources E. R. Wickham, *Church and people in an industrial city* (1957) · P. Bagshaw, *The church beyond the church: industrial mission, 1944–1994* (1994) · J. W. Rogerson, ed., *Industrial mission in a changing world* (1996) · *WWW*, 1991–5 · personal knowledge (2004) · private information (2004) · m. cert.
Likenesses photograph, repro. in *The Independent* (30 Sept 1994) · photograph, repro. in *The Times* (1 Oct 1994)
Wealth at death £163,792: probate, 8 Feb 1995, *CGPLA Eng. & Wales*

Wickham, Sir Henry Alexander (1846–1928), plant collector and planter, was born on 29 May 1846, the son of Henry Wickham, solicitor. His father died when he was four, and he was raised by his mother. He was talented at drawing and undertook some training as an artist.

At twenty Wickham went to Central America, where for three years he engaged in the trade in bird plumage. He returned to England, but a year later was in Colombia and Venezuela dealing in rubber. He made a journey up the Orinoco and down the Rio Negro and Amazon that ended at Santarém in Pará, where he was befriended by some English residents and American Confederate exiles. After returning to England again in 1871, on 29 May he married Violet Cave Carter, daughter of W. H. J. Carter, a Regent Street bookseller who published Wickham's account of his journey. With his wife, his mother, brother, sister, and brother-in-law he sailed out to Santarém to commence life as a sugar and tobacco planter, perhaps financed by his father-in-law.

In 1872 Wickham wrote offering his services as a collector to Sir Joseph Hooker at the Royal Botanic Gardens at Kew. In May 1873 Hooker was approached by Clements Markham of the India Office for assistance in introducing the Pará rubber tree *Hevea Brasiliensis* into India, and thought of Wickham. Encouraged to obtain as many seeds as possible at £10 per 1000, Wickham seized the opportunity not only to gather but to accompany the seeds to England and escape a life that had become unsustainable. His mother and sister had died at Santarém; his plantation

was a failure. In desperate straits it is likely that his and his wife's passages aboard the *Amazonas* were obtained on a promissory note. The seeds had been collected probably in great haste from stands near Boim on the Rio Tapajós, not far from Santarém, in April and May 1876.

To the Brazilian customs Wickham declared his baskets to contain 'exceedingly delicate botanical specimens specially designated for delivery to Her Britannic Majesty's own Royal Gardens'. Though the very size of the shipment might have caused the local Brazilian officials to pause or seek authorization, the deception was more of a precaution. No one on the Amazon at the time could have foreseen that the massive industry about them might one day be eclipsed, or that *Hevea* could be successfully cultivated elsewhere. There was no Brazilian regulation to prevent the export of seed. Wickham later dramatized the deed as a tale of successful smuggling, making the arrival of the *Amazonas* providential—it was actually on a scheduled voyage to Liverpool—and adding a threatening Brazilian gunboat. One thing is certain—that speed had been essential to success, as the oily rubber seeds have brief viability.

Wickham arrived in England with the cargo of 70,000 seeds on 14 June 1876. These were planted in specially prepared beds at Kew, and by August fewer than 4000 had germinated. He received £743 from the India Office and sought a further commission to take the plants to Ceylon. When a response was delayed he decided to take his fee and a quantity of coffee seedlings obtained at Kew and emigrate to Queensland. Acquiring land on the Herbert River north of Townsville he decided on tobacco cultivation. Dogged yet again by misfortune as well as mismanagement he was forced to abandon this venture with little more than the fare home remaining.

In 1886 Wickham returned to Central America. In British Honduras he obtained work initially as an inspector of forests before proceeding to establish a plantation on the Temash River with bananas and local *Castilloa* rubber. A dispute over his lease ended in another débâcle.

In 1895 Wickham turned again to the South Seas in British New Guinea and began by searching for latex-bearing trees and vines offered by its forests. In 1896 he took out a lease in the Conflict Islands, a small atoll of under 1800 acres, 80 miles east of Samarai, and over the next decade developed a coconut plantation.

Wickham had continued to correspond widely, to interest himself in plants that might prove of economic value, and to follow closely developments in the rubber industry and its technology. From 1906, when the success attending the development of rubber plantations in the Far East began to exceed all expectations, his occasional appearances in London received increasing attention from journalists. He was an adept self-publicist. In 1908 he published the embellished account of the 1876 exploit in a book on rubber cultivation and production that contained little that was essentially new. In 1911 he was fêted at an international rubber banquet, presented with 1000 guineas, and provided with an annuity for life by the Rubber Growers' Association and the Planters' Associations of Ceylon and Malaya. His receipts from gifts of money, shares, and other benefactions over subsequent years were substantial. He was able to reside permanently in London in Albion Street, Hyde Park, a frequent attender at meetings of the Royal Colonial Institute, lionized by the rubber companies and demonized by Brazilians. He received a knighthood in 1920. His fame had become international and his name everywhere associated with the rubber industry and the snatch of 1876.

That Wickham had played a crucial role cannot be disputed. It has been established that it was from Wickham's seeds alone that the entire south-east Asian rubber industry was built—though the brilliant work of Henry Ridley in Singapore in the development of the industry was in many ways much more significant. The escapade of 1876 was indeed decisive, but while it may have been undertaken furtively, it was neither illegal nor as remarkable at the time as subsequent events and Wickham's reconstructions were to make of it.

Wickham died on 27 September 1928 at 32 Newton Road, London. His eulogist in *The Times* described him as 'every inch a pioneer, broad-shouldered and heavily built with an extraordinary long wavy moustache, his physical strength ... as great as his resolution'. His shortcomings aside, he remains a paradigm of the nineteenth-century British adventurer and individualist.   D. C. LEWIS

William Wickham (1539–1595), by unknown artist [original, 1591]

Sources W. Dean, *Brazil and the struggle for rubber: a study in environmental history* (1987) · R. Desmond, *Kew: the history of the Royal Botanic Gardens* (1995) · E. V. Lane, 'The life and work of Sir Henry Wickham', *India Rubber Journal* (Dec 1953–Jan 1954) · P. Mason, *Cauchu, the weeping wood: a history of rubber* (1979) · D. C. Lewis, *The plantation dream: developing British New Guinea and Papua, 1884–1942* (1996) · H. A. Wickham, *Rough notes of a journey through the wilderness from Trinidad to Para, Brazil etc.* (1872) · H. A. Wickham, *On the plantation, cultivation and curing of Para Indian rubber* (1908) · m. cert. · d. cert. **Archives** BL OIOC, Caoutchouc · RBG Kew, corresp. relating to smuggling of rubber seeds from Brazil to Kew **Likenesses** group portrait, photograph, repro. in Dean, *Brazil and the struggle for rubber* · photograph, repro. in Wickham, *On the plantation, cultivation and curing of Para Indian Rubber*, frontispiece · portrait, repro. in Desmond, *Kew: the history of the Royal Botanic Gardens* **Wealth at death** £13,235 9s. 8d.: probate, 9 Nov 1928, CGPLA Eng. & Wales

Wickham, Henry Lewis (1789–1864). *See under* Wickham, William (1761–1840).

Wickham [Wykeham]**, William** (1539–1595), bishop of Winchester, was the son of John Wickham of Enfield, Middlesex, and Barbara, daughter and heir of William Parker of Norton Lees, Derbyshire, and Luton, Bedfordshire. What relationship William Wickham had to his great fourteenth-century namesake and predecessor at Winchester is uncertain; he was understandably disposed to hint at some connection. William Wickham was not, however, a Wykehamist, being a king's scholar at Eton from about 1552, proceeding thence to a scholarship at King's College, Cambridge, on 18 September 1556 and a fellowship there on 19 September 1559. He graduated BA

in 1560–61, proceeding MA in 1564 and BTh in 1569; unusually, he never advanced to the doctorate. He was one of many who contributed verses when Martin Bucer and Paul Fagius, anathematized in 1557, were posthumously restored to honour in the university at a ceremony in Great St Mary's on 30 July 1560. On 29 June 1565 Wickham was ordained priest by Bishop Richard Cox of Ely. On 20 June 1568 he was admitted a fellow of Eton, vacating his Cambridge fellowship. About 1570 he served as vice-provost of Eton and, in the occasional absence of the headmaster, taught the scholars; Sir John Harington recalled that he 'shewed as fatherly a care, as if he had been a second tutor to me' (Harington, 65). On 10 August 1570 Wickham was presented to a canonry of Westminster, and on 24 March 1571 he was elected by the dean and chapter as their proctor in convocation, but otherwise he played little part in the abbey's affairs. He vacated his stall there by 19 June 1571, three days later being appointed to one at Windsor, which he retained until he was advanced to the episcopate.

Wickham had become a chaplain to the queen by 1572, when a Latin verse of his was prefaced to Thomas Wilson's *Discourse uppon Usurye*. In April 1574 Archbishop Grindal, writing to Lord Burghley, suggested that Wickham or one 'of like godly zeal towards the poor members of Christ' should be recommended to the queen for the mastership of the Savoy (Nicholson, 349–50). This preferment eluded him, but on 23 July 1574 Bishop Robert Horne of Winchester collated Wickham to the archdeaconry of Surrey (which he vacated by 13 February 1580). On 30 May 1577 he was elected dean of Lincoln, and on 7 September was additionally installed in the prebend of St Botolph in that cathedral. While he was dean musical activity flowered. William Byrd, organist from 1563, left for the Chapel Royal in 1572, but continued to supply Lincoln with new music. Dean Wickham evidently encouraged the copying of music to the extent that vernacular polyphony, hitherto restricted to festivals, would have been in daily use. He may therefore have significantly influenced the characteristic form of Anglican cathedral worship.

On 11 April 1579 (and again on 24 July) Wickham was presented by the crown to the prebend of Eccleshall in Lichfield Cathedral, to which he was admitted on 20 November. On 3 February 1580 he was instituted to the rectory of Cherry Burton, Lincolnshire, at the presentation of Robert Mounson JP. On 11 July in the same year he was presented by Herbert Pelham to the rectory of Withern, Lincolnshire, which he resigned on 8 February 1582.

On 24 October 1584 Wickham was nominated bishop of Lincoln, being consecrated on 6 December. In or about this year he delivered a judgment on a disputed statute of Balliol College, Oxford. During 1586 he was much occupied with discord in the civic leadership at Lincoln; in September he reported that the new mayor (William Scolfield) was 'one of the corruptest in all the towne for his religion' who 'wold thinke that a great glorie to be accoumpted a papiste' (PRO, SP 12/193, no. 51). He was chosen to preach at the funeral of Mary, queen of Scots, which took place on 1 August 1587 in Peterborough Cathedral. Since Elizabeth's government had debated the protocol for this awkward occasion for six months since Mary's execution, the appointment of Wickham as preacher was presumably given some thought, and was not made simply because he was the bishop of the neighbouring diocese. There need have been no fear of his offending the Scottish mourners, who walked out before Wickham began to speak. Taking his text from Psalm 39 ('Lord, let me know mine end'), he thanked God for the 'happie dissolution' of the late queen, 'of whose lyfe and deathe at this tyme I have not muche to saye, bycause I was not acquainted withe the one neither present at the other'. He contented himself with a discourse on the 'generall doctrine of the vanity of all fleshe', though contriving to suggest (by way of a quotation from Luther) that Mary might have atoned for her papist life with a protestant death (Mellows and Gifford, 40). He was nevertheless vilified for allegedly expressing the somewhat contrary hope that the deceased, though an unrepentant papist, might yet be saved.

In 1591 Wickham resolved a long-running dispute in Lincoln Cathedral about the distribution of common revenues among residentiaries and non-residentiaries. On 9 March 1592, along with the earl of Lincoln and other local dignitaries, he was appointed to one of the special commissions for searching out seminary priests and recusants. One of his last acts as bishop of Lincoln, on 19 November 1594, was the issue of a determination on the

statutes of Eton and King's College, Cambridge, of which he was *ex officio* visitor.

Wickham had been offered the see of Winchester following the death of Bishop Thomas Cooper on 29 April 1594. But he was told that his translation would be conditional on his 'passing over certain things' to the crown (*Salisbury MSS*, 5.37). This, it was duly explained to him, meant making a sixty-year reversionary lease of Winchester property to the queen, in favour of Sir Francis Carew. Wickham at first pleaded ignorance of the affairs of his prospective see. On 20 December Sir Robert Cecil flatly told him that his *congé d'élire* had been signed but was not going to be sent to the Winchester chapter until he had submitted to the queen's request. This he did on 24 December, and the *congé* was issued four or five days later. The formal election was on 7 January 1595. The temporalities were withheld from him until he gave (1 March) a further promise that he would honour a customary rent payable to the crown. His temporalities were finally released on 14 March, and on 29 March he was enthroned by proxy. He had, meanwhile, complained to Burghley of the 'extraordinarie and unlawfull leases' he thought he might yet have to grant; he specially feared undeserved repute as a spoiler of the see which 'an honourable bishop ... of the same name and house' had formerly enriched (BL, Lansdowne MS 78, fol. 22). Wickham had long experience of the crown's practice of compelling church landowners to make beneficial leases to courtiers and government officials. As archdeacon of Surrey he had in 1578 made the crown a fifty-year lease of the rectory of Farnham, which in the following year had been granted to William Killigrew, a groom of the privy chamber; and as dean of Lincoln in 1580 he had consented to a ninety-nine-year lease of the rectory of Mansfield, which was subsequently given to the principal secretary (and Wickham's sometime literary associate) Thomas Wilson.

Wickham was prompted to raise the issue of the crown's continuing impoverishment of the church in a sermon before the queen in parliament (seemingly the state opening of 4 February 1589). He observed that the temporalities of English bishoprics and colleges, having been reasonably reduced, were now lower than some in France, Spain, and Germany, but greater than some in Italy; he begged the queen to 'make stay of them at least in this mediocrity', warning that if they should decay in the next thirty years as they had done in the past thirty, hardly a cathedral in England would be found in good repair (Harington, 66). Though Elizabeth is said to have listened graciously to these remarks, Wickham's personal finances were not helped by his oratory, and at his death he owed £1933 to the crown in tenths. Wickham died at Winchester House in Southwark on 2 or 12 June 1595, from an obstruction of the bladder (probably calculus). On 13 June he was buried in Southwark Cathedral. No will survives.

Wickham had married Antonia, youngest daughter of William *Barlow, bishop of Chichester, whose other daughters married bishops Herbert Westphaling of Hereford, William Overton of Coventry and Lichfield, William Day of Winchester, and Archbishop Tobie Matthew of

York, to each of whom Bishop Wickham was, by contemporary usage, brother. Antonia Wickham died on 30 April 1598 and was buried at Alconbury in Huntingdonshire. The eldest son of the marriage, Henry, was made archdeacon of York by his uncle Archbishop Matthew in 1624, retaining this dignity until his death in 1641. Henry's son Tobias was dean of York from 1677 to 1697. Wickham had other sons, Thomas and Barlow (named after his episcopal grandfather, and who died in 1617), and four daughters. A direct descendant, William Wickham, was appointed secretary of state for Ireland in 1802. In 1900 a portrait of Bishop Wickham was reportedly in the possession of his heirs at Binsted Wyck, Hampshire. Thomas Fuller said of him that he was 'equal to any of his order in piety and painfullnesse ... superior to all in patience' (Fuller, *Worthies*, 182).

C. S. KNIGHTON

Sources W. Sterry, ed., *The Eton College register, 1441–1698* (1943), 365 · Wood, *Ath. Oxon.: Fasti* (1815), 832 · *Fasti Angl., 1541–1857*, [Ely], 74 · *Fasti Angl.* (Hardy), 2.34 · *Fasti Angl., 1541–1857*, [Canterbury], 81, 88 · *CPR, 1578–80*, 93, 95, 102, 186, 203 · *CSP dom., 1581–90*, 320, 322, 349, 354, 357; 1595–7, 9, 47 · CUL, EDR, A/1/5, fol. 82 · J. Venn, ed., *Grace book Δ* (1910), 557 (index) · T. Wilson, *A discourse uppon usurye* (1572), sig. Ai · J. Harington, *A briefe view of the state of the Church of England* (1653), 65–7 · C. W. Foster, ed., *Lincoln episcopal records*, Lincoln RS, 2 (1912), 77, 298, 310, 316 · D. M. Owen, ed., *A history of Lincoln Minster* (1994), 67–8, 175 · J. W. F. Hill, *Tudor and Stuart Lincoln* (1956), 228, 231 · F. O. White, *Lives of the Elizabethan bishops of the Anglican church* (1898), 284–6 · F. Heal, *Of prelates and princes: a study of the economic and social position of the Tudor episcopate* (1980), 252–3 · W. T. Mellows and D. H. Giffard, eds., *Peterborough local administration: Elizabethan Peterborough*, Northamptonshire RS, 18 (1956), 39–40 [1956 for 1944] · S. Gunton, *The history of the church of Peterburgh*, ed. S. Patrick (1686); facs. edn (1990), 79 · *Calendar of the manuscripts of the most hon. the marquis of Salisbury*, 5, HMC, 9 (1894), 37–8, 41, 46, 128, 177; 13 (1915), 170 · BL, Lansdowne MS 78, fol. 22 · W. Nicholson, ed., *The remains of Edmund Grindal*, Parker Society, 9 (1843), 349–50 · C. S. Knighton, ed., *Acts of the dean and chapter of Westminster*, 2 (1999), 52 · G. A. J. Hodgett, *Tudor Lincolnshire*, History of Lincolnshire, 6 (1975), 181–2 · Fuller, *Worthies* (1662), 2.182 · Burke, *Gen. GB* (1952), 2709–10 · P. Collinson, *The religion of protestants* (1982) · F. Godwin, *A catalogue of the bishops of England, since the first planting of Christian religion in this island* (1601) · H. Ellis, ed., *The visitation of the county of Huntingdon ... 1613*, CS, 43 (1849)

Archives Hants. RO, Winchester episcopal register, A1/28, fols. 1–3 · Lincs. Arch., Lincoln episcopal register, Reg. XIX, fols. 146v–162

Likenesses portrait, priv. coll.?; in possession of Mrs Wickham, Binsted Wyck, Hampshire, 1900 · portrait (after original, 1591), Wolvesey, Winchester [*see illus.*]

Wealth at death owed £1933 in tenths: Heal, *Of prelates and princes*, 253

Wickham, William (1761–1840), politician, diplomatist, and founder of a British foreign secret service, was the elder son of Lieutenant-Colonel Henry Wickham (1731–1804) and Elizabeth (*d.* 1815), daughter and heir of William Lamplugh of Cottingley, vicar of Dewsbury, Yorkshire. Henry Wickham had been educated at Leipzig and Neuchatel universities and began his military career with two years in the army of Piedmont. William was born in October 1761 at Cottingley, Bingley, Yorkshire, and baptized on 11 November 1761. He was educated at Winchester College (1773–6), Harrow School (1776), and Christ Church, Oxford (1779–82), where he was a younger contemporary of William Wyndham Grenville, John King, and Charles Abbot

(Baron Colchester). At Geneva University (1782–6) he studied law under Amedeo Perdriau, and graduated MA in February 1786. He was called to the bar at Lincoln's Inn in November 1786.

Wickham married Eleanore Madeleine (1763–1836), daughter of Professor Louis Bertrand and Isabella, *née* Mallet, in Geneva Cathedral on 10 August 1788. This linked him with the leading families of Geneva and laid the foundation of his career. His brother-in-law Professor Marc Auguste Pictet was related to Isaac Pictet, British chargé d'affaires at Bern (1772–4), while Eleanore's cousin, the Syndic Rigaud, became an influential friend.

Wickham served as a commissioner of bankrupts from 1790 to 1794. On 7 July 1792 his name (misspelt) appeared in the fiats for appointment of magistrates. He was attached to the Whitechapel police office (PRO, C234/25). Wickham again visited Switzerland in 1792. On his return he wrote to John King, under-secretary at the Home Office, asking to be remembered if anyone was to be sent out to Switzerland and indicating that his communication 'must *be* and *remain* in strict and perfect confidence between you and me' (Wickham to King, 4 Dec 1792, Hants. RO, 38M49/6/5/2). This refutes the long-held belief that it was Lord Grenville's friendship that procured Wickham his diplomatic employment; rather, it was King's friendship with both.

As a government magistrate Wickham worked at the Home Office and employed informers to discover possible treasonable activities. He was commended by ministers for his ability in this field, which included procuring information on the activities of émigrés as well as of the London Corresponding Society. This was probably the secret service carried out for Lord Grenville from August 1793, concerning which Wickham wrote that to avoid commitment all communication passed through the office of the lord chancellor, Lord Rosslyn, and that all trace was removed from the records (27 March 1831, Hants. RO, 38M49/1/56/24). His information led to the arrest of the London Corresponding Society officers in May 1794 (E. Nepean to Wickham, 10 May 1794, Hants. RO, 38M49/6/6/1).

The third duke of Portland, who was then home secretary, appointed Wickham as superintendent of aliens in July 1794. This position officially linked his work as a police magistrate with Lord Grenville and William Pitt. To Pitt, Wickham made regular visits as an intermediary with Portland: 'I was often received in his dressing room, more than once in his bedroom'. Pitt generally 'either minuted down or desired me to report verbally his observations to the Duke of Portland' (Hants. RO, 38M49/1/56/24).

Wickham's diplomatic career began in October 1794. His request for a post in Switzerland was remembered on the arrival of a memoir, forwarded by Lord Robert Fitzgerald from Bern. It purported to be a proposal for peace from two members of the French national convention. Wickham was dispatched on 15 October with Grenville's unsigned instructions to investigate the authenticity of the memoir (Hants. RO, 38M49/1/26/1). The secrecy and haste of his departure precluded any possibility of a secretary to accompany him, and the only funds provided were £200 for travelling expenses. Investigation led Fitzgerald and Wickham to conclude that the memoir was a clever intrigue. But Wickham remained in Switzerland, where he began the build-up of an extensive network of secret service agents throughout central Europe and France. Fitzgerald was granted leave of absence on 9 December 1794. He presented Wickham to the Bern Council as chargé d'affaires, lent him £100, and left in January 1795 (PRO, FO74/4 1794, 38M49/1/27/3).

Wickham had no financial resources, public or private; his immediate necessity was to find a friend, a secretary, and funds with which to entertain 'small quick parties to a few friends. It is liked here, and without it you are without consideration' (Wickham to Grenville, Hants. RO, 38M49/1/27/3). Initially Grenville, with no precedent for funding a foreign secret service, could only pass money through his private account, with the Treasury's obligatory three-month delay. So Wickham had to accept help from his wife's banker relatives. But as an impoverished country gentleman he had a careful approach to money, telling Grenville in March 1795 that his expenses were greater than expected—and rising. His bill at the post office 'regularly exceeded £2 per week … and travel was extravagant'. Wickham hoped that the delay on payments of public funds could be relaxed in his case, 'otherwise I really know not how I must go on'. Two months later his naivety had evaporated, and he was sending Grenville's secretary receipts for £6000—exclusive of his own expenses (Grenville's 'separate account', 24 May 1795-27 Jan 1796).

Promoted to minister-plenipotentiary in March 1795, Wickham resided alternately at Bern and Lausanne, with a privileged position in relation to the Bern councils. By appointing Swiss officials as British officers in the Swiss regiments paid by Britain, Wickham achieved control over passports on the Jura frontier with France (Cavin). He set up a regular correspondence with Lyon and Paris, and, via Francis Drake and John Trevor, British diplomats at Genoa and Turin, also with northern Italy and the Midi (Hants. RO, 38M49/1/10–11). At the same time Lord Grenville directed Lieutenant-Colonel Charles Gregan Craufurd, on a special mission at the Austrian army headquarters, to liaise with Wickham from June 1795 both for political purposes and as a method of passing funds—via army extraordinaries—authorized by parliament. Wickham took on several secretaries—all French—for the different aspects of this work, while Grenville sent the Foreign Office clerk Charles William Flint to assist in May 1795 (PRO, FO 29/5, FO 74/9, nos. 50 and 51; BL, Add. MS 69440, fols. 72–3; Hants. RO, 38M49/1/27/12).

Wickham's intentions were to assist royalist insurrections within France, to provide funds to manipulate elections to the Paris councils, and to suborn a French republican army to support a restoration. By May 1797 he appeared to have achieved his purpose. General Pichegru, supported by senior officers, was well placed to head the overthrow of the Directory, but proved incapable of the revolutionary action required. Wickham's plans were destroyed by the Director Barras, who, advised by General Bonaparte, carried out the coup of 18 Fructidor (4 September 1797). The Director Barthélemy and generals Pichegru and Willot, with a total of forty deputies, were deported to the penal colony of Sinnamary in French Guiana. Wickham's funding of anti-Directory espionage was disclosed, leaving his credibility as a diplomat in shreds and his networks temporarily paralysed. Friends in the Bern Council asked him to 'withdraw quietly without waiting for orders' (Hants. RO, 38M49/6/13/1, 17 Oct 1797, 38M49/1/56/25). He left Switzerland on 7 November to visit the wounded Charles Gregan Craufurd at Frankfurt.

Grenville ordered the withdrawal of the Bern mission, but the continuation of the correspondence with royalists of the interior of France (Bodl. Oxf., MS Talbot c. 14, fols. 60–61, b 21, fols. 71–5). With these arrangements in place, Wickham and his first secretary, James Talbot, returned to London in January 1798, when Portland appointed Wickham under-secretary at the Home Office with John King. But Thomas Carter, Portland's private secretary, disputed the position of superintendent of aliens that he had held in Wickham's absence. This was resolved, and in July 1798 a king's warrant appointed Wickham, John King, and Charles Flint joint superintendents (Hants. RO, 38M49/6/2/1–2; PRO, HO38/7/573). Meantime, the immediate task was to arrange for Talbot's secret return to the Swabian frontier with Switzerland. He left in February 1798, while Wickham reorganized and increased the status of the alien office.

In May 1799 Wickham returned to Switzerland to liaise with the subsidized Russo-Austrian armies and to replace Talbot, who had lost control of the Swabian agency, which included the Paris deputies proscribed in the purge of September 1797, and Swiss émigrés. A coherent force had been formed under General Hotze. The result—the assassination of the French envoys at Rastadt in April 1799—had shocked Europe (Sparrow). Wickham was to control the Swiss corps and liaise with Austria, Bavaria, and Wurtemberg for the supply of further subsidized troops, while continuing the secret networks within France. General Pichegru joined Wickham at Zürich to meet an envoy from Director Barras, who had agreed to a restoration of Louis XVIII in return for a large bribe and letters patent providing a pardon for his regicide. Due to the French victory at Zürich on September 1799, the meeting never took place. Incriminating papers were seized at General Korsakov's headquarters and Pichegru fled (*Fortescue MSS*, vol. 5; Archives Nationales, F7 6217, dos. 4064, 19 Feb 1801).

Wickham's next plan was to raise a French royalist army in the Midi, to be commanded by General Willot, supported by Pichegru. This extremely expensive project was destroyed by Bonaparte's victory at Marengo on 14 June 1800. The apparent defeat of all his plans, combined with the suggestion by George Rose, the secretary to the Treasury, that he had misused public funds, caused Wickham to retreat to a monastery, close to a nervous breakdown. Portland praised his actions, but the second coalition and the Swabian agency were effectively finished. Wickham returned to England in 1801 (Hants. RO, 38M49/8/11, 38M49/1/27/12, 38M49/8/21/1–3).

Wickham hoped for a diplomatic appointment at Berlin. However he was *persona non grata* in Prussia, just as he was in Switzerland. In February 1802 he was appointed a privy councillor and chief secretary in Ireland, and returned as MP for Heytesbury, which he shortly exchanged for Cashel. As chief secretary he continued the work of his predecessor, Charles Abbot, in reducing government expenditure. His resignation in January 1804 was a complicated decision. Although he used the excuse of ill health, his true reasons were horror at the execution of Robert Emmet; a belief that suppression of the Catholics was morally wrong; and a conviction that the duke of York's decision to give Lord Cathcart sole command of the military in Ireland, over the head of the lord lieutenant, was in contempt of the constitution (Hants. RO, 38M49/1/48/6, 7, 38M49/1/56/15–16).

From 1806 to 1807, as MP for Callington and a lord of the Treasury, Wickham defended his use of public funds (Hants. RO, 38M49/1/137, 38M49/1/138). But his resignation as chief secretary had ended his career, and, feeling a failure, he spent much time in later life vindicating that decision. He could not see the far-reaching effects of his secret service organization, not only on the Napoleonic war but also on twentieth-century wars, through the resurrection of its principles in 1908 (Hants. RO, 38M49/1/56/15–16, 31, 35–8; PRO, KV 1/1).

In 1810 Wickham was made an honorary DCL at Oxford. He had a house close to Lord Grenville's Dropmore and bought Binsted Wyck, in Hampshire, but after 1815 he spent much time in southern France or Switzerland, having no settled home for the last fifteen years of his life. He died at Brighton on 22 October 1840.

Henry Lewis Wickham (1789–1864), the Wickhams' only son, was born at Cottingley, Yorkshire, on 19 May 1789. He was educated at Westminster School and Christ Church, Oxford, and called to the bar at Lincoln's Inn on 13 May 1817. He was appointed receiver-general of Gibraltar by Lord Grenville in lieu of an extra pension for his father, and served as principal private secretary to Viscount Althorp (third Earl Spencer) during the latter's stint as chancellor of the exchequer (1830–34). He served as a commissioner of excise enquiry, chairman of the board of stamps and taxes (1838–48), and as a commissioner of public loan. With his cousin John Anthony Cramer he wrote *A Dissertation of the Passage of Hannibal over the Alps* (1820). He married Lucy, daughter of William Markham of Becca Hall, Yorkshire, and they had three children: William of Binsted Wyck, editor of *The Correspondence* (1870) and MP for Petersfield, Hampshire (1892–7); Leonora Emma; and Henry Lamplugh. Henry Wickham died in Chesterfield Street, Mayfair, London, on 27 October 1864 (*GM*, 1864 (vol. 2)). ELIZABETH SPARROW

Sources correspondence, 1794–1840, Hants. RO, Wickham MSS, 38M49 · W. Wickham, ed., *Correspondence of Rt. Hon. William Wickham from 1794* (1870) · PRO, FO 74/4-20, Switzerland; FO 29/5 · *GM*,

2nd ser., 15 (1841), 314–15 · *GM*, 3rd ser., 17 (1864), 794 · *The manuscripts of J. B. Fortescue*, 10 vols., HMC, 30 (1892–1927), vol. 3; vol. 5, pp. 182–4; vol. 6 · E. Sparrow, 'The Swiss and Swabian agencies, 1795–1801', *HJ*, 35 (1992), 861–84 · Foster, *Alum. Oxon.* · J. P. Cavin, 'L'émigration française dans le pays de Vaud au début de la révolution (1789–1793)', mémoire de licence, Université de Lausanne, 1971 · fiats for appointment or removal of justices of the peace, 1708–1837, PRO, C234/25 · 19 Feb 1804, Archives Nationales, F7 6217, dos. 4064 · Lord Grenville's 'separate account', 24 May 1795–27 Jan 1796, Coutts & Co. · PRO, HO 38/7/573, warrant; KV 1/1 · R. G. Thorne, 'Wickham, William', HoP, *Commons, 1790–1820* · *Annual Register* (1841)

Archives Hants. RO, corresp. and papers | Archives du Ministère des Affaires Étrangères, Paris, Mémoires et documents France 588–595 · Archives Nationales, Paris, Série F7 3049 dos. 1/1, 3701–3, 3829, 3831, 4260, 6212; dos. 3652, 6251, 6286; dos. 5841, 6311; dos. 6522/54, 6330; dos. 6953, 6619; dos. 3026, 7589; dos. 35. AF III/59; dos. 231/34. AD 1/116 · BL, corresp. with Francis Drake, Add. MSS 46825, 46833 · BL, corresp. with Lord Grenville and Lady Grenville, Add. MSS 59011–59015, 69048–69049 · BL, corresp. with Lord Hardwicke, etc., Add. MSS 35649–35765, *passim* · BL, Pelham MSS, Add. MSS 33, 107, 1801, 33, 122/116–19, 1803 · BL, corresp. with William Windham, Add. MSS 37865–37880 · BL, corresp. with C. P. Yorke, Add. MS 45037 · Bodl. Oxf., corresp. with third Baron Talbot of Malahide · Devon RO, corresp. with first Viscount Sidmouth · Glos. RO, letters to first Baron Redesdale · NA Scot., letters to Sir Alexander Hope · NL Scot., letters and dispatches to first earl of Minto · PRO, Foreign Office, FO 95/2/5, FO 95/8/13 · PRO, Home Office, HO 5/1-23, HO 36/9/213-214 · PRO, Privy Council, PC 1/21/A35(a), PC 1/42/A.140, PC 1/3117 part 1/2 · PRO, PRO 30/8/140/1; WO 1/749/141-149 · PRO NIre., corresp. with Lord Castlereagh · PRO NIre., corresp. relating to Maynooth College

Likenesses F. H. Fuger, oils, *c*.1801, priv. coll.

Wickham, William Arthur (1849–1929), photographer and Church of England clergyman, was born on 3 February 1849 at Trowbridge, the eldest of the five children of William Wickham (1806–1865), grocer, of Trowbridge, and Emma Sophia (1815–1905), daughter of John Rumming, farmer, of Wingfield, Wiltshire. He was educated privately in Trowbridge until shortly after his father's death, and first earned his living as a schoolteacher at Highgate, Middlesex. There followed itinerant work as a tutor. Wickham inherited his parents' religiosity and later recalled his confirmation as his 'greatest blessing'. In 1873 he entered Lichfield Theological College, and was ordained deacon in 1874 and priest in 1875. Between 1874 and 1878 he held a curacy in the Staffordshire colliery parish of Talke-o'-th'-Hill.

In 1878 Wickham rejected a good living in the west country in favour of a new district in the parish of Wigan, beginning his ministry as vicar of St Andrew's on 3 November. At that time public worship was conducted in a school–church, the benefice was worth less than £200, and there was no vicarage. It was a poor district on the edge of a large industrial town. Wickham achieved much at St Andrew's. He had a church built and consecrated within four years and cleared the debt by 1886. Parish schools and a vicarage followed. His work grew with the population, including the establishment of a host of parish organizations and a parish magazine. His prohibition of drink (and raffles) at bazaars, among parishioners for whom drink was itself a religion, illustrates his principles. During the coal strike of 1893 he established a soup

William Arthur Wickham (1849–1929), by unknown photographer, c.1895

kitchen to alleviate distress. He aired his views on labour relations and on education (as a vociferous opponent of secular board schools), opposed Welsh disestablishment, and was criticized for high-churchmanship.

Wickham was interested in photography as a young man, and his earliest images date from 1869. During the 1880s he put on public lantern shows, using mainly borrowed slides. In 1891, however, he had the idea of using photographs of his parishioners and their surroundings. At the first of these shows on 5 October it was reported that the local views 'were received by the audience with constant rounds of applause as they recognized their friends and neighbours'. This was Wickham's brief period of documentary photography. The most remarkable of these slides (made from dry quarter-plates produced with a bellows camera) were of photographs taken in Wickham's local colliery, Douglas Bank, and 'were examined with the greatest interest, being quite unique in the neighbourhood'. He may have got the idea for these from Arthur Sopwith, whom Wickham might have met while at Talke and who had experimented with flash-lit photography in the Staffordshire pits during the 1880s. Wickham's plates of this type convey graphically the cramped, dirty, and arduous conditions faced daily by the miners. The images of working people above ground are epitomized by a series depicting the St Andrew's soup kitchen. Others include colliers squatting, washing, and awaiting their pay, and some vivid individual portraits of domestic and other occupations, such as those of street vendors. The photographs were deposited with the Wigan Archives Service.

Wickham also undertook ecclesiological researches, producing a number of papers, most of them published by the Historic Society of Lancashire and Cheshire between 1907 and 1916. Typical of these is 'Some notes on Hindley Chappell' (1910).

On 21 June 1892 Wickham married Clara (1862–1926), daughter of John Henry Peck, oilcloth manufacturer of Wigan, and his wife, Martha, at St Andrew's. They had one son, Bernard (d. 1917), and four daughters—Myrtle, Cicely, Monica, and Caroline—who all survived, unmarried, into their eighties, keen to keep alive the memory of their father's achievements. Wickham was described as having a generous disposition and was self-effacing in his career. He was also said to possess a 'domineering will power' and an inability to compromise. His strict teetotalism was well attested, as was his keen and ironical sense of humour.

Failing health and increasing work caused Wickham to leave Wigan in November 1916 for the quiet parish of Ampton, Suffolk, where he remained rector until his death, at the rectory, on 30 May 1929, aged eighty. He was buried on 1 June at Ampton church next to his wife.

In his own time Wickham was known as an industrious clergyman and an ecclesiastical antiquary. His photographic work was not widely known, nor did he ever regard it as other than a hobby and a means to entertain his parishioners and raise funds for the parish. Wickham was no Frank Sutcliffe, certainly, but none the less his lasting significance lies principally in the small but fine legacy of photographic images of working people that his hobby bequeathed, and in his pioneering efforts in underground photography.   NICHOLAS WEBB

Sources K. Ward, *The world of William Wickham: the biography and photography of a remarkable Victorian* (1981) • A. D. Gillies, *Wigan through Wickham's window* (1988) • Wigan Archives Service, Leigh, Wickham papers • Wigan Archives Service, Leigh, St Andrew's, Wigan parish papers • *Wigan Examiner* (8 June 1929) • private information (2004) • d. cert.
Archives Derbys. RO
Likenesses Brown, Barnes & Bell, photograph, 1870–79, Wigan Archives Service, 436/16 • Harrison, photograph, 1873–4, Wigan Archives Service, 436/11 • group portrait, photograph, 1873–4, Wigan Archives Service, 466/8 • photograph, c.1895, Wigan Archives Service, 67884/2,3 [*see illus.*] • photograph, c.1915, Wigan Archives Service, 436/35, 635/16 • photograph, 1926, Wigan Archives Service, 466/7, 67323/7
Wealth at death £4807 10s. 10d.: probate, 5 July 1929, *CGPLA Eng. & Wales*

Wicklow. For this title name *see* Howard, Ralph, first Viscount Wicklow (1726/7–1789) [*see under* Howard, Robert (1683–1740)].

Wicks, Harry (1905–1989), Trotskyist, was born on 16 August 1905 at 37 Lombard Road, Battersea, London, the second son of Frederick Richard Wicks, a municipal carman, railway worker, and trade unionist who died on military service in Egypt in 1918, and his wife, Alice Mary Goddard. He left school in 1919, aged fourteen, and began work on the railways in September of that year. He joined the National Union of Railwaymen (NUR), and the big strike that autumn initiated his radicalization. In his spare time he attended Cedars Road continuation school.

He had his practical education in the vibrant Battersea labour movement, in his NUR branch, in the local *Daily Herald* League, and in the National Council of Labour Colleges, where he encountered working-class autodidacts, such as Jack Clancy, and socialist intellectuals, such as Raymond Postgate.

Wicks was a member of the Labour Party when at fifteen he joined the Communist Party of Great Britain (CPGB), impressed by its analysis of 'black Friday' (15 April 1921), when his union failed to support the locked-out miners. With fellow communists he operated within the Battersea Labour Party and Trades Council—CPGB member Shapurji Saklatvala was the Labour MP from 1922 to 1923 and from 1924 to 1929—until it was disaffiliated by the Labour Party in February 1926 for refusing to expel them. He was active in the NUR, building a party cell at Victoria Station and initiating the rank-and-file paper, the *Victoria Signal*, while developing the Young Communist League (YCL) across London. His horizons were broadened by party intellectuals at the CPGB-dominated Labour Research Department. His interest in the ideas of Leon Trotsky was awakened when he attended classes taught by the dissident communist A. E. E. Reade, who supported the opposition in the Russian party.

Exiled from Victoria to Deal, Kent, in consequence of his role in the general strike, he was elected in 1926 to the executive of the YCL. In 1927 he was selected to spend three years at the International Lenin School in Moscow, a finishing academy for future leaders of world communism. He immersed himself in studying Marxism and the politics of the Comintern. He witnessed the death throes of the 'united opposition' of Trotsky, Zinoviev, and Kamenev, and in 1928 attended the Sixth World Congress of the Comintern, which ushered in the ultra-left policy of class against class and the Stalinization of world communism. Having returned to Britain late in 1930 he was disillusioned to discover the CPGB reduced in membership and marginalized in a new sectarian landscape in which initiatives with other parties were prohibited and former collaborators were pronounced 'social fascists'.

After an unhappy spell as London organizer of the YCL the disenchanted Wicks found employment at Russian Oil Products. He strengthened his links with fellow employee Reg Groves and the Balham Group of the CPGB, who were already in contact with Trotsky. British Trotskyism crystallized around contradictory positions: opposition to the Stalinized Comintern and the imperative for a united front between communists and social democrats to combat fascism mingled with leftist deprecation of the trade unions. Circulation of *The Communist* in May 1932, carrying Trotsky's call for a united front against Hitler, alerted the CPGB leadership. In August, Wicks was expelled, losing his job in the process.

In November 1932 Wicks travelled to Copenhagen to meet Trotsky. But the rejection by Wicks and the majority of the group—the Communist League—of Trotsky's advice that they should enter the Independent Labour Party (ILP) provoked, in 1934, the first of innumerable splits in British Trotskyism. Transformed into the Marxist

League, Wicks and his comrades continued to produce their paper, the *Red Flag*, and work inside the Labour Party and its left-wing, the Socialist League. They were marginalized by Stalin's turn to the popular front as sections of the left stomached the Moscow trials in the interests of anti-fascist unity. Wicks was secretary of the British Committee for the Defence of Leon Trotsky, established in 1936 to answer Stalin's accusations. It was a bitter disappointment: despite support from Bertrand Russell it failed to repeat the success of its American counterpart.

After five years' unemployment Wicks was appointed a municipal clerk in 1937, eventually becoming an electoral registration officer in Battersea. On 18 December 1937 he married Marjorie Edna Loughton, the twenty-four-year-old sister of a YCL friend. They had three sons. Wicks worked closely with the leader of the Trotskyist Marxist group in the ILP, C. L. R. James, on the latter's *World Revolution, 1917–1936*, a development of the Trotskyist world view. Their collaboration influenced the unification in 1938 of most British Trotskyists in the Revolutionary Socialist League (RSL). It was Wicks's last engagement with organized Trotskyism for three decades. He found it difficult to work with young people from a middle-class background and drifted away from the RSL. With members of the original Balham Group he formed the Socialist Anti-War Federation (SAWF) and published a small paper, *The Call*. When the SAWF collapsed, in May 1940, Wicks joined the ILP and helped to produce the *Shop Steward* while contributing to *Free Expression*, a journal of the ILP left.

After 1945 Wicks moved to Twickenham. He was active in the Labour Party and the National and Local Government Officers' Association. His involvement with revolutionary politics and its disappointments was not exhausted. In 1971 he joined the International Socialists, forerunners of the Socialist Workers' Party (SWP), which he left in 1975, as a supporter of an opposition faction. He was subsequently a member of the Workers' League, later reviving links with the SWP. In the 1980s he and his family moved to Marriott, in Somerset. Wicks died in Crewkerne hospital on 26 March 1989, from the effects of a stroke. He had been unassuming, sometimes lacking in confidence, but possessed of integrity and commitment. He had cherished the values of solidarity and class struggle acquired in early twentieth-century Battersea and the opposition to Stalinism embraced in the 1930s. Like other revolutionaries his achievement cannot be measured in terms of political success, but in the contribution that his endeavours made to the militant strand of the British labour movement. JOHN McILROY

Sources H. Wicks, *Keeping my head: the memoirs of a British Bolshevik* (1992) · Russian State Archive of Socio-Political History (RGASPI), Moscow, 495/100 series [scattered but valuable references] · U. Warwick Mod. RC, Wicks papers, MS 102 · U. Warwick Mod. RC, Sara–Maitland papers, MS 15 · U. Warwick Mod. RC, Groves papers, MS 172 · *Harry Wicks: a memorial*, Socialist Platform (1989) · A. Richardson and H. Wicks, interview, 1978 [transcript in J. McIlroy's possession] · S. Bornstein and A. Richardson, *Against the stream: a history of the Trotskyist movement in Britain, 1924–1958* (1986) · S. Bornstein and A. Richardson, *War and The International: a history of* *the Trotskyist movement in Britain, 1937–1949* (1986) · R. Groves, *The Balham Group: how British Trotskyism began* (1974) · B. Hunter, *Lifelong apprenticeship: the life and times of a revolutionary* (1997) · L. Barrow, 'Harry Wicks: a life of heresy', *The Guardian* (3 March 1989) · b. cert. · m. cert. · d. cert.

Archives U. Warwick Mod. RC, papers, MS 102 | U. Hull, Haston MSS · U. Warwick Mod. RC, Groves MSS · U. Warwick Mod. RC, Sara–Maitland MSS | SOUND University of Warwick, Wicks MSS, tapes of interviews with Wicks by Logie Barrow

Likenesses photograph, 1970, repro. in Wicks, *Keeping my head* · photograph, 1970–79, repro. in Bornstein and Richardson, *Against the stream* · photographs, U. Warwick Mod. RC, Sara–Maitland collection · portraits, Russian State Archive of Socio-Political History, Moscow

Wicksteed, Charles (1810–1885), Unitarian minister, was born in Shrewsbury on 10 June 1810, the seventh son and eighth child (of eleven) of John Wicksteed (1774–1837), a starch manufacturer and, after business reverses, manager of a gasworks. Through his mother, Bithia Wicksteed (1775–1819), daughter of John Swanwick of Wem, Shropshire, his descent could be traced from the great dissenting preacher Philip Henry (1631–1707).

In 1818 Wicksteed entered Shrewsbury School, where in time he was admitted to the small group taught directly by the headmaster, Samuel Butler (1774–1839). He thought Butler deficient in the humane side of scholarship, but the classical training was technically superior, and in 1828, assisted financially by the Shrewsbury Chapel and Dr Williams's trust, he entered the University of Glasgow, graduating BA in 1831.

In that year Wicksteed became minister of the Ancient Chapel, Toxteth Park, Liverpool, succeeding John Hamilton Thom (1810–1894), who had moved to Renshaw Street Chapel in the city. In 1835 he became minister at Mill Hill Chapel, Leeds. In 1837 he married Jane Lupton (1815?–1902), daughter of Arthur Lupton of the Leeds mercantile dynasty; they had five sons, including Philip Henry *Wicksteed (1844–1927), and four daughters, one of whom died in infancy.

The theological and literary collaboration forged in Liverpool with Thom, James Martineau (1805–1900) of Paradise Street Chapel, and John James Tayler (1796–1869) of Upper Brook Street Chapel, Manchester, reached its apogee in the joint editorship of the *Prospective Review* in 1845–54, the influential voice of the 'new school' of English Unitarianism, as against the older tradition of eighteenth-century Priestleyanism. Wicksteed published less and exercised a smaller role in the denomination than his friends. He was, however, an erudite and thoughtful man and a popular and important preacher: the 'joyous juvenility' noted by Henry Crabb Robinson (1775–1867) in his travel diary (22 Oct 1849, DWL) may have been a more important portent of later Victorian pulpit style than the rigour and austerity that characterized the preaching of his colleagues in the quadrumvirate.

Wicksteed's health was delicate, and his outward joviality belied deep uncertainties, stemming in part from the loss of his brilliant and adored elder brother Joseph Hartley Wicksteed (*b.* 1803) in a swimming accident in Scotland in 1824. He retired from Leeds for ill health in 1854

and settled in north Wales, where from 1856 he operated a farm, Hafod-y-coed, in the Vale of Clywd. He attended the parish church—but never the morning service, some parts of which Unitarians found offensive—while impressing Unitarian principles on his children. In 1861–3 he supplied the pulpit at Hope Street Church, Liverpool, and in the latter year began a joint ministry with Alexander Gordon (1841–1931); on resigning in 1872 he was enabled by an annuity furnished by friends to become 'minister at large', lecturing around the country until 1881. He had given up the farm in 1875 and in 1877 moved to Croydon, where he died of a stroke on 19 April 1885. He was buried in Norwood cemetery, London.

R. K. WEBB

Sources P. H. Wicksteed, ed., *Memorials of the Rev. Charles Wicksteed, BA* (1886) · *The Inquirer* (25 April 1885) · S. Lawrence, *The descendants of Philip Henry*, ed. J. E. Jones, rev. edn (1925) · minute books, Liverpool, Hope Street Church, Lpool RO · *CGPLA Eng. & Wales* (1885)

Archives Harris Man. Oxf., papers

Likenesses photograph, Harris Man. Oxf. · photograph, DWL, Trustees' Album

Wealth at death £1630 14s. 6d.: probate, 13 June 1885, *CGPLA Eng. & Wales*

Wicksteed, Philip Henry (1844–1927), Unitarian minister and economist, was born on 25 October 1844 at Leeds, one of the nine children of the Revd Charles *Wicksteed (1810–1885), a Unitarian minister, and his wife, Jane Lupton (1815?–1902). Wicksteed was educated at the grammar school, Ruthin, Denbighshire, and University College School, London (1860–61), then at University College (1861–4), and Manchester New College (1864–7), London, where he received the London MA, with a gold medal for classics, in 1867. In April 1868 he married Emily Rebecca Solly, daughter of Henry *Solly, the Unitarian minister at Lancaster and well-known social reformer; they had ten children, two of whom died in infancy. Wicksteed had lived in Leeds, north Wales, London, and Taunton before his marriage; subsequently he lived in Dukinfield (east of Manchester), London (1874–97), and Childrey (near Wantage).

After graduating, Wicksteed became the Unitarian minister at Taunton in Somerset. By late in 1869, however, he was the minister at Dukinfield, and it was here that he came to know the work of Abraham Kuenen, which played an important role in the diffusion of critical study of the Old Testament. Wicksteed was greatly drawn to this Dutch liberal theology, learned Dutch, and translated into English a popular version of Kuenen's findings. In 1886 he published an English translation of the first part of Kuenen's new edition of the *Onderzoek*. In October 1874 Wicksteed became the successor to James Martineau as minister to the Little Portland Street Chapel, London. By 1897, however, the congregation had declined and moreover some distance had opened up between the minister and his charges. Wicksteed decided to concentrate on his lecturing, study, and writing and by 1901 had settled in Childrey.

It was during his years in London that Wicksteed

Philip Henry Wicksteed (1844–1927), by unknown
photographer, c.1874

became involved in the new university extension movement. Between 1887 and 1918 he gave nearly three hundred extension courses for the London Society for the
Extension of University Teaching (founded in 1876) and
the subject matter ranged widely and included Greek
drama, Aristotle, Dante, Wordsworth, economics, and
sociology. It was perhaps as a lecturer on Dante that he
was best-known. Wicksteed also wrote extensively on
Dante and on Dante's relationship to the thought of Aquinas. More popular works included *Six Sermons on Dante*
(1879) and the Temple Classics edition of Dante (1899–
1906), while *Dante and Giovanni del Virgilio* (1902, with E. G.
Gardner) and *From Vita Nuova to Paradiso* (1922) were more
scholarly publications. As a liberal nonconformist able to
enter into medieval thought, Wicksteed published *The
Religion of Time and the Religion of Eternity* in 1899 and then
two works dealing explicitly with Thomist thought, *Dante
and Aquinas* (1913) and *The Reactions between Dogma and Philosophy, Illustrated from the Works of St Thomas Aquinas* (1920). In
these works Wicksteed conveyed, together with his criticisms, his deep appreciation of the significance for the
modern day of the best medieval thought. It was perhaps
in a similar spirit that Wicksteed devoted his last years to
preparing, in collaboration with F. M. Cornford, the Loeb
edition of Aristotle's *Physics*.

A Liberal in his politics, Wicksteed was a familiar figure
on the platforms of London meetings. The pages of *The
Inquirer*, the Unitarian newspaper, carried many of his articles, letters, and reviews relating to current political

issues. While a sympathetic observer rather than an active
supporter of the labour and socialist movements, Wicksteed was an enthusiastic adherent to the Labour church
movement (in 1891) and its journal *The Labour Prophet*, and
a source of inspiration for the movement's founder, John
Trevor.

Wicksteed first came to political economy by reading
Henry George's *Progress and Poverty*. By 1883, however, he
had begun to study the marginal theory of Jevons and by
1884 was expounding that theory to others; it remained
the foundation of all his work in economics.

That work began with Wicksteed's critique of volume 1
of Karl Marx's *Das Kapital* in *To-Day* (October 1884), one of
the earliest critiques of Marx in English. Wicksteed both
rejected Marx's claim that commodities have only
'abstract labour' in common and pointed out that in a
non-slave society there is no competitive force driving the
wage paid for 'labour-force' to the latter's cost of production. For Wicksteed, this destroyed the foundation of
Marx's economic reasoning. Wicksteed's *The Alphabet of
Economic Science* (1888), by contrast, was entirely constructive, expounding in a clear and elementary way the virtues
of a mathematically expressed marginal theory of value
(in effect, the theory of demand). In the famous *Essay on the
Co-Ordination of the Laws of Distribution* (1894) Wicksteed
sought to show how, under certain conditions, the equality of each factor return to the factor's marginal product
could be consistent with 'exhaustion of the product',
there being no unexplained residual. His whole argument
was, however, cast in a partial equilibrium framework.

Wicksteed described his *The Common Sense of Political
Economy* (1910) as the culmination of 'my life effort to do
something real for thought and life'. In Wicksteed's consistently subjective approach, all motives were allowed to
impinge on each human choice and no difference in this
respect was recognized between 'economic' and 'non-
economic' choices; some of Wicksteed's harshest words
are devoted to such concepts as 'the Economic Man'. Yet
subjective was far from meaning egoistic for Wicksteed,
who allowed that motivation would often be other-
directed and perhaps altruistic. The concerns of an economic actor, however, did not include the aims of the
other party to a given transaction; while economic relations need not be egoistic, they are, by Wicksteed's definition, 'non-tuistic'. The *Common Sense* remains a major
statement of a consistently subjective but not asocial
approach to the analysis of choice, whether 'economic' or
otherwise.

Wicksteed was a powerful, vigorous man, who loved to
explore the Norwegian fjords in his small boat, who
cycled in Switzerland at the age of eighty, and who, apart
from a serious illness in 1918–20, enjoyed excellent
health. His later years were graced by honorary degrees at
Leeds (1915) and Manchester (1919). He died at his home,
the Old Manor, Childrey, near Wantage, on 18 March 1927,
aged eighty-two.   IAN STEEDMAN

Sources C. H. Herford, *Philip Henry Wicksteed* (1931) [with extensive bibliography of Wicksteed's work] • R. P. Sturges, *Economists'
papers, 1750–1950: a guide to archive and other manuscript sources for the*

history of British and Irish economic thought (1975) · *CGPLA Eng. & Wales* (1927)

Archives BLPES, papers | BLPES, letters to Graham Wallas · Bodl. Oxf., corresp. with Gilbert Murray · DWL, letters to James Connell · Harris Man. Oxf. · UCL, corresp. with Karl Pearson, etc.
Likenesses photograph, *c*.1874, repro. in Herford, *Philip Henry Wicksteed* [*see illus.*] · A. E. Emslie, portrait, 1887–8, priv. coll. · photographs, repro. in Herford, *Philip Henry Wicksteed*
Wealth at death £11,574 18s. 1d.: probate, 6 May 1927, *CGPLA Eng. & Wales*

Wickwane, William de (*d.* 1285), archbishop of York, is of unknown origins, and his early career is wholly obscure. Although he never held an advanced academic degree, his status as a *magister* has led to the suggestion that he may have been a student at the University of Paris (or possibly Oxford). Whether he was the author of the theological compilation or 'Memoriale' with which he is credited by John Bale, bishop of Ossory, is, however, extremely uncertain. Nor, as far as is known, had he any experience of administrative service on behalf of the English crown. It is accordingly somewhat surprising that Wickwane already held the important dignity of chancellor at York Minster by January 1264, the month in which he was also admitted to the rectory of Ivinghoe in Buckinghamshire. As chancellor and (from at least 1268) canon and prebendary of Newbald, he emerges from Archbishop Giffard's archiepiscopal register as a somewhat truculent member of the York Cathedral chapter, often at odds on financial matters with his superiors. Nevertheless, only two months after Giffard's death in April 1279, Wickwane was elected in his place by an overwhelming majority (eighteen votes out of twenty-one) of the chapter. He lost no time in travelling to Italy where the pope, Nicholas III, set aside the capitular election, and then by papal authority provided Wickwane to the archdiocese of York before consecrating him archbishop at Viterbo on 26 August. The temporalities of his see were restored on 28 October.

Immediately on his return to England, Wickwane began to display a provocative—and characteristic—tenacity in defence of what he took to be the canonical privileges of the church of York. His insistence on having his primatial cross carried before him while travelling through the province of Canterbury from Dover to his enthronement at York, which took place on Christmas day 1279, caused something of a national scandal and permanently embittered his relations with Archbishop Pecham. More dangerously still, and as early as 12 December 1279, Wickwane launched what seems to have been the first full-scale programme of provincial visitation that the northern English church had ever experienced. In 1281 the archbishop deliberately asserted his metropolitan authority over his suffragan see of Durham. On being prevented by force from visiting the cathedral chapter there on 25 June, he had his chair set up in Palace Green and concluded an uncompromising sermon by excommunicating Bishop Robert de Insula as well as Prior Richard of Claxton and his monks, later placing Durham under an interdict. Two years later he took the opportunity of Robert de Insula's death to renew his attempts to conduct a visitation of the Durham chapter, this time *sede vacante*. On 3 July 1283 he dismounted at the cathedral, only to find the church closed against him yet again. Wickwane was forced to leave Durham unceremoniously, after an even more dangerous assault on himself and his retainers than the one he had endured in 1281.

Despite ceaseless endeavours to find a solution to the complex legal issues at stake, Wickwane's attempts to exercise jurisdictional superiority in the diocese of Durham therefore ended in humiliating failure for him. The election of Antony (I) Bek to the bishopric of Durham in July 1283 introduced a new and powerful personality into the confusions of the situation, but the archbishop was now too enmeshed in litigation against the monks of Durham to contemplate a compromise. As his register demonstrates, he was also restlessly active in visiting religious houses and churches within his own diocese. In late 1284 he finally decided to seek justice against the obduracy of the Durham Cathedral chapter by visiting the curia in person. Reported to have arrived at the Cistercian abbey of Pontigny in Burgundy by December 1284, he became fatally ill not long afterwards and returned to Pontigny to die on 26 or 27 August 1285. Miracles were later alleged to have been worked at his tomb there, but in the north of England, Wickwane left a more ambiguous reputation, as an archbishop who was 'lean, harsh and niggardly', but to those who knew him best also 'just in judgement and most tender in conscience' (*Chronicle of Lanercost*, 19).

R. B. DOBSON

Sources *Register of William Wickwane*, Borth. Inst., register 3 · *The register of William Wickwane, lord archbishop of York, 1279–1285*, ed. W. Brown, SurtS, 114 (1907) · R. Brentano, *York metropolitan jurisdiction and papal judges delegate, 1279–1296* (1959) · R. B. Dobson, 'The political role of the archbishops of York during the reign of Edward I', *Thirteenth century England: proceedings of the Newcastle upon Tyne conference* [Newcastle upon Tyne 1989], ed. P. R. Coss and S. D. Lloyd, 3 (1991), 47–64 · W. H. Dixon, *Fasti Eboracenses: lives of the archbishops of York*, ed. J. Raine (1863), 317–27 · C. R. Cheney, 'Letters of William of Wickwane, chancellor of York, 1266–1268', *EngHR*, 47 (1932), 626–42 · H. Maxwell, ed. and trans., *The chronicle of Lanercost, 1272–1346* (1913) · *CEPR letters* · *Historiae Dunelmensis scriptores tres: Gaufridus de Coldingham, Robertus de Graystanes, et Willielmus de Chambre*, ed. J. Raine, SurtS, 9 (1839), 58–69 · G. E. Aylmer and R. Cant, eds., *A history of York Minster* (1977), 50, 69, 75–8, 83 · Emden, *Oxf.*
Archives Borth. Inst., register 3

Widdicomb, Henry (1813–1868), comic actor, born in Store Street, Tottenham Court Road, London, on 14 February 1813, was the son of **John Esdaile Widdicomb** [Widdicumb] (1787–1854), a well-known figure for many years in London, who from 1819 to 1853 was riding-master and conductor of the ring at Astley's Amphitheatre. The elder Widdicomb, before he was at Astley's, played in pantomimes with Grimaldi at the Coburg Theatre, and was said to be an excellent ring-master. When there was no evening performance at Astley's he was frequently seen at Vauxhall. He died in Kennington on 3 November 1854.

When he was fifteen Harry Widdicomb was entered by his father as a clerk at the custom house. Against his father's wish he left this employment in 1831, and obtained an engagement at the Margate theatre under Saville Faucit. He joined the Yorkshire circuit under Down, but moved to London about 1835 and was engaged by Andrew Ducrow. When Astley's was burnt down he went to Liverpool and played leading low comedy parts under Malone Raymond. In March 1842 he was taken on by Benjamin Webster at the Haymarket, his first employment at a West End theatre. In 1845 he became joint manager of the Sheffield and Wolverhampton theatres with Charles Dillon, but three years later he returned to London, and was principal comic actor at the Surrey Theatre from 1848 to 1860. He played, at first occasionally and then regularly, under Fechter at the Lyceum, notably in *Sarah's Young Man* (August 1858), Gilbert's *Uncle Baby* (November 1863), and as the First Gravedigger in *Hamlet* (January 1861 and May 1864), as well as in many other minor roles. He was last seen during 1867 at the Holborn Theatre.

Widdicomb never attained the first rank, but he had a considerable fund of original humour and power of facial expression. He died in Kennington Park Road on 6 April 1868, and was buried at Norwood cemetery.

THOMAS SECCOMBE, rev. NILANJANA BANERJI

Sources *Era Almanack and Annual* (1871) · *The life and reminiscences of E. L. Blanchard, with notes from the diary of Wm. Blanchard*, ed. C. W. Scott and C. Howard, 2 vols. (1891) · Hall, *Dramatic ports.*, vol. 4 · *Daily Telegraph* (7 April 1868) · *The Era* (12 April 1869) · GM, 4th ser., 5 (1868), 689 · *Punch*, 116 (1899), 225 · B. Gaultier [T. Martin], ed., *The book of ballads* (1855) · *Letters of Robert Browning and Elizabeth Barrett Barrett, 1845–1846*, ed. R. W. B. Browning, 2 vols. (1899) · T. Frost, *Circus life and circus celebrities* (1875)
Likenesses portrait?, repro. in *Thespian & Dramatic Record* (8 July 1857) · print, Harvard TC
Wealth at death under £800: probate, 7 May 1868, *CGPLA Eng. & Wales*

Widdicomb, John Esdaile (1787–1854). *See under* Widdicomb, Henry (1813–1868).

Widdowes, Giles (1588/9–1645), Church of England clergyman, the elder son of Thomas Widdowes of Mickleton, Gloucestershire, entered Oriel College, Oxford, probably in 1603 or 1604. He graduated BA on 25 February 1608, proceeded MA on 27 January 1614, and was elected fellow of Oriel on 19 July 1610 by recommendation of William Barlow, who as the bishop of Lincoln was the official college visitor and who overruled objections. In 1614, through the support of Endymion Porter, whose father held land at Mickleton, Widdowes almost obtained from the king Walgrave rectory in Northamptonshire, but it went to John Williams, Lord Chancellor Ellesmere's chaplain. After supporting in 1618 the election as provost of Oriel of William Lewis, chaplain to Lord Chancellor Bacon, Widdowes became college dean in 1619/20. However, when in 1621 Bacon fell from the chancellorship, Provost Lewis, beleaguered by scandal, departed, and John Williams, newly installed as lord keeper, in his role as bishop of Lincoln became the visitor of Oriel. On 14 December Widdowes resigned his fellowship and moved to Gloucester Hall, where he was vice-principal for a time.

In 1619 Widdowes had obtained the rectory of St Martin's at Carfax, Oxford. Here he gradually introduced fuller prayer book worship at his church, Thomas Crosfield noting on 1 January 1628, 'The custome of Common prayer morning & Evening begun at Carfax' (*Diary*, 17). It was later claimed that Widdowes had placed a crucifix in a window. He was an antisabbatarian and danced at Whitsun ales.

Widdowes produced poems for university volumes commemorative of royal occasions. In 1630 he printed a sermon preached at Witney 'concerning the lawfulness of Church-authority, for ordaining and commanding of Rites and Ceremonies to beautifie the Church', entitled *The Schysmatical Puritan*, which he dedicated to Katherine, duchess of Buckingham, as her 'most humble servant and Chaplaine'. It was 'much displeasing to Dr. Abbot archb. of Canterbury' (Wood, 3.179). William Prynne, whom Wood suggests Widdowes had tutored at Oriel, responded in the 1630 edition of his *Anti-Arminianism*. In 1631 Widdowes reprinted *The Schismatical Puritan* and replied to Prynne in *The Lawlesse Kneelesse Schismaticall Puritan*, dedicated to Porter. Prynne countered later that year with *Lame Giles his Haultings*. Wood suggested Widdowes 'was fitted as 'twere on purpose to duel with Prynne (as Don Quixot with the wind-mill which no man else was knight errant enough to encounter)' (Wood, 3.855).

Although Widdowes's anti-puritan stance was sufficiently pronounced to provoke disturbances at St Martin's by puritanical scholars of Lincoln College on 13 December 1637 and by another group on 10 February 1641, he was not successful in gaining further preferment during Laud's time at Canterbury. In 1639 he sought through Porter and the presumed goodwill of Laud the benefice of Islip, Oxfordshire, which was in the gift of the dean and chapter of Westminster. The dean, none other than John Williams, was at that time under suspension, but Islip was given to a fellow of St John's College.

Widdowes was generous to the poor and an energetic pastor towards soldiers during the civil war. He died poor and living in rented accommodation at Oxford, his goods being valued at only £4 17s. 10d. He was buried on 4 February 1645 in the chancel of St Martin's. Wood described him as

a harmless and honest man, a noted disputant, well read in the schoolmen, and as conformable to, and zealous in, the established discipline of the church of England, as any person of his time, yet of so odd and strange parts that few or none could be compared with him. (Wood, 3.179)

W. H. HUTTON, rev. A. J. HEGARTY

Sources Wood, *Ath. Oxon.*, new edn · Foster, *Alum. Oxon.* · G. C. Richards and C. L. Shadwell, *The provosts and fellows of Oriel College, Oxford* (1922) · C. J. H. Fletcher, *A history of the church and parish of St. Martin (Carfax) Oxford* (1896) · R. Atkyns, *The ancient and present state of Glostershire*, 2 pts in 1 (1712) · *The diary of Thomas Crosfield*, ed. F. S. Boas (1935) · CSP dom., 1638–9 · Oxfordshire archives, inventory of goods at death, 1645, PAR 207/9/WI/1 · Calendar of presentation deeds (Oxford diocese), Oxf. diocese papers d. 98, E. R. C. Brinkworth, Oxfordshire archives · Bodl. Oxf., MS Top. Oxon. c. 56 · *The works of the most reverend father in God, William Laud*, 5, ed. J. Bliss (1853), pt. 1 · F. Madan, *Oxford books: a bibliography of printed works*, 3 vols. (1895–1931); repr. (1964)
Wealth at death £4 17s. 10d.: inventory, Oxfordshire Archives, Oxford, PAR 207/9/WI/1, 1 Feb 1645

Widdows, George Henry (1871–1946), architect, was born on 15 October 1871 at Lakenham, Norfolk, the youngest of three children of Henry Francis Widdows (1827–1898), leather merchant, and his wife, Charlotte Belden (1833–1908). His parents were both from Norwich (of which Lakenham is now a part) and Widdows attended King Edward VI School there from 1882 to 1887. From 1887 to 1894 he was articled to Arthur Lacey of Norwich, architect and diocesan surveyor, after which he worked in the offices of W. Henry White of London, Walter Green Penty of York, A. Basil Cottam of Taunton and Bridgwater, and Bradshaw and Gass of Bolton. He became chief architectural assistant to the Derby borough surveyor in 1897. After a couple of years in Derby he married, on 7 June 1899, Mary Thouless (b. 1871/2), also of Norwich.

In 1904 Widdows was appointed building surveyor to the education committee of Derbyshire county council, in whose service he continued until his retirement in 1936. Derbyshire had become an education authority in 1903, at a time when its population had grown very considerably, particularly in the coalmining districts in the east of the county, where Widdows's schools came to be concentrated. Before Derbyshire began its programme of school building, British school design was founded on the idea of a compact building in which classrooms clustered round a central hall from which they could be entered by doors with glazed upper portions, affording a measure of supervision by the head teacher but no through ventilation, and admitting light from one side only. The move from the central hall to the pavilion plan of classrooms opening from well-lighted corridors was led by George Reid and John Hutchings, respectively medical officer of health and architect to the education committee of Staffordshire. In Widdows's own words, in a paper read to the RIBA, Reid 'with Mr. Hutchings, the Staffordshire authority's architect, was the first to break down the bad tradition of the central hall. I think we in Derbyshire may claim to run a close second' (G. H. Widdows, 'School design', RIBA Journal, 28 Nov 1921, 34).

Widdows's most productive periods were 1904–1914 (when he made about forty designs) and 1924–36 (when he produced about twenty-eight). His first attempts at providing properly ventilated schools were marching corridor schools, incorporating wide corridors which could be used as central halls or for drill, with ventilated classrooms at each end of the building; these included Welbeck Road, Bolsover (1906), Highfield, Long Eaton (1911), and Alfreton Road, Tibshelf (1912). The first fully developed veranda or pavilion school was North Wingfield infants' school, designed in 1910 but not completed until after the war. It incorporated the weaving shed window (of the north light roof truss type), which Widdows had probably seen in Lancashire, through which light could flood from one side, more traditional dormers being used on the other. In the early 1920s Widdows designed five Derbyshire schools specifically modelled on North Wingfield, in addition to one at Torquay.

The schools so far discussed were elementary schools, but Widdows also built a number of secondary schools. These quite frequently had the 'hygienic' elements characteristic of his practice, but, unlike the elementary

schools, which were entirely one storey except for teachers' rooms, amounted usually to at least two storeys and were often given a neo-Georgian character: examples include Chesterfield Girls' High School (1909) and Heanor secondary (1910). In Widdows's later years these secondary schools sometimes involved extending historic buildings, which he always handled sensitively. His importance in the history of school architecture is recognized by Seaborne and Lowe, who argue that, 'among the pioneering architects of the early twentieth century, George Widdows was perhaps the most important' (Seaborne and Lowe, 2.85).

As county councils' building responsibilities widened, Widdows worked on hospitals and libraries, while outside his public responsibilities he designed three houses for himself, one at Duffield and two at Allestree, as well as furnishings for St Edmund's Church, Allestree. He seems to have been a deeply religious man: he was a churchwarden and a lay reader at St Edmund's, and for each of his houses he designed a chapel or oratory, where daily prayers were said. He retired in 1936, and died at his home, 21 Park Lane, Allestree, on 11 February 1946; he was survived by his wife, two sons (Bernard and Wystan, both architects), and three daughters. He was buried on 13 February in St Edmund's churchyard, Allestree.   MICHAEL BROOK

Sources Derbyshire Advertiser (15 Feb 1946) · biographical file, nomination papers for ARIBA, 25 July 1904, RIBA BAL · Derby Evening Telegraph (11 Feb 1946) · private information (2004) · Derbyshire RO, D 2200 C/1–71, D 919 C/1/17/1–22 and indexes (1903–1936), C/20/1–22 · R. A. Lowe, 'The medical profession and school design in England, 1902–1914', Paedagogica Historica, 13 (1973), 425–44 · M. Seaborne and R. A. Lowe, The English school: its architecture and organization, 1870–1970 (1977), vol. 2 of The English school: its architecture and organization · 'Some provincial schools', The Builder, 105 (30 Oct 1913), 457–64 · 'The means of architectural expression', The Builder, 107 (10 July 1914), 31–2 · 'County architect', Derby Evening Telegraph (25 Sept 1936)
Archives NRA, priv. coll., personal MSS
Wealth at death £2129 14s. 9d.—probate: 1946

Widdowson, Elsie May (1906–2000), nutritionist, was born on 21 October 1906 at The Ferns, Belmont Road, Wallington, Surrey, one of two daughters of Thomas Henry Widdowson, grocer's assistant, and his wife, Rose, née Elphick. Her younger sister was Dr Eva Crane OBE. Both gained scholarships to the county secondary school, Sydenham, where the remarkably enlightened staff persuaded them to take up science for a career. Since biology was considered a rather 'soft' subject they were encouraged to opt for the more physical sciences. Elsie studied chemistry at Imperial College, London; she graduated BSc (1928) and PhD (1931), and her sister took mathematics and physics, also gaining a PhD degree. Their early love of biology persisted, however: the chemist became a world authority on nutritional physiology and the mathematical physicist on apiculture.

For her PhD Elsie Widdowson studied changes in the carbohydrate chemistry of the developing apple. It then became difficult for her to obtain a permanent job and she was advised that dietetics was a growing profession considered suitable for a woman. It was in 1933, during her postgraduate training in this new subject at King's College Hospital, that she met Robert McCance, a clinical scientist. The scientific partnership was consolidated when in 1938 McCance became reader in medicine at Cambridge and Widdowson joined his team there. The team's ability to define the relevant question and then provide a definitive answer led Widdowson to realize that if nutritional science was to study the effects of diet on physiology it was essential to have a detailed knowledge of the nutrient composition of food as consumed. Filling this fundamental knowledge gap made full use of Widdowson's chemical skills and in 1940 *The Chemical Composition of Foods* was published. As dietary habits changed it was updated in a series of editions and is now known as *McCance and Widdowson's The Composition of Foods*. These food tables have become a factual basis for innumerable nutritional studies throughout the world.

Although very much devoted to fundamental physiology Widdowson and McCance were always prepared to apply their expertise to practical problems. Towards the end of 1939, at the request of the government, they began studies of the potential health consequences that might arise from future food rationing programmes, especially if animal and dairy product supplies had to be cut drastically. An important component was testing the physiological efficacy of the calcium and iron fortification of bread and flour products. These latter investigations built upon pioneering studies which Widdowson and McCance had carried out during the late 1930s and early 1940s on the absorption and excretion of dietary minerals.

In 1946, now permanent members of the Medical Research Council staff, they embarked upon a three-year investigation in war-torn Europe on the nutrition and health of communities, especially children, who had been the victims of chronic under-nutrition. Between 1950 and 1970 this experience prompted Widdowson to encourage prospective investigations of malnourished children in tropical Africa. These were supported by studies in Cambridge on rats and pigs. Widdowson and McCance were the first to demonstrate that the earlier the nutritional deprivation the greater and longer lasting the effect on growth and well-being. This finding inspired others during the 1980s and 1990s to investigate the long-term effects of early growth retardation on susceptibility to both non-communicable and infectious diseases. All acknowledge their indebtedness to Elsie Widdowson for the original idea and subsequent encouragement she generously gave.

Widdowson was president of the Nutrition Society between 1977 and 1980 and of the British Nutrition Foundation from 1986 to 1996. She was, however, equally respected within the field of neonatology and was president of the Neonatal Society from 1978 to 1981. She had begun work on the chemical composition of the human body before the Second World War but in the 1950s and 1960s this work became more focused on early human development. She and her colleagues carried out chemical analyses on whole foetal and newly born cadavers, studies unlikely to be repeated. The results placed our knowledge

of micronutrient accretion during growth on a sounder scientific footing, allowing meaningful dietary recommendations to be made for this critical period. She also became involved in studies on human milk composition, resulting in 1980 in the revision of compositional regulations for breast milk substitutes in the UK.

Following her formal retirement from her Medical Research Council post in 1972 Widdowson pursued her academic interests within the department of investigative medicine at Cambridge. She never lost her curiosity about topics she had investigated at earlier stages during her life. She studied among other things the variability in composition of different mammalian milks. One of her popular party pieces was to talk about milk from mother seals that she was able to study during a visit to Labrador in 1984. She was never afraid of controversy and during the 1980s and 1990s provided strong support for disciplined research using laboratory animals if this was essential for an understanding of human health and disease. As biological research became more and more molecular in emphasis she stressed the continuing importance of whole-body physiology. She remained intrigued by the development of new analytical procedures such as the use of deuterium-labelled water for measuring the breast-milk intake of young babies and doubly labelled water for assessing the energy expenditure of persons unencumbered by the instrumentation traditionally used for this purpose in laboratory-based studies. She could never resist the opportunity to tease the investigator, however, that these marvels of modern science often achieved little more than she herself had done with primitive and less expensive equipment. These comments were always made in a generous spirit and her overriding concern remained the encouragement of the young. She always emphasized that her own career had been enabled by that chance meeting with McCance. Her faith was justified by the subsequent achievements of numerous colleagues she had nurtured throughout her long scientific life.

Elsie Widdowson died, unmarried, at Addenbrooke's Hospital, Cambridge, on 14 June 2000 following a severe stroke while on holiday with her sister on the Dingle peninsula in Ireland. She was buried in Barrington churchyard, Cambridgeshire, on 23 June. A memorial service was held on 20 October 2000 at Great Saint Mary's Church in Cambridge. Although highly respected by all who knew her, and despite having become one of the most famous names in nutritional science, most of the formal trappings of recognition did not come until after Widdowson's retirement from the Medical Research Council. She was elected FRS in 1976, appointed CBE in 1979, and made CH in 1993 at the age of eighty-seven. One reason was the self-effacing nature of her character; another was that her scientific achievements had become inextricably entwined with those of her long-term collaborator Robert McCance. This partnership became so famous that it is inevitable that many have attempted to analyse the nature of their interdependence. McCance was undoubtedly a creative clinical scientist but his ideas needed to be translated into sound experimental studies and this is where Elsie Widdowson's abilities came early to the fore, especially where a sympathetic understanding of the management of junior collaborators was concerned. The fact is that neither could have achieved what they did without the other.   ROGER WHITEHEAD

Sources M. Ashwell, ed., *McCance and Widdowson: a scientific partnership of 60 years, 1933–1993* (1993) · private information (2004) [Eva Crane] · D. Southgate, 'A personal appreciation: Dr Elsie M. Widdowson', *British Journal of Nutrition*, 85 (2001), 513–15 · D. Lister, *The Independent* (16 June 2000), 6a–g · *Daily Telegraph* (22 June 2000) · *The Times* (27 June 2000) · A. Tucker, *The Guardian* (22 June 2000) · *The Scotsman* (19 July 2000) · b. cert. · d. cert.
Archives RS, MSS · Wellcome L., notebooks | FILM MRC Human Nutrition Research, Cambridge, 'McCance and Widdowson: pioneers of nutritional science', videotape made by Margaret Ashwell from historic photographs and sound recordings plus commentary 15 min. | SOUND Nutrition Society, London, compilation of Widdowson Tapes, volumes 1 and 2, prepared by Margaret Ashwell and available from the Nutrition Society, London
Likenesses D. Reed, photograph, NPG; repro. in Southgate, 'A personal appreciation'
Wealth at death £1,246,411—net: probate, 28 Nov 2000, *CGPLA Eng. & Wales*

Widdrington, Ralph (1614/15–1688), scholar, was born at Cheeseburn Grange, Stamfordham, Northumberland, the son of Lewis Widdrington (*d.* 1630) and his wife, Catherine, daughter and heir of William Lawson of Little Usworth, co. Durham. From Morpeth School on 25 June 1632 he was admitted to Christ's College, Cambridge, as pensioner and pupil of John Fenwick. There he graduated BA in 1636, proceeded MA in 1639, and was elected fellow, probably in 1639. He was admitted to Gray's Inn in March 1641 but was ordained and thenceforth tutored actively at Christ's, where his family connections brought him sons of north-country gentry. Fourteen of his younger relatives entered Christ's between 1649 and 1670.

Widdrington was one of three Christ's fellows not removed in March 1644, another being Henry More. Later he denied taking the covenant and claimed to have left college for almost two years, returning only through the influence of 'a relation or two'—presumably his elder brother Sir Thomas *Widdrington, MP and subsequently speaker (Peile, *Register*, 1.421–2). On 24 October 1650 he succeeded Henry Molle as university orator (a position he retained until 1673) and soon after took the engagement, as Samuel Dillingham informed Sancroft on 30 December. Cromwell named him Greek professor on 12 December 1654; Isaac Barrow, who 'had the consent of the University', had to wait for the professorship until Widdrington resigned at the Restoration (J. Aubrey, *Brief Lives*, ed. A. Clark, 2 vols., 1898, 1.90). He attempted in 1659 to displace Ralph Cudworth as master of Christ's. Pepys heard on 21 February 1660 'how he did oppose all the fellows in the college'; a year later he had given up his pupils 'and was now quite out of interest' (Pepys, 1.63, 2.44). Charged with 'failure in trust' and 'fraudulent dealing', he refused to co-operate and in April 1661 'was removed from the college for contumacy and neglect of statutes' (*CSP dom.*, 1660–61, 574–5).

However, Widdrington still had political influence and obtained a king's bench mandamus (20 June 1661), then reinstatement by a privy council committee. In 1665 he unsuccessfully made what Henry More called 'a long rabble of accusations' against Cudworth, and 'collaterally' against More himself (*Conway Letters*, 243, 242). When a fellow was elected in 1667, and a proctor in 1676, Widdrington again sought outside intervention. Meanwhile his personal affairs prospered: he was created DD by royal mandate in 1661 and preferred to the rectories of Thorpe on the Hill, Lincolnshire (6 February 1661), Wendon Lofts, Essex (1666; resigned 1676), Terrington, Norfolk (1673), and Great Munden, Hertfordshire (17 December 1675). Already Lady Margaret preacher (since 1664), he was chosen professor of divinity on the king's recommendation of 30 December 1672.

Widdrington contributed verses to *Justa Edovardo King* (1638), *Luctus et gratulatio* (1658) on the funeral of Oliver and succession of Richard Cromwell, *Sōstra* (1660) on the return of Charles II, and other university collections. He wrote a short treatise on the Lord's supper for the Cambridge edition of Thomas à Kempis's *De Christo imitando* (1688). His long correspondence with Sancroft suggests he was a difficult friend, in particular his letters of 25 November and 3 December 1672 which then reaffirm their friendship. He died in college on 10 June 1688, having made Christ's the beneficiary of his will, dated 19 March 1688, but only after three nephews were dead—an inevitably contentious arrangement, which lost the college most of his substantial estate.   HUGH DE QUEHEN

Sources J. Peile, *Biographical register of Christ's College, 1505–1905, and of the earlier foundation, God's House, 1448–1505*, ed. [J. A. Venn], 1 (1910) · J. Peile, *Christ's College* (1900) · Venn, *Alum. Cant.* · H. Cary, ed., *Memorials of the great civil war in England from 1646 to 1652*, 2 (1842) · J. Hodgson, *A history of Northumberland*, 3 pts in 7 vols. (1820–58), pt 2, vol. 2 · *The Conway letters: the correspondence of Anne, Viscountess Conway, Henry More, and their friends, 1642–1684*, ed. M. H. Nicolson, rev. edn, ed. S. Hutton (1992) · Pepys, *Diary* · J. B. Mullinger, *The University of Cambridge*, 3 (1911) · J. Twigg, *The University of Cambridge and the English Revolution, 1625–1688* (1990) · *CSP dom.*, 1660–61, 574–5; 1667, 220; 1672–3, 327–8; 1676–7, 242–3 · PRO, PROB 11/392, fols. 208r–209r · Bodl. Oxf., MS Rawl. A. 328, fols. 168–9 · Bodl. Oxf., MS Tanner 43, fols. 51, 54
Archives CUL, letters as public orator | Bodl. Oxf., letters, Tanner MSS · CUL, Add. MSS; Adam Wall MSS
Wealth at death supposedly £6000

Widdrington, Roger. *See* Preston, Roland (1567–1647).

Widdrington [*formerly* Cook], **Samuel Edward** (1787–1856), writer on Spain, was the eldest son of Joseph Cook (1759–1844) of Newton Hall, Morpeth, Northumberland, vicar of Chatton and Shilbottle, and sufficiently acquainted with the duke of Northumberland to ask him to be a sponsor for his son. His mother, Sarah Brown, the daughter of E. Brown, was a great-niece and coheir of Nathaniel Widdrington of Hauxley in Northumberland. Samuel Cook entered the navy on 31 December 1802 and saw service in the English Channel, notably in the vicinity of the Camp de Boulogne, where Napoleon was then amassing a flotilla for his projected invasion of England. Cook was later sent to the West Indies, where in June 1805 he obtained special mention for his conduct in the capture of the felucca *La Concepción*. On 10 July 1809, after further service off the coast of Cayenne and Surinam, he was appointed lieutenant to the *Fame* (74 guns). On 16 September 1813, when under the command of Captain Edward Reynolds Sibly in the sloop *Swallow*, he led a successful attack on the *Guerrière*, a French brig, in the neighbourhood of Port d'Anzo in Tuscany. He later served with Captain Charles Dashwood in the *Windsor Castle* (74 guns), on which, in May 1824, when at Lisbon, Dom João VI of Portugal took refuge from his son Dom Miguel, who was putting pressure on him to abdicate. In consequence, Cook was presented by Dom João with the Portuguese Order of the Tower and Sword, and was promoted to the rank of commander. Wearing this insignia he sat for a portrait by the Sevillian artist José Gutierrez de la Vega which was later hung at Newton Hall, Morpeth. He retired from the service shortly after. It would appear that mineralogy and botany were subjects closer to his heart than the navy.

Although he refers to having known Spain from his earliest youth, it was not until 1829 that Cook made his first extensive tour of the country, where he was to remain for over three years. It is difficult from his descriptions to reconstruct the order of his excursions, mostly made from Madrid; but with the possible exception of Richard Ford, whom he met in Seville, Cook explored more remote districts of Spain than any other visitor. Accompanied by Sir Charles Lyell, the geologist, he also made an excursion into the central Pyrenees. While in Madrid, he had shown particular interest in the new mineralogical department added to the museum of natural history. Before leaving Spain he sent home a collection of geological sections together with fir-cones of various species (from which were grown two trees still standing at Newton Hall in the 1990s), and also a number of paintings by Spanish artists, among them a St Catherine by Zurbarán, which he had acquired, for he considered himself a connoisseur. On 18 September 1832, not long after his return to England, Cook married Dorothy, second daughter of Alexander Davison of Swarland Park, Northumberland. In 1834 his *Sketches in Spain during the Years 1829, 30, 31, and 32* was published, and, in 1838, *Observations on the Present State of the [Carlist] War* written from a whig point of view. He also published papers on botany.

In 1840 Cook assumed the surname of Widdrington. He was a fellow of the Royal Society and of the Royal Geographical Society. In October 1842 he revisited Spain, and, *en route* to Andalusia, inspected the phosphorite deposits at Logrosán, the paintings by Zurbarán at neighbouring Guadalupe, and the cinnabar mines of Almadén. On the return journey Widdrington traversed the Asturias and Galicia, provinces he had not explored previously. At Oviedo he met Schultz, a German professor of geology and mining, and remarked on the 'unsaleable' remains he had seen of a consignment of testaments left by George Borrow, whose missionary activities he gratuitously criticized. Widdrington sailed home from Vigo, relieved after having been officiously interrogated at both Santiago and Pontevedra by the police, who, suspicious of his activities,

had accused him of 'examining buildings', which was true enough.

Richard Ford, when acknowledging the invaluable assistance he had received from him while compiling his *Handbook for Travellers in Spain* (1845), described Widdrington as 'a great geologist and stuffer of little birds and stalker of fat women, a tall, stiff man, with a sort of philosophical hat', and as a writer 'dry, painstaking and accurate … [who] understands the people better than the pictures. There he breaks down lamentably … and does not know a Murillo from a mainmast' (*Letters of Richard Ford*). Nevertheless, Widdrington's *Spain and the Spaniards in 1843* (1844), the result of his second tour, was reviewed sympathetically by Ford, who remarked that 'every page discovers good sense, observation, and earnestness, a love of the beautiful and a single-hearted desire to obtain and impart correct information … and like the former [book], must ever be reckoned among the classical works on Spain' (*QR*, 1846).

Widdrington died childless at Newton Hall on 11 January 1856, and was succeeded in his estates by his nephew, Shallcross Fitzherbert Jacson, son of his sister Frances, who also assumed the surname of Widdrington.

E. I. CARLYLE, *rev.* IAN CAMPBELL ROBERTSON

Sources *The letters of Richard Ford*, ed. R. E. Prothero (1905) • I. Robertson, *Los curiosos impertinentes*, rev. edn (1988) • [R. Ford], review of S. E. Widdrington, *Spain and the Spaniards in 1843* (1844), *QR*, 77 (1845–6), 496–526 • private information (2004) • *GM*, 2nd ser., 45 (1856), 305 • O'Byrne, *Naval biog. dict.* • Burke, *Gen. GB*
Likenesses J. Gutierrez de la Vega, oils, *c.*1830, Newton Hall, Morpeth

Widdrington, Sir Thomas (*c.*1600–1664), politician and speaker of the House of Commons, was the eldest son of Lewis Widdrington (*d.* 1630) of Cheeseburn Grange, Stamfordham, Northumberland, who was the 'base-begotten' scion of a venerable Northumbrian family. Widdrington's mother was Catherine, daughter and heir of William Lawson of Little Usworth, co. Durham. The scholar Ralph *Widdrington was a younger brother. He matriculated at Christ's College, Cambridge, in April 1617, and graduated BA at Easter 1620. He was admitted to Gray's Inn on 14 February 1619, called to the bar in 1625, and from 1625 to 1631 reported cases in the court of king's bench. In January 1632 he was appointed recorder of Berwick upon Tweed upon the recommendation of Sir John Fenwick, and in 1633 delivered a loyal speech to the king, who had stopped in the town on his way to Scotland. The following year Widdrington married Frances (1612–1649), daughter of Sir Ferdinando (later second baron) Fairfax, with whom he had six children. Through this alliance he became linked with the Fairfax family's wide network of friends and kinsmen in Yorkshire, which included Thomas, Viscount Wentworth (the future earl of Strafford). In April 1637 Widdrington was appointed recorder of York upon the recommendation of Sir Richard Hutton, and on 30 March 1639 delivered another fulsome address to the king in which he referred to the Scottish covenanters as 'rebels' (Johnson and Bell, 1.348). He was knighted two days later. That same year he was retained as a counsellor-at-law by

Algernon Percy, tenth earl of Northumberland, who commanded Charles's navy in the first bishops' war, and was on close terms with both Wentworth and the Fairfaxes. He also became a bencher and ancient at Gray's Inn in 1639, and on 10 November 1641 was appointed the society's treasurer.

Widdrington was elected MP for Berwick on 11 March 1640, and contributed to several of the debates in the Short Parliament, usually to clarify legal points. In the autumn he stood for election at York as Strafford's nominee, but was rejected by the corporation. He was returned again for Berwick on 3 October. Though never prominent in debate he was one of the most active members of the Long Parliament. Before Pride's Purge he was nominated to almost 300 committees, made numerous reports to the house, managed twenty-three conferences, and was entrusted with drafting almost sixty bills and ordinances. One of his first tasks was to help prepare the Commons case against his former patron, Strafford. He also played a leading role in the attack on the new canons and the Laudian episcopate, and was named to numerous committees for godly reformation and the suppression of recusancy. Having drawn up the articles of impeachment against Bishop Wren, he presented them to the Lords on 20 July 1641, with a 'smart, aggravating speech' (Rushworth, 4.350) in which he accused Wren of suspending 'painful ministers' and of introducing 'dead and venomous ceremonies' (*The Parliamentary … History*, 9.492, 493). When Charles arrived at York in March 1642 Widdrington was reportedly on hand with an address urging the king 'with great boldnesse and vehemencie' to 'condescend unto … Parliament' (*The Kings Entertainment at Yorke*, fol. 3/63). Over the next few months he helped to forward parliament's military preparations, but after being granted leave of absence on 22 July did not return to the house for two years. He spent much of the intervening period in royalist-held York, where he advised the corporation in its dealings with the royalist commander, the earl of Newcastle. In February 1643 he addressed the queen on her arrival at York, urging her to 'bend herselfe, with all her faculties, to a peace' (*Kingdomes Weekly Intelligencer*, 7–14 March 1643, 86, BL, E 93/6). His abandonment of parliament may have stemmed from hostility towards inviting in the Scottish covenanters—a scheme mooted in senior parliamentary circles since 1642. Once the solemn league and covenant had been agreed, however, he may have come to regard Scottish intervention as a necessary evil in reclaiming the north for parliament and counterbalancing the king's use of Irish troops.

Widdrington was readmitted to the Commons on 3 June 1644, and three days later chaired a committee of the whole house concerning the Westminster assembly rules of ordination. He figured prominently in parliament's efforts to settle a godly ministry, and was added to the committee for plundered ministers in November 1644. Through his chairmanship of the northern committee and its successor, the northern association committee (the Commons' standing committees for northern affairs)

he also played a major role in sustaining the parliamentarian war effort. Similarly, he was a key figure in the establishment and maintenance of the New Model Army, under his brother-in-law, Sir Thomas Fairfax, and on 8 May 1645 was added to the committee for the army. His links with the Fairfaxes and apparent dislike of the Scots inclined him strongly towards the anti-Scottish, 'Independent' faction at Westminster, of which Northumberland was a leading member. Perhaps his greatest service to this group was as chairman of the committee of the whole house that drew up the Newcastle propositions over the winter of 1645–6. These were correctly perceived by the Scots as a repudiation of their confederalist terms for settlement in Britain and Ireland.

Appointed a parliamentary commissioner to the army on 12 June 1647, Widdrington was at Fairfax's headquarters when presbyterian rioters 'forced' the two houses late in July, and probably returned to Westminster with the New Model Army early in August. His continuing alignment with the Independents is suggested by his appointment in March 1648 as a commissioner of the great seal—the new commissioners allegedly being chosen 'by the private junto of Cromwell's party beforehand' (Whitelocke, *Memorials*, 2.277). According to his friend and fellow commissioner Bulstrode Whitelocke, Widdrington was far less reluctant to accept the post than he was himself. On 12 October Widdrington was raised to the degree of serjeant-at-law and made one of the king's serjeants. By this stage, however, he was troubled by the increasingly radical turn of army politics, and though he and Whitelocke retained their seats at Pride's Purge, they were 'sad to see such doings' (*Diary of Bulstrode Whitelocke*, 225), and had 'no great mind to sit in the House … as it was then constituted' (Whitelocke, *Memorials*, 2.478). At Cromwell's urging—he having consulted the two men and William Lenthall on 18 and 21 December—they attempted to devise a moderate settlement that would be agreeable to the army, and on 23 December they took part in a fruitless conference at the speaker's house about 'settling the kingdom by the Parliament, and not to leave all to the sword' (Whitelocke, *Memorials*, 2.481).

The two men resolved to have nothing to do with Charles's trial and decided to retire to Whitelocke's house in the country for its duration. Nevertheless, they attended the house on 8 and 23 January 1649, and took the 'dissent', the repudiation of the December vote to continue negotiations with Charles, used as a test for continued membership, just two days after the king's execution. On 8 February they were appointed commissioners of the great seal, but at this point Widdrington's scruples finally got the better of him and he declined the post on grounds of conscience. In respect of his former services he was allowed to practise within the bar and voted an extra quarter's salary. He was named to just thirty committees in the Rump, many of them to do with legal reform or northern affairs. He was appointed serjeant for the Commonwealth on 6 June 1650, and a councillor of state on 10 February 1651. At a meeting called by Cromwell late in

1651 to discuss the settlement of government he advocated some form of monarchy, suggesting the duke of Gloucester as king. On 19 April 1653, at a conference at Whitehall, he spoke strongly against the army's intention of dissolving the Rump.

Regarded by Cromwell's court as a 'very serviceable' man (Thurloe, *State papers*, 5.196), Widdrington was made a commissioner of the great seal on 4 April 1654 and a treasury commissioner the following August. In summer 1654 he was returned MP for York, and supported the Cromwellian interest at Westminster. He faced another moral dilemma in 1655 over the bill for reforming the chancery. Like Whitelocke he regarded the bill as detrimental to the public interest and his oath of office. While insisting that they were 'very unhappy not to satisfy his Highness' (*CSP dom.*, 1655, 152), the two men refused to execute the ordinance and on 8 June they were removed from office. Widdrington retained Cromwell's favour, however, being appointed chancellor of the county palatine of Durham on 3 September 1655. In summer 1656 he was returned MP for both York and Northumberland, and opted to sit for the latter. When parliament assembled on 17 September, John Lisle moved that Widdrington be made speaker, as a 'person of great integrity and experience ... and every way qualified for that service' (*JHC*, 7.423). In fact he proved a poor choice—he was often indecisive, showed a poor grasp of procedure, and was frequently indisposed through ill health. He acquitted himself better on large ceremonial occasions, as, for example, in his speech to Cromwell on 23 January 1657, congratulating him on his deliverance from Sindercombe's plot. His address to Cromwell on 31 March at the presentation of 'The humble petition and advice' was 'at once grave and eloquent and long and prolix' (*CSP Venice*, 1657–9, 37). He urged Cromwell to accept the crown, arguing that it was 'well-known to the nation, agreeable to their constitutions, and necessary to the temperament of the people' (ibid.). He repeated this exhortation in similar addresses on 8 April and 25 May. The high point of his speakership came on 26 June, when he presided at Cromwell's investiture as protector. Exactly a year later he was appointed lord chief baron of the exchequer. He was active in the restored Rump in 1659–60, and was nominated to both the December 1659 and the February 1660 councils of state. On 18 January 1660 he was transferred from the court of exchequer to the post of principal commissioner of the great seal.

At the Restoration, Widdrington lost all the offices and honours that he had gained since the civil war but he was restored to the post of serjeant-at-law on 1 June 1660, and appointed temporal chancellor of the bishopric of Durham on 21 December. He was returned for Berwick and York to the Convention Parliament, and chose the latter seat. He was among those MPs thought to favour a presbyterian church settlement and imposing restrictions on the king's prerogative as the price of his restoration. He also moved (unsuccessfully) that former royalists or their sons be expelled from the house. He was returned for Berwick to the Cavalier Parliament, but by that stage he had

effectively retired from public life. He resigned as recorder of York in December 1661, having given up the recordership of Berwick in 1658. He died on 13 May 1664, and was buried in the chancel of St Giles-in-the-Fields, near his wife and his daughter Dorothy, three days later. His only son, Thomas, had died at The Hague in May 1660, and thus Widdrington's Northumberland estate, valued at £800 per annum, passed to his brother Henry. The rest of his property, which was mainly in Yorkshire, was divided among his four surviving daughters. Despite receiving large salaries in his various employments during the interregnum, he died with debts of £2350. The royalist Sir Philip Warwick sums him up as 'a good lawyer, but naturally a cautious and timorous man' (P. Warwick, *Memoires of the Reigne of King Charles I*, 1701, 381). Widdrington wrote, in or about 1660, 'Analecta Eboracensia', a description and history of York, which remained unpublished until the nineteenth century when it appeared in 1897, edited by C. Caine. DAVID SCOTT

Sources HoP, *Commons* [draft] · *JHC*, 2–7 (1640–59) · *JHL*, 4–10 (1628–48) · *CSP dom.*, 1638–60 · B. Whitelocke, *Memorials of English affairs*, new edn, 4 vols. (1853) · *The diary of Bulstrode Whitelocke, 1605–1675*, ed. R. Spalding, British Academy, Records of Social and Economic History, new ser., 13 (1990) · G. W. Johnson and R. Bell, eds., *The Fairfax correspondence*, 4 vols. (1848–9) · *The parliamentary or constitutional history of England*, 2nd edn, 24 vols. (1751–62), vols. 9, 21 · *The writings and speeches of Oliver Cromwell*, ed. W. C. Abbott and C. D. Crane, 4 vols. (1937–47) · *Diary of Thomas Burton*, ed. J. T. Rutt, 4 vols. (1828) · J. Rushworth, *Historical collections*, new edn, 2–4 (1721) · *A letter written by master Symon Rhodes ... with the substance of Sir Thomas Widdringtons speech* (1642) · *The kings entertainment at Yorke* (1642) · *A fourth word to the wise* (1647) · T. Verax [C. Walker], *Anarchia Anglicana, or, The history of independency*, 2 pts. (1648–9) · [W. Prynne], *A full declaration of the true state of the secluded members case* (1660)

Archives BL, account of procedure in the exchequer, Add. MS 45130 | Berwick RO, Berwick Guild books, B 1/9, 10 · BL, D'Ewes diary, Harley MSS 163, 164 · BL, Fairfax corresp., Add. MS 18979 · BL, Moore diary, Harley MSS 477, 478, 479 · BL, Whitaker diary, Add. MS 31116 · Bodl. Oxf., Fairfax MSS 31, 32 · Gray's Inn, London, ledger book, A 1586 · HLRO, letters to Lord Fairfax · York City Archives, York House books, 35–7

Likenesses T. Athow, wash drawing, AM Oxf.

Wealth at death £800 p.a.; debts of £2350: HoP, *Commons, 1690–1715* [draft]

Widdrington, William, first Baron Widdrington (1610–1651), royalist army officer, was born on 11 July 1610, the only son of Sir Henry Widdrington (*d.* 1623), of Great Swinburne and Widdrington, Northumberland, and his wife, Mary, daughter of Sir Nicholas Curwen, of Workington, Cumberland. His father died on 4 September 1623, when William was thirteen; in February 1627 the king granted his wardship to his kinsman William Cavendish, Lord Mansfield (later earl of Newcastle), with the expectation that he was to marry the daughter of John Steward of Coldingham. In the event the match seems not to have taken place, and on 10 January 1630 he married Mary (*d.* 1676), daughter and heir of Sir Anthony Thorold, of Blankney, Lincolnshire. They had eight sons and two daughters. Widdrington was knighted by the king at Newmarket on 18 March 1632.

From 1635 to 1640 Widdrington took an active part in the administration of Northumberland, and served as

William Widdrington, first Baron Widdrington (1610–1651), by unknown artist

high sheriff in 1636–7; in 1640 he was a deputy lieutenant for the county. He also evidently had a place at court. When the king set up a separate household for the prince of Wales in 1638, with Newcastle as its governor, Widdrington was, according to Clarendon's account, chosen one of the prince's gentlemen of the privy chamber. He was elected MP for Northumberland in both the Short and the Long parliaments. His hostility to the Scots, whose army was quartered in his county, and his loyalty to Charles I was clear at the outset of the Long Parliament, for he had to apologize to the house on 10 November 1640 for calling the covenanting army 'invading rebels' (*JHC*, 25). On 15 March 1641 he presented to the commissioners for the Scottish treaty a petition concerning the depredations in the northern counties caused by the Scots while they awaited pay due from England. He was one of the fifty-six members whose names were posted as 'betrayers of their country' for voting against the attainder of Strafford in May 1641. He has been taken as one of those MPs who, emerging early as an opponent of the Scots, was to become one of 'the inner ring of the Royalist party in the Commons' (C. Russell, *The Causes of the English Civil War*, 1990, 15).

At the outbreak of the civil war Widdrington took up arms for the king, who created him a baronet on 9 July 1642. Five days later he was in Newcastle, apparently raising forces; his steward brought in a company of tenants in arms for the king. In an army list of 1642 he appears as major of Sir Lewis Dyve's regiment. In consequence of his royalism parliament expelled him on 26 August 1642.

During the war Widdrington joined the earl of Newcastle's northern army, serving with him in Yorkshire, Derbyshire, and Lincolnshire, and with particular distinction at Bradford. Following the death of Charles Cavendish in July 1643 he was given command of the southeastern section of Newcastle's command, particularly Lincolnshire and Rutland, and he may have had some role in Nottinghamshire. Margaret Cavendish, duchess of Newcastle, says that he was 'president of the council of war, and commander-in-chief of the three counties of Lincoln, Rutland, and Nottingham' (Cavendish, 166). In August

1643 he was put in command of the garrison at Lincoln, and he and John Henderson were defeated at Horncastle, in Lincolnshire, by the army of the eastern association on 11 October. On 2 November he was created Baron Widdrington of Blankney, Lincolnshire.

In early 1644 Widdrington was a member of the House of Lords at Oxford when it wrote to the Scottish privy council condemning the solemn league and covenant. He assisted in the defence of York in June 1644. After the battle of Marston Moor he accompanied Newcastle to Hamburg, and eventually to Paris. He stayed in France until the summer of 1648, before returning to the Low Countries, where he joined Prince Charles. His extensive coalmines and mills were sequestered from 1646, and the mines sold by the treason trustees. He himself was proscribed by parliament on 14 March 1649 and his estates confiscated; on 17 July his wife was granted a pass to go beyond the sea.

Widdrington crossed over to Scotland with Charles in June 1650 but did not hold command until after the defeat at Dunbar, on 3 September 1650. The committee of estates regarded him as 'wrong principled' and ordered him repeatedly to quit the kingdom, but eventually, on 28 December, gave him leave to stay. He followed Charles into England in 1651, and joined the earl of Derby's forces in Lancashire. Derby's force was routed at Wigan Lane by Robert Lilburne on 25 August, and Widdrington mortally wounded. According to Clarendon he was slain on the field, having been wounded many times and refused the quarter offered him; other accounts suggest that he died a day or two later. He was succeeded by his eldest son, William; a daughter, Jane, married Sir Charles Stanley, Derby's nephew.

Clarendon described Widdrington as 'one of the most goodly persons of that age, being near the head higher than most tall men'. He remembered a man who was quick-tempered but ready to apologize when his anger and indignation had overstepped the mark:

He was a man of great courage and choler, by the last of which he incurred the ill will of many, who imputed to it an insolence of nature, which no man was farther from, nor of a nature more civil and candid towards all in business or conversation. (Clarendon, *Hist. rebellion*, 5.185)

MARTYN BENNETT

Sources CSP dom., 1640–49 • GEC, Baronetage, vol. 2 • M. A. E. Green, ed., *Calendar of the proceedings of the committee for compounding … 1643–1660*, 5 vols., PRO (1889–92) • P. R. Newman, *Royalist officers in England and Wales, 1642–1660: a biographical dictionary* (1981) • JHC, 2 (1640–42) [Readey microprint, NY, 1964] • PRO, court of wards, inquisitions post-mortem, bundle 39, no. 186 • *The manuscripts of his grace the duke of Portland*, 10 vols., HMC, 29 (1891–1931), vol. 1 • GEC, *Peerage* • M. Cavendish, duchess of Newcastle, *Life of William, duke of Newcastle* (1886) • J. Rushworth, *Historical collections*, new edn, 8 vols. (1721–2) • Clarendon, *Hist. rebellion* • Keeler, *Long Parliament*, 394

Archives Northants. RO, Finch-Hatton MS 133

Likenesses A. Van Dyck, oils, c.1630–1639, Townley Hall, Burnley, Lancashire • van Loo, oils, Townley Hall, Burnley, Lancashire • portrait; Sothebys, 20 July 1994, lot 1 [see illus.]

Widdrington, William, fourth Baron Widdrington (1677/8–1743), Jacobite leader, was the son of William

Widdrington, third baron (1656–1695), and Alathea Fairfax (*fl.* 1677–1694), daughter and heir of Charles, fifth Viscount Fairfax of Emley, Yorkshire. He had a staunch Roman Catholic and royalist ancestry. The first baron, his great-grandfather William *Widdrington, was a royalist army officer who was killed at the battle of Wigan (1651). His grandfather served in the army of Charles II, and at the revolution of 1688 his father was dismissed as governor of Berwick and Holy Island and briefly imprisoned. He was kept under surveillance as a likely participant in Jacobite intrigue, but he shortly went into self-imposed exile on the continent, where he died in 1695. He left three sons, William, Charles (*d.* 1756), and Peregrine (*d.* 1749), all of whom became active Jacobites. William, the fourth baron, was educated at Morpeth grammar school and at the Jesuit Collège Louis-le-Grand in Paris, and he became familiar at the Stuart court at St Germain. In 1700 he married Jane Tempest (*d.* 1714), daughter and heir of Sir Thomas Tempest, bt, of Stella Hall, co. Durham, a flourishing Tyneside coaling estate, where he lived because Widdrington Castle, his ancestral seat on the Northumbrian coast, was sacked during a French raid in 1691. He had a rent roll of some £4000 a year and became a leading figure in local Roman Catholic and tory–Jacobite circles, though he did not intervene in local politics or in elections. He was a keen country sportsman and enjoyed a reputation for generous hospitality. His wife died on 9 September 1714 leaving three sons and five daughters.

Widdrington took a leading part in the planning of the northern contribution to the Jacobite rising of 1715. He was passed over for general command because of his Roman Catholicism; he had no military experience or expertise, in any case, but he provided one of the five troops in the Northumbrian Jacobite force, and his brothers Charles and Peregrine joined him in arms. He instigated the plan to transfer operations to the north-west when the planned seizure of Newcastle was thwarted, and he effected the liaison with the Lancastrian Jacobites through his family connections. He was confined to his bed with gout during the action at Preston, and when it was clear that the situation was hopeless he advised Thomas Forster to capitulate. He was tried for high treason by the House of Lords on 19 January 1716. In his defence he maintained that he was not privy to the plan; he had joined hastily and rashly only to keep face with his friends; he had appeared with personal arms only; and he was the first to propose a surrender. He also asked that the plight of his five motherless children be considered. He was found guilty and was sentenced to death, but with only hours to spare he was reprieved at the intervention, it was said, of Lord Carlisle and Lady Cowper, the lord chancellor's wife and a Northumbrian. He and his brothers were released from the Tower in November 1717 under the Act of Grace (3 Geo. I c. 19), but the forfeiture of his estates and the attainder on his barony were not lifted. Peregrine remained in London and, from 1732, lived at Chiswick with Mary, *née* Sherburne, widow of the eighth duke of Norfolk, without benefit of clergy (indeed, she dismissed her chaplain, Thomas Lawson SJ, for his effrontery in querying their marital status). Charles went abroad and died at St Omer in 1756.

In July 1718 Widdrington married Catherine Graham (1677–1757), daughter (and coheir in 1739) of Richard Graham, Viscount Preston, of Nunnington Hall, North Riding of Yorkshire, and granddaughter of Lord Carlisle. In 1719, although the king had no objection, the Commons rejected his petition for an annual allowance of £700 from his late wife's estate to support himself and his 'distressed family'. In 1723 (by 9 Geo. I c. 19, s. 13) he was granted £12,000 from the sale of his estates; in 1733 he successfully petitioned for the restitution of his marital estates. In 1728 Roger Gale described him as 'an infirm valetudinarian' (*The Family Memoirs of the Rev. W. Stukely*, SurtS, 73, 1882, 200). He died at Bath on 19 April 1743, aged sixty-five, and was buried at Nunnington; his widow erected an impressive memorial by James Gibbs to him in the parish church. She died childless in 1757. Notwithstanding the extinction of the title, Henry Francis (1701–1774), his eldest son, was commonly called Lord Widdrington by his fellow Catholics, thus confusing the obituarists at his death in 1774. The Durham estates passed to his nephew, Thomas Eyre of Hassop, and thus out of the family. LEO GOOCH

Sources L. Gooch, *The desperate faction? The Jacobites of north-east England, 1688–1745* (1995) · S. Hibbert Ware, *Lancashire memorials of the rebellion*, 2 pts in 1, Chetham Society, 5 (1845) · GEC, *Peerage* · J. Hodgson, *A history of Northumberland*, 3 pts in 7 vols. (1820–58), pt 3, vols. 1–3 · R. Patten, *The history of the late rebellion* (1865) · C. H. Hunter-Blair, 'The Widdringtons of Widdrington Castle', *History of the Berwickshire Naturalists' Club*, 30 (1947) · F. J. A. Skeet, *History of the families of Skeet, Wilby, Widdrington and others* (1906)
Likenesses British school, oils, repro. in Gooch, *Desperate faction?*, p. 39 · portrait, priv. coll.

Widgery, David John Turner (1947–1992), polemicist and doctor, was born at 17 Wellhouse Lane, Barnet, Hertfordshire, on 27 April 1947, the eldest of four children and only son of John Howard (Jack) Widgery (1923–1997), interior design consultant, and his wife, Margaret Finch (1922–1997), a primary schoolteacher. Widgery was a child of the optimistic, post-Second World War welfare state generation. But he was also a survivor of a scourge of that era: in 1953 he contracted poliomyelitis. He rarely referred to the disease, but in his childhood it caused him great pain and that pain never completely relented. The illness left him with a permanent limp, fired his ambition to become a doctor, and, excluded from most sports—but not swimming—fuelled a voracious, eclectic love of the arts in general, and literature and music in particular.

By the late 1950s the family had moved to Maidenhead, where Widgery attended Maidenhead grammar school, but his publication of an unauthorized school magazine led to his expulsion from the sixth form. He was to regard his real education as taking place in the summer of 1965, when he had a sexual encounter in London with Allen Ginsberg, and a trip to the United States which took in the Watts riots in Los Angeles and the student non-violent co-ordinating committee in the south of the civil rights movement. Via Mexico he went on to Cuba, as a self-appointed representative of British student journalists: chutzpah was one of Widgery's enduring and endearing characteristics. White racism—he was particularly appalled by the treatment he saw meted out to the jazz musician Roland Kirk—accelerated his politicization.

Back in Britain, that autumn Widgery entered the Royal Free Hospital Medical School in London, from which he qualified as a doctor in 1972. It was while a medical student, living in Islington, that he emerged as one of the most talented polemicists and writers of his generation. He was funny, intense, erudite beyond his years (and when wrong amusingly so), and a splendid observer, enthusiast, and scavenger, taking notes from random conversations, from graffiti, and from passers-by. It was an article in the *New Statesman* for 1967, 'Grown-up power', a pyrotechnic meditation on the collision between the post-war consensus and young radicals, which first won him a wider audience.

In the winter of 1966–7 Widgery encountered Richard Neville, one of a group of young Australians who had arrived with the intention of setting up Sydney's *Oz* magazine in London. The British edition became the most interesting among that wave of London 'underground' publications in the late 1960s and early 1970s, and Widgery was one of *Oz*'s most interesting writers. He was briefly its co-editor amid the 1971 *Oz* 'Schoolkids issue' trial. The Australians were outsiders, and Widgery, a quintessential member of that short-lived subculture, the publicly funded post-war grammar schoolboy, alienated by Oxbridge and public school, saw himself as an outsider too. But what was also informing him then, and for the rest of his life, was a libertarian Marxism. In 1967 he joined the International Socialists, precursors of the Socialist Workers' Party. Their hostility to both cold war power blocs and their excavations of some of the revolutionary politics buried under Stalinism provided a structure and a security for Widgery's politics and, particularly through Peter Sedgwick, an inspiration. Marxism focused his sense of history, put muscle into the leaps and links that were characteristic of his writing, his public talks, his conversation. It was a mix of socialism from below, and a bloody-minded dissenting tradition of which the surrealists, Russian futurists, and the beats were twentieth-century examples, as was his suffragette grandmother. The radical year 1968 was important to him, but what was most important within that was that which was closest to home, events such as the London dockers' march in favour of Enoch Powell's 'rivers of blood' speech. By the end of the decade his relationship with the socialist feminist historian Sheila Rowbotham made him sensitive to the birth of the new feminist and gay politics.

After qualifying as a doctor in 1972 Widgery began practising medicine at Bethnal Green Hospital. His first book, *The Left in Britain, 1956–68* (1976), a narrated anthology, was a splendidly unorthodox tour of its subject which settled on the bloody-minded and the arcane corners of politics. The growth of the far-right National Front and some racist utterances from rock musicians led to Widgery becoming a co-founder in 1976 of Rock against Racism. The movement erupted across Britain, and was for him the spirit of 1968, practically applied. It became the subject of his book *Beating Time* (1986).

On 5 February 1982 Widgery married the design historian Juliet Marlande Ash (*b.* 1949). In that year their first daughter, Molly, was born, but she died shortly afterwards. His *New Society* piece on that loss, 'Meeting Molly' (1983), reproduced in his *Preserving Disorder: Selected Essays, 1968–88* (1989), epitomized the candour, controlled emotion, and mixing of the personal and collective that was Widgery's writing at its best. It also reiterated his belief that the spirit of human solidarity was at the core of socialism.

In October 1985, having worked in two other East End practices, Widgery joined what was then the Gill Street Health Centre in Limehouse, east London. Out of that experience and that other, earlier work in the East End came *Some Lives: a GP's East End* (1991). Passionate and at times bleakly funny, *Some Lives* caught the natural, surreal responses of people co-existing with the intolerable, and a sense of the space and time of the East End. It is a classic portrait of late twentieth-century London.

David Widgery died in an accident at his home, 76 Eleanor Road, Dalston, London, on 27 October 1992 and was cremated four days later at the East London crematorium. He was survived by Juliet Ash, his daughter Anny, and his stepson Jess. Widgery had a great capacity to enthuse people. Generous and funny, he was capable of great charm and staggering rudeness—sometimes within the confines of a single sentence.   NIGEL FOUNTAIN

Sources N. Fountain, *Underground: the London alternative press, 1966–74* (1988) · D. Widgery, *Preserving disorder: selected essays, 1968–88* (1989) · A. Gould, *A summer plague: polio and its survivors* (1995) · *The Independent* (30 Oct 1992) · *The Guardian* (29 Oct 1992) · *The Times* (4 Nov 1992) · D. Renton, *David Widgery and the politics of propaganda* [forthcoming] · personal knowledge (2004) · private information (2004) · b. cert. · m. cert. · d. cert.
Archives priv. coll., letters, MS |FILM *Limehouse Doctor* (Diana Tammes, 40 minutes, BBC 2, April 1993) |SOUND BBC, *Year of Dreams pt 1* (BBC R4 documentary 1988) · BL NSA, performance recording
Likenesses photographs, priv. coll.
Wealth at death £9740: probate, 23 May 1996, *CGPLA Eng. & Wales*

Widgery, John Passmore, Baron Widgery (1911–1981), judge, was born on 24 July 1911 at South Molton, Devon, the elder child and only son of Samuel Widgery (*d.* 1940), house furnisher, and his second wife, Bertha Elizabeth Passmore JP. Widgery left Queen's College, Taunton, at the age of sixteen to become an articled clerk, and in 1933 he qualified as a solicitor (John Mackrell prizeman). It was not then thought necessary for a solicitor to be a university graduate. One of Widgery's predecessors as lord chief justice, Rufus Isaacs, had never been to a university, but only Charles Russell had started life as a solicitor.

Perhaps surprisingly, Widgery never practised his profession, but joined the staff of Gibson and Welldon, law

John Passmore Widgery, Baron Widgery (1911–1981), by David J. Poole, 1972

tutors in London. He always retained the clarity of expression required of a good teacher. On 6 April 1935 he married Helen Yates (b. 1911/12), daughter of Baldwin Walker Peel, estate agent, of Campsall Grange, near Doncaster. The outbreak of war in 1939 found him, characteristically, adjutant of his Territorial battalion. He saw active service with the Royal Artillery, in which he became a lieutenant-colonel in 1942. He was made an OBE in 1945, decorated with the Croix de Guerre, and appointed to the order of Leopold. In 1952 he was promoted brigadier in the Territorial Army.

After war ended in 1945, Widgery did not return to the solicitors' profession. He was called to the bar (Lincoln's Inn) in 1946, and quickly built up a substantial practice on the south-eastern circuit, mainly in the areas of rating and town planning. His marriage was dissolved in 1946, and on 3 August 1948 he married Ann Edith (b. 1910/11), daughter of William Edwin Kermode, mining engineer, of the Isle of Man, and former wife of David Willett Fleetwood Dillin Paul. In 1958 Widgery became a QC (the most junior of the sixteen new silks, but the only one to have been called to the bar since the war). He was recorder of Hastings from 1959 to 1961.

In January 1961 Widgery was appointed judge of the Queen's Bench Division and knighted. (The English bench is traditionally clean-shaven, but Widgery retained his military moustache.) He was the first chairman of the senate of the inns of court and the bar. In January 1968 he was promoted to the court of appeal, and appointed a privy councillor. In April 1971 he succeeded Lord Parker of Waddington as lord chief justice, with a life peerage as Baron Widgery.

Widgery was a very good judge for the parties, but hardly a great judge for the jurist. Until struck down by Parkinson's disease, he was always fair and courteous, and quick to see the essential point. He was particularly good in a heavy criminal case, being impatient of subtleties, whether forensic or academic, and his summings-up were models of clarity and soldierly brevity. Although he lacked the legal learning and dominant personality of Lord Goddard, he could write a judgment of quality when his interest was aroused. Few have improved on his explanation of the reasons for imposing some restraint on the recovery of damages for economic loss (*Weller* v. *Foot and Mouth Disease Research Institute*, 1966). But normally problems were resolved by common sense. So when the crown sought an injunction to restrain the publication of the diaries of R. H. S. Crossman, some high-flown rhetoric was made to look foolish by Widgery's decision (since approved by a number of appellate tribunals) that, after ten years, some of the secrets which the former cabinet minister had reported with such relish were of no importance to anyone (*Attorney-General* v. *Jonathan Cape Ltd*, 1976). Some criticized him for sitting too often in the divisional court, but in the 1970s the business of that tribunal had expanded beyond the customary mass of small appeals to include cases of great constitutional importance.

In 1972, as lord chief justice, Widgery agreed to undertake an inquiry into the fatal shooting of thirteen civilians by soldiers of the Parachute regiment in Londonderry earlier that year, an event which came to be known as 'bloody Sunday'. Widgery completed his task with great (as it was later thought, undue) expedition, and exonerated the soldiers from blame. But his findings were never accepted by the nationalist community in Northern Ireland, and prompted a sense of grievance which made it difficult in the 1990s to reconcile the nationalist and loyalist communities. To address this sense of grievance the Blair government, in 1998, established a tribunal under the chairmanship of Lord Saville of Newdigate, a law lord, to review in depth the course of events in Londonderry on the occasion in question and reconsider the responsibility of the soldiers. At the time of writing the tribunal had not yet reported.

Widgery found that the administrative burden of his office, always considerable, was increased by the great structural changes in the courts proposed by Lord Beeching and adopted by parliament. There was something frustrating about having to carry into effect the ideas of another man. After some years Widgery was obviously faltering under the strain, and his resignation in April 1980 (the ninth anniversary of his appointment) was not unexpected.

Well built and ruddy, in manner and appearance Widgery was typical of the west country. He would have finished his game of bowls before dealing with a crisis. Conversely, his devotion to a methodical life meant that at the appointed hour for recreation the papers in even the heaviest case were put aside. Widgery became a bencher of his inn in 1961 and treasurer in 1977. He was awarded honorary doctorates by the universities of Exeter (1971) and Leeds and Columbia (both 1976). He was also, like an ancestor in 1689, a freeman of South Molton (1971). There were no children of either of his marriages. Widgery died at his Chelsea home, 56 Jubilee Place, on 26 July 1981. He was survived by his wife, Ann.

R. F. V. HEUSTON, rev. M. C. CURTHOYS

Sources *The Times* (28 July 1981) · personal knowledge (1990) · private information (1990) · private information (2004) [Lord Bingham of Cornhill] · m. certs. · d. cert. · Sainty, *Judges* · R. Stevens, *The independence of the judiciary* (1993) · W. D. Rubinstein, *The biographical dictionary of life peers* (1991)
Likenesses photograph, 1971, Hult. Arch. · D. J. Poole, portrait, 1972, Lincoln's Inn, London [*see illus.*]
Wealth at death £57,869: probate, 26 Aug 1981, *CGPLA Eng. & Wales*

Widmore, Richard (*bap.* **1681**, *d.* **1764**), historian and librarian, was baptized on 27 June 1681 at St Michael's, Warfield, Berkshire, the son of Christopher Widmore, a bailiff, of Kingsclere in Hampshire, and his wife, Elizabeth. He attended Sedbergh School from about 1693 until 1698 when he was admitted to St John's College, Cambridge. He graduated BA in 1702, MA in 1708.

Widmore was ordained priest by the bishop of London in September 1705 and served as curate at St James's, Dukes Place, in the City of London. By 1711 he was serving as curate of St Margaret's, Westminster, and it was doubtless at this period that he first became familiar with the monastic archive of Westminster Abbey and with its chapter library. In December 1731 the abbey's librarian, Thomas Moore, who had held office for over forty years, was given leave to appoint Widmore as his deputy, doubtless with an understanding that the latter would succeed him. Moore died two years later and Widmore's appointment as librarian was confirmed by the dean and chapter in February 1734. For the next twenty-five years Widmore devoted his efforts to the study of the abbey's history and to the care of its books and records. Hitherto the dean and chapter's library had grown almost exclusively by donation and bequest, but Widmore began to purchase books too, making substantial and important additions to the collections in the course of his custodianship.

About 1735 Widmore began to examine and sort the abbey's records, compiling a catalogue which was finally completed in 1741. From this labour emerged his two publications, both significant contributions to the historiography of Westminster and the first printed accounts to draw their conclusions directly from the original sources. *An Enquiry into the Time of the First Foundation of Westminster Abbey* appeared in 1743 and refuted the then widely held notion that Westminster owed its foundation to King Sebert in the early seventh century. In *An History of the Church of St. Peter, Westminster*, published by subscription in 1751, Widmore provided a more substantial history of the institution, carried down to his own time. An appendix contained transcribed documents and lists of officials.

Widmore also devoted much time to the salvaged collections of the Cotton Library which were still stored at Westminster following the fire at Ashburnham House in 1731. He paid particular attention to the charters, and his reports were heavily relied upon by the committee of trustees of the newly formed British Museum when it surveyed the collections in 1754. The following year, at the request of the trustees, he spent four months cataloguing the 3800 volumes bequeathed to the Cottonian Library by Arthur Edwards (*d.* 1743). In 1756 Widmore was recommended to be one of the librarians of the new museum, but he was never appointed to that office.

Widmore corresponded with the antiquarian Browne Willis and with the biographer John Ward, sending to the latter amendments for a second edition of *Lives of the Professors of Gresham College*. In spite of these and other scholarly connections he was never a fellow of the Society of Antiquaries and his letters (which survive in the British Library) convey little impression of his character beyond that of a studious man, generous with information gleaned from the records in his care.

On 12 May 1760 Widmore preached at the first of two services for the bicentenary of Westminster's foundation as a collegiate church. In the same year he was appointed rector of Lasham in Hampshire where he lived quietly in retirement though retaining both his post and his house at Westminster. He was unmarried. He died at Lasham on 9 November 1764 and was buried there, probably in the chancel, on 15 November. The church at Lasham was completely rebuilt in the nineteenth century and no gravestone or monument has survived. In his will Widmore bequeathed more than forty books to the library at Westminster and there appears to be no foundation for John Nichols's assertion that his private library was sold in 1765.

TONY TROWLES

Sources Venn, *Alum. Cant.* · J. E. B. Mayor and R. F. Scott, eds., *Admissions to the College of St John the Evangelist in the University of Cambridge*, 3 vols. in 4 pts (1882–1931) · *Sedbergh School register, 1546–1909* (1909) · will, PRO, PROB 11/904, sig. 451 · Nichols, *Lit. anecdotes*, 2.618–19; 3.227–8 · A. Prescott, '"Their present miserable state of cremation": the restoration of the Cotton Library', *Sir Robert Cotton as collector: essays on an early Stuart courtier and his legacy* (1997), 391–8 · R. Widmore, *Proposals for printing by subscription an history of the church of St. Peter, Westminster* (1750) · ordination papers, GL, MS 10326/33 · vestry minutes, St Margaret's, Westminster, City Westm. AC · BL, Add. MS 38715, fols. 21, 23 · P. R. Harris, *A history of the British Museum Library, 1753–1973* (1998) · parish register, Warfield, St Michael's, Berks. RO, 27 June 1681 [baptism]
Archives BL, Add. MSS · BL, Lansdowne MSS · Westminster Abbey
Wealth at death over £2000 in family and charitable bequests: will, PRO, PROB 11/904, sig. 451

Wiffen, Benjamin Barron (**1794–1867**), biographer, the second son of John Wiffen (1761–1802), ironmonger, and his wife, Elizabeth, *née* Pattison (1761–1841), was born at Woburn, Bedfordshire, on 28 October 1794. His elder brother was Jeremiah Holmes *Wiffen (1792–1836), whom he followed to the Friends' school, Ackworth, near Pontefract, in 1803. On leaving in 1808 he went into his father's business, and remained in it at Woburn until 1838, when his health failed, and he subsequently retired to Mount Pleasant, near Woburn, with his widowed mother and unmarried sisters. His literary interests were encouraged by his brother and by Richard Thomas How of Aspley Guise, Bedfordshire, the owner of a remarkable library.

Early in 1840 Luis de Usoz y Río, already interested in the Quakers and in Jeremiah Wiffen (now dead) as a translator of Spanish poetry, arrived in London from Italy and was introduced by George Borrow to Josiah Forster. At Forster's request Wiffen called on Usoz y Río in Jermyn Street. There at once sprang up a lifelong friendship between them, and 'henceforward Spain took entire possession' of Wiffen. Late in 1840 or early in 1841 he made his first visit there with George William Alexander (a fellow Quaker and first treasurer of the British and Foreign Anti-Slavery Society) as a deputation to forward the abolition of the slave trade; in 1842 he accompanied Alexander a second time to Spain and Portugal. In 1843 or 1844 Usoz wrote to Wiffen of his plan to recover and republish long lost and long prohibited works by sixteenth-century Spanish religious writers of a broadly Reformation character, and to seek Wiffen's help in this task. Now Wiffen began his book-hunting, of which he gives a most interesting account in his 'Notices and experiences'. He obtained some unique treasures, both in Britain and from the continent. Many rare works he himself copied line for line; of others he obtained transcripts. All was done to assist Usoz, and without his aid the collection of *Reformistas antiguos españoles* (20 vols., 1847–65) could not have been produced. Wiffen himself edited volume 2, the *Epístola consolatoria* (1848), by Juan Pérez de Pineda, contributing also a notice of the author in Spanish and English which was reprinted with the English translation (by John T. Betts) in 1871. He also edited volume 15, the *Alfabeto cristiano* (1861), by Juan de Valdés, in Italian, with modern versions in Spanish and English by Usoz and Wiffen respectively. The remaining volumes were edited by Usoz y Río. Wiffen also wrote the 'Life and writings of Juan de Valdés' (1865) which accompanied the English translation of Valdés's *Hundred and Ten Considerations* by John T. Betts; and a 'Biographical sketch' (1869) of Constantino Ponce de la Fuente, to accompany the English version of his *Confession of a Sinner*, by the same translator. In 1874–1904 Eduard Boehmer printed the *Bibliotheca Wiffeniana* (3 vols.), containing lives and writings of Spanish reformers from 1520, 'according to … Wiffen's plan and with the use of his materials' (as the full title states) but reshaped and with a large contribution by Boehmer himself. The work is a monument to Wiffen's aims and values as stated by himself as early as 1848:

> No merely sectarian or proselytising motive had suggested this course, but something of a love of books, and literature, and a feeling (call it obstinate or generous, as you will) that the persecuted victims of literature should find a voice in after ages, and protectors from the cruelty and bigotry of the ruling powers of their own times. (Pattison, 127)

In early life, and again later, Wiffen wrote verse of some merit but he published nothing separately. He reportedly destroyed his more youthful work. A substantial selection of his later poems (unpublished previously, for the most part) is given in Pattison's *The Brothers Wiffen*. Wiffen died, unmarried, at Aspley Guise on 18 March 1867, and was buried in the Quaker burial-ground at Woburn Sands on 24

March. In Pattison's *The Brothers Wiffen* he is described as 'a small, pale, keen-eyed man' (81), always dressed in Quaker garb, and strict in all observances of the Friends.

R. W. TRUMAN

Sources Wadham College, Oxford, letters from Usoz · M. I. W. Wiffen, 'Memoir', in *Bibliotheca Wiffeniana: Spanish reformers of two centuries from 1520*, ed. E. Boehmer, 1 (1874), 1–20 · B. B. Wiffen, 'Notices and experiences', in *Bibliotheca Wiffeniana: Spanish reformers of two centuries from 1520*, ed. E. Boehmer, 1 (1874), 27–57 · S. R. Pattison, ed., *The brothers Wiffen: memoirs and miscellanies* (1880) · d. cert.

Archives Beds. & Luton ARS, corresp. · Wadham College, Oxford, corresp. and papers | Beds. & Luton ARS, memorial of Richard Thomas How

Wealth at death under £8000: probate, 2 May 1867, *CGPLA Eng. & Wales*

Wiffen, Jeremiah Holmes (1792–1836), poet and translator, was born on 30 December 1792 at Woburn, Bedfordshire, the eldest of the six children of John Wiffen (1761–1802) and Elizabeth, *née* Pattison (1761–1841). Both parents came from Quaker families; his father was a poetry-loving ironmonger and his mother had been a dressmaker on the duke of Bedford's estate, and was reputed to be a visionary. His father died in 1802, leaving his mother to run the large ironmonger's shop next to the George Hotel (later the Bedford Arms), Woburn, and care for five surviving children. His younger brother was Benjamin Barron *Wiffen, and his youngest sister, Priscilla, married Alaric Alexander Watts. After attending three local schools, at the age of nine Jeremiah went to Ackworth School, the Friends' public school near Pontefract, Yorkshire, where he received a sound, if eclectic, education, developing his taste for poetry, learning wood-engraving, and probably acquiring some Latin and Greek.

In 1807 Wiffen was apprenticed to Isaac Payne, a schoolmaster, in Epping, Essex, and in the same year his first published poem, 'Address to the Evening Star', appeared in the *European Magazine* (October 1807). The following year he contributed an account of Broxbourne, Hertfordshire, with an etching of the church by himself to the *Gentleman's Magazine* (1st ser., 78, 1808, 497). In 1811 he returned to Woburn and opened a school in Leighton Road. Studying mostly at night (which became a lifelong habit), he taught himself Hebrew, French, and Italian, and later Spanish and Welsh. Together with James Baldwin Brown the elder and Thomas Raffles he published *Poems by Three Friends* in 1813. These poems and his two independent volumes of poetry, *Aonian Hours* (1819) and *Julia Alpinula … and other Poems* (1820), show the influence of Campbell, and more especially of Byron. On a visit to the Lakes with his brother in the summer of 1819 he called on both Southey and Wordsworth, whose 'white pantaloons' and 'hawk's nose' he described in his diary. He argued amicably with Wordsworth about the merits of Campbell's poetry, and wrote a sonnet to commemorate their meeting.

In the summer of 1821 Wiffen was appointed secretary and librarian to the duke of Bedford at Woburn Abbey. Also in 1821 he issued his 'Proposals' for a new translation of Tasso's *Gerusalemme liberata* in Spenserian stanzas,

Jeremiah Holmes Wiffen (1792–1836), by William Brockedon, 1830

together with a specimen book. His next essay in verse was *The Works of Garcilasso de la Vega* (1823), a translation from the Spanish dedicated to the duke of Bedford, with a life of Garcilasso de la Vega and an essay on Spanish poetry. Publication of *Jerusalem Delivered* (2 vols., 1824) was delayed by a fire in the printing office. Dedicated to the duchess of Bedford, it became his best-known work, running to a number of editions in both Britain and America over the next thirty years. Hogg, in the *Noctes Ambrosianae*, says: 'the best scholar amang a' the Quakers is friend Wiffen, a capital translator, Sir Walter tells me, o' poets wi' foreign tongues, sic as Tawso, and wi' an original vein, too' (Wilson, 243). In a long review in June 1826 the *Quarterly Review* concluded that, as a translator of Tasso, Wiffen could not hope to contend successfully with Fairfax. Wiffen declined an LLD from Aberdeen University in 1827. He contributed poems to magazines and 'albums', and published occasional poetry, often associated with Woburn, throughout his life.

According to his daughter, Jeremiah's 'ideal Love married another', and it was only after her death that he married Mary Whitehead (1789–1872), a Quaker from a Nottingham family, on 20 November 1828 at the Friends' meeting-house in Leeds. They had three daughters: Ida Margaret Wiffen (1829–1865), Mary Isaline Whitehead (*b.* 1831), and Hannah Holinshed (*b.* 1835). On his marriage, he moved from the abbey to a cottage provided by the duke at Froxfield, where he spent the rest of his life. Wiffen took eight years to compile his *Historical Memoirs of the House of Russell* (1833), for which he made extensive researches including a four-month tour in Normandy.

Wiffen remained a lifelong Quaker and was known as a Liberal reformer. His family seems never to have known

poverty, and his post at Woburn brought him not only financial security, but contacts with many of the leading political and artistic figures of the time. Portraits by George Hayter (1824) and William Brockedon (1830) show him with Byronic good looks, but what his friends recalled were his gentleness, courtesy, and good conversation. Following attacks of breathlessness, which he disregarded for some months, he died suddenly at Froxfield on 2 May 1836 and was buried on 8 May in the Quaker burial-ground, Hogsty End, Woburn Sands, Buckinghamshire.

ALEXANDER GORDON, *rev.* CHARLES PLOUVIEZ

Sources [M. F. B. Wiffen], 'The life of J. H. Wiffen, by his daughter', *The brothers Wiffen: memoirs and miscellanies*, ed. S. R. Pattison (1880), 1–76 · *GM*, 2nd ser., 6 (1836), 212–14 · digest registers of births, marriages, and burials, RS Friends, Lond. · 'Dictionary of Quaker biography', RS Friends, Lond. [card index] · J. Smith, ed., *A descriptive catalogue of Friends' books*, 1 (1867), 927–9 · *Biographical catalogue: being an account of the lives of Friends and others whose portraits are in the London Friends' Institute*, Society of Friends (1888) · H. Thompson, *History of Ackworth School, 1779–1879* (1879) · review of *Jerusalem delivered*, *QR*, 34 (1826), 1–19 · J. Wilson, *The works of Professor Wilson*, ed. J. F. Ferrier, vol. 3: *Noctes ambrosianae* (1856) · private information (2004)

Archives Woburn Abbey, Buckinghamshire | Cambs. AS, corresp. with Joseph Beldam · U. Nott. L., corresp. with fourth duke of Newcastle

Likenesses G. Hayter, pen and sepia sketch, 1824, BM; repro. in Wiffen, 'The life of J. H. Wiffen, by his daughter', frontispiece · J. Thomson, stipple, pubd 1824 (after A. Wivell), BM, NPG · W. Brockedon, pencil and chalk drawing, 1830, NPG [*see illus.*]

Wigan, Mrs Alfred. *See* Wigan, Leonora (1805–1884), *under* Wigan, Alfred Sydney (1814–1878).

Wigan, Alfred Sydney (1814–1878), actor, whose father, a teacher of languages, was at one time secretary to the Dramatic Authors' Society, was born at Blackheath, Kent, on 24 March 1814. His early career is obscure, his own accounts of it being contradictory. Since he exhibited some talent for music, he became 'a wandering minstrel', and sang at Ramsgate, Margate, and elsewhere. He was also an usher at a school and assisted his father at the Dramatic Authors' Society. Under the name of Sydney or Sidney he was in 1834 at the Lyceum, and the following year was under Louisa Cranstoun Nisbett at the Queen's Theatre, Tottenham Street. When John Braham opened the newly erected St James's Theatre, Wigan joined him, and, under the name of Sidney, was in September 1836 the original John Johnson in *The Strange Gentleman*, by Charles Dickens. In 1838 he was at a small theatre in the Old Manor House, King's Road, Chelsea, where he played Tom Tug in *The Waterman*, and other musical parts, and sang songs between the acts. With Madame Vestris he appeared in 1839 at Covent Garden, as Mr Wigan, playing the original Sir Otto of Steinberg in Sheridan Knowles's *Love*. On 5 August 1839 he married the actress Leonora Pincott [*see below*].

Wigan continued at Covent Garden until 1844. Some success attended his Montagu Tigg in *Martin Chuzzlewit* and his French usher in *To Parents and Guardians*, but it was not until he was cast for Alcibiades Blague in Jerrold's *Gertrude's Cherries, or, Waterloo in 1835* that he showed, as a guide to the field of Waterloo and a seller of vamped-up

Alfred Sydney Wigan (1814–1878), by Herbert Watkins, late 1850s

relics of the fight, the remarkable finish of his style. On the abrupt closing of Covent Garden, Wigan went to the Strand, where he played Iago in a burlesque of *Othello* and parodied W. C. Macready, and then to the Lyceum, with the Keeleys, having also played at Drury Lane for a while. In later years he produced his own *Watch and Ward* (in which he was the Chevalier Du Guet), *A Model of a Wife* (in which he was Pygmalion Bonnefoi), *Luck's All*, *The Loan of a Wife*, *Next Door*, and *Five Hundred Pounds Reward*, in all of which he took some part.

As a member of Benjamin Webster's company Wigan appeared at the Haymarket in October 1847, playing Sir Benjamin Backbite in a revival of Sheridan's *The School for Scandal*. There he was also the first Osborne in Westland Marston's *The Heart and the World* and the first Hector Mauléon in Webster's *The Roused Lion*. Dudley Smooth in Bulwer-Lytton's *Money*, Goldfinch in Holcroft's *The Road to Ruin*, and Tattle in Congreve's *Love for Love* were his other successful roles at this time. After playing at the Olympic for a while, where he produced his own *Law for Ladies*, he was in 1848–9 at the Haymarket again with Mr and Mrs Charles Kean, playing various Shakespearian characters, in particular the Clown in *Twelfth Night*, Bassanio in *The Merchant of Venice*, and one of the Witches in *Macbeth*. His Achille Talma Dufard in his comedy *The First Night* (adapted from *Le père de la débutante*), seen at the Princess's in October 1849, was one of his finest impersonations. At the Olympic he produced in 1850 his farce *A Dead Take-In*. He continued to play at the Olympic, the Princess's, and the Adelphi until 1857, when, on the plea of ill health, he took a benefit on his retirement from the stage. He reappeared, however, at the Adelphi in March 1859 as Sir Paul Pagoda in *The Bengal Tiger*.

Once more Wigan's career on the stage was in full swing. He opened the St James's in November 1860 and was at the Haymarket once again in April 1861. The following year, with his wife, he gave a series of readings in London, and in October 1867 he opened the newly erected Queen's Theatre in Long Acre with Charles Reade's *The Double Marriage*, adapted from his novel *White Lies*. On the

opening of the Gaiety in December 1868 he was Adolphe Chavillard in *On the Cards*, an adaptation by Alfred Thompson of *L'escamoteur*. Later, for the benefit of Charles Mathews, Wigan played Dangle in *The Critic*. In May 1870, in *The Man of Quality*, an alteration by John Hollingshead of *The Relapse*, he was Lord Foppington. On 6 July 1872, in *The First Night* and *Still Waters Run Deep*, he took a farewell benefit at Drury Lane and retired from the stage. After giving a few private readings, he was seen at the Gaiety at an afternoon performance of *The House or the Home* and *The Bengal Tiger*. In the summer of 1878 he left his house, 33 Brompton Square, and moved to Folkestone, where he died, at 26 Sandgate Road, on 29 November 1878. He was buried in Kensal Green cemetery on 8 December.

Wigan was an admirable actor in a rather narrow groove. He lacked robustness and breadth of style, and could never play a modern gentleman, which part he could not even dress. Humour and pathos were, however, equally at his command. He was a French scholar, and his greatest successes were made in Frenchmen or characters in which he spoke French or broken English—Tourbillon in *To Parents and Guardians*, Château-Renaud, Talma Dufard, Adolphe Chavillard, Hector Mauléon in *The Roused Lion*, and the Marquis de Belleterre in *The Poor Nobleman*. His method was modelled to some extent upon that of Bouffé, a brilliant French actor of the early nineteenth century. Among purely English characters, his John Mildmay in *Still Waters Run Deep* may count as his masterpiece.

Wigan's wife, **Leonora Wigan** [*née* Pincott; *known as* Mrs Alfred Wigan] (1805–1884), was the daughter of Pincott, a showman, and his wife, Elizabeth, who was the daughter of William Wallack and sister of James William Wallack. Leonora was at the outset a rope-dancer and performer on stilts. Her first appearance in London took place on 6 July 1818 at the English Opera House (Lyceum) as Chimpanzee in a pantomime drama, *La Perouse, or, The Desolate Island*, based on Kotzebue; her mother was Umba and J. P. Cooke La Perouse. She also took part in the ballet *Don Juan* and was Ganymede in *Midas*. She was next at Drury Lane, at which her uncle James Wallack was stage-manager from 1826 to 1828, playing pantomime, utility, and walking ladies. In 1831 she was with Madame Vestris at the Olympic, where her Catherine Seton, in a burlesque on *Mary Queen of Scots*, attracted attention. On 5 August 1839 she married Alfred Wigan, whose senior she was by several years, and whom she had nursed during an illness. When in April 1844 the Lyceum opened under the management of the Keeleys, Mrs Wigan spoke the opening lines of Gilbert à Beckett's *Forty Thieves* as a police inspector of fairies; Wigan was Mustapha in the same production. She had a plump figure, a bright eye, and a mass of dark hair, but was not otherwise attractive. To her husband and his associate and partner, Robson, she was of great service, as she had stage knowledge and flair, though with no special expository capacity. She took, after her marriage, some important parts—Mrs Candour in *The School for Scandal* and Mrs Malaprop in *The Rivals*— and obtained applause as Mrs Yellowleaf in *The Bengal Tiger* and Mrs McCann in *Up at the Hills*. Her best part was Mrs Hector Sternhold in *Still Waters*

Run Deep. She supported her husband at most of the theatres at which he appeared, and acquired a reputation in Frenchwomen. She died on 17 April 1884 at her residence, Westwood Lodge, The Avenue, Gipsy Hill, Surrey.

JOSEPH KNIGHT, *rev.* NILANJANA BANERJI

Sources C. E. Pascoe, ed., *The dramatic list* (1879) · C. E. Pascoe, ed., *The dramatic list*, 2nd edn (1880) · *Daily News* (19 April 1884) · *Era Almanack and Annual* (1868) · *Era Almanack and Annual* (1880) · *The Era* (8 Dec 1878) · *The Era* (19 April 1884) · Ward, *Men of the reign* · private information (1900) · personal knowledge (1900) · *Men of the time* (1862) · Hall, *Dramatic ports.* · *The life and reminiscences of E. L. Blanchard, with notes from the diary of Wm. Blanchard*, ed. C. W. Scott and C. Howard, 2 vols. (1891) · H. Morley, *The journal of a London playgoer from 1851 to 1866* (1866) · D. Cook, *Nights at the play* (1883) · Genest, *Eng. stage* · *Theatrical Times* (24 Oct 1846), 174 [memoir] · *CGPLA Eng. & Wales* (1878)

Likenesses attrib. A. C. Sterling, salt print, 1846–9, NPG · H. Watkins, albumen print, 1856–9, NPG [*see illus.*] · C. Silvy, photograph, NPG · portrait, repro. in *ILN* (14 Dec 1878) · portrait?, repro. in *Entr'acte* (7 Dec 1878) · portrait?, repro. in *Theatrical Times* (1 Aug 1846) · theatrical prints, Harvard TC

Wealth at death under £2000: probate, 24 Dec 1878, *CGPLA Eng. & Wales* · £4301 3s. 10d.—Leonora Wigan: administration, 18 Aug 1884, *CGPLA Eng. & Wales*

Wigan, Arthur Ladbroke (*bap.* **1785**, *d.* **1847**), general practitioner and writer, was baptized at Hall Hill, Abbots Bromley, Staffordshire, on 29 April 1785, the second son of the second marriage of Robert Wigan (1743–1803/4), a gentleman farmer, to Elizabeth Eason (1757–1847). He was the uncle of Alfred Sydney *Wigan (1814–1878) and Horace *Wigan (1818/19–1885); his maternal grandfather was Sir Robert Ladbroke (1713?–1773), MP and lord mayor of London in 1747. Wigan apparently attended the local Clarke's Free Grammar School, learning French from French officers imprisoned nearby. He knew Erasmus Darwin as the family doctor. After working as an assistant to an electrical inventor, he was apprenticed to a Croydon practitioner in 1804–7, but was a wilful pupil, and later regretted his poor medical grounding. During this time he became an intimate of Robert Gooch, the physician, then a pupil of Mr James of Croydon. He qualified MRCS in 1807, and he now styled himself A. Ladbroke Wigan. Soon after qualifying he spent time working round the spas, in the hope of acquiring new patients. Following this he joined William Cleveland, a senior apothecary, in his practice based at 2 Dowgate Hill in the City of London. In 1813 Wigan married Cleveland's daughter Lydia Eliza (*d.* 1843/4), with whom he had two sons, and ran the practice after his father-in-law's death.

In 1829 Wigan set himself up in practice in Brighton, where he remained until 1841. During the 1832 cholera epidemic he spent an intensive time visiting practitioners, hospitals, and the poorer districts of London, and reported his findings. In 1835 he bankrupted himself trying to establish a free dispensary for the poor of Brighton, and had to move, but recovered. In 1843 he published *Brighton and its Three Climates*, and also wrote articles for the *Illuminated Magazine*, using the pseudonym Luke Roden. One described local life in his boyhood; another was about a travelling 'mountebank doctor'.

Wigan's main work, *A new view of insanity: the duality of the*

mind proved by the structure, functions and diseases of the brain, and by the phenomena of mental derangement, and shewn to be essential to moral responsibility, was published in 1844. Wigan clearly stressed the double-hemisphere construction of the brain. He explained the usual 'preponderance' (dominance) of one brain, the ability of one brain to substitute for the other, the results of disease of one brain leading to forms of insanity, and effects such as obsessive behaviour, and the 'sentiment of preexistence' (*déjà vu*). He quoted numerous cases from other authors and recalled some of his own. The work followed up articles he had written for *The Lancet*, and contained divagations on education. *A New View of Insanity* was well received, and he acquired some status. His interest in public medicine revived, despite memories of the failure of his free dispensary in Brighton, and he backed Sir James Graham's efforts to reform the medical and surgical professions. In 1846 he made a continental tour; in France he worked briefly with Achille Louis Foville (1799–1878) at Charenton; he also visited Italy, Switzerland, Germany, and the Netherlands, giving a number of medical lectures and visiting many asylums.

Wigan returned to Britain in 1847, when his mother died. He lived in small lodgings in Queen Street, Camden Town, London. He was on close terms with Forbes Winslow, owner of two private asylums. Wigan was taken ill in the West End, developing a severe bronchial complaint; after 'an effusion in the pericardium', he died at his home on 7 December 1847.

Interest in the theory of duality continued during the nineteenth century through the work of Brown-Séquard, W. W. Ireland, and others. Wigan was then largely forgotten, but in the mid-twentieth century work on the 'split brain' renewed interest, and a second edition of *A New View of Insanity* appeared in 1986.   BASIL CLARKE

Sources A. L. Wigan, *A new view of insanity*, 2nd edn (1986) · B. Clarke, 'Arthur Wigan and the duality of mind', *Psychological Medicine* (*c.*1987) [monograph supplement] · *Illuminated Magazine* (1841–3) · HoP, *Commons*

Wigan, Horace (1818/19–1885), actor and playwright, was born in Blackheath, Kent, the son of a teacher of languages who at one time was secretary to the Dramatic Authors' Society. His older brother was the actor Alfred Sydney *Wigan. He was first seen in Dublin, on 1 August 1853, as Billy Lackaday in *Sweethearts and Wives*, and later replaced Webb as King Bruin in *Good Woman in the Wood*. After leaving Dublin he made, under the name Danvers, his first appearance in London, on 1 May 1854 at the Olympic, as Paddy Murphy in Lever's extravaganza *The Happy Man*. He was the original O'Rafferty in Tom Taylor's *A Blighted Being* on 17 October, but failed to win acceptance as a representative of Irishmen, and made no mark for four years. On 5 June 1858, under his own name, he was the first Smythers, a hairdresser, in Taylor's *Going to the Bad*, and on 2 December the first Smoothly Smirk in John Oxenford's *The Porter's Knot*. His next parts included Abder Khan in H. J. Byron's burlesque *Mazeppa*, Horatio Cocles Bric-à-brac in Taylor's *Payable on Demand*, and Mr Cunningham in Taylor's *Nine Points of the Law*. At the Strand on 26 September 1860 he produced an adaptation from the

French entitled *Observation and Flirtation*. He was the original Solomon Probity in H. T. Craven's *The Chimney Corner* (21 February 1861). His own *Change for a Sovereign* was produced at the Strand on 14 March, and on 30 June he created the part of Symptom, an imaginary invalid, in his play from the French *A Charming Woman* (*À trente ans*). His *Friends or Foes*, from Victorien Sardou's *Nos intimes*, was given at the St James's on 8 March 1862, and was the best of his adaptations. While still performing at the Olympic, he was the first Fusell in Watts Phillips's *Camilla's Husband* (14 November 1862) and the first Blush in *Taming a Truant*, his own adaptation of Sardou's *Papillone* (19 March 1863). His first distinct acting success was as the original Hawkshaw, a detective, in Taylor's *The Ticket-of-Leave Man* (27 June 1863).

On 1 November 1864 Wigan undertook the management of the Olympic, the only house in which he had been seen in London, and produced on the opening night Taylor's *The Hidden Hand* and two farces, Oxenford's *The Girl I Left behind me* and John Maddison Morton's *My Wife's Bonnet*—all three adaptations. While manager he continued to act in a variety of parts, and in 1865 brought out his own play *Always Intended*. By 1866, however, he had resigned the Olympic to Benjamin Webster, though he remained acting manager. He was the first Percy Chaffington in Maddison Morton's *If I had a Thousand a Year* (21 October 1867) and Cornelius Tattenham in *From Grave to Gay*, by Ben Webster the younger (2 December 1867). In J. S. Coyne's *The Woman of the World* (*Les coulisses de la vie*) he created the part of the first Golden Bird (18 February 1868). Inspector Javert in *The Yellow Passport* (7 November), an adaptation of *Les misérables*, was another success. *The Life Chase*, an adaptation by Wigan and Oxenford of *Le drame de la rue de la Paix*, was produced at the Gaiety on 11 October 1869, and a melodrama by Wigan entitled *Rag Fair*, in which he played a cheapjack called Brightside, was given at the Victoria on 20 May 1872. At the Gaiety (14 December) he played the Doctor in *Awaking*, Campbell Clarke's version of *Marcel*, and in the Vaudeville's revival of *The Road to Ruin* he was Sulky (1 November 1873). In a performance of *The School for Scandal* at Drury Lane, for Webster's benefit, he was Rowley.

On 24 April 1875, as manager, Wigan opened the Holborn Theatre, renamed the Mirror, with a revival of *The Hidden Hand*, Maltby's *Make yourself at Home*, and James Kenney's *Maids of Honour*. On 29 May he was the original Inspector Walker in *The Detective* (*Le parricide*), adapted by Clement Scott and E. Manuel. However, his speculation was not successful. The theatre passed into other hands and, after frequent changes of name, was demolished. On Wigan's retirement from management a complimentary benefit was given him at Drury Lane. He died on 7 August 1885 at Woodbank, Sidcup, Kent, the house of his daughter Jane Emma Hernu. He was predeceased by his wife, Emma (*b.* 1813/14).

Wigan was a quiet, stolid, undemonstrative actor, whose chief success was obtained in detective parts which called for no display of emotion. Rowley in *The School for Scandal* suited him exactly, and showed the measure of his

intelligence. He was a fair linguist and translated many pieces. Nicoll lists twenty-four plays and adaptations by him. JOSEPH KNIGHT, *rev.* KLAUS STIERSTORFER

Sources *The history of the Theatre Royal, Dublin, from its foundation in 1821 to the present time* (1870) · *The life and reminiscences of E. L. Blanchard, with notes from the diary of Wm. Blanchard*, ed. C. W. Scott and C. Howard, 2 vols. (1891) · C. E. Pascoe, ed., *The dramatic list*, 2nd edn (1880) · *The Era* (8 Aug 1885) · *Era Almanack and Annual* (1886) · *CGPLA Eng. & Wales* (1886) · A. Nicoll, *Late nineteenth century drama, 1850–1900*, 2nd edn (1959), vol. 5 of *A history of English drama, 1660–1900* (1952–9), 622, 823 · census returns, 1881
Likenesses H. Watkins, albumen print, 1856–9 · C. Silvy, photograph, NPG
Wealth at death £384 3*s.* 0*d.*: administration, 1 Jan 1886, *CGPLA Eng. & Wales*

Wigan, John (1696–1739), physician and author, was born on 31 January 1696, the son of William Wigan, rector of Kensington, Middlesex. In 1710 he was admitted to Westminster School, and thence proceeded to Christ Church, Oxford, where he matriculated on 15 June 1714. He graduated BA on 6 February 1719, MA on 22 March 1721, and MB and MD (6 July) in 1727. Some of his poems are included among those written at the time of Queen Anne's death in 1714, and also of Dr Radcliffe's death in the same year. Besides these, he wrote the lines on the death of Dean Aldrich which were published in Vincent Bourne's edition of the dean's poems; and at least four of the exercises in the *Carmina quadragesimalia* (vol. 1, 8, 57–8, 62–3, and 104–5) are ascribed to him. On 5 October 1726 he was admitted principal of New Inn Hall, Oxford, and about the same time was appointed secretary to the earl of Arran, the chancellor of the university.

Wigan was admitted as a candidate at the Royal College of Physicians on 12 April 1731, and as a fellow on 3 April 1732, at which point he resigned his post at New Inn Hall and moved to Craig Court in London. He was elected physician to Westminster Hospital in 1733, a post he retained until 1737. In 1738 he travelled with his friend Edward Trelawny to Jamaica, acting as his physician and secretary. In Jamaica in 1739 Wigan married Mary Wheeler, daughter of John Douce, a planter on the island, and widow of Philip Wheeler of Jamaica, and they had one daughter, Mary Trelawny Wigan.

In his day Wigan was well known as a writer. As early as 1718 he published a translation of a work by Longinus on fever cures. He also produced a respected edition of Aretaeus, published in 1723. When Boerhaave published his edition of the same author in 1735, he referred heavily to Wigan's book, and included a grateful acknowledgement of Wigan's achievement. Wigan also produced a number of other translations and indexes. He died in Jamaica on 5 December 1739, aged forty-three. A black marble slab was laid as a memorial to him in the cathedral church of St Catherine, Spanish Town.

W. W. WEBB, *rev.* CLAIRE L. NUTT

Sources Munk, *Roll* · Foster, *Alum. Oxon.* · J. Welch, *The list of the queen's scholars of St Peter's College, Westminster*, ed. [C. B. Phillimore], new edn (1852)
Likenesses W. Hogarth, portrait; in possession of W. W. Harvey, rector of Ewelme, Oxfordshire, 1900 · oils, NPG

Wigan, Leonora (1805–1884). *See under* Wigan, Alfred Sydney (1814–1878).

Wigg, George Edward Cecil, Baron Wigg (1900–1983), politician, was born at 139 Uxbridge Road, Ealing, on 28 November 1900. He was the eldest of six children (two sons and four daughters) of Edward William Wigg, manager of a dairy business, who declined from a moderately prosperous beginning to losing everything, and his wife, Cecilia Comber, whose family had unbroken non-commissioned army service since the time of Sir John Moore's light division. Wigg was proud of his Wigg ancestors, once prominent in Hampshire, one of whom founded Queen Mary's Grammar School, Basingstoke, to which he won a scholarship when twelve, having attended Fairfields council school. Poverty compelled the end of his formal education when he was fourteen, and after a few inconsequential jobs he joined the Hampshire regiment at eighteen.

Wigg was in the regular army (spending many years in the Middle East) until 1937 and his belief in its virtues never faded, though he was prickly with authority when he thought it unjust. The social prejudices of the time unreasonably prevented his being a commissioned officer until he rejoined in 1940 and became a lieutenant-colonel in the Royal Army Education Corps, where his enthusiasm for current affairs sessions for the troops prompted the jibe, when he was in parliament, that the education corps was 'the only unit of the British Army entitled to include the general election of 1945 among its battle honours'.

Wigg's intelligent, enquiring mind, added to his bitterness at the world's unfairness for which he blamed and loathed the tories, impelled him to read widely and to educate himself politically. While working with the Workers' Educational Association he met in 1933 A. D. Lindsay, master of Balliol College, Oxford. A lasting friendship ensued which greatly influenced Wigg's thinking. Lindsay suggested to Wigg during the war that he should drop his intention of emigrating to Canada in favour of a political career, which he began when elected Labour MP for Dudley in 1945.

A man of swirling emotions prone to hero worship, Wigg attached himself passionately to Emanuel Shinwell, whose parliamentary private secretary he was when Shinwell was minister of fuel and power (1945–7). Shinwell's replacement by Hugh Gaitskell led Wigg irrationally to dislike Gaitskell and often his associates. His knowledge of, and devotion to, the army inspired much of his parliamentary work, and he was a harrier feared by tory service ministers. He could be devastatingly rude. A clash with John Profumo, secretary of state for war, in the autumn of 1962 convinced him of Profumo's deception over army conditions in Kuwait and roused his ire. When the Christine Keeler scandal emerged in 1963 he malevolently pursued Profumo in the Commons until his downfall. An expert in political intrigue (described as wiggery pokery), Wigg was aware of the political advantages to Labour and informed Harold Wilson of his activities throughout. Ironically in 1976 Wigg was charged, on the evidence of

George Edward Cecil Wigg, Baron Wigg (1900–1983), by Mark Gerson, 1971

police officers said by Wigg to be lying, with accosting women from his motor car as he drove slowly near Marble Arch. The Wells Street court magistrate concluded that it was Wigg who was lying, but acquitted him solely because he considered that the 'kerb crawling' of which Wigg had been accurately accused did not amount to an offence.

After Gaitskell's death in 1963 Wigg skilfully managed the campaign for Wilson's election as Labour leader using cajolery and threats to Labour MPs relevant to their future under a probable Wilson regime. In 1964 he became paymaster-general with direct access to the prime minister on security and wider political matters. He was sworn of the privy council at the same time. Voluble in conspiratorial style, whether in person or on the telephone—frequently at unusual hours—he achieved a domination over Wilson which irritated colleagues including Marcia Williams, whose removal from the room he once successfully demanded when he wished to speak confidentially to the prime minister. Eventually Wilson was exhausted by Wigg's constant pummelling and in 1967 adroitly removed him from his presence by making him chairman of the Horserace Betting Levy Board with a seat in the House of Lords as a life peer. Though hipped at this loss of favour and subsequently ungracious about his patron, Wigg was also delighted. Wigg loved racing almost as much as he did the army and political intrigue, and was intermittently a keen owner of indifferent horses. He had been a member of the Racecourse Betting Control Board (1957–61) and of the Horserace Totalisator Board (1961–4).

As dispenser of the statutory levy collected from bookmakers and the tote Wigg was immediately in conflict with the Jockey Club, which considered that he should take their orders as to how the money should be distributed to racing, and told him so at a meeting to which he was summoned. They had mistaken their man. Ferociously Wigg quickened the pace at which the Jockey Club came to realize that their edicts were not as automatically revered as they were at the club's inception in 1752. By shifting the balance of power to the levy board Wigg defused mounting resentment at the Jockey Club's imperious ways. Previously a strong advocate of a tote monopoly, he abruptly reversed his position when he became president of the Betting Office Licensees' Association in 1973, after leaving the levy board. This was not surprising to those familiar with his violent lurches.

Though Wigg maintained deep dislikes, rising to hatreds, he was intensely loyal to his friends and unremitting in his zeal for those he felt were badly treated. He believed fervently that the poorest and most humble in the land had the same right to identity and self-fulfilment as the richest and most powerful, and acted accordingly in his parliamentary and racing career. He employed either considerable charm or hectoring hostility to match his mood or the requirement of the occasion.

Wigg was large and broad-shouldered, with a long and lugubrious face. His beaky nose and wide, tall ears were a cartoonist's delight. In 1930 he married Florence Minnie, daughter of William (Harry) Veal, a stud groom. They had three daughters. There is a bust of Wigg (1984) by Angela Connor placed in the paddock at Epsom racecourse in recognition of his contribution to ensuring into perpetuity the Epsom racecourse and the gallops. Wigg died in London on 11 August 1983.　　WOODROW WYATT, rev.

Sources Lord Wigg [G. E. C. Wigg], George Wigg (1972) · C. Hill, Horse power: the politics of the turf (1988) · private information (1990) · personal knowledge (1990)
Archives BLPES, papers · Bodl. RH, MSS relating to Tanganyika and Zanzibar forestry | PRO, corresp. with colonial secretary, CO 959, 967 | FILM BFI NFTVA, documentary footage | SOUND BL NSA, oral history interview
Likenesses group photograph, 1964, Hult. Arch. · M. Gerson, photograph, 1971, NPG [see illus.] · photographs, 1976, Hult. Arch. · A. Connor, bust, 1984, paddock at Epsom racecourse
Wealth at death £240,291: probate, 17 Jan 1984, CGPLA Eng. & Wales

Wigg, Lilly (1749–1828), botanist, was born at Smallburgh, Norfolk, on 25 December 1749, the son of a poor shoemaker in that village. He received a good village education, and was brought up to his father's trade, but moved to Great Yarmouth before he was twenty, where until 1801 he kept a small school in Fighting-cock Row. He acquired some knowledge of Latin, Greek, and French, was a skilled arithmetician, and wrote a beautifully neat copperplate hand; his love of botany and skill as a collector procured him the acquaintance of Dr John Aikin, Thomas Jenkinson Woodward, Sir James Edward Smith, and Dawson Turner. Wigg restricted his botanizing to the district around Great Yarmouth, where he made several additions to the list of local flowering plants. His main interest was, however, the seaweeds, which he necessarily found cast up on the beaches, and of which he amassed a rich collection.

In 1801 Turner engaged Wigg as a subordinate clerk in Messrs Gurneys and Turner's bank at Great Yarmouth, a position which he occupied for the rest of his life. The sober Wigg was often the butt of his younger colleagues' practical jokes; the ideal bank employee, described by his obituarist as 'laborious and exact, neat and clean in mind and person, honest in word and deed, modest, retiring and diffident' (GM), Wigg was nevertheless stalwart in his beliefs which embraced republicanism, the Baptist faith, and an ardent dislike of papism; he was not, however, a churchgoer.

For nearly twenty years Wigg was collecting material for a history of edible plants, some of which exists in manuscript at the Natural History Museum and at Kew. He also studied the birds and fishes of the Norfolk coast. He was elected an associate of the Linnean Society as early as 1790. He contributed to J. E. Smith's English Botany (1790–1814), and to W. Withering's Botanical Arrangement (1787–92). Dawson Turner named after him Fucus (now Naccaria) wigghii. Wigg died at Great Yarmouth on 28 March 1828.

G. S. BOULGER, rev. ANITA MCCONNELL

Sources H. G. Glasspoole, 'A memoir of Mr Lilly Wigg, F.L.S., of Great Yarmouth', Transactions of the Norfolk and Norwich Naturalists' Society, 2 (1874–9), 269–74 · GM, 1st ser., 100/1 (1830), 184–5
Archives NHM, MS relating to esculent plants · RBG Kew, botanical papers
Likenesses Mrs D. Turner, pencil sketch (aged about sixty), RBG Kew, Wigg MSS

Wigg, Montagu John Stone- (1861–1918), bishop of Papua New Guinea, was born on 4 October 1861 at Tunbridge Wells, the third son of John Stone Wigg, gentleman, sometime mayor of Tunbridge Wells, and his wife, Ellen Matilda Clements. Educated at Winchester College (1875–80), University College, Oxford (BA, 1883; MA, 1887; DD, 1902), and Ely Theological College, he was ordained deacon in 1884 and priest in 1885 by the bishop of London. After serving as non-stipendiary curate of St Andrew's, Wells Street, London (1884), in 1886 he became a missioner for the London Diocesan Home Mission, stationed at Holy Innocents', Hammersmith. He then followed his former vicar, the Rt Revd W. T. T. Webber, to Brisbane as assistant curate (1889), vicar (1891), and canon residentiary and subdean (1892) of St John's Pro-Cathedral. An uncompromising Anglo-Catholic, slight of build, urbane, handsome, and bearded, he continued in Brisbane's inner suburbs the ministry of a slum priest. Here he founded a home for itinerant south sea islanders and in 1892 a philanthropic sisterhood, the Society of the Sacred Advent.

In 1896, 'at the point of a bayonet' (Temple MSS), Webber persuaded the primate of Australia, the evangelical Bishop W. Saumarez Smith, to agree to a bishopric in British New Guinea, where a mission founded in 1891 by the Australian board of missions was languishing. Webber nominated Stone-Wigg, whom he consecrated on 25 January 1898 in Sydney. After touring the Australian colonies, Stone-Wigg was enthroned at Dogura, head-station of the diocese, on 26 May 1898. The board immediately relinquished to him financial responsibility for the mission. He never accepted his stipend. After a fund-raising tour in England in 1902, during which he attended the coronation of Edward VII, he cleared the mission's debts and secured the diocesan endowment. In 1903 he declined nomination to the see of Brisbane and in 1907 he was proposed, among others, as first (and non-stipendiary) bishop of Polynesia.

A halo of 'true romance' (Montgomery to Davidson, 5 Aug 1909, Davidson MSS), inspired by the bishop, came to surround the mission and transcend its poverty, austerity, and insalubrity. Stone-Wigg himself suffered frequent and debilitating bouts of malaria and asthma. Lacking any formal missionary training, he took as his model the Universities Mission to Central Africa. He ran his mission autocratically, with almost monastic discipline and without financial control from any external society. He was a welcome guest at every government house in Australia, and it was claimed by Bishop H. H. Montgomery that there was no ecclesiastic in that country whose opinion held greater weight with governors and premiers. Stone-Wigg respected native custom, praised the Papuan sense of brotherhood and was said in retrospect to have delegated authority too quickly to an indigenous church. At Ganuganuana, near Dogura, he founded a home for children of mixed race. His reading, in theology and ethnography, and his publications, both in Australia and England, particularly an essay, 'The Papuans: a people of the south Pacific', in *Mankind and the Church* (ed. H. H. Montgomery, 1907), show him to have been a man of intellectual interests, tolerance, and caution.

On 21 August 1907 in Sydney, Stone-Wigg married Elfie Marcia (1873–1968), only daughter of James Sutcliffe Mort. After attending the Lambeth conference and the Pan-Anglican Congress in London in mid-1908, he reluctantly resigned his see on medical advice and retired to the fashionable Sydney suburb of Burwood, where he founded two children's homes. Despite protests from within the diocese, until 1915 he constantly assisted the single-handed archbishop of Sydney. The most widely respected Anglo-Catholic in Australia, he chaired the executive of the Australian board of missions until its reconstruction in 1915. In May 1912, as managing director of the Church Publishing Company, he launched the *Church Standard*, published weekly for the ensuing forty years. It was high-church in sympathy and with an Australasian-wide circulation; Stone-Wigg was honorary editor from March 1915. After a prolonged bout of asthma, he died at his home, Ravenna, Appian Way, Burwood, Sydney, on 16 October 1918. He was survived by his wife and two daughters, and was interred in the churchyard of St Thomas's, Enfield, the next day. RUTH FRAPPELL

Sources LPL, Archbishop Frederick Temple MSS, vol. 8, fols. 67–95 · LPL, Archbishop R. T. Davidson MSS, vol. 165, fols. 39, 44–6 · *Church Standard* [Sydney] (25 Oct 1918) · *Sydney Morning Herald* (17 Oct 1918) · H. H. Montgomery, *Church Times* (1 Nov 1918) · D. Wetherell, *Reluctant mission: the Anglican church in Papua New Guinea, 1891–1942* (1977) · Foster, *Alum. Oxon.* · J. B. Wainewright, ed., *Winchester College, 1836–1906: a register* (1907) · parish register (marriage), Sydney, St John's Church, Gordon, 1907 · private information (2004) · *AusDB*

Archives University of Papua New Guinea

Likenesses group photograph, repro. in Wetherell, *Reluctant mission* · photograph, repro. in *Church Standard* · photograph, repro. in *Sydney Morning Herald*

Wiggins, Joseph (1832–1905), Arctic explorer and merchant navy officer, born at Norwich on 3 September 1832, was the son of Joseph Wiggins (*d.* 1843) and his wife, Anne Petty (*d.* 1847). The father, a driver and later proprietor of coaches serving the London–Norwich road, set up in 1838–9 at Bury St Edmunds as innkeeper and coach proprietor but suffered from railway competition. At his death his widow, left with small means, returned with her six sons and three daughters to Norwich, where Joseph was sent to Farnell's School. At the age of fourteen he was apprenticed to his uncle, Joseph Potts, a Sunderland shipowner. He rose rapidly, being master of a ship at twenty-one and subsequently owning cargo vessels. In 1868 he married Annie Potts (*d.* 1904), daughter of his former master, and also became a Board of Trade examiner in navigation and seamanship at Sunderland.

Wiggins became interested in the possibility of establishing a trade route between western Europe and Siberia, by way of the Arctic seas and the rivers which drain into them. The overland route by sledge and caravan was slow, erratic, and expensive, but the sea route was held to be impracticable owing to ice and fog. He argued that a branch of the warm Atlantic drift ought for part of the year to open up the western entrances to the Kara Sea and (in conjunction with the outflow of the great rivers) a route through the sea itself. He chartered and fitted at his own expense a steamer of 103 tons and sailed from Dundee on 3 June 1874; but after reaching the mouth of the Ob, he was compelled to return owing to lack of provisions, expense, and the attitude of his crew. He reached Dundee on 25 September. Although his route was already used by Norwegian fishermen and had been followed by Russian traders as early as the sixteenth century, his voyage called attention to the possibility of establishing a new commercial route with large vessels. He expounded his results in lectures which won him wide fame and thenceforth occupied him when on shore.

In 1875, with private financial support, Wiggins fitted out a sloop of 27 tons and reached Vardö on 27 July, where he met the Russian admiral, Glassenov, and others interested in his work. He accompanied Glassenov (who promised to use his influence with the Russian government and merchants) to Archangel, where he obtained maps, rejoined his sloop, and worked her nearly to Kolguyev Island, but thence turned back, the season being spent. Private British and Russian money financed his third Siberian journey, in a steamer of 120 tons carrying an auxiliary launch. He sailed in July 1876, inspected the Kara River late in August, and by 26 September, having found the Ob inaccessible owing to winds and current, was in the estuary of the Yenisey. On 18 October his ship reached the Kureyka (a right-bank tributary of the Yenisey, which it joins close to the Arctic circle), and was there laid up for the winter. The next year he started for Siberia accompanied by Henry Seebohm the ornithologist, but his ship was wrecked shortly after reaching the Kureyka. In 1878 O. J.

Joseph Wiggins (1832–1905), by Lavender

Cattley, a merchant in St Petersburg, sent Wiggins in command of a trading steamer to the Ob, whence a cargo of produce was successfully brought back. Other vessels performed the same feat; but in 1879–80 the failure of some British and Russian trading expeditions, with which Wiggins declined to be connected (owing to the unsuitability of the vessels), checked public confidence in his schemes, and from 1880 to 1887 he acted as master mariner in other seas.

In 1887–8 the Phoenix company sent Wiggins in the 273 ton *Phoenix* up the Yenisey River to Yeniseysk, far above what was supposed to be the head of navigation for so large a ship. He left his brother Robert, who was his chief officer, on the river as agent. Another ship followed in 1888, but this voyage and the company failed. In 1892 Wiggins was the only one of the polar explorers of the Royal Geographical Society to have confidence in Nansen's plan to explore the Arctic in the *Fram*.

In 1893 Wiggins, by arrangement with the Russian government, took command of the *Orestes*, a larger vessel than any which had hitherto reached the mouth of the Yenisey, and safely delivered a cargo of rails for the Trans-Siberian Railway. For this voyage he was rewarded by the Russian government. The next year, after convoying two Russian steamers to the Yenisey, he was shipwrecked near Yugor Strait and, with his companions, made a difficult land journey home, when the Royal Geographical Society

awarded him the Murchison medal. In 1895 he made his last voyage to the Yenisey, and in 1896 he failed to get beyond Vardö, which involved him in some undeserved censure. From 1897 to 1903 he sailed elsewhere.

In 1905 the Russo-Japanese War brought famine to Siberia. The Russian government planned a large relief expedition by sea. Wiggins took as active a part in the organization of the expedition as failing health permitted, but when the ships sailed he was too ill to accompany them. He died childless at his home, Rossett View, Rossett Drive, Pannal, Harrogate, Yorkshire, on 13 September 1905, and was buried at Bishopwearmouth.

O. J. R. HOWARTH, *rev.* ELIZABETH BAIGENT

Sources H. Johnson, *Life and voyages of Joseph Wiggins FRGS* (1907) · private information (1912) · H. Seebohm, *The birds of Siberia* (1901) · A. H. Peel, *Polar gleams* (1894) · d. cert. · H. R. Mill, *The record of the Royal Geographical Society, 1830–1930* (1930)
Likenesses Lavender, photogravure, repro. in Johnson, *Life and voyages* [*see illus.*]
Wealth at death £715 3s. 9d.: probate, 27 Oct 1905, *CGPLA Eng. & Wales*

Wigginton, Giles (*fl.* 1564–1597), Church of England clergyman and religious activist, was a native of Oundle in Northamptonshire. He entered Trinity College, Cambridge, in October 1564 under the patronage of Sir Walter Mildmay. He was elected a scholar in 1566 and graduated BA in 1569, being elected to a fellowship of the college despite the vigorous opposition of the master John Whitgift, who was already suspicious of Wigginton's puritan sympathies. He took the degree of MA in 1572 and established a reputation for his scholarship in Greek and Hebrew. His puritan views were accompanied by a controversial wit which further alienated Whitgift, who, he alleged, kept him from all college offices and preferments. Wigginton never overcame his sense of injustice at his treatment by Whitgift, so much so that in the mid-1580s, on being offered a handshake by Godfrey Goldsborough, one of Whitgift's protégés, he shrank from it 'as if he had been a serpent, because I knew him to be a corrupt, prophane, proud, nonresident, pluralist pseudo-hierarchist' (Peel, 2.246), an account which is revealing of Wigginton's combative nature. His religious views appear to have attracted the attention of the puritans at Dedham, who tried unsuccessfully to have him appointed to the living there in 1576 or 1577, but in 1579 his college appointed him to the vicarage at Sedbergh in the Yorkshire dales, where his energies could be expended against the common enemy of popery.

Wigginton's character, as much as his views, soon attracted the attention of ecclesiastical authority in the north, and in 1581 Archbishop Edwin Sandys wrote of him that 'he laboureth not to build, but to put down, and by what means he can to overthrow the state ecclesiastical' (Peck, 115). Wigginton had powerful support among a section of the puritan gentry, and on a visit to London in 1584 he was invited to preach before the judges in the church of St Dunstan-in-the-West. News of this came to the notice of his old Cambridge adversary John Whitgift, by now archbishop of Canterbury, who sent an order in the dead of night forbidding him to preach and requiring him under bond to appear before him at Lambeth the next day. There Wigginton was tendered the *ex officio* oath to answer articles as yet undeclared, and on his refusal to take the oath, he was committed to gaol in the Gatehouse, where he remained for nine weeks. On his release he was forbidden to preach in the southern province and returned north to his living. Whitgift continued to pursue him, and on the word of an informant ordered Sandys to initiate proceedings against Wigginton. This Sandys did and Giles was deprived of his living by William Chaderton, bishop of Chester, in 1585. Despite this reputation Wigginton's pastoral involvement bore fruit, and a report on his parish at about that time suggests that he had brought the people of the place to an understanding of reformed principles and practice. This may have owed something to the short catechism he had compiled for his parishioners, which he may have published in 1589 and which was definitely published by his grandson in 1646 as *An Introduction to the Christian Faith*.

Following deprivation Wigginton found himself in York during the trial of the Catholic martyr Margaret Clitherow, with whom he entered into discussion in her prison cell. In the course of the trial he is said to have intervened on her behalf in open court, contesting the legitimacy of the proceedings, and after her sentence he again attempted to persuade her to renounce her views. Wigginton then moved on to London where he once again fell foul of his implacable opponent Whitgift. Brought before the archbishop and again refusing the *ex officio* oath, Wigginton once more found himself in prison, this time the White Lion, and also in chains. Removed to another prison he was degraded from orders, despite the intervention on his behalf of the earls of Warwick and Huntingdon. Wigginton left London on his release and returned to his home town of Oundle where he joined and took a leading role within a group of radical dissenters in the town who withdrew from the parish church to nearby Stoke Doyle, where the squire, Anthony Palmer, was sympathetic. This group, which included the schoolmaster Robert Pamphlin and William Hacket, a local maltster, disrupted the religious life of the town considerably in the years up to 1590.

Wigginton had not severed his connections with the north and returned intermittently to his former parish at Sedbergh where he preached unlicensed. While in Yorkshire, Wigginton was arrested and imprisoned in Lancaster gaol from where, on 27 February 1587, he sought the help of his old patron Mildmay. His treatment by Whitgift figured largely in the first of the Marprelate tracts, *The Epistle*, and this fact, along with his former reputation, made him one of the first suspects for the authorship. He was arraigned before the high commission on 6 December 1588, when he again refused the oath and found himself imprisoned in the Gatehouse once more. Though not the author of the Marprelate tracts Wigginton did pen lively accounts of his earlier confrontations with Whitgift which survive in manuscript and may have provided the

Marprelate source, and he appears also to have transcribed some separatist writings at this time. While in prison he composed a 'Treatise on predestination' and, more in keeping with his style, he also compiled a mock set of visitation articles, purporting to emanate from Whitgift, in which he set out the agenda of the godly while pillorying the archbishop. Wigginton remained in prison for some time and was visited there by his former associate from Oundle William Hacket, whose frenzied response to the crisis within puritanism following the arrest of the leaders of the classes was to prove disastrous. Through Wigginton, Hacket made the acquaintance of Edmund Copinger and they, with Henry Arthington, embarked on the series of events that led to the announcement of the second coming, followed by the suicide of Copinger and the execution of Hacket in July 1591. The extent of Wigginton's knowledge and involvement in what was to prove a calamity to the puritan cause remains obscure, but he is credited with authorship of a pamphlet, *The Fool's Bolt*, distributed by the conspirators, and the authorities were quick to implicate him in the events.

Wigginton was released from prison and sought the support of Burghley in trying unsuccessfully to regain his old living at Sedbergh. His movements thereafter remain obscure: he wrote to Burghley on 4 April 1597 outlining plans for a college to train clergy to engage in controversy with the Roman Catholic missioners and presenting him with a manuscript treatise written against the papists, and in the same year he was presented for preaching unlicensed in his brother's Northamptonshire parish of Collingtree and for disturbing the incumbent of the nearby parish of Blisworth by, characteristically, rushing into the pulpit to preach a sermon of his own. With that he disappears from the record, possibly to the anonymity of his old stamping ground in London where a daughter of his was baptized, at Stratford Bow, later that year.

WILLIAM JOSEPH SHEILS

Sources Cooper, *Ath. Cantab.*, 2.329–31 · M. Marprelate, *The epistle* (1588) · L. H. Carlson, *Martin Marprelate, gentleman: Master Job Throkmorton laid open in his colors* (1981) · W. J. Sheils, *The puritans in the diocese of Peterborough, 1558–1610*, Northamptonshire RS, 30 (1979) · P. Collinson, *The Elizabethan puritan movement* (1967) · J. Morris, ed., *The troubles of our Catholic forefathers related by themselves*, 3 (1877) · 'The examinations of Giles Wigginton', *Transactions of the Congregational Historical Society*, 3 (1907–8), 378–86 · A. E. Platt, *History of the parish and grammar school of Sedbergh* (1876) · I. Green, *The Christian's ABC: catechisms and catechising in England, c.1530–1740* (1996) · A. Walsham, '"Frantick Hacket": prophecy, sorcery, insanity, and the Elizabethan puritan movement', *HJ*, 41 (1998), 27–66 · A. Peel, ed., *The seconde parte of a register*, 2 vols. (1915) · F. Peck, ed., *Desiderata curiosa*, new edn, 2 vols. in 1 (1779)
Archives DWL, Morrice MSS

Wigglesworth, Michael (1631–1705), poet and minister, was born on 18 October 1631, probably in Yorkshire, the son of Edward Wigglesworth, a tradesman, and his wife, Esther, and was taken by his parents to Massachusetts Bay in 1638 during the great puritan migration to New England. After a few weeks at Charlestown, Massachusetts, they went to New Haven, where Michael contracted the illness which weakened his health for the rest of his life.

Aged seven, he was sent to be educated at Ezekiel Cheever's school in New Haven. His education was interrupted to enable him to help his lame father at home, but he was not strong enough to do this and he returned to school in 1644 and went on to Harvard College in 1647.

Wigglesworth studied medicine at Harvard for three and a half years but then felt called to the ministry. After graduating BA in 1651, he undertook his theological training and was a fellow and tutor at Harvard from 1652 to 1654. About 1654 he moved to Malden, Massachusetts, having been offered the position of minister to the congregational church there, but was plagued by spiritual and sexual anxieties, which he recorded in a diary (published in 1951), and was not formally ordained until 1657. In 1655, on 18 May, he married his cousin Mary, daughter of Humphry Reyner of Rowley. They had one child, Mercy, in 1656. Wigglesworth continued to suffer from ill health, a lung ailment which at times prevented him from preaching, and in 1659 his wife died.

From such suffering and doubt came Wigglesworth's poetry. He wrote his verse as a means of serving God by strengthening contemporary belief in the tenets of the Christian religion as he accepted them. His poetic imagination and ability were largely subordinated to his didactic purpose for his untutored readers. His epic poem about judgement day, *The Day of Doom*, begun in 1661 and published in 1662, enjoyed a great and lasting popularity, selling out the 1800 copies of the first edition in a year and going through numerous American and several English editions. It is versified theology, a somewhat pessimistic puritan poetical description of the last judgement with occasional dramatic passages, written in the ballad metre familiar to colonists.

In 1669 Wigglesworth wrote another successful didactic poem, *Meat of the eater, or, A meditation concerning the necessity and usefulness of afflictions unto God's children* (1670), urging Christians to endure tribulation and hope for better times. This was divided into a number of sections of some ten or twelve eight-line stanzas, and shows particularly how his style was in general quaint and harsh. In addition, he published a collection of verses, *Riddles Unriddled, or, Christian Paradoxes*, dealing with such ostensible paradoxes as joy in sorrow or liberty in confinement.

In 1663 Wigglesworth went to convalesce in Bermuda for some seven months, but to little effect. On his return in 1664 he found one Benjamin Bunker had been hired as an associate minister. Thereafter Wigglesworth appears to have left the preaching to Bunker and, putting his medical knowledge to good use, acted as a doctor to the community. He also tutored boys for Harvard. Bunker died in 1670 but Wigglesworth did not immediately return to preaching and in 1674 another minister, Benjamin Blackman, arrived and stayed for four years. In 1679, despite the protests of Increase Mather and others, Wigglesworth married his housekeeper, Martha Mudge (1661/2–1690), a woman much younger than himself. They had six children. The scandal of the marriage prompted Wigglesworth to offer his resignation as Malden's pastor, but the town refused to acknowledge it. He may have been invited to

become president of Harvard in 1684 but probably declined because of illness. Another minister, Thomas Cheever, served as preacher in Malden from 1680 but was dismissed in 1686. Wigglesworth had never officially resigned his post and, his health having improved, he resumed his duties as sole pastor in Malden from 1686. Martha died on 4 September 1690, and on 23 June 1691 Wigglesworth married Sybil (1654/5–1708), daughter of Nathaniel Sparhawk [Sparrowhawk] and widow of Jonathan Avery. They had one child. Wigglesworth's good health continued and he even expanded his activities, joining the Cambridge Association, a society of Boston ministers for improving the religious life of the community, and in 1697, while continuing as Malden's minister, he resumed the position of Harvard fellow and tutor until his death.

Wigglesworth died on 10 June 1705 at Malden and was buried there in the old burial-ground. Cotton Mather wrote his funeral sermon and an epitaph in verse, commending him for his skill in healing all manner of ills and asserting with confidence that he now joyfully awaited his day of doom.   LEONARD W. COWIE

Sources J. W. Dean, *Memoir of the Rev. Michael Wigglesworth*, 2nd edn (1871) · F. O. Matthiessen, 'Michael Wigglesworth, a puritan artist', *New England Quarterly*, 1 (1928), 491–504 · J. W. Dean, *The day of doom, also a memoir of Michael Wigglesworth* (1867) · O. L. Jenkins, *The student's handbook of British and American literature* (1876) · S. A. Allibone, *Great authors of all ages* (1880) · K. B. Murdock, 'Wigglesworth, Michael', *DAB* · J. L. Sibley, *Biographical sketches of graduates of Harvard University*, 1 (1873) · M. C. Tyler, *A history of American literature during the colonial times* (1878) · Allibone, *Dict.*, suppl. · D. P. Corey, *The history of Malden* (1899) · R. Crowder, *No featherbed to heaven: a biography of Michael Wigglesworth, 1631–1705* (1962) · R. Craig, 'Wigglesworth, Michael', *ANB*

Archives Mass. Hist. Soc., MS book of autographical notes; records of religious experiences · New England Historical Genealogical Society, Boston, sermon notes, book of exercises, MSS notes

Wigglesworth, Sir Vincent Brian (1899–1994), entomologist, was born on 17 April 1899 in Kirkham, Lancashire, the second of three children of Sydney Wigglesworth, medical practitioner, and his wife, Margaret Emmeline, *née* Pierce. His father had roots going back to the Yorkshire hamlet of Wigglesworth. He was a general practitioner but also a mechanic and inventor who had studied engineering before changing to medicine. His mother was a painter with an eye for colour who had trained at South Kensington. She came from a family of London solicitors who began as Devon yeomen with business and nautical interests. Pierce Sound in north-west Canada was named after an eighteenth-century ancestor. It was the kind of family that produced famous artists (Wigglesworth's elder brother became a landscape painter, a career cut short by his early death in 1936) as well as scientists. Wigglesworth's father was imaginative, encouraging his children to collect material for microscope demonstrations such as the life in a drop of pond water or the circulating corpuscles in the web of a frog's foot. Many years later, Wigglesworth mentioned the fascination of the frog preparation to Sir Charles Sherrington, saying that he used it to identify potential research students. Less than dedicated students glanced down the microscope and passed on, but future 'physiologists' were unable to tear themselves away from the view of blood cells bustling along capillaries. Collecting was helped by his father's passion for motoring. One of Wigglesworth's earliest memories was of tearing through mud and slush at 18 m.p.h. on his father's new motor tricycle, a Singer Trivoiturette, licence plate B 3, the B designating Lanca-shire. An early edition of *The Motor Car* has a picture of Wigglesworth on this machine. The experience left him with an abiding dislike for motor vehicles, in which he was a notably nervous passenger; he never learned to drive. The boys created a natural history museum, Wigglesworth specializing in butterflies and moths, his brother in beetles. His sister, Dorothy Christine, who car-ried the net, recalled those years as among the happiest of their lives. By the age of five Wigglesworth's observation of the larva to pupa to adult transformation of the magpie moth had given him his lifelong love of insects, an inter-est that was passed on in the family. Later generations grew up with a working knowledge of entomology, know-ing that the best place to find fleas was the cinema, because that was where Uncle Brian went to get live speci-mens to study.

Hardening years began with boarding-school at the age of seven, followed by Repton School, where daily readings of the roll of honour named the boys who had just left for the war but would never now return. Wigglesworth served in France in 1918 as a second lieutenant in the Royal Field Artillery before going up to Gonville and Caius Col-lege, Cambridge, the following year. His double first in natural sciences and physiology earned him the Frank Smart studentship and a chance to work under Gowland Hopkins, who had just founded the department of bio-chemistry in a church basement, with Rudolph Peters, Malcolm Dixon, and Joseph Needham as the first students. Wigglesworth gained an MA in 1921 and his MB BCh in 1926. Vertebrate intermediary metabolism earned him an MD in 1929. In 1926 an opportunity arose for him to follow his passion for insects: Professor Patrick Alfred Buxton invited him to the London School of Hygiene and Tropical Medicine to develop the research base in insect physi-ology, needed for the control of harmful insects. Over the next fifteen years Wigglesworth produced more than fifty papers and was elected to the Royal Society in 1939. In this year, with the publication of *The Principles of Insect Physi-ology*, he created a new science. Meanwhile, in 1928 Wigglesworth married Mabel Katherine Semple (*d.* 1986), illustrator of children's books and daughter of Colonel Sir David Semple of the Indian Medical Service. She became Wigglesworth's lifelong companion, helping him with illustrations for many of his books. They had three sons and a daughter, the youngest son and daughter being twins, as was Wigglesworth's father.

In 1943 Wigglesworth was appointed director of a new agricultural research council unit of insect physiology and moved to Cambridge as reader and head of the sub-department of entomology, and, from 1952, Quick profes-sor of biology. His 'top floor' was an association of twenty to twenty-five academics, staff, students, and visiting workers. Research councils were exceptionally farsighted in recognizing the excellence of people as a basis for gov-ernment support, funding individuals in university set-tings rather than buildings, equipment, and institutes. Wigglesworth could now fully develop his skills, working alone, teaching by example, and eschewing entrepreneur-ial science and laboratory work by proxy. Of his nine books, many translated into other languages, and 264 papers, only nineteen were in collaboration with others. Sixty-three came after his official retirement as professor emeritus in 1966. His drawings and photographs showed his incomparable skill as an observer and interpreter of insect structure and development, the keys to physiology and the understanding of function. From his elegant microscopy came the beautiful and lasting illustrations that added interest and clarity to many standard text-books.

In Wigglesworth's hands insects became more than the objects of beauty or work for the anatomist and system-atist that they had been for centuries of entomologists. His contribution was profound because he recognized that insect tissues lend themselves to simple experiments for the solution of fundamental problems in biology. His success as an experimenter came from using the tools of histology and cytology to read the results of simple experi-ments. His work was supremely economical, giving yes or no answers unencumbered by statistical probabilities. He advised students not to measure anything unless they had to, saying that certainty comes from the design of the experiment and the nature of the observation rather than the number of objects that can be counted. He introduced *Rhodnius*, the blood sucking bug from South America, for his famous experiments on moulting hormones. *Rhod-nius*'s characteristic feature is that it initiates moulting or metamorphosis each time it feeds, requiring no fur-ther sustenance until after ecdysis. He grafted together fed and unfed insects to show that moulting is caused by a hormone borne from the haemolymph of the fed to the unfed larvae. He later showed that the moulting hormone came from the prothoracic glands and that a juvenilizing factor from the corpora allata allowed moulting but pre-vented metamorphosis. He scratched his initials in juven-ile hormone extract on the back of a last instar larva. It emerged as an adult with the letters VBW formed in larval integument on a field with the adult pattern. It was a tri-umphant demonstration of the power of a simple tech-nique and of the value of insects for experiment.

The portrait by C. B. Freeth captures Wigglesworth as a shy man, gentle but single-minded, with a clear brain, skilful hands, and a prodigious memory. He built the new science of insect physiology because it was intellectually satisfying and socially valued. He competed with natural phenomena to find out how insects worked, solving nat-urally posed problems in carefully crafted papers that he wrote and illustrated himself. His achievements came from a man, a time, and an opportunity, that were unique. By the time he died much research in his chosen field had become managed, unpublished, or even hidden, with untested information reserved for industrial gain, business profit, political showmanship, or military power. His life illustrated the lesson that science for the public good comes from giving talented individuals the opportunity to solve problems with free dissemination of the results. The world is richer because he had that opportunity.

Wigglesworth's many honours included the CBE in 1950 and a knighthood in 1964. He was awarded the royal medal of the Royal Society in 1955, and the gold medal for insect morphology in 1992. A medal of the Royal Entomological Society was named after him. He died on 12 February 1994 at Melford Court Nursing Home, near Lavenham, Suffolk, and was survived by his four children. A memorial service was held in the chapel of Gonville and Caius College, Cambridge, on 23 April 1994.

MICHAEL LOCKE

Sources personal knowledge (2004) · private information (2004) [W. R. B. Wigglesworth, Dorothy Christine Edwards, and others] · *WWW*, 1991–5 · *The Times* (15 Feb 1994) · *The Independent* (16 Feb 1994) · M. Locke, *Memoirs FRS*, 42 (1996), 541–53 · V. B. Wigglesworth, 'Some memories', *The Caian* (1978–9), 30–44 · B. L. Gupta, 'VBW 90: a birthday present for the journal', *Journal of the Institute of Physiology*, 36 (1990), 295–305 · S. Maddrell, *The Caian* (1993–4), 80–84 · M. Locke, 'Professor Sir Vincent B. Wigglesworth', *International Journal of Insect Morphology and Embryology*, 21 (1992), 101–15 · M. Locke, 'Professor Sir Vincent B. Wigglesworth', *Insect Physiology*, 40 (1994), 823–6 · J. S. Edwards, 'In memoriam: Sir Vincent Brian Wigglesworth', *Developmental Biology*, 166 (1994), 361–2 · M. Locke, 'V. B. Wigglesworth', *Proceedings of the American Philosophical Society*, 141 (1997), 107–14 · P. A. Lawrence and M. Locke, 'A man for our season', *Nature*, 386 (1997), 757–8 · J. Venn and others, eds., *Biographical history of Gonville and Caius College*, 6–7 (1958–78)

Archives CAC Cam., papers | Bodl. Oxf., corresp. with Torkel Weis-Fogh · ICL, corresp. with John Stodart Kennedy · University of Bristol Library, corresp. with H. E. Hinton

Likenesses W. Bird, photograph, 1961, repro. in Locke, *Memoirs FRS*, 540 · C. B. Freeth, watercolour, 1967, U. Cam., zoology department · photograph, repro. in *The Times*

Wealth at death £781,443: probate, 23 June 1994, *CGPLA Eng. & Wales*

Wigham, Eliza (1820–1899), philanthropist and women's activist, was born at 5 South Gray Street, Newington, Edinburgh, on 23 February 1820, the third of the six surviving children of John Wigham (*c*.1784–1864), a shawl manufacturer, and his wife, Jane Richardson (*d*. 1830) of Whitehaven. Her mother died in February 1830, followed by her eldest sister, Ann, aged sixteen, and one of her younger brothers in 1831. Despite these bereavements, Eliza Wigham had a bright and happy childhood; she was brought up as a member of the Society of Friends and was exposed to the social, political, and philanthropic movements of the city at the Salisbury Road home of her father's cousin, John Wigham, an ardent politician and social reformer. The first cause which she herself espoused was that of the abolition of slavery in the British empire and the USA. As a supporter of the American Anti-Slavery Society, led by William Lloyd Garrison, she worked unceasingly, contributing to fund-raising through the Boston Bazaars, actively corresponding with the American Garrisonian leaders, and writing *The Anti-Slavery Cause in America and its Martyrs* (1863). John Wigham remarried; his second wife was Jane Smeal (1801/2–1888),

the daughter of William Smeal, a grocer and leading Quaker in Glasgow, and secretary of the Glasgow Ladies' Emancipation Society. Stepmother and stepdaughter had a very good relationship and together made the Edinburgh Ladies' Emancipation Society one of the most effective Garrisonian organizations in the UK, much to the chagrin of John Wigham himself.

In 1840 Eliza Wigham's sister, Mary, married Joshua Edmundson of Dublin, and her brother John Richardson *Wigham subsequently joined the business of his brother-in-law. Her brother Henry, who was an anti-slavery agitator, a supporter of the temperance cause and the movement for the abolition of capital punishment, and honorary secretary of the Edinburgh Peace Society, settled in Dublin in 1856, joining his brother's engineering business. But Eliza Wigham remained in the family home in South Gray Street with her stepmother after her father's death in 1864. A committed Christian and a diligent attender of the Edinburgh meeting-house, she conducted a Missionary Helpers' Union from her own house, visited the scattered meeting-houses in Scotland, attended the yearly meeting of the Friends in London, and was recorded as a minister in 1867. She signed the total abstinence pledge in the early years of the temperance movement, and when the British Women's Temperance Association Scottish Christian Union was formed in 1876 she became a vice-president, remaining in post until 1898. One of its foremost workers, she spoke on public platforms and lobbied parliament, town councils, and licensing boards to bring legislation to bear on the drink trade.

Eliza Wigham was also a strong adherent to various movements for securing justice to women, socially and politically, including efforts to further medical education for women and their admission to public boards. Her interest in workhouse management was stimulated by her friendship with Elizabeth Fry, whom she had met at the London meetings of the Friends; for many years she regularly visited St Cuthbert's poorhouse. She acted as secretary to the Edinburgh Society for Women's Suffrage from its establishment and espoused the claims of women for parliamentary franchise in private and public. She was also a member of the purity movement opposing legalized vice, and in 1869 was one of the nineteen women who signed the petition against the Contagious Diseases Acts, being secretary of the Edinburgh Committee, which worked hard for the repeal of the acts (1886). She also made frequent visits to and entertained inmates of the Dean Bank Home, established in Edinburgh to prevent destitute young girls falling into crime. In 1859 she started a 'penny bank' near her home in Causeway Side and a Women's Working Society or mothers' meeting in 1860, running both for thirty-seven years. She was also a fearless advocate for the cause of peace, supporting international arbitration instead of war and actively supporting the victims of the Franco-Prussian War of 1870 and the victims of oppression in Bosnia and Armenia. In November 1888 Jane Wigham died at the age of eighty-six after a long period of illness, during which she had been nursed by her stepdaughter. Eliza Wigham, despite lameness caused by rheumatic gout, continued to live in South Gray Street until after her brother Henry's death in 1897, when she finally gave in to her relatives' entreaties to move to Dublin. She sold up in Edinburgh and moved in with her widowed sister-in-law in May 1898. She continued to attend Quaker meetings for as long as possible but her strength failed in the summer of 1899 and she grew rapidly weaker by the autumn. She moved to her sister Mary's house at Foxrock, near Dublin, ten days before her death on 3 November 1899. Resolute and dauntless in the fight for liberty, progress, and righteousness, Eliza Wigham had been one of the leading citizens of Edinburgh of her era.   LESLEY M. RICHMOND

Sources *Annual Monitor* (1900), 164–87 · *Scottish Women's Temperance News*, 6/2 (June 1898), 85 · E. M. Mein, 'Miss Eliza Wigham', [n.d., *c.*1965], Edinburgh City Library · *Scottish Women's Temperance News*, 12/3 (Dec 1899), 189 · C. E. Robertson, *British Women's Temperance Association Scottish Christian Union: its origin and progress* (1908) · *Annual Report of British Women's Temperance Association, Scottish Christian Union* (1888–1900) · C. Taylor, *British and American abolitionists: an episode in transatlantic understanding* (1974) · C. D. Rice, *The Scots abolitionists, 1833–1861* (1981) · J. Goodfellow, *The print of his shoe: forty years missionary experience in the southside of Edinburgh* (1906) · Boase, *Mod. Eng. biog.*

Archives Boston PL, Boston MSS

Likenesses photograph, 1890–99 (in extreme old age), repro. in Goodfellow, *Print of his shoe* · photograph, repro. in *Scottish Women's Temperance News*, 1/1 (1896), 7 · photograph, repro. in Robertson, *British Women's Temperance Association*, 13

Wealth at death £3634 7s. 7d.: probate, 20 Dec 1899, *CGPLA Ire.*

Wigham, John Richardson (1829–1906), engineer and inventor of gas lighting for lighthouses, was born on 15 January 1829 at 5 South Gray Street, Edinburgh, the youngest of three sons (there were three daughters) of John Wigham (*c.*1784–1864), shawl manufacturer, of Edinburgh and his wife, Jane Richardson (*d.* 1830); his father was a member of the Society of Friends. Eliza *Wigham, the women's activist, was his sister. Eliza *Wigham was his elder sister. Following meagre schooling at Edinburgh, he went in 1843 to Dublin, where he continued his studies privately while serving as apprentice to his brother-in-law, Joshua Edmundson, who ran a hardware and manufacturing business. The business subsequently traded as Joshua Edmundson & Co. and then transferred to Wigham's control on the death of Edmundson.

With Wigham as chairman, Edmundson's Electricity Corporation grew rapidly; a branch was opened in London and taken over by a separate company. In Dublin the firm devoted itself largely to experiments in gas-lighting and Wigham was particularly successful in designing small gasworks suitable for private houses and public institutions. In addition to his private business he held various engineering posts, and as engineer to the Commercial Gas Company of Ireland he designed the gasworks at Kingstown (later Dún Laoghaire). Wigham also played a prominent part in the commercial life of Dublin. He was a director of the Alliance and Dublin Consumers' Gas Company from 1866 until his death; director and vice-chairman of the Dublin United Tramways Company from 1881 to his death; and a member of council (1879), secretary (1881–93), and eventually president (1894–6) of

the Dublin chamber of commerce. Wigham was married, on 4 August 1858, to Mary, daughter of Jonathan *Pim of Dublin, MP for Dublin City from 1865 to 1874; they had six sons and four daughters, of whom three sons and three daughters survived him.

Wigham is remembered mainly as the inventor of important applications of gas to lighthouse illumination. In 1863 he was granted a small sum for experiments by the commissioners of Irish lights, and in 1865 a system invented by him was installed at the Baily lighthouse on Howth Head near Dublin. The gas was manufactured on the spot and the system's main advantages were that it dispensed with the lamp glass essential to the four-wick Fresnel oil lamp of 240 candle-power, in use from 1835, and that the power of the light could readily be increased or decreased: a 28 jet flame, which gave sufficient light for clear weather, could be increased successively to a 48 jet, 68 jet, 88 jet, or 108 jet flame—2923 candle-power—on foggy nights. Although highly valued in Ireland, the system was condemned on trial by Thomas Stevenson, engineer to the Scottish northern lights board. It was made more effective, however, by Wigham's invention of a powerful composite burner in 1868, and in 1869 its further employment in Ireland was strongly advocated by John Tyndall in his capacity as scientific adviser to Trinity House and the Board of Trade. Wigham's ingenuity also acted as a powerful stimulant to rival patentees and led to various improvements in oil apparatus by Sir James Nicholas Douglass and others.

In 1871 Wigham invented the first of the many group-flashing arrangements which enabled mariners to distinguish between different lighthouses. His arrangement was adopted at Galley Head, Mew Head, and Tory Island off the Irish coast. In 1872 a triform light of his invention was installed experimentally at the High lighthouse, Happisburgh, Norfolk; but its further adoption in English lighthouses was discouraged by a committee of Trinity House in 1874. The Irish lights board, however, continued to favour Wigham's system, and in 1878 they installed at Galley Head a powerful quadriform light with four tiers of superposed lenses and a 68 jet burner in the focus of each tier. In 1883 the Board of Trade appointed a lighthouse illuminants committee to consider the relative merits of gas, oil, and electric light. For some years Tyndall had felt that Sir James Douglass had used his influence as engineer to Trinity House for the furtherance of his own patents, to the disadvantage of Wigham's system. He now protested that, as rival patentees, Douglass and Wigham ought both to be members of the lighthouse illuminants committee or ought both to be excluded. His objection was overruled, and consequently he resigned his position as scientific adviser to the Board of Trade in March 1883. A bitter controversy followed in the press between Tyndall and Joseph Chamberlain, president of the Board of Trade. On Tyndall's resignation the lighthouse illuminants committee collapsed. A new committee, of which Douglass was a member, was appointed by Trinity House and, after extensive experiments at South Foreland, it decided to recommend oil and electric light in preference to gas. Wigham protested against his lack of opportunity to demonstrate the advantages of his system, and claimed that his rival Douglass, who had condemned in official reports Wigham's invention of superposed lenses, afterwards employed them for the improvement of his own oil apparatus. Wigham eventually received £2500 from the Board of Trade as compensation for the infringement of his patent. Among Wigham's other inventions were a device for fog signals; a gas-driven siren; a 'sky-flashing arrangement' and a 'continuous pulsating light' in connection with his system of gas illumination for lighthouses; and a lighted buoy or beacon in which, using oil as the illuminant, he obtained, by imparting motion to the wick, a continuous light needing attention only once in thirty days.

Wigham was a member of the Royal Dublin Society and of the Royal Irish Academy, an associate member of the Institution of Civil Engineers, and a fellow of the Institution of Mechanical Engineers. He read papers on gas as a lighthouse illuminant and related subjects before the Society of Arts, the British Association, the Royal Dublin Society, and the Shipmasters' Society. In politics he was a unionist and a member of the Irish Unionist Alliance, and he spoke at public meetings against Gladstone's Home Rule Bill. He was also one of the leaders of the temperance movement in Dublin. As a member of the Society of Friends (the Quakers) he twice refused knighthood in 1887. He died on 16 November 1906 at his residence, Albany House, Monkstown, co. Dublin, after four years of ill health. He was buried on 19 November in the Quaker burial-ground, Temple Hill, Blackrock, co. Dublin. He was survived by his wife. S. E. FRYER, *rev.* R. C. COX

Sources *The Times* (17 Nov 1906) · J. Tyndall, 'A story of our lighthouses', *Nineteenth Century*, 24 (1888), 61–80 · *Nautical Magazine*, 52 (1883), 620 · *Nautical Magazine*, 52 (1884), 547 · *Fortnightly Review*, 50 (1888), 805–28 · *Fortnightly Review*, 51 (1889), 198 · private information (2004) · *Irish Times* (17 Nov 1906)
Likenesses photograph, *c.*1895, Dublin Chamber of Commerce
Wealth at death £7959 10*s.* 3*d.*: Irish probate sealed in London, 2 Jan 1907, *CGPLA Eng. & Wales*

Wigheard [Wighard] (*d.* **664×7**), archbishop-elect of Canterbury, was a Kentish priest and cleric under Archbishop Deusdedit. Following the death of Deusdedit in July 664, he was nominated as archbishop by Ecgberht, king of Kent, and sent to Rome, where he died of the plague before he could be consecrated. The existence of a letter from Pope Vitalian to Oswiu, king of Northumbria, apparently answering a request to appoint an archbishop, led Bede to infer that Wigheard had been sent jointly by both kings. This is unlikely. The pope did, however, probably consult some of Wigheard's companions on the question of filling the vacant see of Canterbury, to which he eventually appointed Theodore in March 668.

MARY BATESON, *rev.* MARIOS COSTAMBEYS

Sources Bede, *Hist. eccl.*, 3.29; 4.1 · J. M. Wallace-Hadrill, *Bede's Ecclesiastical history of the English people: a historical commentary*, OMT (1988)

Wight, Alexander (*d.* **1793**), advocate and writer on election law, was the son of David Wight, writer, of Edinburgh. Wight attended the University of Edinburgh

between 1745 and 1748. He was admitted a member of the Faculty of Advocates on 6 March 1754 and in time established himself as a leading counsel. In 1773 he published, with a dedication to Lord Mansfield, *A treatise on the laws concerning the election of the different representatives sent from Scotland to the parliament of Great Britain, with a preliminary view of the constitution of the parliaments of England and Scotland before the union of the two kingdoms*. Wight revised and updated the *Treatise*, his researches resulting in a more substantial work which appeared in 1784 as *An inquiry into the rise and progress of parliament, chiefly in Scotland; and a complete system of the law concerning the elections of the representatives from Scotland to the parliament of Great Britain*. The work was seen as authoritative; a new and updated edition in two volumes, with cases arranged by William Maxwell Morison, appeared in 1806. It remained the standard work on the subject up to the Reform Act of 1832. Principal Robertson referred to it in his *History of Scotland* when he wrote

> Various questions concerning the constituent members of the Scottish parliament, concerning the era at which the representatives of the boroughs were introduced into that assembly; and concerning the origin and power of the committee of the lords of articles, occur, and have been agitated with great warmth. Since the first publication of this work, all these disputed points have been considered with calmness and accuracy in Mr Wight's *Inquiry*. (Robertson, 188n.)

There are scant details with which to give a truly rounded portrait of Wight's career and character. He was an active member of several faculty committees, and in 1777 he was appointed to the dean's council by the dean of the faculty, Henry Dundas. In 1783 Wight succeeded Ilay Campbell as solicitor-general in the administration of the duke of Portland, to whom the *Inquiry* was dedicated; Wight's interest in electoral reform may have recommended him to the Foxite element in the Portland administration. However, in 1784 William Pitt the younger replaced him by Robert Dundas of Arniston. Wight's distance from his earlier association with Dundas was shown by his subsequent appointment as a counsellor of state to the prince of Wales. Wight was vice-president of the Society of Antiquaries of Scotland and a director of the Musical Society of Edinburgh. He enjoyed a close friendship with another advocate, the gifted but dissipated Andrew Crosbie, and like Crosbie was financially embarrassed by the collapse of Douglas, Heron & Co., the Ayr bank, of which he was a director. Wight was married to Marion Blyth (*d.* 1825), and died in Edinburgh on 18 March 1793. LIONEL ALEXANDER RITCHIE

Sources F. J. Grant, ed., *The Faculty of Advocates in Scotland, 1532–1943*, Scottish RS, 145 (1944), 219 · D. M. Walker, *A legal history of Scotland*, 5 (1998), 25, 349, 826 · D. M. Walker, *The Scottish jurists* (1985), 281 · *Scots Magazine*, 55 (1793), 154 · C. Kidd, *Subverting Scotland's past: Scottish whig historians and the creation of an Anglo-British identity, 1689–c.1830* (1993), 108, 136, 141 · A. Fergusson, ed., *The Honourable Henry Erskine* (1882), 252n. · W. Robertson, *The history of Scotland*, 1 (1802), 188n. · J. Maidment, *The court of session garland* (1888), 68 · A. Stewart, ed., *The minute book of the Faculty of Advocates*, 3: 1751–

1783, Stair Society, 46 (1999) · M. Fry, *The Dundas despotism* (1992) · *IGI*

Wight, Andrew (*bap.* **1719**, *d.* **1792**), farmer and writer on agriculture, was baptized at Ormiston, near Haddington, on 7 January 1719, which was possibly also the day of his birth. He was the son of Alexander Wight (*d.* 1751) and Kathrin Simpson. He married Mary Brown (1740/41–1808) on 29 December 1758, and the couple had six children.

Like his father and grandfather before him, Wight was regarded as a highly innovative and efficient tenant farmer on the Cockburn estate at Ormiston. At the instigation of Henry Home, Lord Kames, he was appointed in 1773 to survey the corn farms under the control of the commissioners to manage the annexed estates. The commissioners were responsible for thirteen estates, which had been forfeited and annexed to the crown through the attainder of their owners' treason after the Jacobite rising in 1745. The commissioners generally took a philanthropic view of their tenants, believing that their principal objective should be to 'civilise the people of the estates, and by kind treatment to make them good subjects' (Wight, 1.v). A key element in this programme of social amelioration was the improvement of tenants' husbandry. Wight's brief was consequently to provide reports on the current material condition of the estates (including such items as soil type, crops sown, implements used, and prices of labour and provisions), and to suggest ways in which the farms might be made more productive. Wight undertook two surveys of the estates in July and August 1773 and 1774. The commissioners were so pleased with the results that they subsequently engaged Wight on an annual basis to undertake general surveys of Scotland for the purpose of both recording and disseminating good farming practice. His findings were published by the commissioners as *Present State of Husbandry in Scotland* (1778–84). In nine years Wight covered more than 4000 miles, and produced agrarian reports on nearly the whole of Scotland (the exceptions are Shetland, Orkney, and Argyll). He died on 11 March 1792, his wife surviving him. Wight is generally regarded as an acute observer of agrarian practices and the changes in the landscape during this period, though the later surveys are slanted heavily in favour of the methods of improvers. The *Present State of Husbandry in Scotland* remains a valuable resource for modern economic historians of eighteenth-century Scotland.

SEBASTIAN MITCHELL

Sources J. A. S. Watson and G. D. Amery, 'Early Scottish agricultural writers (1697–1790)', *Transactions of the Highland and Agricultural Society of Scotland*, 5th ser., 43 (1931), 60–85 · G. E. Fussell, *More old English farming books, … 1731–1793* (1950), vol. 2 of *The old English farming books* (1947–91) · A. Wight, *Present state of husbandry in Scotland*, 4 vols. (1778–84) · A. Young, 'Review of new publications relating to agriculture', *Annals of agriculture and other useful arts*, ed. A. Young, 1 (1784), 357–69 [review of Wight's *Present state of husbandry*] · W. Y. Whitehead, *History of Ormiston* (1937) · parish register (baptism), 7 Jan 1719, Ormiston, Haddingtonshire · parish register (marriage), 29 Dec 1758, Ormiston, Haddingtonshire · J. Donaldson, *Agricultural biography* (1854) · H. Hamilton, *An economic history of Scotland in the eighteenth century* (1963) · H. Hamilton, *The industrial revolution in Scotland* (1932) · A. J. Youngson, *After the Forty-Five: the economic impact on the Scottish highlands* (1973) · monumental inscriptions record, Haddington Local History Society

Wight, James Alfred [*pseud.* James Herriot] (**1916–1995**), writer and veterinarian, was born on 3 October 1916 at 111 Brandling Street, Sunderland, the only child of James Henry Wight (*d.* 1960), a ship plater and accomplished musician, and Hannah, *née* Bell (*d.* 1981), a talented contralto who sang at local concerts. Alf was born in the house owned by his maternal grandfather, Robert Bell, a printer. Immediately after their marriage, James Henry and Hannah moved to Glasgow, where there was much work for a ship plater in the First World War, but Hannah came back to her parents' home to have the baby. Three weeks later, the family moved permanently to Glasgow.

Early years and education The first Wight home in Glasgow was a ground-floor flat of a tenement in the suburb of Yoker. Although working-class, the family was far from the bottom rung of the economic ladder and its relatively spacious accommodation was in no way a slum dwelling. An advantage of living in Yoker was that fields and farmlands were within walking distance. James Henry supplemented his income by leading a cinema orchestra, but with the end of the war, shipbuilding slumped and he lost his job at the yard. He went to work as a joiner and later, when Alf was in his teens, opened a fish and chip shop. Hannah, meanwhile, turned a room of the family home into a dressmaker's and remained in the business for thirty years.

Alf Wight attended Yoker primary school, where he loved history, did well in English, but had trouble with arithmetic. Wight entered Hillhead high school, Glasgow, in September 1928. He was an avid reader and an outstanding student, but he also excelled at sports, especially tennis. As a reward for his excellent schoolwork, Wight was given an Irish setter in 1928, the first of a long line of dogs. The following year he read an article in *Meccano Magazine* describing the career of a veterinarian. As a dog-lover and as a bright young man considering a possible career, he quickly decided to become an animal doctor. A visit to Glasgow Veterinary College, then under the principalship of Dr A. W. Whitehouse, confirmed Wight in his vocation.

On 29 June 1933, in the midst of the great depression, Wight left high school with a higher education leaving certificate and was qualified for admission to veterinary college when four months short of his seventeenth birthday. College life was a surprise, however. The extracurricular part—gambling, partying, drinking, and playing practical jokes—amazed a young man whose parents seldom drank alcohol and who were very circumspect in their use of language. But Wight was a hard-working student and he was well aware that the cost of tuition and his keep was a burden on his family. Although instruction at Glasgow Veterinary College was out of date and the school was not the premier institution in its field, Wight benefited from hands-on experience.

Appointment at Thirsk, marriage, and war years On 14 December 1939 Wight qualified as a member of the Royal

College of Veterinary Surgeons. He took up his first job in January 1940, serving as assistant to a veterinarian named J. J. McDowall in Sunderland. As it was a temporary position, he continued to look for a more permanent appointment. In June a position with the practice of Donald V. Sinclair became available 50 miles away in Thirsk. Wight was offered a junior partnership with a salary and he arrived in Thirsk on 18 July, and lived above the surgery at 23 Kirkgate. Almost immediately, Sinclair joined the Royal Air Force and departed, leaving Wight to run a practice that primarily treated large animals—horses, cattle, sheep—in an unfamiliar area. Under McDowall, Wight had mainly treated cats and dogs, and indeed his interest was in caring for small animals. Yet he worked hard and learned fast. Sinclair was dismissed from the RAF in November 1940 for having lied about his age. He was nearly thirty and too old for pilot training. However, his expertise with large animals was more valuable for the war effort in helping maintain the precious food supply. Brian Sinclair, Donald Sinclair's younger brother and frequent antagonist, came to live with the bachelors during his summers off from veterinary school. Donald and Brian Sinclair became the models for Siegfried and Tristan Farnon in the Herriot saga and Thirsk was transformed into Darrowby.

At a dance in March 1941 Wight met Joan Catherine Anderson Danbury (1918/19–1999), a secretary. Although he had signed up to join the RAF and knew that eventually he would be called for flight training, Wight proposed in July and was accepted. He and Joan married on 5 November 1941 at St Mary Magdalene Church in Thirsk. The couple's first home was on the top floor of the building that housed the surgery. On 3 October 1942 Wight was finally called for active duty. The long delay reflected the fact that veterinary medicine was a reserved occupation, and Britain had a large number of volunteers for the Royal Air Force. Although Wight trained hard and wanted to fly for Britain, he was absent without leave on more than one occasion so he could visit Joan, who was pregnant with their first child; luckily, he was never caught. On 13 February 1943 he was in Thirsk for the birth of James Alexander Wight.

Wight finally learned to fly and took his first solo flight on 7 June 1943. Shortly afterwards, a medical condition from which he had suffered since youth flared up. After surgery and convalescence, followed by dental problems, he decided to apply for a discharge, and on 10 November 1943 he was sent home. Back in Thirsk, Wight found that the business had grown since his departure. He now wanted a full partnership in the practice, but did not receive it until 1949. The Wights' second and last child, Rosemary Beatrice, was born on 9 May 1949. They finally moved to a house of their own in 1953. Wight had bought a plot of land on Topcliffe Road and had a house built to Joan's specifications.

Breakdown and first writings The death of Wight's father on 8 April 1960 was a great psychological blow. The two had always been close, as much friends as father and son. At the time Wight was working extremely hard in the practice and worried about money for the children's

higher education. He suffered a nervous breakdown, underwent psychiatric treatment, and eventually recovered from his depression with the help of his wife, colleagues, and friends. In 1961 he accepted an assignment as a Ministry of Agriculture veterinarian on a trip to the Soviet Union. He fulfilled the same role in Spain in 1962 and in Istanbul in 1963. As more and more the idea of writing a book about his life as a country vet possessed Wight, he began to write seriously. It seems to have helped him to deal with his depression and even to order, soften, and perhaps idealize his memories. He frequently talked to Joan about it, and finally she scornfully informed him that men nearly fifty did not write books. Stung, Wight set out with determination in 1965 to put on paper the book in his head. After a year and a half he had finished a novel, which was rejected. He was, however, encouraged to recast his material in the form of a memoir. He rewrote the novel as a first-person narrative, a fictionalized autobiography called *If Only they could Talk*. After some rejections the book was placed by an agent with Michael Joseph.

Wight was reluctant to use his own name as the author because the Royal Academy of Veterinary Surgeons forbade advertising, and the book could be perceived as such. Watching Birmingham City and Manchester United play football one February evening, Wight hit on the idea of using the name of the Birmingham goalkeeper, James Herriot, as his pen-name. *If Only they could Talk* was published in April 1970. It was modestly successful. A sequel, *It shouldn't Happen to a Vet*, followed in 1972. Newspaper serialization made the character of James Herriot a familiar figure in Britain. *Let Sleeping Vets Lie* appeared in April 1973 and *Vet in Harness* the next year. Reviews were good, and paperback sales were enormous.

Literary success and the Herriot industry In summer 1970 Tom McCormack, the enterprising head of St Martin's Press in New York, was in London looking for books that could rack up significant sales in the US. He was given a copy of *If Only they could Talk* and considered publishing it, but it was too short. When he learned that *It shouldn't Happen to a Vet* had also been published, he was even more interested. The two books together would make a more marketable book in the States. He got Wight to add chapters about Herriot's wedding and they hit on the perfect title for the American publication—a line from the hymn 'All things bright and beautiful'—*All Creatures Great and Small*. The book was published in November 1972 and with McCormack's marketing campaign, the reviews were outstanding. In February 1973 Wight was brought to America twice for successful book tours.

Alf Wight, as James Herriot, had become the most famous veterinarian in the world. His gentle, humorous, compassionate stories set in a somewhat remote place and a distant time had captured the imagination of an enormous number of readers. Mainly through reworking episodes from the memoirs, a Herriot industry was constructed with books about cats and dogs; delightful children's books; *James Herriot's Yorkshire* (1979), a photo-travel book; and *The Best of James Herriot* (1982). But the Herriot saga's greatest success was in film and television. First came a motion picture shot in 1974, *All Creatures Great and Small*, with Simon Ward as Herriot and Anthony Hopkins as Siegfried. *It shouldn't Happen to a Vet* with John Alderton and Colin Blakely was filmed in 1975. In 1977 Wight bought the house in Thirlby that was to be his last home. In that year the BBC began filming the television series *All Creatures Great and Small*, starring Christopher Timothy and Robert Hardy. Four series and forty-one episodes appeared over thirteen years.

Although the stories are part fiction, the life of James Herriot was not so different from that of his creator. Both were healers of animals and both had gentle, self-deprecating senses of humour. Of medium height and weight, Wight had a ruddy complexion, high forehead, and light brown, somewhat wavy hair that turned a silvery white as he aged. In 1979 he was appointed OBE and in that same year received an honorary DLitt from Heriot-Watt University, Edinburgh. Wight was elected a fellow of the Royal College of Veterinary Surgeons in 1982 and was awarded an honorary DVSc from Liverpool University in 1983. In 1992 he was the British Veterinary Association's first recipient of the Chiron award, designed to acknowledge exceptional achievement in the field.

James Alfred Wight died of cancer at Mire Beck, Thirlby, on 23 February 1995. In 1999 Jim Wight published the authorized biography of his father, *The Real James Herriot*. Thirsk, the town known to millions of viewers worldwide as Darrowby, remains a tourist destination. 'Skeldale House' at number 23 Kirkgate, restored to how it was in the 1940s, has become a museum of veterinary science, while the region of north Yorkshire in which it lies is still known as Herriot Country.   SANFORD STERNLICHT

Sources J. Wight, *The real James Herriot* (1999) · S. Sternlicht, *All things Herriot: James Herriot and his peaceable kingdom* (1995) · M. M. Brunsdale, *James Herriot* (1997) · M. J. Rossie, *James Herriot: a critical companion* (1997) · J. Herriot, *James Herriot's Yorkshire* (1979) · C. Moorhead, 'How a country vet turned into a best seller', *The Times* (23 July 1976) · R. R. Lingeman, 'Animal doctor', *NY Times Book Review* (18 Sept 1977), 13 · S. Kanfer, 'The Marcus Welby of the barn yard', *Time* (29 June 1981), 14 · 'Interview with James Herriot', *Maclean's* (29 May 1976), 5
Likenesses photographs, *c.*1970–1975, Hult. Arch.
Wealth at death £5,425,873: probate, 1 Sept 1995, *CGPLA Eng. & Wales*

Wight, (Robert James) Martin (1913–1972), historian and expert on international affairs, was born on 26 November 1913 at 9 Bath Square, Brighton, Sussex, the second of the three children, all sons, of Edward Wight (1879–1959), general medical practitioner, and his wife, Margaretta, *née* Scott (1880–1942). From Prestonville House School, Hove, and Bradfield College (1927–32), Martin, as he was known, went on to take a first in modern history at Hertford College, Oxford, in 1935. He then joined the Royal Institute of International Affairs at Chatham House, London, to work under A. J. Toynbee, for many years a strong influence. A baptized Anglican, he now became a Christian pacifist and worked with the Revd Dick Shepphard. In 1938 he succeeded J. Hampden Jackson as senior history master at Haileybury College, Hertford, where he at once showed a

flair for teaching. His pupils, with whom he had a strong mutual rapport, had considerable successes, winning Oxbridge college scholarships. In 1941 he was granted exemption from military service on condition that he abandoned teaching. His objections to serving were personal: the war was a divine judgement on a backsliding world for whose sins all were responsible. Pacifism was a vocation to which he felt a calling. (He later ignored the Campaign for Nuclear Disarmament, which he regarded as a political campaign.)

From 1941, until he returned to Chatham House in 1946, Wight worked under Margery Perham on the evolution of British African colonial constitutions. The resulting three books were of lasting importance to their subject. When the war ended, he was one of several Christian historians (Herbert Butterfield and Reinhold Niebuhr were others) from whom the experiences of the time drew out eschatological reflections and a prophetic interest in the divine indications of secular history: he was to remain impressed by St Augustine's *City of God*. By 1949, when he moved to the London School of Economics (LSE) as reader in international affairs, his religious beliefs no longer obtruded into his academic work. But his conviction that the true understanding of history lay outside the boundaries of secular experience gave him a magisterial authority with students happy to have their horizons extended beyond the intricacies of post-war international institutions. He continuously refined a course of lectures on what he called international theory, an attempt to categorize the ideas which had influenced the conduct of states in relation to each other. He found three traditions: realist (from Machiavelli to E. H. Carr), rationalist (Grotius and the natural law jurists of the seventeenth century to Gladstone, Lincoln, and F. D. Roosevelt), and revolutionist (from Kant to Lenin and Hitler). The elaboration of his ideas in a wide chronological and geographical sweep was illuminated by anecdotal evidence deftly drawn from a prodigious learning, from Thucydides to *Mein Kampf*. His pupils included Hedley Bull, who edited and published Wight's two unfinished works: *Systems of States* (1977) and, with Carsten Holbrad, *Power Politics* (1978), which was expanded from a 1946 pamphlet with that title which had immediately established Wight's authority. In these books Wight examined historically how sovereign states sought to protect their security and forward their interests by diplomacy, alliance, intervention, war, and, most successfully, by manipulation of the balance of power. The original LSE lectures, edited by his widow and Brian Porter, were published as *International Theory: the Three Traditions* (1991). This now substantial *œuvre* drew from Adam Roberts, Bull's successor in the Montague Burton chair of international relations at Oxford, the comment that Wight was 'perhaps the most profound thinker on international relations of his generation of British academics' (foreword to *International Theory*, xxiv).

In 1958 Butterfield and Wight convened at Cambridge a small body of academics and diplomats, under Rockefeller Foundation patronage, as the British committee on the theory of international politics. From its periodic meetings came, in 1966, *Diplomatic Investigations*, which contained Wight's two most influential essays, 'Why is there no international theory?' and 'Western values in international relations'.

Wight's ideas ran directly against the rising transatlantic tide of behaviourism, systems analysis, and games theory which constructed value- and history-free models from the social sciences to provide techniques for crisis management and the avoidance of war. Wight's concern was with understanding (*Verstehen*), not with predictions or solutions. He believed that this could only be found historically by considering the interplay between ideas (including morals) and events (Wight was an admirer of R. G. Collingwood). In the anarchical world of sovereign states, theory followed rather than determined events and morality was often defined, and monopolized, by sated powers. The most the student or statesman could hope for was intelligent rumination and reflection on the evidence. Though he had a natural propensity for model building, he was always the first to cast doubt on his own findings: 'Classification becomes valuable in humane studies only at the point at which it breaks down' (*International Theory*, 259). Ideal types and paradigms were at best artificial constructs.

In 1961 Wight was appointed, as one of the nine original members of the academic faculty, to the new University of Sussex, as professor of history and founding dean of the school of European studies (the first in Britain). He pioneered an ambitious course, taught in tutorials, involving a language, philosophy, literature, social studies, and thematic history. The rapid proliferation of languages and options may, over time, have given the school a looser intellectual coherence than Wight had intended, but his enthusiasm and dedication ensured that it fulfilled his aim: 'if half of a liberal education in the twentieth century is to gain an understanding of the world we live in, the other half consists in breaking its influence and finding deliverance from the tyranny of the immediate, the novel and the transitory' (D. Daiches, ed., *The Idea of a New University*, 1964, 105).

Wight was a tall, handsome man, with an air of gentle authority (and a strong sense of the ridiculous). He married, on 23 December 1952, Gabriele, *née* Ritzen (*b*. 6 December 1928 in Ulm, Germany), a recent graduate of Reading University. They had six children and lived first in Caterham, Surrey, and from 1960 in Speldhurst in Kent. Wight was not naturally gregarious, but formed lasting close friendships maintained by frequent correspondence in a beautiful hand. He died suddenly at his home at Harwarton, Speldhurst, Tunbridge Wells, Kent, on 15 July 1972 from heart failure following an attack of his chronic asthma, and was buried at Speldhurst. He is commemorated by an annual lecture given, in rotation, at Chatham House, the London School of Economics, and Sussex University. H. G. PITT

Sources *The Times* (17 July 1972) · A. Briggs, *The Times* (19 July 1972) · C. A. W. Manning, *The Times* (21 July 1972) · A. J. Toynbee, *The Times* (3 Aug 1972) · H. Bull, 'Martin Wight and the study of international relations', in M. Wight, *Systems of states*, ed. H. Bull (1977), 1–20 · H. Bull, 'Martin Wight and the theory of international relations', *British Journal of International Studies*, 2 (1976), 101–16 [second Martin Wight memorial lecture] · personal knowledge (2004) · private information (2004)

Archives BLPES, corresp., research notes, and papers

Wealth at death £28,551: probate, 12 Oct 1972, *CGPLA Eng. & Wales* · £197.26: probate, 1973, *CGPLA Éire*

Wight, Robert (1796–1872), botanist, was born at Milton, Duncra Hill, East Lothian, on 6 July 1796, the twelfth of fourteen children of Alexander Wight, a writer to the signet, and his wife, Jane. He was educated at Edinburgh high school and the University of Edinburgh, gaining his surgeon's diploma in 1816 and graduating MD two years later.

Wight went on several voyages as surgeon, including one to America, before entering the East India Company's service in 1819. He was appointed assistant surgeon on 25 May of that year, and attached to the 42nd native infantry stationed at Madras, where he employed Indians to collect plants, and, then knowing little about botany, obtained copies of G. L. Willdenow's *Species plantarum*, C. H. Persoon's *Synopsis*, and an English translation of Linnaeus's *Genera plantarum*. A collection sent by him to Professor Robert Graham in 1823 was lost at sea, but one formed at Samulcotta, Rajahmundry, Vellore, and Madras, reached W. J. Hooker at Glasgow in 1826. In that year Wight was appointed to succeed James Shuter as naturalist in the Madras presidency. He made an extensive tour, lasting nine months, in the southern provinces (his route is marked on the map in N. Wallich's *Plantae Asiaticae rariores*) during which he collected birds, insects, and minerals as well as many plants. In 1828, on the abolition of his Madras office, Wight was appointed garrison surgeon at Negapatam and thoroughly explored that neighbourhood and Tanjore, employing Indian collectors and artists at his own expense.

In 1831, having attained the rank of surgeon on 22 February, Wight contracted jungle fever and returned home on three years' leave, most of which he spent in Edinburgh. He carried with him about 100,000 plant specimens, the duplicates of which he distributed to institutions and individuals in Britain and Europe. He published an account of part of his Indian collection in four articles in W. J. Hooker's *Botanical Miscellany* (vols. 2 and 3, 1830–33). These were included in his *Illustrations of Indian Botany, Principally of the Southern Parts of the Peninsula* (1831–2). This book and three of the four articles incorrectly give Wight's forename as Richard.

However, during his leave Wight was mainly occupied in preparing, with George Walker-Arnott, one of his chief works, the *Prodromus florae peninsulae Indiae orientalis* (1839), which J. D. Hooker and T. Thomson, in their introductory essay to the *Flora Indica* (1855), described as 'the most able and valuable contribution to Indian botany which has ever appeared, and one which has few rivals in the whole domain of botanical literature'. Wight's return

Robert Wight (1796–1872), by Maull & Polyblank, 1855

to India resulted in only the first volume's being published: even so, that work describes nearly fourteen hundred species, using A. P. de Candolle's natural classification, and in 1833–7 Wight issued a lithographic catalogue of 2400 species enumerated in it. While Wight was staying with Hooker in Glasgow he learned the craft of lithography and purchased presses and tools to use in India. With J. E. Smith's and J. Sowerby's *English Botany* (1790–1814) as his model, it was his intention to publish a series of plates of Indian plants.

On returning to India in 1834 Wight was attached to the 33rd native infantry at Bellary, and marched with them to Palamcottai, near Cape Comorin, a distance of some 700 miles. There he recruited three Indian collectors. He then planned a systematic series of plates to illustrate J. R. Ainslie's *Materia medica of Hindustaan* (1813; 2nd edn, 1826), a scheme which he never carried out but in the course of which he published various papers on medicinal plants in the *Madras Journal of Science*. The garden formed by the Agri-Horticultural Society of Madras in 1835 got off to a good start with Wight as its dynamic secretary. The following year he was seized with a severe attack of fever in Tinnevelly and convalesced for a few weeks in Ceylon. In the same year he was relieved of military duties and transferred to the revenue department, with instructions to investigate the state of agriculture in south India, in particular, cotton, tobacco, coffee, senna, and other useful plants. In this capacity he had charge from February 1842 to 1850 of experimental cotton farms at Coimbatore. (A

detailed account of his work there is given in J. F. Royle, *On the Culture and Commerce of Cotton in India*, 1851, 467–523.) On 17 January 1838 Wight married Rosa Harriet, daughter of Lacy Gray Ford of the Madras medical board.

By 1838 Wight had trained a team of Indian craftsmen capable of lithographing two illustrated books almost simultaneously. He embarked on their publication fully convinced that textual descriptions of plants alone were inadequate. *Illustrations of Indian Botany* (1838–50) ceased after only two volumes with 182 crudely hand-coloured plates by Indian artists. The 2101 plates in the companion work, *Icones plantarum Indiae orientalis* (1838–53), were uncoloured. Although the government of Madras subscribed to a small number of copies, Wight lost money on the venture but he had the satisfaction of knowing that 'The Indian Flora can now, I believe, boast of being more fully illustrated than that of any other country under British sway, Great Britain alone excepted' (*Icones*, 6, 1853, v). He selected 200 plates from the *Icones*, depicting plants in the Nilgiri hills in south India, and had them coloured for his *Spicilegium Neilgherrense* (1846–51) in a limited edition of 100 copies.

Wight remained at Coimbatore until March 1853, when he retired, taking with him nearly 10,000 specimens, representing more than 4000 species, which he presented to Kew Gardens in 1871. He then purchased Grazeley Lodge, Shinfield, near Reading in Berkshire, formerly the residence of W. Mitford the historian, and farmed the 66 acres of this property. In 1861 and 1862 he contributed articles on cotton farming to the *Gardeners' Chronicle*, and from 1865 to 1868 he gave information on medicinal uses of Indian plants to Edward John Waring's *Pharmacopoeia of India* (1868). He died at Grazeley Lodge on 26 May 1872; he was survived by his wife, four sons, and a daughter.

A man of exceptional energy, tenacity and industry, Wight was never daunted by the magnitude of the tasks he undertook. He was an outstanding collector who described more than 3000 species of the Indian flora, some of them new to science. His achievements are even more impressive with the limited resources at his disposal in India and the absence of any financial support. He was elected a fellow of the Linnean Society in 1832 and of the Royal Society in 1855 and is commemorated in the names of more than 120 plants (listed by R. K. Basak in *Taxon*, 30, 1981, 787–8).   RAY DESMOND

Sources H. Cleghorn, *Transactions of the Botanical Society* [Edinburgh], 11 (1870–73), 363–88 · R. K. Basak, 'Robert Wight and his botanical studies in India', *Taxon*, 30 (1981), 784–93 · R. Desmond, *The European discovery of the Indian flora* (1992) · I. H. Burkill, *Chapters on the history of botany in India* (Calcutta, 1965) · F. A. Stafleu and R. S. Cowan, *Taxonomic literature: a selective guide*, 2nd edn, 7, Regnum Vegetabile, 116 (1988), 277–81 · J. F. Royle, *On the culture and commerce of cotton in India* (1851), 467–523

Archives NHM, drawings and papers

Likenesses Maull & Polyblank, photograph, 1855, NPG [*see illus.*] · D. Macnee, coloured crayon drawing, RBG Kew · drawing, repro. in Cleghorn, *Transactions* · lithograph, repro. in E. Nelmes and W. Cuthbertson, *Curtis's botanical magazine dedications, 1827–1927*, pp. 142, 931

Wealth at death under £2000: probate, 18 June 1872, *CGPLA Eng. & Wales*

Wight, Sarah (*b.* **1631**), mystic, was born in September 1631, the daughter of Thomas Wight (*d.* before 1643), an official in the auditor's and exchequer's office, and Mary, *née* Purcel. Her mother's first husband, Edward Vaughan, was the king's receiver and surveyor for Northamptonshire and Rutlandshire, with whom she had had a son, Jonathan.

Sarah Wight's account of her own severe illnesses, visions, and miraculous healing are found in the lengthy *Exceeding riches of grace advanced by the spirit of grace, in an empty nothing creature, viz. Mris Sarah Wight* (1647), first published when she was approaching sixteen years of age. The text also contains eyewitness testimonials, including that of her Independent, and later Particular Baptist, pastor, Henry Jessey, in whose name the book was published, corroborating the events which transpired chiefly between the years 1643 and 1647. The narrative gives little information about Sarah's early life except that for seven years her mother suffered from depression and terror of spirit, while living near Londonstone in London with her Irish maid. Unable to care for Sarah, Mary left her rearing to her mother-in-law, with whom Sarah grew up and was 'well trained up in the Scriptures' (Jessey, 5). Sarah was reunited with her mother at the age of nine.

In 1643, while living with her now widowed mother at Lawrence Pountney Lane, London, Sarah began to suffer from deep despair and spiritual angst, a condition which worsened over time. Jessey visited their home almost daily and, during the next four years, witnessed more than sixty ministers try to alleviate Sarah's illness. In February 1647 Sarah's spiritual agitation intensified, spawning a rash of dramatic suicide attempts. She ceased eating and drinking on 27 March 1647 and was apparently struck blind and deaf the following month. At this time she began to have trances during which she quoted texts from scripture and expounded upon them as if from memory; visiting ministers recorded these expositions verbatim. She appeared to be dying, and by 19 April, with the restoration of her sight and hearing, she seemed at peace, assuring her mother that she would no longer do herself harm. On 27 April the first account of her experiences was published, and over the next few months friends gathered to celebrate the spiritual and emotional 'healing' that Sarah had experienced and to hear her quote passages of text, praise God for his mercies, and counsel others in similar circumstances. Theologians quizzed her upon doctrinal points, for explanations of difficult passages, and about the details of her trances. For sixty-five days Sarah fasted and remained in bed; on 11 June, following a dream that she would eat, arise, and walk again, according to the story in Mark 5, she ate her first meal and was able to leave her bed. A fortnight later she was able to walk again, and during the next weeks she celebrated her recovery with friends and family, attended church, and recuperated in a country house at Highgate. By the end of September she was restored to health, with a revised second edition of *The Exceeding Riches of Grace* appearing on 27 September.

Nothing further is known about Sarah Wight and her later life. Her ecstatic experiences as a young woman demonstrate how, during the seventeenth century, pious Englishwomen, particularly among the protestant laity, sought outlets for religious expression other than monastic life. Women prophets, mystics, and theologians published personal accounts of deeply spiritual encounters, and it is within this context that Sarah's own narrative should be read. Her story proved particularly popular: several editions of *The Exceeding Riches of Grace* were issued between 1647 and 1666, and the work was republished at least three times during the eighteenth century.

KAREN O'DELL BULLOCK

Sources [H. Jessey], *The exceeding riches of grace advanced by the spirit of grace, in an empty nothing creature, viz. Mris Sarah Wight*, 2nd rev. edn (1647)

Wight, William (1730–1782), Church of Scotland minister and university teacher, was born in Brampton, Cumberland, on 22 December 1730, the second of nine children of Robert Wight (1684–1764), a dissenting minister who in 1732 became minister of St Michael's Church in Dumfries, and Jean Robeson, daughter of the minister of Tinwald. Wight was educated in arts and divinity at Edinburgh University and Glasgow University, where for a year he superintended the education of the future Archdeacon Hamilton of York. He was ordained to the Capel Street meeting-house (later known as Mary's Abbey), Dublin, on 9 August 1753, and served as co-minister there for nine years.

In September 1759 Wight visited his first cousin and intimate friend the Revd Alexander Carlyle of Inveresk and confessed to being 'heartily tired of his situation as a dissenting clergyman, and of the manner of life in Dublin' (*Autobiography*, ed. Burton, 414). On 1 November 1759 Carlyle and William Robertson wrote a joint letter to Charles Townshend in an attempt to place Wight in the parish of Dalkeith, near Edinburgh, which they mistakenly thought was about to become vacant. Carlyle also wrote letters to Lord Milton and other political patrons in an effort to secure a promise of Wight's appointment to another expected vacancy, the Glasgow University chair of ecclesiastical history, which included a lectureship in civil history. By these means he apparently secured the advance support of Lord Bute and others. When the chair finally became vacant late in 1761, Principal William Leechman informed Baron Mure that most of the Glasgow professors preferred the Revd James Oswald of Methven, whereas Leechman himself favoured his own relative the Revd Patrick Wodrow (NL Scot., MS 4942, fols. 148–9). But he added that Bute was rumoured to be for a third candidate—presumably Wight, Leechman's former pupil. Since the chair was in the gift of the crown, Wight got the appointment in the spring of 1762 in spite of the university's formal recommendation of Oswald, and was admitted on 12 August. The following year he had the honour of preaching before the lord high commissioner and received an honorary DD degree from the University of Edinburgh.

In 1765 Wight became embroiled in an attempt to convert the rotating position of minister to the university chapel into a fixed chaplaincy that he would occupy for

£50 per annum; in letters to William Mure, Leechman turned against the plan because it removed the chaplain from under the principal's authority, and Professor John Anderson charged that it appeared to be 'a Scheme to give Money to a Professor, or to serve a Party' (NL Scot., MS 4942, fols. 187–8, 217–18). Wight did become chaplain, but on 9 June 1766 opponents of the scheme succeeded in stripping away the chaplain's salary, and soon afterwards Wight lost the office itself. His sole publication, *Heads of a Course of Lectures on the Study of History*, first appeared in 1768, and was reprinted in 1772 with a slightly different title and several additions. It outlines more than one hundred lectures on a wide range of topics from pre-Greek to modern European, including a dozen lectures on the progress and improvement of Great Britain in various spheres of culture. In its global sweep, its attention to cultural history, and its inclusion of Scottish history, Wight's course may well have been path-breaking. In 1775 Wight lost out to James Baillie for the Glasgow divinity chair, despite strong support from his friend David Hume, but after Baillie's death in 1778 he competed again, and after narrowly defeating Robert Findlay in a 7–5 vote of the faculty, rector, and dean of the faculty, he was admitted to the divinity chair on 12 June 1778. According to a biographical sketch in the *Edinburgh Magazine*, Wight began to suffer from gout by the time he went to Glasgow, and was so severely afflicted in later life that he had to be carried to his lectures.

Wight was an extremely sociable person whose house in Glasgow College was constantly filled with guests. Carlyle, who considered him 'the most agreeable of all men' (*Autobiography*, ed. Burton, 445), remarkable for his 'brilliancy, vivacity, and smartness' (ibid., 279), described a dinner in Edinburgh in 1759 at which Wight, 'who could talk at random on all sciences without being very deeply skilled in any', impressed Benjamin Franklin, Adam Smith, and the other assembled guests by engaging the great William Cullen on the subject of chemistry and, though but a novice, foiling him 'in his own science' (*Autobiography*, ed. Burton, 414). He also told of a visit to Harrogate in 1763 where Wight was 'enraged' at being snubbed by English guests who regarded him as a stranger, but upon getting his chance quickly charmed the company in his usual way (*Autobiography*, ed. Burton, 454–5). He died, unmarried, on 29 July 1782. RICHARD B. SHER

Sources The autobiography of Dr Alexander Carlyle of Inveresk, 1722–1805, ed. J. H. Burton (1910) · J. Coutts, *A history of the University of Glasgow* (1909) · *The letters of David Hume*, ed. J. Y. T. Greig, 2 vols. (1932) · *Fasti Scot.*, new edn, 2.266, 7.401, 533 · [W. Mure], ed., *Selections from the family papers preserved at Caldwell*, 2 vols. in 3 (1883–5) · T. H., 'Some account of Dr Wight, late professor of divinity in the University of Glasgow', *Edinburgh Magazine, or, Literary Miscellany*, 3 (1786), 260–65 · NL Scot., Caldwell MS 4942
Archives NL Scot., Caldwell MSS (William Mure of Caldwell), MS 4942 · U. Mich., Clements L., Townshend MSS (Charles Townshend)

Wightman, Edward (*bap.* 1580?, *d.* 1612), alleged heretic, may perhaps have been the child baptized on 14 July 1580 by his father John Wightman at Hinckley, Leicestershire; William Burton recorded in 1622 that he was from a family of the manor of Wykin in that parish. A report of his trial describes Wightman as a draper of the parish of Burton upon Trent, Staffordshire, and he was resident there in early 1609, attending the exercises led by the celebrated puritan minister Arthur Hildersam in the town. Here he voiced some very unorthodox views which Hildersam and his friends failed to shake. Wightman then set down his ideas in a manuscript, consisting of eighteen sheets, and delivered the work personally to James I, who was hunting at Royston, Cambridgeshire. The king's commission confirmed the existence of 'a book written and subscribed by him, and given to us', but this has not survived (*A True Relation*, 9). This initiative brought him to the notice of the authorities. According to Samuel Clarke, 'the Bishop and his friends gave out, that Wightman learned his opinions … of the puritans, and of the foresaid exercises, and of Master Hildersham by name'. But Wightman specifically denied this, recalling during his trial, at a public session on 26 November 1611 'in the hearing of five hundred people', that Hildersam had sought to confute his views in private conference, arguing 'that his opinion of soul-sleeping was directly repugnant to the scriptures', and had publicly opposed him on 21 April 1609 (Clarke, 117). Nevertheless, in the following months the bishop of Coventry and Lichfield, Richard Neile, used Wightman's views as a means to denounce Hildersam before the king, in order to justify and authorize the suppression of the exercises with which he was associated, at both Burton and nearby Repton.

By the time of the start of his trial for heresy in November 1611, Wightman had been imprisoned for over six months, having been examined at least five times, on 18 April, 6 May, 9 September, and 8 and 29 October, by Bishop Neile and others including the young William Laud, then president of St John's College, Oxford. Laud also attended the trial, which opened in the consistory of Lichfield Cathedral on 19 November; subsequent sessions were held on 26 and 29 November and from 2 to 5 December. On 2 December, Wightman was said to have recalled that he had abandoned an orthodox Trinitarian position within the previous two years. It is clear from the report of his sentence that he had also adopted what later came to be known as 'seeker' views, apparently identifying himself as one of the new apostles, or extraordinary men, who presaged the return of Christ. By now, he was found to hold 'That Jesus Christ is only man and a mere Creature and not both God and man in one person', but that 'Christ our saviour took not human flesh of the substance of the virgin Mary his mother'. His belief in the sleep of the soul in death applied also to Jesus. Wightman is said to have referred to the Nicene and Athanasian creeds and the 'twelve articles of the belief' as 'inventions of man' (Burrage, 2.218–19).

On 3 December, Bishop Neile asked Wightman to confirm that the account of his views had been given 'freely of his own accord without distraction of mind', to which he replied in the affirmative (Burrage, 2.219–20). His conviction was 'as a heretic' but the punishment was imposed by the civil power through a writ of 9 March issued under the great seal for his execution, and directed to the sheriff of Lichfield (*A True Relation*, 9). Much later, on 9 August 1639, Neile himself recalled Wightman's first ordeal at the stake: 'the fire [having] scorched him a little, he cried out that he would recant. The people thereupon ran into the fire and suffered themselves to be scorched to save him'; after reading a statement abjuring his views, Wightman was unchained and returned to prison. There, for two or three weeks, he considered his captors' demand for a formal written recantation. After refusing, he was brought once more to the consistory, where, reported Neile, he 'blasphemed more audaciously than before'; Neile's further recollection that he had 'died blaspheming' may therefore be taken to signify only that at his execution in April 1612 Wightman died reaffirming his earlier views (*CSP dom.*, *1639–40*, 85). STEPHEN WRIGHT

Sources C. Burrage, *The early English dissenters in the light of modern research, 1550–1641*, 2 vols. (1912) · *A true relation of the commissions and warrants for the condemnation of Bartholomew Legatt and Thomas Withman* (1651) · S. Clarke, *The lives of thirty two English divines*, in *A general martyrologie*, 3rd edn (1677) · *CSP dom.*, 1611–18; 1639–40 · W. Burton, *Description of Leicestershire*, 2nd edn (1777) · P. Collinson, *Godly people: essays on English protestantism and puritanism* (1983) · R. Wallace, *Antitrinitarian biography* (1850) · *IGI*

Wightman, Joseph (*d.* 1722), army officer, was appointed ensign in the 1st foot guards on 29 December 1690. He progressed to lieutenant and captain on 7 August 1693, and to captain and lieutenant-colonel on 8 December 1696. He subsequently transferred to Sir Matthew Bridge's regiment and saw service in Flanders during the Nine Years' War (1689–97). In 1701 Wightman went with the regiment to the Netherlands prior to the onset of the War of the Spanish Succession (1702–13). He saw extensive active service during the duke of Marlborough's initial campaigns, and was promoted to lieutenant-colonel and took command of the regiment in 1702. On the recommendation of Marlborough, Wightman received the brevet rank of colonel on 26 August 1703, with the intention that he should command the contingent of troops earmarked for service in Spain. At this time Marlborough described Wightman as 'a very careful, diligent officer' (Murray, 1.192). In Spain, Wightman served with his regiment (now Holcroft Blood's) in the army of Henri de Massue de Ruvigny, earl of Galway; he was made brigadier-general on 1 January 1707, and fought at the battle of Almanza (25 April 1707). On Blood's death Wightman was appointed, on 20 August 1707, to the colonelcy of the regiment (subsequently the 17th foot, or Leicesters), and on 1 January 1710 he became major-general.

On 12 June 1712 Wightman was appointed the commander-in-chief in Scotland, as the deputy for John Campbell, second duke of Argyll. The appointment came on the recommendation of General John Webb, despite Argyll's preference for Brigadier-General William Breton in the post. Wightman's position was, accordingly, rather awkward and Argyll's attitude toward his lieutenant seems to have been most unco-operative, with official correspondence to Argyll delayed or ignored altogether. Despite this, Wightman made extensive efforts to bolster the

government's position in Scotland, at a time of rising sympathy for the Jacobite cause. At the outset of the 1715 rising Wightman shrewdly drew together his meagre forces and secured Stirling town and castle. Argyll joined him there from London in mid-September. Wightman commanded the infantry in the centre of the army at the battle of Sheriffmuir (13 November 1715) and, although the troops on his left broke, his solid defence held the highlanders' rush. This local success enabled Argyll to employ his cavalry on the right wing to disperse much of the Jacobite army. Rather inevitably there was some dispute between Wightman and Argyll over the meagre honours of the day. Wightman's own account, printed in 1717 as a part of Robert Patten's *History of the Late Rebellion*, was subsequently criticised by admirers of Argyll for being unduly partial.

Wightman continued to serve in Scotland, and he commanded the government army at the small battle of Glenshiel during the Jacobite rising of 1719. His capable tactics, using mortars to unsettle the entrenched highlanders and then sending Campbell's dragoons (subsequently the Royal Scots Greys) to turn the flank of their position, were admirably successful. The rebels dispersed and the accompanying Spanish soldiers surrendered shortly afterwards.

In recognition of his services in Scotland, Wightman was appointed governor of Kinsale in Ireland. Before taking up the post he died of a stroke when in Bath, on 25 September 1722. Probate, granted on 7 November 1722, suggests that he was usually resident in the parish of St James's, Westminster; administration was granted to his widow, Eliza. JAMES FALKNER

Sources *DNB* · C. Dalton, ed., *English army lists and commission registers, 1661–1714*, 6 vols. (1892–1904) · C. Dalton, *George the First's army, 1714–1727*, 2 vols. (1910–12) · *The letters and dispatches of John Churchill, first duke of Marlborough, from 1702 to 1712*, ed. G. Murray, 1 (1845) · N. B. Leslie, *The succession of colonels of the British army from 1660 to the present day* (1974) · C. Petrie, *The Jacobite movement*, 3rd edn (1959) · B. Lenman, *The Jacobite risings in Britain, 1689–1746* (1980) · P. Dickson, *Red John of the battles* (1973) · A. D. Francis, *The First Peninsular War, 1702–1713* (1975) · grant of administration, PRO, PROB 6/98, fol. 235r · R. Cannon, *Records of the 17th foot* (1845)
Archives NA Scot., letters to duke of Montrose

Wightman [*née* James], **Julia Bainbrigge** (1817–1898), temperance activist and author, was born on 23 January 1817 in the Bengal Residency, Cawnpore, India, third daughter of William James, lieutenant-colonel of the East India Company, of Saltford House, Somerset, and his wife, Mary Marshall, daughter of Lieutenant-General Sir Dyson Marshall. Following her mother's death in India, her father returned to England with his family about 1821 and settled at Saltford House, Saltford, Devon. Julia James met and married, on 1 December 1842 in Saltford church, Charles Edward Leopold Wightman (1816–1896), the son of the Revd John Wightman and his wife, Elizabeth Gagaine. With him she moved to Shrewsbury, where his father had the living of St Alkmond's. Charles Wightman was appointed vicar of St Alkmond's Church and took responsibility for the parish. Julia Wightman devoted herself to parish work, including Sunday school and Bible classes. Her first philanthropic undertaking was the rescue of fallen young women: in 1843 she formed a local fund-raising committee, which initially sent girls to local penitentiaries. However, she disliked the existing penitentiary system, with its compulsory two-year residence and regimes of solitary confinement and haircuts upon admittance; after the Chester diocese declined to participate in a joint home with Shrewsbury, she organized the purchase of a house in Wyle Cop, the Salop Home, and was able to use her influence to discontinue such practices. Six years later the penitentiary moved to larger premises on Dogpole, and was eventually taken over by the St Julien's Home in 1866.

Julia Wightman is better known, however, for her temperance work and her book *Haste to the Rescue!*, an account of her temperance activities in Shrewsbury in the form of letters written to her sister, originally published in 1859. A temperance advocate from the early days of her marriage, after she found the cook drunk in the kitchen, both she and her husband attempted a teetotal way of life, although doctors continually prescribed alcohol for her delicate health. Julia Wightman's temperance work in the Shrewsbury community was inspired partly by reading Catherine Marsh's *English Hearts and Minds* (1858), an account of Marsh's work with navvies employed on the construction of the Crystal Palace, and partly by her own experience of the poverty, drunkenness, and associated problems of Butcher's Row, the working-class area of Shrewsbury around St Alkmond's Church. Her own book highlighted the extent of the drink problem and made many aware of the role of total abstinence in alleviating the effects of drink among the working classes.

Throughout her life Julia Wightman was scrupulous in linking all her work with Church of England doctrine and basing it, as she did all her philanthropic activities, around St Alkmond's Church. Despite this Christian-based approach to temperance she did not receive encouragement or support in the early days from the church, but was advised to discontinue the work. However, she was later credited with being one of the major influences in the establishment of the Church of England Temperance Society, founded after the National Temperance League had circulated all clergymen in the Church of England with a copy of her work. Determined to provide an alternative to the public house, Julia Wightman planned a Working Men's Hall to be a 'public house without the drink', first appealing for funds in June 1861. The site of The Fox inn, Shrewsbury, and its adjacent premises were purchased the following year for £700. Royalties from *Haste to the Rescue!* contributed £550 to the fund. The hall opened in April 1863 with further rooms planned. The total cost of the hall, including land, conversion, and new buildings, was to total over £5000. Its opening was a cause for celebration in the town and was attended by 1000 people, including the bishop and a number of clergymen, gaining it the approval of the Church of England. All connected with the hall had to be total abstainers: the conveyance for the former Fox Inn and the new buildings contained clauses ensuring that the hall keepers should be

total abstainers and specifying that all members of the executive committee should be members of the Church of England. The main buildings still exist.

The hall became the venue for many of Julia Wightman's Christian and philanthropic activities, including Bible classes for postmen and policemen, mothers' meetings, sewing classes, and temperance meetings; the church ragged school, founded in 1862, was transferred to it, all teachers and superintendents of the school being required to be teetotallers. After investigating the Irwell Dining Hall in Manchester, which provided cheap meals, Mrs Wightman ensured that the hall would provide a similar service for market people, as well as housing a club and coffee house. It became the venue for meetings of other philanthropic organizations, but no meetings could be held on the premises that condemned the Church of England. The last phase to be built included baths let to members of the public.

Having suffered from delicate health all her life Julia Wightman became unwell for the period 1868 to 1875. Despite her enforced absences from the parish she continued her interest in temperance and other philanthropic activities, writing letters to be read at meetings. After her recovery, in 1882, inspired by a visit from Ellice Hopkins, she founded the Shrewsbury Association for Friendless Girls, making it part of the Lichfield Diocesan Association. She also arranged the purchase of a former eye and ear hospital for conversion into a training school for servants and a free registry for those seeking jobs. Christianity and teetotalism was the bedrock of the training received by the girls. She was instrumental in founding branches of the YMCA and YWCA, despite the fact that she disagreed with the organizations' non-sectarian stance. These, like her other societies, were affiliated to St Alkmond's. In 1882 she began Bible classes for young business-women, and continued to be interested in these classes, writing letters to be read at meetings, until shortly before her death.

Julia Wightman played a significant role in making temperance work an acceptable activity for women. Mrs Sewell and Anna Sewell were inspired by her achievements, and as a result took up aggressive temperance work in Wick. Eleanor Harford Battersby added Christianity to her temperance work after reading *Haste to the Rescue!* and W. S. Caine (1842–1903), later member of the executive of the United Kingdom Alliance, came to visit her and, despite his initial scepticism over the value of teetotalism, signed the pledge with her in 1858.

Julia Wightman's influence on the local Church of England community was great. In 1881 she intervened in the school board elections. There were nine seats available with eleven candidates; five churchmen, five nonconformists, and a Roman Catholic priest. A strong wave of anti-churchmen feeling existed; Mrs Wightman spoke on the issue at the Sunday meeting before the election and sent a letter on the subject to the Revd J. M. J. Fletcher, who circulated it as a handbill. She encouraged all to vote for the principle of religious instruction according to the established church, and, in the event, the five churchmen headed the poll. A firm sectarian, she would not tolerate criticism of the Church of England. Within her work there had to be conversion to the Church of England; unsectarian work was 'spiritual lawlessness'. Her beliefs remained essentially conservative to the end: she was a fervent anti-Darwinist, producing a booklet *Evolution or Special Creation: which?* (n.d.) intended to vindicate the accepted biblical concept of creation. This was inspired by reading sermons advocating Darwinism preached by the bishops of Carlisle, Manchester, and Bedford at the Manchester meeting of the British Association for the Advancement of Science, and was published at the time of the Darwin memorial appeal in Shrewsbury.

Julia Wightman was supported in all her work by her husband, the Revd Prebendary Wightman: he assisted in the foundation of the St Alkmond's schools and did the administrative work in the purchase of the Fox Inn for the Working Men's Temperance Hall. He became a trustee of the hall, and as vicar of St Alkmonds was chairman of the committee for the building of the hall. He remained vicar of St Alkmonds, despite being offered other livings, until two years prior to his death in 1896. After an eleven-day illness Julia Wightman died of cardiac dilation and exhaustion following bronchitis on 14 January 1898 at The Crescent, Shrewsbury. She was buried with her husband in general cemetery, Roman Road, Shrewsbury, on 25 January. MARGARET BARROW

Sources J. M. J. Fletcher, *Mrs Wightman of Shrewsbury: the story of a pioneer in temperance work* (1906) · J. B. Wightman, *Haste to the rescue!* (1859) · J. B. Wightman, *Annals of the rescued* (1861) · *Salopian Shreds and Patches* (16 Sept 1892), 134 · J. E. Rhead, 'The public house without the drink', *Shropshire Magazine*, 18 (April 1966), 25 · *Shrewsbury Chronicle* (21 Jan 1898) · *Bye-Gones Relating to Wales and the Border Counties*, 2nd ser., 5 (1897–8), 283 · *Bye-Gones Relating to Wales and the Border Counties*, 2nd ser., 4 (1895–6), 273 · *Shropshire Magazine*, 2 (Feb 1951), 12–13, 16 · J. B. Wightman, *Ten years' experience of total abstainers* (1871) · m. cert. · d. cert.
Likenesses R. L. Bartlett, photograph, repro. in Fletcher, *Mrs Wightman of Shrewsbury*, 280

Wightman, Sir William (1785–1863), judge, the eldest son of William Wightman, gentleman, of St Clement's, London, a member of an old Dumfriesshire family, and his wife, Elizabeth, was baptized on 2 September 1785 at St Clement Danes, Westminster. He matriculated at University College, Oxford, on 23 March 1801, and in the same year moved to Queen's College as a Michel exhibitioner. He graduated BA in 1805, and MA in 1809. Admitted to Lincoln's Inn on 31 January 1804, Wightman practised initially as a special pleader. In 1819 he married Charlotte Mary, a daughter of James Baird of Lasswade near Edinburgh; they had four daughters.

Wightman was called to the bar in 1821, and in 1830 joined the Inner Temple *ad eundem*. On the northern circuit his reputation as a sound and clear-headed lawyer brought him a large practice. He was engaged in the prosecutions arising out of the Bristol riots of 1831, but owing to his modesty was little known outside the profession. He gave assistance to the law officers of the crown for several years as junior counsel to the Treasury, and was appointed in 1831 to the royal commission on the courts of common

law, and in 1833 to the commission concerned to codify the criminal law.

On the resignation of Mr Justice Littledale, Wightman was appointed a justice of the court of queen's bench on 15 February 1841, and was knighted on 28 April of the same year. He served as a judge for nearly twenty-three years as the trusted colleague of three successive chief justices. He had a sound knowledge of the law, combined with patience, courtesy, and clear reasoning. As at the bar, he did not seek distinction, but fulfilled his duties with dignity and simplicity. Beyond his judicial capacity, he was a pleasant companion, and capable of displaying considerable literary knowledge. He was elected an honorary fellow of Queen's College, Oxford, in 1859. Seized with 'apoplexy' (*GM*), he died on circuit in the judges' lodgings at York on 10 December 1863.

J. A. HAMILTON, *rev.* N. G. JONES

Sources E. Foss, *Biographia juridica: a biographical dictionary of the judges of England … 1066–1870* (1870) · *GM*, 3rd ser., 16 (1864), 250–51 · *The Times* (11 Dec 1863) · J. Arnould, *Memoir of Thomas, first Lord Denman*, 2 vols. (1873), 2, 114–15 · Foster, *Alum. Oxon.* · parish register, St Clement Danes, City Westm. AC · Walford, *County families*
Likenesses oils, Queen's College, Oxford
Wealth at death under £18,000: resworn probate, June 1864, *CGPLA Eng. & Wales*

Wightwick, George (1802–1872), architect and writer on architecture, was born on 26 August 1802 at Alyn Bank, near Mold in Flintshire, the only child of William Wightwick (1775–1811), a country gentleman, and his wife, Anna Maria, *née* Taylor (1779–1864). William Wightwick was accidentally drowned in 1811, and in 1815 George's mother married Walter Damant, a widower with three children. Following the death of his father, George had been sent to board at Wolverhampton grammar school, but after his mother's remarriage the family moved to London, where he attended Dr Lord's school at Tooting until 1817. He trained as an architect, and in 1818 was articled to Edward Lapidge of Grosvenor Square. After completing his pupillage in 1823 he had difficulty obtaining permanent employment, but gained some work through writing and making drawings for *The Public Buildings of London*, by Britton and Pugin. In 1825, following the settlement of his deceased father's affairs, Wightwick made use of the little money available to him for a year's travel in Italy, and in 1828 he privately published *Select Views of Roman Antiquities*, well received but not commercially successful. In 1827 he took employment with Sir John Soane as companion and amanuensis. It was an acrimonious relationship that lasted only eight months, but which none the less resulted in a friendship that was important for Wightwick. Later that year he moved from London to join his family in the west country.

Wightwick established himself in Plymouth, and was then invited to join the practice of John Foulston, the architect who had designed Plymouth's public buildings. The date and terms of this partnership are not known, but Foulston retired some six months later, leaving Wightwick to complete outstanding commissions, particularly work for the earl of Mount Edgcumbe at Stonehouse, as well as continuing with others, notably Bodmin Lunatic Asylum. On 26 August 1829 Wightwick married his step-sister Caroline Damant (1808–1867); that year he became increasingly busy, designing private houses, terraces, public buildings, shops, and churches in the Plymouth area and Cornwall. Many of his commissions emanated from the social network that he energetically cultivated and which was based upon his membership of the Plymouth Athenaeum. In Plymouth he designed the mechanics' institute (c.1827), Athenaeum Terrace (1832), the Esplanade (1836), and the post office at Devonport (1850; dem. 1945). In Devon he designed Calverleigh Court at Tiverton (1844) and Watermouth Castle, near Ilfracombe (1845). His work took him into Cornwall, and his country houses are noteworthy: Luxtowe in Liskeard (1831), Trevarno, near Helston (1839), Penquite at Golant (1848), and particularly the alterations to Tregrehan House at St Blazey (1848).

Although Wightwick's buildings may seem random in variety, eclectic in style, and uncontroversial in execution, they were generally well regarded, but it was the design of his churches that provoked criticism. He designed nine churches, of which eight were built between 1834 and 1844, all to the same formula, a boxlike auditorium with only a shallow chancel and without aisles or pillars. It was Wightwick's belief that Gothic form should be modified to accommodate contemporary, popular requirements, a view he expressed in a series of articles for *Weale's Quarterly Papers on Architecture* (1844–5), and which led to his downfall in the eyes of the ecclesiological establishment. Although his religiosity was later questioned, it was the depth of his convictions that defined his church design. He offended the increasingly ritualistic opinion of the high-church party, expressed in the pages of *The Ecclesiologist*, but Wightwick refused to compromise, and thus censured, his church commissions fell away.

In 1852 Wightwick retired with his ailing wife to Bristol, and three years later moved to Portishead. Caroline Wightwick died on 19 June 1867, and six months later, on 2 January 1868, Wightwick married Isabella (b. 1832), the daughter of Samuel Jackson, the watercolour painter of Clifton. Both his marriages were childless. Wightwick died at his home, 2 Adelaide Terrace, Portishead, on 9 July 1872, and was buried in the graveyard of the local Anglican church, St Peter's, alongside his first wife. His second wife survived him. He left almost all his drawings, watercolours, and papers, including his manuscript lectures, to the RIBA, his architectural work largely contained within six carefully catalogued volumes.

Throughout his professional life as well as in retirement Wightwick wrote extensively, and may be considered one of the first architectural journalists. Early in his career he wrote for two short-lived west country periodicals, *The Philo-Danmonian* (January–June 1830), and the *South Devon Monthly Museum* (January 1833 – June 1836). Later his *Hints to Young Architects* (1846) was reprinted four times, and his terms of employment were printed in *The Architect* (2, 1850). He contributed critical comment on Ruskin's *Seven Lamps of Architecture* in six articles in the *Architect and Building Operative* (November 1849 – January 1850). In retirement he contributed a series of articles on architecture to *The Critic* between January 1852 and May 1858, and another series to the *Edinburgh Building Chronicle* between May 1854 and May 1857. He wrote prolifically for other national journals, including *Bentley's Miscellany*, which published his autobiography 'The life of an architect' in parts between 1852 and 1854, and in 1852 contributed a monthly series on local architectural matters to the *Bristol Times* under the pseudonym Robert Ramble. He was awarded the RIBA silver medal for his essay 'A critical study on the architecture and genius of Sir Christopher Wren' in 1859. Wightwick may now be remembered as an architect, but he was also a romantic pragmatist who sought to entertain as well as to educate through writing and lecturing. In 1840 *The Palace of Architecture: a Romance of Art and History* was published, his work of fantasy that embraced all architectural styles, a volume that represented this gregarious man as truly as his functional but ideologically incorrect churches.   ROSAMUND REID

Sources *Bentley's Miscellany*, 45–64 (1859–68) · RIBA BAL, Wightwick MSS · RIBA BAL, Drawings collection, Wightwick MSS · *Proceedings of the Plymouth Athenaeum* · *Weale's Quarterly Papers on Architecture* (1843–5) · *The Ecclesiologist*, 1–29 (1842–68) · grants for churches, LPL, records of the ICBS · *The Critic* (1844–63) · *Transactions of the Royal Institute of British Architects* · *Bristol Times and Bath Advocate* (1839–53) · will · *CGPLA Eng. & Wales* (1872) · d. cert. · Boase & Courtney, *Bibl. Corn.* · parish register (baptism), 16 Nov 1802, Mold, St Mary's · *Devon and Cornwall Notes and Queries*, 26 (1954–5) · Colvin, *Archs.*

Archives RIBA BAL, lectures and lecture notes for planned lectures; biographical extracts from printed sources | Devon RO, letters to Sir Thomas Dyke Acland

Likenesses E. Scriven, stipple (after R. R. Scanlan), BM, NPG; repro. in Arnold's *Library of the Fine Arts* (1832)

Wealth at death under £7000: probate, 15 Aug 1872, *CGPLA Eng. & Wales*

Wiglaf (*fl.* 827–c.840), king of the Mercians, succeeded to the kingdom in 827, in very difficult circumstances. His predecessors Beornwulf and Ludeca had been killed in battle against the East Angles in 826 and 827; at the same time, King Ecgberht of Wessex had conquered the provinces of Kent, Surrey, Sussex, and Essex, formerly under Mercian control. Mercia's sudden decline seems to have been due to a continuing leadership crisis, which began with the death of King Cenwulf in 821 and was exacerbated by the deposition of Ceolwulf in 823. The origins of Beornwulf, Ludeca, and Wiglaf are obscure; they were probably regional rulers, strong enough to establish themselves on the throne, but not necessarily in a position to command the loyalty of all the Mercian factions. In 829 Ecgberht of Wessex conquered Mercia, deposed Wiglaf, and went on to receive the submission of the Northumbrians; he struck coins at the Mercian mint of London and a king-list indicates that he was briefly regarded as king of Mercia. But the annal for 830 in the Anglo-Saxon Chronicle remarks: 'In this year Wiglaf again obtained the kingdom of the Mercians' (*ASC*, text A, s.a. 828, *recte* 830). There is no real evidence that Wiglaf rebelled against Ecgberht's authority; nor can it be shown that he was a client king of Ecgberht, despite the impression given by the Anglo-Saxon Chronicle (essentially a West Saxon source for the ninth century), that Ecgberht's victories in 829 established him as overlord of all of southern England. This and other evidence does suggest, however, that some kind of political settlement arose between Wiglaf and Ecgberht.

There is no overt indication of West Saxon interference in Mercian affairs in the years immediately after 830 (the invasion of Wales by Ecgberht in that year would have had to have been launched from Mercia, but it may well have taken place before Wiglaf's restoration). Wiglaf had control of Middlesex in 831 and would therefore seem to have regained the vital port of London, but the London mint became moribund early in his reign and no Mercian coinage was produced until the early 840s. Wiglaf disposed of land and issued charters without reference to Ecgberht; the earlier of the two surviving diplomas in his name is dated to 'the first year of my second reign', which shows that Wiglaf was prepared to acknowledge the fact of his temporary deposition. It must remain an open question whether Wiglaf was restored in 830 by his own efforts or by those of Ecgberht; whatever the circumstances, Wiglaf's 'second' reign appears to signal the beginning of a change in the relationship between Mercia and Wessex. The keynote is no longer a perennial hostility marked by frequent clashes, but rather a growing accommodation which matured into occasional alliances against the growing viking threat.

Perhaps bolstered by an understanding with Ecgberht, Wiglaf managed to secure his position in Mercia and went on to rule until about 840. The exact date of his death has not been preserved, but it is known that he was buried in a mausoleum at Repton. The eighth-century Mercian ruler Æthelbald (d. 757) had also been interred at Repton; Wiglaf may have been a kinsman or descendant of Æthelbald, but it is also possible that the place of his burial was chosen simply to associate him and his family with earlier greatness. His queen, Cynethryth, may have represented an alliance with another Mercian faction (Offa's queen had the same name), but she is known only from her attestations to Wiglaf's two diplomas. The earlier of these, which dates from 831, is also attested by Wiglaf's son, Wigmund. According to the Passio sancti Wigstani, which may be based on a ninth-century source, Wiglaf arranged for Wigmund to marry a daughter of King Ceolwulf named Ælfflæd; they had a son, *Wigstan, who was later murdered and venerated as a saint at Repton. The passio suggests that Wigmund did indeed become king after Wiglaf's death. There is no independent evidence to support this claim (although it must be admitted that the sources for this period are very poor indeed), and the fact that Wigmund does not attest Wiglaf's diploma of 836 may indicate that he died before his father.

S. E. KELLY

Sources ASC, s.a. 829, 830 [texts A, E] · AS chart., S 188, 190 · S. Keynes, 'The control of Kent in the ninth century', Early Medieval Europe, 2 (1993), 111–32, esp. 122–4 · S. Keynes, 'King Alfred and the Mercians', Kings, currency and alliances: history and coinage of southern England in the ninth century, ed. M. A. S. Blackburn and D. N. Dumville (1998), 1–46 · P. Grierson and M. Blackburn, Medieval European coinage: with a catalogue of the coins in the Fitzwilliam Museum, Cambridge, 1: The early middle ages (5th–10th centuries) (1986), 292 · A. Thacker, 'Kings, saints and monasteries in pre-viking Mercia', Midland History, 10 (1985), 1–25, esp. 12–14 · D. W. Rollason, 'The cults of murdered royal saints in Anglo-Saxon England', Anglo-Saxon England, 11 (1983), 1–22, esp. 5–9 · M. Biddle, 'Archaeology, architecture, and the cult of saints in Anglo-Saxon England', The Anglo-Saxon church: papers on history, architecture, and archaeology in honour of Dr H. M. Taylor, ed. L. A. S. Butler and R. K. Morris, Council for British Archaeology Research Report, 60 (1986), 1–31, esp. 16–22

Likenesses coin, BM

Wigmore. For this title name see Mortimer, Roger (III) de, lord of Wigmore (1231–1282).

Wigmore [alias Campion], **William** (c.1599–1665), Jesuit, a native of Herefordshire, was the son of Sir William Wigmore and his wife, Anne, daughter of Sir John Throckmorton of Gloucestershire. His mother was a committed Catholic, his father at times a conformist. Several of his brothers and sisters were members of religious orders, most of them adopting the alias Campion in honour of the martyred Jesuit Edmund Campion. His sister Catherine Campion (née Elizabeth Wigmore) was professed a Benedictine nun at the pro-Jesuit convent of Ghent in 1628. She helped establish the filiation at Boulogne in 1652, acting as abbess from August 1653 until her death in October 1656. Another sister, Winifred Wigmore, was one of Mary Ward's initial companions, and was sent by her to settle the institute's troubled house at Liège in the period leading up to its suppression in 1631.

William Campion was educated at St Omer, entered the Society of Jesus at the Watten noviciate on 25 August 1624, undertook further studies in the society's college at Liège, and was ordained priest about 1632. He held various offices at the Jesuit college at St Omer and was professed there on 20 August 1640. He served on the English mission from 1644, from 1653 to 1655 acting as rector of the college of St Francis Xavier, which covered Wales and parts of the west of England. He wrote The Catholicke Doctrine of Transubstantiation (1657), which appears to have grown out of debates in Paris with exiled Church of England bishop John Cosin as part of a struggle for the spiritual allegiance of the exiled Irish nobleman Murrough O'Brien, earl of Inchiquin. As published it addressed the question of the interpretation of the church fathers in regard to current controversy. He may have been the Father Campion reported as procurator for the society in Paris in July 1659, who sought to distance the society from the English Commonwealth and align it with the exiled monarchy. In 1659 he was appointed confessor to the Benedictine convent at Pontoise, the successor of his sister's house at Boulogne and of which he was a benefactor. From 1664 he acted as rector of the Jesuit tertiary house at Ghent and died there on 28 September 1665.

R. M. ARMSTRONG

Sources H. Foley, ed., Records of the English province of the Society of Jesus, 7 vols. in 8 (1875–83) · T. M. McCoog, English and Welsh Jesuits, 1555–1650, 2 vols., Catholic RS, 74–5 (1994–5) · [W. Wigmore], The Catholicke doctrine of transubstantiation (1657) · CSP dom., 1659–60 · A. Kenny, ed., The responsa scholarum of the English College, Rome, 1,

Catholic RS, 54 (1962) · *Miscellanea, V*, Catholic RS, 6 (1909) · *Miscellanea, X*, Catholic RS, 17 (1915) · P. Guilday, *The English Catholic refugees on the continent, 1558–1795* (1914)

Wigner, George William (1842–1884), analytical chemist, was born on 19 October 1842 at Norfolk Street, King's Lynn, the eldest son of John Thomas Wigner, minister of the local Baptist church, and his wife, Harriett Louisa (née Ovenden). He was educated at Lynn grammar school before becoming a clerk in a private banking firm in London in 1859.

Wigner spent his leisure time studying chemistry, and, following a lecture he gave on the subject, was offered, in 1864, a post in the Deptford chemical works of Frank Hills. In 1867, in conjunction with the bullion brokers W. C. and R. G. Sillar, Wigner developed the ABC process of sewage treatment, which was patented in June 1868. Using a mixture of alum, blood, and clay, the patentees hoped to purify sewage and at the same time produce a powerful manure. In the same year that the patent was granted, Wigner became managing director of the Native Guano Company, set up to work the process. Despite the insinuation by the royal commission on river pollution in 1870 that the ABC process was fraudulent, it remained the most durable of chemical sewage treatment processes, and was still operating in the late 1880s.

In the early 1870s Wigner ceased to be active in the Native Guano Company, and in 1872 he began practice in Great Tower Street as a chemical analyst, specializing in commercial materials and foodstuffs. On 4 April in the same year he married Fanny Louisa (1850/51–1884), daughter of William Harrison, wholesale grocer. In 1878 Wigner carried out a programme of analyses of the waters of seaside towns, sponsored by the *Sanitary Record*, and published as *Seaside water: an examination into the character of the water-supply at the watering places of England and Wales* (1878). Wigner's salutary warning that many places to which holiday makers were resorting for health were unhealthy brought forth hostile criticism from local medical men and partisan chemists.

Wigner was a promoter of the Sale of Food and Drugs Act of 1875 and principal founder of the Society of Public Analysts in the same year. He served as public analyst for Plumstead, Greenwich, and Deptford. Recognizing that prosecutions often failed due to disagreement over proper methodology, he was an early leader in the movement for standard methods. In 1876 Wigner and John Muter became proprietors as well as editors of *The Analyst*. Wigner's editorial criticism of some of his colleagues' methods strained the fellowship of the young society but strengthened the profession. As editor, as secretary of the society from its beginning until 1883, and as president during the last year of his life, Wigner made the society and the journal a clearing-house of information in the fight against adulteration, compiling annual reports from public analysts in Britain and America, reviewing trends in adulteration, and undertaking analytical and legal efforts against it. A definition of adulteration drafted by Wigner won a prize from the United States national board of health in 1880 and was incorporated into legislation passed by several states. In 1878 he proposed a point system that would sum the results of several tests and allow ready comparison of waters from different towns. Comparisons using a simplified version of the scale were published annually in *The Analyst* during the early 1880s.

Wigner was a fellow of the Chemical Society and of the Institute of Chemistry. Most of his approximately fifty scientific papers were contributions to *The Analyst* on many aspects of food and water chemistry. He died at his home, 82 Wickham Road, Brockley, of stricture of the œsophagus on 17 October 1884, a few months after the death from rheumatic fever of his wife, and was buried in Brockley cemetery five days later. The couple were survived by their two small children.

CHRISTOPHER HAMLIN

Sources *JCS*, 47 (1885), 344–5 · *The Analyst*, 9 (1884), 193 · 'Inaugural address', *The Analyst*, 10 (1885), 42 · R. C. Chirnside and J. H. Hamence, *The 'practising chemists': a history of the Society for Analytical Chemistry, 1874–1974* (1974) · C. Hamlin, *A science of impurity: water analysis in nineteenth century Britain* (1990) · E. W. Stieb and G. Sonnedecker, *Drug adulteration: detection and control in nineteenth-century Britain* (1966) · 'Royal commission to inquire into … the pollution of rivers', *Parl. papers* (1870), 40.1, C. 37; 40.157, C. 109; 40.499, C. 181 [reports 1–2] · *Catalogue of scientific papers*, Royal Society, 19 vols. (1867–1925) · b. cert. · m. cert. · d. cert. · d. cert. [F. L. Wigner]
Likenesses photograph, repro. in Chirnside and Hamence, *The 'practising chemists'*
Wealth at death £2544 8s. 6d.: probate, 5 Dec 1884, *CGPLA Eng. & Wales*

Wigram, Clive, first Baron Wigram (1873–1960), soldier and courtier, was born on 5 July 1873 at Madras, the eldest of three sons of Herbert Wigram (1842–1914), of the Madras civil service, and Amy Augusta (d. 1935), daughter of Lieutenant-General John Wood Rideout, of the Indian army. He was educated at Winchester College (1886–91), where he excelled at games, most notably cricket, and at the Royal Military Academy, Woolwich (1891–3). In 1893 he was commissioned in the Royal Artillery and two years later he was appointed aide-de-camp to Lord Elgin, viceroy of India. He served with the 18th Bengal lancers in the Tirah campaign on the north-west frontier in 1897–8, and in 1900 joined Kitchener's horse in the Second South African War, where he was mentioned in dispatches. Life in a vice-regal establishment suited Wigram and he returned to India as aide-de-camp to Lord Curzon, who succeeded Elgin as viceroy. When the prince of Wales (later George V) visited India in 1905 his chief of staff, Sir Walter Lawrence, invited Wigram to be his assistant. Wigram became military secretary to the commander-in-chief at Aldershot in 1908 but, upon the accession of George V in 1910, he exchanged a promising military career to be equerry and assistant private secretary to the king. Sporty and down-to-earth, with chauvinist views typical of many army officers, Wigram suited the king's taste for simplicity and directness in his aides. Tall, handsome, and athletic, he was the model of the soldierly courtier.

George V's reign was marked by war, industrial unrest, and the advent of socialism and universal suffrage, all of which the king took to be a danger to the crown. Given the

Clive Wigram, first Baron Wigram (1873–1960), by Frank O. Salisbury, 1921

many crises of the reign the office of the private secretary became increasingly important to the monarchy. For most of his career in royal service Wigram served as assistant to the sagacious Arthur Bigge, Lord Stamfordham, from whom he learned the niceties of the king's constitutional position and the need to be well informed and trusted by all parties. At the end of the First World War social malaise and the drift of democratic politics galvanized the monarchy into defending its position more vigorously. The king's advisers felt obliged to consider a more coherent strategy of self-defence than palace precedent provided. In view of the constitutional constraints this meant forging bonds of affection at home and across the empire. Wigram was among the palace reformers and once described those who opposed any changes in the dignity and status of the sovereign as 'Palace Troglodytes' (Rose, 227). A master of propaganda and imaginative gestures, he wanted greater publicity given to imperial tours and welfare missions to working-class communities. He called for a full-time press officer, who was appointed in 1918, and urged the royal family to widen its social circle. Behind the scenes he monitored expressions of republicanism in the Labour Party and, through contacts outside government, kept the king informed of Communist Party activity. He was created KCVO in 1928, later promoted GCVO.

Wigram was appointed private secretary to the king after Stamfordham's death in 1931, and the following year was sworn of the privy council. He lacked Stamfordham's intellectual gifts or skill as a draftsman, but beneath the bluff exterior of an Indian army colonel there was shrewdness and purpose. He knew the king's mind and could draw on a wide circle of friends and contacts for advice. Within months of his appointment as private secretary, in the depths of the depression, he had to face a political crisis of the first magnitude. Personally, he favoured setting up an emergency government and supported the king's decision to intervene to that end. The use of the royal prerogative led to the formation of the National Government, with Ramsay MacDonald at its head. Though he acted on advice the king's role was contentious, not least because it led to a division in the Labour Party. At the time several Labour MPs accused him of political meddling.

George V was highly sensitive to what he felt to be encroachments on his prerogative and threats to the integrity of the empire, and in the final years of his reign Wigram had to deal with, among other issues, the appointment of governors-general, the rise of Indian nationalism, and German rearmament. More agreeably he oversaw the festivities surrounding the king's silver jubilee in 1935, an event which he described as 'a dream—a miracle arranged by Providence' (Royal Archives, GV P633/324). In jubilee year he was made a peer (25 June) and appointed keeper of the privy purse. Within months of the celebrations his duties extended to nursing the ailing king. It was to Wigram that George V spoke his dying words, asking about the state of the empire.

Wigram stayed on as private secretary, to settle in the new king, but their relations were uneasy from the start. Edward VIII regarded Wigram as a courtier of the old school, which did not recommend him. For his part Wigram was all too familiar with the king's failings and soon came to believe that his state of mind bordered on insanity. He left Edward's service in July 1936 but was recalled by George VI, albeit briefly, after the abdication and appointed permanent lord-in-waiting and extra equerry. During his career as a palace official he also served as deputy constable and lieutenant-governor of Windsor Castle, and keeper of the Royal Archives. For many years he and his family lived in the Norman tower at Windsor. A keen gardener and fellow of the Royal Horticultural Society, he converted the moat garden into a botanical showpiece. He retired to London in 1945.

During and after his long period in royal service Wigram was active in charitable and educational institutions, where his connections and buoyant humour were much valued. He was a fellow of his old school, Winchester, and a governor of Wellington College and Haileybury College. He served as president of the Westminster Hospital, vice-president of King Edward VII's Sanatorium, vice-president of the National Association of Boys Clubs, and was on the board of King George's Jubilee Trust. On 5 December 1912 he had married Nora Mary, only daughter of Colonel Sir Neville Chamberlain. They had two sons, the younger of whom was killed in action in 1943, and a daughter. Lady Wigram died on 5 January 1956 and their daughter two years later. Thereafter Wigram's mental and physical powers declined. He died in London on 3 September 1960 and was succeeded in his title by his surviving son, George Neville Clive. It would be easy to underrate his career in royal service. Not only was most of it spent in the shadow of Lord Stamfordham but the discretion and secrecy surrounding court life cloaked the machinations behind the throne. But in an era in which the monarchy felt threatened Wigram, despite his conservatism, was among the principal architects of its transformation into an institution more in tune with social democracy. There is a tablet to his memory in the north choir aisle of St George's Chapel, Windsor. FRANK PROCHASKA

Sources *DNB* · *The Times* (5 Sept 1960) · K. Rose, *King George V* (1983) · H. Nicolson, *King George V: his life and reign* (1953) · Royal Arch., George V papers · P. Ziegler, *King Edward VIII* (1990) · F. Prochaska, *Royal bounty: the making of a welfare monarchy* (1995) · F. Prochaska, *The republic of Britain, 1760–2000* (2000) · V. Bogdanor, *The monarchy and the constitution* (1995) · R. Allison and S. Riddell, eds., *The royal encyclopedia* (1991) · S. Bradford, *George VI* (1989) · GEC, *Peerage* · *CGPLA Eng. & Wales* (1960) · Burke, *Peerage*
Archives Royal Arch., MSS | BL OIOC, corresp. with Sir Edmund Barrow, MS Eur. E 420 · BL OIOC, letters to Sir W. R. Lawrence and Lady Lawrence, MS Eur. F 143 · Bodl. Oxf., corresp. with Samuel Bickersteth · Bodl. Oxf., corresp. with Sir Horace Rumbold · Bodl. Oxf., corresp. with Lord Simon · Commonwealth War Graves Commission, Maidenhead, papers relating to his appointment as member of the Imperial War Graves Commission · CUL, corresp. with Lord Hardinge, etc. · CUL, corresp. with Sir Samuel Hoare · NAM, corresp. with Lord Rawlinson · NL Aus., corresp. with first Viscount Stonehaven · U. Newcastle, Robinson L., corresp. with Walter Runciman
Likenesses F. O. Salisbury, drawing, 1921; Christies, 25 Sept 1985, lot 95 [*see illus.*] · L. Calkin, portrait, 1925; in possession of his family, 1971
Wealth at death £48,176 9s. 7d.: probate, 20 Dec 1960, *CGPLA Eng. & Wales*

Wigram [*née* Watts], **Eleanor**, **Lady Wigram** (1767–1841), philanthropist, was born on 1 April 1767, one of at least two daughters and one son of John Watts of Southampton, later secretary to the victualling office, and his wife, Eleanor Wyatt (*d.* 1811). On 23 June 1787 she married Robert *Wigram (1744–1830), a ship's surgeon turned drug merchant, at St Botolph's Church, Aldgate, London.

Robert Wigram already had six children from his marriage to Catherine Broadhurst (1750–1786) of Mansfield in 1772. He and Eleanor had sixteen surviving children, twelve sons and four daughters, and one son who died in infancy. Eleanor's offspring included James *Wigram (1793–1866), later vice-chancellor, and Joseph Cotton *Wigram (1798–1867), later bishop of Rochester.

From 1788 the Wigrams lived at Walthamstow House, Walthamstow, Essex, Robert's former residence. After the death of John Watts, Eleanor's mother moved there, staying until she died; Eleanor Wigram also lived there until her death. As adults, her sons Octavius, George, and Edward occupied houses adjoining hers in the 'Wigram enclave'.

Robert Wigram's 'second marriage was a very happy one; his wife became the "Lady Bountiful" of Walthamstow, besides being an excellent mother and a first-rate mistress' (Bosworth, 4). One surviving portrait represents her as an elegant society lady, another as a matriarch. She had other qualities: her husband reputedly said of her, 'I never did undertake any business of moment without

consultation with my wife, and I can truly say it has much promoted my fortune' (Green and Wigram, 1.54). That fortune proved to be considerable. By 1805 Wigram had partnerships in Reid's brewery, Huddart's rope works, the Blackwall shipbuilding yard, and his own business in Crosby Square. In 1810 he was chairman of the East India Docks. He was elected MP for Fowey in 1802, for Wexford in 1806, and was created a baronet in 1805.

Lady Wigram played a pioneering role in the provision of education and welfare services in Walthamstow. In 1807 she was funding a charity school for twelve children. This was the only recorded Anglican day school for the poor in the parish, besides the workhouse and endowed grammar schools. In 1815 she arranged for the mistress of the girls' endowed school to be instructed, at no expense to the parish, in the Madras system, the monitorial method of teaching used in national schools. In 1818 she suggested that the parish vestry form a new school by merging existing charity schools. Her plan was adopted in 1819, and the first national school in Walthamstow built, for boys and girls. In 1825 she was one of the seven 'special superintendents' of the girls' national school.

Lady Wigram's most striking achievements were associated with voluntary associations connected with the Anglican church. In 1815 she founded the Walthamstow Female Benefit Society (WFBS), the first recorded voluntary association in the parish, of which she remained sole patron and treasurer for twenty-six years. A sizeable proportion of local women became benefited members, often joining with young children and remaining in the society until widowhood or death. Benefits included free medical attendance and a weekly payment in times of sickness for a subscription of a shilling a month. The financial stability of this society was due in large part to Lady Wigram's ability to command the support of a wide cross-section of the local élite, many of whom contributed 1 guinea a year as honorary members. Consequently, the WFBS seems to have been more successful than the equivalent benefit society, founded in 1824 and run by a local curate.

Lady Wigram also founded, in 1824, the ladies' auxiliary of the Walthamstow branch of the Church Missionary Society, which was very successful, raising over four times as much money in, for example, 1839–40 as the male-run branch. The auxiliary survived only until 1848, and records of the WFBS are extant only until 1844. In 1840 she became one of the proprietors of the newly founded Walthamstow Proprietary Library, one of the few local cultural facilities for the well-to-do inhabitants.

Lady Wigram died on 23 January 1841 at Walthamstow House. She was buried in St Mary's churchyard, Walthamstow, in the same vault as her husband, on 29 January 1841. At his death in 1830 Robert Wigram had settled £6000 per annum on her, together with the Walthamstow House estate, which included 30 acres of land in 1820. These were divided among her children and stepchildren on her death, the estate being entailed on Wigram's eldest son.

Although Lady Wigram was described as 'a Lady Bountiful', no details have been found of regular informal giving, and no bequests to charities are listed in her will. By contrast, her recorded philanthropic work was characterized by the creation of associations and institutions, some of which were more effective than those run by men. Her biography illustrates how early nineteenth-century élite women could play a key role in local institutional philanthropy. MARY CLARE MARTIN

Sources M. C. Martin, 'Women and philanthropy in Walthamstow and Leyton, 1740–1870', *London Journal*, 19 (1994), 119–50, nn. 125–35, 139–41 · R. S. Wigram, *Biographical notes relating to certain members of the Wigram family* (1912), 18–35 · H. Green and R. Wigram, *Chronicles of Blackwall Yard* (1881), 50–54 · G. F. Bosworth, *Some Walthamstow houses and their interesting associations*, Walthamstow Antiquarian Society Official Publications, 12 (1924), 1–6 · probate, PRO, PROB/11/1942, quire no. 155, ff. 38–40, no. 46 [Lady Wigram's will] · probate, NMM, Wigram MSS, Wig/3/12 (1825) [Sir Robert Wigram's will] · Waltham Forest Archives (LBWF), St Mary's Walthamstow, register of burials (1768–1817), W83.1 RBU.1 12/2/1811 and R.BU.4 29/1/1841 · d. cert., General Register Office for England · marriage register of St Botolph without Aldgate, 1779–95, GL, MS 9230/5 · 'Walthamstow National Schools Rules and Regulations', LPL, Howley letters, 46 (1825), 70 · *Proceedings of the Church Missionary Society for Africa and the East* (1824), 41 · *Royal Kalendar* (1776–94)
Archives Vestry House Museum, Vestry Road, London, Walthamstow Female Benefit Society MSS
Likenesses Thomson, engraving (from miniature by Chalon), Vestry House Museum, Vestry Road, London; repro. in E. Ball, *La Belle assemblée*, 91, new series (1832) · G. Turner, engraving (*Wigram family*; after G. Smart), Vestry House Museum, Vestry Road, London · silhouette, priv. coll.

Wigram, George Vicesimus (1805–1879). *See under* Wigram, Joseph Cotton (1798–1867).

Wigram, Sir James (1793–1866), judge and legal writer, was born at Walthamstow House, Essex, on 5 November 1793, the third son of Sir Robert *Wigram (1744–1830) and his second wife, Eleanor *Wigram (1767–1841), daughter of John Watts of Southampton. Wigram's father, a merchant and shipowner, and MP for Wexford and Fowey, was created baronet in 1805. His elder brother, the second baronet, changed his name to Fitzwygram in 1832. Another of his brothers was Joseph Cotton *Wigram. Wigram was educated privately before matriculating in 1811 at Trinity College, Cambridge, where he graduated BA as fifth wrangler in 1815, and proceeded MA in 1818. He gained a fellowship at Trinity in 1817 but vacated this on his marriage on 24 December 1818 to Anne (*d.* 1844), daughter of Richard Arkwright of Willersley Castle, Derbyshire, and granddaughter of Sir Richard Arkwright. The couple had four sons and five daughters.

Wigram was admitted to Lincoln's Inn on 18 June 1813, and called to the bar on 18 November 1819. He practised in the court of chancery with such success that he was appointed king's counsel on 27 December 1834 and was elected a bencher of his inn in January 1835. In 1831 he published his *Examination of the rules of law respecting the admission of extrinsic evidence in aid of the interpretation of wills* which went through four editions in his lifetime, and appeared in a fifth edition in 1914. This was followed in 1836 by his *Points in the Law of Discovery* (2nd edn., 1840). These books led to an interesting correspondence with

some of the American judges, including the eminent commentator Joseph Story who regarded them as 'works of extraordinary merit, ability, and learning, and eminently useful to the profession' (*Life and Letters of Joseph Story*, ed. W. W. Story, 2 vols., 1851).

Wigram's wife's family owned considerable property in the neighbourhood of Leominster, Herefordshire, and supported by this Wigram stood as parliamentary candidate for Leominster as a tory in 1837. He was unsuccessful, but was returned for the borough without opposition at the next general election on 28 June 1841, but sat only until his appointment to the bench as a vice-chancellor on 30 October 1841, following the statute 5 Vict. c. 5 which provided for the appointment of two further vice-chancellors. He was knighted on 15 January 1842 and sworn of the privy council, becoming a member of its judicial committee. His decrees, well reported by Thomas Hare, were remarkable for their lucid exposition of legal principle and were generally admired. He resigned on 26 October 1850 as a result of an illness which led to complete blindness, and was granted a pension of £3500 a year. He died at his home, 68 Portland Place, London, on 29 July 1866. W. R. WILLIAMS, *rev.* N. G. JONES

Sources E. Foss, *Biographia juridica: a biographical dictionary of the judges of England … 1066–1870* (1870) · *Law Journal* (3 Aug 1866), 432 · *GM*, 4th ser., 2 (1866), 417–18 · Venn, *Alum. Cant.* · *Law Times* (4 Aug 1866), 699 · Burke, *Peerage* · *CGPLA Eng. & Wales* (1866)
Likenesses W. Walker, mezzotint, pubd 1849 (after J. W. Gordon), BM · G. Richmond, crayon, Trinity Cam.
Wealth at death under £70,000: probate, 7 Sept 1866, *CGPLA Eng. & Wales*

Wigram, Joseph Cotton (1798–1867), bishop of Rochester, was born at Walthamstow, Essex, on 26 December 1798, the fifteenth child of Sir Robert *Wigram, first baronet (1744–1830), an eminent Irish merchant and shipowner of London and Wexford. His mother, Sir Robert's second wife, was Eleanor *Wigram (1767–1841), daughter of John Watts of Southampton. Joseph was educated privately at Fulham and proceeded to Trinity College, Cambridge, where he graduated BA as sixth wrangler in 1820, MA in 1823, and DD in 1860. He was ordained deacon in November 1822 by the bishop of Ely and priest in May 1823 by William Howley, bishop of London. He served as a curate of Leytonstone, Essex, from 1822. In 1827 he became a district clergyman in the parish of St James, Westminster, under the Revd J. G. Ward. His twelve years of devoted work saw five new schools built and teams of visitors established. The chapel of ease for which he was responsible was rebuilt and opened as St Luke's Church, Berwick Street. He was also appointed secretary of the National Society from 1827, a position he held until 1839. On 1 March 1837 he married Susan Maria (1816–1864), daughter of Peter Arkwright of Willersley in Derbyshire. On 28 March 1839 he was appointed by James Scott rector of East Tisted in Hampshire, and in 1850 removed to the rectory of St Mary's, Southampton, which was in the gift of Charles Sumner, bishop of Winchester. On 16 November 1847 he was collated archdeacon of Winchester. He also held a canonry at Winchester Cathedral from 1850 until his consecration as bishop of Rochester on Ascension day 1860 in the parish church of St Mary, Lambeth. Bishop Charles Sumner wrote: 'my right arm is cut off to furnish Rochester with its chief ruler' (G. H. Sumner, 397). He died in London at 15A Grosvenor Square on 6 April 1867 and was buried at Latton parish church in Essex alongside his wife. They had six sons and three daughters.

Wigram's qualities as a Christian leader have been somewhat underestimated. His archidiaconal report on the problems of Portsea (1851) demonstrated a far-sighted awareness of the problems of a naval parish and how they might be addressed. As a bishop Wigram was a resolute opponent of non-residency in his diocese, which then included Essex and most of Hertfordshire. He was a conscientious pastor to his clergy and worked to raise their minimum salary to £250 per annum. He was staunchly committed to the parochial system and a decided advocate of mission women to assist the clergy. He argued that infants be baptized at public worship and that confirmation candidates should be given careful and full instruction. Wigram also promoted national day schools and evening institutions for adults. Although appointed by Lord Palmerston, Wigram was not quite 'of his politics', as Owen Chadwick observed (1.472). One explanation for this was Palmerston's overriding concern to have bishops who, regardless of their political allegiance, would make an active contribution to the debates in the House of Lords on church affairs. Wigram was a conscientious bishop of evangelical views, who on one occasion somewhat rashly denounced his clergy for wearing moustaches and playing cricket with their parishioners on village greens. Wigram's strong advocacy of lay agents to assist the incumbent in the parish and his teaching on the second advent suggest that his sympathies were with the Recordites. When he died Bishop Charles Sumner wrote that 'he was one of the most single-minded, straightforward men I have ever known, somewhat cold in manner, but full of energy and devotion to his work. The diocese will never have a more disinterested and unselfish head' (Sumner, 397 n.).

Wigram was essentially a pastor rather than a scholar and the bulk of his published writing related to practical and ministerial topics. In addition to a number of sermons and pamphlets he wrote *Elementary Arithmetic* (1831), *The Geography of the Holy Land* (1832; 5th edn, 1855), *Practical Hints on the Formation and Management of Sunday Schools* (1833), *The Cottager's Daily Family Prayers* (1862), and *Daily Hymns for the Month* (1866).

His younger brother, **George Vicesimus Wigram** (1805–1879), writer and lexicographer, was born in Walthamstow, Essex, on 28 March 1805, the twentieth child of Sir Robert Wigram, and the fourteenth with his second wife, Eleanor, née Watts. Converted in 1824 as a young officer he left the army and entered Queen's College, Oxford, in 1826, but did not graduate. He intended to take orders in the Church of England but Bishop Blomfield declined to ordain him on the grounds of his extreme evangelical views. In 1827 he met with John Nelson Darby in Oxford and joined the (Plymouth) Brethren, devoting

himself at the same time to the study of the biblical text. In 1831 Wigram published *A Protest Against the National Establishment of England*, and towards the end of the same year organized the first Brethren congregation in London. In 1834 his first wife, Fanny, died. She was daughter of Thomas Cherbury Bligh. He later made a second marriage, to Catherine, only daughter of William Parnell of Avondale and aunt of Charles Stewart Parnell.

In his youth Wigram lavished his immense wealth on clothes and horses; at Oxford he kept a close carriage. Latterly he used his inheritance for religious publishing. He became dissatisfied with Alexander Cruden's biblical concordance because it gave no clues as to the Greek language. In 1839 he therefore financed and published *The Englishman's Greek and English Concordance of the New Testament*, a second edition of which appeared in 1844 and an index in the following year. This work was based on the concordance of E. Schmidt and contained an alphabetical arrangement of every word in the Greek text. It was followed in 1843 by *The English's Hebrew and Chaldee Concordance of the Old Testament*. Later, in 1867, he edited with W. Chalk *The Hebraist's Vade Mecum*, which was the first attempt at a complete verbal index to the contents of the Hebrew and Chaldee scriptures.

The close friend and associate of John Nelson Darby, Wigram sided with him in the split with the (Plymouth) Brethren which resulted in the setting up of the separate Exclusive Brethren in 1849. Indeed it is clear that Wigram's unbending disposition inclined Darby to maintain his differences with Plymouth groups. Wigram initiated and edited a new journal for the Exclusives under the title of *Present Testimony*. Along with Darby he contributed articles and teaching which helped to generate the rapid expansion of Exclusivism in the middle Victorian years.

Wigram died on 1 January 1879 at his house, 45 Great Cumberland Place, London, leaving more than £50,000 of the money he had inherited from his father's estate. Seven or eight hundred people, 'almost entirely well-to-do middle class', attended his funeral at Paddington cemetery.　　　　　　　　　　　　　NIGEL SCOTLAND

Sources *The Times* (9 April 1867) · *Record* (8 April 1867) · Boase, *Mod. Eng. biog.* · Venn, *Alum. Cant.* · G. H. Sumner, *Life of Charles Richard Sumner DD, bishop of Winchester* (1876) · O. Chadwick, *The Victorian church*, 1 (1966) · D. W. Bebbington, *Evangelicalism in modern Britain: a history from the 1730s to the 1980s* (1989) · E. Dennett, *Memorials of the ministry of G. V. Wigram*, 3 vols. (1880–81) · *Daily News* (7 Jan 1879) · M. S. Weremchuk, *John Nelson Darby* (1990) · N. Noel, *The history of the Brethren*, 2 vols. (1936) · W. G. Turner, *John Nelson Darby* (1901) · H. H. Rowden, *The origins of the Brethren, 1825–1850* (1967) · B. W. Newton, *Letters and accounts of early years of the Brethren in the so called Fry manuscripts* · H. Pickering, *Chief men among the Brethren: a series of brief records of Brethren beloved collected from many sources* (1932) · *DNB* · *CGPLA Eng. & Wales* (1867)
Archives LPL, letters to Charles Golightly
Likenesses portrait?, repro. in *ILN*, 36 (1860), 357
Wealth at death under £45,000: probate, 13 May 1867, *CGPLA Eng. & Wales* · under £60,000—George Vicesimus Wigram: probate, 12 March 1879, *CGPLA Eng. & Wales*

Wigram, Ralph Follett (1890–1936), diplomatist, was born on 23 October 1890 at Egginton House, Egginton, Bedfordshire, the only son of Eustace Rochester Wigram, retired army officer, of Mount Sandford, Barnstaple, Devon, and his wife, Grace Mary, daughter of Lieutenant-Colonel Ralph Bradford-Atkinson, of Angerton, Morpeth, Northumberland. His paternal grandfather was the Rt Revd J. C. Wigram, bishop of Rochester. Educated at Eton College and University College, Oxford, Wigram obtained a second-class degree in modern history in 1912. He served in the War Office from 1914 to 1916 as a captain on the special list, in which capacity he accompanied a military mission to the Caucasus. He was decorated with the Russian order of St Anne. From 1916 to 1919 he was employed at the British embassy in Washington and in September 1919 he passed into the Foreign Office where, as a third secretary in the central department, he acquired an expert knowledge of the peace settlement and attended many of the post-war conferences in France, Italy, and Belgium. Promotion to second secretary in December 1920 was followed in 1923 by a posting to the British embassy in Paris where he quickly developed a range of important contacts in French social and political life. Following a further promotion to first secretary in July 1924, and marriage in 1925 to Ava Bodley, daughter of the author John Edward Courtenay *Bodley, Wigram was struck down with polio in 1927, an event which some believed would mark the end of his career. Nevertheless, after a long period of recuperation he returned to Paris to resume his duties. In recognition of his services he was appointed CMG in January 1933.

Following Hitler's accession to the German chancellorship Wigram was recalled to London to become head of the central department with the rank of acting counsellor, and in July 1934 he was promoted counsellor. Working closely with Sir Robert Vansittart and Orme Sargent, whose views of the Nazi menace he shared, Wigram watched with mounting anxiety the growth of the German armed forces in contravention of part V of the treaty of Versailles. He was unmoved by Hitler's professed desire for co-operation with Britain and contemptuous of those who favoured an accommodation with a resurgent Germany at the expense of Britain's other European friendships. He was equally appalled by the apparent indifference of cabinet ministers and other politicians to the warnings about the pace and scope of Hitler's rearmament which he and his department provided. The minutes and memoranda he wrote after 1933 are a fitting testament to his understanding of Hitler's designs and the dangers to which Britain would be exposed if she failed to stand squarely with France and simultaneously to make adequate preparation for her own defence. He was especially anxious about the growth of German air power and in the spring of 1935, following the announcement of the existence of the Luftwaffe, he secured Vansittart's permission to leak information to the *Daily Telegraph* about the expansion of the German air force. In April he visited Winston Churchill at Chartwell and informed him of the rising concern felt in the Foreign Office about Hitler's rearmament and intentions. This was the first of numerous meetings over the next eighteen months in the course of which Wigram supplied Churchill on a regular basis

with information about actual and potential German aircraft production for use in his campaign for accelerated British rearmament. Wigram was not opposed to the idea of a multilateral settlement with Germany but shared Vansittart's conviction that a worthwhile agreement could only be negotiated from a position of strength. He was also convinced of the necessity to uphold the balance of power in Europe which Hitler was manifestly aiming to destroy. For these reasons he was anxious to maintain Italian friendship against Hitler, but saw his hopes dashed when Mussolini invaded Abyssinia in October 1935 and thus set in train the series of events which eventually culminated in Anglo-Italian estrangement and the declaration of the Rome–Berlin axis. Wigram saw the reoccupation of the Rhineland in March 1936 as a crucial turning point and believed it would now be impossible to stop Hitler without resort to force. 'War is now inevitable', he famously remarked to his wife at their London home, 'and it will be the most terrible war there has ever been. I don't think I shall see it, but you will. Wait now for bombs on this little house' (Churchill, 178). Thereafter he considered his work a failure, but like his mentor Vansittart he had done all in his power to alert the British government to the threat posed by Nazi Germany. His untimely death deprived the Foreign Office of one of its most astute and intelligent analysts of the European political scene. The sense of loss shared by his colleagues was profound and sincere. Suffering from lung cancer, Wigram died suddenly of a pulmonary embolism at his country home at Seaford, Sussex, on 31 December 1936. His funeral took place at Holy Trinity Church, Cuckfield, Sussex, on 4 January 1937.

G. T. WADDINGTON

Sources *The Times* (1 Jan 1937) · *The Times* (2 Jan 1937) · *The Times* (5 Jan 1937) · PRO, FO 371 · M. Gilbert, *Winston S. Churchill*, 5: 1922–1939 (1976) · M. Gilbert, ed., *Winston S. Churchill*, companion vol. 5/2 (1981) · N. Rose, *Vansittart: study of a diplomat* (1978) · I. Colvin, *Vansittart in office: an historical survey of the origins of the Second World War based on the papers of Sir Robert Vansittart* (1965) · W. S. Churchill, *The Second World War*, 1 (1948) · V. Lawford, *Bound for diplomacy* (1963) · W. K. Wark, *The ultimate enemy: British intelligence and Nazi Germany, 1933–1939* (1985) · Lord Vansittart [R. G. Vansittart], *The mist procession: the autobiography of Lord Vansittart* (1958) · A. Eden, earl of Avon, *The Eden memoirs*, 1: *Facing the dictators* (1962) · *FO List* (1936) · private information (2004) [librarian, Eton College] · *WWW*, 1929–40 · b. cert. · d. cert.
Archives PRO, lectures on British foreign policy, FO 800 | CAC Cam., corresp. with E. L. Spears

Wigram, Sir Robert, first baronet (1744–1830), merchant and shipbuilder, was born on 30 January 1744 in Wexford, Ireland, son of John Wigram (*d.* 1746) of Wexford, merchant and master of the privateer *Boyne*, and his wife and cousin Mary, daughter of Robert Clifford of Wexford. His father drowned at sea when he was two, and he was brought up in Wexford by his maternal uncle, a doctor, before going to London in 1762. After two years' apprenticeship to a Dr Allen of Dulwich he qualified as a surgeon in 1764, joined the East India Company as a surgeon's mate, and sailed to India. He worked as a ship's surgeon until 1772, when he had to stop practising: an eye infection he developed in China had permanently damaged his eyesight. In 1772 he married Catherine (d. 1786), daughter of John Broadhurst of Mansfield, Nottinghamshire, a Unitarian, and under her influence he became a Unitarian. They had four sons and two daughters. In 1787 he married Eleanor [see Wigram, Eleanor, Lady Wigram (1767–1841)], widow of Captain Agnew and daughter of John Watts of Southampton, secretary to the victualling office, and they went on to have thirteen sons and four daughters.

Wigram opened a drug business in 1774 at 4 White Lion Court, Cornhill, London, and became one of the leading drug importers in the country, putting into practice his knowledge of the trade of India and China. He moved the business nearby to 3 Crosby Square, Bishopsgate, in 1782, and bought Walthamstow House in Essex.

As his fortune grew Wigram began to buy shares in East India Company ships. The first was the *General Goddard*, in 1788, and in 1790 he bought the *True Briton*, built by the Wellses of Rotherhithe. As well as owning several ships Wigram became one of the leading ship's husbands in the port of London. At the same time he was acquiring land, part of the Orchard House estate, belonging to the East India Company, on the Thames near Blackwall Yard. He was also a partner in Reid's Brewery, which supplied beer to the Indiamen, and in Huddart's Rope Works, at Limehouse. Wigram was a leader of the group of shipowners who pressed the government to establish the East India Dock Company in 1803 and build docks at Blackwall, on the Thames, for East India Company ships; he was also one of the original subscribers to the company. A member of the committee for constructing the docks, he chaired the East India Dock Company from 1810 and became a director in 1815, at the time when he was buying the freehold of several parts of the Orchard House estate.

Wigram was elected MP for Fowey in 1802 and held this seat until 1806, when he became MP for Wexford. He was a strong supporter of William Pitt and was rewarded with a baronetcy in 1805, for which he himself had applied, mentioning the expense to which he had gone as lieutenant-colonel of the 6th Loyal London volunteers and in fitting out ships for the navy. He left parliament in 1807.

In 1805 Wigram bought a large share in Blackwall Yard from John Perry and the Wells brothers. The first shipyard to be built on the left bank of the Thames, Blackwall Yard was originally created by the East India Company for the building and repair of its ships, but it was sold in 1650 and developed in the eighteenth century into one of the largest shipyards on the Thames. During the Napoleonic wars it was the place of embarkation for regiments going overseas, and ships were built there for the navy: in 1813 alone, ten frigates were built there. Part of the yard was sold to the East India Company in 1803 for the new docks, which opened in 1806. When Perry retired in 1810, the Wells brothers sold the property to Wigram, with John Wells retaining a quarter share, but with no active role, until he sold it to Wigram in 1813. Wigram ran the yard with the help of two of his sons, Money and Loftus. He retired from active control at Blackwall Yard in 1819 and sold the yard to Money and Loftus Wigram, and George Green, the son-in-law of John Perry, former owner of the yard. The firm became Wigrams and Green, and in 1821 it launched the first steam vessel to be built at Blackwall Yard. Sir Robert Wigram died at Walthamstow, Essex, on 6 November 1830.

Wigram was a man of great energy. According to the diarist Joseph Farington, occupation was essential to him, and he 'should be miserable if in a morning he should not awake with his head full of ideas of business for the day' (*Farington Diary*, ed. Greig, 6 Oct 1811). Several of his sons were successful, including his eldest son, Sir Robert Wigram (knighted in 1818), a director of the Bank of England and an MP for many years; George Vicesimus *Wigram (1805–1879) [see under Wigram, Joseph Cotton], a writer and a member of the Plymouth Brethren; Sir James *Wigram (1793–1866), barrister and author of legal works; and Joseph Cotton *Wigram (1798–1867), bishop of Rochester.

ANNE PIMLOTT BAKER

Sources S. Porter, ed., *Poplar, Blackwall and the Isle of Dogs: the parish of All Saints*, [2], Survey of London, 44 (1994), 553–74 • H. Green and R. Wigram, *Chronicles of Blackwall Yard* (1881) • HoP, *Commons* • P. Banbury, *Shipbuilders of the Thames and Medway* (1971), 114–26 • *The Farington diary*, ed. J. Greig, 8 vols. (1922–8) • *GM*, 1st ser., 100/2 (1830), 563–4 • Burke, *Peerage*

Archives NMM, business and legal papers | NL Scot., corresp. with Thomas Graham Stirling

Likenesses C. Turner, group portrait, etching, 1826 (after J. Smart), BM • J. H. Watt, engraving (after T. Lawrence), BM

Wealth at death est. wealth over £500,000 in 1809: *Farington diary*, ed. Greig

Wigram, William Ainger (1872–1953), advocate of the Assyrian church and people, was born on 16 May 1872 at the vicarage in Furneaux Pelham, Hertfordshire, one of the seven children of Woolmore *Wigram (1831–1907), vicar of Brent Pelham with Furneaux Pelham, and his wife, Harriet Mary (d. 1927), daughter of the Revd Thomas *Ainger, of Hampstead. A baronetcy in the Wigram family descended to William's older brother Edgar in 1920. Wigram was educated at King's School, Canterbury, and matriculated at Trinity Hall, Cambridge, in 1891. He took his degree in 1893 and became a pupil of Bishop B. F. Westcott of Durham. He was ordained deacon in 1896 and priest in 1897, and served two assistant curacies in the Durham diocese, the latter at St Barnabas, Sunderland. There he was recruited by O. H. Parry in 1902 for the Archbishop of Canterbury's Mission to the Assyrian Christians. The archbishop's mission worked to sustain the Assyrian Church of the East (more commonly called the Nestorian church) in Persia and Turkey by means of schools, printing, parish work, and support for the patriarch. Wigram served ten years in the mission, the last five (1907–12) as its head. His chief responsibility was to conduct a school for boys and ordinands in Van in eastern Turkey. In 1910 he removed the school to Bibaydi in the mountains north of Mosul in an attempt to challenge the Catholic dominance over the local Christians. A tireless walker, he toured villages, making frequent visits to the patriarch's remote home of Kochanes. Wigram's experiences in the country of the Church of the East, recorded in anecdotal style, can be read in his book *The Cradle of Mankind* (1914, with illustrations by Edgar Wigram).

Unlike some others associated with the mission, Wigram never became discouraged about the future of the Church of the East. He remained a trusted adviser of Archbishop Randall Davidson, who awarded him the Lambeth degree of DD in 1910. Wigram's most notable success was in bringing the Assyrian Church of the East into contact with the wider ecclesiastical world. His book *The Assyrian Church, 100–640 A.D.* (1910) popularized this name for the church among English speakers. The book also argued that the Nestorianism of the Church of the East was merely nominal. Others had come to this conclusion before, but Wigram gave it practical effect. Legislation to allow intercommunion between the Anglican churches and the Church of the East, taken up by the Lambeth conference of 1910 and finally passed in 1920, was largely the result of his diplomacy among the bishops on both sides.

Seeking other work with eastern churches, Wigram left the Assyrian mission in 1912 for a chaplaincy in Constantinople. There he was overtaken by the First World War and interned. In 1918 he was intercepted on his way home and posted to Mesopotamia as a political officer to help manage the resettlement of the displaced Assyrian people in their old lands. The resettlement failed, however, as did all efforts to re-start the archbishop's mission. With the election of an eleven-year-old boy to the patriarchate in 1920 the church further weakened itself, but Wigram continued to support the patriarch as the only credible political leader of the whole people. After five years in Greece (1922–6) as chaplain to the British legation, Wigram visited Iraq again in 1928. His conviction that the British government owed the Assyrians a settlement as an autonomous people (expressed in a number of occasional writings, although toned down for his book *The Assyrians and their Neighbours*, 1929) made him unwelcome to the authorities there. After the end of the British mandate in 1932, the treatment of the Assyrians by the new Iraqi government confirmed his belief that Britain had betrayed them. Wigram accompanied the young patriarch Mar Eshai Shimun to Geneva to plead his cause before the League of Nations in 1933. Wigram's intransigence lost him the confidence of Archbishop Cosmo Gordon Lang, and when in 1938 Lang finally gave over responsibility for relations with the Assyrians to the bishop of Jerusalem, Wigram retired from Anglican–Assyrian affairs in disgust.

Wigram held a canonry of St Paul's Church, Malta, from 1928 to 1936. He was a well-known lecturer for the Hellenic Travellers' Club and author of *Hellenic Travel* (1947). He never married, and from about 1929 lived with his sister at Green Acres, Wells, Somerset. He died on 16 January 1953 at the Old Manor, Salisbury, Wiltshire. One of the last visitors to call on him before his death was Mar Eshai Shimun.

J. F. COAKLEY

Sources Assyrian Mission MSS, LPL · *W. A. Wigram: a fragment of autobiography*, ed. J. F. Coakley (1985) · St Ant. Oxf., Middle East Centre, Jerusalem and the East Mission MSS · Wigram file, American School of Classical Studies, Athens, Gennadius Library · private information (2004) · b. cert. · d. cert.

Archives American School of Classical Studies, Athens, Gennadius Library | LPL, Assyrian Mission MSS · St Ant. Oxf., Middle East Centre, Jerusalem and the East Mission MSS
Likenesses photographs (as a young man), priv. coll. · three photographs (in rather old age), American School of Classical Studies, Athens, Gennadius Library; repro. in J. F. Coakley, *The Church of the East and the Church of England* (1992)
Wealth at death £18,540 15s. 4d.: probate, 22 May 1953, *CGPLA Eng. & Wales*

Wigram, Woolmore (1831–1907), Church of England clergyman and campanologist, was the fifth son of ten children of Money Wigram (1790–1873), director of the Bank of England, of Manor Place, Much Hadham, Hertfordshire, and Mary, daughter of Charles Hampden Turner, of Rooks Nest, Godstone, Surrey. He was born on 29 October 1831 at Devonshire Place, London. His father's mother was Eleanor *Wigram, Lady Wigram. His father was the elder brother of Sir James Wigram, Joseph Cotton Wigram, and George Vicesimus Wigram. Of his own brothers, Charles Hampden (1826–1903) was knighted in 1902, and Clifford (1828–1898) became director of the Bank of England. Wigram entered Rugby School in August 1844, and in 1850 matriculated at Trinity College, Cambridge, where he graduated BA in 1854 and proceeded MA in 1858. Among his close friends at Cambridge was John Gott (1830–1906), afterwards bishop of Truro. After taking holy orders in 1855, Wigram was curate of Hampstead (1855–64), vicar of Brent Pelham with Furneaux Pelham, Hertfordshire (1864–76), and rector of St Andrew's with St Nicholas's and St Mary's, Hertford (1876–97). From 1877 to 1897 he was rural dean of Hertford, and in 1886 was made honorary canon of St Albans, where he lived from 1898 until his death, and was an active member of the chapter. A highchurchman, Wigram was for a long time a member of the English Church Union. He married on 23 July 1863 Harriet Mary (d. 1927), daughter of the Revd Thomas *Ainger of Hampstead; they had four sons, including William Ainger *Wigram, who became an advocate of the Assyrian church and people, and three daughters.

Wigram was an enthusiastic campanologist, and became an authority on the subject. A series of articles in *Church Bells* was collected in 1871 under the title *Change-Ringing Disentangled and Management of Towers*.

In his earlier days Wigram was an enthusiastic alpine climber. He was a member of the Alpine Club from 1858 to 1868. His most memorable feat was the first successful ascent, in the company of Thomas Stewart Kennedy (with Jean Baptiste Croz and Josef Marie Krönig as guides), of La Dent Blanche, near Zermatt, on 18 July 1862.

Wigram died from the effects of influenza at his home, Watling House, Watling Street, St Albans, on 19 January 1907, and was buried in St Stephen's churchyard there. His wife survived him.

W. B. OWEN, *rev.* ELIZABETH BAIGENT

Sources *The Times* (22 Jan 1907), 12 · Venn, *Alum. Cant.* · H. M. Wigram, *Memoirs of Woolmore Wigram, canon of St Alban's ... 1831–1907* (1908) · E. Whymper, *Scrambles amongst the Alps in the years 1860–69*, 5th edn (1900) · *CGPLA Eng. & Wales* (1907) · WWW
Likenesses portrait, repro. in Wigram, *Memoirs of Woolmore Wigram*

Wealth at death £39,809 18s. 4d.: probate, 18 Feb 1907, *CGPLA Eng. & Wales*

Wigstan [St Wigstan] (*d.* 849), martyr, is most reliably documented in what is probably the ninth-century section of an early eleventh-century list of saints' resting places, *Secgan be þam godes sanctum þe on Engla lande ærost reston*, which has an entry 'Then St Wigstan rests at the monastery of Repton near the River Trent' (Liebermann, 11). This record may be corroborated by architectural study at St Wystan's Church, Repton, which shows that during the Anglo-Saxon period two corridors were pierced to give access to the crypt, possibly to allow access to a saint's shrine, presumably Wigstan's. Archaeological excavation has shown a cluster of richly fitted graves around the east end of the church, possibly representing persons wishing to be buried close to the saint. According to Thomas of Marlborough (*d.* 1236), prior of Evesham and author of the abbey's chronicle, King Cnut translated Wigstan's remains to Evesham, although a portion was later returned to the newly founded canons of Repton. The same writer asserts that Wigstan was the son of Wigmund, king of Mercia in the early ninth century, and his queen, Ælfflæd. On Wigmund's death, Wigstan refused to become king, preferring a life of religion. When his relative Beorhtfrith asked permission to marry the widowed queen, however, Wigstan refused and Beorhtfrith accordingly had him murdered. John of Worcester, writing in the early twelfth century, gives a brief mention of Wigstan's parentage, death, and burial (at Repton), and gives the date of his death as 1 June 849. Finally, a slightly different version of Wigstan's life and death is preserved in two fourteenth-century manuscripts, Gotha, Forschungsbibliothek, MS I. 81, and London, British Library, Harley MS 2253, which came originally from Herefordshire. Because this version does not refer to the translation of Wigstan's relics to Evesham in the time of Cnut it is possible, but by no means certain, that they derive from an early *passio*, possibly of ninth-century date.

If the information contained in these texts is reliable, it appears that Wigstan was a victim of dynastic conflict in early ninth-century Mercia, specifically between the family of King Wiglaf, whose son Wigmund was, and the family of King Beorhtwulf, father of Wigstan's killer Beorhtfrith. Wigstan's subsequent veneration as a saint is part of a wider pattern of the veneration of kings and princes killed for what appear to have been political motives. That veneration may have been prompted by the church at large as a means of drawing attention to the crimes of the murderers; or it may have emanated from the desire of the victims' families to perpetuate their memory and the iniquity of their enemies. Repton seems to have been the centre of a royal estate, for in later centuries it had a large parish with dependent chapelries; and Wigstan's cult seems also to have been fostered on the neighbouring royal estate of Glen, where churches at Wigston and Wistow, Leicestershire, were dedicated to the saint. In the later middle ages, Wistow was supposed to have been the site of Wigstan's murder. The cult appears never to have been widely diffused, and its relationship with these royal estates suggests that it was sponsored from within the Mercian royal family.   DAVID ROLLASON

Sources D. Rollason, *The search for St Wigstan, prince-martyr of the kingdom of Mercia*, Vaughan Paper, 27 (1981) • D. W. Rollason, 'The cults of murdered royal saints in Anglo-Saxon England', *Anglo-Saxon England*, 11 (1983), 1–22 • M. Biddle, 'Archaeology, architecture, and the cult of saints in Anglo-Saxon England', *The Anglo-Saxon church: papers on history, architecture, and archaeology in honour of Dr H. M. Taylor*, ed. L. A. S. Butler and R. K. Morris, Council for British Archaeology Research Report, 60 (1986), 1–31 • A. Thacker, 'Kings, saints and monasteries in pre-viking Mercia', *Midland History*, 10 (1985), 1–25 • F. Liebermann, *Die Heiligen Englands* (1889) • John of Worcester, *Chron.*

Wigtown. For this title name *see* Fleming, Malcolm, first earl of Wigtown (*d.* in or before 1363); Fleming, John, first earl of Wigtown (*c.*1567–1619) [*see under* Fleming, John, fifth Lord Fleming (*d.* 1572)]; Fleming, John, second earl of Wigtown (*bap.* 1589?, *d.* 1650).

Wihtgar (*d.* 544?), king of Wight, was the eponymous founder of the dynasty which ruled the Isle of Wight until 685 and from which King Alfred's mother, Osburh, claimed descent. Wihtgar is said in the Anglo-Saxon Chronicle to have fought with Stuf against the British in 514, following the arrival of the West Saxons with three ships at 'Cerdicesora'. In 534 Stuf and Wihtgar are recorded as receiving the Isle of Wight from their kinsmen *Cerdic and *Cynric; in 544 Wihtgar is said to have died and been buried at 'Wihtgarabyrig'.

Wihtgar is one of several examples in the early annals of the chronicle of presumably mythic individuals whose names seem to be derived from places with which they were associated. The first element of his name is an Anglicization of Vecta, the Latin name of the Isle of Wight, whose inhabitants were sometimes referred to in Anglo-Saxon sources as Wihtgara. The genealogy of the royal house of Kent also incorporated names in Wiht-, and there seems to have been an early association between Kent and Wight. Bede believed that both were areas of Jutish settlement and finds from Anglo-Saxon cemeteries on the Isle of Wight have their closest parallels in Kent. It is difficult to disentangle any truths about the origins of the kingdom of Wight from the entries in the chronicle, which clearly follow established conventions for foundation myths, though it should be noted that Stuf, unlike Wihtgar, is an acceptable personal name. The linking of the myths of Stuf and Wihtgar with those of Cerdic and Cynric is likely to have occurred after 685 when Cædwalla, king of the West Saxons, conquered the island and had its last king, Aruald, and his two brothers, put to death.

BARBARA YORKE

Sources ASC, s.a. 514, 534, 544 • *Asser's Life of King Alfred: together with the 'Annals of Saint Neots' erroneously ascribed to Asser*, ed. W. H. Stevenson (1904), ch. 2 • Bede, *Hist. eccl.*, 1.15; 4.15–16 • P. Sims-Williams, 'The settlement of England in Bede and the *Chronicle*', *Anglo-Saxon England*, 12 (1983), 1–41 • B. A. E. Yorke, 'The Jutes of Hampshire and Wight and the origins of Wessex', *The origins of Anglo-Saxon kingdoms*, ed. S. Bassett (1989), 84–96 • C. J. Arnold, *The Anglo-Saxon cemeteries of the Isle of Wight* (1982) • B. A. E. Yorke, *Kings and kingdoms of early Anglo-Saxon England* (1990)

Wihtred (*d.* 725), king of Kent, was the son of *Ecgberht I (*d.* 673) [*see under* Eorcenberht] and the brother of *Eadric (*d.* 686) [*see under* Hlothhere], both rulers in Kent. For several years after Eadric's death Kent had been at the mercy of foreign invaders, who had set their own candidates on the throne: Mul (*r.* 686–7), brother of the West Saxon king Cædwalla; Swæfheard (*r.* 687/8–*c.*692), son of the East Saxon king Sæbbi; and Oswine (*r.* 688/9–690?), backed by the Mercian king Æthelred. Eventually Wihtred managed to build up enough support to make good his claims to the kingship. In July 692 Swæfheard and Wihtred were ruling together in Kent; they may have been joint rulers, or the kingdom may have been divided between them. Bede's calculations about the length of Wihtred's reign suggest that he first came to power in the autumn of 690, but some of Wihtred's charters indicate that the beginning of his reign was usually reckoned from the summer or autumn of 691. By 694 Swæfheard had disappeared from the scene, for in a charter of that year Wihtred made a grant of land without reference to a joint ruler, and explicitly gave thanks to God 'who has extended our boundaries as they were in our father's time' (*AS chart.*, S 15). In this charter, Wihtred's wife Cynegyth is presented as co-donor; no earlier Kentish queen had been given this status in a charter, and after Wihtred's reign they once more sink into obscurity, so it may have been the case that Cynegyth was given additional importance because Wihtred relied on the support of her kindred.

In the early years of Wihtred's sole reign there is evidence for close relations between Kent and Wessex. In 694 the people of Kent 'made terms with Ine' (king of the West Saxons from 688 to 726) and presented him with 30,000 pence in compensation for the killing of the West Saxon usurper Mul in 687 (*ASC*, s.a. 694); it may be significant that the Anglo-Saxon Chronicle links this event with Wihtred's succession to the kingdom of Kent. Either in 695 or in 696 Wihtred proclaimed a set of laws in the course of a Kentish assembly at an unidentified place called 'Berghamstyde'. In comparison with other seventh-century law-codes, Wihtred's laws seem particularly preoccupied with ecclesiastical matters, such as the position of the church and churchmen in secular society, and the enforcement of lay observance of ecclesiastical rules. Towards the end Wihtred turns to the more worldly matter of the treatment of thieves, and closes with a prescription that strangers and foreigners should keep to the road or be assumed to be thieves. Remarkably this same provision is to be found in the law code of King Ine (issued between 688 and 694), which implies that the two rulers had come to some agreement about the treatment of foreigners in their respective kingdoms.

After its difficult beginning, Wihtred's long reign seems to have been remarkably uneventful; but the sources are poor for this period and certain triumphs and calamities may have slipped from the record. It has been suggested that in the 690s the kingdoms of Anglo-Saxon England arrived at an involuntary balance of power, which led to a period of relative stability; Northumbria was in decline and Mercia was deterred from trying to conquer south-eastern England by the existence of strong kings (with a mutual understanding) in Wessex and Kent. Possibly this impression of relative peace is a product of inadequate source material; there is a hint of troubles in the preamble of the grant of privileges which Wihtred made to the Kentish churches in 699. Nevertheless, it is clear that Wihtred must have been a very able (or very fortunate) king to rule the wealthy kingdom of Kent for more than thirty years, apparently without challenge, and to be able to hand it on to his sons. He may well have made judicious use of alliances, regularly cemented by marriage. His first wife, Cynegyth, seems to have died or to have been repudiated very quickly, for in a charter of 696 there is a new royal consort named Æthelburh, again presented as co-donor of the estate; she appears prominently in Wihtred's other charters from the late 690s. Towards the end of his reign Wihtred was associated with a third queen, named Wærburh, who attested with her husband and her son Alric the proceedings of a synod that took place at Bapchild, probably in 716 (*AS chart.*, S 22); the charter as it stands is spurious, but the forger has made use of witness lists from a genuine document or documents. Wihtred also seems to have strengthened his position by winning the firm support of the Kentish churches. In his law code he exempted them from the payment of royal tribute, a concession strengthened by a charter of privileges issued in 699. He is also known to have made land grants to the monastery of St Peter and St Paul (later St Augustine's) in Canterbury, and to the ministers in Thanet and Lyminge; in some late sources he is remembered as the founder of the minster at Dover.

Wihtred died on 23 April 725 and was buried in St Mary's Church in the monastery of St Peter and St Paul, Canterbury. He was succeeded by his three sons: *Æthelberht II (*d.* 762), *Eadberht I [*see under* Æthelberht II], and Alric. Nothing more is heard of Alric after Wihtred's death, which suggests that he may have been denied power by his half-brothers (he was evidently the son of a different wife, Wærburh); his elder brothers ruled jointly until Eadberht's death in 748. S. E. KELLY

Sources Bede, *Hist. eccl.*, 4.26; 5.8, 23–4 · *AS chart.*, S 10–16, 18–22 · 'The laws of Wihtred, king of Kent', *English historical documents*, 1, ed. D. Whitelock (1955), 361–64, no. 31 · *ASC*, s.a. 694 · S. Keynes, 'England, 700–900', *The new Cambridge medieval history*, 2, ed. R. McKitterick (1995), 18–42 · S. E. Kelly, ed., *Charters of St Augustine's Abbey, Canterbury, and Minster-in-Thanet*, Anglo-Saxon Charters, 4 (1995), appx 3, 'The kings of Kent' · F. M. Stenton, *Anglo-Saxon England*, 3rd edn (1971), 62, 203 · N. Brooks, *The early history of the church of Canterbury: Christ Church from 597 to 1066* (1984), 78, 182 · K. H. Krüger, *Königsgrabkirchen der Franken, Angelsachsen und Langobarden bis zur Mitte des 8. Jahrhunderts: ein historischer Katalog*, Münstersche Mittelalter-Schriften, 4 (1971), 264–87 · R. U. Potts, 'The tombs of the kings and archbishops in St Austin's Abbey', *Archaeologia Cantiana*, 38 (1926), 97–112

Wikeford, Robert (*d.* 1390), archbishop of Dublin and administrator, was probably born at Wickford Hall, Essex. A scholar and fellow (1344) of Merton College, Oxford, he subsequently studied abroad and became doctor of laws. He was a king's clerk and acquired interests in Henley and elsewhere in Surrey. He was rector of Avington church,

Hampshire, in 1351 and held numerous other preferments, including the prebends of Scamblesby in Lincoln (1363), Ludington in Shaftesbury (1368), and North Newbald in York (1370). In October 1361 Wikeford was collated to the archdeaconry of Winchester. He was also, by 1380, dean of the king's free chapel in Penkridge, Stafford. He served the king overseas, first on a mission in November 1368 to Pope Urban V, and then on diplomatic assignments in various locations, including Brabant (1370), Flanders and the Flemish cities (1371), and Aquitaine (1373). He held the post of constable of Bordeaux from 7 March 1373 until 23 July 1375. On 12 October 1375 Wikeford was promoted by papal provision to the archbishopric of Dublin, the temporalities being restored on 30 January 1376. He was appointed chancellor of Ireland on 18 July 1376 but did not, apparently, take up office immediately. He was reappointed on 26 September 1377, after the accession of Richard II, but was replaced on 15 December 1378 by Robert Sutton, nominated keeper of the seal. In 1378 Wikeford was active in the defence of Dublin against the Irish of Leinster. He successfully petitioned in 1380 for the restoration to his see of the manor of Swords, seized in 1377 in the course of investigations by Nicholas Dagworth.

In March 1384 Wikeford went to England on business concerning both the king's interests and those of his see. Following this he was reappointed chancellor on 10 September 1384, with special privileges reserving to the king any complaints against him. In December 1384 he was rebuked for exceeding his authority and acting without the consent of Philip Courtenay, lord lieutenant, and was relieved of his office before 27 March 1385. He was, however, chosen with Alexander Balscot, bishop of Ossory, to report to the king from the great council in October 1385, which asked for royal intervention to defend the lordship. Wikeford was absent from Ireland from January 1386 until 27 September 1387. He was among the advisers to Richard II witnessing the Shrewsbury statement of the judges in September 1387 which declared illegal the proceedings of the recent commission; and, according to the monk of Westminster, he betrayed the judgment to the duke of Gloucester. Wikeford died on 28 August 1390, leaving money to Merton College for all the altars in the college chapel.   D. B. JOHNSTON

Sources *The whole works of Sir James Ware concerning Ireland*, ed. and trans. W. Harris, rev. edn, 2 vols. in 3 (1764) · *Chancery records* · E. Tresham, ed., *Rotulorum patentium et clausorum cancellariae Hiberniae calendarium*, Irish Record Commission (1828) · *Fasti Angl., 1300–1541*, [Lincoln] · *Fasti Angl., 1300–1541*, [Monastic cathedrals] · *Fasti Angl., 1300–1541*, [Chichester] · *Fasti Angl., 1300–1541*, [Exeter] · Rymer, *Foedera*, new edn, vol. 3 · *RotP*, vol. 3 · *Polychronicon Ranulphi Higden monachi Cestrensis*, ed. C. Babington and J. R. Lumby, 9 vols., Rolls Series, 41 (1865–86), vol. 9, p. 103 · Emden, *Oxf.* · G. C. Brodrick, *Memorials of Merton College*, OHS, 4 (1885) · H. G. Richardson and G. O. Sayles, eds., *Parliaments and councils of mediaeval Ireland*, IMC, 1 (1947) · G. O. Sayles, ed., *Documents on the affairs of Ireland before the king's council*, IMC (1979)

Wilberforce, Ernest Roland (1840–1907), bishop of Chichester, was born on 22 January 1840 at his father's rectory at Brighstone in the Isle of Wight, the third son of Samuel *Wilberforce (1805–1873), bishop successively of

Oxford and Winchester, and his wife, Emily Sargent (1807–1841). His childhood was spent at Lavington and Cuddesdon, where he acquired his lifelong love of country sports. From 1854 he attended Harrow School, but left in 1857 without attaining any great distinction. After two years with a private tutor he matriculated at Exeter College, Oxford, in May 1859. His Oxford career was noted more for his prowess as an oarsman than for academic work, and he graduated BA in 1864 with an honorary fourth. He proceeded MA in 1867, and was awarded his BD and DD in 1882.

Wilberforce's marriage on 23 June 1863 to Frances Mary, third daughter of Sir Charles Anderson, bt (1804–1891), resulted in a more serious attitude to life and work. Upon graduation he went to Cuddesdon College, then under Edward King, to train for the ministry. In December 1864 he was ordained deacon by his father, and priest the following year. After brief curacies at Cuddesdon and Lea in Lincolnshire, in 1868 he was presented to the living of Middleton Stoney, near Bicester. However, he resigned in 1870 on account of his wife's poor health; she died from tuberculosis in San Remo in October 1870. In the same year he became domestic chaplain to his father, then bishop of Winchester, and in 1871 was made sub-almoner to Queen Victoria.

In 1873 Gladstone appointed Wilberforce to the living of Seaforth, a suburb of Liverpool and a traditionally evangelical parish. Here his moderate high-churchmanship led him to introduce a daily service and a weekly celebration of holy communion, but with such tact as to avoid any serious friction with the congregation. On 14 October 1874 he married Emily, only daughter of George Connor, afterwards dean of Windsor. They had three sons and three daughters. While at Seaforth Wilberforce became an active supporter of the temperance movement, he and his wife both taking the pledge in 1876. It was also while at Seaforth that he first became renowned for his strong voice and powerful sermons.

In 1878 Wilberforce was appointed a residentiary canon of Winchester, and to the wardenship of the Wilberforce Mission, formed and endowed as a memorial to his father. Most of his missionary work was done in Portsmouth and Aldershot, but in 1881 a legal ruling finally removed the mission to the diocese of Rochester. Following a brief missionary journey to Quebec, in 1882 he was offered by Gladstone the new see of Newcastle.

At the time of his consecration on 25 July 1882 in Durham Cathedral, Wilberforce was the youngest diocesan bishop in the Church of England. The act forming the new diocese has been passed in 1878, but it had taken four years to raise sufficient funds to support a bishop, a measure of the problems faced by Wilberforce in restoring the position of the church in an industrial area long neglected and now dominated by nonconformity. The 1881 census had shown a town of nearly 150,000 persons, but a contemporary local religious census revealed that fewer than 6500 attended Anglican services, a decline even on the 1851 figure. Wilberforce realized that the key to restoration was financial, and his Bishop of Newcastle's Fund raised nearly £250,000 in its first five years. Within ten years eleven new churches and seven new vicarages had been built in the city, and the clergy increased by twenty-eight. At the same time Wilberforce was determined to make his presence felt throughout the diocese, travelling great distances in rural Northumberland to perform confirmations. In the first four years of his episcopate he confirmed twice as many candidates as had been confirmed in the four years before his arrival. And despite early opposition from local nonconformists, his tactful manner of proceeding gradually won many of them to his support. In many ways Wilberforce's work in Newcastle is comparable to that of W. F. Hook in Leeds in the previous generation.

By the mid-1890s Wilberforce's unrelenting work was starting to affect his health, and in 1895 he moved to become bishop of Chichester. However, here he soon found himself faced with a different set of problems. A number of the churches on the Sussex coast had become notorious for their ritualistic practices. Starting in 1898 the evangelicals launched a fresh campaign against ritualism, resulting in the Lambeth judgment against the use of incense and processional lights in the following year. Wilberforce persuaded five of the nine ritualist incumbents in his diocese to comply with the ruling, and attempted to avoid prosecution in the other cases. While personally unmoved by ritual practices, he was aware that legal proceedings and imprisonment following the 1874 Public Worship Regulation Act had largely failed to achieve anything but a legacy of bitterness and division, which he hoped to avoid. In 1905 he appeared as a witness before the royal commission on the state of ecclesiastical discipline, and in his evidence both criticized what he saw as the prejudiced and inaccurate claims of the evangelicals and defended the work of the ritualist clergy in his diocese.

In 1896 Wilberforce's work for the temperance movement was recognized when he became chairman of the Church of England Temperance Society. In 1904, despite his age, he joined the 'mission of help' to southern Africa to aid in the process of reconciliation in the aftermath of the Second South African War. Following a short illness Wilberforce died on 9 September 1907 at Bembridge in the Isle of Wight. He was buried at West Hampnett, near Chichester, on 14 September. GEORGE HERRING

Sources J. B. Atlay, *The life of the Rt. Revd. Ernest Roland Wilberforce* (1912) · *DNB* · Burke, *Peerage* · A. R. Ashwell and R. G. Wilberforce, *Life of the right reverend Samuel Wilberforce … with selections from his diary and correspondence*, 3 vols. (1880–82) · *Chronicle of Convocation* (Feb 1908) · 'Royal commission on ecclesiastical discipline: minutes of evidence', *Parl. papers* (1906), 34.173–84, Cd 3071 · *Church Times* (13 Sept 1907) · *The Guardian* (11 Sept 1907) · *Temperance Chronicle* (13 Sept 1907) · Gladstone, *Diaries*

Archives BL, corresp. with W. E. Gladstone, Add. MSS 44439–44787, *passim*

Likenesses C. Goldsborough Anderson, oils (copy), bishop's palace, Chichester; copy, bishop's palace, Chichester · wood-engraving, NPG; repro. in *ILN* (29 July 1882)

Wilberforce, Henry William (1807–1873), Roman Catholic convert and journalist, the youngest son of William *Wilberforce (1759–1833), politician and philanthropist,

and his wife, Barbara Ann Spooner (1777–1847), was born at Clapham, Surrey, on 22 September 1807. Two of his elder brothers were Robert Isaac *Wilberforce and Samuel *Wilberforce. At the age of nine Henry was sent for private tuition to the Revd John *Sargent, rector of Graffham, Sussex. He was transferred six years later with his brother Samuel to the Revd F. R. Spragge's establishment at Little Bounds, Bidborough, Kent. He matriculated at Oriel College, Oxford, on 16 March 1826, going into residence the following Michaelmas term. During four long vacations he read with John Henry Newman, whose intimate friend he became. He was active in the debates of the Oxford Union, of which he was elected president. He graduated BA in 1830 with a first class in classics and a second class in mathematics. Initially intending to become a barrister, he was admitted to study at Lincoln's Inn in 1831, but he continued to reside at Oxford, where he won the Ellerton theological prize and took his MA degree in 1833.

Under Newman's influence Wilberforce decided to give up the law and take holy orders. He was ordained deacon in 1834 and immediately appointed by his relative Charles Richard Sumner, bishop of Winchester, perpetual curate of Bransgore, on the edge of the New Forest. He had just married, on 24 July 1834, Mary (1811–1878), the fourth daughter of his former tutor John Sargent. One of her sisters married his brother Samuel; another married Henry Edward Manning. They had five sons and four daughters; four of the children died young. Wilberforce was an ardent supporter of the Tractarian movement, with advanced liturgical ideas which he put into practice in his parishes. In 1838 he published *The Parochial System: an Appeal to English Churchmen*, a plea for church extension and lay stewardship. In 1841 the archbishop of Canterbury nominated him to the vicarage of Walmer, near Deal. In 1843, on the suggestion of the prince consort, he was presented by the lord chancellor to the wealthy vicarage of East Farleigh, near Maidstone, held some years earlier by his brother Robert.

Preceded by his wife, Wilberforce was received into the Roman Catholic church on 15 September 1850, resigning his vicarage. He published *Reasons for Submitting to the Catholic Church: a Farewell Letter to his Parishioners* in 1851, which led to a controversy and reached its sixth edition in 1855. As a married former parson, he was excluded from both his clerical and legal vocations. There was little employment for him in his new church, and he was often in financial difficulties; but his spirits were never dampened. In 1852 he became secretary of the newly founded Catholic Defence Association in Dublin. This led to the publication of *Proselytism in Ireland* (1852), a correspondence between him and the Revd Alexander Dallas on the latter's Irish church missions. In 1854 Wilberforce became proprietor and editor of a London weekly newspaper, the *Catholic Standard*, renamed in 1855 the *Weekly Register*. In the politics of Roman Catholic journalism the *Weekly Register* was the Liberal rival of the tory *Tablet*. Wilberforce was cautiously supportive of the liberal Catholics Sir John Acton and Richard Simpson and their *Rambler* and *Home and Foreign Review*. Wearying of the burden of editing a weekly, Wilberforce put the *Weekly Register* up for sale in 1863 and sold it in 1864. Thereafter he confined his journalism to writing more than twenty articles and reviews for the *Dublin Review*, seven of which were posthumously published by his sons as *The Church and the Empires* (1874), with a biographical memoir by Newman. Throughout his life it was this good man's fate to be overshadowed by more distinguished connections. A journey to Jamaica having failed to restore his health, Wilberforce died on 23 April 1873 at his residence, Chester House, Stroud, Gloucestershire, and was buried in the nearby Dominican churchyard at Woodchester.

JOSEF L. ALTHOLZ

Sources D. Newsome, *The parting of friends: a study of the Wilberforces and Henry Manning* (1966) · *The letters and diaries of John Henry Newman*, ed. C. S. Dessain and others, [31 vols.] (1961–), vols. 2–27 · J. H. Newman, 'Memoir of Henry W. Wilberforce', in H. W. Wilberforce, *The church and the empires* (1874), 1–16 · M. G. Holland, *The British Catholic press and the educational controversy, 1847–1865* (1987) · J. L. Altholz, *The religious press in Britain, 1760–1900* (1989)
Archives Bodl. Oxf., family corresp. · Oriel College, Oxford, theological notebook · St Mark's vicarage, Harrogate, Yorkshire, Sandwith MSS · Ushaw College, Durham, corresp. | Birmingham Oratory, letters to John Henry Newman · BL, corresp. with W. E. Gladstone, Add. MSS 44353–44391 · CUL, letters to Lord Acton · U. Birm. L., letters to Harriet Martineau
Likenesses photograph, repro. in H. W. Wilberforce, *The church and the empires* (1874), frontispiece · photograph (with his wife), repro. in Newsome, *Parting of friends*

Wilberforce, Lionel Robert (1861–1944), physicist, was born on 18 April 1861 in Munich, Bavaria, the elder son (there was also a daughter) of Edward Wilberforce (1834–1914), barrister and from 1899 master of the Supreme Court, and his wife, Fannie, daughter of Alexander Flash of New Orleans. He was educated at the London International College, Isleworth, and at City and Guilds College, London, matriculating in 1879 at Trinity College, Cambridge, where he graduated thirteenth in the mathematics tripos in 1883 and with a first in the natural sciences tripos in 1884. He then began research on electrostatics with J. J. Thomson at the Cavendish Laboratory, Cambridge, and published a number of papers on the development of new experimental techniques and the mathematical analysis of physical phenomena such as viscosity and the vibrations of springs.

Wilberforce was appointed assistant demonstrator at the Cavendish Laboratory in 1887 and demonstrator in 1891, the year in which he married, on 13 August, a fellow student, Margaret (1864/5–1929), second daughter of the Revd W. Raynes, a prominent Cambridge University figure; they had no children. This was a time of rapid increase in the numbers of students studying experimental physics. Wilberforce was heavily involved in managing this expansion, which he described in his chapter, 'The development of the teaching of physics in Cambridge', in the commemorative volume *A History of the Cavendish Laboratory, 1871–1910* (1910). With T. C. Fitzpatrick he wrote *A Laboratory Note Book of Elementary Practical Physics* (1896).

Shortly after his promotion to university lecturer in physics in 1900 he was appointed Lyon Jones professor of physics at University College, Liverpool (from 1903 the University of Liverpool), in succession to Sir Oliver Lodge. He held this post until his retirement in 1935.

Faced with a heavy teaching load and a small staff, one of Wilberforce's first tasks at Liverpool was the planning of a new physical laboratory. Opened in November 1904, the George Holt Physics Laboratory was a fully equipped modern laboratory in which Wilberforce took great pride. Here Wilberforce oversaw the gradual growth of the department in both teaching and research. With the aid of his laboratory assistant E. F. Welch, whom he brought with him from Cambridge in 1900, Wilberforce was an inspiring lecturer who greatly enjoyed illustrating his lectures with experiments and who went to great lengths to make physics accessible to his students. He was also a noted popular lecturer.

Much of Wilberforce's scientific work at Liverpool was concerned with the development of apparatus and techniques for teaching, including the Wilberforce spring, on which he published a short book in 1909, and a ripple tank for the demonstration of wave phenomena (which was borrowed for demonstration at the British Empire Exhibition in Wembley in 1924). A keen proponent of kinematic instrument design, he also devised a set of kinematic clamps and boss head which found widespread use in many laboratories. Though he himself took little more than a tolerant interest in the 'modern' physics of atoms and quanta, he promoted a succession of talented younger colleagues (among them C. G. Barkla, J. Rice, E. A. Stewardson, C. A. Beevers, and H. Lipson) whose interests lay in these areas. In the early 1930s he renewed his interest in electrical and magnetic units, attending an international conference in Paris and publishing several papers on the subject. His research output was not large by comparison with some of his contemporaries, however, and it was for his teaching that Wilberforce was chiefly recognized.

A witty, courteous, and genial man, Wilberforce was widely regarded as an excellent administrator with sound judgement. He served on many university committees; he was acting vice-chancellor of the University of Liverpool in 1926/7 and wrote a short history of the university to celebrate its twenty-fifth anniversary in 1928. On his retirement in 1935 he was made emeritus professor; he continued to serve on the committees of several local institutions and took an active interest in church matters. In his leisure time he was a keen mountaineer and skater; he was also a regular fell walker in the Lake District. Wilberforce died at 2 York House, Kensington Church Street, London, on 1 April 1944. A memorial service was held in Liverpool Cathedral on 25 April.

JEFFREY A. HUGHES

Sources R. W. Roberts, 'Prof. L. R. Wilberforce', *Nature*, 153 (1944), 517–18 · G. K. Perrin, '100 years of physics teaching: Liverpool University physics department, 1881–1981', MSc diss., U. Lpool, 1997 · *A history of the Cavendish Laboratory, 1871–1910* (1910) · T. Kelly, *For advancement of learning: the University of Liverpool, 1881–1981* (1981) · Venn, *Alum. Cant.* · R. W. Ditchburn, 'Reminiscences', *The making of physicists*, ed. R. Williamson (1986), 12–20 · H. Lipson, 'Physics in a minor department, 1927–1936', *The making of physicists*, ed. R. Williamson (1986), 94–100 • 'New buildings of the University of Liverpool: the George Holt Physics Laboratory', *Nature*, 71 (1904–5), 63–5 • Trinity Cam. • *WWW* • D. B. Wilson, 'Experimentalists among the mathematicians: physics in the Cambridge natural sciences tripos, 1851–1900', *Historical Studies in the Physical Sciences*, 12 (1981–2), 325–71 • A. B. Wood, 'Lionel Robert Wilberforce', *Proceedings of the Physical Society*, 57 (1945), 585 • private information (2004) • m. cert. • d. cert. • *CGPLA Eng. & Wales* (1944)

Archives U. Lpool, principal's letter-books, S2320 • U. Lpool, council minutes, S2210 • U. Lpool, senate minutes • U. Lpool, press cuttings • U. Lpool, faculty of science report book 17 • U. Lpool, annual reports of council and the university

Likenesses group photograph, *c.*1935, repro. in *Annual report*, Liverpool University • group photograph, *c.*1935, repro. in Kelly, *For advancement of learning* • portrait, U. Lpool

Wealth at death £32,928 16*s.* 4*d.*: probate, 14 June 1944, *CGPLA Eng. & Wales*

Wilberforce [*née* Ogilvie-Forbes], **Marion Katherine** (1902–1995), aviator, was born at Boyndlie House, Fraserburgh, Aberdeenshire, Scotland, on 22 July 1902, the daughter of John Charles Mathias Ogilvie-Forbes (1850–1941), ninth laird of Boyndlie, and his second wife, Anne Marguerite Prendergast (*d.* 1950). Her father had originally studied for the Anglican priesthood but was received into the Roman Catholic church by Cardinal Newman, later becoming privy chamberlain to four popes. There were five children from his second marriage. Educated at Boyndlie House by a succession of French governesses, from an early age Marion also became involved in the day-to-day running of the estate. At fourteen she was entrusted with collecting rents from tenants. At sixteen she went to the Convent of Jesus and Mary at Stony Stratford, Buckinghamshire, and from there to Somerville College, Oxford, where she obtained a degree in agriculture in 1922. Through her agricultural interests she became involved in the work of the Fairbridge Farm Schools, a charitable organization that settled orphan children in agricultural communities in the dominions. Before her marriage she travelled widely, inspecting farm schools in Canada and Australia.

Marion knew Robert William Francis Wilberforce (*d.* 1984), who had been a contemporary of her brother David at Ampleforth College. After Oxford he was torn between life as a priest and matrimony. After six months testing the strength of his vocation as a monk at Ampleforth Abbey, he decided against it. Marion was waiting to collect him at the abbey gates when he emerged. They married in 1932 and bought their Essex farm, Nevendon Manor, where she kept chickens and bred pigs and cattle. The piglets she named after her brothers, reserving the name of her youngest brother, Malcolm, for the runt of the litter. Robert Wilberforce became a solicitor and a company director.

Encouraged by her two aviator brothers, Marion learned to fly at Stag Lane, gaining her pilot's licence in 1930. After successfully investing on the stock exchange she was able to buy her first aircraft, a de Havilland Cirrus Moth, later replaced by a Hornet Moth. These aircraft were registered as farm implements for tax purposes and used to ferry livestock. A trip to Europe to visit friends for lunch would be an opportunity to bring back some chickens or a calf placed in bags behind her seat. Flying with the minimum of instrumentation and navigating visually, if uncertain of her whereabouts she would land to ask the way or read a signpost. When civilian flying ceased in 1939, she had accrued 900 flying hours in this way.

In December 1939 Pauline Gower won her battle to form a women's section of Air Transport Auxiliary (ATA). Though limited to fly non-operational aircraft and on 20 per cent less pay than males of equal rank, this signalled a breakthrough in the prejudice against female pilots. Wilberforce was invited to go to Whitchurch for flight testing and on 1 January 1940 she became one of the first eight women to report for duty at Hatfield no. 5 ferry pool. At first pilots were engaged in ferrying RAF Tiger Moths from the de Havilland factory at Hatfield to maintenance units and RAF stations as far afield as Scotland. However, the loss of pilots in the battle of Britain, allied to increased aircraft production, brought about a radical change and by the end of 1941 Marion was piloting Hurricanes, Spitfires, and twin-engine types and had taken over command of no. 5 ferry pool, Hatfield. Early in 1943 she moved to no. 12 ferry pool, Cosford, to take command of the second all-women pool of ATA, becoming in 1944 one of only eleven women qualified to fly the four-engine Lancaster and Stirling bombers. Often required to ferry many different types in a day, ATA pilots needed the versatility usually demanded only of test pilots. By mid-1945, on leaving the ATA, Wilberforce had flown some 2400 hours and over 100 different aircraft types. Characteristically, she declined the offer to become an MBE and proceeded to immerse herself in country life and peacetime flying, rarely speaking of her wartime exploits.

Wilberforce had begun hunting in 1933; on returning to Nevendon Manor she served on the committee of the Essex union hunt (1962–82), becoming the only woman master of foxhounds in the hunt's 236-year history. A fearless rider, she hunted into her eighties, and having little faith in doctors, would obtain her medicines from the vet, claiming her horse was sick. In 1947 she co-owned a Hornet Moth G-ADKM with her brother Neil. Though the skies had become more regulated, Marion continued to fly around the British Isles visiting friends in the same happy-go-lucky way of pre-war days. Her post-war logbook indicates that she visited most European countries. She might lunch in Luxembourg, listen to music at the Vienna Staatsoper, or even take a sister-in-law to Paris to pick up Molyneux couture. On 5 May 1949 she set off to visit her brother Neil, then an air attaché in Moscow. Travelling via Amsterdam, Copenhagen, and Stockholm, she arrived in Helsinki two days later. To her annoyance she had to leave the aircraft there and go by other means to Moscow. Acquiring another Hornet Moth G-AEZG in 1964, she continued flying until the age of eighty. By this time she had become disenchanted by all the rules and regulations imposed on the private pilot.

Having no children of her own, Marion Wilberforce continued a particular interest in the Fairbridge Farm Schools and was for many years chair of the child care committee.

She often had Fairbridge children to stay with her. Though she could seem quite formidable at first, she is remembered as being kind and mothering the younger girls in the ATA ferry pool. On her husband's death in 1984 she returned to live with her brother Malcolm in the family home at Boyndlie. Now dilapidated with gardens overgrown and the family chapel derelict, they lived happily amid the decay. A stoic in old age and impatient of physical frailties, she refused to wear hearing aids. Her last months were spent in Stratford Park Nursing Home, Stroud, where she died on 17 December 1995. She was cremated at Stroud, but her ashes were interred at Markington Roman Catholic Church, Harrogate, Yorkshire, near the Wilberforce family home.   ENID DEBOIS

Sources private information (2004) [James Ogilvie-Forbes, nephew and executor] · private information (2004) [John Lumsden, nephew] · L. Curtis, *The forgotten pilots* (1971) · private information (2004) [Geoffrey Horrocks, neighbour at Nevendon] · m. cert. · *CGPLA Eng. & Wales* (1996)
Archives Fairbridge Trust, London, pre-war and post-war logbooks · Maidenhead Heritage Trust, Air Transport Auxiliary collection, wartime logbooks
Wealth at death £339,865: probate, 16 Feb 1996, *CGPLA Eng. & Wales*

Wilberforce, Octavia Margaret (1888–1963), physician, was born on 8 January 1888 at Lavington House, Petworth, West Sussex, the eighth and youngest child of Reginald Garton Wilberforce (1838–1914), army officer and barrister, and his wife, Anna Maria (*d.* 1938), daughter of the Hon. Richard Denman of Sussex. Octavia was proud of her heritage as great-granddaughter of William Wilberforce, emancipator of the slaves, and granddaughter of Samuel *Wilberforce, bishop of Oxford and Winchester. At times of achievement in her life she visited Westminster Abbey in London to tell the good news to William Wilberforce, 'sitting benignly in his chair' (*Octavia Wilberforce: the Autobiography*, 81).

Although Octavia was the least welcome of her parents' children, she recalled her childhood as happy, because she was allowed to run wild. Her education consisted primarily of sporadic lessons in music, history, and literature, from occasional tutors, with only one year of formal education at the age of sixteen. After presentation at court in 1907 she drifted into an undisciplined way of life, playing golf, growing roses, and helping with the housekeeping. By the age of twenty-one she was depressed and frustrated at the alternative prospects of marriage to a wealthy man or looking after elderly parents. An unwelcome marriage proposal in 1911 forced her to recognize that she was '*not* cut out for' marriage but wanted instead to 'mean something in the world' (*Octavia Wilberforce: the Autobiography*, 28).

Octavia Wilberforce's life was transformed in 1909 by her meeting Elizabeth *Robins (1862–1952), the famous American actress, writer, and suffragette, who became the most important person in her life. Octavia described her meeting with the charismatic feminist, twice her age, as 'a turning-point in my life … hero worship at first sight'. Elizabeth challenged her protégée to seek the education

denied her and to fulfil her dream to become an independent doctor. Octavia's upbringing was so sheltered and restricted that at twenty-three her mind was untrained and she was still innocent and inexperienced. Even so, Elizabeth recognized her sterling qualities of honesty, integrity, humour, zest for life, and determination, reinforced by her strong sense of her own identity. Octavia matured rapidly after 1913 with Elizabeth as her 'adopted mother', and came to share her mentor's belief that economic independence was essential if women were to control their own lives. Years later Octavia's friend Leonard Woolf was impressed by 'the fineness and genuineness' of her character, complex yet rocklike, generous but without illusions. He saw her as a remarkable individualist who required great strength of mind to liberate herself from the bonds of family and class (*Octavia Wilberforce: the Autobiography*, xx, 14, 73; Woolf, 29–31).

Octavia needed these qualities in her struggle to become a doctor, especially in withstanding her parents' intense resistance and ridicule. The campaign for general acceptance of women doctors was still being fought when she began medical studies at the London School of Medicine for Women in 1913. Only 3 per cent of qualified doctors were female in 1913 and prejudice persisted against women in private practice. Octavia's parents argued forcefully that medicine was 'unsexing' for women, that she would never make a living, and that she would wreck her prospects of domestic happiness. Her father refused to pay for her medical training and cut her out of his will, leaving her entirely dependent on the financial support of loyal friends, especially Sydney Lord Buxton and Elizabeth Robins.

An even greater obstacle was Octavia's ignorance in several subjects which constituted the minimum entrance requirements for medical school. Despite special coaching and immense effort, she was twenty-seven before she passed in all subjects, after seven failures. She was determined both to prove that women medical students were just as capable as men and to help consolidate women's position in medicine. Octavia qualified MRCS LRCP in 1920. She particularly enjoyed her clinical training in London in 1917–18 at St Mary's Hospital, Paddington, which accepted only a few women students as a wartime experiment. She was so highly regarded there as a diagnostician that she was appointed clinical clerk to Dr Wilfred Harris, an outstanding neurologist, and after qualifying became his house physician in 1921–2. Throughout Octavia's training Elizabeth's support was 'protective, far-seeing, ambitious for my success', but once Octavia qualified their long-term relationship became an equal one (*Octavia Wilberforce: the Autobiography*, 116).

In 1923 Octavia established her own general medical practice at 24 Montpelier Crescent, Brighton, rejecting the dream of a London consultancy as too risky and expensive. General practice in Brighton offered her a life of great rewards, allowing her to be self-supporting in her beloved Sussex and to convince her sceptical family of her success. In time she also became a full physician at the New Sussex Hospital for Women and Children in Brighton and at the Marie Curie Hospital in London. From 1927 Octavia developed Elizabeth Robins's fifteenth-century farmhouse, Backsettown, in Sussex, as a convalescent home for overworked professional women and exhausted housewives, who enjoyed fresh dairy produce from Octavia's pedigree herd of Jersey cows. In 1940–41 her wide circle of friends extended to include Virginia Woolf, who confided her fear that the war would reactivate her terrible mental affliction. Octavia was devastated that she could not avert the tragedy of Virginia's suicide, but consoled herself that she brought occasional peace to a deeply troubled mind.

Octavia officially retired two years after Elizabeth Robins's death in 1952, and spent her last nine years seeing patients and her many friends and farming at Backsettown, besides working on the West Sussex county council. She died at the New Sussex Hospital for Women and Children on 19 December 1963. A private cremation followed, and a memorial service for her was held at Hove parish church, on 3 January 1964.   PAT JALLAND

Sources *Octavia Wilberforce: the autobiography of a pioneer woman doctor*, ed. P. Jalland (1989) · O. Wilberforce, 'The eighth child', U. Glas. L., MS · A. V. John, *Elizabeth Robins: staging a life, 1862–1952* (1995) · L. Woolf, 'Octavia Wilberforce', *Backsettown, Elizabeth Robins and Octavia Wilberforce* (privately printed, 1952) · b. cert. · d. cert. · *Medical Directory* (1962) · Burke, *Gen. GB*

Archives Women's Library, London, corresp. and typescript autobiography · Women's Library, London, typescripts of speeches and notes | U. Sussex, corresp. with Leonard Woolf · U. Sussex, corresp. with Virginia Woolf

Wealth at death £44,817: probate, 15 April 1964, *CGPLA Eng. & Wales*

Wilberforce, Robert Isaac (1802–1857), Roman Catholic convert, was born on 19 December 1802 at Broomfield, on Clapham Common, the fourth child and second son of William *Wilberforce (1759–1833) and his wife, Barbara Ann (1777–1847), eldest daughter of Isaac Spooner of Elmden Hall, Coventry. Two of his three brothers (William, the eldest, and Henry *Wilberforce, the youngest) were later received into the Roman church, and Samuel *Wilberforce—three years his junior—became successively bishop of Oxford and of Winchester.

Wilberforce was educated at a private school owned by the Revd E. G. Marsh at Nuneham Courtenay, near Oxford, proceeding thence to Oriel College, Oxford, in 1820. He obtained first-class honours in both classics and mathematics in 1823, and three years later gained the prestigious prize of a fellowship at Oriel, becoming the colleague of the future leading spirits of the Oxford Movement: John Keble, John Henry Newman, Edward Pusey, and Richard Hurrell Froude. He proceeded to deacon's orders after taking up his fellowship and was ordained priest in 1828.

At this time Wilberforce's religious views were in a state of flux. He had experienced an abortive love affair shortly after taking his degree and had seriously considered becoming a missionary. In addition, his first meeting with Keble in the summer of 1823, while studying under him at a reading party at Southrop parsonage in the company of

Robert Isaac Wilberforce (1802–1857), by unknown photographer

Froude and Isaac Williams, had caused him some perplexity, as he encountered for the first time the high Anglican tradition of churchmanship so utterly different in its emphasis and spirituality from the evangelicalism of his father and his Clapham friends. Cautious by nature, he reserved his judgement. In 1827, however, after reading Keble's newly published *The Christian Year*, all his misgivings disappeared, and he was prepared to declare his total devotion to its author. Up to that point he had been most closely in sympathy with Pusey, and had determined to emulate him in acquiring a command of German and Hebrew; to this end he had obtained from Pusey letters of introduction to the disciples of Schleiermacher at the universities of Göttingen and Bonn. On the eve of his departure for Germany in the winter of 1827, however, circumstances at Oxford intervened. Edward Copleston, provost of Oriel, was appointed bishop of Llandaff, and Wilberforce—anxious to see Keble at the head of his college—remained in Oxford to press his claims at the ensuing election. In the event Edward Hawkins was elected provost, and Wilberforce subsequently accepted a post as college tutor.

For the next three years the relationship between Wilberforce and Newman (and R. H. Froude, another recently appointed tutor) became closer—they had been so close, indeed, that Newman offered Wilberforce a curacy at St Mary's in 1829, which he declined; shared family social occasions aroused speculation that a match was imminent between Wilberforce and Newman's sister Jemima.

Conflict at Oriel between the three junior tutors and the new provost began in the summer of 1828. Wilberforce broached a proposal, soon militantly championed by Newman and Froude, that tutorial responsibility, hitherto little more than that of a college lecturer, should be rendered more appropriate to a scholar in orders by the giving to each tutor of special charge for a limited number of serious students ('reading men' as opposed to the idle gentlemen commoners), over whom they would exercise both academic and moral supervision. Hawkins, at first sympathetic, became uneasy at what he suspected—not without reason—might encourage favouritism and provide an opportunity to indulge in religious proselytism. Disagreement turned into conflict in 1829 when Sir Robert Peel resigned as MP for the university on the question of Catholic emancipation, and Newman and Hawkins found themselves on opposite sides in the consequent bitter parliamentary election. Peel—to Hawkins's chagrin—failed to regain his seat, and the provost interpreted Newman's opposition to him as yet another attempt to undermine his authority. His decision to refuse to assign new pupils to Newman, Wilberforce, and Froude effectively led to the termination of their tutorships in 1831.

Wilberforce had been loath to support Newman in his campaign against Peel. He was not by nature a fighter. Unlike his dearly loved brother Samuel, he was a shy, self-effacing man—unambitious, studious, slow to commit himself. For him, release from college duties meant the opportunity, at last, to study in Germany, and he left for Bonn in the summer of 1831. However, German student life appalled him; he could read German but felt too embarrassed to speak it. Being slightly deaf, he could not understand it when spoken to him, so his attendance at lectures induced instant sleep. Also he felt homesick. He returned to England in December 1831, sought out a lady who had stirred his heart on their first meeting at the Wilberforce home in 1828—Agnes Wrangham, the daughter of the archdeacon of Cleveland—and duly proposed to her. They were married in June 1832. It was entirely in his character that he spent the first day of their honeymoon in embarking upon the writing of a book.

There followed the quest for a suitable living, the outcome of which cooled Wilberforce's relations with Newman. There was no shortage of offers. It was even suggested that he might become first bishop of Calcutta, prudently taken no further. The most attractive proposal, which he eventually accepted, came from his father's friend Lord Brougham, the whig lord chancellor, who on hearing that the Wilberforce family fortune had virtually collapsed offered him the substantial living of East Farleigh in Kent. It gave Newman no pleasure that a friend of his had accepted preferment from an infamous whig.

Members of this generation of the Wilberforce circle seemed blighted by the untimely deaths of their wives. Samuel Wilberforce and his brothers-in-law Henry Manning and George Dudley Ryder (all of whom had married daughters of John Sargent of Lavington) suffered agonies of early bereavement. So it was to be with Robert too.

Agnes died in November 1834, following the birth of their second son, Edward. Their first-born, William, was only one year old. A Yorkshire cousin of Agnes, Jane Legard, came to look after the stricken family, and in April 1837 she and Wilberforce were married. Three years later, in August 1840, the family moved to Yorkshire, Wilberforce securing the living of Burton Agnes, near Beverley, through an exchange sanctioned by the lord chancellor. In January 1841 he was appointed archdeacon of the East Riding, succeeding his father-in-law by his first marriage, Francis Wrangham, who was retiring.

In the intervening years Wilberforce had been much occupied in the writing of the five-volume *Life and Letters* of his father, who died in 1833—a joint task in collaboration with his brother Samuel, published in 1838. It was not congenial work, and the less so because of Robert's growing antipathy to almost every aspect of evangelicalism, an attitude not entirely shared by his younger brother. He found himself, if not actually within the Tractarian camp, in full sympathy with Newman's *Lectures on Justification* (1838) and his attempt to represent Anglicanism as the *via media* between Roman Catholicism and continental protestantism. This view was reinforced when he came to study Lutheran doctrines more closely in his first book on a theological theme, *The Five Empires*, published in 1841. The move to Yorkshire and the tiresome archidiaconal duties, undertaken with characteristic conscientiousness, made him feel increasingly isolated from the mainstream of ecclesiastical events. He could not share Samuel's growing estrangement from Newman, but still less was he prepared to endorse Henry's devoted discipleship. It was with his brother-in-law, Henry Manning, archdeacon of Chichester from 1840, that he came to find the closest kinship, especially after a visit Manning paid to Burton Agnes in 1843. From that time on they corresponded regularly, at once sanguine in their expectations of Samuel Wilberforce's advancing ecclesiastical fortunes, but utterly downcast by a momentous event in October 1845—Newman's reception into the Roman church.

Not from his own choosing, but very much at the instigation of Gladstone, Manning found himself cast in the role of the new leader of the shattered Tractarian ranks, and he looked to Wilberforce for help and advice at every turn, acknowledging his superior scholarship. While Wilberforce did not entirely share Manning's preoccupation with the high calling of the sacerdotal commission and his views on the importance of sacramental confession, he was at one with him in three respects: the centrality of the sacraments; the conviction that the Church of England, if it were to be seen truly as a teaching church, must be freed from all state interference in matters of doctrine; and the need within the church for a systematic corpus of theology. Both Manning and Gladstone were convinced that Wilberforce was the one man capable of producing this theological synthesis, and in the years between 1845 and 1853 he duly accepted the challenge in the form of three substantial volumes: *The Doctrine of the Incarnation* (1848), *The Doctrine of Holy Baptism* (1849)—a rather more polemical work, directed against the writings of the evangelical William Goode—and *The Doctrine of the Holy Eucharist* (1853). In these works, the doctrine of baptismal regeneration is set forth starkly and uncompromisingly: so too the doctrine of the real presence in the eucharist, though Wilberforce did not go so far as to accept the Catholic doctrine of transubstantiation. Most significantly, Tractarian incarnationalism receives its climactic interpretation as 'the great objective fact of Christianity' (*Doctrine of the Incarnation*, 4).

Wilberforce's grand design in the three related volumes is also expounded in his series of sermons preached between 1847 and 1850, and published as *Sermons on the New Birth of Man's Nature* (1850). Each deals with a particular aspect of the incarnation and the sacramental system, representing the doctrine of the incarnation as the very essence of Christianity (challenging the evangelical contrary emphasis on the centrality of the atonement). Wilberforce describes the sacraments as 'the natural outworks' of the incarnation, in accordance with the teaching of St John who declared 'mediation to be the great law of the Gospel Kingdom, the central fact in the economy of grace' (p. 225). This massive dogmatic compendium could be taken as the swansong of mid-Victorian high-church theology. A completely new interpretation of the doctrine of the incarnation was soon to appear in the post-Darwinian decades, when Tractarian teaching and the insights of F. D. Maurice fused in the works of the Lux Mundi group, and of Charles Gore in particular. It was also a swansong in a more personal sense. While he was writing his *magnum opus* Wilberforce endured the same agonies as his friend Manning as he witnessed the seemingly inescapable proof of the inherent Erastianism of the Church of England in two successive blows: the appointment in 1847 of the allegedly heterodox R. D. Hampden to the bishopric of Hereford by Lord John Russell, and the consequent failure of the church's protests to carry the slightest weight; and the even more devastating exhibition of the church's impotence when the judicial committee of the privy council overruled the court of arches in the notorious Gorham judgment of 1850. In this case, a secular court presumed to define the doctrine of the Church of England by requiring the high-church bishop of Exeter, Henry Phillpotts, to institute to a living within his diocese a Calvinist who rejected the doctrine of baptismal regeneration. In desperation Wilberforce watched Manning, his closest friend and ally, fight and fail, and eventually accept the inevitable by seeking reception into the Roman church in 1851. His own brother Henry had already made the same decision.

From 1851 onwards Wilberforce entered into a period of spiritual anguish as his brother Samuel, together with Gladstone, Pusey, and Keble, strove to keep him faithful to the church of his baptism, while Newman, Manning, and his brother Henry advanced every possible argument to entice him to join them. His situation rapidly became intolerable. In January 1853 his wife died after months of illness, during which he had done his utmost to conceal the turmoil in his mind. There were rumours too that a

prosecution was afoot over his extreme views on the nature of the eucharist. In the end it was the question of the authority of the church and the inadmissibility of the royal supremacy that resolved his dilemma, and he published his conclusions in what was to be his last publication, *An Inquiry into the Principles of Church Authority* (1854). He resigned his preferments in August that year, and in October left the country for Paris, where he was received into the Roman Catholic church on All Saints' eve. Gladstone, on hearing the news, wrote to Samuel Wilberforce: 'He stands at the head of our living divines. His withdrawal from the Church of England could be compared to nothing but that of Newman and Manning, and I am not sure that the blow would not be as great as either' (Newsome, *Parting of Friends*, 402).

Wilberforce's initial intention was to retire as a layman to a small estate in Connemara in Ireland (purchased against this eventuality), and to lose himself in his books. Manning pressed him to seek ordination, hoping that he would join him in the community of priests (the Oblates of St Charles Borromeo) that he had been commissioned to found in order to undertake missionary work in the poorest quarters of London. In 1856 Wilberforce entered the Accademia Ecclesiastica in Rome on the pope's nomination. While in minor orders he was taken ill with gastric fever. He died in Albano on 3 February 1857, and was buried in Rome in the St Raymond's Chapel of the church of S Maria sopra Minerva. Manning, who had been at his friend's bedside until the end, reported to Henry Wilberforce: 'In Rome the one thing remarked in him … was his childlike humility. He had in truth entered the kingdom of God as a little child' (Newsome, *Parting of Friends*, 409).

DAVID NEWSOME

Sources D. Newsome, *The parting of friends: a study of the Wilberforces and Henry Manning* (1966) · R. Fairweather, ed., *A library of protestant thought: the Oxford Movement*, 5 (1964) · A. Härdelin, *The Tractarian understanding of the eucharist* (1965) · E. S. Purcell, *Life of Cardinal Manning*, 2 vols. (1896) · A. R. Ashwell and R. G. Wilberforce, *Life of the right reverend Samuel Wilberforce … with selections from his diary and correspondence*, 3 vols. (1880–82) · D. Newsome, *The convert cardinals: John Henry Newman and Henry Edward Manning* (1993) · P. Toon, *Evangelical theology, 1833–1856: a response to Tractarianism* (1979) · G. Rowell, 'Christ and the church in Robert Isaac Wilberforce's *Doctrine of the incarnation*', *By whose authority? Newman, Manning, and the magisterium*, ed. V. A. McClelland (1996), 259–72 · Bodl. Oxf., MSS Wilberforce

Archives Bodl. Oxf., corresp. | Birmingham Oratory, letters to John Newman · BL, Gladstone MSS · BL, letters to W. E. Gladstone, Add. MSS 44356–44527 · Bodl. Oxf., corresp. with Henry Manning · Emory University, Atlanta, Georgia, Manning archives

Likenesses photograph, repro. in Newsome, *Parting of friends*, facing p. 370 [*see illus.*]

Wilberforce, Samuel (1805–1873), bishop of Oxford and of Winchester, was born on 7 September 1805 at Broomfield, Clapham Common, fifth child in the family of four sons and two daughters of William *Wilberforce (1759–1833), MP and philanthropist, and his wife, Barbara Ann (1777–1847), eldest daughter of the evangelical Birmingham banker Isaac Spooner (1735–1818) and his wife, Barbara, *née* Gough-Calthorpe (1744–1826), of Elmdon Hall, Warwickshire. His brothers were William (1798–1879),

Samuel Wilberforce (1805–1873), by Herbert Watkins, late 1850s

Robert Isaac *Wilberforce (1802–1857), and Henry William *Wilberforce (1807–1873), his sisters Barbara (1799–1821) and Elizabeth (1801–1831). In 1808 the family removed to Kensington Gore, then after 1821 moved several times before settling in 1825 at Highwood Hill in Mill Hill, Middlesex. Here they remained until the younger William's debts forced its sale in 1831.

Samuel was educated privately by a series of clerical schoolmasters: in 1817 he was sent to Stephen Langston at Hastings and then to Edward Garrard Marsh at Nuneham Courtenay, Oxfordshire. In 1819 he was removed to George Hodson, at the time chaplain to William Wilberforce's friend Lewis Way at Stanstead Park, Sussex (fellow pupils included Henry Hoare), with whom he remained when Hodgson removed to Maisemore, Gloucestershire, in 1820. In 1822 Samuel was sent to Francis Spragg at Bidborough, Kent, to prepare for university. As befitted the son of a leading member of the Clapham Sect, Wilberforce's happy childhood was characterized by the strong evangelicalism of both his home and his schools. His parents took an intense interest in the spiritual and moral development of their children, and Samuel appears to have experienced particularly intense scrutiny as William's favourite. His father wrote to his nine-year-old son: 'I am anxious to see decisive marks of your having begun to undergo the *great change*' (Newsome, *Parting of Friends*, 49).

University and marriage In 1823 Wilberforce followed his brother Robert to Oriel College, Oxford, as a commoner.

Here he formed a close circle of friends, including George Prevost and Charles Anderson, known as the Bethel Union on account of its religiosity. Unlike Robert and his younger brother Henry, however, he did not become intimate with John Keble; though close to Hurrell Froude, Wilberforce was 'stigmatized as a humbug' by the latter and John Henry Newman (Ward, 247), differing from them not least on the question of celibacy. A keen rider and hunter, Wilberforce also took a prominent part in the proceedings of the nascent Union Society. Here he adopted a liberal stance, arguing that the deposition of Charles I had been justified and favouring Catholic emancipation. In 1826 he graduated BA with a first in mathematics and a second in classics, proceeding MA in 1829 (he was subsequently awarded a DD in 1845 and an honorary fellowship of All Souls in 1871). In November 1826 he was an unsuccessful candidate for a Balliol fellowship. Any further attempt was pre-empted by Wilberforce's eagerness to marry Emily (1807–1841), daughter of a close friend of the Wilberforces and Hodsons, John *Sargent (1780–1833), evangelical rector of Lavington, Sussex, and his wife, Mary (1778–1861), daughter of the banker Abel Smith. The marriage, on which Wilberforce had set his heart in 1821, was celebrated by Charles Simeon on 10 June 1828; during the next six years Henry Wilberforce, Henry Edward Manning, and George Dudley Ryder married Emily's sisters. Four sons and one daughter survived infancy, including Ernest Roland *Wilberforce (1840–1907), later bishop of Chichester.

Young clergyman Fulfilling his father's hopes, Wilberforce took deacon's and priest's orders in 1828 and 1829 respectively. He was appointed to his first post, a curacy at Checkendon, Oxfordshire, in January 1829. Close to Oxford and with fewer than 300 inhabitants, the living was carefully selected to suit an inexperienced pastor; among others rejected as too demanding were a curacy at Chiddingfold, Surrey, and later the vicarage of Ribchester, Lancashire, offered by his father's two evangelical episcopal cousins, Charles Richard and James Bird Sumner. None the less, as clergyman in charge, Wilberforce was an active pastor, instituting Sunday afternoon lectures on the gospels and special services on saints' days. It appears that his encounter with dissent, continued contacts with Oxford associates, and dismay at the prospects for the established church combined to reinforce the respect for church order characteristic of Claphamite evangelicalism in a development towards high-churchmanship; simultaneously, his response to contemporary politics led him now to speak of himself as 'a very high Tory' (Ashwell and Wilberforce, 1.45), condemning Peel's acceptance of Catholic emancipation.

In January 1830 Wilberforce left Checkendon when C. R. Sumner presented him to the rectory of Brighstone, Isle of Wight. Worth £700 a year, and with 700 inhabitants, this was a more challenging post, and brought the advantage of comparative proximity to Lavington. The climate also suited Emily's poor health—the string of christenings at

Brighstone being punctuated by miscarriages and a still-birth. Wilberforce soon impressed Sumner with his qualities. He proved a model parochial clergyman, introducing evening and cottage services, and founding Sunday and day schools, an infirmary and dispensary, and an allotment ground. In 1833 Wilberforce formed a clerical society on the island, effectively establishing himself as one of the leading clerics in the diocese, a position recognized in 1836 when Sumner appointed him rural dean, and earlier by his selection as preacher at the 1833 visitation. His status was further enhanced by his inheritance of the Lavington estate on the death of Henry Sargent in 1836, Wilberforce thus becoming Manning's squire.

The 1833 visitation sermon, *The Apostolical Ministry*, alarmed some evangelicals with its emphasis on the apostolical succession and 'high-church principles'. Wilberforce still retained great respect for the evangelical tradition, admiring Sumner and strongly supporting the Church Missionary Society ('my favourite society') while trying to bring it into closer association with the Society for the Propagation of the Gospel (SPG). Nevertheless, he was increasingly uncomfortable with Calvinism and the low-church tendencies of mid-1830s evangelicalism, and welcomed the publication of the Tracts for the Times, both for their emphasis on episcopacy and holy living, and as a protest against the Erastian policy of the state. In 1835 Wilberforce claimed to 'belong to no school' (Ashwell and Wilberforce, 1.90), and was in effect forging his own version of the *via media*. His support for the Tractarians could not extend to a repudiation of the Reformers (and effectively his father), and he was troubled by their neglect of justification, their severe line on post-baptismal sin, and the doctrine of reserve. He regarded these as deviations from the teachings of high-churchmen such as Richard Hooker and William Beveridge, to whom he professed his allegiance. Moreover, the publication of Hurrell Froude's *Remains* in 1838 disturbed Wilberforce deeply: whereas a university sermon preached in 1837 owed much to Newman, Wilberforce's two sermons as select preacher in 1838 both warned of the danger of Oxford teaching. Newman's subsequent refusal to publish Wilberforce in the *British Critic*, and the reluctance of Tractarians to subscribe to the Martyrs' Memorial in Oxford, confirmed his misgivings in their unacceptable display of party spirit.

From the mid-1830s, Wilberforce was establishing a wider reputation. This led to offers of further preferment, including a preachership in Tunbridge Wells Chapel (1834); St Dunstan-in-the-West, from Charles Simeon; the important vicarage of Leeds from Sir Robert Inglis in 1837; and Walter Farquhar Hook's proposed swap for his living of Leamington in 1838. Although Wilberforce was impatient of further advancement, these were all declined on Sumner's advice or medical grounds.

Wilberforce's reputation was in part acquired as an author. His portrait of evangelical sanctity in an anonymous *Notebook of a Country Clergyman* (1833) was echoed in an edition of Henry Martyn's journals prefaced with a memoir of John Sargent (1837), and it was probably Samuel who

prevented Robert playing down their father's evangelicalism in their joint *Life of William Wilberforce* published in 1838, followed in 1840 by an edition of his correspondence. The influence of a young family is apparent in *Agathos* (1839) and *The Rocky Island* (1840), collections of improving stories for the young, and by the end of the decade Wilberforce was engaged on the history of the Episcopal church in the USA published in 1844.

More important than his writings, however, were Wilberforce's frequent and accomplished appearances in pulpits and on platforms. His most significant speaking engagement came with a preaching tour for the SPG in Devon and Cornwall in 1839, which won him the lasting admiration of Henry Phillpotts. With his speech on colonial bishoprics at the Mansion House on 8 April 1840—which prompted Charles James Blomfield to observe 'I do not quite like hearing you, for you make me cry' (Ashwell and Wilberforce, 1.160)—this tour established him as a leading speaker of the day.

Archdeacon of Surrey and dean of Westminster Wilberforce's obvious talents were acknowledged when Sumner made him archdeacon of Surrey in November 1839, an appointment which entailed promotion to a canonry at Winchester the following August. Wilberforce took avidly to his new responsibilities, organizing ruridecanal chapters, attempting to establish a consolidated fund for the revenues of all church societies in the archdeaconry, and delivering widely read charges which William Ewart Gladstone, at least, worried adopted a tone more appropriate to a bishop than an archdeacon. In October 1840 the bishop presented him to the rectory of Alverstoke, Hampshire, a parish of some 13,000 inhabitants embracing both the military and naval establishments of Gosport and the resort of Stokes Bay. Outside commitments made him more dependent than previously on curates. Once more, however, Wilberforce was an active pastor, instituting additional services, schools, and district visiting. The curates (including his friend Richard Chevenix Trench) themselves were organized into an effective team ministry, and the parish attracted candidates for ordination seeking practical experience. More recognition came when a speech on the slavery issue won the favour of Prince Albert, who made Wilberforce a chaplain in January 1841; he became a favourite preacher at court, being appointed sub-almoner to the queen in October 1844, and then high almoner in 1847 (he served in this post until 1869).

Wilberforce was invited to deliver the Bampton lectures for 1841, but withdrew after Emily's death on 10 March 1841. This tragedy permanently marked Wilberforce. For the remainder of his life the anniversary, her birthday, and chance references to the past always provoked strong emotions, providing the occasion for self-examination and the renunciation of the worldly ambition which Wilberforce recognized in himself. Another source of distress in the early 1840s was the evident divergence in the theological positions of his circle as revealed by the contest for the Oxford poetry professorship (in which Wilberforce backed James Garbett) in 1841. During the same year Wilberforce welcomed the Anglo-Prussian scheme for a Jerusalem bishopric as a means of introducing episcopacy into the national church of Prussia. In each case Wilberforce found himself ranged against his brothers and other high-churchmen who had expected his support; given his association with Sumner and Baron von Bunsen at court, and his rapid advancement, there were inevitably accusations of trimming. As with his support for the degradation of William George Ward in February 1845, however, Wilberforce's stance owed more to his distaste for the divisions in the Church of England fostered by the Tractarians. It nevertheless did no harm to his prospects, and in March 1845 Wilberforce was promoted to the deanery of Westminster, his decision to retain Alverstoke provoking further criticism.

Bishop of Oxford Wilberforce's Westminster career was short-lived. In October 1845 Sir Robert Peel offered him the bishopric of Oxford, overriding Blomfield's misgivings at the appointment of a high-churchman in the context of the Tractarian controversy. His new office, to which he was enthroned on 13 December 1845, thrust Wilberforce into national prominence, but much of his subsequent reputation rests on his work within his diocese. In 1845 Oxford was effectively a new diocese, Buckinghamshire being appended to an already recently enlarged bishopric. Part of the challenge confronting the new bishop was consequently to consolidate the jurisdiction.

Wilberforce's high estimation of the episcopal office and his commitment to the preservation of unity in the visible church ideally suited him for this task. The stress on unity also appeared in a memorandum drawn up on his appointment, which emphasized the need to 'Be a "father in God" to men of *all* opinions amongst my clergy' (Ashwell and Wilberforce, 1.319). Wilberforce sought to improve and invigorate diocesan institutions and clerical performance, and also to promote the corporate life of the diocese and counter the polarizing effects of church party. Many of the methods he employed had already been introduced by others—notably Sumner, from whom Wilberforce learned much—but sheer force of personality and energy combined with the systematic thoroughness of his reorganization of diocesan activity to convince many contemporaries that Wilberforce was 'inaugurating *a new era in the history of the English episcopate*' (Burgon, 2.12).

Central to Wilberforce's achievement was his own presence throughout the diocese. He travelled incessantly, increasing the number of confirmation centres from the nine employed by Bagot to 188 by the 1860s, each visited triennially; numerous consecrations, society meetings, and informal descents on individual clergy also took the bishop out into the diocese. In 1850 Wilberforce inaugurated annual Lenten missions, in which a week-long residency in a major town incorporated daily services and often an ordination. Wilberforce regarded ordinations as one of his most important responsibilities, and enforced rigorous standards. He ensured more personal contact with ordinands during a period of residence at the rebuilt episcopal palace at Cuddesdon. Candidates were thus

introduced into the diocesan clerical community focused on its bishop. Wilberforce fostered this community through encouraging the calling of ruridecanal chapters, annual assemblies of rural deans at Cuddesdon, an embryonic diocesan synod summoned in protest at the 'papal aggression' in 1850, and from 1860 a clerical retreat at Cuddesdon. Cuddesdon was also the site for a theological college founded in 1854. Here students participated in a round of daily services and were trained in a highly clerical environment in close proximity to the episcopal palace, in contrast to the earlier foundations at Wells and Chichester, where no such common life had been practised.

Episcopal authority over the diocese was enforced through the accumulation of more diocesan patronage (the fourteen livings in episcopal hands in 1845 had increased to ninety-five in the diocese alone by 1869), and the careful selection of able men of all parties as archdeacons and rural deans. These officers assisted in the investigation of sensitive issues of doctrine or liturgical irregularity and in Wilberforce's determined effort to discipline inefficient or immoral clergy (he gleaned the names of those attending hunt balls from the newspapers). As in his own parishes, Wilberforce tried to increase the provision of services, insisting on monthly, and encouraging weekly, celebrations of holy communion. The diocesan machinery was completed by a series of diocesan societies and charities, under the auspices of which more than £2 million were expended in the diocese.

National prominence: 'Soapy Sam' Wilberforce's oratory and vigour promised increasing prominence in an episcopate the brightest ornaments of which were a generation older. His public speeches broadly accorded with the advice Prince Albert tendered the new bishop, in abstaining '*completely* from mixing himself up with the politics of the day' (Newsome, *Parting of Friends*, 306) save when humanitarian concern dictated otherwise, as on the issue of slavery which had been so dear to his father. His views on the whigs—'shabby, word-eating, pocket-picketing … sacrilegious villains'—were consequently reserved for private occasions (Soloway, 261–2). He made a successful maiden speech in the Lords on the subject of transportation in March 1846, and soon after was the main spokesman among bishops identified with conservatism who supported the repeal of the corn laws. If he thought of himself as a 'Liberal Tory', however, he remained an opponent of 'modern liberalism … a heartless steam engine' (ibid., 260) and what he regarded as the evils of industrial society. He strongly supported the Ten Hours Movement and purchased a suit from the Christian socialists' tailors co-operative. His charge of 1848 ranged widely across social issues, calling on the clergy to fight prostitution and blood sports while championing improved sanitation, amelioration of the poor law, and prison reform. If Wilberforce's social thought ultimately harked back to a pre-Victorian, hierarchical rural world, he also believed current social problems to be partly a result of the inadequate efforts of the Hanoverian church to bind the classes. This created a tension reflected in his support for additional free seating in churches while he remained less convinced than some other bishops of the need to dispense with appropriated pews altogether. Another consequence was his determined effort to promote church education, both nationally (he helped to arrange a compromise between the government and the National Society over inspection in 1846) and in his diocese, where his initiatives included the foundation of a diocesan training college for teachers, which opened at Culham in 1852.

The auspicious opening of Wilberforce's episcopate was swiftly followed by a severe set-back. In November 1847 Lord John Russell nominated Renn Dickson Hampden as bishop of Hereford. In 1836 Wilberforce had joined the outcry at Hampden's appointment as regius professor of divinity at Oxford; now he signed the episcopal protest initiated by Henry Phillpotts, and then individually suggested to Lord John Russell that Hampden's orthodoxy be determined before a special tribunal. Since Hampden was rector of Ewelme, Oxfordshire, it was to Wilberforce that William Henry Ridley and others gave notice of their intention to file articles against him. On 16 December 1847 Wilberforce signed letters of request to initiate a hearing before the court of arches, and wrote to Hampden, quizzing him on his theology and asking him to withdraw his Bampton lectures and *Observations on Dissent* from circulation. Hampden's answer failed to satisfy the bishop, but Wilberforce was later disquieted to discover that Hampden had already attempted to withdraw the *Observations*, leaving the less controversial Bampton lectures as the only basis for the charge of heterodoxy. Wilberforce now read the Bamptons for the first time, found no heresy, and was also advised that he should not have issued letters of request (which he had regarded as an administrative act) unless he believed there was a *prima facie* case to answer. Withdrawing the letters, Wilberforce unsuccessfully urged Hampden to expunge the offending passages, and then, in a letter of 28 December 1847 subsequently published in *The Times*, absolved Hampden of error. While close associates appreciated the courage of his public admission of error and determination to follow his conscience, Charles C. F. Greville spoke for many others in declaring that 'Sly Sam of Oxford … has covered himself with ridicule and disgrace' (*Greville Memoirs*, 6.118). His final efforts to extract concessions from Hampden were regarded as desperate attempts to save face. Highchurchmen felt that Wilberforce had presumed to judge the case himself and then betrayed the cause from self-interest; liberals and evangelicals marked the bishop as an intolerant and impetuous high-churchman. The incident appears to have cost Wilberforce his favoured position at court, and, in his own view, his chance of promotion to Canterbury on the death of William Howley in 1848. As the queen informed Gladstone on Wilberforce's death, she had 'admired and liked him *most before* he became a Bishop, and before he leant so much to those High Church views which did harm' (*Letters of Queen Victoria*, 2.264). It was at this time that Wilberforce acquired his enduring nickname of 'Soapy Sam'.

Wilberforce's position was also complicated by a series of conversions to Roman Catholicism in his close family. The defection of the Ryders in 1846 was followed in 1850 by that of his brother Henry and his wife. In 1851 the Gorham case provoked the secession of Manning; three years later it was the turn of Robert Wilberforce, and in 1863 the eldest brother, William, was received. Alongside Gladstone, with whom an association had developed during the early 1840s, Wilberforce struggled unsuccessfully to prevent this final disintegration of the Lavington circle. The conversions caused Wilberforce great personal distress, costing him some of his most sustaining friendships and sources of counsel. They also provoked suspicion as to the sincerity of Wilberforce's own Anglicanism. Robert's secession prompted Wilberforce to contemplate resigning his see 'in order that without reproach of remaining in the English Communion for the sake of my preferments I may testify … against the accursed abominations of the Papacy' (Newsome, *Parting of Friends*, 401).

The context of the conversions lay behind the close scrutiny applied to Wilberforce's response to Tractarianism and ritualism in his own diocese. He took a strong line on what he regarded as Romanizing excesses. Thomas William Allies repeatedly troubled his bishop, until in 1849 the publication of his *Journal of the Tour in France* led Wilberforce to demand a retraction, which was shortly followed by Allies's secession. A similarly uncomfortable relationship with Edward Bouverie Pusey culminated in a dispute over the latter's distribution of devotional manuals and the practice of regular confession. In 1850 Wilberforce informally inhibited Pusey from preaching in the diocese, only rescinding his ban after publicly condemning the manuals in his 1851 charge. None the less, where admonition was required Wilberforce preferred to act informally, and his inclusive vision of the national church made him determined to accommodate practices which he believed did not in themselves promote secession or might help to restrain those tempted to abandon the national church. His resolve in this respect was only hardened by evangelical demands that he should take punitive action; he consequently experienced fierce criticism, particularly from *The Record*. In 1849 Wilberforce gave his support to a proposal by William John Butler and Elizabeth Crauford Lockhart to create a sisterhood for the reclamation of fallen women at Wantage. In 1852 another house of mercy was established in the diocese, this time at Clewer on the initiative of Thomas Thelluson Carter. Although Wilberforce imposed strict restrictions on both institutions, there was inevitably controversy, not least when Lockhart seceded to Rome. Wilberforce was similarly vulnerable over developments at the theological college at Cuddesdon, where Henry Parry Liddon, appointed vice-principal in 1854, encouraged liturgical variations unacceptable to Wilberforce. Forced by the efforts of Charles Portales Golightly and public concern into initiating an inconclusive inquiry in 1858, Wilberforce continued to shelter Liddon from criticism while privately cautioning him that Cuddesdon graduates were 'too peculiar'. The appointment of Henry H. Swinny as principal in

1858 finally led Wilberforce to acknowledge the incompatibility of their positions, and he accepted Liddon's resignation.

These difficulties made the 1850s and early 1860s frustrating for Wilberforce, and his discomfort was increased by his lack of sympathy with most of the governments of the period and in particular his outrage at the episcopal appointments of Russell and Palmerston. With Gladstone supportive but powerless, he also recognized the unlikelihood of his own promotion; his enmity with Palmerston dated back to an incautious attack on the future premier at a meeting of the Winchester Diocesan Church-Building Society in 1837. In 1862 he dared to dream of York, but was disappointed, as he was in 1868 when, despite his growing distance from Gladstone over politics and the Irish church, Benjamin Disraeli failed to promote him to London, the vacancy cruelly coinciding with a further apostasy, that of Wilberforce's surviving daughter, Emily (Ella), and her husband, J. Henry Pye.

Throughout this period Wilberforce was an important figure in national debates on ecclesiastical issues. His interventions had three overall objectives. The first was the preservation of the connection of church and state, and with it the Christian character of the nation. To this end Wilberforce resisted Jewish emancipation, changes in marriage and divorce law, the conscience clause in education, Sunday opening of museums and exhibitions, and the total abolition of church rates. He none the less accepted the need for adjustments to reflect changing circumstances, such as university reform, and on church rates his preferred solution was a voluntary rate if, in return, control of the parish church could be restricted to those prepared to pay.

This last proposal would have contributed to Wilberforce's second purpose, the strengthening of the church's capacity for independent action and self-determination. The same objective prompted his call for an expansion of the episcopate. Wilberforce also sought to ensure that missionary bishops should be appointed by the church and not the state, sponsoring an unsuccessful bill to this effect in 1853. While Wilberforce was less disconcerted by the Gorham judgment than many in his circle—'a mere state decision' (Ashwell and Wilberforce, 2.40)—it nevertheless gave an important impulse to his efforts in this direction. He supported Blomfield's efforts of 1850–51 to secure a more satisfactory final court of appeal in ecclesiastical causes than the judicial committee of the privy council. From the mid-1850s onwards Wilberforce argued that, in order more clearly to demonstrate that lay judges did not exercise authority over the church's doctrine, the ecclesiastical element should be removed from the judicial committee, with bishops sitting separately to determine doctrinal matters referred to them by the court of appeal.

In 1850 Blomfield's solution was to refer ecclesiastical causes to the upper house of a revived convocation. Wilberforce had previously argued against reviving convocation, but now emerged alongside Henry Hoare as a leading campaigner for its restitution. In 1852 Wilberforce persuaded the bishops convened for the formal business of convocation to petition to be heard on a pending Clergy Discipline Bill, and secured an agreement that Archbishop J. B. Sumner, who opposed the revival, would not prorogue the session without the agreement of his suffragans. From then on the revival progressed steadily but slowly as the archbishop's resistance was gradually eroded. While Sumner remained at Canterbury, Wilberforce was the leading figure in convocation, and, with Blomfield failing and then retiring, this helped to establish his pre-eminence among the episcopate, as did his early involvement in the church congress.

The defence of orthodoxy Wilberforce's third aim was to resist challenges to doctrinal orthodoxy emerging from liberal churchmen and new scientific theories. An exception was his standing by Frederick Denison Maurice when he was dismissed for heterodoxy by King's College, London, in 1853. More characteristically Wilberforce was prominent in the orthodox response to the publication of *Essays and Reviews* in 1860. His anonymous review for the *Quarterly Review* (109, January 1861, 248–305), which sent the issue through five editions, condemned the essayists collectively for arguing away revelation and dogma in placing too much reliance on Rowland Williams's 'verifying principle' and already discredited German thought. Wilberforce drew up the collective episcopal response published in *The Times* (12 February 1861) and subsequently organized a volume of *Replies to Essays and Reviews* (1862). In February 1864 he moved the synodical condemnation of the volume in convocation, described by Lord Westbury as 'a well-lubricated set of words, ... so oily and saponaceous that no one can grasp it' (*Hansard 3*, 176, 1864, col. 1546), an oblique reference to Wilberforce's nickname. It was also Wilberforce who in 1863 persuaded the bishops to inhibit his former friend John William Colenso and who secured the condemnation of the *Pentateuch Critically Examined* (that is, demonstrated to be a collection of fabulous stories) in convocation.

Wilberforce had a lifelong interest in natural history, being vice-president of the British Association and serving on the council of the Geological and Zoological societies. It was therefore as a keen amateur scientist as well as a theologian that he reviewed Charles Darwin's *On the Origin of Species* for the *Quarterly Review* (108, July 1860, 225–64). Relying heavily on the work of his friend Richard Owen he dismissed the book as bad science with distressing theological implications; Darwin thought the review 'uncommonly clever' (*Correspondence*, 8.293). When the British Association met in Oxford in 1860, Wilberforce flippantly asked if anyone would be prepared to trace their descent from an ape on their grandmother's side. The joke elicited a stinging off-the-cuff riposte from Thomas Henry Huxley, who (in one version) claimed such ancestry was preferable to descent from a 'man highly endowed by nature and possessed of great means and influence and who yet employs those faculties for the mere purpose of introducing ridicule into a grave scientific discussion' (Jensen, 168). The incident has subsequently acquired fame as a dramatic landmark in the supposed Victorian triumph of rational science over obscurantist religion, but caused no great stir at the time, Wilberforce himself believing he had got the better of the exchange.

Bishop of Winchester Wilberforce's stance as defender of orthodoxy in the early 1860s moderated the hostility of his evangelical critics; moreover Anglo-Catholics, starved of episcopal representation, increasingly forgot their reservations and adopted Wilberforce as a champion. By the time of Gladstone's appointment as prime minister, therefore, he was a less controversial figure, whose stature in the church was unquestionable. The political differences between premier and bishop were also diminished as Wilberforce accepted the inevitability of Irish disestablishment after the 1868 election. Gladstone at last gave Wilberforce the recognition he craved: in December 1869 he was enthroned as bishop of Winchester. Wilberforce at once busied himself with diocesan affairs, combined now with his role as a member of the commission on ritual appointed in 1867 (on which he moderated proposals to discipline ritualists and resisted alteration of the Athanasian creed). In 1870 he was appointed president of a committee of convocation charged with revision of the translation of the New Testament, and became embroiled in a characteristic controversy over the involvement of the Unitarian scholar George Vance Smith. The demands of the new diocese strained his health: Wilberforce suffered three heart attacks during 1870 and 1871. He was still fully active, however, when on 19 July 1873 he suffered a riding accident near Abinger, Surrey, while accompanying Lord Granville to Holmbury to meet Gladstone. Wilberforce died almost immediately. On 25 July in accordance with his own wishes, he was buried next to his wife in Lavington churchyard.

Assessment Frequently caricatured during his own lifetime (for example by Disraeli in *Lothair*, and as the third son of Archdeacon Grantly in Anthony Trollope's *The Warden*), Wilberforce's considerable posthumous reputation was established in a predominantly Anglo-Catholic historiography which exaggerated the originality, if not the vigour, of his diocesan activity. Sabine Baring-Gould, writing in 1914, for example, claimed that 'He was the first of the Bishops of the Victorian age to show what the duties of a bishop were. ... He may truly be said to have recast the whole idea of the Episcopate, and to have successfully raised the tone of clerical life' (Baring-Gould, 175). Later in the twentieth century he was most frequently remembered for his confrontation with Huxley, in which he was unjustly cast in the role of a pompous, privileged, and ignorant obscurantist. His prominence in so many aspects of Victorian religious history (not to mention the remarkable and moving family history so minutely documented in the Wilberforce family papers) nevertheless ensured that with the revival of academic interest in the subject from the 1960s onwards he received more scholarly attention than any other member of the nineteenth-century episcopate.

Wilberforce's most striking quality was his energy (not least as a letter writer: his son estimated that he completed an average of 6430 letters a year, and on one occasion he simultaneously dictated four letters to secretaries while writing a fifth himself). This lay behind his remarkable achievement of establishing himself as a leading national figure while simultaneously gaining a reputation for a uniquely intimate relationship with his own diocese. As a public speaker he had few clerical rivals. His charm and what Liddon called 'the force of conscious sympathy' won him influence and loyalty, if also feeding his reputation for 'soapiness'. His public manner gave little hint of the personal griefs so movingly recorded in his private papers and somehow caught in the sober portraits of Wilberforce in later life. He himself recognized many shortcomings, without being able to overcome them. He was ambitious: in 1846 Benjamin Jowett observed harshly that Wilberforce never lost sight of the spiritual in pursuing the temporal (*Life and Letters of Benjamin Jowett*, ed. E. Abbott and L. Campbell, 1, 1897, 152). He was impatient of the complexities of issues, his impetuosity leading him into positions which on later reflection he could not conscientiously sustain. The early Victorian church required the confident, non-partisan, and invigorating leadership at which Wilberforce excelled. Later in the century, however, Wilberforce's own uncomplicated faith ill equipped him for the necessary formulation of a constructive response to the challenge of liberal theology.

ARTHUR BURNS

Sources A. R. Ashwell and R. G. Wilberforce, *Life of the right reverend Samuel Wilberforce … with selections from his diary and correspondence*, 3 vols. (1880–82) • D. Newsome, *The parting of friends: a study of the Wilberforces and Henry Manning* (1966) • S. Meacham, *Lord Bishop: the life of Samuel Wilberforce* (1970) • R. K. Pugh, 'The episcopate of Samuel Wilberforce, bishop of Oxford, 1845–69, and of Winchester, 1869–73, with special reference to the administration of the diocese of Oxford', DPhil diss., U. Oxf., 1957 • *The letter-books of Samuel Wilberforce, 1843–1868*, ed. R. K. Pugh (1969) • J. W. Burgon, 'Samuel Wilberforce: the remodeller of the episcopate', *Lives of twelve good men*, [new edn], 2 (1889), 1–70 • A. Burns, *The diocesan revival in the Church of England, c.1800–1870* (1999) • R. A. Soloway, *Prelates and people: ecclesiastical social thought in England, 1783–1852* (1969) • O. Chadwick, *The Victorian church*, 2 vols. (1966–70) • J. L. Altholz, *Anatomy of a controversy: the debate over 'Essays and Reviews', 1860–1864* (1994) • J. V. Jensen, 'Return to the Wilberforce–Huxley debate', *British Journal for the History of Science*, 21 (1988), 161–79 • *The Greville memoirs*, ed. H. Reeve, new edn, 6 (1888) • *The letters of Queen Victoria*, ed. G. E. Buckle, 3 vols., 2nd ser. (1926–8), vol. 2 • *The correspondence of Charles Darwin*, ed. F. Burkhardt and S. Smith, 8 (1990) • S. Baring-Gould, *The church revival* (1914) • M. Ward, *Young Mr. Newman* (1948) • D. Newsome, 'How soapy was Sam? A study of Samuel Wilberforce', *History Today*, 13 (1963), 624–32 • Gladstone, *Diaries*

Archives Bodl. Oxf., corresp. and diaries; letters • Duke U., Perkins L., corresp., mainly relating to missionary activities • W. Sussex RO, corresp. and papers relating to his Sussex estate and family affairs | BL, Aberdeen MSS • BL, corresp. with Lord Carnarvon, Add. MS 60839 • BL, corresp. with W. E. Gladstone, Add. MSS 44343–44345 • BL, letters to Mrs W. E. Gladstone, Add. MSS 46227–46228 • BL, corresp. with Sir Arthur Hamilton-Gordon, Add. MSS 49210–49214 • BL, letters to Sir R. I. Murchison, Add. MS 46128 • BL, corresp. with Sir Robert Peel, Add. MSS 40423–40603 • Bodl. Oxf., corresp. with Sir Charles Anderson; letters to Benjamin Disraeli; corresp. with Lord Kimberley; corresp. with H. E. Manning • CKS, letters to duke of Cleveland and duchess of Cleveland; letters to fifth Earl Stanhope and Countess Stanhope · Exeter Cathedral, letters to Henry Phillpots · LPL, Blomfield MSS, corresp. with Baroness Burdett-Coutts; corresp. with C. P. Golightly; letters to C. T. Longley; letters to Charles Marriott; corresp. with A. C. Tait; corresp. with C. Wordsworth · Lpool RO, letters to fourteenth earl of Derby · LUL, corresp. with Lord Overstone · Oriel College, Oxford, letters to R. D. Hampden · PRO, corresp. with Lord John Russell, PRO 30/22 · Pusey Oxf., letters to H. P. Liddon · St George's Chapel, Windsor, corresp. with Dean Wellesley · Trinity Cam., letters to W. Whewell · U. Nott. L., Denison MSS · University of New Brunswick, corresp. with Sir Arthur Hamilton-Gordon · W. Sussex RO, letters to duke of Richmond

Likenesses R. Woodman, stipple, 1843 (after G. Richmond, 1843), NPG · H. Robinson, stipple, pubd 1845 (after drawing by G. Richmond), BM, NPG · F. R. Say, oils, exh. RA 1846, LPL · E. M. Ward, group portrait, oils, 1855 (*Queen Victoria investing Napoleon III with the Order of the Garter at Windsor Castle*), Royal Collection · C. Pusey, pen-and-ink sketch, c.1856, NPG · C. Pusey, pencil and watercolour sketch, c.1856, NPG · H. Watkins, photograph, 1856–9, NPG [*see illus.*] · G. Richmond, oils, 1864–5, Cuddesdon College, Oxfordshire; study, NPG · G. Richmond, charcoal and chalk drawing, 1868, NPG · G. Richmond, oils, 1868, RA; version, The Deanery, Westminster · E. W. R., oils, 1873, Society for the Propagation of the Gospel, London · wooden bust, 1876, Christ Church Oxf. · H. H. Armstead, recumbent effigy, 1890, Winchester Cathedral · Ape [C. Pellegrini], caricature, NPG; repro. in *VF* (24 July 1869) · W. Holl, stipple (after drawing by G. Richmond, c.1851), BM, NPG · Maull & Polyblank, photograph, NPG · oils, Oriel College, Oxford · photographs, NPG · photographs, LPL · woodcuts and engravings, NPG

Wilberforce, William

Wilberforce, William (1759–1833), politician, philanthropist, and slavery abolitionist, was born on 24 August 1759 at the Wilberforce house in High Street, Hull, the third child and only son of Robert Wilberforce (1728–1768), merchant, and his wife, Elizabeth (d. 1798), daughter of Thomas Bird, of Barton, Oxfordshire. His paternal grandfather, William Wilberforce (1690–1776), established the family fortunes through the Baltic trade, acquired Yorkshire landed property, and was twice mayor of Hull. The younger William had three sisters, but only one of these, Sarah (1758–1816), survived to adulthood.

Education and early career, 1759–1784 William was a small and delicate child, but precocious. He was first educated, in 1767–8, at Hull grammar school. There, under the tuition of Joseph and Isaac Milner, he was set on a table and made to 'read aloud as an example to the other boys' (Wilberforce and Wilberforce, 1.4). In 1768, because of his father's premature death, he was sent to live with an uncle, also William Wilberforce, and his wife, Hannah, at their homes in St James's Place, London, and in Wimbledon. During the following two years he attended Mr Chalmers's school in Putney, which he later described as 'very indifferent' (Harford, 197). Meanwhile his aunt Hannah, an admirer of George Whitefield and friendly with the Methodists, influenced him towards evangelicalism. His grandfather and mother, however, took fright, and brought him back to live in Hull, where every effort was made to distract him from such enthusiastic religion. In the short term these endeavours appeared successful, and during his teenage years William spent his holidays immersed in the lively social round of Hull while continuing his education, from 1771 to 1776, as a boarder at Pocklington School.

William Wilberforce (1759–1833), by Sir Thomas Lawrence, 1828 [unfinished]

Wilberforce entered St John's College, Cambridge, in October 1776. His quick intelligence and substantial fortune, augmented by the deaths of his grandfather in 1776 and his childless uncle William in 1777, relieved him of any necessity for applying himself to hard study. His undergraduate years were therefore spent in an atmosphere of easy-going sociability, although he regarded the more dissipated extremes of university life with distaste. He took his BA in 1781 and his MA in 1788.

Wilberforce showed little inclination to involve himself actively in the family business, and while still at Cambridge he resolved to pursue a political career. In September 1780, when barely twenty-one, he was elected MP for Hull. In the House of Commons, free from any financial need to obtain public office, he adopted an independent stance from the outset. His earliest recorded interventions in debate, on smuggling and on naval shipbuilding, reflected the maritime interests of his constituency. He became a member of several clubs, notably Goostree's, the focus for a circle of about twenty-five young members. A particularly significant friendship was established with his Cambridge contemporary William Pitt the younger, who regularly stayed with Wilberforce at his house in Wimbledon inherited from his uncle. Pitt, Wilberforce, and Edward Eliot travelled to France together in autumn 1783.

After Pitt became prime minister in December 1783, Wilberforce, albeit without government office, was a key supporter of his minority government in its difficult early months. In particular, on 25 March 1784 he delivered a powerfully effective speech at the Yorkshire county meeting in the Castle Yard at York, being dramatically interrupted by the arrival of a messenger with news of the dissolution of parliament, which Wilberforce himself announced to the assembled freeholders. Having thus brought himself prominently to public attention, Wilberforce rapidly emerged as a compromise Pittite candidate for Yorkshire at the ensuing general election. On 6 April the Foxites conceded defeat, and he returned to the Commons as a representative of England's largest county—a remarkable achievement for a man without major landed interests who was not yet twenty-five. At the time this success seemed fully to open his way to the fulfilment of conventional ambition; in the event it was to provide him with the independent political weight required for a career that took a very different course.

Launching Christian reform, 1785–1789 Wilberforce's boyish encounter with evangelicalism appeared in his late teens and early twenties to have been a passing phase, and he later recalled that he 'had imbibed sceptical notions, and had hired a sitting at Lindsey's Unitarian Chapel' (Harford, 206). In 1785, primarily through the influence of Isaac Milner, later dean of Carlisle, with whom he travelled on two extended continental tours, he became convinced that mainstream Christian doctrine was true. He then went through an evangelical conversion experience, lamenting the perceived futility of his past life, absorbing 'the infinite love, that Christ should die to save such a sinner' (Wilberforce and Wilberforce, 1.91). From this followed a resolution to commit his future life wholly to the service of God. He sought spiritual advice from the leading evangelical clergyman John Newton, whom he had encountered as a boy, and who now strongly counselled him to remain in politics. This influence was reinforced from a different quarter by that of Pitt, who warned him against rendering his 'talents useless both to yourself and mankind' (Pollock, 38). Hence Wilberforce resolved not to withdraw from public life, but rather to perform his parliamentary duties 'with increased diligence and conscientiousness' (Bodl. Oxf., MS Wilberforce c. 49, fol. 14).

The gregariousness, generous hospitality, and liveliness in conversation that had characterized Wilberforce before 1785 persisted after his conversion. Though he himself was prone to regard such attributes as evidence of spiritual declension, they were in fact powerful tools for motivating others and gaining affection and co-operation. His effectiveness as a parliamentary leader, and more broadly as an agent of national religious and moral revival, stemmed from his capacity to combine spiritual earnestness with charm, tact, and lightness of touch in human relationships. At the same time his Christian convictions, and his sense of the ultimate significance and rightness of his causes, ensured a fundamental integrity and a dogged readiness to persist in the face of repeated set-backs.

In the short term, however, there were some false starts. In the parliamentary session of 1786 Wilberforce brought forward a bill on the criminal law designed to reduce the sentence on women convicted of treason from burning to hanging, and to extend dissection after execution from murderers to rapists, arsonists, burglars, and robbers. It passed the Commons but was thrown out by the Lords. He also introduced a Registration Bill, providing for the registration of all freeholders, and for the taking of polls in several centres across a county on the same day, rather than—as then happened—only in the county town over several days. Again the measure was lost in the Lords. The

tentative and unsuccessful nature of these forays into humanitarian and parliamentary reform was a sign of Wilberforce's good intentions, but also of his lack of experience and his inability immediately to find compelling causes on which to focus his energies.

Nevertheless, at the end of 1786 Wilberforce demonstrated the strength of his commitment to political life by taking the lease of a house in Old Palace Yard, Westminster, close to parliament, and deciding to sell the house in Wimbledon that had hitherto been his main home. For the next five years he lacked any other permanent residence of his own, and when away from Westminster drew on the extended hospitality of his numerous friends. In particular John Thornton, a fellow evangelical and half-brother of his aunt Hannah, gave him the regular use of a room at his home in Clapham.

It was in 1787 that the concerns that dominated the rest of Wilberforce's life became clear. First, through a variety of channels, particularly association with the circle around Sir Charles and Lady Middleton, and visits from Thomas Clarkson, Wilberforce's hitherto vague concern for the welfare of slaves was transformed into sustained leadership of the parliamentary campaign for the abolition of the slave trade. He had already begun to collect evidence when his decision was catalysed by a conversation with Pitt and William Grenville in May 1787, under what came to be called the 'Wilberforce oak' at Holwood in Kent, when the prime minister urged Wilberforce to make the cause his own. While others, notably Clarkson, worked on gathering evidence and mobilizing public opinion through the committee for the abolition of the slave trade, Wilberforce complemented their work through his exertions in the House of Commons. Second, he meanwhile purposefully lobbied bishops and prominent laymen to secure the issue by the king on 1 June 1787 of a proclamation for the encouragement of piety and virtue; this followed earlier precedents, but reflected the perception of Wilberforce and others that the tide of vice and immorality was rising. He then in the latter part of 1787 engaged in hectic travelling around the country, soliciting the support of further notables. He successfully established a society to promote the implementation of the proclamation and hence to be an agency of moral reformation. On 28 October he wrote in his journal that 'God Almighty has set before me two great objects, the suppression of the slave trade and the reformation of manners' (Wilberforce and Wilberforce, 1.149).

Wilberforce gave notice of a parliamentary motion on the abolition of the slave trade for early in 1788, but his exertions in 1787, following on the upheaval of his spiritual crisis of 1785–6, precipitated in February 1788 a serious stress-related illness, probably ulcerative colitis, that incapacitated him for several months. At one point he was thought to be dying, but he slowly recovered, spending his convalescence at Bath and Cambridge. At this time he began the regular moderate use of opium, which continued for the remainder of his life, and proved an effective treatment for his recurrent nervous and intestinal disorders.

In Wilberforce's absence, Pitt advanced the anti-slave-trade cause by ordering an investigation by the privy council, and then, in May 1788, moving for one by the House of Commons. The subsequent debate revealed considerable support for abolition. Also passed was a bill, promoted by Sir William Dolben, to regulate the capacity of slave ships in order to improve the conditions of the slaves. Following the publication of the privy council report on 25 April 1789, Wilberforce marked his own delayed formal entry into the parliamentary campaign on 12 May with a closely reasoned speech of three and a half hours, using its evidence to describe the effects of the trade on Africa and the appalling conditions of the middle passage. He argued that abolition would lead to an improvement in the conditions of slaves already in the West Indies, and sought to answer the economic arguments of his opponents. For him, however, the fundamental issue was one of morality and justice. He concluded by moving twelve resolutions condemning the trade. These, though, were never discussed. Concerns about economic consequences rendered the house receptive to the stance of the trade's supporters: that more evidence was needed before a responsible decision could be taken. The matter was adjourned to the next session, but Wilberforce had convincingly launched the parliamentary campaign that dominated his life for the next eighteen years.

Labours and set-backs, 1790–1797 In January 1790 Wilberforce secured a select committee to examine the evidence on the slave trade. Throughout the ensuing parliamentary session he assiduously participated in its proceedings, while his house in Old Palace Yard was a centre of activity for the abolitionists. The general election of June 1790, in which he was returned again for Yorkshire without a contest, prevented further progress that year. In October and November, however, his usual autumn wanderings were broken by an extended stay at Yoxall Lodge in Staffordshire, the home of his Cambridge friend Thomas Gisborne. Here, with the assistance of Thomas Babington, Wilberforce worked extremely hard to assimilate and condense the vast quantity of information generated by the select committee.

The select committee resumed its deliberations in February 1791, and Wilberforce, encouraged by a letter from the dying John Wesley, returned to his assiduous gathering of material. On 18 April, in a four-hour speech that showed his mastery of the evidence and arguments, he moved for leave to bring in an Abolition Bill. Subsequent debate was lively and extended over two evenings, but when the house divided at 3.30 on the morning of 20 April Wilberforce was defeated by 163 votes to 88. The outbreak both of revolution in France and, early in 1791, of a slave rebellion in the French colony of San Domingo (Haiti) had heightened insecurities and led the majority of MPs to oppose a measure that they perceived as potentially destabilizing.

This set-back demonstrated that victory would not be easy, and so the anti-slavery campaigners sought to broaden their base of support. Wilberforce became more

aware than hitherto that activity outside parliament was important. Hence in summer and autumn 1791 he worked with his close friend Henry Thornton to launch the Sierra Leone Company, which aimed to resettle former slaves on the west coast of Africa and to advance legitimate trade with the region. He also began to take a greater direct interest in the work of the committee for the abolition of the slave trade, attending one of its meetings for the first time in December 1791.

On 2 April 1792 Wilberforce again moved in the Commons for abolition. The ensuing all-night debate was one of the memorable occasions of the unreformed parliament, drawing great eloquence from Pitt, Fox, and Wilberforce himself. The decisive intervention came from Henry Dundas, the home secretary, who proposed the compromise of gradual abolition, which passed by 230 votes to 85. Yet it proved a pyrrhic victory, partly because the word 'gradual' could be used as a cover for indefinite delay, partly because in the ensuing years further progress was obstructed in the Lords. Wilberforce's troubles were augmented by the threats of John Kimber, a slave-ship captain whom he had named in the Commons as having flogged a slave girl to death. Kimber was consequently arrested and tried for murder, but, having been acquitted because of poorly presented prosecution evidence, he pursued Wilberforce for an apology and compensation, menacing him with physical violence.

Despite such frustration and antagonism, Wilberforce's commitment to abolition never wavered. On 26 February 1793 he narrowly lost a vote in the Commons whereby he had been hoping to put pressure on the Lords. During the sessions of 1793 and 1794 he unsuccessfully promoted a Foreign Slave Bill, which would have prohibited the use of British ships to carry slaves to the territories of other countries.

Meanwhile, though, other interests developed. Wilberforce believed that insufficient efforts were made to prevent the outbreak of war with France in February 1793, a source of tension in his hitherto close friendship with Pitt. The war continued to concern him greatly, and he was also worried by radical agitation at home, although he did not identify with alarmist reactions. He was, however, the more convinced of the need for national moral and spiritual revival, and in autumn 1793 he began to write material for a 'tract' on 'practical Christianity' which he saw as a requisite response to the needs of the times. Meanwhile in May 1793 he took the opportunity provided by the renewal of the East India Company's charter to attempt to obtain a legislative commitment to the promulgation of Christianity in India. His clauses were initially included in the bill, but then struck out after lobbying from the directors of the company, who feared that religious confrontations would damage their commercial and political interests.

Wilberforce's disquiet about the war increased, and on 30 December 1794 he moved an amendment to the address urging the government to try to secure peace. On 26 January 1795 he supported an opposition motion with a similar purpose. He thereby further strained his friendship with Pitt, but Wilberforce had no intention of making lasting common cause with the opposition whigs. His position was one of independence on the basis of convictions arrived at through prayer and belief in divine guidance. Pitt did not bear a grudge, and on 26 February supported Wilberforce when he proposed another unsuccessful motion against the slave trade. When Wilberforce again moved for peace on 27 May, Pitt was privately sympathetic, although more hawkish members of the government, notably Dundas and William Windham, remained antagonistic.

By autumn 1795 Wilberforce and Pitt were fully reconciled, on the basis of a desire for peace but also a recognition that it was unrealistic in the short term, coupled with serious concern at growing unrest at home. Hence Wilberforce fully supported Pitt when in November he brought forward the 'gagging' bills against seditious meetings and treasonable practices. When Wilberforce received news that Christopher Wyvill was mobilizing Yorkshire against the measures, he made a dramatic dash up the Great North Road in a coach borrowed from Pitt. He arrived in York just in time to deliver a decisive speech at the county meeting on 1 December, when he claimed that the provisions of the bills had been misrepresented, and argued that they offered the best possible balance between 'the security of the constitution, and … every reasonable toleration to the subject'. His intervention was crucial in securing a loyal address rather than a hostile petition.

Wilberforce's support for the government at this crucial juncture served to reduce fears that the anti-slave-trade campaign was potentially subversive. Certainly, when he renewed the parliamentary struggle in February 1796 he met with more success than in recent years, with his Abolition Bill proceeding as far as a third reading on 15 March. It was then narrowly defeated because some of his supporters were at the opera. The session of 1796 was curtailed by the general election in June, when Wilberforce was again returned for Yorkshire without a contest. On 15 May 1797 he yet again proposed a motion against the slave trade, but once more lost the vote.

Wilberforce's interests in social reform expanded during the mid-1790s. He energetically supported Jeremy Bentham in his abortive plans for a panopticon that would have improved conditions for prisoners. He encouraged medical and educational initiatives and also the Society for Bettering the Condition and Increasing the Comforts of the Poor, formed in 1796. For Wilberforce, though, the nation's most pressing needs were moral and spiritual, and in April 1797 he at last completed and published *A practical view of the prevailing religious system of professed Christians in the higher and middle classes of this country contrasted with real Christianity*. This work was the tract begun in 1793 and now expanded into a full-length book. As the title implies, Wilberforce expounded his interpretation of New Testament teachings as a basis for a critique of the lukewarm and inadequate practice of Christianity he observed around him. He called for religious revival as an essential means of reversing national moral decline. Despite its unfashionable theme and diffuse and discursive style, the book was extensively read and very influential. It was repeatedly reprinted and translated. It was both 'the manifesto of the evangelical party of the time' (*DNB*) and Wilberforce's own personal testimony, which provided a powerful rationalization of his philanthropic and political exertions over the preceding decade.

Marriage, family, and religious life Wilberforce's single-minded commitment to his chosen causes led him during the late 1780s and early 1790s to resist romantic involvements, and there is little doubt that he remained not only single but celibate until his thirty-eighth year. Then on 15 April 1797, while at Bath, he met Barbara Ann (1777–1847), the third child and eldest daughter of Isaac Spooner of Elmdon Hall, Warwickshire, a Birmingham banker, and his wife, Barbara Gough-Calthorpe, the sister of the first Lord Calthorpe. Barbara had come to Wilberforce seeking spiritual advice. He was immediately smitten and, with characteristic impulsiveness, proposed within a fortnight of their first encounter. The couple were married quietly at Walcot church, Bath, on 30 May 1797. The relationship was characterized by enduring mutual devotion, and Barbara's attentiveness helped to sustain Wilberforce's increasingly frail health, although her associated tendency to a narrow-minded possessiveness was also a constraint upon him. Following a near-fatal attack of typhoid in 1800, her own health was never robust. The first child, William, had been born in July 1798, to be followed by Barbara (1799), Elizabeth (1801), Robert Isaac *Wilberforce (1802), Samuel *Wilberforce (1805), and Henry William *Wilberforce (1807). Wilberforce loved children and was a devoted and playful father, cultivating a warm family life in the midst of his hectic political activities. Unusually for the period, all the children survived to adulthood.

In 1792 Wilberforce had accepted an invitation from Henry Thornton to share his home at Battersea Rise in Clapham, an accessible refuge from his hectic life at Old Palace Yard. Following his marriage he leased Edward Eliot's nearby house, Broomfield, and after Eliot's death in late 1797 he bought it. Wilberforce, however, retained something of the nomadic spirit of his youth, and continued to travel extensively around the country during the parliamentary recess. His visits to Bath, beneficial to his health and appealing to his innate sociability, were frequent and prolonged.

Wilberforce's Christian commitment remained fundamental to his life. Private prayer and Bible reading were central to his daily routine, and his surviving diaries and journals illustrate the depth of his continual quest for holiness and obedience to the call of God. In the period after his conversion he regularly sought and received counsel from Isaac Milner and John Newton, and as the years passed he himself became a valued spiritual counsellor, notably to the agriculturalist Arthur Young, who had been much stirred by reading the *Practical View*. Wilberforce cultivated a strongly religious tone in family life through holding daily family prayers and anxiously watching over the spiritual development of his children.

When in London he worshipped at the Anglican proprietary Lock Chapel near Hyde Park Corner, whose minister from 1785 was the biblical commentator Thomas Scott; at Clapham he attended the parish church, where John Venn was incumbent. Despite its intensity, Wilberforce's religion was never austere: while reverencing Scott's ministry he did not imbibe his Calvinism, and, while strongly upholding the observance of Sunday as a day of rest, he saw it as a time for recreation with family and friends as well as for spiritual duties.

The 1790s and 1800s marked the heyday of what was later labelled the Clapham Sect, the group of wealthy evangelicals around Wilberforce and Henry Thornton whose other notable members included Edward Eliot, Charles Grant, Zachary Macaulay, John Shore (Lord Teignmouth), and James Stephen. Stephen's second marriage to Wilberforce's sister, Sarah, in 1800 meant that the two close friends became brothers-in-law, and the Wilberforces were linked to another leading religious and literary family. This circle of friends was of great importance to Wilberforce in providing emotional and practical support for the ongoing anti-slave-trade campaign. It was also a focal point for religious initiatives in which he played an important role, notably the formation in 1799 of what became the Church Missionary Society, the launch in 1801 of the magazine *Christian Observer*, and the establishment in 1804 of the British and Foreign Bible Society.

Wilberforce was intensely loyal to the Church of England, seeing it as the essential safeguard of the Christian fabric of the state. Initially, therefore, he opposed the repeal of the Test and Corporation Acts. One of the key reasons for the success of the *Practical View* was that its call for national spiritual and moral renewal could be read in broad Anglican as well as specific evangelical terms. At the same time he had a natural affinity with dissenters and Methodists, and in 1800 his influence was important in deflecting Pitt from a measure to restrict the licensing of preachers.

Even before his conversion Wilberforce had been generous in his charitable giving, but after 1785 he became more energetic and systematic in sharing his considerable wealth with others. For example in 1798, the year after his marriage, he gave away more than £2000. He was willing to assist individuals in straitened circumstances even when he had not been previously acquainted with them. He also gave extensive support to Anglican clergy. In 1789, while staying with Hannah More, he had visited the Mendips, and his appalled reaction to the destitution and lack of education of the local people gave a further focus to his philanthropic aspirations. He undertook to fund More in promoting moral and social improvement in the neighbourhood, and maintained a long-term commitment to supporting her work.

The path to abolition, 1797–1807 The closing years of the eighteenth century were unpropitious for the anti-slave-trade cause. Not only did a sense of national crisis engender a political atmosphere unreceptive to reform and innovation, but the passing in 1797 of a measure that referred the matter to the colonial legislatures further frustrated Wilberforce's efforts. Hence his annual motions in 1798 and 1799 were defeated by narrow majorities. In 1799, however, an act was passed that further restricted overcrowding on slave ships. In 1800 and 1801 Wilberforce refrained from proposing his normal motion, a change of tactics arising initially from hopes for an agreed suspension of the trade and then for an international agreement on abolition as part of a peace settlement. But such expectations proved unfulfilled, and Pitt's resignation in 1801 and replacement as prime minister by the less sympathetic Henry Addington was a further discouragement. In 1802 Wilberforce's readiness to defer to a motion by George Canning against the settlement of slaves in Trinidad meant that his own motion became a mere token gesture at the end of the session.

Meanwhile the moral and social condition of Britain greatly concerned Wilberforce. He supported measures to contain unrest, including the further suspension of habeas corpus, and the Combination Acts of 1799–1800. His sense of a parallel need for moral reform was evident in his disapproval of Pitt's duel with George Tierney in 1798 and in efforts to promote Sunday observance. When the bad harvests of 1799 and 1800 resulted in much scarcity of food and severe distress among the working class, he assiduously participated in the work of the parliamentary committee charged with finding solutions. His motivation was quite as much compassion as fear of disaffection: his vision was for a stable Christian social order in which the wealthy fully accepted their spiritual, moral, and financial obligations to those less fortunate than themselves.

In the general election of July 1802 Wilberforce was for a fourth time returned unopposed for Yorkshire. The new parliament proved much readier than its predecessor to contemplate abolition of the slave trade, but in the short term any progress was further delayed by the fear of French invasion after the breakdown of the peace of Amiens in 1803. Wilberforce initially opposed the renewal of the war, believing British retention of Malta to be unjustified, but he came to accept that Napoleon's imperialistic ambitions made conflict inevitable.

In the parliamentary session of 1804 the prospects for abolition at last improved. Pitt's return to Downing Street did not help much, but the anti-radical hysteria of the 1790s had receded, and the Irish MPs brought to Westminster by the union of 1801 helped to shift the weight of opinion in the Commons. Hence, on 20 May, Wilberforce obtained leave to bring in a bill by a margin of 124 to 49, and this bill passed through all its stages in the Commons before the end of June. Once again, however, the dawn proved false: it was too late in the session to attempt to get the bill through the Lords that year. Wilberforce had to reintroduce the measure in the Commons in February 1805, only this time to be defeated on the second reading. In the meantime Wilberforce in July 1804 persuaded Pitt to use an order in council to stop the slave trade to Dutch Guiana, which had been captured by Britain. Although the government procrastinated and did not issue the order until September 1805, it did suggest that the trade's days were numbered. A further promising development in 1805 was closer communication between Wilberforce and the whig abolitionists.

Parliamentary resolutions in April 1805 for the impeachment of Lord Melville (Dundas), the first lord of the Admiralty, for condoning the misappropriation of naval funds, presented Wilberforce with a painful tension between his personal loyalty to Pitt and his independent upholding of public morality. Wilberforce, who feared for 'the purity of our political system' (Wilberforce and Wilberforce, 3.228), said that Melville's admission of the truth of the key charge against him gave him no option but to vote for the impeachment resolutions. His speech turned the finely balanced debate against Melville. It also greatly distressed Pitt, but the friendship between him and Wilberforce was unbroken, and the latter, profoundly moved by the prime minister's premature death in January 1806, carried a banner at his public funeral.

Wilberforce supported the Grenville–Fox ministry formed after the death of Pitt. This reflected his general preference for sustaining the government of the day as far as was consistent with his own independence, but he also recognized that, with two longstanding supporters of abolition now in power, the situation was promising. Adopting a tactic suggested by James Stephen, he persuaded the government to reintroduce the unsuccessful Foreign Slave Bill of the 1790s under the guise of procedural legislation to confirm Pitt's Guiana order in council of the previous year. The measure passed rapidly through both houses, and then, on 10 June 1806, Fox—to whom Wilberforce deferred for the sake of the cause—eloquently moved a resolution for general abolition. It too passed, and Wilberforce moved the subsequent address to the king.

Fox's death in September again destabilized the political situation and was a set-back for abolition. Grenville called a general election with a view to strengthening his position, and after a tense campaign Wilberforce once more carried Yorkshire without a poll. He spent the time before parliament met working on *A Letter on the Abolition of the Slave Trade*. Like the *Practical View*, his other substantial literary work, this was a pamphlet that grew into a book. It consolidated and restated the formidable array of evidence and argumentation against the trade that Wilberforce had developed over the previous two decades. Its publication on 31 January 1807 served to inform the final phase of the struggle, which had already begun with Grenville's introduction of an Abolition Bill in the Lords. When it had passed the upper house by unexpectedly large majorities, Viscount Howick (Charles Grey) moved its second reading in the Commons on 23 February. Wilberforce, though, was the real hero of the evening, as it became clear that this phase of his labours was at last coming to a triumphant end. Eloquent tributes were made to his efforts, and the bill passed by 283 votes to 16. It received the royal assent on 25 March.

Embodying the national conscience, 1807–1825 Wilberforce's public standing in the wake of slave-trade abolition was immediately tested severely when the incoming tory government called another general election in May 1807, and for the first and only time in his career he faced a poll for Yorkshire. Confronting as he did the great wealth and influence of both the Fitzwilliam and the Harewood interests, it was a testimony to the personal esteem in which he was held, and to his effectiveness in representing the county over the previous quarter-century, that he was returned at the head of the poll. It was alleged, however, that Wilberforce had compromised his independence by a coalition with Henry Lascelles, the tory candidate. Wilberforce denied the charge and defended himself in a published letter to the electors. He acknowledged that some of his supporters had indeed also solicited votes for Lascelles, but this was without his sanction, and it would have been improper for him to constrain their actions. The experience appears to have confirmed Wilberforce's sense of the need for moderate electoral reform, which he continued to advocate.

Wilberforce's continuing concern over slavery was now carried into creating the African Institution, which aimed to ameliorate conditions in the West Indies, and to develop the Sierra Leone project as a foundation for disseminating Christianity and civilization in Africa. He also sought to prevent slaves being carried in foreign ships. Freed, though, from the immediate pressures of the campaign for British abolition, he was able to exercise his strong moral authority in diverse ways. During these years members of the government readily sought and received his advice, but he maintained his independent stance, even after his friend and fellow evangelical Spencer Perceval became prime minister in 1809. He continued until 1812 assiduously to attend the Commons, with an influential voice on issues such as the duke of York scandal in 1809, the failure of the Walcheren expedition in 1809 and the subsequent parliamentary inquiry, and the regency arrangements consequent on the king's final breakdown in health in 1810–11. His role as leader of the group of evangelical 'Saints' in parliament was recognized but informal.

In 1808, anxious to limit his expenses so as better to finance his philanthropy, and weary of continual commuting between Westminster and Clapham, Wilberforce had sold both Broomfield and Old Palace Yard. He purchased a lease of Gore House in Kensington (on the site where the Albert Hall was later built), which provided a relatively rural lifestyle within walking distance of parliament. It also became a centre for his burgeoning extraparliamentary activities, helping many individuals and acting as an office-bearer and leading supporter for numerous evangelical societies.

At the general election of 1812 Wilberforce, conscious of advancing age and declining energy, decided not to contest Yorkshire, and was returned instead for Bramber in Sussex, a pocket borough controlled by a cousin of his wife, Lord Calthorpe. This change greatly reduced his constituency responsibilities while enabling him to remain in the Commons and to continue to advocate his central concerns. He sat for Bramber for the remainder of his parliamentary career.

Wilberforce's advocacy of religious liberty now came to the fore. He had agonized much on the Roman Catholic question, but now his dislike of perceived prejudice and his belief that concession would strengthen Irish loyalty led him in March 1813 to support emancipation, a stance that put him at odds with many of his evangelical supporters. The renewal of the East India Company's charter then gave him an opportunity to revive his campaign of 1793 to secure the admission of missionaries into India. For him this was a cause analogous to the abolition of the slave trade. He held that it would be the means to liberate India from the 'moral and social ignorance and degradation' that he saw as inherent to Hinduism, by opening the way to 'Christian light and moral improvement' (W. Wilberforce, *Substance of the Speeches … on the East India Bill*, 1813, 48, 106). He was supported by extensive petitioning, and on 22 June 1813, in one of his most compelling Commons speeches, he persuaded the house to pass the necessary resolutions. The foundation of the bishopric of Calcutta ensued.

In the meantime Wilberforce maintained the campaign against slavery by promoting a bill, suggested by Stephen, to set up a register of slaves already in the West Indies so as to provide leverage for improving conditions and to make it easy to prevent additions by illicit trading. In 1814, as the war with France appeared at last to be ending, he strongly urged that a general abolition of the slave trade should be incorporated into the peace settlement. He addressed an open letter to Talleyrand on the matter, and also a lengthy personal letter to Alexander I of Russia, who was sympathetic and granted him a private audience when in London in June 1814. Already, however, Wilberforce had been bitterly disappointed by Castlereagh's initial failure to obtain such a provision. He led a campaign, supported by the African Institution and a wave of petitioning, to secure the revision of the treaty. On 27 June he proposed and carried unanimously an address to the regent that committed the government to the cause and ensured that, despite limited short-term success, it remained firmly on the diplomatic agenda, in relation to Spain, Portugal, and the United States, as well as France. A further dimension of Wilberforce's concern to improve conditions in the West Indies came between 1815 and 1820, when he supported and advised Henri Christophe, a former slave who had proclaimed himself king of Haiti, in efforts to promote the educational and religious advance of his people.

In response to the hardship and unrest that followed the end of the Napoleonic wars Wilberforce reluctantly sided with the measures adopted by the Liverpool government. Although his philanthropic and compassionate impulses remained strong, he lacked a first-hand understanding of the extent of the distress of the poor, and regarded radical agitation as subverting the stability of the constitution. He also perceived it as linked to anti-Christian beliefs and believed that 'democrats' squeezed out spiritual interest by laying too 'great a stress on the concerns of this world' (Wilberforce and Wilberforce, 5.36). His vote in favour of

the corn laws in 1815 led to fears that his house would be attacked. In June 1817 his support for the suspension of habeas corpus caused Sir Francis Burdett ironically to tag him 'the honourable and religious member', provoking Wilberforce into a robust defence of his own stance. In 1819 the Peterloo massacre heightened his fears of subversion, and he approved of the subsequent Seditious Meetings Act. In 1820, when George IV's estranged wife, Caroline of Brunswick, sought her rights as queen, Wilberforce, preoccupied with the dangers to constitutional stability and public morality, tried unsuccessfully to mediate a settlement. Radical attacks on his perceived hypocrisy indirectly testified to his status as a national moral arbiter.

These years saw failing health and painful bereavements. As he aged, Wilberforce's slight figure became increasingly hunched, and he began to wear a steel corset to support his body. His eyesight, never good, steadily deteriorated, he continued to have bowel problems, and he also suffered recurrent chest complaints. Henry Thornton, whom Hannah More judged 'a great part of himself' (Pollock, 248), died in 1815, Wilberforce's sister, Sarah, in 1816, and his elder daughter, Barbara, in 1821. Meanwhile in 1819 his eldest son, William, now grown into an amiable but feckless young man, distressed his father by his manner of life as a Cambridge undergraduate.

Amid these public and private burdens Wilberforce, fortified by his Christian convictions, retained an underlying emotional equanimity and a brightness and warmth of manner that impressed his acquaintances. Radicals might dislike him, but he was enormously venerated by the evangelicals, and the appearance of his increasingly frail and bent figure at religious meetings was greeted with great adulation.

By the early 1820s Wilberforce was limiting his public activities. In 1821 his decision to sell Gore House and move to Marden Park in Surrey, 15 miles from Westminster, signified a growing disengagement from parliamentary affairs. Conscious, however, that his active career was nearing its close, he still sought to give renewed impetus to the campaign against slavery. Hopes that the end of the slave trade would lead to an amelioration of conditions in the West Indies had been disappointed, and the proposal for a register of slaves failed to make progress. Emancipation appeared to be the only effectual way forward. In May 1821 Wilberforce approached Thomas Fowell Buxton to be his coadjutor and eventual successor in the Commons leadership of the campaign to free the slaves. Little was done until early in 1823, when the Anti-Slavery Society was formed, and Wilberforce published his *Appeal to the religion, justice and humanity of the inhabitants of the British empire in behalf of the negro slaves in the West Indies*. In this pamphlet he dwelt on the moral and spiritual degradation of the slaves and presented their emancipation as a matter of national duty to God. It proved to be a powerful inspiration for the anti-slavery agitation in the country. It also stirred William Cobbett into a virulent published attack on Wilberforce for his alleged failure to acknowledge the extent of the deprivation and oppression suffered by the 'free British labourers' whose lot he had contrasted favourably with that of the slaves.

Wilberforce's anxiety to participate in the parliamentary campaign was indicated by a move back to London, to Grove House in Brompton, but it was now Buxton who took the lead in the Commons, by moving a resolution against slavery on 15 May 1823. Wilberforce spoke in his support and also participated in anti-slavery debates on 16 March and 11 June 1824, when in his last speech in the Commons he urged that the matter should not be left to the colonial governments. While it was clear that he no longer had strength for protracted and extensive activity, he had provided an invaluable initial impetus to this new phase in the anti-slavery movement.

Retirement, death, and reputation, 1825–1833 Wilberforce suffered two bouts of serious illness in 1824, and early in 1825 he bowed to the inevitable and resigned his parliamentary seat. He purchased Highwood Hill, a house with a small estate at Mill Hill in Middlesex, in a rural situation but accessible to London, and moved there in 1826. Free from the stress of public life, his health improved somewhat, and he passed an active retirement, rejoicing in the beauties of nature, maintaining his extensive correspondence, continuing to travel extensively on visits to numerous friends, and cultivating his devotional life. Although generally withdrawing from politics, he retained his passionate commitment to the anti-slavery cause, offering counsel and occasional public support to its active leaders.

Wilberforce's family was a source of both pride and pain. He delighted in the academic success of his three younger sons and in their decisions to take Anglican orders. Although Robert and Henry later converted to Roman Catholicism, during their father's lifetime the evangelicalism of the family appeared secure. Meanwhile, Wilberforce supported William in a speculative dairy business, the failure of which in 1830 caused him disastrous financial losses. The death of the younger daughter, Elizabeth, in 1832, brought further grief to her parents.

The severe financial retrenchment forced upon Wilberforce in 1830 led him to let Highwood and to spend his closing years in a peripatetic existence, focused on the vicarages of two of his sons. He divided the bulk of his time between Brighstone on the Isle of Wight, where Samuel, later bishop of Oxford and Winchester, was incumbent, and East Farleigh in Kent, to which Robert had recently been presented by Lord Chancellor Brougham out of concern for Wilberforce's financial situation.

Wilberforce's final decline in health began early in 1833 with a severe attack of influenza. He went to Bath, where the waters had so often in the past appeared beneficial to him, but this time he experienced no relief, suffering 'much from pain and languor' (Wilberforce and Wilberforce, 5.355). In mid-July he was moved to London, where for some days he seemed to improve. Late on 26 July he

was thrilled to hear that the bill for the abolition of slavery had passed its third reading in the Commons, the culmination of his life's work. On the following evening he became much weaker, and after a series of fainting fits he died, early in the morning of 29 July at 44 Cadogan Place, Sloane Street.

Wilberforce had wished to be buried at Stoke Newington with his sister and elder daughter, but following a requisition—at the instigation of Lord Brougham, from many peers and MPs—the family consented to interment in Westminster Abbey. The funeral took place there on 3 August, with the lord chancellor, the speaker of the House of Commons, and the duke of Gloucester among the pallbearers. The distinguished and numerous attendance from both houses of parliament and the extensive interest of the general public were 'exalted testimony of the esteem in which he was held … and of the friendship which his mild manners and noble qualities had won him' (*The Times*). He was laid to rest on the same day in the north transept, close to three other great parliamentarians of his generation: Pitt, Fox, and Canning. A striking seated statue by Samuel Joseph was erected in Westminster Abbey in 1840, and a commemorative column was erected in Hull in 1834.

The five-volume life of Wilberforce by his sons Robert and Samuel was published in 1838. It was copiously documented, but thin on interpretation; strong on insight into its subject's religious life, weak on understanding of the context of his political achievements. It gave rise to an unedifying controversy with the veteran Thomas Clarkson, who felt that his own role in the abolition campaign had been denigrated. Two prominent tendencies in subsequent perceptions of Wilberforce had already been presaged during his lifetime. To evangelicals he was a seminal leader and inspiration, a man of committed faith and integrity, who at great personal cost followed the call of Christ to help the oppressed abroad and proclaim the moral and spiritual imperatives of the gospel at home. In the eyes of secular radicals and socialists, however, his concentration on overseas slavery, his spiritual and moral preoccupations, and his underlying social conservatism caused him to disregard the deprivation and injustice suffered by his own countrymen. Behind both perceptions, though, lay an awareness of his undoubted stature as a leader who stirred the conscience of the nation and upheld the human rights and dignity of the slaves. Many others contributed to the campaign against slavery, but Wilberforce's role was essential and unique precisely because he was a fully integrated and respected member of the political and social élite. While he challenged the attitudes of his class, he did not transcend them, but by his residual conformity he secured his enduring influence. In religion the legacy of his evangelistic zeal and spiritual earnestness helped to shape the Victorian age he did not live to see; in politics he maintained a courage, independence, and incorruptibility that has given lasting inspiration to British public life. JOHN WOLFFE

Sources Bodl. Oxf., MSS Wilberforce · R. I. Wilberforce and S. Wilberforce, *Life of William Wilberforce*, 5 vols. (1838) · J. Pollock,

Wilberforce (1977) · J. S. Harford, *Recollections of William Wilberforce, esq, MP for the county of York during nearly thirty years; with brief notices of some of his personal friends and contemporaries*, 2nd edn (1865) · *The correspondence of William Wilberforce*, ed. R. I. Wilberforce and S. Wilberforce, 2 vols. (1840) · *Family prayers by the late William Wilberforce, esq*, ed. R.I. Wilberforce (1834) · T. Clarkson, *Strictures on a life of William Wilberforce, by the Rev. W. Wilberforce and the Rev. S. Wilberforce* (1838) · W. Cobbett, 'Wilberforce', *Cobbett's Weekly Political Register* (30 Aug 1823) · J. C. Colquhoun, *William Wilberforce: his friends and his times* (1867) · J. J. Gurney, *Familiar sketch of the late William Wilberforce* (1838) · [J. Stephen], review of *Life of William Wilberforce*, *EdinR*, 67 (1838), 143–80 · *The Times* (5 Aug 1833) · D. Wilson, 'Introduction', in W. Wilberforce, *Practical view*, 3rd edn, Select Christian authors with introductory essays, 29 (1829) · *Yorkshire election: a collection of the speeches, addresses, and squibs* (1807) · R. Anstey, *The Atlantic slave trade and British abolition, 1760–1810* (1975) · L. W. Cowie, *William Wilberforce, 1759–1833: a bibliography*, Bibliographies of British Statesmen, 17 (1992) · R. S. Drewry, *William Wilberforce, 1759–1833* (1959) · E. M. Forster, *Marianne Thornton: a domestic biography* (1956) · R. G. Thorne, 'Wilberforce, William', *HoP, Commons, 1790–1820* · J. Brooke, 'Wilberforce, William', *HoP, Commons, 1754–90* · D. Newsome, *The parting of friends: the Wilberforces and Henry Manning*, 2nd edn (1993) · *DNB* · C. Tolley, *Domestic biography: the legacy of evangelicalism in four nineteenth-century families* (1997) · E. G. Wilson, *Thomas Clarkson: a biography* (1989)

Archives Bodl. Oxf., corresp. and papers, incl. diary · Boston PL, letters and papers · Duke U., Perkins L., corresp., bank account books · Hull Central Library, corresp. · Hunt. L., letters · Rutgers University, New Brunswick, letters · St John Cam., corresp. · W. Sussex RO, family papers · Wilberforce House and Georgian Houses, Hull, family corresp. and legal papers | BL, corresp. with Jeremy Bentham, Add. MSS 33542-33544 · BL, corresp. with William Eden, Add. MS 34427 · BL, corresp. with Lord Grenville, Add. MSS 58978, 69038 · BL, letters to third earl of Hardwicke, Add. MSS 35424, 35649 · BL, corresp. with Lord Holland, Add. MS 51820 · BL, corresp with second earl of Liverpool, Add. MSS 38191, 38288, 38323, 38416, 38566, 38742 · BL, corresp. with first Viscount Melville, Add. MS 41085 · BL, letters to Lady Sparrow, Egerton MS 1964 · BL, letters to Lord Wellesley, Add. MSS 37308–37310 · BL, letters to A. Young, Add. MSS 35127-35133, *passim* · Bodl. Oxf., corresp. with J. F. Barham · Bodl. RH, letters to Thomas Fowell Buxton · Bristol RO, corresp. with J. S. Harford · CKS, letters to William Pitt and others · CUL, letters to Thornton family and Charles Forster · Derbys. RO, letters to Sir R. J. Wilmot-Horton · Devon RO, letters to Sir Thomas Dyke Acland · Devon RO, corresp. with Henry Addington · Duke U., Perkins L., letters to William Smith · East Riding of Yorkshire Archives Service, Beverley, letters to John Grimston and Thomas Grimston · Glos. RO, corresp. with Granville Sharp · Hants. RO, letters to Lord Calthorpe · Hants. RO, corresp. with George Malkin and Mary Malkin · Hants. RO, corresp. relating to Charles Singleton of Winchester · Harrowby Manuscript Trust, Sandon Hall, Staffordshire, letters to Ryder family, earls of Harrowby · Hunt. L., letters to Edward Locker · Hunt. L., letters to Zachary Macaulay · Hunt. L., letters to Elizabeth Montagu · N. Yorks. CRO, corresp. with Christopher Wyvill · NAM, letters to James Chisholm · PRO, letters to William Pitt, PRO 30/8 · Sheff. Arch., letters to Samuel Roberts · St Deiniol's Library, Hawarden, letters to Sir John Gladstone · U. Birm. L., letters to Henry Venn · U. Hull, Brynmor Jones L., corresp. with Sir Charles Hotham-Thompson · UCL, corresp. with Lord Brougham · W. Yorks. AS, Leeds, letters relating to Luddites

Likenesses J. Russell, oils, 1770, NPG · J. Rising, portrait, 1789, Wilberforce House Museum, Hull · R. Newton, caricature, 10 May 1792 · stipple and line engraving, pubd 1792 (after J. Davies), BM, NPG · J. Sayers, etching, pubd 1795, BM · J. Sayers, caricatures, *c*.1795–1806 · J. Gillray, caricatures, *c*.1795–1809 · I. Cruickshank, caricatures, 1797 · J. Russell, oils, *c*.1801, Leeds City Art Gallery · J. Russell, pastel drawing, 1801, priv. coll. · C. Williams, caricatures, 1801-20 · T. Rowlandson, caricatures, 1805-23 · T. Webb,

medal, 1807 · portrait, 1808 (after etching by H. Edridge), Courtauld Inst., Witt Library · I. and G.? Cruickshank, caricature, 1809 · J. Vendramini, engraving, 1809 (after portrait, 1808), Courtauld Inst., Witt Library · G. Cruickshank, caricatures, 1813–21 · J. Marryat, caricature, 1819 · S. Vowks, caricature, 1820 · L. Marks, caricature, 1821 · F. Marryat, caricature, 1822 · T. Lawrence, oils, 1828, NPG [*see illus.*] · W. Heath, caricature, 1830 · S. Joseph, marble bust, 1833, City Art Gallery, York · G. Richmond, oils, 1833, St John Cam. · G. Richmond, watercolour drawing, 1833, National Gallery, London · S. Joseph, marble statue, 1838, Westminster Abbey · Hickel, group portrait, oils (*The House of Commons, 1793*), NPG · Hickel, oils, Wilberforce House, Hull · J. Rising, oils, Wilberforce House, Hull · C. Williams, caricature, etching, V&A · caricatures, repro. in M. D. George, *British Museum catalogue of political and personal satires*, 6–11 (1793–1832) · caricatures, repro. in M. D. George, *English political caricature* (1960) · caricatures, repro. in R. J. H. Douglas, *The works of George Cruickshank* (1903) · caricatures, repro. in E. B. Krumbhaar, *Isaac Cruickshank* (1966) · caricatures, repro. in T. Wright and R. H. Evans, *Account of the caricatures of James Gillray* (1851) · caricatures, repro. in T. Wright, *The works of James Gillray* (Chatto & Windus, [n.d.]) · pastel drawing, Wilberforce House, Hull · portrait (aged eleven; after J. Russell), Wrangham collection

Wilbraham, Sir Philip Wilbraham Baker, sixth baronet (1875-1957), ecclesiastical lawyer and administrator, was born at Rode Hall, Scholar Green, Cheshire, on 17 September 1875, the younger and only surviving son of Sir George Barrington Baker, fifth baronet (1845–1912), who took the additional surname of Wilbraham by royal licence in 1900, and his wife, Katharine Frances (*d.* 1945), only child of General Sir Richard Wilbraham. A descendant of Sir George Baker, the physician who demonstrated the possibility of poisoning through the use of leaden vessels, notably in the manufacture of Devonshire cider, Wilbraham succeeded his father in the baronetcy in 1912. He was educated at Harrow School, where he was a scholar and head of the school, and at Balliol College, Oxford, where he was an exhibitioner and obtained a first in classical moderations (1896) and second classes in *literae humaniores* (1898) and jurisprudence (1899). Standing as a candidate in law he was elected a fellow of All Souls College in 1899 but having married in the meantime was unable to renew his fellowship when it expired in 1906; he retained a deep affection for All Souls throughout his life. On 8 August 1901 he married Joyce Christabel (*d.* 1958), daughter of Sir John Henry Kennaway, third baronet. They had three daughters and one son.

Entering the chambers of Charles Sargant, Wilbraham was called to the bar by Lincoln's Inn in 1901 and practised, though not with the compulsion which lack of means might have supplied. Confining his interest to ecclesiastical matters, he was appointed chancellor of the diocese of Chester (1913), chancellor and vicar-general of York (1915), and chancellor of the dioceses of Truro (1923), Chelmsford (1928), and Durham (1929). He held these offices until his appointment in 1934 as dean of the arches, master of the faculties, and vicar-general of the province of Canterbury, and auditor of the chancery court of York. These appointments he resigned in 1955 owing to failing health. As dean of the arches Wilbraham became a judge of the highest ecclesiastical court. His reputation is overshadowed among lawyers by that of his immediate predecessor Sir Lewis Dibdin. Few appeals came before him and throughout the war the court was little used. A pre-war case (St Hilary) was heard by deputy since Wilbraham himself had already been consulted as chancellor of the diocese of Truro. The three reported judgments of Wilbraham were Ogbourne St George (1941), St Saviour's Walthamstow (1950), and Lapford (1954).

Wilbraham was one of the original members of the church assembly and its first secretary (1920); he resigned the secretaryship in 1939 on accepting from the crown the office of first church estates commissioner, remaining, however, an active member of the assembly. His influence on the assembly during its formative years was very great. His co-operation with Lord Hugh Cecil produced the rules for conducting the assembly's business, the one supplying the legal experience and the other knowledge of parliamentary procedure. As member and secretary of the assembly he was also member and secretary of all the committees; he used the power thus given so constructively as to earn everybody's complete trust. It fell to him not only to prepare reports and the preliminary drafts of measures, work he especially enjoyed, but also to expound often complicated clauses to the assembly. This he did in short, careful sentences, impossible to misunderstand and entirely convincing by their reasoned impartiality. In the verbatim record his speeches stand out from others in the debates. His refusal to fight and his advocacy of acceptable compromises counteracted that divisive tendency, induced by suspicions between differing schools of churchmanship, which might have marred the assembly's work.

To administration, as first church estates commissioner, Wilbraham in 1939 came late. He entered office expecting to carry through amalgamation of the ecclesiastical commissioners and Queen Anne's bounty, plans for which had already been laid. And as a countryman who owned farmland in Cheshire he especially looked forward to visiting the estates. But with the outbreak of war came instead adaptation of curtailed activities to war conditions and the evacuation of sections of the two offices to different parts of the country. Estate visits proved impracticable and he had to give up his London house. Case work and preparation for the future occupied him. Yet it was a period of greatest happiness; gradualness suited his inclination. He had time to grow into the work and to love it. When the delayed amalgamation matured after the war he was qualified as nobody else (and not even he earlier) to complete it. Trying negotiations were followed by legislation which might easily have become dangerously controversial. The successful launching of the church commissioners in 1948 and their harmonious development over the first five critical years testify to his skill and patience in leadership. He liked to carry everybody with him. The deliberately slower pace he preferred provided a firm foundation for greater advances to follow. Nevertheless, it was in his time that the commissioners' over-large agricultural holdings were reduced and their reinvestment of

securities began. He put through the assembly the measure (diocesan stipends funds, 1953) which freed large holdings of trustee stocks for profitable reinvestment. He retired in 1954 and was appointed KBE in the same year.

By virtue of tenure of the Rode estate Wilbraham was high steward of Congleton from 1912; he was a JP for the county of Cheshire from 1919; he was appointed commissary by the dean and chapter of St Paul's in 1942. Archbishop Lang conferred on him the Lambeth degree of DCL in 1936 and he was elected a bencher of Lincoln's Inn in 1942. He died at his home, Rode Hall, on 11 October 1957; his son Randle John Baker Wilbraham (1906–1980) succeeded in the baronetcy.

Tall, somewhat forbidding, Wilbraham exhibited the gravity of innate shyness covering natural friendliness. He lost his reserve in the Athenaeum billiard-room. At home at Rode with his wife, who was of the utmost help to him, he was a delightful host. That the church formed the centre of his interests was no accident. He was in the best sense a good churchman, deeply religious, conducting family prayers each morning in the old tradition.

JAMES BROWN, rev. MARK POTTLE

Sources *The Times* (14 Oct 1957) · personal knowledge (1971) · private information (1971) · Burke, *Peerage* (1967)
Likenesses O. Birley, oils, 1940, Church House, Westminster; replica, Rode Hall, Scholar Green, Cheshire
Wealth at death £34,916 17s. 5d.: probate, 29 Nov 1957, *CGPLA Eng. & Wales*

Wilbye, John (*bap.* 1574, *d.* 1638), composer and musician, was baptized at Diss in Norfolk on 7 March 1574, the third son of Matthew Wilbye (*d.* 1605), a prosperous tanner and also, it seems, an amateur lutenist. Nothing is known of his early life or musical training. It was probably through the Cornwallis family of nearby Brome Hall that he was introduced to the Kytson family of Hengrave Hall, near Bury St Edmunds. Elizabeth Cornwallis was the wife of Sir Thomas Kytson, master of Hengrave, and Wilbye entered the Kytsons' service at some time during the early to mid-1590s, remaining at Hengrave until Lady Kytson's death in 1628. He also benefited from periods of residence in London, for the Kytsons had a house in Austin Friars which would have afforded him ready contact with London musical circles; it was from their town house that he inscribed his first publication, *The First Set of English Madrigals to 3, 4, 5, and 6 Voices* (1598), dedicated to Sir Charles Cavendish, a son-in-law of Sir Thomas and Lady Kytson. Such a location also enabled Wilbye to involve himself with the capital's music business, and in 1600 he was involved with Edward Johnson (another musician and composer employed at Hengrave) in negotiations for the publication (and, subsequently, in the proof-reading) of John Dowland's second book of lute songs. The following year Wilbye contributed a madrigal, 'The Lady Oriana', to *The Triumphs of Oriana*, the collection of madrigals published in 1601 in praise of the aged Queen Elizabeth.

Within the Kytson family itself Wilbye seems to have gained the status of an honoured retainer. By 1603 he had his own comfortably furnished room ('Wilbye's chamber': an inventory of that year enables the room to be identified), and in her later will Lady Kytson made him a substantial bequest of furniture and linen. Even before this he must have acquired considerable means, for in 1613 he obtained the lease of a valuable sheep farm in the neighbourhood. In the meantime his second, and final, collection, *The Second Set of Madrigals to 3, 4, 5, and 6 Parts, Apt both for Viols and Voices* (1609) was published, and though he lived a further twenty-nine years this proved to be his last major publication. In 1614 he contributed two pieces to Sir William Leighton's *The Tears or Lamentations of a Sorrowful Soul*, but nothing else of his has survived except a handful of mostly unimportant compositions (many incomplete) for voices and/or instruments.

Thus Wilbye's reputation rests squarely upon his two volumes of madrigals. His first volume appeared one year after that of Thomas Weelkes, who was about the same age. Though the two composers were the greatest of the English madrigalists, their personal biographies suggest they were very different characters. While Weelkes started brilliantly but finally declined into a sadly disordered state, Wilbye's life story suggests a worthy, thrifty man who won his employers' trust and respect to a degree far greater than might have been expected of a servant, and who ended his days in honoured and comfortable retirement. His music lends support to this view; where Weelkes's was sturdy, ground-breaking, and powerfully rhetorical, Wilbye's was balanced, polished, and refined, never seeking to startle, let alone shock, the listener. In his verse (whether written by himself or selected) he was the more discriminating.

In his 1598 volume Wilbye started cautiously, appropriating, but then evolving further, the madrigal style as it had been naturalized into English music in the works of Thomas Morley. But already, especially in the four-voice works of this first collection, Wilbye showed a quiet enterprise that was turning the madrigal into something more characterful and individual, often in very simple but telling ways. To cite just one instance: in perhaps the most perfect piece in the whole thirty-work collection, 'Adieu, sweet Amaryllis', Wilbye perceived that a shift at the end into the major key for the final farewells would, far from brightening the mood, here bring a tone of resignation tinged with melancholy. It was a kind of subtlety that had no place in Weelkes's madrigals. Wilbye exploited this shift much more widely in his second volume.

It is in this collection that Wilbye achieved his full stature, its thirty-four pieces adding up to the greatest of all the English madrigal volumes. In this remarkably consistent publication two works are nevertheless outstanding, between them exhibiting all the main virtues of his style. In the joyful love song 'Sweet honey-sucking bees' Wilbye employed the lightest of madrigalian idioms, but through his characteristic inventiveness, rhythmic variety, and (very important) constant contrasts in scoring and texture, he contrived to build a piece as impressive for its imposing scale as for its lively detail. 'Sweet honey-sucking bees' is another madrigal that, on its last page,

slips its plangent music, here setting 'Ah, then you die!', into the major key—surely a deliciously ambivalent touch that points the current *double entendre* of 'die'—that is 'to expire' or 'to achieve sexual intercourse'. But 'Draw on, sweet night', a work of pervasive melancholy, alternates major and minor, the latter colouring the poet's pain, the former fortifying the soothing balm of the darkness in which he seeks release. Wilbye's profoundly moving setting is probably the most perceptive treatment of a text among all the English madrigals, and it is this quality above all that makes 'Draw on, sweet night' surely the greatest of all English madrigals.

There must be a strong suspicion that Wilbye's worldly affairs interested him increasingly after about 1610, which may account for his virtual abandonment of composition during his last three decades. But this may not be the whole story. By the first decade of the seventeenth century the fashion for the madrigal was already passing, and the newer trends emerging in English tastes were for a different kind of music employing more radical styles. It is perfectly plausible that Wilbye, whose beautifully poised and tasteful madrigals consistently suggest that their composer never had any interest in the more extreme technical and stylistic explorations going on around him, decided that he no longer had anything to offer. And so, his employers requiring no new compositions from him and himself being now in no need of supplementary income from his music, he fell silent. On Lady Kytson's death in 1628 the Hengrave establishment broke up, and for the last ten years of his life Wilbye was in the service of the Kytsons' daughter Mary, Countess Rivers, at her house in Colchester. Wilbye, who was unmarried, had a close friendship with the countess until his death, and it was almost certainly in Holy Trinity Church facing the house that he was buried in the autumn of 1638. His will (in which he styles himself 'gentleman'; previously he had designated himself 'yeoman') was made on 10 September and proved on 30 November. It shows that he died with substantial assets, for there were several legacies of property and land as well as two musical bequests: his 'best long bow' to a friend, John Barkar, and—intriguingly—his 'best viol' to the eight-year-old prince of Wales (the future Charles II). He also left some £400, which included a legacy of £20 to Countess Rivers—a sign, perhaps, of the degree of personal friendship in his relationship with his nominal employer.　DAVID BROWN

Sources E. H. Fellowes, preface, *The English madrigal school*, ed. E. H. Fellowes, 6 (1914); rev. edn pubd as *First set of madrigals*, rev. T. Dart (1966) · D. Brown, *Wilbye* (1974) · J. Kerman, *The Elizabethan madrigal: a comparative study* (1962) · M. Ross, 'The Kytsons of Hengrave: a study in musical patronage', MMus diss., U. Lond., 1989
Wealth at death £400, plus land and property, and personal items: Fellowes, *First set of English madrigals*

Wilcocks, Joseph (1673–1756), bishop of Gloucester and dean of Westminster, born on 19 December 1673 at Bristol, was the son of Joseph Wilcocks, a physician of Bristol. He entered Merchant Taylors' School in the City of London on

11 September 1684, and matriculated from St John's College, Oxford, on 25 February 1692. From 1692 to 1703 he held a demyship at Magdalen College, and from 1703 to 15 February 1722 a fellowship. He graduated BA on 31 October 1695, MA on 28 June 1698, and BD and DD on 16 May 1709. For a while from about 1709 he served as chaplain to the English factory and embassy at Lisbon, where his devoted ministry throughout an outbreak of smallpox earned widespread admiration. His wife, Jane (d. 1725), was the daughter of John Milner, the British consul at Lisbon. On his return to England, Wilcocks was appointed chaplain-in-ordinary to George I and preceptor to the daughters of the prince of Wales. On 11 March 1721 he was installed a prebendary of Westminster, and on 3 December 1721 he was consecrated bishop of Gloucester, holding his stall in commendam.

Over the next few years Wilcocks published several sermons, which reflected his enthusiasm for the Hanoverian succession and his keen interest in the work of the Society for the Reformation of Manners and the charity school movement. On 21 June 1731 he was installed dean of Westminster, and on the same day was nominated bishop of Rochester. He was a conscientious diocesan, who steadily refused further promotion, declining even the archbishopric of York. At Westminster he devoted himself to completing the restoration of the abbey and to finishing the building of Sir Christopher Wren's two west towers. He died on 28 February 1756, at Westminster and was buried on 9 March in Westminster Abbey under the consistory court, where his son erected a monument to his memory in 1761.

Wilcocks's only son, **Joseph Wilcocks** (1724–1791), antiquary and philanthropist, was born in Dean's Yard, Westminster, on 4 January 1724. He was admitted to Westminster School in 1731, becoming a king's scholar in 1736. He was elected to Christ Church, Oxford, in 1740, matriculating on 10 June and graduating BA in 1744 and MA in 1747. He was scholarly by nature, winning several college prizes, and after leaving Oxford he undertook serious antiquarian work in Italy. 'An account of some subterraneous apartments, with Etruscan inscriptions, discovered at Civita Turchino in Italy' was published in *Philosophical Transactions* in 1763, and the posthumously published *Roman Conversations, or, A Short Description of the Antiquities of Rome* (2 vols., 1792–4), which contains many biographical details of himself and of his father, reflected his extensive knowledge of Roman history and archaeology. He was elected FSA in 1765. His considerable wealth, which was supplemented by the bequest of an aunt's lottery winnings, was largely devoted to works of piety and benevolence. During his time in Rome, Pope Clement XIII was said to have referred to him as 'the blessed heretick' (Bickerstaffe, xli), and he was noted for support of several hospitals and his kindness to the poor and to the animal creation. He lived for some time in Barton, Northamptonshire. His friends included Edmund Burke, Benjamin West, Granville Sharp, and Adolphus Kempenfelt, in whose estate at Hurley, Berkshire, Wilcocks had a life interest; he never married. He died of an

apoplectic stroke at The Crown inn, Slough, on 23 December 1791, and was buried in Westminster Abbey on 31 December, in his father's vault.

E. I. CARLYLE, rev. RICHARD SHARP

Sources W. Bickerstaffe, 'Memoir', *Roman conversations, or, A short description of the antiquities of Rome*, 2nd edn (1797) · J. R. Bloxam, *A register of the presidents, fellows … of Saint Mary Magdalen College*, 8 vols. (1853–85), vol. 6, pp. 120–27 · Foster, *Alum. Oxon., 1500–1714*, 1.1630; 2.1552 · *GM*, 1st ser., 26 (1756), 150 · *GM*, 1st ser., 61 (1791), 1237 · *Old Westminsters*, 2.993 · J. Ingamells, *The English episcopal portrait, 1559–1835: a catalogue* (privately printed, London, 1981)
Likenesses J. Vanderbank, oils, 1737, Magd. Oxf. · R. Graves, line engraving, BM, NPG · S. Phillips, stipple (Joseph Wilcocks; after B. West), repro. in Bickerstaffe, 'Memoir', frontispiece · E. Seeman, portrait (Joseph Wilcocks), priv. coll. · J. Simon, mezzotint (Joseph Wilcocks; after portrait by E. Seeman), BM, NPG

Wilcocks, Joseph (1724–1791). *See under* Wilcocks, Joseph (1673–1756).

Wilcox, Herbert Sydney (1890–1977), film producer and director, was born at Norwood, London, on 19 April 1890, of Irish parents. He was the third of the four sons and the fourth of the five children of Joseph John Wilcox, sculptor and manager of a billiard hall, and his wife, Mary Healy. He was educated at a succession of Brighton elementary schools and subsequently embarked on a career as a billiards professional in London. On the outbreak of the First World War he enlisted as a private in the 17th battalion, Royal Fusiliers, and was later commissioned as a second lieutenant in the East Kents. He transferred to the Royal Flying Corps in 1916. At the end of the war he became a film salesman in Leeds and in 1922 entered film production in London.

Wilcox's first production, *The Wonderful Story*, a rural drama, received great critical acclaim but was a box office failure. A second film, the highly coloured melodrama, *Flames of Passion*, was a success with the public. This experience decisively shaped Wilcox's philosophy of filmmaking for the rest of his career. 'No more stark realism', he wrote later: 'My objective now was escape entertainment of pleasant people in pleasant surroundings doing pleasant things' (H. Wilcox, 53). He began directing films with *Chu Chin Chow* in 1923 and demonstrated his instinct for showmanship by importing established Hollywood stars and by shooting some of his films in Germany to take advantage of superior technical facilities there.

From 1928 to 1935 Wilcox was head of production for the newly formed British and Dominions Film Corporation. Having mastered the new techniques of sound on a trip to Hollywood, he launched an annual production schedule of thirty films. For one of them, *Goodnight Vienna* (1932), he signed the comparatively inexperienced Anna *Neagle (1904–1986), whom he was later to marry and with whom he formed a partnership unique in British film history: he directed her in thirty-two films over the next twenty-seven years. She achieved her first great success in Wilcox's *Nell Gwyn* (1934), then in 1936 he decided that she should play the title role in a full-scale biographical film about Queen Victoria. Unable to find a backer,

Herbert Sydney Wilcox (1890–1977), by Howard Coster, 1936

Wilcox shot the film with his own money in five weeks. Released in the coronation year of 1937, *Victoria the Great* won both critical and popular acclaim. Wilcox followed it with an even more successful Technicolor sequel, *Sixty Glorious Years*. Released in 1938, the year of Munich, this film answered a popular mood of nostalgia for a more settled age, one of moral and political certainty when Britain successfully policed the world. Hollywood beckoned and there Wilcox directed Anna Neagle in *Nurse Edith Cavell* (1939) and a trio of musicals before they returned to Britain to film the life of Amy Johnson, *They Flew Alone* (1941).

With the war over, Wilcox once again implemented his film-making creed by providing glamour, romance, and escapism for a public in the grip of austerity. He teamed Anna Neagle with Michael Wilding in what became the much loved 'London series': *Piccadilly Incident* (1946), *The Courtneys of Curzon Street* (1947), *Spring in Park Lane* (1948), and *Maytime in Mayfair* (1949). These were essentially light-hearted and undemanding pieces. But Anna Neagle's stature as a dramatic actress was confirmed when she played the French resistance heroine in *Odette* (1950), the film Wilcox said he would most like to be remembered by, and Florence Nightingale in *The Lady with a Lamp* (1951). These years saw the Wilcox–Neagle partnership at its peak critically and financially. For six consecutive years from 1947 to 1952 Anna Neagle was the top British film actress at the cinema box office, and four of the Wilcox–Neagle films won the *Daily Mail* national film award.

But the 1950s saw the beginning of the lean years. A combination of financial misfortune and changing audience tastes led eventually to the bankruptcy court. The films Wilcox was making in the 1950s still had the look and feel of the 1930s about them. He directed his last film, *The Heart of a Man*, in 1959. Subsequent film projects failed to reach the screen and in 1964 Wilcox was made bankrupt. Revealing that he had had to borrow £341,800 since 1955, he said that 'the so-called realistic vogue was upon us' but he refused to make 'films about unpleasant themes and unpleasant people'. Plans for a comeback were hampered by a coronary thrombosis which he suffered in 1965. He regained his health, was discharged from bankruptcy in 1966, and in 1967 published his autobiography, *Twenty-Five Thousand Sunsets*. He was to make no further films.

Wilcox was a Roman Catholic and intensely proud of his Irish background. He liked to believe that he may have been born in Cork and repeated the story so often that it found its way into many of his obituaries. He had many of the qualities traditionally associated with the Irish. He was loyal, sentimental, charming, shrewd, and tenacious. He was fond of telling stories and willing to back his judgement up to the hilt. As a film-maker he was a showman and an entertainer rather than an artist. As a producer, he was able instinctively to gauge the public's taste in films for thirty years and he proudly provided 'mass entertainment for mass audiences', furnishing escapism in the depression and the period of post-war austerity and inspiration before and during the war. As a director, he was painstaking rather than exciting, visually unadventurous but technically proficient. His entire output over more than thirty years was never less than highly professional and in the best of taste, the two qualities he most prized.

Wilcox was appointed CBE in 1951. He was married three times. In 1916 he married Dorothy, daughter of Ernest Addison Brown, retired captain, of the merchant marine; they had no children. The marriage was dissolved in 1917 and in 1918 he married Mrs Maude Violet Clark, daughter of Ernest David Bower, a dentist. There were three daughters and one son of this marriage, which was dissolved in 1943. In that year he married Anna Neagle, who was born Florence Marjorie Robertson, daughter of Captain Herbert William Robertson. They had no children. Wilcox died in London on 15 May 1977.

JEFFREY RICHARDS

Sources H. Wilcox, *Twenty-five thousand sunsets* (1967) · A. Neagle, *There's always tomorrow* (1974) · P. Wilcox, *Between hell and Charing Cross* (1977) · private information (1986) · *WWW* · *The Times* (16 May 1977)
Likenesses H. Coster, photograph, 1936, NPG [*see illus.*]

Wilcox, Thomas (*c*.1549–1608), Church of England clergyman, is first recorded in 1564, when he matriculated at St John's College, Oxford, suggesting that he was born about 1549; much later in his career he was listed in a formal ecclesiastical document as a non-graduate. He became one of the preachers entertained in the peculiar London parish (in both the formal and informal senses) of Holy Trinity Minories, and he served the cure of All Hallows,

Honey Lane. Towards 1570 he became part of a militant tendency of younger London preachers, led by John Field, curate of St Giles Cripplegate. In an attack published in 1581 against a certain I.B., a 'libertine', or freewiller, he would own the designation of 'Puritan' even while repudiating it, 'a worde of a doubtfull signification', attributing its invention to the Catholic exile Nicholas Sander (Wilcox, *The Unfouldyng of Sundry Untruthes*, 80–83).

In 1571 Wilcox had joined with another radical spirit, William White, in replying to attacks on the nonconformists made in Paul's Cross sermons by bishops John Jewel and Robert Horne. Jewel was told that they would pray that God would put it into the queen's heart to remove Jewel from his 'over quiet estate, pompous livings and lordly titles' (Peel, 1.79–80). In June 1572 Field and Wilcox wrote and published, anonymously, the outspoken presbyterian manifesto *An Admonition to the Parliament*. The *Admonition* proper, relatively measured and carefully structured in its argument, was the work of Wilcox, the more heated and satirically inventive *View of Popishe Abuses* which accompanied it Field's handiwork. So much is clear from exchanges with Archbishop Parker's chaplain, when Wilcox disowned responsibility for 'the bitternes of the stile', which Field freely acknowledged (Peel, 1.89–90). Both were imprisoned on the authority of the archbishop. The admonitioners became famous overnight and were visited by many of the leading nonconformist clergy, which is not to say that their extreme views were universally approved. After three months Field and Wilcox were sentenced by the lord mayor and aldermen to a further year's imprisonment in Newgate, which, in spite of petitions to the privy council, Lord Burghley, and the earl of Leicester from themselves and their impoverished wives, they appear to have served. At an appearance before the privy council in the summer of 1573 they were threatened with banishment. Bishop Edwin Sandys of London, who suffered much opprobium on their account, complained that London would never be quiet until 'these authors of sedition who are now esteemed as gods' were removed far from the city. 'The people resort unto them as in Popery they were wont to run on pilgrimage' (BL, Lansdowne MS 17, no. 43, fols. 96–7). Eventually the pair were released into the care of Archdeacon John Mullins. In the autumn of 1573 Wilcox went off on a tour of puritan centres in the midlands, but by February 1574 he was back in London, replacing Field, who was now perhaps overseas, as the regular correspondent of 'Father' Anthony Gilby at Ashby-de-la-Zouch, reporting from his house in Coleman Street the latest oppressions of the bishops.

John Field always took the upper hand in his dealings with Wilcox. In December 1572 both men had composed 'a breife confession of Faythe', which, if wisdom had not prevailed, they would have attempted to promulgate as a formal affirmation by the entire presbyterian movement, an intrinsically schismatic gesture. 'Brother Wilcox' seems to have acted on Field's instructions, which ended: 'Studie to be breife' (Peel, 1.83–4). But in 1583 the relationship turned sour. This is revealed by some correspondence that fell into the hands of Richard Bancroft, and which he

exploited in 1593 in his book *Daungerous Positions*. The letters in Bancroft's hands may have mentioned the particulars of the offence, but the future archbishop, with his unfailing tabloid instincts, thought it not fit to rehearse 'any mans private behaviour or infirmities', leaving the prurient reader to suspect the worst. But it does sound as if the transgression was moral rather than theological or professional. For his part, Wilcox told Field that he had been dealt with 'disorderly', and hinted that 'hee had perhaps concealed as great infirmities of Fields', specifying six. Field retorted: 'If God hath made you an instrument, to seeke for the advancement of Christs scepter: kisse it your selfe and bee subject unto it.' It was the private opinion of Tomson and Thomas Cartwright that Wilcox should be 'for ever' suspended from his ministry (Bancroft, 117–19). It is perhaps significant that Wilcox in many of his writings was somewhat over-zealous in declaring himself a sinner, making much of 'the grievousnes of mine offences' (Wilcox, *Summarie and Short Meditations*, epistle). No less than six of his dedicatory prefaces and many of his letters were subscribed: 'Thomas Wilcocks [or "T.W."] the Lordes unworthie [or "most unworthie"] servant [or "minister"]', in effect his trademark.

In 1577 a new bishop of London, John Aylmer, had recommended that Wilcox and others be sent off to Lancashire, to wear out their zeal on the papists. However, Wilcox had already moved, but only as far as Hertfordshire, where he became curate of Bovingdon, a chapelry of Hemel Hempstead. In 1584 he was one of five clergy in the archdeaconry of Huntingdon, 'recusants', who evaded subscription to Archbishop Whitgift's three articles. He neither appeared nor subscribed, but was presumably protected by some of the many powerful friends whom he had by now acquired. Soon after this Wilcox was reported as attending a presbyterian conference in Oxford, which included some of the Scottish ministers then in exile in England. In March 1596 'T.W.', who may have been Wilcox, preached in a combination lecture or prophesying at Southwell in Nottinghamshire, but his presence so far from his usual haunts is not otherwise accounted for. Aylmer and his successors were not entirely rid of Wilcox's presence. He signed prefaces to published works from London in 1581, 1587, 1591, 1595, 1599, 1600 (giving his address as Lothbury), and 1604.

In spite of his own alleged 'infirmity', or even because of it, Wilcox became one of the most sought after of puritan casuists, a pioneer in the art of 'practical' or 'comfortable' divinity. Long after his death he would receive the tribute of a volume of collected *Works* (1624), something which never happened to Field. In 1589 he published *Large Letters, Three in Number*, dedicated to eight named London citizens 'and all the rest of his Christian acquaintance in London'. Many more of his pastoral letters survived in manuscript in a large folio volume until the late seventeenth century, when they were listed by the dissenting divine Roger Morrice: 'most of them containing little but godly, plain and necessary exhortations and directions for the exercise of godlynesse' (Morrice MSS, 'Letters of eminent persons',

2.617(2)), although a letter written to the countess of Sussex on 24 February 1577 asked her to use her influence at court on behalf of the silenced puritan ministers, himself included.

Wilcox was one of the most committed, active, and socially and politically well connected of Elizabethan puritan ministers, and the tally of his correspondents reads like an Elizabethan *Who's Who*. It includes Sir Francis Walsingham and his wife, Fulke Greville ('several' letters), the MP Peter Wentworth, Lady Anne Bacon, the wife of the clerk of the council, Robert Beale, Lord and Lady Zouche, and Sir Richard Knightley's sister and Sir John Harington's mother-in-law, Lady Rogers. Most of these letters were written in 1577–8. Wilcox's dedicatory epistles are distinctive for their emphasis on Christian friendship. His particular patrons, besides many wealthy Londoners, were Martin Harlackinden of Woodchurch, Kent, the recipient of scores of letters, who at his death in 1585 left Wilcox and his wife, Annah, an annuity for life of £13 6s. 8d., plus £6 13s. 4d. for their son, Elijah; the third earl of Bedford and his wife, Lucy, the great patroness of poets, described as his 'very Christian friends' (Amandus Polanus, preface, *Substance of Christian Religion*, trans. T. Wilcox, 1600); and Lady Anne Bacon. He dedicated his *Discourse Touching the Doctrine of Doubting* (1598) to the Bedfords and the countess's brother Sir John Harington (later Lord Harington of Exton) and his wife from Woburn, and in 1595 published a moralized account of 'a fearefull fire' at Woburn (Wilcox, *A Short yet a True and Faithfull Narration*). Other books, written or translated by Wilcox, were dedicated to Sir Francis and Lady Walsingham, Sir John Popham, Sir William Pelham, Sir John Brocket, Sir John Cutts, and Sir Charles Morison.

In 1604 Wilcox presented the ten-year-old Prince Henry with Philippe de Mornay's *A Woorke Concerning the Trewnesse of the Christian Religion*, his revision of a translation begun by Sir Philip Sidney and completed by Arthur Golding. The dedication included a fulsome declaration of loyalty to 'your most loving father, and my only dear and dred Soveraigne and gracious Lord and Master, here upon earth'. There is evidence that Wilcox had acted as some kind of intermediary between the English puritan interest and James at about the time of his accession. Later he was one of the ministers who met behind the scenes at the Hampton Court conference in 1604, in order to brief the four principal puritan spokesmen.

Wilcox seems to have spent much time at Gorhambury as a chaplain and pensioner of Lady Anne Bacon. A servant of Anthony Bacon reported on one occasion that 'Mr Willockes had a paper with a grete delle of gould in it' (LPL, MS 650, no. 169). There is strong internal evidence that the puritan archives published in 1593 as *A Parte of a Register* and the larger manuscript collections known as 'The seconde parte of a register', an enterprise begun by John Field, were assembled by Wilcox, and perhaps at Gorhambury. An item in 'The seconde parte', the account of the interrogation in 1572 of Field and Wilcox by Andrew Pearson, Archbishop Parker's chaplain, was written up by Wilcox after Field's death in 1588.

Wilcox wrote or translated some twenty-five books (if various publications attributed to 'T.W.' are all his). Some of his *Works* were posthumously published in 1624 by the staunchly puritan divine and physician Dr John Burges, who had married Wilcox's eldest daughter, Sara, in 1621. It was a daughter of Burges's first marriage who married the celebrated puritan divine William Ames.

PATRICK COLLINSON

Sources *A parte of a register* [1593] · A. Peel, ed., *The seconde parte of a register*, 2 vols. (1915) · [R. Bancroft], *Daungerous positions and proceedings* (1593) · CUL, MS Mm.1.43 (Baker MS 32) · W. H. Frere and C. E. Douglas, eds., *Puritan manifestoes: a study of the origin of the puritan revolt, with a reprint of the 'Admonition to the parliament', and kindred documents, 1572* (1907); repr. (1954) · 'Letters of eminent persons', DWL, Morrice MSS, 2.617 (2) · *The works of that late Reverend and learned divine, Mr Thomas Wilcocks*, ed. [J. Burges] (1624) · P. Collinson, *The Elizabethan puritan movement* (1967); pbk edn (1990) · C. W. Foster, ed., *The state of the church in the reigns of Elizabeth and James I*, Lincoln RS, 23 (1926) · W. Urwick, *Nonconformity in Hertfordshire* (1884) · *DNB* · T. Wilcox, *Large letters, three in number* (1589) · BL, Lansdowne MS 17, no. 43, fols. 96–7 · LPL, MS 650, no. 169 · G. Donaldson, 'The relations between the English and Scottish presbyterian movements to 1604', PhD diss., U. Lond., 1938 · T. Wilcox, *The unfouldyng of sundry untruthes* (1581) · T. Wilcox, *Summarie and short meditations* (1580) · T. Wilcox, *The summe of a sermon* (1596) · T. Wilcox, *A short yet a true and faithfull narration* (1595) · P. de Mornay, *A woorke concerning the trewnesse of the Christian religion*, ed. T. Wilcox, trans. P. Sidney and A. Golding (1604)

Wild. *See also* Wilde, Wyld, Wylde.

Wild, Charles (1781–1835), watercolour painter, was born in London. He was apprenticed to the draughtsman Thomas Malton the younger and, like his master, he specialized in architectural subjects. It was from Malton's house that Wild exhibited his first works, at the Royal Academy in 1803, two views of Christ Church, Oxford. In total he showed nine works at the academy but it was at the Society of Painters in Water Colours that he was to make his mark, exhibiting 165 architectural subjects between 1809 and 1833. These comprised internal and external views of the great English cathedrals and, after 1821, the churches, first of northern France and subsequently of Belgium and of Germany. Works such as *View in the East Transept of Worcester Cathedral* (exh. Society of Painters in Water Colours, 1823; V&A) combine a close attention to architectural detail with an attractive picturesque treatment. Wild's work was generally well received by the critics, who appreciated his ambition to raise the status of the architectural subject. *A View in Canterbury Cathedral*, exhibited in 1810, included pilgrims and was accompanied by a quotation from Chaucer; *The Penance of Jane Shore, in the Old Cathedral of St Paul's* (exh. Society of Painters in Water Colours, 1827), a reconstruction from archaeological evidence, was accompanied in the exhibition catalogue by lines from Sir Thomas More. In addition to supporting the society's exhibitions Wild was its treasurer from 1823 to 1826, and its secretary from 1827 to 1831.

Wild's work as an engraver and publisher of architectural views earned him a place in the history of the Gothic revival. Beginning with *Twelve Perspective Views of the Exterior and Interior Parts of Canterbury*, in 1807, he produced a series of aquatints—sometimes coloured—of English cathedrals, which were praised for their accuracy. The Canterbury series was followed by York in 1809, Chester in 1813, Lichfield in 1813, Lincoln in 1819, and Worcester in 1823. Wild's travels on the continent also resulted in a number of publications, including *Twelve select examples of the ecclesiastical architecture of the middle ages, chiefly in France* (1826) and a series of etched outlines from *Architectural Sketches Made in Belgium, Germany and France* (1833). Wild was particularly adept at publicizing his publications and many of the original watercolours appeared at the society's exhibitions. Wild is perhaps best remembered, however, for his contribution to one of the most sumptuous publications in hand-coloured aquatint, William Henry Pyne's *History of the Royal Residences* (3 vols., 1819). He produced watercolours for fifty-eight of the hundred views, including large groups of Windsor Castle and Carlton House, some of which provide a unique record of lost interiors (Royal Collection). He also painted four highly detailed watercolours, now in the Victoria and Albert Museum, for Whittaker and Nayler's *Coronation of George IV* (1821–41).

Wild's career was seriously affected by failing eyesight after 1827, and he became blind in 1832. He died, on 4 August 1835, at 35 Albemarle Street, Piccadilly, where he had lived since 1820. Among his children with his wife, Margaret, was the architect James William *Wild.

GREG SMITH

Sources *The Royal Watercolour Society: the first fifty years, 1805–1855* (1992) · Graves, *RA exhibitors* · J. L. Roget, *A history of the 'Old Water-Colour' Society*, 2 vols. (1891) · *DNB*
Archives BL, letters to J. Elmes, Add. MS 42864

Wild, (John Robert) Francis (1873–1939), Antarctic explorer, was born at Skelton in Cleveland, Yorkshire, on 18 April 1873, the son of Benjamin Wild, schoolmaster, of Newcastle upon Tyne, who later kept a school at Eversholt in Bedfordshire. His mother was Mary (Pollie), daughter of Robert Cook, of Sheriff Hutton, Yorkshire. Robert Cook may have been a grandson of Captain James Cook, the circumnavigator, through the latter's son James who, according to the unconfirmed family tradition, was not drowned, as officially reported, but deserted from the Royal Navy and had therefore every inducement to conceal his identity. James abandoned his wife, and a man representing himself to Robert Cook as his father was in later years turned away from his putative son's door. At the age of sixteen Francis or Frank Wild (as he was known) went to sea in the merchant service, which he left as a second officer, transferring to the navy as a rating in 1900.

In 1901 Wild was accepted as an able seaman volunteer for the 1901–4 National Antarctic Expedition of Robert Falcon Scott in the *Discovery*. He was a member of Albert Borlase Armitage's sledge party to the high plateau reaching an altitude of 8900 feet, the first high-level journey on the Antarctic plateau, and when a member of the party was lost over an ice-cliff in a blizzard, Wild demonstrated the resilience in the face of adversity that was to be his hallmark, keeping his head and leading the party back to safety. Wild became an experienced sledger on this expedition, gaining the skills that made him so valuable to

future explorations. In 1907, on Ernest Shackleton returning to the Antarctic in the *Nimrod*, Wild was invited to join him and was one of the party of four that made the long southern sledge journey across the Ross Barrier, up the Beardmore Glacier, and over the high plateau to the record latitude of 88°23′ S, one of the greatest sledge journeys ever made. He showed himself to be an incomparable sledger, wiry, energetic, and buoyant, with great lasting powers and unusual muscular strength. It was this alone that saved him when, on the Beardmore Glacier, he narrowly avoided being dragged into a crevasse by a pony falling to its death. In 1911 Douglas Mawson, a member of Shackleton's 1907–9 expedition, chose Wild as one of the few non-Australasians for his Australian Antarctic Expedition (1911–14) in the *Aurora*. Wild was placed in charge of a party of eight which occupied the Western Base on the Shackleton Ice Shelf, from which useful sledge journeys were made into Queen Mary Land and to Kaiser Wilhelm Land. This was one of the most daring winterings in Antarctic history, since the base camp was 17 miles from the land, on floating ice.

Wild's next Antarctic expedition was as Shackleton's second in command on the British Imperial Trans-Antarctic Expedition, which aimed to cross the continent from the Weddell Sea to the Ross Sea passing the pole *en route*. Obeying direct orders from the Admiralty, the expedition departed from Plymouth in the *Endurance* on 8 August 1914, after the outbreak of war in Europe. But after the wreck of the ship by ice pressure in November 1915 the explorers sought a desperate refuge on Elephant Island, whence Shackleton and five others made a boat journey to South Georgia for help. Wild had wanted to share the dangers of this voyage with Shackleton, but the latter relied upon him to lead the party of twenty-two men left on Elephant Island. There they inhabited little more than a sand-spit, 'a precarious foothold between the grim ice-fields and the treacherous, ice-strewn sea' (Shackleton, *South*, 173). Faced with meagre resources Wild kept up morale by constantly watching for the ice to clear and, when it did, confidently proclaiming: 'Roll up your sleeping-bags, boys; the boss may come to-day' (ibid., 191). On 30 August, four months after he had left, and at his fourth attempt, Shackleton returned. To Wild's 'energy, initiative, and resource' Shackleton attributed the survival of all twenty-two of the Elephant Island party: 'He showed wonderful capabilities of leadership and more than justified the absolute confidence I placed in him' (ibid., 190).

On his return to England Wild was commissioned as temporary lieutenant RNVR early in 1917, and served as a transport officer on the North Russian front. In 1918–19 he wintered in Spitsbergen with a small party in charge of an English coalmining property. He was appointed CBE in the 1920 new year's honours, in recognition of his war service and his role in the 1914–16 Antarctic expedition. An attempt at tobacco planting in Nyasaland was cheerfully abandoned when in 1921 Shackleton prepared a new expedition to the Weddell Sea in the *Quest*. On the way south Shackleton died suddenly at South Georgia on 5

January 1922 and Wild took over command. A crack in the furnace of the *Quest* had already threatened the expedition, which was in any case 'a hybrid affair; a strange medley of the quest of lost islands and of the exploration of once-glimpsed ice-infested coasts such as no other polar leader than Shackleton … would have conceived' (*GJ*, 239). Under Wild it became an unexciting but worthy exercise in mapping and surveying, although without knowing it he moved within 60 miles of the Antarctic continent. This was Wild's fifth and last expedition. On 24 October 1922 he married Vera Alexandra (*b.* 1881/2), daughter of Theodore Bogosoff, tobacco broker. He had rescued her from Russia where she had been left stranded after the death of her husband, Granville Altman, a Borneo tea planter; there were no children. Wild reluctantly settled in South Africa and resumed for a time his farming, eventually moving to Klerksdorp, Transvaal, where, after a period of ill health, he died of pneumonia, on 20 August 1939. The award of a civil-list pension of £170 in May had come too late to alleviate the penury of his last years. In 1924 Wild was awarded the patron's medal of the Royal Geographical Society for his outstanding services to Antarctic exploration; he had been awarded the society's Back grant in 1916.

R. N. RUDMOSE BROWN, *rev.* MARK POTTLE

Sources R. F. Scott, *The voyage of the 'Discovery'*, 2 vols. (1907) · E. Shackleton, *The heart of the Antarctic: being the story of the British Antarctic expedition, 1907–1909* (1909); new edn (1999) · E. Shackleton, *South: the story of Shackleton's 1914–1917 expedition* (1921) · D. Mawson, *The home of the blizzard: being the story of the Australasian Antarctic expedition, 1911–1914*, 2 vols. [1915]; new edn (2000) · F. Wild, *Shackleton's last voyage: the story of the 'Quest'* (1923) · R. E. P., *GJ*, 90 (1940), 238–40 · *The Times* (1 June 1923); (21 Aug 1939); (29 Aug 1939) · private information (1949) · m. cert.
Archives Scott Polar RI, corresp., journals, and papers · State Library of New South Wales, Sydney, memoirs
Likenesses photograph, repro. in *The Times* (21 Aug 1939), 12b · photograph, repro. in *The Times* (27 Aug 1921), 10d · photograph, repro. in *The Times* (2 Aug 1922), 12g · photograph, repro. in Shackleton, *South*, facing p. 176 · photographs, Scott Polar RI

Wild, George (1610–1665), Church of Ireland bishop of Derry, was born on 9 January 1610 in Middlesex, the son of Henry Wild, a citizen of London. He entered the Merchant Taylors' School, London, in 1619, and was elected scholar of St John's College, Oxford, in 1629. He matriculated on 13 November 1629, was elected fellow of his college in 1631, graduated BCL on 7 February 1635, and was incorporated at Cambridge in the same year. While at Oxford he wrote plays, unpublished in his lifetime, including *Euphormus*, a Latin comedy, *The Converted Robber*, and *Love's Comedy*, the latter acted before Charles I at St John's on 30 August 1636 to celebrate the opening of Archbishop Laud's new quadrangle there, the expensive production being paid for by the archbishop. Wild became chaplain to Laud, and was presented by him to the vicarage of St Giles, Reading, and in 1640 to the rectory of Biddenden, Kent. With the outbreak of civil war he became chaplain and preacher to the king at Oxford, the degree of DCL being conferred upon him on 23 November 1647. In March 1643

he preached in St Mary's before those MPs who had joined Charles I at Oxford, subsequently publishing the sermon.

Wild was turned out of his fellowship by the parliamentary visitors in 1648, having been sequestered from his living at Biddenden before 20 May 1645. During the interregnum he continued to officiate as a clergyman where he could, John Evelyn being present for his Easter sermon at St Gregory's, London, on 15 April 1655. Evelyn was present again on 30 December following, when Wild 'preached the funeral Sermon of preaching' in advance of the planned implementation of Cromwell's proclamation against the ministrations of Anglican clergy or the use of the prayer book; 'so pathetic was his discourse, as drew many tears from his auditory' (*Diary of John Evelyn*, 2.107). Thereafter he conducted prayer book services and administered communion in a house in Fleet Street, London, and at some point appears to have suffered imprisonment.

After the Restoration, Wild was appointed bishop of Derry, and was one of twelve bishops consecrated by Primate Bramhall in St Patrick's Cathedral, Dublin, on 27 January 1661. He and Jeremy Taylor, who preached at the consecration, were the only appointees without previous ecclesiastical careers in Ireland. Both men appear to have been considered unsuitable for English bishoprics, where the composition of the bench was determined, in large measure, by the need to placate 'moderate' presbyterian opinion and to win as broad support as possible for the restored hierarchy. Wild and Taylor were, however, appointed to Irish dioceses with large numbers of protestant nonconformists, and Wild proved himself energetic in moving to enforce laws on conformity. In 1665 he boasted that he had 'brought very many [dissenters] of late to a peaceable conformity' (*Hastings MSS*, 4.125). Considered to have been 'of great piety, and charity and to have stinted himself and spent most of the revenues of his see on acts of benevolence and hospitality' (Leslie, 9), he was somewhat of an ascetic in his later years. Visiting Dublin to attend parliament, he died of heart disease on 29 December 1665, and was buried in the choir of Christ Church, Dublin. He was unmarried, and left modest bequests to the Merchant Taylors' School, St John's College, and to the poor of Derry, London, and Kent. His funeral sermon was preached by Robert Mossom, who succeeded him at Derry.

RICHARD BAGWELL, *rev.* JASON Mᶜ ELLIGOTT

Sources J. B. Leslie, *Derry clergy and parishes* (1937) · Foster, *Alum. Oxon.* · H. Cotton, *Fasti ecclesiae Hibernicae*, 6 vols. (1845–78) · R. Mossom, *A narrative panegyrical of the life, sickness and death of George, lord bishop of Derry* (1666) · *The works of the most reverend father in God, William Laud*, ed. J. Bliss and W. Scott, 7 vols. (1847–60) · *The diary of John Evelyn*, ed. A. Dobson, 3 vols. (1906) · A. Ford and others, eds., *As by law established: the Church of Ireland since the Reformation* (1995) · *Report on the manuscripts of the late Reginald Rawdon Hastings*, 4 vols., HMC, 78 (1928–47), vol. 4 · *Walker rev.* · J. R. Elliott, 'Drama', *Hist. U. Oxf.* 4: *17th-cent. Oxf.*, 641–58
Archives BL, Add. MS 14047 · Hunt. L., corresp.
Wealth at death left £200 to charity and church: Leslie, *Derry clergy*

Wild, James William (1814–1892), architect, son of Charles *Wild (1781–1835), watercolour painter, and his wife, Margaret, was born on 9 March 1814 in Lincoln, and baptized there in St Peter's, Eastgate. In 1830 he was articled to George Basevi. Already familiar with the Gothic style through his father's work he made rapid progress and at the conclusion of his pupillage was entrusted with the design and erection of a small country church. Independent practice rapidly followed, and Wild was elected an associate of the Royal Institute of British Architects on 29 May 1837, proposed by George Basevi, C. Fowler, and J. B. Papworth; he gave his address as 35 Albemarle Street, London (his parental home). Before 1840 Wild had built six churches, including Holy Trinity, Blackheath Hill (1839; a design was exhibited at the Royal Academy, 1838); Holy Trinity, Coates, Cambridgeshire (1839); St Lawrence, Southampton (1839–42; design exhibited at the Royal Academy, 1839); and a church at Barton, Yorkshire (1840).

In Christ Church, Streatham (1841), Wild designed a church of remarkable originality, often described as being in a Byzantine manner but in fact richly eclectic, combining Early Christian, Italian Romanesque, Islamic, and moorish elements. He relied on simple decoration, with innovatory brick and terracotta polychromy for the exterior details, to secure a distinctive building at the low cost to which his employers restricted him. He was assisted in the internal decoration of the church by Owen Jones, who later became his brother-in-law (by marrying Wild's sister Isabella in 1842).

It was perhaps through his friendship with Jones that Wild became interested in Near Eastern studies and was motivated to join Dr Karl Lepsius's great expedition to Egypt and Nubia, under the patronage of the king of Prussia, from 1842 to 1845. Wild was hired as an architectural draughtsman and a promising orientalist. Lepsius described him as 'a young architect, full of genius, [who] seeks with enthusiasm in the East a new field for the exercise of the rich and various gifts with which he is endowed' (C. R. Lepsius, *Letters from Egypt, Ethiopia and the Peninsula of Sinai*, 1853, 35). Among the other members of the expedition was Joseph Bonomi, the second curator of Sir John Soane's Museum. Lepsius and his team drew monuments and inscriptions as far south as Meroe in the Sudan and conducted excavations at Hawara. Wild worked hard on Egyptology during the course of the expedition and contributed a number of letters to *The Athenaeum*, in one of which he explained for the first time the method by which the Great Pyramid was constructed. On reaching Cairo in October 1842 he was captivated by Cairene domestic building and threw himself into the study of medieval Islamic architecture. He also joined the circle of orientalists around Edward William Lane and thereby gained access to many Islamic residences occupied by Europeans which he studied painstakingly, one of the first Western architects to devote himself to this subject.

After a short hiatus Wild left Lepsius's expedition and returned in April 1844 to Cairo, where he remained for most of the next three years, until the spring of 1847, continuing to explore mosques and Arab houses, living among the people, and making meticulous sketches and drawings. He was also given a number of commissions in Cairo, including a design for a gateway to the British cemetery (1844) for which a design survives in the Public Record Office, Kew. His most important work in Egypt was the Anglican church of St Mark in Alexandria. Wild was appointed as its architect in 1845 but the church was only completed, after changes to the design during construction and long periods of inactivity, in 1855. In its final form the church is eclectic in style, combining an Early Christian plan and English inscriptions with Islamic detailing (decoration derived from architectonic forms, geometrical and flattened foliage ornament) and symbols of faith (the cross and the six-pointed star). By using Islamic detailing Wild not only utilized his studies of Islamic forms but also tried to ensure that the building would be unlikely to give offence in a Muslim city. Mark Crinson has described the building of St Mark's as 'an unprecedented event: the first public statement of Anglican presence in the Near East that was also recognised … as a statement of religious toleration' (Crinson, 'Leading into captivity').

An obituary of Wild (*Art Journal*, 97, 1893, 120–21, signed T. P.) describes how, as a result of his work on St Mark's, Wild was brought into contact with Turkish officials and succeeded in obtaining a firman from the Porte granting an inspection of the great mosque at Damascus in Syria. The obituary recounts that when, after leaving Cairo in 1847, Wild arrived in Damascus and requested the help of the British consul in using this permission

> the official was horrified at the proposal [as] such a desecration of the sacred building by an infidel would mean death … if discovered … Mr. Wild was not to be deterred from making the attempt, and next morning the Consul accompanied him to the door of the mosque leaving him, with much anxiety, to his fate. The Arabic language, native dress and a certain ascetic appearance were … an ample disguise and he had the gratification of seeing the entire Holy Place without exciting the slightest suspicion, no European ever before having been successful in doing so. (*Art Journal*, 120)

The same obituary also explained other techniques Wild resorted to in the course of his travels, explaining that

> drawing in the East involves no inconsiderable amount of inconvenience, not to say danger, from the great suspicion of the natives of the use which may be made of their treasures: here again he had to resort to stratagem, and what could not be done in the daytime had to be accomplished in the night. From time to time in his wanderings he 'marked in' the objects he desired to copy, prepared his damped paper for squeezes and in the darkness set forth and obtained impressions with such perfect exactness of details as could not be obtained by drawing under an umbrella without intrusion. (ibid., 120–21)

Many of the meticulous drawings made by Wild during his travels are now in the Victoria and Albert Museum (presented by his daughter Elizabeth Wild in 1938). Although Wild's Cairo notebooks were never published, they did become a source for later writers. Owen Jones's celebrated *Grammar of Ornament* (1856–7) used Wild's drawings of Cairo for the illustrations of Arabian details.

Wild returned to Britain permanently in 1848, visiting

Constantinople, Italy, and Spain *en route*. He resumed practice and in 1849 won a competition for the design of the St Martin's northern schools in Castle Street, Long Acre, London (dem.), which, after Christ Church, Streatham, were his most important work and an influential example of the secular use of the Gothic. A plain frontage onto a narrow side street allowed Wild to demonstrate how he could achieve a façade of great beauty using only the simplest of elements, creating a fine rhythmic composition by means of arcuated treatment of the lower storeys.

In 1851 Wild was appointed decorative architect to the Great Exhibition, working with Owen Jones, who had been appointed one of the superintendents of works, on the interior decoration of the Crystal Palace. Wild's brother Charles Heard Wild was also employed there, checking calculations and testing the structural elements. In the same year, 1851, Wild's health broke down and this eventually compelled him to retire from active practice in 1857. In 1852 he designed the great water tower at Grimsby docks, a red brick structure 230 feet high, inspired by Italian and oriental towers. An obituary of Wild by Reginald Stuart Poole (unsourced copy, Sir John Soane's Museum archive) noted that exactly 1 million bricks had been used in its construction and described it as 'the most original and simplest structure of its kind in the United Kingdom'.

From 1853 Wild was retained by the South Kensington Museum as an expert on Arabian art. During this period he designed a Cairene window (now removed) for the oriental courts at the museum, designed by Owen Jones in 1863–5, and also assisted Lieutenant-Colonel Henry Scott in the design of the architectural cast courts (1868–73) and the Huxley Building in Exhibition Road (1867–71). When the iron and glass buildings which had formed the first home of the South Kensington Museum (now the Victoria and Albert Museum) were dismantled and re-erected in east London to form the Bethnal Green Museum (1872), Wild was responsible for the new masonry façade, although the forecourt and campanile that he intended were never built. He also designed the British legation buildings at Tehran in Persia (1869) and produced a design for the British consulate at Alexandria (exhibited at the Royal Academy in 1870), which was accepted but never built owing to lack of funds.

In 1878 Wild was appointed curator of Sir John Soane's Museum at 13 Lincoln's Inn Fields, where he carried out many alterations to Soane's interiors. In 1889–90 he constructed the ground-floor Ante-Room and the domed New Picture Room. The intended painted ceiling decoration for the latter remained on paper at the time of Soane's death and was executed, based on the original drawings, only in 1992. Below the Ante-Room and New Picture Room Wild also modified the Catacombs and the West Chamber. Between 1890 and 1892 he inserted glass pavement lights on the ground floor of the museum and widened the small Study, the Dressing Room, and the stairs down to the basement storey. In the same period he made major alterations to Soane's crypt, removing the flat, low stone ceiling and much of the south wall, altering a series of arches,

and inserting a large glass window onto the Monument Court, with a deep sill on which he arranged a large group of John Flaxman's models to form the Flaxman Recess. Wild also made proposals to remove Soane's famous dome area skylight and demolish the architectural drawing office to form one large top-lit modern gallery across the rear of the museum: this was a proposal too far for the trustees of the museum. At the time of his death Wild was busy with proposals to put an extra storey onto the main house.

Wild died at the museum on 7 November 1892 and was buried on 11 November at Kensal Green cemetery. He was survived by his wife, Ellen, and two daughters.

HELEN DOREY

Sources *Building News*, 63 (1892), 664 · *The Builder*, 63 (1892), 384 · T. P., 'The late curator of Sir John Soane's museum', *Art Journal*, new ser., 13 (1893), 120–21 · *Journal of Proceedings of the Royal Institute of British Architects*, new ser., 9 (1892–3), 275–6 · *The Times* (11 Nov 1892), 10 · *Dir. Brit. archs.* · M. Crinson, *Empire building: orientalism and Victorian architecture* (1996) · M. Crinson, 'Leading into captivity: James Wild and his work in Egypt', *Georgian Group Journal*, [5] (1995), 51–64 · J. N. Summerson, 'An early modernist: James Wild and his work', *Architects' Journal* (9 Jan 1929), 57–62 · Graves, *RA exhibitors* · G. Stamp and C. Amery, *Victorian buildings of London, 1837–1887: an illustrated guide* (1980) · *The Athenaeum* (25 Feb 1843), 189–90 · biographical file, RIBA BAL · R. S. Poole, obituary, source unidentified; copy, Sir John Soane's Museum · M. Darby, 'The Islamic perspective', *World of Islam festival trust* (1983) · H. S. Goodhart-Rendel, 'Rogue architects of the Victorian era', *RIBA Journal*, 56 (1948–9), 251–9 · census returns, 1891 · *CGPLA Eng. & Wales* (1893) · *IGI* · N. Jackson, 'Christ Church, Streatham, and the rise of constructional polychromy', *Architectural History*, 43 (2000), 219–52
Archives Bodl. Oxf. · LMA · Sir John Soane's Museum, London, curatorial papers · Sir John Soane's Museum, London, papers · St Mark's Church, Alexandria, Egypt, archives · U. Oxf., Griffith Institute, archaeological papers incl. notebooks, drawings, and plans · V&A | CUL, letters to Joseph Bonomi
Wealth at death £9663 7s. 6d.: probate, 18 Feb 1893, *CGPLA Eng. & Wales*

Wild, Jonathan (*bap.* 1683, *d.* 1725), thief-taker, was born in Wolverhampton, Staffordshire, and baptized on 6 May 1683. He was the eldest of five children of 'mean but honest Parents': his father, possibly John Wyld, was a carpenter who probably died about 1699; his mother (*d.* c.1721), a fruit seller (*Authentick Narrative*, 3). After learning to read, write, and cast accounts at the Wolverhampton charity school Wild, at about the age of fifteen, was bound apprentice to a Birmingham buckle-maker. Most accounts agree that the man who would become the greatest criminal mastermind of the eighteenth century served out his time 'honestly enough' (*Life of Jonathan Wild*, 2), returning about 1705 to Wolverhampton, where he married, and 'work[ed] very diligently for some time' as a buckle-maker (*True and Genuine Account*, 230). However, less than two years later Wild abandoned his wife and infant son and set out for London.

Marriages and the making of a criminal Only a few months after his arrival Wild was arrested for debt and thrown in the Wood Street compter where, according to his own account, he was to spend 'above … four Years' (Wild, ii). Wild languished for a time in the common side of the prison; however, such was his 'Address' that he soon

Jonathan Wild (*bap.* 1683, *d.* 1725), by Thomas Cook, pubd 1819 (after unknown artist, 1725)

earned the confidence of the keepers, and was not only granted the 'Liberty of the Gate', but was appointed 'Underkeeper' to those 'disorderly Persons' kept in the compter until they could be brought before a magistrate (*Lives of the most Remarkable Criminals*, 17). Here Wild cultivated the acquaintance of prostitutes and petty criminals—not least of whom was one Mary Milliner, a 'common Street-Walker' who was to become both Jonathan's 'first instructor' in the ways 'of the sharping and thieving world' (*History of the Lives*, 7; *Select Trials*, 1735, 2.54; *True and Genuine Account*, 232), and the first of his many mistresses (he was reported to have had six 'wives' altogether—the last of whom, Mary Dean, he formally married in 1719, although his first wife was then still living).

Wild was discharged from the compter in December 1712, apparently taking advantage of a recent parliamentary act for the relief of debtors, and promptly set up house (or, according to some accounts, a brothel) with Mary Milliner in Lewkenor's Lane; several months later they moved to Cock Alley, Cripplegate. Their relationship came to an end about 1714. A liaison with Judith Nun about 1714/15 produced a daughter, born at this time. Both were said to have survived Wild. Another short-term relationship *c.*1714/15 was with Sarah Perrin, alias Gregstone or Grigson, who also survived him. There were no children of

this relationship and several accounts suggest that Wild had become sterile as a result of mercury treatment for syphilis. His relationship with Elizabeth Man, or Mann, was deeper and more lasting. Wild had not lived with Nun or Perrin, but treated Man as his common law wife and lived publicly with her for perhaps four years. She died in late 1718 or early 1719 and was buried in St Pancras churchyard. Wild lost no time in mourning but went through a marriage ceremony on 13 February 1719 at St Pancras Church with Mary Dean, *née* Brown, widow of John 'Skull' Dean, executed for burglary in 1717; she may have died in or before 1732. The 'wedding' was well attended, but Howson could find no record of it, presumably because Wild had it omitted or destroyed to avoid a bigamy charge.

Wild's London career began while he was living with Mary Milliner. Initially he seems to have cobbled together a living from the proceeds of prostitution and from sporadic work as a bailiff's assistant; however, he soon graduated to racketeering and dealing in stolen goods. It seems he was initiated into this line of work by none other than Charles Hitchen, who had recently been suspended from the office of under city marshall after being accused of receiving and various other shady practices. Some time in the spring or summer of 1713 Hitchen, who was still empowered to act as a constable, approached Wild, asking him to accompany him as an assistant in his nightly 'Rambles'—ostensibly to reform disorderly houses, but in reality to extort protection money and to traffic in stolen goods (Wild, 13). After Hitchen was reinstated to his office in April 1714 he and Wild 'fell to Loggerheads' and 'parted … each of them separately pursuing the Business of Thief-taking' (*Select Trials*, 1735, 2.57).

Thief-taker and maker It was then that Wild began his career as a thief-taker and receiver in earnest. By the end of 1714 he had moved his quarters to the Little Old Bailey, where 'at length his House became an Office of Intelligence for lost Goods' (*History of the Lives*, 37). Skilfully evading a 1706 act which made receiving stolen property a felony Wild acted as a kind of middleman who helped the victims of theft recover their goods, but without ever keeping them in his possession. The newspapers were 'daily cramm'd' with advertisements 'calling loudly out for all Sorts of strayed Valuables to be brought in to Mr. Wild's in the Old Baily, upon Promise of great Rewards and no "Questions"' (*Authentick Narrative*, 18). In the eyes of many contemporaries Wild performed a vital public service, especially by arranging the return of various paper notes and bills which were of little use to thieves but of great value to their owners. Initially, at least, Wild was cautious enough to refuse any fees (although he took a large cut from the thieves); and often, to cement his 'reputation for a mightily honest man', he would take measures to have the thieves—or at least those whom he could not 'bring to comply' with him—apprehended and prosecuted (*True and Genuine Account*, 237, 235). Thus Wild played a wily double game in which he acted both the part of a receiver and a thief-taker who earned not only 'public applause' for bringing 'offenders to justice', but the rewards offered by parliament for the successful conviction of burglars and highwaymen (ibid., 238).

Wild's credit soared in the spring of 1716, when he apprehended several street robbers who had murdered a gentlewoman in the course of an assault. In May 1716 he inserted an advertisement in the government newspaper, the *London Gazette*; other notices placed around the same time describing him as a man who '[made] it his Business to apprehend [thieves], and bring them to Justice' (*Daily Courant*, 22 June 1716), furthered the impression that Wild was acting in a semi-official capacity. 'Mr. Jonathan Wild' began to 'make a considerable Figure in the World': he began to 'stile himself Esquire', wore a sword, kept a carriage and footmen, and became so successful in his 'Business', that 'a vast Resort of People of all Ranks and Conditions', now flocked to his 'Office' (*Weekly Journal, or, Saturday's Post*, 19 Jan 1718; *History of the Lives*, 14). By January 1717 Wild was openly proclaiming himself to be the 'Head Theif Catcher', or 'Thief-catcher General of Great Britain' (*Weekly Journal, or, British Gazetteer*, 19 Jan 1717; *Weekly Journal, or, Saturday's Post*, 28 Feb 1719, 5).

In early 1718 Hitchen, evidently piqued at his old rival's success, published several pamphlets denouncing Wild as 'the Regulator' of a vast network of thieves and fences (Hitchen, *Regulator*, 5). Moreover, the 'Thief-Taker' was a 'Thief-Maker', who 'pervert[ed] the good Intention … of Parliament' (in granting immunity to robbers who turned evidence against two or more accomplices) by manipulating and stifling the testimony of witnesses to protect his 'Pensioners' on the one hand, or to hang those criminals who had outlived their usefulness or defied his authority on the other (ibid., 16). Wild promptly responded with a pamphlet of his own accusing his old 'Grand Master in Iniquity' of being 'guilty of more flagrant Crimes' than his former 'servant' (Wild, ii). Wild enumerated all 'of the dealings, and good Correspondence between the M[arsha]l and the Thieves' (ibid., 23), with a particular emphasis on Hitchen's attachment to 'his beloved Subjects, the Pickpockets' (ibid., 7–8), and his intimate acquaintance with the 'Sodomitish Academy' (ibid., 41). (Hitchen was indeed convicted of attempted sodomy in 1727.) Wild emerged on all fronts the clear victor of this paper war: a series of exchanges printed in the weekly newspapers ended with one editor refusing to be further bullied by 'Tom Teltruth' (Hitchen), whose 'Truth' was now called into question (*Authentick Narrative*, 7; *Weekly Journal, or, Saturday's Post*, 12 April 1718).

The Jonathan Wild Act and its aftermath The timing, if not the wisdom, of Hitchen's attack on Wild may be explained by the fact that a clause in the 1718 Transportation Act would make it a felony to accept a reward for recovering stolen goods without attempting to prosecute the thief. Many have seen this legislation as directly aimed at Wild: indeed, the City recorder, Sir William Thomson, the principal architect of this act, had begun to look askance at Wild. Several accounts claimed that in 1718 Thomson had taken Wild aside to warn him 'against going

any longer at his old Rate' now that it had 'become a capital crime' (*Lives of the most Remarkable Criminals*, 46). However, all the evidence suggests that Wild, far from heeding this caution, 'went on in his wicked trade … with more impudence and shameless boldness than ever' (*True and Genuine Account*, 251).

This raises the question of why, for nearly seven years after the passage of the so-called Jonathan Wild Act, Wild not only continued but flourished in his trade of receiver–thief-taker. This has often been explained in terms of the corruption of early eighteenth-century society in general and the system of private prosecution in particular: contemporaries and later commentators alike saw Wild as 'in league with several trading justices' as venal as himself (Place MSS, fol. 13), while Gerald Howson, Wild's modern biographer, has suggested that even such high-ranking City officials as Thomson long turned a blind eye to the thief-taker's double-dealing. It is possible that after Wild's and Hitchen's paper war the authorities were unwilling to further expose the degree to which they themselves were implicated in questionable activities, although it is more likely that, as 'Philanthropos' (Bernard Mandeville) implied, magistrates 'made use of [Wild] for an Evidence', and were 'beholden to him in the Administration of Justice', simply because in a period of mounting anxiety about violent crime and gang activity he was viewed as a necessary evil (*British Journal*, 27 Feb 1725).

Perhaps, after 1718, to 'support his Credit with the Magistrates' and to divert attention away from his effective role as a receiver, perhaps simply because he had become hardened by his success, Wild focused more and more on the very public business of gang breaking and thief-taking (*Lives of the most Remarkable Criminals*, 2.46; *True and Genuine Account*, 237). This was, moreover, a business which became more lucrative after a 1720 royal proclamation offered rewards of £100 (over and above those granted by parliament) for the successful conviction of robbers in the vicinity of London. Wild became a fixture at the Old Bailey and other criminal courts where 'scarce an Assize or Sessions past but Jonathan slew his Man'—appeared as an evidence for the prosecution (*Authentick Narrative*, 7). Wild's divide and conquer tactics began to elicit complaints from defendants—one of whom in 1723 loudly descried Wild as a villain who 'gets his Livelihood by … swear[ing] away honest Men's Lives' (*Select Trials*, 1742, 1.345).

Public opinion turned sharply against Wild in the autumn of 1724 with his involvement in the arrest and prosecution of two of the most famous criminals of the day—Jack Sheppard and his accomplice Joseph 'Blueskin' Blake. The press championed Sheppard's cause, casting him as a kind of underdog hero who had resisted having any dealings with Wild and employing him as a mouthpiece to denounce 'the Scandalous Practice of Theifcatching' (*Narrative of the Robberies*, 164). Conversely, Blueskin served as an example of one of the many 'foster children' whom Wild 'had [bred] … up to be thieves' and later brought to the gallows (*True and Genuine Account*, 252). On 14 October, while Blueskin was awaiting trial, Wild casually informed him that he could do nothing for him short of paying for his coffin; enraged, Blake fell on the thief-taker and slit his throat with a clasp-knife. While Wild survived the wound his reputation was not so easily salvaged: the *Newgate's Garland* ballad, prematurely celebrating Jonathan's demise, broadcasted the 'Good News' that 'Honester poor Rogues' could, like their betters, now rob with impunity.

Trial, execution, and reputation The Blueskin incident 'made People a little more inquisitive into [Wild's] Honesty'; indeed, it would seem that Jonathan had now become so notorious that the authorities found 'themselves obliged ... to take Notice of Him' (H. D., iv; *Lives of the most Remarkable Criminals*, 2.50). On 15 February 1725 Wild was arrested for assisting one of his henchmen, Roger Johnson, 'to make his Escape from a Constable' (*Select Trials*, 1735, 2.44). Wild was held on a warrant of detainer, consisting of eleven articles accusing him of, among other things, being both a receiver and a confederate of thieves; of having 'form'd a kind of Corporation of Thieves'; and of having 'often sold human blood, by procuring false Evidence' (ibid., 2.44–5). There was as yet no precise charge against Wild, and it seems that the authorities were still casting about for prosecution witnesses when on 10 March Wild 'saved them that Trouble by committing a Felony while ... in Newgate' (*Select Trials*, 1742, 2.206): he had accepted 10 guineas for returning some stolen lace to one Mrs Statham without attempting to prosecute the thieves (who had, in any case, committed the robbery on his instructions). On 15 May 1725 Wild was tried at the Old Bailey for 'privately stealing' the lace, and for 'helping' Statham 'to the said Lace' for a reward (*Select Trials*, 1735, 2.46). In a vain attempt to influence the jurors Wild 'dispers'd' a list of names of seventy-five 'Persons' he had 'discover'd, apprehended and convicted' to the courtroom (a modest estimate; some contemporaries put the figure as high as 120; ibid., 2.46). Neither this, nor all the art employed by Wild's counsel in the course of his four-hour trial, could save him; although acquitted of the theft he was convicted of the second indictment—a charge made capital by the clause of the 1718 act supposedly drafted with him in mind—and sentenced to hang.

After conviction 'Jonathan's Cunning and Courage forsook him'; he refused even to attend chapel for fear of being 'insult[ed]', or worse, by enemies (*Select Trials*, 1735, 2.108, 111). Wild appeared 'disorder'd' and almost stupefied, complaining that 'he thought he deserved well' for having 'regain'd Things of great Value for Dukes, Earls and Lords' and for his strenuous efforts to apprehend 'the greatest and most pernicious Robbers', which had left his body covered with 'Wounds and Scars' (ibid., 110–11). The night before his execution Wild attempted to commit suicide by taking a large dose of laudanum—so large, in fact, that he 'vomited it up in a great measure, and liv'd to be hang'd' (*Evening Post*, 25 May 1725).

On 24 May 1725 Wild, still 'almost insensible' from the effects of the drug, embarked on what would prove to be an arduous journey to Tyburn. A 'numerous Crowd' of hostile spectators greeted him with triumphant jeers—some, according to one account, 'calling out *Blewskin*,

&c'—and pelted him so violently with stones that 'Blood flew from him plentifully' (*Mist's Weekly Journal*, 29 May 1725; *Parker's Penny Post*, 26 May 1725). At the place of execution Wild was hastily turned off after it became clear that the mob would brook no delays. Such was Wild's unpopularity that 'the Noisy Multitude' only 'acquiesc'd' in allowing his body to be carried off in a coach after it was 'given out that it was design'd for the Surgeons' (*London Journal*, 29 May 1725; *Evening Post*, 25 May 1725). Wild had desired to be buried next to Elizabeth Man and was quietly interred late the following night at St Pancras churchyard, but early in the next month his body was 'dug up from the grave and carried off' by persons unknown (*Original Weekly Journal*, 5 June 1725). Many years later a skeleton believed to be Wild's resurfaced and was eventually donated to the Royal College of Surgeons in 1847.

If Wild's remains belonged to posterity, his name had long been the property of satirists and pamphleteers. As Peachum in John Gay's *Beggar's Opera* (1728), or Henry Fielding's *Jonathan Wild the Great* (1743), Wild—and by analogy, his counterpart in high life, Robert Walpole—had become a byword for hypocrisy and corruption in high places, an illustration of the old dictum that great rogues prosper while little rogues hang. In Harrison Ainsworth's *Jack Sheppard* (1839), Wild was resurrected as Sheppard's evil nemesis and the embodiment of the corruption and brutality of a bygone age. The real Jonathan Wild, however, rivals any of his fictional incarnations: there were thief-takers before and after Wild, but none of them, as Mandeville pointed out, reigned 'with such an absolute Sway, or so long and successfully as himself', or 'was ever more universally known in his Occupation' (*British Journal*, 17 April 1725). Those who wish to learn more about this Jonathan Wild are referred to Gerald Howson's excellent biography, *Thief-Taker General: the Rise and Fall of Jonathan Wild* (1970).　　ANDREA MCKENZIE

Sources [J. Wild], *An answer to a late insolent libel entitled, 'A discovery of the conduct of receivers and thief-takers, in and about the City of London ...' written by C—s H—n* (1718) • *An authentick narrative of the life and actions of Jonathan Wild, citizen and thief-taker of London* (1725) • *The history of the lives and actions of Jonathan Wild, thief-taker. Joseph Blake alias Bleuskin, foot-pad. And John Sheppard, housebreaker*, 3rd edn (1725) • [H. D.], *The life of Jonathan Wild, from his birth to his death*, 2nd edn (1725) • *The lives of the most remarkable criminals*, 3 vols. (1735) • *A narrative of the robberies, escapes, &c. of John Sheppard ... The whole publish'd at the particular request of the prisoner*, 6th edn (1725) [often attributed to D. Defoe; repr. in H. Bleackley and S. M. Ellis, *Jack Sheppard* (1933)] • *The proceedings on the king's commission of the peace* (1723–4) [Old Bailey sessions papers, 14–21 Oct 1724] • [C. Hitchen], *The regulator, or, A discovery of the thieves, thief-takers, and locks, alias receivers of stolen goods in and about the City of London* (1718) ['By a prisoner in Newgate'] • *Select trials ... at the sessions house in the Old Bailey*, 2 (1735), 44–112 • *Select trials at the sessions house in the Old Bailey*, 4 vols. (1742) • A. Smith, *Memoirs of the life and times, of the famous Jonathan Wild, together with the history and lives, of modern rogues, several of 'em his acquaintance, that have been executed before and since his death* (1726) • *The true and genuine account of the life and actions of the late Jonathan Wild, not made up of fiction and fable, but taken from his own mouth, and collected from papers of his own writing* (1725) [attributed to D. Defoe; repr. in H. Fielding, *Jonathan Wild*, ed. D. Nokes (1982), 223–57] • [C. Hitchen], *A true discovery of the conduct of the receivers and thief-takers in and about the City of London* (1718) • BL, Francis Place MSS, Add. MS 27826, fol. 13 • J. Dobson, 'The college criminals', *Annals of* *the Royal College of Surgeons of England*, 9 (1951), 339–46 · G. Howson, *Thief-taker general: the rise and fall of Jonathan Wild* (1970) · F. J. Lyons, *Jonathan Wild, prince of robbers* (1936)

Likenesses T. Cook, line engraving, pubd 1819 (after unknown artist, 1725), BM, NPG [*see illus.*] · caricature, repro. in *The life and glorious actions … of Jonathan Wild* (1725) · execution ticket, BM · portrait, repro. in Defoe, *The true and genuine account … of Jonathan Wild*, frontispiece · portrait, repro. in *History of the lives and actions of Jonathan Wild*, frontispiece · portrait, repro. in H. D., *Life of Jonathan Wild*, frontispiece

Wealth at death fairly prosperous from *c*.1716 until death: *Weekly Journal, or, Saturday's Post* (5 March 1718) · est. £200–£300 p.a.: H. D., *Life of Jonathan Wild*, 16 · est. £400–£500 p.a.: *History of the lives*, 10 · left son £300; sums to widow and daughter: *London Journal* (29 May 1725)

Wild, Robert (1615/16–1679), nonconformist minister and satirical poet, was born at St Ives, Huntingdonshire, the son of Robert Wild, shoemaker. After attending a private school at St Ives he was admitted as a sizar at St John's College, Cambridge, on 26 January 1632, aged sixteen, and named a scholar on 6 November 1634. He graduated BA in 1636 and proceeded MA in 1639. He was ordained a deacon at Peterborough on 18 February 1638 and a priest on 22 December 1639. For a time he apparently could find employment only as an usher in a free school. In spite of having proceeded BD at Oxford in November 1642, by order of the House of Commons Wild was appointed rector of Aynho, Northamptonshire, on 22 July 1646, and James Long, the previous incumbent, was sequestered on 10 December 1646. By 1644 Wild had married; he and his wife, Joyce (*d*. 1687), had at least three children—Robert (1644/5–1691), John (*d*. 1682?), and James.

A definitive canon of Wild's works has not been established. Indeed, the author of *A Scourge for the Libeller* (1672) complained, with exaggeration, that every anonymous 'sheet' was attributed to Wild. One of his earliest works appears to have been 'The combat of the cocks', which appeared without attribution in Thomas Randall's *The High and Mighty Commendation* (1642), and then anonymously as *A Horrible, Terrible, Troublesome, Historical Narration of a Duel* (1660); it was identified as Wild's work in the second edition of his *Iter boreale* (1661) and in Charles Cotton's *The Complete Gamester* (1674). Another early work, although not published until 1689, may have been *The Benefice: a Comedy*; in the tradition of the Elizabethan Marprelate tracts, it recounts the bitterness of the Book-worm, a young divine, toward the patron Marchurch who is interested only in selling a clerical living, not in the learning of a prospective incumbent. *The Incomparable Poem Gondibert, Vindicated* (1655), which praises Sir William Davenant, has been attributed to Wild. His erudition is manifest in *The Arraignment of a Sinner at the Bar of Divine Justice* (1656), a sermon preached at the assizes in Oxford and dedicated to his patron, John Cartwright of Aynho, sheriff of Oxfordshire.

A friend of Richard Baxter, Wild shared his dislike of sectaries though not his interest in theological debate. The execution of the presbyterian minister Christopher Love in 1651 inspired Wild to write *The Tragedy of Christopher Love* (1660), in which he denounced 'cruell *Cromwell*, whelp of that mad Star' Sirius, likening him to Herod.

Wild later again vented his dislike of the former lord protector in *Oliver Cromwells Ghost* [1678?]. He welcomed George Monck's restoration of monarchy, on which he wrote '*Exit Tyrannus* over *Lambert*'s dore'. His praise for Monck as the saviour of the nation from tyranny and the sectaries was effusive:

> *Monck*! the great *Monck*! That syllable out-shines
> *Plantagenet*'s bright name, or *Constantine*'s. …
> He took Rebellion rampant, by the Throat,
> And made the Canting *Quaker* change his Note.

The poem from which these lines are taken, *Iter boreale* (p. 5), was published on St George's day, 23 April 1660, and achieved wide popularity, with eight editions appearing by 1674, including two in 1668. Its success inspired others to write sequels: *Iter boreale, the Second Part* (1660), by T. H., and *An Essay to a Continuation of Iter boreale* (1660).

At the Restoration Long regained his cure at Aynho, but Charles II, undoubtedly wanting to reward Wild for his support, presented him with the rectory of Tatenhill, Staffordshire, where he was inducted on 1 September 1660. He was created DD by Oxford on 9 November 1660 and by Cambridge the following year. The publication of a second edition of *Iter boreale* in 1661 enabled Wild to append a number of shorter poems, most of which were elegies to the earl of Essex and puritan ministers such as Richard Vines, 'our English *Luther*' (p. 35), Jeremiah Whitaker, Stephen Marshall, and Jeremiah Burroughs. The works of Edward Reynolds, who conformed and became bishop of Norwich, received special praise. Refusing to conform himself, Wild was ejected from his living at Tatenhill in 1662 and moved to Oundle, Northamptonshire. A corpulent man, he suffered so severely from gout that he was incapacitated from preaching for months at a time, yet he retained a sense of humour, comparing his confinement at the hands of Bishop Gout to Edward Calamy's incarceration for preaching illegally following his ejection. This became the subject of Wild's *A Poem upon the Imprisonment of Mr. Calamy* [1663], in which he castigated the bishops:

> … see them Steeple upon Steeple set,
> As if they meant that way to Heaven to get.

In *Anti-boreale* [1663] Bishop Laurence Womock retorted by calling Wild '*one* of Geneva-*Basan Bulls fat breed*' and assigning him partial responsibility for the regicide (fol. a3r–v). No less acerbic was *On Calamy's Imprisonment, and Wild's Poetry* [1663], which prematurely wrote Wild's epitaph:

> This *Presbyterian Brat* was *born* and *cry'd*,
> Spit in his *Mothers Face*, and so he *dy'd*.

This work has been unconvincingly attributed to George Sacheverell, presumably because he copied it into his commonplace book (BL, Add. MS 28758), and to Samuel Butler, who denied authorship in *On the Answer to Dr Wilds Poem* (1663) and condemned the anonymous writer for having vilified Wild and Calamy. The other replies to Wild's poem on Calamy's imprisonment were *To R. W., D.D.* (1662 [1663]), *Dr. Wild's Echo* [1663], *An Answer for Mr Calamie* (1663), *To the Ark in Newgate* (1663), and *An Answer to Wild* [1663], the last of which portrayed him as 'a poor *Erratick*'. His defenders lashed back at 'Hudibras', the reputed author of *On Calamy's Imprisonment*, in *Hudibras Answered by True de Case* [1663] and *Your Servant Sir* [1663].

In the meantime, in *The Recantation of a Penitent Proteus* [1663] Wild wrote a biting satire about Nathaniel Lee, effectively making him a representative of puritans who had conformed to the established church:

> If the *great Turk* to *England* come, I can
> Make *Gospel* truckle to the *Alcoran*.

Wild took aim as well at Roger L'Estrange, surveyor of the press, whom he linked to the turncoat Lee:

> Our Names ty'd taile to taile make a sweet Change
> Mine onely is St[r]ange Lee, and his *Le-Strange*.

He was not finished with L'Estrange, whom he ridiculed in *The Grateful Non-Conformist* (1665) for his readiness to 'smell a Plot, a *Presbyterian* Plot' (p. 67). Nevertheless, L'Estrange licensed *An Essay upon the Late Victory Obtained by ... the Duke of York* (1665), in which Wild effused patriotic fervour for James's naval triumph over the Dutch. The poem was reprinted in Edinburgh the same year as *A Gratulatory Verse*.

Although Wild has been described as a royalist, his principles harmonized with those of most protestant dissenters. In *The Loyal Nonconformist* (1666) he professed loyalty to monarchical government and his readiness to take an oath not to alter it, but he repudiated the oath abjuring the solemn league and covenant, the enforced usage of the Book of Common Prayer and the surplice, and episcopal polity. A defender of Anglicanism responded in *Swearing and Lying* (1666), averring that Wild's professions of loyalty notwithstanding, he 'yield[ed] all things but obedience'. When Calamy died the following year, Wild saluted him as a prophet and martyr in *On the Death of Mr Calamy* (1667). Wild again came under attack in *A Sovereign Remedy for the Presbyterian's Maladie* [1667], and in an exchange of verse with Nathaniel Wanley, vicar of Trinity Church, Coventry, published as *The Fair Quarrel* (1666; repr. 1668). Here, too, Wild defended nonconformists, in part by satirizing the Five Mile Act:

> Nor is there any Statute of our Nation
> That sayes, *in five miles* of a *Corporation*
> If any *Outed-man* a Fart should vent,
> That you should apprehend the *Innocent*.

He apparently preached when he could, for in July 1669 he was indicted for holding a conventicle at Nuneaton, Warwickshire. Despite his differences with the government, he favourably contrasted Charles II with the popes in *Upon the Rebuilding the City* (1670).

When the king issued a declaration of indulgence in 1672, Wild expressed his gratitude but pointedly noted that dissenting clergy, unlike the '*Jack-dawes*' who held livings in the established church, were interested in preaching rather than material gain: '*Peter* shall preach, *Judas* shall bear the purse.' Published as *Dr Wild's Humble Thanks for his Majesties Gracious Declaration* (1672), it elicited hostile responses in *An Answer to the Author of Humble Thanks* (1672), *Dr. Wild's Squibs Return'd* (1672), and *Poor Robin's Parley with Dr. Wilde* (1672). In *A Letter from Dr. Wild to his Friend Mr. J. J.* (1672) he enthusiastically referred to the declaration as 'a second *Magna Charta*' and expressed hope that parliament

would approve it (p. 6), not least because he thought it was economically beneficial. Anglican apologists promptly responded in *An Answer to Old Doctor Wild's New Poem* [1672?], *Moonshine, or, The Restauration of Jews-Trumps and Bagpipes* (1672), and *Flagellum poeticum* (1672), which chided Wild for having denigrated Anglicans. Other satirists were directing barbs at him, as in *A Wipe for Iter-boreale Wilde* (1670) and *The Wild Goose Chas'd* [1672?]. Taking advantage of the indulgence, he obtained a licence as a presbyterian in August 1672 to preach in his house at Oundle. Optimistic about England's prospects in the Third Anglo-Dutch War, he suffused *A Panegyrique Humbly Addrest to the Kings most Excellent Majesty* (1673) with patriotism:

> Heav'n, that hath plac'd this *Island*, to give Law,
> To Ballance *Europe*, and for *States* to Aw.
> (p. 2)

Advancing years slowed Wild's pen. In *The Poring Doctor* (1674) he denounced a doctor of the church as a '*doting Fool*' who could neither pray nor preach, and who confused the names of Jesus and Judas. Responding to reports of the Popish Plot, he threw down the gauntlet to the papacy in *An Exclamation Against Popery* (1678):

> Plot on Proud *Rome*! And lay thy damn'd Design
> As low as Hell, we'll find a Countermine.

He also attacked Rome in *Dr. Wild's Poem: In nova fert animus* [1679], composed as the First Exclusion Parliament met. *Dr. R. W.'s Last Legacie* [1679] is usually regarded as his last poem, but *A Copy of the Last Verses Made by Dr. Wild* (1679) may also be his work. In it the author denounced 'Papists' as traitors and repudiated the efforts of the court's supporters to draw parallels between 1679 and 1641.

Following his death in July 1679, apparently from apoplexy, Wild was buried at Oundle on the 30th. In the works that marked the occasion, *A Dialogue between Death and Doctor Robert Wyld* (1679) observed that 'Great Wyld is slain!' and *A Pillar Set upon the Grave of the Reverend Dr. Robert Wilde* [1679] praised him as a prophet and a poet, but noted that his verse was sometimes too light and his sermons 'too home, Phanatick-like'. His will, dated 10 August 1678 and proved on 17 February 1680, provided bequests of £1050, part of which was used to purchase six bibles each year for winners of a lottery in which six women and six men participated. He was survived by his wife, his sisters Elizabeth Acton, widow, and Esther Wild, and his sons, Robert, John, and James, a London linen-draper. Robert (BA, Brasenose College, Oxford, 1665; MA, King's College, Cambridge, 1668) served as vicar of Chiddingly, Sussex (1661–1672?), rector of Blyborough, Lincolnshire (1672–1674?), and rector of Toppesfield, Essex (1674–91). John (BA, St Catharine's College, Cambridge, 1667; MA, Pembroke College, Oxford, 1670) was vicar of Weekley, Northamptonshire (1678–82), and chaplain to Lord Montagu of Boughton. According to Richard Winwood, an old friend of Wild's, the latter was pleased by John's position in Montagu's family.

One of the most popular satirists of the Restoration era, Wild was described by Eugenius in John Dryden's *Of Dramatick Poesie* (1668) as 'the very [George] *Withers* of the City: they have bought more Editions of his Works then would serve to lay under all their Pies at the Lord Mayor's *Christmass*' (p. 5). When Samuel Pepys read *Iter boreale* in August 1663, he 'like[d] it pretty well but not so as it was cried up' (Pepys, 4.285), and he spent part of Christmas day 1667 listening to a friend read Wild's poems. In 1679 John Oldham also associated Wild with Wither:

> Should Parts, and Nature fail, yet very spite
> Would make the arrant'st *Wild*, or *Withers* write.
> (Oldham, 3)

Several of Wild's poems were included with those of John Wilmot, earl of Rochester, in *Rome Rhym'd to Death* (1683), and an incomplete edition of his *Poems*, edited by John Hunt, was published in 1870.   RICHARD L. GREAVES

Sources *Calamy rev.*, 529 · *CSP dom.*, 1663–4, 379; 1664–5, 143–4; 1668–9, 430; 1672, 239, 302, 473; 1672–3, 340–41; 1673–5, 501 · R. Wilde, *Poems*, ed. J. Hunt (1870) · Venn, *Alum. Cant.* · G. de F. Lord and others, eds., *Poems on affairs of state: Augustan satirical verse, 1660–1714*, 7 vols. (1963–75), vols. 1–2 · Pepys, *Diary*, 4.285; 8.589 · Wood, *Ath. Oxon.*: *Fasti* (1820), 35–6 · *Report on the manuscripts of Lord Montagu of Beaulieu*, HMC, 53 (1900), 187 · *Walker rev.*, 282 · [J. Oldham], *Satyrs upon the Jesuits*, 2nd edn (1682) · R. Pirie, 'Two editions of *Iter boreale*, 1668', *Book Collector*, 12 (1963), 204–5 · will, PRO, PROB 11/362, sig. 32
Archives BL, Add. MS 28758, fols. 103, 106
Wealth at death £1050: *Calamy rev.*; will, PRO, PROB 11/362, sig. 32

Wilde, Sir Alfred Thomas (1819–1878), army officer, of Kirby Cane Hall, Bungay, third son of Edward Archer Wilde (*d.* 1871), solicitor, of College Hill, Queen Street, London, and his wife, Marianne, daughter of William Norris, physician, was born on 1 November 1819. He was a brother of James Plaisted *Wilde, Lord Penzance, and nephew of Thomas *Wilde, Lord Truro. Educated as a commoner at Winchester School from 1834 to 1837, he obtained a commission as ensign in the East India Company's army on 12 December 1838, and joined the 15th Madras native infantry in April 1839. He was transferred to the 19th Madras native infantry in June, was promoted to lieutenant on 9 July 1842, qualified as interpreter in Hindustani in March 1843, and served with his regiment through the 1843 disturbances on the Malabar coast.

In January 1847 Wilde was appointed adjutant, and in February became quartermaster and interpreter to his regiment. In March 1850 he was transferred to the adjutancy of the 3rd Punjab native infantry, and qualified as interpreter in the Telugu dialect. In April 1851 he was appointed second in command of the 4th Punjab native infantry, and was in field command of the regiment and other troops at the occupation of the Bahadur Khel valley, Kohat district, in November, receiving the thanks of government for defeating a night attack of a body of Wazirs upon the fort of Bahadur Khel. He was promoted to brevet captain on 12 December, took part in the capture of the village of Allah-dad-Khan in 1854, was promoted to captain on 23 November 1856, and was thanked by the government of India for valuable service in the great inundation of the Indus in that year.

In March 1857 Wilde commanded the 4th Punjab native infantry in the successful expedition under Brigadier Neville Chamberlain against the Bozdar Baluchis. His regiment remained loyal, and Wilde was engaged throughout the Indian mutiny. He was at the siege of Delhi, and in the storming parties which captured the Delhi magazine and palace on 16 and 20 September, when he was wounded. He took part in the actions of Gangari, Patial, and Mainpuri in December, and in that of Shamsabad on 27 January 1858. He was promoted to brevet major for his services at Delhi on 19 January, and was thanked by government.

Wilde commanded the 4th Punjabis in the first victorious assault on the entrenchments in front of Lucknow at the siege of that city in March 1858, led a storming party at the capture of the begum's palace on 14 March, and was wounded on 21 March at the attack on Goal Masjid, in the heart of the city. This secured the capture of Lucknow, and in May he went on leave to England to regain his health. He was mentioned in dispatches, promoted to brevet lieutenant-colonel on 20 July, and made CB, military division, on 16 November 1858.

Wilde returned to India in 1859. In March 1860 he commanded his regiment in the expedition against the Mahsud Wazirs, and was thanked for his services. He was promoted regimental major on 18 February 1861, and on 3 March 1862 he was appointed commandant of the corps of guides, and commanded them in the expedition to Ambala against the Sitana and Mandi fanatics in 1863. On 20 July he was promoted colonel in the army, made an aide-de-camp to the queen, and was given command of the 2nd brigade of the Usafzai field force, which harried the villages of Sitana and Mandi. He was promoted regimental lieutenant-colonel on 12 December 1864, and on 8 February 1865 succeeded to the command of the Punjab irregular force with the rank of brigadier-general.

Wilde married, in 1866, Ellen Margaret, third daughter of Colonel Godfrey T. Greene CB, Royal (late Bengal) Engineers; they had at least one daughter and three sons. On 12 June 1866 he was made CSI. In 1868 he commanded the field force in the Hazara Black Mountain expedition, and received the thanks of government for his services. He was made a KCB, military division, on 2 June 1869, and was promoted major-general on 18 July. On his final return from India in 1871 he was awarded a good-service pension. In 1877 he was appointed a member of the Council of India, and promoted lieutenant-general on 1 October 1877. He died at his residence, Donoon House, Clapham Common, London, on 7 February 1878; he was survived by his wife.   R. H. VETCH, *rev.* JAMES FALKNER

Sources *Army List* · *The Times* (9 Feb 1878) · *Annual Register* (1878) · *Hart's Army List* · *East-India Register* · J. W. Kaye and G. B. Malleson, *Kaye's and Malleson's History of the Indian mutiny of 1857–8*, 6 vols. (1888–9) · Boase, *Mod. Eng. biog.* · Walford, *County families* (1875) · *CGPLA Eng. & Wales* (1878)
Wealth at death under £4000: probate, 1 March 1878, *CGPLA Eng. & Wales*

Wilde, George James De (1804–1871). *See under* Wilde, Samuel De (*bap.* 1751, *d.* 1832).

Wilde, Henry (1833–1919), electrical engineer and inventor, was born in Manchester. He may be the Henry

Wilde who was the son of Horatio Wilde and his wife Hannah, and who was baptized on 17 February 1833. At the age of sixteen, he was left without parents in charge of a younger brother and sister. After being educated in private schools, he was apprenticed to a mechanical engineer, and before the age of twenty-one had attained a position of responsibility in the works. At this time he was already experimenting with voltaic cells, electrical machines and kites, and the electro-deposition of metals.

In 1856 Wilde established a business in Manchester as an electric-telegraph and lightning-conductor engineer, and spent some years on the development of a magneto-electric alphabetic telegraph, which was demonstrated at the international exhibition in London in 1862. In December 1863 he patented a twin-armature machine in which a magneto-electric generator provided excitation current for the field winding of another generator. These machines were made in quantity by Wilde & Co., but in use they had the disadvantage of becoming very hot. In 1867 he patented an entirely different type of multipolar machine, which was used for electro-deposition and arc lighting. Among his other patents was one in 1875 for the making of copper rollers for calico printing.

Wilde nearly discovered the principle of self-excitation, but other inventors achieved it first, notably Charles Wheatstone and the Siemens brothers. In 1898, having since 1871 styled himself 'electrical engineer', he was elected an honorary member of the Institution of Electrical Engineers, and the following year contributed the sum of £1500 to a benevolent fund for the benefit of their members. At the same time, he thought it desirable to submit to them an autobiographical statement, which was published in the *Journal of the Institution of Electrical Engineers*.

Wilde published many other papers in the *Proceedings of the Royal Society* and elsewhere, especially after his retirement in 1884, on a wide variety of subjects, including the magnetization of iron, atomic weights, the spectrum of thallium, the moving force of celestial bodies, aerial locomotion, and the velocity with which air rushes into a vacuum. He made arclights as searchlights for the Royal Navy (1874); after the *Titanic* disaster in 1912 he strongly urged that mercantile vessels should be fitted with searchlights. He invented the magnetarium for reproducing the phenomena of terrestrial magnetism and the secular variation of the mariner's compass (1890).

He was elected a fellow of the Royal Society in 1866, and was awarded the Albert gold medal of the Royal Society of Arts in 1900. He had an honorary DSc from the Victoria University of Manchester (1900), and a DCL from Oxford University (1903). He was a liberal benefactor, during his lifetime and in his will, of the Manchester Literary and Philosophical Society, the University of Oxford, and the Académie des Sciences, Paris. He died of heart failure 'accelerated by want of medical attention' at his residence, The Hurst, Macclesfield Road, Alderley Edge, Cheshire, on 28 March 1919. He had been a widower for twenty-six years, and had no children.

RONALD M. BIRSE, *rev.* BRIAN BOWERS

Sources H. Wilde, *Journal of the Institution of Electrical Engineers* (1899), 3–11 [autobiographical letter] · *Journal of the Institution of Electrical Engineers*, 57 (1919), 625–6 · *Nature*, 103/2581 (17 April 1919), 129–30 · D. S. L. Cardwell, 'Faraday and the dynamo', *Annals of Science*, 49 (1992), 479–87 · W. W. Haldane Gee, 'Obit of Henry Wilde', *Manchester Memoirs*, 5 (1920), 1–16
Archives CUL, letters to Sir George Stokes
Wealth at death £9,154 10s. 9d.: probate, 14 June 1919, *CGPLA Eng. & Wales*

Wilde, James Plaisted, Baron Penzance (1816–1899), judge, was born in London on 12 July 1816, the second son of Edward Archer Wilde (1788–1871), solicitor, and his wife, Marianne Norris. Sir Alfred Thomas *Wilde was his brother. He was educated at Winchester College and later at Trinity College, Cambridge, where he matriculated in Michaelmas term 1834 and took his BA in 1838 and his MA in 1842. On 15 April 1836 he was admitted as a student at the Inner Temple, where he was called to the bar on 22 November 1839, and elected bencher on 15 January 1856.

A pupil of Barnes (afterwards Sir Barnes Peacock), and 'devil' to his uncle Sir Thomas *Wilde (later Lord Truro), Wilde was rapidly launched into practice. In 1840 he was made counsel to the commissioners of customs, and thereafter made a successful career both on the northern circuit and at Westminster. He took silk on 6 July 1855, was made counsel to the duchy of Lancaster in 1859, and in 1860 became a baron of the exchequer and was also invested with the coif and knighted (on 13 and 24 April respectively). On 20 February 1860 Wilde married Mary Pleydell Bouverie, the youngest daughter of William Pleydell-*Bouverie, third earl of Radnor; they had no children.

After the death of Sir Cresswell Cresswell in 1863 Wilde was transferred to the court of probate and divorce (28 August), and on 26 April 1864 was sworn of the privy council. He soon showed himself worthy of his new office and did much to shape both the substantive law and the procedure of the court, being very much involved in the proceedings under the Legitimacy Declaration Act (21 & 22 Vict., c. 93). He was created Baron Penzance on 6 April 1869 and on 23 April took his seat in the House of Lords.

Wilde was an active peer, concerned with issues of social change. In his maiden speech he justified the disestablishment of the Church of Ireland on the broad ground of equity (15 June 1869). He also helped the government to push through legislation enabling the evidence of the parties to be taken in actions for breach of promise of marriage and adultery proceedings. In the following session he supported the measures in amendment of the laws relating to absconding debtors, married women's property, and the naturalization of aliens, and moved on 27 March 1871 the second reading of the bill for the controversial legalization of marriage with a deceased wife's sister. He also took an active part in the discussions on the judicature bills of 1872 and 1874.

Wilde retired from judicial office in November 1872 because of ill health and took a pension of £3500. In 1874, however, he accepted the position of judge under the Public Worship Regulation Act (37 & 38 Vict., c. 85). He was invested with the statutory jurisdiction by sign manual on

14 November 1874, without anything more than a formal nomination by the archbishops of Canterbury and York. By virtue of the statute he succeeded to the offices of dean of the arches court of Canterbury, master of the faculties, and official principal of the chancery court of York on the retirement in October the following year of Sir Robert Phillimore and Granville Harcourt Vernon. However, a mere declaration of churchmanship was substituted for the oath and subscription to the Thirty-Nine Articles required by the 127th canon of 1603–4. This meant that his jurisdiction lacked moral authority, his monitions could be and were often disregarded, and his Erastianism was treated with contempt. Nor was his position in the judicial hierarchy clearly defined: the statute did not expressly constitute his court a superior court of law or invest him with power to commit for contempt, and the court of queen's bench asserted the right to review his decisions and restrain their enforcement by prohibition. Eventually these questions were determined in Penzance's favour by the House of Lords in 1881 and 1882, but by that time his position as ecclesiastical judge was emasculated. The bishops discouraged recourse to his court, while the laity generally doubted the morality or practical sense of prosecuting ritualists and so converting them into martyrs. For these reasons Penzance's court came eventually to be all but deserted for that of the archbishop of Canterbury.

Penzance retired from the bench in March 1899, and died at his seat, Eashing Park, Godalming, Surrey, on 9 December 1899. He was buried on 15 December at Shackleford, near Godalming. His wife died less than a year later on 24 October 1900.

Penzance also served on various royal commissions, including those on the marriage laws (1865), the courts of law (1867 and 1869), claims to compensation consequent on the abolition of purchase in the army (1873), the retirement and promotion of military officers (1874), the customs of the stock exchange (1877), and the condition of Wellington College (1878). He seldom took part in judicial deliberations in the House of Lords. His favourite pastime was gardening, and his favourite flower the rose, which he hybridized with remarkable success.

J. M. RIGG, rev. SINÉAD AGNEW

Sources Venn, *Alum. Cant.* · L. G. Pine, *The new extinct peerage, 1884–1971: containing extinct, abeyant, dormant, and suspended peerages with genealogies and arms* (1972), 215 · E. Foss, *Biographia juridica: a biographical dictionary of the judges of England … 1066–1870* (1870) · Boase, *Mod. Eng. biog.* · *Law Magazine*, 5th ser., 25 (1899–1900), 212–27 · *Law Times* (10 April 1869), 450 · *Law Times* (18 Feb 1871), 307 · *Law Times* (8 Aug 1874), 259 · *Law Times* (27 Nov 1875), 72 · *Law Times* (16 Dec 1899), 161–2 · *Law Journal* (16 Dec 1897), 688 · *Annual Register* (1886), 222 · *Annual Register* (1899), 13, 179–80 · Allibone, *Dict.* · H. P. Liddon, *The life of Edward Bouverie Pusey*, ed. J. O. Johnston and others, 4 vols. (1893–7), vol. 4, pp. 282–8 · W. Ballantine, *Some experiences of a barrister's life*, 7th edn (1883), 172 · *Guardian* (13 Dec 1899) · *The Times* (11 Dec 1889) · *The Times* (12 Dec 1889) · *Men and women of the time* (1899), 845–6 · *Leading men of London: a collection of biographical sketches* (1895), 4–5 · A. T. C. Pratt, ed., *People of the period: being a collection of the biographies of upwards of six thousand living celebrities*, 2 (1897), 260 · L. C. Sanders, *Celebrities of the century: being a dictionary of men and women of the nineteenth century* (1887), 822 · Burke, *Peerage* · GEC, *Peerage* · Lord Selborne, *Memorials*, 4 vols. (1896–8) · *Hansard 3*, 196–212, 208–26, 235– · 'Royal commission on … laws of marriage', *Parl. papers* (1867–8), vol. 32, no. 4059 · 'Royal commission to inquire into the operation of … courts', *Parl. papers* (1868–9), vol. 25, no. 4130; (1872), 20.217, C. 631; 20.245, C. 631-I; (1874), 24.1, C. 957; 24.13, C. 957-I; 24.183, C. 984; 24.191, C. 984-I; 24.307, C. 1090 [reports 1–5] · 'Royal commission to inquire into memorials from officers', *Parl. papers* (1874), vol. 12, C. 1018 [abolition of purchase] · 'Royal commission on army promotion and retirement', *Parl. papers* (1876), 15.77, C. 1569 · 'Royal commission on … the London stock exchange', *Parl. papers* (1878), 19.263, C. 2157 · 'Royal commission to inquire into Wellington College', *Parl. papers* (1880), 13.215, C. 2650 · *VF* (18 Dec 1869) · 'Judges and law officers', *Law reports: appeal cases*, 12 (1887), xviii

Archives LPL, corresp. with A. C. Tait

Likenesses carte-de-visite, 1860–69, NPG · Ape [C. Pellegrini], caricature, watercolour study, NPG; repro. in *VF* (18 Dec 1869) · Barraud, print, NPG; repro. in *Men and Women of the Day*, 4 (1891) · Lock & Whitfield, woodburytype photograph, NPG; repro. in T. Cooper, *Men of mark: a gallery of contemporary portraits* (1883) · Spy [L. Ward], chromolithograph caricature, NPG; repro. in *VF* (12 March 1896) · lithograph, NPG; repro. in *VF*, 1 (1869), pl. 2 · photograph, NPG; repro. in T. Cooper, *Men of mark: a gallery of contemporary portraits*, 4 (1880), pl. 19 · portrait, repro. in *Green Bag*, 13 (1901), 478 · portrait, NPG; repro. in *ILN*, 114 (1899), 373 · portrait, NPG; repro. in *ILN*, 115 (1899), 863 · wood-engraving, NPG; repro. in *ILN* (19 May 1860) · wood-engraving (after photograph by J. & C. Watkins), NPG; repro. in *ILN* (26 Sept 1863)

Wilde [*née* Elgee], **Jane Francesca Agnes**, Lady Wilde [*pseud.* Speranza] (**1821–1896**), writer and Irish nationalist, was born on 27 December 1821 in Dublin, the last of the four children of Charles Elgee (1783–1824), attorney, and his wife, Sarah (*d.* 1851), daughter of Thomas Kingsbury, commissioner of bankruptcy. Her parents were both Irish. Her early years are unrecorded. She dismissed enquiries into her date of birth and birthplace as impertinence, saying 'There is no register of my birth in existence. It was not the fashion then, nor compulsory in Ireland as it is now' (letter, priv. coll.). She juggled with her birth date (as her son Oscar was to do) and wove romantic mysteries about her background. Asserting, for example, that Elgee was a corruption of the Italian name Algiati, she went on to claim relationship with the poet Dante Alighieri. Jane's father died in India (his reason for going there is unknown) and where and how Sarah Elgee and her children lived after his death is uncertain. Jane was well educated, becoming fluent in French, German, and Italian, and well-grounded in Greek and the classics.

Despite her respectable, protestant background, Jane allied herself in her twenties with the revolutionary Young Ireland movement. In 1846 she began contributing rousing nationalistic poetry and prose to its weekly journal, *The Nation*. She did so under the pseudonym of Speranza, to avoid family wrath. An inflammatory leader she wrote for the 29 July 1848 edition, 'Jacta alea est' ('The die is cast'), while the editor, Charles Duffy, was in prison, called for armed insurrection ('Oh, for a hundred thousand muskets'), and caused an uproar. The journal was shut down for sedition. Jane's verse expressed anger at the causes and effects of the great famine. Emotional poems such as 'The Stricken Land', in which she attacked the English for taking Irish corn ('Weary men, what reap ye?— Golden corn for the stranger'), 'Courage' ('Lift up your pale faces, ye children of sorrow'), and the compassionate,

Jane Francesca Agnes Wilde, Lady Wilde (1821–1896), attrib. George Morosini

'The Voice of the Poor' ('Before us die our brothers of starvation; around are cries of famine and despair') fired audiences throughout Ireland. When her son Oscar toured America in 1882, he was welcomed by the Irish there not as the famous aesthete, but as 'Speranza's boy'.

Jane's appearance was striking: nearly 6 feet tall, she had a Junoesque figure, good features, long blue-black hair, and expressive brown eyes. An admirer, Sir William Rowan Hamilton, astronomer royal for Ireland and world-renowned mathematician, found her 'almost amusingly fearless and original' who 'likes to make a sensation' (Hamilton letters, NL Ire., 905). Although she claimed that 'a Joan of Arc was never meant for marriage' (MS letter, November 1852, U. Reading L.), Jane married Dr William Robert Wills *Wilde (1815–1876) on 12 November 1851. They had three children: William Charles Kingsbury (b. 1852), Oscar Fingal O'Flahertie *Wilde (1854–1900), and Isola Francesca Emily (1857–1867). Despite a self-mocking cry of 'Behold Speranza making gruel' (MS letter, November 1854, U. Reading L.), she adored her children, and gave her family absolute support and loyalty all her life.

Jane's Saturday salon or *Conversazione* was famous. The Wildes' house in Dublin's Merrion Square, according to the *Irish Times*, 'was known as the house where a guest met all the Dublin celebrities in literature, art and the drama' (11 March 1878). Jane disliked 'the fatal miasma of the commonplace' (Lady Wilde, *Notes on Men, Women and Books*, 1891). A friend, Henriette Corkran, remembered her as hostess looking like a tragedy queen in a long crimson silk

gown with flounces of Limerick lace, a vast crinoline, floating scarves, a gilt crown of laurels, and so many portrait-brooches she resembled a 'walking family mausoleum' (Corkran, 137–8). Emulating writer Charles Maturin, her uncle by marriage, she entertained in rooms darkened by closed shutters and lit only by dim, red-shaded lamps.

Jane was an early, fervent, and constant advocate of women's rights: campaigning for better education for women; inviting the suffragist Millicent Fawcett to her home to speak on female liberty; and criticizing the different moral codes for men and women. She praised the passing of the Married Women's Property Act, 1883, preventing women from having to enter marriage 'as a bond slave, disenfranchised of all rights over her fortune' (Lady Wilde, 'A new era in English and Irish social life', *Gentlewoman*, January 1883).

Jane, with her linguistic ability, became a translator of importance: her first publication was *Sidonia the Sorceress* (a German terror-tale by J. W. Meinhold, 1849) which was Oscar's favourite childhood reading. Two translations from Alphonse de Lamartine followed: *Pictures of the First French Revolution* (1850) and *The Wanderer and his Home* (1851). Then there was *The Glacier Land* (from Alexandre Dumas père, 1852); *The Future Life* (from Emanuel Swedenborg, 1853); and finally *The First Temptation* (from Wilhelmine Canz, 1863).

Dr Wilde was knighted in January 1864. But the celebrations this provoked, together with Jane's first published collection, *Poems*, were followed by a series of disasters. That year Sir William and Lady Wilde were the principals in a sensational Dublin court case regarding a young woman called Mary Travers with whom Sir William had become involved. Then, in 1867, Isola died of fever at the age of nine. In 1871 the two illegitimate daughters of Sir William were burnt to death and in 1876 Sir William himself died. The family, shocked, found he was virtually bankrupt.

Jane left Dublin for London in 1879, to join her two sons. Oscar was establishing an artistic circle; her elder son, Willie, was a journalist. To earn money she began writing for publications such as the *Pall Mall Gazette*, *The Queen*, the *Burlington Magazine*, and the *Lady's Pictorial*. She recalled her travels with her husband in *Driftwood from Scandinavia* (1884), and drew on material left by Sir William, a notable folklorist, for her next two books: *Ancient Legends, Mystic Charms and Superstitions of Ireland* (1887), which W. B. Yeats called a 'most imaginative collection' (*Letters of W. B. Yeats*), and *Ancient Cures, Charms and Usages of Ireland* (1890). Her last publications were collections of her articles: *Notes on Men, Women and Books* (1891) and *Social Studies* (1893).

For most of her life in London, Lady Wilde lived with her eldest son in rented houses in Mayfair and Chelsea. She revived her weekly salon and guests included the Irish novelist George Moore; Bernard Shaw, who admitted 'Lady Wilde was nice to me in London'; and W. B. Yeats— who said of her that 'London has few better talkers' (W. B. Yeats, *Letters to the New Island*, 1970, 76–7). Oscar attended her salons and the links between the two remained strong: she wrote constantly to him, treating him as her close confidant and signing her letters when depressed La Madre Dolorosa.

Lady Wilde successfully applied for a £100 grant from the Royal Literary Fund in 1888 and received a civil-list pension of £70 a year in 1890 in recognition of her husband's services to statistical science and literature. She lived in poverty, sometimes having to ask Oscar for money. He paid her most pressing bills but his involvement with Lord Alfred Douglas severely strained his income.

Lady Wilde never forgot Speranza's place in Ireland. After Oscar's overwhelming success she wrote to him only half-jokingly to say 'I suppose I shall now be known as the Mother of Oscar' (Lady Wilde to Oscar Wilde, William Andrews Clark Memorial Library). His arrest in 1895, his vilification in the papers and subsequent imprisonment, devastated her. She was to write, 'I only feel the agony and loss of all that made life endurable and my singing robes are trailed in London clay' (MS letter, New York Public Library, Berg Collection). Yet when friends urged Oscar to leave England, she told him: 'If you stay, even if you go to prison, you will always be my son, it will make no difference to my affection, but if you go, I will never speak to you again' (Yeats, Autobiographies, 289). Her Irish pride was strong. Her son must show moral courage.

The events took their toll. Lady Wilde contracted bronchitis in January 1896 and, failing, asked to see Oscar. Her request was refused. She died at her home, 146 Oakley Street, Chelsea, on 3 February 1896. Her elder son was penniless and Oscar paid for her funeral on 5 February at Kensal Green cemetery in London. A headstone proved too expensive and she was buried anonymously in common ground. JOY MELVILLE

Sources J. Melville, Mother of Oscar (1994) [incl. bibliography of Lady Wilde's printed works] · T. de Vere White, The parents of Oscar Wilde (1967) · C. J. Hamilton, Notable Irishwomen (1904) · C. G. Duffy, Four years of Irish history, 1845–1849: a sequel to 'Young Ireland' (1883) · H. Corkran, Celebrities and I (1902) · R. Ellmann, Oscar Wilde (1987) · B. de Breffny, 'Speranza's ancestry: Elgee—the maternal lineage of Oscar Wilde', Irish Ancestor, 4 (1972), 94–103 · T. G. Wilson, Victorian doctor: life of Sir William Wilde (1942) · H. Wyndham, Speranza (1951) · Anna, comtesse de Bremont, Oscar Wilde and his mother (1911) · P. Byrne, The Wildes of Merrion Square (1953) · W. B. Yeats, Autobiographies (1955) · R. H. Sherard, The life of Oscar Wilde (1906) · The letters of W. B. Yeats, ed. A. Wade (1954) · d. cert. · U. Cal., Los Angeles, William Andrews Clark Memorial Library · Kensal Green cemetery records · letters, U. Reading, archives · NL Ire., Hamilton letters · letter, NYPL, Humanities and Social Sciences Library, Berg collection

Archives NL Ire., corresp. relating to her pension · U. Cal., Los Angeles, William Andrews Clark Memorial Library · U. Reading, letters | Kungliga Bibli);eket, Stockholm, letters to Lotten von Kraemer · NL Ire., letters to Mrs Olivecrona [copies] · NYPL, Humanities and Social Sciences Library, Berg collection

Likenesses B. Mulrenin, portrait, exh. Royal Hibernian Academy 1864; now lost · attrib. G. Morosini, crayon drawing, NG Ire. [see illus.] · coloured ambrotype, Merlin Holland Collection

Wealth at death virtually nil; although the rents from Moytura House, co. Mayo, should have come to her, tenants in Ireland were mostly refusing to pay rents and Lady Wilde rarely got any: letters, U. Reading

Wilde, Johannes [János] (1891–1970), art historian, was born in Budapest on 2 June 1891, the sixth and youngest child of Richard Wilde (d. 1912), a tailor, and his wife, Rosa Somlyaky (d. 1928). His parents were devout Roman Catholics who brought him up in an atmosphere of piety and simplicity. He suffered bereavement with the early death of his father and his elder brother Paul, who had greatly influenced him. Educated at the state Gymnasium in Budapest for eight years, he entered the university there in September 1909 to study art, archaeology, and philosophy under Gyula Pasteiner. The summer term of 1911 was spent at the University of Freiburg-im-Breisgau, and, with a scholarship from the Hungarian ministry of education, he continued his studies, under Max Dvořák, at the University of Vienna from October 1915 to July 1917. He was awarded a doctorate in philosophy by Vienna University summa cum laude in July 1918 for his thesis 'Die Anfänge der italienischen Radierung'.

Wilde's first publication, in 1910, was a translation into his native Hungarian of Adolf Hildebrand's Das Problem der Form in den bildenden Künsten, which is an interesting pointer to his own approach to the visual arts. He was also to gain a reputation as a connoisseur of Hungarian poetry and literature, but his first allegiance was to art, and in August 1914 he became a voluntary assistant at the Museum of Fine Arts in Budapest. After gaining his PhD, he returned to the museum's department of prints and drawings as an assistant keeper under Simon Meller, a post he was to hold until December 1922. Here were laid the foundations of Wilde's interest in connoisseurship and the study of old master drawings. It seems likely that Meller nurtured Wilde's interest in Michelangelo, on whom he had himself published.

During the short-lived Hungarian Soviet Republic of 1919, Wilde and Frigyes (Friedrich) Antal, among others, were directed by the commissar of public education to sequestrate those privately owned works of art regarded as of national importance. However, in September 1920 Wilde was granted six months' study leave to enable him to accept Dvořák's invitation to lecture at Vienna University. This leave was prolonged to allow Wilde to prepare, in collaboration with Karl Swoboda, an edition of the collected works of Dvořák, whose death in February 1921 was a cruel personal loss to Wilde. Too young to succeed Dvořák as professor, Wilde was invited to join the Kunsthistorisches Museum, Vienna, in 1923; he accepted Austrian citizenship in 1928.

Despite his demanding museum duties, Wilde continued to lecture and supervise students until the crisis of the Anschluss and his subsequent resignation from the museum for reasons of conscience in November 1938. He had by then decided to leave Austria, impelled largely by fear for the safety of his Hungarian-Jewish wife, Dr Julia Gyárfás (d. 1970), also an art historian, whom he had married on 6 February 1930. Assisted by a former pupil, Count Antoine Seilern, the couple left Austria ostensibly to visit an exhibition in Holland in April 1939, afterwards flying to England where they were the guests of Kenneth Clark and his wife at Port Lympne. A few months later, at the outbreak of war with Germany, Wilde went to Aberystwyth to look after Seilern's pictures, stored in the university library. At the director's request, he began to assist in cataloguing the National Gallery pictures which were in store there, together with the Italian drawings from the British Museum. This happy coincidence led to his friendship with A. E. Popham, with whom he was later to collaborate in preparing the published catalogue of Italian fifteenth- and sixteenth-century drawings in the Royal Collection (1949). Popham persuaded the British Museum trustees, in June 1940, to invite Wilde to compile the catalogue of the collection's Michelangelo drawings. But in the same month, during the panic caused by the Nazi offensive in France, Wilde was interned. Despite strong protests from English friends, he was deported to Canada and only survived the rigours of the concentration camp through the care of a fellow detainee, Otto Demus.

In May 1941 Wilde was freed and allowed to live in Buckinghamshire as the guest of Count Seilern, who had done much to secure his release. He resumed his Michelangelo studies and began teaching at London University. On 12 March 1947 he had become a British subject, and in 1948 he was appointed reader in the history of art at London University and deputy director of the Courtauld Institute of Art. He officially retired in 1958, although he continued to teach part-time until his seventieth birthday. The title of professor was conferred on him in 1950; he was elected a fellow of the British Academy in 1951, appointed CBE in 1955, and awarded the Serena medal of the British Academy in 1963.

Wilde gained an international reputation for his work on the Italian, especially the Venetian, paintings at the Kunsthistorisches Museum, and his many contributions to the problems of dating, style, attribution, and condition appeared in the 1928 Gemäldegalerie catalogue and in the Vienna *Jahrbuch*. His first major work was the reconstruction of the San Cassiano altarpiece of Antonello da Messina from three surviving fragments in Vienna. One of his most important achievements was the systematic use of X-rays as a tool for discovering not only the physical condition of a picture but also as a guide to the individual artist's creative process. His collaboration with the restorer Sebastian Isepp was crucial to this work, and in 1930 Wilde established at the Kunsthistorisches Museum what was probably the first museum X-ray laboratory for the examination of paintings in Europe. By 1938, more than 1000 X-rays of works in the collection had been made under his supervision.

The study of Michelangelo's art was, however, the most profound intellectual passion of Wilde's life, and his catalogue of the Michelangelo drawings in the British Museum his greatest achievement. Published in 1953, it was supplemented by Wilde's six lectures on Michelangelo (published posthumously in 1978). These lectures skilfully guide the reader, not only through the complexities of Neoplatonism and traditional Christian theology as they shape the subject matter of Michelangelo's major commissions, but also through the even more complex

processes by which Michelangelo evolved them. In 1952 Wilde also worked on the Michelangelo drawings in the Teylers Museum, Haarlem, but his catalogue of these has not survived. His impressive lectures on Venetian painting appeared in 1974. It was one of Wilde's fundamental principles to ask not only why a work of art was conceived in a particular way, but also to try to discover the extent to which its original location determined the artist's formal solution.

A tall, sparely built man, Wilde had a grave gentle manner that masked a rigorous intellect and an incorruptible spirit. Those who knew him during his years in England remember his strong jaw and aquiline features, kindly grey eyes behind gold-rimmed spectacles, his silver hair brushed back from a broad forehead. His lectures were delivered with a clear deep voice, in an English enriched by the slow soft drawl of Vienna. Students who may at first have felt in awe of him at tutorials quickly learned of his willingness to share knowledge and give wise counsel, although he could be crushingly ironic on occasion. Kenneth Clark rightly described him as the most beloved and influential teacher of art history of his time. Wilde died at his home, 131 Burbage Road, Dulwich, on 13 September 1970, within three months of his wife's death. They had adopted a son, whom they left behind in Vienna in 1939, and who died during the war. Wilde bequeathed a drawing by Rembrandt, his library, and all his manuscripts and notes to the Courtauld Institute.   DENNIS FARR

Sources M. Kitson, *The Times* (15 Sept 1970), 12 · M. Hirst, *Burlington Magazine*, 113 (1971), 155–7 · private information (2004) [Anthony Blunt; Paul Levi; Michael Hirst; Kenneth Clark; Count Antoine Seilern; Klára Garas; Jan Van Gelder; Countess Karla Lanchkoronska; home office, London] · biographical notes, c.1947, Courtauld Inst., Wilde file · K. Clark, 'Johannes Wilde', *Burlington Magazine*, 103 (1961), 205 · personal knowledge (2004) · D. Farr, *The Times* (21 Sept 1970), 10 · *CGPLA Eng. & Wales* (1970)
Archives Courtauld Inst., corresp. and papers · UCL, school of Slavonic and east European studies, corresp. and papers
Likenesses group photograph, c.1930, Courtauld Inst. · photographs, c.1950 · Ferenczy, bronze statue (as a young man)
Wealth at death £13,456: probate, 21 Dec 1970, *CGPLA Eng. & Wales*

Wilde, John (1590–1669), barrister and politician, was the son and heir of George Wilde of Kempsey, Worcestershire, serjeant-at-law, JP, and MP for Droitwich, and Frances, daughter of Sir Edmund Huddleston of Sawston, Cambridgeshire. Wilde matriculated at Balliol College, Oxford, on 18 January 1605. He graduated BA on 20 October 1607 (being incorporated at Cambridge, 1608) and MA on 4 July 1610. Admitted as a student of the Inner Temple about November 1602, he was called to the bar in 1612, elected a bencher in 1628, created a serjeant-at-law in 1636, and appointed under-steward of Kidderminster on 4 August of that year. From 1627 he was a legal counsel to the city of Worcester, and in March 1640 he became its recorder.

Wilde served Droitwich as an MP in every parliament from that of 1621 to the Short Parliament of 1640. He was an active member from the beginning, with particular interests in law reform, commerce, and foreign policy. In

1621 and again in 1624 he brought in a long list of grievances against novel and exorbitant fees, particularly in the court of exchequer, where he practised, and against the abuse of licences and writs. On 27 November 1621, during the debate on Lord Digby's unsuccessful mission to secure the return of the Palatinate, he launched a passionate attack against Spain, describing it as 'Hanniball *ad portas*', and concluding, 'Let this Carthage be destroyed'. Wilde went so far as to declare King James I 'deluded' in his belief that Spain could be trusted as a diplomatic interlocutor, and the house shouted him down, perhaps less in dissent than to shield him from the consequences of his rash words.

By the parliament of 1626 Wilde had emerged as a leading figure in the House of Commons, speaking in critical debates and chairing committees. On 28 February he delivered a major speech on the mismanagement of the Spanish war, citing the refusal of 'the cordial counsel of Parliament' and warning of policy made 'by single counsel or private respects' (Bidwell and Jansson, 2.149). The latter was a clear allusion to the duke of Buckingham, whose impeachment on 'common fame' he supported later in the session. After a sombre address on 12 May calling for a remonstrance against the imprisonment of Sir John Eliot and Sir Dudley Digges in the Tower, it was the speaker who was cried down for breaking the long silence that followed. Wilde spoke less frequently in the parliament of 1628, but he stoutly defended habeas corpus and supported the bill to confirm the subject's ancient liberties.

Wilde finally secured the county seat for Worcestershire in the Long Parliament on 21 October 1640 when he defeated a royalist opponent, Sir Thomas Littleton. His parliamentary experience and legal expertise pushed him rapidly to the fore. He was appointed chairman of the impeachment committee against the thirteen bishops involved in promulgating the canons of 1640, and on 3 August 1641 he made its report to the House of Lords. In April he staunchly supported the bill of attainder against the earl of Strafford. In December he was appointed to chair the committee investigating the alleged army plot, and on 6 January 1642 he was named to head the committee appointed to consider measures for the security of the kingdom and the City of London in the wake of the attempted arrest of the five members. Later in the month he conducted the impeachment hearings against the attorney-general, Sir Edward Herbert. Along with Bulstrode Whitelocke, Wilde frequently during this time chaired the house when it went into committee. He shepherded the bill to raise £400,000 for the defence of Ireland and the kingdom through to passage on 11 March 1642. On 18 March the house recommended him for appointment as a deputy lieutenant in Worcestershire, and in June, after being granted permission to buy arms formerly belonging to the recusant Lord Windsor for his own use and that of his county, he subscribed two horses and £1000 for the parliamentary cause.

Throughout the months that preceded the outbreak of the civil war, Wilde was among the most active figures in the house. In addition to the impeachment of Herbert, he undertook those of Sir Thomas Gardiner, recorder of London, and the lord mayor, Sir Richard Gurney, as well as prosecuting George Benion and John Weld, high sheriff of Hampshire. In June he was prominently involved in securing ordinance for parliament and mustering the livery companies, as well as in preparing the charges to the deputy lieutenants of Lancashire and Warwickshire. Always one of the more godly members of the house, he chaired the committee to establish the Westminster assembly, in which he was to serve as a lay member, and was appointed to draw up bills to confine and disarm recusants, to employ fines collected from them for the Irish war, and to provide for raising their children in the protestant faith. (Yet neighbourliness was important to him as well; he stoutly defended a Catholic gentry family in Warwickshire in December 1640.)

A majority of the Worcestershire gentry declared for the king as the summer began, leading to a hasty intervention by Wilde and his fellow knight for the shire, Humphrey Salway. They headed off a muster that had been fixed for the quarter sessions on 13 July, and instigated a petition to the justices to execute the militia ordinance, as well as one by the freeholders in support of parliament. Their efforts were unavailing, however, and on 12 August the county mustered 'for the king's safety and honour' outside Worcester.

In February 1643 parliament nominated Wilde as chief baron of the exchequer as part of its proposals to the king for an accommodation. On 5 April a bill was introduced to recompense him, along with Sir William Strickland, for losses to his estate. Presumably his recovery was aided by his appointment as a sequestration commissioner for Worcestershire. As a member of the Westminster assembly he prosecuted Archbishop Laud with zeal, employing against him the same argument of constructive treason that he had supported in Strafford's attainder. On 19 June 1646 he was appointed an assize judge, in July he became recorder of Worcester, and on 12 October he became chief baron of the court of the exchequer. He left the house on 14 November to take up this post, receiving much acclaim for his services. On the bench Wilde remained a committed partisan. Clarendon called him an 'infamous judge' for presiding at the condemnation of Captain John Burley, who had tried to free Charles I from captivity in Newport, and for securing the exoneration of Charles's would-be assassin, Captain Edmund Rolfe. Toward Charles himself he remained implacable. He promoted petitions against further treaty with him in Somerset in March and September 1648, and on 10 October he joined Cornelius Holland and Thomas Hoyle in demanding justice against all delinquents 'without exception' in the House of Commons.

Like his fellow justices Wilde declined to serve on the high court of justice to try the king. He embraced the Commonwealth with alacrity, however, and served on its first two councils of state while continuing to preside over the court of the exchequer. On 17 March 1649 he delivered a 'gallant speech' on behalf of the new government at Exeter, though only seven of forty JPs attended it. When the mayor of Exeter threw the proclamation of the Commonwealth into the gutter, Wilde fined him £200. Wilde prospered during these years, allegedly trafficking in forged debentures for fee-farm rents. After leaving the council of state, he was appointed a militia commissioner for Worcestershire on 25 September 1651.

Wilde inherited a number of houses and other properties in Droitwich, and some thirty other buildings in Worcester and the surrounding shire. He profited perhaps even more handsomely from his legal practice, and was accused of peculation during the civil war and after. He married a coheir, Anne, daughter of Sir Thomas Harries, bt and serjeant-at-law, of Tong Castle, Shropshire; they had one daughter, also named Anne. Through Harries he was also related to William Pierrepont, who served with him in the Long Parliament.

Cromwell removed Wilde from the bench in October 1653 in favour of William Steele, who had served as Captain Burley's prosecutor. This dismissal in favour of a junior colleague was particularly galling, and he vainly enlisted the services of his old friend and colleague Whitelocke in seeking to win the protector's favour. Wilde retired to Worcestershire for the next several years, where he served as a JP and as a commissioner for raising the county assessment in 1656. In January 1659 he was returned for his old seat of Droitwich in Richard Cromwell's parliament, where he petitioned for the restoration of his former position and the payment of £1300 arrears in salary. He was granted his recompense, but was restored to the judicial circuit only with the return of the Long Parliament, in which he took his former place. On 17 January 1660 he was at last reinstated as chief baron, but was again replaced in May by Charles II, who appointed Sir Orlando Bridgeman in his place. Wilde's last service was to advise the Convention Parliament in smoothing the transition to the Restoration. He was absolved by the Act of Indemnity and retired to his house in Hampstead, Middlesex, where he died in 1669. Wilde was buried on the estate of his son-in-law, Charles West, Lord De La Warr, at Wherewell, Hampshire.

Wilde's greatest eminence was as chief baron of the exchequer, and the gain, loss, recovery, and final surrender of this position preoccupied him for the last seventeen years of his career. His larger historical importance may lie in the role he played in the events of the civil war. Wilde was in the vanguard of those who affirmed parliament's assumption of sovereign powers in an emergency, for example its right to raise military forces and to execute the great seal on its own authority. In the aftermath of the attempt on the five members, he spoke of the king as having laid hands on 'the horn of the altar', a phrase which, as Conrad Russell notes, had been previously used to describe the royal sovereignty. Although he cannot be described as a parliamentary legitimist in the manner of William Prynne, his unwavering support of parliament's

claims to authority in 1642–3, and the legal prestige he brought to them, made him a central figure at the beginning of the civil war.   ROBERT ZALLER

Sources W. B. Bidwell and M. Jansson, eds., *Proceedings in parliament, 1626*, 4 vols. (1991–6) · A. Steele Young and V. F. Snow, eds., *The private journals of the Long Parliament*, 2–3 (1987–92) · A. Fletcher, *The outbreak of the English civil war*, rev. edn (1985) · S. R. Gardiner, *History of the Commonwealth and protectorate, 1649–1656*, new edn, 4 vols. (1903) · Greaves & Zaller, *BDBR* · Clarendon, *Hist. rebellion* · R. C. Johnson and others, eds., *Proceedings in parliament, 1628*, 6 vols. (1977–83) · Keeler, *Long Parliament* · W. Notestein, F. H. Relf, and H. Simpson, eds., *Commons debates, 1621*, 7 vols. (1935) · C. Russell, *The fall of the British monarchies, 1637–1642* (1991) · *DNB* · W. R. Williams, *The parliamentary history of the county of Worcester* (privately printed, Hereford, 1897)

Wilde, Oscar Fingal O'Flahertie Wills (1854–1900), writer, was born on 16 October 1854 at 21 Westland Row, Dublin, the second of the three children of William Robert Wills *Wilde (1815–1876), surgeon, and his wife, Jane Francesca Agnes *Wilde, *née* Elgee (1821–1896), writer and Irish nationalist, daughter of Charles Elgee (1783–1824), solicitor, and his wife, Sarah Kingsbury (*d.* 1851), whose sister Henrietta married the Revd Charles Robert Maturin (1780–1824), author of *Melmoth the Wanderer* (1820). Wilde, his father, and his elder brother, William Charles Kingsbury (1852–1899), afterwards added the name Wills as a forename, asserting kinship to William Gorman Wills, a playwright famous after Henry Irving's title-role performance of his *Charles I* (1872). Wills was the son of the Revd James Wills (1790–1868), poet and man of letters, whose *The Universe* (1821) was wrongly attributed to his friend Maturin, thus symbolizing linkage between the Wilde and Elgee families.

Boyhood and education, 1854–1874 Wilde's immediate family was more clerical than any of his fellow writers' of the Irish Renaissance: in addition to Maturin, two paternal uncles proper and one by marriage, a maternal uncle, and maternal grandfather were ordained in the (established) Church of Ireland. These and some of their lay relatives and friends participated in the Romantic flowering of Irish evangelicalism (1815–45) which sought to convert the Irish Catholic masses where predecessor protestant episcopalians were content to subordinate them. All the major Irish Renaissance writers of protestant origin showed some evangelical inheritance, substituting cultural for spiritual leadership: Wilde, Shaw, Yeats, Synge, O'Casey. All retained the self-confidence and authoritarianism of Irish protestant evangels. Wilde's Iokanaan in *Salomé* (1893) and Canon Chasuble in *The Importance of being Earnest* (1895) reflect that family clerical background, as do Wilde's 'Poems in Prose'.

Wilde was baptized by his father's brother Ralph in St Mark's Church, Dublin, on 26 April 1855. Five or six years later he was baptized into the Roman Catholic church, at his mother's instance, by the Revd L. C. Prideaux Fox (1820–1905), chaplain to the juvenile reformatory at Glencree, co. Wicklow, where the family were on holiday. Wilde violated no Irish protestant taboo as great as that broken by his mother for him in thus perverting him (as

Oscar Fingal O'Flahertie Wills Wilde (1854–1900), by Elliott & Fry, 1881

her relatives would have termed it). During the great Irish famine (1845–52) William Wilde had directed the census from local medical reports giving him unique mastery of famine mortality and his folklore researches showed its cultural toll, while Jane Elgee as poet and polemicist on the Dublin *Nation* declared that the million-odd victims owed their fate to her fellow protestant landlords. Wilde's dialogue between Death and Avarice in 'The Young King' (*Lady's Pictorial*, Christmas 1888) echoes her indictment while his *Ballad of Reading Gaol* (1898) has recollections of her poem 'The Famine Year'. He would have understood the symbolism of her consecration of her sons to the church whose children had died in such horror and such numbers. He reaffirmed her defence of the Irish revolutionaries of 1848 when lecturing in San Francisco in 1882. Filial devotion made him a rebel, with some uncertainty as to his cause.

Wilde's Irish-speaking father took his family on vacations to Galway in quest of folklore, later written up by his widow: Wilde himself retained enough Irish to sing abstruse Gaelic lullabies to his children. Wilde would also draw on his parents' mastery of ghost, curse, and fairy lore to inspire his first prose fiction, 'The Canterville Ghost' and 'Lord Arthur Savile's Crime' (*Court and Society Review*, Feb–March and May 1887), and *The Happy Prince and other Tales* (1888). The wish of human vanity whose fulfilment brings ultimate damnation, characteristic in Gaelic story-telling, dominates Wilde's *The Picture of Dorian Gray*

(1890, 1891). Wilde would duly win his greatest social success as oral narrator. His parents' choice of Gaelic heroic names for him (including what may have been a claim of descent from the 'wild' O'Flaherties, memorable threats to English settlers) heightened his alienation. Fenian legend supposedly survived in the bard Ossian, son of the Odysseus-like contriver Fingal, and father of the Achilles-like hero Oscar: Wilde fulfilled all three roles in his life. But Fenian names sounded ominous in Irish protestant ears after 1858, and Wilde may have suffered from it as a boarder at Portora Royal School, Enniskillen, co. Tyrone, a bastion of English imperial culture where Ireland was virtually obliterated from formal educational allusion. Wilde seems to have detested his time there (1864–71), although winning scripture prizes in 1869 and 1870. But it taught him how to conceal the Irish identity he had inherited.

On 23 February 1867 Wilde was told that his little sister Isola Francesca (*b.* 1857) had just died. He mourned her unconsolably, memorialized her ten years later in the poem 'Requiescat' (later anthologized by Yeats), carried a lock of her hair as best he could until his death, and haunted his literary work with images of girls unknowing of their incipient womanhood, for example in *Vera* (1880, 1882), 'The Canterville Ghost', 'The Birthday of the Infanta' (*Paris Illustré*, 30 March 1889), *The Picture of Dorian Gray*, each of his four great comedies, and *Salomé*, the keynote always innocence expressed in extreme terms, whether of courage, kindness, or cruelty. His earliest surviving letter (to his mother, 5 September 1868) shows his hunger at Portora for home and its culture, asking for the current number of James Godkin's *National Review*, then an outlet for her patriotic verse, and seeking news of her poems' possible republication (subsequently realized) by the Glasgow Irish nationalist firm Cameron and Ferguson. From Portora he won a scholarship to Trinity College, Dublin, in 1871.

Wilde's mother by now held a literary salon at 1 Merrion Square, Dublin, the Wilde family home from 1855, with visitors such as the poets Aubrey de Vere and Samuel Ferguson, the great peasant story-teller William Carleton, and the Dublin historian John Gilbert. At Trinity, Wilde's chief mentors were the classicists John Pentland Mahaffy and Robert Yelverton Tyrrell. Mahaffy proved a stimulating challenge in his witty contempt for Roman Catholicism, Irish nationalism, democracy, liberalism, socialism, and Gaelicism, on none of which he influenced Wilde: but both men helped make him a great Greek scholar. He won a foundation scholarship in 1873 and the Berkeley gold medal for Greek in 1874. Mahaffy germinated Wilde's first great dramatic character, Prince Paul Maraloffski, the tsar's premier in *Vera*, cruel, treacherous, and endlessly amusing. Wilde's juvenile cult of Shelley weathered the editorial austerity exuded by Edward Dowden from Trinity's chair of English literature. Wilde was then too shy for much student friendship but activity in college societies threw him together with Edward Carson.

Poet and intellectual in Oxford, 1874–1879 In June 1874 Wilde won a demyship in classics to Magdalen College,

Oxford, where he studied until 1879, having graduated BA in November 1878 with a double first in classical moderations and *literae humaniores* or greats (classics). Dublin probably educated him better than Oxford, but Oxford gave him a new world of expression and audience. In place of the Dublin wits and scholars vying to outsmart one another, he found intellectuals whose oratorical articulacy was declining as his own developed: Walter Horatio Pater and John Ruskin. In Wilde's last Dublin year Pater published his *Studies in the History of the Renaissance*. Its conclusion induced academic malice and was withdrawn by him in the second edition (1877), but Wilde was fascinated by its agenda: 'not the fruit of experience, but experience itself … success in life … [is] to burn always with this hard gemlike flame' (W. Pater, *Studies in the History of the Renaissance*, 1873, 210). Ruskin recruited Wilde into a group of social activists trying to build a road, and his anger at social cruelty found fallow soil in the boy from the famine-writers' house. Pater and Ruskin shaped Wilde's thought and its expression: they did not originate it. Initially he brought their ideas and his glosses into the market-place in lectures on aesthetics in the UK and the USA. Thereafter he embedded them, begirt in his own wit and charm, in fictions such as *The Happy Prince and other Tales* and *The Picture of Dorian Gray*. To Wilde ideas had to assert themselves dramatically: Yeats saw him as 'a man of action' (O'Sullivan), Chesterton as 'an Irish swashbuckler—a fighter' (*The Victorian Age in Literature*, 1913), and even Whistler's sneer 'Oscar has the courage of the opinions—of others' (*Truth*, 2 Jan 1890) realized it.

Wilde's first literary stage was Irish, finding outlets for his Oxonian perceptions in poetry and prose in the *Dublin University Magazine* (protestant evangelical), *Kottabos* (edited by Tyrrell), the *Irish Monthly* (Jesuit), and the Boston *Pilot* (Catholic and Irish nationalist). He celebrated the new temple of aesthetic rebellion, the Grosvenor Gallery (*Dublin University Magazine*, June 1877), and made a lengthy appeal for a starving Irish artist Henry O'Neill (1800–1880) in *Saunders's News-Letter* (29 December 1877), reprinted in his mother's old Dublin journal, *The Nation*. David (later the Rt Revd Abbot Sir David) Hunter-Blair (1853–1939), a close friend at Magdalen, was converted to Roman Catholicism in 1875, graduated in 1876, and entered the Benedictine order in 1878. Wilde's Catholic self was most notably expressed to him, although Wilde deferred a full Catholic identity until his deathbed (D. H. Blair, *In Victorian Days*, 1939). Wilde's Catholic consciousness permeates his stories, his prison and post-prison writings pursue its realization, and his poem *The Sphinx* (1894), begun at Oxford, shows warring attractions for him of paganism and Catholicism.

Wilde was happy at Oxford, apart from financial pressures and disciplinary measures following his protracted vacation in Greece in April 1877 with Mahaffy. Sir William Wilde's death on 19 April 1876 was a severe psychological blow, and left the family much poorer than they had expected. Wilde won Oxford's Newdigate prize for his poem 'Ravenna' in 1878 and declaimed it in the Sheldonian Theatre on 26 June. It was published as his first book.

Its laments for the sufferings of Dante and Byron proclaimed admiration and anticipation. His graduation was delayed by the requisite divinity test to satisfy requirements as to his Anglican status, which he deliberately failed until it was a laughing-stock. He then worked on 'Historical criticism among the Ancients', for the chancellor's English essay prize. No award was made. Posthumously published as *The Rise of Historical Criticism* (1909) it shows a remarkable grasp of historiography, a subject then in its infancy. It shows history as the foundation of his thought, with a judicious scepticism. It also stands on the cusp of Victorian confidence and its collapse. It sees history's motive as 'the discovery of the laws of the evolution of progress' (O. Wilde, *Complete Works*, introduced by M. Holland and others, [1994], 1207). Its author's doubts about whether history was progress grew to illuminate works as different as his *The Importance of being Earnest* and *The Ballad of Reading Gaol*.

Literary apprentice, dandy, and lecturer at large, 1879–1885
Wilde settled in London early in 1879; his mother and brother also moved there. The land war developing in Ireland made their few remaining properties uneconomic, but Oscar and his mother were none the less firm supporters of home rule and Charles Stewart Parnell. They still cut a wide swathe in society, assisted by her new salon. He won friendships with three great rivals in beauty and celebrity in and out of the theatre, Emily Charlotte Le Breton (Lillie) Langtry, Ellen Terry, and Sarah Bernhardt, writing poems to all three. He frequented the theatre and dressed in the aesthetic role, the better to evangelize beauty in modern life. The knee-breeches, the great bowties, and the ornate hats became famous; they were guyed and caricatured in *Punch* and bad plays and ultimately in the new Gilbert and Sullivan opera *Patience*, for whose opening on 23 April 1881 Wilde bought a 3 guinea box. He knew their work, and he intended not to protest against its satire on aestheticism, but to latch on to it. His physique, mannerisms, opportunism, salesmanship, female admirers, and even background of Irish landholding inspired George Grossmith as Bunthorne to put more and more of Wilde into the part. Wilde, tall, growing plumper, drawling, almost affecting affectation, developed his own performance on Bunthorne lines. Unlike Bunthorne, Wilde was not a fraud: he was fascinated by beauty from classicism to Keats, he correlated reform in dress and house decoration with beauty and respect in human relations, and he saw philistinism as tyranny in taste and politics. But he enjoyed self-mockery—from his difficulty at Oxford in living up to his blue china to his deathbed insistence that the wallpaper was killing him. His *Poems* were published by David Bogue at his own expense a few weeks after *Patience* opened, and like Bunthorne's they were often derivative (for which the Oxford Union, despicably, rejected his presentation copy). The book sold out four editions of 250 copies at half a guinea within the year. Amid much that had been tried, there was a little that rang true—'Requiescat', 'Magdalen Walks', 'Hélas!', 'Humanitad', respectively saluting Isola, Oxford, Christianity, paganism. Many of the poems have a value as

social documents—giving us incisive glimpses of the theatre, politics, cosmopolitanism, and parochialism of their time. Gladstone, Matthew Arnold, Swinburne, and Oscar Browning complimented him on all or some of the poems, but reviewers were rude. Individual verses acquired new meanings in the light of his later life, such as 'Roses and Rue—to L[illie] L[angtry]':

> But strange that I was not told
> That the brain can hold
> In a tiny ivory cell,
> God's heaven and hell.

Yet Wilde's tragic forebodings were constantly balanced by the growth of his comic genius. His tragedy *Vera* found its early drafts undermined by the hilarity induced by the evil Prince Paul's epigrams. Wilde had studied Polish and Russian literature under his mother's influence, but *Vera's* hidden Irish resonance, however smothered by the tsar's court and its pursuing nihilists, gave the hardbitten worldly wisdom on which the play turns. The play argued, wisely from either Irish or Russian contexts, that political intransigence ensures worse repression and worse revolution, and that political extremes induce one another's success at the expense of rational solutions. *Vera* was scheduled for a London production in December 1881 with Mrs Bernard Beere, *née* Fanny Mary Whitehead (1856–1915), a lifelong friend of Wilde, in the title role but it was cancelled since its nihilist assassination of the tsar might seem to reflect on its real-life counterpart the previous March, the murder of Tsar Alexander II.

Wilde contracted with the producer of *Patience*, Richard D'Oyly Carte, to lecture in the USA, whose people might otherwise fail to understand what the opera was satirizing. He sailed on the *Arizona* on 24 December 1881, landing in New York on 2 January 1882, delivering nearly 150 lectures throughout the USA and Canada, and receiving $6000 over the next twelve months. His lectures were entitled 'The decorative arts', 'The house beautiful', 'The English Renaissance', and 'Irish poets and poetry in the nineteenth century'. He improved in both brevity and force as he travelled from the east to the west coast. He sailed home on the *Bothnia* on 27 December 1882, docking in Liverpool on 6 January 1883. His was a theatre performance, and it furthered theatre links. His friendship with Dion Boucicault guided the early weeks of his tour and gave him contacts for *Vera*. Boucicault proved in his case as in those of all his major fellow playwrights of the Irish Renaissance the vital precursor in technique, craftsmanship, and wit. *Vera* was taken by Marie Prescott (1853–1923), who played the title role at the Union Square Theatre in New York from 20 August 1883 for a week (to hostile notices) with later touring in upper New York state. Wilde returned to the USA for the production (11 August to 11 September). Meanwhile Mary Anderson commissioned a play from him which he sent her from Paris in March 1883, a historical tragedy in Shakespearian verse, *The Duchess of Padua*. She rejected it. Her brother Joseph (1863–1943?) later married Gertrude, daughter of the American actor–manager Lawrence Barrett (1838–1891), who staged it in

New York from 21 January 1891 as *Guido Ferranti*, with considerable success cut short by Barrett's death in March.

Wilde lived in Paris from January to May 1883, meeting Hugo, Verlaine, Mallarmé, Edmond de Goncourt, Degas, Zola, Daudet, and his own first major biographer, Robert Harborough Sherard (Kennedy) (1861–1943), a Francophile revolutionary enthusiast whom he saw almost every day, and who brings him vividly to life in these days. Wilde then resumed his lectures, adding 'Impressions of America', and performing all over the British Isles. On 25 November 1883 he became engaged to Constance Mary Lloyd (1858–1898), a protestant Dublin girl, whom he had known since 1881. They married at St James's (Church of England) Church, Sussex Gardens, Paddington, London, on 29 May 1884. The honeymoon was spent in Paris, where Sherard had to cut short private confidences on the delights of the wedding night from an ecstatic Wilde. Wilde's sexual experiences to date seem to have been entirely heterosexual. The speed with which he took up homosexual activity after introduction to it some three years later by Robert *Ross is evidence in itself against any previous acquaintance with it; he astounded his later lover Lord Alfred *Douglas by stating that no such thing existed in Portora. Sherard later recalled Wilde's mention of syphilis at Oxford after experience with a female prostitute. Wilde thought himself cured of this (if it ever happened) although it is possible, as Ellmann speculates, that he later feared it lingered (the enchanted portrait of Dorian Gray seems to reveal syphilis among other physical evidence for the foul life lived by its perfectly preserved original). His marriage was sexually vigorous, with his son Cyril born on 5 June 1885, at the Wildes' new home in London, 16 Tite Street, Chelsea, while his son Vivian (later altered by its owner to Vyvyan) Oscar Beresford was born on 3 November 1886. The resultant strain on the Wildes' finances led them to abstain from sexual intercourse. Constance inherited £900 a year from her grandfather John Horatio Lloyd QC, but Wilde's earnings were entirely freelance and involved contributions to his mother's upkeep. Remembering his father's sexual infidelities (resulting in at least three bastards), Wilde recoiled from the thought of sexual solace with other women, and Ross seems to have exploited his sexual hunger and refusal to betray his heterosexual bed. Wilde never seems to have engaged in anal penetration either actively or passively.

The artist as critic, 1885–1891 From early in 1885 Wilde was a regular book critic for the *Pall Mall Gazette*. Under the pressure of rapid book reviewing Wilde began to make his comic genius serve his aesthetic evangelism in print, as he had been doing on the lecture platform and at the dinner table. Constance Wilde took up her husband's beliefs in dress reform, displayed rational dress to advantage, and spoke fluently on the subject. Wilde's own maturity in prose dates from his marriage. Significantly, his first timeless successes as a writer came in fields also cultivated by his wife: costume, and fairy-stories. His first major essay, 'Shakespeare and stage costume' (*Nineteenth Century*, May 1885) brought his prose comedy into its own. Later revised as 'The truth of masks' for inclusion in his essay collection

Intentions (1891), it was Wilde's first presentation of his masque of masks whose reader can never be sure how seriously to take the author—and neither, apparently, can the author. It coincided with his best verses before the *Ballad*: 'To my Wife with a Copy of my Poems', a miniature of egocentric tenderness, and 'The Harlot's House', which launched the decadence of the 1890s five years early.

'The Canterville Ghost' and 'Lord Arthur Savile's Crime' (spring 1887) used society comedy as skilfully as Irish folklore, foreshadowing Wilde's return to playwriting. Edmund Wilson in *Classics and Commercials* (1950) diagnosed 'a sense of damnation, a foreboding of tragic failure' (p. 336) even in Wilde's earlier work. Lord Arthur confronts horrors of possible social disgrace and criminal trial when a fortune-teller predicts he will commit a murder; the ghost enjoys haunting American purchasers of his family home by Irvingesque theatrical performances but suffers for his life's crimes in the purgatory from where the Isola-like Virginia finally rescues him. The two stories make excellent use of modern forms, the former originating in the first of Wilde's delicate and deadly dissections of English aristocratic social gatherings, while the latter arises hilariously from Wilde's shrewd witness to British–American social confrontations.

To raise an income Wilde became editor of Cassell's monthly magazine the *Lady's World*, which he promptly renamed the *Woman's World*, serving for its issues from November 1887 to October 1889. *The Happy Prince and other Tales* was published by Alfred Nutt in May 1888: its origin in Irish oral narrative is affirmed by his subsequently reciting the stories to his sons, weeping for 'The Selfish Giant' when the child befriended by the giant becomes the crucified Christ who takes his protector to paradise. Their permanent place in child affections refutes the vulgarism that Wilde's literary reputation arose from his legal notoriety. In all cases they are on the child's side, celebrating the courage and generosity of the poor and vulnerable, while their satire mocks the kind of pomposity and hypocrisy children can recognize. January 1889 saw publication of his 'Pen, pencil, and poison' (*Fortnightly Review*), an aesthetic 'study in green' of the forger, artist, and poisoner Thomas Griffiths Wainewright and of 'The decay of lying' (*Nineteenth Century*), an elegantly Platonic dialogue supposedly denouncing the renunciation of invention by modern story-tellers while actually dissecting them in a succession of hilarious but profound epigrams. The Wainewright essay startlingly reveals Wilde's criminologist credentials long before his acquisition of practical experience of prison. Forgery also dominated 'The portrait of Mr W. H.', whose first draft in *Blackwood's Edinburgh Magazine* (July 1889) Wilde expanded to book length. It was not returned by its intended publisher, John Lane, when Wilde's trials put paid to its publication (realized in a limited New York edition in 1921 and a London commercial publication in 1958). A painting is forged to provide evidence for the existence of a boy actor as recipient of Shakespeare's sonnets and creator of his heroines: does the forgery impair the thesis or provide proof of its perpetrator's conviction, all the more when its discovery

induces suicide? 'No man dies for what he knows to be true. Men die for what they want to be true, for what some terror in their hearts tells them is not true' (O. Wilde, *Complete Works*, 349). The story is gratifyingly post-modern in its doubts about scholarly certainties: the zealot loses faith having converted his target. It also points out that the place to look for a male lover for Shakespeare must initially be in his own profession, and the sonnets might be expected to have some relevance to the plays.

Wilde relinquished the *Woman's World*, much enlivened by his literary notes, and left book reviewing after a review-essay (*The Speaker*, 8 February 1890) on the fourth-century BC Chinese sage Chuang Tzŭ. He extolled the philosopher who saw perfection in ignoring oneself, divinity in ignoring action, and sagacity in ignoring reputation, silently marking the contrast from himself by thoughts on how disturbing Chuang Tzŭ would be at dinner parties (at which Wilde himself was now London's leading lion). His valedictory to criticism (*Nineteenth Century*, July and September 1890) was reprinted in *Intentions* as 'The critic as artist', where he transformed remunerative hackwork into a creative creed. The critic's response to the work of art under review should be to make another. This was set out in a gorgeous profusion of epigram and paradox, ostentation and learning, frivolity and wisdom, but few critics reached deeper into the heart of their business than Wilde's evangel.

In July 1890 *Lippincott's Magazine* published Wilde's first version of *The Picture of Dorian Gray*. His critic's interest in Stevenson's *Dr Jekyll and Mr Hyde* ('reads dangerously like an experiment out of the *Lancet*': 'Decay of lying') induced the idea of age and its spiritual effects expressing themselves in the portrait whose model walks free of either. 'The decay of lying' had nature imitating art: in *Dorian Gray* nature imitates art with—literally—a vengeance, when in knifing the portrait Dorian kills himself and becomes the final horror to which its successive changes have evolved. Dorian Gray himself became a name as immortal as those of Jekyll and Hyde, his picture in the attic baring his self-obsessed soul as vital a symbol as the 'madwoman in the attic', the discarded first wife established in Charlotte Brontë's *Jane Eyre* (1847). The story itself, so far from vindicating art for art's sake, asks what it profiteth a man to gain the whole world, and suffer the loss of his own soul. His sexual sins, so far as we know them, are firmly heterosexual. He attracts two men, the artist Basil Hallward who has fallen in love with his appearance, and Lord Henry Wotton, whose scruples might be philosophically less nice than Hallward's but who never seems to go beyond repainting Dorian in epigrams. The fervent expression of Hallward's love (arguably the finest sentiment in the story) unleashed the venom of Wilde's Oxford classicist contemporary Samuel Henry Jeyes (1857–1911), who in the *St James's Gazette* (20 June 1890) demanded that the book be burnt and hinted that its author or publisher were liable to prosecution in terms which suggested more familiarity with homosexuality than his vehemence warranted; comparably, Charles Whibley in the *Scots Observer* accused Wilde of writing for 'none but outlawed noblemen and perverted telegraph boys'. Wilde revised it, toning down a few passages for book publication, adding six new chapters to the book and about nineteen years to the action. His preface disposed of his critics in an epigram sequence. Technically the amendments are improvements. Wilde, contrary to what he liked to say, was a very hard worker when it came to revising his writings, and from *Vera* onwards could be ruthless in what he removed. Despite, or possibly because, W. H. Smith refused to stock it ('filthy' was his description), it was the most famous novel of its time. On its appearance in April 1891, the critics were quieter, but still confused, apart from Pater, who reviewed it enthusiastically for *The Bookman* (November 1891).

Politics and the theatre: the years of mastery, 1891–1895 Wilde moved more fully into social criticism with his 'The soul of man under socialism' (*Fortnightly Review*, February 1891), perhaps the most memorable and certainly the most aesthetic statement of anarchist theory in the English language. In 1891 Wilde was hard at work on a play, and also published *Intentions* and *Lord Arthur Savile's Crime and other Stories*. In November came *A House of Pomegranates*—more ornate fairy-stories than the *Happy Prince* collection and more directly socialist: the happy prince wanted to use his adornments to relieve suffering but the young king discovers his to be the cause of it. The general effect is more tragic, the infanta's dwarf dying of grief when he realizes she likes him only as an object of ridicule for his ugliness, the fisherman and his soul corrupted in their separation, the star-child's expiation for his snobbery and cruelty ending in his life as ruler cut short and his successor ruling evilly. The elegiac, doom-laden note accords with the new spirit of *fin de siècle* which a character in *Dorian Gray* had equated with *fin du globe*.

Lady Windermere's Fan opened under George Alexander's direction and lead male performance at the St James's Theatre, London, on 20 February 1892. It anticipates Ibsen's *A Doll's House* twenty years after. Ibsen was the crucial influence that turned Wilde from a melodramatist into a dramatist: Wilde was as much his pupil as was Shaw, with whom he linked himself as playwright. Mrs Erlynne, like Ibsen's Nora, has left her husband and offspring and returns to blackmail Lord Windermere, her son-in-law, on the threat of self-disclosure to her daughter who believes her to have died a loving wife. Lady Windermere, led by suspicion that her husband's payments to Mrs Erlynne are recompense to his mistress, leaves her home to elope with Lord Darlington, from which decision Mrs Erlynne rescues her at further cost to her own reputation. Mrs Erlynne is a figure of potential tragedy, but she is also much the wittiest person in the play and ultimately deals herself a happy ending with an infectious cynicism. She endangers her own future to save her daughter from the brittle, loveless life into which her bid for freedom had enmeshed her. The play was revolutionary in its mingling of the vocabulary of comedy, the potential of tragedy, and the insistence on realism.

Herbert Beerbohm Tree was actor–manager for Wilde's next play, *A Woman of No Importance*, after *Lady Windermere's Fan* had run to delighted audiences and enraged critics (save for the Ibsenite William Archer) in London and on tour through almost all of 1892. The title role for Tree's production described an unmarried mother doing exactly what Mrs Erlynne denied modern life would permit: to become a dowdy, having been victimized by a dandy. Mrs Bernard Beere played Mrs Arbuthnot while Tree played Lord Illingworth, the treacherous dandy, who encounters his former mistress and their son twenty years after, while he is conducting a flirtation with Mrs Allonby (played by Mrs Tree), who recalls Mrs Erlynne's conversation without her complication. Tree had more in common with Wilde than any other actor and thus may have been more alive to the dangers of his more liberated epigrams, some of which were deleted, notably when Tree sidetracked a seventeen-year-old blackmailer named Alfred Wood, for which Wilde gratefully gave Mrs Allonby the entrance line 'The trees are wonderful, Lady Hunstanton. But I think that is rather the drawback of the country. In the country there are so many trees one can't see the temptations', that is, one could not see the Wood for the Trees. Only the first four words remained in the text, which may be all Wilde intended to happen: uttered by Mrs Tree, they must have raised a fine laugh from the regular customers at the Haymarket Theatre, where the play opened on 19 April 1893, running until 16 August. For all of Wilde's cult of the dandy, Illingworth is defeated and discredited at the play's end, at the hands of the somewhat absurd American puritan girl who makes a man of Illingworth's bastard. Wilde assigned his savage indictments of modern society to her, answered by the elegant English society ladies in the finest feline form; but at the play's end they are hollow and she is victrix. William Archer was once again its sole defender.

In late 1891 Wilde wrote *Salomé*, partly in Paris. Sarah Bernhardt had begun rehearsals of it at the Palace Theatre in London by June 1892 but the play was banned from performance by the lord chamberlain for infringing protestant Reformation legislation against medieval miracle or otherwise religious plays. The play's censor, Edward Frederick Smyth Pigott (1824–1895), was in no doubt that however pagan Wilde might currently be feeling, he was too Catholic to be staged. That the play was in French no doubt made matters worse: that was half-way to Latin. It is apparently untranslatable into English: various attempts were made by Lord Alfred Douglas, Aubrey Beardsley, Wilde himself revising Douglas, Wilde's son Vyvyan Holland, Jon Pope, Steven Berkoff, and others, but it demands reading and performance in French to make its impact. Beardsley illustrated the French text in a series of drawings proclaiming the decadence of the day. Both Wilde and Beardsley privately belittled one another's work for the published play (February 1893) but their impact was mutually inspirational. They seem in accord as to Herodias and Herod: her no longer irresistible voluptuosity, his predatory, questing eyes. Beardsley's sophisticated Salomé in *toilette* and dance is far removed from Wilde's idea of terrifying innocence enraged, and even befouled, by the prophet obsessed by the omnipresence of guilt (as Émile Vernadakis has established). Yet Beardsley's hungry devourer of Iokanaan and vampirical ascendant with his head seems the vital stimulus for Richard Strauss in creating his opera in 1905, and Beardsley's experienced Salomé rather than Wilde's virgin child dominated most subsequent performances of the play. It was Beardsley more than Wilde who followed the tradition of Flaubert and Maeterlinck on the theme. Wilde's Salomé is a human being, as opposed to a sex object in (or out of) seven veils. Bernhardt toyed with the idea of a Paris production, but dropped it when Wilde's scandal overtook him. *Salomé* was first produced on 11 February 1896 by Aurélien Marie Lugné-Poe (1869–1940), who played Herod to Lina Munte's Salomé, for the Théatre de l'Œuvre in Paris. News of it rescued the imprisoned Wilde from utter despair.

From October 1893 Wilde worked on *An Ideal Husband*, whose highly political plot he elaborated from an anecdote told by Frank Harris. Sir Robert Chiltern, saved by his friend Lord Goring from blackmail over his sale of a cabinet secret in the remote past, leaps at the first chance of forbidding Goring's marriage to his sister because Goring had entertained the lady from whom he obtained the document. Although now known to Goring as thief and traitor, Chiltern once secure becomes the House of Commons moralist, reclaiming moral superiority regardless—or perhaps mindful—of what Goring must think of him. Shaw, now the *Saturday Review* theatre critic, hailed Wilde as 'our only thorough playwright. He plays with everything: with wit, with philosophy, with drama, with actors and audience, with the whole theatre' (12 Jan 1895). Lewis Waller played Chiltern in his production at the Haymarket, with Julia Neilson as his wife: they opened on 3 January 1895. Charles Brookfield (playing Goring's valet, Phipps), helped gather evidence that might implicate Wilde in recently criminalized homosexual relations. Wilde had found the theatre a haven where homosexuality found acknowledgement if not acceptance. It also meant that enemies could discover more, quicker.

Wilde's last play, *The Importance of being Earnest*, opened at the St James's on 14 February 1895 with George Alexander as John Worthing and Allan Aynesworth (E. Abbot-Anderson; 1865–1959) as Algernon Moncreiff. Although hurriedly reduced from four acts to three because of Alexander's insistence on a curtain-raiser, it won critical unanimity of applause (save for Shaw) and the twentieth century in general, when permitted to view it, hailed it as the greatest English comedy of all time. Wilde's first two comedies had been published in November 1893 and October 1894 respectively, but their successors had to await his release, and *The Importance of being Earnest* was published by Leonard Smithers in February 1899, by which time Wilde's sufferings had caused him to lose all his regard for the play, to which he gave little annotation and no hint of the original four-act text, which did not appear until 1956. Wilde's notes for *An Ideal Husband*, published by Smithers in July 1899, included likening of its characters to models for appropriate painters, to culminate in the blackmailer

Mrs Cheveley: 'A work of art, on the whole, but showing the influence of rather too many schools'. These notes were the last creative work Wilde ever wrote.

Imprisonment and *De Profundis*, 1895–1897 On 28 February 1895 Wilde received a card at his club, the Albemarle, ten days after it had been left by John Sholto Douglas, eighth marquess of Queensberry, accusing Wilde of being 'ponce and somdomite' or of 'posing as somdomite'. Wilde took out a warrant against him for criminal libel. Queensberry entered a plea of justification on 30 March. Having belatedly assembled evidence found for Queensberry by very recent recruits, it declared Wilde to have committed a number of sexual acts with male persons at dates and places named. None was evidence of sodomy, nor was Wilde ever charged with it. Queensberry's trial at the central criminal court, Old Bailey, on 3–5 April before Mr Justice Richard Henn Collins ended in Wilde's attempt to withdraw the prosecution after Queensberry's counsel, Edward Carson QC, MP, sustained brilliant repartee from Wilde in the witness-box on questions about immorality in his works and then crushed Wilde with questions on his relations to male youths whose lower-class background was much stressed. Collins demanded that Queensberry be found not guilty and Queensberry's solicitors sent the plea of justification and its supporting evidence to the public prosecutor, on which Wilde was arrested at 6.10 p.m. and lodged in Holloway prison. Next day, 6 April, Wilde was charged with offences under the Criminal Law Amendment Act (1885), section XI together with Alfred Taylor, owner of a male brothel Wilde had used, and who went to penal servitude rather than inform against Wilde. Bail was refused. Of ten alleged sexual partners Queensberry's plea had named, five were omitted from the indictment at Wilde's first trial (26 April – 1 May) before Mr Justice Arthur Charles (1839–1921), where a sixth was dismissed for perjury, a seventh denied any impropriety, and an eighth required a verdict of not guilty during Wilde's second trial. The trial under Charles ended in jury disagreement after four hours. Wilde was granted bail, for £5000; his case was separated from Taylor's on 20 May. Taylor was found guilty on 21 May; Wilde was tried on 22–25 May, and found guilty on 25 May. Both prisoners were sentenced by Mr Justice Alfred Wills to two years' penal servitude with hard labour. The two known persons with whom Wilde was found guilty of gross indecency were male prostitutes, one of them the blackmailer Wood. Wilde was also found guilty on two counts charging gross indecency with a person unknown on two separate occasions in the Savoy Hotel. These may in fact have related to acts committed by Queensberry's son, Lord Alfred Douglas, who had also been Wood's lover. But Wilde had had sexual relations in 1893–4 with the remaining prostitute, Charles Parker (now a soldier), on which he was found guilty on four counts.

Far more severe than any court verdict was the utter social destruction of Wilde. His blameless, and somewhat neglected, family were utterly innocent sufferers. His entertainment of homosexual friends in hotels and abroad had sometimes coincided with economic privation and credit embarrassment for his wife and children. The house at 16 Tite Street was given over to the bailiffs at Queensberry's demand (non-payment of costs awarded him after his trial), and Wilde's family possessions, library, art collection, autographed gifts, and even children's toys including a rabbit hutch were put up for auction with a view to selling as much as possible for as little as possible. Constance Wilde took the children, Cyril and Vivian, to her brother Otho Holland Lloyd (1856–1943) in Switzerland. She decided against divorcing Wilde, whom she visited in prison in September 1895 and February 1896, but changed her children's and her own surname to Holland. She was dying from spinal injury caused by a fall in Tite Street.

Wilde's first prison month was in Pentonville, where R. B. Haldane (on a Home Office committee under Herbert Gladstone investigating prison conditions) saw him on 12 June 1895. Haldane managed to get books for Wilde (to be read through the prison library). Wilde was transferred to Wandsworth (from 4 July to 20 November) before being sent to the much smaller Reading gaol (administered by the Berkshire authorities). Robert Sherard visited Wilde first in Wandsworth where he supported Constance Wilde's anxiety that he repudiate his homosexual friends. But when Wilde was taken to the bankruptcy court in Carey Street for his first hearing at Queensberry's suit on 24 September 1895, Robert Ross (now returned after a self-protecting flight to the continent during the Wilde trials) waited in a corridor to raise his hat, which moved the friendless convict to the heart. Arthur Clifton (1862–1932), a solicitor friend of both, saw Wilde during these hearings (resumed on 12 November when Wilde was declared bankrupt), and Ross's friend William More Adey (1858–1942) became a consultant, visiting Wilde on 30 November ten days after Wilde's horrific experience in being transferred to Reading when he was subjected to half an hour of mobbing, including being spat upon, although handcuffed and guarded, while waiting for a change of trains. Ross now became Wilde's most constant prison visitor, turning Wilde's desire to repudiate his former lifestyle into a rejection of the lover who had supplanted Ross and who for fear of indictment was still on the continent, Lord Alfred Douglas, to whom the letter posthumously named *De Profundis*, was written between December 1896 and March 1897.

Wilde's prison experience was physically and psychologically destructive, particularly between November and July when the Reading governor was Lieutenant-Colonel Henry Bevan Isaacson (1842–1915): not a Jew, as commentators assumed. He had a kindlier successor, Major James Osmond Nelson (1859–1914), but Reading was dominated by its doctor, Oliver Calley Maurice JP (1838–1907). Governors came and went: Maurice was a permanent power-broker. Wilde's medical condition had become dangerous from a fall in Wandsworth which exacerbated middle-ear disease, from which he died five years later. Maurice dismissed any anxieties, and Wilde's petitions to the home secretary asking for release on medical grounds were

ignored on Maurice's advice. As the son of one of the world's greatest aurists, Wilde knew his ear condition was serious, and that Maurice's diagnosis was faulty. But when on release Wilde denounced existing prison conditions in the *Daily Chronicle* (28 May 1897) he highlighted other prisoners in mortal danger from Maurice ('It is a horrible duel between himself and the doctor. The doctor is fighting for a theory. The man is fighting for his life. I am anxious that the man should win') as well as children and other tragic victims of the system.

This transition was made possible by Wilde's spiritual regeneration, which worked its way out in *De Profundis*. It did not deny his own culpability for the wreck of his and his family's lives, but it made his obsession with Douglas the leading count in his own self-indictment. It attacked Douglas for hatred of his father, acknowledged his love for Wilde, but saw that love, like Wilde himself, enslaved in the work of hate. Ross was held up as a model of friendship and stimulus. Yet the power and profundity of *De Profundis* itself asserted Douglas's far more cataclysmic inspirational effect. Nor was the contrast accurate in all respects. Both Ross and Douglas were demanding, self-centred, and indiscreet, and Wilde's relationship to both of them was more that of an indulgent but exploited uncle than of the physical lover he seems to have been for a relatively brief time in each case. Both Ross and Douglas were homosexual liberationists, Ross more constructively, Douglas more flamboyantly: *De Profundis* justly denounced the egotism of Douglas in using Wilde's imprisonment to publicize the launch of his own book of verse, but Douglas also tried to show the utter injustice of Wilde's fate in particular and the punitive legislation in general. But *De Profundis* is also an extraordinary record of a man hurled from the pinnacle of literary success to the uttermost public degradation, and of the spiritual means by which he turned away from despair. Wilde fixed his mind on Christ, first as a person, then (in *The Ballad of Reading Gaol*) as a redeeming god. The sublime elimination of himself in the thought of the suffering of his fellow prisoners, in his time and in all time, permeates the letters to the *Daily Chronicle* and the *Ballad*, all written after his release. *De Profundis* is less reflective of this than the proof of how it was happening. Its universal quality is more evident if it is read as a man addressing himself, the Douglas of the letter being Wilde as well as Douglas.

The elimination of self had its apogee in *The Ballad of Reading Gaol* which Wilde began to write at the end of May, the month in which he was released, completing it in October, and seeing it published by Smithers in February 1898, initially signed C. 3. 3. Its theme was the man hanged in Reading while Wilde was there, Charles Thomas Wooldridge (1866–1897), trooper of the Royal Horse Guards, who had murdered his wife in what today seems a clear attack of mental illness. With high dramatic sense Wilde turned the sufferings of all the other convicts into a subordinate but supportive chorus. The poem made no denial of guilt, although its hanged prisoner ultimately suffered more than the rest, and embodied their agonies more intensely. The *Ballad* followed the advice of *De Profundis* to

Douglas, and sustained itself by love, ultimately the redeeming love of Christ, rather than hatred of custodians such as Maurice (though he figured prominently enough to worry the printers about a possible libel action). Hatred of the prison system and of the human oppression that created it animated the *Ballad*: but the poem confronted that cruelty with the love of Christ against which it offended. Chesterton would see the *Ballad* as 'a cry for common justice and brotherhood very much deeper, more democratic' than the most radical protest of the age (G. K. Chesterton, *Victorian Age in Literature* [1913], 227).

Wilde was released from Reading on 18 May, being handed *De Profundis* by Nelson, and was transferred for a night to Pentonville, where he was met by Adey. He travelled to Dieppe, where he was met on 20 May by Ross. For some months Wilde called himself Sebastian Melmoth (*d.* 288?), after the Christian martyr under Diocletian—transfixed by arrows, whence a cult figure in homoerotic art—and the doomed hero of *Melmoth the Wanderer* (1820) by his mother's maternal uncle-in-law Charles Maturin, which had influenced *The Picture of Dorian Gray* and which Ross had re-edited in 1892. Wilde settled for a time in Berneval, near Dieppe, but left for Naples in September, having been reconciled with Douglas, who advised on final revisions and additions to the *Ballad*—Douglas was a poet, after all. They did not, apparently, discuss *De Profundis*, which Wilde evidently thought Douglas had read (Ross was to have sent it to him after having had it typed: if Douglas ever got it, or any part of it, he destroyed that text without reading much of it). The withdrawal of their incomes by Wilde's wife and Douglas's mother ended their Naples Indian summer. Wilde returned to Paris in February and on 23 March 1898 the *Daily Chronicle* published his last public prose work, a second prison letter (signed as the *Ballad*'s author) intervening in the current debate on the Prisons Bill.

Apart from passing his plays for the press, Wilde's writing life was over. Constance had been very moved by the *Ballad* and by both prison letters, but she died on 7 April 1898. Wilde's life became a helpless drift from place to place, centring on Paris. From London, with limited resources and occasionally guilt-ridden impatience, Ross struggled to manage his survival. Wilde went to Rome and received the blessing of Leo XIII in April 1900. His medical condition became worse and he was rescued from dying in a Paris street by a former landlord, Jean Dupoirier, proprietor of the Hôtel d'Alsace, rue des Beaux-Arts, where he died on 30 November 1900. An Irish priest, Cuthbert Dunne, obtained by Robert Ross, had conditionally baptized him, and given him extreme unction and absolution, being satisfied that Wilde, although now speechless, understood and approved. Wilde was buried at Bagneux on 2 December 1900 by Ross, Douglas, Dunne, Dupoirier, and a few other friends. In 1909 his uncorrupted body was moved to Père Lachaise cemetery, Paris, with a monument by Jacob Epstein over the grave. Ross's ashes were placed in the grave at his request after his death in 1918.

Posthumous reputation Although still unmentionable in most circles at the time of his death, Wilde had an obituary in *The Times* and a notice in the *Dictionary of National Biography*. Sherard published a touching memoir, *Oscar Wilde: the Story of an Unhappy Friendship* (1902), followed by *The Life of Oscar Wilde* (1906) and *The Real Oscar Wilde* (1915). Ross issued less than half of *De Profundis* in 1905, shorn of any allusion to Douglas although occasionally addressing an unspecified friend identifiable with Ross. Douglas reviewed it favourably, and others proclaimed it a classic. Wilde's reputation soared from the depths, and Ross planned and brought out a comprehensive fourteen-volume edition of Wilde's known published writings with the aid of Christopher Sclater Millard in 1908, emended in 1909, followed by many republications in cheap editions by the publisher, Methuen. Millard under the name Stuart Mason produced an invaluable, if somewhat ragbag, *Bibliography of Oscar Wilde* (1914), abounding in instructive tangents; several other Mason volumes covered the *Dorian Gray* controversy (*Art and Morality*, 1907, 1912, reproducing the major reviews from Jeyes to Pater and the ensuing correspondence), and further bibliographical problems. Anonymously Millard issued an edition of the trial transcripts, *Oscar Wilde Three Times Tried* (1912). Ross, as Wilde's named literary executor, cleared the estate of bankruptcy in July 1906 and administered it for the sons of Wilde, both of whom served in the First World War, in which Cyril was killed (1915). Vyvyan Holland took over the estate after Ross's death in 1918. Wilde's vast sales were unaccompanied by critical assessment of much value: academic respectability, masquerading as integrity, dominated intellectual opinion to insist that Wilde would have been forgotten had it not been for the scandal. The First World War was made an excuse to argue that Wilde fostered a cult of national degeneracy which the Germans would exploit for blackmailing, morale, and other purposes, climaxing in the sensational and ludicrous trial *R. v. Billing* (1918). The British Isles alone pursued this thesis: Wilde was by now a major literary figure in Europe, North America, and ultimately Asia. His reputation in Latin American countries would follow, with significant influence on writers such as Jorge Luis Borges. Biographies of varying degrees of unreliability kept his story before the public, though significantly the two most substantial up to the Second World War were by a Frenchman, Léon Lemonnier (1931), and a Russian, Boris Brasol (1938). In 1946 Hesketh Pearson produced the best *Life of Oscar Wilde* to date, a collage of memoirs and memories by a former actor drawing on many personal recollections given him over thirty years. More impressionistic than scholarly, it remains a sparkling narrative, a fine introduction to the theatre world of Wilde, and a stimulating, sympathetic critique from the polarity of an English, agnostic, heterosexual tory.

Wilde's critical reputation in the British Isles came into its own when Rupert Hart-Davis published his authoritative edition of *The Letters of Oscar Wilde* (1962). It included the first reliable text of *De Profundis*, whose status as a letter to Douglas had become known when a Ross-inspired work, *Oscar Wilde: a Critical Study* (1912) by Arthur Ransome, led Douglas to sue for libel against implications of having betrayed Wilde. Douglas was then forced to listen in the witness-box to Wilde's laceration of him. This was read from the manuscript which Ross had given to the British Museum (now the British Library) in 1909 on condition of its remaining closed for fifty years; there, after being called in evidence in 1913, it remained. Douglas pursued a vendetta against Ross thereafter, denouncing Wilde in *R. v. Billing* but renewing affection in his *Oscar Wilde: a Summing-Up* (1941). Portions of *De Profundis* had been republished in the USA and as appended matter to Frank Harris's *Oscar Wilde: his Life and Confessions* (1916, 1918, 1938) whose vivid pages and largely invented conversations (Wilde's supposed reiteration of 'Frank' is one obvious inauthenticity) added their plenty to the inventions in circulation, complicated by some endorsement from Harris's one-time drama critic on the *Saturday Review*, Shaw, which allowed the book's publication in Britain for the first time in 1938. After Douglas's death Vyvyan Holland published the full text of *De Profundis* (1949) from a transcript copy, and it replaced the fragment of 1905 in most editions of Wilde's works. Only when Hart-Davis and his future wife, Ruth Simon, scrutinized the British Museum manuscript did it become clear that Ross had not had a true copy made, nor had he employed an accurate typist. Hart-Davis at last established the true text, and Wilde's life swam into full focus in his own narration from his Oxford days when the letters began.

Wilde still awaited a satisfactory biographer, and it seemed that in Richard Ellmann he had found him. Ellmann was a brilliant critic of Wilde's and his mother's protégé William Butler Yeats, and a definitive biographer of Wilde's posthumous scrutinizer, James Joyce. Ellmann pursued Wilde's life for several decades, but the onset of fatal illness obliged him to publish his (posthumous) biography in unrevised form. Ellmann had been anxious to let the multitude of divergent voices be heard on Wilde, and sought what now seems a post-modernist approach, in harmony with Wilde's exuberant denunciation of the tyranny of fact in 'The decay of lying' but without the distillation of possibility from probability in all cases which he would have wished. Nor was Ellmann able to incorporate his own final researches or those most recently communicated to him. He became preoccupied by what is now known to be a baseless thesis of Wilde suffering from continued syphilis. The result is a work of towering artistic insight, elegant prose, critical genius, but not the authoritative biography in all respects. Since Ellmann, his pupil Declan Kiberd has greatly advanced awareness of Wilde's Irish heritage in his books *Inventing Ireland* and *Irish Classics* and his student Jarlath Killeen has greatly advanced understanding of Wilde as a Catholic author in his doctoral dissertation (2001). Among many other academic studies may be singled out Émile Vernadakis *Les prétextes de Salomé* (3 vols., Paris, 1987), showing the origins of Wilde's French play in his English writing as well as in his French studies.

Visually Wilde has been before the public since 1936 when Robert Morley starred in the play *Oscar Wilde* by Leslie Stokes and Sewell Stokes (1936) in a version of which he starred in the eponymous film (1960). He was perhaps a little too remote, but he captured Wilde's dignity and, more unusually, his slightly pedagogic manner. Peter Finch in *The Trials of Oscar Wilde* gave a more orthodox version, stressing Wilde's self-possession and coolness under threat, if rather less of the artist. The classic realization will always be that in Mícheál Mac Liammóir's *The Importance of being Oscar* (1961), a work of genius, bringing together man, work, reputation, and above all performance, sometimes being Wilde, sometimes his creations from Herod to Lady Bracknell. The film starring Stephen Fry (1997) made for a more English Wilde but met with interest and appreciation, especially because the relaxation of censorship enabled more unrestrained depiction of aspects of Wilde's private life. A fine bust of Wilde by the sculptor Patrick O'Connor (1955) survives in the best private collection of Wildeana, that of Donald Hyde and Mary Hyde at Princeton. The best collection in the world is that at the William Andrews Clark Library of the University of California at Los Angeles.

The popular and critical successes of Wilde in the twentieth century interplayed significantly with the struggle for decriminalization and social acceptance of homosexuality. Homosexual or bisexual actors found their self-respect reaffirmed by direction or performance of Wilde's plays, obvious instances being John Gielgud's John Worthing in *The Importance of being Earnest* (1922, 1930, 1939, 1942, 1947), Michael Redgrave's in Anthony Asquith's film of that play (1952)—whose conquest of mass audiences owed more, however, to Edith Evans as Lady Bracknell and Margaret Rutherford as Miss Prism—and Mac Liammóir in Dublin Gate Theatre productions of Wilde including his dramatized *Dorian Gray* (1956) when he played Lord Henry Wotton. Mac Liammóir designed the bilingual marble plaque affixed to Wilde's birthplace at his birth centenary, and supported the London centenary commemoration, led by Sir Compton Mackenzie. Growing police persecution of homosexual offences met increasingly angry protest after 1954, as did the failure to implement the Wolfenden report's demand for decriminalization. Wilde, as the most conspicuous UK victim at the cost of many more possible works of genius, was a clear rallying point, and the widespread popular dissemination of his writings by Collins (1948), Penguin (1954), and others undoubtedly made converts otherwise unready to bestir themselves for such legal reform. The *Letters* and consequent critical re-evaluation in the UK strengthened such sentiment, and facilitated the achievement of substantial though not total removal of legal penalties for homosexual intimacies (by the Wilson government). Gay liberation in 1971 in the USA obtained rapid UK discipleship and the growth in academic study of sexuality necessarily made much of Wilde as a well-known and now well-recorded case whose literary achievement continued to pose its mysteries as well as its revelations. Gay bookshops in various cities in USA and UK frequently made use of his name; amateur plays about him and productions of his works became more and more numerous in theatre festivals led by Edinburgh Festival Fringe (annually in August); Ellmann's biography led the literary fare for general consumption, winning a mass audience for academic criticism on the highest level. Various Wilde societies and symposia continued to flourish, and to encourage both greater liberalism in public attitudes and greater promiscuity among devotees. As cultural hero and literary icon, Wilde beguiles scholars and fascinates the public at large; this ability shows no signs of abating in the twenty-first century. OWEN DUDLEY EDWARDS

Sources R. H. Sherard, Oscar Wilde: the story of an unhappy friendship (1902) · R. H. Sherard, The life of Oscar Wilde (1906) · [C. S. Millard], Oscar Wilde three times tried (1912) · R. H. Sherard, The real Oscar Wilde [1916] · L. Lemonnier, La vie d'Oscar Wilde (1931) · B. Brasol, Oscar Wilde: the man, the artist (1938) · H. Pearson, The life of Oscar Wilde (1946) · A. Douglas, Oscar Wilde: a summing-up (1941) · F. Harris, Oscar Wilde: his life and confessions (1916); (1918); (1938) · R. Ellmann, Oscar Wilde (1987) · D. Kiberd, Inventing Ireland (1995) · D. Kiberd, Irish classics (Cambridge, MA, 2001) · J. Killeen, PhD diss., University College Dublin, 2001 · É. Vernadakis, Les prétextes de Salomé, 3 vols. (Paris, 1987) · The complete letters of Oscar Wilde, ed. M. Holland and R. Hart-Davis (2000) · M. Holland, The Wilde album (1997) · V. Holland, Son of Oscar Wilde (1954) · I. Small, Oscar Wilde revalued (1993) · I. Small, The aesthetes: a sourcebook (1979) · N. Page, An Oscar Wilde chronology (1991) · H. Montgomery Hyde, The trials of Oscar Wilde (1948) · H. Montgomery Hyde, Oscar Wilde: a biography (1982) · R. Merle, Oscar Wilde (1948) · V. O'Sullivan, Aspects of Wilde (1936) · W. B. Yeats, Autobiographies (1955) · H. Montgomery Hyde, Oscar Wilde: the aftermath (1962) · L. Finzi, Oscar Wilde and his literary circle: a catalogue (1957) · private information (2004)

Archives Bodl. Oxf., legal corresp. and papers · Bodl. Oxf., papers · Bodl. Oxf., papers relating to his literary estate · Hunt. L., letters, literary MSS · L. Cong., corresp., literary MSS, and papers · NYPL, letters and literary MSS · Ransom HRC, papers · U. Cal., Los Angeles, William Andrews Clark Memorial Library, corresp., literary MSS and papers | BL, corresp. with Society of Authors relating to his estate, Add. MSS 56854–56859 · Bodl. Oxf., letters to various members of the Lewis family and others · Harvard U., Houghton L., telegrams to A. Leverson · Magd. Oxf., letters to R. Harding [copies] · Magd. Oxf., letters to William Welsford Ward

Likenesses Elliott & Fry, photograph, 1881, NPG [see illus.] · N. Saromy, photograph, 1882, U. Texas · N. Saromy, two photographs, 1882, NPG · Twym [A. S. Boyd], pencil drawing, 1883, NG Ire. · S. P. Hall, pencil sketch, 1888–9, NPG · W. & D. Downey, photograph, woodburytype, 1891, NPG · A. Beardsley, caricature, 1894, Tate collection · M. Beerbohm, drawing, 1894, AM Oxf. · M. Beerbohm, drawing, 1898, Princeton University Library · photograph, 1898, NPG · M. Beerbohm, drawing, 1916, Tate collection · M. Beerbohm, drawing, 1926, U. Texas · Ape [C. Pellegrini], caricature, NPG; repro. in VF (24 May 1884) · J. A. MacNeill Whistler, pen-and-ink drawing, U. Glas. · J. A. MacNeill Whistler, two pen-and-ink sketches, U. Glas. · F. Pegram, pencil sketch, V&A · O. Wilde, self-portrait, drawing, Bibliothèque Nationale, Paris, Cabinet des Estampes

Wilde, Samuel De (bap. 1751, d. 1832), portrait painter, was baptized at the Dutch church of Austin Friars, London, on 28 July 1751, the eldest of the two sons of a Dutch woodcarver, also Samuel De Wilde (d. 1753), who had settled in England by 1748 when he married De Wilde's mother, Frances Havart, at St James's Church, Westminster, London. On 19 November 1765 De Wilde was apprenticed for seven years to his godfather, Samuel Haworth, a woodcarver in Denmark Street, Soho. However, he soon showed a talent for painting, broke his apprenticeship,

and entered the newly formed Royal Academy Schools on 9 November 1769. At the Royal Academy he would have encountered artists such as Johann Zoffany, whose theatrical portraiture later became a major influence.

We know little of De Wilde's early work: etchings signed P. Paul and mezzotints inscribed S. Paul produced in the 1770s have been attributed to him, but with no real justification. He first exhibited his small portraits at the Society of Artists in 1776 and continued showing there until 1778. From that date onwards he exhibited at the Royal Academy, broadening his œuvre from 1782 onwards with scenes of banditti and fancy pictures. However, he became best-known for his theatrical portraits, which were exhibited almost every year at the academy from 1792 until 1821. He also sent three paintings to the British Institution in 1812.

De Wilde's career in theatrical portraiture began with the start of the publication by John Bell (1745–1831) of the second issue of the British Theatre in January 1791. Before this the only painting by De Wilde with a theatrical connection seems to have been William Shuttlewood, the Actor, Aged 21 (1788; Yale U. CBA), but this represents an actor in everyday dress. Each number of the British Theatre consisted of a play accompanied by a vignette and a full-length portrait of a leading actor or actress of the day as one of the characters. Bell chose De Wilde as the portraitist and puffed him in his newspaper, The Oracle, on 8 April 1791 with the statement: 'Zoffany has hitherto been considered as the most celebrated Painter of small whole lengths, but comparison now gives DE WILDE a place as his superior' (Mayes, 'John Bell', 101). He provided his protégé with a studio in the British Library, his bookshop on the Strand, and invited potential subscribers to visit the artist at work. De Wilde was extremely productive, painting no fewer than thirty-six character portraits in 1791 and thirty-three in 1792. These paintings show actors and actresses in costume with props, set against a theatrical backdrop. Thomas Blanchard as Ralph in 'The Maid of the Mill' (engraved 1791; Garrick Club, London) is a good example of the series, inspired by Zoffany's theatrical portraits of the 1760s. In total De Wilde provided ninety-three pictures for the series before Bell ran into financial problems and both employer and employee were evicted from the British Library by George Cawthorn, a rival bookseller. The last number of the British Theatre to bear Bell's imprint was published in August 1795. Only two of De Wilde's plates appeared under Cawthorn's regime and it is likely that these were found in the British Library after the seizure.

By this date, however, De Wilde's career was established. In 1804 business was thriving to the extent that, despite having a studio at his home in Leicester Square, he began to rent additional rooms from the duke of Bedford at 9 Tavistock Row, Covent Garden. Many actors and actresses came from the nearby Drury Lane and Covent Garden theatres to sit to him there and his theatrical portraits adorned numerous publications, including the Monthly Mirror, John Cawthorn's Minor British Theatre, and

William Oxberry's *New English Drama. Sarah Harlowe as Beatrice in 'The Anatomist'* (1805; Royal Collection) is typical, representing a single figure against a plain background. These portraits were also published independently as prints and highly sought after by collectors such as Charles Mathews, whose collection now forms the basis of that of the Garrick Club. As well as painting in oil, De Wilde came to specialize in soft pencil or crayon with light washes of watercolour. His usual fee in 1810 and 1811, as noted in his diary, was £2 12s. 6d. for a watercolour drawing while oil paintings varied upwards in price from a few guineas.

De Wilde's success was clearly wavering by 1810, however, as the diary also records financial loans from friends and he stopped exhibiting at the Royal Academy almost a decade before his death. Some suggest this was due to failing eyesight while others ascribe it to old age and a sense of lack of recognition, particularly as he was never a candidate for election to the Royal Academy (Mayes, *De Wildes*).

Samuel De Wilde died on 19 January 1832 and was buried in the burial-ground adjoining Whitefield's Tabernacle in Tottenham Court Road, London. All that is known about his wife is that she was called Eleanor and that they had two children, Louisa Harriet (*b.* 1801) and **George James De Wilde** (1804–1871). George was born in London on 19 January 1804 and was originally intended for an artistic career. However, he soon showed a predilection for writing and, following a temporary post at the Colonial Office, began working for the *Northampton Mercury* c.1830. He became editor for the paper and a major figure in Northampton society, serving as governor to the local infirmary and helping to found the Northampton Central Art Gallery. In 1825 he married Mary Caroline Butterworth, with whom he had five children; after her death he married, in 1845, Louisa Packer, with whom he had a further two children. He died in the *Mercury* offices on 16 September 1871. KATE RETFORD

Sources DNB · I. Mayes, *The De Wildes* (1971) · G. Ashton, 'De Wilde, Samuel', *The dictionary of art*, ed. J. Turner (1996), 8.840–41 · I. Mayes, 'John Bell, the *British Theatre* and Samuel De Wilde', *Apollo*, 113 (1981), 100–03 · I. Mayes, 'Curtain call: portraits by Samuel De Wilde', *Country Life*, 154 (15 Nov 1973), 1530–34 · B. Stewart and M. Cutten, *The dictionary of portrait painters in Britain up to 1920* (1997), 167–8 · G. Ashton, *Pictures in the Garrick Club*, ed. K. A. Burnim and A. Wilton (1997) · Graves, *RA exhibitors*, 2 (1905), 317–18 · Graves, *Soc. Artists*, 76 · Mallalieu, *Watercolour artists*, 1.82 · D. Foskett, *A dictionary of British miniature painters*, 1 (1972), 243–4 · Waterhouse, *18c painters*, 111 · Redgrave, *Artists*, 125

Likenesses S. De Wilde, oils, c.1870 (after self-portrait by S. De Wilde), repro. in Mayes, 'John Bell', 101; priv. coll. · stipple, BM

Wilde, Thomas, first Baron Truro (1782–1855), lord chancellor, was born in Warwick Square, Newgate Street, London, on 7 July 1782, the second son of Thomas Wilde, attorney, of London and Saffron Walden, Essex, and his wife, Mary Ann, *née* Knight. He was uncle of Lord Penzance and younger brother of Sir John Wilde (*d.* 1859), chief justice from 1827 of the Cape of Good Hope.

Wilde was educated at St Paul's School in London from 1785 until 1796, when he left to be articled to his father.

Thomas Wilde, first Baron Truro (1782–1855), by George Zobel, pubd 1851 (after Sir Francis Grant, 1850)

Although he once ran away to try his hand at commerce, he was admitted attorney in 1805, and for some years practised as such on his own account. In March 1811, however, he entered himself at the Inner Temple and was called to the bar on 7 February 1817. By then he had already practised as a certificated special pleader for two years, and on 18 April 1813 married Mary, daughter of William Wileman and widow of William Devaynes, a banker; they had a daughter and three sons, one of whom died in infancy.

Wilde had none of the personal advantages which heighten the effect of oratory. He was small and thick-set with irregular features, his voice was unmusical and his delivery monotonous. He had a speech impediment, which he evaded rather than overcame by the use of synonyms, but his mastery of the technicalities of pleading, his connections, and experience, joined to great talent and industry, all assisted his success. Retained in 1820 for the defence of Queen Caroline during the progress through parliament of the bill of pains and penalties, he readily surmounted the prejudice with which he was at first received by Brougham and Denman, and distinguished himself in cross-examination. The celebrity thus early gained opened the way to an extensive common-law practice, and Queen Caroline expressed her gratitude by making him, with Stephen Lushington, one of her executors. Wilde was made serjeant-at-law (13 May 1824), and in Trinity term 1827 he was advanced to the rank of king's serjeant.

On 31 May 1831 Wilde was elected for Newark-on-Trent as a whig. He won the seat only at the fourth attempt, lost it at the general election of December 1832, but recovered it on 5 January 1835 and retained it until the dissolution of 23 June 1841. Having unsuccessfully sought a puisne judgeship on account of his poor health, from 1841 to 1846 he represented Worcester. Like most great lawyers, Wilde was unfitted to carry the House of Commons by storm, and at first he confined himself to the discussion of points of detail in the measures for the reform of the representative system and the law of bankruptcy. On 2 April 1835 he made a rambling speech displaying more rancour than vigour in support of Lord John Russell's motion for a committee on Irish church temporalities. On his party's return to power on 8 April he devoted himself at first chiefly to election petition business, and on 16 February 1836 was appointed to serve on the Carlow election petition committee as legal nominee to examine witnesses without power of voting. On the question of privilege (the reporting of debates in the Commons) raised by the great case of *Stockdale* v. *Hansard* (*Hansard* 3, 38, 1837, 1299; 48, 1839, 356) he maintained from the first the highest possible view of the dignity and authority of the House of Commons. During this controversy he succeeded Sir Robert Monsey Rolfe (afterwards Baron Cranworth) as solicitor-general (2 December 1839), and was knighted (19 February 1840). The tension between the House of Commons and the court of queen's bench was then extreme. Wilde was prepared for the most violent measures, and, though his excessive zeal was curbed on the whole by the attorney-general, John (later Lord) Campbell, he nevertheless opposed the legislative settlement of the question on the ground that it involved a tacit waiver of the privilege that it affirmed. He was no less jealous of the privileges of the serjeants-at-law. He opposed, and succeeded in obstructing Brougham's attempt, by means of the prerogative, to admit queen's counsel to equal rights of audience with serjeants in the court of common pleas, but reverence for the past did not blind him to the demerits of Westminster Hall as a setting for the law courts, and it was under his auspices that the first steps were taken towards their relocation in the Strand (*Hansard* 3, 57, 1849, 1162). He succeeded Campbell as attorney-general on 3 July 1841, but went out of office on the fall of Lord Melbourne's administration in the following September.

Wilde was one of the earliest converts to Rowland Hill's scheme of postal reform, which he introduced to the House of Commons on 27 June 1843. He also supported the measure of the same year for the more effectual suppression of the slave trade. His professional knowledge and skill showed to advantage in the discussions which arose on the report from the committee on the forged exchequer bills (4 April 1842), the reversal of the judgment against O'Connell (5 September 1844), and the question of privilege raised by the case of *Howard* v. *Gossett* (30 May 1845; *Hansard* 3 61, 1842, 1222; 70, 1844, 399; 76, 1844, 2007; 80, 1845, 1099).

Wilde's first wife died on 13 June 1840, and on 13 August 1845 he married Augusta Emma D'Este (1801–1866), daughter of *Augustus Frederick, duke of Sussex, and his wife, Lady Augusta Murray, daughter of the fourth earl of

Dunmore. Wilde met his second wife while acting for her brother in litigation which sought to establish his legitimacy. It was a romantic match, and her royal connections supplied a useful cachet in his subsequent career. There were no children of the marriage.

On the formation of Lord John Russell's administration in July 1846 Wilde was reappointed attorney-general, but, in consequence of the sudden death (6 July) of Sir Nicholas Conyngham Tindal, he was at once appointed chief-justice of the court of common pleas. On 30 October he was sworn of the privy council. As a judge, he displayed the same strengths as at the bar—an amazing attention to detail and acuteness in applying the law—but was prone to losing the important amid the unimportant in the detail at his disposal. The chief-justiceship, for which the experience of a lifetime had eminently fitted him, he held for little more than four years, being induced in 1850 to become lord chancellor. He was sworn in on 15 July, was created Baron Truro of Bowes, Middlesex, and took his seat in the House of Lords.

Notwithstanding his age and inexperience of equity business, Wilde proved a competent chancellor, mastering the rules of equity in the same manner as he had earlier those of the ecclesiastical courts. But his success was achieved at the cost of intense study—his judgments were invariably written—and his health suffered in consequence. His period as lord chancellor saw the creation of the lords justices of appeal in chancery, who could hear appeals from the master of the rolls or the vice-chancellors with or without the lord chancellor being present. Thus was achieved the dual triumph of freeing the chancellor for the legislative business of the House of Lords and his duties as a minister, without severing his link with the actual administration of justice. Wilde also supported the Common Law Procedure Act, 1852, which ended the need to cite a specific cause of action in the writ which commenced proceedings at common law. For the future, the cause would appear in the pleadings, which unlike the writ could be amended. Effectively, therefore, the old forms of action were abolished.

Wilde was relieved of the burdens of office by the fall of the government in February 1852, and in 1853 ceased to attend the House of Lords. After two years of suffering he died at his residence, 13 Eaton Square, London, on 11 November 1855. His remains were interred on 17 November in the Dunmore vault in the churchyard of St Lawrence, near Ramsgate. His widow presented his law library to the House of Lords and his portrait to St Paul's School.

J. M. RIGG, rev. T. G. WATKIN

Sources J. B. Atlay, *The Victorian chancellors*, 1 (1906) · *JHC* · *JHL* · *Hansard* 3 · J. Manning, T. C. Granger, and J. Scott, *Common bench reports: cases argued and determined in the court of common pleas* (1846–57), vols. 3–10 · C. Clark, *House of Lords cases on appeals and writs of error*, 3 (1853) · J. P. De Gex, S. Macnaghten, and A. Gordon, *Reports of cases heard and determined by the lord chancellor*, 8 vols. (1853–64), vols. 1–3 · GEC, *Peerage* · *The Times* (13 Nov 1855) · *The Times* (30 Jan 1860) · Baker, *Serjeants* · J. Manning, *Serviens ad legem* (1840) · A. Pulling, *Order of the Coif* (1884)
Archives HLRO, legal notebooks and papers | BL, corresp. and papers, incl. papers relating to defence of Queen Caroline, Add.

MSS 43727–43728 • PRO, corresp. with Lord John Russell, PRO 30/22
Likenesses T. Wright, stipple, pubd 1821 (after A. Wivell), BM, NPG • F. Grant, oils, 1850, St Paul's School, London • G. Zobel, mezzotint, pubd 1851 (after F. Grant, 1850), BM, NPG [*see illus.*] • T. Y. Gooderson, oils (after F. Grant), NPG; copy, Palace of Westminster, London • G. Hayter, group portrait, oils (*The trial of Queen Caroline, 1820*), NPG; two pen, pencil, and wash studies, 1820, NPG • H. Linton, woodcut (after Thomas), NPG • H. Weekes, bust, Middle Temple, London • H. Weekes, marble bust, Palace of Westminster, London • engraving (after sketch), BM

Wilde, Sir William, first baronet (*c.*1611–1679), judge and politician, was the son and heir of William Wilde (*d.* 1650), a vintner of Bread Street, London. Admitted to the Inner Temple from Clifford's Inn on 13 February 1630, Wilde married, on 6 July that year, Hannah Terry, the daughter of another London vintner; their relationship was ended prematurely by Hannah's death two months later. Called to the bar on 21 May 1637, Wilde may have been practising in chancery and king's bench the following year, although his professional career was soon disrupted by political crisis and civil war. In summer 1643 William Wilde junior of the Temple was assessed at a mere £50 by the parliamentarian committee for advance of money. Two years later he claimed that his net worth was only £500, disregarding lands held by his father for life, and that over the previous eighteen months he had made less than £15 as exigenter of Yorkshire, an office connected with the court of common pleas which Wilde may have held since 1631.

Despite the obscurity of the next few years of Wilde's life, his acquisition of an additional chamber in Figtree Court in 1649, election to the bench of the Inner Temple in November 1652, and second marriage that same year or earlier to Jane Wilson (*d.* 1661) of Hanwell, Middlesex, who would bear his son and heir, Felix, all point to a steadily expanding practice. With the revival of royalist City presbyterianism following the military coup which overthrew Richard Cromwell's protectorate, Wilde was elected on 3 November 1659 to the politically sensitive post of recorder of London. His personal standing and influence were further enhanced early next year when he was returned unopposed as one of the members for London in the Convention Parliament, where he busied himself with committee work and delivered at least eight speeches. As a member of the committee appointed to prepare parliament's response to the royal declaration of Breda, Wilde also joined the MPs who waited on Charles II in the Netherlands, and was knighted there together with London's other representatives after presenting a loyal address which he had helped to draft.

After his return to England, Wilde continued to play a linking role between parliament and the City. As recorder he served on the commission for the trial of the regicides, after moving successfully in the Commons that Sir Arthur Hesilrige not be indicted, and was raised to a baronetcy during the September adjournment. Created serjeant-at-law in October (when the patrons of his count were the earl of Northumberland and the lord mayor of London), Wilde was appointed king's serjeant on 10 November 1660. He also served in such local offices as justice of the peace and assessment commissioner, not only for London (where he became deputy lieutenant in 1662), but also for Middlesex and Kent. These reflected his extensive landed property, both leased and freehold, at Ash, Dunmow, and Lewisham, where he lived when not occupying his town houses at Great St Bartholomew's Close and Lincoln's Inn Fields, or his chambers at the Temple and Serjeants' Inn. However, Wilde did not stand for the Cavalier Parliament, perhaps because his failure to oppose the excise had damaged his political standing in London.

Following the death of his second wife in August 1661, Wilde married for a third time in October 1662. His bride was a 32-year-old spinster, Frances Barcroft (*d.* 1719), of St Michael Bassishaw, London. Their only son, William, was confusingly given the same baptismal name as both his father and his older half-brother, Wilde's second son by Dame Jane, the first Lady Wilde (BL, Add. MS 5520, fol. 251). In April 1668 Wilde was made a puisne justice of common pleas; his appointment 'during pleasure' signalled a major policy shift, since from 1641 onwards virtually all judges had been appointed 'during good behaviour'. The significance of this change became apparent six years after his transfer to the court of king's bench in 1673, when Charles II revoked the patents of Wilde and three other judges. According to Burnet the dismissal of this 'worthy and ancient judge' (*Burnet's History*, 2.199) in April 1679 followed Wilde's judicial censure of perjured testimony by a key witness to the supposed Popish Plot.

Wilde died on 23 November 1679 and was buried on 2 December in the Temple Church (despite an expressed wish for his 'fraile body' to lie in St Bartholomew's 'neere my deceased vertuous wife Dame Jane' (PRO, PROB 11/361, fol. 333). His large estate of lands and leases, loans and mortgages, plate, fine furniture, jewellery, books, and musical instruments comprised the accumulated fruits of parental inheritance, marriage settlements, and a successful legal career. Wilde had been friendly with the learned physician Sir George Ent and was known to Sir John Evelyn. His only significant publication was as editor of Sir Henry Yelverton's king's bench reports (1661, and four subsequent editions). WILFRID PREST

Sources M. W. Helms and E. Cruickshanks, 'Wilde, William', HoP, *Commons, 1660–90* • *DNB* • W. R. Prest, *The rise of the barristers: a social history of the English bar, 1590–1640*, 2nd edn (1991) • R. L. Lloyd, ed., 'Admissions to the Inner Temple to 1659', typescript, 1954, Inner Temple Library, London • will, PRO, PROB 11/361, fols. 333–5 • Foss, *Judges*, 7.193–5 • Baker, *Serjeants* • M. A. E. Green, ed., *Calendar of the proceedings of the committee for advance of money, 1642–1656*, 3 vols., PRO (1888) • *Burnet's History of my own time*, ed. O. Airy, new edn, 2 vols. (1897–1900) • *Report on the manuscripts of Allan George Finch*, 5 vols., HMC, 71 (1913–2003), vol. 2, p. 53 • J. L. Chester and J. Foster, eds., *London marriage licences, 1521–1869* (1887) • Evelyn, *Diary*, 4.45
Archives BL, holograph letter to Sir Richard Browne, Lewisham, Add. MS 15858, fol. 205
Likenesses T. Athow, wash drawing (after J. M. Wright), AM Oxf.
Wealth at death substantial: will, PRO, PROB 11/361, fols. 333–5

Wilde, William James [Jimmy] (1892–1969), boxer, was born on 12 May 1892 at 8 Station Road, Pont-y-gwaith, in the parish of Craig Berth-lwyd, near Tylorstown in south Wales, the son of James Wilde, a coalminer, and his wife,

William James [Jimmy] **Wilde** (1892–1969), by unknown photographer, 1919

Margaret Ann Evans, a miner's daughter. Known from birth as Jimmy, he was the second child, with an elder sister named Mary Anne and several younger than himself. After being educated at a local council school, he was able to leave school at the age of thirteen by passing a modest examination that gave him a labour certificate, and he went to work in the pits as a boy-helper at the rate of half a crown per day. To add to the family budget and to find the money to buy a few luxuries, such as cigarettes, he engaged in boxing bouts at the fairground booths, for which he received 5s. if he won. As he was rarely defeated in this hazardous profession after an arduous week in the pits, he soon built up a reputation for himself as a glove fighter under the marquess of Queensberry rules, but also took part in illegal bare-fist contests staged in secret in the Welsh mountains on a Sunday.

Just before his nineteenth birthday Wilde had become a star performer in Welsh rings and decided to leave the mines and devote his whole time to a boxing career. By now he had married Elizabeth Davies, daughter of Dai Davies, a miner under whom Wilde had served in his apprentice days in the pits. Himself an ardent boxer, Davies had coached Jimmy and taught him the rudiments in the small confines of his bedroom. Wilde's marriage took place at Pont-y-gwaith in 1910 and two sons were subsequently born: David, who later took up boxing, and Verdun, who had no inclination for the sport. Wilde reigned as undisputed flyweight champion of the world from 24 April 1916 until 18 June 1923, and although the weight limit for his class was 8 stone, he never went to scale at more than 6 stone 10 pounds, which meant that he was always called upon to meet opponents far bigger and heavier than himself. Among heavyweights the difference of a stone does not present anything like the handicap that it does among smaller men. Although he did not weigh much, Wilde possessed long legs and arms, with powerful shoulder muscles. He moved fast and punched with devastating power; his defence was confined to unorthodox bobbing and swaying that made him a difficult target to hit with any accuracy. He owed his amazing muscular development to his early days as a miner when, because of his small size, he could squeeze himself into the narrowest seam to hack away at the coal-face with his pickaxe.

Wilde's last paysheet at the Ferndale no. 8 pit owned by D. Davies & Sons Ltd, dated 1 April 1911, showed him earning the sum of £6 7s. 9d. for a fortnight's work, from which was deducted 1s. due to his check-weigher and 1s. 7d. for the services of a doctor, leaving a total of £6 5s. 2d. from which he had to pay his 'boy' 2s. 6d. a day. It was not much on which to buy a house and bring up a family—hence Wilde's decision to become a professional boxer. In the next twelve years he was to earn thousands of pounds with his fistic talent. By 1911 Wilde could claim, without risk of repudiation, that he had taken part in over 800 contests, but from 1911 until his retirement in 1923 his official record shows 138 well-paid bouts, which included seven British or world title contests, and the winning outright of a Lord Lonsdale challenge belt. Seventy-eight of his contests during this period, mostly against bantamweights and featherweights, ended within the scheduled number of rounds, and his phenomenal punching power earned him such colourful names as the Mighty Atom, the Tylorstown Terror, and the Ghost with a Hammer in his Hands. He became a great favourite in the principal boxing arenas throughout the country, especially at the famous National Sporting Club in Covent Garden, London; at the height of his fame his name became a household word. In a triumphant tour of America, from 1919 to 1920, he earned $100,000. He was beaten only four times: once when he fought against doctor's orders, once by a disputed decision, once by an American far heavier than himself, and in the final defence of his world title in New York against the Filipino Pancho Villa, who at twenty-two was Wilde's junior by nine years. For this contest Wilde received his largest purse, of £13,000.

On returning to Britain, Wilde announced his retirement from active boxing, but he continued to be interested in the sport, both as a manager of boxers and as a promoter of boxing tournaments. He died at Whitchurch Hospital in Cardiff, on 10 March 1969, just two months before his seventy-seventh birthday. The cause of death was given as acute influenza and severe mental abnormality.   GILBERT ODD, *rev.*

Sources *The Times* (11 March 1969) · *CGPLA Eng. & Wales* (1970)
Archives FILM BFI NFTVA, documentary footage · BFI NFTVA, news footage · BFI NFTVA, sports footage
Likenesses G. Belcher, caricature, coloured etching, 1919, NPG · photograph, 1919, Sci. Mus., Science and Society Picture Library [*see illus.*] · photographs, 1921–36, Hult. Arch. · H. Robinson, group portrait

Wealth at death £6653: administration, 20 March 1970, *CGPLA Eng. & Wales*

Wilde, Sir William Robert Wills (1815–1876), surgeon, was born at Kilkeevin, near Castlereagh, co. Roscommon, the youngest of the three sons and two daughters of a prominent local medical practitioner, Thomas Wills Wilde, and his wife, Amelia (*d. c.*1844), daughter of John Fynn. From his family background and schooling in Roscommon—the Royal School at Banagher and the Church of Ireland diocesan school at Elphin—Wilde acquired an idealized if scholarly devotion to the folk traditions and topography of the west of Ireland. His introduction to surgery came from accompanying his father on his rural rounds. In 1832, however, Wilde was bound as an apprentice to Abraham Colles, the pre-eminent Irish surgeon of the day, at Dr Steevens' Hospital in Dublin. He was also taught by the surgeons James Cusack and Sir Philip Crampton and the physician Sir Henry Marsh. Wilde also studied at the private and highly respected school of anatomy, medicine, and surgery in Park Street (later Lincoln Place), Dublin. Wilde's close and significant friendships with the physicians Robert Graves and William Stokes came about as a result of his being taught by Graves at Park Street. He completed his Dublin training with a year's midwifery at the Rotunda Hospital under Evory Kennedy, where he won the annual prize examination with a treatise on spina bifida.

A collapse in health preceded Wilde's appointment as a licentiate of the college of surgeons in March 1837. For either reasons of health or as a consequence of his having fathered a child out of wedlock, his mentors arranged for him to absent himself temporarily from Dublin in September of that year to travel as surgeon to a consumptive Glasgow merchant bound for Madeira and the Levant on the steam yacht *Crusader*. The numerous cases of ophthalmic trachoma Wilde encountered on the streets of Alexandria and Cairo were decisive for his later orientation towards eye surgery. The notes on the climate, natural history, topography, and state of medicine in the places he visited were later published as the two-volume *Narrative of a Voyage to Madeira, Teneriffe and Along the Shores of the Mediterranean* (1840). This work, which became known popularly as Wilde's *Voyage*, established him as a Dublin savant and led to him becoming a regular contributor to, and close associate of, the editorial coterie behind the *Dublin University Magazine*. It also introduced Wilde to the 'gentlemen of science' who made up the British Association for the Advancement of Science (BAAS). His attendance at its 1839 Birmingham meeting marked the start of a long and fruitful association with the natural history and anthropological sections of the BAAS.

The £250 fee Wilde received for *Voyage* allowed him to extend his medical education by a period of study abroad, first in London for three months in 1839 at the Royal London Ophthalmic Hospital (Moorfields) and the Hunterian Museum, and then at the Allgemeines Krankenhaus in Vienna. At Moorfields his teachers were John Dalrymple, Frederick Tyrell, and George Guthrie. He also made the acquaintance of Richard Owen, the Hunterian professor of comparative anatomy at the Royal College of Surgeons. His London circle included Queen Victoria's physician Sir James Clark, his fellow Dublin expatriate, the surgeon and later founder of King's College Hospital, Robert Bentley Todd, and Sarah Lee, illustrator and author of *Memoirs of Baron Cuvier* (1833) and numerous works of travel, African exploration, and natural history. Through the novelist Maria Edgeworth, Wilde was brought into London literary society. Although Wilde had gone to Vienna primarily to extend his knowledge of ophthalmic and aural surgery he quickly discovered that the latter was as neglected by the Allgemeines Krankenhaus as it was by Moorfields. With the treatment of eye disease, however, he followed a six-month course on practical surgery in the Viennese medical faculty, which in 1812 had established a chair and clinic of ophthalmology. Here Wilde observed the clinical and teaching practices of Anton Rosas (1791–1855), the second holder of the ophthalmology chair, and Friedrich Jaeger (1784–1871), professor of ophthalmology at the Joseph's academy, where surgeons were trained for service in the imperial army. Vienna also afforded him access to Josef Skoda (1805–1881), renowned for his diagnosis of diseases of the chest, and the pathological anatomist Karl Rokitansky (1804–1878).

From Vienna, Wilde travelled to Munich, and from there to Prague, Dresden, and Heidelberg, where he attended the university for several months as an independent scholar before to going to Berlin to study at the clinic of Johann Friedrich Dieffenbach (1792–1847), founder of plastic surgery. The letters of introduction he carried from Maria Edgeworth were a passport to the political and intellectual élites, most notably to the Berlin Geographical Society, at which he read a paper on Irish ethnology and which brought him to the attention of Alexander von Humboldt (1769–1859).

Wilde returned to Dublin in 1841 to open a practice as an eye and ear specialist from his home at 15 Westland Row. As his practice grew he moved in 1848 to 21 Westland Row, and then in 1855 to 1 Merrion Square. On 12 November 1851, in St Peter's Church, Dublin, he married the poet and critic Jane Francesca, known as Speranza (1821–1896) [*see* Wilde, Jane Francesca Agnes], the daughter of the Dublin attorney Charles Elgee (1783–1824) and Sarah (*d.* 1851), daughter of the Revd Thomas Kingsbury LLD, of Lisle House, Dublin. They had two sons, the barrister and later journalist William Charles Kingsbury Wills (1852–1899) and the writer, critic, and journalist Oscar Fingal O'Flahertie Wills *Wilde, and a daughter, Isola Francesca (1857–1867). Wilde also fathered three illegitimate children, one of whom, a son whom he called Henry Wilson (*c.*1838–1877), a name thought to have been a play on 'Wil(de's) son', was trained by his father as an oculist. Wilson was the author of *Lectures on the Theory and Practice of the Ophthalmoscope* (1868), and, after Wilde's death, succeeded him as senior surgeon to St Mark's Hospital for Diseases of the Eye and Ear. Wilde's two other natural children, Emily (1847–1871) and Mary (1849–1871), were adopted as wards by his eldest brother, the Revd Ralph Wilde.

Wilde established in Dublin a specialist eye and ear hospital modelled on Moorfields but including aural practice. He acquired the lease of a disused stable on South Frederick Lane, off Molesworth Street, and converted it into a dispensary for treating the eye and ear complaints of the poor of Dublin. The reputation he quickly acquired from the popularity of his dispensary both enhanced his private practice and led to his being appointed lecturer in ophthalmology and otology at the Park Street school. Wilde's dispensary paid for itself through monthly subscriptions from each of his patients, but further expansion into the treatment of in-patients and the development of teaching required a larger building. In 1844 Wilde purchased the building on Mark Street that had formerly housed a general hospital. As St Mark's Hospital and Dispensary for Diseases of the Eye and Ear this became the first hospital in the British Isles to teach aural surgery, and the first in Ireland to combine treatment of the eye with that of the ear. Funded partly from a realization of the assets of the former general hospital, partly from a grant from the Dublin grand jury, and partly from private subscriptions, it appointed Robert Graves as consultant physician and Sir Philip Crampton as consultant surgeon. Its success was such that it soon outgrew the Mark Street building. The closing of the Park Street school in 1848 provided Wilde with a timely opportunity for further expansion. He bought the building for £1100 and put £200 into structural work, which enabled it to become a hospital for twenty public patients, with three private rooms, outpatient facilities, an operating theatre, a lecture room, and rooms for a resident surgeon. In 1862 Wilde formally delegated the management of St Mark's as a voluntary hospital to a board of trustees to safeguard its facilities for the poor of Ireland. It merged in 1897 with the National Eye and Ear Infirmary to form the Royal Victoria Eye and Ear Hospital, on Adelaide Road.

Under Wilde's direction St Mark's became a centre for research and teaching in ophthalmic and aural practice. Wilde followed the continental teaching techniques of clinical instruction at the patient's bedside in what was effectively a specialist teaching hospital. As a surgeon he followed the methodology of the schools of Paris and Vienna in seeking to apply to surgery the localized insights offered by pathological anatomy. He was a regular attender of the Saturday afternoon meetings of the Dublin Pathological Society. Wilde's *Observations on Aural Surgery and the Nature and Treatment of Diseases of the Ear* (1853) drew on the wealth of detailed clinical case reports he had amassed at St Mark's. It was also the first textbook to provide practitioners with a reliable nosology and pathology for scientific diagnosis and treatment. The book, in which Wilde classified ear diseases by pathology rather than symptomatology, was bitterly attacked in *The Lancet* by Wilhelm Kramer, who advocated the older symptomatological classification. The attack was supported by *The Lancet*'s editor, who said that the reviewer had 'consigned [Wilde's] book to the trunkmakers'. Nevertheless, in 1853 the appointment of surgeon oculist-in-ordinary to the queen in Ireland was conferred on him.

Wilde's bedside investigations were crucial in establishing the role of the tympanic membrane and the middle ear in aural infections. Wilde introduced into Irish medical practice the unsplit ear speculum designed by the Viennese otologist Ignaz Gruber (1803–1872) for examination of the tympanic membrane. He also developed the first dressing forceps specifically for use with the ear, an aural snare, and a new incision to be used in the surgical treatment of mastoiditis. As 'Wilde's snare' and 'Wilde's incision', these became the first otological additions to the existing stock of Irish medical eponyms.

In his other specialism, eye surgery, Wilde was a keen proponent of the use of atrophine in the treatment of corneal ulcer and cataracts. He followed Jaeger's technique for the removal of cataracts by upward incision, and performed numerous operations to relieve squint by tenotomy, cutting and then stitching to divide the internal rictus muscle of the eye. He regarded the granulations of ophthalmic trachoma as the most frequent cause of blindness in Ireland and believed it was the same condition he had seen in Egypt. He independently (with Thomas Wharton Jones, a London ophthalmologist, confirmed the cause of astigmatism as being the asymmetry of the cornea. Wilde shared with many of his contemporaries an ambiguity about anaesthetics, though he did support the use of chloroform for plastic operations on the face and the tear ducts.

In 1843 Wilde initiated an extended series of clinical communications in the *Dublin Journal of Medical Science*, questioning received medical opinion on eye and ear surgery and issues of public health. Having added the word *Quarterly* to its title when he became editor in 1845, he used the journal to campaign vigorously on behalf of his profession, publishing as an open letter the 1847 attack by Robert Graves on the central board of health for the inadequacy of the financial provision it had made for doctors involved in famine work. In *Medico-legal observations upon infantile leucorrhea, arising out of the alleged cases of felonious assaults on young children, recently tried in Dublin* (1854), he argued that leucorrhea in minors was not necessarily associated with venereal infection and did not therefore provide conclusive proof of sexual assault; *On the Physical, Moral, and Social Condition of the Deaf and Dumb* (1854) drew on the statistics he had compiled from the 1851 Irish census. These represented the first attempt anywhere in Europe to classify the total number of persons in a given geographical area suffering from disease, either permanent or temporary, on a given day.

In the 1850s Wilde also enjoyed lucrative part-time employment in the emergent life-insurance industry, in his case as medical referee for the Victoria Assurance Company. He was an early member of the Statistical and Social Inquiry Society of Ireland, and in 1844 he had instituted at St Mark's an annual series of hospital reports distinguished by their level of statistical detail. The statistical abilities he had demonstrated in his book *Austria: its Literary, Scientific and Medical Institutions* (1843) drew him to the attention of the organizers of the material collected in the 1841 census of Ireland and led to his appointment as medical adviser and compiler of the table of deaths for the census report. He went on to become assistant commissioner for the censuses of 1851, 1861, and 1871, service which earned him a knighthood in 1864.

Wilde viewed the Irish countryside as a national asset which was threatened by famine, emigration, and education. His early writing on this topic was to have been expanded into a 'History of Irish medicine and popular cures', but this remained uncompleted at the time of his death. Some of the material he had assembled was published in his *Irish Popular Superstitions* (1852) and, posthumously, in Lady Wilde's *Ancient Cures, Charms and Usages of Ireland* (1887). Through his wife and her contributions to *The Nation*, Wilde was linked to the nationalist politics of Young Ireland; he himself was a quasi-nationalist, and in his final years looked favourably on Isaac Butt's campaign for Irish home government. Wilde became part of the inner circles of the Royal Irish Academy, the British Association for the Advancement of Science, and the Celtic Society of Dublin. The first volume of his *Descriptive Catalogue of the Antiquities … in the Museum of the Royal Irish Academy* (3 vols., 1857–62) was published to coincide with the association's meeting in Dublin in 1857. At its 1874 meeting in Belfast, Wilde gave an address entitled 'On the ancient races of Ireland'. Other publications reflected his interests in natural history and travel. In 1849 he also published *The Closing Years of Dean Swift's Life*, one of the earliest refutations of Swift's insanity.

Wilde's reputation became tarnished by scandal. Mary Travers, a long-term patient of his and the daughter of a colleague, had for some time been engaged in an increasingly public campaign of harassment against Wilde, claiming that he had seduced her. This culminated in her writing, and then distributing outside the building where Wilde was about to give a public lecture, a pamphlet crudely parodying himself and Lady Wilde as Dr and Mrs Quilp, and portraying Dr Quilp as the rapist of a female patient anaesthetized under chloroform. Lady Wilde complained to Mary's father, Robert Travers, which resulted in Mary bringing a libel case against her. Mary Travers won her case but was awarded a mere farthing in damages by the jury. The case, however, was the talk of all Dublin. Wilde's refusal to enter the witness box during the trial was widely held against him as ungentlemanly behaviour and provided his fellow oculist and medical editor Arthur Jacob with a further opportunity publicly to campaign against the man he had earlier accused of rapacity as a gentlemanly entrepreneur of surgery.

From this time onwards Wilde began to withdraw from Dublin to the west of Ireland, where he had started in 1864 to build what became Moytura, his house overlooking Lough Corrib in Connemara. His declining health and persistent and prolonged bouts of depression during much of that time were exacerbated by deaths of his daughter Isola from fever in 1867, and of his natural daughters Emily and Mary in a fire in 1871. Moreover, the trial cost Wilde dear, with costs of £2000 awarded against his wife, and this may have started the downward spiral which left his family in virtual penury after his death. Wilde returned to Dublin to die on 19 April 1876 at 1 Merrion Square surrounded by his family, and, Oscar Wilde later recalled, a former lover who sat with Lady Wilde's permission, shrouded in a veil at his bedside. He was buried three days later in the Church of Ireland cemetery of Mount Jerome in Harold's Cross, Dublin.

JAMES McGEACHIE

Sources J. Sproule, 'Sir William Wilde, MD, MRIA: surgeon oculist to the queen in Ireland', *Dublin University Magazine*, 85 (1875), 570–89 · R. M. Gilbert, *Life of Sir John Gilbert* (1905) · T. G. Wilson, *Victorian doctor: being the life of Sir William Wilde* (1942) · T. de Vere White, *The parents of Oscar Wilde* (1967) · B. de Breffney, 'The paternal ancestry of Oscar Wilde', *The Irish Ancestor*, 5 (1973), 96–9 · E. Lesky, *The Vienna medical school of the 19th century*, trans. L. Williams and I. S. Levij (1976) · J. H. Story, 'Sir William Robert Wills Wilde (1815–1876)', *British Journal of Ophthalmology*, 2 (1918), 65–71 · L. B. Somerville-Large, 'Dublin's eye hospitals', *Irish Journal of Medical Science*, 225 (1944) · 'The development of ophthalmology in Ireland', *Irish Journal of Medical Science*, 411 (1960) · P. Froggatt, 'The demographic work of Sir William Wilde', *Irish Journal of Medical Science*, 478 (1965), 213–30 · E. M. Crawford, 'William Wilde's table of Irish famine, 900–1950', *Famine, the Irish experience, 900–1950: subsistence crises and famines in Ireland*, ed. E. M. Crawford (1989), 1–30 · J. McGeachie, '"Normal" developments in an "abnormal" place: Sir William Wilde and the Irish school of medicine', *Medicine, disease and the state of Ireland, 1650–1940*, ed. G. Jones and E. Malcolm (1999), 85–101 · N. Weir, *Otolaryngology, an illustrated history* (1990), 79 · J. Hirschberg, *The history of ophthalmology*, trans. F. C. Blodi, 8b (1988), 119–43 · F. C. Blodi, 'William R. Wilde (1815–1876) in Vienna', *Documenta Ophthalmologica*, 81 (1992), 59–73

Archives NA Ire., chief secretary's MSS, corresp. with chief secretary for Ireland, hospital records · NL Ire., Colonel Thomas Larcom MSS · Royal College of Physicians of Ireland, Dublin, Kirkpatrick biographical file on Irish doctors · Royal College of Surgeons, Edinburgh, letters to Sir J. Y. Simpson on use of chloroform

Likenesses T. H. Maguire, oils, 1847, NL Ire. · E. Nicol, watercolour drawing, 1854, NG Ire. · H. Furniss, caricature, BL · J. H. Lynch, lithograph (after daguerreotype by L. Gluckman), NG Ire. · T. H. Maguire, lithograph (after drawing, 1847), NG Ire. · photographs, Royal College of Physicians of Ireland, Dublin · plaster bust, Royal Victoria Eye and Ear Hospital, Dublin

Wealth at death under £7000: probate, 29 May 1876, *CGPLA Ire.*

Wildeblood, Peter (1923–1999), journalist and campaigner for homosexual law reform, was born on 19 May 1923 in Alassio, Italy, the only child of Henry Seddon Wildeblood (*b.* 1863), a retired engineer from the Indian public works department, and his much younger second wife, Winifred Isabel, *née* Evans, the daughter of a sheep rancher in Argentina. He was brought up in his parents' cottage near Ashdown Forest and won scholarships first to Radley College and then to Trinity College, Oxford, where he postponed his studies until after the Second World War. He served as a meteorologist in the RAF in Southern Rhodesia, appreciating the dilution in wartime service life of class-consciousness, for which he had a lifelong hatred. Repatriated at the end of September 1945, he read French at Trinity, graduated in 1947 with a second-class degree in modern languages, and enjoyed an affair with a foreign prince whom he had met 'during one of my frequent week-ends in London' and in whose company he became part of a social scene ranging 'from Cabinet Ministers to the proprietress of a Mayfair brothel' (Wildeblood, 27).

On leaving Oxford, Wildeblood took a job as a waiter while writing for such magazines as *Punch* and *Vogue*. His first play, *Primrose and the Peanuts*, about Britain's failed groundnuts scheme in Africa, was well received when produced at the Bedford Theatre in Camden Town in 1950. He was taken onto the staff of the *Daily Mail*, starting in Leeds and rising within five years from general reporter to gossip columnist, festival of Britain correspondent, drama critic, court reporter, coronation columnist, and finally diplomatic correspondent. Meanwhile he explored the homosexual social scene in London and met Peter McNally, an RAF corporal with whom he conducted a passionate affair and to whom he wrote love letters. It was this correspondence which proved a crucial part of the evidence leading to Wildeblood's conviction for conspiracy to incite acts of gross indecency (the first use of the charge since the trials of Oscar Wilde) on 24 March 1954. The case, in which his friend Lord Montagu of Beaulieu was a co-defendant, became a *cause célèbre*, winning for Wildeblood the notoriety, sympathy, abuse, and respect which his stand attracted in equal measure, and upon which his most famous book, *Against the Law* (1955), was centred. 'Very faintly', he wrote:

> as though at the end of a tunnel, I could see what I must do. I would make a statement ... I would simply tell the truth about myself. I had no illusions about the amount of publicity which would be involved. I would be the first homosexual to tell what it felt like to be an exile in one's own country.   (Wildeblood, 55)

The facts of the Montagu case (as it became known) are complicated, though well documented in contemporaneous accounts. This was Lord Montagu's second trial; his first, which did not lead to a conviction, involved allegations by boy scouts. His second, in which Wildeblood was a co-defendant, was often later muddled with the scouting affair, but centred this time around a party in 1953 in a beach house belonging to Montagu, in which the peer, Wildeblood, Michael Pitt-Rivers, McNally and his friend John Reynolds, and others took part. Reynolds and McNally turned queen's evidence against Wildeblood, Pitt-Rivers, and Montagu. The theatre critic Kenneth Tynan (a friend from Oxford days) stood bail for Wildeblood. Peter Rawlinson QC defended him. In simple, direct, and readable style, *Against the Law* told a story of oppressive police behaviour, harassment, public humiliation, distorted evidence, ghoulishly sanctimonious press coverage, conviction, dismissal from the *Daily Mail*, and an eighteen-month prison sentence, of which Wildeblood served a year. The book was also a moving and lively account of the pointless and unconstructive nature of prison life. On its publication, it was widely saluted, though many booksellers refused to display it, and some refused to stock it. 'A courageous, honest book which can do a great deal of good, even to the most prejudiced', said the *Daily Telegraph* (16 November 1999). The book did much to fuel the public and political disquiet about the law on homosexuality which the trial itself had ignited, a disquiet which led to the establishment of the Wolfenden committee on homosexual offences and prostitution, to which, out of gaol, Wildeblood then gave evidence. That

committee's report led eventually to the limited decriminalization of homosexual behaviour between adults in private, the first reform of its kind in that century, and one which in time led to further movement towards equalizing the law in Britain.

Wildeblood seems to have irritated Sir John Wolfenden, and a few homosexual contemporaries, by a forwardness which some saw as attention seeking and others found 'self-hating'. His central allegation, that something amounting to an almost McCarthyite witch-hunt of homosexuals was being consciously orchestrated by the British state, was and remains disputable. It is just as likely, as Patrick Higgins argued in *Heterosexual Dictatorship* (1996), that the first stirrings of a homosexual consciousness and self-confidence, and the increased visibility of homosexual men, were bringing with them a public reaction. What is indisputable is that Wildeblood was part of these stirrings, and that the valiant and at first lonely personal stand he took contributed importantly to the new mood. It is true that he never sought prosecution, tried to avoid conviction, and, once convicted, had nothing left to lose and some sort of status to gain by proclamation. But the same can be said of countless men who had been caught momentarily in the light before him, and who had shrunk back into the shadows. Wildeblood was one of the first writers in the English-speaking world to identify himself as a homosexual (as opposed to confessing to homosexual acts) and to proclaim himself part of a group deserving of respect and the acknowledgement of ordinary human rights.

Wildeblood went on to a solid career in writing, theatre, and scriptwriting. Drawing on experience from the Soho drinking club he opened, he wrote a fictionalized biography, *A Way of Life* (1956), and two novels, *The Main Chance* (1957) and *West End People* (1958). A gangland musical based on this last—*The Crooked Mile* (1959)—met a measure of success. Drawn into television, Wildeblood joined Granada as a producer in 1969, and was responsible for a string of generally light television productions. He was well regarded for his professionalism, but became disenchanted with Britain and in the 1970s moved to Toronto to begin a new career with the Canadian Broadcasting Corporation, settling eventually in Vancouver. He took Canadian citizenship. In 1994 he suffered a devastating stroke. Paralysed, he learned to use a computer keyboard with his chin. Friends spoke of his cheerful and positive attitude.

In 1999 *Against the Law* was republished by its original publishers in Britain, Weidenfeld and Nicolson. Few readers recognized the England Wildeblood had described in 1955, and the persecution he catalogued had faded in the public memory. The new edition of his once-famous book evoked little interest, seeming to come from a world that was hardly remembered. But Wildeblood's obscurity, even irrelevance, in 1999 was a tribute to the cultural change he had so fearlessly championed half a century before. A few weeks after his book's republication he died, on 13 November 1999, in Victoria, British Columbia.   MATTHEW PARRIS

Sources P. Wildeblood, *Against the law* (1955) · M. Parris, preface, in P. Wildeblood, *Against the law*, 2nd edn (1999) · *The Times* (16 Nov 1999) · *Daily Telegraph* (16 Nov 1999) · *The Guardian* (16 Nov 1999) · *The Independent* (25 Nov 1999) · b. cert.

Likenesses photograph, 1954, repro. in *The Times* · photograph, repro. in *The Guardian* · photograph, repro. in *The Independent* · photograph, repro. in *Daily Telegraph*

Wilder, Philip van (*d.* 1554), musician, was born probably in the Low Countries at the close of the fifteenth century. During the second quarter of the sixteenth century he oversaw secular music-making at the English court; in particular his position brought him close to Henry VIII, who was himself an enthusiastic and proficient musician. As a composer, van Wilder is of only modest significance within a broad European context, but his works were widely known and influential in sixteenth-century England. He seems to have belonged to a musical family; two other musicians of the name van Wilder also served the Tudor court during Henry VIII's reign. Nothing is known about him before about 1522, when he is first recorded as being resident in London. By 1525 he was serving as a lute player to the king and commanded a substantial salary implying special status. He was granted licences to import wine from Gascony and woad from Toulouse; he also received income from property granted in London and Dorset, and gifts from the king and from Princess Mary. His denization was granted on 10 April 1539. He lived in the London parish of St Olave, from 1537 with his wife, Frances, with whom he had two daughters and four sons; one son, Henry, also became a musician in the privy chamber.

As a member (later a gentleman) of the privy chamber, van Wilder occupied a position of high rank. His own instrument was the lute, which he not only played but also taught to Henry's children, Mary and Edward. He had charge of a group of singers, men and boys, unconnected to the choir of the Chapel Royal, and it was presumably for them that the majority of his vocal works were composed. He was also responsible for the upkeep of the royal instruments at Westminster. The scope of that last position is made clear from the great inventory of Henry VIII's possessions at his death; it lists thirteen organs, nineteen other keyboard instruments (virginals and clavichords), and several hundred smaller wind and string instruments including viols, lutes, and recorders.

Virtually no lute music by van Wilder is known to exist. Instead, his surviving works are mainly *chansons* to French texts, some thirty in number. A few of these were printed in Antwerp during his lifetime, but the majority are found only in Elizabethan manuscript sources, where they are largely transmitted either without text, as if for instrumental performance, or as *contrafacta* adapted to sacred or secular English words. Stylistically they range from compact settings in the manner of Claudin de Sermisy to more densely polyphonic works for as many as seven voices. Several motets by him also survive; one of them, *Sancte Deus*, is written in a recognizably English idiom. Van Wilder's works circulated largely under the name Philip or Phillips, a fact that until recently caused confusion

between him and the later English composer Peter Phillips.

Philip van Wilder died in London on 24 February 1554, and was buried at St Olave, Hart Street. The following anonymous tribute to him was printed four years after his death in Richard Tottel's poetic miscellany *Songs and Sonettes*:

> Bewaile with me, all ye that have profest
> Of musicke, th'arte by touche of coarde or winde;
> Laye downe your lutes and let your gitterns rest.
> Phillips is dead whose like you can not finde,
> Of musicke much exceeding all the rest.
> Muses, therefore, of force now must you wrest
> Your pleasant notes into an other sounde.
> The string is broke, the lute is disposest,
> The hand is cold, the bodye in the grounde.
> The lowring lute lamenteth now therefore
> Phillips her frende that can her touche no more.
> (Tottel, sig. XIv)

Until the late twentieth century van Wilder was rarely given more than passing mention by British musicologists, whose writings on the Tudor period tended to concentrate on the achievements of native musicians. His rehabilitation has been brought about largely by American scholarship.   JOHN MILSOM

Sources A. Ashbee and D. Lasocki, eds., *A biographical dictionary of English court musicians, 1485–1714*, 2 vols. (1998) · *Philip van Wilder: collected works*, ed. J. A. Bernstein, 2 vols. (New York, 1991) · J. M. Ward, *Music for Elizabethan lutes*, 2 vols. (1992) · D. Starkey, ed., *The inventory of King Henry VIII: the transcript* (1998) · R. Tottel, *Songs and sonettes* (1557)

Wealth at death see will, proved 24 Jan 1555, PRO, PROB 11/36, fol. 1

Wilderspin, Samuel (1791–1866), educationist, was born on 23 March 1791 in Hornsey, London, the son of Alexander and Ann Wilderspin. His father, a follower of Swedenborg, was a member of the Church of the New Jerusalem, founded in London in 1787. Wilderspin was separated from his parents at the age of seven, sent to a school in central London, and later apprenticed as a calenderer in the textile trade. About 1819, while serving as a clerk to the minister of a New Jerusalem church in south London, he met James Buchanan, a fellow Swedenborgian, recently arrived from Robert Owen's famous school in New Lanark to open the first London infant school at Brewer's Green, Westminster. When Joseph Wilson, a London silk merchant, decided in 1820 to open a similar infant school in Spitalfields, Buchanan recommended Wilderspin and his wife, Sarah Anne (whom he married in 1811), as master and mistress. With some help from Buchanan and occasional visits from Owen, Wilderspin evolved innovative methods of teaching large groups of children from two to six years of age. These were described in his first book, *On the Importance of Educating the Infant Children of the Poor*, published in 1823, which also emphasized the need for education as a means of combating juvenile crime and raising the social level of the poor.

Wilderspin's school in Spitalfields attracted many visitors and led to the formation of the Infant School Society,

Samuel Wilderspin (1791–1866), by George T. Payne, pubd 1848 (after John Rogers Herbert)

a middle-class philanthropic organization, in 1824. Wilderspin became the society's agent, travelling on horseback or by gig throughout Britain to found and popularize infant schools on his model. On the demise of the society in 1828, he settled in Cheltenham and began a career as a freelance educator. From early 1828 to late 1830 he spent most of his time in Scotland, perfecting his system and devising novel means of publicity, involving public lectures, examinations, and parades of children through the streets. Following the death of his first wife, he married in 1826 Jane Mary Peacock, who probably died in 1828.

Wilderspin relinquished his active role in the New Jerusalem church in 1825, and later became a nominal Anglican, but he remained a Swedenborgian at heart. Swedenborg's educational theory rested on his conviction that infancy was a state of innocence, that the child was endowed with curiosity and a love of knowledge, and that education was a developmental process from a blank mind to wisdom. Although Wilderspin was inspired by the practice of Owen and Buchanan, and was familiar with the concepts of Pestalozzi and the phrenologists, he derived most of his principles from the Swedenborgian canon, combining them with his own practice to produce a new, if not entirely consistent, system of infant teaching. This was based on short classroom lessons in an inclined gallery, the stimulation of the senses of the child by the use of apparatus, pictures, and objects, and an emphasis on play, using the playground both as an arena for activity and a site for the formation of character. His ultimate aim was to inculcate moral principles based on Christian love and charity but without religious dogma or ceremony. Although sometimes burdened by an excess of inert knowledge and repetitive memory work, his system at its best was far in advance of the methods of his time and anticipated much of twentieth-century early childhood education.

After twelve years of travel throughout England, Scotland, Ireland, and Wales (during which time some 270 infant schools were established, mostly on his model), Wilderspin accepted a series of important educational engagements. In 1836–7 he organized the non-denominational school system of Liverpool town council, introducing progressive changes which aroused the fierce opposition of Anglican and conservative forces. Early in 1838, at the invitation of the commissioners of national education in Ireland, he took charge of the Dublin model infant school, and subsequently of all three of the model schools; but after an altercation with one of the Catholic commissioners his contract was not renewed and he left Dublin in August 1839. Between these two engagements, in the latter part of 1837, he had taken part in the Central Society of Education's campaign for a state-supported national system of education, incurring the wrath of influential evangelicals in his home town of Cheltenham.

On his return to England from Dublin in August 1839, Wilderspin found that his difficulties in Ireland, and his three-year absence from his work as a travelling infant school missionary, had diminished his reputation. Both church and state refused to employ him, but many of his ideas and practices were adopted, without acknowledgement, by both the largely evangelical Home and Colonial School Society and the committee of council on education. His fame in Britain rested not only on his practical work as an educational innovator but also on his numerous books. In addition to *On the Importance of Educating the Infant Children of the Poor*, which went through seven further editions (with varying titles and added content) between 1823 and 1852, Wilderspin published *Early Discipline*, an account of his travels, in 1832 (second edition 1834); *A System of Education for the Young* (1840); and, with his son-in-law T. J. Terrington, *A Manual for the Religious and Moral Instruction of Young Children in the Nursery and Infant School* (1845). His reputation spread abroad, and infant schools on his model were opened in France, Austria, Hungary, Italy, Switzerland, Sweden, and the USA.

In the early 1840s lack of employment forced Wilderspin to the edge of destitution. He was saved by the patronage of Daniel and Mary Gaskell of Lupset Hall, Wakefield, in Yorkshire, who supported him both morally and materially. After a short time as master of the infant school at Barton upon Humber, Lincolnshire, with his third wife, Mary Dowding (they had married in 1838), he retired to Wakefield in 1848. There he spent an active retirement as a prominent member of the local mechanics' institute. In 1846 he had been granted a civil-list pension of £100 per annum, and also received an annuity of

£40 from the interest on £1818 collected as a 'national tribute' by the efforts of the Gaskells. Wilderspin died in Wakefield on 10 March 1866, and was buried in Thornes churchyard.   W. P. McCANN

Sources P. McCann and F. A. Young, *Samuel Wilderspin and the infant school movement* (1982) · private information (2004) · PRO, RG 4/4239
Archives LUL, Goldsmiths' Library of Economic Literature, notes, pamphlets, minute books, etc. · LUL, papers | LUL, Goldsmiths' Library of Economic Literature, Young papers
Likenesses G. T. Payne, mezzotint, pubd 1848 (after J. R. Herbert), BM, NPG [*see illus.*] · J. R. Herbert, portrait, priv. coll. · G. T. Payne, oils, BM

Wilding, Anthony Frederick (1883–1915), tennis player, was born on 31 October 1883 at Opawa, near Christchurch, New Zealand, the second of the five children of Frederick Wilding QC (1852–1945) and his wife, Julia Anthony (1854–1936), who had emigrated from England in 1879. Frederick Wilding, an accomplished sportsman, gave his eldest son lessons in rugby, cricket, and lawn tennis, games in which the young schoolboy soon excelled. Anthony Wilding attended Wilson's School at Christchurch, where he captained the football team and began winning tennis tournaments in his teenage years. In 1902 he was admitted to Trinity College, Cambridge, where he studied law. He was an able scholar, but made a name for himself on the tennis court. During his first summer term he won the freshmen's lawn tennis tournament; in 1904 he was secretary of the university lawn tennis club; in 1905 he was the club president; and he represented Cambridge University against Oxford in both of these years, when he was their best singles player.

On graduating from Cambridge in 1905, Wilding read for the bar and was called by the Inner Temple in 1906, before qualifying as barrister and solicitor of the supreme court of New Zealand in 1909. Yet he retained a strong interest in lawn tennis, at which he had made steady progress. From 1903 onwards he won championships in virtually all parts of the tennis world. He was very fond of travelling to compete in tournaments, and sometimes journeyed half-way across Europe on his motorcycle to do so. From 1905 he represented Australasia in the Davis cup, a prize which, alongside Norman Brookes, he captured from Great Britain in 1907 and retained in 1908, 1909, and 1911. Wilding's record at Wimbledon was particularly impressive. In 1910 he won the All England singles championship by defeating the title-holder, A. Wentworth Gore; then he retained the title for the next three years (1911–13), defeating in turn H. Roper Barrett, A. W. Gore, and M. E. McLoughlin in the final. Wilding also won the Wimbledon championship doubles in 1907 (partnered by Brookes), in 1908 and 1910 (partnered by M. J. G. Ritchie), and in 1914 (partnered again by Brookes).

It was by constant practice and rigorous physical training that Wilding made himself into one of the great players of his era. In his early days he would hit a tennis ball for hours against a wall. He was not regarded as one of the most brilliant or graceful of lawn tennis players, but was reckoned one of the most difficult to beat. His main strengths were concentration, determination, and physical fitness; his main weaknesses were a suspect backhand and somewhat erratic overhead play. His autobiography, *On the Court and Off* (1912), was published at the height of his tennis fame. By then he was having to concentrate on his business career in Britain and New Zealand.

In July 1914, at New York, Wilding and Brookes regained the Davis cup for Australasia from the United States. Shortly afterwards the outbreak of the First World War brought a halt to Wilding's tennis heroics. He joined the Royal Marines, and in October 1914 was gazetted second lieutenant at headquarters intelligence corps. His knowledge of European roads was potentially valuable, and he was keen to work with armoured vehicles. He volunteered for an auxiliary armoured squadron in the Royal Naval Air Service, and in March 1915 was posted to France with the rank of lieutenant. In early May 1915 Wilding was promoted captain, and his team was moved to the front line near Neuve Chapelle, France. Just one week later, on 9 May 1915, he was killed when a shell exploded adjacent to the dug-out in which he was sheltering. He was unmarried. He was buried the following day and reinterred after the war at a Rue-des-Berceux military ceremony.

                DARYL ADAIR

Sources A. F. Wilding, *On the court and off* (1912) · A. Wallis Myers, *Captain Anthony Wilding* (1916) · *DNB* · *DNZB*, vol. 3
Wealth at death £651 12s. 6d.: administration, 11 Jan 1916, *CGPLA Eng. & Wales*

Wilding, Dorothy Frances Edith (1893–1976), portrait photographer, was born on 10 January 1893 at 5 Westfield Terrace, Longford, Gloucestershire, the youngest of nine children of Richard Wilding, a commercial traveller, and his second wife, Mary Martha Edwards (*b.* 1866). She was sent to live, aged four, with her childless aunt and uncle Thomas and Fanny Hayter in Cheltenham. Extrovert in character, her early ambitions were to be an actress or a painter.

Through an early interest in picture postcards Wilding, aged only sixteen, bought her first camera and tripod. She moved to London in 1910 and after an apprenticeship with the retoucher Ernest Chandler, who was associated with the fashionable portrait photographer H. Walter Barnett, she managed to save £60 by the time she was twenty-one. With this money she opened her first studio at 67 George Square, just off Portman Square, in 1914.

Building on early success, Wilding moved to a top-floor studio at 264 Regent Street in 1918, employing seven staff to cope with the steadily growing demand for her work. Her loyal and talented staff (almost always women) were to grow in number throughout her career and number nearly forty at her peak during the 1930s. The idiosyncratic Wilding style was adopted by many who worked for her and assistants would be responsible for many famous portraits attributed to her.

A Dorothy Wilding portrait is distinctive not only in style but also in presentation. The photograph, mounted

Dorothy Frances Edith Wilding (1893–1976), self-portrait, 1930s

on different layers of tinted card, was interlaced with tissue paper; a thick crayon outline surrounded the photograph which was embellished by her characteristic signature. The Wilding art nouveau logo was printed on the back. On 28 July 1920 Wilding married the leather merchant Walter Oscar Portham (b. 1867); it was a seemingly loveless marriage which ended in divorce eleven years later. On 4 June 1932, aged thirty-nine, she married the interior decorator Thomas (Rufus) Leighton Pearce (1882/3–1940) who was responsible for much of the modernist and striking design in her Bond Street studio.

From 1923 onwards Wilding began to show her work both in Britain and abroad and became involved in commercial work including for the Condor Hat Company. She also began to supply leading periodicals with images of leading actresses—defining the iconography of Tallulah Bankhead and Gladys Cooper. Wilding's portraits made her subjects beautiful, striking, and modern but also classical and sensual in a quintessential art deco style. Bright lighting, dramatic retouching, distinctive props, and her strict rules for posing, such as folding of hands and double profiles, characterized her style of iconic and idealized portraiture.

Prosperity was guaranteed by a series of royal sittings starting in 1928 with the duke and duchess of Kent, leading to the official coronation portraits of George VI (1937; NPG) and Elizabeth II (1952; NPG). In 1937 Wilding opened a second studio in New York. Her Bond Street studio was bombed in the blitz in 1940, which destroyed almost all

the early negatives, prints, and records. Wilding continued to work in New York, and her American subjects such as Yul Brynner (1951; NPG) and Harry Belafonte (1954; NPG) inspired some of her best later work. The duke and duchess of Windsor became regular clients.

Wilding's style of studio portraiture became less fashionable by the late 1950s and she exhibited her work for the last time at the London Salon of Photography in 1957. The following year her autobiography, In Pursuit of Perfection, was published and she sold her business for £3000 to one of her assistants, Tom Hustler, who kept the studio going until 1973.

Wilding died on 9 February 1976 of heart failure at 1 Knaresborough Place, Kensington, London, leaving an estate of £54,000 with bequests to many of her longserving assistants. The National Portrait Gallery holds over 900 of her original negatives and prints. Her work is also represented in, among other places, the Royal Photographic Society collection at the National Museum of Photography, Film and Television, Bradford.

SUSAN BRIGHT

Sources T. Pepper, Dorothy Wilding: in pursuit of perfection (1991) • V. Williams, Women photographers: the other observers, 1900 to the present (1986) • D. Wilding, In pursuit of perfection (1958) • private information (2004) • V. Williams and L. Heron, Illuminations (1996) • G. Howell, In Vogue: six decades of fashion (1975) • J. Scholfield, 'Dorothy Wilding', Zoom (Aug 1987), 37 • G. Greig, 'Exposed: secrets of a royal photographer', Sunday Times (28 July 1991) • W. Packer, 'Dated portraits', Financial Times (13–14 July 1991) • T. Hustler, 'Perfect poses', British Journal of Photography (18 July 1991), 20 • interview, Energine newsreel, 12 May 1937, NPG, Heinz Archive and Library [printed copy] • interview, National Broadcasting Company, Inc., 1941, NPG, Heinz Archive and Library [printed copy] • d. cert. • m. certs.
Archives National Museum of Photography, Film and Television, Bradford, Royal Photographic Society collection • NPG, works, papers, articles, and general ephemera
Likenesses D. Wilding, self-portraits, photographs, c.1920–1929, NPG • D. Wilding, self-portraits, photographs, 1930–39, NPG [see illus.] • D. Wilding, self-portraits, photographs, c.1950–1959, NPG
Wealth at death £54,000: Pepper, Dorothy Wilding: in pursuit of perfection

Wilding, Michael Charles Gauntlet (1912–1979), actor, was born on 23 July 1912 in Leigh-on-Sea, the son of Henry Wilding, a soldier and businessman who claimed descent from John of Gaunt and William Howley, archbishop of Canterbury, and his wife, Ethel Thomas (c.1870–c.1946), who acted with Sir Ben Greet's company before her marriage. On the outbreak of revolution in Russia in 1917 Wilding's father, who had been working in military intelligence in Moscow, returned to England and Wilding enrolled at Christ's Hospital. He briefly studied art at the London Polytechnic, and then spent a year in Bruges as a café portraitist before accepting a clerking job with the commercial art firm Garlands.

In 1934, exploiting the fact that a girlfriend's father had shares in the British and Dominion Film Company, Wilding was hired as an extra at Elstree Studios and soon found himself serving as stand-in to Douglas Fairbanks junior on Catherine the Great. Having taken his first featured role in Late Extra (1935), he sought stage experience, first with

Watford Repertory and then with Fay Compton's company on its 1937 tour of Australia.

Wilding married the actress Kay Young in 1938 (the marriage ended in divorce about 1941). He worked exclusively on stage until the closure of West End theatres during the 'phoney war' prompted a return to acting in films. Initially he took supporting roles in morale-boosters such as *Tilly of Bloomsbury* (1940) and *Sailors Three* (1941) but Noël Coward was suitably impressed with his performance in *Ships with Wings* (1942) to cast him as Flags in the naval combat classic *In which we Serve* (1942).

Classified as unfit for military duty, Wilding performed with an Entertainments National Service Association party in Gibraltar. Yet despite his taking the lead in *English without Tears* (1944) his career seemed to have stalled. Indeed, Elspeth Grant of the *Daily Graphic* proclaimed she found him 'overwhelmingly modest and singularly lacking in ambition' (Wilding, 45). Fate then intervened. With first choice John Mills still in the forces, Wilding was hired against his better judgement by director Herbert Wilcox to star opposite his wife, Anna Neagle, in *Piccadilly Incident* (1946). It proved a huge success, and over the next six years Neagle and Wilding formed the most profitable romantic partnership in the history of British cinema.

With Wilcox constantly at the helm the couple oozed sophistication in *The Courtneys of Curzon Street* (1947), *Spring in Park Lane* (1948), and *Maytime in Mayfair* (1949). But Wilding was keen to spread his wings and take his chances in Hollywood; although Wilcox refused all transatlantic offers, he did loan out his star to Sir Alexander Korda for *An Ideal Husband* (1948) and to Alfred Hitchcock for *Under Capricorn* (1949) and *Stage Fright* (1950). Wilding's liaison with actress Marlene Dietrich finally forced Wilcox into negotiating an American project. But Greer Garson's frostiness meant *The Law and the Lady* (1951) was an uncomfortable experience. Moreover, it received a critical mauling, although Leonard Mosley of the *Daily Express* felt that 'Mr Wilding carries the Union Jack right into the heart of Hollywood. He is truly an international star' (Wilding, 62).

After returning to Britain, Wilding co-produced *Into the Blue* (1951) with Wilcox and followed the Neagle vehicles *The Lady with a Lamp* (1951) and *Derby Day* (1952) with a new twenty-year contract. However, it was terminated almost immediately as he married the film star Elizabeth Taylor on 27 February 1952; that month he and his new bride moved to Hollywood. A three-year deal was signed with MGM, but Wilding's refusal to accept such sub-standard assignments as *Latin Lovers* quickly led to his suspension. Studio mogul Jack Warner considered him 'the biggest romantic discovery since Rudolph Valentino' (Wilding, 103), yet films such as *Torch Song* (1954)—in which he played a blind pianist opposite a ceaselessly hostile Joan Crawford—*The Egyptian* (1955), and *The Glass Slipper* (1956) did little to enhance his reputation.

Only Wilding's private life seemed of interest. Even though Wilding had fathered two sons, Michael and Christopher, gossip columnist Hedda Hopper insinuated that he was having an affair with another expatriate actor, Stewart Granger. The fact he won an out-of-court settlement from the all-powerful termagant earned him considerable kudos, but that was quickly dissipated by the news that Taylor had left him for producer Mike Todd and that he had been dismissed from an MGM pirate adventure film for forgetting his lines. Wilding and Taylor divorced in 1957.

Wilding was becoming increasingly prone to blackouts, which had been affecting him since the mid-1930s. Convinced that his acting days were over, he began working for Jerry Hogan as a talent agent. Feeling miscast, Wilding nevertheless returned to Britain, where in the late 1950s he married the millionairess Susan Nell, who set him up as the host of her Brighton restaurant, the Three Little Wilding Rooms. However, he detested the work and the marriage quickly collapsed.

In 1962 Hogan asked Wilding to help reintroduce the actress Margaret *Leighton (1922–1976) to British audiences after an indifferent spell in the United States. The couple married in 1964 and, although Wilding took occasional film roles in *Waterloo* (1970) and *Lady Caroline Lamb* (1972), he was content to devote himself to her career. In his autobiography, *Apple Sauce* (1982), the man once tipped to be the new Cary Grant admitted that he had always been afraid of performing: 'I was not a born actor and the art of acting never came to me easily' (Wilding, 176). After a long battle with multiple sclerosis, Margaret Leighton died in 1976. Wilding never fully recovered from her loss and, following a blackout-induced fall, he died near Chichester from a long-formed blood clot on the brain on 8 July 1979. He was cremated at Chichester on 22 July.

DAVID PARKINSON

Sources M. Wilding, *Apple sauce* (1982) · D. Spoto, *Elizabeth Taylor* (New York, 1995) · www.uk.imdb.com [M. Leighton] · *CGPLA Eng. & Wales* (1979)
Likenesses photographs, c.1942–1959, Hult. Arch. · F. W. Daniels, bromide print, 1946, NPG · portraits, Kobal collection, London · portraits, Ronald Grant archive, London · portraits, Huntley archive, London
Wealth at death £147,392: probate, 10 Sept 1979, *CGPLA Eng. & Wales*

Wildman, Sir John (1622/3–1693), Leveller and conspirator, was possibly the son of Jeffrey Wildman, yeoman, of Wreningham, Norfolk. According to Clarendon, Wildman, whom he knew personally, studied at Cambridge, though surviving records do not mention him. He also reputedly pursued legal studies in London, and though he never became a barrister he provided legal assistance to various people and was knowledgeable in property law. Medicine also interested him. Pepys erred in labelling Wildman a Fifth Monarchist, and although Burnet regarded him as a deist in his later life, Wildman welcomed the Independent minister George Cokayne into his home to preach, suggesting that he had congregationalist sympathies. Before 1646 Wildman married Frances, daughter of Sir Francis Englefield, a Catholic baronet in Berkshire; they had one son, John (d. 1710). By 1655, shortly after Frances's death, Wildman had married Lucy (d. 1692), daughter of Lord Lovelace.

Military service and Leveller activity By 1647 Wildman was serving in the army, and in July he professed to have inside knowledge about negotiations concerning 'The heads of proposals'—the army's terms for a settlement with Charles I. On 4 September the general committee of officers recommended that he be appointed governor of Poole and Brownsea, but nothing came of this, perhaps prompting his decision to leave the army. In late September, Wildman and Maximilian Petty began helping agents who represented five regiments articulate their grievances. The result was *The Case of the Armie Truly Stated*, to which Wildman may have contributed. Presented to Sir Thomas Fairfax on 18 October, it accused the generals of not keeping faith with the soldiers by purging parliament and called for a radical extension of the franchise, biennial parliaments, the abolition of tithes and the excise, repeal of recusancy and conventicle statutes, and law reform. Wildman almost certainly helped compose the *Agreement of the People*, setting forth the Levellers' call for a unicameral legislature, biennial elections, expanded suffrage, and religious freedom. He was a principal spokesman for the agreement in the debates held at Putney in the general council of the army. On the eve of the debates he may have written the first of the *Two Letters from the Agents of the Five Regiments*, encouraging soldiers to demand reform; he also probably wrote *A Cal to All the Souldiers of the Army*, distributed on 29 October, accusing Cromwell and Henry Ireton of betraying the soldiers' trust. On the contentious issue of suffrage, he argued in the debates that 'every person in England hath as cleere a right to Elect his Representative as the greatest person in England' (Firth, 1.318). He also denied any power in the House of Lords or monarch to veto legislation approved by the Commons, insisting that all authority be vested in the Commons, and called for Charles's trial. Shortly thereafter the general council of the army appointed Wildman (the only citizen to be included) to a committee assigned to examine the extent to which *The Case of the Armie* and the agreement were compatible with the army grandees' position. In the meantime Wildman and John Lilburne were organizing a campaign in London against the grandees and parliament. Writing under the anagrammatic pseudonym John Lawmind, in late December Wildman published *Putney Projects*, attacking the grandees as pretended patriots and accusing Cromwell of attempting to impose slavery on England. Early the following year Wildman, Lilburne, and others wrote to supporters in Kent urging them to stand firm. At a meeting in Smithfield, Wildman warned that civil war would resume if the government were not quickly settled, and he again assailed Cromwell.

Arrested on charges of sedition, Wildman (alias Wenman) and Lilburne appeared at the bar of the Commons on 20 January 1648, where they denied the house's jurisdiction and demanded trial by common law. The house committed them to prison, where they remained without trial for six months. In *Truths Triumph* (1648) he protested his arrest, called for national unity on behalf of freedom and justice, depicted the plight of textile workers in the west, and cited food riots in Wiltshire to exhort

parliament to implement reforms. At Lilburne's request Wildman also composed *The Laws Subversion* (1648), pleading the case of the presbyterian MP Sir John Maynard, who had also been imprisoned without trial. Following a petition from London supporters and Maynard's address to the Commons, parliament released Wildman and Lilburne on 2 August. At the Nag's Head tavern on 15 November, Wildman explained the 'just ends of the war' to Levellers and Independents, following which the group resolved to convene a committee to draft another agreement (*Writings and Speeches of Oliver Cromwell*, 1.688–9). In late November, Wildman and Lilburne conferred at Windsor with Colonel Thomas Harrison, and it was agreed to set up a committee comprising radicals from London and parliament as well as from the army and the Leveller leadership to prepare a new *Agreement of the People*. In reaction, this helped to precipitate the vote in the House of Commons to accept the king's latest answer to the parliamentary peace proposals as the basis of a settlement, and this in turn precipitated Pride's Purge and the trial of the king. The committee did indeed meet throughout mid-December (the 'Whitehall debates') and drew up a new agreement, but to the disgust of Wildman and other Levellers, when the army presented this document to the Rump of the Long Parliament on 15 January 1649 it had significantly diluted it, above all in weakening the commitment to religious liberty as a natural right. Later allegations that Wildman was on the scaffold with Charles I are baseless, but claims that he differed significantly from other Leveller leaders in his refusal to denounce the king's trial as a sham and in his willingness to work with the new Commonwealth regime are correct.

In May the government was preparing to send Wildman as a commissioner to Guernsey, but for unknown reasons this fell through. The same year he was commissioned as an officer in Sir John Reynolds's regiment of horse, though he did not accompany it to Ireland in August. *The Clarke Papers* lists a Captain Wildman as commanding a troop of sixty men in Cheshire, and a Major Wildman in charge of a troop of Reynolds's horse in Hampshire. For Wildman's refusal to condemn the new regime, Lilburne and Richard Overton castigated him in July.

Wildman's estrangement from his fellow Levellers was brief, for in 1650 he and Lilburne advised in the exchequer the fenmen who were protesting the draining of the marshes around the Isle of Axholme, in Lincolnshire. In the autumn Wildman and Lilburne went to Lincolnshire, but they apparently made no attempt to organize support for the *Agreement of the People*, nor did they participate in or encourage the riots and destruction of crops. In October 1651 Wildman and Lilburne entered into an agreement with the fenmen, promising to defend them from lawsuits and fines stemming from the riots in return for 1000 acres each. While Lilburne was responsible for surveying this land, Wildman defended the commoners' interests in London, but he and Lilburne failed to persuade parliament to hear the fenmen's case. There is no reliable evidence that the fenland involvement of the two men was intended as a precursor of a Leveller inspired insurrection.

In the meantime Wildman and John Price represented London freemen in December 1650 as they endeavoured to make the London Common Hall representative of the citizens rather than the livery companies, but their efforts ultimately failed. Nor was Wildman successful in December 1651 when he sought to represent Gloucester in seeking reparations from parliament for damages sustained in the siege of August 1643; for his services he wanted a third of any reparations, which the mayor and aldermen deemed excessive. During the early 1650s he was active in the land market, purchasing property in twenty counties, mostly as an agent for others. The properties included Becket House, Shrivenham, Berkshire, which he acquired from Henry Marten. Of the fifty transactions in which he participated, most involved property in Lancashire and Yorkshire; through such dealings he obtained substantial wealth.

Conspiracy and espionage during the protectorate In the elections to the first protectorate parliament Wildman stood for Westminster and Scarborough, losing the former but winning the latter. However, proprietors of reclaimed land in Lincolnshire successfully petitioned against his sitting on the grounds that he had lied about the contract awarding him 1000 acres for defending the fenmen. Wildman now turned against the government, drafting the petition of three republican colonels—Thomas Saunders, John Okey, and Matthew Allured—against rule by a single person and in favour of the fundamental rights outlined in the agreement. Wildman and other Levellers met with excluded parliamentary republicans, and he was also in contact with Major-General Robert Overton, who was implicated in a plot against Monck in Scotland. With Edward Sexby, Wildman not only sowed discontent among army units but plotted to assassinate Cromwell. He was arrested in the second week of February 1655 as he was dictating 'The declaration of the free and well-affected people … in arms against the tyrant Oliver Cromwell'. In it he called for a constitutional settlement with free and regular parliaments. He was confined in Chepstow Castle and then transferred to the Tower on 10 March. Through his friend Colonel Henry Bishop he made contact with royalists prior to Penruddock's insurrection the same month. Cromwell accused Wildman of being one of the uprising's managers. In fact Wildman was prepared to sell himself to either side, offering his services to John Thurloe as a spy while pursuing contacts with the royalist agents William Rumbold, an incarcerated Leveller, and Sir Robert Shirley. Apparently in return for agreeing to spy on royalists Wildman was released on 26 June 1656 on a bond of £10,000, and his estates were restored.

Acting as a double agent, Wildman, William Howard, and eight other Baptists and Levellers signed a petition to the exiled future Charles II pledging to venture their lives for him if he promised to restore the Long Parliament, abolish tithes, grant amnesty, and provide religious freedom. For their services they unsuccessfully sought £2000

from Charles. In January 1657 Wildman again plotted with Sexby to assassinate Cromwell, to which end they commissioned Miles Sindercombe. Wildman approved a plan to burn Whitehall Palace, killing Cromwell and signalling an uprising. Following the arrest of Sexby in July 1657, perhaps owing to Wildman's betrayal, the latter assumed responsibility for negotiating with the Spaniards as part of the conspiracy; for this purpose he travelled to Flanders several times in the summer and early autumn. He professed to want an invasion of England, but Charles lacked money and men. Negotiations between Levellers and royalists ceased in December 1657 when Howard was arrested.

After Richard Cromwell succeeded his father as protector in September 1658 Wildman sought to forge an alliance between Levellers, Baptists, royalists, and Spaniards; his principal co-conspirators were the duke of Buckingham and Peter Talbot, an Irish Jesuit. Wildman was possibly a co-author in February 1659 of *The Leveller*, which echoed James Harrington's call for a government of laws rather than men. When the army ousted Cromwell in May, Wildman gave up on his plot; by this point Hyde had lost confidence in him in any event. With Marten, Henry Nevile, John Lawson, Samuel Moyer, and John Jones, Wildman wrote two letters to the army leader Charles Fleetwood in early May calling for a bicameral legislature, with a senate to debate issues and a popular assembly to enact laws. Two months later he helped Nevile draft a humble petition to the restored Rump Parliament opposing a unicameral legislature. The petition, which had been written in Nonsuch House, represented Harrington's views. With other republicans, Wildman and Nevile founded the Rota Club in Michaelmas term. In recognition of Wildman's keen interest in polity Fleetwood invited him to sit on a committee to draft a new constitution in the wake of the army's recent expulsion of the Rump, and he did so with zeal, though the effort failed. When John Lambert went to Scotland to heal a rift with Monck over the army's actions Wildman threw his support to Lambert's parliamentarian foes, persuading Colonel Henry Ingoldsby and Major Robert Huntington to seize Windsor Castle. For this the Rump, restored once more, thanked Wildman on 28 December, and he was appointed colonel of the Berkshire militia and a commissioner for the assessment at Westminster in January 1660. The same month he received the council of state's thanks for his service in suppressing dangerous meetings in Berkshire.

Disaffection, imprisonment, and parliamentary service His republican principles notwithstanding, Wildman was initially regarded with favour by the Restoration regime, undoubtedly because of his royalist links in the 1650s. He must have helped himself as well by terminating the Rota Club in February 1660. Drawing on his substantial wealth, he may have assisted Bishop pay £21,000 for the postmaster-generalship, and for a time he exercised considerable influence over Bishop. In the undated 'Brief discourse concerning the business of intelligence' he provided the government with suggestions on how to use the

Post Office to conduct espionage. Simultaneously, however, he participated in the republican club that gathered in his own Nonsuch House, which William Parker managed for him. For allegedly plotting with Harrington, John Ireton, and others, Wildman was imprisoned in the Tower on 26 November 1661. The government suspected them of conspiring to restore the Long Parliament or electing a new one, seizing London and other key towns, and opposing a standing army, but a parliamentary committee could not find substantial evidence of a conspiracy. Apparently to avoid a writ of habeas corpus he was moved to St Mary's in the Isles of Scilly in July 1662. Accusations that he helped to plot the northern rebellion in 1663 are baseless. Moved to Pendennis Castle in early 1666, he was finally released in October 1667, probably through Buckingham's intervention. The duke made Wildman his secretary and legal adviser. Samuel Pepys heard in December that Wildman had been nominated to the commission to investigate the public accounts, but nothing came of this, probably owing to substantial opposition from Sir William Coventry and Sir John Talbot. Citing ill health, Wildman took his family to the continent in July 1670. Upon his return in 1675 he resumed his close relationship with Buckingham, serving as his solicitor and a trustee of his will. He and Nevile accompanied the duke to Paris in August 1678 in an unsuccessful attempt to obtain money from Louis XIV to support their political activities. Although Wildman's endeavour to win a seat in parliament for Marlborough failed in the first election of 1679, he succeeded in the second election, only to be rejected by the election commission. As MP for Great Bedwin, Wiltshire, in the Oxford parliament he voted against exclusion, preferring to impose limitations on James.

The Rye House plot, Monmouth's rebellion, and exile Frustrated by the king's treatment of parliament Wildman apparently engaged in reckless talk of assassinating Charles, or so the informer Charles Rea claimed in April 1681. Wildman was now working closely with Algernon Sidney and Silius Titus. When Sidney persuaded Monmouth, Essex, and Russell to tell Wildman about their proposed insurrection, the latter repudiated assassination. At their request he drafted a revolutionary manifesto; no copy survives. He played a key role in discussions with Scottish dissidents, especially Robert Baillie, but Robert Ferguson subsequently accused Wildman of failing to persuade the Scots to support a commonwealth. He was also in touch with Robert West's Rye House cabal through Richard Rumbold, but he refused to give Rumbold money to purchase weapons for an assassination party. Following disclosure of the plotting Wildman was incarcerated in the Tower, on 28 June 1683. Before his apprehension he had sent word to his wife to destroy any incriminating papers. In late July the government considered trying him, but it had insufficient evidence, notwithstanding Howard of Escrick's claim that Wildman knew about the proposed uprising. Two cannons and their carriage, which James thought were suitable for use in the streets, were found in the cellar of Wildman's London house, hidden under straw and wood; in October the state investigated

their origin (Wildman had obtained them from Buckingham). Appearing in king's bench on a writ of habeas corpus on 28 November, Wildman was released on bail. At his home he celebrated the same day with John Hampden and Francis Charlton. He was formally discharged on 12 February 1684.

By late February 1685, following the accession of James II, Wildman and his cousin William Disney were in contact with Monmouth, urging him to reach an agreement with Argyll regarding an invasion. With the whig Goodwin Wharton, Wildman, seeking funds for Monmouth, searched for treasure in Somerset House and a home in Holborn, purportedly with the aid of an executed felon's spirit. Monmouth asked Wildman to communicate with Macclesfield, Delamere, and Gerard of Brandon about co-ordinating a rebellion in Cheshire with the duke's invasion; at the least, he consulted with Delamere in London. When Monmouth was about to sail he sent Robert Cragg to inform Wildman and to ask that the latter send five or six good horses to the west for the duke's use. Monmouth relied on Wildman, Henry Danvers, and Matthew Meade to lead an uprising in London as soon as government troops left for the west, but this the three men failed to do. Wildman refused to consult with Danvers or make plans until the duke landed, thus betraying the confidence Monmouth had placed in him. By this point Wildman was a wanted man, a warrant for his arrest having been issued on 19 May. Proclamations for his apprehension were published on 4 June and 26 July, but he escaped to the continent. In October he was seen in Cleves, where John Locke joined him the following month. The general pardon issued by the king in March 1686 excluded Wildman, as did James's subsequent pardons. In exile Wildman associated with such fellow dissidents as Francis Goodenough, John Manley, John Matthews, and Sir Robert Peyton. Through Gilbert Burnet he established ties to William, becoming one of his chief propagandists. In the *Memorial from the English Protestants* (1688), ostensibly from suffering protestants in England to Willem Bentinck, Wildman called on the prince to protect protestantism and the fundamental rights of Englishmen. To win the support of the English for William, he also wrote *Ten Seasonable Queries* (1688). Dissatisfied with William's proposed declaration, he drafted an alternative (now lost), castigating Charles's and James's violations of English law. Although Macclesfield and Mordaunt shared his criticism, Shrewsbury, Burnet, and Henry Sidney did not. However, Wildman and Burnet jointly drafted forty or fifty articles condemning James that were to be distributed in the Netherlands if the invasion succeeded.

The Convention and political activities in the age of William III Wildman's stature as a prominent Williamite led to his appointment in December to the assembly of past members of the Commons' committee of thirteen that invited William to exercise civil government. Before the Convention met Wildman articulated his views in *A Letter to a Friend* (1689), arguing that the government had been dissolved and all power vested in the people, and calling for a figurehead monarch devoid of a veto. Elected to the Convention for Great Bedwin, he demanded James's permanent exclusion from the throne, argued that government by a Catholic was inconsistent with England's independence, and averred that making William and Mary sovereigns would prevent anarchy. A member of the rights committee, he proposed that the declaration be sent directly to William, bypassing the Lords. He chaired the committee that investigated Philip Burton and Richard Graham, the crown's solicitors in the Rye House trials. Altogether Wildman was named to sixty-four committees, including those to examine the public accounts, consider the oaths of supremacy and allegiance, prevent excessive expenses in electing MPs, and draft an address supporting William's foreign alliances. He made fifteen recorded speeches, in one of which (on 2 November 1689) he contended that the war against James was to defend England against popery and slavery; France, he thundered, was 'the Bottom of all Slavery' (Grey, 9.391). With the Commons' permission, he testified to the Lords' committee investigating the deaths of Sidney, Essex, and Russell. Perhaps because of his previous ties to the army's rank and file, in early 1689 he received numerous petitions from soldiers in Berkshire protesting their poor condition. He continued to defend his political views in print, publishing *Good Advice before it be Too Late* and *A Defence of the Proceedings of the Late Parliament* the same year. In addition to serving in the Convention, Wildman was appointed postmaster-general at a salary of £1500 p.a. (1689–91), justice of the peace for Middlesex (1689–93), and commissioner of assessment for Westminster (1689) and Berkshire and Wiltshire (1689–93). A member of the Skinners' Company beginning in 1689, he served as an alderman of London (1690–93), having been nominated by Sir Thomas Pilkington and Sir Patience Ward.

In June 1690 Carmarthen accused Wildman of complicity in Sir James Montgomery's plot to restore James to the Scottish throne, but the evidence was inconclusive. The earl of Monmouth charged Wildman with fabricating letters to discredit the tories, an accusation endorsed by Mary. William finally dismissed him as postmaster-general in February 1691, provoking Hampden's ire. The king sought to mend political fences by appointing Wildman deputy lieutenant of Middlesex in March 1692 and knighting him in the Guildhall on 29 October of the same year. Following Wildman's death on 4 June 1693, aged seventy, he was buried in St Andrew's, Shrivenham, Berkshire.

Historical assessment Interpretations of Wildman have ranged widely, from Buckingham's reputed claim that he was one of England's wisest statesmen to Sir William Coventry's damning indictment that he had been false to everyone. According to Cragg, Monmouth complained that Wildman had insisted on governing everyone and blamed him for the lack of sufficient support in England in 1685. Disraeli, on the other hand, absurdly praised Wildman as 'the soul of English politics in the most eventful period of this kingdom' and a man who 'seemed more

than once to hold the balance which was to decide the permanent forms of our government' (B. Disraeli, *Sybil, or, The Two Nations*, 1881, 18). As a political thinker and a legal practitioner Wildman was second rate, though his vision of law reform, including codification of common law, limitations on the power of judges, simplification of property law, and a substantial reduction in the use of capital punishment, was bold. Nevertheless, claiming to champion the rights of Englishmen, he seized every opportunity to profit from the misfortunes of others. His irresistible attraction to political intrigue, which proved to be his defining characteristic, overrode both political convictions and friendships.   RICHARD L. GREAVES

Sources *The Clarke papers*, ed. C. H. Firth, 4 vols., CS, new ser., 49, 54, 61–2 (1891–1901) · *The writings and speeches of Oliver Cromwell*, ed. W. C. Abbott and C. D. Crane, 4 vols. (1937–47) · A. Grey, ed., *Debates of the House of Commons, from the year 1667 to the year 1694*, new edn, 9 (1769) · *JHC*, 5 (1646–8) · *JHC*, 7 (1651–9) · *JHC*, 8 (1660–67) · *JHC*, 10 (1688–93) · M. Ashley, *John Wildman, plotter and postmaster: a study of the English republican movement in the seventeenth century* (1947) · R. L. Greaves, *Secrets of the kingdom: British radicals from the Popish Plot to the revolution of 1688–89* (1992) · A. Woolrych, *Soldiers and statesmen: the general council of the army and its debates, 1647–1648* (1987) · *CSP dom.*, 1649–50; 1654–6; 1659–70; 1676–7; 1680–84; 1689–92 · J. P. Ferris, 'Wildman, John', *HoP, Commons, 1660–90* · W. A. Shaw, ed., *Calendar of treasury books*, 8, PRO (1923); 9 (1931); 10 (1935) · M. A. E. Green, ed., *Calendar of the proceedings of the committee for compounding … 1643–1660*, 1, PRO (1889) · *Seventh report*, HMC, 6 (1879) · *The manuscripts of the House of Lords*, 4 vols., HMC, 17 (1887–94), vol. 2 · *Calendar of the Clarendon state papers preserved in the Bodleian Library*, 3: 1655–1657, ed. W. D. Macray (1876); 4: 1657–1660, ed. F. J. Routledge (1932) · Clarendon, *Hist. rebellion* · J. Frank, *The Levellers* (1955) · D. Underdown, *Royalist conspiracy in England, 1649–1660* (1960) · B. Whitelocke, *Memorials of English affairs*, new edn, 4 vols. (1853) · R. L. Greaves, *Deliver us from evil: the radical underground in Britain, 1660–1663* (1986) · N. Luttrell, *A brief historical relation of state affairs from September 1678 to April 1714*, 6 vols. (1857) · A. B. Beaven, ed., *The aldermen of the City of London, temp. Henry III–[1912]*, 2 vols. (1908–13) · K. Lindley, *Fenland riots and the English revolution* (1982) · C. Holmes, 'Drainers and fenmen', *Order and disorder in the English revolution*, ed. A. Fletcher and J. Stevenson (1984), 166–95 · R. Spalding, *Improbable puritan* (1975), 238

Archives Blenheim archives | PRO, State MSS 31/1/25, 40
Likenesses J. Hoskins, miniature, 1647, V&A · W. Hollar, etching, 1653, BM; repro. in Ashley, *John Wildman*
Wealth at death see will, PRO, PROB 11/415, sig. 105

Wilds, Amon Henry (*bap.* 1790, *d.* 1857). *See under* Busby, Charles Augustin (1786–1834).

Wilds, Sarah (*d.* 1692). *See under* Salem witches and their accusers (*act.* 1692).

Wildy, (Norman) Peter Leete (1920–1987), virologist, was born on 31 March 1920 at Tunbridge Wells, Kent, the only child of Eric Lawrence Wildy (1890–1973), electrical engineer, and Gwendolen Leete (1890–1982). He was educated at Eastbourne College and then went on to study medicine at Cambridge University and St Thomas's Hospital medical school in London. He qualified MRCS, LRCP (1944) and MB, BChir (1948). In 1945 he married Joan Audrey Kenion, daughter of Geoffrey Cadwalladwr Kenion (1881–1945), tea planter, and Beatrice Aitcheson Pyper (1884–1973); they had a son and two daughters.

From 1945 to 1947 Wildy served in the Royal Army Medical Corps in India, Egypt, and west Africa, before returning to a fellowship at St Thomas's Hospital medical school. Appointed to a lectureship there in bacteriology in 1952, he soon became interested in the rapidly growing field of virology and went to study with Sir MacFarlane Burnet at the Walter and Eliza Hall Institute in Melbourne, at that time one of the great centres for virology. It was there that he started work on herpes, which was to be his major research interest for the remainder of his career. He continued this work on returning to St Thomas's and was appointed senior lecturer in bacteriology in 1957. Next he went to Cambridge, and then to Glasgow, where with Michael Stoker as director he created the Medical Research Council's new Experimental Virus Research Unit. Wildy was assistant director of the unit from 1959 to 1963.

However, it was in the short stay in Cambridge that Wildy established his name among virologists worldwide. With Sydney Brenner and Bob Horne, at that time the doyen of electron microscopists, he applied the technique of negative staining to the study of viruses. For the first time some of the structural details, and not just their outlines, could be seen. The interest created by this work led Wildy into virus classification, and his paper 'What's in a virus name?' (*Nature*, 29 Jan 1966, 450–54), with Adrian Gibbs, Bryan Harrison, and Douglas Watson, set out a logical scheme for classifying viruses. This led in turn to the formation of the International Committee for Virus Nomenclature (later the International Committee for the Taxonomy of Viruses), of which Wildy was the first chairman. This unified virus classification and led to the publication, updated every three years, of the *Classification and Nomenclature of Viruses*.

In 1963, after five years in Glasgow, during which the unit he and Stoker had created became an internationally recognized centre of virology, Wildy became professor of virology and bacteriology at the University of Birmingham, where he put together an excellent herpes virology team. Clearly the housekeeping chores of a university department occupied a lot of his time, but he still had the vision to introduce an MSc course in virology which was copied by several other universities. At this time too he started with Colin Kaplan a new journal, *The Journal of General Virology*, which from its humble beginnings in 1967 became a well-established and well-regarded addition to the virology scene. As though that was not enough, together with Joseph Melnick of the USA he initiated the International Congresses of Virology. As with the *Journal of General Virology*, from the first meeting in Helsinki in 1968 these congresses became major events in the international virology calendar. Wildy also founded, with Bernie Roizman of the USA, the annual Herpes Virus Workshop.

In 1975 Wildy moved to the chair of pathology at Cambridge, and became a fellow of Gonville and Caius College. He had clear ideas about how the department should move forward and he was making arrangements at the time of his death to secure the study of parasitology within both the university and the Molteno Institute.

Because of his many contributions to microbiology Wildy had been elected a fellow of the Royal Society of Edinburgh in 1962; he was also president of the Society for General Microbiology from 1978 to 1981 and became an honorary member in 1986. He served on the board of the Public Health Laboratory Service, as well as being an adviser to the World Health Organization and a member of several governing bodies of research council institutes. His wide knowledge and equable personality led to his chairing many (perhaps too many) committees involved in rationalizing British microbiology. Clearly this diverted him from his own research activities far too much, but his breadth of knowledge and vision shone through in what was to be his last grant application to the Medical Research Council for funds to support his research.

Wildy was a countryman at heart and usually found a house in or near a village in which to spend a very full family life, surrounded by plants and animals. He was a large man physically, but this did not give him an overpowering presence. On the contrary, his manner was friendly and kind and it was this manner, together with his generous spirit, which made him the father figure of British virology during his later years. He was also a man of many parts, able to turn his hand to many activities. Aside from his skill on the flute and piccolo, he became involved in the spinning and dying of wool (he actually made a spinning-wheel), reroofed a barn, rebuilt several of the rooms in his house in Abberley in his Birmingham days, and looked after the church clock next to his home when he lived at Hinxton near Cambridge. On top of all these activities, he had a wonderful sense of humour, which enabled him to defuse many difficult professional situations. He was a mimic with quite professional skills and an excellent after-dinner speaker.

Wildy died from lung cancer in Papworth Hospital, Cambridge, on 10 March 1987 and was buried at Hinxton. He was survived by his wife and children.

FRED BROWN

Sources private information (2004) [J. A. Wildy; D. Watson] · personal knowledge (2004) · *The Times* (16 March 1987) · *Daily Telegraph* (3 April 1987) · *The Lancet* (23 May 1987) · WWW
Likenesses portrait, repro. in *The Lancet*
Wealth at death £348,233: probate, 5 June 1987, *CGPLA Eng. & Wales*

Wilenski, Reginald Howard (1887–1975), art critic and historian, was born at 16 Upper Westbourne Terrace, Paddington, London, on 7 March 1887, the son of Abraham Arthur Wilenski, merchant, and his wife, Alice (*née* Simeon), of 16 Upper Westbourne Terrace, Paddington. The surnames suggest a Polish ancestry, and Jewish descent on both his father's and mother's sides. Elected a foundation scholar at St Paul's School, London, he won the John Watson art prizes three years running, in 1902–5 (a fellow premiate in 1904 was Eric Kennington). He won the Smee science prize in 1903; and in 1904 both the Truro prize, for an essay on epic poetry, and the Butterworth prize for English literature. His headmaster observed in his final report that Wilenski was 'very rigorous and capable, has shown power in a great many directions', but added that 'if he were to read for Moderations with profit, he must apply himself to Classics' (private information). Wilenski left St Paul's in July 1905 and went up to Balliol College, Oxford, to read classics, but stayed only a year before leaving, without a degree, to study painting in Munich and Paris. He returned to London in 1909.

He exhibited at the International Society, the Royal Society of Portrait Painters, and the Salon d'Automne, Paris, but achieved no reputation as a painter, although he always described himself as 'artist and art critic'. He presumably enjoyed financial support from his father, since on 5 August 1914 he married, at Kensington register office, Marjorie Isold Harland (1889–1965), a university graduate and daughter of Robert Wilson Harland, civil engineer. By now Wilenski *père* described himself as of independent means, and lived at Maida Vale. Wilenski spent the years of the First World War in the War Office intelligence department.

After the war Wilenski devoted himself to art criticism and wrote exhibition reviews for the *Evening Standard* between 1923 and 1926. Encouraged by the publisher Geoffrey Faber, Wilenski wrote his first polemical book, *The Modern Movement in Art* (1927), in which he saw the modern movement as a return to the architectural or classical idea, especially in the work of the cubists and their followers (he ignored German expressionism, Dada, and surrealism). French critics had earlier made a similar claim. Wilenski considered the study of art history useful only in so far as it shed light on contemporary art, and all his books were aimed at the interested, educated layman. Perhaps his best didactic book is *The Meaning of Modern Sculpture* (1932), where he attacked those who thought the ancient Greek sculptors were the 'first and last to achieve perfection'. He called this the 'finality-complex' and was adept at inventing categories and catch-phrases, which, allied to a pithy style and short sentences, proclaimed his journalistic skills. He defended contemporary sculptors' search for fresh inspiration from non-classical sources.

Wilenski wrote substantial historical surveys of Dutch, French, and English painting in 1929, 1931, and 1933 respectively, to coincide with the large-scale Royal Academy winter exhibitions of those national schools held in 1929, 1932, and 1934. These all followed a similar pattern: the span covered by each exhibition was broken down into periods, and Wilenski wrote a general introduction, followed by a more detailed discussion of individual artists and their works. He adopted the same approach for *Modern French Painters* (1940), and for his two-volume *Flemish Painters, 1430–1830* (1960), the last a carefully researched synthesis of known material presented in layman's language. These popular volumes ran to many revised editions. He ventured into psychological analysis in *John Ruskin: an Introduction to Further Study of his Life and Work* (1933), and suggested Ruskin's madness had begun, not in old age, but in early manhood.

Wilenski, if less influential and profound than Roger Fry, or less infectiously enthusiastic than Clive Bell or Herbert Read, nevertheless provided soundly based, well-illustrated accounts of subjects not catered for elsewhere at that time. In 1945 he began editing the Faber Gallery series of paperbound coloured picture albums, with eminently readable introductions by either himself or other notables, as in *Florentine Paintings*, by Kenneth Clark; some forty titles eventually appeared under his editorship.

Wilenski became a special lecturer in art at Bristol University (1929–30), and a special lecturer in the history of art at Manchester University (1933–45); Manchester University conferred an honorary MA on him in 1938. A press censor from 1939 to 1941, Wilenski also served in the BBC European Services in 1941–4. He was appointed chevalier of the Légion d'honneur in 1967.

Wilenski died of bronchopneumonia at Marlow Cottage Hospital, Buckinghamshire, on 19 April 1975, and was cremated.　　　　　　　　　　　　　　　DENNIS FARR

Sources private information (2004) · I. Elliott, ed., *The Balliol College register, 1900–1950*, 3rd edn (privately printed, Oxford, 1953) · b. cert. · m. cert. · d. cert. · *WW* (1972) · *WWW, 1971–80* · *The Times* (22 April 1975)
Archives King's Lond., Liddell Hart C., corresp. with Sir B. H. Liddell Hart · Tate collection, corresp. with Leon Underwood
Wealth at death £54,192: probate, 11 Sept 1975, *CGPLA Eng. & Wales*

Wilford [*née* Gale], **Elizabeth** (*d.* 1559), merchant, was probably born in the parish of St George, Botolph Lane, London, the only surviving child of Thomas Gale (*d.* 1540), a freeman of the Haberdashers' Company of London, and his wife, Elizabeth (*d.* 1546), the daughter of William Wilkinson, of the parish of St Dionis Backchurch, and his wife, Elizabeth. Her father was active in Iberian commerce, and possessed connections to the prominent London merchants William Locke and Sir George Barnes. She married on or around 1 September 1529 Nicholas Wilford (*d.* 1551), a freeman of the Merchant Taylors' Company, the fifth son of James Wilford, a merchant taylor, sheriff, and alderman of London, and was identified in her marriage indentures as the principal beneficiary of her father's substantial estate. Her husband began his career as a merchant in Bilboa, Spain, in the 1520s, became a substantial English cloth exporter, served as auditor of the City of London (1545–7), represented London in the 1542 parliament, and became a governor of St Bartholomew's Hospital. Following her marriage Elizabeth resided first in the parish of St Bartholomew-the-Less and later, after her mother's death, in her parents' capital tenement and shops in Botolph Lane. She and her husband were also parishioners and property holders of Wandsworth, Surrey. They had four sons and seven daughters: Thomas, who in 1560 married Elizabeth, the daughter of Sir James Hawes; William, who died childless; Robert, who in 1575 married Mary Watson; Edmond, who died in infancy; Elizabeth, who married, first, John Kidderminster and, second, Robert Gage; Anne, who married, first, John Webbe, alias Killiho, and, second, Gabriel White; Parnell, who c.1565–6 married William Towerson; another Elizabeth; Grace; Martha, who married Francis Cressett; and Joyce. Several of the children and their spouses became nationally prominent. The eldest son, Thomas, a freeman of the Merchant Taylors' Company, was a common councilman (1561–99) and chamberlain of the City (1591–1603). William Towerson (d. 1584) was the noted developer of commerce with equatorial west Africa whose exploits were described by Richard Hakluyt in his *Principal Navigations*; Gabriel Towerson (1576–1623), a grandson of Elizabeth Wilford, was the chief factor of the East India Company executed by the Dutch at Amboyna.

Elizabeth Wilford was active as a cloth exporter in her widowhood following her husband's death in the London outbreak of the sweating sickness of 1551. She was one of only two women to appear among the 201 founding members of the Muscovy or Russia Company in 1555, and the only one to invest in her own right, without a spouse. In the absence of business or family papers, she can rarely be viewed outside the circumstances of her domestic life during marriage and widowhood. Her last will of 1559 is typical of her position and sex for this period in its elaborate disposal of possessions within her extended family. Although she moved in socially prominent circles (one nephew was Sir James Wilford MP, and a distinguished mid-Tudor soldier; her brothers-in-law included Sir John (later Lord) Mordaunt; and among her husband's business associates were three lord mayors of London), her first known public act was as executrix for the estate of her deceased husband. Under the terms of Nicholas Wilford's will she probably received in excess of £1000, besides a life interest in all the property in Surrey and the London family residence. In view of the Wilford family's close association with the two innovative long-distance trading destinations of the 1550s, Russia and west Africa, investment in the Russia voyages was a logical move in her widowhood.

Wilford dated her will 31 March 1559; she must have died shortly afterwards, as it was proved on the following 19 April. She was buried beside her husband in the parish church of St George, Botolph Lane. She was evidently raised by Catholic parents and died in the old faith, requesting prayers for the health of her soul.

J. D. ALSOP

Sources T. S. Willan, *The Muscovy merchants of 1555* (1953), 91, 127 · J. D. Alsop, 'The career of William Towerson, Guinea trader', *International Journal of Maritime History*, 4 (1992), 45–82 · PRO, PROB 11/28, fols. 153–4 [will of Thomas Gale] · PRO, PROB 11/31, fols. 27–8 [will of Elizabeth Gale] · PRO, PROB 11/34, fols. 68–9 [will of John Wilford the elder] · PRO, PROB 11/34, fols. 171v.–172v. [will of Nicholas Wilford] · PRO, PROB 11/34, fol. 244 [will of William Wilford the elder] · PRO, PROB 11/42B, fols. 17v.–18v. [will of Elizabeth Wilford] · PRO, PROB 11/125, fol. 107 [will of Anne White] · A. D. K. Hawkyard, 'Wilford, Sir James', HoP, *Commons, 1509–58*, 3.616–17 · R. Cooke, *Visitation of London, 1568*, ed. H. Stanford London and S. W. Rawlins, [new edn], 2 vols. in one, Harleian Society, 109–10 (1963), 55, 143 · R. R. Sharpe, ed., *Calendar of wills proved and enrolled in the court of husting, London, AD 1258 – AD 1688*, 2 (1890), 633 · F. F. Foster, *The politics of stability: a portrait of the rulers in Elizabethan London*, Royal Historical Society Studies in History, 1 (1977), 167, 188 · CPR, 1548–9, 418; 1554–5, 56 · R. Hakluyt, *The principal navigations, voiages, traffiques and discoveries of the English nation*, 2 (1589); facs. edn Hakluyt Society, extra ser., 39 (1965), 98–130 · C. Welsh, ed., *Register of freemen of the City of London in the reigns of Henry VIII and Edward VI* (1908), 56 · probate act book, PRO, PROB 8/3, fol. 23v.
Wealth at death over £1000 presumed; excl. property: will, PRO, PROB 11/28, fols. 153–4; 11/31, fols. 27–8; 11/34, fols. 171v–172v; 11/42B, fols. 17v–18v; Hawkyard, 'Sir James Wilford'

Wilford, Sir James (*b.* in or before **1517**, *d.* **1550**), soldier, was the only son of Thomas Wilford (d. 1553), landowner, of Hartridge, Kent, and his first wife, Elizabeth (d. in or before 1530), daughter of Walter Culpepper of Bedgebury, Kent, and his wife, Anne. His grandfather James Wilford (d. 1526), merchant tailor, sheriff and alderman of London, established the family's fortunes in London and Kent. Thomas Wilford, the eldest son, inherited the Kent estates and, following the death of his first wife, married Rose, daughter of William Whetenhall, of Peckham, Kent. The couple had three sons: Sir Thomas *Wilford (c.1530–1610), soldier, of Heding, Kent, governor of Ostend, deputy lord lieutenant of Kent, and MP for Winchelsea, Sussex; William; and Francis, of Nonington, Kent; and a daughter, Cicely (d. 1611), later the wife of Edwin Sandys, archbishop of York.

James Wilford should not be confused with his first cousin James Wilford, of Broad Street ward, London, and Surrey, eldest son of John Wilford (d. 1551). The first public reference to Wilford is found for 1538, when he was considered for the post of daily waiter in the household of Sir Thomas Cromwell, Henry VIII's secretary. By 1542 Wilford was a servant of the king, when pardoned for an assault enacted with his lifelong friend Thomas Wyatt the younger. He was patronized by Sir John Baker, under-treasurer and chancellor of the exchequer, who was also from Kent. Wilford married Joyce (d. 1580), daughter of John Barrett of Aveley, Essex, by 1543. The couple had a son and two daughters. Baker and Barrett enjoyed a close friendship, cemented by family marriages. Wilford's brother-in-law, Thomas Barrett DCL (d. 1544), was canon of St Paul's Cathedral and a royal chaplain; his sister-in-law, Anne Barrett (d. 1553), married Sir Martin Bowes, under-treasurer of the royal mint and lord mayor of London from 1545 to 1546.

Wilford established his reputation in the wars of the late 1540s, beginning with service in the army royal at Boulogne in 1545. He declined to command at Basse Boulogne under Adrian Poynings in June 1546, but was none the less well respected. A note in the state papers for about 1547 listed him among gentlemen, 'whiche either for ther experyens wysdom lernyng or languages ar mete to serve in the most part of things' (PRO, SP 46/162, fol. 53r). In 1547 he was appointed provost-marshal of the army for the Scottish campaign of the lord protector, Edward Seymour, duke of Somerset. On 10 September 1547 he distinguished himself at the battle of Pinkie, placing himself among the foremost of the vanguard. He was knighted on 28 September for this action. With his star on the rise, Wilford sat in the parliament that met on 4 November, representing Barnstaple, Devon, raised recruits for the army, and returned north, arriving at Newcastle upon Tyne on 12

Sir James Wilford (b. in or before 1517, d. 1550), by unknown artist, 1547

March 1548. Placed briefly in command of Lauder, Berwickshire, in April he participated in the capture of Haddington. This town was to become the key to the English control of the lowlands, and on 28 April William Grey, thirteenth Lord Grey of Wilton, recommended Wilford for the command, informing Somerset, 'there is no man among us so apte for that charge' (CSP Scot., 1547–63, 111). The English occupiers worked feverishly to improve the fortifications, constructing a trace italienne or low-lying artillery fort, but the garrison was overlooked by high ground, victuals were scarce, and the enemy too near. On 3 June Wilford and Thomas Wyndham successfully led a sortie to capture Dalkeith, Edinburghshire, but on 26 June the French army began to move into position for a siege. Wilford's subsequent defence of Haddington, against superior, better equipped forces and in the face of desertion, chronic supply problems, and epidemic disease, was the most celebrated action of the war. The commander was short of powder, shot, victuals, money, and men, and his condemnation of English relief efforts was unremitting. On 11 December Somerset gave free rein to his own frustrations: 'mary we cannot but marvell that ye shuld demaunde so much as ye doo' (PRO, SP 50/4/120, fol. 595). Nevertheless, Wilford's defence was masterly until, early in 1549, upon leading an attack on Dunbar Castle, Haddingtonshire, he was wounded and taken prisoner. Haddington held out until the garrison was evacuated on 1 October 1549, a critical event that led to the end of hostilities in early 1550. The young captain, released on exchange, arrived at York in November in a weak state. He never recovered. Wilford was awarded the keepership of

Otford Park, Kent, made steward of the manor of Gravesend, Kent, and awarded an annuity of £133 6s. 8d. However, his will of 18 November 1550 revealed a broken constitution, 'very weake, feeble and sicke in bodye' (PRO, PROB 11/33, sig. 28). Wilford's death was not long delayed; he died at the Crutched Friars, London, and was buried at St Bartholomew by the Exchange on 24 November. Miles Coverdale preached the funeral sermon. His widow soon after married Thomas Stanley, later an under-treasurer of the Elizabethan mint. Stanley acquired in 1553 the wardship of Sir James Wilford's only son, Thomas.

J. D. ALSOP

Sources HoP, Commons, 1509–58, 2.125; 3.616–17 • will, PRO, PROB 11/33, sig. 28 • CSP Scot., 1547–63 • PRO, state papers Scotland, SP 50/2; PRO, SP 50/3; PRO, SP 50/4 • PRO, state papers, domestic, addenda, SP 15/2 • PRO, state papers, domestic supplementary, SP 46/162, fols. 53r–54v • BL, Add. MSS 32, 657 • exchequer, pipe office, declared account, PRO, E 351/145 • G. W. Marshall, 'Sir James Wilford, Kt.', The Genealogist, 4 (1880), 1–5 • W. Patten, The expedicion into Scotlande of the most woorthely fortunate prince Edward, duke of Soomerset (1548) • M. L. Bush, The government policy of Protector Somerset (1976) • M. Merriman, The rough wooings: Mary queen of Scots, 1542–1551 (2000) • T. Churchyard, A generall rehearsall of warres (1579), sigs. H1r–H1v, H3r • DNB

Archives PRO, SP 15, 46, 50
Likenesses oils, 1547, Coughton Hall, Warwickshire [see illus.] • attrib. J. Belkamp, oils, Knole, Kent • portrait, St George's Hospital, London • portrait, repro. in The Genealogist, 4 (1880), facing p. 1; in possession of A. W. Hall, 1900

Wilford, John (fl. 1706–1747), bookseller, was apparently the stationer apprenticed for seven years to the London bookseller George Sawbridge, on 4 February 1706; this might locate his birth date about 1689. Wilfords are well represented in the seventeenth-century book trade, but John's precise family connections remain obscure. He opened a shop at the Three Flower de Luces in Little Britain about 1715, the year in which he entered The Memorial of the Church of England in the Stationers' Company's register, but his earliest surviving imprint dates only from 1719. It seems that he began as a retail bookseller and only later turned to publishing. All three titles in an advertisement of 'Books sold by John Wilford' at the end of Clarendon's History of the Rebellion … in Ireland (1720) were printed for others, including two for George Sawbridge.

Wilford's most original production was the Monthly catalogue, or, General register of books … printed or reprinted either at London or the two universities (March 1723–December 1729). Previous registers of new titles had been chiefly devoted to promoting the properties of the advertisers (like the Term Catalogues, 1668–1711) or the publisher (like Bernard Lintot's Monthly Catalogue, 1714–17), whereas Wilford's compilation is truly general, indiscriminate, and disinterested—if not, inevitably, exhaustive. In 1730 the Gentleman's Magazine imitated the scheme in a regular monthly department and, to meet this competition, Wilford continued his catalogue as a department of the newly founded rival London Magazine (1731–80). Wilford's Monthly Catalogue remains an indispensable bibliographical guide to the books of its period.

Beside the London Magazine, Wilford published or co-published other important periodicals: the Daily Post

Boy (1728–35), the *Grub Street Journal* (1730–37), and *Fog's Weekly Journal* (1728–37). These occasionally brought him into conflict with government authority—particularly *Fog's Journal* and the foreign news reports featured in the *Daily Post Boy*. Other libels for which he was arrested were Swift's reflections on 'Sir R[ober]t Brass' (that is, Walpole) and 'the Hirelings of St S[tephen]s' in his *Epistle to a Lady who Desired the Author to Make Verses on her in the Heroic Style* (1734), and an advertisement of Pope's *Letters* (May 1735), naming the poet's titled correspondents (considered a breach of privilege).

A list of Wilford's publications may be found in the *Daily Courant* (7 January 1734). From 1731 to 1741 he published a number of titles in parts by subscription, of which the most interesting are two duodecimo volumes of *Select Trials … at the Sessions-House in the Old Bailey* (1734), covering some 'hair-raising varieties of crime' (Wiles, 207). This is the first *Newgate Calendar* and reprints or condenses not only the usual sessions paper and ordinary's account, but also some scarce ephemera. The emphasis is on the sensational and bizarre, but the facts are reliably reported; a reprint with two more volumes (not by Wilford) of a continuation appeared in 1742.

Wilford's last serial publication was *Memorials and characters, together with the lives of divers eminent and worthy persons* (1600–1740), published in twenty-six irregular monthly folio numbers from 1739 to 1741. It contains about 240 lives, one-third of them women's, compiled by the clergyman John Jones (c.1700–1770) and others, chiefly from funeral sermons. The title-page announces that the compilers drew on 'above 150 different Authors, several scarce Pieces, and some original Manuscripts'; there is an appendix of monumental inscriptions.

Wilford declared bankruptcy in 1735 and, though he continued business in Little Britain, published relatively little thereafter. His last imprint is dated 1747, and possibly he died soon afterwards. He is probably not the John Wilford of Southampton Street who died on 2 January 1764.   HUGH AMORY

Sources private information (2004) [M. Treadwell, Trent University] · D. F. McKenzie, ed., *Stationers' Company apprentices*, [3]: 1701–1800 (1978), 307 · F. T. Wood, 'Notes on London booksellers and publishers, 1700–1750', *N&Q*, 161 (1931), 291–3 · *DNB* · R. M. Wiles, *Serial publication in England before 1750* (1957) · D. F. McKenzie and J. C. Ross, eds., *A ledger of Charles Ackers* (1968) · M. Harris, *London newspapers in the age of Walpole* (1987)

Wilford [Wulford], **Ralph** (c.1479–1499), impostor and claimant to the English throne, was the son of a cordwainer who lived at the Black Bull in Bishopsgate Street, London. He was encouraged by an Augustinian friar named Patrick to challenge Henry VII's possession of the throne by impersonating the imprisoned *Edward, earl of Warwick, nephew of Edward IV, as Lambert Simnel had done in 1487. Later he is said to have confessed that the idea of the impersonation originated in dreams he had had while at school in Cambridge. From East Anglia his mentor seems to have taken him into Kent, where he began to confide in individuals that he was the earl

escaped from the Tower of London; the friar then proclaimed him from the pulpit. Wilford was soon arrested and taken first before the earl of Oxford, to whom he confessed his true identity, and then before the king. He was imprisoned, tried, and executed by hanging at St Thomas Watering on the Old Kent Road on Shrove Tuesday (12 February) 1499. Chronicles record his age at death as nineteen or twenty. His body was not taken down and buried until four days later. Friar Patrick, protected by benefit of clergy, was sentenced to perpetual imprisonment.

S. J. GUNN

Sources A. H. Thomas and I. D. Thornley, eds., *The great chronicle of London* (1938) · *The Anglica historia of Polydore Vergil, AD 1485–1537*, ed. and trans. D. Hay, CS, 3rd ser., 74 (1950) · *Hall's chronicle*, ed. H. Ellis (1809)

Wilford, Robert (d. 1396), merchant and mayor of Exeter, may have originated at Nottingham (where his illegitimate son John sold property in 1413), or at Wilford, a village a few miles south of Nottingham. But he came to be closely associated with Exeter, where he is first recorded in 1363, by when he had married Elizabeth, widow of John Hull, a wealthy and politically prominent draper of the latter city. John Hull left one daughter and three sons, one of whom, Henry Hull, served as Robert Wilford's apprentice, and also as executor for both Robert and Robert's son William [see below]. No doubt his marriage provided the material basis for Wilford's trading career. He was the richest and most active merchant in Exeter during the last three decades of the fourteenth century. From 1367 he regularly imported wine, dyestuffs, iron, oil, salt, herring, and other commodities, often transporting these goods in one of three ships he co-owned. His exports of cloth and numerous imports of woad, madder, brasil, alum, and potash reflected his investments in the cloth industry, as did his regular business dealings with dyers, drapers, and merchants in Devon, Somerset, and London. He accumulated extensive property holdings in Exeter and its suburbs, including many shops in prime commercial locations. In 1377 he paid the highest murage tax in the city (15s.); as Exeter's leading citizen he lent money to the city on several occasions, to finance such projects as the construction of a new barge and the paving of the streets.

Not surprisingly Wilford came to dominate the city government of late fourteenth-century Exeter. He served as mayor an extraordinary thirteen times between 1373 and 1394, and also acted as receiver (the city's chief financial officer) twice, steward once, councillor fifteen times, and elector sixteen times. MP for Exeter in 1377 and 1381, he also officiated three times as mayor of the city's staple. His influence outside the city is evident in his appointment as controller of customs at the port of Exeter in 1364, collector of the poll tax in Exeter and its suburbs in 1377, justice of the peace, and member of several commissions of oyer and terminer in Devon. He enjoyed particularly close connections with the Courtenay earls of Devon; listed as an esquire of Earl Edward (d. 1419) in the latter's livery roll of 1384/5, Wilford was also paid for unspecified services on several occasions between 1381 and 1396. Indeed his links with the family covered several generations; Earl

Edward's grandmother, the dowager Countess Margaret (d. 1391), named Wilford as one of her executors, and Wilford later made arrangements in his own will for prayers for the souls of Margaret, her husband Earl Hugh (d. 1377), and their son William Courtenay, archbishop of Canterbury (d. 1396).

Robert Wilford died at Exeter between 7 July and 28 August 1396. In his will he left one third of his estate to be sold for prayers for his soul and for the souls of relatives and friends, another third to his wife, Elizabeth, for the term of her life, and the remaining third to his son William, who also inherited his mother's share when she died some time after 1404. His executors included John Wilford (d. 1417), who was probably his natural son. Although John seems never to have married and to have died without heirs, his birth was no impediment to success as a merchant oligarch in Exeter, where he served in such high city offices as receiver, councillor, steward, and elector on many occasions between 1395 and 1414, and was constable of the staple in 1413 and member of parliament in 1414.

Inevitably, however, John Wilford was overshadowed by his half-brother **William Wilford** (d. 1413), who enjoyed a political and commercial success similar to his father's. Elected mayor of Exeter seven times between 1400 and 1412, he too served the city as receiver, steward, councillor, elector, constable, and mayor of the staple, and as member of parliament five times between 1395 and 1411. Like his father he was appointed to commissions of inquiry and oyer and terminer, and had connections with the Courtenays, acting as a witness to a quitclaim of Sir Edward Courtenay, son of the Earl Edward whom his father had served, although William also wore the livery of Bishop Stafford of Exeter (d. 1419). William Wilford continued his father's interests in the cloth trade, exporting cloth overseas and aulnaging it for domestic sale. His imports, however, were less varied, concentrating largely on wine and woad for dyeing textiles. A shipowner like his father, he was probably the same William Wilford who gained the attention of chroniclers for his exploits as admiral of a fleet of west-country ships which captured numerous French ships loaded with rich cargoes off the coast of Brittany in 1403. Besides seizing the cargoes and burning many of the ships, Wilford also landed at Penmarch on the south-west coast of Brittany, and led his troops some 18 miles inland, ravaging the surrounding villages and countryside.

The Wilfords' standing in Devon allowed William to marry Margaret, widow of Robert Cruwys of Morchard, Rackenford, and East Anstey in Devon, and daughter of Sir Robert Cornu of Thornbury. When William Wilford died in 1413, probably before 26 April, he left a daughter, Elizabeth, who by then had married John Parker of Exeter, and an under-age son, Robert, who eventually received the bulk of his property, including 100 marks reserved exclusively for his support as a minor. His executors included his wife, Margaret, and his half-brother, Henry Hull. To another half-brother, William Hull, he left part of his share in a ship, while to his bastard half-brother, John, Wilford bequeathed a jewel worth 4 marks. His other

bequests included £10 and the revenues from a croft outside the south gate to build and maintain a water conduit in Exeter, along with gifts to the local religious houses, and 4 marks for forgotten tithes. At his death, his goods were valued at £228 6s. 8d.; in 1412 his estates, which included extensive possessions in Exeter inherited from his father, as well as his wife's properties and lands he had acquired in Frogmore and Crediton, yielded an annual income of at least £22. MARYANNE KOWALESKI

Sources Devon RO, Exeter city archives · Devon court rolls, account rolls and deeds, Devon RO · Chancery records · PRO, Chancery extents for debts, C131 · PRO, Chancery certificates of statute merchant and statute staple, C241 · PRO, Court of common pleas, CP40 · PRO, Exchequer aulnage rolls, E101 · PRO, Exchequer K.R. customs accounts, E122 · PRO, Exchequer K.R. memoranda rolls, E159 · PRO, Ministers' accounts, SC6 · BL, Additional charters · F. C. Hingeston-Randolph, ed., *The register of Edmund Stafford, 1395–1419* (1886) · Exeter Cathedral, dean and chapter archives · *Johannis de Trokelowe et Henrici de Blaneforde … chronica et annales*, ed. H. T. Riley, pt 3 of *Chronica monasterii S. Albani*, Rolls Series, 28 (1866) · Nottingham borough court rolls, Notts. Arch. · *Inquisitions and assessments relating to feudal aids*, 6 vols., PRO (1899–1921) · M. Cherry, 'The liveried personnel of Edward Courtenay, earl of Devon, 1384–5', *Devon and Cornwall Notes and Queries*, 35 (1982–6) [151–9, 189–93, 219–25, 258–63, 302–10] · F. B. Prideaux, 'Cruwys of Morchard and East Anstey', *Devon and Cornwall Notes and Queries*, 13 (1924–5), 134–7 · HoP, *Commons* · J. Vowell [J. Hooker], *The description of the citie of Excester*, ed. W. J. Harte, J. W. Schopp, and H. Tapley-Soper, 3 pts in 1, Devon and Cornwall RS (1919–47) · *The register of Edmund Lacy, bishop of Exeter*, ed. G. R. Dunstan, 5 vols., CYS, 60–63, 66 (1963–72) · F. Devon, ed. and trans., *Issue roll of Thomas de Brantingham*, RC (1835) · E. Lega-Weekes, 'An account of the Hospitium de le Egle, some ancient chapels in the close, and some persons connected herewith', *Report and Transactions of the Devonshire Association*, 44 (1912), 480–511 · M. M. Rowe and A. M. Jackson, eds., *Exeter freemen, 1266–1967*, Devon and Cornwall RS, extra ser., 1 (1973)

Wealth at death in 1377 paid 15s. in an Exeter murage tax based on value of goods and lands: Devon RO, misc. roll. 72 · £228 6s. 8d.—William Wilford: will, Hingeston-Randolph, ed., *Register*, 402 · in 1412 estates were conservatively est. to yield £22 p.a.—William Wilford: *Inquisitions and assessments*, vol. 6, p. 419

Wilford, Sir Thomas (c.1530–1610), soldier, was the third son of Thomas Wilford (d. 1553) of Hartridge, Kent, merchant and landowner, and his second wife, Rose, daughter of William Whetenhall of Peckham. His elder half-brother, Sir James *Wilford (b. in or before 1517, d. 1550), had a distinguished military career. Like him, Wilford was brought up as a soldier, but nothing is known of his education. He was a beneficiary of his brother's will.

Wilford was a committed protestant and went into exile with his brother James Wilford during Mary I's reign. They both signed the 'new discipline' at Frankfurt am Main in 1557. Wilford was appointed captain of Camber Castle, Sussex, in 1566 and was much involved in politics and administration in Winchelsea, Sussex, between 1566 and 1572. He was MP for the borough in 1571 and 1572. In 1573, already an experienced soldier, he acted as the marshal for the expedition undertaken by Walter Devereaux, first earl of Essex, during the ill-fated attempt to establish a plantation in co. Antrim. The expedition was strongly opposed by the local Irish chief, Brian mac Phelim O'Neill, and it was largely due to the experience and courage of

Wilford that it survived the winter. His outstanding service to the force was acknowledged by Essex.

Wilford was a strong advocate of English intervention in the Low Countries, and wrote to his protestant patrons, Sir Francis Walsingham, principal secretary, and Robert Dudley, earl of Leicester, on the subject. He was captain of a cavalry company at Ostend in 1585, one of many English officers and men serving in the Low Countries before Leicester's 'official' expedition was sanctioned by the treaty of Nonsuch in August 1585. Leicester reorganized the structure of the English troops, removed Wilford from the official payroll, and transferred him to the payroll of the states general. This caused him acute financial hardship, from which he had not recovered five years later. He was garrison sergeant-major of Ostend in 1586. On Leicester's departure, he served his successor, Peregrine Bertie, Lord Willoughby de Eresby, was made sergeant-major of the entire English force in the Netherlands in 1587, and was appointed a member of the council of war in December 1587 and sergeant-major of the field in February 1588. Willoughby frequently followed his advice. He played a prominent part in the successful defence of Bergen op Zoom, which was attacked in September 1588. Willoughby knighted Wilford for his distinguished service during the siege.

Early in 1589 Wilford was sent to England to report to the privy council on the problems that Willoughby was facing. Sir John Norris bemoaned his absence because he felt that Wilford would be more able to persuade Willoughby to release soldiers for the Portuguese expedition. In September 1589 Wilford was appointed high marshal of the expedition to support Henri of Navarre in Normandy, with Willoughby as commander. He was also colonel of the Kent regiment. The force landed at Dieppe and marched to support Henri at Paris. It supported Henri throughout November and December and played a key part in the capture of Vendôme, Le Mans, and Alençon. During the siege of Alençon on 5 December 1589, Wilford devised an engine that utilized an iron hook to pull down the drawbridge of one of the defensive ravelins defending the town. He then led the assault force into the work and slaughtered the garrison of thirty-four men. The town surrendered the next day, claiming they feared the English behind them more than the French in front of them.

Wilford joined the debate about the correct strategy for opposing a Spanish invasion force, and rejected the notion proposed by Thomas Digges that every landing site should be held and defended with fieldworks and troops. He favoured concentrating forces for an effective counter-attack, and rebutted Digges's work line by line in *A military discourse whether it be better for England to give an invader present battle or to temporise and defer the same.*

After Wilford's return from Normandy his finances appear to have been gradually restored and he became heavily involved in the military administration of Kent. He was appointed the deputy lieutenant of the county in October 1589 and, in addition to taking responsibility for the county musters, he superintended the admiralty works at Dover harbour in 1590–91. He was JP for Kent

from about 1592. He became the governor of Camber Castle in 1593. In July 1595 he was commissioned to exercise martial law in the county, with the draconian power to arrest and summarily execute vagrants and others. In 1597 Wilford was commissioned to survey the castles of the downs, which guarded the sheltered anchorage behind the Goodwin Sands, Kent, following an invasion scare, and in August 1599 was appointed one of the sergeant-majors of the force planned to meet a further invasion threat.

On 17 March 1595 Wilford was admitted as a member of Lincoln's Inn. He died intestate at his manor of Hedding, Kent, on 10 November 1610 and was probably buried there. He had married Mary, the only daughter of Edward Poynings, who had been killed during the defence of Boulogne in January 1546. They had three sons, including Sir Thomas Wilford (who succeeded him and married Elizabeth, the eldest daughter of Sir Edwin Sandys), and a daughter.

M. A. STEVENS

Sources CSP Ire., 1571–5 · CSP for., 1580–90 · APC, 1590–97 · HoP, Commons, 1558–1603 · J. L. Motley, History of the United Netherlands— from the death of William the Silent to the 12 year truce (1609), 4 vols. (1875), vol. 1, pp. 375, 376, 382, 384 · C. G. Cruickshank, Elizabeth's army, 2nd edn (1968) · P. E. J. Hammer, The polarisation of Elizabethan politics: the political career of Robert Devereux, 2nd earl of Essex, 1585– 1597 (1999) · L. Boynton, 'The Tudor provost marshal', EngHR, 77 (1962), 437–55

Archives Leics. RO, corresp. with Robert Dudley, earl of Leicester

Wealth at death owed over 2000 livres in 1589 due to expenditure made at Ostend in 1587; petitioned for redress and was made lieutenant of Kent and captain of Camber Castle; debt probably paid off by time of death: CSP for., 1589, p. 420, fol. 893.

Wilford, William (*d.* **1413**). *See under* Wilford, Robert (*d.* 1396).

Wilfrid [St Wilfrid] (*c.*634–709/10), bishop of Hexham, played a central role in the political and ecclesiastical life of later seventh-century England.

Upbringing and first journey to Rome Born the son of a minor Northumbrian nobleman, Wilfrid was sent at the age of fourteen to the court of the Northumbrian king Oswiu (*d.* 670). There he first demonstrated his ability to elicit the patronage of the great, a quality he retained throughout his life, by attracting the attention of Queen Eanflæd, who placed him at Lindisfarne under the monk Cudda, a former companion of her husband. Within a few years he was sent by Eanflæd to her kinsman, King Eorcenberht of Kent, at whose court he lived for a year or so before taking up with another of the queen's associates, the Northumbrian Biscop Baducing (later Benedict Biscop), in order to make the pilgrimage to Rome. When, about 653, he and Biscop arrived at Lyons, they parted company, not perhaps entirely amicably, Biscop continuing to Rome and Wilfrid remaining under the patronage of the bishop, Aunemund (known to Wilfrid's biographer, Stephen of Ripon (Eddius Stephanus), as Dalfinus). According to Stephen, who is not entirely to be trusted on this matter, the bishop offered to marry Wilfrid to his niece and make him governor of a Frankish province. Wilfrid, however, rejected his offer and proceeded to Rome.

The buildings, ceremonies, and above all the relics of the Holy See had an enormous impact upon the impressionable young pilgrim. He made daily visits to the shrines of the martyrs and conceived (or at least consolidated) there what was to prove a lifelong devotion to the apostolic brothers Peter and Andrew, vowing, before St Andrew's altar in the rotunda attached to St Peter's, to become, like them, an evangelist. Almost as formative was his education in the most recent teaching about the calculation of Easter and other matters of ecclesiastical observance by the archdeacon Boniface with whom he evidently struck up a close friendship. In due course, having been presented to the pope and in possession of a collection of relics, he returned to Lyons. There, according to Stephen of Ripon, he remained for three years, during which he received the tonsure and was further instructed in orthodox practice. More fantastically, Stephen also alleges that he was present at Aunemund's murder, a chronological impossibility since Wilfrid had returned to England by the end of 658 and the murder did not take place until 660. Nevertheless, whatever the precise course of events at Lyons, there can be little doubt that Wilfrid's early visits there left an impression almost as profound as Rome itself, and had a lasting impact upon his notions of episcopal authority and status.

Ripon Abbey and the Northumbrian bishopric, c.658–669 On his return to England, Wilfrid was recommended by the West Saxon king, Cenwalh, to Oswiu's son, the *regulus* (under-king) Alchfrith, by whom he was granted the monastery of Ripon and estates assessed at 40 hides. The monks recently installed there, who included the young Cuthbert and his abbot Eata, were expelled, to be replaced at Wilfrid's invitation by Abbot Tondbehrt and his kinsman Ceolfrith, both from the important royal foundation at Gilling in Northumbria.

In 663 Wilfrid reaffirmed his continental connections by seeking ordination at the hands of the Frankish Agilbert, former bishop of the West Saxons. The young abbot's rising reputation was boosted in 664 when, in conjunction with Agilbert, he proved a skilful spokesman for the victorious Roman party at the Synod of Whitby. By then, however, Wilfrid was making enemies as well as friends. His intrusion into Ripon was almost certainly controversial and the departure of Bishop Colman of Lindisfarne and a substantial portion of his household in the aftermath of Whitby also aroused hostility in powerful quarters within the Northumbrian establishment. Nevertheless, when shortly afterwards the see of Northumbria again became vacant, Alchfrith was able to secure Wilfrid's appointment, with a view to removing the see centre from the now discredited Lindisfarne to Paulinus's church at York. Characteristically, Wilfrid sought unimpeachably orthodox credentials before entering into his inheritance; deeming there to be insufficient bishops in England to perform a valid consecration, he obtained the consent of Oswiu and Alchfrith to go to Francia, where, during a splendid ceremony at the Merovingian royal palace of Compiègne, presided over by his friend Agilbert and eleven other bishops, he was publicly enthroned and

carried shoulder-high in a golden chair. The episode is a clear illustration of the continuing impact of the ideals and aesthetic of episcopal grandeur which Wilfrid had imbibed during his earlier sojourn at Lyons.

According to Bede, Wilfrid 'lingered' abroad seeking consecration. Certainly he seems not to have returned until 666 and then was further delayed when his ship was beached on the pagan shore of Sussex, a potential catastrophe from which he and his followers emerged with honours, having slain the high priest and fought off the South Saxon host before escaping with the returning tide. When the new bishop eventually reached Northumbria, he found his position much changed: his patron Alchfrith had been eclipsed and he himself had been superseded at York by Ceadda (Chad), a figure strongly linked with Lindisfarne. Wilfrid was forced to withdraw to his monastery of Ripon, his base for the next three years from which, resourceful as ever, he exercised his episcopal authority in Mercia and Kent by permission of their friendly kings. In Mercia in particular he seems to have acquired considerable estates from Wulfhere, on which he established religious communities, including perhaps Oundle, where he dedicated a church to St Andrew. The situation was resolved only in 669 after the arrival at Canterbury of a new archbishop, Theodore. Wilfrid was restored to his see and Ceadda, who was consecrated afresh, was made bishop of the Mercians. According to Stephen of Ripon, Ceadda's appointment was largely due to Wilfrid's good offices, his see being based upon the great estate of Lichfield, initially granted to Wilfrid himself. Doubtless, Wilfrid wished to remove a potential rival from the Northumbrian scene; but even so the episode points to a certain large-mindedness, apparent elsewhere in his career.

Episcopal power on the continental model, 669–678 The years which followed his restoration, 669–678, were Wilfrid's most successful and illustrate his aims and ideals most clearly. In accordance with what he had seen in Francia, he replaced the remote island monastery of Lindisfarne with a genuine see city; Paulinus's cathedral at York was splendidly brought back from ruin, adorned with glass windows, whitewashed walls, and new fittings. At Ripon, Wilfrid invested yet more heavily in building, constructing there a new church of stone, dedicated to St Peter at an elaborate ceremony conducted according to Gallic rites and attended by King Ecgfrith and his brother Ælfwine. In addition, by 672 his ecclesiastical patrimony was enriched with the grant by Ecgfrith's queen, Æthelthryth, of a large estate at Hexham, where Wilfrid founded his second great monastery and built another stone church, remarkable for its grandeur and complexity and dedicated to his especial patron, St Andrew. The new buildings reflected Wilfrid's travels. Although vague and confusing, Stephen of Ripon's descriptions suggest that they were aisled basilicas, no doubt influenced by the great churches Wilfrid had seen in Rome and elsewhere; indeed in the twelfth century returning pilgrims expressly declared that the church at Hexham re-created the splendours of the Holy See.

Wilfrid intended the contents of these churches also to

evoke what he had seen abroad. Above all, they were to house relics of the Roman martyrs in an appropriate environment; the strange surviving crypts are perhaps best explained as an attempt to re-create the catacombs in which Wilfrid had seen the corporeal remains of the saints whose relics he had brought back to England. Other objects, equally redolent of Frankish or Roman magnificence, included the gospel book commissioned for Ripon, with its purple-stained pages and letters of gold, the jewelled shrine in which it was stored, and the gold, silver, and purple hangings and altar vestments which adorned his two great churches.

The liturgy within these churches looked to the same cultural milieux. Like Benedict Biscop, Wilfrid was particularly concerned to enhance their ceremonial with appropriate music, bringing to Ripon in the late 660s a Kentish singing master trained in the Roman tradition, the first to practise there since the early seventh century. The importance which the bishop attached to his liturgical achievements is apparent from the fact that, when defending himself at a hostile council some thirty-five years later, he expressly claimed to have introduced into Northumbria the double choir to sing liturgical antiphons and responsions 'according to the rite of the primitive church' (Eddius Stephanus, *Life of Bishop Wilfrid*, c.47). Equally significant was his claim to have been the first Northumbrian to patronize the rule of St Benedict, which he promoted in his two great houses and in the numerous other communities which placed themselves under his direction. His own monastic observance, however, was almost certainly coloured by customs imbided in the Frankish milieux whose eclectic rules provided his earliest introduction to Benedict's work.

Wilfrid was also one of the first English churchmen to appreciate the importance of the written charter as a means of guaranteeing monastic possessions. He caused a list of the gifts made to Ripon to be written down, witnessed, and publicly read at the dedication ceremony and from the 670s he seems to have been associated with a number of innovative charters which adopt a new incarnational dating linked with the Dionysiac Easter tables. He thereby championed two important practices which he encountered abroad: written authentication of land grants and the Easter tables so recently introduced into Rome.

During these successful years Wilfrid enlarged his monastic connection. His possessions increased as Ecgfrith expanded the boundaries of his kingdom; besides his two great houses of Ripon and Hexham, he acquired lands in and to the west of the Pennines, formerly held by the Britons, and in the conquered territories of the Picts and Scots to the north. Moreover, his monastic connection continued to transcend political boundaries; indeed, in the 670s he probably added to his holdings outside Northumbria, in particular in the kingdom of the Hwicce. Wilfrid's pretensions at that period are indicated by his claim at the Roman synod, convened by Pope Agatho to condemn Monotheletism in 680, to represent the whole of northern Britannia and Hibernia, and

the islands settled by the English, British, Scots, and Picts. That he could indeed mobilize wide-ranging contacts is indicated by his response in 676 to a request from the Franks of Austrasia to secure the return from Ireland of the exiled Merovingian prince, Dagobert. Wilfrid more than fulfilled his task, sending Dagobert on his way with a suitable entourage drawn from his own followers. He was then, it seems, in especially close contact with Irish communities which observed the Roman Easter, for only shortly afterwards his monk Willibrord left Ripon to settle among them for a prolonged period of study.

Although Stephen of Ripon dilates upon Wilfrid's temporal glories—his innumerable followers arrayed in royal vestments and arms, his many monasteries, his personal wealth—he also stresses his hero's personal asceticism and pastoral assiduity. Wilfrid is depicted as modelling himself on biblical prophets and apostles, travelling around his diocese, baptizing and confirming in accordance with current models of episcopal sanctity. Though he apparently ordained numerous priests and deacons to help him in the administration of the sacraments, significantly, he consecrated no episcopal coadjutors. Probably he felt that his vast see was best left undivided if he was to maintain the outward show he believed appropriate to his office. As a result he never, as might have been expected, sought the revival of Gregory the Great's scheme for a northern metropolitan with twelve subordinate bishops, nor, apparently, did he openly challenge Theodore's growing pretensions, which culminated in his assumption of the title of archbishop of the island of Britain in 679 or 680. On the other hand Wilfrid certainly aspired to an independence greater than the bishops south of the Humber: in 672, for example, he merely sent legates to the synod which Theodore convened at Hertford. Above all, his claim to represent northern Britain at the synod of 680 looks like a covert assertion of metropolitan, even archiepiscopal, authority. It may be that Wilfrid's fall frustrated (or indeed was precipitated by) such grandiose plans and that he was never thereafter in a position to revive them. That, however, they were not forgotten is perhaps suggested by Stephen's twice referring to York's metropolitan status.

It is significant that Wilfrid never sought to buttress the case for a northern ecclesiastical province by appealing to the authority of Pope Gregory the Great. Interestingly, the cult of the apostle of the English was most vigorously promoted by Wilfrid's opponents; like his Roman mentors, Wilfrid himself appears to have been comparatively uninterested in Gregory, whose teachings on episcopal rule, based as they were upon small dioceses and an avoidance of show, conflicted with his Frankish-derived notions of episcopal power and splendour.

Deposition and first appeal to Rome, 678–680/81 In 678 Wilfrid's fortunes underwent a dramatic reversal: Ecgfrith turned against him and he was driven from Northumbria. The reasons for the king's change of attitude are unclear. Possibly they were connected with Wilfrid's friendly relations with the kings of Mercia with whom Northumbria was generally at variance in the later 670s. A powerful interest within the Northumbrian establishment focused on the great royal foundation of Strensall–Whitby was also hostile to Wilfrid; Strensall–Whitby's abbess, Hild, not only supported the Lindisfarne community at the synod of 664 and Archbishop Theodore in Rome in 680, but had connections with monasteries and aristocrats in western Francia, bitterly opposed to Wilfrid's Austrasian (eastern Frankish) friends. Above all, Ecgfrith himself had strong personal reasons for disliking his bishop, who had supported his first queen, Æthelthryth, in her determination to remain celibate. After she had received the veil from Wilfrid in 672 the king married again, and, according to Stephen of Ripon, his new consort sought to undermine Wilfrid by making the king envious of his outstanding riches. In a deliberate act of provocation, Archbishop Theodore was called in to divide the great Northumbrian diocese. New sees were established at Ripon and Hexham, under figures unsympathetic to Wilfrid and his followers, and York itself was given to a pupil of Hild of Strensall–Whitby, the bishop's old enemy.

Wilfrid determined to appeal in person to the pope against his deprivation and set out for Rome on a leisurely and circuitous progress, apparently intended to avoid the lands of the hostile Ebroin, mayor of the palace and effective ruler of Neustria (western Francia). Having crossed to Frisia, where he paused to preach to the heathen inhabitants, the bishop made his way to the court of his friend Dagobert II, then king of Austrasia, where he was offered and refused the see of Strasbourg. By 679 he had arrived in Rome, where preparations for the synod which was to condemn the Monothelete heresy were in progress. There he claimed (with justification) to have been uncanonically deprived of his see and sought full restitution, or, if that was denied, that any new sees should be occupied by men drawn from the clergy of his churches. The pope and council found in Wilfrid's favour, but worded their judgment with considerable care. Wilfrid was to be restored to the diocese which he had lately held and with the aid of a church council was to choose fellow bishops who were to be consecrated by Theodore. The intruding bishops were to be expelled. Pope Agatho thus allowed Wilfrid a special position in the north but stopped short of awarding him metropolitan status. Wilfrid's position was, however, further strengthened by a privilege exempting his monasteries from the authority of the diocesan and ascribing them directly to the Holy See.

Armed with this verdict Wilfrid returned to Northumbria. Ecgfrith was, however, unmoved by the pope's judgments, and according to Stephen of Ripon cast his former bishop into prison, an episode ignored by Bede and difficult to accommodate with evidence that by 680 Wilfrid had departed to Mercia. The exile was given land for a small monastery by Berhtwald, nephew of King Æthelred and probably sub-king of a Mercian dependency in north Wessex. Those arrangements were, however, soon terminated by pressure from Ecgfrith and perhaps from the West Saxon king, Centwine, Ecgfrith's brother-in-law. Wilfrid, his fortunes at their lowest ebb, was forced to take refuge in Sussex. The Mercians' only concession to

their former protégé was to allow Oshere, king of the Hwicce, to grant land at Ripple (in modern Worcestershire), originally given to the monastery of Ripon, to one of his monks.

Conversion of Sussex and bishop of the West Saxons, 680/81–686 When Wilfrid arrived in Sussex in 680 or 681, the king, Æthelwalh, and his people were, according to Stephen of Ripon, entirely pagan. Bede, however, relates that Æthelwalh himself had married a Christian princess and accepted the Christian faith at the instigation of Wulfhere of Mercia some five to ten years earlier; he also mentions, somewhat dismissively, a little community of Irish monks at Bosham, the later history of which suggests that it may have been more important than he allowed. Nevertheless, Wilfrid must be credited with a major role in converting the still largely pagan population of Sussex. He was able to capitalize on a severe drought, the end of which apparently coincided with his arrival in the kingdom. Characteristically making the most of his opportunities, he not only urged the new faith upon a people who felt deserted by their ancient gods with notable persuasiveness, but also taught practical remedies, in particular new methods of fishing, to counteract the famine which the drought had induced. When Æthelwalh gave Wilfrid a large estate at Selsey, upon which he established a monastery, he further insinuated the new religion by manumitting all the slaves.

Some time in the early 680s Wilfrid seems to have transferred his allegiance to Cædwalla, an exiled and still pagan prince of the West Saxons who invaded Sussex and slew Æthelwalh. When Cædwalla became king of the West Saxons in 685, he summoned Wilfrid, making him bishop in his kingdom and giving him 300 hides in the newly conquered Isle of Wight. The South Saxons, who quickly regained their independence, were it seems abandoned or subjected to the West Saxon bishopric, while the still pagan inhabitants of the Isle of Wight were placed under the care of Wilfrid's nephew Beornwine, who was one of his clergy, and the priest Hiddila. This murky episode, which scarcely redounds to Wilfrid's credit, is treated with considerable circumspection by both Bede and Stephen of Ripon.

Renewed dissension and second appeal to Rome, 686–705 Shortly after his removal to Wessex, Wilfrid's fortunes changed yet further for the better. With the death of Ecgfrith in 685, the elderly archbishop, Theodore, determined to make peace and in 686 he sent letters recommending a settlement to the new king of Northumbria, Aldfrith, to Abbess Ælfflæd of Whitby (who appears to have inherited her predecessor's mantle as leader of the anti-Wilfridians), and to Æthelred of Mercia. According to Stephen of Ripon, Theodore also sought to nominate Wilfrid his successor at Canterbury, an offer which Wilfrid magnanimously suggested was best referred to a church council.

Aldfrith fell in with the archbishop's proposals and Wilfrid was restored to his privileged monasteries of Hexham and Ripon and to the diocese of York, from which the intruder Bosa was expelled. His new diocese was, however, only a shadow of the great see which he had administered in the 670s. To the south Lindsey had been lost to Mercia and to the north Abercorn to the Picts. Moreover, in Bernicia the sees of Lindisfarne and Hexham, created since 678, remained in being. Although Wilfrid administered both temporarily for about a year, following the deaths of their bishops, Eata and Cuthbert, by 688 both sees had new incumbents. The partial nature of the settlement made further dissension inevitable and matters came to a head in 691, according to Stephen of Ripon because of the king's insistence on implementing the late archbishop's controversial decrees and more especially because of plans to despoil the monastery of Ripon of its lands and turn it into an episcopal see. By 692 Wilfrid had left for Mercia, and Bosa, it seems, had been restored to York.

Wilfrid remained in Mercia under the protection of King Æthelred for some eleven years, serving as bishop at Leicester and assisting in the translation ceremonies at Ely of his friend and patron, the queen–abbess Æthelthryth. In 703 Berhtwald, Theodore's successor at Canterbury, presided over a church council which, with Aldfrith's consent, sought to resolve Wilfrid's anomalous position by depriving him of all his possessions except the monastery of Ripon, where he was to remain without exercising his episcopal office.

In consultation with Æthelred, who continued to guarantee Ripon's Mercian endowments, Wilfrid determined on a further appeal to Rome, a move to which his enemies responded by excommunicating him and all his supporters. By 704 both Wilfrid and his party and the envoys of Archbishop Berhtwald were in Rome. Basing himself on earlier papal judgments in his favour, Wilfrid appealed to Pope John VI (r. 701–5) for a confirmation of Agatho's privilege for his two great monasteries. The pope found Wilfrid personally guiltless of the charges alleged against him and confirmed the judgments of his predecessors; anxious to avoid dissension in Britain, he ordered that the matter be resolved at a synod convoked by Berhtwald 'with Bishop Wilfrid', and attended by Bosa of York and John of Hexham.

Settlement, last years, and death Wilfrid, as always tempted to linger abroad, remained in Rome for several months, visiting the shrines of saints and collecting relics, ecclesiastical vestments, and ornaments. As he returned he suffered a seizure at Meaux, from which he perhaps never fully recovered and during which he received a vision indicating that he had been saved by the intercession of the Virgin, whose cult he had hitherto neglected in favour of the apostles Peter and Andrew. He arrived in Kent in 705, was reconciled with Berhtwald, and, attended by his abbots, made his way to London and thence to the former king, Æthelred, by then abbot of Bardney, who greeted him with renewed friendship. Aldfrith, who refused to accept the judgment of the Holy See, died shortly afterwards, leaving a minor as his heir and apparently expressing regret for his obduracy. Wilfrid was much involved in

the political upheaval which followed. Aldfrith's successor, Eadwulf, was of a different lineage, and evidently was regarded by Wilfrid (whose entourage at Ripon included Eadwulf's son) as a friend. Eadwulf, however, rejected Wilfrid's advances, ordering him to leave the kingdom. Shortly afterwards the king himself was expelled, after a reign lasting only two months, and Aldfrith's young son, Osred, succeeded. By then, in a sudden *renversement*, Osred had become Wilfrid's adopted son (*filius adoptivus*); the bishop, so long at variance with the house of Ecgfrith, had been transformed into the guardian of its heir. It is perhaps at this period that Hexham, under Wilfrid's episcopal control, espoused the cult of the saint–king Oswald, a leading member of Osred's lineage. The fruits of the realignment became apparent in 706 when, at a synod presided over by Archbishop Berhtwald and attended by Northumbria's leading nobles and clergy, Ripon and Hexham with all their possessions were restored to Wilfrid. Shortly afterwards Bosa of York died, and the opportunity arose to reinstate Wilfrid in his original see. The ageing and probably ailing bishop did not, however, press his claims, acquiescing instead in the translation of John of Hexham, a move which left Wilfrid with episcopal as well as abbatial authority at Hexham. Significantly, Stephen of Ripon never discusses the episode, which he perhaps regarded as a defeat.

Wilfrid survived a further four years. Some eighteen months before he died he suffered a second stroke, after which he made a final disposition of his possessions, choosing suitable superiors to rule his monasteries and, it seems, deciding on the distribution of his lands. Not long afterwards he shared out his portable treasure, kept at Ripon. His mode of doing so casts an interesting light on the ideals and practice of Rome's great champion. According to Stephen of Ripon, he summoned two of his abbots and a number of monks, before whom he divided his treasure into four parts. The best portion was offered to two Roman churches, the Liberian basilica, Santa Maria Maggiore, and the shrine–church of the apostle Paul, San Paolo fuori le Mura; of the three remaining portions, one was to be devoted to the poor, a second to the abbots of Ripon and Hexham 'to purchase the friendship of kings and bishops' (Eddius Stephanus, *Life of Bishop Wilfrid*, c.63), and a third to rewarding those followers who had accompanied the bishop into exile but had not yet received treasure or estates. Although the exact sequence of events is unclear, it seems that Wilfrid went on to nominate his kinsman Tatberht as co-ruler and eventual successor at Ripon and Acca as his successor at Hexham. All this, it need hardly be said, is a world away from ideal Benedictine practice as recommended by the rule, which laid especial emphasis on the community's role in electing its superior regardless of the claims of the founder's kin. Indeed, Wilfrid's actions at this particularly crucial moment of his life look like those of a contemporary secular aristocrat. In particular, his sharing out of his treasure evokes the actions of a Germanic lord in the midst of his *comitatus* (following), rather than the traditional deathbed scenes of a Christian bishop and abbot. Significantly, none of this appears in Bede, whose own ideals of episcopal behaviour as set forth, for example, in his letter to Ecgberht or his life of Cuthbert are markedly different and more austere.

After making these dispositions, Wilfrid received a deputation asking him to confer with King Ceolred about the position of his monasteries in Mercia. He therefore left for that kingdom, where he again confirmed his will, distributing land and possessions among his monks. He then proceeded to his monastery at Oundle, where he was seized with a final sickness and shortly afterwards died. It was the forty-sixth year of his episcopate and the fourth year of Osred's reign: almost certainly, therefore, 709 or 710. After due preparation his body was placed in a cart and brought to Ripon for burial on the south side of the altar in the church of St Peter. Bede records the elaborate epitaph inscribed on his tomb.

Assessment and cult Undoubtedly ambitious, probably pugnacious and opinioned, Wilfrid was from an early age deeply and enthusiastically involved in controversy. His career divided contemporaries and has engendered debate among historians ever since the early eighth century, when Stephen of Ripon and Bede produced their divergent accounts. That Wilfrid could elicit fierce loyalty is sufficiently indicated by the admiring and committed tone of Stephen's biography. That, on the other hand, his was a somewhat ambiguous career, is suggested by Bede's account with its significant omissions and discreet distortions. Clearly Bede could not ignore a figure who played so large a part in establishing the church in his own kingdom and elsewhere, who had championed Roman orthodoxy so successfully, and who was, moreover, the patron of his friend and diocesan Acca. His account represents a carefully edited summary of those episodes in Stephen which were most relevant to his own purposes in writing his *History*. It need not necessarily be read as disapproving, although it is perhaps worth remembering that it was before Wilfrid, who for some six years was his diocesan, that Bede was accused of heresy, a charge which stimulated a furious letter stigmatizing the bishop's entourage as drunken boors, and barely veiling an attack on the bishop himself.

One aspect of Wilfrid's career which Bede unquestionably plays down is his involvement in earthly concerns. Undoubtedly, Wilfrid could in many ways be described as worldly; he was fond of display and a great builder and collector of fine objects; he clearly shared many of the values of the secular nobility, whose sons were to be found in his entourage, and treated his friends and followers with an open-handed generosity appropriate to a great lord; he was at home in royal courts and spent time and effort in winning the good opinions of kings and princes. Yet he was more than this. His support of Æthelthryth in her pursuit of virginity suggests a concern for ascetic values sufficient to put at risk his most significant royal friendship. The controversies in which he was embroiled were clearly not all of his making; and his apparent willingness in 680

to accept the division of his diocese, provided his colleagues were drawn from his own clergy, seems reasonable. Above all, his evangelizing activities at the low points in his career suggest a genuine and continuing concern to fulfil his early vow before St Andrew's altar.

Wilfrid was one of the most cosmopolitan figures of his age: his monastic communities represent a network transcending English political boundaries; his diplomatic contacts extended from Ireland to Austrasian Francia, Lombard Italy, and Rome; his architectural, liturgical, and collecting interests mark him as among the foremost English patrons of the arts in the later seventh century, rivalled only by Benedict Biscop. Such wide-ranging activities left a lasting impact, especially apparent in his missionary work. Not only did he do much to speed up the final phases of the conversion of the English kingdoms in the 680s, but in Frisia his preaching, followed up by the work of his pupil Willibrord, and his consecration of Willibrord's companion Swithberht as bishop in the early 690s, initiated Anglo-Saxon intervention in the pagan areas on the Frankish periphery.

All in all, Wilfrid was a remarkably complex figure. The defender of Roman orthodoxy was educated in an Irish-influenced milieu and built up a monastic confederation not unlike those of his Irish contemporaries. The earliest Northumbrian exponent of the Benedictine rule probably himself followed eclectic Gallic observance. Paradox and ambiguity also characterized his personal life. Clearly ambitious, he declined several offers of advancement, including, apparently, the English primacy. Worldly and rich, he seems to have practised private austerities. Such contradictions help to explain the ambivalent discretion of Bede's portrait.

Among his followers Wilfrid became the object of a cult immediately after his death. At Oundle, in ceremonies which resemble those accorded to other early English saints, the body was brought into a marquee and laid out, washed, and clothed in appropriate ecclesiastical vestments. Water used in washing the body was ritually poured away at a carefully marked site which became the scene of miracles, and the robe on which Wilfrid's body had been laid out was also preserved and esteemed a holy relic capable of working wonders. At Ripon the whole community came out bearing relics to greet the funeral cortège in a ceremony again modelled on those for the reception of a saint. Tatberht, Wilfrid's heir, established the formal apparatus of a cult, celebrating a daily private mass in Wilfrid's honour and keeping Thursday, the day on which he died, as a feast day equivalent to Sunday. The anniversary of the saint's death became an even more solemn feast attended by a great gathering of his abbots and followers. There were vigils at the tomb and on at least one occasion the event was marked by a sign which was taken by Stephen of Ripon as proof that in death Wilfrid had joined the company of the apostles in heaven.

In pre-conquest England, Wilfrid was commemorated by two feasts, 12 October and 24 April. In 709 neither date was a Thursday, the death-day which Stephen of Ripon expressly says was kept as Wilfrid's feast. Although the

October date has traditionally been regarded as the main commemoration, marking Wilfrid's death or deposition, the April feast is in fact earlier—it alone occurs in the eighth- and ninth-century calendars; 24 April was a Thursday in 710, and is therefore probably the date of Wilfrid's death. The emphasis on the October feast perhaps developed because that in April was likely to conflict with Lent and Easter.

Although Wilfrid's cult started early, it did not spread particularly rapidly. Stephen of Ripon's life survives in only two manuscripts and probably never had a wide currency outside Wilfrid's foundations. One reason for its limited circulation is that the Wilfridian confederation soon broke up; almost certainly, it suffered a severe blow when Wilfrid's heir at Hexham was driven from his see in 731. Thereafter, the main cult centre seems to have been at Ripon, where, following its sack by Eadred in the mid-tenth century, the cult was revived and patronized by Oda, archbishop of Canterbury, and his nephew Oswald, archbishop of York. There were, allegedly, two *inventiones* (discoveries), the accounts of which are mutually contradictory. Oda was believed to have brought Wilfrid's body from Ripon to Canterbury, whereas Oswald elevated the relics *in situ* and re-established a community at Ripon to look after them. Those events issued in a verse reworking of Stephen's life, by Frithegod, a member of Oda's household, again a work which achieved only a very limited circulation. Thereafter relics were distributed to other great centres, including Peterborough.

By the conquest Wilfrid's cult was relatively well-established; his feast is to be found in most of the early calendars, although curiously he was rarely invoked in the litanies. In England at least eleven religious communities claimed to possess a relic, and some forty-eight ancient churches were dedicated to him. ALAN THACKER

Sources E. Stephanus, *The life of Bishop Wilfrid*, ed. and trans. B. Colgrave (1927) · E. Stephanus, 'Vita sancti Wilfridi I, episcopi Eboracensis', *Passiones vitaeque sanctorum aevi Merovingici*, ed. B. Krusch and W. Levison, MGH Scriptores Rerum Merovingicarum, 6 (Hanover, 1913), 193–263 · Bede, *Hist. eccl.*, 3.25; 4.12–14; 5.19 · *Venerabilis Baedae opera historica*, ed. C. Plummer, 2 vols. (1896) · D. P. Kirby, ed., *St Wilfrid at Hexham* (1974) · D. P. Kirby, 'Bede, Eddius Stephanus and the "Life of Wilfrid"', *EngHR*, 98 (1983), 101–14 · H. Mayr-Harting, *The coming of Christianity to Anglo-Saxon England*, 3rd edn (1991) · E. John, 'The social and political problems of the early English church', *Land, church and people*, ed. J. Thirsk (1970), 39–63 · J. Campbell, 'Bede I' and 'Bede II', *Essays in Anglo-Saxon history*, ed. J. Campbell (1986), 1–48 · W. Goffart, *The narrators of barbarian history* (1988), 235–328 · G. Isenberg, *Die Würdigung Wilfrieds von York in der Historia ecclesiastica gentis Anglorum Bedas und der Vita Wilfridi des Eddius* (Münster, 1978) · A. T. Thacker, 'The social and continental background to early Anglo-Saxon hagiography', DPhil diss., U. Oxf., 1976, 235–78 · W. T. Foley, *Images of sanctity* (1992) · W. T. Foley, '*Imitation apostoli*: St Wilfrid of York and the Andrew script', *American Benedictine Review*, 40 (1989), 13–31 · M. Gibbs, 'The decrees of Agatho and the Gregorian plan for York', *Speculum*, 48 (1973), 213–46 · C. Cubitt, 'Wilfrid's "usurping bishops": episcopal elections in Anglo-Saxon England', *Northern History*, 25 (1989), 18–38 · C. Cubitt, *Anglo-Saxon church councils, c.650–c.850* (1995) · P. Sims-Williams, 'St Wilfrid and two charters dated AD 676 and 680', *Journal of Ecclesiastical History*, 39 (1988), 163–83 · I. N. Wood, 'Ripon, Francia, and the Franks' casket in the early middle ages', *Northern History*, 26 (1990), 1–19, esp. 8–17 · I. N. Wood, 'Northumbrians and Franks in the age of Wilfrid', *Northern History*, 31 (1995), 10–21 · P. Fouracre and R. A. Gerberding, *Late Merovingian France: history and hagiography, 640–720* (1996), 172–6 · S. Coates, 'The role of bishops in the Anglo-Saxon church', *History*, new ser., 81 (1996), 177–96 · *Frithegodi monachi breviloquium vitae beati Wilfredi et Wulfstani*, ed. A. Campbell (Zurich, 1950) · Bede, *Opera de temporibus*, ed. C. W. Jones (1943), 132–5, 307–15 · Eddius Stephanus, *Het Leven van Sint Wilfrid*, ed. H. Moonen (1946)

Wiliam Dafydd Llywelyn (*b.* **1525/6**, *d.* in or after **1606**), scribe of Welsh manuscripts, described himself as of Llangynidr, Brecknockshire. His patronymic tells all that is known of his father, Dafydd Llywelyn. In a manuscript he wrote in 1604 (NL Wales, MS 15542) he records his age as seventy-eight.

The earliest reference to Wiliam is as customary tenant of a meadow in Llangynidr in 1561. His surviving manuscripts, probably written for his own use, show interest in Welsh literature and, unusually, in early texts on Welsh music. The earliest of them appears to be NL Wales, MS Peniarth 147, written not before 1566. Of the ten manuscripts that he wrote, wholly or in part, several are fragmentary, and only one identifies the scribe, in a dated colophon (as did one other known only from a copy). Annotation in two of his manuscripts which contain medical texts in Welsh, NL Wales, MS 5280 and BL, Add. MS 15078, shows that he must have been a practising physician.

Wiliam's copies of recusant texts first appear in manuscripts datable to the 1580s. Swansea City Library MS A.1.57 contains a miscellany of Welsh devotional texts, some of Welsh origin and others translated, including Richard Bristowe's *Manuall, or, Meditation* (printed clandestinely three times between 1580 and 1592), a translation which Wiliam also copied in NL Wales, MS Llanstephan 13, evidence that he was producing copies other than for his own use. The most substantial recusant work which he preserved is in NL Wales, MS 15542, written in 1604. This work, known only from this manuscript, is Robert Gwyn's *Lanter Gristnogawl*, book 1, composed in 1580 (published in 1970 by Geraint Bowen as *Gwssanaeth y gwŷr newydd*), and book 2, composed in 1574. In a colophon to this manuscript, written when he was seventy-eight, Wiliam Dafydd declares that he wrote this book 'not for myself but for those who would come after me'.

NL Wales, MS 13250, a literary miscellany evidently dating from Wiliam's last years, reflects an abiding interest in earlier Welsh literature, including poetry relating to the Tristan legend, while also containing a carol to the Virgin and the unique text of a Welsh translation, by Arthur ap Huw (*d.* 1570), vicar of Tywyn, Merioneth, of an attack on the reformers dating from Marian times, George Marshall's *A Compendious Treatise in Metre*, published in 1554. This little miscellany exemplifies the complex amalgam of his inheritance.

Wiliam's most personal remarks, and a reminder of the anxiety that could be felt even in a remote part of Wales by an eighty-year-old recusant scribe, come in his colophon, preserved in a copy in NL Wales, MS Llanstephan 17, fols. 312–13, to a lost transcript by him of the metrical psalms of William Midleton which he made in 1606:

the head white, the eye dull, the hand heavy, the house smoky, the master busy, the wife bitter, the bed hard, the bread tough, the drink sour, friends far, the purse empty, acquaintance small, trust smaller, and in slight fear that some wandering rascal should see me in that smoky corner and proclaim abroad that I was doing other than what I was.

DANIEL HUWS

Sources D. Huws, 'Wiliam Dafydd Llywelyn', *Y Cylchgrawn Catholig*, 12 (2000), 23–9 · G. Bowen, ed., *Gwssanaeth y gwŷr newydd* (1970) · R. G. Gruffydd, ed., *A guide to Welsh literature*, 3: *c.1530–1700* (1997) · Badminton manorial records, NL Wales, 58 and 405 Archives BL, Add. MS 15078 · NL Wales, 471; 13250; 15542 · NL Wales, Llanstephan 13; 24 · NL Wales, Peniarth 147 · Swansea City Library, A.1.57

Wiliam Llŷn (1534/5–1580), Welsh-language poet, may have hailed from Llŷn in Caernarvonshire: the name adopted by Wiliam, and by his brother and fellow poet Huw Llŷn, and references by contemporary poets, support this supposition. In spite of several conjectures—one links Wiliam with the Griffith family of Cefnamwlch—the exact nature of his connection with Llŷn remains a mystery. What is known is that by 1569 he had married and settled in Oswestry (his son, Richard, was baptized there that year), and a lease of 1574 shows that he was residing in Willow Street in a house that he later bequeathed to his wife, Elizabeth, and which she subsequently leased (1587) to Llŷn's bardic pupil and elegist, Rhys Cain.

The earliest poem by Wiliam that can be accurately dated is a series of *englynion* to Gruffudd Dwnn of Ystradmerthyr, Carmarthenshire, composed in 1557. Thomas Wiliems claims that Dwnn, who was renowned for his patronage and learning, instructed both Wiliam and his brother Huw in the poetic art (Cardiff Central Library, Cardiff MS 4.330, 223). Wiliam himself acknowledges his debt to the poet Siôn Brwynog of Llanfflewin, Anglesey, who died in 1562 (Stephens, poem 101), but his most important bardic teacher, and the figure with whom he is invariably associated, was Gruffudd Hiraethog. Of Gruffudd's numerous pupils it was Llŷn who gained preeminence [*see also* Cywyddwyr (*act. c.*1330–*c.*1650)]. According to the master, 'Nid oes dim yn anwybodus i Wiliam Llŷn' ('There is nothing that Wiliam Llŷn does not know'; Bowen, 242). After his death in 1564 many of Gruffudd's books found their way to Wiliam's home in Willow Street. Wiliam followed in his mentor's footsteps, and, having previously graduated as *disgybl disgyblaidd* ('amenable apprentice'), won recognition as *pencerdd* ('chief of song'), and possibly as bardic teacher, at the Caerwys eisteddfod of 1567. Wiliam's poignant elegy to Gruffudd is regarded as his most outstanding composition.

Gruffudd's books contained genealogical and heraldic material. Wiliam annotated and augmented these; he likewise compiled genealogical and heraldic books which now form part of the Peniarth collection at the National Library of Wales, Aberystwyth, as well as historical, grammatical, and astronomical texts, which have not survived. His vocabulary (Cardiff Central Library, Cardiff MS 3.12) was patterned on Gruffudd's, and he exemplified individual words with quotes from his own poems and those of

contemporary and earlier poets. Wiliam in turn bequeathed 'all the bookes and rolls that I have' to his pupil Rhys Cain (Morrice, xx–xxi), who paid tribute to his instructor in a moving elegy, as did another pupil, Siôn Phylip.

Between 1557 and 1580 Wiliam composed about 175 *cywyddau* and *awdlau*, half of which are safeguarded in two manuscript collections in his own handwriting (Cardiff Central Library, Cardiff MSS 2.103, 5.167). In many cases the year of composition is conveniently recorded. The note 'Wm llyn ai k ar diwaytha y kafodd dal am dano 1580' ('Composed by Wiliam Llŷn; the last for which he received payment 1580') follows the *cywydd* to Edward Llwyd of Plas Is-y-clawdd, Chirk. These pieces are mostly eulogies and elegies to members of the gentry, and occasionally to church dignitaries such as Richard Davies, bishop of St David's, and to lesser lights, such as Owain ap Gwilym, curate of Tal-y-llyn in Merioneth. In keeping with the poet's social role in late medieval Wales, Wiliam composed verse soliciting gifts on behalf of his patrons; he also had cause to thank two of his patrons for gifts—a peacock and a bow—that he received.

Wiliam seems to have been reluctant to travel far from Oswestry in his search for patronage. The greatest number of his poems by far were addressed to families in the counties of Flint and Denbigh, Merioneth and Montgomery, and visits to Caernarvonshire and Anglesey in the north, and to south Wales, were noticeably less frequent. On one occasion he was induced to seek reconciliation with one Wiliam Gruffudd of Caernarfon. Reading between the lines, it appears that Wiliam had failed to keep an engagement, and, significantly, his two other conciliatory poems sought to appease patrons who lived across the Menai Strait in Anglesey. It is not inconceivable that their evident displeasure could have been the result of a broken promise by the poet.

Welsh poets in the second half of the sixteenth century used the *englyn* form to a far greater degree than their predecessors, and Wiliam Llŷn was no exception. About 100 of his *englynion* have been recorded. Those describing the hospitality he received in individual homesteads naturally belong to the same genre as his more formal praise poetry. Others convey his dealings with fellow poets such as Morys Dwyfech, Raff ap Robert, and Simwnt Fychan. Many can be loosely described as love and religious verses, two themes that are given no prominence in the *cywyddau* and *awdlau*. Wiliam is credited with only one religious *cywydd*, which is somewhat reminiscent of Siôn Cent, and one love poem (Gruffudd Hiraethog again comes to mind), an *awdl*, which effectively demonstrates his technical dexterity even if its content lacks passion.

Wiliam Llŷn's importance as an elegist has long been recognized. J. C. Morrice claimed that he was 'the best elegist not only of the sixteenth century but, perhaps, of all Welsh bards' (Morrice, xxxix). The acute expression given to the poet's personal lamentation at the loss of a patron and acquaintance and to the grief felt by family and society alike is in keeping with this particular genre. In

Wiliam's elegies, stark and candid comments of the inevitability of death and man's helplessness in view of his impending fate recur with unnerving consistency, all conveyed in a dignified yet sparing and proverbial style that complements the *cywydd*'s compact couplets. The two most remarkable elegies were composed to Gruffudd Hiraethog and to fellow poet, Owain ap Gwilym, the latter recorded in over ninety manuscript sources. Both feature a dialogue between the dead and the living, a device employed by Rhys Cain when he had cause to mourn Wiliam Llŷn's death, and copied by several poets during the course of the following century, especially in connection with the death of a member of the bardic fraternity. Saunders Lewis and other critics have argued that Wiliam's elegies are an expression of Renaissance stoicism.

Nine poems by Wiliam (including the two elegies mentioned) were included in *Gorchestion beirdd Cymru* (1773) and about 100 in *Cynfeirdd Lleyn* (1905). The most comprehensive collection of his works, Morrice's *Barddoniaeth Wiliam Llŷn* (1908), unfortunately contains verse that cannot now be safely attributed to the poet.

The registers of Oswestry parish church record the death and burial there of 'Will'm Llyn Bardus' on the last day of August 1580. According to Rhys Cain, Wiliam Llŷn died before reaching the age of forty-six.

A. CYNFAEL LAKE

Sources R. Stephens, 'Gwaith Wiliam Llŷn', PhD diss., U. Wales, 1983 · J. C. Morrice, *Barddoniaeth Wiliam Llŷn* (1908) · M. Fardd [J. Jones], *Cynfeirdd Lleyn, 1500–1800* (1905) · R. Jones, *Gorchestion beirdd Cymru* (1773) · D. Huws, 'Wiliam Llŷn, Rhys Cain a Stryd Wylow', *National Library of Wales Journal*, 18 (1973–4), 147–8 · D. J. Bowen, 'Disgyblion Gruffudd Hiraethog', *Studia Celtica*, 10–11 (1975–6), 241–55 · G. A. Williams, 'Galwedigaeth Wiliam Llŷn', *BBCS*, 26 (1974–6), 36–7 · S. Lewis, *Detholion o waith Ieuan Glan Geirionydd* (1931), 16–24 · R. M. Jones, *Llên Cymru a chrefydd* (1977), 274–80 · B. Jarvis, *Llinynnau* (1999), 36–44 · parish register, Oswestry [death, burial]

Wiliems [Williams], **Thomas** (*b.* 1545/6?, *d.* in or before 1623?), Welsh lexicographer, was the son of Wiliam ap Tomos ap Gronwy, and Catherine, the illegitimate daughter of Meredydd ab Ifan, founder of the Wynn family of Gwydir and great-grandfather of its historian, Sir John Wynn. Born in Ardda'r Mynaich in Arllechwedd, probably in 1545 or 1546, and possibly on 20 April, Wiliems probably went to the school kept by the Wynn family primarily for its sons and also attended by William Morgan, the future translator of the Welsh Bible, but instead of proceeding to Cambridge as the latter did, he went to the University of Oxford, although there are no clear records of his stay there owing to confusion with others of the same name. He must have left Oxford without a degree to take holy orders, hence the 'Sir' usually prefixed to his name (the title traditionally accorded to clergymen in Wales). He served for a while as curate in Trefriw, not far from his home. There he remained for the rest of his life, although he later became a recusant and thereafter practised as a physician, a calling that at that time required no special training and at best only book- or manuscript-learning, of

which he had much, having started transcribing manuscripts when he was twenty-one years old, if not earlier. Wiliems was fortunate to be born into a generation of gentry better educated owing to the influence of the Renaissance than ever before and for some time afterwards, a generation well represented as such by the *generosi* of the Vale of Clwyd and its vicinity, who seem to have had in their possession some of the most important extant Welsh manuscripts. This meant for Wiliems easier, although not easy, access to manuscripts, to read and/or transcribe which he was prepared to make every effort.

Naturally Wiliems could not disregard medical manuscripts such as Llanstephan MS 10 and BL, Add. MS 14913 (with its text of *Meddygon Myddfai*), both of which passed through his hands, and it is not surprising to learn from Bishop Humphrey Humphreys that there existed in his time 'a pretty large Herbal in Latin, Welsh and English' written by Wiliems; parts of this may survive in Thomas Evans's hand in Cardiff MS 2.973.

Like some of his fellow recusants denied access to the press, Wiliems took part in transcribing their works to secure their preservation and circulation. Father Vincenzo Bruno SJ's *Trattato del sacramento della penitenza* was apparently translated by him into Welsh. A section of the second part of Gruffydd Robert's grammar was copied by him in Peniarth MS 62. Wiliems was free from the prejudice which led some protestant Renaissance scholars to disregard the documents relating to the history of the medieval church.

But Wiliems's interest in Welsh manuscripts was wider even than that of the poets, their traditional conservationists, for it was the catholic interest of one who must have been planning at an early age to write a dictionary of the Welsh language. There is evidence enough to prove that he examined, transcribed, and/or used all kinds of manuscripts comprising genealogical texts (witness 'Prif Achæ Holh Gymrû Benbaladr', NL Wales, MSS 16962 and 16963), historical texts (transcripts of 'Brut y Brenhinedd' and 'Historia Dared', NL Wales, MS 5281), legal texts (a transcript of a Latin text of the Welsh Laws, Peniarth MS 225, and signs of having read Peniarth MS 29 and Peniarth MS 30), linguistic, including grammatical, lexicographic, and other pertinent texts (transcripts of 'Pum Llyfr Cerddwriaeth' in Peniarth MS 62, of two bardic grammars in Mostyn MS 110, and his copious summary of Welsh proverbs in Mostyn MS 204, although not in his hand), and selections from the corpus of late medieval professional poetry (Peniarth MS 77, Havod MS 26). Peniarth MS 188 is described by J. Gwenogvryn Evans as Wiliems's 'Common place book or dictionary-in-the-making', 'the whole having no apparent system or arrangement'. Although Wiliems does not mention Thomas Thomas's Latin–English dictionary (first edn, 1587), he found in it the system he could follow: all he had to do was to substitute Welsh equivalents for Thomas's English. It took him several years (4 May 1604–2 October 1607, although the date on the title-page is 1608) to write up his 'Thesaurus linguae Latinae et Cambrobritannicæ', the three quarto volumes of Peniarth MS 228.

The strenuous efforts of his friend John Edwards, Plas Newydd, Chirk, extending even to the making of a more legible partial copy (Brogyntyn MSS 9 and 10) to ensure publication, proved to be unsuccessful and Wiliems turned to his kinsman, Sir John Wynn, in whose possession the manuscript was (from 13 August 1623) after Wiliems had died. Sir John Wynn did not survive Wiliems for many years, but he quickly appealed to John Davies, Mallwyd, for his help, promising financial support providing Davies would see the work through the press and on condition that full recognition be given to the author and the dedication be to Sir John. Davies was known to be engaged on a Welsh dictionary, and eventually published the *Dictionarium duplex* (1632) comprising a Welsh–Latin part composed by himself and a Latin–Welsh which is admittedly and obviously based on a very much abridged and revised version of Wiliems's 'Thesaurus'. Perhaps Davies should not be too harshly criticized for taking advantage of the circumstances, and especially of the support of the Gwydir family, but one must regret that Wiliems has been denied the recognition and honour he so richly deserves as the author of the 'Thesaurus' and as one of the greatest lexicographers of the Welsh language.

J. E. CAERWYN WILLIAMS

Sources DWB · J. E. Caerwyn Williams, 'Thomas Wiliems, y Geiriadnowr', *Studia Celtica*, 16–17 (1981–2), 280–316 · J. E. C. Williams, *Geiriadurwyr y Gymraeg yng nghyfnod y dadeni* (1983) · G. Harries, 'Blwyddyn geni Syr Thomas Wiliems', *Llên Cymru*, 2 (1952–3), 259 · G. Bowen, 'Lhyuran or Sacranen o Benyd, Thomas Wiliems o Drei friw', *National Library of Wales Journal*, 13 (1963–4), 300–05 · M. J. Burdett-Jones, 'Sacrafen Tenyd', *Ysgrifau Beirniadol*, 13 (1985), 227–31 · C. G. Thomas, 'Oan gyfeiriad at Syr Tomas Wiliems, Trefriw, ym mhafunrau'r Sesiwn Fawr am Sir Odinbych', *National Library of Wales Journal*, 23 (1984–5), 425–7 · *Report on manuscripts in the Welsh language*, 2 vols. in 7, HMC, 48 (1898–1910) · G. Tibbott, W. L. Davies, and E. D. Jones, 'Introduction to handlist of Peniarth manuscripts', *Handlist of manuscripts in the National Library of Wales*, 1 [1940], iii–xxiii · NL Wales, Peniarth MS 62, 119

Wilkes, John (1725–1797), politician, was born in St John's Square, Clerkenwell, London, on 17 October 1725, the second son of the six children of the malt distiller Israel Wilkes (1698–1761) of Clerkenwell and his wife, Sarah (1700–1781), the daughter of John Heaton, a tanner from Bermondsey. This plebeian though prosperous background was not a promising one for a man with social and political pretensions, but the Wilkes family evidently marked out the clever and charming John for such advancement, and there never seems to have been any suggestion that he should manage the distillery. That task fell to his younger brother Heaton after the eldest son, Israel, had declined it. Having been sent to a school in Hertford in 1734, Wilkes had mastered Latin and Greek by the age of fourteen, and remained a scholar throughout his life. His Presbyterian mother was the dominant figure in the household, but John took the opportunity to break free of moral restraint when he went to the University of Leiden in 1744; he later boasted to James Boswell of his incessant whoring and drinking there. This Dutch interlude ended when he was summoned back for an arranged marriage on 23 May 1747 to a bride some ten years older

John Wilkes (1725–1797), by Johan Zoffany, 1779–82 [with his daughter Mary Wilkes]

than himself, Mary Mead (d. 1784), whose dowry from her wealthy widowed mother was the manor of Aylesbury in Buckinghamshire. While it was evidently intended by his parents to establish his fortune, this betrothal was a mismatch between a simple, devout woman and a sophisticated rake, one that not even the birth of a daughter, Mary (known as Polly), in 1750 could save. For some years Wilkes played a dual role of country squire—he served as a local magistrate in Aylesbury—and London man about town (he was elected to two prestigious clubs, the Royal Society in 1749 and the Beef Steak Club in 1754). Wit and generosity gave him the entry into society his parents had sought for him.

In Buckinghamshire, Wilkes joined the Hell Fire Club, as locals dubbed the society of 'the monks of St Francis' at Medmenham, and doubtless regaled members with the 'Essay on woman', an unpublished obscene parody of Alexander Pope's *Essay on Man* which he wrote in 1754. His evil genius was Thomas Potter, who not only strengthened Wilkes's addiction to vice but also introduced him into politics. Before the parliamentary general election of 1754 Potter deceptively flattered him with the idea of a joint candidature for the two seats at Aylesbury, where Wilkes had an important interest—only for Wilkes to find himself being palmed off with the honorific sop of being county sheriff while Potter was elected with another candidate. The prime minister, the duke of Newcastle, noting his interest in politics, sent Wilkes to fight, at his own expense, the distant borough of Berwick upon Tweed, a hopeless and costly quest. Such political adventures incurred almost as much disapproval by his thrifty and puritanical wife as his fashionable lifestyle, and the marriage broke up. A trial separation in 1756 became permanent the next year, when Wilkes retained the Aylesbury estate and agreed to pay his wife £200 a year. Their daughter chose to live with her father, and their loving relationship was thought even by his severest critics to be a redeeming feature of Wilkes's life.

Entry into politics, 1757–1763 Wilkes now decided to exploit his electoral influence at Aylesbury, and the opportunity came in 1757, when Potter moved to another seat on being given office by a new ministry headed by the elder William Pitt. Wilkes already knew Pitt as the brother-in-law of his Buckinghamshire neighbours Lord Temple and George Grenville, and enrolled under his banner after an unopposed by-election. Pitt in reply congratulated him 'on your being placed in a public situation of displaying more generally to the world those great and shining talents which your friends have the pleasure to be so well acquainted with' (John Wilkes MSS, BL, Add. MS 30877, fol. 5). But Wilkes, so sparkling a companion, was not a fluent public speaker and remained anonymous and silent in parliament. This failure to live up to expectations doomed his various patronage requests to be a lord of trade, ambassador to Constantinople, and governor of Quebec. At the next general election, in 1761, he avoided a contest for his Aylesbury seat by crude bribery, offering 300 of the 500 voters £5 each. Before the new parliament met Pitt resigned office over the cabinet's refusal to back his demand for a Spanish war. Wilkes took Pitt's side, and made his maiden speech supporting him on 13 November 1761, being deemed a follower of Lord Temple. He spoke several more times that session, but soon realized that he would not make his mark in debate. Horace Walpole was disparaging about his performance: 'His appearance as an orator had by no means conspired to make him more noticed. He spoke coldly and insipidly, though with impertinence; his manner was poor, and his countenance horrid' (Walpole, *Memoirs*, 1.142).

The political talent of Wilkes lay in his pen. After an anonymous pamphlet of 9 March 1762, *Observations on the Spanish Papers*, and some essays in *The Monitor*, he made his name by his political weekly the *North Briton*, founded on 5 June 1762 to attack the new ministry of George III's Scottish favourite, Lord Bute. The very name was chosen to adopt a satirical guise of Scottish approval of Bute's take-over of England. Wilkes was personally responsible for most of the text, though the poet Charles Churchill was also an important contributor. The paper, which soon achieved a circulation of nearly 2000, escaped prosecution by shrewd political calculation and legal advice: but individuals offended included Lord Talbot, lord steward of the royal household, who fought a pistol duel with Wilkes on 6 October 1762, and the cartoonist William Hogarth, who was to exact revenge in 1763 by his savage caricature *John Wilkes Esquire*. This portrayal of an impudent demagogue with a hideous squint was to be the visual image of Wilkes conveyed both to contemporaries and to posterity. More conventional portraits show that he was not quite

that ugly, but he himself was famously wont to say that it took him half an hour to talk his face away.

During the Bute ministry (1762–3) the main focus of opposition attack was the peace of Paris ending the Seven Years' War, condemned as far too generous to defeated France. The *North Briton* commented on 1 January 1763 that the treaty had 'saved England from the certain ruin of success', and the paper constantly reminded readers of the old Scottish alliance with France against England. The journalistic talent of Wilkes soon came to appear the sole recourse of Bute's enemies as opposition in parliament faded early in 1763. Ministerial attempts to silence the paper were unavailing, for government lawyers could find no ground for prosecution.

The *North Briton* case When Bute resigned on 8 April 1763 he was succeeded as prime minister by George Grenville, who had broken with Pitt and Temple in 1761. Wilkes momentarily held his fire, but when Grenville ended the parliamentary session by a king's speech commending the peace, *North Briton* no. 45 on 23 April denounced the 'ministerial effrontery' of obliging George III 'to give the sanction of his sacred name' to such 'odious' measures and 'unjustifiable' declarations. Immediate prosecution of the paper for seditious libel ensued. But the Grenville ministry made a legal blunder by arresting Wilkes and his associates under a general warrant directed against 'the authors, printers and publishers' without naming any persons. The story initially became confused when Wilkes himself was released on the ground of parliamentary privilege. When the crowd in Westminster Hall, ignorant of legal niceties, saw their hero being freed on 6 May, the building echoed with shouts of 'Wilkes and liberty'. Wilkite mobs on London streets became a common phenomenon during the next dozen years. Wilkes now challenged the legality of the general warrant by actions for damages and false arrest. There already existed doubts on that point; but an expensive and sustained legal challenge was now made possible by the deep purse of Lord Temple, ironically the prime minister's eldest brother.

The ministerial campaign against Wilkes preceded legal decisions on general warrants. Wilkes had unwisely given a hostage to fortune by privately printing off a few copies of the *Essay on Woman*. The ministry obtained a copy, and further blackened his already unsavoury reputation by having it read out to a crowded House of Lords when parliament met on 15 November 1763. The House of Commons resolved on the same day that the *North Briton* was a seditious libel, and on 24 November that parliamentary privilege did not cover seditious libel, thereby exposing Wilkes to punitive legal action. The Commons debate of 15 November, moreover, had resulted in a pistol duel the following day in Hyde Park between Wilkes and an MP, Samuel Martin, who had impugned his personal courage. Wilkes was so badly wounded in what many thought a plot against his life that he was unable to attend any further legal or parliamentary proceedings. Before the end of the year he had fled from justice: he crossed to France on 25 December and took up residence in Paris. Pleading ill health, he refused to attend either parliament or the law courts.

The House of Commons on 19 January 1764 received evidence that Wilkes had published the *North Briton*, and so expelled him as unworthy to be a member, without a vote. Politicians concerned about the issues he had raised were not willing to defend the man himself. But the legality of general warrants was a matter of widespread concern, and after a run of acrimonious debates the ministry avoided a parliamentary defeat on 17 February by only fourteen votes, 232 to 218. The trial of Wilkes for libel followed four days later in the court of king's bench. He was convicted of publishing the *North Briton* and the *Essay on Woman*, but no attempt was made to prove his authorship. After he had failed to answer five summonses to attend, he was outlawed on 1 November. The *North Briton* case nevertheless produced a victory for 'liberty' in the total condemnation of general warrants. Already on 6 December 1763 Chief Justice Charles Pratt had ruled in the court of common pleas that general warrants could not be used as search warrants of unspecified buildings. This verdict was complemented by judgments of Chief Justice Lord Mansfield in the court of king's bench on 18 June 1764 and 8 November 1765 that ended the use of general warrants for the arrest of persons.

Wilkes was to remain abroad for four years, since his return to Britain would have meant imprisonment. Later he recalled, admittedly to a Paris correspondent, that he was 'never so happy' as in his French exile (Wilkes MSS, U. Mich., Clements L., III, no. 26). He entered the dazzling intellectual society of Paris through the salon of Baron D'Holbach, a former fellow student at Leiden, and was lionized as a champion of liberty. He acquired a tempestuous Italian mistress in the nineteen-year-old dancer Gertrude Corradini, but on a journey to Italy in 1765 she decamped with all she could carry. Wilkes stayed for four months in Naples, and then made his way to Geneva, spending two months in the company of Voltaire. He returned to Paris in the hope of help from the first Rockingham ministry, former opponents of Grenville, for his affairs were now desperate. Afraid of the financial consequences of debt and outlawry, he had liquidated his assets in Britain: the manor of Aylesbury was sold for £4000, his library for £500. But the friend, Humphrey Cotes, to whom he had entrusted the management of his finances, proved neither competent nor honest. After Wilkes received £1000 in the first half of 1764, he obtained not a penny more from Cotes. Numerous requests to the Rockingham ministry for a pardon and patronage, backed by a mixture of flattery and threats, produced only a precarious income of £1000, voluntarily subscribed by friends in that administration. Wilkes unofficially visited Britain in May 1766 in a vain attempt to extort a pardon, and did so again in the autumn after the duke of Grafton took over the Treasury on behalf of Lord Chatham, the former Pitt. Grafton declined to help him, and a furious Wilkes returned to France to write a scathing pamphlet, *Letter to the Duke of Grafton*, an attack on 'flinty heart' Chatham, that served to bring Wilkes back to public attention and to

pave the way for his return to Britain. News of the bankruptcy of Cotes in the summer of 1767 may have been the final spur, if credence may be attached to this apocryphal statement: 'What the devil have I to do with prudence? I owe money in France, am an outlaw in England … I must raise a dust or starve in a gaol' (Bleackley, 185). Wilkes intended to obtain a parliamentary seat at the general election due by March 1768, and to do so through popular election, not by purchase or gift from an admirer. He visited London briefly in December 1767, and returned in February 1768, living quietly under the name of Osborn until parliament was dissolved on 11 March. No answer was made to a request for pardon that he submitted to the king on 4 March, but neither was there any attempt to apprehend him. Wilkes, to resolve this anomalous situation, formally announced his intention to surrender himself to justice when the court of king's bench next met, on 20 April, and meanwhile busied himself with securing a parliamentary seat.

The Middlesex election Wilkes defied the advice of his friends and stood for the City of London in the election on 25 March 1768, but he came last of seven candidates for the four seats, with a mere 1247 votes, as against 2957 for the lowest successful candidate. He blamed his failure on the shortness of his campaign, and dropped a bombshell by promptly announcing that he would challenge the two sitting members for the county of Middlesex (in effect Greater London with a rural surround). A clockwork campaign organized both propaganda and transport to the county town of Brentford, 10 miles from the City. Superb organization was reinforced by popular enthusiasm, as crowds intimidated supporters of his two opponents, the Chathamite George Cooke and the independent Sir William Proctor. In a low poll on 28 March, Wilkes triumphed by 1292 votes to 827 for Cooke and 807 for the defeated Proctor.

The cabinet, headed by the duke of Grafton, promptly decided to expel Wilkes from parliament on the assumption that he would be imprisoned after his court appearance on 20 April. But Lord Mansfield deemed his attendance in court voluntary, and the ministry feared a riot if he was arrested. Wilkes, anxious to resolve the legal situation, delivered himself into custody on 27 April, only to be freed by a mob. In a farcical sequel to this episode he stole into prison in disguise, giving rise to obvious jokes. On 8 June his outlawry was revoked on a technicality, but six days later he was sentenced for his 1764 convictions, a year each for publishing the *North Briton* and the *Essay on Woman*. The whole Middlesex election case was played out while he remained in king's bench prison.

That famous saga was preceded by a by-election caused by Cooke's death. John Glynn, Wilkes's leading counsel, defeated Proctor in a poll in December 1768 by 1542 votes to 1278, a result that signified the Wilkite hold on Middlesex more obviously than the snap victory of Wilkes himself. A petition from Wilkes about his treatment in 1764, and a newspaper piece by him on 10 December, accusing the ministry of having deliberately planned a military attack on a Wilkite crowd outside his prison on 10 May that resulted in several fatalities, provoked the wavering Grafton cabinet into a renewed determination to expel him from parliament. This was achieved on 3 February 1769 by a composite resolution listing five libels, two as seditious and three as obscene, the former being the newspaper item of 10 December 1768 and the *North Briton*, and the latter drawn from the *Essay on Woman*. Many deemed this mode of proceeding unfair, but the expulsion was carried by 219 votes to 137. Wilkes was not the man to accept such treatment, and he was returned unopposed at a by-election on 16 February 1769. Next day the House of Commons resolved Wilkes to be 'incapable' of election, since he had been expelled, and later again voided his return in a second by-election on 16 March. To end this monthly ritual, the ministry, for the third by-election on 13 April, produced a rival candidate, Colonel Henry Luttrell, who was well protected by soldiers. Although Wilkes defeated Luttrell by 1143 votes to 296, the latter was awarded the seat by the Commons two days later. The episode became a major political controversy, as the parliamentary opposition challenged the decision both at Westminster, where the ministerial majority fell to 54 over the seating of Luttrell, and in a summer petitioning campaign throughout England. The topic dominated the opening of the new parliamentary session in January 1770, and Grafton resigned as prime minister when his Commons majority fell to forty; however, Lord North stepped into the breach, to become prime minister for the next twelve years. Wilkes had felled one prime minister, but had not brought down the king's government.

Wilkes had no intention of being the cat's-paw of the parliamentary opposition. Deprived of a Commons seat until the next general election, he intended to make London his power base, for the democratic structure of City government was open to exploitation by such a popular hero. The 7000 liverymen annually chose the City officials and the court of common council, and also, within each of the twenty-six wards, the aldermen for life as vacancies arose. But before the political career of Wilkes could be relaunched, his finances had to be put in order, if his release from the king's bench prison in April 1770 was not to be followed by immediate imprisonment for his debts, estimated at £14,000 in February 1769. That month the Society of Supporters of the Bill of Rights was formed, and made the settlement of these debts its first task, a herculean one in the face of Wilkes's continued extravagance even in prison. Already Wilkes himself had secured election as alderman, for the ward of Farringdon Without in January 1769, and that year saw Wilkites procure City offices and become aldermen. But a split among Wilkites resulted from the intention of a group led by John Horne to make the Bill of Rights Society a truly radical organization and not merely a vehicle for the payment of Wilkes's debts. An escalating quarrel led on 9 April 1771 to secession by Horne and his supporters, who formed a new Constitutional Society. However, despite this quarrel, both factions co-operated in the simultaneous contest with the House of Commons over parliamentary reporting.

The reporting of parliamentary debates Hitherto parliamentary reporting had been suppressed by direct action by both houses against newspapers and magazines. The successful challenge to this censorship in 1771 followed a tactical coup masterminded by Wilkes. The political excitement generated by the Middlesex election had led to a significant expansion of the London press, and by early 1771 this had resulted in extensive reporting of parliamentary debates. The attempt by the Commons to stop this practice was initiated by two ministerial supporters, and the North administration soon gave it official backing. On 7 February 1771 two printers were summoned to appear, and on 26 February their non-attendance led to orders for their arrest. Wilkes, realizing that the campaign would be extended to other newspapers, devised a plan to thwart this policy. He would pit against the power of parliament the privilege of the Wilkite-dominated City of London, which claimed an exclusive right of arrest within its own boundaries, and where printers would be encouraged to take refuge. The beauty of the scheme was that secrecy was not necessary. Once the House of Commons had embarked on its course of action, confrontation would be inevitable. And so it proved. Six more printers were added to the list on 12 March, and three days later an attempt to arrest one of them in the City, John Miller of the *London Evening-Post*, a Wilkite newspaper, was frustrated by City magistrates. It was in vain that the Commons imprisoned the Wilkite Lord Mayor Brass Crosby and another alderman. Wilkes himself, the third official directly concerned, refused to obey the summons before the house, and the Commons chose not to pursue the matter; Chatham was informed on 24 March that 'the ministers avow Wilkes too dangerous to meddle with. So his Majesty orders: he will have "nothing more to do with that devil Wilkes"' (*Correspondence of William Pitt*, 4.122–3). In London even ministerial supporters deemed it prudent to support the City's privilege, and parliamentary reporting continued from within this safe haven. The North ministry tacitly conceded defeat, and thenceforth newspaper reporting of parliament was established. The administration had been outmanoeuvred by the astute Wilkes, even though the parliamentary opposition had shunned the project. Once the fatal step into the City had been taken the government was unable to extricate itself from the trap. There was a sequel to this episode in 1775 when Wilkes, then lord mayor, threw down the same gauntlet to the House of Lords, which declined a confrontation, for the consequences of committing him to the Tower were too horrendous to contemplate. This freedom of the press to report parliament was a significant long-term gain for 'liberty' in ensuring responsibility of MPs to their constituents.

City politician This so-called *Printers' case* was the greatest triumph of Wilkes arising from his power within the City of London, but during the next few years he further exploited the political situation there to embarrass government. It was a three-sided contest, for the secession group led by John Horne competed with the Wilkites in radical zeal and for City posts, while the North ministry sought to exploit the split among its opponents. Wilkes did not himself draft the political programme put forward by the Bill of Rights Society on 23 July 1771, but he endorsed it and personally advocated annual parliamentary elections and the abolition of pocket boroughs. In the 1771 election of City sheriffs he and his acolyte Frederick Bull defeated two ministerial candidates. As sheriff, Wilkes adopted a high profile, out of a genuine concern for 'liberty' as well as to cultivate his public image. He sought to prevent government 'packing' of juries, and criticized the multiplicity of death sentences for trivial crimes. This role was a preliminary to the 1772 election of lord mayor. Wilkes duly headed the poll, but the court of aldermen exercised its right to choose the second candidate, the Hornite James Townsend. 'Wilkes was thunderstruck, and, for once, angry in earnest', noted Horace Walpole (Last Journals of Horace Walpole, 1.158). A year later the ministry stood aside as Wilkites fought Hornites. Wilkes and Bull came first and second, only for an alliance of ministerialists and Hornites in the court of aldermen to choose Bull, a treatment of Wilkes that proved counterproductive, as Walpole commented: 'This proscription of Wilkes, though for two years together he was first in the poll, did but serve to revive his popularity from the injustice done him' (ibid., 1.250).

For most of 1774 the inevitable candidature of Wilkes for lord mayor dominated London politics. The situation was complicated by the ministerial decision to call a general election in the autumn of 1774, but Wilkes gained by a bargain with John Sawbridge, hitherto a leading Hornite. Sawbridge was promised Wilkite support for a London parliamentary seat, and in return prevented radical opposition at the mayoral elections to Wilkes and Bull, who defeated two ministerial candidates. This time the court of aldermen accepted Wilkes, again top of the poll. Soon afterwards Wilkes re-entered the Commons, being returned unopposed with Glynn for Middlesex, to the vain fury of king and ministers.

The mayoralty of Wilkes was one of the most splendid in London's history. His generosity, popularity, and flair for publicity combined to make it memorable; and affection for his daughter, Polly, an elegant lady mayoress, also explained why he put on such a show. He gave frequent and lavish entertainments—his expenses of £8226 exceeding by £3337 his official allowances—and he ended heavily in debt. Wilkes, as when sheriff, took his duties seriously. He concerned himself with the regulation of food prices and with charity for prisoners, and he initiated a campaign against prostitutes, thereby gaining respect and respectability; the archbishop of Canterbury attended one of his functions. Genial host and busy administrator, Wilkes hoped to take advantage of his popularity by securing election to the lucrative if onerous post of City chamberlain, manager of London's finances. But, after persuading the incumbent to resign, he was defeated in 1776 by a ministerial candidate, for by then his seemingly unpatriotic opposition to the American War of Independence was proving to be a solvent of Wilkite control of the City.

Wilkes and America Contrary to legend, Wilkes never championed the cause of American independence in principle. Nor was he even always sympathetic to colonial grievances. His reaction, when in France, to news of the Stamp Act crisis in 1765 was to comment to his brother Heaton that 'there is a spirit little short of rebellion in several of the colonies' (Wilkes MSS, U. Mich., Clements L., I, no. 91). But during the next few years colonial adulation of Wilkes as a hero of liberty led him to adopt the idea of a common cause on both sides of the Atlantic. He offered words of encouragement to America, commending resistance to the 1767 import duties on tea and other items, and deploring the use of soldiers in Boston, by an analogy with events in London. After the Boston Tea Party of 1773 had reignited the American question, the colonial cause afforded new ground on which to attack government as the Middlesex election lost its appeal. Wilkes took little part in London agitation against ministerial policy in 1774, but once he was lord mayor he busied himself in organizing a series of City petitions. When he presented a remonstrance to George III on 10 April 1775 his conduct was such that it was said 'the King himself owned he had never seen so well-bred a Lord Mayor' (Last Journals of Horace Walpole, 1.456). But George III then foiled this propaganda tactic of Wilkes by vetoing any repetition of such ceremonies. As the colonial crisis escalated Wilkes shifted his ground from merely supporting American resistance to taxation, as in a Commons speech of 6 February 1775, to endorsement of the colonial denial of parliament's authority, as on 26 October; but the final demand for independence he did not accept. In parliament, urging conciliation rather than coercion, he therefore denounced the American war only as bloody, expensive, and, above all, futile, telling the Commons on 20 November 1777 that 'men are not converted, Sir, by the force of the bayonet at the breast' (Almon, 8.8). After news of Burgoyne's surrender at Saratoga, Wilkes on 10 December 1777 moved repeal of the Declaratory Act of 1766 as a final attempt to save the colonial link, but secured only ten votes. The failure of the 1778 peace commission led him to urge recognition of American independence, in a speech of 26 November 1778: 'A series of four years disgraces and defeats are surely sufficient to convince us of the absolute impossibility of conquering America by force, and I fear the gentle means of persuasion have equally failed' (Almon, 11.21). That he believed American independence to be inevitable was misinterpreted then, and later, as support for the idea: the case was rather that his realism anticipated majority British opinion by several years. But the outbreak of the American war had proved the kiss of death to City radicalism. Deprived of that power base, Wilkes became more active in Westminster politics.

Parliamentary politician The parliamentary behaviour of Wilkes on his return to the Commons in 1774 confounded all expectations. He did not create his own radical party, as he lacked the reputation and resources to do so—and indeed sufficient supporters, once dubbing them his 'twelve apostles'. Nor did he enlist in either of the opposition parties led by lords Rockingham and Shelburne. But he was not the silent backbencher many expected from his earlier spell in the house. He spoke regularly in debate, delivering prepared speeches, marked by detailed research and literary polish, that, though designed for the press rather than parliament, fully merited the attention his character and reputation secured for them. The diarist Nathaniel Wraxall recalled that

> he was an incomparable comedian in all he said or did; and he seemed to consider human life itself as a mere comedy … His speeches were full of wit, pleasantry, and point; Yet nervous, spirited, and not at all defective in argument. (Wraxall, 2.296–7)

Every session Wilkes moved to rescind the resolution of 17 February 1769 declaring him incapable of election after expulsion. On the first occasion, 22 February 1775, the North ministry was pushed harder than on America, winning only by sixty-eight votes, but thereafter the motion became one of form until the resignation of North in 1782. That Wilkes made the first ever motion for parliamentary reform, on 21 March 1776, established his radical credentials for posterity. He urged the transfer of seats from rotten boroughs to London, the more populous counties, and the new industrial towns. The motion was defeated without a vote, and afterwards, in the 1780s, Wilkes, while remaining a reformer, allowed others to take the lead.

'Liberty' for Wilkes embraced wider objectives than political aims. Although brought up a dissenter, from the 1750s he was a professed Anglican, but he held extremely liberal views on religious toleration, expounding them when supporting a Dissenters Relief Bill on 20 April 1779. After pointing out that a person's religion was due to accidents of time and place of birth, Wilkes declared:

> I wish to see rising in the neighbourhood of a Christian cathedral … The Turkish mosque, the Chinese pagoda, and the Jewish synagogue, with a temple of the Sun. … The sole business of the magistrates is to take care that they did not persecute one another. (Almon, 12.311)

Wilkes was a conspicuous absentee when fellow radicals organized City protests against the Quebec Act of 1774 for establishing the Catholic church in Canada, and he had scant sympathy with the anti-Catholic Gordon riots in London during June 1780. He took an active role in their suppression, receiving accolades from supporters of government but incurring unpopularity in London. It signified his final transformation into respectability, one underpinned at last by financial security. The City chamberlain who had defeated him in 1776 died on 9 November 1779, and Wilkes routed a ministerial candidate by 2343 votes to 371, formally taking office on 1 December 1779.

When Lord Rockingham succeeded North as prime minister in 1782 Wilkes was at last able, on 3 May, to carry his motion to erase the 1769 resolution on the Middlesex election, thereby belatedly establishing the right of voters to choose any eligible candidate. But soon there occurred a seismic change in his political career. After Rockingham's death on 1 July 1782, Charles James Fox led the bulk of his party back to opposition when George III chose Shelburne as the new prime minister. Wilkes disliked Fox's attempt to bully the king and chose to support Shelburne, demonstrating that his frequent professions of loyalty to the crown had not been mere formality. He therefore opposed the Fox–North coalition of 1783, denouncing their East India Bill in a much-admired speech as confiscation paving the way for corruption, and became a follower of the younger Pitt, not least because he was a parliamentary reformer. At the general election of 1784 he fought Middlesex as a ministerial candidate and scraped home by sixty-six votes. Thenceforth he was an occasional and silent Pitt supporter, and made only one more recorded speech, seeking in 1787 to prevent the impeachment of his friend Warren Hastings. But unpopularity for both his support of government and his neglect of parliamentary duties cost him his seat without a contest at the 1790 general election. His political career ended in irony. He detested the violence and political extremism of the French Revolution; but on 11 June 1794 a loyalist mob, perhaps from folk memory, smashed the windows of his house. Wilkes refused to prosecute, saying, 'they are only some of my pupils, now set up for themselves' (*Morning Post*, 24 June 1794).

The man in the round 'Mr. Wilkes was the pleasantest companion, the politest gentleman, and the best scholar he knew' (John Wilkes MSS, BL, Add. MS 30874, fol. 92). This 1783 tribute from Wilkes's old adversary Lord Mansfield serves as a reminder that politics never filled his life. Pursuit of women engrossed much of his attention; he was a man of culture; and from 1779 he had duties as City chamberlain. All this activity took place against a background of financial difficulty, eased but not solved by his chamberlain's income, which fluctuated between £1500 and £3000, and at least ended his earlier dependence on private donations. He always spent freely, without heed for the morrow, was often pressed for money, and died virtually insolvent.

The post of City chamberlain was no sinecure. Wilkes supervised a staff of seven, to administer official and charitable funds, and had various other duties, such as the admission of freemen. He worked hard, visiting the Guildhall several days a week to the end of his life, and contemporaries attested to his efficiency. His zeal as an administrator, already displayed as a Buckinghamshire magistrate, London alderman, City sheriff, and lord mayor, was a facet of his character often overshadowed by his political and social activities.

So also was the cultural thread of his life. Wilkes amassed a personal library of altogether nearly 3000 books and pamphlets. He read and wrote in French, and knew both Latin and Greek. His correspondence and speeches alike were laced with classical and other literary allusions. In a debate of 28 April 1777 on the British Museum he made a far-sighted plea for the establishment of a copyright national library and national art gallery. During the last decade of his life he gave fuller vent to his literary turn of mind, publishing editions of Catullus in 1788 and Theophrastus in 1790, respectively in Latin and Greek.

But the wider contemporary world knew Wilkes only as a profligate. That he loved all women except his wife was his famous boast. His overt sexual promiscuity, which was emphasized by bawdy language and lack of shame, began before his arranged marriage, from which there could be no escape of divorce and which he gave as an excuse for his conduct to his daughter when he assured her, 'I have since often sacrificed to beauty, but I never gave my heart except to you' (John Wilkes MSS, BL, Add. MS 30880B, fol. 71). He did not remain faithful even to his current mistresses, of whom the most enduring was Amelia Arnold (b. 1753). He set her up in a nearby house for the last two decades of his life, and she was mother of an acknowledged daughter, Harriet Wilkes, born in 1778. An earlier illegitimate child, born in 1760 to his housekeeper, was passed off as his nephew John Smith, a papal nephew joked Wilkes, who in 1782 obtained for him a post in India.

Somehow Wilkes contrived to fit in a conventional social life among all these interests. He did not hunt or gamble, and indeed boasted that he had 'no small vices'. Instead he simply enjoyed company. His engagement diary records numerous occasions when he was either at private houses or at public dinners. Wraxall recalled how 'in private society, particularly at table, he was pre-eminently agreeable, abounding in anecdote, ever gay and convivial … He formed the charm of the assembly' (Wraxall, 2.297). Wilkes, a tall and thin man, enjoyed good health, and preferred to walk the 3 miles from his Westminster home to Guildhall rather than hire a carriage. Towards the end of his life he became emaciated, and the reputed cause of his death on 26 December 1797, at his house, 30 Grosvenor Square, Westminster, was marasmus, a disease of malnutrition. He was buried in Grosvenor Chapel, South Audley Street, Westminster, on 4 January 1798.

Posterity has been reluctant to accept that Wilkes, a womanizer and blasphemer, and a man with a cynical sense of humour, could have possessed genuine political principles, a verdict seemingly confirmed by such stories as his comment to George III that he had never been a Wilkite, and his rebuke to an elderly woman who called out 'Wilkes and liberty' on seeing him in the street: 'Be quiet, you old fool. That's all over long ago' (Bleackley, 376). Nor did his overnight conversion in 1782 from radical to courtier do his reputation any good, even though he received no reward in honour or office. That last twist to his career is irrelevant to his earlier political record. For two decades Wilkes fought for 'liberty', whether freedom from arbitrary arrest, the rights of voters, or the freedom of the press to criticize government and report parliament. He suffered exile, financial ruin, and imprisonment for his principles, and by a combination of political courage and tactical skill won notable victories over government. He thereby earned respect from Lord North. In a debate of 27 November 1775 the prime minister declared that one Wilkes was enough, 'though, he said, to do him justice, it was not easy to find many such' (Almon, 3.214–30). After Wilkes British politics would never be the same

again: his career permanently widened the political dimension beyond the closed world of Westminster, Whitehall, and Windsor. PETER D. G. THOMAS

Sources P. D. G. Thomas, *John Wilkes: a friend to liberty* (1996) • H. Bleackley, *Life of John Wilkes* (1917) • BL, John Wilkes MSS, Add. MSS 30865–30896 • U. Mich., Clements L., Wilkes MSS • J. Almon, ed., *The parliamentary register, or, History of the proceedings and debates of the House of Commons*, 17 vols. (1775–80) • H. Walpole, *Memoirs of the reign of King George the Third*, ed. G. F. R. Barker, 4 vols. (1894) • *The last journals of Horace Walpole*, ed. Dr Doran, rev. A. F. Steuart, 2 vols. (1910) • N. W. Wraxall, *Historical memoirs of his own time*, new edn, 4 vols. (1836) • N. W. Wraxall, *Posthumous memoirs of his own time*, 2nd edn, 3 vols. (1836) • *Correspondence of William Pitt, earl of Chatham*, ed. W. S. Taylor and J. H. Pringle, 4 vols. (1838–40) • G. Nobbe, *The North Briton: a study in political propaganda* (1939) • W. P. Treloar, *Wilkes and the city* (1917) • C. C. Trench, *Portrait of a patriot: a biography of John Wilkes* (1962)
Archives BL, corresp. and papers, Add. MSS 30865–30896 • GL, corresp. and papers • U. Mich., Clements L., corresp. and literary MSS | Bodl. Oxf., letters to John Dell, MS Eng. Lett. c57 • Derbys. RO, letters to William Fitzherbert • Yale U., Beinecke L., corresp. with James Boswell
Likenesses W. Hogarth, etching, pubd 1763, BM, NPG • J. S. Müller, line engraving, pubd 1763 (after his earlier work), BM, NPG • J. Wilson, mezzotint, pubd 1764 (after R. E. Pine), NPG • R. Houston, group portrait, oils, c.1768, NPG • R. E. Pine, oils, 1768, Palace of Westminster, London • W. Dickinson, mezzotints, pubd 1768–74 (after R. E. Pine), BM, NPG • J. Zoffany, double portrait, oils, 1779 (with his daughter), priv. coll. • J. Zoffany, double portrait, oils, 1779–82 (with his daughter), NPG [*see illus.*] • J. Sayers, etching, pubd 1782 (after his earlier work), NPG • T. Cook, line and stipple engraving, pubd 1800 (after W. Hogarth), NPG • D. D'Angers, bronze medallion, Musée des Beaux Arts, Angers, France • R. Earlom, pencil drawing, NPG • T. Hudson, portrait, Aylesbury Museum • L. F. Roubiliac, bust, GL • J. Watson, mezzotint (after R. E. Pine), House of Commons Library • group portraits, repro. in Bleackley, *Life* • line and stipple engraving (after unknown artist), NPG • sculpture, Chelsea porcelain figure, BM • silver medal, NPG
Wealth at death estate did not cover bequests

Wilkes, Joseph (*bap.* 1733, *d.* 1805), industrialist and entrepreneur, was the fourth of nine children and second son of Joseph Wilkes (1698–1769), grocer, of Overseal, Derbyshire, and Elizabeth, his wife (*d.* 1762). His grandfather was another Joseph Wilkes (1670–1749), a nailer, of Barton under Needwood, Staffordshire, and Overseal. Wilkes was baptized at Seal church, Derbyshire, on 3 September 1733. Later, three of his brothers, John (1728–1790), William (1737–1781), and Thomas (1745–1795), and one of his nephews, Joseph Pycroft (1758–1833), were partners in his commercial, industrial, and banking enterprises.

Little is known of Joseph Wilkes's early life, but the family's prosperity increased in the mid-eighteenth century. This prompted a local tradition that at the time of the Jacobite rising in 1745, when the rebels penetrated as far south as Derby, one of the Wilkeses, possibly Joseph's father,

> purchased a barrel of nails which had been taken from his [Bonnie Prince Charlie's] adherents, and upon emptying it, found that the top and bottom only were nails, but the middle was all gold. Thus enriched [Joseph and Thomas Wilkes] became able to take part in or originate various schemes for the improvement of trade which shortly

afterwards presented themselves. (Gresley, historical notes, Derbyshire RO, D809 A/PI 431)

Wilkes married Elizabeth (known as Bessy) Wood (*d.* after 1774) at Seale on 11 September 1759. They had three surviving daughters. Joseph moved from Overseal to nearby Measham in Leicestershire about 1780.

Support for a transport network to open up markets was a lifelong interest of Joseph Wilkes. He and his brother John, both described as 'cheese factors', were partners in the new syndicate that obtained the lease after 1762 of the Trent Navigation which linked Burton upon Trent, Staffordshire, with river and canal wharves throughout the region. New waterways made it economically viable to exploit local coal and ironstone seams, and in 1767 Joseph leased coal mines in Measham and Oakthorpe, Leicestershire, which included rights to dig clay. Brickmaking enabled Wilkes to prosper, but also later encouraged him to develop the innovation still characteristic of his local buildings, the production of double-sized bricks, popularly called 'Wilkes's gobs', to reduce liabilities under the brick tax introduced in 1785. Wilkes diversified into banking, founding in 1780 in Ashby-de-la-Zouch, Leicestershire, the first bank outside the county town, together with similar businesses in Burton upon Trent, Measham, and his native Overseal.

Wilkes was linked in the 1760s with the Sampson Lloyds, senior and junior, ironmasters and later bankers of Birmingham; but his most significant business and financial partnership was from 1780 to 1798 with Robert 'Parsley' Peel (1723–1795) and his son Robert, first baronet (1750–1830). The Peels' cotton-spinning mills in Burton upon Trent opened in 1780 and were followed ten years later by a large-scale textile complex at Fazeley in Staffordshire on a site purchased and developed by Wilkes and Peel, whose activities were further cemented by the formation of the new London and Tamworth bank of Peel, Wilkes, Dickenson, and Goodall.

Independently at Measham, Wilkes initiated an even greater transformation: in the 1780s he built two spinning mills, many weaving shops, large brickworks and limeworks, and an iron foundry where iron barges, steam-engine boilers, and other metal goods were produced. Local agriculture was improved, in part because water drained from Wilkes's coalmines was used for irrigation, and the town, largely rebuilt, became briefly an important business centre. Wilkes was an early but cautious investor in steam power, buying two Boulton and Watt engines for Measham corn and cotton mills, in 1786 and 1787 respectively; another winding engine, the first in the midlands coalfield, for the Oakthorpe coal pit, in 1787; and in 1802 a fourth engine, at that time the largest in the region, for his original Measham corn mill. Coalmining in Brinsley near Nottingham and in Oakthorpe and Measham continued alongside Wilkes's other activities, and his last major project was to promote the Ashby Canal, completed in 1804, and its connection with the Coventry Canal near Bedworth in Warwickshire, and to open up coal markets further afield, not only for himself but also for neighbouring landowners.

Joseph Wilkes was a leading figure in a group of relatives and colleagues in the forefront of business innovation and development in and around south Derbyshire in the later eighteenth century. In addition to the Peels the group included William Wyatt (1701–1773), estate steward and member of the Staffordshire family of architects; Nathaniel Curzon of Breedon on the Hill, Leicestershire; and the agricultural and livestock improver Robert Bakewell (1725–1795), after whose death Joseph Wilkes became a founder and the first president of the Smithfield Cattle and Sheep Society in London. Where Wilkes differed from contemporaries was in the importance he gave to integrating industrial, commercial, agricultural, financial, and transport facilities to maximize potential markets.

An energetic and determined character, Wilkes was 'possessed of a strong, intelligent, original and active mind and, whatever he took in hand, was conducted with a spirit which overcame all obstacles' (Pitt, 185).

Over a period of forty years from the early 1760s he was a prime mover in the midlands in improving communication networks, opening up new markets, exploiting mineral resources, developing banking facilities, introducing new machinery, ameliorating land by drainage and water management, creating innovative building materials, and planning new large-scale manufacturing complexes. All this was achieved without the advantages of high social status or, apparently, a good education.

Joseph Wilkes moved to Croydon, Surrey, about 1804, and he died there in May 1805. Before his death he transferred his Derbyshire property to his widowed sister, Mrs Elizabeth Gresley (1735–1816), and her children by her first marriage, Joseph and Elizabeth Pycroft.

MARGARET O'SULLIVAN

Sources parish register, Overseal, Seale, 3 Sept 1733, Derbys. RO, D 809 [baptism] · parish register (baptism), Barton under Needwood, Staffordshire, 1698? · Derbys. RO, Gresley family papers, D 77 · J. M. Gresley, historical notes, Derbys. RO, D 809 A/PI 431 · W. Pitt, *Agriculture and minerals of the county of Leicestershire* (1809) · J. Farey, *Agriculture and minerals of the county of Derbyshire*, 1 (1811) · M. Stratton and B. Trinder, 'Foundations of a textile community: Sir Robert Peel at Fazeley', *Textile History*, 26 (1995), 185–201 · J. Nichols, *The history and antiquities of the county of Leicester*, 3/2 (1804) · M. Palmer and P. Neaverson, 'Early years of steam power in Leicestershire', *Leicestershire Historian*, 4/4 (1996), 30–44 · M. Palmer and P. Neaverson, *Industrial landscapes of the east midlands* (1992) · C. P. Griffin, 'The economic and social development of the Leicestershire and south Derbyshire coalfield, 1557–1914', PhD diss., U. Nott., 1969 · J. Nichols, ed., *Bibliotheca topographica Brittanica*, 10 vols. (1780–1800), vol. 8; repr. (1968)
Archives Derbys. RO, Gresley family MSS, D 77 · Derbys. RO, Wilkes and Kettle cheese trade and farm accounts, 1790–1805, D 2444

Wilkes, Richard (1691–1760), physician and antiquary, the eldest of the three sons of Richard Wilkes (1666–1740/41), and Lucretia, *née* Astley (*c.*1670–1717), of Wood Eaton, Staffordshire, was born at Willenhall, Staffordshire, on 16 March 1691. The family, originally from Hertfordshire, had lived in Staffordshire for three centuries. Wilkes was educated at Trentham and at Sutton Coldfield, Warwickshire, and entered St John's College, Cambridge, on 13 March 1710, gaining a BA in January 1714 and an MA three years later. He was elected a fellow of St John's on 21 January 1717; he resigned on 23 March 1723. At Cambridge he attended the mathematics lectures of Nicholas Saunderson, to whose *Algebra* he contributed a memoir in 1740. In 1718 Wilkes was chosen as Linacre lecturer at the college. Briefly in deacon's orders at Stow by Chartley, Staffordshire, he failed to secure a living and began practising medicine at Wolverhampton on 12 February 1720. There is no evidence of his having an MD degree.

On 24 June 1725 Wilkes married an heiress, Rachel (1695–1756), the eldest daughter of Rowland Manlove of Abbots Bromley, and moved to the Wilkes family estate of some 450 acres at Willenhall. His father had built their house, the Old Hall, on the Walsall Road; it was demolished in 1934. Wilkes's younger brother John was already practising there as a surgeon; his sister Anne committed suicide in 1744. As a physician, Wilkes kept detailed patient case notes; he also wrote a diary, too personal to have been intended for publication, of which the first and second volumes have survived, although the county antiquarian, Stebbing Shaw, referred to a third volume, now apparently lost. Wilkes was actively involved in founding a chapel of ease at Willenhall in 1748, and was chapel warden there until his death; he was also a trustee of the town's workhouse. He owned the Wolverhampton waterworks, and in 1750 actively promoted the healing qualities of the springs at Willenhall, long reputed for eye and skin conditions, having already carried out his own experiments on the mineral waters.

Rachel Wilkes died in May 1756 and on 9 October Wilkes remarried; his second bride was Frances (1711–1798), widow of Heigham Bendish (1680–1723), a former Essex physician, and sister of the Revd Sir Richard Wrottesley, head of the leading local family. Wilkes was said to live in considerable state after this second marriage. Apart from his diaries, Wilkes wrote *A Treaty on Dropsy* (1730), *A letter to the gentlemen … of Staffordshire on the treatment of the distemper now prevalent among horned cattle* (1743), and *An Essay on the Smallpox* (1747). He is credited with creating an epitaph in Wolverhampton church for Claudius Phillips (*d.* 1732), a musician. He had wide antiquarian interests and wrote part of a history of Staffordshire, which Shaw incorporated in his own *History and Antiquities of Staffordshire* (1798–1802). Wilkes was also planning a new edition of Samuel Butler's *Hudibras*. When seriously ill in 1747 he wrote his own epitaph in eighteen rhyming couplets:

Here, reader, stand awhile, and know
Whose carcase 'tis that rots below.
A Man's, who walk'd by Reason's rule,
Yet sometimes err'd and play'd the fool;
A Man's, sincere in all his ways,
And full of the Creator's praise;
Who laugh'd at Priestcraft, pride, and strife,
And all the little tricks of life.
He lov'd his king, his country more,
And dreadful party-rage forebore:
He told nobility the truth,
And wink'd at hasty slips of youth.
The honest poor man's steady friend,
The villain's scourge in hopes to mend.
His father, mother, children, wife,

His riches, honours, length of life,
Concern not thee. Observe what's here.
He rests in hope, and not in fear.
(S. Shaw, *History and Antiquities of Staffordshire*, 2.148)

Wilkes's journals describe many of his experiments, as well as showing his considerable scientific and antiquarian interests. They are of particular value, however, as a record of his patients, therapies, and professional acquaintances across the midlands. His patients ranged from the local gentry (the Vernons of Sudbury, the Leveson-Gowers of Trentham) to the poorest, whom he treated for the medical interest of their symptoms, many described in great detail. One patient criticized him as 'little lamented but for his judgment in physick. He was without doubt a good physician but no charity' (Wyndham, 1.170), and he twice refused to attend William Shenstone's dying brother.

Wilkes had been visiting patients in Wolverhampton on the day he died, 6 March 1760, in Willenhall, apparently from 'a Return of the Gout in his Stomach' (*Aris's Birmingham Gazette*, 10 March 1760), and was buried on 20 March at St Giles, Willenhall, where a monument was erected in 1800. He died a very wealthy man. Both marriages were childless and by his will, made on 22 February 1759, the estate was to pass eventually after his wife's death to his cousin, the Revd Thomas Unett (1732–1785) of Stafford. Frances Wilkes made her will in 1784, having won a chancery lawsuit with Thomas Unett over the estate. She died at Froxfield, Hampshire, on 24 December 1798.

JOAN LANE

Sources R. Wilkes, diary and case notes, Wellcome L., MSS 5005, 5006 · R. Wilkes, journal, 1735–8, Staffs. RO, 5350, D 3118 · S. Shaw, *The history and antiquities of Staffordshire*, 2 vols. (1798–1801) · F. W. Hackwood, *The annals of Willenhall* (1908) · N. W. Tildesley, *A history of Willenhall* (1951) · N. W. Tildesley, 'Dr Richard Wilkes of Willenhall, Staffordshire: an eighteenth-century doctor', *Lichfield and South Staffordshire Archaeological and Historical Society Transactions*, 7 (1965–6), 1–10 · M. Wyndham, *Chronicles of the eighteenth century*, 2 vols. (1924) · P. J. Wallis and R. V. Wallis, *Eighteenth century medics*, 2nd edn (1988) · *The letters of William Shenstone*, ed. M. Williams (1939) · G. J. Armytage and W. H. Rylands, eds., *Staffordshire pedigrees*, Harleian Society, 63 (1912), 247–8 · Venn, *Alum. Cant.* · *Aris's Birmingham Gazette* (10 March 1760) · T. Baker, *History of the college of St John the Evangelist, Cambridge*, ed. J. E. B. Mayor, 1 (1869), 303 · T. Baker, *History of the college of St John the Evangelist, Cambridge*, ed. J. E. B. Mayor, 2 (1869), 1008 · T. Baker, *Admissions to St John's College*, 2 (1893), 196 · BL, Stowe MS 753, fols. 70, 242, 248, 286 · parish register (burial), St Giles, Willenhall, Staffordshire, 20/3/1760
Archives Staffs. RO, medical journal · Wellcome L. | BL, letters to Charles Lyttelton, Stowe MS 753
Likenesses engraving (after oil painting), repro. in Shaw, *History and antiquities of Staffordshire*, vol. 2, facing p. 146 · oils, priv. coll.; known to have been at the Wilkes family house at Willenhall in 1908
Wealth at death very wealthy; £1062 bequests: will, PRO, PROB 11/861, sig. 485; bequests printed in Tildesley, *History of Willenhall*, 156–7

Wilkes, Sir Thomas (*c.*1545–1598), diplomat, was already an adult when first recorded in 1572. It is not known whether he originated from Sussex, as stated by Anthony Wood, from Wiltshire, or from the west midlands. His parentage and family are obscure, but he had relatives both in London and the Wolverhampton area. Seventeenth-century genealogies are demonstrably wrong. That a new coat of arms was devised for him implies obscure origins.

Wilkes stated that he spent eight years travelling in France, Germany, and Italy before settling in Oxford. Although nothing is known of his earlier education, he had surely been studying in Oxford for several years before he graduated BA in February 1573 and was appointed probationary fellow of All Souls College. He was immediately appointed secretary to Dr Valentine Dale, the newly appointed ambassador to Paris, doubtless on the strength of his continental experience and contacts. It may also be significant that he was already acquainted with and a correspondent of Sir Francis Walsingham, principal secretary, who was to be his patron until he died in 1590. A letter from the privy council of 24 May 1573, perhaps originating with Dale, perhaps with Walsingham, secured Wilkes leave of absence from his fellowship.

Early diplomatic service, 1574–1582 It was only briefly that Wilkes played second fiddle to Dale. Never a resident ambassador responsible for continuing relations, he was constantly employed on special missions that required initiative and intrigue, and involved risks, not least to himself. In 1584 he stated that he had served Elizabeth I without regard for his life, reputation, or the difficulty of the task. Like Walsingham, he was a committed protestant and supported an aggressive foreign policy as a result. He understood military matters and was not averse to involving himself in them, he had a good grasp of complex affairs, and his reports are both lucid and contain sound recommendations. Late in life he admitted to his 'boldness oftentime used in presuming to yield my rude and raw opinion' on matters of state to political superiors. He apologized while still pressing his case (BL, Stowe MS 296 fol. 7r).

An early instance of the sort of mission at which Wilkes excelled occurred in 1574. In April he was commissioned directly to assure the Huguenot Henri Bourbon, king of Navarre, and François Valois, duke of Alençon, then incarcerated by the dowager queen, Catherine de' Medici, of Elizabeth's support. Having accomplished the mission Wilkes was placed in considerable danger when Alençon exposed him to Catherine: Navarre's intervention alone saved him from arrest. He was expelled from France and found himself disowned by Elizabeth, whose response to Catherine's complaint of 10 July was to blame Wilkes and instruct him to explain his actions to Catherine. Returning to France, he received a personal interview on 7 September at which he denied any plot and in doing so secured permission to remain in France.

Wilkes was recalled to England in February 1575 to embark on a sustained period of pro-Huguenot diplomacy. Dispatched first to the Rhineland, ostensibly to meet Sir Philip Sidney, Wilkes's main objective was to consult the Calvinist Frederick III Simmern, elector palatine, about how best to help the French Huguenots. He returned in April bearing the elector's preference for military intervention in support of Henri (I) de Bourbon, prince de Condé, and a request for a subsidy of £150,000.

This sum was whittled down and agreed to in further missions from August 1575. Wilkes himself remained with the elector and participated in the ensuing invasion with his own men at his own charge until peace was agreed in June 1576. He went on a further mission to Spain in December 1577 to negotiate a compromise in the Netherlands. He was instructed to inform Philip II that Elizabeth favoured his rule in the Netherlands providing that his approach was conciliatory rather than coercive. In particular, the queen demanded that Don John of Austria be recalled. If Philip agreed, Elizabeth would help him overcome the rebels; if not, she would be obliged to help them. Although Wilkes secured no answer to his unpalatable and unacceptable message, he was treated quite well: Wilkes was not to know that Philip wanted him to depart 'before he commits some indiscretion that will force us to burn him' (MacCaffrey, 313). Returning via France on 16 February 1578, he was dispatched on 4 April via William the Silent, prince of Orange, to Don John of Austria to offer mediation and advocate a cease-fire, both of which suggestions were firmly declined.

Domestic duties, 1582–1586 Bar a further mission to the Netherlands in 1582, Wilkes spent the next seven years in England. During these years he established his fortunes and started a family. About 1578 he had married Margaret (c.1562–1596), daughter of Ambrose Smith, a London mercer, and his wife, Joan, of Coggeshall, Essex. Wilkes was rewarded in 1576 with the office of queen's printer, which he sold to Christopher Barker, and with one of the four clerkships of the privy council, which carried a salary of £50 a year. In January 1579 a rota was agreed for the clerks, as was standard practice, Wilkes being assigned for duty during the months of May to August and November to December. His office placed him at the heart of decision making but provided him with only limited opportunity to pursue his own interests. Thus in 1581, when he pressed his own suit to the privy council, he was furiously berated for his impropriety by William Cecil, Baron Burghley, lord treasurer. Further efforts to advance his own interests were similarly unsuccessful. He complained to Robert Dudley, earl of Leicester, on 12 July 1584, after a request for preferment was interpreted by the queen as a plea to leave her service. Exaggerating his poverty somewhat and claiming that he had been paid only £350 for twelve years' service, whereas £400 had been received from the clerkship alone and as much again from Downton parsonage, Wilkes lamented how much he had depended on the largesse of his father-in-law and on his creditors. He claimed he had incurred debts of £500 that he could not repay and asked that he be permitted to reduce his costs by removing from Brentford, Middlesex, to Downton, Wiltshire. Since he was also unsuited to clerical work, he sought employment in some other capacity so that he could repair his credit or at least asked for the appointment of a third clerk to the privy council to enable him to retrench in other ways. He was still pursuing the balance of his wife's portion in 1587.

In 1585, perhaps in response to his complaints, Wilkes was granted a twenty-one-year monopoly on the import of white salt through King's Lynn, Boston, and (from 1586) Hull: regrettably it was not trouble-free and placed him at odds with popular opposition to monopolies in 1587–8, when the Commons were induced to drop their attacks. In 1593 he had to discuss the matter with his parliamentary critics before a committee of the privy council. He could not afford to give the monopoly up. A further aspect of his domestic duties began in 1584 when Wilkes was elected MP for Downton. Wilkes's clerkship also entitled him to absences from government. Apparently he first settled at Brentford in Middlesex. It was as clerk of the privy council, not a resident, that he became a freeman of Southampton in 1581: he was three times elected Southampton's MP, in 1586 (when he declined), 1589, and 1593. Wilkes was fairly active in parliament. In 1582 the queen induced a reluctant Winchester College to lease him Downton rectory for forty years. Subsequently he presented his cousin Dr William Wilkes (d. 1637), a fellow of Merton College, Oxford, to the vicarage. He was re-elected MP for Downton in 1586. He was JP for Wiltshire from about 1583 to 1593, when he moved to Rickmansworth in Hertfordshire, at which time he assigned his property at Downton to Carew Ralegh, elder brother of Sir Walter Ralegh. He was JP for Hertfordshire from about 1593, reflecting his establishment of himself in that county. He was employed on various important tasks, for example, in examining the Jesuit Edmund Campion on the rack in the Tower of London in 1581, seizing the books and papers of Thomas Norton, and inquiring into a minor conspiracy in the west midlands in 1583.

The veteran ambassador, 1586–1598 Wilkes's diplomatic career reached its apogee in the Netherlands in 1586–7. Leicester, dispatched to the Netherlands in 1585, accepted the role of governor-general of the Netherlands, contrary to Elizabeth's specific instructions, but she was persuaded during the spring of 1586 to accept the *fait accompli*. When she selected Wilkes in July 1586 to report on the state of the Netherlands, Leicester was at first highly enthusiastic. 'Wilkes hath exceedingly wisely and well behaved himself', he wrote. 'Her majesty does not know what a jewel she hath of him' (Bruce, 360, 383). His colleague Thomas Sackville, Baron Buckhurst, observed next year that Wilkes was 'so sufficiently practised in the estate of other countries and so well trained in your affairs at home, with such excellent gifts of utterance, memory, wit, courage and knowledge and with so faithful a heart to serve your majesty' (HoP, *Commons, 1558–1603*). It was not therefore surprising that Wilkes was chosen to fill the English vacancy on the council of state. His own preference, set out in a lengthy discourse, opposed any accommodation with Philip and favoured the independence of the recently declared United Provinces. He argued that Elizabeth should accept sovereignty. Such views were not easily reconciled with his complex brief from the government, not fully known to Leicester, to reduce English expenditure, and promote harmony between the earl and the states general. Bolstering Leicester's authority was difficult when Wilkes fundamentally disagreed with aspects of his policy, notably the earl's solicitation of popular support against the town regents on whom alone, Wilkes thought, stability depended. Wilkes's independence and frank reports exposing Leicester's intrigues and errors were resented by the earl, who counter-attacked with malicious rumours that Wilkes had maligned Burghley. Wilkes also found himself at odds with Jan van Oldenbarneveldt, advocate of the states general of the United Provinces. In the face of Leicester's growing hostility to all his leading subordinates and the English embarrassment at Sir William Stanley's betrayal of Deventer, Wilkes, troubled by poor health, decided, in company with the general Sir John Norris, to take the extreme step of abandoning their posts without royal licence or informing Leicester, and returned to England in June 1587. They were ill-received: Norris was banned from the court and Wilkes was imprisoned briefly in the Fleet, then placed under house arrest with a friend.

Wilkes was felt to have at least partly justified his behaviour and his integrity was not long in doubt. Walsingham ordered 'he should be well-used for that he was not to be a close prisoner, but was only done for and upon a slightt displeasure conceived by her Majesty' (C. Read, *Mr Secretary Walsingham and the Policy of Queen Elizabeth*, 3 vols., 1925, 3.252). Such punishment, Leicester felt, was quite inadequate. 'Surely there was never a falser creature, a more seditious wretch, than Wilkes', he railed. 'He is a villain, a devil, without faith or religion' (*DNB*). Leicester, using his influence as the queen's favourite, was able to deny Wilkes his clerkship. Wilkes's petitions, even Walsingham admitted, could not avail against him—and it was only on 4 August 1589, following Leicester's death, that he was returned to favour and was allowed to resume his clerkship. In September 1589 he took part in the renegotiation of England's treaties with the Netherlands.

Yet Wilkes's misdemeanour may have been disastrously mistimed. His recent disgrace no doubt disadvantaged him when the secretaryship of state fell vacant in 1590 on the death of Walsingham. Though repeatedly mooted for the post in 1590–91, it was taken by Burghley himself and largely delegated to his son Sir Robert Cecil, who was duly appointed in 1596. Between 1596 and 1598 Wilkes wrote his 'Brief and summary tractate' on the duties of a councillor. He dedicated it to Cecil. It is extant in a manuscript in the British Library's Stowe collection and detailed the qualities of an able royal servant, including diligence and professionalism.

Wilkes was dispatched to the Netherlands again in May 1590. One objective of this mission was to address England's ongoing military and financial commitment to her Dutch ally and to pressure the rebel leaders to make a greater contribution to the cost of England's war effort in the Netherlands. Wilkes was also instructed to ascertain the truth behind rumours that the Dutch had offered Henri IV sovereignty of the United Provinces in return for French support against Spain. Additionally he was to learn whether or not Philip had made peace overtures towards the rebel leaders. Apart from gaining the reassurance that neither report was true, the mission achieved little and

Wilkes sailed for England in August. He was knighted in 1591.

Wilkes was sent once again to France in March 1592 to secure possession of several towns guaranteed by Henri in return for Elizabeth's assistance. He returned the following year to persuade Henri not to convert to Catholicism and to ensure that he maintained his anti-Catholic stance alongside Elizabeth. In September 1594 Wilkes was chosen to lead an embassy to Archduke Ernest, Spanish governor-general of the Netherlands. However, due to French and Dutch opposition, the mission proved abortive. He married Frances (b. c.1576, d. in or after 1598), daughter of Sir John Savage of Rocksavage, Cheshire, and his wife, in or after 1596. They had a daughter, Margaret (b. 1596x8), who outlived her parents. In February 1598 he accompanied Cecil on his final mission to France, but he died en route at Rouen on 2 March. Presumably he was buried there.

Wilkes took some care over his will before his death. He was anxious to fulfil his relatively minor obligations to the children of the Italian Giacomo Manetti, of whom he himself had been executor. His will dealt only with the leasehold and copyhold estate in Rickmansworth, which he left with plate, jewels, stock, and chattels to his widow, whom he made responsible for the education and marriage of their daughter. He left only £13 6s. 8d. to his servant George Baynham and made no other legacies. That he doubted whether his moveables amounted to Margaret's £300 marriage portion without restricting Frances's share and that he owed £400 in short-term loans suggests that he died in far less affluent circumstances than might be expected of such a distinguished and prominent government servant. His will was proved on 12 May.

MICHAEL HICKS

Sources DNB · HoP, Commons, 1558–1603 · R. B. Wernham, Before the Armada: the growth of English foreign policy, 1485–1588 (1966) · W. T. MacCaffrey, Queen Elizabeth and the making of policy, 1572–1588 (1981) · PRO, PROB 11/91, sig. 96 · C. Read, Lord Burghley and Queen Elizabeth (1960) · R. B. Wernham, After the Armada: Elizabethan England and the struggle for western Europe, 1588–1595 (1984) · R. E. Battle, 'The Rev. William Wilkes, DD, rector of Barford St Martin, Wiltshire, 1585–1637, and John Marston, dramatist', Wiltshire Archaeological and Natural History Magazine, 61 (1966), 47–62 · J. Bruce, ed., Correspondence of Robert Dudley, earl of Leycester, CS, 27 (1844) · VCH Staffordshire · VCH Wiltshire · CPR, 1563–82 · APC, 1581–2, 1589–92, 1596–8 · BL, Stowe MS 296, fol. 7r

Archives BL, treatise on duties of a councillor, MS Stowe 296, fols. 7–20 | BL, diplomatic corresp., Cotton MSS · BL, Lansdowne MSS · BL, letters to Lord Leicester, Egerton MS 1694 · PRO, state papers, letter-book of mission to the Netherlands, SP 105/91

Wilkes, Wetenhall (1705/6–1751), poet and author, was born in Killdrumfetran, Kilmore, co. Cavan, the son of Thomas Wilkes, gentleman, and Mary Martha Moylan. It seems likely that the family had some association with Bishop Edward Wetenhall (1636–1713). Wilkes attended Mr Lane's academy in Dublin before going to Trinity College in 1721, aged fifteen; he married Mary Berrill on 24 September 1727 in the parish of St Andrew in Dublin.

Wilkes moved to Carrickfergus, co. Antrim, where he wrote An Essay on the Existence of God, published by subscription in Belfast in 1730. This orthodox and worthy essay

might have signalled the auspicious start of a career in the church or public service but five years later Wilkes was working as a gauger at the whiskey distillery in Bushmills. In 1735 he sold his inheritance from his father of a bishops' lease on land in Kilmore for £167 to his friend, the portrait painter Alex De Lanauze, but he continued to have money problems, and was confined for debt in the Dublin prison known colloquially as the Black-Dog.

Wilkes's ingenious answer to his plight was the composition of The Humours of the Black-Dog … by a Gentleman in Confinement, printed and sold in the Marshalsea of the four courts in 1737, and dedicated to Swift, whom Wilkes might have met through Swift's connection to the Sheridans in Cavan. Wilkes later claimed implausibly that he sold 17,000 copies in two months. A second part appeared in 1737, followed in the same year by Tom in the Suds, or, The Humours of Newgate: a New Poem, with a prefatory letter dated 3 October 1737 addressed to 'Tom' the Newgate and Black-Dog gaoler. More cantos of Tom in the Suds appeared in 1738, satirically describing Tom's genealogy and several of the apartments at the gaol.

In the summer of 1738 Wilkes wrote The Mourning Muse, a Verse Elegy, dedicated to the memory of Robert Craighead, minister to the dissenting congregation in Capel Street, Dublin. Wilkes himself was probably not a dissenter, considering his family background and his dedication to the Church of Ireland primate, Dr Hugh Boulter, of his popular A letter of genteel and moral advice to a young lady: being a system of rules and informations, digested into a new and familiar method, to qualify the fair sex to be useful, and happy in every scene of life, published by subscription in Dublin in 1740. Swift subscribed for twenty copies. The book is a lively collection of opinionated and fond advice which reveals a lot about the personality of Wilkes. It was written for his sixteen-year-old niece before, as the introduction states, he leaves his 'native Country in hopes of becoming useful to others'.

On settling in London in 1741 Wilkes published An Essay on the Pleasure and Advantage of Female Literature. He had taken Anglican orders by 1746, when he published a work intended to illustrate and explain scripture to children, A short history of the state of man with regard to religion and morals, from the beginning of the world to the reformation.

Hounslow-Heath: a Poem (1748), in which Wilkes celebrated the glories of angling, coursing, and hunting, carried an advertisement for a 'tenth edition' of the Humours of the Black-Dog, but no edition after the second (1737) has been traced. A few months later appeared The Prisoner's Ballad, or, Welcome, Brother Debtor, with a disingenuous advertisement which claimed that the poem had been pirated by shorthand when performed at a concert in Dublin in 1737. At the time of his death on 25 March 1751 Wilkes was rector of South Somercote, near Louth, Lincolnshire.

KATHERINE O'DONNELL

Sources Burtchaell & Sadleir, Alum. Dubl. · D. F. Foxon, ed., English verse, 1701–1750: a catalogue of separately printed poems with notes on contemporary collected editions, 2 vols. (1975) · A. Carpenter, Verse in English from eighteenth-century Ireland (1998) · Office of the Irish Registry of Deeds, Henrietta Street, Dublin 1, 99.14.67693 · parish register, Dublin, St Andrew's, 24 Sept 1727 [marriage] · *London Magazine*, 20 (1751), 188

Wilkie, Sir David (1785–1841), painter of genre, historical subjects, and portraits, was born on 18 November 1785 in the manse at Cults, in the parish of Pitlessie, Fife, where he was baptized on 4 December 1785, the third of the five children of the Revd David Wilkie (1738–1812), and his third wife, Isabella (c.1762–1824), daughter of James Lister, farmer at Pitlessie Mill.

The early years in Fife and Edinburgh Wilkie's schooling, locally at Kettle and Cupar, drew nothing out of him. His conspicuous gift, precociously apparent, lay in the observation of human behaviour. His way forward was to turn this to advantage, and so, helped by influential neighbours, he applied for admission to the Trustees' Academy in Edinburgh—so called for being administered by the Board of Trustees for Fisheries, Manufactures, and Improvements in Scotland. He was there from 1799 to 1804, under the mastership of John Graham, who had recently returned from London and established a curriculum which involved not only drawing but, unusually, painting. Among fellow pupils were John Burnet and William Allan. Graham instituted prizes for small history pictures, and in 1803, with John Clerk of Eldin as examiner, Wilkie took the first with *Diana and Callisto* (Chrysler Museum, Norfolk, Virginia). In Fife he kept himself by painting portraits cheaply, adopting the fashionable style of Henry Raeburn in a number of them; the grandest and most original is *William Bethune-Morison and Family* (1804; NG Scot.). His creative energy, on the other hand, went into furthering his ambition, already set, to tell stories of common life on the patterns offered by David Allan, and by the seventeenth-century Dutch and Flemish genre painters; they were, chiefly, Adriaen van Ostade and David Teniers the younger, known to him then almost wholly through prints. The summit of his achievement in this direction, premonitory of much to come, was the panoramic *Pitlessie Fair* (1804–5; NG Scot.), an uneasy aggregate of rustic incident, yet full of observant and inventive passages. By the time it was finished, Wilkie realized that Scotland offered no future, and had decided on going to London.

London, 1805–1812 Wilkie arrived in London on 20 May 1805, and by early July he had informally attached himself to the Royal Academy Schools, where he threw himself into study, and was formally enrolled on 28 November. He was now twenty-one.

Wilkie had come with little money, and lived in penury such that after a few months he feared he would have to desert his one talent and return home. Again to support himself he resorted to what he called his old trade in portraiture, an art for which he always felt himself unfitted. Nevertheless, he had brought with him *Pitlessie Fair*, which he appears to have lent to the royal piano maker William Stodart, the first to order portraits from him. Through him the picture was seen by others, leading to a commission in January 1806 from the third earl of Mansfield for *Village Politicians* (exh. RA, 1806; priv. coll.). In the exposition and control of its subject it marks a rapid advance. Its

Sir David Wilkie (1785–1841), self-portrait, 1805–6

text was taken from 'Scotland's skaith', a versified plea for temperance by Hector McNeill, but it was not for any social topicality that the picture drew immediate attention among academicians. The hanging committee for that year's exhibition placed it in a prime position, and Henry Fuseli, lately the professor of painting, said, 'Young man, that is a dangerous work' (Cunningham, 1.116). He sensed, without doubt, that this fierce declaration of naturalism, shaped in the old manner of the Low Countries, questioned the Franco-Italian values of history painting, promulgated for a century; equally, it challenged the sweet ruralism of Francis Wheatley, W. R. Bigg, and George Morland. Some likened Wilkie's early pictures to the poems of George Crabbe. The present picture quickly attracted two substantial and later friendly patrons: Sir George Beaumont, who commissioned the *Blind Fiddler* (exh. RA, 1808; Tate collection); and Lord Mulgrave, who commissioned *Rent Day* (exh. RA, 1809; priv. coll.). In 1807 the president of the Royal Academy, Benjamin West, had considered Wilkie 'already a great artist', and *Card Players* (exh. RA, 1808; priv. coll.) was commissioned for William Frederick, second duke of Gloucester.

This group of pictures had its culmination in two works, larger and more complex, aimed at the top of the market. In 1809 Wilkie began the *Village Festival* (exh. RA, 1812; Tate collection) as a speculation, having become wary of the exigencies that commissions could impose; J. J. Angerstein added it to his collection of old masters in 1811. In that year Wilkie began *Blind-Man's-Buff* (exh. RA, 1813; Royal Collection), commissioned by the prince regent through West. This act of patronage, in keeping with the prince's taste for Dutch pictures, was to have an effect on

Wilkie's later career. These works show progressive mastery, not only in Wilkie's management of the relationships, in mind and action, between the people in the scenes he created, but especially in the rendering of their individualities. This latter skill, widely appreciated at the time, owed much to the researches being made into the physiognomy of expression by Charles Bell.

In 1809 Wilkie—encouraged by Fuseli, Joseph Farington, and others—put his name down for election as an associate of the Royal Academy, and was admitted on 6 November, although a year short of the statutory age of twenty-five; he did not cease to draw in the Academy Schools. Despite a hostile faction, using Edward Bird as its stalking-horse, he was elected Royal Academician on 11 February 1811. Also in 1811 he moved to the first of four successive addresses in the suburb of Kensington (none surviving), for the sake of better air than that north of Oxford Street, where he had lodged before. In 1812 Wilkie took public stock of himself by holding a one-man exhibition, an unusual procedure. Of the twenty-nine pictures, seven had been exhibited before. The more important he borrowed; the earliest was *Pitlessie Fair* and the most recent the *Village Festival*. Among the others was a deeply felt and loving portrait of his parents (priv. coll.), painted on a visit home in 1807.

During the exhibition, subscriptions were taken for a forthcoming engraving by Abraham Raimbach after *Village Politicians*. In 1809 Wilkie had begun to have engravings made from a number of his pictures. This fairly common practice was valuable in keeping an artist's work in the public eye. For Wilkie there must also have been the hope that the need to paint portraits would be reduced by the sale of prints; bread and butter was certainly to come from this source for the rest of his life. His first and best interpreters were Burnet and Raimbach, who worked in the line manner he preferred; early on they joined him as publishers, but later this and the business of distribution went into commercial hands. In his lifetime, prints went to France, the Low Countries, Germany, Spain, America, and India. At home especially they became the source of many copies and pastiches.

London, 1812–1825 Wilkie's first seven assertive years in London were followed by a decade or so as active, his work now conveying a sense of having been painted with the confidence of an established master. The texture of his paint became creamier, his colour more mellow—tone was to become an absorption—his line more beguiling, his penetration of character more searching. The period may be said to open with the *Letter of Introduction* (exh. RA, 1814; NG Scot.), a composition of two figures in which a gulf of acute awkwardness is opened between a complacent youth and the suspicious recipient of the letter, a tetchy old man of taste. Their arrangement echoes examples from the Low Countries, but not now the peasantry of Ostade and Teniers; rather, and significantly, Dutch painters of comfortable interiors—in this case, openly enough, Gerard ter Borch. Burnet wrote: 'It was a common practice with Wilkie to adopt a part of a celebrated work as a point to work from … The spectator, by

this means, was drawn into a predisposition of its excellence' (J. Burnet, *Rembrandt*, 1849, 40). The allurement had warrant in the example of Sir Joshua Reynolds, of whom Wilkie was a constant admirer.

Among Wilkie's finest achievements, for its large groupings and emotional range, is *Distraining for Rent* (exh. RA, 1815; NG Scot.), a 'sadly real' subject, open to political interpretation, although not intentionally. Bought by the directors of the British Institution, who collected to encourage British artists and to provide examples for students, it was the first of Wilkie's pictures to enter a public collection; he was to have the then singular distinction of having pictures in the National Gallery during his lifetime, when Angerstein's and Beaumont's collections went there in 1824 and 1826.

Wilkie returned to Scotland only intermittently, and never without purpose. In 1817, in search of subject matter, he made his only visit to the highlands, where the way of life was strange to him, a lowlander. He had asked advice on what to see from Walter Scott, whom he visited at Abbotsford on the way back. The major outcome of this ethnographic tour was to be *Highland Whisky-Still at Lochgilphead* (exh. British Institution, 1820; priv. coll.), bespoken in 1819, on the strength of a sketch, by Major-General Sir Willoughby Gordon, a lasting patron.

The prince regent had already asked for a second picture, and in 1817 Wilkie's consummately vivacious *Penny Wedding* (exh. RA, 1819; Royal Collection) was begun. The subject, from the lowlands, looks back to the century before, fixing details of a disappearing way of life, as in novels by Scott and John Galt. Before work on this was finished, an order came from Maximilian I of Bavaria, likewise for a subject of Wilkie's own choosing, and in 1819 he began *Reading a Will* (exh. RA, 1820; Neue Pinakothek, Munich). In the catalogue of the exhibition at the Royal Academy he tagged it with a reference to an episode in Scott's story of *Guy Mannering* (1815), which it does not illustrate, but which he re-created in his own manner. Although the opening of a will had been proposed to Wilkie as a subject a decade earlier by the actors John Liston and John Bannister—he had a taste for plays—this does not account for a staginess in the picture. This almost certainly came from his use, for some years about this time, of a device in the formation of a composition, old but not much used in his day. Into a small box with an open side were placed clay models, as in a theatre; this allowed their arrangement and lighting to be considered before transfer to the canvas. It was noticed of this picture that the proportion of the figures to their setting was larger than before. The development became conspicuous in *Parish Beadle* (exh. RA, 1823; Tate collection), also noticeable in which are a loosening in the handling of the paint and a forcefulness of light and shadow; Fuseli detected a look of Guercino, others of Rembrandt. The change of style thus adumbrated was not, however, apparent in his small, genially domestic portrait of the *Duke of York* (exh. RA, 1823; NPG), also painted for Gordon.

If Wilkie had misgivings about his competence to be a

portrait painter, he had a less understandable lack of confidence in his ability to paint landscape. He felt his inexperience while painting the trees and sky in the *Village Festival*, and set out to improve himself. For ten years or so he exercised himself in the art, and made a number of accomplished studies, stimulated by an amateur landscapist, his friend Perry Nursey. He chose to exhibit only one landscape, the large *Sheepwashing* (exh. British Institution, 1817; NG Scot.), having explained to Beaumont, another amateur: 'My ambition is not more than that of enabling myself to paint an out-door scene with facility' (Cunningham, 1.454). But only a handful of his subjects had landscape backgrounds, and after 1825 he gave up landscape painting altogether.

In 1820 Wilkie began the work by which he is most widely known, *Chelsea Pensioners* (exh. RA, 1822; Apsley House, London). The duke of Wellington, who was to become a friend, had come to him in 1816 for a picture, saying, 'the subject should be a parcel of old soldiers assembled … at the door of a public-house, chewing tobacco and talking over their old stories'. Agreeing that this would make a picture, Wilkie added that 'it only wanted some … principal incident to connect the figures together' (*Life of Benjamin Robert Haydon*, 1.246). The outcome was a subject pretending to represent the reception of the news from Waterloo by pensioners and others outside the public houses near Chelsea Hospital. It is, in effect, a history picture with an invisible hero, the popular joy being in the victory of the nation rather than of a commander. Of great intricacy, 'composed rather than inspired', a contemporary remarked (*The Athenaeum*, 1842, 585), it was admired for its 'expressions touchantes' by the French painter Théodore Géricault (C. Clément, *Géricault*, 1867, 202), and at the exhibition it had to be protected from the crowds by a rail; the entrance-money taken at the Royal Academy that year was the highest ever. The duke paid the exceptional sum of £1260 for the picture, in cash.

Later in 1822 George IV went on a state visit to Edinburgh, to be presented there as the king of Scotland at home in his Scottish capital. Wilkie went also, hoping to find in the pageantry of the occasion, largely orchestrated by his friend Scott, a subject for a second modern history picture. At about the same time he was giving thought to a subject from Presbyterian history. Both were to come. In 1823 Wilkie was informed by the home secretary, Sir Robert Peel, who was to become a patron, that the king had chosen him to succeed Raeburn as limner for Scotland. A state portrait of the king was thus expected from him, although he had never painted a formal portrait, indeed any at full length and of life size. An opportunity for trying his hand came in 1824, when an invitation came from Fife to paint the earl of Kellie for the county hall. He went to Scotland again that year and got the portrait well under way, also gathering materials for his two pictures of Scottish history, present and past.

On the continent, 1825–1828 Each of the years from 1824 to 1826 brought calamity. Since his father's death Wilkie's mother had become the centre of his London home. She died in 1824; the year in which his eldest brother, John, also died, in India. His other older brother, James, died in 1825. Both brothers left children to be taken care of, some of whom Wilkie had already been supporting. He had long been prone to nervous illness, brought on by anxiety; now he had fresh financial responsibilities. Professionally, he worried over his burden of work, not least that arising from his royal appointment. By the spring of 1825 he had become too tense to write, or to paint. Travel was advised as a relief. While he was abroad, his income from engravings was to be undermined by the failure of his print publisher in the crash of 1826.

Wilkie had travelled before, to Paris in 1814 and to the Low Countries in 1816, essentially to see pictures. Although he was alert to work done recently by the French, his chief interest on both journeys had been in Dutch and Flemish painters of the seventeenth century; the grandeur of Rubens was a particular revelation. Now, in July 1825, he set off on a grand tour, centred on Rome, with an excursion into Germany in 1826. The high Renaissance painters who impressed him greatly were Raphael, Michelangelo, and Fra Bartolommeo, and of the later sixteenth century, Titian and Correggio. Returning, he made a diversion into Spain, then scarcely known to painters. He went there not least in the hope of finding old masters for Peel, as he had been doing in Italy. He spent six months over the winter of 1827 in Madrid, making a trip to Seville; new and exciting to a British painter, was the encounter with major works by Velázquez and Murillo. It may be judged that of all these painters, Raphael, Titian, Correggio, and Murillo had the most evident effect on his practice, although by other means he had already arrived at an understanding of the discipline of Raphael and the colouring of Titian.

In Rome, Wilkie painted three modest scenes of pious observances seen during Holy Week, to which he added a fourth, painted at Geneva during a lengthy pause after leaving Italy, over the summer of 1827. At Madrid, where he enjoyed the company of Washington Irving, he finished a picture, and began three others, on the subject of Spanish resistance to the French occupation. These four clearly announce a new stylistic ambition. They are generous in scale, the figures large and forward in the picture space, the whole executed, as never before, with rapidity and freedom. Each of these characteristics was virtually imposed in consequence of his illness; his old ability to paint small and in detail had been taken from him. His achievement on the continent of a new style and a way forward was in accord with his previously apparent pursuit of old masterliness. Materially, he tried for richness and transparency by using bitumen. After two or three decades this treacherous tarry compound almost invariably degenerated, so disfiguring many of his larger late pictures, and making their original impact hard to judge nowadays.

London, 1828–1840 After an absence of three years Wilkie was home again in July 1828. The king received him generously, buying two of the Italian pictures, as well as all four of the Spanish ones, the largest and most vigorous of which is the *Defence of Saragossa* (exh. RA, 1829; Royal Collection). The intermediary in this was Sir William Knighton, who himself became a patron and a confidant.

Of the work Wilkie had left unfinished in 1825, the *Earl of Kellie* (exh. RA, 1829; County Hall, Cupar, Fife) was soon completed. A portrait, *George IV in Highland Dress* (exh. RA, 1830; Royal Collection), the fulfilment of his duty as limner, was not judged a very good likeness, but Wilkie thought the tartan outfit in which he had seen the king at Edinburgh so rich 'that one might fancy Velásquez, Rembrandt, and Titian ambitious of such a model' (letter to Prince D. Dolgoruky, 1839, Yale University Library, New Haven, Connecticut). The history picture commemorating the king's visit to the city, begun a year after the event, was the *Entrance of George IV at Holyrood House* (exh. RA, 1830; Royal Collection), over 6 feet long. Although incorporating portraits, it has almost no documentary value, being a fancy kindred to Scott's when he invented the spectacle for the occasion; none the less the picture remains a serious construction, Rubensian in derivation.

The fourth unfinished work was the other history picture begun in 1823, the large *Preaching of Knox before the Lords of the Congregation* (exh. RA, 1832; Tate collection); it went to Peel. Wilkie was shortly to write: 'The question of Catholic and Protestant I have considered a theme for art' (Cunningham, 3.113); his interest in the theme had been deepened by his observations on the continent. The picture was critically received as an assured achievement in the historical branch of art.

The king appointed Wilkie his painter in ordinary in 1830, in succession to Sir Thomas Lawrence; he was confirmed in the office later that year by William IV, and in 1837 by Queen Victoria. He found state portraits difficult; they, and repetitions from them, took much time. With Queen Victoria he failed, and lost favour. His office under the crown, as well as the need of money despite his economical way of life, made it difficult for him to avoid requests for full-length formal portraits of persons of eminence, among them *Viscount Melville* (exh. RA, 1831; University of St Andrews); the *Duke of Wellington as Constable of the Tower* (exh. RA, 1834; Merchant Taylors' Company, London); and a lord mayor of London, *M. P. Lucas* (exh. RA, 1839; Guildhall Art Gallery, London). He continued to paint private portraits.

Although Wilkie had returned from the continent with a new style, it would appear that for the next ten years or so he had an imperfect sense of direction. This is, in a manner, indicated by the increase in the variety and originality of his subject matter: *Columbus in the Convent of La Rabida* (exh. RA, 1835; North Carolina Museum of Art, Raleigh) is one of six pictures on Spanish themes, one commissioned from New York; the *First Earring* (exh. RA, 1835; Tate collection), painted for John, sixth duke of Bedford, was the first of five pictures treating upper-class female domestic life. Reversions to scenes of cottage domesticity are represented by the *Cotter's Saturday Night* (exh. RA, 1837; Glasgow Art Gallery), a pious and moralizing subject found in the poem by Robert Burns and painted for the print publisher F. G. Moon. *Napoleon and the Pope* (exh. RA, 1836; NG Ire.)—

an encounter of 1813—was painted for John Marshall, the Leeds linen manufacturer. Restricted to the two figures, 'my largest picture' attracted remarks on matters of detail and on the nature of history painting, but none arising from the politics of the event shown. As surely as the picture of Knox preaching, this was a statement on the conflict between temporal and spiritual power. Thematically akin, and of a more immediate political pertinence, was the *Peep-o'-Day Boy's Cabin* (exh. RA, 1836; Tate collection), painted for Robert Vernon. Wilkie's Spanish subjects had been novel in British painting, and a success. In 1835, looking for more new material, he went to Ireland, until then visited only by a few English topographers. There, as in the highlands in 1817, his attraction was to the primitive in rural life. The picture described this; further, by centring the narrative on one of the old protestant bands, still at odds with the indigenous Catholic population, it opened the sensitive issue of political responsibilities in London.

Since Wilkie's return in 1828 a large number of his critics—and of his public too, no doubt—had felt disappointed when they found that he had abandoned his old subject matter and manner of presentation, above all the strong characterization that outshone his seventeenth-century models. Many had seen in Wilkie an heir to Hogarth; few can have been aware of the nervosity that had lowered his manual capacity. The feeling was, and persists even now, that a source of enlightening entertainment went when Wilkie Europeanized his style. Yet in this he was to venture further.

Wilkie had not been unwilling to enter into portraiture when he could blend it with history, so to invest it with anecdote; 'portraits in action' was his phrase. One such picture had been that of George IV at Holyrood; another was to be the *First Council of Queen Victoria* (exh. RA, 1838; Royal Collection). Also of the sort, although the portrait in it was posthumous, is *Sir David Baird Discovering the Body of Tippoo Saib* (exh. RA, 1839; NG Scot.). Over 11 feet high, and the result of four years' work, this heroic image was begun in 1835 at the request of Baird's widow. Wilkie regarded it as a commission 'of first rate consequence' (Wilkie, MS letter to Knighton, 20 Sept 1834, Mitchell Library, Glasgow). If his phrase was portentive it might be explained by his interest in what he had seen of the revival of fresco painting in Rome and in Germany, and which, since the burning of the houses of parliament in 1834, had become a prospect in England.

In 1839 Wilkie began a still more forward-looking picture, *John Knox Dispensing the Sacrament at Calder House* (NG Scot.), a commercial undertaking to give Moon a subject for engraving as a companion to the existing print after the picture of Knox preaching. In formal contrast to the latter, this carefully deliberated composition is overtly formed on high Renaissance precedent. For Wilkie the scene concerned 'the restoration of a holy ordinance to its primitive simplicity' (Cunningham, 3.232). The painting was not to be finished.

The Holy Land, 1840–1841 As Wilkie was beginning the picture of Knox, he also began one of *Samuel Ministering before*

Eli. Always careful to lend truth to his historical works by working from evidences of their period, this subject provoked questions about what the world of the Old Testament had looked like. On the continent he had already wondered at anachronisms in biblical paintings. Now he wrote to Gordon, who had commissioned the subject: 'The researches of travellers must assist greatly in the representation of Scripture subjects' (Wilkie, MS letter to Gordon, 21 Oct 1839, priv. coll.). David Roberts had shown him drawings he had recently made in Palestine, but Wilkie's allusion was rather to the rising number of illustrated accounts of the Levant published in the 1830s—themselves part of a wider popular attraction to the region, raised by political, military, and missionary interests there.

On 15 August 1840 Wilkie left London for the Holy Land. Like most travellers then, he used the Bible as his guidebook. Intending only to gather authentic materials for further engagements in scriptural subjects, he limited his painting equipment to that necessary for making studies. He was to express his larger purpose in writing to Peel of 'the great work to be essayed of representing Scripture history' (Cunningham, 3.415); behind this was a democratic wish that, with government help, painting should be enjoyed at large in public places.

The war in Syria delayed Wilkie at Constantinople from October to January, so that he did not reach Jerusalem until February 1841. There his attention was largely drawn to remains associated with the life of Christ and to the manners of the existing Jewish community. At Jerusalem he made small compositions in oil, two of which survive in private collections. In them he presents scenes from the life of Christ in which the physical types, costumes, and settings are those about him in the city. At the age of fifty-six Wilkie seemed on the verge of a significant new departure.

Wilkie left Jerusalem for home in April. Waiting for a steamer at Alexandria he used the time to paint a small portrait, *The Pacha of Egypt* (Tate collection), as he had painted *The Sultan of Turkey* (Royal Collection) at Constantinople. Wilkie died of a sudden illness on 1 June 1841, aboard the SS *Oriental*; he was buried at sea, off Malta. At the Royal Academy, in the following year, his loss was marked by two imaginary representations of burial at sea: the *Funeral of Sir David Wilkie* (priv. coll.) by his friend George Jones, and *Peace: Burial at Sea* (Tate collection) by his old sparring partner J. M. W. Turner.

Afterword Wilkie was held in high esteem as a man and as an artist. Among artists, some particular friends were William Allan, Francis Chantrey, William Collins, John Constable, Andrew Geddes, B. R. Haydon, John Jackson, C. R. Leslie, and Thomas Phillips. When Lawrence died, Wilkie was near to succeeding him as president of the Royal Academy, but knew he was not constituted for so contentious an office. He was an honorary member of foreign academies; was made doctor of civil law at Oxford on 13 June 1834; was knighted on 15 June 1836; and in 1841 was nominated a chevalier of the Légion d'honneur. On his death a public subscription was raised for a memorial, and

in the end a marble statue by Samuel Joseph was presented to the National Gallery in 1844 (Tate collection). An extensive retrospective exhibition was mounted at the British Institution in 1842.

Wilkie revealed almost nothing of his private life, which was essentially domestic. In congenial surroundings he could be amusing; in his earlier years at least he played the fiddle. He did not marry, although he had at least one hope. By inference, he lost his Presbyterianism to the Church of England; his patriotism was as a Briton pleased to be Scottish. In the 1830 he went, if not very attentively, to meetings of the British Association for the Advancement of Science; he does not appear to have been much given to reading, and he mastered no foreign language.

Of a number of surviving portraits of Wilkie, the most valuable are by William Beechey (exh. RA, 1809; Scot. NPG), Andrew Geddes (exh. RA, 1816; Scot. NPG), and Thomas Phillips (exh. RA, 1829; Scot. NPG); each was engraved. There is also a life mask of uncertain date (Scot. NPG). Of the few self-portraits, notable are those from 1805–6 (Scot. NPG), 1813 (NPG), and 1840 (Musée des Beaux-Arts, Pau).

Wilkie painted a total of some 500 works in oil, including some 170 portraits; many of these works were small studies and sketches, and about half the total can no longer be accounted for. Of the total, he exhibited in London eighty-seven subject pictures and thirty-seven portraits. He was a prolific and distinguished draughtsman, for figures perhaps the finest of his age; he exhibited six drawings at the Royal Academy. His will, made on 21 July 1825 and proved on 10 August 1841, provided that the contents of his studio, copyrights in prints, and personal effects—his house was evidently leased—should be sold, the proceeds to be held in trust for his sister Helen and brother Thomas, then portioned among nephews and nieces. The arrangement, complicated in its care for equity, resulted in sales by his trustees at Christies on 25–30 April and 3–4 May 1842, and on 20–21 June 1860; the catalogues of these are greatly informative.

Latterly, Wilkie employed assistants, among them John Ballantyne, J. Z. Bell, Alexander Fraser, John Simpson, and W. S. Watson. He took an interest in the training of young painters, and gave them advice and letters of recommendation. Some painters, of genre in particular, developed from him. C. W. Cope, Daniel Maclise, and John Phillip are examples; others, such as Thomas Webster and Thomas Faed, simply followed in his footsteps. Wilkie's considerable influence on Victorian painting, which remains to be charted accurately—so too his influence abroad—was depressed variously by the aesthetic values of John Ruskin, J. A. M. Whistler, and Roger Fry. A reassessment was begun with the Wilkie exhibition at the National Gallery of Scotland and the Royal Academy in 1958.

Much of Wilkie's writing—letters (many survive), journals (lost), and his 'Remarks on painting'—was published in 1843 by his first biographer, Allan Cunningham, whose account, although he made excisions and alterations on occasion, remains indispensable. The major collections of

Wilkie's paintings are in the National Gallery of Scotland, Edinburgh, and the Tate collection. There are substantial holdings of his drawings in Aberdeen Art Gallery, the Fitzwilliam Museum, Cambridge, the National Gallery of Scotland, Edinburgh, the British Museum, the Courtauld Institute, and the Victoria and Albert Museum, London, and the Ashmolean Museum, Oxford.

HAMISH MILES

Sources A. Cunningham, *The life of Sir David Wilkie*, 3 vols. (1843) · 'Sir David Wilkie', *The Athenaeum* (1841), 459–60 · 'Sir David Wilkie and his friends', *Fraser's Magazine*, 24 (1841), 443–54 · 'Wilkie's letters to Perry Nursey', *The Academy*, 14 (1878), 323–4, 345–6 · J. Burnet, *Practical essays on various branches of the fine arts. To which is added, a critical inquiry into the principles and practice of the late Sir David Wilkie* (1848) · 'Autobiography of John Burnet', *Art-Journal*, 12 (1850), 275–7 · W. W. Collins, *Memoirs of the life of William Collins, Esq., R.A., with selections from his journals and correspondence*, 2 vols. (1848) · L. Errington, *Sir David Wilkie: drawings into paintings* (1975) [exhibition catalogue, Edinburgh, NG Scot., 1975] · Farington, *Diary* · *The reminiscences of Solomon Alex. Hart*, ed. A. Brodie (1882) · *Life of Benjamin Robert Haydon, historical painter, from his autobiography and journals*, ed. T. Taylor, 2nd edn, 3 vols. (1853) · *Benjamin Robert Haydon: correspondence and table-talk*, ed. F. W. Haydon, 2 vols. (1876) · *The diary of Benjamin Robert Haydon*, ed. W. B. Pope, 5 vols. (1960–63) · C. R. Leslie, *Autobiographical recollections*, ed. T. Taylor, 2 vols. (1860) · *Memoirs and recollections of the late Abraham Raimbach*, ed. M. T. S. Raimbach (1843) · R. Redgrave and S. Redgrave, *A century of painters of the English school*, 2 vols. (1866) · W. J. Chiego, ed., *Sir David Wilkie of Scotland* (1987) [exhibition catalogue, North Carolina Museum of Art, Raleigh, 1987] · H. Miles, *Fourteen small pictures by Wilkie* (1981) [exhibition catalogue, Fine Art Society, London, 1981] · L. Errington, *Tribute to Wilkie from the National Gallery of Scotland* (1985) [exhibition catalogue, NG Scot., Edinburgh, 1985] · D. B. Brown, *Sir David Wilkie: drawings and sketches in the Ashmolean Museum* (1985) [exhibition catalogue, AM Oxf. 1985] · N. Tromans, *David Wilkie, painter of everyday life* (2002) [exhibition catalogue, Dulwich Picture Gallery]
Archives Hunt. L., letters · NL Scot., corresp. and papers · NL Scot., letters · NL Scot., letters, diaries · NRA Scotland, priv. coll., letters · V&A, papers | Beds. & Luton ARS, letters to Samuel Whitbread · BL, letters to Perry Nursey, Add. MS 29991 · BL, corresp. with Sir Robert Peel, Add. MSS 40355–40608 · CKS, letters to Lord Stanhope · Hunt. L., letters to A. Raimbach · Mitchell L., Glas., letters to Sir W. Knighton and his son · Morgan L., letters to Sir G. Beaumont · NA Scot., minutes of trustees' academy · NL Scot., letters to Sir G. Beaumont · NL Scot., corresp. with Robert Liston · NL Scot., letters to T. Macdonald · priv. coll., letters to Sir J. W. Gordon · RA, corresp. with Thomas Lawrence · U. Glas., letters to Sir William Knighton and his son · Yale U., letters to Prince D. Dolgoruky
Likenesses D. Wilkie, self-portrait, oils, 1805–6, Scot. NPG [*see illus.*] · J. Jackson, black lead drawing, 1807, BM · C. B. Leighton, lithograph, 1807 (after B. R. Haydon), NPG · W. Beechey, oils, exh. RA 1809, Scot. NPG · G. H. Harlow, pencil and wash drawing, 1812, NPG · D. Wilkie, self-portrait, oils, 1813, NPG · A. Geddes, oils, 1816, Scot. NPG · B. R. Haydon, pencil drawing, 1816, NPG · C. C. Vogel von Vogelstein, pencil drawing, 1826, Kupferstichkabinet, Dresden, Germany · T. Phillips, oils, exh. RA 1829, Scot. NPG · D. Wilkie, self-portrait, oils, 1840, Musée des Beaux-Arts, Pau, France · S. Joseph, marble bust, 1842 (after plaster bust, 1824), Scot. NPG · S. Joseph, marble statue, 1843, Tate collection · E. McInnes, mezzotint, pubd 1843 (after T. Phillips), BM, NPG · F. Holl, stipple and line engraving (after T. Phillips), BM, NPG · W. H. Hunt, watercolour drawing, NPG · J. Jackson, watercolour drawing, NPG · Smith, plaster life mask, Scot. NPG · D. Wilkie, self-portrait, oils, Yale U. CBA · D. Wilkie, self-portraits, Scot. NPG · P. C. Wonder, group portrait, study (*Patrons and lovers of art*), NPG

Wilkie, Sir David Percival Dalbreck (1882–1938), surgeon, was born at Kirriemuir, Forfarshire, Scotland, on 5 November 1882, the younger son of David Wilkie, jute manufacturer, and his wife, Margaret Lawson Mill. Given his background, the reasons he opted for a medical career are unknown but he proceeded from the Edinburgh Academy (secondary school) to the University of Edinburgh, from which he graduated MB in 1904 and MD in 1908. He became FRCS (Edin.) in 1907 and FRCS (Lond.) in 1918. After graduation he held house appointments in Edinburgh at the Royal Infirmary, the Royal Hospital for Sick Children, and the Chalmers Hospital; thereafter, as was customary for those of his time who had adequate financial resources, he visited surgical clinics at Bonn, Bern, and Vienna. He was appointed to the surgical staff of Leith Hospital in 1910, and in 1912 he became assistant surgeon to the Royal Infirmary, Edinburgh. In 1911 Wilkie married Charlotte Ann Erskine, eldest daughter of James Middleton MD, of Stow, Midlothian; there were no children.

In Edinburgh, Wilkie joined a formidable surgical organization inspired by Francis Caird, one of the pioneers of abdominal surgery in Scotland and a figure who has lacked recognition in the history of surgery in Edinburgh. Through him Wilkie served, along with others, such as Harold Styles and Sir James Fraser, to create a scientific school of clinical surgery. His researches won him the Victoria jubilee prize of the Royal College of Surgeons of Edinburgh, in 1918. Wilkie was an instigator of thought about such matters as the cause and development of acute appendicitis and he made other contributions to abdominal surgery, though his views on such controversial matters as diverticulosis and gall bladder disease have not stood the test of time. His hypothesis was that chronic illness with abdominal symptoms could originate from the gall bladder, from duodenal ulcer, from 'chronic' appendicitis, or from diverticular disease. This unitary concept did not have any basis in anything other than clinical observation of the often co-presence of two or more of these disorders. However, he may have been observing, and correlating with his clinical observations, data about patients who, though diagnosed differently in later years, were nevertheless suffering from what to them were real abdominal conditions.

As a member of the Royal Naval Volunteer Reserve, Wilkie joined the navy on the outbreak of the First World War in 1914. He served on the hospital ship *St Margaret of Scotland* (Portland) and thereafter in Salonika and on the western front as a surgeon to a casualty clearing station. He was appointed OBE in 1919.

Because of his association with Harold Styles, Wilkie's place in clinical teaching grew so that when the chair of systematic surgery at Edinburgh became vacant in 1924 (on the suicide of Alexis Thomson) he was the obvious successor. Previously such chairs had been largely devoted to the pursuit of clinical practice that would support status rather than science. However, Wilkie negotiated a different contract because he considered that in the past chairs of surgery did not have a high academic content and (*pace* Joseph Lister) had been mainly appointments that could be exploited rather than carry a near or total commitment to research and teaching. Wilkie, having travelled widely on the continent and in the USA, saw the need for compromise between practice and science, and he threw himself with characteristic zeal into his role, which had been the subject of fresh negotiation between him and the university. Nevertheless he retained the right of private practice—in the late twentieth century called 'maximum parttime'—which he did not need financially but which he felt formed an element of his status as a surgeon. Even late in his surgical career he would think nothing of going to North Berwick (20 miles from Edinburgh) to remove an appendix for a large fee. His gift of lucid expression served him well as a lecturer, while his cheerful, dignified, yet modest presence won the hearts of his students.

Wilkie's particular interest, derived from his experiences in the USA, was in developing surgical research, and he gathered around him a group of young surgeons both from the UK and from the USA (the latter were rare in the 1930s) who were proud to be regarded as 'Wilkie's young men'. The surgical research tradition that he fostered was significant in starting a new wave of surgical study in Scotland after the Second World War, under Charles F. W. Illingworth, James Learmonth, William Wilson, and others. Despite Wilkie's other preoccupations—he was involved in many committees and was a recipient of a number of honorary awards—he remained primarily concerned with impressing his personal qualities on his associates, and he was regarded by his coevals and his younger colleagues with something akin to reverence. Wilkie's personal characteristics, derived from his liberal principles and his interpretation of religion in its broadest sense, made him someone who could be sympathetic to the troubles, anxieties, and ambitions of others. One of his junior colleagues said that 'his simple almost boyish charm commanded a positive joy in sharing service with him'. He was also actively involved with the army medical advisory board, the British Empire Cancer Campaign, and the Medical Research Council (1933–7). He was knighted in 1936.

Wilkie did not enjoy uniform good health. He had a severe gastrointestinal haemorrhage in 1937 and some time after this found a mass in his own abdomen. An attempt by his colleague Gordon Gordon-Taylor to remove this gastric cancer was unsuccessful, and Wilkie died in London on 28 August 1938. Much of his estate was gifted to the University of Edinburgh, to continue support for the department of surgery, and he is remembered *inter alia* by the Wilkie Laboratory, which the university court, in recognition of his services, caused to be so known.

HUGH DUDLEY

Sources *University of Edinburgh Journal*, 9 (1937–8), 257–9 • *British Journal of Surgery*, 26 (1938), 390–92 • *BMJ* (10 Sept 1938), 598–600 • H. W., *Edinburgh Medical Journal*, 3rd ser., 45 (1938), 726–8 • *The Times* (30 Aug 1938) • private information (2004) • J. A. Ross, *The Edinburgh school of surgery after Lister* (1978) • *DNB*
Likenesses D. Foggie, pencil drawing, 1933, Scot. NPG • photograph, Wellcome L. • portrait, repro. in *BMJ* • portrait, repro. in *British Journal of Surgery*
Wealth at death £200,167 13s. 5d.: confirmation, 7 Dec 1938, CCI

Wilkie, William (1721–1772), Church of Scotland minister and poet, was born on 5 October 1721, the son of James Wilkie, a farmer at Echlin in the parish of Dalmeny, 10 miles north-west of Edinburgh. He was educated at the local school and then at the University of Edinburgh, where he studied arts and prepared for the ministry in association with the William Robertson circle of young clergymen of letters. His father's death during his student days obliged him to run the family farm, 2 miles west of Edinburgh, for the benefit of his three unmarried sisters, and farming would continue to be his primary occupation for eight years after obtaining his licence to preach from the presbytery of Linlithgow on 29 May 1745. In September 1745 he enlisted in the college company, formed to defend Edinburgh from the Jacobite army of Charles Edward Stuart, but he never saw action in that conflict. He was befriended by a neighbour, George Lind, the sheriff-substitute of Edinburghshire, who introduced him to the third duke of Argyll, Lord Milton, and the earl of Lauderdale, patron of the nearby parish of Ratho. Thanks to Lauderdale, Wilkie was called to Ratho on 15 February 1753 and was ordained as assistant; he became successor three months later, finally becoming the sole minister there after the death of the aged incumbent, John Guthrie, on 28 February 1756. At Ratho he used sophisticated enclosures and drainage systems to increase yields from the glebe allotted to the minister, and he founded the Husbandry Club for rural improvement.

In late May 1757 Wilkie published anonymously in Edinburgh, with a dedication to Argyll, the *Epigoniad*, a long, ponderous epic that was harshly criticized in the London reviews as well as in a pamphlet, *A Critical Essay on the 'Epigoniad'*. Among his Scottish admirers, however, the epic earned him the epithet the Scottish Homer, just as his lifelong passion for agricultural improvement spawned such nicknames as Potato Wilkie and the Potato Minister. Blaming the failure of the *Epigoniad* on the prejudice of English readers and a conspiracy of English booksellers, Wilkie's friend David Hume encouraged the publication of a second edition in London early in 1759, and he praised it in the April issue of the *Critical Review*. The title-page of the second edition identifies Wilkie as the author and calls the work 'carefully corrected and improved', meaning the deletion of Scotticisms and some self-serving critical remarks about Pope in the preface, and the addition of 'A Dream, in the Manner of Spenser'. But the second edition also sold poorly, and the surplus stock was reissued ten years later with two different cancelled title-pages.

Wilkie took an interest in geometry and history as well as poetry, and his scientific ability, along with the influence of Professor Robert Watson, helped him to win election to the chair of natural philosophy at the University of St Andrews in July 1759, after several unsuccessful attempts to obtain academic positions at Glasgow and Aberdeen. He was admitted to the university on 12 November and resigned his clerical charge at Ratho three days later. Although he never published in his academic field, he acquitted himself well in the classroom, focusing his attention on scientific principles of agriculture, which he practised on a few acres of farmland that he purchased in the vicinity of St Andrews. In late March 1768 he is believed to have interceded with Principal William Tullidelph to reinstate the future Scots poet Robert Fergusson after the principal had expelled him for a prank. Shortly after this event Wilkie published in London his second book of poetry, *Fables*, with a dedication to the earl of Lauderdale. Declaring himself a little 'disappointed' after reading this work, James Beattie wondered, in a letter of 1 July 1768, how 'a man of good sense' could demonstrate 'such a poverty in his language and versification' (Aberdeen University Library, MS 30/1/15). Similarly, Henry Mackenzie, who considered the *Epigoniad* a work of 'great merit', judged *Fables* harshly (Mackenzie, *Account*, 15–16). *Fables* attracted little attention and never went to a second edition, but both of Wilkie's books were reprinted in 1795, along with an important biographical sketch, in volume 11 of Robert Anderson's *Complete Edition of the Poets of Great Britain*.

Wilkie, who was unmarried, was a man of extraordinary eccentricity. He dressed shabbily, went about dirty and unkempt, was absent-minded in the extreme, employed grotesque gestures, chewed tobacco excessively, and slept under a large pile of heavy blankets in an effort to stave off the feverish chills to which he was prone. Mackenzie states that his circle of Edinburgh literati considered him 'superior in original genius to any man of his time, but rough and unpolished in his manners, and still less accommodating to the decorum of society in the ordinary habits of his life' (Mackenzie, *Account*, 15). One member of that circle, Alexander Carlyle, recounted a remarkable evening of verbal jousting in 1759, after which the English visitor Charles Townshend said that 'he had never met with a man who approached so near the two extremes of a god and a brute as Wilkie did' (*Autobiography*, ed. Burton, 413). Yet Sir Robert Liston, while admitting that Wilkie was slovenly in his dress and personal hygiene, asserted that he was gentle, kind, and good-humoured, and deserved Mackenzie's description as 'rough and unpolished' only in the sense that 'he abstained from every thing like flattery or compliment, and perhaps too frankly spoke the truth' (Mackenzie, *Account*, 183–4). Liston's insistence that Wilkie was an excellent companion is supported by his role as a participant in a philosophical dialogue by Adam Ferguson, set on a highland jaunt with David Hume and others.

Wilkie was elected to the Select Society of Edinburgh on 4 December 1754, and was a member of the general assembly of the Church of Scotland in 1758 and 1762; he received honorary DD degrees from St Andrews University in 1766 and from Marischal College, Aberdeen, in 1767. Owing to his agricultural efforts, he accumulated an estate worth between £2000 and £3000, which he left to his two unmarried sisters. His manuscripts were bequeathed to his friend the Revd Robert Liston of Aberdour, but they do not seem to have survived. Shortly after his death on 10 October 1772, from an undisclosed 'lingering indisposition' (Anderson, xiii), he was eulogized by Robert Fergusson in 'An Eclogue to the Memory of Dr William Wilkie', which appeared in the *Weekly Magazine* on 29 October.   RICHARD B. SHER

Sources R. Anderson, 'The life of Wilkie', *A complete edition of the poets of Great Britain*, 13 vols. (1792–5), vol. 11, pp. v–xxiv · *The autobiography of Dr Alexander Carlyle of Inveresk, 1722–1805*, ed. J. H. Burton (1910) · Chambers, *Scots.* (1855) · D. Daiches, *Robert Fergusson* (1982) · *Literature and literati: the literary correspondence and notebooks of Henry Mackenzie*, ed. H. W. Drescher, 2 vols. (1989–99), vol. 1 · R. L. Emerson, 'The social composition of Enlightened Edinburgh: the Select Society of Edinburgh, 1754–1764', *Studies on Voltaire and the Eighteenth Century*, 114 (1973), 291–329 · A. Ferguson, *Collection of essays*, ed. Y. Amoh (1996), 39–65 [incl. Ferguson's dialogue of a highland excursion with Wilkie and others] · H. G. Graham, *Scottish men of letters in the eighteenth century* (1901) · *The letters of David Hume*, ed. J. Y. T. Greig, 2 vols. (1932) · S. Lafon, 'La fable dans l'Écosse des Lumières: William Wilkie et Allan Ramsay', *Écosse des Lumières le XVIIIe siècle autrement*, ed. P. Morère (1997), 73–85 · H. Mackenzie, *An account of the life and writings of John Home* (1822) · E. C. Mossner, *The forgotten Hume: le bon David* (1943) · E. C. Mossner, *The life of David Hume*, 2nd edn (1980) · E. C. Mossner, 'Adam Ferguson's "Dialogue on a highland jaunt" with Robert Adam, William Cleghorn, David Hume, and William Wilkie', *Restoration and eighteenth-century literature*, ed. C. Camden (1963), 297–308 · *Fasti Scot.*, new edn, 1.182–3 · R. B. Sher, *Church and university in the Scottish Enlightenment: the moderate literati of Edinburgh* (1985) · R. Crawford, ed., *Heaven-taught Fergusson: Robert Burns's favourite Scottish poet* (2003) · J. Hall, *Travels in Scotland*, ed. [W. Thomson], 2 vols. in 1 (1807)
Archives NL Scot., letters to Lord Milton, MSS 16676, 16702, 16712, fols. 213, 214, 216
Wealth at death over £2000–£3000

Wilkin, Simon Wilkin (1790–1862), publisher and literary scholar, was born at Costessey (Cossey), Norfolk, on 27 July 1790, the second of the three children of William Wilkin Wilkin (1762–1799), a Norfolk flour miller, and his wife, Cecilia Lucy (d. 1796), daughter of William Jacomb of London. On his father's death Wilkin moved to Norwich to live with his guardian, Joseph *Kinghorn, who educated him at home. At twenty-one Wilkin was an expert entomologist, a fellow of the Linnean Society, and a member of the Wernerian Society of Edinburgh. His niece Cecilia Lucy Brightwell quotes her father's description of him as 'a good scholar … attractive in manner, and agreeable in personal appearance'.

Two major crises affected Wilkin's life: having inherited substantially in 1811, he lost everything in 1816, when the paper mill in which he was a partner failed, and in 1832 his guardian's death was a severe blow. Bankruptcy compelled him to sell his outstanding entomological collection, which was purchased by the Zoological Society. Soon after, however, he established a well-respected printing and publishing business in Norwich, his authors including Harriet Martineau, Amelia Opie, George Borrow, and William Taylor. On 18 July 1825 he married Emma, daughter of John Culley of Costessey, and they had two daughters and a son.

In 1834 Wilkin moved with his family to London, increasingly estranged from the Baptist church to which he had been a generous benefactor, through disagreement with its policy on communion. He had played a major role in the development of the Norfolk and Norwich Literary Institution and Norwich Museum, but once he left Norwich, much of his energy seems to have faded.

Wilkin's greatest achievement was his four-volume edition of Sir Thomas Browne (1836; reissued 1852). He collated manuscripts and early editions meticulously so as to produce the best possible text, exhaustively researching Browne's vast correspondence in the British Museum and Bodleian Library. Geoffrey Keynes saw his work as the foundation of all subsequent editions, praising him as 'the ideal editor for Browne' (*Works*). Wilkin also wrote a textbook on the use of the globes (1823–6), and contributed to his son Martin Hood Wilkin's biography of his guardian, *Joseph Kinghorn of Norwich* (1855).

Wilkin's London years, spent at Cossey Cottage, Pilgrim Lane, Hampstead, were saddened by doctrinal disputes with the Norwich Baptists. He died at home on 28 July 1862, and was buried in his native village of Costessey.

M. H. WILKIN, *rev.* ANN MARGARET RIDLER

Sources C. B. Jewson, *Simon Wilkin of Norwich* (1979) [incl. work list printed by Wilkin] · C. L. Brightwell, *Memorials of the life of Mr Brightwell of Norwich* (1869), 25 · M. H. Wilkin, *Joseph Kinghorn of Norwich: a memoir* (1855) · *The works of Sir Thomas Browne*, new edn, ed. G. Keynes, 1 (1964), 9 · C. L. Brightwell, diary, Norfolk RO, MS 69 · Norfolk RO, Norfolk and Norwich Literary Institution papers · *The Athenaeum* (9 Aug 1862), 182 · d. cert.
Likenesses oils, repro. in Jewson, *Simon Wilkin of Norwich*, frontispiece
Wealth at death under £7000: probate, 11 April 1863, *CGPLA Eng. & Wales*

Wilkins, Augustus Samuel (1843–1905), classical scholar, was born in Enfield Road, Kingsland, Middlesex, on 20 August 1843, the son of Samuel J. Wilkins, a schoolmaster in Brixton, and his wife, Mary Haslam of Thaxted, Essex. His parents were Congregationalists. After being educated at Bishop's Stortford collegiate school, Wilkins attended the lectures of Henry Malden, professor of Greek, and of F. W. Newman, professor of Latin, at University College, London. He entered St John's College, Cambridge, with an open exhibition in October 1864, becoming a foundation scholar in 1866, and winning college prizes for English essays in 1865 and 1866, and the moral philosophy prizes in 1868. He distinguished himself as a fluent speaker at the union, and was president for Lent term 1868. In the same year he graduated BA as fifth in the first class of the classical tripos. Both as an undergraduate and as a bachelor of arts he won the members' prize for the Latin essay, while his skill as a writer of English was attested by the three university prizes he won—the Hulsean for 1868, the Burney for 1870, and the Hare for 1873—for essays respectively entitled 'Christian and pagan ethics', 'Phoenicia and Israel', and 'National education in Greece'.

As a nonconformist, Wilkins was legally disqualified for a fellowship. Although the religious disability was cancelled by the Tests Act of 1871, Wilkins remained disqualified by his marriage in 1870 to Charlotte Elizabeth, the second daughter of W. Field of Bishop's Stortford. Moreover, he could not benefit from the removal of this second disability under the statutes of 1882, since these precluded

from eligibility anyone who had taken his first degree more than ten years before, as he had.

In 1868 Wilkins took the MA degree in the University of London, receiving the gold medal for classics, and in the same year was appointed Latin lecturer at Owens College, Manchester, where he was promoted in the following year to the Latin professorship. For eight years he also lectured on comparative philology, and for many more he undertook the classes in Greek Testament criticism. In the University of London he was examiner in classics from 1884 to 1886, and in Latin from 1887 to 1890 and from 1894 to 1899. He was highly successful as a popular lecturer on literary subjects in Manchester and in other large towns of Lancashire. He was of much service to education in Manchester outside Owens College, particularly as chairman of the Lancashire Independent college, and of the council of the High School for Girls. Within Owens College he was a strong supporter of the claims of women to equal educational rights with men, and of the establishment of a theological department in the university. In 1903, after thirty-four years' tenure of the Latin professorship in Manchester, a weakness of the heart compelled him to resign, but he was appointed to the new and lighter office of professor of classical literature. He died on 26 July 1905 at the seaside village of Llandrillo-yn-Rhos, in north Wales, and was buried in the cemetery of Colwyn Bay.

Wilkins was one of the first classical scholars to introduce to English readers the results of German investigations in scholarship, philology, and ancient history. His chief independent work was his excellent edition of Cicero's *De oratore* (bks i–iii, 1879–92) which continued to be regularly consulted a century later. A much appreciated critical edition of the text of the whole of Cicero's rhetorical works followed in 1903. He also issued commentaries on Cicero's *Speeches Against Catiline* (1871), and the speech *De imperio Gnæi Pompeii* (1879), and on Horace's *Epistles* (1885); he contributed to Postgate's *Corpus poëtarum Latinorum* a critical text of the *Thebais* and *Achilleis* of Statius (1904); and he produced *Roman Antiquities* (1877) and *Roman Literature* (1890), as well as a book on Roman education (1905). He contributed important articles to various works of reference, including the ninth edition of the *Encyclopaedia Britannica*. He joined H. J. Roby in preparing an elementary Latin grammar in 1893.

Wilkins dedicated his edition of the *De oratore* to the University of St Andrews, which conferred on him an honorary degree in 1882; he received the same distinction at Dublin in 1892, and took the degree of LittD at Cambridge in 1885. J. E. SANDYS, *rev.* RICHARD SMAIL

Sources J. F. S., *The Eagle*, 27 (1906), 69–84 · S. A. Burstall, *The story of the Manchester High School for Girls, 1871–1911* (1911) · Venn, *Alum. Cant.* · *CGPLA Eng. & Wales* (1905)
Likenesses J. Collier, oils, *c*.1904, University of Manchester
Wealth at death £5741 12s. 0d.: probate, 16 Sept 1905, *CGPLA Eng. & Wales*

Wilkins, Sir Charles (*bap.* 1749, *d.* 1836), orientalist, born at Frome, Somerset, where he was baptized on 21 June 1749, was the son of Hugh Wilkins and Mary Wray. His mother was niece of the engraver Robert Bateman Wray

Sir Charles Wilkins (*bap.* 1749, *d.* 1836), by John Sartain, pubd 1830 (after James Godsell Middleton)

and of Charles Wray, a partner in Hoare's Bank in London, who procured a writership in the East India Company's Bengal establishment for his great-nephew. In 1770 Wilkins proceeded to Bengal and became superintendent of the company's factories at Malda. Following the example of his friend Nathaniel Brassey Halhed, and with the encouragement of Warren Hastings, the governor-general, he took up the study of Sanskrit and became the first Englishman to master the language. Wilkins was one of the pioneer orientalists of British India who, under the leadership of Sir William Jones, made Calcutta the centre of a new type of orientalism, focusing on India and the Sanskrit language, which had a considerable vogue in Europe in the late eighteenth and early nineteenth centuries; the study of Sanskrit and Indian antiquities, according to an idea widely prevalent in Europe, would bring about an 'Oriental Renaissance' similar to the Renaissance that had been brought about by the revival of Greek letters.

Wilkins's contributions to the new orientalism began with the leading role he played in establishing, in 1778, a printing press for oriental languages, for which he was (in the words of Halhed) 'metallurgist, engraver, founder, and printer' of types for Bengali and Persian. His Bengali types were used in Halhed's *Grammar of the Bengali Language* (1778), the first English primer for that language, at a time when knowledge of Bengali among company servants was rare; his press had a profound effect upon the people of Bengal, ushering Bengali literature into the era of printing. The same year, he tells us, his curiosity excited by the example of Halhed (who had begun the study of Sanskrit, and who had published a few brief characterizations of that language, including comparisons with

Greek), he took up the study of Sanskrit. Halhed did not get very far in his study of the language, and continued to rely on Persian translations for his knowledge of the content of Sanskrit literature. Wilkins, however, succeeded, and after the arrival in Calcutta of Sir William Jones, who was already famous for the brilliance of his accomplishments in Persian and Arabic, became fast friends with Jones and assisted him in learning Sanskrit. In 1784 Wilkins was one of a small band of company servants who founded the Asiatic Society in Calcutta, with Jones as president. His publications in the first volume (1788) of the society's journal, *Asiatic Researches*, comprised three articles translating ancient inscriptions of India, which launched the modern study of Indian epigraphy, and a brief description of the Sikh religion; the second volume (1790), published after his departure from India, contained translations of two more inscriptions.

Besides his contributions to Indian typography and epigraphy, Wilkins undertook three projects which, though not fully realized, were to provide the foundations for the new orientalism: a Sanskrit grammar, a Sanskrit dictionary, and a translation of the great epic, the *Mahabharata*. Each of these projects was a massive undertaking in its own way: the grammar because it would have to include an extensive vocabulary, because there was no published Sanskrit–English dictionary, and because a Devanagari typeface would have to be devised, the dictionary because of the vastness of the Sanskrit language and its literature, and the *Mahabharata* because it is the longest epic poem in the world, conventionally reckoned to consist of 100,000 verses. Ultimately he published the grammar but not the dictionary (of which there are some manuscript remains), and translated as much as a third of the *Mahabharata*, publishing, however, only parts of it.

The first of these projects to appear was his translation of a part of the *Mahabharata*, the *Bhagavad gita*, an important text of Hindu devotionalism, which was published in London (as *The Bhagvat-Geeta*) by the East India Company in 1785. He had sent it to Warren Hastings who, apparently without consulting him, forwarded it to the court of directors with a recommendation to publish, and who supplied a preface for it. It enjoyed a great response in Europe and in America (especially among the transcendentalist writers of New England), and was much translated, French and Russian versions appearing more or less immediately, in 1787.

Wilkins left India and the company service in 1786, for reasons that are not wholly clear but which seem to include the departure of his friend and patron Hastings, the state of his own health, and private affairs; in 1787, soon after returning to England, he married Elizabeth Keble, in London. They resided at Bath for a time, and then returned to London, where they were living in 1788 when Wilkins was elected to the Royal Society in recognition of his pioneering Sanskrit studies and his typographical achievements. His first wife died about that time, and late in 1789 he married Lucy Shingler at Hawkhurst in Kent. During this period he published a translation of the *Hitopadesha* (1787), a book of political wisdom presented through animal fables and popular tales which has ever since played a large role in the learning of Sanskrit in the West, and another part of his *Mahabharata* translation, the story of Shakuntala (1794, 1795). (At about the same time Sir William Jones published a translation of Kalidasa's dramatic version of this story which was well received in Europe and translated into many European languages.) In 1800 Wilkins re-entered the service of the East India Company as librarian, an office then established mainly for the care of its collection of manuscripts, many of them taken in the victory over Tipu Sultan at Seringapatam. On the establishment in 1806 of East India College at Hertford Castle (later Haileybury College) he accepted the offices of examiner and visitor, and continued the duties up to his death in London on 13 May 1836; he was interred in the graveyard of St John's Wood Chapel. He left three daughters; the eldest, Elizabeth, was married to the philologist William *Marsden (1754–1836), with whom Wilkins shared many scholarly interests.

Wilkins's literary achievements were recognized by his election to the Royal Society and by the award in 1825 of the society's gold medal, inscribed 'Carolo Wilkins literaturae Sanskritae principi'; and by his creation of DCL of Oxford in 1805; he was also an associate of the Institut de France. He was knighted in 1833.

European knowledge of ancient Indian literature and the Sanskrit language owes a great deal to the pioneering efforts of Charles Wilkins. He was greatly esteemed by Sir William Jones, who stated that he took up Sanskrit himself only because Wilkins's determination to return to Europe left him without a guide in Sanskrit literature; and after Wilkins's departure he more than once described him, only slightly inaccurately, as the only person in Europe who knew Sanskrit. In addition to highly regarded translations of Sanskrit works, Wilkins soon set about establishing Sanskrit learning in England. In 1795 he designed and cast a fount of type in the Devanagari script for the Sanskrit grammar he was writing, but it was destroyed when his house burnt down; it would have been the first of its kind. He abandoned the project, but resumed it after the formation of East India College, having been encouraged by Alexander Hamilton, Sanskrit professor of the college, publishing the grammar in 1808 for the use of its students. Two others had been published in Bengal nearly simultaneously, by William Carey (1804) and Henry Thomas Colebrooke (1805). Hitherto Sanskrit could only be learned in India, from pandits, and Calcutta had had a virtual monopoly of the new orientalism; now it could be learned from books, in Europe, at a time when Sanskrit instruction had been inaugurated by Hamilton's appointment to the first European professorship in Sanskrit.

Although Wilkins never completed his dictionary of Sanskrit, he produced three lexicographical publications, the first of which seems to be a fragment of that project: it was a treatise on the roots of Sanskrit (1815). The second was a glossary of words in Indian languages having to do with land revenue, which was attached to the so-called fifth report on the East India Company (1812), a work that was later elaborated upon and superseded by H. H. Wilson's extensive dictionary of Indian revenue terminology. The third was his revision of John Richardson's *A Dictionary: Persian, Arabic, and English* (1806); Persian was the lingua franca of Indian diplomacy, and the medium through which the new orientalism made its first approaches to knowledge of Sanskrit literature.

THOMAS R. TRAUTMANN

Sources M. Lloyd, 'Sir Charles Wilkins, 1749–1836', *India Office Library and records: report for the year 1978* (1979), 9–39 · *DNB* · N. B. Halhed, *A code of Gentoo laws* (1776), preface · N. B. Halhed, *A grammar of the Bengal language* (1778) · W. Jones, *Sacontala* (1792), preface · *The letters of Sir William Jones*, ed. G. Cannon, 2 vols. (1970) · R. Rocher, *Orientalism, poetry and the millennium: the checkered life of Nathaniel Brassey Halhed, 1751–1830* (1983) · T. R. Trautmann, *Aryans and British India* (1997) · R. Schwab, *The oriental renaissance: Europe's rediscovery of India and the East, 1680–1880* (1984) · *GM*, 2nd ser., 6 (1836), 97–8 · C. Wilkins, *Grammar of the Sanskrita language* (1808), preface

Likenesses J. Sartain, mezzotint, pubd 1830 (after J. G. Middleton), BM, NPG [*see illus.*]

Wilkins, David (1685–1745), Coptic scholar, was born of Prussian parentage in Memel, Lithuania, on 11 June 1685. His original name was Wilke, which he Latinized as Wilkius and Anglicized into Wilkins. Little is known about his education in Germany (probably in Berlin) or how he acquired his knowledge of ancient and Semitic languages, which was extensive rather than profound. He referred to the antiquarian Ezechiel Spanheim, the elector of Brandenburg's ambassador in England from 1701 to 1710, as his former teacher (Wilkins, 92). By 1707 Wilkins was studying at the Bodleian Library in Oxford and had encountered a group of clerical protectors in London. In 1709, engaged in preparing a history of the patriarchs of Alexandria (which remained in manuscript) and the *editio princeps* of the Coptic (Bohairic) New Testament, the *Novum Testamentum Aegyptium* (1716), he left for the continent. He called on scholars, examined manuscripts in Vienna, Rome, and Paris, and stopped in Amsterdam in 1714 to see to the publication of his first works—an edition of the Aramaic paraphrasis of the books of Chronicles and an Armenian version of the apocryphal third epistle to the Corinthians (1715)—and of John Chamberlayne's polyglot edition of the Lord's prayer, to which he contributed.

By then Wilkins was a well-known figure in the republic of letters, acquainted with the French orientalist in Berlin, Mathurin Veyssière de Lacroze, and in correspondence with numerous European intellectuals who shared his interest in languages and the early church. In England his reception was mixed. Oxford refused him an MA (23 May 1712), but he was created DD at Cambridge in October 1717, and in 1724 was appointed lord almoner's reader of Arabic, a post he resigned in 1729. He was elected FSA on 13 January 1720.

Like one of his first patrons, John Ernest Grabe, another Prussian immigrant, Wilkins converted to Anglicanism. His main patron was William Wake, archbishop of Canterbury. After employing him for some years as an amanuensis, Wake made him librarian at Lambeth Palace in 1715, and gave him the Kentish rectories of Mongeham Parva (30 April 1716) and Great Chart (12 September 1719). Wilkins resigned them both on obtaining the rectories of Hadleigh and Monks Eleigh in Suffolk in November 1719, and the place of joint commissary of the archiepiscopal deanery of Bocking in Essex. On 21 November 1719 he became Wake's domestic chaplain. He acquired the twelfth prebend in the church of Canterbury on 26 January 1721 and on 19 December 1724 the archdeaconry of Suffolk.

Wilkins was an industrious scholar. In the three years he spent as librarian at Lambeth he made important contributions to the cataloguing of manuscripts. In 1721 he edited the Anglo-Saxon laws, in 1725-6 the complete works of John Selden, and in 1731 the Coptic Pentateuch. His main work was his *Concilia Magnae Britanniae et Hiberniae*, an account of British church councils from 446 to 1717 (4 vols., 1737).

The quality of Wilkins's output was uneven. He was primarily a copyist and a compiler, often lacking thoroughness and discrimination. His edition of Selden is careless, but credit must be given to his diligence in assembling unpublished material. Despite his assurance to Lacroze that he read Coptic as easily as Latin (*Thesaurus epistolicus Lacrozianus*, 1.376), his Bohairic New Testament, as Lacroze himself observed (ibid., 3.97, 154-61), betrays an inadequate familiarity with the language and suffers from an arbitrary use of different manuscripts with no indication which they are. His *Concilia* was indebted to Henry Spelman and Thomas Tanner, and still more to Wake. It can be criticized for the mistakes in Anglo-Saxon, the use of inferior manuscripts, and the treatment of chronology, but remains a formidable achievement and has provided the basis for much later work.

Wilkins had many detractors—John Gagnier, the professor of Arabic at Oxford, who deplored his incompetence in Arabic and Hebrew (*Remarks*, 8.50, 11.296), Edward Harley, who described him as 'a very great scoundrel' (Yoewell, 420), and the cantankerous Thomas Hearne, who, as librarian at the Bodleian, had watched him turn from a young man 'of a civil, Courteous and modest behaviour' (*Remarks*, 2.108) into 'a vain ambitious man, of little judgement, tho' great industry' (*Remarks*, 11.115), ready to 'do anything in the World for a little Money' (*Remarks*, 7.283). Wilkins's pomposity emerges from his portrait and his correspondence, and suspicions of his mercenary nature were strengthened by his marriage on 15 November 1725 to Margaret (*c*.1692-1750), the half-witted eldest daughter of Thomas, fifth Lord Fairfax, of Leeds Castle, Kent, with a dowry of £4000. Yet there was another side to Wilkins. He had loyal friends, and behaved generously to the son of Bishop Tanner, whose offer of £50 for copying out his father's *Bibliotheca Britannica* he refused to accept before the book was published. Wilkins had no children. He died of gout at Hadleigh on 6 September 1745, leaving his wife as his sole heir. He was buried in the chancel of Hadleigh church. ALASTAIR HAMILTON

Sources D. C. Douglas, *English scholars, 1660-1730*, 2nd edn (1951) · E. F. Jacob, 'Wilkins's *Concilia* and the fifteenth century', *TRHS*, 4th ser., 15 (1932), 91-131 · *DNB* · *Remarks and collections of Thomas Hearne*, ed. C. E. Doble and others, 11 vols., OHS, 2, 7, 13, 34, 42-3, 48, 50, 65, 67, 72 (1885-1921) · *Thesaurus epistolicus Lacrozianus*, 3 vols. (1742-6) · B. M. Metzger, *The early versions of the New Testament: their origin, transmission, and limitations* (1977) · É. Quatremère, *Recherches critiques et historiques sur la langue et la littérature de l'Égypte* (1808) · *Jean Le Clerc: epistolario*, ed. M. G. Sina and M. Sina, 4 vols. (Florence, 1987-97) · J. Nichols, ed., *Letters on various subjects ... to and from William Nicolson*, 2 vols. (1809) · F. M. Powicke, 'Sir Henry Spelman and the Concilia', *PBA*, 16 (1930), 345-79 · J. Yoewell, 'Notes on books and men by Edward Harley, earl of Oxford', *N&Q*, 2nd ser., 9 (1860), 417-21 · A. W. Haddan and W. Stubbs, eds., *Councils and ecclesiastical documents relating to Great Britain and Ireland*, 3 vols. (1869-71) · D. Wilkins, *Dissertatio de lingua Coptica, Dissertationes ex occasione sylloges orationum dominicarum scriptae ad Joannem Chamberlaynium* (1715) · PRO, PROB 11/743 · A. J. Arberry, *The Cambridge school of Arabic* (1948)

Archives BL, Harley MSS 3779 · BL, Sloane MSS 4046 · BL, Stowe MSS 748, 750 · BL, Add. MSS 6185, 6190, 6468, 32415, 32556, 34265 · Bodl. Oxf., collections and papers, MSS, Add. MSS A 179-184, Add. C 64 · Bodl. Oxf., MS AUTOGR. c. 8 · Bodl. Oxf., sermons · Chetham's Library, Manchester, sermons, MS A. 2. 99 · LPL, corresp. and papers · Suffolk RO, Ipswich, notes and papers | BL, collections relating to Tanner's *Bibliotheca Britannico-Hibernica*, Add. MSS 46683-46686 · Christ Church Oxf., Wake papers · LPL, letters to William Beauvoir; corresp. with bishop of Derry

Likenesses J. Cole, oils, 1740-44, S. Antiquaries, Lond. · oils (as a young man), LPL

Wilkins, David Livingstone [Dave] (**1914-1990**), trumpeter and singer, was born in Bridgetown, Barbados, on 25 September 1914, the fourth son and the youngest of the ten children of the Revd Frank Reginald Wilkins (1867-1945), a Methodist preacher and missionary with the Bethany Methodist Mission, and his wife, Ella Gertrude (Gertie) (*b*. 1870), a singer in the church choir. Both parents were Barbadian. Wilkins attended Wesley Hall Boys' School, Bridgetown, and at the age of twelve learned to play the cornet in a Salvation Army band. After becoming proficient on this instrument, he joined his brothers in a group that played for parties. He took a correspondence course in sight-reading, then when he was seventeen left home to work as a professional musician. He spent two years in St Vincent, where he studied American jazz recordings and learned to improvise, and worked in Martinique before moving to Trinidad in 1934. There he joined the pianist Bert McClean, whose Jazz Hounds accompanied Ken 'Snake Hips' Johnson when the Guyanese dancer made local theatre appearances in 1935. Wilkins, who was now playing the trumpet, impressed Johnson by his grasp of the African-American vernacular idiom and was promised a job with the 'all-coloured' band he proposed leading in England. By 1937, however, he had joined the Trinidad constabulary band and was surprised when Johnson's contract arrived.

Wilkins made an immediate impression in London. Shortly after his arrival he recorded with the American pianist Fats Waller; he was chosen for this and other recording sessions by the critic and musician Leonard Feather, who wrote that '[his] flair for improvisation is quite remarkable' (*Melody Maker*, 2 July 1938). He was not a flamboyant trumpeter. While he lacked the resilient embouchure or 'lip' of a brass player such as Louis Armstrong, he compensated for this by his sensitive and imaginative interpretation. He was soon in demand to play at impromptu jam sessions and as a guest at the regular meetings of the Rhythm Club movement. For the younger generation of aspirational jazz musicians who lionized Johnson's West Indians, he was the orchestra's most inventive individual.

A slight, reddish-skinned man whose resemblance to the American comedian had earned him the nickname in Trinidad of Joe E. Brown, Wilkins was himself a natural comic and a popular member of Johnson's band. He was featured both as trumpet soloist and singer in their broadcasts, thereby becoming known to those unable to patronize London nightclubs. In March 1941 he escaped injury on stage at the Café de Paris when it was destroyed by a German bomb, killing Johnson. The Café de Paris tragedy was something of a watershed in the black musicians' community and the band members scattered to find work wherever they could. Wilkins was never unemployed. He was hired by 'hot' jazz musicians such as the trumpeter Johnny Claes, the saxophonist Kathy Stobart, and, most prominently, the clarinettist Harry Parry, and also filled prestigious nightclub residencies with, among others, the bandleader Bert Ambrose. He recorded prolifically and became an indispensable part of the wartime jam sessions that were inspirational to listeners and young musicians alike. Meanwhile, on 26 June 1941 he married Henrietta Emma (Etta; b. 1921/2), the daughter of John William Loughton. The marriage was short-lived, and she later married the trombonist George Chisholm.

In 1944 Wilkins was a founder member of the All-Star Coloured Band, formed by Leslie 'Jiver' Hutchinson, his colleague in Johnson's trumpet section. Recruited primarily from musicians who had played with Johnson, this was an attempt to maintain the momentum he had initiated and stood as an assertion of black autonomy. When this disbanded, Wilkins joined the popular bandleader Ted Heath, then the pinnacle of achievement for a dance-band musician. From 1947 he increased his personal popularity by singing comedy numbers with Heath—although he came to resent being forced into the racially stereotyping role this required. Eventually, however, he became debilitated by the constant touring. He left Heath in April 1949 on doctor's orders and took undemanding dance-band engagements, but he continued to play with Heath's band unofficially and to make scheduled guest appearances. Despite medical advice, he kept a high profile at jam sessions in places such as the Caribbean Club and even flirted with bebop, the new modern-jazz movement. He also played for a new generation of Caribbean settlers when, as a member of Cab Kaye's band, he accompanied the Trinidadian calypso singer Lord Kitchener at community dances. He travelled to Europe with Kaye and in Amsterdam met, and on 7 October 1952 married, Wilhemina Hendrika (Willie) de Kater (b. 1928); they had one daughter, Carole Ann (b. 1953), but divorced in 1960. He was also the father of David Howarth (b. 1952), later known as David Scott.

On his return to Britain, Wilkins's health deteriorated. Hard living and the insecurities of the travelling life had taken their toll and, avoiding the limelight, he looked for steady, if anonymous, employment in dance-halls and for summer seasons. He emerged in the early 1960s to work with several imaginative musicians who played in the style rooted in his own swing era and known as mainstream jazz, but by the middle of that decade he had suffered an emotional collapse. After intermittent hospitalization he moved into a residential hospital. He continued to play music occasionally, but by 1971 his professional career was over.

Wilkins was one of the most influential British trumpeters of his generation. In whatever field he worked, his playing was marked by the freshness and rhythmic audacity that characterizes the authentic jazz musician. As a popular artist and entertainer he was widely admired, and, through reaching out to a wider public, he helped to maintain a Caribbean profile at a time when few local black figures were visible. In 1981 he returned to living in the community, was interviewed extensively, and recorded his history for posterity. He remained a recipient of fan mail until his death, despite having been out of the music business for almost two decades. He died on 26 November 1990 in the Whittington Hospital, Islington, London, of heart failure, and was cremated at Islington crematorium on 10 December. VAL WILMER

Sources V. Wilmer, *The Independent* (1 Dec 1990) · D. L. Wilkins and Val Wilmer, interview, BL NSA · J. P. Green, 'Bix in Barbados—Dave Wilkins, trumpet', *Storyville* (April–May 1985), 136–48 · L. Feather, 'West Indian cleric who had nine children and a trumpet player', *Melody Maker* (2 July 1938) · 'Local musicians for England', *Port-of-Spain Gazette* (6 April 1937) · E. Charles, 'Spotlight on the boys, no. 14: Dave Wilkins', *The Beat*, 1/8 (1947) · private information (2004) · personal knowledge (2004) · m. cert. · d. cert.
Archives SOUND BL NSA, oral history, 1988
Likenesses J. Maycock, photographs, *c.*1938, priv. coll. · V. Wilmer, photographs, 1960, priv. coll. · V. Wilmer, photographs, 1988, priv. coll. · photographs, priv. coll.

Wilkins, George (d. **1618**), playwright and pamphleteer, was the son of George Wilkins, identified at his death in 1603 as 'George Wilkins the Poet'. Together with his father he may have written the two sonnets signed 'G. W. Senior' and 'G. W. I.' (Junior) that preface the volume of Spenser's *Amoretti* published in 1595. The evidence suggests that he was an ambitious and, for a time, well-connected writer who none the less failed to make a prosperous living at his craft. He published all his known work in a brief period of intense activity between 1606 and 1608, but was probably writing for a decade before that. By 1610 he had set up as an innkeeper in the seedy district of St Sepulchre's in London.

Of Wilkins's early life nothing is known. He was probably the George Wilkins who married Katherine Fowler at St Lawrence Jewry on 13 February 1602, and the union produced a son, Thomas, baptized at St Giles Cripplegate on 11 February 1605. Wilkins regarded himself as a man of education, and projects himself more than once in his writings in the stock image of the poor and unregarded scholar, but he is not known to have attended a university. His first known published work was a translation of a

Roman chronicle, *The History of Justine* (1606), in which he extensively plagiarized an earlier translation by Arthur Golding. He then moved downmarket to collaborate with Thomas Dekker on the pamphlet *Jests to Make you Merrie*, published in 1607. By this time Wilkins was also active as a freelance writer for the stage. *The Miseries of Enforced Marriage*, his only known unaided play, was first acted by the King's Men probably in the middle of 1607, since on publication in the late summer of that year (having been registered in July) it was described on the title-page as a current production. Also entered on the Stationers' register that summer was *The Travels of the Three English Brothers*, on which Wilkins worked with John Day and William Rowley. It was performed by the Queen's Men at the Red Bull in Clerkenwell, and described on its title-page 'As it is now played'.

The Miseries of Enforced Marriage is based on the sensational story of Walter Calverley, which also provided the plot of another and better-known King's Men play, *The Yorkshire Tragedy*. Wilkins's play was a popular one, and new editions were published in 1611, 1629, and 1637. He probably also collaborated with John Day in the writing of the play *Law Tricks* in 1608. But his chief claim to modern fame rests on his association with Shakespeare's *Pericles*. Scholarship has confirmed Wilkins's authorship of the first nine scenes of the play, and has constructed a plausible narrative from initial collaboration to its first publication in 1609. Following the success of *Miseries*, Wilkins was employed by the King's Men to work on the new play, which was either a collaborative project from the outset, or one that Shakespeare took over after Wilkins had roughed out a plot and written the opening scenes. The subject matter could be described as a new departure for either writer, though its peripatetic theme recalls *The Travels of the Three English Brothers*, which dramatizes the wanderings of the Sherley brothers; and the two plays may be connected also by their popularity with Catholic private audiences. *Travels* and *Pericles* were both in the repertory of Cholmeley's Players, a Yorkshire-based company of recusant players, who performed them on tour in the homes of Catholic families in 1608–10. It is quite possible that Wilkins himself was a recusant: Roger Prior suggests that he may have been the 'George Wilkinson' who was convicted of not going to church in 1608, though firm evidence of his religious affiliations is lacking. Wilkins's pamphlet *Three Miseries of Barbary* (probably published in 1607) may have owed some of its information to Sir Anthony Sherley, who was in north Africa in 1605–6 and was by then a formal convert to Rome.

The latter pamphlet was published by Henry Gosson, who also brought out the first edition of *Pericles* in 1609. The defects of this edition are generally thought to be the result of its being a memorial text, unauthorized by the company and surreptitiously reported by one or more of its actors. Wilkins may have been the means by which Gosson obtained the copy for his edition (though Gosson does not credit Wilkins on the title-page, perhaps because ascribing the play solely to Shakespeare would improve

sales). The publisher had secured a lucrative title, for *Pericles* was a very popular play, holding the stage into the 1620s; and this could explain why Gosson was later prepared to stand bail for Wilkins on an assault charge in 1611.

Wilkins had already found another way to capitalize on the play's success when in 1608 he published a prose romance, *The Painful Adventures of Pericles Prince of Tyre*. This explicitly claims to be based on the play, and has a good deal in common with it; but all the signs are that Wilkins was working from memory rather than from a manuscript—as junior collaborator he would probably not own a copy of the playtext, which was the sole property of the King's Men. *Pericles* was officially registered for publication by Edward Blount in 1608, but no book under his imprint emerged, and the entry may have been designed to block Wilkins or others from publishing without the company's consent. It is notable that, despite having created two major successes for the King's Men in 1607–8, Wilkins's connection with them was severed after the publication of *Pericles*, and as far as is known he did no further work for the stage.

The King's Men may have had other reasons to distrust George Wilkins. Records show that he was in trouble with the law as early as 1602, and he was regularly in court from 1610 until the end of his life. His later belligerence was probably aggravated by disappointment at the termination of his writing career, as he struggled to make a living as a victualler in an insalubrious urban quarter—the area around Cow Cross and Turnmill Street, notorious for thieves and prostitutes. But it is likely that Wilkins was always a difficult and untrustworthy character. The case in which he was bailed by Henry Gosson was one in which he was accused of 'abusing one Randall Borkes and kicking a woman on the belly which was then great with child' (Prior, 'Life of George Wilkins', 144), and this was not the only time he was arraigned for violence against women. In 1611 Wilkins was arrested for helping a prostitute suspected of theft to escape justice, and after his release on bail was accused of abusing a constable in the execution of his office. The tangled story that emerges from the court records prompts the suspicion that Wilkins's tavern also operated as a brothel. In another case in 1614 involving his wife, a witness testified that Wilkins's house was frequented by lewd women. This is supported by a later misfortune that befell Wilkins: in 1616 he was in court to testify against a group of rioters who had pulled down 'a great part' of his house—almost certainly an example of the action habitually directed against theatres and brothels.

In 1612, as a result of his misdemeanours, Wilkins temporarily lost his licence to operate as a victualler. During the next two years he avoided further charges, though he himself was the object of assault. Having regained his licence, however, he was once more in trouble in 1616, when he was fined for assaulting one John Parker and stealing his hat and cloak. The final chapter of his life, like several earlier ones, is written in court records. In 1618 he was accused of harbouring a felon and, having been bailed, was recorded as discharged on 2 October 'because he is dead'. His death must have taken place after the sessions on 3 September, when his case was postponed. Wilkins died intestate, and his estate was awarded to his widow on 14 October. ANTHONY PARR

Sources R. Prior, 'The life of George Wilkins', *Shakespeare Survey*, 25 (1972), 137–51 · R. Prior, 'George Wilkins and the young heir', *Shakespeare Survey*, 29 (1976), 33–9 · M. Eccles, 'George Wilkins', *N&Q*, 220 (1975), 250–52 · S. Wells and G. Taylor, *William Shakespeare: a textual companion* (1987) · W. le Hardy, ed., *Middlesex sessions records*, 1–4 (1935–41) · M. P. Jackson, '*Pericles*, acts I and II: new evidence for George Wilkins', *N&Q*, 235 (1990), 192–6 · E. A. J. Honigmann, *The stability of Shakespeare's text* (1965) · J. Crow, ed., *Law-trickes* (1950) · W. Schrickx, '*Pericles* in a book-list of 1619', *Shakespeare Survey*, 29 (1976), 22–32 · C. J. Sisson, 'Shakespeare quartos as prompt-copies', *Review of English Studies*, 18 (1942), 129–43

Wilkins, George (1785–1865), Church of England clergyman, born at Norwich in May 1785, was the third son of William Wilkins (1751/2–1815), an architect, and his wife, Hannah Willett, and the younger brother of William *Wilkins. He was educated at Bury St Edmunds grammar school, and in 1803 entered Gonville and Caius College, Cambridge, graduating BA in 1807, MA in 1810, and DD in 1824. Ordained in 1808, Wilkins became curate of Great Plumstead, Norfolk, and then of Hadleigh, Suffolk, under Dr Edward Auriol Hay-Drummond (d. 1829), uncle of the earl of Kinnoull. He married Hay-Drummond's daughter Amelia Auriol on 3 September 1811, having first run away with her to Gretna. That year he published *Lines Addressed to Mrs Hay Drummond*. The first Earl Manvers presented him to two Nottinghamshire vicarages: Laxton, on 1 December 1813, and Lowdham, on 19 January 1815. On 8 November 1817 the second earl presented him to the important parish of St Mary's, Nottingham; he continued to hold Lowdham in plurality until 1839. In 1823 he was collated by the archbishop of York to the prebendal stall of Normanton in Southwell collegiate church. Lord Eldon presented him to the rectory of Wing in 1827, mainly on the strength of his book *Body and Soul* (1822), though its publication provoked some controversy, especially with Revd J. H. Browne, archdeacon of Ely. An earlier publication, *The History of the Destruction of Jerusalem as Connected with the Scripture Prophecies*, appeared in 1816.

On 24 April 1832 Wilkins became archdeacon of Nottingham in succession to William Barrow. His ministry at Nottingham, a parish with a population of 28,000 souls, was controversial. He took an active interest in the Nottingham dispensary for the sick poor (1831), and established an elementary school for girls (1835). But his relations with the large number of dissenters in his parish were not harmonious; he attacked dissent in his archidiaconal charges of 1834 and 1837. His attempt to collect tithes in 1833 failed. The refusal in 1843 of the vestry, dominated by dissenters, to vote a rate to pay for essential repairs to the tower of St Mary's Church caused the church to be closed, and demonstrated the unenforceability of church rates in many parishes. Wilkins announced his resignation as vicar in October 1843, accepting in its place the rectory of Beelsby, Lincolnshire, in the gift of the Southwell collegiate church, though he never resided there. He concentrated instead on the assiduous discharge of his archidiaconal duties, building two chapels of ease in Nottingham itself, and collecting £2000 to restore St Mary's Church and provide sittings for 2000 people.

Tall, active both in body and mind, and of a fine presence, Wilkins was famous for his pulpit oratory. He wrote various sermons, charges, letters, and addresses. The latter part of his life was spent at Southwell as the last canon residentiary. There he devoted himself for many years to the restoration of both the services and the fabric of Southwell church. He died at the residence, Southwell, on 13 August 1865, and was buried south-east of the church. Of his sons, Henry St Clair *Wilkins was a general, John Murray Wilkins (d. 1881) was the last rector of Southwell collegiate church before it became a cathedral, and George Dashwood Wilkins (d. 1885) was in the service of the East India Company.

M. G. WATKINS, rev. M. C. CURTHOYS

Sources *Nottingham Journal* (14 Aug 1865) · *Nottingham Journal* (18 Aug 1865) · *The Guardian* (16 Aug 1865) · Boase, *Mod. Eng. biog.* · Venn, *Alum. Cant.* · A. C. Wood, 'An episode in the history of St Mary's Church, Nottingham', *Transactions of the Thoroton Society*, 56 (1952), 60–76
Archives BL, corresp. and accounts with A. Spottiswoode, etc., Add. MS 48903
Likenesses photograph, repro. in *Church of England photographic portrait gallery* (1859), pl. 52
Wealth at death under £9000: probate, 23 Oct 1865, *CGPLA Eng. & Wales*

Wilkins, Henry St Clair (1828–1896), army officer, son of George *Wilkins (1785–1865), archdeacon of Nottingham, and his wife, Amelia Auriol, *née* Hay-Drummond, niece of the ninth earl of Kinnoul, was born on 3 December 1828. After attending Addiscombe College, he was commissioned lieutenant in the Bombay Engineers on 11 June 1847. His further commissions were: captain, 27 August 1858; lieutenant-colonel, 1 March 1867; colonel, 15 August 1870; major-general, 21 December 1877; lieutenant-general, 31 December 1878; and general, 18 January 1882, when he retired on a pension.

Wilkins served with the field force from Aden against Arab dissidents in 1858. He commanded the Royal Engineers throughout the Abyssinian expedition of 1868, where the difficult terrain required engineering skills of the highest order. He was mentioned in dispatches by Lord Napier of Magdala for his 'invaluable and important services', and was appointed aide-de-camp to the queen, with the rank of colonel in the army.

As well as an able soldier Wilkins was an accomplished draughtsman and artist. Employed in architectural and engineering works in the public works department of India, his designs were considered notable for their fitness and beauty. Among them were: at Aden, the restoration of the ancient tanks in the Tawella valley; at Bombay, the government and the public works secretariats (he also won the first prize in a competition for his design for the European general hospital); at Poona, the Sassoon Hospital, the Deccan College, the Jewish synagogue, and the mausoleum of the Sassoon family; and at Bhuj, the palace of the rao of Kach.

Wilkins married, in 1856, Eliza Violet, daughter of Colonel Colin Campbell McIntyre of the 78th highlanders. Wilkins published *Reconnoitring in Abyssinia* (1870) and *A Treatise on Mountain Roads, Live Loads, and Bridges* (1879). Wilkins died suddenly, on 15 December 1896, at his residence, 77 Queen's Gate, South Kensington, London, and was survived by his wife. R. H. VETCH, *rev.* JAMES FALKNER

Sources *Indian Army List* · *Army List* · *The Times* (Dec 1896) · *Royal Engineers Journal* (1897) · H. Wilkins, *Reconnoitring in Abyssinia* (1870) · Boase, *Mod. Eng. biog.* · Kelly, *Handbk* · *CGPLA Eng. & Wales* (1897)
Wealth at death £16,379 10s. 10d.: resworn probate, Sept 1897, *CGPLA Eng. & Wales*

Wilkins, Sir (George) Hubert (1888–1958), polar explorer and climatologist, was born at Mount Bryan East, South Australia, on 31 October 1888, the thirteenth and youngest child of Harry Wilkins, grazier, and his wife, Louisa Smith. Until 1903 he lived and worked on his parents' sheep station where outdoor activities, coupled with his early experience of the devastation caused by drought, laid the foundations for his lifelong interest and work in the natural sciences, climatology, and meteorology.

From 1903 to 1908, at the Adelaide School of Mines, Wilkins studied electrical and general engineering, extending his studies also to photography and cinematography. In 1908 he left Australia as a ship stowaway and commenced his career of adventure in Algiers. Later he worked in London as a newspaper reporter and cameraman with assignments in many countries, the most interesting being some months in 1912 spent filming the fighting between the Turks and the Bulgarians. Over this general period he found time also to take flying lessons and to experiment in aerial photography.

The year 1913 saw the beginning of Wilkins's career as a polar explorer with his appointment as photographer to Vilhjalmur Stefansson's Canadian Arctic expedition. Thereafter, until early 1916 when he returned to Australia to enlist, he acquired much experience in the techniques of living, travelling, and working in the Arctic region, adding greatly to his knowledge of the natural sciences. He became convinced that the aeroplane could be used to explore and map the polar regions, and developed a plan to set up a series of permanent weather stations in those regions as part of a worldwide scheme for systematic and co-ordinated weather forecasting.

With a commission in the Australian Flying Corps, in May 1917 Wilkins was sent to Europe, where he was appointed assistant to the official photographer to the Australian forces, Captain Frank Hurley, of Antarctic fame. His subsequent work as a war photographer in France was of such quality that he rose to the rank of captain, received the MC and bar, and was twice mentioned in dispatches. He was several times wounded and acquired a reputation for daring, courage, and leadership.

The war over, Wilkins gained further flying experience, first as navigator on an unsuccessful attempt to fly from England to Australia in late 1919, then in British airships. Later he was appointed photographer to a mission sent to the Dardanelles to reconstruct the Gallipoli campaign. On his discharge from the services he immediately took steps to further his own plans for polar exploration. But his scheme for polar weather stations was rejected by the Royal Meteorological Society, while a proposal to fly an airship in the Arctic received no support in either England or Germany. Finally, in 1920–21 he had his first taste of work in the Antarctic as second-in-command of J. L. Cope's ill-fated expedition working in the Graham Land area. This was followed by service as naturalist with Sir Ernest Shackleton in his *Quest* expedition, and later by a period in Soviet Russia spent surveying and filming the effects of drought and famine—subjects close to his mind since they reiterated the need for an international weather forecasting service. Next came an expedition (1923–5) for the British Museum through northern Australia, to carry out a biological survey and to collect specimens of the rarer mammals. His book *Undiscovered Australia* (1928) shows clearly the extent and high quality of his work, the collections made including plants, birds, insects, fish, minerals, fossils, and Aboriginal artefacts, as well as mammals. The expedition also proved Wilkins's skill as a project organizer and leader of men.

After plans for an Antarctic expedition failed through shortage of funds, Wilkins turned his attention to the Arctic, where he successfully carried out a remarkable programme of pioneering air exploration with the American army pilot Carl Ben Eielson. On one expedition they experienced engine failure during a blizzard and were forced to make a landing on pack ice 550 miles from their point of departure, Point Barrow in Alaska. They endured a fourteen-day walk to safety, during which they drew heavily on the survival experience that Wilkins had gained with Stefansson's Arctic expedition. With stretched finances Wilkins managed somehow to acquire a new plane and in April 1928 the pair set out in a Lockheed Vega on their historic flight from Barrow eastward over the Arctic Ocean, to Spitsbergen. The purposes behind this remarkable exploit (as indicated in his book *Flying the Arctic*, 1928) were to prove the value of the aeroplane for polar exploration; to demonstrate the viability of air passenger routes over polar lands; and to further Wilkins's cherished plan for polar meteorological stations. In June of that year Wilkins was knighted by the king in London.

Wilkins next revived his plans for aerial exploration in the Antarctic where between 1928 and 1930 he led two expeditions, making, with Eielson, the first flight in that area on 16 November 1928, as well as numerous significant geographical observations and discoveries from the air. Wilkins's reputation as a pioneer of the air age in polar regions was by now firmly established.

In 1929 Wilkins married a fellow Australian then working in New York as an actress, Suzanne Bennett (Bennett was a stage name), daughter of John Evans, a mining engineer of Victoria, Australia. They had no children. It was a happy marriage in which both parties by mutual agreement pursued their chosen careers.

In 1931 came Wilkins's famous venture by submarine in Arctic waters, made, as he explained in *Under the North Pole:*

the *Wilkins–Ellsworth Submarine Expedition* (1931), with the twofold purpose of exploring the region from Spitsbergen westwards via the north pole to the Siberian coast, and experimenting with the craft as a weather station, both above and below the ice and in radio contact with the outside world. For this expedition Wilkins was lent a submarine by the United States navy, which he renamed *Nautilus*. The submarine suffered engine failure during the Atlantic crossing and eventually left Bergen for the Arctic circle on 5 August. When an attempt was made to dive under the ice, on 22 August, it was discovered that *Nautilus* had been sabotaged by crew members, who had detached the diving rudders. Wilkins refused to be put off by the unwillingness of his crew to follow and kept the submarine on the edge of the ice pack, conducting useful scientific experiments over previously unexplored seabed. Then, early in September, he achieved his objective by filling the ballast tanks and diving slowly at the ice edge, forcing *Nautilus* under, where she remained for more than an hour in spite of the terrifying noise of the ice rending on the hull. On 8 September the radio masts were re-erected and Wilkins ended five days of radio silence to communicate to the outside world that the voyage was over. The transmission ended speculation that a disaster had overtaken the expedition. Having failed to reach the North Pole, Wilkins found himself branded a failure and 'pilloried as an irresponsible adventurer': nothing, though, 'could shake his belief in the principles of submarine exploration' (Grierson, 148). It was entirely due to his resolve that *Nautilus* had become the first vessel ever to operate beneath the Arctic ice pack, and he had led a scientific programme that revealed the potential for future research, achievements that fully justified the endeavour.

The thirties also saw Wilkins working with the American Lincoln Ellsworth on four expeditions to the Antarctic continent, using the ship *Wyatt Earp* and aeroplanes. He also played a major role in the search operations for the Soviet aviator Sigismund Levanevsky and his crew, who were lost over the Arctic Ocean in August 1937. Wilkins offered his services to the Soviet government, and was accepted, and spent until March 1938 engaged in the search. At the same time he carried out pioneering work in moonlight flying under winter conditions; a large programme of meteorological work; and constant studies of ice movements from the air. In June 1938 he was received by Stalin in Moscow, as a gesture of Soviet gratitude, and addressed a meeting of the Russian Academy of Sciences.

When war broke out in 1939 Wilkins, who was in the United States, was rejected by the British and Australian governments for war work, on account of his age. But he was subsequently employed by the American government, first in missions concerned with aircraft manufacture on behalf of the allied powers; and later in missions through the office of strategic services, work which took him to the Middle and Far East. With the entry of America into the war he served from 1942 onwards as a geographer, climatologist, and Arctic adviser with the US

quartermaster-general's corps, being particularly concerned with the development of efficient operational and survival techniques and equipment for the Arctic and sub-Arctic regions. After the war he served first with the US Navy office of scientific research (1946–7), then in an advisory capacity with the US weather bureau, later with the Arctic Institute of North America. Finally in 1953 he was appointed geographer to the research and development command, specializing in studies and research connected with human activities in the polar regions.

Wilkins had the restless mind and outlook of the true pioneer. He possessed tremendous mental and physical drive—assets which, joined to a vivid imagination and a supreme faith in his purpose, enabled him to overcome all obstacles. He was continually on the move, being irresistibly drawn to new ideas and practical projects. He rarely concerned himself with the more obvious results, implications, and significance of an achievement and consequently the published records of his many projects and expeditions were unfortunately scanty. Some of his findings were later proved to be erroneous, most notably his 'discovery' during the 1928–9 aerial Antarctic expedition that Graham Land was an archipelago and not a peninsula as previously thought. Evidence put before the Royal Geographical Society in London in 1940 proved conclusively that Wilkins was wrong, but he appeared not to be unduly concerned. The error, and Wilkins's lack of interest in its cause, led to him being regarded with some suspicion in scientific circles, but he was primarily a field explorer and trail-blazer, working to a clear if long-range plan, based upon his conviction of the necessity for a worldwide meteorological organization. He was convinced that a direct relationship existed between the meteorology of the polar regions and weather conditions elsewhere and that a full knowledge of polar geography would be required before his plan for polar weather stations could be realized. In these fields he was a pioneer, as he was in polar exploration by air and submarine.

Wilkins was reticent, self-sufficient, and infinitely adaptable. Interested in everything, he enjoyed the company of his fellows, yet found it easy to live and work among primitive peoples, if only because he shared their intense awareness of nature in all her moods. He had a strong religious background and was actively interested in such matters as telepathy and life after death. Solitary by nature and by no means the ordinary gregarious man, he was yet a good mixer and companion both on and off the job.

Wilkins was a fellow of the Royal Meteorological Society and of the Royal Geographical Society, which awarded him its patron's medal. Among the many other medals which he received were the Samuel Finley Breese Morse medal from the American Geographical Society, the gold medal of the International League of Aviators, and the Norwegian Air Club's gold medal of honour. He was a companion of the order of St Maurice and St Lazarus of Italy and in 1955 received the honorary degree of DSc from the University of Alaska.

On 30 November 1958 Wilkins died suddenly in his

hotel at Framingham, Massachusetts. He had lived to see the under-ice transits of the Arctic Sea by the American nuclear submarines *Nautilus* and *Skate*, in August 1958, and it was particularly fitting that the latter vessel should facilitate Wilkins's often expressed wish that his ashes might be scattered near the north pole. In March 1959 *Skate* effected this rite, breaking through the polar ice after a long and hazardous voyage, of the kind Wilkins himself had pioneered.

R. A. SWAN, rev. MARK POTTLE

Sources *The Times* (2 Dec 1958) · private information (1971) · L. Thomas, *Sir Hubert Wilkins: his world of adventure* (1961) · *AusDB* · J. Grierson, *Sir Hubert Wilkins: enigma of exploration* (1960) · V. Stefansson, *The friendly Arctic* (1921) · F. Wild, *Shackleton's last voyage* (1923) · J. G. Hayes, *The conquest of the south pole* (1932) · *National Geographic Magazine* (Aug 1938) · C. E. W. Bean, *Gallipoli mission* (1948) · E. W. Hunter Christie, *The Antarctic problem* (1951) · R. A. Swan, *Australia in the Antarctic* (1961) · C. E. W. Bean and others, *The official history of Australia in the war of 1914–1918*, 12 vols. (1921–43) · T. Eliassen and S. Nasht, *Voyage of the Nautilus*, film, Norway, 2001
Archives Dartmouth College, Hanover, New Hampshire, papers · NHM, MSS and photos: 'Undiscovered Australia' · Scott Polar RI, journals and notes | NL Scot., corresp. with Sir James M. Wordie | FILM BFI NFTVA, documentary footage · BFI NFTVA, news footage
Likenesses photographs, c.1920–1921, Hult. Arch. · R. Mason, portrait, US Army Research Center, Natick, Massachusetts, Wilkins Arctic Test Chamber · R. H. Perry, portrait, priv. coll. · J. P. Quinn, portrait, priv. coll. · V. Vuchnich, portrait, priv. coll. · Lady Wilkins, portrait, Museum of the Marine Historical Association, Mystic, Connecticut · Lady Wilkins, two portraits, priv. coll.

Wilkins, John (1614–1672), theologian and natural philosopher, was probably born at Canons Ashby, Northamptonshire, the eldest of the five children of Walter Wilkins (*d*. 1625), an Oxford goldsmith, and Jane (*d*. 1633), daughter of the noted puritan divine John *Dod. After his father's death, his mother married another Oxford man, Francis Pope. She gave birth to a daughter, who did not survive childhood, and to Walter *Pope, who became close to her eldest son and was the successor to Christopher Wren as professor of astronomy at Gresham College.

Education and early career Wilkins entered Edward Sylvester's grammar school in Oxford at the age of nine. He matriculated at New Inn Hall, Oxford, in May 1627, but soon transferred to Magdalen Hall; he took the degrees of BA in 1631 and MA in 1634, and for a brief period was a tutor in his college. His moderate puritan background may have influenced his move to Magdalen Hall, where Laudian Arminianism was resisted longer than at other colleges. Even there, however, Laudianism prevailed, and this may have precipitated Wilkins's decision to leave Oxford in 1637. In view of his mature theological position it seems reasonable to infer that he was influenced early on by his grandfather John Dod. Described as a passive nonconformist, Dod focused on the unanimity of certain beliefs rather than on those things that caused difference and strife, and (like Wilkins later) he emphasized the importance of practical morality.

Wilkins was instituted as vicar of Fawsley, near Daventry, Northamptonshire, on 2 June 1637, and ordained as a priest at Christ Church Cathedral, Oxford, on 18 February

John Wilkins (1614–1672), by Mary Beale, c.1670–72

1638. The previous vicar at Fawsley was John Dod, who took up the post again shortly after, when Wilkins resigned to become private chaplain to William Fiennes, first Viscount Saye and Sele, a leading puritan and anti-Laudian. Wilkins's brief tenure at Fawsley, while his grandfather stepped down, may have been a stratagem to circumvent a Laudian policy of limiting ordination to those granted a benefice (to prevent would-be puritan clerics from becoming lecturers and private chaplains).

By 1641 Wilkins was in London acting as private chaplain to George, eighth Lord Berkeley, a moderate in both religious and political outlook. In late 1644 he entered the service of Charles Louis, prince elector palatine, but their rapport seems to have been based more on mutual scientific interests than on a similarity of religious perspective. He must also have made a reputation for himself as a theologian or preacher by this time, because he was appointed preacher to Gray's Inn in 1645 and also seems to have been a regular preacher at the Savoy Chapel. His first published religious work, *Ecclesiastes* (1646), was subtitled *A Discourse Concerning the Gift of Preaching*, and was intended as a handbook for preachers.

Scientific interests, 1638–1648 Wilkins's interest in the latest developments affecting natural philosophy was apparent in his earliest publications. In 1638 he published *The discovery of a new world, or, A discourse tending to prove, that ('tis probable) there may be another habitable world in the moon*. He added to this in 1640 his *Discourse concerning a new planet; tending to prove, that ('tis probable) our earth is one of the planets*. Powerful and influential works of popularization, these books aimed to expound and defend the new world picture developed by Copernicus, Galileo, and Kepler. The first book argued that the earth was not uniquely different from other heavenly bodies, while the second tried to remove philosophical and religious objections to the earth's motion and show how it might be physically possible.

In 1641 Wilkins published *Mercury, or, The secret and swift messenger: shewing how a man may with privacy and speed communicate his thoughts to a friend at any distance*. Concerned primarily with means of encoding or otherwise protecting the secrecy of communications, orally or in writing, it also discussed how messages may be secretly and swiftly conveyed over great distances. In the course of this work Wilkins briefly considered the possibility of a 'Universal Character' that would be legible to readers in any language. This was a theme to which he would later return.

While in London, Wilkins became a regular member of a group devoted to the study of natural philosophy and the sciences related to it, such as geometry, mechanics, magnetism, chemistry, and medicine. This group has been seen as one of the forerunners of the Royal Society. Its principal convener may have been Theodore Haak, but it seems clear that Wilkins was a leading member of the group as it broke up in 1648, at about the time that he moved to Oxford. Shortly after this Wilkins became a prominent member of a similar group that began to meet in Oxford with some of the same personnel as the London group.

In 1648 Wilkins published *Mathematical Magick, or, The Wonders that may be Performed by Mechanical Geometry*. The first part of the book, on mechanical powers, showed how simple machines like the lever, pulley, and screw could be used to bring about remarkable effects, while the second part, on mechanical motions, discussed among other things flying machines, the submarine, automata, and perpetual motion. Offered as a practical manual rather than as a work of theoretical exposition, it can nevertheless be seen as a foreshadowing of the mechanical philosophy and of the increasing importance of the geometrical approach to an understanding of nature. It was influenced by the work of Guidobaldo del Monte and Marin Mersenne, and formed an attractive and highly effective medium of popularization.

Warden of Wadham College, 1648–1659 Wilkins was chosen in 1648 as warden of Wadham by the visitors appointed by parliament to reform the University of Oxford. The committee included Lord Saye, Lord Berkeley, and Richard Knightley, another of Wilkins's early patrons, but why they should have thought of Wilkins in this connection remains a mystery. The warden was required to be a doctor of divinity, but Wilkins was given a year's dispensation because of his service to the elector palatine. He took the degrees of BD in April 1648 and DD in December 1649. In the interim he accompanied the elector palatine to The Hague and Heidelberg.

Wilkins proved to be an excellent warden and Wadham thrived under his direction. It was during this period that the practical implications of his latitudinarian theological outlook became evident. Under his tolerant and conciliatory regime Wadham became a place where scholars of different political and religious persuasions could live and work together. Because of Wilkins the college also became attractive to scholars with an interest in the new philosophy. Seth Ward and Lawrence Rook left Cambridge to take up fellowships at Wadham, while John Wallis, Jonathan Goddard, William Petty, Ralph Bathurst, Thomas Willis, and Robert Boyle moved to Oxford to attend the scientific meetings that Wilkins encouraged as a continuation of those he used to attend in London. He also attracted some brilliant students, most notably Christopher Wren, but also his stepbrother, Walter Pope, William Neile, Thomas Sprat, William Lloyd, and Samuel Parker. He created a formal garden at Wadham, which included a number of scientific instruments, a statue that appeared to talk, and transparent apiaries from which the honey could be extracted without the bees' being killed.

Wilkins was also influential in the university at large. In October 1652 he was appointed to a five-man committee to which Cromwell effectively delegated his powers as chancellor. Wilkins used this position to fight against the visitors for the restoration of the independence of the university and the colleges, to mediate between contending factions within the university, and to defend the university from outside threats. The most visible example of the last was *Vindiciae academiarum* (1654), a response written by Wilkins and Seth Ward to John Webster's *Academiarum examen* (1654). Representing radical sectarian views of a rather antinomian and illuminist kind, Webster called for an end to the standard university education of clergymen: in its place he called for a reformed curriculum that would concentrate on a practical utilitarian knowledge of nature. Wilkins and Ward responded to both of these issues, defending the role of education in fitting men for the ministry and refuting Webster's charges about the inadequacy of the scientific and mathematical education available at Oxford.

During this period Wilkins published two further religious works. *A Discourse Concerning the Beauty of Providence* of 1649 was a sermon intended to bring comfort to those adversely affected by the recent upheavals in church and state. Showing the influence of Senecan Stoicism, Wilkins advocated patient submissiveness to Providence in times of suffering. *A discourse concerning the gift of prayer: shewing what it is, wherein it consists and how far it is attainable by industry* (1651), like the earlier *Ecclesiastes*, was intended as an advice manual to aid in the organization of thoughts and in effective communication between man and God. These three religious works proved highly influential in the contemporary shift to a plainer, clearer, and more simply ordered style in sermons and other forms of writing.

In 1656 Wilkins married the lord protector's youngest sister, Robina (d. 1689), and became stepfather to her two daughters. Robina was the recent widow of Peter French, canon of Christ Church, who was, like Wilkins, one of the five men to whom Cromwell delegated his powers as chancellor. The marriage seems to have been an opportunistic move by Wilkins, some said to preserve or promote the university's interests, others suggested it was for his own. Even Wilkins himself (though admittedly after the Restoration) implied that he married Robina under duress, but he did not make clear who was exerting this pressure.

When Richard Cromwell was appointed chancellor of the university in 1657, Wilkins became his closest adviser at Oxford. Late in 1658 there were rumours that Wilkins would be appointed provost of Eton or that he would be made vice-chancellor at Oxford, but these came to nothing. He was, however, appointed as master of Trinity College, Cambridge, on 17 August 1659 (he resigned from Wadham on 3 September). Although this may have been initiated by Richard Cromwell, the new lord protector, it was the fellows of Trinity who petitioned for Wilkins to be appointed master, and this was granted by parliament. Wilkins immediately began reforms at Trinity and made such a success of his mastership that the fellows petitioned Charles II for his retention after the Restoration. Charles, however, was obliged to fulfil a promise made by his father to Henry Ferne, who replaced Wilkins on 3 August 1660. At the end of that same month, however, Wilkins was installed as dean of Ripon Cathedral, and was also made a prebendary of York Minster.

Activities after the Restoration After leaving Cambridge Wilkins took up residence in London and again became preacher at Gray's Inn. Lord Berkeley granted him the living of Cranford in Middlesex at the end of 1661, and in April 1662 he became vicar of St Lawrence Jewry, London. Effectively excluded from active participation in ecclesiastical politics (since he seemed a turncoat to all sides), Wilkins unhesitatingly accepted the Act of Uniformity in 1662 and tried to persuade moderate dissenters like Richard Baxter, John Howe, and Edmund Calamy that it was in the best interests of the church. He now began to emerge as the leader of the growing latitudinarian party, which argued in favour of allowing a broad measure of theological and philosophical dissent where there was agreement on key basic principles, formulated so as to gain the ready assent of the majority of ordinary Christians.

Wilkins was also influential once again in the organization of natural philosophy in England, being a founder member and extremely active fellow of the newly formed Royal Society of London. He chaired the initial meeting on 28 November 1660 to discuss the nature of the society, and was subsequently elected fellow (22 April 1663) and one of the society's two secretaries, a position he held until leaving London for Chester in 1668. He was a council member until just before his death, and was even sometimes referred to as the society's vice-president (an unofficial title). He was not only an active contributor to the scientific meetings and an indefatigable member of the various investigative committees that were a prominent feature of the society, but was also a busy administrator and fundraiser. Furthermore, he was one of the leading shapers of the society's characteristic experimental method. Perhaps the most influential way in which he did this was through his close and detailed supervision of Thomas Sprat's official *History of the Royal Society* (1667), which was not so much a history (Sprat and Wilkins began work on it

as early as 1663) as a manifesto of the society's aims and methods.

During these years Wilkins also produced what is perhaps his most significant work, his *Essay towards a Real Character and a Philosophical Language*. This was published in 1668, though it seems that he began work on it with the help of Seth Ward shortly after their collaboration on *Vindiciae academiarum*. Calls for a universal language had increased as a result of the flourishing of vernacular literature and an increasing dissatisfaction with Latin, partly with regard to the difficulty of learning it, but also with regard to its ambiguities and complexities. Wilkins rejected the approach of those who believed that the supposed language of Adam might be recovered, but tried to develop an artificial equivalent based upon a classification of knowledge. The vocabulary of this new language was to be built up by systematic modifications of the basic generic terms that were deemed to cover all the major categories of existence. A knowledge of the system would enable the reader, or listener, not just to recognize the signification of a word but also to understand how the referent fitted into the entire scheme of things. This is what made Wilkins's artificial language 'philosophical', not just universal in the sense that a unanimously agreed upon lingua franca would be.

During the final stages of work on his *Essay* Wilkins lost his house, and most of his belongings and papers, in the great fire of London, but being eager to complete his scheme he enlisted the help of John Ray and Francis Willoughby to improve the botanical and zoological nomenclature. This was a major factor in stimulating Ray to develop his own classificatory studies. Similarly, Samuel Pepys reported that he helped to draw up a table of naval terms, such as the names of rigging. Even with this and other help, Wilkins admitted his scheme's shortcomings and called upon the Royal Society to improve it. Although various fellows of the society spoke highly of the scheme for a while, only Robert Hooke showed any lasting commitment to it, and the committee established to improve on the *Essay* never reported. Scholars have argued about the major influences upon Wilkins's linguistic studies. There is little evidence that the universal language schemes of Amos Comenius played any significant role; Mersenne may have been an inspiration but George Dalgarno, to help whom Wilkins had begun to draw up classificatory tables of knowledge after 1657, was a more direct influence.

Wilkins re-entered ecclesiastical politics after the fall of Clarendon. Supported by the duke of Buckingham, he drew up proposals for the comprehension of dissenters within the framework of church and state, based on the principles of the declaration of Breda (1660). Thanks largely to information supplied by Wilkins's close friend Seth Ward, parliamentary opposition was able to organize itself and reject the proposals in February 1668. In spite of the damage this did to Wilkins's reputation in the eyes of the high-church party he continued to find favour with Buckingham and the king. He had been appointed as one of the king's chaplains in July 1667 and by May 1668 it was widely believed that he would be made a bishop at the next opportunity.

On 15 November 1668 Wilkins was consecrated bishop of Chester. The diocese was a stronghold of both Roman Catholicism and Presbyterianism, but the bishop's tolerant and conciliatory approach to dissenters succeeded in bringing some nonconformists back to the Church of England, and ensured good relations with those who remained recalcitrant. During this period Wilkins lived in the episcopal palace in Chester, though he occasionally made protracted visits to Wigan, a rich parish that supplemented the bishop's income. He was also active in the House of Lords, and served on at least fifty parliamentary committees before his death. He was a major organizer of opposition to the Conventicle Act of 1670. He still managed to maintain his scientific interests: Ray and Willoughby were frequent visitors to Chester, and he continued to support the Royal Society.

With Buckingham's continued patronage and the flourishing of latitudinarianism, it was often assumed that Wilkins would rise above Chester, if only to a more lucrative and important diocese, but ill health overtook him. Having suffered throughout 1672 from what were supposed to be 'fits of the stone' (though this was not confirmed at autopsy), he died on 19 November in London, at the house in Chancery Lane of John Tillotson, husband of Wilkins's stepdaughter Elizabeth French. On his deathbed he was said to have declared himself to be 'prepared for the great experiment'. He was buried at St Lawrence Jewry, London, on 12 December 1672. His widow was buried there on 17 June 1689. He bequeathed about £700 to his widow, £400 to the Royal Society, and £200 to Wadham.

Wilkins's last book, *Of the Principles and Duties of Natural Religion*, was prepared for publication in 1675 by Tillotson. Arguing that the existence of God, knowledge of his attributes, and the requirement of a suitable demeanour towards him could all be established by the use of reason, the book also included a discussion of religious epistemology. Wilkins insisted that 'moral certainty', as opposed to physical or mathematical certainty, is all that can be expected in religion. The book was a major statement of latitudinarian principles.

Wilkins was described by Aubrey as 'lustie, strong growne, well sett, and broad-shouldered', and even those who opposed or disapproved of him acknowledged his considerable talents and merits. He made a profound contribution to English ecclesiastical history and theological method, being a major figure in the forging and the promotion of latitudinarianism and one of the earliest contributors to the English tradition of natural theology. He also played a crucially important role in the establishment of the Royal Society's self-professed experimental methodology, and thus in the establishment of the characteristic method of English scientific empiricism. Finally, as a result of his strong interest in and commitment to the development of so-called universal language schemes, he made an important contribution to the history of linguistics.   JOHN HENRY

Sources B. J. Shapiro, *John Wilkins, 1614–1672: an intellectual biography* (1969) · H. Aarsleff, 'Wilkins, John', *DSB* · J. L. Subbiondo, ed., *John Wilkins and 17th-century British linguistics* (1992) · M. M. Slaughter, *Universal languages and scientific taxonomy in the seventeenth century* (1982) · J. Knowlson, *Universal language schemes in England and France, 1600–1800* (1975) · J. Wilkins, *Mercury, or, The secret and swift messenger*, 3rd edn (1708), pt 3 of *The mathematical and philosophical works of … John Wilkins* ; repr. with introduction by B. Asbach-Schnitker (1984), ix–cix · M. Cohen, *Sensible words: linguistic practice in England, 1640–1785* (1977) · V. Salmon, *The study of language in 17th-century England* (1979) · H. R. McAdoo, *The spirit of Anglicanism: a survey of Anglican theological method in the seventeenth century* (1965) · H. G. Van Leeuwen, *The problem of certainty in English thought, 1630–1690* (1963) · *DNB* · parish register (burial), 17 June 1689, St Lawrence Jewry · *Corrections and additions to the Dictionary of National Biography*, Institute of Historical Research (1966) · P. B. Wood, 'Methodology and apologetics: Thomas Sprat's *History of the Royal Society*', *British Journal for the History of Science*, 13 (1980), 1–26

Likenesses M. Beale, oils, *c*.1668, Wadham College, Oxford · M. Beale, oils, *c*.1670–1672, Bodl. Oxf. [*see illus.*] · M. Beale, oils, *c*.1670–1672, RS · A. Blooteling, line engraving (after M. Beale, 1668), BM, NPG · Sturt, engraving · R. White, engraving · oils, Wadham College, Oxford

Wealth at death over £1300: Shapiro, *John Wilkins*, 303

Wilkins, Leslie Thomas (1915–2000), criminologist, was born on 8 March 1915 at 107 High Street, Colchester, the third son and third child of Henry John Wilkins (*d*. 1930), manager and later proprietor of shoe shops, and his wife, Catherine Emma, *née* Hobey (*d*. 1950). He despised his school education, and the fundamental Christianity of his early life evoked a lifelong antipathy to formal religion. His training as a probation officer had to be discontinued when his widowed mother could no longer afford it. His later academic career makes it surprising that he never took a degree. A clerical job in the Ministry of Labour was followed, on the outbreak of war, by work at Folland Aircraft, Hamble, and later service in the RAF. He married on 2 January 1945 Barbara Lucy (*b*. 1920), daughter of Felix Gerald Swinstead, professor of music.

By spring 1945 Wilkins was acting squadron leader, posted to Oslo. He returned to the Air Ministry as flight lieutenant in the air accident prevention branch. Tailgunners, he found, sometimes survived severe crashes because they faced backwards. This led him to lobby unsuccessfully for backward-facing seats in passenger aircraft. His research on the handling characteristics of Gloster Meteors (why wait until the pilot was dead to look for problems?) was discontinued by an air marshal with the remark 'I will not have junior officers criticizing their equipment' (*The Times*, 2 June 2000, 25). Wilkins resigned his commission. Then and later he was buoyed up by his wife and their family of two sons and two daughters.

In 1946 Wilkins was elected fellow of the Royal Statistical Society and joined the government social survey. One of the more arcane tasks assigned to him was estimating the demand from ex-service personnel for campaign stars and medals. Eighty per cent said they would 'definitely apply'; Wilkins calculated that only 35 per cent would actually do so. His estimate was 0.5 per cent out. The saving of metal in straitened post-war times was no trivial matter. An epidemiological study of deafness at this stage led to the award of the Francis Wood memorial prize by the Royal Statistical Society. Working with Herman Mannheim of the London School of Economics, he found that those sent for youth custody (then called borstal training) showed differences in reconviction outcome attributable to the regime, having factored out individuals' propensity to reoffend. Published in 1955, the Mannheim–Wilkins monograph was the first product of the newly established Home Office research unit. Wilkins moved to that unit, and a rich period of highly original research followed. Alongside his unrivalled technical mastery of operational research, he had a strong sense of what was right, about which he was unfailingly vocal. He was appalled that attempted suicide was regarded as a crime, and by the lack of practical concern for the victims of violent crime.

Wilkins's departure from the Home Office was acrimonious. It resulted from his alleged comments to *The Times* on the Drugs (Prevention and Misuse) Bill then before parliament. The *Times* editorial of 20 April 1964 read, 'A leading authority on juvenile crime suggested that people found in unauthorized possession of the drug should be put on probation with compulsory medical treatment.' Unwilling to apologize for the leak (an internal minute had been passed to the paper by someone else), Wilkins left the Home Office in 1964, and soon afterwards took an appointment with the United Nations in Tokyo, then in 1966 took up a chair (and later deanship of criminology) at the University of California, Berkeley. The backdrop was campus turbulence about the Vietnam War, and the California governorship of Ronald Reagan. Wilkins refused to supply the university with details of staff who had crossed picket lines. This led to his nickname, the 'dissident dean', and his resignation.

Wilkins moved in 1969 to become dean of the school of criminal justice at the State University of New York, Albany. Sabbaticals in Australia and British Columbia preceded retirement (he called it semi-retirement) in 1982, and a return to the UK. He and Barbara first lived at Old Sodbury, which he claimed was a mnemonic (people will ask 'where's the old sod now' and remember), then moved to Cambridge, where he reconnected with academic life at the university's Institute of Criminology. He retained the title of research professor at Albany, which remained his preferred title until his death from heart disease on 8 May 2000 in Addenbrooke's Hospital, Cambridge. A moving humanist ceremony at his home preceded his cremation. His wife survived him.

Wilkins will be remembered for technical brilliance, as in his demonstration of a travelling wave of criminality among those who were very young at the outbreak of the Second World War. His American work on the development and use of statistical guidelines for sentencing, and release on parole, separated case facts from judicial/parole board caprice. This work remains relevant for sentencing reform worldwide. Perhaps centrally, he will be remembered for separating the problem of crime from the problem of how to deal with offenders. Wilkins was scathing about the notion that a crime was solved when someone to blame had been identified. By analogy with air accident investigation, all factors making a crime possible had to be considered before one could think about solutions and undertake remedial action. This perspective is increasingly influential in applied criminology.

KEN PEASE

Sources privately published memoirs [available from the librarian, Institute of Criminology, 7 West Road, Cambridge, CB3 8DT] · personal knowledge (2004) · private information (2004) · B. Burnham and C. Nuttall, *The Guardian* (3 July 2000) · *The Times* (2 June 2000), 25 · b. cert. · m. cert. · d. cert.
Archives BLPES, papers relating to published works
Wealth at death £337,159—gross; £330,208—net: probate, 13 Oct 2000, *CGPLA Eng. & Wales*

Wilkins [*née* Jebb], **Louisa** (1873–1929), agricultural administrator, was born on 8 August 1873 at The Lythe, Ellesmere, Shropshire, the daughter of Arthur Trevor Jebb (1839–1894), barrister, and his wife, Eglantyne Louisa, *née* Jebb (1845–1925). Her parents were cousins, and her mother's brother was Sir Richard *Jebb, regius professor of Greek at Cambridge. Her younger sisters were Eglantyne *Jebb and Dorothy Frances *Buxton. Educated at home before going to Newnham College, Cambridge, then under the principalship of Mrs Sedgewick, Louisa Jebb was one of a select minority of women to take the agricultural diploma. A friendship at Newnham with Victoria Buxton (later Mrs Victoria de Bunsen) led to the two embarking on a journey through Asia Minor. This entailed travelling from Constantinople via Tarsus to the headwaters of the Tigris, sailing down to Baghdad, and returning to Damascus through the Syrian Desert. The adventure was described in Louisa's subsequent book, *By Desert Ways to Baghdad* (1907), and the experience stimulated her interest in Eastern qualities, particularly in the value of silence, a virtue which she pursued for the rest of her life.

The primary focus of Louisa's life, however, proved to be agriculture, an interest stemming from her studies at Cambridge. This led her not only to take responsibility for the management of a 125 acre farm, but also to embark on a detailed investigation into prevailing agricultural conditions. She gave evidence to the parliamentary smallholdings committee in 1906–7, and her study resulted in the publication of *The Small Holdings of England: a Survey of Various Existing Systems* (1907). This work was at this time one of the most definitive treatments of small-holdings and their functioning.

In 1907 Louisa Jebb married a civil servant, Roland Field (1872–1950), son of A. S. *Wilkins, professor of Latin. The marriage heralded her move to London in order that her husband might continue his work at the Treasury. In spite of this, and the birth of their two daughters, Louisa's interest in agriculture continued unabated. She became a governor of the Agricultural Organisation Society, as well as undertaking a key role in the committee of the Board of Agriculture and Fisheries, which had the responsibility for the agricultural education of women.

Following the outbreak of the First World War, Louisa became an active member of the wages board. Under the auspices of the Women's Farm and Garden Union she conducted an investigation into the opportunities for educated women to work in agriculture or horticulture. Her report, *The Work and Employment of Educated Women in Horticulture and Agriculture* (1915), was published in the *Journal of the Board of Agriculture*, and also separately: it heralded the development of greater national awareness of the problems faced by women seeking agricultural employment. Louisa was also instrumental at this time in the establishment of the Women's National Land Service Corps, the forerunner of the Women's Land Army. During the war she played a significant role in administering the operation of the corps, helping to improve relations with farmers and persuading more of them to accept women labourers in the agricultural sector. Following the takeover of this organization by the Board of Agriculture and Fisheries she was offered the post of director of the women's section; but she declined for personal reasons.

Louisa's interest in agriculture continued after the war and, in addition to a number of articles for *The Times*, in 1927 she published a revised edition of her report for the Board of Agriculture and Fisheries. Her practical work continued with a women's farm colony at Lingfield. This was an experiment undertaken by the Women's Farm and Garden Association to enable women to gain practical experience in running their own farms.

Throughout her career Louisa played an important role in enabling countrywomen of all classes to appreciate their worth. In doing so, she significantly enhanced the recognition of the real potential of women in the agricultural sector and her work may be compared with that of Meriel Talbot and Gladys Potts. An indefatigable and enthusiastic person she was also the outstanding pioneer of the small-holding movement, or at least its revival at the beginning of the twentieth century. She was appointed OBE.

Louisa Wilkins died of cancer on 22 January 1929 at 24 Aubrey Walk, Campden Hill, London, following a prolonged illness. She was survived by her husband, who retired in 1935, having been assistant paymaster-general at the Treasury from 1924 to 1935.   JOHN MARTIN

Sources *The Times* (25 Jan 1929) · *The Times* (29 Jan 1929) · L. Wilkins, 'The work and employment of educated women in horticulture and agriculture', *Journal of the Board of Agriculture*, 22 (1915–16), 554–69, 616–42; pubd separately as *The work and employment of educated women in horticulture and agriculture* (1915) · P. Horn, *Rural life in England in the First World War* (1984) · J. Thirsk, ed., *The agrarian history of England and Wales*, 8, ed. E. H. Whetham (1978) · P. E. Dewey, *British agriculture in the First World War* (1989) · P. King, *Women rule the plot: the story of the 100 year fight to establish women's place in farm and garden* (1999) · *WWW* · L. Jebb, *The small holdings of England: a survey of various existing systems* (1907) · b. cert. · d. cert.
Wealth at death £11,907 17s. 9d.: resworn probate, 11 March 1929, *CGPLA Eng. & Wales*

Wilkins, William (1778–1839), architect and antiquary, was born on 31 August 1778 in the parish of St Giles, Norwich, the son of William Wilkins (d. 1815), a successful building contractor in East Anglia who in 1780 moved the family to Cambridge and became agent to Viscount Newark (later Earl Manvers), and his wife, Hannah (née Willett).

William Wilkins (1778–1839), by Edward Hodges Baily, 1830

George *Wilkins was his brother. Architectural design and history increasingly occupied his father's interest. Partner to Humphrey Repton between c.1785 and 1796, the elder Wilkins then established an independent practice designing houses in the neo-Gothic and neo-classical styles, most notably Donington Park, Leicestershire (1798–1800), and Pentillie Castle, Cornwall (with his son; c.1810; dem.). Thereby he founded the intellectual and professional foundations of his son's more distinguished career as architect and scholar. Moreover, the financial competence Wilkins senior displayed in his architectural business and management of a profitable circuit of theatres in Norfolk and Suffolk enabled him to support his son's scholarly bent and consequent social elevation to the ranks of the gentry. In this respect William Wilkins typifies proto-professional architectural practice, combining the skills of the artisan with the learning of the antiquary, but also anticipates the incorporation of gentrified social and academic values which elevated the status of architecture to that of a profession within the Victorian period.

At Norwich school, Wilkins was a talented draughtsman and a scholar, in both classics and mathematics; he entered Gonville and Caius College, Cambridge, in 1796, shortly after his father repaired the master's lodge; he graduated sixth wrangler in mathematics in 1800. In 1798 he had begun a fine set of drawings of King's College chapel which were contemporaneous with its repair by his father, and twice exhibited at the Royal Academy, in 1810 and in 1837. These heralded a profound respect for medieval design further indicated in his first publication, 'Some account of the prior's chapel at Ely' in 1801 in *Archaeologia*, the journal of the Society of Antiquaries of London, to which he had been elected in 1796.

Scholarship and early practice In 1799 Wilkins made his first set of architectural designs for improvements to Earl Manvers's seat, Thoresby Park, Nottinghamshire, which demonstrated his growing interest in classicism and formed the earliest example of what was to become a pattern of aristocratic patronage. Wilkins's gregarious, amiable, and inoffensively ambitious personality, matched by a commanding stature and bluff good looks, later remarked upon in the obituaries published by the *Gentleman's Magazine* (*GM*, 426–7) and *Civil Engineer and Architect's Journal* (1839, 388–9), undoubtedly assisted him in securing commissions from distinguished patrons. His intelligence drew the attention of George Gordon, fifth earl of Aberdeen, who became a friend and later collaborator, and led to his being awarded the Worts travelling bachelorship in 1801. The bursary funded his tour of the ancient Greek empire (mainly the modern Sicily and Greece) that lasted until 1803. His regularly dispatched letters, written in Latin, testify to his dedicated if conventional mind, which he occupied in studying the inconsistently documented Greek remains in Italy and Sicily.

In 1807, supported by a fellowship at Gonville and Caius and a mastership of the Perse School, Wilkins published *The Antiquities of Magna Graecia*, which sealed his reputation as a scholar. During the preparation of this work, he applied the fruits of his studies to his pioneeringly consistent Greek revival scheme of 1805 for the projected Downing College at Cambridge. Backed by influential alumni, including Sir Busick Harwood of Downing, who had nominated him for the Society of Antiquaries, and endorsed by the collector and virtuoso Thomas Hope, Wilkins won a reconstituted competition with a typically lucid design. The requisite facilities and accommodation were efficiently arranged in four separated blocks forming an innovative campus plan. Only the side ranges housing the fellows, the undergraduates, and the common room were built (1807–13 and 1818–22), owing to budgetary restrictions which prohibited the construction of the northern entrance and the lecture-room block, modelled on the Athenian Propylaea, and the southern library, chapel, and dining hall block, fronted by porticoes adapted from the Erechtheum, which were imitated more modestly on the completed buildings. Wilkins's pragmatically learned approach, whereby he organized the required space into appropriate three-dimensional volumes, themselves moderated by the scale and form of his chosen ancient models, and then applied the identifying motifs to the main façades, was necessarily somewhat less deft in contemporary additions to Osberton House, Nottinghamshire, but yielded an even more harmonious construction for the East India College, Haileybury (1806–9; now Haileybury School). This last commission possibly led to his

meeting Alicia Carnac Murphy, daughter of Matthew Murphy of Ravendale, Lincolnshire, who held a senior post with the East India Company; the couple married in 1811.

Stylistic qualities Wilkins's pure style, informed by classical study and enabled by mathematical acuity, clarified contemporary neo-classical practice. Yet if Wilkins gave preference to pure form rather than architectural expression he was genuinely interested in matters of ideology and technology. The construction of Downing College extended the facilities for legal and medical education at Cambridge, and East India College was the institution where reforms in the government of Britain's major imperial possession could be studied. In the Nelson Pillar at Dublin (1807; dem.) and in revised form at Great Yarmouth (where the Doric column has a statue of Britannia atop a globe and peristyle of caryatid figures of victory in synthetic Coade stone) he combined Roman and Greek motifs. He also embarked upon a series of Gothic revival country houses beginning with the Tudor Gothic Dalmeny House, Linlithgowshire (1814–17), for the fourth earl of Rosebery, after also drawing a neo-Greek scheme that recalled his remarkable attic transformation of Grange Park, Hampshire (1808–9), for his friend the antiquary Henry Drummond. He turned again to East Anglian Tudor architecture when enlarging Tregothnan, Cornwall (1816–18), for the fourth Viscount Falmouth and designing the more austere Dunmore Park, Stirlingshire (1820–22; dem.), for the fifth Earl Dunmore.

Wilkins and the classical style Where appropriate, however, Wilkins reverted to the Periclean forms of his formative years. He fronted the fashionable Freemason's Hall, Bath (1817–18), with a handsome Ionic recessed (antis) portico, and dignified the economical commissioners' church of St Paul's, Nottingham (1821–2; dem.), with a portico and steeple adapted from the Athenian octagonal Tower of Winds and circular choragic monument of Lysicrates. His compilation with Lord Aberdeen in 1812–13 of *The Civil Architecture of Vitruvius*, published in 1817, and his participation in the Elgin marbles debate of 1816, bear witness to Wilkins's continuing interest in classical design. His reservations about the presumed unique and preeminent qualities of the sculptures, reiterated in *Atheniensia, or, Remarks on the Topography and Buildings in Athens* (1817) and in *Memoirs Relating to European and Asiatic Turkey*, edited in 1820 by his Cambridge friend the Revd Robert Walpole of Trinity College, were troubled by evidence of Greek realism and polychromy. None the less, Wilkins reproduced the Panathenaic frieze in the salon of Argyll House, London, which he altered in 1809 for Lord Aberdeen, and for the staircase of his fashionable United University Club, London (1821–6; dem.), another work in which he was aided by J. P. Gandy. Wilkins was also assisted by the young Irish designer James Gallier, and he superintended the training of G. F. Jones, J. H. Stevens, and the better-known Benjamin Ferrey.

Major works Such assistance was important, since Wilkins was by then heavily involved with three major works at Cambridge and the editorship of the Society of Dilettanti, to which he had been elected in 1809. Since 1814 he had been preparing *The Unedited Antiquities of Attica* (1817), a finely illustrated volume that would be cited in the testimonial presented toward his successful election to the Royal Society in 1831. He gathered the remaining findings of the 1811–13 Dilettanti expedition into the five-part revised edition of the society's *Antiquities of Ionia* (1769–1915), the third part of which was completed shortly after his death. From 1822 to 1830 Wilkins acted as secretary of the Dilettanti in lieu of his more hard-pressed friend Sir Thomas Lawrence. During these years Wilkins was elected an associate of the Royal Academy and then Royal Academician in 1823 and 1826 successively.

Three Cambridge college commissions, at King's (1824–8), Trinity (1823–5), and Corpus Christi (1823–7), brought greatest professional satisfaction, succinctly recorded in a remark to the Revd Christopher Wordsworth, master of Trinity College, that Gothic was 'my forte' (Liscombe, 131). Not that Wilkins abandoned the classical ideal. In 1821 he had designed a neo-Greek scheme to marry with Wren's work at Trinity, and completed a striking if unbuilt design for Bylaugh Hall, Norfolk, which was still at the forefront of the English Renaissance revival when exhibited at the Royal Academy in 1818. He had the greatest latitude in terms of site, specification, and budget at Corpus Christi. There the new quadrangle designed in 1822 and completed by 1827 added a new chapel, hall, library, and accommodation for the master, fellows, and undergraduates alongside the Old Court, part of which he preserved. The visual effect and spatial ambience of the quadrangle and main interiors won Wilkins recognition as an accomplished Gothic revivalist. By comparison, Trinity New Court (1823–6) is less substantial, and his additions to King's College, notwithstanding the remarkable felicity of his screen and hall, are compromised by the divergent size of the quadrangle and the style of James Gibbs's building. Respect for medieval architecture informs the thorough restoration scheme he drew up for the vestry of the abbey church of St Mary, Sherborne, in 1828, where he envisaged the installation of wrought-iron beams in the tower to ensure the conservation of the ancient fabric.

Non-professional interests Midway through this productive period Wilkins sought to record his fortunate position. Over several weeks in 1824 A. E. Chalon painted his portrait and that of his wife of thirteen years, Alicia, surrounded by their children Henry Robert (*b.* 1813), Alicia (*b.* 1817), and William Bushby (*b.* 1822) in the drawing-room of his main residence at 36 Weymouth Street, London. (His sons would both enter the Anglican ministry, Henry after working as an architect, while Alicia married Ruskin's friend the Revd William Kingsley.) He could afford a fashionable address and to entertain quite lavishly, owing to his successful practice and also to the theatrical business he had inherited. This consisted of a chain of theatres in East Anglia, which remained profitable over much of the decade, as Wilkins stated in evidence before the 1832 parliamentary select committee on dramatic literature. The theatres included houses in Cambridge (designed with his

father in 1814; remodelled), Great Yarmouth (reconstructed by Wilkins in 1816; dem.), Norwich (Theatre Royal, refurbished including a Greek Doric colonnade, 1825–6; des.), and the Bury St Edmunds Theatre (1818–19), which has been restored to its original neo-classical elegance. Wilkins engaged companies that presented plays by contemporary playwrights as well as Shakespeare, and attracted talented actors including Irving, Kean, and Macready. His taste for theatre and for art, each coloured by his fascination with cultural history, is evident in the Carolingian costumes in which he and his family are attired in the 1824 family portrait by Chalon. Behind them are displayed pictures from his collection of mainly Dutch and Italian painting with, most prominently, a copy of Raphael's *Transfiguration*. Besides indicating his relatively conventional connoisseurship (the catalogues of the sales of his collection at Christies in May 1830, April 1838, and May 1840 number several pictures subsequently identified as copies), the visual reference to Raphael's painting reflects a religious conviction, which, interwoven with stoicism, would course through the letters Wilkins wrote through the final months of his life.

From Cambridge to London The enlargement of King's College was finished by 1828 but did not lead to further college commissions despite the expansion of both Cambridge and Oxford. The restrained style of Wilkins's designs was losing popularity, and his neo-Greek and neo-Gothic designs for the 1821–2 and 1825 competitions for a university observatory and new quadrangle for St John's College at Cambridge were placed second. His resulting frustration is evident in letters on redevelopment at Cambridge addressed to the editor of the *Cambridge Chronicle* (November 1826 and March 1828), followed by two surprisingly critical pamphlets, *A Letter to the Members of the Senate of the University* (February 1831) and *An Appeal to the Senate on the Subject of the Plans for the University Library* (April 1831). The pamphlets were composed after the double rejection, in 1829 and 1830, of a well-conceived neo-Greek design for the Cambridge University Library that was eclipsed by the more dynamically composed revivalism of C. R. Cockerell. The rejection of Wilkins's learned but moderate historicism signalled the decline of his career at Cambridge, though he did receive a large commission in 1825 to complete the reconstruction of East India House, London, started by Cockerell's father. Completed in 1830, this work coincided with less extensive additions to the company's military seminary at Addiscombe, Surrey (1825–7; both dem.).

The depth of Wilkins's disappointment in the library competitions derived from his erstwhile fame within Cambridge, where he maintained a home at Lensfield House, Lensfield Road (remodelled with a Greek Doric antis portico, 1811; dem.), and success elsewhere. Besides the prestigious East India House, however, he had recently finished the new St George's Hospital at Hyde Park Corner, London (1825–8; now redeveloped as the Lanesborough Hotel). He was also supervising realization of his impressive classical edifice for University College on Gower Street (1825–32), in which he was assisted by J. P.

Gandy, and transforming a proposal to convert the old Royal Mews in Trafalgar Square into a design for a combined National Gallery and Royal Academy. Each of these commissions reflected the enlargement of Wilkins's understanding of architectural function and of the social space in which it operated, which had been stimulated by reading the works of John Howard, Jeremy Bentham, and continental Enlightenment authors. His growing awareness of the social distress and activism precipitated by post-war recession and reactionary politics had an impact on the design of the new Norfolk gaol and shire house in Norwich (1822–4) and the county gaol at Huntingdon (1826–8). Here Wilkins endeavoured to implement the improvements advocated by Howard in order to increase ventilation and sanitation but reduce communication between petty and hardened criminal. The Norfolk gaol was the most innovative, inserting a radial penitentiary within the castle walls alongside the historic keep. The penitentiary contained separate cells, categorized by gender and degree of criminality, central supervision of eating, worship, and exercise, together with a treadmill engineered by his friend the ironmaster T. J. Bramah. In the case of Huntingdon gaol Wilkins surely also came to appreciate the curtailing of professional opportunity experienced by his clerk of works, James Gallier. Within three years Gallier, lacking the connections to attract patronage, was forced to emigrate with many other British architects to North America.

The impact of industrial society similarly affected Wilkins's plans for St George's Hospital and University College, London. An 'H' plan layout, curtailed for the college, ensured ample ventilation and lighting, both to combat contagion in the former and nurture learning in the latter. His use of the simpler square columns of the Athenian choragic monument and Thrasyllus signified his acceptance of a more scientific functionalism paralleled by the adaptation of Bramah's structural ironwork and water closets, both incorporated at the college. It was the first non-sectarian and faculty-centred university in Britain. The neat disposition of internal space facilitated the provision of diverse departmental needs, later mirrored in miniature in the Yorkshire Philosophical Society Museum (1827–30; superintended by R. H. Sharp), where Greek ornamentation was combined with functional exhibition and study rooms supplied with gas lighting. Wilkins had intended a much grander urban presence for the university, with porticoed wings and a domed great hall projecting forward onto Gower Street, an intention which was curtailed by insufficient capital consequent upon strident conservative opposition. The elevated central portico, deriving from the Hadrianic Temple of Jupiter Olympus at Athens, was built, however, and remains a testament to his considerable powers of design. Breaking rank with several among his circle, not least Lord Aberdeen, Wilkins embraced liberal views in his lively *Letter to Lord Viscount Goderich on the Patronage of the Arts by the English Government* (1832), in which he advocated government support of the creative arts and more comprehensive state education. He maintained always a belief in the need for

traditional academic training: in evidence to the 1836 parliamentary select committee on arts and manufactures he commended the study of pre-eminent ancient models. Such orthodoxy can also be discerned in the brief allusion to his proposed teaching strategies as professor of architecture at the Royal Academy, a post to which he was elected in 1837, in his last scholarly book, *Prolusiones architectonical, or, Essays on subjects connected with Grecian and Roman architecture* (1837).

Prolusiones was dedicated to the second Earl Grey who had supported Wilkins in the fulfilment of the gallery and academy commission (the academy opened in 1837 and the gallery in 1838). The constraints imposed by the government, and by the duke of Northumberland, who owned adjacent property, limited Wilkins's naturally unostentatious architectural vision. He was obliged to reuse the Corinthian columns from Carlton House, diminishing the scale of the façade, and to insert two public lanes through the building, partly to ensure rapid deployment in Trafalgar Square of troops from the extant barracks at the rear, for which he also had to supply further accommodation in the basement of the gallery wing. The consequence is an insufficiently imposing and fractured edifice, surmounted by an attenuated and inelegant drummed dome, that, despite surviving to become an icon of late twentieth-century international tourism, belittled Wilkins's contemporary reputation—although John Constable considered it 'a very noble house' (*Constable's Correspondence*, 37). The technical innovations of the Bramah-manufactured cast- and wrought-iron skylighting of the major galleries and the economical provision of diverse accommodation for both institutions did nothing to mitigate criticism of the exterior. Two competitive schemes he prepared in 1835 both foundered; one, now lost, was for the Fitzwilliam Museum, Cambridge, and the other for the Houses of Parliament competition, was memorable for a ceremonial entrance court to the Thames and as the subject of his final polemic, *An Apology for the Designs of the Houses of Parliament Marked Phil-Archiamedes* (1836; repr. 1837).

Later years By this date Wilkins was suffering from the early phase of his terminal kidney disease, first diagnosed as gout. The condition could have been precipitated by recent anxieties and obliged him to withdraw from the professorship of architecture at the Royal Academy and to return to Cambridge in late 1838. He endured an increasingly painful illness with surprising good humour, to judge by correspondence with his old friend Hudson Gurney and the accounts of visitors such as Joseph Romilly. He lived to finish a suitably studious essay on 'The Lydo-Phrygian inscription' for the 1834 volume of the *Transactions of the Royal Society of Literature of the United Kingdom*. He died at his Cambridge home, Lensfield House, on 31 August 1839, the sixty-first anniversary of his birth. He was buried under the sacrarium of the chapel at Corpus Christi College, and in his obituary in the *Gentleman's Magazine* prominence was given to a view expressed in *The Athenaeum* that though his works 'bespeak taste and genius … the opinions as to the degree of merit to which these may be thought entitled are various' and concludes that

> perhaps of all his public buildings, none was so generally admired and approved of, and none upon which he prided himself more, than the College of Corpus Christi … it was in this work that he was left to the full scope of his genius, without restraint, his employers resting wholly upon the responsibility of his professional character. (*GM*, 426–7)

Wilkins's achievement as a scholar–architect continued to be undervalued until the revival of interest in Enlightenment and Romantic architecture that culminated in the 1972 Council of Europe exhibition *The Age of Neo-Classicism*, though the taint of calculation and copyism, summed up by James Elmes as 'so much Greek, so much cold' (*Civil Engineer and Architect's Journal*, 10, 1847, 382), still distorts recognition of his measured contribution to early nineteenth-century architecture and culture.

R. WINDSOR LISCOMBE

Sources R. W. Liscombe, *William Wilkins, 1778–1839* (1980) [with full bibliography] · Colvin, *Archs.* · J. M. Crook, *The Greek revival: neo-classical attitudes in British architecture, 1760–1870* (1972) · D. Watkin, *Thomas Hope, 1769–1831, and the neo-classical idea* (1968) · D. Watkin, *The triumph of the classical: Cambridge architecture, 1804–1834* (1977) · C. Sicca, C. Harpum, and E. Powell, *Committed to classicism: the building of Downing College, Cambridge* (1987) · *GM*, 2nd ser., 12 (1839), 426–7 · *Civil Engineer and Architect's Journal*, 2 (1839), 388–9 · *Civil Engineer and Architect's Journal*, 10 (1847), 382 · *John Constable's correspondence*, ed. R. B. Beckett, 5, Suffolk RS, 11 (1967) · private information (2004)
Archives BL · BL OIOC · CCC Cam. · Church commissioners, London · Col. U., Rare Book and Manuscript Library, Phoenix collection · CUL · Downing College, Cambridge · Gon. & Caius Cam. · King's Cam. · NL Ire. · priv. coll. · PRO · RA · RIBA · S. Antiquaries, Lond. · St Mary's Abbey, Sherborne · Suffolk RO, Bury St Edmunds, corresp. relating to Theatre Royal, Bury St Edmunds · Suffolk RO · Trinity Cam. · UCL · Yale U. CBA · Yorkshire Philosophical Society | Norfolk RO, corresp. with Hudson Gurney and Gurney family relating to Keswick Hall
Likenesses A. E. Chalon, group portrait, 1824, priv. coll. · E. H. Baily, marble bust, 1830, Trinity Cam.; on loan to FM Cam. [*see illus.*]
Wealth at death £20,000–£30,000; £50 to wife; houses in London and Cambridge; theatre circuit; art collection: will, 1839, item 663, piece 1919

Wilkins, William Henry (1860–1905), biographer, born at Compton Martin, Somerset, on 23 December 1860, was the son of Charles Wilkins, farmer, of Gurney Court, Somerset, and afterwards of Mann's Farm, Mortimer, Berkshire, where Wilkins passed much of his youth. His mother was Mary Ann, *née* Keel. After private education, he was employed in a bank at Brighton; he then entered Clare College, Cambridge, in 1884 with a view to taking holy orders, and graduated BA in 1887, proceeding MA in 1899. At the university he developed literary tastes and interested himself in politics. An ardent Conservative, he spoke frequently at the union, of which he was vice-president in 1886. After leaving Cambridge he settled down to a literary career in London.

For a time Wilkins acted as private secretary to the earl of Dunraven, whose proposals for restricting the immigration of undesirable foreigners Wilkins embodied in *The Alien Invasion* (1892), with an introduction by R. C. Billing, bishop of Bedford. The Aliens Act of 1905 followed many of its recommendations. Also in 1892 he edited, in conjunction with Hubert Crackanthorpe, whose acquaintance he had made at Cambridge, a short-lived monthly periodical called *The Albemarle* (nine issues). He next published four novels (two alone and two in collaboration) under the pseudonym De Winton. *St. Michael's Eve* (1892; 2nd edn, 1894) was a serious society novel. Then followed *The Forbidden Sacrifice* (1893), *John Ellicombe's Temptation* (1894; with the Hon. Julia Chetwynd), and *The Holy Estate: a Study in Morals* (with Captain Francis Alexander Thatcher). With another Cambridge friend, Herbert Vivian, he wrote under his own name *The Green Bay Tree* (1894), which boldly satirized current Cambridge and political life and passed through five editions.

Wilkins's best literary work was done in biography. He formed a close acquaintance with the widow of Sir Richard Burton, and after her death wrote *The Romance of Isabel, Lady Burton* (1897), a sympathetic memoir founded mainly upon Lady Burton's letters and autobiography. Wilkins also edited in 1898, by Lady Burton's direction, a revised and abbreviated version of her *Life of Sir Richard Burton*, and her *Passion Play at Ober-Ammergau* (1900), as well as Burton's unpublished *The Jew, the Gypsy, and el Islam* (with preface and brief notes; 1898), and *Wanderings in Three Continents* (1901). These were poorly edited and Burton's executors did not ask him to undertake further work. Some years later, when Wilkins fell on hard times, Burton manuscripts appeared on the market and were traced back to Wilkins (Lovell, 790).

Ill health did not deter Wilkins from original work in historical biography which involved foreign travel. Patient industry, an easy style, and good judgement atoned for a limited range of historical knowledge. At Lund University in Sweden he discovered in 1897 the unpublished correspondence between Sophie Dorothea, the consort of George I, and her lover, Count Philip Christopher Königsmarck, and on that foundation, supported by research in the archives of Hanover and elsewhere, he based *The Love of an Uncrowned Queen: Queen Sophie Dorothea, Consort of George I*, which was well received (2 vols., 1900; rev. edn 1903). Wilkins's *Caroline the Illustrious: Queen Consort of George II* (2 vols., 1901; new edn, 1904) had little claim to originality. *A Queen of Tears* (2 vols., 1904), a biography of Caroline Matilda, queen of Denmark and sister of George III of England, embodied researches at Copenhagen and superseded the previous biography by Sir Frederic Charles Lascelles Wraxall. For his last work, *Mrs. Fitzherbert and George IV* (2 vols., 1905), Wilkins had access, by Edward VII's permission, for the first time to the Fitzherbert papers at Windsor Castle, besides papers belonging to Mrs Fitzherbert's family. In 1901 he edited *South Africa a Century Ago*, valuable letters of Lady Anne Barnard, written from 1797 to 1801 while with her husband at the Cape of Good Hope. Wilkins also published *Our King and Queen* [Edward VII and Queen Alexandra]: *the Story of their Life* (2 vols., 1903), a popular book, copiously illustrated, and he wrote occasionally for periodicals. He died unmarried on 22 December 1905 at his home, 3 Queen Street, Mayfair, London, and was buried in Kensal Green cemetery.

G. LE G. NORGATE, rev. H. C. G. MATTHEW

Sources *The Times* (23 Dec 1905) · *EdinR*, 193 (1901), 56–86 · R. Gerds, *Supplement to Allgemeine Zeitung*, 77 (1902) · *WWW* · M. S. Lovell, *A rage to live: a biography of Richard and Isabel Burton* (1998) · private information (1912) · personal knowledge (1912) · *CGPLA Eng. & Wales* (1906)
Archives King's AC Cam., letters to Oscar Browning
Wealth at death £6673 16s. 1d.: resworn probate, 5 Jan 1906, *CGPLA Eng. & Wales*

Wilkinson [*née* Seward], **Catherine** [Kitty] (1786–1860), philanthropist, was born in 1786, probably in Londonderry. There is no authoritative record of her early years, but she appears to have been one of several children of an English soldier named Seward (or Seaward) and his Irish wife, and to have come to Liverpool—after surviving a shipwreck, if the tale is to be believed—as a small child with her widowed mother or stepmother. The family was befriended by Mrs Lightbody, of the prominent Liverpool Unitarian family of that name, who first employed the young girl as a servant and then apprenticed her at the age of eleven to a cotton textile mill. This mill is identified variably as Low Mill at Caton near Lancaster, which was owned sequentially by Thomas Hodgson and Samuel Greg (both of whom had married into the Lightbody family), or as Quarry Bank Mill at Styal in Cheshire, also owned by Samuel Greg. Kitty Seward remained at the mill until the age of eighteen, when she returned to Liverpool to earn her living and to care for her ill and unstable mother.

In 1812 Kitty Seward married a French sailor named John De Monte (or Dimont) and had two sons, but was widowed before the second child's birth. A period of great hardship followed, as Kitty attempted to support her children and her deranged mother through charring, nail-making, and the weekly 2s. granted her by the parish. In 1823 she married Thomas Wilkinson, a porter in a cotton warehouse owned by the Rathbone family (who were also linked by marriage to both the Lightbodys and the Gregs). Thomas and Kitty Wilkinson had no children, but over the course of several decades Kitty would care for and raise many ill or destitute children. She also visited the poor and acted as almoner for Elizabeth Rathbone, the daughter of Samuel Greg and wife to the fifth William Rathbone, who was closely involved in philanthropic activities in Liverpool, and who had great confidence in Mrs Wilkinson's judgement and principles.

Although the care of orphans would occupy many years of Kitty Wilkinson's life, it was her role in the cholera epidemic of 1832 that turned her into a local legend. Not only did she devote herself to tending the sick (and to caring for orphaned children, for whom she founded a school) but she also offered the use of her kitchen as a wash-house, and began—on a surgeon's advice—to wash and disinfect bedding using chloride of lime. Her efforts were noticed and encouraged by William and Elizabeth Rathbone, and with the aid of the local District Provident Society the wash-house was kept open after the epidemic was

over. During the next few years Rathbone sought to persuade the city council of the merits of public wash-houses, where poor residents could come to bathe or wash clothing at a nominal cost, and the first such establishment was opened under the council's auspices in 1842. The experiment was a success and spread, both in Liverpool and nationally. Kitty Wilkinson acted (with her husband) as superintendent of one wash-house, and after his death in 1848 continued active in neighbourhood and philanthropic work.

Although a figure of real importance in the development of Liverpool's municipal services, Kitty Wilkinson never controlled the terms on which her life and work came into the public eye. Even during her life, Wilkinson's story was retailed by those local social reformers (and notably members of the Unitarian Rathbone, Greg, and Lightbody families) concerned to chastise the indifferent rich and demonstrate that a spirit of self-sacrifice and civic concern could flourish even among the poor. It was this representation of Wilkinson that won public acclaim: in 1846 Wilkinson was presented with a silver tea service from the queen, the queen dowager, and ladies of Liverpool; a biographical portrait appeared in *Chambers's Miscellany*; and, in 1910, a stained-glass window portrait of Wilkinson was installed in Liverpool Cathedral. Because these early biographers were so concerned to tell a morally uplifting tale, however, Wilkinson's own motivations and personality remain elusive. The sole surviving photograph, much reprinted, shows a heavy-set woman much worn by work, with a prominent brow and a clear and unsmiling countenance. Kitty Wilkinson died in Liverpool on 11 November 1860, and was buried in St James's cemetery there.

SUSAN PEDERSEN

Sources *Memoir of Kitty Wilkinson of Liverpool, 1786–1860*, ed. H. R. Rathbone (1927) · W. R. Rathbone, *The life of Kitty Wilkinson: a Lancashire heroine* (1910) · 'Catherine of Liverpool', *Chambers's miscellany*, new edn, 4 (1872) · H. Channon, *Portrait of Liverpool* (1970)
Likenesses photograph, 1833, repro. in Rathbone, ed., *Memoir of Kitty Wilkinson of Liverpool, 1786–1860*, frontispiece · stained-glass window, 1910 (after photograph, 1833), Liverpool Cathedral; destroyed during World War II and replaced

Wilkinson, Charles Smith (1843–1891), geologist, was born at Potterspury, Northamptonshire, on 22 August 1843, the fourth son of David Wilkinson, civil engineer, and his wife, Elizabeth, *née* Bliss. He early gained enthusiasm for geology from his uncle, a Gloucestershire quarryman. After the family migrated to Melbourne, Australia, in 1852, he attended T. P. Fenner's Collegiate School and, from 1859, was employed by the geological survey of Victoria, carrying out geological mapping in various parts of the colony. He published on the formation of nuggets and experimented on the treatment of ores.

In 1868 lung inflammation caused Wilkinson's resignation from the survey, and he moved to Wagga Wagga, New South Wales, to recover. In 1871 he moved to Sydney, where he became a licensed surveyor in that colony's surveyor-general's department. The previous year to a royal commission on the goldfields he made a case for the close relations between geology and mining, recommending the formation of a department of mines. Appointed geological surveyor in the department of lands in 1874, he transferred to the newly created department of mines in the following January and formed a geological survey. Following the work of Samuel Stutchbury and W. B. Clarke, he began systematic mapping, publishing the first geological map of New South Wales in 1880. Wilkinson travelled widely in the colony, as government geologist and for the prospecting board, and encouraged the development of a mining museum to educate the public and assist prospectors.

On 4 May 1887 Wilkinson married Eliza Jane Leitch at Berry Jerry near Wagga Wagga; there were two sons from the marriage. Although often absent from Sydney, Wilkinson was active in the colony's cultural life as an office holder in scientific bodies and a commissioner for international and intercolonial exhibitions. He was a fellow of the Geological and Linnean societies of London, and the Victoria Institute, the last-named reflecting his interest in the relations between science and religion, about which he frequently lectured. Wilkinson died of cancer at Burwood, Sydney, on 26 August 1891, cutting short a fine career as geologist and administrator. He was buried in the Anglican cemetery at Enfield, Sydney, the next day. Tall and with a handsome presence, Wilkinson was liked and admired as an unostentatious but enthusiastic worker, and his more than ninety maps and reports remain widely used a hundred years after his death. He produced numerous articles for the popular press, and at his home gave classes on geology for working men. He is remembered in the names of numerous fossils. D. F. BRANAGAN

Sources *Daily Telegraph* [Sydney] (27 Aug 1891), 5 · H. C. Russell, 'Anniversary address', *Journal and Proceedings of the Royal Society of New South Wales*, 26 (1892), 6–9 · private information (2004) [family] · *Town and Country Journal* [Sydney] (16 Feb 1889), 24 · *Town and Country Journal* [Sydney] (29 Aug 1891), 18 · *Town and Country Journal* [Sydney] (5 Sept 1891), 27 · *Sydney Mail* (29 Aug–5 Sept 1891) · E. J. Dunn and D. J. Mahony, 'Biographical sketch of the founders of the geological survey of Victoria', *Bulletin of the Geological Survey of Victoria*, 23 (1910), 30–31 · *Mining Journal* (17 Oct 1891) · J. Adrian, 'Charles Smith Wilkinson and the geological survey of New South Wales, 1875–1891', *Earth Sciences History Group, Geological Society of Australia, Newsletter*, 15 (July 1992), 3–6
Archives priv. coll. · State Archives of New South Wales, Sydney, department of mines
Likenesses etching (after photograph by Kerry), repro. in *Sydney Mail* (5 Sept 1891), p. 525 · etching (after photograph), repro. in *Town and Country Journal* (16 Feb 1889), 24 · etching (after photograph), repro. in *Town and Country Journal* (5 Sept 1891), 27 · photograph, repro. in Dunn and Mahony, 'Biographical sketch of the founders of the geological survey of Victoria', facing p. 30
Wealth at death shares in mining companies in Queensland, Australia

Wilkinson [*née* Gifford], Elizabeth (1612/13–1654), spiritual autobiographer, was the daughter of Anthony Gifford and his wife, Elizabeth Cottle, of Halsbury, Devon. Closer identification of the parents is risky. She married Dr Henry Wilkinson (1616–1690), principal of Magdalen Hall from 1648 to 1660, in 1646 or 1647.

Elizabeth Wilkinson's 'Narrative of God's Dealings with her' was written before her marriage and published posthumously. It appears in an account of her life and death appended to a sermon preached by Edmund Staunton at her funeral, and catalogued under his name (1659). Copies may include elegies. The narrative also appears in a rearranged but substantially the same 'life and death' in Samuel Clarke's *Ten Eminent Divines … whereunto is Added … other Eminent Christians* of 1662 (pp. 512–35). Her life, presented as the very pattern of presbyterian female piety, is by Robert Harris. However, her own narrative comes to the reader unmediated, unlike the slightly later oral conversion testimonies of Congregational women, which were abridged while recorded. In a period of widespread female illiteracy Elizabeth's narrative is a rarity.

The young Elizabeth Gifford was educated by godly parents during her minority; then for about twenty years she lived with an aunt, described as an 'Old Disciple'. Life with her aunt appears to have been outwardly uneventful and solitary, but the docile and diligent child became a natural intellectual, and the events of a troubled spiritual life are signposted by her reading.

At twelve Elizabeth Gifford read Lewis Bayly's popular *Practise of Piety* (1612), which describes vividly the sufferings of the damned and the bliss of the elect. She was terrified into a cold goodness, succeeded by a crisis of faith. She was rescued from the threat of atheism by God's directing her to read Calvin on creation. But now she feared she had committed the sin against the Holy Ghost, and was forever damned. The Lord however directed her to read *The Christian's Daily Walke* (1627) by Henry Scudder, and his analysis of the nature of that sin convinced her that she had not committed it. She might yet be one of the elect. Joy did not last long. Awareness of sin and doubt dogged her. 'I found it the hardest thing to believe' (Clarke, 518). Yet often in adverse conditions, as for example in a serious illness, God vouchsafed her glimpses of his love. At last she felt encouraged to confide her condition to spiritual friends, and through them, through sermons, through books, she found a more settled faith, and her text becomes heavy with biblical quotations of God's promises to be faithful.

As the administration of the Lord's supper had lapsed in Gifford's parish, probably because of the civil war, she ended her narrative with an appeal to Robert Harris (a lifelong friend of Scudder's) to be admitted to the Lord's supper at the Oxford church where he administered it. This was about 1646 or 1647 (Clarke, 524).

Elizabeth Gifford married Henry *Wilkinson (1616/17–1690) shortly after. On 8 December 1648 'a child of Mr Wilkinson of Magd. Hall' was buried at St Peter-in-the-East, Oxford, and a daughter, Elizabeth, followed it in early 1654. It was, though, a happy marriage. They were well matched, and Elizabeth adopted the full regime of the puritan wife and mother. She died at her home, near Magdalen Hall, Oxford, on 8 December 1654 and was buried next day at St Mary's Church, Great Milton, Oxfordshire. She was forty-one, as her monument (which still survives) confirms. Probably she died in childbirth:

Here lies Mother and Babe without sins
Next birth will make her and her infant twins.

It was erected by her husband 'as a memorial of his entire love to his dearly beloved'. Three children survived (Bodl. Oxf., MS Lat. misc.C. 19, 86–7). Her husband sadly ended his elegy:

Oh that I could submit with thankful mind
Now God hath much made up my losse in kind.
(BL, Staunton, 44)

Remarriage was a near necessity.   MARY PRIOR

Sources E. Staunton, *A sermon preacht at Great Milton … at the funeral of Mris Elizabeth Wilkinson … whereunto is added a narrative of her godly life* (1659) · S. Clarke, *A collection of the lives of ten eminent divines* (1662), 512–35 · *The life and times of Anthony Wood*, ed. A. Clark, 1, OHS, 19 (1891), 188 · M. Burrows, ed., *The register of the visitors of the University of Oxford, from AD 1647 to AD 1658*, CS, new ser., 29 (1881), 3 · W. D. [W. Durham], *The life and death of … Robert Harris* (1660) · H. F. Giffard, 'Giffard's jump', *Report and Transactions of the Devonshire Association*, 34 (1902), 648–703 · parish registers, Oxford, St Peter-in-the-East, Oxon. RO · parish registers, Great Milton, Oxon. RO · Bodl. Oxf., MS Wood E. 1, fol. 281b [monumental inscription] · Bodl. Oxf., MS Wood F. 29A, fol. 353 [monumental inscription] · Henry Wilkinson's commonplace book, Bodl. Oxf., MS Lat. misc. C.19, 86–8, 116
Likenesses mural monument, St Mary the Virgin, Great Milton, Oxfordshire

Wilkinson, Ellen Cicely (1891–1947), politician, was born on 8 October 1891 at 41 Coral Street, Ardwick, Chorlton upon Medlock, Manchester, the second daughter and the third among the four children of Richard Wilkinson, a cotton worker and later insurance agent, and his wife, Ellen Wood (*d.* 1916). The family lived in a terrace house with an outside privy, but they were moving up socially: three of the children went to college, two obtaining university degrees. Richard Wilkinson, from an Irish family, had a keen sense of justice and a quick temper, but he was a serious-minded pillar of his Methodist church: he gave up drink, and his wife kept the front doorstep white with regular stoning. Ellen Wilkinson inherited her father's concern for justice, whose socialist outcome reflected her Methodist background, reinforced by knowing that poor medical treatment at her own birth had produced 'a life of agonizing suffering' for her mother: 'all my childhood was dominated by the fact of mother's illness', she later recalled (Wilkinson, *Myself when Young*, 399–400).

Early life and entry to politics: 1891–1924 The urge to speak in public came early: as a small child, Ellen and her grandmother, who was caring for her, held Sunday services together during which Ellen would stand on a chair and preach. There was much talk within the home about sermons, as well as many opportunities at religious functions for recitations, debates, and speech-making. Yet Wilkinson was not a tractable child. She resented being ousted as the youngest child by the late advent of her younger brother, just as she resented the special educational privileges boys then enjoyed. Educated at Ardwick higher elementary school and Stretford Road secondary school, she was a self-confident and rebellious pupil whose formal education was supplemented by accompanying her father to lectures on theological subjects, and in later life she

Ellen Cicely Wilkinson (1891–1947), by Howard Coster, 1945

continued to attend Methodist chapel whenever possible. 'By the time I was fourteen', she recalled, 'I was reading Haeckel, and Huxley and Darwin with my father' (Wilkinson, *Myself when Young*, 405). She won a pupil teacher bursary which enabled her to attend as a pupil teacher for two and a half days a week at the pupil teachers' centre in Manchester, while spending the other half of the week teaching in elementary schools.

By winning the Jones history entrance scholarship to Manchester University in 1910, Wilkinson opened herself up to gaining an upper second-class honours degree in history (in 1913), but much more importantly to a host of new and powerful political influences. Not the least among these was that of the one man to whom she ever became engaged, J. T. W. Newbold, the ungainly Quaker who probably first introduced her to Marxism and who strengthened her pacifism. The engagement was broken off in 1913, but there were other socialist influences, most notably the speeches of Mrs Bruce Glasier and the writings of Robert Blatchford. Wilkinson became a Fabian, joined the Independent Labour Party in 1912, and gained experience in the university's debating society which made her a confident, effective speaker and a vivid, fluent writer.

Thereafter Wilkinson gravitated towards public life through becoming active in a host of pressure groups and reforming organizations. Soapbox oratory, journalistic experience, assiduity in research, broadened contacts within the labour movement—all this and more now came her way. In 1913 she became an organizer with the (non-violent) National Union of Women's Suffrage Societies in Manchester. In 1915 she became the first national women's organizer for the Amalgamated Union of Co-operative Employees (later the Union of Shop, Distributive and Allied Workers), retaining the post for the rest of her life; from 1919 to 1925 she represented the union on four trade boards. Active in the Women's International League for Peace and Freedom, she opposed the First World War and was a member of the league's mission sent in 1920 to investigate the Black and Tans' activities in Ireland; its report urged an immediate truce, with the release of Irish political prisoners. She joined the Communist Party on its formation in Britain in 1920 and visited Russia in 1921, but in 1923—though still a member of the Communist Party—she stood as an official Labour candidate for Ashton under Lyne, winning more than a quarter of the votes cast in a three-cornered contest but coming bottom of the poll. In the same year, however, she was elected to the Manchester city council, where she remained until 1926.

Back-bencher on the left: 1924–1940 In 1924 Wilkinson resigned from the Communist Party, and in three-cornered contests at the general elections of 1924 and 1929 she won Middlesbrough East for Labour. As the only woman Labour MP in the parliament of 1924, elected while still lacking the household qualification that would have qualified her to vote, she was inevitably drawn into speaking up for women. 'I feel sometimes that I am the Member for widows rather than the Member for Middlesbrough', she told MPs on 22 February 1928, when championing the cause of women over seventy who had been excluded from the government's pension scheme (*Hansard 5C*, 22 Feb 1928, col. 1646). Like most Labour MPs at this time she championed women's interests without seeing these as distinct from those of the men in their social class, and in the split between the old and new feminism in the mid-1920s she naturally took the interventionist rather than the individualist side: equal opportunity for women to pursue careers seemed less important to her than the need to defend both sexes against economic exploitation. If she had been forced to choose between feminism and socialism, she would have chosen socialism, but so great was the democratic overlap between the two that the choice never presented itself, and she spoke up vigorously for equal franchise in 1928 and for equal pay in 1936. But when in March 1944 she had to choose between backing equal pay and supporting the wartime coalition government, it was the government that she backed in the three confidence votes held on the issue.

Overriding everything for 'our Ellen', as they called Wilkinson, was a deep and passionate loyalty to her working-class constituents. 'God make us worthy of the men we lead!', Dalton reported her as saying in 1926, a year in which she worked hard for the miners in the general strike (*Political Diary of Hugh Dalton*, 40). Striking a firm note of class loyalty, she drew heavily in her parliamentary speeches on local information laced with an amusingly

sarcastic wit, and was never slow to 'take up the cudgels', as she put it. Dorothy Elliott recalled that 'she was stirred by individual events and by her love of people. If she heard of oppression, wherever it might be, she had to go and see for herself, and take action'. Within the labour movement 'her intense loyalty to people, her integrity, directness, courage, and the strength of her emotions gave her a great influence' (*DNB*). In her speeches Wilkinson repeatedly tried to bring home to MPs the realities of working-class life—for example, by enhancing a speech on 29 June 1926 with a display of the rope and chain that Somerset miners used to drag their tubs. Like Winifred Holtby's headmistress Sarah Burton in *South Riding*, partly modelled on her, Wilkinson 'believed in fighting. She had unlimited confidence in the power of the human intelligence and will to achieve order, happiness, health and wisdom' (Holtby, 66). This stance prompted sharp parliamentary exchanges with Conservative women MPs, including Lady Astor, who none the less behind the scenes gave her practical help when she badly needed rest in 1929. It was in that year, in the minority Labour government, that Wilkinson became parliamentary private secretary at the Ministry of Health to Susan Lawrence, whom she admired.

By the late 1920s Wilkinson had complemented her rapport with the extra-parliamentary labour movement by building up a reputation within the House of Commons. With her red hair and her distinctive appearance—she was the first woman MP to wear a brightly coloured dress and shingled hair—she could hardly be ignored. Her slight figure—she was only 4 feet 10 inches tall—made her perkiness seem all the more courageous, for she was afraid of nobody. She could immediately warm up a debate with her jauntily irreverent manner, yet at the same time retain parliament's respect because it knew that the respect was mutual. So immersed was she in the life of the house that she published a light-hearted book of parliamentary sketches, *Peeps at Politicians* (1930), and a detective story, *Division Bell Mystery* (1932). With her vitality and her disarmingly wry sense of humour, unaccompanied by self-consciousness or vanity, she was a good debater who could spark humour in others. Her lightly sarcastic, sometimes even skittish speeches were ever incredulous that the Conservatives could really think as they did.

Yet Wilkinson was more than a good constituency MP and lively back-bencher, as Beatrice Webb in February 1927 had already perceived. Predicting 'a big political career' for Wilkinson, Webb saw that she was 'becoming, unknown to herself, moulded for the Front Bench and eventually for office': she would make a good departmental minister, more efficient and popular than those Labour stateswomen Susan Lawrence and Margaret Bondfield (Webb, *Diaries, 1924–1932*, 133). Political commentators were impressed with how carefully Wilkinson prepared her case when speaking in parliament on women's pensions in 1925, and she displayed the same grasp of detail when with all-party support in 1938 she piloted through her Hire Purchase Bill, which ensured a fairer deal for the customer. Her commitment and knowledge were nourished by her close identification with her constituencies, Middlesbrough and Jarrow, deeply involved as they were in heavy industry. Local loyalties lay behind her eagerness in the mid-1920s, for instance, to resume trade with Soviet Russia. 'I happen to represent in this House one of the heaviest iron and steel producing areas in the world', she told MPs in 1928: 'I know I do not look like it, but I do' (*Hansard 5C*, 1 Mar 1928, col. 734).

At the general election of 1931 Wilkinson's percentage of the votes cast at Middlesbrough fell only slightly, but this time she faced only a single, Liberal, opponent and so was soundly defeated. 'Just like you middle-class people', was her retort when her Labour colleague Edith Picton-Turbervill said she would abstain in the National Government's confidence debate on 8 September 1931 (Picton-Turbervill, 258). For political and personal reasons, Wilkinson's morale in the early 1930s was low, and for a time she seems to have found consolation in Christian Science, with further help from Lady Astor. Impulsive, emotional, and an erratic judge of character, Wilkinson experienced some difficulties that were of her own making. Her domestic life was disorganized and hurried, complicated greatly by her tendency to over-commit herself to good causes and by difficulty in meeting journalistic deadlines. Things were rendered manageable only by the devoted help of her sister Annie. In 1936 the two sisters bought a cottage in Penn, a bolt-hole which brought much-needed peace and privacy. Wilkinson's personal life was also in difficulties: she asked Beatrice Webb in July 1931 whether a woman in public life should remain celibate if she had found a congenial friend with an uncongenial wife; Webb interpreted this as referring to the Labour MP and journalist, J. F. Horrabin, with whom Wilkinson had a short-lived affair.

Yet Wilkinson was nothing if not resilient, and in 1935 she became Labour MP for Jarrow in a straight fight. The stage was now set for one of the twentieth century's most famous identifications between MP and constituency. 'Nowadays', she told MPs in November 1938, 'any Member of Parliament for one of the distressed areas has become a kind of glorified commercial traveller for his area' (*Hansard 5C*, 28 Nov 1938, col. 157). Two years earlier she had led the famous march from Jarrow to London, herself walking for most of the way, and learning much from her fellow marchers about the realities of poverty. She informed parliament that a Jarrow vicar had told her how the young men there were 'just like eggshells. They looked all right outside, but when they were faced with the infection and cold of the winter they just cracked like eggshells' (*Hansard 5C*, 8 July 1936, col. 1269). On 11 November 1936 she begged MPs themselves to learn from the marchers by allowing them to appear at the bar of the house, but in vain. Three years later she educated the nation in the most important of her books, *The Town that was Murdered*, published by the Left Book Club complete with a substantial bibliography. There she used the decline of local shipbuilding to illustrate how monopoly capitalism precluded

efficiency in the local iron and steel industry, and rendered irrelevant the type of 'remedy' for Jarrow's poverty and sickness that blamed the conduct of the individual rather than a defective economic system. The remedy lay only through socialism—that is, through nationalization, tax reform, and planning. 'Jarrow's plight is not a local problem', she wrote, 'it is the symptom of a national evil' (Wilkinson, *The Town that was Murdered*, 283). For a busy back-bencher to write such a well-documented and eloquent book was a formidable achievement.

Wilkinson had never been narrowly preoccupied with domestic policy, and in 1932 she visited India as part of a delegation from the India League; when contributing to the parliamentary debate on India on 18 April 1940 she felt able to refer to the many Indians who were her friends, including Nehru. She pleaded eloquently against using authoritarian methods against nationalists there, if only because of the bad image of Britain that this would project in the United States. Her main inter-war concern with overseas policy, however, lay closer to home: as early as April 1933 she was urging British feminists to resist Nazi discrimination against women's employment. She opposed fascism in every way open to her: helping refugees, passionately opposing non-intervention in Spain, which she visited, and seeing appeasement in 1938–9 as an outcrop of upper-class self-interest. Her House of Commons attack on Chamberlain's policy on 24 August 1939 was scathing, striking a divisive note which even some of her sympathizers in parliament found distasteful, yet it was one of the most impressive parliamentary speeches on foreign policy made by any woman MP up to that date.

In government: 1940–1947 In May 1940 Wilkinson became parliamentary secretary to the Ministry of Pensions. The office narrowed her debating front within the House of Commons, but her contributions were crisp and well informed. In October 1940 she became joint parliamentary secretary to the Ministry of Home Security, which involved her more deeply in civil defence issues. She was not the sort of minister whose effectiveness with paperwork pleases civil servants, nor was she always even-tempered. But she was good at publicity, and set an example to others with her energy and courage. She spent days and nights in bomb shelters when conditions were at their worst, and was prominent in organizing civil defence and the fire service. Wilkinson, like her party, was being edged away from opposition-mindedness by the war. Her patriotism made her intensely proud of having served in the wartime coalition, and she alone among Labour MPs gave Churchill a sympathetic cheer when he entered the House after his defeat at the general election of 1945.

Wilkinson never married, but her close relations with Herbert Morrison had probably become more than platonic in the late 1930s. In identifying closely with his political ambitions she made enemies on the left of the Labour Party, and she made more by backing him strongly late in 1943 when he allowed Mosley's release from prison. 'Little Ellen … is apt to be much too publicly emotional abt her

Chief', wrote Dalton in his diary on 24 November of a discussion in the national executive committee; she 'makes an impassioned defence, with sobs in her throat, but it really isn't very convincing, except to the purists for civil liberty' (War Diary, 674). She was still backing Morrison's designs on the leadership in 1945, but she was too passionately committed to make a successful conspirator, and in this she ultimately failed. Once more she was returned for Jarrow in a straight fight, her percentage of the votes cast rising to two-thirds, and she found that her conspiracies against Attlee did not preclude her admission to his cabinet as minister of education.

Wilkinson's seventeen months in cabinet constituted something of an anticlimax. She was accused later of failing to advance comprehensive schools, but this is doubly anachronistic: the movement for comprehensives could not then compete with the traditional Labour Party policy of providing equal opportunity within the existing educational system; besides, the first priority at a time of postwar reconstruction and scarce resources was inevitably to implement the Education Act (1944). Choosing a few key areas for special effort, she won the resources and provided the necessary drive and organization to ensure free school milk and school meals, smaller classes, extensive school building, a school-leaving age raised to fifteen, and an expansion in the county colleges which would help win acceptance for education up to the age of eighteen. But she had too little time: she was severely handicapped as a minister by poor health. She had neglected her health during the war, and had inherited her father's bronchial asthma. The situation was not helped by her being prone to accidents, especially while driving, which she did in hair-raising fashion. She died at St Mary's Hospital, Paddington, London, on 6 February 1947, of heart failure following an overdose of medication which was almost certainly accidental, while suffering from emphysema with pneumonia and acute bronchitis. Until her death she was living in a flat at Hood House, Dolphin Square, Westminster.

For Dorothy Elliott the effect of Wilkinson's work 'was rather the sum of a long series of isolated efforts than the working out of any sustained policy' (DNB). Beatrice Webb would not have been surprised. Her shrewd analysis of 1927 did not find in Wilkinson a capacity for hard thinking or spiritual insight: she would therefore be only 'an interpreter of other people's thoughts and intentions' (Webb, Diaries, 1924–1932, 133). Rare is the politician who is more than this, but at least as rare is the politician who combines a capacity for hard-working and generous-minded protest against injustice with skill at channelling it towards parliamentary institutions, and who then goes on in a ministerial capacity to defend democracy energetically and courageously at its time of greatest danger.

BRIAN HARRISON

Sources The political diary of Hugh Dalton, 1918–1940, 1945–1960, ed. B. Pimlott (1986) · The Second World War diary of Hugh Dalton, 1940–1945, ed. B. Pimlott (1986) · W. Holtby, South Riding: an English landscape, paperback edn (1954) · E. Picton-Turbervill, Life is good: an autobiography (1939) · Beatrice Webb's diaries, 1924–1932, ed. M. Cole (1956) · The diary of Beatrice Webb, ed. N. MacKenzie and J. MacKenzie, 4 vols. (1982–5), vol. 4 · E. Wilkinson, contribution, Myself when young: by famous women of to-day, ed. countess of Oxford and Asquith (1938), 399–416 · E. Wilkinson, The town that was murdered: the life-story of Jarrow (1939) · DNB · R. Betts, 'Parliamentary women: women ministers of education, 1924–1974', Women, educational policy-making and administration in England: authoritative women since 1880, ed. J. Goodman and S. Harrop (2000) · M. Francis, 'A socialist policy for education? Labour and the secondary school, 1945–51', History of Education, 24/4 (1995) · B. D. Vernon, Ellen Wilkinson, 1891–1947 (1982)

Archives Labour History Archive and Study Centre, Manchester, corresp. with R. Palme Dutt | SOUND BL NSA, 'The fiery particle', BBC Radio 4, 23 Oct 1991, B8750/3 · BL NSA, performance recording · BL NSA, recorded talk

Likenesses E. Kapp, chalk drawing, 1930, Barber Institute of Fine Arts, Birmingham · H. Coster, photograph, 1945, NPG [see illus.] · W. Stoneman, photograph, 1945, NPG · H. Coster, photographs, NPG · N. Hepple, portrait, priv. coll. · photographs, Hult. Arch.

Wealth at death £7253 16s. 11d.: administration with will, 18 Oct 1947, CGPLA Eng. & Wales

Wilkinson, (James John) Garth (1812–1899), Swedenborgian writer and homoeopath, born in Acton Street, Gray's Inn Lane, London, on 3 June 1812, was the eldest son of **James John Wilkinson** (bap. 1780, d. 1858), lawyer, the eldest son of Martin Wilkinson, attorney, and Jane Rawling. James Wilkinson was baptized at St Mary-le-Bow, Durham, on 19 June 1780, and entered Gray's Inn, London, on 26 November 1802; he practised as a special pleader and was also a judge of the county palatine of Durham. On 4 September 1811 he married Harriet Robinson of Sunderland. By 1849 he had married again; his second wife, Anne Wilkinson, wrote a number of legal works. She predeceased him. He died at 8 Church Row, London, on 25 December 1858.

Garth Wilkinson was educated at a school in Sunderland, and afterwards at a private school at Mill Hill kept by John Charles Thorowgood and at Totteridge in Hertfordshire. At the age of about sixteen he was apprenticed by his father to Thomas Leighton, senior surgeon of the infirmary at Newcastle upon Tyne. In 1832 he went to London to train at various hospitals, and in June 1834 he became a member of the Royal College of Surgeons of England and a licentiate of the Society of Apothecaries. On 4 January 1840 he married Emma Anne, daughter of William Marsh, a jeweller. They had one son and three daughters.

Wilkinson was attracted by the writings of William Blake, and in 1839 he edited his Songs of Innocence and of Experience, with considerable alterations. A volume of his own poems, entitled Improvisations from the Spirit, which appeared in 1857, showed many traces of Blake's influence. Early in life Wilkinson was also introduced, by his maternal uncle George Blakiston Robinson, to the writings of Emanuel Swedenborg, and he became a member of the committee of the Swedenborg Society and of the subcommittee for promoting the issue of a uniform edition of Swedenborg's works. From 1839 he devoted most of his literary energies to the translation and elucidation of Swedenborg's writings.

When in 1840 Wilkinson began to contribute to the

(James John) Garth Wilkinson (1812–1899), by Robert Faulkner, c.1867

Monthly Magazine the originality of his philosophic intellect immediately attracted attention. A paper which appeared in 1841 dealing with Coleridge's comments on Swedenborg's *De oeconomia regni animalis* and his *De cultu et amore Dei* gained him the admiration of the American writer Henry James, father of the novelist. James corresponded with Wilkinson at length, and two of his works, *The Church of Christ not an Ecclesiasticism* (2nd edn, 1856) and *Christianity the Logic of Creation* (1857), were composed of letters originally addressed to Wilkinson. In 1843 and 1844 Wilkinson published his translation of Swedenborg's *De oeconomia regni animalis* as *The Animal Kingdom Considered*. These volumes were followed by further translations, one of which, *Outlines of a Philosophic Argument on the Infinite*, won him the friendship of Ralph Waldo Emerson. Wilkinson's translations were accompanied by preliminary discourses which were declared by Emerson to 'throw all contemporary philosophy of England into shade' (*Representative Men*, 1882, 65; cf. *English Traits*, 1857, 140). Besides enjoying the esteem of Emerson, Wilkinson was intimate with Thomas Carlyle, James Anthony Froude, Charles Dickens, Alfred Tennyson, and the Oliphants, and he was the friend of Edward Augustus Freeman, who was a relative.

For Wilkinson, Swedenborg promised not merely a linkage (mystical in some definitions) between everything natural and supernatural but also a new organization of knowledge and thus of medical and social relations. 'All power' (as he worded one sentence of his own translation of the Swede's *Animal Kingdom*, xxxix) 'resides in the least things'. This core principle made him a readier listener when Emma Anne refused, on homoeopathic grounds, to administer a drug he himself had just prepared for their first baby. Her mutiny precipitated his conversion to homoeopathy. (This incident is recounted in Wilkinson's own words in his biography by C. J. Wilkinson on pages 247–9.) Wilkinson then established himself as a homoeopath in Wimpole Street, London.

The same Swedenborgian principle helped make Wilkinson, along with Swedenborgians such as William White but unlike some homoeopaths, into a furious opponent of vaccination. This, for him—along with the Contagious Diseases Acts and vivisection—exemplified an already current misdevelopment in the natural sciences and in any version of medicine that claimed to derive from them. This misdevelopment was, he believed, compartmentalization, and one of its silliest results was materialism; its ghastliest was, towards the lay and powerless in general and towards women and animals in particular, a coldly objectifying arrogance, or 'specialism' as he called it. This had social (not least anti-woman) dimensions. Crucially it applied primogeniture to the terrain of knowledge:

> aim[ing] rather at increasing intellectual property in a few hands, and transmitting it unimpaired from generation to generation, than … [at] the public service. … All the … fences, and other arrangements of intellectual estates, are especially adapted for the system of individual proprietorship, and would be useless under a different mode of tenure. (*Science for All*, 1847, 3–16)

By contrast Wilkinson agreed with most plebeian medicators in wanting every person to be their own and their neighbour's healer, unintimidated by what he called the 'corporate quackery' of orthodoxy.

All this made Wilkinson, despite his membership of the Royal College of Surgeons, not merely someone for whom surgery had become 'ever an abomination' (Wilkinson, 264) but also an increasingly shrill Cassandra against the dominant intellectual and social trends in medicine. His own allegiance to 'leasts' harmonized with spiritualists and with many medical heretics in their belief in the power of what came to be called 'imponderables'. In common with mid-nineteenth-century medical botanists and others, he attempted to work out the democratic implications of this apparent power. In the 1880s he was still looking forward to 'new doctrines' which would renew 'all business, all property, all relations' and would amount to 'the Second Coming of Christ' (*Swedenborg's Doctrines and the Translation of his Works*, 1882, 5, 7). During the 1840s he had been stirred by Fourierism and in 1848 he had visited Paris and felt sympathy with its insurgent workers.

Wilkinson was versed in Icelandic and Scandinavian literature. He was a member of the Icelandic Society of Copenhagen, and corresponded with Gunnar Rudberg, the Scandinavian philologist. He was associated with Jón A. Hjaltalín in translating Swedenborg's *Divine Love and Wisdom* into Icelandic (1869). He visited the United States, and about 1850 was the English correspondent of several New York and Boston papers. His earliest residence in London was 25 Church Row, Hampstead. About 1848 he moved to Finchley Road. He died at 4 Finchley Road, London, on 18 October 1899, and was buried on 21 October in Hampstead cemetery.

E. I. CARLYLE, *rev.* LOGIE BARROW

Sources L. Barrow, 'An imponderable liberator: J. J. Garth Wilkinson', *Studies in the history of alternative medicine*, ed. R. Cooter (1988), 89–117 · C. J. Wilkinson, *James John Garth Wilkinson* (1911) · m. cert. · d. cert. · private information (1900) · private information (1988) · *The Times* (23 Oct 1899) · *Morning Light* (23 Oct 1899) · 'Contemporary portraits, new series no. 18', *University Magazine: a Literary and Philosophic Review*, 3 (1879), 673–92 · *Fraser's Magazine*, 55 (1857), 178 **Archives** Swedenborg Society, London, corresp. **Likenesses** R. Faulkner, photograph, *c.*1867, NPG [*see illus.*] · F. Leifchild, bust; Swedenborg Society, Bloomsbury Street, London (in 1900) · portrait; Swedenborg Society, Bloomsbury Street, London (in 1900) · portrait, repro. in Wilkinson, *James John Garth Wilkinson* **Wealth at death** £5302 4s. 7d.: probate, 9 Nov 1899, *CGPLA Eng. & Wales* · under £5000—John James Wilkinson: probate, 1859, *CGPLA Eng. & Wales*

Wilkinson, Sir Geoffrey (1921–1996), inorganic chemist, was born on 14 July 1921 at 506 Halifax Road, Springside, near Todmorden, Yorkshire, the eldest of three children of Henry Wilkinson (1885–1975), master painter and decorator, and his wife, Ruth, *née* Crowther (1891–1962), weaver. Both his parents came from Yorkshire and moved to the centre of Todmorden in 1926, to 4 Wellington Road: the house is marked by a blue plaque erected in his honour in 1990, and in 1997 another plaque was erected in the town hall.

Early life and education Wilkinson's interest in chemistry came early: he was fascinated by watching his father mixing his painting materials, and by visiting the laboratory of his uncle, the manager of a small chemical factory making Epsom and Glauber's salts in Todmorden. He won a West Riding county scholarship in 1931 to Todmorden secondary school; the school had many other pupils later to become famous, including Sir John Cockcroft, who became in 1951 the first of its two Nobel laureates. Though at different times, Cockcroft and Wilkinson had the same physics teacher. Wilkinson was a brilliant pupil and won a royal scholarship to Imperial College, London, starting there in 1939.

Wilkinson found life at Imperial competitive: in the year before his was another future Nobel laureate, Derek Barton, who like Wilkinson later rejoined the college as a professor. He read chemistry but also studied geology as an ancillary subject. He did so well at this that he won the prestigious Murchison prize in geology—indeed he thought at one point of giving up chemistry in favour of geology. He graduated in 1941 with the top first-class honours BSc of the year, and started work towards his PhD under H. V. A. (Henry) Briscoe (then the only professor of inorganic chemistry in the country) on 'Some physicochemical observations on hydrolysis in the homogeneous vapour phase'. This rather Delphic title concealed the fact that the main substance studied (probably part of

Sir Geoffrey Wilkinson (1921–1996), by Liam Woon, 1990

Briscoe's war research) was the intensely toxic phosgene. Wilkinson remarked that Briscoe 'directed his Ph.D. research from a safe distance'.

North America Towards the end of 1942 Wilkinson was selected by the Joint Recruiting Board to join the British contingent on the atomic energy division of the Canadian National Research Council (part of the 'Tube Alloys' atomic bomb project). He sailed out on the RMS *Andes* from Greenock to Halifax, Nova Scotia, on 11 January 1943—recalling that the scientists were supposed to travel first class, but that his room, clearly marked 'for one seaman only', had to be shared with three other scientists. Some interesting incidents occurred while he was on the project. He witnessed an accident in which a glass vessel containing heavy water (then a virtually priceless material used for moderating nuclear reactions), which had been smuggled from the Norwegian heavy water plant out through occupied France, had been dropped so that all the liquid spilled on the floor. Most of it was recovered by hurriedly mopping it up with handkerchiefs. Some time later a solution containing a precious 20 mg of the intensely toxic and radioactive plutonium nitrate boiled over onto a wooden bench and soaked into it; it was retrieved by sawing up the bench and extracting the wood and sawdust with boiling water. Safety was not a prime consideration: Wilkinson would routinely pick up intensely radioactive radium-beryllium neutron sources with his fingers. In Montreal and at Chalk River he worked with many celebrated names—among them Pierre Auger, John Cockcroft, Charles Coryell, Bertrand Goldschmidt, Jules Guéron, Alfie Maddocks, and two figures later to find notoriety as Soviet spies, Alan Nunn May and Bruno Pontecorvo.

In 1946 Wilkinson became a research fellow at the Radiation (Lawrence Livermore) Laboratory, University of Berkeley, California, where he worked with his good friend and future Nobel laureate, Glenn Seaborg, on the production of new isotopes. In 1950 he moved to the Massachusetts Institute of Technology as a research associate, and in September 1951 he was appointed assistant professor of chemistry at Harvard. It was there that his interest in organometallic chemistry developed and where he did the research which was later to be the main source of his Nobel prize. On 17 July 1952 Wilkinson married Dr Lise Sølver Schou (b. 1924), a Danish plant physiologist and medical historian, and daughter of Svend Aage Schou, professorial rector of the Pharmaceutical High School, Copenhagen; theirs was a long and happy marriage. They had two daughters, Anne and Pernille. In 1954, with the help of a Guggenheim fellowship, Wilkinson spent a nine-month sabbatical leave at the University of Copenhagen, where he worked in a laboratory in which the necessary upward draught in the fume cupboard was still accomplished by having flaming gas burners at the top. His research necessitated the use of flammable organic solvents and he had several spectacular fires. Despite this he continued pioneering research in the field of organometallic hydride chemistry.

Return to Imperial College In 1955 Wilkinson was appointed professor of inorganic chemistry at Imperial College, taking up his position there in January 1956 at the early age of thirty-four. One of the first things that he did on arrival was to cajole a grant of £20,000—a very large sum in the mid-1950s—from the authorities to purchase a nuclear magnetic resonance (NMR) instrument, the first such commercial spectrometer in Britain. Sir Alexander Todd, then chairman of the advisory committee on scientific policy, had the remarkable prescience to recommend that the grant should be made, and it was a wise investment for research in Britain. Wilkinson and his students used the machine tirelessly and to very good effect. He was elected a fellow of the Royal Society in 1965, received its royal medal in 1981 and its Davy medal in 1996 (in the course of his life he received some fifteen medals and nine honorary degrees). He was knighted in 1976.

In those rather formal days Wilkinson was remarkable in that he dressed casually, adopted some American habits, addressed his students by their first names and expected them, and the departmental staff, to call him Geoff. He was as popular with the cleaners—his office and laboratories needed their particular attention—as with his students and the academic staff. Although he had little interest in administration and really rather despised administrators ('apparatchiks', he called them) he was, from 1976 to 1988, to everyone's surprise a very effective head of the chemistry department. This he accomplished largely by inspired delegation and having an open-door policy for staff and students alike.

In 1988 Wilkinson became professor emeritus and the college commissioned a striking portrait in oils of him by the artist Keith Grant. In the same year the firm Johnson Matthey plc provided a laboratory for him on the top floor of the chemistry building. There he continued to run a small, creative research group until the day before his death, producing some ten high-quality, innovative research papers a year, an astonishing record for someone who had supposedly retired.

Wilkinson's chemistry Wilkinson's work covered a wide range, but a common factor was that metals played a central role in almost all the compounds which he studied. The radiochemistry of isotopes was the topic of his early research years, from 1943 to 1951; isotopes are forms of an element with the same atomic number (number of protons) but different mass numbers (sum of the number of protons and neutrons in the atom). He amassed during this time a vast knowledge of inorganic chemistry, since radiochemists had to know in great detail the practical chemistry of the transition metals, the lanthanides, and the actinides in order to separate their isotopes. He believed that his greatest contribution in those early days was to measure the rates of formation of the products formed by fission of uranium-235, the material used in the first atomic bomb. With Glenn Seaborg at Berkeley he worked on nuclear taxonomy, the production of neutron deficient isotopes of the transition elements and the lanthanides, using the cyclotrons at the Radiation Laboratory at Berkeley, and there he made more artificial isotopes than anyone else before or since—no less than eighty-nine. He was particularly proud of his nuclear transmutation of platinum to gold, which caught the public imagination after a report in 1948 in the *San Francisco Chronicle*.

Wilkinson was most famed for his fundamental contributions to organometallic chemistry, the study of compounds containing a direct metal-to-carbon bond. It is fair to say that his work launched modern organometallic chemistry. The realization of the unique sandwich structure of ferrocene (bis-cyclopentadienyliron) by him and Robert B. Woodward at Harvard eventually led to a Nobel prize in 1973, awarded jointly to Wilkinson and Professor E. O. Fischer of the Technische Hochschule, Munich. In ferrocene, so named because of certain similarities with benzene, an iron atom lies between two parallel cyclopentadienyl (C_5H_5) rings. Although ferrocene had been made before, no one, before this pioneering work, knew or understood its unique structure. Having established the structure of ferrocene, Wilkinson went on to make analogous materials with other metals, and many other novel organometallic compounds, thereby revolutionizing perspectives on the subject. Although he did not investigate their industrial potential, many of the sandwich compounds have remarkable and useful properties, being used now in sensors and as catalysts for olefin polymerization. It was during this period too that he made creative use of the then fledgeling technique of nuclear magnetic resonance. Later he turned to the chemistry of metal alkyls and aryls, and did some remarkable work in this essentially new area—it is typical of him that, in his Nobel speech, he spoke on this rather than on the ferrocene work that gave him his prize.

Although principally remembered as an organometallic chemist, Wilkinson made an enormous contribution to co-ordination chemistry (which, unlike organometallic chemistry, involves compounds containing no metal–carbon bonds). This thread ran through his entire research career, for co-ordination chemistry had a crucial role to play in the separational aspects of his radiochemistry. Outstanding in this area was his work on homogeneous catalysts—materials which in solution accelerate a chemical reaction without themselves being destroyed. His discovery in 1966 of the remarkable complex $RhCl(PPh_3)_3$, which catalyses addition of hydrogen to organic compounds, was seminal. It became universally known as Wilkinson's catalyst, and both it and its analogues were widely used in chemical and biomedical reactions. About the same time he showed the compound $RhH(CO)(PPh_3)_3$ to be a very effective and selective catalyst for the reaction of organic olefins with hydrogen and carbon monoxide (syngas) to give aldehydes. This became a widely used industrial process for converting propylene to n-butyraldehyde, a precursor for plasticizers and many other useful organic compounds. His work on these and other catalysts revolutionized understanding of homogeneous catalysis by transition-metal complexes.

Publications Wilkinson produced 557 scientific papers on fundamental chemical research, and wrote or edited a number of books still in use many years later. Of these the most internationally influential was *Advanced Inorganic Chemistry: a Comprehensive Text* (1962), which he and his ex-student F. Albert Cotton produced. It is no exaggeration to say that this revolutionized the presentation of inorganic chemistry to undergraduates, postgraduates, and chemists everywhere. The book was translated into many languages, much to his irritation in some cases, for he had difficulty in retrieving royalties for some of those translated versions which had been pirated. There was a hilarious correspondence between him and the Soviet authorities on this matter; for some obscure reason the recipient of these letters at the Soviet embassy was the agricultural counsellor, later to be expelled by Sir Alec Douglas-Home as a spy. Wilkinson insisted on sending copies of his letters and the deadpan replies from the agricultural counsellor to all universities and, to its extreme discomfiture, the Foreign Office. Subsequent editions of Cotton and Wilkinson, as it was universally known, were published in 1966, 1972, 1980, and 1988. The sixth edition (with Cotton, Murillo, and Bochmann) was published in 1999; two days before he died Wilkinson handed in his final, typically untidy, manuscript for typing.

Important too for research chemists everywhere were the six-volume *Comprehensive Coordination Chemistry* (1987), for which Wilkinson was the chief editor with R. D. Gillard and Jon McCleverty as editors, and the nine-volume *Comprehensive Organometallic Chemistry* of 1982, revised and reissued in fourteen volumes in 1995, which he edited with F. G. A. Stone and E. W. Abel. He also launched in 1982, with Don Bradley, the successful inorganic chemistry journal *Polyhedron*.

The scientist and the man If ever a chemist lived out E. M. Forster's dictum 'only connect', it was Wilkinson. For over fifty years he made fundamental contributions to nuclear, organometallic, co-ordination, and catalytic chemistry, and much of his brilliance lay in his extraordinary ability

to interlink these topics, one fertilizing the other. His obituarist in *The Independent* said that 'The spirit in his research group was more like that of an urgent gold rush in the West than the scholarly and disciplined calm expected in academia' (*The Independent*, 1 Oct 1996). If anything this understates the truth: he expected his students to work as hard as he did—seven days a week or at least six, from early morning to late evening. He was, however, remarkably tolerant of eccentric and individual behaviour, perhaps because he himself showed such traits (for example, he made remarkably ingenious and creative use of expletives). He was an excellent supervisor, communicating his own enthusiasm, but always giving the student the space to develop his or her own ideas. A valuable and all-too-rare aspect of his training of students was to insist that they write scientific papers of their results for publication, which he would then invariably return to them, after ruthless editing and alteration, for rewriting: an iterative process.

Wilkinson's research was always original and he had limitless enthusiasm and energy for new chemistry. His work clearly demonstrated one of his dearest beliefs: that imaginative and curiosity driven exploratory synthesis provides a pivotal approach for the creative development of new science. Although he had some industrial collaboration, his work was never directed towards immediate short-term applications, and he sought (and received) little financial support from industry. One of the keys to his success was his encyclopaedic knowledge of chemistry, and particularly of what was significant in it to his own research. He rapidly assimilated techniques that were new to him, found good experts in these areas, and enthused them to collaborate with him.

It is perhaps significant that in 1978 Wilkinson named his chair at Imperial College the Sir Edward Frankland chair of inorganic chemistry. Frankland (1825–1899) was the second professor at the Royal College of Chemistry, from 1868 to 1885. There are parallels between Wilkinson and Frankland: both came from humble backgrounds, Frankland in Lancashire and Wilkinson from very close to Lancashire. Both were organometallic chemists (Frankland is often called the father of organometallic chemistry); and both were relatively uncharismatic lecturers but gifted experimentalists. Wilkinson was amused later to receive letters addressed not to him but to Sir Edward.

Wilkinson was fiercely protective of British science and research; despite his enormous international standing he insisted on publishing almost all his research papers in British scientific journals. He became the scourge of those responsible for higher education and research in the country: a succession of prime ministers received a flow of letters from him on this and other subjects, as did ministers of education, functionaries in research councils, university vice-chancellors, and others. His work was always original and he had limitless enthusiasm and energy for new chemistry; he wore his fame lightly and was accessible to all.

Wilkinson was of medium height, and had a wiry figure

and blue eyes which lit up and sparkled when he recognized a friend or spoke of something close to his heart, such as his beloved Yorkshire. His accent was a curious mixture of his native Yorkshire with a strong hint of the transatlantic twang which derived from his thirteen years in North America. He had a keen sense of the mischievous and, when he felt he was in the right company, would express seemingly outrageous opinions and with delight enthusiastically defend them. Although he had a forceful personality there was a certain shyness and even defensiveness in his nature—he would only with extreme reluctance make after-dinner speeches and rarely attended conferences or gave international lectures. A happy family man, when his children were young and particularly outside term time, he went every weekend with his wife to his house in Sussex, where chemistry was entirely eschewed; he proudly claimed to have planted more than 2000 trees there. He had a great sense of fun, was an excellent raconteur, and had many interests: a favourite pastime was walking on the moors and fells of his native Yorkshire, and he had a keen interest in music.

Some two months before Wilkinson's death an informal dinner was held at Imperial College to celebrate his forty years (1956–96) at the college; more than a hundred people attended from all over the world, and his remarkable memory was evident by his instant recognition of collaborators from the distant past. It was a happy and memorable occasion for all. He died on 26 September 1996 at his home, 14 Passmore Street, London, of coronary thrombosis, and was cremated on 8 October at Putney Vale. He was survived by his wife, Lise, and their two daughters.

Assessment Wilkinson's contributions to many areas of chemistry were immense. He was lucky to have been part of what came to be seen as a golden age of chemical research, when pressure to obtain funds was far less insistent than later, and when there was positive encouragement to do what he did so well—research for the sake of it, rather than for material rewards. He was fortunate too to have been associated with the atomic energy project, to which he gave much but from which he also received much in experience and in knowledge. The timing and circumstances of his first and perhaps most fundamental discovery (recognition of the true nature of ferrocene) were a great help, as was being at an institution, Harvard, where the first NMR instrument was sited and where there were so many distinguished chemists. He was fortunate also to have selected such excellent collaborators at Imperial College. Nevertheless, it needed a certain genius to have used this good fortune creatively, to have harnessed it constructively, and to have exercised the remarkable instinct which he had for the new experiment, the new area of research, which would produce really original and creative new science.

BILL GRIFFITH

Sources M. L. H. Green and W. P. Griffith, *Memoirs FRS*, 46 (2000) · M. A. Bennett, A. A. Danopoulos, W. P. Griffith, and M. L. H. Green, 'The contributions to original research by Professor Sir Geoffrey Wilkinson FRS 1921–1996', *Journal of the Chemical Society, Dalton Transactions* (1997), 3049–79 · G. Wilkinson, autobiographical sketch, *Les prix Nobel en 1973* (Stockholm, 1974), 147–8 · M. L. H. Green and W. P. Griffith, 'Geoffrey Wilkinson and platinum metals chemistry', *Platinum Metals Review*, 42 (1998), 168–73 · W. P. Griffith, *Chemistry in Britain* (Jan 1997), 52–3 · G. Wilkinson, 'The iron sandwich: a recollection of the first four months', *Journal of Organometallic Chemistry*, 100 (1975), 273–8 · *The Independent* (1 Oct 1996) · *The Guardian* (2 Oct 1996) · *The Times* (4 Oct 1996) · *Daily Telegraph* (12 Oct 1996) · *Nature* (21 Nov 1996) · *WWW* · personal knowledge (2004) · private information (2004)

Archives ICL, college archives, papers, corresp., etc · priv. coll., handwritten autobiographical memoir | FILM ICL, interview footage, 1988 · ICL, interview footage, 1990 | SOUND BL NSA, recorded lecture, H7931-2

Likenesses cartoon, 1974?, repro. in F. A. Cotton, 'Geoffrey Wilkinson as a research mentor', *Polyhedron*, 16 (1997); priv. coll. · K. Grant, oils, 1988 · K. Grant, sketch, 31 May 1988 (after his oil painting), priv. coll. · L. Woon, photograph, in Cibachrome, 1990, NPG [*see illus.*] · family photographs, priv. coll. · photograph, repro. in Green and Griffith, *Memoirs FRS*, 147 · photograph, repro. in *The Independent* · photograph, repro. in *The Guardian* · photograph, repro. in *The Times* · photograph, repro. in *Daily Telegraph* · photograph, repro. in *Nature* · photograph, repro. in Griffith, *Chemistry in Britain* · photograph, repro. in G. Wilkinson, autobiographical sketch · photographs, ICL · photographs, priv. coll.

Wealth at death £510,542: probate, 5 Feb 1997, *CGPLA Eng. & Wales*

Wilkinson, George Howard (1833–1907), Scottish Episcopal bishop of St Andrews, Dunkeld, and Dunblane, was born at Durham on 12 May 1833, the eldest son of George Wilkinson of Oswald House, Durham, and his wife, Mary, youngest child of John Howard of Ripon, Yorkshire. On his father's side he was from a long-established gentry family in co. Durham and Northumberland. Educated at Durham grammar school, Wilkinson went to Brasenose College, Oxford, in October 1851, but in November was elected to a scholarship at Oriel College. He obtained second-class honours in *literae humaniores*, graduated BA in 1855, and proceeded MA in 1859 and DD in 1883. After a year spent in travel he was ordained deacon (1857) and priest (1858) and licensed to the curacy of St Mary Abbots, Kensington, London. On 14 July 1857 he married Caroline Charlotte, daughter of Lieutenant-Colonel Benfield des Voeux, fourth son of Charles des Voeux, first baronet. They had three sons and five daughters.

In 1859 Lady Londonderry, widow of the third marquess, presented Wilkinson to the living of Seaham Harbour, co. Durham, and in 1863 the bishop of Durham, C. T. Baring, appointed him vicar of Bishop Auckland in the same county. Wilkinson had been untouched at Oxford by the Tractarian movement, but during the 1860s he moved away from his moderate evangelicalism which subordinated the sacraments to personal conversion. Under the influence of Canon T. T. Carter and others he espoused Anglo-Catholicism, though he remained ambivalent about aural confession until the 1870s. Difficulties followed with the bishop, who was an evangelical. Wilkinson's health suffered from the strain, and in 1867 he accepted the incumbency of St Peter's, Great Windmill Street, London. In this small and poor parish he began to refine the basic thrusts of his very successful parochial ministry. These included open-air preaching, then a novelty; widespread involvement of laity and particularly women as district visitors responsible to the clergy; and evangelical preaching in the context of Catholic liturgy and ritual. One of the earliest to take up parochial missions, he helped to organize the innovative high-church twelve-day mission to London in 1869. During its progress he accepted the offer by Bishop John Jackson of London of St Peter's, Eaton Square. His incumbency there, beginning in January 1870, was widely known for its success in a parish which included both wealthy, influential parishioners and poorer housing areas.

Active in church affairs generally, Wilkinson spoke at church congresses; sought in the years of ritual trouble (1870–80) to act as an interpreter between the bishops and the ritualists; and zealously advocated foreign missions, the day of intercession for which owed its establishment to him. In 1877 the bishop of Truro, E. W. Benson, made him an examining chaplain; on 6 September of the same year his wife died. In 1878 he refused to be nominated suffragan bishop for London. Select preacher at Oxford from 1879 to 1881, in 1880 he was elected a proctor in convocation and gave evidence before the royal commission of 1881 on ecclesiastical courts. In 1882 he declined an invitation from the bishop of Durham, J. B. Lightfoot, to become canon missioner.

In 1883, on Benson's translation to Canterbury, Gladstone appointed Wilkinson to succeed him at Truro, and he was consecrated at St Paul's on 25 April 1883. At Truro he completed the building of the cathedral and saw it consecrated on 3 November 1887, founded a sisterhood, the Community of the Epiphany, and did much for the clergy of poorer benefices. In 1885 he declined the see of Manchester. He took part in the 1888 Lambeth conference. In April 1891, after a mental collapse, he announced his resignation; he was perennially subject to depression caused by over-scrupulosity and an acute sense of sin, which existed in tension with personal vanity.

Restored by a visit to South Africa, Wilkinson was on 9 February 1893 elected to succeed Charles Wordsworth as bishop of St Andrews, Dunkeld, and Dunblane, and was enthroned in St Ninian's Cathedral, Perth, on 27 April. In 1904 the bishops of the Scottish Episcopal church elected him primus. As a diocesan he created a fund for church extension and raised £14,000 for extensions and renovations to St Ninian's Cathedral; and he fostered interest in home and foreign missions. As primus this concern became focused especially on South Africa, which he again visited. Instrumental in establishing the Episcopal church's Temperance Society, he also took the lead in working towards closer relations between the Episcopal and Presbyterian churches, but was misunderstood because of his refusal to gloss over historic differences between the two bodies. He ministered to Gladstone during the latter's terminal illness in 1898.

Despite his later Anglo-Catholicism, Wilkinson retained a firm belief in the need for personal conversion, which allied him with other Anglo-Catholics such as Richard Meux Benson and Charles Bodington. His Catholic evangelicalism was attested to in his many minor works of practical spirituality, including *Instructions in the Devotional Life* (1871), *Instructions in the Way of Salvation* (1872), and *Lent Lectures* (1873). One of the foremost preachers of his day, Wilkinson had a wide circle of influence which included Lord Balfour of Burleigh, Donald MacLeod, one-time moderator of the Church of Scotland, and Adeline, duchess of Balfour. He died of a heart attack at 13 Queen Street, Edinburgh, on 11 December 1907, and after funeral services at Edinburgh and Perth was buried in Brompton cemetery, London. A. R. BUCKLAND, *rev.* ROWAN STRONG

Sources A. J. Mason, *Memoir of George Howard Wilkinson*, 2 vols. (1909) · G. T. S. Farquhar, *The late bishop of St Andrews* (1908) · J. Storrs, 'In memoriam' George Howard Wilkinson …: substance of a sermon preached at St Peter's, Eaton Square … 1907 [1908] · *Memorials of the Most Rev. George H. Wilkinson D.D.* (1908) · H. S. Holland, *George Howard Wilkinson, bishop of St Andrews* (1908) · C. L. Shadwell, *Registrum Orielense*, 2 (1902) · *CGPLA Eng. & Wales* (1908)
Archives BL, letters to W. E. Gladstone, Add. MSS 44479–44526 · LPL, corresp. with E. W. Benson · LPL, corresp. with A. C. Tait · LPL, corresp. with F. A. White
Likenesses G. Frampton, effigy, c.1905, St Ninian's Cathedral, Perth · W. Dower, photogravure, repro. in Mason, *Memoir of George Howard Wilkinson*, vol. 2, frontispiece, 417 · Lock & Whitfield, photogravure, repro. in Mason, *Memoir of George Howard Wilkinson*, vol. 1, frontispiece · Spy [L. Ward], caricature, watercolour study, NPG; repro. in *VF* (26 Dec 1885) · photograph, NPG · wood-engraving (after photograph by Lock & Whitfield), NPG; repro. in *ILN* (10 Feb 1883)
Wealth at death £25,391 5s. 5d.: probate, 14 Jan 1908, *CGPLA Eng. & Wales*

Wilkinson, Henry (1610–1675), Church of England clergyman and ejected minister, was born on 4 March 1610 at Waddesdon, Buckinghamshire, the son of Henry Wilkinson (1566–1647) and his wife, Sarah, daughter of Arthur Wake of Salcey Forest, Northamptonshire, and sister of the diplomat Sir Isaac *Wake. The elder Henry Wilkinson, born in Halifax, matriculated in 1582 at Queen's College, Oxford, graduated BA in 1585, was elected fellow of Merton College, Oxford, in 1586, and proceeded MA in 1590 and BD in 1597. From 1601 until his death on 19 March 1647 he was rector of Waddesdon. He published *A Catechism* (which went through four editions between 1623 and 1637) and *The Debt Book* (1625) and was a member of the Westminster assembly from 1643. The younger Henry Wilkinson was one of a family of six sons and three daughters. He matriculated from Magdalen Hall, Oxford, aged twelve, on 14 February 1623, graduating BA on 25 November 1626, and proceeding MA on 11 June 1629 and BD on 16 November 1638.

Wilkinson preached in and about Oxford, but, because of his outspoken puritanism, at first the bishop of Oxford refused to ordain him. In his *Sermon Against Lukewarmness in Religion*, preached at St Mary's on 6 September 1640, Wilkinson challenged hearers to be zealous in their faith, condemned superficial and formalistic worship, and proclaimed the Scots' taking of Newcastle to be God's judgment upon England's empty religiosity. For this he was suspended from his divinity lectureship at Magdalen Hall and all priestly functions in the university until he should recant. He appealed to the Long Parliament, which restored him on 23 December 1640 and ordered the sermon to be printed. Wilkinson moved to London, was appointed minister of St Faith's under St Paul's in August 1644, chosen as a member of the Westminster assembly, and on 29 August 1645 became rector of St Dunstan-in-the-West. On three occasions he preached official sermons before parliament and had them published. There was a touch of irony in his last one: *Miranda stupenda* was delivered on 6 July 1646 in thanksgiving for the fall of Oxford to the army.

In 1646 parliament dispatched Wilkinson to Oxford, where he was chosen senior fellow of Magdalen and deputed a parliamentary visitor. The next year he signed 'A testimony to … the solemn league and covenant'. On Dr Thomas Iles's expulsion, parliament appointed him, on 1 March 1648, canon of Christ Church, Oxford, where he was installed on 12 April. When the medieval stained glass was taken out of the cathedral windows, Anthony Wood records, Wilkinson 'stampt upon many parts of [it] and utterly defaced them' (*Calamy rev.*, 530). Wilkinson was created DD on 24 July 1649 and elected Lady Margaret professor of divinity in the place of his fellow visitor, Francis Cheynell, on 12 July 1652. In 1654 he was an assistant to the commission for ejecting scandalous ministers in Oxfordshire. By then he had married Lady Vere Ker (or Carr), daughter of Robert *Ker, first earl of Ancram, and his second wife, Anne, daughter of William Stanley, sixth earl of Derby. They had four children. He was known at Oxford as Long Harry or Senior to distinguish him from Henry Wilkinson (1616/17–1690), the principal of Magdalen Hall.

At the Restoration, though his predecessor was dead, Wilkinson's petition for royal confirmation of his prebendary failed. After ejection as canon in favour of Jasper Mayne (27 July 1660) and as professor in favour of Thomas Barlow (1 September), Wilkinson preached at All Hallows, Lombard Street, London, then at Clapham, Surrey, where he occupied a large house of fourteen hearths. A conventicle of sixty or more persons to whom he was preaching was broken up at Camberwell in August 1665, and some of his congregation were arrested. On 2 April 1675 Wilkinson took out a licence under Charles II's declaration of indulgence for either his house or the schoolhouse at Clapham to be used as a presbyterian meeting-house.

Wilkinson was a renowned preacher; three of his sermons were published after he delivered them at Cripplegate and Southwark in Samuel Annesley's popular *Morning Exercises* (1661 and 1674). When he died on 5 June 1675, either at Deptford or Putney, hundreds of people attended his funeral at Drapers' Hall and his burial in St Dunstan-in-the-West Church. Wilkinson was survived by his wife, one son, Robert, and two daughters, Ann and Elizabeth. His will, made at Clapham on 2 April 1675 and proved on 1 July, showed that he still owned a leasehold in Oxford and was able to leave £600 to each of his daughters. He should not be confused with the Roman Catholic apologist Henry Wilkinson of the same period who published *Meditation upon the Marks of the True Christ* (1655). JIM SPIVEY

Sources *The nonconformist's memorial … originally written by … Edmund Calamy*, ed. S. Palmer, 1 (1775) · *Calamy rev.* · Wood, *Ath. Oxon.*, new edn, vol. 3 · Wood, *Ath. Oxon.: Fasti*, new edn · Foster, *Alum. Oxon.* · *The life and times of Anthony Wood*, ed. A. Clark, 1, OHS,

19 (1891); 2, OHS, 21 (1892); 4, OHS, 30 (1895) · W. Kennett, *A register and chronicle ecclesiastical and civil* (1728) · *DNB* · R. Jeffs, ed., *Fast sermons to parliament … 1640/1–1653*, 34 vols. (1970–71), notes in vols. 8, 14, and 24 · H. Wilkinson, *A sermon against lukewarmness in religion* (1641), preface · J. Nichols, ed., *The morning exercises at Cripplegate, St Giles in the Fields and in Southwark*, 5th edn, 1 (1844) · *Walker rev.* · CSP dom., 1671–2 · *Scots peerage*, 5.468

Archives Hertford College, Oxford, theological notes and sermons

Wealth at death leasehold in Oxford; £600 to each of two daughters

Wilkinson, Henry (1616/17–1690), college head and ejected minister, was the son of William Wilkinson, curate or chaplain of Adwick-le-Street, Yorkshire, where he was born. John Wilkinson (*d.* 1650), principal of Magdalen Hall and president of Magdalen College, Oxford, was his uncle. After studying under John Langly in Gloucester and Edward Sylvester in Oxford, Henry matriculated at Magdalen Hall on 10 October 1634 aged seventeen. His tutor was Dr Henry Wilkinson, later canon of Christ Church, Oxford. He graduated BA on 28 November 1635, proceeded MA on 26 May 1638, and became tutor and dean of his college.

When the civil war started Wilkinson left Oxford, joined the Westminster assembly, and became a popular preacher. He became lecturer or minister of Buckminster, Leicestershire, in 1642; lecturer at Carfax church, Oxford, on 10 October 1642 (albeit that he was hardly in a position to exercise while the town was the royalist headquarters); and vicar of Epping, Essex, on 30 October 1643, upon the sequestration of Martin Holbeach. He was appointed a parliamentary visitor of Oxford University on 1 May 1647. Created BD on 14 April 1648 he became fellow and vice-president of Magdalen College on 25 May, principal of Magdalen Hall on 12 August, and Whyte's professor of moral philosophy on 24 March 1649. He was known as Dean Harry, to distinguish him from his former tutor. A strong parliamentarian, Wilkinson signed the Essex 'Testimony … to the solemn league and covenant' (1648) and entertained Oliver Cromwell and his commanders at Magdalen Hall on 19 May 1649. Preaching before them next day he 'prayed hard for the army' (Bloxam, 2.cviii).

In 1652 Wilkinson was created DD and was elected prebendary of Worcester Cathedral, though he was never installed. Wilkinson's wife, Elizabeth (1612/13–1654) [*see* Wilkinson, Elizabeth], the daughter of Anthony Gifford of Devon, died on 8 December 1654, and on 4 September 1655 he married Anne Benson (*d.* 1698) of Hackney, Middlesex. On 27 May 1658 the council of state voted him a salary of £60 for his Carfax lectureship. Reputed for his scholarship he catalogued the Magdalen Hall Library (published in 1661), published six Latin sermons and treatises between 1654 and 1660, and regularly preached in the university church. He fervently pleaded presbyterian reform against all 'prophane' influences: rising Socinianism; Antinomian 'spirits' and unordained sectarians who were 'self-conceited Seducers'; and Arminians, who were a blend of Jesuits and superficial protestants. Wilkinson was fearless. In 1660 he offended returning episcopal powers with his *Three Decads of Sermons* urging readers not to 'hanker after superstitious Ceremonies, a formal Service Book, [or] a Lordly Prelacy'.

After the Restoration Wilkinson's petition to remain in place was successful (29 March 1661), but in September the chancellor of the university, the earl of Clarendon, chided Wilkinson for the nonconformity of Magdalen, complaining that it contained only 'factious and debauched persons'. Wilkinson was ejected from his livings by the Act of Uniformity in August 1662, though some university officials desired to retain him because he was a good disciplinarian. He preached at Buckminster, Leicestershire, until he was gaoled on erroneous charges of complicity in the Farnley Wood plot. Upon release, in September 1665, he settled at Gosfield, Essex, when, between the tenures of Thomas Wardener and Henry Elliot (1669–72), apparently he officiated at the parish church. An entry in the visitation book of the archdeaconry for 9 June 1671 notes his citation for reading divine service not according to the rubric. On 19 July he was pronounced contumacious and was excommunicated.

After Charles II's declaration of indulgence he got licences, dated 16 May 1672, for himself as a presbyterian teacher at Gosfield and for his house as a presbyterian meeting-house. When these were revoked he wrote to Anthony Wood in Oxford, in July 1672, seeking employment as a Latin translator to eke out a living. In 1673 or 1674 he moved to Sible Hedingham, Essex, where his library was distrained on his refusing to pay the fine for unlawful preaching. Afterwards he occasionally relied on charity from patrons such as Mary Rich, countess of Warwick, to sustain him. His last years were in Suffolk: at Great Cornard near Sudbury (1680), and at Castle Honingham (1690). He died on 13 May 1690 and was buried on the 15th at Milding, near Lavenham. His widow, Anne, moved to Dedham, Essex, where she lived with her daughter, Martha, the wife of the vicar, William *Burkitt, until her death in November 1698. JIM SPIVEY

Sources *The nonconformist's memorial … originally written by … Edmund Calamy*, ed. S. Palmer, 1 (1775) · *Calamy rev.* · Wood, *Ath. Oxon.*, new edn, vol. 4 · Wood, *Ath. Oxon.: Fasti*, new edn · Foster, *Alum. Oxon., 1500–1714*, vol. 4 · *The life and times of Anthony Wood*, ed. A. Clark, 5 vols., OHS, 19, 21, 26, 30, 40 (1891–1900), vols. 1–2, 4 · J. R. Bloxam, *A register of the presidents, fellows … of Saint Mary Magdalen College*, 8 vols. (1853–85) · *DNB* · H. Wilkinson, *Three decads of sermons* (1660), preface · E. Staunton, *A sermon preacht at Great Milton, at the funerall of … E. Wilkinson* (1659) · W. Kennett, *A register and chronicle ecclesiastical and civil* (1728) · T. W. Davids, *Annals of evangelical nonconformity in Essex* (1863) · *CSP dom.*, 1660–61

Archives Bodl. Oxf., commonplace book · Bodl. Oxf., notes on Merton College | Bodl. Oxf., letters to Anthony Wood

Wilkinson, Isaac (*bap.* **1695**, *d.* **1784**), iron-founder, was baptized on 6 May 1695 at Washington, co. Durham, the son of John Wilkinson and his wife, Margaret Thompson. He was the fifth child, his mother dying after his birth. His father having died by 1704, Isaac was brought up by his elder brother John, a wool merchant. His education is unknown; he had a rough literacy and could keep accounts, sometimes creatively. He was apprenticed to the iron trade, probably at the Swalwell works near his home. About 1721–3 he moved to Little Clifton furnace near Workington, where he stayed until 1735. On 9 November 1727, described as iron-founder, he married Mary (*d.* 1786), daughter of Henry and Margaret Johnson of Briggham, Cumberland. She was a dissenter, and Wilkinson is henceforward referred to as a Presbyterian. Their seven children included the ironmasters John *Wilkinson and William *Wilkinson.

A highly skilled iron-founder, Wilkinson commanded high wages before going to Clifton. The furnace there had converted to smelting with coal and charcoal; and Wilkinson cast on contract. In 1735 he moved to Backbarrow furnace, again smelting with coke as a specialist founder. As well as casting on contract, he bought iron from the firm, casting for sale on his own account. In 1738 he obtained a patent, partly for cast box smoothing-irons, though he must have known that Baddeley of Birmingham had a similar 1722 patent, which had lately expired. Isaac, with his brother John as partner, subsequently bought a mill for finishing the irons. However, he cheated his brother over the profits due to him, and their partnership in consequence ended. He had additional works, possibly a furnace, at Wilson House, Cartmel, where he may have lived.

In 1747, with the Rowlinson family and others, Wilkinson set up the Lowwood iron company on a site very close to Backbarrow. In the course of the following year he ceased to cast for the Backbarrow Company. In 1749 he withdrew from the Lowwood Company too, but bought iron for casting from them. He went to law with the Lowwood Company and others over his box iron patent and their enticement of his workers, when it became clear his patent was not original. In 1753 Isaac Wilkinson left Lancashire and took over a furnace at Bersham, near Wrexham, Denbighshire, earlier used for both charcoal and coke smelting. His elder son John became superintendent of the coke-iron furnace; and Isaac's partners were his brother-in-law William Johnson, the Liverpool merchant Samuel Green, and the Shrewsbury capitalist Edward Blakeway. Railed ways, air furnaces, and mills for working iron were built, while a nearby furnace at Ruabon was bought. As well as overseeing these developments, Isaac continued to charge separate fees for casting.

In 1757 Wilkinson took out a patent for a cylinder-blowing engine. Its development is obscure, but originally the blast was to be produced by water columns, recalling the French *trempe* system. The blast could supposedly be provided by pipes at some distance from the power source. Tried at Bersham, New Willey, Shropshire (where his son John was a partner), and at the furnaces Isaac later used in south Wales, it does not appear to have been effective. Yet Charles Wood, the manager of the Cyfarthfa ironworks, saw Wilkinson's cylinders in action at neighbouring Dowlais in 1766 and was impressed: 'they are by much preferable to any Leathern Bellows, & require much less water in proportion to their Blast' (Charles Wood's journal, 22 May 1766). John Wilkinson had ironed out the problems by the mid-1770s, however, when he was successfully using steam-powered and cylinder-blown blast in his furnaces. Isaac Wilkinson's Bersham partner Blakeway went bankrupt in 1759, and the latter's shares passed to his sister-in-law Mary Lee. She became the main shareholder in 1762, and married Wilkinson's son John in 1763, giving him control at Bersham. The works there subsequently acquired an international reputation for quality castings, especially for steam engine cylinders and solid-bored cannon. In 1758 Isaac took out a patent for dry sand moulding in a flask or box, which seems to have had real originality.

As early as 1762 Wilkinson sued his partners, including his son John, over his remuneration for casting. When the partnership broke up in the post-war depression Isaac sued the others over the finances. He then moved to Bristol, and Bersham was put up for sale. However, John Wilkinson emerged as effective owner in 1766. Isaac was awarded over £1000 and costs, but after renewed litigation settlement was reached in 1767. At the same time John Wilkinson agreed payments to his father for his casting and blowing patents, though Isaac remained in legal dispute with another partner.

Isaac Wilkinson was subsequently an iron-founder at Bristol, but had brief but interesting involvements with the Dowlais and Plymouth ironworks in south Wales. He also introduced the Guest family to the south Wales industry. Local master colliers supplied him with coal for his furnace at Cyfarthfa, but this led to further lawsuits, which showed Wilkinson in financial difficulties. In the 1770s he sued the Bersham and New Willey companies, both now run by his son John, over patent fees; and as late as 1779 he was again at law about a bad investment in a Gloucestershire furnace. He died in London on 31 January 1784, but was probably buried at Bristol.

Isaac Wilkinson's career was long, complex, and often fraught. A great craftsman, his business sense often did not equal his technical skill, and he was invariably involved in disputes that led to litigation. His headstrong nature was inherited by his more famous sons, John and William. Wilkinson had some genuine inventive talent; and the frequency with which he was admitted to new coke-smelting partnerships in the 1750s, 1760s, and 1770s, though he had very little in the way of money to contribute, suggests that his new blowing technology, to which his partners gained privileged access, was seen as having value. J. R. HARRIS

Sources W. H. Chaloner, 'Isaac Wilkinson, potfounder', *Studies in the industrial revolution presented to T. S. Ashton*, ed. L. S. Presnell (1960) · W. H. Chaloner, 'John Wilkinson, ironmaster (1728–1808)', in W. H. Chaloner, *People and industries* (1963) · A. S. Davies, 'Isaac Wilkinson (c.1705–1784) of Bersham, ironmaster and inventor', *Transactions* [Newcomen Society], 27 (1949–51), 69–72 · A. Birch, *The economic history of the British iron and steel industry, 1784–1879* (1967) · J. V. Beckett, *Coal and tobacco: the Lowthers and the economic development of west Cumberland, 1660–1760* (1981) · Ironbridge Gorge Museum Library, Coalbrookdale, Shropshire, Janet Butler MSS · Journal of Charles Wood, 22 May 1766, Glamorgan Archive Service · C. Evans, 'Failure in a new technology: smelting iron with coke in south Gloucestershire in the 1770s', *Transactions of the Bristol and Gloucestershire Archaeological Society*, 109 (1991), 199–206
Archives Ironbridge Gorge Museum Library, Coalbrookdale, Shropshire, Janet Butler MSS · Lancs. RO, Backbarrow MSS, DDMC

Likenesses double portrait (with John Wilkinson), priv. coll.; repro. in Chaloner, 'Isaac Wilkinson, potfounder', facing p. 28

Wilkinson, James Hardy (1919–1986), mathematician, was born on 27 September 1919 in Strood, Kent, the third child in the family of two sons and three daughters of James William Wilkinson, dairyman, and his wife, Kathleen Charlotte Hardy. The family, impoverished when their dairy business failed in the 1930s, was close and happy. As a boy Wilkinson's exceptional qualities secured him a foundation scholarship to Sir Joseph Williamson's Mathematical School in Rochester before he was eleven. He won a major scholarship to Trinity College, Cambridge, which he entered just after his seventeenth birthday in 1936. He won college prizes in 1937 and 1939 for being the most distinguished student of his year in any subject, became a wrangler in part two of the mathematics tripos in 1938, and took his part three in 1939.

After the Second World War broke out in 1939 Wilkinson, together with other leading young mathematicians, was drafted into the Ministry of Supply. After working mainly on pedestrian calculations he sought a more demanding mathematical environment as soon as the war ended. In May 1946 he joined the mathematics division of the National Physical Laboratory (NPL), where E. T. Goodwin led a desk machine computing section, and where A. M. Turing was busy designing the automatic computing engine (ACE). After a brief spell of desk machine work Wilkinson devoted himself to Turing's machine. The ACE project was hampered by erratic leadership from Turing and misdirection from above. But after Turing's departure in 1948 and the establishment of a new NPL regime, Wilkinson took a leading role in the development of a modified machine, known as Pilot ACE; this proved highly successful from its inception in May 1950. In that year Wilkinson was promoted to principal scientific officer and by 1974 he had become chief scientific officer.

The results that Wilkinson obtained from programs run on the Pilot ACE and later machines spurred him to develop new analytical and numerical techniques. In succeeding years he described the fruits of his research in publications which came to form the very foundation of numerical linear algebra. He wrote more than 100 papers and was the author of *Rounding Errors in Algebraic Processes* (1963) and the monumental *The Algebraic Eigenvalue Problem* (1965). In 1960 George Forsythe of Stanford, one of the most eminent numerical analysts of his generation, wrote: 'In my opinion Wilkinson is single-handedly responsible for the creation of almost all of the current body of scientific knowledge about the computer solution of the problems of linear algebra.' This judgement was made when Wilkinson's most productive period still lay in the future. He spent his working life at NPL, but also made many visits to the USA. In particular he was an annual consultant to the Argonne National Laboratory for some twenty years, a visiting professor at Ann Arbor, Michigan (1957–73), and a professor at Stanford (1977–84). His lectures were legendary; his meticulous clarity owed much to painstaking preparation concealed by a highly individual, informal delivery.

Wilkinson obtained an ScD from Cambridge in 1962. He was elected FRS in 1969, and in the following year became the first person ever to receive both the A. M. Turing award of the Association for Computing Machinery and the J. von Neumann award of the Society for Industrial and Applied Mathematics in the same year. In the next fifteen years honours and distinctions (including honorary doctorates from Brunel, 1971, Heriot-Watt, 1973, Waterloo, 1978, and Essex, 1979) came regularly. Posthumous honours included the establishment of the J. H. Wilkinson fellowship at Argonne, and also the triennial Wilkinson prize sponsored jointly by NPL, the Numerical Algorithms Group, and Argonne.

Wilkinson was a jovial, round-faced, ruddy-complexioned man, once described as having 'all the aspects of a sailor on shore leave and ready to do the town'. He certainly had a great capacity for enjoying himself, and his ready wit enlivened any gathering. He appeared to be interested in everything and everybody; boredom was impossible in his company. Of his specific interests, perhaps the greatest outside mathematics was music, of which his knowledge was wide and profound. He was also very knowledgeable about the wines with which he entertained his friends and which he consumed with such pleasure. Very many people felt that they knew Wilkinson, though in fact few knew him well; beneath the jocularity he was a very private individual.

In 1945 Wilkinson married Heather Nora, daughter of William Henry Ware, buyer for a drapery warehouse. They had a daughter, who died in 1978, and a son. Wilkinson died at his home, 40 Atbara Road, Teddington, Middlesex, on 5 October 1986, from a heart attack.

CHARLES CLENSHAW, rev.

Sources L. Fox, *Memoirs FRS*, 33 (1987), 671–708 · personal knowledge (1996) · *CGPLA Eng. & Wales* (1987)
Likenesses photograph, repro. in *Memoirs FRS*, 33 (1987), 670
Wealth at death £149,365: probate, 1987, *CGPLA Eng. & Wales*

Wilkinson, James John (bap. **1780**, d. **1858**). *See under* Wilkinson, (James John) Garth (1812–1899).

Wilkinson, Jeannette Gaury (1841–1886), trade unionist and suffragist, was born on 19 March 1841 at 40 Long Lane, Bermondsey, London, the daughter of George Henry Wilkinson, a foreman clerk in a large merchant's warehouse, and his wife Jane (*née* Lane). She had several brothers, one of whom was blind. Jeannette Wilkinson was educated at a private school in Queen Street, City of London, and from the age of seventeen earned her own living as an upholsteress.

Jeannette Wilkinson was determined to improve her education and attended evening classes at the Birkbeck Institute where she studied economics, history, and English literature. It was here that she became close friends with one of the tutors, J. H. Levy, who recalled that she was hampered in her scholastic achievements by poor handwriting which resulted from years of heavy upholstery work, in particular carpet sewing. He 'could not but

admire the patience with which she fought against the stiffness her former occupation had induced in the joints of her fingers' (*Women's Union Journal*, 83). Levy helped her to improve her handwriting and a string of prizes followed, including first prize of the Society of Arts for political economy in 1873.

In 1875 Jeannette Wilkinson became involved in the women's trade union movement. She was elected as secretary of the London Upholsteresses' Society which was affiliated to the Women's Protective and Provident League, an organization formed by Emma Paterson in 1874 to promote female trade unionism. Jeannette Wilkinson attended the Trades Union Congress nine times as a delegate from the society. Her speeches demonstrated a detailed, first-hand knowledge of women's work conditions and were well received, although her opposition to protective legislation for women, a view shared by other feminists within the league, was not acceptable to the majority of male delegates.

Jeannette Wilkinson had always been determined to be a schoolteacher. After passing the queen's scholar examination of the education department at Birkbeck she was helped by Helen Taylor, a member of the London school board, to gain a position as an assistant mistress. In 1876 she became a certificated teacher and a year later obtained employment in the Westcott Street board school at Southwark. Two years of teaching in a very poor neighbourhood, however, took its toll of Jeannette Wilkinson's health and she left Westcott Street to take up other teaching posts. These were only short-lived and by 1882 she was thinking of returning to her old trade when J. H. Levy found her a position as a clerk with the Vigilance Association for the Defence of Personal Rights. A secularist in religion and a radical individualist in politics, Jeannette Wilkinson agreed with the aims of the association, but in Levy's opinion she was not a very good clerk.

It was fortunate, therefore, that an opportunity soon arose for Jeannette Wilkinson to take up employment with the women's suffrage movement. She had long taken an interest in women's emancipation and the claim for the vote. In 1884 she was asked to support a resolution in favour of women's suffrage at a meeting at St James's Hall. She was an impressive speaker, 'saying what she wanted to say in short, pithy sentences, and never lulling her audience to sleep with musical platitudes. Every sentence was needed in the chain of logical argument' (Orme, 389–90). On the strength of her speaking skills Jeannette Wilkinson was asked to become an organizing secretary and lecturer for the Bristol Society for Women's Suffrage where she worked closely with the secretary, Helen Blackburn. Early in 1885 she was transferred to London and helped to organize meetings in the area for the National Society for Women's Suffrage. In the same year she moved an amendment at the Trades Union Congress which called for the direct representation of women in parliament. Despite bitter opposition from a small group of delegates the amendment was supported by a majority of seventy to ten.

Jeannette Wilkinson firmly believed that women

should have opinions on all the political questions of the day and her support for home rule for Ireland led her to join her local Liberal Association in 1885. She was elected to the executive council and during the general election campaign addressed numerous meetings in favour of Liberal candidates. During this period she continued to be active in the trade union movement, attending meetings of the Women's Trade Council, the Upholsteresses' Society, and the committee of the Women's Protective and Provident League. She also found time to write letters and short pieces for the *Women's Union Journal* and to complete an article for the *Charity Organisation Review* entitled 'The inspection of workshops in London'.

Jeannette Wilkinson was one of a small minority of working-class women who became active as organizers and speakers in the trade union movement in the 1870s and 1880s and who also held strong feminist beliefs. As Helen Blackburn noted:

> instances of working men who have forged their way, through hard study, high up the ladder of achievement are frequent … but the instances in which women have done so are comparatively rare. Jeannette Gaury Wilkinson was one of these … Truly of her it might be said, 'She loved her fellow-*women*'. (Blackburn, 166)

Jeannette Wilkinson was always earnest in promoting reforms, but was judicious in her treatment of opponents who, even when they disagreed with her views, appreciated the accuracy of her statements and her open-mindedness.

> Her manner was pleasant and cheery at all times. Her small body never seemed strong enough for the tasks she set it to do, but the bright eye and determined mouth showed where the strength came from to supply physical deficiencies. (Orme, 389)

Ill health cut short Jeannette Wilkinson's political and trade union activities. She died after a severe attack of asthmatic bronchitis on 22 August 1886 at 115 Westmoreland Road, Walworth, London, the home she shared with her brother and his wife. She was buried in Forest Hill cemetery, London, on 27 August. A memorial fund was established by members of the women's suffrage movement to pay for a marble slab to mark her grave and to provide assistance for the education of a niece.

JUNE HANNAM

Sources E. Orme, 'Jeannette Wilkinson', *Englishwoman's Review*, 17 (1886), 385–91 · 'Our loss', *Women's Union Journal* (Sept 1886) · J. H. Levy, 'Jeannette G. Wilkinson', *Women's Union Journal* (Sept 1886) · H. Blackburn, *Women's suffrage: a record of the women's suffrage movement in the British Isles* (1902) · b. cert. · d. cert.

Wilkinson [*née* North], **Joan** (*d.* 1556), religious radical, was the daughter of Roger North (*d.* 1509) and his wife, Christian. Roger was a citizen of London; Christian was the daughter of Richard Warcup of Sinnington, Yorkshire, and widow of Ralph Warren. Joan Wilkinson was married to an alderman of the city of London, but nothing further is known about either him or their marriage, except that they had three daughters: Christian and Frances, who predeceased their mother, and Jane, who was unmarried at the time of Joan's death and served as executor of her will. Mrs Wilkinson's brother, Edward *North, first Baron

North, however, may have benefited from his sister's marriage and Alderman Wilkinson's connections in the city of London. (Lord North apparently did not share his sister's faith, since he was a member of the commission for the suppression of heresy in 1557.) Mrs Wilkinson was a silkwoman in Anne Boleyn's household between 1533 and 1535, and in that capacity she would have been exposed to the evangelical beliefs espoused by Anne and her chaplains. The source of Joan Wilkinson's education is not known, but clearly she could read and write. The queen kept a large Bible open and available for her servants to read, and she also sponsored numerous trips to the continent (including a number by her chaplains) to buy evangelical texts that were banned in England. In 1535, after Anne had been imprisoned, her chaplain William Latymer was returning with one such shipment when he was apprehended at Sandwich. Although he was detained, he was allowed to send his books on to London for the attention of none other than Joan Wilkinson.

Mrs Wilkinson held property at King's Stanley in Gloucestershire, as well as a residence in Soper Lane in London, and she was probably living in Gloucestershire by 1551, when John Hooper, a radical protestant, became bishop there. She had clearly developed a friendship with Hooper by the end of Edward's reign. Following Mary's accession as queen in 1553 and the subsequent restoration of Catholicism, Joan Wilkinson took on a new and important role: that of nurse or caregiver for the protestant divines imprisoned and eventually martyred for their beliefs, including Bishop Hooper. She was one of a number of gentlewomen, including her cousin Anne Warcup, who continued to work for the new religion in this way, even in the face of the threat of personal danger. Those who benefited from her largesse included John Hooper, John Bradford, Nicholas Ridley, Hugh Latimer, and Thomas Cranmer. She interceded on their behalf to obtain more healthy accommodation when they became ill, and provided them with food and clothing. Bishop Latimer probably gave voice to a common sentiment held by all when he wrote to her to thank her, exclaiming, 'If the gift of a pot of water shall not be in oblivion with God, how can God forget your manifold and bountiful gifts when he shall say unto you, "I was in prison, and you visited me"?' (*Sermons*, 444). In addition to letters of gratitude such as Latimer's, Mrs Wilkinson, along with the other female caregivers, received written sermons in the form of letters from the future martyrs: long meditations and exhortations based on scripture. These were clearly intended for dissemination among the followers of protestantism who were still in England, thus providing a means whereby the protestant divines' voices could continue to be heard by the followers of the new religion, albeit in written form.

In addition to writing letters to spread the protestant message and to thank Mrs Wilkinson, the divines also gave her advice on what to do after they were gone. John Bradford thought that she should step forward and offer herself as a martyr, but he was alone in this. The others urged her to flee before it was too late, to preserve her life so that she could continue to promote protestantism. Archbishop Cranmer exhorted her to withdraw:

> from the malice of your and God's enemies, into some place where God is most truly served: which is no slandering of the truth, but a preserving of yourself to God and the truth, and to the society and comfort of Christ's little flock.
> (*Miscellaneous Writings*, 445)

This she did, seeking shelter among the English exiles in Frankfurt am Main. There she continued her active support of protestantism, support that became particularly significant after her death in 1556. In her will, which opens with the declaration that she was 'in voluntarie exile for the true religion of Cryst', she left money for the 'vertuos education' of Hooper's son Daniel. She then went on to leave 'all those my bokes which Mr Hooper hadde the use of during his lif' to the various English protestant congregations in exile on the continent, and left £100 to the poor of those congregations. She also tried to ensure that her daughter Jane persevered in her evangelical faith, providing that she would lose a substantial proportion of her inheritance if she made an inappropriate marriage. (PRO, PROB 11/42B, fols. 233–5). Joan Wilkinson died in Frankfurt, but her will was subsequently proved in the prerogative court of Canterbury, on 23 June 1559. Her place of burial is unknown.

CAROLINE LITZENBERGER

Sources *The writings of John Bradford*, ed. A. Townsend, 1 vol. in 2 pts, Parker Society, 31 (1848–53) • *Miscellaneous writings and letters of Thomas Cranmer*, ed. J. E. Cox, Parker Society, [18] (1846) • M. Dowling, 'Anne Boleyn and reform', *Journal of Ecclesiastical History*, 35 (1984), 30–46 • 'William Latymer's chronicklle of Anne Bulleyne', ed. M. Dowling, *Camden miscellany, XXX*, CS, 4th ser., 39 (1990) • *Later writings of Bishop Hooper*, ed. C. Nevinson, Parker Society, 16 (1852) • *Sermons and remains of Hugh Latimer*, ed. G. E. Corrie, Parker Society, 20 (1845) • *LP Henry VIII* • PRO, PROB 11/42B, fols. 233–5 • *The works of Nicholas Ridley*, ed. H. Christmas, Parker Society, 1 (1841) • S. Brigden, *London and the Reformation* (1989) • 'North, Edward', *DNB*

Wealth at death bequests of over £120; manor in Kings Stanley, Gloucestershire, and property in two other parishes in Gloucestershire: will, PRO, PROB 11/42B, fols. 233–5

Wilkinson, John (*fl.* 1652–1683), Quaker schismatic, was from Millholme, New Hutton, Westmorland. Little else is known of his background, except that he was a husbandman and was convinced by George Fox in 1652 near Sedbergh. As one of the early Quakers, he travelled with John *Story of Preston Patrick from about 1654 to spread the Quaker message in the south and west of England, and the two were 'Instrumentall to Convince many in sevrall parts' and were 'greatly beloved of the Brethren', while in 'unity with the ffriends' (Penney, 267). In July 1654 he and Story wrote to George Fox from Cinderhill Green on the Yorkshire–Derbyshire border, relating details of their meetings in Derbyshire and Nottinghamshire. They may have passed into Cumberland and Durham as an undated letter expresses their wish to visit these areas. In 1655 both were in Wiltshire, the centre of their early work, where they convinced several Baptists. Wilkinson wrote to fellow Quakers Edward Burrough and Francis Howgill,

reporting that, 'Many falls from them; they have no courage left' (Braithwaite, *Beginnings*, 387). In the same year both Wilkinson and Story were imprisoned in Gloucester gaol and at some point in the 1650s they spent time in Bristol. A letter of 1655 suggests that Wilkinson was married, evidence reinforced by the Quaker digest registers which record the birth of Sarah Wilkinson on 30 January 1661 whose father was named as John Wilkinson of Millhome and member of Kendal monthly meeting. In 1662 Wilkinson and a fellow Quaker, John Audland, were arrested in Westmorland for refusing the oath of allegiance. During his imprisonment, Wilkinson wrote a short piece on persecution entitled 'Some queries to any that profess themselves Christians' which was included in Audland's *The Suffering Condition of the Servants of the Lord* (1662). It is likely that he was the John Wilkinson who visited Ireland in 1669 along with William Penn, Solomon Eccles, and John Banks.

About the end of 1672, Wilkinson rejoined Story, who was leading a group of dissatisfied Preston Patrick Friends in opposition to the movement's stance of meeting openly in defiance of the second Conventicles Act of 1670. The breakaway group was also opposed to Fox's establishment of women's meetings and other Quaker practices such as the recording of papers of condemnation against errant Quakers, and the insistence that the tithe testimony should be upheld even if individual Friends did not feel moved to do so. It would appear that Wilkinson was initially reluctant to break with mainstream Friends as in October 1671 he had approved of the establishment of a women's meeting at Kendal 'for unity's-sake' (Wilkinson, 38), and the following year he had specifically criticized Preston Patrick Friends for neglecting meetings. Quaker records state that he 'at first seemed tendrly to accord with ffaithfull ffriends in Incorageing faithfull womens Meetings' and 'allso in ffriends Care and Inspection' and 'that all their Xtian [Christian] testemonys might be ffaithfully kept up' but eventually 'quickly Joyned' with Story after the latter returned from a visit in the south (Penney, 267). Even so, Wilkinson has been judged as playing a smaller role than Story in the events that followed and what was to become known as the Wilkinson–Story separation.

In January 1675 Wilkinson and Story met George Fox at Worcester Castle to discuss the divisions, but soon after they openly separated from the movement. A paper condemning them was issued by the 1675 yearly meeting, and they refused to attend two further meetings which had invited them to Westmorland Friends. While in Bristol with William Rogers, who later wrote *The Christian Quaker* (1680) in their defence, Wilkinson and Story were asked to attend a meeting at Draw-well in April 1676 with leading Quakers at which Wilkinson and Story maintained their reasons for separation but did admit to wrongdoing in opposing Friends 'in the practice of those things that they testify are commendable in the Church of God' (Braithwaite, *Second Period*, 306). The two then visited Fox at Swarthmoor but their resentment at the way in which mainstream Quakers had misrepresented their actions at

Draw-well prevented a lasting reconciliation. After the 1677 yearly meeting issued another strong condemnation of the Wilkinson–Story separation, the Westmorland quarterly meeting removed meetings for worship from the homes of dissident Friends. A number of Quaker meetings thus became wholly separated and at Hutton, Wilkinson himself was apparently able to carry with him the entire meeting of about six families.

Little has been recorded of Wilkinson in his later years except that he remained loyal to his friend John Story, who died in 1681. He wrote 'A brief relation concerning the life and death of John Story' in *The Memory of that Servant of God, John Story, Revived* (1683), which also contained the testimonies of other sympathetic Friends. In his remaining years Wilkinson appears to have carried on travelling and holding meetings, visiting Reading in 1678 and Bristol about the same time. He seems never to have been reconciled with the rest of the movement: 'he was … laboured with and visited by sevrall Brethern, & sometimes seemed somewt softer, yet did not Joyne againe in unity' (Penney, 268). He is believed to have died and been buried at Kendal a few years after Story's death.

CAROLINE L. LEACHMAN

Sources W. C. Braithwaite, *The beginnings of Quakerism*, ed. H. J. Cadbury, 2nd edn (1955); repr. (1981) · W. C. Braithwaite, *The second period of Quakerism*, ed. H. J. Cadbury, 2nd edn (1961); repr. (1979) · N. Penney, ed., *The first publishers of truth* (1907) · RS Friends, Lond., Swarthmore MS vol. 1.32, 33, 36 (MS vol. 351); vol. 4.63 (MS vol. 355) · J. Besse, *A collection of the sufferings of the people called Quakers*, 1 (1753) · Quaker digest registers, RS Friends, Lond. · 'The judgement of J. W. and J. S. … publicly read in meeting at Drawell', J. Wilkinson, *The memory of that servant of God, John Story, revived* (1683), 37–9 · R. L. Greaves, *God's other children: protestant nonconformists and the emergence of denominational churches in Ireland, 1660–1700* (1997)

Archives RS Friends, Lond., Swarthmore MSS 1, 32–36 (MS vol. 351, 32–36) · RS Friends, Lond., Swarthmore MSS 4, 63 (MS vol. 355, 63) · RS Friends, Lond., Port. MS 23, 145 · RS Friends, Lond., Port. MS 41, 88

Wilkinson, John (1728–1808), ironmaster and industrialist, was born in Clifton, Cumberland, the eldest son of Isaac *Wilkinson (*bap.* 1695, *d.* 1784), ironmaster, and his wife, Mary Johnson (*d.* 1786); William *Wilkinson was his brother. In the 1720s Isaac Wilkinson was iron-founder at Clifton furnace; in the 1730s he moved to Backbarrow furnace and later to Lowwood in Furness, north Lancashire. John was sent to the dissenting academy at Kendal, run by Dr Caleb Rotherham. On leaving the academy at the age of seventeen, he was apprenticed to a Liverpool merchant for five years and then returned to enter into partnership with his father. When his father moved to Bersham furnace in north Wales in 1753 John remained behind in the north, living at Kirkby Lonsdale in Westmorland, perhaps to wind up their local business. There, on 12 June 1755, he married Ann Maudesley, the coheir to two manors. In the following year a daughter, Mary, was born at Kirkby Lonsdale. Ann died on 17 November 1756, shortly after the couple moved to Bersham to join Isaac Wilkinson.

Severnside ironworks From 1755 John Wilkinson is named as a partner in the Bersham concern, but he soon operated

John Wilkinson (1728–1808), by Thomas Gainsborough, *c.*1776

partly independently, becoming a managing partner in the New Willey Company of 1757 which took over the early coke-iron furnace at Willey, near Broseley in Shropshire. New furnaces and casting-houses produced a wide range of coke-pig castings, including cannon and shot, pipes, and cylinders; wagon-railways delivered raw materials to the works and carried finished goods to the Severn. While it is difficult to date, it was probably at the end of the 1750s that Wilkinson erected a furnace at Bradley, in Bilston parish, Staffordshire, but this was only of local importance until redeveloped in 1772. New Willey and Bradley were operated as coke furnaces, and Bersham for some time alternated between coke and charcoal iron but turned permanently to coke-pig after a difficult period during which Wilkinson developed his father's patented blowing engine successfully at all three works. He was operating New Willey with blowing-cylinders powered by a Newcomen engine before 1776, at which time a Watt engine was installed. Bersham in particular became an important producer of ordnance, Wilkinson selling through agents until 1770. Bersham and New Willey became producers of quality steam engine cylinders, making a price agreement for their sale with the original producers, the Darbys of Coalbrookdale, in 1762.

A key business change came from the bankruptcy of Edward Blakeway, partner in Bersham, New Willey, and Bradley, entailing the take-over of his shares by his sister-in-law, Mary Lee, who became the main shareholder. She married John Wilkinson in December 1763. In the depression following the end of the Seven Years' War there were disputes at Willey and also at Bersham, from where Isaac Wilkinson left to embark on foundry and furnace projects in Bristol and south Wales; but by 1766 John Wilkinson had emerged in control of both. Bersham became celebrated for high-quality casting and its guns sold well. Wilkinson developed a technique for boring iron guns from the solid, rotating the gun barrel rather than the boring-bar. Patented in 1774, this method produced guns less likely to explode and with a more accurate bore. While bronze cannon were already being bored from the solid, the boring of large naval iron cannon from the solid was a new method. The navy sought to overthrow the patent, though on the grounds that it was against the national interest and created a monopoly rather than on any technical invalidity. It was quashed in 1779, but this did not prevent Wilkinson remaining a major manufacturer of ordnance of high repute.

Making cylinders for Boulton and Watt In 1775 Wilkinson made his first steam engine cylinder for the firm of Boulton and Watt, which proved very satisfactory when other ironmasters had been unable to meet Watt's specifications. He built a Watt engine for his New Willey works, but quickly devised a new lathe, the cylinder lathe, for the more accurate casting of cylinders—an invention of great importance which secured him a virtual monopoly, for Watt would not recommend other cylinder makers to those who wished to install his engines. For many years there were good personal and business relations between Wilkinson and the engine partners. Wilkinson continued to improve the cylinder lathe until 1779; he did not patent it, and it was copied by the Coalbrookdale Company and others. In 1774 Wilkinson had made his younger brother William a partner in Bersham, but during the visit of the Frenchman Marchant de la Houlière to his Broseley works in 1775 he recommended William to him to go to France to set up ordnance works on his own pattern, which William did, at Indret, near Nantes. Subsequently, William was the technological adviser to the scheme to set up great coke-iron furnaces and associated plant at Le Creusot in Burgundy. It is clear that John acted as consultant to his brother in both projects. During the 1780s the works under John Wilkinson's control expanded and became more important. Bersham was less significant in furnace output but became outstanding for high-quality castings, ordnance, and calendered and other engineering goods, while its requirements in pig iron were satisfied from Wilkinson's other furnaces. These included one at Snedshill, Shropshire, in which he became a partner in 1777, and he soon added a second there; both furnaces were cylinder-blown by Boulton and Watt engines, and they were said to be very large for their time.

From 1772 the Bradley works was further extended and additional furnaces and rolling mills built. In the 1780s,

first at Broseley, Wilkinson began to set up forges at his works to employ the Wright and Jesson 'stamping and potting' process for the conversion of coke-pig to wrought iron, thus expanding the market, and in 1782 he set up forges for this process at Bradley, too, his forges being provided with steam-powered hammers worked by Boulton and Watt engines. The association with Boulton and Watt was very close from the late 1770s. It provided the engines for the Paris water company of which J.-C. Perier was the engineer and leading entrepreneur; Wilkinson made the cylinders for the engines and great quantities of iron water pipes. The engine parts were shipped to Paris with the collaboration of both governments, despite France joining in the American War of Independence; and the presence of Wilkinson's water pipes on British wharves gave rise to the belief that he supplied the French with cannon during the war. He was involved with Boulton and Watt, and even more the copper magnate Thomas Williams, in the intense negotiations over the future of the copper industry in the 1780s. At this period the main market for Boulton and Watt engines—Wilkinson supplying the cylinders—was the Cornish copper mines, and they, and Wilkinson, had invested in them. Wilkinson invested £25,000 in the Cornish Metal Company of 1785 and he and Williams were decisive in the trade agreements of that year and their revision in 1787. Wilkinson became a shareholder in two of the subsidiaries of the Anglesey mines managed by Williams, and he was a partner in a Birmingham metal warehouse with him and Boulton and Watt.

New foundries and new techniques The important innovation of the 1780s in the iron industry was Henry Cort's puddling and rolling process for converting coke-pig to wrought iron. It had a period of difficult development under the patronage of Richard Crawshay. Wilkinson did not adapt it at once, though by 1789 he had himself produced improved rolls and dispensed with the old second, or chafery, stage of forging. He was experimenting with puddling itself by 1790. After nearly abandoning the experiment he began to succeed in the same year and was using it extensively by the mid-1790s. Bradley was further extended around 1790 with great use of steam power for furnace-blowing, boring, and turning, and for rolling mills and slitting mills.

In 1792 Wilkinson bought the Brymbo Hall estate in Denbighshire, where furnaces and other plant were installed. This great phase of expansion, well in place for the war demand after 1793, meant that he was producing in 1796 about one-eighth of the nation's iron (15,274 tons). Bersham alone was valued at over £40,000 in 1789. Wilkinson was also important in the lead industry, being a major investor in Minera and other mines in north Wales, and he had several smelters, one of which was at Bersham. He had devised a process for producing lead pipe and had a works and depot for this at Rotherhithe, London.

In the 1790s Wilkinson was involved in two bitter disputes. One was with his brother William, and it related to William's shares in Bersham, which John had offered to let him increase, but only at a new and realistic valuation. William seems to have resented the expansion in other works, especially the nearby Brymbo, in which he did not have an interest, and the terms for renewed investment in Snedshill, in which he did. John may have been resentful at paying William his due share of the profits when he had long taken no part in management but had earned large sums from the French government by an arrangement secured for him by John. William believed that John's accounts for Bersham were drawn up in a way unfavourable to him, and that John had concealed profitable transactions with Thomas Williams and others. The quarrel went to chancery in 1794, and John put Bersham up for sale, which led to an action in king's bench. Eventually John bought out William's share in Bersham fairly cheaply, but arbitrators awarded William over £8000 in dividends owed.

This suit tangled with a more celebrated one, between John Wilkinson and Boulton and Watt, and William moved into the latter's camp, recruiting key Bersham workers for its new engine-building works, Soho Foundry. It also acted as arbitrator in another quarrel between the brothers relating to lead mining in north Wales. Its own quarrel with John Wilkinson arose because he supplied a number of firms with 'pirate' Boulton and Watt engines which he did not declare to the partnership, and the proprietors of these firms did not pay Boulton and Watt engine premiums (a fee for the use of their engines based on the fuel savings of Boulton and Watt engines in comparison with ordinary Newcomen engines). The partners probably knew of the piracies by 1795, but it was only in that year that Boulton was able to discharge a debt of £5000 to Wilkinson. Some of the engines were owned by industrialists with low coal costs, certain to pay low premiums, and to such orders Boulton and Watt was believed to give low priority. Eventually Wilkinson had to compound with them for the payments on nineteen engines he had supplied to others and for some he had built for himself, but it was not until after 1798 that Boulton and Watt was able to dispense with his cylinders. While William and the Boulton and Watt circle tended to report with glee on John's business problems, John himself was building new furnaces in 1803–4, and Bradley was certainly flourishing in the early years of the nineteenth century.

Diversification One of John Wilkinson's last inventions was the cupola furnace; originally thought of as a small smelter, it became popular for remelting pig for casting. He was a great advocate of the increased use of iron as a raw material, and while his more eccentric creations, such as his own coffin and memorial column, are often cited, he was an original subscriber to the world's first iron bridge of 1779—that over the Severn at Ironbridge— though he withdrew in favour of Abraham Darby III, its main advocate and constructor. He had two iron canal barges and a river barge built, the first iron cargo-carriers. Like many contemporary industrialists Wilkinson overcame the shortage of regal coin by issuing his own trade tokens, which were of high quality and displayed his own head and the inscription 'John Wilkinson Ironmaster'. The first, of 1787, was struck by Thomas Williams, and

later issues by Boulton and by Westwood. A silver version of the token was struck in small numbers. Wilkinson invested in two banks; one, a Shrewsbury bank, had been founded in 1792, Wilkinson entering it in 1795 when it was having difficulties. He joined a new Birmingham banking partnership in 1801. At his death he was still an investor in both banks.

Wilkinson was attracted to the profits to be made from canals. He was particularly involved in promoting the Flint Coal Canal, the Shropshire Canal, and the Shrewsbury Canal, and in the Glamorgan Canal primarily promoted by his friend Richard Crawshay. He was a leading shareholder in the less successful Chester and Ellesmere Canal. He was a committed agricultural improver, especially near his principal residences. In the late 1770s he bought Castlehead Hill near Grange over Sands, north Lancashire, building a mansion and improving 1000 acres of nearly worthless mossland surrounding it, typically developing new techniques to drain it so that it could produce crops. He seems to have been more interested in the achievement than in any economic return. At Brymbo he enhanced the value of the infertile land, largely by liming, so that it produced worthwhile yields. He employed a very early steam-powered threshing machine there by 1798. As well as Brymbo Hall and Castlehead, he had The Lawns (a much used house at Broseley), and a house at Bradley.

Personal life and personality While Wilkinson was sometimes referred to by other industrialists making representations to government, particularly on the iron trade, he tended to dislike any interruption to his iron making and generally wanted government to leave industry alone. His political attitudes surfaced rarely. He was very friendly with his brother-in-law, the scientist Joseph Priestley, who had married his sister Mary in 1762. When Priestley moved to take charge of the Unitarian New Meeting in Birmingham in 1780 Wilkinson bought him a house, and for a time he tried to train Priestley's son as a manager in the iron trade. Wilkinson seems to have shared Priestley's early enthusiasm for the French Revolution, and he gave him immediate and continuing financial aid after his house was burnt down in the Birmingham Church and King riots of 1791; he also made large investments in French *assignats*, mainly for Priestley's benefit. His own use of countersigned *assignats* as a form of token payment at Bersham was stopped by parliament in 1793.

Originally a Presbyterian, Wilkinson is thought to have moved to the Unitarianism of Priestley, and his early approval of the French Revolution is even taken as indicating deism or atheism. But while his burial memorial at Castlehead, an abbreviation of his own draft epitaph, dedicates his achievements to the glory of God, the full version also hoped for 'a Heavenly Mansion as promulgated by Jesus Christ, in whose gospel he was a firm believer'—seeming evidence that he was thus neither atheist nor deist. His sexual morals were easy-going. He and his second wife Mary had no children, she being about forty at the time of their marriage; however, he had a series of mistresses, some of whom were his servants. From 1800 he had a regular mistress, Ann Lewis, by whom he had three children when in his seventies. After his wife's death at Castlehead, probably in 1806, he legitimized these children and bequeathed his property in trust to them, but he left Castlehead to Ann. His nephew Thomas Jones, whom he had trained as a manager in the iron industry, was now only residuary legatee when he had expected to be sole heir.

After a short illness Wilkinson died at Bradley on 14 July 1808. He was buried at Castlehead, where an iron obelisk was erected in his memory. His nephew then contested the will in chancery, and with lawsuits continuing to 1823 and reaching the House of Lords at a time of depression and change within the iron industry, the works declined, the property was sold off, and Wilkinson's great industrial empire ingloriously disappeared. The only works that was bought was Brymbo, in 1842 by the railway engineer and investor William Robertson and others. It became once again an important works, and in the 1850s Robertson became a founder partner in Beyer Peacock, the well-known locomotive builders of Manchester. Wilkinson's son John, after attending Cambridge University and undergoing a spell in the army, was said to be profligate and to have emigrated to the United States. His daughters married well; the elder married William Legh, and their son became the first Lord Newton of Lyme.

Wilkinson is said to have been strongly built; he had a long, heavy face badly scarred by smallpox, and a strong deep voice. In the first great period of technology-driven expansion in the British iron industry—even with contemporaries such as Abraham Darby III, Richard Crawshay, Richard Reynolds, and William Reynolds—Wilkinson was the dominant figure, making a great impression on contemporaries at all levels and combining technological leadership and inventiveness with business ability. His confidence in his technical lead meant that his works were normally open to the inspection of foreigners. His imperious, almost despotic, attitude made him disliked by some contemporaries, but his excellent relations with Richard Crawshay, William Reynolds, and Thomas Williams are in contrast; too much weight, not unnaturally, has perhaps been put on the evidence of the Boulton and Watt correspondence. Though at times ruthless, he was generally considerate to good workmen, and alone among contemporary ironmasters he was a folk hero, celebrated in popular song, and the subject of myth, so that thousands are said to have gathered seven years after his death to await his prophesied reappearance. J. R. HARRIS

Sources 'John Wilkinson, ironmaster', W. H. Chaloner, *People and industries* (1963) · W. H. Chaloner, 'The Wilkinsons and the iron trade', *Industry and innovation: selected essays*, ed. D. A. Farnie and W. O. Henderson (1990) · W. H. Chaloner, 'Isaac Wilkinson, potfounder', *Studies in the industrial revolution*, ed. L. S. Pressnell (1960), 23–51 · W. H. Chaloner, 'The hazards of trade with France in time of war, 1776–1783', *Industry and innovation: selected essays*, ed. D. A. Farnie and W. O. Henderson (1990) · H. W. Dickinson, *John Wilkinson, ironmaster* (1914) · A. Birch, *The economic history of the British iron and steel industry, 1784–1879* (1967) · A. H. Dodd, *The industrial revolution in north Wales* (1933) · B. Trinder, *The industrial revolution in Shropshire*, 2nd edn (1981) · J. R. Harris, *The copper king: a biography of Thomas Williams of Llanidan* (1964) · J. D. Marshall, *Furness and the industrial revolution* (1958) · J. Tann, ed., *Selected papers of Boulton and Watt* (1981) · E. Roll, *An early experiment in industrial organisation: being a history of the firm of Boulton & Watt, 1775–1805* (1930); repr. (1968) · *GM*, 1st ser., 78 (1808)
Archives Inst. CE, memoranda | Birm. CA, corresp. with Boulton family · Birm. CA, corresp. of Wilkinson and his brother William with Boulton and Watt · Gwent RO, Cwmbrân, Richard Crawshay letter-book · Ironbridge Gorge Museum Library, Janet Butler MSS · NL Wales, Priestley–Wilkinson MSS
Likenesses double portrait, 1730–39 (with Isaac Wilkinson), Pennybridge Hall, Cumbria · T. Gainsborough, oils, *c.*1776, Gemaldegalerie, Berlin [*see illus.*] · oils, *c.*1790, Ironbridge GMT · oils, *c.*1790, Wolverhampton Art Gallery · after L. F. Abbott, oils, *c.*1795, NPG; copy, Ironbridge GMT · T. G. Harper?, portrait, Bilston Art Gallery · sculpture token, NPG
Wealth at death defective list of landed estate, 1808, excl. Castlehead and Brymbo; additional land in Cartmel parish, Lancashire, Beetham parish, Westmorland (*c.*1500 acres), Denbighshire (several holdings, *c.*2000 acres), Flintshire (*c.*200 acres), Hadley, Wellington parish, Shropshire (300 acres), Staffordshire around Bradley (*c.*1000 acres), Surrey, Rotherhithe estate, small acreage but largely works and workshops (probably valuable)

Wilkinson, Sir **John Gardner** (1797–1875), Egyptologist, born on 5 October 1797, probably at Little Missenden Abbey, Buckinghamshire, and baptized at Chelsea, London, on 17 January 1798, was the only surviving child of the Revd John Wilkinson and his wife, Mary Anne, daughter of the Revd Richard Gardner. From his father, a fellow of the Society of Antiquaries, Wilkinson derived his early interest in the scholarship of the past. His mother was also a classical scholar. She taught him how to draw—the only artistic training he ever received. He was orphaned at an early age; his parents left him a small income, which later financed his researches. He became the ward of the Revd Dr Yates. In 1813 Wilkinson entered Harrow School where he came under the influence of its headmaster, George Butler, who encouraged his interests. He matriculated at Exeter College, Oxford, in 1816, but left three years later without taking a degree, to begin his grand tour. He planned to make a leisurely journey through Europe followed by a voyage to Egypt, then a subject of great popular attention, before returning to England and purchasing a commission in the army. As Wilkinson passed through Italy, however, he impressed the accomplished classical scholar Sir William Gell with the depth of his interest in the past and his artistic ability. Gell, who was well connected to scholarly developments, convinced him that he could make a contribution to the study of ancient Egypt and gave him a course of preparatory instruction to that end.

Wilkinson arrived in Egypt on 22 November 1821. He soon became so fascinated with the land that he abandoned all thoughts of an army career and spent the next twelve years there. During that time he travelled widely throughout Egypt, twice ascending the Nile into Nubia and exploring both the eastern and the western deserts. He accomplished an extraordinary amount of work at most of the major archaeological sites then known in Egypt and recorded them in his numerous notebooks and sketchbooks. His sketches are rendered with an accuracy and consistency that make them valuable evidence for monuments that were damaged or destroyed after he

Sir John Gardner Wilkinson (1797–1875), by Henry Wyndham Phillips, 1840–44

drew them. He was among those at the forefront of the field of Egyptology, a discipline so new that its very name had yet to be coined. He followed the decipherment of the hieroglyphs closely and corrected some of Jean François Champollion's early translations, though the latter's contribution is by far the more important.

The primary focus of Wilkinson's work in Egypt was at ancient Thebes. It was he who initiated the numbering system for the tombs in the Valley of the Kings: some of the numbers that he painted over their entrances may still be seen. He was especially interested in the Tombs of the Nobles on the hill of Shaykh ʿAbd al-Gurna, recognizing that their naturalistic mode of representation made them evidence for daily life in ancient Egypt. He remodelled one of the tombs (TT 83) into a comfortable habitation that became a well-known landmark for the rest of the century.

During his Egyptian years Wilkinson published several works, among them an account of some of his earliest eastern desert explorations in the *Journal of the Royal Geographical Society* in 1832. He also published two short Egyptological books, both quite rare, *Materia hieroglyphica* (1828) and *Extracts from Several Hieroglyphic Subjects* (1830). The Royal Geographical Society sponsored the publication of his map of Thebes (1830), an extraordinarily accurate and detailed survey, but so large and expensive as to limit its circulation.

Wilkinson returned to Britain in 1833 and soon afterwards published a survey of both ancient and modern Egypt entitled *Topography of Thebes and General View of Egypt* (1835), the most substantial work on Egypt since the French *Description de l'Égypte*. Wilkinson's greatest published work was *Manners and Customs of the Ancient Egyptians* (1837), a profusely illustrated description of ancient Egyptian society. Drawing upon his work in the tombs at Gurna, Wilkinson was able to present a poignant picture of daily life in ancient Egypt that instantly caught the popular imagination. Praised by one reviewer as a 'restoration to life, as it were, of the ancient Pharaohs, and their subjects' (*QR*, Jan 1839, 120), it passed through many editions, influencing generations of English-speaking readers. Melbourne's government recognized Wilkinson's accomplishments with a knighthood on 26 August 1839. Many observers were impressed that Wilkinson, unlike many continental scholars, had received no government assistance for his researches.

The two decades following the publication of *Ancient Egyptians* were years of travel and writing. In Britain, Wilkinson ranged widely and was a frequent guest at country houses. He made several trips to Europe and through the Mediterranean, resulting in numerous publications. For example, a trip into south-eastern Europe in 1844 provided material for *Dalmatia and Montenegro* (1848). While it displayed naïvety about the region's ethnic conflicts, it also contained much significant material, such as documentation of regional costume and a description of the Paulician heresy. Wilkinson returned to Egypt in 1842, 1844, and 1848–9. While these trips hardly matched the first one in range or intensity of research, they provided new experiences, such as an exploration of the eastern delta on one occasion and an ascent of the Nile as far south as Jebel Berkel on another. His last trip to Egypt was in 1855–6; during it he suffered sunstroke while sketching a monument at Thebes. Wilkinson published several other works about ancient Egypt including *The Architecture of the Ancient Egyptians* (1850) and *The Egyptians in the Time of the Pharaohs* (1857), but none of these matched *Ancient Egyptians* in originality or scope. His popular *Handbook for Travellers in Egypt* (1847) for John Murray's series of travellers' guides went through many editions.

On 16 October 1856 Wilkinson married Caroline Catherine Lucas (1822–1881), botanical author, daughter of Henry Lucas, of Uplands, Glamorgan. After some years of searching, the Wilkinsons found a permanent residence at the village of Reynoldston in Gower, near Lady Wilkinson's childhood home. In the course of thoroughly renovating their house, named Brynfield House, Wilkinson added a large library where he arranged and rearranged his collections, especially his notebooks and sketchbooks, which he believed still contained unrealized potential. During his Gower years Wilkinson became deeply involved in British antiquities, many of which were only a short walk from his home. He was an officer in the Cambrian Archaeological Association and a contributor to its journal. In 1867 he lent his influential support to the successful effort to save the medieval gate at Tenby. Wilkinson died at Llandovery on 29 October 1875 while returning from an extended visit to his relatives, the Harpur-Crewes, at their estate, Calke Abbey, in Derbyshire. He was buried on 3

November in the churchyard at Llandingad, under a monument of his own design, an obelisk atop a pedestal.

A revised edition of *Manners and Customs of the Ancient Egyptians* was published in 1878, brought up to date by Samuel Birch of the department of Egyptian antiquities at the British Museum. Lady Wilkinson's plans for publishing various of her husband's manuscripts came to naught, however. Particularly regrettable in that regard is his 'Desert plants of Egypt', which was drawn in colour on stone, and was ready for publication in every way when a misunderstanding with the printer over the subvention caused the project to be cancelled. The stones were erased soon after, leaving just one lovely lithograph on the prospectus to the never published work. Wilkinson's most enduring legacy to scholarship is probably his notebooks, sketchbooks, and other Egyptological papers, the full value of which has yet to be assessed. These, with most of his other papers, Wilkinson willed to be deposited at Calke Abbey; they subsequently went to the Bodleian Library, Oxford. His collections of antiquities, including his excellent collection of Greek vases, were donated to Harrow School, an indication of his lifelong affection for that institution.

Wilkinson was a member of many scholarly societies and, besides his knighthood, received numerous other honours, more than any Egyptologist of his day. He also published many works in addition to those mentioned above and in many different fields, but his most important contribution by far was to the study of ancient Egypt. With some justice he has been referred to as 'the real founder of Egyptology in Great Britain' (Dawson and Uphill, 443). JASON THOMPSON

Sources J. Thompson, *Sir Gardner Wilkinson and his circle* (1992) · W. R. Dawson and E. P. Uphill, *Who was who in Egyptology*, 3rd edn, rev. M. L. Bierbrier (1995), 443–5 · J. Thompson, 'Sir Gardner Wilkinson's house at Sheikh Abd al-Qurna in Thebes', *KMT*, 7 (1996), 52–9 · J. Thompson and R. Lucas, 'Sir Gardner Wilkinson in Gower', *Journal of the Gower Society*, 46 (1995), 6–14 · parish register, London, Chelsea, St Luke, 17 Jan 1798, LMA [baptism], 17 Jan 1798 **Archives** Bodl. Oxf., corresp., sketchbooks, journals, and papers · Harrow School, Middlesex · priv. coll. · U. Oxf., Griffith Institute, journal and corresp. | BL, letters to Charles Babbage, Add. MSS 37183–37201 · BL, corresp. with Francesco Carrara, Add. MS 38650 · BL, letters to Robert Hay, Add. MS 38094 · Bodl. Oxf., corresp. with Lord Lovelace and Lady Lovelace · NL Wales, letters to Johnes family · Yale U., Beinecke L., letters to T. J. Pettigrew **Likenesses** sketch, 1830–1839?, repro. in C. Hobson, *Exploring the world of the pharaohs* (1987) · W. Brockedon, chalk drawing, 1838, NPG · Count D'Orsay, pencil and chalk drawing, 1839, NPG · H. W. Phillips, oils, 1840–44, Calke Abbey, Derbyshire [*see illus.*] · E. Edwards?, photograph, 1865?, AM Oxf. · photograph, 1870–79, priv. coll. · photograph (probably at about the time of his marriage), Bodl. Oxf. · photographs (in later life), Bodl. Oxf. **Wealth at death** under £10,000: probate, 28 Dec 1875, *CGPLA Eng. & Wales*

Wilkinson, John Joseph Tate (1769/70–1846), actor and theatre manager, was the first of the five surviving children of Tate *Wilkinson (1739–1803), the manager of the York circuit of theatres, and his wife, Jane, *née* Doughty. Already from 1797 a member of the company, Wilkinson assumed its management on his father's death and, although his active role ended with his bankruptcy in 1814, he remained closely associated with and financially dependent on the (diminishing) circuit until his own death in 1846.

According to his father's memoirs, *The Wandering Patentee*, Wilkinson had 'a genteel education' and was 'proficient a little in music'. Sometimes he would supplement an evening's bill by dancing a minuet. However he was 'too diffident' to shine on the stage, despite being a favourite with a perennial patron, the countess of Mexborough. He never performed with the regularity of the majority of the company and rarely took a leading role: he customarily played Paris in *Romeo and Juliet*, doubled as Tyrrel and the duke of Norfolk in *Richard III*, and took the role of Cromwell in *Henry VIII*. But he made the part of the eponymous George Barnwell his own, chose Blusherly in Richard Cumberland's *The Natural Son* for one of his benefits, and appeared most frequently as Jack O'Connor in O'Keefe's *Prisoner at Large*.

In February 1794 Wilkinson married Sarah Maria Reynolds (1771/2–1832), who had first come from Covent Garden to play with the company in November 1790, and who was a permanent member from January 1792 onwards. Both before and after her marriage she performed far more often than Wilkinson himself, her preferred roles including Polly in *The Beggar's Opera* and Rosetta in *Love in a Village*.

Initially John Wilkinson's management was little different from his father's—the company progressed on the same basis from Hull to York, Leeds, Pontefract, Wakefield, and Doncaster in the course of the year—but he obtained fewer bespeaks, engaged fewer stars, and began, in an effort to retain audiences, to mount more extravagant spectacles. By 1809 there were reports of his financial difficulties, and Pontefract was dropped from the circuit. At the same time, having been criticized for the condition of his Hull theatre, Wilkinson contracted with the Hull corporation for £1260 to buy land for a new one in Humber Street; he made a down payment of £500 and agreed to pay interest at 5 per cent on the remainder. His new theatre, capable of holding 1700 and designed by Charles Mountain the younger, was financed by subscriptions and opened on 1 May 1810 with Stephen Kemble in James Thomson's *Tancred and Sigismunda*. But Dorothy Jordan, writing from Wakefield in 1811, complained that Wilkinson did not have the money to pay her. In 1813 the Leeds theatre, in Hunslet Lane, the only one in the circuit to which Wilkinson had the absolute title, was offered unproductively for sale. Later the same year the circuit was advertised, abortively, as to be auctioned as a whole.

Wilkinson's bankruptcy in 1814 placed the administration of the circuit in the hands of trustees at York and at Hull, where they represented the interests of the shareholders in the new theatre. Wilkinson held the key assets of the royal patents for Hull and York, the freehold of the Leeds theatre, a financial stake in the theatre at Hull, and leases—for various periods of time and on various conditions—for the theatres at Doncaster, Wakefield, and York. While the circuit was sub-let to a series of actor-managers, and Doncaster and Wakefield were lost in the 1830s, Wilkinson was able to retire, with his wife, three of his four daughters, and his son, to live a quiet life as an independent gentleman at Acomb, York, drawing an income principally from rents paid by sub-lessees and from the annual, and often lucrative, benefits held on his behalf. Wilkinson died at his home in Front Street, Acomb, on 20 January 1846. C. M. P. TAYLOR

Sources T. Wilkinson, *The wandering patentee, or, A history of the Yorkshire theatres from 1770 to the present time*, 4 vols. (1795) [facs. edn (1973)] · S. Rosenfeld, 'The York theatre', 1948, York City Library · Hailstone collection of playbills, Minster Library, York · letters from trustees of the Hull and York theatres, Hull Central Library · A. Aspinall, ed., *Mrs Jordan and her family* (1951) · 'List of all Performers at the Hull Theatre Royal', Hull Central Library · T. Sheppard, *Evolution of the drama in Hull and district* (1927) · L. Fitzsimmons, 'The Theatre Royal, York', *York History*, 4 · W. Senior, *The old Wakefield Theatre* (1894) · 'Theatrical memoirs and anecdotes of actors who have appeared at Hull, York etc.', Hull Central Library · *Wakefield Star* · *Wakefield and Halifax Journal* · *Hull Rockingham* · *York Gazette* · Pontefract Magistrates Quarter Sessions order books · d. cert. · probate, 1848 · C. M. P. Taylor, *Right royal: Wakefield theatre, 1776–1994* (1995)

Wealth at death £300: probate, 1848

Wilkinson, Joshua Lucock (*bap.* **1769**, *d.* in or after **1802**), travel writer, was baptized on 9 August 1769 in the parish of St Nicholas, Liverpool, the son of George Wilkinson (*d.* 1783), captain in the Royal Navy, and his wife, Rebecca (*d.* 1801), whom he had married on 24 September 1767. His maternal grandfather, Joshua Lucock, had resided in Cockermouth and at Lorton Hall (just outside that town) in Cumberland, and had in 1745 built the Cockermouth house in which William Wordsworth was born and lived until 1783. Part of Wilkinson's youth was spent at Cockermouth—he recalls that in his 'school-boy' days he had 'frequently seen the mountains and lakes' of 'Cumberland' (*The Wanderer*, 2.131)—and he may have attended Hawkshead grammar school with Wordsworth. Captain Wilkinson seems to have been often at sea, and was drowned in 1783 when the *Ville de Paris*, sailing with 'the homeward-bound fleet from Jamaica', was crippled by a heavy gale off Newfoundland and later sank in the North Sea (*GM*, 52, 499; *GM*, 53, 267). Thereafter his widow seems to have made Cockermouth her permanent residence, and Wilkinson probably lived with her until in 1790 or 1791 he moved to London, where he was eventually enrolled (on 2 May 1793) at Gray's Inn.

Wilkinson may already have been acquainted with Wordsworth's brother Richard; in any case, the two became friendly when they both entered Gray's Inn in the early 1790s, and shared rooms as well as chambers. They probably did so until the summer of 1793 (shortly after Wilkinson's enrolment at Gray's Inn), when Richard Wordsworth moved to set up his own office at Staple Inn. In September 1792, William Wordsworth, returning from France, wrote to his brother that:

> I look forward to the time of seeing you Wilkinson and my other friends with pleasure. I am very happy you have got into Chambers, as I shall perhaps be obliged to stay a few weeks in town about my publication you will I hope with Wilkinson's permission find me a place for a bed. Give Wilkinson my best Complts I have apologies to make for not having written to him, as also to almost all my other friends. (*Letters of William and Dorothy Wordsworth*, 81)

In 1791 Wilkinson had returned from a continental tour similar to that undertaken by Wordsworth. In 1795 he published a two-volume account of this and of a 1793 tour (which took in the Low Countries, France, Switzerland, Germany, and Italy), as *The Wanderer, or, A Collection of Anecdotes and Incidents*. Meanwhile, in 1793 he had published a short, polemical work entitled *Political facts, collected in a tour, in the months of August, September, and October, 1793, along the frontiers of France*. This outspoken volume—part travelogue, part reportage—is critical of the conduct of the German allies of the British in the war against republican France, and concludes with an appeal for British neutrality. In 1794 Wilkinson translated a pamphlet by the comte de Montgaillard, a French émigré, entitled *The State of France, in May 1794*, which displays an ambivalent attitude to the revolutionary war.

The Wanderer is a long, reflective work, describing Wilkinson's travels on foot around Europe during the separate excursions of 1791 and 1793. As with *Political Facts*, the pedestrian mode of travel facilitates intimate contact with a wide range of people, and Wilkinson presents a fascinating tapestry of European characters and attitudes. He narrowly escapes being pressed into the imperial army on several occasions, and at one point is mistaken for Louis XVI, who has just escaped to Varennes. He consistently displays contempt not only for Catholic superstition, but for religious belief in general, and contemporary reviews of *The Wanderer* criticized this 'grossly indecent' tendency (*Monthly Review*, 115). In the second volume, he alludes to an incident which is later developed by Wordsworth into the story of Vaudracour and Julia in *The Prelude* (book 9), and he may well have discussed this story with the poet. In any case, it is almost certain that Wordsworth during late 1792 read the first part of the manuscript of *The Wanderer*. Wilkinson's travelogue provides an interesting prose counterpart to the European books of *The Prelude*, and may have suggested to Wordsworth several of the motifs of solitary travel, reflection, and revisiting which characterize his poem.

In October 1794 Wilkinson witnessed Richard Wordsworth's signature on an important bond drawn up to protect from the claims of creditors the £600 bequeathed to the poet by Raisley Calvert. He may have married: there is a record of a marriage between a Joshua Wilkinson and Alice Ashworth on 14 December 1796 in Rossendale, Lancashire. Thereafter the letters and papers of the Wordsworth household provide only brief glimpses of Wilkinson. Early in 1802 Dorothy reports that she and William met him at Keswick during Christmas 1801, and that William and Wilkinson supped at the Royal Oak inn together. Wilkinson's presence in the Lakes at this time was necessitated by the recent death of his mother, who had died at Lorton Hall on 1 December 1801 (her death is noted in *GM*, 71, 1154). He was back in London by 19 January 1802, when he proved her will. Nothing is known of his subsequent life and career. KATHERINE TURNER

Sources C. L. Shaver, 'Wordsworth's Vaudracour and Wilkinson's *The wanderer*', *Review of English Studies*, new ser., 12 (1961), 55–7 · *The letters of William and Dorothy Wordsworth*, ed. E. De Selincourt,

2nd edn, rev. C. L. Shaver, M. Moorman, and A. G. Hill, 8 vols. (1967–93), vol. 1, p. 656 • J. Wilkinson, *The wanderer, or, A collection of anecdotes and incidents, with reflections, political and religious, during two excursions in 1791 and 1793, in France, Germany, and Italy*, 2 vols. (1795) • *GM*, 1st ser., 52 (1782), 499 • *GM*, 1st ser., 53 (1783), 267 • *GM*, 1st ser., 71 (1801), 1154 • J. Foster, *The register of admissions to Gray's Inn, 1521–1889, together with the register of marriages in Gray's Inn chapel, 1695–1754* (privately printed, London, 1889), 398 • J. L. Wilkinson, *Political facts, collected in a tour, in the months of August, September, and October, 1793, along the frontiers of France* (1793) • *Monthly Review*, new ser., 16 (1795), 115–16 • D. Wu, *Wordsworth's reading, 1770–1799* (1993), 148–9 • *IGI* • PRO, PROB 11/1369, sig. 71, fols. 105v–106v [mother's will]

Wilkinson [née Lumsden]**, Dame Louisa Jane** (1889–1968), military nurse, was born Louisa Jane Lumsden on 11 December 1889 at 5 Peel Street, Sunderland. She was the daughter of James Lumsden, merchant seaman, and his wife, Louisa, *née* Benskin; she had at least one brother, Robert, but little else is known about her family or her early life. She was educated at Bede Collegiate School, Sunderland, and Thornbeck Collegiate School, Darlington, and she embarked upon her nursing career in 1911, aged twenty-two.

Louisa had just completed her training at the Royal Infirmary, Sunderland, when the First World War was declared, and she immediately joined Queen Alexandra's Imperial Military Nursing Service (QAIMNS) as a reservist. Established by royal warrant in March 1902 under the patronage of Queen Alexandra, the QAIMNS combined the forces of army nurses and those of the Princess Christian's Army Nursing Service Reserve, and was responsible for the nursing of sick and wounded soldiers at home and abroad. Louisa's postings at military hospitals in the United Kingdom were followed by a tour of duty on Malta, but by late 1917 she had returned to Britain. On 20 December 1917 she married Robert John Wilkinson (1884–1918), an acting captain with Queen Victoria's first Royal Irish Fusiliers. The marriage, which took place at Fulham register office, was tragically short, for her husband was killed on active service on 2 June 1918.

After the war, childless and widowed, Wilkinson joined the QAIMNS as a regular. She rose quickly through the ranks from staff nurse to sister, serving first in the United Kingdom and then, after 1926, as one of the pioneer nurses posted to India. Shortly after the outbreak of the Second World War she returned to London as principal matron at the War Office, and for two years was involved in setting the army nursing services on a wartime footing. In 1942 she returned to India to take up what proved to be her most challenging post, that of chief principal matron. Her remit was to organize all the Indian military nursing services and auxiliary nursing centres—a daunting task given the severe shortage of trained nurses in the country. In typical fashion, and with her usual efficiency, Wilkinson founded a nurses' training scheme for Indian women, and succeeded in making India one of the largest nursing commands in the world. She was also responsible for establishing the postgraduate school of nursing administration in the country, which ensured that the improved standards of training in Indian military hospitals was maintained. On her return to the United Kingdom in May

Dame Louisa Jane Wilkinson (1889–1968), by Bassano, 1944

1944 she was appointed matron-in-chief of the QAIMNS at the War Office, a position she held with great dignity until her retirement in October 1948.

Throughout her lifetime Wilkinson's vivid personality earned her the respect of her many friends and admirers. She was renowned for being cheerful and warm-hearted, practical as well as courageous. Her contribution to nursing services earned her a number of decorations. In 1919 she was awarded the British Empire Medal and made ARRC, the second-class nursing decoration instituted by Queen Victoria in 1883. In 1941 she was awarded the first-class honour, Royal Red Cross (RRC), in recognition of special services rendered in nursing the sick and wounded of the army and navy, and as a result of her exceptional work in India she was made an OBE in 1943. After being appointed CBE in 1946 she was then made dame commander in the military division of the Order of the British Empire in 1948.

In retirement Dame Louisa was elected president of the Royal College of Nursing in 1948, a unique honour for a service matron, and significant in that it maintained the link between military and civil nursing. In 1949 she was also deeply involved in the establishment of Queen Alexandra's Royal Army Nursing Corps (QARANC), which brought together the QAIMNS and the Territorial Army Nursing Service (the TANS, which dated from 1907), and she served as first controller commandant QARANC until 1954. The foundation and early running of the QARANC Association, in which Queen Mary took such an interest, was also the result of Dame Louisa's devotion and hard work.

On 4 December 1968 Dame Louisa Wilkinson suffered a coronary thrombosis, and was pronounced dead on arrival at the War Memorial Hospital, Crowborough, Sussex. Her funeral took place at All Saints' Church, Crowborough, nine days later, and her remains were interred in the town's garden of remembrance, in Herne Road. A fitting tribute was made at the thanksgiving service held in her honour at Millbank, London, on 15 January 1969:

> her great love for the QA's and indeed of the nursing profession made her an outstanding figure in our time, and now at her passing we reflect on her as a person and are thankful for her example and work. (*QARANC Association Gazette*, 3)

The beneficiaries of her estate, which amounted to £33,301, included members of her family, the Church of England Children's Society, London, Dr Barnardo's Homes, and the QARANC Association Benevolent Fund.

SUSAN L. COHEN

Sources *QARANC Association Gazette*, 6/1 (1969), 1–9 · WWW · L. Wilkinson, letters to Queen Mary, Royal Arch., RA, GV/cc.49/199/200 · *Army List* (1884) · *Army List* (1914–48) · QAIMNS register, 1903–26, PRO, WO25/3596, fol. 2/10/276 · *The Times* (10 Dec 1968) · *Nursing Times* (26 June 1948), 1 · J. Piggott, *Q.A.R.A.N.C.* (1990), 87–8 · *British Journal of Nursing* (Aug 1944), 91 · b. cert. · d. cert.
Archives Royal Arch., letters to Queen Mary
Likenesses Bassano, photograph, 1944, NPG [*see illus.*] · group portrait, photograph, 1948, Archives of the Royal School of Nursing, Scottish Board, 42 South Oswald Road, Edinburgh, P/9/AGM/24 · photograph, repro. in *Nursing Times* (8 July 1944), 467 · photograph, repro. in *British Journal of Nursing*, 91 · photograph, repro. in *Nursing Times* (26 June 1948), 458 · photograph, repro. in *Q.A.R.A.N.C. Association Gazette*, 1 · portrait, Wellcome L., RAMC 801/22/45
Wealth at death £33,301: probate, 4 March 1969, *CGPLA Eng. & Wales*

Wilkinson, Sir (Robert Francis) Martin (1911–1990), stockbroker, was born on 4 June 1911 in Blackheath, London, the elder son and eldest of four children of Sir Robert Pelham Wilkinson, a partner of De Zoete and Gorton from 1913 to 1960 and deputy chairman of the stock exchange from 1936 to 1946, and his wife, Phyllis Marion Bernard. He was educated at Repton School.

Wilkinson joined De Zoete and Gorton straight from school in 1930 and became a partner in 1936, having become a member of the stock exchange in 1933. During the Second World War he served in the Royal Air Force in radar intelligence in Northern Ireland and Italy, and at Bushey Priory, attaining the rank of squadron leader. In 1946 he married Dore Esme, daughter of William John Arendt, timber trader; they had three daughters.

Wilkinson returned to De Zoete and Gorton after the war and was elected to the council of the stock exchange in 1959. He became deputy chairman in 1963 and was elected chairman in 1965, having acted as chairman for the year before he took office, when he stood in for the third Baron Ritchie of Dundee during his illness. He became senior partner of De Zoete and Bevan following the merger of his firm with David A. Bevan and Simpson in 1970. He retired from the chairmanship of the stock exchange in March 1973 and from De Zoete and Bevan in 1976.

Wilkinson chaired the stock exchange during a difficult period. It was a time when international pressures were beginning to exert influence and reform was becoming necessary. He was himself not a natural reformer, being steeped in the traditions of the exchange and the City. He was, however, open to ideas of reform and he encouraged his younger colleagues to come forward with them. He grasped ideas quickly and thoroughly and was a natural leader in the implementation of change.

During Wilkinson's period of office the settlement of stock exchange business was centralized, and stock exchanges throughout the United Kingdom and the Republic of Ireland came together in one organization. These two changes were interlinked. A single market authority was essential. Only one exchange could achieve the most efficient system of settlement and transfer of securities which was recommended by the City-wide Heasman committee in 1970. The exchanges were amalgamated in 1973 and this achievement led to the full computerization of the settlement procedures after Wilkinson's retirement. Furthermore, only one exchange could ensure the imposition of the best regulatory standards across the whole country and thus satisfy investors that their business was being fairly conducted and settled.

During Wilkinson's term of office the stock exchange's historic building, which had been extended many times on the same site since 1801, was pulled down and rebuilt, an extensive project which required the full backing of the voting members. He patiently achieved the necessary backing, explaining how essential the rebuilding was for the efficiency of the market place and particularly its worldwide communications.

Other reforms during Wilkinson's tenure of office included the abolition of the requirement of British nationality for membership of the stock exchange, the relaxation of some of the restrictions preventing member firms from competing in overseas markets, the easing of restraints on advertising, the tightening of the financial reporting requirements imposed on firms, the admission of women to the membership and to the trading floor, and the introduction of rules which allowed firms for the first time to seek external capital through the formation of limited partnerships or companies. These reforms arose from the need for stock exchange firms to be internationally competitive. It was no mean achievement to lead the exchange through these changes in the face of much internal criticism from members who preferred to think of the exchange more as a club than an international market place. He strongly opposed attempts by the merchant banks, who were large fund managers, to set up an alternative market place for the matching of trades by computer under the name Ariel, which he saw as a threat to the orderly conduct of the central market.

Wilkinson's years in office were also difficult because attitudes in Westminster towards the City of London and to the exchange were hostile. Politicians were apt to describe the exchange as a 'casino' and to draw unflattering comparisons between the paper shuffling of stock markets and the real world of manufacturing industry. Wilkinson continued the work of his predecessors in encouraging a greater public knowledge of the workings and *raison d'être* of the exchange. He did not enjoy such public platforms, being himself a very private man, but he was not afraid to stand up and do his public duty as chairman. He left his listeners in no doubt about the role of the exchange as the market through which industry could raise long-term risk capital and as the regulatory authority which demanded high standards of disclosure from listed companies and financial probity and ethical behaviour from its members, thus serving the interests of investors. He was a major influence on the introduction of legislation to make insider trading a criminal offence, having initiated this with a speech (of which he gave his colleagues no prior warning) in which he said it was 'no better than theft'.

Wilkinson served as chairman of two investment trusts—Altifund (1976–81) and the City of London Brewery Trust (1977–8). He was the seventh generation of his family to be a liveryman of the Worshipful Company of Needlemakers. He was knighted in 1969.

Wilkinson was of medium height, well built, and well groomed. His movements and gestures were restrained, almost self-conscious. His somewhat aquiline features could be severe, but they frequently relaxed into a ready, impish smile. When he retired he lived part of the year near Cortona in Italy and indulged his passion for gardening at his home in England (Hurst Anclays, Ship Street, East Grinstead, Sussex) while continuing to act as consultant to De Zoete and Bevan. He died on 22 January 1990 in Pembury Hospital, Kent. NICHOLAS GOODISON, rev.

Sources *The Times* (24 Jan 1990) · stock exchange archives, GL · personal knowledge (1996) · private information (1996) · *CGPLA Eng. & Wales* (1990)
Archives GL, stock exchange archives
Likenesses photograph, repro. in *The Times* (24 Jan 1990) · portrait, stock exchange, London
Wealth at death £685,295: probate, 1990, *CGPLA Eng. & Wales*

Wilkinson, Sir **Nevile Rodwell** (1869–1940), army officer, artist, and herald, was born on 26 October 1869 at Highgate, Middlesex, the third son of Colonel Josiah Wilkinson, a barrister practising at the parliamentary bar, and his wife, Alice Emma, daughter of Thomas Smith, of Highgate. He had an idyllic childhood with much yachting as a family sport and spells of living in the south of France; it was there, among the cypresses, that he executed his first serious drawing. Having been educated at Harrow School, he entered the Royal Military College, Sandhurst, in 1889, before being gazetted to the Coldstream Guards. He had something of a giant's physique, standing 6 feet 5 inches in his stockinged feet and 7 feet 6 inches when wearing his bearskin.

After a period in Dublin, Wilkinson undertook guard duties at Buckingham and St James's palaces. In addition he enrolled and worked hard at the National Art Training School (later the Royal College of Art, South Kensington).

During this period he was fortunate to meet both Sir John Millais and John Singer Sergeant. On the outbreak of the Second South African War in 1899 he was sent to South Africa, where he served with credit, and was decorated and received four clasps. His marriage on 29 April 1903 to Lady Beatrix Frances Gertrude (*d.* 1957), elder daughter of Sydney Herbert, fourteenth earl of Pembroke, took him once again to Ireland as he and his wife set up house at Mount Marrion, a property near Dublin belonging to his father-in-law. The couple had two daughters. Wilkinson's ten-year residence paved the way for his later appointment to the office of Ulster king of arms.

The old sycamore tree on the Mount Marrion estate, into the roots of which his three-year-old daughter said she had seen a fairy queen disappear, was significantly to be the inspiration for Wilkinson's celebrated *Titania's Palace*. This *chef-d'œuvre en miniature*, completed over some eighteen years, was unique in being neither a luxurious dolls' house nor a model of an existing or possible future structure. It covered a space of 63 square feet, and was finished in every conceivable detail. Wilkinson developed, with the aid of an etchers' glass, a technique for decoration he called 'mosaic painting': minute dots of watercolour, irregular in shape like mosaic tesserae, about 1000 to the square inch. The palace was opened in 1923 by Queen Mary and was much admired by the public. It was exhibited not only in the United Kingdom but also in the Netherlands, Canada, the United States, Argentina, Australia, and New Zealand, raising thousands of pounds for children's charities: the *raison d'être* of the entire exercise.

In 1908 Wilkinson was appointed to succeed Sir Arthur Vicars as Ulster king of arms, the latter having been forced to resign following the scandal of the theft of the Irish crown jewels (the jewelled insignia of the Order of St Patrick) from the Ulster office in Dublin Castle. Untainted by any previous connection with the Ulster office, Wilkinson was well known in Dublin and ideal for the post: a man of commanding presence and stature, he was also an artist of repute who had developed a knowledge of heraldry. Within a few days of taking over he had to break open the strong room in the Ulster office—his predecessor would not hand over the keys—in order to produce the symbols of state to be used at a forthcoming levee. The maces and sword of state were thus retrieved, in the presence of witnesses, while the lord lieutenant and Lady Aberdeen entertained their guests to dinner in another part of the castle.

In the course of his duties Wilkinson proclaimed the accession of George V and attended his coronation. Because of Wilkinson's height a new tabard had to be made for the Ulster king of arms. He was greatly involved in the 1911 visit of the king to Dublin, being the mouthpiece, so to speak, of the lord lieutenant—almost all correspondence on this subject passing between Dublin and London went through the Ulster office. Upon this visit he was made a CVO. With the outbreak of war in 1914 Wilkinson rejoined the army, and served in France and Gallipoli, earning a mention in dispatches and a brevet majority. Notwithstanding war service he returned to Dublin on several occasions for official duties. Following the evacuation of Gallipoli, Wilkinson was sent to Switzerland to look after British interests.

After the war Wilkinson returned to full-time duties at the Ulster office. In 1921 he attended upon the first Catholic lord lieutenant for several centuries, Viscount Fitzalan of Derwent, at his taking up office. In the following year he arranged the first opening of the parliament of Northern Ireland by George V which took place in the Belfast City Hall. Such a location required the greatest tact and diplomacy, as the prime minister of Northern Ireland was thus the guest of the lord mayor, but it was, nevertheless, an opening of parliament. In consequence of the success of the event Wilkinson was advanced in the Royal Victorian Order and made a KCVO. He personally designed the obverse of the great seal of Northern Ireland, which was modelled by Cecil Thomas, and exhibited in the sculpture gallery of the Royal Academy exhibition of 1924: and he wryly observed that this was the first time his work had penetrated into the sacred precincts of Burlington House. He also designed and granted arms for each of the six counties of Northern Ireland. In addition, Wilkinson established the heraldic museum at the Ulster office in 1909—the first of its kind in the world. He also wrote several books, including his reminiscences (1925), *Wilton House Pictures* (1907), *Wilton House Guide* (1908), and *The Guards' Chapel, 1838–1938* (1938).

In his capacity as Ulster king of arms, and so the sovereign's lieutenant in matters armorial within his area of jurisdiction, Wilkinson was destined to serve during an extraordinarily difficult period of Irish history. Throughout the 1920s and 1930s he functioned from the official Ulster premises in the Bedford Tower within Dublin Castle. Despite the difficult political circumstances he managed to preserve the armorial and genealogical heritage of Ireland. Indeed, so successful was he in this that not long after the establishment of the Irish republic, followed by his death, the republic created the office of chief herald of Ireland to carry on the work so carefully fostered by Wilkinson. He was the last of the permanent royal officers to function from Dublin Castle. He ensured the preservation of records, making it possible for the new chief herald to start with registers dating back some 400 years. Wilkinson died in Dublin on 22 December 1940. His widow subsequently married the seventh earl of Wicklow. CONRAD SWAN

Sources N. R. Wilkinson, *To all and singular* (1925) · records of the Ulster Office, Dublin, Ireland · records, Coll. Arms · *The Times* (24 Dec 1924) · *DNB* · private information (2004) [A. J. Toppin] · b. cert.
Likenesses W. Stoneman, photograph, 1931, NPG · group portrait, oils (*Proclaiming in Dublin the accession of George V*), Tower of London

Wilkinson, Norman (1882–1934), stage designer, was born at Handsworth Wood, Birmingham, on 8 August 1882, the second son of Howard Wilkinson, of Handsworth Wood, a partner in the firm of Wilkinson and Riddell, textile wholesalers in Birmingham, and his wife, Jessie Caroline Bragg. He was educated at the New School, Abbotsholme, Derbyshire, which had Swedenborgian affiliations. Here he benefited from an enlightened policy which replaced the usual patriotic heroes of conventional teaching with the great thinkers and artists. He thus gained an early familiarity with the works of, among others, Shakespeare, Blake, and Bach, and was familiar with the writings of Edward Maitland, Anna Kingsford, and other mystics.

On leaving school Wilkinson entered the Birmingham School of Art, which was then at its peak under the able administration of Edward R. Taylor. The brilliant staff included Arthur Gaskin and Henry Payne, who were both at that time working with William Morris. Wilkinson was able to indulge and develop his highly individual taste and acquired possessions such as a sixteenth-century harpsichord, a Kelmscott *Chaucer*, and old Welsh furniture with which he furnished in part a house designed for the family by W. R. Lethaby. Although he already had a small room fitted up as a model theatre, on the stage of which he produced scenery for Shakespearian dramas, his bent was really that of the collector and producer. He composed charming musical settings for the early lyrics of W. B. Yeats and for old carols, and he played the harpsichord with taste. Naturally of a generous and affable disposition, Wilkinson was also shy and self-conscious, and though he possessed great and diverse talents, he lacked the intense application and ability necessary to make the most of them.

There followed periods spent in Paris and Italy with an especially intensive study of Gothic art and Tudor design. Wilkinson's enthusiasm for Elizabethan drama did not, however, rule out the work of Maeterlinck, Stephen Phillips, and Bernard Shaw, and he was drawn to the less commercial stage. He began designing costumes in 1910 for Charles Frohman's repertory season at the Duke of York's Theatre, and followed this up with sets for *A Winter's Tale* and *Twelfth Night* (1912), and *A Midsummer Night's Dream* (1914) for Harley Granville Barker at the Savoy Theatre. Wilkinson's memorable design for the production of the *Dream* featured an iridescent forest and 'gold-faced fairies, their eyebrows picked out in crimson'. William Bridges-Adams, with whom Wilkinson would later collaborate on another famous production of the play at Stratford, objected to this 'stylistic treatment', which he thought rendered the play too 'stylish, sophisticated, *towny*' (Brock and Pringle, 42). He likened Wilkinson's fairies to 'static little figurines on a London mantlepiece' rather than the ethereal creatures of Shakespeare's imagination (Speaight, 91). The design nevertheless put Wilkinson 'in the vanguard of the rebellion against nineteenth-century stage realism' and won for him an international reputation as a stage designer (Brock and Pringle, 41–2). He had further success in 1914 with his settings for Granville Barker's production of *The Dynasts* at the Kingsway Theatre.

The First World War had a powerful impact on Wilkinson's life and work, and he never fully recovered from the effects of its brutalities upon his sensitive and essentially pacifist nature. For a time afterwards he continued his work at the Lyric Theatre, Hammersmith, which was then under the management of Nigel Playfair, and designed sets for *The Rivals*, *Lionel and Clarissa*, and *The Would-Be Gentleman* in 1925–6. To this period also belong his designs for plays produced by the Phoenix Society and the Stage Society.

In 1932 Bridges-Adams invited Wilkinson to design the settings and costumes for his production of *A Midsummer Night's Dream* at the Stratford Memorial Theatre, of which Wilkinson had become a governor in 1920. It was the last play to open in the 1932 festival spring season and it proved to be the high point, principally because of the stage design. Bridges-Adams gave Wilkinson a free hand and the 'glitter of gold' of the pre-war Granville Barker production now 'mellowed to softest silver' (Brock and Pringle, 42). The players wore robes of white and dove-grey and the overall effect was one of 'memorable and satisfying beauty' (Kemp and Trewin, 165). The next year Wilkinson and Bridges-Adams enjoyed another successful collaboration with an acclaimed production of *Romeo and Juliet*, in which they created an Elizabethan atmosphere on the apron stage with a setting notable for its simplicity. It ranked as one of the best productions of the play seen at Stratford.

Wilkinson had proved an important source of new inspiration at the festival, though his influence there was destined to be short-lived. He died, unmarried, in London on 14 February 1934. At the time of his death he was working on designs for *The Tempest* at Stratford, and Bridges-Adams paid tribute to his artistry: 'He was something of an Elizabethan, and his taste was catholic, embracing everything, old or new, that was first rate. Modernity held no terrors for him' (*The Times*).

MAXWELL ARMFIELD, rev. MARK POTTLE

Sources *The Times* (16 Feb 1934) · personal knowledge (1949) · private information (1949) · J. Parker, ed., *Who's who in the theatre*, 7th edn (1933) · S. Brock and M. J. Pringle, *The Shakespeare memorial theatre, 1919–1945* (1984) · T. C. Kemp and J. C. Trewin, *The Stratford festival: a history of the Shakespeare memorial theatre* (1953) · R. Speaight, ed., *A Bridges-Adams letter book* (1971) · CGPLA Eng. & Wales (1935)
Likenesses M. Armfield, portrait, *c*.1901, priv. coll.
Wealth at death £77,493 1s. 8d.: resworn probate, 1935, CGPLA Eng. & Wales

Wilkinson, Sir Peter Allix (1914–2000), army officer and diplomatist, was born on 15 April 1914 in India, the only son of Captain Osborn Cecil Wilkinson (*d*. 1915), an army officer, and his wife, Esmé, *née* Wilson, daughter of Sir Alexander Wilson. He came from a military family, a grandfather and two uncles being generals, and his middle name recalling another ancestor who was one of Napoleon's generals. His father, an officer in the East Yorkshire regiment, was serving in India at the time of Wilkinson's birth. He was sent to France at the outbreak of the First World War and when Wilkinson was only ten

months old was killed in action at Ypres. Wilkinson's early childhood was lonely with a background of financial difficulties and ill health. When he was seven, his mother remarried; her new husband was an Englishman working in the Egyptian irrigation service, and later they could afford to send Wilkinson to school, at Scaitcliffe preparatory school and then Rugby School. He spent holidays either in Egypt or with an aunt who was a painter and from whom he developed an interest in art. From Rugby he went to Corpus Christi College, Cambridge, where he read first modern languages and later military studies. Possibly because of glandular fever, he failed to achieve the first-class degree expected of him.

After leaving Cambridge in 1935 Wilkinson was commissioned into the Royal Fusiliers, where he intended to follow the family military tradition. He quickly tired of peacetime soldiering and managed to get sent to Czechoslovakia to learn the language. He was there by coincidence and in plain clothes when the Germans marched into Prague in March 1939. It was his first experience of intelligence work, and he made careful and coded notes of the German units involved. This led in turn to his being included among a dozen British officers trained in irregular warfare and attached to General Carton de Wiart's mission to Poland. Once again he witnessed a German invasion, this time the blitzkrieg attack on Poland in September 1939 which triggered the Second World War. He managed to escape from Warsaw and wrote a report on the German offensive which, though ignored at the time, was later recognized by a mention in dispatches.

Wilkinson was now accepted as a budding expert on intelligence and irregular warfare matters. He was sent on a further military mission, to Budapest, and was later attached to the free Polish headquarters in Paris, being responsible for evacuating General Sikorski by flying boat. After the fall of France he worked with Colin Gubbins and Peter Fleming to establish potential 'stay behind' parties in southern England who would disrupt German communications in the event of an invasion of the UK in 1940. When this threat receded Wilkinson joined the Special Operations Executive (SOE) and did a parachuting course before being sent to Crete, once again arriving just before the German invasion. He was in action there, before being evacuated by sea. Back in the UK, he was involved in planning various clandestine activities inside occupied Europe, including the assassination of Reinhard Heydrich, the brutal Nazi Reichsprotektor of Bohemia and Moravia, in 1942. Eventually he gained consent for a daring penetration of the German Reich, and led the first offensive ground patrol into Germany/Austria since 1940. For this operation he had first to cross Bosnia, Croatia, and Slovenia (calling at Tito's partisan headquarters *en route*). The journey through the rugged and hostile mountains would have tried the physique of anyone, and was the more remarkable as he was suffering from asthma and sinusitis throughout. This bold and valuable reconnaissance was rewarded by an immediate DSO. In the same year (1944) he was appointed a military OBE. He also received for his wartime activities the Polish cross of valour, the Czech order of the white lion, and (much later) the order of the Yugoslav banner. He ended the war with the rank of lieutenant-colonel and a heroic reputation. He married, on 14 March 1945, (Mary) Theresa Villiers (1917–1984), daughter of Algernon Hyde Villiers, an officer in the Lothians and Border horse, killed in action in 1917, and great-granddaughter of George William Frederick Villiers, fourth earl of Clarendon, foreign secretary during the Crimean War. They had two daughters.

Not surprisingly, Wilkinson found the prospect of peacetime soldiering no more appealing in 1945 than in 1935. In 1947 he was recruited by the Foreign Office and posted to Vienna, where he was involved with the Allied Control Commission. He was moved as first secretary to Washington in 1952, and in 1955 seconded to Geneva as secretary-general to the four powers' heads of government conference; this was followed by five years (1955–60) as counsellor in Bonn. After a period in the Foreign Office, he was seconded to the Cabinet Office in 1963 as under-secretary, and from there he was in 1964 appointed senior civilian instructor at the Imperial Defence College in London. In this post his familiarity with military life and his distinguished war service added greatly to his authority.

In 1966 Wilkinson received his first ambassadorial appointment, to Vietnam. With the shadows of war over that country, his military experience was once again highly relevant to the difficult task he faced. It was a measure of his high reputation within the diplomatic service that on his recall from Vietnam in 1967 he was appointed chief clerk (the deputy under-secretary of state in charge of personnel and administration). In this role he demonstrated a cool and realistic assessment of his colleagues' capabilities which was often more astringent than they imagined. His final diplomatic appointment, in 1970, was as ambassador to Austria, a country he knew well. He was created KCMG in the same year (having been made CMG in 1960).

Wilkinson's career might well have gone further, but in 1971 his wife suffered severe injuries in a car accident which left her with brain damage. Wilkinson decided to retire prematurely in order to nurse her and provide closer companionship. He briefly accepted a London appointment as co-ordinator of intelligence at the Cabinet Office (1972–3), where once again his wartime activities stood him in good stead. His wife died in 1984. He later found time to write (in conjunction with Joan Bright-Astley) *Gubbins and SOE* (1993), a biography of his wartime companion, and an account of his own early life, *Foreign Fields* (1997). He had retired to the village of Charing in the weald of Kent. Though tall and spare, he had always suffered from indifferent health, and he lost his eyesight almost entirely in the last years of his life. He nevertheless retained his lively interest in people and affairs, and also in fly-fishing. He died of pneumonia at the William Harvey Hospital, Ashford, Kent, on 16 June 2000 survived by his two daughters. He was a shrewd and modest diplomat whose quiet manner betrayed nothing of his dramatic wartime persona. But in matters physical, mental, and

emotional throughout his life he proved himself more robust and determined than many apparently tougher characters.   JOHN URE

Sources *The Times* (20 June 2000) · *Daily Telegraph* (28 June 2000) · *WWW* · Burke, *Peerage* · personal knowledge (2004) · private information (2004) · d. cert.
Archives IWM, diary of mission to Poland
Likenesses photograph, repro. in *The Times* · photograph, repro. in *Daily Telegraph* · photographs, priv. coll.
Wealth at death £483,147: probate, 31 Oct 2000, *CGPLA Eng. & Wales*

Wilkinson, Richard James (1867–1941), colonial administrator and Malay scholar, was born on 29 May 1867 at Salonika, the eldest son of the British consul, Richard Wilkinson (d. 1894), and his wife, Jane Whittall. He spent much of his boyhood in Spain, where his father was consul at Malaga (1872–81), and learned to speak French, German, Spanish, Italian, and Greek. In 1881 his father was transferred to Manila, and Wilkinson and a brother were sent to Felsted School in Essex. At Trinity College, Cambridge (1886–9), he was an exhibitioner, won five prizes, rowed, was president of the union, and obtained second-class honours in the history tripos. In the combined civil service entrance examination he passed high, heading the list in French, but he failed the riding test required for entry to the Indian Civil Service. Perhaps as a result of this disappointment he left Cambridge without being formally admitted to his BA—an omission which he remedied in 1901.

He joined the Straits Settlements civil service in 1889, and passed the government examinations in Malay (1891) and in Hokkien (1895). He learned Chinese with a view to joining the consular service in China, but was persuaded to remain in the Straits Settlements. William Maxwell, then Straits Settlements colonial secretary and himself an outstanding scholar, had noted Wilkinson's talents and persuaded him to take over the preparation of a much-needed comprehensive Malay–English dictionary. At Cambridge, Wilkinson's friends included Walter Skeat, son of one of the group of academics associated with James Murray in compiling the *Oxford English Dictionary*, which may have been Wilkinson's model in adopting a system of demonstrating the meaning of words by citing them in quotations. In the 1890s the younger Skeat, also in the local civil service, collaborated with Wilkinson in collecting his material, but Skeat later went off to pursue his outstanding research in Malay and Aborigine ethnography. Wilkinson's dictionary, a massive two volumes, was published in Singapore in 1901–2 and for the ensuing century has been the definitive work on classical Malay.

Wilkinson had found his métier in the government education service. His annual report on the Straits Settlements education department for 1899 won high praise in the Colonial Office for its 'many far-reaching observations' and he helped to found the first Malay teacher training college. He was also invited to write a paper entitled 'The education of Asiatics', laid before parliament in 1902. Then came his *triennium mirabile* (1903–6) as head of the education department of the Federated Malay States, in which he launched a wide-ranging series of textbooks and Malay classical texts, until then not in print, and took a leading part in founding the Malay College at Kuala Kangsar—the 'Malay Eton'—for the better education of the sons of the ruling Malay élite. But he fell out with unimaginative superiors who eased him out of education in favour of a less innovative senior colleague. He then (1907–9) became in effect deputy to the energetic resident of Perak, Ernest Birch, and they collaborated in producing the Papers on Malay Subjects, a series of monographs, intended for the use of government officials, on Malay history and culture. In addition to being general editor, Wilkinson wrote nine of the sixteen publications in the first series. A selection of these papers has been reprinted (1970–71); they remain definitive studies.

In 1910 Wilkinson was appointed resident of Negri Sembilan, which has an unusual matrilineal social system; two of his monographs relate to this state. In 1911 he was given accelerated promotion to become colonial secretary Straits Settlements, and in this capacity, under a 'hands off' governor, he administered the colony. At the outbreak of war in August 1914 he dealt effectively as acting governor with the serious crises in the local food supply and the tin market. His willingness first to seek advice and then to accept responsibility for action which he judged necessary earned him praise from the business community. In 1912 he was appointed CMG, and on 23 October that year he married Edith Sinclair Baird; they had no children. From 1916 to 1922 he was governor of Sierra Leone. In wartime Freetown was an active naval base at which ships assembled to form homeward convoys through dangerous waters. The aftermath of war brought scarcity of food and high prices, leading to serious riots and damage to the shops of unpopular Levantine traders. After coping with these troubles Wilkinson promoted the construction of a feeder road system in rural areas as links with the railway, but he left to his successor the problem of how best to tackle overdue reform of the constitution.

Wilkinson contemplated retirement in Smyrna, where he had family connections—possibly in its export trade. But the devastation of Smyrna in the Graeco-Turkish War led him to settle at Mytilene on the Aegean island of Lesbos. Here he produced a completely new edition of his dictionary, typed in its entirety by his wife, and resumed writing on Malay subjects. When Germany invaded Greece in 1941 the Wilkinsons withdrew to Smyrna, where he died on 5 December, survived by his wife. In manner Wilkinson was a 'retiring scholar', but he was decisive in action and could be incisive, albeit with a touch of humour, in his comments. He is one of the few British colonial officials still remembered in Malaya for their outstanding scholarship. J. M. GULLICK

Sources R. O. Winstedt, *Journal of the Malayan Branch of the Royal Asiatic Society*, 20/1 (1947), 143–4 · *The Times* (11 Dec 1941) · *WWW* · W. Makepeace, G. E. Brooke, and R. St J. Braddell, *One hundred years of Singapore*, 2 vols. (1921); repr. (1991) · R. Stevenson, *Cultivators and administrators: British education policy towards the Malays, 1875–1906* (1975) · b. cert. · d. cert. · m. cert. · private information (2004) [Felsted School; Trinity College, Cambridge] · J. S. Sidhu, *Administration in the Federated Malay States, 1896–1920* (1920) · P. Loh Fook Seng,

Seeds of separatism: educational policy in Malaya, 1874–1940 (1975) · W. R. Roff, *The origins of Malay nationalism* (1967); 2nd edn (1994) · F. Wong Hoy Kee and Gwee Yee Hean, *Perspectives: the development of education in Malaya and Singapore* (1972) · T. N. Goddard, *The handbook of Sierra Leone* (1925) · will of R. J. Wilkinson, Sept 1941 · R. J. Wilkinson, correspondence, 1922–3, CUL, Add. MSS 6468179, 6468186 · *CGPLA Eng. & Wales* (1943)

Archives CUL, letters to the librarian, Add. MSS 6468179, 6468186

Likenesses photograph, before 1907, repro. in A. Wright and H. A. Cartwright, eds., *Twentieth century impressions of British Malaya* (1908), 860 · photograph (when older), Arkib Negara Malaysia, Kuala Lumpur; repro. in K. Johan, *The emergence of the modern Malay administrative elite* (1984)

Wealth at death £1885 13s. 8d.: administration with will, 13 Aug 1943, *CGPLA Eng. & Wales*

Wilkinson, Robert (b. c.1470, d. in or after 1515), composer, is of unknown parentage and upbringing. At Michaelmas 1496 he was appointed to the staff of Eton College as clerk of the parish of Eton, whose church was the college ante-chapel. From this humble beginning his musical talents took him, with surprising rapidity, to appointment as a lay singing-man of the chapel choir in January 1499, and as master of the choristers one year later. His occupation of this office seems to have been entirely uneventful; his stipend was increased on two occasions. An episcopal visitation of the college in April 1515 found no fault with the choir under Wilkinson's direction (its unclean surplices excepted). The degree of conscientiousness informing the choir's work in his time is suggested by the necessity for a visitation four years after his departure to require more of the singing-men to be diligent about their duties.

Wilkinson's principal surviving monument for posterity is the wonderful collection of late fifteenth-century church polyphony known as the Eton choirbook. Compiled c.1502–5 for performance by his choir, it contained ninety-three Marian antiphons and Magnificats, most being of great length and technical virtuosity. Its original inclusion of seven of Wilkinson's own compositions indicates the degree of influence which he exercised in its compilation. It is a tribute to contemporary standards of training that this ambitious collection was assembled for a body of singers consisting of but four or five chaplains, Wilkinson and four or five singing-men, and eight or nine chorister-boys (possibly enhanced by a handful of competent supernumeraries from among the fellows and schoolboys).

While enterprising in their choice of texts, two of Wilkinson's compositions included within the original layer are now wholly lost, and three exist only as fragments. One survives complete, as does the second half of another; both appear to be early works, manifesting somewhat imperfect integration of their stylistic components. Three of the lost or fragmentary pieces were for six voices, exhibiting already Wilkinson's particular delight in sheer sonority. His masterpiece was the *Salve regina* for nine voices, added to the Eton choirbook after his death and now one of the greatest splendours of the collection. Its unique scoring for two trebles, alto, four tenors, and two basses lends massive sound to its full passages, and affords scope for much resource in its kaleidoscopic display of combinations of voices for reduced ensembles. Also added to the choirbook was Wilkinson's setting of the apostles' creed as a canon thirteen-in-one over a plainsong ostinato; however, though highly diverting to sing, this is not of great musical consequence. Wilkinson vacated his offices at Eton College early in August 1515. No further trace has been found, but the manner in which he received a generous gratuity during his final year there suggests that his departure was not by death but to other employment, now unknown.

ROGER BOWERS

Sources Eton · F. L. Harrison, ed., *The Eton choirbook*, 2nd edn, 3 vols., Musica Britannica, 10–12 (1967–73), nos. 9, 18, 50, 54, 57, 60, 63 · Lincs. Arch., Lincoln diocesan archives · C. Hocking, 'Cantus firmus, mode, and text in the Eton choirbook', PhD diss., U. Cam., 1995, chap. 5 · A. H. Thompson, ed., *Visitations in the diocese of Lincoln, 1517–1531*, 3 vols., Lincoln RS, 33, 35, 37 (1940–47) · F. L. Harrison, *Music in medieval Britain*, 2nd edn [1963]
Archives Eton College, Eton choirbook, MS 178

Wilkinson, Sarah Scudgell (d. c.1830), writer, was the author of at least seventy separate publications, over fifty of which were chapbook romances. She wrote at least six more extended novels, one of which, *The Thatched Cottage* (1806), gained two reviews, and earned sufficient money for Wilkinson to open a library. A school textbook and a series of Valentine Writers in verse are also known. Of the romances, about a third are acknowledged condensations of existing romances or plays, including work by Sarah Fielding, Matthew (Monk) Lewis, Sir Walter Scott, and Amelia Opie. Her 'original' Gothic fiction diversified the 'castle spectre' formula with Persian, Polish, and even 'aquatic' settings; she has been called 'one of the most productive and gifted of female fiend-mongers' (Tymn, 171). Her work tends to emphasize the plight of women victimized for sexual failings. Her efficient command of standard Gothic crises led in *The Spectre of Lanmere Abbey* (1820) to a degree of playful generic mockery reminiscent of Austen's *Northanger Abbey* (1818). Her most frequently reprinted work was *The Tragical History of Miss Jane Arnold, Commonly called Crazy Jane*; an ostensibly moral tale of seduction, madness, and suicide, it was originally issued about 1818 and was very popular on the northern provincial circuit. She petitioned the Royal Literary Fund for aid for herself and her 'fatherless child' in 1821, declaring that poor health and 'a painful tumour under my right arm' rendered her incapable of any employment beyond writing and needlework. She was apparently receiving £1 per month for her part in the *Lady's Monthly Museum* (Royal Literary Fund, case 375, 12 Dec 1821). About the same time she began to add Scudgell to her name on title-pages, for reasons not known. The last work ascribed to her and clearly dated is *Adeline, or, The Victim of Seduction* (1828). The date of her death is thought to be about 1830.

PAUL BAINES

Sources Blain, Clements & Grundy, *Feminist comp.*, 1167 · M. B. Tymn, ed., *Horror literature: a core collection and reference guide* (1981), 171–3 · M. Summers, *A Gothic bibliography* (1940), 213–14, 268, 273, 333, 438, 458, 517, 531, 557 · G. Kelly, *English fiction of the Romantic*

period (1989), 59 · S. Curran, ed., *The Cambridge companion to British Romanticism* (1993), 202 · W. S. Ward, *Literary reviews in British periodicals, 1798–1820: a bibliography*, 2 (1972), 563 · Royal Literary Fund Archive, case 375, 12 Dec 1821

Wilkinson, (Henry) Spenser (1853–1937), military historian, was born on 1 May 1853 at 9 Wilberforce Terrace, Preston Street, Hulme, the second son of Thomas Read Wilkinson, a banker, and his wife, Emma Wolfenden. He was educated at Owens College, Manchester, and (from 1873 to 1877/8) Merton College, Oxford. He read for the bar at Lincoln's Inn and was called in 1880. In 1888 he married Victoria, the eldest daughter of Sir Joseph Archer *Crowe (1825–1896). There were six children of the marriage: two sons and four daughters. The marriage was close and loving, and Victoria's death in 1929 was a devastating blow to Wilkinson from which he never completely recovered.

In 1874, while on vacation from Oxford, Wilkinson chanced to read an article upon European armies. This inspired a lifelong interest in military affairs. He had joined the volunteers at Oxford, and took a commission when he returned to Manchester in 1880. With six other enthusiasts, in 1881 Wilkinson founded the Manchester Tactical Society. This was intended to remedy the volunteers' ignorance of military theory and to improve their outdated drill. Wilkinson, by selecting and translating suitable foreign texts, provided more realistic tactical exercises. While still extending and enhancing his own military education, he established his reputation as the volunteers' spokesman.

Wilkinson had supposed that he would earn his living as a lawyer, but for more than a quarter of a century journalism was his principal vocation, providing both an income and a platform from which to promote his ideas. From 1881 he had contributed the occasional article on military subjects to the *Manchester Guardian*, and in 1883 C. P. Scott offered him a short-term engagement to cover Wolseley's Egyptian campaign. His unique gift as a newspaper writer who understood military matters was immediately recognized, even by the army's high command. Nevertheless, Scott doubted whether Wilkinson ought to be retained by the *Manchester Guardian*. W. T. Arnold, who taught Wilkinson the art of leader writing, took his part against Scott. Wilkinson's formidable command of detail rested upon exhaustive researches and he wrote with care on a range of disparate subjects. But in 1892 Scott decided Wilkinson had to leave because of his 'lack of a real hold of Liberal principles' (Ayerst, 239). Wilkinson was not sympathetic to every nuance of the radicalism that inspired the columns of the *Guardian*. He was no Gladstonian Liberal, nor was he always the easiest of colleagues. But his work had undoubtedly added distinction to the columns of the *Guardian*, while his comments upon military affairs were counted influential. Several years of penury as a freelance journalist followed.

It was his friend Lord Roberts who eventually helped Wilkinson to secure a place with the *Morning Post*, where he rapidly established himself as chief leader writer on imperial and military affairs. The *Post*'s traditions—high tory, patrician, self-consciously English, and blatantly imperialist—were the opposite of those that informed the *Guardian*. This did not discomfort Wilkinson, who could, on occasion, as over the infamous Kruger telegram (4 January 1896), play the ardent jingoist. Lord Glenesk, the owner of the *Morning Post*, was a sympathetic, loyal supporter and friend to Wilkinson. Not so his daughter Lilias Bathurst, who succeeded her father as proprietor. At the behest of Fabian Ware, the rabid tariff-reform editor of the *Post*, she allowed Wilkinson's copy to be censored. Ware accused Wilkinson of holding destructive views and providing material that was stale and out of date. Though Wilkinson continued writing for the *Morning Post* until 1914, he did so with waning enthusiasm.

Ware's comments had not been without substance. Until the Second South African War, a pragmatic progression had been evident in Wilkinson's thinking and writing. This was reflected, first, in his desire to improve the efficiency of the volunteers. Then he sought to solve the problems of leadership at command level by seeking inspiration from Germany's example. Next, imperial defence absorbed his thoughts, and then naval theory, to which he applied his earlier thinking on the functions of a general staff. Imperial defence questions necessarily involved him in the controversy over India. Finally, all problems combined in the one consuming question 'How might the nation best conduct the affairs and responsibilities of its great empire?' For years, often alone, Wilkinson condemned public and governmental indifference and demanded that the diplomatic, naval, and military consequences of Britain's changing imperial and global responsibilities be addressed seriously. He argued that naval and military preparations were inappropriate and insufficient. But it was only the initial defeats of the Second South African War that provided 'the political education … that has been utterly neglected'. Now Wilkinson enjoyed his greatest influence with the army, the 'thinking officers' rejoicing at his well-aimed censures. His influence extended to the Foreign Office, where his work was much admired, particularly by his brother-in-law Sir Eyre Crowe. Crowe's seminal memorandum of 1 January 1907 on British relations with France and Germany was in large part a summary of Wilkinson's main arguments in *The Nation's Awakening* (1896).

Among the many other books Wilkinson wrote before the Second South African War, the most important and influential were: *Citizen Soldiers* (1884), concerning the volunteers; *The Brain of an Army* (1890), his *magnum opus*, a brilliant description and analysis of the working of the German general staff system; and *Imperial Defence* (1891), which was written in collaboration with Sir Charles Dilke and demonstrated Wilkinson's thinking on naval power. Although Wilkinson's attempts to reorganize the Admiralty proved futile, he became a moving spirit in the foundation of the navy league (1894), whose subsequent actions and campaigns he did not altogether approve. It is notable that although he was encouraged and supported particularly by Lord Roberts, and despite his long-standing, frequent, and trenchant campaigns in print to

improve the volunteers, it was not until 1904 that Wilkinson was at last given an official voice when appointed a member of the Norfolk commission. He used that rare opportunity effectively, if without immediate result.

In 1909 Wilkinson was elected to a fellowship of All Souls, and became the first Chichele professor of military history at Oxford University. For years he had hoped for an academic appointment and since the Second South African War his interests had turned increasingly to history. He enjoyed teaching and could inspire the able and dedicated. They, sadly, proved fewer at Oxford than he had expected. His lectures, abstract and detailed, were delivered in a monotone, and made even less intelligible by his habit of chewing his beard. He wrote much. As a historian he was thorough, direct, and honest. He emphasized the practical and eschewed theory, aiming to prepare his students for the direction of war.

The years of the First World War cast a tragic blight upon Wilkinson. Time and again he volunteered his services to the Admiralty and War Office only to be turned down. He grew ever more frustrated and disheartened by this cruel official neglect that confirmed he was now one of 'yesterday's men'. He had the ear of neither Westminster nor Whitehall. His lectures were attended by dwindling audiences. Deep personal pain was added to frustration when one of his sons was killed in action. All that was left was to make patriotic speeches and seek mental and spiritual consolation by looking backwards in his researches to earlier wars. Though he retired from Oxford in 1923, he continued writing military history until 1930, when he completed a trilogy on the Napoleonic wars. In 1932 he confided to Basil Liddell Hart that he was 'getting rather tired of war', and instead was writing his recollections and translating Homer. An autobiographical fragment, *Thirty-Five Years, 1874–1909*, was duly published in 1933, and in the year he died Wilkinson completed a translation in blank verse of the *Odyssey*. He died at the Acland Home, Banbury Road, Oxford, on 31 January 1937.

Wilkinson was a prolific and influential military writer. As a reformer, his bent was always practical rather than theoretical, and his overriding preoccupation, to establish the appropriate mechanism—a properly organized general staff—to decide questions of tactics and strategy. A unique pedagogic distinction was that Wilkinson was both a pioneer of university military education and, in Sir John Colomb's words, 'the greatest instructor of the public mind'.   A. J. A. MORRIS

Sources H. S. Wilkinson, *Thirty-five years, 1874–1909* (1933) • *The Times* (1 Feb 1937) • J. Luvaas, *The education of an army: British military thought, 1815–1940*, new edn (1965), 253–90 • *WWW* • D. Ayerst, *Guardian: biography of a newspaper* (1971) • K. M. Wilson, *The Morning Post, 1905–26* (1998) • b. cert. • *DNB* • *CGPLA Eng. & Wales* (1937)
Archives NAM, corresp. and papers; research notes | BL, corresp. with Sir Charles Dilke, Add. MSS 43915–43916 • BL, corresp. with Miss G. M. Tuckwell relating to Sir Charles Dilke, Add. MS 43967 • JRL, letters to the *Manchester Guardian* • King's Lond., Liddell Hart C., corresp. with Sir B. H. Liddell Hart • NAM, letters to Earl Roberts • Queen's University, Belfast, letters to Otto Kyllmann • Richmond Local Studies Library, London, Sladen MSS •

U. Leeds, Brotherton L., letters to Lilias, Countess Bathurst • War Office Library, Manchester Tactical Society minutes
Wealth at death £3709 8s. 10d.: probate, 16 Feb 1937, *CGPLA Eng. & Wales*

Wilkinson, Tate (1739–1803), actor and theatre manager, was born in London on 27 October 1739, the son of the Revd John Wilkinson (d. 1757) and his wife, Grace, *née* Tate (d. 1763), the daughter of an alderman of Carlisle. His father was chaplain to the Savoy, chaplain to Frederick, prince of Wales, rector of Coyty in Glamorgan, and curate of Wise in Kent. Wilkinson's own life and the anecdotal sweep of his colourful stage career can be found recorded, in considerable detail, in the four volumes of his *Memoirs of his Own Life* (1790) and in the four volumes of *The Wandering Patentee, or, A History of the Yorkshire Theatres from 1770 to the Present Time* (1795).

Wilkinson's early education was provided by the schooling of a Mr Bellas in Church Lane, and later that of a Mr Tempest, near Wandsworth. He might have been expected to follow dutifully the example of his father and enter the church, but at the age of ten he became unexpectedly stage-struck. The theatre housekeeper of Covent Garden, a family acquaintance, allowed him privileged access to rehearsals and productions in what must have seemed to the young boy the most hallowed of secular surroundings. At the age of thirteen he was sent to Harrow School, where the zeal he now displayed for things theatrical found outlet in his skill at mimicry and in the performance of roles such as Lady Townly in Vanbrugh's *The Provok'd Husband* and Romeo. When he was seventeen his father was sentenced to fourteen years' transportation to America for the illegal conduct of marriages by his own licence at the Savoy, and in March 1757 his father died when storms forced the convict ship to put in for shelter at Portsmouth. Although Wilkinson and his mother were close to destitution, the young man now surprised and offended Jonas Hanway, a close friend of his father, by spurning the security of an arranged commission in the army. Wilkinson, ambitious for a stage career, applied instead to John Rich, manager of Covent Garden Theatre, who offered him some instruction then promptly admonished him as being incapable of acting. The prospect of employment with Rich was further diminished by making an enemy of Covent Garden's renowned leading lady, Margaret Woffington. Believing she had heard Wilkinson mimic her one evening, Mrs Woffington had insisted on his dismissal. Wilkinson's *Memoirs* capture the off-stage drama of the green room confrontation with Woffington:

> Mr Wilkinson, I have made a visit this morning to Mr Rich to command and to insist on his not giving you any engagement whatever—no, not of the most menial kind in the theatre.—Merit you have none—charity you deserve not,—for if you did my purse should give you a dinner … I heard you echo my voice when I was acting, and I sincerely hope in whatever barn you are acting as an unworthy stroller, that you will fully experience the same contempt you dared last night to offer me.

Ned Shuter, a comic player and friend of Wilkinson's, invited him, however, to play a role, that of the Fine

Tate Wilkinson (1739–1803), by Stephen Hewson, 1791

Gentleman, in Garrick's farce *Lethe*, staged for Shuter's benefit performance on 28 March 1757. Wilkinson was introduced 'as a person who had never appeared'. On the second evening, playing the same role in a benefit for the actor James Bencraft, he was taunted and hissed off the stage. A few weeks later he was present as an onlooker in the wings when Woffington suffered the collapse and paralysis that was to end her career. He went to the assistance of the actress and later recorded the incident in his memoirs, recalling her kind words as he helped her from the stage.

With the help of aristocratic patrons, Wilkinson managed to gain an audience with David Garrick, the revered actor–manager of Drury Lane. Garrick was so taken with his mimicry and impersonation of his rival Samuel Foote that he engaged him for Drury Lane's autumn season 1757–8 at 30s. a week. At this same time Wilkinson also joined a company under the management of Wignall in Maidstone, Kent, opening as Aimwell in Farquhar's *The Beaux' Stratagem*. He played other roles without much success and on appearing at Drury Lane under Garrick was given only walk-on parts. The unpredictable Garrick, now cold towards Wilkinson, encouraged him to leave for Ireland with Foote. Towards the end of 1757 he appeared with Foote at Smock Alley Theatre, Dublin, under Sheridan, playing the part of Puzzle in Foote's then popular entertainment *Tea*. The role gave Wilkinson scope for his imitations of contemporary performers, which proved a great success with Dublin audiences. The suggestion to Sheridan that he now add an imitation of the manager himself was, however, coldly received. Sheridan dismissed Wilkinson from the stage until his contracted benefit performance on 25 February 1758. The measure, though, of his popularity was in the considerable takings of 130 guineas. He returned to London, flushed with his Irish success, to find himself still denied acceptance by Garrick. With the help of influential friends he managed to find employment from 9 June to 14 August 1758 in Portsmouth, where the fleet was then stationed. With the Portsmouth company he extended his repertory with roles such as Romeo, Hotspur, Richard III, Lear, Hamlet, and Orestes.

Wilkinson's first appearance under Garrick at Drury Lane took place with Foote in October 1758 in Foote's two-act farce *Diversions of the Morning*. In the role of Bounce, Wilkinson again gave a range of imitations of well-known actors, to the delight of audiences. One of his victims, the actor Luke Sparks, complained to Garrick and demanded that the imitations be withdrawn. Garrick consented to this, but the reaction of the audience to the censorship of the imitations was so riotous that Garrick immediately capitulated. In an attempt to pacify feelings in the theatre community, Garrick submitted now to Wilkinson's additional impersonation of Garrick himself. Garrick's outrage was softened, however, by the obvious success at the box office. At the close of the season in May 1759, for his benefit performance, Wilkinson played his imitation of Foote, and also acted Othello, to a crowded, distinguished, and appreciative audience.

Wilkinson continued to enjoy theatrical success in Dublin and Winchester. In November 1760 he made his first appearance at Covent Garden in Foote's *The Minor*, a satirical comedy which made fun of Sheridan's schemes to set up an academy and which played in direct competition with Foote's own production at Drury Lane. As well as parodying Foote's style of playing, Wilkinson also imitated Garrick to such effect that Garrick never again spoke to him.

Wilkinson's fame was now spreading, and for three years, from 1762 onwards, he lived a peripatetic life with appearances at Birmingham, Bath, Chester, London, Portsmouth, and Bristol. He also played for the first time at Norwich and York, and in February 1765 in Edinburgh, once again performing in *The Minor*. In York he had come into contact with Joseph Baker, the owner and manager of a newly built and unlicensed theatre, who had once been an actor as well as a painter of church interiors and theatrical scenery. This relationship proved to be one of the most significant in Wilkinson's life. Baker's warmth and affection towards him was such that he came to feel like an adopted son. Baker was heavily in debt, partly due to investment in a new theatre, when it was suggested that he consider taking on Wilkinson as a business partner. At the age of twenty-six, Wilkinson joined Baker's enterprise, eventually investing some £1400, attending to refurbishment, reordering costumes with richer fabrics, and generally improving the theatrical stock. He also developed an ethical approach to the employment and working practice of the acting profession, introducing much needed reforms such as an end to the custom of actors knocking on doors to solicit for their benefit performances.

On 11 October 1768 Wilkinson married Jane Doughty in York, and in August 1769 the first of their seven children was born. Baker died in 1770, leaving Wilkinson sole manager of the York circuit, a mixture of Yorkshire-based theatre buildings, including, additionally, those of Hull and Newcastle. Wilkinson abandoned Newcastle a year or two later but built and opened, at considerable expense, a new theatre in Leeds in 1774. Company performances were given in the race week at Doncaster and, at other times, in Beverley, Halifax, Pontefract, Sheffield, and Wakefield. But managerial responsibilities did nothing to diminish Wilkinson's appetite for acting. He continued to make visits and appearances in Dublin, Birmingham, Edinburgh, Glasgow, Norwich, and elsewhere. In January 1778 he returned to Covent Garden at the invitation of Mr Harris, his friend and manager of the theatre:

This journey with others, was the occasion of my adopting the title of the WANDERING PATENTEE, as from my quitting my Yorkshire home to trip to Dublin, Edinburgh, Glasgow, and other places, occasioned Mr Woodfall's whimsically favouring me with that appellation. (Wilkinson, *The Wandering Patentee*, 278)

In 1780 Wilkinson took an additional responsibility for the management of the Edinburgh theatre, resulting in his command now of three patent theatres, his royal trio of York, Hull, and Edinburgh. In 1788 he broke his leg and suffered feverishly for many months. Although he continued to move around the circuit in pursuit of his duties, sometimes carried in a litter, his more active and juvenile roles had now to be abandoned and visits to fellow managers limited. A bad attack of gout in 1792 signalled deteriorating health. By the mid-1790s he was quite worn down with the stress of management and excessive travel, and he made use of the enforced rest to pursue his writing and reminiscences for *The Wandering Patentee*. He also contributed a series of articles, with lively anecdotes of actors, to the theatrical periodical the *Monthly Mirror*. None of this, after such an active and varied life, could quite prevent the tendency to bouts of depression in his final years.

Wilkinson still acted on occasion until 1801 and continued to control the affairs of his northern circuit until his death, in York, on 25 August 1803. He was buried shortly afterwards at All Saints' Church, York. (His monument inscription remains at All Saints' Pavement.) He left five surviving children, one of whom, John Joseph Tate *Wilkinson, like himself an actor, succeeded him in the management of the York circuit. Little exists by way of critical commentary on Wilkinson's achievements as an actor. His reputation was founded on enormous popularity as a gifted mimic of exceptional skill and ability. He caught the very appearance of the people he imitated, even if they were young women. His friend Stephen Kemble once called him 'the ugliest man he ever saw'. George Anne Bellamy, however, described him as 'tall, his countenance rather sportive than beautiful, and his manners agreeable'. In retrospect it may be Wilkinson's remarkable thirty-seven years' tenure as a theatrical manager that stand as his most formidable achievement. As Highfill points out: 'Few indeed were the British actors of the latter half of the century who were not at some point in their careers beneficiaries of the alternate cosseting and scolding of "the wandering patentee"' (*BDA*). In his lifetime, Wilkinson came to be admired and respected for his probity and his fairness in the conduct of a profession that had long endured fraudulent practice, exploitation, and desperate insecurity. ERIC PRINCE

Sources T. Wilkinson, *Memoirs of his own life*, 4 vols. (1790) · T. Wilkinson, *The wandering patentee, or, A history of the Yorkshire theatres from 1770 to the present time*, 4 vols. (1795) · C. B. Hogan, ed., *An index to 'The wandering patentee' by Tate Wilkinson* (1973) · Genest, *Eng. stage* · Highfill, Burnim & Langhans, *BDA* · G. W. Stone, ed., *The London stage, 1660–1800*, pt 4: 1747–1776 (1962) · C. B. Hogan, ed., *The London stage, 1660–1800*, pt 5: 1776–1800 (1968) · C. B. Hogan, 'One of God's almighty unaccountables', *The theatrical manager in England and America*, ed. J. W. Donohue (1971)
Archives York Minster, personal collection of playbills from 1766
Likenesses S. Hewson, oils, 1791, Garr. Club [*see illus.*] · W. Ridley, stipple, 1799 (after F. Atkinson), BM, NPG; repro. in *Monthly Mirror* (1799) · T. Wright, engraving, 1820 (as Simkin; after Wageman), York City Art Gallery · M. U. Sears, mezzotint, pubd 1829, NPG · Atkinson?, portrait, Garr. Club · I. Cruikshank, caricature, engraving (*The wandering patentee*), Harvard TC · attrib. S. Hewson, oils, York City Art Gallery · engraving, York City Art Gallery
Wealth at death left goods, etc. value £2000: will, 14 Nov 1800

Wilkinson, Thomas (*fl.* 1609–1612), composer, is of unknown parentage. Although there may be two composers named Thomas Wilkinson in the musical sources, the more important is the man who replaced John Hilton as organist and master of the choristers at Trinity College, Cambridge, some time between March and September 1609 and was still in post in May 1612, but is never mentioned by his first name in the college archives. He worked at Trinity in a period of great musical activity and had ample opportunity to compose, possibly for inclusion at the appropriate place in morning and evening prayer in college chapel services, verse anthems with viol accompaniment, as well as three five-part pavans for these instruments for domestic use in college. This music is skilfully written and, although it does not equal that of his more illustrious contemporaries for richness and sustained invention, deserves to be more widely known. The anthems, while conservative in style, show signs of madrigalian influence, and some of his music remained popular, especially in eastern England. When, in March 1642, Dr John Cosin's wife, having died in childbirth, was buried at Peterborough Cathedral, the precentor (Francis Standish) selected part of 'The Burial Service composed by Mr Wilkinson' to be sung at her funeral service. Asked by Cosin why he had chosen it, Standish replied, 'It is a good anthem, and you have not yet heard it' (Payne, *Provision and Practice*, 165–6).

Wilkinson's activities before his appointment to the Trinity post are uncertain. He may well be identifiable with a man of that name who had served as a lay clerk at Norwich Cathedral between 1575 and 1580, and at King's College, Cambridge, between 1580 and 1595. It seems likely that there date from this period two dull and old-fashioned full five-part anthems attributed to 'Wilkinson', 'O Jerusalem' and 'Why art thou so full of heaviness?' Alternatively, though less probably, the Trinity musician

may have been recruited from the membership of his college. In 1602–3 one 'Wilkinson' took the part of a lute player (named Citharaedus) in the college play *Labyrinthus* performed in that year; and in 1605–6 an identically named individual appears in the list of choristers (who were often young men with broken voices rather than genuine choirboys at Trinity at this period) for that financial year. This Wilkinson may, in turn, be the man who graduated BA (1605–6) and MA (1609), although Venn's claim that this graduate became vicar of Langtoft, Lincolnshire, in 1613, if correct, makes it unlikely that he is identical with the Trinity musician. It was probably this individual 'Mr Tho. Wilkinson' of Trinity, who early in 1611 gave evidence in the aftermath of riots that had taken place between members of Trinity and St John's colleges, allegedly caused by the Trinity stage-keepers at two recent college plays. A copy of *Cantiones sacrae* (1575) by Tallis and Byrd, now owned by the Royal College of Music, bears the signature of a Thomas Wilkinson.

Wilkinson, although replaced by one Mason on 20 May 1612, had not vacated the Trinity post by his death; nothing further is known about him. IAN PAYNE

Sources I. Payne, *The provision and practice of sacred music at Cambridge colleges and selected cathedrals, c.1547–c.1646* (1993) · A. H. Nelson, ed., *Cambridge*, 2 vols. (1989) · Trinity Cam. · I. Payne, 'Instrumental music at Trinity College, Cambridge, c.1594–c.1615: archival and biographical evidence', *Music and Letters*, 68 (1987), 128–40

Wilkinson, Thomas Turner (1815–1875), mathematician and local historian, was born on 17 March 1815 at Abbot House, Mellor, near Blackburn, one of two sons of William Wilkinson, farmer, and Mary Turner. His mother died when he was nearly two and his father cared little for his sons, so Wilkinson and his brother remained with his grandparents, under the care of his aunt Ann. His father remarried and took Wilkinson to live with him, without his brother. Wilkinson was educated from seven to twelve at his cousin's school, where his ability in reading and arithmetic were noted. He assisted on his father's farm and neglected his studies for four years but revived them when he saw his brother's arithmetical ability. His uncle, John Wilkinson, encouraged him in mathematics and let him use his extensive library, and he then worked through several mathematical textbooks. He met with a local group of mathematicians where his interest in astronomy was kindled.

Wilkinson's discovery of the *Ladies' Diary* in 1835 stimulated him to start a collection of English periodicals containing mathematics, which he claimed was the largest outside London. He contributed many solutions and mathematical essays to the *Ladies' Diary* and its successor, the *Lady's and Gentleman's Diary*, and was awarded its mathematical prize in 1852. He and several of his pupils contributed to the mathematical section of the *York Courant*, the *Northumbrian Mirror*, and the *Preston Chronicle*. He contributed a major series of articles on English mathematical periodicals in the *Mechanics' Magazine* which led to his election as a fellow of the Royal Astronomical Society in December 1850. Through mathematical periodicals he became acquainted with Augustus De Morgan, James Cockle, and Thomas Stephen Davies, the latter encouraging him to write on a school of Lancashire geometers.

Wilkinson said he was involved with the *Educational Times* from its inception, and was mainly responsible for introducing the mathematical department into that journal, to which he was a major contributor. He gained its two mathematical prizes and also wrote a lengthy paper on porisms (theorems, usually in geometry, arising during the investigation of some other proposition). Wilkinson became involved with a Blackburn group of mathematicians who formed a short-lived journal, the *Student's Companion*. One later member of the group was John Garstang, former deputy headmaster of Blackburn grammar school and teacher of the Revd Robert Harley. Many of the group contributed to the *Ladies' Diary* and Garstang to the *Educational Times*.

Wilkinson worked in W. and J. Statter's cotton mill as a bookkeeper until the firm became bankrupt. He was then appointed deputy headmaster of Burnley grammar school, a post he held for two short stretches, followed by a long term of office of thirty years. In between his teaching at Burnley, he started three schools—the national school at Crawshawbooth, the parish school at Habergham Eaves, and the private Mount Pleasant School. While under his direction, the parish school was the first in the district to be inspected by the government. He also had a pawnbroking business in Cheapside, Burnley.

About 1830 Wilkinson had become involved in the instigation of a mutual improvement society in the village of Mellor and he was also connected with the Burnley Mechanics' Institute in many capacities for over thirty years. He was a member of many local societies. He wrote extensively on local history, and his works on Burnley parish church and Burnley grammar school are still standard. In collaboration with John Harland he chronicled the ballads, songs, folklore, and legends of Lancashire, although he professed himself not much interested in the work. The Burnley Literary and Philosophical Society was inaugurated in 1861; the educational pioneer Sir James Kay-Shuttleworth became president and Wilkinson vice-president. Wilkinson held many positions in local office: member of the corporation of Burnley, councillor, chairman of the finance committee, alderman, and overseer of Habergham Eaves.

Wilkinson was married twice, first to Agnes Ward of Preston in 1837, and then to Angelina Harrison of Burnley, who was connected to the first Lord Ribblesdale. He had five children, two of whom died, leaving one son and two daughters. He was devoted to his second wife and never recovered following her sudden death on 13 April 1874. The prostate disease which had troubled him for several years ended his life on 6 February 1875, at his home, in Pickup Terrace, Habergham Eaves.   JANET DELVE

Sources W. A. Abram, 'Memorial of the late T. T. Wilkinson, FRAS, of Burnley', *Transactions of the Historic Society of Lancashire and Cheshire*, 3rd ser., 4 (1875–6), 77–94 • T. T. Wilkinson, 'Mathematical periodicals', *Mechanics' Magazine*, 48–59 (1848–53) • T. T. Wilkinson, 'Lancashire geometers and their writings', *Memoirs of the Literary*

and Philosophical Society of Manchester, 2nd ser., 11 (1854), 123–57 • T. T. Wilkinson, *History of the parochial church of Burnley*, another edn (1869) • T. T. Wilkinson, 'The grammar school, Burnley', *Transactions of the Historic Society of Lancashire and Cheshire*, new ser., 10 (1869–70), 19–34 • T. T. Wilkinson, *Lancashire songs and ballads, ancient and modern* (1875) • 'Lancashire workers of the past: Alderman T. T. Wilkinson, F.R.A.S.', *Lancashire and Cheshire Naturalist*, 7 (1914–15) • d. cert.

Archives Chetham's Library, Manchester, corresp. | Col. U., Butler Library, letters to W. J. C. Miller, MF 95–142

Wealth at death under £3000: probate, 23 June 1875, *CGPLA Eng. & Wales*

Wilkinson, William (*c*.1551–1613), religious writer and ecclesiastical lawyer, was a Yorkshireman by birth. His precise origins are unclear, though it is known that his family held land in Bradford. His university education began when he matriculated as a pensioner at St John's College, Cambridge, in 1571. He took his BA degree in 1575. Shortly afterwards, Wilkinson began to make intensive investigations of the Family of Love, a mystical religious fellowship; he would become one of its principal opponents.

Wilkinson became a fellow of St John's in 1577, by which time he was also working as a schoolmaster in Cambridge. His plans to publish a book criticizing the Family of Love were already well advanced, and he sought and received encouragement from Richard Cox, bishop of Ely. In 1578 he took his MA degree and busied himself with his research. He knew several members of the Family of Love personally, and responded to their request for written articles setting out his objections to their theology. In 1579 this document, accompanied by the Family's responses, was published in Wilkinson's *Confutation of Certain Articles Delivered unto the Family of Love*. The work was dedicated to Bishop Cox, who added a short commendation on the cover, and it also included notes written against the Family by John Young, bishop of Rochester. The *Confutation* drew attention to what Wilkinson regarded as the Family's gross doctrinal and moral errors. These included a belief in human perfectibility, a penchant for allegorizing scriptural facts, and a collective lifestyle characterized by extreme secrecy. Wilkinson warned that the Church of England was in terrible danger, and rebuked its ministers for the general laxity of their religious attitudes.

Wilkinson's sympathy with puritanism in this phase of his life was demonstrated again in 1580, when he wrote the dedicatory epistle in *A Very Godly and Learned Treatise, of the Exercise of Fastyng*, which was almost certainly by Thomas Cartwright. Wilkinson's dedication was addressed to the Lady Paget and to Mr Edward Carie, a member of the queen's privy chamber, and was written 'at my Poore house' in St Botolph, Aldersgate, London.

From 1588 Wilkinson held the prebend of Fridaythorpe in York Cathedral, receiving a dispensation so that he could do so despite being a layman. His future, however, lay in the southern province. Early in 1589 he was awarded a doctorate in law at Cambridge. Wilkinson was then elected, with Lord Burghley's support, to the chancellorship of the diocese of Salisbury. He took up the post in 1590 and held it until the end of his life. Throughout this period he discharged his functions with admirable skill and sensitivity. It was also in 1590 that Wilkinson became an advocate in the court of arches, and received a warrant from the archbishop of Canterbury for admission to Doctors' Commons. His academic allegiance subsequently shifted from Cambridge to Oxford, where in 1593 he took a doctorate in civil law (by incorporation). Wilkinson was probably the W. W. who, at some point before 1594, translated and published passages from Luther in A Methodicall Preface Prefixed before the Epistle to the Romanes. Between 1608 and 1613 he also served as a justice of the peace for the county of Wiltshire.

Wilkinson died in October 1613, and his will was granted probate by the prerogative court of Canterbury. He bequeathed his lands in the parish of West Wellowe, Wiltshire, to Mary, his 'loving and welbeloved wife', during her lifetime. The date of his marriage has not been established. Mary was also granted the right to occupy his dwelling house, held by lease from the vicars-choral of Salisbury Cathedral. There were no surviving children, and Wilkinson consequently made cash bequests totalling £216 to a number of siblings, nephews, nieces, and servants. CHRISTOPHER MARSH

Sources B. P. Levack, The civil lawyers in England, 1603–1641 (1973) · G. D. Squibb, Doctors' Commons: a history of the College of Advocates and Doctors of Law (1977) · M. Ingram, Church courts, sex and marriage (1987) · C. W. Marsh, The Family of Love in English society, 1550–1630, another edn (1994) · Venn, Alum. Cant. · Foster, Alum. Oxon. · R. Cox, letterbook, Gon. & Caius Cam., MS 53/30 · will of William Wilkinson, PRO, PROB 11/122, sig. 110 · CSP dom., 1581–90 · STC, 1475–1640 · W. Wilkinson, A confutation of certain articles delivered unto the Family of Love (1579) · A. Peel and L. H. Carlson, eds., Cartwrightiana (1951)

Wealth at death bequests of £216 cash; plus estate in Wiltshire: will, PRO, PROB 11/122, sig. 110

Wilkinson, William (1744–1808), ironmaster, was the youngest son of the iron-founder Isaac *Wilkinson (bap. 1695, d. 1784) and his wife, Mary Johnson (d. 1786), and brother of the more famous John *Wilkinson. At the time of his birth his parents were living at Backbarrow in Lancashire. He entered the celebrated dissenting academy at Warrington, probably in 1759. The scientist Joseph Priestley joined the staff, and in 1762 married Mary, sister of John and William. William's training was probably at the family ironworks at Bersham, Denbighshire, where in 1774 his brother John admitted him to a partnership on very favourable terms. The works had already a great reputation for the casting of steam engine cylinders, guns, pipes, and many other products. William briefly became managing partner at Bersham, though the advanced technology applied there was developed by John.

In 1775 the French brigadier Marchant de la Houlière, who was trying to develop iron smelting with coal in France, visited John Wilkinson at his New Willey (Broseley, Shropshire) works. He was particularly interested in John's achievement in the boring of cast-iron guns from solid, and wished to bring him to France. John could not go, but proposed the services of William, who agreed enthusiastically.

William Wilkinson made a preliminary visit to France within weeks. It was probably at this early stage that the Isle of Indret on the Loire near Nantes was identified as a site for water-powered mills to bore cannon. Early in 1777 he returned to France, Indret works was built, and Wilkinson was granted 12,000 livres salary, soon rising to 50,000. He supplied all the plans for Indret, but quickly had difficulties with French associates who complained of 'le despotisme anglais'. However he established better relations with the engineer Pierre Toufaire, who executed the works Wilkinson planned in France. The 2 million livres Indret had cost produced but few cannon, and this failure was investigated. The great artillery expert Jean-Baptiste Vaquette de Gribeauval recommended Ignace de Wendel, an artilleryman, and from a great family of ironmasters, to examine the situation. He took over Indret and decided that the problem was caused by the lack of coke iron for solid-bored cannon, not obtainable when England and France were at war. The answer was to be the creation of a great coke ironworks in France, and Wilkinson was considered to be the only man available to accomplish it.

The site chosen was Le Creusot near Montcenis in Burgundy. Wilkinson's payment was to be 216,000 livres, plus living and travelling expenses. His contract showed that he would need to consult his brother John and to refresh his knowledge of the rapidly changing technology in England. Le Creusot as finished had four coke-iron blast furnaces with steam-powered blast, reverberatory furnaces, large coking facilities, and 5 leagues of iron railway. Curiously Wilkinson was only on site for nine months during its building over 1781–4. The Wilkinsons supplied three steam engines at high prices. The investment was enormous and the crown a major shareholder. The furnaces came into blast in 1785 but the iron made was poor, and within a few years the cannon-boring mills there were occupied with charcoal iron and bronze cannon. For several decades Le Creusot was a 'contre-exemple' (Woronoff, 335), dissuading the further take-up of British coke-iron technology in France.

After a return to Britain in 1786 Wilkinson made some further extensive European journeys, finally settling again at Plas Grono near Wrexham in 1789. He soon quarrelled with his brother John over the management of Bersham, and particularly his accrued profit from his share in this highly successful works during his absence abroad. Lawsuits began in 1794, and he was at law with John Wilkinson and other family members until his death. Wilkinson objected to John's continued development and diversification of his own industrial interests outside Bersham, and wanted the maximum return from Bersham and associated enterprises. During the dispute Wilkinson became an ally of Boulton and Watt, with whom John had long worked as a supplier of cylinders for their engines. Their interests changed, they were no longer allies of John Wilkinson and his friend Thomas Williams in the copper trade, they had just discharged a large debt to John, and were now ready to sue him over his illegal 'pirate' sales of their patent engines. They hoped William Wilkinson would be of use to them in creating their own engine-making works at Soho, Birmingham, begun in 1795. He made available to them John's newly invented cupola furnace. John arranged to sell Bersham, moving much equipment to his new works at Brymbo. William set about seducing Bersham workers for Boulton and Watt. The case went to arbitration, and the works were put up for sale, being taken over by Thomas Jones, nephew to William and John, with capital supplied by John. Subsequently there were bitter lawsuits of great complication between the brothers over their north Wales lead-mining interests, William Wilkinson being a partner with John in the Minera mine. There were smelters at Bersham and Brymbo, the latter owned solely by John. Eventually John sold his share of the mine, ceding it to his partners. Wilkinson and his associates were not very successful in its subsequent management and it was again under John's control at the time of William's death.

Wilkinson married late in life, in 1791. His wife was Elizabeth Kirkes (d. 1808) of Liverpool, a widow, and daughter of James Stockdale of Cark Hall, Cartmel, a district with which the Wilkinsons had long associations. The Stockdales had extensive business interests, including a cotton mill. A daughter, Mary Anne, was born in 1795, and a second daughter, Elizabeth Stockdale, in 1799, the elder marrying Matthew Robinson Boulton, only son of the great Birmingham industrialist, in 1813.

William Wilkinson is significant for his part in the attempted transfer of a large part of British coal-iron technology to France. While eventually the cannon-boring technology devised by his brother was successfully transferred, the great iron smelter at Le Creusot was largely a failure, and Wilkinson's supercilious and overbearing manner and his failure to give enough personal supervision must take some blame. Like his father he seems to have pursued litigation too readily, and he at least matched his brother in his arbitrary disposition, while having none of his inventive or innovative ability, or the capacity to manage a large and diverse business empire. He died at Plas Grono in March 1808, having appointed the younger James Watt to be guardian to his daughters.

J. R. HARRIS

Sources W. H. Chaloner, 'The brothers John and William Wilkinson in their relations with French metallurgy, 1775-1786', *Industry and innovation: selected essays*, ed. D. A. Farnie and W. O. Henderson (1990), 19–32 · W. H. Chaloner, 'Marchant de la Houlière's report to the French government on British methods of smelting iron ore with coke and casting naval cannon', *Edgar Allen News* (Dec 1948–Jan 1949) · W. H. Chaloner, 'The Stockdale family, the Wilkinson brothers, and the cotton mills at Cark in Cartmel, c.1782–1800', *Transactions of the Cumberland and Westmorland Antiquarian and Archaeological Society*, new ser., 44 (1964), 356–72 · H. W. Dickinson, *John Wilkinson, ironmaster* (1914), 49–55 · D. Woronoff, *L'industrie sidérurgique en France pendant la révolution et l'empire* (1984), 335–9 · D. Ozanam, 'La naissance du Creusot', *Revue d'Histoire de la Sidérurgie*, 4 (1963), 103–18 · J. Tann, ed., *The select papers of Boulton and Watt*, 1 (1981), 10, 121–2, 126 · E. Roll, *An early experiment in industrial organisation: being a history of the firm of Boulton & Watt, 1775–1805* (1930); repr. (1968), 157–9 · J. R. Harris, 'The diffusion of English metallurgical methods to eighteenth century France', *French History*, 2/1 (1988), 22–44
Archives Birm. CA, Matthew Boulton MSS · Birm. CA, Boulton and Watt collection · Birm. CA, James Watt MSS · Ironbridge Gorge Museum Library, Coalbrookdale, Shropshire, Janet Butler MSS

Wilkinson, William Boutland (1819–1902), concrete manufacturer and builder, was born on 2 January 1819 in St Peter's district, Newcastle upon Tyne, one of three children of Joseph Wilkinson (1772–1837), potter, and his wife, Sarah Boutland (1786–1856). Following three years' technical and general secondary education at Dr Bruce's academy, Newcastle, where he won a medal for industriousness, Wilkinson was apprenticed to a local plasterer, Robert Robson. He subsequently established his own business, including an early trade in manufacturing 'artificial stone'. The firm advertised Wilkinson's Improved Granite Concrete, staircases, and fireproof floors. Wilkinson patented diverse inventions, such as non-slip treads for concrete stairs, and extended the business to include them. He formed a registered company, W. B. Wilkinson & Co., which by 1897 had its head office in Newcastle, works in Kent, and managers in London and Liverpool.

Wilkinson's most significant invention was the first design in Britain, or elsewhere, for reinforced concrete in 1854–5 (no. 2293, 1854) which was intended to improve the construction of fireproof buildings. This differed from previous combinations of iron and concrete which had not taken proper account of the complementary strengths of the two materials. Wilkinson's patent, and subsequent statements, demonstrate an understanding of the principle of distributing the iron in order to take advantage of its tensile strength. His system used 'as little iron as possible and that wholly in tension, thereby preventing waste' (*Architect and Contract Reporter*). In a letter to *The Builder* in 1884 Wilkinson claimed economy for his system, rather than the status of a new building material, although he recognized its superior strength. He suggested using wire rope for reinforcement because it was plentiful and cheap. This was secured in the concrete by looping or twirling the ends.

W. B. Wilkinson & Co.'s office records of works and tests were unfortunately destroyed by fire so that little is known of Wilkinson's uses of reinforced concrete. The earliest recorded example was for a two-storeyed cottage near Ellison Place, Newcastle, built about 1865. This was demolished in 1954, but first photographed and the construction described. Visually uninteresting outside, the cottage had a coffered ceiling to the ground floor composed of a reinforced concrete slab and beams with wire rope disposed according to the patent of 1854. Although referred to as 'entirely reinforced concrete' (Cassie, 25), possibly only the floors, beams, chimney, and stairs were of that material. Wilkinson's patent does not refer to exterior walls and their thickness here could indicate plain concrete.

Instead of this work representing a 'local and temporary' application of Wilkinson's system (Singer and others, 5.488), it is likely that his company regularly employed reinforced concrete from the time of the patent until the early 1900s, advertised simply as 'fireproof' construction.

Wilkinson in his 1884 letter to *The Builder* referred to the use of his patent, and papers by the managing director of W. B. Wilkinson & Co., Philip Hobbs, in the early 1890s make it clear that the company was then testing and employing reinforced concrete with only slight changes to the original patent.

Wilkinson lived with his mother until her death. On 30 January 1866, when he was forty-seven, he married Elizabeth (b. 1835/6), daughter of Thomas Wilkinson, mason (her mother's name is unknown); the couple had four daughters and two sons. From humble beginnings, Wilkinson became a wealthy businessman and civic dignitary. He was a JP and a director of several companies, including the Newcastle and Gateshead gas and water companies and the Redheugh Bridge Company. His household in 1881 included three female servants; he owned homes in Newcastle and Whitley, and 'rode in a carriage and pair with his own footman' (Brown, 140). Wilkinson died, aged eighty-three, on 13 October 1902 at his home, Belvedere House, Whitley, Northumberland. The beneficiaries of his estate included, in addition to his family, various societies, especially for promoting the Anglican faith. He was buried in Jesmond old cemetery, Newcastle, on 15 October and commemorated with a stained glass window in St Nicholas's Cathedral.   TRICIA CUSACK

Sources P. Cusack, 'Reinforced concrete in Britain, 1897–1908', PhD diss., U. Edin., 1981 · J. M. Brown, 'W. B. Wilkinson, 1819–1902, and his place in the history of reinforced concrete', *Transactions* [Newcomen Society], 39 (1966–7), 129–42 · W. F. Cassie, 'Early reinforced concrete in Newcastle upon Tyne', *Magazine of Concrete Research* (March 1955), 25–30 · W. B. Wilkinson, 'Iron and concrete', *The Builder*, 46 (1884), 42 [letter] · *Architect and Contract Reporter*, 57 (5 Feb 1897), 30 [advert] · census returns for Newcastle upon Tyne, 1881, PRO, RG 11/5059/100 · 'The late W. B. Wilkinson', *Builders' Journal*, 16 (22 Oct 1902), 168 · 'Funeral of Mr W. B. Wilkinson', *Newcastle Daily Chronicle* (16 Oct 1902), 5 · 'Will of the late W. B. Wilkinson', *Newcastle Daily Chronicle* (24 Nov 1902) · 'Early use of reinforced concrete', *Builders' Journal*, 23 (20 June 1906), 17 · C. Singer and others, eds., *A history of technology, 5: The late nineteenth century, c.1850 to c.1900* (1958) · T. Potter, *Concrete: its uses in building* (1877) · m. cert. · d. cert. · *CGPLA Eng. & Wales* (1902)

Archives British Patent Office · Tyne and Wear Archives Service, Newcastle upon Tyne, business records of W. B. Wilkinson & Co.

Likenesses engraving (after photograph by R. E. Ruddock), repro. in *Newcastle Daily Chronicle* (16 Oct 1902), 5 · portrait (*W. B. Wilkinson in old age*), repro. in Brown, 'W. B. Wilkinson', pl. xxvi(a)

Wealth at death £171,494 19s. 10d.: probate, 6 Nov 1902, *CGPLA Eng. & Wales*

PICTURE CREDITS

Wellesley, Arthur, first duke of Wellington (1769–1852)—V&A Images, The Victoria and Albert Museum

Wellesley, Gerald Valerian (1809–1882)—© National Portrait Gallery, London

Wellesley, Henry Richard Charles, first Earl Cowley (1804–1884)—© National Portrait Gallery, London

Wellesley, Richard, Marquess Wellesley (1760–1842)—The Royal Collection © 2004 HM Queen Elizabeth II

Wells, Herbert George (1866–1946)—© National Portrait Gallery, London

Wells, John Campbell (1936–1998)—© Lewis Morley, courtesy of The Akehurst Bureau; collection National Portrait Gallery, London

Wells, Mary Stephens (1762–1829)—© National Portrait Gallery, London

Wells, Sir Thomas Spencer, first baronet (1818–1897)—reproduced by kind permission of the President and Council of the Royal College of Surgeons of London

Wells, William Thomas [Bombardier Billy Wells] (1887–1967)—Getty Images - Hulton Archive

Wellwood, Sir Henry Moncreiff, eighth baronet (1750–1827)—© National Portrait Gallery, London

Welsh, Elizabeth (1843–1921)—by courtesy of Felix Rosenstiel's Widow & Son Ltd., London, on behalf of the Estate of Sir John Lavery; the Mistress and Fellows, Girton College, Cambridge

Welwitsch, Friedrich Martin Josef (1806–1872)—© Royal Botanic Gardens, Kew: reproduced by kind permission of the Director and the Board of Trustees

Wemyss, David Douglas (1760–1839)—© National Portrait Gallery, London

Wemyss, Rosslyn Erskine, Baron Wester Wemyss (1864–1933)—© National Portrait Gallery, London

Wentworth, Benning (1696–1770)—New Hampshire Historical Society

Wentworth, Charles Watson-, second marquess of Rockingham (1730–1782)—St Osyth's Priory, Essex; photograph National Portrait Gallery, London

Wentworth, D'Arcy (1762–1827)—Mitchell Library, State Library of New South Wales

Wentworth, Sir John, first baronet (1737–1820)—Hood Museum of Art, Dartmouth College, Hanover, NH; gift of Mrs. Esther Lowell Abbott, in memory of her husband, Gordon Abbott

Wentworth, Mary Watson-, marchioness of Rockingham (bap. 1735, d. 1804)—by kind permission of Mrs P. Gordon-Duff-Pennington of Muncaster Castle. Photograph: Photographic Survey, Courtauld Institute of Art, London

Wentworth, Thomas, first Baron Wentworth (1501–1551)—© National Portrait Gallery, London

Wentworth, Thomas, second Baron Wentworth and de jure seventh Baron Le Despenser (1525–1584)—© National Portrait Gallery, London

Wentworth, Thomas, first earl of Strafford (1593-1641)—Petworth House, The Egremont Collection (The National Trust) / NTPL / Derrick E. Witty

Wentworth, William Charles (1790–1872)—La Trobe Picture Collection, State Library of Victoria

Wernher, Sir Julius Charles, first baronet (1850–1912)—© reserved

Wesley, Charles (1707–1788)—Trustees of Epworth Old Rectory

Wesley, John (1703–1791)—© National Portrait Gallery, London

Wesley, Samuel (bap. 1662, d. 1735)—© National Portrait Gallery, London

Wesley, Samuel (1766–1837)—© National Portrait Gallery, London

Wesley, Samuel Sebastian (1810–1876)—© National Portrait Gallery, London

West, Sir Algernon Edward (1832–1921)—© National Portrait Gallery, London

West, Benjamin (1738–1820)—The Baltimore Museum of Art: Gift of Dr. Morton K. Blaustein, Barbara B. Hirschhorn and Elizabeth B. Roswell, in Memory of Jacob and Hilda K. Blaustein, BMA 1981.73

West, Lionel Sackville Sackville-, second Baron Sackville (1827–1908)—© National Portrait Gallery, London

West, Sir Raymond (1832–1912)—© National Portrait Gallery, London

West, Sarah (1790x95–1876)—© National Portrait Gallery, London

West, Victoria Mary Sackville- (1892–1962)—© Cecil Beaton Archive, Sotheby's; collection National Portrait Gallery, London

Westall, Richard (1765–1836)—© reserved; private collection

Westall, William (1781–1850)—© National Portrait Gallery, London

Westcott, Brooke Foss (1825–1901)—Macmillan Publishers Ltd; photograph National Portrait Gallery, London

Westcott, Foss (1863–1949)—© National Portrait Gallery, London

Westermarck, Edvard Alexander (1862–1939)—by courtesy of London School of Economics

Westfaling, Herbert (1531/2–1602)—by kind permission of the Lord Bishop of Hereford and the Church Commissioners of England. Photograph: Photographic Survey, Courtauld Institute of Art, London

Westmacott, Sir Richard (1775–1856)—© National Portrait Gallery, London

Weston, Dame Agnes Elizabeth (1840–1918)—© National Portrait Gallery, London

Weston, Frank (1871–1924)—© National Portrait Gallery, London

Weston, Richard, first earl of Portland (bap. 1577, d. 1635)—Kingston Lacy,

The Bankes Collection (The National Trust). Photograph: Photographic Survey, Courtauld Institute of Art, London

Weston, Thomas (1737–1776)—Garrick Club / the art archive

Wetenhall, Edward (1636–1713)—© Copyright The British Museum

Wethered, Joyce (1901–1997)—© reserved; National Trust Photographic Library / John Hammond

Wetherell, Sir Charles (1770–1846)—© National Portrait Gallery, London

Whale, James (1889–1957)—Getty Images - Hulton Archive

Wharton, Arthur (1865–1930)—private collection; photograph © National Portrait Gallery, London

Wharton, Sir George, first baronet (1617–1681)—© National Portrait Gallery, London

Wharton, Henry (1664–1695)—© National Portrait Gallery, London

Wharton, Philip, fourth Baron Wharton (1613–1696)—private collection. Photograph: Photographic Survey, Courtauld Institute of Art, London

Wharton, Philip James, duke of Wharton and Jacobite duke of Northumberland (1698–1731)—private collection in England. Photograph: Photographic Survey, Courtauld Institute of Art, London

Wharton, Thomas (1614–1673)—by permission of the Royal College of Physicians, London

Wharton, Thomas, first marquess of Wharton, first marquess of Malmesbury, and first marquess of Catherlough (1648–1715)—© National Portrait Gallery, London

Whateley, Dame Leslie Violet Lucy Evelyn (1899–1987)—© Estate of Henry Lamb; The Imperial War Museum, London; photograph National Portrait Gallery, London

Whately, Richard (1787–1863)—© National Portrait Gallery, London

Wheatcroft, Harry (1898–1977)—© Lewis Morley, courtesy of The Akehurst Bureau; collection National Portrait Gallery, London

Wheatley, Dennis Yates (1897–1977)—© Paul Joyce / National Portrait Gallery, London

Wheatley, Francis (1747–1801)—© National Portrait Gallery, London

Wheatley, John (1869–1930)—© National Portrait Gallery, London

Wheatley, John Thomas, Baron Wheatley (1908–1988)—© National Portrait Gallery, London

Wheatstone, Sir Charles (1802–1875)—© National Portrait Gallery, London

Wheeler, Anna (1785?–1848x50)—© National Portrait Gallery, London

Wheeler, Sir (Robert Eric) Mortimer (1890–1976)—© National Portrait Gallery, London

Wheldon, Sir Huw Pyrs (1916–1986)—© Bob Collins; collection National Portrait Gallery, London

Whewell, William (1794–1866)—© National Portrait Gallery, London

Whichcote, Benjamin (1609–1683)—by permission of the Master, Fellows, and Scholars of Emmanuel College in the University of Cambridge

Whillans, Donald Desbrow (1933–1985)—Alpine Club Photo Library, London

Whistler, Daniel (1618/19–1684)—by permission of the Royal College of Physicians, London

Whistler, James Abbott McNeill (1834–1903)—Arrangement in Gray: Portrait of the Painter, c.1872, James Abbott McNeill Whistler, Bequest of Henry Glover Stevens in memory of Ellen P. Stevens and Mary M. Stevens, Photograph © The Detroit Institute of Arts

Whistler, Reginald John [Rex] (1905–1944)—© Estate of Rex Whistler 2004. All rights reserved, DACS; collection National Portrait Gallery, London

Whiston, William (1667–1752)—© National Portrait Gallery, London

Whitaker, John (1735–1808)—© National Portrait Gallery, London

Whitbread, Samuel (1720–1796)—© National Portrait Gallery, London

Whitbread, Samuel (1764–1815)—private collection. Photograph: Photographic Survey, Courtauld Institute of Art, London

Whitby, Daniel (1637/8–1726)—© National Portrait Gallery, London

White, Charles (1728–1813)—© Manchester City Art Galleries

White, Sir Dick Goldsmith (1906–1993)—© News International Newspapers Ltd

White, Francis (1563/4–1638)—© National Portrait Gallery, London

White, Sir George, first baronet (1854–1916)—Royal Aeronautical Society Library

White, Sir George Stuart (1835–1912)—© National Portrait Gallery, London

White, (William) Hale (1831–1913)—Cecil Higgins Art Gallery (Bedford Borough Council), Bedford, England

White, John (1570–1615)—© National Portrait Gallery, London

White, Joseph (bap. 1746, d. 1814)—© National Portrait Gallery, London

White, Joseph Blanco (1775–1841)—© National Portrait Gallery, London

White, Richard (1539–1611)—© Copyright The British Museum

White [Blacklo], Thomas (1592/3–1676)—© National Portrait Gallery, London

White, Thomas (1628–1698)—reproduced by kind permission of the Bishop of Peterborough; photograph: The Paul Mellon Centre for Studies in British Art

White, Sir William Henry (1845–1913)—courtesy of the Institution of Civil Engineers Archives

Whitefield, George (1714–1770)—© National Portrait Gallery, London

Whitehead, Alfred North (1861–1947)—© National Portrait Gallery, London